For use wi

GW00390793

Distance	Age	Mar.	Apr.							
5f	4	10-0	10-0	10-0	10-0	10-0	10-0			
	3	9—0	9—2	9—4	9—6	9—8	9-10	9—11	9-12	9-13
	2	6—8	6-13	7—3	7—7	7-11	8—1	8—5	8—8	8-11
6f	4	9-13	10-0	10-0	10-0	10-0	10-0	10-0	10-0	10-0
	3	8-11	9—0	9—2	9—4	9—6	9—8	9-10	9—11	9-12
	2		6-13	7—3	7—7	7-11	8—1	8—5	8—8	
7f	4	9-12	9-13	10-0	10-0	10-0	10-0	10-0	10-0	10-0
	3	8—8	8-11	9—0	9—2	9—4	9—6	9—8	9-10	9—11
	2				7—4	7—8	7-12	8—2	8—5	
1m	4	9-11	9-12	9-13	10-0	10-0	10-0	10-0	10-0	10-0
	3	8—6	8—9	8-12	9—1	9—3	9—5	9—7	9—9	9-10
	2						7—9	7-13	8—2	
9f	4	9-11	9-12	9-13	9-13	10-0	10-0	10-0	10-0	10-0
	3	8—4	8—7	8-10	8-13	9—2	9—4	9—6	9—8	9—9
1¼m	4	9-10	9—11	9-12	9-13	10-0	10-0	10-0	10-0	10-0
	3	8—2	8—5	8—8	8-11	9—0	9—3	9—5	9—7	9—8
11f	4	9—9	9—11	9-12	9-13	9-13	10-0	10-0	10-0	10-0
	3	8—0	8—4	8—7	8-10	8-13	9—2	9—4	9—6	9—7
1½m	4	9—9	9-10	9—11	9-12	9-13	10-0	10-0	10-0	10-0
	3	7-12	8—2	8—5	8—8	8-11	9—0	9—3	9—5	9—7
13f	4	9—8	9-10	9—11	9-12	9-13	9-13	10-0	10-0	10-0
	3	7-11	8—1	8—4	8—7	8-10	8-13	9—2	9—4	9—6
1¾m	4	9—7	9—9	9-10	9-12	9-13	9-13	10-0	10-0	10-0
	3	7—9	7-13	8—3	8—6	8—9	8-12	9—1	9—3	9—5
15f	4	9—6	9—8	9-10	9—11	9-12	9-13	10-0	10-0	10-0
	3	7—8	7-12	8—2	8—5	8—8	8-11	9—0	9—2	9—4
2m	4	9—6	9—8	9-10	9—11	9-12	9-13	10-0	10-0	10-0
	3	7—7	7-11	8—1	8—5	8—8	8-11	9—0	9—2	9—4
2¼m	4	9—6	9—8	9—9	9—11	9-12	9-13	9-13	10-0	10-0
	3	7—6	7-10	8—0	8—4	8—7	8-10	8-13	9—1	9—3
2½m	4	9—5	9—7	9—9	9-10	9—11	9-12	9-13	10-0	10-0
	3	7—5	7—9	7-13	8—3	8—6	8—9	8-12	9—1	9—3

For 5-y-o's and older, use 10-0 in all cases.

to guarantee
daily full form
data and every
racing fact the
leading experts
can provide...
**ORDER The
Sporting Life**
to be delivered
to you *every day*

The Sporting Life

2

3

- Full cards and form
- Colours for TV races
- Latest information from Newmarket and Lambourn
- Exclusive Speed-Plus ratings only in the

Sporting Chronicle

No other paper gives you all these features PLUS

- Reports and details of the bloodstock sales
- Runners and results for the big overseas races
- Formcards for the afternoon greyhounds
- Full-page football pools guide

Your trump card.

The PTS Laurels

Nationwide network of credit telephone offices

Starting Price and Tote. Stakes from 5p

Ante post and board prices, shows and results

Unique PTS multiple bets

Betting up to the off for TV racing

Free 112 page betting guide – Winning Ways

SALES DATES IN
1977

Europe's leading bloodstock sales organisation will hold sales in 1977 on the following dates—

(Subject to alteration)

Spring (Mixed) Sales
APRIL 27

July (Mixed) Sales
JULY 5-7

September (Mixed) Sales
SEPTEMBER 5

October Yearling Sales
SEPTEMBER 26 - OCTOBER 1

Houghton Yearling Sales
OCTOBER 11-15

Autumn (Mixed) Sales
OCTOBER 24 - OCTOBER 29

Newmarket December Sales
NOV 24-26 & NOV 28 - DEC 2

Tattersalls

KNIGHTSBRIDGE GREEN, LONDON, S.W.1

Tel: 01-584 8771   Telex: 918039

Europe's leading monthly horse publication:—

Subscriptions:

Twelve issues: £9. OVERSEAS RATES: Surface mail £10 (U.S.A. $17.50). Airmail: U.S.A. $44.00; Australia and New Zealand £25.75.

Pacemaker and The Horseman,

P.O. Box 90, London S.W.3. Tel: 01-730 0701/2

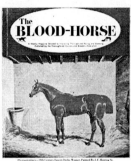

THE BRITISH RACEHORSE

Glossiest of all racing publications, The British Racehorse is required reading for every keen student of breeding. Under the Directorship of John Hislop, this lavishly produced magazine is profusely illustrated throughout. Each issue carries a pictorial review of recent flat racing while articles on all aspects of racing and breeding (except betting) are contributed by leading experts. Five issues are published each year in March, July, August, September and November, the latter three being timed to cover the principal international bloodstock sales.

A year's Subscription by post from the address below £10.

16

A Timeform Publication

RACEHORSES
of 1976

Price: £15.00

Compiled and Produced under the direction of
Phil Bull, B.Sc., and Reg Griffin

by members of the Timeform Organisation
J. G. Clarke (Director), G. Greetham, B.A.
(Director), G. F. Walton, Dip.A.D. (Associate
Director), J. D. Newton, B.A., (Editor), D. P.
Adams, P. Carey, A. M. Caulfield, A. C. W. Cook,
B.A., A. P. Johnson, B.A.. J. C. McGrath, P.
Stansfield and Q. G. Fox, L.S.I.A. (Advertising).

Published by Portway Press Limited, Timeform House,
Halifax, Yorkshire, and Printed by Walter Pearce & Co.,
Brentford, Middlesex.

18

CONTENTS

Foreword

"Racehorses of 1976" deals individually, in alphabetical sequence, with every horse that ran under Jockey Club Rules in 1976, plus a number of French and Irish horses that did not race here. For each of these horses is given (1) its age, colour and sex, (2) its breeding, (3) a form summary giving details of all its performances during the past three seasons, (4) a rating of its merit, (5) a commentary upon its racing or general characteristics as a racehorse, with some suggestions, perhaps, regarding its potentialities in 1977, and (6) the name of the trainer in whose charge it was on the last occasion it ran.

The book is published with a twofold purpose. Firstly, it is designed to provide the betting man with data for practical use in analysing the racing programmes from day to day, and instructions as to its use in this capacity will be found in the Explanatory Notes which follow this Foreword; and secondly, the book is intended to have some permanent value as a review of the exploits and achievements of the more notable of our thoroughbreds in 1976. Thus, while the commentaries upon the vast majority of the horses are, of necessity, in note form, the best horses are more critically examined, and the short essays upon them are illustrated by half-tone portraits and photographs of the finishes of some of the races in which they were successful.

The attention of foreign buyers of British bloodstock, and others who are concerned with Timeform Ratings as a measure of absolute racing class in terms of a standard scale, is drawn to the section headed "The Level of the Ratings" in the Explanatory Notes on page 37.

February, 1977.

22

INDEX TO PHOTOGRAPHS
PORTRAITS & SNAPSHOTS

25

Horse		Breeding	Copyright	Page
Pampapaul	.. 2 b.c.	Yellow God–Pampalina (Bairam II)	*Patricia Vigors*	538
Pawneese	.. 3 b.f.	Carvin–Plencia (Le Haar)	*P. Bertrand*	548
Piney Ridge	.. 2 ch.f.	Native Prince–Makeacurtsey (Herbager)	*Patricia Vigors*	563
Polly Peachum ..	5 b.m.	Singing Strand–Bolton Girl (Blue Lightning)	*A. Russell*	568
Quiet Fling	.. 4 b.c.	Nijinsky–Peace (Klairon)	*Fiona Vigors*	585
Raffindale	.. 4 gr.c.	Raffingora–Wharfedale (Wilwyn)	*Fiona Vigors*	590
Record Token ..	4 ch.c.	Jukebox–Bare Costs (Petition)	*Fiona Vigors*	598
Relkino ..	.. 3 b.c.	Relko–Pugnacity (Pampered King)	*R. Anscomb*	609
River Dane	.. 2 ch.f.	Tyrant–Audrey Joan (Doutelle)	*P. Bertrand*	617
Riverqueen	.. 3 b.f.	Luthier–Riverside (Sheshoon)	*P. Bertrand*	620
Rowantree	.. 3 b.f.	Silly Season–Calvine (Prince Chevalier)	*W. W. Rouch & Co.*	634
Rudella ..	.. 2 b.f.	Raffingora–Goldarella (Goldhill)	*R. Anscomb*	643
Secret Man	.. 3 b.c.	Breton–Secret Harbour (Ribot)	*P. Bertrand*	669
Sky Ship..	.. 2 ro.c.	Roan Rocket–Bedeni (Parthia)	*R. Anscomb*	687
Smuggler	.. 3 ch.c.	Exbury–Hiding Place (Doutelle)	*R. Anscomb*	691
Solar ..	.. 3 ch.f.	Hotfoot–L'Anguissola (Soderini)	*W. W. Rouch & Co.*	694
So Sharp	.. 3 b.c.	So Blessed–Cutle (Saint Crespin III)	*R. Anscomb*	699
Sporting Yankee	2 b.c.	Vaguely Noble–Sale Day (To Market)	*Fiona Vigors*	704
St Joles ..	.. 3 b.c.	Welsh Saint–Gleniffer Braes (Hard Tack)	*R. Anscomb*	713
Swagger ..	.. 2 b.f.	Prominer–Twaddle II (Tim Tam)	*W. W. Rouch & Co.*	724
Tachypous	.. 2 b.c.	Hotfoot–Stilvi (Derring-Do)	*W. W. Rouch & Co.*	731
Taffytina	.. 2 b.f.	Caerdeon–Tina II (Tulyar)	*Fiona Vigors*	732
Teddington Park	2 b.c.	Mill Reef–Hecla (Henry the Seventh)	*W. W. Rouch & Co.*	736
The Hertford	.. 5 b.g.	Supreme Sovereign–Emerald Velvet (Sheshoon)	*W. W. Rouch & Co.*	742
Thieving Demon	3 b.c.	Burglar–Hell's Angels (Hook Money)	*Press Association Photos*	747
Trepan ..	.. 4 b.c.	Breakspear II–Quiriquina (Molvedo)	*A. Russell*	761
Twig Moss	.. 3 b.c.	Luthier–Top Twig (High Perch)	*P. Bertrand*	771
Ubedizzy	.. 3 b.c.	Carnival Dancer–Ermyn Lass (Ennis)	*A. Russell*	774
Vitiges ..	.. 3 ch.c.	Phaeton–Vale (Verrieres)	*P. Bertrand*	783
Walk By ..	.. 4 b.f.	Tower Walk–L'Anguissola (Soderini)	*W. W. Rouch & Co.*	786

RACE PHOTOGRAPHS

31

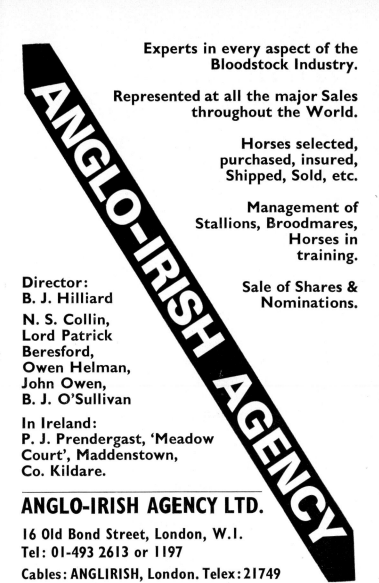

Airlie .... *for*
the best selection of stallions in Europe and the best care that money can buy

The seven studs under the control of Captain A. D. D. Rogers comprise over 2,000 acres of fenced and watered lands. There is a permanent staff of over 100 including two veterinary surgeons and a resident farrier. The vets are immediately contactable around the clock by telephone or shortwave radio.

For the convenience of overseas patrons we can offer accommodation for mares prior to the start of the covering season. This enables mares visiting the stallions **HABITAT, NONOALCO, CROWNED PRINCE, MALACATE, MANADO, SANDFORD LAD, SIMBIR, TARGOWICE** and **TUMBLE WIND** to settle in their new surroundings.

Also under the management of Captain A. D. D. Rogers

Grangewilliam Stud
Maynooth, Co. Kildare

Simmonstown Stud
Celbridge, Co. Kildare

Baroda Stud
Newbridge, Co. Kildare

Ballyowen Stud
used solely for Yearlings

Williamstown Stud
for southern hemisphere stock

Newtown Stud
a strict isolation yard

THE BROWNSTOWN STUD
CURRAGH CO. KILDARE
One of the World's Great Breeding Establishments

Weavers' Hall wins the Irish Sweeps Derby

BROWNSTOWN mares have produced:

Levmoss
(8 races, £143,483, including Prix de l'Arc de Triomphe, Prix du Cadran and Ascot Gold Cup)

Sweet Mimosa
(Prix de Diane, 1970, £76,407)

Arctic Prince
(Derby Stakes; leading broodmare sire)

Panastrid
(Irish 1000 Guineas)

Panaslipper
(Irish Derby; a leading sire)

Lucero
(Irish 2000 Guineas)

Solar Slipper
(Champion Stakes, broodmare sire of Royal Palace)

Royal Danseuse
(Irish 1000 Guineas)

Allangrange
(Irish St Leger)

Mart Lane
(St Simon Stakes 1976)

Weavers' Hall
(Irish Sweeps Derby and £67,757)

Silken Glider
(Irish Oaks, 2nd Epsom Oaks)

Feevagh
(Yorkshire Oaks; dam of Feemoss; grandam of LEVMOSS and SWEET MIMOSA)

Sixpence
(leading two-year-old; dam of Four-and-Twenty, won Santa Anita and Hollywood Derbys)

Arctic Sun
(leading two-year-old; dam of Arctic Prince)

Le Levanstell
(Queen Elizabeth II Stakes; a leading sire and grandsire)

Discipliner
(dam of Skymaster, Martial and El Gallo)

Bog Road
(Gallinule Stakes, Ballymoss Stakes and £37,419)

Silk Buds
(Silken Glider Stakes)

Small World
(Park Stakes)

The Brownstown Stud was founded in 1941. At present there are four stallions and 50 mares in residence.

All enquiries to Joseph McGrath, Brownstown Stud, Curragh, Co. Kildare.   Tel. Curragh 41303

1977 SALES PROGRAMME

Two-year-old In-Training Sale	March 21st
March Mixed Sale	March 22nd
Sale of Showjumpers, Event Horses & Jumping Ponies	March 23rd/24th
Derby Sale of Top Steeplechasers	June 24th
Dublin Horse Show Sale of Hunters & Showjumpers	August 4th/5th/6th
August Mixed Sale	August 12th
September Yearling Sale of High-Class Flat Bred Yearlings	September 12th/13th/14th
Sale of Showjumpers, Event Horses & Hunters	November 7th
November Sale of National Hunt Stock	November 8th/9th/10th/11th
December Sale of Flat-Bred Stock	December 5th/ 6th/ 7th

EXPLANATORY NOTES

To assess the prospects of any horse in a race it is necessary to know two things about him: first, how good he is; and second, what sort of horse he is. In this book the merit of each horse is expressed in the form of a *rating* (printed on the right); and the *racing character* of the horse given in the commentary.

TIMEFORM RATINGS

The Timeform Rating of a horse is simply the merit of the horse expressed in pounds. More precisely, it is *the number of pounds which, in our opinion, the horse would be entitled to receive in an average Free Handicap*. Thus, a horse which we regard as worth 9 st 7 lb in an average Free Handicap, i.e., 133 lb, would receive a rating of 133: and one regarded as worth 8 st (112 lb) would receive a rating of 112; and so on.

This explains what the ratings are; but of course individual ratings are not actually allocated in this way, merely by "inspection." The rating of any horse is a result of careful examination of its running against other horses. We maintain a "running" handicap of all horses in training throughout the season, or, to be strictly accurate, two handicaps, one for horses aged three years and over, and one for two-year-olds.

THE LEVEL OF THE RATINGS

At the close of each season all the horses that have raced are re-handicapped from scratch, and each horse's rating is revised. It is also necessary to adjust the general level of the handicap, so that the mean of all the ratings is kept at the same standard level from year to year. Left to itself, the general level of the ratings, in each succeeding issue of Timeform, tends to rise steadily. For technical reasons it is desirable to allow it to do so during the season: but, in the winter, when the complete re-handicap is done, the ratings must, of course, be put back on their proper level again.

This explains why, in this book, the ratings are, in general, different from those in the final issue of the 1976 Timeform series.

RATINGS AND WEIGHT-FOR-AGE

These matters, however, are by the way. What concerns the reader is that he has, in the ratings in this book, a universal handicap embracing all the horses in training it is possible to weigh up, ranging from tip-top classic performers, with ratings from 130 to 145, down to the meanest selling platers, rated around the 40 or 50 mark. And what we now have to explain is the practical use of these ratings in the business of weighing up a race.

Before doing so, it is important to mention that all ratings are at weight-for-age, so that equal ratings mean horses of equal merit: perhaps it would be clearer if we said that the universal rating handicap is really not a single handicap, but four handicaps side by side: one for 2-y-o's, one for 3-y-o's, one for 4-y-o's and one for older horses. Thus, a 3-y-o rated, for argument's sake, at 117 is deemed to be identical in point of "merit" with a 4-y-o also rated at 117: but for them to have equal chances in, say, a mile race in June, the 3-y-o would need to be receiving 13 lb from the 4-y-o, which is the weight difference specified in the Age, Weight and Distance Table on the page facing the front cover. However, let us to cases!

USING THE RATINGS

In using Timeform Ratings with a view to discovering which horses in any race have the best chances at the weights, we have two distinct cases, according to whether the horses taking part are of the same age or of different ages. Here is the procedure in each case:—

A. Horses of the Same Age

If the horses all carry the same weight there are no adjustments to be made, and the horses with the highest ratings have the best chances. If the horses carry different weights, jot down their ratings, and to the rating of each horse add one point for every pound the horse is set to carry less than 10 st, or subtract one point for every pound he has to carry more than 10 st. When the ratings have been adjusted in this way the highest resultant figure indicates the horse with the best chance at the weights.

Example (any distance: any month of the season)

2 Happy Sound (9-6)	..	Rating 119	....	add 8	 127
2 Emeraldo (9-4)	..	Rating 113	....	add 10	 123
2 Yellow Sky (8-11)	..	Rating 107	....	add 17	 124
2 The Charmer (8-7)	..	Rating 108	....	add 21	 129
2 Bossman (8-2)	..	Rating 100	....	add 26	 126
2 Mr Hodgkiss (7-7)	..	Rating 92	....	add 35	 127

The Charmer (129) has the best chance; Happy Sound (127) and Mr Hodgkiss (127) are next best.

B. Horses of Different Ages

Take no notice of the weight any horse receives from any other. Instead, consult the Age, Weight and Distance Table on the page facing the front cover. Treat each horse separately, and compare the weight it has to carry with the weight prescribed for it in the table, according to the age of the horse, the distance of the race and the month of the year. Then, add one point to the rating for each pound the horse has to carry less than the weight given in the table: or, subtract one point from the rating for every pound he has to carry more than the weight prescribed by the table. The highest resultant figure indicates the horse most favoured by the weights.

Example (1½ miles in July)

(Table Weights: 5-y-o 10-0; 4-y-o 9-13; 3-y-o 8-11)

6	Staretta (9-12)	.. Rating 115	.... add	2	 117
4	Peaceville (9-9)	.. Rating 114	.... add	4	 118
6	Swift Cheetah (9-5)..	Rating 115	.... add	9	 124
3	Comanchero (8-12) ..	Rating 120	subtract	1	 119
4	Lady Luck (8-11)	.. Rating 101	.... add	16	 117
3	Heather Downes (8-7)	Rating 112	.... add	4	 116

Swift Cheetah (124) has the best chance at the weights, with 5 lb in hand of Comanchero (119).

JOCKEYSHIP AND APPRENTICE ALLOWANCES

There is just one further point that arises in evaluating the chances of the horses on the basis of their ratings: the question of jockeyship in general, and apprentice allowances in particular. The allowance which may be claimed by an apprentice is given to enable apprentices to obtain race-riding experience against experienced jockeys. For the purposes of rating calculations it should, in general, be assumed that the allowance the apprentice is able to claim (3 lb, 5 lb, or 7 lb) is nullified by the boy's inexperience. Therefore, the *weight adjustments to the ratings should be calculated on the weight allotted by the handicapper, or determined by the conditions of the race*, and no extra addition should be made to a rating because the horse's rider claims an apprentice allowance.

The above is the general routine procedure. But of course there is no reason why the quality of jockeyship should not be taken into account in assessing the chances of horses in a race. Quite the contrary. Nobody would question that the jockeyship of a first-class rider is worth a pound or two, and occasionally an apprentice comes along who is riding quite as well as the average jockey long before he loses the right to claim. There is no reason whatever why, after the age and weight adjustments have been made to the ratings, small additional allowances should not be made for these matters of jockeyship. This, however, is a matter which must be left to the discretion of the reader.

WEIGHING UP A RACE

It having been discovered, by means of the ratings, which horses in a particular race are most favoured by the weights, complete analysis demands that the racing character of each horse, as set out in the commentary upon it, shall be checked to see if there is any reason why the horse might be expected not to run up to his rating. It counts for little that a horse is thrown in at the weights if he has no pretensions whatever to staying the distance, or is unable to act on the prevailing going.

These two matters, suitability of distance and going, are, no doubt, the most important points to be considered. But there are others. For example, the ability of a horse to accommodate himself to the conformation of the track. Then there is the matter of pace versus stamina: as between two stayers of equal merit, racing over a distance suitable to both, firm going, or a small field with the prospect of a slowly-run race, would favour the one with the better pace and acceleration, whereas dead or soft going, or a big field with the prospect of a strong gallop throughout the race, would favour the sounder stayer. There is also the matter of temperament and behaviour at the start: nobody would be in a hurry to take a short price about a horse with whom it is always an even chance whether he will consent to race or not.

A few minutes spent checking up on these matters in the commentaries upon the horses concerned will sometimes put a very different complexion on a race from that which is put upon it by the ratings alone. We repeat, therefore, that the correct way to use Timeform, or this annual volume, in the analysis of individual races is, first to use the ratings to discover which horses are most favoured by the weights, and second, to check through the comments on the horse to discover what factors other than weight might also affect the outcome of the race.

Incidentally, in setting out the various characteristics, requirements and peculiarities of each horse in the commentary upon him, we have always expressed ourselves in as critical a manner as possible, endeavouring to say just as much, and no whit more than the facts seem to warrant. Where there are clear indications, and definite conclusions can be drawn with fair certainty, we have drawn them: if it is a matter of probability or possibility we have put it that way, being careful not to say the one when we mean the other; and where real conclusions are not to be drawn, we have been content to state the facts. Furthermore, when we say that a horse *may not* be suited by hard going, we do not expect the reader to treat it as though we had said that the horse is *not* suited by hard going. In short, both in our thinking and in the setting out of our views we have aimed at precision.

THE FORM SUMMARIES

The form summary enclosed in the square brackets shows for each individual horse the distance, the state of the going and where the horse finished in each of its races on the flat during the previous three seasons. Performances are in chronological sequence, the earliest being given first.

The distance of each race is given in furlongs, fractional distances being expressed in the decimal notation to the nearest tenth of a furlong.

The going is symbolized as follows: h = hard or very firm; f = firm; fg = fairly good, or on the firm side of good; g = good; d = dead, or on the soft side of good; s = soft, sticky or holding; v = heavy, very heavy or very holding.

Placings are indicated, up to sixth place, by the use of superior figures, an asterisk being used to denote a win.

Thus, 1976 12f³ 11.7g signifies that the horse ran twice in 1976, finishing third over 12 furlongs on firm going first time out, and then unplaced, not in the first six, over 11.7 furlongs on good going. N.R. means that the horse did not race.

Included in the pedigree details are the highest Timeform Annual ratings during their racing careers of the sires, dams and sires of dams of all horses, where this information is available.

THE RATING SYMBOLS

The following symbols, attached to the ratings, are to be interpreted as stated:—

p   the horse is likely to make more than normal progress and to improve on his rating.

P   there is convincing evidence, or, to say the least, a very strong presumption that the horse is capable of form much better than he has so far displayed.

+   the horse may be rather better than we have rated him.

d   the horse appears to have deteriorated, and might no longer be capable of running to the rating given.

§   a horse who is somewhat ungenerous, faint-hearted or a bit of a coward, one who may give his running on occasions, but cannot be relied upon to do so.

§§   an arrant rogue or a thorough jade; so temperamentally unsatisfactory as to be not worth a rating.

?   if used in conjunction with a rating this symbol implies that the rating is based upon inadequate or unsatisfactory data, upon form which it is impossible to assess with confidence. The use of a query without a rating implies that although the horse has form, its merit cannot be assessed on the data at present available.

RACEHORSES OF 1976

Horse	Commentary	Rating

ABERCATA 4 br.g. Aberdeen 109–Toccata (Kythnos 126) [1974 N.R. 1975 **71**
8g⁵ 8fg* 10f³ 10.5g³ 8f⁵ 8f 8f 1976 10g 12f⁶ 10.6f³ 10s⁴ 8g* 8.2v³] strong
gelding: quite a moderate handicapper: winner at Lanark in October by 2 lengths
from Romance at Sea: stays 1¼m: acts on any going. *E. Collingwood.*

ABERCORN 4 ch.c. Aberdeen 109–Golden Ears 94 (Gratitude 130) [1974 5fg **74**
5s⁴ 6d 5v⁵ 5g⁶ 6s³ 6v 1975 6v* 6f⁴ 7.2fg 6g³ 6g⁶ 6s⁴ 6g⁴ 6g² 1976 5fg³ 6g* 7.2d
6fg⁵ 6g⁴] strong colt: quite a moderate handicapper: narrow winner at Carlisle
in May and ran creditably on first and fourth outings: best form at 6f: appears
to act on any going but is suited by some give in the ground. *E. Collingwood.*

ABERDONNA 4 b.f. Aberdeen 109–Maona (Narrator 127) [1974 5s 5v 1975 **—**
N.R. 1976 12fg] lightly raced and seems only plating class. *R. Vibert.*

ABERGWIFFY 4 ro.c. Precipice Wood 123–Dugo 90 (Dumbarnie 125) [1974 **64**
7d 8s 6s⁶ 1975 10.8s⁴ 14f 11.5f⁵ 12g⁵ 13g⁵ 16h⁴ 16h³ 14g⁴ 12f⁴ 16s 10.8g 1976
13.8g² 12f³ 16.1d⁶ 8f³ 9f² 9fg³ 12g³ 13.8f* 7f⁶ 7f* 8fg 12s⁵] well-made colt:
winner of poor maiden race at Catterick in August and minor event at Lanark
the following month: effective at 7f and stays well: seems to act on any going:
blinkered second outing: dwelt start final appearance. *M. Camacho.*

ABERKLAIR 2 br.f. Klairon 131–Abercourt 89 (Abernant 142) [1976 5f* 5f³ **67**
5fg⁶ 5f 6fg 7fg] neat filly: half-sister to three winners, including fairly useful 1974
2-y-o 5f winner Court God (by Red God): 540 gns foal: dam won four times over
6f at 2 yrs: won 12-runner maiden race at Teesside in April but is only plating
class: should be suited by 7f and 1m: action suggests give in the ground will suit
her. *M. W. Easterby.*

ABEROAN 2 gr.f. Roan Rocket 128–Abergrove 103 (Abernant 142) [1976 5fg **86**
5h* 5v³] first foal: 3,600 gns yearling: dam best at 6f: made all to win 11-runner
maiden race at Bath in July by 2½ lengths from Billycombe: not seen out again
until October when 8 lengths third of seven to Mummy's Darling in minor event
at Leicester: will probably stay 1m: seems to act on any going. *J. Nelson.*

ABODE 2 ch.c. Habitat 134–A-Bye 116 (Abernant 142) [1976 5d 5f 5f⁵ 5d* **101**
5s²] robust colt: second foal: dam, a smart 5f performer at 2 yrs, is sister to
good sprinter Abwah and half-sister to Owen Dudley: took some time to find his
form but showed useful form in the autumn: made all when winning maiden race
at Nottingham comfortably by 3 lengths from Sallow and was caught close home,
after being clear 1f out, when neck second to Kingsfold Trooper in nursery at
Sandown: suited by soft ground: speedy: sold 8,800 gns Newmarket Autumn
Sales, reportedly for export to Australia. *N. Murless.*

ABOMA 3 b.c. Balidar 133–Romany 87 (King's Bench 132) [1975 6fg³ 5fg³ 5f² **75**
5.1g³ 6g 1976 6fg⁴ 6g² 6fg² 5fg² 5.3f² 5.8h* 6f² 6f³] first foal: dam best at
sprint distances: in frame on all outings and won maiden race at Bath in July by
3 lengths from Snug: stays 6f: acts on hard ground: consistent. *J. Winter.*

ABROVIAN 3 ch.f. Reliance II 137–Lady Hazel (Hornbeam 130) [1975 6fg **—**
7g³ 7g⁴ 8f 6g 1976 12g⁵ 12d 16fg³ 12fg 13fg⁴ 16g⁵ 14d 14.7d⁵ 16v 12g⁵ 10.6v⁵
10.2s] smallish filly: best run at 2m: sold 850 gns Ascot December Sales. *W.
Elsey.*

ABS 2 ch.c. Red God 128 §–La Duchesse (Prince Bio) [1976 5.1fg* 6f⁴ 6fg*] **110**
tall, lengthy colt: half-brother to three winners, including Breeders Dream (by
Tudor Melody), a smart performer at around 1m: 4,000 gns yearling: dam won
over 11f in France: won maiden race at Yarmouth in June and put up a very
creditable performance to win seven-runner New Ham Stakes at Goodwood the
following month, producing a fine turn of foot in final furlong to beat Haveroid
¾ length: 6 lengths fourth of 12 to Cawston's Clown in Coventry Stakes at Royal
Ascot in between: got loose at exercise in August and injured his head and a fore-
leg: should stay 1m if able to race again. *J. Hindley.*

ABU DHABI 3 ch.g. Gulf Pearl 117–Silver Perch 58 (High Perch 126) [1975 —
5f 6fg 6fg 8g 1976 8.2f 12.2g 12fg 10.1fg 10fg⁵] poor plater: blinkered last two
outings: bought by B.B.A. 500 gns Ascot June Sales for export to Sweden. *G.
Smyth.*

ABYSSINIA 2 b.c. So Blessed 130–Addis Ababa 102 (Pardal 130) [1976 5g⁴] — p
strong, useful-looking colt: half-brother to several winners, notably smart 9f and
1¼m handicapper Negus (by Grey Sovereign): 4,400 gns yearling: dam won at
1½m: made a good first appearance when 6 lengths fourth of nine to And Behold
in maiden race at Kempton in May, going on steadily throughout, but did not race
again: will stay at least 1m. *G. Harwood.*

ACADEMIA 2 b.f. King Emperor–Grecian Nymph (Parthia 132) [1976 8s 10v] —
third foal: 760 gns yearling, resold 1,025 gns Ascot June 1976 Sales: dam showed
only moderate form: little sign of ability in end-of-season events at Sandown
(slowly away) and Nottingham. *D. Dale.*

ACCELERATE 2 br.c. Hotfoot 126–Acclio 102 (Acropolis 132) [1976 6g³ 6v²] **100**
half-brother to several winners, including smart sprinter Acquit (by Sing Sing)
and very useful miler Acquaint (by Midsummer Night II): dam a sprinter: ran
very well for a newcomer when 5½ lengths third of seven to more-experienced
Etienne Gerard in Clarence House Stakes at Ascot in September, showing up all
way and staying on well: favourite for £2,600 event at York the following month
but went down by ½ length to Our Jimmy, keeping on well without being given a
very hard race when held by winner: will probably stay 1m: sure to win races.
P. Walwyn.

ACERNOON 3 b.g. Acer 123–Noon Cloud (Nimbus 130) [1975 N.R. 1976 12s —
10v] half-brother to 1m seller winner Abernoon (by Aberdeen): dam of little
account: backward when well beaten in maiden event at Chepstow and claiming
race at Nottingham (tried in blinkers) at end of season. *R. Sturdy.*

ACES HIGH 4 b.f. Acer 123–Nosh (Court Martial) [1974 5g³ 5f² 5h 5f⁶ 5fg³ **39**
5fg² 6s 5g⁴ 5s 5.9s 1975 5f 5h 6f 1976 7g² 8f 6f⁴ 6g⁴ 5g⁶ 6g*] poor plater: not
seen out after winning at Hamilton in June (no bid): best form at up to 7f. *K.
Stapleton.*

ACLAND 2 bl.f. Mandamus 120–Gloriosa 102 (Aureole 132) [1976 6v 8.2s] —
strong filly: sixth produce: 600 gns foal: dam, a stayer, is half-sister to Aberdeen:
well behind in October in £2,100 event at York and minor race at Haydock
(tailed off). *R. Hollinshead.*

ACOMA 3 b.f. Rheffic 129–Almyre (Wild Risk) [1975 N.R. 1976 10g* 12g⁵ **121**
12g*]
'Acoma is the best filly I've ever had: absolutely fantastic.' That was the
remarkable tribute paid by Acoma's owner Daniel Wildenstein when he spoke to
us on Prix Vermeille day at Longchamp in September. Praise indeed from the
man who owns Allez France and Pawneese! Unfortunately we shall never know
just how good Acoma really was. She has been retired to stud, having seriously
injured a leg when winning the Prix de Minerve at Evry in July on only her third
racecourse appearance.
    Acoma's racing career spanned only forty days. Following an effortless six-
length success in a newcomers race at Saint-Cloud in June she was aimed at the
Irish Guinness Oaks in which among her seventeen rivals she encountered the
French Oaks third Lagunette and the Irish One Thousand Guineas winner Sarah
Siddons, the latter fifth in the French Oaks. Acoma started a heavily-backed
favourite. However, the form-book choice Lagunette won the race, at the
generous odds of 3/1, with Acoma just over two and a half lengths back in fifth
place. There's no doubt that Acoma was a better filly than the result of the Irish
Oaks showed. After holding a prominent position for just over a furlong she lost
her pitch and dropped back to the rear of the field. By the time the runners swung

Prix de Minerve, Evry—Acoma outclasses the opposition

into the home straight she had made up ground to be within a length or so of Lagu-nette, but whereas Lagunette was switched and found an opening on the outside Acoma was taken inside and couldn't get a clear run until inside the last furlong. Acoma finished like a train but Lagunette had gone beyond recall. In another few strides Acoma would have been at least third, probably second. The blame for Acoma's defeat could not be laid entirely at her jockey's door: her 'greenness' showed clearly as Saint-Martin asked her for her effort. Signs of inexperience were again evident when Acoma won the Group 3 Prix de Minerve. This time Saint-Martin wisely sent her on from the start and she was never out of a canter in beating the very useful Lady and Co by five lengths. Tragically, as Acoma crossed the line she injured a hind leg, and that was that.

Acoma (b.f. 1973)	Rheffic (b 1968)	Traffic (ch 1961)	Tomy Lee or Traffic Judge
			Capelet
		Rhenane (br 1961)	Tanerko
			Rhea II
	Almyre (b 1964)	Wild Risk (b 1940)	Rialto
			Wild Violet
		Ad Gloriam (b 1958)	Alizier
			Ad Altiora

By the French Derby and Grand Prix de Paris winner Rheffic, Acoma is a half-sister to Ashmore (by Luthier) in whose commentary can be found other family details. Acoma would have been very well suited by distances in excess of a mile and half, and after the Irish Oaks she was being talked about as the Wildenstein representative in the St Leger won ultimately by her stable-com-panion Crow. It's arguable that with better luck Acoma would have been a classic winner, and she was obviously a high-class filly, although whether she was anywhere near as good as her reputation we are not in a position to judge. *A. Penna, France.*

ACQUAINT 5 ch.g. Midsummer Night II 117–Acclio 102 (Acropolis 132) [1974 7fg² 8g³ 8.2f* 8fg* 8g⁵ 8f 8d⁵ 8s* 8s³ 9d 1975 8v 8s 8fg 9fg⁵ 8f² 8g⁴ 8g³ 8v² 8g* 1976 10g] compact gelding: very useful handicapper (rated 113) in 1975: well beaten in Littlewoods Spring Cup at Liverpool in April, only outing as a 5-y-o: stays 9f: acts on any going. *P. Walwyn.* —

ACQUITTAL 2 b.c. Hopeful Venture 125–Capital Charge 103 (High Treason 126) [1976 7fg 7f 8g⁴ 8fg* 8s] strong, good-bodied colt: half-brother to two winners, including fairly useful 1m winner Cab (by Abernant): dam a sprinter: odds on, unimpressive when winning 14-runner maiden race at Beverley in September by 1½ lengths from Velvet Boy: favourite for nursery at Pontefract the following month but didn't seem to have a good chance at weights and never got into race: looks short of pace and will probably stay at least 1½m. *B. Hobbs.* 82

ACRANIAN GOLD 2 ch.f. Acrania 110–Indigold (Indigenous 121) [1976 5s] fourth foal: dam never ran: started slowly when tailed-off last of 18 in maiden race won by Military Queen at Warwick in October. *G. Gadd.* —

ACRONYM 3 b.c. Roan Rocket 128–Aberangell 96 (Abernant 142) [1975 7g 7g 1976 7fg 8h* 8g* 8f* 8s³ 8h² 8f³ 10h*] well-made colt: good mover: had a successful season, winning maiden race at Teesside and handicaps at Carlisle, Beverley and Pontefract: had a neck to spare over Merry Tudor on last-named course in August: stays 1¼m: best served by a sound surface and acts on hard going. *Sir Mark Prescott.* 86

ACTIONED 4 b.g. Dewan–Court Action (Court Martial) [1974 5g⁶ 1975 7s 10.4g 8fg 1976 8v⁶] well-made American-bred gelding: well behind in maiden race at Ayr in April, only outing as a 4-y-o. *A. Barclay.* —

ADAGIO 4 b.c. Tudor Melody 129–Darlene 117 (Dante) [1974 N.R. 1975 8v 10d* 1976 9fg⁶ 10g⁵ 12g³ 12f² 12fg* 12.3fg⁴ 11.7f* 10fg⁶ 14fg⁶] neat colt: fairly useful handicapper: successful at Newbury in June and Windsor the following month: had very poor run when creditable fourth to Warbeck at Newcastle in between: stays 1½m: appears to act on any going: wears blinkers. *R. Hern.* 92

ADAMIO 3 ch.g. Sole Mio–Ad Adama (Palestine 133) [1975 5g 5.1f 1976 7.2g 8f⁵ 8f² 7fg³(dis) 7f³ 10.6g² 9fg⁴ 8.2f*] useful plater: modest plater: attracted no bid when successful at Haydock in August: well suited by 1m although evidently stays 1¼m: acts on firm going: blinkered last three outings. *W. A. Stephenson.* 62

ADAM VAN VIANEN 3 b.c. Abdos 134–Nabua (Le Fabuleux 133) [1975 8s² 8.5s* 10s⁶ 1976 10.5s⁶ 11g³ 12s* 12g⁴ 13.5g⁶ 15.5s³] lengthy French colt: 121

Beenham Stakes, Newbury—a narrow win for Ad Lib Ra
(nearer camera) over Night Before

second foal: brother to useful French middle-distance winner Antipas: dam never ran: made much of running and kept on really well in straight when beaten 4 lengths and ½ length by Exceller and Sir Montagu in Prix Royal-Oak at Longchamp in September: had earlier won minor event at Chantilly and not been disgraced when 4 lengths fourth to Diagramatic in Grand Prix de Vichy and when about 7½ lengths sixth to Ashmore in Grand Prix de Deauville: evidently suited by a test of stamina: acts on soft going. *A. Paus, France.*

ADDIE 3 br.f. Klairon 131–Elia (Narrator 127) [1975 6g 6fg 7g 1976 8.2d 8.2d 11.1s] probably of no account. *M. James.* —

AD LIB 2 b.g. Free Boy 96–Adha 111 (The Phoenix) [1976 8fg 8.2s⁶ 8v] compact gelding: brother to plater Free Girl, a winner from 1m to 11f: showed a little ability in sellers in September, finishing seventh of 23 at Leicester and sixth of 22 at Nottingham. *R. Vibert.* **59**

AD LIB RA 2 b.c. Droll Role–Libra 97 (Hyperion) [1976 6g³ 6fg 8d*] neat, strong, good-bodied American-bred colt: very good mover: half-brother to several winners, including Oaks second Roses for the Star (by Stage Door Johnny) and Ribocco, Ribero and Libra's Rib (all by Ribot): dam, half-sister to Edmundo and Gloria Nicky, won at 2 yrs: favourite, held on well in a driving finish when winning 17-runner maiden race at Newbury in September by a head from Night Before, the pair finishing clear: will stay at least 1½m: likely to make a smart 3-y-o. *F. J. Houghton.* **106 p**

ADMIRAL COUNT 3 b.g. On Your Mark 125–Follette (Amour Drake 129) [1975 5fg 6f³ 7g² 6fg 7f⁵ 8.2g³ 1976 8.2d³ 8fg 8f* 12h³ 11f² 8f² 8f⁶ 10g 8g] lengthy gelding: made all when winning maiden race at Edinburgh in July by ½ length from Ascot Weather: effective at 1m and stays 11f but seemed to find 1½m beyond him: appears to act on any going: blinkered last two outings in 1975: **77**

suitable mount for a lady rider: sometimes has his tongue tied down: ran poorly last three outings. *H. Bell.*

ADMIRAL KANARIS 2 b.c. Great Nephew 126–Sardinia (Romulus 129) [1976 **87** 7.2fg⁵ 7g³ 7fg⁴ 7s 8v] lengthy, attractive colt: good walker: first foal: 8,400 gns yearling: dam won over 5f and 1m in France: ran well when 2½ lengths third of eight to Catiline in Donnington Castle Stakes at Newbury in July: did not reproduce that form, starting odds on on next outing and finishing well beaten in two nurseries (had stiff tasks): should stay 1m: seemed completely unsuited by heavy ground on final outing. *C. Brittain.*

ADORABELLA 3 ch.f. High Line 125–Orabella II 111 (Set Fair 129) [1975 **82** 5f 7g³ 8f⁶ 8g³ 8g⁶ 7g⁶ 1976 10f 10f* 12g⁴ 11.7fg² 12f⁴ 13.1h² 12f*] lightly-made filly: won handicap at Bath in May and claiming race at Newmarket in August, latter by 2½ lengths from Charles Martel: will probably stay further than 1½m (beaten 1½ lengths in two-horse affair over 13f): acts on firm going. *P. Cole.*

ADVISER 2 ch.c. Green God 128–Maureen's Slipper (Gratitude 130) [1976 5f² **121** 6fg* 6f* 6g* 6d² 6g⁴]

Adviser did not make it to the top in his first season but he is a good colt all the same, and the three races he won, he won running away. It was at Goodwood in July, in the Foxhall Maiden Stakes, that he gained his first success. Second favourite to Conifer on the strength of a promising second to the speedy filly Metair in the Myrobella Stakes at Salisbury two weeks previously, he went into the lead a furlong and a half from home and drew away, winning unchallenged. A fortnight later Adviser followed up this success by taking the Bulford Stakes at Salisbury by twelve lengths from a bad field, after which he was sent to Kempton, where he made nothing of the useful youngsters—Aspect, Local Knowledge and Swift Hussar—opposing him in a field of nine for the Sirenia Stakes, and led throughout, quickening below the distance and coming home clear by three lengths.

On the evidence of these performances there was every reason to believe that Adviser was capable of dealing with opposition much more exacting than that which he had been called upon to meet thus far, and on his next appearance he was made favourite, at 11/10 on, for the Mill Reef Stakes at Newbury in September. Of his five opponents, only Man in the Moon, a winner at Ascot and Haydock before finishing a good second to Nice Balance in the Seaton Delaval Stakes at Newcastle, and Anax, who had won the Champion Two-year-old Trophy at Ripon on his most recent appearance, were seriously backed against him. Anax beat him. As at Kempton, Adviser was in the lead from the start, but

Foxhall Stakes, Goodwood—Adviser wins in fluent style from Quick Retort, Donzel and the grey Village Swan

Mr Leonard Sainer's "Adviser"

under hard riding he could find no more in the last furlong, and went under by half a length. That Adviser was perhaps not at his best on this occasion was suggested by his behaviour in the paddock—he was very much on his toes and broke out into a sweat—and two weeks later he succeeded, by a head, in turning the tables on Anax in the William Hill Middle Park Stakes at Newmarket. Racing next to the stand rails, which at that particular meeting seemed to constitute something of a disadvantage, he showed good speed from the start only to find Tachypous, Nebbiolo and Mandrake Major just too strong in the last furlong. He was beaten a little over two lengths.

Adviser (ch.c. 1974)	Green God (ch 1968)	Red God (ch 1954)	Nasrullah / Spring Run
		Thetis II (ch 1957)	Guersant / Three Rock
	Maureen's Slipper (br 1967)	Gratitude (ch 1953)	Golden Cloud / Verdura
		Sabot D'Or (b 1957)	Princely Gift / Amber Slipper

By Green God and the second produce of a Gratitude mare who won over five furlongs in Ireland as a two-year-old, Adviser has the pedigree of a sprinter pure and simple, and we fancy that's what he'll turn out to be. An attractive, well-made individual, who cost 7,200 guineas as a yearling, Adviser probably acts on any going (he has yet to encounter the really soft stuff) and races most genuinely. He has been exported to South Africa. *P. Walwyn.*

AEGEAN PRINCE 2 ch.c. Crowned Prince 128–Mary Charlotte 93 (Charlottes- **75** ville 135) [1976 8s 8.2s³] useful-looking colt: third foal: half-brother to a minor winner in the U.S.A. by Sword Dancer: 4,300 gns foal and resold for 8,600 gns as a yearling: dam successful over 1¼m in Ireland at 3 yrs, and also won two races in the U.S.A.: not disgraced when 10 lengths third of 12 to Hot Grove in minor event at Haydock in October: lost chance at start on previous outing: should stay 1¼m. *C. Brittain.*

AERAS 2 br.c. So Blessed 130–Villa Tenata 73 (Vienna 127) [1976 5fg* 5f⁵ 5f³ 5fg* 5f² 6fg³ 6f³ 6fg⁶ 6g] robust colt: second living foal: dam stayed well: won 10-runner minor event at Leicester in March and came out best in a very tight finish to a well-contested event at Windsor in May, beating The Dundass a short head: close up on three other occasions: stays 6f: genuine and consistent but disappointed at Brighton on second outing (possibly unsuited by a switch-back track) and was well beaten last time out: sold 3,300 gns Newmarket Autumn Sales. *M. Smyly.*   **93**

AERELKO 3 b.c. Relko 136–Clouds Away (Nashua) [1975 6fg 7fg 8d 8g⁶ 8g 1976 8v 10g 10v 16f⁵ 12g² 13.8d* 13f⁵ 12.2g] compact colt: sweated up prior to winning 13-runner maiden race at Catterick in May all out by ¾ length from Harry Hedges: stays well: seems to need some give in the ground: usually wears blinkers nowadays: finished lame final outing. *D. Sasse.*   **66**

AERIAL FLIGHT 2 ch.g. Bally Russe 113–Way Up (Three Wishes 114) [1976 7fg 8fg] strong gelding: third foal: brother to two minor winners: dam never ran: backward when last in maiden races at Chester and Beverley in September. *D. Plant.*   **—**

AERIAL KIT 2 b.f. Communication 119–Liliberto (Umberto 118) [1976 5f 5fg 5d 7fg 5fg 8s] leggy filly: bad plater: sold 550 gns Doncaster October Sales. *L. Shedden.*   **—**

AERO 2 gr.f. Capistrano 120–Sinne (Tin Whistle 128) [1976 5d 5g] half-sister to Shepherd's Crook (by Current Coin), a winner from 5f to 1¼m: 200 gns yearling: dam never ran: last in minor events at Newcastle in April and Ayr in May: very unruly at Carlisle later in May and was withdrawn after getting loose: not seen out again. *T. Walker.*   **—**

AEROSOL 2 br.c. Great Nephew 126–Psalmodie (Nasram II 125) [1976 5.5d* 6d³ 6.5s*] French colt: first foal: dam won twice over 1¼m at 3 yrs and is daughter of sister to French Derby winner Sanctus II: successful in a newcomers race at Chantilly and in Group 3 Prix Eclipse at Saint-Cloud: having first race for over two months, led well inside final furlong when beating Angarius by 1½ lengths in latter race in October: will stay at least 1¼m: acts on soft going. *F. Boutin, France.*   **112**

AFFIDAVIT 2 br.f. Sahib 114–Lamplight 92 (Pall Mall 132) [1976 5fg 5f] small filly: first foal: dam won twice over 5f at 2 yrs, and stayed 9f: last in maiden races in the spring, starting slowly in first of them: trained by R. Simpson on first outing. *Miss N. Wilmot.*   **—**

AFFIRMATIVE 4 b.f. Derring-Do 131–Hayat 71 (Never Say Die 137) [1974 5g² 5g³ 1975 8g* 7f² 8fg* 8g² 8f⁴ 8f* 8f* 8g* 8g⁴ 1976 8d⁵ 7f³ 8g* 8.2g⁶ 9fg* 10.2f² 8.2g* 10f² 8h* 8g² 9g] compact filly: fairly useful handicapper: had another good season, winning at Thirsk, York, Nottingham and Pontefract: ran well on most of her other outings: stays 1¼m: acts on hard going: good mount for an apprentice: very tough, genuine and consistent: said to be in foal to Workboy. *M. H. Easterby.*   **90**

AFRICAN BEAT 3 b.c. Sing Sing 134–Tamergene 100 (Tamerlane 128) [1975 5s⁶ 5g⁴ 5.3f* 5fg⁵ 5f 6g 1976 5fg⁶ 5fg³ 6g³ 6f² 6fg³ 6f 5g⁴ 6g 6d³] small colt: quite a moderate handicapper: stays 6f: appears to act on any going: ran well when tried in blinkers on final outing. *C. Dingwall.*   **72**

AFRICAN DANCER 3 b.f. Nijinsky 138–Miba 109 (Ballymoss 136) [1975 6g 6fg 1976 7f⁶ 10fg⁵ 12.3s* 12g³ 12fg³ 12g 12fg² 14.6g* 12.5d 12v] Hardly a season goes by without Harry Wragg producing a smart three-year-old filly. Now, to a list which in recent years has included Lacquer, Sovereign, Full Dress II, Popkins, Favoletta, Cheveley Princess and Furioso, there must be added African Dancer. Unplaced but not disgraced in her two races as a youngster, she improved steadily through quite an arduous second season to end it probably the best filly of her age in this country racing at distances of a mile and a half or more. It must be said, though, that the English staying fillies weren't a particularly bright lot.   **116**

African Dancer first came into prominence in the Cheshire Oaks. The outsider of the party, as had been her stable-companion Old Bill when winning the previous day's Chester Vase, African Dancer relished the soft ground and ran

Cheshire Oaks, Chester—African Dancer is out on her own at the finish

away from her four opponents in the straight. The opposition could easily have been of sterner stuff, but next time out African Dancer started third favourite for the Oaks. After making the early running, she played second fiddle to Pawneese over a greater part of the final mile; she was beaten easily for speed, but in the end she held on to third place from her stable-mate Laughing Girl and Centrocon, nine lengths behind the winner. On terms 5 lb better Centrocon beat African Dancer into third place, with Catalpa intervening, in Haydock's Lancashire Oaks the following month, while in the Irish Guinness Oaks later in July African Dancer could finish only ninth to the French filly Lagunette.

Consequently, when African Dancer turned out for the Yorkshire Oaks she was easy to back at 16/1, with the Irish fillies I've A Bee and Sarah Siddons, third and second respectively in the Irish Guinness Oaks, heading the market. Sent on from the start at a brisk pace, African Dancer was ridden from half a mile out, but she responded well, beating off one challenge after another up the long straight until she finally succumbed to Sarah Siddons almost on the line. With no overseas challenge for the Park Hill Stakes at Doncaster the following month, African Dancer took her opportunity to win an important prize. There was still

Park Hill Stakes, Doncaster—African Dancer reverses Epsom Oaks placings with Roses for the Star. The third horse is Centrocon

a competitive field, with all the best of the English-trained staying fillies taking part. Favourite was Roses for the Star who had looked an unlucky loser when finishing a length behind African Dancer at York. Second favourite was the lightly-raced Mayo Girl, a close-up fifth in the Yorkshire Oaks when having her first outing for three months. African Dancer came next in the betting. Also in the field were the Ribblesdale winner Catalpa, Centrocon, Laughing Girl, the handicappers Iona and Lamb's Tale and Highclere's half-sister Christchurch.

For a time it looked as though the race would start without African Dancer: she was very difficult to en-stall. Nevertheless she did go in, and she jumped off safely, settling down in the middle of the field as Catalpa and Centrocon made the running at a good lick. By the time the straight was reached almost all the runners, including African Dancer, were off the bridle. As Catalpa dropped back over three furlongs out, African Dancer started to make a steady run which took her to the front at the distance. Staying on well, she won by a length and a half from Roses for the Star with Centrocon two lengths further back. African Dancer was reported by the starter, which meant that it would have been impossible for her to take part in the St Leger two days later (she had been declared to run at the four-day stage) even if her owner had wanted to run her; at least twenty-four hours notice must be given of a stalls test, and the test cannot be taken on the day of an intended race. African Dancer did run twice after the Park Hill, but added little to her reputation, being beaten about six lengths by Paint the Town in the Prix de Royallieu and finishing well back in the St Simon Stakes.

African Dancer (b.f. 1973)	Nijinsky (b 1967)	Northern Dancer (b 1961)	Nearctic
			Natalma
		Flaming Page (b 1959)	Bull Page
			Flaring Top
	Miba (b 1962)	Ballymoss (ch 1954)	Mossborough
			Indian Call
		Stop your Tickling (bl 1949)	Jock II
			Senatrix

African Dancer is easily the best produce of her dam Miba. Of Miba's five previous foals, four won, the pick being those quite useful performers Taxco (by

Sir Philip Oppenheimer's "African Dancer"

Silver Shark), a winner at up to a mile and a quarter, and Shaba (by Shantung), a winner at up to a mile and three quarters. Miba was one of the best English middle-distance fillies of her year; she won the Princess Elizabeth Stakes at Epsom and the Pretty Polly Stakes at Newmarket and gained a place in the Ribblesdale and Park Hill. Incidentally, Miba finished just behind Mabel in her Park Hill; Mabel became the dam of the 1975 Park Hill winner May Hill. Miba comes from a good winner-producing family; her half-sisters Ticklish and Proper Pretty have produced, respectively, those well-known performers Caius and Duboff, while one of her daughters, Ya Ya, has produced Fluellen.

A strong, shapely, attractive filly, African Dancer was a great credit to her trainer who invariably turned her out looking really well. It says much for her constitution that she maintained her form and enthusiasm for most of a long campaign (she was on the go from early April to late October) and she is as genuine a filly as you could hope to find. She should do very well as a broodmare and will visit Welsh Pageant in 1977. *H. Wragg.*

AFRICAN VIOLET 2 b.f. Amber Rama 133–St Brigid 81 (Molvedo 137) [1976 5fg 5g 5f² 5.8f* 5fg³ 5s⁴] small, sturdy filly: fourth foal: half-sister to winners abroad by Raffingora and Tycoon II: dam stayed 1m: favourite when winning eight-runner maiden race at Bath in September by 2½ lengths from May Bride: ran creditably in nurseries afterwards: will stay 7f+: acts on any going: sold 5,200 gns Newmarket Autumn Sales. *P. Walwyn.* **83**

AFRICA STAR 4 br.c. Tobrouk–Kelly Castle (Kelly 122) [1974 5fg⁶ 5fg 1975 6s 7s⁶ 8g 6v⁶ 7f⁶ 10f⁶ 11f⁴ 11d* 15g⁴ 11h⁵ 10h 1976 8.2v² 10f² 8g³ 8d⁴ 10f² 8f* 11g³ 9f* 10.6g⁴ 8f⁴ 8g² 8g 8s*] selling handicapper: winner at Doncaster in July and at Wolverhampton in August and October: will stay 1¼m (had no chance at weights when well behind over 15f): acts on any going: has won without blinkers but wears them nowadays: suitable mount for an apprentice: consistent. *A. Balding.* **53**

AHDEEK 4 b.c. Reindeer 124–Pocahontas II (Roman) [1974 7s* 9s⁵ 7.3s³ 1975 8.5d⁵ 10g⁵ 12g 10g* 1976 12fg* 12d² 12g* 10g⁵ 12fg³ 16.1fg⁴ 16g⁴ 12g⁴] strong, good-looking colt: particularly good mover: made a very fine start to season, winning Dean Swift Handicap at Epsom, Ladbroke Handicap at Kempton and finishing good second to Ribellaro in David Dixon Gold Cup at York (all before end of May): most disappointing afterwards and showed little enthusiasm on seventh outing when fourth to Night In Town in Brown Jack Stakes at Ascot in July: best form at up to 1½m: probably acts on any going: blinkered fourth start: sold 10,500 gns Newmarket December Sales. *R. Armstrong.* **108**

AINSLEY BOY 4 ch.c. Virginia Boy 106–Lady Player (Ballyciptic 122) [1974 5d 5.1g 5g 1975 5v 6s* 6g² 8f⁴ 6h* 5fg³ 8g⁴ 6f* 6fg⁶ 6fg⁴ 6g 6f 1976 7fg 5g² 6fg 7.2d³ 6f 8f 6g⁴ 7f 8f] useful sort of colt: quite a moderate handicapper: no worthwhile form after fourth outing: stays 7f but has shown best form at 6f: acts on any going: suitable mount for an apprentice: blinkered seventh and eighth appearances: trained by V. Mitchell first two starts in 1976: sold 2,000 gns Newmarket September Sales. *F. Dever.* **70 d**

AINTREE PALS 3 gr.g. Pals Passage 115–Dorstar (Star Moss 122) [1975 5g⁶ 5v⁴ 5f 7f⁵ 6fg³ 7f 7g⁴ 1976 10.8f 10f⁵] light-framed gelding: showed some ability at 2 yrs: lightly raced and no worthwhile form in 1976. *Mrs R. Lomax.* **—**

AIR PERUVIAN 2 ch.c. Sadair–Anglo Peruvian (My Babu 136) [1976 8s*] American-bred French colt: fifth produce: half-brother to a minor winner in U.S.A.: 29,000 dollars foal: dam, a stakes winner at up to 6f at 2 yrs, is half-sister to French 1,000 Guineas winner Pampered Miss (by Sadair) and to Empery: favourite for 23-runner newcomers event at Saint-Cloud in October and put up a promising effort to win by a length from Natchitoches: will probably stay 1¼m: sure to go on to better things. *A. Head, France.* **?**

AIR TROOPER 3 ch.c. King's Troop 118–Aries (Acropolis 132) [1975 7d 6fg² 7g⁵ 7g⁴ 1976 8f⁶ 8g⁶ 7g³ 8.2f* 8f* 10fg⁴ 10fg³ 9f² 8g⁶ 10g³] compact colt: won 12-runner maiden race at Nottingham in June and handicap at Salisbury in July, latter by a head from Lord Elect: first past post in £2,000 handicap at Ripon in August, having 3 lengths to spare over Confessor, but was relegated to second place following a stewards' inquiry and an objection as he had accidentally hampered runner-up when crossing to rails 2f out (was most certainly winner on merit in our opinion): ran easily better subsequent race on final appearance: needs further than 7f and stays 1¼m: acts on firm going. *W. Wightman.* **84**

AIRWAYS 4 br.f. Bally Russe 113–Way Up (Three Wishes 114) [1974 5f 5f 5f 5fg* 6h⁴ 6g⁵ 5fg 1975 8s⁵ 8g⁴ 9fg⁶ 8.2fg 8h³ 9fg 9fg⁴ 7.2fg 8fg 8g 9fg⁴ 8f 8.2s **—**

1976 7g 8f 10fg] small filly: poor plater: acts on hard going: has worn blinkers but didn't as a 4-y-o. *S. Nesbitt.*

ALACRITER 3 b.f. Mountain Call 125–Rubella (Buisson Ardent 129) [1975 **98** 5fg* 5f* 5fg* 5fg² 5g* 5fg² 5g⁵ 1976 6fg 8g⁵ 8fg³ 8g 8h³ 7g⁶ 5.8f] well-made filly: good mover: useful as a 2-y-o and won four races: unsuccessful in 1976, often facing stiff tasks, and became disappointing (blinkered last three outings): probably stays 1m: sold 5,000 gns Newmarket December Sales. *J. Nelson.*

ALANROD 3 gr.c. Gala Performance–Miss Fenton 98 (Palestine 133) [1975 **103** 5s² 5d* 5s² 1976 5fg 5fg 6g³ 6fg 7.6g⁵ 7g 7f² 7d⁶ 5d 6v* 5s³] useful-looking colt and a nice mover: showed useful form from time to time, but didn't manage to win until October when beating Oudalia convincingly by 3 lengths in handicap at Newbury, wearing a hood for first time: stays 7f: acts on any going but is particularly well suited by soft: blinkered eighth and ninth starts, hooded last two: trained until after third outing by S. Ingham. *R. Hannon.*

ALBA RETTER 3 b.f. Alba Rock 107–Half Price (Counsel 118) [1975 N.R. — 1976 12s] half-bred filly: dam lightly-raced novice hurdler: sweating and dwelt when behind in maiden race won by Tudor Wynk at Chepstow in October. *L. Kennard.*

ALBION PRINCE 2 b.c. Prince Regent 129–Albionia 85 (Faberge II 121) **69 p** [1976 8d 8s] quite attractive, compact colt: second foal: 8,600 gns yearling: dam won at up to 1m: unquoted and distinctly in need of race, ran well considering his lack of peak fitness when eighth of 17 to Ad Lib Ra in maiden race at Newbury in September: in rear in 28-runner maiden race won by Royal Boxer at Newmarket the following month: should stay middle distances: sure to do better in time. *M. Jarvis.*

ALBRIGHTON 4 b.c. Alcide 136–Peep of Dawn 76 (Constable 129) [1974 7fg **105** 8s* 1975 10v* 12s³ 13.4g³ 11fg⁴ 14.8g* 13fg² 16g⁴ 16g² 1976 16fg*(w.o.) 14fg* 16fg* 16fg⁵ 16.1fg² 19fg² 16.1f³ 19s⁶] smallish, good-looking colt: useful handicapper: winner at Yarmouth in May, Ascot in June and Newmarket the following month: creditable second (had no chance with winner but finished well clear of remainder) to Sea Anchor in Goodwood Stakes later in July: well beaten last two outings: stays well: seems to act on any going but is well suited by top-of-the-ground conditions: genuine and consistent. *H. Cecil.*

ALCAYDE 4 b.g. Burglar 128–Little Alice (Djefou) [1974 5g 6g 7v⁴ 7g⁴ 8s* 8g — 1975 7s 7s² 10s⁴ 9g³ 7f⁴ 12.2f⁶ 12f 8g 8g 10fg 1976 8.2s 10.2s 10v 12v] big, tall, rangy gelding: little worthwhile form since his early 3-y-o days: seems to stay 1¼m: acts on any going. *B. Richmond.*

ALCIDETTE 3 br.f. Alcide 136–Bamford Queen (Rise 'N Shine II) [1975 5s **110** 1976 6s 8s 6g 10f² 10f³ 9g² 8f* 10f³ 11f³ 8f⁵ 12f³ 12f² 12f* 12s 10s²] second foal: half-sister to The Nadi Royale (by My Swanee), quite a useful handicapper at up to 1m: dam won four races from 9f to 13f in Ireland and also won over hurdles: won maiden race at Thurles in June: showed much improved form against stiffer opposition subsequently, finishing 5½ lengths third to Northern Treasure in Blandford Stakes and neck second to Slap Up in Brownstown Stakes, both races at the Curragh, and then trouncing some useful fillies in minor event at Limerick in September, beating Extravaganza by 5 lengths: well suited by middle distances and will stay further: acts on any going. *P. Mullins, Ireland.*

ALCOCK 3 b.g. Alcide 136–Bird 80 (Firestreak 125) [1975 N.R. 1976 12.2fg — 14.7d⁴ 16.1v] first foal: dam won at 1m: showed only worthwhile form when 6 lengths fourth of nine to Ruddy Sam in minor event at Redcar in September. *W. Elsey.*

ALDBURY GIRL 6 ch.m. Galivanter 131–Fire Song 107 (The Phoenix) [1974 — N.R. 1975 N.R. 1976 7fg 6g 7f] of little account nowadays: not raced after May and was sold to T. Craig 1,100 gns Newmarket Autumn Sales. *Mrs R. Lomax.*

ALDIE 10 gr.g. Goose Creek 116–Elegy (Our Babu 131) [1974 9f⁶ 10g 10g 10f **70** 10f* 10g³ 9d⁶ 9s* 10g³ 10s 10d² 1975 9v⁵ 10g 10g 10f* 8fg 10f² 10h³ 10fg³ 10g⁴ 10fg³ 10.2f* 10f³ 10.2g 10g 10g 1976 10f² 9g 10f 10f 10f² 12h³ 10h² 10fg³ 9g⁴ 10f⁶ 10.2f³ 10f 10.2s⁴ 10s] one-time useful handicapper but has deteriorated considerably: best at 1¼m: acts on any going but is well suited by firm ground: suitable mount for a boy: normally a front runner. *I. Balding.*

A-LEVEL GIRL 3 b.f. Behistoun 131–Requisite 87 (Prince Chevalier) [1975 **51** 8f 8g 1976 10f⁶ 9f 14d⁶ 12fg⁵ 15.5s⁶] poor form in maiden and minor events. *D. Weeden.*

ALEXANDA THE GREAT 2 br.c. So Blessed 130–Arkadia 74 (Larkspur 128)   89
[1976 6d⁶ 6s²]   second foal: 10,500 gns yearling: dam, winner over 1¼m, is half-sister to very smart Tesco Boy: put up a good first effort when sixth of 23 to Running Bull in maiden race at Newmarket in October, finishing in good style to be beaten only about 1½ lengths: again ran on strongly when length second to Tudor Jig in 24-runner minor event at Teesside the following month: will be suited by 1m+: sure to win races in the north. *S. Hall.*

ALFIE ROSE 3 b.c. St Alphage 119–Dixie Rose (Le Dieu d'Or 119) [1975 N.R.   —
1976 5g⁶ 7g]   big, tall, well-made colt: half-brother to three winners here and abroad: 1,000 gns foal and resold 700 gns yearling: dam won over 1m in Ireland: showed signs of ability in maiden races at Kempton in August but probably needs more time: sold 680 gns Doncaster September Sales. *R. Price.*

ALGORA 4 gr.c. Raffingora 130–Alsvider (Zimone) [1974 5h³ 5f* 5fg* 5g⁴   81
6fg³ 5fg³ 5d² 5s⁴ 5s 5v*   1975 5v 5d 5g 6f⁴ 5fg² 5fg⁴ 5g² 5g 5f 5f² 5g⁴ 5d 6d 5g
1976 6f 5fg 6g 6fg² 5d* 6f³ 5fg⁴ 6f³ 5fg³]   strong, compact colt: moderate handicapper on his day: odds on when winning at Redcar in June by 5 lengths from Anton Lad: ran creditably afterwards: stays 6f: acts on firm going but is extremely well suited by heavy: wears blinkers: didn't get the best of breaks on final appearance (July). *M. W. Easterby.*

ALHIB 3 br.c. Sahib 114–Altruism 71 (Alcide 136) [1975 5g 6f 8f 8v   1976   82
10.8fg² 10f* 9d⁵ 10fg² 10g* 11s* 10f⁶]   smallish colt: much improved from 2 yrs to 3 yrs and won maiden race at Beverley and handicaps at Leicester and Ayr: just held off Princely on last-named course in June: well beaten under a stiff weight on final outing later in month: possibly finds 9f on sharp side and will stay 1½m: acts on any going: genuine: sold 1,350 gns Ascot November Sales. *G. Pritchard-Gordon.*

ALIANTE 3 ch.c. Busted 134–Glider 82 (Buisson Ardent 129) [1975 N.R.   1976   99
10f* 10fg* 10fg* 10.6g² 11s³ 10g 8v]   well-made, useful sort of colt: closely related to very useful middle-distance performer Donello (by Crepello), and half-brother to several other winners, including Juggernaut (by Ragusa), a very useful performer at up to 1½m: 17,500 gns yearling: dam won over 1m: short-priced favourite when winning minor events at Yarmouth and Leicester and handicap at Newmarket in August: creditable second to Chemin de Fer in £4,000 handicap at Haydock in August: subsequently sent to race in Italy and finished good third in a pattern event at Milan in September: will stay 1½m: said to have had leg trouble and to require some give in the ground to be seen to best advantage: trained by H. Cecil in England. *S. Cumani, Italy.*

ALICE DECOY 3 b.f. Decoy Boy 129–Alice (Parthia 132) [1975 5s 5d 5f⁵ 5f⁴   57
5h⁴ 7f⁵ 7g²   1976 8d⁴ 6g 6d 7g³ 7.2fg]   small, strong-quartered filly: plater: appears to stay 1m: suited by some give in the ground and ran as though feeling hard going on fifth outing in 1975: blinkered last two outings (ran creditably on first): sold to H. Blackshaw 460 gns Newmarket July Sales. *F. Carr.*

ALI-DEE 2 b.c. Native Prince–Welcome Dona 82 (Fighting Don) [1976 5s 6d   77
6f*]   well-grown colt: won seven-runner auction seller at Pontefract in June by 1½ lengths from Lillivanter: sold afterwards for 1,650 gns for export to Belgium where he won at least twice: wore blinkers in this country. *P. Haslam.*

ALI FOREVER 3 b.g. Brave Invader–Royal Account (Henry the Seventh 125)   70 d
[1975 6g 7g 8g   1976 9f 12.3s 12.2f⁴ 12g* 12.2g⁶ 12f² 13g⁴ 12f⁶ 12f⁵ 13.8g⁴ 10g 13g]
well-grown, long-striding gelding: won maiden race at Hamilton in May: ran poorly in most of his other races and is not one to rely on: stays 1½m: sometimes sweats up: very slowly away penultimate start (lady ridden). *K. Payne.*

ALINE MARGARET 4 b.f. Cagirama 103–Lady Forlorn (Lord of Verona 120)   —
[1974 5g 5g⁵ 5f⁴ 5f⁴ 5g⁵   1975 12s⁶ 8g 11g 8g 8f 8g⁵ 8g 11g³ 8f² 12g 9g⁶ 8g⁵ 7g
1976 8g 8f 13g 15f⁵ 11g⁵ 20f]   plater: no worthwhile form as a 4-y-o: acts on firm going: not raced after July. *T. Craig.*

ALISON SARAH 3 ch.f. Mountain Call 125–Maiden's Blush (Fortino II 120)   —
[1975 5fg 5g 7f 7v 6g   1976 8h 6f 8fg 6f³ 8h² 8f⁶ 7f² 10h]   poor plater: stayed 1m: blinkered third outing: destroyed after breaking leg at Pontefract in September. *J. Mulhall.*

ALISON'S JEWEL 4 b.f. Carlemont 132–Nisi 95 (Krakatao 130) [1974 5f 5g   57
5s⁵ 8s   1975 6f⁶ 8f 8f³ 5.8f⁵ 10.2h⁴ 8d 10fg   1976 8h³ 7f 13.1s]   rangy American-bred filly: poor maiden: ran her best race of season over 1m (should stay further):

has worn blinkers but didn't at 4 yrs: sold 340 gns Ascot October Sales. *R. Turnell.*

ALISON'S MY GIRL 3 b.f. Appiani II 128–Flaunt (Soleil II 133) [1975 7f 6g **59** 7f 7f⁵ 7f 9fg⁵ 9g⁴ 10g* 1976 12f⁵ 13fg⁵ 10f 11.1f⁴ 12.2g² 13f⁴ 12fg⁵ 10f² 10f 12f³] poor handicapper: stays 1½m: has worn blinkers but does better without: has occasionally started slowly: trained by J. Harris first two outings. *R. Hollinshead.*

ALL AMBER 2 ch.c. Amber Rama 133–Doushiska 78 (Hornbeam 130) [1976 8g **66** 8d] well-made colt: half-brother to 1½m winner Habitual (by Habitat): dam won at 1½m: showed a little ability, finishing eighth to Royal Flume in £2,400 event at York in September and being prominent for 6f in maiden race won by Ad Lib Ra at Newbury later in month: sold 1,800 gns Ascot October Sales. *J. Nelson.*

ALLAN WATER 3 b.c. Allangrange 126–Miss Jones 61 (March Past 124) **77** [1975 N.R. 1976 8f⁵ 10g⁶ 8.2g⁶ 8f* 8f2] strong, workmanlike colt: good mover: half-brother to three minor winners: 2,200 gns yearling: dam ran only twice: having first race since May, turned in a game performance when winning 21-runner maiden event at Ripon by ½ length from Henry Stuart: odds on when narrowly beaten by Loudly in minor event at Thirsk the following month: will be well suited by further than 1m (had stiff task when tried at 1¼m): acts on firm going. *R. Price.*

ALL BONUS 3 br.g. All Tan–Maiden Venture (Eastern Venture 107) [1975 — N.R. 1976 12s] first foal: dam poor novice hurdler: unquoted when behind in maiden race won by Tudor Wynk at Chepstow in October. *J. S. Evans.*

ALL BOY 2 b.c. Right Boy 137–Earall (Khalkis 127) [1976 5s 5v] third foal: — half-brother to fair middle-distance handicapper Lochranza (by Highland Melody) and 3-y-o 1½m winner Chebbie (by Chebs Lad): dam tailed off on both outings: well behind in October in maiden races at Doncaster and Nottingham. *W. Wharton.*

ALLEGED 2 b.c. Hoist the Flag–Princess Pout (Prince John) [1976 7s*] first **112 p** living foal: $34,000 yearling, $175,000 2-y-o: dam won 13 races in U.S.A., most of them at 4 yrs and 5 yrs, and showed high-class form on grass at up to 9f: co-favourite for 15-runner maiden race at the Curragh in November and ran out an impressive 8-length winner from Asante Sana: will stay 1½m: sure to go on to better things. *V. O'Brien, Ireland.*

ALLEVIATE 3 b.f. Levmoss 133–Anxious Call (Whistler 129) [1975 7.6g⁶ — 1976 12f 8fg 8g⁵ 8fg 12g] no worthwhile form in maiden and minor events: sometimes sweats up. *S. Woodman.*

ALLEYDATE 3 ch.f. Twilight Alley 133–Candydate 86 (Canisbay 120) [1976 — 5s 5fg 6f⁴ 7f⁶ 6h] very unimpressive both in appearance and performance. *S. Norton.*

ALLEY TOR 2 b.c. Carrara–Smock Alley (Grandmaster) [1976 8s 7v] half- — brother to winning plater: tenth of 19 to Nordman in maiden race at Sandown in October: collapsed and died at Lingfield the following month. *M. Francis.*

ALLEZ BRITAIN 3 ch.g. Double-U-Jay 120–Incendo (Ionian 128) [1975 5f⁴ **92** 5f⁶ 5fg 1976 6g 6g 5g 6fg⁴ 6g² 5.3f* 5f³ 6f* 6fg* 6f² 6h* 5g 5fg² 7s 7s] attractive, strong, compact gelding: quite a useful handicapper: in good form in the summer and won at Brighton (twice, one a maiden race), Folkestone and Windsor: best form at 5f or 6f on a sound surface. *B. Swift.*

ALLEZ STANWICK 3 b.f. Goldhill 125–Stone's Throw (Tenerani 135) [1975 **64** 5g 5f⁶ 7g³ 6g² 6h⁵ 1976 8fg 7g⁶ 8f 6g 9.4h⁴ 7f* 7f⁵ 7g] leggy filly: won seller at Catterick in August (no bid): should stay 1m: acts on firm going. *Denys Smith.*

ALL FRIENDS 4 gr.c. Don II 123–Radio Manx 84 (Tudor Melody 129) [1974 **116** 5g* 5f² 5f* 6.3g³ 6.3s* 8s² 5v* 1975 7v 8.5fg* 8f⁴ 7g 8g 8f⁶ 8fg³ 8fg 10d⁶ 1976 8f³ 7.6d* 7g⁴ 8.5g* 8f⁵ 7.6fg² 8f² 7.3fg 8fg2] strong, shapely, good-topped colt: good walker: a smart animal as he showed when winning Group 3 Diomed Stakes at Epsom in June for second year in succession, holding off Sauceboat in most game fashion throughout the final furlong: successful earlier in season in Earl of Chester Handicap at Chester: ran well on nearly all his other outings, notably when ½-length second to Nearly New (rec 26 lb) in Watney Mann Stakes at Lingfield in July and when runner-up to Waldlaufer in valuable Spreti-Memorial at Munich later the same month: stays 1m: acts on any going: particularly well

Diomed Stakes, Epsom—All Friends just holds the renewed challenge of Sauceboat (left). Homeboy finishes third

suited by a sharp track: blinkered last three outings in 1975: very genuine and consistent. *N. Vigors.*

ALL HOPE 3 b.c. My Swallow 134–Let's Hope (One Count) [1975 6g* 7fg³ **104** 1976 7fg 8.5g³ 6d⁶ 8fg² 7f 8f⁵ 8h⁵ 9f 8d² 8v⁴ 7s²] strong, well-grown, most attractive individual: good walker and mover: put up some very useful perform-ances, including when runner-up in two races at Newbury, Hermitage Stakes in June (to Dominion) and Arlington Stakes in September (to Patris), and when second of 12 to wide-margin winner Fleur d'Amour in Playboy Bookmakers Handicap at Sandown in October: also ran moderately many times and is inconsis-tent: stays 1m: possibly unsuited by heavy ground. *M. Jarvis.*

ALLOWAY TREASON 3 br.g. Alloway Lad 103–Never Miss (Never Dwell 89) — [1975 5fg 1976 8f] evidently of no account. *G. Wallace.*

ALLREY 3 ch.g. Roan Rocket 128–Scottish Circuit 87 (King's Bench 132) [1975 **73** 6g³ 6g⁴ 8s⁵ 8g 1976 9f 10f⁴ 12.3fg³ 10f² 12.2f⁴ 10fg*] strong, compact, robust gelding: showed improved form when winning nine-runner maiden race at Ripon in August all out by a neck from Alvage, the pair finishing clear: had run respect-ably in blinkers previous two outings: evidently stays 1½m: best form on a sound surface: sold to D. Barons 4,300 gns Newmarket Autumn Sales. *J. Etherington.*

ALL SERENE 2 br.f. Le Levanstell 122–Fortunal (Fortino II 120) [1976 6g⁶ **104** 6f* 6f² 7f* 6f] Irish filly: second foal: half-sister to very useful Irish 3-y-o Festive Morn (by Gala Performance). a winner over 6f at 2 yrs: dam, placed over 1m at 2 yrs, is half-sister to Chamozzle and Richard Grenville: successful twice at Phoenix Park, winning 10-runner maiden race in July by short head and 11-runner Park Stakes in September by ½ length from Miller's Lass: also ran well when length second to Regal Ray in Moyglare Stud Stakes at the Curragh in between but finished last of 15 to Lordedaw when short-priced favourite for valuable nursery at Naas in October: will stay 1¼m: acts on firm going. *V. O'Brien, Ireland.*

ALLSPICE 3 b.f. Frankincense 120–Alecto 76 (Combat 123) [1975 5fg 5fg — 1976 9f 10.6g 11.5d] tall, leggy filly: well behind in maiden races: sold 280 gns Ascot December Sales. *T. Molony.*

ALLTYRE 2 b.c. Tamerlane 128–Pyelogram 65 (Umberto 118) [1976 5fg 5g **97** 5f⁶ 7g⁵ 6g 6g² 6s 8s 6s⁴ 7s³ 7s* 7.6v] neat colt: half-brother to a winner over jumps in France: 750 gns yearling: dam a stayer: inconsistent but is fairly useful on his day: made virtually all to win 19-runner minor event at Chepstow in October by 1½ lengths from Nobody's Fool: stays 7f well and should stay further: acts on soft going: trained by D. Keith on first two outings. *D. Underwood.*

ALOFT 2 br.f. High Top 131–Over the Water II (Doutelle 128) [1976 6g³] **88 p** strong filly: half-sister to a winning sprinter by Mountain Call: dam won over 11f in France: 25/1 and backward, put up a promising first effort when 1½ lengths third of 30 to Rheola in maiden race at Newmarket in September, keeping on well over final 2f to be nearest at finish: will be suited by 1m or more: was nowhere near peak fitness at Newmarket and is a useful filly in the making. *B. Hills.*

ALOHA PRINCE 4 b.c. Native Prince–Welcome Jess 82 (Ballymoss 136) [1974 **—** N.R. 1975 8g 8g⁴ 8.2g 1976 10.2s] of little account. *H. Westbrook.*

ALPHA ELK 3 ch.g. St Alphage 119–Elka (Pardal 130) [1975 5f 6g⁶ 7g⁶ 1976 **—** 9v] leggy gelding: quite moderate form in 1975, when well-backed favourite on last two outings: 25/1 and in need of race when tailed off in minor event at Newcastle in October on only outing in 1976. *G. Richards.*

ALPHERAT 2 gr.c. Amber Rama 133–Pearlemor 93 (Gulf Pearl 117) [1976 5g* **115** 5g* 5f² 6g³ 7s³ 8d⁴ 8v⁴] strong, rather hollow-backed Italian colt: second foal: half-brother to fair sprint winner Grey Ghost (by Yellow God): 10,000 gns foal: dam won three times over 5f and is half-sister to Steel Heart: won his first two races, both at Rome, in the style of a very useful colt, cantering away with Premio Kariba and then scoring by 6 lengths from previous winner Maierato in Premio Aniene: in frame subsequently in good races, finishing 4 lengths second to Gods-walk in Norfolk Stakes at Royal Ascot, third to Blushing Groom in both Prix Morny at Deauville (beaten 3¼ lengths) and Prix de la Salamandre at Longchamp (beaten 2¾ lengths), and fourth in Grand Criterium at Longchamp and Premio Tevere at Rome: stays 1m: acts on any going. *A. Perrone, Italy.*

ALPINE CALL 2 ch.c. Mountain Call 125–Sticky Wicket (Quorum 126) [1976 **—** 6g 6d 6v] well-grown colt: only poor form in maiden and minor events. *A. Johnson.*

ALSBURG 2 ch.f. Burglar 128–Alsaga 86 (Alcide 136) [1976 5fg 6d 7f] ap- **—** parently of no account. *W. Gray.*

AL STANZA 2 gr.f. Al Hattab–Light Verse (Reverse) [1976 5fg² 5fg* 6fg² 6g* **112** 6fg⁶ 6v² 8s]
European owners and trainers interested in racing American stock but unable to afford the prices at the show-piece Saratoga and Keeneland Sales may find a visit to the Hialeah Sales of two-year-olds in training worthwhile. Al Stanza was bought there by Robert Armstrong in January for 11,500 dollars, a modest

Princess Margaret Stakes, Ascot—Al Stanza has the measure of Swagger (right), Great Flight and Rings (partly obscured by the winner)

sum by American standards and, now that she has been raced, a bargain by any standards. She came out of a strenuous first season with wins in two races at Ascot to her credit, as well as second place in pattern races at Newmarket (the Cherry Hinton Stakes) and Baden-Baden (the Zukunfts-Rennen). She is not out of the top drawer, not a classic prospect, but she is, nevertheless, more than useful.

Al Stanza took the Erroll Stakes and the Princess Margaret Stakes at Ascot, in the latter paying a compliment to the highly-regarded Ampulla, who had beaten her, receiving 3 lb, in the Cherry Hinton in between. For all that she had less than a length to spare over Swagger in the Princess Margaret, Al Stanza won decisively, never seeming likely to be headed after gaining the lead at the distance, and her win counted for a lot more than her previous one on the track, when she had very little to beat for a race worth as much as the Erroll Stakes. Al Stanza, Ampulla and Swagger were each put in their place in their next race, the Lowther Stakes at York in August, where in finishing fifth, sixth and seventh respectively to Icena they all ran as though finding six furlongs on top of the ground on the sharp side for them.

Al Stanza got her chance at a longer distance in the Criterium des Pouliches at Longchamp in October. Before then she was presented with the opportunity to race over a testing six furlongs when rain soaked the course for the Zukunfts-Rennen; and she ran a splendid race in the mud, losing narrowly to the home-trained Cagliostro, with Faridetta about three lengths behind her carrying the same weight. Al Stanza tackled a mile at Longchamp and was well beaten, but in all fairness to her she didn't have much of a chance of winning a race of that description. She is some way below the standard usually required, she started at 47/1 and she finished out of the first ten behind Kamicia.

Al Stanza (gr.f. 1974)	Al Hattab (ro 1966)	The Axe (gr 1958)	Mahmoud Blackball
		Abyssinia (gr 1953)	Abernant Serengeti
	Light Verse (b 1970)	Reverse (b 1962)	Turn-to Miss Grundy
		Brighton View (ch 1962)	Tuscany Evening Sun

As a three-year-old Al Stanza will almost certainly show that she stays a mile, and she will probably stay further, although her sire's best-known runner, the Poule d'Essai des Poulains second Roan Star, has been a disappointment over longer distances. The sire, Al Hattab, winner of sixteen races including the nine-furlong Jersey Derby, was one of the leading sires of two-year-olds in the United States in 1976. The dam never ran and Al Stanza is her first foal. Light Verse's sire, Reverse, was runner-up in the Jersey Derby; her dam Brighton View won a five-furlong claiming race as a three-year-old but was by Tuscany, whose biggest winner by far was the champion steeplechaser Tuscalee. Light Verse is a half-sister to two winners at up to a mile in the States, including the stakes winner Weekend Fun. Al Stanza is a genuine filly and she seems to be able to act on any going. *R. Armstrong.*

ALTA 4 ch.c. Midsummer Night II 117–Thoughtful Light 85 (Borealis) [1974 **55** 6g 5fg 7g 1975 9v 7fg³ 8fg³ 8.2f* 10fg³ 8.2f² 8g³ 8g 8g 1976 8d⁴ 9g 8f⁵ 8f 8f⁵ 8h⁶] poor handicapper: has yet to show conclusively that he stays further than 1m: acts on firm going and a soft surface: tried in blinkers on fourth outing (ran freely): inconsistent: sold 5,200 gns Newmarket Autumn Sales. *R. D. Peacock.*

ALTEZZA 3 ch.c. Busted 134–Fortezza 106 (Botticelli 129) [1975 N.R. 1976 — 8fg 10.5s] strong, lengthy colt: half-brother to two winners, including very useful 1m to 2m winner Hurrah (by Exbury): dam a miler: backward when behind in Wood Ditton Stakes at Newmarket in April (eighth of 14 to Danestic) and Glasgow Stakes at York the following month, dwelling on first occasion: sold 840 gns Newmarket Autumn Sales. *H. Wragg.*

ALTOGETHER NOW 2 b.f. Tamerlane 128–Altogether 91 (Faberge II 121) **52** [1976 5s 5g 5f⁶ 6fg 7fg⁵ 7s] small, light-framed filly: second foal: 420 gns yearling: dam won Chester Cup: only poor form in sellers: will stay well. *J. Powney.*

ALUIZA RIVER 3 b.g. The Bo'sun 114–Clover Bloom (Solon Morn 109) [1975 — N.R. 1976 10.8fg 12g 10fg 8g 8v] workmanlike gelding: probably of little account. *K. Ivory.*

Freemen of York Handicap, York—Alverton (No. 11) wears down Chas Sawyer

ALUMIA 2 br.f. Great Nephew 126–Carcosa 103 (Sovereign Lord 120) [1976 — 5f 6fg⁶ 5.9g] first foal: dam won over 6f and 7f at 2 yrs: no worthwhile form in varied company. *H. Smyth.*

ALUMISS 2 ch.f. Henry the Seventh 125–Annie Ackleton (Shackleton 119) — [1976 6f 6fg 8s] shapely filly: first foal: dam lightly-raced N.H. mare: unquoted when behind in large fields of maidens. *W. Wightman.*

ALVAGE 3 br.f. Alcide 136–Soie Sauvage (Shantung 132) [1975 6f 6g⁵ 1976 **69** 9f 8s⁵ 8f⁴ 10fg² 8h² 10g⁴ 8s⁵ 10g² 10.2s*] lightly-built filly: 20/1 when winning 27-runner maiden race at Doncaster in November staying on by 1½ lengths from Falcon's Heir: finds 1m on sharp side nowadays and will be suited by 1½m: acts on any going. *Denys Smith.*

ALVERTON 6 ch.g. Midsummer Night II 117–Alvertona 89 (Saint Crespin III **99** 132) [1974 N.R. 1975 12s 12g⁴ 12.5g* 1976 12g* 12s* 13s* 12fg* 13g* 14fg² 16g² 14.6d* 13g* 14.6s⁴] strong, workmanlike gelding: had a most rewarding season, winning three times at Ayr and twice at Doncaster and York for first-place prize-money of over £16,500: gained his most valuable successes on eighth and ninth outings when winning J. W. Chafer Great Yorkshire Handicap at Doncaster (trounced sole opponent Swing Through by 12 lengths) and Bogside Cup at Ayr (held off Plenty Spirit in dogged fashion), both in September: plugged on valiantly (had no chance with very easy winner) when second to Sir Montagu in Tote-Ebor Handicap at York and when runner-up to Shangamuzo in Top Rank Club Handicap at Newcastle (both in August): stays 2m: seems to act on any going: has worn blinkers (not in 1976): usually wears bandages: suitable mount for an apprentice: a most game, genuine and consistent racehorse. *M. H. Easterby.*

ALWESTON 4 b.c. Alcide 136–Mollymawk 88 (Fairey Fulmar 124) [1974 8d **76** 1975 11v² 10d 12f 1976 12d 10.2fg³ 8f² 8f* 8h* 8f 8d⁴ 12s² 11s²] attractive, lengthy colt: good walker: quite a moderate handicapper: winner of apprentice events at Yarmouth in July and Redcar the following month: stays 1¼m: acts on any going: sold to D. Barons 4,000 gns Newmarket Autumn Sales. *R. Armstrong.*

AMADINA 3 br.f. Great Nephew 126–Java Sparrow 96 (Mossborough 126) **96** [1975 5f 6fg* 6fg² 6d 1976 8.5fg* 10fg 8fg² 7fg* 8g⁴ 7fg⁵ 7.6fg³ 7.3d⁶ 7s⁵] shapely filly: made all when winning handicaps at Epsom in April (from Honey Blossom) and Salisbury in June (from Star Walk): creditable third to Sportsky in similar event at Chester in September: stays 1m (well beaten in Pretty Polly Stakes at Newmarket on only attempt at 1¼m): appears to act on any going. *F. J. Houghton.*

AMADOU 4 ch.f. Hotfoot 126–Grande Fille 83 (Fortino II 120) [1974 6fg³ 6fg* 6g³ 6v³ 1975 8g⁵ 8s 6f* 6fg* 6f² 6f* 6f* 6fg² 5g⁵ 1976 6s 6g 7g⁶ 5d² 6g⁵ 6d 5v⁵] compact filly: much improved as a 3-y-o, winning four times: raced in France for most of 1976, running her best race on fourth outing when 2 lengths second of 12 to Baradaan in handicap at Deauville in August: well-beaten fifth of eight to Baildon in handicap at Newbury in October, only outing in this country as a 4-y-o: best form at 6f: appears to act on any going but is particularly well suited by firm: suitable mount for an apprentice: genuine: trained in France by J. Lyon. *B. Hanbury.* **93**

AMATI 4 ch.c. Forli–Sofaya II (Sicambre 135) [1974 N.R. 1975 8s 10.4d² 11.1fg³ 12fg⁴ 12.3fg² 10fg* 10f² 12f* 10f* 14f³ 16fg 10f5 1976 9fg] fairly useful performer (rated 90) at 3 yrs: stayed 1½m: showed best form on a soft surface: dead. *B. Hills.* **—**

AMBA PRINCESS 3 b.f. Amber Rama 133–Miss Blandy 86 (Major Portion 129) [1975 7f⁵ 8f 1976 8f² 10f6] lengthy filly: stays 1m: sold 2,000 gns Newmarket December Sales. *H. Cecil.* **—**

AMBERETTA 3 ch.f. Supreme Sovereign 119–French Bread (Klairon 131) [1975 5fg⁶ 6d 1976 7g 8f⁵ 6f⁵ 6h 6f³ 6g 6v* 7v² 6s⁶] quite a moderate performer: came into her own on heavy ground at back end of season, winning selling handicap at Newcastle (no bid) by 4 lengths from Rossella Bella and running creditably in stronger company: best form at up to 7f but should stay further: ran poorly when tried in blinkers on sixth appearance. *M. Camacho.* **72**

AMBER GODDESS 3 b.f. Yellow God 129–Mene Mene Tekel (Premonition 130) [1975 N.R. 1976 9f 8.2g⁵ 8fg⁵ 12.2fg] rangy filly: should stay 1¼m: sold 800 gns Newmarket December Sales. *E. Cousins.* **50**

AMBER LADY 2 br.f. Amber Rama 133–Lady Bingo (Match III 135) [1976 5f] lightly-built filly: half-sister to 3-y-o 7f winner Lotto (by Derring-Do): 200 gns yearling: dam won seven races in Italy: tailed-off last of 18 in maiden auction race won by Luke Splendid at Thirsk in April, only outing. *Hbt Jones.* **—**

AMBERREN 3 ch.c. Amber Rama 133–Renoir Picture 90 (Relko 136) [1975 5f 5f² 5f 6g³ 5f³ 6f* 8f⁵ 7g⁶ 1976 7f³ 6g 8g⁴ 6fg⁴ 7f 7fg 7g 7s 8s] quite a moderate handicapper: stays 1m: acts on firm going and ran poorly on soft on last two outings. *S. James.* **67**

AMBER SAM 3 ch.g. Levanter 121–Lucille Belle (Alcide 136) [1975 5g 8g 8g 8g⁶ 8d⁴ 8v 1976 8g 12d* 12d6 14fg³ 16.9f 15.8fg 12d 16s6 12v] quite a moderate performer: won weakly-contested maiden race at Haydock in April: ran creditably on next two outings but subsequently showed little worthwhile form: probably stays 1¾m: acts on a firm and a soft surface: sometimes sweats up: well behind when pulled up on fifth and sixth starts. *R. Hollinshead.* **66**

AMBER'S FLIGHT 3 b.f. Pony Express 85–Ambersfield (Amber X 133) [1975 N.R. 1976 8f] third foal: dam ran only at 2 yrs: tailed-off last in 12-runner maiden race won by The Four Hundred at Bath in June. *G. Cottrell.* **—**

AMBER VALLEY 3 b.g. Forlorn River 124–Jackies Joy (Skymaster 126) [1975 N.R. 1976 9f 8g³ 9.4h² 10.2g* 9v* 10.2s 10v* 8s²] first foal: dam well beaten in four maiden races: in good form in the autumn and won maiden race at Doncaster, minor event at Newcastle and handicap at Teesside: trotted up from Petit Eclair (value of win 10 lengths) on last-named course in October: stays 1¼m well: very well suited by heavy ground. *J. Hanson.* **98**

AMBLEY WOOD 4 br.f. Honour Bound 109–Diana (Dornot) [1974 N.R. 1975 N.R. 1976 14.7d 16f4 15.5h6] apparently useless. *P. Mitchell.* **—**

AMBOISE 3 b.c. Royal Palace 131–Parlez-vous 88 (Pardal 130) [1975 7g³ 7fg* 7fg* 8s⁴ 7.3g³ 1976 12fg4 10d* 12fg³ 10f* 10h* 10fg³ 11.7f* 11.7g² 12g³ 11fg*] well-made colt: had a successful season and won minor events at Redcar (two) and Windsor and handicaps at Ripon and Pontefract: defied a 10-lb penalty and won his second race in three days when beating Funny Valentine ¼ length in Darley Brewery Handicap on last-named course in July: in frame on all his other outings and ran Royal Match to ¾ length in £2,400 handicap at Windsor in August: stays 1½m: appears to act on any going with possible exception of really soft. *H. Cecil.* **113**

AMBRINA 4 ch.f. Ambernash–Mandolina 102 (Aureole 132) [1974 5v 1975 7s 8.2g 1976 8f 8f 8d] seemingly of no account. *M. Ryan.* **—**

AMERDALE 2 br.c. Bold Lad (Ire) 133–Coral Beach 118 (Relko 136) [1976 **71**
6f 8g 8fg⁶] well-made, attractive colt: first foal: 6,000 gns yearling: dam smart
middle-distance filly: showed only quite modest form in varied company but lost
ground at start on each appearance: will probably be suited by middle distances.
J. Hindley.

AMIABILITY 6 br.m. Appiani II 128–Sudden Thought 98 (Pardal 130) [1974 —
N.R. 1975 5.9f 1976 6g] lightly raced since 1973 and apparently of little
account. *Mrs L. Dingwall.*

AMIR 3 ch.c. Frankincense 120–Gillysweet 89 (Honeyway 125) [1975 5g 1976 **55**
8f 9fg² 8f²] lengthy, lightly-made colt: plater: runner-up at Kempton and Bath
in April: stays 9f. *S. Ingham.*

AMITY 2 ch.f. Amber Rama 133–Clarity 98 (Panaslipper 130) [1976 5f 6g⁶ 6v*] **91**
neat, strong-quartered filly: half-sister to three winners, including useful 1975
2-y-o Blessed Martin (by So Blessed) and quite useful middle-distance winner
Clarenceux (by Great Nephew): dam, half-sister to Santa Claus, won at up to
1½m: put up easily best effort when staying on really well, after coming under
pressure at halfway, to win 23-runner maiden race at Newbury in October by
¼ length from Brig of Ayr: will be suited by 1m+: acts well on heavy going. *R.
Hern.*

AMORE MARE 3 ch.f. Varano–Come Aboard 82 (Whistler 129) [1975 5s⁵ 5d* **67**
6fg⁶ 6f 6fg 6g 1976 5fg³ 5fg³ 5fg 5fg 10g 5s] strong filly: showed no worthwhile
form after second outing: form only at 5f: acts on a firm and a soft surface:
sometimes wears blinkers. *A. Johnson.*

AMORE MIO 2 ro.f. Sole Mio–Portia's Pick (Counsel 118) [1976 5f 5g 6g 6fg **62**
7.2f 6s 7s⁴ 7s² 8.2v 8v] small filly: moderate plater: suited by 7f and should stay
1m: acts on soft going: ran poorly when tried in blinkers: sold 200 gns Ascot
November Sales. *J. Haine.*

AMOROUS SONG 3 ch.c. Song 132–Amorella 106 (Crepello 136) [1975 5f* —
6fg³ 1976 7h⁵] half-brother to useful miler The Moorings (by Parthia): won
15-runner maiden race at Bath in July, 1975: not disgraced in handicap at Bath
in July on only outing at 3 yrs: may stay 1m. *J. Nelson.*

AMORZIER 2 b.c. Crozier 117–Amorchow (Chou-Chin-Chow 99) [1976 6f 7fg —
6h] useless. *D. Plant.*

AMPULLA 2 b.f. Crowned Prince 128–A.1.76 (Abernant 142) [1976 5fg* 6fg* **110**
6fg⁵ 7g³]
   That Ampulla is very highly regarded is obvious from the company she
was asked to keep as a two-year-old. She moved in the best circles after an impressive win first time out in the George Lambton Stakes at Newmarket in May,
following up with runs in the Cherry Hinton Stakes at Newmarket, the Lowther
Stakes at York and the Laurent Perrier Champagne Stakes at Doncaster, taking
on stronger opposition each time. She won the Cherry Hinton by a length and a
half from Ascot winner Al Stanza, but she was beaten about three lengths into
fifth place behind Icena in the Lowther and eleven lengths into third place behind
J. O. Tobin in the Champagne. The Cheveley Park Stakes winner Durtal finished
in front of her in the last two races, and Al Stanza was giving her 3 lb at Newmarket, so it looks as though Ampulla was around 10 lb behind the leading two-
year-old fillies. Nevertheless she should train on and do well as a three-year-old,
probably as a sprinter but perhaps at distances up to a mile.

Ampulla (b.f. 1974)	Crowned Prince (ch 1969)	Raise A Native (ch 1961)	Native Dancer
			Raise You
		Gay Hostess (ch 1957)	Royal Charger
			Your Hostess
	A.1. (gr 1963)	Abernant (gr 1946)	Owen Tudor
			Rustom Mahal
		Asti Spumante (ch 1947)	Dante
			Blanco

   Ampulla's first season didn't shed much light on what her best distance might
be. In the Lowther Stakes she ran as though six furlongs on fast ground was by
then too sharp for her, but in the Champagne Stakes she seemed to find seven
furlongs too far; in the latter she sprawled badly and went to pieces after showing
near the front for six furlongs. Yet her run behind Icena is probably a fair
reflection of her merit, and if it is, she hadn't a hope of finishing anywhere near
J. O. Tobin in the Champagne. An examination of Ampulla's pedigree leads

one to anticipate that she may well have a stamina problem, although the possibility of her getting a mile cannot be ruled out altogether. Without exception her dam's other five winners were speedy animals. Pearlemor (by Gulf Pearl), Bold Ron (by Bold Lad), Chili Girl (by Skymaster), Steel Heart (by Habitat) and Harrapan Seal (by Habitat) all won as two-year-olds, and only Harrapan Seal gave any indication that she stayed beyond six furlongs. Steel Heart, the best of the five, was a high-class sprinter. Crowned Prince, of whose first crop as a stallion Ampulla is a member, stayed seven furlongs as a two-year-old but raced only once, when beaten over a mile, at three. His brother Majestic Prince stayed a mile and a quarter. Bred as Ampulla is, and with the looks to match her breeding (she is a big, most attractive filly), her sale price as a yearling of 41,000 guineas was no surprise; at the same age Steel Heart fetched 71,000 guineas and Harrapan Seal fetched 44,000 guineas. Even at the price Ampulla is worth the money. *C. Brittain.*

AMUN'RA 3 b.c. Red God 128 §–Star Boarder (Porterhouse) [1975 5fg 5g⁴ 5d* **100** 5f* 5f² 6fg⁶ 5v² 6g² 1976 8g⁵ 7fg 5s⁵ 6fg⁵ 6d³ 5f* 5fg² 5.6g⁶ 6g] strong, shapely colt: useful handicapper: put up a good performance when winning under top weight at Nottingham in June, beating Gold Rupee by a head: creditable neck second to Sweet Nightingale in Singleton Handicap at Goodwood the following month: best at sprint distances: acts on any going: occasionally sweats up: consistent: changed hands 6,600 gns Newmarket Autumn Sales. *Denys Smith.*

AMYNTOR 2 b.c. Sir Gaylord—Crepellana 121 (Crepello 136) [1976 8s* 8d²] **122** p
The French had every reason to be delighted with the result of their most valuable race for two-year-olds, the Grand Criterium. Beforehand there had looked to be a real danger of the prize going to an English stable by way of J. O. Tobin but he could finish only third, beaten by the home-trained colts Blushing Groom and Amyntor. Blushing Groom's four-length victory established that he was the best two-year-old to race in Europe in 1976, and he is a top-notch miler in the making; Amyntor's run was that of a potentially top-class middle-distance colt. In the paddock Amyntor, a strong, well-grown sort, looked one of the nicest in the ten-strong field, and he ran far better than his starting price of 27/1 would have led one to expect. About three furlongs out Amyntor became involved in some scrimmaging, but once he got clear he stayed on in really good style to pip J. O. Tobin by a head for second place. Piggott, the rider of the third, lodged an objection to Amyntor for having hampered his mount but the placings remained unaltered.

Amyntor's only prevous outing had been in the Prix de Fontenoy, a valuable race for newcomers at Longchamp in September which since 1968 has been chosen for the début of such high-class animals as Djakao, Gyr, Bourbon, Targowice, Kalamoun, Mount Hagen, Caracolero and Youth. Amyntor justified his position of favourite in a seven-strong field, winning by a head, but was lucky to do so; the second favourite, Monseigneur, a brother to the 1975 Belmont Stakes winner Avatar, looked to be going the better when coming through to head the front-running Amyntor only to throw away his winning chance by drifting badly left near the finish.

The form of the Fontenoy looks well up to standard; Monseigneur ran twice in good company afterwards, being beaten two and a half lengths in the Prix Saint-Roman and going down by only half a length to the highly-regarded El Criollo in the Prix de Conde; the third horse, another very well-related American-bred colt called Quiet Zone, who was beaten fully six lengths, ran out a comfortable winner of a maiden race at Longchamp on his next appearance.

Amyntor (b.c. 1974)	Sir Gaylord (b 1959)	Turn-to (b 1951)	Royal Charger / Source Sucree
		Somethingroyal (b 1952)	Princequillo / Imperatrice
	Crepellana (ch 1966)	Crepello (ch 1954)	Donatello II / Crepuscule
		Astana (b 1956)	Arbar / Theano

Amyntor's style of running as a two-year-old suggests that he will be markedly better as a three-year-old; he is sure to be extremely well suited by longer distances judging by the way he finished over a mile. His breeding is that of a middle-distance performer. His sire Sir Gaylord produced such outstanding horses as Sir Ivor and Habitat while at stud in the United States and Amyntor comes from the first of four crops sired in France before his return to his native country in 1976. Crepellana, Amyntor's dam, had only one previous foal, an unraced colt by Royal Palace. She had an excellent record on the racecourse, winning the French Oaks, running Saraca to a short head in the Prix Vermeille and, the following year, finishing third to Derby winners Nijinsky and Blakeney in the King George VI and Queen Elizabeth Stakes. Crepellana comes from one of the best Boussac families; her dam Astana won the Prix du Conseil Municipal and was a half-sister to the French Derby winner Philius. Other top-class animals from this family are the dual Prix de l'Arc winner Corrida and the Epsom Derby winner Galcador. Clearly Amyntor has a lot to live up to but he has given every indication he will make his mark in the top French races. Remember his name, you'll hear a good deal more of it! *R. Mesme, France.*

ANAX 2 b.c. Right Tack 131–Paltrasse 84 (Palestine 133) [1976 6fig4 5g* 6fig4 **120** 6g* 6d* 6g5]

Like most good trainers, Bruce Hobbs does not believe in having his two-year-olds fully wound up for their first racecourse appearance, and of the fourteen individual two-year-old winners sent out by the Palace House Stables, only Shardia was successful at the first time of asking: first time up Tachypous, after drifting out from 3/1 to 15/2, was beaten into eighth place in an ordinary maiden event at Newmarket.

Newmarket was also the scene of Anax's racecourse début. And in the Fulbourn Maiden Stakes at the July meeting he caught our eye running a most promising race when fourth of twenty-three to J. O. Tobin. A 14/1 chance, Anax came out of the stalls very slowly, and was well behind until making strong and highly significant progress on the bridle racing into the last two furlongs. At the post, where he had improved to within eight lengths of the winner, he was going on in tremendous style. A big, strong, good-topped colt, who was backward and would obviously be much better for the experience, Anax had caught our eye in the paddock too, and we left Newmarket with the strong feeling that here was a good two-year-old. And so it proved. Anax won three races, including the Champion Two-year-old Trophy at Ripon and the Mill Reef Stakes at Newbury, from five more racecourse appearances.

At Ripon Anax had among his opponents Haveroid, who had created a favourable impression when giving weight and a comfortable beating to some useful youngsters in the Prince of Wales's Stakes at York, Claddagh, who had run the speedy filly Mummy's Darling to a short head, when conceding her 8 lb, in the Chesterfield Stakes at Newmarket, Birkholm, a progressive American-bred colt who had won his last two races, and Stradey Park, who had finished a good second to Paddington in the Rous Memorial Stakes at Goodwood. Star

Mill Reef Stakes, Newbury—Geoff Lewis forces Anax up to take the lead from Adviser near the finish

Attention completed the field. In this company Anax found the early pace faster than he could manage in comfort, but to his credit he stuck to his task under pressure, and with Haveroid, who had led on the bridle with the race apparently won a furlong out, faltering near the finish, he was able to get up and pass him close home. A game performance!

Anax ran much the same sort of race in the Mill Reef Stakes, taking some time to warm up but running on strongly to master the favourite Adviser well inside the last furlong. That Adviser, who had been sweating and ill at ease in the paddock, had not run right up to his best mark was suggested by the proximity of Haighall in third place, and when the pair met again, Anax finished behind Adviser in the William Hill Middle Park Stakes at Newmarket. But only by a head, and apart from the winner, Anax's stable-companion Tachypous, nothing finished better, Anax improving from eighth to fifth place under hand riding from Baxter, and making up at least two lengths on Adviser in the space of the last half-furlong. At a mile we would have no hesitation in backing Anax to beat all those who finished in front of him here, except perhaps Tachypous.

		Hard Tack	Hard Sauce
	Right Tack	(b 1955)	Cowes
	(b 1966)	Polly Macaw	Polly's Jet
Anax		(br 1959)	Listowel
(b.c. 1974)		Palestine	Fair Trial
		(gr 1947)	Una
	Paltrasse	Sinna	Birikan
	(b 1967)	(b 1956)	Inisheer

Anax, who cost 9,800 guineas as a yearling, is a son of the Two Thousand Guineas winner Right Tack, out of a mare by the Two Thousand Guineas winner Palestine. Paltrasse, whose first living produce Anax is, won over a mile as a three-year-old, and is a sister to Pal Sinna, the dam of Bay Express. Anax's breeding confirms the impression that he will be suited by a mile, and at that distance we expect him to show himself a better three-year-old than he was a two-year-old and to win some good races. He acts well on a soft surface. *B. Hobbs.*

ANCHOR WOOD 2 gr.f. Precipice Wood 123–Debra C 72 (Combat 123) [1976 **57** 5.8f⁶ 7s 10v⁵ 8.2v⁶] quite a moderate plater: stays 1¼m. *J. Hill.*

ANCHOVY TOAST 4 b.f. Firestreak 125–Ancarjen 93 (Poaching 115) [1974 **56** 5g 6fg 6s 8d 7s 1975 8g 8g 8fg* 8fg⁵ 10h⁵ 8fg³ 10f² 10g* 10fg 8f² 10g³ 12g 12f* 12g 1976 12.2f 11.7fg⁴ 10fg⁴ 10f⁶ 12fg] compact filly: poor handicapper: sold, covered by No Mercy, 2,600 gns Newmarket December Sales. *R. Jarvis.*

ANDBECCA 3 b.f. First Phase 97–Smokey Mine 91 (My Smokey 125) [1975 **—** N.R. 1976 11f] second foal: dam effective at 6f to 1m: tailed-off last of 10 to Main Chance in maiden race at Hamilton in September. *J. Mulhall.*

AND BEHOLD 2 gr.c. Sovereign Path 125–Dino 82 (Vienna 127) [1976 5g* **108** 6f³ 7fg² 6fg 7.3v⁵] lengthy, attractive colt: third foal: 4,800 gns yearling: dam, who stayed 1m, is half-sister to Double Jump: won nine-runner maiden race at Kempton in May by a neck from Oppressor: placed in much better company on next two outings, finishing 2 lengths third to Cawston's Clown in Coventry Stakes at Royal Ascot and head second to Sky Ship in Lanson Champagne Stakes at Goodwood, but then ran poorly in Gimcrack Stakes at York (blinkered) and finished only fair fifth to Fair Season in Horris Hill Stakes at Newbury: stays 7f well and should stay 1m: acts on firm going. *R. Akehurst.*

ANDURA 2 b.c. Amber Rama 133–Pleaseme 100 (Javelot 124) [1976 5g 5s³ **61** 5f³ 6fg⁵ 5g 8v⁶] short-coupled colt: plater: ran easily best race on second outing when 3 lengths third to Maritime Diver at Ayr in June: beaten long way when tried over 1m but had little chance at weights. *T. Craig.*

ANDY REW 3 b.c. Lear Jet 123–Chantel-Gold 74 (Chantelsey 130) [1975 **95** 5g 5g⁴ 6fg 7g 7f³ 7f* 8g* 8d³ 1976 8f⁴ 10s⁶ 10fg⁶ 12g⁴ 10f* 10f² 8f* 8h² 8.2f² 8g³ 10d³] well-made, good sort of colt: good mover: quite a useful handicapper: comfortable 4-length winner at Bath in June and Brighton in July: ran respectably afterwards, including when tried in blinkers on tenth outing: stays 1¼m (well beaten on only attempt at 1½m but was not knocked about when chance had gone): acts on any going but is well suited by firm: suitable mount for an apprentice. *P. Cole.*

ANEGADA 2 ch.f. Welsh Pageant 132–Antigua 100 (Hyperion) [1976 6g 6v⁴] **79** strong, robust filly: half-sister to three winners, including fairly useful stayer

Cedar Grove (by Relko): dam won at 1½m: showed ability in large fields of maidens in the autumn, in October showing up all way when 5 lengths fourth of 23 to Amity at Newbury: will stay 1¼m. *Doug Smith.*

ANEMOS 3 b.c. Derring-Do 131–Folle Fete 73 (Vieux Manoir 132) [1975 5g⁴ **101** 5f* 6fg* 6g* 6fg² 6g² 6fg* 6g* 1976 7fg⁵ 6f 6d 6g³ 7s] strong, useful sort of colt: dam won over 1½m: showed very useful form as a 2-y-o and won five of his eight races: favourite, finished creditable fifth to Man of Harlech in Tote Free Handicap at Newmarket in April: did not run up to his best afterwards and was tailed off on final outing: will stay 1m: evidently needs a sound surface. *P. Walwyn.*

ANGEL ABOARD 6 ch.h. Angel's Head 106–P & O 63 (Doutelle 128) [1974 — 10g⁶ 11.7fg 10d⁴ 10fg 8.3g⁶ 10.2v 1975 N.R. 1976 17.1s 10s] of no account. *H. Payne.*

ANGELAS RAFF 2 b.f. Raffingora 130–La Liz (Lauso) [1976 5g⁶ 5g⁵ 6f⁴ 7fg⁵ **75** 7g⁵ 7h 6s] strong filly: second reported foal: 2,000 gns yearling: dam ran only once: quite a moderate filly: probably stays 7f: blinkered in her later races but has done better without. *P. Ashworth.*

ANGELOS 2 gr.f. Town Crier 119–Angel Beam 115 (Hornbeam 130) [1976 **97** 5fg⁴ 5fg⁴ 5.3f* 5g* 5fg 5f³ 5f*] neat, attractive filly: first foal: dam, a smart winner over 5f and 6f at 2 yrs, needed 1¼m+ at 3 yrs: winner of maiden race at Brighton and minor events at Sandown and Folkestone: put up a useful performance on last-named course in September, running on gamely to catch Miss Diver close home: bred to stay at least 1m but is evidently thought to be a sprinter: acts on firm going: genuine and consistent. *P. Walwyn.*

ANGELS PATHWAY 3 ch.c. Sky Gipsy 117–Nasira 94 (Persian Gulf) [1975 5f **82** 5fg⁶ 5f² 5g* 5f² 1976 6g 6fg³ 6fg 6g⁵ 6fg 7g 6f⁴ 6f] strong, compact colt: mainly disappointing, putting up best effort when third of 16 to Broxted in handicap at Newmarket in April: stays 6f: acts on firm going: well beaten when tried in blinkers on fourth outing but had a stiff task: exported to U.S.A. *R. Price.*

ANHYDROUS 5 b.g. Fleet Nasrullah–Countess Albie (Pet Bully) [1974 8.2fg⁶ — 10.4g⁵ 10g* 10s² 10d³ 10.1g² 11.7g 1975 8fg 8v⁵ 12.2fg 12s 15.8f⁴ 16h 13fg 12f⁶ 12f 12.2f³ 9fg 8f⁴ 12.2g⁶ 1976 12.2f 12fg 12s³ 12.5s] big, good-looking American-bred gelding: poor handicapper nowadays: prone to breaking blood vessels: probably stays 1½m: acts on any going: sometimes wears blinkers. *E. Collingwood.*

ANNA NATASHA 4 b.f. Prince Tenderfoot 126–Shelduck 70 (Dicta Drake 126) — [1974 5.1f³ 5.1f 6g 5.1s 7.2s 1975 6s 6s⁴ 7s 7g 7f 6fg 6f 1976 8fg 6g] light-framed filly: poor plater: has been tried in blinkers: not seen out after April. *P. Allingham.*

ANNANDALE LADY 2 ro.f. Leander 119–Dotty Belle (Coronation Year 124) — [1976 5f 5g] fourth foal: dam never ran: behind in September in maiden race at Thirsk and well-contested seller at Ayr. *G. Richards.*

ANNA'S PRINCESS 3 b.f. Derring-Do 131–Lady Anna 85 (Panaslipper 130) — [1975 6f 6h⁶ 7f⁵ 7f 8.2d 8g 10g² 8v⁶ 1976 12v³ 10f⁵ 12f⁴ 14.7f⁵ 12f³ 14fg⁵ 10.6g 12f⁵] strong, compact filly: plater nowadays: stays 1½m but possibly not 1¾m: usually wears blinkers: sold 1,150 gns Newmarket Autumn Sales. *M. H. Easterby.*

ANNA'S RICHES 2 ch.c. Richboy 117–Lady Anna 85 (Panaslipper 130) [1976 — 5g⁶ 5f 5d 5f 5f] bad plater: has worn blinkers: sold 170 gns Doncaster June Sales. *M. H. Easterby.*

ANNEGONI 2 b.c. Will Hays (USA)–Amber Witch (King's Troop 118) [1976 **77** 6fg⁵ 8g 7v³ 8s⁵] well-grown, rangy colt: first foal: dam poor maiden in Ireland: beaten some way on last two outings but showed definite ability, finishing third of 19 to Mackelly at Newcastle and fifth of 20 to Lady Rhapsody at Sandown: probably stays 1m; acts on heavy going. *C. Brittain.*

ANNELINE 2 b.f. Caliban 123–Anassa 108 (Pardal 130) [1975 7fg 7g 7s⁴ 1976 **64** 10fg 7g 12g⁴ 12f³ 12f⁴ 12s 10.2s] small filly: in frame in maiden races at Brighton in the summer: suited by 1½m: ran poorly last three outings. *J. Dunlop.*

ANNEMARY 4 gr.f. Runnymede 123–Fair Nina 91 (Set Fair 129) [1974 5g — 5.1s* 5fg 6s³ 1975 6g 7fg 7f³ 6fg 6fg 7fg 7.6fg 7s 10g⁵ 10g⁵ 12g 1976 10fg 7g 8fg] neat filly: poor handicapper nowadays: stays 7f: acts on any going: has been tried in blinkers. *Mrs R. Lomax.*

Mrs J. W. Jennings' "Angelos"

ANNES GIFT   2 ch.f. Ballymoss 136–Pamaloo 93 (Pall Mall 132)   [1976 7s 5s 7s]   —
half-sister to a minor 2-y-o winner by Celtic Ash: dam won from 6f to 1¼m: beaten
long way on all outings.   *O. O'Neill.*

ANNE'S PRETENDER   4 ch.c. Pretense–Anne la Douce 123 (Silnet 131) **122**
[1974 7fg* 7g 8g5   1975 8g 12g2 12fg4 12fg3 10g2 11g* 8s3 10fg   1976 10g4 10f3
10g* 10f* 10fg4 10d]
   The hottest and driest summer on record kept many horses off the course
in 1976 but thanks mainly to the artificial watering systems that are now general
on our important racecourses racing survived the drought very well.   In August
a number of jumping fixtures and Chepstow's Bank Holiday flat meeting had
to be cancelled because of the iron-hard ground.   Epsom was also affected and its
August Bank Holiday fixture was transferred to Kempton.   However, most of
the meetings attracted a reasonable number of runners.   Twenty-one runners for
six races at Lingfield in July was the lowest turnout: later there were only
twenty-four runners for a six-race card at Pontefract, twenty-five for one at
Folkestone and twenty-eight for others at Brighton and Redcar.   But these
were the only flat meetings at which there were fewer than thirty runners.
   Compare the situation with that before artificial watering was used.   Let's
take a look back at 1934 and 1935, two seasons taken at random.   In 1934 on firm
going Hamilton attracted seventeen runners for one card of six races, nineteen
for another and twenty-six for another.   Liverpool, Worcester, Edinburgh and
Nottingham all drew fewer than thirty runners in a day, as did Pontefract and
Epsom—and that does not exhaust the examples of pitifully small fields.   It was
the same picture in 1935.   Redcar, Wolverhampton, Haydock, Folkestone,
Chepstow, Worcester, Lanark, Hamilton and Ayr all attracted fewer than thirty
runners on one day, and probably there were several others.   So much for the
myth that in the days before artificial watering horses were turned out whatever
the going!   Going back even further we can find evidence that the trainers of fifty
or sixty years ago were just as averse to running their horses on firm going as are
their counterparts today.   George Lambton, writing of the mighty Diadem, said:

'That year the going at Ascot was terribly hard, and I had some doubts about running her.'

The desirability of watering racecourses is still argued about today although many more racecourses have been equipped with watering systems in the past ten years or so. The most often-used argument against artificial watering is that in the long run it leads to a 'softening' of the breed. However, if our horses are indeed getting soft we can think of other, much more plausible explanations for it. In France watering has been the order of the day for a very long time and yet we didn't hear the pessimists who denigrated our English racehorses in 1976 bemoaning the softness of the French thoroughbred! A better argument is that the 'complete' racehorse should be capable of racing on any sort of going, that inability to act on hard ground is therefore a shortcoming in a racehorse and, hence, ability to act on a hard surface a desirable attribute. If this is agreed it may justifiably be held that watering is wrong, at least in principle. It is also argued that watering is unfair to the owners of those horses that are only at their best on firm or hard going; our climate usually provides ample opportunities each season for the mudlarks so why tamper with nature when it provides a surface favourable to the top-of-the-ground performer? However, those who favour watering point out that very few horses are really at home on the extremes of going. They argue that where there are conflicting interests it is surely reasonable to be guided by the principle of giving benefit to the greatest number. And if one is guided by that principle one must accept watering as desirable. But, whatever the pros and cons of artificial watering, surely the crux of the matter is that the majority of owners and trainers are loathe to race horses on ground so hard that they risk injury by galloping on it. We have seen how, in the past, this attitude led to pitifully small fields when the going was firm or hard. Artificial watering when conditions are dry definitely helps to raise the size of fields to a level where they offer enough entertainment to maintain the interest of the public. And we have stressed before that racing cannot afford to be so blind as to ignore the requirements of the public, particularly the betting public. If it did it would die.

Let no-one get the idea that we are whole-heartedly in favour of the present arrangements for watering courses in this country. The first essential of any

Sir Charles Clore's "Anne's Pretender"

watering system is that it should be efficient and there are systems in operation on some of our tracks where water is applied unevenly and at some courses not all of the width of the track is watered. It is idiotic to employ a handicapper to ensure that as far as possible all the horses in a race have an equal chance and then allow Mr Clerk of the Course to come along with his watering can and give a considerable advantage to one side of the course over the other. This state of affairs must be brought to an end. Uneven watering, apart from being grossly unfair, has unfortunate and potentially dangerous side-effects which we should be better without, such as jockeying for position and subterfuges for getting on to the fastest ground. There is also much that could be done to equalise the effects of watering at some of our courses where there is a relatively efficient system. There are some where after watering it has often seemed that one particular side or part of the track is markedly faster or slower than the rest. Those racecourse executives concerned should investigate the soil composition and drainage at their tracks.

Sandown's watering system had many critics after the Whit Monday meeting at which the stand side of the track, which is out of range of the sprinklers of the watering system, rode considerably faster than the far side; the wide strip of unwatered ground showed up clearly. The first jockey to exploit the faster ground was Piggott on the favourite for the Brigadier Gerard Stakes, Anne's Pretender. Anne's Pretender had had a couple of outings in the current season and the Brigadier Gerard Stakes, a Group 3 race, was the first important objective of his four-year-old campaign. As soon as the field reached the turn into the straight Piggott left the leader Battlecry, with whom he had kept in close touch from the start, and steered Anne's Pretender to the stand side. Most of the others followed his example, while Battlecry continued to race up the far side. Anne's Pretender kept up a strong gallop to win by a length and a half from the consistent Chil the Kite. Battlecry, a horse with smart form who was fourth favourite for the race at 5/1, toiled in well behind, having raced on ground much softer than that taken by his main rivals. The Sandown executive answered its critics by constructing a false running rail in the straight to ensure at later meetings that horses raced on the watered ground. This reduced the width of the straight in parts to fourteen yards and is unlikely to be adopted as a long-term solution.

Anne's Pretender and Chil the Kite met again a fortnight later in the Prince of Wales Stakes at Royal Ascot. Neither was expected to give the odds-on favourite Rose Bowl much of a race, but, in the event, the race was won by a French horse whose form beforehand had seemed inferior to that of Anne's Pretender and Chil the Kite. The name of the French invader who swept past the front-running Anne's Pretender a furlong out, brushing him aside as if he were a nonentity, was soon to become very well known. It is now history that Trepan was disqualified after winning the Prince of Wales Stakes and his next race the Joe Coral Eclipse Stakes as a result of traces of an illegal stimulant being found in his system after each event. Anne's Pretender, who had finished seven lengths clear of third-past-the-post Chil the Kite at Royal Ascot, was awarded the Prince of Wales Stakes. A further result of the Trepan inquiry was that Anne's Pretender was moved up to third place in the Joe Coral Eclipse Stakes in which he finished twelve lengths behind Trepan, ten lengths behind Wollow and six lengths behind the St James's Palace Stakes winner Radetzky. There were good horses behind Anne's Pretender, including Chil the Kite and the Derby runner-up Relkino, but the Eclipse confirmed the opinion formed of Anne's Pretender at the end of his three-year-old career that he is about 14 lb behind the best. He was off the course for more than three months after the Eclipse, during which time he left Price's stable to be trained by Peter Walwyn. He led the stand-side group for seven furlongs before finishing a long way behind on softish ground in the Champion Stakes on his final appearance.

Anne's Pretender (ch.c. 1972)	Pretense (br 1963)		Endeavour II (b 1942)		British Empire	
					Himalaya	
			Imitation (ch 1951)		Hyperion	
					Flattery	
	Anne la Douce (b 1958)		Silnet (b 1949)		Fastnet	
					Silver Jill	
			Sweet Anne (ch 1950)		Tehran	
					Cheerful Anne	

Anne's Pretender's ancestry was examined in detail in *Racehorses of 1975*. His sire Pretense was an extremely versatile, good-class American racehorse who won over six furlongs as a five-year-old after showing as a four-year-old that he probably stayed a mile and three quarters. Anne la Douce was third in the Oaks and dead-heated for first place in the Prix Vermeille in 1961. Before Anne's Pretender she bred four winners, all of whom were successful at middle-distances. Anne's Pretender raced only at a mile and a quarter in 1976 but we should have liked to have seen him tried again at a mile and a half. His third to Grundy in the Irish Derby and his fourth to the same horse in the Derby are performances which rate among his best in our book. The 'catch-us-if-you-can' tactics employed on Anne's Pretender in the Derby and in some of his other races suit him admirably and he acts well on a firm surface. He is an attractive, good-bodied colt who made fine physical progress as a four-year-old and always stood out in the paddock. He is to continue his racing career in the United States. *P. Walwyn.*

ANNINA 3 ro.f. Roan Rocket 128–Nedda 113 (Alcide 136) [1975 5g4 5g* 6fg 5fg2 5f4 5g6 6g4 6f6 1976 7fg 10fg5 8.5fg2] small filly: favourite and tried in blinkers, appeared none too keen when going under by a short head to Back One Eleven in seller at Epsom in June: had earlier run respectably in handicaps: probably stays 1¼m. *B. Hobbs.* **75**

ANNS DREAM 4 b.g. Sahib 114–Dumana 96 (Dumbarnie 125) [1974 6g 5.8v 6s3 5.9v2 1975 5f 5f 5.9fg 7.6g 1976 10g6 12s 12s3] small, workmanlike gelding: poor maiden nowadays: stays 1½m: acts on heavy going: had very stiff task when tried in blinkers. *E. Reavey.* **60**

ANOTHER CHAPTER 2 b.c. Tower Walk 130–Karen Chase 82 (Will Somers 114 §) [1976 5s 5fg5 5f6 6g] useful-looking colt: half-brother to three winners, including useful middle-distance performer Mr Fordette (by Gulf Pearl): 4,200 gns yearling: dam, a maiden sprinter, is half-sister to useful stayer Cagirama: ran respectably when 6 lengths sixth of 19 to Petard in minor event at Ripon in August, penultimate outing: form only at 5f but should stay further. *K. Payne.* **77**

ANOTHER DEBONA 3 b.g. Majetta 115–Panamaid (Panaslipper 130) [1975 5f 5fg 1976 8.2d] leggy gelding: in rear in maiden races: unseated rider at start on first outing in 1975: not seen out in 1976 until October. *S. Nesbitt.* **—**

ANOTHER FIDDLER 5 ch.g. Burglar 128–Izeste (Lavandin 128) [1974 5g4 5g 5g6 5g5 5fg4 5.3f4 5.8g5 5fg2 5g2 5g 5.8v 1975 5.8g2 6g 5.8h3 5.3f6 5.8f5 5.8f2 6fg* 5f5 5fg 5.8f6 6g 6f5 1976 5.9f5 6g* 6fg2 6f2 6f2 7fg5 6f* 5.8h4 6f* 7d 5.8f 6d4 6s] dipped-backed gelding: good mover: fairly useful plater: winner at Catterick and Windsor (twice): long odds on when accounting for two opponents on last-named course in August: also ran creditably on some of his other outings, including in three non-sellers: stays 6f: acts on any going: sometimes wears blinkers: good mount for an apprentice. *G. Balding.* **70**

ANOTHER FROLIC 4 ch.f. Star Combine 109–Court Frolic (Fairplay) [1974 N.R. 1975 N.R. 1976 18s] sister to poor hurdler Commonwealth Games and half-sister to moderate chaser Mexican Frolic (by Crespin Rouge): dam never ran: 20/1 when well beaten in poor maiden race (amateur riders) at Doncaster in October, only outing. *J. Powney.* **—**

ANOTHER GRAND 2 br.g. Another River 89–Grand Mistress (Grandmaster) [1976 8fg 7s] half-brother to 5f to 1m winner Henry Dee (by Marcus Superbus): dam a point-to-pointer: in rear in maiden races at Beverley (backward and dwelt) in September and Edinburgh (finished last) the following month. *Denys Smith.* **—**

ANOTHER MORLEY 4 ch.g. Whistling Wind 123–Diamonds Galore 95 (Luminary 132) [1974 5f6 5g 5.9g 5fg 1975 6g 8s 6f 6h 7.6g 6fg3 5f5 1976 10d] leggy gelding: stays 6f: acts on a firm surface: usually wears blinkers. *D. Yeoman.* **—**

ANOTHER NATIVE 3 b.f. Native Prince–Another Flutter 75 (Credo 123) [1975 5s* 5fg2 5g3 5f4 5h2 5f2 5d 5h2 5h4 5g 5g 1976 5v5 5f6 6d] small filly: showed fair form at 2 yrs but appeared not to train on: should have stayed at least 6f: acted on any going, but showed best form on a sound surface: exported by B.B.A. to Brazil. *F. Carr.* **64**

ANOTHER PATHAN 2 b.c. Tribal Chief 125–Athanatos (Never Say Die 137) [1976 5g 5fg4 5fg 7fg2 7g] compact colt: brother to fairly useful miler Proud Pathan: 4,000 gns yearling: dam unraced half-sister to smart handicapper London Gazette: showed a little ability in varied company: will stay 1m. *D. Sasse.* **74**

ANOTHER PINTA 4 b.f. Typhoon 125–Drinka Pinta 101 (Court Feathers 120) [1974 6g 6g5 7g6 1975 7v6 9g 10.1s4 10fg 10fg* 8h4 11.1fg4 8g 10f3 8g6 12d6 10fg **—**

1976 8g 10h⁶ 10g 8f]   compact filly: plater: no worthwhile form at 4 yrs: best
form at up to 1¼m: seems to act on any going: sometimes wears a hood: sold 900
gns Doncaster June Sales, since a winner in Holland.   *R. Bastiman.*

ANOTHER PLUM   3 br.f. So Blessed 130–Sugar Plum 103 (Zucchero 133 §)   —
[1975 6g   1976 9f 10.1f⁵ 12g]   leggy, unfurnished filly: little worthwhile form in
maiden races: sold 4,500 gns Newmarket December Sales.   *H. Candy.*

ANOTHER REVENGE   2 ch.c. Sweet Revenge 129–Callidice 77 (Worden II   —
129)   [1976 6fg 5d 6d]   half-brother to three winners, including useful 1974
2-y-o Athelstan (by Derring-Do): cost 6,800 gns as a yearling but showed no sign
of ability in maiden races: blinkered third outing.   *A. Corbett.*

ANOTHER SPRING   2 gr.f. Town Crier 119–Kingdom Come 77 (Klondyke Bill   **66**
125)   [1976 7fg 6fg 6f 7.2f⁵ 6fg³ 6g]   leggy, unfurnished filly: first foal: dam won
over 6f at 3 yrs: only plating class: stays 7f.   *G. Toft.*

ANOTHER WARRIOR   2 gr.c. Green God 128–Solviliana (Vilmorin) [1976   **74**
5fg 6d 5g³ 5.6f⁴ 6fg 5f² 5f⁶ 5fg*]   leggy colt: attracted no bid after winning 17-
runner seller at Ripon in August by a length from Raffondo: has yet to show he
stays beyond 5f.   *G. Toft.*

ANTIMACASSAR   3 b.f. Tudor Melody 129–Loose Cover 106 (Venture VII   **72**
129)   [1975 7g² 6s³ 7fg   1976 8d⁴ 8g⁴ 8f² 8fg 8g 10d⁴ 12.2s³ 12g⁴]   rangy filly:
showed fair form at 2 yrs, but is disappointing: has yet to show conclusively
she stays further than 1m: ran moderately when tried in blinkers on second and
final outings.   *R. Armstrong.*

ANTON LAD   6 br.h. Anton 106–Castleway 77 (Lucero 124)   [1974 6f³ 6g 6f 5f³   —
5fg³ 5f³ 5fg* 5g⁶ 5g² 5fg* 6s* 5d² 6s 5s² 5s*   1975 6g 5d 5f* 5f³ 6g⁴ 5s 5g⁵   1976
5s⁵ 5d² 5v 5s 5s]   leggy horse: useful handicapper (rated 101) at 5 yrs: 5 lengths
second of five to Algora at Redcar in June: subsequently off course until October
and was well beaten (had stiffish tasks): stays 6f but is possibly at his best at 5f:
acts on any going and on any track: has worn blinkers: usually wears a tongue
strap: suitable mount for an apprentice: genuine.   *J. Mulhall.*

ANTRONA   3 gr.f. Royal Palace 131–Ileana 113 (Abernant 142)   [1975 6fg*   **116**
6.5d² 8s* 8s⁴   1976 8fg³ 8fg⁴ 10g³ 10.5d⁴ 10g* 10d* 10.5d² 10g⁶]
   At the back-end fillies can run all sorts of strange races.   Look at Antrona
for instance: on her final racecourse appearance she trailed in a well-beaten sixth
of ten behind Ranimer in the Sun Chariot Stakes at Newmarket in September.
Her display was totally out of character—she had been a model of consistency,
never out of the frame in eleven previous races, and had shown herself a match for
all but the best fillies.   Her two successes in 1976 came in the Group 3 Prix de
Malleret at Longchamp in June and the Prix de Psyche at Deauville in August.
In the former race she settled matters in a few strides and came home two lengths
clear of Ranimer, a fact which in itself underlines just how much below form
Antrona ran in the Sun Chariot.   In the Prix de Psyche Antrona, conceding 7 lb
to all her six rivals, again scored decisively and had two and a half lengths to spare
over the unpredictable Imogene.   Amongst her other good efforts Antrona
numbered a fourth place in two classics, the One Thousand Guineas in which she
was beaten just over one and a half lengths by Flying Water and the Prix de
Diane in which she was six and a half lengths behind Pawneese; and she also
finished a close third to Riverqueen in a semi-classic, the Prix Saint-Alary.   To
emphasise Antrona's consistency it's worth mentioning that she met Theia five
times in her life, twice at two years and three times in 1976.   The score was four
—one in Theia's favour but on no occasion was there more than 2 lb in it either
way.

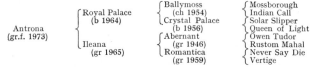

Antrona (gr.f. 1973)	Royal Palace (b 1964)	Ballymoss (ch 1954)	Mossborough
			Indian Call
		Crystal Palace (b 1956)	Solar Slipper
			Queen of Light
	Ileana (gr 1965)	Abernant (gr 1946)	Owen Tudor
			Rustom Mahal
		Romantica (gr 1959)	Never Say Die
			Vertige

   Antrona is a half-sister to two winners in France, namely the nine-furlong
winner Valdo (by Salvo) and Trentino (by Crepello), successful at up to a mile
and a half.   The dam Ileana, a daughter of the good stayer Romantica, was a very
useful miler.   Antrona didn't grow a great deal from two to three years but was

nonetheless an attractive filly. She was better suited by a mile and a quarter than by a mile and might well have stayed a mile and a half. Probably she acted on any going. She visits Nonoalco. *F. Boutin, France.*

ANYA YLINA 2 b.f. Bold Reasoning–Goofed (Court Martial) [1976 8d* 8s]   **?**
American-bred French filly: half-sister to top-class French 7f to 1¼m winner Lyphard (by Northern Dancer), top-class 1m to 1½m filly Nobiliary (by Vaguely Noble) and very useful French and American winner Barcas (by Sailor): $145,000 yearling: dam a stakes winner at up to 1½m: put up a very promising display in seven-runner newcomers race at Longchamp in September, making most of running and not being seriously troubled to win by 3 lengths from Desert Pet: favourite for Group 1 Criterium des Pouliches on same course the following month but faded in the straight and finished in rear behind Kamicia: almost certainly much better than her Pouliches running suggests. *M. Zilber, France.*

ANYONE NOT DANCING 4 br.c. Lear Jet 123–Kiata (Will Somers 114 §)   **—**
[1974 5f 5fg 5.9g 1975 12.2f 1976 8g 12g 13.8d] of no account. *S. Norton.*

ANY TIME 2 b.c. Petingo 135–Green Chiffon 83 (Crepello 136) [1976 8s⁶]   **79 P**
quite an attractive colt: third foal: 9,000 gns yearling: dam twice a winner over 1¼m from four starts: 20/1, caught our eye when just under 11 lengths sixth of 28 to Royal Boxer in maiden race at Newmarket in October, coming with a good run in final 2f and not being given a hard race when held: will stay 1¼m: sure to do a good deal better. *L. Cumani.*

APERITIF 2 br.f. My Swallow 134–Mrs Hauksbee 102 (Pindari 124) [1976 6fg   **—**
8s] big, workmanlike filly: second foal: dam won over 1¾m: behind in large fields of maidens at Newbury in August (very backward, started slowly) and Sandown in October: trained by A. Jarvis on first outing: sold 400 gns Ascot December Sales. *R. Hannon.*

APOLLO 2 b.g. Green God 128–Medaea 90 (Darius 129) [1976 5f 5fg 5g 5f 6g⁴   **75**
6fg⁶ 6h* 6d³ 8f] plater: attracted no bid after showing improved form to win seven-runner seller at Brighton in August by 2 lengths from Princess Rose: suited by 6f but appeared not to stay when tried at 1m: ran badly in blinkers on fourth outing. *P. Haslam.*

APOSTROF (SWE) 7 ch.g. Moderne 121–Altamira (Ringjostallet) [1976 8fg⁵]   **—**
Swedish-bred gelding: finished second in Swedish Derby in 1972: 33/1, started slowly and was always tailed off in minor event won by Dominion at Goodwood in September, first outing in this country. *N. Guest.*

APPERSETT 4 br.g. Appiani II 128–Indian Music 82 (Dalesa 109) [1974 7g⁴   **—**
6d 8s 1975 12f⁶ 10h 12f 10f 1976 13.8g 8g] poor maiden: well beaten both outings as a 4-y-o, including in a seller: possibly needs at least 1½m: has been tried in blinkers: not raced after May: sold 825 gns Ascot July Sales. *Denys Smith.*

APPIADER 5 b.g. Appiani II 128–Snake Charmer 87 (St Paddy 133) [1974   **—**
10.8fg 14f 10g 1975 N.R. 1976 8g] of no account nowadays. *G. Wallace.*

APPLALTO 2 br.g. Alto Volante 109–Pomme (Polic 126) [1976 8s⁵ 8v*]   **86**
robust, attractive gelding: first live foal: dam unraced half-sister to useful 1970 2-y-o Apple Sauce: made some late headway when about 10 lengths fifth of 28 to Royal Boxer in maiden race at Newmarket in October: favourite for minor event at Teesside later in month and won comfortably by a length from Robin's Song after always going well: will stay middle distances. *Sir Mark Prescott.*

APPLEFORD 3 b.c. Reform 132–Crepellina (Crepello 136) [1975 6fg 7g⁶ 7d   **63**
7f 8g 1976 8.5fg 10fg 8.3fg⁶ 10g 7s² 8s] lengthy colt: plater: ran easily best race when neck second to The Headman at Brighton in October when blinkered first time: ran moderately when again blinkered on final outing: should stay middle distances: well suited by soft going. *D. Whelan.*

APPLE PEEL 2 ch.f. Pall Mall 132–Eden (Gulf Pearl 117) [1976 6fg 7s³   **72**
6v⁶ 7v⁵] sturdy filly: half-sister to a minor winner at up to 1¼m by Laser Light: dam never ran: quite a modest maiden: will stay 1¼m. *H. Williams.*

APPLE PRINCESS 3 ch.f. Major Portion 129–Granny Smith 76 (Tiger 125)   **—**
[1975 7h 6fg 7fg 8f 8g 1976 12g⁵ 16f 12.2f⁴ 10fg³ 8h³] poor plater: probably stays 1½m: usually wears blinkers. *W. Atkinson.*

APPY NELL 2 b.f Appiani II 128–Galloping Nell 68 (Worden II 129) [1976   **—**
6d 5g] second produce: 400 gns foal: dam ran only twice: tailed-off last in June at Ripon (backward) and Doncaster (slowly away). *L. Shedden.*

APRES DEMAIN 3 ch.c. King Emperor–Domani 106 (Mourne 126) [1975   **96**
6fg 6fg* 7g* 7fg³ 1976 8fg* 9.8fg 10.5s 10fg⁴ 8g³ 8g³ 8g] attractive, well-made,

long-striding colt: showed very useful form in 1975: long odds-on, easily won minor event at Leicester in March: raced inconsistently afterwards but put up a creditable effort when third of 12 to Sousa in handicap at Kempton in August: stays 1¼m: acts well on a firm surface and is possibly unsuited by soft going: wears blinkers nowadays: sold privately for export to South Africa. *P. Walwyn.*

APRIL DAYS 2 b.f. Silly Season 127–Maina 118 (St Paddy 133) [1976 6g 7s] very attractive filly: second foal: dam, second in 1971 Oaks, needed at least 1½m: 25/1 when seventh of 19 to Lady Oriana in maiden race at Newmarket in October, second outing and better effort: will do better with time and longer distances: to be trained by H. Cecil in 1977. *N. Murless.* **69 p**

APRIL LUCKY 3 b.g. St Alphage 119–Susceptible 86 (Supreme Court 135) [1975 5s* 5g 7g6 1976 6f 6fg 6g 6g3 7f 6g2 6d6 7v4 6s5] leggy gelding: in frame in varied company, including when good second to Touch of Silver in well-contested seller at Ayr in September: stays 7f: needs some give in the ground and acts on heavy going: blinkered fourth and fifth outings: sometimes sweats up. *C. Crossley.* **63**

APRIL MAGIC 3 b.f. Silent Spring 102–Magic Fin (Magic Red) [1975 5g 1976 11.7f 8f 12.2fg] plain filly: showed no signs of ability in maiden races in first half of season. *W. Williams.* **—**

ARAGLIN 2 ch.f. Rarity 129–Emerald Isle 97 (Kelly 122) [1976 6fg6 6fg 7g] half-sister to several winners, including fair 6f to 1½m winner Kerry Blue (by Tamerlane): dam, half-sister to Sound Track and Flyover, won over 5f: little worthwhile form in maiden races: sold 370 gns Ascot November Sales. *A. Corbett.* **62**

ARAGOSTA 3 b.f. Henry the Seventh 125–Lobster Quadrille 79 (Neptunus 132) [1975 8g 1976 11.7f 12.2f 10f 16f4 13.8g5] poor plater: blinkered last two outings: sold to T. Craig 600 gns Doncaster November Sales. *J. Bethell.* **—**

ARAPAHO 3 b.c. Huntercombe 133–Persuader 118 (Petition 130) [1975 6fg4 7d4 1976 7fg* 8g* 8d 10fg4 7g3 8g 10g* 8s] fine, big, good-looking, rangy colt: won maiden races at Newmarket (by 3 lengths from Silversmith) and **108**

Lady Beaverbrook's "Arapaho"

Sandown (by 5 lengths from Premier Bond), both in April, in good style: gained a further success when beating Shelahnu 2 lengths in £1,700 minor event on latter course in September: usually took on stronger opposition in his other races, putting up a good effort when fifth of nine (subsequently promoted to fourth on disqualification of winner on technical grounds) to Trepan in Joe Coral Eclipse Stakes, also at Sandown, in July: stays 1¼m: acts on a firm surface and is possibly not at his best on a soft one (moved poorly to post on final outing). *R. Hern.*

ARCH SCULPTOR 3 b.c. Habitat 134–Money For Nothing 104 (Grey Sovereign **123** 128 §) [1975 5s⁶ 5d⁶ 6g⁶ 5d* 6g⁴ 1976 8fg 6d 5d² 6.5g* 6.5d² 6g² 6g 6d 8.2v] strong, powerful, good-bodied colt: half-brother to high-class sprinters Mummy's Pet (by Sing Sing) and Parsimony (by Parthia) and to fairly useful sprinter Pennycuick (by Celtic Ash): 35,000 gns yearling: dam useful 5f sprinter: developed into a very smart sprinter and finished runner-up in three pattern races, Prix du Gros-Chene (beaten 2 lengths by stable-companion Kala Shikari) at Chantilly, and Prix Maurice de Gheest (went under by a length to Girl Friend) and Prix de Meautry (this time beaten ½ length by Girl Friend), both at Deauville: 4-length winner of Prix Hampton at Evry in between: ran poorly on both outings in this country, in Duke of York Stakes at York and Challenge Stakes at Newmarket: best at sprint distances: acted on a soft surface: sold at Deauville November Sales 460,000 francs (approx £55,400): stands at Grange Stud, Co. Cork, fee 650 gns. *A. Breasley, France.*

ARC ROUGE 2 ch.c. Supreme Red 93–Irene's Gift (Malfaiteur) [1976 5f **62** 6f⁴ 7fg 7fg⁶ 8s 8.2v] second foal: dam never ran: little worthwhile form and was well beaten in seller on final outing: sold 290 gns Ascot November Sales. *T. Marshall.*

ARCTIC BUNNY 3 b.c. Crisp and Even 116–Brush Off (Arctic Star) [1975 **45** 8d 8g 7g⁶ 1976 11.1fg⁴ 10.1fg⁶ 8fg⁶ 9fg⁴] plater: best run at 11f: blinkered last two outings. *P. Taylor.*

ARCTIC JOHN 6 br.g. Arctic Kanda 111–Malton Hope 92 (High Treason 126) —
[1974 N.R. 1975 N.R. 1976 16f⁵ 14fg⁵ 13.4fg] poor staying maiden: blinkered second and third outings. *M. Bradley.*

ARCTIC RASCAL 5 b.g. Arctic Kanda 111–dam by Port Corsair 98 [1974 **73** N.R. 1975 8v⁴ 10f 12f 8g² 8f³ 8g 8h 11.7f* 10.1fg⁴ 10f 8.2d 10.8g⁵ 10g⁵ 10g² 8g³ 1976 11.7fg⁴ 9f⁴ 12.2f* 10.4fg 10.2f* 16d* 10s* 14d] quite a moderate handicapper: winner at Warwick in August, at Bath and Nottingham the following month and at Chepstow in October: effective at 1¼m and stays 2m well: acts on any going: suitable mount for an inexperienced rider: genuine and consistent. *M. Bradley.*

ARCTIC SPORT 2 b.c. Blakeney 126–Bell Crofts 79 (Arctic Time 127) [1976 —
7v] quite attractive colt: half-sister to two winners, including useful miler Posy (by Major Portion): 7,400 gns yearling: dam won at 9f: virtually pulled up in 16-runner maiden race won by Peace Symbol at Leicester in October, only outing. *M. Jarvis.*

ARCTIC TERN 3 ch.c. Sea-Bird II 145–Bubbling Beauty (Hasty Road) [1975 **126** 6g² 7g² 6.5v* 7.7d* 1976 8s* 8g⁵ 10.5g² 12g 10g⁵ 11d² 12s 12s⁴ 8.2v⁵] French colt: half-brother to several moderate animals: dam, from a good family, ran only twice: put up a good performance when successful in Prix de Fontainebleau at Longchamp in April, beating Roan Star (levels) by ¾ length: ran best subsequent races when second to Youth in two important events at Longchamp, Prix Lupin (beaten ¾ length at levels) and Prix Niel (beaten by same margin, this time in receipt of 4 lb) and when just over 2 lengths fourth to On My Way in Group 2 Prix du Conseil de Paris on same course in October: somewhat disappointing in his other races, Poule d'Essai des Poulains (favourite when fifth of 11 to Red Lord), Prix du Jockey-Club (ninth to Youth), Prix Eugene Adam (favourite when fifth to Crow), Prix de l'Arc de Triomphe (twelfth to Ivanjica) and Prix Perth (fifth to Dominion): stays 1½m: acts well on heavy going: sometimes wears bandages: a high-class colt on his day. *J. Fellows, France.*

ARCTIC TRIBUNE 2 ch.c. Sallust 134–Arctrullah (Great Captain) [1976 **92 p** 5s 5s*] strong, rangy colt: half-brother to several winners, including good Italian 3-y-o Art Style (by Le Levanstell): sold twice as a yearling, for 4,000 gns and 6,000 gns: dam won twice at 2 yrs: 25/1 and still bit backward when running on strongly to win 13-runner maiden race at Sandown in October by 1½ lengths from Tinsley Green: will stay further than sprint distances: has the scope to make a useful colt. *R. Jarvis.*

Queen Anne Stakes, Ascot—Ardoon is strongly pressed by Record Token

ARDEMA 5 b.m. Armistice 131–Demonia (Phil Drake 132) [1974 10f 13.3g — 12f 8d 10g 10s 16v 8d⁵ 1975 8f 10fg⁶ 12f⁴ 12f⁴ 15.8g² 18g⁶ 1976 16f 17.1s⁴] big, strong French-bred mare: plater: evidently suited by a good test of stamina nowadays: probably acts on any going: has run well in blinkers. *R. Sturdy.*

ARDENT PORTION 6 ch.g. Double-U-Jay 120–Fiery Kitten (Buisson Ardent 80 129) [1974 10s 12.2f⁶ 11.7fg 12g⁵ 11.7fg 1975 12f² 12fg* 12fg⁴ 12fg* 12f⁵ 1976 12g 12g 12g⁴ 12fg² 12fg* 13fg* 12fg³ 12f² 12fg² 12d³] strong, medium-sized gelding: moderate handicapper: goes well at Leicester and gained his third victory on that course when beating Molly's Beau 3 lengths in July: awarded race after finishing 1½ lengths second to Zarzaitine at Nottingham later in month: stays 1¼m: appears to act on any going: wears blinkers: consistent. *G. Harwood.*

ARDEUR 3 gr.f. Roan Rocket 128–Softly Glowing 90 (Tutankhamen) [1975 — 5d 5g 6g⁶ 5fg 1976 9d 8fg 8f³ 8h] strong, compact filly: cost 7,000 gns as a yearling but showed only poor form: covered by Mummy's Pet. *J. W. Watts.*

ARDOON 6 b.h. Track Spare 125–Sweet Jewel (Will Somers 114§) [1974 **124** 5v 5s² 5g² 7fg* 6fg 8g² 6fg⁴ 7.3d 6s 1975 8g 7s⁶ 8v³ 7.2g* 8f* 8fg² 8g* 7.2fg² 1976 8f* 8g² 8g³ 7.2d² 8f* 8fg⁴ 8f² 7.3fg*] Since arriving from Ireland in the second half of **1974**, Ardoon has never

Hungerford Stakes, Newbury—another close finish, as Ardoon again holds the challenge of Record Token

stopped improving. As a five-year-old he won three good handicaps, one of them the Royal Hunt Cup, and as a six-year-old, in his final season, he developed into a horse good enough to hold his own in top company at distances around a mile.

Ardoon got off to a flying start. In April he won the Newbury Spring Cup in good style by a length and a half from Yamadori, giving weight to all his eleven opponents except Record Token; and between Newbury and Royal Ascot he ran well to be placed three times, including when going down by two and a half lengths to Record Token, at level weights, in the John of Gaunt Stakes on dead ground at Haydock. Ardoon's chosen engagement at Ascot was the Queen Anne Stakes. Though the race lacked a top-class miler of the calibre of such outstanding recent winners as Welsh Pageant, Sun Prince and Sparkler it was a highly competitive affair. Record Token opposed Ardoon again and of the nine who went to post only the three-year-old Right So appeared to have little chance of success. Ardoon forged clear below the distance but Record Token harried him relentlessly throughout the final furlong, and it was only by a neck that Ardoon took his revenge for defeat at Haydock. Boldboy ran on to be third, four lengths behind Record Token and a length and a half in front of the French challenger Monsanto.

After Royal Ascot Ardoon reached the frame in the Sussex Stakes at Goodwood and the William Hill Gold Cup at Redcar, running well both times, before going on to Newbury to win the last race of his long and splendid career, the Hungerford Stakes. At Goodwood he found the three-year-olds Wollow, Free State and Poacher's Moon too strong for him, but was beaten less than four lengths by Wollow; at Redcar he started favourite, even with 10-0, and went down by only half a length to Claudio Nicolai. As in most of Ardoon's races, his admirable battling qualities were tested to the full at Newbury where, once again, his old rival Record Token proved hardest to beat among fourteen opponents. Forcefully ridden by Taylor, Ardoon took a definite advantage about three furlongs from home and got the better of another final-furlong tussle with Record Token by the same margin as at Ascot—a neck. Behind the first two came a strong field led by Thieving Demon, Scott Joplyn and Super Cavalier.

Ardoon (b.h. 1970)	Track Spare (b 1963)	Sound Track (ch 1957)	Whistler
			Bridle Way
		Rosy Myth (b 1958)	Nearco
			Rosy Dolly
	Sweet Jewel (b 1965)	Will Somers (br 1955)	Tudor Minstrel
			Queen's Jest
		Diamond Deuce (ch 1950)	Windsor Slipper
			Lilting Lady

Ardoon is the first foal of Sweet Jewel, an Irish mare who raced until she was three and won at up to a mile. Sweet Jewel is a half-sister to the winners Staysail, successful thirteen times in the United States, and All of a Kind, a very useful two-year-old in this country. The second dam, Diamond Deuce, won over five furlongs as a two-year-old and was placed over a mile and a half the following season. Sweet Jewel's foals to race since Ardoon include Ardallen (by Wolver Hollow) who won four times at up to a mile and a half in Ireland. Track Spare has sired other tough, honest performers besides Ardoon, Record Run being the most notable. Ardoon commences stallion duties appropriately enough at his owner-breeder's stud, the Ardoon Stud, at Newbridge, Co. Kildare, at a fee of 800 guineas with an October 1st concession.

A strong, good-topped individual, he acted on any going although he was particularly well suited by a firm surface. *G. Pritchard-Gordon.*

ARGO 3 ch.f. Decoy Boy 129–Maid of Athens (Acropolis 132) [1975 5fg 5f^6 5f^5 5g^6 5g 6g 1976 8.2f 8fg 6g^4 6g 5.9fg 5g 5s 5s^6 6s] big, lengthy filly: modest plater: stays 6f: slipped and unseated rider final outing: trained part of season by K. Ivory. *A. W. Jones.* —

ARGUMENTAL P 3 ch.c. Green God 128–Lovely Woman 81 (Primera 131) [1975 5d 5.1f^3 5f* 5fg^2 5.1g^4 5f 6v 1976 7fg 6f^3 5.8f^4 6fg* 5.1fg^4 6h] well-grown colt: modest handicapper: winner at Yarmouth in May: runs as though he will stay further than 6f: ran moderately final outing (July). *R. Hollinshead.* **80**

ARI MOU 3 br.g. Prevailing–Lake Shore Drive (Master Owen) [1975 N.R. 1976 12fg 10.1g 10g] compact gelding: first produce: 1,700 gns foal, resold 360 gns Ascot May Sales: dam a winning stayer in Ireland: behind in maiden races at —

Newbury, Windsor and Sandown (very slowly into stride) and was sold again 600 gns Ascot November. *J. Old.*

ARISTOTLE 3 b.c. St Paddy 133–Bee Keeper 90 (Honeyway 125) [1975 5f   **67** 5g³ 6g² 7fg 7fg 5d 1976 6.5s⁶ 6.5g 6.5g⁶ 5v 8.2f 5f³ 6fg³ 5g⁴ 6fg³ 7fg 5h² 5.8h³ 5fg 5g⁴ 5f* 5g⁶ 5h² 6g] strong, good-bodied colt: good mover: quickly drew clear in last furlong when winning apprentice handicap at Haydock in August by 3 lengths from Panglima: best form at 5f and 6f but is bred to stay middle distances: acts on hard ground: usually wears blinkers. *D. Sasse.*

ARKENGARTHDALE 2 b.f. Sweet Story 122–Fortzeno 78 (Fortino II 120)   — [1976 7s] third reported foal: sister to a poor animal and half-sister to a winning plater: dam won over 6f at 3 yrs: unquoted when behind in 20-runner maiden race won by Brightly at Newmarket in October. *J. Powney.*

ARMELLE 2 b.f. Tribal Chief 125–Rosaberry 84 (Rockefella) [1976 5fg 5f* 5f⁴   **87** 5.9f² 6h³ 5g⁵ 6s⁴] small, sturdy filly: fifth foal: half-sister to a winner in Malaysia: dam a moderate 2-y-o: won 14-runner maiden race at Nottingham in June by 3 lengths from Elizabeggs: ran consistently well afterwards, including when neck second to Jenny Splendid in nursery at Wolverhampton in August: well suited by 6f: probably acts on any going. *H. Candy.*

AROCHE 2 b.f. Forli–Rock Diamond (Princely Gift 137) [1976 5fg* 6fg⁵]   **85** American-bred filly: sister to 3-y-o French 1m and 9f winner Radetzky March, and half-sister to several minor winners in U.S.A.: 14,000 gns yearling: dam won at 2 yrs and 3 yrs in U.S.A.: quickened to lead inside final furlong when winning 10-runner maiden race at Haydock in July by ¾ length from Galloway Wold: favourite for £2,200 nursery at Newmarket later in month but finished only fifth of 11 to Charley's Revenge: should stay 1m. *B. Hills.*

ARONIA 2 gr.f. Roan Rocket 128–Rosyta 85 (Reform 132) [1976 5d] first foal: — dam winner at up to 1½m: blinkered when tenth of 11 to Stephandre in maiden race at Doncaster in May: sold 5,400 gns Newmarket December Sales. *R. Hern.*

ARONTA 2 b.f. Town Crier 119–Miss Twist 84 (Major Portion 129) [1976 7v]   — closely related to fairly useful 1972 2-y-o Regal Miss (by Sovereign Path) and half-sister to two winners: 4,200 gns yearling: dam won at 1¼m: 20/1 when in rear in 15-runner minor event won by North Stoke at Lingfield in November, only outing. *B. Swift.*

ARRAS JEWEL 2 b.f. Willipeg 112–Wildeye 85 (Solonaway 128) [1976 5g 5s   — 5s] half-sister to moderate miler Arras Gem (by Three Wishes): dam best at 6f or 7f: behind in maiden and minor events in the autumn. *A Smith.*

ARROWSMITH 2 ch.f. Sky Gipsy 117–Grand Velvet 83 (Grand Roi 118)   **71** [1976 5f 7fg 7g 7g⁴] second foal: dam stayed well: finished strongly when 3 lengths fourth of 21 to Sosue Me in £1,600 seller at Newmarket in September: will be better suited by 1m or more. *R. Smyth.*

ARTAIUS 2 b.c. Round Table–Stylish Pattern (My Babu 136) [1976 8d²] **110** p American-bred Irish colt: half-brother to several winners, including Ascot 1,000 Guineas Trial winner Embroidery (by Double Jay) and stakes winner Stylish Genie (by Bagdad): $110,000 yearling: dam half-sister to smart middle-distance colt Arthurian (by Round Table): failed by 2 lengths to beat Orchestra when long odds on for six-runner Beresford Stakes at the Curragh in October but nevertheless ran very well for a newcomer, comfortably accounting for some useful animals after having anything but a clear run: will stay middle distances: clearly has a big reputation and looks sure to make a smart performer. *V. O'Brien, Ireland.*

ARTHUR LEES 4 b.c. Jimmy Reppin 131–Margravine 75 (Nimbus 130) [1974   — 5g³ 7s⁵ 7v* 6v² 1975 8s⁵ 8fg 8g 1976 10fg 8d 10g] big, strong, good sort of colt: useful performer at 2 yrs: mainly disappointing afterwards: stayed 1¼m: showed all his form on an easy surface: well beaten in blinkers final outing: dead. *J. Sutcliffe.*

ARTIFICE 5 b.g. Master Owen–Lady Artist II (Artist's Son) [1974 N.R. 1975   — 16v* 16v² 16v⁴ 12g* 1976 11.1g⁵] ex-Irish gelding: brother to 13f winner Art Mistress and half-brother to several winners, including dual Irish Cesarewitch winner Bigaroon (by Bowsprit): dam won over 2m: respectable fifth to Irish

Harmony in amateur riders race at Kempton in May, only outing on flat (better known as a useful hurdler nowadays): stays well: acts on heavy going. *J. Thorne.*

ASAMA 4 gr.c. Ribero 126–Field Mouse 108 (Grey Sovereign 128 §) [1974 **101** 8d5 7v 1975 10.1f 11.1fg 12d4 14fg* 15g2 12f* 16g3 1976 16.1d2 13s6 16g2 19fg3] well-made colt: good walker: quite a useful performer: ran well on three of his four outings, finishing 2½ lengths second of five to Mr Bigmore in Lymm Stakes at Haydock in May, neck second to Night In Town in Brown Jack Stakes at Ascot in July and 8½ lengths third to Sea Anchor in Goodwood Stakes later in July: stays well: acts on any going with the possible exception of very soft (very disappointing when hot favourite on second appearance). *R. Price.*

ASAPH'S BOY 3 b.g. Cornhill 60–St Asaph 68 (Dunoon Star 110) [1975 N.R. — 1976 10f 12d 16f6 8f 8h] leggy, light-framed gelding: only poor form. *J. Leigh.*

ASA YOLSON 3 b.c. Luthier 126–Bernina (Prudent II 133) [1975 5.9f* 7h4 **97** 7f* 7g* 1976 7g* 7fg 7g4 8fg 10.5s 7.6h4 7fg5 7.6g 7.6g 7s6] leggy, useful sort: won £1,200 event at Folkestone in March by ½ length from Egalaloon: ran well from time to time afterwards, notably when good fourth of 15 to Royal Boy in James Lane 2,000 Guineas Trial at Kempton the following month: should stay 1m (out of his depth in 2,000 Guineas and Mecca-Dante Stakes on only attempts at 1m or more): acts on firm going: occasionally sweats up. *D. Marks.*

AS BLESSED 2 b.f. So Blessed 130–Asmara 94 (Alycidon 138) [1976 5d* 5g* 5f4 **101** 6g 5s] rangy, quite attractive filly: keen walker: closely related to fair sprinter Bless Me (by Princely Gift) and half-sister to useful performers Tudoron (by Tudor Melody) and Ashabit (by Habitat): 4,600 gns yearling: dam won at 1¼m: won £1,700 maiden race at York in May and Arabella Stakes at Kempton later in month, beating Blue Linnet going away by 2½ lengths after being bit slowly into stride in latter race: had a very bad run when fourth to Cramond in Queen Mary Stakes at Royal Ascot the following month and did very well to be beaten only 1½ lengths: off course some time afterwards and then finished in rear in William Hill Cheveley Park Stakes at Newmarket and a well-contested race at Doncaster: will probably stay 1m. *C. Brittain.*

ASCENSURE 10 b.g. Conwyn 88–Ascension 87 (Sol Oriens) [1974 N.R. — 1975 N.R. 1976 12g6] moderate N.H. performer: well-beaten sixth of 15 to Commandant in amateur riders race at Leicester in April, first outing on flat. *J. Spearing.*

ASCOT DANDY 3 b.g. Taste of Honey 92–Radio City (Bleep-Bleep 134) [1975 — N.R. 1976 7g 8f6] half-brother to very useful 6f and 7f winner Welsh City (by Maestoso): dam poor plater: never showed in maiden races at Leicester in April and Brighton in May. *B. Swift.*

ASCOT ROYALE 5 gr.g. Track Spare 125–Petite Path 106 (Sovereign Path **68** 125) [1974 8g 8fg 10g 12g6 10fg6 8g 10g* 9d 8fg 12.2g 9d6 9g4 8s 8s 1975 8s* 8f 8f 8g 8fg5 7.6g 8d6 8.2fg3 10g 10g2 8fg5 9fg* 10g2 10fg2 10g3 7d2 1976 8g3 10f 8d 8fg5 8fg 10fg3 8f* 8f3 10fg3 8h2 9g5 8f 8fg4 8v 7v] strong, compact gelding: quite a moderate handicapper: won eight-runner apprentice handicap at Lingfield in June: not disgraced afterwards: stays 1¼m: appears to act on any going: has been tried in blinkers: suitable mount for a lady rider. *R. Mason.*

ASCOT WEATHER 3 b.f. Silly Season 127–Partridge 65 (Mossborough 126) **73** [1975 N.R. 1976 8f5 8fg5 8f5 8f2 10f* 10fg* 10fg5 10g5 10g] neat filly: quite a good mover: first foal: dam, suited by a distance of ground, is sister to five winners, including smart 1½m filly Beaufront: short-priced favourite when winning handicaps at Redcar and Newcastle in July, on both occasions having race in her pocket from 2f out: will probably stay 1½m: acts on firm going: blinkered third outing: ran below her best last three appearances: sold 3,000 gns Newmarket December Sales. *J. W. Watts.*

ASCURRY MILL 3 b.g. Bilsborrow 85–Dance Hall Tramp (Polic 126) [1975 — N.R. 1976 15f6 15g4] apparently of little account. *T. Craig.*

ASDIC 5 b.g. Astec 128–Boat Hook 103 (Hook Money 124) [1974 12g2 12g* — 14g6 12fg3 11.7fg5 12g3 14s2 12g6 16d 1975 12s3 12d* 12s2 12fg2 12fg 12fg3 11.6g 12d 12fg 1976 12fg 12g6 12fg6] shapely gelding, and a very nice mover: most disappointing on flat since fourth start as a 4-y-o: stays 1¾m: appears to act on any going: has run creditably for an apprentice but is ideally suited by strong handling. *S. Ingham.*

ASHABIT   3 b.c. Habitat 134–Asmara 94 (Alycidon 138)   [1975 5fg³ 6f² 6fg* **103**
6fg² 6fg² 7g*   1976 7fg 8d 8.2d 8f⁴ 8fg*]   small, attractive, sturdy colt: showed
useful form at 2 yrs: returned to his best when winning handicap at Sandown in
July, quickening in good style to beat Mossberry by 3 lengths: may stay further
than 1m: evidently not at his best on softish ground: genuine: exported by
B.B.A. to New Zealand. *P. Walwyn.*

ASHBRO LADDO   3 ch.c. Roi Soleil 124–Rajput Rose (Buisson Ardent 129) **114**
[1975 5f² 6g⁴ 7g*   1976 8d² 8.2d⁶ 8g 8g* 10d⁴ 8s*]   attractive, quite well-made
colt: useful handicapper: won valuable William Hill Trophy at Sandown in
September by 1½ lengths from Game Lord: went clear in a few strides when
successful on same course the following month, beating Yamadori most decisively
by 4 lengths: stays 1m but appeared not to stay when tried at 1¼m: acts on soft
going: suited by a strong gallop. *R. Price.*

ASHDOWN FOREST   4 b.f. Bivouac 114–Hammerwood (Combat 123)   [1974   —
5f 5v⁶ 1975 10.1f 8g 6fg   1976 12g⁵ 12g⁵]   small filly: only poor form: possibly
needs soft ground. *J. Edwards.*

ASHEN LIGHT   2 ch.f. Shiny Tenth 120–Rao Ash (Celtic Ash) [1976 5g 6g   **76**
5.9f* 6g² 7g⁶ 8s⁵]   first foal: 500 gns yearling: dam never ran: showed improved
form when winning nine-runner maiden race at Wolverhampton in August by ¾
length from Burnished Gold: had no chance with easy winner Breast Stroke in
nursery at Windsor later in month but finished clear of nine others: should stay
beyond 6f: acts on firm going. *A. Johnson.*

ASHINGORA   4 b.f. Raffingora 130–Hopton Ash 97 (Celtic Ash) [1974 5fg
5f 6s⁴ 6fg 6fg 1975 8v³ 9.4g⁵ 11f* 11f⁵ 12h 12f 1976 10g⁵ 13f 10f 10fg 8d]
strong, compact filly: poor plater: stays 11f: acts on any going: has been tried in
blinkers: not raced after May. *A. Dent.*

ASHMORE   5 b.h. Luthier 126–Almyre (Wild Risk) [1974 12g² 12g* 11s⁴ **125**
15.5s⁶ 12.5g³ 13.5d* 13.5g* 15.5g³ 12v 1975 12v⁵ 12g* 12f² 12.5g² 12f⁶ 1976
12.5g² 12g 13.5d* 13.5g* 12g]
    The Wildenstein racing stables housed a wealth of talent in 1976. Flying
Water, Pawneese and Crow carried the Wildenstein colours to success in three
English classics and, with Pawneese also taking the King George VI and Queen
Elizabeth Diamond Stakes, M Wildenstein's horses won for him in Britain
during the season £244,500, easily a record in this country for an owner. And to
think that at one point in the previous season he was saying that he might not run
any more horses in England because they were always unlucky here!

    Ashmore, the best middle-distance horse above the age of three in the
Wildenstein string, raided these shores only once in 1976, being well beaten by
Pawneese at Ascot. English racegoers will remember him better as the horse
who gave Bustino a good race in the 1975 Coronation Cup. Bustino broke the
track record that day but Ashmore stuck gamely to him all the way in the
straight and went down only by a length. That must rank as one of Ashmore's
very best performances, along with his two successes in the Grand Prix de
Deauville, his win as a four-year-old in the valuable Prix Jean de Chaudenay at
Saint-Cloud and his two close seconds in the Grand Prix de Saint-Cloud. As this
record suggests Ashmore is not quite in the same league as some of his more
illustrious stable-companions; but he's a very good horse nonetheless as a glance
at the Handicap Libre, published in October, will show. The French handicapper
rated Ashmore the second-best horse above three years to race at distances of
a mile or more in France in 1976, behind only the Prix de l'Arc winner Ivanjica.

    Ashmore didn't run as a five-year-old until July when he lined up for the
Grand Prix de Saint-Cloud. It was his first time out since finishing sixth to
Grundy in the King George VI and Queen Elizabeth Stakes almost a year before.
The stable had two runners in the Grand Prix and the stable-jockey elected to
ride the in-form Maitland; but it was Ashmore who ran much the better race,
losing by half a length to the filly Riverqueen, who had won the Poule d'Essai
des Pouliches (French Guineas) and had suffered her only defeat up to that time
when runner-up to Pawneese in the Prix de Diane (French Oaks). The English
challengers for the Grand Prix, the four-year-olds Quiet Fling and Libra's Rib,
who had finished first and second in the Coronation Cup, were no match for
Riverqueen and Ashmore. At Deauville in August Ashmore picked up two races,
the Prix de Reux, the weights for which greatly favoured him, and the much more
important Grand Prix de Deauville. Ashmore had won the Grand Prix de

Grand Prix de Deauville—a decisive win for Ashmore over Diagramatic and Duke of Marmalade

Deauville as a three-year-old when he was awarded the race after being hampered by Admetus who was first past the post. Nothing was near enough to Ashmore in the closing stages of the race in 1976 to cause him any trouble—he was out on his own at the end, four lengths clear of the hitherto-unbeaten three-year-old Diagramatic with some other good animals further behind.

		Luthier (br 1965)	Klairon (b 1952)		Clarion III Kalmia
			Flute Enchantee (b 1950)		Cranach Montagnana
Ashmore (b.h. 1971)		Almyre (b 1964)	Wild Risk (b 1940)		Rialto Wild Violet
			Ad Gloriam (b 1958)		Alizier Ad Altiora

An admirably bold policy has always been pursued with M Wildenstein's top horses and in October Ashmore was sent to race in North America. Saint-Martin went to ride him in the Jockey Club Gold Cup at Belmont Park, passing up the mount on the William Hill Futurity runner Juge de Paix on the same day. The race was run on dirt and Ashmore failed to distinguish himself, coming home ninth of the ten runners. Ashmore is a really good sort of horse who stays well and acts on any going (although reportedly he missed the Prix de l'Arc because his connections considered the ground too soft for him). If he stays in training he should win more high-class races. In point of merit he is about as good a racehorse as was his sire Luthier who, however, seemed best at distances short of a mile and a half and showed very good form at a mile and a mile and a quarter as a three-year-old. Ashmore is the second foal of Almyre who subsequently bred the smart filly Acoma (by Rheffic) whose highly promising career was cut short by injury in 1976. Almyre was a very useful staying mare, a winner at up to thirteen furlongs. The grandam Ad Gloriam didn't win a race but is a half-sister to the 1963 French One Thousand Guineas winner Altissima. *A. Penna, France.*

ASHTEAD 2 ch.c. Shiny Tenth 120–Crincan 83 (Tesco Boy 121) [1976 5.3fg 5f **67** 6g 6g 7g 7s⁴ 10v³] poor mover: plater: ran best races on last two outings: will probably stay 1½m: evidently needs a soft surface and acts well on heavy going: pulled up lame on second start: blinkered fifth appearance. *D. Whelan.*

ASHTON AUTO 2 ch.f. Mountain Call 125–Gaol Bird 84 (High Treason 126) **—** [1976 6v] maiden first foal: 2,500 gns yearling: dam, winner over 1¼m, is sister to Tower Walk: unquoted and in need of outing when behind in 23-runner maiden race won by Amity at Newbury in October. *J. Nelson.*

ASPECT 2 b.c. Huntercombe 133–High Order 102 (Hugh Lupus 132) [1976 **115** 5fg² 6f* 6g² 6h* 6s*] Three wins and two seconds from five starts was Aspect's record in his first season, and the indications are that he will train on and continue to do well as a three-year-old. Card Player and Adviser were the two to beat him—Card Player by four lengths in the May Maiden Stakes at the Newmarket Spring meeting, and Adviser by three lengths, when conceding 3 lb, in the Sirenia Stakes at Kempton in August. Of his successes, two—those at Yarmouth in August on his second appearance and at Pontefract in September on his fourth outing—were gained easily from weak opposition, and it was his performance in the Potter Trophy at Newmarket in October on his final appearance which stamped him as a smart two-year-old. Taking the lead approaching the distance, Aspect ran on resolutely to hold off Crimson Silk by a length and a half, the pair drawing right away from the four-times winner Jenny Splendid in the last furlong. Swift

Hussar, who had come out much the same horse as Aspect in their races against Card Player and Adviser, was beaten over ten lengths into sixth place.

		Huntercombe		Derring-Do		Darius
		(br 1967)		(br 1961)		Sipsey Bridge
Aspect				Ergina		Fair Trial
b.c. 1974)				(br 1957)		Ballechin
				Hugh Lupus		Djebel
		High Order		(b 1952)		Sakountala
		(b 1964)		Bride Elect		Big Game
				(b 1952)		Netherton Maid

It will be noticed that Aspect, a well-grown, leggy colt, who cost 4,100 guineas as a yearling, has yet to race beyond six furlongs, but we'll be surprised if another furlong proves beyond him, even though his sire, Huntercombe, was essentially a sprinter. Indeed we expect Aspect to be suited by seven furlongs, and to show improved form at that distance. His dam, a sister to the St Leger winner Hethersett, won at nine furlongs, and to Kashmir II has bred Hari Singh, a winner over a mile in France. Other factors in Aspect's favour are that he can, apparently, give his running whatever the state of the ground, and that he had the benefit of an easy first season: so everything considered it would indeed be surprising were he not to train on and do well as a three-year-old. Make a note of him for the Free Handicap! *Doug Smith.*

ASPIRE 5 ch.g. Crocket 130–Time Bomb (Supreme Court 135) [1974 8fg⁴ 9f⁴ **68** 10f⁵ 12d 12.2fg³ 12d 13s 10g 1975 11.7g⁶ 12d 11.1g 12d³ 1976 13g* 12.2f² 12.2d* 12f³] neat gelding: very good mover: quite a moderate performer: won seller at Nottingham in April and 11-runner handicap (non-seller) at Catterick the following month: stayed 13f: seemed to act on any going: dead. *H. Williams.*

ASSET 5 b.g. Birdbrook 110 or Acer 123–Chantel-Gold 74 (Chantelsey 130) [1974 11.2f³ 12f* 14.7f* 14.6g² 14.7g* 14.7g⁴ 14fg 14.6fg* 15s² 16v⁶ 1975 13d² 13f* 16fg⁵ 12h⁴ 16f⁵ 1976 15fg⁶] strong gelding: quite a useful handicapper (rated 92) in 1975: 20/1 when remote sixth of seven to Beechwood Lad at Edinburgh in September, only outing as a 5-y-o: needs a test of stamina: appears to act on any going but is particularly well suited by firm: sometimes wears blinkers (didn't at Edinburgh). *G. Richards.*

ASSEZ CUITE 2 b.f. Graustark–Clinkers 111 (Relic) [1976 5d* 7s² 8s] **114** American-bred French filly: half-sister to winners here and in France, including very useful French middle-distance performer Chavin (by Herbager) and fairly useful 1974 2-y-o 7f winner Bloody Tower (by Forward Pass): dam, very useful at 5f and 6f, is daughter of smart sprinter La Fresnes: put up a smart performance when taking on colts in Prix de la Salamandre at Longchamp in September, making most of running and keeping on so well when headed that she kept second place, 2 lengths behind Blushing Groom: had previously come out best in close finish in Prix Yacowlef at Deauville in August, winning by ½ length from Captains Queen: fourth favourite for 14-runner Criterium des Pouliches at Longchamp in October but could finish only 6 lengths seventh to Kamicia: suited by 7f and should stay further: acts on soft going. *J. Fellows, France.*

ASSURANCE 4 b.c. Astec 128–Shawlie 91 (St Paddy 133) [1975 5v⁶ 5f⁶ 6g⁴ **94** 6fg 7f² 7d² 7g² 7g³ 8fg⁴ 8g 1976 10.8fg* 10g² 10.8f* 10fg* 11.7f² 10fg* 10g⁴ 10fg 10.5g⁵ 10d] good sort: quite a useful handicapper: showed much improved form in first part of season and won at Warwick (twice, maiden race and minor event), Lingfield (Cosmopolitan Cup, narrowly after a ding-dong battle with Prince Pepe) and Epsom (beat Little Tern ½ length): ran well below his best afterwards: should stay 1½m: goes very well on fast ground and a sharp track: has been tried in blinkers but does better without. *G. Harwood.*

ASSURED 3 b.g. Reliance II 137–Qualm 91 (Royal Palm 131) [1975 6fg 8g **97** 7g⁶ 8g 1976 12g² 13.4s* 16fg² 16g³ 16g³ 14s*] tall, fair sort of gelding: quite a useful handicapper: put up a good performance when winning at Chester in May by ¾ length from Crimson Coon: ran creditably afterwards, particularly on last two outings, and gained a further success when coming with a well-timed run to beat Light Lager at Sandown in October: very well suited by a test of stamina: appears to act on any going but goes particularly well on soft. *H. Candy.*

ASTON FIRS 2 br.f. Linacre 133–Rose Vale (Valerullah 113) [1976 6f⁶ 7f² 6fg² **97** 6h* 7d 6s*] compact filly: half-sister to two winners here and abroad, including 1966 Irish 2,000 Guineas third Not So Cold (by Arctic Time): 260 gns yearling: dam placed over 5f in Ireland at 2 yrs: successful twice, trotting up from poor

opposition: n maiden race at Carlisle in August and beating Greek Myth 4 lengths
in eight-runner minor race at Catterick in October (scored with something in
hand): should stay 1m: acts on any going: ran moderately on fifth outing.
N. Adam.

ASTOR BOY 4 ch.c. Skymaster 126–Shawlie 91 (St Paddy 133) [1974 5g **99**
5f⁶ 6v 1975 6s 7s² 6f² 7fg³ 8.3fg 7d 8g 9g* 7.6s 8g* 1976 7fg⁵ 7fg* 10h* 7g*
11.7fg* 8fg*] rangy colt: fairly useful handicapper: had a fine season, winning
five races in a row, at Newbury, Windsor, Kempton and Lingfield (twice),
before the end of August: effective at 7f and stays 1½m: acts on any going and
on any track: ran poorly when tried in blinkers at 3 yrs: suitable mount for
an apprentice or lady rider: genuine and consistent. *Miss A. Sinclair.*

ATHENA ROYALE 2 b.f. Athens Wood 126–Imperatrice (Bold Ruler) [1976 **78**
6fg 6f³ 6g 7g] rather hollow-backed filly: half-sister to 9f winner Cleo (by
Vimy) and to a prolific winner in France and Italy: dam lightly raced: quite
modest form in maiden and minor events: should be suited by 1¼m+. *B.
Hobbs.*

ATHENIA PRINCESS 2 b.f. Athens Wood 126–Pytchley Princess 107 (Privy **80**
Councillor 125) [1976 7g⁶ 7fg⁵ 7.2f³] strong, lengthy filly: third living foal:
half-sister to Hunting Man (by Mandamus), a winner in Belgium and over
1¼m in France: dam a miler: moderate maiden: 4½ lengths third of 11 to Shardia
in minor event at Haydock in August: will be suited by 1¼m+. *D. Morley.*

ATHENS GOLD 2 ch.g. Athens Wood 126–Golden Handshake 92 (Golden —
Cloud) [1976 6g 8g] half-brother to six winners, including fair sprinter Gay
City (by Forlorn River): 2,000 gns yearling: dam won at 1m: dwelt when well
behind in maiden races at Newcastle in August and Ayr in September. *L.
Shedden.*

ATHLETE'S FOOT 2 br.f. Prince Tenderfoot 126–Persian Pie (Tamerlane **115**
128) [1976 5d⁴ 5g* 5f 5g*]
     Contagious ringworm of the feet, athlete's foot for short, seems an unlikely
and unfortunate source of name for an expensive racehorse, even one by Prince
Tenderfoot. There have been more indelicate namings than Athlete's Foot—
Tape Worm is one that springs to mind—but they have usually been redeemed
by their underlying wit, as with Tape Worm who was by Sound Track out of
Creepy Crawley by The Bug. But what's in a name when it comes to performances? Inelegant handle or not, Athlete's Foot has proved an extremely
speedy filly, one of the fastest of her age and sex seen out in 1976.
     Athlete's Foot's last race of the season produced by far her best performance.
She was the only two-year-old to take on older sprinters in the Sir Gatric Stakes
at Doncaster's St Leger meeting and she seemed to have a very stiff task;
her rivals included the Palace House Stakes winner Polly Peachum, the smart
Irish filly Thrifty Trio, the good ex-Italian colt Madang and the King George
Stakes winner Music Boy. She was far from friendless in the market though,
and comfortably justified the confidence behind her. After travelling very
smoothly all the way next to the stand rails, she quickened well to lead one and
a half furlongs out and was in no danger from then on, crossing the line two
and a half lengths clear of the three-year-old Minstrel. A length and a half
further back came Thrifty Trio who ran on to beat the favourite Polly Peachum
by half a length. This was an excellent run by Athlete's Foot, especially as
it was her first outing for nearly three months and she was also reported to

*Sir Gatric Stakes, Doncaster—Athlete's Foot beats
her seniors Minstrel and Thrifty Trio*

have come in season on the morning of the race, but the result doesn't put her in the top class. Minstrel is no more than a very useful handicapper, and Polly Peachum, who was meeting Athlete's Foot on terms worse than weight-for-age, was almost certainly past her best after a strenuous campaign. It would have been most enlightening to see how Athlete's Foot fared against the top European sprinters in the Prix de l'Abbaye de Longchamp, her proposed objective, but soon after Doncaster it was reported that she had suffered a setback and was out for the season.

Athlete's Foot's other runs require little describing. Her trainer pitched her in at the deep end on her first outing, letting her take on the previous winners Godswalk, Digitalis and Piney Ridge on weight-for-sex terms in the Marble Hill Stakes at the Curragh in May. She was beaten about eleven lengths into fourth place but really impressed us for a newcomer, matching strides with Godswalk for three furlongs. Twelve days later she went some way towards fulfilling this promise, comfortably winning a small race at Naas by three lengths, but at Royal Ascot she proved a great disappointment in the Queen Mary Stakes, being beaten soon after three furlongs and finishing only ninth of twelve behind Cramond. Obviously this was not her true form and it might be significant that she was off the course for so long afterwards. Possibly the firm ground did not suit her.

Athlete's Foot (br.f. 1974)	Prince Tenderfoot (b 1967)	Blue Prince (b 1951)	Princequillo / Blue Denim
		La Tendresse (b 1959)	Grey Sovereign / Isetta
	Persian Pie (b 1963)	Tamerlane (br 1952)	Persian Gulf / Eastern Empress
		Honey Pie (b 1956)	Combat / Sweet Pickle

Persian Pie, Athlete's Foot's dam, went to stud in 1967 and produced a foal in each of the next eight years. Of her seven foals of racing age, six have run and all of them have won a race of some description. The best of them before Athlete's Foot was undoubtedly the very speedy Whistling Wind colt Persian Breeze, top weight in the 1975 Northern Free Handicap; but Masandra (also by Whistling Wind) and Crusty Shah (by Tyrant) both showed useful form over sprint distances. Persian Pie's eighth foal, a colt by that successful young sire Northfields, fetched 36,000 guineas as a yearling and may well improve his dam's already notable record. Persian Pie's racing career gave little indication that she possessed any ability—she failed to reach the first six in any of her six outings from five furlongs to eleven furlongs—and her immediate family achieved little of note; Honey Pie won a small five-furlong race at two years and bred one winner, and the next dam failed to win before producing four ordinary winners in the British Isles.

The 12,000 guineas Athlete's Foot cost as a yearling now looks money well spent. In appearance she is most attractive, being strong and good-quartered, and she looks the type to make a very smart sprinter at three years. Smart though she may be, she may find worthwhile races hard to come by at three; Ireland still doesn't stage many good-class sprint events and she will have to improve quite a few pounds to beat the best of the colts in England's top races. *P. Prendergast, Ireland.*

ATLANTIC BRIDGE 2 gr.c. Dike–Crossing (Le Haar 126) [1976 7v²] fourth   **96 p**
foal: half-brother to a winning plater by Beau Garcon: 4,800 gns yearling: dam, half-sister to very smart French colt Crossen, won over 1½m in France: 12/1, put up an excellent effort for a newcomer in nine-runner minor event at Lingfield in November, holding every chance 2f out and staying on so well that he failed by only a short head to catch Imperial Guard: will stay 1½m: sure to improve and win races. *R. Price.*

ATLANTIC CROSSING 2 b.c. Tribal Chief 125–Poppy Day 78 (Soleil II 133)   **77**
[1976 5.1fg⁵ 5f⁵ 5g 5g³ 5s⁶ 6d] good-bodied colt: second foal: brother to 1975 2-y-o 5f winner Noble Memory: 1,250 gns yearling: dam a sprinter: quite a moderate maiden: best form at 5f: probably acts on any going. *K. Ivory.*

ATLANTIC PRINCE 2 b.c. Four Burrow 91–Newstead Belle 74 (Chamier 128)   **76**
[1976 6fg⁵ 8f⁴ 8g 8s] brother to 1m to 1½m winner Atlantic Princess: dam of little account: narrowly-beaten fourth of eight in maiden race awarded to

Cabin Boy at Bath in September, best effort: will stay 1½m: acts on firm going. *P. Cole.*

ATOP 4 b.f. Aureole 132–Tudor Top 104 (Tudor Minstrel 144) [1974 7v — 1975 12f 12f 1976 11.7f] seems of little account. *J. Cann.*

ATREFS 3 ch.c. Continuation 120–Flying Vail (Valerullah 113) [1975 6fg — 6g 1976 7g 7g] brother to two winners, including fair 1970 2-y-o 7f winner Harvedothos: no worthwhile form in maiden races. *M. Smyly.*

ATREK 9 b.g. Crocket 130–Caspian Sea 95 (Tehran) [1974 6g⁶ 6g⁴ 6g³ 6fg⁴ 7f **53** 6g⁴ 6fg 6g* 7fg 6s 6s 1975 6g 5v⁴ 6fg 6g³ 7f 6h⁴ 7.6g⁴ 6g⁴ 6g 5f 5f² 5g⁶ 7fg 1976 5f 8v² 8g⁶ 8f 10s⁵ 7.6fg⁵ 6f⁶ 7v] poor handicapper: best at up to 1m: acts on any going: usually wears blinkers: goes well on a sharp track: very inconsistent. *E. Collingwood.*

ATTIVO 6 b.g. Appiani II 128–El Galgo 64 (Miralgo 130) [1974 18.4g* 16fg* **84** 16d⁵ 1975 N.R. 1976 18fg⁴ 14s⁴] useful handicapper in 1974 (rated 102): ran by far his better race since when strong-finishing fourth of 10 to Assured at Sandown in October: stays extremely well: acts on any going: has been tried in blinkers: usually apprentice ridden: off course over five months between outings. *P. Mitchell.*

ATTRACTIVE THIEF 5 b.g. Burglar 128–Romantic Colleen (St Paddy 133) — [1974 7fg 5fg⁵ 5f 8d 5.3fg³ 8g 5.9g³ 1975 N.R. 1976 10f 8fg] lengthy gelding: rated 65 at 3 yrs: well beaten both outings, including in a seller, as a 5-y-o: best at 5f: acts on a firm surface: sold 410 gns Ascot June Sales. *K. Bridgwater.*

ATTYMON PLACE 3 b.c. Mummy's Pet 125–Bashi 73 (Zarathustra 131) **88** [1975 5s⁴ 5f* 5f 5fg³ 5.9f² 5f² 5f* 5fg⁶ 5.3f³ 5g 5g 1976 5g⁵ 5d 5fg 8f 5h⁵ 5f*] neat colt: quite a useful handicapper on his day: put up a good performance when winning narrowly under 10-0 at Warwick in August: best form at 5f: acts well on firm going: blinkered (second time) at Warwick. *P. Cole.*

ATWOOD 2 gr.c Athens Wood 126–Luciennes 108 (Grey Sovereign 128 §) **104** [1976 7f 7fg³ 7f 7h 7d² 7fg² 8s² 8s⁶] workmanlike colt: half-brother to two winners, including very smart 3-y-o sprinter Broxted (by Busted): 600 gns yearling: dam won her first two races at 2 yrs: second in maiden race and nurseries: put up a useful effort on last occasion, going down only by a short head to Rutlow in 17-runner £1,800 nursery at Brighton in October: well suited by 1m at 2 yrs and will stay further: has run creditably on a firm surface and goes very well on soft ground: swerved badly at start on third and fourth outings, unseating rider on second occasion: wore blinkers fifth to seventh outings and ran creditably without them on last appearance: exported to Norway. *C. Brittain.*

AUDELA 2 b.f. Sovereign Path 125–Au Revoir 79 (Ballymoss 136) [1976 7g⁴ **76** 7s] first foal: dam, from a very successful family, won over 1½m: unquoted, missed break in 23-runner maiden race at Newmarket in October but made late progress to finish promising 7½ lengths fourth to Windy Sea: weak 7/1 shot when in rear behind stable-companion Brightly in similar race, again at Newmarket, later in month: should stay 1¼m. *B. Hobbs.*

AUDRAN 2 b.g. Appiani II 128–Ardria 76 (Major Portion 129) [1976 8s] — half-brother to two minor sprint winners and to two N.H. winners: 1,400 gns yearling: dam won over 5f and appeared to stay 1¼m: 16/1 when never·dangerous ninth of 19 to Nordman in maiden race at Sandown in October, only outing. *M. Jarvis.*

AUGUST 3 gr.f. Silly Season 127–Addis Ababa 102 (Pardal 130) [1975 7d⁵ — 6f 8.2g² 8f⁵ 1976 10g 12d] useful-looking filly: showed some ability at 2 yrs but ran moderately in large fields of maidens in first part of season: should stay 1¼m: sold 1,800 gns Newmarket December Sales. *H. Candy.*

AULD ACQUAINTANCE 2 gr.c. Happy New Year–Amaryllis 92 (Tudor **64** Melody 129) [1976 5fg 5f³ 6fg⁴] second foal: dam won over 5f at 2 yrs: claimed for £1,050 when 6 lengths fourth of 12 to King's Verdict in claiming event at Brighton in June, reportedly for export to Belgium. *J. Nelson.*

AUNT AUGUSTA 5 br.m. Counsel 118–Pinjarra 97 (Pinza 137) [1974 14fg⁶ **64** 14fg³ 12.2v² 14fg 12.2s* 14s* 12v³ 16.1v² 1975 14f 15.8f⁵ 15g 12s 12g 1976 15.8g 10h 8f⁴ 14d] tall, rangy mare: showed her only worthwhile form of season when 5½ lengths fourth of seven to Alweston in apprentice handicap at Yarmouth in July: effective at 1m and stays well: acts on any going but goes particularly well in the mud: sweated up on reappearance. *A. Bacon.*

AUNT BETTY 2 ch.f. Great Nephew 126–Kythrea 56 (Alycidon 138) [1976 **83**
5g² 5g³ 7g 6s³] small, lengthy filly: half-sister to quite moderate 2m winner
Moonlight Chase (by Midsummer Night II): dam lightly-raced half-sister to
very useful stayer Staghound: placed in maiden races, on last occasion finishing
2¼ lengths third of 13 to High Value at Chepstow in October: should stay middle-
distances. *I. Balding.*

AUNTIE GRACE 2 b.f. Great Nephew 126–Gay Barrettstown (Santa Claus —
133) [1976 6d] fair sort: second foal: 1,500 gns yearling: dam half-sister
to Bruni: moved poorly on way to start and missed break when behind in
17-runner minor event won by Maternal at Haydock in June: had refused to
enter stalls on same course the previous month: sold 760 gns Doncaster October
Sales. *L. Shedden.*

AUNT JEAN 4 ch.f. Great Nephew 126–Genoveva (Parthia 132) [1974 5g —
5f⁴ 6g³ 6g⁶ 7g² 7.2g³ 6v⁴ 6d 1975 8v⁶ 10s 8h³ 8fg⁴ 8f⁶ 10fg* 10fg⁴ 10.8f* 1976
10f⁵] small filly: quite a moderate handicapper (rated 78) in 1975: in need of
race when last of five to Long Love at Redcar in August, only outing as a 4-y-o:
stays 1¼m: acts on hard going: has been tried in blinkers but has done much
better without them. *T. Kersey.*

AUNT PEGGY 4 b.f. Royal Palm 131–Delayed Cheers (Three Cheers 119) —
[1974 5g 5fg 5.3d 5d 1975 N.R. 1976 5g 10.1fg 10f] worthless plater. *J.
Long.*

AUNT THEA 2 gr.f. Capistrano 120–Tuned-in (Tamerlane 128) [1976 5fg⁶ —
6d] neat filly: first foal: 2,100 gns yearling: dam twice-raced sister to smart
out-and-out stayer Lawrence T: having first outing since March when ninth of
24 to Mint Condition in seller at Windsor in September. *J. Hill.*

AUR 3 ro.f. Aureole 132–Vif (Nimbus 130) [1975 5fg 1976 12.2fg] half- —
sister to two winners, including useful sprinter Drabant (by Set Fair): blinkered
and having first race for a year when behind in maiden event at Wolverhampton
in June, only outing. *W. Stephenson.*

AUREA VIS 3 b.f. Aureole 132–Ultra Violet 84 (Sunny Brae 121) [1975 N.R. —
1976 9f] half-sister to two winners, including useful miler Dawn Review
(by March Past): dam won over 5f at 2 yrs: tailed off in 23-runner maiden race
won by Blue Rag at Wolverhampton in May. *G. Pritchard-Gordon.*

AUSTHORPE HILL 3 b.f. Hopeful Venture 125–Herods Palace 95 (Palestine **46**
133) [1975 5g⁴ 7g 7fg 1976 8f³ 10.6d⁵ 8f⁴ 8g⁶ 7d* 16f 7.2fg] plater: made
all when winning at Redcar in June (no bid): best form at around 1m: usually
wears blinkers. *D. Chapman.*

AUTOWAY 3 ch.c. Astec 128–Sam's Daisy 91 (Super Sam 124) [1975 5g⁶ 6f⁴ **89**
7f* 7f⁵ 7g 1976 7fg 8g 12g 10fg³ 8f 12.2f³ 12fg² 10d 12g³ 10s⁶ 12s⁶] compact
colt: fair handicapper on his day: stays 1½m: best form on a sound surface:
well beaten under a stiffish weight when blinkered on last outing. *W. Stephenson.*

AUTUMN GLOW 3 b.c. Pongee 106–September Fire (Firestreak 125) [1975 **95**
5f² 5g* 6f⁵ 6h* 6d 6fg 5fg³ 6h³ 6f² 1976 7f 6f 7fg⁶ 8f⁶ 6fg 7f 7f³ 6f⁶ 8f 8g³ 8d³
11s* 8s⁵ 8.2s* 12v] strongly-made, useful sort: fair handicapper: at his best
in the autumn and won at Redcar and Haydock in October: stays 11f: acts
on any going: ran moderately when tried in blinkers on sixth outing: suitable
mount for an apprentice. *T. Fairhurst.*

AUTUMN SONG 4 b.g. Star Moss 122–Song O' the Mist 82 (Tenerani 135) —
[1974 N.R. 1975 N.R. 1976 12v] half-brother to poor novice hurdler Mr
Moke (by Crown Law): 33/1 when well beaten in minor event won by Chance
Belle at Lingfield in November, only outing. *N. Wakley.*

AVAHRA 4 br.f. Sahib 114–Sabot D'Or 112 (Princely Gift 137) [1974 5fg* 5g⁵ —
5f⁴ 5fg² 5g* 5g 1975 5fg 6v*(dis) 6d² 6g³ 7g 1976 6f] lengthy filly: useful
handicapper (rated 108) in 1975: well beaten when beaten two lengths by
Roman Warrior at Thirsk in April, only outing at 4 yrs: stays 6f (had little
chance at weights when well beaten over 7f): appears to act on any going.
P. Rohan.

AVARAY 3 b.c. Val de Loir 133–Torbella III 118 (Tornado) [1975 7g* 8d⁵ 8s² **123**
1976 10fg* 11g⁴ 8g* 10g² 8d⁶ 8s⁴] French colt: brother to good-class French
stayer Tourangeau, and half-brother to several winners, including top-class
miler Carlemont (by Charlottesville): dam finished second in Irish Oaks: won
Prix de Courcelles (by ½ length from Twig Moss) and Prix de la Jonchere (by
a neck from Ricco Boy), both at Longchamp, in the spring: narrowly beaten
afterwards in Prix Eugene Adam (short-head second to Crow) and Prix Jacques

le Marois at Deauville (sixth to Gravelines in a blanket finish): fourth of nine to Gravelines in Prix du Moulin de Longchamp in September: best form at up to 1¼m: appeared to act on any going: stud in New Zealand. *A. Head, France.*

AVEC AMOUR 2 ch.f. Jolly Jet 111–Stellario (Indian Hemp 124) [1976 **69** 5fg 5.1fg 7f 9fg 7g⁶ 8s³ 8.2v³] short-coupled filly: half-sister to two minor winners in U.S.A.: 520 gns foal: dam unraced half-sister to Le Levanstell: plater: third in October at Redcar and Nottingham: will stay 1¼m: blinkered fourth outing. *G. Blum.*

AVGERINOS 2 ch.c. Welsh Pageant 132–Kinnerton Street (Accordant) [1976 **121** 6g* 6f² 7g*]

Avgerinos had his introduction to racing at Ascot in July, when he took part in, and won, the Granville Stakes for newcomers, but he made only two appearances afterwards, his trainer regarding him as more of a three-year-old than a two-year-old, and racing him accordingly. But although Avgerinos was looked upon primarily as a colt for the future, that did not prevent his starting favourite for the Granville Stakes, nor his being ridden out for it, even though a slow exit from the stalls meant that he was immediately at a serious disadvantage. Eddery admitted afterwards that he was in two minds whether or not to accept the position but, happily for those who had backed the horse, he persevered and Avgerinos came through to master Mandrake Major well inside the last furlong, winning by half a length.

Of those behind Avgerinos, Mandrake Major went on to win a maiden event at Newmarket and the Flying Childers Stakes at Doncaster on his next two appearances, Birkholm, who finished fourth, also went on to take his next two races, and Casino Boy, sixth, next time out easily accounted for eighteen rivals in a maiden race at Lingfield. Avgerinos, on the other hand, went next all the way up to Newcastle to get beaten, at 11/2 on, by Pub Spy in the £1,000 Wansbeck Stakes on firm going, racing with his head up and seemingly putting little heart into his work as Pub Spy held him at bay over the last furlong.

Although one couldn't ignore the possibility of his feeling the ground, Avgerinos' performance led to his honesty being questioned, but three weeks later he redeemed himself with an exemplary display in the Intercraft Solario Stakes, run over seven furlongs at Sandown. Ninth of the ten runners in the early stages, he threaded his way through on the inside in the straight, led entering the final furlong, and stormed clear to win by three lengths from Mr Nice Guy, with Oriental Rocket third.

After such an impressive victory the temptation to go on with Avgerinos must have been strong, but Walwyn resisted it, stating that the colt was weak

Granville Stakes, Ascot—Avgerinos wins this newcomers race a shade comfortably in the end from Mandrake Major and Ad Lib Ra

Mr C. Karpidas' "Avgerinos"

and inexperienced, and needed time to develop, adding that he would be entered for the Two Thousand Guineas. Whether Avgerinos can be produced to his trainer's satisfaction in time for this race is a matter for conjecture—a big, strong, good sort of horse, he will obviously not be hurried—and whether he has the ability to win it even if he can be got ready, is also open to question. By our reckoning his performance in the Solario Stakes, impressive as it was, leaves him with a lot to find before he can be regarded as up to classic-winning standard. Mr Nice Guy and Oriental Rocket are second-raters.

Avgerinos (ch.c. 1974)	Welsh Pageant (b 1966)	Tudor Melody (br 1956)	Tudor Minstrel
			Matelda
		Picture Light (b 1954)	Court Martial
			Queen of Light
	Kinnerton Street (ch 1967)	Accordant (ch 1960)	Ace Admiral
			Midi's Mom
		Danae (ch 1947)	The Solicitor
			Justitia

Nor is his breeding, on the dam's side at any rate, all that it might be. Of the three mares on the tail-female side, only Danae saw a racecourse. She was a five-furlong sprinter, and a useful one. At stud Danae has produced eleven individual winners, of whom Rambunctious (by Rasper) was successful in a pattern race, winning the World's Playground Stakes over seven furlongs. Kinnerton Street has bred two winners besides Avgerinos, Relent (by Crimson Satan), whose nine successes from his first twenty-seven starts includes two stakes races over sprint distances, and Leinster Lady (by Diplomat Way), who won a small race over seven furlongs in Ireland. From a classic viewpoint the family is an undistinguished one, with little indication of stamina to be found in it, and it is not to be anticipated that Avgerinos, who cost 15,500 guineas as a yearling, has it in him to make the improvement necessary to put himself on the map where the Two Thousand Guineas is concerned. A mile will probably prove to be the limit of his stamina, and it might be that he is not at his best on firm going. *P. Walwyn.*

AVIATOR 4 b.c. Frankincense 120–Brief Flight 108 (Counsel 118) [1974 6fg⁴ 6g* 6fg⁵ 5s⁵ 6d² 1975 7g⁶ 7g 8fg 8f⁶ 8d⁶ 10g* 9g* 8g* 1976 8s 10d 8.2f³ 10.5fg 8fg 11g 8d] strong, good sort of colt: formerly a smart performer: ran his only worthwhile race in 1976 on third outing when third to Gracious Melody at Haydock in July: most disappointing on his other starts and put up a sour display on final appearance when blinkered for first time, dropping himself out soon after halfway and coming in tailed off behind Charta Pearl in apprentice handicap at Redcar in September: stays 1¼m: appears to act on any going. *S. Hall.*   **98§**

AVIEMORE 3 ch.f. Murrayfield 119–Ice Carnival (Arctic Prince 135) [1975 N.R. 1976 11g 8f] compact filly: half-sister to useful miler Isis (by Ennis): dam a middle-distance performer: behind in maiden race at Newbury in May and minor event at Leicester the following month. *W. Payne.*   **—**

AVITUS 2 br.f. Murrayfield 119–Tartown 89 (Gratitude 130) [1976 5g⁶ 5f² 6g² 5g² 6g] compact filly: second foal: 1,250 gns yearling: dam fair sprint handicapper: well beaten in a seller on first outing but ran well in better company afterwards, on fourth outing finishing ¾-length second to Fast Delivery in four-runner nursery at Newcastle in August: effective at 5f and 6f, and may get further. *T. Craig.*   **82**

AVON ROYALE 5 ch.m. Remainder 106–Avon Princess 70 (Coronation Year 124) [1974 6fg 7fg 8g 6f 8fg 7.2d⁴ 6fg 7fg* 7fg 8s 1975 7s⁴ 8f³ 7f² 7f 5.9f⁵ 6fg 8g* 8.3fg³ 7f³ 8fg² 8f⁴ 7f 1976 7fg 8f 7f³ 7fg³ 7g⁵ 7f² 7f* 7f* 6h³ 7f* 7f] smallish mare: stands up to her racing well and won three times at Catterick, on final occasion beating Landscaper in a driving finish in August: stays 1m: acts on any going: ran moderately when tried in blinkers: good mount for an apprentice: genuine and consistent: trained by N. Guest until after fifth start. *D. Ringer.*   **63**

AWASH 3 br.f. Busted 134–Fluke 117 (Grey Sovereign 128 §) [1975 7g³ 1976 12g⁴ 10g⁵ 8s 8s] well-made, quite attractive filly: showed signs of ability on first two outings, but was off course four months afterwards and was well beaten on her return: blinkered final outing. *R. Hern.*   **—**

AWAY SWALLOW 2 ch.c. My Swallow 134–Clouds Away (Nashua) [1976 6f 7g 8s] quite an attractive colt: second foal: half-brother to 3-y-o winning stayer Aerelko (by Relko): dam placed over 1½m in France: behind in large fields of maidens at Newmarket in August and October (two). *P. Robinson.*   **—**

AXEHOLME PRIDE 3 b.f. Majority Blue 126–Hardihood (Hard Ridden 131) [1975 6g 7fg 8v 1976 8g 8d⁴ 8.2d] workmanlike filly: poor maiden. *A. Bacon.*   **—**

AYTIDEFS 3 br.c. Lear Jet 123–Will o' the Wisp 98 (Hornbeam 130) [1975 6g³ 1976 8d⁶ 10s] half-brother to a minor winner here and to a winner in Germany: showed ability on only outing at 2 yrs, but was off course almost a year afterwards and showed no worthwhile form in 1976: should stay at least 1m. *D. Ringer.*   **—**

AZANIA LAD 4 b.g. Acrania 110–Fair Lady 83 (Pink Flower) [1974 N.R. 1975 N.R. 1976 10fg 12f 10.1fg] probably of no account. *G. Gadd.*   **—**

B

BABADAO 2 ch.f. Stardao 83–Babulass (Babu 117) [1976 5g 5f 5f 5g 5d⁵ 5g⁵ 5v] light-framed filly: half-sister to two winners, including Ma's Baby (by Ashford Lea), a fair winner over 5f at 2 yrs in 1974: dam well beaten on both outings: only plating class: will stay 1m: best form on a soft surface. *E. Collingwood.*   **75**

BABBACOMBE 2 b.f. Petersham 67–Cream Tea 59 (Seafront) [1976 5f 5g 5f⁵ 5f 6h⁴ 8f 8.2h⁶] bad plater. *P. Poston.*   **44**

BABBLING 2 ro.f. Birdbrook 110–Bore Da (Manucheir 97 §) [1976 5g 5g 5fg] third foal: dam a winning chaser: in rear in seller at Goodwood and maiden races at Salisbury. *L. Hall.*   **57**

BABY BEN 2 ch.f. Royben 126–Dorbe 80 (Tudor Melody 129) [1976 5f 5f⁵ 5g⁴ 5fg⁵ 5fg² 7f³ 5fg² 6g⁴] neat filly: half-sister to 3-y-o middle-distance winner Our Anniversary (by Prince Regent) and to two winners in Italy: third in maiden race at Beverley and went down by a neck in two sellers at Newcastle: stays 7f: blinkered final outing. *M. W. Easterby.*   **67**

BABY BLAIR   4 b.g. Forlorn River 124–Parthica 98 (Parthia 132)   [1974 5g 5f²   **75**
5fg² 5g 6s⁵ 5.3f³ 5s   1975 5s 5d⁵ 6f² 6fg 6fg² 5.3g* 5g⁴ 5.8f⁴ 5g³   1976 5.9fg⁶ 5f
7fg⁶ 7g 7f* 7g 8.3fg* 8g* 8fg⁵ 10f 8.2d 6s]   lightly-made gelding: useful plater:
winner at Leicester, Windsor and Kempton as a 4-y-o: heavily backed on last two
occasions: stays 1m: acts on firm going: suitable mount for an apprentice: bought
out of G. Balding's stable 800 gns after winning at Leicester: retained 560 gns at
Windsor, 1,600 gns at Kempton. *L. Hall.*

BABY ELLI   2 b.f. Diplomat Way–Magic Singing (Alibhai)   [1976 6f 5f]   half-
sister to seven winners in England and the U.S.A., including fair 11f winner King's
Choir (by Crepello): 5,600 gns yearling: dam winning half-sister to top-class
sprinter Secret Step and Belmont Stakes winner Quadrangle: well behind in
maiden races at Lingfield in June and Folkestone in July. *M. Masson.*

BABY RAT   3 b.f. Reliance II 137–Water Rat 83 (Hard Tack 111 §)   [1975   **52**
7d 6g 7.2s 6g⁶   1976 6.5g 8g⁴ 8.5g 7.5s 11.1fg³ 8.2f 13fg* 13.4s⁴ 11.1f 16.9f⁶ 16f 12f]
small filly: made most when running out game winner of handicap at Nottingham
in April: did not run up to her best afterwards and was well beaten in a seller on
final outing: sold 520 gns Newmarket September Sales. *D. Marks.*

BACCARAT ROSE   2 b.f. Meadow Mint 120–Rosy Morn (Roan Rocket 128)   **74**
[1976 5f* 5d 6fg⁵ 6fg⁶ 5fg⁶]   workmanlike filly: first foal: 1,750 gns yearling: dam
showed no worthwhile form: won 10-runner maiden race at Newcastle in April
by ½ length from Silver Cygnet: ran best subsequent race when sixth to Meadow
Monarch in minor event at Thirsk in July on penultimate outing: will stay 1m:
possibly unsuited by a soft surface. *F. Carr.*

BACKGAMMON BOY   2 ch.g. Richboy 117–Pal Greta 76 (Palestine 133)   —
[1976 5f 5fg 6g 6fg 8.2h]   workmanlike gelding: bad plater: blinkered final
outing: sold 320 gns Doncaster September Sales. *K. Payne.*

BACK ONE ELEVEN   3 ch.c. Frankincense 120–Arabian Conquest 97 (Constable   **78**
129)   [1975 6fg 7fg⁵ 6g⁵ 7f³ 7g² 7fg⁶ 7g 7.6g   1976 8.5g*]   shapely colt: won
seller at Epsom in June by a short head from Annina: sold 3,800 gns afterwards,
presumably for export to Belgium: stays 1m well: ran moderately when blinkered
on final outing at 2 yrs. *R. Hannon.*

BADAJOS   2 b.c. Royal Palace 131–Lerida 119 (Matador 131)   [1976 7fg⁶ 7fg² **104**
7f⁴]   lengthy colt: half-brother to two good winners by Tudor Melody in Philip of
Spain and Spanish Air, and to another winner by Abernant: dam a smart 2-y-o:
in frame in August in 18-runner maiden race at Newbury (beaten ½ length by
Oriental Rocket) and £3,100 event at Newmarket (2½ lengths fourth to Card
Player): will be suited by 1m+. *H. Cecil.*

BADA'S BROOK   2 ro.f. Roan Rocket 128–Prudent (Silly Season 127)   [1976 6g⁵   **64**
6fg 6g 8s 7s]   workmanlike filly: first foal: dam, of little account, is half-sister to
very smart Silver Cloud and Jupiter Pluvius: little worthwhile form in good-class
maiden races, but showed up for 5f when eleventh of 27 to Sporting Yankee at
Newmarket in October on penultimate outing. *B. Hobbs.*

BADGERS GLORY   4 br.g. Dairialatan 111–Little Tot (Flush Royal 127)   [1974   —
N.R.   1975 N.R.   1976 10.1fg 17.7f]   third produce: dam never ran: well beaten
in maiden races at Windsor in June and Wolverhampton in August. *J. Old.*

BAD LOVE   2 gr.c. Town Crier 119–Tiger Doll 85 (Tiger 125)   [1976 6fg⁶ 8s]   **74** p
second foal: 4,400 gns yearling: dam won over 5f at 2 yrs: unquoted when sixth of
12 behind easy winner Habeebti in maiden race at Newmarket in August: made
some late headway when behind in 27-runner maiden race won by Sporting
Yankee also at Newmarket in October: should do better. *B. Hanbury.*

BAGDAD GOLD   4 br.g. Bagdad–Candida Gold 96 (Relic)   [1974 N.R.   1975   —
5d 6f 8.2g 10f 10.1f⁶ 10.1f³ 8g 10.8g   1976 10g 10s]   very attractive, shapely
gelding: poor maiden: best runs at 1¼m. *D. Nicholson.*

BAGSHOT   3 b.c. Connaught 130–Grisbi 96 (Grey Sovereign 128 §)   [1975 5g⁶   **94**
7g² 8d⁴ 8g² 8f⁴   1976 12fg² 12fg* 12.2f* 12g⁴ 16f⁶ 12g⁵]   strong, good-bodied,
useful sort: won early-season minor events at Newmarket and Wolverhampton:
had some stiff tasks afterwards: may well stay further than 1½m: acts on firm
going: sometimes sweats up: not seen out after July. *B. Hobbs.*

BAG SNATCHER   2 b.c. Burglar 128–Miss Pinza 95 (Pinza 137)   [1976 5f 5h³
6f]   useful-looking colt: half-brother to a winning stayer: 3,400 gns yearling:
dam stayed 1¼m: no worthwhile form in minor events: sold 2,000 gns Newmarket Autumn Sales. *R. D. Peacock.*

BAHRAIN PADDY   3 b.c. The Brianstan 128–Judana 72 (Pirate King 129)   **82**
[1975 5f⁵ 5fg⁵ 7f 7g*   1976 8fg⁴ 11fg⁴ 13.4s⁵ 12fg 12.2g⁴ 12f*]   sturdy colt:

good mover: enterprisingly ridden, showed improved form when winning five-runner handicap at Ripon in June by 7 lengths from Pass the Port: stays 1½m: goes well on firm ground: dwelt when tried in blinkers on fourth outing. *R. Hollinshead.*

BAILADOR 4 ch.c. Le Haar 126–Lakme (La Varende 125) [1974 N.R. 1975 **71** 10.5s³ 12g⁵ 12g⁴ 1976 13g² 12g⁴ 12fg* 16fg 12d⁵ 14s⁶ 14d⁶] ex-French colt: favourite, won amateur riders race at Newmarket in May by 1½ lengths from Tour de Force: will stay further than 13f: has worn blinkers (ran well in them on reappearance) but didn't at Newmarket. *G. Balding.*

BAILDON 6 br.h. Will Somers 114 §–Delian 84 (Delirium 126) [1974 5g⁵ 6g² **90** 5f³ 5g⁵ 5fg² 5s³ 6fg⁶ 5d* 5s* 5v⁴ 5s⁴ 1975 5g³ 5d⁶ 5d⁴ 5g* 5f⁵ 5f⁵ 5g² 5g² 6f 5fg⁵ 5g 5s⁵ 5g 5g³ 1976 5g³ 5g⁵ 6fg* 6f⁵ 6g⁴ 6g² 5.8f⁴ 6fg⁴ 6f⁴ 6f⁵ 5g⁵ 5v* 5s 5s] strong, lengthy horse: good mover: quite a useful handicapper: successful at Epsom in April and at Newbury in October, on latter course just getting the better of a driving finish with Murrmatch: also ran creditably in some of his other races, notably when 2¾ lengths fourth of 17 to Jimmy The Singer in Spillers Stewards' Cup at Goodwood in July (eighth start): stays 6f: acts on any going: has been tried in blinkers: sometimes wears a bandage on near-fore: frequently held up: genuine but needs strong handling. *G. Harwood.*

BAINBRIDGE 3 ch.c. Siliconn 121–Spaniard's Darling (Darling Boy 124) **69** [1975 N.R. 1976 7fg 7g⁵ 9f 8fg³ 10fg⁵] compact colt: second produce: 1,000 gns foal: dam of little account: close-up third to dead-heaters Fly High and The Frummer in maiden race at Brighton in June: stays 1m (well beaten when tried at 1¼m): not seen out after June. *J. Winter.*

BAKERS FOLLY 2 b.g. Sweet Revenge 129–Court Whisper 83 (Queen's Hussar — 124) [1976 5f] second foal: half-brother to Evedor (by Firestreak), a useful winner at up to 7f at 2 yrs: sold twice as a yearling, for 500 gns and 1,200 gns respectively: dam stayed 1½m: badly away when remote ninth of 10 in maiden race won by The Bowler at Bath in April: sold 300 gns Ascot October Sales. *J. Hill.*

BAKEWA 2 b.g. Sit In The Corner–Bestwitch 104 (Borealis) [1976 5f⁶ 6fg] — seventh reported living foal: dam 6f sprinter: in rear in minor events at Newcastle in April and June (last of 10). *J. Etherington.*

BALANCOIRE 2 b.f. Swing Easy 126–Graceful 83 (Grey Sovereign 128 §) — [1976 5g 5fg] first foal: dam won over 7f at 2 yrs: in rear in maiden races at Salisbury in May and June (blinkered). *R. Hern.*

BALANTE 2 ch.f. Balidar 133–Smoking Room (Pall Mall 132) [1976 6fg 5fg* **90** 6f⁵ 6d* 7d³ 8v³] strong, useful sort: second foal: half-sister to a winning plater by Track Spare: 1,750 gns yearling: dam never ran: successful in maiden race and a nursery at Windsor, putting up easily better effort in latter race when winning by 1½ lengths from Little Thruster: stays 7f well, and should stay 1m (probably unsuited by very heavy going on only attempt at trip): suited by some give in the ground but has won on a firm surface. *S. Woodman.*

BALDUR 4 br.c. Breton 130–Night Off 124 (Narrator 124) [1974 7.2g³ 7d* 7s³ **86 §** 1975 8v* 8.5d³ 10.5d⁵ 12fg² 12g⁵ 12f 8g⁴ 1976 7.2d⁴ 8g 12fg² 12d³ 13g* 16.1fg² 12g 13g 15fg² 12.2v⁵] well-made, robust, good sort of colt: trounced moderate opposition when winning handicap at Hamilton in June, but is none too keen on racing: stays 2m: appears to act on any going: ran below his best when tried in blinkers. *Denys Smith.*

BALI BREEZE 4 b.f. Balidar 133–Windy Breeze 77 (Pindari 124) [1974 N.R. **45** 1975 6g 5g 7g 8g 8d 1976 7fg 5.9g 8g⁶ 8fg² 10d] compact filly: poor maiden: stays 1m: sold 500 gns Newmarket Autumn Sales. *J. Benstead.*

BALIDON 3 ch.c. Balidar 133–Blue Stocking (Chamossaire) [1975 5f⁶ 6fg* 6f⁴ **94** 6g* 7g 7d* 1976 7f 7g 6fg 8fg 8h² 10g²] close-coupled, strong-quartered, attractive colt: useful handicapper: took some time to find his form, putting up easily his best effort on final outing when good second to Tiger Trail in handicap at Kempton in August: stays 1¼m: probably acts on any going: twice showed a tendency to hang left as a 2-y-o and needs strong handling. *S. Woodman.*

BALIGARI 2 b.c. Balidar 133–Judith's Bairn (Double-U-Jay 120) [1976 5fg **55** 6fg 6g 7s] neat colt: behind in maiden races and a Chepstow seller. *A. Pitt.*

BALIGREAT 3 b.f. Great Nephew 126–Bali 70 (Ballymoss 136) [1975 5g² — 5.9fg⁴ 7f 6g 7f* 6d 8g 1976 7fg⁶ 7fg 5f 12f⁶] lengthy, dipped-backed filly:

won maiden event at Leicester in September, 1975: little worthwhile form since: sold 1,200 gns Ascot August Sales. *N. Adam.*

BALIMENE 2 b.f. Balidar 133–Mene Mene Tekel (Premonition 130) [1976 6d] — half-sister to useful 1973 French 2-y-o Wolves (by Wolver Hollow) and to two winners in Ireland: 220 gns yearling: dam won two races at up to 1¼m in Ireland and is half-sister to smart French stayer Roi de Perse: 20/1 and ridden by 7-lb claimer when eighteenth of 23 to Running Bull in maiden race at Newmarket in October. *W. Holden.*

BALITA 3 ch.f. Balidar 133–La Derelitta (Botticelli 129) [1975 5f³ 5g* 5g⁶ 6d⁵ 86 5.3f 6d⁶ 6g⁴ 6g 1976 6g 5g⁴ 5fg² 5.8h⁵ 5fg⁵ 6f⁵ 6h⁴] neat, lightly-made filly: modest handicapper: probably acts on any going: trained until after fourth outing by J. Dunlop. *S. Woodman.*

BALLAD SINGER 6 br.h. Prince Dual–Dusky Legend (Experiment) [1974 70 10.8f⁵ 12g⁴ 10g³ 10g⁴ 10g* 10f* 11.7fg 9d* 10g² 10s³ 8g³ 8s⁵ 10v² 1975 9v* 10v³ 10g⁵ 10f² 10g* 9fg² 12d³ 10g⁴ 10g² 1976 8g 10g⁶ 8fg 10g 11.1g⁶ 10h³ 10g⁶ 10f⁴] quite a moderate handicapper: ran best race in 1976 when creditable third to Astor Boy at Lingfield in June: best form at around 1¼m: acts on any going: has worn blinkers: excellent mount for a boy. *R. Akehurst.*

BALL AND CHAIN 2 ch.f. Manacle 123–Impassioned Plea 91 (Counsel 118) — [1976 5.8f⁴ 5s 5v⁵] fifth foal: 1,650 gns yearling: dam won from 7f to 1½m: little worthwhile form in maiden races in the autumn: slowly away on first outing. *R. Price.*

BALLOON 3 b.g. Ballyciptic 122–Winchester (Sica Boy 132) [1975 5g 6fg 52 7g⁴ 7g 8d 7g 1976 8.2g 7g 7.6fg⁶ 7fg 7f 7fg⁵ 9f⁵ 8f⁴ 10fg⁵ 10d⁵ 10.8s 11.1s⁵] narrow, leggy, unfurnished gelding: selling handicapper nowadays: stays 1¼m: changed hands 725 gns Ascot February Sales. *F. Wiles.*

BALLY BABU 3 b.g. Ballyciptic 122–Aspasie (Milesian 125) [1975 6fg 8g 8s — 5d 1976 8fg 11.1g 12fg 12h³ 12f] lengthy, light-framed gelding: poor plater: blinkered final outing. *T. Gosling.*

BALLYCALL 3 ch.g. Ballymoss 136–Kitty's Pet 59 (High Treason 126) [1975 47 5s⁵ 5v 5g⁴(dis) 5fg⁵ 6f 7fg 8f⁵ 9fg 10g 1976 10g³ 10.6d⁴ 8fg 10h³ 12f⁵ 8f] strong gelding: stays at least 1¼m: ran badly in seller on second outing and possibly needs a sound surface. *M. Stevens.*

BALLY CREEK 3 b.f. Ballymoss 136–Creek Alley 91 (Klairon 131) [1975 N.R. — 1976 12g] third foal: 420 gns yearling: dam stayed at least 1¼m: unquoted when tailed-off last of 13 behind Spey in maiden race at Newmarket in September. *W. Stephenson.*

BALLYDAMUS 5 br.g. Mandamus 120–Westmorland Jane 76 (Vimy 132) 49 [1974 11g⁶ 12g² 10f² 12g 14fg⁴ 14.7f* 16d 16d 1975 13g 16d³ 17.7fg⁴ 16fg³ 17.1f 16f² 16f² 14fg 16d 1976 16f³ 17.7f³ 12f 17.1f⁵ 15.5f⁴ 17.1h] strong gelding: poor handicapper: ran creditably on first two outings: stays well: has run respectably on softish ground but is ideally suited by firm: sometimes wears blinkers. *N. Vigors.*

BALLY HONEY 4 ch.c. Ballymoss 136–Come On Honey 94 (Never Say Die 137) 53 [1974 N.R. 1975 12d 1976 12fg⁴ 10fg³] strong, attractive colt: an extremely well-bred individual but has been lightly raced and shown only poor form: sold 3,600 gns Newmarket Autumn Sales. *N. Murless.*

BALLY KNOUD 3 b.f. Hill Rise 127–Irish Rule (Court Splendour 117) [1975 7d³ 84 1976 10g 10fg² 10g³ 10.2g² 10g² 10.2s] big American-bred filly: quite moderate form in varied company: stays 1¼m and has given us impression she will be suited by 1½m: ran poorly final outing: sold 3,300 gns Newmarket December Sales. *R. Armstrong.*

BALLYLANEEN 5 br.m. Master Buck–Shareamore Again (Arctic Slave 116) — [1974 N.R. 1975 N.R. 1976 16v⁶ 16v 17s⁴ 16v³ 16g² 16.1f³] first foal: dam never ran: in frame in bumpers events in Ireland in early part of season: well-beaten third to Frisky Scot in bad maiden race at Haydock in August, only appearance in this country: stays. *J. Edwards.*

BALLY PRINCE 4 b.g. Continuation 120–Empress of Scotland (Ratification — 129) [1974 5fg 6s 6g⁴ 7fg⁶ 8d 1975 8v 7.6g⁴ 8g⁴ 7f⁴ 6fg⁴ 6g² 6f⁵ 7g³ 7fg* 1976 7fg 7f] lengthy gelding: showed quite moderate form at 3 yrs: had stiffish tasks when well beaten in two handicaps before end of April, only starts in 1976: stays 7f: acts on a firm surface: best in blinkers: suitable mount for an apprentice. *L. Kennard.*

BALLY TUDOR   3 b.f. Henry the Seventh 125–Ballyseedy 73 (Dicta Drake 126)   **75**
[1975 6f⁴ 8.2d   1976 7.6s³ 8fg³ 12.2g² 10fg³ 10g 10g⁶ 10d³ 8.2d² 8s² 8.2v³ 8v⁵]
lengthy, sparely-made filly: quite a moderate maiden: possibly does not stay
1½m: appears to act on any going: blinkered seventh to tenth outings and ran
poorly without them on final appearance: one paced.   *C. Brittain.*

BALRANALD   4 b.c. Burglar 128–Margaret Ann 83 (Persian Gulf)   [1974 N.R.   **74**
1975 8fg 1976 8g⁶ 8fg* 10g⁵ 8g 10s 10d 13v] strong, well-made colt: won 14-runner
apprentice event at Newmarket in August by ¾ length from Spring Storm, the
pair finishing well clear: stays 1¼m: blinkered last two outings.   *B. Hobbs.*

BALSA   3 b.f. Irish Ball 127–Alisarda (Aureole 132)   [1975 7.2fg 8.2g 7g   1976   —
12.2f 14fg 10f 13fg 16f⁴ 12f]   bad plater.   *T. Molony.*

BALSARROCH LADY   2 b.f. Manacle 123–Balsarroch Girl (Whistler 129)   **56**
[1976 5g⁵ 5s³ 6f 7f³ 7f⁶ 8f]   small filly: placed in sellers at Ayr and Redcar in
first half of season: evidently stays 7f but is not certain to stay 1m.   *J. Carr.*

BALTEUS   2 b.c. Baldric II 131–Honerko 112 (Tanerko 134)   [1976 7.5d 7.5g*   **116**
9s*]   French colt: first foal: dam a very useful middle-distance winner here and
in France: a smart performer and won two of his three races, a maiden race at
Deauville in August by 2 lengths from Hermodore and Group 3 Prix Saint-
Roman at Longchamp in October by a short head from Numa Pompilius: put up
a game effort in latter race, leading from the start and then rallying well when
headed 50 yards out: will probably stay 1½m: acts on soft going.   *J. Cunnington,
jnr, France.*

BALTIC LOVE   4 b.g. Current Coin 118–Arctic Villa (Arctic Star)   [1974 5fg⁶   **65**
5g 7g⁵ 8s² 10s³   1975 11.1s*   1976 12g² 14.7d³]   well-made gelding: poor handicapper: ran creditably in two early-season amateur riders events: one paced and
stays well: acts on soft going.   *P. Rohan.*

BALTOIS   2 ch.c. Balidar 133–Honi Soit (Above Suspicion 127)   [1976 5g 5fg³   **83**
6fg² 5f 5fg 5s* 5s]   well-made colt: first foal: 1,500 gns yearling: dam poor Irish
maiden: showed improved form when winning nursery at Folkestone in October
by a neck from Sky Jump: not disgraced under a penalty on final outing: stays
6f: evidently well suited by some give in the ground.   *S. Woodman.*

BALUSTRADE   3 b.g. Balidar 133–Glen Helen 69 (Tudor Melody 129)   [1975   **71**
5d 7d 6g 6g 5f⁴ 7g 6g   1976 7g⁶ 10f 8fg 10fg 10fg⁵ 8fg* 8.3f² 8g 10.6g* 10g³]   neat
gelding: selling handicapper: decisive winner at Wolverhampton in June (bought
in 1,300 gns) and Haydock in August (no bid): stays 1¼m well: wears blinkers
nowadays: trained until after Haydock by H. Williams.   *J. Edwards.*

BALY ROCKETTE   4 ch.c. Crocket 130–Baletta 107 (Ballymoss 136)   [1974   **115**
7.5g² 1975 8g² 6.5g* 8.5v³ 10v³ 8g* 8g* 8g* 8g* 9.2g 8g* 6g⁵ 1976 7d⁵ 8f 8d⁶
7.5d⁶ 8v⁴]   strong, shapely, muscular French colt: second foal: brother to Bala,
a winner in Italy: dam, useful at 3 yrs, stayed well: raced mainly in Italy in 1975
and was rated best 3-y-o at distances up to 1m, winning several good prizes and
beating Three Legs when winning Premio Resegone: 4½ lengths fifth of 11 to
Gravelines in Prix du Palais Royal at Longchamp in May on reappearance, but
didn't reproduce that form: well beaten behind Ardoon in Queen Anne Stakes at
Royal Ascot: stays 8.5f.   *C. Milbank, France.*

BAM BAM   4 gr.c. Raffingora 130–Nicky B 82 (Rockefella)   [1974 6g⁶ 5s⁴ 6s²   —
7v² 1975 8fg⁴ 8v 8f 8.2g 8f³ 12f 10fg 8h 8f⁵ 10fg⁵ 1976 9fg 10f⁵ 8fg] strong
colt: plater nowadays: stays 1m: acts on any going.   *A. Davison.*

BAMSTAR   3 ch.f. Relko 136–Aura 92 (Aureole 132)   [1975 N.R.   1976 12g⁴   —
13.1f 15.5s⁴ 12s³]   well-made, quite attractive filly: second foal: dam fairly
useful winner at 1m and 1½m: showed a little ability in maiden races: should stay
beyond 1½m: possibly unsuited by firm going: blinkered last two outings.   *J.
Nelson.*

BANDYKE   2 ch.c. Dike–Banning (Crafty Admiral)   [1976 6d 7s]   half-brother   —
to three winners, including smart French middle-distance stayer Balompie (by
Pardao): 4,400 gns yearling: dam ran only three times: behind in maiden races at
Redcar in June and Edinburgh in October.   *W. A. Stephenson.*

BANFF   2 b.c. Rarity 129–Spice Road (Gallant Man)   [1976 6v 10d]   half-   —
brother to French 3-y-o Diplomat Spy (by Diplomat Way) and a winner in
U.S.A.: 4,200 gns yearling: dam won at up to 1m in U.S.A.: in rear in end-of-
season maiden and minor events at Newbury and Newmarket.   *D. Keith.*

BANG AHEAD 2 b.f. Pinsun 108–Roychateau (Royal Record II) [1976 5g **40**
5g 5fg 5d 5f⁶ 5h³ 5g 5f²] small filly: bad plater: wears blinkers: sold 200 gns
Doncaster August Sales. *T. Fairhurst.*

BANGORS GREEN 3 b.c. Busted 134–Atonement 109 (Palestine 133) [1975 —
5g 5f 1976 9f 8fg 9.4g⁵] leggy, lightly-made colt: little worthwhile form in
northern maiden races. *G. Richards.*

BANJO BONES 3 gr.g. Supreme Sovereign 119–Mirth (Tamerlane 128) [1975 —
N.R. 1976 12fg⁵] second produce: half-brother to a winner in Holland: 1,350
gns foal: dam never ran: 33/1 when distant fifth of 15 to Ribo Pride in weakly-
contested amateur riders race at Leicester in September. *G. Kindersley.*

BANNER 2 b.f. Blakeney 126–Quarterings 104 (Princely Gift 137) [1976 7d] — p
well-made filly: fourth foal: sister to 3-y-o out-and-out stayer Belfalas, and half-
sister to useful 11f winner Royal Quarter (by Royal Palace): dam stayed 1½m:
25/1 when thirteenth of 30 to Guama in maiden race at Newbury in September:
will need a test of stamina: should do better. *R. Hern.*

BARBARA BEE 2 b.f. Sharpen Up 127–Exhibition 109 (Nearula 132) [1976 —
6fg 7g 5d 8d] of no account: changed hands 320 gns Ascot October Sales. *G.
Blum.*

BARBECUE 6 ch.h. Bivouac 114–Honey Bun 109 (Honeyway 125) [1974 13g³ **66**
10.2g² 12.3g² 12f⁵ 12f⁴ 14.6g* 12.3g⁶ 16.9g* 16g* 1975 14s 16d⁴ 18.4g⁵ 16g⁵ 16fg
16fg³ 16.2s 13g 13g 13fg³ 16fg² 17f⁵] workmanlike horse: quite a useful
handicapper at his best: creditable second to Eric Stuart at Newbury in April:
finished lame when tailed off behind Heracles at Bath the following month:
stays 2m well: said by stable to need top-of-the-ground conditions: good mount
for an inexperienced rider: well suited by forcing tactics. *R. Hollinshead.*

BARCLAY'S OWN 5 ch.g. Great Nephew 126–Alycida (Alycidon 138) [1974 —
8fg 12.2fg³ 14.7f³ 16g⁵ 1975 14.7s 14g 12g 1976 12.5v] plating-class gelding:
stays 1¾m: usually wears blinkers. *J. Leigh.*

BARGATE LADY 2 b.f. Highland Melody 112–Vivacity (Port Corsair 98) **58**
[1976 5f 5g² 5f 6h⁵ 7fg 7fg] light-framed filly: 6 lengths second to Mariners Girl
in seller at Ayr in August, only indication of ability: should stay further than 5f.
M. Naughton.

BARGILLEAN 3 b.g. Hul a Hul 124–Black Stocking (High Hat 131) [1975 5f —
6f 1976 8h⁵] of no account. *G. Wallace.*

BARIOLE 3 ch.c. Barbare II 128–Little Bird (Fr) (L'Epinay 126) [1975 5.1f⁵ **66**
5.1f 8fg 1976 8.2g⁶ 12g² 12.2d⁴ 13g⁵ 15.8f⁴ 12fg*] neat colt: plater: winner at
Newmarket in July by a length from Redhead: sold 1,100 gns afterwards,
reportedly for export to Belgium: best form at up to 13f: often wears blinkers
(did so when successful) but does just as well without. *R. Armstrong.*

BARJAC 2 ch.c. Dapper Dan (USA)–Barbarossa (Cambremont 121) [1976 8g] —
narrow French-bred colt: brother to Barbaranne, a winner over 6f and 7f at 2 yrs
in France: 70,000 francs yearling (approx. £7,500): dam, who never ran, is closely
related to high-class French 6f to 1¼m performer Barbare: missed break when
well behind in £2,400 event won by Royal Plume at York in September. *M.
Jarvis.*

BARLEYCROFT STAR 4 b.g. Forlorn River 124–Lucker Jewel (Lord of **48**
Verona 120) [1974 N.R. 1975 8h 8g⁶ 7fg 1976 8f* 8f² 10f⁴ 12g⁶ 8f³ 8f 8.2fg⁵
9f² 8f³] well-grown gelding: springer in market, showed much improved form
when winning selling handicap at Pontefract in April: ran respectably on some
of his subsequent outings: best form at up to 9f: acts on firm going. *W.
Stephenson.*

BARLINE 3 b.f. Lauso–Barwin 102 (Wilwyn 129) [1975 6g 8f 1976 10f 12f* **59**
10fg⁴ 16f²] well-grown filly: 25/1 when winning maiden race at Folkestone in
June: beaten 1½ lengths by sole-opponent Forgotten Dreams in handicap at
Warwick in August: runs as though 1¾m is a minimum trip for her: sold to P.
Allingham 3,000 gns Doncaster October Sales. *W. Stephenson.*

BARMY 7 b.g. Silly Season 127–Bewilder 87 (Crepello 136) [1974 16fg² 16fg⁴ **63**
17.1g 16fg⁵ 16.9g³ 16g⁴ 16g* 15.5s⁴ 1975 16v* 17.1f³ 17.7fg³ 12f* 1976 16.1d⁵
16f⁴ 16fg⁴] strong gelding: effective at 1½m but is well suited by extreme
distances: acts on any going: not raced after April. *I. Balding.*

BARNABY BECK 3 b.c. Forlorn River 124–Lunar Princess 109 (King's Bench **73** d
132) [1975 5fg 5g 5fg⁶ 6f* 6f³ 7f 6d⁶ 8g⁶ 8fg⁵ 6v⁶ 1976 8g 8f* 10.6d² 8fg* 8fg

8f 9fg² 9f 9fg 9fg 8s 8d] light-framed colt: in good form early in season:
was well backed when winning seller at Teesside and handicap (by 6 lengths) at
Pontefract, both in April: raced inconsistently afterwards: stays 1¼m well:
appears to act on any going: seems best in blinkers: sometimes wears bandages.
R. Bastiman.

BARNACLE 2 b.g. Quayside 124–Charybdis (Chanteur II 135) [1976 6d] half- —
brother to several winners, including fairly useful 3-y-o miler Calor (by Caliban)
and high-class 6f to 1m horse Joshua (by Welsh Rake): dam slow maiden: 20/1
when twenty-first of 23 to Running Bull in maiden race at Newmarket in
October. *W. A. Jarvis.*

BARNY 2 b.c. Irish Ball 127–Love is Blind 90 (Hasty Road) [1976 6f 6g² 6fg⁶ **81**
7v⁵ 8v⁴ 6s] neat colt: first foal: 1,550 gns yearling: dam won over 6f at 2 yrs:
stayed on well when 2½ lengths second to Latest Model in maiden race at
Newcastle in August: ran respectably afterwards, including in a nursery: will
stay 1m+: seems to act on any going. *W. A. Stephenson.*

BARON BUNCH 3 b.c. Stephen George 102–Whiphand 83 (Supreme Court 135) **64**
[1975 5d⁵ 5fg* 6fg⁵ 5fg 5fg⁴ 5fg 6g 1976 8s 8g 8.5g 10g 8g 8.2d⁶ 7f² 7f⁵] quite
useful-looking colt: best form at up to 7f: acts on firm going: sold 2,300 gns Ascot
May Sales and has since won in Belgium. *C. Bewicke.*

BARONCINO 2 b.g. Barron's Court–Golden Tradition (Mossborough 126) —
[1976 6fg⁴ 6f] compact gelding: half-brother to a winner in Greece by Atan: dam
never ran: swerved at start when remote fourth to King Elect in seven-runner
event at Yarmouth in June: out of his depth at Royal Ascot later in month and
was not seen out again. *R. Supple.*

BARONCROFT 4 br.c. High Hat 131–Dark Finale (Javelot 124) [1974 8s 8d **82**
1975 10f 10.1s 12f³ 10.1fg 11.7f² 12f² 10fg* 11.7fg* 12f* 12g³ 12fg* 13.3g⁴ 1976
12f⁵ 12fg 12fg³ 10g⁶ 14s³ 12s] strong, sturdy colt: useful handicapper (rated 101)
at 3 yrs: 4¾ lengths third to Assured at Sandown in October, best effort in 1976:
stays 1¾m: acts on any going: has been tried in blinkers: bandaged last two
outings: well suited by front-running tactics. *S. Ingham.*

BARON DE HOLLAND 2 gr.c. Supreme Sovereign 119–Light Jumper 100 (Red **62**
God 128 §) [1976 5g 6fg 5g 5d 6v 5s] scraggy colt: seemed to show ability when
seventh of eight to Hedge School in minor event at Haydock on fourth outing
but showed nothing like that form in sellers on three other occasions, including
when blinkered once. *D. McCain.*

BARONET 4 b.c. Huntercombe 133–Chagrin Falls 101 (Polic 126) [1974 6g⁵ **87**
1975 8s 7.6g* 8.2g* 8fg 7g 8fg⁶ 7.3d⁴ 1976 8g 10.2g³ 10fg⁴ 10g] lengthy,
attractive colt: ran best race at 4 yrs when creditable 4 lengths fourth of 10 to
Kunpuu in Playboy Bookmakers Handicap at Newmarket in April: stays 1¼m:
acts on a firm surface: not raced after May. *N. Callaghan.*

BARON HOPKINS 2 ch.c. Frankincense 120–Jolie 64 (Jolly Jet 111) [1976 —
5fg 6v 7v] neat, strong colt: little sign of ability, including in a seller: blinkered
first outing. *A. W. Jones.*

BARONIAL 3 ch.g. Barron's Court–Eglee 99 (Norseman) [1975 N.R. 1976 —
10.1f⁴] third foal: half-brother to Mugatpura (by Floribunda), a fair handicapper
at up to 1¼m on Flat and also a high-class hurdler: dam won at up to 1½m in
Ireland: 33/1 when remote fourth of nine to Ragotina in maiden race at Windsor in
August. *F. Walwyn.*

BARONS CHARTER 3 ch.g. Runnymede 123–Judiciary 74 (Above Suspicion **50**
127) [1975 N.R. 1976 6g 10g 9f 8f⁴ 8f 10g⁴ 10s 10s³] fair sort: half-brother
to three winners, including Legal Eagle (by Manacle), a very smart performer
at up to 1m: showed signs of some ability in varied company, but ran poorly in
selling handicap on penultimate outing: evidently stays 1¼m: sold 600 gns Newmarket Autumn Sales. *G. Harwood.*

BARRY LYNDON 2 ro.c. Silly Season 127–Courting (Quorum 126) [1976 6d] — p
strong, lengthy colt: half-brother to five winners, notably high-class sprinter
Apollo Nine (by Skymaster): 1,800 gns foal, 1,500 gns yearling: dam half-sister
to very smart miler Miletus: unquoted and very backward when thirteenth of 23
in maiden race won by Rings at Newmarket in October: will do better in time.
M. Masson.

BARSALOI 3 br.g. Lorenzaccio 130–Mara River 116 (Gratitude 131) [1975 —
N.R. 1976 6fg 8s] half-brother to two fairly useful animals, namely sprinter
Lake Victoria (by Stupendous) and 1972 2-y-o Regatta (by Silly Season):

dam 6f to 1m handicapper: in rear in maiden events at Goodwood and Warwick in the autumn: should stay at least 1m. *R. Hern.*

BARTOLOZZI 3 ch.c. Lorenzaccio 130–Sharondor 84 (Matador 131) [1975 **82** N.R. 1976 9g* 10.5s 9fg 10f 11.7fg³ 11.7f⁶ 14f⁴ 12g⁴] strong colt: fourth produce: half-brother to three winners, including useful 1972 2-y-o 7f winner Altiora (by Taj Dewan): 8,000 gns foal, resold privately 7,000 gns as a yearling: dam 6f sprinter: heavily-backed favourite when running out an impressive 8 lengths winner of newcomers event at Wolverhampton in May: put up easily best effort afterwards when creditable third to Princely in handicap at Windsor the following month: stays 1½m (ran poorly over 1¾m): dwelt but soon recovered when tried in blinkers on fourth outing. *N. Callaghan.*

BARTON MILLS 9 b.h. Privy Councillor 125–Jane Barnie 73 (Dumbarnie 125) **68** [1974 6g⁴ 6f⁴ 7f* 7f³ 7g 8f* 9d 1975 7f 16g⁶ 1976 8fg 20f 10f³] quite a moderate handicapper: stays 1m: acts on any going: usually wears blinkers: very trouble-some on second outing and was withdrawn, not under orders, after twice un-seating rider. *J. Hindley.*

BASALT 4 b.g. Tribal Chief 125–Balisland's Queen 93 (Abernant 142) [1974 — N.R. 1975 6s⁵ 6v 8d 5g 12f⁶ 10g 1976 5.9fg 5fg 6g 5f 5fg 5s 6d] of no account. *R. Ward.*

BASILDON BOND 2 ch.f. Good Bond 122–Ennis Royal 65 (Ennis 128) [1976 **49** 5f 6fg⁶ 7s 7s 8v⁶] poor plater. *H. Nicholson.*

BATH MISS 3 ch.f. Appiani II 128–Glittering Prize 79 (Luminary 132) [1975 — 5g 5f 5g² 6fg² 7g* 6f⁵ 7f 1976 10.4fg 8.2d 8s 8s] plater: won maiden race at Edinburgh in 1975 but was well beaten on all outings at 3 yrs: wears blinkers. *D. Williams.*

BATTENVILLE 2 ch.c. Shoolerville 121–Lovely Lady II (My Love 133) [1976 — 6g] half-brother to several winners, including quite useful middle-distance performers Patron Saint and St Columbus (both by Saint Crespin III): dam ran only once: 20/1, made some late progress when behind in 18-runner maiden race won by Reclamation at Newmarket in July, only outing. *R. Armstrong.*

BATTLECRY 4 ch.g. Bold Lad (Ire) 133–Grenadiere 111 (Right Royal V 135) **111** [1974 7d 6d⁴ 1975 10s² 9d³ 10.5g* 10fg² 10g* 10.5fg² 1976 10g 10fg³ 10.4d* 10.5d* 10g⁵ 9fg² 11.5g² 15g* 11.5g⁴ 11.5g* 18g³ 12g²] rangy gelding: winner of handicaps at Chester and York in May, making all and keeping on well on both occasions: also ran well on last-named course the following month when second to Affirmative: bought out of H. Wragg's stable after this run to race in France and did well for his new stable, winning at Bordeaux in August and the following month: stays 15f but has yet to prove he gets further (well beaten over 2¼m on penultimate start): appears to act on any going: blinkered fourth outing in France: genuine and consistent. *M. Laborde, France.*

BATTLEMENT 4 b.c. Tower Walk 130–Aspasie (Milesian 125) [1974 5f 5s* **66** 5v³ 1975 6v³ 6v* 5g⁴ 6g* 6g 5fg 6f 6g² 6g* 7fg 6fg 6fg 6d⁴ 6fg 1976 5f 6g⁴ 7fg 7fg⁴ 7g 6g 7g 8d⁵ 8v⁴ 8v⁴] neat colt: best form at up to 6f: needs an easy surface, and acts well on heavy going: sometimes wears blinkers: ran wide on turn on seventh start: sold out of N. Callaghan's stable 600 gns Doncaster August Sales after sixth outing: disappointing on Flat, but winner over hurdles. *E. Collingwood.*

BATTY 4 b.g. Welsh Saint 126–Kateth 104 (Sammy Davis 129) [1974 6g — 1975 N.R. 1976 10.2fg] lengthy gelding: good walker: well-beaten eighth of 14 to Bobbins in maiden race at Doncaster in June, only outing since his 2-y-o days. *P. Rohan.*

BAUDELAIRE 2 ch.c. Klairon 131–Pinchbeck (Chanteur II 135) [1976 6h* **118** 7g⁵ 8g 7s² 7.3v² 8v*]
Baudelaire's stable, which has had rather a quiet time since winning the Benson and Hedges Eclipse Stakes with Coup de Feu in 1974, received fitting reward for enterprise when Baudelaire picked up the Group 2 Premio Tevere at Rome in November. On his form in this country Baudelaire wouldn't have been seriously considered for races of a similar category such as the Coventry Stakes, Gimcrack, Richmond or Champagne. His only success had come in a maiden race at Carlisle in July; he had been well beaten under 7-10 when favourite for a nursery at Ayr; and on each occasion he had taken on good-class opposition he had found at least one too good for him. Avgerinos had him about seven lengths behind in fifth place in the Intercraft Solario Stakes; the newcomer Princess Tiara (in receipt of 8 lb) got up to beat him a

length in the Somerville Tattersall Stakes; and Fair Season had little difficulty in holding him off by four lengths in the Horris Hill Stakes.

In both of the last two races Baudelaire had shown that he was very much at home in the mud, and conditions were in his favour in Rome, where the ground became so heavy that the Premio Tevere came very close to being abandoned. What the form of the race amounts to is difficult to say with any accuracy—Baudelaire, a two-and-a-half-length winner, was chased home by a French colt, Hasty Reply, who had won at Saint-Cloud on his only previous appearance, and an Italian colt, My Royal Prima. Bolkonski won the Tevere in his time, but we'll be surprised if Baudelaire's performance is within 10 lb of the top.

Baudelaire (ch.c. 1974)	Klairon (b 1952)	Clarion III (b 1944)	Djebel / Columba
		Kalmia (b 1931)	Kantar / Sweet Lavender
	Pinchbeck (b 1959)	Chanteur II (b 1942)	Chateau Bouscaut / La Diva
		Metallic (b 1945)	Nasrullah / Platinum

Baudelaire, a 7,600-guinea yearling, is a brother to Pinchbelle, a minor winner over a mile and a half in Ireland, and half-brother to two more winners, the better of them being the 1968 Lingfield Oaks Trial winner Our Ruby (by Pardao). His dam, Pinchbeck, showed only poor form in Ireland but is a half-sister to Ironic, a smart performer at around seven furlongs. The family has produced little else of note in recent years.

Judging by Baudelaire's running as a two-year-old, he will be well suited by a mile and a quarter, or more, at three years. Admirable though his Italian win was, it doesn't, we feel sure, entitle him to be seriously considered as a classic colt and to win races he'll need to avoid the best of his age. His success at Carlisle came on hard going but by far his best displays have been put up when there was plenty of give in the ground. _D. Sasse._

BAYBERRY   2 b.f. Henry the Seventh 125–Caprice 90 (King's Leap 111)   **77** [1976 5fg^4 5g^2 5fg^2 5g^3 6g^5 7.2g^4 7g 7fg] lengthy filly: first foal: dam won twice over 5f at 2 yrs: moderate maiden: stays 7f: blinkered final outing. _T. Molony._

BAYDON BELLE   2 b.f. Watteau–Anturia 87 (Aureole 132)   [1976 8s] half-   — sister to two winners here and abroad, including fair stayer Sweet Boronia (by Mandamus): 500 gns yearling: dam ran only at 2 yrs, when winner at 7f: started slowly when tailed-off last of 16 to Billion (U.S.A.) in maiden race at Bath in October. _P. Taylor._

BAY GEM   3 b.f. Sterling Bay–Irish Pearl (Gulf Pearl 117)   [1975 N.R. 1976   — 10g] first foal: dam moderate Irish maiden: started slowly when tailed-off last of 19 behind Frankie in minor event at Ayr in September. _L. Docker._

BAY SQUIRE   3 b.g. Sahib 114–Frigid Flower (Arctic Prince 135)   [1975 6g^3 **59** 6g 5g^3 6g^5 6g^4 1976 8fg 7.3g 8.2g^4 8.2d 10s^4 8s^4] quite a useful sort: seems to stay 1¼m: acts on soft going: blinkered last two outings. _P. Cundell._

BAYSTONE   4 b.g. Kibenka 119–Wild Cat 95 (Eastern Venture 107)   [1974   — N.R. 1975 N.R. 1976 13.1s 14s] probably of no account. _G. Cottrell._

BAY TEMPEST   2 b.c. Swing Easy 126–Quite a Storm 87 (Quorum 126)   **75** [1976 5f 5fg^4 5f 5f 5f* 5.3f^3] workmanlike colt: third foal: 4,100 gns yearling: dam best at up to 1m: showed first worthwhile form when winning 12-runner seller at Wolverhampton in August by neck from Princess Rose: bought in 1,000 gns afterwards: will stay at least 6f: blinkered second outing. _P. Haslam._

BAY TREE'S GIRL   3 br.f. Prince Regent 129–Julie de Carneilhan (Le Haar   **63** 126) [1975 5s^4 5fg 7f^2 7g^6 7g 1976 8f 5g 6g* 6f^6 7g^4 10f^6 11.7f 8f^5 8v] neat filly: won 16-runner apprentice maiden event at Salisbury in May by ¾ length from Bede House: ran moderately last three outings: seems to stay 1¼m: acts on any going: sold 600 gns Newmarket December Sales. _R. Smyth._

BEACON WOOD   2 b.f. Clever Fella 117–Bowerswood Rose (Premonition 130)   **45** [1976 5f 5s^6 5d 5d 6f 5fg 5g 5s 6s] small filly: poor plater. _T. Walker._

BEAMING LEE   8 br.h. Le Levanstell 122–Beaming Lady 87 (Hornbeam 130)   — [1974 10fg^2 12g^4 10g 10h^3 12f^3 1975 10f 10g 1976 10f] lengthy horse: lightly raced and no worthwhile form since 1974: stays 1½m: acts on any going:

has been tried in blinkers, but does at least as well without: good mount for
an inexperienced rider. *J. Thorne.*

BEAM SPLITTER 3 b.f. Busted 134–Westerlands Prism (Primera 131) [1975 —
N.R. 1976 10g] big, workmanlike filly: third foal: dam showed only poor
form: slowly away when tailed-off last of 21 behind Lamb's Tale in maiden race
at Sandown in April: sold 430 gns Ascot October Sales. *Mrs F. Nagle.*

BEARRUE 2 b.c. Twilight Alley 133–Jini 110 (Nosca) [1976 9s 5.9s 8.2s] well- —
made colt: half-brother to winners in France and Ireland: dam high-class French
sprinter: only plating class on form so far. *R. Hollinshead.*

BEAU BRIGG 3 b.g. New Brig 120–Minibelle (Straight Cut 103) [1975 8g —
1976 8fg⁵ 9.4g] plating-class maiden: unruly in stalls final outing. *R. Cross.*

BEAU BRUMMIE 2 b.c. Northfields–Bow Mite (Gun Bow) [1976 5fg 5g 6f² 88
7h⁵ 7h* 7f² 7f⁴ 8fg* 8s 8s] leggy, light-framed colt with poor forelegs: second foal:
half-brother to a winning plater by Tower Walk: 1,000 gns yearling: dam won
four times at up to 6f in U.S.A.: won two nurseries at Redcar, having his field well
strung out when beating Westwood Boy 4 lengths in August and just holding on
when beating Naughty Lass a head in September: stays 1m: acts on hard going:
ran moderately at Bath, Brighton and Pontefract and evidently needs a straight
course. *J. Powney.*

BEAU BUCK 5 ch.h. Buckpasser–Blue Norther (Windy City 142) [1974 122
10.5s* 1975 10v³ 12g5 10fg 11g* 12s 12s² 1976 12.5g* 12fg 13g* 12.5g 11s⁴ 12s⁶
12s² 12.5v²] rather lightly-made American-bred French horse: high-class performer: winner at Saint-Cloud in April and at Longchamp the following month, on
latter course beating Luenge a length in Group 3 La Coupe: ran well in most of his
subsequent races (rather disappointing on fourth appearance), notably when
fourth to Kasteel in Prix Foy, sixth to Ivanjica in Prix de l'Arc de Triomphe and
second to On My Way in Prix du Conseil de Paris all at Longchamp: stays 13f:
possibly needs an easy surface, and acts on heavy going: sometimes bandaged
in front: genuine and consistent. *J. Cunnington, France.*

BEAU CASTEL 3 br.c. Bold Lad (Ire) 133–Lady Wong (Black Tarquin 136) —
[1975 6f 6g 8g 1976 9f 12h³] strong, dipped-backed colt: only poor form. *J.
Dunlop.*

BEAU DUTCH 3 ch.g. Ribocco 129–Dutch Maid (Piet) [1975 7g⁶ 7f² 8g* 8fg* 103
1976 12g⁴ 12g* 12g⁵ 12f⁴ 14.8fg* 13.3g 14fg² 14fg] big, useful sort: useful handicapper: won at Newbury in May (put up an excellent performance to beat Grey
Baron a head) and Newmarket in July (by a neck from Tutu): ran easily best
subsequent race when runner-up to Tug of War at Goodwood in July when tried
in blinkers: did not wear blinkers on final outing: stays 1¾m well: acts on firm
going. *M. Stoute.*

BEAUFORT STREET 5 gr.g. Right Boy 137–Toccata (Kythnos 126) [1974 80
5s⁶ 5fg 5fg² 6g⁴ 5g* 5d⁵ 5d³ 6d 6g 5.8v 5v⁶ 5s* 6d 1975 5d² 5.8g 5g⁶ 5g⁵ 6fg⁵
7f 5.9f³ 5f³ 5h⁴ 5h* 5.8f 5g⁴ 5g 5g 1976 7fg² 5.1fg 5g* 6f² 5.9f² 5f* 6h⁴ 5fg⁵ 5g 5s⁴
5s 7s⁵] neat gelding: fair handicapper: winner twice at Warwick, on second
occasion beating What A Picture 1½ lengths in July: stays 7f: acts on any going:
used to wear blinkers but didn't at 5 yrs: often bandaged near-fore. *A. Dalton.*

BEAU HUSSAR 3 b.c. Queen's Hussar 124–Lisabella (Right Royal V 135) 48
[1975 7g 1976 10g²] second produce: 920 gns yearling: dam, daughter of Irish
Guinness Oaks winner Aurabella, won over 9f and 1¼m in France: had none too
clear a run when 1½ lengths second to Oisin in maiden race at Folkestone in
March: was not seen out again and was sold to F. Yardley for 1,700 gns
Ascot June Sales. *S. Ingham.*

BEAU JAMIE 3 b.g. Galivanter 131–Stevie 79 (The Phoenix) [1975 5f 8.2g 70
1976 6fg 6g³ 6fg² 6d² 5fg⁴ 5f³ 5fg* 5f⁴ 5g²] quite a moderate handicapper: raced
consistently through the season and won 22-runner maiden race at Nottingham
in July by 1½ lengths from Endeared: stays 6f: appears to act on any going: best
in blinkers. *J. Hardy.*

BEAUJELLAS DARISTO 3 b.f. Dairialatan 111–Bisto §§ (Polkemmet 91) —
[1975 N.R. 1976 10g] half-sister to minor 7f winner Chesil Bank (by Silver
Kumar): dam temperamental: last of 13 behind Oisin in maiden race at Folkestone in March. *J. Holt.*

BEAUMEL BOARD 2 gr.f. Tribal Chief 125–Welsh Coral 93 § (Welsh Abbot 100
131) [1976 5fg⁶ 5g³ 5f² 5g* 5f* 5f* 5g⁴ 5f⁴ 5.1f² 5fg* 5fg⁴ 5fg⁵ 5g⁴] leggy filly:

second living foal: 2,800 gns yearling: dam temperamental sprint maiden: stood up well to a busy campaign and won £1,200 event at Ripon, two small races at Folkestone and £2,000 event at Newcastle: made all to beat Jewelled Turban a length on last-named course in July: usually wears blinkers but ran well without them on ninth outing: tough and consistent: sold 70,000 gns Newmarket Autumn Sales, reportedly for export to Trinidad. *G. Blum.*

BEAUNE 2 ch.f. Lyphard 132–Barbra (Le Fabuleux 133) [1976 8d* 8s⁴] 114 p French filly: first foal: dam, a useful performer at up to 1¾m, is sister to French St Leger winner Bourbon and half-sister to French Derby second Beaugency: favourite when winning 11-runner newcomers race at Evry in September by 4 lengths from Tarbette: again favourite when faced with a much stiffer task in 13-runner Prix des Reservoirs at Longchamp the following month but was beaten about 1½ lengths into fourth place behind Edinburgh: will stay 1½m: should make a good-class 3-y-o. *C. Datessen, France.*

BEAU SOVEREIGN 6 ch.g. Supreme Sovereign 119–Adeelah 79 (Persian — Gulf) [1974 9s⁵ 12f 8f 1975 N.R. 1976 12s] narrow gelding: poor maiden: has worn blinkers. *V. Lay.*

BEAUTIFUL PARK 3 ch.f. Keren 100–Beautiful Sally (Sallymount 125) — [1975 6g 5s⁵ 6g 7fg 7.2s 1976 7g 11fg³ 9v⁵ 12g 15v] tall filly: only poor form. *M. Naughton.*

BEAU WONDER 3 b.f. Veiled Wonder–Beauatire 86 (Beau Sabreur 125) [1975 — 6f 7g 5s⁵ 1976 15.5s] poor form in maiden races. *G. Beeson.*

BECKHAM 3 ch.c. Gala Performance–Right Now 100 (Right Royal V 135) — [1975 5.1f 7g 1976 8fg 10fg 16h⁶] poor maiden: trained until after second outing by G. Pritchard-Gordon. *R. Murphy.*

BEDAZZLED 2 b.c. Shiny Tenth 120–Sagacious 74 (Persian Gulf) [1976 6f 6fg 65 6fg 7s⁴] robust colt: poor mover: half-brother to several winners here and abroad: 1,000 gns yearling: dam middle-distance maiden: showed first worthwhile form when 3½ lengths fourth of 10 to What-A-Secret in maiden race at Edinburgh in October: will stay 1m+: sold 3,600 gns Doncaster November Sales. *Denys Smith.*

BEDE HOUSE 3 ch.g. Songedor 116–Gay Amanda 75 (Counsel 118) [1975 5f 58 5f² 6g⁴ 5g⁶ 7g 1976 8f 6g² 6g 7s³ 6s⁵ 6d] lightly-made gelding: showed modest form at 2 yrs and is only a plater nowadays: stays 7f. *R. Akehurst.*

BEDFELLOW 3 b.f. Crepello 136–Seventh Bride 109 (Royal Record II) [1975 94 6f* 7d⁵ 8d² 1976 12fg⁵ 12fg 13g³ 16g 16s*(w.o.) 14s] shapely, attractive filly: third foal: half-sister to two winners by Reform, namely Oaks winner Polygamy and Cheshire Oaks winner One Over Parr: didn't reproduce her 2-y-o form and became disappointing: gave a lot of trouble at stalls, eventually rearing over backwards, when withdrawn, not under orders, on intended reappearance: stayed at least 1½m (had stiff task when well beaten over 2m): probably acted on any going: stud. *P. Walwyn.*

BEDFORD LODGE 2 ch.g. Allangrange 126–Primrose Hill 82 (Red God 128 §) 89 [1976 5fg 6d 5f⁵ 7f* 7f* 7f⁵ 7fg* 8g] rather leggy gelding: second foal: 2,300 gns yearling: dam a sprinter: won maiden race and £2,000 nursery at Brighton and seven-runner nursery at Chester: made all when beating Another Pathan by a very wide margin on last-named course in September: should stay 1m: acts well on firm going. *N. Callaghan.*

BEDLAM HILL 2 b.c. Mummy's Pet 125–Acton Sattalite 79 (Gilles de Retz 132) 100 [1976 5f³ 6g* 6g] useful-looking colt: second living foal: half-brother to 3-y-o 1¼m winner Good Manners (by Mandamus): 700 gns yearling: dam won from 1m to 1½m: finished clear of six others when dead-heating with Jona for maiden race at Ayr in July: in rear in nursery on only outing afterwards: stays 6f well and may get further. *J. W. Watts.*

BEDOUIN DANCER 2 ch.f. Lorenzaccio 130–Persian Poem 58 (Darius 129) 79 [1976 6d⁶ 7g⁶] quite attractive filly: half-sister to fairly useful 1974 2-y-o 6f winner Double Nap (by Double Jump): 4,600 gns foal, resold 3,000 gns yearling: dam poor plater: put up a pleasing first effort when staying on to finish 4 lengths sixth of 17 to Maternal in minor event at Haydock in June: not seen out again until September when 9 lengths sixth of 21 to Nana's Queen in maiden race at Ayr: should stay 1¼m. *J. Hanson.*

Molecomb Stakes, Goodwood—Be Easy leads inside the last furlong to beat Faridetta (left), Japora (right), Brightelmstone and Geopelia (partly obscured by winner)

BE EASY   2 gr.f. Be Friendly 130–Easy to Love 90 (Infatuation 129)   [1976 5fg² **109** 5g* 5fg* 6fg 6g²]

It was not surprising to see Be Easy start at 33/1 for the William Hill Cheveley Park Stakes. Although she had won two of her four previous races, including a pattern event, she seemingly had had her limitations exposed when finishing only eighth of thirteen to Icena in the Lowther Stakes at York, never being able to get into the race. Prior to this she had looked to be a steadily-improving filly, following up a maiden-race win at Kempton with a win in the Molecomb Stakes at Goodwood. Held up at Goodwood in contrast to Kempton, she came through to take the lead off the long-time pacemaker Faridetta inside the final furlong and beat her by half a length, with such as Japora, Brightelmstone and Geopelia close up behind.

Favourite for the Cheveley Park was the French filly Haneena with Durtal next in the market and 10/1 bar. The race can be simply described. Durtal jumped out well on the far side, made all the running and won decisively. Be Easy was settled down last of the group on the far side. She made steady progress from halfway, on the rails, went into second place a furlong out and held Rings for second place, three lengths behind the winner. Normally a filly who finishes runner-up in the Cheveley Park must be regarded as a serious contender for the One Thousand Guineas but we do not hold Be Easy in such high esteem. With such as Athlete's Foot, Metair, Cloonlara and Icena absent the Cheveley Park did not look up to standard, and the winner Durtal had proved no match for J. O. Tobin in the Laurent Perrier Champagne Stakes at Doncaster on her previous outing. In the Molecomb, Be Easy had not been the best filly at the weights—Faridetta gave her 3 lb. To become a live prospect for the Guineas Be Easy has a lot of improvement to make during the winter.

Be Easy (gr.f. 1974)	Be Friendly (ch 1964)	Skymaster (ch 1958)	Golden Cloud Discipliner
		Lady Sliptic (ch 1954)	Preciptic Persian Slipper
	Easy to Love (gr 1961)	Infatuation (br 1951)	Nearco Allure
		Vilmorina (gr 1950)	Vilmorin Foliage

Be Easy is the seventh foal and third winner of her dam, who was quite a useful handicapper at a mile and a mile and a quarter. Easy to Love was purchased, carrying Be Easy, for 6,000 guineas at the December Sales. Be Easy is closely related to Nelski (by Skymaster), a moderate handicapper at up to seven furlongs, and she is also a half-sister to a winner in Malaysia by Sammy Davis and to the disappointing Vibrate (by Charlottown). Easy to Love is a half-sister to numerous minor winners produced by Vilmorina, a modest winner herself. Be Easy will probably stay a mile as a three-year-old. A useful-looking filly, she acts on a firm surface although her trainer was reported as saying after the Molecomb that he thought such conditions were against her. She has yet to race on anything softer than good. *J. Dunlop.*

BEE BUMBLE 2 b.f. Sterling Bay–Quippy 66 (Quorum 126) [1976 5f⁴ 5g³ 5h³ **67**
5s⁴ 5fg* 5d² 5fg] neat filly: good walker: second foal: half-sister to a winning
2-y-o plater: 600 gns yearling: dam half-sister to Cambridgeshire winner Siliciana:
won maiden auction event at Pontefract in May: finished only seventh (eased
right up once chance had gone) behind stable-companion Bowsquare Lady in
seller at York in June: will stay 6f: acts on any going: sold 820 gns Doncaster
August Sales. *K. Payne.*

BEECHWOOD LAD 4 ch.c. Skymaster 126–Sanaara (Mourne 126) [1974 6fg⁶ **67**
7v 10s* 8g⁶ 1975 10d* 10s³ 12g⁴ 12.2f 14f² 12f 12h 12g³ 12f 12d 1976 11d*(dis)
13g² 10f³ 12s 12g³ 13g² 12fg⁵ 12fg* 12.2f³ 15.8fg² 15fg* 16.1d 12.5v³ 12.5s⁵]
strong colt: quite a moderate performer: disqualified and placed last after
passing post first in seller at Edinburgh in April: ran creditably in most of his races
afterwards, and won non-selling handicaps at Thirsk in July and Edinburgh in
September: stays well: acts on any going: sometimes wears blinkers: suitable
mount for an apprentice: sometimes wears bandages: trained by R. Bastiman
until after seventh outing. *M. H. Easterby.*

BEE SPLENDID 2 b.f. John Splendid 116–Ardent Worker 88 (Buisson Ardent **80**
129) [1976 5fg² 5fg⁴ 6fg⁵ 5.3g⁴ 5fg* 5f* 5.3h⁵ 5g⁴] strong, lengthy filly: half-
sister to three winning sprinters, notably very smart Lazenby (by Bleep-Bleep),
and to a winner abroad: 700 gns foal, 1,750 gns yearling: dam stayed 1m: made
all to win seller at Sandown in July (very comfortably) and nursery at Folkestone
the following month (by a neck from Miss Init): best form at 5f. *S. Ingham.*

BEETHOVEN 2 b.c. Song 132–Devon Night 100 (Midsummer Night II 117) **107**
[1976 5fg² 5fg³ 5f* 5f* 5f* 5fg 5d³] lengthy colt: half-brother to two winners,
including 1m and 1¼m winner Devoted (by Roan Rocket): dam won at up to 7f
at 2 yrs: a speedy colt who made all when winning maiden race at Windsor and
minor events at Wolverhampton and Redcar: good third to Song of Songs and
Rahesh in Highclere Nursery at Newbury in September: should stay 6f: useful.
P. Walwyn.

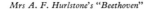

Mrs A. F. Hurlstone's "Beethoven"

BEFORE THE MAST 5 ch.g. Restless Wind–Courageously (Endeavour II) —
[1974 8s⁴ 8.2g⁶ 8.2v 6g 8.2v 1975 5fg 6g 7fg⁴ 8f⁶ 7fg 8g* 6f⁴ 8f⁴ 9h⁶ 1976 7g 8g]
selling handicapper: needs further than 6f and stays at least 1m: acts on any
going except very soft: has worn blinkers: suitable mount for an apprentice: not
raced after April and was sold 400 gns Doncaster May Sales. *J. Turner.*

BEHOLD 2 br.g. So Blessed 130–Collyria 127 (Arctic Prince 135) [1976 7fg] —
unimpressive-looking gelding with a round action: well bred but finished last of
26 in seller won by Supreme Penny at Redcar in September: sold 200 gns Doncaster November Sales. *H. Blackshaw.*

BEHOLDEN 5 b.g. Current Coin 118–Aequanimitas (Infatuation 129) [1974 8f —
8h² 9.4fg 12.2s⁴ 10fg 16d 12s* 12v 15.8s* 1975 15.8d 15v⁴ 16h⁴ 12g 16d 1976
15f⁴] compact gelding: fair plater in 1974: has since raced in better company
and has usually been well beaten, on only outing at 5 yrs finishing well behind
Tamashoon at Teesside in April: stays 2m: acts on any going: best in blinkers:
sold 600 gns Ascot April Sales. *R. Bastiman.*

BEL AZUR 3 b.g. Aglojo 119–Vidamour (Ossian II) [1975 5s 5fg 5g 5f 6f 1976 —
9f 11v² 16f⁴ 16g 12fg] plater: showed only sign of ability on second outing:
possibly unsuited by firm going: sold 1,000 gns Doncaster September Sales. *E.
Collingwood.*

BELDALE GODDESS 2 ch.f. Green God 128–Near One (Crepello 136) [1976 —
5f⁶] first foal: bought privately as a foal for 1,000 gns: dam Irish middle-distance
maiden: sixth of 13 to easy winner I Don't Mind in seller at Beverley in June,
only outing. *M. W. Easterby.*

BELDALE HOMES 2 ch.c. Deep Diver 134–Pukekohe (Larkspur 128) [1976 **76**
5f 5d 5s³ 5f 5fg³ 5fg] strong, good-looking colt: second produce: 2,300 gns foal:
dam lightly-raced half-sister to very useful 1972 2-y-o April Bloom: third in
maiden races at Doncaster and Newcastle (4½ lengths behind Durtal) in first half
of season: subsequently exported to Canada and won there: usually sweats up.
M. W. Easterby.

BELFALAS 3 b.c. Blakeney 126–Quarterings 104 (Princely Gift 137) [1975 **108**
6g⁴ 7g⁵ 8d 1976 12g² 16d² 16.1d* 16f⁵ 20.9fg² 14fg³ 18d²] strong, well-made,
good-looking colt: particularly good mover: an out-and-out stayer who needs
really long distances to be seen to best advantage: ran race of his life when length
second to Mr Bigmore in 2½m Goodwood Cup in July, pressing winner hard in
final furlong and finishing a long way clear of remainder: creditable second to John
Cherry in S.K.F. Cesarewitch at Newmarket in October when tried in blinkers,
having no chance with most impressive 5-length winner but comfortably accounting for twelve others: had gained his success in maiden race at Haydock earlier
in season: acts on a firm and a soft surface. *R. Hern.*

BELIEVED 3 b.f. Blakeney 126–Authenticated (Above Suspicion 127) [1975 **66**
6g 7f 1976 10.8f⁴ 12g⁵ 10f⁴ 10h* 10f⁴ 10.8g² 11.7d² 10.5v 10s] lightly-built
filly: won weakly-contested maiden event at Redcar in July: runner-up in
handicaps at Warwick and Windsor afterwards, just being caught by Veracious on
latter course in September: should stay well: appears to act on any going. *B.
Hanbury.*

BELINDA MEDE 2 gr.f. Runnymede 123–Belinda Pocket 84 (Pampered King **86**
121) [1976 5fg 5g² 5fg 5fg⁵ 5f³ 5d] compact, good sort: third living foal: sister
to 1975 2-y-o 5f winner Shernden, and half-sister to another 2-y-o winner: dam
won over 5f at 2 yrs: fair performer: ran well in a couple of nurseries: acts on
firm going. *W. Payne.*

BELLA CANTO 3 ch.f. Crooner 119–Bella Sandra 88 (Botticelli 129) [1975 **82**
N.R. 1976 8fg 8f* 8f⁴ 10.8h 10fg* 10.2f* 10d³ 10.6d* 10d] well-grown, useful
sort of filly: fourth foal: half-sister to a winner in Norway: dam won over 13f:
had a successful season and won maiden race at Chepstow and handicaps at
Leicester, Bath and Haydock: beat Hydrographic ¾ length, the pair finishing
clear, on last-named course in October: stayed 1¼m well: appeared to act on any
going: stud. *P. Walwyn.*

BELLA CLOSE 2 b.f. Saintly Song 128–Wether Fell (Klairon 131) [1976 5g³ **78**
5fg* 5f² 5g²] second foal: half-sister to 3-y-o 9f winner Krugerrand (by Goldhill):
860 gns yearling: dam once-raced half-sister to 1,000 Guineas second Marisela:
won minor event at Pontefract in April: close-up second to Pandu at Catterick
and Hard-To-Woo at Ayr subsequently: exported to Brazil by B.B.A. *R. D.
Peacock.*

BELLA NOVA 2 b.f. Right Boy 137–Orbenita (Orbit 106) [1976 5f 5f 5g 5v] —
neat filly: poor plater. *J. Mulhall.*

BELLAPAIS 3 ch.c. Welsh Abbot 131–Summer Day 117 (Golden Cloud) [1975   —
6g 6f 1976 10.1fg 13.8d 8.2g⁵ 9.4h³ 7f] big colt: only poor form: sold 1,650 gns
Ascot August Sales: dead. *Sir Mark Prescott.*

BELLA ROSETTA 3 b.f. Willowick–Snow Bunny (Hard Ridden 131) [1975   **58**
5g⁵ 5s 6fg 7f 1976 5g 6g 6f⁵ 6f² 7h³ 7fg] lightly-made filly: quite a modest
plater: stays 7f: tried in blinkers third outing: sold 390 gns Ascot August Sales.
T. Gosling.

BELLE BERGERE 6 ch.m. Faberge II 121–Beau Rouge (Beau Sabreur 125)   —
[1974 N.R. 1975 N.R. 1976 12fg⁵ 14fg] probably of no account nowadays.
T. Gosling.

BELLE BRETONNE 5 b.m. Celtic Ash–Belle-Dame 92 (Primera 131) [1974 **90**
11.7fg⁵ 12g* 12fg 12f² 16s³ 16d 16v⁴ 1975 12f⁴ 22.2fg6 19f³ 16fg³ 14d* 14s² 19s*
14g⁵ 1976 14g 18.4s6 16g⁵ 20f6 16f* 19fg⁵ 16g⁵ 14fg⁵ 16d² 19s* 18d] quite
attractive mare: fair handicapper: successful at Lingfield in June and Goodwood
in September, on latter course beating Night In Town by 2 lengths: stayed on
well when 2½ lengths second to John Cherry in Joe Coral Newbury Autumn Cup
earlier in September: needs at least 2m to be seen to best advantage: acts on any
going: suitable mount for an apprentice: genuine and consistent. *S. Woodman.*

BELLE VUE 3 b.g. Track Spare 125–Royal Camp 91 (Sovereign Path 125)   **76**
[1975 5s 5f 5fg⁵ 5fg⁴ 6g 5fg² 5g 5g⁴ 5g 5g⁴ 1976 6g 6g 5fg 7g² 8.2f⁵ 7.6fg* 7fg²
7.2g² 8h6 8f⁵ 8g² 8g 8.2s 8s 8.2s⁵ 6s²] neat gelding: won apprentice handicap at
Chester in July: raced most inconsistently afterwards but had two good performances to his credit in minor events at Doncaster: effective at 6f and stays
1m: probably unsuited by hard ground: usually blinkered at 2 yrs, but did not
wear them in 1976: suitable mount for a boy. *R. Mason.*

BELLS AGAIN 2 b.c. Siliconn 121–Peal of Bells (Rising Light) [1976 5fg 7fg   **71**
7g 5fg6 5f] strong colt: half-brother to several winners, including useful stayer
Dutch Bells (by Poaching): staying-on 3½ lengths sixth of 17 to Quimay in
valuable seller at York in August, best effort. *W. Marshall.*

BELL-TENT 5 b.g. Bivouac 114–Chilcombe Belle 75 (Robert Barker 125)   **94**
[1974 8f 8s 6g⁴ 1975 8fg⁴ 10f* 10fg* 8fg² 10g⁵ 10f* 1976 8g 10f⁵ 8f 10g* 10f*
10fg* 10.5fg 10fg⁵ 10d³ 8g³] strong gelding: fairly useful handicapper: successful at Salisbury and Chepstow in May and at Sandown the following month,
trotting up from Sweet Reclaim on last-named course: stays 1¼m: acts on firm
going: ran very freely seventh start: pulled very hard for his head on ninth
appearance: didn't get the best of runs on final outing. *W. Wightman.*

BELPER 7 ch.g. Busted 134–Maurine 98 (Worden II 129) [1974 12s³ 10g* 11g⁴ **102**
10.8g⁵ 10h* 10f 12f* 12g* 10.5fg 12g² 12g 10.2g 12g 1975 10s 10g* 8fg⁴ 12f*
12f* 12f⁵ 12f* 12f⁴ 12fg⁴ 10g 10g 11d* 1976 12fg⁵ 10fg⁵ 11g² 10fg² 10g² 12fg*
10fg² 11fg³ 12f² 10.5fg⁴] attractive gelding: good mover: useful handicapper:
was arguably his sixth course victory when winning Operatic Society Challenge
Cup at Brighton in June, beating Don Fortune 1½ lengths: stays 13f: appears
to act on any going: suitable mount for an apprentice: blind in nearside eye and
is ideally suited by a tight, left-handed, undulating track such as Brighton or
Epsom: does best with forcing tactics: a thoroughly game, genuine and consistent
old campaigner. *J. Dunlop.*

BELSTON 4 b.c. Blakeney 126–Flower of India 76 (Aureole 132) [1974 N.R.   —
1975 N.R. 1976 11f⁴ 13.8f⁴] probably of no account. *J. Barclay.*

BE MY FRIEND 3 b.c. Be Friendly 130 Chicuelina 74 (Matador 131) [1975 **63**
5f 6d 7g 1976 8g 6fg6 7fg³ 5g* 6g 8s⁵ 8s 6s] strong, useful-looking colt: won
maiden race at Warwick in August: ran badly on last two outings, including in
a seller: promises to stay 1m: sometimes sweats up. *E. Reavey.*

BE MY GUEST (USA) 2 ch.c. Northern Dancer–What a Treat (Tudor Minstrel **100** p
144) [1976 6g 6s*] half-brother to two winners, including stakes-placed
Bendara (by Never Bend): 127,000 gns yearling: dam, champion 3-y-o filly in
U.S.A., won at up to 1¼m: 5/2 on, won 13-runner maiden race at the Curragh
in October in good style, going on at halfway and scoring comfortably by 3
lengths from Classic Line: had veered left at start on previous outing, back
in June: will stay 1½m: has the makings of a very smart colt. *V. O'Brien,
Ireland.*

BEN DONACHAN 3 ch.c. Reform 132–Valdesta 106 (Persian Gulf) [1975   **82**
N.R. 1976 8g 10fg* 11.7d 12v²] well-made colt: fifth reported foal: dam,
closely related to Zabara and Rustam, won three times at 7f: won three-runner
minor event at Lingfield in August all out by ½ length from Fine Blue: creditable

second to Make a Signal in handicap at Leicester in November, easily better subsequent effort: stays 1½m: probably acts on any going. *R. Price.*

BENDY BABY 3 b.c. Burglar 128–Quenilda 101 (Fair Copy) [1975 5f 5s² 5g² **76** 5f 5.8h² 6f⁴ 5g² 6f 6s² 1976 6fg⁴ 8fg 6g⁵ 6g* 8g⁶ 7g] lightly-made, quite attractive colt: put up easily best effort when winning seller at Kempton in May by 5 lengths from Brightest and Best: subsequently bought in 3,300 gns: did not reproduce that form but was not raced after June: stays 6f but probably not 1m: acts on any going. *P. Haslam.*

BENELECTRIC 2 br.f. Ben Novus 109–My Worry 72 (March Past 124) [1976 — 5fg 5g] light-framed filly: third foal: half-sister to a plater: dam placed over 5f at 2 yrs: behind in maiden races at Thirsk and Lanark in May. *J. Turner.*

BENEVOLENCE 3 b.c. Never Bend–Amicable 117 (Doutelle 128) [1975 6fg³ **72** 7d 1976 8f² 9f³ 10f 11g] lengthy colt: good mover: placed in maiden races at Ascot in April (beaten 1½ lengths by True Shot) and Lingfield in June (close third to Tutorial): finished last in both subsequent races, on final outing running very freely when tried in blinkers: best form at up to 9f, although should be suited by further: sold 2,100 gns Ascot August Sales. *I. Balding.*

BEN HALL 2 b.c. Frankincense 120–Loppy Luv 67 (Soueida 111) [1976 5fg **73** 5d³ 5g⁴ 5h² 6g 6f 6g] light-framed colt: poor mover: placed in seller at Redcar and maiden auction event at Carlisle in first part of season: should stay 1m. *J. Vickers.*

BEN MACDUI 2 gr.g. Siliconn 119–Stolen Rocket (Roan Rocket 128) [1976 **57** 5s 5d 6f] leggy gelding: quite a modest plater: should stay 6f: sweated up final outing. *M. W. Easterby.*

BENNACHIE 3 b.g. Firestreak 129–Leuze (Vimy 132) [1975 6f 6fg 8g 1976 — 10.2s 10.2s] big, rangy gelding: has shown signs of ability in maiden races when backward: will stay well: not seen out until October in 1976. *M. W. Easterby.*

BENNY WREN 2 b.c. Royben 125–Tudor Wench 72 (Tudor Jinks 121) [1976 — 5g] small, sturdy colt: half-brother to quite useful Irish sprinter Paddy's Choice (by Runnymede): 500 gns yearling: tailed-off last of 10 in good-class auction event at Newbury in May, only outing. *F. Walwyn.*

BENT STREET 3 br.g. Burglar 128–Once For All (Quorum 126) [1975 5f⁵ — 5f 5f³ 5d² 1976 8g 8h 5.8h 10.1fg] lengthy gelding: showed quite moderate

Debenham Handicap, Kempton—Berkeley Square wins hands down from Creetown

form at 2 yrs but was well beaten on all outings in 1976: should stay at least 6f: tried in blinkers third outing: trained by J. Bethell until after third appearance. *Mrs A. Finch.*

BERBERRY 5 gr.m. Abernant 142–Blaeberry 100 (Hook Money 124) [1974 **44** N.R. 1975 8g 1976 6fg⁶ 7g 8f⁵ 6h⁴ 7d] poor plater: stays 6f: sold 760 gns Newmarket Autumn Sales. *P. Robinson.*

BERIOSOVA 2 ch.f. Lorenzaccio 130–Cloudbreak 95 (Nimbus 130) [1976 **108** 5.1fg* 6d⁴ 5fg⁴ 7f* 7f³ 8d⁴] small, rather dipped-backed filly: good mover: half-sister to winners in Italy and France: 5,800 gns yearling: dam won over 5f at 2 yrs: twice a winner at Yarmouth, picking up a maiden race in May and nine-runner nursery in August: creditable fourth of five to Triple First in May Hill Stakes at Doncaster in September: will probably stay 1¼m: probably acts on any going. *H. Cecil.*

BERKELEY BELLE 2 ch.f. Runnymede 123–Dart River 87 (Darius 129) **65** [1976 5f⁵ 5g⁵ 5g 5g 5f⁴ 5.9f 6d 8s] lengthy filly: plating-class maiden: stays 6f but is not certain to stay 1m. *H. Nicholson.*

BERKELEY SQUARE 4 ch.c. Midsummer Night II 117–Sweet Sonnet 72 **112** (Honeyway 125) [1974 6fg 6fg⁴ 6d* 1975 7fg⁶ 10g² 8fg⁴ 9g 9g 8g⁵ 1976 8g 7fg* 7fg⁴ 7g² 8g⁴ 7fg² 7g* 7fg* 7.2g* 7d 7v] lengthy, quite attractive colt: smart handicapper: did very well for his new stable: won at Kempton, Newbury, Newmarket and Haydock: put up a particularly fine effort (overcame difficulties in running) on last-named course in August, storming clear in final furlong to beat Boldboy 1½ lengths in Joe Coral Handicap: stays 1¼m but seems best at around 7f nowadays: appears to act on any going: genuine: unplaced last two outings but is likely to do well again at 5 yrs. *G. Harwood.*

BERMONDO 5 gr.g. Cumshaw 111–Amber Mona (Amber Light 114) [1974 **70** 7d* 7h 10fg 8d² 8s* 8.2s* 8v⁵ 1975 7d 7.6g 8f³ 8fg 7fg⁶ 8fg 8g⁵ 1976 7fg⁵ 7.6fg 8fg 8g⁴ 10fg² 10g⁴ 8.3d² 8g⁵ 10d] quite a moderate handicapper: ran well in several of his races and on seventh start was disqualified and placed second (hampered Pagos Boy inside final furlong) after beating that horse in a tight finish at Windsor in September: stays 1¼m: extremely well suited by soft going: suitable mount for an apprentice: sometimes wears a bandage on near-hind. *J. Benstead.*

BERNADINE 2 b.f. Farm Walk 111–Love Seat (King's Bench 132) [1976 5f 5h⁶ **58** 5h* 8f 8fg 8s] small filly: second foal: half-sister to 3-y-o Resin (by Frankincense), a winner at 5f and 6f: attracted no bid after getting up to beat stable-companion Habbershaw a short head in eight-runner seller at Beverley in July: had stiff tasks in nurseries afterwards: should stay middle distances. *M. W. Easterby.*

BERNICE CLARE 3 ch.f. Skymaster 126–Darya 104 (Darius 129) [1975 N.R. **68** 1976 7g³] fourth foal: half-sister to a winner in Greece: 4,100 gns yearling: dam best at 6f: 8/1, turned in a very respectable first effort when 1½ lengths third of nine, staying on well, to River Belle in minor event at Ayr in September: will stay 1m: sold 5,000 gns Newmarket December Sales. *J. Hanson.*

BEROSTINA 5 ch.m. Ribero 126–Polistina 106 (Acropolis 132) [1974 10s **—** 8.2s 8v 1975 12.3d⁵ 10fg⁵ 8.2f 6h⁵ 15.5fg³ 14fg 12d 13.1g⁶ 13g 12v 1976 12f⁴ 8g 11.7h] fair 2-y-o but has shown only poor form since: has been tried in blinkers. *D. Hanley.*

BE ROYAL 2 b.f. Royal Palm 131–Besides 105 (Naucide) [1976 5v 5v*] **97** p strong filly: half-sister to four winners, including very useful 5f to 13f winner Costmary (by Grey Sovereign): dam showed useful form at up to 7f: made all and was not extended when winning maiden race at Leicester in November by 4 lengths from Grain of Truth: will stay 7f. *N. Adam.*

BE SATISFIED 2 b.f. Silly Season 127–Lucyrowe 125 (Crepello 136) [1976 5g³ **81** 5f⁴ 6f³ 6f⁵] neat filly: half-sister to fairly useful Lady Rowe (by Sir Ivor), a winner at up to 7f, and to 3-y-o middle-distance winner Rowe Residence (by Royal Palace): dam, very smart winner at up to 1¼m, was best at 1m: only moderate at her best and seemed to get steadily worse: ran badly when blinkered on final outing: stays 6f: sold 10,500 gns Newmarket Autumn Sales, reportedly for export to Australia. *P. Walwyn.*

Houghton Stakes, Newmarket—Bessie Wallis justifies favouritism to score handsomely from Daviot

BESSIE WALLIS 2 b.f. Prince de Galles 125–Love for Sale 104 (Crepello 136) **106 p** [1976 7d*]

Jeremy Hindley had some very promising two-year-old fillies in 1976. On the opening day of the Houghton meeting he produced the unraced Princess Tiara to win the well-contested Somerville Tattersall Stakes in style, and two days later he ran another newcomer, Bessie Wallis, in the Houghton Stakes. Rumour had it that this latest newcomer was superior to Rings, another filly in the stable who had finished a good third to Durtal in the William Hill Cheveley Park Stakes, and she started clear favourite. Among the other twenty-four runners in the race were Million, by far the most expensive yearling ever sold in England or Ireland, and promising animals by such stallions as Sir Ivor and Nijinsky. For once racecourse rumour proved an accurate guide. Bessie Wallis soon showed in front on the far side, had the measure of the large field some way out and kept on so strongly that she never looked like being caught. Daviot ran on to be second, two and a half lengths behind, with previous winner Windy Sea a length and a half further back in third place.

Bessie Wallis (b.f. 1974)	Prince de Galles (b 1966)	Welsh Abbot (br 1955)	Abernant / Sister Sarah
		Vauchellor (b 1959)	Honeyway / Niobe
	Love for Sale (ch 1964)	Crepello (ch 1954)	Donatello II / Crepuscule
		Tudor Love (ch 1957)	Owen Tudor / Amora

The Houghton Stakes is won more often than not by a very good animal: Roses for the Star, Shebeen, Long Row, Guillotina, Levanter and Blakeney have all won it in recent years. The horse who ran Blakeney close was Bessie Wallis' sire Prince de Galles and two years previously the race went to her dam Love for Sale. Prince de Galles has had limited success at stud. By far the best horse by him is the Norwegian colt Noble Dancer who ran so well to be fourth to Ivanjica in the Prix de l'Arc de Triomphe; his best winners in this country are the fairly useful fillies Lily Langtry and Mistress Clare, both of whom stay quite well, and the useful two-year-old Haighall. In 1975 his seven yearlings auctioned averaged only 1,544 guineas and evidently the only reason Bessie Wallis' breeder and part-owner did not sell her, as he does most of his yearlings, was that he was advised that she was unlikely to fetch more than £700. She'd fetch a great deal more than that now!

Love for Sale didn't run again after her Houghton Stakes success. She had two winners from four foals before Bessie Wallis. To Celtic Ash she produced Bretton Woods, who finished second to Attica Meli in the 1973 Doncaster Cup, and to the American horse Tyrant she foaled the filly Amerusa who has won

104

several races in Italy, including the nine-furlong Premio Fiuggi in 1975 when she was rated the second-best two-year-old filly. The grandam Tudor Love showed useful form at a mile and a mile and a quarter, and was a daughter of Amora, winner of the Cheshire Oaks from only three starts. There is a good deal of stamina in the family and Bessie Wallis should stay a mile and a half; indeed her trainer was said to regard her more as an Oaks filly than a One Thousand Guineas candidate. Of course she still has quite a lot of improvement to make before she can be regarded as up to classic standard but with there being few high-class staying fillies yet established Bessie Wallis must be kept in mind. *J. Hindley.*

BEST OFFER 2 ch.f. Crepello 136–Floral Gift 84 (Princely Gift 137) [1976 6g 7fg² **96** 7g*] rangy, good-bodied filly: second foal: half-sister to moderate 1975 2-y-o Durbar (by Native Prince): dam lightly-raced winner over 5f at 2 yrs: improved with racing and won minor event at Lingfield in September by 2½ lengths from Rare Beauty: will stay 1m. *R. Hern.*

BE TRUE 6 ch.m. Tudor Treasure 119–Tijuana 91 (Floribunda 136) [1974 N.R. — 1975 N.R. 1976 14g 11.7fg] quite a moderate handicapper (rated 71) in 1973: well beaten in two sellers as a 6-y-o, only outings since: best form at 1m, but stays 1¾m: extremely well suited by a soft surface. *H. O'Neill.*

BETSY MAY 3 gr.f. Fleece 114–Betty Belle 65 (Dual 117) [1975 5f 5f 7f 5g⁴ 6d* — 6v 1976 7fg 7f 6d 7g 6f 5.8f 5s 6s 10v] neat filly: poor mover: useful plater at 2yrs but showed no worthwhile form in 1976: blinkered last two outings in 1975 and sixth start. *K. Bridgwater.*

BETSY ROSS 2 gr.f. Petingo 135–Clear Path (Sovereign Path 125) [1976 6v] **69 p** tall, well-grown filly: second foal: half-sister to useful Irish middle-distance winner Silvery Blue (by Sea Hawk II): dam won over 7f in Ireland on her only start at 2 yrs: 10/1, showed promise when eighth of 23 to Amity in maiden race at Newbury in October: will be suited 1m: sure to do better. *R. Price.*

BETTER BLESSED 2 br.c. So Blessed 130–Ribetta (Ribocco 129) [1976 5fg⁴ **92** 5g³ 7fg⁴ 7g³ 8.2d³ 7d⁴ 8v⁶] leggy colt: first produce: 1,650 gns foal, resold 2,700 gns yearling: dam placed over 1⅓m: fair maiden: stays 1m: acts on a soft surface but is probably unsuited by heavy going. *P. Ashworth.*

BETTER LATE 3 b.f. Sterling Bay–Too Soon 73 (Sheshoon 132) [1975 5f — 5s 5f* 5f² 6fg³ 5f³ 5g 1976 5fg⁴ 5v⁴] neat ex-Irish filly: has a rather round action: fourth foal: 2,000 gns yearling: dam a stayer: showed quite useful form in Ireland at 2 yrs, but could finish only fourth to Mon Fleur when well-backed favourite for seller at Beverley in September (was having first run for a year but looked fit) and has clearly deteriorated considerably: stays 6f: acts on firm going: left on first outing at 2 yrs. *S. Wainwright.*

BE TUNEFUL 4 ch.f. Be Friendly 130–Alchorus 78 (Alcide 136) [1974 7s² 7s* **120** 8.2v³ 1975 7g* 7d² 6g* 6g 7.3g³ 6g³ 6fg* 1976 8g 6f² 6fg⁵ 6.5d⁶ 7.3fg 7g² 6g² 6d² 6v³] most attractive filly: won Challenge Stakes at Newmarket in 1975: put up her best performance of 1976 in that race in the autumn, finishing strongly to run Star Bird by ½ length: was unable to win as a 4-y-o but was usually thereabouts in good company and gained a place on four other occasions, when 3 lengths second to Gentilhombre in Cork and Orrery Stakes at Royal Ascot, 1½ lengths second to Boldboy in Sanyo Stakes at Doncaster, ¾-length second to Honeyblest in Diadem Stakes at Ascot and 1¾ lengths third to Record Token in Vernons Sprint Cup at Haydock: best at up to 7f: acts on any going: best form on a galloping track: usually a strong finisher: genuine and consistent. *J. Hindley.*

BEVERLEY BOY 4 b.c. Chebs Lad 120–Painful Details (Shantung 132) [1974 **80 d** 5d⁵ 6f⁴ 7g² 7g* 6fg² 8s* 1975 8f⁵ 10.6fg 8d 10g⁵ 1976 10.2g⁵ 12.3d² 12f³ 12d* 13g* 12f² 13g⁶ 14fg 13g 12d 12v³ 12.5v⁵] compact colt: moderate handicapper nowadays: winner twice at Hamilton at 4 yrs: stays 13f: appears to act on any going except firm: no worthwhile form last six outings. *W. Gray.*

BEYOND THE FRINGE 2 b.f. Queen's Hussar 124–Outward Bound 79 (Sing — Sing 134) [1976 6g 8fg] small, strong filly: sister to two winners, including Boundless a winner at up to 7f, and half-sister to another winner: dam ran only at 2 yrs: seventh of 13 to Princess du Rhone in maiden race at Beverley in September, second and better effort. *B. Hanbury.*

BIBURY ASH 7 br.g. Celtic Ash–Callidice 77 (Worden II 129) [1974 8fg⁶ 10g — 10.4g 8g 12fg 12g⁵ 12d² 11.7fg⁶ 1975 12.2s 11.7g 14f 1976 10fg 11.7fg 14fg] strongly-built gelding: mainly disappointing since 1972 and has his fair share of temperament nowadays (refused to race on final start): started slowly when tried in blinkers: not an easy ride and needs strong handling. *T. Marshall.*

BICENTENNIAL 2 br.c. Blakeney 126–Bananaquit 103 (Prove It) [1976   **—** 6g6 5f] leggy, quite attractive colt: first foal: 14,000 gns yearling: dam, a winner twice over 5f at 2 yrs, comes from a speedy family: very coltish in paddock, showed some promise when 11 lengths sixth of 17 to Roi-des-Toits in maiden race at Haydock in August: in rear in minor event won by Top Soprano at Goodwood later in month: unlikely to be effective at sprint distances. *F. J. Houghton.*

BICOQUE 3 gr.c. Fric 128–Pavillon 88 (French Beige 127) [1975 N.R. 1976   **86** 7fg 12fg* 12f5 14d 16s] good sort: first foal: dam won at 1¼m: 33/1 and having first run since April when winning six-runner minor race at Newmarket in July by a neck from Palace Royal: didn't reproduce that form: has yet to show he stays further than 1½m: has reportedly been difficult to train: sold 1,400 gns Newmarket Autumn Sales. *B. Hobbs.*

BIDDESDEN 3 b.g. Reform 132–Tin Mary 96 (Tin King 126) [1975 N.R. 1976   **—** 9g3 9.4h6 8f] small, quite useful sort of gelding: first foal: dam stayed 1m: remote third to Bartolozzi in newcomers event at Wolverhampton in May, best effort: blinkered final outing: sold 280 gns Doncaster September Sales. *J. Etherington.*

BIG CLIVE 3 b.c. Charlottown 127–Mount Rosa 98 (Hill Gail) [1975 6g 5g6 7s   **70** 1976 8f 12g 12g 11.7fg4 15.5s* 12s2] neat colt: showed much improved form on last two outings when raced in blinkers, narrowly winning maiden race at Folkestone in October and then finishing excellent second to Solo Reign in handicap at Newmarket later in month: effective at 1½m and stays well: probably acts on any going but is well suited by soft. *R. Smyth.*

BIGRIBO 5 b.h. Ribero 126–Palmavista 120 (Royal Palm 131) [1974 8fg   **89** 10g* 12g*(dis) 8f 10fg 12s 1975 12s 12g5 10fg 12fg4 12f2 12f2 14g2 16fg5 12g3 1976 12g 13f5 11.7fg4 10fg3 10f6] sturdy, strong-quartered horse: fairly useful handicapper: very narrowly beaten when creditable third to Whirlow Green at Yarmouth in May, best effort as a 5-y-o: stays 1¾m but possibly not 2m: acts on firm going: usually wears blinkers but didn't on last two starts: sometimes sweats up: not much of a battler and is a difficult ride: sold 2,800 gns Newmarket July Sales. *M. Jarvis.*

BIG RUFUS 2 b.c. Ribero 126–Polistina 106 (Acropolis 132) [1976 7g 7v] big   **—** colt: half-brother to fairly useful 1974 2-y-o 6f winner Creptina (by Crepello): 5,000 gns yearling: dam stayed 7f: behind in minor events at Ascot (last of 17) and Lingfield in the autumn. *C. Brittain.*

BIG TREAT 2 ch.c. Hotfoot 126–Crepinette 64 (Saint Crespin III 132) [1976   **96** 5g5 5fg4 7h* 7h* 7f2 8g4] compact, attractive colt: good mover: half-brother to four winners here and in Italy: 9,200 gns yearling: dam won at 11f: showed improved form when tried over longer trips, winning maiden and minor events at Warwick and Bath in July and finishing good fourth to Cosy Bar in nursery at York in September: acted on hard going: sold 8,400 gns Newmarket Autumn Sales: dead. *P. Walwyn.*

BILL CAWGRAVES 4 b.g. Alcide 136–Copper Gold (Democratic 124) [1974   **—** 5fg 7g 7f 1975 9v3 11d5 16g3 16h 14.7g 15fg* 1976 8f] lengthy, unfurnished gelding: sweating, took charge of his rider on way to post prior to finishing last in amateur riders event at Pontefract in June, only outing at 4 yrs: dead. *C. Tinkler.*

BILLIEJO 3 b.f. Bilsborrow 85–Tropic Romance (Tropique 128) [1975 6g 7g   **—** 1976 8s 8f 8f] poor maiden. *T. Kersey.*

BILLIE'S PAL 2 b.f. Breeders Dream 116–Raflex 72 (Skymaster 126) [1976 5f6   **90** 5g* 5f* 5f* 6fg3 6s] second foal: half-sister to 1975 2-y-o 6f winner Gay Sahib (by Sahib): 1,600 gns yearling: dam placed at 5f and 6f: improved greatly after winning seller at Wolverhampton in May (bought in 1,250 gns) and showed herself to be quite a useful filly when beating much stronger opposition at Brighton later in month and at Chepstow in June: off course three months prior to finishing behind in nursery on final outing: should stay 6f: acts on firm going. *J. Hill.*

BILLION 2 ch.c. Amber Rama 133–Auburn Lady 106 (High Treason 126)   **59** [1976 5fg6 5g 7f4 7h5 7d] rather hollow-backed colt: only plating class: stays 7f. *N. Callaghan.*

BILLION (USA) 2 ch.c. Restless Wind–Festiva (Espace Vital) [1976 7fg⁵ 7g⁶   **88**
8d² 8s* 8v²] tall, attractive American-bred colt: good mover: half-brother to
Irish middle-distance winner Falaise (by Pretendre) and Chilean Oaks winner
Figura (by Sun Prince): dam won Chilean One Thousand Guineas: favourite when
scrambling home by a short head from Piccolo Marat in 16-runner maiden event
at Bath in October: also second in maiden race and a nursery at Newbury: runs
as though he will be suited by middle distances: appears to act on any going.
J. Dunlop.

BILLS BIRTHDAY 2 ch.c Bluerullah 115–Big Mary (Dicta Drake 126) [1976   **—**
5f 5f 5f 5g⁶] leggy colt: poor plater: dead. *G. Richards.*

BILL'S SONG 3 b.c. Song 132–Beamless 73 (Hornbeam 130) [1975 5fg⁶ 5s²   **91**
6g³ 5v⁴ 1976 6fg² 6fg* 6fg³ 5g² 5d* 5fg³ 5fg⁴ 6h* 5fg⁵ 5g 5g] neat colt: quite
a useful handicapper: had a good season and won at Warwick (twice, including
a maiden event) and Sandown: very good fourth to Rundontwalk in Tote Sprint
Trophy at Ascot in June: runs as though 6f is his trip: acts on any going: suitable
mount for an apprentice: lost his form at the back-end and was sold 1,500 gns
Newmarket Autumn Sales: exported to Hong Kong. *J. Holt.*

BILLYCOMBE 2 b.f. Sovereign Bill 105–Heathcombe (Langton Heath 97)   **77**
[1976 5fg⁵ 5f³ 5h²] second foal: dam a winning point-to-pointer: quite a
moderate maiden: not seen out after July: will stay 1m. *J. Thorne.*

BILLY LIAR 4 b.g. Lauso–Kushi 65 (Paridel 112) [1974 N.R. 1975 5g⁴ 8g   **75 d**
6fg*(dis) 8.2s⁵ 6d 1976 5f³ 6g² 5.9f⁶ 6s² 5.1fg⁶ 6f⁵ 7f 6h 6f 6h 6g 5s] dipped-
backed gelding: quite a moderate handicapper on his day: ran creditably on first
few outings, but became very disappointing: evidently best at sprint distances:
acts on any going. *V. Mitchell.*

BINES BRIDGE 3 ch.f. Lorenzaccio 130–Mockbridge 106 (Bleep-Bleep 134)   **94**
[1975 6f 7g* 7g³ 1976 7fg 10fg² 13g²] lengthy filly: only lightly raced:
finished runner-up in handicap at Brighton in May (to Via Con Vente) and
Royal Caledonian Hunt Cup at Ayr in September (looked light in paddock and
was no match for Broken Record): probably stays 13f: acts on a firm surface:
sold 6,200 gns Newmarket December Sales. *N. Murless.*

BINGO LIZ 2 br.f. Enbrage 78–Flashena 72 (Cash and Courage 116) [1976 7f   **52**
7f² 7f⁵ 7.2f] big filly: poor plater. *S. Wainwright.*

BINHAM 3 b.c. Blakeney 126–Tenura (Prince Bio) [1975 7g⁵ 10f⁶ 1976 12g   **—**
10fg⁵ 14g] neat colt: fair maiden at 2 yrs but showed little worthwhile form in
1976 (heavily-backed favourite on first outing): should stay at least 1½m. *J.
Bethell.*

BIRDCAGE WALK 6 ch.g. Pall Mall 132–Wichuraiana (Worden II 129) [1974   **—**
N.R. 1975 N.R. 1976 16f⁵] staying hurdler: half-brother to Wollow but has
shown no worthwhile form himself on flat: bandaged only outing in 1976. *T.
Kersey.*

BIRD CHERRY 3 br.f. Falcon 131–Betula 89 (Hornbeam 130) [1975 N.R.   **59**
1976 8fg 8f² 8h*] good-quartered filly: third living foal: dam won at 6f at 2 yrs
and 1¼m at 3 yrs: landed odds by ½ length from Saddler's Queen in eight-runner
maiden race at Chepstow in June: stays 1m: acts on hard going: bought by
D. Dartnall 1,050 gns Newmarket December Sales. *F. Maxwell.*

BIRETTA 9 gr.g. St Paddy 133–Sun Cap 123 (Sunny Boy III) [1974 N.R.   **—**
1975 N.R. 1976 12s] quite a moderate handicapper in 1973: having first outing
on flat since when well beaten in ladies race at Chepstow in October: stays well:
acts on firm going: has been tried in blinkers. *Mrs J. Pitman.*

BIRKHOLM 2 b.c. Mickey McGuire–To My Lady (Amber Morn) [1976 6g⁴ 5g*   **113**
6fg* 6g⁴ 6g²] American-bred colt: lengthy, good sort and a good mover: second
foal: brother to Haut Brion, three times a winner at 2 yrs in 1975 in U.S.A.:
$6,500 yearling: dam won at up to 1m in U.S.A., including a stakes race: won
two races in good style in August, beating Viscount 2 lengths in minor event at
Haydock and needing to be kept going only with hands and heels to score by
same margin from Hedge School in £1,500 event at Leicester: ran well afterwards,
finishing 2 lengths fourth of six to Anax in Champion 2-y-o Trophy at Ripon
and 3 lengths second to Etienne Gerard in Clarence House Stakes at Ascot: will
stay 1m. *R. Armstrong.*

BISHOP'S JEWEL 3 ch.g. St Chad 129–Julie Glitters (Nice Guy 123) [1975   **—**
7g 6g 1976 10.1fg 10.1f 12fg] poor maiden. *A. Pitt.*

BISHOPSWOOD 3 ch.g. Salvo 120–Star of Gold 102 (Nimbus 130) [1975 N.R.   **63**
1976 10fg 13g⁶ 15.5h³ 16.1f⁵] half-brother to several winners at home and

abroad, including fairly useful stayer Parthian Star (by Parthia): dam a middle-distance performer: showed some ability in maiden events: stays well: ran moderately in amateur riders event on final outing and was sold 1,000 gns Ascot October Sales. *J. Dunlop.*

BIT OF A MADAM 2 b.f. Richboy 117–Swinburn (Coliseum 116) [1976 6f6 5.9f4 6f 7fg] first foal: dam last in a point-to-point: only plating class: will stay 1m+. *N. Adam.*　**55**

BITTER SPARE 2 b.f. Track Spare 125–Shady Walk 72 (Gratitude 130) [1976 5h 5f5 5f 5s2 6s3 7v6 7v] leggy filly: fourth produce: 300 gns foal, resold 160 gns yearling: dam stayed 11f: quite a moderate maiden: best form at 6f but should stay 1m: evidently needs a soft surface. *W. Gray.*　**77**

BITTY BOY 4 b.g. Habitat 134–Court Caprice 107 (Court Martial) [1974 6f 6fg 5.9g 8s 8s 1975 8s 8v 5fg 7f 6f 1976 7fg 8fg] useless. *N. Wakley.*　**—**

BIVVIE 2 b.f. Bivouac 114–Brocette 60 (Brocade Slipper 116) [1976 6fg3 5.9f 7f 7g5 8f 8.2s] small filly: bad plater. *G. Blum.*　**46**

BLACKADDER 2 b.f. High Top 131–Silly Symphony 100 (Silly Season 127) [1976 5fg* 6g* 5fg2 6g3 6g] neat, well-made filly: first foal: dam won from 6f to 1m: won maiden race at Salisbury in June by 2 lengths from Be Easy, and St Catherine's Stakes at Newbury the following month by 1½ lengths from subsequently-disqualified Rahesh: placed afterwards in two well-contested events, going down by ½ length to Haraka in St Hugh's Stakes at Newbury in August and finishing 3¾ lengths third to Lady Mere in £3,300 event at York the following month, but was beaten 11 lengths by Durtal when equal ninth of 15 in William Hill Cheveley Park Stakes at Newmarket in September: best form at 5f but is bred to be suited by 7f and 1m. *P. Walwyn.*　**109**

BLACK ALICE 4 bl.f. Sahib 114–Betsy Cluppins 68 (Soueida 111) [1974 N.R. 1975 10.1fg 10.1f 8f 8.2g 8g 1976 6fg 5.9fg] of no account: sold out of V. Cross's stable 430 gns Ascot January Sales. *P. Arthur.*　**—**

BLACK CROW 2 b.f. Sea Hawk II 131–Café Au Lait 97 (Espresso 122) [1976 6f5 6v 7s] fair sort: second foal: half-sister to 3-y-o Petit Eclair (by Major　**71** p

Mr Duncan Davidson's "Blackadder"

BLA

Portion), a winner at 7f and 10.8f: dam stayed 1½m: showed ability in maiden races, finishing eighth of 20 to Brightly at Newmarket in October: apprentice ridden last two outings: a stoutly-bred filly who will probably do better over distances more in keeping with her breeding. *Doug Smith.*

BLACKFOOT GIRL 3 b.f. Prince Tenderfoot 126–Soot (Black Tarquin 136) **64** [1975 5s 5g⁶ 5fg 5.3f⁶ 6g 5f⁴ 7g 8d⁶ 7g⁵ 1976 5h⁵ 5.8h 5g² 7g⁵ 6fg] sturdy filly: finished strongly when ½-length second to Power Girl in maiden race at Kempton in August, best effort: bred to stay 1¼m: blinkered fifth and sixth outings at 2 yrs: sold 1,000 gns Newmarket Autumn Sales. *R. Smyth.*

BLACK ICE 2 b.c. Frigid Aire–Toys (Sammy Davis 129) [1976 6fg 6fg] first — foal: 1,050 gns yearling: dam never ran: in rear in June in maiden auction event at Epsom and seller at Windsor. *A. Pitt.*

BLACKJACK STREET 3 br.c. David Jack 125–Red Border (Border Legend — 119) [1975 6fg 1976 10fg 10fg] tailed off in maiden races at Salisbury in first half of season. *O. O'Neill.*

BLACK JIM 3 ch.c. Jimmy Reppin 131–Dark Helen 111 (Black Tarquin 136) **62** [1975 6f⁶ 6f 6g⁵ 7g 8v⁵ 1976 6v² 8d 8f⁴ 10f 6g⁵ 7g* 7f⁵ 7g 6s⁴ 5h⁵] lightly-built colt: bought in 950 gns after winning seller at Catterick in June: twice not disgraced in better company afterwards: should stay 1¼m: evidently acts on any going. *H. Bell.*

BLACK MINSTREL 2 b.c. Luthier 126–Innocent Air 75 (Court Martial) [1976 **95** 7fg 7f³ 7.2f² 7g⁴ 7fg] big colt: half-brother to Invariable (by Snob), a useful winner at around 9f in France: dam ran in U.S.A., England and France, winning three small French races at up to 10.5f: ran well in two minor events in August, finishing 2 lengths third to Fast Frigate at Salisbury and 1½ lengths second to Do Better at Haydock, but put up easily best effort when remote fourth to J. O. Tobin in Laurent Perrier Champagne Stakes at Doncaster in September: will stay 1½m: suited by some give in the ground. *D. Sasse.*

BLACK PATE 4 b.g. Laser Light 118–Amanda Jane 75 (Rustam 127) [1974 — 5d 5d⁴ 5g 7g 7g 7s⁴ 8g 6g⁴ 8s³ 1975 6v⁶ 8d³ 10d⁵ 10s 9g 8g 1976 11d 8fg⁶] sturdy gelding: bad maiden: stays 1m but gives impression that 7f may suit him better: best in blinkers. *H. Bell.*

BLACK RAY 3 b.c. Blakeney 126–Blue Ray 82 (Royal Record II) [1975 6f⁴ **66** 6f 8.2g⁴ 7d 10g* 1976 9fg 12fg³ 11.7f⁴ 12g³ 12f 13fg⁴ 16g 11.7d⁶ 12s 16s 13v] smallish colt: quite a moderate handicapper: stays 13f: well beaten when tried in blinkers on ninth outing. *C. Brittain.*

BLACK SABBATH 3 b.c. Typhoon 125–Petemoss (Bounteous 125) [1975 7d⁵ 7g 8g 1976 12g⁶ 10fg³ 12fg² 12g 14fg* 12h* 14fg³ 14fg⁴ 12g³ 14.6d 12s 16g] workmanlike colt: successful in maiden event at Sandown and minor event at Lingfield, both in June: had earlier finished excellent second to Norfolk Air in Ladbroke Derby Trial Stakes, also at Lingfield, and afterwards finished creditable third in handicaps at Sandown (to Grey Baron) and Kempton (to Merry Kerry): stays 1¾m: acts on hard ground: lacks a turn of foot and is suited by front-running tactics: stumbled and unseated rider tenth outing: much improved. *M. Francis.*

BLACKSBOAT 7 br.g. Stupendous–Margaret Ann 83 (Persian Gulf) [1974 — 6fg⁶ 12h² 10h⁴ 8f⁴ 1975 8g 8g⁵ 8fg⁴ 8.3fg² 8fg 7d 1976 10f 8fg] strong gelding: plater: appears to stay 1½m but does the bulk of his racing at shorter distances: acts on any going: sometimes wears blinkers and bandages: sold 440 gns Ascot June Sales. *R. Carter.*

BLACQUAY 3 br.g. Quayside 124–What's Left 73 (Remainder 106) [1975 — 5f 5g 6fg 1976 12v⁴ 8fg 8.2g] no worthwhile form in maiden and minor events. *Denys Smith.*

BLADING 3 ch.f. Admiral's Boy–Ballast (Polic 126) [1975 5d⁶ 5s⁴ 5f 5.8h 8g 8g **53** 8d 1976 11.1fg³ 10.1fg⁴ 10.1fg⁵ 10.6d*] leggy, unfurnished filly: plater: showed improved form when winning at Haydock in May (no bid): stays 11f: suited by some give in the ground: has worn blinkers but does better without. *G. Balding.*

BLAGOSLAV 4 b.c. Baldric II 131–La Montespan (Tantieme 136) [1974 6g **96** 6g 7g⁴ 7s² 1975 8v 8g* 9s 8fg² 8f 1976 16fg⁶ 12fg² 14fg 14f 12fg*(dis) 16fg⁵ 10fg 12fg⁵] strong colt: fairly useful handicapper: disqualified for hampering third horse after winning seven-runner Durdans Handicap at Epsom in June (made virtually all) by a neck from Paper Chase: well beaten afterwards: best form at up to 1½m: appeared to act on any going: sold to Australia as a stallion. *D. Dale.*

109

BLAIR ELECT 4 b.f. Ovid 95–Poaching's Folly (Poaching 115) [1974 N.R. — 1975 N.R. 1976 10s] second foal: half-sister to poor animal Tambourina (by Drumbeg): dam of no account: 50/1 when last of 14 behind Chartered Course in minor event at Teesside in November, only outing. *K. Stapleton.*

BLAKENEY BELLE 3 b.f. Blakeney 126–March Spray 101 (March Past 124) — [1975 6d 1976 7.6s 8fg 7fg 5fg 12g⁶ 12v] neat, short-legged filly: poor maiden: sold 1,450 gns Newmarket December Sales. *J. Bethell.*

BLAKENEY BREEZE 2 br.c. Blakeney 126–Bloomers 93 (Floribunda 136) — [1976 8g 7s 8s] brother to poor animal Blak-en-Bloo, and half-brother to quite useful sprinter Gold Loom (by Goldhill) and fair 1975 2-y-o 6f winner Hopeful Bloom (by Hopeful Venture): 13,000 gns yearling: dam stayed 1¼m: prominent 5f when remote seventh of 14 to Crown Bowler in minor event at Lingfield in September, second and probably best effort. *R. Price.*

BLAKEWOOD 3 b.f. Blakeney 126–Wind Break 81 (Borealis) [1975 7d 8.2d **75** 1976 11.7f 17.7f² 16f⁶ 16f⁴ 17.7f* 16f² 16g* 16d⁴ 16s] neat filly: won maiden race at Wolverhampton in August: afterwards ran well in handicaps and won one at Warwick later in month by 2½ lengths from Super Jennie: stays well: acts on any going with the exception of really soft: wears blinkers. *H. Candy.*

BLAKEY 3 b.f. Blakeney 126–Psidjet (Psidium 130) [1975 N.R. 1976 12d³ — 16.1f⁴ 16g⁶ 15.8g 14.7d³ 16.1v⁶] strong filly: first foal: dam unraced half-sister to very smart French 1m to 1¼m performer Prince Jet: slow maiden. *M. Camacho.*

BLAKEY RIDGE 3 b.c. Busted 134–Lowna 120 (Princely Gift 137) [1975 N.R. **80** 1976 8fg 8.2g 10d* 8v³] leggy, rather narrow colt: closely related to Gospill Hill (by Crepello), a smart performer at up to 1¼m, and half-brother to 1974 2-y-o 6f winner The Hobman (by Tudor Melody): dam won Molecomb Stakes: having first outing for four months and blinkered first time when wide-margin winner of moderate maiden event at Yarmouth in September: heavily-backed odds-on shot and again blinkered when well-beaten third to Petrina in minor event at Newcastle the following month (raced on apparently slower going in straight): stays 1¼m: acts on a soft surface: sold 6,000 gns Newmarket Autumn Sales. *N. Murless.*

BLA-KROSS 2 b.c. Blakeney 126–Cross Tree (Crepello 136) [1976 8v 8s] — small colt: half-brother to three winners, including very useful sprinter Precious Drops (by Great Nephew): dam never ran: little worthwhile form in end-of-season minor events at Teesside and Doncaster. *W. Elsey.*

BLANC RIVAGE 2 ch.c. Riverman 131–Tour Blanche (Le Fabuleux 133) [1976 **114** 8g* 8s*] French colt: fourth foal: half-brother to Valmur (by Val de Loir), a useful winner at up to 13.5f: 150,000 francs yearling (approx. £16,000): dam never ran but comes from a very successful family: successful twice at Maisons-Laffitte in October, winning 18-runner newcomers race by a neck and putting up a good effort in a well-contested event, giving Irodos 6 lb and beating him comfortably by 2 lengths: will probably stay 1½m. *A. Head, France.*

BLASKETTE 5 br.m. Blast 125–Merok (Eastern Venture 107) [1974 9f* 10h* **99** 10fg* 12fg 10g⁴ 12g 1975 10d² 10fg² 12f³ 10g⁶ 10f² 10.5fg³ 9g⁵ 10.8g³ 1976 10g 10fg² 10fg* 10g* 10fg² 10fg³ 10.5fg* 10f* 10d 10g] rangy mare: did really well as a 5-y-o, winning four races, including good handicaps at Epsom (Daily Mirror Handicap by ½ length from Belper), York (impressive winner of Falmouth Handicap) and Goodwood (floored odds on Chil the Kite by 2 lengths): gained her other success when trotting up in minor event at Brighton: effective at 9f and stays 1½m:

Chesterfield Cup, Goodwood—Blaskette is too good on the day for Chil the Kite

Mrs R. Owen-George's "Blaskette"

probably acts on any going: goes well on a switchback track: has a good turn of foot: admirably game, genuine and consistent. *N. Vigors.*

BLASTAVON 7 b.g. Blast 125–Avonella 73 (Rockavon 120) [1974 6g³ 6g* 5.9g⁵ 6f⁵ 6g⁶ 6fg* 6g* 6g* 6fg⁵ 6f 6g² 6g 6d³ 6g* 7.3d⁵ 6s* 5v³ 5v 1975 6s 6s 6f³ 6fg 6fg³ 7.2g² 6g⁶ 6f⁵ 1976 6fg 6g⁴ 6f⁵ 6f³ 7fg 6f 7g⁶ 5.9f 7d 6v] one-time fair handicapper: well beaten in 1976, including in sellers: stays 7f: acts on any going and on any track: sometimes wears blinkers: suitable mount for an apprentice: occasionally starts slowly. *G. Hunter.* **67**

BLAZINGFORTH 3 b.c. Bally Russe 113–Ballyforth 79 (Ballylinan 118) [1975 N.R. 1976 18s] half-brother to three sprint winners by Dignitary, including fair sprinter Shepherd's Tartan, and to useful hurdler/chaser Santon Brig (by New Brig): dam won over 5f at 2 yrs: tailed off in amateur riders maiden event won by Brother George at Doncaster in October. *J. Berry.* **—**

BLEJAUNE 2 ch.c. Miracle 116–Copper Corn 79 (Vilmorin) [1976 5fg 5f⁴ 5f⁵ 5.9f⁴ 6g 6f] big, strong, close-coupled colt: fifth foal: 1,300 gns yearling: dam, a sprinter, is sister to very speedy Poplin: quite a moderate maiden: stays 6f: sold 1,600 gns Doncaster November Sales. *N. Adam.* **76**

BLESSED BOY 4 br.g. So Blessed 130–Borana 105 (Aureole 132) [1974 5fg 6g⁴ 5v³ 5v⁵ 1975 10.8s⁵ 9fg 12fg 10fg² 10.1fg³ 10g⁴ 10d² 10.8g² 10d² 10g³ 1976 9f 8fg 8g⁴ 8f] tall gelding: poor maiden: stays 1¼m: acts on any going: ungenerous. *D. McCain.* **§§**

BLESSED MARTIN 3 br.c. So Blessed 130–Clarity 98 (Panaslipper 130) [1975 5f⁴ 5f 7f³ 7g⁵ 7g* 8f* 7g⁵ 1976 10v² 7d 8g³ 7fg 10f⁵ 7f⁶ 8fg 11s] useful performer at 2 yrs but ran moderately in 1976 and has deteriorated: should stay 1¼m: probably needs a sound surface: trained until after third outing by N. Angus. *G. Blum.* **69**

BLESS MY SOUL 3 b.f. So Blessed 130–Aurelia 68 (Aureole 132) [1975 8.2d⁴ 1976 12.2fg⁴ 7g³] well-made filly: in frame in maiden races at Wolverhampton **56**

111

in April and Edinburgh in May (tried in blinkers): should stay 1½m but has shown better form at shorter distances: exported by B.B.A. to Brazil. *B Hanbury.*

BLESS MY STARS 3 br.f. So Blessed 130–Life Belt 75 (Only for Life 126) — [1975 5g 5h 1976 8fg 10fg 10f5 8g] leggy filly: poor maiden: blinkered first race in 1975 and final outing. *H. Collingridge.*

BLICKLING HALL 4 b.g. Blakeney 126–Grove Hall 66 (Hook Money 124) — [1974 7s 7g5 8s 1975 10s 16g5 12g5 14fg 1976 12g 9f 14f 22.2f] moderate Irish maiden: remote seventh to Coed Cochion in Queen Alexandra Stakes at Royal Ascot on final appearance: stays quite well: sold out of W. Robinson's stable 4,800 gns early in year and was resold for 5,600 gns at Ascot October Sales. *M. O'Toole, Ireland.*

BLITZ 6 b.g. Pall Mall 132–Wild Bee (Hill Gail) [1974 10.2s2 10.8g 9d4 10g5 70 1975 10g3 10g 10.2g 8g 1976 14g* 12g 12g 14fg5] strong gelding: moderate handicapper: won apprentice selling handicap at Sandown in April by ¾ length from Dellwood Prince: well beaten in non-selling company afterwards: stays 1¾m: acts on any going: blinkered last two outings. *Dr A. Jones.*

BLONDEL 3 br.c. King Log 115–Street Singer 122 (Kingsway) [1975 6fg6 7fg — 1976 5.9fg 9d 8g 8g 8g 8g 8f5 8f6 7g 13.1s] workmanlike colt: plating-class maiden: stays 1m: blinkered penultimate outing: sold to D. Jermy 540 gns Newmarket Autumn Sales. *D. Sasse.*

BLONDE WARRIOR 2 b.c. Military 112–Premium Blonde (Pindari 124) [1976 — 5f 5g 6d 5s 7v 7s] apparently of no account, although hasn't yet run in a seller. *P. Allingham.*

BLOOMINGDALE 6 gr.m. Stoic–Blooming Hills (Hillsdale) [1974 N.R. 1975 — N.R. 1976 12f6] moderate performer (rated 81) in 1972: tailed-off last of six in handicap at Folkestone in May, only outing since: possibly unsuited by firm going. *J. Long.*

BLOU HEMEL 3 b.f. Virginia Boy 106–The Real Thing (Sayajirao 132) [1975 — N.R. 1976 11f 11g5 8fg6 10g 11f6 6v 8v6] of little account. *T. Craig.*

BLUE BRAID 2 gr.f. No Mercy 126–Braida (Tissot 131) [1976 5g 7fg 5v] — well-made filly: first foal: 900 gns yearling: dam placed in Italy at 3 yrs: well behind in maiden races: blinkered final outing. *M. Smyly.*

BLUE BRIGAND 3 ch.c. Majority Blue 126–Marennes 89 (Pearl Diver 130) — [1975 6fg2 7fg* 6d 1976 8g 7fg 7.6s] attractive well-made colt: showed useful form as a 2-y-o, but ran well below his best in 1976: will stay 1m: possibly not at his best on a soft surface: tried in blinkers final outing: sold 4,900 gns Newmarket July Sales. *P. Walwyn.*

BLUE CHROME 4 br.g. Hot Brandy 119–Narratus 94 (Narrator 127) [1974 76 N.R. 1975 13.8f6 16fg2 12f4 16g- 16f2 16 1fg* 14fg2 15s2 16g 16g 1976 13g3 12g 14.7d2 16f4 14.7f4 16h4 20f5 15.8f* 16f2 15fg3 15.5s*] big gelding: quite a moderate handicapper: most decisive winner at Catterick in August and Folkestone in October, on latter course beating Floating Penny by 12 lengths in amateur riders event: well suited by long distances: acts on any going: ideal mount for an amateur: sweated up sixth and eighth outings: genuine and consistent. *Miss S. Hall.*

BLUECON 2 b.f. Majority Blue 126–Consequently 101 (Con Brio 121) [1976 — 5d 6s 7s] third produce: 300 gns foal, 800 gns yearling: dam stayed 1m: in rear in Scottish maiden and minor events in first half of season. *H. Bell.*

BLUE DREAM 2 b.f. Blue Streak 99–Dream Buck (Pinturischio 116) [1976 69 5f 5fg6 5f5 5.8f4 5.9f*] first foal: dam never ran: blinkered first time, showed improved form to win 12-runner seller at Wolverhampton in July by ½ length from Leyburn Lady (no bid): not seen out again: will probably stay 1m. *R. Hannon.*

BLUE FIRE 8 b.g. Majority Blue 126–Light Blaze (Borealis) [1974 N.R. 1975 — N.R. 1976 15.5s] little worthwhile form on flat in 1971: having first outing since when well behind in amateur riders race at Folkestone in October won by Blue Chrome. *H. O'Neill.*

BLUE GIPSY 5 b.m. Sky Gipsy 117–Borage 77 (Cagire II 122) [1974 8d 10.2g — 1975 8v 10fg 12f 12h 10fg 8g 1976 12h 8fg] of no account: dead. *H. F. Freeman.*

BLUEHILL 3 gr.f. Blue Streak 99–Tamblast (Tamerlane 128) [1975 6s2 6g 5g 80 5g3 6g3 5v3 1976 6fg* 6g3 6fg2 6g6 6f2 5fg] small, stocky filly: won maiden race at Leicester in March: subsequently ran well when placed in handicaps: should stay 7f: appears to act on any going: gave a lot of trouble on last three appearances and was twice withdrawn: sold out of T. Marshall's stable 660 gns Ascot August Sales. *F. Wiles.*

BLUE JET 3 b.g. Blue and Grey 93–Whistlewych 40 (Whistler 129) [1975 5v 5g 6f3 6f* 7fg2 6f* 7g5 5f 7f6 6g4 1976 9g 12g 8s 8f 7.2fg3 7f3 6f4 6g6] narrow gelding: modest plater: should stay 1m: acts on any going: sometimes wears blinkers. *J. Carr.* **63**

BLUE LINNET 2 b.f. Habitat 134–Golden Linnet 96 (Sing Sing 134) [1976 5g5 5fg2 5fg* 5g2 5g2 6g 5g 5d4] lengthy filly: half-sister to two winners, including useful 1974 2-y-o Circus Song (by Hill Clown): dam won over 5f and 6f, and is half-sister to good sprinter Monet: won maiden race at Newmarket in April in good style by 4 lengths from Cramond: creditable second in well-contested events on next two outings, going down by 2½ lengths to As Blessed at Kempton in May and by 3 lengths to Brightelmstone in Acorn Stakes at Epsom the following month: lightly raced afterwards but returned to her best when fourth to Self Portrait in nursery at Newmarket on final outing: should stay 6f. *S. Ingham.* **89**

BLUE MOONLIGHT 3 b.f. Bluebeard–Lune d'Avril (Sailing Light 119) [1975 7g 10g 1976 8.2d 5.9s6] leggy, sparely-made filly: poor maiden. *M. Salaman.* —

BLUE MYSTIC 4 ch.g. Ballyciptic 122–Bluemantle (Right Royal V 135) [1974 N.R. 1975 11.7f 17.7f 1976 13g 17f4 12fg 14fg] probably of no account. *M. Haynes.* —

BLUE OAK 4 ch.f. Blue and Grey 93–Oak Cliff Girl (Tudor Cliff) [1974 N.R. 1975 8g 1976 8fg] probably of little account. *M. Bradley.* —

BLUE PIMPERNEL 3 gr.g. Blakeney 126–Empress of Britain 93 (Amber X 133) [1975 N.R. 1976 8g 10.1fg5 10g] compact gelding: second foal: dam prolific winner at up to 1¼m: going on finish when remote fifth of 21 in maiden race won by Saturnus at Windsor in May, best effort: off course four months afterwards and was well beaten on his return: will stay 1½m. *Miss A. Sinclair.* —

BLUE PROSE 3 b.f. Blue Streak 99–Prosody 71 (Epigram) [1975 5.8f 7fg 6g5 5.8f 6s 1976 10.1fg 8f 8h5 8h5] quite a moderate plater at 2 yrs, but showed no worthwhile form in 1976: sold 390 gns Ascot July Sales. *R. Hannon.* —

BLUE RAG 3 b.f. Ragusa 137–Blue Butterfly 105 (Majority Blue 126) [1975 5g 1976 7fg 9f* 8f 10g6 8s 8s] first foal: 4,700 gns yearling: dam a useful performer over 5f at 2 yrs: won 23-runner maiden race at Wolverhampton in May by ½ length from Va d'Isere: off course some time after next outing and put up best subsequent effort on her return: evidently stays 1¼m. *J. Bethell.* **70**

BLUES AGAIN 4 ch.c. Majority Blue 126–Incarna 82 (The Phoenix) [1974 5fg4 5g4 6fg5 6g4 6fg6 5g4 5s3 6s6 6v3 1975 5d 6d 6f* 6fg6 7f 6fg 6fg5 7g* 7fg 6g2 7.3d5 7g 6g2 6g 1976 8g 7fg4 6g 6g 6f4 6f4 7fg4 6f3 7fg3 6f 8f2 7f 7f3 8d3 8g2 7.6s* 6d 8v6] strong colt: fair handicapper: gained a well-deserved success when winning ladies race at Lingfield in September by 12 lengths from King Ocar: put up probably his best other effort of season when 4 lengths third of six to Raffindale in minor event at Lingfield in June on eighth outing: in lead when unseated rider (saddle slipped) 2f out on fourth start: stays 1m: seems to act on any going: wears blinkers: suitable mount for an apprentice or lady rider: sold 2,600 gns Newmarket Autumn Sales. *K. Ivory.* **81**

BLUE SONG 2 ch.f. Majority Blue 126–Palakada 88 (Palestine 133) [1976 5s 8v] cost only 200 gns as a yearling and seems to possess little ability. *A. Neaves.* —

BLUE SOUL 2 b.f Blue Streak 99–Clarito 84 (Dumbarnie 125) [1976 5.8f] seventh foal: dam at her best at 2 yrs: 66/1 when last of nine in seller at Bath in June: sold 230 gns Ascot August Sales. *J. Pullen.* —

BLUE TOWN THANKS 5 b.g. Bluerullah 115–Park Scene 87 (Pall Mall 132) [1974 10.1g 10.8fg 13.8f* 1975 N.R. 1976 10.6d] plater (rated 58) in 1974: having first outing since when tailed off in amateur riders event at Haydock in October (blinkered): stays well: acts on firm going. *C. Boothman.* —

BLUE WITH COLD 3 b.c. Hardicanute 130–Mary D 99 (Vigo 130) [1975 N.R. 1976 10.1fg3 10g2 10fg* 10.2h* 12f2 10fg3 11.7h3] strong, rangy colt: half-brother to two winners, including very useful 1971 Irish 2-y-o 5f winner Supercede (by Super Sam): 1,600 gns yearling: dam 5f sprinter: placed in all his races and won maiden event at Sandown and minor contest at Bath (trotted up) in the summer: probably stays 1½m: acts on hard ground. *F. Maxwell.* **86**

BLUFFER 3 b.c. Busted 134–Grande Fille 83 (Fortino II 120) [1975 N.R. **97**
1976 8fg 12fg³ 12fg³ 16f⁴ 12.3fg*] well-made colt: good walker: second produce:
half-brother to useful sprinter Amadou (by Hotfoot): sold privately 5,500 gns
as a foal, resold 40,000 gns as a yearling: dam won over 5f at 2 yrs: odds on
when wide-margin winner of weakly-contested maiden race at Newcastle in
June: subsequently bruised a tendon and was not seen out again: had earlier
shown useful form when in frame in Warren Stakes at Epsom, Ladbroke Derby
Trial at Lingfield and Queen's Vase at Royal Ascot: pushed along much of way
in last-named race but made tremendous headway in straight and was going on
really well at finish, being beaten only just over 4 lengths into fourth place
behind General Ironside: runs as though he will be suited by extreme distances:
acts on firm going. *C. Brittain.*

BLUMENBACH 3 b.c. Dr Fager-Bonnie and Gay (Sir Gaylord) [1975 6f 7f **72**
6fg 1976 10.8fg 10.8f 6fg* 6g⁴ 5.8h 6fg 7h⁶] American-bred colt: put up easily
best effort when game winner of maiden race at Brighton in May: ran moderately
last three outings: evidently suited by 6f. *J. Welch.*

BLUNDER 2 ch.f. Blast 125–Necora 79 (Royal Record II) [1976 5f 6d 6g 6s] **58**
first foal: plater: showed only sign of ability when ninth of 21
to Burley in £1,400 event at Newmarket on penultimate start: unseated rider
final outing: sold 660 gns Newmarket Autumn Sales. *R. Jarvis.*

BLUSHING BRIDE 3 gr.f. Veiled Wonder–Bromhead (Sovereign Path 125) **—**
[1975 5d 5s 5d 5f⁵ 6fg 6fg³ 6g 1976 10f⁶ 8d] of little account. *P. Poston.*

BLUSHING GROOM 2 ch.c. Red God 128 §–Runaway Bride (Wild Risk) **131**
[1976 5g³ 5.5d* 5.5g* 6g* 7s* 8d*]
The only race Blushing Groom lost in six starts as a two-year-old was his
first, and the races he won included the Prix Robert Papin (5.5f), the Prix Morny
(6f), the Prix de la Salamandre (7f) and the Grand Criterium (1m), the big four
races in France for two-year-olds. My Swallow, in 1970, was the first to accomplish this feat, and no other horse has done so. Had Blushing Groom been
trained in England and won instead, say, the Richmond Stakes (6f) at Goodwood,
the Gimcrack Stakes (6f) at York, the Laurent Perrier Champagne Stakes (7f) at
Doncaster, and the William Hill Futurity (1m) at Doncaster, what would we think
of him? Well, to start with he would be unique, for no horse has won all four of
these races. In fact, since the inception of the William Hill Futurity, as the
Timeform Gold Cup, in 1961, in which year the distance of the Champagne Stakes
was extended from the six furlongs to seven, no horse has won any three of these
races, and one has to go all the way back to Palestine in 1949 to find the last
horse to win the Richmond Stakes, the Gimcrack Stakes and the Champagne
Stakes. J. O. Tobin, who won the Richmond Stakes and the Champagne Stakes
in 1976, was generally regarded as the best two-year-old to have raced in this
country for years, until Blushing Groom cut him down to size in the Grand
Criterium.
Yet, outstanding as Blushing Groom's record is, it is doubtful whether

Prix Robert Papin, Maisons-Laffitte—Blushing Groom defeats River Dane

Prix Morny, Deauville—a convincing success for Blushing Groom over Water Boy and the grey Alpherat

anyone in this country would have been prepared to regard him as a better horse than J. O. Tobin, had the latter not been allowed to take his chance in the Grand Criterium. J. O. Tobin had won the Richmond Stakes impressively from Priors Walk and Tachypous, and in the Champagne Stakes he had defeated the subsequent Cheveley Park Stakes winner, Durtal, in a canter. Few who saw his victories doubted that he was an exceptionally brilliant two-year-old. But J. O. Tobin was no match for Blushing Groom. Taking the lead on the turn for home, Blushing Groom strode away in tremendous style in the straight to win, virtually unchallenged, by four lengths from Amyntor, who beat J. O. Tobin by a head for second place. Not since 1962, when Hula Dancer was successful, has the Grand Criterium been won by such a wide margin.

J. O. Tobin was not the only English-trained two-year-old to receive this sort of treatment from Blushing Groom. Sunny Spring, an easy winner of the Windsor Castle Stakes at Royal Ascot, couldn't get within eight lengths of him when third in the Prix Robert Papin, whilst Nice Balance, who had won the Group 3 Seaton Delaval Stakes at Newcastle on the second of two previous appearances and who was regarded as a pretty good colt, was beaten almost fifteen lengths in the Prix de la Salamandre. Blushing Groom won the Robert Papin very comfortably by three quarters of a length from the filly River Dane, and the Salamandre by two lengths, apparently all out, from another filly, Assez Cuite. He had no English challenge to contend with in the Morny, and pulled away from the distance to win easily by three lengths.

By his successes in these races, worth incidentally a total of £141,039 to add to the £3,882 he picked up for a runaway win in the Prix de Rochefort at Evry on his second appearance, Blushing Groom is entitled to be regarded as the outstanding two-year-old in Europe. outstanding in terms of pace in that he possessed the speed to beat high-class opposition at sprint distances, and outstanding

Prix de la Salamandre, Longchamp—yet another important win for Blushing Groom, who is followed home by Assez Cuite, Alpherat and King of Macedon

Grand Criterium, Longchamp—Blushing Groom shows himself the best two-year-old in Europe. Four lengths behind comes Amyntor (No. 2), who heads English challenger J. O. Tobin near the line

in terms of stamina in that he was able to win a top-class race over what is regarded as a stayers' course for first-season performers. He was the complete two-year-old.

So much for Blushing Groom in 1976. How do we see his future? Well, the first thing to strike us when we saw him in the parade ring before the Prix de la Salamandre was that he was an attractive, well-grown individual, who already had the physical development of a three-year-old, and there must be a real possibility that he will be unable to maintain his progress relative to some of his contemporaries. Not that we would expect any of them to be forward enough or fast enough to overthrow him in the French Two Thousand Guineas. We say the French Two Thousand Guineas advisedly. Mathet rarely has a runner in this country nowadays, and the probability is that Blushing Groom will be raced exclusively in France as a three-year-old. And then there is the question of his stamina. Let's take a look at his breeding.

Blushing Groom (ch.c. 1974)	Red God (ch 1954)	Nasrullah (b 1940)	Nearco
			Mumtaz Begum
		Spring Run (b 1948)	Menow
			Boola Brook
	Runaway Bride (b 1962)	Wild Risk (b 1940)	Rialto
			Wild Violet
		Aimee (b 1957)	Tudor Minstrel
			Emali

A son of Red God, who has given us another two-year-old champion in Jacinth, in addition to a host of other winners, Blushing Groom is out of the Wild Risk mare Runaway Bride, and thus a full brother to Bayraan, a very smart performer in France from six furlongs to a mile. Runaway Bride, who was placed over a mile and a half in Ireland as a four-year-old, is a half-sister to two winners in France, and a granddaughter of Emali, who won the Ulster Cambridgeshire. Emali, in turn, was a daughter of Eclair, whose full sister, Infra Red, was the fourth dam of Mill Reef and the third dam of Wollow. Thus Blushing Groom, who was purchased through Keith Freeman for 16,500 guineas as a foal at the December Sales, comes from one of the most successful families in the Stud Book, and he is going to have tremendous appeal as a stallion when his days on the racecourse are over. Blushing Groom's yearling half-brother, by Zeddaan, fetched 25,000 guineas at the 1976 December Sales, having failed to reach his reserve at Deauville three months previously. Few good horses by Red God stay beyond a mile, and we fancy that Blushing Groom will be no exception. He acts well on soft going. *F. Mathet, France.*

BLUSTERY 4 b.g. Busted 134–Esquilina 89 (Romulus 129) [1974 5fg 5g 6f 7s⁵ 7g* 7.3d 8g³ 7s* 1975 10v² 8v 8d³ 11.7s³ 11fg² 11fg 12fg 1976 12fg 10.2g³ 8g 7s⁴] sturdy gelding: had stiff tasks in handicaps but showed some form: stays 1½m: possibly best served by some give in the ground and acts well on soft going. *M. Smyly.* **85**

BLYTH ENDEAVOUR 2 b.g. Prince Tenderfoot 126 Silba II (Ragusa 137) [1976 5fg 5g] first foal: 2,800 gns yearling: dam placed at up to 2m: behind in maiden races at Newmarket in May and Leicester (second favourite, finished eleventh of 18 to Tudor Lilt) in June: sold 520 gns Newmarket Autumn Sales. *H. Cecil.* **60**

BLYTH'S FOLLY 3 b.f. Prince Tenderfoot 126–Genazzano (Shantung 132) [1975 5f 6g 5g³ 5g² 1976 5g² 6g⁶ 5.3f⁵ 5g⁵ 8fg² 8fg 10.1d* 10s² 10s* 10v*] good-bodied, attractive filly: in good form in the autumn and won maiden race at **89**

116

H. H. Aga Khan's "Blushing Groom" (H. Samani)

Windsor (by 6 lengths), minor event at Sandown and handicap at Lingfield: came
with a strong last-furlong run when beating Grecian Bond by 3 lengths on last-
named course in November: well suited by 1¼m and may well stay further:
probably acts on any going but seems best served by some give in the ground.
R. Price.

BOBBINS 3 ch.f. Bold Lad (Ire) 133–Popkins 120 (Romulus 129) [1975 N.R. **70**
1976 7fg 10g 7.6s 10fg³ 10fg⁵ 10.2fg* 10g⁵ 12fg] small, strong filly: second foal:
dam very smart at up to 1¼m: decisive 4-length winner of maiden race at Doncaster in June: ran poorly afterwards: stays 1¼m well: acts on a firm surface:
sold 7,400 gns Newmarket December Sales. *H. Wragg.*

BOBBY KEMPINSKI 2 ch.g. Right Tack 131–Tuna 63 (Silver Shark 129) **82**
[1976 5v* 5f⁵ 5f⁴ 6g 6g³ 7fg⁵ 6f² 6v* 7d 6s³] useful sort: first foal: dam showed
only poor form at 1m: 7-length winner of maiden race at Ayr in April: ran well in
nurseries later in season, quickening really well when winning one at York in
October in a blanket finish by a neck from dead-heaters Broon's Secret and Gnos:
will stay 1m: acts on any going but is well suited by heavy. *E. Collingwood.*

BOCO 7 b.h. Ribocco 129–Co-Optimist (Never Say Die 137) [1974 12.2fg⁶ **§§**
18.4g⁵ 16g⁴ 18.4g⁶ 16g* 19g⁴ 16g 18g² 17.4s 16s   1975 18.4g 17.7fg* 16fg* 18.4g
18f⁵ 16g⁶ 16d 16f⁶ 1976 16.1d 16f⁴ 16g⁴ 17.7f 15.8fg⁵] strong, deep-bodied
American-bred horse: formerly a moderate handicapper (rated 81 as a 6-y-o) but
is only poor nowadays: needs long distances: acts on any going: wears blinkers:
a moody customer and is best left alone. *F. J. Houghton.*

BODENSEE 2 b.f. Wolver Hollow 126–Lake Constance 85 (Star Gazer 123) **102**
[1976 5fg² 5f 5f* 6fg⁶ 6f* 6g² 6g²] shapely filly: third produce: 1,900 gns foal,
resold 4,600 gns yearling: dam best at sprint distances: not extended when
winning four-runner maiden race at Nottingham in June: showed much improved
form in nurseries afterwards and won one at Goodwood in August by a neck from
Petinara: will stay 7f: acts on firm going. *B. Hobbs.*

BODY BLOW 2 b.c. What A Pleasure–Roman Meadow (Roman) [1976 6g 7s] **—**
American-bred colt: half-brother to three winners in U.S.A., notably smart 1966
2-y-o Forgotten Dreams (by Royal Note): $17,000 yearling: dam placed in

117

U.S.A.: ninth in a newcomers race (second favourite) and £1,500 event, both at Goodwood in September. *R. Price.*

BOG OAK 3 gr.f. Sassafras 135–Betty Burke 95 (Prince Chevalier) [1975 N.R. 1976 10g] half-sister to three winners, namely very useful stayer Arisaig and useful middle-distance performer Pseudonym (both by Acropolis) and very useful 1m winner Stirling Castle (by Royal Palace): dam won at 5f and 6f: 20/1 when in rear in 15-runner maiden race won by Sousa at Nottingham in April: sold 2,200 gns Newmarket December Sales. *H. Cecil.*

BOHEMIAN 4 b.c. Busted 134–Moondaisy 94 (Wilwyn 129) [1974 7s⁴ 7v 1975 10d 9d 12f⁶ 13.3fg⁶ 12.2f³ 10fg 13g² 16g 9fg² 1976 10.2fg⁶ 13.4fg⁶] attractive, rangy colt: no worthwhile form in 1976: stays 13f: acts on firm going: ran very freely when tried in blinkers (only attempt at 2m): has run well for an apprentice. *D. Sasse.*

BOIS LE DUC 3 b.f. Kalydon 122 or March Past 124–Mattinata 90 (Matador 131) [1975 5d 7fg 1976 10.1d 5s] small, lightly-made filly: poor maiden. *Miss N. Wilmot.*

BOLDARO 5 b.g. Bold Lad (Ire) 133–Etoile de France (Arctic Star) [1974 8fg 8g 6g 1975 8fg 8f 10g 1976 15g] attractive, good sort of gelding: little worthwhile form: sold to M. Tate 775 gns Ascot November Sales. *G. Richards.*

BOLD ARROW 4 b.c. Bold Lad (Ire) 133–Loidien 95 (Ribot 142) [1974 6fg **65** 1975 8g 10f³ 8g⁴ 8fg⁴ 5g⁴ 7fg 7s 7g 8g 1976 9fg² 8g² 9g² 10f³ 11.1g⁴ 10f² 12fg* 10f⁵ 10f⁴ 10g 12s 10s 10s⁶] strong, good-looking ex-Irish colt: quite a moderate handicapper: beat Dyscole ¾ length when winning at Doncaster in June: stays 1½m: acts on firm going: sometimes wears blinkers: sold 2,000 gns Newmarket December Sales. *M. Haynes.*

BOLD AURA 2 b.c. Aureole 132–Blue and Silver (Blue Tom 127) [1976 8s — p 8.2s⁶] big, strong colt: first foal: dam won three small races over middle distances in France and is half-sister to Irish Guinness Oaks winner Aurabella (by Aureole): made some late progress when remote sixth of 12 to Hot Grove in minor event at Haydock in October: will stay 1½m: the type to do much better at 3 yrs. *P. Walwyn.*

BOLD AUSTRIAN 2 b.c. Bold Lad (Ire) 133–Austria 93 (Henry the Seventh — p 125) [1976 6g 7g] first foal: 6,000 gns yearling: dam stayed 1½m: behind in newcomers race at Goodwood in September and maiden race at Newmarket (twelfth of 22) in October. *G. Harwood.*

Ladbroke Abernant Stakes, Newmarket—the blinkered Boldboy gets the verdict by a head from Honeyblest

BOLDBOY 6 b.g. Bold Lad (Ire) 133–Solar Echo (Solar Slipper 131) [1974 **126**
6fg* 8g* 7s⁴ 6fg⁴ 8g² 6s³ 1975 6v² 7d⁵ 8f³ 7g⁴ 8g² 7 3g 7g³ 1976 6fg* 8g 7.2d³
8f³ 7g⁴ 7.2g² 8f² 7g* 6g⁴ 6d³]
After a slightly disappointing season as a five-year-old, in which he failed to
win, Boldboy found a new lease of life at six and overtook Petty Officer's record
winning total of almost £45,000 for an English-trained gelding. Two of Boldboy's performances stand out as at least as good as anything he has achieved.
The first came on his seventh outing, in the Waterford Crystal Mile at Goodwood
in August. Up against five three-year-olds, including the second and third in
the Sussex Stakes, Free State and Poacher's Moon, Boldboy went down by only
a short head to Free State, to whom he was conceding 10 lb more than weight-
for-age. His task at the weights appeared so difficult that he was unquoted in
the betting. Less than a fortnight later, Boldboy gave Be Tuneful 10 lb and
beat her a length and a half in the Sanyo Stakes at Doncaster—another cracking
performance.
Boldboy gained his other win of the season very narrowly, in the Ladbroke
Abernant Stakes at Newmarket on his first appearance, at the chief expense of
Honeyblest. Having his first run at a distance as short as six furlongs since he
finished second in the race the previous year, he fared far better than we anticipated at the trip on top-of-the-ground and made virtually every post a winning
one. He later ran creditably over six in the Diadem Stakes and the Challenge
Stakes but we get the impression that seven furlongs or a mile suits him better
nowadays. Boldboy finished in the frame in all his other races except the
Lockinge Stakes (he ran poorly that day in the absence of his regular partner
Mercer), among those races being the Queen Anne Stakes at Royal Ascot and
the Prix de la Porte Maillot at Longchamp. Boldboy has run some splendid
races in France in his time, and his performance in the hotly-contested Maillot
was another good one: he was beaten less than half a length although only
fourth to Son of Silver. He also gave a good account of himself in his first
appearance in a handicap: carrying 13 lb more than Berkeley Square in the
Joe Coral Handicap at Haydock, he went down by a length and a half.

		⎧ Bold Ruler	⎧ Nasrullah
	⎧ Bold Lad	⎨ (b 1954)	⎨ Miss Disco
	⎪ (b 1964)	⎩ Barn Pride	⎧ Democratic
Boldboy	⎨	(ch 1957)	⎨ Fair Alycia
(b.g. 1970)	⎪	⎧ Solar Slipper	⎧ Windsor Slipper
	⎪ Solar Echo	⎨ (b 1945)	⎨ Solar Flower
	⎩ (b 1957)	⎩ Eastern Echo	⎧ Colombo
		(b 1938)	⎨ Singapore's Sister

Since Boldboy's pedigree was last dealt with in depth, in *Racehorses of 1973*,
his dam has produced the useful filly Seminar (by Don II), a winner three times
as a two-year-old, and Call of the Deep (by Captain's Gig), a name to remember
for 1977. Boldboy is a good-looking gelding, who carries his years well, and the
signs are that he will be a tough nut to crack for some time yet. Sometimes
he sweats up, and he used to wear blinkers but he does at least as well without
them nowadays. Boldboy acts on any going. *R. Hern.*

BOLD FANTASY 2 b.f. Bold Lad (Ire) 133–Ribot's Fantasy 99 (Ribot 142) **89 p**
[1976 7g*] Irish filly: first foal: dam won over 1½m and is sister to Ragusa:
second favourite for 13-runner newcomers event at Phoenix Park in October
and put up a promising display to win by 1½ lengths from Paper Bag: will stay
1¼m: likely to develop into a very useful performer. *P. Prendergast, Ireland.*

BOLD JACK 2 ch.c. Bold Lad (Ire) 133–Gallissa (El Gallo 122) [1976 5fg⁶ 5g **§§**
6fg 5.3fg⁶ 7g 6s] well-made colt: second foal: half-brother to a winner in Italy
by Crocket: 5,200 gns yearling: dam a fairly useful winner over 5f at 2 yrs in
Ireland: ran to 95 when 9 lengths seventh of 10 to Avgerinos in Intercraft
Solario Stakes at Sandown, but ran poorly in his other races and is clearly
untrustworthy: evidently suited by 7f: blinkered fourth and fifth outings.
R. Hannon.

BOLD PIRATE 4 b.c. No Robbery–Venture (Tulyar 134) [1974 7g* 6g² 7g³ **114**
9s* 1975 10f⁶ 10fg 10g 10s⁵ 12g 1976 10g³ 12f 10.5fg* 10fg 10.5fg⁴] lengthy,
quite attractive colt: held on gamely when winning John Smith's Magnet Cup
at York in July by a head from Fool's Mate: also ran well when in frame in
Brigadier Gerard Stakes at Sandown in May (third to Anne's Pretender) and
Benson and Hedges Gold Cup at York in August (finished well to take fourth
place, 10 lengths behind Wollow): best form at up to 1¼m and appears not to

John Smith's Magnet Cup, York—Bold Pirate wins a thrilling duel with Fool's Mate.
The third horse is True Shot

stay 1½m: probably acts on any going: has worn a tongue strap: ran very poorly on fourth outing. *R. Hern.*

BOLD TACK 5 b.h. Bold Lad (Ire) 133–Albercaro 88 (Hard Tack 111 **§**) [1974 **100** 6f* 8s 6fg⁵ 6.3g² 6g⁴ 6.3g* 6f⁵ 6f² 7fg 6d² 1975 5g 6g⁴ 6fg⁴ 6f² 6.3fg* 6g 6g* 6g 1976 6fg⁴ 6g⁶ 6d⁵ 7g⁶ 6fg⁵ 6fg³ 7fg³ 7.2f⁴ 8g² 8g] strong ex-Irish horse: good mover: very useful performer at 4 yrs but was mainly disappointing in 1976: best form at 6f but seems to stay 1m: seems to act on any going: has worn

Sir Michael Sobell's "Bold Pirate"

blinkers (hooded ninth start) but is better without: sold out of W. Robinson's stable 9,200 gns Goffs February Sales: not one to rely on. *B. Hills.*

BOLD WARRIOR 5 b.g. Brave Invader–Natty 98 (Narrator 127) [1974 N.R. 1975 12s 9f 9f 8g 8h* 10fg⁵ 8g 1976 10g 12g] workmanlike gelding: best form at 1m but should stay further: acts on hard going: suitable mount for a lady rider: blinkered final start. *J. Berry.*

BOLLIN TARA 2 ch.f. St Paddy 133–Bollin Charlotte 79 (Immortality) [1976 **64** 6f⁶ 6g 8v 8.2s] strong, compact filly: third foal: half-sister to Immortal Knight (by Midsummer Night II), a useful winner at up to 9f: dam a miler: showed a little ability on first outing but was well beaten afterwards: should stay at least 1m. *M. H. Easterby.*

BOLTBY 3 b.g. The Brianstan 128–Cherry Pie 81 (Rockavon 120) [1975 N.R. **—** 1976 12f⁶ 10h⁵ 10.6g 10f 12f] workmanlike gelding: half-brother to two minor winners: bought 2,600 gns Doncaster May Sales: dam won over 7f at 2 yrs: well beaten in varied company, including selling: sweated up fourth outing: blinkered final start: sold 1,100 gns Ascot November Sales. *W. A. Stephenson.*

BOMBARDIER 3 ch.g. Sing Sing 134 or King's Troop 118–Taranto 90 (Major **87** Portion 129) [1975 N.R. 1976 10g⁴ 12fg* 12f² 12g³] workmanlike gelding: good mover: first foal: dam middle-distance handicapper: won 14-runner maiden race at Newbury in August, quickening very smoothly to beat Greenstead Lad by 4 lengths: ran creditably when placed in minor events at Ripon and Goodwood afterwards: stays 1½m. *J. Dunlop.*

BOMBAY DUCK 2 ch.f. Ballyciptic 122–Hindu Curry (Hindostan 119) [1976 **65** 5s⁵ 6d 7fg⁴ 7fg] compact, robust filly: half-sister to several winners, notably smart Irish sprinter Clever Fella (by Le Levanstell): 3,000 gns yearling: dam never ran: ran best race when 8 lengths fourth of 13 to May Song in maiden race at Chester in July: will be suited by 1m. *P. Rohan.*

BOMBE 3 gr.f. Roan Rocket 128–La Melba 99 (Chanteur II 135) [1975 N.R. **82** 1976 8fg³ 8fg⁶ 12.2g² 10f³ 9.4h³ 8h⁶ 12.2f² 9.4h* 10f² 9.4h* 10f* 10g⁴ 8.2h* 10fg²(dis)] half-sister to numerous winners, including top-class French horse Breton, winner at up to 1m: dam won at up to 1¾m: only moderate but won four small races, at Carlisle (two), Beverley and Hamilton: made all to beat Ochil Hills Star 2 lengths on last-named course in September: stays 1½m: acts on hard ground: wears blinkers: often runs freely to post and unseated rider on way down on seventh outing. *M. W. Easterby.*

BONA-MIA 2 b.c. Good Bond 122–My Mary 93 (French Beige 127) [1976 5g **107** 5g⁶ 6fg² 7f* 7g* 7s 8g*] compact colt: half-brother to three winners, including fairly useful 6f to 1m performer Candles (by Firestreak): dam a stayer: won minor event at Salisbury in August and good-class nurseries at Doncaster and Newmarket the following month: held off Court House by a neck on last-named course: will stay 1¼m: acts on firm going and is probably unsuited by soft. *T. Gosling.*

BONDED GIFT 3 b.c. Divine Gift 127–Jane Merryn (Above Suspicion 127) **—** [1975 6fg 6f⁵ 1976 7fg 8fg 7g 10fg⁴] lengthy colt: little worthwhile form in varied company: possibly finds 1¼m too far for him: sold 1,500 gns Ascot July Sales. *H. Smyth.*

BOND'S BEST 2 ch.f. Good Bond 122–Izeste (Lavandin 128) [1976 6g 6fg] **—** well-made filly: half-sister to two winners, including sprinter Another Fiddler (by Burglar): dam placed at up to 9f in France: unquoted, made no show when in rear in 17-runner maiden race won by Miellita at Goodwood in July: unseated rider on first outing. *R. Price.*

BONK 5 br.g. Bing II–Monamolin 109 (Golestan 127 §) [1974 8v 1975 8f⁵ **—** 8.3fg³ 8f 1976 10.1fg⁴] leggy, light-framed gelding: quite a moderate plater: remote fourth of 15 to Doubly Hopeful in maiden race at Windsor in September, only outing at 5 yrs: apparently stays 1¼m. *M. Bolton.*

BONNIE DE LYON 3 ch.f. Jukebox 120–Gorgeous Gael (Atan) [1975 5d 5.9g **42** 7.2s 6g² 1976 8fg 9f 8f 10f 10h⁴] small filly: probably stays 1¼m: blinkered third and final outings. *J. H. Peacock.*

BONNIE LOLA 2 b.f. Gulf Pearl 117–Bonnie Bird 73 (Aureole 132) [1976 5g **—** 5d 7.2f 8v 7v 5s] small filly: of little account. *P. Farrell.*

BONSOIR 3 br.f. Realm 129–Goodbye 73 (Linacre 133) [1975 5g 5g⁴ 1976 **—** 6v⁶ 6f 5f 8f 7fg 6g 10v³] poor plater: ran best race over 1¼m: sold to D. Chapman 450 gns Doncaster October Sales. *S. Hall.*

BONVICINO 3 b.c. Charlottown 127–Rotisserie 106 (Tesco Boy 121) [1975 — N.R. 1976 12g 12fg] good-looking colt: first foal: 3,500 gns yearling: dam won Fred Darling Stakes: behind in maiden races at Kempton and Newmarket (led 1m) in April. *B. Hanbury.*

BOOM QUAY 2 ch.c. Quayside 124–Blasllyn 88 (Blast 125) [1976 5g 5f 5d⁴ 6fg 70 6g⁵ 6f 8f*] leggy colt: dam appeared to stay 1½m: bought in 800 gns after dead-heating with Eightsome in 22-runner seller at Thirsk in September: will stay 1½m: appears to act on any going: sold 2,600 gns Doncaster September Sales. *K. Payne.*

BOOTHFERRY LADY 2 b.f. Marcus Superbus 100–Quibble 59 (Quisling 117) — [1976 8fg 8.2s 8s 10s 8v] bad plater: blinkered final outing. *D. Williams.*

BOOTLACES 2 b.g. So Blessed 130–Gated 79 (Worden II 129) [1976 7fg 6fg 69 6v⁴ 6d] half-brother to three winners, including useful stayer Padlocked (by Pardao): 3,000 gns yearling: dam a staying half-sister to Remand: showed signs of ability, finishing seventh of 23 to Running Bull in maiden race at Newmarket in October on final outing: will be suited by 1m+. *P. Robinson.*

BORAK 2 b.c. Deadly Nightshade 107–Gingell (Damremont 121) [1976 6f 8.2s 10v 8.2v] leggy colt: worthless plater. *F. Dever.*

BORDELLO 2 ch.f. Crepello 136–Eternal Love 102 (Ratification 129) [1976 89 6d² 7d] very good-looking, lengthy filly: half-sister to several winners, notably smart No Alimony (by Alcide), a winner at up to 1¼m, and very useful middle-distance performer Loyal Guard (by Worden II): dam won over 5f at 2 yrs: second favourite for seven-runner Blue Seal Stakes at Ascot in September and put up a very encouraging effort, finishing length second to Circlet after being slowly into stride and showing signs of greenness: second favourite, raced on disadvantageous stands side when only twelfth of 25 to Bessie Wallis in Houghton Stakes at Newmarket the following month: should be suited by middle distances: sure to win a race. *P. Walwyn.*

BORDER PALACE 2 b.f. Royal Palace 131–Near The Line 88 (Nearula 132) — [1976 7g 8d 8v] sister to Pink Palace, a fair winner at up to 1¾m: no sign of ability, including in a Newmarket seller. *P. Robinson.*

BORDER RIVER 3 b.g. Forlorn River 124–Kelso Girl (Royal Palm 131) [1975 85 5f² 5f* 5h⁴ 6d⁵ 5g⁶ 6f³ 6f³ 5g 6s 7g⁶ 1976 7f 6fg⁴ 6fg³] strong gelding: moderate handicapper: probably stays 7f: best form on a sound surface: blinkered sixth outing in 1975: consistent. *W. C. Watts.*

BOSTON FLYER 2 b.f. Mansingh 120–Spare Pin 68 (Track Spare 125) [1976 57 5f 5f* 6d⁶ 6f 8fg 6v] small filly: first foal: 820 gns yearling: dam placed at up to 13f: won 16-runner maiden auction event at Beverley in April by a length from Jolly Joe: no better than a plater on the rest of her form however and finished well behind on last two outings, including in a valuable seller: probably stays 6f. *H. Blackshaw.*

BOTANIST 3 ch.g. Ballymoss 136–Larkspur's Love (Larkspur 128) [1975 5g² 86 6f² 6f⁵ 8f 1976 10.8f³ 16d⁴ 11.5g* 12.2f* 12fg² 12fg* 14fg⁶] fair performer: in good form in the summer and won maiden race at Yarmouth, minor event at Wolverhampton and handicap at Lingfield: beat Autoway a neck, the pair finishing clear of four others, on last-named outing in August: best form at 1½m and appeared not to stay when tried at 2m: acts on firm going: sold to J. Old 4,200 gns Ascot October Sales. *G. Pritchard-Gordon.*

BOUCHER GARCON 2 b.c. Galivanter 131–Lucky Deal 93 (Floribunda 136) 74 [1976 5g 5g 6fg 5.9s⁴ 7v³ 7v⁶] neat colt: second foal: half-brother to winning 3-y-o sprinter Pickwood Sue (by Right Boy): 2,200 gns yearling: dam won over 5f

Timeform Charity Day Selling Plate, York—no danger to Bowsquare Lady

at 2 yrs: quite a moderate maiden: suited by 7f and will stay further: acts on heavy going. *S. Norton.*

BOUCHETTE 5 b.m. Current Coin 118–Umgeni Poort 109 (Botticelli 129) — [1974 9d 8h 8g 7g 8fg³ 7d* 7fg* 8g⁴ 7d 1975 8.2g 8f 7f⁵ 9fg 6g² 7f⁵ 8f 1976 5f 10f 7f⁶ 5h⁶ 7f] leggy, rather lightly-made mare: poor handicapper: stays 1m: seems to act on any going. *A. Smith.*

BOUNDLESS 7 br.g. Queen's Hussar 124–Outward Bound 79 (Sing Sing 134) **83** [1974 7g 7s 6s⁵ 1975 5.8g⁴ 7f 6fg⁴ 6f* 5.8h* 6fg⁴ 5fg⁵ 5.8f* 7f 6g⁶ 6g 1976 7fg 5.8f⁵ 7fg 6g² 6g* 6g⁵ 5.8f² 6f⁴ 7g⁶ 6fg⁵ 7f⁵ 7fg⁴ 5.8f⁵ 5v] strong, shapely gelding: fair handicapper: narrow winner at Salisbury in May: stays 7f but best form at 6f: acts on any going but goes particularly well on firm: has been tried in blinkers but does better without: consistent. *G. Peter-Hoblyn.*

BOUNTIFUL 2 b.f. Richboy 117–Zidda (Zarathustra 131) [1976 5g⁵ 5d⁶] **57** half-sister to a winner abroad by Tin Whistle and to a winning stayer by Never Say Die: 320 gns yearling: dam won over 6f at 2 yrs in Ireland: only poor form in small races at Hamilton in May. *N. Robinson.*

BOURTON LAD 2 b.c. Jimmy Reppin 131–Susan 88 (Hard Tack 111 §) [1976 — 7g 8g] small, sturdy, short-legged colt: half-brother to two winners, including fair sprinter Sally Jane (by Royal Palm): dam 5f sprinter: behind in minor event at Kempton in August (very backward) and maiden race at Goodwood the following month. *M. Haynes.*

BOVICK 4 ch.f. Compensation 127–Singleton 61 (Tudor Melody 129) [1974 5g⁵ — 5f⁶ 6g⁶ 6g⁶ 1975 5s⁴ 5f² 5fg³ 6g³ 6f* 7f 8f* 10f* 8g⁵ 10fg 1976 10g 10h⁵ 9g] quite useful plater at her best: showed form in a non-seller in 1976 but didn't race after May: best form at up to 1m, but stays 1½m: seems to act on any going: sold 500 gns Doncaster Autumn Sales. *T. Craig.*

BOWERBIRD 2 ch.f. Herbager 136–Bayonne (Bold Ruler) [1976 6fg 6f 7.2f*] **88** American-bred filly: second foal: half-sister to a winner in U.S.A. by Hoist the Flag: dam, who won three races at up to 7f as a 3-y-o in U.S.A., is daughter of 1957 champion American 3-y-o filly Bayou: showed first sign of ability when winning 13-runner minor event at Haydock in August, making all and keeping on most gamely to hold off Roxwell by a neck: should stay 1½m: ridden by 7-lb claimer on first two outings. *H. Wragg.*

BOWER CLUB 6 b.m. Ron 103–Wotwunit (Torbido) [1974 5fg 5f 6g 6f 5g **47** 5g⁵ 5s 5s² 5g 1975 5fg 6g 5g 5f² 5g² 5g² 5f4 5f* 6g⁶ 5f 5g 1976 5f 5fg⁵ 5g² 6d 5g* 6g³ 5f⁵ 5h 5f⁶ 5f 5s³] poor sprint handicapper: won seller at Edinburgh in June: best form at 5f: acts on any going: usually wears blinkers: good mount for an apprentice. *A. Balding.*

BOWLING ALLEY 3 ch.c. St Alphage 119–La Ponderosa (Kelly 122) [1975 **94** 5g⁵ 5fg⁴ 5d² 5g² 5g 1976 5g 5.9fg* 5g₄ 6d⁶ 5d⁴ 5fg³ 7g 6d³ 6g⁵ 6d* 7s] rangy, long-striding colt: quite a useful handicapper: winner at Wolverhampton in April (maiden race) and Newmarket in October: came with a very strong run from 2f out to lead near finish when beating Oudalia ¾ length on latter course: probably finds 5f on sharp side and may stay 7f: acts on a firm and a soft surface: sometimes wears blinkers (did so at Newmarket): very slowly into stride and never going at all on seventh outing and was eventually pulled up. *G. Smyth.*

BOWSHOT 2 ch.c. Salvo 129–Look Here 92 (Ratification 129) [1976 7fg 8d 8s²] **93** tall, quite well-made colt: third foal: half-brother to 1¼m winner What (by I Say): 2,900 gns yearling: dam won over 6f: proved no match for easy winner Lady Rhapsody in 20-runner maiden race at Sandown in October but finished well clear of third horse: will be suited by middle distances: acts well on soft going. *R. Smyth.*

BOWSQUARE LADY 2 b.f. Swing Easy 126–Mercury 74 (Pardal 130) [1976 **89** 5d* 6d 5fg* 5s² 5fg³ 5f⁵ 5fg 5f 5.9fg] half-sister to a minor winner by Sing Sing: 260 gns foal, resold 100 gns yearling: dam won seven times in Belgium: won maiden auction event at Pontefract in May and was bought in for 4,000 gns after winning seller at York the following month in very good style by 5 lengths from Gold Pot: twice ruined her chance in nurseries afterwards by starting slowly: form only at 5f: acts on any going with possible exception of very firm: blinkered penultimate outing and is not one to trust implicitly. *K. Payne.*

BOW-WOW 2 br.f. Buff's Own 113–Parley 79 (Armistice 131) [1976 5f 6f* 7f² **103** 8g 7fg* 8g 8v² 8s 8s* 8s³] leggy filly: second foal: half-sister to a minor 2-y-o winner by Frankincense: dam a stayer: bought out of B. Hobbs's stable for 1,800 gns after winning 17-runner seller at Ripon in June and proved a very good buy, winning nurseries at Yarmouth, Beverley and Doncaster: stayed on

123

strongly to lead close home when beating Revlow a neck on last-named course in October: will stay well: acts on any going: occasionally starts slowly: tough, genuine and consistent. *R. Hollinshead.*

BOY DAVID   2 br.c. Welsh Saint 126–Hot Baby (Tropique 128)   [1976 5d]   —
tall, good-bodied colt: half-brother to three winners here and abroad, including fairly useful Sure Loser (by Falcon), a winner at up to 1¼m: 3,700 gns yearling: dam of little account: very backward indeed when tailed-off last of 25 to Union Card in maiden race at Newbury in September. *G. Hunter.*

BOY MARVEL   3 b.g. Richboy 117–Miss Marvel 59 (Palestine 133)   [1975 5v   **69**
5g⁵ 6f² 7f   1976 7g 7f 7g 8f 7f 6f⁴ 6h 7g⁴ 5s 6s]   plain gelding: quite a moderate handicapper at his best: probably finds 5f too sharp for him but is not certain to stay 1m: blinkered fifth outing. *L. Shedden.*

BRA   2 b.f. Busted 134–Lagoon Girl (First Landing)   [1976 7d]   half-sister to a   — p
winner by Kentucky Pride in U.S.A.: dam stakes-placed half-sister to very smart American horse Atoll: unquoted when tenth of 25 in Houghton Stakes won by stable-companion Bessie Wallis at Newmarket in October: will do better over longer distances at 3 yrs. *J. Hindley.*

BRACKLESHAM BAY   6 ch.g. Palestine 133–Elba (Cagire II 122)   [1974 7h⁶
7.6g 8g 7s² 7.3d⁶ 7g⁵ 7d⁵ 7.6v⁴   1975 7.6g⁵ 7f⁴ 7f⁵   1976 12s]   strong, quite attractive gelding: fair handicapper (rated 85) in 1974: raced in Jersey most of his 6-y-o days: 33/1 when well beaten in handicap at Folkestone in October won by Raratonga, only outing in this country in 1976: best form at up to 7f: acts on any going. *G. Vibert, Jersey.*

BRACLE   2 b.g. Manacle 123–Bronze Seal 79 (Privy Councillor 125)   [1976 5d   —
6v 6v]   light-framed gelding: fourth produce: dam quite a moderate staying 2-y-o: behind in maiden races in the autumn. *G. Balding.*

BRAEMAR   6 b.g. Royal Avenue 123–Sara Tal (Cagire II 122)   [1974 12.3f   —
13g² 12fg³ 16g³ 18g³ 20g* 22.2g⁵ 18g³ 17v* 17.4s³ 16v⁴   1975 15s   1976 12.5s] workmanlike gelding: quite a moderate handicapper in 1974: lightly raced and no worthwhile form since: one paced and needs a really stiff test of stamina: acts on heavy going: sometimes wears blinkers but does as well without. *S. Hall.*

BRAG   3 ch.g. Falcon 131–Lost Angel 99 (Parthia 132)   [1975 5f 6f 5f 5f⁴ 6f⁴ 6f⁴   **67**
1976 6f⁶ 7g 9.4h² 10f* 12fg⁶ 12f]   lengthy gelding: won poor maiden race at Redcar in July by a head from fast-finishing Allrey: stays 1½m (has twice run badly over 1¾m): blinkered fourth appearance at 2 yrs: has given us impression that he isn't completely genuine. *W. A. Stephenson.*

BRAHMS   2 b.c. Round Table–Moccasin (Nantallah)   [1976 7f* 6.3f*]   **114** p
Here, in Brahms, we have a brother to Apalachee, the outstanding two-year-old of 1973 who ranked 5 lb clear in both the English and Irish Free Handicaps of that year.   It's unfortunate for the younger brother that comparison with his illustrious predecessor is inevitable, especially since, with human nature being what it is, there is a tendency to glorify the past and belittle the present in racing.   We are sure, however, that we are being fair when we say that Brahms's form at two years, good though it is, comes nowhere near that of Apalachee.   Perhaps he will redress the balance at three years, at which age Apalachee was something of a disappointment, running only twice and being beaten by Nonoalco and Giacometti when the shortest-priced favourite for the Two Thousand Guineas for forty years.

Brahms ran only twice in his first season, taking on quite useful animals in a minor event at Leopardstown early in August and then facing a much stiffer task in the Railway Stakes at the Curragh.   His more impressive performance came in the minor race.   Three previous winners, Delicia, Yemshik and Oakland, were among the six runners but all were penalised 5 lb for their successes and Brahms beat them in really good style.   After being last to leave the stalls he was given time to find his stride and then came through in excellent fashion in the straight to win by two and a half lengths from Delicia.   There was little doubt after this race that Brahms was a colt of great potential but even so it came as a surprise to see Robert Sangster quoted in *The Irish Field* as saying that Brahms had been re-syndicated for 1,400,000 dollars, an increase of 900,000 dollars on the horse's purchase price as a yearling.   The members of the new syndicate seemed to be taking a big risk considering that the race Brahms won was worth only £1,206 to the winner, that he beat nothing out of the ordinary and that he was receiving weight.

After Brahms's run in the Railway Stakes twelve days later some, at least, in the syndicate must have doubted whether he was worth it.   All five runners were

Railway Stakes, the Curragh—Brahms (left) is flat out to short-head the subsequently-disqualified Roman Charger, with Pampapaul close up in third place

winners but such was Brahms's reputation that he started at 7/2 on. His jockey on this occasion was Piggott, over in Ireland for three mounts for the O'Brien stable. All three won and it was on Brahms that Piggott had to work his hardest; again the horse was one of the slowest to leave the stalls but he improved after halfway and ran on after being given a couple of cracks to catch Roman Charger in the last stride. A length back in third place came Pampapaul who looked the unlucky horse of the race, having been badly hampered in the final furlong when Roman Charger veered across him. The stewards moved Roman Charger down to third place in favour of Pampapaul. One correspondent went so far as to describe Brahms's running as extremely disappointing but this seems harsh. The extended six-furlong trip of the Railway Stakes, a trip shorter than that of Brahms's first outing, seemed too sharp for him; and the very firm ground might not have suited him judging by the way he was hanging in the closing stages. Against Brahms though are the facts that Roman Charger was giving him 2 lb and is not in the top flight on his other form, and that Pampapaul strengthened his claim to be considered unlucky by easily turning the tables on Roman Charger in the National Stakes. This race was to have been Brahms's next but he was reported to have had a slight temperature the previous weekend and was not risked. He was also entered in the Middle Park, the Dewhurst and the William Hill Futurity but was scratched well in advance of the running dates.

		Princequillo (b 1940)	Prince Rose Cosquilla
	Round Table (b 1954)	Knight's Daughter (b 1940)	Sir Cosmo Feola
Brahms (b.c. 1974)		Nantallah (b 1953)	Nasrullah Shimmer
	Moccasin (ch 1963)	Rough Shod (b 1944)	Gold Bridge Dalmary

Brahms bears a distinct resemblance to Apalachee, and he fetched the second-highest price for a yearling at auction in the United States in 1975. His breeding is top class. Round Table, his sire, still holds second place in the list of leading money winners although he raced in the late 'fifties, and he has also been a big money-spinner at stud, producing the winners of over 11,000,000 dollars in the USA alone. Moccasin, the dam, was the best two-year-old filly of her year in the United States, winning all eight of her starts from five and a half furlongs to eight and a half. As well as Apalachee and Brahms she has produced Indian, another son of Round Table, who won a minor stakes race over a mile at six years but who had to be destroyed shortly before going to stud, and the smart but lightly-raced Irish three-year-old Nantequos (by Tom Rolfe), who has won twice over nine furlongs.

We stated confidently in *Racehorses of 1973* that Apalachee would stay a mile and a half. He never got the chance to show whether he did or not but we can see no reason to change our opinion; Brahms we also expect to stay that distance. As we have already said, we can't rate him highly on his two-year-old form but even if he falls short of classic standard he should make a decent three-year-old. *V. O'Brien, Ireland.*

BRANCASTER 2 b.c. Huntercombe 133–Cigarette Case 89 (Faberge II 121) — [1976 6fg 6fg] well-made colt: first foal: dam won from 1m to 11f: behind in maiden race at Salisbury in June and Convivial Stakes at York (still in need of outing) in August: should stay 1m. *J. Bethell.*

BRANDED 5 b.g. Meldrum 112–Well Matched 79 (Niccolo Dell'Arca) [1974 8fg⁴ 7f³ 7fg³ 8f* 9.4fg* 8g³ 10d⁵ 8.2g² 8g* 8g⁵ 1975 10.2g² 8.2s² 8g* 8f* 8h* 8g* 8h² 10g 7.6g⁴ 8g⁴ 8g 1976 8fg²] strong, close-coupled gelding: fair handicapper: ran creditably when second of 10 to Chuconte in amateur riders race at Salisbury in June, only outing on flat in 1976: effective at 1m to 1¼m: best suited for top-of-the-ground conditions, and acts on hard going: suitable mount for an apprentice: genuine and consistent. *S. Mellor.* **75**

BRANDEN 4 gr.g. Sea Hawk II 131–Emerald Isle 97 (Kelly 122) [1974 8d 8s⁶ 1975 14f⁶ 16g* 14fg² 1976 12f 12.3f⁶ 16g 13.8g] well-grown, rangy gelding: quite a moderate handicapper (rated 82) at 3 yrs: no worthwhile form in 1976: needs a stiff test of stamina: blinkered third outing and wore bandages on first two. *T. Fairhurst.*

BRANDON HILL 3 b.c. Wolver Hollow 126–Debatable 84 (Counsel 118) [1975 5s 6f 7.5f⁴ 7.5f² 6f 7g* 6g² 8g² 7g⁴ 7.5g* 1976 7s 9v⁶ 10f* 8g 10g⁵ 12g* 12f⁶ 9f 12g² 12f³ 10f³ 8fg 12fg² 10d² 12s²(dis) 12s] first produce: 3,000 gns foal: dam stayed 1¾m: won handicaps at Phoenix Park and the Curragh, prior to finishing excellent sixth, beaten just under 7 lengths, to Malacate in Irish Sweeps Derby: continued to run well afterwards, especially when runner-up in three races at the Curragh, minor event in July (beaten a length by Lane Court), Autumn Free Handicap (top weight when beaten 1½ lengths by Finsbury) and Trigo Stakes (disqualified after running Countess Eileen to a neck), both in October: stays 1½m: acts on any going: wore blinkers at 2 yrs. *P. Mullins, Ireland.* **118**

BRANDONS BELL 2 b.f. Foggy Bell 108–Green Edge 76 (Border Legend 119) — [1976 6g 9fg 6v] leggy, unfurnished filly: poor mover: bad plater. *P. Bevan.*

BRANDS HATCH 3 b.c. Track Spare 125–November (Firestreak 125) [1975 6f⁴ 7g* 7s 1976 7fg⁵ 9g² 9fg* 8fg³ 10f⁴ 10.2f⁴ 10fg³ 10fg⁴ 8g] useful sort: useful handicapper: comfortable winner at Ripon in May by 3 lengths from Take Aim: continued to run well afterwards and finished close-up third to Il Padrone in Extel Handicap at Goodwood in July: stays 1¼m: acts on any going: got rather hot in paddock and then dwelt in stalls at Goodwood: ran badly final outing. *L. Cumani.* **102**

BRANDYLAND 3 b.c. Farm Walk 111–Corvoisier Queen (Coronation Year 124) [1975 7g 1976 10.1fg 12g⁵ 12fg⁵ 12f³ 12f³ 12f³] well-made colt: stays 1½m. *Mrs D. Oughton.* **56**

BRAVADE 3 b.f. Blast 125–Rhodia (Parthia 132) [1975 6g 7f² 7fg⁶ 6g 6g⁴ 1976 8fg* 8g 10fg² 8f³ 8s] good walker: bought in 2,400 gns after winning seller at Newmarket in May by 3 lengths from Legal Advice: evidently stays 1¼m: occasionally wears blinkers but does just as well without: trained until after third outing by J. Hindley: covered by Goldhill to Southern Hemisphere time. *F. Carr.* **69**

BRAVE ELBOW 3 ch.c. Salvo 129–Brilly 94 (Acropolis 132) [1975 N.R. 1976 10g 8s⁵ 12s² 12v⁴] second foal: half-brother to fair 5f winner Midgetina (by Silly Season): dam won over 6f: 10 lengths second of 19 to Tudor Wynk in maiden race at Chepstow in October: stays 1½m. *R. Vibert.* **66**

BRAVE HUNTER 2 b.c. Caliban 123–Molvitesse 75 (Molvedo 137) [1976 5fg 5f⁴ 6f⁴ 7fg 6g⁴ 6f* 5.9fg] well-grown colt: brother to 3-y-o Calaburn, a winner at up to 1¼m: 1,400 gns yearling: dam won over 1m: made all when winning seller at Nottingham in August (no bid): will stay 1¼m. *W. Marshall.* **76**

BRAVE LASS 2 ch.f. Ridan–Bravour II (Birkhahn) [1976 5fg* 5d⁴ 6g* 6g* 5g*] **114**
The Ballygoran Stud and Mr W. J. McEnery made a shrewd move in 1973 when importing the stallion Ridan to stand in Ireland. He had been a top-class racehorse at two, three and four years in the United States, showing good form at all distances from three furlongs (in thirty-three seconds) to a mile and a quarter, and ending his career with a tally of thirteen wins, six seconds and two thirds from twenty-three starts. By the end of 1972 he had sired the

Bradgate Park Nursery Handicap, Doncaster—a stylish win by Brave Lass

winners of over 2,700,000 dollars and since he left the United States his appeal to breeders over here was greatly increased by the exploits of his near relatives; his sisters Moccasin and Thong have between them produced Apalachee, Nantequos, Brahms, Thatch, Lisadell, King Pellinore and Marinsky while others from the family include Cellini and Take Your Place. Ridan did well too, siring the 1974 French St Leger winner Busiris and Stamen, a smart performer at a mile and a half and a mile and three quarters in 1975, from very few runners over here. The 1976 season saw his first Irish crop reach the racecourse and it included the very speedy Brave Lass, but unfortunately Ridan died before the 1977 covering season.

Brave Lass looked promising when getting home by a neck from Mofida in a maiden race at Newmarket early in the season but then she put up a moderate display in the Wilkinson Memorial Stakes at York in May, finishing only fourth to the 20/1-shot Laser Lady and all of five lengths behind Mofida. Perhaps she didn't act on the softish ground but the chances are that all was not well with her as it was nearly sixteen weeks before she again saw a racecourse. The rest, whether enforced or otherwise, proved a blessing; by the time she reappeared the nursery season had started and the handicapper, with the evidence of only two runs to go on, gave her the mark of a moderate animal. Moderate she most certainly isn't, and her trainer took full advantage of her lenient treatment, running her three times in nurseries in the space of twenty-four days and giving the handicapper little chance to catch up.

All three races resulted in comfortable wins. At Kempton she quickened very smoothly to lead inside the last two furlongs and came home two lengths clear of Haighall with seven others well beaten off; at Doncaster a 5 lb penalty proved totally inadequate, and her nearest pursuer, Bodensee, was five lengths behind at the line; and at Ascot, where she started at 2/1 on with a 7 lb penalty, she was most impressive, cruising into the lead running into the final furlong and being still on the bridle at the finish. The one-and-a-half-length margin over Rushley Bay at Ascot gives little indication of her superiority; she had quite a lot in hand, and she has been rated accordingly. On that rating she would have had a chance in the bigger races in the autumn, but she wasn't entered for any of them.

		Nantallah	Nasrullah
	Ridan	(b 1953)	Shimmer
	(b 1959)	Rough Shod	Gold Bridge
Brave Lass		(b 1944)	Dalmary
(ch.f. 1974)		Birkhahn	Alchimist
	Bravour II	(br 1945)	Bramouse
	(b 1963)	Barcarole	Organdy
		(b 1951)	Bereitschaft

Brave Lass's dam, Bravour II, has had a varied life. At two years she raced

127

in her native Germany, winning all three of her races and being rated the best of the fillies. At three years she started very well, winning the Schwarzgold-Rennen, the German equivalent of the One Thousand Guineas, but in both her subsequent races she gave the impression that a mile and a quarter was beyond her best although she finished third in the Preis der Diana (German Oaks). She then changed hands and at four years she ran twice in France, finishing third in a small race over eleven furlongs and then fifth in an apprentice race. At stud in France she produced three moderate animals by Bon Mot III and to Stupendous she foaled a filly called Voura whose only win on the flat came in a mile-and-a-quarter seller at the provincial track Mauron. Brave Lass is Bravour's first foal for her latest owner, Mr Joel. The grandam, Barcarole, also produced another very successful filly called Brisanz who won both the Schwarzgold-Rennen and the Preis der Diana.

On breeding there is no reason why Brave Lass should not stay at least a mile. In appearance she is a leggy filly and looks at her best on the move—she has a particularly good action and really stretches out. As to her prospects as a three-year-old, she is still some way below the best and it would be extremely optimistic to expect any mercy from the handicapper. She has a good turn of foot though and she'll win a race or two. *T. Waugh.*

BRAVE MARY 3 b.f. Derring-Do 131–Ulmaria (Immortality) [1975 6g 7g* **82** 1976 7f 8d* 10f4] neat filly: finished strongly when winning handicap at York in May by 1½ lengths from Swakara: came off a true line in closing stages and would have won by a considerably greater margin had she kept straight: should stay further than 1m: best form on an easy surface: sold 4,000 gns Newmarket December Sales. *B. Hills.*

BRAVE PRINCE 2 ch.c. Yellow God 129–Queen Caroline 86 (Ragusa 137) **84** [1976 5fg6 5f5 5f 5d3 5s* 5d] second foal: 1,000 gns yearling: dam placed over 6f at 2 yrs: favourite, won 18-runner maiden race at Warwick in October by 2 lengths from Stay With Me: should stay at least 1m: evidently needs some give in the ground. *B. Lunness.*

BRAVE TALK 7 b.g. Derring-Do 131–Chatting 109 (Arctic Star) [1974 12g **53** 11.7fg 11.7fg 11.7g3 11.7g* 10fg6 10s6 1975 9v 10v 11.7f 12fg* 12g3 10fg3 11.7f3 12fg2 11.7fg3 1976 13f 12f 11.7fg 12g 14fg 12fg4 17.1h4] shapely, attractive gelding: poor handicapper nowadays: suited by middle distances: acts on firm going and is probably unsuited by heavy. *P. Haslam.*

BRAWBY LAD 5 b.g. Shooting Chant–Ginger Puss (Worden II 129) [1974 **64** 7fg 7.6g 6h5 6f 10f6 10.1fg4 10g 6g2 6s4 6s 6v2 1975 6v2 6s 7s 6f 6f 7f 8f3 8g4 7g5 5f3 8g3 6d 8f 1976 7g3 6fg2 6g* 5fg 6g 7fg] compact gelding: won apprentice handicap at Leicester in April by 1½ lengths from White Wonder: effective at 6f to 1m: acts on any going: has been tried in blinkers: suitable mount for an apprentice. *D. Weeden.*

BREAST STROKE 2 b.f. Divine Gift 127–Paddling 66 (St Paddy 133) [1976 **90** 5fg* 5f2 6fg2 6f2 6g* 5fg4 6g2] rather unfurnished filly: first foal: 800 gns yearling: dam placed over 1¼m: won maiden auction event at Pontefract in May and ran out an easy 7-length winner of nursery at Windsor in August: also has some other excellent efforts to her name, on final outing finishing neck second to Red Johnnie in £2,000 nursery at Leicester: will stay 1m: acts on firm going. *J. Hindley.*

BREATH EASY 2 br.c. Swing Easy 126–Breathalyser (Alcide 136) [1976 **83** 5f 5s 6g3 7h 7f 8.2d 6v5 6s 7v] well-grown colt: third living foal: half-brother to very useful middle-distance stayer Major Green (by Double-U-Jay): 240 gns yearling: dam daughter of very useful sister to 1,000 Guineas winner Abermaid: ran easily best race when about ½-length fifth of 10 to Bobby Kempinski in nursery at York in October: form only at 6f and ran badly when tried at 1m: goes well on heavy ground: ran poorly when blinkered on final outing. *N. Adam.*

BREATHING EXERCISE 3 ch.g. Pall Mall 132–Karen Chase 82 (Will Somers **96** 114 §) [1975 5g3 6fg3 8d 7g3 7f2 1976 6.5g* 6.5g5 8.5g5 7g3 6fg 6g* 7f* 7g5 7.6fg5 6d* 6v4] well-made gelding: particularly good mover: won minor event at Cagnes-sur-Mer in February: most disappointing in early-season handicaps at Doncaster and Newmarket and was subsequently off course three months during which time he was gelded: in fine form on his return and won handicaps at Nottingham, Redcar and Haydock: beat Cudgel ½ length on last-named course in October despite showing a tendency to hang: best form at 6f and 7f: appears to act on any going: blinkered third and fourth outings: has occasionally sweated up. *R. Armstrong.*

BREEZE WAGON 3 b.g. Firestreak 125–Immortelle (Never Say Die 137)   **74**
[1975 5s 5d 6f⁶ 6g⁶ 6fg⁵ 7g⁶ 1976 10fg⁵ 11f² 10g* 12g² 12f² 10fg* 11g³ 9f³ 10g³]
strong, attractive gelding: quite a moderate handicapper: won at Kempton
(in good style by 6 lengths) and Newcastle (very confidently ridden when beating
Regal Tudor comfortably by 2 lengths): creditable third to Tiger Trail at Kempton in August on final outing, making up a tremendous amount of ground after
being tailed off at half-way: probably finds 1¼m on sharp side nowadays and will
be suited by a return to racing over 1½m: acts on firm ground. *G. Peter-Hoblyn.*

BREEZY GIRL 3 b.f. Whistling Wind 123–Ribocana (Molvedo 137) [1975   **50**
5f 7f 6f 7f 6f⁴ 8g⁵ 8g³ 7g 1976 9g 13.8d⁶ 12.2g 9fg⁴ 10g³ 10h⁵ 15.8f⁵] sturdy
filly: poor mover: plater: stays 1¼m: blinkered third outing: sold 520 gns Doncaster September Sales. *Miss S. Hall.*

BREFFNI PRINCE 2 b.g. Prince Regent 129–Golden Harp 69 (Aureole 132)   **56**
[1976 5g 6fg 6fg⁶ 7g 6g 8fg] small, dipped-backed gelding: showed a little
ability in maiden race on first outing but was well beaten in sellers afterwards.
E. Reavey.

BREMO 3 gr.g. Quadrangle–Rose River (Sailor) [1975 N.R. 1976 9fg² 11.7f²   **83**
11.7f* 14g 13.1h³ 12.2f² 12f⁴ 14fg 12.2s³ 12v⁶ 12s⁵] lengthy, attractive American-
bred gelding: second produce: dam unraced half-sister to smart animals Goose
Creek and Berkeley Springs: won maiden race at Bath in May: ran creditably
from time to time afterwards: stays 1½m (ran poorly over 1¾m): acts on any
going but action suggests he will always be best with some give in the ground:
blinkered seventh outing: suitable mount for an apprentice. *I. Balding.*

BREWMASTER 3 br.c. John Splendid 116–Ronelda (Tyrone 130) [1975   **—**
5g 5f 5f 5d 6g 8g 1976 6f 6g 8d 6v] short-backed colt: moderate plater at 2 yrs:
no worthwhile form in 1976 but had some stiff tasks: stays 6f: blinkered final
outing. *J. Mulhall.*

BRIANA 2 b.f. The Brianstan 128–Siciliana 77 (Sicilian Prince 126) [1976   **64**
5d 5g⁶ 5g⁴ 5f² 5f³ 5f⁶] workmanlike filly: half-sister to winning 1975 2-y-o
plater Hilliana (by Goldhill): cost 900 gns at Doncaster January 1976 Sales:
dam a stayer: placed in maiden races won by Hand Canter and Royal Princess
at Catterick in July: not raced after August: should stay 1m. *E. Collingwood.*

BRIANSUE 2 br.f. The Brianstan 128–Preston Sue 73 (Sicilian Prince 126)   **—**
[1976 5f⁶ 5s] neat filly: second foal: dam stayed well: well beaten in small
races in the north: will probably be suited by middle distances. *Denys Smith.*

BRIARDOWN 3 b.g. Doon 124–Early Rose 61 (Will Somers 114 §) [1975   **54**
N.R. 1976 8g 8s³] second foal: half-brother to useful sprinter Briarvanter
(by Galivanter): dam of little account: 5½ lengths third of 18 to Penchand in
maiden race at Warwick in October: stays 1m. *M Masson.*

BRIAREUS 2 b.g. The Brianstan 128–Villa Vera (Gilles de Retz 132) [1976   **77**
5f 6d 6g⁴ 7f² 8g⁶ 7g⁵] compact gelding: good mover: first reported living foal:
sold twice as a yearling, for 600 gns and 1,500 gns: dam won three times over
1½m in Ireland: quite a moderate maiden: suited by 7f and should stay further.
J. Fitzgerald.

BRIAR PATCH 4 ch.c. Porto Bello 118–Delsa 69 § (Delirium 126) [1974   **95**
5.3d³ 5d⁵ 5g* 6s* 5s* 1975 6g 6f³ 6fg 1976 6fg³ 6g³ 6g³ 6s 5.3f² 5g 5g*] strong,
attractive colt: fairly useful handicapper: ran on very well under strong pressure
to pip Relative Ease on post when winning at Kempton in August: ran creditably
on most of his earlier outings, starting heavily-backed favourite on second, third
and fourth starts: stays 6f: acts on any going: sweated up fourth appearance.
R. Price.

BRIARVANTER 5 b.h. Galivanter 131–Early Rose 61 (Will Somers 114 §)   **92**
[1974 6f* 6g 6fg² 6g⁴ 6d 6v² 1975 6f 6g* 6fg 7fg 7f⁵ 6d³ 7f* 6g 6d 6s⁴ 1976 6fg
6f⁶ 6g* 6f* 7fg³ 7fg⁴ 6f* 6fg³ 6fg² 6f* 5g⁴ 6d*] strong, deep-girthed horse:
had a cracking season, winning handicaps at Goodwood, Folkestone, Salisbury,
Haydock and Redcar: gamely resisted Sonnenblick's strong last-furlong challenge when winning at Redcar in September on final appearance: stays 7f: acts
on any going: good mount for an apprentice and has won four times for claimer
H. Ballantine: genuine and consistent. *M. Masson.*

BRICLIC 2 b.c. Frigid Aire–Gala Premiere § (By Thunder! 122) [1976 5g⁵ 7fg*]   **71**
well-grown colt: half-brother to fair sprinter Helenita (by Right Boy) and to
two winners abroad: 1,200 gns yearling: won 11-runner seller at Thirsk in July
by 2 lengths from Nimbullion, never looking in danger of defeat despite starting
slowly: bought in 625 gns afterwards: will stay 1¼m. *W. A. Stephenson.*

BRICOL BOY 2 b.g. Communication 119–Princess Karen 70 (Bounteous 125)   —
[1976 5g 5v]   poor form in sellers. *C. Crossley.*

BRIDGE FOUR 2 br.f. Roi Soleil 125–Toblerone (Honeyway 125) [1976 7d]   — p
big, well-made filly: half-sister to two winners, including very smart Irish
sprinter Cinerama Two (by Sound Track): 5,000 gns yearling: dam never ran:
showed up for 5f from a poor draw when behind in 30-runner maiden race won
by Guama at Newbury in September: sure to do better. *J. Hindley.*

BRIDGEWATER 2 b.c. Yukon Eric–Lingala (Pinturischio 117) [1976 5f 5g⁵   **64**
5f⁴ 5f 6f³ 5f 6f 6fg² 5f]   plater: ran easily best race when ¾-length second to
Peak Princess at Ayr in July: stays 6f: blinkered fifth and final outings: changed
hands 800 gns Doncaster August Sales. *K. Payne.*

BRIDLE LANE 3 b.f. Track Spare 125–Leca 77 (Soderini 123) [1975 5g 1976   —
8v 10v] lightly raced and no worthwhile form although still did not look
ready on final outing. *J. Hill.*

BRIDSTOW 3 br.g. Breeders Dream 116–Nancy 106 (Tamerlane 128) [1975   **65**
6fg 6f*(dis) 7v⁴ 8g 7d 7g 1976 8f 8g³ 7h² 8h³ 8g²] workmanlike gelding: good
walker: placed in modest company: stays 1m: blinkered final outing in 1975.
G. Balding.

BRIGHT ANNE 3 b.f. The Brianstan 128–Bright Vienna (Vienna 127) [1975   —
N.R. 1976 5f 8f 7fg] neat filly: of no account. *H. Wharton.*

BRIGHT BID 3 br.f. The Brianstan 128–Winning Bid 93 (Great Captain) [1975   **60**
5d⁵ 6g 6g 1976 8g⁶ 10s 12fg³ 14fg⁵ 16fg³ 16h⁴ 16fg² 14.7f* 14g 16fg³ 16s]
tall filly: half-sister to Eclipse winner Coup de Feu (by White Fire III) and
St Leger victor Peleid (by Derring-Do) but is only moderate herself: showed a
good deal of courage when winning maiden race at Redcar in July all out by
a length from Rough River: stays well: blinkered second to fourth outings:
sold 6,400 gns Newmarket Autumn Sales, reportedly for export to Australia.
W. Elsey.

BRIGHT BIRD 5 ch.m. Laser Light 118–Cuckoo 86 (Cagire II 122) [1974 5s   **83** d
5g⁵ 6fg⁴ 5g² 5fg³ 5f 5d 7fg 1975 5g⁵ 5g 5f⁴ 5.1f⁶ 5f⁶ 5.3f⁵ 5f* 5f* 5f⁴ 5g⁵ 1976
5fg* 5g⁵ 5.1fg⁵ 5g 5f⁴] tall, useful sort of mare: poor mover in her slower paces:
quite a moderate handicapper: successful at Thirsk in May: best form at 5f:
acts well on firm going: sometimes wears blinkers, although didn't when successful: sometimes races with tongue tied down and did so at Thirsk. *W. O'Gorman.*

BRIGHT CAP 5 ch.g. Florescence 120–Capua 69 (Darius 129) [1974 5g 6f⁴   —
7.9g² 9f⁴ 8g 7s 1975 9v⁶ 10v 9s 8s 8f 8g⁶ 9f⁴ 7f 8.2fg⁶ 10h³ 1976 8g] poor
plater: stays 1¼m: probably requires a sound surface, and acts on hard going:
blinkered on only outing in 1976. *D. Chapman.*

BRIGHT COMET 4 b.c. Derring-Do 131–Santa Anita 78 (Pardao 120) [1974   —
7.9g 7s⁵ 7s 8g 1975 9v³ 8s² 10s⁴ 8f³ 8f⁶ 11.7f⁴ 12.2f⁵ 10g³ 10fg² 16f² 14g* 14.7f²
16g³ 16g 1976 16fg⁶ 18fg⁶] strong colt: no worthwhile form at 4 yrs, but used
to be a fair performer: stays well: probably acts on any going: blinkered last
outing at 2 yrs: trained by H. Nicholson on first outing. *A. Jarvis.*

BRIGHT DECISION 3 ch.f. Busted 134–Miss Klaire II 104 (Klairon 131)   **80**
[1975 N.R. 1976 7fg⁴ 10g 7g³ 8fg² 8f* 8f² 8fg³ 10f³ 10f² 12g⁶] fair sort: good
mover: sister to useful middle-distance handicapper Buss and half-sister to
several winners, including very useful miler Miracle (by High Hat): dam a
sprinter: favourite, hacked up by 7 lengths from Panda's Gambol in 11-runner
maiden race at Yarmouth in June: good ½-length second to Sanguine in handicap
on same course in August: best form at up to 1¼m: acts on firm going. *J. Winter.*

BRIGHTELMSTONE 2 br.f. Prince Regent 129–Sweet Reason (Elopement 125) **102**
[1976 5fg² 5fg* 5g* 6f² 5fg⁴ 7f] strong filly: good mover: half-sister to 3-y-o
7f winner Welsh Reason (by Welsh Saint) and useful sprinter Exemplary (by
Sovereign Lord): dam unraced half-sister to two very useful stayers: easy
winner of maiden race at Salisbury in May and of valuable Acorn Stakes at
Epsom the following month: took on five other winning fillies at Epsom and
beat them well, drawing away to win by 3 lengths from Blue Linnet: in frame
in two good races afterwards, looking likely winner of Chesham Stakes at Royal
Ascot until caught near finish by Limone, and not being disgraced when 1¾
lengths fourth to Be Easy in Molecomb Stakes at Goodwood: stays 6f but not
7f. *R. Smyth.*

130

BRIGHTEST AND BEST 3 b.f. Laser Light 118–Posh 80 (Migoli 132) [1975 **68**
5g 5g[5] 5fg 7f[6] 7f 6g 5d[6] 1976 6fg 7fg 6fg[4] 6g[2] 7.2g[5] 6g[2] 5h2] fair sort: runner-up
in sellers at Kempton and Leicester and an apprentice event at Bath in first
half of season: gives us impression 6f is her limit: ran creditably in blinkers on
last outing at 2 yrs. *C. V. Miller.*

BRIGHT FINISH 3 b.c Nijinsky 138–Lacquer 118 (Shantung 132) [1975 7fg **121**
1976 10.5fg* 12g* 12fg* 14v* 16s*]
This most attractive, beautifully-bred individual is probably a very good colt
capable of running well in the best company as a four-year-old. At this stage of
his career it is impossible to be any more definite about his merit and prospects.
He has spent the greater part of his time on the racecourse picking off minor
prizes—the Daniel Prenn Plate and the Middlethorpe Stakes at York, the St
James's Stakes at Kempton and the Running Gap Stakes at Newmarket—in
so doing twice brushing aside third-rate opposition and twice being stretched
by a better stamp of animal, by Swing Through over a mile and a quarter at
York and by Ivory Girl over a mile and a half at Newmarket. In gaining the
last of his five successive victories as a three-year-old, in the Jockey Club Cup
at Newmarket, Bright Finish undoubtedly produced the high-class performance
usually required to win that end-of-season pattern race for stayers, trotting up
by eight lengths from Shangamuzo, but it would almost certainly be misleading
to regard him full value for the eight lengths. Bright Finish had the benefit of
impeccable handling from his jockey, Piggott, that day. While the jockeys on
the other fancied runners dawdled, Piggott kept Bright Finish in close touch
with the front-running no-hoper Homefield, and sent him into a clear lead
seven furlongs from home. May Hill, a light of other days, was the only other
near enough to have the opportunity to challenge; she was a spent force with
two furlongs to go and it was left to Shangamuzo to run on from a poor position
to claim second place to a winner who quickened impressively over the last two
furlongs or so. Shantallah, who declined to exert himself, and Major Green,
who ran badly, completed what was, for a race worth more than £13,000, a weak
field.
Bright Finish strikes us as a better prospect for races over the Cup distances
than over distances as short as a mile and a half, particularly after seeing the way
he came home in the Jockey Club Cup. There is plenty of speed in his pedigree,
though. His dam, Lacquer, winner of the Cambridgeshire and Irish One
Thousand Guineas, was never raced over a distance longer than nine furlongs;
his grandam, Urshalim, was a very speedy daughter of five-furlong sprinter
Horama. The family has, in fact, produced a notably high number of fast
horses in the last thirty years, possibly the best of them Lacquer's half-sister

*Daniel Prenn Plate, York—a game win for Bright Finish on his first outing of the season.
Swing Through is second*

Sovereign (by Pardao). Lacquer had two foals before Bright Finish: they were
Paint Job (by Pretendre) and Brilliantine (by Stage Door Johnny), the former
a winning hurdler of no great shakes on the flat, the other, by John Cherry's
sire, a very useful winner at up to a mile and a quarter who stayed at least
thirteen furlongs.

Bright Finish (b.c. 1973)	Nijinsky (b 1967)	Northern Dancer (b 1961)	Nearctic
			Natalma
		Flaming Page (b 1959)	Bull Page
			Flaring Top
	Lacquer (b 1964)	Shantung (b 1956)	Sicambre
			Barley Corn
		Urshalim (b 1951)	Nasrullah
			Horama

Until August Bright Finish was trained by Jeremy Tree: he was sent to
Newmarket when the Beckhampton gallops became, in his trainer's opinion,
too hard for serious work. That Bright Finish was not risked on hard ground
at home does not necessarily mean that he will be unable to show his form on
hard going on the racecourse; we will just have to wait and see. The evidence
of the form book is that Bright Finish has won twice from two starts on a firmish
surface (he has never tackled anything firmer) but he has shown far and away
his best form on soft ground, when winning the Jockey Club Cup. Lacquer,
incidentally, acted on any going; the sire, Nijinsky, acted well on firm going
and never had the opportunity to race on soft. *M. Stoute.*

BRIGHT FIRE 8 b.g. Firestreak 125–Light Case 107 (Borealis) [1974 10fg⁶   **92**
10fg³ 10g 10fg 10fg⁵ 10d⁶ 10v² 8s⁴ 1975 10s 10f⁴ 10g² 10f 10fg⁶ 10g⁴ 10.8g*
10.6v⁵ 1976 10g⁴ 12fg⁴ 10g² 12fg² 12g⁵ 10d³ 10.8s² 11v*] quite a useful
handicapper and a very good mover: rather a moody and inconsistent old-timer,
not so good as in his youth: rallied close home when getting the better of Rolfe
at Newbury in October: ran creditably on most of his other outings, notably
on sixth appearance when 3 lengths third of nine to Chil the Kite in Peter
Hastings Stakes at Newbury in September (made a lot of running): stays 1½m:
acts on any going: sometimes loses ground at start: found little under pressure
on fourth outing. *H. Blagrave.*

BRIGHTLY 2 br.f. Aureole 132–Merry Sunshine (Santa Claus 133) [1976 6d 7s*]   **92 p**
quite an attractive filly: second foal: dam never ran: drew clear final furlong when
winning 20-runner maiden race at Newmarket in October by 3 lengths from
Olympic Visualise: a very useful staying filly in the making. *B. Hobbs.*

BRIGHT MASTER 3 b.g. Sahib 114–Bight of Peru 100 (Denturius) [1975   **66**
6h⁵ 6fg⁵ 6f⁶ 5.9g 1976 8fg⁵ 10g³ 10h⁶ 10.1f] lengthy gelding: good mover:
plater: good third to Onedin Line at Leicester in May: ran moderately in non-
sellers afterwards, including when tried in blinkers on final outing: stays 1¼m:
trained until after second outing by J. Nelson. *P. Haslam.*

BRIGHTON JET 3 ch.f. Jolly Jet 111–Brighton Girl 96 (Right Boy 137)   **69**
[1975 5d 6g 1976 7fg 8fg 7.6s 6g 6g* 7g 6fg⁴ 6f 5fg⁴ 5f 7f* 8d⁴ 8s] neat filly:
plater: winner at Leicester in June and Beverley in August, on neither occasion
attracting a bid: stays 1m: appears to act on any going. *R. Hollinshead.*

BRIGHT STREAK 2 ch.f. Firestreak 125–Gleaming Horn 97 (Hornbeam 130)   **68**
[1976 5fg 7f 6fg⁴ 6f⁶] sister to Firehorn, a winner at 1m and 1¼m in France and
also successful in Italy, and half-sister to a winner by Birdbrook: dam a miler:
showed some ability in varied company: will stay at least 1m. *D. Morley.*

BRIGHT SWAN 2 br.f. Will Hays (USA) or Meadow Mint 120–Frenship IV   **83**
(Worden II 129) [1976 6fg 7fg 8s 8s²] tall filly: half-sister to a 1¼m winning
plater by Road House II: 200 gns yearling: dam lightly raced: improved with
racing, finishing 2½ lengths second of 19 to Nordman in maiden race at Sandown
in October on final outing: will stay middle distances: acts on soft going: suited
by forcing tactics. *R. Hannon.*

BRIGHTY 3 b.f. Connaught 130–Aunt Florrie (Delirium 126) [1975 N.R.   **—**
1976 10.1fg] half-sister to several winners, including Irish Cambridgeshire
winner Mighty Quin (by Never Say Die): 5,400 gns yearling: dam won at 2 yrs
in Ireland: started slowly when in rear in 21-runner maiden race won by Saturnus
at Windsor in May: sold 300 gns Ascot December Sales. *M. Ryan.*

BRIG OF AYR 2 b.f. Brigadier Gerard 144–Gospel Truth 95 (Above Suspicion   **90 p**
127) [1976 6v²] neat filly: third foal: half-sister to fair 3-y-o middle-distance
winner Veracious (by Astec) and to True Word (by Blakeney), a winner from

9f to 2m: dam stayed well: 20/1, put up a fine first effort when $\frac{3}{4}$-length second to Amity in 23-runner maiden race at Newbury in October, being in front coming to final furlong and not being knocked about unnecessarily when headed by her more-experienced rival: will stay 1$\frac{1}{2}$m: sure to win races. *J. Dunlop.*

BRIL 4 ch.g. Double Jump 131–Narrow Escape 112 (Narrator 127) [1974 7fg 8d 1975 12g 1976 12fg 15.5s 12s⁴ 12s] well-made gelding: lightly raced but showed a little ability when 9 lengths fourth of 14 to Burleigh in apprentice event at Chepstow in October: sold 2,600 gns Newmarket Autumn Sales. *G. Harwood.* **57**

BRILLIANT GEM 3 b.f. Charlottown 127–Topaz 102 (Honeyway 125) [1975 7g⁵ 7g 8g⁴ 1976 8.5fg] lightly-made filly: showed moderate form at 2 yrs: broke blood vessel and was pulled up in Princess Elizabeth Stakes at Epsom in April on only outing in 1976: sold 4,000 gns Newmarket July Sales. *T. Waugh.* **—**

BRILLIANT REPARTEE 2 ch.c. Caerdeon 98–Mary Francis (Elopement 125) [1976 5fg 5g 6s 5f] good mover: little worthwhile form in varied company, including selling: sweating and blinkered final outing. *H. Cecil.* **43**

BRIQUESSARD 2 br.c. Forlorn River 124–Evergreen (Buisson Ardent 129) [1976 5s³ 5s⁴ 6d] brother to poor 3-y-o plater Reve and half-brother to four minor winners: dam unraced half-sister to London Gazette: showed ability in maiden races, putting up probably best effort when just over a length third to Duke's Girl at Folkestone in October on first outing: will stay 7f. *H. Collingridge.* **78**

BRISBANE QUEEN 2 ch.f. Double Jump 131–Bobelle 62 (Pirate King 129) [1976 5v² 5g⁵ 5g⁴ 7f³ 8f 5g] first foal: dam placed over 5f at 2 yrs: showed a little ability in small races in Scotland but was well beaten in a well-contested seller on final outing: stays 7f (ran moderately when tried at 1m): sold 320 gns Doncaster October Sales. *N. Angus.* **63**

BROCADED 2 ch.f. Meldrum 112–Brocatelle 71 (Brocade Slipper 116) [1976 5s 5g] third foal: half-sister to a winning plater by Sailing Light: dam quite a moderate handicapper at around 1m: behind in Scottish maiden and minor events in October. *R. Stubbs.* **—**

BROKE 4 b.c. Busted 134–Mahwa 82 (Match III 135) [1974 6g⁶ 7fg 7g 8s 1975 10f 10.1f 8g 12g² 12g 12g⁶ 1976 14g 14fg 10f² 12f⁴ 10f* 10.1f⁵ 12g] useful-looking colt: quite a moderate handicapper: outsider of four, beat Outrage a neck at Folkestone in August: well beaten afterwards: should stay further than 1$\frac{1}{2}$m: acts on firm going: trained by Mrs F. Nagle until after fourth outing. *D. Underwood.* **66**

BROKE EVEN 3 b.c. Busted 134–Equal Chance 95 (Hitting Away) [1975 N.R. 1976 8fg 10g 11.1g 13.3fg 13.1f 12v] strong colt: third foal: half-brother to a minor winner: dam a sprinter: no worthwhile form in maiden races: blinkered fourth and final outings. *G. Hunter.* **—**

BROKEN CAST 5 ch.g. Busted 134–Die Cast 69 (Never Say Die 137) [1974 12f³ 12g 1975 15f⁶ 14.7f⁶ 12f² 16f* 12s⁴ 14f⁵ 1976 15f² 16f⁶ 16s 16f* 16h⁵ 16.9f⁴ 18fg⁶ 16fg* 14d] rangy gelding: quite a moderate handicapper: goes well at Beverley and won twice on that course in 1976, beating Pontresina 2$\frac{1}{4}$ lengths in September on second occasion: well beaten in between: needs further than 1$\frac{1}{2}$m and stays well: acts on any going: sometimes wears blinkers but does at least as well without them. *R. D. Peacock.* **70**

BROKEN DATE 3 b.f. Busted 134–Arrival 102 (Henry the Seventh 125) [1975 5g⁴ 5f³ 5g² 5g 1976 10f⁶ 8g 6fg² 6g 7s] lengthy, shapely, attractive filly: best run at 6f but should stay at least 1m: blinkered final outing in 1975: sold 1,100 gns Newmarket December Sales. *W. Wightman.* **61**

BROKEN RECORD 3 b.f. Busted 134–Sam's Song 99 (Narrator 127) [1975 8g 1976 12f* 12fg² 12fg⁴ 12f² 13g*] big, well-made filly: won maiden race at Goodwood in May and Royal Caledonian Hunt Cup at Ayr in September: drew clear inside final 2f to beat Bines Bridge impressively by 7 lengths on latter course: ran creditably in between, notably when good second to Lighter in handicap at Goodwood in August: will be well suited by 2m: acts on firm going. *J. Winter.* **99**

BROKEN STRING 2 b.c. Nice Music 115–So Unlikely 60 (Blast 125) [1976 5g 5f⁴ 5f² 6d 6f⁵ 5f⁵ 7g] plater: showed ability on third outing when blinkered first time but did not run up to that form afterwards, including when again blinkered: should stay 6f+. *R. Hannon.* **58**

BROKOPONDO 9 gr.g. Mongo–Aces Swinging (Native Dancer) [1974 N.R. 1975 N.R. 1976 12h⁴ 17.1h⁵] fairly useful but temperamental handicapper **59**

in 1971: showed a little ability in two races at 9 yrs, only outings on flat since: sold 1,000 gns Doncaster Autumn Sales and resold privately for 500 gns later same day. *H. Payne.*

BROMPTON SQUARE 3 b.c. Charlottown 127–Tinted (Kythnos 126) [1975 **94** 7g⁵ 7fg 9fg* 7f⁵ 8g 1976 10fg 8fg⁶ 14fg⁴ 12g* 12g 16g] lengthy colt: hung right in final furlong but got up near finish when winning handicap at Newmarket in July by ¾ length from London God: probably stays 1¼m (ran moderately when tried at 2m): acts on a firm surface: sold 5,200 gns Newmarket Autumn Sales. *P. Robinson.*

BRONINGTON 2 b.c. Prince de Galles 125–Hidrilene 81 (High Perch 126) **84 p** [1976 6g⁵] strong, well-grown colt: second produce: half-brother to 1972 2-y-o 1m winner Bisque (by Hardicanute): 2,000 gns foal, resold 4,500 gns yearling: dam half-sister to successful broodmares Fran, Petite Marmite and Camanae: 10 lengths fifth of seven to Avgerinos in Granville Stakes at Ascot in July, making up ground in closing stages after being a long way behind: will stay 1¼m: sure to do better. *R. Hern.*

BRONSON 3 ch.g. Saintly Song 128–My Audrey 100 (Pall Mall 132) [1975 **60** N.R. 1976 6fg 8f 8fg⁶ 7.6fg 10g⁵ 8.2d 10v*] fair sort: fourth living foal: half-brother to a winner in Italy: 2,500 gns foal, resold 1,450 gns yearling: dam stayed 1m: favourite and dropped in class when winning seller at Leicester in October by a length from Sambrook: sold 2,300 gns afterwards: stays 1¼m. *H. Williams.*

BRONTE BOY 2 ch.c. Good Bond 122–Meadow Wood (Meadow Court 129) — [1976 5.9s] first foal: 200 gns yearling: dam unraced half-sister to very useful sprinter Robinski: behind in 18-runner maiden race won by Fear Naught at Wolverhampton in October. *L. Barratt.*

BRONZE MINK 4 ch.f. Foggy Bell 108–Chaseme Mink 69 (Tin Whistle 128) — [1974 5f 5fg 5g 5g 5fg 6s⁵ 1975 6v² 8fg 8f 7g 8f 8g 1976 8fg 5.9f 10.6d 8fg 8fg 8s] short-backed, unfurnished filly: poor plater: stays 6f: seems to need the mud: blinkered fifth outing: disappointing. *L. Barratt.*

BRONZE REEL 5 ch.m. Doudance 99–Bronze Bouquet (Wilwyn 129) [1974 8.2s 12s 12g 1975 10.1fg 1976 12f 17.1f⁶] strong, lengthy mare: poor staying maiden. *V. Cross.*

BROOKENDER 3 b.g. Klairon 131–Little Rapide 90 (Rapace 130) [1975 7g **43** 8.2g 8d 1976 16f 14f⁶ 15d⁵ 16.1v 18s⁴] tall, useful-looking gelding: has a round action: poor maiden: one paced and needs long distances: sold to C. Dingwall 1,000 gns Newmarket Autumn Sales. *R. Jarvis.*

BROOKFIELD MISS 2 b.f. Welsh Pageant 132–Focal 92 (Faubourg II 127) **73** [1976 7fg 8fg⁵] compact, quite useful sort: half-sister to several winners, including useful 1967 2-y-o The Industan (by El Gallo): 9,000 gns yearling: dam won from 6f to 2m: showed some ability in maiden races at Salisbury and Beverley (favourite) in September: will stay 1¼m. *Sir Mark Prescott.*

BROOMLEY 3 b.c. Blakeney 126–Blue Line 98 (Blue Peter) [1975 6g² 1976 **75** 9d⁴ 12.3d⁵ 10.5s⁵ 12fg⁴ 12.3fg* 12fg⁵ 10.6g 13v 12.5s⁶] useful-looking colt: good walker: started the season in good company but is only moderate and struggled to land odds in minor event at Newcastle in July: will stay well: wears blinkers nowadays. *W. Elsey.*

BROON'S SECRET 2 b.g. Most Secret 119–Vaudaville 77 (Vigo 130) [1976 5f⁴ **93** 5g* 5g 5f² 7f⁴ 5f² 6g³ 6g* 6v²] strong gelding: half-brother to a winning sprinter by Constable: dam ran only at 2 yrs: won minor event at Hamilton in May and picked up quite a valuable prize when winning 10-runner nursery at Ayr in September by a length from Prince of Jarva: also had some other good efforts to his credit, going down by a neck to Bobby Kempinski in blanket finish to a nursery at York in October on final outing: not disgraced when tried over 7f but gives impression 6f is his trip: acts on any going. *M. H. Easterby.*

BROTHER GEORGE 3 b.g. Native Prince–Lily Elsie 74 (Our Babu 131) [1975 ? N.R. 1976 10.2fg 12f 15.8g 18s*] lengthy gelding: first foal: 780 gns yearling: dam won over 1¼m: 10-length winner of weakly contested amateur riders maiden contest at Doncaster in October: needs extreme distances. *S. Hall.*

BROTHER HENRY 2 ch.c. Henry the Seventh 125–Intolerable Burden 91 — (Palestine 133) [1976 5fg⁶ 5g 6fg] third foal: brother to fair 1968 2-y-o 5f winner Oh Henry: 580 gns foal and resold 1,300 gns yearling: dam stayed 7f: no sign of ability in maiden and minor events in first part of season: sold 600 gns Ascot November Sales. *M. Masson.*

BROTHER SOMERS 9 ch.h. Will Somers 114 §–Freya 88 (Fair Trial) [1974 **55**
8g 8f 8g 7g⁵ 8g 7fg* 7g 8.2s³ 8d 8g 8s⁴ 8g⁴ 8g² 8.2s 8.2s 1975 8s 8s 8g³ 7s 8fg²
8f⁴ 8fg² 7fg² 8fg³ 8g⁵ 8.3fg³ 8f² 8g 8d 7d 1976 9fg⁶ 8fg² 7g 8g² 8fg 9g⁴ 8g]
poor handicapper nowadays: has been fired: stays 1m well: acts well on firm
going and is unsuited by heavy: acts on any track: has run respectably in
apprentice events, but is ideally suited by strong handling. *G. Harwood.*

BROUGHTY HARBOUR 5 ch.g. Typhoon 125–Queen Mab (Twilight Alley **—**
133) [1974 12g⁴ 13g² 13g* 12fg 12.3s⁵ 13.8s³ 14.6s* 1975 16v⁶ 14.7s* 15s⁴
14.7f³ 20g² 16fg* 14.6fg* 18g* 13g* 14g⁵ 1976 16s 16g⁶] rangy gelding: quite
a useful handicapper (rated 91) at 4 yrs: made only two appearances in 1976
and still didn't look fully wound up when sixth to Echo Summit at Ripon in
May on second of them: lacks pace and is suited by a good test of stamina:
acts on any going: suitable mount for an apprentice: sometimes sweats up:
very genuine. *S. Hall.*

BROWN MINT 2 br.c. Meadow Mint 120–Reach for the Sky 87 (Skymaster **98**
126) [1976 5fg* 6f* 6fg⁵] neat, strong colt: first foal: 1,900 gns yearling: dam
a sprinter: won 16-runner maiden race at Salisbury in June (by 3 lengths from
Beethoven) and minor event at Windsor in July (by short head from Shush):
moved poorly to post when well-beaten fifth of six to Paddington in Rous
Memorial Stakes at Goodwood later in July and was not seen out again: should
stay beyond sprint distances. *P. Cole.*

BROWN OAK 5 ch.g. Pall Mall 132–Golden Darling 86 (Darling Boy 124) **—**
[1974 N.R. 1975 N.R. 1976 8g] always behind in 11-runner amateur riders
event at Ripon in May, only outing. *K. Ivory.*

BROXTED 3 gr.c. Busted 134–Luciennes 108 (Grey Sovereign 128 §) [1975 **120**
5g² 6f* 6f² 7d² 7.3g 1976 6g⁵ 6fg* 6fg* 6d² 5g⁴ 6f⁶ 6fg⁵] well-grown colt: has
been hobdayed: closely related to Leonello, a winner at up to 2m: 4,600 gns
yearling: dam ran only at 2 yrs, when winner of her first two races: developed
into a smart sprinter and won well-contested handicaps at Newmarket and
Lingfield early in season in fine style, on latter course beating Bluehill 1½ lengths
in Johnnie Walker Stakes: afterwards in frame in Duke of York Stakes at York
(2⅓ lengths second to Three Legs) and Temple Stakes at Sandown (just under
3½ lengths fourth to Lochnager) and finished excellent fifth to Jimmy The Singer
in Spillers Stewards' Cup at Goodwood in July: subsequently beaten three times
in U.S.A.: best form at 6f: appeared to act on any going: standing at Emral
Stud, Wrexham, £350 n.f., n.f. *N. Callaghan.*

BRUNI 4 gr.c. Sea Hawk II 131–Bombazine 110 (Shantung 132) [1974 7d 1975 **131**
8d² 10f* 10g² 12fg 10fg* 14.6g* 12s 1976 14d* 12f² 12g² 12g* 12s⁵]
The St Leger is often won by a horse with top-class pace, a horse fast enough
to win a Derby, a horse whose career will not suffer if it is asked to come back
to racing at middle distances. Such were Ragusa, Ribocco, Nijinsky and the
latest winner Crow. Sometimes the St Leger is won by a horse decidedly lacking
in pace, a horse like Provoke or Athens Wood. And sometimes it's won by
a horse who possesses the pace to make him a power in middle-distance races,
but who at the same time would certainly be better suited by a long-distance
programme. Such were Hethersett and Bustino.
There's little doubt which of these categories Bruni belongs to. He was as
likely as any recent St Leger winner to make up into a Cup horse. But had he
been aimed at the Cup races as a four-year-old what benefit, comparatively
speaking, would it have been to his owners? Nearly all the big money, not to
mention the prestige, goes to the middle-distance races. We have something
to say in our comments on Sagaro about the lack of balance in the pattern of
racing. Suffice to say here that the authorities are doing English racing a
disservice by encouraging the constriction of the race-distance pattern. On the
evidence of his runaway victory in the St Leger Bruni could have turned out to
be a world-beater at distances beyond two miles, another Alycidon. That Bruni
was denied the opportunity to show his worth over long distances was one of the
saddest features of the 1976 season.
Bruni showed top-class form as a four-year-old against the specialist middle-
distance horses, winning two of his five races and being the victim of misfortune
in two others, including the King George VI and Queen Elizabeth Diamond
Stakes in which some regarded him as an unlucky loser. His campaign began
with an impressive victory in the Yorkshire Cup in May when, giving weight all
round, he toyed with Mr Bigmore, Sea Anchor, Dakota and the modest handicapper Migelitto. Mr Bigmore and Sea Anchor went on to prove themselves two
of the best out-and-out stayers in a vintage season for long-distance horses;

Yorkshire Cup, York—Bruni saunters home with Piggott motionless. Mr Bigmore (right) finishes second, ahead of Sea Anchor and the blinkered Dakota

Dakota was to meet Bruni again in the King George VI and Queen Elizabeth Diamond Stakes in July. Little attention was paid to the fact that Bruni hadn't left the stalls as well as the others at York, but slow-starting was to become a characteristic of most of Bruni's later performances and was to merit much greater consideration after his next race. After a brief flirtation with the idea of running Bruni in the Gold Cup his owners opted to run the horse in the Hardwicke Stakes at Royal Ascot where only four took him on. His most dangerous rival appeared to be the Italian Derby winner Orange Bay, who was sent to be trained by Walwyn at the end of his three-year-old days and had already gained a good win in the Jockey Club Stakes. Also in the field was Libra's Rib who on his latest appearance had run a close second in the Coronation Cup, a race Bruni by-passed because his connections didn't want him to race on firm going at Epsom where he had jarred himself badly in the Derby. Bruni went off with odds of 5/2 laid on him but right from the start he was in trouble. As the stalls opened he literally ambled out and was soon some way behind the others. At one point he was ten or twelve lengths behind the leader Libra's Rib and half a dozen lengths behind Orange Bay. Orange Bay took up the running before the final turn with Bruni in pursuit. Bruni drew up to Orange Bay below the distance and got in front for a stride or two in the last furlong before the effort of making up so much ground took its toll on him and Orange Bay went on again to win by a head. Libra's Rib was four lengths adrift in third place with the others in the next parish. Piggott came in for criticism for allegedly hanging too far back on Bruni and not taking advantage of the poor early pace to make up some of the ground given away at the start. Maybe Piggott should shoulder some of the blame but it is evident from the way he rides Bruni that he considers that the horse does not take kindly to being hustled along. Piggott should know Bruni almost as well as anyone, seeing that he rode him in all his races during the season.

The feeling that Bruni had been unlucky in the Hardwicke seemed wide-

Cumberland Lodge Stakes, Ascot—Bruni is far too good for Illustrious Prince

spread and he was again preferred in the betting to Orange Bay when the pair met in the King George VI and Queen Elizabeth Diamond Stakes at Ascot in July. The race is England's most important all-aged weight-for-age event, and appropriately there was an extremely strong field which included three classic winners from the current generation of three-year-olds. Bruni was third favourite, behind the French Derby winner Youth and Pawneese who had completed the English-French Oaks double. The Irish Derby winner Malacate was also among the ten runners. Again Bruni started slowly, losing about five lengths; when the stalls opened he was backing against the rear doors of his stall and seemed to be paying more attention to trying to dislodge Piggott than to the business in hand. Bruni's behaviour caused Piggott momentarily to lose an iron leaving the stalls. After such a chapter of accidents it was no surprise to see Bruni about ten lengths behind the leader Pawneese in Swinley Bottom, about a mile from home. And there was further misfortune in store for Bruni. He soon improved several positions on the inside but as the field approached the straight he had to forfeit ground when the struggling three-year-old Coin of Goid dropped back into his path. Turning for home Bruni seemed in a hopeless place and he had a poor passage before Piggott finally got him free to begin a challenge. Unfortunately for Bruni, by the time he got going Pawneese already had the race won. Bruni finished very fast, faster than anything else in the field, flying along to peg back Orange Bay, Dakota and Malacate near the post and failing by a length to catch Pawneese. Bruni took second place by a short head from Orange Bay. Whenever the loser is travelling faster than the winner in a close finish there is always a temptation to regard him as unlucky. Piggott was not inclined to rue his luck. 'Bruni doesn't have the speed to get out of a troublesome situation' he said. The implication of Piggott's remark is that had Bruni possessed top-class middle-distance pace he would have been able to side-step trouble on the home turn. Be that as it may there's no room to doubt that with any sort of luck in running Bruni would have given Pawneese a good fight. What a pity they didn't meet again when both were at the top of their form.

When a horse develops a reluctance to start there is always the possibility that one day he may refuse to race at all. Which is what almost happened to Bruni at Ascot in September in the Cumberland Lodge Stakes, a race chosen as part of h's preparation for the Prix de l'Arc de Triomphe. There was no runner of the calibre of Orange Bay and Bruni was odds on. Once again he didn't budge from the stalls until the others had got away and for a few strides it looked as if he was in two minds about whether to set off. But, patiently ridden, he settled down behind the rest, giving them something like a dozen lengths start, and then motored past them easily in the straight, like a Rolls passing a group of wheel-chairs. Piggott didn't put him into the lead until well inside the last furlong but so fast was he travelling in relation to the opposition that at the line he had five lengths to spare over the runner-up, the three-year-old Illustrious Prince. Strangely, the French betting public, which seldom looks beyond its own horses and hardly ever weighs the enemy more mighty than it seems, rated Bruni's chance in the Prix de l'Arc de Triomphe more highly than did the betting public on this side of the Channel. Bruni started second favourite for the Arc at 5/2, behind only the Bunker Hunt pair Youth and Exceller, who were coupled for betting purposes. Bruni jumped off with the others at Longchamp and was in a forward position all the way. His performance was almost a repetition of his running in the race as a three-year-old. He looked as likely as anything to win on the home turn but after challenging for the lead early in the straight he dropped back to fifth, two places higher than in 1975, more than six lengths behind the winner Ivanjica. An invitation to run Bruni in the Washington International in November was declined but Americans will have the chance to see him over there, for he has been sent to race in California.

		Sea Hawk II		Herbager		Vandale
Bruni		(gr 1963)		(b 1956)		Flagette
(gr.c. 1972)				Sea Nymph		Free Man
				(gr 1957)		Sea Spray
		Bombazine		Shantung		Sicambre
		(b 1963)		(b 1956)		Barley Corn
				Whimsical		Nearula
				(br 1958)		Whimbrel

Bruni's sire Sea Hawk II is a strong influence for stamina and his dam Bombazine, who was a very useful racemare, stayed a mile and a half well. If by some circumstance Bruni should be found in a longer distance race in future he would not fail for want of the necessary stamina. But the only circumstance

137

that we can foresee is if Bruni's habit of losing ground at the start persists and becomes too serious an obstacle to success in the top middle-distance races in the States where races are nearly always run at a very strong pace throughout.

Apart from his erratic behaviour at the start Bruni has never done anything wrong on the racecourse and has always run his races out in most genuine fashion. He acts on any going although he has a light action which suggests that he may be more at ease when the going is on top than when it is soft. He is a strong, slightly short-backed colt. *R. Price.*

BRYONY 2 br.f. Connaught 130–Lupulin 68 (Romulus 129) [1976 6fg 7g 8s]   — smallish, compact filly: good mover: dam won over 11f from three starts: little sign of ability in maiden races. *P. Walwyn.*

BRYTON 3 b.g. Frankincense 120–Dalmary 58 (Lucky Brief 128) [1975 5v 5s 1976 7g 7.2g] probably of little account: sold 240 gns Ascot August Sales. *D. Williams.*

BUBBLES 3 b.f. Ballymoss 136–Brief Flight 108 (Counsel 118) [1975 N.R.   **76** 1976 10f 16f 16.1v⁴ 12.5v²] lengthy filly: poor mover: half-sister to three winners, including smart Aviator (by Frankincense): dam won Northern Free Handicap: caught on line by Chartered Course in maiden race at Teesside in October, easily best effort: stays 1½m but not 2m: fell on second outing. *S. Hall.*

BUCKIE 6 ch.g. Crocket 130–Cullen 80 (Quorum 126) [1974 10g 8s 10.2v² 12s*   **84** 12v* 1975 12d6 10fg* 12fg* 14d³ 12d* 1976 10g 12f³ 10g⁵ 11.7h* 14f⁶ 12g⁴ 14fg* 12d⁴ 11v⁶] lightly-made gelding: moderate handicapper on his day: winner at Bath in August and Salisbury the following month, getting home by a length from Rushmere on latter track: may well stay further than 1¾m: probably acts on any going: excellent mount for a boy. *R. Turnell.*

BUCK'S CLUB 3 b.c. Buckpasser–Amerigo Lady (Amerigo 116 §) [1975 6f⁴   **79** 6g⁵ 5g⁴ 7fg 1976 6fg⁶ 5f⁴ 8fg 8f* 8f 8h⁴ 10.8g* 10.2f] good sort: won apprentice event at Pontefract in June by a length from Gilda and handicap at Warwick in August by ½ length from Believed: stays 11f: unseated rider leaving stalls fifth outing: inconsistent: exported to USA. *I. Balding.*

BUGLE BOY 5 b.g. Cracksman 111–Belle-Lettres (Cagire II 122) [1974 12.2f²   **69** 12f³ 13s³ 14.8fg⁶ 12g⁶ 12g³ 16v⁶ 10.6v 1975 N.R. 1976 16.1d⁶ 12s*] narrow gelding: fair handicapper on his day (rated 89) as a 3-y-o: lightly raced since but won apprentice race at Pontefract in October by a length from Stormy Princess: stays well: acts on any going. *P. Rohan.*

BUGLE CALLING 2 br.f. The Brianstan 128–Colours 115 (Torbido) [1976 6h³   **71** 7fg 6h³] small filly: half-sister to several winners, including fairly useful 1972 2-y-o Queen's Justice (by Mandamus), a prolific winner in Italy subsequently: 960 gns foal: dam won 1960 Manchester Cup: showed a little ability when third in maiden races at Carlisle in July: should stay 7f+. *J. Fitzgerald.*

BULBUL 3 b.f. Sing Sing 134–Bibi Mah 108 (Tehran) [1975 N.R. 1976 7s   — 8.2v⁶] sister to very smart sprinter Jukebox and half-sister to useful winners by Abernant and So Blessed: dam, middle-distance performer, is half-sister to Lord of Verona: blinkered and ridden by 7-lb claimer when well beaten in maiden races at Wolverhampton (started slowly) and Nottingham in October. *S. Nesbitt.*

BULLWHIP 5 b.h. Stephen George 102–Whiphand 83 (Supreme Court 135)   — [1974 8s⁶ 7f⁵ 7fg 8g 7fg⁶ 1975 8.2g² 8.3fg 8g⁶ 8g⁵ 8.2s⁵ 1976 7fg 7fg⁶ 8fg 8h⁵] neat horse: plater nowadays: stays 1m: appears to act on any going: reared up in stalls and was slowly away third start: retained 480 gns Ascot July Sales. *D. Jermy.*

BUNMOOR 3 b.f. Golden Dipper 119–Bunberry (Le Sage 128) [1975 N.R.   — 1976 8f 8h] half-sister to moderate 1m winner Smokey's Girl (by Spartan General): dam of little account: seems to possess little ability: sold 350 gns Doncaster November Sales. *W. Charles.*

BUNNY BOY 4 br.c. Right Boy 137–Baggage 86 (Zeus Boy 121) [1974 5g³   **75** 5f* 5f* 5g⁵ 5g⁴ 6fg⁴ 5fg 5g 1975 5d⁵ 6v 5g* 5g 5f⁶ 5h 5h³ 5h³ 5g 5h² 5fg⁵ 6g 5g⁴ 1976 5f³ 5g* 6s⁶ 5g⁵ 5g³ 5fg⁵ 5.9f⁶ 5fg* 5s³] useful sort: quite a moderate handicapper: finished well when winning at Doncaster in April and at Redcar in September: didn't show the same form in between: stays 6f: acts well on firm going: does just as well with or without blinkers: sold 1,550 gns Newmarket Autumn Sales. *P. Rohan.*

BUNNY TALK 3 b.g. Solar Topic 97–Midnight Bunny (Midsummer Night II   **56** 117) [1975 8fg 8s 8f⁶ 1976 8h 5fg⁵ 6f⁵ 5g² 5g 5s] big, well-grown gelding:

plating-class maiden: best form at up to 6f and is not certain to stay 1m. *F. Carr.*

BUNWELL 3 b.g. Lucky Brief 128–Flying Line (Linesman 111) [1975 5g 5f 6g⁶ 1976 8g 8d] well-grown gelding: poor form in maiden races and a seller: trained first outing by N. Guest. *D. Ringer.*   —

BURCOM BUOY 3 b.g. St Paddy 133–Jeanne D'Ex (Exar 130) [1975 6g 8g 1976 9g 12d* 12f³ 16v⁵] strong, useful sort: won maiden race at Ripon in June all out by ¾ length from Roseanne: should stay well: acts on a soft surface and is possibly not at his best on a firm one (hung under pressure on third start): well tailed off on final outing (first run for over three months). *M. Camacho.*   **78**

BURELOR 3 b.c. Timmy My Boy 125–Be Lively (Tyrone 130) [1975 7g 7.2fg 7g 7v⁴ 1976 8f 10s 10fg 11g⁴ 14fg⁴ 16f³ 16fg⁴] strong, compact French-bred colt: fair fourth of eight to Legal Advice in seller at York in July (fifth outing): evidently stays 1¾m but possibly not 2m: sometimes wears blinkers but seems to do as well without. *D. Sasse.*   **55**

BURLEIGH 4 ch.g. Charlottown 127–Running Blue 115 (Blue Peter) [1974 8d* 7d² 1975 10d⁶ 10g⁴ 12g 1976 10.2g 12g 10f² 12f* 8fg³ 10fg⁴ 8g 12fg³ 10fg 10g³ 12g⁶ 12fg⁶ 14fg³ 10g² 12s*] quite moderate nowadays: easy winner of apprentice races at Chepstow in May and October, and is used by stable for educating its apprentices: stays 1¾m: acts on any going: sometimes starts slowly: usually wears blinkers: sometimes sweats up: inconsistent. *R. Hern.*   **74**

BURLEY 2 b.c. Lear Jet 123–Forest Row (Royal Highway 117) [1976 5fg 6h 5.9f 7g⁶ 6g* 8v⁵ 6s*] first foal: 1,800 gns yearling: dam lightly-raced hurdler: made all when winning seller (33/1) at Newmarket in September (bought in 2,100 gns) and nursery at Haydock the following month (in no danger from halfway when beating Gold Bar by 7 lengths): has yet to show he stays further than 6f: suited by some give in the ground but was beaten long way on only outing on heavy going. *J. Hill.*   **87**

BURMA PINK 3 gr.c. Gulf Pearl 117–Magna 107 (Runnymede 123) [1975 5fg 6fg 1976 7g⁵ 7g* 8fg* 8.2d 8fg² 8fg³ 6fg⁵ 8g⁶ 7f* 7g⁵ 7s] strong, lengthy colt: good walker: won maiden race at Leicester in April and handicaps at Salisbury (overcame difficulties in running) in May and Newmarket in August: quickened clear in final furlong when beating Alanrod 3 lengths on last-named course: possibly finds 6f on sharp side and stays 1m: probably needs a sound surface: often wears blinkers nowadays. *G. Harwood.*   **93**

BURNISHED GOLD 2 b.f. Breton 130–Vive la Reine (Vienna 127) [1976 5fg 6fg 5.9f² 5g⁴ 5f⁶ 7s] quite a good sort but unfurnished at present: first foal: dam, a winner over 1½m in France, is sister to outstanding racehorse and sire Vaguely Noble: quite a moderate maiden: needs much further than 5f and should be well suited by 1¼m+: possibly not at her best on soft ground: sold 27,000 gns Newmarket December Sales. *H. Candy.*   **74**

BURNISHED LIGHT 2 ch.f. Gold Rod 129–Cumbrae Light (Luminary 132) [1976 5f* 5fg⁴ 6fg 6fg] half-sister to a winning hurdler: dam poor winning chaser: won seller at Warwick in April (no bid): ran creditably next time out but was then off course for over two months, having stiff tasks on her return: should be suited by 6f+. *Miss N. Wilmot.*   **69**

BURNOX 3 b.or br.c. Alloway Lad 103–Xynias 78 (Kythnos 126) [1975 N.R. 1976 11s 13s 12h⁴ 13fg⁶ 15g³ 11h³] plating-class maiden: dead. *N. Angus.*   —

BURNT BROWN 2 bl.c. Firestreak 125–Glorious Hour (Le Dieu d'Or 119) [1976 6fg 6f 7v 10v] big, strong colt: no worthwhile form in varied company: started slowly first outing, unseated rider coming out of stalls on third and wore blinkers on final outing. *Hbt Jones.*   —

BUSEH 2 b.f. Royben 125–Windsor Maid (Can.) (Victoria Park) [1976 5g 6d⁶ 7fg 6fg² 7f² 7.2f³ 7fg³ 7g⁵ 7g] lengthy filly: placed in three sellers prior to finishing 3½ lengths third of 15 to Topling in maiden race at Salisbury in September: stays 7f: acts on firm going: wears blinkers: suitable mount for a boy: sold to D. Williams 400 gns Ascot November Sales. *P. Cundell.*   **68**

BUSHBRANCH 2 br.f. John Splendid 116–Deacons Hay (Constable 129) [1976 5g 6f 6fg 6g 6d 8v] little worthwhile form, including in sellers. *G. Balding.*   **54**

BUSHLEY SPARK 3 br.f. Calpurnius 122–Mernian 100 (Counsel 118) [1975 5f 1976 9f] half-sister to winning middle-distance stayer Apple Of My Eye (by Silver Cloud): dam genuine and consistent miler: behind in minor event and maiden race: sold 250 gns Ascot June Sales. *R. Hannon.*

BUSHY PIECES 2 b.c. Ribero 126–Lavington 64 (Ratification 129) [1976 6fg⁵ 7f* 7g² 7f⁵ 8f] fourth foal: half-brother to a minor winner over 5f and to 3-y-o 1m winner Selham (by Derring-Do): dam, placed twice at 1m, is half-sister to top sprinters Lucasland and So Blessed: odds on, won maiden race at Edinburgh in July by ½ length from Forensic, the pair finishing well clear: 6 lengths second to Signale in minor event at Ostend the following month: should stay middle distances. *Sir Mark Prescott.* **80**

BUSINESS GIRL 2 b.f. Huntercombe 133–Tumbrel 113 (Djebe) [1976 5d 5s 5v] workmanlike filly: well beaten in end-of-season maiden races. *R. Vibert.* **—**

BUSMAN'S HOLIDAY 4 ch.g. Silly Season 127–Clippie 99 (Nimbus 130) [1974 N.R. 1975 8d² 8s² 7fg⁴ 8h⁴ 8f² 9.4f² 10fg⁶ 1976 8g³ 10s² 9g* 10g³ 8f* 8.2f² 8g] quite a moderate performer: ran well as a 4-y-o winning amateur riders events at Hamilton and Pontefract, both in June: stays 1¼m: probably acts on any going: has been tried in blinkers: genuine and consistent. *H. Bell.* **73**

BUSTABILITY 2 br.c. Busted 134–Farzana (Faristan 123) [1976 7g] neat, quite attractive colt: third foal: half-brother to Irish 1½m winner Montpellier (by Hopeful Venture) and to a winner in France: 1,600 gns yearling: dam won minor 9f event at 3 yrs in France: backward when in rear in 17-runner £2,900 event won by Royal Plume at Ascot in September. *P. Cole.* **—**

BUSTED FIDDLE 4 ch.c. Busted 134–Dolina (Saint Crespin III 132) [1974 N.R. 1975 8d 10f* 12g⁶ 16f 12f* 14fg³ 14g³ 13g 1976 12fg 11.7fg* 12d⁶ 12g⁵ 12fg² 12f³ 12.3fg⁴ 12f³(dis) 12fg² 16fg 12h² 12g 12d² 12d⁶ 12v²] neat, strong, attractive colt: fair handicapper: successful at Windsor in May: promoted to second (didn't get much room when challenging 1f out) after finishing about ½-length third to subsequently-disqualified Blagoslav at Epsom in June: best form at up to 1½m and appears not to stay 2m: acts on firm going and a soft surface: had very poor run on seventh start: blinkered tenth to twelfth outings: inconsistent. *R. Price.* **90**

BUSTELLO 4 b.g. Busted 134–Radio Caroline 109 (Sing Sing 134) [1974 6fg 6s 8s 7g 1975 8f 10.5g 9f² 8f* 8g* 8.2h* 8g³ 9g 1976 8g 8f 9fg 8f 7f 8fg³ 9fg 12fg⁴ 12.2f⁴ 10f²] tall, rather leggy gelding: useful handicapper (rated 101) at 3 yrs: mainly disappointing in 1976 but put up a fair performance when ½-length second of 10 to Upanishad at Beverley in August: appears to stay 1½m: acts on hard going: tailed off when tried in blinkers on fifth start: sweated up third outing: found little off bridle on sixth and eighth appearances: exported to Switzerland where he has since been successful. *M. W. Easterby.* **85**

BUSTIFFA 4 ch.f. Busted 134–Sniff 81 (Espresso 122) [1974 N.R. 1975 12fg⁵ 16fg³ 12g 1976 12.5g* 16f² 16fg² 12g* 17.7f⁴ 14.7d* 14fg⁴ 12h 20g*] big filly: did well after winning poor maiden race at Teesside in April and gained further successes in minor event and amateur riders race, both at Edinburgh, and £4,000 event at Ostend: beat Chiran when winning Gladiateur d'Ostende in August on final outing (reportedly broke down inside final furlong): stays really well: appears to act on any going except possibly very firm: genuine and consistent: sold 8,600 gns Newmarket December Sales. *Sir Mark Prescott.* **72**

BUSTLE ON 2 b.f. Busted 134–Antonietta Corsini (Herbager 136) [1976 5.1f⁶] half-sister to 3-y-o Connaught Square (by Connaught) and very smart middle-distance stayer Relay Race (by Relko): dam, winner of eight races in Italy, is sister to Italian Derby winner Appiani II: never-dangerous sixth of seven to Lizzylyn in maiden race at Yarmouth in August: will need at least 1¼m: to be trained by H. Cecil in 1977. *N. Murless.* **—**

BUSTLE UP 3 b.f. Prince Regent 129–Doral 97 (Darius 129) [1975 7f 7.2fg 8f 1976 12.5g⁴ 12.3s 16.1d⁴ 13s*] quite a moderate performer: not seen out after winning maiden race at Ayr in June by a length from Roseanne: stays well: acts on soft going: has twice worn blinkers, but does better without. *E. Weymes.* **71**

BUSTLING 5 b.g. Busted 134–Mahwa 82 (Match III 135) [1974 7h 7fg⁵ 10f⁴ 8d² 8g³ 8fg⁵ 10.1fg³ 10v 1975 10s⁶ 8fg 10.1fg⁵ 8f⁵ 10.1fg³ 12f* 12.2g⁵ 1976 12g 11.7fg 12f* 12f] rangy gelding: poor handicapper: made all and ran on well when winning at Folkestone in May by a short head from Mantop, the pair finishing clear: suited by 1½m: seems to act on any going: suitable mount for an apprentice: game. *Mrs F. Nagle.* **61**

140

BUTTERSCOTCH 2 ch.c. Alcide 136–Warehead Candy (Canisbay 120) **92**
[1976 7f 7fg⁶ 7fg 7fg*] compact, good sort: third foal: 220 gns yearling: dam
never ran: showed much improved form and had field well strung out when
winning 12-runner maiden race at Edinburgh in September by 5 lengths from
Money In: will be suited by 1½m. *C. Bewicke.*

BUTTON BOY 3 br.g. Major Portion 129–Teller Vif (Narrator 127) [1975 5g³ **73**
5d* 5g⁴ 5d⁵ 6g⁵ 7h 7f* 8fg 7f 1976 10f⁴ 9f 7f⁶ 8.2d 10.6d 8f² 7fg⁶ 10h⁶ 8f* 10fg*]
plater: ridden by 7-lb claimer, won at Redcar and Nottingham in space of four
days in August: sold 1,300 gns on latter course: stays 1¼m: acts on any going:
ran badly when tried in blinkers at 2 yrs: inconsistent. *K. Payne.*

BYKER BANK 3 br.c. Hul a Hul 124–Jennybell (High Hat 131) [1975 5f 5f⁵ **—**
5g 6g 6g 5v 1976 5f 7f 7f 8fg 10fg 10h] poor plater: sold 280 gns Doncaster
November Sales. *S. Wainwright.*

BY-WAY 3 b.f. Blakeney 126–Appian Way 89 (Romulus 129) [1975 N.R. **65**
1976 12g⁶ 12g³ 12g] small, lightly-made filly: first foal: dam won three times
over middle distances: co-favourite when just over 7 lengths third to Expadeo
in 10-runner maiden race at Haydock in August, best effort: will stay well. *J.
Bethell.*

C

CABAR FEIDH 4 b.g. Aggressor 130–Fashion Wear (Hard Tack 111 §) [1974 **—**
N.R. 1975 10f 12f 1976 12v⁵] poor maiden on flat but has shown himself
a fairly useful hurdler. *P. Calver.*

CABARITA 4 b.f. First Landing–Chary (Revoked) [1974 N.R. 1975 8f³ 8g **63**
8g² 8g 6g* 6g 6d 1976 5f 6g⁵ 8g 5.9g⁶ 5.9f⁴ 5f⁵ 7fg⁶ 5.9f 5.9fg 6g] rangy, attractive American-bred filly: fair handicapper (rated 88) at 3 yrs: didn't run up to
her best in 1976 and was tailed off on final appearance (blinkered first time):
best form at 6f: acts on firm going. *R. Cambidge.*

CABIN BOY 2 b.g. Seaepic 100–Tinted Venus 74 (Tudor Minstrel 144) [1976 **96**
6fg³ 6f⁴ 8f* 8f³ 8s] half-brother to numerous winners, including smart 1958
2-y-o Fortune's Darling (by Fair Trial): failed by a neck to catch Sovereign
Lane in eight-runner maiden race at Bath in September but was awarded race
by stewards: good third to Tudor Lilt in nursery on same course later in month:
will stay 1¼m: acts on firm going: ran moderately in blinkers on second outing.
R. Hern.

CABOTAGE 2 gr.f. Sea Hawk II 131–Cab 86 (Abernant 142) [1976 8s] well- **— p**
made filly: first foal: dam won twice over 1m: remote ninth of 20 to Lady
Rhapsody in maiden race at Sandown in October, only outing: should do better.
J. Tree.

CACHE CACHE 5 b.h. Alcide 136–Hiding Place 109 (Doutelle 128) [1974 **76**
8g⁵ 10g⁶ 10.1fg² 10s² 10s³ 1975 12.2s 9g 10g⁴ 10g* 12fg 10f³ 10fg* 9g³ 9f* 1976
10.4d⁴ 10g⁵ 10g 9g⁴] neat horse: fairly useful handicapper (rated 93) at 4 yrs
but has deteriorated and ran his only worthwhile race in 1976 on final appearance:
stays 1¼m but evidently not 1½m: acts on any going: has worn blinkers, including
when successful: sold 9,600 gns Newmarket December Sales. *I. Balding.*

CADOGAN LANE 6 br.h. Tamerlane 128–Astrellita 112 (Pardal 130) [1974 **87**
10.2s 13g⁴ 16fg⁵ 13.3g* 20g² 14.6g⁴ 19g⁶ 16s 18g³ 18d⁶ 1975 16s⁶ 18d⁴ 16g³
20f 16fg 18.4g* 22.2f⁴ 19f² 20g² 19s⁴ 16g³ 18fg⁴ 1976 14.6g² 14g³ 18.4s 13.3fg⁵
20f⁵ 16fg⁴ 18.4fg⁴ 16g³ 19fg⁴] neat horse: fair handicapper nowadays: ran
creditably in several of his races in 1976: well suited by extreme distances:
needs a sound surface to be seen to advantage: has been tried in blinkers: does
best when held up: sold to D. Kent 1,250 gns Newmarket Autumn Sales. *B.
Hills.*

CAELIDH 2 br.f. Silly Season 127–Angello 87 (Crepello 136) [1976 6g³ 6g² 6g³ **98**
6v²] tall, lengthy filly: sister to Royal Lodge Stakes winner Adios, and half-
sister to another winner: dam won at 1m: found one or two too good for her on
all her outings, but was beaten by very useful fillies when runner-up at York in
September (beaten 3 lengths by Lady Mere in £3,300 event) and Newcastle
in October (beaten a length by Mofida): will stay 1¼m: acts on heavy ground:
sure to win a maiden race: to be trained by H. Cecil. *N. Murless.*

CAERDEON LINE 2 ch.c. Caerdeon 98–Inklet (Never Say Die 137) [1976 **97**
5f 5f 7fg⁵ 6d* 7s³] quite a good-looking colt: half-brother to quite useful 1974
2-y-o Taw and Torridge (by Sayfar), a winner at up to 7f: 340 gns yearling: dam,
a twin, is unraced daughter of smart sprinter Ink Spot: 20/1 when winning 25-

runner maiden race at Newmarket in October by 2 lengths from Lady Mason: will stay 1m: acts on soft going. *R. Smyth.*

CAERINION 3 ch.f. Royal Palace 131–Caergwrle 115 (Crepello 136) [1975 **76** 6fg 1976 7fg 7.6s⁵ 8g²] lightly-built filly: sister to useful miler Caer-Gai: dam won 1968 1,000 Guineas: good second to Katie May in minor event at Sandown in June: will stay further than 1m: sold 13,000 gns Newmarket December Sales. *N. Murless.*

CAERNARVON KING 2 b.c. Mummy's Pet 125–Chiltern Miss 85 (Hook Money **79** 124) [1976 5d⁴ 5f⁴ 5f³ 5fg⁵ 5d⁵ 5.9s* 6v⁵ 6s⁵] useful sort: fourth produce: 600 gns foal, 1,800 gns yearling: dam won over 1m: won all-aged event at Wolverhampton in October by a short head from Four Lawns: stays 6f: acts on any going. *R. Hollinshead.*

CAIRNFOLD 3 b.f. Never Bend–Charvak (Alcibiades 95) [1975 6d 1976 10g **68** 10fg⁴ 12.2fg² 11.7h* 12fg⁴ 12f³] lengthy, attractive American-bred filly: comfortable winner of maiden race at Bath in July: stayed 1½m: acted on hard ground: exported to Australia. *P. Walwyn.*

CAIRNS 2 b.f. Derring-Do 131–Authors Correction 68 (Narrator 127) [1976 — 8fg 8s 10d] compact, strong-quartered filly: second foal: 2,600 gns foal and resold 3,000 gns yearling: dam won 17f amateur riders event: behind in maiden and minor events in the autumn. *D. Dale.*

CAKE POPPER 2 b.f. Connaught 130–Dilly 89 (Princely Gift 137) [1976 **103** 5.3f⁵ 5fg² 6f* 6f 7g* 8v⁴] third foal: half-sister to moderate 1974 2-y-o Yllid (by St Chad): dam placed at 5f: won maiden race at Brighton in August and nursery at Goodwood in September, latter gamely by a length from Who Cares: stays 1m: probably acts on any going: to be trained by H. Cecil. *N. Murless.*

CALABURN 3 b.f. Caliban 123–Molvitesse 75 (Molvedo 137) [1975 5f⁶ 5g² **71** 5f⁴ 6g* 6g² 8fg³ 1976 11f 10s 9fg* 7f 9fg 10h³ 9fg 10h⁴ 8d⁵ 8s 10g* 8s*] small filly: plater: winner at Newcastle in June, Lanark in October and Teesside in November (bought in 1,050 gns): stays 1¼m: acts on any going. *Hbt Jones.*

CALCUTTA 2 br.f. Sahib 114–Last Summer 66 (Will Somers 114 §) [1976 **65** 5fg³ 5fg* 7f⁶ 7g 8g] neat filly: half-sister to a winning 2-y-o plater by Golden Dipper: 300 gns yearling: dam fair plater at 2 yrs: bought in 680 gns after winning four-runner seller at Pontefract in April: not seen out again until September and had stiff tasks in nurseries. *E. Reavey.*

CALENDAR 2 b.c. Mansingh 120–Grey Miss 72 (Grey Sovereign 128 §) [1976 **61** 5s 6fg 6f⁶ 6fg 8.2v⁴] small, fair sort: modest plater: ran easily best race when tried in blinkers on final outing: suited by 1m: acts on heavy ground: sold 360 gns Newmarket Autumn Sales. *P. Rohan.*

CALERICA 3 ch.f. Caliban 123–Manerica (Mandamus 120) [1975 6fg 5fg 8g — 8g 1976 6g 9f] poor maiden. *S. Matthews.*

CALETA PRINCE 8 br.g. Kythnos 126–Lilis (Windsor Slipper) [1974 N.R. — 1975 10d 12.2fg 12.3d³ 12g⁶ 12h 15fg⁴ 12f² 10.4f 12g* 12.2g 1976 16.1d 12.5v⁶] quite a moderate handicapper: best form at around 1½m: acts on any going: ran poorly when tried in blinkers: sometimes wears bandages: suitable mount for an apprentice: inconsistent. *D. Plant.*

CALHIVE 4 br.f. Caliban 123–Honey House (Road House II) [1974 7d 7d 7v⁴ — 1975 10f² 10g 8f² 7fg⁵ 8f⁴ 8g 1976 12f 12fg 10d⁵] lengthy filly: poor maiden: acts on firm going: ran poorly when tried in blinkers: none too consistent: not seen out after May. *J. Harris.*

CALIBINA 4 ch.f. Caliban 123–Right Prospect 77 (Right Boy 137) [1974 **98** 5s*5v* 5s³ 1975 7fg⁴ 8.2fg² 8fg 8f² 10f⁵ 8d 7fg* 7.6g* 6d² 7g 1976 7g 7fg⁵ 7fg² 6fg* 7fg* 6f* 6h² 6f* 5.8f* 7s] lightly-made filly: good walker: had a fine season winning five handicaps, at Windsor, Brighton, Catterick, Goodwood and Bath: best at up to 1m: acts on any going: good mount for an apprentice or lady rider: acts on any track: genuine and consistent. *P. Cole.*

CALIBRATION 3 br.c. Caliban 123–Fair Jinks 65 (Tudor Jinks 121) [1975 **87** 5f 6fg 6f 8g 8d 1976 8fg 7g⁶ 10.1fg* 10fg³ 9g² 11.7d³ 12s*] attractive colt: much improved at 3 yrs and won maiden race at Windsor in July and handicap at Brighton in October: made all to beat Veracious 4 lengths on latter course: effective from 9f to 1½m: appears to act on any going: has worn blinkers but does better without: trained until after second outing by M. Francis. *R. Akehurst.*

CALIBRE 4 ch.f. Caliban 123–Stay 62 (Never Say Die 137) [1974 7d 7g 1975 — 11v 11.7g 1976 10.1fg] well-made filly: poor maiden: should stay well. *P. Taylor.*

CALICOURT 2 b.c. Caliban 123–Scorton Court 65 (Le Levanstell 122) [1976 **88** 5f 5d³ 5.9g 7fg* 8g⁴ 8.2d⁵] lightly-made colt: has a round action: third foal: brother to moderate 1974 2-y-o sprint winner Dancing Tara: dam stayed 1m: made all to win maiden race at Chester in September by 6 lengths from Nekasim: ran creditably in nurseries afterwards: will stay 1¼m: acts on a firm and a soft surface. *R. Murphy.*

CALISOLON 2 b.g. Caliban 123–Solensister 100 (Ennis 128) [1976 7d] half- **73 p** brother to a middle-distance winner by Midsummer Night II: dam a sprinter: unquoted when ninth of 25 in Houghton Stakes won by Bessie Wallis at New-market in October: may stay 1¼m: should do better. *P. Cundell.*

CALJOBO 3 ch.c. Calpurnius 122–Bojo 89 (Vilmorin) [1975 6g 6fg² 5.9fg* **116** 6fg³ 1976 6fg³ 7fg 7.6s⁶ 8fg* 6f² 10g³ 10g⁴ 10g⁵ 8g²] smart handicapper: made all when scoring by 2¼ lengths from Chop-Chop at Newmarket in May: went under by a head when excellent second to Import in 12-runner Wokingham Stakes at Royal Ascot the following month: subsequently raced without success in French provinces: best form at up to 1m: well suited by a sound surface: trained by J. W. Watts until after fifth outing. *M. Laborde, France.*

CALLIMOOR 2 br.c. Calpurnius 122–Mellormoor (Forlorn River 124) [1976 **89** 5d⁶ 5d⁶ 5f² 6g* 7f⁴ 6fg 6f⁵ 6fg 6v 7s⁴] neat, strong colt: first foal: 150 gns yearling: dam placed over 5f at 2 yrs: won maiden auction event at Doncaster in June by 2½ lengths from Glazepta Rework: creditable fourth to Rose Melody in £1,700 event at Redcar the following month, next outing and best subsequent effort: suited by 7f: acts on firm going and is probably unsuited by heavy: blinkered seventh outing. *S. Nesbitt.*

CALLING CARD 3 ch.g. Mountain Call 125–Lady Extra 95 (Exbury 138) **76** [1975 5g 7g 1976 8.2d⁴ 8fg³ 7g⁴ 10g* 10g* 12g 11.5g] lengthy gelding: creditable third of 14 to Burma Pink in handicap at Salisbury in May: coltish in paddock and tried in blinkers when moderate fourth to Glorified in similar event at Kempton later in month: subsequently raced in French provinces and won there twice: stays 1¼m (had stiff tasks when tried at further): gave us impression that he is none too keen: trained by P. Walwyn until after third outing. *P. Swann, France.*

CALL OF THE DEEP 2 b.c. Captain's Gig–Solar Echo (Solar Slipper 131) **105 p** [1976 6d²] wiry, useful sort: half-brother to several winners, notably high-class 6f to 1m gelding Boldboy (by Bold Lad, Ire) and smart 1966 Irish 2-y-o Sovereign Slipper (by Fortino II): 21,000 gns yearling: dam ran only once: second favourite for 23-runner maiden race at Newmarket in October and ran very well, going down by only ¾ length to Rings after holding every chance 1f out and keeping up a determined challenge: will be suited by 1m+: a promising colt who looks sure to win races. *H. Cecil.*

CALMIN 4 ch.c. Caliban 123–Ermina 94 (Courville 107) [1974 7s 6d 6s 1975 **50** 7d 8d 6fg* 7g² 6f² 8g 6g 6g 1976 6fg 8fg⁵ 7fg⁵ 7f 7f 6f⁶] tall, rangy colt: plater: stays 7f: acts on firm going: blinkered fourth outing: well backed final appearance (July). *A. Dalton.*

CALOR 3 b.c. Caliban 123–Charybdis (Chanteur II 135) [1975 7d 8g⁵ 8g² 8v* **79** 1976 10fg 8fg 10fg⁶ 8f³ 8d* 8s² 8s* 8s 8s] moderate handicapper: won at Yarmouth (ladies race) in September and at Bath in October, latter by 6 lengths from Paper Rich: best form at 1m but should stay further: acts on any going but is very well suited by some give in the ground: sold 6,800 gns Newmarket December Sales. *R. Jarvis.*

CALSPEA 2 ch.f. Calpurnius 122–Speadon 75 (Eudaemon 129) [1976 6fg³ **81** 7.2f⁵ 7d] good-bodied filly: second foal: dam won 5f seller as a 2-y-o: ran well when 6½ lengths third of 27 to Home Fire in maiden race at Newbury in August but did not reproduce that form (badly drawn final outing): should be suited by 7f. *N. Vigors.*

CALYPSO ROSE 3 ch.f. Crocket 130–Thereby 99 (Star Moss 122) [1975 5.1f — 7g⁶ 5g 1976 7fg 8.2g] quite an attractive filly: lightly raced and little worth-while form: should stay 1m. *M. Stoute.*

CA MARCHE 4 b.c. Gulf Pearl 117–Marching 86 (Aureole 132) [1974 N.R. **93** 1975 11v 11s³ 11s⁴ 13.3g6 16fg³ 12g* 14fg* 12g* 16g* 1976 12d³ 12f² 16fg 12g 12fg] strong colt: useful handicapper (rated 101) at 3 yrs: creditable second to Royal Match in Bessborough Stakes at Royal Ascot on second outing but was most disappointing afterwards: stays well: seems to act on any going: usually wears blinkers (didn't on fourth outing): suited by forcing tactics: possibly needs strong handling: ran very freely on third outing. *J. Tree.*

CAMBERLAD 3 gr.g. Young Emperor 133–Ambage (Pappa Fourway 139) **46** [1975 5s 5d 6f 1976 6f 10f² 15.8f 12g 8fg 8f⁶ 6f⁴ 8.2h⁵ 8f] plater: effective from 6f to 1¼m and does not stay 2m: tried in blinkers at 2 yrs. *G. Wallace.*

CAMBERWELL BEAUTY 2 b.f. Saintly Song 128–Papillon Rouge 60 (Klairon **67** 131) [1976 5fg² 5f² 5g² 6s⁶ 8d⁵ 6s⁵ 8v³] narrow, light-framed filly: fair plater: suited by 1m: seems to act on any going: sold 400 gns Newmarket December Sales. *R. Hannon.*

CAMBRIDGE GOLD 2 b.c. Sassafras 135–Greyia (Grey Sovereign 128 §) **70** [1976 6f* 6fg⁴ 8f 7g 8v] leggy colt: half-brother to fairly useful 1972 2-y-o Halesia (by High Hat): 1,000 gns yearling: dam won at 1m and 1¼m in France: bought in 880 gns after narrowly winning seller at Redcar in July: not disgraced in better company afterwards: will stay 1¼m+: acts on firm going. *K. Payne.*

CAMBRIDGE STAR 2 ch.g. Dike–Clariden 82 (Hook Money 124) [1976 5g* **100** 5fg² 7f* 7f⁴ 7d³] brother to 3-y-o King St Clare and half-brother to useful 5f to 7f performer Yonge St Clare (by Queen's Hussar): 1,500 gns yearling: dam moderate over 5f at 2 yrs: won maiden event at Folkestone in March: gelded and off course four months after second outing: showed much improved form on his return, running out an 8-length winner of five-runner nursery at Yarmouth in August and finishing creditable third to Whitby Jet in £1,600 event at Redcar the following month (would have been closer but for being squeezed out at distance): will probably stay 1m. *W. O'Gorman.*

CAMERADERIE 2 br.f. Polyfoto 124–Gay Biddy 48 (Khalkis 127) [1976 5f] — small filly: second foal: 1,500 gns yearling: dam poor plater: backward and always behind in small race at Thirsk in April, only outing. *H. Blackshaw.*

CAMPERO 3 b.c. A Tempo 127–Neptambre (Neptunus 132) [1975 5.5s⁴ 6g* **117** 8g 8d 7.5s 9s² 1976 10v³ 12g* 10.5g⁴ 15d² 12g⁴ 15d* 13.5d² 14.6d 12s] good-looking French colt: good mover: dam won two 6f sellers at 2 yrs and seemed to stay 1½m at 3 yrs: developed into a good stayer and won handicap at Saint-Cloud in March under top weight and Group 3 Prix Berteux at Chantilly in July by 2 lengths from Fresnay: twice finished close second to Secret Man, in Prix de l'Esperance at Longchamp and Prix de Menneval at Deauville, but was well behind him when eleventh to Crow in St. Leger at Doncaster in September on eighth outing (looked hard trained): stays very well: acts on soft going: trained until after sixth start by G. de Mola. *M. Zilber, France.*

CANBERRA 7 b.g. Canisbay 120–Lyre Bird 93 (Tudor Minstrel 144) [1974 **62** 12g⁶ 14.7g⁵ 12s* 12.3v³ 1975 N.R. 1976 12f² 12.3f* 12s⁵] strong gelding: won handicap at Newcastle in April by 3 lengths from Revertis: stays well: acts on any going. *N. Crump.*

CANCELLO 7 ch.g. Rosyth 94 or Coliseum **116**–Rose Gate (Exodus 112) [1974 — N.R. 1975 14.7f³ 12g⁵ 10g³ 1976 14.7d] big, strong gelding: very useful chaser, but is only moderate on flat: needs further than 1¼m: backward and sweating on only outing in 1976. *N. Crump.*

CANDID QUEEN 3 ch.f. Good Bond 122–Queen Julia 85 (Pampered King 121) **80** [1975 6d⁴ 7s⁵ 1976 10g⁵ 10.1fg 10g 10fg 10g² 10g³ 10s* 10s] compact filly: won maiden race at Goodwood in September by a length from Helcia: runs as though she may stay 1½m: seems to need some give in the ground. *D. Keith.*

CANDLES 4 b.c. Firestreak 125–My Mary 93 (French Beige 127) [1974 8d 7v — 1975 10g 10s 8g³ 6.5g* 8s⁴ 10.2g 5fg 8fg 8f 8fg² 8f 6g 8g² 7.6fg 8f 1976 8g 10.6d] strong, sturdy colt: well beaten in two amateur riders events at 4 yrs: suited by 1m and should stay further: suitable mount for an inexperienced race-rider. *J. Powney.*

CANDYMAY 2 b.f. Maystreak 118–Cield 70 (Nimbus 130) [1976 5g 5fg 5f 5g⁵ **61** 5d 5f⁶ 5f⁵ 5f⁵ 6g 5d 7v] compact filly: plating-class maiden: should stay 7f: trained by T. Walker most of season. *S. Wainwright.*

CANDY MILL 3 b.c. Sweet Story 122–Meanwhile (Star Moss 122) [1975 N.R. — 1976 8s 12g] first foal: dam poor maiden: well beaten in maiden races in Scotland. *N. Angus.*

CANICULE 3 b.f. Canadel II 126–Sunday Out 95 (Lord of Verona 120) [1975 **75** 5f 5f⁶ 6f³ 5h⁴ 8f⁵ 1976 8f 8fg² 9.4g* 9f² 12f⁴ 10f 10fg² 10v³ 11s⁴ 12v⁵] smallish filly: won maiden race at Carlisle in May by 2 lengths from Romany Charter: had some stiffish tasks afterwards but was not disgraced: probably stays 1½m: acts on any going. *W. Gray.*

CANMARLIN 3 ro.f. Double Jump 131–Sister Agnes 90 (St Paddy 133) [1975 —
5g 5fg 5.1f⁴ 5g⁵ 5f² 1976 8fg 7g] lengthy filly: plater: fell, broke leg and was
subsequently destroyed at Catterick in June: should have stayed at least 6f:
blinkered final outing in 1975. *R. Bastiman.*

CANTHARIDES 2 b.f. Philip of Spain 126–Kermene 89 (Persian Gulf) [1976 **71**
5fg* 5d⁵ 5f⁶ 6d] neat filly: third foal: half-sister to a minor winner: dam won at
1¼m and 11f: raced alone on far side when winning 10-runner maiden race at
Wolverhampton in April by a length from odds-on Can-U-Bid: exported to
Trinidad by B.B.A. *P. Cundell.*

CANTLIE 10 b.g. Le Levanstell 122–Nature Myth 84 (Zarathustra 131) [1974 **70**
12h⁶ 12f² 14fg⁵ 11g³ 12h³ 10g⁵ 12g 12g⁶ 10.2v 14s 1975 12s* 17.1f 12f⁵ 12h⁴ 16.9f³
14g⁵ 12f³ 1976 12.2fg 12f⁴ 12h² 12f⁴ 17.1s⁶] quite a moderate handicapper
nowadays: stays 2m but is effective at much shorter distances: acts on any going.
L. Kennard.

CAN'T REASON 3 ch.c. Treason Trial 80–Carnisio (Dionisio 126) [1975 5d —
5fg 5fg 8g 7g 1976 8f 10fg 8f 12s 12g 12s] poor maiden: blinkered third outing.
Mrs L. Dingwall.

CAN-U-BID 2 b.c. Lear Jet 123–Klondyke Fire (Klondyke Bill 125) [1976 **71**
5g³ 5fg² 5d⁴ 5fg² 5s⁵ 6s⁶] useful-looking colt: first foal: 2,500 gns yearling: dam
unraced half-sister to very smart 1975 French 2-y-o French Swanee: quite a
moderate maiden: stays 6f: appears to act on any going: consistent except for
below-par effort in blinkers on third outing: not seen out after June. *K. Payne.*

CANVEY ISLAND 3 ch.f. Continuation 120–Our Judy (Sicilian Prince 126) **49**
[1975 5fg⁴ 5g⁶ 6f⁴ 5fg 5g 7g 1976 5f 6h⁶ 6h 5h⁶ 10h⁵ 8.2h⁴ 16f] neat filly: poor
plater: suited by 1m+ but does not stay 2m. *P. Poston.*

CAPE RACE 2 b.f. Northern Dancer–Sticky Case 116 (Court Martial) [1976 **88**
6fg⁶ 6fg 8g² 8g] American-bred filly: half-sister to several winners, including
very smart 7f to 1¼m performer Lord Gayle (by Sir Gaylord) and good-class
middle-distance winner Never Return (by Ribot): dam won at up to 1¼m: put up
best effort when 1½ lengths second of 12 to Mined Illusion in maiden race at
Leicester in September: slowly away only subsequent outing: will stay 1¼m. *R.
Armstrong.*

CAPITAL 2 b.f. Richboy 117–Anna Boleyna 84 (Right Royal V 135) [1976 —
7d 10v] tall filly: second live foal: half-sister to very useful French middle-
distance filly La Route Millard (by Busted): dam won over 1¼m: behind in
maiden races at Newbury and Nottingham in the autumn. *R. Mason.*

CAPORELLO 2 b.c. Crepello 136–Golden Keep 77 (Worden II 129) [1976 6fg⁶ **101**
7g* 7g] attractive, well-made colt: third foal: 25,000 gns yearling: dam won
from 1¼m to 13f: disputed lead much of way when winning £1,900 event at
Sandown in September by 2½ lengths from Tully: second favourite for £2,900
event at Ascot later in month but finished only eighth of 17 to Royal Plume: will
stay 1½m. *G. Pritchard-Gordon.*

CAPPUCCILLI 3 b.f. Lorenzaccio 130–Bora Bora 91 (Hethersett 134) [1975 —
6g* 7d* 8g² 1976 7f 8fg 11.7f³ 12g⁶ 12fg³] first foal: dam probably stayed 1½m:
showed very useful form at 2 yrs but did not train on and looked lean and light
when tailed off on final appearance: trained until after second outing by H. Cecil.
D. Morley.

CAPRICIOUS 3 ch.f. Snob 130–Caravella (Prince Taj 123) [1975 7f* 1976 **105**
10f⁶ 8g 12g 12g⁵ 12f² 12f³ 12fg* 12f⁴] lengthy, attractive French-bred filly: half-
sister to minor winners in France by Traffic and Cadmus: dam a smart miler in
France: won Galtres Stakes at York in August by a short head from Laughing
Girl, coming from behind with a smooth run to lead inside final furlong but
eventually being all out to hold off runner-up's renewed challenge: not disgraced
on most of her other starts: stays 1½m: acts on firm going: ran moderately in
blinkers on third outing. *P. Prendergast, Ireland.*

CAPTAIN CHEEKO 2 ch.c. Military 112–Sunny Belle (Windsor Sun 116) **68**
[1976 5f 5.1g 5s 7s⁶ 6s⁶ 8v³] fair plater: well suited by 1m and will stay further:
acts on heavy ground. *P. Allingham.*

CAPTAIN FLASH 3 b.c. Irish Ball 127–Feather Bed 111 (Gratitude 130) **73**
[1975 7fg 1976 8g⁶ 11.1g⁴ 13.3fg³] strong, attractive colt: in frame in maiden
races at Kempton in May (just over 4 lengths fourth of 17 to Shangamuzo) and
Newbury in June (5½ lengths third of 13 to Sunbelt): suited by a test of stamina.
H. Wragg.

Galtres Stakes, York—Capricious just holds off the blinkered Laughing Girl

CAPTAIN FRANCES 3 b.f. Captain's Gig–Arbour (High Hat 131) [1975 —
N.R. 1976 6f] third produce: 1,250 gns foal: dam unraced daughter of good
stayer Alcove: poor mover: 50/1 and in need of race, slow into stride and ran very
green when last of 19 in maiden race at Thirsk in April. *J. Cousins.*

CAPTAIN GREENE 2 ch.c. Jimmy Reppin 131–Corsley Bell 96 (Owen Tudor) **72**
[1976 6g⁵ 6fg] half-brother to smart miler Town Crier (by Sovereign Path):
8,200 gns yearling: dam won over 5f at 2 yrs and is half-sister to very speedy
Krakenwake: ran promisingly when 7 lengths fifth of 19 to Casino Boy in minor
event at Lingfield in August: still looked as though race would do him good when
behind in Convivial Stakes at York later in month: will stay 1m. *I. Balding.*

CAPTAIN JAMES 2 b.c. Captain's Gig–Aliceva (Alcide 136) [1976 5f² 6f* **117**
5g² 7f* 7f² 7g²]
   One of the most interesting features of the bloodstock sales in 1976 was the
method used by the Brownstown Stud, which bred Captain James, to sell half its
crop of yearlings. In the past the majority of the stud's animals went into
training with Seamus McGrath but in 1976 it was decided that the numbers
must be reduced. How to reduce them posed a problem. If the stud had made
the selection prospective buyers would, naturally enough, have assumed that the
ones put up for auction were the least promising, and would have bid accordingly.
Therefore the Brownstown Stud used an idea pioneered in Canada, whereby all
the yearlings that are sound enough to sell are carefully matched and then offered
in pairs. Once the bidding is completed the successful bidder takes the horse of his
choice and the other goes into training with the McGrath racing stable. Captain
James's yearling half-sister by Tyrant, who was matched with a filly by Home
Guard, was the selected one at a price of 17,000 guineas. It will be fascinating to
see who comes off the better, the McGraths or the buyers at the sale who included
such expert judges as Vincent O'Brien and Paddy Prendergast. As one com-

146

mentator pointed out, there is an old proverb that 'nothing can make a fool of a man like a horse' and the chances are that two horses will do the job even more comprehensively!

Captain James was one of several good-class, consistent two-year-old colts in Ireland in 1976. While there may have been several better than he there were few more consistent animals around; in six runs, mostly against tough opposition, he won twice and finished second four times. Good as his winning performances were—he showed great determination to win a minor event at Phoenix Park in June after being hampered more than once, and beat Lordedaw by a length and a half in the Mullion Stakes at Leopardstown the following month—his efforts in defeat were better. It was in a small race that Godswalk proved too good for him by two lengths early in the season but his other three placings came in pattern races. In the Curragh Stakes Captain James put in a very strong late run and was considered unlucky by some to go down by a head to Nebbiolo; in the £16,000 National Stakes at the Curragh he started favourite but Pampapaul beat him by two and a half lengths after the pair had veered sharply left in the closing stages; and in the Larkspur Stakes at Leopardstown Captain James found the task of giving weight all round too much for him, and The Minstrel went past in the final furlong to beat him a length.

			Turn-to		Royal Charger
	Captain's Gig		(b 1951)		Source Sucree
	(br 1965)		Make Sail		Ambiorix
Captain James			(br 1951)		Anchors Aweigh
(b.c. 1974)			Alcide		Alycidon
	Aliceva		(b 1955)		Chenille
	(b 1966)		Feevagh		Solar Slipper
			(b 1951)		Astrid Wood

Captain James hails from the most successful McGrath family in recent years. His dam Aliceva is a half-sister to Feemoss, who has bred both Levmoss, winner of the Ascot Gold Cup, French Gold Cup and the Prix de l'Arc de Triomphe, and Sweet Mimosa, winner of the French Oaks. Aliceva was moderate herself, winning a mile-and-a-quarter-maiden race, but it is likely that she would have stayed very well given the chance. Her sire, Alcide, was a stayer of the highest class and her half-brother by Saint Crespin III, Laurence O, was a top long-distance handicapper who won the Queen Alexandra Stakes and finished second in the Cesarewitch. Both of Captain James's winning half-brothers showed a fair amount of stamina, the three-year-old Vivar (by Le Levanstell) being placed over a mile and a half and the Faberge II colt Celtic Barge winning at up to two miles. We would be confident of Captain James's prospects of staying a mile and a half but for his style of running on his last two starts; in the National Stakes he pulled hard both on the way down and in the race, and in the Larkspur Stakes he fought for his head and was allowed to go on. It is to be hoped that he doesn't become headstrong, for he has the makings of a good three-year-old. *S. McGrath, Ireland.*

CAPTAIN LARK 3 ch.g. The Bo'sun 114–Dumbridie (Dumbarnie 125) [1975 **39** 5fg 5g5 5f4 5g5 5f4 5.8h6 10g 7g 1976 8fg 11.1fg5 8.2f6 8f5 7g6 5g 5h 7f] poor plater: blinkered third and fourth outings: sometimes starts slowly. *M. Stevens.*

CAPTAIN MAINWARING 2 ch.c. Ridan–Lass O'Morelands 76 (High Treason **86** 126) [1976 6g6 5.3s2 5s4] lengthy, lightly-made colt: good mover: half-brother to two winners, including useful 6f to 1¼m winner Smart Sam (by Super Sam): 10,500 gns yearling: dam won 5f seller at 2 yrs: went down by 2 lengths to First Swallow in five-runner minor event at Brighton in October: blinkered when 6 lengths fourth of 13 to Arctic Tribune in maiden race at Sandown later in month: should stay further than sprint distances. *P. Walwyn.*

CAPTAIN MIDNIGHT 2 br.c. Meadow Mint 120–Karin Maria 86 (Double Jump **65** 131) [1976 5s 5g5 6fg 7f6 8f 8.2s4 10s] leggy colt: fair plater: stays 1m but is not certain to stay 1¼m: possibly unsuited by firm going. *K. Whitehead.*

CAPTAIN PAGET 3 gr.c. Captain's Gig–Jasamaran § (Vilmorin) [1975 5d4 **97** 6fg* 6fg* 7g3 7fg6 1976 7fg 7fg 8.2d2 8f 8fg6 10fg5 8fg2 8g5 7f4 8g*] good sort: had mainly stiff tasks prior to just holding off Belle Vue by ⅓ length in apprentice event at Doncaster in September: ran well earlier when runner-up in Cecil Frail Handicap at Haydock (beaten 8 lengths by Gunner B) and well-contested event at Newcastle (beaten ¾ length by Fluellen): best form at up to 1m: acted on a firm and a soft surface: dead. *G. Hunter.*

CAPTAIN POLDARK 2 br.c. Prevailing–Roxane (Ger) (Masetto) [1976 5g⁵ — 6d] workmanlike colt: second foal: dam placed at up to 1¾m in France: beaten some way in small races in the spring. *F. Dever.*

CAPTAINS GLORY 2 b.g. Captain's Gig–Henco (High Hat 131) [1976 5g 5d] plain gelding: backward when behind in maiden races at Catterick and Nottingham in September. *G. Vergette.*

CAPTAINS MATE 2 b.c. Ridan–Fair Astrologer 81 (Relic) [1976 5d⁴ 5f³   88 6fg⁵ 6g² 5.1g*] neat colt: second foal: half-brother to fair Klairio (by Klairon): 3,500 gns yearling: dam, half-sister to very smart Fair Astronomer, stayed 7f: fairly useful: dwelt at start of 16-runner maiden race at Yarmouth in September but came through to win by 1½ lengths from Mister Quilp, the pair finishing clear: will stay 1m. *B. Hobbs.*

CAPTAIN'S TABLE 4 ch.c. Habitat 134–Ship's Biscuit 96 (Doutelle 128) §§ [1974 6g 6fg 6d³ 6fg² 6fg² 6d³ 1975 8.5d 8fg* 8d⁵ 8f 8.3fg 1976 12d 9g³] strong, well-made colt: one-time fair performer but has shown an unwillingness to exert himself: should stay at least 1¼m: appears to act on any going: usually wears blinkers: best left alone. *V. Thompson.*

CAPTAIN'S WINGS 3 br.c. Captain's Gig–Rising Wings (The Phoenix) [1975   83 5f 6fg* 6fg* 6d³ 7fg² 7f 7g 6g 1976 7fg 8.2d 8t 12f⁶ 11g 10g 10.6d] lengthy colt: showed quite useful form at 2 yrs: usually had stiff tasks in 1976, running easily best race on third outing: bred to stay middle distances: sold 2,600 gns Doncaster October Sales. *F. Carr.*

CAPTIVE KNIGHT 3 br.c. Manacle 123–Nocturnal (Combat 123) [1975 5f 5f   70 d 1976 8fg² 8fg 7fg 7g 6g 5fg 8h³ 8s] strong colt: seems only plating class: stays 1m: sold to H. Collingridge 1,200 gns Newmarket Autumn Sales. *F. Maxwell.*

CARABINIER 4 br.c. Queen's Hussar 124–Floss 94 (Counsel 118) [1974 7s — 7d⁶ 7v³ 1975 8s 10f⁵ 12f² 14fg² 10g⁴ 11g 10s 12g 1976 12s] rangy colt: poor maiden on flat but is a fairly useful hurdler: seems to stay 1¾m (definitely stays 1½m): probably acts on any going: wears blinkers: sold privately out of Mrs R. Lomax's stable 4,000 gns Ascot January Sales. *J. Edwards.*

CARA GO DEO 3 ch.g. Whistling Wind 123–Ana de Mendoza (Royal Challenger   68 129) [1975 5g 5s 5g 7f² 8g³ 8g³ 1976 10s 10s 12f⁵ 12g⁴ 8.6f² 12f² 12f² 10f* 10g³ 10fg³ 16d] half-brother to two winners in Ireland: 10,500 gns yearling: dam stayed well: odds-on, 6-length winner of maiden race at Tralee in August: third to wide-margin scorer Frankie in minor event at Ayr the following month: stays 1½m (unplaced in Irish Cesarewitch on only attempt at 2m): acts on firm going: wears blinkers. *P. Prendergast, jnr, Ireland.*

CARANX 2 ch.f. Double Jump 131–Cavally (Major Portion 129) [1976 6g] — third foal: dam never ran: backed from 20/1 to 12/1 when behind in 19-runner minor event won by Casino Boy at Lingfield in August, only outing. *Miss A. Sinclair.*

CARA'S TRUMP 2 b.c. Kibenka 119–Yanoula 79 (Nosca) [1976 6f 7d 6d³]   82 half-brother to two winning platers: dam showed form over 7f at 2 yrs: dead-heated with Gentle God for third place, 5½ lengths behind Rocket Symphony, in maiden race at Newmarket in October, easily best effort: will stay 1m: changed hands 350 gns Doncaster October Sales, after second outing. *W. Stephenson.*

CARAVAN CENTRE 4 b.f. Nelcius 133–Princesse Moss (Mossborough 126) — [1974 8s 8s 1975 10v 12g 12.2f⁶ 16h⁴ 16fg⁴ 13.8fg⁵ 16h⁵ 13.8f² 15.8g* 12g² 1976 15.8g 16f 10fg] leggy filly: selling handicapper: well beaten all outings at 4 yrs: suited by long distances: acts on firm going: has been tried in blinkers but has done better without. *W. Gray.*

CARBERRY GIRL 3 b.f. Hard Man 102–Will's Girl 76 (Will Somers 114 §)   38 [1975 5d 5fg 5g³ 5f⁴ 1976 5f 7f 5h⁵ 5s] poor plater at 2 yrs: little worthwhile form in better company in 1976. *T. Craig.*

CARBURTON 3 gr.c. Runnymede 123–Fiddlers Too 80 (Neron 121) [1975   71 5d 5g* 5h* 5.6g⁴ 6fg⁵ 5f⁵ 5fg⁵ 5h³ 5g 1976 5fg 6f³ 5f⁴ 6d⁵ 6fg 5g⁶ 5fg 6fg 5g³ 6d⁴] quite useful at 2 yrs: nowhere near as good in 1976 and is only quite a moderate handicapper nowadays: stays 6f: best form on a sound surface: ran below his best when tried in blinkers on fifth outing. *V. Mitchell.*

CARDINAL PUFF 2 ch.c. St Alphage 119–Cartlone (Escart III) [1976 8s] — good-looking colt: second foal: 4,300 gns yearling: dam, daughter of Cesarewitch winner Prelone, won 17f amateur riders event in Ireland: never-dangerous eighth of 20 to Lady Rhapsody in maiden race at Sandown in October. *N. Vigors.*

148

The Queen's "Card Player"

CARD PLAYER   2 ch.c. Crepello 136–Albany 120 (Pall Mall 132)   [1976 5fg* **111**
6d* 7f* 8d⁶]   neat, attractive colt who carries plenty of condition: third foal:
dam, daughter to high-class stayer Almeria, showed smart form at 1¼m: a useful
colt who won at Newmarket in April and August and at Haydock in between:
gained his most valuable success on last occasion when running on well to win
£3,100 event by ½ length from Crown Bowler: weakened from 2f out when last
of six to Gairloch in Royal Lodge Stakes at Ascot in September: will stay at
least 1¼m: appears to act on any going: genuine.   *I. Balding.*

CARD SHARP   4 br.g. Chebs Lad 120–Quicken (Falls of Clyde 126)   [1974 6g   —
7d   1975 8h⁵ 7fg 8h⁵ 8fg 8fg⁴ 8g⁶ 10g⁶   1976 12fg⁵]   small gelding: plater:
best form at up to 1m: acts on a firm surface: has worn blinkers: blinkered final
outing 1975 and on reappearance: sold 600 gns Ascot April Sales for export to
Belgium where he subsequently won.   *G. Balding.*

CAREG-WEN   2 ch.f. Stephen George 102–Can't Wait (Eudaemon 129)   [1976   —
5g 5f 6fg 6fg 7f]   big, strong filly: no sign of ability in minor and maiden events
in first half of season.   *J. O'Donoghue.*

CARELESS PRINCESS   2 b.f. Prince Regent 129–Takawin 109 (Takawalk II   **84**
125)   [1976 6f 5g 5g² 6f 5s² 5s⁴ 5v²]   big, strong filly: first foal: dam won at
up to 6f: runner-up in three maiden races at Lingfield, failing by only a neck to
hold off Tinsley Green in November: should stay 6f: acts on heavy ground.
J. Benstead.

CARIBBEAN   3 ch.c. Habitat 134–Sunland 108 (Charlottesville 135)   [1975   **94**
6d⁶   1976 8f 8fg 11.1g² 11fg* 12f]   strong, attractive colt: good mover: put
up good performance when winning handicap at Newbury in June by 3 lengths
from Sir Montagu: well-beaten seventh under a penalty to Shangamuzo in King
George V Stakes (handicap) at Royal Ascot later in month: stays 11f: best in
blinkers: exported to Australia.   *R. Hern.*

CARIBBEAN BOY   7 b.g. Cintrist 110–Blue Hawaii 75 (Royal Palm 131)   **70**
[1974 8s 6g⁵ 8fg³ 7fg⁴ 7f* 7g* 6f² 6fg* 7g² 6d 6s 6s 7s⁴   1975 6v 5g 7f* 8g⁶ 7f*
6g 6h² 5.9fg 7g³ 8f⁶ 8g* 8f 8g 6g   1976 7g 6fg 6f⁵ 8f 7fg 7fg* 7fg² 7f⁴ 10h 8f³ 7f⁵

149

8f 8d 8g] strong gelding: poor handicapper nowadays: goes well at Yarmouth and was gaining his sixth victory on that course when beating Beaufort Street 3 lengths in May: in frame on three other occasions at Yarmouth, only other worthwhile efforts in 1976 (rarely shows his form on other tracks nowadays): effective at 6f and stays 1m: seems to act on any going but best form on a sound surface: sometimes wears blinkers: excellent mount for a boy: sold 1,600 gns Doncaster October Sales. *R. Bastiman.*

CARITA 3 b.f. Captain's Gig–Tacora (Cernobbio 123) [1975 7g 7.2fg⁵ 8s 8g 5g⁵ 1976 8fg 6f 6g⁴ 7g 8.2d] plating-class maiden: should stay middle distances. *J. Carr.*   **54**

CARLQUEST 4 br.f. Don Carlos–Last Bequest (Bounteous 125) [1974 5fg 5.8s 5v 1975 7v 12.2fg 10h 1976 10.1fg] of little account. *J. Gibson.*   **—**

CARLWOOD 6 b.g. Big Timber §§–Carle's Girl 83 (Merry Boy) [1974 N.R. 1975 10s 12g 11fg⁵ 14fg 12f⁴ 1976 10f 12.2f] of no account. *M. Bolton.*   **—**

CARMELLA 2 b.f. Connaught 130–Hormuz (Persian Gulf) [1976 6fg⁶ 7fg 6fg⁵ 5fg 6g] poor plater: sold 220 gns Doncaster October Sales. *G. Blum.*   **55**

CARNAL GIFT 2 b.f. Divine Gift 127–Incarna 82 (The Phoenix) [1976 5d 5f] plain filly: in rear in sellers at Redcar (blinkered) and Beverley in first part of season. *D. Williams.*   **—**

CARN GREY ROCK 3 b.g. Jimmy Reppin 131–On Safari (King Hal) [1975 7g 7fg 8g 6g⁴ 8fg² 8d 1976 10g 10.1f 13.3fg 10g⁴ 8.3fg 10.1fg 12f³ 12fg* 12v⁴] smallish, sturdy gelding: quite a modest plater: won five-runner claiming race at Leicester in September by 2 lengths from Panda's Gambol: stays 1½m well: possibly requires a sound surface: lost all chance at start sixth outing: wears blinkers nowadays. *P. Cole.*   **57**

CARNIVAL SOVEREIGN 9 br.g. Carnival Dancer 113–Honey Girl 82 (King-stone) [1974 5f 5g⁵ 5g² 5fg³ 5g⁶ 5fg⁶ 5v⁴ 5s² 5v 1975 5g 5g 5g³ 5g 5fg³ 6g⁶ 5g* 5h³ 5f³ 5f² 5f³ 5f⁶ 5g⁴ 1976 5f 5g⁴ 5.9f* 5g³ 6f⁶ 5f⁴ 6f² 5h⁴ 6v 5s⁴ 6v] poor handicapper: successful at Wolverhampton in May by a head from Micted: not disgraced most outings afterwards: stays 6f: acts on any going: suitable mount for an apprentice: has sometimes worn bandages behind. *E. Weymes.*   **59**

CARNLEA HOUSE 4 b.c. Reindeer 124–Vesper Bell (Larkspur 128) [1974 6d 7g 7g* 8g⁴ 7g* 1975 12g 12.2f⁴ 10f* 12f³ 10g³ 9g 10d² 12g 11g³ 12g 12g⁶ 1976 10h⁴ 10d 12f⁴ 11s⁵ 12fg⁵ 12.3fg² 11fg 12f³ 10g* 12.3fg* 10fg⁴ 12d 12.2s⁵] compact colt: fair handicapper nowadays: winner at Newcastle in August and Chester the following month, on both occasions keeping on really well: stays 1½m: appears to act on any going but goes well on a sound surface: suitable mount for an apprentice: effective with or without blinkers: suited by forcing tactics: ran badly last two outings. *Denys Smith.*   **87**

CAROLINA MOON 4 ch.f. Grey Dawn 132–Irish Sword (Irish Lancer) [1974 6g* 5d* 5s³ 7v⁴ 1975 9g² 9g* 10g⁵ 8d⁵ 8g 1976 9d⁶ 8d* 8d* 8d 8d⁵] French filly: very useful performer: won Prix de Sevres at Longchamp in June and Prix d'Astarte at Deauville the following month, in latter event beating Dona Barod 2 lengths: put up better subsequent effort when about 2 lengths fifth of eight to Monsanto in Prix du Rond-Point at Longchamp in September on final appearance: stays 1½m: acts on soft going: exported to Canada. *M. Clement, France.*   **116**

CAROLINE'S MELODIE 2 b.f. Typhoon 125–Pilicina (Milesian 125) [1976 5fg 6f² 6fg 7g] second foal: dam of little account: 2½ lengths second to Master Wrekin in minor race at Windsor in July, easily best effort: should be suited by 7f+. *D. Underwood.*   **72**

CAROLINIAN 3 ch.g. Charlottown 127–Crepe Myrtle 80 (Crepello 136) [1975 N.R. 1976 8f 10s⁵] well-made gelding: second foal: dam won over 1m at 3 yrs: blinkered and having first outing since April, showed a glimmer of ability when just over 9 lengths fifth of 11 to Candid Queen in maiden race at Goodwood in September: will stay 1½m: sold to T. Forster 5,200 gns Newmarket Autumn Sales. *J. Tree.*   **—**

CARON 3 b.c. Caro 133–Arme d'Or (Armistice 131) [1975 9d⁴ 9d 1976 11g* 11g² 12.5g* 12g³ 15.5g³] second foal: half-brother to useful French 1¼m performer Oreste (by Luthier): 70,000 francs (approx. £6,400) yearling: dam very useful middle-distance performer in France: won maiden race at Maisons-Laffitte in April and minor event at Saint-Cloud the following month: placed in much stronger company on his other outings, finishing ¾-length second to Twig Moss in Prix Noailles at Longchamp and third to Exceller in Prix du Lys at Chantilly and in Grand Prix de Paris also at Longchamp, putting up better effort in latter   **121**

event in June when beaten only about 5½ lengths: stays well: very smart. *J. Cunnington, jnr, France.*

CARPAULANA 2 b.c. Double-U-Jay 120–Jingling Jane 77 (Sing Sing 134) **50** [1976 5v⁵ 5g 5h 8f 8.2h⁵ 5g] lightly-built colt: poor plater. *N. Angus.*

CARRIAGE WAY 2 br.c. Track Spare 125–Polyandrist 92 (Polic 126) [1976 **107** 6g 6d* 6g⁵ 7.6v⁴] robust, well-made colt: second living foal: half-brother to 3-y-o Trigamy (by Tribal Chief), a very useful winner over 5f: dam best at up to 1¼m: held off Rachmaninoff by a neck after a driving finish to eight-runner Ribero Stakes at Doncaster in September: had plenty to do subsequently: will stay 1m. *R. Price.*

CARRIGBEG PRINCE 3 ch.c. Roll of Honour 130–Irish Gem (Princely Gift **75** 137) [1975 7g 1976 16f³ 16g⁴ 16.1d³ 16f² 16f* 15g⁶] deep-bodied colt: scraped home by a short head from Nation Wide in 11-runner maiden race at Nottingham in June: had little chance at weights when well beaten on only subsequent outing (September): stays very well: appears to act on any going. *W. Elsey.*

CARRIGEEN 2 b.f. Royalty 130–Ennis Rock 97 (Ennis 128) [1976 7d 8s] **72 p** well-made, good sort: half-sister to four winners, including very useful 1974 2-y-o Good News (by Crooner): dam won over 5f at 2 yrs: quite prominent on both outings, finishing eighth of 30 to Guama in maiden event at Newbury in September and seventh of 19 to Nordman in similar race at Sandown the following month. *R. Hern.*

CARTRIDGE SPEED 3 b.c. Vitriolic–Solid Thought (Solidarity) [1975 5g **60** 5.1f⁶ 5g 7g³ 8g* 7fg² 1976 12.2g 10.4s 8d⁴ 8.2g⁵ 8s⁵ 7.2fg 8fg²] smallish American-bred colt: fair handicapper at his best but deteriorated in 1976 and raced in sellers on last two outings: best form at 7f and 1m and ran moderately over longer distances: possibly not at his best on soft ground. *Denys Smith.*

CARTWRIGHT 7 b.g. Ribotlight 100–May Wyne (Dogger Bank 122) [1976 **65** 14g² 15.5s] ex-New Zealand gelding: won two races over 10.5f as a 4-y-o: having first outing on flat in this country, made a lot of running when 2 lengths second of 13 to Ringed Aureole in amateur riders race at Goodwood in September: well beaten in similar event at Folkestone the following month: stays 1¾m: promising jumper. *S. Mellor.*

CARVERS CORAH 2 br.f. Easter Island 101–Marieran (Pappatea 114) [1976 **—** 5g 6fg 8f 7f] bad plater. *P. Felgate.*

CASAQUE NOIRE 3 ch.f. Welsh Pageant 132–Runzara 100 (Runnymede 123) **81** [1975 5fg 5fg* 5fg³ 5f 6g 6g 1976 5f⁴ 5g⁵ 6g] neat filly: good fourth to Minstrel in handicap at Newbury in April, best effort: stays 6f: not seen out after June. *J. Winter.*

CASARRI 2 b.c. Upper Case–Arrival 102 (Henry the Seventh 125) [1976 5g **72** 6g 6fg 6g³ 7d 7g⁵ 7s² 7v] fair sort: quite a useful plater: will probably stay 1¼m: best form in blinkers. *W. Holden.*

CASERTA 2 b.f. Royal Palace 131–Jibuti 111 (Djebe) [1976 6fg] half-sister to **—** five winners, notably very useful middle-distance winner Cesarea (by Raeburn II): dam very useful from 1m to 1¼m: fell and broke a leg at Salisbury in September and had to be destroyed. *P. Walwyn.*

CASE STUDY 3 b.c. Reliance II 137–Kaiserin (Carapalida) [1975 N.R. 1976 **78** 10s 15.5s⁶ 12.5v³] lengthy colt: third reported foal: half-brother to winning stayers by Shantung and Royal Palace: dam won five races in Argentina and was placed in Argentinian 1,000 Guineas and Oaks: close-up third to Chartered Course in maiden race at Teesside in October: stays 1½m. *R. Price.*

CASINO BOY 2 b.c. Levanter 121–Gleann Buidhe (Pampered King 121) **110** [1976 6g⁶ 6g* 6fg³ 7s³ 6s*] strong, well-grown colt: half-brother to a winning 2-y-o plater by Harken: 3,600 gns yearling: dam won twice over hurdles: won minor event at Lingfield in August (by 3 lengths from Haighall) and nursery at Newmarket in October: held on really well when pressed when winning latter event in a very close finish by a neck from Freight Forwarder: third in between in Acomb Stakes at York (beaten 3 lengths by Padroug) and £4,400 nursery at Lingfield (beaten 4½ lengths by Lady Constance): will stay 1¼m: probably acts on any going. *R. Price.*

CASINO GRANDE 3 b.g. So Blessed 130–Moghari 78 (Djebe) [1975 6f 6g 6g **60** 7g 1976 9d 8h 10.6d⁴ 10.6d⁵ 9fg 7.2fg² 7fg⁴ 7f³ 8f⁶ 8d³] neat, strong gelding:

selling handicapper: best form at up to 1m but probably stays 1¼m: wears blinkers. *J. Etherington.*

CASONA 2 ch.f. Upper Case–Never Say No 105 (Never Say Die 137) [1976 10v] half-sister to two winners here and abroad, including very useful 1969 2-y-o Sayes (by Sing Sing): 760 gns yearling: dam stayed 1¼m: behind in maiden race won by Morning Lee at Nottingham in October. *P. Cole.* —

CASPARDALE 5 ch.g. Frankincense 120–Wasdale 97 (Psidium 130) [1974 7g³ 10.8g⁴ 8g³ 7d 12.2g* 12.3d² 14d 12s² 1975 11.7f 12f⁴ 12f⁴ 12.2g* 12.2g 1976 15.8g⁵ 12d* 12f] attractive, well-made gelding: won handicap at Edinburgh in April: best form at up to 1½m: needs some give in the ground to be seen to best advantage: has been tried in blinkers: suited by front-running tactics: inconsistent. *G. Richards.* 66

CASSIO 4 ch.c. Continuation 120–Candlelight 98 (Gratitude 130) [1974 5fg 7v 7s 8s 7s 6s⁴ 1975 6s² 6s² 6s⁵ 6fg 7fg³ 7f⁴ 8h* 7f² 8g 8.2f 8g 8.3fg 6g³ 6f 1976 8fg 8g] plater: showed no form in 1976: stays 1m well: acts on any going: wears blinkers: sold 300 gns Newmarket Autumn Sales. *K. Ivory.* —

CASTLE CULLEN 2 b.f. Polyfoto 124–Pu-Ush 66 (Galivanter 131) [1976 5f 7f*] sister to a poor animal: 500 gns yearling: dam, a plater, stayed 1¼m: 33/1 and apprentice ridden, made all when winning 10-runner seller at Catterick in July (no bid): will stay 1m. *L. Shedden.* 56

CASTLE IN SPAIN 3 b.g. Royal Palace 131–Costmary 108 (Grey Sovereign 128 §) [1975 7g 8f³ 8g 7.2v⁴ 1976 12fg 11s* 12.3fg⁴ 15.8f⁶ 16v³ 16s³ 16v³] well-grown gelding: quite a moderate handicapper: won maiden race at Ayr in May by 1½ lengths from Glenturk: runs as though he now needs extreme distances: best form with some give in the ground: ran creditably in blinkers on final outing: sweated up and ran badly on fourth start. *S. Hall.* 71

CATALPA 3 b.f. Reform 132–Ostrya 116 (Hornbeam 130) [1975 6g⁴ 7.2fg² 7v* 7g² 1976 10fg³ 10g 12f* 12fg² 14.6g] 115
Catalpa's success in the Ribblesdale Stakes at Royal Ascot was about as unexpected as that of her dam Ostrya in the race thirteen years before. Nothing Catalpa had achieved suggested that she was up to beating Gilding, Countess

Ribblesdale Stakes, Ascot—Catalpa wins unchallenged from Roses for the Star

Eileen or My Fair Niece, never mind the red-hot favourite Roses for the Star, and she started at 16/1. What's more, Catalpa's owner had been contemplating running her instead in a minor race at Warwick! Surprisingly, Catalpa went ahead before the home turn and opened up a substantial lead which none of her six rivals seriously threatened, and at the line she had four lengths to spare over Roses for the Star, with My Fair Niece a similar distance away third. Catalpa had one other performance to rank with her Ribblesdale victory; that was on her next outing when she lost a desperate battle with Centrocon, to whom she was conceding 5 lb, in the Lancashire Oaks at Haydock in July. By the time of her only subsequent race, the Park Hill Stakes at Doncaster in September, Catalpa had trained off; at least that's what her performance suggested. After causing trouble at the start she trailed in the best part of twenty lengths behind African Dancer whom she'd beaten in the Lancashire Oaks.

Catalpa (b.f. 1973)	Reform (b 1964)	Pall Mall (ch 1955)	Palestine / Malapert
		Country House (br 1955)	Vieux Manoir / Miss Coventry
	Ostrya (b 1960)	Hornbeam (ch 1953)	Hyperion / Thicket
		Malcolmia (b 1952)	Sayani / Silvery Moon

Catalpa's dam Ostrya was very lightly raced. Apart from winning the Ribblesdale she ran second to Outcrop in the Park Hill Stakes. At stud Ostrya has produced a collection of minor winners, including a sister to Catalpa called Rosyta who won over a mile and a half. Ostrya's most notable relative is her half-brother Oncidium (by Alcide), winner of the Jockey Club Cup and the Coronation Cup and an outstandingly successful stallion in Australasia. Catalpa, a leggy filly, stayed a mile and a half really well and acted on any going. She has been retired, and visits Habitat. *H. Cecil.*

CATAMARAN 4 ch.f. Lauso–Oceania (Aureole 132) [1974 N.R. 1975 10fg 11g 14fg 13f 16g 12g⁵ 12v* 1976 16f⁵ 16g⁵ 14g 16f⁶ 17.1s] close-coupled filly: moderate performer (rated 82) at 3 yrs: mainly disappointing in 1976: suited by a good test of stamina: acts on heavy going: suitable mount for an apprentice: fell third start and was pulled up final appearance. *W. Wightman.* —

CATCH ME UP 3 ro.c. Decoy Boy 129–Shall Do (Passenger 122 or Derring-Do 131) [1975 6f 5g 5g³ 6g³ 5f⁶ 5f 5d 7g 5fg 1976 5t⁴ 6d* 5f* 6f⁵ 7fg² 6h⁵ 5fg 6v³ 5s 6v 6s] small, sturdy colt: plater: winner at Ripon and Redcar in June: sold out of J. Carr's stable 1,350 gns on latter course: well beaten in better company on last three outings: effective at 5f to 7f: appears to act on any going: sometimes wore blinkers at 2 yrs but did not wear them in 1976: reluctant to go to start on seventh appearance and bolted on way to post on penultimate start. *S. Nesbitt.* 60

CATCHWORD 2 b.f. Mountain Call 125–Ensnarer (Bold Ruler) [1976 5s⁶ 5g⁴ 6fg⁴ 7fg⁴ 7g⁶ 7.2f³ 7fg 8fg² 8s² 8g 8v*] neat filly: first foal: 940 gns yearling: dam unraced daughter of top 1967 Brazilian filly Embuche: won nursery at Teesside in October by 1½ lengths from Jason, the pair finishing clear: suited by 1m and will probably stay further: acts on any going: used to wear blinkers. *W. Elsey.* 82

CATHERINE STREET 3 b.f. Pall Mall 132 Yesterday 83 (Sayajirao 132) [1975 N.R. 1976 8fg 8fg 10fg 10s] well-made filly: second living foal: dam stayed 1½m: no worthwhile form in maiden races: sold 525 gns Ascot November Sales. *B. Swift.* —

CATHMARIA 2 ch.f. Great Heron 127–Macaw 85 (Narrator 127) [1976 6v*] second foal: dam won over 1m and is daughter of Yorkshire Oaks winner Sea Parrot: won 20-runner seller at Haydock in October by 2½ lengths from Northgate Lass: bought in 1,950 gns afterwards: will stay 1¼m: capable of holding her own in better company. *R. E. Peacock.* 75 p

CATILINE 2 b.c. Native Prince–Kesh 104 (Tamerlane 128) [1976 5g 6fg* 7g* 6fg⁴ 7g] big, well-made colt: half-brother to fairly useful 1¼m to 13f winner Irish Word (by Worden II): dam won over 5f and 6f at 2 yrs: won maiden race at Salisbury in June and quickened well to lead in final furlong when beating Our Jimmy a length in eight-runner Donnington Castle Stakes at Newbury the following month: fair fourth of five to J. O. Tobin in Richmond Stakes at Goodwood later in July, better subsequent effort: will stay 1m. *R. Hern.* 97

CATSPOINT 4 br.f. Murrayfield 119–Crystal Belle (Pandofell 132) [1974 N.R. —
1975 6s⁵ 8v 7d⁶ 6fg 1976 12fg] small filly: poor plater: should stay at least
1¼m. *R. Hannon.*

CAVALIER'S BLUSH 3 ch.f. King's Troop 118–Buff Beauty 92 (Mossborough **75**
126) [1975 6g 6f⁵ 7g 1976 12fg⁴ 10.1f⁴ 13fg² 14f* 12f³ 13s³ 16s² 16v² 16v*]
modest performer: won minor event at Yarmouth in August and handicap at
Lingfield in November, latter by 2 lengths from Nation Wide: suited by a good
test of stamina: acts on any going: consistent. *T. Waugh.*

CAVALRY QUEEN 2 ch.f. Queen's Hussar 124–High Corinda 85 (High Treason —
126) [1976 5g] lengthy, lightly-made filly: second foal: dam won over 5f at
2 yrs: got loose prior to start and then missed break when in rear in maiden race
won by Faridetta at Haydock in May, only outing: sold 240 gns Ballsbridge
December Sales. *E. Cousins.*

CAVEWOMAN 2 b.f. Caliban 123–Beauklairon (Klairon 131) [1976 9d² 10v] **72**
third foal: dam showed only poor form: 1½ lengths second of nine to Saratoga
Kid in maiden race at Wolverhampton in October, better effort: should stay
1¼m. *Hbt Jones.*

CAWSTON'S CLOWN 2 b.c. Comedy Star 121–Cawston's Pride 131 (Con Brio **110**
121) [1976 5g⁴ 5g* 5d* 6f* 6fg⁵ 5d⁶]
    The standard of racing for older horses at Royal Ascot is probably as high
now as it has always been, but it is becoming increasingly apparent that the
quality of two-year-old drawn to the meeting is steadily on the decline. This
is particularly so in the case of the Coventry Stakes. Recent winners of the
Coventry Stakes—Perdu, Doleswood, Whip It Quick and Galway Bay, to name
those successful in the race from 1972 to 1975—do not begin to compare with
the cracking good horses—Rock Sand, The Tetrarch, Diadem, Fairway, Tudor
Minstrel and Palestine, for example—who have won it over the years, and
Cawston's Clown, the 1976 Coventry Stakes winner, is no-one's idea of a tip-top
two-year-old. Nebbiolo beat him by twelve lengths in the Gimcrack Stakes
at York, and Mandrake Major by ten lengths in the Flying Childers Stakes at
Doncaster. Admittedly Cawston's Clown might not have been at his best on
either occasion following a two-month absence with the cough, but even his
performance in the Coventry Stakes does not speak all that highly for him,
seeing that it was only by a head that he held on to beat Lordedaw, an Irish
colt destined to lose five races before winning a nursery at Naas.
    But although Cawston's Clown was no match for the top two-year-olds,
and although he is a moderate horse as Coventry Stakes winners go, he was a
speedy colt early on in the season. Six lengths was the verdict in his favour

*Coventry Stakes, Ascot—Cawston's Clown (far side) leads throughout and resists
the challenge of Lordedaw. The third horse is And Behold*

when he won the Little John Maiden Stakes at Nottingham in April on his second appearance, and five lengths the distance by which he won when [he smashed up a big field in the Tattersall's Yorkshire Stakes at York a month later. On the strength of these performances, Cawston's Clown started third favourite at Ascot, and, after leading from the start, he held on bravely as Lordedaw came at him in the last furlong. There wasn't an ounce left in him at the finish.

Cawston's Clown (b.c. 1974)	Comedy Star (b 1968)	Tom Fool (b 1949)	Menow
			Gaga
		Latin Walk (br 1960)	Roman Tread
			Stall Walker
	Cawston's Pride (ch 1968)	Con Brio (ch 1961)	Ribot
			Petronella
		Cawston Tower (gr 1956)	Maharaj Kumar
			Silver Ribbon

Cawston's Clown's hard race in the Coventry, coupled with the fact that he did not show his form afterwards, raises the possibility that he might never again be so good as he was in his early days as a two-year-old. His dam, the fastest two-year-old filly of 1970, won the One Thousand Guineas Trial on her reappearance but was taken out of training after refusing to start in the King's Stand Stakes at Royal Ascot: she died from a twisted gut in the spring of 1976. Her 1976 yearling, a brother to Cawston's Clown, was sold for 75,000 dollars at Saratoga. Should Cawston's Clown, who cost 7,200 guineas as a yearling and is a half-brother to Katie May, regain his form, we would think it unlikely that he would be effective beyond seven furlongs. He appears to act on any going. *N. Adam.*

CEDAR EMERALD 2 b.c. Green God 128–Parkhurst (Sing Sing 134) [1976 5fg⁶ 5g 5s 7fg 6g* 6g* 7d] strong, good-bodied colt: third foal: 1,700 gns yearling: dam never ran: made all to win seller at Lingfield in August (no bid) and nursery at Warwick later same month: not certain to stay 7f: has worn bandages: sold to M. Tate 800 gns Ascot November Sales. *J. Winter.* **84**

CEDAR GRANGE 2 b.c. Mansingh 120–Evendo 83 (Derring-Do 131) [1976 5g 5f 5fg 5v*] second foal: dam showed ability at 2 yrs but failed to train on: having first run for three months, won all-aged event at Nottingham in October by 5 lengths from Elusive Character: will stay 6f: acts on heavy ground: reared up in stalls and was withdrawn under orders on third outing. *C. Bewicke.* **94**

CELEBRATION DAY 2 b.g. Upper Case–Elizabeth of York 66 (Henry the Seventh 125) [1976 5fg 6d⁵ 7s] second foal: 700 gns yearling: dam won over 7f: apprentice ridden when 10 lengths fifth of 24 to Mint Condition in seller at Windsor in September, best effort: should stay at least 7f. *J. Hill.* **50**

CELESTIAL GEM 2 ch.c. Gulf Pearl 117–Purple Goddess 69 (Red God 128 §) [1976 6g⁶] neat colt: first foal: 6,600 gns yearling: dam placed over 5f at 2 yrs: 9/1, made little show when remote sixth of 10 to Sunfish in maiden race at Newbury in July, only outing. *R. Price.*

CELESTIAL GIFT 2 ch.f. Divine Gift 127–Trusian (Milesian 125) [1976 5fg 5g* 5fg² 5g³ 5.1fg⁴ 5g 5d] leggy, light-framed filly: half-sister to two minor winners on flat: 800 gns yearling: dam lightly-raced daughter of Irish 1,000 Guineas winner Princess Trudy: won maiden auction event at Kempton in April by neck from Raffingo: ran well in better company afterwards, going down by a neck to Mr Nice Guy at Lingfield, but was well beaten in nurseries under stiff weights on last two outings (off course much of summer beforehand): will stay 6f. *R. Hannon.* **86**

CELTIC GODDESS 2 ch.f. Green God 128–Pop Ash (Celtic Ash) [1976 6g²] first foal: dam of little account: 16/1, ran creditably when 1½ lengths second of 14 to Magenta in newcomers event at Goodwood in September: will stay 7f: should win a race. *C. Brittain.* **83 p**

CELTIC QUERY 3 br.g. Prince de Galles 125–Cantella (Never Say Die 137) [1975 N.R. 1976 10v³ 12h⁴ 14fg⁶ 10v³ 10v⁴] lengthy gelding: bad plater: sold 330 gns Ascot December Sales. *P. Cundell.* **42**

CELTIC SCENE 3 b.c. Irish Ball 127–Red Sea 70 (Zimone) [1975 N.R. 1976 9g⁴ 12d⁵] neat colt: half-brother to two winners, including useful 1m and 1¼m plater Take It Easy (by Great Nephew): 3,000 gns foal: dam won 1¼m seller: well beaten in newcomers event at Wolverhampton in May and maiden race at Ripon in June: sold 620 gns Newmarket July Sales. *W. Wharton.* **—**

CELTIC TRACK 3 ch.g. Track Spare 125–Celtic Flower 93 (Celtic Ash) [1975 6f⁵ 1976 11.7f 11.7f 11g⁵] plating-class maiden. *M. Stevens.* **—**

Lancashire Oaks, Haydock—Centrocon battles on gamely to ward off Catalpa and African Dancer

CENSUS 7 ch.g. Blueroy 93–Moyvite (Alibi II 117) [1974 13f^5 1975 8g 13g — 10.6fg 12.2fg 12.2g 1976 14fg] compact gelding: poor selling handicapper: blinkered last two outings in 1975: usually wears bandages. *F. Muggeridge.*

CENTROCON 3 ch.f. High Line 125–Centro 86 (Vienna 127) [1975 6g 8f* **112** 7.6g^2 1976 10fg^4 10g^2 12g^5 12fg* 12fg^4 14.6g^3] attractive filly: ran well in high-class fillies races and won Lancashire Oaks at Haydock in July by ½ length from Catalpa, leading 3½f out and battling on with great gusto to win all out: in frame in Pretty Polly Stakes at Newmarket, Sandleford Priory Stakes at Newbury (1½ lengths second to Sarania), Yorkshire Oaks at York (just over a length fourth to Sarah Siddons) and Park Hill Stakes at Doncaster (3½ lengths third to African Dancer): good fifth to Pawneese in Epsom Oaks on her other start: stays 1¾m: acts on firm going: occasionally sweats up: very game and genuine. *H. Candy.*

CEPPO 2 b.c. Manacle 123–Nocturnal (Combat 123) [1976 5v^2 5d^5 5f 5s 5f* 5h* **72** 5g 5f^5] quite a moderate colt: successful twice at Hamilton, racing alone when winning seller in July and getting best of a very close finish to a nursery the following month: will stay 6f: best form on a sound surface: wears a hood: suitable mount for a boy. *N. Angus.*

CERAN'S BOY 2 ch.c. Military 112–Ceran (Brocade Slipper 116) [1976 5fg **60** 5.9g 5fg 6g 5f^3 6g 6d] tall colt: quite a modest plater: should be suited by 6f: wears blinkers nowadays. *J. Benstead.*

CERUA 2 b.c. Nashua–Cerisette (My Babu 136) [1976 7g^3 10d^4] American- **88** bred colt: half-brother to 3-y-o Please Turn Over (by Turn-to) and very smart stayer John Cherry (by Stage Door Johnny): dam, placed at 2 yrs, comes from same family as Secretariat: in frame in maiden races at Newmarket in October, finishing 3½ lengths third of 23 to Windy Sea and 5½ lengths fourth of 12 to subsequently-disqualified Gunbad: will stay well. *B. Hills.*

CESARINE 3 b.f. Royal Palace 131–La Paiva 92 (Prince Chevalier) [1975 — N.R. 1976 7f 8g^5 8fg] small, close-coupled filly: half-sister to several winners, notably Brigadier Gerard (by Queen's Hussar): dam effective at 1m to 1¼m: showed some signs of ability, finishing fifth of eight to Katie May in minor event

156

at Sandown in June: will stay middle distances: sweated up first two outings. *H. Candy.*

CESSY 4 ch.f. Burglar 128–Clarabella 94 (Klairon 131) [1974 5f 5s² 5g⁵ 5fg 5d **54** 6v 5v 6s⁶ 5d 1975 6s⁵ 6s⁴ 5s³ 6f⁶ 6fg 6g 1976 6g² 5g² 5s 5s] lengthy filly: sprint plater: ran creditably on first two starts: acts on soft going: usually wears blinkers: retained 520 gns Doncaster Autumn Sales. *A. Doyle.*

C'EST FINI 2 br.g. Another River 89–Fairworth 74 § (Fair Seller 126) [1976 — 5fg 5fg] light-framed gelding: in rear in 17-runner sellers at Ripon in August and Edinburgh in September. *W. A. Stephenson.*

CESTREFELD 2 gr.f. Capistrano 120–Brig O'Doon 57 (Shantung 132) [1976 **94** 5f⁵ 5s⁵ 5d* 7f⁴ 7fg⁵ 7g³ 6v*] rather leggy filly: half-sister to 3-y-o What a Find (by Hul a Hul), a winner at up to 1¼m: 200 gns yearling: dam poor maiden: won maiden auction event at Redcar in May and bettered that effort when staying on to win nursery at Leicester in October by ¾ length from Sylvia's Dream: will stay 1m: suited by some give in the ground and goes particularly well on heavy. *S. Hall.*

CHADACRE 4 ch.g. St Chad 120–Nuage Rouge 93 (Nimbus 130) [1974 6s — 1975 6s⁵ 9s⁴ 8s 6g 8.7s 7.5s³ 10s² 9s 1976 12g] ex-Irish gelding: moderate maiden: stays 1¼m: acts on soft going. *R. E. Peacock.*

CHADFORTH 4 b.g. St Chad 120–Heather Lane (Tamerlane 128) [1974 6s — 1975 8s⁵ 8g⁶ 11g 7f⁶ 7g⁵ 1976 8f] lengthy gelding: plater: stays 1m: acts on firm going. *T. Kersey.*

CHADLEIGH 9 b.g. Alcide 136–Red Chorus 103 (Chanteur II 135) [1974 — 16fg⁶ 16f⁴ 16g⁶ 18fg* 17.7f* 20g⁵ 16g² 16g⁴ 1975 13g 17.7fg 1976 17.7f 15.8g⁴ 22.2f⁵ 16.1fg⁶] one-time fair staying handicapper: no worthwhile form since 1974: needs long distances: has won on easy ground but is best served by a sound surface: sold 575 gns Ascot August Sales. *W. Wharton.*

CHAD'S HOUR 2 b.f. St Chad 120–Ebnal Hour (Tacitus 124) [1976 5s³ 5f 5f] **59** light-framed filly: only poor form, including in a seller. *P. Rohan.*

CHADVILLE 3 b.g. St Chad 120–Tail Oats (Vilmoray 126) [1975 5d 5g 8fg — 8.2g 1976 10f 12f⁶ 12.2d] of no account: sold 300 gns Doncaster June Sales. *F. Carr.*

CHAIN OF REASONING 2 b.c. Hail to Reason–Daisy Chain 103 (Darius 129) **94** [1976 5fg² 5fg² 6fg² 5g² 7fg* 7g] big, good-looking American-bred colt: particularly nice, easy mover: half-brother to French 6f to 1m winner Hampton Court (by Tudor Melody) and 3-y-o 1m winner Ground Work (by Graustark): dam won at 1m: made all when winning 11-runner maiden race at Chester in September by 6 lengths from Kolyma: second on all previous outings, coming up against a useful animal each time: will be suited by 1m+: wears blinkers nowadays and gave strong impression that he was none too interested in racing on final outing. *R. Hern.*

CHALLONER 8 ch.g. Ron 103–Wunownlee (Rondo II 81) [1974 N.R. 1975 **54** N.R. 1976 12s⁵ 8g⁵ 8g⁵ 7fg⁶ 10fg³ 15.5s⁴ 12.2s] poor maiden: 5½ lengths third of 16 to Deep River in handicap at Leicester in September (apprentice ridden), easily best effort: best form at 1¼m. *J. Webber.*

CHALLOW 3 br.f. My Swallow 134–Not for Portia 68 (King's Bench 132) — [1975 5f 6f⁶ 8f⁶ 8g 8v 1976 12.2f 16fg 12.2fg 13.4fg 13g 17.7f⁶ 12g 9.4h² 11.1g² 12fg 12.2s⁵ 12v] lengthy filly: plating-class maiden: probably stays 11f but is not certain to stay further. *R. Hollinshead.*

CHAMBER MAID 2 b.f. Don II 123–Crown Passage 90 (Pall Mall 132) [1976 **99** 5g⁵ 5f 5fg³ 5fg 5g⁵ 5fg*] neat, early sort: half-sister to three winners, including fairly useful 1973 2-y-o 5f winner Kingly Street (by Native Prince): 2,000 gns yearling: dam won over 5f at 2 yrs: ran by far her best race when winning 14-runner event at Windsor in June by wide margin from Virginia Lad: not seen out again: should stay 6f: wears blinkers. *F. J. Houghton.*

CHAMPAGNE WILLIE 2 b.c. The Brianstan 128–Sparkling Jewel (Faberge II **102** 121) [1976 6fg⁴ 6g² 6fg² 6f* 6d⁵] well-grown, lengthy, long-striding colt: first produce: 520 gns foal, resold 1,200 gns yearling: dam of little account: made all when easily disposing of four moderate animals in maiden race at Yarmouth in August: also ran well in much better company, including when 1½ lengths second to Town and Country in Hyperion Stakes at Ascot and when going down by only a neck to sole-opponent King Elect in £1,900 event at Newmarket: stays 6f: headstrong and is not an easy ride. *N. Callaghan.*

CHANCE BELLE 3 ch.f. Foggy Bell 108–Chancer 78 (Chamier 128) [1975 N.R. 85
1976 12g⁵ 12v* 12v*] well-grown filly: first produce: 780 gns foal, resold 600 gns
2-y-o: dam, a winner at up to 1¾m on Flat, showed useful form over hurdles and
fences: won maiden race at Leicester in October and minor event at Lingfield in
November: had her field well strung out when beating Contarini Fleming by
7 lengths on latter course: will stay further than 1½m: acts on heavy going: ridden
by apprentice J. Bleasdale when successful. *R. Jarvis.*

CHANCEL 2 b.c. Great Nephew 126–Law and Impulse 104 (Roan Rocket 128) 69
[1976 5g⁶ 7v] close-coupled colt: second foal: half-brother to useful 1974 2-y-o
Cardinal Wolsey (by Henry the Seventh), subsequently a winner in Spain and
over 1¼m in France: dam won over 5f at 2 yrs: showed a little ability in maiden
races at Newbury in May and Leicester in October: will stay 1m. *H. Candy.*

CHANDA 3 br.c. Tamerlane 128–Romula (Romulus 129) [1975 5s⁴ 5f 6f* 6h⁴ 57
7f⁴ 7f⁵ 7f⁵ 7g 8fg⁴ 7d* 1976 12.2g⁵ 12f³ 12g 12s⁴ 12.2d³ 13g⁵ 12f* 13.8f³] small
colt: rated 79 at 2 yrs but is only really a modest plater nowadays: won at
Haydock in July (no bid): stays 1¾m: acts on any going: wears blinkers nowadays: sold 575 gns Ascot September Sales. *J Vickers.*

CHANGING ERA 3 b.g. Reform 132–Ever Swinging 104 (Immortality) [1975 —
6g 1976 8g] sturdy gelding: behind in maiden races: backward and blinkered
on only outing in 1976. *J. Nelson.*

CHANTINGHALL 3 b.c. Sweet Story 122–Make Believe 93 (Fairey Fulmar 124) —
[1975 7g 7fg 8.2f 8.2g 1976 11f 12f⁴ 16fg³ 9g 16g 13.8g] of little account:
pulled up lame final outing. *L. Docker.*

CHANTRO 6 b.h. Sing Sing 134–Tropical Kit 87 (Umidwar) [1974 5fg⁵ 6fg⁴ 76
6f* 6fg⁶ 6f* 6fg² 5f² 6g 5fg 6s 6s 1975 6g⁵ 5f 6fg² 6g 6g³ 6g⁵ 6g* 6g 6fg 6f 6f
1976 6g⁶ 7f⁵ 6g 6fg] quite a useful handicapper (rated 91) at 5 yrs: disappointing
form in 1976: stays 6f: best suited by top-of-the-ground conditions: has run
creditably in blinkers but does at least as well without them: suitable mount
for an apprentice: needs things all his own way: has won five times at Ripon.
J. W. Watts.

CHAPEAU VERT 3 ch.c. Green God 128–Mon Chapeau (High Hat 131) [1975 53
5v 5v 5f 5fg 1976 6f³ 6g⁴ 7fg 6f²] small, sturdy colt: plater: put up a good
effort when head second to Shanghai Lady in non-selling handicap at Windsor in
July on final outing: best at 6f. *T. Marshall.*

CHARENTE 5 ch.g. Charlottown 127–Wind Break 81 (Borealis) [1974 12g —
11.7g⁴ 12f³ 16.9g* 16fg 16d⁶ 16.9s 1975 N.R. 1976 15.8s⁵] short-backed
gelding: quite a moderate handicapper (rated 77) in 1974: tailed off in seller at
Catterick in October, only outing since: very well suited by a good test of stamina:
acts on a firm surface and seems unsuited by a soft one: used to wear blinkers but
didn't at Catterick. *F. Yardley.*

CHARITES 3 ch.f. Red God 128 §–Thetis II (Guersant 129) [1975 5.1f⁴ 5fg —
7g 1976 5fg 6h⁴] small, light-framed filly: sister to top-class sprinter Green
God, but has shown little worthwhile form herself. *I. Walker.*

CHARLES MARTEL 4 ch.c. Charlottown 127–Safety Fast 76 (Abernant 142) 85
[1974 6fg⁵ 6g⁶ 8d 1975 10g* 10g* 10g 12h⁵ 14.8g³ 12g 13g 15s⁵ 14g 1976 12fg²
12f* 12d⁴ 12fg³ 12f* 12f* 12f² 12g³ 14g 10d⁴ 12.2s⁶ 12s] lengthy colt: good
walker and mover: fair performer: successful three times at 4 yrs, including twice
at Folkestone: stays 1¾m: acts on firm going: good mount for an apprentice:
trained by H. Wragg until after seventh outing: sold 2,300 gns Newmarket
Autumn Sales. *P. Cole.*

CHARLEY'S BAIRN 3 br.f. Prince de Galles 125–Scottish Double (Dual 117) 77
[1975 6g⁵ 7fg⁴ 1976 8f³ 8.2f⁴ 8g⁴ 7f⁵ 7g³ 8s⁶] lengthy filly: ran well in handicaps
on fourth and fifth outings, finishing good third to Panorealm at Goodwood in
September: ran moderately on only outing afterwards and is possibly not at her
best on soft ground: will stay 1¼m. *M. Masson.*

CHARLEY'S REVENGE 2 b.c. Runnymede 123–Constance Spry (Gentle Art 102
121) [1976 5fg* 5g* 5f⁴ 5fg² 5d² 6g³ 5f* 6h² 6fg* 6g⁵] smallish, attractive colt:
good walker: half-brother to a minor winner by Sayfar: 2,300 gns yearling: dam
never ran: comfortable winner of maiden race at Newmarket and minor event at
Doncaster early in season and trained on well, adding further successes in well-
contested race at Beverley in June and £2,200 nursery at Newmarket in July:
stays 6f: acts on both a firm and a soft surface: genuine and consistent: good
mount for a boy: exported to U.S.A. *R. Armstrong.*

CHARLIE BATTLE 4 b.g. Le Prince 98–Guerra (Milesian 125) [1974 N.R.   **57**
1975 10.8f 8f 12f   1976 10.1fg* 11.7fg 13.8g* 16f⁵ 16f⁵ 18.1g]   poor handicapper:
winner of seller at Windsor in May and handicap (non-seller) at Catterick the
following month: well beaten afterwards: stays 1¾m: acts on a firm surface. *G.
Blum.*

CHARLIE CLAIRE 2 b.c. The Brianstan 128–Vodwen 71 (Busted 134) [1976   **52**
5g⁴ 5.9g 7h 7.2f 8s]   small colt: only poor form, including in a seller: trained most
of season by B. Hills. *D. Barons.*

CHARLIE HARRY 2 b.f. Gala Performance–Chocolate 69 (Pall Mall 132) [1976   **61**
5g⁶ 5f⁶ 5f⁵ 6f⁶ 6g 5g⁶ 5d 6v 6v⁶ 5s]   small, strong filly: showed a little ability in
varied company, including selling: seems to find 5f too sharp and will stay 7f+:
blinkered eighth and ninth outings: sold 450 gns Doncaster November Sales. *R.
Hollinshead.*

CHARLIE M 4 ch.c. Major Portion 129–Cherry Brandy (Tenerani 135) [1974   **75**
6g⁵ 7d 6s   1975 10.1s 6f* 6f 6g 7g 8fg³ 8.3g³ 7.6g⁶   1976 7fg 10fg*]   lightly-made
colt: quite a moderate handicapper: narrow winner from Lucky Seventeen at
Yarmouth in June: stays 1¼m: possibly needs a sound surface and acts on firm
going: has been tried in blinkers. *M. Masson.*

CHARLIESTRATFORD 8 ch.m. Silver Cloud 121–Chateau Ogilvie 87   —
(Cortachy 107) [1974 N.R.   1975 N.R.   1976 7fg 10h⁶]   of little account nowadays. *R. Keenor.*

CHARLOTTE BEACON 3 b.f. Charlottown 127–Linum 81 (Takawalk II 125)   —
[1975 5v⁶ 5v⁶ 6f⁵ 6fg   1976 10.1fg 10fg⁶ 10.1fg⁶ 16f⁵]   neat filly: poor plater:
sometimes wears blinkers: sold 350 gns Ascot August Sales. *D. Keith.*

CHARLOTTE'S DEN 3 ch.f. Charlottown 127–Denosa 109 (Worden II 129)   **55**
[1975 N.R.   1976 7f 11.7h³ 11.1g³ 13.1s² 12s³]   neat filly: first living foal: dam
stayed at least 1m: showed a little ability in maiden and minor events: will be
well suited by really long distances: trained by J. Tree until after third outing.
P. Cole.

CHARM FAIR 3 b.f. March Past 124–Bridge of Stories 80 (Appian Bridge 111)   —
[1975 5fg³ 5f⁴ 5g⁴ 5h⁴ 7g 6g   1976 7f 6d⁶ 5fg 5f 6f⁵]   strong, workmanlike filly:
little worthwhile form at 3 yrs: should stay 7f: missed break fourth outing and
swerved coming out of stalls on final appearance. *H. Wharton.*

CHARMING WEATHER 2 ch.f. Song 132–In Arcady 92 (Gratitude 130)   **72**
[1976 6g 5s⁴ 5s]   half-sister to a winner abroad: 800 gns yearling: dam won at up
to 1m: showed a little ability in maiden races in the autumn: should stay 6f. *I.
Walker.*

CHARTA PEARL 4 gr.c. Gulf Pearl 117–Magna 107 (Runnymede 123) [1974   **92**
N.R.   1975 5d³ 6v 6fg⁴ 8fg 8g⁵ 7.6f² 7f* 8.3g² 7s* 7g²   1976 8f⁶ 8g* 8f³ 8h³
8.2g³ 7f* 8fg* 8f* 8d* 8v⁵]   big, strong, good-looking colt: fairly useful handicapper: winner five times at 4 yrs, at Lanark, Beverley, Ripon, Thirsk and
Redcar (apprentice race), last four in the space of a month: stays 1m: acts on any
going: bandaged third start: genuine and consistent. *J. Etherington.*

CHARTER BELLE 4 b.f. Runnymede 123–Parbloom (Pardal 130) [1974   **56**
N.R.   1975 5g 5.3g 5.9fg 7s⁴ 8g⁴ 6d   1976 6g 8f³ 6f⁵ 8.2d³ 10v⁴]   workmanlike
filly: quite a modest plater: stays 1m but has yet to show she gets further: acts on
any going. *P. Robinson.*

CHARTERED COURSE 3 b.g. Charlottown 127–Stellaria 75 (Robert Barker   **79**
125) [1975 6g⁵ 7.2g   1976 12fg 12.3f⁵ 10h⁶ 9v² 12.5v* 10s*]   rangy gelding:
showed vastly improved form when racing on very soft ground at the back-end
and won maiden race and minor event at Teesside: beat Wolver Valley 3 lengths
in latter race in November: stays 1½m well. *M. W. Easterby.*

CHARTERED LADY 2 b.f. Runnymede 123–Vazzeda (Klairon 131) [1976   **89**
5fg⁵ 5d⁶ 6g² 6s* 7.2v]   lightly-made filly: half-sister to a winner in Italy: 320 gns
foal: dam never ran: showed improved form when raced at 6f and won maiden
race at Chepstow in October by 1½ lengths from So Cutting: had very stiff task in
nursery on only subsequent outing: should stay 7f: acts on soft going. *D. Keith.*

CHARTERMEDE 3 b.c. Runnymede 123–Flying Feathers 98 (Pardal 130)   **70**
[1975 6g 8.2g⁵   1976 8v² 9d⁶ 8.2d³ 8.2g* 8f⁴ 8.2f⁵ 10fg⁵ 8.2h³ 8.2h⁴ 8s]   leggy
colt: won maiden race at Hamilton in June by 1½ lengths from Princess Modesty:
stays 1m (ran poorly when tried at 1¼m): acts on any going. *W. Gray.*

CHARTWIN 3 b.f. Richboy 117–Darwin Tulip (Campaign 106 or Pirate King   —
129) [1975 N.R.   1976 6v 7g 8fg]   backward when behind in northern maiden
races: blinkered and started slowly first time out. *A. Balding.*

CHARVILLE 5 b.m. Town Crier 119–Charline 93 (Charlottesville 135) [1974 **71**
6g 7g 7g 8.2g² 8g* 12.2g* 11g⁴ 11.7g³ 12d 10v⁶ 10s² 12v⁵ 1975 10.8d⁴ 10g³ 10g⁴
12fg² 12h² 15f³ 12f² 11.7fg⁴ 11.7f⁵ 10g 13.1f² 12fg³ 10.2g 1976 10fg* 12.2f⁴
12f² 10f⁴ 10f* 10f* 10f* 10.8h² 10h⁴ 10h* 10.2f² 10f²] a really tough mare
who won five handicaps in 1976, including three at Nottingham: best form at up
to 1½m: acts on any going: wears blinkers: ideal mount for a boy: most game,
genuine and consistent. *P. Cundell.*

CHAS SAWYER 4 b.c. Pall Mall 132–Distant Horizon 92 (Nimbus130) [1974 **96**
5fg 6fg 1975 8g⁶ 10d³ 10fg* 10fg³ 12f² 12g* 1976 12fg² 12fg⁶] neat colt:
fairly useful handicapper: good second to Alverton at York in June on reappearance: finished very sore when well-beaten sixth of eight to Peaceful
in Old Newton Cup at Haydock the following month on only other outing:
stays 1½m: acts on firm going: genuine and consistent: bandaged both outings,
and is difficult to train. *G. Pritchard-Gordon.*

CHASSE 2 b.f. Mountain Call 125–Kentucky Blues 83 (Royal Record II) [1976 —
5s 5s 5.9s 6d] third foal: half-sister to 3-y-o middle-distance winner Shuwaiman
(by Alcide): dam showed ability over sprint distances at 2 yrs: little worthwhile
form in maiden races. *R. Boss.*

CHASSEUR 4 br.g. Queen's Hussar 124–First Huntress 64 (Primera 131) [1974 **62**
8d 1975 8g 7fg⁴ 10g 8g⁶ 8.2s* 8g³ 10g² 1976 8f⁵ 12g² 12d 10.6d³ 12.2s 12s⁴
12v⁴] leggy gelding: poor handicapper nowadays: stays 1½m: seems to act
on any going: sold 3,700 gns Doncaster November Sales. *R. Jarvis.*

CHATILLON 3 gr.g. Runnymede 123–Florecilla 90 (Matador 131) [1975 5v⁶
5s³ 5g³ 6d 6g 7s 1976 10.8f 7fg] probably of little account nowadays. *M.
Tate.*

CHAYZE 2 br.f. Seaepic 100–River Scene (Coronation Year 124) [1976 5fg
5g 5s 5.9s 6s 6s 5v] fourth foal: dam of no account: in rear in maiden races
and an all-aged event. *K. Bridgwater.*

CHEBBIE 3 ch.g. Chebs Lad 120–Earall (Khalkis 127) [1975 N.R. 1976 **83**
12d³ 15f³ 12fg* 12f⁴ 12f* 12f² 12.2g⁴] second foal: half-brother to Lochranza
(by Highland Melody), a prolific winner from 5f to 13f: dam tailed off on both
outings: in frame on all outings and won minor event at Ripon in July and handicap at Beverley the following month, latter by 3 lengths from Pass the Port:
best form at 1½m: acts on firm going: consistent. *J. Fitzgerald.*

CHEBS BOW 2 b.f. Chebs Lad 120–Elf's Bow (Elf Arrow 117) [1976 5g —
6h] first foal: dam of little account: no worthwhile form in maiden races at
Catterick in June and Carlisle in July. *G. Richards.*

CHEB'S HONOUR 3 ch.f. Chebs Lad 120–Queens Evidence 95 (King's Bench
132) [1975 5.1f 5g 5fg³ 5g 5g 5.1g² 6g 5fg⁵ 5v³ 1976 7fg 6f] tall filly: fairly
useful plater at 2 yrs: little worthwhile form in better company in first part of
1976: should stay 1m: probably acts on any going: slowly away when tried
in blinkers on second outing in 1975. *W. Holden.*

CHEBS SONG 2 b.f. Chebs Lad 120–Song of May 79 (Sing Sing 134) [1976 —
5fg 5fg 5fg] leggy, unfurnished, unattractive filly: poor plater: not seen out
after May. *J. Carr.*

CHEDDAR PINK 3 ch.f. Olden Times–Dianthus (Your Host) [1975 6g 6f³ **69**
7g⁴ 6g⁵ 1976 10f³ 10f⁵] compact American-bred filly: showed moderate form
at 2 yrs: put up better effort in 1976 on first outing: stays 1¼m: not seen out
after May. *B. Hills.*

CHEERING ROCKET 2 b.f. Cratloe Rocket 95–Cheering Crowds 75 (Entente —
Cordiale 119) [1976 5fg⁴ 5f⁶ 5f⁶ 7g] bad plater. *M. Bradley.*

CHEERS 4 b.g. Be Friendly 130–No Court (Court Harwell 130) [1974 6g 8.2s —
8s³ 1975 N.R. 1976 9g 12.5h³ 12s 10.2fg 8f] well-grown gelding: poor maiden:
stays 1m but has yet to show he stays 1½m: sweating and blinkered on second
start: sold 580 gns Doncaster August Sales. *A. Bacon.*

CHELLA 2 b.f. March Past 124–Nimble Beauty 86 (Nimbus 130) [1976 5.1f⁵ **44**
6f 6f⁴ 7g⁴ 8fg] leggy filly: bad plater. *G. Blum.*

CHELTENHAM 3 ch.f. Connaught 130–Look Here 93 (Ratification 129) [1975 **55**
7fg 8f 1976 12f⁵ 12g⁴ 12fg⁵ 16f⁴ 13.1f 16s] rangy filly: plating-class maiden:
suited by a test of stamina. *P. Mitchell.*

CHEMIN DE FER 3 br.c. Mummy's Pet 125–Monte Carlo 78 (Pandofell 132) **95**
[1975 5d 5f⁴ 5g³ 5f⁵ 6fg³ 6fg⁶ 5g⁴ 5g⁴ 1976 10.8f* 10.8f⁴ 8g* 8fg³ 7fg⁴ 10g*

10.6g* 10fg⁴ 10.5g³ 10g² 10.5v] well-made colt: had a good season and won maiden race at Warwick and handicaps at Salisbury, Nottingham and Haydock: came from behind and quickened well to beat Aliante decisively by 1½ lengths in valuable Harvey Jones Handicap on last-named course in August: effective at 1m and will probably stay 1½m: acts on firm going and ran well below his best on heavy on final outing: has worn blinkers but does better without: usually held up. *F. Maxwell.*

CHENNEL LANE 2 b.c. Caerdeon 98–Glebe 83 (Tacitus 124) [1976 5fg   **89**
5g 6d 7s⁵ 7v* 6s] first foal: dam who won over 2m at 4 yrs, is half-sister to high-class filly Bringley: fair performer: won weakly-contested maiden race at Leicester in October driven out by 1½ lengths from Muston Copse: will stay 1½m: acts on heavy going: suitable mount for an apprentice. *W. Holden.*

CHENNEY GIRL 3 b.f. Prince de Galles 125–Naval Patrol 105 (Blue Peter)   —
[1975 N.R. 1976 9fg³ 14fg⁶] leggy, sparely-made, unfurnished filly: half-sister to seven winners, including very useful 6f or 7f handicapper Air Patrol (by King's Bench) and quite useful stayer Sea Robber (by Pirate King): dam won at up to 1¼m: little worthwhile form in newcomers event at Wolverhampton in April and maiden race at Sandown in June: sweated up badly and was apparently upset in stalls on latter course. *R. Akehurst.*

CHERIE LOVE 2 ch.f. Green God 128–Party Love (Parthia 132) [1976 5fg   **52**
5d 7f 7fg 6f 8f] looks a fair sort but showed little worthwhile form, including in sellers: sold 420 gns Doncaster November Sales. *K. Payne.*

CHERRY CAKE 2 ch.f. Pieces de Galles 125–Angel Cake 66 (Supreme Court   —
135) [1976 5fg⁵ 6h⁵ 7fg⁵ 8v] unfurnished filly: half-sister to four minor winners here and abroad: 2,800 gns foal, resold 3,700 gns yearling: dam stayed 11f: plating-class maiden. *M. W. Easterby.*

CHESSWOOD 3 ch.g. Levanter 121–Regal Princess 73 (Royal Palm 131) [1975   **49**
7f 7g 7g⁶ 7g 8g 6g 1976 8fg 12f⁵ 12.3fg³ 14.7h² 15v⁴] strong gelding: only poor form: evidently suited by a test of stamina: blinkered third and fourth outings. *W. A. Stephenson.*

CHESTERTON 3 br.g. Stupendous–Sandray 99 (Sheshoon 132) [1975 5s 6g⁶   —
1976 10fg 10.5s] strong gelding: little worthwhile form: will stay 1½m: action suggests that give in the ground will suit him best: retained by trainer 500 gns Doncaster June Sales. *M. H. Easterby.*

CHESTNUT WALK 2 ch.f. Weepers Boy 124–Paidfor 58 (Preciptic 122)   —
[1976 6h 7h 7f] second foal: dam won over hurdles: behind in maiden races in the summer: slowly away second outing. *M. McCourt.*

CHEVELLE 2 b.f. Cheval 117–Betty Belle 65 (Dual 117) [1976 5fg] neat   —
filly: second foal: half-sister to a winning plater by Fleece: dam won over 1¼m: missed break when tailed off in maiden race won by Gaelic God at Thirsk in May. *P. Buckley.*

CHEVULGAN 3 b.f. Cheval 117–Nicky's Vulgan (Vulgan 123) [1975 N.R.   —
1976 10.1f 10.1fg⁵ 16f⁵] first foal: dam won 2m bumpers race in Ireland: plating-class maiden. *Miss N. Wilmot.*

CHEYENNE 3 gr.f. Sovereign Path 125–Ardneasken 84 (Right Royal V 135)   **58**
[1975 6fg 6f* 6g⁵ 1976 10d⁵ 10fg⁴ 9fg 8.2h 10v] fairly useful sort and a good walker: sister to very useful middle-distance handicapper Warpath: showed winning form at 2 yrs but was disappointing in 1976, running easily best race on second outing: started slowly when tried in blinkers on penultimate appearance. *S. Hall.*

CHEYENNE QUEEN 2 ch.f. Yellow God 129–Jasamaran § (Vilmorin) [1976   **87**
5g⁵ 5fg* 5fg⁶] big, strong filly: good mover: half-sister to three winners, including useful sprinter Trem Blay (by Sovereign Lord): 6,000 gns yearling: dam ungenerous sister to top-class sprinter Gay Mairi: made all when winning 20-runner maiden race at Newbury in June by 1½ lengths from Bodensee: last of six to Al Stanza in Erroll Stakes at Ascot later in month when giving weight all round: not seen out afterwards: will stay 6f. *Miss A. Sinclair.*

CHICHESTER BIRD 2 gr.c. Birdbrook 110–Fair Marina 93 (Hethersett 134)   **78**
[1976 5fg⁶ 5g² 6f² 7.3d⁵ 8s] rangy colt: good walker: second living produce: brother to 3-y-o 7f seller winner Swift Marina: dam won over 6f as a 2-y-o: quite a moderate maiden: stays 7f but possibly not 1m. *R. Hern.*

CHICO'S SPECIAL 4 br.g. Gala Performance–Big Beauty (Big Game) [1974   —
5fg 5g⁴ 5s³ 5s 5g 5fg³ 6f³ 1975 N.R. 1976 8g] of little account nowadays. *D. Chapman.*

CHIEF EXECUTIVE 2 br.c. Tribal Chief 125–Solly Graham 82 (Romulus 129) —
[1976 6d 5v] strong, useful sort of colt: second foal: dam stayed 1m: behind in
maiden race (last of 25) at Newmarket and all-aged event at Nottingham in
October. *P. Cundell*

CHIEF MARTIAL 3 b.c. Chieftain–Polly Toogood 117 (Darius 129) [1975 5fg⁴ —
1976 7g] strong American-bred colt: only lightly raced but has shown signs
of ability: should stay 1m. *J. Nelson.*

CHIEF SCOUT 6 ch.g. Sheshoon 132–Chief Danger 80 (Primera 131) [1974 —
12fg 16g³ 12g 14g⁵ 14s³ 15.5s 1975 16d 10g 1976 14g³] fair sort: has a
round action: plater: blinkered only appearance in 1976: suited by a good test of
stamina: acts on soft going: sold 640 gns Ascot June Sales. *T. M. Jones.*

CHILLI WILLI 3 b.f. Jukebox 120–Solinda (Soleil II 133) [1975 5s* 5f 6fg 6g⁴ 69
1976 6g 6fg 7g⁵ 8.5fg³ 8fg² 7fg* 8f³ 6g⁵ 7s⁴ 8d⁵] lightly-made filly: fair plater:
bought in 1,550 gns after winning at Newcastle in July: stays 1m: appears to act
on any going: suitable mount for an apprentice: sold 1,900 gns Newmarket
December Sales. *P. Cole.*

CHILTERN RED 3 ch.f. Red God 128 §–Ashton Jane 86 (Gratitude 130) —
[1975 6g 5s⁴ 1976 6fg 7fg 6g 6g⁵] third foal: sister to Red Alert, a high-class
performer at up to 7f, and to useful 5f sprinter Martianess, but showed little
worthwhile form herself: blinkered last two outings. *P. Cundell.*

CHIL THE KITE 4 b.c. Kalydon 122–Dipper 108 (Donore 119) [1974 5fg³ 121
5h³ 7g³ 7g* 8s* 7s 1975 8d* 8.2g⁴ 10fg² 8fg* 10.5d⁵ 8f* 8fg* 8g⁴ 1976 9fg*
8g⁴ 10g² 10f² 10fg⁶ 10fg* 10f² 10d*]
    What a plucky little customer Chil the Kite is! Three hard seasons haven't
dampened his enthusiasm for racing in the slightest, and he has won nine of
his twenty-two races and finished in the frame on ten other occasions. In
Racehorses of 1975 we said that Chil the Kite was capable of giving a good
account of himself in decent company outside handicaps: he didn't take long
to prove us right, winning the Earl of Sefton Stakes at Newmarket in April
on his reappearance. Running on really well up the hill he had two lengths
to spare over Dominion at the line with Orange Bay and Jumping Hill res-

*Peter Hastings Stakes, Newbury—a splendid shot of Chil the Kite
humping top weight to victory*

pectively a further length and a half and three quarters of a length behind. Decent company to say the least! Chil the Kite won two more races. At Ayr in July he took the Land of Burns Stakes by one and a half lengths from Swell Fellow and at Newbury in September he rounded off his season in great style, galloping his rivals into the ground in the Peter Hastings Handicap, winning by two lengths from The Tista who was receiving 24 lb. Although Chil the Kite faced stiff tasks on most of his other appearances, he finished out of the money on only one occasion. He put up a splendid effort to get within one and a half lengths of Anne's Pretender in the Brigadier Gerard Stakes at Sandown in May on his third outing, but in both the Prince of Wales Stakes at Royal Ascot and the Joe Coral Eclipse Stakes at Sandown Chil the Kite was soundly beaten behind Trepan. At Ascot Chil the Kite was promoted to second place (he finished nine and a half lengths back in third) upon the disqualification of Trepan.

Chil the Kite (b.c. 1972)	Kalydon (b 1956)	Alycidon (ch 1945)	Donatello II
			Aurora
		Lackaday (b 1947)	Bobsleigh
			Lackadaisy
	Dipper (b 1959)	Donore (gr 1947)	Fair Trial
			Zobeida
		Lark (b 1952)	Chanteur II
			Laurel

Chil the Kite is by Park Top's sire Kalydon out of Dipper, who was a useful sprinter at her best. Dipper has had several foals to race, including Dipthong (by Acropolis), successful over seven furlongs as a two-year-old. Lark, Dipper's dam, was a good racemare, winner of the Cheshire Oaks and the Cornwallis Stakes, the latter in the days when the race was run over a mile. Chil the Kite, as some of the other good horses in his family including Dipper and Lark, is physically unimposing, perhaps most accurately described as neat. He stays a mile and a quarter and acts on any going. He should do well on the Californian tracks where he has now been sent to race. *B. Hobbs.*

CHINA GOD 3 b.c. Cumshaw 111–White Goddess 65 (Red God 128 §) [1975 6fg 7f 8f 6d* 1976 8.2f 8g2 12d4 11g* 12f 10.8f5 8fg 10.6d6 8.2v4 10v] quite a moderate handicapper: wide-margin winner at Hamilton in June: possibly needs further than 1m and stays 11f: needs an easy surface. *R. Cambidge.* **76 d**

CHINAR TREE 3 b.c. Wolver Hollow 126–Mary Kelly 102 (Kelly 122) [1975 7g 7g 8f3 9g6 8g5 1976 10.1fg 8fg5 8d3 8f 10.4fg2 10f3 10.1fg* 10f4 12.3fg5 8.3d 12v3] attractive, shapely colt: 7-length winner of maiden race at Windsor in August: stays 1¼m and seems to find 1½m too far for him (ran moderately in seller over that trip on final outing): possibly unsuited by heavy ground: sometimes wears blinkers but does just as well without (did not wear them at Windsor): has raced with his tongue tied down. *B. Hanbury.* **68**

CHINA STAR 3 ch.f. Doon 124–Belle Blonde (Kelly 122) [1975 7.6g 1976 12fg 13.1s] fair sort: no sign of ability. *D. Dale.* **—**

CHINA TEA 3 br.f. Round Table–Jan Jessie (Turf Charger) [1975 5fg* 6g6 1976 7.3f5 8fg] neat, attractive American-bred filly: good mover: ran well when 3½ lengths fifth to Rowantree in Fred Darling Stakes at Newbury in April (looked on backward side): seventeenth of 25 to Flying Water in 1,000 Guineas at Newmarket later in month and was not seen out again: should stay at least 1m: acts on firm going: sold 28,000 dollars Keeneland November Sales. *H. Cecil.* **95**

CHINCHILLA 2 b.f. On Your Mark 125–Lintola 101 (Constable 129) [1976 5f 5fg6 6d 6s] strong, shapely filly: half-sister to three minor winners: 4,800 gns yearling: dam won at 5f and stayed 1m: just under 5 lengths seventh of 25 to Caerdeon Line in maiden event at Newmarket in October, third and best effort: will stay 7f. *B. Hanbury.* **80**

CHINESE FALCON 3 ch.f. Skymaster 126–Oriental Touch (Parthia 132) [1975 5v 5s6 5g 7g6 7g4 6fg4 6f* 6s3 6g2 7f2 7g 1976 8f 8g5 7g 8s6 6s 6fg 6f 8fg] moderate handicapper at 2 yrs but showed no worthwhile form in 1976: should stay 1m: acted on any going at 2 yrs: often wears blinkers: sometimes starts slowly. *M. Naughton.* **—**

CHINESE ROYAL 2 b.c. Ribero 126–Ming Vase 84 (Princely Gift 137) [1976 7g] small colt: half-brother to Nighttime Glory (by Breeders Dream), a winner in both England and Belgium at 2 yrs in 1975: 6,000 gns yearling: dam won over 5f **—**

at 2 yrs: appeared to refuse to race when last of 14 to Filipachi in minor event at Kempton in August, only outing. *F. J. Houghton.*

CHIQUERA 4 b.g. Falcon 131–Chinchilla II (Sicambre 135) [1974 6g⁵ 5v 6s⁶ 6g 8s 1975 8g 12f 16h² 16fg⁵ 15fg³ 20g* 14.6fg³ 18g 15s³ 15d⁶ 1976 12f⁴ 17.7f⁵ 16f³ 16h⁶ 20f⁶ 15g⁵ 13v] sturdy gelding: suited by really long distances: acts on any going: has run well in blinkers. *J. Turner.* **62**

CHIRP 2 ch.c. Crooner 119–Our Polly 85 (Henry the Seventh 125) [1976 5f 5f⁵ 6g 7s* 7.2v⁵] first reported foal: 320 gns yearling: dam a sprinter: won 14-runner seller at Warwick in October by 2½ lengths from Husseinia, the pair finishing clear (no bid): suited by 7f and will stay 1m: acts on any going. *R. Vibert.* **70**

CHITTERLING 2 b.f. Blakeney 126–Conchita 113 (Matador 131) [1976 6g⁶ 7g³ 7s] neat filly: half-sister to four winners, including quite useful sprinter Fish and Chips (by Major Portion): 6,000 gns yearling: dam won five times at 6f: led for over 5f when 5½ lengths third of 19 to Best Offer in minor event at Lingfield in September, best effort: will stay 1m+. *J. Dunlop.* **83**

CHOCOLATE IMP 3 br.g. Doudance 99–Jane Somers 64 (Will Somers 114 §) [1975 6g 6fg 8.2d 8g 7g 1976 5fg 6g⁵ 7fg 12.2s] well-grown gelding: gives impression that he needs further than 6f and will stay 1¼m (had stiff task and was having first race after a long absence when tried at 1½m on final outing). *M. Tate.* **—**

CHOCOLATE OLIVER 3 br.g. Le Dieu d'Or 119–Sacratic (Democratic 120) [1975 N.R. 1976 6g] half-brother to two minor winners: 480 gns foal: dam of little account: last but one behind Hot Bird in 14-runner maiden race at Hamilton in May. *Mrs A. Finch.* **—**

CHOP-CHOP 3 br.c. Birdbrook 110–Flying Escape 74 (Hook Money 124) [1975 5v² 5s 6fg⁶ 7fg³ 6fg 7fg 8f⁴ 6g* 7d³ 8d* 1976 8fg* 10fg³ 8fg* 10fg⁵ 8fg² 8g² 8f 7.6g 8g² 8g³ 8g⁴ 8g² 9g] small, useful-looking colt: fairly useful handicapper: won two early-season races at Newmarket, first of them an apprentice event, and kept his form well, on penultimate outing running Sweet Reclaim to ½ length at Ascot in September: best form at 1m: acts on any going: genuine and consistent. *J. Benstead.* **92**

CHORAL 3 b.f. So Blessed 130–Tinkling Sound 93 (Sound Track 132) [1975 5.9f 5g 1976 6g] narrow filly: no sign of ability in maiden races. *Sir Mark Prescott.* **—**

CHORUS MASTER 3 b.c. Ragusa 137–Sing a Song 115 (Sing Sing 134) [1975 6fg 7g 8g 8g⁶ 1976 11.7f³ 11.7f³ 14g⁶ 16f⁴] useful-looking colt: third in maiden race at Bath in April and handicap at Windsor in May: evidently stayed 1½m but appeared not to get 2m on final outing: dead. *S. Ingham.* **65**

CHRISDEDOR 3 b.f. Forlorn River 124–Laird's Lass 99 (Proud Chieftain 122) [1975 5.1f 6g 5f³ 6f³ 5.1g³ 5fg³ 5g³ 5f 5.9g³ 6g 1976 6fg 5fg 6g⁶ 6f⁴ 5.8h⁴ 6f² 5fg⁴ 5f 5.3h² 5g³ 6fg 5.8f⁴] small filly: poor handicapper: ran below her best in sellers on last two appearances: stays 6f: suitable mount for an apprentice: ran moderately when tried in blinkers on eighth outing: sold 500 gns Newmarket Autumn Sales. *K. Ivory.* **63**

CHRISTCHURCH 3 b.f. So Blessed 130–Highlight 107 (Borealis) [1975 N.R. 1976 7f 10fg² 10g⁴ 12.2fg* 15g² 14.6g] lengthy French-foaled filly: half-sister to five winners, including 1,000 Guineas and French Oaks winner Highclere (by Queen's Hussar), good-class 1m to 1½m performer Gloss (by Stupendous) and very useful middle-distance filly Light Duty (also by Queen's Hussar): dam won at 1½m: won maiden race at Wolverhampton in June: had run very well against much stronger opposition at Goodwood, finishing about 3 lengths fourth of nine to Laughing Girl in Lupe Stakes: no match for Du Maurier in minor event at Ayr in July and was well beaten in Park Hill Stakes at Doncaster in September (prominent to 3f out): probably stays 15f: acts on a firm surface. *R. Hern.* **88**

CHRISTINE JANE 2 b.f. King's Leap 111–Dixies Wonder 69 (Blue Lightning 114) [1976 5fg 5f³ 5f³ 5fg³ 6d² 6f* 7h² 6f* 8g 7.2v³ 7g] light-framed, leggy filly: half-sister to fairly useful handicapper Edwards Hill (by Weepers Boy), a winner at up to 1½m: 650 gns yearling: dam a stayer: twice a winner at Redcar, picking up a maiden auction event in June and beating Lucky Prize going away by 1½ lengths in £1,200 race the following month: should stay at least 1m: appears to act on any going: consistent. *T. Fairhurst.* **81**

CHRISTMAS CANDLE 4 br.c. Tycoon II–Christmas Pageant (March Past 124) [1974 7g 7g 7v³ 1975 12v² 12g⁵ 12g³ 12fg³ 12g⁵ 12.2g⁴ 13.3g⁵ 12s³ 12v³ 1976 12g²] strong, compact colt: moderate maiden: favourite, beaten a head by Commandant in amateur riders race at Leicester in April, only outing in this **65**

country at 4 yrs: stays 1½m: seems to act on any going: exported to Belgium. *F. Winter.*

CHRISTMAS COMET 4 br.g. Pia Star–Perilla (Sword Dancer) [1974 7s 8.2d⁶ 8s² 9s⁴ 1975 12v 12.2g 9fg² 1976 13g⁶ 10g 10s] lengthy gelding: should stay further than 9f: acts on soft going: blinkered last two outings in 1975: disappointing. *D. Nicholson.*   —

CHRISTMAS TIME 2 b.f. Silly Season 127–Wartime 70 (Martial 131) [1976 7s] third foal: dam stayed quite well: 12/1 when thirteenth of 20 to Brightly in maiden race at Newmarket in October, only outing. *W. Elsey.*   —

CHRISTMAS VISIT 2 br.c. Daring Display 129–Aya Sofia (Milesian 125) [1976 7g 7g⁵ 7d⁶] neat, attractive colt: half-brother to 1972 2-y-o winner Carmoni Prince (by Le Prince): 9,800 gns yearling: dam winning Irish sprinter: creditable 7 lengths fifth of 17 to Royal Plume in £2,900 event at Ascot in September: had a stiff task when sixth to The Minstrel in William Hill Dewhurst Stakes at Newmarket the following month but was still going well when badly hampered about 2f out and is much better than his finishing position would suggest: clearly well thought of and looks sure to win races at 3 yrs. *B. Hills.*   **94 p**

CHRISTOPHER 2 gr.g. Pals Passage 115–Planetarium (Abraxas 97) [1976 5f 5f⁴ 6fg 7fg] unfurnished gelding: well beaten in maiden and minor events. *G. Richards.*   —

CHRISTOPHERS GIRL 2 br.f. Joshua 129–First Court 82 (Primera 131) [1976 5s⁵ 6s 7v] second foal: 200 gns yearling: dam won over 1½m: showed signs of a little ability on first outing but was well beaten afterwards. *V. Cross.*   —

CHUCONTE 3 b.c. Gladwin–Ad Lib Honey (Honeys Alibi) [1975 6fg 6g* 7f 6fg² 6f⁴ 1976 7fg 8g 8fg* 8f² 8h² 8h* 10g* 10g* 8g] strong, good-looking American-bred colt: won apprentice race at Pontefract and amateur riders events at Salisbury, Kempton and Newcastle: all out when beating Two Bells 2½ lengths on last-named course in August: stays 1¼m: acts on hard ground: effective with and without blinkers: ran as though there was something wrong with him on final outing: exported to U.S.A. *B. Hills.*   **88**

CHUKAROO 4 b.c. Kibenka 119–Wild Words 76 (Galivanter 131) [1974 6s 1975 7s 8g 7fg* 7g* 7g⁶ 7f⁴ 7.6g 8g 7d 1976 7f³ 7fg⁵ 7fg* 7f* 7f² 7.2f² 7fg² 7.3d 8s⁵] well-made, quite attractive colt: moderate handicapper: successful at Brighton and Chepstow in May and ran creditably in most of his other races afterwards: best form at 7f: acts on firm going: suitable mount for an apprentice: genuine and consistent. *W. Payne.*   **81**

CHUM-CHUM 5 b.c. On Your Mark 125–Tack 88 (Tacitus 124) [1975 5v 5v⁴ 6fg 6f 6f* 6fg 1976 5f⁵ 6g⁶ 6fg⁶ 8fg³ 7g³ 6f 8g⁶ 7fg 8.3d⁴ 8s* 8v³] well-made colt: good mover: fairly useful handicapper: put up a good performance when winning at Goodwood in September by 2 lengths from Calor: stays 1m: acts on any going: ran respectably when tried in blinkers on ninth outing but didn't wear them when successful: sold 7,800 gns Newmarket Autumn Sales, reportedly to race in U.S.A. *R. Smyth.*   **92**

CHURCHILLIAN 3 b.g. Tamerlane 128–Word Perfect (Worden II 129) [1975 5g⁶ 5fg 5fg² 5g⁴ 5g 6g 1976 8.2f⁵ 8f⁵ 8g⁵ 9f³ 8f³ 7.6fg² 8fg³ 8s*] compact colt: favourite, won maiden race at Edinburgh in October by a length from Miss Damus: will stay 1¼m+: acts on any going: ran below his best when tried in blinkers on fourth start: has given us impression he is none too genuine. *C. Bewicke.*   **79**

CIDER DRINKER 2 b.f. Space King 115–Chocolate Pot (Hook Money 124) [1976 7s] first live foal: dam of little account: tailed off in minor event won by Alltyre at Chepstow in October. *G. Vallance.*   —

CIEL D'OR 3 ch.f. Sky Gipsy 117–Minimoose (Klondyke Bill 125) [1975 5s³ 1976 6.5s 6.5g 5v 7fg⁵ 5fg 5f 6f 7g 6d 7s 6v] poor maiden: sold out of J. Dunlop's stable 460 gns Ascot April Sales after third outing. *F. Wiles.*   —

CILKSHOE 2 ch.f. Shoemaker 121–Cecilka (Porterhouse) [1976 6g 7s] strong, quite attractive French-bred filly: half-sister to French 3-y-o Cidrax (by Yellow God), a winner at up to 9.5f: 4,000 gns yearling: dam won 17f bumpers event at 4 yrs: behind in newcomers event at Lingfield in September and minor race at Sandown in October (eleventh of 12 to Sleeper). sold 420 gns Ascot December Sales. *Miss A. Sinclair.*   —

CILLA 2 b.f. Highland Melody 112–Rockazar 85 (Master Rocky 106) [1976 6d 5g 7f 5f 7f⁵ 7g] lengthy filly: poor plater. *R. Cambidge.*   **53**

CINDASONG 2 b.f. Saintly Song 128–Lucinda Anne (Abernant 142) [1976 5fg **45** 5g 5.9f 5g 5s 7s⁵] leggy filly: bad plater. *D. Nicholson.*

CINDERMOUSE 2 b.f. Blast 125–Melodor 103 (Songedor 116) [1976 5g 5fg] — third foal: dam a miler: behind in sizeable fields of maidens at Leicester in May and Nottingham in July. *C. V. Miller.*

CINDERS 3 br.f. Firestreak 125–Princess Nefertiti (Tutankhamen) [1975 **72** 5s⁵ 1976 8fg² 8fg⁴ 8f⁴ 8h⁶ 8f⁵] quite moderate: should stay further than 1m: acts on firm going: raced with tongue tied down on third outing. *Doug Smith.*

CINDY-CATION 2 gr.f. Fleece 114–Georgie Lass 58 (Bleep-Bleep 134) [1976 — 5s 5s 7v] first foal: dam, who barely stayed 5f, is sister to very smart sprinter Lazenby: no worthwhile form in maiden and minor events in the autumn. *J. Powney.*

CINQUAPACE 4 br.f. Tudor Melody 129–New Move 112 (Umberto 118) [1974 **61** N.R. 1975 7fg⁴ 8g 1976 5.9fg 8fg 7g 7g* 7f* 7f² 8h⁶ 7f 7h 7f³] quite a moderate handicapper: successful at Edinburgh and Folkestone in June: stays 7f: acts on firm going: good mount for an apprentice: sold 8,000 gns Newmarket December Sales. *P. Cole.*

CIRCLET 2 b.f. Baldric II 131–Highlight 107 (Borealis) [1976 6g 6d*] rather **97** lightly-made filly: half-sister to several winners, notably 1,000 Guineas and French Oaks winner Highclere (by Queen's Hussar), smart 1m to 1¼m horse Gloss (by Stupendous) and very useful middle-distance filly Light Duty (also by Queen's Hussar): dam won at 1½m: favourite and just about fittest of seven-strong field, stayed on well to win Blue Seal Stakes at Ascot in September by a length from newcomer Bordello: will stay 1¼m. *R. Hern.*

CIRCUS SONG 4 b.c. Hill Clown–Golden Linnet 96 (Sing Sing 134) [1974 — 5fg 5.1f⁴ 5f⁴ 6g* 5d³ 6g* 6v⁴ 1975 7s 10g 8f⁴ 7f⁶ 8f³ 7g 1976 10fg 8f] lengthy colt: fair handicapper (rated 89) in 1975: lightly raced and no worthwhile form at 4 yrs: stays 1m but isn't certain to stay 1¼m: appears to act on any going. *T. Waugh.*

CITOYEN 4 b.c. Above Suspicion 127–Tomorrow (Citation) [1974 N.R. 1975 **124** 10s* 10v* 10g³ 12g 15.5g² 13.5g 15.5s² 12s 1976 10v* 15.5s⁴ 15.5g* 20g³ 12.5g⁵ 15d* 20s² 12s] French colt: high-class stayer: did well in 1976, winning Prix Exbury at Saint-Cloud in March (over a distance short of his best), Prix Jean Prat at Longchamp in April (beat Luenge easily) and Prix Kergorlay at Deauville in August (by 3 lengths from Olmeto): far from disgraced on three of his other starts, finishing 5¼ lengths fourth of 12 to Sagaro in Prix de Barbeville, 3¾ lengths third of 10 to same horse in Prix du Cadran and 2 lengths second to Knight Templar (rec 7 lb) in Prix du Pont de Flandre, all at Longchamp: effective at 1¼m when

Blue Seal Stakes, Ascot—a Royal success as Circlet beats the stable-companions Bordello (hidden) and Lady of the Moon, with Sally Bowles (left) a close fourth

conditions are testing but is particularly well suited by a test of stamina: acts on heavy going. *J. de Choubersky, France.*

CITY AFFAIR 2 ch.c. Veiled Wonder–Treasure Boat 54 (Hook Money 124) [1976 5f⁶ 5g 6fg 6fg 6g] compact colt: of no account: sold 310 gns Ascot November Sales. *D. Kent.* —

CITY CHAMP 2 b.g. Crozier 117–System 86 (Galivanter 131) [1976 5fg 5f 6f 6f 6d 7fg] leggy gelding: bad plater: blinkered final outing: sold 420 gns Doncaster October Sales. *R. Hollinshead.* —

CITY LIGHTS 3 gr.f. Town Crier 119–Lovely Beam 87 (Infatuation 129) [1975 N.R. 1976 8g 8g] strong, good sort of filly: half-sister to two winners, including very useful sprinter Lovelight (by Bleep-Bleep): dam a sprinter: in rear in maiden races at Newbury and Sandown in July. *Miss N. Wilmot.* —

CITY SAINT 2 b.c. Saintly Song 128–Goodytwoshoes (Above Suspicion 127) [1976 6d 6f] lengthy colt: half-brother to two winning 2-y-o platers: 620 gns yearling: dam showed poor form at around 1½m: in rear in maiden race at Redcar and £1,200 event at Leicester, both in June. *J. Berry.* —

CIVIL LIST 4 b.c. Royal Palace 131–The Creditor 127 (Crepello 136) [1974 7d 1975 10.8g³ 1976 12fg 16d 12s] rather light-framed colt: beautifully bred but is lightly raced and seems only plating class: should stay at least 1½m. *E. Jones.* —

CIVIL SERVANT 4 br.g. Frigid Aire–Pink Tape 83 (Supreme Court 135) [1974 7.2s⁵ 7v² 7s⁴(dis) 1975 10.8s 12g⁴ 10f⁵ 10.1f³ 10f⁵ 10d⁵ 1976 12fg 8fg 10.1fg 10g 8f⁵ 8.3f³ 8.3fg⁴ 8f³ 8g] poor plater: seems to stay 1½m: acts on any going: has run creditably both in blinkers and without them. *A. Johnson.* **44**

CLADDAGH 2 b.c. Bold Lad (Ire) 133–Clarina (Klairon 131) [1976 5s 5fg* 5fg² 5g⁵ 6g³ 6d⁶] strong, good-looking, most taking individual: American foaled: excellent mover: first foal: dam won twice over 1½m in Ireland: won £1,300 event at Sandown in June by 4 lengths from Regal Flash after quickening impressively 1f out: placed in two quite valuable events afterwards, going down by a short head to Mummy's Darling in Chesterfield Stakes at Newmarket and finishing well when 1¾ lengths third to Anax in Champion 2-y-o Trophy at Ripon: will stay 1m: acts on a firm surface. *H. Wragg.* **110**

CLAIRONCITA 3 br.f. Don Carlos–Miss McLairon 96 (Klairon 131) [1975 6d 1976 10.1f 8g 10.1fg² 10.1fg⁵ 10.1f² 10.1g* 11.7fg* 12g* 10g* 10s* 14s] unfurnished filly: improved greatly in second part of season and won small races at Windsor (two), Goodwood, Lingfield and Nottingham within a month in the autumn: comfortably beat Blyth's Folly 3 lengths on last-named course in September: stays 1½m: acts on any going. *F. J. Houghton.* **97**

CLANE 2 b.c. So Blessed 130–Hermosita 70 (Matador 131) [1976 8s³ 8.2s²] strong, well-made colt: closely related to fairly useful sprinter Princie Pooh (by Princely Gift) and half-brother to a winner: dam, winner at up to 13f, is half-sister to Irish Derby winner Your Highness: placed in maiden event at Sandown and minor event at Haydock in October, chasing home 3-length winner Hot Grove on latter track: will stay middle distances: sure to win a race. *H. Cecil.* **92**

CLAPHAM TESS 2 ch.f. Varano–Blitzmaid (Technion 96) [1976 5s 5f 5.9f 5g⁶ 7f] short-coupled filly: bad plater: blinkered last two outings: sold 310 gns Ascot August Sales. *D. Williams.* **45**

CLARANNLYN 3 ch.f. Jimmy Reppin 131–All Shy 64 (Alcide 136) [1975 5g 5fg³ 6fg⁶ 7g⁴ 6f³ 6g* 7g 6d 7f 1976 7f 10fg⁵ 8s 12f 8f 8f⁴ 7f 7d 7s 10g⁵] plater: rated 75 at 2 yrs but showed no worthwhile form in 1976: should stay 1¼m: best form at 2 yrs in blinkers. *D. Weeden.* —

CLARE 3 ch.f. Saintly Song 128–Mellow (Woodcut 114) [1975 5g 5fg 6g 1976 10.1fg 10s] well-made, quite attractive filly: little worthwhile form in maiden races *D. Keith.* —

CLASSIC EXAMPLE 2 ch.c. Run The Gantlet–Royal Saint 117 (Saint Crespin III 132) [1976 6v 7v³] half-brother to three winners, including smart middle-distance 3-y-o Illustrious Prince (by Le Levanstell): dam, a smart miler, is sister to Altesse Royale: had every chance when third of 15 behind easy winner North Stoke in minor event at Lingfield in November: will stay middle distances: will do better at 3 yrs. *P. Walwyn.* **76 p**

CLAUDE LORRAIN 2 b.c. Tarbes 125–Cynorodon (Val de Loir 133) [1976 6f⁵] French-bred colt: cost 32,000 francs as a yearling (approx. £3,400): dam placed second over 1m at 2 yrs, her only start: started slowly when about 5 **69 p**

William Hill Gold Cup, Redcar—in a driving finish Claudio Nicolai holds off Ardoon and Lord Helpus

lengths fifth of seven to Master Wrekin in maiden race at Windsor in July: will stay middle distances: sure to do better at 3 yrs. *J. Dunlop.*

CLAUDIO NICOLAI 3 br.c. Diatome 132–Capricciolo (Saint Crespin III 132) **113** [1975 5s⁵ 6g* 6g⁵ 7f* 7.2fg⁶ 1976 8g* 8fg 10f⁵ 10.5fg⁴ 10fg³ 8f* 8g³ 8g⁵ 7s⁵ 7.2d⁶] strong, good-looking American-foaled colt: smart performer: ran on well under pressure when winning William Hill Gold Cup (handicap) at Redcar in August by ½ length from Ardoon: performed creditably on most of his other outings, notably when winning Roseberry Stakes at Teesside in April and when finishing fourth of nine to Bold Pirate in John Smith's Magnet Cup at York in July: best form at 1m: acts on firm going and is possibly not at his best on soft: apprentice ridden when running respectably seventh outing but is suited by strong handling. *Denys Smith.*

CLEAN CANASTA 3 ch.f. Silly Season 127–Canasta Girl 90 (Charlottesville **81** 135) [1975 7f* 7g² 1976 8fg⁵ 10h³ 10d⁵ 10.6d] unfurnished filly: showed quite useful form at 2 yrs but is only a moderate performer nowadays: will probably stay further than 1¼m. *H. Cecil.*

CLEAR MELODY 5 b.g. Highland Melody 112–Cape Clear 63 (Fastnet Rock **95** 123) [1974 5fg 5fg⁵ 5f⁵ 6fg 5f² 5fg 5f 5f* 5g* 5g 5g³ 5g⁶ 5g² 5fg 5fg⁴ 5s³ 5g⁵ 5f* 5s⁴ 5g* 5g 5d 5s 1975 5v³ 5s⁴ 5d* 6g² 5d* 5f 5f 5fg 5g³ 5d³ 6f³ 5h* 6g² 5fg 5.6g 6d⁵ 5f³ 5g² 6s⁶ 5v⁵ 1976 6fg 6g 5d* 5fg⁶ 5s 5d⁴ 5fg² 5fg² 5h⁵ 6fg 6f² 6fg* 5fg 6f² 6g² 6f⁴ 6g⁴ 6d³ 5v⁶ 5s 5s] fairly useful handicapper: a really hardy customer who has had seventy races in the last four seasons but nevertheless retains his form and enthusiasm remarkably well: successful twice at 5 yrs, at York in May and Nottingham in August (Nottingham Stewards' Cup): in frame on nine other occasions, notably on seventeenth start when about 3 lengths fourth of 18 to Last Tango in Burmah-Castrol Ayr Gold Cup at Ayr in September: stays 6f: acts on any going: often wears blinkers: suitable mount for an apprentice: game and genuine. *S. Nesbitt.*

CLEAR SONG 2 br.f Saintly Song 128–Sylphide 113 (Supreme Court 135) **67** [1976 5f⁴ 5f* 6fg 5g 6g 5fg⁵ 5s] neat filly: half-sister to several winners, including very useful middle-distance performer Dieu Soleil (by Crepello): 960 gns yearling: dam very useful at around 1m: won maiden auction event at Catterick in April by ¾ length from Beaumel Board: not seen out again until August and had some stiff tasks, running easily best race on sixth outing: best form at 5f but should stay 1m: sold 520 gns Doncaster November Sales. *R. Hollinshead.*

CLEMS BOY 4 br.g. Space King 115–Cloudari (Pindari 124) [1974 N.R. **74** 1975 9g⁴ 8fg 10h² 10f* 12f³ 8h* 11.7fg³ 8g 8d⁶ 12g² 10.2g* 12g⁴ 1976 8g⁴ 10g⁶ 8d 9g⁵ 8fg⁵ 8f⁵ 10f³ 12f² 10.2fg² 12f⁴ 13.8f* 12.3fg² 12fg³ 15.8f⁴ 12f⁵ 10f⁵] lightly-made gelding: quite a moderate handicapper nowadays: successful at Catterick in July by 1½ lengths from Hill Station: stays 1¾m but appeared not to stay further on fourteenth appearance: acts on hard going and may be unsuited by soft: goes well for apprentice P. d'Arcy. *G. Toft.*

CLINTWOOD 4 gr.g. Lauso–Evelina 99 (Floribunda 136) [1974 6f 6fg⁴ 6g³ **95** 6g⁵ 5g* 5g³ 5fg² 5g 6s 1975 8s 7g 6f* 7f 5f* 6f* 6fg* 6h⁴ 6g⁵ 6f⁵ 6fg 1976 6s* 7f⁴ 6g* 6g 5s* 6d² 6f³ 6fg 6fg⁶ 5fg* 6f³ 5fg² 6f⁴ 5fg² 5g² 5fg³ 5s 5s⁶] well-grown

Nottingham Stewards' Cup—the blinkered Clear Melody gets the verdict by a short head from Briarvanter, with White Wonder and Maxi's Taxi (right) the next to finish

gelding: has an enlarged knee: fairly useful handicapper: a tough individual who won at Newcastle, Ayr (twice) and Thirsk at 4 yrs: best at up to 6f: acts on any going: excellent mount for an apprentice: genuine and consistent. *W. A. Stephenson.*

CLIVEDEN REACH 3 b.f. Creme dela Creme–Stream (Ridan) [1975 6g² 6g³ 8g⁶ 1976 8fg⁵] rangy American-bred filly: rated 81 at 2 yrs but ran moderately on only outing at 3 yrs (May): will stay 1¼m *J. Nelson.*   —

CLOCHE 3 br.f. Klairon 131–Wind Song 112 (Tudor Melody 129) [1975 7fg 1976 7.6s 10.5d 8g 6f⁴] quite attractive filly: rated 82 at 2 yrs but showed only a little ability in 1976: should stay 1m. *B. Hills.*   **61**

CLOONLARA 2 b.f. Sir Ivor 135–Fish Bar (Baldric II 131) [1976 5f* 6.3g* 5f*]   **130**

J. A. Mulcahy has owned several top-class horses in the past few years but classic success has so far eluded him. His Thatch headed the Irish Free Handicap at two years and shared top place in the English Free Handicap at three years yet finished only fourth to Mon Fils in the Two Thousand Guineas; Apalachee, an outstanding two-year-old, found Nonoalco and Giacometti too good for him when 9/4 on for the race the following year; King Pellinore, who has proved a great success since being sent to race in the United States, met his match in Grundy in the Irish Sweeps Derby and in Bruni in the St Leger. His Cloonlara, though, a filly with a middle-distance pedigree who has shown exceptional speed, looks like developing into an outstanding filly at three years, and a classic win seems very much on the cards.

Cloonlara's three races were in Ireland, all within the space of two months in the summer. Her last race, the Phoenix Stakes at Phoenix Park, provided by far her stiffest task and her most impressive win. The odds-on favourite was Godswalk, a colt with a record of four wins from five outings, the latest being the Norfolk Stakes in which he easily accounted for Alpherat, The Andrestan, Royal Diver and Pandu, winners between them of eleven of their fourteen starts. Of the others in the betting Tamariscifolia and Ring Leader had each won twice from their last three starts; Tamariscifolia ran out a five-length winner of an eighteen-runner maiden race before landing the odds in a small race that contained three other winners, and Ring Leader comfortably beat a large field of maidens prior to running out a ten-length winner in a field of four. The only other to be quoted at less than 66/1 was Margardave, winner of a maiden race on his previous outing by five lengths and four. Understandably, some people suspected that the easy five furlongs on fast ground might prove too sharp for Cloonlara, who had already won over an extended six furlongs, but she shot out of the stalls and soon held a clear advantage over Godswalk. The rest of the field were in trouble before halfway and at the line she had extended her lead over the favourite to six lengths, with Ring Leader just getting the better of Tamariscifolia for third place, four lengths further away. After the race Paddy Prendergast, who has trained ten winners of the Phoenix Stakes, gave his opinion that Cloonlara was the best filly (presumably in Ireland) since the days of Arctic Sun, the outstanding two-year-old of 1943. An interesting thought, but one difficult to substantiate.

Unfortunately, we didn't get another chance to see Cloonlara; she injured herself and pulled up lame after the Phoenix Stakes. She was soon sound again, and there was said to be an outside chance of her running in the William Hill Cheveley Park Stakes but the race went by without her. The firm going at Phoenix Park could have caused her injury; it is worth noting that over two months went by before Godswalk reappeared, and neither the third nor fourth was seen out again.

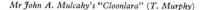

Cloonlara (b.f. 1974)	Sir Ivor (b 1965)	Sir Gaylord (b 1959)	Turn-to
			Somethingroyal
		Attica (ch 1953)	Mr Trouble
			Athenia
	Fish Bar (b 1967)	Baldric II (b 1961)	Round Table
			Two Cities
		Fisherman's Wharf (ch 1959)	Alycidon
			Herringbone

Cloonlara's other wins were easily gained. In the Hurry-On Stakes at Phoenix Park she soon had the measure of her eight opponents and came home five lengths clear of Success at Last; in the three-runner Probationers Stakes at the Curragh she started at 10/1 on and won by the same margin. Cloonlara

Mr John A. Mulcahy's "Cloonlara" (T. Murphy)

gave her stable its seventh victory in the Probationers Stakes during the last
ten years; it was in this race that her sire, Sir Ivor, gained his first win.

Cloonlara's pedigree is top-class; even so, it is somewhat surprising to find
her possessing such speed that she was able to trounce sprint-bred animals at their
own game. Sir Ivor only once attempted a trip shorter than seven furlongs and
that was when he finished only sixth over six furlongs on his first appearance as
as a two-year-old. He started his stud career over here, siring a number of
very good horses, and he has met with similar success, mostly with fillies, since
going to the States. In 1976 his daughter Optimistic Gal increased her earnings
to nearly 700,000 dollars and finished second in all three of the Triple Crown
races for fillies; Fascinating Miss and the ex-Irish Miss Toshiba both won 100,000
dollar-added stakes races and Ivanjica won the Prix de l'Arc. Of Sir Ivor's
runners here, nearly all have stayed a mile and a large number have been suited
by middle distances; most of those with stamina limitations have been out of
sprint-bred mares. The distaff side of Cloonlara's pedigree is chock-full of
stamina. Her dam, Fish Bar, a very useful filly, won over an extended mile
and a half in France. The next dam, Fisherman's Wharf, was out of the One
Thousand Guineas and St Leger winner Herringbone, as were those very smart
stayers Dogger Bank and Entente Cordiale. Fisherman's Wharf stayed well,
and she finished second in the Brown Jack Stakes. Fish Bar has had only two
other foals. One, a filly called Dapping, a three-year-old sister to Cloonlara,
ran only once, finishing fourth to Sarah Siddons at two years. The other, the
Habitat colt Denizen, did much better, at two years showing smart form over
six furlongs and the following season running Boone's Cabin to a head over that
distance from only three starts. Evidently Denizen was regarded as a sprinter
and as he, like Cloonlara, is by a son of Sir Gaylord, there seems some reason to
question whether she is going to stay. We think she will, for Sir Ivor is a much
stronger influence for stamina than is Habitat. We certainly expect Cloonlara
to stay a mile, and at this stage she is the filly we would want to be on for the
One Thousand Guineas: she is a worthy favourite. *V. O'Brien, Ireland.*

CLOTHES LINE   2 b.f. High Line 125–Double Clip 69 (Double Red 122)   [1976   **71**
7f 5.9fg⁴ 8g]   first foal: dam a winning hurdler: quite a moderate maiden: will
stay 1½m.   *J. Hardy.*

CLOUD NINE   4 ch.f. Skymaster 126–Spare Filly 95 (Beau Sabreur 125)   [1974   **82**
5g 5s* 6s 6s⁴   1975 6f 7g⁶ 7fg* 7f⁵ 7g² 8d* 9d⁴   1976 8g 7fg⁵ 8g 7.6f³ 7g⁵ 8fg⁴
10s* 10s]   compact filly: good walker: fair handicapper: beat Just Revenge ¾
length when winning at Goodwood in September: ran well in some of her other
races, including when 3¾ lengths fifth of 14 to Record Token in Top Rank Club
Victoria Cup at Ascot in May on second outing: stays 1m: appears to act on
any going: wears blinkers.   *J. Bethell.*

CLOVE HITCH   5 b.h. Charlottown 127–Slip Stitch 120 (Parthia 132)   [1974   —
12g⁴ 12g 12g⁵ 14g⁵ 12v   1975 12s 12d 11.7f 15.8f 12fg⁶ 15s 12g²   1976 12fg]
sturdy, short-legged horse, and a good mover: mainly disappointing since his 2-y-o
days: stays 1½m: acts on soft going and is possibly unsuited by firm: has twice
been tried in blinkers: sold 2,000 gns Ascot June Sales.   *D. Morley.*

CLOVER PRINCESS   3 b.f. Right Tack 131–Rose Noir (Floribunda 136)   [1975 **110**
6f² 6f 6f²   1976 7s* 7f⁴ 7g⁴ 6f⁵ 8g² 7g* 8f³]   big, strong filly: second foal: 800
gns yearling: dam lightly-raced sister to Florescence: developed into a smart
performer, winning Warmlife Stakes at Phoenix Park in March by 3 lengths from
Lady Singer and minor event at the Curragh in June: also ran extremely well
when length second to Sarah Siddons in Irish 1,000 Guineas on latter course
and when just over 2½ lengths third to Kesar Queen in Coronation Stakes at
Royal Ascot in June on final outing: stays 1m well: acts on any going: consistent.
L. Browne, Ireland.

CLUED UP   8 ch.g. Smartie 102–Sage Warbler (Le Sage 128)   [1974 12g⁶ 10fg⁴   **64** d
13g 11g² 11g* 13s⁵   1975 11g⁵ 11g⁴ 12.3f⁴ 11v 13d* 13g⁵ 12g 12d⁴ 12v   1976
11g³ 12s 13s³ 11s⁴ 11fg 11fg⁶ 13g 12g 15fg⁵ 16.1d 12.5v]   poor handicapper
nowadays: stays 13f: appears to act on any going: goes well for an apprentice
but is far from consistent.   *R. Mason.*

CLUNY HILL   6 b.g. Le Dieu d'Or 119–Mountain Path 91 (Bobsleigh)   [1974   —
N.R.   1975 N.R.   1976 6g 8g 10.1fg 8fg]   of little account.   *T. Marshall.*

CLYSON   2 b.c. Marcus Superbus 100–Gill Breeze (Farm Walk 111)   [1976   **55**
5g 5s⁶ 5f⁴ 6f⁵ 5f* 5f 5f]   small colt: attracted no bid after winning bad seller

at Lanark in July: sold 550 gns Doncaster October Sales: retired to stud as a pony stallion. *S. Nesbitt.*

C MINOR 3 gr.c. B Major (U.S.A.)–Paella II (Ballymoss 136) [1975 5s 5g 5.1f 6fg 8.2g 9fg 8.2d⁶ 8g 10g 10f 1976 14f⁴] small colt: rated 73 at 2 yrs: beaten some way in maiden race at Yarmouth in August, only outing: will probably need a really stiff test of stamina: has worn blinkers. *R. Boss.*

CNOCH BHUI 4 b.c. Continuation 120–Flowing Lava §§ (Krakatao 130) [1974 **82** 6g 6.3g⁵ 6f⁴ 7v⁶ 7g 1975 8s² 10g* 10s⁶ 9f⁴ 10f* 12f* 9f² 12f² 9g 10g 10s⁶ 12g 1976 9s² 10s³ 13g⁴ 12g³ 14f 12g⁴ 13f⁵ 8f² 10f⁶ 9f⁵ 12fg⁶ 12fg⁴ 10v] Irish colt: fair handicapper: ran creditably in some of his races at 4 yrs, including in apprentice events but disappointed when heavily-backed favourite for minor race won by Royal Fanfare at Liverpool in April on third appearance: stays 1½m: acts on any going: was tried in blinkers as a 2-y-o: sold 4,300 gns Newmarket Autumn Sales. *C. Magnier, Ireland.*

COAL BAG KATE 3 b.f. Frankincense 120–Gypsey Race 84 (Romulus 129) **64** [1975 6g 8f 8g 1976 7g 8.2g 6fg 6g³ 6g 6g] lengthy filly: plater: showed only sign of ability on fourth outing: should stay 1m: blinkered final outing. *P. Metcalfe.*

COATHAM 3 ch.f. Divine Gift 127–Eutrippa 101 (Eudaemon 129) [1975 5s⁵ **—** 5g 6h 5g⁶ 5f⁴ 5g* 5f 5g⁴ 1976 5fg⁵ 5g⁵ 5h⁴ 5fg 7f³ 6g 6v 7v] leggy filly: plater: bred to stay 1m: ran poorly last two outings. *H. Blackshaw.*

COBBLERS MARCH 9 b.g. New Brig 120–Ballybay (Wood Cot) [1974 N.R. **—** 1975 12d* 10g 12.2fg] poor performer: stays 1½m: acts on a soft surface: front runner. *W. Charles.*

COCKADE 3 b.f. Derring-Do 131–Camanae 72 (Vimy 132) [1975 6f³ 6fg² **82** 1976 8f 8fg* 7s] neat, stocky filly: sister to 2,000 Guineas and Observer Gold Cup winner High Top: dam won at 1¾m: showed useful form at 2 yrs: favourite, won maiden event at Salisbury in September driven out by ½ length from Musical Prince: stays 1m: started slowly on final outing. *R. Hern.*

COCOBOY 3 ch.g. Connaught 130–Coconut 75 (Tesco Boy 121) [1975 N.R. **60** 1976 8f 8fg 10s⁴] good-looking gelding: first foal: dam stayed 1m: 25/1 when fourth of 11 to Brandon Bay in minor event at Leopardstown in November, first sign of ability: sold out of M. Jarvis' stable 780 gns Newmarket July Sales after second outing. *J. Murphy, Ireland.*

CODEBREAKER 3 br.c. Burglar 128–Anagram 76 (Vilmoray 126) [1975 6s 5g* **92** 5d³ 1976 5f² 5f³ 5g* 5g* 5fg* 5fg³ 5f² 6fg 5fg⁶ 5v⁶] useful-looking colt: useful handicapper: successful at Sandown in April and June and Goodwood in between: not certain to stay 6f: acts on firm going and ran respectably on softish ground at 2 yrs: wears blinkers: genuine and consistent but benefits from strong handling: off course three months before final outing. *W. Payne.*

Lonsdale Handicap, York—Coed Cochion draws away from Franc Flinders and Night In Town (right)

CODED SCRAP 3 b.c. Mummy's Pet 125–Autumn Breeze (King's Bench 132) **80**
[1975 6f 5g 6fg⁵ 6d³ 5d* 5s³ 1976 5g* 5g⁶ 5g⁴ 6g 5fg⁵ 6d⁵ 6v 5s³ 5s⁴ 6s*] sturdy
colt: moderate handicapper: won at Doncaster (Batthyany Handicap) in March
and Teesside in November, latter by 3 lengths from Tabernacle: stays 6f: evidently
needs an easy surface and acts well on soft going: twice ran moderately when
tried in blinkers. *T. Fairhurst.*

COED COCHION 4 gr.c. Lauso–Grecian Garden 76 (Kingstone) [1974 7g 9s* **111**
10s² 1975 12s² 13.4g² 14fg² 16f² 14d⁴ 14fg 18g² 16g* 1976 12fg⁴ 18.4s 20g⁶
20f³ 22.2f* 20.9fg³ 16fg* 16g⁵ 18g²] good-looking, rangy colt: very useful
performer: successful in Queen Alexandra Stakes at Royal Ascot (beat Masqued
Dancer 2½ lengths with rest of field well strung out) and Lonsdale Handicap
at York in August (most impressive, drawing right away from his field to beat
Franc Flinders comfortably by 5 lengths): ran his best other races when good
sixth of 10 to Sagaro in Prix du Cadran at Longchamp in May and when ¾-length
second to Sea Anchor in Doncaster Cup in September on final appearance:
had an abundance of stamina and was suited by extreme distances: acted on
any going: retired to Longfield Stud, Tipperary, fee around £200. *J. Hindley.*

COFFEE BOY 4 b.g. Kalydon 122–Lady Stone 67 (Zarathustra 131) [1974 **80**
N.R. 1975 N.R. 1976 12s*] good sort: second foal: half-brother to poor
stayer Mandarelle (by Mandamus): dam won at 1¼m: 14/1, trotted up from
Derry Town when winning maiden race at Haydock in October, only outing:
stays 1½m. *S. Hall.*

COIGNAFEARN 6 b.g. Current Coin 118–Doin Foine 65 § (Quorum 126) **73**
[1974 8d⁵ 8f 10f 8f⁴ 10f³ 9fg⁴ 8g² 10f* 10.4g 11g² 9g* 10g² 8fg* 10.5fg³ 10.5s*
10.2g³ 10d² 11s* 10.6v⁶ 1975 8h⁶ 12g 10.5d 10g⁶ 9fg 12.2g 12g 1976 12f²
11s* 12.3fg⁵ 10f³ 12f⁴ 11fg² 11fg⁵ 12f³] strong, shapely gelding: tough and
consistent handicapper: successful at Ayr in June: stays 1½m: acts on any going:
has worn blinkers, but does better without them: excellent mount for an inexperienced rider. *H. Bell.*

COIN CASE 6 b.h. Current Coin 118–Vanity Case 77 (Counsel 118) [1974 **—**
N.R. 1975 N.R. 1976 10s 10f] poor selling handicapper: stays 1m: appears
to act on any going: blinkered final appearance. *M. Naughton.*

COIN OF GOLD 3 ch.c. Welsh Pageant 132–Mesopotamia 126 (Zarathustra **114**
131) [1975 5g⁴ 6f⁶ 7fg* 7fg⁶ 8g³ 8s² 8g 1976 12.3d⁴ 10.5s 12g 12fg* 12fg²
12g⁶ 12fg⁴ 14.6d] useful-looking colt: half-brother to useful 5f to 1m performer

Churchill Stakes, Ascot—Coin of Gold (rails) regains the lead from Lost Chord near the line

Belitis (by Tudor Melody) and useful Guest Night (by Sir Ivor), a winner up to
9f: put up an excellent performance when sixth of 10 to Pawneese in King George
VI and Queen Elizabeth Diamond Stakes at Ascot in July, being beaten only
about 7 lengths: had earlier won Churchill Stakes on same course by a head from
Lost Chord and run Peaceful to a head in Old Newton Cup at Haydock and
afterwards finished fourth to Hawkberry in Great Voltigeur Stakes at York:
well beaten in Epsom Derby (tried in blinkers) and St Leger: suited by 1½m and
should stay further: showed best form on soft at 2 yrs but ran well on a firm
surface in 1976 and appears to act on any going. *C. Brittain.*

COLD BRONZE 4 br.f. Frigid Aire–Arodstown Tan (Atan) [1974 5fg 5fg* —
5f⁶ 1975 N.R. 1976 8f⁶ 8f⁵ 8s] seems of little account nowadays. *P.
Robinson.*

COLD CREAM 4 ch.f. Silver Shark 129–Cheek to Cheek 99 (Alycidon 138 or   53
Infatuation 129) [1974 8g 6.5v² 1975 8.5g 10.5g 10.5g⁶ 9g 12g⁶ 1976 13.8g
8g⁶ 8fg⁴ 11d⁶] ex-French filly: showed quite useful form at 2 yrs, but deteriorated considerably, although won in Sweden at 4 yrs: blinkered on reappearance.
H. Blackshaw.

COLDITZ CAPTIVE 2 b.c. Royal Captive 116–Fire and Ice 78 (Zucchero 133 §)   ?
[1976 5g 5g⁵ 5fg⁵ 6fg 6d] deep-bodied colt: half-brother to five winners, including very smart 1975 French 2-y-o 6f and 1m winner French Swanee (by
My Swanee): 1,200 gns yearling: dam won 5f seller at 2 yrs: appeared to run
a good race and was not beaten all that far when last of five behind useful
animals in £2,600 event at Newmarket in July on third outing but was well
beaten on all other starts: should stay 6f+. *W. Marshall.*

COLD JUSTICE 3 br.c. Arctic Judge 94–Rimelo (Richard Louis 116) [1975   59
7.6g 8g 7s⁶ 1976 10g⁶ 11.1fg⁶ 13fg² 10g 17.7f⁴ 16f⁴ 16h* 16f⁴] well-made
colt: good walker: narrow winner of five-runner maiden race at Lingfield in
June: stays well: acts on hard going. *J. Benstead.*

COLET COURT 2 ch.g. Saintly Song 128–Diello (Crepello 136) [1976 5g²   71
6fg⁶ 6g⁶ 7fg 7.3d 8s] useful-looking gelding: quite a moderate maiden: will
stay 1¼m. *G. Smyth.*

COLEUS 4 ch.g. Crocket 130–Tannhausa (Summer Tan) [1974 5f⁶ 5fg 5fg* 6g   83
5g 6d⁶ 5g⁶ 7.2g 8s⁵ 1975 7v² 7d² 7g⁵ 7f³ 7fg* 8h² 7f² 8.2fg⁵ 7g³ 10fg² 10g 9fg
1976 10.2g⁴ 9fg³ 8d² 10h* 10f² 10d³ 10f⁵ 8.2fg⁵] well-grown, plain gelding:
fair handicapper: successful at Teesside in April by 3 lengths from Long Love:
stays 1¼m: appears to act on any going: has been tried in blinkers: consistent:
sold 3,000 gns Doncaster August Sales. *J. Hardy.*

COLLABORATOR 4 ch.g. Quisling 117–Bright and Breezy 91 (Set Fair 129)   60
[1974 5fg 6g 7fg 8v⁴ 1975 8v⁶ 8.5d² 8f⁴ 8.5f³ 8g 10.1fg 8fg 12s 10g 1976
12g³ 12f³ 12f² 12f² 15.5h² 12f³] well-made gelding: quite a moderate maiden:
placed at Folkestone on all his outings at 4 yrs: stays well: probably acts on
any going: has been tried in blinkers. *A. Pitt.*

COLLECTORS DREAM 2 br.f. Breeders Dream 116–Cameo 114 (Como 120)   83
[1976 5fg³ 5s⁴ 5fg* 5fg⁴ 5.3h⁶ 5d 5d⁵] strong, good-bodied, shapely filly: closely
related to useful 6f and 7f winner Tudor Fox (by Tudor Melody) and half-
sister to several other winners, notably top-class sprinter Raffingora (by Grey
Sovereign): dam 5f sprinter: easy winner of 13-runner maiden race at Leicester
in June, beating Al Stanza 3 lengths: ran respectably in nurseries afterwards:
a speedy filly who is best served by a sound surface. *Doug Smith.*

COLOMBADE 3 b.f. Boldnesian–Imperial Hill (Hill Prince) [1975 N.R.   89
1976 8f² 8.2f* 8fg* 7h* 8g³] lengthy, quite attractive American-bred filly: half-
sister to useful 6f winner Irish 2-y-o 5f winner Happy Boy (by Never Bend) and to
several minor winners in U.S.A.: $45,000 yearling: dam stakes-winning half-
sister to dam of Secretariat and Sir Gaylord: a progressive filly who won maiden
race at Haydock and minor events at Newmarket and Redcar in the summer, on
last-named track beating Pay Roll with a good deal more in hand than length
margin suggests: slow into stride when fair third to Intermission in valuable
fillies handicap at Ascot in September: may stay further than 1m: acts on hard
going. *L. Cumani.*

COLOMBE 2 b.f. So Blessed 130–Bird In The Hand 82 (Major Portion 129)   84
[1976 5g² 5fg³ 5f³ 5f* 5f 5.3s⁴] lengthy, lightly-made filly: first foal: dam won
over 7f: odds on, made all to win nine-runner maiden race at Warwick in August
by 1½ lengths from African Violet: will be well suited by 6f: sold 3,000 gns
Newmarket Autumn Sales, reportedly for export to Sweden. *H. Candy.*

COLONEL TAJ 3 b.c. Prince Taj 123–Egualita 111 (Democratic 124) [1975 **66**
5f⁶ 5f 6fg⁴ 7g⁶ 1976 8f² 8fg² 11s⁴ 10s] compact colt: runner-up in early-season
races but was off course a long time after third outing and ran poorly on final
appearance (November): stays 11f: acts on any going: twice wore blinkers at
2 yrs: trained first three outings by W. Haigh. *H. Blackshaw.*

COLOURFUL CONNIE 2 ch.f. Green God 128–Blue Lobelia 72 (Majority Blue **80**
126) [1976 5f² 5g 5f² 5.1f* 5g⁶ 5g] strong, well-made filly: first foal: 620 gns
yearling: dam won 7f seller at 3 yrs: made all when winning nine-runner maiden
race at Yarmouth in August by 1½ lengths from Lantern Light: will stay 6f. *A.
Corbett.*

COLYTON LASSIE 2 b.f. Pharaoh Hophra 94–Pushti Kuh (Le Dieu d'Or 119) —
[1976 8s] first living foal: dam useless on Flat, over hurdles and in point-to-
points: tailed-off last of 16 to Wester Win in maiden race at Bath in October.
R. Hannon.

COMAK 2 br.g. Counsel 118–Makin 86 (March Past 124) [1976 6fg 6g 7s 6v] **63**
third foal: half-brother to fairly useful 1969 2-y-o 5f and 6f winner Makinroy (by
King's Bench) and Makinlau (by Lauso), a fair winner at up to 1½m: dam won
over 5f at 2 yrs and stayed at least 1m: plating-class maiden. *G. Smyth.*

COMEDY FLO 2 b.f. Comedy Star 121–Fiery Flo 78 (Firestreak 125) [1976 —
5fg] half-sister to two winners, including Dad (by Constable), a fairly useful
winner from 5f to 1¼m: 400 gns yearling: dam sprint maiden: tailed off in auction
event won by Mia Saint at Leicester in April: sold 360 gns Doncaster October
Sales. *W. Stephenson.*

COMEDY SQUARE 2 b.f. Comedy Star 121–Alsike 71 (Cagire II 122) [1976 —
6fg 6f] attractive filly: half-brother to useful miler Campari (by Bleep-Bleep)
and two other winners: 1,600 gns yearling: dam of little account: behind in
maiden races at Newmarket and Yarmouth in July, wearing blinkers and
swerving at start on latter course. *N. Callaghan.*

COMEDY TURN 4 gr.g. Court Fool–Lebanon 87 (Palestine 133) [1974 5g 6fg —
6s 7g 6fg 7fg 7s 1975 10.1f⁵ 10.1s 12f⁵ 15.5f² 15.5f⁵ 15.3d³ 16.5fg 1976 15.5h
15.5s] workmanlike gelding: poor maiden: stays well: acts on firm going:
sometimes wears blinkers. *T. Gates.*

COMERAM 3 ch.c. Amber Rama 133–Comely (Boran) [1975 5.5fg* 5g 5.5g³ **118**
5.5g⁶ 6.5d² 7.5s* 7g* 7s³ 8g² 7.7d² 1976 10.5s⁵ 8g³ 8d² 8d* 7g² 8g⁴] big, strong,
good sort of colt: third foal: half-brother to French 1m to 11f winner Comezeda
(by Zeddaan) and French minor winner Lybar (by Barbare II) and to good
French 2-y-o Pharly (by Lyphard): 75,000 francs (approx. £6,900) yearling: dam
very useful middle-distance filly: went under by a short head to Northern
Treasure in Irish 2,000 Guineas at the Curragh in May, soon coming under whip
after taking lead 2f out but responding very gamely to strong riding in last few
yards and only just failing to pull race out of fire: gained compensation when
making all to win Prix de Pontarme at Chantilly the following month by 1½
lengths from The Chaplain: also placed in two important races at Longchamp,
Poule d'Essai des Poulains (third to Red Lord) and Prix de la Porte Maillot (very
close second to Son of Silver): probably does not stay 1¼m: appears to act on any
going: genuine and consistent: exported to U.S.A. *R. de Tarragon, France.*

COMET KOHOUTEK 4 b.c. Le Levanstell 122–Armenia (Buisson Ardent 129) **74**
[1974 6fg 6s 1975 8v² 10s 10g⁴ 10fg* 11.7fg³ 12f³ 12f 12v 12g⁶ 12d 1976 12g*
11.7fg 12g⁶ 12g* 13.3fg⁶] lengthy colt: quite a moderate performer: winner of
apprentice handicaps at Ascot and Leicester in May: stays 1½m: acts on any
going. *G. Harwood.*

COMEUPPANCE 2 b.f. Baldric II 131–High Rise (Ballymoss 136) [1976 5g **62**
5d 6f⁵ 6g 8s] lightly-built filly: only plating class: blinkered fourth outing. *N.
Adam.*

COME UP SMILING (U.S.A.) 3 b.f. Amber Rama 133–Misty Light 112 (Ribot **106**
142) [1975 5d⁶ 5.5s⁴ 5s⁴ 4.5g* 6.5d³ 5s⁵ 6.5g⁵ 1976 7s² 7g² 8fg 8d² 8g⁴ 8g⁴ 8g⁵
8v⁶ 8v⁵ 8s³ 8v] first foal: dam very useful at up to 1½m: failed to win a race in
1976 but nonetheless showed herself a useful filly, running several good races,
including when runner-up to Guichet in Prix Imprudence at Maisons-Laffitte in
April and when just over a length fifth to Anne Palatine in Prix de la Calonne at
Deauville in August: about 9 lengths seventh of 25 to Flying Water in 1,000
Guineas at Newmarket: stays 1m: appears to act on any going: sometimes wears
blinkers but does just as well without. *J. Fellows, France.*

COM

COME WEEWANDA 3 b.f. Communication 119–Weewanda 94 (Cagire II 122) [1975 8f 7d 5g 1976 8f6 6g 6fg 7s] light-framed filly: well beaten, including in sellers. *C. Brittain.* —

COMMANDANT 4 b.g. Nelcius 133–Silk Tabbard (Court Harwell 130) [1974 N.R. 1975 N.R. 1976 12g* 12s] half-brother to fair middle-distance handicapper Firesilk (by Firestreak) and poor stayers Bedouin (by Bivouac) and Hard Silk (by Hardicanute): dam never ran: successful in amateur riders event at Leicester in April by a head from Christmas Candle, starting at 25/1: subsequently off course until October when well behind in similar race at Chepstow: stays 1½m. *G. Balding.* **65**

COMMAND FREDDY 2 b.c. My Swallow 134–Vanga (Rockavon 120) [1976 7d4 8d* 8d] well-grown French colt: third foal: half-brother to fairly useful 3-y-o middle-distance winner Sanguine (by Sanctus II): 10,500 gns yearling: dam won three races at up to 1½m in France: had 16-runner field well strung out when winning newcomers event at Chantilly in July and put up a smart performance in 12-runner Prix la Rochette at Longchamp six weeks later, coming through to win by 2 lengths from Juge de Paix (gave 6 lb) after being in rear for long time: 5/1 for Grand Criterium at Longchamp in October but never looked like getting into race and finished only seventh of 10 to Blushing Groom: will stay 1¼m. *M. Clement, France.* **114**

COMMON LAND 4 br.c. Klairon 131–Short Commons 109 (Hard Tack 111 §) [1974 5g2 6f2 6g4 6fg2 7g* 7d6 1975 7g 9s6 10fg 8f* 8f5 8g2 8g2 9g 8.2s 1976 7fg 8s6 8fg6 8fg3 8.3f3 7fg2 8fg 8g 8s3 10v3] attractive colt: very smart handicapper (rated 121) at 3 yrs: has deteriorated considerably and disappointed on several occasions in 1976 (gives us impression he doesn't relish a struggle): suited by 7f or more: seems to act on any going: usually wears blinkers nowadays: sold 4,600 gns Newmarket December Sales. *M. Jarvis.* **102 §**

COMMUNE 2 b.f. Communication 119–Paul's Plume 96 (Stephen Paul 131) [1976 5g 5g 5s] small filly: in rear in Scottish maiden races. *J. Barclay.* —

COMMUNICANT 3 ch.g. Communication 119–Diamond Talk (Counsel 118) [1975 5f4 5fg* 5d2 5g 1976 7fg6 8fg 8fg6 11.7d] tall, sparely-made gelding: won maiden race at Salisbury at 2 yrs: had very stiff tasks and was well beaten in 1976 when racing over distances possibly beyond his optimum: appeared to act on any going at 2 yrs: very slow into stride on second outing. *F. Maxwell.* —

COMMUNICATE 2 b.c. Communication 119–Vivel (Vienna 127) [1976 5fg 6fg 5g6 5f 5h2 5g 5.1g 5d 5s3 5s4 5v] neat colt: in frame in varied company, including selling: should stay 6f: acts on any going: blinkered last three outings: bolted before start final appearance. *D. Dale.* **76**

COMMUTER 2 b.f. Communication 119–Spare Maid (Track Spare 125) [1976 5.9f 5g 7g 6s] first foal: dam never ran: little worthwhile form, including in a seller. *W. Stephenson.* —

COMTAR 3 b.f. Communication 119–Attar (Honeyway 125) [1975 5fg6 5fg3 5f5 1976 6g 5.8f5 5fg] plater at 2 yrs: little worthwhile form in better company in 1976: should stay 6f: sold 300 gns Ascot July Sales. *Mrs L. Dingwall.* —

COMTEC 2 b.c. Communication 119–Tecllyn 97 (Technion 96) [1976 5f 5fg 5fg2 6fg4 6fg2 6g 8f 6g5 6s3 6s5] plater: ½-length second to Virginia Lad at Goodwood in July, best effort: did not reproduce that form although ran respectably from time to time: suited by 6f but is unlikely to stay 1m: best form on a sound surface: inconsistent and does best when blinkered. *R. Hannon.* **79**

CONCILIATION 3 ch.f. St Paddy 133–Mitigation 91 (Milesian 125) [1975 5s 6f 6f2 7f* 6fg* 6d 1976 8d5 7g4 8.5g4 7fg4 8.3fg2 8.2fg6 7g3] attractive filly: quite a useful handicapper: will stay 1¼m: evidently needs a sound surface: found very little when tackled when tried in blinkers on final outing. *R. Hern.* **93**

CONCORDE LADY 2 b.f. Hotfoot 126–Terex (Khalkis 127) [1976 7g 9s6] third foal: half-sister to two winners, including fairly useful 3-y-o stayer Ventrex (by Henry the Seventh): 720 gns yearling: dam half-sister to two good animals: beaten about 5 lengths when sixth of nine to Saratoga Kid in maiden race at Wolverhampton in October: will stay 1½m. *C. Brittain.* **66**

CONCRETE 2 b.g. Gold Rod 129–Ballast (Polic 126) [1976 8f 8g 8s] plain gelding: poor plater: blinkered second outing (slowly away): apprentice ridden first two starts. *D. Holmes.* —

CONEYCROFT 2 b.g. The Brianstan 128–Sunbelle 77 (Lauso) [1976 5f 5g 6f] workmanlike gelding: behind in maiden races and a seller in first half of season. *W. Wharton.* —

176

CONFESSOR 3 br.c. So Blessed 130–Compulsion 56 (Aggressor 130) [1975 6f* **93**
6s⁵ 6d 1976 7d 6d 6fg⁶ 8fg* 8fg⁵ 8g⁵ 9f* 10g³ 8g³ 9g] leggy colt: put up a very
game performance when making most to win handicap at Doncaster in June by
2 lengths from Burma Pink: appeared beaten on merit when 3 lengths second to
Air Trooper in similar event at Ripon in August but was awarded race following
a stewards' inquiry and an objection: stays 1½m: acts on any going: sold 6,600 gns
Newmarket Autumn Sales, reportedly for export to Scandinavia. *J. W. Watts.*

CONFIDANTE 3 ch.f. Gulf Pearl 117–Abigail 103 (Abernant 142) [1975 6d —
1976 8s 10s] neat, good-quartered filly: behind in maiden and minor events.
J. Bethell.

CONFLEUR 4 b.f. Compensation 127–French Flower 89 (Le Lavandou 111) —
[1974 6g 6g⁴ 5.1s³ 7d 7g 5v² 5v³ 1975 6g 6s⁴ 6f⁴ 6fg* 5f³ 6fg 5h⁵ 6g 1976 6fg
5.9f 5.9g 6f 6g 6d] well-made filly: poor handicapper nowadays: stays 6f: acts
on any going: sometimes wears blinkers and did so when successful. *W.
O'Gorman.*

CONFLUENCE 5 br.h. Forlorn River 124–River Moy (Niagara Falls 104) **75** d
[1974 6d* 5f 6d 6fg² 6s 6g³ 7s 6v⁴ 6d 1975 8g⁵ 6fg⁴ 7g⁴ 8fg³ 8h* 8fg* 8d² 8.2fg²
8fg⁶ 8s 8f² 8f³ 8fg⁴ 1976 7f⁶ 7f² 7.2f 8fg⁵ 7g 8.2f 10v⁵ 8g⁵] tall, short-backed
horse: poor handicapper nowadays: stays 1m (ran badly when tried at 1½m): acts
on any going except perhaps very soft: sometimes wears blinkers but does as well
without: inconsistent. *W. Haigh.*

CONGENIAL 4 b.c. Alcide 136–My Jean 84 (Macherio) [1974 6f 7g³ 7g 8d² —
8s³ 8v² 8.2s⁶ 1975 12s 12.2fg*(dis) 11s* 12h⁴ 12f* 12f² 16h⁴ 12g 1976 12g 12g⁵
12.2g 12fg] workmanlike colt: fair handicapper (rated 88) in 1975: well beaten
all four starts at 4 yrs: well suited by 11f and 1½m, but ran as though failing to
stay when tried at 2m: acts on any going: sweated up third start: bandaged last
two appearances. *M. H. Easterby.*

CONGLOMERAT 2 gr.c. Zeddaan 130–Belle Bella (Milesian 125) [1976 6d³ **129**
6.5g* 8d 8d* 10v*]
    The Criterium de Saint-Cloud, a Group 2 race run over a mile and a quarter,
poses a severe test to a two-year-old especially on heavy going, and is hardly
likely, one would think, to bring out the best in a colt whose sire, Zeddaan, had
definite stamina limitations, and whose maternal grandsire, Milesian, was a
sprinter. But Conglomerat comes from stout stock on the distaff side—his dam,
who never ran, is a half-sister to the Irish Oaks winner Lynchris—and he revelled
in the conditions, going clear from the start and winning unchallenged by what
looked to be a margin much wider than the six lengths returned by the judge.
El Criollo, the favourite, was left toiling many lengths adrift in fifth place. This
was some performance—El Criollo had won the important Prix de Conde on his
previous appearance—and it is impossible to escape the conclusion that Conglomerat must be a very good horse indeed. Nor, it seems, is he one for whom
really testing conditions are essential. On his second outing he had scored
easily in maiden company over six and a half furlongs on good ground at Evry,
and two appearances later he had trotted up by four lengths, after being several
lengths clear on the turn, in the Prix Herod run over a mile on a soft surface on
the same course. We have a strong feeling that Conglomerat is going to be
concerned in the finish of some important races in 1977, at distances upwards
of a mile and a quarter.

    Conglomerat is a half-brother to the Sea-Bird II filly Beautiful Sea, who won
over nine furlongs at two years, and was placed second, three quarters of a length
in front of Ivanjica, in the Prix Vanteaux at Longchamp on the first of two
appearances as a three-year-old. The dam, Belle Bella, in addition to being a
half-sister to the Irish Oaks winner Lynchris, is a half-sister to Irish Lass, the dam
of the Irish Sweeps Derby winner Irish Ball. The next dam, Scollata, was a
half-sister to the Irish Cesarewitch winner and Queen Alexandra Stakes runner-up
Strait-Jacket (by Straight Deal) and a granddaughter of the distinguished mare

Criterium de Saint-Cloud—Conglomerat is out on his own at the finish

Schiaparelli, the dam of the One Thousand Guineas and St Leger winner Herringbone, Swallow Tail and Shantung's dam Barley Corn. *F. Boutin, France.*

CONIFER 2 b.c. Tudor Melody 129–Fircone 106 (Mossborough 126) [1976 6fg⁵ 6fg 7d] strong, rather hollow-backed, good sort: good walker: closely related to 1970 2-y-o 5f winner Land of Song (by Sing Sing), and half-brother to several winners, including smart out-and-out stayer Celtic Cone (by Celtic Ash) and very useful middle-distance winner Flame Tree (by Roan Rocket): dam useful 2-y-o: backward, ran very promisingly when about 8 lengths fifth of 14 to J. O. Tobin in £2,000 maiden race at Newmarket in July: finished only eighth of 14 to Adviser when favourite for similar race at Goodwood later in month and had a very stiff task when ninth of 11 to The Minstrel in William Hill Dewhurst Stakes at Newmarket in October: will stay at least 1¼m: obviously thought much better than form so far would indicate. *B. Hobbs.* **87** p

CONNAUGHT SQUARE 3 b.f. Connaught 130–Antonietta Corsini (Herbager 136) [1975 6g⁵ 8g* 1976 12.3s² 8g 8g 10d⁴] strong, lengthy, shapely filly: half-sister to very smart stayer Relay Race (by Relko): showed herself a useful filly at 2 yrs: 10 lengths second to African Dancer in Cheshire Oaks at Chester in May: not seen out again until the autumn and lost her form completely: probably stayed 1½m: sweated up last three outings: blinkered final appearance: stud. *N. Murless.* **—**

CONNORS 2 ch.c. Bold Lad (Ire) 133–Arenaria 102 (Aureole 132) [1976 6v] brother to very useful 1m to 1¼m performer Redesdale, and half-brother to another winner: 14,000 gns yearling: dam, winner at 7f and 1m, is closely related to Miralgo and Parnell: 9/1 when never-dangerous eighth of 22 to Good Company in maiden race at Newbury in October: sure to be better for this experience. *R. Price.* **—** p

CONSISTER 3 ch.f. Burglar 128–Ulupi's Sister 86 (Combat 123) [1975 5f³ 5g³ 5fg*(dis) 6fg³ 5fg⁴ 5g* 5h* 5g³ 5d 1976 6f⁵ 5h⁵ 7f 6f² 6h⁵ 6fg 7f⁵ 6g 6f] leggy filly: showed fair form at 2 yrs but is only quite moderate nowadays: possibly best at 6f nowadays: acts on hard going: often wears blinkers: sometimes sweats up. *J. Etherington.* **82**

CONTARINI FLEMING 4 br.f. Abdos 134–Samisk (Auriban 133 §) [1974 N.R. 1975 N.R. 1976 12s⁵ 13.1s⁵ 15.5s⁵ 12v²] poor maiden: ran best race on final appearance: stays 1½m: acts on heavy going. *D. Kent.* **68**

CONTINUING STORY 2 b.f. Double-U-Jay 120–Village Flirt 77 (Galivanter 131) [1976 5g⁶] second foal: half-sister to a poor animal by St Alphage: 780 gns yearling: dam 5f plater: remote sixth of seven to stable-companion Billie's Pal in seller at Wolverhampton in May, only outing. *J. Hill.* **—**

CONTRARY 4 b.g. Song 132–Mary 93 (Tamerlane 128) [1974 6fg 6fg⁴ 6g* 1975 7d 8g 12f 10g 10f 10.1fg⁴ 8g 1976 10v 11d 13g] strong, well-made gelding: poor plater nowadays: tailed off when pulled up in amateur riders race at Nottingham in April on final appearance at 4 yrs: slowly away when tried in blinkers: sold 470 gns Doncaster May Sales. *M. Naughton.* **—**

CONTRIBUTION 2 b.f. Connaught 130–Discernment 66 (Pan II 130) [1976 5g 7g⁴ 7f] lengthy, good sort: half-sister to two minor winners: dam lightly-raced half-sister to very useful 1½m horse Buff's Own: beaten 6½ lengths by **77**

178

Taffytina in maiden race at Newbury in May and in £2,100 event at Newmarket in July: had stiff task on only subsequent outing: will stay 1½m. *B. Hobbs.*

CONVERSANT 2 ch.f. Be Friendly 130–Poem 82 (Pall Mall 132) [1976 5fg 5fg³ 5fg 5g] small filly: bad plater. *G. Blum.* —

COOL CAT 2 br.g. Frigid Aire–Super Cat 80 (Epaulette 125) [1976 5g] half-brother to a minor 2-y-o winner by Be Friendly: 130 gns foal, resold 940 gns yearling: dam won 6f seller at 2 yrs: last of nine behind Cambridge Star in maiden race at Folkestone in March, only outing. *R. Smyth.* —

COOL HAND 2 gr.c. Gold Rod 129–Baroda Glory (Palestine 133) [1976 5s] — p half-brother to fair 1973 2-y-o 7f winner Jennifer Juniper (by Jolly Jet): 3,600 gns yearling: dam of little account: 8/1, lost ground at start and was some way behind at halfway, but made up a fair amount of ground from then on without ever threatening to get on terms, when eighth of 12 to Waterbuck in maiden race at Haydock in October: will stay 1m: will do a lot better at 3 yrs. *R. Price.*

COOL HAND LUKE 4 br.c. Town Crier 119–Tibby's Amigo (Sammy Davis 129) **42** [1974 5f 5fg 7g 7f 8d³ 8s 8s 7s² 6s* 7g⁵ 6d 1975 8s⁶ 8s⁵ 7s 9fg⁵ 8f⁴ 8h 8f 10fg⁶ 8g² 1976 6g 8g 10fg⁴ 10d⁵ 7f⁵ 7f 7g] poor plater nowadays: seems to stay 1¼m: acts on firm going but is ideally suited by some give in the ground: sometimes wears blinkers. *W. Murray.*

COOL SHULA 3 ch.f. Lord Gayle 124–Clancool (Beau Sabreur 125) [1975 5f — 6fg⁵ 5g² 7f⁴ 7f 6g 6d 1976 8fg 6d⁵ 7.2fg 6fg⁴ 7g 6v] lightly-made filly: plater: no worthwhile form in 1976: broke a leg at Newcastle in October and was destroyed. *C. Crossley.*

COPANBLEW 3 ch.g. Midsummer Night II 117–Miss Fidelity (Fidalgo 129) **65** [1975 5g 6fg 5.9f⁵ 7g⁶ 7h 8g 10g 1976 10.8fg 8fg 8h⁴ 12d] modest plater: seems to stay 1m: not seen out after May. *J. Hardy.*

COPLOW KATE 3 ch.f. Sovereign Gleam 117–One Rose (Pall Mall 132) [1975 **65** 5d 5v² 5s 5f⁵ 5.1f* 5f² 5f 5.9fg* 6d 6g 1976 5g⁶ 6f 5.8h³ 6fg⁵ 6f⁵ 6f⁵ 6g] workmanlike filly: should stay 1m: acts on any going, but goes particularly well on firm. *W. Wharton.*

COPPER 3 ch.f. Manacle 123–Siceliot (Sicilian Prince 126) [1975 5h 5s 5g 5fg⁴ **58** 5g³ 1976 8g 6v² 6d 6f² 6g³ 5f⁶ 6g 7fg³ 6f⁶] plain filly: placed in varied company, including selling: should stay 1m: best form on a sound surface: wears blinkers. *E. Collingwood.*

COPPERGATE 2 b.c. Hotfoot 126–All Shy 64 (Alcide 136) [1976 5fg 5fg⁶ **52** 5fg 6f⁴ 7f 7.2f] strong, good-bodied colt: poor plater: will stay at least 1¼m. *M. W. Easterby.*

COPPER SEA 7 br.g. Sea Wolf 116–Bonnie Bladnoch (Lord of Verona 120) — [1974 N.R. 1975 N.R. 1976 16fg⁴ 9f⁵ 13.8f⁵ 15g] useless. *K. Payne.*

COPTHORNE POLLY 3 b.f. Double-U-Jay 120–Polar Polly 88 (Arctic Storm — 134) [1975 7d 7.6g 1976 12g 16f 16g] lengthy, useful sort: no worthwhile form in varied company: sold 330 gns Ascot December Sales. *D. Dale.*

COQUITO'S PRINCE 2 b.c. Crowned Prince 128–Belgian Bullet (Vimy 132) **89** [1976 7g 8s³] big, rangy colt: third foal: half-brother to very useful miler Golden Aim (by Yellow God): 15,000 gns yearling: dam won four times over 1½m in Ireland: always thereabouts and stayed on well when 5½ lengths third of 28 to Royal Boxer in maiden race at Newmarket in October: will stay 1¼m+: sure to win a race. *B. Hanbury.*

CORDERAY 3 gr.f. Swing Easy 126–Pallah (Palestine 133) [1975 6g² 6f² **63** 7fg³ 8g⁴ 1976 10fg⁶ 11.1fg² 10f⁵ 10h³ 11.5d⁶ 9v⁵ 10.2s] leggy filly: best run at 11f: ran poorly last three outings, once in blinkers: evidently needs a sound surface: sold 1,200 gns Newmarket December Sales. *H. Cecil.*

CORNAGE 4 b.f. Candy Cane 125–Sound Recordo 95 (Sound Track 132) [1974 **71** 5g² 5d² 6s 1975 7s* 7f³ 7f² 8.2fg⁵ 8g 1976 8fg 7f³ 7.2f⁶] compact filly: quite a moderate handicapper: unlucky in running when narrowly-beaten third to Avon Royale at Catterick in August, best effort at 4 yrs: best form at up to 7f and has yet to prove she stays further: acts on any going. *J. Etherington.*

CORNET JOYCE 3 b.g. Derring-Do 131–Heather Grove (Hethersett 134) **51** [1975 5fg² 5fg⁵ 7.2g⁵ 7g⁶ 7f 7f⁶ 8.2d 1976 6g 8fg 10f⁴ 10.2h⁴ 12fg⁶ 6fg 10s² 7s⁵ 10v⁶ 10v⁶] small, lightly-made gelding: plater: seems best at 1¼m: probably acts on any going: best form in blinkers. *R. Sturdy.*

CORNISH RHAPSODY 2 br.f. Typhoon 125–Royal Deb (Flush Royal 127) **68**
[1976 6fg 7fg 7d 7s] workmanlike filly: half-sister to a minor winner by Runnymede and to smart chaser Soloning (by Solon Morn): dam never ran: showed
a little ability in maiden race at Salisbury on second outing but was well beaten
afterwards. *M. Smyly.*

CORPORAL 2 br.c. Queen's Hussar 124–Mae West 82 (Never Say Die 137) **64**
[1976 6g 7g 7v] third foal: half-brother to 1¼m winner Bontecou (by Reform):
dam ran twice at 2 yrs: backward when behind in maiden races, on final outing
finishing last of 15 in a weakly-contested event at Leicester in October. *H.
Candy.*

CORRECT APPROACH 2 b.f. Right Tack 131–Vi 90 (Vilmorin) [1976 **77**
6fg 5f⁵ 7s 6s⁶] strong, good type of filly: half-sister to 3-y-o 1¼m winner Vigrey
(by Supreme Sovereign) and to three other winners, including useful 1973
2-y-o 5f winner Leodora (by Manacle): 2,100 gns yearling: dam best at sprint
distances: showed signs of ability in varied company, at Chepstow in October
finishing about 4 lengths sixth of 20 to Nobodys Fool in minor race: will stay
1m. *P. Cole.*

CORRIDOR 3 b.f. Crocket 130–Floradora 106 (French Beige 127) [1975 6f **—**
7fg 1976 8g 8f 8f 7f⁴] unfurnished filly: poor plater *F. Wiles.*

CORRIEFEOL 3 br.f. Jaipur–Easily Fooled (Tom Fool) [1975 5g² 5s³ 5.1f* **91**
5f 5.6g* 6fg² 6f² 6g² 1976 7fg 8g⁶ 8f⁵ 6h³ 7fg⁵ 7f] neat American-bred filly:
quite a useful handicapper: best form at 1m and will stay further: probably
acts on any going: brought down on first outing and was withdrawn under
orders after giving trouble in stalls on final appearance. *H. Cecil.*

CORTOWN LADY 3 b.f. Sovereign Gleam 117–Miss Dorothy 87 (Major Portion **56**
129) [1975 5fg 5fg 5fg* 5fg³ 5g 1976 5g 5fg 5f 6f⁵ 5h² 5.9f⁵ 5f 5g⁵ 6d 8s] light-
framed filly: plater: stays 6f: sold 400 gns Ascot November Sales. *D. Weeden.*

CORYLUS 2 ch.f. Calpurnius 122–Royal Nutmeg (Entanglement 118) [1976 **50**
5.9f⁶ 5.9f 6f 8fg 8.2s] poor plater. *D. Nicholson.*

COSTA BECK 2 b.f. Forlorn River 124–Mataloo 57 (Matador 131) [1976 5g² **54 d**
5g³ 5f 5h⁴ 5g⁴ 5h⁶] small, unimpressive filly: good second in seller at Doncaster
on first outing, but disappointed afterwards (twice tried in blinkers) and evidently
went the wrong way: sold 240 gns Ascot December Sales. *W. C. Watts.*

COSTA MINT 2 b.g. Meadow Mint 120–Recap 80 (King's Troop 118) [1976 **—**
6g⁵ 7f 7f⁵ 8.2f] of no account. *T. Craig.*

COSY BAR 2 b.c. Be Friendly 130–Red Barrel 95 (Aureole 132) [1976 5d **110**
6fg* 6fg⁴ 7fg⁴ 8g* 8g] well-made colt: half-brother to useful stayer Reviver
(by Only for Life): 12,500 gns yearling: dam won at 1¼m: a very useful performer who put up a fine display under top weight to win £1,800 nursery at
York in September by 1½ lengths from Prince Carl: had earlier won a maiden
race at Newmarket and finished 1½ lengths fourth to Sky Ship in 7f Lanson
Champagne Stakes at Goodwood: well beaten in nursery at Newmarket in
September on final outing: better suited by 1m than shorter distances. *B.
Hobbs.*

COUNTERFEIT LADY 3 b.f. Bold Lad (Ire) 133–Forgery 90 (Sing Sing 134) **88**
[1975 5f* 5fg⁵ 5v 5f 1976 5.9g 5fg⁴ 5.1fg 5f⁵ 5.3f* 6h² 5g] shapely, attractive
filly: good mover: ran easily her best races at Brighton, winning handicap by
3 lengths from Dusky Damsel and finishing in frame on her other two runs
there: brought wide on each occasion: stays 6f: acts on hard going: ran moderately when tried in blinkers on fourth outing: well suited by an undulating track.
M. Stoute.

COUNTERPART 2 b.c. Baldric II 131–Counterstroke (Saint Crespin III 132) **71**
[1976 7fg 8s 7s] shapely colt: good mover: French-bred colt: second foal:
dam, a very useful performer in France, won at up to 1¼m: showed ability
in maiden race on first outing but was well beaten afterwards: possibly unsuited
by soft going. *I. Balding.*

COUNTESS EILEEN 3 b.f. Sassafras 135–Smash Hit (Roan Rocket 128) [1975 **111**
7f⁵ 9.5g³ 8g* 1976 10f³ 12fg³ 12f⁴ 12g 12f* 12f⁴ 12fg 14fg³ 12v⁵ 12s*] lengthy,
useful-looking Irish filly: first foal: 1,700 gns yearling: dam won over 6f in
Ireland at 3 yrs: won handicap at Galway in July by 2½ lengths from Capricious

and Trigo Stakes at the Curragh in October by a neck from subsequently-disqualified Brandon Hill: in frame in four well-contested races, including Lingfield Oaks Trial (just over 1½ lengths third to Heaven Knows) and Ribblesdale Stakes at Royal Ascot and also ran well when seventh of 18 to Lagunette in Irish Guinness Oaks (tried in blinkers) and when 11 lengths third to Meneval in Irish St Leger, both races at the Curragh: stays 1¾m: acts on any going: genuine: sold 30,000 gns Newmarket December Sales, and has been exported to Germany. *L. Browne, Ireland.*

COUNTESS LOR 2 b.f. Lorenzaccio 130–Countess Decima (Sir Gaylord)   **77** P
[1976 6v³] lengthy filly: first foal: 3,300 gns yearling: dam unraced half-sister to four stakes winners: 12/1, showed considerable promise when beaten about 5½ lengths by subsequently-disqualified Picatina in 15-runner £2,100 event at York in October, being badly drawn and losing quite a lot of ground when switched to race on apparently better ground after 2f, but keeping on well in closing stages without being unnecessarily knocked about: will stay at least 1m: certain to have derived considerable benefit from the outing and should win races at 3 yrs. *H. Cecil.*

COUNTESS RAGUSA 3 ch.f. Caliban 123–Palvee 73 (Queen's Hussar 124)   —
[1975 6f 7f⁶ 6fg 1976 7fg 10f 12.2fg 7fg] small, lightly-built filly: little worth-while form. *M. Tate.*

COUNTY BOY 2 b.c. Richboy 117–Romancing 82 (Romulus 129) [1976   **78**
5fg 6fg* 6f⁴ 8f] half-brother to two winners, including fairly useful 1975 2-y-o 7f winner Stormy Affair (by Prevailing): 300 gns yearling: dam won at 6f at 2 yrs: won 15-runner maiden race at Windsor in July by 4 lengths from Baltois: should stay 1m. *P. Cole.*

COUP DE SOLEIL 2 b.c. Roi Soleil 125–Black Gnat (Typhoon 125) [1976   **81**
5g 6fg 6s³ 7s 6v⁴] well-made colt: second foal: half-brother to fair 1975 2-y-o Wild Hunter (by Whistling Wind): 1,000 gns yearling: dam won seven times from 5f to 9f in Ireland: moderate maiden: will stay 1m: best in blinkers. *R. Vibert.*

COURT CIRCUS 6 b.h. Floribunda 136–On Probation 92 (King's Bench 132)   **97**
[1974 8f³ 11.2fg³ 12g 7f³ 7g⁴ 8g³ 8g* 11.2f* 7g 8s⁴ 7fg⁵ 12g 8g 8.2v 8g 11.2s⁴ 11.1s

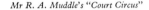

Mr R. A. Muddle's "Court Circus"

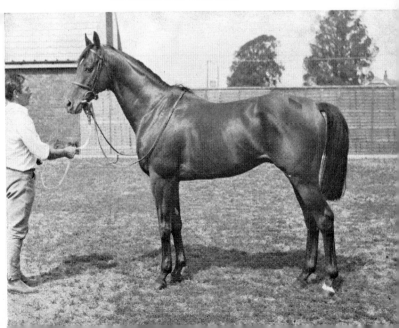

8.2v   1975 10 1g 12fg² 10fg* 12f* 12f* 12f² 14fg* 12f 14g³ 13g⁶ 12g 12f⁵ 16g⁶ 13g²
14f⁶   1976 12g⁴ 16fg⁴ 14g² 12fg* 12g* 13s⁵ 13.3fg³ 12f⁴ 11.7fg² 12f* 12fg² 12fg*
12.3f² 12h* 12g] well-made horse: an admirably game, genuine and consistent
handicapper who won five races in 1976, including two at Goodwood and at
Brighton: gained his most important success in Warren Stakes at Goodwood in
July, making all and beating Busted Fiddle 3 lengths: stays 1¾m but has twice
disappointed over 2m: acts on any going: has worn blinkers: usually ridden by
claimer R. Muddle: sold only 1,000 gns Ascot December Sales. *B. Hanbury.*

COURTEENHALL 2 gr.c. Queen's Hussar 124–Eightsome Reel 78 (Atan)   —
[1976 6g 5.9f 7fg] rangy colt: bad mover: first foal: dam won over 5f at 3 yrs,
and stayed 7f: little worthwhile form in maiden races. *A. Corbett.*

COURT HOUSE 2 ch.c. My Swanee 122–Windy Rush (Whistling Wind 123)   90
[1976 5g 5fg³ 6g⁴ 6fg⁶ 8g* 8g² 8s*] lengthy colt: first foal: dam moderate at 2 yrs
in Ireland: off course much of summer but showed fair form in nurseries on his
return in the autumn, winning at Yarmouth and Wolverhampton and failing by
only a head to catch Bona-Mia in £1,800 event at Newmarket in between: well
suited by 1m: acts well on soft going. *W. Marshall.*

COURTING DAY 4 gr.f. Right Boy 137–Sunday Out 95 (Lord of Verona 120)   63
[1974 5f⁴ 5g² 5g⁶ 6s² 5d² 5s⁶ 5v²   1975 8f 8h⁴ 8h² 8f² 8h⁶ 8g⁶ 8h*   1976 7f³ 8f⁴
8fg² 7g² 8f² 10f⁶ 9f³ 9h² 11h² 8fg³ 8.2f* 8g 8v] lightly-made filly: ran consistently in handicaps in the north at 4 yrs and gained a well-deserved success
when winning at Hamilton in September: stays 1m but probably not 1¼m: acts
on any going: best in blinkers. *W. Gray.*

COURT LANE 4 br.c. Mandamus 120–Jemake 85 (High Treason 126)   [1974   94
5fg⁶ 5d² 5fg⁴ 5d* 5g⁴ 6d² 6d   1975 6v 5s³ 6d³ 5.8f⁴ 6g⁶ 8d² 8f* 8.2fg⁴ 8d* 10g*
8v³ 8g⁵ 10f³   1976 10fg* 10g³ 10g⁶ 10fg² 9g⁴ 9fg⁴ 8f⁴ 8.2g* 8fg³ 8g³ 10.2g* 9g]
strong, compact colt: fairly useful handicapper: successful at Leicester in March,
Haydock in August and Doncaster the following month: ran well on most of his
other outings, including on eighth start when narrowly-beaten third to Silver
Steel in Rose of York Handicap at York: stays 1¼m well: acts on any going:
suitable mount for an apprentice or lady rider: tough, genuine and consistent:
unseated rider final appearance. *G. Hunter.*

COURT MELODY 6 b.g. King's Leap 111–Sea Melody 79 (Tudor Minstrel 144)   —
[1974 7.6g 8f² 7fg² 8g⁵ 8fg² 10g⁴   1975 8g 8fg* 8f* 8f³ 8d³ 8fg⁶   1976 9g] big,
strong gelding: quite a useful handicapper (rated 92) in 1975: well beaten behind
Tintoretto at Wolverhampton in May, only appearance at 6 yrs: well suited by
1m but has yet to show he stays 1¼m: probably acts on any going: has been tried
in blinkers: suitable mount for an inexperienced rider. *E. Fisher.*

COY GIRL 3 b.f. Decoy Boy 129–Frilly Flaxon 57 (Chamier 128) [1975 5f 5f   45
6h   1976 6d 6f 5fg⁶ 5h⁴] compact filly: poor plater: ran badly when tried in
blinkers: sold 300 gns Doncaster August Sales. *S. Nesbitt.*

CRACKED LIPS 2 b.f. Crowned Prince 128–Neiva (Abdos 134) [1976 6v]   —
neat, strong filly: second reported foal: half-sister to French 3-y-o Naive Grunter
(by Gyr): dam won over 7f at 2 yrs in France and is sister to Grand Prix de
Marseille winner Arinda: 20/1 and in need of run when behind in 23-runner
maiden race won by Amity at Newbury in October: should be suited by longer
distances. *B. Hills.*

CRACKLE 4 b.f. Nelcius 133–Miracle Girl 75 (Sing Sing 134) [1974 N.R.   1975   —
8d 10fg 10fg⁴ 12.2g⁶ 8g² 8d³   1976 12fg 12fg] strong, well-made filly: sweated
up and ran badly both outings at 4 yrs: best form at 1m: none too resolute. *W.
Wightman.*

CRACK OF LIGHT 2 ch.f. Salvo 129–Clear Day 84 (Crepello 136) [1976 8g⁴]   74 p
lengthy filly: first foal: dam placed twice over 5f at 2 yrs: 10/1, chased leaders all
way when 7 lengths fourth of 12 to Mined Illusion in maiden race at Leicester in
September: should do better. *H. Cecil.*

CRAIGELLACHIE 6 b.g. Royal Palm 131–Berryfield Beauty 62 (Gratitude   82
130)   [1974 5f⁴ 5f² 5fg⁵ 5g 5g* 5g⁴ 5s³ 5s⁴ 5s³ 5v⁵   1975 5g 5f* 5g² 5.1f⁴ 5f² 5d²
5g² 5g* 5v* 5f³ 5s³ 5g⁶   1976 5f⁶ 5f* 5f³ 5f* 5g³ 5fg⁶] strong gelding: fair
handicapper: winner at Ostend in July and at Catterick the following month:
speedy and is best at 5f: acts on any going: has been tried in blinkers: good
mount for an apprentice: tough, genuine and consistent. *K. Whitehead.*

Queen Mary Stakes, Ascot—a near thing between Cramond (No. 5), Piney Ridge and Easy Landing (far side). The unlucky As Blessed is fourth, ahead of Triple First (light colours) and Japora

CRAIGTON LAD 3 ch.g. probably Foggy Bell 108–Morag (Our Babu 131) —
[1975 N.R. 1976 10g] first foal: dam never ran: in rear behind Frankie in minor race at Ayr in September: sold 260 gns at Doncaster Sales the following month. *J. Turner.*

CRAMOND 2 b.f. Porto Bello 118–Annie May (Aggressor 130) [1976 5fg² 5f* **105**
5f* 5fg⁶] strong filly: first ₒal: 460 gns foal and resold for 2,200 gns as a yearling: dam of little account: 25/1 for 12-runner Queen Mary Stakes at Royal Ascot in June but was always prominent and got up close home to win by a head and a neck from Piney Ridge and Easy Landing: had previously landed the odds in maiden race at Wolverhampton in May: not disgraced when giving weight all round in St Hugh's Stakes at Newbury in August on final outing, finishing 5 lengths sixth to Haraka: will stay 6f: useful. *R. Boss.*

CRASH COURSE 5 b.h. Busted 134–Lucky Stream 99 (Persian Gulf) [1974 **126**
10f* 13.3g² 12s⁵ 14fg* 14.6g 1975 12fg³ 20f* 16fg⁴ 21f 16fg* 18g* 16g² 1976
16g² 20f² 16fg²]
This fine, genuine stayer was difficult to train as a five-year-old and had only three races, all of them in June, before a tendon injury forced his retirement. Two days before the Gold Cup at Royal Ascot, Crash Course was lame in his near hock and seemed most unlikely to be in the field. Fortunately, he was galloped sound the day before the Gold Cup and was able to show in the race that he was one of the best long-distance horses of the year in Europe. Although no match for Sagaro, who had something in hand of his one-length winning margin, Crash Course beat the rest decisively. In third place, a couple of lengths behind Crash Course, came Sea Anchor who had beaten a very backward Crash Course by two lengths in the Henry II Stakes at Sandown a fortnight earlier. Crash Course was seen out only once more. He made a valiant effort when conceding between 14 lb and 35 lb to ten rivals in the Joe Coral Northumberland Plate at Newcastle; only Philominsky, in receipt of 28 lb, was too good on the day for him,

and at the finish there was only a length and a half between the pair of them.

Crash Course (b.h. 1971)	Busted (b 1963)	Crepello (ch 1954)	Donatello II
			Crepuscule
		Sans le Sou (b 1957)	Vimy
			Martial Loan
	Lucky Stream (b 1956)	Persian Gulf (b 1940)	Bahram
			Double Life
		Kypris (b 1950)	Victrix
			Phinoola

Crash Course's sire Busted had another excellent year, being responsible for 27 individual winners of 43 races and £70,685 in Britain and Ireland. Had Crash Course stayed sound there is not much doubt that he would have boosted his sire's magnificent record, possibly by repeating his 1975 win in the Doncaster Cup, a race which in his absence went to the Gold Cup third Sea Anchor. Crash Course is a half-brother to four useful winners—Stock Beck (by Saint Crespin III), Paddle Boat and Lucky Paddy (both by St Paddy), and Deep River (by Tudor Melody). All won at a mile and a half and all except Deep River gave the impression that they would have been suited by longer distances. The dam Lucky Stream was quite a useful winner at up to eleven furlongs and is a half-sister to Sultry Day, a very useful stayer in this country in the late 'fifties who showed even better form after being sent to France. The grandam Kypris won the Prix de la Salamandre and finished fourth in the French Oaks. Crash Course, a powerful, good-looking, deep-bodied horse, acted very well on firm going and ran badly the only time he encountered the mud. He has been retired to the Irish National Stud at a fee of £250 with the live foal concession. *J. Hindley.*

CRAZY CREATURE 2 b.c. Stephen George 102–Dicentra 101 (Infatuation 129) **73**
[1976 5fg 5fg³ 5g² 5f⁴ 5s⁶ 5f⁴ 5d* 6fg³ 5.9f 5fg⁵ 5f⁵ 5fg³ 5.9fg⁴ 6s³] smallish colt: half-brother to fair middle-distance handicapper Setra (by Setay): 500 gns yearling: bought in 1,450 gns after winning seller at Doncaster in May: ran creditably in nurseries on last few outings: stays 6f: appears to act on any going: genuine and consistent. *R. Murphy.*

CRAZY HARVEST 3 br.g. Crocket 130–Harvest Dream 95 (Premonition 130) **77**
[1975 6fg 1976 7fg 10g⁴] strong gelding: showed only form when just over 5½ lengths fourth of nine to Lucky Mickmooch in maiden race at Epsom in June: evidently suited by 1¼m. *W. Stephenson.*

CRAZY HORSE 4 b.g. Jukebox 120–French Doll (Worden II 129) [1974 7g **73**
7d 8d 1975 8fg³ 8fg⁶ 7f⁶ 8g² 7f² 8.3fg* 12g³ 10g⁵ 1976 10fg 10f 12g 10fg 7g⁴
7f 8g⁶ 8f 8s² 6d³ 7v*] neat gelding: poor handicapper: successful at Leicester in November: best at up to 1m: acts on any going: wears blinkers. *R. Sturdy.*

CREAMILINE 2 ch.c. Net 116–Syr Daria (Mincio 127) [1976 6d 7g 8s] half- **74**
brother to French middle-distance winner Syr Violon (by Violon d'Ingres): dam won six times over middle distances in France: in mid-division in maiden races at Yarmouth and Newmarket (two): will stay 1½m. *A. Goodwill.*

CREETOWN 4 b.c. Tower Walk 130–Lavella (Le Lavandou 111) [1974 6s⁶ 5s* **112**
1975 6v⁴ 7v⁴ 6g² 6s⁵ 6fg³ 6fg⁵ 6g⁶ 8d³ 1976 6.5g 6.5g 7fg* 7f* 7fg² 8g³ 7fg* 7g*
7.6h 6f* 7.3fg 7h⁴] attractive, well-made colt: very useful handicapper: had a highly successful 4-y-o campaign, winning five races, including three at Brighton (one of them Brighton Sprint Handicap) and Craven Handicap at Epsom (by 3 lengths from Yunkel): stays 1m but best form at shorter distances: acts on any going: blinkered fifth outing at 3 yrs (ran well) and second start in 1976 (ran badly): goes well on switchback tracks: genuine and consistent: had stiff tasks last two outings. *J. Nelson.*

CREPANI 3 b.c. Crepello 136–Trip to the Moon 84 (Sicambre 135) [1975 N.R. —
1976 10fg 11g] small, sturdy, quite attractive colt: brother to Derby fourth Great Wall and to a minor winner, and half-brother to several winners including Derby fourth Moon Mountain (by Mourne): 31,000 gns yearling: dam ran only at 2 yrs: never in with a chance when ninth in early-season maiden races at Kempton and Newbury. *I. Balding.*

CREPE PAPER 2 b.c. Crepello 136–Pelting 98 (Vilmorin) [1976 6f 6g³ 7f² 8f³ **85**
8s] strong, good-bodied colt: half-brother to numerous winners, notably very smart 1973 2-y-o Splashing (by Petingo): 8,400 gns foal, resold 23,000 gns yearling: dam 5f sprinter: moderate maiden: probably stays 1m but ran best race at 7f: sent to France. *P. Walwyn.*

CRICKET BAT 3 ch.f. Indigenous 121–Sister Willow 95 (Premonition 130) —
[1975 5s 5f 5fg⁵ 6f² 6fg² 6f* 1976 6f 5h⁵] tall, good sort: fair handicapper at
2 yrs: had stiff tasks and showed little worthwhile form on only two outings in
1976: not seen out after June: should stay 7f. *R. Hannon.*

CRI DE COEUR 4 ch.g. Weepers Boy 124–Courtly Girl 74 (Supreme Court 135) —
[1974 N.R. 1975 8g 1976 7g 16.1d] big, strong gelding: of little account:
sold 350 gns Ascot June Sales and exported to Sweden. *P. Makin.*

CRIME BUSTER 4 b.g. Busted 134–County Court 98 (Grey Sovereign 128 §) —
[1974 8d 7v⁵ 1975 8g 10d 11.1fg 8fg² 8g² 8g* 8fg* 8g 8fg⁶ 8g 1976 10.2g
10.6d] good-bodied gelding: said to have been hobdayed: possibly best at around
1m but should stay further: ran poorly in blinkers (gave impression that something had gone wrong with him) final outing in 1975 and at 4 yrs (finished tailed
off). *S. Nesbitt.*

CRIMSON COON 3 br.c. Tycoon II–Crimson Belle (Red God 128 §) [1975   **65**
5f⁶ 6f 7f⁶ 7s² 7f⁴ 7.6s 7g* 1976 12f⁵ 13.4s² 12fg² 11.7f⁵ 14g 12h² 12fg 10d 12s⁶
12s³ 16v 12v] compact colt: suited by a test of stamina: acts on any going:
won in blinkers at 2 yrs but showed form without in 1976: suitable mount for
an apprentice: not particularly consistent. *R. Sturdy.*

CRIMSON SILK 2 ch.c. Counsel 118–La Muleta (Matador 131) [1976 5g⁴ **104**
5s⁶ 6fg⁶ 6d² 5v² 6s²] strong, workmanlike colt: first foal: 3,200 gns yearling:
dam once-raced daughter of very speedy Crimson: 1½ lengths runner-up in three
races in the autumn, £2,200 nursery at Ascot (to Our Jimmy), £1,800 maiden
race at York (to Don) and Potter Trophy Nursery at Newmarket (to Aspect):
will probably stay 7f: very well suited by soft ground: sure to win a race. *R.
Mason.*

CROCK OF ALE 3 br.g. Crocket 130–Check Royale (Meadow Court 129) [1975   **57**
5.1f 5.1f³ 5.9f⁶ 5.1f* 1976 7f 8fg³ 7fg⁶] plater: has worn blinkers, but seems
to do better without: exported by B.B.A. to Belgium and is a winner there.
W. O'Gorman.

CROFT CLOSE 2 br.g. Sit In The Corner–Open Arms 77 (Dignitary 121) [1976   **72**
5fg 5g 5g⁵ 5f³ 5f³ 5fg⁴ 5fg⁴] small, compact gelding: fairly useful plater: should
stay 6f: goes well for apprentice G. Skeats. *J. Cousins.*

CROFTING 3 ch.f. Crepello 136–Heathfield 99 (Hethersett 134) [1975 6d* **98**
1976 7.3f 10.5d² 10fg² 10fg² 12fg 8g³] well-made, attractive filly: second in
three good races, Musidora Stakes at York (beaten 2½ lengths by Everything
Nice), Twyford Stakes at Newbury (beaten ¾ length by stable-companion Silken
Way) and Durham Stakes at Newcastle (blinkered first time, went under by ¾
length to St Joles): again blinkered when running poorly on final outing: should
be suited by 1½m (out of her depth when tried at trip in Yorkshire Oaks): acts
on a firm and a soft surface. *R. Hern.*

CROISETTE 4 br.f. Sunny Way 120–Solar Telegram (Solar Slipper 131) [1974 **92**
7g 6s³ 6d² 1975 7s* 6d* 8.2g⁴ 9fg³ 6f² 8.2fg³ 9fg⁵ 8g⁵ 10fg³ 8.2v* 1976 8.2v*
8d* 8f⁵ 10g* 10s* 8f³ 8g⁵ 10g⁴ 10.6d⁴ 10.5v² 10.2s⁶] compact filly: fairly useful
handicapper: winner at Hamilton and Newcastle, both in April, and twice at Ayr
(amateur riders events) the following month: stays 1½m: acts on any going,
but is particularly well suited by some give in the ground: ideal mount for an
apprentice or amateur rider: genuine and consistent. *S. Hall.*

CROPFALL 6 ch.m. Acropolis 132–Fallacious 68 (Never Say Die 137) [1974 —
N.R. 1975 N.R. 1976 16fg] quite a moderate stayer (rated 79) in 1973: always
behind when well beaten in handicap at Warwick in April, only outing since:
stays 1¾m: seems to act on any going. *J. Powney.*

CROSBY SIMON 2 ch.c. Green God 128–Treacle Tart 71 (Aureole 132) [1976   **52**
5f 5d 6fg 5h⁶ 6f⁵ 6h⁶ 7fg 8s 5v] neat colt: poor plater: blinkered penultimate
appearance. *J. Calvert.*

CROSS BIRD 2 b.f. Fury Royal 108–Artist's Lover (Botticelli 129) [1976   **49**
5f 5fg⁶ 5fg 6fg³] compact filly: first reported foal: dam won over 1½m and
also ran in point-to-points: 3¾ lengths third of nine to Hardy Maid in seller at
Lingfield in June: subsequently exported to Belgium and has won over there.
R. Smyth.

CROSS GATE 2 ch.g. Chestergate 111–Catherine's Stones (Henry the Seventh —
125) [1976 6fg 5.9s 5v] small gelding: no worthwhile form, including in a
seller. *S. Nesbitt.*

CROW 3 ch.c. Exbury 138–Carmosina (Right of Way 117) [1975 N.R. 1976 **134** 8.5g* 10v⁴ 12g² 10g* 10.5fg² 14.6d* 12s² 10d]

Crow's emergence as a very good horse was one of the highlights of the second half of the season. For years we have waited for Exbury to sire something as good as himself, and now our wait is almost at an end if Crow, who remains in training, shows even half the amount of improvement from three to four that Exbury did. Exbury was a great horse at the age of four, one of the best to have raced over middle distances in Europe in the last thirty years, just as brilliant over a mile and a quarter as a mile and a half, unbeaten in five races, including the Prix de l'Arc de Triomphe and the Prix Ganay. The previous season he finished only sixth in the Arc and third in the French Derby, his merit apparently fully exposed, and his record at that age doesn't match Crow's. Crow has already won the St Leger and finished a clear second in the Arc. There is no knowing whether Crow has the improvement in him still needed to put him firmly in the Exbury class but the signs are encouraging. Until he ran poorly in the Champion Stakes on his final appearance of the season he had a record of significant and sustained progress from the time he returned to the track in July after an absence of sixteen weeks; he has had comparatively little racing in the best company and probably he is not yet fully exposed. Persevering with him at distances as short as a mile and a quarter may hinder his development and harm his reputation but, barring accidents, he is the one they all will have to beat at the top races at a mile and a half or more.

Unlike his sire, Crow did not run as a two-year-old and did not show high-class form until halfway through his third year, by which time his stable-companions Pawneese and Flying Water had already won three classics between them. His first win of significance came in the Prix Eugene Adam at Saint-Cloud in July, by a short head from the Prix de la Jonchere winner Avaray, a colt very near to the top of the tree who was giving him 4 lb. Before the Prix Eugene Adam, Crow had been out only three times, his absence from the course from March to July reportedly being the result of a blood disorder. Two runs at Maisons-Laffitte in the early spring brought him a win from Youth's lead-horse Oilfield in the Prix Northeast for newcomers and a defeat, apparently on merit, behind Nillaos, Kano and Campero in the Prix Lagrange. On his return a much stiffer task faced him in the Grand Prix de Compiegne. Racing at Compiegne is usually of a modest standard but the Grand Prix offers a purse big enough to attract runners as good as Hunza Dancer, the Epsom Derby third and still capable of high-class performances, and Inis-Gloire, the Irish Cambridgeshire winner. For one of his limited experience Crow did well to divide the two four-year-olds; the margin of defeat was only half a length, although Hunza Dancer gave the impression that it could easily have been increased. Crow, ridden by Dubroeucq in place of Saint-Martin who had the mount on Luenge at Newmarket, made the running until Hunza Dancer collared him in the last furlong.

Saint-Martin rode Crow in the Prix Eugene Adam twelve days later, and he handled him beautifully. The Eugene Adam is a pattern race contested by horses of, or near to, classic standard and run over a distance of a mile and a quarter, two furlongs less than the Grand Prix de Compiegne. The presence in the field of front-runners of the calibre of Vitiges and French Friend, the latter making his first appearance of the season, gave Saint-Martin the opportunity to settle Crow; he had him in fourth or fifth place in the fourteen-strong field, moved him up gradually from the home turn into a narrow lead at the distance from Avaray, French Friend, Arctic Tern and Happy Tim, and kept just enough up his sleeve to hold on, riding with hands and heels.

Crow was improving rapidly; as he improved so did the tasks set him increase in difficulty. Next time out he had to take on what seemed to be the

Prix Eugene Adam, Saint-Cloud—Crow (far side) and Avaray almost together, followed by French Friend, Happy Tim, Arctic Tern, Vitiges and Riboboy

St Leger Stakes, Doncaster—French challengers first and second, with Crow winning decisively from Secret Man. The grey Scallywag takes third place, ahead of Oats

best horses in France or England over a mile and a quarter, Trepan and Wollow, in the Benson and Hedges Gold Cup at York. Against such opposition his chance of winning appeared remote: he held sounder credentials for a race of this nature than the stayers Quiet Fling and Patch, but as well as Trepan and Wollow to contend with he had Twig Moss, second in the French Derby and effective at the shorter trip. Crow once again reached new heights. He ran Wollow to a length, the only one of Wollow's six opponents anywhere near him at the finish, making headway in the straight without ever threatening to win and closing steadily in a manner that suggested he would be suited by a return to a longer distance.

At the time, the value of Crow's performance at York tended to be underestimated; the fact that Trepan and Twig Moss ran well below their best probably led many to discount the margin of Crow's superiority over the rest of the field—five lengths or more. So when he was returned for the St Leger, accompanied by Secret Man, Campero, French Friend and the pacemaker Vital Hunter, he came as part of what was widely regarded as a French 'second team,' although he started one of the three joint-favourites along with General Ironside and Oats. The numerical strength of the French challenge, unusual nowadays, was a tribute to the regard in which Exceller and Youth, probables for the French St Leger, were held; it was also an indication of a suspected overall weakness in the English and Irish opposition.

There seemed good reason for a certain amount of French optimism behind their so-called 'second team,' although there were stamina doubts about Crow, whose dam's only win had been over five furlongs as a three-year-old, and doubts about the form of French Friend, who had been beaten easily by Citoyen at Deauville since his third in the Prix Eugene Adam. Secret Man had lost only one of his five races during the season, beaten four lengths by Exceller in the Grand Prix de Paris; he was proven over the distance as was Campero, twice just behind him in important races in France. The English challenge was a strong one in the sense that most of the best stayers in the country turned out, but there was clearly little between the leading English horses and none except Marquis de Sade had looked in recent weeks as though he had more than normal improvement in him. Norfolk Air and General Ironside had been beaten by Hawkberry at York; Scallywag had been well beaten by Marquis de Sade at Goodwood and had since been tubed; Smuggler, winner of the Gordon Stakes from Oats, General Ironside and Norfolk Air, is not at his best on ground as soft as that which prevailed on Leger day; Oats, third in the Derby, had lost to the older Swell Fellow at Newbury last time out; and Marquis de Sade, ante-post favourite a week before the race, took a walk in the betting after rumour got round that all was not well with him.

Crow murdered the lot of them for pace. Approaching the two-furlong marker there was little to choose up in front between, from the inside, Norfolk Air, Smuggler, Oats, Crow and Secret Man, but Saint-Martin had been biding his time, having turned for home halfway down the field, and almost as soon as he asked Crow for an effort the horse quickened clear of all except Secret Man, showing that extra gear that few of the English three-year-olds had revealed in the top middle-distance races. For a short while it seemed as though Secret Man

187

would be a danger on the outside; not because he was moving anywhere nearly so well as Crow, but because he threatened to barge into him. Quickly the danger receded. Crow, pushed along into a comfortable lead, stayed on for a very decisive win, ears pricked, by two lengths from Secret Man, completing a career record of victories in every English classic for his jockey. There were excuses of varying plausibility made for several of the vanquished; the outsider Black Sabbath fell more than a mile out, Tierra Fuego was struck into, eighth-placed Marquis de Sade and eleventh-placed Campero were clearly not seen at their best, but there isn't any doubt in our mind that the winner was easily the best animal in the field. He is one of the best winners of the race in the last few years and different from some of them in that he has proved capable of showing his form over a shorter distance since his win.

Crow made his return to a shorter distance in the Prix de l'Arc de Triomphe and emerged the best of four Leger winners in the field, the others being Bruni, Exceller and the Norsk St Leger winner Noble Dancer. He did much more than beat those horses, of course; he beat all except Ivanjica and once again showed a fine turn of foot, bursting into the lead two furlongs from home. At that point he appeared to have the race won, comfortably holding Youth and Bruni, but Ivanjica, who had had nothing like so strenuous a season as he, quickened past him inside the last furlong and won by two lengths. Trained as a four-year-old with the Arc in view Crow may go one better, particularly if conditions are similarly testing.

As other Arc runners before him, Crow was started for the Champion Stakes and ran poorly. He is unlikely to be the last to do so. The Champion Stakes comes too soon after the Arc for many horses, and it came too soon, we think, for Crow. He showed his races in the paddock beforehand. There are other hypotheses to be considered why Crow finished only thirteenth, and a remote thirteenth at that, behind Vitiges after toiling all the way. The first, that he failed because he raced on the slower side of the course, carries little weight, for he didn't even put up a show against his own group, led by Malacate. Crow, at his best, is better than Malacate. The second, that he found the distance of ten furlongs too sharp by that stage of the season may well prove correct. Nevertheless, in view of the fact that we have accepted that the race came too soon after the Arc, it is only fair to Crow to reserve judgement—until he has run again over a similar trip (perhaps in the Prix Ganay or the Eclipse). After all, his two previous runs at the distance, while not his very best runs, produced a second in the Benson and Hedges Gold Cup and a win in the Prix Eugene Adam.

Crow (ch.c. 1973)			
	Exbury (ch 1959)	Le Haar (ch 1954)	Vieux Manoir / Mince Pie
		Greensward (b 1953)	Mossborough / Stargrass
	Carmosina (ch 1963)	Right of Way (ch 1957)	Honeyway / Magnificent
		Sixtina (ch 1956)	Aristophanes / La Dogana

The achievements of Crow and fellow classic winner Empery helped to re-focus attention on the scale of operation undertaken by some of the most successful owner-breeders nowadays, a scale of operation that a number of French racing's protectionists are foolishly striving to limit. Crow's dam Carmosina was purchased in Argentina, for 10,000 dollars, after winning one small race from four starts as a three-year-old; Empery's dam, a top-class Peruvian mare, cost five times as much when bought just out of training in Lima. Such enterprise deserves the reward it has reaped, in our opinion. The reward was a long time in the reaping with Carmosina, and she was one of a batch of fifty-one Wildenstein mares sold in Kentucky four months before Crow set foot on a race-course. The batch fetched 623,300 dollars, to which sum Carmosina, in foal to French Derby winner Rheffic, contributed only 9,200 dollars; in the same batch Flying Water's dam, Formentera, in foal to Shantung, contributed 32,000 dollars; Earth Spirit's dam Eagle Eye, in foal to French Two Thousand Guineas winner Faraway Son, contributed 12,000 dollars.

Carmosina produced one runner before Crow, the filly Cofimvaba (by Verrieres), and has produced one since, the colt Catus (by New Chapter). Cofimvaba won decent races over the jumps in France but she disappointed in a subsequent hurdling career in England and has been retired to stud. Catus ran a promising third in the race in which General made an impressive first appearance on Prix de l'Arc day. Carmosina one wouldn't regard as bred in the purple, with the handicapper Right of Way for her sire, but it is easy to appreciate that she

M D. Wildenstein's "Crow" (Y. Saint-Martin)

would have appeal to the international breeder, for her dam, Sixtina, is a close relative of the outstandingly successful stallion Forli. Sixtina, a good winner in Argentina and the dam of two good winners over there, including a brother to Carmosina called Manfred, is by Forli's sire Aristophanes out of a sister to Forli's dam Trevisa. There is plenty of speed in the family. Sixtina and Manfred, as well as Carmosina, showed form over five furlongs, and even Right of Way, who stayed eleven furlongs, was regarded as a miler for the best part of his career.

It is a near certainty that Crow will be trained for a middle-distance programme as a four-year-old, but in the event of his being aimed at a Cup race the fact that some of his most notable relatives on the distaff side of his pedigree were speedy animals may still be of relevance when estimating his stamina. Probably he will stay further than a mile and three quarters, but he is not a horse who needs a thorough test of stamina to be seen to best advantage as are nearly all the Cup horses nowadays. Far from it! He has a turn of foot; that's where he has the advantage over most of the horses of his generation who race over middle distances, and that's the main reason why his emergence was one of the highlights of the second half of the season. Crow goes particularly well on soft ground. His ability to handle very firm going has to be taken on trust; he did well enough against Wollow on a firmish surface to suggest that firmer going in itself will not inconvenience him, but presumably the shorter the distance the more desirable soft ground will be for him. In appearance Crow is an attractive, short-backed colt, reminiscent of his sire although noticeably taller. He will make a tip-top four-year-old. *A. Penna, France.*

CROWN BOWLER 2 ch.c. Supreme Sovereign 119–Ali Drake (Dicta Drake 126) **110**
[1976 5g* 5g2 5d3 6fg2 7f2 7g 7s* 7d3] rangy colt: half-brother to two winners by Major Portion, including fairly useful 1974 2-y-o Glorious Devon: 6,200 gns yearling: dam twice-raced daughter of Irish Oaks runner-up Indian Melody: won minor events at Sandown in April (by ¾ length from Ratamataz) and Lingfield in September (led close home when beating Swagger a short head): ran well on

most of his other starts, including when 8 lengths third of 11 to The Minstrel in William Hill Dewhurst Stakes at Newmarket in October: will stay 1m: acts on any going. *B. Hills.*

CROWN MAJOR 4 b.c. Majority Blue 126–Tiara III (Persian Gulf) [1974 5g⁴   **59**
6fg³ 6fg⁶ 5g⁵ 6fg⁵ 6g⁴ 1975 10f 7f* 8.2g⁶ 8.3fg² 8f⁴ 7g⁶ 8.3fg³ 8.3fg⁵ 7f 7.6g 7s 1976 10.2g 7fg 7fg⁶ 6fg² 6f 6g³ 7fg⁵ 6fg 7fg⁶ 7g 9f 7f] big, strong colt: poor handicapper: stays 1m: acts on firm going: has run well in blinkers but does better without. *M. Bolton.*

CROWN MATRIMONIAL 4 b.c. Right Royal V 135–Le Magicienne (Val de   —
Loir 133) [1974 6g 7g⁶ 6g 7.2d 1975 N.R. 1976 14f 12fg] useful hurdler but is only a poor performer on flat. *I. Dudgeon.*

CRUCIAL DECISION *2 ch.f. Damascus–Slapton Sands (First Landing)   **92**
[1976 5fg³ 7fg* 7g² 7g⁵] half-sister to smart 3-y-o Riboboy (by Ribot) and to French filly Sea Sands (by Sea-Bird II), a smart winner at up to 1¼m: $75,000 yearling: dam, a winner over 6f at 3 yrs in U.S.A., is half-sister to four stakes winners: 3/1 on for three-runner event at Lingfield in July and made all to win by 1½ lengths from Tudor Lilt: placed behind useful fillies on two other outings, running well when 1½ lengths second to Taffytina in £2,100 event at Newmarket later in July: will stay 1¼m. *B. Hills.*

CRUISING 2 gr.c. Habitat 134–Running River 77 (Crocket 130) [1976 5f   —
5.1g⁴] third foal: half-brother to Rippling (by Derring-Do), a useful winner at up to 6f as a 2-y-o in 1975: dam twice-raced half-sister to smart sprinter Turnkey: showed a little ability when remote fourth of 16 to Captains Mate in maiden race at Yarmouth in September: should stay 6f. *M. Stoute.*

CRUSTY SHAH 3 ch.c. Tyrant–Persian Pie (Tamerlane 128) [1975 5h⁶ 5d⁵   **92**
5g⁴ 5f* 5d* 5f⁴ 5v⁶ 1976 5f⁴ 7fg 6d 7fg⁵ 7g⁴ 6f* 6fg 5g 5f⁶ 6g⁶] good-looking, full-quartered colt: half-brother to smart 2-y-o Athlete's Foot (by Prince Tenderfoot): fairly useful handicapper: had some stiff tasks in 1976 and put up easily best effort when making all to beat Resin in good style by 2½ lengths at Redcar in July: best form at sprint distances: acts on any going with possible exception of heavy: exported to Hong Kong. *N. Angus.*

CRY FOR HELP 2 ch.f. Town Crier 119–Palestra 92 (Palestine 133) [1976   —
6fg 5fg 7fg 8s] half-sister to 3-y-o Penny God (by Red God), the best 2-y-o in Hungary in 1975, and to a winner abroad: 675 gns foal: dam stayed 7f: well beaten in maiden races. *V. Cross.*

CRY FOR JOY 3 b.g. Town Crier 119–Mahal 101 (Tutankhamen) [1975 5f 6g   —
6f 6g 1976 6f 14g 10f] leggy gelding: bad plater: has worn blinkers: sold 400 gns Ascot August Sales. *A. Neaves.*

CRY NO MORE 3 b.c. Weepers Boy 124–Balfour Lass 81 (My Smokey 125)   **81**
[1975 5v⁵ 5s* 5d⁵ 5f² 5g* 6f 5fg⁵ 6fg 6g³ 5g 1976 8f 7fg 5f 5fg² 6f⁴ 5fg 6h⁵ 5fg² 5.8f 5s² 6s*] hollow-backed colt: modest handicapper: won minor event at Doncaster in November by a length from Belle Vue: best at sprint distances: acts on any going: occasionally wears blinkers but does just as well without. *R. Hannon.*

CRY OF JOY 2 br.f. Town Crier 119–Artemesia 56 § (Martial 131) [1976   **50**
5f⁴ 5d] lightly-built filly: showed only poor form in sellers: not seen out after May. *K. Payne.*

CRY OF MARCH 2 gr.f. Town Crier 119–March Stone 84 (March Past 124)   —
[1976 5s 5v] small, sturdy filly: half-sister to two 2-y-o winners, including fairly useful 5f winner Riotous (by Silver Cloud): 2,200 gns yearling: dam soft ground 1¼m to 2m handicapper: backward when behind in end-of-season maiden races at Sandown and Lingfield. *D. Keith.*

CRYPTOMERIA 2 ch.f. Crepello 136–Miss Glen 107 (Abernant 142) [1976   **80**
5g⁵ 6fg² 8g³] rather unfurnished filly: closely related to fairly useful 3-y-o 1¼m winner Index (by Busted) and half-sister to three minor winners: dam a miler: moderate maiden: will stay 1¼m. *H. Candy.*

CRYSTAL FJORD 2 b.f. Midsummer Night II 117–Voluntary Salute (March   —
Past 124) [1976 5fg 6g] plain, narrow filly: in rear in maiden race at Leicester in March and seller at Warwick in June. *Miss N. Wilmot.*

CRYSTAL HALO 2 b.f. St Chad 120–Lumina (Nimbus 130) [1976 5h 6fg   **78**
8s³ 10v] lightly-made filly: half-sister to two winners, including fair 1½m winner Palace Rose (by Aureole): dam disappointing half-sister to Royal Palace: quite a moderate maiden: well suited by 1m and should stay further. *P. Walwyn.*

CUCKMERE ISLAND 3 ch.c. Easter Island 101–Cuckmere Beacon 67 (Casmiri — 107) [1975 7g⁵ 8f 1976 15.5s] of no account. *B. Wise.*

CUDGEL 3 br.g. The Brianstan 128–Pelta (Border Chief 101) [1975 5g² 5f* **92** 5f² 1976 5f⁶ 5d* 5g* 6f 6fg² 6d² 6d 6s⁵] well-grown, leggy gelding: quite a useful handicapper: won at Chester (by a head from Pascualete) and Haydock (by 4 lengths from Lanark Birk) in May: ran very well when ½-length second to Breathing Exercise at Haydock in October (ridden by 7-lb claimer and having first run since July) but ran moderately on last two outings: stays 6f: probably acts on any going. *P. Rohan.*

CULBERGE 5 b.g. Faberge II 121–Mia Culpa (Le Levanstell 122) [1974 8s⁵ **44** 8g 10f⁵ 8g⁴ 8s² 8fg⁵ 8s³ 10d³ 10g² 12g⁴ 8s 10.8v⁴ 1975 15.8d³ 12.2fg 8g 1976 12.2s 8s 12s⁵] compact gelding: poor maiden. *Dr A. Jones.*

CULLODEN KING 2 b.c. Night Life 92–Culloden Queen (Fleche Bleu 84) — [1976 6s] second reported foal: dam never ran: 33/1 and ridden by 7-lb claimer when behind in 24-runner minor event won by Tudor Jig at Teesside in November. *W. Elsey.*

CUMBERNAULD 9 br.g. Ribot 142–Gazpacho 120 (Hard Sauce 131) [1974 **88** 18.4g³ 22.2f⁶ 22.2fg* 19g⁵ 18g³ 16.2v⁵ 18d 16.1v 1975 16.1g⁴ 20f² 22.2fg* 18.4g² 22.2f⁵ 21f⁴ 1976 18d⁵ 20f 18.4fg⁵ 19fg 16.1f² 20g⁴ 18fg³ 18g² 18.1g² 19s⁵ 18d] small gelding: not the animal he was but is far from being a backnumber and showed fairly useful form from time to time in 1976: requires a thorough test of stamina: acts well on firm ground and does not act on very soft: sometimes wears blinkers: genuine: sold to C. Dingwall 1,000 gns Ascot December Sales. *B. Hanbury.*

CUMNOCK SCOUSE 3 bl.g. Bluerullah 115–Sweet Morning Breeze (Vic Day **72** 126) [1975 N.R. 1976 10f 6g⁵ 8.2g 6g* 8v⁵ 6s] fifth foal: half-brother to two minor sprint winners: dam won at 1m: won weakly-contested maiden race at York in September all out by a short head from Palm Court Joe: had stiffish tasks afterwards: should stay 1m: started slowly first two outings. *G. Richards.*

CUNNING TRICK 4 ch.c. Decoy Boy 129–Derry Willow (Sunny Way 120) **52** [1974 5fg 5f 5d 5g 5s* 7g 5g⁵ 5v³ 1975 6v 6fg⁵ 5g⁶ 6g⁶ 6fg⁶ 5g 6h 8g 8g⁴ 7g 8fg³ 9fg⁶ 1976 8g³ 8g⁴ 8.3f² 8fg* 8f] strong colt: poor mover: poor handicapper: sold out of M. Francis's stable 750 gns after winning seller at Yarmouth in May (favourite): stays 1m: seems to act on any going except perhaps very firm: has run well in blinkers but didn't wear them in 1976: sometimes wears bandages: sold 360 gns Ascot September Sales. *R. Bastiman.*

CUPIDS DEW 2 b.c. Taj Dewan 128–Valcupid (Dan Cupid 132) [1976 7fg **91** 7g² 8g³ 8d 8v] small, close-coupled, attractive colt: first foal: dam twice-raced daughter of Oaks winner Valoris: placed in minor event at Kempton in August (length second to Filipachi) and £2,400 race at York the following month (beaten 3 lengths by Royal Plume) but was well beaten in a maiden race (favourite) and a nursery afterwards: will stay 1¼m: seems to need a sound surface. *B. Hills.*

CURLEYWEE 3 b.f. Paddy B 105–Ryans Daughter (Rise 'N Shine II) [1975 — 5d 6fg⁶ 1976 11g 7.2g 7f] neat filly: no worthwhile form, including in sellers: not seen out after June: blinkered final outing. *P. Cundell.*

CURRENT 2 b.c. Tudor Melody 129–Coulomb 108 (Crepello 136) [1976 7d 7s] — second foal: dam useful miler: ninth of 19 to Alltyre in minor event at Chepstow in October, second and better effort: will stay 1m. *Sir Mark Prescott.*

CURRENT MAGIC 6 b.h. Current Coin 118–Phosphorescence 92 (Aureole 132) — [1974 12s² 18fg³ 16g³ 12.2fg* 14f³ 12d 11s⁵ 12v² 12v 1975 N.R. 1976 16fg] quite a moderate handicapper (rated 75) in 1974: well-beaten seventh of nine to Piccadilly Etta at Lingfield in May, only outing since: stays well: acts on any going: used to wear blinkers but didn't at Lingfield. *M. Tate.*

CUSTARD 3 b.f. Darling Boy 124–Serein (Prince Chevalier) [1975 N.R. — 1976 10.1f 14d 12g] half-sister to three minor winners here and abroad: 800 gns foal, resold 340 gns yearling: dam, lightly-raced half-sister to Hotfoot, has been in Belgium: no sign of ability in maiden races. *N. Callaghan.*

CUT AND RUN 2 b.g. Run The Gantlet–Waterford Glass 97 (St Paddy 133) — p [1976 8s] well-grown, very attractive gelding: third foal: dam, winner over 1¼m, is half-sister to Royal Palace, Selhurst and Prince Consort: in rear in 27-runner maiden race won by Sporting Yankee at Newmarket in October: should do better in time if looks are anything to go by. *T. Waugh.*

CYCLAMATE 8 b.g. Runnymede 123–Zugela 90 (Zucchero 133 §) [1974 8g **48** 9g² 8.3fg³ 7g² 7fg 8g² 8s⁴ 1975 7fg 9g 8g 7f⁶ 8f 1976 7f⁴ 8fg² 7fg³ 7f 7g*] selling handicapper: successful at Brighton in August by ½ length from Doris's Choice (no bid): best at up to 9f: seems to act on any going: sometimes wears blinkers. *W. Wightman.*

CZARIST 5 b.h. Faberge II 121–Kitty Wake (Milesian 125) [1974 10g* 12g⁵ **64** 9g³ 12g² 12g 10f² 8g 11s 10v 1975 9s 8s 8f 10.2g 10g 8g 9f⁶ 9fg⁴ 10f⁶ 1976 11.7f³] poor handicapper nowadays: creditable third of 10 to Winged Dagger at Bath in April, only outing in 1976: stays 1½m: acts on firm going: sometimes wears blinkers but didn't at Bath. *I. Wardle.*

D

DAINTY DELIGHT 2 ro.f. My Swanee 122–Glenunga (Faberge II 121) [1976 **65** 5f⁶ 5g³ 5f*] sturdy filly: second foal: sold twice as a yearling, for 580 gns and 780 gns: dam won over 1¼m in Ireland: bought in 950 gns after winning seller at Beverley in June: not seen out again: will stay 1m+: apprentice ridden at Beverley. *K. Payne.*

DAISY BUTTONS 2 ch.f. Most Secret 119–Red Form (Reform 132) [1976 **52** 5fg 6f 6f⁵ 7fg³] plater: 6 lengths third of 11 to Briclic at Thirsk in July when blinkered first time: probably stays 7f: exported to Holland. *M. W. Easterby.*

DAISY WARWICK 3 br.f. Ribot 142 or Sir Gaylord–White Pearl (Aureole 132) — [1975 5fg³ 5fg² 7d⁴ 6d 1976 10g] sparely-made American-bred filly: quite useful form at 2 yrs when trained by P. Walwyn: not seen out until September when running poorly behind Frankie in minor race at Ayr: should stay 1¼m: best form on a firm surface. *F. Carr.*

DAKOTA 5 br.h. Stupendous–Ardneasken 84 (Right Royal V 135) [1974 7d **120 §** 10f 12f* 12f* 12fg* 14.7d² 14fg 9v⁵ 12g 14.6s² 1975 13.4d⁴ 12d⁴ 12fg 15g* 14.7f² 14fg* 16fg² 12g² 12d* 1976 12f⁵ 12fg³ 14d⁴ 12g⁴ 13.3fg⁴ 11g⁶ 12s]

Dakota's temperament finally got the better of him as a five-year-old and in seven races he only twice showed any semblance of the form that had earned him wins as a four-year-old in three good races, including the Ebor Handicap and the St Simon Stakes. As anticipated Dakota was weighted out of the big handicaps in 1976 and was raced exclusively in high-class weight-for-age events. In April he went down by a neck and a head to Orange Bay, who was conceding him 7 lb, and Libra's Rib in the Jockey Club Stakes at Newmarket, but he reserved by far his best performance for the King George VI and Queen Elizabeth Diamond Stakes at Ascot in July. Almost ignored in the betting at 80/1 Dakota ran a magnificent race, putting in a powerful challenge, after being held up as usual, to be fourth, about two lengths behind Pawneese. The home-trained four-year-olds Bruni and Orange Bay were the only others to beat him in a field that included the French Derby winner Youth, the Irish Derby winner Malacate and Ashmore, the best middle-distance horse over the age of three in France. Dakota veered across the course in the closing stages when holding second place, and finished against the rails; had he kept a straight course he might have been placed.

			Bold Ruler	Nasrullah
Dakota	Stupendous		(b 1954)	Miss Disco
(br.h. 1971)	(br 1963)		Magneto	Ambiorix
			(br 1953)	Dynamo
	Ardneasken		Right Royal V	Owen Tudor
	(br 1964)		(br 1958)	Bastia
			Alice Delysia	Alycidon
			(ch 1956)	Daring Miss

Dakota, who was an erratic character but a pretty consistent racehorse as a four-year-old, wasn't often in racing humour in 1976 and on his last three outings he seemed most unwilling to exert himself. He ended the season ignominiously, tailed-off last in the Prix de l'Arc de Triomphe. Dakota is a half-brother to three winners, including Warpath (by Sovereign Path) who has been popular with northern breeders in his first three years at stud. Dakota, a strong, well-grown, rather burly horse, stayed well and acted on any going. He was a difficult ride and went best for his regular jockey Barclay. Blinkers became standard equipment on the racecourse for Dakota after he caused mayhem

Mr Guy Reed's "Dakota"

before the start of a race at Epsom as a four-year-old. Dakota came up at the December Sales and was knocked down for 42,000 guineas to the British Blood-stock Agency, acting for the Polish National Stud. *S. Hall.*

DALAL 2 b.f. My Swallow 134–Haunting Melody 96 (Sing Sing 134) [1976 **78** 5f 5h2 5d 5s2] half-sister to three winners, including 1975 2-y-o Daring Song (by Derring-Do) and useful 6f to 1m winner Little Sir Echo (by Silver Cloud): 8,200 gns yearling: dam a miler: runner-up in small race at Folkestone in August and seller at Warwick in October: will stay 6f. *M. Masson.*

DALETTA 3 br.g. Majetta 115–Dale Way (Sunny Way 120) [1975 5s* 6fg 7f3 **103** 7f 7g 7.5g 8s6 7s3 1976 8s2 12g3 10g3 8f3 9f2 10f* 8f5 11.5f5 10f* 9f3 7f 11g] Irish gelding: second produce: 620 gns foal: dam never ran: useful handicapper: winner at Navan in June and Phoenix Park the following month (beat Imperial Fleet 2 lengths): performed creditably on most of his other appearances, notably when short-head second to Ballymountain Girl in Irish Lincolnshire at the Curragh in April and when about 4 lengths fifth to Gododin in well-contested minor event on the same course in June: last of seven to Gunner B in Doonside Cup at Ayr in September on final outing: effective from 1m to 1½m: acts on any going: wears blinkers: suitable mount for an apprentice. *T. Nicholson, Ireland.*

DAME CLARA 3 ch.f. Manacle 123–Madam Clare 66 (Ennis 128) [1975 5s **92** 5g5 6h3 7f 6fg2 6fg 6g 5d2 6g3 6g* 1976 6f 6f4 6fg5 7fg 5.8h* 6fg* 6g2 7g 6f* 7.6g3 6v] small, light-framed filly: fairly useful handicapper: apprentice ridden when successful at Bath and Lingfield in July and Folkestone in September: made all when beating Red Counsel 1½ lengths on last-named course: stays 7f: acts on hard ground and is probably unsuited by heavy: best in blinkers (ran poorly when tried without them). *P. Cole.*

DAME FOOLISH 3 b.f. Silly Season 127–Major Barbara 90 (Tambourine II **99** 133) [1975 5fg* 6g* 5f5 6d2 1976 7fg2 8g5 8g4 10d2] neat, quite attractive filly: one of best English 2-y-o fillies in 1975: wasn't so good in 1976, but was off course for a long time after finishing 3 lengths second to Flying Water in

Ladbroke Nell Gwyn Stakes at Newmarket in April: put up best effort afterwards when 5½ lengths fourth of 12 to Manilata in Severals Stakes, also at Newmarket, in October: probably stayed 1m: seemed to act on any going: visits Brigadier Gerard. *H. Cecil.*

DAMNATION 3 ch.f. New Chapter 106–Shearer (Shantung 132) [1975 7g² 7f³ **77** 7f 8g⁵ 1976 9f² 10f* 12f* 10f³ 11.7f 12g*] lengthy filly: won maiden race at Lanark and minor event at Beverley (trotted up) in April and £1,250 event at Ostend in August: subsequently sold privately for £1,900 to continue racing in Belgium: stays 1½m: acts on firm going. *Sir Mark Prescott.*

DAM WATER 2 b.c. Forlorn River 124–Blessed Beauty 97 (Rustam 127) **73** [1976 5g 5g² 5g³ 5s* 6d 5g] first foal: 2,200 gns yearling: dam winner at up to 7f: won maiden race at Ayr in May by head from Double Secret: lightly raced and well beaten afterwards, including in a nursery: should stay 6f: acts on soft going. *T. Fairhurst.*

DANCE IN THE DARK 2 b.c. Most Secret 119–Bright Vienna (Vienna 127) — [1976 5f 5.1fg⁵ 6d 7g] bad plater: apprentice ridden all outings: sold to S. Cole 340 gns Newmarket Autumn Sales. *Sir Mark Prescott.*

DANCE MAJOR 2 ch.c. Majority Blue 126–Tap Dance 91 § (Panaslipper 130) **74** [1976 5fg⁴ 5f 5d 5d⁴] robust colt: half-brother to two minor winners: 1,050 gns yearling: dam a miler: good fourth to Brown Mint in maiden race at Salisbury in June: did not reproduce that form, and sweated up when 8 lengths fourth to Jacado in similar race at Nottingham in September: will stay 6f. *P. Makin.*

DANCING CIRCUS 2 ch.c. St Chad 120–Dance Away (Red God 128 §) [1976 **76** 5f⁴ 5.1fg² 5f 5g 5g 5fg] small, compact colt: second foal: half-brother to 3-y-o middle-distance winner Tidal Dance (by Hardicanute): 1,400 gns yearling: dam fairly useful winner over 5f at 2 yrs in Ireland: ½-length second to clever winner King Elect in maiden race at Yarmouth in May, only worthwhile form: well beaten in £1,900 seller at Sandown when tried in blinkers on penultimate outing: will stay 6f. *R. Hannon.*

DANCING HILL 3 b.f. Hillary–Stage Fright (Native Dancer) [1975 N.R. **80** 1976 10fg 8g² 8g² 11.5d² 12g² 12v³] quite an attractive American-bred filly: sister to a minor winner and half-sister to four other winners in U.S.A.: dam a minor winner in U.S.A.: disappointing maiden: gives impression 1½m is minimum trip for her nowadays: exported to U.S.A. *N. Murless.*

DANCING LEAVES 2 ch.f. Galivanter 131–Queen of Autumn (Pindari 124) **54** [1976 5fg 5.1fg 5.1fg⁵ 5h 5g 8f⁵ 6d 8.2s 7s³] quite a modest plater: stays 1m. *M. Ryan.*

DANCING PARTNER 5 ch.m. Hul a Hul 124–Crusheen (Typhoon 125) [1974 **52** 5g 6fg⁵ 6g 5g 8.5g 1975 5h 6g 5.3f 7g⁶ 5g 1976 5f 5g⁶ 9g 7fg⁵ 6s 5h 10f⁴ 6h* 8h* 8g 8.2f 10.6d] poor handicapper: showed much improved form when winning six-runner apprentice selling handicap at Folkestone (bought in 500 gns) and handicap at Carlisle, both in August: stays 1m: acts on hard ground: has worn blinkers: ridden by claimer F. Curley when successful. *P. Poston.*

DANCING QUEEN 4 b.f. Shooting Chant–Dellie Douglas (Le Levanstell 122) — [1974 N.R. 1975 N.R. 1976 6f 8.3fg 8h] evidently of no account. *Dr A. Jones.*

DANCING ROBE 2 ch.c. Habitat 134–Dancing Rib 87 (Sir Ribot) [1976 **86** 5.1g³ 6d⁴ 6v⁴] first foal: 13,000 gns yearling: dam won over 1m as a 2-y-o: poorly drawn when in frame in maiden races, finishing fourth in October in large fields at Newmarket (7 lengths behind Rings) and Newbury (6 lengths behind Good Company when favourite): will stay 1m. *R. Armstrong.*

DANCING SONG 2 b.f. Ridan–Carol Song (Sing Sing 134) [1976 5d 5fg 5fg² **87** 5v] tall filly: half-sister to 3-y-o Song God (by Red God), a winner twice over 5f at 2 yrs: cost 5,800 gns Doncaster March 1976 Sales: dam, winner twice over 1m in France as a 3-y-o, comes from same family as Faberge II: put up easily best effort when length second to Home Fire in eight-runner minor event at Goodwood in September: will be suited by 6f: acts on a firm surface and may be unsuited by heavy ground. *C. Brittain.*

DANCING TULIP 2 b.f. Double-U-Jay 120–Pretty Tulip (Miralgo 130) [1976 — 6d] third foal: half-sister to Irish 1¾m winner Pretalgo (by Candy Cane): 500 gns yearling: dam won over 1¼m in Ireland: sixteenth of 23 to Running Bull in maiden race at Newmarket in October. *J. Powney.*

DANDY SCOT 4 br.g. Behistoun 131–Rose Blanche 89 (French Beige 127) **67** [1974 N.R. 1975 8fg 12.2f³ 12.3fg 12.3f⁴ 1976 12f² 13.8d⁵ 16f² 16f³ 16h² 16fg³

Wood Ditton Stakes, Newmarket—Danestic beats Illustrious Prince and Mossberry

14.7f³ 12fg* 16.1d]   poor handicapper: showed improved form when winning at
Beverley in September by ¾ length from Night Nurse: stays well: acts on firm
going: sold to M. Tate 3,900 gns Ascot December Sales. *W. Elsey.*

DANEBURY PONGEE 3 gr.g. Pongee 106–Rimfire Queen 98 (Appian Bridge   —
111) [1975 5g 1976 12.3f 12.2fg]   workmanlike gelding: lightly raced and no
sign of ability in maiden events: raced with tongue tied down on first outing. *J.
Fitzgerald.*

DANESTIC 3 b.c. Majestic Prince–Dana (Dan Cupid 132) [1975 N.R. 1976 **114**
8fg* 10.5fg² 10.5g⁶ 12g 8d⁴ 10v 8v²]   good sort of colt: American-bred: well-
brother to fair 1m winner Dana's Return (by Turn-to): dam never ran: well-
backed second favourite, won Wood Ditton Stakes at Newmarket in April by a
neck from Illustrious Prince: ran well behind Youth in two important races at
Longchamp, namely Prix Daru (4 lengths second) and Prix Lupin (6¾ lengths
sixth) and was not disgraced when ninth of 23 to Empery in Epsom Derby in
June: off course afterwards until autumn and was disappointing in good-class
company in England and France on his return, being beaten 7 lengths by impressive winner Jellaby at York in October on final outing: seems to need further
than 1m nowadays: evidently needs a sound surface: exported to South Africa.
B. Hills.

DANISH KING 2 br.c. Hardicanute 130–Rustling Waters 72 (Ballymoss 136)   **98**
[1976 5d⁶ 6fg 7f* 7g 8g⁵ 8g⁴]   strong, attractive colt: half-brother to useful filly
Shallow Stream (by Reliance II): dam disappointing half-sister to St Leger winner
Cantelo: led close home to win six-runner minor event at Brighton in July by ¼
length from The Dundass: not disgraced afterwards and finished respectable
fourth to Revlow when blinkered in valuable nursery at Ayr in September on
final outing: will stay 1¼m: to be trained by H. Cecil. *N. Murless.*

DANNY'S SISTER 3 ch.f. Whistling Wind 123–Liberdad 61 (Matador 131)   **53**
[1975 N.R. 1976 5f 5fg]   third foal: half-sister to a 1½m winner in Ireland by
Fleece: dam lightly raced: seventh of 11 to Friendly Jester in apprentice maiden
event at Edinburgh in July, first and better effort. *K. Whitehead.*

DARCY 4 b.c. Crooner 119–Sprightly Sprite 80 (Babur 126) [1974 6fg 6d²   **73**
6g⁶ 5v 5s⁴ 1975 7s 8g 7fg 7.6g 8g⁶ 10.8g* 1976 12f* 14fg⁵ 12g* 12f⁴ 12g*
11.7fg³ 12g²]   medium-sized, lengthy colt: quite a moderate handicapper:
successful at Chepstow in April, Leicester in June and Kempton the following
month: stays 1½m: acts on any going: genuine and consistent. *V. Cross.*

DARDANELLA LADY 5 gr.m. Samothraki 108–Lindholme Lady (Prince   —
Royal 115) [1974 7d⁶ 8s³ 7.2fg⁴ 11.1f⁴ 13f⁴ 11.2f⁶ 10h⁶ 8fg 8s 1975 8f 1976 8f]
neat, lightly-made mare: plater: stays 11f: seems best in blinkers: needed race on
only outing at 5 yrs. *S. Norton.*

DARING DAN 2 b.c. Run The Gantlet–Regal Winnie 88 (Royal Avenue 123)   **89**
[1976 5d* 6fg⁴ 7f³ 6s 8s]   useful sort: first foal: dam, successful at up to 1¼m, is
half-sister to smart sprinter Hard Water: won maiden race at Haydock in May by
2 lengths from Piety: in frame in quite valuable events at York and Redcar
afterwards, but was well beaten in nurseries on last two outings: will stay 1¼m:
possibly not at his best on very soft ground: sold 2,600 gns Doncaster November
Sales. *W. Wharton.*

DARING MARCH 2 br.c. Derring-Do 131–March Spray 101 (March Past 124)   **86**
[1976 5fg³ 6fg³ 6fg²]   big, strong, well-grown colt: brother to very smart sprinter
Daring Boy: dam a sprinter: placed in maiden races, in July finishing 6½ lengths

195

third of 14 to J. O. Tobin in £2,000 event at Newmarket and 1½ lengths runner-up to Sequoia at Nottingham: will stay 7f. *J. Bethell.*

DARING SONG   3 b.f. Derring-Do 131–Haunting Melody 96 (Sing Sing 134)   **109**
[1975 5fg³ 5f 5g* 1976 7.3f⁶ 5g² 6fg]   compact filly: only lightly raced but showed herself a very useful filly, finishing about 3 lengths sixth to Rowantree in Fred Darling Stakes at Newbury in April and failing by only ½ length to catch September Sky in handicap at Sandown in July on first two outings: should stay 1m: acts on firm going. *A. Corbett.*

DARK GREY   6 gr.g. Grey Sovereign 128 §–Treacle 86 (Hornbeam 130)   [1974   —
12s⁵ 10fg 8fg 12g⁵ 10fg 12g 14s 12g³ 10.6v   1975 11fg 10fg 10fg 8f⁶ 10f⁶ 12f² 10g 14s 15.5s⁶ 12g²   1976 11.1g 10f]   poor handicapper: evidently suited by 1¼m: acts on firm going: often wears blinkers: suitable mount for a lady rider. *T. Gates.*

DARK SEAL   5 ch.g. Privy Seal 108–Terry Pat 55 (Mossborough 126)   [1974   —
8s 8.5g⁶ 8g 12.2v 16fg⁴ 16s   1976 N.R.   1976 16.1d⁴ 16f 16f]   poor staying handicapper: tried in blinkers final outing at 3 yrs: pulled up lame final start in 1976: dead. *R. Hollinshead.*

DARK STRANGER   2 br.c. Royalty 130–Sylvanite 86 § (Rockefella)   [1976   **83**
5g 5s⁴ 5f³ 6d⁵ 6s⁴ 7.2fg 7fg⁴ 6g⁴]   useful-looking colt: half-brother to several winners, including speedy Treasure Hunt (by Wilwyn): sold for 440 gns as a foal and for 300 gns when reoffered at same sale: dam ungenerous sprinter: moderate maiden: ran very well when fourth of 14 to Downholme in nursery at Newcastle in August, penultimate outing: will stay 1m: acts on any going. *Denys Smith.*

DARK WARBLER   2 b.c. Song 132–Beamless 73 (Hornbeam 130)   [1976 5d]
neat colt: third foal: brother to useful 3-y-o sprinter Bill's Song: 5,400 gns yearling: dam stayed 1½m: showed up to past halfway when twenty-second of 25 to Union Card in maiden race at Newbury in September: sold 700 gns Ascot October Sales. *J. Tree.*

DARLEY DALE   3 b.c. Derring-Do 131–Pearl Barley 79 (Pinza 137)   [1975   **84**
7g 7fg⁵ 1976 8.2d* 10g⁶ 10.4s 8.2f⁵ 12fg⁶ 8g⁴ 8s⁵]   rangy, good-looking colt: made virtually all to win minor event at Haydock in April by 1½ lengths from Malin Court: ran best race afterwards when 5 lengths fourth to Silver Steel in Autumn Cup at Doncaster in September, holding every chance until squeezed out 1f out: ran moderately in most of his other races but had some stiff tasks: should stay 1¼m: sold 3,600 gns Newmarket Autumn Sales. *B. Hills.*

DARLING ALICE   3 ch.f. My Swanee 122–Sweet Heart V (Honeyway 125)   —
[1975 N.R.   1976 12.2fg 12g]   seems of no account. *R. Cambidge.*

DARLING BOB   4 br.g. Darling Boy 124–Makbuba 86 (Dumbarnie 125)   [1974   **69**
5d 5f² 5f* 5f⁴ 6fg⁶ 6d² 5g 5g* 5.9g²   1975 5fg 6s⁵ 5d⁴ 8.2g² 8f² 8.2f* 7g 10h* 8h 8g⁶ 8g² 8.2fg   1976 10g⁴]   useful sort: quite a moderate handicapper: creditable fourth to Royal Match in Littlewoods Spring Cup at Liverpool in April, only start at 4 yrs: stays 1¼m: seems to act on any going: has been tried in blinkers. *G. Balding.*

DARLING EVE   4 ch.f. Darling Boy 124–Christmas Eve 86 (Rockefella)   [1974   **63**
5g² 5fg³ 7g² 6d⁵ 8s⁶ 7s   1975 8g 8g⁴ 8.2f³ 8g 10f 10fg   1976 12.5g²]   strong, workmanlike filly: not seen out after finishing second to Bustiffa in poor maiden race at Teesside in April: stays 12.5f well: evidently acts on firm going. *N. Crump.*

DARTON BOY   2 b.c. Another River 89–Sagana Song 54 (Songedor 116)   [1976   —
5f 8fg]   light-framed colt: last in maiden races at Lanark and Beverley and seems to be of little account. *S. Wainwright.*

DARWEN LAD   2 ch.c. Galivanter 131–Gown Tab 88 (Taboun 128)   [1976   **78**
5d 5s 5fg 6f² 5f⁴ 6h² 7f* 8f² 7g 7g²]   lightly-built colt: dam won at up to 11f: attracted no bid after winning seller at Redcar in July by 3 lengths from Selborne: close-up second in two nurseries at Lanark afterwards, being caught close home both times: very well suited by 7f and 1m: acts on hard going. *M. H. Easterby.*

DASHING DAVID   2 ch.c. Realm 129–Hariota 73 (Hook Money 124)   [1976   **62**
5f 5f 5.3fg 5.1f² 5g² 5f⁵ 5f]   small colt: modest plater: runner-up at Yarmouth and Nottingham (missed break) in the summer: will be suited by 6f+. *W. Marshall.*

DASHING HUSSAR   4 ch.g. Queen's Hussar 124–Macadamia 87 (Martial 131)   —
[1974 5.1f* 6fg* 7d⁶ 1975 10d 7g 8f³ 8f⁶ 7.6f³ 1976 8g 7fg 7g 7g]   strong, good-looking gelding: fairly useful handicapper (rated 96) at 3 yrs but deteriorat-

ed considerably and showed little worthwhile form in England in 1976, including in a seller: stays 1m (badly hampered 2f out in only race over a longer distance): appears to act on any going: blinkered second and fourth starts: not raced in this country after May and was exported to Jersey where he was subsequently successful. *P. Haslam.*

DASTINA 2 b.f. Derring-Do 131–Omentello 91 (Elopement 125) [1976 5g 6g 7h[2] 7g] neat filly: seventh foal: sister to smart 7f performer Tudor Mill, and half-sister to five winners: dam won over 13f: showed only sign of ability when going down by short head to Mrs Wife in maiden race at Brighton in August: will stay 1m: sold to E. Reavey 2,500 gns Newmarket Autumn Sales. *P. Walwyn.* **80**

DAVENTRY SEALINK 2 b.f. Seaepic 100–D.J.B. 68 (Djebel) [1976 6fg] half-sister to a winner over fences by Mossy Face: dam placed over 5f at 2 yrs: tailed-off last of 16 to Sipit in maiden race at Windsor in July. *K. Ivory.* —

DAVES EQUAL 3 br.g. Murrayfield 119–Equal Rights (Persian Gulf) [1975 5v 5s[6] 5s[2] 5s[5] 5g 5f 5f[4] 6h[2] 6h[4] 5f[3] 5f[3] 6g[3] 5f[6] 8f[5] 1976 10fg 10g 8s[5] 10.2s[5]] compact gelding: fair plater at 2 yrs: showed only a little ability in better company in 1976: should stay further than 1m: probably acts on any going: sometimes wears blinkers. *T. Fairhurst.* —

DAVETT 7 b.m. Typhoon 125–Phrygia (Mossborough 126) [1974 11.2d[6] 12g* 12.2d4 13f* 12f[4] 12fg 12g[3] 14.6fg[5] 12g[2] 15g[6] 13s[5] 12g[2] 12d[3] 1975 13d[4] 12s* 11fg* 12g[2] 12f[2] 12h[5] 12g[2] 13h[4] 12f[2] 12g[2] 12.2g 1976 10v[3] 12d[5] 11g[2] 12.2d 12f[5] 11s[2] 12.3fg[2] 12f* 12f* 13g 12.2f* 10g[2] 12f[3] 12.2g] fair handicapper: successful at Edinburgh and Hamilton in July and at Catterick the following month: best form at up to 13f: acts on any going: occasionally wears blinkers but didn't when successful in 1976: suitable mount for an apprentice: genuine and consistent. *T. Craig.* **80**

DAVID'S CITY 6 b.g. David Jack 125–Mary Escart (Escart III) [1974 N.R. 1975 N.R. 1976 11.7h] first produce: dam never ran: last of nine in minor event won by Lucky Devil at Bath in July, only outing. *N. Guest.* —

DAVID'S FOLLY 3 b.g. High Line 125 or David Jack 125–Red Folly 68 (Double Red 122) [1975 N.R. 1976 13.1s[6] 16.1v] fourth foal: half-brother to fair 1972 2-y-o 7f winner Sinner Man (by Right Boy): 500 gns (privately) yearling: dam a winning stayer: well beaten in end-of-season maiden and minor events. *M. McCourt.* —

DAVIDSON 5 b.g. David Jack 125–Fair Jacqueline 79 (Fortino II 120) [1974 12g 10f[5] 8g* 8h* 8g[2] 8d[4] 1975 N.R. 1976 6fg[5]] well-made gelding: fair handicapper (rated 87) in 1974: hung badly all way when well beaten behind Hei'land Jamie at Nottingham in April, first outing since: needs further than 6f nowadays and should stay further than 1m: seems to act on any going: ran badly when tried in blinkers: needs strong handing. *W. Clay.* —

DAVID TUDOR 3 b.g. David Jack 125–Elizabeth Tudor (Tudor Jinks 121) [1975 5s[6] 5.1f[3] 6g[4] 5d[3] 5.9fg 7fg 1976 10.8fg[4] 10f 12fg[6] 8.2g] workmanlike gelding: should stay 1½m (had stiff task when tailed off on only attempt at trip): occasionally wears blinkers. *N. Guest.* —

DAVIOT 2 b.c. Roan Rocket 128–Tomboy 95 (Sica Boy 132) [1976 8d[3] 7d[2]] big, rangy colt: brother to very useful middle-distance winner Melantha, and half-brother to four other winners, two of them useful: dam stayed 1½m: put up two promising efforts, finishing 7 lengths third of 17 to Ad Lib Ra in maiden race at Newbury in September when on backward side, and making good progress to finish 2½ lengths second to Bessie Wallis in 25-runner Houghton Stakes at Newmarket in October: will stay 1½m: a very useful colt in the making. *G. Smyth.* **103**

DAVOUT 2 b.c. Ridan–Croix du Risque (Wild Risk) [1976 7f 8d] rangy colt: half-brother to several winners, notably 3-y-o Free Ridden (by Shantung) and high-class French middle-distance winner Free Ride (by Free Man): dam won at up to 1½m in France: behind in minor event at Salisbury in August and maiden race at Newbury in September. *D. Sasse.* —

DAWLISH 5 b.g. Double-U-Jay 120–Druid's Desire (Welsh Abbot 131) [1974 7fg[5] 12.3g 8.2f 8f[6] 7.2g* 8g 8s[2] 8g 8.2s 1975 8d[3] 7s 8v[4] 7g 7.2s 1976 8g 10g 7.6d[6]] strong, well-grown gelding: one-time fairly useful handicapper: ran poorly in 1976 and appears far from trustworthy nowadays: stays 1m: seems to act on any going but is ideally suited by some give in the ground: has been tried in blinkers. *E. Cousins.* —

DAWN AFFAIR 6 ch.m. Entanglement 118–Fairey Dawn 71 (Fairey Fulmar **45**
124) [1974 7f^5 7g 10g^6 10.2g 8.5fg 7g^4 7g 7fg 8f^3 8g 7.6v 10v^4 1975 10s^4 10.1g
10f^4 7f 1976 9g^6 10f^5 10s^5] small mare: good mover: poor handicapper: best
form at up to 1¼m: acts on any going: bandaged in front on first outing in 1976:
trained by B. Wise until after second outing. *V. Cross.*

DAWN CRYER 3 ch.c. Weepers Boy 124–Fairey Dawn 71 (Fairey Fulmar 124)   —
[1975 N.R. 1976 6f^5 7s^6] half-brother to two winners, including fair middle-
distance handicapper Dawn Reign (by Perfect Sovereign): dam won at 1¼m:
beaten just over 12 lengths when sixth of 12 to The Headman in seller at Brighton
in October. *T. Gates.*

DAYTIME GLORY 2 b.c. Breeders Dream 116–July Mist 79 (High Treason 126) **58**
[1976 5g 5d^5 5g^6 6h 6f^3 7f^6 7f 7g 8fg] plater: narrowly-beaten third to Turn
The Corner at Ripon in July: probably stays 7f: wears blinkers nowadays:
sold 560 gns Newmarket Autumn Sales. *A. Johnson.*

DAY TWO 7 ch.g. Blast 125–Rovira 83 (Luminary 132) [1974 8d 6g 7f 5f^4 6fg **57**
6fg^6 6g 6fg^3 7g 8g 6s^6 7d 6s^3 7v^4 1975 8d 6v* 6s^3 7f^2 6fg 7f 6g^2 6g^5 6g 6f 6s^6 6g
6g^2 1976 5f 6g^4 6f^3 6fg^6 7g 5g 5fg 6v 6v 7v] rangy gelding: one-time fair handicapper: nothing like the force he was and ran poorly most outings in 1976: best
at 6f or 7f: acts on any going. *V. Mitchell.*

DEAN 2 b.c. Dark Tiger–Fairy Moonbeam 86 (Fairey Fulmar 124) [1976 7g **71** p
8s^5] strong, good-looking French-bred colt: brother to French 3-y-o Dark Moon,
and half-brother to French middle-distance winner Spy Man (by Spy Well):
dam stayed 1¼m well: unquoted but showed up prominently in large fields of
maidens at Newmarket in October, on second occasion leading far side for 6f
when about 14 lengths fifth of 27 to Sporting Yankee: will stay 1¼m: sure to
win races in time *J. Hindley.*

DEAN'S GUY 2 b.c. Double Jump 131–Misylda 100 (Faubourg II 127) [1976   —
6v] half-brother to several winners, including quite useful but unreliable miler
Sky Lord (by Behistoun): 1,000 gns yearling: dam won at 6f and 1¼m: apprentice
ridden when behind in 22-runner maiden race won by Good Company at Newbury
in October. *D. Keith.*

DEAREST ALICE 3 b.f. Alcide 136–Pleasaunce 84 (Petition 130) [1975 N.R.   —
1976 11.1g 13.3fg^5 13g] well-made, good-topped filly: third foal: half-sister to
fairly useful sprinter Pleasure Garden (by Jolly Jet): dam stayed 1m: showed
only a little ability, running easily best race on second outing. *G. Pritchard-
Gordon.*

DEAR REMUS 4 br.g. Darling Boy 124–Wolfsburg (Neckar) [1974 7fg^5 7g   —
10s 1975 11.1g 12f^2 17.7f^4 12f^3 12g* 13f^5 13f^6 16g 1976 12.2f 12g] tall gelding:
probably needs at least 1½m: has been tried in blinkers: sold 540 gns Doncaster
May Sales. *R. Edwards.*

DEB 3 b.f. Decoy Boy 129–Pepstep 88 (Polic 126) [1975 5fg^4 5f^4 5fg 5s 1976   **57**
6f^4 6f] plating-class maiden: sold to P. Felgate 580 gns Newmarket Autumn
Sales. *D. Gandolfo.*

DEBENTURE 6 br.g. Tycoon II–Wild Words 76 (Galivanter 131) [1974 10d^2 —
8g* 10f^2 10g* 7s* 6g^3 7.6v^3 1975 N.R. 1976 7g 7fg 7fg^6 8g 10fg 8fg 8g] poor
handicapper nowadays: stays 1¼m and finds 6f on the sharp side: well suited by
some give in the ground: has been tried in blinkers: excellent mount for an
apprentice: bandaged third start. *P. Taylor.*

DEBONA GIRL 2 ch.f. Continuation 120–Sabra's Star 65 (Midsummer Night II   —
117) [1976 5fg 5f 5d 5s] workmanlike filly: behind in minor and maiden events.
S. Nesbitt.

DEBUTANTE 2 ch.f. Silly Season 127–Grove Hall 66 (Hook Money 124)   — p
[1976 7s] half-sister to numerous winners, including smart stayer Hazard (by
Sheshoon) and useful sprinter Abergrove (by Abernant): 4,100 gns yearling:
dam won over 1m: 10/1 when fourteenth of 19 to Lady Oriana in maiden race
at Newmarket in October: should do better at 3 yrs. *M. Stoute.*

DECADE 2 b.f. Deck Hand–Lady Citation (Citation) [1976 6g 8g^5 7s^3] **72**
American-bred filly: half-sister to three minor winners in U.S.A.: dam won twice
in U.S.A.: quite a moderate maiden: stays 1m. *B. Hills.*

DECEPTIVE 3 b.f. Great Nephew 126–Deceiver 101 (Borealis) [1975 N.R.   —
1976 8f^6 10fg^5 8v] half-sister to four winners, including quite useful 1¼m and
1½m winner Calvine (by Prince Chevalier): dam best at 1¼m: just under 8 lengths
sixth of 12 behind Regal Romance in maiden race at Salisbury in August, first
and best effort: should stay middle distances. *I. Balding.*

DECISION 6 b.g. Gala Performance–Cis (Eudaemon 129) [1974 8fg* 8g 8g 12g —
9.5g* 8.5s 1975 8s⁶ 8fg⁵ 8h⁶ 10fg 8.3fg⁵ 8fg 1976 9fg] workmanlike gelding:
stays 9f well: appears to act on any going: sometimes wears blinkers: backward
and always behind on only outing in 1976. *D. Marks.*

DEENAIR 2 b.f. Track Spare 125–Psidjet (Psidium 130) [1976 6fg 7.2f 7d 10v] —
well-made filly: little worthwhile form in maiden and minor events. *D. Sasse.*

DEEP BLUE 2 br.f. Deep Diver 134–Quality Girl (Quorum 126) [1976 5d 5s] —
lengthy filly: half-sister to a minor winner: 4,000 gns yearling: dam, of little
account, is half-sister to very useful filly Broadway Melody: well behind in
maiden races at Newbury in September and Bath (20/1) in October. *P. Haslam.*

DEEP DIVIDE 4 b.f. Precipice Wood 123–Tacadora 73 (Tacitus 124) [1974 —
5g* 5f³ 5f⁶ 6g⁴ 7s 6g³ 6v 1975 8d⁶ 7.2fg 6f 8.2fg² 9g* 8.2s⁴ 7fg² 1976 8v⁵ 8fg]
workmanlike filly: plater: will stay further than 9f: probably unsuited by heavy
ground though appears to act on any other: has been tried in blinkers: sold
640 gns Newmarket July Sales. *E. Cousins.*

DEEP RIVER 4 b.c. Tudor Melody 129–Lucky Stream 99 (Persian Gulf) [1974 **89**
7d 7v⁴ 1975 8.2g 8f² 10h* 10f* 10f* 10f¹ 13.5s³ 13.5s³ 11g⁵ 10s* 10.6v 1976 10fg
10.5d⁵ 10fg⁶ 10fg³ 10.2f³ 10f³ 10f³ 10.5g⁴ 10fg* 12d* 12.2v² 12s⁴] attractive,
well-made colt: fairly useful performer on his day: winner at Leicester in September and at Haydock the following month and ran creditably in his races
afterwards: stays 1½m: acts on any going: suitable mount for an apprentice:
blinkered eighth appearance: has a fair turn of foot. *I. Walker.*

DEEP WATERS 2 ch.f. Green God 128–Cashka 63 (Celtic Ash) [1976 6d] — p
first produce: 3,100 gns foal: dam poor maiden: 8/1 when twelfth of 22 to Rocket
Symphony in maiden race at Newmarket in October: evidently thought to have
ability and should do better at 3 yrs. *L. Cumani.*

DELARUM 4 b.g. Creme dela Creme–Rumpled (Free for All) [1974 5.1f 5s⁵ 8s —
1975 10.2fg⁶ 8g³ 10.1fg³ 10g⁶ 1976 10.4fg] angular American-bred gelding:
best form at 1m: blinkered only appearance in 1976: sold out of D. Morley's
stable 840 gns Doncaster March Sales. *H. Morris.*

DELAWARE BAY 3 b.c. Saratoga Skiddy 113–Linloskin (Hard Sauce 131) **64**
[1975 5f 5.8f 5fg⁶ 5f 7g 1976 6g³ 6f 5f 5.8h 7fg*] modest plater: came out best in
a desperate finish when winning at Leicester in August: sold to M. Tate 825 gns
afterwards: stays 7f: blinkered penultimate appearance. *F. Maxwell.*

DELAYED ACTION 3 b.f. Jolly Jet 111–Oversight (Tudor Melody 129) [1975 **108** d
5fg* 5s* 5d* 5s³ 5g* 5d⁵ 5g² 5h² 5f* 5g⁴ 5fg² 5fg* 1976 5d* 6f⁴ 5d 5s 5f⁵ 5f⁶
5fg 6f⁵ 6f³ 5.6g 6g⁴ 6d] rather unfurnished filly: nowhere near so successful as in
1975 and won only her first race, Field Marshall Stakes at Haydock in April
by 4 lengths from Rundontwalk: ran moderately on most of her other outings
and is not so good as she was: stays 6f: acts on any going: suitable mount for
a boy. *G. Toft.*

DELICIA (FR) 2 ch.f. Sovereign Path 125–Relicia (Relko 136) [1976 5g* 6f² **105**
7f² 8g²] Irish filly: sister to French 1m winner Patricia: 10,000 gns yearling:
dam, from a very successful family, showed smart form over middle distances
in France: won maiden race at the Curragh in April by ½ length from Western
Tyranny: runner-up to very useful animals on all outings afterwards, going
down by a head to Captain James in £1,250 event at Phoenix Park in July, by
2½ lengths to Brahms in £1,200 event at Leopardstown the following month
and by 2 lengths to Nanticious in Silken Glider Stakes, also at Leopardstown,
in September: stays 1m: acts on firm going. *J. Oxx, Ireland.*

DELLWOOD PRINCE 4 b.g. Mandamus 120–Lazzarone 60 (Sica Boy 132) **56**
[1974 5.1g 5v⁵ 5s 1975 7s 6s⁵ 10fg 10g 10d⁴ 10g³ 1976 12fg* 14g² 12g 14d 10fg
12s 10v* 12.5s] strong, sturdy, short-legged gelding: selling handicapper:
winner at Leicester in March and October, on both occasions attracting no bid
afterwards: stays 1¾m: acts on any going: best in blinkers. *W. Holden.*

DELTA SONG 3 br.c. Delta Judge–Broadway Melody 118 (Tudor Melody 129) **117**
[1975 5fg² 6f* 6fg 7fg 1976 5g 5f 6g 6fg² 6fg* 6f 6g² 7d 6g] big, rangy American-bred colt: good mover: showed himself a smart 3-y-o when length second
to Jimmy The Singer in Spillers Stewards' Cup at Goodwood in July, finishing
strongly without being able to trouble winner: gained compensation when
beating Sonnenblick by a length in Northumberland Sprint Trophy at Newcastle
the following month: 4 lengths second to impressive winner (stable-companion)
Sandford Lady at York in September, best subsequent effort: stays 6f very

well and should stay 7f: pulled up (thought to have dislocated a joint) on final appearance. *R. Price.*

DEMANDING 3 ch.f. Tyrant–Daisy Jane (Epaulette 125) [1975 N.R. 1976 **64** 6v⁵ 5.9g⁵ 6g⁴] third foal: half-sister to an Irish bumpers winner: 2,400 gns yearling: dam won at 1m: showed only sign of ability when tried in blinkers on final outing: will probably stay 1m: sold 400 gns Newmarket July Sales. *E. Cousins.*

DEMELZA 2 gr.f. Sovereign Bill 105–Court Victory 62 (Juvenile Court 112) **65** [1976 5f 5g⁴ 6g 6h³ 5.9f³ 6g 6h⁵ 5f⁴ 6s⁴ 8v²] modest plater: stays 1m: acts on any going: wears blinkers. *C. Dingwall.*

DE MILO 3 ch.f. Busted 134–Eternal Love 102 (Ratification 129) [1975 6g³ 6fg⁴ **89** 1976 7fg* 8.5fg² 10.4d³ 8g⁴ 8f] quite an attractive filly: impressive 7-length winner of maiden race at Wolverhampton in April: 5¾ lengths third of 10 to So Sharp in minor event at Chester in May, best subsequent effort: would have stayed 1¼m: acted on a firm and a soft surface, but was possibly not at her best on really firm: ran moderately when tried in blinkers on final outing: exported by B.B.A. to Australia. *P. Walwyn.*

DEMPSEY 4 ch.g. My Swanee 122–Orestia (Orestes) [1974 6g⁵ 1975 6s* 7v² **83** 7v* 8g 1976 10g 10f⁵ 10d² 8fg 7fg³] strong, well-made gelding: very useful performer in Ireland at 3 yrs, winning Tetrarch Stakes at the Curragh: didn't show the same form in this country in 1976 but ran respectably when placed in handicaps at Pontefract in May and Sandown (blinkered) in July: stays 1¼m: best form on a soft surface. *J. Dunlop.*

DENANEER 3 ch.f. Green God 128–Shelduck 70 (Dicta Drake 126) [1975 5g² **72** 5f⁵ 5s⁵ 6g⁴ 1976 6fg 6g⁴ 5g⁶ 6fg⁵ 5fg⁵ 5h³ 5.8h 7h³ 8f² 10f* 12g 10v⁵] moderate filly: won maiden race at Nottingham in August in good style by 4 lengths from Twist of Lemon: ridden by 7-lb claimer when first past post in handicap at Ripon earlier in month, but wandered left in straight, hampered runner-up, and was subsequently relegated to second after a stewards' inquiry: stays 1¼m (started slowly and ran moderately when tried at 1½m): acts on firm going and ran poorly on heavy on final outing: blinkered twice, running creditably on first occasion but moderately on second. *R. Price.*

DERAB 3 b.g. Green God 128–Sundalgo 82 (Fidalgo 129) [1975 5fg⁶ 5d⁵ 5g **60** 1976 9fg 10.1f 12fg 10fg*] tall, good-topped gelding: won selling handicap at Newmarket in June impressively by 5 lengths: sold 2,300 gns afterwards, reportedly for export to Belgium: stays 1¼m: acts on a firm surface: best in blinkers. *J. Sutcliffe.*

DERRINGO 3 b.c. Derring-Do 131–Telouet 90 (Sing Sing 134) [1975 5s³ **96** 6fg⁴ 5fg² 5g* 6g 5g⁶ 1976 6fg 5s 5g 6fg⁶ 6fg 5f² 5fg 5d³ 5g* 5v 6d] workman-like colt: good walker: quite a useful handicapper on his day: won £2,400 handicap at Ascot in September decisively by 1½ lengths from Raffia Set: stays 6f: best form with some give in the ground and moved very short to post on firmish surface on fifth and seventh starts: blinkered last outing at 2 yrs: very inconsistent: exported to Hong Kong. *C. Brittain.*

DERRY TOWN 4 b.c. Charlottown 127–Derry Lass (Derring-Do 131) [1974 **66** 8d 8d 1975 11v 10.1f 12g 12g 15fg⁴ 1976 12fg 12f⁵ 13.8g 15.5h² 13.1f⁵ 12.2s 12s⁶ 12s²] neat colt: poor staying maiden: acts on hard going: blinkered sixth outing. *G. Smyth.*

DESERT WARRIOR 2 b.c. Realm 129–Dorrit 98 (Zucchero 133 §) [1976 **88** 5g³ 5f² 6fg 5d 6g] strong, compact colt: half-brother to two winners, including quite useful 1m and 1¼m winner Grandiflora (by Supreme Sovereign): 7,800 gns yearling: dam disappointing and temperamental maiden from same family as Romulus and Sostenuto: put up two good efforts in June, being beaten only about a length by Hemsworth at Hamilton (after jockey mistook winning post and dropped his hands) and going down by 3 lengths to Sunny Spring in Windsor Castle Stakes at Royal Ascot: lame after running badly on third outing later in month and was well beaten in two races in the autumn: should stay 6f+: sure to win races in the north if he can reproduce his Royal Ascot running. *J. Hanson.*

DESPERATION 2 ch.f. Be Friendly 130–Severn Bridge 81 (Hornbeam 130) **68** [1976 5d⁶ 5f⁶ 5f⁴ 5.9fg⁶ 6s 7s⁴ 7g] robust filly: fourth foal: 850 gns yearling: dam, from same family as Dibidale, won over 9f: plating-class maiden: will stay 1m: possibly not at her best on very firm going: sold 600 gns Newmarket Autumn Sales. *Sir Mark Prescott.*

DESSIMA 2 b.f. Prince de Galles 125–Sally Dancer (Sammy Davis 129) [1976 **57** 5s 5s 5.9s] second foal: dam of no account: behind in maiden races in the midlands, finishing ninth of 18 to Fear Naught at Wolverhampton in October on final outing. *C. Brittain.*

DESTINO 5 b.h. Salvo 129–Villa Marina 96 (Tudor Melody 129) [1974 10fg **74** 12.2f 12d 12fg 12.3s³ 12g⁵ 10d* 1975 13s² 12g⁴ 12g³ 10fg² 10.2g* 8f* 9fg³ 1976 10fg³ 8f² 10f³ 10fg* 10g] useful sort: good walker: quite a moderate handicapper: trotted up from Bermondo in apprentice event at Newbury in August: best form at 1m to 1¼m but stays further: acts on any going: possibly unsuited by a sharp track: ideal mount for inexperienced race-rider. *H. Wragg.*

DESTINY HILL 5 b.h. Power of Destiny–Scotts Hill (Colonel O'F) [1974 **60** 8g 8.2g 8g⁴ 10g 8s 1975 15fg* 16.9f⁵ 16f⁴ 1976 16.1d² 16fg³ 16.1d] strong American-bred horse: suited by a good test of stamina: acts on firm going and a soft surface: often wears blinkers: sold out of F. Rimell's stable 1,050 gns Doncaster May Sales. *S. Holland.*

DESTINY'S DAUGHTER 2 b.f. Manacle 123–Harp (Ennis 128) [1976 **75** 5fg 5f⁵ 5h 5s⁴ 5v 5v⁵] neat filly: first living produce: dam never ran: quite a moderate maiden: acts on any going. *P. Makin.*

DEVA ROSE 4 br.f. Chestergate 111–Sunburst Rose 87 (Solonaway 128) [1974 **70** 5g 5fg⁶ 6g 5g² 5d 5d⁴ 6v³ 6v 5.9v⁵ 1975 7.6g 8g 7fg 5h⁴ 5h 5f⁶ 5.9fg 5f* 5fg³ 5f 5g 5g 6g³ 6d 1976 6fg⁴ 5f⁴ 6g 5fg³ 5.9f⁴ 5.9g² 5.9g³ 5f* 5f* 5fg² 5h*] neat, strong filly: in cracking form in midsummer, winning three races in the north: gained her final success when beating My Chopin a neck at Carlisle: best at sprint distances: acts on any going: has worn bandages: good mount for an inexperienced race-rider. *R. Hollinshead.*

DEVAS 3 ch.c. Red God 128 §–Fierte (Relic) [1975 N.R. 1976 8g 13.3fg — 12fg] lengthy colt: half-brother to fair middle-distance performer Expensive (by Exbury): dam half-sister to top-class French stayer Zamazaan: no form in maiden races at Sandown and Newbury (two): blinkered second outing. *I. Balding.*

DEVIL'S CUB 3 b.c. Falcon 131–Vahred 114 (Mirza II) [1975 5d 5s 6g **57** 1976 7fg 6fg 6fg⁵ 6fg⁵ 7fg² 6d⁴ 5f⁴ 8fg³] lengthy colt: quite a modest plater: stays 1m: found very little off bridle when tried in blinkers on third outing: not seen out after July. *W. O'Gorman.*

DEVIL'S DIKE 3 b.f. Dike–Kazannka (Wild Risk) [1975 6g 6f² 7g⁵ 1976 **88** 8.2f 10f² 12.2g* 13f² 12f* 12h* 12fg² 12fg] short-backed, close-coupled filly: ran well in 1976 and won maiden race at Catterick in June, and handicap at Beverley (by 7 lengths) and two-runner minor event at Pontefract in July: good second to Honeypot Lane in handicap at Goodwood later in month: stays 13f: acts on hard going: sold 5,200 gns Newmarket December Sales. *H. Cecil.*

DEVIL'S DOUBLE 4 ch.g. Double-U-Jay 120–Beaming Lady 87 (Hornbeam — 130) [1974 N.R. 1975 16f² 16g³ 12.3fg 1976 12.5s] big, lengthy gelding: has raced only once since June 1975: suited by long distances. *R. D. Peacock.*

DEVIL'S MOON 2 ch.f. Sheshoon 132–Moon Saint 82 (Saint Crespin III 132) — [1976 5g 5f 10v] first foal: dam apparently best at sprint distances: in rear on all outings: off course April to October. *J. Leigh.*

DEVIS 4 b.g. Manacle 123–Windsor Pearl 91 (Pearl Diver 130) [1974 6d 6g **63** d 1975 7fg² 8s⁵ 8g⁵ 8g⁴ 6g* 6f³ 6g 7d 1976 6v* 8g⁶ 6d 8f⁶ 6s³ 7.6fg 7g 5s] fair plater: favourite, successful at Ayr in April by 5 lengths from Shy Meld (no bid): stays 1m: acts on any going: best in blinkers: good mount for an apprentice. *D. Williams.*

DIAGRAMATIC 3 b.c. Sir Wiggle–Miss Suzy (Agasajo) [1975 N.R. 1976 **116** 10g* 10d* 12g* 12g* 13.5g²⁻ 12s] American-bred French colt: half-brother to minor winners in U.S.A. and France: dam won Chilean Oaks: won newcomers event at Saint-Cloud and minor events at Evry and Vichy prior to winning Group 3 Grand Prix de Vichy in August in good style by 3 lengths from Cavalcadour, with Hunza Dancer third: 4 lengths second to Ashmore in Grand Prix de Deauville, later in month, better subsequent effort: stays 13f well: acts on a soft surface: smart. *F. Mathet, France.*

DIAMOND DAY 2 ch.f. Welsh Pageant 132–Diamond Wedding (Never Say Die **76** 137) [1976 6f⁵ 6f⁵ 7g⁴] fourth foal: half-sister to Tudor Jewel (by Henry the Seventh), winner at up to 9f: dam unraced half-sister to Major Portion: quite a moderate maiden: will stay 1m. *T. Waugh.*

DIAMOND DIVINE 3 b.f. Divine Gift 127–Diamond Brooch 71 (Gilles de Retz 132) [1975 N.R. 1976 7f 6g 6g 7g 6f³ 5g 6fg 7s³ 6v⁶] rangy filly: half-sister to useful sprinter Le Vingt-Huit (by Jukebox): 2,500 gns foal, resold 3,100 gns yearling: dam half-sister to Raffingora: showed a little ability in varied company: stays 7f: acts on any going: blinkered final outing: sold 825 gns Ascot December Sales. *B. Swift.* **56**

DIAMOND GIFT 3 ch.f. Roan Rocket 128–Diamond Wedding (Never Say Die 137) [1975 5fg⁵ 6s 1976 8fg 6fg 6f 6g 5g 6f] workmanlike filly: bad plater: should stay at least 1m. *M. Bradley.* **—**

DIAMOND SPRAY 3 ch.f. Roan Rocket 128–Sirpech (High Hat 131) [1975 6f⁴ 6g 6d³ 1976 7fg 7g⁵ 12g 10.1f⁵ 6g] small filly: poor walker: disappointing as a 3-y-o. *Doug Smith.* **—**

DICKIES RISING SUN 2 b.f. Roi Dagobert 128–Island Princess (Raise A Native) [1976 5fg 5g⁵ 5fg⁵ 5fg⁴ 5f 5f 6g 6g² 6s] leggy filly: 33/1, put up easily best effort when dead-heating for second place, 2 lengths behind Burley, in 21-runner seller at Newmarket in September: will be suited by 7f+. *D. Weeden.* **76**

DIDDY GIRL 2 b.f. Comedy Star 121–Linton Spring 84 (Khalkis 127) [1976 5fg 5fg 6fg⁴ 5.8f⁵ 7fg] strong filly: well beaten in maiden races and seller: blinkered second and third outings: sold out of N. Callaghan's stable 280 gns Doncaster August Sales. *Dr A. Jones.* **42**

DIDDY'S TREASURE 3 ch.f. Richboy 117–Diddy Duck 53 (Dicta Drake 126) [1975 N.R. 1976 12s] third foal: half-sister to a winning hurdler: dam stayed 1m: in rear in maiden race won by Tudor Wynk at Chepstow in October, only outing. *S. Holland.* **—**

DIDO'S HILL 2 b.f. Sharpen Up 127–Dido's Granddaughter (By Thunder! 122) [1976 5fg 5f 9fg] tailed off in two of her three races and is of little account. *M. Bradley.* **—**

DIFFERENT STORY 3 ch.f. Crisp and Even 116–Peggytub 54 (Will Somers 114 §) [1975 6f 5g 1976 6g] compact filly: no signs of ability in maiden races and a seller: sweated up and very much in need of race on only outing in 1976 (May). *J. Hayward.* **—**

DIKARO LADY 3 b.f. Dike–Karo Dame (Tudor Melody 129) [1975 6fg 7v⁶ 6g 1976 12 3s 10f⁶] big, strong filly: only lightly raced but gave indications of having a little ability: not seen out after May. *Denys Smith.* **—**

DIKES DAUGHTER 2 gr.f. Dike–Atonement 109 (Palestine 133) [1976 5.8f³ 5s⁶ 5s⁶] half-sister to five winners, including useful 1971 2-y-o 6f winner Fresh Start (by Busted): 2,100 gns yearling: dam, speedy 2-y-o, is sister to Pall Mall: 25/1, ran creditably when 2¾ lengths third of eight to African Violet in maiden race at Bath in September: did not reproduce that form and is possibly unsuited by soft going: will stay 6f. *G. Smyth.* **76**

DIKUSA 3 b.c. Dike–Miss Upward 77 (Alcide 136) [1975 6g⁶ 7g 8s⁴ 1976 10fg* 10fg⁴ 12g³ 12fg² 14fg²] big, tall colt: won minor event at Lingfield in May by 3 lengths from Galahad II: finished lame when 4 lengths second to Mark Hush in handicap at York in July and was not seen out again: stays 1¾m: trained until after second outing by C. Brittain. *B. Hills.* **94**

DINAH'S SLIPPER 4 br.f. Marcus Brutus 108–Dancing Slipper (Cabrach) [1974 N.R. 1975 N.R. 1976 8g 12f⁵] probably of little account. *I. Jordon.* **—**

DINKUM CHIEF 2 gr.g. Tribal Chief 125–Sara Lady 81 (Roan Rocket 128) [1976 5f⁶ 5g⁴ 6fg 5d 5s 5s] workmanlike gelding: only plating class: should stay 6f. *R. Mason.* **58**

DIORINA 2 b.f. Manacle 123–Dior 80 (Dionisio 126) [1976 5fg³ 5fg² 5g² 5h² 5fg⁴ 5.3f* 6f 7s⁶] neat, compact, attractive filly: half-sister to three winners, including fairly useful 1975 2-y-o Flying Colours (by King's Company): dam, placed at up to 1½m, won over hurdles: second in three maiden races prior to winning seven-runner nursery at Brighton in August by a head from Good Try: probably stays 7f: not disgraced when tried in blinkers on final outing (had stiff task). *W. Wightman.* **91**

DIP STICK 2 b.f. Right Boy 137–Mustard Spoon (Silver Kumar 112) [1976 7h 5f 7fg 7s] no form in varied company, including selling: blinkered first three outings. *W. Williams.* **—**

DISC JOCKEY 2 b.c. Tudor Music 131–Fei-Hoo 65 (Dionisio 126) [1976 6g⁵ 6g* 6g⁶ 7g] dipped-backed colt: half-brother to two winners, including useful miler **95**

Thrifty (by Continuation): dam of little account: won five-runner minor event at Newcastle in August going away by 4 lengths from Red Seed: fair sixth to Region in £1,600 event at Ayr the following month, better subsequent effort: will probably stay 1m: action suggests a soft surface will suit him well. *N. Angus.*

DISCOUNT CYCLES   2 ch.f. Sovereign Gleam 117–Debatable 84 (Counsel 118)   —
[1976 6fg 8g]   second foal: half-sister to Irish 3-y-o Brandon Hill (by Wolver Hollow), a very useful winner at up to 1½m: dam stayed 1¾m: in rear in maiden races at Nottingham in August and Leicester in September.   *G. Pritchard-Gordon.*

DISMASTED   4 b.c. Busted 134–Martinetta 77 (Ballymoss 136)   [1974 N.R.   **64**
1975 12v 10f 8f 11.5g⁶ 10g   1976 12fg² 12fg³ 12s* 12g⁶ 12g⁶ 13.5d]   good-looking, rangy colt: favourite, won 16-runner amateur riders event at Doncaster in May: well beaten afterwards, including in France (last of seven behind Valmur in valuable amateur riders race at Deauville in August): should stay 2m: appears to act on any going: sold to D. Barons 6,400 gns Newmarket Autumn Sales.   *G. Pritchard-Gordon.*

DISTANT COUSIN   4 br.g. Ballyciptic 122–Catherines Sister 96 (Petition 130)   **61**
[1974 6g⁵ 7d⁴ 7d 8v⁵   1975 8s⁵ 7v* 8g* 8.3s* 7g³ 10fg⁶ 8h² 9g* 8f⁵ 9f 8f⁵ 12f⁵   1976 12fg⁶ 8g 12s 10fg* 10f⁵ 8f² 8f³ 7d 8fg 10d]   small gelding: plater: successful at Pontefract in May (bought in 680 gns): stays 1¼m but appears not to stay 1½m: acts on any going: suitable mount for an apprentice: blinkered sixth to eighth outings: ran badly final appearance and was sold 580 gns Doncaster October Sales.   *R. Bastiman.*

DIVERS EXPRESS   2 b.c. Lucky Sovereign–Sam's Baby (Sammy Davis 129)   —
(1976 5fg 5fg 5.1fg⁶ 6g 8.2s]   bad plater.   *T. Molony.*

DIVINE FIZZ   3 ch.c. Yellow God 129–Fille de Fizz (Ragusa 137)   [1975 N.R.   **67**
1976 8.2g 5f⁵ 5fg 7fg 7v 8 2s⁶]   robust colt: showed a little ability and was far from disgraced when sixth under a very stiff weight in handicap won by Autumn Glow at Haydock in October: probably stays 1m.   *J. Etherington.*

DIVINE KING   4 ch.c. Divine Gift 127–Mrs Binks (Whistling Wind 123)   [1974 **110**
5s² 5f² 5g* 5g² 5h* 6f⁵ 5fg³ 6d* 5d² 5s⁶   1975 7s 6g⁵ 6d* 6d 6s⁴ 6fg 6g³ 6v⁴   1976 6fg⁶ 5fg 6d⁴]   strong colt: very smart performer (rated 122) at 3 yrs: lightly raced in 1976 but ran respectably in two of his three races, finishing close seventh to Polly Peachum in Palace House Stakes at Newmarket in April and 3¾ lengths fourth of nine to Sandford Lady in Spring Handicap at York in May: best form at 6f (had a fair chance at weights when tried over 7f): won on hard ground as a 2-y-o but has shown his best form on a soft surface: has worn bandages: not particularly consistent.   *R. Hannon.*

DIVINE PENNY   2 ch.f. Divine Gift 127–Bronze Alloy 82 (Hook Money 124)   **65**
[1976 5fg 5d⁶ 5s 6s⁴]   second living foal: 400 gns yearling: dam stayed 5f: fair plater: ran best race on final outing and is suited by 6f.   *R. Akehurst.*

DIVINE SUNSHINE   2 ch.f. Divine Gift 127–Hopeful Sunshine (Red God 128 §)   **53**
[1976 5g 5f 5d⁵ 6h³ 6f]   small filly: poor plater: will stay 7f.   *W. Wharton.*

DIVINITY   2 ch.c. Divine Gift 127–Sweet Patsy (Nice Guy 123)   [1976 6g 6d 6g   **79**
7s³ 8d*]   third reported living foal: 3,000 gns yearling: dam never ran: improved with distance and was awarded race by stewards after finishing ½-length second of 14 to East Plaistow in £1,400 seller at Newmarket in October: bought in 2,100 gns afterwards: well suited by 1m: acts on soft going.   *N. Callaghan.*

DIVISION BELL   2 b.f. New Member 119–Please Go (Tangle 121)   [1976 5g 6fg]
first foal: dam N.H. performer: in rear in maiden races at Salisbury in May and June.   *J. Old.*

DO BETTER   2 br.c. Derring-Do 131–Mary Mine 102 (Infatuation 129)   [1976 **106**
7.2f* 7fg² 7s 7d]   neat, strong colt with plenty of quality: brother to moderate Mary Minor: dam won from 1m to 1½m, and is half-sister to Pasty: impressive winner of 13-runner minor event at Haydock in August, starting none too well and soon being 15 to 20 lengths behind leader but really finding his stride in closing stages to get up and win going away by 1½ lengths from Black Minstrel: put up a similar effort when neck second to Gairloch in minor event at Goodwood the following month: well beaten in good-class nurseries on last two outings: needs

Mr G. P. Williams' "Do Better"

at least 7f and will stay 1¼m+: acts on firm going and is probably unsuited by soft: worth following. *P. Walwyn.*

DOCKET 2 br.f. Swing Easy 126–Lady Advocate 116 (King's Bench 132) [1976 **88** 5fg⁵ 5d 5d³ 5d⁴ 5fg³ 5f² 5g² 5fg* 5g³ 5s*] big filly: half-sister to several winners here and abroad: 2,000 gns yearling: dam smart sprinter: raced consistently and won maiden race at Chester and minor event at Edinburgh: made virtually all when beating Warrior's Sister by 1½ lengths on latter course in October: will be suited by 6f: blinkered last three outings: exported to U.S.A. *M. H. Easterby.*

DOCTOR FEELGOOD 3 gr.g. Roan Rocket 128–Mrs Hauksbee 102 (Pindari **52** 124) [1975 5s 5v 5g 5g⁴ 5g⁴ 8d 7g² 7g⁵ 8v 1976 12d³ 12g³ 12g 14f² 8f⁴] small gelding: seems to stay 1½m: usually wears blinkers, but didn't do so on last two outings: sold out of C. Bewicke's stable 2,000 gns Ascot July Sales after fourth start. *R. Carter.*

DOCTOR'S CHOICE 2 br.f. Petingo 135–Just a Moment (Ballymoss 136) **116** [1976 8g* 7.7s²] French filly: first foal: 2,600 gns yearling: dam placed twice over 1½m in France: won 14-runner newcomers event at Saint-Cloud in October by a short head from Belle Kali: 38/1 for Group 3 Prix Thomas Bryon at Saint-Cloud later in month but ran very well indeed against the colts, finishing 1½ lengths second of 13 to General: will stay middle distances: acts on soft going. *R. Carver, France.*

DOCTORS DILEMMA 3 gr.c. Veiled Wonder–Lady Patient (Dumbarnie 125) **73** [1975 5v 5d 5.9fg⁵ 6fg⁴ 5f⁶ 1976 5fg* 5f* 5d⁵ 5fg⁶ 5h³] compact colt: quite a modest handicapper: won at Warwick in April and Wolverhampton in May: stays 6f but seems best at 5f on a sound surface: wears blinkers: goes well for H. Ballantine. *H. Smyth.*

DOCTOR WALL 3 ch.c. Porto Bello 118–Second Sight 99 (Premonition 130) **101** [1975 5f 5fg³ 6fg⁶ 6fg* 1976 5g⁵ 6fg² 6d 6fg³ 6f 7g 7.3d 7s] rangy colt: useful handicapper: placed at Newmarket in April (1½ lengths second to Broxted) and Newbury in June (3 lengths third to Gwent): stays 6f well: evidently needs a sound surface: has been tried in blinkers but does better without. *J. Tree.*

DOCTOR WIN 4 gr.g. Right Boy 137–Vital Win 65 (Harwin 119) [1974 —
6f 6fg⁶ 6f 6d 1975 8.2f⁵ 5g 8h³ 9f² 9.4f³ 1976 10.2s] poor maiden. *M W.
Easterby.*

DOE'S GIRL 3 gr.f. Donibristle 96–Solina (Ocarina 131) [1975 6d 1976 8f —
10.8f] small filly: apparently of no account. *R. Cambidge.*

DO GOOD 2 b.c. Derring-Do 131–Good Conduct (Sing Sing 134) [1976 6fg **107**
6fg² 7f³ 7h* 7f* 8g⁶ 8s 8.2v³] strong, well-grown colt: first foal: dam unraced
half-sister to four winners: successful twice at Bath, winning a maiden race in
July and putting up a really good effort when coming home 6 lengths clear of
Slick Chick under top weight in nursery in September: stays 1m: acts on any
going: sold 9,400 gns Newmarket Autumn Sales: exported to Canada. *P. Walwyn.*

DOGS OF WAR 2 ch.c. Shoolerville 121–War Talk 90 (Assagai) [1976 5.1g 7d] —
lengthy colt: first foal: dam won over 6f and 1m: apprentice ridden when behind
in maiden race at Yarmouth in September and 25-runner Houghton Stakes at
Newmarket in October: sold 1,500 gns Newmarket Autumn Sales. *R. Armstrong.*

DOHA 2 ch.f. New Chapter 106–Sea Plane (Neptune II 127) [1976 5.5d⁵ 6g³ **113**
6s⁴ 6.5d² 6.5g² 7s 7g³ 8s²] French filly: half-sister to fair 3-y-o stayer Forgotten
Dreams (by Shoemaker) and to a winner in France: 20,000 francs yearling
(approx. £2,100): dam a minor 1¼m winner in France: still a maiden but gained
places in four good races: beaten less than a length by Perello in Group 2 Criterium
de Maisons-Laffitte in September and finished 3 lengths second of 14 to Kamicia
in Group 1 Criterium des Pouliches at Longchamp the following month: will
stay 1½m: acts on soft going. *G. Serpereau, France.*

DOLBEN LAD 4 b.c. Lauso-Viana (Privy Councillor 125) [1974 N.R. 1975 **70**
10d 1976 12fg* 12fg² 12d² 22.2f⁶ 14f² 18.1g] strong colt: won minor event at
Pontefract in April and ran creditably in most of his races afterwards: stays well:
probably acts on any going. *J. Harris.*

DOLBEN LASS 7 b.m. Rockavon 120–Spring Star 52 (Sermon) [1974 N.R. —
1975 N.R. 1976 12f] plating-class maiden: stays 11f. *J. Harris.*

DOLLIE CASE 3 br.f. Jukebox 120–Miss Patsy 96 (Olein's Grace 127) [1975 —
5h 7f³ 7f 6f⁵ 7g* 8g 7g 8fg 1976 12.2s⁵ 10v] light-framed, narrow filly: stays
1m: possibly requires some give in the ground. *J. Vickers.*

DOLLY DICKINS 2 br.f. Double-U-Jay 120–Romula (Romulus 129) [1976 —
5f 5d 5g 7f⁶ 7fg 7g 10v] lengthy filly: no worthwhile form, including in auction
events. *R. Hollinshead.*

DOLPHIN SAFARI 3 br.f. Huntercombe 133–Dolphinet 96 (Big Game) [1975 **98**
5d³ 6g 5fg² 1976 5f² 5g³ 6g* 6d* 7g* 7f⁶ 6fg³ 7fg⁴ 7.3d] strong, dipped-
backed filly: ran up a hat-trick of wins in May, scoring in handicaps at Salisbury
(from Monymusk) and York (from Pitboy) and minor event at Kempton (very
comfortably by 4 lengths from Star Walk): possibly finds 6f on fast ground on
sharp side nowadays and may well stay 1m: appears to act on any going:
suitable mount for an apprentice: consistent: sold 7,800 gns Newmarket December Sales. *M. Smyly.*

DOMINION 4 b.c. Derring-Do 131–Picture Palace 83 (Princely Gift 137) **123**
[1974 5fg² 6g⁶ 6fg⁵ 5d² 7.3s⁶ 1975 8v* 8g³ 12fg 10fg⁶ 8f⁴ 8d* 9g 1976 9fg²
10g² 8g² 8fg* 8fg* 8fg⁵ 7.3fg 8fg* 8d³ 8d² 8.2v*]
Three cheers for Dominion! His success in the Prix Perth at Saint-Cloud
in November was the only outright victory by a British-trained horse in a
French pattern race in 1976. In the sense that Dominion has long been knocking
at the door in good races, there could scarcely have been a more deserving
winner. Favoured by the weights he took full advantage of his opportunity,
beating Mittainvilliers in good style by two and a half lengths with Tyrant's
Vale and Jellaby next. Full of Hope, Earth Spirit, Arctic Tern and Ranimer,
all high-class winners earlier in the year, were among the also-rans.
Dominion's ten outings as a four-year-old before the Prix Perth brought
wins in the Hermitage Stakes at Newbury and lesser events at York and Goodwood as well as place-money in important races, notably the Lockinge Stakes,
the Queen Elizabeth II Stakes and the Grosser Kaufhof Preis, the last-named
run at Cologne. As in the previous season, when he finished third to Bolkonski

Prix Perth, Saint-Cloud—a fine win for Dominion

in the Guineas, facing uphill work was his customary lot but Dominion has retained commendable enthusiasm for his job.

Dominion (b.c. 1972)	Derring-Do (br 1961)	Darius (b 1951)	Dante
			Yasna
		Sipsey Bridge (b 1954)	Abernant
			Claudette
	Picture Palace (b 1961)	Princely Gift (b 1951)	Nasrullah
			Blue Gem
		Palais Glide (b 1948)	King Legend
			Side Slip

Picture Palace has produced other good winners besides Dominion in Prominent (by High Hat, who was still winning races at nine years of age, Projector (by Hopeful Venture) and Jeune Premier (by Primera). Dominion appears not to stay beyond a mile and a quarter and in our opinion he's best at around a mile. A robust, attractive colt, he acts on any going and is a credit to a family noted for producing genuine and workmanlike racehorses. He has been sold to race in America. *I. Balding.*

DOMITOR 4 b.c. Busted 134–Red Goddess 84 (Red God 128 §) [1974 6fg⁶ **80** 7g*(dis) 7d² 7g 1975 9v⁶ 9d² 10.6fg³ 10fg* 12g* 15g* 14fg⁵ 12g⁶ 1976 10.6d 12.3d⁴ 10.6d⁶ 12.3fg*(w.o.) 12fg⁴ 10.5g² 10.2g² 11g⁶] strong, good-bodied colt: fair handicapper: ran best race at 4 yrs when runner-up to Parsifal at York in September on sixth outing: has won at 15f, but gives impression that he is best at up to 1½m: seems to act on any going: sold to R. Armstrong 820 gns Newmarket December Sales. *M. W. Easterby.*

DON 2 ch.c. Yellow God 129–Dogana (Zank) [1976 6d³ 6fg⁴ 5v* 5s⁵] rangy, **98** good-looking colt: second foal: 1,600 gns yearling: dam won over 9f at 3 yrs in Ireland: battled on well to win £1,800 maiden race at York in October by 1½ lengths from Crimson Silk, the pair finishing clear: remote fifth of nine to La Ville de Rire in well-contested event at Doncaster later same month: should stay beyond 6f: probably best suited by a soft surface and acts well on heavy going. *W. Elsey.*

DONA BAROD 4 gr.f. Don II 123–Baroda Princess (Skymaster 126) [1974 **121** 7.5d* 8v* 1975 8g* 8d 10g⁴ 9.2s³ 8s* 7d 8s⁵ 1976 8d⁶ 8g⁵ 9.7d⁵ 8g* 8d² 8d 8s² 9.2s* 10d] French filly: closely related to Grey Gaston (by Fortino II), a fairly useful performer at up to 1½m: 10,000 gns yearling: dam, lightly raced, is daughter of sister to Milesian: ran well against high-class opposition several times at 4 yrs, including when winning Prix Messidor at Maisons-Laffitte in July by 1½ lengths from Monsanto and Prix de l'Opera at Longchamp in October by ¾ length from Pollenka: creditable second in Prix d'Astarte at Deauville (beaten 2 lengths by Carolina Moon) and Prix du Moulin de Longchamp (2½ lengths behind Gravelines) and wasn't disgraced (raced on slower stands side) when eighth of 19 to Vitiges in Champion Stakes at Newmarket, also in October, on final outing: stays 1¼m: acts on soft going. *J. Cunnington, jnr, France.*

DON AMIGO 2 br.c. Relko 136–Donna Lydia 110 (Hyperion) [1976 7d] **— p** brother to useful stayer Donna Nook, and half-brother to stallion Don Carlos (by Charlottesville) and two minor winners: dam middle-distance performer: unquoted, showed up to past halfway when nineteenth of 25 to Bessie Wallis in Houghton Stakes at Newmarket in October: will do better over long distances. *J. Winter.*

DONESSA 2 ch.f. Doon 124–Pardilly 71 (Pardao 120) [1976 5f⁵ 7g 7s⁶] first **60** foal: dam stayed 1½m: showed a little ability in maiden races: will stay 1¼m: sold 260 gns Doncaster November Sales. *J. W. Watts.*

DON FORTUNE 4 b.c. Kalydon 122–Fortunella 110 (Pinza 137) [1974 7fg **94** 7g² 7fg* 7s³ 8g* 1975 12s⁶ 10g 12f³ 12f³ 12h* 14f³ 14fg⁶ 1976 12fg⁶ 12fg⁵ 11g⁴ 11.1g* 12fg⁵ 12fg² 12h² 12.3fg⁵] strong, well-made colt: fairly useful handi-capper: successful at Kempton in May by ¾ length from So They Say: ran creditably in most of his races afterwards: stays 1½m (has twice run below his best at 1¾m): acts on hard going. *M. Ryan.*

DONNACHANT 5 ch.m. Shooting Chant–Donnarose (Fighting Don) [1974 **—** 6f 8f 8g 8fg³ 6s⁴ 6d 6d 8g 1975 N.R. 1976 8f 8g 8fg] of little account nowa-days. *M. Camacho.*

DON PHILIPE 4 b.g. Don Carlos–Lantern (Relic) [1974 5.8g 5d 1975 16s⁴ **71** 17.7fg⁶ 16h³ 1976 12fg⁴ 16f⁶ 14g 12.2f* 10f³ 10f* 12f⁴ 11g² 10f³ 10.6g 13v] plater: successful at Wolverhampton in May and Nottingham the following month, being bought in for 825 gns on latter course: stays 1½m: acts on firm going: suitable mount for an apprentice: wears blinkers. *A. Davison.*

DONRAE 3 gr.f. Don II 123–Brief Chorus 105 (Counsel 118) [1975 5g⁵ 5g* **93** 6f⁵ 5fg³ 5h* 1976 8f³ 10.5d⁵ 8.2d³ 8f⁶ 6fg 8g⁴ 8g⁶] lengthy, leggy filly: good walker: ran best races when in frame in Cecil Frail Handicap at Haydock in May (9½ lengths third to Gunner B, having a very poor run in straight) and Northern Goldsmiths' Handicap at Newcastle in August (just over 2 lengths fourth to Lyncathal): best at 1m: appears to act on any going: gave impression at New-castle that she may be best suited by waiting tactics: blinkered final outing (ran moderately). *W. Gray.*

DON REVIE 3 ch.g. Laser Light 118–Pretest 87 (Premonition 130) [1975 6f 6d **—** 5g² 5.9g 5v 1976 10.1f 12fg 10fg 8.3f] strong-quartered gelding: plater: should be suited by 7f+: wore blinkers at 2 yrs but didn't do so in 1976: sold out of R. Hollinshead's stable 575 gns Ascot January Sales. *M. Goswell.*

DONSHARLOTTA 2 gr.c. Don II 123–Sharlotta 84 (Sheshoon 132) [1976 **70** 6fg 6f 8fg⁶ 6v 8s⁴] lightly-built colt: first foal: dam needed a test of stamina: suited by a test of stamina himself and ran best races at 1m, on final outing finishing 4 lengths fourth of 18 to Mischiefmaker in seller at Redcar in October: will stay 1½m: appears to act on any going: blinkered last two outings. *D. Williams.*

DON'T TOUCH 2 b.g. Taj Dewan 128–Coals of Fire 86 (Firestreak 125) [1976 **90 p** 10d*] second living foal: half-brother to moderate 1973 2-y-o Celtic Fire, a winner of a 5.8f seller: 3,000 gns yearling: dam exported to Denmark after winning over 5f at 2 yrs: well-backed favourite, went down by a short head to stable-companion Gunbad in £2,100 event at Newmarket in October but was carried left in final furlong and was awarded race by stewards: will stay well: almost certainly has improvement in him and should make a useful 3-y-o. *J. Hindley.*

DONZEL 2 br.c. Don II 123–Say Gwen (Never Say Die 137) [1976 5g² 6fg³ **100** 6f 8s⁴] lengthy, workmanlike colt: third foal: half-brother to useful Irish middle-distance filly Extravaganza (by Sovereign Gleam) and useful miler Always Faithful (by Super Sam): 8,600 gns yearling: dam lightly raced: ran only three times after a promising début in May, putting up easily best effort when 5½ lengths fourth of 17 to Rutlow in nursery at Brighton in October: will stay middle distances: probably acts on any going, with the possible excep-tion of very firm: will win a race. *G. Harwood.*

DOOGALI 2 ch.f. Doon 124–Rogali 80 (Royal Avenue 123) [1976 7fg⁵] half- **70 p** sister to 1974 2-y-o 7f winner Dualvi (by Dual) and 3-y-o 7f winner Norton Falcon (by Birdbrook): dam a sprinter: outsider of party, showed promise when 4 lengths fifth of nine to Prince Carl in maiden race at Ayr in July, making steady progress in closing stages: likely to do better. *N. Angus.*

DOON DAHLIA 3 ch.f. Doon 124–Summer Plumage (Midsummer Night II **—** 117) [1975 N.R. 1976 8s 8g] first foal: dam never ran: last in maiden races at Ayr in June and July. *J. Barclay.*

DOONELLA 3 ch.f. Doon 124–Double Babu (My Babu 136) [1975 7.6g 1976 **—** 10.2s] half-sister to minor 1¼m winner Carlos Boy (by Don Carlos): tailed off in maiden race at Doncaster in November. *P. Cole.*

DOON LAD 3 b.c. Hard Man 102–Miss Dunoon 83 (Dunoon Star 110) [1975 **50**
7g 6g 7g 6d 7g⁵ 8g 1976 6v⁴ 8f³ 7g⁴ 7g] workmanlike colt: ran best race on
third outing: off course some time afterwards and was bandaged near-fore on
only subsequent outing: probably stays 1m. *L. Docker.*

DOON PALACE 3 ch.f. Doon 124–Dux Girl 99 (Bewildered 102) [1975 5d —
5s⁵ 6fg 1976 6s 10f] no worthwhile form in maiden events and a seller: sold
400 gns Doncaster September Sales. *H. Bell.*

DOONSIDE 4 b.c. Doon 124–Easterbury (Privy Councillor 125) [1974 8.2d² —
9s 8s 1975 10v* 10s* 9g* 9d* 10fg 13g³ 14fg 10f* 10d⁵ 10f 1976 12fg² 13v⁵]
leggy colt: lightly raced at 4 yrs and wasn't seen out after April: stays 1½m: acts
on any going but is particularly well suited by soft: genuine. *K. Whitehead.*

DOORLOCK 2 gr.c. Tudor Melody 129–Hozelock 86 (Vilmorin) [1976 7g —
7d 8v] good-looking colt: beaten some way in maiden races at Newmarket
(two) and Teesside in October: sold 900 gns Doncaster November Sales. *Sir
Mark Prescott.*

DOORMAT 3 b.c. Tudor Music 131–Lady Matador 108 (Matador 131) [1975 **85**
5fg 5.9f 5fg 5g* 5d 6v³ 1976 8g⁶ 5g 6d 5s 5s² 5s] strong colt: ran easily best
race when length second to Faridina in handicap at Haydock in October: stays
6f: acts on heavy ground. *D. Ancil.* -

DOREEN'S BID 4 b.f. Fine Bid 106–Doreens Choice 53 (King's Bench 132) —
[1974 N.R. 1975 8f 8h 9fg³ 11 1f⁴ 10g 8.2d 10.8g 8d 1976 9fg] poor maiden:
seems to stay 11f. *L. Barratt.*

DOREEN'S SILVER 3 gr.f. Goldhill 125–Tiny Rose 73 (Palestine 133) [1975 **46**
5fg 5g⁵ 5g³ 6g³ 7g⁶ 5g³ 6g⁶ 1976 8g⁵ 8h 8fg 6d 8g 8d⁶ 6v⁶ 7v⁴] leggy, narrow
filly: plater: stays 7f (had stiff tasks when tried at 1m): sometimes wears blinkers:
trained until after fourth outing by J. Calvert. *J. Etherington.*

DORIS'S CHOICE 3 gr.g. Doon 124–Dalcourt 72 (Fidalgo 129) [1975 5f 5g **58**
6f⁴ 6g 5g 6g 7g⁴ 1976 10g 11.1fg 16f 8fg 7f⁴ 7f² 7g³ 8fg 7s²] quite a modest
plater: ran well when runner-up to easy winner Qui Va La in all-aged event
(non-seller) at Folkestone in October on final outing: best at 7f although
runs as though he would be suited by further: acts on any going: has shown
a tendency to swerve (did so when blinkered on fifth outing). *D. Underwood.*

DOUBLE BLUFF 3 b.g. No Argument 107–Over Called 70 (Fine Bid 106) **71**
[1975 8d 8g 1976 12d 10fg 13fg³ 16fg 14f* 14fg 13.1f⁶] strong, compact,
quite attractive gelding: won maiden race at Yarmouth in August a shade
comfortably by 2½ lengths from Pinewood Grange: stays 1¾m but possibly
not 2m: acts on firm going: sold 6,800 gns Newmarket Autumn Sales. *M.
Smyly.*

DOUBLE COMEDY 4 b.g. Double Jump 131–Comedy Girl 103 (Ujiji) [1974 —
5d 6h⁵ 7.2d⁴ 8.2g 1975 7s 8g 7f 8h 7f 7fg 1976 11d 8g 10f] plain, unfurnished
gelding: poor plater: has been tried in blinkers. *J. W. Watts.*

DOUBLE EAST 3 ch.c. Levanter 121–Samarra (Milesian 125) [1975 N.R. **96**
1976 10.1fg² 11g* 12fg* 12h* 12s³] attractive colt: half-brother to fairly
useful miler Starlit Night (by Midsummer Night II): dam won over 1m in
Ireland: won maiden race at Newbury (overcame difficulties in running), minor
event at Leicester and handicap at Lingfield in first half of season: held on by
a head from Konrad on last-named course in June after ding-dong battle:
not seen out again until late September when well-beaten third of five to Warbeck
in handicap at Ascot: stays 1½m: acts on hard ground. *R. Price.*

DOUBLEGLOW 7 b.g. Double-U-Jay 120–Gleyre (Whistler 129) [1974 7g **88**
8g* 14g 10.4d* 12d 10d 10.2g 1975 10v⁵ 9v 12.2g⁴ 10.6s 10.6v 1976 10.2g*
12f* 12g* 11.1g² 12f 8g 11.7fg⁵ 11.7f⁴] compact, good-bodied gelding: fair
handicapper: successful at Doncaster and Thirsk (twice) in 1976: stays 1½m:
appears to act on any going: excellent mount for an inexperienced rider: trained
by B. Hills first four outings. *F. J. Houghton.*

DOUBLE LIE 4 b.g. Double Jump 131–Lead On (Aureole 132) [1974 5fg **56 d**
5.1g⁴ 1975 10g 1976 8.2v* 8fg 10.4fg 10h 8s] lengthy gelding: plater:
narrow winner at Hamilton in April (no bid): no worthwhile form afterwards
(pulled up lame on second outing): stays 1m: acts on heavy going: wears blinkers:
trained by M. James until after third outing. *D. Plant.*

DOUBLE LIGHT 2 b.c. Double Jump 131–Twilight Time (Abernant 142) **77**
[1976 5.9g⁶ 6fg 7f⁵ 7g² 6d²] plater: second to Sloane Ranger at Warwick
in August and to Mint Condition at Windsor in September, both times finishing
well clear of rest of sizeable fields: stays 7f: sure to win a seller. *P. Robinson.*

DOUBLE LOVE 3 b.g. Prince Tenderfoot 126–Sum Toy (Chieftain) [1975 7g 1976 10g] strong, compact gelding: well-backed favourite when eighth of 13 to Oisin in maiden race at Folkestone in March, only outing: sold 290 gns Ascot June Sales. *B. Hanbury.* —

DOUBLE PACK 3 b.f. David Jack 125–Inheritance 81 (Compensation 127) [1975 N.R. 1976 10f6] second foal: half-sister to 1m winner Royal Legacy (by Prince de Galles): dam stayed 1½m: dwelt when remote sixth of nine to Welsh Relic in maiden race at Yarmouth in July, only outing. *P. Robinson.* —

DOUBLEPHOTO 3 b.c. Vaguely Noble 140–Double Steel (Gustav Dore 114) [1975 8.2d 8g 1976 11g3 12d 12fg5 10s 10.2s2] big, strong American-bred colt: quite moderate form in varied company: runner-up to Flying Diplomat in 17-runner maiden race at Doncaster in October when blinkered first time: probably stays 1½m: appears to act on any going. *J. Dunlop.* 77 d

DOUBLE POPPY 3 br.f. Double Jump 131–Porpora (Andrea Mantegna) [1975 N.R. 1976 9.4g 8f 12f 12fg5 14.7h5 16f3] plating-class maiden: ran best race fourth outing: sold 320 gns Ascot December Sales. *J. Leigh.* —

DOUBLE SANDS 3 ch.f. Double Jump 131–Silver Sand 86 (Grey Sovereign 128 §) [1975 N.R. 1976 8.2f] small filly: half-sister to three winners, including very smart sprinter Workboy (by Firestreak): dam fair winner at 1m and 1½m: tailed-off last of 12 behind Air Trooper in maiden race at Nottingham in June, only outing. *G. Vergette.* —

DOUBLE SECRET 2 b.c. Most Secret 119–Double K 72 (Goldhill 125) [1976 5f2 5fg4 5s2 5fg4 5fg* 5g2 5fg3 5g4] strong, quite attractive colt: second foal: half-brother to useful winning plater Kaymay (by Maystreak): dam won over 5f at 2 yrs: won maiden event at Ayr in July by 1½ lengths from Guard Duty: ran well afterwards in nurseries at Ayr (two) and York, wearing blinkers on last two outings: will stay 6f. *M. H. Easterby.* 94

DOUBLE STAR 4 ch.c. Star Moss 122–Corypha (Royal Palm 131) [1974 5fg 7g 6g3 8.2s 1975 10fg 11.5f 12f4 12f3 1976 12fg6] plain colt: stays 1½m: acts on firm going: bandaged only outing at 4 yrs. *D. Ringer.* —

DOUBLE SWEET 3 b.f. Sing Sing 134 or Double Jump 131–Neat and Sweet 81 (Narrator 127) [1975 5.9f 1976 10fg 9f5 7.6fg 9fg 10d] poor plater. *L. Barratt.* —

DOUBLETTE 2 ch.f. Double Jump 131–Florabette (Floribunda 136) [1976 5g3 5f4 5h2 6g*] workmanlike filly: first foal: dam never ran: won claiming race at Ostend in July by 2½ lengths from ex-English filly Cross Bird: claimed for £2,600 afterwards and is now trained in Belgium. *Sir Mark Prescott.* 67

DOUBLE TWENTY 4 b.c. Tribal Chief 125–Andromache 112 (Delirium 126) [1974 N.R. 1975 8v 7v 6s 6f 6s 6f 10g 1976 6g6 8g2 8.3f5 8fg] poor plater: stays 1m. *J. Benstead.* 46

DOUBLE-U-JUSTICE 3 b.f. Double-U-Jay 120–Miss Tring 94 (Mustang) [1975 N.R. 1976 6d] half-sister to four winners, including Apollo Eight (by Faberge II), a prolific winning stayer on the Continent: dam a stayer: last of nine in maiden seller at Haydock in April. *J. Cousins.* —

DOUBLE VENTURE 3 ch.f. Double-U-Jay 120–Evening Sky 74 (Skymaster 126) [1975 6g 8g5 1976 8fg 6g 5fg 6v] lengthy filly: plating-class maiden. *A. Potts.* —

DOUBLE YOU 2 b.f. Double Jump 131–Veryowen (Fleet Discovery) [1976 5d 5fg 6h3 6fg 5fg] neat filly: second produce: 660 gns foal: dam twice-raced sister to a stakes-placed winner: showed a little ability in minor event on third outing but was well beaten in a valuable seller (blinkered) on final appearance: stays 6f. *J. W. Watts.* 68

DOUBLY DOUBTFUL 2 br.f. Forlorn River 124–Misfired 101 (Blast 125) [1976 5f 5fg 6f 6h3 8s 6s] unimpressive individual: bad plater. *Hbt Jones.* 48

DOUBLY HOPEFUL 3 ch.f. Double Jump 131–Vaguely Hopeful 65 (Fortino II 120) [1975 N.R. 1976 7fg 10f2 12.2f 12d6 10.2fg 10f2 12.3f4 10f2 10.1fg* 10g* 10g2 10.8s3 10.2s4 10v* 8s*] big filly: first foal: 2,900 gns yearling: dam ran only three times: had a successful time in the autumn and won maiden race at Windsor and minor event at Yarmouth in September, apprentice event at Nottingham the following month and handicap at Doncaster in November: put up an excellent performance when beating Amber Valley 2 lengths on last-named course: stays 1½m but not 1½m: seems to act on any going: ran poorly in blinkers on third outing: suitable mount for an apprentice: a tough individual. *B. Lunness.* 98

DOU

DOUBTFUL GEORGE 2 b.c. Breeders Dream 116–Chivalrous 104 (Prince —
Chevalier) [1976 5f 5fg] half-brother to Irish 1¼m winner Egyptian Prince (by
Tutankhamen): 1,000 gns yearling: dam won at 1½m: behind in auction event at
Pontefract in April and seller at Ripon in May. *M. W. Easterby.*

DOUVAINE 2 ro.f. Don II 123–Diaphane (Dark Star) [1976 5f⁴ 6g* 6fg² 6fg⁴ **86**
6f⁴] active sort: French bred: first foal: dam, winner over 7.5f, is daughter of
sister to Match III and Reliance II: having first race for over 3 months, landed a
gamble in 18-runner maiden event at Nottingham in July by 1½ lengths from
Menin: ran well when fourth in nurseries at York and Haydock the following
month: will stay 1m. *B. Hills.*

DOVE 3 ch.f. Sea Hawk II 131–Righteous Girl 93 (Right Boy 137) [1975 5f⁴ **78**
6f⁴ 6g⁴ 7.3d⁴ 7g 1976 7s 8f⁴ 10f³] useful-looking, good-bodied filly: in frame in
well-contested minor event at Beverley in June and handicap at Brighton in July:
will stay 1½m: acts on firm going. *H. Candy.*

DOWNHOLME 2 ch.c. Charlottown 127–Tailor Donore 83 (Donore 119) [1976 **97**
5g 6f³ 5fg⁵ 5f⁶ 7fg* 8g 8fg³ 8v* 8s³ 7.2v] neat, attractive colt: half-brother to
three winners, including 3-y-o Master Cutter (by Hard Tack), a fairly useful
winner over 5f at 2 yrs: dam 5f sprinter: successful in nurseries at Newcastle in
August and York in October, making all in very testing conditions on latter
course to win by a wide margin from Bow-Wow: needs at least 7f and stays 1m:
acts on any going and goes very well on heavy ground: blinkered second to fourth
outings: trained by Denys Smith on first four appearances. *J. W. Watts.*

DOWNSTAIRS 2 ch.f. Linden Tree 127–Nigretta (Ribot 142) [1976 6fg 6g **73**
9fg²] compact filly: half-sister to a winner over jumps in France by Neckar: dam
good-class winner in Italy: showed first worthwhile form when 4 lengths second
of 20 in maiden race won by Identity at Wolverhampton in September on final
outing: will stay well. *P. Cole.*

DOYENNE 4 b.f. Don II 123–Cayenne (Hornbeam 130) [1974 5s⁴ 5.9s² 1975 **67**
6s* 7g 6fg* 6f 6f 6fg* 7fg 7s 6s 1976 6f 6f³ 6fg⁴] leggy, light-framed filly:
quite a moderate handicapper: ran best race at 4 yrs when creditable third of
seven to Calibina at Goodwood in August: best at 6f: seems to act on any going:
ran moderately when tried in blinkers on final outing in 1975. *P. Cundell.*

DRAGON KING 3 ch.c. Crepello 136–Miss Hong Kong 69 (Mossborough 126) —
[1975 N.R. 1976 11f 12fg 12fg] big, strong colt: third foal: dam, half-sister to
good 5f sprinter Caterina and Eclipse winner Scottish Rifle, won over 1¼m:
showed up well for a long way in maiden races at Newbury and Newmarket in
April and Ladbroke Derby Trial at Lingfield in May, but was not seen out again:
should stay 1½m. *Doug Smith.*

DRAGON LASS 2 b.f. Cheval 117–Penstemon (Pendragon) [1976 7fg 8s⁶ 7s] —
poor plater. *J. Thorne.*

DREAM COUNTY 3 b.f. Sing Sing 134 or Breeders Dream 116–Hants 111 **76**
(Exbury 138) [1975 6g⁴ 6f³ 6g⁶ 7f⁶ 1976 10f³ 10f³ 12.2f* 12.2g⁵ 12.2s* 12s³ 12v⁴]
neat filly: won modest maiden race at Catterick in August: improved on that form
when winning handicap at Wolverhampton in October by a length from Alweston:
stays 1½m well: acts on any going but is evidently well suited by plenty of give in
the ground: sold 6,000 gns Newmarket December Sales. *Doug Smith.*

DREAM DANCER 2 b.c. Sword Dancer (USA)–Quick Dream (Crepello 136) —
[1976 6d] French-foaled colt: dam lightly-raced half-sister to very useful miler
Quebracho: unquoted and ridden by 7-lb claimer when last but one in 23-runner
maiden race won by Running Bull at Newmarket in October. *L. Cumani.*

DREAM DAYS 2 b.f. Breeders Dream 116–Topless 67 (Epaulette 125) [1976 **61**
5fg 5fg⁵ 5f⁶ 5f⁵] small filly: little worthwhile form and will do better in sellers.
C. Bewicke.

DREAMING 3 b.f. Breeders Dream 116–Brief Note 92 (Counsel 118) [1975 —
5s 5g² 5f³ 6f⁴ 5.9f² 7g⁴ 6g⁶ 6g⁶ 7g³ 7.6s 1976 6fg 8fg 6fg⁵] neat filly: ran best
race in claiming event on final outing (May): should stay 1¼m. *B. Swift.*

DREAM LOVER 2 ch.c. Long Till 113–Manicou's Dream (Manicou) [1976 5f] —
first foal: dam fair hurdler: 16/1 when behind in 15-runner minor event won by
subsequently-disqualified Ground Cover at Lingfield in June: needs much
further and will stay middle distances. *R. Smyth.*

DRED SCOTT 4 b.c. Tom Rolfe–Free Model (Phideas) [1974 N.R. 1975 **66**
8v 8g³ 9d⁴ 10fg² 10f* 10.2h* 12g⁵ 10g² 12g² 10d⁶ 1976 12g 12f⁶ 10f³ 10fg⁶ 8.2g³
8.2fg² 8h² 10.1f³ 10.6f 10s⁴ 12v²] strong, compact, quite attractive American-

bred colt: poor handicapper: stays 1½m: seems to act on any going: probably best in blinkers: trained by D. Morley first two outings at 4 yrs. *D. Sasse.*

DRINK UP 2 ch.c. My Swallow 134–Warsite 101 (Relic) [1976 5g 6g 6fg 8g 7g] **66**
strong colt: brother to 3-y-o Sporty Girl, a good winner in Belgium, and half-brother to two minor winners: backward when beaten some way in maiden and minor events. *R. Smyth.*

DROLI 4 ch.f. Starry Halo 122–Kaye Sister 81 (Royal Palm 131) [1974 6s —
7d⁵ 7d⁵ 7g³ 1975 10fg 8g⁵ 12s 1976 10.1fg 10f] bad plater. *A. Davison.*

DROP OF A HAT 3 b.f. Midsummer Night II 117–Nonsensical 99 (Silly Season **83**
127) [1975 5fg³ 5.9fg* 6fg³ 6fg* 7f* 7d² 7g³ 7.2s* 7g³ 1976 8.5fg⁵ 12fg 8fg 10f⁶ 8f⁴ 8f 7s] tall American-bred filly: enjoyed an excellent first season (rated 105): showed nothing like that form in 1976, putting up best effort when tried in blinkers on fifth outing: possibly does not stay 1½m: acts on any going: again blinkered final outing. *I. Balding.*

DRUMADOLL 4 b.f. Meldrum 112–Adolphus Street 51 (Planchado) [1974 5fg **51**
5fg 5fg 6g⁴ 1975 8g 7.2g 9fg 7fg⁵ 10h 9f 7g 8h² 1976 8f⁴ 10f* 12.2f² 12.2f⁵ 10f 10g 12fg 12.2s 11.1s²] strong filly: apprentice ridden when winning seller at Beverley in May by 2½ lengths from Africa Star (no bid): good second to Voucher Book in minor event at Catterick in July on third start, best other effort at 4 yrs: stays 1½m: acts on any going. *P. Wigham.*

DRUM MAJOR 5 ch.g. Ballymoss 136–Soldier's Song 104 (Court Martial) —
[1974 8g⁴ 10fg³ 11.1g² 11g³ 12fg 12g³ 12g³ 1975 N.R. 1976 16fg] quite a moderate handicapper (rated 78) in 1974: last of nine in handicap won by Piccadilly Etta at Lingfield in May, only outing since: should stay further than 1½m: ran respectably in blinkers on last outing at 3 yrs. *D. Underwood.*

DUBOFF 4 br.f. So Blessed 130–Proper Pretty 62 (Worden II 129) [1974 5g⁵ **120**
6v⁵ 6g⁵ 1975 7g* 8f* 8h* 10.1fg* 9f* 8f* 12g 10f* 8fg* 10.5g⁵ 10g* 1976 10g 8f* 12f⁴ 8f⁶ 8fg* 8g⁵ 10fg 7g⁴ 10g² 10d]
 Duboff's record in 1976 well illustrates the problem trainers usually encounter in placing high-class four-year-old fillies in England. Duboff was every bit as good and as keen as in the previous season, and for most of the year she had the top-of-the-ground conditions that suited her so well, but from ten starts, of which only one was out of her distance range, she added only two more victories to her magnificent tally. Of the two races she won, one was a contest of very little consequence at Beverley. The other, the Child Stakes at Newmarket, was worthy of a filly of her ability and gave her owner adequate reward for the enterprise in keeping her in training. Duboff nearly missed winning the Child Stakes, having experienced great difficulty in obtaining a clear passage before squeezing home by a short head from Red Ruby; had she lost she would have been

*Child Stakes, Newmarket—Duboff catches Red Ruby (noseband) in the
final strides.   The other runners are (left to right) Roussalka,
Sauceboat, Intermission and Heaven Knows*

Mrs C. R. Radclyffe's "Duboff"

desperately unlucky, and justice appeared to be done when the stewards allowed the result to stand.

In nearly all of her other races Duboff was simply taking on more than she could handle; so she lost no caste in defeat, and on two notable occasions she underlined just how good a filly she was. Giving weight to all except Raga Navarro in the Prix Messidor, she finished fifth of thirteen behind Dona Barod, to whom she was conceding 9 lb, in a very strong field. Monsanto was second, Gravelines third, Comeram fourth; and Duboff was beaten less than six lengths. In the Sun Chariot Stakes in the autumn, a race she won the previous season, Duboff accounted for every horse except the French three-year-old Ranimer, whom she ran to two and a half lengths on terms 6 lb worse than weight for age. A distance of four lengths separated second and third: behind Duboff were Sauceboat, Everything Nice and Antrona.

Duboff (br.f. 1972)	So Blessed (br 1965)	Princely Gift (b 1951)	Nasrullah / Blue Gem
		Lavant (b 1955)	Le Lavandou / Firle
	Proper Pretty (b 1961)	Worden II (ch 1949)	Wild Risk / Sans Tares
		Stop your Tickling (bl 1949)	Jock II / Senatrix

Duboff's dam, Proper Pretty, is a staying half-sister to two better-known staying fillies in Miba and Ticklish. Miba is the dam of African Dancer, Ticklish produced the miler Caius. Duboff has twice been tried over a mile and a half, and on the evidence of those runs she is much better at shorter distances, although she is usually to be seen going on strongly at the end of her races at a mile and a quarter. Duboff is an attractive, rangy filly, and a very genuine one, too. She was ideally suited by firm going. She was sold for 100,000 guineas at the December Sales and visits Brigadier Gerard. *B. Hills.*

DUCK BUSTER 4 b.c. Busted 134–Zarwood 88 (Pinza 137) [1974 5g 6fg³ 7d — 7g⁶ 8v* 8s* 1975 10d⁵ 10g⁴ 12f 1976 14g 12s 12g 10fg⁵ 10f³ 10f⁵ 10h⁵ 10g]

212

lengthy, lightly-made colt: fairly useful performer at 2 yrs but became disappointing and descended to sellers in 1976: well suited by soft going: sold 900 gns Ascot September Sales: dead. *W. Wightman.*

DUCKDOWN 3 b.f. Blast 125–Clay Duck 61 (Dicta Drake 126) [1975 N.R. —
1976 8f 10.2h³] first foal: dam needed long distances: remote third of four to Blue With Cold in minor event at Bath in July. *D. Gandolfo.*

DUKE ELLINGTON 3 br.c. Prince Tenderfoot 126–Zanzara 113 (Fairey Fulmar **111**
124) [1975 5h² 5g* 5v* 6g² 1976 7f³ 8fg] strong, attractive colt: good walker and mover: showed good form at 2 yrs and finished runner-up in William Hill Middle Park Stakes at Newmarket: ran only twice in 1976, finishing behind Wollow both times, when fifth of 10 in Clerical, Medical Greenham Stakes at Newbury in April and seventh of 17 in 2,000 Guineas at Newmarket later in month: evidently stays 1m: seems to act on any going. *R. Price.*

DUKE OF CAWSTON 3 gr.g. Ribero 126–Cawston Tower 112 (Maharaj **65**
Kumar 124) [1975 5s⁴ 5g² 6g² 5fg² 5g⁵ 1976 9.4h² 8h⁴ 8g 8f⁵] strong, good-quartered gelding: disappointing maiden: may well stay 1½m: dwelt last two outings: sold 2,100 gns Newmarket Autumn Sales. *T. Fairhurst.*

DUKE OF HOPEFIELD 2 ch.c. Queen's Hussar 124–Vision Splendid (Aureole —
132) [1976 7d 7v⁶] brother to Trance, a winner at up to 11f, and half-brother to three winners: 4,200 gns yearling: dam never ran: moderate sixth of 15 to Chennel Lane in weakly-contested maiden race at Leicester in October, better effort. *M. Stoute.*

DUKE OF MARMALADE 5 b.h. Vaguely Noble 140–Mock Orange (Dedicate) **117**
[1974 10fg* 12f³ 12g² 12d* 14fg² 12s 12s* 1975 10g* 15g² 12g* 12g³ 12g² 12.5g³ 10g³ 13.5g⁵ 11s² 12s 12g³ 12.5s* 1976 12g* 10g³ 12g³ 12g 13.5g³ 12s 12v³ 14v*] tall American-bred horse: good-class performer: won Premio Ellington in May and Premio Roma in November, both at Rome: ran well in most of his other races, gaining places in Premio Presidente della Republica on same course later in month (beaten 3 lengths by Shamsan), Gran Premio di Milano in June (beaten by Rouge Sang and Art Style), Grand Prix de Deauville in August (about 4 lengths behind Ashmore) and Gran Premio del Jockey Club at

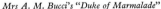

Mrs A. M. Bucci's "Duke of Marmalade"

Milan in October (about 1½ lengths behind Infra Green): last of 10 behind Pawneese in King George VI and Queen Elizabeth Diamond Stakes at Ascot and sixteenth of 20 to Ivanjica in Prix de l'Arc de Triomphe on only other outings: effective at middle distances and stays well: appears to act on any going: genuine and consistent: blinkered at Ascot: had positive dope-test at Ascot. *M. Bertini, Italy.*

DUKERY 2 ch.c. Marmaduke 108–Eringa 101 (Saint Crespin III 132) [1976 8s 6d] first living foal: dam disappointing half-sister to Huntercombe: in rear in maiden races at Newmarket in October but was very backward on first outing. *J. Bethell.*
—

DUKE'S GIRL 2 gr.f. Town Crier 119–Audros 96 (Panorama) [1976 5fg 5f5 5f 6fg 5fg3 5s*] light-framed filly: half-sister to several minor winners: 220 gns yearling: dam won at 7f and 1m: put up best effort when winning maiden race at Folkestone in October by a length from Jill Somers: should stay 7f: seems to act on any going but is well suited by soft: trained until after fifth outing by K. Ivory. *R. Hannon.*
79

DULAS VALLEY 4 br.f. Kibenka 119–Quissante (Buisson Ardent 129) [1974 N.R. 1975 8f 8f6 8g 8f 8f 1976 10v5] of little account. *M. Bradley.*
—

DULCIDENE 2 b.f. Behistoun 131–Debach Game 69 (Darius 129) [1976 6d2 6g] second foal: half-sister to 3-y-o 9f winner Game David (by David Jack): dam stayed 1¼m: ¾-length second to Valley of Diamonds in seller at Yarmouth in September, the pair finishing 4 lengths clear, first and better effort: will stay 1¼m: sold 800 gns Newmarket Autumn Sales. *A. Goodwill.*
71

DULSIE BRIDGE 2 b.f. Runnymede 123–Erisca 88 (Doutelle 128) [1976 5f 6fg] half-sister to three winners, including smart miler Murrayfield (by Match III): dam won at 1½m: in rear in maiden races at Windsor in July. *I. Balding.*
—

DU MAURIER 3 ch.c. Busted 134–Trilby (Pinza 137) [1975 N.R. 1976 11g2 11.1g2 10fg* 12f* 15g* 16fg*] strong, good-bodied colt: sixth foal: half-brother to five winners, including smart middle-distance performer Paper Cap (by Silly Season) and useful 1m to 1½m handicapper Welsh Rarebit (by Abernant): 9,600 gns yearling: dam unraced half-sister to very smart stayer Fighting Ship: won maiden race at Newmarket in June and ran out an easy winner of minor events at Ripon, Ayr and Newcastle in space of a week in July: not seen out again: stays well: acts on firm going. *J. Dunlop.*
96

DUMBUNNY 2 br.f. Sit In The Corner–Pontings 101 (Polic 126) [1976 6fg* 6fg* 6g4] strong, robust filly: good mover: half-sister to two winners abroad: dam 5f sprinter: won maiden race at Nottingham and minor event at Ripon in August in good style, on latter course coming home 8 lengths clear of Firemaiden: started short-priced favourite for Firth of Clyde Stakes at Ayr in September but was beaten 3 lengths into fourth-of-nine place behind Mofida: stays 6f. *H. Cecil.*
100

DUM SPIRO SPERO 2 ch.f. Blast 125–Lady Magellie 63 (Lord of Verona 120) [1976 5g 5f 5f 7fg] small filly: no sign of ability: sold 300 gns Doncaster October Sales. *K. Stapleton.*
—

DUNFERMLINE 2 b.f. Royal Palace 131–Strathcona 81 (St Paddy 133) [1976 7fg3 8d2 8g2] rangy filly: third foal: dam, half-sister to Eclipse winner Canisbay, won at 1m: put up a useful effort in five-runner May Hill Stakes at Doncaster in September, looking likely to win 2f out but still being ½ length behind all-the-way winner Triple First at line: turned in a similar display in Argos Star Fillies Mile at Ascot later in month, this time going down by ½ length to Miss Pinkie: will stay 1½m: suited by an easy surface (has a round action): sure to win a race. *R. Hern.*
112

DUNMURRY BOY 3 br.c. Tudor Music 131–Wilhelmina (Proud Chieftain 122) [1975 5s2 5g* 6fg6 7g* 7f6 7f3 6f* 1976 7d* 8d6 6fg4 7f 6fg 6fg5 8g] big, rangy, useful sort: well-backed favourite, won Northern Free Handicap at Newcastle in April by ¾ length from Fighting Lady: faced some stiff tasks afterwards but three times ran creditably: gave impression that 6f on fast ground was on sharp side for him and stayed 1m: acted on any going: broke a fetlock at Ripon in August and was destroyed. *S. Wainwright.*
103

DUNQUETZAL 4 b.g. Khalkis 127–Vullamond (Vulgan 123) [1974 N.R. 1975 N.R. 1976 17g 16.1f4 14g] ex-Irish gelding: probably of little account. *G. Balding.*
—

DUNRETZ 4 b.g. Duneed 84–Havering (Gilles de Retz 132) [1974 N.R. 1975 10.1s 12.2fg2 16f5 12.2f4 10fg4 10.8f3 10.1fg4 10g4 10s2 12.2g* 10g 12d3 12g*
67

1976 12fg 12.2fg^2 12f^3 12f^3 12g 10f^3 12.2s^4 12.2s^3 10s^2 10s^3] useful-looking gelding: poor handicapper: ran creditably most outings at 4 yrs: stays 1½m: acts on any going. *P. Makin.*

DUOTONE 2 gr.f. Sweet Revenge 129–Anchusa (Acropolis 132) [1976 5.1f 5s] — half-sister to several winners, including Cambridgeshire winner King Midas (by Pampered King): dam unraced daughter of top-class sprinter Abelia: well beaten in maiden races at Yarmouth in August and Nottingham in September but still looked in need of race at Nottingham: sold 500 gns Doncaster November Sales. *M. Stoute.*

DURHAM LAD 3 b.g. Tycoon II–Miss Scribbler 82 (Counsel 118) [1975 5f* **56** 7f^4 7g^3 6fg 7f 5g^4 5d 1976 6f 9g 8.2d 8f 10f^3] moderate gelding: plater: ran best race over 1¼m: blinkered fourth outing. *D. Williams.*

DURHAM LEGEND 2 b.c. John Splendid 116–Liza Goblin 83 (King Legend) — [1976 5f 5fg] half-brother to three minor winners and to a good winner in Norway: dam best at around 1m: behind in maiden races at Warwick in April (very backward) and Windsor in May. *K. Ivory.*

DURHAM RIVER 3 gr.g. Rugantino 97–Liza Goblin 83 (King Legend) [1975 — 5f 5fg 6g 6fg 6g 10g 1976 8fg 14fg 10.1fg] of little account *K. Ivory.*

DURHAM WARRIOR 2 ch.c. Decoy Boy 129–Killona (Pardal 130) [1976 — 5fg^5 5g 7f 8f] workmanlike colt: in rear in minor and maiden events. *K. Ivory.*

DURTAL 2 b.f. Lyphard 132–Derna II (Sunny Boy III) [1976 5fg* 6fg* **120** 6fg^2 7g^2 6g*]
    As a three-length winner of the William Hill Cheveley Park Stakes, Britain's only Group 1 race confined to two-year-old fillies, Durtal would be considered, in normal circumstances, one of our leading hopes of keeping the One Thousand Guineas at home. Judging by statements made soon after her win, though, she is by no means certain even to run in the Guineas; she may well run instead in the French equivalent, the Poule d'Essai des Pouliches. The Pouliches carries substantial premiums for the owners and breeders of the first four horses, providing the horses are French bred, the idea being to encourage owners to support the French sales and to establish studs there. Durtal, a product of the Haras d'Etreham, provides Robert Sangster a clear opportunity of picking up the winning owner's premium but is it really worth missing the One Thousand Guineas for it? The 1976 values were £39,447.50 to the winner of the One Thousand Guineas, and £34,965 for the Pouliches to which was added a sum of £10,490 for the owner and £8,741 for the breeder. If these figures are repeated in 1977 Mr Sangster would be about £6,000 better off should his filly win the French race, a useful amount of money to be sure, but not a particularly significant amount nowadays in the world of bloodstock breeding and racing. Is it really worthwhile to forego the greater prestige attached to winning the One Thousand Guineas in order to run in France? We doubt it.
    Durtal's record as a two-year-old was an admirable one of three wins and two highly creditable seconds from five outings. We took a great liking to her on her first appearance when she ran out a four-length winner from the more-experienced Hand Canter in a maiden race at Newcastle in June. That here was a very promising filly was clear from the way Durtal quickened right away from her field. She quickly followed up by winning the Rose of Lancaster Stakes at Haydock, a £5,000-plus race run for the first time in 1976. Judging by the turnout the race may not be long-lived, for only the Mill Reef filly Grain of Truth took on Durtal and she was unable to make it a contest. Durtal won by seven lengths and finished so strongly that her jockey took three furlongs to pull her up.
    After these highly satisfactory introductory runs Durtal took on much stiffer company. In both the Lowther Stakes at York and the Laurent Perrier Champagne Stakes at Doncaster she found one too good for her, but we thought her a little unlucky at York. Normally York is one of the best and fairest courses in the country but the results on the straight course at the August meeting suggested that horses racing on the stand side, which is where Durtal raced, were at a disadvantage. Although she drew away from her group, she was half a length behind Icena at the line. Bad luck played no part in her Champagne Stakes defeat; she met a much better horse in J. O. Tobin and in the last furlong she was left toiling in his wake. Durtal put up a game fight after making the running, and although she was beaten four lengths it was another

William Hill Cheveley Park Stakes, Newmarket—Durtal makes all the running and beats Be Easy (left) by three lengths. The third horse, Rings, is not on the picture, and the fourth, Haneena, is obscured by Be Easy

seven back to the third, the filly Ampulla, who had been much closer to her at York.

The field for the Cheveley Park Stakes was not a fully representative one with Icena, Cloonlara and Athlete's Foot absent. The French filly Assez Cuite, who had run so well against Blushing Groom in the Prix de la Salamandre, also dropped out after being said to be a likely starter. Of the fourteen runners to take on Durtal only Piney Ridge, a narrow winner of the National Stakes, Regal Ray, successful in the Moyglare Stud Stakes, and Be Easy, who beat Faridetta half a length in the Molecomb Stakes, had won a pattern race. The French filly Haneena, who had passed the post four lengths clear in the Prix d'Arenberg on her previous outing only to be disqualified controversially, started a clear favourite from Durtal. The latter was never headed in the race. Nothing looked like getting to her in the final furlong and her winning margin of three lengths has been bettered by only Jacinth and Lalibela in the Cheveley Park in the last ten years. Be Easy finished second, two lengths ahead of Rings and slightly more in front of Haneena. Rings's prominent showing seems to devalue the form. Less than three weeks later she got home by only three quarters of a length from the newcomer Call of the Deep in a maiden race over the same course and distance.

Durtal (b.f. 1974)	Lyphard (b 1969)	Northern Dancer (b 1961)	Nearctic
			Natalma
		Goofed (ch 1960)	Court Martial
			Barra II
	Derna II (b 1961)	Sunny Boy III (b 1944)	Jock II
			Fille de Soleil
		Miss Barberie (b 1950)	Norseman
			Vaneuse

Durtal showed speed at two years that was surprising, perhaps, for a filly of her breeding; if she proves to have the stamina at three years that one would expect, then she will do very well. Durtal is one of the first crop of Lyphard, a top-class French horse at distances up to a mile and a quarter whose achievements in France are probably less well remembered over here than his run in the Epsom Derby, in which he careered round Tattenham Corner like a car with no steering. He hasn't had many runners, but in addition to Durtal he has sired the Prix de la Foret winner Pharly and very useful animals in Beaune and Oestrine. Both he and his contemporary Riverman look to have the makings of tip-top stallions and should be great assets to the French breeding and racing industry. Durtal's dam, Derna II. was placed at a mile and a quarter to thirteen furlongs. From five previous runners she produced three winners, notably Darcounette (by Dapper Dan) and Valderna (by Val de Loir) who were useful fillies at around a mile and a half. The grandam, Miss Barberie, was very useful at up to thirteen furlongs and one of her two winners, a filly called Miss Molydal, won at up to two and a half miles.

By our reckoning Durtal still has improvement to make before she catches up with the Irish filly Cloonlara. When she gets her chance at a mile or more she may well make that improvement, and she seems sure to figure prominently in the classics, especially the Oaks. A well-made filly, she cost as a yearling 145,000 francs, approximately £15,500. *B. Hills.*

DUSKY DAMSEL 3 br.f. Sahib 114–Serejose 72 (Gratitude 130) [1975 5fg 1976 6fg 8f 6f 6g* 6fg 5.3f² 5fg 8.3d 5s⁵] rangy filly: heavily-backed favourite, showed much improved form when winning handicap at Brighton in June in runaway style by 6 lengths from Allez Britain: did not reproduce that form: stays 6f but probably not 1m. *L. Hall.* **68**

DUSKY MELODY 2 gr.g. Grisaille 115–Little Singer (Sing Sing 134) [1976 5fg 5f 5g⁵ 5f 5f 5fg 6d 6s] compact gelding: poor mover: bad plater: blinkered nowadays. *D. Yeoman.* **44**

DUSKY WARRIOR 2 b.c. Hul a Hul 124–Inki Dinki (Rustam 127) [1976 5g³ 5f³ 5h³ 5f⁶ 6fg 5f 5.1g] useful-looking colt: half-brother to two minor winners here and abroad: sold with dam for 2,900 gns as a foal and resold 1,800 gns yearling: dam placed in France: quite a moderate colt at his best: should be suited by 6f+: blinkered fourth and final outings: trained by P. Rohan on first two appearances. *N. Callaghan.* **74**

DUST-UP 2 b.c. Shiny Tenth 120–Mary Read 95 (Pindari 124) [1976 5d 5fg 6fg 6d 5v⁶ 5s³] third foal: 3,000 gns yearling: dam stayed 7f: just over 4 lengths third of 12 to Waterbuck in maiden race at Haydock in October, best effort: will stay 7f: suited by some give in the ground. *R. Hollinshead.* **82**

DUSTY BLUEBELL 3 b.f. Sky Gipsy 117–Worldly Miss (Worden II 129) [1975 6g 7.3g 7s 6g 1976 6.5s 10g 6.5g 8g 6fg 5.9g] behind in varied company, including at Cagnes-sur-Mer: blinkered final outing (May): sold, covered by Shiny Tenth, 1,700 gns Newmarket July Sales. *D. Marks.* **—**

DUTCHMAN 2 gr.c. Roan Rocket 128–Old Dutch 91 (Fastnet Rock 123) [1976 8s] brother to useful 1m to 1½m winner Malleny, and half-brother to smart 3-y-o Frankie (by Crooner) and three other winners, including Oaks winner Sleeping Partner (by Parthia): 6,400 gns yearling: dam half-sister to top-class stayer Donald: 20/1 when never-dangerous eighth of 19 to Nordman in maiden race at Sandown in October: sure to be better for this experience. *J. Dunlop.* **— p**

DUTCH MARTYR 3 b.c. Coliseum 116–Going Dutch 75 (Shantung 132) [1975 5f 5fg* 7g³ 6f² 6f* 6fg 5g⁶ 1976 10v³ 9s 7g⁵ 8s 6f² 6f⁵ 8.2f 6s 8g 6s] strong, workmanlike colt: fair handicapper at 2 yrs but is only quite moderate nowadays: bred to stay middle distances but seems best at up to 7f: best form on a sound surface: inconsistent. *N. Robinson.* **64**

DUTCH MAY 4 ch.f. Maystreak 118–My Old Dutch 76 (Technion 96) [1974 5f⁵ 5g⁵ 5f⁵ 6d 5s² 5s² 5v⁴ 5s² 6v² 5d* 1975 6s* 6g 7f⁶ 5g⁵ 6g* 6f² 6fg* 5fg* 6v* 5d* 6g⁵ 1976 5d⁵ 6fg 5fg 5fg 6f 6g⁴ 6g⁶ 7v⁶ 6s] small filly: fairly useful sprinter: mainly disappointing in 1976 and ran easily her best race of season on seventh outing when about 5 lengths sixth of 18 to Last Tango in Burmah-Castrol Ayr Gold Cup at Ayr in September, going on well in closing stages: best form at up to 6f: acts on any going: good mount for an apprentice: blinkered final appearance. *M. W. Easterby.* **96**

DUTCH SILVER 2 br.g. Meldrum 112–Dutch Again 62 (Cash and Courage 116) [1976 8g 8 2f 8g] leggy gelding: half-brother to two winners, including fairly useful miler Shieldfield (by Constable): cost 720 gns Doncaster May Sales: dam stayed 1¼m: behind in maiden and minor events. *J. Calvert.* **58**

DUTCH TREAT 3 b.c. Le Levanstell 122–Northern Beauty (Borealis) [1975 **112**
7g⁴ 7.2fg* 7g* 1976 7f 10.5s³ 12g⁵ 12s³ 12s* 14.6s⁵] good-looking colt: creditable third to Trasi's Son in Mecca-Dante Stakes at York in May: didn't race again
until the autumn, best efforts when 5 lengths third of nine to Jolly Good in
minor event at Lingfield and when cantering over Valuation and three moderate
animals in minor race at Redcar: stays 1½m (well beaten under a stiffish weight
over 1¾m): appears to act on any going but goes particularly well on soft. *R.
Price.*

DU TONNERRE 3 br.f. Caliban 123–Gun Powder Plot 83 (Conspirator 114) **55**
[1975 6f 8.2g 8f 1976 8fg 7f⁶ 6f 6f⁴ 7fg* 7g 10f 7h] selling handicapper: favourite, made all when winning unchallenged at Newmarket in May (bought in
1,500 gns): no form in better company afterwards: stays 7f but possibly not
1¼m: acts on firm going: best in blinkers: changed hands 2,400 gns Newmarket
July Sales. *Miss N. Wilmot.*

DYSCOLE 4 ch.g. Sassafras 135–Madina 119 (Beau Prince II 131) [1974 N.R. **68**
1975 10s 1976 8d 12fg³ 14fg³ 12fg² 12g⁵ 11.7fg 12.2s] rangy French-bred
gelding: poor handicapper: stays 1¾m: acts on a firm surface: suitable mount
for an apprentice: blinkered sixth outing. *P. Mitchell.*

E

EAGLE'S RIGHT 4 br.f. Mr Right–Eagle's Tryst (Bald Eagle 119) [1974 —
N.R. 1975 12g 16.1fg⁶ 12g⁵ 12f² 12f* 14.7g³ 12d 1976 16s 14fg 17.7f 15g⁶]
strong American-bred filly: lightly raced and no worthwhile form at 4 yrs: stays
1¾m: best form on a sound surface and acts on firm going. *A. Johnson.*

EARLY DAWN 3 b.c. Red God 128 §–Tomorrow (Citation) [1975 5g* 5fg² **100**
6f⁴ 6fg 7g⁵ 1976 7fg 8d⁵ 8d³ 8g² 10.6v⁴ 12s] attractive, shapely colt: ran
extremely well when 1½ lengths third of eight to Patris in Arlington Stakes at
Newbury in September and 1½ lengths second of 12 to Manilata in Severals
Stakes at Newmarket the following month: suited by 1m but seems not to stay
middle distances: appears to act on any going: has been tried in blinkers, including on final outing, and has given impression of being none too keen on a couple
of occasions. *M. Jarvis.*

EARLY MORNING 6 b.m. Dual 117–Fury 88 (Faubourg II 127) [1974 11.2d²
8.2g⁶ 8fg 11g⁶ 12h 12.2fg³ 10f⁵ 13.8f⁵ 12g⁵ 8fg 12g⁴ 12.2fg 1975 10.1g 12s 10h
8f 10g 8.2g 10.6fg⁶ 8f 10f 10.8g 11.1g² 10g 1976 10.6d 10f⁴ 10f⁵ 10.6g 10g
10v] poor selling handicapper: probably stays 1¾m: appears to act on any
going: has run poorly when blinkered: usually wears bandages. *F. Wiles.*

EARLY SUMMER 4 b.f. Silly Season 127–Viburnum 102 (Guersant 129) [1974 —
5g 6d 1975 5v 5fg 8f 8f 8g 8g 1976 8fg 12.2f] of no account. *S. Holland.*

EARTH SPIRIT 3 br.c. Amber Rama 133–Eagle Eye (Victory Morn) [1975 5g **121**
5g* 5g 5.5g² 5.5g 8s* 8g⁵ 7s 7s* 8g² 1976 9g* 8f² 8fg⁶ 8s 8.2v] good-looking
French colt: dam placed ten times at up to 10.5f in France: showed very good
form as a 2-y-o, winning three races, including Criterium de Maisons-Laffitte:
put up a fine performance when winning Prix Jean Prat at Chantilly in June
on reappearance by a nose from Ricco Boy, making all the running: performed
respectably on next two outings, both in this country, finishing length third to
dead-heaters Radetzky and Patris in St James's Palace Stakes at Royal Ascot
(subsequently promoted to second on disqualification of latter) and just over
6½ lengths sixth of nine to Wollow in Sussex Stakes at Goodwood in July, but
ran badly in Prix du Moulin de Longchamp and Prix Perth at Saint-Cloud on
last two outings: should stay 1½m: acts on any going: has worn blinkers, but
runs better without them. *A. Penna, France.*

EASBY SAINT 3 b.f. Saintly Song 128–Memoire Cheri 76 (Mossborough 126) —
[1975 5v 5f 5g³ 6f² 6g² 7h² 7f² 7.2fg 8f⁴ 1976 7.2fg 7fg] small, compact filly:
plater: ran moderately both outings as a 3-y-o (needed race and slowly into stride
first time out): bred to stay 1¼m: acts on hard going: sold to D. Chapman 1,000
gns Doncaster September Sales. *M. H. Easterby.*

EASTCOTE 4 ch.f. Lauso–Eastern Cham (Chamossaire) [1974 N.R. 1975 14fg —
12h 10g 1976 12f⁴ 13.8f⁶ 15.5h 11h] probably of no account. *P. Poston.*

EASTER JEWEL 3 b.f. Easter Island 101–Highland Jewel (Scotch Sauce) —
[1975 5s 5s 5g³ 5fg⁶ 1976 8fg 8.2d] plating-class maiden: slowly away first
time out (April): wasn't seen out again until September (dwelt and tailed off).
S. Underhill.

EAS

EASTERN GIFT 4 br.c. So Blessed 130–Singapura 103 (Grey Sovereign 128 §) —
[1974 5d³ 6s³ 1975 7.6g⁴ 8f 8g* 9g² 10.4f³ 10d⁴ 12g 1976 10fg⁶ 12g] lengthy
colt: quite a useful handicapper (rated 90) at 3 yrs: made only two appearances
in 1976, second of these when well behind Darcy at Leicester in June (blinkered):
has yet to show he stays further than 1¼m: possibly best on an easy surface:
sold 1,350 gns Newmarket Autumn Sales. *I. Balding.*

EASTERN PALACE 2 gr.c. Habitat 134–Al-Burak 103 (Silver Shark 129) 88 p
[1976 6g³] first foal: dam won from 5f to 1½m in Ireland and France: third
favourite, ran promisingly when staying-on 2½ lengths third of 18 to Greenjacket
in newcomers event at Lingfield in September: will be suited by 7f+: will improve and win a maiden race. *I. Balding.*

EASTERN ROMANCE 2 b.f. Sahib 114–Lovelorn 56 (Forlorn River 124) 73
[1976 5fg 5h⁶ 6f 6h³ 6g* 5.9s⁶ 7v] leggy filly: first foal: dam stayed 7f: attracted
no bid after coming out best in close finish to 14-runner seller at Goodwood in
September: will stay 7f. *G. Balding.*

EASTERN SILK 3 gr.f. Zeddaan 130–Fine Soie (Le Fabuleux 133) [1975 88
N.R. 1976 8f* 10g² 10g] first foal: dam from a good staying family: favourite,
won seven-runner maiden race at Goodwood in August, leading 2½f out and
drawing clear to beat Sunburst in good style by 8 lengths: long odds-on, did not
go through with her effort when ¾-length second to Turnpike in three-runner
minor event on same course the following month: out of her depth only
subsequent outing: stays 1¼m. *R. Hern.*

EASTERN SPRING 2 br.c. Queen's Hussar 124–Arawak 109 (Seminole II) 91 p
[1976 8s²] half-brother to fair 1973 2-y-o 1m winner Relka (by Relko) and quite
moderate 1½m winner Rag (by Ragusa): 14,500 gns yearling: dam, winner
over 1m at 2 yrs, finished third in Irish Guinness Oaks and Yorkshire Oaks: 12/1,
came out best of those racing on far side and was going on well at finish when
4 lengths second of 27 to Sporting Yankee in maiden race at Newmarket in
October: will stay 1¼m: a good first effort by a colt who is sure to win races.
L. Cumani.

EASTER SURPRISE 3 ch.f. Communication 119–Starsetter 75 (Aureole 132) —
[1975 5v 1976 5f 6g] no worthwhile form, including in a seller at 2 yrs. *B.
McMahon.*

EAST PLAISTOW 2 b.c. Manacle 123–Silver Comb (Silver Cloud 121) [1976 85
6h² 5f⁶ 7h⁴ 8.2d 8s⁴ 8d³ 8s² 7.2v⁴] lengthy colt: second foal: 2,900 gns yearling:
dam a plater: well-backed favourite for £1,400 seller at Newmarket in October
and made all to win by ½ length from Divinity only to be moved down to third
place by stewards for accidentally hampering placed horses: blinkered on both
outings afterwards, putting up better effort on first of them when neck second to
Court House in nursery at Wolverhampton later in month: suited by 1m and
forcing tactics: best form on a soft surface. *J. Hill.*

EAST RIDING 3 b. or br.g. High Table 105–Little Audrey (Damascus 86) —
[1975 N.R. 1976 13h³ 12s⁴ 12g] sixth foal: dam of little account: no worthwhile
form in minor events and maiden race in the north. *D. Holmes.*

EASY ANNA 2 ch.f. Swing Easy 126–Annabelle 73 § (Exbury 138) [1976 71
5d 5s 6v 6s 5v] second living foal: half-sister to a winner in France and Italy
by Hopeful Venture: 2,000 gns yearling: dam temperamental half-sister to very
useful miler Seventh Hussar: showed some ability in maiden races in the autumn:
should stay 7f. *O. O'Neill.*

EASY BOY 3 ch.c. Swing Easy 126–Hi-Baby 102 (High Treason 126) [1975 60
5d⁶ 5v* 6fg 5.9fg⁶ 5d⁶ 1976 6v³ 5h 5f⁵ 6fg³ 6g² 6v⁴ 7v*] light-framed colt:
plater: sweated up badly prior to winning at Teesside in October: sold to H.
Blackshaw 620 gns afterwards: stays 7f: goes well on heavy ground and is unsuited by hard: trained until after third start by K. Payne. *G. Richards.*

EASY LANDING 2 b.f. Swing Easy 126–Land Ho (Primera 131) [1976 5g² 110
5s* 5fg* 5fg* 5f³ 5g² 6fg³ 5d] lengthy, good-quartered filly: first foal: dam
lightly-raced daughter of very smart sprinter Lucaslaud: winner of maiden race
at Chester, minor event at Goodwood and Kingsclere Stakes at Newbury: beat
Lady Eton 2 lengths on last-named course in June: ran very well on next three
outings, going down by a head and a neck to Cramond and Piney Ridge in Queen
Mary Stakes at Royal Ascot and by a head to Piney Ridge in National Stakes at

219

Sandown and then finishing excellent 2 lengths third of 13 to Icena in Lowther Stakes at York after hanging left under pressure: stays 6f: has won on soft going but has shown her best form on firm: game and consistent until running moderately in blinkers on final outing. *J. Tree.*

EBB AND FLO 3 b.f. Forlorn River 124–Dam N'Blast 83 (Blast 125) [1975 **75** 5g³ 5fg³ 6f* 6d⁵ 5.9f³ 1976 8fg⁴ 9fg⁵ 10f³ 10g³ 8.2fg³ 8f⁶ 8f² 12g² 12.2s²] neat filly: quite a moderate handicapper: effective at 1m to 1½m: acts on any going: consistent. *H. Collingridge.*

ECHO SUMMIT 4 b.c. Hill Rise 127–Jib (Gulf Stream 120) [1974 N.R. 1975 **99** 11s 14f* 14g² 12g* 12fg² 12f* 1976 14fg² 16g* 16fg* 16g* 18d3] big, tall, lengthy colt: useful performer: won three good handicaps early in season, namely Campbell-Gray Queen's Prize at Kempton in April, March Handicap at Newmarket later in month and R. W. Armstrong Memorial Challenge Cup at Ripon in May: not seen out after finishing third to Tall Lad at Doncaster later in May: needs a good test of stamina: appears to act on any going but is well suited by top-of-the-ground conditions. *H. Cecil.*

EDGERLY GOLD 3 b.g. Acrania 110–Golden Fraternity 89 (Brunel) [1975 **—** N.R. 1976 10.1fg 12g 12.2g⁴ 10.1fg] half-brother to several poor animals: dam, a useful plater on Flat, also won over hurdles and fences: plating-class maiden: should stay middle distances: off course three months after third outing. *R. Vibert.*

EDINBURGH 2 b.f. Charlottown 127–Queen's Castle 98 (Sovereign Path 125) **117** [1976 7.5g* 8s 7s⁴ 8s*] first foal: dam stayed at least 1½m and is half-sister to Reform: successful in newcomers event at Deauville in August and in Group 3 Prix des Reservoirs at Longchamp in October: 20/1 for latter race but came through strongly, after being waited with, to win going away by a length from Sanedtki: showed nothing like her Reservoirs form on her other outings, finishing eighth of 11 behind Proud Event in Prix d'Aumale at Chantilly and being beaten 4½ lengths by Lancastera in Prix de l'Obelisque at Longchamp: will stay 1½m: acts on soft going. *J. Cunnington, jnr, France.*

EDINBURGH ROCK 3 ch.c. High Line 125–Erisca 88 (Doutelle 128) [1975 **—** 7d 7g 8g⁵ 8d 1976 10.6d3] lightly-built colt: plating-class maiden: blinkered only outing in 1976. *I. Balding.*

Mr J. H. Whitney's "Easy Landing"

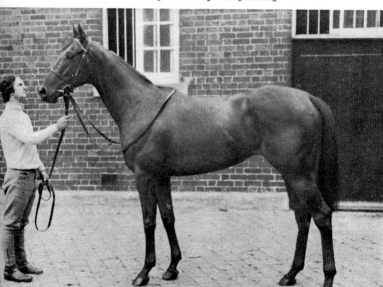

EDINGTON 2 b.g. Swing Easy 126–Golden Tessa 69 (Rapace 130) [1976 5f **78** 6h³ 7fg 7fg] fourth foal: dam effective from 1m to 13f: quite a moderate maiden: should stay beyond sprint distances. *T. Marshall.*

EDMUND BURKE 3 b.c. Advocator–Section (Ambiorix 130) [1975 7g 1976 — 12fg 12v 10.2s] rangy American-bred colt: no worthwhile form in maiden races (tailed off last two outings). *I. Balding.*

EGALALOON 3 gr.c. My Swanee 122–Monagram 77 (Mon Fetiche 120) [1975 **76** 6s³ 6f⁵ 1976 7g² 6fg 7.6fg⁶ 8g 8f³ 7g] tall, narrow colt: modest form in varied company, but became disappointing: possibly needs further than 6f, and stays 1m. *M. Masson.*

EIGHTH LEGION 3 b.f. Communication 119–Seventh Legion 66 (Atlas 126) — [1975 N.R. 1976 9.4g 8.2g 9.4h⁶] probably useless. *R. Titterington.*

EIGHT OF DIAMONDS 3 b.f. Silent Spring 102–Six of Diamonds (Sayajirao — 132) [1975 N.R. 1976 10.1d] half-sister to winning stayers Black Diamond (by Black Tarquin), Crystal Clear and The Holt (both by Chamossaire): dam won over 7.8f in Ireland as a 2-y-o: unquoted, started slowly and finished tailed off in 17-runner maiden race won by Blyth's Folly at Windsor in September. *J. Cann.*

EIGHTSOME 2 ch.f. Pieces of Eight 128–Little Elsa 91 (Pindari 124) [1976 **69** 5d 6f 7f 8f* 8v] well-grown filly: second foal: 1,300 gns yearling: dam lightly-raced winner over 6f at 2 yrs: put up easily best effort but attracted no bid after dead-heating with Boom Quay in 22-runner seller at Thirsk in September: beaten very long way in nursery on only outing afterwards: will stay 1½m: acts on firm going and is evidently unsuited by heavy: blinkered last two appearances. *M. H. Easterby.*

EIRENE 3 b.f. Dschingis Khan–Egina (Alycidon 138) [1975 7g* 6.8g³ 8s* 8s* **?** 1976 8g 8fg 9g 10.5g 11g 10g 9g] German-bred filly: officially rated 3 lb superior to Manilata as a 2-y-o in Germany, her victories including Alexander Rennen at Frankfurt: nowhere near so good as a 3-y-o and finished well in rear behind Flying Water in 1,000 Guineas at Newmarket in April on only appearance in this country: stays 1m: acts on soft going. *M. Biermann, Germany.*

ELAINE MARY 2 b.f. Hard Man 102–La Veuve 90 (Roi de Navarre II 123) **76** [1976 5fg 5f⁵ 5f³ 5.9f⁴ 5g⁴ 6fg⁵ 6d³ 5fg*] fourth reported foal: dam a stayer: made all and put up easily best effort when winning 17-runner seller at Edinburgh in September by 2 lengths from Prima Tempo: sold 600 gns afterwards: possibly better suited by 5f than 6f but should stay further: blinkered fifth and final outings. *A. Jarvis.*

EL ARGENTINO 3 bl.c. Melodic Air 111–Conville Beauty 69 (Constable 129) **48** [1975 5s 5g 5fg 5fg² 5f⁶ 5g⁴ 5g⁴ 5g²] leggy colt: poor plater: should stay 1m: tried in blinkers at 2 yrs: sold 240 gns Ascot September Sales. *S. Norton.*

ELBAYGO 2 b.c. Comedy Star 121–Skippy 54 (Miralgo 130) [1976 6d] half- — brother to a winning 2-y-o plater by Grisaille: 380 gns yearling: dam of little account: in need of race when behind in 23-runner maiden event won by Whitby Jet at Redcar in June. *W. Gray.*

EL CABALLERO 2 ch.c. Tudor Music 131–Phosphorescence 92 (Aureole 132) **78** [1976 5fg 6fg 7h² 7h⁵ 7.2f³] shapely colt: half-brother to two winners, including Current Magic (by Current Coin), a winner at up to 1½m: 3,500 gns yearling: dam won at 1m: in frame in maiden race at Bath and seller at Haydock (blinkered) in August: needs at least 7f and will probably stay middle distances: acts on hard going. *N. Vigors.*

EL CAPITAN 3 br.c. Captain's Gig–Capule (Middleground) [1975 6fg⁶ 6f* 7g* **92** 1976 8g 7fg⁴ 7g⁴ 6fg 6f] attractive, good-quartered colt: good walker: fairly useful handicapper: should stay at least 1m: ran moderately in blinkers final outing and was sold 2,000 gns Ascot October Sales. *J. Dunlop.*

EL CRIOLLO 2 b. or br.c. Blue Prince 123–Los Incas (Tropique 128) [1976 8s* **123** 10s* 10v⁵] American-bred French colt: half-brother to two winners in U.S.A., including El Diablito (by The Scoundrel), a stakes winner at up to 1m, and to a winner in Venezuela: $9,700 foal, resold $8,000 as a yearling: dam, placed at 3 yrs, is daughter of half-sister to Angelola, Hypericum, Above Board and Kingstone: ran out an impressive 6-length winner of a valuable newcomers event at Longchamp in September, but had to struggle to hold off Monseigneur by ¼ length when odds on in Prix de Condé on same course the following month: evens favourite for Group 2 Criterium de Saint-Cloud in November but probably found very bad ground against him and was well beaten into fifth place behind Conglomerat: will stay 1½m: acts on soft going. *R. Carver, France.*

EL HIPPY 2 gr.c. Sea Hawk II 131–Light Opera 101 (Vienna 127) [1976 6fg **65** 6fg6 7f3] second foal: brother to 3-y-o Little Tern, **a** fairly useful winner at up to 1m: 7,000 gns yearling: dam, closely related to Laser Light, stayed 7f: showed only a little ability in maiden races: will stay 1m. *N. Vigors.*

ELIE MARINE 3 ch.f. Firestreak 125–Anna Lisa (Petition 130) [1975 5v5 5v4 **—** 5f 5fg 8fg 7f* 7f4 7.2d2 7g 1976 7f 9g 7f 9fg 8f5 8.2f 10v 6s] short-coupled filly: showed only worthwhile form as a 3-y-o when fifth of 10 to Palustra in handicap at Ripon in June: should stay 1¼m: probably acts on any going. *H. Blackshaw.*

ELIZABEGGS 2 b.f. Burglar 128–Rose de Soleil 68 (The Bo'sun 114) [1976 **70** 5g 5fg 5fg 5f2 5h3 6f6 6f2 6d 5fg3] first foal: sold privately 200 gns yearling: dam stayed 1m: placed in maiden races and sellers, finishing 2 lengths third of 17 to Elaine Mary in a seller at Edinburgh in September on final outing: stays 6f: acts on hard going. *T. Marshall.*

ELIZABETHAN 3 br.f. Tudor Melody 129–Ash Lawn 86 (Charlottesville 135) **89** [1975 N.R. 1976 8s*] tall filly: fourth foal: half-sister to 1m and 9f winner Star Tail (by Roan Rocket): dam, fair middle-distance performer, is sister to Selhurst and half-sister to Royal Palace: favourite, put up a highly satisfactory first effort when winning moderate maiden race at Sandown in October quite comfortably by 3 lengths from Bally Tudor despite hanging badly right when challenging: will stay 1½m: sold to B.B.A. *N. Murless.*

EL KITALA 5 b.g. Raise You Ten 125–Nine and Four 85 (Spy Song) [1974 **—** 6fg2 7fg5 1975 N.R. 1976 8g 8f 12f 10f] lengthy gelding: plater: has worn blinkers: sold 1,800 gns Ascot July Sales. *J. Haine.*

ELLAND ROAD 2 b.c. Red God 128 §–Angelic Spree 78 (Busted 134) [1976 **104** 6fg4 7d2 7g2 7s4] strong colt: first foal: 10,500 gns yearling: dam half-sister to Soft Angels, Sweet Moss and Sucaryl: ran very well when close-up second at Yarmouth and Ascot in September, going down by ½ length to The Czar on former course and by a neck to Royal Plume in £2,900 event on latter: started favourite for Somerville Tattersall Stakes at Newmarket the following month but ran moderately, finishing about 10 lengths fourth to newcomer Princess Tiara: will stay 1¼m. *R. Armstrong.*

ELLORA 4 b.c. What A Pleasure–Dark Design (Dark Star) [1974 won two **121** races from four starts in U.S.A. 1975 6g6 6d 8d2 6g4 7d 6v 1976 8d 8fg* 8g* 9.7d 8d6 8d5 8g* 8s] lengthy American-bred colt: good mover: very smart performer: winner three times at 4 yrs, including in Group 3 events at Longchamp in May (beat El Rastro a nose in Prix du Muguet) and Deauville in August (ran out a comfortable winner from Monsanto in Prix Quincey): far from disgraced when last of six to Full of Hope in Prix du Chemin de Fer du Nord at Chantilly in June and finished very good fifth to Gravelines in Prix Jacques le Marois (also at Deauville in August): gained his other win at Evry in April: stays 1m: probably acts on any going: racing in U.S.A. *A. Breasley, France.*

ELM 2 b f. Realm 129–High Beech (High Hat 131) [1976 5g* 5fg* 5g6 5v5 5s] **88** well-made filly: first foal: dam won over 7f and 1¾m at 3 yrs in Ireland: quickened in good style when winning minor races at Sandown in April and Lingfield in May, on latter course beating Bee Splendid 2 lengths: last but one on all outings afterwards, but was off course over four months after third appearance and had a very stiff task on final start: will stay 6f: acts on a firm surface and is probably unsuited by heavy ground. *B. Hills.*

EL MUCHACHO 4 gr.g. Right Boy 137–Elche (Flush Royal 127) [1974 5s **—** 5g 8s 1975 8g 9fg 12.2fg 1976 10.1fg 10f 14f 12g 10d] of no account. *H. O'Neill.*

EL RASTRO 6 br.h. Breakspear II–Raillery II (Rasper) [1974 8s* 8g* 8s2 **120** 7s* 8d 7v2 8v* 1975 8s2 8d* 8g3 7d4 8s 1976 8g3 8d* 8s2 8g* 9.7d2 9.2g4 8d] high-class French horse: a really consistent performer who was winning Prix de Ris-Orangis at Evry for the third successive year when beating Full of Hope by a length in April: rather hampered and was awarded race on the disqualification of Sauceboat when 1½ lengths second to that filly in Lockinge Stakes at Newbury the following month: also ran well on all his other outings, notably when finishing second in Prix du Muguet and Prix Dollar (beaten 2 lengths by Kasteel on fifth start), both at Longchamp, and when seventh of 13 to stable-companion Gravelines in Prix Jacques le Marois at Deauville in August on final appearance (beaten less than 2 lengths in a blanket finish): stayed 1¼m: acted on any going: usually held up: stud in Florida. *A. Penna, France.*

EL RONDO 5 ch.g. Ron 103–Miel Dore (Rockavon 120) [1974 8g 6fg 6f 5g 5g — 6fg⁴ 7g 6h 6fg 5s 5s 8s² 1975 9v 10.6s 1976 13g 10f⁶ 17.7f] compact, workmanlike gelding: poor handicapper nowadays: probably stays 1¼m but is unlikely to stay long distances: acts on any going: sometimes wears blinkers: sold 520 gns Ascot October Sales. *M. Tate.*

ELTHAM 2 b.g. Royal Palace 131–Electric Blue 91 (Sing Sing 134) [1976 6g **87** 6h² 7fg² 8g] second foal: half-brother to quite moderate 1975 2-y-o Grill Room (by Connaught): dam stayed 1m well: fair maiden: should stay 1m+. *E. Weymes.*

ELTON ABBESS 2 b.f. Tamerlane 128–Tragara (Buisson Ardent 129) [1976 **86** 5g 5g 5g² 5fg 5fg⁵ 7g 6s⁶ 5s*] good sort: half-sister to Bill The Black (by Levmoss) quite a useful but temperamental 2-y-o in 1973: 3,600 gns yearling: dam, daughter of smart stayer Romantica, won in Italy: 25/1 and apprentice ridden, won maiden race at Folkestone in October by a length from So Cutting: best form at 5f, but should stay 1m: seems to act on any going. *P. Allingham.*

ELUSIVE 2 b.c. Blakeney 126–Pavillon 88 (French Beige 127) [1976 7fg⁵ 7g³ **97** 7fg² 8g² 8g⁴ 7d] lengthy, attractive colt: second foal: half-brother to 3-y-o middle-distance winner Bicoque (by Fric): dam won at 1¼m: still a maiden but is a fairly useful colt as he showed when 4 lengths fourth of 13 to Bona-Mia in £1,800 nursery at Newmarket in September: will stay 1½m. *B. Hobbs.*

ELUSIVE CHARACTER 4 b.c. Galivanter 131–Palouci 59 (Palestine 133) **69** [1974 5g⁶ 5f 5g³ 5fg² 5g³ 5g⁴ 5s³ 5d 1975 5.9v 5f⁶ 6g 5g 5g⁶ 5g⁴ 1976 5s 5v²] lengthy colt: poor maiden: best form at 5f: probably acts on any going: ran well when blinkered final outing at 3 yrs and second appearance in 1976. *D. Whelan.*

ELVENA 2 b.f. Burglar 128–Lemania's Pride (Vigo 130) [1976 5fg 5.1fg 5g⁶ **47** 5.1f⁵ 6fg 6d 6g] small filly: bad plater: has worn blinkers: sold 420 gns Newmarket Autumn Sales. *G. Blum.*

ELVERS 3 br.c. Swing Easy 126–Impassioned Plea 91 (Counsel 118) [1975 — N.R. 1976 10s 8s⁶ 12s⁶ 12v] fourth produce: 4,200 gns foal, resold 460 gns yearling: dam won at up to 1¼m: little worthwhile form in maiden and minor events at the back-end. *N. Callaghan.*

ELYSIAN FIELDS 2 ch.f. Northfields–Suir-Delight (Precipitant 113) [1976 **81** 5g 5h* 5f⁶ 5g] useful-looking filly: half-sister to three winners, including useful French middle-distance winner Suirelko (by Relko): 3,700 gns yearling: dam won 2m bumpers race and is half-sister to Golden Horus: having first race for four months, made all to win five-runner maiden race at Folkestone in August by 6 lengths from Dalal: ran moderately on both outings afterwards: should be much more at home over 7f+. *B. Swift.*

EMERGENCY CALL 4 br.f. Bleep-Bleep 134–Love-Lies-Bleeding 74 (Javelot **41** 124) [1974 5s⁵ 5g² 5h² 5fg⁴ 6f 5fg⁴ 6s⁶ 1975 6s 6fg⁶ 5f 7f⁶ 8.3fg 1976 5g³] plater: best form at 5f, although has run respectably over 6f. *P. Cole.*

EMIJO 3 ch.f. Gulf Pearl 117–Shady Side 82 (Pall Mall 132) [1975 N.R. 1976 **71** 7g 8f⁵ 7g 6fg 5s² 7s⁵ 8v*] strong filly: second foal: half-sister to Red Pool (by Forlorn River), placed in 6f and 7f sellers as a 2-y-o: 4,300 gns yearling: dam won over 5f at 3 yrs from only three starts: showed improved form at the back-end and won seven-runner maiden race at Leicester in November by ¾ length from Miss Kung Fu: stays 1m: acts well on heavy ground. *S. Ingham.*

EMINENCE 2 bl.c. Sahib 114–Guilpath 77 (Sovereign Path 125) [1976 5d⁴ 5s⁴ **79** 6d⁶ 6h² 7f² 7.2g* 8g 8fg 8v⁴] well-grown colt: half-brother to Guiltrack (by Track Spare), a useful winner over 5f and 6f at 2 yrs: 2,800 gns yearling: dam stayed 7f: only moderate but picked up quite a good prize when beating Haybale 2½ lengths in £2,200 nursery at Haydock in August: disqualified after winning maiden race at Lanark by short head on previous outing: suited by 7f, but has yet to prove he stays 1m: probably acts on any going. *M. H. Easterby.*

EMMIE'S GEM 3 ch.f. Hul a Hul 124–Glenashee (Arctic Storm 134) [1975 — N.R. 1976 7g 5f 9f 6f⁵] second foal: 220 gns yearling: dam poor Irish maiden: had very stiff task at weights when 7 lengths fifth of eight to Portrayal in selling handicap at Catterick in July, only glimmer of ability. *R. Ward.*

EMPEROR OF GHANA 3 b.c. King Emperor–Ghana II (Botticelli 129) [1975 **71** 6fg 6fg 6d⁵ 8g³ 8fg² 1976 10.8fg 8.2f⁶ 8g 8f³ 10fg⁴ 8fg² 14.7h³ 14.7f² 10fg⁴ 12f³ 12.2fg 14.7d⁶ 14v¹] lengthy, unfurnished colt: inconsistent maiden: seems to stay 15f but has shown best form at shorter distances: sometimes wears blinkers: finds little off bridle: trained until after third outing by C. Brittain. *S. Nesbitt.*

EMPERY 3 b.c. Vaguely Noble 140–Pamplona II (Postin) [1975 8s* 8g⁶ 7.7d³ **128** 1976 8g⁴ 9g⁵ 10.5g³ 12g* 12f²]

The Epsom Derby, though it can seldom be regarded as the most important horse race in Europe nowadays, remains one of the most searching and significant tests in the world for a three-year-old; winning the Derby and obtaining the winner's stud services are still burning ambitions of most owners and breeders. In the face of intense competition from the Prix du Jockey-Club, the Irish Sweeps Derby, the King George VI and Queen Elizabeth Stakes and, above all, the Prix de l'Arc de Triomphe, the race has succeeded in maintaining a very high standing; it has been won by six genuinely outstanding horses in Relko, Sea-Bird II, Sir Ivor, Nijinsky, Mill Reef and Grundy, two of them trained in France, two in Ireland and two in England, in the fourteen years since the inauguration of the Sweeps Derby. Another winner in the period, Santa Claus, can have been little behind the least able of that group of six, but the race does sometimes produce a winner that seems ordinary by comparison, although, of course, not ordinary in any other sense. Such were Larkspur, Charlottown, Blakeney, Morston and Snow Knight; and such, on all the evidence available, was Empery, who would, we feel sure, have made a bigger name for himself had he been raced over longer distances before being retired.

The first thing that strikes one about Empery is his lack of success. He won only two races, one of the two a contest restricted to newcomers; in six other starts he managed second place once, when beaten easily by Malacate in the Irish Sweeps Derby. He finished down the field in France's best race for staying two-year-olds, the Grand Criterium, third of ten to Arctic Tern at the same age in the Prix Thomas Bryon, third of twelve to Youth in France's most important classic trial, the Prix Lupin, fourth of eleven to Red Lord in the Poule d'Essai des Poulains, the French equivalent of the Two Thousand Guineas, and fifth of thirteen to Happy New Year in another classic trial, the Prix Daphnis. These are the bare bones of his record. For a Derby winner they are an unimposing sight, but in assessing Empery it is essential to take account of two points. First, that he was a stayer; second, that as a stayer he was trained with the Derby as his main objective. If these points are recognised, then he will be seen in a better light.

That Empery was regarded as a stayer by his brilliant trainer was made fairly clear from the minute he set foot on the racecourse. He began his career in the one-mile Prix de Villebon, run in the mud at Longchamp in September, and after the easiest of victories from six opponents he was kept at around the

Derby Stakes, Epsom—the field at Tattenham Corner—Vitiges leads Radetzky and Relkino (left); Empery comes next, ahead of Norfolk Air (immediately behind Radetzky) and Oats (quartered cap)

same distance for the rest of the season, tackling top company in the Grand Criterium and the Prix Thomas Bryon. Second favourite to Manado, ahead of Vitiges, in the Grand Criterium, Empery never seemed likely to improve from the middle of the field. Less than three weeks later he showed much more prominently in the Prix Thomas Bryon at Saint-Cloud; he fought a long battle with the Grand Criterium runner-up Comeram before the pair of them were pounced on inside the last furlong by Arctic Tern, who was receiving weight. Few of those watching who understand racing would have been left in much doubt that Empery would be a better horse with further to go. At the end of the year he received a mark 10 lb behind the top-weighted Manado in the Handicap Optional, and only fifteen two-year-olds were officially regarded his superior in France.

Empery began his second season still racing at a distance of a mile, a distance then on the sharp side for him in an event as well-contested as the 1976 Poule d'Essai des Poulains. Taking account of the restriction the distance placed on him, Empery gave a highly encouraging display in the Poulains. He settled down in second place, and as in the Prix Thomas Bryon he had a long battle with Comeram for the lead in the straight; in the end he was outpaced by Red Lord, a colt by the sprinter Red God, who went clear in the last furlong. Empery finished almost alongside Roan Star and Comeram, just in front of Arctic Tern. In view of this performance, his running in the Prix Daphnis over nine furlongs at Evry two weeks later was disappointing: he came home in the middle of a large, closely-bunched group headed by the winner, Happy New Year. The winner's achievement in improving from last to first in the straight was in marked contrast to Empery's; the latter failed to quicken at all in the last two furlongs. Probably the fairly slow pace early on contributed to his disappointing show, but he should have done better.

Eight days later, in the middle of May, Empery fulfilled his promise at the second time of asking and put himself right in the Derby picture by running third to his stable-companion Youth and Arctic Tern in the Prix Lupin at Longchamp. Youth had already won two classic trials, the Prix Greffulhe and the Prix Daru, the latter so impressively that many regarded him as potentially the best three-year-old colt in France, yet Empery finished less than two lengths behind him. Significantly, Empery ran the best race of his career up to that time. The presence of an effective pacemaker, Oilfield, and the distance of the Prix Lupin, only about a half-furlong under eleven furlongs, suited him. He laid close up from the jump-off and galloped on extremely well up the entire length of the home straight, although he never looked like taking the lead from Youth in the last two furlongs. The announcement soon came that Youth would go for the Prix du Jockey-Club and Empery would take his chance at Epsom, a chance that improved considerably four days later when Piggott accepted to ride him.

Piggott had a record of winners in the Derby unequalled by any jockey living and equalled by only two jockeys, Robinson and Donoghue, in the history of the race. He had ridden six winners in a span of twenty-two years—Never Say Die, Crepello, St Paddy, Sir Ivor, Nijinsky and Roberto—employing similar tactics on each in so far as he always had them close to the leaders approaching the bottom of Tattenham Hill. With Empery he did the very same thing. Probably several of Piggott's winners could have afforded a greater start to the opposition in the straight granted a clear run, for, after all, most of them were horses endowed with an exceptional turn of speed, but there is not the shadow of a doubt that the tactics pursued with the stayer Empery were exactly right. It is virtually certain that Empery could not have won from behind.

Piggott rode him beautifully. The horse was never worse placed than fifth in the twenty-three-strong field and rounded Tattenham Corner poised on the heels of the front-running Vitiges, with Radetzky and Relkino alongside, and Oats and Norfolk Air just behind. If the hot favourite Wollow was going to be the main danger, as Piggott was entitled to assume, then at least he would have Empery to catch. But where was Wollow; how had he fared? Unlike Empery he had not had the advantage of a smooth run, and coming down the hill his chance of success did not appear bright. In the middle of the field soon after the start from his draw towards the inside, he made up a few places very quickly and then, almost as quickly, he dropped back to his original position; and at the point where Empery's jockey prepared to launch an assault on the leader with the turn nearly behind him, Wollow had at least nine horses to pass, of whom only Illustrious Prince looked done for. Once into the straight Wollow did make good progress on the outside but he never had Empery in his sights. Empery, ridden to go third two furlongs out as Vitiges began to weaken at last, and put under very strong pressure approaching the distance, found more acceleration than he had ever found before. He wrested the lead from Relkino, and kept on so well in the

Derby Stakes, Epsom—Empery pulls away from Relkino and Oats. Hawkberry finishes fourth, followed by Wollow (left) and Vitiges (right)

final furlong that at the line he had three lengths in hand, a convincing margin that didn't seem in prospect two furlongs from home. Oats, sixth into the straight, kept on steadily under hard driving to run Relkino very close for second place, ahead of Hawkberry, Wollow and Vitiges.

For the first time since 1965, Sea-Bird's year, a French-trained horse had won the Derby. Four days after Empery's win Youth took the Prix du Jockey-Club by the same margin, three lengths, completing for his owner a double not achieved since M Boussac's heyday when, in 1950, Galcador and Scratch II won the respective races. Youth's win raised the important question of which stable-companion was the better, a question of importance not least to those twenty investors who had contracted to pay 300,000 dollars for a share in both horses. The pair were to be retired at the end of the season to Gainesway Farm in Kentucky, with every member of the syndicate entitled to one nomination per year to each horse; Nelson Bunker Hunt retained twenty shares for his own use. The question is easy enough to answer now Youth's best performances have outstripped Empery's in quality and quantity; but in the middle of June it was not so easy to answer, although most people, including ourselves, would have come down in Youth's favour. At the end of the season the Derby field could justifiably be said to have been below its normal strength. Wollow and Vitiges, the best horses in the race behind the winner, clearly did not give their true running. And the three that divided the winner and Wollow Relkino, Oats and Hawkberry—were beaten often enough subsequently to show that, as three-year-olds at any rate, they could not be regarded as outstanding opposition by the very best standards.

At the time, however, matters had a different complexion. Wollow had won the Two Thousand Guineas and five other races, and Empery had been the first to lower his colours; Vitiges, 8 lb above Empery in the Handicap Optional, had been second in the Two Thousand Guineas; Relkino, a respectable sixth (for a stoutly-bred horse) in the Guineas, might well have been a late-developing type similar to his former stable-companion Bustino; Oats, said to be the best in Peter Walwyn's string, could have been a very good horse for all anyone knew to the contrary, having won the Ladbroke Blue Riband Trial over a distance palpably on the sharp side for him on his previous appearance; Hawkberry, not long out of the maiden stage, came from a stable well known for its patience with its best horses and its ability to improve them in a relatively short time. And although Empery's record could not be described as imposing, it was obviously that of an improving three-year-old. Other Derby winners in living memory, good Derby winners, too, had less than he to boast about. Had not Arctic Prince's only win before the Derby been in a £200 maiden race at Redcar? Airborne was still a maiden only three weeks before the Derby. And what about Never Say Die and Psidium; were they any better than Empery beforehand?

The race for the Irish Sweeps Derby went a long way towards resolving the question of the relative merit of Empery and Youth, at least at a distance of a mile and a half. Malacate, third and beaten fair and square in the Prix du Jockey-Club, won easily by two and a half lengths from Empery. Piggott again rode Empery beautifully, tracking Oilfield until pushing ahead entering the straight, only to be left standing in the last three hundred and fifty yards. Hawkberry, in fourth place, more than halved the distance between himself and Empery, which at Epsom stood at about four lengths, and he seemed still to be on the upgrade. Empery had every chance of beating Malacate had he been good enough, and one has to draw the conclusion that Malacate was the better horse on the day. Conditions on the day were very fast—firm going and Oilfield in to make the pace—and bearing in mind that Empery was essentially a stayer one may properly make allowances for his defeat without taking credit from the winner. Malacate was the speedier type, and on what we saw at the Curragh we should have contemplated backing Empery to beat him over a mile and half only under testing conditions. Over a longer distance Empery would have been another proposition, and it's a great pity the St Leger went by without him.

Empery remained in training in France during the summer without meeting any of his engagements. He would have run in the Benson and Hedges Gold Cup but for sustaining a slight injury. In the autumn he was flown to the United States, missed running in the Man o'War Stakes after a reported loss of condition in quarantine, and retired to Kentucky. Youth, in the meantime, continued to add to his reputation.

		Vienna	Aureole
	Vaguely Noble	(ch 1957)	Turkish Blood
	(b 1965)	Noble Lassie	Nearco
Empery		(b 1956)	Belle Sauvage
(b.c. 1973)		Postin	Hunter's Moon
	Pamplona II	(ch 1940)	Quinta
	(b 1956)	Society's Way	Kingsway
		(b 1950)	Society's Vote

The majority of French breeders are delighted to see the last of Empery on

Mr N. B. Hunt's "Empery"

French racecourses, though they don't put it quite so bluntly, and would also be glad to see the back of all other American-bred horses anywhere near as good as he. They have become increasingly resentful in the last few years of the lifting of a huge amount of French prize money (at the chief expense of the locals, of course) by horses bred in the United States; they have become so incensed that in August the 1,600-member French Thoroughbred Breeders Association proposed the introduction of a scheme to ban from all French races, except pattern races, horses foaled outside the Common Market and sired by stallions standing outside the Common Market, beginning with two-year-olds in 1978, followed by two-year-olds and three-year-olds in 1979 and then horses of all ages until 1983. The real significance of the restriction was to owners of American-breds; they would have to prepare their American-breds outside France and ship them in just for the big races, or prepare them by running solely in the big French races, or forego racing them in France. Presumably the French breeders would prefer the last alternative. Fortunately, sense has prevailed, and the scheme will not be put into effect. At a meeting of international breeders held in Ireland in September the proposal met strong opposition from the Earl of Harrington, representing the Irish breeders, The Hon J. J. Astor, representing the English breeders and, naturally, from the American representatives. They objected to the principle of protectionism, as also did M Boussac at the traditional dinner on the eve of the Prix de l'Arc de Triomphe and as also do we. There is no doubting that the restriction would benefit French owners—it's self evident; with the field virtually to themselves far more purse money would surely be won by French horses. And the restriction would benefit the French breeders, in that the demand in France for their produce, especially at the Deauville Yearling Sales, would increase. But the restriction could not possibly, either in the short term or the long, improve the quality of French racing. Far from it. Shorn of the best American-breds, racing on the top French tracks would have been of a considerably lower quality in the last few seasons and would continue to be so. The real answer to the French breeders' problem is to be found in the old adage 'if you can't beat 'em, join 'em.' Why not follow Alec Head's example? Recognise the value of the American thoroughbred and invest in it.

Empery's sire, Vaguely Noble, needs no recommendation to French breeders from us. He must be just about the best-known stallion in the world by now, and he is certainly one of the most successful. Ironically, he did much of his racing in France, and but for his first owner's death he would almost certainly be standing in Europe. Empery's dam, Pamplona II, was bred in Peru. She proved the best of her generation in Peru, winning the triple crown, the last leg of which, the Gran Premio Nacional, is run over fifteen furlongs. She also won in Argentina, where racing was considered to be of a higher standard, and ran respectably there behind the outstanding Brazilian colts Escorial and Farwell in the Gran Premio 25 de Mayo. Her sire Postin was a top racehorse in Peru, and became leading sire for six seasons, while her dam Society's Way was English, the winner of five races in the north for trainer T. H. Dent. The next dam, Society's Vote, was a daughter of the Irish Oaks winner Conversation Piece. Pamplona, purchased by Mr Hunt at the end of her distinguished racing career, would have been acknowledged an outstanding broodmare even without Empery to represent her. Five earlier foals are winners, two of them, Sports Event (by T.V. Lark) and Anglo Peruvian (by My Babu), goodish fillies in the United States, and the other three, Pampered Miss (by Sadair), Always Loyal (by Pretendre) and Empery's brother Pelopides, winners in France. Pampered Miss is the pick of the five. In 1970 she won the Poule d'Essai des Pouliches and ran third behind Sweet Mimosa and Highest Hopes in the Prix de Diane. Sports Event, the winner of a stakes race, has produced two stakes winners, Anono and Vagabonda; she is also the dam of Sportsky.

Empery is a deep-bodied colt and a good, fluent mover. There is nothing in his action to suggest that ground as firm as that on the Irish Sweeps Derby Day would in itself inconvenience him, and he probably acted on any going, though, as he was essentially a stayer, the speedier the opposition the more likely he would be to benefit from an easy surface. In this respect he was lucky to find good ground at Epsom. *M. Zilber, France.*

EMPRESSARIA 2 br.f. Tycoon II–Empress of England (Constable 129) [1976 5g⁵] narrow filly: third foal: dam never ran: about 10 lengths fifth of eight in seller won by Mia Saint at Doncaster in March, only outing. *M. H. Easterby.*

EMPRESS CHANDA 2 b.f. King Emperor–Glorious Light 53 (Alcide 136) 78 [1976 7fg 7g⁵ 7g⁴ 8s⁵ 7s⁶] strong filly: third foal: closely related to a bumpers winner by Stupendous: 960 gns yearling: dam slow maiden: quite a moderate maiden: will stay middle distances. *I. Walker.*

EMPRESS OF RUSSIA 4 b.f. Royal Palace 131–Nagaika 117 (Goyama 127) **72** [1974 N.R. 1975 10fg⁵ 10f² 1976 9g 12fg² 12h*] leggy, unfurnished filly: not seen out after accounting for two poor opponents (unimpressively) in maiden race at Brighton in August (long odds on): stayed 1½m: acted on hard going: stud. *N. Murless.*

EMPRESS REGENT 3 b.f. Prince Regent 129–Shot Gold (Vimy 132) [1975 **97** 6fg 7g⁴ 8.2g* 1976 12.2g² 14f² 12f* 12g² 18g* 18d⁶] leggy filly: developed into a fairly useful handicapper: won at Ripon in August (gamely) and Doncaster the following month (comfortably by 2½ lengths from Cumbernauld): appeared winner on merit at York in between when beating Lochranza a shade comfortably by 2½ lengths but slightly hampered runner-up when hanging on to rails 2f out and was subsequently relegated to second place: fair sixth of 14 to most impressive winner John Cherry in S.K.F. Cesarewitch at Newmarket in October: stays extremely well: appears to act on any going. *J. Hindley*

ENCHANTED 3 b.f. Song 132–Nymph 81 (Never Say Die 137) [1975 5fg² 5h* **94** 5f² 5g* 5f² 5fg⁴ 6fg² 6d⁶ 1976 6fg⁴ 5g 5fg 5d² 5v²] neat filly: dam won over 1m and seemed to stay 1½m: showed very useful form as a 2-y-o: ran respectably, though beaten some way, when fourth of 13 to Broxted under a stiff weight in Johnnie Walker Handicap at Lingfield in May on reappearance: put up easily her best subsequent effort when head second to Minstrel in minor event at Newbury in September (first outing for three months and blinkered first time): again blinkered when running below her best final appearance: may stay further than 6f: possibly not at her best on heavy ground but acts on any other. *H. T. Jones.*

ENDEARED 3 ch.f. Derring-Do 131–Hopiana 116 (Hook Money 124) [1975 **62** N.R. 1976 5fg⁶ 5fg² 5g³ 5d] useful-looking filly: first living foal: dam smart 5f performer: placed in maiden races at Nottingham in July and Kempton in August: had very stiff task on final appearance: taken down early to start on first outing: sold 1,500 gns Newmarket December Sales. *J. Bethell.*

ENDLESS ECHO 3 ch.c. Mountain Call 125–St Lucia 116 (Alycidon 138) [1975 **88** 5g³ 6fg 6g⁴ 6fg³ 6fg 6g² 7g² 1976 6fg⁵ 5g⁵ 6d³ 6fg² 6f* 7.2g⁴ 6f⁴ 6d 6d] well-grown, good-bodied colt: modest handicapper: comfortable winner at Yarmouth in July: will stay 1m: best form on a sound surface, and acts on firm going: has worn blinkers but seems better without: sold 7,400 gns Newmarket Autumn Sales and is to be trained by A. Pitt. *Doug Smith.*

ENDORSMENT 3 b.c. Falcon 131–Traffic Offence 61 (Traffic Judge) [1975 **63** 5s 5g⁶ 5g 5.1f* 5f³ 6g⁶ 5f 5fg⁵ 1976 8.2f* 10.4s 8f 7.6fg 8h²] dipped-backed colt: modest plater: won gamely (made virtually all) at Nottingham in April (no bid): stays 1m well: acts on hard going and is possibly unsuited by soft: bandaged third outing. *P. Milner*

ENEMY 3 b.c. Le Prince 98–Envy 98 (Princely Gift 137) [1975 7f⁵ 7.5g* — 1976 8g⁵ 8fg⁴ 10f²] good-looking ex-Irish colt: third foal: brother to Right Regal, winner of a bumpers race in Ireland: dam won at 1m: showed quite useful form in Ireland in 1975: heavily-backed favourite, appeared to have every chance when fifth of 11 to easy winner Stellenbosch in apprentice event at Kempton in May: had little chance at weights when well beaten both subsequent outings: should stay further than 1m. *B. Swift.*

ENGLISHMAN'S BOND 2 ch.c. Good Bond 122–Hot Spot (Vienna 127) **77** [1976 6g 6f⁴ 6g 8s⁵ 7s⁵] compact colt: ran best race when apprentice ridden at 6 lb overweight in £1,800 nursery at Brighton in October, finishing fifth of 17 to Rutlow: will stay 1¼m. *Mrs D. Oughton.*

ENGLISH ROSE 3 gr.f. Samothraki 108–Joyce's Girl (Zeus Boy 121) [1975 — N.R. 1976 9fg 10g] small, short-legged filly: well beaten in sellers. *W. Clay.*

ENNIS TOWN 2 b.c. Charlottown 127–Pat 98 (Ennis 128) [1976 6f⁴ 6fg³] **93** workmanlike colt: half-brother to 1974 2-y-o 5f winner Royal Pat (by King's Troop) and to a winner in Jersey: 2,500 gns yearling: dam 5f sprinter: in frame in minor event at Ripon and £2,000 race at York, both in June, on latter course finishing 5 lengths third of eight to Great Oak: will stay 7f+. *M. H. Easterby.*

ENRYCO MIEO 4 ch.c. David Jack 125–Bag of Bones (Relic) [1974 6f 6g⁶ **58** 6f⁵ 6fg⁴ 6s⁶ 7s 8s 1975 12v* 12.2s³ 12fg* 12fg⁶ 13f⁵ 11fg 12g⁴ 13.8fg 16g 15d* 16d 13.8g 1976 15.8g⁶ 13v⁶ 12d⁶ 13s⁶ 13.8g 13g 16fg⁵] lightly-made colt: didn't run up to his best at 4 yrs: well suited by a thorough test of stamina: appears to act on any going: has worn blinkers but has done better without them: inconsistent: off course three months before final outing. *K. Payne.*

ENSIGN STEEL 4 gr.f. Majority Blue 126–Red Sails 87 (Vilmorin) [1974 **57**
N.R. 1975 8h 8f⁶ 7d⁶ 8.2d 1976 9g⁶ 6s² 8f⁵] useful-looking filly: plating-
class maiden: best form at 6f: evidently best suited by a soft surface: sold 620
gns Doncaster October Sales. *S. Wainwright.*

EPISODE 2 b.c. Lampardal 92–Pretty Story 89 (Premonition 130) [1976 6g **65**
7h⁴ 7f⁴ 8fg 8s] fair sort: half-brother to a winning plater by Galivanter: dam
won four times at 1¼m: showed a little ability in small races at Beverley and
Lanark in July: should be suited by 1¼m or more: blinkered final outing. *J.
Etherington.*

EPSOM IMP 3 br.g. St Alphage 119–Sarah Jane 80 (Pardao 120) [1975 5v 5d⁴ **90**
5f* 5fg⁶ 5g³ 6s 1976 7fg³ 7.3g 7d 5d* 5fg* 5fg³ 5g³ 5g⁴ 5g⁶ 5v*] strong gelding:
fairly useful handicapper: winner at Haydock in June (apprentice race) and
July and at York in October (narrowly beat Hot Bird): best form at 5f, although
has run creditably over 7f: acts on any going: blinkered last outing at 2 yrs:
good mount for an apprentice. *M. Tate.*

ERIC STUART 4 br.g. Precipice Wood 123–Hot Seat 73 (Sing Sing 134) [1974 **76**
5g 5f 6g 6fg 5g⁵ 8s* 8g⁵ 8s 1975 10fg 8f 11.7fg 11.7f⁴ 11.7fg⁴ 14s* 16s* 1976
12g 16fg* 16fg⁵ 14f⁶ 16f⁵ 16fg⁴ 14fg* 16fg³ 18f² 16g⁶ 16f³ 14s 12s] tall gelding:
quite a moderate handicapper: successful at Newbury in April and Salisbury
in June (amateur riders event): extremely well suited by a good test of stamina:
acts on any going: suitable mount for a lady rider. *J. Holt.*

ERMINIA 3 b.f. Gulf Pearl 117–Miss Etta (King's Troop 118) [1975 N.R. **61**
1976 6d* 8f⁵] half-sister to useful sprinter Maccaboy and French 11f winner
Corporal Major (both by Will Somers): 480 gns yearling: dam never ran: bought
in 725 gns after winning maiden seller at Haydock in April by 2 lengths from
Walter: not seen out again until July when running moderately in better company: should stay further than 6f: refused to enter stalls and was withdrawn
not under orders on final appearance. *J. Hill.*

ERNEL 2 ch.c. Sassafras 135–Belaying Pin (Iron Peg §§) [1976 6v] first **— p**
produce: 3,600 gns foal: dam won up to 7f in U.S.A.: second favourite for
22-runner maiden race at Newbury in October but made little show, eventually
finishing thirteenth to Good Company: should stay middle distances: evidently
quite well thought of and should do better at 3 yrs. *G. Hunter.*

ERNYDEE 2 b.c. Frontin 125–Belle de Bal (Emerson) [1976 5f 6f] light- **—**
framed colt: behind in maiden auction event at Thirsk (tailed off) and seller at
Ripon in first part of season. *E. Magner.*

ERSTUNG 2 b.f. Shantung 132–Bonkers 86 (Sallymount 125) [1976 6fg 5fg **83**
7h⁴ 8g⁵ 8s²] narrow filly: half-sister to a winner in Italy by Burglar: 200 gns
yearling: dam won over 2m: in rear in seller on first outing but ran well in better

Clarence House Stakes, Ascot—a smooth success for Etienne Gerard over Birkholm

company afterwards, finishing 4 lengths second of 20 to Money to Spare in nursery at Pontefract in October: will stay 1½m: acts on any going. *W. Holden.*

ESCAPOLOGIST 4 b.c. Derring-Do 131–Escape 93 (Gilles de Retz 132) [1974   **99** 6g³ 6s* 7v* 7d*   1975 7s² 8g 7.3g 8d⁴ 10s* 8g 8s   1976 9fg⁵ 10.4d² 10g 8f 12v 10.6v⁶] well-made colt: useful handicapper: good second to Battlecry in Ladbroke Chester Handicap in May: faced stiffish tasks subsequently: stays 1¼m: acts well on heavy going: tried in blinkers final outing at 3 yrs and fourth appearance in 1976: sold out of G. Pritchard-Gordon's stable 8,000 gns Ascot August Sales after fourth outing. *I. Wardle.*

ESCAROLE 5 b.h. Herbager 136–Landmark (Revoked) [1974 N.R.   1975 13d²   **—** 12s² 16.1fg* 12f* 12g³ 14fg 16g   1976 14.6g⁶] fair handicapper (rated 86) in 1975: has run only once since: stays well: acts on any going: wears blinkers but has run well without: suitable mount for an amateur. *G. Balding.*

ESLA 2 ch.f. Doon 124–Oca (O'Grady) [1976 5g 5fg 7h⁶ 7fg⁴ 7v] first produce: **65** dam a plater: ran best race when 4½ lengths fourth of 15 to Topling in maiden race at Salisbury in September: will stay 1¼m. *M. Smyly.*

ESPRIT D'OR 4 b.f. Jolly Jet 111–Bantam 64 (Combat 123) [1974 5fg 5g³ 6g² **64** 7g³ 7g 6s   1975 8s 8g 7fg 7fg 6g 8f⁶   1976 8g 10f 8fg* 8f² 7f³ 8g] small filly: good mover: made all when winning amateur riders maiden race at Thirsk in July by 7 lengths from Winscombe: best at up to 1m: acts on firm going: wears blinkers nowadays. *Miss N. Wilmot.*

ESQUINADE 3 br.f. Silly Season 127–Esquilina 89 (Romulus 129) [1975 6fg⁶ **68** 7g⁴ 6g* 6g⁴ 7d   1976 8.2d³ 8g 8f] useful-looking filly: won minor event at Pontefract in 1975: lightly raced in 1976, running easily best race on first outing: stays 1m. *B. Hanbury.*

ESS-DEE-CON 2 b.c. Grisaille 115–Wee Song (Weepers Boy 124) [1976 5g   **—** 5d 5f 5s] no worthwhile form, including in a valuable seller, early in season. *S. Nesbitt.*

ESSOUAIRA 4 b.f. Aureole 132–Parthian's Way (Parthia 132) [1974 6fg⁶ 7d   **—** 7g 6s⁴ 7g² 6v³   1975 10f 8f² 8.5f 8h³ 8d⁵ 8f   1976 8f 7g 10h] small filly: poor maiden: best at 1m: acts on any going. *M. Bradley.*

ESTATE AGENT 3 b.g. Candy Cane 125–Creel Inn 75 (Premonition 130) [1975 **80** N.R.   1976 10s*] second foal: half-sister to quite moderate 1973 2-y-o Kelfield (by Galivanter): 1,900 gns 2-y-o: dam showed form only at sprint distances: 20/1, won 12-runner minor event at Teesside in November staying on by 3 lengths from Ornamental Night: will probably stay 1½m: acts on soft going. *M. W. Easterby.*

ESTRALITA 3 gr.f. Prince de Galles 125–Veejlee 101 (Vilmorin) [1975 5fg⁶   **—** 5f⁶   1976 6f] sparely-made filly: well beaten in varied company, including selling: dead. *D. Gandolfo.*

ETIENNE GERARD 2 ch.c. Brigadier Gerard 144–Oh So Fair (Graustark) **118** [1976 6fg* 7f⁶ 6g* 6g]

Imagine you were the rider of a highly-regarded two-year-old which had just run disappointingly in an important race, what would you say to the owner on returning to the unsaddling enclosure? Would you tell him that his horse, for which he might perhaps have laid out a considerable sum of money, had had every chance, had been beaten entirely on merit, and was therefore by inference not the high-class performer he had hoped or had perhaps been led to believe; or would you seek instead to sweeten the bitter pill of defeat by stating something to the effect that the horse had been unable to give its running on this occasion, and that given time, better luck or different circumstances, there was still reason to hope that it would eventually make good? Remember owners are optimists by nature—they have to be—and without the optimism of owners, where would jockeys be? Indeed, where would any of us be? So one should always be prepared for reasons to be advanced in explanation of defeats sustained by highly-regarded two-year-olds, and one would be well advised to take those reasons with the proverbial pinch of salt.

Etienne Gerard, a highly-regarded two-year-old if ever there was one, had reasons advanced in explanation of failure on two occasions in his first season. And he ran only four times. Appearing in public for the first time with a reputation which said he was a potential classic colt for owner P. A. Philipps, Etienne Gerard was made favourite at 6/5 to beat fifteen rivals in the Pegasus Maiden

Stakes at Newmarket in July. Always travelling smoothly just in behind the leaders, he tended to wander off a true line up the hill but came away in the closing stages to win comfortably by a length and a half, doing nothing wrong that could not be excused on the grounds of inexperience. He impressed all the critics most favourably. Accordingly, Etienne Gerard was made a hot favourite on his next appearance to beat such useful youngsters as Card Player, Crown Bowler and Our Jimmy in the Fitzroy House Stakes over seven furlongs on the same course. He was never well placed nor racing smoothly, and dropped right away in the last furlong to finish sixth of eight, beaten over ten lengths. This defeat must have come as a bitter blow to those who had visualised Etienne Gerard as a worthy son of his illustrious sire, but when Etienne Gerard reappeared at Ascot just under a month later his reputation, seemingly, was still very much intact. According to his jockey, the seventh furlong had been Etienne Gerard's undoing in the Fitzroy House Stakes, and he was confidently expected by those who knew him best to defeat his six opponents in the Clarence House Stakes over six furlongs. Etienne Gerard couldn't have accomplished his task more impressively. Responding immediately when asked to go about his work from the distance, he stormed into the lead in the final furlong and won handsomely by three lengths. Birkholm was second. This performance, impressive as it was, did not give Etienne Gerard an outstanding chance in the William Hill Middle Park Stakes on his next appearance, but he should have run much better than he did. Co-favourite at 5/1 with Tachypous, he recovered from a tardy beginning to be well on terms at halfway, but dropped out again inside the last two furlongs to finish tenth of eleven, the explanation this time being that he had 'swallowed his tongue.'

Etienne Gerard
(ch.c. 1974)

- Brigadier Gerard (b 1968)
  - Queen's Hussar (b 1960)
    - March Past
    - Jojo
  - La Paiva (ch 1956)
    - Prince Chevalier
    - Brazen Molly
- Oh So Fair (b 1967)
  - Graustark (ch 1963)
    - Ribot
    - Flower Bowl
  - Chandelle (b 1959)
    - Swaps
    - Malindi

Those then were Etienne Gerard's races in his first season—a finely balanced

Mr P. A. Philipps' "Etienne Gerard" (P. Cook)

mixture of performances good and bad. Perhaps he didn't stay the seventh furlong of the Fitzroy House Stakes, perhaps he did swallow his tongue in the Middle Park, but in the quest for the Two Thousand Guineas winner of 1977 no-one in his right mind is going to be impressed by the claims of a colt whose lot it was to have reasons advanced in explanation of failure every other time he set foot on a racecourse. Frankly, we shall be surprised if Etienne Gerard one day realises his reputation as a top-class colt, whether he proves able to stay beyond six furlongs or not.

There is no reason on his breeding why Etienne Gerard should be all that lacking in stamina. Brigadier Gerard, his sire, stayed a mile and a half well enough to win the King George VI and Queen Elizabeth Stakes at Ascot and is responsible for the promising French colt General, who has won at a mile; whilst Roussalka and My Fair Niece, Etienne Gerard's half-sisters by Habitat and Great Nephew respectively, have both won at a mile and a quarter. Oh So Fair, the dam, was also successful at a mile and a quarter. If breeding considerations were the only considerations to be taken into account, one would expect Etienne Gerard to get a mile and a quarter at least. On the other hand Etienne Gerard's performance at Ascot was that of a colt with a fine burst of speed at his command and it may be that he won't stay so far as his breeding suggests, though one would certainly expect him to have no trouble in getting seven furlongs, even on his second outing as a two-year-old. No-one watching him at Ascot needed telling that this was a far different colt from the one which had failed so ignominiously in the Fitzroy House Stakes, and it could well be that Etienne Gerard was unable to stride out freely on the firm ground at Newmarket. But the going won't do as an excuse for his failure to make much of a show in the Middle Park Stakes—it was perfect. To reconcile this disappointing display with his impressive performance at Ascot is difficult to say the least; so difficult that some observers saw fit to question his honesty. They may be right, but really it is a case of wait and see. A fine, big, well-developed colt, Etienne Gerard certainly looks a good horse. *M. Stoute.*

ETOILE GRISE 4 gr.f. Sea Hawk II 131–Place d'Etoile 93 (Kythnos 126) — [1974 N.R. 1975 10d 12.3g 11s 14g⁵ 1976 13v² 16s 12s] strong filly: half-sister to Irish 2,000 Guineas winner Northern Treasure (by Northfields): stays well: acts on heavy ground: sold 16,500 gns Newmarket December Sales. *R. Mason.*

ETRUSCAN MAID 5 b.m. Arrigle Valley 98–Jungle Lady 78 (Lion's Roar 94) — [1974 N.R. 1975 N.R. 1976 12f] well behind in maiden race won by Allan Water at Ripon in August, only outing. *S. Norton.*

EULALIE 2 b.f. Queen's Hussar 124–Sounion 69 (Vimy 132) [1976 5g⁴ 6fg² 85 7fg*] shapely, rather unfurnished filly: half-sister to three winners, including very useful middle-distance performer Honorius (by Hornbeam): dam won at 1½m: favourite, got gamely when winning 15-runner maiden race at Salisbury in September by a head from Best Offer: will stay 1m+. *P. Walwyn.*

EUSTON 4 gr.f. St Alphage 119–Japhette 79 (Vilmorin) [1974 5s 1975 6s 58 6f⁴ 6f² 6fg* 6f 6fg³ 6fg² 7fg 8g 7.6s 1976 7fg⁵ 6g⁵ 7g² 6f 6f⁴ 7fg 6f 7f] poor handicapper nowadays: backed at long odds when ¾-length second of 17 to The Old Pretender at Leicester in June, easily best effort at 4 yrs: stays 7f: acts on firm going: has worn blinkers and ran creditably in them on second outing in 1976: good mount for an apprentice: ran very badly final outing. *G. Harwood.*

EVA ANNE 2 b.f. Acrania 110–Duanna (Songedor 116) [1976 5f⁶ 5f⁶ 6g] bad 40 plater. *R. Vibert.*

EVE 4 ch.f. Quisling 117–Little Apple (Sovereign Lord 120) [1974 5f 5f* 6g⁴ 81 5g³ 5fg⁵ 6g⁴ 5g 5.3g² 5g³ 1975 5s⁵ 6f⁵ 5f 5h 5g⁵ 5g⁴ 5.3f 5.3f 5f 5f³ 1976 5f 7g 8f⁴ 8f* 8f 8f* 8h⁴ 8f* 7f*] leggy filly: winner four times at Yarmouth in 1976, including in three selling handicaps (bought in on second and third occasions): gained her final win when beating Sound Jiff ¾ length in non-seller in August: stays 1m: acts on firm going: has worn blinkers (not when successful): needs things all her own way and was brought wide and raced alone on each occasion when winning at 4 yrs. *T. Molony.*

EVEN TEMPERED 2 ch.c. Sweet Revenge 129–Plumtree Plain (Primera 131) — [1976 5s⁶] second produce: 2,100 gns foal, 2,800 gns yearling: dam a minor winner over 9f in France: outsider of party when remote last of six to Kilavea in newcomers event at Goodwood in September. *P. Haslam.*

Musidora Stakes, York—Everything Nice has too much pace for Crofting and Love Story (rails)

EVENTURA 3 ch.f. Huntercombe 133–High Acres (High Perch 126) [1975 **77**
6fg 6f³ 1976 7f* 7g 7s 7s 6s] rangy filly: half-sister to useful 7f and 1m winner
Super Red (by Hill Clown) and useful sprinter Running Jump (by Runnymede):
won maiden race at Ayr in May by a neck from Midsummer Madness: ran
creditably under stiff weights in handicaps on last two outings: stays 7f: acts
on any going. *G. Pritchard-Gordon.*

EVER SO COOL 2 ch.f. Never Say Die 137–Cool Harmony 63 (Arctic Storm 134) —
[1976 6fg 6v] big, strong French-foaled filly: half-sister to 6f and 1m seller
winner Cool Melody (by Right Boy): dam a middle-distance performer: well
behind in large fields of maidens at Newbury in August (very backward, finished
last of 27) and October: will need time and longer distances. *G. Hunter.*

EVERYTHING NICE 3 gr.f. Sovereign Path 125–Emma Canute 93 (Hardi- **107**
canute 130) [1975 5g³ 5d* 5f 6g* 6f* 7fg⁵ 6d 1976 7fg 10fg² 10.5d* 10f² 10fg⁶
12fg 10g* 10g⁴] neat, quite attractive filly: good mover: put up a tremendous
performance under top weight when winning Virginia Fillies Handicap at
Newcastle in August, cruising up to leader in straight and quickening right
away from her field in final furlong to beat Gay Jennie 2½ lengths: ran well in
most of her other races, notably when winning Musidora Stakes at York in May
by 2½ lengths from Crofting and when in frame in Pretty Polly Stakes at the
Curragh in June (2 lengths second to Lady Singer) and Sun Chariot Stakes
at Newmarket in September (just over 6½ lengths fourth to Ranimer): best form
at 1¼m: acts on any going: thoroughly genuine and consistent: sold 64,000
gns Newmarket December Sales. *B. Hobbs.*

EVROS RIVER 4 b.g. Forlorn River 124–Fergus Lily 73 (Ennis 128) [1974 **58**
6fg 6fg 6g⁴ 6g 6d 1975 6g 8f² 8g⁴ 8g 7fg³ 8.2g* 7.6g² 1976 7g 7fg³ 7f⁶ 7fg 7f³
8g 7f] strong gelding: poor handicapper nowadays: stays 1m well: acts on
firm going: suitable mount for an inexperienced rider: tried in blinkers as a
2-y-o: sold to D. Jermy 560 gns Ascot September Sales. *G. Balding.*

EXACUM 3 ch.c. Exbury 138–Crassula (Canisbay 120) [1975 6f 7g 8.2g 8.2d⁴ **74**
8fg 10g³ 1976 12.3s² 12fg 16f] lightly-made colt: creditable second to Ribarbaro in 16-runner apprentice maiden event at Newcastle in April but was moderately both subsequent outings and was sold 420 gns Doncaster August Sales:
should stay further than 1½m: evidently needs some give in the ground. *S.
Hall.*

234

EXCELLER 3 b.c. Vaguely Noble 140–Too Bald (Bald Eagle 119) [1975 7.5g 9d* **129**
8s³ 10s³ 1976 10.5g² 10g* 12g* 15.5g* 15.5s* 12s]

Nelson Bunker Hunt held a strong hand in the Prix de l'Arc de Triomphe
with his runners Exceller and Youth, as also did the Head family with their pair
Ivanjica and Riverqueen, and the Wildenstein stable with Crow and Pawneese.
But weaknesses could be seen in each card in every hand, perhaps the most
obvious concerning the fillies Pawneese and Riverqueen, whose form had to be
taken on trust after their poor showing in the Prix Vermeille last time out, and
the most serious concerning Exceller, who, although unquestionably one of the
best horses in the field with wins in the Grand Prix de Paris and the Prix Royal-
Oak behind him, had never given any indication that he possessed the speed to
cope with top-class opposition over middle distances.

The Grand Prix de Paris and the Prix Royal-Oak, the latter the equivalent
of the St Leger, are the best races over two miles in France for three-year-olds.
We saw Exceller hand out a four-length beating to the Ebor winner Sir Montagu
in the Royal-Oak, and we left the course that day with the strong impression that
the winner was the type for whom long distances were almost certainly essential
if he were to be seen to best advantage; furthermore, assessing him on what we
had seen that day and on his record as a whole, we came to the firm conclusion
that he wouldn't be fast enough to be placed in the Arc, not even if, as could be
expected, he got a strongly-run race and testing conditions. In the event,
Exceller ran poorly in the Arc; so poorly (he finished tailed off and was never
going) that it is quite possible to argue that the nature of the race had little or no
bearing on his performance; afterwards report had it that he would be tested
privately for dope. Nevertheless, we are pretty sure that Exceller will never
make a top-class middle-distance horse. If all is well with him he should be aimed
at the Cup races as a four-year-old, in which he will, to say the least, provide
formidable opposition for Sagaro.

Exceller's record is clearly that of a stayer: the further he has gone, the
better his form. He finished his season as a two-year-old with a good performance over ten furlongs in the mud at Longchamp, taking third place to French
Friend in the Prix de Conde. Earlier he had won a nine-furlong maiden at Evry
and passed the post first in the one-mile Prix Herod on the same course; the
stewards, on an objection, put him down to third place in the Prix Herod for
hampering Happy Tim. In the Handicap Optional he was rated within a stone
of the best of his age.

As a three-year-old Exceller had a fairly easy run-up to the Grand Prix de
Paris at Longchamp in June. He had three outings, the first two at around ten
furlongs, the other at a mile and a half. He lost the Prix de Suresnes at Longchamp to a much speedier type, to none other than Malacate, but by only a
length; he won the Prix Matchem at Evry by two and a half lengths from second-
raters and then ran clean away with the Prix du Lys at Chantilly, accounting for
a small field that included Caron, second in the Prix Noailles, and Kano, third in
the Prix de Guiche, but no top-class horse except Exceller. Most of the leading
French middle-distance horses missed the Prix du Lys in favour of the Prix du
Jockey-Club, the French Derby, earlier on the same day's card. Exceller came
six lengths clear when pushed right out in the second half of the straight at
Chantilly, and on the strength of that performance he started at 5/2 on for the
Grand Prix de Paris, in which one of his eight opponents was Caron.

The low turn-out for the Grand Prix caused some concern in France, but

*Grand Prix de Paris, Longchamp—Exceller wins in great style from
Secret Man and Caron*

it's much too early to say that the race is losing its appeal to owners, although by and large there seems a growing reluctance on the part of owners to support long-distance races, especially with high-class three-year-olds. The most likely explanation for the low turn-out is to be found in the fact that staying three-year-olds good enough to run in the Grand Prix de Paris were very thin on the ground in 1976. Of course, there is little doubt that the race has had to share more of the limelight with the Prix du Jockey-Club in recent years; since 1966 the Jockey-Club's purse has been the more valuable, whereas before 1965 it was always less. In 1939 the prize money for the Grand Prix was twice the Jockey-Club's, and over a hundred years ago the race was claimed to be the richest in the world. However, the size of the prize offered by the Grand Prix is, in all conscience, still enormous at around £100,000; as long as it remains at around the same level in the next few years the fields should return to their usual strength. The previous season, incidentally, twenty-two runners went to post, including the second, fourth, fifth, seventh and eighth in the Prix du Jockey-Club; so if the Grand Prix has lost any appeal it has lost it almost overnight!

Two of the Jockey-Club runners opposed Exceller; the fourth-placed Ydja, beaten about five lengths by Youth, and Yule Log, whose only hope seemed to lie entirely in the resource of his new jockey Piggott. Ydja again finished fourth, this time beaten nearly ten lengths after injuring himself in the closing stages; Yule Log finished last, just behind the Queen's Valuation and some twenty-five lengths behind Exceller, who strung out the field like washing in the straight. Secret Man, narrow winner from Campero in a long-distance trial at Longchamp, the Prix de l'Esperance, chased him home at four lengths, never able to get within effective reach; Caron finished third, a length and a half back. Saint-Martin rode Exceller, temporarily renewing his outstandingly successful partnership with Mathet which had ended five years before. Mr Hunt had sent Mathet about a dozen horses from Zilber's stable at the beginning of the year; one of them was Exceller, another the Grand Prix de Vichy winner Diagramatic. Mathet's jockey Dubroeucq usually rides Exceller, and he rode the horse in his next race, the Prix Royal-Oak at Longchamp in September, in which Saint-Martin partnered one of Mr Tikkoo's two runners, the Prix de la Cote Normande fourth Zamp.

Exceller started at 5/1 on for the Royal-Oak, opposed by only six others of whom Sir Montagu appeared to have the best form. Youth had been taken out in favour of Exceller, the home team had been weakened considerably by the formidable French assault on the St Leger which had resulted in a win for Crow from Secret Man, and by this time Exceller was looking an outstandingly good animal. Caron and Ydja did not race after the Grand Prix de Paris but Secret Man's performances held the form up; as well as beating most of the top English stayers at Doncaster he had won, on his only other start, a fairly important long-distance race at Deauville, the Prix de Menneval, from Campero.

Exceller again succeeded in stringing out his field, and won by four lengths without being touched with the whip. Unlike most who have expressed an opinion on the race, we do not believe he had anything in hand of second-placed Sir Montagu; nevertheless, four lengths better than Sir Montagu is top-class staying form in our book, for Sir Montagu had won the Ebor running away by eight lengths with 8-0 on his back. Exceller took over early in the straight after tracking Adam van Vianen, a respectable sixth to Ashmore in the Grand Prix de Deauville, and Sir Montagu from the start. He remained in front, pushed along, to the finish. As he was entering the final furlong an incident took place well behind him that earned the French jockey Paquet a month's suspension. Bold Bird, Paquet's mount who had been behind throughout, hampered Zamp's stable-companion Nuclear Pulse, who also had never been at the races; he hampered him so badly that he came down. The incident had no bearing on the result, nor did an apparent brush between the second and third in the closing stages which led Piggott, the rider of the third, Adam van Vianen, to object.

Prix Royal-Oak, Longchamp—another emphatic victory by Exceller who has English challenger Sir Montagu and Adam van Vianen well held

Mr N. B. Hunt's "Exceller"

Exceller's win was the seventh in the race for trainer Mathet, following Vamour, Match III, Relko, Reliance II, Sassafras and Henri le Balafre; Exceller became the first horse since Pleben in 1972 to land the Grand Prix and Royal-Oak double.

		Vienna (ch 1957)	Aureole
	Vaguely Noble (b 1965)		Turkish Blood
		Noble Lassie (b 1956)	Nearco
Exceller			Belle Sauvage
(b.c. 1973)		Bald Eagle (b 1955)	Nasrullah
	Too Bald (br 1964)		Siama
		Hidden Talent (b 1956)	Dark Star
			Dangerous Dame

    Exceller cost 25,000 dollars as a yearling at the Keeneland Summer Sale, a small sum one would have thought for a well-grown colt by Vaguely Noble out of a stakes-winning, winner-producing daughter of a Kentucky Oaks winner. Too Bald, the dam of minor winners Bagayo (by Turn-to) and Mauna Loa (by Hawaii) besides Exceller, won thirteen races and more than 174,000 dollars between the age of three years and five. Her dam, the Kentucky Oaks winner Hidden Talent, produced another stakes winner called Turn to Talent. Hidden Talent was a daughter of a winner in the United States and a granddaughter of Lady Kells, a half-sister to Solonaway.
    Exceller shows the high action that often betokens the soft-ground performer, and indeed, he acts on soft going. There is no evidence that he needs some give in the ground—he has yet to race on anything firmer than good and is unlikely to do so if he remains in France—but if he is sent to this country he may be put out of court in the Gold Cup by firm going. We shall have to wait and see. *F. Mathet, France.*

EXEAT   3 b.f. Quartette 106–Long Term 76 (Sing Sing 134) [1975 N.R. 1976   —
7f 5.3f 5.8h 10.1fg6] compact filly: sister to moderate 1¼m winner Singlet: dam best at sprint distances: well beaten in newcomers and maiden events. *J. Holt.*

EXPADEO 3 b.f. St Paddy 133–Expresso 76 (Roan Rocket 128) [1975 7d 82 1976 12fg⁵ 11g⁵ 12g* 12f² 11.7fg³] fair sort: won 10-runner maiden race at Haydock in August by 7 lengths from No Fear: odds on when 2½ lengths second to Wounded Knee in three-runner minor event at Newmarket later in month, better subsequent effort: stays 1½m. *R. Hern.*

EXPLOITEUR 2 b.c. Sharpen Up 127–Best Exhibit (Kalydon 122) [1976 5fg 95 5f² 5f 7f³ 6f³ 7h*] second foal: dam never ran: put up a good effort to win maiden race at Brighton in August by 4 lengths from Pedlar: stays 7f well: acts on hard going: wears blinkers. *P. Haslam.*

EXPOSED 2 br.c. Polyfoto 124–Belle of Sark (Daybrook Lad 104) [1976 88 5.1g⁶ 5f⁵ 5f* 6fg² 5g⁵ 5f² 5g 5d 5s⁴] workmanlike colt: first foal: dam won over 9f as a 3-y-o in Ireland: made all to win minor event at Lingfield in June by short head from Colourful Connie: ran quite well in nurseries afterwards: should stay 6f: sold 4,200 gns Newmarket Autumn Sales. *C. Brittain.*

EXTRAVAGANZA 3 b.f. Sovereign Gleam 117–Say Gwen (Never Say Die 137) 102 [1975 7g 6g 8.5g² 8s 1976 10s* 12f 10f* 12fg⁴ 10f⁵ 16f² 10f* 10f* 12fg 12f* 9f 12f² 9g⁵ 10d⁶ 10v] second foal: half-sister to useful miler Always Faithful (by Super Sam): 2,000 gns yearling: dam ran only twice: won maiden race at Phoenix Park early in season: subsequently showed quite useful form in handicaps, winning at Leopardstown (twice), Navan and Clonmel: ninth of 17 to Capricious in Galtres Stakes at York in August: stays 1½m: acts on any going: wears blinkers: suitable mount for an apprentice. *K. Prendergast, Ireland.*

EXTROVERT 4 b.c. Bon Mot III 132–Exhibition 109 (Nearula 132) [1974 6d 8d 1975 8g⁶ 8v⁵ 10g² 8.5v² 7.5v² 10g* 8f⁴ 11.7fg* 13.5s² 12g² 1976 14.6g 12f⁶ 11.1g⁶ 12fg⁵] good sort: quite a useful handicapper (rated 96) at 3 yrs: lightly raced and little worthwhile form in 1976: stays well: seems to act on any going: has been tried in blinkers. *P. Haslam.*

F

FABRICA 2 gr.f Supreme Sovereign 119–High Meadow 105 (High Treason 126) — [1976 6fg⁶ 6g] first foal: 2,200 gns 2-y-o: dam won at up to 7f: not fully fit when beaten some way in minor event at Ripon in August and maiden race at Doncaster in September. *M. H. Easterby.*

FABRICON 2 b.g. Sigebert 131–Doreen (Zank) [1976 5fg 7.2f 8f] strong, — deep-bodied gelding: behind in sellers but was backward on first two outings and carried 8 lb overweight on only other start: sold 240 gns Doncaster September Sales. *K. Payne.*

FACULTY 4 ch.g. Right Royal V 135–Miss Glen 107 (Abernant 142) [1974 7g 67 8.2d⁵ 7s 8d 1975 12.2v 10f⁵ 10.1s² 12f* 12.2fg³ 11.7fg 12fg⁵ 12f 13d 12.2g⁶ 12d* 1976 12g⁶ 12g⁴ 12g⁵ 12f² 10fg⁵ 11.7fg² 11.7fg⁶] sturdy gelding: poor handicapper nowadays: most disappointing final outing at 4 yrs: stays 1½m: acts on any going: ran below his best when tried in blinkers: excellent mount for an apprentice. *H. Candy.*

FAIRAMA 2 ch.f. Amber Rama 133–Miel (Pall Mall 132) [1976 5fg 6f 5g] — first foal: dam unraced half-sister to smart 1960 2-y-o King's Son: no worthwhile form in maiden and minor events: sold 540 gns Newmarket September Sales. *W. Wightman.*

FAIR BRUTUS 3 b.c. Marcus Brutus 108–Family Affair 87 (Pappageno II) — [1975 N.R. 1976 13.1s⁶ 16.1v 12s] half-brother to Fair Kitty (by Saucy Kit), a winner over 5f and 2m, and to some winning hurdlers: dam best at 1½m: bought for 2,000 gns Ascot August Sales: well beaten in end-of-season events at Bath, Haydock and Chepstow. *D. H. Jones.*

FAIR DANDY 6 b.g. Carnival Dancer 113–Dick's Yarn 80 (Peter's Yarn 106) 71 [1974 5f 6fg 5fg 5fg* 5fg⁴ 5g 5fg⁴ 5.6d 5s⁶ 5v 5v* 5s⁴ 5v² 1975 5f³ 5fg⁵ 5d⁴ 6f⁵ 6g⁵ 5f² 5s⁴ 5g 6g 5g 1976 5g⁵ 6fg³ 5h³ 6g³ 6fg⁴ 5fg⁵ 6d³ 6s⁶ 5s² 6v⁵] compact gelding: quite a moderate handicapper nowadays: ran creditably most outings in 1976: has shown his best form at 5f: acts on any going: has been tried in blinkers: sometimes loses ground at start. *W. Haigh.*

FAIRFIELD PRINCE 2 ch.c. Songedor 116–Chinese Fern 54 § (Spartan General — 109) [1976 7v 6s] first foal: dam temperamental plater: very backward when in mid-division in maiden races at Teesside in October and November: will do better when fitter. *W. A. Stephenson.*

FAIRFIELDS 2 b.f. Sharpen Up 127–Arctic Jewel (Mandamus 120) [1976 5fg 73 5fg⁶ 5f 5.1f* 5fg⁴ 5g] third foal: dam unraced half-sister to high-class German horse **Luciano**: attracted no bid after winning four-runner seller at Yarmouth in August: respectable fourth to Petard in nursery at Beverley the following month, better subsequent effort, but had little chance at weights on final outing: will be suited by 6f: sold privately 700 gns Doncaster October Sales, resold 450 gns Doncaster November Sales. *N. Callaghan.*

FAIRGOLD 5 ch.g. St Alphage 119–Gold Ingot 90 (Golden Cloud) [1974 6d 6fg³ 6g⁴ 5f³ 5fg⁴ 7g 5g² 5s² 6fg 6s 5.9g 5d 1975 5fg* 5f⁴ 5f* 5f* 5s* 5g⁴ 5g³ 5g⁶ 1976 5f 5s 5s] big, strong, lengthy gelding: fair handicapper (rated 88) in 1975: lightly raced and no worthwhile form at 5 yrs (off course May to October between first and second outings): best form at 5f and ran poorly when tried at 7f: acts on any going: has sometimes worn a bandage on near-hind. *T. Fairhurst.* —

FAIR HEAD 3 ch.f. High Line 125–Fair Winter 111 (Set Fair 129) [1975 7d 7.6g* 1976 10.4s 10s⁶ 10d 10.6d⁶] useful-looking filly: should stay at least 1½m: possibly unsuited by very soft ground. *H. Candy.* **65**

FAIR KITTY 5 ch.m. Saucy Kit 76–Family Affair 87 (Pappageno II) [1974 8g 8s 1975 16h⁵ 1976 15.8g³ 16f*] compact mare: poor handicapper: beat Bustiffa 2 lengths at Beverley in April: stays 2m: acts on hard going. *J. Fitzgerald.* **52**

FAIR LOUISE 2 b.f. Blakeney 126–Louisine 94 (Blue Peter) [1976 8v 8g³ 8v] half-sister to fair miler March Cavalier (by March Past): 2,400 gns yearling: dam won three 6f races at 3 yrs, and is daughter of fastest 1951 2-y-o filly Constantia: made good late progress when 2¾ lengths third of 20 to Harriet Air in minor event at Lanark in October: will be suited by further than 1m. *W. A. Stephenson.* **72**

FAIRLY EVEN 3 b.f. Crisp and Even 116–Fairy Princess 92 (Solonaway 128) [1975 N.R. 1976 11g 13.3fg 8fg] rangy filly: half-sister to three winners, including useful miler Pytchley Princess (by Privy Councillor) and useful middle-distance handicapper Royal Sanction (by Ratification): dam 6f to 1m handicapper: made no show in maiden races at Newbury (two) and Salisbury: sold 520 gns Newmarket Autumn Sales. *W. Wightman.* —

FAIRLY HOT 2 b.f. Sir Ivor 135–Full Dress II 115 (Shantung 132) [1976 7d 6d²] strong, good-bodied, attractive American-foaled filly: second living foal: dam won 1969 1,000 Guineas and is half-sister to three good staying fillies: 4 lengths runner-up to Rocket Symphony in maiden race at Newmarket in October: will stay 1½m: should win a race. *H. Wragg.* **83 p**

FAIRMAN 3 ch.c. Manacle 123–Fairabunda 59 (Floribunda 136) [1975 5f 5f³ 5f 5f⁶ 5f⁵ 5fg 5g 7v 7g 6g 1976 6fg 8d* 9g* 8.2d² 10g⁴ 10f⁶ 10g 10f² 10fg⁶ 10fg 9h* 10f* 10.1fg 12fg³ 12s* 12v³] small colt: only a modest handicapper but had a successful season, winning at Edinburgh (twice, including a maiden race), Hamilton (twice) and Newmarket: held off fast-finishing Voucher Book by 1½ lengths on first-named course in October: stays 1½m: acts on any going: has been tried in blinkers but does much better without: a tough individual. *W. Marshall.* **80**

FAIR NIC 4 b.f. probably Romancero 100–Grey Colleen (Our Charger 119) [1974 N.R. 1975 N.R. 1976 12h²] first foal: dam of little account: 5 lengths second to long odds-on Empress of Russia in three-runner maiden race at Brighton in August, only outing. *J. Old.* —

FAIR OPAL 3 ch.f. Typhoon 125–Fair Marilyn (Macherio) [1975 6g 7g 1976 9f 8g 10f⁶ 12v] compact filly: little worthwhile form in maiden and minor events: tailed off when blinkered on second outing: swerved and unseated rider leaving stalls on final appearance. *H. Collingridge.* —

FAIR PERSON 4 ch.c. Gala Performance–Milosun 79 (Milesian 125) [1974 5f⁶ 6fg⁶ 5g 8d 5fg 5v 1975 10f 1976 12.5g] lengthy colt: of little account. *H. Blackshaw.* —

FAIR SALUTE 3 ch.f. Salvo 129–Hascombe Fair 93 (Gentle Art 121) [1975 8g 8g 10g 1976 7f 7fg⁶ 6f⁵ 6h⁶ 8f⁶ 7f 6fg⁶] poor plater: evidently stays 7f: blinkered final outing. *D. Marks.* **47**

FAIR SARITA 3 b.f. King's Troop 118–Fair Samela 108 (Constable 129) [1975 5fg⁴ 5fg* 6fg² 6s 1976 8.2d 6d 6fg 6fg⁵ 5fg* 5f² 6fg³ 5g⁶] strong, useful sort: fairly useful handicapper: winner at Chester in July by 1½ lengths from Prevailing Love: subsequently ran well when placed at Redcar and Newcastle, on latter course finishing third to Delta Song in Northumberland Sprint Trophy: should stay 7f: well suited by a firm surface and is not at her best on a soft one. *Denys Smith.* **95**

Horris Hill Stakes, Newbury—Fair Season makes all the running and is clear of Baudelaire

FAIR SEASON 2 b.c. Silly Season 127–Fairy Ring 91 (Quorum 126) [1976 **120** 6fg³ 6fg³ 7fg* 7f* 8g² 7s² 7.3v*]

Until he ran in the Horris Hill Stakes at Newbury in October Fair Season had been campaigned, with a measure of success, against handicappers and second-raters. He had, however, lost twice as many races as he had won, and it was not to be anticipated that he would come home alone at Newbury, four lengths ahead of the rest of the field, after making all the running. It was a meritorious win. Baudelaire, who had tried unsuccessfully to keep up with him in the straight, went on to beat some pretty smart youngsters—Alpherat included—in the Premio Tevere in Rome, and it is evident that Fair Season is a good colt when conditions are testing. Easily his best previous performance had been his second on soft going, a length and a half behind Lady Constance and three lengths in front of Casino Boy, in the hotly-contested John Sutcliffe Trophy Nursery at Lingfield.

In all Fair Season ran seven times and he was never out of the first three. At Newmarket in July he won the Exeter Stakes by three lengths from Elusive, and at Ostend a month later he took the Grand Criterium International d'Ostende, a £5,000 race, by a length and a half from Mofida, who was receiving 4 lb. This latter performance looks a good one on paper, but Mofida is not at her best over seven furlongs, and the form is devalued by the proximity of the ex-English

Col J. Berry's "Fair Season"

colt Flaming Temper, who was two lengths away in third place. As a matter of interest, when details of this race first appeared in the English Press, Fair Season was variously reported as having won by half a length, by a length and by five lengths. The distances as we have given them are those measured from a side-on photo of the finish published in *Sport et Turf*. One shouldn't leave the Grand Criterium without adding that this valuable race is at the mercy of any decent English-trained youngster, and in his heyday as an owner Mr David Robinson regularly used to win it. In general, Belgian-trained horses are of very poor quality. Belgium, incidentally, is one country in Europe which will accept English flat racers straight away into handicap company, and Timeform ratings are used as a guide to determining their weights.

Fair Season (b.c. 1974)	Silly Season (br 1962)	Tom Fool (b 1949)	Menow
			Gaga
		Double Deal (b 1946)	Straight Deal
			Nonats
	Fairy Ring (gr 1967)	Quorum (gr 1954)	Vilmorin
			Akimbo
		Royal Myth (ch 1951)	Marsyas II
			Eleanor Cross

Although the ground was returned officially as firm when he won the Grand Criterium, we are satisfied that Fair Season is at his best on an easy surface, and one should be wary of backing him to run to his rating when the going is on the fast side. A strong, attractive colt, Fair Season is the third foal of his dam, Fairy Ring, and a half-brother to the moderate three-year-old maiden Roundtown (by Connaught) and the Sing Sing filly Fairy Song, who won over five furlongs as a two-year-old in 1974. Fairy Ring won over a mile on softish going as a three-year-old, and stayed at least a mile and a quarter: she is a half-sister to Tudor Tale (by King of the Tudors), a very useful stayer. Fair Season will probably stay at least as well as his dam did. It is not to be expected that he will make the improvement necessary to be considered seriously for the Two Thousand Guineas. But he is, as we have said, a good colt, and it will be surprising if he doesn't win more races when conditions are testing. *I. Balding.*

FAIRSINGH   2 ch.g. Mansingh 120–Fair Nina 91 (Set Fair 129) [1976 5d]   — leggy gelding: behind in 18-runner minor event at Catterick in May, only outing: dead. *L. Shedden.*

FAIR STRIPPER   2 b.f. Veiled Wonder–Fairennis (Ennis 128) [1976 5fg 5f6   **55** 5.1f3 5f6 6d 5s]   poor plater: should stay 6f: blinkered fourth and fifth outings: sold 440 gns Newmarket Autumn Sales. *G. Blum.*

FAIR VICTORY   3 ch.f. Double Jump 131–Bright Windsor 81 (Narrator 127)   — [1975 5v5 5d* 6fg 8d 7fg   1976 8s]   lengthy filly: won small race at Sandown as a 2-y-o: not seen out in 1976 until October and was well beaten (had stiff task, was bandaged in front and needed race): not certain to stay 1m: acts on a soft surface and is possibly unsuited by a firm one. *Lady Herries.*

FAIRY CARAVAN   3 ch.f. Sky Gipsy 117–Cherry Burton 79 (Kalydon 122)   **73** [1975 5d2 5g4 5g3 5g5 5fg2 7f 5g3 6g3   1976 6v5 5d5 5g3 6g 5fg4 7f4 8.2g 8d* 8.2d5 6v 8s 8s*]   leggy, light-framed filly: quite a moderate performer: won seller at Redcar in September (bought in 1,000 gns) and handicap at Chepstow the following month (beat Orange Gin 2½ lengths): probably needs further than 6f nowadays, and stays 1m: acts on any going: sold 550 gns Doncaster November Sales. *E. Cousins.*

FAIRY FISHERMAN   2 b.c. Captain's Gig–Pixie Jet 105 (Polly's Jet) [1976   **98** 7fg2 7f* 7d 6v]   strong, deep-bodied colt: half-brother to four winners, including 7f and 9f winner Texas Boy (by Astec): 4,400 gns yearling: dam 5f sprinter: odds on for 14-runner minor event at Yarmouth in July and made all to win easily by 3 lengths from Aston Firs: not seen out again until October when in rear in nurseries at Newmarket (well-backed favourite) and Nottingham but had stiffish tasks: will stay 1m: acts on firm going. *J. Hindley.*

FALCON'S HEIR   4 br.c. Falcon 131–Aunt Cathy (Khalkis 127) [1974 5d 6fg   **68** 6s   1975 6s 7s2 6f3 7f 5h5 5.8f4 5g 6d 6f 9g   1976 6fg 6g 8s5 10.2s2]   strong colt: ran best race at 4 yrs on final appearance: needs further than 5f and stays 1¼m: acts on any going: ran poorly when tried in blinkers. *R. Akehurst.*

FALIRAKI 3 b.c. Prince Tenderfoot 126–Super Flower 64 (Super Sam 124) **125**
[1975 5s⁵ 5v 5d⁴ 5s* 5g⁴ 5f² 5f* 5g⁴ 1976 7f 5fg² 5g³ 5f⁵ 5fg² 5s]
The three-year-old sprinters in Europe were the least inspiring collection
since 1966, and Faliraki, who had some claim to be considered the best of them,
went through the season without a win. Of the nineteen sprint pattern races
run in England, Ireland and France open to three-year-olds and upwards,
only seven fell to three-year-olds. Of these seven one was the Prix de l'Abbaye
de Longchamp in which Gentilhombre only shared the spoils with the year-
older Mendip Man and another was the Ballyogan Stakes, recently established
as Ireland's solitary pattern-race sprint, but in 1976 carrying a first prize of
only £2,378 and as yet of no international significance. A sharp contrast
indeed with 1969 when the three-year-olds, headed by Song, Tudor Music,
Tower Walk and Burglar, carried off fifteen of the important sprints! It wasn't
as though the older sprinters in 1976 were, as a group, of extraordinarily high
quality. Lochnager was outstanding, but the likes of Roman Warrior, Three
Legs, Record Token, Honeyblest, Girl Friend, Hillandale, Polly Peachum,
Be Tuneful and Import are hardly our idea of exceptional sprinters.
Faliraki came closest to winning when runner-up in the William Hill Sprint
Championship at York in August. He went to post with three respectable
efforts behind him: he had run Polly Peachum to three quarters of a length
in the Palace House Stakes at Newmarket, and had twice been beaten by
Lochnager, by just over two lengths into third place in the Temple Stakes at
Sandown and by just under five lengths into fifth in the King's Stand Stakes
at Royal Ascot. Faliraki started at 16/1 at York. After losing ground by
switching behind the leaders on to the far rail early on, he looked likely to
be run off his feet at halfway, but responded really well to strong riding and
produced a last-furlong rattle which must have given Lochnager's supporters
palpitations even though Lochnager had half a length to spare at the post.
This was a fine effort by Faliraki, particularly as beforehand he had spread a
plate which was taken off and not replaced.
In the absence of Lochnager, Faliraki started a heavily-backed favourite
for his only subsequent race, the Prix de l'Abbaye at Longchamp. We've
never seen him look better—he was outstanding in the paddock—and, of course,
his run at York gave him an obvious chance. However, after breaking well
he came under the whip at halfway and folded up very quickly. He finished
eighth of ten, about five lengths behind the dead-heaters Gentilhombre, who
had finished just over two lengths behind him in the William Hill, and Mendip
Man.

Faliraki (b.c. 1973)	Prince Tenderfoot (b 1967)	Blue Prince (b 1951)	Princequillo
			Blue Denim
		La Tendresse (b 1959)	Grey Sovereign
			Isetta
	Super Flower (b 1968)	Super Sam (br 1962)	Above Suspicion
			Samaria
		Kingsworthy (b 1953)	Kingstone
			Sotades

Faliraki is from the second crop of the sprinter Prince Tenderfoot who is
proving a valuable addition to the Irish stallion ranks, having sired Duke
Ellington, Icing, Lord Henham, Tender Camilla and the two-year-olds Athlete's
Foot, winner of the Sir Gatric Stakes, and Silk Slipper, winner of the Prix
des Chenes. Faliraki is the first foal of Super Flower, a moderate half-sister
to the high-class two-year-old Typhoon and the very successful American
broodmare Moment of Truth. A strong, well-made colt who cost 6,200 guineas
as a yearling, Faliraki should certainly stay six furlongs, although he is evidently
regarded by connections as a five-furlong horse. His one attempt at a distance
beyond five furlongs was in the seven-furlong Vauxhall Trial at Phoenix
Park, when far from cherry-ripe he finished a well-beaten ninth behind Lucky
Wednesday. Faliraki won on soft going as a two-year-old but subsequently
showed much better form when winning the Norfolk Stakes at Royal Ascot on
firm, and in the light of his failure in the Longchamp mud it's reasonable to suppose that he is best suited by top-of-the-ground conditions. He will be racing
in the United States as a four-year-old. *M. O'Toole, Ireland.*

FALL TO PIECES 3 ch.f. Forli–Durani (Bold Ruler) [1975 6g 7g³ 7g* 1976 **101**
8d² 8fg* 8fg⁶ 8d⁶ 8.2v] big, strong, quite well-made American-bred filly: showed
improved form to win Fern Hill Handicap at Ascot in June by 6 lengths from
Solar: didn't reproduce that running, and ran poorly behind Handycuff in

handicap at Haydock in October on final outing: stayed 1m: acted on a firm surface and was probably unsuited by heavy ground: stud. *P. Walwyn.*

FALSECHO 2 b.f. Relko 136–Silent Swindler 59 (Tacitus 124) [1976 7h 7g 7.5g 7v 6.5v 7.5d 8.2v] first foal: dam won 1½m seller: 20/1 when remote seventh of 13 to Do Good in maiden race at Bath in July: little worthwhile form, including in sellers, in France subsequently: trained by D. Hanley on first outing. *W. Gill, France.* —

FAMILY PORTRAIT 3 ch.f. Henry the Seventh 125–Mura 68 (Romulus 129) [1975 6g5 6g4 6f 6g 1976 6v 6fg 6d] leggy, light-framed filly: poor plater: will stay 1m: sold 340 gns Newmarket July Sales. *E. Cousins.* —

FANCY SOVEREIGN 2 b.c. Lucky Sovereign–Fancy Star 87 (Star Gazer 123) [1976 5.9s] half-brother to two winners by Dunoon Star: dam fair winner at 2 yrs: tailed off in 16-runner maiden race won by Fear Naught at Wolverhampton in October. *L. Barratt.* —

FANCY STREAK 3 ch.f. Firestreak 125–Fanciful (Infatuation 129) [1975 5s5 5s4 5f* 6fg3 6h2 6fg3 5g4 6d 1976 8fg 7fg] unfurnished filly: narrow winner of maiden event at Catterick in 1975: broke leg in seller at Sandown in June and was destroyed. *R. Keenor.* —

FANLINGERER 2 ch.c. Swing Easy 126–Candytuft 110 (Mossborough 126) [1976 5fg6 6g 7v] lengthy colt: good mover: half-brother to several minor winners: 4,500 gns yearling: dam very useful at 2 yrs: poor form in maiden races: blinkered final outing: sold 300 gns Ascot December Sales. *N. Vigors.* 67

FANTASY ROYALE 2 b.f. Breeders Dream 116–Queen's Penny (Queen's Hussar 124) [1976 5fg 5g 5fg2 5.1f2 6g 5s4] tall filly: second foal: half-sister to very smart Hillandale (by Crossing The T), a winner at up to 7f: dam never ran: moderate maiden: good fourth of nine to La Ville de Rire in Doncaster Stakes in October: will stay 7f: acts on any going: trained by D. Keith on first outing. *N. Adam.* 84

FARCROFT 2 br.f. Country Retreat 91–Dunwen (Dumbarnie 125) [1976 5fg 7g 6fg 5.8f] third foal: 200 gns yearling: dam ran only once: in rear in minor and maiden events. *F. Walwyn.* —

FAR CRY 5 ch.h. Weepers Boy 124–Warning Note (Premonition 130) [1974 7.6g 5f6 5g* 5fg 5g2 5g4 5g 1975 5.8g 6g4 6fg2 6f2 6fg5 5.8f2 5f3 6d 7fg2 5.8f 1976 5.8f2 6f* 6g6 6fg 7f4] big, strong horse: won handicap at Folkestone in May by 1½ lengths from Talarea: evidently stays 7f: acts on firm going: suitable mount for an apprentice. *S. Woodman.* 68

FARE 3 b.f. Le Dieu d'Or 119–Sue's Last (Como 120) [1975 N.R. 1976 9v 10.2s] strong filly: fourth foal: half-sister to a winning hurdler: dam of no account: backward when tailed off in maiden races at York and Doncaster in October: retained 1,200 gns Doncaster November Sales. *N. Crump.* —

FAREWELL BLEEP 4 b.g. Bleep-Bleep 134–Night Final 78 (Darius 129) [1974 5d* 5f2 5f3 5f3 5f5 5fg 5g5 6fg 5d 6g 5d 1975 6g6 5g 6f* 6fg 7f5 6d 1976 7g 6v3 7g2 7f4 6g] robust, well-made gelding: plater: ran respectably on a couple of occasions at 4 yrs but is inconsistent: was sold to M. Tate 850 gns Ascot July Sales: stays 7f: seems to act on any going. *W. Marshall.* 62

FARFISA 3 ch.f. Sassafras 135–Music Mistress (Guide 118) [1975 6g 1976 12f3 14fg* 16f5 14f* 14f* 16.9f3 14f* 14f3 14d6] leggy, unfurnished filly: successful four times at Yarmouth, on last occasion putting up a particularly good effort when beating Dolben Lad ¾ length in handicap in August: stays well: acts well on firm going: genuine but ran below her best last two outings. *M. Stoute.* 86

FARIDETTA 2 gr.f. Good Bond 122–Farida Jinks 106 (Tudor Jinks 121) [1976 5d4 5g* 5fg* 5fg* 5fg* 5fg2 5fg4 6v4 5g6] quite well-made filly: half-sister to four winners, including useful sprinter Faridina (by Sky Gipsy): dam 5f sprinter: a useful and speedy filly who kept her form well and won at Haydock, York (twice) and Newcastle, her last three wins coming in events worth at least £2,000 to the winner: also put up a very good effort when favourite for Molecomb Stakes at Goodwood in July, going down by only ½ length to Be Easy after making running: probably stays 6f: genuine and consistent. *I. Walker.* 107

FARIDINA 4 b.f. Sky Gipsy 117–Farida Jinks 106 (Tudor Jinks 121) [1974 5fg 5.9fg 5d* 5s 5d3 1975 5s3 5fg 5g6 5g5 5s4 5g3 5s* 5g* 5g* 1976 5fg3 5d6 5fg 5g 5g3 5g3 6d6 5s* 5s* 5s4] lengthy, short-legged filly: fair handicapper: winner at Doncaster and Haydock in October: also ran well when third (badly 88

Dick Turpin Stakes, York—Faridetta keeps Petinara at bay

hampered and was possibly an unlucky loser) to Overtown in Crocker Bulteel Stakes at Ascot in May on reappearance: best form at 5f: extremely well suited by some give in the ground: suitable mount for an apprentice: genuine. *I. Walker.*

FARMER'S GLORY 3 br.g. Behistoun 131–Miss Alice 80 (High Hat 131) [1975 5g 7g 7g 1976 12g] tall, fair sort of gelding: well beaten in minor and maiden races. *T. M. Jones.*   —

FARM GAZER 5 b.m. Star Gazer 123–The Farmer's Wife 86 (Royal Challenger 129) [1974 6f 7fg² 6f* 7fg* 6f² 1975 5v6 6g⁴ 6fg6 5.9t² 5fg² 5f⁵ 5.8f⁵ 7f* 6f 6g 7fg⁴ 1976 8g 7g 8f 7fg 7f⁴ 6f 7f⁴] leggy mare: poor handicapper nowadays: stays 7f: seems to act on any going but goes particularly well on firm: ran creditably when tried in blinkers: has worn bandages: sold to F. Yardley 470 gns Ascot September Sales. *R. Bastiman.*   **45**

FAR MUK LAN 5 ch.m. Bluerullah 115–Sagaris (Milesian 125) [1974 5v 7s 8s 1975 8f 8h 1976 9f] poor plater: has been tried in blinkers. *W. Williams.*   —

FAR NORTH 3 b.c. Northern Dancer–Fleur (Victoria Park) [1975 7g⁴ 8g* 9s* 1976 8g* 10.5fg 12f⁵ 10g] American-bred French colt: brother to top-class 2-y-o The Minstrel: showed very smart form at 2 yrs, winning Group 3 Prix Saint-Roman at Longchamp by 2½ lengths from Youth: made all when winning Prix Omnium at Saint-Cloud in March: put up easily best effort after-wards when 6½ lengths fifth of 17 to Malacate in Irish Sweeps Derby at the Curragh in June (ran poorly in Prix Daru and Prix de la Cote Normande on his other two starts): apparently stays 1½m: seems to act on any going: tends to get very worked up before his races. *J. Fellows, France.*   **119**

FARTHING 2 b.f. Maystreak 118–Clouds of Gold (Goldhill 125) [1976 6f 6g 5f⁴ 5s] small filly: first foal: dam never ran: little worthwhile form in maiden and minor events: should be suited by 6f. *W. Elsey.*   —

FASCHING 2 b.f. Silly Season 127–Ostrya 116 (Hornbeam 130) [1976 7g²] half-sister to several winners, including Ribblesdale Stakes winner Catalba (by Reform): dam won 1963 Ribblesdale Stakes: favourite for 18-runner maiden race at Yarmouth in September and ran well, finishing 2½ lengths second to Unella after leading from 2f out to inside final furlong: will stay 1¼m: sure to be better for this experience and will win a race. *H. Cecil.*   **80 p**

FASCINATING RHYTHM 2 ch.f. Porto Bello 118–Lovely Evening 85 (Henry the Seventh 125) [1976 6fg 7fg⁴ 6fg 6d⁴] quite a modest plater: stays 7f. *S. Ingham.*   **54**

FASSAROE 2 ch.c. Sassafras 135–Silken Yogan 115 (Ballyogan) [1976 7f 7g⁴*] Irish colt: half-brother to several winners, including very useful 1973 Irish 2-y-o 7f and 1m winner Silk Buds (by Busted): dam 5f sprinter, at her best at 2 yrs: got up close home when winning eight-runner maiden race at Leopardstown in August by a head from Mississipi, the pair finishing 10 lengths clear: will be suited by 1m: started slowly on first outing: probably a very useful colt in the making. *S. McGrath, Ireland.*   **102 p**

FAST DELIVERY 2 b.c. Yellow God 129–Sens Unique 79 (Faubourg II 127) [1976 5f⁴ 5f 5s² 6fg 6f* 6fg⁵ 5f³ 6fg 5g* 5fg 5g 5fg] small, robust colt: comfort-   **81**

FEA

able winner of seller at Nottingham in June (no bid) and put up a really good effort to win four-runner nursery at Newcastle in August when apprentice ridden at 12 lb overweight: stays 6f but has shown best form at 5f: acts on any going: to be trained by S. Wainwright. *K. Payne.*

FAST FLO 3 ch.f. Clear River 114–Quicken (Falls of Clyde 126) [1975 6g 5f 5f 1976 8h⁶ 10.2h⁴ 5.8h] lightly-made filly: well beaten in maiden races and sellers. *L. Kennard.* —

FAST FRIGATE 2 gr.c. Sea Hawk II 131–Swift Protectress (Court Martial) [1976 7g* 7f* 7g⁶ 8s²] well-made, very attractive colt: fourth foal: 8,000 gns yearling: dam won three minor races at around 1m in France: successful on first two outings, making up a lot of ground in straight when scoring by 4 lengths from Sovereign Ford in minor event at Sandown in July and giving weight all round when beating Crepe Paper a head in similar race at Salisbury the following month: proved no match for Night Before in eight-runner minor event at Goodwood in September and went down by 5 lengths: will stay 1¼m+: acts on any going. *I. Balding.* **96**

FAST JOKER 2 b.c. Fast Hilarious–Fortress (Hill Prince) [1976 5fg⁵ 6g⁴ 7f⁶ 8g 7s] compact American-bred colt: half-brother to three minor winners in U.S.A.: cost $15,000 at Hialeah 2-y-o's in Training Sales: dam won one of her 28 starts: showed ability in maiden and minor events in the summer: off course two months after third outing and had stiffish tasks in nurseries on his return: should be suited by 1m. *R. Armstrong.* **80**

FAST MOVER 4 b.c. Runnymede 123–Emma Peecher (Quorum 126) [1974 5f 5f* 5fg⁵ 6d 7v 1975 7s⁴ 8g 10s 9fg⁵ 10h⁴ 8fg² 8f³ 8f² 8fg 10g⁴ 9fg² 10f³ 10g 1976 8fg* 8.2v³] small colt: poor plater: successful at Leicester in March (no bid): stays 1¼m: best form on a sound surface: does best in blinkers. *J. Hardy.* **53**

FAST SOVEREIGN 3 br.f. Track Spare 125–Smart Sovereign 72 (Smartie 102) [1975 5fg 5d 5d 1976 7fg 7fg 6fg 6g 8.2f] poor plater: should stay 1m: blinkered last two outings: sold 330 gns Ascot September Sales. *R. Mason.* —

FATHER FIGURE 3 ch.g. Majority Blue 126–Metrovision (Golden Vision 105) [1975 5fg 6f⁶ 1976 10.1fg 10.1f⁶ 9f 10fg 10.1fg³ 10f² 10.1fg³ 10.1fg³ 10s³ 10v²] half-brother to three winners by Gulf Pearl, including Ebor winner Anji: showed a little ability in maiden races: stayed 1¼m: blinkered eighth outing: dead. *A. Pitt.* **66**

FATHERLESS 3 b.f. Ragusa 137–Clippie 99 (Nimbus 130) [1975 N.R. 1976 10.1d³ 8.2d⁴] half-sister to several winners, including quite useful stayer Harridan (by Fighting Charlie) and quite useful 2-y-o 6f winners Crowdie (by Crepello) and Erebus (by Sammy Davis), 13,500 gns yearling: dam won at up to 1m: in frame in maiden races at Windsor and Nottingham in September: gives impression she needs further than 1m and will stay 1½m. *F. J. Houghton.* **63**

FAVEDO 7 b.g. Molvedo 137–Afdera (Cranach) [1974 12f* 12g* 12g 12g⁶ 12g⁶ 10g³ 1975 12f⁵ 12f⁴ 12f⁵ 1976 17.7f 12fg⁵ 14fg] unfurnished gelding: quite a moderate handicapper: best at up to 1½m: acts on firm going. *R. Akehurst.* —

FAWN 2 b.f. Tom Rolfe–Chocolate Beau (Beau Max) [1976 6fg³ 6f*] neat, strong American-bred filly: half-sister to several winners, including stakes winners Satin Gold (by Tulyar) and Olmec (by Pago Pago): dam a stakes winner at 2 yrs: fulfilled the promise of her first outing when running out a comfortable winner of 19-runner maiden race at Ripon in August, making all to beat Great Sign 3 lengths: will stay 1m. *H. Cecil.* **93**

FEARLESS BOY 3 ch.c. Yellow God 129–Madam Clare 66 (Ennis 128) [1974 5s³ 5v³ 5g⁴ 6d* 1975 5.9g³ 6s* 6fg⁵ 6g² 6f 6fg 6g⁶ 6g³ 5v² 1976 5.9fg⁵ 6s² 7f* 7g³ 7d* 7f³ 7fg⁴ 7g² 6d 7v 7v] strong, attractive colt: moderate handicapper: successful at Newcastle in April and at Redcar the following month and ran well in some of his other races: needs further than 5f to be seen to advantage nowadays and may well stay further than 7f: acts on any going: genuine: sweated up sixth start. *M. Jarvis.* **81**

FEARLESS LAD 2 b.c. Gold Rod 129–Fearless Lady 92 (Privy Councillor 125) [1976 6f 5fg 5d 5d] good-looking colt: third foal: dam genuine sprinter: little worthwhile form in maiden races and his ability does not match his looks. *G. Smyth.* —

FEAR NAUGHT 2 b.f. Connaught 130–Brave Huntress (Big Game) [1976 7v 5.9s*] half-sister to three winners, including fairly useful 1½m handicapper Noirmont Point (by Hornbeam): 1,900 gns yearling: dam of no account: backed **82**

245

from 20/1 to 6/1, got up close home to win 18-runner maiden race at Wolverhampton in October by a neck from Venturus: will stay 1¼m. *J. Etherington.*

FEATHER TOP 5 b.m. Falcon 131–Invermore (Anwar 120) [1974 7fg 9f⁴ **60** 10.8g² 10.2g* 10g⁴ 10fg⁴ 10fg³ 10g 12s² 12v* 1975 12g 12g³ 1976 12g⁵] strong, well-made mare, and a good mover: ran respectably in apprentice handicap at Ascot in May on only outing in 1976: suited by 1½m nowadays: seems to act on any going: suitable mount for an inexperienced rider. *D. Underwood.*

FELCOURT 3 b.g. Long Till 113–Light Gold (Le Dieu d'Or 119) [1975 N.R. — 1976 16h⁵] second foal: dam poor novice hurdler/chaser: 25/1 when tailed-off last of five behind Cold Justice in maiden race at Lingfield in June. *M. Bolton.*

FELICE 2 ch.c. Porto Bello 118–Cherio Honey (Macherio) [1976 5fg³ 5f² 5f⁵ **78** 6fg⁴ 5.9f⁴ 7g] attractive colt: good mover: first reported foal: 1,800 gns yearling: dam half-sister to 1,000 Guineas runner-up Super Honey: quite a moderate maiden: should stay 7f (had plenty to do when well beaten over that distance). *Doug Smith.*

FELL SWOOP 5 b.m. Falcon 131–Aurora Polaris (Borealis) [1974 10.1fg 10f 7f **51** 8d 7fg 10g³ 12s⁶ 10d³ 1975 13s 10g 1976 14f² 15.5s] small mare: only a poor performer on Flat but is a fairly useful hurdler: stays 1¾m: acts on any going: best in blinkers. *J. Benstead.*

FEMINIST 2 b.f. Reform 132–Joan of Arc 94 (Never Say Die 137) [1976 6g⁴ **65** 6fg³ 6fg 7g 8fg⁶] shapely, good-bodied, attractive filly: has a round action: half-sister to two minor winners abroad: 11,000 gns yearling: dam, half-sister to eleven winners, won at 1¼m: in frame in maiden races in July at Newmarket (18-runner event) and Windsor (4¾ lengths third of 15 to Haighall): should stay 1¼m: usually blinkered. *B. Hanbury.*

FENNY BOY 2 b.c. Dedini–Petite Charlotte 74 (Charlottesville 135) [1976 5fg⁵ **83** 5f² 5g* 5f⁴ 6fg 6fg 6d 5s² 5s⁶] strong colt: first produce: 220 gns foal: dam won over 1½m: had field quite well strung out when winning 16-runner maiden race at Salisbury in May by 1½ lengths from Chichester Bird: put up by far his best effort afterwards when blinkered first time, finishing neck second to Karella in nursery at Warwick in October: again blinkered on final outing: form only at 5f but should be suited by 6f+: acts on any going. *G. Cottrell.*

FERBAIN FLYER 4 b.c. Prince des Loges 73–Santa Marta 51 (Lavandin 128) — [1974 N.R. 1975 N.R. 1976 16g⁶ 16.1d 22.2f 14s⁵] tall, rangy colt: poor staying maiden: trained first three races by R. Sturdy. *M. Haynes.*

FERRYBRIDGE 3 ch.f. St Paddy 133–Queensferry 81 (Pindari 124) [1975 6g **84** 7fg² 1976 8.5fg³ 10fg⁴ 10fg⁶ 10.2s² 10.6v*] lengthy filly: won weakly-contested maiden race at Haydock in October by 10 lengths: will stay 1½m: appears to act on any going: blinkered last two outings: sold 8,800 gns Newmarket December Sales. *N. Murless.*

FERRY POINT 6 b.g. Forlorn River 124–Tudera (Primera 131) [1974 N.R. — 1975 N.R. 1976 13.1s] rated 62 in 1973: having first outing since when well behind in minor event at Bath in October won by Regalian: stays 9f: acts on firm going. *L. Kennard.*

FESTIVAL HALL 3 b.c. Habitat 134–Symphonie (Tambourine II 133) [1975 **82** 6fg 1976 8fg 10.1f⁴ 8fg 8.2d* 10s²] very attractive, neat colt: tried in blinkers, showed first worthwhile form when winning 17-runner maiden race at Haydock in October by 2 lengths from Bally Tudor, the pair finishing clear: again blinkered when creditable second to Blyth's Folly in minor event at Sandown later in month: stays 1¼m: acts on soft going: sold to R. Armstrong 5,800 gns Newmarket Autumn Sales. *H. Wragg.*

FETCHING 2 b.f. Falcon 131–Only a Game (Whistling Wind 123) [1976 5f 5f² **87** 5f³ 5fg⁴ 5f*] Irish filly: second foal: half-sister to fairly useful 1975 Irish 2-y-o 5f winner Only a Take (by Takawalk II): 1,900 gns yearling: dam quite useful Irish sprinter: 3½ lengths fourth of six to Al Stanza in Erroll Stakes at Ascot in June: not seen out again until late-August when winning four-runner maiden race at Down Royal by ¾ length from Mrs Bee: should stay 6f: sold 4,500 gns Goffs August Sales. *M. O'Toole, Ireland.*

FETTERCAIRN 2 b.c. Manacle 123–Miss Atalanta 83 (Hethersett 134) [1976 **71** 5s³ 8g⁶] fourth produce: 780 gns foal and resold 19,000 gns yearling: dam placed over 7f at 2 yrs: close-up third of nine to Dam Water in maiden race at Ayr in May: not seen out again until October when co-favourite for 20-runner minor event at Lanark and ran respectably to finish 4½ lengths sixth to Harriet Air: probably stays 1m. *N. Angus.*

Hilary Needler Trophy, Beverley—Feudal Wytch is chased home by La Raine

FETTERED 2 b.c. Manacle 123–Anatevka (Privy Councillor 125) [1976 5fg **70**
6d³ 7h⁶ 7fg⁴ 6f⁴ 8fg⁵ 7v⁶ 6s] useful-looking colt: quite a moderate maiden: best
form at 7f (had stiff task and was hampered 1f out when tried at 1m): ran poorly
on hard going but probably acts on any other. *M. W. Easterby.*

FEUDAL WYTCH 2 b.f. Tribal Chief 125–Whistlewych 40 (Whistler 129) **108**
[1976 5fg 5d* 5f* 6fg⁶ 6g³ 7g⁴ 6fg* 6g⁴ 6g⁵ 6v³] useful-looking filly: half-sister
to 1975 2-y-o 6f winner Blue Jet (by Blue and Grey): dam of little account: had
an excellent season, winning a maiden race at Redcar, Hilary Needler Trophy at
Beverley and £2,100 nursery at York: put in a strong late run to catch Hand
Canter when winning last-named race by a neck in August: probably stays 7f,
but best form at 6f: appears to act on any going, except perhaps heavy. *J. Carr.*

FIANDRA 6 b.m. Linacre 133–Gay Rita (Eudaemon 129) [1974 N.R. 1975 **—**
N.R. 1976 18s] useless. *J. Twibell.*

FIBEEL 2 b.f. Most Secret 119–Maudavil 82 (Ennis 128) [1976 5fg⁶ 5g² 5g³ **72**
5h*] neat, strong filly: won three-runner maiden event at Carlisle in July very
smoothly by 5 lengths from Doublette: will probably stay 6f. *M. H. Easterby.*

FIDELIS 3 ch.f. Communication 119–Menith Wood (Lancewood) [1975 N.R. **—**
1976 8h 9f] half-sister to fair 1m selling handicapper Miss Renworth (by Blast):
dam of no account: tailed off in maiden races. *O. O'Neill.*

FIELD MARSHALL 3 gr.c. St Paddy 133–Field Mouse 108 (Grey Sovereign **61**
128 §) [1975 5g⁴ 5d³ 5s 5f 6f² 6f 6fg 7f 8f² 8f 1976 7g 11.1fg 10f 10f⁵ 16f⁴ 12g⁵
8.2d⁶ 12g⁴ 11f⁴ 8.2g⁶ 16fg 12g 8g 12.2fg⁶ 12v 12s] powerful, well-grown colt:
half-brother to smart 2-y-o Triple First (by High Top): poor maiden: best form
at around 1½m: acts on firm going and is probably unsuited by soft: occasionally
wears blinkers but does better without. *M. Stevens.*

FIELD MOSS 4 gr.g. Levmoss 133–Just Alice (Worden II 129) [1974 6s 7g 8s **—**
9s³ 8s 1975 9v 10f 10.1s⁵ 12g⁴ 13d 16.1d⁵ 16g⁴ 1976 9fg 10.1fg 12s 13.8g 15.8f⁴
12.2f] of little account. *J. Twibell.*

FIERY LADY 2 b.f. Firestreak 125–Panama Rag 77 (Welsh Rake 118) [1976 **43**
5f⁶ 5h 5f] small filly: bad plater: sold 320 gns Doncaster June Sales. *J. Carr.*

FIERY RING 4 b.c. Round Table–Napalm (Nilo 101) [1974 6g⁶ 7d 1975 8d⁵ **—**
10g³ 12f⁶ 10g* 12fg* 12fg² 12d² 11.7g 1976 12fg⁴ 14g] very attractive
American-bred colt: very good mover: quite useful handicapper (rated 95) at
3 yrs: raced only twice in 1976 and appeared to take little interest in proceedings
when well beaten on second start (blinkered): stays 1½m: acts on a firm surface
but might be best suited by an easy one. *R. Hern.*

247

Washington Singer Stakes, Newbury—Fife and Drum takes care of his two opponents Regency Bill and Mr Nice Guy

FIFE AND DRUM   2 b.c. Queen's Hussar 124–Heathfield 99 (Hethersett 134) **111 p** [1976 6g* 6fg*].

A slight illness prevented Fife and Drum taking his chance in the Mill Reef Stakes at Newbury in September, and so denied us the opportunity of getting a clearer idea of his ability.   A race against the likes of Anax and Adviser would have told us much more about him than his two previous runs. We know that he's a very useful colt but is he a classic prospect?   He certainly looked one on his first appearance, in the valuable Strathclyde Stakes at Ayr in July, when he ran on strongly from halfway, caught Forty Winks inside the final furlong and strode away to win by two and a half lengths.   Further back were some good horses, among them Feudal Wytch and La Ville de Rire.   It had to be borne in mind, though, that Fife and Drum was receiving a fair amount of weight from most of the others; Forty Winks was giving him the best part of a stone.

Fife and Drum met two rivals at level weights on his next outing, in the Washington Singer Stakes at Newbury in August, and wasn't nearly so impressive.   The two that took him on were those tough colts Regency Bill and Mr Nice Guy but, admirable as each of these is, neither is anywhere near top class. Fife and Drum was expected to beat them easily and started at 5/2 on.   He was tucked in behind as Regency Bill made the running, and was pulled out to challenge at halfway.   He needed a fair amount of driving to hit the front coming to the final furlong but then kept on well enough, despite flashing his tail a couple of times, to beat Regency Bill by a length.   He can't be regarded as a potential classic horse on this performance, but our race-reader thought he looked still very big and burly in the paddock, and attributed his tail-swishing to greenness.   There is improvement in Fife and Drum, but we doubt whether it will be enough to put him among the best three-year-olds.

Fife and Drum (b. c. 1974)	Queen's Hussar (b 1960)	March Past (br 1950)	Petition / Marcelette
		Jojo (gr 1950)	Vilmorin / Mary Jane
	Heathfield (b 1966)	Hethersett (b 1959)	Hugh Lupus / Bride Elect
		Court Caprice (b 1956)	Court Martial / Whimbrel

Fife and Drum is the fourth foal and third winner produced by Heathfield, who has proved well worth the 11,000 guineas she cost the Queen at the end of her racing days.   Heathfield is a product of extremes, being by the St Leger

248

winner Hethersett out of the useful Court Caprice who ran exclusively at five furlongs. Her connections tried her from five furlongs to a mile and a half, and her three wins were between six furlongs and a mile. Her first foal, the Sovereign Path colt Ascot Heath, won a small race at Nottingham for the Queen and showed much better form in France the following year, winning four times at up to a mile and finishing third to Lianga in the Prix Maurice de Gheest. Heathfield's other winner, the three-year-old filly Crofting (by Crepello), didn't quite live up to expectations but showed useful form over a mile and a quarter. Fife and Drum's third dam Whimbrel is the third dam of Bruni, but we don't expect Fife and Drum to stay anything like as well as he. A mile should suit him admirably and he may get a furlong or two more. A strong, deep-girthed, well-made colt, he is said by his connections to need a bit of give in the ground. *W. Hern.*

FIGHTING BRAVE 4 b.c. Huntercombe 133–Alemena (Acropolis 132) [1974 **87** 5s 5.8g² 7g² 6fg² 7s 6v² 6s* 1975 7s* 8s³ 7d³ 7.6g² 7s² 7fg 9g* 8.3fg³ 8g³ 8.3g⁴ 8g⁴ 7.6s 1976 8g* 9fg* 8fg 8f⁴ 9g² 7.6f⁴ 8f² 9g³ 8fg* 8.2v⁵ 7.6v⁶] small, sturdy colt: fair handicapper: did well at 4 yrs, winning at Doncaster, Wolverhampton and Salisbury, gaining his final success when beating Track Hero ¾ length on last-named course in September: stays 9f: acts on any going but is particularly well suited by soft: good mount for an apprentice: genuine and consistent. *G. Harwood.*

FIGHTING KING 5 b.g. probably Timber King 95–Die Fighting (Fighting **49** Don) [1974 N.R. 1975 9v³ 8g⁴ 8fg⁵ 12g⁴ 1976 7fg³] strong gelding: poor maiden: lacks pace and is ideally suited by further than 7f: retained 2,400 gns Ascot October Sales. *Denys Smith.*

FIGHTING LADY 3 br.f. Chebs Lad 120–Donnarose (Fighting Don) [1975 5d³ **103** 5h³ 5f* 5f² 5f⁴ 7g⁶ 7f 6d 1976 7d² 7fg* 7s⁶ 8.2d⁵ 8f⁶ 7fg* 7fg* 6g] quite a useful sort: improved through season and picked up two good handicaps at Newmarket (the Glenlivet by a short head from The Hand and the Duchess of Montrose by a head from Net Call) and one at Newcastle (Beeswing Handicap by a neck from Running Jump): ideally suited by 7f on top-of-the-ground, although has run well over 1m on softish ground: blinkered final appearance in 1975: ran way below her best on final outing. *E. Collingwood.*

FIGHTING QUEEN 2 br.f. Gala Performance–Sutherland 73 (Typhoon 125) **58** [1976 5f 5d 5g 5d 5g⁴ 5fg⁶ 5fg⁶] moderate plater: will be better suited by 6f+: sold 390 gns Ascot October Sales. *Denys Smith.*

FIGURE OF SPEECH 3 br.g. Breeders Dream 116–Metaphor 79 (Nimbus 130) **51** [1975 5f 5fg 5g 1976 6fg² 8fg] small gelding: poor plater: blinkered both starts in this country in 1976: sold 1,500 gns Ascot May Sales and subsequently won in Belgium. *T. M. Jones.*

FILIPACHI 2 b.c. Great Nephew 126–Righteous Girl 93 (Right Boy 137) [1976 **97** 7g* 7s⁴] neat colt: half-brother to several winners, including fairly useful 1975 2-y-o 6f winner Dove (by Sea Hawk II): 5,400 gns yearling: dam ran only at 2 yrs, when winner at 5f and 6f: disputed lead all way when winning minor event at Kempton in August by a length from Cupid's Dew: had stiff task at weights but ran well when fourth to Lady Constance in £4,400 nursery at Lingfield the following month: will stay 1m. *B. Hanbury.*

FINAL BID 2 b.c. Busted 134–Pale Carnation (Palestine 133) [1976 6g⁵ 6fg] **66** strong, lengthy, very attractive colt: half-brother to three winners, including useful middle-distance performer Lightning Trial (by Parthia): 6,400 gns yearling: dam won over 1m and 1½m in Ireland: put up a promising first effort when fifth of eight to Mr Nice Guy in Woodcote Stakes at Epsom in June but ran moderately in maiden race at Nottingham the following month and was not seen out again: will stay 1¼m. *J. Sutcliffe.*

FINAL CALL 5 br.g. Town Crier 119–Marchella 62 (March Past 124) [1974 7fg **58** 9f⁶ 10f* 10g* 11s 8f* 10g 1975 10g 10fg⁴ 10f* 10f*(dis) 11.7fg² 12f² 12.2f⁵ 1976 12.2fg⁴ 12.2f⁶ 11.7f 11.7f] strong gelding: stayed 1½m but showed best form at 1¼m on firm going and seemed unsuited by soft: dead. *J. Cann.*

FINAL GIRL 2 br.f. Dadda Bert 95–Golden Mall (Pall Mall 132) [1976 5f 6f⁵] **—** neat filly: poor plater. *J. Hardy.*

FINE BLUE 3 br.c. French Vine 111 Devon Card (Devon Prince 99) [1975 **80** 6fg 7f 9g 1976 10fg 10fg² 8g* 10fg² 7fg³ 10d⁵ 8s 8.2v⁵] strong colt: won 19-runner maiden race at Newbury in July comfortably by 3 lengths from Hum: went under by ½ length to Ben Donachan in minor event at Lingfield the following month, best subsequent effort: needs further than 7f and will probably stay 1¼m. *P. Makin.*

FINE SPECIAL 2 b.f. Seaepic 100–Anasayra (Sayajirao 132) [1976 5fg 5d* 6d 7f⁵ 8.2d] light-framed filly: bought in 1,400 gns after winning seller at Hamilton in May: should stay 1m: reportedly exported to Trinidad. *P. Rohan.* **64**

FINEST WINE 2 b.c. Connaught 130–Alizarina (Ragusa 137) [1976 5d 7.2fg 7fg³ 7g] close-coupled colt: quite a moderate maiden: dead. *F. Carr.* **69**

FINGORA 3 b.c. Raffingora 130–Frisky Molly 64 (Dumbarnie 125) [1975 6g 5f* 5g³ 5h 6fg 1976 5fg 5f⁵ 6d⁵ 6g 6g 5fg⁵] strong colt: won maiden race at Ripon in 1975: had stiff tasks as a 3-y-o and showed no worthwhile form: stays 6f: tried in blinkers fourth outing. *W. C. Watts.* **—**

FINITE 2 b.c. American Native–Regilla (Fine Top 125) [1976 5g⁴ 5fg⁴ 6d² 5fg⁴ 6f* 6h* 7fg* 7f⁵ 7d] shapely colt: half-brother to two winners: 3,900 gns yearling: dam won over 1¼m in France at 3 yrs: won at Brighton in June and at Pontefract and Newcastle in July: beat four other previous winners at Pontefract, scoring by a neck from Charley's Revenge, and kept on well to land the odds by a head from Gio in £1,800 event at Newcastle: will stay at least 1m: appears to act on any going: sweated up considerably fourth outing: did well physically in 1976 and should be worth following as a 3-y-o *M. Stoute.* **103**

FINOCCHIO 3 gr.c. Reform 132–Twinkling Star § (Never Say Die 137) [1975 8g 1976 12fg 11g 14fg³ 14fg³] compact, short-legged colt: evidently suited by 1¾m: sold 2,100 gns Newmarket Autumn Sales. *H. Cecil.* **43**

FINTALEX 3 b.g. Prince Tenderfoot 126–All England 93 (St Paddy 133) [1975 5g 6fg 8.2d 1976 10g 6f 7fg 8f² 8d] plating-class maiden: stays 1m: sold to W. Clay 880 gns Doncaster September Sales. *D. Weeden.* **60**

FINTONA 3 ch.f. Galivanter 131–Tyrona 76 (Tyrone 130) [1975 N.R. 1976 9g 12g 12.2d² 12.2g⁶ 13s³ 14.7f⁵] lengthy filly: poor plater: seems to need long trips: sold 600 gns Doncaster November Sales. *R. D. Peacock.* **50**

FIRBY 2 b.c. Sit In The Corner–Monica Rose (Forlorn River 124) [1976 5g 5fg 6d 5fg⁶ 6f⁵ 7f⁵ 6f³ 6f²] well-made colt: quite a modest plater: best form at 6f: usually wears blinkers: exported to Denmark and is a winner there. *M. W. Easterby.* **59**

FIREBOAT 2 b.f. Firestreak 125–Saucy Moll 94 (Hard Sauce 131) [1976 5fg 5d 7f⁶ 6f⁴ 8f⁵ 6g⁶ 8fg 6v⁶ 8v] leggy filly: second foal: sister to 1975 2-y-o 6f winner Raggen: dam a stayer: quite a moderate maiden: effective at 6f to 1m: best form on a sound surface (ran below her best on heavy ground on last two outings, including in a seller): blinkered final appearance. *Hbt Jones.* **73**

FIREBREAK 3 b.f. Firestreak 125–Dike 54 (Petition 130) [1975 7g 6g 1976 7g⁶ 7fg⁴ 7f 6fg 7fg 6f 8d 12g] workmanlike filly: poor maiden: blinkered sixth start. *W. O'Gorman.* **—**

FIRE FAIRY 6 b.m. Firestreak 125–Fair Exchange II (Swaps) [1974 10g 12f⁵ 10f⁴ 14s 1975 10.1g³ 10fg* 12f² 10g⁵ 10.6fg⁶ 12f⁴ 1976 10f 12f⁵ 10h⁶] dipped-backed mare: little worthwhile form since winning ladies race at Sandown in 1975: probably stays 1½m: acts on firm going. *R. Sturdy.* **—**

FIRE GLAZE 3 ch.g. Laser Light 118–Nobody's Child (Skymaster 126) [1975 5d 5v² 5v⁴ 5g 5f⁶ 5g 1976 7.6fg] small gelding: poor plater: bolted before start on only outing, when apprentice ridden, and needs strong handling. *P. Milner.* **—**

FIREMAIDEN 2 b.f. Firestreak 125–Evvoia 53 (Khalkis 127) [1976 5f² 5f⁶ 6g⁴ 6f* 6f* 6fg² 6s⁵ 6v] fair sort: first foal: dam of no account: won maiden race at Redcar in August and put up an excellent effort under a penalty in nursery at Windsor later in month, getting up to win by a head from odds-on Breast Stroke: creditable **fifth** to Casino Boy in nursery at Newmarket in October: will stay 1m+: acts on any going: missed break sixth outing. *M. Jarvis.* **94**

FIREPATH 2 ch.f. Hotfoot 126–Lochailort 100 (Doutelle 128) [1976 5fg 5f 5s 7v] half-sister to four winners, including Norwegian Derby winner Tuloch (by Tudor Melody): 3,700 gns yearling: dam needed at least 1¾m: well beaten in maiden and minor events: will stay 1¼m: slowly into stride first two outings. *W. A. Stephenson.* **—**

FIRE PLAN 3 b.c. King's Troop 118–Daydreamer 78 (Star Gazer 123) [1975 5g⁴ 5.1f 7fg⁴ 7g³ 7f⁵ 6g⁴ 6fg 1976 7fg⁴ 7g⁵ 8f² 8.2f⁴ 10fg² 10f² 10fg 10.8f²] **58**

lightly-made colt: disappointing maiden: best form at 1m: acts on firm going: wore blinkers at 2 yrs and on seventh start. *J. Winter.*

FIRE-SCREEN 3 gr.f. Roan Rocket 128–Indolent 97 (Tyrone 130) [1975 6fg **76** 6s² 6fg⁵ 1976 8g 8f³ 7fg³ 8f² 10.2h*] rangy filly: won four-runner maiden race at Bath in August by 2 lengths from Springboard: stays 1¼m: acts on hard going: sold 3,500 gns Newmarket December Sales. *J. Winter.*

FIRESILK 5 b.g. Firestreak 125–Silk Tabard (Court Harwell 130) [1974 7.2f **74 ?** 8g 10f³ 10f* 10.6g⁵ 10g³ 12g² 10v² 1975 N.R. 1976 10g 8fg 10f⁵ 10s* 10.2s* 10v⁴ 12v⁵] moderate handicapper: enterprisingly ridden when winning amateur riders event at Brighton in October: well backed when winning apprentice handicap at Doncaster later in month by ½ length from Whirlow Green: stays 1¼m well: acts on any going. *G. Balding.*

FIRESTORM 3 br.c. Firestreak 125–Zizi (Nimbus 130) [1975 5s⁵ 5f³ 5s* **91** 6fg* 6fg³ 7g⁵ 7f⁶ 7fg⁴ 6s* 7d 1976 7fg⁴ 8fg 7g⁵ 10fg⁶ 8g] short-backed colt: creditable fourth of eight to dead-heaters Gimri and Le Deux in handicap at Epsom in April, best effort: best form at up to 7f but is bred to stay 1¼m: acts on any going: not seen out after July. *G. Balding.*

FIREWINE 2 ch.f. Porto Bello 118–Hot Number 75 (Firestreak 125) [1976 **45** 5f 5f 6g 7v 6s] lightly-built filly: poor plater. *H. Wharton.*

FIR'S HILL 3 b.c. Jukebox 120–Luluna (Pinza 137) [1975 5v³ 5g* 5s* 8g 8g² **93** 7.2d* 8g³ 7.2v² 1976 9fg 8f⁶ 8fg² 10f⁴ 8f³ 10g* 10.5v³ 10.2s³ 10.6v² 12s³] compact colt: fairly useful handicapper: successful at Ayr in September, beating Hydrographic ½ length: ran well afterwards, particularly when runner-up to Fluellen in £4,000 Vernons Organisation Stakes at Haydock the following month: seems to stay 1½m: goes extremely well in the mud: suited by a left-handed course. *M. W. Easterby.*

FIRST BEND 4 b.g. Track Spare 125–Panderwick 69 (Pandemonium 118) **63** [1974 5f⁴ 5g 5fg⁴ 6d² 5g³ 5d⁶ 5v⁵ 1975 6v 7fg 7f⁶ 6fg² 7g 6g² 7g* 7.2fg⁴ 5.9fg⁵ 7.6fg³ 8g 1976 7fg² 7f² 7g 6g⁶ 7g⁴ 8g 5.9fg⁶ 6d³ 6v 6d] leggy gelding: poor handicapper nowadays: runs as though 7f is his trip: seems to act on any going: suitable mount for an apprentice. *R. Mason.*

FIRST OFFER 2 b.f. Welsh Saint 126–Xmas Cracker 66 (Roan Rocket 128) **—** [1976 7s] first foal: 200 gns yearling: dam stayed 7f: last of 19 in maiden race won by Lady Oriana at Newmarket in October. *M. Jarvis.*

FIRST QUAY 3 ch.c. Quayside 124–Halkissimo 61 (Khalkis 127) [1975 5d* **89** 5d² 6d⁴ 1976 7d 9g 6g⁴ 6h* 6h⁶ 6d 6s] strong, good sort of colt: ran best race when winning handicap at Carlisle in June decisively by 2 lengths from Peter Culter: ran below his best afterwards (tried in blinkers final outing): best form at sprint distances: appears to act on any going: sold 4,000 gns Newmarket Autumn Sales, reportedly for export to Sweden. *Denys Smith.*

FIRST SWALLOW 2 b.f. My Swallow 134–Bantam 64 (Combat 123) [1976 **95** 5fg⁵ 6f⁵ 5g* 5g² 5.3s* 6s 5d] sister to 3-y-o 1m and 1¼m winner Fly High, and half-sister to several winners, notably high-class 1m to 1¼m performer Gold Rod (by Songedor): 2,600 gns yearling: dam won 5f seller at 2 yrs: won maiden race at Warwick in August (by 5 lengths) and minor event at Brighton in October: possibly unlucky not to win on outing in between, going down by only ½ length to Metair in £1,800 nursery at Newmarket after being carried right by third horse: probably stays 6f but is better at 5f: acts on soft going. *J. Hill.*

FIRST UP 2 br.c. Balidar 133–Dusky Princess (Sayajirao 132) [1976 5f³ 6g* **114** 6.3f⁵ 5g² 5g* 5d² 5s³] Irish colt: half-brother to two winners, including very useful Irish sprinter Excessive (by Experiment): 800 gns foal, resold 4,200 gns yearling: dam ran only twice: made much of running when winning 17-runner maiden race at the Curragh in July and nursery at Phoenix Park three months later, in latter race beating Jeremy Fisher 1¼ lengths: second favourite when going down by 4 lengths to odds-on Godswalk in eight-runner Waterford Testimonial Stakes at the Curragh later in October: stays 6f: useful. *S. McGrath, Ireland.*

FISHER 4 br.c. So Blessed 130–Beamless 73 (Hornbeam 130) [1974 5s 6s⁶ **51** 1975 6f 8g 1976 10f⁵ 10.6d 7fg 8fg⁵ 6f⁶] neat colt: poor plater: evidently stays 1¼m: probably acts on any going. *W. Payne.*

FIVE BELLS 3 b.g. Foggy Bell 108–Beautiful Time (Arctic Time 127) [1975 **57** N.R. 1976 13.8d 12f² 12.2fg⁵ 14.7d] well-grown gelding: runner-up in seller at Thirsk in September: stays 1½m. *J. Fitzgerald.*

FIXBY GOLD   6 b.g. Goldhill 125–Gongoozler 66 (Dickens 125)   [1974 12v⁵   —
12.2s⁵ 12g³ 10.2s⁵   1975 N.R.   1976 12s]   neat, strong gelding: poor performer
(rated 68) in 1974: having first outing on flat since when tailed off in ladies race
at Chepstow in October: stays 1½m: tried in blinkers at 2 yrs and at Chepstow.
W. Williams.

FIXED TARGET   4 br.c. Random Shot–Likely Mite (Mito)   [1974 5g³ 7s 5v   —
1975 5f 5fg⁴ 6g 8h* 7.6fg*   1976 8g 7f⁶]   strong American-bred colt: fair performer (rated 89) at 3 yrs: lightly raced in 1976: suited by 1m and will stay
further: acts on hard going: sold 1,000 gns Newmarket July Sales. *Denys
Smith.*

FLAME BIRD   4 gr.f. Birdbrook 110–Ablaze 94 (Abernant 142)   [1974 5g 5g   —
5fg* 5fg³   1975 7fg 6f 5fg 5d   1976 5f 5f 12fg]   tall, good-topped filly: won
maiden race at Windsor as a 2-y-o: well beaten since and was never in race when
tried over 1½m on final outing (although should stay further than 5f): blinkered
final appearance at 3 yrs. *M. W. Easterby.*

FLAMEPROOF   3 b.f. Prince de Galles 125–Burning Deck 56 (Fighting Ship 121)   ?
[1975 6d⁴ 8g³ 8g⁶   1976 10.2s⁴ 8fg 11g* 12f 11g 10s⁴ 11v⁴]   well-grown, long-
striding filly: won £1,100 event at Cologne in June: ran best race in this country
when creditable fourth to Gold Claim in handicap at Sandown in October: stays
1¼m: acts on soft going: trained when racing in Germany by W. Ostmann: sold
to H. Nicholson 5,000 gns Newmarket Autumn Sales. *Mrs R. Lomax.*

FLAMETHROWER   2 br.f. Forli-Lighted Lamp (Sir Gaylord)   [1976 6fg]   — p
quite attractive, rangy filly: half-sister to three winners, notably smart French
7f to 1¼m winner Lighted Glory (by Nijinsky): 29,000 gns yearling: dam half-
sister to Crocket: 15/2, showed up quite well for 4f when behind in 27-runner
maiden race won by Home Fire at Newbury in August: sure to do better in time.
H. Cecil.

FLAME TREE   4 gr.g. Roan Rocket 128–Fircone 106 (Mossborough 126)   [1974 **108**
7g 7d² 8d* 7.6v*   1975 10d³ 10g 10fg³ 12g⁴ 12g⁴ 10g* 12g   1976 12fg³ 11g*
12d²]   useful performer: ran out an impressive winner of Ladbrokes Ayrshire
Handicap at Ayr in September, strolling into the lead 2f out, after being last in
early stages, and having only to be pushed out with hands and heels to beat
Kafka 1½ lengths: took a strong hold after leaving stalls (had little left in reserve
when winner came at him) when 5 lengths second to Mister Geoffrey (rec 23 lb)
at Newmarket the following month: stays 1½m and usually runs as though he
will be well suited by further: seems to act on any going: genuine. *B. Hobbs.*

FLAMING TEMPER   2 ch.c. Tyrant–Smoke Signal 77 (Bleep-Bleep 134)   **81**
[1976 5g² 5fg² 5g² 5f6 5fg2]   compact, robust colt: second foal: 1,750 gns yearling: dam won over 5f at 2 yrs: runner-up in four of his five outings in this
country, going down by a short head to Red Johnnie at Doncaster and to Regency
Bill at Leicester in March: subsequently raced in Belgium, winning at least
twice and finishing excellent third behind Fair Season and Mofida in 7f Grand
Criterium International d'Ostende in August: ran respectably in blinkers on
third outing. *B. Swift.*

FLARE SQUARE   3 ch.f. Red God 128 §–Alberta 98 (Douteelle 128)   [1975 5f⁴   —
1976 8f 6f]   neat, strong filly: lightly raced and no worthwhile form, including
in a seller (at 2 yrs). *D. Nicholson.*

FLASHBACK   5 b.h. Polyfoto 124–Hiprim 62 (Primera 131)   [1974 6g 5.8g 5.8g   —
5g³ 6g* 5v²   1975 7s³ 6g 5fg* 6g 5g* 6d⁴ 5g* 5d⁶ 5g* 5g2   1976 6g 5s⁴]   fairly
useful handicapper (rated 99) at 4 yrs: lightly raced in 1976 but ran respectably
on his second outing (May): has won at 6f but is a speedy animal and is best at
5f: acts on any going. *A. Davison.*

FLASH FIRE   2 b.c. Caerdeon 98–Twinkling Hill 77 (Hillary)   [1976 5f⁵ 6fg⁴]   **62**
first foal: dam won over 1¼m: showed only a little ability in minor events at
Lingfield in June and July: sold to Denys Smith 2,000 gns Newmarket Autumn
Sales. *N. Murless.*

FLASH FLIGHT   2 b.c. Polyfoto 124–Shelduck 70 (Dicta Drake 126)   [1976   **68**
6fg 7s⁶ 7v⁵]   half-brother to two winners, including Fend Lahoule (by Hul a
Hul), a winner at up to 1m in France: 4,100 gns yearling: dam won over 9f:
backward, but showed a little ability, finishing fifth of 15 to Chennel Lane in
weakly-contested maiden race at Leicester in October. *J. Nelson.*

FLASH IMP   7 bl.g. Bing II-Double Magnum (Gigantic 102)   [1974 16g² 14s⁴   **99**
16d 15s⁵ 18d   1975 16s⁵ 14s² 18d* 16g² 12d⁵   1976 18.4s⁴ 18d⁴ 16v²]   big,
strong gelding: useful handicapper: creditable second of five to French Princess

at York in October: extremely well suited by a thorough test of stamina and some give in the ground: excellent mount for an apprentice: sometimes sweats up. *M. Tate.*

FLASH PAST 3 b.c. Indiaro 83–Fanfare (Fair Risk 114) [1975 N.R. 1976 12fg⁴ 15.5s] smallish colt: first living foal: dam quite useful hurdler: 33/1 and in need of race when remote fourth of five to Carn Grey Rock in claiming race at Leicester in September: last of 16 in amateur riders event at Folkestone the following month. *A. Davison.* —

FLASH POLY 2 b.f. Polyfoto 124–Flying Fifteen 105 (Fairey Fulmar 124) [1976 5fg⁶ 5f 5f⁴] neat, lightly-built filly: seems only plating class: not seen out after May. *J. Powney.* —

FLAVELLE 3 gr.f. Lucky Sovereign–Gingell (Damremont 121) [1975 5g 6f 5fg 5f 1976 13.8g] of no account. *F. Dever.* —

FLAWLESS 2 ch.f. Jefferson 129–My Sapphire (My Babu 136) [1976 6f 7d 10s⁴] good sort of filly: French bred: ninth of 30 to Guama in maiden race at Newbury in September: started favourite for seller at Pontefract the following month but could finish only fourth to Sleigh Bells: seems to stay 1¼m. *Doug Smith.* **64**

FLAXTON 5 b.g. Track Spare 125–Fly Baby Fly (Tangle 121) [1974 N.R. 1975 N.R. 1976 10s] half-brother to moderate sprinter Samba (by Sammy Davis): dam won over hurdles: 25/1, led for some way prior to finishing well-beaten seventh of 14 behind stable-companion Chartered Course in minor event at Teesside in November, only outing. *M. W. Easterby.* —

FLECHE ROUGE 3 b.g. Indiaro 83–Fidau (Alcastus 118) [1975 N.R. 1976 13fg] first live foal: dam quite a moderate hurdler: unquoted when tailed-off last in 11-runner maiden race won by Super Jennie at Nottingham in July. *A. Davison.* —

FLEECE ALLEY 2 ch.f. Twilight Alley 133–Miss Fleece All 69 (Tangle 121) [1976 7v 6s] poor maiden: last on both outings but started slowly on first. *G. Wallace.* —

FLEETING SPIRIT 2 b.c. Tower Walk 130–Spirit in the Sky 106 (Tudor Melody 129) [1976 5.6f 5fg 7fg³] lengthy colt: first foal: 4,600 gns yearling: dam won from 6f to 1½m: moved badly on way to post prior to finishing 9 lengths third of 12 to Calicourt in maiden race at Chester in September: will stay 1m. *F. Carr.* **65**

FLEETLINE 2 b.f. Supreme Sovereign 119–Caronia 90 (Petition 130) [1976 5s 6s 6s] evidently of no account. *R. Mason.* —

FLEET ST FLOSSIE 4 br.f. Linacre 133–Danesby Lady (Appian Bridge 111) [1974 N.R. 1975 N.R. 1976 18s 12.5v] fourth foal: dam of no account: well beaten in maiden races at Doncaster (amateur riders event) and Teesside in October. *D. McCain.* —

FLEETWAY 2 gr.f. Major Portion 129–Berengaria 79 (Martial 131) [1976 8f 8fg 6v 10s] plain filly: bad plater. *J. Mulhall.* —

FLEORA 3 gr.f. Fleece 114–Oram Belle (Quorum 126) [1975 5g 5g 6s 1976 7g 8fg 12fg⁴ 10f⁴ 10.1d⁴ 10s³ 9s] small, sturdy filly: showed a little ability in maiden and minor events but ran poorly on final outing: suited by middle distances. *R. Akehurst.* **62**

FLEUR AMI 3 b.g. Be Friendly 130–Hilldyke Flower 79 (Klondyke Bill 125) [1975 5s 6f 8fg 1976 8f⁴ 8g 10.1fg 7d³ 7fg 16f 12.2fg] strong, good sort: bad plater: trained until after sixth outing by P. Mitchell. *S. Holland.* —

FLEUR D'AMOUR 3 br.f. Murrayfield 119–Dorothy Darling 76 (Red God 128 §) [1975 5v⁴ 5f² 5f 6fg⁵ 7f² 8.2g 6s* 1976 8f 8fg 7.3g 5.8h² 6fg² 6fg⁴ 7fg² 7g² 7s² 7s* 6v²] small filly: gained a well-deserved success when winning Playboy Bookmakers Handicap at Sandown in October, turning race into a procession from over 2f out and coming home 8 lengths clear of All Hope: stays 7f: acts on any going but goes particularly well on soft: best in blinkers: occasionally sweats up: consistent. *P. Cundell.* **83**

FLEUR DE FLANDRE 2 b.f. Raisingelle–Flamante (Big Brave) [1976 6fg 6f⁶ 6g 6d² 6g] good-looking French-bred filly: first foal: dam ran once at 3 yrs in France: staying on when 10 lengths second of 15 to Supernaculum in maiden race at Yarmouth in September: will be suited by 7f+. *R. Armstrong.* **68**

FLINT CROSS 3 b.f. Songedor 116–Why Dorrit (Question) [1975 5d 1976 **49** 8fg 6g 7g 8fg⁴ 8f⁶ 6f³ 8fg⁴] sturdy filly: poor plater: will stay 1¼m. *N. Callaghan.*

FLIRTER 4 ch.g. Saucy Kit 76–Pelta (Border Chief 101) [1974 6f 7g* 7g³ **67** 1975 12.2d² 12s* 12s⁴ 12g* 12.2f³ 15.8fg⁴ 12g 12s 1976 13g* 12g 15.8g 15g⁴ 16.1fg⁵] rangy gelding: won amateur riders race at Nottingham in April by 1½ lengths from Grand Display: best form at up to 13f: acted on any going: blinkered last two starts: sold to Miss S. Morris 1,700 gns Doncaster August Sales: dead. *P. Rohan.*

FLOATING PENNY 5 b.g. Pieces of Eight 128–Cinders 105 (Combat 123) — [1974 10.1fg 11.7fg 8fg 8.2g⁴ 1975 8fg 1976 15.5s²] quite attractive American-bred gelding: fair 2-y-o: raced most of his 5-y-o days in Jersey, winning once: 33/1, beaten easily by Blue Chrome when second of 16 to that horse in amateur riders race at Folkestone in October: stays 2m. *S. Arthur, Jersey.*

FLORABONDA 2 ch.f. Good Bond 122–Florecilla 90 (Matador 131) [1976 5f **57** 6g 5g 6g 7g 7s] good-bodied filly: quite a modest plater: blinkered final outing: sold 620 gns Newmarket Autumn Sales. *B. Swift.*

FLORAL ROYAL 3 ch.f. Irish Ruler–Flowery (Farnsworth) [1975 5g* 6fg* **84** 5d² 6f² 1976 6fg 5g⁴ 5fg 5fg 5.3f³ 6d 5fg⁶] leggy, rather narrow American-bred filly: ran best race as a 3-y-o when third to Peranka in minor event at Brighton in August, but never recaptured her very useful 2-y-o form: gave impression on final outing that she needs further than 5f nowadays, and will stay 1m: tried in blinkers third start. *R. Armstrong.*

FLORA TWICE 3 ro.f. Double Jump 131–Princess Flora 64 (Floribunda 136) **68** [1975 5g 6f³ 6fg 6f² 6fg 6g 6g 1976 8fg 8.5fg 6f 6g⁴ 6f 6f*] lightly-made filly: plater: sold 760 gns after winning at Folkestone in July: should stay 1m: blinkered last three outings: sweating and dwelt at start on second appearance. *J. Benstead.*

FLOREFINA 2 br.f. Floriana 106–Fiona Jane 92 (Sing Sing 134) [1976 5f⁶ **60** 5fg⁴] workmanlike filly: led until weakening quickly approaching distance when 7 lengths sixth of 14 in maiden race won by Heckle at Newbury in April: dropped right out in final 2f when distant last of four to Hunnylyn in minor event at Epsom later in month and was not seen out again. *G. Hunter.*

FLORESSA 3 br.f. Sassafras 135–Florentia (Relic) [1975 8g³ 7.5s³ 8g⁴ 8s* **120** 1976 10g 10.5f⁴ 10.5d* 10g³ 12g 13.5g⁵ 12s³ 12s 10.5s] French filly: half-sister to a lightly-raced animal by Yorick: 54,000 francs yearling (approx. £5,000): dam won over 1m in France at 4 yrs: put up a good performance when winning Group 3 Prix de Royaumont at Chantilly in June by ¾ length from Doll Dreams, finishing strongly after being waited with: raced inconsistently afterwards, but had three other fine efforts to her credit, notably when third to Lagunette and Sarah Siddons, beaten only a nose and a length, in Prix Vermeille at Longchamp in September: stays 13f: evidently acts on any going. *P. Lallie, France.*

FLORIMAN 3 b.g. Floriana 106–Mandane (Eastern Venture 107) [1975 7d — 1976 12fg] poor maiden. *J. Pullen.*

FLO SUPREME 2 br.f. Swinging Junior 118–Askalot (Javelot 124) [1976 5fg **66** 6fg³] second foal: bought privately 250 gns as a yearling: dam won over 1½m in Ireland: claimed for £1,000 after finishing third to King's Verdict in claiming race at Brighton in June and has since won in Belgium. *D. Hanley.*

FLUELLEN 3 b.g. Welsh Pageant 132–Ya Ya 84 (Primera 131) [1975 5g³ 6g² **117** 6fg⁴ 7g* 1976 7fg⁴ 7g 9s⁵ 8fg⁵ 8fg* 9g³ 10.6v*] tall, useful-looking gelding: good mover: showed improved form after being gelded in the summer and won £2,400 event at Newcastle in August (by ¾ length from Captain Paget) and £4,000 Vernons Organisation Stakes at Haydock in October (decisively by a length from Fir's Hill): excellent third of 29 to Intermission in Irish Sweeps Cambridgeshire at Newmarket in between: suited by 1¼m and will probably stay further: probably acts on any going: out of his depth when tried in blinkers on second outing: genuine and consistent: should make a very good 4-y-o. *H. Wragg.*

FLY BYRD 9 b.g. Sing Sing 134–Mosquito 106 (Mossborough 126) [1974 14.7f — 8d⁶ 8g 7.6g 5g 1975 8fg 1976 5.9f 15g 10.6d] useless. *W. Clay.*

FLYER 6 b.h. Skymaster 126–Claree 104 (Royal Palm 131) [1974 6h 6fg⁵ 7.6fg **70** 6f 5.8g⁴ 5.8g⁵ 7fg 6d⁶ 5s* 6s 1975 5d² 7s* 5g⁴ 5d* 6g* 5f 5f 6g 5s² 8g 6g 1976 6v² 7d⁵] strong, shapely horse: good mover: fair handicapper (rated 87) in 1975: ran only twice at 6 yrs but wasn't disgraced when second to Messenger

Vernons Organisation Stakes, Haydock—a win for Fluellen over Fir's Hill (left) and Gale Bridge

Boy at Ayr in April on reappearance: effective at 5f to 7f: needs an easy surface to be seen to advantage, and acts well on soft going: wears blinkers nowadays: sold 1,200 gns Newmarket April Sales. *H. Bell.*

FLY HIGH 3 b.c. My Swallow 134–Bantam 64 (Combat 123) [1975 6fg⁶ 6fg⁴ 8d 7.2d⁶ 1976 8f² 8f² 9f² 8fg* 10fg² 10f* 11.7f² 10.1fg 12s⁴] small, neat colt: only moderate, but ran quite well and picked up maiden race at Brighton (dead-heated) and minor event at Folkestone in the summer, starting odds on both times: stays 1½m: acts on any going: consistent. *R. Price.* **73**

FLYING BRIDGE 5 ch.m. Bleep-Bleep 134–Paddygrino (St Paddy 133) [1974 10d 7.6v 10v 8v 1975 7g 7f⁵ 7f* 7.6fg⁴ 8fg 7g 1976 8fg 7fg 7f² 8.3fg² 8f* 8g* 8s⁶ 8.2v] selling handicapper: successful twice at Warwick in August: bought out of G. Smyth's stable 1,050 gns after first win; changed hands 1,000 gns after second: stays 1m: acts on firm going: best in blinkers: suitable mount for an inexperienced rider. *G. Gadd.* **55**

FLYING COLOURS 3 b.f. King's Company 124–Dior 80 (Dionisio 126) [1975 5v 5v³ 5f³ 5.8h⁴ 7f* 7g 8g² 1976 8.5g 8f 8g 10f⁵ 7g] lightly-made filly: ran very well in nurseries at 2 yrs but showed little worthwhile form in 1976: stays 1m (ran poorly over 1¼m): seems to act on any going: sold to S. Cole 460 gns Ascot November Sales. *W. Wightman.* **—**

FLYING DICE 4 b.g. Skymaster 126–Ardicella (Botticelli 129) [1974 6fg 6d 6d* 6v⁴ 1975 7d 8fg² 10.8f⁵ 8fg* 8.3g⁶ 8.2d² 8d⁵ 1976 7fg⁶ 8g* 8.2g² 8fg 7g⁶ 8g⁴ 8v] strong, rangy gelding: narrow winner of handicap at Leicester in April: stays 1m: seems to act on any going, except perhaps heavy: blinkered last two appearances. *H. Candy.* **70**

FLYING DIPLOMAT 5 b.g. Diplomat Way–Plaintiff II (Ribot 142) [1974 6fg² 8f 1975 8s³ 10.2g 7fg 6h 1976 10.4fg 8v² 10.2s* 10s⁵] compact gelding: stayed on well when winning maiden race at Doncaster in October: stays 1¼m: probably acts on any going: tried in blinkers final outing in 1975. *A. Smith.* **78**

FLYING ECHO 8 b.m. Flyover 109–Court Curtsey (Distinctive 118) [1974 N.R. 1975 N.R. 1976 8f] well-beaten last of seven in amateur riders race won by The Hand at Newmarket in August, first outing on flat. *W. Marshall.* **—**

FLYING EMPRESS 2 gr.f. Young Emperor 133–Flying Fancy (King of the Tudors 129) [1976 6d] well-grown filly: half-sister to very useful Flight to Glory (by Native Charger), a stakes winner at up to 7f in U.S.A.: 2,300 gns yearling: dam, a winner, is daughter of very speedy Krakenwake: 33/1 when just over 9 lengths fourteenth of 25 behind Caerdeon Line in maiden race at Newmarket in October: sold to A. Johnson 4,800 gns Newmarket Autumn Sales. *I. Balding.* **69 p**

FLYING FABLE 3 ch.f. Skymaster 126–Gold Fable (Faberge II 121) [1975   **69**
5s 5g 5g⁴ 5v 1976 6fg⁵ 8.2d⁵ 8v*] well-made filly: decisive winner of 11-
runner maiden race at Leicester in October, beating Smithfield Lady 2½ lengths:
stays 1m: acts on heavy ground. *F. Maxwell.*

FLYING FUR 3 b.f. Comandeer 101–Cape Sable (French Beige 127) [1975   **—**
N.R. 1976 12fg] rangy filly: second foal: dam of little account: 33/1 and
backward, made little show behind Ribo Pride in weakly-contested, 15-runner
amateur riders race at Leicester in September. *W. Holden.*

FLYING JOHN 2 br.c. John Splendid 116–Twite (Chanteur II 135) [1976   **—**
5f 6fg 6g] bad plater: blinkered first outing: sold 230 gns Ascot June Sales. *Sir
Mark Prescott.*

FLYING ORDERS 3 ch.g. Meadsville–Hamlet's Queen (Royal Hamlet 115)   **62** d
[1975 5fg³ 5f⁴ 5.9fg 5h 1976 6d³ 5g 5f 6f 6g 6v⁵ 5s 7v] sturdy gelding: good
third of 12 to Gold Topaz in handicap at Catterick in May but did not reproduce
that form and ended season in sellers: stays 6f. *H. Blackshaw.*

FLYING PRINCE 7 b.g. Skymaster 126–Mene Mene Tekel (Premonition 130)   **—**
[1974 N.R. 1975 N.R. 1976 12s 15.5s] seemingly of little account. *J.
O'Donoghue.*

FLYING SOVEREIGN 2 b.f. Sovereign Bill 105–Hat Girl (High Hat 131)   **74**
[1976 5fg³ 5f³ 5fg* 5d⁴] half-sister to fairly useful 1973 2-y-o Desperate Dan
(by Sica Dan) and two winners abroad: 1,200 gns yearling: dam of little account:
comfortable 1½ lengths winner from Sole Agent in maiden auction event at
Epsom in April, despite hanging badly at distance: moderate fourth to Jewelled
Turban in minor race at Catterick the following month and was not seen out
again: will be suited by 6f: trained by R. Hannon until after third outing.
M. H. Easterby.

FLYING SWALLOW 2 b.c. My Swallow 134–Senna (Sica Boy 132) [1976   **—**
6fg 7fg 7fg⁵ 8d] strong colt: brother to 3-y-o 1¼m winner Sweet Swallow,
and half-brother to three winners, including fairly useful 1¾m winner Widower
Brown (by Mourne): 2,000 gns yearling: dam won over 11f in France: little
worthwhile form in maiden races but showed up well for 6f on final outing.
N. Callaghan.

FLYING TACKLE 3 b.f. Murrayfield 119–Love-Lies-Bleeding 74 (Javelot 124)   **83** d
[1975 5d⁵ 5f 5fg 6f 6f 6fg 5fg⁶ 5g 5g 5g⁴ 7fg* 6s 1976 8.5fg⁵ 7g² 8g 10.1fg⁶
7fg⁴ 6f 8g 7f 8.3d] compact filly: creditable second to Glorified in handicap
at Kempton in May but subsequently lost her form completely: stays 7f: has
been tried in blinkers. *M. Haynes.*

FLYING WATER 3 ch.f. Habitat 134–Formentera (Ribot 142) [1975 6g*   **120**
1976 7fg* 8fg* 10g]
    For once, the previous season's form provided no obvious pointer to the
outcome of the One Thousand Guineas except to those most closely concerned
with the three principals. The winner, Flying Water, was virtually an unknown
quantity until she beat the Cheveley Park Stakes second Dame Foolish in the
Ladbroke Nell Gwyn Stakes three weeks before the Guineas. Her only appearance in public as a two-year-old came in a race confined to newcomers over six
furlongs at Chantilly in July, shortly after which she threw a splint. She won the
race by two lengths from Imogene, who went on to finish second in the Prix
Morny, but one couldn't assess with any precision the value of Flying Water's
performance; there was little definite to be said about her except that she showed
great promise and would stay a mile. She did not appear in the Handicap
Optional at the end of the season. The second in the Guineas, Konafa, and third,
Kesar Queen, did not receive a weight in the Two-Year-Old Free Handicap in
England. Konafa, after winning at Yarmouth second time out, was well beaten
in the Argos Star Fillies Mile and beaten nearly nine lengths by Obstacle at level
weights in the Tattersall Nursery. Kesar Queen spent her time as a two-year-old
in maiden races, winning on her fifth and last start by two and a half lengths in a
seventeen-strong field at Newmarket. In sharp contrast Pasty, the winter
favourite for the Guineas, had gone unbeaten through her five races at two years,
holding off Dame Foolish, Solar and Outer Circle in the last and best of them,
the William Hill Cheveley Park Stakes, a race which is often a pointer to the
Guineas.
    The race for the Nell Gwyn Stakes, at Newmarket in April, put a different
complexion on matters. Dame Foolish, looking plenty fit enough to do herself
justice, proved no match for Flying Water and went down by three lengths.

Ladbroke Nell Gwyn Stakes, Newmarket—Flying Water has no difficulty coping with Dame Foolish (left) and Katie May

Behind came eight fillies of varied achievements, among the eight Outer Circle, who was the pick of the paddock, and the northern-trained Woodsome (8-9 in the Free Handicap). Flying Water, light of build and looking small and insignificant at the side of a strong filly like Outer Circle, showed that size isn't always everything when it comes to winning good races, coasting through to make her challenge running into the Dip after being held up. Soon she went clear and she won very smoothly, so smoothly that she supplanted Pasty as favourite for the Guineas. Konafa, incidentally, finished last of the ten runners. The following day Pasty blotted her copybook in the Fred Darling Stakes, finishing fourth behind the outsider Rowantree, Solar and Manilata. Nothing turned up in the period between the Craven meeting and the Spring meeting to shake public confidence in Flying Water, although Kesar Queen's second to Riverqueen in the Prix de la Grotte, in front of Antrona, showed her a vastly improved filly, and when the field came under orders for the Guineas Flying Water lay out on her own in the betting at 2/1. Pasty at 12/1 was second favourite just ahead of Antrona and Kesar Queen.

Flying Water faced the largest field assembled for the One Thousand Guineas for nearly fifty years; twenty-four runners opposed her, most of them, if the betting or the form book could be taken as a reliable guide, running for a place. Apart from Flying Water only the Ascot Trial winner Gilding, Rowantree and Petalca (as a two-year-old) had won last time out. Two fillies came over from Germany, one of them Eirene, officially rated superior to Manilata the previous season, but neither succeeded in taking a hand. Flying Water's jockey rode a remarkable race, especially for one riding in a classic, coolly allowing so much start to most of his opponents that he gave the impression he had Allez France under him. Fortunately for him, perhaps, the field split into two groups, increasing his prospects of getting a clear run from the back. Flying Water, racing on the far side as did all of the first seven home, was soon well behind along with Konafa, and she gave the front-running Kesar Queen at least a dozen lengths start from halfway. Even two furlongs from the finish, she had a great deal to do, but by that time, to her credit, she appeared good enough to do it; she was picking up ground on the outside of her group without the jockey as much as moving for his whip. A furlong later she had the race in the bag. Quickening very smoothly, she deprived Kesar Queen of the lead well inside the last furlong

1,000 Guineas Stakes, Newmarket—Flying Water and the runner-up Konafa come from well behind to catch Kesar Queen (rails) and Antrona

M D. Wildenstein's "Flying Water"

and held on by a length from 66/1-chance Konafa, who, although she also finished very strongly, was under the whip whereas Saint-Martin exuded confidence to the end. Kesar Queen and Antrona, a close third and fourth respectively, were at least six lengths clear of the remainder.

How good is this filly who could afford Kesar Queen a start of at least a dozen lengths in four furlongs? If one is prepared to make allowance for the spectacular manner in which victory was achieved one can make Flying Water almost anything, but this course of action seems unwise. Don't forget that Konafa recovered just as much ground. Strictly on the result of the race Flying Water strikes one as being less than outstanding among One Thousand Guineas winners —the form of the third and fourth is reliable enough a yardstick even if the form of the second isn't—but at the time of her victory she certainly looked set to establish herself as one of the top fillies in Europe at around a mile. Unfortunately, Flying Water made only one more appearance, and she lost a little of her shine through defeat in the Prix Saint-Alary, in which race Riverqueen, not Flying Water, started favourite. Antrona and Kesar Queen both beat Flying Water that day and Riverqueen, the winner, beat her by around five lengths. There was no zip about Flying Water here; disappointingly she remained among the backmarkers throughout and was afterwards reported by her stable to have been amiss.

Flying Water (ch.f. 1973)	Habitat (b 1966)	Sir Gaylord (b 1959)	Turn-to
			Somethingroyal
		Little Hut (b 1952)	Occupy
			Savage Beauty
	Formentera (ch 1968)	Ribot (b 1952)	Tenerani
			Romanella
		Fighting Edie (b 1956)	Guersant
			Edie Kelly

The first thing to be accepted about Flying Water's defeat is that she may well not have been good enough to win the Prix Saint-Alary: there weren't many fillies around in Europe better than Riverqueen. However, she did, we think, fail to show her form, probably because she was in season, possibly because she

258

found the longer distance beyond her. Habitat, her sire, is not a strong influence for stamina although he has got good fillies that stay at least a mile and a quarter —Rose Bowl and Roussalka, for instance. There is plenty of stamina on the dam's side. Formentera is a half-sister by Ribot to the Grand Prix de Saint-Cloud winner Felicio II, and is out of a half-sister to St Paddy and the Park Hill winner Parmelia. Formentera was so moderate a racemare that her racing character is difficult to pin down, but she appeared to stay at least a mile and a quarter. Flying Water is her first foal. On balance, one would expect Flying Water to stay a mile and a quarter; perhaps she will show as a four-year-old that she does so. Flying Water injured herself in the summer, and injured herself pretty seriously by all accounts, but it is hoped to get her back on the racecourse in 1977. Flying Water goes well on firm ground. She has a low, daisy-cutting action and she may not prove so well suited by soft if she is ever risked on it.
A. Penna, France.

FOB 5 b.g. Lauso–Belinda Pocket 84 (Pampered King 121) [1974 N.R. 1975 N.R. 1976 12g 10f 10f 8h⁴ 14fg⁵] poor performer nowadays: blinkered at 2 yrs and on final appearance in 1976. *P. Calver.* — **46**

FODEN'S EVE 2 ch.f. Dike–Kable (Bleep-Bleep 134) [1976 5f² 5fg* 5f² 6g³ 6fg³ 6fg] lengthy, light-framed filly: half-sister to three minor winners: 360 gns yearling: dam half-sister to Kibenka: made all to win 23-runner maiden auction event at Salisbury in May by a length from Running Account: ran well afterwards until finishing in rear in nursery in August on final outing: should stay 7f. *R. Hannon.* — **80**

FOLIO 4 ch.g. Jolly Jet 111–French Maid 89 (Shantung 132) [1974 N.R. 1975 9fg 12g 10g 14g 1976 12f⁴ 11.2f² 12g² 11.4g² 14g* 17f⁴] Irish gelding: won maiden plate at Gowran Park in June by a length from Zorayah: 5½ lengths fourth to Grand Orient in similar event at Beverley on reappearance, only outing in this country: one paced and stays well: trained by P. Prendergast until after fifth outing. *P. Norris, Ireland.* — **70**

FOLLOW THE LEADER 3 gr.f. Gilded Leader 75–Albine 72 (Amber X 133) [1975 N.R. 1976 5g 5v⁶] compact filly: first foal: dam poor plater: showed no sign of ability in maiden race at Kempton in August and minor event at Haydock in October. *B. McMahon.* — —

FONDOON 4 b.g. Doon 124–Found 70 (Delirium 126) [1974 N.R. 1975 12v 1976 12d] probably of little account. *A. Bacon.* — —

FOOL'S MATE 5 b.g. Busted 134–Spring Fever 110 (Botticelli 129) [1974 10.8fg* 12f² 14fg² 14.8fg* 16g² 14g⁴ 1975 14s 16g*(w.o.) 12fg 12f* 12g* 12f* — **122**

P.T.S. Laurels Stakes, Goodwood—the enterprisingly-ridden Fool's Mate pulls out extra when pressed by Royal Match

13.3g³ 12fg² 12g 1976 12f 12fg⁴ 13.4s⁴ 10g⁴ 10f 10.5fg² 12g* 10fg*] big, lengthy gelding: very smart handicapper: in frame on all his four outings in handicap company at 5 yrs, winning Trundle Stakes and P. T. S. Laurels Stakes (held off Royal Match by a length) within the space of five days at Goodwood in July, and finishing close fourth in Daily Mirror Handicap at Epsom in June (fourth appearance) and second in John Smith's Magnet Cup at York earlier in July (failed by a head to hold Bold Pirate): faced stiffish tasks on most of his other starts, but put up a good performance on second outing when about 2 lengths fourth to Orange Bay in Jockey Club Stakes at Newmarket: has won at 15f but has shown best form at up to 1½m: suited by sound surface and acts well on firm going: genuine and consistent. *H. Cecil.*

FOOLS RUSH IN 3 ch.c. Roan Rocket 128–Flibbertigibbet 97 (Klairon 131) **73** [1975 N.R. 1976 8fg 10g 8d 10fg 10fg² 10fg* 10fg³ 12g⁵ 10d 10fg 16s] lengthy colt: half-brother to very useful middle-distance handicapper Funny Man (by Jolly Jet), useful stayer Pot Luck (by Hopeful Venture) and fair 1¼m winner Lennox Gardens (by Pall Mall): dam won at up to 1½m: made all when winning four-runner maiden race at Sandown in July by a neck from On Course: well beaten afterwards: should stay 1½m but is not certain to stay 2m: sometimes wears blinkers, and did so when successful: sold 2,900 gns Newmarket Autumn Sales. *R. Armstrong.*

FORAGE 2 gr.c. Hopeful Venture 125–Abelia 128 (Abernant 142) [1976 8s **109** 7v* 8s] brother to fair 1¼m winner Future Chance and half-brother to several good winners, including smart milers St Padarn (by St Paddy) and Casabianca (by Never Say Die): 9,000 gns yearling: dam top-class sprinter: put up an impressive display when making all to win minor event at Lingfield in November by 10 lengths from Merchant Tubbs: started favourite for similar event at Doncaster four days later but could finish only seventh of 26 to Lucent and had possibly not recovered from his Lingfield exertions: will probably stay 1¼m: acts on heavy ground. *P. Walwyn.*

FORCE TEN 6 br.h. Crest of the Wave 95–Beira (Targui) [1973/4 placed four **55** times from twelve starts in New Zealand 1975 10fg 8g⁶ 16s 12.2g 10.2g³ 1976 12.2g² 12f² 15.5s⁴ 12s³] New Zealand-bred horse: poor maiden: probably stays 2m: acts on any going. *W. Stephenson.*

FOREIGN EMBASSY 2 b.c. Mandamus 120–Foreign Bird 92 (Lauso) [1976 **63** 5g 6d 6fg⁶ 7g 7.2f 7fg⁵ 7v] strong colt: only plating class on form so far: will stay 1m: blinkered final outing. *W. A. Stephenson.*

FORENSIC 2 b.c. Firestreak 125–Elia (Narrator 127) [1976 5g 5g⁶ 6fg 6f⁴ 7f² **79** 7f⁶ 7h⁴ 7.2f⁵] lightly-made colt: quite moderate form in maiden races, but ran below his best in a seller on final outing: should stay 1m. *W. Marshall.*

FOREST MOOR 3 br.g. Right Tack 131–Abercourt 89 (Abernant 142) [1975 **86** 5s 5f⁶ 5g³ 5h³ 5f³ 1976 6fg⁴ 6d* 6f* 8f 6g⁵ 6f² 6h 6g⁴ 6fg³ 6v] useful sort: won maiden race at Pontefract in May going away by 1½ lengths from Beau Jamie and handicap on same course the following month by 2 lengths from Consister: appeared not to stay 1m on fourth outing but wasn't ridden to conserve his stamina: appears to act on any going: sold out of M. H. Easterby's stable only 600 gns Ascot September Sales and ran below his best on first appearance for new stable. *O. O'Neill.*

FOREST PLAYBOY 3 b.g. Candy Cane 125–Forest Fun (Pardao 120) [1975 — N.R. 1976 9f 16.1v] big gelding: third foal: 220 gns yearling: dam won over 1½m in Ireland: 25/1 and backward when unplaced behind Sweet Lad in minor event at Ripon in June: in rear behind Glenalema in maiden race at Haydock in October. *M. Camacho.*

FORGETS IMAGE 4 b.f. Florescence 120–Zenoelg 84 (El Gallo 122) [1974 **68** 5.1g 5s⁶ 8d⁶ 7s² 1975 7s⁴ 8g⁴ 8g* 9.4g⁵ 8f² 8.2s* 7fg⁵ 1976 8g⁵ 10g⁴ 8f* 8f⁵ 8g⁴ 7fg 8f² 7.2d⁵ 7f³ 8g⁴ 8h 7f⁴ 8f⁵] quite a moderate handicapper: stood up well to a busy early-season campaign (ran thirteen times before the middle of July): was very enterprisingly ridden when winning apprentice event at Thirsk in April by ¾ length from Barleycroft Star: stays 1m: acts on any going: blinkered last two starts. *S. Nesbitt.*

FORGOTTEN DREAMS 3 b.f. Shoemaker 121–Sea Plane (Neptune II 127) **82** [1975 7fg 7f 1976 10f⁴ 11.7f² 11.1f⁵ 16f* 16.9f* 16f* 16g³ 16g³] leggy French-bred filly: won maiden race at Beverley and handicaps at Wolverhampton and Warwick: put up best performance when beating Popsi's Poppet hard held by 3 lengths at Wolverhampton in July: stayed well: acted on firm going: wore blinkers: stud. *P. Walwyn.*

'OR HIRE   2 b.f. Roll of Honour 130–La Mistrale (Le Levanstell 122)   [1976 5d   **68**
5fg 7f 6f⁵ 6f² 7fg 8fg⁶]   small filly: first foal: 750 gns yearling: quite a moderate
maiden: will stay 1¼m+.   *G. Toft.*

'ORITA   3 br.f. Irish Ball 127–Forini 79 (Fortino II 120)   [1975 N.R.   1976 9v   **—**
15v⁶]   second foal: half-sister to a winner in Austria by Tamerlane: dam won at
up to 1½m: well beaten in minor event at Newcastle and maiden race at Teesside
in October.   *S. Hall.*

'OR KEEPS   3 b.f. Track Spare 125–Bench Game (King's Bench 132)   [1975   **57**
N.R.   1976 10fg 10fg⁴ 10fg³ 8f² 8s 9s⁴]   light-framed filly: sister to very smart
1m to 1¼m performer Record Run and half-sister to three winners, including
useful miler Do Justice (by Fortino II): dam half-sister to smart 1961 2-y-o
Gustav: put up best effort when neck second to Supreme Vista in six-runner
maiden race at Yarmouth in August, the pair finishing clear: has yet to show
conclusively she stays 1¼m: possibly needs a sound surface.   *G. Pritchard-
Gordon.*

'ORLIANA   2 b.f. Forli–Hail to Vail (Hail to Reason)   [1976 6g⁵ 6g]   neat,   **75**
attractive filly: second reported produce: half-sister to Hariana (by Reviewer),
a winner at up to 9f in France: 8,200 gns foal: dam unraced daughter of Snow
Scene II, a stakes winner of $112,000 at up to 9f: started at 33/1 when taking on
some useful fillies in nine-runner minor event at Kempton in August but ran
promisingly to finish 6½ lengths fifth to Rockery (Fr): easy in market and a bit
disappointing in paddock, never got into race and finished behind in 26-runner
maiden event won by Sarasingh at Doncaster the following month: should
stay 1¼m.   *B. Hills.*

FORLORNA   2 b.f. Forlorn River 124–Sweet Serenade 93 (High Perch 126)   **72**
[1976 5.1f 5.1f⁴ 5.1f⁴ 6d]   third foal: 540 gns yearling: dam won over 6f at 2 yrs:
fourth in maiden races at Yarmouth in August, being beaten 2¾ lengths by
Colourful Connie on second occasion: should stay 6f+.   *G. Blum.*

FORLORN CLOUD   3 b.f. Forlorn River 124–Playful Cloud 103 (Nimbus 130)   **—**
[1975 5fg 5g   1976 8s 10g]   light-framed filly: no worthwhile form, including in
sellers.   *J. Barclay.*

FORLORN KING   2 b.c. Forlorn River 124–Virgin Queen 78 (Welsh Rake 118)   **68**
[1976 5f 6fg 5f 5f 6fg 5v³ 5v³ 6s]   neat colt: third in £1,600 event at Newcastle
(8 lengths behind Last Sale) and seller at Teesside (beaten 1½ lengths by Thornhill
Fanciful) in October: evidently suited by heavy going.   *W. A. Stephenson.*

FORLORN LASS   2 b.f. Forlorn River 124–Pamardia 77 (Pampered King 121)   **—**
[1976 5g 5d 5s]   lightly-made filly: behind in maiden races: sold 410 gns
Ascot November Sales.   *H. Westbrook.*

FORLORN QUEEN   3 b.f. Forlorn River 124–Virgin Queen 78 (Welsh Rake 118)   **—**
[1975 5fg³ 5f⁴ 5g⁴ 5f   1976 8fg 6s⁶ 8f 8s⁶ 7v]   leggy filly: plater: best form at 5f
or 6f: sometimes sweats up.   *W. A. Stephenson.*

FORLORN RAID   5 b.m. Forlorn River 124–Tholen Raid (Bewildered 102)   **—**
[1974 11.7fg 11.7g² 11.1g 12g 14d⁶ 16g⁵ 12g 8v*   1975 7s   1976 12f⁶]   light-
framed mare: lightly raced and no worthwhile form on Flat since her 3-y-o days.
L. Kennard.

FORLORN SCOT   2 b.c. Forlorn River 124–Kelso Girl (Royal Palm 131)   [1976   **94**
5g 5fg³ 5fg⁴ 6f 5g³ 6fg 6s² 5v* 6s⁶]   light-framed colt: brother to fairly useful
1975 2-y-o 5f winner Border River, and half-brother to a minor winner: dam never
ran: won minor event at Teesside in October by ¾ length from Pandu: stays 6f
but seems better at 5f: well suited by a soft surface and acts on heavy going:
blinkered last three outings.   *W. C. Watts.*

FORMLAND   3 b.c. Reform 132–Filandria 90 (French Beige 127)   [1975 7g 8g   **72**
1976 10f 17.7f⁶ 12fg 14.7f³ 14g⁵ 12.2fg⁴ 16fg² 12v² 15v²]   lightly-built colt:
placed in varied races, including a York seller: suited by long distances: seems
to act on any going: sold 1,500 gns Newmarket Autumn Sales.   *C. Brittain.*

FORMULA   3 b.f. Reform 132–Alesia 104 (Alycidon 138)   [1975 5fg⁴ 6f 5fg⁵   **72**
1976 8fg⁶ 8g* 8fg³ 10d 10s⁵ 10v³]   lengthy filly: 33/1 when winning 18-runner
maiden race at Sandown in July, quickening really well to beat Dancing Hill
1½ lengths: has yet to show she stays further than 1m but should do so.   *R.
Akehurst.*

FORTIMBRAS   2 gr.c. Swing Easy 126–La Cilla 98 (Milesian 125)   [1976 5fg⁴   **80**
5g⁴ 6fg⁶ 7g⁶ 8.2d 8s]   rather lightly-built, somewhat unfurnished colt: first foal:
dam won three times over 5f at 2 yrs: quite moderate, running best race when
about 7 lengths sixth of 17 to Gala Lad in nursery at Catterick in September

after dwelling at start: suited by 7f but has been well beaten when tried at 1m. *B. Hills.*

FORTISSIMAID   3 gr.f. Fortissimo 111–Arnes Maid 81 (March Past 124)   **65**
[1975 6g 7.6g⁶ 8g   1976 10g 16.1d 12fg⁵ 13.8g*]   workmanlike filly: plater: winner at Catterick in September: sold to W. C. Watts 1,200 gns afterwards: stays well.   *R. Jarvis.*

FORTRITION   5 b.m. David Jack 125–Fortlet (Fortina)   [1974 N.R.   1975   —
N.R.   1976 14fg 10f 12v]   seemingly of no account.   *S. Matthews.*

FORTUNE COOKIE   4 b.c. St Paddy 133–Candy Gift 97 (Princely Gift 137)   —
[1974 N.R.   1975 N.R.   1976 10s 12s⁴ 10.2s]   rangy colt: half-brother to four winners, including good middle-distance horse Candy Cane (by Crepello): dam, daughter of top-class miler Kandy Sauce, won at 1m: ran freely when 10½ lengths fourth to Coffee Boy in maiden race at Haydock in October.   *G. Balding.*

FORTY THIEVES   3 ch.g. Tobrouk–Grand Larceny (Supreme Court 135)   **53**
[1975 8.2g 7g 8.2g 8g   1976 10f* 12g 12f⁶ 10f⁵ 10f 16d]   plater: attracted no bid after winning six-runner event at Lanark in April all out by ½ length from Camberlad: stays 1¼m: acts on firm going: trained until after second outing by E. Collingwood.   *E. O'Grady, Ireland.*

FORTY WINKS   2 br.c. Philip of Spain 126–Siesta Time 107 (Ommeyad 120)   **119**
[1976 5fg² 5d² 5d² 5fg³ 6d² 5s* 6g² 5g³ 6fg² 6g* 5g² 7s³]
       Forty Winks's two-year-old career can be broken down into two distinct phases, with the dividing line between the eighth and ninth outings.   Phase one saw him competing with little success and less distinction in varied company mainly in the north: Aeras beat him in a small race at Leicester, Jameson gave him weight and a beating in a minor event at Haydock, Cawston's Clown slammed him in the Tattersalls' Yorkshire Stakes at York, and Lady Eton and Sunny Spring, the latter of whom was making his first appearance, proved far too good for him in a maiden race at Newmarket.   Forty Winks's only success during this period came on his sixth appearance, when he wore blinkers for the first time and experienced no difficulty in beating five undistinguished northerners— Guard Duty, Sandicroft, Jewelled Turban, Lucky Prize and K'Ang Hsi—in the Bellisle Stakes at Ayr.   The general level of his form, confirmed by his third to Trackally and Double Secret in the Underwood Nursery at Ayr in August on his eighth appearance, was that of a colt over two stone behind the best of his age.
       And so to phase two, and a much improved Forty Winks.   And a much improved Forty Winks for no apparent reason.   Starting at 20/1, he made Nebbiolo pull out all the stops to get the better of him by two and a half lengths (Cawston's Clown was well behind in fifth place) in the Gimcrack Stakes at York, followed up by taking the Ouseburn Nursery on the same course, a race which

Ouseburn Nursery Handicap, York—Forty Winks wins from Jenny Splendid (hidden)

was a present for him on the evidence of his Gimcrack form, failed two weeks later by only a short head to hold off He Loves Me, who was receiving 11 lb, in the Harry Rosebery Challenge Trophy at Ayr, and then ran third to Princess Tiara and Baudelaire, beaten a length and six lengths, in the Somerville Tattersall Stakes at Newmarket. The Somerville Tattersall Stakes marked Forty Winks's first attempt at a distance greater than six furlongs. Held up, he improved almost to reach a challenging position at the distance, only to find the first and second, both of whom were receiving a deal of weight, much too strong in the last furlong. Forty Winks had a tough task at the weights, but the distance was the principal cause of his failure to run to form. Seven furlongs is beyond him.

		Tudor Melody	Tudor Minstrel
	Philip of Spain	(b 1956)	Matelda
	(b 1969)	Lerida	Matador
Forty Winks		(b 1961)	Zepherin
(br.c. 1974)		Ommeyad	Hyperion
	Siesta Time	(b 1954)	Minaret
	(b 1961)	Time Call	Chanteur II
		(b 1955)	Aleria

The Somerville Tattersall Stakes also marked Forty Winks's last appearance in England. He has been exported to South Africa. A tall colt, half-brother to the minor winner Noddy Time (by Gratitude), he cost 2,700 guineas as a yearling, was best at up to six furlongs, and probably acted on any going. *D. Thom.*

FOUNDRY BOY 3 ch.g. Richboy 117–Pal Greta 76 (Palestine 133) [1975 N.R. 1976 6f 5.9g 6fg 5fg 8f] seems of no account, although has yet to race in a seller. *G. Vergette.* — —

FOUNT OF HONOUR 3 b.g. Sheshoon 132–Regal Fountain 84 (Grey Sovereign 128 §) [1975 N.R. 1976 11g 12g 11g*] rangy gelding: half-brother to three winners, including high-class French 2-y-o King of Macedon (by Diatome): dam stayed 7f: stayed on strongly when winning nine-runner maiden race at Newbury in July by 4 lengths from Piccadilly Line: will probably stay 1½m: sold 4,100 gns Newmarket Autumn Sales. *R. Hern.* **78**

FOUR ALLS 2 gr.c. Raffingora 130–Putli II (Fast Fox 123) [1976 6fg 5fg 5s 5s] strong, good-bodied colt: little worthwhile form in maiden races. *N. Adams.* —

FOUR BILLS 2 ch.c. Sovereign Bill 105–Maona (Narrator 127) [1976 5f 7v] useless. *G. Wallace.* —

FOUR DAYS 2 b.g. Quadriga 97–My Day (Vasant 111) [1976 5g 5f] bad plater. *D. Plant.* —

FOUR FATHOMS 2 ch.c. Gulf Pearl 117–Capule (Middleground) [1976 6fg⁴] third foal: half-brother to useful 1975 2-y-o 6f and 7f winner El Capitan (by Captain's Gig): dam a minor winner over 5f at 2 yrs in U.S.A.: 16/1, ran promisingly when about 4 lengths fourth of 12 to Tudor Lilt in minor event at Lingfield in June, leading for 5f: will stay 1m: sure to be better for this experience. *J. Dunlop.* **67 p**

FOUR JETS 3 b.g. Jolly Jet 111–Saucy Flirt 102 (King's Troop 118) [1975 5.1f 7g 1976 10fg 17.7f⁵ 16g 14d 16s 15.8s*] workmanlike gelding: all out when winning selling handicap at Catterick in October: sold to H. Blackshaw 875 gns afterwards: stays 2m: acts on soft going: usually wears blinkers nowadays. *D. Weeden.* **62**

FOUR LAWNS 3 b.f. Forlorn River 124–Ever Grateful 95 (King's Bench 132) [1975 5v² 1976 6fg³ 5g⁴ 5d⁵ 6d⁴ 5.9s² 5s* 5s] compact filly: ran out decisive winner of all-aged maiden event at Warwick in October (beat Emijo 1½ lengths): stays 6f: probably acts on any going: twice played up before start and was withdrawn not under orders. *D. Marks.* **77**

FOVERAN 3 b.f. Forlorn River 124–Three Feathers 98 (Tenerani 135) [1975 5f 6f⁶ 7g 1976 8g 8f 12.2f⁵] well-made filly: in rear in maiden and minor events: should stay middle distances: sold to R. Edwards 330 gns Ascot July Sales. *W. A. Stephenson.* —

FOX DIVER 2 b.c. Welsh Saint 126 Lady Faberge (Faberge II 125) [1976 6s 6f] June foal: first produce: 720 gns yearling: dam won at up to 7f in Ireland: in rear in maiden races at Ayr in June and Yarmouth in August: sold 410 gns Doncaster September Sales. *R. Supple.* —

FOX

FOXHUNT 3 b.f. Hopeful Venture 125–Daylight 92 (Princely Gift 137) [1975 **72**
N.R. 1976 10.1fg 12g 12.2fg⁵ 13g² 16fg⁵ 12g⁶] sister to winning stayer Happy
Heart, and half-sister to four winners, including useful middle-distance performer Parlight (by Parthia) and useful stayer Grey God (by Busted): dam a
miler: went under by a head to Impulsora in 13-runner maiden race at Nottingham in July: ran moderately afterwards: stays 13f: sold 1,050 gns Newmarket
Autumn Sales. *J. Dunlop.*

FOXWOOD BOY 3 ch.g. Virginia Boy 106–Narsia (Narrator 127) [1975 5g **66**
5fg 5fg⁵ 6h² 5.9f³ 5g⁵ 6g⁴ 7fg 6g⁶ 5g* 5.9g⁵ 6g 8fg 1976 8fg⁴ 11.1fg* 8fg⁵ 8g*]
workmanlike gelding: fair plater: apprentice ridden when successful at Wolverhampton in April and Ripon in May, on latter course being sold for 1,300 gns:
stays 11f: acts on hard ground: has been tried in blinkers but does better without.
A. Jarvis.

FRAASH 3 ch.g. Frankincense 120–Desert Ash (Celtic Ash) [1975 7g 8fg⁶ 7s **68**
1976 8.2f 10fg 12.2f 10g 7g 8fg 8fg 7f 7d⁵ 10s* 12v³] lengthy gelding: plater:
attracted no bid after scoring by 10 lengths at Lingfield in September: not
disgraced in better company on final outing: stays 1½m: needs plenty of give
in the ground: ran respectably when tried in blinkers on ninth outing: retained
by trainer 310 gns Doncaster August Sales. *B. Lunness.*

FRAGONARD 3 b.g. Swing Easy 126–Fair Charmer 77 (Court Martial) [1975 **71**
6g 6g⁵ 1976 8f 8fg⁶] quite a moderate gelding: suited by 1m. *P. Makin.*

FRAGRANT CLOUD (FR) 3 ch.f. Balidar 133–Rossana II (Saint Crespin III **69**
132) [1975 5g 6fg 6f 5f⁵ 1976 7f 8g 7d⁶ 7g⁵ 5f 5f² 5h³ 5f⁶ 5f³ 6f² 5g* 5f² 5fg⁴
5g 5v³ 5s 5s⁴ 6s 6s] neat filly: poor mover: quite a moderate handicapper:
successful at Wolverhampton in August: best form at 5f and 6f: acts on any
going: wears blinkers: suitable mount for an apprentice. *S. Nesbitt.*

FRAGRANT COFFEE 2 ch.f. Frankincense 120–French Coffee (Espresso 122) **80**
[1976 5fg 5f 5f 5fg² 5f³ 5.3h 5s⁶] lightly-built filly: first foal: bought privately
for £1,000 as a yearling: dam well behind in three maiden races: placed in
maiden races at Nottingham and Catterick in the summer, finishing 1½ lengths
second of 16 to My Therape on former course: will stay 1m: acts on firm going.
D. Dartnall.

FRANCA 2 b.f. Frankincense 120–Maltese Cat 58 (Pall Mall 132) [1976 5fg **96**
5fg² 5d³ 5f* 7f² 7g* 7f* 7f⁴ 7.3d] lightly-made filly: half-sister to winning
stayer Lutyens (by Alcide): 800 gns yearling: dam a poor performer: winner of
maiden race at Pontefract in June and nurseries at Lingfield and Catterick
in August: made all, under a 5-lb penalty, when scoring by 4 lengths from Frisco
Bay on last-named course: suited by 7f: acts on firm going: acts well on a sharp
track:genuine and consistent but did not run up to her best form on last two
outings. *P. Haslam.*

FRANC BOIS 3 b.c. Faraway Son 130–Jacinthe de Bois (Tyrone 130) [1975 —
N.R. 1976 9fg 12g 16g] strong, lengthy, good sort of colt: half-brother to
several winners abroad: 35,000 francs yearling (approx. £3,200): dam a smart
performer at up to 7f as a 2-y-o: plating-class maiden: blinkered first two outings.
D. Sasse.

FRANC FLINDERS 5 ch.g. Current Coin 118–Polly Flinders (Polly's Jet) **95**
[1974 8fg² 9f⁶ 9f⁴ 10g³ 12f² 12s³ 13.8s² 1975 14.7s² 12v² 12s² 12s* 12f* 12fg*
10.4g³ 12f* 12.3f² 12g² 12d⁴ 1976 10.2g² 12g⁴ 12s² 12d⁶ 13s³ 12f* 14.7f* 16fg²]
strong gelding: quite a useful handicapper: quickened well when winning at
Redcar in July by 4 lengths from Guido Fawkes: had previously won amateur
riders race at Beverley and run creditably in apprentice events: stays well:
acts on any going: excellent mount for an inexperienced race-rider: very consistent: not seen out after August and has since been fired. *P. Rohan.*

FRANCISCO 2 br.g. Don Carlos–Sing On 81 (Sing Sing 134) [1976 8.6f 8.6f —
7s 8.2h 8fg] ex-Irish gelding: gambled on in seller at Hamilton in September
on fourth outing but finished well-beaten seventh of 10 to Little Gadge: trained
by P. Doyle on first three outings. *D. Dale.*

FRANCOIN 4 ch.g. Current Coin 118–Dionut (Dionisio 126) [1974 N.R. —
1975 N.R. 1976 6f 10f] strong gelding: half-brother to fair sprint handicapper
Tanaria (by Track Spare) and to two N.H. winners: dam never ran: 50/1,
missed break and was outpaced throughout in high-class company at Thirsk
in April: broke leg and was subsequently destroyed at Folkestone the following
month. *O. O'Neill.*

FRANKENSTEIN 2 ch.g. Frankincense 120–Freuchie (Vulgan 123) [1976 — p
6v⁶] first foal: dam winning hurdler: unquoted when never-dangerous 12

264

lengths sixth of 22 to Good Company in maiden race at Newbury in October: will be better suited by longer distances. *S. James.*

RANKIE 3 br.c. Crooner 119–Old Dutch 91 (Fastnet Rock 123) [1975 8s³ 8g⁴ 8g⁶ 1976 10s⁶ 8fg⁵ 10.5s 12g 10g* 9g 7v⁵] well-made colt: half-brother to Oaks winner Sleeping Partner (by Parthia): trotted up from moderate opposition at Ayr in September: raced in pattern races on his previous three starts, running race of his life when about 5 lengths fifth of 17 to Wollow in 2,000 Guineas at Newmarket in April: moderate fifth of nine to Jane's Joker in £3,200 handicap at York in October on final outing: stays 1¼m (well-beaten fourteenth of 23 to Empery in Epsom Derby on only attempt at 1½m): requires a sound surface. *J. Hanson.* **117**

RANKILYN 3 b.f. Frankincense 120–True Dresden 58 (Vilmoray 126) [1975 5s* 5f² 5g⁴ 5g 5g 1976 6h⁶ 5f³ 5fg 5f⁴ 5f 5s⁵] dipped-backed filly: creditable third to My Chopin in handicap at Hamilton in July, best effort: speedy and will probably always be best at 5f: acts on any going: sold out of T. Gosling's stable 230 gns Ascot January Sales. *T. Craig.* **63**

RANKLIN HYDE 2 b.g. Mandamus 120–Queen's Footsteps 93 (Sovereign Path 125) [1976 5f 6f⁶] lengthy gelding: twice well behind at Pontefract, including in an auction seller. *M. H. Easterby.* **—**

RANKLY YES 3 br.g. Frankincense 120–Luscinia 73 (Sing Sing 134) [1975 6fg³ 6f 1976 8fg⁶ 10f 8fg] leggy, unfurnished gelding: little worthwhile form: should stay 1m: unseated apprentice rider before start on final outing. *Miss S. Hall.* **—**

FRATINI 3 b.f. Reliance II 137–Frangipani 77 (Crepello 136) [1975 N.R. 1976 14g⁴ 12g⁶ 16g³ 15.8g² 16.1v] lengthy filly: third foal: half-sister to quite moderate middle-distance performer Queen's English (by Salvo): dam, lightly raced, is out of half-sister to Hethersett: quite a moderate maiden: ran moderately on heavy ground last time out: needs long distances: started slowly second outing. *N. Vigors.* **69**

FREDHA 4 ch.f. Free Boy 96–Adha 111 (The Phoenix) [1974 N.R. 1975 10.1g⁶ 12.2g 10.6v 1976 13.8d] poor form in maiden races: dead. *R. Vibert.* **—**

FREDICULATE 2 ch.f. Articulate 121–Freddie's Friend (Amber Light 114) [1976 5f 6fg 6f] strong filly: last on all outings but still looked burly on final appearance. *P. Buckley.* **—**

FREE 3 gr.f. Varano–Independence 64 (Runnymede 123) [1975 5g 1976 10g 7fg 6s 8fg⁵ 10g*] very small filly: poor plater: winner at Newmarket in July by ¾ length from Game David: sold 1,600 gns afterwards, presumably for export to Belgium: stays 1¼m: bandaged in front second outing. *D. Thom.* **55**

FREE COSSACK 3 gr.c. Right Royal V 135–Idover 95 (Fortino II 120) [1975 8g 8f 1976 10g⁴ 12g 10fg⁵ 11.5fg⁴ 12f] lengthy colt: showed a little ability in maiden races: blinkered final outing: dead. *M. Masson.* **—**

FREE GIRL 6 b.m. Free Boy 96–Adha 111 (The Phoenix) [1974 7d⁴ 8g 8fg² 11.2f* 10h* 12.2f 11.2fg⁵ 8f⁶ 8g 8.2g* 8.2v 1975 8d 8g 8.2d⁵ 8f 10fg³ 8h³ 10g² 8f 10.6fg 11.1g⁴ 1976 10f] dipped-backed mare: plater: evidently suited by further than 1m nowadays and stays 11f: acts on hard going. *J. Cousins.* **—**

FREE RIDDEN 3 b.f. Shantung 132–Croix du Risque (Wild Risk) [1975 7g 7g* 1976 10g 12g 10fg 14g⁴ 12fg⁶ 8g⁶ 10d 10 6d³] light-framed ex-Irish filly: half-sister to several winners, notably high-class French middle-distance winner Free Ride (by Free Man): dam won at up to 1½m in France: quite a moderate handicapper: should stay 1½m (gave impression she needs further than 1m on sixth appearance): blinkered third and fourth outings. *D. Sasse.* **—**

FREE STATE 3 b.c. Hotfoot 126–Born Free 105 (Alycidon 138) [1975 6g² 6g* 1976 8f* 8g* 8f² 8fg² 8fg² 8f*] **125**

This most attractive colt was one of two by his sire, the other was Tachypous, whose physical appearance made a lasting impression on us at Goodwood on Sussex Stakes day, and there's no doubt that Hotfoot is getting some fine-looking animals. Some of them can run a bit, too! Free State himself, who started the season in handicaps, took on Wollow in the big race and came closer to beating him than any other English-trained horse came on the four occasions during the year that Wollow showed winning form. He went down by only a length. He stuck to Wollow over the last two furlongs, although always having the worse of the battle and, in the end, being beaten a shade comfortably. This was Free State's best performance, and on the strength of it he is fully entitled to be regarded as one of the best of a less-than-outstanding generation of milers in this country.

Free State's performance made all the more regrettable his absence, through injury, from the Irish Two Thousand Guineas. He would have given a good account of himself there, although around that time, and indeed up to Goodwood, he was taking on horses below classic standard in handicaps. The day before Wollow won the Clerical, Medical Greenham Stakes at Newbury in the spring Free State had made a winning reappearance in the Stroud Green Handicap at the same meeting, beating The Tista with impressive ease. Between then and Goodwood he ran three times and never failed to show improvement despite the fact that he won only once—when taking the Esher Cup at Sandown from Spade Guinea and Obstacle with an even greater ease than the Stroud Green Handicap. At Royal Ascot he came out of a very tight finish to the Britannia Stakes with third place (and afterwards got second at the expense of Lord Helpus in the stewards' room) and at the Newmarket July meeting he finished a half-length second to Trusted in the William Hill Silver Vase. Free State had to give 18 lb to such a useful three-year-old as Trusted, so now that he had arrived at the top of the handicap there seemed everything to gain and little to lose by switching him to races like the Sussex Stakes, especially as there were so few really good milers around.

Free State made only one appearance after the Sussex Stakes, probably because on that one appearance he not only had a desperately hard race but had a much harder race than might reasonably have been anticipated. His chance in the Waterford Crystal Mile at Goodwood in August was there for everyone to see. Conditions were ideal, and he received weight from all his five opponents—18 lb from the older Boldboy, 9 lb from Radetzky, 5 lb from Niebo and Poacher's Moon (he had beaten the latter at levels in the Sussex Stakes) and 4 lb from Super Cavalier whom Murray rode at overweight. Free State saw off Poacher's Moon, Niebo and Super Cavalier without too much trouble but Radetzky, who took the field along at a fast pace, and Boldboy proved very tough opponents. Third into the straight, Free State came under pressure around a furlong and a half out, at the time that Boldboy was taking over from Radetzky in front, and it needed all Eddery's power in the saddle to

Mrs D. McCalmont's "Free State"

Waterford Crystal Mile, Goodwood—Free State (left) has to pull out all the stops to wear down Boldboy

get him home. Radetzky couldn't quicken with the other two in the last furlong but Boldboy remained ahead of Free State until in the shadow of the post.

Free State (b.c. 1973)	Hotfoot (br 1966)	Firestreak (br 1956)	Pardal / Hot Spell
		Pitter Patter (br 1953)	Kingstone / Rain
	Born Free (ch 1960)	Alycidon (ch 1945)	Donatello II / Aurora
		Queen of Sheba (b 1948)	Persian Gulf / Ojala

If Free State takes after his sire he will be even better at four years than three, and he will stay a distance of a mile and a quarter. The probability is that he will follow his sire in both respects, although it might be argued that a less dry summer than the last two could jeopardize his prospects. Free State has proved extremely well suited by firm going and he has never once raced on ground any easier than good. Born Free, his dam, stayed a mile and a quarter and she acted on any going. Her form in two starts at a mile and a half did not measure up to her best—surprisingly for a daughter of Alycidon—although she finished second in the Cheshire Oaks. The next dam Queen of Sheba was a versatile racemare: she won the Cheshire Oaks and came within a neck of taking the Irish Oaks, and she also won the Irish One Thousand Guineas and the Royal Hunt Cup. Perhaps the best-known and most important of her eight winners is Menelek (by Tulyar), a stayer in his racing days and now a prolific sire of jumping winners. Born Free produced three winners before Free State; they were Simonstown (by High Treason) who stayed a mile, Living Free (by Never Say Die) who stayed a mile and a half, and For Ever Free (by Reform) who stayed nine furlongs. If Free State does not succeed in making more than the normal improvement he may be difficult to place as a four-year-old, but if and when he is beaten he is still likely to be thereabouts at the finish, and he will not go down without giving of his best. He is that sort of horse—as tough and genuine as they come. *P. Walwyn.*

FREEZE THE SECRET 2 b. or br.f. Nearctic–Secret Practice (Native Dancer) **90 p** [1976 6d³] attractive American-bred filly: half-sister to What a Beauty (by Swaps), a winner at up to 7f: $30,000 yearling: dam won over 6f at 3 yrs in U.S.A.: 14/1, took the eye in paddock prior to finishing promising 4¾ lengths third of 23 to Rings in maiden race at Newmarket in October: will stay 7f: likely to improve and win races. *L. Cumani.*

FREIGHT FORWARDER 2 b.c. Calpurnius 122–Wig and Gown (Mandamus **100** 120) [1976 5g 6fg⁶ 6f* 6fg⁴ 7f⁵ 7g⁴ 7s 6s² 6s] neat colt: first foal: 2,000 gns yearling: dam never ran: showed improved form when winning minor event at

Folkestone in July by 1½ lengths from Sauve Qui Peut: bettered that effort in New Ham Stakes at Goodwood later in month, finishing about 3 lengths fourth to Abs and also ran well when neck second to Casino Boy in close finish to nursery at Newmarket in October: best at 6f: acts on any going. *A. Pitt.*

FRENCH FOX 4 b.g. Prince de Galles 125–Foxy Countess (Stone Fox 106) **54** [1974 N.R. 1975 8g⁶ 9g 8g⁴ 1976 9fg 7fg 8fg 8f³ 10f³ 8f⁶ 8h⁵ 7fg 8fg] neat gelding: poor handicapper: stays 1¼m: acts on firm going: sold out of R. Turnell's stable 1,400 gns Ascot August Sales after eighth outing. *J. Berry.*

FRENCH FRIEND 3 b.c. Herbager 136–Take a Stand (Amerigo 116 §) [1975 **118** 7.5g 7s⁶ 8.5d² 8g* 10s* 1976 10g³ 15d³ 14.6d 10v] American-bred French colt: good sort: showed very smart form at 2 yrs and won Prix de Conde at Longchamp: just over 2 lengths third to Crow and Avaray in Group 2 Prix Eugene Adam at Saint-Cloud in July on his first outing in 1976 but didn't fulfil promise of that run, subsequently finishing 5 lengths third to Citoyen in Prix Kergorlay at Deauville, tenth of 15 to Crow in St Leger at Doncaster and ninth of 14 to Iron Duke in La Coupe de Maisons-Laffitte: possibly best at distances short of 15f: acts on soft going. *R. de Tarragon, France.*

FRENCH GIPSY 3 ch.f. Sky Gipsy 117–Joie de France (Reliance II 137) — [1975 N.R. 1976 10f⁵ 8g 8h⁴ 7h] first foal: 2,500 gns yearling: dam won over 1¼m in Ireland: plating-class maiden: best run at 1m. *A. Pitt.*

FRENCH HARMONY 4 br.c. Tudor Melody 129–Belle Affaire 96 (Elopement **72** 125) [1974 6s² 6s³ 1975 7g⁵ 8s⁶ 7.6g⁵ 8g 8fg 6g⁶ 10fg² 10g⁶ 8h* 8f² 10g* 10g 11g 1976 12g⁵ 12g 11.7fg⁶ 11.7fg³ 11.7fg* 11.7f⁵ 10g 12f⁴ 12s⁶ 10s 10s] strong, quick-actioned colt: quite a moderate handicapper: successful at Windsor in August by a short head from Pass the Port: stays 1½m: acts on any going: best in blinkers: inconsistent. *D. Underwood.*

FRENCH PRINCESS 4 b.f. Prince Regent 129–Queen Dido 104 (Acropolis 132) **84** [1974 6fg 8s³ 8d⁴ 8v 1975 12s⁵ 16s³ 16f* 16f* 16fg* 16f² 16g² 16g⁴ 16g² 18fg 1976 14fg⁵ 16g³ 18.4s 16g⁴ 20f 16fg 16fg⁶ 18f³ 16v* 14s³] fair handicapper: having her first race for three months, held off Flash Imp by 1½ lengths when winning at York in October: probably feeling the effects of that run when well beaten on same course two days later: suited by long distances: acts on any going: blinkered seventh start: sold 3,500 gns Newmarket December Sales. *M. Ryan.*

FRENCH REVERSE 3 ch.g. Military 112–Bouleversee (Napoleon Bonaparte **58** 114) [1975 7d 7g 7f 8f⁶ 9g 7g 7g³ 1976 10.1fg 8fg⁴ 7fg³ 7g² 10.1fg] lengthy gelding: modest plater: has yet to show he stays further than 7f (ran poorly over 1¼m on final outing): ran creditably in blinkers on third appearance. *R. Hannon.*

FRENCH SAINT 2 b.g. Saintly Song 128–Montserrat 59 (Trouville 125) [1976 — 7f⁶] leggy gelding: fourth live foal: dam won at 1m: 25/1 and in need of race, always struggling when sixth of seven to The Bowler in minor event at Catterick in July. *Miss S. Hall.*

FRENCH TYRANT 3 b.g. Tyrant–French Dame 80 (French Beige 127) [1975 — 5s⁴ 5f 6g 6fg 1976 10.2s] big, strong gelding: good walker: showed a little ability at 2 yrs: backward only outing in 1976 (November). *M. W. Easterby.*

FRIDAY BROWN 3 ch.f. Murrayfield 119–Nemea 98 (Ommeyad 120) [1975 **84** 5f 5f 6g⁶ 6s 1976 9f⁴ 10.1fg³ 10fg* 10g⁴ 8.2fg 6h* 8d* 8fg* 8s³] small, sharp sort of filly: successful in maiden race at Lingfield in July and handicaps at Folkestone, Yarmouth and Leicester: was particularly impressive, quite one of easiest winners we saw all season, when beating Il Ruffino by 5 lengths (could have doubled that margin) on last-named course in September: effective at 6f to 1¼m: possibly not at her best on soft ground (ran below form last time out): goes well for apprentice H. Ballantine. *M. Masson.*

FRIDAY'S MEADOW 3 ch.c. Continuation 120–Tamer Flash 71 (Tamerlane — 128) [1975 7f 8.2g 7g 1976 10.2g 10.8f⁶] leggy, light-framed colt: only poor form: blinkered final outing. *H. Williams.*

FRIDOLINA 2 b.f. Frigid Aire–Zaza 85 (Pinza 137) [1976 7f⁶ 7g 9fg 8d 8v] **63** modest plater: sold 190 gns Ascot November Sales. *A. Corbett.*

FRIENDLY 2 ch.f. Bold Lad (Ire) 133–Joey 110 (Salvo 129) [1976 5g² 5g⁶ 5d² **77** 6s 6v] small, well-made filly: first foal: dam, winner over 5f and 7.6f, stayed 1¼m: quite a moderate maiden: runner-up to Great Flight at Sandown in June and to Miss Knightsbridge at Haydock in October: should be suited by further than 5f: sold 4,700 gns Newmarket December Sales. *H. Wragg.*

FRIENDLY BOY 4 b.c. Be Friendly 130–Quantity 77 (Quorum 126) [1974 5g⁶ —
6fg 6fg 8s* 7s⁵ 8g³ 8v⁶ 1975 8v* 10v 8v⁶ 9s 1976 8g 10g 10v⁶ 8fg⁶ 10g⁵] strong,
robust colt: most disappointing since winning handicap at Pontefract in April as
a 3-y-o: possibly best at up to 1m: very well suited by soft going: has worn
blinkers. *F. Carr.*

FRIENDLY BUILDER 3 b.f. King's Leap 111–Nitsi (Final Score 113) [1975 **78**
5g 5g² 5g* 5g² 6fg⁴ 6fg⁴ 6f 6v 1976 6g 7fg 6g 8fg 10s³ 10fg⁶ 10.2g⁶ 10d⁶ 10g⁴
12.2s 8d²] useful sort: blinkered first time when runner-up to The Four
Hundred in claiming race at Newmarket in October: apparently stays 1¼m but
not 1½m. *N. Callaghan.*

FRIENDLY CHOICE 2 b.f. Be Friendly 130–Elected 74 (Red God 128 §) **80**
[1976 5g⁶ 6d 5.3f² 5fg² 6f⁴] strong filly: half-sister to Sunset Value (by Current
Coin), a winner at up to 1m: 2,000 gns yearling: dam won at 1m: runner-up in
maiden races at Brighton (to Angelos) and Chester (to Rahesh) in July: possibly
better suited by 5f than 6f: acts on firm going. *P. Haslam.*

FRIENDLY CHORUS 2 ch.f. Be Friendly 130–Alchorus 78 (Alcide 136) [1976 **71**
5g² 5g] second foal: sister to top-class filly Be Tuneful, a winner at 6f and 7f:
dam won over 9f: ran respectably for a newcomer when second to wide-margin
winner First Swallow in 10-runner maiden event at Warwick in August, but was
well beaten in a similar event at Lanark (favourite) in October: will stay 7f.
B. Lunness.

FRIENDLY GODDESS 2 ch.f. Green God 128–Pal Sinna 80 (Palestine 133) **80**
[1976 6fg 5fg² 5s] rangy, unfurnished filly: very good mover: third foal: half-
sister to two winners, including top-class sprinter Bay Express (by Polyfoto):
14,500 gns yearling: dam placed at up to 1¼m: ran well from a low draw when
4 lengths second of 19 to Right of Light in maiden race at Salisbury in September:
started favourite for similar event at Folkestone the following month but ran
badly and is probably unsuited by soft going: will stay 6f. *J. Nelson.*

FRIENDLY HOPPITY 2 ch.f. Be Friendly 130–Hoppity 72 (Negotiation) —
[1976 5fg 5d⁵] neat filly: first foal: dam half-sister to smart sprinter Hopiana:
in rear in sellers at Ripon and Redcar in May. *J. W. Watts.*

FRIENDLY JESTER 3 ch.f. Be Friendly 130–Lady Jester 108 (Bleep-Bleep 134) **90**
[1975 5s² 1976 6v⁶ 5f* 5fg*] rangy filly: having first outing for three months,
won apprentice maiden event at Edinburgh in July: put up a much better performance when spreadeagling her field in seven-runner handicap at Goodwood
later in month, coming home 6 lengths clear of Cry No More: not seen out again:
speedy and probably best at 5f on top-of-the-ground. *T. Fairhurst.*

FRIENDLY KISS 2 b.f. Be Friendly 130–Stolen Kiss 75 (Lord of Verona 120) **78**
[1976 5s³ 5g⁵ 5fg³ 5fg³ 6f 5d] strong filly: third foal: dam a middle-distance
performer: third in maiden races at Chester (two) and Nottingham, on latter
course being beaten 2¼ lengths by My Therape in July: will stay 7f. *M. Salaman.*

FRIENDLY NOW 2 ch.c. Be Friendly 130–Right Now 100 (Right Royal V 135) **107**
[1976 7fg 6f 6d* 6fg* 7v² 8v⁶] big, good-looking colt: third foal: 3,700 gns
yearling: dam, half-sister to Mon Fils and Son of Silver, won twice over 1½m
and stayed well: won maiden race at Yarmouth (well-backed favourite) and
25-runner minor event at Redcar in September: made all and held on well under
pressure when beating Supernaculum by ½ length in latter event: sixth
to Baudelaire in Premio Tevere at Rome in November: should stay 1m: seems
to act on any going. *L. Cumani.*

FRIENDLY SOUND 3 b.f. Be Friendly 130–Sweet Sound 74 (Sound Track 132) **82**
[1975 5g⁶ 5.1f³ 5f 6g 6g⁴ 1976 6g⁵ 6g⁴ 7fg* 7fg³ 7f* 7g] quite well-made
filly: won minor event at Epsom and handicaps at Newmarket and Yarmouth:
had 1½ lengths to spare over Jackoleon on last-named course in August: stays 7f:
acts on firm going: ran poorly final appearance. *G. Pritchard-Gordon.*

FRIENDLY SPECIAL 2 ch.f. Be Friendly 130–Retsillac M 76 (St Chad 120) —
[1976 6v] first foal: 1,150 gns yearling: dam showed quite moderate form at
2 yrs: slow into stride and never got into race when remote tenth of 20 to Cathmaria in seller at Haydock in October. *P. Cole.*

FRIENDLY SYLVAN 2 b.f. Be Friendly 130–Sylvan Angle (Ragusa 137) —
[1976 5g 6f⁶ 5s] compact filly: first produce: 2,600 gns yearling: dam won in
Germany at 2 yrs and 3 yrs: well behind in maiden races: sold 320 gns Doncaster
November Sales. *B. Lunness.*

FRIGID D'OR 3 br.g. Frigid Aire–Hannah d'Or (Rockefella) [1975 N.R. —
1976 7g] second foal: 180 gns yearling: dam placed over 9f in France at 3 yrs:

tailed-off last of 14 behind Lotto in maiden race at Kempton in August. *M. Haynes.*

FRINTON LODGE 3 b.c. Laser Light 118–Long Shadow 77 (Royal Palm 131) **?** [1975 5s 5fg 5fg6 6f 6g 7d4 7g3 7f2 7.6s6 1976 9fg4 8f4 9g2 7.5g3 8.5g4 8.5g2 10g* 8.5g* 11.5g 8.8g 9.5g] neat colt: won two small races at Divonne-les-Bains in August: stays 1¼m: probably acts on any going: has been tried in blinkers: trained until after second outing by R. Akehurst. *P. Swann, France.*

FRISCO BAY 2 b.c. Realm 129–Rockspray 77 (Roan Rocket 128) [1976 5fg **91** 5g6 6fg5 6fg* 7g2 7f2 7f3 7s* 7v2] small colt: second foal: 540 gns yearling: dam, a plater, appeared to stay 2m: successful in seller at Leicester in July (no bid): showed much improved form in the mud in nurseries on last two outings, winning at Sandown in October (made all) by 5 lengths from Loyal Deed and finishing 1½ lengths second of 18 to Royal Audition at Leicester the following month: will stay 1m. *P. Cole.*

FRISKY SCOT 5 ch.g. Crocket 130–Babble On 79 (Acropolis 132) [1974 10s **52** 7.2s6 8v6 1975 8f4 12.3fg 8fg 1976 12g2 14.7f3 15.8f3 17.7f2 15.8f2 16.1f* 18.1g3] workmanlike gelding: a twin: poor performer: won bad maiden race at Haydock in August by 1½ lengths from Owen Glyndwr: needs long distances: acts on firm going: sold 3,500 gns Newmarket Autumn Sales. *W. Elsey.*

FRIVOLITY 3 ch.f. Varano–Primlace 84 (Chamossaire) [1975 5f 7f6 7f 7fg **70** 10g6 1976 10fg 12g3 12g 16f5 16f3 16f* 15g4 16d2 16s] quite a modest performer: wide-margin winner of poor maiden race at Ripon in August: good second to Arctic Rascal in handicap at Nottingham the following month but ran poorly final outing: a thorough stayer who will be suited by extreme distances: possibly unsuited by really soft going: sold 6,000 gns Newmarket December Sales. *W. Marshall.*

FRUITY 3 ch.f. Galivanter 131–Fair Game 84 (Big Game) [1975 N.R. 1976 **—** 5f] lightly-built filly: half-sister to useful handicapper Big Venture (by Hopeful Venture) and to four other winners: dam ran only at 2 yrs: unquoted and ridden by 7-lb claimer, missed break and always behind in 19-runner maiden race at Beverley in June. *D. Sasse.*

FULBECK 2 ch.c. Charlottown 127–Cantadora 107 (Matador 131) [1976 **79** 5fg3 5fg* 5g5 7g6 7f 5g6 5.9s5 5d] rather light-framed colt: half-brother to four winners, notably useful 3-y-o sprinter Rory's Rocket (by Roan Rocket): 3,500 gns yearling: dam a sprinter: won maiden race at Newmarket in April in good style by 4 lengths from Gold Bar but is only a moderate performer: best form at up to 6f: seems to act on any going. *D. Marks.*

FULL FRONTAL 2 b.c. Daring Display 129–Ducklet (Epaulette 125) [1976 **61** 5g 5f 6g 6s6 5v] poor performer: showed little in varied company, including selling: should stay 7f+: blinkered last two outings: sold 550 gns Ascot November Sales. *G. Hunter.*

FULL OF FUN 2 b.f. Galivanter 131–Her Ladyship 90 (Prince Chevalier) **—** [1976 6fg] sister to a winning sprinter, and half-sister to several other minor winners: dam middle-distance performer: behind in 13-runner maiden race won by Dumbunny at Nottingham in August. *D. Morley.*

FULL OF HOPE 6 b.h. Great Nephew 126–Alpine Bloom 123 (Chamossaire) **125** [1974 7.5g* 10g6 8d2 7.5s* 7v2 8v 1975 7.8v* 10g* 8g5 8s2 10d6 7s2 8s2 1976 8g* 8d2 8g3 9.7d4 8d* 9.2g* 8d 7s6 8.2v] French horse: half-brother to several winners, including useful stayer Rising Falcon (by Gyr): dam third in 1958 1,000 Guineas: a high-class animal who was in tremendous form in first half of season, winning three important events, namely Prix Edmond Blanc at Saint-Cloud in March (beating Trepan easily by 3 lengths), Prix du Chemin de Fer du Nord at Chantilly (narrowly from Gravelines) and Prix d'Ispahan at Longchamp (beat Ivanjica 2½ lengths) in June: most disappointing last three appearances: stays

Prix d'Ispahan, Longchamp—Full of Hope beats Ivanjica, Ricco Boy and El Rastro

1¼m: acts on heavy going: suited by forcing tactics: genuine. *G. Delloye, France.*

FULLSTOP 2 ch.f. Salvo 129–Full Toss 108 (Ballymoss 136) [1976 6fg⁶ 7g 7g 8s] **68 p**
lengthy filly: good walker: half-sister to 1¼m winner Hopefully (by Reform): dam won over 1½m: showed ability, finishing seventh of 23 to Windy Sea and tenth of 28 to Royal Boxer (made some late headway) in maiden races at Newmarket in October: should do much better over middle distances at 3 yrs. *H. Wragg.*

FULL VALUE 5 br.h. Relko 136–How Far 107 (Hethersett 134) [1974 7.6g⁵ **54**
10.1fg³ 10g⁴ 9.4f⁴ 1975 8g² 7f* 7f⁵ 7f 8f 1976 10fg⁴ 9fg³ 12fg⁶ 8f⁶ 8f⁵] very short-backed horse: stays 1¼m: acts on firm going. *D. Ringer.*

FUNNY HAT 2 b.f. Will Hays (U.S.A.)–Tiny Toque (High Hat 131) [1976 —
7d 8s 7s] strong filly: half-sister to a winning hurdler: 300 gns yearling: dam poor Irish maiden: 33/1 on all outings but showed a little ability, finishing tenth of 19 to Lady Oriana in maiden race at Newmarket in October on final outing. *B. Hanbury.*

FUNNY LADY 2 b.f. Comedy Star 121–Marcida 85 (Alcide 136) [1976 5g 6f⁵ —
6fg] evidently of no account. *C. Dingwall.*

FUNNY VALENTINE 3 b.c. Silly Season 127–Anippe 102 (Aggressor 130) **85**
[1975 5f⁴ 5.9f 6fg⁴ 7g 6fg⁶ 1976 8fg⁶ 8g⁵ 10fg* 10f* 11.7fg² 10f⁴ 10h² 10g³ 10h³ 10f² 12h⁴ 10g] dipped-backed colt: modest handicapper: winner at Yarmouth and Pontefract in June: suited by 1¼m (did not run up to his best when tried at 1½m): acts on firm going: blinkered third outing at 2 yrs and tenth start: dwelt sixth and seventh appearances: consistent (although ran moderately final outing): doesn't find a great deal off bridle and is suited by waiting tactics. *J. Powney.*

FURLEY 2 b.f. Decoy Boy 129–Cecilia Gallerani (Pinturischio 117) [1976 **91**
5fg 6fg 5fg⁴ 5h* 5f² 5fg] leggy filly: first foal: dam showed only poor form: made all when winning five-runner maiden race at Pontefract in August by 4 lengths from Quimay: creditable second under a penalty in nursery won by Rahesh at Nottingham later in month: quite speedy and is not certain to stay 6f: badly hampered on final outing. *J. Winter.*

FUSILIER 4 b.g. Shantung 132–Fusil 105 (Fidalgo 129) [1974 7fg 7d³ 7fg **63**
1975 12v⁴ 1976 12.5g 12fg 12.5h⁴ 12.3fg² 12fg⁶ 15g² 16f* 12.2g³ 12h⁴ 13v²] lengthy gelding: poor stayer: won bad maiden race at Beverley in August by 3 lengths from Morning: acted on any going: sold 2,600 gns Newmarket Autumn Sales: dead. *H. Wragg.*

FUTURE FOREST 3 ch.c. Continuation 120–Sylvan Wood (Red God 128 §) **104**
[1975 5g³ 5g* 5g⁴ 5g* 5g³ 5g* 5s* 1976 6fg 5s² 5s* 6g⁶ 5.6g⁵ 5v⁴ 6s] shapely, attractive colt: useful sprinter: ran out a comfortable winner of valuable Amoco Handicap at Doncaster in May, beating Last Tango by a length: wasn't seen out again until September but had two fair efforts to his credit in the autumn: should stay 6f: best form on an easy surface and is very well suited by soft going. *N. Angus.*

G

GABLES END 3 ch.f. Roi Soleil 125–Treaty 86 (Ratification 129) [1975 5s² —
5s⁴ 5s 5v 5f² 5g² 5f⁵ 5f* 5f³ 5f⁴ 5fg⁶ 5f 6f⁶ 1976 5f 8f 5f⁴ 7f 5f] ex-Irish filly: fair performer at 2 yrs: had stiffish tasks in 1976 and showed no worthwhile form. *J. Fitzgerald.*

GAEA 2 b.f. Charlottown 127–Ticklish 112 (Greek Star) [1976 5f 5g 5h 7f⁵ —
7fg] half-sister to three winners, including very useful miler Caius (by Romulus): 1,000 gns yearling: dam a stayer: little worthwhile form, including in maiden auction events: blinkered last two outings. *T. Fairhurst.*

GAELIC 4 b.c. Busted 134–Parlez-vous 88 (Pardal 130) [1974 7fg³ 7fg² 7s* **90**
8s² 1975 8s² 8v⁵ 8f³ 10fg⁵ 12g⁵ 10.6s* 1976 10g 10.6d² 12.3s² 10.5d] neat, compact, good-bodied colt: good mover: fairly useful handicapper: good second at Haydock in April and Chester the following month, but wasn't seen out after running poorly at York later in May: stays 1⅓m: acts on any going, but is particularly well suited by soft: not particularly consistent: sold 6,100 gns Doncaster May Sales. *Denys Smith.*

GAELIC BEAU 5 ch.g. El Cid 109–Gaelic Belle 69 (Ossian II) [1974 9.4f —
11.2f 8fg 7g 8.2v 1975 N.R. 1976 16.1f] plain gelding: of little account. *J. Cousins.*

GAE

GAELIC GOD 2 b.c. Green God 128–Whistler's Sister 75 (Tin Whistle 128) **84**
[1976 5fg* 6d 6f 5h⁴ 5h³ 5f⁵ 5g⁵] robust colt: second produce: 1,200 gns foal,
resold 3,000 gns yearling: dam sprint plater: won maiden race at Thirsk in May
by a neck from Hemsworth: close-up third in nursery won by Ceppo at Hamilton
in August and finished fair fifth of 18 to stable-companion Imari in £1,900
seller at Sandown the following month on final outing: stays 6f: acts on hard
ground. *K. Payne.*

GAELIC MELODY 5 b.m. Highland Melody 112–Ennis Royal 65 (Ennis 128) —
[1974 8fg³ 10g 8f³ 8f⁵ 8h³ 8.2g* 8fg 8g⁶ 8g 8s³ 8v³ 1975 N.R. 1976 7h] quite
a moderate handicapper (rated 69) in 1974: slowly into stride and always
behind in amateur riders event won by Sunset Value at Brighton in August,
only outing since: stays 1m but probably not 1¼m: seems to act on any going:
wears blinkers. *R. Supple.*

GAETANO 2 b.c. Bold Lad (Ire) 133–Daphne 106 (Acropolis 132) [1976 —
6d 8s 7v] strong, good-bodied, rather plain colt: half-brother to two winners
in Ireland: 7,800 gns foal and resold 1,100 gns as a yearling: dam, who stayed
1½m. is half-sister to 1,000 Guineas runner-up Gwen: no worthwhile form but
looks the sort to do better at 3 yrs. *C. Brittain.*

GAFFER 4 b.g. Giolla Mear 113–Bavelin (Javelin) [1974 N.R. 1975 N.R. —
1976 10.2s 12s] big gelding: second foal: half-brother to Irish hurdler Slieve
Bloom (by No Argument): dam Irish staying maiden: behind in maiden races
at Doncaster and Haydock in October. *M. W. Easterby.*

GAIRLOCH 2 ro.c. Roan Rocket 128–Nettlebed 84 (Hethersett 134) [1976 7g* **121 p**
7fg* 8d*]

Gairloch's life story reads rather like that of an equine ugly duckling. At
the tender age of eight months he was sent by his breeders to the December Sales.
Two Lorenzaccio fillies which accompanied him fetched nearly 8,000 guineas
between them but Gairloch, whose two-year-old half-sister looked to be of little
account, fetched only 1,900 guineas. If his breeders regretted selling him for this
price they had cause to feel sorrier when Gairloch's year-older brother Whistlefield made his first appearance; this colt, whom they had retained, showed a deal
of promise in finishing third in a good-class maiden race. Nevertheless, just
before Whistlefield had his second race Gairloch made his second appearance in
the sale-ring, coming up at the Ballsbridge Yearling Sales. The catalogue made
no mention of Whistlefield, and Gairloch's breeders, represented by Jack Doyle,

*Royal Lodge Stakes, Ascot—Gairloch does just enough
to beat Pampapaul*

were able to buy him back for 6,400 guineas. They have since had every reason to be pleased with their change of mind; Whistlefield has shown smart form and Gairloch, with three wins in as many starts, has turned out to be a 'swan'.

Gairloch had his first race in August. His starting price of 14/1 in maiden company at Kempton suggested that he wasn't expected to win, but win he did and in impressive style too; he came through very smoothly to take the lead approaching the distance and soon went clear to win by four lengths from Region. At Goodwood eleven days later he and Do Better, the two winners in a seventeen-strong field for the Pilleygreen Stakes, drew right away in the final furlong with Gairloch getting the verdict by a neck.

Gairloch met much stronger opposition on his final outing of the season, in the Royal Lodge Stakes at Ascot later in September. Of the six runners Gairloch, Card Player, Hot Grove and the July Stakes winner Sky Ship were unbeaten after ten outings between them, and the other two, Pampapaul and Millionaire, had never finished out of the first two in nine starts. The Irish colt Pampapaul was made favourite on the strength of an excellent win in the £16,000 National Stakes on his last outing and it was he, pulling hard, who made the running. Gairloch was settled in last place until approaching halfway, then improved steadily on the outside, and it was clear early in the straight that he was travelling very strongly. He moved up in fine style to join Pampapaul at the distance and drew ahead steadily to win by three quarters of a length. This was a splendid effort by Gairloch, even though Pampapaul may have run a bit too freely for his own good in the early stages. Not once did Gairloch's jockey resort to his whip and we got the impression, as at Goodwood, that Gairloch did just enough to win and no more. He almost certainly has improvement in him; if so he will make a high-class three-year-old.

		Roan Rocket (ro 1961)	Buisson Ardent (b 1953)	Relic
Gairloch (ro.c. 1974)				Rose O'Lynn
			Farandole II (gr 1947)	Deux pour Cent
				Faramoude
		Nettlebed (b 1967)	Hethersett (b 1959)	Hugh Lupus
				Bride Elect
			Joyce Grove (b 1946)	Bois Roussel
				Samovar

How far will Gairloch stay? Unfortunately Whistlefield, who might have shed some light on the matter, ran only once as a three-year-old, putting up a good performance at a mile. The dam, Nettlebed, was tried over all sorts of distances but not until she was a four-year-old, and in foal, did she gain her one success, in a seven-furlong handicap. Her dam, Joyce Grove, was a daughter of the Queen Mary Stakes winner Samovar and a half-sister to the One Thousand Guineas winner Zabara and the high-class 1955 two-year-old Rustam. As a race-horse she was moderate, winning only a six-furlong maiden at three years, but she did much better at stud; ten of her foals won here and in the United States, the best of them being the Petition horse Day Court whose wins in the States included the ten-furlong Hawthorne Gold Cup. Roan Rocket made his name as a miler but was beaten only a short head in the Eclipse. Gairloch should stay a mile and a quarter and possibly further, judging by his relaxed style of racing. He's a well-made colt, a very good mover and has a fine turn of foot. By far his best form is on an easy surface, but it's much too early to tell if an easy surface suits him best. *R. Price.*

GALA DISPLAY 2 b.c. Daring Display 129–Sabotage 96 (High Treason 126) **78** [1976 5s2 5s3 5s 6s] well-made Irish colt: half-brother to two minor winners: 6,600 gns yearling: dam won at 5f and 1m: beaten favourite on first two outings, going down by 5 lengths to Digitalis when odds on at Phoenix Park in March and being beaten 4¼ lengths by Jump To It in maiden race at Chester in May: off course over five months before final outing: should stay 6f: trained by P. Prendergast on first three starts. *P. Norris, Ireland.*

GALADRIEL 5 b.m. Track Spare 125–Magical Maid (Premonition 130) [1974 **64** 8f5 8h* 8d 8fg3 8fg 8h4 7g4 8d5 8s 1975 8fg6 7g 8.2f6 8f 8h3 8g5 8h4 8g 8f 8f 6g 8.2d5 8g2 8g6 1976 9fg 8fg* 10.1fg2 7g 8fg* 7fg2 8g 10f2 8f4 8.2fg2 8.2fg3 8f3 8g2 8.3g3 8g* 10g5 8s] small filly: fair selling handicapper: well backed when success-ful at Warwick in April, Brighton in May and Wolverhampton in August, being bought in for 560 gns on last-named course: stays 1¼m: seems to act on any going: has been tried in blinkers. *E. Reavey.*

GALAHAD II 3 ch.c. Gala Performance–Nymphea 91 (Nearula 132) [1975 **102** 5g 6f 7g2 8g3 8g2 1976 10f4 10fg* 10fg2 12g6 12v* 12v*] strong, good-looking colt: well-backed favourite, won 13-runner maiden race at Nottingham in April: sold out of R. Price's stable 10,000 gns Newmarket Autumn Sales and subsequently won handicaps at Haydock and Lingfield in space of four days, on latter course defying a 4 lb penalty when beating Busted Fiddle 10 lengths: stays 1½m: acts on a firm surface but goes particularly well on heavy ground. *D. Underwood.*

GALA LAD 2 ch.g. Gala Performance–Land 62 (Baldric II 131) [1976 5f³ 5f 5fg³ **91** 6d* 7f⁵ 7.2f* 7g*] leggy gelding: blind in right eye: second foal: 1,200 gns yearling: dam of little account: put up a fine performance in 17-runner nursery at Catterick in September, coming from last to first and winning going away by 1½ lengths from Gnos: twice successful earlier in plating company at Haydock: will stay 1m: probably acts on any going. *M. H. Easterby.*

GALA PRINCESS 3 ch.f. Midsummer Night II 117–Gala Queen 90 (Darius 129) **54** [1975 6f 6d 8g 1976 12f² 12g] big filly: stays 1½m: bought by B.B.A. 1,200 gns Newmarket July Sales for export to Australia. *J. W. Watts.*

GALE BRIDGE 3 ch.f. Vaguely Noble 140–Mrs Gotrocks (Bold Bidder) [1975 **115** 7s* 1976 7.3f 12fg 8g* 8g³ 10.6v³ 12s*] big, rangy, good-looking American-bred filly: first produce: 28,000 gns foal: dam, daughter of leading American racemare Oil Royalty, won once over 6f from five starts at 3 yrs: quite lightly raced but is a smart filly, as she showed when winning three-runner Atlanta Stakes at Sandown in September very smoothly by 4 lengths and 8 lengths from Solar (gave 11 lb) and Crofting (levels), and £8,000 William Hill November Handicap at Doncaster by 3 lengths from stable-companion Shelahnu with rest of field well strung out: very well suited by 1½m and will stay further: needs some give in the ground. *R. Price.*

GALE FORECAST 4 b.f. Eborneezer 105–Northerly 78 (Twilight Alley 133) — [1974 N.R. 1975 N.R. 1976 14f 14g⁵ 15.5s] big, workmanlike filly: first foal: dam stayed 1¼m: poor form in maiden race and two amateur riders events. *Mrs D. Oughton.*

GALENIST 3 b.f. Behistoun 131–Galosh 86 (Pandofell 132) [1975 N.R. — 1976 12fg] lengthy filly: second foal: dam needed long distances and soft ground to show to advantage: tailed off in 17-runner Galtres Stakes won by Capricious at York in August: dead. *W. Elsey.*

GALIANO 7 b.h. Galivanter 131–Queen's Rock 85 (Souverain 135) [1974 **101** 8g³ 7g* 8fg 8g⁴ 7fg 8g 1975 7fg² 8f 1976 8g³ 7fg⁶ 7fg 8s] strongly-made horse: useful handicapper: ran well when third, beaten a length and a head by The Hertford, in Irish Sweeps Lincoln at Doncaster in March on reappearance: not disgraced when sixth of 11 to Berkeley Square in Debenham Handicap at Kempton the following month, but ran poorly last two outings (not raced after May): stays 1m: acts on any going: sometimes sweats up: usually comes with a late run: bought by B.B.A. for export to South Africa. *B. Hills.*

GALLANT CSAR 2 ch.c. Czar Alexander 112–Ally Ant (Leanant) [1976 5f — 5g⁶ 6fg 6f 7fg 7v⁴] small colt: only poor form in varied company: blinkered fourth outing: trained by P. Mitchell on first five starts: sold 600 gns Newmarket Autumn Sales. *C. Brittain.*

GALLANT WELSH 2 br.c. Welsh Pageant 132–Tin Mary 96 (Tin King 126) **103** [1976 6f³ 7.9f* 7g⁵] second foal: 1,000 gns yearling: dam stayed 1m: odds on for 16-runner event at Dundalk in September and won like a useful colt, coming home 8 lengths clear of Before Eight: had a much stiffer task on final outing and was beaten just over 4 lengths into fifth place behind The Minstrel in Larkspur Stakes at Leopardstown: suited by 1m. *P. Prendergast, jnr, Ireland.*

GALLERY ROYAL 2 b.c. Gala Performance–Balabukha (Sayajirao 132) — [1976 5g 7g] neat, rather lightly-built colt: half-brother to three winners, including Irish 3-y-o Bay God (by Yellow God), successful at around 1m: 3,500 gns yearling: dam never ran: behind in large fields of maidens at Salisbury in May (started slowly) and Newmarket in October. *B. Hills.*

GALLETTO 2 b.f. Nijinsky 138–Gaia 116 (Charlottesville 135) [1976 8v*] **88 p** American-bred Irish filly: half-sister to useful stayer Sir Daniel (by Sir Ivor): dam won 1969 Irish Guinness Oaks: odds on, finished well to get up close home when winning 12-runner maiden race at Leopardstown in October by ¾ length from Tristan da Cunha: sure to improve and should make a smart staying filly. *V. O'Brien, Ireland.*

GALLICO 5 br.h. El Gallo 122–Bare Costs (Petition 130) [1974 5g 6g⁵ 6fg⁴ **91** 5fg* 6fg⁵ 5s⁴ 5d⁵ 6d 1975 6g⁵ 5g³ 5.1f* 5.3f³ 5fg³ 6f 5f⁴ 5g³ 5g 5g³ 1976 5fg²

5fg 5fg³ 5fg⁵ 5.3fg* 5fg* 6fg⁶ 5fg 5g 5g² 5s⁵ 5v⁴] lengthy horse: fairly useful handicapper: successful at Brighton in June and Newmarket the following month, beating Peranka in a tight finish on latter occasion: stays 6f: acts on any going but best form on a sound surface: suitable mount for an apprentice: blinkered third outing. *S. Woodman.*

GALLIC REBEL 7 br.h. Galivanter 131–Clarabella 94 (Klairon 131) [1974 N.R. 1975 N.R. 1976 15.5h] probably of no account. *J. Long.* —

GALLOWAY WOLD 2 b.c. The Brianstan 128–Blue Whirlwind 80 (Never Say Die 137) [1976 5f⁶ 5d⁶ 5f⁶ 5fg² 5f² 5f⁵ 5h² 5f] neat, strong colt: first foal: dam won over 5f as a 2-y-o: second three times, on final occasion going down by ½ length to odds-on Lutomer Riesling in three-runner event at Redcar in July: also twice ran badly when short-priced favourite and is an inconsistent customer. *E. Weymes.* 81

GALWAY BAY 3 b.c. Sassafras 135–Windjammer 95 (Hard Tack 111 §) [1975 5f* 6f* 6fg* 6fg³ 1976 7f 7g 10.4s⁵] compact colt: was a smart 2-y-o, winning three races, including Coventry Stakes and Hyperion Stakes at Ascot: didn't do well physically from 2 yrs to 3 yrs and ran very disappointingly in 1976: tried in blinkers second outing: not seen out after May. *I. Balding.* —

GAMBLING GIPSY 3 ch.f. Sky Gipsy 117–Good as Gold (Nimbus 130) [1975 6fg 6f 1976 8fg 8fg 8s* 8fg² 8f⁵ 8g 8s⁵] particularly attractive filly: half-sister to Whistling Wind (by Whistler): showed much improved form when winning minor event at Doncaster in May by a length from Streaker King: respectable second to Lucastown in similar race on same course the following month but ran below her best afterwards: stays 1m well: appears to act on any going. *G. Pritchard-Gordon.* 78

GAME COLLEEN 3 b.f. Double-U-Jay 120–Ol' Kalou 71 (Ballymoss 136) [1975 8g 1976 7fg 10.8f] tall filly: plating-class maiden. *B. Lunness.* —

GAME DAVID 3 ch.g. David Jack 125–Debatch Game 69 (Darius 129) [1975 5.1f 8.2d 9g 1976 10fg 10g² 12fg³ 12f⁴ 11.5d³ 16s 9s*] plater: ridden by 7-lb claimer when winning nine-runner maiden race at Wolverhampton in October by 6 lengths from Laurel Lark: best form at 9f but should stay well (well beaten when tried at 2m but was not ridden to conserve his stamina): sold to D. Barons 3,000 gns Newmarket Autumn Sales. *A. Goodwill.* 68

GAME LORD 3 b.c. Lord Gayle 124–Princess Ru (Princely Gift 137) [1975 6g 1976 8.2f* 9d 10fg* 10fg⁵ 8f³ 10f³ 8fg⁴ 9fg* 10fg³ 9f⁵ 8g² 9g] well-made colt: fairly useful handicapper: winner at Nottingham (maiden race), Newmarket and Newcastle: quickened well when beating Silver Steel a neck in Harry Peacock Challenge Cup on last-named track in July: 1½ lengths second to Ashbro Laddo in valuable William Hill Trophy at Sandown in September: stays 1½m: probably needs a sound surface: wears blinkers nowadays: sweating sixth outing: needs to be held up: consistent. *J. Hindley.* 94

GAN ON GEORDIE 4 br.c. On Your Mark 125–Miss Dalston (Sayajirao 132) [1974 5d* 5d* 6fg 5fg⁶ 1975 7d⁴ 6d 6f* 7fg* 6d⁴ 7g² 6fg⁴ 6fg* 6d 6fg⁴ 6g⁶ 5s⁴ 1976 5s³ 6fg² 6s² 7d⁵ 5fg³ 6g⁴ 6fg⁴ 6f* 6f³] well-grown, useful sort: fairly useful handicapper: successful at Redcar in August by a length from Clear Melody: ran well on some of his other outings, including on final appearance when 7½ lengths third of 14 to Honeyblest in Great St Wilfrid Handicap at Ripon in August: stays 7f: seems to act on any going: acts on any track: genuine: excellent mount for an apprentice: blinkered sixth start. *Denys Smith.* 93

GARAWIND 2 ch.f. Whistling Wind 123–Shangara (Credo 123) [1976 5.9g] third foal: half-sister to useful middle-distance stayer Pal's Bambino (by Pals Passage): sold twice as a yearling, for 1,500 gns and 2,500 gns: dam won twice over 5f at 2 yrs in Ireland: 20/1 and apprentice ridden when last of 25 in maiden race at Wolverhampton in June. *R. Murphy.* —

GARDEN PARTY 4 b.f. Reform 132–Pageant 80 (Santa Claus 133) [1974 6fg 7d* 7.2v* 8s² 1975 7.3v⁴ 10.2g 11fg³ 12g 1976 12.3d 13g 11s⁶ 11fg⁴ 8g³ 10f⁴ 10g⁶ 8fg³ 8fg² 8.2f⁴] lightly-made, lengthy filly: fair handicapper on her day: didn't manage to win at 4 yrs but ran respectably on several occasions: effective at 1m and should stay 1½m: acts well on heavy going: effective with and without blinkers: sold to M. Stevens 2,100 gns Ascot December Sales. *T. Craig.* 81

GARDONE 3 b.f. Petingo 135–Golden Keep 77 (Worden II 129) [1975 N.R. 1976 7f 11g 12g 8fg] attractive, close-coupled filly: second foal: 4,500 gns yearling: dam won from 1¼m to 13f: no worthwhile form in maiden races: sold 1,800 gns Newmarket Autumn Sales. *G. Harwood.* —

GARN 4 b.g. Sing Sing 134–Town House 91 (Pall Mall 132) [1974 5g 1975 7.2g 5g 7.2fg 6f⁶ 5.9fg⁵ 5f⁵ 5g 7fg⁵ 8g 1976 6fg 8g* 7f⁵ 10f 8fg⁴ 5f⁴ 8d 7s] tall 47 gelding: plater: successful at Ripon in April (no bid): stays 1m: acts on firm going. *A. W. Jones.*

GARRICK   2 ch.c. Reform 132–Pantomime Star (Silly Season 127)   [1976 5fg⁴ **66** 7g 7v⁴ 6d]   neat, strong colt: first foal: dam won over 11f and 1½m in France: 7½ lengths fourth of 15 to Chennel Lane in weakly-contested maiden race at Leicester in October, best effort: will stay 1¼m: ran badly in blinkers on final outing. *I. Balding.*

GARRISON GIRL   3 ch.f. Queen's Hussar 124–Persian Dancer 75 (Persian Gulf)   **67** [1975 N.R. 1976 8fg² 8fg⁴ 8fg⁵ 10fg³ 8fg 10.6d³]   neat filly: fourth foal: half-sister to a winning plater: dam won over 1¾m: only plating class: should stay 1¼m. *W. Elsey.*

GARTREE HILL   3 br.c. Stupendous–La Fresnes 126 (Court Martial)   [1975 **60** N.R. 1976 8g 10g⁶ 10.1fg⁵ 10.1f³ 12.2fg 10s]   big, tall, useful-looking colt: half-brother to five winners, including very useful sprinter Clinkers (by Relic) and useful 5f sprinter Top Security (by Sing Sing): dam a very smart sprinter: 2½ lengths third of nine to Kyriakos in maiden event at Windsor in July, best effort: started slowly first two outings: sold 2,200 gns Ascot October Sales. *J. Dunlop.*

GAUNLESS GIRL   3 ch.f. Quayside 124–Comprella 54 (Compensation 127)   — [1975 N.R. 1976 10f 8fg 11f]   plating-class maiden: sold 390 gns Ascot July Sales. *Denys Smith.*

GAVEL   2 ch.c. High Line 125–Psomma 59 (Psidium 130)   [1976 7h 10v]   first   — foal: dam placed at up to 1¼m: in rear in maiden race at Brighton in August (slowly away) and seller at Leicester in October. *R. Sturdy.*

GAY ALICE   2 b.f. Royal Palm 131–Balandra Star 92 (Blast 125)   [1976 5g⁴ **72** 5fg 5f³ 5.1g² 7fg⁶ 5.3f⁵ 5f* 5fg]   small filly: attracted no bid when winning seller at Windsor in August by 3 lengths from Matnat Saba: not certain to stay 7f: blinkered last two outings: sold 240 gns Ascot December Sales. *R. Hannon.*

GAY BIRD   4 gr.f. Birdbrook 110–Fanciful (Infatuation 129)   [1974 6fg 6fg 5s³ 5g⁴ 6s* 6v² 1975 8d³ 8s⁴ 8g 10.5s⁵ 12.2f³ 8f 10.8g 8fg² 8.2v⁶ 1976 8g 9fg⁴ 12fg³ 12g⁵ 9g³ 12g 9g]   lengthy filly: most disappointing at 4 yrs (not seen out after early June): best form at up to 1¼m: acts on a firm surface but is particularly well suited by soft going: disappointed when tried in blinkers: sold, covered by Spanish Gold, 1,000 gns Newmarket December Sales. *R. Hollinshead.*

GAY ELEANOR   3 ch.f. Jukebox 120–Princess Lointaine (Milesian 125)   [1975 5d 5g⁶ 7f 1976 10fg⁶]   big filly: little worthwhile form in maiden races: needed race only outing at 3 yrs: sold out of M. H. Easterby's stable 480 gns Doncaster March Sales. *G. Richards.*

GAY HAZARD   2 b.f. Falcon 131–Wallis III (Black Gang)   [1976 7g 7g 7s]   half-sister to three winners, including useful Irish stayer Burn the Candle (by Midnight Sun): 1,300 gns yearling: dam won at 2 yrs in U.S.A.: no worthwhile form, including in a seller: sold 350 gns Doncaster November Sales. *N. Callaghan.*

GAY HERON   2 gr.g. Great Heron 127–Lingay 99 (Sing Sing 134)   [1976 5f 5f 5f* **75** 6fg 7f 8g⁵ 6v⁴ 8s]   compact gelding: showed first worthwhile form when winning seller at Thirsk in May by 3 lengths: sold out of M. H. Easterby's stable 1,100 gns afterwards: ran well in nurseries at York on sixth and seventh outings, making much of running and rallying close home when about ½-length fourth to Bobby Kempinski in October: stays 1m but may be better suited by shorter distances: blinkered third to fifth starts: trained by D. Holmes fourth to sixth outings: sold 2,000 gns Doncaster October Sales. *D. Chapman.*

GAY JENNIE   3 b.f. Lord Gayle 124–Jeannette (Whistler 129)   [1975 6fg⁵ **69** 1976 8fg 8g² 12g* 10g² 12fg⁶]   well-grown filly: won 14-runner amateur riders race at Kempton in August by 1½ lengths from Welthi: good second to Everything Nice in Virginia Fillies Handicap at Newcastle later in month: stays 1½m: bandaged in front final appearance (well beaten): sold 1,600 gns Ascot December Sales. *Miss S. Hall.*

GAY JUDE   3 b.f. Manacle 123–My Rhonda 75 (Nulli Secundus 89)   [1975 5f² **82** 5fg² 5g* 5f³ 5f² 5.3g² 1976 5d⁴ 5fg⁵ 6fg 7g 5g 6h⁶ 6v]   small filly: no worthwhile form after finishing fifth of six to Virginia Wade in Ladbroke Club Handicap at Epsom in April: probably best served by 5f on a sound surface: tried in blinkers on fifth outing. *H. Westbrook.*

GAY MINNIE   3 b.f. Divine Gift 127–Gay Frolic 83 (Coalition 110)   [1975 5g **65** 5f³ 5g 5g 5.9g 5g⁴ 1976 5fg 6f³ 8f* 8g³ 10f² 11.7f⁴ 8s⁴]   lightly-made filly: sold out of T. M. Jones's stable 1,300 gns after winning five-runner seller at Bath in April comfortably by 4 lengths from Amir: subsequently ran creditably in handicaps: stays 11f well: probably acts on any going: has worn blinkers but does better without: unseated apprentice rider before race on fifth appearance. *I. Wardle.*

GAY PAT   4 ch.f. Hessonite 88–Gay Cavell 66 (Night and Day II)   [1974 7s 7g   **41** 6d   1975 8g 8.2g 7f 9fg² 10f³ 9fg* 10h⁴ 8g⁴ 10f³ 12g³ 8g   1976 8f* 8h⁴ 6h 10f 10.6g 8f² 10h⁵ 8s⁴]   small filly: plater: bought in for 600 gns after winning at Pontefract in June by a head from Adamio: effective at 1m and stays 1½m: acts on firm going: blinkered fourth start: sold 420 gns Doncaster October Sales.   *W. Haigh.*

GAY ROBERT   3 b.g. Chebs Lad 120–Gay Cavell 66 (Night and Day II)   [1975   — N.R.   1976 10f 8f 8.2d]   robust gelding: third foal: half-brother to a winning plater: dam stayed 1½m: well beaten in maiden and minor events: ran very wide into straight on first two outings.   *W. Haigh.*

GAY SHADOW   3 b.f. Northfields–Riddels Bay (Primera 131)   [1975 5.1f* 6fg*   **86** 6d 5f⁶ 6fg 6g⁵   1976 6fg 6fg 5g 7f⁵ 7f⁶]   robust, quite well-made filly: respectable fifth to Friendly Sound in handicap at Yarmouth in August: had stiff tasks on most of her other starts: bred to stay 1¼m+: acts on firm going: blinkered third outing.   *Doug Smith.*

GAY STREAKER   2 br.f. Firestreak 125–Fanciful (Infatuation 129)   [1976   **§§** 5.1fg 5h 7f 6f]   most unsatisfactory temperamentally and was sold for 240 gns at Ascot September Sales.   *H. Collingridge.*

GAY TWENTIES   2 b.f. Lord Gayle 124–Schull (Yorick II 127)   [1976 6g 7d   **69** 6s⁶]   fair sort: half-sister to very useful 6f and 7f performer Step Ahead (by Continuation) and to very successful French jumper With Honours: dam never ran: showed first sign of ability when 7 lengths sixth of 12 to Chartered Lady in maiden race at Chepstow in October: should stay 1m.   *G. Smyth.*

GAY VIXEN   2 b.f. Healaugh Fox–Bonnie Hellen 80 (Falls of Clyde 126)   [1976   — 5fg 6f 7h 7h 7f 8s]   leggy, unfurnished filly: no worthwhile form in varied company.   *T. Marshall.*

GEDERA   3 gr.f. Palestine 133–Lilac Beauty (Alcide 136)   [1975 6g 7g⁶   1976   **80** 7fg³ 8fg* 9f³ 10g⁴ 10s* 10fg⁴]   neat filly: quite a modest handicapper: winner at Warwick (maiden event) and Doncaster in the spring: stays 1¼m: acts on any going: sold 10,500 gns Newmarket December Sales.   *G. Pritchard-Gordon.*

GEE-DEE   3 ch.g. Doon 124–Margessa (Florus 110)   [1975 5d 5.1f   1976 10.8f   — 8fg 6g]   useless.   *G. Wallace.*

GEETEEBEE   2 b.c. Impecunious–Quick Speech (Articulate 121)   [1976 7v]   — second foal: half-brother to a poor animal: dam poor hurdler: in rear in maiden race won by Forage at Lingfield in November.   *J. Benstead.*

GELLINA   5 b.m. Gelert 93–Collina 88 (Matador 131)   [1974 5fg 5g 5f³ 5g 6g⁴   — 5.3g⁵ 7s   1975 6g⁵ 7f⁴ 7f⁵ 8.3fg⁵ 8.3fg⁵ 8fg   1976 12.2fg 7f 5h⁴ 5f 5.3f⁶ 6h⁶]   bad plater: probably stayed 1m: acted on firm going: suitable mount for an apprentice: dead.   *J. Pullen.*

GEMINA   3 b.c. So Blessed 130–Brilliant Stone 106 (Borealis)   [1975 5v³ 5s   **101** 5f⁶ 7.2g³ 6f² 6f* 6fg* 6fg* 6g²   1976 8g² 7d 6d 6d⁴ 8fg⁶ 8f² 6fg 7fg⁴ 8g⁶ 8g³ 8g² 10g 9g]   rangy, attractive colt: useful handicapper: ran well when in frame at Beverley, Newcastle, Doncaster and Ayr, on last-named course in September going under by 1½ lengths to Malin Court: stays 1m (ran poorly over 1¼m, but was possibly feeling effects of hard race the previous day): well suited by a sound surface: best in blinkers: exported to U.S.A.   *M. H. Easterby.*

GEMINI MISS   4 b.f. My Swanee 122–Free Time 89 (Sayajirao 132)   [1974   **65** 6f² 6fg 6v   1975 9g² 10g* 10fg³ 12f 10d 10g   1976 10g 10f⁴ 8fg⁶ 10f 8g 8s³ 8v²]   lengthy filly: ran well in handicaps on last two outings: promises to stay further than 1¼m (had a stiff task when unplaced over 1½m): acts on any going: sold 1,000 gns Ascot November Sales.   *P. Taylor.*

GENERAL   2 b.c. Brigadier Gerard 144–Mercuriale (Pan II 130)   [1976 8d*   **122** p 7.7s*]   The first foals of Brigadier Gerard and Mill Reef reached racing age in 1976. The debate still goes on about the relative merit of the two great contemporaries, and this served to heighten the interest that always exists when the progeny of brilliant racehorses arrive on the scene.   Which would be the better stallion? Bearing in mind that the chances of either siring a horse as outstanding as himself in his lifetime, let alone in a first crop that is usually smaller numerically than most succeeding ones, are statistically minute, each can be said to have made a satisfactory beginning to his new career.   Mill Reef, from only seven runners,

Prix Thomas Bryon, Saint-Cloud—the very promising General is too good for Doctor's Choice and Hermodore

produced useful winners in Miller's Lass, Millionaire, Silver Shoals, Sunfish and Teddington Park while Brigadier Gerard, with fewer winners from more runners, sired the smart Etienne Gerard and General, one of France's main hopes for classic success in 1977.

General's first appearance came in a maiden race at Longchamp in October, on the same day that his stable-companion Blushing Groom added a win in the Grand Criterium to those already gained in the Prix Robert Papin, Prix Morny and Prix de la Salamandre. With rumours abounding that General had finished upsides Blushing Groom in a gallop earlier in the week, he started odds on to beat his six more-experienced rivals. His scintillating performance suggests that the rumours were well founded; he was never headed and strode clear of his field in the straight to win unchallenged by five lengths from Loguivy with Crow's half-brother Catus a further four lengths back in third. This was a highly promising effort, but too much was read into the fact that General's time was four-fifths of a second faster than Blushing Groom's, over the same course and distance, later in the afternoon. Few people noticed, or seemed to care, that the third race over a mile on that day, a race for maiden fillies, also produced a faster time than the Grand Criterium's.

General's second race, the Prix Thomas Bryon at Saint-Cloud later in October, provided a much more significant test. All thirteen runners had won at least once, and they included Numa Pompilius, beaten a short head in the Prix Saint-Roman on his previous appearance, Aigle Blanc, who had gone down by a head to Perello in the Criterium de Maisons-Laffitte on his last start, and Doctor's Choice, Granlieu, Hermodore, Saint Irial, Silgar and Zinov, all of whom had won their last race. So impressive had General been at Longchamp that he started at 2/1 on. He justified his market position but gave his supporters a few anxious moments in doing so. This time tactics were changed and instead of making the running he was only about sixth behind Casaque as they made the home turn. Early in the straight his jockey found himself shut in and it wasn't until a furlong out that he saw daylight. General quickened when asked to go for the gap and, lengthening his stride in impressive fashion, he soon hit the front and went on to win comfortably by a length and a half from the filly Doctor's Choice. Third place, a short head further back, went to the 20/1-shot Hermodore who finished fast after having none too clear a run. General would almost certainly have finished further ahead with a clearer run and there was a lot to like about the way he quickened.

General (b.c. 1974)	Brigadier Gerard (b 1968)	Queen's Hussar (b 1960)	March Past
			Jojo
		La Paiva (ch 1956)	Prince Chevalier
			Brazen Molly
	Mercuriale (ch 1965)	Pan II (b 1947)	Atys
			Pretty Girl
		Sirrima (ch 1955)	Hyperion
			Mixed Blessing

General is a strong, lengthy colt with a look of quality about him. He is the

278

GEN

fourth foal, and second runner, of Mercuriale; the first runner, a colt by Exbury
called Exceptionnel, showed smart form in France, finishing a close-up third in
the Criterium de Saint-Cloud at two years and winning the one-and-a-half-mile
Grand Prix de Nantes the following season.   Mercuriale was no mean performer
herself, being successful at up to a mile and a half as well as finishing second to
La Lagune at two years and third to Roseliere at three.   She is one of several
winners in France out of Sirrima, a half-sister to the Ebor winner Die Hard; the
most successful of the others were the **very smart** filly Haltilala, who won the
1966 Prix Vermeille, and Sophora, a son of Exbury who won the Grand Prix de
Vichy.   Sirrima won over five furlongs from only two starts but her brother,
Bless You, stayed two miles well.   The next dam was a thorough stayer, and
General will not fail in his likely target, the French Derby, for want of stamina.
We expect to hear a lot more of him at three years and he may well provide
Brigadier Gerard with his first classic winner.   *F. Mathet, France.*

GENERAL AUGUSTUS   3 gr.c. Star Moss 122–Welsh Way 108 (Abernant 142)   **66**
[1975 N.R.   1976 7fg 8fg 10fg⁴ 10g³ 10fg 10.2fg⁶ 12f² 13fg 12f*]   lengthy colt:
half-brother to three winners, including high-class sprinter Welsh Saint (by St
Paddy): 5,400 gns yearling: dam useful at up to 7f: only moderate but managed
to win five-runner maiden race at Brighton in August by a head from Linden Dolly:
stays 1½m (ran poorly over 13f when tried in blinkers): sold 4,000 gns Ascot August
Sales.   *M. Stoute.*

GENERAL IRONSIDE   3 gr.c. Sea Hawk II 131–Come Dancing (Can)   91 **121**
(Northern Dancer)   [1975 7g* 7fg² 8g⁵ 8d²   1976 12fg* 16f* 12fg³ 12fg³ 14.6d
14fg²]
    The exportation of Sea Hawk II to Japan in 1973 has been made to appear
highly regrettable by events over the last few seasons.   Just look at the horses
he left behind him: he sired Seafriend, winner of the Royal Lodge Stakes, the
Nijinsky Stakes and the King Edward VII Stakes; Erimo Hawk, the Ascot Gold
Cup and Goodwood Cup winner; Irvine, winner of the Jockey Club Cup and the
Premio Roma; Paulista, one of the best fillies in France in 1974; La Zanzara,
winner of the Italian One Thousand Guineas and subsequently a top-class
racemare in North America, rated ahead of Dahlia, Comtesse de Loir and
Nobiliary in the Turf Handicap; Matahawk, the Grand Prix de Paris winner;
Claire Valentine, successful in the 1976 Italian Oaks; Sharper, shock winner of
the 1976 Grosser Preis von Baden; Bruni, Scallywag, Hawkberry and last but not
least, General Ironside, whose contribution includes a win in both the Predominate Stakes and the Queen's Vase.
    Like most of Sea Hawk's stock, General Ironside improved from two years
to three years and improved when given the opportunity of racing over distances
of a mile and a half or more.   He wasn't seen out until late spring, by which
time he'd already been taken out of the Derby and had the St Leger as his long-
term objective.   In his first race, the Predominate Stakes at Goodwood, he
brushed aside some Derby hopefuls; apparently in need of the outing, he ran
out a well-merited four-length winner from Kafue Park.   General Ironside, not
surprisingly, started a short-priced favourite for his next race, the Queen's Vase
at Royal Ascot.   The result was never in much doubt, although he was restrained
for a long way.   Giving weight to twelve of his thirteen rivals, he made good
headway when given the office to lead a furlong from home.   From then on he
needed only to be pushed out, and at the line he had two lengths to spare over
Valuation, impressing with the way he went about his work.   General Ironside
now earned himself a 6/1 quote for the St Leger; 6/1, in fact, was the price at
which he started in the race three months later.   In the interim he finished third
in two races over a mile and a half, to Smuggler and Oats in the Gordon Stakes at
Goodwood and to Hawkberry and Norfolk Air in the Great Voltigeur Stakes at
York.   In the former race General Ironside was, perhaps, unlucky to lose: he
was given a great deal to do, surprisingly for a known stayer, and found himself
somewhat short of room in the last fifty yards.   At the post he was less than a
length behind Smuggler.   General Ironside took the field in the Leger accompanied by a pacemaker, Vital Hunter.   Connections were no doubt influenced by
the fact that General Ironside had been beaten for speed in rather a slowly-run
Great Voltigeur.   Vital Hunter did his job adequately, but once he'd dropped
out General Ironside was unable to quicken up to get to grips with the leading
group, merely plodding on into a distant seventh-of-fifteen place behind Crow.
A week later General Ironside was sent on a retrieving mission in the Irish St
Leger.   He was equipped with blinkers but had been forsaken by Piggott, who
was aboard the odds-on favourite Meneval.   General Ironside, ridden by Durr,

279

Queen's Vase, Ascot—General Ironside is suited by this test of stamina and wins in good style from (left to right) Valuation, Ormeley and Bluffer

ran a better race than at Doncaster and finished second, three lengths in front of Countess Eileen, but he didn't reproduce his best form and proved no match for Meneval.

General Ironside (gr.c. 1973)	Sea Hawk II (gr 1963)	Herbager (b 1956)	Vandale
			Flagette
		Sea Nymph (gr 1957)	Free Man
			Sea Spray
	Come Dancing (b 1967)	Northern Dancer (b 1961)	Nearctic
			Natalma
		Come in Please (b 1958)	Narrator
			Blue Cross

A strong colt, and a good walker, General Ironside is the second foal of Come Dancing, a winner over six furlongs and a mile as a three-year-old. At stud she has also produced a moderate French performer Banacek (by Le Levanstell) and the two-year-old Welsh Dancer (by Welsh Pageant), winner of a seven-furlong race at Yarmouth in 1976. Come Dancing is a half-sister to several winners, including Come In Dad, a stakes winner at up to a mile and a half,

Cork and Orrery Stakes, Ascot—Gentilhombre quickens to go clear of Be Tuneful and Pascualete

and she comes from the same family as the top-class miler King's Bench. General Ironside's future lies in the long-distance races, and that future is rosy, in our opinion, provided he spends a lot more of his time at two miles or beyond than he did as a three-year-old. As we said, he was impressive in the Queen's Vase. He has shown his best form on a sound surface, although he ran well on easy ground as a two-year-old. *H. Cecil.*

GENERAL PATTERNS 2 b.c. Meldrum 112–Tre-Ami 70 (High Treason 126) **70**
[1976 5s⁵ 5fg⁵ 5h⁴ 6fg 6g 5g⁴ 7v⁵ 6s] plain, rather leggy colt: half-brother to 1967 2-y-o 5f winner Shane-Kop (by Road House II) and to a winner in Denmark: quite a moderate maiden: probably stays 7f: looked unsuited by the hard ground when running poorly on third outing. *F. Carr.*

GENESIS 4 ch.f. Ribero 126–Star Story 117 (Red God 128 §) [1974 6s² 1975 **—**
7s⁴ 8f³ 8d² 8fg³ 1976 10f⁶ 10g⁴ 7g⁶] attractive, lengthy filly: fairly useful performer at her best: well beaten at 4 yrs: stays 1m: acts on any going: sold 5,000 gns Newmarket December Sales. *F. J. Houghton.*

GENOVESE 4 b.g. Ribero 126–Gold Frame (Royal Serenade 132) [1974 6g **65**
8s³ 8.2s³ 8v² 7g 1975 10.8s⁴ 10f 12.2f 14.7f² 12fg 12f² 12g² 12.5fg³ 1976 13.8g* 12d⁴ 12.2f⁵] well-made gelding: won poor maiden race at Catterick in March: stays well: acts on any going: has been tried in blinkers but is better without them: sold 525 gns Ascot September Sales. *F. Carr.*

GENTILHOMBRE 3 ch.c. No Mercy 126–Kirisana 82 (Darius 129 or Kribi 110) **125**
[1975 5s 5f* 6f* 6s* 6fg³ 1976 7f³ 8fg 6f* 6fg⁶ 5fg⁵ 6g⁵ 5s* 6v⁶]
    The top three-year-old sprinters had to take a back seat behind their elders more often than not in 1976. Gentilhombre, arguably the best English sprinter of his age and unquestionably one of the best, found gaining a place beyond him in four of the six races in which he met the older horses. He finished sixth to Lochnager in the July Cup and fifth to him in the William Hill Sprint Championship, fifth to Honeyblest in the Diadem Stakes and, finally, sixth to Record Token in the Vernons Sprint Cup. Not once did we see an excuse for Gentilhombre, and it does seem that he was beaten on merit in all four races.
    Nevertheless, the two races that Gentilhombre won were important ones: the Cork and Orrery Stakes at Royal Ascot and the Prix de l'Abbaye de Longchamp, the first run over six furlongs on firm going in midsummer, the second run over five furlongs on soft in the autumn. The two races were also well-contested ones despite the fact that leading fancies ran poorly in both: Three Legs (the favourite), Honeyblest and Petipa disappointed at Ascot, while the William Hill Sprint Championship second Faliraki (the favourite) and Kala Shikari trailed in towards the back of the field at Longchamp. Gentilhombre started at 17/2 at Ascot and at 38/1 at Longchamp, his big odds on the second occasion no doubt a consequence of his three defeats in between; at 38/1 he was the outsider but one in a field of ten, whereas Faliraki was returned at 2/1. In both races Gentilhombre led virtually from start to finish, the main difference between them so far as he was concerned being that in the Cork and Orrery he succeeded in shaking off his strongest challenger, Be Tuneful, in the last furlong and won in good style by three lengths, whereas in the Prix de l'Abbaye three opponents, Mendip Man, Raga Navarro and Girl Friend, bore down on him fast in the closing stages and one of them, Mendip Man, forced a dead-heat. Perhaps one should say that Mendip Man was adjudged to have forced a dead-heat, for

Prix de l'Abbaye de Longchamp—in a blanket finish, Gentilhombre (No. 3) dead-heats with Mendip Man. Also involved are Raga Navarro (rails) and Girl Friend (No. 7) with King of Macedon a close fifth

in the opinion of some visiting racegoers a low-quality photo-print appeared to show Gentilhombre the outright winner. Be that as it may, the most important point to anyone not financially involved is that the first two home were almost locked together; Mendip Man had again reserved his best performance of the season for the Prix de l'Abbaye (he finished two short heads behind Lianga in 1975), and holding him was Gentilhombre's best performance too. Without Lochnager in the field the race could not be regarded as having as significant a place as it usually does in the sprint championship, but Gentilhombre's performance looks the equal of anything accomplished by an English three-year-old sprinter in the course of the season.

Gentilhombre (ch.c. 1973)	No Mercy (gr 1968)	Fortino II (gr 1959)	Grey Sovereign
			Ranavalo
		Crowning Mercy (ch 1960)	Supreme Court
			Mistress Grace
	Kirisana (ch 1966)	Darius or Kribi (ch 1953)	Alycidon
			Sweet Marie
		Tolosana (ch 1959)	Botticelli
			Tokamura

Gentilhombre changed hands towards the end of the year but remains in training under the same management, all set to continue to demonstrate, by winning good races, the kind of bargain his previous owner struck when he bought him for 1,000 guineas as a yearling. Gentilhombre's best performances are likely to continue to be restricted to distances up to six furlongs, although, like his sire No Mercy, he has form at seven furlongs. He finished a creditable third to Wollow in both the Laurent Perrier Champagne Stakes (as a two-year-old) and the Clerical, Medical Greenham Stakes. He failed to get the extra distance of the Guineas. No Mercy had two other three-year-old winners worth mentioning, both of them in Ireland, the sprinter Grande Prairie and the miler Crowning Issue. The dam, the stayer Kirisana, visited Arctic Kanda, Lorenzaccio, No Mercy, Sahib and St Paddy in her first five years at stud, producing to Arctic Kanda the winning plater Edgar's Plan, fatally injured in a hurdle race at Stratford, and to St Paddy a colt who will be a two-year-old in 1977. Gentilhombre, a strong, sprint type in appearance and an excellent mover, acts on any going. *N. Adam.*

GENTLE GOD 2 ch.c. Yellow God 129–Flattering 117 (Abernant 142) [1976 **82** 6g 6v³ 6d³] half-brother to three winners, notably 1,000 Guineas winner Humble Duty (by Sovereign Path): 1,500 gns yearling: dam at her best at 2 yrs: third in maiden races at Newbury (to Good Company) and Newmarket (to Rocket Symphony) in October: will stay 7f. *M. Francis.*

GENTLEMAN AT ARMS 2 b.c. Major Portion 129–Stormy Venture (Arctic **72** Storm 134) [1976 6g 7g 7.3v] neat colt: good walker: third foal: half-brother to two winners, including very useful stayer Carolus (by King Log): dam won 9f apprentice race in France: showed promise when eighth of 15 to Petlady in maiden race at Kempton in August: had stiff tasks on both outings afterwards: will stay 1m. *R. Price.*

GENUINE MYSTIC 7 b.h. Pirate King 129–Tudor Myth 82 (King of the Tudors — 129) [1974 17.7f⁴ 12fg 16f⁵ 16s 16.5g⁶ 16s 12.2v 1975 N.R. 1976 12.2f 10.6d] poor handicapper: stays 2m: acts on hard going and is probably unsuited to soft. *R. Murphy.*

GEOFFREY'S GREY 8 gr.g. Runnymede 123–Lovely Beam 87 (Infatuation 129) — [1974 9s* 12fg 10.2g⁴ 1975 N.R. 1976 12d 8v] poor handicapper: stays 9f: acts on soft going. *M. Camacho.*

GEOPELIA 2 b.f. Raffingora 130–Little Bird 87 (Only for Life 126) [1976 **109** 5f* 5f* 5d² 5f* 5f³ 5fg² 5fg⁵ 5fg²] useful-looking, strong-quartered filly: third foal: half-sister to winners in France and Malta: dam won over 5f at 2 yrs: winner of maiden race at Nottingham and minor events at Thirsk in first part of season: kept her form well afterwards, finishing 2 lengths fifth to Be Easy in Molecomb Stakes at Goodwood and excellent second to Self Portrait in nursery at York in August on final outing: unlikely to stay 6f: probably acts on any going: sometimes a bit slow into stride: genuine and tough: sweated up badly at Goodwood. *T. Molony.*

GEORGIAN GIRL 2 b.f. Prince Tenderfoot 126–Primed (Primera 131) [1976 **72** 6f 7fg⁶ 7d 8s⁵] useful-looking filly: third foal: 1,500 gns yearling: dam well bred but of little account: showed a little ability in maiden races, on final outing finishing about 6 lengths fifth of 16 to Billion (U.S.A.) at Bath in October: stays 1m. *R. Smyth.*

GEORGIE STEPHENS 5 b.g. Stephen George 102–Dicentra 101 (Infatuation **31**
129) [1974 8d 7d⁵ 10g⁵ 12.2g 12s⁶ 10s⁶ 10v⁵ 1975 8s 10.1f⁶ 10.1f⁴ 8.3f 1976
10f³] neat gelding: poor plater: ran creditably on only outing in this country
at 5 yrs: stays 1¼m: ran badly when tried in blinkers: exported to Switzerland.
D. Hanley.

GERAGHTY GIRL 2 ch.f. Frankincense 120–Tina's Way 61 (Palestine 133) **54**
[1976 5g 5f 5f 5fg] small filly: no worthwhile form in maiden race and sellers:
sold 210 gns Doncaster October Sales. *G. Blum.*

GERAGHTY RACING 2 b.c. Hul a Hul 124–Allegria (Bullrush 106) [1976 **76**
5d 5d 5f⁵ 5f⁴ 5h* 7fg³ 7fg 5h⁴] well-grown, rangy colt: third living produce: 1,000
gns yearling: dam won over 5f at 2 yrs in Ireland: won weakly-contested maiden
race at Pontefract in July: excellent third to Triple First in minor event at Thirsk
later in month and ran well in nursery at Hamilton in August: stays 7f well:
wears blinkers nowadays. *J. Etherington.*

GERANIUM 3 b.f. Ragusa 137–Delphinium 93 (Tin King 126) [1975 N.R. —
1976 12.2f 11f] quite a good walker: first foal: dam stayed 6f: tailed off in
maiden races at Catterick in August and Hamilton the following month. *S. Hall.*

GERARD 2 b.c. Brigadier Gerard 144–La Mirabelle 92 (Princely Gift 137) **91**
[1976 6fg 6g² 6fg⁵ 7d⁴ 7g⁴ 6d³ 6d³] smallish, quite attractive colt: third foal:
half-brother to 3-y-o 1½m winner Palace Royal (by Royal Palace): 8,400 gns
yearling: dam won over 6f at 2 yrs and is half-sister to several winning stayers:
ran well when in the frame in maiden and minor events, on final outing going
down in a desperate finish to Running Bull and Haco at Newmarket in October:
will stay middle distances. *C. Brittain.*

GERI'S JEWEL 2 b.f. Seaepic 100–Zendarood (Sayajirao 132) [1976 6h 6g] —
fifth reported living produce by a thoroughbred sire: dam useless: little worthwhile form in maiden races at Chepstow in June and Nottingham (ninth of 18)
in July. *J. Spearing.*

GERPOORA 4 ch.c. Laser Light 118–Sky Green (Skymaster 126) [1974 5g 5g³ **78**
6fg² 7fg⁴ 7g 7s⁵ 7g² 8s² 8s 7v² 1975 8s* 8s³ 10fg² 10.1fg⁴ 10fg² 10d³ 10d³ 12g 10s
1976 10fg²] rangy colt: fair handicapper: did not impress in paddock, but
nevertheless ran well when second to Court Lane at Leicester in March on only
outing in 1976: best form at up to 1¼m: appears to act on any going: consistent:
exported to U.S.A. *R. Akehurst.*

GERRARD'S CROSS 2 b.c. Brigadier Gerard 144–Queen's Keys 84 (Right **75** p
Royal V 135) [1976 7s⁶] neat colt: fourth foal: dam, winner over 1¼m from
two starts, is half-sister to very useful Abbie West: second favourite, finished only
about 7 lengths sixth of 12 to Sleeper in minor event at Sandown in October but
was far from disgraced, having been a bit slowly into stride and still nearly last
turning into straight: will stay 1½m: sure to do better. *P. Walwyn.*

GERSHWIN 3 b.c. Town Crier 119–Dream of Olwen 85 (Tehran) [1975 7g 6g³ **93**
5v² 1976 6v* 5d* 6f⁴ 5g² 5f* 6fg² 6f 6g 5v⁵] tall, close-coupled colt: won small
races at Ayr and Edinburgh in April and handicap at Doncaster in July (beat
Codebreaker 1½ lengths): dead-heated for second place with Sonnenblick when
beaten ¾ length by Roman Warrior in Canada Dry Shield (handicap) at Ayr
later in month, best effort afterwards (had stiff tasks last two outings): will stay
1m: acts on any going. *J. W. Watts.*

GET INVOLVED 2 b.f. Shiny Tenth 120–Shoulder Flash 89 (Epaulette 125) **64**
[1976 5fg 5f⁴ 5f 5fg 6s⁵ 5s⁶ 5s⁶] leggy filly: modest plater: stays 6f: probably acts
on any going. *D. Marks.*

GET READY 3 b.f. On Your Mark 125–La Corsaire 86 (Pirate King 129) [1975 **91**
5g* 5fg⁶ 1976 5g 5f³ 5s 5fg 5.3f 5f 6f⁶] neat, sharp sort: ran easily best race at
3 yrs when third of six to Urray Harry in handicap at Ascot in April: had stiff
tasks afterwards: best at 5f: acts on firm going. *M. Jarvis.*

GETTA FELLA 2 b.f. Umbrella Fella–Noble Nugget (Klondyke Bill 125) **72**
[1976 5fg 5g⁴ 5f 5f 8s 6s] leggy filly: first foal: dam won three races at up to
10.7f at 4 yrs in France: 7½ lengths fourth of six to Royal Diver in Great Surrey
Stakes at Epsom in June, only worthwhile form: should stay 1m: sold 250 gns
Doncaster November Sales. *D. Hanley.*

GETTON 3 b.f. Yukon Eric–Brunhilde 84 (Combat 123) [1975 N.R. 1976 10s —
16.1v] half-sister to quite useful staying handicapper Franwin (by Fidalgo):
dam showed ability at 2 yrs: tailed off in minor event at Nottingham in September
and maiden race at Haydock the following month. *J. Gilbert.*

GHENT 6 bl.g. Linacre 133–Gort Na Fluir (Pendragon) [1974 N.R. 1975 —
N.R.] 1976 13g] useless: sold 600 gns Ascot May Sales. *P. Ransom.*

GIFT ACRE 5 br.g. Linacre 133–Qualm 91 (Royal Palm 131) [1974 8.2fg² — 10f³ 9f* 8f³ 9fg⁶ 10fg 12g² 10fg⁶ 8.5d³ 12s⁶ 1975 10f⁵ 12f 10fg 12h 7.6fg⁶ 8g 1976 8g 10f] compact gelding: poor performer nowadays: probably finds 7f on sharp side and stays 1½m: seems best suited by a sound surface, and acts on firm going: often wears blinkers: suitable mount for a lady rider. *J. Berry.*

GIFT OF GOLD 3 b.f. Frankincense 120–Raymonda 107 (Primera 131) [1975 **74** 5g 5g 6f 6d⁶ 1976 8fg 7g² 7g³ 8fg] leggy filly: quite moderate form in varied company: claimed out of Newmarket seller in July and subsequently won in Belgium. *J. Dunlop.*

GIFFORD LASS 2 ch.f. Cheveley Lad 105–Falderal 72 (Darling Boy 124) **56** [1976 5s 5s³ 6s 5v] strong filly: made much of running when 5¾ lengths third of 18 to Military Queen in maiden race at Warwick in October, best effort: should stay 6f. *M. Bradley.*

GILDA 3 b.f. Connaught 130–Rigoletta (Ragusa 137) [1975 6g⁴ 8g 7f 1976 **65** 10g³ 10.4d 10.1f 8f² 8fg* 8g³ 8d⁵ 8v] lightly-built filly: overcame all sorts of difficulties in running when winning selling handicap at Newmarket in July by ½ length from Chilli Willi: sold out of R. Boss's stable 2,900 gns afterwards: respectable third to Golden Gayle in amateur riders event on same course later in month: should stay 1½m: possibly unsuited by heavy ground: runs well for an apprentice. *P. Robinson.*

GILDING 3 gr.f. Kauai King–Guinea Sparrow 119 (Grey Sovereign 128 §) **103** [1975 6f 7d* 8d³ 1976 7f* 8fg 10g⁶ 12f⁶ 8g⁶] lengthy, attractive filly: put up good performances when winning Ascot 1,000 Guineas Trial in April by 2 lengths from Icing and when just over 4 lengths sixth of nine to Sarania in Sandleford Priory Stakes at Newbury the following month: eighteenth of 25 behind Flying Water in 1,000 Guineas at Newmarket in between: ran moderately last two outings, once wearing blinkers. *I. Balding.*

GILEASTAR 3 b.f. Gilded Leader 75–Branston's Star (Pollards 104) [1975 — N.R. 1976 8f 12f³ 12fg] sixth foal: dam maiden hurdler: probably plating class. *W. Gray.*

GILLIAN ROSEMARY 3 br.f. John Splendid 116–Royal Bit (King's Troop 118) — [1975 5s 5fg 5fg 6f⁵ 7f 7g 6s⁵ 1976 7f⁶ 8fg 7f 8.5fg 10fg 12f⁵] strong filly: plater: no worthwhile form as a 3-y-o and was sold 370 gns Ascot October Sales: has worn blinkers. *J. Benstead.*

GIMRI 3 ch.g. Quayside 124–Conita 94 (Constable 129) [1975 5v 5d* 5g⁵ 7f⁴ **80** 6fg 6g⁶ 1976 8f³ 7fg* 10fg 7.3g² 10fg⁴ 8g 8f 8fg 6v⁵] workmanlike gelding: apprentice ridden, dead-heated with Le Deux in handicap at Epsom in April: creditable ½-length second to Scott Joplyn in similar event at Newbury the following month, best subsequent effort: appears to act on any going: unseated rider leaving stalls on third outing. *R. Smyth.*

GINARA 3 ch.f. Treason Trial 80–Sweet Gina (Privy Councillor 125) [1975 — N.R. 1976 10.8f] leggy filly: second produce: 450 gns foal: dam of little account: tailed-off last of 13 in maiden race at Warwick in April. *C. Dingwall.*

GINGER 3 b.f. Red God 128 §–Hedgerow (Hornbeam 130) [1975 5f 5f 5.8f³ **76** 5fg* 5fg² 6f³ 8g 1976 8fg⁵ 8g 11fg⁴ 6h⁴ 6f⁵ 6h³ 8d² 7.6s⁵ 8s⁶] leggy, light-framed filly: quite a moderate handicapper: raced alone when head second to Calor in ladies event at Yarmouth in September, best effort: stays 1m: probably acts on any going with exception of really soft: best in blinkers nowadays: sold 12,000 gns Newmarket December Sales. *P. Cole.*

Ascot 1,000 Guineas Trial Stakes—Gilding has two lengths to spare over Icing

GINGER FRINGE 2 ro.g. By Rights 100–Tropical Bird (Tropique 128) [1976 —
6g 7.2f] tall gelding: always well behind in maiden and minor events at Haydock in August. *D. McCain.*

GINGER KEN 4 b.g. Brave Invader–Condicote Lane (Sunny Way 120) [1974 **60**
N.R. 1975 10g 10s⁴ 1976 10f² 12fg⁶ 10.1fg 13.1s⁴ 15.5s³] small gelding:
poor maiden: stays well: acts on any going. *S. Woodman.*

GINGER KNIT 3 b.c. Prevailing–Bedecked 104 (Rockefella) [1975 5f 6fg* **83**
7g⁶ 6s² 6g 1976 7g 8f³ 10s² 10fg⁴ 12g⁵ 10f⁵] good-bodied, deep-girthed colt:
modest handicapper: placed at Newbury and Newcastle, on latter course chasing
home easy winner Palatable in X.Y.Z. Handicap: gives impression he will stay
further than 1¼m but ran moderately only attempt at 1½m so far: acts on any
going: not seen out after June. *B. Hills.*

GINGERMEDE 3 b.f. Runnymede 123–Ginger Puss (Worden II 129) [1975 **73**
6g 5.8f³ 7fg 5g 5.8f* 6g 6g 1976 7fg³ 6fg⁵ 6h² 6f 6h³ 7g⁴ 5.8f⁶ 8s] quite a
moderate handicapper: stays 7f: acts on hard ground and is possibly unsuited
by soft (ran moderately final outing). *G. Balding.*

GINIA 2 ch.f. Virginia Boy 106–Follette (Amour Drake 129) [1976 5g 6f] —
half-sister to three winners, including Current Folly (by Current Coin), successful
at up to 9f in Ireland: 400 gns yearling: dam ran only once: behind in maiden
races at Warwick and Lingfield (last of 16) in June. *J. Sutcliffe.*

GIO 2 ch.c. Dictus 126–Blue Command (Bold Commander) [1976 5d⁵ 6fg 6f⁴ **94**
6fg³ 7.2fg* 6fg² 7fg² 7f³ 8g] strong, rangy colt: first foal: 3,200 gns yearling:
dam useful French middle-distance winner: made all and was not hard pressed
to win maiden race at Haydock in July by 2 lengths from Wayland Prince:
runner-up on next two outings, being only just caught by Finite in £1,800 event
at Newcastle on seventh start: should stay 1m: suited by front-running tactics:
wears blinkers nowadays, having swerved very violently at start on second
appearance. *B. Hills.*

GIPSY LAST 3 ch.c. Sky Gipsy 117–Maushe Joan § (Major Portion 129) [1975 **62**
5v 5g⁵ 5fg³ 6f⁶ 5fg⁴ 6g³ 5d⁵ 6g⁵ 6g⁵ 1976 7g 8.2f² 8g⁵ 7f² 8g⁶] modest plater:
stays 1m: appears to act on any going, although has a round action which
suggests soft ground may suit him best: best in blinkers. *J. Hardy.*

GIPSY MARAMICK 2 b.f. Mummy's Pet 125–Spring Gipsy 75 (Sky Gipsy 117) **75**
[1976 5g⁴ 5g* 5g⁴ 5d⁵ 5g 5.9f 5f 5f⁶] small filly: first foal: 640 gns yearling:
dam placed over 6f at 2 yrs: won maiden race at Liverpool in April by 1¼ lengths
from Rose of Baydon: creditable fifth to Luke Splendid in minor event at
Ripon two months later but finished last on three of her four outings afterwards:
sold to G. Wallace 390 gns Doncaster October Sales. *R. Hollinshead.*

GIPSY'S SPELL 4 ch.f. Sky Gipsy 117–Nuit d'Or 87 (Doutelle 128) [1974 5g **70**
5g 5s 6v 1975 7g 10.1f 8g 1976 6fg⁶ 6fg 6f² 6fg* 6v 6s² 7v] strong filly: fair
plater: bought in for 1,200 gns after winning 12-runner event at Windsor in
August by 2 lengths from Rossella Bella: best form at 6f: acts on any going:
tried in blinkers as a 2-y-o. *Miss N. Wilmot.*

GIRL FRIEND 4 b.f. Birdbrook 110–View Mistress 113 (King's Troop 118) **126**
[1974 5.5g* 5.5g* 5.5g⁵ 5.5d* 7v 1975 7v* 8g² 8fg⁶ 8g⁴ 6g³ 8v² 6d⁴ 7s³ 8.2v⁶
1976 8d 5f* 7d² 7g⁵ 6.5d* 8d 6d* 6g⁵ 5s⁴ 5s* 6v⁵]

Girl Friend was undoubtedly the best sprinter of her sex in Europe in
1976. She contested six of the seven pattern races for sprinters open to her
in France, won four of them and finished a close fourth in another. We didn't
see the best of her on her one appearance in this country as a four-year-old,
when she finished only fifth to Record Token in the Vernons Sprint Cup at
Haydock in October.

Girl Friend was at the top of her form in the summer, hitting a purple
patch at Deauville in August, where, unusually for a top-class racehorse, she
was asked to turn out three times in the space of twelve days. She won both
her sprint races, the Prix Maurice de Gheest and the Prix de Meautry and, in
between, she ran extremely well over a mile in the Prix Jacques le Marois,
finishing eighth to Gravelines, beaten less than two lengths. In both the Prix
Maurice de Gheest and the Prix de Meautry Girl Friend ran out a convincing
winner from high-class opposition. In the first-named she sailed past Arch
Sculptor in the final furlong and beat him by a length. Ile, in turn, finished
ahead of Realty, Manado, Three Legs and Be Tuneful. Arch Sculptor also
opposed Girl Friend in the Prix de Meautry. This time, on terms slightly
worse, he got half a length closer but had no chance of preventing her com-

pleting a sprint double last achieved by Midget in 1957. It wasn't surprising to see Girl Friend run so well in the Prix Jacques le Marois. The previous season she had proved herself no mere speed merchant, losing the One Thousand Guineas to Nocturnal Spree only in the last stride, and earlier in 1976 she had finished second to Gravelines in the Prix du Palais Royal and a close fifth to Son of Silver in the Prix de la Porte Maillot, both run over seven furlongs at Longchamp.

After her Deauville exertions Girl Friend was off the racecourse until late September. Following a respectable fifth to Kala Shikari in the Prix de Seine-et-Oise at Maisons-Laffitte she lined up for France's only Group 1 sprint, the Prix de l'Abbaye de Longchamp, and finished hot on the heels of Mendip Man, Gentilhombre and Raga Navarro after a tardy start. Girl Friend's two other successes as a four-year-old were gained over the same course and distance as the Prix de l'Abbaye. In May she caught Polly Peachum on the line in the Prix de Saint-Georges, and in October she coasted home from Kala Shikari in the Prix du Petit Couvert.

Girl Friend (b.f. 1972)	Birdbrook (gr 1961)	Mossborough (ch 1947)	Nearco / All Moonshine
		Game Bird (gr 1955)	Big Game / Sweet Pepper
	View Mistress (b 1964)	King's Troop (b 1957)	Princely Gift / Equiria
		My Margaret (b 1951)	The Phoenix / Cracknel

Like Birdbrook, her sire, Girl Friend has improved with racing. Birdbrook was a tough, consistent, front-running handicapper who raced until he was seven, winning sixteen times at up to a mile and a quarter. For one nowhere near the top flight as a racehorse Birdbrook has done extremely well at stud, siring good-class performers, apart from Girl Friend, in Star Bird and Brook. Magibrook and Ferrer, who have done well in Italy, and Partridge Brook and Apple King are other notable winners of his. Girl Friend is the only winner that View Mistress has so far produced. View Mistress showed her best form as a two-year-old when she won four races in the north over five furlongs. Her dam, My Margaret, also successful over the same distance, was a sister to six winners and a half-sister to four more, including the Irish Derby winner Chamour. Girl Friend is an attractive, well-made, consistent and versatile filly who is suited by some give in the ground. She is also very tough, and she remains in training for another season. *P. Lallie, France.*

GIRL OF SHIRAZ 2 br.f. Hotfoot 126–Queen of Twilight 107 (Off Key 121 or   **75 p**
Twilight Alley 133) [1976 6d] strong, attractive filly: second foal: 4,300 gns
yearling: dam won at up to 1¾m, including Jockey Club Stakes: weak in market
but looking well, about 7 lengths tenth of 25 to Caerdeon Line in maiden race
at Newmarket in October: will do better over a longer trip. *F. J. Houghton.*

GIVE ME TIME 5 b.g. Birdbrook 110–Lady Magistrate 105 (Privy Councillor   **54**
125) [1974 8fg⁵ 8.5s 10s 1975 7g 10g³ 12fg 8g 1976 7fg³ 8fg⁴ 6f³ 6g] strong
gelding: poor handicapper: stays 1¼m: possibly unsuited by soft going: has worn
bandages: suitable mount for an apprentice: sold 4,000 gns Ascot June Sales
(reportedly to race abroad). *R. Smyth.*

GIVEN 4 ch.g. Jolly Jet 111–Gift Token 107 (Firestreak 125) [1974 5f³ 6f³   **—**
1975 N.R. 1976 12fg⁵ 14fg] of little account. *G. Beeson.*

GLANFIELD 4 b.f. Eborneezer 105–Light Gold (Le Dieu d'Or 119) [1974 6s   **—**
7v 1975 10g 10f 1976 10.1fg] of no account. *M. Bolton.*

GLANOE 3 b. or br.f. Green God 128–Europeana 84 (Dual 117) [1975 5s⁴   **108**
6f³ 6f* 7f² 6f² 7f³ 8g* 8d² 1976 7g⁶ 8g 8f* 10g 10d⁵ 8s*] Irish filly: showed
useful form and won well-contested minor event at the Curragh in September
by a short head from Louboff and handicap on same course in November by
1½ lengths from Parole: best form at 1m (well-beaten eighth of 10 to Ranimer in
Sun Chariot Stakes at Newmarket on first of two attempts at 1¼m): acts on
any going: sweated up at Newmarket: trained part of season by K. Prendergast.
M. Kauntze, Ireland.

GLASSMOOR 3 b.f. Hopeful Venture 125–Night Lark (Larkspur 128) [1975   **—**
N.R. 1976 9v 8.2v] third produce: half-sister to Next Step (by March Past),
a winner over 5.9f at 2 yrs and subsequently a winner in Malaya: 980 gns foal:

*Prix Maurice de Gheest, Deauville—Girl Friend beats Arch Sculptor,
the blinkered Realty and Manado (left)*

dam ran only twice: made no show in maiden races at York and Nottingham
in October. *W. Wharton.*

GLAZEPTA 2 ch.c. Deep Diver 134–Laikipia 89 (St Paddy 133) [1976 5f 5f **65**
5s 5fg⁵ 5g⁵ 5f⁴ 5fg 5.9fg 6v 10s] neat, strong colt: good walker: third foal:
cost 5,000 gns as a yearling but has shown only a little ability in varied company,
including selling: unlikely to stay 1¼m: usually blinkered nowadays: trained by
H. Nicholson on first three appearances. *A. Jarvis.*

GLAZEPTA REWORK 2 br.c. Caliban 123–Benedetta da Castello (St Paddy **93**
133) [1976 5g 6g² 7h⁵ 7fg³ 6fg³ 5.9f² 5f³ 5.9g² 6f⁵ 7d³ 8g³ 8.2d² 7.2v² 10v³ 7v³]
close-coupled colt: half-brother to winners in Italy and Brazil: 240 gns foal
and resold for 880 gns as a yearling: dam never ran: placed in twelve of his
fifteen starts but didn't manage to win, coming closest to success when length
second to Sloane Ranger in nursery at Nottingham in September: best form at
up to 1m but should stay middle distances: suited by an easy surface and is
possibly not at his best on hard: suitable mount for an apprentice: trained by
H. Nicholson on first outing. *A. Jarvis.*

GLEAMING WAVE 2 b.c. Sovereign Gleam 117–Sapphire Spray (Floribunda **103**
136) [1976 5g⁶ 7f 7fg³ 5.9f⁶ 7g* 7d 7g* 7.6v²] half-brother to two winners
abroad, including 3-y-o Pako Dark (by Linacre), a fairly useful winner in Italy:
3,100 gns yearling: dam won over 6f at 3 yrs in Ireland: successful in nurseries
at Warwick in August and Lanark in October, on latter course leading close
home to beat Darwen Lad by ¾ length: will stay 1m: acts on any going. *B.
Lunness.*

GLENALEMA 3 ch.c. Levmoss 133–Windy Gay 118 (Whistling Wind 123) **74**
[1975 N.R. 1976 14g 12.2fg² 16.1v* 12v³] strong colt: second foal: dam a
smart performer, winner of both her races at 2 yrs: won 18-runner maiden event
at Haydock in October by 2½ lengths from Ragusa Bay: moderate third (short-
priced favourite) to Chance Belle in minor event at Lingfield the following month
when put back to 1½m: extremely well suited by a thorough test of stamina:
dwelt first outing. *R. Price.*

GLEN ALN 6 ch.g. Fez 107–Green Label (Taj Ud Din) [1974 N.R. 1975 —
N.R. 1976 10.2g] well behind in apprentice race won by Doubleglow at
Doncaster in April, only outing on flat: poor novice hurdler. *J. Haine.*

GLENDOR 3 ch.f. Canadel II 126–Hyperion Rose 54 (Cash and Courage 116) —
[1975 N.R. 1976 8g 8h 7f⁶] of little account. *S. Wainwright.*

GLENHOWAN 3 b.g. Tamerlane 128–Criffel 99 (Malhoa) [1975 N.R. 1976 —
11.1g 11.1g 12fg] compact gelding: fourth foal: dam won at 1¼m and 1¾m:
unquoted when in rear in maiden races at Kempton (two, tailed off both occasions)
and Lingfield (blinkered). *J. Dunlop.*

GLENPATRICK 5 ch.h. Birdbrook 110–Glenshee 80 (Vilmorin) [1974 7g —
10.1fg 7g² 8d⁵ 8g⁴ 7fg⁵ 1975 11.7g 8f 7f* 7f 7.6g 8fg³ 7g* 8.2fg* 6h³ 8g 1976
8fg 6d 6s 8v] strong-quartered horse: quite a moderate handicapper (rated 74)
at 4 yrs: no worthwhile form in 1976: possibly needs further than 6f and stays
1m well: suited by a sound surface, and acts on firm going: best in blinkers:
suitable mount for an apprentice: sold 330 gns Doncaster October Sales. *R.
Bastiman.*

287

GLENSILVER 2 gr.c. Capistrano 120–Catnip 65 (Hornbeam 130) [1976 5f **90** 5fg² 5fg⁴ 5g 6g 6fg 6f³ 6fg* 6g⁵ 7fg 6fg 6f 6g] small, attractive colt: half-brother to fairly useful 1975 2-y-o winner Friendly Chief (by Be Friendly): 340 gns foal, resold 5,800 gns yearling: dam stayed 1¼m: looked thoroughly unsatisfactory temperamentally in first part of season but then settled down and won small race at Lingfield in July by 2 lengths from Regal Flash: not disgraced when seventh of eight to Sky Ship in Lanson Champagne Stakes at Goodwood later in month, but was well beaten in nurseries on last three outings: should stay 1m: blinkered penultimate appearance: trained by S. Ingham on first five outings. *M. Bolton.*

GLENSMERE 3 gr.c. Current Coin 118–Pardwin (Pardal 130) [1975 5g⁵ 5g⁶ **71** 6fg 5g² 5.9fg⁴ 7g 6g 7d⁴ 6g² 6v 1976 8g³ 10.8fg³ 8.2f 10g 9g 10f⁵] tall colt: stays 11f: ran poorly final outing (June). *A. Jarvis.*

GLEN STREAM 2 b.c. Paddy's Progress 113–Sally Peel (John Peel) [1976 5fg **64** 5f²] blinkered when head second of eight to Henry Hotfoot in seller at Chepstow in June: trained by M. Salaman on first outing: dead. *D. Dartnall.*

GLENTRESS 3 br.f. Prince de Galles 125–Prim Dot (Primera 131) [1975 6g⁴ **63** 6f⁵ 1976 10.2g 10s⁶ 9v² 10.2s³ 10.6v³] half-sister to two winners, including useful stayer Outpoint (by Fighting Charlie): placed in end-of-season maiden races in the north: will probably stay 1½m: evidently suited by heavy ground. *H. Collingridge.*

GLENTURK 3 b.c. Petingo 135–Donna Lollo 102 (Donatello II) [1975 8fg 6d **68** 1976 8g 8v³ 7g 16g³ 11s² 16fg⁴ 16f⁴ 13fg*] strong colt: won weakly-contested maiden race in July by a head from Sage: evidently stays 2m: acts on any going: wears blinkers. *Denys Smith.*

GLENTURRET 2 b.c. Habitat 134–First Round 97 (Primera 131) [1976 5f 5d² **109** 6g² 5g* 6f*] third foal: half-brother to Tuparamaro (by Astec), a useful winner at up to 1¼m in England and France: dam won at up to 1½m: second in maiden races at the Curragh, going down by 1½ lengths to Rumson in May and by 3 lengths to Pampapaul in 16-runner event in July: off course until October but won both his races on his return, maiden race at Phoenix Park (by 5 lengths from Katayeff) and 15-runner minor event at Naas (by 4 lengths from Uncle Pokey), starting odds on both times: will stay 1m. *D. Weld, Ireland.*

GLIMMER 3 b.c. Ragusa 137–First Light 82 (Primera 131) [1975 N.R. 1976 **60** 8f 10.1fg 8fg 6f²] compact, good sort of colt: second foal: dam effective from 5f to 1m: showed only form when runner-up in maiden seller at Folkestone: should stay 1¼m: sold to W. Clay 1,100 gns Ascot July Sales. *J. Dunlop.*

GLISSANDO 3 b.g. Quadrangle–Lucretia Bori (Bold Ruler) [1975 8f 1976 **74** 11g 14f* 12f² 16f⁵ 16g] tall, lengthy American-bred gelding: odds on when easily accounting for two rivals in maiden race at Salisbury in July: stays 1¾m but has yet to show he stays 2m: ridden by 7-lb claimer when successful: sold to D. Morley 7,800 gns Newmarket Autumn Sales. *I. Balding.*

GLITTERING CASCADE 4 ch.g. Silent Spring 102–Glittering Star 80 (Poet's — Star 81) [1974 N.R. 1975 N.R. 1976 13.1s] fourth foal: dam won over 6f: behind in minor event won by Regalian at Bath in October, only outing. *R. Vallance.*

GLOOM 3 br.g. Sahib 114–Unpredictable 103 (Pardal 130) [1975 7d 1976 10h*] **65** second reported foal: dam won over 6f as a 2-y-o: made all when winning nine-runner apprentice race at Chepstow in June by 2½ lengths from Harvest Bounty: stays 1¼m: sold 3,200 gns Doncaster September Sales. *P. Cole.*

GLORIFIED 3 b.c. So Blessed 130–Moment Supreme 102 (Supreme Court 135) **105** [1975 6g 6f³ 7g⁶ 7g 1976 7g² 8.2f* 7s* 7g* 7.6fg 8g 7s] strong, compact colt: in cracking form early in season and won handicaps at Nottingham, Chester and Kempton, showing useful form: held off Flying Tackle by a neck on last-named course in May: off course subsequently until September and had stiff tasks in all races after his return, running respectably in first of them: stays 1m: acts on any going. *J. Bethell.*

GLORIOUS DEVON 4 ch.c. Major Portion 129–Ali Drake (Dicta Drake 126) — [1974 6fg³ 6s⁵ 6s* 1975 8.5d⁶ 7s³ 10fg 8fg 8fg² 8f⁴ 8fg 8fg⁶ 7.6g⁶ 9g 10g⁴ 1976 7f 7.6fg 10g 7fg 7f⁴ 8g] strong colt: quite a moderate handicapper: should stay 1¼m: appears to act on any going: has been tried in blinkers: not particularly consistent: trained by D. Whelan until after fifth start. *M. Goswell.*

GLOSS 6 br.h. Stupendous–Highlight 107 (Borealis) [1974 10d 10g* 8f* 12f² — § 8g²(dis) 8g 8g⁵ 8g⁴ 8fg³ 10d 10d 1975 8d 10s 12d 8fg⁶ 10fg 8f 9d 8fg³ 10fg* 10f⁵

8s[6] 9g 1976 18fg[3] 16g[6] 12f 10.2f[5]] rangy horse: one-time smart performer: ran moderately in 1976: effective at 1m to 1½m but didn't stay extreme distances: required a sound surface: sometimes wore blinkers: sometimes sweated up badly (did so on third start): showed little enthusiasm: dead. *Mrs R. Lomax.*

GNOS 2 b.c. Song 132–No Recall 85 (Tutankhamen) [1976 5fg 5f[6] 6fg[3] 5fg[3] 5fg **86** 8f[6] 7g[2] 6fg 6v[2]] strong colt: half-brother to Amber Call (by Cheval), a winner over 7f in Belgium as a 2-y-o: 700 gns foal and resold for 850 gns as a yearling: dam, half-sister to good stayer High Line, won over 5f at 2 yrs: runner-up in nurseries at Catterick and York, going down by a neck to Bobby Kempinski in a blanket finish at York in October (blinkered first time): well suited by 6f and 7f, but seemed not to stay when tried over 1m: ridden by 7-lb claimer at Catterick and York. *P. Wigham.*

GO ABOUT 3 br.f. Whistling Wind 123–Tackienne (Hard Tack 111 §) [1975 **67** 5g[3] 5h[3] 7g[3] 7fg[2] 8g 1976 8.2f[6] 10.4s[3] 8.2d[3] 8.2d[5] 7g* 7.6fg 9fg[3] 6g[3] 8.2d 6v] small filly: fair plater nowadays: landed a gamble when winning at Doncaster in June by 3 lengths from Port-le-Boy: bought in 1,550 gns afterwards: evidently stays 1¼m: acts on any going: sweated up badly eighth outing but ran creditably: tailed off when tried in blinkers on final appearance but lost her chance when stumbling early in race and run is best ignored. *P. Rohan.*

GO BROOKHIRE 3 br.g. Klairon 131–Bodega 87 (Espresso 122) [1975 7f 7g — 8g 1976 10.1fg 10.1fg] first living foal: dam won over 6f: in rear in minor and maiden events, twice starting slowly. *D. Barons.*

GOD AEOLUS 3 br.g. Hotfoot 126–Sylvan Path 69 (Sovereign Path 125) [1975 **60** 7g 6fg 1976 8f 11.7f[5] 10f[5] 8h[4] 10.8f[2] 8.3fg[4]] small, sturdy gelding: moderate plater: needs further than 1m and will stay 1½m: blinkered last two outings. *B. Hills.*

GODILA 2 ch.f. Green God 128–La Romantica III (Nagami 124) [1976 5g[3] **93** 5fg[6] 7f[3] 6g[4] 6d[5] 7.2d*] small filly: half-sister to three winners, including very useful stayer Sofonisba (by Soderini): 2,000 gns yearling: dam won in Italy: looked to have a good chance in four-runner nursery at Haydock in October and won well, coming home 3 lengths clear of Hyver Hill: will stay 1m: acts on a soft surface. *W. Gray.*

GODNAR 2 ch.c. Green God 128–Narita 86 (Narrator 127) [1976 5.1g] half- — brother to 1972 2-y-o 1m winner Sovereignity (by Supreme Sovereign): dam won over 7f and 1m as a 2-y-o: 50/1 when behind in 16-runner maiden race won by Captains Mate at Yarmouth in September. *W. Stephenson.*

GODODIN 3 b.c. Green God 128–True Course 124 (Hill Gail) [1975 5g 6f[4] **113** 6.3f[3] 5g 6f 1976 6g[4] 7g* 8d 7f* 7.9g[5] 8f* 8f* 10g[4] 7t[3]] strong, well-grown colt: half-brother to four winners, including smart 1969 2-y-o sprinter True Rocket (by Roan Rocket): dam won 1961 Convivial Stakes on only outing at 2 yrs: successful in minor event at Limerick in May but subsequently showed much better form and gained another three victories, on last occasion putting up a smart performance when beating Wolverlife (rec 4 lb) by a short head in French Furze Stakes at the Curragh in June: stays 1m and ran below his best when tried at 1¼m: acts well on firm going. *S. McGrath, Ireland.*

GODSTAR 2 b.c. Red God 128 §–Reinstar 83 (Sovereign Path 125) [1976 5fg **79** 5fg[4] 5f[4] 6f[5] 7g[3] 7d] second foal: dam won over 1½m: quite a moderate maiden: ran poorly in nursery on final outing: will stay 1m. *J. Winter.*

GODSWALK 2 gr.c. Dancer's Image–Kate's Intent (Intentionally) [1976 5s[3] **123** 5s* 5f* 5d* 5f* 5f[2] 5d*]
  The 61,000 dollars paid for this Dancer's Image colt at the Saratoga Yearling Sales proved to be money exceptionally well spent. In 1976 he won five of his seven races, was allotted the second-highest weight in both the English and Irish Free Handicaps for two-year-olds and in November was resold for a sum in excess of £300,000; a happy train of events that few could have foreseen when Godswalk made his first appearance, distinctly backward, as early as the first day of the Irish season.
  Godswalk's most important win came in the Norfolk Stakes at Royal Ascot in June. By then he had already had four races, finishing third first time out and then winning at the Curragh, Phoenix Park and once more at the Curragh. All three races in Ireland were impressive, and his last one, in the Marble Hill Stakes on Irish Two Thousand Guineas day, left us with little room for doubt that he was the best two-year-old yet seen out in either Ireland or England. Among

Norfolk Stakes, Ascot—Godswalk shows Alpherat a clean pair of heels

the nine runners in the Marble Hill Stakes were Piney Ridge and Digitalis, both of whom had already shown useful form, and the newcomer Athlete's Foot who started second favourite. Godswalk, the favourite, beat them with ease, always racing in touch, joining the leaders on the bridle at halfway and then showing a splendid turn of foot to go five lengths clear of Digitalis and Piney Ridge.

Only four took on Godswalk at Ascot but they represented good early-season form, and had won eleven of their fourteen races. Godswalk started odds on after his performance in the Marble Hill Stakes and put up the best performance by a two-year-old at the Royal meeting; he pulled his way to the front in the last two furlongs and beat the Italian colt Alpherat by four lengths, with his jockey needing to do no more than sit still. This was a really good effort by Godswalk. Alpherat went on to be placed behind Blushing Groom in two of France's top races, just over three lengths behind him in the Prix Morny and two and three quarter lengths behind in the Prix de la Salamandre; The Andrestan, beaten six and a half lengths, subsequently won two more races besides gaining a place in the National Stakes and the Prince of Wales's Stakes; and the other runners, Royal Diver and Pandu, beaten eight lengths and twelve lengths respectively, put up some useful performances afterwards.

Unfortunately Godswalk raced only twice after Ascot and on one occasion, in the Phoenix Stakes at Phoenix Park in August, he was trounced by the filly Cloonlara. The betting was close between Godswalk and Cloonlara but he never got near her, and although he easily disposed of the rest of the field, he was beaten six lengths. Cloonlara has every right to be considered the better after this run, but we doubt whether Godswalk showed his form against her; it may well be significant that he was off the course for some time afterwards. The wet weather deprived us of another chance of seeing Godswalk in England when the Cornwallis Stakes at Ascot in October had to be abandoned. Had the race been run we would surely have learned more about him, up against probable runners such as Forty Winks, Song of Songs, Be Easy and Metair, than we did when Godswalk was switched to the Waterford Testimonial Stakes at the Curragh a week later. Godswalk started at 3/1 on and never gave his supporters an anxious moment; he cruised home four lengths ahead of First Up, winner of a £2,000 nursery under 9-4 on his last appearance. This was Godswalk's third win on softish ground, and as he has also won two races on firm, including the Norfolk Stakes, it seems obvious that he has the ability to act on any going.

Godswalk (gr.c. 1974)	Dancer's Image (gr 1965)	Native Dancer (gr 1950)	Polynesian
			Geisha
		Noors Image (b 1953)	Noor
			Little Sphinx
	Kate's Intent (b 1964)	Intentionally (bl 1956)	Intent
			My Recipe
		Julie Kate (b 1957)	Hill Prince
			Doggin' It

All of Godswalk's races at two years were over five furlongs, which suggests strongly that his connections regarded him as a sprinter, and his style of racing is that of a sprinter. Normally with a colt as good as Godswalk there is the temptation to run at a mile, over which distance there is much more money and prestige to be won than in sprints; Wollow's win in the Two Thousand Guineas alone brought in more than all Lochnager's wins in the King's Stand Stakes, the July Cup and the William Hill Sprint Championship put together. But there are two good reasons for anticipating that Godswalk will be kept to sprinting: first, he will be running in 1977 in the colours of Robert Sangster, the owner of a well-fancied Two Thousand Guineas candidate, The Minstrel, who is much more certain to be suited to the trip than is Godswalk; second, Lochnager's retirement leaves the sprinting field wide open.

Godswalk's sire Dancer's Image has already sired two top-class European winners in Lianga and Saritamer, both of whom were successful at up to a mile although Saritamer's best distance was six furlongs. From a previous mating with Kate's Intent, Dancer's Image sired a filly called Kabylia who showed useful form at two years in France, winning over five furlongs and five and a half furlongs, and at three years ran creditably over seven furlongs and a mile. Kate's Intent has also had sprint winners in the States by Snob and Majestic Prince but neither was out of the ordinary. Both Godswalk's dam and grandam were good winners; Kate's Intent was one of the best three-year-old fillies of her year in Canada, winning two seven-furlong stakes races, and at three years Julie Kate won the six-furlong Misty Isle Stakes and the slightly longer La Centinela Stakes. While we don't rule out the chance of Godswalk's staying a mile, we believe his future lies as a sprinter and we can't think of another two-year-old of 1976 likely to make a better one. His new trainer, Vincent O'Brien, looks sure to win top-class races with this strong, compact colt. *C. Grassick, Ireland.*

GO GO GUNNER 5 ch.g. Firestreak 125–Flying Fifteen 105 (Fairey Fulmar 124) **60**
[1974 8fg⁶ 9f⁵ 7g² 7g⁶ 8v 1975 8d 6f* 6fg⁶ 6f⁶ 6g⁶ 6f⁶ 6s³ 6g⁵ 1976 9g³ 13g³ 10h³ 12s] sturdy, deep-bodied gelding: good mover: poor handicapper nowadays: ran badly final outing at 5 yrs: stays 13f: acts on any going: has been tried in blinkers. *J. Turner.*

GOLDANIA 4 br.f. Weepers Boy 124–Golden April 71 (Sovereign Lord 120) **66**
[1974 5v 6s⁶ 1975 8.2g 10fg⁴ 12s 11.1g³ 10d 1976 14g⁵ 10f* 10.6d² 10.1fg² 8f 10.2h* 10f² 10h⁵ 13.1f³] light-framed filly: fair placer: winner at Folkestone and Bath, being bought in for 750 gns on latter course in July: stays 11f and probably finds 1m on short side nowadays: probably acts on any going: suitable mount for an apprentice. *P. Cole.*

GOLD BAR 2 b.g. Pieces of Eight 128–Moeru Bara 107 (Firestreak 125) [1976 **74**
5fg⁴ 5fg⁴ 5fg² 7g⁶ 6fg 6g* 6g 6v 6s²] strong, robust, good sort: half-brother to two winners by Salvo, notably very useful middle-distance stayer Fire Red (by Salvo): dam 5f sprinter: sold out of P. Cundell's stable 1,700 gns after winning £1,500 seller at Haydock in August by ½ length from Rivock: runner-up to wide-margin winner Burley in nursery at Haydock in October, easily best effort afterwards: will stay 1m: acts on any going: blinkered sixth to eighth outings. *W. Elsey.*

GOLD CHEB 3 b.f. Chebs Lad 120–Goldwyn 107 (Goldhill 125) [1975 5g² 5s² **88**
5g² 6f⁶ 7f* 7f* 7fg² 8f³ 6g³ 1976 7g* 7f 6fg² 8f⁴ 6fg² 7g³ 6fg⁴ 8g⁶ 6g 6s] well-made filly: fair handicapper: 25/1 when successful at Thirsk in May: ran creditably afterwards, finishing in frame at York (twice), Beverley, Ayr and Newcastle: effective at 6f to 1m: seems to act on any going: genuine and consistent: good mount for an apprentice: occasionally sweats up: had a bad run on second outing and had little chance at weights last two starts. *M. W. Easterby.*

GOLD CLAIM 4 ch.c. Lucky Brief 128–Gold Cypher 76 (Pardao 120) [1974 **85**
5f* 5g 5fg⁶ 6f⁵ 7g* 7.3d 1975 10g² 10s* 10s* 10.4d⁴ 10fg⁴ 10fg⁴ 10fg³ 10d 10.6s² 12.2g² 10.2g 1976 11s³ 12g⁴ 10g⁴ 10g⁵ 11v² 10.6d⁶ 11g* 12s 12g 11fg⁶ 10g* 12.3fg⁶ 11g 10s⁶ 10s*] compact colt: fair handicapper: successful at Edinburgh in May and at Sandown in July and October, on last-named course making most of the running and keeping on well both times: stays 1½m: acts on any going but is particularly well suited by soft: suitable mount for an apprentice: genuine. *C. Bewicke.*

GOLD CLASP 2 ch.f. Goldhill 125–Tuesday Eve 98 (Silnet 131) [1976 5f³ 6fg **78**
7g 7f² 7fg⁶ 8f⁶ 8s⁶] well-made, deep-girthed filly: half-sister to several winners, including very useful 1m and 1½m winner Evening Venture (by Hopeful Venture): bought privately 4,500 gns as a yearling: dam stayed 1½m: quite a moderate maiden: stays 1m: acts on firm going. *S. Ingham.*

GOLDEN AIM 4 b.c. Yellow God 129–Belgian Bullet (Vimy 132) [1974 5v 5g² **101**
1975 8v⁴ 8g⁵ 7.3g 7.6f* 7g 8.2s 1976 8g 9fg 8g⁶] strong, rangy, slightly dipped-backed colt: smart performer (rated 116) at 3 yrs: lightly raced in 1976 but showed form in two of his races, finishing eighth of 26 in Irish Sweeps Lincoln (raced on disadvantageous far side and must have gone close with a better draw) in March, and sixth of 12 in William Hill Easter Handicap the following month,

both won by The Hertford at Doncaster: ridden by 7 lb claimer on latter occasion and gave us impression that stronger handling would suit him better: stays 1m: acts on heavy going: sweated up when tried in blinkers: retained 8,200 gns Newmarket Autumn Sales. *P. Robinson.*

GOLDEN APPLE 2 b.f. Athens Wood 126–Granny Smith 76 (Tiger 125) — [1976 7.2f 7g 8v] stocky filly: behind in maiden and minor events but was backward on first two outings: will need a thorough test of stamina. *L. Shedden.*

GOLDEN BIRD 3 b.g. Golden Dipper 119–Goldilocks 71 (Golden Vision 105) — [1975 5d 5v⁴ 5s⁶ 5g 6fg 8f 8.2f³ 1976 12fg] small, sturdy gelding: out of his depth only outing in 1976: stayed 1m: dead. *W. Marshall.*

GOLDEN DELICIOUS 3 ch.f. Calpurnius 122–Dreamland (Atlas 126) [1975 — N.R. 1976 8h] half-sister to moderate sprinters Royal Victoria (by Royal Grey) and Hodden Grey (by Silver Kumar): dam ran only twice: started slowly when tailed off in apprentice event won by Indian Warrior at Bath in August. *J. Holt.*

GOLDEN DUCKLING 5 ch.g. Celtic Ash–Golden Harmony 105 (Aureole 132) — [1974 11g² 11.7fg 12g 16g² 16g⁶ 1975 10g 14s⁴ 16g 1976 14fg⁶ 16.1fg] strong, well-made gelding: poor maiden: suited by long distances: possibly not at his best on a firm surface: blinkered both outings at 5 yrs. *P. Cundell.*

GOLDEN ENSIGN 4 ch.c. Golden Dipper 119–Misty Ensign 65 (Premonition 50 130) [1974 5fg 5s⁶ 5v 5.9s⁵ 1975 8fg 7fg* 7g⁶ 7f⁴ 7f 7f 5g 7d⁶ 1976 7fg 8.3f 7g 7f 7fg 8.3fg 8.3fg³ 8g 8g³ 8fg⁴ 7d 10d 8s⁶ 10v⁵ 10v⁵] small colt: plater nowadays: best form at up to 1m: seems to act on any going: saddle slipped on twelfth start: blinkered final appearance. *D. Dale.*

GOLDEN GAYLE 4 ch.g. Lord Gayle 124–Golden Samantha 88 (Sammy Davis 80 129) [1974 6f 7g 8s³ 1975 8s 11g² 1976 12g 12s² 8g² 8g* 10h² 10g⁴ 10d³ 10d*] strong, sturdy gelding: winner twice at Newmarket at 4 yrs, beating Gay Jennie narrowly in amateur riders event in July and trotting up from My Polyanna in apprentice handicap in October (backed at long odds): acts on soft going and appeared unsuited by hard on fifth outing. *P. Rohan.*

GOLDEN GIGGLE 3 ch.f. Golden Dipper 119–Miss Hilarity (No Worry 105) — [1975 8v 1976 10.1fg 16.1d 10.1fg⁵ 10g⁶] of little account. *R. Vibert.*

GOLDEN GROVE 2 ch.f. Roan Rocket 128–Persian Dancer 75 (Persian Gulf) 72 [1976 5fg⁴ 5f⁶ 5fg 7f³ 7f⁵ 7f³ 7g⁵ 8fg⁵ 8f 8s 7s³] plain filly: half-sister to a winning plater: 720 gns foal, resold 540 gns yearling: dam won over 1¼m: in frame in varied company but ran below her best when third in seller at Chepstow in October on final outing (blinkered): should stay 1m. *E. Reavey.*

GOLDEN GUN 3 br.g. Kashmir II 125–Courrai Je (Silly Season 127) [1975 5f⁶ — 6f³ 6fg⁶ 5.9f 8f 1976 6d 8v⁶] strong, compact gelding: plater nowadays: tailed off in claiming race at Leicester in October on final appearance but was in need of race: should stay 1m: sold 500 gns Newmarket Autumn Sales. *J. Hardy.*

GOLDEN HALL 2 ch.c. Great Nephew 126–Alpine Bloom 123 (Chamossaire) — [1976 7g 7s] tall colt: brother to very smart French 7f to 1½m performer Full of Hope, and half-brother to several other winners: 1,600 gns yearling: dam third in 1,000 Guineas: behind in maiden race and Somerville Tattersall Stakes (looked rather lean and finished tailed off) at Newmarket in October. *R. Armstrong.*

GOLDEN LANE 2 b.c. Goldhill 125–Pronuba (Sica Boy 132) [1976 5s 5d⁶ 5v 73 6d] attractive colt: half-brother to a winning plater and to a winner in Belgium: 1,800 gns yearling: dam placed over 1¼m in Ireland: having first race for over five months, showed only worthwhile form when about 3½ lengths sixth of eight to Hedge School in minor event at Haydock in October, staying on after dwelling at start: should stay 6f. *J. Etherington.*

GOLDEN LANIA 3 b.f. Sea Hawk II 131–Lania 69 (Ribot 142) [1975 7fg⁴ 7g² 69 8d 1976 10g⁴ 12fg⁴ 10g⁵ 12f² 12fg³] tall filly: ran easily best race when fast-finishing fourth, beaten just over 1½ lengths, to Heaven Knows in Oaks Trial at Lingfield in May: didn't reproduce that form, including when tried in blinkers on fourth outing: probably needs further than 1¼m and will be suited by further than 1½m: acts on a firm surface. *C. Brittain.*

GOLDEN LAVA 3 br.c. Amber Rama 133–Lavant 101 (Le Lavandou 111) 69 d [1975 6fg 1976 8f³ 9f⁵ 10fg⁶ 10.6g⁴] compact, good-quartered colt: good mover: 3 lengths third of 17 to True Shot in maiden race at Ascot in April:

ran moderately afterwards: stays 1m: sold 2,200 gns Newmarket Autumn Sales. *M. Jarvis.*

GOLDEN MURRY   3 ch.f. Murrayfield 119–Golden Silhouette (Twilight Alley —
133)   [1975 N.R.   1976 12s 10v]   strong, compact filly: third foal: 280 gns
2-y-o: dam well beaten in maiden races: well beaten in maiden race at Chepstow
and claiming race (tailed off) at Leicester at end of season.   *M. Tate.*

GOLDEN POLLEN   2 ch.f. Meldrum 112–Anna Capri 82 (Luminary 132) —
[1976 5.1fg]   pulled up on début at Yarmouth in May and was subsequently
destroyed.   *R. Jarvis.*

GOLDEN RIFLE   4 ch.c. Goldhill 125–Bisley (Polic 126 or Punchinello 97)   **46**
[1974 5d 5f⁵ 5f³ 5fg 6fg 5d⁵ 5v   1975 7v 8f 8.3g 7g   1976 16f⁴]   poor plater:
stays 2m: acts on firm going.   *C. Dingwall.*

GOLDEN ROCK   4 br.g. Double-U-Jay 120–Quarry (Quorum 126)   [1974 6fg —
6g* 6f* 7g 7g² 7.2s²   1975 10g³ 10g³ 10g 10f⁵ 7.2s³ 8g*   1976 10s 7s]   well-made,
compact gelding: lightly raced and no form in two end-of-season handicaps at
4 yrs, wearing blinkers on first occasion: stays 1¼m: probably acts on any going:
bandaged both starts in 1976.   *P. Arthur.*

GOLDEN SEABIRD   2 ch.f. Seaepic 100–Shades of Purple (Blackness 107) —
[1976 8g]   third foal: dam of no account: backward and apprentice ridden
when tailed-off eleventh of 12 to Mined Illusion in maiden race at Leicester in
September.   *E. Magner.*

GOLDEN TRIBE   3 b.f. Tribal Chief 125–Scorton Gold 101 (Reverse Charge 115) —
[1975 5s⁵ 5h 6g 6d 6f³   1976 7g 10fg 8fg⁵ 14g 10.1fg⁵ 10d 10s 8s]   small, compact
filly: little worthwhile form and was well beaten under a stiff weight in selling
handicap at Lingfield in September on seventh outing: blinkered sixth start:
sold 240 gns Newmarket Autumn Sales.   *K. Ivory.*

GOLDEN VELVET   2 b.f. Golden Monad 116–Spanish Stone (Don Carlos) —
[1976 7s]   first foal: dam never ran: 25/1 when fourteenth of 20 to Brightly
in maiden race at Newmarket in October.   *W. Marshall.*

GOLDEN VOW   2 b.c. Good Bond 122–Sunsaly 75 (Sallymount 125)   [1976 6fg   **88**
6g² 6fg³ 5f⁴ 7d⁴]   strong, short-backed colt: third foal: 2,700 gns yearling:
dam won 5f seller at 2 yrs: placed in maiden races at Newmarket, going down
by short head to Reclamation in July and finishing 5¾ lengths third to Habeebti
in August: will stay 1m.   *G. Pritchard-Gordon.*

GOLDEN ZACCIO   3 ch.c. Lorenzaccio 130–Golden Plate 87 (Whistler 129)   **83**
[1975 5d* 5s² 5fg 6fg³ 7g⁴ 6f² 5fg⁴ 5v   1976 7g 7g⁵ 5f⁴ 6d 6fg 10fg³ 12f* 8h⁴
14fg 10g]   useful sort: won five-runner minor event at Redcar in July by
3 lengths from Petalca: ran moderately afterwards: stays 1½m (tailed off when
tried at 1¾m but had stiff task): appears to act on any going: wears blinkers
nowadays: suitable mount for an apprentice: sold 4,200 gns Newmarket Autumn
Sales.   *T. Fairhurst.*

GOLD FLIGHT   3 ch.c. Goldhill 125–Northern Flight (Borealis)   [1975 5.8f⁶   **87**
5.9fg³ 5.9f⁶ 6g⁴ 5s³ 6g² 5g*(dis) 5v⁵   1976 5g 6g⁶ 6g³ 8.2d* 7g* 8f* 7f² 8.2g* 8g²
7f⁶ 7.6fg⁵ 9f* 8.2f⁴ 8f⁵ 7f² 7.6g 10g 8g 12f⁵]   strong, compact colt: only a fair
handicapper but had highly successful season and won five races, including three
at Hamilton: kept his form well until last four outings when probably feeling
effects of his arduous campaign: stays 9f well: acts on any going: has won for
an apprentice: tough and genuine.   *M. Stevens.*

GOLDHILLS PRIDE   2 b.c. Goldhill 125–Belligerent 74 (Roan Rocket 128)   **79**
[1976 5f⁵ 5g 5fg³ 5fg² 5h⁵ 5fg³ 7.2v 6v⁵]   small colt: first foal: 2,000 gns yearling:
dam placed over 5f at 2 yrs: moderate maiden: probably best at 5f: trained by
I. Walker on first three outings.   *T. Craig.*

GOLD KESTREL   2 b.c. Gold Rod 129–Spring Romance 83 (Silly Season 127)   **61**
[1976 5fg 5fg⁶ 5fg 6f 5f 6f⁵ 7s³ 6s⁴ 5v]   small colt: plater: suited by 7f and will
stay further: acts on any going: trained by P. Buckley on first six outings.
E. Collingwood.

GOLD LOOM   7 b.g. Goldhill 125–Bloomers 93 (Floribunda 136)   [1974 8s 6s*   **81**
5fg 6g⁶ 6f⁴ 6fg⁵ 6f³ 6g* 6d⁶ 7fg² 6s³ 7fg⁴ 6s⁴ 8v⁵ 6s* 6s² 7s⁵   1975 6v² 5v⁵ 6fg*
6v⁴ 6g² 6f² 6fg² 6h* 6g* 6fg⁵ 6h* 7f⁴ 6f⁵ 6g   1976 6f² 6v⁶ 6fg 6g* 6g⁶ 7d⁴ 6fg³
6f 6g⁴ 6h⁴ 6g³ 6fg² 7.2f⁵ 6f 6s²]   strong gelding: once fair handicapper:
dead-heated for first place with Rundontwalk at Ripon in May: ran creditably
in most of his races afterwards: best at 6f: acts on any going: bandaged on first
outing: good mount for a boy: slowly away eighth start.   *W. Gray.*

GOLD MARK 4 ch.c. Jimmy Reppin 131–Juli Girl 82 (Saint Crespin III 132) **83**
[1974 6fg 6fg² 6s² 8g 6d⁵ 1975 10v⁶ 6f* 6g* 6s 6fg⁶ 6f² 6g* 5.8f 6d⁵ 6d⁵ 6g³
6d⁶ 1976 6fg 6fg* 6f 6fg² 6f³ 6g] good-looking colt: fair handicapper: put up a
good performance when winning at Goodwood in July by a neck from Scattered
Scarlet: apparently best at 6f: acts on any going: suitable mount for an apprentice: consistent: fell third outing. *S. Ingham.*

GOLD PEARL 2 ch.c. Gulf Pearl 117–Dark Dolores 83 (I Say 125) [1976 5f* **78**
5f⁵ 5g⁶ 6fg⁴] useful-looking colt: second foal: half-brother to 3-y-o 1m winner
The Four Hundred (by Pall Mall): dam won over 5f at 2 yrs: won maiden race at
Lanark in April by 1½ lengths from Hard-To-Woo: distant last of four to
Regency Bill in minor event at Chester in July and was not seen out again:
should be suited by 6f. *M. Stevens.*

GOLD PLAN 6 ch.g. Goldhill 125–Adolphus Street 51 (Planchado) [1974 N.R.
1975 N.R. 1976 8fg] well behind in 11-runner amateur riders maiden race
at Thirsk in July, only outing. *P. Wigham.*

GOLD POT 2 ch.c. Goldhill 125–Baburtula (Babur 126) [1976 5s⁵ 5fg³ 5fg² **65**
5fg² 5fg⁶ 5f⁶ 5fg⁴ 5f⁴ 6f³] moderate plater: claimed for export after finishing
2 lengths third of 18 to Swing Right at Ripon in August: suited by 6f: has worn
blinkers but does better without. *D. Williams.*

GOLD REVENGE 2 ch.c. Sweet Revenge 129–Goldwyn 107 (Goldhill 125)
[1976 5d] strong colt: second foal: half-brother to fair 3-y-o Gold Cheb (by
Chebs Lad), a winner at 7f: dam, winner seven times over 5f at 2 yrs, is sister
to smart sprinter High Award: unquoted and in need of race, started slowly and
in circumstances performed creditably to finish eleventh of 15 to Cawston's
Clown in £2,200 event at York in May: refused to enter stalls and was withdrawn
at Ripon the following month and was not seen out again. *M. W. Easterby.*

GOLD RIVER 3 gr.g. My Swanee 122–Golden Mist 76 (Denturius) [1975 6g
6g 8d 8g 7s 1976 8g 6f] strong, compact gelding: poor maiden: sold 900 gns
Doncaster August Sales. *G. Pritchard-Gordon.*

GOLD RUPEE 3 b.f. Native Prince–Petty Cash 99 (Pindari 124) [1975 5fg³ **86**
5f⁴ 1976 5g* 5g³ 5d² 5fg² 5f² 5f² 5g³ 5g⁵ 5g] lengthy filly: won 14-runner
maiden race at Sandown in April: ran well in handicaps afterwards, on seventh
outing finishing third to Peranka at Kempton in August: should stay 6f: appears
to act on any going: blinkered sixth to eighth outings and ran moderately
without blinkers on final appearance. *J. Winter.*

GOLD SHOW 4 ch.f. Le Dieu d'Or 119–Ballerine 99 (Borealis) [1974 5g⁵ 5g⁵ —
6fg 5.8g² 5.1g⁴ 5d² 6v⁶ 1975 8f⁵ 10h⁵ 10g 8g 10g 1976 8fg 7f⁶] plater: best
form on an easy surface: has been tried in blinkers. *P. Taylor.*

GOLD SPARK 2 ch.c. Gold Rod 129–Sparkle 82 (Alycidon 138) [1976 7fg² **80**
7g 6d 8v⁴] good-looking colt: 5 lengths runner-up to Paddington in six-runner
£1,600 event at Newmarket in July, only form: should be suited by 1m: acts
on a firm surface: sold 3,300 gns Newmarket Autumn Sales. *A. Corbett.*

GOLDSPUR 7 b.g. Goldhill 125–Miss Fivefootwo (Borealis) [1974 N.R. —
1975 9v⁵ 8fg 10.1f 9f 1976 12g 12fg] probably of no account. *J. Gibson.*

GOLD STREAK 4 br.c. Firestreak 125–Golden Wedding 107 (Sunny Brae 121) **60**
[1974 6g 6s⁴ 6s 7g³ 7v⁶ 7v 1975 8s² 9v⁵ 8d³ 8f 8g* 8f⁴ 8g³ 8g 1976 9g³ 10g*
10g 10fg 8.2d 10s] compact colt: favourite when winning handicap at Lanark
in May by a length from Over The Moon: well beaten afterwards, including in
a Haydock seller on penultimate outing: stays 1¼m: acts on heavy going and
seems unsuited by firm: used to wear blinkers but didn't at 4 yrs. *A. Johnson.*

GOLD TIPPED 6 ch.h. Hook Money 124–Lady in Trouble 112 (High Treason
126) [1974 7f⁶ 7fg 8f 8h 5.9g² 5.8g⁵ 6g* 5g³ 7g 6s 6s 6s 6g 1975 6fg⁴ 5d³ 6g
6f³ 6f 6f⁵ 7f 6s 8g 6g 1976 5.9f 6g 12f] strong, good-looking horse: poor
handicapper nowadays: well beaten at 6 yrs: sold 410 gns Ascot October Sales.
H. Payne.

GOLD TOPAZ 3 ch.f. Goldhill 125–True Delirium 87 (Delirium 126) [1975 **76**
5g⁶ 5g⁶ 5g⁵ 1976 5fg³ 6d* 5g 6s² 6g³ 6g 6d 6s] sturdy filly: quite a moderate
handicapper: overcame difficulties (last of all into stride) when winning at
Catterick in May going away by 1¼ lengths from River Petterill: suited by 6f
and a soft surface. *J. W. Watts.*

GOLD TV 2 ch.c. T.V. Lark–Faith in Gold (Nashua) [1976 5fg 5g 5fg⁶ 7fg 7.2f **81**
7fg⁴ 8g³ 8.2d 8s³ 10v⁵] compact, strong-quartered American-bred colt: good

mover: $65,000 foal: dam won twice at up to 1m at 3 years in U.S.A. and is half-sister to $309,000 earner Seaneen: third in maiden races at Ayr and Warwick, putting up better effort on former course when beaten 4½ lengths by Jam: should stay 1¼m: sometimes wears blinkers but does just as well without. *F. J. Houghton.*

GOLD VALE 2 br.g. Goldhill 125–Hillvale 60 (Narrator 127) [1976 5f 5fg⁴ 7fg]   **62**
neat gelding: modest plater: reportedly exported to Singapore. *P. Rohan.*

GOLLYWOG 3 br.g. Mandamus 120–Arak 74 (Rustam 127) [1975 7g 1976   —
7g 8fg 7fg 8fg 10.2s] tall gelding: plating-class maiden. *M. Smyly.*

GONE FOR A BURTON 6 br.g. Galivanter 131–Burtonwood 106 (Blue Peter)   —
[1974 N.R. 1975 N.R. 1976 7f 8fg] fair plater (rated 65) in 1973: well beaten both outings since: stays 1m: appears to act on any going: has worn blinkers, including on second appearance: sold 600 gns Ascot October Sales. *J. Welch.*

GONE ON 3 ch.g. Farm Walk 111–Fiametta (High Hat 131) [1975 8fg⁴   **76**
1976 10.5fg 12fg² 10f* 10g⁵ 12.2g² 16v] tallish gelding: won minor race at Ripon in August by 1½ lengths from Bombe: stays 1¾m well (ran badly over 2m): acts on firm going and is possibly unsuited by heavy. *Miss S. Hall.*

GONESH 4 ch.c. Amber Rama 133–Sea Lichen 106 (Ballymoss 136) [1974 5fg   —
6d 1975 9v 7s 7g³ 7f⁵ 1976 12s] robust, attractive colt: poor handicapper: has yet to show he stays further than 7f: best in blinkers. *F. Winter.*

GONE SPARE 3 br.c. Track Spare 125–Fadmoor (Primera 131) [1975 6fg 5g   **44**
5g 5.9f 6g 1976 6d⁵ 8h 7fg⁴ 7g 6d³] rangy colt: plater: stays 7f: blinkered last two outings, running creditably on final appearance: sold 820 gns Doncaster June Sales. *K. Payne.*

GOOD ALIBI 3 b.f. Fleece 114–Rosie Crucian (Polkemmet 91) [1975 6f 5fg⁵   —
5f⁶ 7g 7.6g³ 10g⁵ 7.6s⁵ 1976 10g 12f 12g 8f3] narrow, leggy filly: little worthwhile form in 1976: stays 1¼m. *P. Ashworth.*

GOOD ARGUMENT 6 b.g. No Argument 107–Melitta 98 (Honeyway 125)   —
[1974 10g⁵ 12.2f⁵ 17.1f⁴ 16s⁴ 1975 12g 14fg 1976 11.7fg] poor plater: sold 600 gns Ascot November Sales. *W. Marshall.*

GOOD BIRD 3 ch.f. Good Bond 122–Whirlibird 78 (The Pelican) [1975 5fg   —
5f⁶ 6s³ 6g⁴ 8fg* 1976 10f 12fg 9fg] very useful plater at 2 yrs when trained by B. Hills: no worthwhile form in 1976: best form at 1m: sold 750 gns Doncaster August Sales and resold 620 gns Ascot September Sales. *H. Blackshaw.*

GOOD COMPANY 2 b.c. King's Company 124–Pendlehill 119 (The Phoenix)   **94 p**
[1976 7g 6v*] lengthy, good sort: closely related to top Italian performer Caspoggio (by King's Troop) and half-brother to three winners: 10,000 gns yearling: dam a smart sprinter: backed from 25/1 to 11/1, disputed lead all way when winning 22-runner maiden race at Newbury in October by 2 lengths from Riberry: will stay 7f: acts on heavy going: a useful colt in the making. *P. Cole.*

GOOD FELLOW 3 b.c. Queen's Hussar 124–Favoletta 115 (Baldric II 131)   **66**
[1975 N.R. 1976 8fg⁴ 8g 8f⁴ 8s³ 9v³ 8s² 10.2s3] strong, medium-sized colt: first foal: dam won Irish 1,000 Guineas: didn't fulfil the promise he showed when fourth to Danestic in Wood Ditton Stakes at Newmarket in April and is only moderate: probably stays 1¼m: tried in blinkers final start: off course four months after second outing. *H. Wragg.*

GOOD INTENT 2 ch.c. Be Friendly 130–Indian Error 64 (Seminole II) [1976   **63**
5f 5g 6fg 6d] small, good-topped colt: unplaced in maiden races but showed signs of ability: will stay 7f. *M. Masson.*

GOOD MANNERS 3 b.c. Mandamus 120–Acton Sattalite 79 (Gilles de Retz 132)   **71**
[1975 6g 6f 7g⁶ 1976 8fg 7g⁵ 10f3 10fg³ 10.8f* 10fg⁴ 10.8fg⁶ 10.1fg⁵] neat, strong, good-bodied colt: good mover: comfortable winner of apprentice handicap at Warwick in July: stays 11f: acts on firm going. *S. Ingham.*

GOOD OUTLOOK 3 b.f. Pregonero 103–Sunny Forcast (Manicou) [1975 6d   —
1976 11g 8fg 12g] good sort: behind in maiden races: sold 360 gns Ascot December Sales. *R. Hannon.*

GOOD TRY 2 ch.f. Good Bond 122–Try-Gun (Combat 123) [1976 5f3 5d⁶ 5g*   **92**
6f3 5.3f² 5fg⁵] robust filly: half-sister to several winners, including fairly useful 1967 2-y-o 7f winner Flint-Lock (by Rockavon): dam of no account: made all to win maiden race at Warwick in June by 2 lengths from Elton Abbess: ran well afterwards, going down by a head to Diorina in nursery at Brighton in August: will stay 1m: possibly not at her best on a soft surface. *H. Candy.*

295

GOOLAGONG 6 b.m. Bargello–Coolnagratten (Flamenco or Vulgan 123) — [1974 N.R. 1975 N.R. 1976 12g 12s⁴ 16.1d] poor maiden: probably stays 1½m. *N. Crump.*

GOOSED AGAIN 2 gr.f. Birdbrook 110–Damsel in Distress 75 (Sir d'Orient — § 90) [1976 5f 7g] temperamental plater: sold 330 gns Ascot September Sales. *T. Marshall.*

GOOSE PIMPLE 3 gr.g. Birdbrook 110–Damsel in Distress 75 (Sir d'Orient 90) — [1975 N.R. 1976 8g] brother to fair 1972 2-y-o plater Dolly Bird and half-brother to two winning sprint platers by Blason and Welsh Abbot: dam, a plater, showed best form at sprint distances: 16/1 when well-beaten seventh of 11 behind Loudly in maiden race at Warwick in August. *T. Marshall.*

GO STEADY 2 b.c. Balidar 133–Calm Sea 83 (Set Fair 129) [1976 5fg 5g⁵ 5f⁵ **59** 5fg³ 6fg⁶ 7h⁶] small, lightly-made colt: good walker: only plating class: probably stays 7f. *J. Winter.*

GO SURFING 3 b.f. Go Marching–Surfing (Noor 123) [1975 N.R. 1976 8f⁴ — 8f] leggy, light-framed, unfurnished filly: fourth foal: half-sister to three winners, including Joe Gaylord (by Sir Gaylord), a stakes winner at around 1m: $22,000 yearling: dam never ran: nearest at finish when 4½ lengths fourth to Grey Sail in maiden race at Beverley in April: ran badly in similar event at Thirsk later in month and gave us impression that she was going the wrong way temperamentally. *L. Cumani.*

GRACCHUS 5 b.m. Grand Roi 118–Gala Premiere § (By Thunder! 122) [1974 — 12f⁵ 10f⁴ 12.2f⁶ 10d 1975 N.R. 1976 7.6fg 6f⁴ 17.7f 10f 10.4fg] workmanlike mare: of little account nowadays. *M. James.*

GRACIOUS MELODY 6 b.h. Golden Horus 123–Esconaba (Chamier 128) **96** [1974 8d³ 7f³ 7f² 8f* 9f⁶ 7fg² 8s 8fg³ 8s² 8s* 8s² 1975 8d 8v* 8v³ 7s 8g² 8f⁴ 8f⁵ 8fg⁴ 9f* 9g⁶ 8f³ 9fg² 8fg 1976 8g* 8f 8g³ 8g⁴ 8fg⁴ 8.2f* 10fg³ 8fg³ 8f⁶ 8fg 7.2f* 8g* 8g* 9g] neat, strong, shapely horse: fairly useful handicapper: had a good season, winning at Haydock (twice), York and Ayr: gained his most valuable success on last-named track in September, getting the better of a drawn-out battle with Affirmative by a head: stays 9f but appeared not to stay 1½m on seventh start: acts on any going: has worn blinkers: genuine: sold 3,200 gns Newmarket Autumn Sales. *Denys Smith.*

GRADIVA 2 ch.f. Lorenzaccio 130–Fanghorn 117 (Crocket 130) [1976 5g⁴ 5fg **110** 5g² 5f* 6g⁶ 6fg* 6f³ 7g² 6d²] lightly-made filly: third reported foal: dam placed in French 1,000 Guineas: won maiden race at Wolverhampton in July and £1,800 nursery at Windsor the following month, latter by 2 lengths from Breast Stroke: good second on last two outings, carrying top weight when beaten 2 lengths by Bona-Mia in £1,800 nursery at Doncaster in September and rallying well when going down by ¾ length to 4-y-o Sandford Lady in Vernons Sprint Trial at Haydock the following month: will stay 1m: appears to act on any going: ran creditably in blinkers on third outing. *F. J. Houghton.*

GRAIN OF TRUTH 2 b.f. Mill Reef 141–Village Gossip 69 (Narrator 127) **84** [1976 5fg³ 6fg² 5fg³ 5f³ 6d 6s³ 5v²] neat, attractive filly: good walker: seventh reported foal: dam stayed 1¼m: placed on all but one of her outings, going down by 4 lengths to Be Royal in maiden race at Leicester in November: will be suited by 7f or 1m: blinkered fifth and final outings and has given impression she is none too keen on racing. *I. Balding.*

GRAND ATTRACTION 7 ch.g. Attractive 72–Grand Fabric 62 (Grandmaster) — [1974 8.2g 11g 9fg⁵ 12fg 1975 8g⁶ 10g 9f 6fg³ 8f⁵ 10g 16h 7g 8g 1976 8v³ 8g 8g] bad plater: stays 1½m: has worn bandages: sold 300 gns Doncaster October Sales. *G. Wallace.*

GRANDCHANT 3 br.c. Grandier 127–Singing Queen (Chanteur II 135) [1975 **120** 7.8s² 8v* 1976 9.8fg* 12f* 12g⁵] French colt: half-brother to Merlin (by Fine Top), placed on flat and over jumps in France: dam won over 1m in France at 2 yrs: developed into a smart 3-y-o and won two good races at Longchamp, Group 3 Prix de Guiche (by a length from No Turning) and Group 2 Prix Hocquart (by ¾ length from Lodovico): beaten just over 5 lengths when fifth of 18 to Youth in Prix du Jockey-Club at Chantilly in June but would have finished much closer had he not been badly hampered 1f out: stays 1½m: acts on any going. *J. Cunnington, jnr, France.*

GRAND CHAT 4 ch.c. Grand Roi 118–Kitten 102 (Pardal 130) [1974 7.6v⁶ **100** 1975 8v 11v⁴ 11.7g* 12g* 12f⁴ 12f* 12g² 12fg² 14fg 16g 1976 12fg² 16g² 16fg⁴] really attractive, well-made colt: fairly useful handicapper: good second at

Newmarket and Kempton early in season, on latter course in April going down by a neck to Echo Summit in Campbell-Gray Queen's Prize: effective at 1¼m and stays 2m well: acts on firm going: genuine and consistent. *S. Ingham.*

GRAND DISPLAY 5 br.m. Stupendous–French Parade 113 (March Past 124) **52**
[1974 8.2f 10.1fg³ 8g 10g⁵ 12.2s² 10d² 10g⁴ 11.2fg² 9s* 10s⁴ 1975 10.2g 9v 12fg⁵ 13fg⁵ 12fg⁵ 12fg⁶ 10fg⁵ 10f³ 10.6s 1976 16f 13g² 12g³ 12g⁵ 10s 13.8g 12fg⁴ 12h* 12f³ 12h⁴ 12.2f 15.5s] tall mare: poor performer: won amateur riders race at Carlisle in June: stays at least 13f: acts on any going: tried in blinkers at 2 yrs: sweated up eleventh start. *D. Weeden.*

GRANDE PRAIRIE 3 gr.g. No Mercy 126–Search 79 (High Perch 126) [1975 **111**
5f⁶ 5f² 6d 6fg* 5d 1976 5s 5s 5f³ 6.3f* 5f* 5f* 5f² 6f²] third foal: half-brother to 1973 2-y-o 7f seller winner Largesse (by Compensation): 2,600 gns yearling: dam won at 1½m: improved at a tremendous rate in the summer and won three handicaps withing a month, at the Curragh (Midsummer Scurry), Phoenix Park and Leopardstown (comfortably defied 14-lb penalty): runner-up twice at Phoenix Park afterwards, on final outing going under by a length to Kashiwa in Herbertstown Stakes in August: should stay 1m: needs a sound surface: blinkered last two outings at 2 yrs: usually apprentice ridden: one of the best sprinters in Ireland. *P. Prendergast, jnr, Ireland.*

GRAND GOLDA 3 gr.f. Supreme Sovereign 119–Silver Phantom 82 (Right —
Boy 137) [1975 5g 5g 1976 8f 5g 6g⁶ 10f⁴ 8fg] lengthy filly: poor maiden: ran best race over 1¼m. *R. Smyth.*

GRAND HOPE 4 ch.g. Grand Roi 118–Malton Hope 92 (High Treason 126) —
[1974 6fg 6fg³ 5g* 6g² 6s⁴ 5g 6v 1975 7s 6s⁵ 7f³ 8.2fg³ 8f* 8.2fg² 10.6s⁵ 7fg 8.2v 1976 8v] smallish, stocky gelding: moderate handicapper (rated 82) at 3 yrs: ran badly when last of seven in seller at Ayr in April on only outing in 1976: best form at up to 1m: acts on firm going and is unsuited by heavy ground: usually wears blinkers nowadays: sold to D. McCain 700 gns Doncaster May Sales. *M. H. Easterby.*

GRAND NIECE 2 b.f. Great Nephew 126–Vhairi 115 (Narrator 127) [1976 5f **80 p**
6g⁶] half-sister to two middle-distance winners in France: 4,800 gns yearling: dam smart and thoroughly genuine performer at up to 1¾m: 25/1 when creditable sixth of nine to Mofida in valuable and well-contested Firth of Clyde Stakes at Ayr in September, second outing and easily better effort: likely to show further improvement, particularly when tackling middle distances: sold to J. W. Watts 4,600 gns Doncaster November Sales. *W. Elsey.*

GRANDO KING 7 br.g. Negotiation–Yellow Streak (Shantung 132) [1974 18h —
1975 N.R. 1976 17.7f] very useful hurdler: well beaten in handicap at Wolverhampton in May, first outing on flat since 1974. *M. Tate.*

GRAND ORIENT 5 b.h. Prince des Loges 73–Rina's Tale (Narrator 127) [1974 **58**
12g⁶ 10fg⁶ 12f 12f⁵ 10g⁴ 12g 8.2v 1975 6f³ 10fg 8g 7.6g 1976 12f* 14fg⁶ 14fg⁴ 12g 8g] won poor race at Beverley in April by ½ length from Princely Chief: stays 1¾m: has been tried in blinkers: sweated up on reappearance. *R. Sturdy.*

GRAND SWING 2 b.c. Swinging Junior 118–Grand Daughter (Tamerlane 128) —
[1976 6fg 5.9s 5v 5s] lightly-built colt: behind in varied company, including selling. *A. W. Jones.*

GRASS CURRENCY 2 b.c. Meadow Mint 120–Lindos (Acropolis 132) [1976 **63**
6f⁶ 7g 8.2h² 8s] second foal: half-brother to smart Irish 6f to 9f winner Gentleman James (by Right Tack): 1,000 gns yearling: dropped in class, ran best race when ¾-length second of 10 to Little Gadge in seller at Hamilton in September: suited by 1m. *T. Craig.*

GRAVELINES 4 gr.c. Cadmus 124–Gray Dove (T.V. Lark) [1974 N.R. 1975 **130**
8g* 7.5g* 8g 7s* 7s 1976 8g* 7.5g² 9g* 7d* 8d² 8g³ 8d* 8s*]
The late but expected withdrawal of Gravelines from the Champion Stakes line-up deprived us of the opportunity of seeing in action in this country the leading French miler above the age of three. Two weeks earlier Gravelines, a recent clear-cut winner of the Prix du Moulin de Longchamp, fetched the equivalent of £114,700 (950,000 francs) at the Polo Club sale in Paris, the top price at the sale. He has now been put into training with Arnold Winick in the United States. The special attraction of Gravelines to an American buyer is clear: a European horse up for sale with better prospects of making the top grade over there at the highly popular distances around a mile would be hard to find, and in addition he is a horse from a family well known in the States, his dam being a full sister to a notable filly, the Santa Barbara Handicap winner Pink Pigeon. Gravelines' form is not such that it sets him much above the

Prix du Moulin de Longchamp—Gravelines wins in fine style from Dona Barod and Manado

best of his contemporaries in France, yet at today's prices he doesn't look an expensive purchase.

Gravelines did not reach the top straight away; his first high-class performance came towards the end of May in the Prix du Palais Royal, almost twelve months after he made his first appearance on the racecourse. He improved greatly as a four-year-old, as did his sire Cadmus who at the same age won the Prix d'Harcourt from Prominer. At three, Gravelines was beaten on the two occasions he was put in against high-class opposition, in the Prix Messidor and the Prix du Pin, and at four he was brought out much earlier in the season than the recognised top horses are brought out. If his stable thought they had better tackle, no-one could blame them. He began at Saint-Cloud in February and was aimed at second-rate prizes until running in the Prix du Palais Royal. In one of his three races during this period he was beaten—a horse called Lanargo, who had been racing at Cagnes-sur-Mer, beat him half a length at Saint-Cloud.

From the time he won the Prix du Palais Royal—by two lengths from Girl Friend, with such as Monsanto, Mendip Man, Realty and Thieving Demon also in the field—Gravelines was kept in the best races. If the riding arrangements made for him afterwards are a reliable guide, his connections experienced some difficulty in keeping up with his rate of progress; until the autumn the stable's Monsanto was evidently regarded, not without reason, as the better horse. Following a neck defeat for Gravelines by Full of Hope in the Prix du Chemin de Fer du Nord at Chantilly in June (he finished in front of Lanargo this time) stable-jockey Saint-Martin switched to Monsanto in the Prix Messidor, leaving Gravelines for Pyers to ride. The Prix Messidor, a pattern race run at Maisons-Laffitte in July, a race in which Boldboy had finished second and Girl Friend fourth the previous season, attracted a strong field although only Comeram represented the three-year-olds and only Duboff represented England. Monsanto beat Gravelines by three parts of a length after the latter came late and on none too straight a course, but Dona Barod, receiving 8 lb, comfortably accounted for them both. Comeram finished fourth, about five lengths behind the winner, and Duboff, giving 11 lb to Monsanto and Gravelines, did well to finish within a neck of Comeram in fifth place.

The Prix Jacques le Marois attracted an even stronger field than the Messidor; the race is not only one of the most important of the Deauville season, it's one of the most important in the French Calendar. Lianga won it by six lengths in 1975 and the Two Thousand Guineas winner Nonoalco just scraped home the year before. Gravelines again went to post accompanied by a stable-companion, not Monsanto this time—he was in reserve for the Prix Quincey—but El Rastro, whom Saint-Martin chose to ride. Pyers rode Full of Hope, so Gravelines had a new partner, G. W. Moore the son of the famous Australian jockey. Having provided a sensational finish two years running, the Prix Jacques le Marois had a lot to live up to in 1976. It did not fail. The first seven of the thirteen starters crossed the line almost as one, and eighth-placed Girl Friend missed fourth prize by little more than a length. Gravelines won; El Rastro came in seventh, their proximity at the finish underlining the difficulty facing the stable in choosing between its milers. Three three-year-olds followed Gravelines home, Radetzky and Vitiges dead-heating for second place in front of Manado. A head separated the runners-up from the winner and from the fourth; a head further back came Ellora, followed by the three-year-old Avaray. Then El Rastro. Dona Barod, 5 lb worse off, ran disappointingly.

Gravelines, Manado, Ellora, Avaray and Dona Barod met again in the Prix du Moulin de Longchamp in September, a race of much the same standing as the Prix Jacques le Marois. Saint-Martin, with Gravelines, Monsanto and Earth Spirit to pick from, made the correct decision. He rode Gravelines, who produced a most impressive turn of foot in the last furlong and won easily from another strong finisher Dona Barod, who met him on the same terms as at Deauville. The result showed a further improvement in Gravelines; he beat Dona Barod by two and a half lengths and his superiority over the other horses who ran in the Marois was more marked than at Deauville in every instance. In addition he beat the consistent Monsanto by at least six lengths. The following Sunday Dona Barod won the big race for fillies on Prix de l'Arc day, the Prix de l'Opéra, and she subsequently ran eighth of nineteen in the Champion Stakes.

Gravelines (gr.c. 1972)	Cadmus (b 1963)	Supreme Court (b 1948)	Persian Gulf or Precipitation
			Forecourt
		Covert Side (gr 1958)	Abernant
			Cub Hunt
	Gray Dove (gr 1966)	T.V. Lark (b 1957)	Indian Hemp
			Miss Larksfly
		Ruwenzori (gr 1956)	Oil Capitol
			Ruanda

Without Gravelines, Cadmus would have a sorry record at stud and the French let him go in 1975. Gray Dove, Gravelines' dam, is a mare of unusually high quality to be sent to him. Although she never ran she is, as we said, a sister to the stakes winner Pink Pigeon, who won not only the Santa Barbara Handicap but five other handicaps now rated as pattern races. She is also a sister to at least four other winners in the United States, two of them placed in stakes races, and is a half-sister to another winner. The next dam, Ruwenzori, finished third in the Hollywood Oaks and she won four times. Gravelines is a half-brother to a filly by Sigebert called Guadaloupe who showed useful form at distances up to around a mile in France. He has shown by far his best form at a mile but he has won at nine furlongs; with Cadmus, a horse who stayed a mile and a half, for his sire there is a fair chance that he will stay a mile and a quarter. He acts on any going. *A. Penna, France.*

GRAY BUTTONS 2 ch.c. Gulf Pearl 117–Martial Air 113 (Court Martial) [1976   **— p** 8s] closely related to useful winner Nadir Shah (by Persian Gulf), and half-brother to many winners, including Sound the Bugle and Mironton (both by Alcide): dam a miler: 10/1, prominent for 5f when behind in 27-runner maiden race won by Sporting Yankee at Newmarket in October: should do better. *J. Tree.*

GREAT BALL 4 ch.c. Major Portion 129–Blaeberry 100 (Hook Money 124)   **84** [1974 6d5 7fg 6fg* 8g3 1975 7v3 10g 10.6fg4 12f6 12g 12fg4 14fg 12g3 12f3 12s 12g6 1976 8g 10.4d 10d* 10f4 10g4] strong colt: useful performer (rated 104) at 3 yrs: ran by far his best race in 1976 when winning minor event at Pontefract in May by ½ length from Dempsey: stays 1½m: seems to act on any going: has worn blinkers (including on last two outings): unreliable: bought out of D. Hanley's stable 1,800 gns Ascot January Sales. *W. Clay.*

GREAT BIRNAM 5 b.g. Celtic Ash–Aldegonde (Nimbus 130) [1974 12g3 12g*   **86** 14f4 14d 12g 1975 12s4 12g2 12fg4 13.3fg4 12fg5 14f* 12g 14g3 14g5 14g* 1976 14g 12fg6 14.7d4 14f2 16.1fg3] good-looking, well-made gelding: fair handicapper: stays well: acts on firm going: ran freely when tried in blinkers: requires strong handling: sold 1,250 gns Ascot November Sales. *G. Pritchard-Gordon.*

GREAT BROTHER 4 b.c. Great Nephew 126–Limuru 83 (Alcide 136) [1974   **95** 6fg* 7d2 8g 1975 8g* 1976 6.5g6 11g 10g 7.5g 8d* 8g* 11g2 9g* 8g5 8g 9g 7v4 8v] rangy colt: good mover: lightly raced at 2 and 3 yrs, but ran eleven times in France in first half of 1976 season, winning amateur riders events at Rambouillet (two) and Evry: having first race in this country since his 3-y-o days (and first outing since June) when 12½ lengths fourth of nine to Jane's Joker in handicap at York in October: tailed off in similar event at Newbury later in month: stays 11f: seems to act on any going: trained in France by C. Milbank. *C. Brittain.*

GREAT ECHO 6 b.g. Great White Way–Miss Echo (Chamier 128) [1974 5v4   **70** 12g* 10d6 7fg4 7f2 5.9g3 8fg3 7fg4 8fg4 10.4d3 7s* 7s 1975 7s 7.6g2 7.2g2 7f2 7.2fg3 6fg3 6g3 6f 7f6 5.9fg3 7g 10.2g 1976 10g6 8s4 12h2 5f 12f4] quite a moderate handicapper: very narrowly beaten by Grand Display in four-runner amateur riders race at Carlisle in June: best form at 6f or 7f but stays 1½m: acts on any going and on any track: has worn blinkers: bandaged off-fore final outing. *H. Bell.*

GREAT ESCAPE 2 b.c. Tower Walk 130–Sovereign Court 87 (Sovereign Path — p
125) [1976 6d] big, strong, good sort: half-brother to several winners here and
in Italy, including quite useful miler Almagest (by Star Gazer): 18,500 gns yearling: dam won over 7f at 2 yrs: unquoted and very backward when sixteenth of
23 in maiden race won by Rings at Newmarket in October: looks the type to make
a very nice 3-y-o. *G. Harwood.*

GREAT FLIGHT 2 ch.f. Great Nephew 126–Crescent Dart 103 (Sing Sing 134) 105
[1976 5g² 5g* 6fg³ 6g³ 6fg 6fg] small, quite attractive filly: third foal: half-sister
to smart 1974 2-y-o sprinter Double Dart (by Songedor): dam a sprinter: won
nine-runner maiden race at Sandown in June by 1½ lengths from newcomer
Friendly: ran well to finish third in two good-class races the following month, being beaten less than 2 lengths by Ampulla in Cherry Hinton Stakes at Newmarket
and 1½ lengths by Al Stanza in Princess Margaret Stakes at Ascot: ran moderately
on last two outings, including when tried on blinkers on penultimate start: well
suited by 6f. *R. Hern.*

GREAT IDEA 3 b.c. Great Nephew 126–Divine Thought 102 (Javelot 124) 104
[1975 5.1f* 6fg* 6h² 7g* 7f⁴ 1976 8.2d³ 7g⁵ 10.4s* 12f⁴ 10fg 10g⁵ 8g 8g⁵] strong,
compact colt: good mover: put up best effort when winning nine-runner Dee
Stakes at Chester in May, finishing strongly to score narrowly from dead-heaters
Gunner B and Radetzky: ran respectably on three of his subsequent outings,
including when about 3½ lengths fifth behind Iron Duke in Prix de la Cote
Normande at Deauville in August: should stay 1½m: acts on any going. *H. Cecil.*

GREAT LAD 4 ch.c. Great Nephew 126–Lovely Lady 81 (Never Say Die 137) 61
[1974 6g 7s 7g⁴ 9s* 1975 12s 12g⁶ 10fg 8f 10fg 14fg⁴ 12v 17.1g² 16g 12d* 1976
12fg⁴ 12d⁵ 12f⁵ 14f⁴ 12fg] strong colt: very well suited by a test of stamina: acts
on soft going: has been tried in blinkers: suitable mount for an apprentice: trained
by W. Marshall until after third outing. *B. Richmond.*

GREAT MEMOIRS 2 ch.f. Great Nephew 126–Blue Book 101 (Majority Blue 97
126) [1976 5f* 6g² 6fg⁵] small, useful-looking filly: third foal: half-sister to two
2-y-o 5f winners by Burglar, including useful La Voleuse: dam, winner twice over
5f at 2 yrs, stayed 1m: won maiden race at Salisbury in August by ¾ length from
Quick Retort: ran better subsequent race when excellent second, beaten 2 lengths
to Rockery (Fr), in minor event at Kempton later in month: suited by 6f and will
probably get further. *P. Walwyn.*

GREAT OAK 2 b.c. Athens Wood 126–Lady Astronaut (Polly's Jet) [1976 5fg 107
6fg* 6fg² 6fg² 5f⁴ 7f 7d³ 6g⁴] well-made, good-looking colt: first produce: 460
gns foal, resold 1,600 gns yearling: dam, placed at 2 yrs in France, is sister to high-
class performer Turbo Jet and half-sister to Faberge II: put up a good performance to win eight-runner £2,000 event at York in June, coming home 2 lengths
clear of Millionaire despite being eased: second to Man in the Moon on next two
outings, going down by 3 lengths in Fenwolf Stakes at Ascot and by 1½ lengths
when meeting him on terms 11 lb better in Cock of the North Stakes at Haydock:
ran best race afterwards when length third of 16 to The Czar in minor event at
Yarmouth in September: should stay 1½m. *H. T. Jones.*

GREAT PAL 2 ch.c. Great Nephew 126–Smokey Sue 67 (Never Say Die 137) 73
[1976 7fg 7g 8s] big, strong, attractive colt: third foal: half-brother to 6f winner
Romoke (by Romulus) and to a winner in Italy: 5,000 gns foal, and resold 18,000
gns yearling: dam placed over 1m at 3 yrs: ran respectably for a newcomer when
about 11 lengths eighth of 17 to Gairloch in minor event at Goodwood in September: behind in well-contested events at Ascot and Doncaster afterwards: the
type to do better in time. *C. Brittain.*

GREAT SENSATION 2 b.c. Malicious–Ricky's Rita (Trentonian) [1976 7h 7h⁶ 72
7.2f² 7.3d⁴ 8s] small colt: half-brother to three minor winners in North America:
dam won once from 11 starts: showed ability in varied company, including
selling: should stay 1m: acts on firm going. *P. Haslam.*

GREAT SIGN 2 b.c. Wolver Hollow 126–Austrian Girl (Vienna 127) [1976 5f⁶ 85
6f²] strong, compact colt: fourth foal: 2,800 gns yearling: dam never ran: 3
lengths second to Fawn in 19-runner maiden race at Ripon in August: will stay
at least 1½m: should find a winning opportunity in the north. *S. Hall.*

GREAT SOMERFORD 5 gr.g. Right Royal V 135–Idover 95 (Fortino II 120) —
[1974 11.7fg 11.7fg 1975 12s⁶ 1976 8fg 10f] neat gelding: bad plater: wears
blinkers. *W. Williams.*

GREAT SURPRISE 7 gr.g. Zeus Boy 121–Veronica Franchi (Tenerani 135) —
[1974 N.R. 1975 18g 1976 12g] probably of little account. *K. Ivory.*

Dee Stakes, Chester—Great Idea (left) finishes fast to overhaul Gunner B and Radetzky (rails)

GREAT THINGS 3 ch.g. Major Portion 129–Perimoss 75 (Mossborough 126) **57**
[1975 6g 6fg 1976 8fg 12g 10g⁶ 10g² 10s⁴ 11.1s⁴] strong, medium-sized gelding: showed first worthwhile form when runner-up to Noeletta in claiming race at Kempton in August but subsequently ran moderately in sellers: should stay 1½m: possibly unsuited by soft going: blinkered third to fifth outings. *J. Sutcliffe.*

GRECIAN BOND 3 b.f. Good Bond 122–Clytemnestra 81 (Bullrush 106) **81**
[1975 6g 7fg⁵ 7f 1976 10.4s* 11f³ 12d⁶ 8f² 8.2f³ 10.1fg 10g⁵ 10v* 10v²] big filly: won handicaps at Chester in May and Newcastle in October, on latter course beating Shady Desire 7 lengths: probably finds 1m on sharp side for her and stays 1½m well: acts on any going but goes particularly well in the mud: sold 3,800 gns Newmarket December Sales. *B. Hills.*

GRECIAN CLOUD 3 ch.f. Galivanter 131–Anthela 76 (Acropolis 132) [1975 **64**
5s² 5g 5s³ 7fg⁶ 7.2s 8g 7g* 7d 1976 11.1fg⁵ 10f² 12.2g³ 13g² 12f³] lengthy filly: stays 13f: probably acts on any going. *J. Edwards.*

GREEK FLAME 2 b.f. Athens Wood 126–Land of Fire 99 (Buisson Ardent 129) — p
[1976 7s] third foal: dam genuine performer at up to 1m: 16/1 when ninth of 19 to Lady Oriana in maiden race at Newmarket in October: should improve. *G. Pritchard-Gordon.*

GREEK MONARCH 4 ro.c. Monarca–Thracia 83 (Pindari 124) [1974 8v⁵ **72**
7g⁴ 8s⁵ 1975 12v 12.2s⁶ 11.7f* 10fg³ 12f⁴ 12f 12g⁵ 1976 12fg⁶ 13f⁴ 12.2f² 11.7f⁴ 11.7fg* 12g⁴ 12f 11.7h²] strong colt: quite a moderate handicapper: ran consistently at 4 yrs, winning at Windsor in May by 4 lengths from Winged Dagger: stays well and needs at least 1½m: acts well on firm going: wears a tongue strap: suitable mount for an apprentice. *R. Vibert.*

GREEK MONEY 6 gr.m. Sovereign Path 125–Go Go Girl (Romulus 129) [1974 —
9g³ 9g² 9f² 11.9g² 12s² 1975 12f³ 9f³ 8.7f⁴ 12f* 10f² 8g 10g* 1976 10f⁵ 12.3fg⁴ 11fg⁴ 13g⁵ 12h³ 13f⁵ 12.5v] poor handicapper: raced in Ireland at 4 and 5 yrs, and showed moderate form there, winning maiden plate at Dundalk and handicap at Listowel in 1975: little worthwhile form in this country as a 6-y-o: stays 1½m: blinkered in 1975. *E. Collingwood.*

GREEK MYTH 2 ch.f. Green God 128–Idle Chatter (Romulus 129) [1976 5s **82**
5f⁵ 5h 5f⁵ 6h* 6f 6f 6s²] neat filly: 190 gns yearling: dam Irish staying maiden:
attracted no bid after winning seller at Pontefract in July all out by 1½ lengths
from Darwen Lad: showed improved form when 4 lengths second of eight to
Aston Firs in minor event at Catterick in October: will stay 7f: acts on any
going but is very well suited by soft: blinkered, sweating and very much on toes
when refusing to race on third outing. *J. Fitzgerald.*

GREEN-FINGERED 2 ch.c Green God 128–Flower Show 85 (Supreme Court **85**
135) [1976 5fg 7h² 7h* 7s] brother to a French plater, and half-brother to
three winners, including fairly useful 1½m handicapper Poppy (by Ballymoss):
1,100 gns foal, resold 2,400 gns yearling: dam best at around 1½m: odds on, won
maiden race at Bath in August by 2½ lengths from El Caballero: will stay 1m:
acts on hard ground. *B. Hills.*

GREENHILL GOD 2 b.c. Green God 128–Hill Queen 75 (Djebe) [1976 6fg] — p
closely related to top-class sprinter Sandford Lad (by St Alphage), and half-
brother to several winners, including very useful sprinter Sandford Lady (by
Will Somers): 10,000 gns yearling: dam stayed 1¼m: 16/1, got well behind in
early stages but was going on very much better at finish when in rear in £2,000
maiden race won by Adviser at Goodwood in July: has the scope to do better
at 3 yrs. *R. Price.*

GREENJACKET 2 b.c. Salvo 129–Courtlier 89 (Supreme Court 135) [1976 6g*] **96 p**
brother to fairly useful 1974 2-y-o 1m winner Miss Evo, and half-brother to three
winners, including very useful Irish miler Courtwell (by Court Harwell): 800 gns
yearling: dam stayed 1¾m: 33/1, put up an encouraging display for such a
stoutly-bred colt when winning 18-runner newcomers event at Lingfield in
September by ½ length from Waterbuck: sure to improve over longer distances
and will stay at least 1½m. *C. Bewicke.*

GREEN LADY 2 ch.f. Green God 128–Plot (Never Say Die 137) [1976 5f³ 5fg **55**
5fg 7f 6g] useful-looking filly: ran promisingly on first outing but was well
beaten afterwards and was sold 760 gns Newmarket Autumn Sales. *F. Carr.*

GREEN LAUREL 3 ch.f. Sassafras 135–Green Chiffon 83 (Crepello 136) [1975 **65**
6f⁵ 6f 1976 10g 10.5d 11.1g⁶ 12d⁵ 12g³ 11g 16fg⁶] well-made filly: showed a
little ability in varied company but ran poorly last two outings: should be
suited by 1½m+: wears blinkers nowadays. *F. J. Houghton.*

GREEN MADONA 2 ch.f. Green God 128–Joan's Gallery (Sunny Way 120) —
[1976 5.1f⁵ 5fg] third foal: dam never ran: 6 lengths fifth of seven to Lizzylyn
in maiden race at Yarmouth in August: well beaten in seller at Ripon later in
month. *M. Jarvis.*

GREEN MANSIONS 2 ch.c. Levmoss 133–Emerald Velvet 76 (Sheshoon 132) —
[1976 6g⁶ 7fg] lengthy colt: half-brother to three winners, including useful 7f
and 1m winner The Hertford (by Supreme Sovereign): 4,300 gns yearling: dam
a stayer: showed a little promise on first outing but finished last in a weakly-
contested event at Edinburgh on only other start: should stay well. *Denys
Smith.*

GREENSTEAD LAD 3 b.c. Caliban 123–Breathalyser (Alcide 136) [1975 6g⁵ **78**
1976 8fg⁴ 11g² 10g⁶ 12fg² 12s⁶] lengthy, useful sort: runner-up in maiden
races at Newbury in May (to Double East) and August (to Bombardier): not
disgraced under stiff weight in handicap at Newmarket on final outing: suited
by 1½m. *J. Winter.*

GREEN TURTLE DIVER 2 br.c. Deep Diver 134–Samarra (Milesian 125) **82**
[1976 5d⁵ 5f⁶ 5fg 5f³ 5g² 6g] strong, workmanlike colt: 4 lengths third of 25
to Spring Dive in maiden event at Thirsk in September: favourite for sellers on
next two outings, putting up easily better effort when failing by a short head
to catch Show Stealer in 21-runner event at Ayr: evidently best at 5f. *F. Carr.*

GREENWOOD 4 gr.c. Habitat 134–Grey Goose 113 (Grey Sovereign 128 §) —
[1974 6g 1975 N.R. 1976 9g] ex-French colt: backward, wearing blinkers
and having first outing since July, 1974 when behind in maiden race at Ripon
in April. *R. Boss.*

GRESHAM GIRL 3 b.f. Right Tack 131–Granville Greta 115 (Grandmaster) **78**
[1975 5f 5f 5.1g⁵ 5f² 6g* 6d* 6g⁵ 6g³ 6f² 6v 1976 7fg 6g 5.9g⁴ 6f³ 6f³ 6fg⁶
6h⁵ 5.9f 6g* 6f 6v] small filly: quite a moderate handicapper: narrow winner
at Ripon in August from Sunset Song: runs as though she will stay 7f: acts on
any going with possible exception of really soft: has worn blinkers but does
better without: goes well for apprentice N. Crowther. *G. Vergette.*

GRETTA'S GIRL 3 b.f. Arctic Kanda 111–Little Twink (Little Buskins 119) —
[1975 N.R. 1976 8g 9.4h³ 12f⁵] first foal: dam won over hurdles: poor plater:
sold 900 gns Ascot November Sales. *Denys Smith.*

GREY AGLOW 5 gr.m. Aglojo 119–P.L.G. (Anwar 120) [1974 8fg 8fg 11.2f⁶ **80**
14f 12.2fg 8g 8s 8v 7s 6s⁶ 7s³ 1975 12.2fg⁴ 10f³ 12f³ 12h³ 12g⁵ 12.2fg³ 12f*
15.8fg* 12.2f 16.2s² 13.8g⁵ 12v* 1976 16.1d* 16s⁶ 15f³ 17.7f 15.8g⁶ 16fg³ 16.1d
12s⁵ 12s* 12.5v* 12.5s⁴] modest handicapper: successful at Haydock in
April and at Doncaster and Teesside in October: stays 2m: acts on any going
but is well suited by plenty of give in the ground: effective with or without
blinkers: goes well for 7-lb claimer B. Hood. *J. Etherington.*

GREY BARON 3 gr.c. Alcide 136–Chysanthia (Ballymoss 136) [1975 6f³ **120**
6g⁶ 8g⁴ 8s³ 8g* 8d⁴ 10f³ 1976 12f³ 12fg² 12g² 14g* 14fg* 15g* 14fg 16g 14g² 14s²]
Bruce Hobbs secured a bargain when he purchased Grey Baron at the
Doncaster Yearling Sales for only 2,800 guineas, a sum substantially less
than the horse had fetched as a foal. Hobbs paid 11,000 guineas for Grey
Baron's year-older half-brother Tolmiros, who has won races but is not so
good a horse. Grey Baron has shown very smart form, and judging by the
progress he has been making he won't be far behind the best stayers in 1977.
Grey Baron went from strength to strength during his second-season
campaign, and finished out of the first three only twice in ten starts, but not
until he was raced over a mile and three quarters did he manage to get
his head in front. His first two
successes were gained in almost
identical fashion in handicaps run
over the same course and distance.
At Sandown on the last day of May,
giving upwards of 12 lb to his seven
rivals, he was always pulling over
his field and won very smoothly by
three lengths from Ribarbaro. A
month later, again under top weight,
Grey Baron trounced Spring Frolic,
to whom he was conceding 20 lb,
by four lengths. He was improving,
as can be fairly gauged by the fact
that earlier in the season at Newmarket Grey Baron, on terms 6 lb
better, had failed by one and a half
lengths to cope with Spring Frolic.
After Sandown Grey Baron's mettle
was really put to the test: he took
on a strong field of older horses in
the valuable Tennent Trophy
Handicap at Ayr in July, and

*William Hill Handicap, Sandown—Grey
Baron is not extended to beat Spring Frolic
and Black Sabbath (rails)*

appeared to have a very stiff weight.
However, he turned in a splendidly
game performance and won by a
neck from Ribellaro.

Grey Baron was charged very highly for his three wins in succession and
he cut no ice in his next two races, the Tote-Ebor at York in August and the
Top Rank Club Handicap at Newcastle later in the month. However, he
returned to form in grand style when runner-up on his last two outings, going
under by two lengths to Unsuspected in a Newmarket handicap and by three
lengths to Roses for the Star in a minor event at Sandown. On both occasions
he was giving lumps of weight to the winner; to Roses for the Star, a classic-
placed filly, no less than 16 lb.

Grey Baron (gr.c. 1973)	Alcide (b 1955)	Alycidon (ch 1945)	Donatello II
			Aurora
		Chenille (br 1940)	King Salmon
			Sweet Aloe
	Chysanthia (gr 1963)	Ballymoss (ch 1954)	Mossborough
			Indian Call
		Abelia (gr 1955)	Abernant
			Queen of Peru

By the top-class stayer Alcide, Grey Baron is the sixth foal of Chysanthia,
an unraced daughter of the brilliantly speedy Abelia. All of Chysanthia's

previous foals are winners, the best of them being Tolmiros, useful at a distance of a mile and a quarter. Chysanthia is a half-sister to numerous winners, notably the smart milers Casabianca and St Padarn. The third dam Queen of Peru (by Big Game) is a half-sister to a good stayer called Dubonnet (by Papyrus) who won the Goodwood Cup. A strong, attractive colt, Grey Baron stays very w_ll and acts on any going. He is very genuine and is the type of horse to go on improving as a four-year-old. He is invariably held up, and possesses a good turn of speed for a stayer which should stand him in good stead in high-class company. *B. Hobbs.*

GREY BLOSSOM 2 gr.f. Grisaille 115—Coral Flower (Quorum 126) [1976 5g 5fg 6f3 6fg3 6fg4 7f4 8.2s3 7s2 6s 6s 8v*] small filly: fair plater: won at Leicester in November by a length from Demelza (no bid): needs at least 7f nowadays and stays 1m well: acts on any going: blinkered second to ninth outings. *A. Goodwill.* **67**

GREYGORA 2 gr.f. Raffingora 130—Grey Streak 85 (Palestine 133) [1976 5d3 5.6f 6f2 6f] robust filly: half-sister to 3-y-o 1m winner Streaker King (by King's Troop): dam a miler: placed in maiden race at Doncaster in May and minor event at Catterick in July, on latter occasion looking not at home on the course when going down by ½ length to clever winner Hand Canter: stays 6f: appears to act on any going. *J. Fitzgerald.* **74**

GREY GOWN 2 gr.f. Galivanter 131—Drip Dry 87 (Coronation Year 124) [1976 5g 7g] lightly-built filly: half-sister to two winners, including fair sprinter Moor Lane (by Tin Whistle): 520 gns foal: dam won twice over 1m: behind in maiden races at Newcastle in August (missed break) and Ayr in September. *E. Weymes.* **—**

GREY MORLEY 3 gr.f. Pongee 106—Nasca 81 (King's Bench 132) [1975 5fg3 6f 1976 5f 6f 6f 7g5 8f] rather lightly-made filly: ran poorly as a 3-y-o. *E. Collingwood.* **—**

GREY MOUNTAIN 3 gr.g. Town Crier 119—Abernette 102 (Abernant 142) [1975 5fg 6fg 5d 5g 5g 1976 6fg 7f* 8fg5 8f 7g5 8fg 7f 8.2h5 12f2 10f3 10d6 12s5] leggy gelding: fair plater on his day: winner at Beverley in April by a length from Solar Saint: bought in 1,550 gns afterwards: stays 1½m: acts on any going: retained by trainer 1,600 gns Ascot July Sales. *W. Marshall.* **66**

GREY PRESTO 4 gr.c. Fortissimo 111—Frisco Kid (I Say 125) [1974 8s 1975 8d 9g6 10.1fg 10g 8g 10g5 1976 8.3f3 8d2 7fg4 8fg5 8g3 8f2 8fg5 7d 10d2 8s6] poor plater: stays 1¼m: appears to act on any going: effective with or without blinkers: sold to D. Jermy 600 gns Ascot October Sales. *P. Makin.* **49**

GREY SAIL 3 gr.c. Grisaille 115—Dareth 64 § (Dara §§) [1975 5s5 5s4 5f3 5h2 6g4 6f3 5g 6f 5g 7g4 6g6 1976 8f* 6f* 8f2 9f 8h6 8f5 8f4 8f* 10g6 8g4 8v4 8s* 8s6] leggy colt: winner of maiden race at Beverley and minor event at Thirsk early in season and subsequently picked up ladies race and handicap at Redcar, latter in October by a neck from Shady Desire: stays 1m well: acts on any going: suitable mount for an apprentice. *J. Calvert.* **86**

GREY TIGER 3 gr.c. Willowick—Tigerin (Prodomo) [1975 7.5g5 6g 1976 8s6 10f* 12f* 9g* 10f2 16f 14f2 12g 12f3 14f2 14f5 13f2 10s 12g] Irish colt: second living foal: half-brother to Irish 7f winner Townsman (by Henry Higgins): 7,000 gns yearling: dam top-rated 3-y-o filly in Germany in 1965: won maiden race at Navan in May and handicaps at Killarney and Mallow later in month: odds on and won by a short head on last two occasions: runner-up in four handicaps afterwards: subsequently sent to race in Italy: stays 1¾m: acts well on firm going: seemed badly hampered about 5f out when well beaten behind General Ironside in Queen's Vase at Royal Ascot on sixth start. *K. Prendergast, Ireland.* **98**

GREY TRILBY 2 gr.f. Don II 123—Judy O'Grady (Whistler 129) [1976 6g 5fg6 6s 6s 5v4] robust filly: showed ability only at 5f but should stay 6f. *B. Swift.* **70**

GRIM LASS 4 ch.f. Above Suspicion 127—Irish Rising 71 (St Paddy 133) [1974 5f* 6fg 7fg4 7d5 7.2g5 8s 1975 6g4 6f* 6fg6 6h2 6h5 7g4 6fg2 7.6fg 1976 7g 8f3 8fg4 7fg* 8g2 7g6 7g 5h4 6h 6h] compact filly: made all when winning handicap at Thirsk in May by 1½ lengths from Strathoykel: stays 1m and wasn't disgraced over 5f on eighth start: appears to act on any going but is particularly well suited by firm: suited by a sharp track and front-running tactics. *J. Berry.* **65**

GRINLING GIBBONS 4 br.c. Bagdad—Angel Falls (Sir Gaylord) [1974 N.R. 1975 8v 11v3 16s2 14g2 16f 16f* 16g2 16f* 14fg* 16g 18fg3 1976 14.6g* 14fg3 16g4 **101**

304

16g³ 20f⁴ 16fg³ 19fg 16g⁴ 18d⁵] attractive, well-made American-bred colt: useful handicapper: put up a splendid performance on reappearance, beating Cadogan Lane very easily by 5 lengths at Doncaster in March: ran creditably in most of his races afterwards, on sixth start finishing 2¼ lengths third of 11 to Philominsky in Joe Coral Northumberland Plate at Newcastle in June: stays very well: acts on any going: genuine and consistent: blinkered sixth and eighth outings: sold to G. Vergette 7,800 gns Newmarket Autumn Sales. *G. Harwood.*

GRITTI PALACE 7 b.g. Appiani II 128–Queen of Connemara (Prince Chevalier) [1974 10.1g 8d* 10h² 10f* 12s 10d⁴ 12s² 10v* 10d* 12g* 1975 N.R. 1976 14fg⁴] useful handicapper (rated 101) in 1974: tailed-off last of four behind Top Straight at Yarmouth in June, first outing since: stays 1½m: acts on any going: good mount for an apprentice: has a splendid turn of foot: presumably difficult to train. *P. Robinson.* —

GRITTLE 2 br.f. Great Nephew 126–Little Hexa (Exar 130) [1976 5f 5d⁴ 6g⁶ 5f 6h* 7f 8f⁵] small filly: 4-length winner of seller at Pontefract in August (bought in 640 gns): should stay 1¼m. *F. Carr.* 65

GROOVYMAN 2 br.g. Mansingh 120–Groovy 86 (Sound Track 132) [1976 5f 5d 5h 5g 5v] lengthy gelding: well beaten in maiden races and a seller. *J. Vickers.* —

GROUND COVER 2 b.c. Huntercombe 133–Crepe Myrtle 80 (Crepello 136) [1976 5g 5fg* 5d⁶ 5f² 5fg³ 5fg 6g⁵ 6v⁴] neat colt: third foal: dam, daughter of sister to Goodwood Cup winner Double Bore, won over 1m: impressive winner of maiden race at Windsor in May: apprentice ridden when successful at Lingfield the following month but was moved down to second by stewards for hampering Noirima: will probably stay 7f: seems to act on any going: sold 9,000 gns Newmarket Autumn Sales, reportedly for export to Canada. *J. Tree.* 100

GROUNDSEL 2 b.f. Reform 132–Guilded Moss 75 (Ballymoss 136) [1976 8fg 9s³] third foal: half-sister to 1974 2-y-o 1m winner Gilliflower (by Great Nephew): dam stayed at least 1¾m: 1½ lengths third of nine to Saratoga Kid in maiden race at Wolverhampton in October: will stay middle distances: lost ground at start on both outings. *E. Weymes.* 72

GROUND WORK 3 b.f. Graustark–Daisy Chain 103 (Darius 129) [1975 6fg⁵ 7d 1976 8fg* 8g⁴ 8s] well-made, attractive American-foaled filly: overcame difficulties in running when winning 16-runner maiden race at Newcastle in June in good style by 1½ lengths from Love Story: odds on for handicap at Ayr the following month but could finish only fourth to Indianira, and ran poorly (tailed off) when tried in blinkers on only outing afterwards (September): will stay at least 1¼m: acts on a firm surface and is possibly unsuited by soft going: sold 11,000 gns Newmarket December Sales. *R. Hern.* 82

GROVE'S BOY 3 b.c. King's Leap 111–Camilla Mary (Molvedo 137) [1975 5g² 5.1f⁵ 5g 5fg² 6f³ 7g² 7g 8.2d² 8g⁴(dis) 8.2g³ 7g 1976 8g 8f* 8.2g² 9f⁴ 8fg⁴ 8fg* 10f² 8g³ 8f² 8.2f* 8g⁴ 8h⁴ 8g 8g⁶ 9g 8.2v³] neat, lightly-made colt: fairly useful handicapper: successful at Brighton, Yarmouth and Windsor: apprentice ridden when beating London Glory ¾ length on last-named course in July: stays 1¼m: best form on a sound surface: suitable mount for an apprentice: consistent most of season but was below form last four outings: sold 8,800 gns Newmarket Autumn Sales. *C. Brittain.* 91

GRUMPY 2 ch.c. Leander 119–Spotty Bebe 83 (Credo 123) [1976 5g³ 7f⁴ 7h³ 7h 7fg 6g⁶] strong, lengthy colt: first foal: dam a sprinter: in frame in maiden races at Salisbury (two) and Bath: fair sixth of 21 to Burley in £1,400 seller at Newmarket in September on final outing after swerving at start (blinkered first time): stays 7f. *E. Reavey.* 66

GRUNHILDE 2 b.f. Mountain Call 125–Roller Bird 69 (Ribocco 129) [1976 6fg 5fg 7d] neat filly: first foal: 5,400 gns yearling: dam middle-distance maiden: unplaced in large fields of maidens, twice apprentice ridden, finishing eleventh of 30 to Guama at Newbury in September on final outing. *P. Cundell.* —

GUAMA 2 b.f. Gulf Pearl 117–Cremoria (Crocket 130) [1976 7d*] attractive, shapely filly: first foal: dam, winner over 1½m in France, is sister to smart French filly Red Wood and half-sister to Celtic Ash: 25/1 for 30-runner maiden race at Newbury in September but put up a very promising performance, joining leaders going very easily ¼m out and then staying on, without being at all hard ridden, to win by 1½ lengths from Misalliance: will stay 1½m: impressed us as the best-looking filly in the paddock at Newbury but looked as though race was needed and she should show considerable improvement at 3 yrs. *M. Jarvis.* 89 P

GUARD DUTY 2 b.c. Tower Walk 130–Baltarq (Tarqogan 125) [1976 5v⁴ **86**
5f² 5s² 5fg² 6g³ 5f² 5d³] strong colt: first foal: 4,800 gns yearling: dam won over
7.9f at 2 yrs in Ireland: fair maiden: runner-up four times, on final occasion finishing strongly when beaten 2½ lengths by Whenby in nursery at Hamilton in
September: will stay 7f: probably acts on any going. *N. Angus.*

GUFFAW 3 br.c. Prince Regent 129–Blueit 96 (Final Score 113) [1975 6s⁶ **76**
1976 8f 8fg⁴ 8g⁴ 7g⁴ 8fg⁴ 8s² 8s 12v² 12s⁴ 10.2s] short-backed colt: quite moderate
form in maiden races: runs as though he may stay further than 1½m: ran poorly
when tried in blinkers on final outing. *W. Wightman.*

GUICHET 3 b. or br.f. Jacinto–Croquet (Court Martial) [1975 5.5s* 5.5g⁵ 6d **117**
5d³ 1976 7g* 8g⁶ 8g* 8g* 8f² 8d⁶ 9.2s 7s] workmanlike American-bred French
filly: sister to two stakes winners, namely Silver Mallet, smart winner at up to
1m, and Buzkashi, a very useful middle-distance performer, and half-sister to a
stakes-placed winner: dam won three races in America and is half-sister to California Oaks winner Flying Fur: won Prix Imprudence at Maisons-Laffitte in April
by ½ length from Come Up Smiling: could finish only sixth to Riverqueen in French
1,000 Guineas the following month, but then won Prix de Bagatelle by 1½ lengths
from Start The Game and Prix de Sandringham by a length from Kesar Queen,
both races at Longchamp: given too much to do when going under by a head to
Kesar Queen in Coronation Stakes at Royal Ascot (made up at least 5 lengths in
last 2f and only just failed to get up): ran poorly afterwards: should stay further
than 1m: acts on any going: exported to U.S.A. *F. Boutin, France.*

GUIDO FAWKES 3 ch.c. Sea Hawk II 131–Spoiled Wine (Pampered King **97**
121) [1975 7fg⁵ 8s⁴ 7.3g⁶ 1976 12fg³ 10.4d² 14fg* 16f 16f² 14f²] shapely,
attractive colt: good walker: beat Modern Times by 4 lengths when successful in
maiden race at Newmarket in May: excellent second to Belle Bretonne in handicap
at Lingfield the following month but was disappointing odds-on favourite only
subsequent outing: probably needs further than 1¾m nowadays, and will stay
extreme distances: appears to act on any going: sold to E. Jones 3,100 gns Newmarket Autumn Sales. *B. Hills.*

GUILSWAY 3 gr.f. Track Spare 125–Guilpath 77 (Sovereign Path 125) [1975 **—**
5fg 5g⁶ 6g 6g 1976 7g 8fg⁶ 8h³ 8.2f 8fg⁵ 8fg 10.4fg⁴ 8.2d 9v 9s 10v⁶] strong,
useful sort: only poor form, and was well beaten in claiming race at Leicester on
final outing: easily best run at 1¼m: evidently needs a sound surface: ran moderately in blinkers on sixth appearance. *R. Mason.*

GUINEAPIG 2 b.c. Sovereign Path 125–West Virginia (Charlottesville 135) **85**
[1976 6fg⁵ 7fg⁶ 8d⁴ 7v⁶] leggy, light-framed colt: half-brother to 9f and 1¼m
winner Shore Captain (by Skymaster): 8,200 gns yearling: dam lightly-raced
half-sister to St Leger winner Provoke: 8 lengths fourth of 17 to Ad Lib Ra in
maiden race at Newbury in September, best effort: possibly unsuited by heavy
ground: dead. *H. Candy.*

GULF OF CORINTH 2 ch.c. Gulf Pearl 117–Gwen 114 (Abernant 142) [1976 **— p**
7g 8d 8s] strong, well-made, attractive colt: very good walker: half-brother
to three winners, including useful 1m to 1½m performer Timon (by Acropolis):
10,500 gns yearling: dam, thoroughly genuine filly, finished second in 1,000
Guineas: little worthwhile form in useful maiden company but was distinctly
backward on first two outings and looks capable of much better. *B. Hobbs.*

GULF ROYAL 2 ch.c. Gulf Pearl 117–Ennel (Seminole II) [1976 6f⁵] half- **— p**
brother to three winners, including very useful 3-y-o Super Cavalier (by Tower
Walk) and very smart miler Fastacre (by Linacre): 9,600 gns yearling: dam
never ran: 10/1, showed up for 4f when fifth of nine behind wide-margin winner
Adviser in minor event at Salisbury in August: will do better, probably over
7f+. *G. Harwood.*

GULLIVER LAD 4 ch.g. Manacle 123–Starsilk 83 (Counsel 118) [1974 N.R. **66**
1975 6s* 6s 6g 6fg⁶ 8.2d 8g 6g 1976 8f 7f 7g⁴ 6fg⁴ 5.9fg 6f⁶ 6f²] lightly-made
gelding: quite a moderate performer: caught close home when second to Another
Fiddler in seller at Windsor in July: stays 7f: has worn blinkers: suitable mount
for an apprentice. *D. Dale.*

GUNBAD 2 ch.c. Welsh Pageant 132–Nick of Time 104 (Nicolaus) [1976 7g³ **93**
8s 10d²] quite an attractive colt: half-brother to four winners, including
good stayer Erimo Hawk (by Sea Hawk II): 13,000 gns yearling: dam won at
up to 7f, and is half-sister to Kashmir II: first past post, short head in front of
stable-companion Don't Touch, in £2,100 event at Newmarket in October, but
hung left in final furlong hampering runner-up and was moved down a place
by stewards: stays 1¼m: should gain compensation at 3 yrs. *J. Hindley.*

Andy Capp Handicap, Redcar—Gunner B shows all his courage to peg back Move Off, with Seadiver, Brands Hatch and Claudio Nicolai also in attendance

GUNNER B 3 ch.c. Royal Gunner–Sweet Councillor (Privy Councillor 125) **121**
[1975 5g³ 5s*(dis) 7f² 7f³ 6fg² 6g* 6g* 1976 10.2g* 10s⁴ 10.4s² 10.5s² 8.2d*
12f* 10f* 8f³ 12fg⁶ 11g*]

What a grand horse Gunner B is! Having been kept on the go since winning a small race at Doncaster on the first day of the season, he turned in his best performance on his final outing when winning the Doonside Cup at Ayr in September. His task at Ayr looked formidable—he was giving 5 lb to the older Dakota, Patch and Rymer and 17 lb to the three-year-old filly My Fair Niece—but he won without his rider having to use the whip. Sent on two furlongs out after tracking the leader Patch for most of the way, Gunner B beat Rymer by half a length with Swell Fellow, whom he was meeting on terms close to weight-for-age, the same distance away third. Even conceding that Dakota and Patch ran way below their best it was still a very impressive performance from Gunner B at the weights.

At the end of his two-year-old days Gunner B had looked to be no more than a useful handicapper, and his ability to gain a place in the Dee Stakes and the Mecca-Dante Stakes early in the new season was taken generally to highlight the poor quality of the three-year-olds rather than signal any great improvement in Gunner B. The result of the valuable and competitive Cecil Frail Handicap, run over a mile at Haydock at the end of May, made most people change their minds. Gunner B won it by eight lengths! Following an

Doonside Cup, Ayr—Gunner B puts up his best performance on his final outing, beating Rymer (left), Swell Fellow and My Fair Niece, with Patch (right) a disappointing fifth

easy victory over two vastly inferior animals in the Watt Memorial Plate at Beverley, Gunner B tried for his hat-trick in the Andy Capp Handicap at Redcar, carrying an 8 lb penalty. He put up a really game performance, getting up by half a length from Move Off after coming under the whip two furlongs from home, and earned a less-than-generous 8/1 quotation for the St Leger which was said to be his long-term objective.

Gunner B continued his unorthodox preparation for the St Leger with a run in the one-mile Welbred Handicap at Beverley. Set to carry 10-1 and giving lumps of weight all round, he finished a creditable third to Lord Helpus who was meeting him on terms 26 lb better than in the Cecil Frail only five weeks previously! Gunner B was then sent for the Gordon Stakes at Goodwood— a much more significant test for a Leger candidate. In it, he ran his only poor race of the year, being beaten two furlongs out and coming home last of the six runners, some fifteen lengths behind the winner Smuggler. Our first re-action was that he did not stay a mile and a half in good company, and his connections must have had similar thoughts, for they didn't run him in the Leger, but after his performance over eleven furlongs in the Doonside Cup we are not so sure, and he is well worth another chance at the trip.

Gunner B (ch.c. 1973)	Royal Gunner (ch 1962)	Royal Charger (ch 1942)	Nearco
			Sun Princess
		Levee (ch 1953)	Hill Prince
			Bourtai
	Sweet Councillor (b 1968)	Privy Councillor (ch 1959)	Counsel
			High Number
		Sugarstick (b 1956)	Zucchero
			York Gala

A strong, deep-bodied colt, Gunner B is the first foal of the unraced Sweet Councillor. His grandam Sugarstick, a winner over a mile and a half in Ireland as a four-year-old, is a half-sister to the Cambridgeshire winner Sterope and to the useful stayer Wyresdale who produced those very useful performers Knight of the Dales, Starry Halo and Yellow River. Gunner B is the best progeny of his sire, the North American horse Royal Gunner, a very tough and smart performer who won six and was placed in seventeen of his thirty-one races. Since being retired in 1967 Royal Gunner has stood in America, England and Ireland and is now in Greece.

Gunner B has a lot to recommend him. He is honest and tough, he has the ability to handle any type of going and track, and is effective at distances from a mile to at least eleven furlongs. Horses of his kind are not easily beaten, and despite the fact that he has yet to show he is up to taking on the best at level weights and that he is right at the top of the handicap he is likely to pick up more races. *G. Toft.*

GUN TOWER 3 b.f. Tower Walk 130–Bow Mite (Gun Bow) [1975 5fg 1976 **60** 5f6 6f 7f4 9.4h4 8fg 9fg 8f4 9fg* 10g2 10d4] light-framed filly: plater: spread-eagled her field when winning at Wolverhampton in September (bought in 650 gns): stays 1¼m: best form on a sound surface: sometimes bandaged off-fore: sold 480 gns Newmarket Autumn Sales. *F. Carr.*

GUR AMIR 8 b.g. Tamerlane 128–Blood Royal (Princely Gift 137) [1974 8g* **70** 8f3 7fg 8d3 7g* 8s* 8g3 8v2 8v6 1975 8g 7.2fg5 8g2 8f 7g6 8g5 1976 8d3 8fg 7fg 8d2 8v 8.2v)] useful handicapper at his best but is not the force he was and showed only quite moderate form in 1976: stays 1m: acts on any going: has worn blinkers: excellent mount for a boy. *G. Pritchard-Gordon.*

GURGLING 3 gr.f. Town Crier 119–Rockpool 83 (Nimbus 130) [1975 6fg **58** 1976 8.2f 8f 7g2 7g6] quite attractive filly: good walker: length second of 16 to Mr Metal in maiden race at Edinburgh in May, best effort: may be better suited by 1¼m+. *J. Hindley.*

GUSTY'S GIFT 2 ch.c. Divine Gift 127–Gusty Girl 71 (Darling Boy 124) **87** [1976 5fg 5.9g* 6d3 5.9s4 5s5 7.6v] lengthy, good-topped colt: good mover: brother to a winner in Germany and Switzerland, and half-brother to two winners: 3,800 gns yearling: dam won over 6f at 2 yrs: having first race for three months but well-backed favourite, put up quite a useful effort when winning maiden event at Wolverhampton in August by 2½ lengths from Glazepta Rework: ran respectably in nurseries afterwards: should stay 7f: acts on soft going. *B. Swift.*

GUSTY SOMERS 5 b.g. Will Somers 114 §–Gusty Girl 71 (Darling Boy 124) — [1974 N.R. 1975 8f 6g 1976 8.2f] fair plater (rated 66) at 2 yrs: lightly raced

Jersey Stakes, Ascot—the much improved Gwent is too good for Wolverlife and Scott Joplyn

since, and was well beaten in handicap at Nottingham in August won by Somerville Queen on only outing in 1976. *B. Richmond.*

GWENJOY 3 ro.f. Healaugh Fox–Patchwork (Cash and Courage 116) [1975 5f   —
5f 8g 10g 10g 1976 10.8fg 12.2fg⁶ 9f 10g 12fg 10.8f 9f 8g⁶] of no account.
K. Bridgwater.

GWENT 3 b.c. Welsh Pageant 132–Mamzelle 85 (King's Troop 118) [1975 6g **118**
6g⁴ 7g 7d³ 6fg* 1976 7f 8fg 8d⁴ 6fg* 6fg* 7f* 6fg 6fg 7.3fg] lengthy, good-
quartered colt: half-brother to smart French 2-y-o Haneena (by Habitat):

Mr A. Villar's "Gwent"

put up an impressive performance when winning Jersey Stakes at Royal Ascot in June, soon putting issue beyond doubt when sent into lead inside final furlong and beating Wolverlife by a length: had previously won Great Eastern Handicap at Newmarket by ½ length from Ubedizzy and George Smith Memorial Handicap at Newbury by 1½ lengths from May Beck: probably stays 1m but has shown best form at 6f and 7f: acts on a soft surface but is very well suited by top-of-the-ground conditions: wears blinkers: does best when held up: sometimes gets above himself in paddock: ran below his best last three outings, including under a very stiff weight in Spillers Stewards' Cup. *B. Hobbs.*

GYPSY BECK 2 ch.f. Sky Gipsy 117–Glittering Prize 79 (Luminary 132) [1976 5f 5fg] evidently of no account. *D. Williams*   —

H

HABANERA 2 br.f. Habitat 134–Sandarey 94 (Darius 129) [1976 5s 5v] good-looking filly: half-sister to four winners, including 3-y-o Sousa (by March Past), a winner from 7f to 1¼m: 6,200 gns yearling: dam won at 1m and 11f: behind in end-of-season maiden events at Sandown (in need of race) and Lingfield (springer in market). *Miss A. Sinclair.*   —

HABBERSHAW 2 b.f. Tribal Chief 125–Reddish 94 (Red God 128 §) [1976 5g 5g 5fg 5g 5f² 5h² 5g* 5g 6f² 5fg 5fg] strong, compact filly: 5-length winner of seller at Ayr in July (retained by stable 720 gns): raced in nurseries subsequently, putting up a good effort when running Mrs McArdy to a length at Thirsk in September but ran badly in three others and is inconsistent: evidently better suited by 6f then 5f nowadays: wears blinkers. *M. W. Easterby.*   80 ?

HABBERSUPREME 2 b.c. Supreme Sovereign 119–Dencombe (Ballymoss 136) [1976 5g 5f⁴ 6fg⁶ 7h 7.2f 8fg 8v⁶ 10v*] half-brother to Air Major (by Majority Blue), a winner over 7f in Ireland: bought in 750 gns after showing improved form to win seller at Leicester in October by a neck from Maharanee: stays 1¼m well: acts on heavy ground. *F. Carr.*   74

HABEEBTI 2 br.f. Lorenzaccio 130–Dugo 90 (Dumbarnie 125) [1976 6fg* 6f* 6g] strong filly: sister to 1975 2-y-o Veruschka, a winner over 6f in Ireland, and half-sister to several winners, notably high-class sprinter Abergwaun (by Bounteous): 14,000 gns yearling: dam best at around 7f: won two races at Newmarket in August in good style, quickening impressively to beat San Bernadino 5 lengths in 12-runner maiden race and not being hard pressed to account for Red Light District in a 13-runner minor event: had her limitations exposed when only twelfth of 15 to Durtal in William Hill Cheveley Park Stakes, also at Newmarket, the following month: will probably stay 1m: acts on firm going. *H. Cecil.*   108

HABERDASHER 4 ch.c. Habitat 134–Fleeting Interest (Buisson Ardent 129) [1974 5d² 5g⁴ 5g⁴ 5fg² 6s 5g 1975 6s⁶ 6s 6f 6g 5d² 5g* 5h³ 5fg⁶ 5f³ 5g⁶ 5fg* 5g 5g 6g 5g 1976 5g⁵ 5f³ 6g 5f* 6fg³ 5fg⁶ 6g 5g³ 5.1fg* 6fg 6fg⁶ 5fg 5fg⁵ 5f 5fg] strong colt: quite a moderate handicapper: successful at Beverley in May and Yarmouth the following month: best at 5f: appears to act on any going: wears blinkers: ran moderately last few outings. *G. Peter-Hoblyn.*   79

HABITUS 2 b.c. Habitat 134–Rebus 97 (Busted 134) [1976 7g*] first foal: $45,000 yearling: dam stayed well: 3/1 on for nine-runner newcomers event at Phoenix Park in October and fully justified the confidence, coming home 3 lengths clear of Lord of the Silk with the rest well beaten off: will stay 1¼m: clearly a very useful colt in the making. *V. O'Brien, Ireland.*   108 p

HACO 2 br.f. Tribal Chief 125–Jolie Etoile 95 (French Beige 127) [1976 6g 6d²] first living foal: 11,000 gns yearling: dam won over 1½m and is half-sister to the dams of Royal Palace, Welsh Pageant and Crocket: ran on well from below distance but just went down in a desperate finish when short-head second to newcomer Running Bull in 23-runner maiden race at Newmarket in October: will stay 1m: sure to win a race. *B. Hobbs.*   87

HAGAR HALL 2 b.c. Tower Walk 130–Tul a Dee (Tulyar 134) [1976 8d 7g⁴] attractive colt: half-brother to two winners in Ireland: 2,100 gns yearling: dam won over 1½m in Ireland: unquoted, ran creditably when 8½ lengths fourth of 22 to Sin Timon in maiden race at Newmarket in October: will stay 1m. *P. Haslam.*   79

HAIGHALL 2 b.c. Prince de Galles 125–French Seam 80 (French Beige 127) [1976 5fg 7fg² 6fg* 6g² 6g² 6d³ 6d⁵] tall colt: half-brother to quite useful 1975 2-y-o 7f winner Rusthall (by Midsummer Night II): 2,800 gns yearling: dam   104

HAM

once-raced half-sister to smart 1966 2-y-o Slip Stitch: made all to win maiden race at Windsor in July by ¾ length from Midsummer: ran well on next three outings, putting up a particularly fine effort when staying on to finish 4½ lengths third of six to Anax in Mill Reef Stakes at Newbury in September, but ran poorly when short-priced favourite for nursery at Ascot later in month on final outing: will stay 1¼m. *G. Hunter.*

HALF A PORTION 2 ch.f. Major Portion 129–Miss Lollypop (St Paddy 133) — [1976 7fg 6g 7d 5s] lengthy filly: half-sister to 3-y-o 1¼m winner Lace Basket (by Silly Season): bought privately 750 gns as a foal: little worthwhile form in varied company. *D. Jermy.*

HALF MOON BAY 3 b.f. Behistoun 131–Summersoon 89 (Sheshoon 132) **56** [1975 5s 5s 5s 7g 7.2fg 10g 10g 1976 13fg⁴ 16g 13g 15.8f² 13.8g³] plater: suited by a good test of stamina: sold to J. Berry 420 gns Doncaster November Sales. *L. Shedden.*

HALF TRUTH 8 b.m. Straight Lad 110–Grey Rose 58 (Grey Sovereign 128 §) — [1974 N.R. 1975 12s 1976 15.5s] half-sister to smart chaser Clear Cut (by Articulate): no form in two amateur riders races. *H. O'Neill.*

HALICAS 4 b.c. Habitat 134–Lania 69 (Ribot 142) [1974 5fg⁵ 7d 1975 7g* — 8v³ 10.4d⁵ 8.5fg² 8f 8v 8g 8.2s 1976 8g] attractive colt: very useful performer (rated 110) at 3 yrs: looked well but finished well behind in Irish Sweeps Lincoln at Doncaster in March, only outing in 1976: apparently best at up to 1m: seems to act on any going: has been tried in blinkers: exported to Australia. *C. Brittain.*

HALLAH 3 b.g. Halation 82–Rose of Ennis 78 (Ennis 128) [1975 6fg 5f⁵ 5.9f⁴ **66** 5.8f³ 7g⁴ 5fg³ 5d* 5v* 1976 8g⁴ 6v⁴ 7fg 7f³ 8f⁶ 8g 6h⁵ 5h⁴ 8fg⁶] leggy gelding: smart plater at 2 yrs: raced mainly in stronger company in 1976, best effort when third of 15 to Porcupine Pie in handicap at Wolverhampton in May: evidently stays 7f: goes well in the mud but is not inconvenienced by firm going. *A. Jarvis.*

HALLING 3 b.f. Inclination 96–Emulate (Dante) [1975 5s² 5f⁵ 5g 5g 5d 1976 — 10.1fg 6f 6f⁵ 7s] disappointing plater. *R. Blakeney.*

HALLS TREASURE 2 b.c. Quisling 117–Aggvus 86 (Aggressor 130) [1976 6f³ **82** 6f 6g 7g⁵] first foal: 180 gns yearling: dam won over 6f at 2 yrs: quite a moderate colt: stays 7f and will probably get 1m. *W. Marshall.*

HALMA 3 b.f. Hallez 131–Immaculate (Sovereign Path 125) [1975 N.R. 1976 — 8g 10s 13.1s⁵ 12v] half-sister to three winners here and abroad, including Spanish Oaks winner Delfica (by Hardicanute): dam lightly raced: no worthwhile form in maiden and minor events. *I. Wardle.*

HALMAHERA 3 ch.g. Crosby Don 95–Sugar and Spice 73 (Articulate 121) — [1975 6g 7g 8f 1976 10.1fg 10.1fg] little worthwhile form in maiden races: blinkered last two outings in 1975. *D. Barons.*

HALOMATA 2 b.f. Hallez 131–Carromata (St Paddy 133) [1976 6g] compact — filly: half-sister to high-class French stayer Matahawk (by Sea Hawk II): dam daughter of Oaks winner Carrozza: 25/1 and backward, started slowly and beat only two home in 30-runner maiden race won by Rheola at Newmarket in September: will probably need at least 1¼m. *B. Hills.*

HALSALL 4 br.c. Hotfoot 126–Jeanne D'Ex (Exar 130) [1974 6f 6s⁵ 6f* 6s⁴ **94** 8s 8.2s 1975 7d 8v² 8d* 11s³ 9fg* 9g² 10g² 10g³ 10g³ 10.5fg⁴ 12f⁴ 1976 7g 12.2f² 13g² 12.2d³ 12h² 12f* 11fg* 13g² 12fg*] workmanlike colt: fairly useful handicapper: successful at Redcar, Ayr and Leicester inside a month: relegated to second on fifth outing of season: stays 13f: acts on any going: genuine and consistent. *T. Craig.*

HAMADAN 2 b.c. Maushe Joan 78 § (Major Portion 129) [1974 — 10fg⁵ 11g* 10.5g⁴ 12h³ 12d 1975 N.R. 1976 10f 12.2f 12fg 14fg 12fg] strong, good sort of horse: poor handicapper nowadays: stays 11f: best form on a sound surface. *S. Cole.*

HAMISH 5 gr.g. Sayfar 116–Constance Spry (Gentle Art 121) [1974 10fg 12fg⁵ — 12g* 10d 12s⁵ 12d³ 1975 16d 12f 15.5f³ 15.5f 14g 10fg⁴ 12.2fg 12f⁶ 1976 8g⁶ 12f⁶ 10f⁵ 12g² 15.5s] small gelding: poor handicapper: remote second to effortless winner Red Regent in Moet and Chandon Silver Magnum at Kempton in August: lacks pace and needs 1½m +: suitable mount for an amateur rider. *G. Pritchard-Gordon.*

HAMPSHIRE 2 b.c. Silly Season 127–Pirate Queen 77 (Pirate King 129) [1976 **77** 6g 7g⁵ 7g 7v²] strong, compact colt: third foal: half-brother to useful 3-y-o

311

Stainley Nursery Handicap, Ripon—the blinkered Hand Canter wins his sixth race.
Stanwick Maid leads the chasing group

stayer Tug of War (by Reliance II) and fairly useful 1¼m winner General Custer (by Derring-Do): dam placed over 7f at 2 yrs: stayed on when second to easy winner Peace Symbol in 16-runner maiden race at Leicester in October: will stay at least 1¼m. *D. Whelan.*

HAND CANTER 2 b.c. Mummy's Pet 125–Sound Number 103 (Sound Track **105** 132) [1976 5fg 5fg⁵ 5fg² 5f* 6f* 6f* 5fg* 6h* 6fg² 5g* 5g⁶] neat, strong, attractive colt: half-brother to fair miler Sound Jiff (by Never Say Die) and to two winners in France: 3,800 gns yearling: dam, a sprinter, is half-sister to smart Some Hand: a great credit to his trainer and was cleverly placed to win at Catterick (twice), Hamilton, Ripon and Pontefract, all in the space of a month in the summer: ran well in nurseries on next two outings, adding another success to his tally when winning £1,300 event at Ripon in August by 2 lengths from Stanwick Maid: stays 6f: acts on firm going: wears blinkers but is tough and consistent: very well suited by sharp tracks: has won five times for apprentice N. Crowther. *J. Hindley.*

HANDYCUFF 4 b.g. Manacle 123–Black Rage 91 (My Babu 136) [1974 5g⁴ **89** 5g³ 5g* 6s* 6fg³ 6s* 1975 6v 6d 6f⁶ 8d² 7f* 8g 8d⁴ 7.2s⁴ 8g⁶ 8.2s 7d⁴ 1976 6f 7f⁴ 8fg* 8f 7g⁵ 8d² 8v* 8.2v*] tall gelding: quite a useful handicapper: winner at Thirsk, Newcastle and Haydock at 4 yrs: stays 1m: acts on any going but is ideally suited by an easy surface: sometimes wears blinkers: had a poor run on sixth outing: sold 4,600 gns Doncaster October Sales. *L. Shedden.*

HANEENA 2 b.f. Habitat 134–Mamzelle 85 (King's Troop 118) [1976 6d* **118** 6g 5d² 6g⁴] strong, good-bodied French filly: third foal: half-sister to two winners, notably smart 3-y-o 6f and 7f performer Gwent (by Welsh Pageant): 17,000 gns yearling: dam won over 5f at 2 yrs: 3-length winner of maiden race at Evry in July and showed herself a smart filly when winning Group 3 Prix d'Arenberg at Chantilly in September easily by 4 lengths from Black Sulphur (moved down to second by stewards at Chantilly for hampering runner-up although winner on merit): beaten in Group 1 races on her other outings, finishing 10 lengths ninth of 11 to Blushing Groom in Prix Morny at Deauville and 5½ lengths fourth of 15 to Durtal in William Hill Cheveley Park Stakes at Newmarket (heavily-backed favourite): will stay 7f: acts on a soft surface: exported to U.S.A. *A. Breasley, France.*

HANETA 3 br.f. Native Prince–Elizabeth of York 66 (Henry the Seventh 125) — [1975 5v 1976 10.1f 8f] no worthwhile form in maiden races: sold 360 gns Ascot June Sales. *J. Hill.*

HANGSENG 4 b.g. Sing Sing 134–Miss Charisma 104 (Ragusa 137) [1974 **41** 5fg 5g 5.1g 1975 8g 7g⁵ 5f⁵ 1976 5f⁵ 5fg⁶ 5.9f 7g 6s⁶ 8g 12v⁶] strong, well-grown gelding: poor handicapper: had stiffish tasks at 4 yrs: probably stays 7f: tried in blinkers on third and sixth starts. *R. Supple.*

HANLEY SWAN 4 ch.g. Fischio–Vidi's First (Vidi Vici 112) [1974 N.R. — 1975 N.R. 1976 10fg⁶ 12fg] probably of little account. *Mrs J. Pitman.*

HANNS CHRISTOF 5 br.g. Major Portion 129–Ceol Abu (Vimy 132) [1974   —
7s 12f² 11f 12g 10fg 9.4s 14.7g 1975 N.R. 1976 12.5g] probably of little
account. *W. Haigh.*

HAPPY COMBINATION 2 gr.c. The Parson 119–France (Milesian 125)   **82**
[1976 5f² 6fg⁵ 6g³ 7fg 7f* 7g⁵ 8g 7g] robust colt: brother to French 1975 2-y-o
7f seller winner Steel Dust: dam ran only once: won seven-runner maiden race
at Warwick in August by a head from Vaguely James: should stay at least 1m:
acts on firm going: blinkered fifth, sixth and eighth outings. *F. J. Houghton.*

HAPPY FAMILIES 3 ch.f. Swaps–Mirthful (Jaipur) [1975 7f⁶ 7f⁵ 8.2g 1976   —
11f] plating-class maiden: should stay middle distances. *Sir Mark Prescott.*

HAPPY HOLLOW 3 b.g. Wolver Hollow 126–Joyful Scene 104 (Vilmorin)   **61**
[1975 6fg⁶ 7.2g⁶ 7f³ 7f² 7f 7g⁵ 1976 8fg⁵ 10fg⁴ 10f 9.4h⁵] strong, compact,
useful sort: good walker: disappointing maiden: probably stays 1¼m: sold
1,650 gns Ascot July Sales. *M. Jarvis.*

HAPPY NEW YEAR (FR) 3 b.c. Poleax–Ramolina (Klairon 131) [1975 8g⁶   **116**
8d³ 8g³ 1976 9g* 9.8fg 9g* 10g⁶ 9g⁵ 10g⁶ 8g³ 10g⁶] French colt: brother
to two winners in France, including Pardner, a useful performer at around
9f, and half-brother to another winner: dam won over 1m in France at 4 yrs:
won minor event at Maisons-Laffitte in March and Group 3 Prix Daphnis at
Evry in May (by ½ length from Habitancum): had some stiff tasks afterwards,
but continued to run well, especially when 3 lengths third to Ellora in Prix
Quincey at Deauville in August and when 3½ lengths sixth to 4-y-o Monsanto
(levels) in Prix Ridgway on same course later in month: stays 1¼m: smart.
J. Cunnington, France.

HAPPY OCCASION 2 ch.f. Sky Gipsy 117–Sovereign Gate 81 (Sovereign   —
Path 125) [1976 5fg] first reported foal: dam a sprinter: ninth of 14 to
Blackadder in maiden race at Salisbury in June: dead. *P. Cole.*

HAPPY SWALLOW 2 ch.f. My Swallow 134–Happy Georgette (Crepello 136)   —
[1976 5.9s] second living foal: dam once-raced half-sister to very useful 1967
2-y-o Covey: tailed off in 18-runner maiden race won by Fear Naught at Wolverhampton in October. *G. Blum.*

HAPPY THOUGHT 3 b.f. Kauai King–Grenadiere 111 (Right Royal V 135)   **57**
[1975 N.R. 1976 8f 10s 12fg 12f 12fg⁶ 12h² 14f³ 10fg⁶] well-made, attractive
filly: has only a little ability: probably stays 1¾m: blinkered last three outings:
sold 5,000 gns Newmarket December Sales. *H. Wragg.*

HAPPY VICTORIOUS 9 ch.g. Gratitude 130–Eastern Bloom (Full Bloom)   **88**
[1974 7f 7.6g⁴ 7f* 6g³ 8g² 7.6d* 7g⁴ 1975 7.6g⁴ 7fg 7f² 6g⁴ 7fg⁴ 8g⁵ 7.6f² 7g⁵
1976 7f⁴ 7.6d³ 7fg⁵ 7f* 7fg⁵ 7h³ 7.6fg² 7g] just a fair handicapper nowadays:
winner at Brighton in 1976 and ran creditably in most of his subsequent races:
stays 1m: acts on any going: wears blinkers: front runner who is very well
suited by a sharp track and has won four times at Chester. *Doug Smith.*

HARAKA 2 br.f. Hul a Hul 124–Palencia (Palestine 133) [1976 5f* 5f* 5fg*   **110**
6f⁴ 7f⁶] small, useful-looking Irish filly: half-sister to useful 1973 Irish 2-y-o
5f winner Facile (by Faberge II) and to a winner in France: dam sister to very
useful sprinter Coney Island: took on several speedy fillies in St Hugh's Stakes
at Newbury in August and showed herself to be very useful, quickening in
fine style to lead at distance and win by ½ length from Blackadder: successful
earlier at Phoenix Park in April and July, being moved up by stewards to
joint first on latter occasion: 2¼ lengths fourth of eight to Regal Ray in Moyglare
Stud Stakes at the Curragh, better subsequent effort: best form at 5f and almost
certainly doesn't stay 7f: acts on firm going. *E. Harty, Ireland.*

HARD ATTACK 4 b.c. Hard Tack 111 **§**–Shashana (Khalkis 127) [1974 5.3f⁶   **95**
6g³ 8v* 1975 10f⁶ 11.7s⁶ 11.7g 12g* 1976 13s* 14.6fg* 15g³ 16d] fairly
useful handicapper: winner at Ayr (William Hill Scottish Handicap) and Doncaster in June: well-backed favourite, didn't get the best of runs when about
2 lengths third of nine to Grey Baron in Tennent Trophy at Ayr the following
month: stays well: appears to act on any going but is possibly best suited by
some give in ground (hung as though feeling ground at Doncaster): pulled up
lame (reportedly with a dislocated shoulder) on final appearance. *R. Price.*

HARD HELD 4 ch.c. Manacle 123–Ange d'Or (Golden Cloud) [1974 5g⁶ 5fg⁴   **72**
5s³ 5s² 6v⁶ 1975 8g 5d² 5v* 5s⁶ 6f 7f 5f 5f* 6g 7g 5g⁵ 6g 1976 7g⁶ 5f⁴ 5f⁴
7fg⁶ 6d⁴ 8f² 8fg⁶ 8d⁶ 5s* 7v⁶ 7v² 6s⁴] strong colt: quite a moderate handicapper:
successful at Pontefract in October by ½ length from Fair Dandy: stays 1m:

St Hugh's Stakes, Newbury—Haraka holds off Blackadder

acts on any going: suitable mount for an apprentice: ran respectably in blinkers on fifth start. *W. Gray.*

HARDIRONDO 3 b.f. Hardicanute 130–Rotondo (Royal Buck) [1975 6f⁴ 8g² 8s⁵ 1976 12fg⁶ 11.1g⁵ 12g² 14g* 14f⁴ 14fg⁴ 16g² 17.1s 16v⁴] very lightly-made filly: won 12-runner maiden race at Sandown in July by a length from Riboﬂeur after a hard battle, the pair ﬁnishing clear: stays well: best form on a sound surface. *S. Woodman.*　　**77**

HARDIVIM 6 b.h. Hardicanute 130–Vimagraph 80 (Vimy 132) [1974 17.1g⁵ 16fg³ 16s³ 18g² 15.5s² 16.5g⁴ 16d² 16s* 18.1g* 16.1s⁴ 1975 16d 17.7fg 17.1h³ 16fg 16.9f* 16fg³ 1976 17.1s] very small horse: quite a moderate handicapper: tailed off on only outing in 1976: stays extremely well: acts on any going: sometimes wears blinkers: sold 320 gns Ascot December Sales. *D. Gandolfo.*　　**—**

HARD LUCK 2 br.f. Hardicanute 130–Lucky Air 79 (Tudor Melody 129) [1976 5f 6f 6f⁶ 5f⁴ 6d 7s 8.2v*] neat ﬁlly: plater: attracted no bid after winning at Nottingham in October: stays 1m well: acts on heavy ground: ran below her best when tried in blinkers on ﬁfth outing. *D. Hanley.*　　**71**

HARDLY REGAL 3 br.f. Hardicanute 130–Rigel (Star Gazer 123) [1975 6g 5s 1976 7.6s 7fg] leggy, unfurnished ﬁlly: will probably stay 1¼m: sold 300 gns Newmarket July Sales. *E. Cousins.*　　**—**

HARD PENNY 3 b.g. Hard Tack 111 §–Bookie's Money (Sunny Way 120) [1975 5f 7f 5g 1976 10fg 10fg] strong gelding: no worthwhile form in varied company. *R. Hannon.*　　**—**

HARD SAILOR 6 b.h. Hard Tack 111 §–Denise Marie 63 (Monet 127) [1974 7s⁶ 5s 7fg⁵ 7f⁴ 7.9f³ 6.3fg 10.6g⁵ 12d⁴ 10.2d⁵ 8.2v³ 6g³ 8s⁵ 5v³ 1975 8fg⁵ 7v² 7.6g* 8.2g 7.2g⁶ 9g 7.2g⁴ 10.4g⁵ 8fg⁴ 7.6f⁵ 8.2g⁶ 8g 10.6s³ 1976 10.6d 8fg 10.6d

8g] poor handicapper: disappointing since winning at Chester in 1975: best form at up to 1m but stays further: acts on any going: sometimes wears blinkers. *J. Calvert.*

HARD SCHOOL 2 b.g. Green God 128–Good Taste (French Beige 127) [1976 — 5f 5f 5g] of little account: sold 240 gns Doncaster May Sales. *J. Turner.*

HARD TO TELL 3 b.f. Buckpasser–Close Up 117 (Nearula 132) [1975 5g6 68 1976 7g4 8g 8fg4 10.6g2] big, rangy, attractive filly: half-sister to Irish 1,000 Guineas second Silky (by Nijinsky), Derby third Freefoot (by Relko) and high-class middle-distance performer Moulton (by Pardao) but showed only a little ability herself: possibly best at 1m. *H. Wragg.*

HARD-TO-WOO 2 br.f. Tyrant–Marble Court 108 (Petition 130) [1976 5f2 5g* 93 6d2 6g* 7g3 6fg] fourth living produce: sold with dam for 4,000 gns as a foal: dam stayed 1m: twice a winner in minor races in Scotland, beating Bella Close a head at Ayr in May and landing odds by 4 lengths from Old Court at Hamilton the following month: 5 lengths third of five to In Haste in £3,100 event at Ayr in August: stays 7f: sold 8,400 gns Newmarket Autumn Sales, reportedly for export to South Africa. *N. Angus.*

HARDWOOD 3 b.f. Queen's Hussar 124–Eastwood 81 (Shantung 132) [1975 — N.R. 1976 11g 11.1g] rangy filly: fourth foal: half-sister to two minor winners: dam a stayer: apprentice ridden when behind in maiden races at Newbury (dwelt) and Kempton (tailed off) in May: exported by B.B.A. to New Zealand. *P. Haslam.*

HARDWOOD LAD 2 ch.c. Royal Palace 131–Nedda 113 (Alcide 136) [1976 6d 63 6fg 7.2fg 8fg 8s 8s] neat colt: plating-class maiden: will stay 1½m. *R. Hollinshead.*

HARDY MAID 2 b.f. Hardicanute 130–La Miranda 80 (Miralgo 130) [1976 73 5fg 5g6 6fg* 6fg5 6f6 7f3 6fg 8f 7s 8s4] first foal: dam best at up to 7f: attracted no bid after winning seller at Lingfield in June by ¾ length from Royal Communique: good seventh of 17 when carrying 11 lb overweight in nursery won by Tudor Lilt at Bath in September, best subsequent effort: stays 1m: acts on firm going and ran below her best on soft on last two outings: sold 1,250 gns Newmarket Autumn Sales. *P. Makin.*

HARDY TURK 3 b.h. Hill Clown–Turkhan Law (Turkhan) [1974 8g 12.2f3 71 11.7fg4 12g* 17.1f3 12g 14g6 1975 10.5fg 16f 13d5 12.2g5 1976 12g 12d2 12f4 13g* 12d5 15.8g 15fg 12d 12s] neat horse: made most of running and stayed on well when winning handicap at Ayr in May by 4 lengths from Halsall: most disappointing in his races on Flat afterwards but subsequently did well over hurdles: stays well: acts on firm going and a soft surface: wears blinkers nowadays: suitable mount for an apprentice. *S. Hall.*

HAREM 4 b.f. Tribal Chief 125–Shari (Rustam 127) [1974 5g* 5fg6 5d2 5fg* 114 5s2 1975 5d 5f3 5fg* 5f* 5f* 5fg3 5g2 5s4 5g4 1976 5fg 5f 5s5 5f 5fg4 5fg* 5fg4] compact filly: good mover: very useful performer: turned in a good effort when winning eight-runner handicap at York in July, beating Clear Melody ½ length (the pair finishing clear): respectable fourth to Music Boy in King George Stakes at Goodwood later in month: exceptionally speedy and has yet to race beyond 5f: acts on any going: genuine and consistent: exported to Australia. *R. Mason.*

HARGRAVE ROGUE 3 ch.c. Stephen George 102–Sweet Minuet (Setay 105) 71 [1975 6g 5fg6 5fg5 5fg6 5.1g* 6g 6g5 8.2g5 7d3 6v* 1976 7fg 8.2f3 10fg6 10fg3 11f5 10fg 8.2d* 14f3 8g4] quite a modest handicapper: won amateur riders race at Haydock in June all out by a head from Mayswing: stays 1¼m (ran below his best at longer trips): acts on any going: suitable mount for an inexperienced rider. *D. Thom.*

HARISSA 3 b.f. Bold Hour–Honey Lake (Spy Song) [1975 5g2 5v* 5g6 1976 96 8f2 8fg2 7g4 7f5] neat ex-Italian filly: American bred: half-sister to two winners by Never Bend, including useful Irish sprinter Honey Bend: $30,000 yearling: dam won at 2 yrs in U.S.A. and at 3 yrs over 6f in Ireland: won Premio Garda at Milan in May 1975: having first outing for a year, turned in an excellent performance when head second to Venus of Stretham in well-contested minor event at Beverley in June: did not reproduce that form although was not disgraced when 6½ lengths last of four behind Thieving Demon in £3,100 event at Newmarket the following month: stays 1m: acts on any going: sold 6,000 gns Newmarket December Sales. *L. Cumani.*

HARRIET AIR 2 b.f. Hardicanute 130–Inquisitive Girl 97 (Crepello 136) 80 [1976 5fg 6fg 6g 6d 8g*] half-sister to three winners abroad: 3,800 gns yearling: dam stayed 1m: led close home to win 20-runner minor event at Lanark in

October by $\frac{3}{4}$ length from Royal Declaration: better suited by 1m than shorter distances and will stay further. *S. Hall.*

HARRIET ROYALE 4 b.f. Silver Chest 95–Royal Godess 64 (King's Coup 108) — [1974 N.R. 1975 8g 1976 10h⁴ 10fg] probably useless. *E. Magner.*

HARRY CHURCHILLS 6 ch.g. Quisling 117–Athene 64 (Supreme Court 135) — [1974 7g 7g⁵ 7fg² 7g 7g⁴ 7fg 7g 8s⁴ 8d⁵ 6s 1975 7fg 7fg³ 6fg 6f⁶ 7h⁶ 5f 1976 8g] neat, strong gelding: poor performer: needs further than 6f and stays 1m: probably unsuited by soft ground: has twice run badly in blinkers: has raced with his tongue tied down: unreliable. *D. McCain.*

HARRY HALL 3 ch.g. On Your Mark 125–Penny Wise (Hook Money 124) §§ [1975 5g² 5f⁴ 6g⁵ 7d⁶ 8g* 1976 8fg³ 8fg² 12fg⁶ 10.6d* 10f⁴ 12f 10.8f 10.4fg 8fg 10d 11.1s] neat gelding: sold out of G. Blum's stable 1,800 gns after winning selling handicap at Haydock in June by 2 lengths from Goldania: lost his form completely afterwards and became temperamental, refusing to race on last three outings: stays 1¼m: usually wears blinkers: best left alone nowadays: sold 450 gns Doncaster November Sales. *M. James.*

HARRY HEDGES 4 b.c. Tiffauges 124–La Viola (Guersant 129) [1974 6d 62 1975 10d⁵ 1976 13.8g² 12g 12h* 12v⁴] attractive, neat colt: won poor race at Pontefract in September, beating Ice King fairly comfortably by 2½ lengths: fair fourth to Tour de Force at Haydock the following month: stays 1¾m: acts on any going: tailed off throughout and was virtually pulled up on second outing. *R. Jarvis.*

HARRYS FIZZALE 3 ch.c. Levanter 121–Katie Boyle (Whistling Wind 123) 68 [1975 5d⁵ 5v³ 5s⁴ 5fg² 5f* 6f⁴ 6fg⁴ 7f³ 1976 8g 10v* 12g 12fg 8.2g⁶ 11s⁵ 8fg⁵ 10fg²] leggy colt: wide-margin winner of three-runner handicap at Ayr in April: descended to selling company last two outings, chasing home stable-companion Button Boy at Nottingham in August: claimed by B. Richmond afterwards: possibly does not stay beyond 1¼m: acts on any going. *K. Payne.*

HARVEST BIRD 4 g-.c. Birdbrook 110–Welsh Harvest 108 (Welsh Abbot 131) 76 [1974 N.R. 1975 8f 1976 8g⁵ 8fg 7g* 6s* 7v 6s] compact colt: moderate handicapper: winner at Catterick in September and at Chepstow the following month: stays 7f: acts on soft going. *I. Walker.*

HARVEST BOUNTY 3 b.g. Cumshaw 111–Corn Dolly 85 (Midsummer Night II 57 117) [1975 5v 5f 5fg 7g 6g⁵ 1976 10.8fg 11.7f 10.1fg⁶ 10.1f 10h² 8g 8f 10.1fg⁵ 8.3d] useful-looking gelding: plating-class maiden: stays 1¼m. *J. Cann.*

HARVEST BOY 2 b.c. Richboy 117–Bonny Lesley (Shantung 132) [1976 5v² — 5s⁶ 5.1f⁶ 5g 5g 8s] bad plater. *G. Wallace.*

HASNA 2 ch.f. Brigadier Gerard 144–Arethusa 94 (Acropolis 132) [1976 6g 7d] — half-sister to two minor winners by Fighting Ship: 7,400 gns yearling: dam stayed 1¼m: little worthwhile form in newcomers race at Lingfield in September and Houghton Stakes at Newmarket in October. *M. Masson.*

HASTY REPLY 2 b.c. Pronto–So Social (Tim Tam) [1976 7.5d* 8v²] 113 American-bred French colt: half-brother to winners in France and in U.S.A., including Ward McAllister (by Bold Ruler), a very useful stakes winner at up to 9f, and Snobishness (by Forli), a winner at up to 1¼m: dam won three times at up to 1m at 3 yrs in U.S.A.: 38/1 and apprentice ridden, finished fast to win 16 runner newcomers race at Saint-Cloud in October by short head from Crystal Palace: went down by 2½ lengths to Baudelaire in Premio Tevere at Rome the following month: will stay 1½m: a smart colt in the making. *F. Boutin, France.*

HATFIELD HEATH 5 b.m. French Beige 127–Paridel Queen (Paridel 112) — [1974 8s 8f⁵ 8.2fg 8g 8g 1975 8.2s 12g 10f 8h 10g 8g 1976 10g 12f 10h⁵] of no account. *P. Poston.*

HATHEBH 2 b.f. Native Prince–Gay Sylvia (Sayajirao 132) [1976 5v] half- — sister to four winners, including useful 1975 Irish 2-y-o 5f to 1m winner Gucumatz (by Green God): sold twice as a yearling, for 1,500 gns and 1,800 gns: dam never ran: 16/1 when behind in 20-runner maiden race won by Scented Air at Leicester in October. *R. Price.*

HAUNTING MUSIC 3 b.c. Ragusa 137–Chat-Haunt (Faberge II 121) [1975 60 8fg 8f 1976 10.8f² 16f² 11h⁶ 16f² 15.8g⁴] poor maiden: stays 2m: ran below his best in blinkers on final outing: sold 2,300 gns Newmarket Autumn Sales. *M. Jarvis.*

*Prince of Wales's Stakes, York—Haveroid beats The Andrestan (hidden)
and Scops Owl impressively*

HAVEROID   2 b.c. Tycoon II–Marton Lady 103 (March Past 124)   [1976 5f³ 5f* **122**
5f* 5f* 6fg² 5fg* 6g² 6d⁶ 5s⁵]

Haveroid won four of his nine races in his first season and showed himself
to be a very speedy colt, the equal of any two-year-old in the country over five
furlongs.   But not over six furlongs.   At six furlongs Haveroid twice failed to
last home after looking all over the winner.   In the New Ham Stakes at Goodwood, he led on the bridle at the distance, but couldn't hold off Abs in the last
furlong.   Similarly, in the Champion Two-year-old Trophy at Ripon he was pulling over his opponents when taking up the running a furlong from home, but tired
perceptively a hundred yards later.   Anax got up to beat him a neck.   These
two performances just referred to were both on fast ground.   The going was on
the soft side when Haveroid made his third and last attempt at six furlongs, in the
Challenge Stakes at Newmarket, and he never held out any hope of being concerned in the finish.

Over his ideal distance the ground seems not to be a factor where Haveroid
is concerned, for on going returned officially as soft (the winner's time suggests that
it might not have been so soft as all that) he ran an excellent race, quite up to
his best form, when close-up fifth behind Girl Friend in the Prix du Petit Couvert
at Longchamp in October on his final appearance.   Even so we would rather have
him on firm ground than on anything else.   On firm going Haveroid won three
races in a row—at Edinburgh, Beverley and Ripon—following a promising third
first time out, and the ground was also on the firm side when he gained his most
important success, in the Prince of Wales's Stakes at York in August.   On paper
Haveroid's task in this race was a formidable one for a colt whose previous best
performance was a comfortable win over Pandu in the Horn Blower Stakes at
Ripon, but Haveroid made light of it.   Conceding none of his opponents less than
7 lb, he came through in typical Piggott fashion inside the last furlong to beat
The Andrestan comfortably by a length.   Scops Owl, Jameson and Priors Walk
were among those behind.

Haveroid (b.c. 1974)	Tycoon II (br 1962)	Tamerlane (br 1952)	Persian Gulf / Eastern Empress
		Djebel Idra (b 1957)	Phil Drake / Djebellica
	Marton Lady (b 1966)	March Past (br 1950)	Petition / Marcelette
		Maid of Kintail (ch 1960)	Atlas / Icewater

Haveroid's pedigree is unprepossessing to say the least.   Tycoon II, successful in smart company in France at up to a mile, and a half-brother to Bon Mot III,
who won the 1966 Arc, has sired a number of winners, but none so good as

Haveroid; whilst Marton Lady, whose second foal Haveroid is, was the only winner bred by the unraced Maid of Kintail, whose own dam, Icewater, was the sole winning product of Early Rivers, a non-winning half-sister to two moderate winners. One would have to go some way to find a horse of Haveroid's considerable ability with such undistinguished parentage. A strong, compact colt, Haveroid will probably always be best at five furlongs, though he is obviously capable of winning at six, and he acts particularly well on a firm surface. *N. Adam.*

HAWKBERRY 3 b.c. Sea Hawk II 131–Khalberry 109 (Khaled) [1975 7f **123** 1976 7g 10g* 12g⁴ 12f⁴ 10f* 12fg* 10g⁵]

Hawkberry and Sir Montagu ran races a Leger prospect could be proud of at the York August meeting, one winning the Great Voltigeur and the other the Ebor. Alas, neither was entered in the Leger! The logic behind the alternative programme announced for Hawkberry—the ten-furlong Joe McGrath Memorial Stakes followed, perhaps, by the Champion Stakes—was less easy to appreciate than that behind the plan to run Sir Montagu in the Prix Royal-Oak. Missing the Leger may well pay dividends in the long run with what Hawkberry's trainer called 'a green baby of a horse' after the Voltigeur, and yet it is difficult to see what advantage could be gained by running him in top-class company at a mile and a quarter. Hawkberry is not a Champion Stakes horse. In the end he did not appear in the Champion Stakes but he did take on Malacate in the Joe McGrath Memorial and had his limitations at so short a distance ruthlessly exposed. He couldn't quicken with the first four in the last two furlongs and was beaten seven lengths behind Malacate, beaten also by Mart Lane, Niebo and Northern Treasure. As with most of Sea Hawk's runners, Hawkberry has more stamina than speed.

We wouldn't like anyone to get the idea that Hawkberry has no speed—only that he hasn't enough to go racing with in the top flight at distances under a mile and a half. He had quite enough speed to cope with a decent handicapper like Spanish Doubloon at a mile and a quarter in the Mulhuddart Stakes at Phoenix Park two weeks before York; and at a mile and a half in the Great Voltigeur Stakes, he not only made animals like General Ironside and Scallywag appear leaden-footed but also came from last to first in the straight and caught Norfolk Air, who had led clear into the final furlong, near the post.

Hawkberry made his first appearance in this country in the Derby. A big, strong, good-topped colt, he impressed both in the paddock and in the race, his performance in the race being particularly noteworthy for a colt just out of maiden company. He had won for the first time only four weeks earlier, in the

Great Voltigeur Stakes, York—Hawkberry (left) comes with a strong run and heads Norfolk Air near the finish. General Ironside finishes third

Mayflower Maiden Stakes at Phoenix Park. In the Derby Hawkberry went down by little more than four lengths to Empery, battling on in the straight like a seasoned campaigner to keep Wollow out of fourth place. He ran practically the same race in the Irish Sweeps Derby and again took fourth place, beaten about the same distance behind Malacate although on this occasion he finished much closer to Empery. His form is only 7 lb to 10 lb behind the best of the middle-distance form, and if he can improve on it over longer trips, as we are certain he can, then his progress as a stayer will be worth watching.

Hawkberry (b.c. 1973)	Sea Hawk II (gr 1963)	Herbager (b 1956)	Vandale
			Flagette
		Sea Nymph (gr 1957)	Free Man
			Sea Spray
	Khalberry (b 1967)	Khaled (b 1943)	Hyperion
			Eclair
		Brown Berry (b 1960)	Mount Marcy
			Brown Baby

Anyone familiar with the racing record of Hawkberry's dam would be perfectly in order to question whether Hawkberry will make a stayer. Khalberry, also trained by Paddy Prendergast incidentally, had six races as a two-year-old and four races as a three-year-old without once going further than five furlongs. She was pretty effective at five furlongs, too; she finished a good fourth in the Queen Mary Stakes and won a handicap under 9-7 at Phoenix Park. She was, however, a very free-running individual, temperamentally unsuited, apparently, to racing over the longer distances her breeding suggested she would be able to manage. Khalberry is a half-sister, by the miler Khaled, to the Belmont Stakes winner Avatar and the California Derby winner Unconscious; she is also the daughter of a full sister to the Washington International winner Fisherman.

In that he is amenable to restraint and is well suited by a mile and a half Hawkberry is much more the son of his sire than his dam, and the fact that Khalberry was a five-furlong sprinter carries little weight with us now that Hawkberry has run eight times. He'll stay all right. As many other three-year-olds, after two unusually dry seasons, Hawkberry has yet to race on ground easier than good. He acts well enough on firm. *P. Prendergast, Ireland.*

HAYBALE 2 b.c. Hardicanute 130–Pardala (Pardal 130) [1976 6d 7.2fg³ 7f³ **79** 7.2g² 6f 7g 7v] rangy colt: first foal: dam, winner over hurdles, is half-sister to Irish 1,000 Guineas and Irish St Leger winner Pidget: moderate maiden: will stay middle distances: acts on firm going. *W. Elsey.*

HAY BRIDGE 5 br.g. Mandamus 120–Centellear 75 (Arctic Star) [1974 7d² — 7f 8f 8g⁵ 7fg 8g 8.3fg 6g² 7fg 1975 14d⁶ 1976 14fg] plater: dwelt start when behind in apprentice race at Goodwood in September, only outing since April 1975: best form at up to 7f: needs an easy surface: sometimes wears blinkers: inconsistent. *Miss N. Wilmot.*

HAYLOFT (FR) 3 b.f. Tudor Melody 129–Haymaking 115 (Galivanter 131) **100** [1975 5f* 5f³ 5fg* 5f* 6d 1976 7.3f 6fg 6fg 8f³ 7.6fg² 6f 6fg⁴] attractive filly: showed very useful form as a 2-y-o and won three races, including Mole-comb Stakes at Goodwood: not particularly consistent in 1976 but ran credit-ably when fourth of 12 to Sonnenblick in Wykeham Handicap at York in August on final outing: effective at 6f and stays 1m: acts on any going: blinkered last three appearances. *F. J. Houghton.*

HAYWIRE 2 br.c. Galivanter 131–Haybells (Klairon 131) [1976 5d 7g 6v] **80** strong colt: first foal: 4,700 gns yearling: dam lightly-raced half-sister to very useful filly Haymaking (by Galivanter): unquoted when seventh of 21 to Nobodys Fool in maiden race at Newmarket in October, second outing and best effort. *P. Haslam.*

HAZY MELODY 4 br.c. Tudor Melody 129–Heliosian (Helioscope) [1974 — 6d⁵ 6g³ 6g 7d⁴ 9s⁶ 8g 1975 8d⁴ 10s³ 9g⁴ 11.7fg* 12h³ 12.2f⁶ 12g² 10f⁶ 10.2g 1976 17.1s] quite a moderate handicapper: tailed off on only outing in 1976: stays 1½m: seems to act on any going. *L. Kennard.*

HEAD FIRST 2 br.f. Welsh Pageant 132–Guillotina 118 (Busted 134) [1976 **83** p 6v³] leggy filly: first foal: dam, smart middle-distance stayer, is half-sister to very successful broodmare Pristina: weak in market, put up an encouraging first effort in 23-runner maiden race at Newbury in October, running on really well after being behind in early stages and finishing 3 lengths third to Amity: will be well suited by middle distances: certain to benefit from this experience and will make up into a useful filly. *P. Walwyn.*

319

HEATHER TOPS 3 ch.f. Astec 128–Menloe (Charlottesville 135) [1975 7g **73**
9½fg⁴ 8.2d⁶ 1976 12fg 11.5d*] quite a modest performer: 33/1 and having
first run since April, won 11-runner maiden race at Yarmouth in September
by 2½ lengths from Dancing Hill: stays 1½m. *N. Callaghan.*

HEATH WOOD 2 ch.c. Murrayfield 119–Recce (Donore 119) [1976 5f 5.1fg³ **89**
5f² 5.9g* 5.6f² 5.1f⁵ 5fg⁴ 5g³ 5.9fg] compact colt: sixth foal: dam never ran:
made all when winning 25-runner maiden race at Wolverhampton in June
by 4 lengths from Juli's Son: creditable third of nine to Hand Canter in nursery
at Ripon in August: stays 6f well: acts on firm going: has run well for an apprentice. *C. Brittain.*

HEAVEN KNOWS 3 b.f. Yellow God 129–Dialora (Diatome 132) [1975 5v² **113**
5s* 5g⁵ 7g⁵ 7s* 7g⁵ 8g⁶ 1976 7f³ 8fg⁵ 12fg* 12g 8fg³ 10fg 12fg 8g² 9g] sturdy
filly: quickened really well to win Oaks Trial at Lingfield in May by 1½ lengths
from Spiranthes: ran well afterwards when placed in Child Stakes at Newmarket
in July (1½ lengths third to Duboff) and valuable fillies handicap at Ascot in
September (3 lengths second to Intermission) and had put up a good performance
earlier in year when fifth of 25 to Flying Water in 1,000 Guineas at Newmarket:
stays 1½m but has shown best form at 1m: acts on any going and on any track.
R. Smyth.

HEAVENLY CHOIR 2 ch.f. St Alphage 119–Tra-La-La (Penhurst) [1976 **79**
6g 5s⁵ 5g²] half-sister to Irish 3-y-o Extra La (by Exbury), a winner at up
to 1m: dam Spanish bred: put up easily best effort when going down by a short
head to Sharpway in 12-runner maiden race at Lanark in October: will stay 6f.
D. Weeden.

HEAVENLY HARVEST 3 b.g. Solar Topic 97–Peach Fair (Lord of Verona **—**
120) [1975 6g⁵ 6d⁶ 8.2g⁴ 8g 1976 9g 8fg⁴ 12g 10s] dipped-backed gelding:
probably stays 1m. *J. Etherington.*

HEAVENLY SONG 2 ch.f. Mansingh 120–Heavenly Dancer 83 (Skymaster 126) **73**
[1976 5g⁵ 5h⁴ 6g 5s 6s² 5s²] neat filly: first foal: bought privately 2,000 gns
as a yearling: dam a sprinter: runner-up in sellers at Doncaster and Haydock
at end of season: stays 6f: acts on soft going: blinkered fourth outing. *J.
Fitzgerald.*

HEAVEN'S EYES 2 b.f. Green God 128–Tropicana 80 (Krakatao 130) [1976 **74**
5fg⁵ 5f⁴ 5g⁴ 5f⁴ 5h⁴ 5f³ 5s⁴] half-sister to four winners, including useful sprinter
Condora (by Matador): 1,500 gns yearling: dam won at 1m: moderate maiden:
will be suited by 6f: acts on firm going and is possibly not at her best on soft.
M. Masson.

HEAVENS HILL 3 b.f. Sassafras 135–Past Tense 98 (Relic) [1975 6f 5f* 6fg⁴ **79**
1976 8.5fg⁴ 10g] neat filly: about 8 lengths fourth of five finishers to Memory
Lane in Princess Elizabeth Stakes at Epsom in April: last behind Sarania in
Sandleford Priory Stakes at Newbury the following month and was not seen
out again: should stay at least 1¼m. *H. Blagrave.*

HECKLE 2 gr.f. Birdbrook 110–Cap Estel 104 (Fortino II 120) [1976 5f* **83**
5fg² 5fg⁵ 6f⁴ 5fg⁶ 5g⁴ 6f⁶ 5g] strong filly: third foal: dam ran only at 5f: finished
strongly to win 14-runner maiden race at Newbury in April by ½ length from
Swinging Girl: ran creditably in several nurseries afterwards (off course some
time after third outing): stays 6f: wears blinkers. *H. Smyth.*

HEDGE SCHOOL 2 ch.c. Swinging Junior 118–Queen's Pet (Pall Mall 132) **96**
[1976 5g* 5g 5d³ 5f³ 6fg² 5fg⁶ 5d*] second produce: 100 gns yearling: dam
never ran: proved a bargain, winning a maiden auction event at Catterick
in March and minor race at Haydock in October, on latter course staying on
extremely well to win in very good fashion by ¾ length from Hutton Barns:
effective at 5f and 6f: acts on any going but is well suited by a soft surface:
consistent. *Denys Smith.*

HEIDELBERG 7 b.g. Miralgo 130–Western Sun (Golden Cloud) [1974 12v **—**
14s 1975 14g⁴ 1976 14s] well-made gelding: poor performer: stays well:
suited by an easy surface. *Mrs D. Oughton.*

HEIGHT OF SEASON 2 b.c. Silly Season 127–Persina (Tamerlane 128) **103**
[1976 5f 5f⁵ 6g² 7d³ 7f* 8fg*] Irish colt: second foal: half-brother to 3-y-o
Zoroaster (by Zeddaan): 21,000 gns yearling: dam lightly-raced sister to three
winners: easy winner of 14-runner maiden plate at Galway in September and
put up a useful display when winning £1,800 Unidare Apprentice Nursery at
the Curragh later in month by ¾ length: will be suited by 1¼m+. *D. Weld,
Ireland.*

Oaks Trial Stakes, Lingfield—Heaven Knows is followed home by Spiranthes,
Countess Eileen (right) and Golden Lania (left)

HEI'LAND JAMIE 5 b.g. Highland Melody 112–Mary Newall 69 (Coronation **111**
Year 124) [1974 6f² 6h* 6f³ 5fg* 5g² 5g⁴ 5d³ 6fg² 6fg⁴ 6s* 6s³ 5v⁵ 1975 8d
6s² 5v³ 6v* 6fg* 6f⁵ 6f* 6g⁴ 6fg³ 6fg³ 6d⁶ 6f⁴ 5g⁴ 6g³ 5v³ 1976 6f* 6v⁴ 6g²
6fg* 6g⁶ 6fg² 6f³ 6fg 6fg 5.6g* **6g²** 6s] workmanlike gelding: very useful handicapper: put up a fine performance when winning William Hill Portland Handicap at Doncaster in September, making all and holding off Last Tango and
High Award gamely in final furlong: excellent second to Last Tango under

William Hill Portland Handicap, Doncaster—Hei'land Jamie (nearest camera)
is strongly pressed by Last Tango and High Award (far side), with
May Beck a close fourth

an 8-lb penalty in Burmah-Castrol Ayr Gold Cup at Ayr the following week: successful earlier in season at Teesside and Nottingham: best at 6f but wasn't disgraced when tried over 1m on first outing in 1975: acts on any going: good mount for an apprentice: very tough, genuine and consistent: trained by T. Fairhurst first three outings in 1976. *N. Adam.*

HEI'LAND MARY 3 br.f. Highland Melody 112–Mary Newall 69 (Coronation Year 124) [1975 5fg 5f³ 5g³ 5g² 1976 6fg* 6v² 5h² 6g³ 6g 5s⁶ 6v] quite a modest performer: won 18-runner maiden race at Leicester in March by 1½ lengths from Bill's Song: placed in three handicaps afterwards but was then off course most of summer, putting up best effort after her return on penultimate outing: stays 6f: acts on any going: trained until after second start by T. Fairhurst. *N. Adam.* **76**

HEI'LAND QUEEN 2 br.f. Highland Melody 112–Mary Newall 69 (Coronation Year 124) [1976 5d 5s⁵ 6d] compact filly: sister to very useful sprinter Hei'land Jamie and to 3-y-o 6f winner Hei'land Mary: dam won sellers over 6f and 1m: put up easily best effort when about 3 lengths fifth of 13 to Jon George in maiden race at Doncaster in October: should stay 6f. *N. Adam.* **76**

HELCIA 3 b.f. Habitat 134–Rhevona (Rockavon 120) [1975 6fg² 6g⁶ 7g² 8g⁵ 1976 10g⁶ 11.5fg² 10fg³ 12fg³ 10f² 10d⁵ 10s² 10d⁵] attractive filly: usually found one or two too good for her: possibly best at distances short of 1½m: acted on any going: best in blinkers: visits Welsh Pageant. *H. Cecil.* **79**

HELDORTY 2 b.g. Tycoon II–Dornob 64 (Dornot) [1976 5fg 5g 6fg⁴ 7.2g⁵ 7.2d⁴ 8.2v] first foal: 640 gns yearling: dam a winning chaser: ran well in a nursery on fourth outing but showed only poor form in his other starts, including a seller: will stay 1¼m. *R. Hollinshead.* **62**

HELIOTROPE 3 ch.f. King Emperor–Zardia 96 (Zarathustra 131) [1975 5g 7fg 1976 12g 12f 11.1g 12.2s⁴] good-bodied filly: poor maiden: tried in blinkers second outing: sold out of W. Wightman's stable 725 gns Ascot June Sales after third start. *M. Killoran.* **—**

HELLBECK 3 br.g. Sea Moss–Tarqueta (Tarqogan 125) [1975 N.R. 1976 12.2f] rangy gelding: first foal: dam of little account: 20/1 and in need of run when last of seven in minor event won by Ringed Aureole at Catterick in April. *E. Weymes.* **—**

HELL BENT 2 ch.g. Busted 134–Benita 94 (Roan Rocket 128) [1976 8g] strong gelding: first foal: dam a sprinter: 10/1 and in need of race, started none too well and never got into race when tenth of 13 to Royal Plume in £2,400 event at York in September: should come on a lot as a result of this outing and do better at 3 yrs. *H. Cecil.* **— p**

HELLO DAR 2 b.c. Never Say Die 137–Arzemdokt 74 (Persian Gulf) [1976 8s] half-brother to two winners, including fair stayer Persian Twilight (by Twilight Alley): 840 gns yearling: dam effective at 1m and 1¼m: unquoted and backward when behind in 26-runner £2,200 event won by Lucent at Doncaster in November. *S. Norton.* **—**

HELLO LOVE 3 ch.f. Stephen George 102–Can't Wait (Eudaemon 129) [1975 5d 5g 1976 10g 8s 7s] good-bodied filly: behind in all races. *J. O'Donoghue.* **—**

HELM 3 ch.f. Royal Palace 131–Ripeck 90 (Ribot 142) [1975 6d 1976 10fg* 12g²] lightly-made filly: half-sister to four winners, including very good stayer Buoy (by Aureole) and smart sprinter Fluke (by Grey Sovereign): won 16-runner maiden race at Salisbury in June by 2 lengths from Fine Blue: outclassed by Bright Finish in minor event at Kempton the following month but finished clear of three others: stays 1½m. *R. Hern.* **81**

HE LOVES ME 2 b.c. Sovereign Path 125–Short Commons 109 (Hard Tack 111 §) [1976 6f⁴ 5g*] tall, lengthy colt: closely related to Om (by Grey Sovereign), a very useful winner in Italy, and half-brother to two winners, notably very smart miler Common Land (by Klairon): 14,000 gns yearling: dam won Free Handicap: well-backed favourite for nine-runner Harry Rosebery Challenge Trophy at Ayr in September and came through very late to beat Forty Winks a short head after being a long way off leaders in early stages: received the best part of a stone from Forty Winks but is a very useful colt in the making: will be suited by 6f or more. *J. Hindley.* **108 p**

HELPING HAND 2 b.f. Right Boy 137–Skerne Glory 58 (Pinza 137) [1976 6f 5f⁶ 5f² 7g² 6v] fair sort: first foal: dam won 1¼m seller: second in maiden **77**

races at Beverley in August and Ayr in September, on latter course finishing 3 lengths behind Nana's Queen in 21-runner event: stays 7f well. *A. Smith.*

HELVELLYN 2 b.f. Mountain Call 125–Westmorland Jane 76 (Vimy 132) **72** [1976 6f⁶ 7f 7f⁴ 7f*] third foal: sister to Sharp Fellah, a middle-distance winner in France and half-sister to another winner: dam, half-sister to St Leger second Canterbury, placed at up to 17f when named Ciboulette: sold to W. Stephenson 1,450 gns after showing improved form to win six-runner seller at Newmarket in August by 2 lengths from Buseh: will probably stay beyond 1m: blinkered last two outings. *J. W. Watts.*

HELVETICA 2 b.f. Upper Case–Colwyn Bay 81 (Klairon 131) [1976 5g 6d — 6fg 6g 5s 6s] well-made filly: no worthwhile form in maiden and minor events: blinkered last two outings. *D. Sasse.*

HEMSWORTH 2 ch.c. Native Prince–Lady Matador 108 (Matador 131) [1976 **80** 5f⁵ 5fg² 5f 5g*] strong, useful sort: half-brother to three winners, including 1975 2-y-o 5f winner Doormat (by Tudor Music): 3,100 gns yearling: dam a sprinter, at her best at 2 yrs: made virtually all when winning minor event at Hamilton in June by a head from Keira: will probably stay 6f: withdrawn under orders on third outing after ducking under stalls. *M. W. Easterby.*

HENDRABURNICK 3 b.c. Military 112–Sixes and Sevens (Democratic 124) — [1975 6fg 7d 7g² 7f⁵ 1976 9fg⁵ 10.1fg 7f 8fg⁶] compact colt: quite a useful plater at 2 yrs: no worthwhile form in 1976: stays 7f: sold to P. Ransom 440 gns Ascot July Sales. *C. Dingwall.*

HENLEY FAIR 2 b.c. Leander 119–Marly Fair 95 (Constable 129) [1976 — 5g] half-brother to a good juvenile hurdler: dam won over 5f and 6f at 2 yrs: backward, moved poorly to post and was always behind in maiden race won by Marching On at Carlisle in May. *G. Richards.*

HENRIETTA LOUISA 2 gr.f. Pongee 106–September Fire (Firestreak 125) — [1976 5f³ 5f 5fg⁶ 7fg] lightly-made filly: only plating class: blinkered last two outings. *T. Fairhurst.*

HENRIETTE RONNER 3 b.f. Yellow God 129–Welcome Dona 82 (Fighting — Don) [1975 5s 5.1f³ 5fg* 1976 5f⁵ 12.2s 6s] well-made, attractive filly: quite moderate form at 2 yrs when trained by J. Winter: sold 1,000 gns Ascot June Sales and was well beaten on all outings for new stable, including when blinkered on final outing. *F. Yardley.*

HENRY HOTFOOT 2 b.c. Hotfoot 126–Tudor Cream 73 § (Tudor Melody 129) **65** [1976 5f 5fg 5f* 7g] fourth foal: 640 gns yearling: dam disappointing at 2 yrs: showed only worthwhile form when winning eight-runner seller at Chepstow in June by head from Glen Stream: off course nearly three months afterwards: will stay 1m. *J. Hill.*

Harry Rosebery Challenge Trophy, Ayr—He Loves Me (near side) draws up to Forty Winks. The third horse is Latest Model

HENRY STREET 2 ch.c. Henry the Seventh 125–Wigmore Street 80 § (Aureole 67
132) [1976 5fg 6g 5fg 6d 8s³ 8g 7s 7v] half-brother to a winning plater by
Negotiation: sold with dam for 2,100 gns as a foal: dam sister to very useful
Hotroy: 2½ lengths third of 10 to What-A-Secret in maiden race at Edinburgh in
October, only sign of ability: will stay 1¼m+ : trained by G. Vergette on first two
outings. *Mrs L. Dingwall.*

HENRY STUART 3 b.g. Bold Lad (Ire) 133–Fotheringay 101 (Right Royal V 76
135) [1975 7g⁴ 6g 1976 8fg⁴ 7fg 8g² 8f²] very good-looking, well-made
gelding: runner-up in maiden races at Ayr and Ripon in the summer, going down
by ½ length to Allan Water in large field on latter course in August: will stay
further than 1m. *J. Dunlop.*

HERACLES 3 b.c. Breeders Dream 116–Papillon Rouge 60 (Klairon 131) [1975 92
5.1f² 5.9f² 6fg³ 5.9fg² 7fg* 8g 8.2d 7fg 1976 7fg⁶ 7.3g⁴ 7g* 8g 7.2g³ 7.2f⁵ 7.6fg
7.6g² 8s] dipped-backed colt: quite a useful handicapper: decisive winner at
Epsom in June by 1½ lengths from Meritable: good second to Panorealm at
Lingfield in September but ran badly when tried in blinkers on final outing:
should stay 1m: possibly unsuited by soft going: lost ground at start on first
two appearances. *I. Walker.*

HERACLES (SPA) 6 b.h. Alfidir–La Maja II (Goyaz) [1974 11g* 12g 15.5d 60
1975 12f⁵ 12fg 1976 17f* 14g⁶ 16g⁴] Spanish-bred horse: successful in handicap at Bath in May by a neck from Tamashoon, first worthwhile form on flat in
this country: well beaten afterwards: stayed well: dead. *F. Winter.*

HERGEST RIDGE 2 gr.f. Grey Love 103–Mary's Twiggy (Queen's Hussar 124) —
[1976 5f] dam never ran: started slowly when tailed-off last of nine
in seller won by Rose of Baydon at Chepstow in April. *P. Ransom.*

HERIOT 4 b.g. Mandamus 120–Henry's Daughter 95 (Tudor Jinks 121) [1974 75
7g* 6s⁵ 6s 8g³ 1975 8f³ 8.2f³ 10g⁵ 9.4g³ 8g 12f³ 12f⁴ 8g⁴ 8f* 8g² 1976 7d³
8fg* 8g⁵ 8g 8h⁴ 8f³ 11fg** 12h² 12f² 13g 12s] quite a moderate handicapper:
successful at Carlisle in May and Ayr in July: stays 1½m: acts on firm going
and a soft surface: sold 4,500 gns Doncaster October Sales. *N. Angus.*

HERITON 3 ch.c. Connaught 130–Hayrake 98 (Galivanter 131) [1975 7g 7d 7g 58
1976 8.2f 10fg⁴ 8g⁵ 7fg 8g 8g 10g⁴] good-looking, rangy colt: probably stays
1¼m: dwelt last two appearances, wearing blinkers on first of them: sold 2,200 gns
Doncaster November Sales. *G. Peter-Hoblyn.*

HERMODORE 2 br.c. Luthier 126–Noche de Ronda (Cambremont 121) [1976 119
6d⁵ 7.5g² 7.5v* 7.7s³] French colt: second foal: half-brother to Persa (by
Bald Eagle), a minor winner at around 1¼m in France: dam won over 10.5f:
developed into a smart colt and, after winning a 17-runner maiden race at Saint-
Cloud in October, ran very well to finish 1½ lengths third to General in Prix
Thomas Bryon on same course despite having none too clear a run: will stay
at least 1¼m: acts on heavy going. *R. Touflan, France.*

HERONRY 2 b.c. Great Heron 127–Two in Love (Bolero) [1976 5g⁵ 5g⁴ 6g² 97
7fg* 7f² 7f] neat colt: brother to a winner in Italy and half-brother to four
minor winners: 6,000 gns yearling: dam never ran: improved with distance and
won maiden race at Newmarket by 2 lengths from Fairy Fisherman: good second
to Bedford Lodge under top weight in £2,000 nursery at Brighton the following
month but ran poorly in similar event at Newmarket later in August and was not
seen out again: will stay 1m. *S. Ingham.*

HERON'S COPPER 2 ch.c. Nice Music 115–Heron's Dolly (Combat 123) 49
[1976 5f 5.9g 5g 8.2s 7s⁴ 10v] small colt: poor plater: blinkered third outing.
J. H. Peacock.

HE'S A GENT 2 b.c. Good Behaving–Riga (Branding) [1976 8d² 7.5g* 8d⁵] 111
leggy American-bred French colt: half-brother to several minor winners in
U.S.A.: 9,500 dollars yearling: dam won in Argentina: put up a very useful
effort when winning 13-runner maiden race at Maisons-Laffitte in September by
¾ length from Pharly, the pair finishing well clear: 27/1 when 9 lengths fifth to
Blushing Groom in Grand Criterium at Longchamp the following month: blinkered
first two outings. *R. Carver, France.*

HESSIAN 3 ch.g. Military 112–Empress of England (Constable 129) [1975 —
N.R. 1976 10.1f⁶ 10.1g 8s 8s⁴] second foal: dam never ran: showed only
sign of ability when 7½ lengths fourth of 18 to Penchand in maiden race
at Warwick in October. *J. Webber.*

HETHERDERRY 2 br.f. Derring-Do 131–Hethersent 71 (Hethersett 134) [1976 —
7s] fourth foal: sister to a poor filly: dam won at 1¼m: unquoted and dwelt when
seventeenth of 20 to Brightly in maiden race at Newmarket in October. *D.
Weeden.*

HETHER FOX 3 br.c. Healaugh Fox–Lilian Langley 75 (Bleep-Bleep 134) —
[1975 N.R. 1976 9g 8f] workmanlike colt: bad mover: seems of no account and
was tried in blinkers on final outing: sold 460 gns Ascot November Sales. *J.
Turner.*

HEY ROMEO 5 ch.h. Midsummer Night II 117–Princess Gretel 97 (The Phoenix) **72**
[1974 8.5h⁶ 7.6g 8g 7g* 1975 7g 7f 1976 6s³ 8v 6v³] good-looking horse:
lightly raced since his 3-y-o days but showed he still has some ability on first and
third starts: stays 7f: acts on soft going. *N. Guest.*

HEY WILLIE 2 b.f. Richboy 117–Hay-Hay 62 (Hook Money 124) [1976 5g 5f² **71**
5d² 5f² 5.1f² 6g⁵ 8f 5f] compact filly: second foal: 420 gns yearling: dam stayed
1¼m: second in maiden auction events, coming closest to success on third outing
when short-headed by Bowsquare Lady at Pontefract: should be suited by 6f:
blinkered penultimate outing. *B. Hills.*

HIDDEN TALENT 4 b.c. Divine Gift 127–Our Shadow 75 (Our Babu 131) **74**
[1974 5fg 5g 5g⁶ 5fg 6fg 6fg* 7g⁵ 6g⁶ 1975 8.2s³ 8s 7d⁶ 8g 7f³ 8.2f* 8fg⁴
10fg² 10fg* 10.1fg⁵ 1976 10fg 10f² 10g² 11.1g³ 10fg⁵ 11.7f⁵ 13fg³ 16.1h* 16g⁵
18.1g⁵ 16d³ 13v⁶] compact, good-bodied colt: quite a moderate handicapper: ran
creditably on several occasions in 1976 and gained a well-deserved success when
trouncing Hill Station at Folkestone in August: stays 2m: acts on firm going:
blinkered last two outings at 3 yrs: sold 2,300 gns Ascot November Sales. *J.
Sutcliffe.*

HIGH AWARD 5 ch.h. Goldhill 125–Gay Treasy (High Treason 126) [1974 6s* **113**
6fg⁴ 6g* 7h² 7g² 7g 7g³ 6s 6v³ 1975 6v⁵ 6g 6s 6f* 5fg* 6fg 6g⁵ 6f⁶ 6g⁶ 5fg* 6fg*
5g³ 6d 5g⁵ 6fg⁵ 6v⁶ 1976 6fg³ 7fg 5d² 5s⁶ 5g⁵ 6f⁴ 5fg³ 6fg 6f⁴ 5fg* 6f 5.6g³ 6g 5s⁶]
strong horse: poor mover in his slower paces: very useful handicapper: was
winning race for second year in a row when beating Clintwood a length in Harewood Handicap at York in August: ran well on several other occasions, including
on twelfth outing when close third to Hei'land Jamie in Portland Handicap at
Doncaster in September: effective at 5f to 7f: acted on any going: went well for
R. Wernham: tough, genuine and consistent: standing at Sandling Stud, Kent,
fee £200 or £300 n.f.n.f. *R. Supple.*

HIGH BALL 2 ch.c. Bold Lad (Ire) 133–High Day (High Hat 131) [1976 7g 8g —
7v] shapely colt: 12,000 gns yearling but was beaten some way on all outings,
finishing last of 18 on final appearance. *M. Jarvis.*

HIGH CALIBRE 2 br.f. Caliban 123–Wimpole Street 102 (Reverse Charge 115) **80**
[1976 5fg³ 7h⁵ 7fg⁴ 6s 6s⁴] rather light-framed filly: half-sister to several
winners, including French 3-y-o 1m winner Wimswinga (by Swing Easy): 1,800
gns yearling: dam, half-sister to Wrekin Rambler, stayed 1⅜m: moderate maiden:
will stay 1¼m+. *P. Cole.*

HIGH CHARGE 2 ch.f. High Line 125–In Command 115 (March Past 124) **78** p
[1976 7g³] third foal: dam smart winner at up to 1½m: weak 10/1-shot, put up an
encouraging first effort in 18-runner maiden race at Yarmouth in September,
showing up all way and finishing 3 lengths third to Unella: will stay 1½m: sure to
improve. *G. Pritchard-Gordon.*

*Harewood Handicap, York—High Award wins for the second successive year. Behind him
come Clintwood, Spanish Air and the grey Overtown*

HIGHDOWN 3 b.c. Queen's Hussar 124–Tudor Gal 106 (Henry the Seventh 125) [1975 N.R. 1976 8s⁶ 12v⁶] rangy colt: poor mover: fourth foal: half-brother to moderate stayer Linkenholt (by Reliance II): dam useful winner at up to 1¼m: little worthwhile form in maiden races at Warwick and Newbury in October. *H. Blagrave.* —

HIGH DRAMA 4 gr.f. Hill Clown–Addis Ababa 102 (Fardal 130) [1974 7g⁶ 7fg 7d 1975 13.3fg⁴ 14d² 16f² 16f² 16f* 17.1g* 1976 14.6g 16.1d 13g 15f⁴ 14fg³ 14.7f² 16.1f* 16g³ 18g³ 16fg⁶ 14d⁴] useful-looking filly: quite a moderate handicapper on her day: came back to form when winning at Newmarket in August by 1½ lengths from Cumbernauld: well suited by long distances: seems to act on any going: sold 4,000 gns Newmarket December Sales. *Denys Smith.* 77

HIGH FINALE 2 b.f. High Line 125–Dark Finale (Javelot 124) [1976 7d⁶ 7s⁶] third foal: sister to French 3-y-o filly Ancholia, very useful winner at up to 14.5f, and closely related to useful middle-distance winner Baroncroft (by High Hat): dam won at up to 1½m in Ireland: sixth in maiden race at Newbury (to Guama) and minor event at Chepstow (to Alltyre) in the autumn: will be suited by middle distances. *H. Candy.* 71

HIGHLAND DRUMMER 3 gr.g. My Swanee 122–Willow Run (Chamossaire) [1975 N.R. 1976 9f] half-brother to several winners here and abroad, including quite moderate 1971 2-y-o 5f winner Faded Glory (by Will Somers) and 2m bumpers winner Glenone (by Signa Infesta): 560 gns yearling, resold three times at 2 yrs fetching 420 gns on last occasion: dam of little account: apprentice ridden at 7-lb overweight, always last behind Sweet Lad in minor event at Ripon in June: sold 340 gns Doncaster November Sales. *H. Blackshaw.* —

HIGHLAND JIG 5 b.g. Ben Novus 109–Gala Dance (Solar Slipper 131) [1974 10fg 9f⁵ 9f² 11.2f² 14f 12f⁵ 12fg⁴ 10s³ 10fg⁴ 1975 10fg² 10h⁴ 12g⁴ 10f* 1976 12fg 13g⁵ 12.2f⁵ 10fg⁵] big gelding: stays 1½m: acts on any going: suitable mount for an apprentice: sold to W. Page 1,000 gns Ascot August Sales. *R. Hollinshead.* 64

HIGHLAND SPICE 2 br.g. Highland Melody 112–Sugar Sweet 87 (Zucchero 133 §) [1976 5fg⁴ 7fg⁶ 6f⁶] well-grown gelding: dam stayed 2m: showed ability in varied company, including selling: will stay 1m. *M. W. Easterby.* 64

HIGH LEE 2 ch.f. Will Hays (U.S.A.)–Luluna (Pinza 136) [1976 6f 7.2fg⁴ 7g 7.2f] lengthy filly: quite a moderate maiden: will stay 1m+: blinkered final outing: retained by trainer 460 gns Ascot November Sales. *S. Norton.* 71

HIGH LIFE 3 b.c. My Swallow 134–Particule II (Vieux Manoir 132) [1975 N.R. 1976 10.5s 11.1g 10fg] tall colt: 10,500 gns yearling but was beaten some way in useful company at York, Kempton and Salisbury in first half of season and was sold 825 gns Ascot November Sales. *I. Balding.* —

HIGH LINNET 2 b.f. High Table 105–Plimsoll Line (Sailing Light 119) [1976 6g 8fg 7v] small filly: plating-class maiden. *J. Etherington.* —

HIGHLY DELIGHTED 2 b.c. High Top 131–Lady R.B. (Gun Shot) [1976 6fg 5fg⁵ 5.9f³ 7g*] half-brother to J.C.'s Shadow (by Iron Ruler), a winner at up to 1m in U.S.A.: dam, unplaced in six starts, is sister to top-class American horse Gun Bow: won eight-runner maiden race at Wolverhampton in August comfortably by 1½ lengths from Mary Green: will stay 1m. *G. Pritchard-Gordon.* 85

HIGH OPINION 3 ch.c. Siliconn 121–Amour-Propre (High Perch 126) [1975 N.R. 1976 6f⁴] second foal: 340 gns yearling: dam never ran: started slowly but made good progress from distance when just over 4½ lengths fourth of seven to Another Fiddler in seller at Windsor in July, only outing: sold 200 gns Doncaster September Sales. *R. Price.* —

HIGH POLISH 2 ch.c. High Line 125–Expo 80 (Sheshoon 132) [1976 6g 6fg⁴ 7s 6v] second foal: 5,200 gns yearling: dam won over 7f at 2 yrs and stayed at least 1¼m: 11 lengths fourth of six to Millionaire in minor event at Windsor in September: will stay well. *R. Smyth.* —

HIGH PRAISE 3 ch.f. Swing Easy 126–Omnia Opera 83 (Major Portion 129) [1975 5s⁶ 5.9fg⁶ 5fg 6f 1976 10.8f⁵ 8g 6fg 5.8f⁶] showed a little ability in maiden company at 2 yrs but was well beaten in sellers in 1976: blinkered final outing in 1975 and 1976. *Mrs R. Lomax.* —

HIGH PRINCE 3 b.c. Saintly Song 128–Yours and Mine 83 (Tin Whistle 128) [1975 8g 1976 6f 6d] workmanlike colt: lightly raced and no worthwhile form (heavily-backed favourite on reappearance in August): will stay 1m. *J. Hardy.* —

HIGH SEASON 4 b.c. Silly Season 127–Tabulator (Never Say Die 137) [1974 7fg* 7g² 7fg* 7g⁶ 1975 8v 7f 7g 8g⁵ 1976 14.6g 14g 12f* 12f⁶] tall, rather leggy 92 colt: very useful 2-y-o: ran his best race since when winning six-runner handicap at Beverley in May by a neck from Pot Luck: stays 1½m: acts on firm going and is apparently unsuited by heavy: not raced after early June. *W. Marshall.*

HIGH STEWARD 3 b.c. Taj Dewan 128–Fervent (French Beige 127) [1975 6d 7g⁴ 1976 10f 12d³ 12g² 12g⁴ 13g⁴ 13s] robust, well-made colt: capable of producing good form, as he showed when quite close-up fourth to Ivory Girl in Fitzwilliam Stakes at Doncaster in September but did not reproduce that run and was well beaten on final outing: should stay further than 1½m: acts on a soft surface. *F. Dever.* **75**

HIGH VALUE 2 b.f. Forlorn River 124–Caernarvon Castle (Charlottesville 135) [1976 5fg⁶ 5fg 5f⁴ 5f⁴ 5f⁴ 5s² 6s* 6s] small filly: first produce: 800 gns foal: dam never ran: showed improved form in the autumn and won maiden race at Chepstow in October by a neck from Olympic Visualise: will probably stay beyond 6f: acts on firm going but is evidently better on soft. *R. Supple.* **85**

HIGHVIEW LORD 4 ch.g. Yellow God 129–Super Storm (Arctic Storm 134) [1974 5fg 1975 8.2g 10f 10d 10g⁵ 12v 1976 9fg⁶ 8g² 7fg] strong gelding: poor performer: stayed 1¼m: dead. *I. Walker.* **52**

HIGH WALK 4 b.f. Tower Walk 130–Irish Antics 82 (Gigantic 102) [1974 N.R. 1975 8s³ 8v 8v 7fg 9g 1976 10fg 8s 7f 8f⁶] leggy filly: plater: stays 1m. *A. Smith.* **—**

HIGH WOLD 2 b.g. Saintly Song 128–Annbella (Acropolis 132) [1976 8v] big, strong gelding: second foal: dam unraced half-sister to several winners: unquoted and backward when behind in 24-runner minor event won by The Czar at York in October. *J. Fitzgerald.* **—**

HIGSON'S FOLLY 2 b.f. Sahib 114–Fashion Wear (Hard Tack 111 §) [1976 5g 5f⁶ 5fg 5d 5f 7f³ 6f 7f 7f 7.2f] very unimpressive-looking filly: bad plater: stays 7f: blinkered fifth outing: sold 180 gns Doncaster September Sales. *W. Murray.* **50**

HILLANDALE 4 b.c. Crossing The T–Queen's Penny (Queen's Hussar 124) [1974 5g⁴ 5g⁴ 5g² 5d* 5fg* 5fg⁴ 5d⁵ 6v* 5v² 1975 7v* 7v⁶ 6d⁵ 7fg⁴ 7f³ 7g 7g⁴ 7.3g⁵ 7g⁵ 6fg⁶ 1976 8v² 6.5s* 7fg³ 7fg 7g⁴ 6d⁶ 6s³ 6d* 7.2d⁴ 6s* 6v²] attractive, compact colt: stood up well to a busy season and improved tremendously, on final outing running Record Token to a length in Vernons Sprint Cup at Haydock in October, with some very good sprinters behind: successful three times earlier in season, at Cagnes-sur-Mer in February, at Evry in September (amateur riders race) and at Doncaster the following month (beat Last Tango 2½ lengths in handicap): also ran well on some of his other starts, including when third to Kronenkranich in Goldene Peitsche at Baden-Baden and when sixth behind Girl Friend in Prix de Meautry at Deauville: best form at up to 7f: acts on any going but revels in the mud: very smart. *D. Keith.* **125**

HILLBORN 3 b.f. Good Bond 122–Ulador (Sovereign Lord 120) [1975 N.R. 1976 8v 8.2v 8v] third foal: dam of no account: well beaten in end-of-season maiden races. *H. Wharton.* **—**

Allendale Handicap, Doncaster—Hillandale takes care of Last Tango (right) and Walter

HILLIANA 3 b.f. Goldhill 125–Siciliana 77 (Sicilian Prince 126) [1975 5s 5s 5s 5f² 5g* 5h⁵ 7f⁶ 1976 6g 7g 5f⁴ 6h 9f⁴ 8.2f⁴ 10g³ 8s⁶] poor plater: seems to stay 1¼m: sometimes dwells at start. *J. Cousins.* **58**

HILL OF TARA 3 b.f. Royal Palace 131–Corbalton 103 (Milesian 125) [1975 N.R. 1976 7f 9f] good-looking, well-made filly: half-sister to four winners, including very smart middle-distance performer Knockroe (by Fortino II): dam winner at up to 11f: little worthwhile form in newcomers event at Newbury (made a lot of the running) and maiden race at Wolverhampton in the spring. *J. Nelson.*

HILL'S DOUBLE 2 b.c. Derring-Do 131–Pinelopi (Prince Bio) [1976 6fg 6f 7s* 7v*] useful sort: half-brother to three winners, notably very smart 7f to 1¼m winner Relpin (by Reliance II): 9,000 gns yearling: dam never ran: short-priced favourite when runaway winner of maiden race at Edinburgh (by 8 lengths) and minor event at Teesside (value of win 12 lengths) in October: will stay 1¼m: acts on heavy ground: trained by R. Price on first two outings: a very useful colt in the making. *M. Stoute.* **105**

HILL SERENADE 3 b.f. Hill Clown–Greek Serenade (Grey Sovereign 128 §) [1975 N.R. 1976 8s] sister to a poor animal and half-sister to three winners, including useful sprinter Princess Runnymede (by Runnymede): 440 gns yearling, resold 400 gns 2-y-o: dam sister to top-class 1958 2-y-o Greek Sovereign: last of 12 in maiden race won by Churchillian at Edinburgh in October. *J. Berry.*

HILL STATION 4 ch.g. Sheshoon 132–Space Suit 100 (Roan Rocket 128) [1974 6v 1975 11v⁴ 14fg⁴ 10h² 12f* 12f³ 14fg² 12.2g³ 1976 12.2f 12f² 14fg⁴ 14fg 12f² 15.5f* 13.8f² 16.9f² 16.1h² 14fg] attractive, rangy gelding: quite a moderate handicapper: successful at Folkestone in July by a length from Tug of War: runs as though he needs at least 2m nowadays: acts on hard going: started slowly and always tailed off when tried in blinkers on fourth outing: sold out of J. Nelson's stable 5,000 gns Ascot July Sales after seventh start. *M. Bolton.* **74**

HILLTOP LASS 3 gr.f. Precipice Wood 123–Hot Seat 73 (Sing Sing 134) [1975 N.R. 1976 8fg 10.1fg 16h 11.7h 10.1fg] probably of little account. *J. Holt.* —

HIMLEY GIRL 4 br.f. Hill Clown–The Dowager 79 (Relic) [1974 5fg 5g³ 5h³ 5f 5g 5v 5g 1975 9fg 10h 7f 8.2fg 8g 12f 1976 7g 6g⁴ 6fg] bad plater. *C. Crossley.* —

HIPPARION 4 gr.g. Sayfar 116–Grecian Palm 78 (Royal Palm 131) [1974 6fg 6fg* 7d³ 7fg² 7g 1975 8g⁶ 10f² 10g² 10.6s 1976 7.6s⁶ 10s² 12s²] leggy, rather lightly-made gelding: useful handicapper at 3 yrs: disappointing in 1976: stays 1½m: appears to act on any going. *S. Mellor.* —

HIPPOCRAT 2 b.c. Huntercombe 133–Tien Shan 67 (Busted 134) [1976 5fg 6fg] strong, short-legged colt: first foal: bought privately 1,500 gns yearling: dam, half-sister to top-class sprinters So Blessed and Lucasland, stayed 1½m: behind in maiden race at Salisbury in June and minor event at Chester in September: dead. *A. Johnson.*

HIS MASTERS ROCKET 2 ch.c. Roan Rocket 128–Lady Jester 108 (Bleep-Bleep 134) [1976 5f 5g 6fg⁴ 7fg³ 7fg⁵ 7f* 7g 8f⁵] lengthy, useful-looking, strong-quartered colt: half-brother to fairly useful sprinter Trickster (by Major Portion) and 3-y-o 5f winner Friendly Jester (by Be Friendly): 3,300 gns yearling: dam won seven races, all at 5f: made all to win 15-runner maiden race at Warwick in July by a length from Vaguely James: stays 1m: none too consistent. *B. Hills.* **83**

HIS'N HERS 2 ch.f. Good Bond 122–Tang-Hiloa (Rockefella) [1976 5fg 6s 6s] leggy, unfurnished filly: well behind in minor events and a seller. *D. Yeoman.* —

HI SNOOP 5 ch.m. High Hat 131–Royal Snoop (King of the Tudors 129) [1974 8g⁴ 6fg 8d⁵ 8s⁵ 8v⁴ 10v³ 1975 8f 10g⁶ 8.3f 8g 1976 6s] light-framed filly: bad plater. *A. Davison.* —

HISTON GREEN 2 b.g. Major Portion 129–Queen of the Winds (Borealis) [1976 5fg 6d⁴ 7f⁵ 7h³ 8.2d⁴ 8s⁵ 7v⁶] half-brother to four winners, including Whistling Shaft (by Breakspear II), a useful performer at up to 1½m: 820 gns yearling: heavily-backed favourite for 19-runner nursery at Nottingham in September and showed improved form in finishing 3 lengths fourth to Sloane Ranger: ran respectably in blinkers in similar company on last two outings: suited by 1m and will stay further: retained by trainer 2,300 gns Doncaster June Sales. *M. H. Easterby.* **71**

HISTORIC MYTH 7 b.g. Tacitus 124–Dodone 98 (March Past 124) [1974 —
N.R. 1975 16s⁶ 14d 12f⁶ 13.3fg 16fg 12f 7f 10.2g 16g⁴ 1976 15.8f⁶] poor
handicapper nowadays: stays well: sometimes wears blinkers (didn't on only
appearance in 1976). *A. Jones.*

HIT THE ROOF 2 b.c. Upper Case–Hardiemma 81 (Hardicanute 130) [1976 6f —
6d 7g] first produce: 1,700 gns foal and resold 4,000 gns yearling: dam won at
up to 11f: little worthwhile form in maiden races at Newmarket (two) and
Yarmouth. *R. Jarvis.*

HITTITE GLORY 3 b.c. Habitat 134–Hazy Idea 118 (Hethersett 134) [1975 **119**
5fg⁵ 6g* 6f⁶ 6fg 5g* 6g* 7fg⁵ 1976 7.5g 8g 5f³ 6fg 5fg 6g]
    The high hopes entertained for Hittite Glory as a three-year-old were never
fulfilled. Only once in six starts did he show anything approaching the high-
class form that had enabled him to win three races in his first season, including
two of England's most important contests for two-year-olds, the Flying Childers
Stakes at Doncaster, in which he beat Music Boy by half a length, and the
William Hill Middle Park Stakes at Newmarket, in which he prevailed by a
short head from Duke Ellington. Along with most of Mr Tikkoo's horses Hittite
Glory was transferred to Chantilly at the beginning of 1976; by September just
about all that Hittite Glory had acquired was £2,300 for finishing third in the
King's Stand Stakes and a badly tarnished reputation. His performance in
the King's Stand Stakes at Royal Ascot was a very good one. He was beaten
three quarters of a length and three lengths behind Lochnager and Realty,
staying on really well after getting outpaced in the early stages. However,
with the possible exception of a seventh-of-twelve placing to The Chaplain in
the Prix Montenica at Maisons-Laffitte on his seasonal début, when he was
giving weight all round and was beaten about five lengths, Hittite Glory's other
efforts make depressing reading: last of eleven in the French Two Thousand
Guineas, last of ten in the July Cup, ninth of eleven in the William Hill Sprint
Championship and ninth of ten in the Prix de Seine-et-Oise.

Hittite Glory (b.c. 1973)	Habitat (b 1966)	Sir Gaylord (b 1959)	Turn-to / Somethingroyal
		Little Hut (b 1952)	Occupy / Savage Beauty
	Hazy Idea (b 1967)	Hethersett (b 1959)	Hugh Lupus / Bride Elect
		Won't Linger (ch 1961)	Worden II / Cherished

    In October Hittite Glory was syndicated at £4,000 per share, and he now
stands at the New Ground Stud, Newmarket, at a fee of £1,200 with the no
foal concession. In spite of his disappointing second season we have every
confidence that Hittite Glory can make a name for himself as a stallion. He is
physically a most impressive individual, a powerful, round-bodied bundle of
muscle. By the top-class racehorse and stallion Habitat out of the Hethersett
mare Hazy Idea, Hittite Glory is a half-brother to Rubric (by Red God) who
won over five furlongs in this country as a two-year-old and who has since won
several times in Spain, and to the French two-year-old Corviglia Boy (by
Crepello), winner of a newcomers race at Chantilly in 1976. Hazy Idea was a
smart racemare who had the speed to win over six furlongs as a two-year-old
and the stamina to win over a mile and three quarters in her second season.
Although a mile should have been within his capabilities on breeding, there's no
doubt Hittite Glory's forte was sprinting. He acted on firm going and never
encountered ground softer than good. Hittite Glory was far from consistent
but on his day he was a very good horse. *A. Breasley, France.*

HOBNOB (FR) 4 ch.c. Gyr 131–Forever 68 (Never Say Die 137) [1974 6f² —
7fg* 7d² 7d* 7d⁴ 7.3s 1975 10g² 10.5d* 12fg 12fg 15g³ 14fg³ 14.6g⁴ 12g 1976
16g⁶] leggy, quite attractive colt: good mover: smart performer at 3 yrs: made
only one appearance in 1976, running promisingly when sixth to Night In Town
at Ascot in July, forcing pace for much of way and weakening only in final 2f
(looked very backward): stays very well: seems to act on any going: bandaged
at Ascot and is evidently difficult to train: sold 10,000 gns Newmarket December
Sales. *H. Wragg.*

HOHE-MUNDE 2 br.f. Crooner 119–Gay Frolic 83 (Coalition 110) [1976 6g] —
sister to Spring Fling, a winner at up to 1¼m, and half-sister to 3-y-o Gay Minnie
(by Divine Gift), a winner over 1m: 240 gns yearling: dam won from 1¼m to 1¾m:
tailed off in newcomers event won by Greenjacket at Lingfield in September
Mrs N. Whitfield.

HOLDFORTH BOY 2 ch.c. Swinging Junior 118–Maiden's Blush (Fortino II **72**
120) [1976 5g 5g5 5fg 5g2 7f* 8f4 8fg] quite useful-looking, leggy colt: won seller
at Redcar in August (no bid): good fourth to Moon Express in a nursery at
Thirsk the following month: stays 1m: acts on firm going. *Denys Smith.*

HOLLOW AWAY 2 b.c. Wolver Hollow 126–Pim-Pam (Acropolis 132) [1976 —
5f 6s 6f 8g] fourth foal: 3,400 gns yearling: dam once-raced half-sister to
Swinging Junior: in rear in maiden races and a £2,400 event. *K. Payne.*

HOLLY DOON 3 b.f. Doon 124–Miltown Lass (Panaslipper 130) [1975 6f —
1976 8fg 8fg 8fg 5f 8f 8d] small filly: no worthwhile form, including in a seller,
and refused to race on penultimate outing: blinkered at 2 yrs and on fifth start.
D. Holmes.

HOLMWOOD LEAP 3 b.g. King's Leap 111–Sidam 79 (Psidium 130) [1975 —
5d 5s 5f5 5g6 7h 7g 7f 1976 7f 8f] worthless plater. *T. Craig.*

HOLY BIDDY 2 b.f. Divine Gift 127–Postbridge (Fighting Ship 121) [1976 **52**
5fg6 5f4 5d6 5.9f5 6h] small, light-framed filly: poor plater: sold 400 gns Ascot
August Sales *J. Edwards.*

HOMEBOY 3 b.c. King's Troop 118–Reita 87 (Gilles de Retz 132) [1975 6g* **113**
6g2 7g4 1976 8g6 8.5g3 8f4 7s] strong, compact, robust colt: ran well when in
frame in Diomed Stakes at Epsom (third of seven to All Friends) and St James's
Palace Stakes at Royal Ascot (2½ lengths fourth of eight to dead-heaters Radetzky
and Patris) in June: not seen out again until the autumn when not disgraced in
handicap at Newmarket: stays 1m: acts on firm going: trained by I. Balding
until after third outing. *M. Jarvis.*

HOMEFIELD 8 ch.g. El Cid 109–Part Exchange 78 (Faubourg II 127) [1974 **73**
N.R. 1975 16s5 15s 13f6 12fg 14f6 12h 16fg 16g 1976 15f 12f 12d2 12d6 13g4
13g3 12h 20f* 12h* 17.1h* 12.2f2 16.1h3 12h* 14fg* 18.1g6 16.1d 16s6] quite
a moderate handicapper: a really tough customer who took on a new lease of
life in 1976 and won five races: gained his final success when beating Mister
Geoffrey 2½ lengths in valuable George Todd Apprentices Challenge Trophy at
Goodwood in September: effective at 1½m and stays extremely well: appears to
act on any going: a most game, genuine and consistent front runner: ridden by
apprentice F. Curley when successful in 1976. *P. Poston.*

Lady Beaverbrook's "Homeboy"

HOME FIRE 2 ch.f. Firestreak 125–Meg Swerie (Whistler 129) [1976 5g **99**
5f² 5fg*(dis) 6fg* 6g⁴ 5fg*] well-made filly: second living foal: half-sister
to moderate Let's Pretend (by Pretendre): 1,900 gns yearling: dam second three
times from 6f to 1m at 3 yrs in Ireland: a useful filly who won 27-runner maiden
race at Newbury in August (very easily by 6 lengths from Rheola) and eight-
runner minor event at Goodwood the following month (beat Dancing Song a
length): also first past post in maiden race at Goodwood in July, ¼ length in
front of Scarcely Blessed, but was moved down to last place by stewards: will
stay 1m: acts on a firm surface. *L. Hall.*

HOMELY LASS 3 b.f. Galivanter 131–Justice II (Umberto 118) [1975 6g **—**
1976 7.2g] lightly-raced plater. *R. Edwards.*

HOME WATERS 3 b.f. Gulf Pearl 117–Last Lap 75 (Immortality) [1975 5g **83**
6f⁶ 7g 7fg* 8d² 7.2s⁶ 1976 8.2f 10g⁵ 10g 8g⁴ 8.2g⁶ 10d² 12s⁴ 10s²] narrow filly:
ran well when runner-up in handicaps at Newbury (to Renda) and Chepstow
(to Word of Honour) in the autumn: best form at 1¼m but should stay 1½m:
appears to act on any going: sold 2,300 gns Newmarket December Sales. *H.
Candy.*

HOME WIN 2 b.c. Habitat 134–Triumphantly (Bold Ruler) [1976 6v] second **— p**
foal: half-brother to 3-y-o 7f winner Suffragette (by Reform): dam, winner at up
to 1m at 3 yrs in U.S.A., is daughter of Oaks winner Sicarelle: weak 9/1-shot
when behind in 22-runner maiden race won by Good Company at Newbury in
October: should do better. *R. Hern.*

HONE 2 ch.f. Sharpen Up 127–Lucy 83 (Sheshoon 132) [1976 5fg* 5g⁴ 5f³] **79**
lightly-made, leggy filly: third foal: half-sister to a winning plater by Sky Gipsy:
220 gns foal: dam won over 1¼m: won maiden race at Windsor in May by 2
lengths from Sole Agent: ran creditably on both subsequent outings: exported
to Belgium by B.B.A. *F. Maxwell.*

HONEGGER 2 b.c. King's Troop 118–Honey Palm 86 (Honeyway 125) [1976 **95 p**
8s²] strong colt: half-brother to 1972 2-y-o 6f winner Miss Casanova (by
Galivanter): 5,800 gns yearling: dam a sprinter, at her best as a 2-y-o: 20/1 and
looking well, showed good speed to go clear of far-side runners when 3 lengths
second to Royal Boxer in 27-runner maiden race at Newmarket in October:
stays 1m well: an excellent first effort by a colt who is sure to win races. *L.
Cumani.*

HONEST BUILDER 2 b.c. Irish Ball 127–Miss Jessica 90 (Milesian 125) [1976 **—**
5g 7h 6fg 8f 7s 10v] small colt: bad plater: blinkered final outing: sold 250 gns
Ascot December Sales. *K. Ivory.*

HONEYBLEST 4 br.c. So Blessed 130–Riddels Bay (Primera 131) [1974 5f* **120**
6g 6g² 5fg* 5.5fg 5v² 1975 5fg⁴ 5d 6d 6fg* 6g* 6g* 6f 6fg³ 6fg* 6g⁵ 6fg⁴ 6g²
1976 6fg² 6f² 6d⁶ 6f 7g² 6f* 6g* 6d⁴ 6v]

Honeyblest has been a marvellous servant of his stable. As a three-year-old
he won four sprint handicaps against horses of his own age, carrying big weights
to victory at Newmarket in July and York in August, and afterwards ran
creditably in the Diadem Stakes and the Challenge Stakes. These performances
ensured that Honeyblest would strike off almost at the top of the handicap as
a four-year-old and in fact he took part in only one such race all season, the
valuable Great St Wilfrid Handicap at Ripon in August. By that time Honeyblest was without a win in the current season, although he had three times been

*Great St Wilfrid Handicap, Ripon—Honeyblest is always going better
than Jimmy The Singer*

*Diadem Stakes, Ascot—Honeyblest stays on well to beat Be Tuneful
and the blinkered Royal Boy*

second, in the Ladbroke Abernant Stakes at Newmarket in April (beaten a
head by Boldboy when in receipt of 3 lb), in the Thirsk Hall Stakes a week later
(beaten a neck by Roman Warrior when in receipt of 8 lb) and in the Fen Ditton
Stakes over seven furlongs at Newmarket in July (beaten two lengths by the
Two Thousand Guineas third Thieving Demon).   Honeyblest was set to receive
more than a stone from Lochnager in the original handicap for the Great St
Wilfrid and with 8-13, on the same mark as the three-year-old Broxted and set
to receive weight also from Roman Warrior, Polly Peachum, Pascualete and
Lazenby, he seemed well in. With Lochnager, Roman Warrior and Polly
Peachum engaged in more important business at York two days earlier, and
with Broxted in America and Pascualete on the sidelines, Honeyblest landed the
£6,206 first prize without much difficulty, winning in fine style and having only
the Spillers Stewards' Cup winner Jimmy The Singer within half a dozen lengths of
him at the line.

Mr John Slade's "Honeyblest"

Just how leniently Honeyblest had been treated by the handicapper at Ripon was shown when he beat some good sprinters in the Diadem Stakes at Ascot a month later. Honeyblest disputed the lead most of the way with the Cork and Orrery winner Gentilhombre, who afterwards dead-heated for the Prix de l'Abbaye de Longchamp. Honeyblest took a narrow advantage entering the last furlong and struggled gamely to hold off several challengers. He won by half a length and a length from Be Tuneful and Royal Boy, with Boldboy fourth. Honeyblest, sold after the Diadem Stakes for a sum reported to be in excess of £50,000, had two more races and ran slightly below form on unsuitable going in the Challenge Stakes and the Vernons Sprint Cup in October.

Given a sound surface to race on Honeyblest was a good sprinter. He was genuine and consistent but was a headstrong, free-running animal which made him a difficult ride. Baxter, his regular jockey, got on best with him, although Honeyblest threw him off on the way to the start of the Portland Handicap causing injuries to Baxter which led to the horse being withdrawn. Even Piggott had difficulty anchoring Honeyblest when he had the mount on him in the Cork and Orrery Stakes at Royal Ascot; the horse took charge on the way to the start, running away onto the round course and using up so much energy that when the time came for racing he had little left and there was nothing for Piggott to do but bring him back at the tail of the field.

Honeyblest (br.c. 1972)	So Blessed (br 1965)	Princely Gift (b 1951)	Nasrullah / Blue Gem
		Lavant (b 1955)	Le Lavandou / Firle
	Riddels Bay (br 1962)	Primera (b 1954)	My Babu / Pirette
		Heron Bay (br 1954)	Honeyway / Borobella

Honeyblest, a well-made, quite attractive colt, who always looked a picture in the paddock, is now at stud in Greece. He is one of the best horses sired so far by the Princely Gift stallion So Blessed who had another fine season in 1976. So Blessed was a top-class sprinter but most of his offspring stay better than he. Seeing that Honeyblest's dam won over two miles it may seem a little surprising, therefore, that Honeyblest should turn out to be a sprinter. However, it should never be forgotten that every mating presents a high number of different possibilities and we must always turn to the horse himself to tell us by his conformation, his action and his racecourse performances which of the possibilities presented by his pedigree has materialised in him. *Doug Smith.*

HONEY BLOSSOM 3 b.f. Connaught 130–Honey Bee 103 (Honeyway 125) **105** [1975 5fg* 6f2 6fg2 7g2 1976 8.5fg2 10f4 10f5 10f*] useful handicapper: put up an excellent performance when tried in blinkers on final outing, winning Park Top Handicap at Brighton by 5 lengths from Shortbread: stays 1¼m: acts on firm going: sold 7,600 gns Newmarket July Sales. *P. Walwyn.*

HONEY BLUE 8 br.g. Better Honey 110–Blue Penny (Hello Peter) [1976 12f5] — ex-New Zealand gelding: successful twice from his 22 starts in that country, winning maiden race over 1m, and 11f event: backed at long odds when well behind in amateur riders event at Beverley in July won by Franc Flinders, only outing on flat in this country. *R. Cambidge.*

HONEY BOWL 2 ch.c. Tower Walk 130–Twinkling Star § (Never Say Die **91** 137) [1976 5fg4 5.9f* 7.2f4] lengthy colt: half-brother to several winners, including useful 1973 2-y-o Space Shot (by Reform): 6,000 gns yearling: dam disappointing daughter of Irish 1,000 Guineas winner Even Star: won seven-runner maiden race at Wolverhampton in August by 3 lengths from Glazepta Rework: should stay 1m: retained by stable 5,600 gns Doncaster November Sales. *N. Vigors.*

HONEY BRIGHT 5 br.m. Right Boy 137–Heather Honey (Honeyway 125) — [1974 8fg 7g 8f3 8f6 7fg2 8g6 8g6 11.5g 8.2s 7s 6v 1975 8.2s 6s6 7s 8.2d* 7f 7g* 8fg4 8h5 8g4 9f* 11g3 7f 9h 8g 1976 8.2v6 7d 8f 7g 7f 8.2g4 10f4 8.2f] compact mare: poor handicapper: well beaten in 1976: best form at up to 9f: unsuited by very soft ground. *B. Richmond.*

HONEY MAJOR 2 ch.c. Major Portion 129–Once for All (Quorum 126) [1976 **82+** 5fg* 6f2] half-brother to two minor winners by Royal Avenue: 900 gns yearling: dam never ran: lost about 5 lengths at start and so did really well to win £1,800 maiden race at York in July by a length from Portal Lad: 3 lengths second to odds-on Hand Canter in three-runner event at Hamilton later in month but again dwelt at start and is almost certainly better than the bare result suggests: will stay 1m. *F. Carr.*

HONEYMOOR 5 br.m. Pardao 120–Hethersent 71 (Hethersett 134) [1974 — 11.1f 5fg 7fg6 11.5g 12d4 10v4 1975 13.8d 13.8fg 1976 18s6] probably of no account. *F. Dever.*

HONEYPOT LANE 3 b.f. Silly Season 127–Sweet Hour 91 (Primera 131) **91** [1975 N.R. 1976 7f3 10.1fg* 10.6d5 10g2 12fg* 12fg6] lengthy filly: first foal: dam won over 5f and 6f at 2 yrs: short-priced favourite, won maiden race at Windsor in May by a length from Double East: ran well afterwards and won handicap at Goodwood in July by a length from Devil's Dike: stays 1¼m well: acts on a firm and a soft surface. *R. Hern.*

HONEY TOWER 2 br.f. Tower Walk 130–La Reine Margot 76 (Pampered — King 121) [1976 7s] second foal: 6,600 gns foal: dam, placed over 7f at 2 yrs, is half-sister to top-class middle-distance filly Paulista: 12/1 when behind in 20-runner maiden race won by Brightly at Newmarket in October. *B. Hills.*

HOOKED AGAIN 7 br.g. Hook Money 124–Game Maria 106 (Big Game) — [1974 14.6s 12g4 12.2d5 14.7f* 12fg3 13g* 13g* 16g 12g 12g 1975 N.R. 1976 13g4] tall gelding: moderate handicapper (rated 82) in 1974: well-beaten fourth of six to Hardy Turk at Ayr in May, only outing since: stays well: well suited by firm ground: sometimes wears blinkers: good mount for an apprentice. *G. Richards.*

HOPE ANCHOR 3 b.c. Hopeful Venture 125–Time Call (Chanteur II 135) — [1975 7f 8g 7g 1976 8g5 12.3s] half-brother to high-class stayer High Line (by High Hat): little worthwhile form in varied company, but finished very lame on final outing (April) and was said to have severed tendons in near-fore. *P. Robinson.*

HOPE ETERNAL 2 b.g. Veiled Wonder–Yellow Streak (Shantung 132) [1976 **60** 5f 6h4 5.9g 5f4] half-brother to very useful hurdler Grando King (by Negotiation): dam once-raced half-sister to very speedy Ink Spot: little worthwhile form in varied company. *N. Angus.*

HOPEFUL BLOOM 3 b.g. Hopeful Venture 125–Bloomers 93 (Floribunda 136) **77 d** [1975 5g6 5f3 6g* 8fg3 8g6 7g6 1976 10f2 12g2 10f6 12fg 12.2g 12.3fg5 12fg 12.3v3 10v6] strong gelding: creditable second in early-season handicaps at Beverley and Ripon but ran moderately in most of his other race: stays 1½m: sold to W. A. Stephenson 3,000 gns Doncaster November Sales. *W. Gray.*

HOPEFUL CID 2 ch.c. El Cid 109–Freda's Hope (Fighting Don) [1976 6d 6f 6f2 **69** 6h4 7f3 7.2f6 8fg4 8.2s 10s3] workmanlike colt: fair plater: will stay 1½m: acts on any going: has run well both with and without blinkers. *S. Norton.*

HOPEFUL STORY 2 b.c. Hopeful Venture 125–Paperback 94 (Hard Ridden **76 p** 131) [1976 7s4] attractive, good-bodied colt: third foal: half-brother to two quite useful 2-y-o winners, including 3-y-o Paper Rich (by Richboy): 2,000 gns yearling: dam best at up to 7f: unquoted for 11-runner minor event at Sandown in October but showed considerable promise, running on in very good style in straight to finish about 9 lengths fourth of 11 to Imperial Guard: will be well suited by 1m+: has quite a lot of improvement in him. *B. Hills.*

HOPEFUL WAY 3 b.f. Hopeful Venture 125–Artway 82 (Articulate 121) [1975 **63** 7.2fg3 7v 6d 8g 1976 8fg 12g 10f6 12fg3 12f*] workmanlike filly: well-backed favourite, put up easily best effort when running out comfortable winner of eight-runner seller at Thirsk in September (no bid): runs as though she will stay further than 1½m: acts on firm going. *F. Carr.*

HOPE OF GLORY 2 b.f. So Blessed 130–Time of Hope 98 (Matador 131) **65** [1976 6g 6s4] strong, attractive filly: half-sister to a 2-y-o winner by Privy Councillor: dam a sprinter: third favourite when 9 lengths fourth of 11 to Port Ahoy in minor event at Pontefract in October: stays 6f. *Sir Mark Prescott.*

HORA ROYALE 2 b.f. Kibenka 119–Princess's Time (Arctic Time 127) [1976 **82** 5g3 5g4 5g 6fg3 7f2 7f 8fg4] tall filly: good mover: half-sister to two fairly useful performers by Lauso, including middle-distance stayer Lousy Time: 1,700 gns yearling: dam half-sister to Irish St Leger winner Allangrange: moderate filly: should stay 1¼m: ran badly on third and sixth outings, on latter occasion wearing blinkers and ridden by 7-lb claimer: inconsistent. *R. Hannon.*

HORNEL 3 ch.g. Double Jump 131–Miss McWorden 75 (Worden II 129) [1975 **59** 5s 5s 7f4 7f 8f 8g6 1976 12.2d5 10f 13.8f*] leggy gelding: plater: winner at Catterick in July by 4 lengths from Matsui: sold to A. Bacon's stable 525 gns afterwards: stays well: blinkered final outing in 1975: sometimes sweats up. *D. Yeoman.*

HORSEGUARDS 4 ch.c. Pall Mall 132–Teresa Aguesca (Saint Crespin III 132) **101**
[1974 5f⁴ 6g⁵ 7s³ 8s* 8g² 8v* 1975 10g⁶ 10s⁶ 10v* 12g* 11.1v* 12v* 12g² 11v⁵
12g 12g 12g⁶ 12d⁴ 12v 12g 1976 12g⁵ 12f 12.3s* 12g² 12fg³] lengthy colt:
useful handicapper: stayed on gamely when winning at Chester in May by 2½
lengths from Gaelic: ran well in his two races afterwards but wasn't seen out
after being beaten about ½ length when third of seven to Slim Jim in Newbury
Summer Cup in June: will stay further than 1½m: acts well on heavy going:
game and genuine: sold to J. Haine only 940 gns Newmarket Autumn Sales.
P. Walwyn.

HORTON BOY 2 b.c. Siliconn 121–Andrea 88 (Kingstone) [1976 5fg 8.2s 7s] —
compact colt: bad plater. *S. Cole.*

HOT BELLE 3 br.f. Hotfoot 126–Caveletta 82 (Buisson Ardent 129) [1975 **48**
5v² 5s 5d⁶ 6f⁴ 6fg* 5f³ 5f⁵ 5.9fg² 6g 5d 7g³ 1976 7f⁴ 7g 10f 8.3f 6f³ 6v]
small filly: plater: should stay 1m: ran moderately when tried in blinkers:
suitable mount for an apprentice: sold out of N. Adam's stable 425 gns Ascot
August Sales after fifth outing. *A. Neaves.*

HOT BIRD 3 ch.f. Birdbrook 110–Ablaze 94 (Abernant 142) [1975 5fg⁴ 5.8g⁶ **98**
5fg² 5d⁵ 5g⁵ 5g² 5d² 1976 6f⁵ 6g* 6d 5g* 5g³ 5f² 5f* 5fg* 6fg⁶ 5fg⁴ 5g²
5v² 5s³] big filly: useful handicapper: much improved and had a good season,
winning at Hamilton, Catterick, Redcar and Thirsk: scored comfortably on last
two occasions, at Redcar picking up John Player Handicap by 3 lengths from
Fair Sarita: good second to Panglima at Doncaster in September and to Epsom
Imp at York the following month: stays 6f but has shown best form at 5f: acts on
any going: has shown form with and without blinkers. *M. W. Easterby.*

HOTCAKES 3 ch.c. Virginia Boy 106–Golden Hostess (Kythnos 126) [1975 5s **72**
5g 6fg³ 7g 5g* 5f 5f² 5h² 6fg 5g* 5f 5g 5g 1976 5g 6d⁴ 7d 5d 5g⁶ 5f 5s⁶ 6f 5f⁶ 5h³
5f⁶ 5f⁵ 5f 6v⁴ 6s] strong colt: showed quite useful form at 2 yrs and won at
Lanark (seller) and Edinburgh: nowhere near so good in handicap company in
1976: best form at 5f and probably does not stay 7f: suited by a sound surface
and acts on hard ground: has been tried in blinkers but does better without:
suitable mount for an apprentice: sometimes sweats up: trained most of season
by K. Payne. *G. Blum.*

HOT CROSS BUN 3 b.g. So Blessed 130–Tartlet 83 (Primera 131) [1975 **79**
N.R. 1976 8.2g 9f 8fg³ 8g⁶ 8f² 8f* 8.3g³ 8fg⁶ 8s³ 8.2v⁶] useful-looking gelding:
second foal: 1,800 gns yearling: dam placed at up to 1½m: won maiden race at
Beverley in August: ran respectably in handicaps afterwards: will stay 1¼m+:
acts on any going: wears blinkers nowadays: sold to M. Francis 2,800 gns Newmarket Autumn Sales. *C. Brittain.*

HOT FUDGE MONDAY 2 gr.c. Raffingora 130–Queensboro 85 (Quorum 126) **75**
[1976 5fg 6g 5.9f³ 7fg 6fg] June foal: strong, robust colt: half-brother to a
winner over hurdles: 1,700 gns yearling: dam won over 1¼m: quite a moderate
maiden: stays 6f but possibly not 7f. *R. Jarvis.*

HOT GROVE 2 b.c. Hotfoot 126–Orange Grove 81 (Aggressor 130) [1976 6fg* **113**
6fg* 8d³ 8.2s*]
With 8-7 Hot Grove is to be found in the Two-Year-Old Free Handicap on
the same mark as Saros, who ran second in the William Hill Dewhurst Stakes,
and Mandrake Major, who won the Flying Childers Stakes and finished third
in the William Hill Middle Park Stakes. Well, we would have no hesitation in
backing either of these horses to beat him at level weights, but that Hot Grove
is a pretty good colt admits of no argument. His third to Gairloch and Pampapaul in the Royal Lodge Stakes at Ascot represents the only occasion on which
he was beaten in four starts, and though his successes were gained in relatively
unimportant events at Salisbury, Chester and Haydock, Hot Grove could do no
more than win them. At Haydock he had very little to beat, but he gave over
a stone to such as he had to beat and won in style by three lengths and seven.

Hot Grove (b.c. 1974)	Hotfoot (br 1966)	Firestreak (br 1956)	Pardal
			Hot Spell
		Pitter Patter (br 1953)	Kingstone
			Rain
	Orange Grove (b 1967)	Aggressor (b 1955)	Combat
			Phactonia
		Orange Girl (b 1962)	Grey Sovereign
			Mistress Gwynne

A well-made colt, Hot Grove is a son of Hotfoot, who is doing well as a stallion, out of Orange Grove, who distinguished herself as a juvenile hurdler. Orange Grove, who comes from the same family as Gay Time and Elopement, won over a mile and a half on the flat, and from what we have seen of Hot Grove we should think that stamina rather than speed is his strong point even though he did win twice over six furlongs. Distances upwards of a mile and a quarter will give him his best chance of winning races as a three-year-old. He appears to act on any going. *F. J. Houghton.*

HOT HEIR 2 br.c. Whistling Wind 123–Flaming 95 (Fidalgo 129) [1976 5fg 5.1fg[2] 6f* 6fg[2] 6g[3] 7d] useful-looking colt: good mover: fifth produce: 220 gns foal: dam won over 5f and 6f at 2 yrs: won well-contested event at Pontefract in June by 1½ lengths from Mofida: placed in two quite valuable races the following month, running creditably when 4½ lengths third of five to Town and Country in Hyperion Stakes at Ascot: should stay further than 6f but ran well below his best when tried at 7f: acts on firm going. *L. Cumani.* **94**

HOT PAD 2 b.f. Hotfoot 126–Padrona 103 (St Paddy 133) [1976 6g 6d] useful-looking filly: first foal: 18,000 gns yearling: dam, half-sister to numerous winners, won over 5f and 6f at 2 yrs: showed some ability in maiden races at Newmarket, finishing 5½ lengths seventh of 30 to Rheola in September and eighth of 23 to Rings in October: will stay 1¼m. *B. Hobbs.* **78**

HOTRUNNA 2 ro.f. Hotfoot 126–Tetroana 85 (Palestine 133) [1976 5g 5fg[3] 5f[4] 5.1f[3] 6fg 6g[3] 6s] lengthy filly: half-sister to two winning platers: 780 gns yearling: dam best at 6f or 7f: quite a moderate maiden: will stay 1m: acts on firm going. *W. Holden.* **71**

HOT SHOT 4 ch.g. Maystreak 118–Isobel-Anne 78 (Lord of Verona 120) [1974 5s[5] 5s[3] 5fg[2] 5f[2] 5f[3] 6fg 5f* 6fg* 6d* 6s[2] 5s 1975 7g 7f 6f* 6f[2] 7fg[2] 7f[4] 7h[4] 8g 8d 8g 1976 6g 6g[4] 6f 7fg[4] 6h[6] 6d] leggy, light-framed, narrow gelding: didn't run up to his best in 1976: best at up to 7f: acts on any going: suitable mount for an apprentice: sweated up second and third starts. *W. C. Watts.* **68**

HOT STEEL 3 gr.g. Taste of Honey 92–Steel Fever (Delirium 126) [1975 5f[6] 5fg 6fg[5] 5fg 7f 1976 8g 6fg 6d] of little account. *D. Hanley.* **—**

HOT SYMPHONY 3 b.c. Hotfoot 126–Gloriosa 102 (Aureole 132) [1975 6g[3] 6g[2] 7fg[3] 7g 7.2d 1976 8s 6.5g 8g 8.5g 7g 8g 10s 8g 7.2g 7g] good-looking colt: showed moderate form at 2 yrs but was well beaten in 1976: often wears blinkers: sold 260 gns Newmarket Autumn Sales. *D. Sasse.* **—**

HOT VENTURE 3 gr.g. Hotfoot 126–Queens Port (Umberto 118) [1975 N.R. 1976 9f 8f 12g 12.2d] leggy gelding: poor plater: sometimes starts slowly: blinkered first outing: sold 280 gns Doncaster June Sales. *W. Gray.* **—**

HOUSE BREAKER 2 b.f. Burglar 128–Leonora's Legend 83 (Rockefella) [1976 5fg 5fg[5] 6fg 6g 8fg 8.2s 7s[6] 8v*] plater: 20/1 when successful at Leicester in November (no bid): stays 1m well: acts on heavy ground: sometimes wears blinkers (did so at Leicester). *M. Haynes.* **75**

HOWE LANE 2 b.f. Tamerlane 128–Future Hope 85 (Mossborough 126) [1976 6f 7g[3] 8g 8v[3] 8v[5]] compact filly: half-sister to four minor winners: 420 gns foal: dam placed over 1½m: moderate maiden: will stay middle distances: acts on heavy going. *J. Calvert.* **73**

HUL A FIRE 3 br.f. Hul a Hul 124–Gilwayte 81 (Gilles de Retz 132) [1975 N.R. 1976 6f 6f 7.6fg 12v] seems of little account. *W. Clay.* **—**

HULEH VALLEY 2 b.f. Hul a Hul 124–Cotoneaster (Never Say Die 137) [1976 5f 5s[6] 5fg 6fg* 7d 5fg 6s 6v] workmanlike filly: bought in 1,000 gns after winning four-runner seller at Yarmouth in June: faced very stiff tasks in nurseries afterwards: stays 6f: wears blinkers. *R. Bastiman.* **54**

HUM 3 b.f. Crooner 119–Tiara II (Sunny Boy III) [1975 N.R. 1976 8fg[4] 8.2f[2] 8g[2] 10fg[3] 8s 12v[4]] half-sister to four winners here and in France, including stayers Charivari (by Charlottesville) and Charlotson (by Charlottown): dam won over 7f in France: quite a moderate maiden: runner-up to Colombade at Haydock and Fine Blue at Newbury in July: stays 1¼m: evidently needs a sound surface. *P. Cundell.* **69**

HUMBALUNG 2 b.c. So Blessed 130–Rosie Bacardi (Ballymoss 136) [1976 6g 8s[4] 8s[4]] closely related to fair middle-distance performer Chinese God (by Princely Gift): 680 gns yearling: dam won over 1¼m at Haydock: fourth in maiden races in October, being beaten 7 lengths by Royal Boxer at Newmarket and just under 4 lengths by Nordman at Sandown: will be suited by further than 1m. *D. Keith.* **86**

HUMBER PILOT 5 b.h. Young Christopher 119–Magibbillibyte 77 (Constable — §
129) [1974 7d⁵ 8fg* 10f 8g⁵ 8g³ 8h³ 8.2g 8s 8s 1975 7v⁵ 7f 8f³ 10f⁴ 8h 8.2fg 8f
1976 10fg⁶] big, strong, well-made horse: one-time fair handicapper but has
deteriorated considerably and is far from trustworthy: stays 1m but probably
not 1¼m: acts on hard going and seems unsuited by soft. *J. Hardy.*

HUMBIE 2 gr.c. My Swanee 122–Humatune (Tin Whistle 128) [1976 5f 5g² 5f⁵ **75**
5fg] first living produce: 260 gns foal, resold 1,700 gns yearling: dam ran only
four times: went down by ½ length to Spanish Baron in maiden race at Edinburgh
in June, best effort: will stay 6f. *N. Angus.*

HUMDOLEILA 2 ch.c. Green God 128–Stay Nice 85 (Nice Guy 123) [1976 **81**
6g⁴ 7g] half-brother to two winners by Hard Tack, including useful sprinter
Nice Tack: 5,600 gns yearling: dam won at 1m: 20/1 when 3 lengths fourth of 14
to Magenta in newcomers event at Goodwood in September: eighth of 21 to
Nobodys Fool in maiden race at Newmarket the following month. *B. Hills.*

HUMPTY DUMPTY 4 gr.c. Right Boy 137–Shilly Shally 89 (Sallymount 125) —
[1974 7d 6s 1975 8v 8g² 8f 10.1fg⁵ 7f³ 7d⁴ 8.3fg 8.2g² 10d⁶ 10.8g⁴ 1976 13.8g⁴]
rangy colt: best form at up to 1m: best form on a sound surface, and acts on firm
going: has been tried in blinkers but has done better without: looks a difficult
ride. *G. Richards.*

HUNAN 3 b.g. Caliban 123–Moeru Bara 107 (Firestreak 125) [1975 5f 6fg 7g **65**
6fg² 6g 7d³ 6s³ 6g 1976 6fg⁶ 6fg⁶ 6g 10fg⁶ 10.4fg³ 10fg⁵ 10.1fg⁴ 8fg³] strong gelding: became disappointing, and descended to selling company on final outing:
stays 1¼m: probably acts on any going but is well suited by soft. *P. Cundell.*

HUNDALEE 9 br.g. Tutankhamen–Straight Off 88 (Straight Deal) [1974 **61**
12g 16f* 15g² 13g² 15g* 20v* 17v² 18g² 18d⁵ 1975 14.8g 18g 1976 15f⁵
16f³ 22.2f 18fg⁵] fair handicapper at his best: lightly raced in 1976 but ran
respectably when third of eight to Sea Kestrel at Lingfield in June: stays
extremely well: acts on any going. *H. Bell.*

HUNNYLYN 2 ch.f. Huntercombe 133–Lady's Walk (Pall Mall 132) [1976 5g* **95**
5fg* 5g⁵ 5fg⁶] light-framed, very small filly: second foal: half-sister to 3-y-o
Scott Joplyn (by Tower Walk), a useful winner at up to 7f: dam lightly raced:
favourite, made all when winning £1,200 event at Doncaster in March by 1½
lengths from May Bride, and four-runner minor event at Epsom the following
month by 3 lengths from Heckle: in rear in two well-contested races in June and
was not seen out again: such a small filly that we have probably seen the best of
her. *C. Brittain.*

HUNTERCOMBE LAD 3 b.g. Huntercombe 133–Lesson Two (Sheshoon 132) **69**
[1975 5s 5s 5fg⁶ 5g² 5f² 6h* 6f³ 8f 8g⁴ 1976 8f² 7f² 6fg³ 8.2g* 9g² 8s² 9fg 8h⁶]
leggy, unfurnished gelding: plater: sold out of K. Whitehead's stable 960 gns
after winning at Hamilton in May: stays 9f: acts on any going: not seen out after
July. *H. Bell.*

HUNTING CRY 2 b.g. Huntercombe 133–Rahat-Lakoum (Sayajirao 132) **75**
[1976 8s⁴ 6s] half-brother to a minor winner: dam, winner over 11f in Ireland,
is sister to 1,000 Guineas third and Irish Oaks runner-up Indian Melody: well
backed in both his races, finishing 3 lengths fourth of 14 to Wester Win in maiden
race at Bath and seventh of 20 to Nobodys Fool in small race at Chepstow, both
in October: will probably be suited by a return to racing over 1m. *D. Hanley.*

HUNTING TOWER 8 b.g. Henry the Seventh 125–Welsh Huntress 106 (Big **42**
Game) [1974 8fg 10fg* 8.2fg³ 8g³ 12g² 7.6g⁵ 10.4g 9g⁶ 12.2s⁵ 10.4d⁴ 10s 1975
12f 8h 10fg 11d² 9g 10.6fg 10.4f 9f⁴ 1976 7.6fg 10h⁴ 10f⁶ 10.4fg 11h⁴] poor
handicapper: stays 1¼m: acts on any going: needs a hood and blinkers and twice
ran badly without them in 1975: good mount for an apprentice. *C. Crossley.*

HUNTING WILLY 2 b.c. Willywonty 100–Miss Cheshunt (Miralgo 130) [1976 **77**
5.9s⁶ 5v⁶] first reported foal in this country: dam has been in Sweden: sixth in
maiden race at Wolverhampton in October (beaten only 2 lengths) and in
minor event at Leicester in November. *N. Guest.*

HUNTSMAN'S LEAP 3 ch.c. Welsh Pageant 132–Sunsuit 116 (Alycidon 138) **92**
[1975 5g⁶ 6h* 7.2fg⁵ 7g³ 8g 7fg 1976 7fg³ 7fg⁶ 7s 8g⁶ 8f* 8f* 8fg³] good-looking
colt: successful in minor events at Wolverhampton and Brighton in the summer:
made all when beating Mountain Rescue ½ length on latter course in August:
took on much stronger company when well-beaten third of six to Fluellen in
Greenhead Stakes at Newcastle later in month: not seen out again: should stay
1¼m+: acts on hard ground and is evidently unsuited by soft. *J. Winter.*

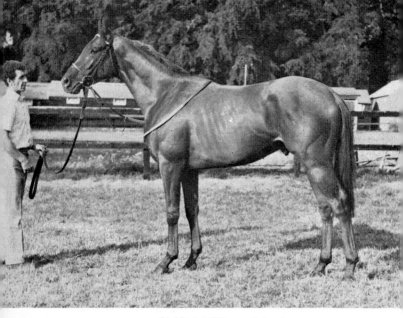

Lord Derby's "Huntsman's Leap"

HUNT THE GUN   3 ch.c. Royal Gunner–Brave Huntress (Big Game)   [1975   **65**
5v 7.6g 6g   1976 10g⁶ 8.5fg 12fg⁴ 10.1f⁴ 10fg 10.1fg² 12g]   plating-class maiden:
suited by middle distances: blinkered last two outings: exported to U.S.A.
D. Hanley.

HURRY ON HOSTESS   3 gr.f. St Alphage 119–Nice Hostess (Nice Guy 123)   **68**
[1975 5s 5s² 5f* 5g³ 6fg 5g⁵ 5f   1976 5v³ 5h⁴ 5fg 5g² 5f³ 6fg 5fg³ 5f⁵ 5f⁶ 5fg]
quite a modest handicapper: best form at 5f: acts on any going: suitable mount
for an apprentice: sometimes wears blinkers. *E. Collingwood.*

HURRY ROUND   6 b.h. Farm Walk 111–Phantom Star 119 (Persian Gulf)   —
[1974 N.R.   1975 N.R.   1976 12fg⁶ 10f 12f⁴ 12f² 8fg³ 10h⁵]   quite a moderate
handicapper: narrowly beaten by Franc Flinders in amateur riders event at
Beverley in July, the pair finishing well clear of six others: well-beaten third to
easy winner Dominion in minor event at York later in month: stayed 1½m: acted
on firm going: dead. *J. Calvert.*

HUSSEINIA   2 ch.c. King's Company 124–Purlane (Kashmir II 125)   [1976 5f   **63**
6f 6g 7s 7s² 8.2v]   first foal: dam seemed to need long distances: modest plater:
stays 7f but possibly not 1m: blinkered last two outings. *J. Sutcliffe.*

HUTNAGE   3 ch.c. Lorenzaccio 130–Quaker Girl 94 (Whistler 129)   [1975 5f   **67**
6fg 5.8f²   1976 8f 8fg⁵ 7fg⁵ 7fg* 7h² 7f³ 8.2fg⁵ 8.3f³ 8s]   workmanlike colt: led
close home when winning handicap at Leicester in June by a neck from Pam's
Gleam: probably stays 1m: possibly needs a sound surface, and acts on hard
ground: ran creditably in blinkers on third outing: sold 4,000 gns Newmarket
Autumn Sales. *F. Maxwell.*

HUTTON BARNS   2 ch.f. Saintly Song 128–My Song 85 (Songedor 116)   [1976   **92**
5fg⁶ 5g² 5f* 5f² 5d²]   small filly: third foal: dam, best at 5f, is
half-sister to Chebs Lad and Reet Lass: showed improved form when running
out 4-length winner of maiden race at Catterick in August: runner-up in minor
events afterwards, going down by a length to Imperial Jade at Thirsk and by
¾ length to Hedge School at Haydock: should stay 6f: best form on top-of-the-
ground conditions. *W. Haigh.*

338

HYDROGRAPHIC 3 ch.c. Quayside 124–Belle of Rannoch 73 (Golden Cloud) **77**
[1975 6fg 7fg 7g 8.2g⁵ 6g 6g⁴ 5v 1976 10s³ 8h³ 12d⁵ 11g* 9f⁵ 11f² 11g² 13.8f³
10.4fg 10g² 10.6d² 10v] strong, compact colt: favourite, won maiden race at
Edinburgh in June by ½ length from Tilton Boy: runner-up in four handicaps
afterwards, on final occasion going down by ¾ length to Bella Canto at Haydock
in October: probably needs further than 9f and stays at least 11f: evidently acts
on any going but is possibly best served by an easy surface: apprentice ridden
when successful. *Denys Smith.*

HYPERION GIRL 3 b.f. Royal Palm 131–Hyperion Lass (Punchinello 97) **—**
[1975 5.9fg² 7fg⁶ 7f 9g 1976 8f 12.2s⁶ 12v] strong filly: no worthwhile form
since first outing at 2 yrs. *W. Wharton.*

HYPERNAN 2 gr.c. Hopeful Venture 125–Pall Nan 86 (Pall Mall 132) [1976 **55**
5f 6f⁶ 6g 6f 6fg] robust, lengthy colt: only plating class: will be better suited
by 7f+. *K. Payne.*

HY TUDOR 6 b.m. Bounteous 125–Tudor Request 87 (Tudor Minstrel 144) **—**
[1974 10v 10s⁵ 1975 N.R. 1976 14fg⁶ 16f] poor plater: stays 1½m: acts on
firm going and a soft surface: has worn blinkers. *J. Hayward.*

HYVER HILL 2 ch.c. Porto Bello 118–Alydea (Alycidon 138) [1976 6fg⁶ 6fg⁵ **114**
6g* 7.2d² 6v*] strong, lengthy, good-looking colt: half-brother to several minor
winners: 5,200 gns yearling: dam never ran: winner of maiden race at Kempton
in August and £2,000 event at Leicester in October, putting up a really good effort
when holding off Our Jimmy by ¾ length in latter race, the pair finishing clear:
went down by 3 lengths to Godila in four-runner nursery at Haydock in between
when giving away lumps of weight: best form at 6f: acts on heavy ground.
R. Price.

I

IBZAN'S DAUGHTER 2 b.f. Tyrant–Bethlehem (Santa Claus 133) [1976 5s **—**
5v] second reported foal: sold twice as a yearling, for 400 gns and 1,200 gns:
dam never ran: well behind in seller at Haydock (missed break) and claiming
race at Leicester at end of season: sold 350 gns Ascot December Sales. *A.
Johnson.*

ICE KING 4 br.c. King Emperor–Anticham 98 (Chamossaire) [1974 6g 7.2g² **67**
7v 1975 8d 1976 11.7fg 10fg⁴ 10h⁴ 10.1f² 12g² 15.5h* 14g 12h²] workmanlike colt: won weakly-contested maiden race at Folkestone in August by 7
lengths from Derry Town: stays well: acts on hard going and is possibly unsuited
by heavy. *B. Hills.*

ICENA 2 ch.f. Jimmy Reppin 131–Boudicca 101 (Combat 123) [1976 6fg* **117**
6g 6fg*]
There was a Jekyll and Hyde look about Icena's first two runs. Her
first, at Newmarket in July, was full of promise. In the paddock we thought

*Lowther Stakes, York—Icena is followed on this side by the third horse Easy Landing,
whilst the runner-up Durtal is out of the picture on the far rails*

Icena a very attractive filly, big, lengthy and deep-bodied, but she also looked well short of peak fitness. That she was able to come through in the final furlong to win her race, a good-class maiden worth nearly £2,000 to the winner, appeared to show her a smart filly in the making. Her next outing, in the Princess Margaret Stakes at Ascot, was very much an anti-climax; she swerved badly left at the start, was never racing on an even keel, and came home last of eight behind Al Stanza. Forgive her for her lapse, though; greenness was probably its sole cause.

In the circumstances it was not surprising that Icena should start at 25/1 on her next outing, in the Lowther Stakes at York's August meeting. We mentioned in our commentary on Pasty in *Racehorses of 1975* that this race attracted disappointingly small fields towards the end of the 'sixties. In fact from 1967 to 1971 the race averaged only three runners a year. A change in the conditions raised the average to around seven runners over the next four years, but this was not entirely satisfactory and in 1976 the distance was altered from five furlongs to six. The upshot was thirteen runners, the largest field since Pourparler won in 1963, and the field included Al Stanza, Swagger and Great Flight, all of whom had finished well ahead of Icena at Ascot. Most fancied in the betting were the Cherry Hinton Stakes winner Ampulla, the Murless-trained filly Paddington who had won three of her four starts, the unbeaten Durtal and the consistent Easy Landing, who had been beaten only narrowly in both the Queen Mary Stakes and the National Stakes. By the time the Lowther was run the fact had not yet become apparent that horses racing on the stand side were at a disadvantage. All except Easy Landing and Icena came up the stand side, and it was clear some way out that this pair held the advantage. Easy Landing led inside the final furlong but she weakened quickly and Icena ran on strongly to win by half a length from Durtal, whose good finishing effort took her to the head of the stand-side group. Exactly how much Icena benefited from racing over towards the far rails we wouldn't like to guess, but we do consider Durtal a little unlucky not to have won. Nevertheless, this was a smart performance by Icena, one that suggested she would have had a big say in races such as the Argos Star Fillies' Mile in the autumn. Unfortunately a slight setback in training prevented her from running again.

			Djeddah
		Midsummer Night II (ch 1957)	Night Sound
	Jimmy Reppin (ch 1965)	Sweet Molly (ch 1958)	Chamier
Icena (ch.f. 1974)			Cockles and Mussels
		Combat (br 1944)	Big Game
	Boudicca (br 1959)		Commotion
		Bronze Vixen (ch 1941)	Donatello II
			Silver Fox II

Icena's sire, Jimmy Reppin, hasn't had the standard of mares at stud that his racing record deserved; he was a top-class horse both at three and four years. He hasn't done at all badly though, siring other good fillies in Joking Apart and the French One Thousand Guineas third Curtain Bow, as well as the Spillers Stewards' Cup winner Jimmy The Singer. Jimmy Reppin was at his best at around a mile, but there is a good deal of stamina in the bottom half of Icena's pedigree. Her dam, the useful winner Boudicca, was better suited by a mile and a half than shorter trips, and she is a sister to Bronzamazon who needed at least that distance. The best of Boudicca's four previous winners were In Command (by the six-furlong to one-mile horse March Past), who showed smart form over middle distances, and Relentless, who was a useful performer at up to a mile and a half although his sire was the miler Ratification. The grandam, Bronze Vixen, was a sister to the useful stayer Good Company and to Donah, the dam of the top-class stayer Donald and the tough long-distance horse Cunningham. Oncidium, Sleeping Partner and Falkland all come from this family and we expect Icena to be well suited by middle distances at three years. She has the physical scope to make an even better three-year-old and she may well develop into a leading Oaks candidate. We hardly need add that her connections secured a bargain when they bought her for 5,400 guineas as a yearling. *H. T. Jones.*

ICICA 3 b.g. Frankincense 120–Sandby 81 (Klairon 131) [1975 6g 5g* 6h* **77 d**
6f³ 6s 1976 8f⁶ 7g 5s⁴ 6h³ 6g⁶ 6h⁴ 7g⁵ 9h 6g] quite useful at 2 yrs: became
disappointing in 1976 and descended to selling company on final outing: should
stay 1m: acts on hard ground and may be unsuited by soft: sold to J. Fitzgerald
580 gns Doncaster October Sales. *N. Angus.*

ICING 3 b.f. Prince Tenderfoot 126–Cake (Never Say Die 137) [1975 5g⁴ 5f* **98**
6f* 7f* 8d* 1976 7f² 8fg 10f 6.3g] neat, attractive filly: one of best of 1975
staying 2-y-o fillies and won Argos Star Fillies' Mile at Ascot: 2 lengths second
to Gilding in Ascot 1,000 Guineas Trial and twelfth of 25 to Flying Water in
1,000 Guineas at Newmarket, both in April: off course two months afterwards
and ran below her best, including when blinkered on third outing, on her return:
should stay further than 1m: appears to act on any going. *P. Prendergast,
Ireland.*

ICKYBOK 4 ch.f. Canadel II 126–Ganga (Sallymount 125) [1974 5f 5h 5h 7d —
1975 N.R. 1976 12.2f 8fg] of little account. *N. Guest.*

IDENTITY 2 gr.f. Roan Rocket 128–Idover 95 (Fortino II 120) [1976 7fg **83**
9fg*] half-sister to fair 1973 2-y-o 1m winner Great Somerford (by Right Royal
V) and to a winner in Italy: dam a sprinter: led some way out when winning
20-runner maiden race at Wolverhampton in September by 4 lengths from
Downstairs: stays better than her pedigree might suggest. *E. Weymes.*

IDLE GENIUS 3 br.g. Welsh Abbot 131–Sing Saucey (Hard Sauce 131) [1975 —
5g 5f⁶ 5g 6g 1976 6fg 5fg⁶ 8g⁶ 6g⁶ 8.2s 8s 6v] leggy gelding: poor plater:
blinkered final outing (slowly away and swerved right soon after start). *A.
Jarvis.*

I DON'T MIND 2 b.f. Swing Easy 126–Va Beni (Infatuation 129) [1976 5f* **78**
5fg 5d⁴ 5v⁴] well-grown filly: half-sister to three minor winners: 520 gns
yearling: dam won over 1¼m in Ireland: well backed, won seller at Beverley in
June easing up by 5 lengths from Victoria Blue Boy and was so impressive that
she cost 3,700 gns to buy in: off course some time afterwards and was not disgraced in minor events at Haydock and Leicester after her return: will stay 6f:
appears to act on any going. *J. Berry.*

IGLOO FIRE 3 ch.g. Firestreak 125–Igloo Maid (Arctic Slave 116) [1975 7f **81**
5f 6fg 6g* 7.2d 7.2v 1976 7f 8d² 9.4h* 10f³ 12fg⁴ 12s³] well-grown gelding:
moderate handicapper: won at Carlisle in July by ½ length from Shy Meld: ran

Mrs V. Hue-Williams' "Illustrious Prince"

well afterwards, especially when 2 lengths third to Fairman at Edinburgh in October on final outing: stays 1½m well: acts on any going: often sweats up. *W. A. Stephenson.*

ILLUSTRIOUS PRINCE 3 b.c. Le Levanstell 122–Royal Saint 117 (Saint **115** Crespin III 132) [1975 N.R. 1976 8fg² 10.5s* 12g 12fg 12g² 12v³] lengthy colt: half-brother to fair 1¼m winner William The Red (by Relko) and fairly useful middle-distance performer Holy Prince (by Ballymoss): dam, a miler, is sister to Altesse Royale: created a very favourable impression early in season and won 15-runner Glasgow Stakes at York in May going away by 5 lengths from Navigator: well beaten next two races, Epsom Derby (reportedly stumped up after finishing eighteenth of 23) and Great Voltigeur Stakes at York (last of seven), but confirmed himself a good horse, gaining a place in Cumberland Lodge Stakes at Ascot (second to impressive winner Bruni) and St Simon Stakes at Newbury (staying-on third to Mart Lane) in the autumn: will be suited by further than 1½m: seems to act on any going: should make up into a very smart 4-y-o. *P. Walwyn.*

IL MAGNIFICO 5 ch.h. Supreme Sovereign 119–Villa Medici 82 (Panorama) **78** [1974 5g 6fg⁵ 7.6g⁵ 6fg⁵ 6f² 6g³ 7fg* 7fg 6d 7.6v 1975 7.6f² 8f 7fg⁵ 8h⁵ 7.6g³ 10.6s⁵ 1976 7.6fg⁵ 7g⁵ 8g⁶ 7fg* 8fg⁶ 10g⁴ 10.4fg³ 10d*] well-made horse: quite a moderate handicapper: narrow winner of 18-runner seller at Sandown in June (no bid): subsequently ran well in ladies races and won one at Newbury in September: stays 1¼m: appears to act on any going: has been tried in blinkers but has done better without them: trained by G. Harwood until after sixth outing. *C. Tinkler.*

IL PADRONE 3 b.c. St Paddy 133–Ragirl (Ragusa 137) [1975 7fg³ 1976 **105** 10f* 12fg⁵ 12fg⁶ 12g 10.5fg⁵ 10fg* 10d 10g³ 12s] fine, big, good-looking colt: good mover: won early-season maiden race at Nottingham and Extel Handicap at Goodwood in July: came from some way back in latter race, and held off Kafue Park by a head in a driving finish: third to Partridge Brook in £2,400 event at Ascot in September (hung right and found little under pressure after looking likely winner when taking up running 2f out): probably stays 1½m: acts on firm going and is possibly unsuited by soft: seems well suited by waiting tactics. *J. Sutcliffe.*

IL RUFFINO 3 br.c. Prince Regent 129–Maragay 65 (Match III 135) [1975 5g* **65** 6f⁶ 6s⁴ 7g 1976 10fg 7g⁵ 8h 8.2fg⁵ 6h⁶ 6g⁵ 7g 8fg² 10s⁴ 8g 8s 7v] quite a modest handicapper: probably needs further than 6f and should stay at least 1¼m: appears to act on any going: often wears blinkers nowadays: inconsistent. *D. Sasse.*

IMARI 2 b.f. Welsh Saint 126–Till 85 (Hook Money 124) [1976 5h⁴ 5fg³ 5g* 6fg⁴ **75** 5fg² 5f 5g* 6g⁵ 5fg⁶] robust filly: third foal: half-sister to a winner in Norway: sold twice as a yearling, for 1,200 gns and 2,500 gns: dam won at 1m: won weakly-contested maiden race at Lanark in May and was bought in for 2,100 gns after winning sixth of eight seller at Sandown in September: stays 6f. *K. Payne.*

IMMATATION 2 b.f. Polyfoto 124–Pargio 77 (Parthia 132) [1976 5f 5g³ **?** 5d⁶ 5g⁶ 4g* 5g* 5d* 5g⁶ 6g 5d⁵ 4.5g⁴ 5g² 7.7v] French-foaled filly: first foal: dam placed over 7f and 10.8f: moderate plater in this country but won her first three races in France, namely a small race at Le Touquet and sellers at Maisons-Laffitte and Deauville: bought in for approximately £4,700 after last two wins: should stay 6f: wears blinkers: trained by D. Hanley on first five outings. *W. Gill, France.*

IMMORTAL KNIGHT 6 b.h. Midsummer Night II 117–Bollin Charlotte 79 **89** (Immortality) [1974 8s 8fg 8f⁶ 7fg⁵ 7.2g 7g⁴ 7g* 7.2s³ 8fg* 7g⁶ 8s⁵ 8.2s³ 9v* 1975 8d 10d² 8v² 8v* 1976 8g⁶ 10g² 8g 8.2g 8fg] neat horse: quite a useful handicapper: made only five appearances in 1976: ran really well on first two of them, finishing sixth of 26 to The Hertford in Irish Sweeps Lincoln at Doncaster in March and 1½ lengths second to Royal Match in Littlewoods Spring Cup at Liverpool the following month: stays 1¼m: acts on any going: genuine: wears a tongue strap: had a poor run on third start: off course nearly four months before fourth outing. *M. H. Easterby.*

IMPERIAL GUARD 2 b.c. Brigadier Gerard 144–Altesse Royale 126 (Saint **106** Crespin III 132) [1976 6g⁵ 7g⁴ 7s* 7v*] good-looking colt: second foal: half-brother to 1975 2-y-o 6f winner Pocket Hercules (by Baldric II): dam won 1,000 Guineas, Oaks and Irish Guinness Oaks and is half-sister to Yaroslav and Imperial Prince: won minor events at Sandown and Lingfield at the back-end, disputing lead all way when beating Tamanaco 3 lengths on firmer course and running on under hard driving to hold off Atlantic Bridge by a short head on latter: will stay middle distances: acts on heavy ground. *P. Walwyn.*

Extel Stakes, Goodwood—a near thing between Il Padrone and Kafue Park, with Brands Hatch, Trusted and The Tista next to finish

IMPERIALIST 3 ch.g. King Emperor–Daisy 92 (Abernant 142) [1975 7g 8g — 1976 10fg 12g 12.2fg³ 12s⁵] lengthy gelding: stays 1½m: ran moderately in blinkers on second outing: sold out of I. Balding's stable 1,300 gns Ascot July Sales after second start. *P. Mitchell.*

IMPERIAL JADE 2 b.c. Huntercombe 133–Dunmore Lass II 94 (Nashua) **98** [1976 5s 6f⁴ 5f 5f* 6g⁶] good sort: half-brother to two winners, namely 1972 2-y-o Exmoor Lass (by Exbury) and Dun Habit (by Habitat), successful at up to 1m: 12,000 gns yearling: dam won at up to 9f: 50/1, showed much improved form when winning quite well-contested six-runner minor event at Thirsk in September by a length from Hutton Barns: well-backed favourite when carrying a penalty in valuable nursery at Ayr later in month but didn't have a very good run and never got into race, finishing only sixth to Broon's Secret: best form at 5f but should be suited by further: acts on firm going. *M. W. Easterby.*

IMPERIAL MISS 2 b.f. Philip of Spain 126–Irish Queen (Hauban 132) [1976 **75** 5f* 5f² 6fg 5f³ 5.3h² 7g³ 6d⁶ 6s] small, lightly-made filly: first foal: 150 gns yearling: dam well beaten in three races: won four-runner seller at Warwick in April (bought in 420 gns): twice second in better company at Brighton afterwards: stays 7f: acts on hard ground. *R. Hannon.*

IMPORT 5 ch.h. Porto Bello 118–Immortelle (Never Say Die 137) [1974 8s³ 7d⁶ **127** 5fg² 6g² 5f⁴ 6g* 5f³ 6fg⁴ 6g 5s² 5.6d³ 5v⁶ 1975 6s⁵ 6g 5g 6fg³ 6f* 6fg⁴ 6f* 6d² 5.6g³ 6d² 5g² 1976 6fg³ 6d⁶ 6g* 6f* 6fg³ 6fg]

Import has replaced Highland Melody, who had to be put down in 1976, at the Hunsley House Stud at Little Weighton in Yorkshire. Import was a better sprinter than his predecessor, better by around a stone; he was a tip-top handicapper by the end of a four-year career in which he improved every season, and during that career he won two of the best sprint handicaps in the Calendar, the Wokingham at Royal Ascot and the Spillers' Stewards Cup at Goodwood.

	Porto Bello (ch 1965)	Floribunda (b 1958)	Princely Gift Astrentia
Import (ch.h. 1971)		Street Song (b 1956)	Le Lavandou Theme Song
	Immortelle (ch 1960)	Never Say Die (ch 1951)	Nasrullah Singing Grass
		Thunder (b 1952)	Hyperion Chenille

Import's best form in his last season left his best of previous years well behind, although earlier victories had included one from Polly Peachum in the Stewards Cup of 1975 and one of his earlier defeats, by Roman Warrior in the Burmah Castrol Ayr Gold Cup of the same year, had been by only the narrowest of margins. In May he won a handicap at Kempton under 9-3, in June he won the Wokingham Stakes under 9-4 and then he ran the race of his life in the July Cup at Newmarket. The July Cup is no handicap; it's a pattern race, one of the most important sprints in the country, but Import managed to take third place in a ten-horse field, ahead of Roman Warrior, Be Tuneful, Gentilhombre, Kala Shikari, Petipa, Hittite Glory and Gwent. He even had his head in front for a furlong from about two and a half furlongs out after being up with the leaders from the start, and at the finish he was within a length of the winner, Lochnager, and only a neck behind Three Legs. Import had only one outing afterwards. He appeared to hold a great chance of gaining another win in the Stewards' Cup,

Wokingham Stakes, Ascot—the blinkered Import continues Bill Wightman's fine record in big handicap sprints, beating Caljobo very gamely by a head

started a heavily-backed favourite under 9-4 and was turned out looking a picture. However, he finished only seventh of seventeen to Jimmy The Singer. From what this and later results at the meeting showed to be an unfavourable starting position, he led or disputed the lead until losing his place shortly after passing the two-furlong pole.

Import is by Porto Bello, the sire of Roman Warrior and the Queen Mary Stakes winner Cramond. Porto Bello was a precocious sprinter, and he is a strong influence for speed. Probably Import as a stallion will also be a strong influence for speed, although his dam comes from a high-class staying family. Immortelle, the dam, is a lightly-raced sister to the Irish Sweeps Derby runner-up Lionhearted; her grandam Chenille was the dam of Alcide and of Parthia's dam

Major H. S. Cayzer's "Import"

Lightning. Easily the best of Immortelle's five runners besides Import is the middle-distance handicapper Breeze Wagon (by Firestreak). Import ran his best races over six furlongs on a sound surface; he was ideally suited by six furlongs but he was capable of useful performances over five, and he acted on any going. A strong, muscular horse, he was an extremely good mover. Thoroughly genuine, he was best in blinkers and he wore them in nearly all of his races in his last two seasons. *W. Wightman.*

IMPULSORA 3 b.f. Royal Palace 131–Belle Sicambre 120 (Sicambre 135) **73**
[1975 N.R. 1976 7f 10g 13.3fg⁴ 16h² 13g* 17.1h⁶ 16f] lengthy filly: sister to very useful French middle-distance winner Royal Empire and half-sister to two winners, including good-class middle-distance horse Belbury (by Exbury): dam won French Oaks: favourite, won maiden race at Nottingham in July by a head from Foxhunt: ran only twice afterwards, running well on first occasion but moderately on second: suited by a test of stamina: acted on hard ground: stud. *P. Walwyn.*

INCANDESCENCE 4 ch.c. Frankincense 120–Strawberry Moon 97 (Midsummer —
Night II 117) [1974 6fg 8s* 8v⁴ 1975 9fg 8f 11g² 10g* 10f³ 10fg⁵ 10d* 12v 1976 12s] strong, rangy colt: quite useful at 3 yrs: last of 10 to Grey Aglow in handicap at Doncaster in October: stays 11f: acts on any going: ran moderately when tried in blinkers on final outing at 3 yrs. *E. Weymes.*

INCA PRINCE 3 b.c. Kibenka 119–Coya 57 (Lauso) [1975 N.R. 1976 8fg 10fg⁵ **67**
11.5d⁴ 10.2s] first foal: dam a middle-distance plater: showed a little ability in maiden company: will stay 1½m: changed hands 420 gns Doncaster October Sales. *W. Stephenson.*

INCA PRINCESS 2 b.f. Incas 88–War Shore (Warrens Pride 81) [1976 5fg —
5fg 5f 5g 7f] useless. *M. Tate.*

INCHMARLO 3 ch.f. Nashua–Cherryville (Correspondent) [1975 6f* 6fg² 8g⁵ —
1976 10fg] attractive American-bred filly: won Virginia Water Stakes at Ascot in July, 1975, in style of a useful filly: did not look particularly well when ninth of 10 (made running until headed inside last 2f) behind Spiranthes in Pretty Polly Stakes at Newmarket in April, only outing: should stay 1¼m: exported by B.B.A. to New Zealand. *P. Walwyn.*

INDEX 3 ch.f. Busted 134–Miss Glen 107 (Abernant 142) [1976 6g⁶ 7fg² 1976 **72**
10fg* 10g⁶ 12fg⁵] rangy filly: won 12-runner maiden race at Kempton in April in good style by 3 lengths from Leventis: not seen out after June: stays 1¼m but possibly not 1½m: acts on a firm surface. *H. Candy.*

INDIAN CAPTIVE 5 b.g. Manacle 123–Hot Curry (Sayajirao 132) [1974 —
N.R. 1975 N.R. 1976 7fg 10fg⁶] moderate performer (rated 83) at 2 yrs: well beaten in two races at Yarmouth since. *P. Robinson.*

INDIANIRA 4 br.c. Chieftain–Foxie Walker (Olympia) [1974 won one race **94**
from three starts in U.S.A. 1975 6g 1976 6f 8f 7g* 7g⁵ 6fg* 6g² 8g* 6fg* 8fg⁴ 6g² 6g* 6f* 7g⁴ 6d⁴] strong, good-looking American-bred colt: came on by leaps and bounds after winning seller at Lanark in May (bought in 4,200 gns) and gained five further successes in handicaps, including three at Newcastle: heavily-backed favourite, defied a penalty in very comfortable style when gaining his final victory, beating My Chopin 1½ lengths at Thirsk in September: effective at 6f and stays 1m well: acts on firm going: blinkered and bandaged behind at Lanark: dwelt start last appearance. *M. W. Easterby.*

INDIAN MARK 5 br.h. On Your Mark 125–Indian Music 82 (Dalesa 109) —
[1974 8s⁴ 6d 8g 7.3g⁴ 7g⁶ 7g* 7s 7s 7.6v 1975 8fg 10v⁴ 10s 10g* 10.5s 10fg⁵ 12f 10g³ 12f⁶ 11.7fg 1976 10g] neat horse: fair handicapper (rated 87) in 1975: made only one appearance at 5 yrs: best form at up to 1¼m on a sound surface: suitable mount for an apprentice. *J. Old.*

INDIAN MISTRESS 3 b.f. Sahib 114–Willing 77 (Wilwyn 129) [1975 5d 6fg —
6f³ 6fg⁶ 6f² 6g 6g⁴ 7g 1976 10.1fg 7fg 7g] lightly-made filly: fair plater at 2 yrs: well beaten in three outings in similar company in May: should stay 1m: blinkered last two starts in 1975 and final outing. *M. McCourt.*

INDIAN SOL 4 b.f. Sahib 114–Solvilium (Vilmorin) [1974 5fg 5g 5g 6s 5.9s* —
1975 6f 7fg 6fg 8fg 1976 7fg 6f⁴] rangy filly: little worthwhile form since winning maiden race in 1974: stays 6f: acts on soft going. *L. Hall.*

INDIAN STREAK 2 ch.g. Maystreak 118–Indian Sing 69 (Seminole II) [1976 —
5f 5fg 7f] lightly-built gelding: bad plater: sold 260 gns Doncaster October Sales. *M. H. Easterby.*

INDIAN TEA 4 br.f. Taj Dewan 128–Tea Break 102 (Ballymoss **136**) [1974 —
N.R. 1975 11.5f 12.2g⁵ 12g 1976 13g⁶ 15.5s] poor maiden: evidently needs
long distances. *J. Haine.*

INDIAN WARRIOR 3 gr.c. Sing Sing 134–Intent 102 (Vilmorin) [1975 N.R. **91**
1976 5g⁶ 6g* 7g² 7g⁴ 7h* 8h* 7fg⁴ 8g* 8g⁵ 8s⁶ 8s²] lengthy colt: brother to
top-class sprinter Song and half-brother to several other winners, including very
useful 6f to 1m performer Ifni (by Petingo): dam a sprinter: had a successful
season and won at Ayr (maiden race), Bath (twice, handicap and apprentice
event) and Kempton (handicap): put up a particularly good effort on last-named
course in August when making all and holding on narrowly from Oriental Star:
stayed 1m: acted on any going: sold 18,000 gns Newmarket December Sales,
and is at stud in Victoria. *P. Walwyn.*

INDISCREET 4 b.f. Stupendous–Past Folly 90 (Narrator **127**) [1974 N.R.
1975 N.R. 1976 12fg] big, rangy filly: half-sister to four winners, including
fair French stayer Bravado (by Aggressor): dam middle-distance performer:
bandaged in front, finished ninth of 11 in maiden race won by Saragusa at
Kempton in April, only outing. *H. Smyth.*

INDUSTRIOUS 3 b.f. Bold Lad (Ire) 133–Export 81 (Exbury **138**) [1975 5g³ **69**
5.9f² 1976 8fg⁵ 10f] neat, attractive filly: has ability but was not seen out after
May: should stay 1¼m: sold 8,200 gns Newmarket December Sales. *R. Hern.*

INFRA GREEN 4 ch.f. Laser Light 118–Greenback II (Fric **128**) [1974 6.3g **120**
5g 6s* 7.5s 7s 1975 8v⁴ 9g* 10.5d⁶ 8fg² 10g* 8d* 10.5g² 9.2s⁶ 1976 10fg³ 10.5g*
12g⁵ 10s⁵ 12s 12v*]
   The Prix Ganay, run at Longchamp in May, is the most valuable race in
Europe in the first part of the season for horses above the age of three; in 1976
it carried a first prize of £46,620, more than double that for its English counterpart, the Coronation Cup. Just how hard a race the Prix Ganay is to win can be
judged from the quality of the horses that have been successful in it in the past
fifteen years—Javelot, Misti IV, Exbury, Relko, Free Ride, Diatome, Behistoun,
Taj Dewan, Carmarthen, Grandier, Caro, Mill Reef, Rheingold and Allez France,
in that order. Allez France won the race in successive years.
   Though Infra Green falls a long way short of matching up to the recent
Prix Ganay winners she was a worthy winner on the day, getting home in a
blanket finish from the front-running colt Kasteel and the two other fillies in the
field, Ivanjica and Rose Bowl. Ivanjica turned the tables on Infra Green in the
autumn, beating her in both the Prix du Prince d'Orange and the Prix de l'Arc de
Triomphe. In the Arc, won by Ivanjica, Infra Green was prominent all the way
and came home seventh of the twenty runners, about eight lengths behind the
winner. In her only race afterwards Infra Green landed the odds in the Gran
Premio del Jockey Club, one of Italy's major international races, run at Milan in
October.
   We did not see the best of Infra Green on her only outing in this country.
She was struck into and damaged a fetlock in the Coronation Cup. The injury
put Infra Green on the easy list for several weeks and it was more than three
months before she ran again.

Infra Green (ch.f. 1972)	Laser Light (ch 1966)	Aureole (ch 1950)	Hyperion
			Angelola
		Ruby Laser (ch 1961)	Red God
			Dilly Dilly
	Greenback II (b 1967)	Fric (br 1952)	Vandale II
			Fripe
		Mrs Green (b 1960)	Honeyway
			Brilliant Green

   Infra Green has improved with age. As a two-year-old she won once from
five starts in Ireland and was given 7-10 in the Irish Free Handicap. In the next
season, when she was raced in France, she developed into one of the leading
fillies of her age, winning the Prix Chloe, the Prix de Malleret and the Prix
d'Astarte, all important events for three-year-old fillies. Infra Green is the
best horse sired by Laser Light who was retired to stud in Ireland in 1970.
Laser Light, the result of a union between a stayer and a sprinter, turned out to
be a sprinter pure and simple. Few of Laser Light's offspring stay beyond
a mile and a quarter, although, as one would expect with his pedigree, a
good proportion of them possess more stamina than their sire. Infra Green's
dam Greenback II didn't race but she was stoutly bred, by the Coronation
Cup winner Fric out of the modest winning stayer Mrs Green. Mrs Green,
who raced only as a four-year-old, was very one paced and needed at least

Prix Ganay, Longchamp—a driving finish between Infra Green, Kasteel (No. 9), Ivanjica (hidden), Rose Bowl and Tip Moss (hidden)

a mile and a half. The third dam Brilliant Green was a very useful stayer as a three-year-old when she won the Gordon Stakes and the Jockey Club Stakes. She is the dam of that genuine and consistent stayer Gaberdine who was by the sprinter Abernant. Infra Green, an attractive filly, stays a mile and a half well and acts on any going. *E. Bartholomew, France.*

INGHAM 4 ch.g. Silver Shark 129–Australe (Sicambre 135) [1974 6g 8s⁴ 9g 1975 12v 10.1s 16f 10h* 10fg 1976 15.8g] lightly-made gelding: very slowly away only outing at 4 yrs (apprentice ridden): stays 1¼m but not 2m: acts on hard going: wears blinkers. *S. Nesbitt.* —

INGOLDSBY 2 ch.c. Tower Walk 130–Anona-Anona 73 (Alcide 136) [1976 5g 5fg 5fg 5d 7f 7f 7g] narrow, light-framed colt: poor maiden: wears blinkers: sold to Hbt Jones 440 gns Ascot October Sales. *G. Blum.* 55

IN HASTE 2 ch.c. Hotfoot 126–Caroline of York 55 (Saint Crespin III 132) [1976 6fg* 6fg* 7g* 7g] shapely colt: third foal: 1,300 gns yearling: dam a stayer: took on four very useful animals in £3,100 Heronslea Stakes at Ayr in August and put up a very good display, coming through smoothly to lead over 1f out and winning cleverly by a length from Taffytina, the pair finishing clear: had earlier won auction events at Newcastle: favourite for 10-runner Intercraft Solario Stakes at Sandown in September but could finish only eighth of 10 to Avgerinos after appearing to have every chance (subsequently reported to have pulled a muscle in hind-quarters): will stay 1¼m: very useful. *J. W. Watts.* 113

INISHLACKEN 2 b.c. Connaught 130–Jenny 99 (Red God 128 §) [1976 8s⁶ 8s⁶] half-brother to Irish 3-y-o Sea Lore (by Sea Hawk II), a fairly useful performer at 2 yrs: dam won at up to 7f in England and France: sixth in maiden race at Sandown (to Nordman) and £2,200 event at Doncaster (to Lucent) at end of season: will do better at 3 yrs. *I. Balding.* 76 p

INJUDICIOUS 4 b.f. Quorum 126–Wayward Damsel (Pay Up) [1974 5.8g 5fg 5.8s 5.8v 8v³ 1975 N.R. 1976 8fg 10f⁶ 11.7h⁴ 8f⁶ 8g* 8s⁵] poor handicapper: 33/1, showed first form for a long time when winning apprentice handicap at Ascot in September: ran respectably on only subsequent outing: best at 1m: suited by some give in the ground. *R. Turnell.* 67

INSOLVENT 3 ch.c. Busted 134–Julieta 108 (Ratification 129) [1975 8g 8f* 1976 10g⁵ 12fg⁶] strong colt: won 20-runner maiden race at Newmarket as a 2-y-o: ran creditably on both outings early in season, finishing fifth of seven (beaten 10 lengths) to Riboboy in Sandown Classic Trial and sixth of eight (beaten 8½ lengths) to Norfolk Air in Ladbroke Derby Trial at Lingfield: should stay 1½m. *Doug Smith.* 96

INTERMISSION 3 ch.f. Stage Door Johnny–Peace 113 (Klairon 131) [1975 N.R. 1976 7f² 12.3s⁴ 8fg* 8fg 8g* 9g*] 117

As a racemare Peace never managed to fulfil the immense promise she showed when cantering up in the Blue Seal Stakes on her only outing as a two-year-old but already she has more than atoned as a broodmare. Her first three foals, Peaceful (by Crepello), Quiet Fling (by Nijinsky) and Intermission (by Stage Door Johnny), were all racing in 1976 and between them they won eight races worth £64,483. Peaceful developed into a very useful middle-distance stayer, his wins including the Vaux Gold Tankard and the Old Newton Cup; Quiet Fling won the John Porter Stakes and the Coronation Cup, and Intermission showed

Vernons Maiden Plate, York—Intermission romps home

herself a smart filly, ending her racing career with a win in the Irish Sweeps Cambridgeshire. Peace's two-year-old filly by Mill Reef, Quiet Harbour, didn't make the racecourse in 1976, but this is no surprise for Quiet Harbour split a pastern. She will be making a name for herself in 1977 if only breeding counts.

It was in the autumn that Intermission struck form with a vengeance. Before then her record was that of an improving, lightly-raced filly. She had trotted up from moderate opposition in the Vernons Maiden Plate at York, and finished a fair seventh to Duboff in the Child Stakes at Newmarket when ridden by an apprentice unable to claim his 5 lb allowance. Her only poor performance had been in the Cheshire Oaks, a race run over a mile and a half in testing conditions. In retrospect it seems reasonable to conclude that either she didn't stay the trip or was unsuited by the conditions. She ran as though she didn't stay. In August Intermission's trainer, Jeremy Tree, found himself unable to

Irish Sweeps Cambridgeshire Handicap, Newmarket—Intermission holds off the fast-finishing The Hertford (checks) by a short head, with Fluellen a close third

train her on the rock-hard Beckhampton gallops, and along with Bright Finish she was sent to Michael Stoute at Newmarket, to work on the all-weather gallop. The move paid handsome dividends. When Intermission turned out for the Taylor Woodrow Charity Handicap at Ascot in September she looked very well, perfectly fit despite her eleven-week absence from the racecourse, and after cruising smoothly into the lead just under two furlongs out she went on to win very easily indeed by three lengths from Heaven Knows, from whom she was receiving 10 lb. A 7 lb penalty brought Intermission's weight up to 8-6 in the Irish Sweeps Cambridgeshire, the same weight as that carried by Lacquer, the last three-year-old filly to win the Cambridgeshire. Intermission came to the front of the twenty-nine-runner field two furlongs out and looked sure to win decisively, but after mastering Fluellen she had to call on her last reserves of courage to repel The Hertford's late challenge. Following a stewards' inquiry the placings remained unaltered and Intermission retired to stud with the valuable prize that her tenacity surely deserved.

By the American stallion Stage Door Johnny, normally a strong influence for stamina, Intermission apparently stayed nowhere near so well as her half-brothers Peaceful and Quiet Fling. Her strong suit was her speed and in the Cambridgeshire it looked very much as though nine furlongs was the limit of her stamina. A neat, attractive filly, she acted on firm going. Intermission should make another excellent broodmare for her owner. She visits Nonoalco. *M. Stoute.*

INTERPATAN 2 b.f. Communication 119–Spearley (Dairialatan 111) [1976 **67** 6s³ 5s 6v] first produce: dam ran over hurdles while carrying this foal: 1¾ lengths third of nine to Liberty Lass in seller at Goodwood in September, first and best effort: will stay 7f. *O. O'Neill.*

INTO HARBOUR 3 gr.f. Right Tack 131–Headland (Sovereign Path 125) — [1975 N.R. 1976 7fg 7fg⁴ 5fg] attractive, stocky filly: half-sister to two winners in Ireland: 1,200 gns yearling: dam won over 1m in Ireland: plating-class maiden. *G. Pritchard-Gordon.*

INTORENO 2 br.f. Inclination 96–Silver Palace 53 (Martial 131) [1976 5g 7f — 6h⁵] close-coupled filly: in rear on all outings, finishing tailed-off last in maiden race on final appearance. *D. Dale.*

INTOXICATED 2 ch.c. Caruso 112–Well Laced (Devonian) [1976 5g 7v³ 7s⁵ 5s⁴ **82** 6s⁴] short-backed colt: half-brother to a winning chaser: dam an Irish hunter chaser: moderate maiden: better at 6f and 7f than 5f and will stay 1m: acts on heavy ground: trained part of season by H. Nicholson. *S. Holland.*

INVENTORY 8 b.g. Royal Record II–Sonsa 115 (Hyperion) [1974 16g² 14fg — 16g* 16g 16s⁴ 16g 16g² 16d² 14s⁴ 16d* 16v² 1975 16d² 14fg⁵ 16fg⁶ 16g⁵ 14fg 16g 16d* 14g⁴ 16d² 14g 1976 16fg⁵ 14g 16d] fairly useful handicapper (rated 92) in 1975, but is inconsistent and none too generous nowadays: stays well: acts on any going but is best on an easy surface: usually wears blinkers but has run creditably without: sold to M. Salaman 800 gns Newmarket Autumn Sales. *G. Smyth.*

INVERGAYLE 4 ch.c. Lord Gayle 124–Invermore (Anwar 120) [1974 7g 8s³ — 8d⁵ 1975 12.2v⁵ 12s* 12g³ 10d³ 10g⁴ 10g⁵ 12h³ 13g⁴ 16g 16g 1976 12f⁵] well-made colt: good walker and mover: has been hobdayed: well beaten only appearance on flat in 1976: well suited by 1½m or more: acts on any going: wears blinkers nowadays but hasn't shown his best form in them: sold to J. Old 1,750 gns Newmarket Autumn Sales. *H. T. Jones.*

IOLE 3 b.f. Alcide 136–Spree 117 (Rockefella) [1975 N.R. 1976 10g] small — filly: sister to quite useful middle-distance performer Algarve and half-sister to three other winners here and abroad: dam finished second in 1963 1,000 Guineas and Oaks: 25/1 when in rear in 21-runner maiden race won by Lamb's Tale at Sandown in April, only outing: exported by B.B.A. to Australia. *J. Tree.*

ION

IONA 3 b.f. Kalydon 122–Island Woman 76 (King's Troop 118) [1975 6f⁴ 8g⁶ **92** 1976 14fg* 12fg⁶ 12fg³ 14fg* 14g 16g] strong, good-bodied filly: put up a most impressive performance when winning Melrose Handicap at York in August, quickening to go clear 2f out and winning easing up by 5 lengths from Rowe Residence: had earlier trotted up in a slowly-run maiden race at Yarmouth: suited by a good test of stamina: acts on a firm surface. *J. Hindley.*

IPPOLYTI 3 b.f. Derring-Do 131–Sandfly (French Beige 127) [1975 5fg* 5f* **97** 7g* 7fg* 1976 8g⁴ 10fg⁴ 10g* 10fg 12fg] lightly-made, strong-quartered filly: showed useful form at 2 yrs when unbeaten in four starts: showed herself nearly as good in 1976 and won five-runner handicap at Newbury in July by 2 lengths from Honeypot Lane, staying on really strongly: gave impression she would have been suited by further than 1¼m but did not run up to her best when tried at 1½m (attempted to make all): acted on firm going: stud. *P. Walwyn.*

IRENE'S GIRL 3 br.f. Swing Easy 126–Viota 86 (Klairon 131) [1975 7fg 7d³ **—** 7d⁶ 8g* 7.6s³ 1976 8.5fg⁶ 10g 16fg] rangy filly: won maiden race at Bath at 2 yrs: no worthwhile form in 1976 and ran badly over 2m on final appearance: dead. *R. Smyth.*

IRISH CLOVER 3 b.f. John Splendid 116–Shamrock's Beauty 79 (Primera 131) **—** [1975 N.R. 1976 8f 8f 8fg 7s] last in all her races, including a Brighton seller. *G. Balding.*

IRISH GIRL 2 b.f. Sallust 134–Glad One 111 (Milesian 125) [1976 7fg³ 7.5s*] **87 p** Irish filly: half-sister to two middle-distance winners by Ballymoss: 8,400 gns foal: dam, daughter of top-class stayer Gladness, was placed in Irish 1,000 Guineas, Epsom Oaks and Irish Guinness Oaks: fulfilled promise of a good debut run, when third to Marinsky in newcomers event at the Curragh, by winning 17-runner maiden race at Punchestown in October by 1½ lengths from Dream World: will be suited by 1m or more: probably acts on any going. *J. Oxx, Ireland.*

IRISH HARMONY 5 br.h. Tudor Melody 129–Miss Ireland 83 (Grey Sovereign **89** 128 §) [1974 8fg 8f* 8f 8g⁵ 8g² 10d 1975 11v⁴ 10f* 8g⁴ 9d⁶ 8f⁴ 1976 11.1g* 10s⁴ 9g² 12.3fg³ 12.3f³] quite a useful handicapper: 20/1-winner of amateur riders race at Kempton in May, beating Doubleglow and Our Manny: ran respectably in most of his races afterwards: stayed 11f really well: acted on any going: sold as a stallion to Venezuela. *P. Rohan.*

IRISH MORN 3 br.g. Irish Ball 127–First Watch (Primera 131) [1975 8g 1976 **—** 12.5v 10s] sturdy gelding: well behind in maiden races at Teesside at the back end. *R. Lamb.*

IRISH MUSIC 3 b.g. Tudor Music 131–Petario (Golden Cloud) [1975 5d⁵ 7g² **63** 8g 8g³ 1976 8f 8fg] plating-class maiden: not seen out after June: stays 1m: blinkered final outing in 1975. *F. Carr.*

IRISH POET 2 ch.c. Allangrange 126–Christina Rossetti 102 (Monet 127) **—** [1976 8s] big colt: half-brother to two winners, including smart miler My Drifter (by Le Levanstell): 3,000 gns foal, resold 3,900 gns yearling: dam won over 5f at 2 yrs: unquoted when tailed off in 27-runner maiden race won by Sporting Yankee at Newmarket in October. *B. Lunness.*

IRISH PRINCE 3 b.c. Irish Ball 127–Miss Jessica 90 (Milesian 125) [1975 **70** 5f⁴ 5g³ 6g 5g 1976 12.5g³ 12.3s⁶ 12f² 10f² 12g 11s⁵ 9.4h* 10f⁶ 8fg 12f] neat colt: all out when winning six-runner maiden race at Carlisle in June by 1½ lengths from Brag: effective at 9f and stays 1½m: needs a sound surface, and acts on hard ground: blinkered second and fourth outings in 1975: sold 1,200 gns Doncaster October Sales. *E. Collingwood.*

IRONBRIDGE 3 gr.g. Grisaille 115–Seven Sisters 88 (Supreme Court 135) **48** [1975 5g⁶ 5d⁴ 5g³ 7f 7g⁶ 6fg 7f 6d 1976 7g 6fg⁶ 7fg⁶ 8d³ 9f⁶ 10.4fg 9fg² 10s 10d⁶ 8s⁴ 15.8s² 10v²] poor plater: stays 2m: appears to act on any going: often wears blinkers: sometimes starts slowly. *M. Bradley.*

IRON DUKE 3 b.c. Sicambre 136–Insulaire (Aureole 132) [1975 7v⁴ 7.5s* 7.7s⁴ **122** 1976 10.5s 9g² 10.5g* 10g* 11d⁴ 10v* 12.5v⁶] French colt: first foal: 85,000 francs (approx £7,300) yearling: dam showed very useful form in France at up to 1½m: an improving sort who won three races, minor event at Maisons-Laffitte and two Group 3 events, Prix de la Cote Normande at Deauville in August (by 1½ lengths from Cheraw) and La Coupe de Maisons-Laffitte the following month (by a length from Twig): not disgraced when about 7 lengths fourth to Youth in Prix Niel at Longchamp in between: best form at 1¼m but should stay 1½m: acts on heavy ground. *F. Palmer, France.*

IRONY 2 ch.c. Crowned Prince 128–Diamond Spur (Preciptic 122) [1976 5d³ **105** 5g* 6.3g² 7g³ 8d³] Irish colt: half-brother to top-class miler Sparkler (by Hard Tack): 14,500 gns yearling: dam ran four times in Ireland: odds on, won 12-runner event at Naas in May by ¾ length from Ring Leader: off course some time afterwards but ran well on return, gaining places in Anglesey Stakes (length second to Readjust), Larkspur Stakes (4 lengths behind The Minstrel) and Beresford Stakes (4½ lengths behind Orchestra): stays 1m: exported to U.S.A. *P. Prendergast, Ireland.*

ISEULT 4 ch.f. Songedor 116–Peggy Jones 91 (Davy Jones) [1974 N.R. 1975 — 13g 12.2g³ 12g 1976 12fg 16fg⁶ 12f 12g] slow maiden. *F. Dever.*

ISLAND DEGREE 3 br.f. Hawaii–Double Laureate (Double Jay) [1975 7g* **100** 7g³ 7d⁶ 7f 1976 10.2f* 12.3s³ 12g 12fg⁴ 10fg⁵ 10fg⁵ 8g² 8g²] American-bred filly: raced mainly in high-class fillies races after easily landing odds in three-runner minor event at Bath in April and put up an excellent performance when just over 3 lengths fifth of ten behind Roussalka in Nassau Stakes at Goodwood in July: runner-up in Strensall Stakes at York (to Sauceboat) and Devonshire Stakes at Doncaster (to Welsh Flame) in September: effective at 1m but is probably better suited by middle distances: acts on firm going: racing in U.S.A. *B. Hills.*

ISLAND MIST 3 b.g. Foggy Bell 108–Dry Island 73 (Miralgo 130) [1975 5g **79** 6f 7g³ 8fg⁵ 8s 1976 12g* 10.5fg 12f⁴ 10f²] well-grown maiden: won 14-runner maiden race at Lanark in May by 2½ lengths from Schoolhouse Dale: chased home easy winner Soudno in minor event at Lanark in September (first run since June): stays 1½m well: sold 5,500 gns Doncaster September Sales. *W. Haigh.*

ISLAND STAR 3 b.g. Kalimnos 94–Barney's Star 71 (Doubtless II 111) [1975 — N.R. 1976 10fg 10.2fg 8f] evidently of no account although has yet to race in a seller. *G. Wallace.*

ISLE OF MAY 3 br.f. Decoy Boy 129–Shining Rock 88 (Rockefella) [1975 — N.R. 1976 12.2s 8s 12s] half-sister to winning platers by Tycoon II and Silver Cloud: dam stayed 1m: well beaten in end-of-season maiden races. *Dr A. Jones.*

ISOBEL'S CHOICE 2 ch.f. Green God 128–Philistia (Palestine 133) [1976 5f **58** 5f 5fg* 6f 5fg 6d 6v 6v 5v⁵] lengthy filly: plater: attracted no bid after beating sole opponent Red Tune at Leicester in June: form only at 5f. *R. Hollinshead.*

ISOLATE 3 br.c. Sir Ivor 135–Incommunicado (Double Jay) [1975 7g² 7g² 8g* **89** 1976 12fg⁴ 8g⁴ 10.6g⁶ 10g³ 10d 10s 10.8s] neat American-bred colt: good walker: very good 2 lengths second to Arapaho in £1,700 minor event at Sandown in September but hung badly right under pressure, hampering third horse and was put down a place after a stewards inquiry: will probably stay further than 1¼m (had very stiff task when tried at 1½m): possibly not at his best on softish ground: ran badly in ladies race on fifth appearance when blinkered first time: again blinkered on last two outings, on both occasions being pulled up, reportedly having injured himself: one to be wary of. *P. Walwyn.*

ISOMER 4 ch.f. Runnymede 123–Primeapple (Primera 131) [1974 5f⁶ 1975 **43** 8f 8h 6fg³ 5h² 6fg³ 6fg² 5f² 6s⁴ 6f* 6s⁴ 5g 1976 7g* 7fg 6g 7g 7f] lengthy filly: selling handicapper: narrow winner at Catterick in March: bought out of R. Carter's stable 950 gns afterwards: stays 7f: acts on any going: sweated up final appearance. *S. Nesbitt.*

IT MUST BE HIM 5 b.h. Aberdeen 109–Bridge of Clyde 96 (Falls of Clyde 126) **60** [1974 6g³ 7f² 5g 6g⁴ 5fg² 6g* 5g⁶ 5.8v 6d 6s² 1975 6f 5.1f 6f⁶ 8.2g 6f 5g 6g 1976 6fg⁶ 5g 5f 5g³ 5s⁴ 6v] big, robust horse: finished well when in frame in handicaps at Catterick in September (third to What A Picture) and Warwick the following month (close fourth to Offa's Mead): stays 7f: acts on any going: blinkered last two outings in 1975. *N. Guest.*

IT'S BUBBLES 2 br.f. Golden Dipper 119–Suds 64 (Hardicanute 130) [1976 **76** 5f 5f 6fg 6f³ 7g² 8d² 8.2v⁵] small filly: first foal: dam placed over 5f and 7f at 2 yrs: runner-up in good-class sellers at Newmarket in September and October: stays 1m: suited by some give in the ground. *W. Marshall.*

IVAN 3 gr.c. Le Prince 98–Russia (Palestine 133) [1975 7g 7g 8s 1976 8.5fg — 8fg 10.1fg] compact ex-Irish colt: behind in maiden and minor events but was backward on first two outings: blinkered final appearance (May). *B. Swift.*

Prix du Prince d'Orange, Longchamp—Ivanjica trots up from Sea Sands

IVANJICA 4 b.f. Sir Ivor 135–Astuce (Vieux Manoir 132) [1974 8s* 8v⁶ 1975 **132** 9.5v³ 8g* 9.2g⁵ 10.5g* 12s* 12s 1976 10fg⁶ 10.5g³ 9.7d 9.2g² 10s* 12s* 12s³]
It took until the autumn for Ivanjica to recover her best form. Her performances in the early part of the season, although they included a third place in the Prix Ganay and a second in the Prix d'Ispahan, fell short of those which had earned her decisive wins as a three-year-old in the Poule d'Essai des Pouliches and the Prix Vermeille. In winning both of these races decisively, Ivanjica showed a highly impressive turn of finishing speed, cutting down her rivals in the straight after being waited with. Runner-up to her on each occasion was another excellent filly Nobiliary who finished second to Grundy in the Derby in between her clashes with Ivanjica and then went on to win the Washington International. Ivanjica and Nobiliary stood head and shoulders above the rest of the staying three-year-old fillies of their year and it was a surprise when neither managed to finish in the first five in the most important middle-distance race in Europe, the Prix de l'Arc de Triomphe. Ivanjica, who started second favourite for the Arc, finished in the middle of the field, behind her less-fancied stable companion Green Dancer and also beaten by Nobiliary. One of the reasons advanced in explanation of Ivanjica's failure in the Prix de l'Arc was that she had a disadvantageous draw on the outside of the field. We ourselves made it clear in *Racehorses of 1975* that we wouldn't dream of laying any of the blame for a horse's defeat in a race over a mile and a half on the draw. A lot of rubbish has been talked and written about the effect of the draw in the Prix de l'Arc de Triomphe and after the success in 1974 of Allez France (drawn fifteen of 20) and the victory in the latest running of the Arc of Ivanjica (drawn fourteen of 20) we hope we shall have heard the last of it.
Ivanjica was brought out fresh after a summer's rest and was an impressive winner of her only race before the Prix de l'Arc, the Prix du Prince d'Orange, an all-aged race run over a mile and a quarter at Longchamp in September, a fortnight before the big race. She sauntered through the small field in the straight to win very easily by four lengths and we formed the opinion there and then that she was a live candidate for the Prix de l'Arc. Our enthusiasm was dampened a little when we were told that some among her connections thought her inferior to Riverqueen, who had gone on to success against older horses in the Grand Prix de Saint-Cloud after following in Ivanjica's footsteps by winning the Poule d'Essai des Pouliches. On the day that Ivanjica won the Prix du Prince d'Orange Riverqueen failed badly in the Prix Vermeille. If Ivanjica was back to her best she had a good chance in the Arc, notwithstanding the fact that the field was first-rate. There were nine classic winners in the line-up, counting the Norwegian St Leger winner Noble Dancer, the others being Ivanjica and Riverqueen, the French Derby winner Youth, the St Leger winners Bruni, Crow and Exceller, and the Oaks winners Pawneese and Lagunette. Pawneese had won England's most important all-aged weight-for-age race, the King George VI and Queen Elizabeth Diamond Stakes, in addition to both the English and French Oaks. There were plenty more good horses, too, among the twenty runners.
The official weight-for-age scale was reviewed before the start of the 1976 flat season; the amended scale generally sets older horses to meet three-year-olds on terms a pound or two better than before. In the Prix de l'Arc the older horses met the three-year-olds on terms 2 lb better than twelve months earlier. The composition of the field was roughly the same as in 1975: there were ten three-year-olds, six four-year-olds, three five-year-olds and one six-year-old, the 1975 Arc runner-up On My Way. The three-year-olds Youth and Exceller, coupled for betting purposes, headed the pari-mutuel returns at 2/1 with the leading English four-year-old Bruni next best at 5/2. Crow and Pawneese, and Riverqueen and Ivanjica (both pairs coupled in the betting) were the only others

352

in the field to start at odds of less than 14/1. Pawneese, like Riverqueen, had run badly in the Prix Vermeille and the stable-jockey Saint-Martin chose to ride Crow in the Arc, being replaced on Pawneese by the English champion Eddery.

Pawneese and the outsider Kasteel broke quickly from the stalls and immediately went into the lead. Most of the best horses were kept near the front from the start but Ivanjica was brought sharply over from her outside draw to race against the rails behind the others. After a furlong she was last and she continued to hang back as Kasteel and Pawneese began to draw clear approaching halfway. At one time the leaders had an advantage of half a dozen lengths over Youth who headed the chasing group which included both Crow and Bruni. Coming down the hill towards the home turn the big lead set up by Pawneese and Kasteel was gradually whittled away, and although Pawneese was still in front at the entrance to the straight she was passed at once by Kasteel. With Youth, Crow and Bruni breathing down his neck, Kasteel wasn't good enough to hold on for long and Youth soon took over with Crow and Bruni at his quarters. Ivanjica, meanwhile, had had the immense good fortune coming down the hill to enjoy an uninterrupted run along the rails which had taken her into eighth place on the final bend, about four lengths behind the leaders. Crow's jockey decided to push on with a quarter of a mile to go and his mount quickly took the measure of Youth and Bruni, going a length up and looking for all the world like a winner. Then Ivanjica arrived on the scene full of running. She accelerated superbly to pass Youth and Bruni at the distance and then unleashed a brilliant finishing burst inside the last furlong to catch Crow and win going away by two lengths. Youth came third, three lengths behind Crow, followed by the strong-finishing Noble Dancer, who didn't have the best of runs, Bruni, and the French older horses Beau Buck and Infra Green. Then there was a five-length gap before the main body of the field crossed the line; tailed off were Exceller and one of the English challengers Dakota.

On the way back to the unsaddling enclosure Ivanjica shied at the photographers, deposited Head on the ground and galloped away down the course. Although Ivanjica collided with a plastic rail before being caught she suffered only superficial cuts on her flank and seemed none the worse for the escapade. Ivanjica's was a notable triumph for the Head family. For Alec Head it was the third time he had saddled an Arc winner, his previous successes being with Nuccio in 1952 and Saint Crespin III in 1959. For Freddie Head, son of the trainer, Ivanjica was a third winning ride in the Arc, following those on Bon Mot III and San San. Not surprisingly in so big a field, there were hard-luck stories about some of the losers. The ones with most validity seemed to be those concerning Noble Dancer and On My Way. Noble Dancer would undoubtedly have finished closer but for having to be checked and switched inside the last furlong to avoid running into the back of Youth; On My Way came back with a badly-twisted shoe.

On My Way, Ivanjica, Youth and Noble Dancer met again in the Washington International at Laurel in November. Since its inception in 1952 the Washington International has succeeded in attracting very few winners of the Prix de l'Arc de Triomphe and no horse has completed the double. The tight Laurel track, which is less than a mile round and has a run-in of only about a furlong and a half, has often been criticised as being an unsuitable test for a top middle-distance performer who has made his reputation on the broad acres of Longchamp. Connections of an Arc winner have everything to lose and little to gain by going to Laurel. So the appearance of Ivanjica in the field for the twenty-fifth Washington International was something of a scoop for the Laurel executive. For Ivanjica it was the first time she had raced at any track other than Longchamp. She started joint-favourite but was beaten into third place by Youth and On My Way. Nevertheless she was the first Arc winner to gain a

Prix de l'Arc de Triomphe, Longchamp—Ivanjica wins going away from Crow, Youth and the Norwegian challenger Noble Dancer

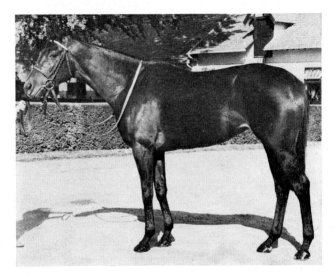

M J. Wertheimer's "Ivanjica"

place in the Washington International since Ballymoss in 1958. In the intervening period Puissant Chef, San San and Star Appeal all failed, though Puissant Chef, who unseated his rider at the start, and San San, who was hampered by fallers, had valid excuses for doing so.

Ivanjica's win in the Prix de l'Arc de Triomphe earned for her owner £144,928. Had Ivanjica been bred in France she would also have qualified for a breeders' prize of £36,232 and an owners' bonus of £43,478. In fact there are extra prizes for all French-bred winners and placed horses in races in France. Currently, more than two million pounds a year is paid out in France in breeders' premiums. A submission by the Thoroughbred Breeders' Association to the Levy Board in July for the introduction of breeders' prizes in England from the start of the 1977 flat season was turned down. The Thoroughbred Breeders' Association wanted a ten per cent breeders' prize for English-bred winners in all two-year-old races, except sellers and claiming races, in 1977, to be followed in 1978 by additional similar prizes for the first four in pattern races and for the winners of all other races restricted to fillies (excluding sellers, amateur riders races, etc.). It was also suggested that from the start of the 1977/78 season, the breeders of winners of steeplechases with an added value of £1,000 or more (excepting sellers, etc.) should also be eligible for a prize. The maximum cost to the Levy Board for breeders' prizes in 1977 was estimated at a little over £120,000, rising to around £425,000 in 1978. The Thoroughbred Breeders' Association reckoned that fewer than half of the qualifying races would be won by English-bred horses.

Is there a case for breeders' prizes? We have never been favourably disposed towards them. The breeder is engaged in a commercial enterprise; he gets his price when he sells his product. The argument that if a horse sold for a relatively paltry sum subsequently wins the Derby or the Prix de l'Arc de Triomphe the breeder is entitled to feel hard done by at not receiving a financial cut from the owner's windfall, carries no weight with us. Breeders frequently sell for substantial sums yearlings which subsequently prove incapable of winning a race of any description. Do they offer any recompense to the unfortunate purchasers of these yearlings, who paid for them so much more than they proved to be worth? They do not. It has never been known. Very well: breeders cannot have it both ways.

We make two further observations. First, that there is a finite amount available in prize money, and that if you give some of it to the breeder of a horse, you must necessarily do so at the expense of the owner. Second, we believe that whether you award premiums or you don't is a purely arbitrary decision of no real consequence for the health of racing. A simple law of economics will regulate the supply of breeders, owners and horses. Horses in short supply means higher sale prices for the breeders: owners in short supply means lower sale prices. A self-adjusting situation.

Ivanjica (b.f. 1972)	Sir Ivor (b 1965)	Sir Gaylord (b 1959)	Turn-to
			Somethingroyal
		Attica (ch 1953)	Mr Trouble
			Athenia
	Astuce (b 1964)	Vieux Manoir (b 1947)	Brantome
			Vieille Maison
		Ashleen (b 1956)	Alizier
			Asheratt

Ivanjica, a most attractive filly, was bred in the United States where she was sold as a yearling for 180,000 dollars. Her sire Sir Ivor was a magnificent racehorse whose exploits will still be remembered vividly by most European racegoers. As a three-year-old he won the Two Thousand Guineas, the Derby, the Champion Stakes and the Washington International and was second to Vaguely Noble in the Prix de l'Arc de Triomphe. He is at stud at Claiborne Farm, Kentucky. Ivanjica's dam Astuce, who raced in France, was a very useful stayer. Ivanjica herself was extremely well suited by a mile and a half. There is no doubt, either, that the conditions on Arc day were in her favour; she acts well on soft going. She was tried in blinkers on her fourth outing in 1976 but there is no question of her being anything but a thoroughly genuine racehorse. As we said in *Racehorses of 1975* her main asset was a first-class turn of foot. Ivanjica raced in America after running at Laurel and is to visit Secretariat in 1977. *A. Head, France.*

I'VE A BEE 3 ch.f. Sir Ivor 135–Honey Portion 107 (Major Portion 129) [1975 **114** 7g⁵ 8d* 1976 7g* 8g 12g³ 12fg] short-backed, attractive Irish filly: half-sister to several winners, including smart French stayer Honeyville (by Charlottesville) and very useful stayer Honey Crepe (by Crepello): dam a miler: ran easily her best race when 2½ lengths third of 18 to Lagunette in Irish Guinness Oaks at the Curragh in July, making very good headway from rear on home turn and finishing strongly to fail narrowly to take second place: started favourite for Yorkshire Oaks at York the following month but again got behind and was never in race, finishing very disappointing last of 13 behind Sarah Siddons: all out when gaining her success in Group 3 Mulcahy Stakes at Phoenix Park in April by a head from Lady Singer: stays 1½m: possibly requires an easy surface. *V. O'Brien, Ireland.*

I'VE A JAY 2 br.f. Double-U-Jay 120–Hi Tess 65 (Supreme Court 135) [1976 — 5s 7g] third foal: sister to Irish 9f winner Hi Jay: dam plating class: little worthwhile form in maiden races at Phoenix Park in March and Yarmouth (remote eighth of 14) in September: trained by C. Magnier on first outing. *C. Brittain.*

IVER 5 b.g. Tacitus 124–Goldella 60 (Golden Cloud) [1974 8d 10.8f⁴ 11.7fg³ **81** 10fg* 10f⁴ 11.7fg 12.2fg* 12fg² 14g 11.7g⁵ 12s⁴ 12g³ 10d 12v⁶ 1975 12d⁵ 12s⁴ 14f⁶ 10g 12f² 12f⁵ 11.7fg⁶ 12.2f* 12f 10.2f⁴ 12g* 13g³ 1976 12f* 12g² 12f* 13.3fg² 12fg³ 12f⁵ 12s⁵ 14g] fair handicapper: successful at Folkestone in May and Chepstow the following month: probably stays 13f: seems to act on any going but is well suited by firm: good mount for an apprentice. *R. Akehurst.*

IVORS 5 ch.g. Perspex–Colines Bride (Nearcolein) [1974 N.R. 1975 N.R. — 1976 18f³ 16g⁴ 17g² 14g] ex-Irish gelding: brother to Spy Glass, a winner over hurdles in Ireland: in frame in three bumpers races in May: having first outing in this country when eighth of 13 to Ringed Aureole in amateur riders race at Goodwood in September: stays well. *G. Balding.*

IVORY GIRL 3 b.f. Sir Ivor 135–Treacle 86 (Hornbeam 130) [1975 6g 7fg⁴ **107** 7.2fg 8f* 8g² 1976 10fg 12fg² 12fg⁶ 12g* 10g] strong, shapely, deep-bodied, attractive filly: won Fitzwilliam Stakes at Doncaster in September by a short

Fitzwilliam Stakes, Doncaster—a ding-dong battle between (left to right) Ivory Girl Pass the Port and The Hand

head from Pass the Port, holding on well under pressure to win all out: had run very well on her two previous outings, finishing 1½ lengths second to Bright Finish in well-contested minor event at Newmarket and just over 3½ lengths sixth to Sarah Siddons in Yorkshire Oaks at York: probably finds 1½m too short for her and stays 1½m: probably best in blinkers but did not wear them at Doncaster: exported to U.S.A. *H. Cecil.*

IZZY FAST 3 b.c. Good Apple 91–Pretty (The Pelican) [1975 N.R. 1976 —
9g6] first foal: dam never ran: started slowly when tailed-off last of six behind Bartolozzi in newcomers race at Wolverhampton in May. *H. Westbrook.*

J

JACADO 2 b.c. Captain's Gig–Tackaway 77 (Hard Tack 111 §) [1976 5g3 6g3   89
5fg3 5d* 5s] lengthy, good sort: third foal: half-brother to useful middle-distance performer Noble Bay (by Lord Gayle): 16,000 gns yearling: dam won over 1m: sweated up prior to winning 12-runner maiden race at Nottingham in September by a head from Ravelston: should be suited by 7f+: acts on a firm and a soft surface: consistent. *J. Sutcliffe.*

JACKALLA 2 b.g. David Jack 125–Candy Girl (Tutankhamen) [1976 5g 6g   64
7fg 6d6 8fg5 8d6] neat gelding: will stay middle distances: acts on a firm and a soft surface. *P. Robinson.*

JACKIE'S PROMISE 2 ch.c. Miracle 116–Zabbotina (Welsh Abbot 131)   70
[1976 5fg 5f4 5f3 5f 5f 5.8f* 6g5 5g 5.9s3 5s6 7v] quite a moderate colt: attracted no bid after winning seller at Bath in June by 2 lengths: not disgraced in better company afterwards: stays 6f: acts on any going: usually blinkered nowadays but has run well without them: good mount for a boy. *Dr A. Jones.*

JACK JIGGS 4 b.g. Welsh Rake 118–Melpomene 96 (Pardal 130) [1974 5f   62
6fg 6g 1975 6s5 8f4 8f3 7f 7f* 6g2 1976 8g 8g* 7f6 7g2 7g4 7fg6 7g5 7fg6 7d6 8.2d] lightly-made gelding: modest plater: apprentice ridden when winning at Salisbury in May: finds 6f on sharp side for him and stays 1m: acts on firm going. *B. Wise.*

JACKOLEON 3 ch.c. Major Portion 129–Royal Academy 99 (Golden Cloud)   76
[1975 5.1f 6f 6f3 7g2 7f 8.2d 1976 6fg 7g* 8d6 8fg 7fg 7f5 7f2 7g2 8f4 7f4 8d2 7s4] compact, good sort: won maiden race at Doncaster in April by 1½ lengths from Jimmy The Singer, starting at 25/1: runner-up in handicaps at Yarmouth (two) and Kempton afterwards: stays 1m: possibly not at his best on really soft going. *A. Dalton.*

JACK'S BIRTHDAY 2 br.c. Caliban 123–Queen's Rose 85 (Queen's Hussar 124)   78
[1976 5fg 6h4 6d3 7s5 6v] first reported foal: dam won over 7f at 2 yrs and appeared to stay 1¾m: quite a moderate maiden: will stay 1m+. *M. Masson.*

JACKSMATE 4 b.g. Panco 91–Rocky Trail (Black Rock 113) [1974 N.R. —
1975 N.R. 1976 10s] half-brother to a couple of N.H. winners: dam placed
over hurdles: 33/1 when behind in minor event at Nottingham in September,
first outing. *D. Nicholson.*

JACK SOMERS 2 br.c. Will Somers 114 §–Jane Shaw (Galivanter 131) [1976 —
6fg 5f 6f 8fg 7v] workmanlike colt: plating-class maiden. *J. Etherington.*

JACK'S PRINCESS 3 ch.f. Varano–Attraction (Petition 130) [1975 N.R.
1976 10d 12.2g 12.2f] unfurnished filly: probably of little account. *R. E.
Peacock.*

JACMEL 4 b.c. Double Jump 131–Haiti 79 (Relic) [1974 5g 5g³ 6g³ 6g² 7d⁴ 6g —
6s* 1975 7d* 8s² 8d⁵ 7.2g³ 7fg* 7fg⁴ 7g⁶ 7.6g⁴ 1976 8.2v 8v] lengthy, strong-
quartered colt: good walker: fair handicapper in 1975: well beaten both outings
at 4 yrs (didn't reappear until October): stays 1m really well: appears to act on
any going: bandaged both outings. *B. McMahon.*

JACOBA 2 br.f. Royal Palm 131–Eve Darlin 50 (Arcticeelagh 119) [1976 5f **40**
6f³] leggy filly: 5½ lengths third of seven to Market Fresh in seller at Nottingham
in June: will be suited by 7f. *J. Hardy.*

JACYKING 3 ch.c. Aureole 132–Pyrola 87 (Psidium 130) [1975 8.2d 1976 12f **63**
10fg² 15g*] big, strong colt: easily accounted for three poor opponents in
maiden race at Ayr in August: stays well. *S. Hall.*

JAGLO 2 b.c. Aglojo 119–Viennese Puppet (Tudor Melody 129) [1976 6fg⁵ 6g*] **79**
half-brother to winning Irish sprinter Whistling Waltz (by Whistler): attracted
no bid after winning seller at Warwick in June by 2½ lengths from Sloane Ranger
but looked useful for a plater: will stay 1m. *M. Jarvis.*

JAILER 3 b.g. Maystreak 118–Senior Warden 78 (Eudaemon 129) [1975 6h⁶ —
6f⁶ 1976 12.5v⁶] lightly raced and no worthwhile form in maiden company.
J. Vickers.

JALALI 3 ch.g. River Beauty 105–Armenia (Buisson Ardent 129) [1975 7g³ **114**
7g⁴ 7.5g² 1976 10g² 10f* 12f* 12f* 11g²] closely related to moderate middle-
distance handicapper Comet Kohoutek (by Le Levanstell) and half-brother to a
bumpers winner: dam never ran: improved apace and won three races, maiden
event at Navan in July, minor event at Listowel in September (easily) and
handicap at Naas in October (easily defied 7-lb penalty): narrowly failed to defy
a similar impost in handicap at Naas later in month and went down by ¾ length
to Mr Kildare (rec 17 lb): stays 1½m: acts on firm going: very useful. *C. Magnier,
Ireland.*

JAM 2 ch.c. Fric 128–Still Room 84 (Major Portion 129) [1976 5.9g⁵ 7f⁵ 7g³ **90**
8g* 8.2v⁶] small, stocky colt: first foal: dam won over 7f at 2 yrs: won 12-runner
maiden race at Ayr in September by 2½ lengths from Rostov: had very stiff task
on final outing: will stay 1¼m. *B. Hobbs.*

JAMAR 5 br.m. Kashmir II 125–Soie Sauvage (Shantung 132) [1974 6g³ 6g⁴ **59**
8g 5g 1975 5f⁵ 5g³ 5h² 5f³ 5f* 5g 5g 1976 6f 6v⁵ 5f⁴ 5fg 5fg⁵ 5f³ 5h* 5f⁴ 5h⁶]
rather leggy mare: narrow winner of handicap from Musical Piece at Beverley in
July (well-backed second favourite): best form at sprint distances: acts on any
going: suitable mount for an apprentice or lady rider: has worn blinkers: sweated
up fourth outing. *Denys Smith.*

JAMES JUNIOR 3 ch.c. Jimmy Reppin 131–Our Alyce (Our Babu 131) [1975 **60**
5g⁶ 5fg² 5.9f³ 6fg³ 6g 6g 7g³ 7s 1976 8f 8.2f 7.3g⁵ 7g⁵ 7g 7g² 7s 8s 8.2s] workmanlike colt: should stay 1m: possibly best served by a sound surface. *R. Akehurst.*

JAMESMARK 2 b.c. Firestreak 125–Lucky Number (River Chanter 121) [1976 —
7g 7g] rangy, workmanlike colt: no worthwhile form in minor events at Kempton in August. *P. Ashworth.*

JAMESON 2 ch.c. Huntercombe 133–Trekker 86 (Grey Sovereign 128 §) [1976 **107**
5g* 5d* 5d⁵ 5d² 5f* 5g⁴ 5fg⁴ 5g] strong, good-bodied, compact colt: first foal:
3,700 gns yearling: dam won twice over 1¼m: out early in season, winning at
Catterick and Haydock, and gained another success in 10-runner Robert B.
Massey Group Trophy at Beverley in June, beating Trackally more comfortably
than length margin suggests: fair fourth of six to Piney Ridge in National Stakes
at Sandown the following month and raced on apparently slower ground when
remote fourth to Haveroid in Prince of Wales's Stakes at York in August: will

Robert B. Massey Group Trophy, Beverley—Jameson beats Trackally

stay 6f: appears to act on any going: ran badly when tried in blinkers on final outing: sometimes loses a little ground at start. *W. Wharton.*

JAMES THREE 4 ch.c. Jimmy Reppin 131–Queen's Evidence 95 (King's Bench 132) [1974 5d 5g 5g⁵ 7s³ 7.2g 8s³ 1975 8s 9g* 8g 10fg⁵ 9fg* 8fg⁶ 8g⁵ 7s 8d³ 7.6s 1976 9fg 9g] tall, quite attractive colt: stays 9f: seems to act on any going: suitable mount for an apprentice. *D. Keith.*

JAM SESSION 2 b.f. Jukebox 120–Springview (Vimy 132) [1976 5fg⁶ 5fg 5f 5g — 5f 6f] leggy filly: cost 9,000 gns as a yearling but is only a poor performer: blinkered third and fourth outings: trained by F. J. Houghton on first four appearances. *F. Carr.* 57

JANE LOUISE 3 gr.f. Queen's Hussar 124–Diamond Pin 89 (Princely Gift 137) — [1975 7d 6g 1976 10.8f 11.7f⁴ 12fg 11.7fg⁵ 10.1fg⁵] big, tall filly: poor maiden: blinkered last two outings: sold 250 gns Ascot December Sales. *J. Bethell.*

JANE'S GIRL 2 b.f. Joshua 129–Fairstar 86 (Star Moss 122) [1976 5fg 5d 5h³ 61 5f² 7h⁵ 7f 6g] plain filly: second foal: 180 gns yearling: dam stayed at least 1m: placed in maiden auction events at Carlisle and Doncaster (5 lengths runner-up to Jenny Splendid) in the summer but ran poorly afterwards: should be suited by 7f. *V. Mitchell.*

JANES JOKER 4 b.c. Court Fool–Star-Call 90 (Bleep-Bleep 134) [1974 5fg 103 5g⁶ 7g⁵ 6s* 6fg 6d² 8g* 8g² 8s² 8s* 8v⁴ 1975 8s* 8g³ 8v² 8d² 8.2g⁵ 10.6fg⁶ 8fg 7.6g² 9g³ 8g 8d⁶ 9g⁴ 8g³ 8d 8.2s* 1976 8g 7.2d* 7.6d⁴ 8s³ 6d* 8fg* 7fg⁵ 7.2g⁵ 8fg 7.6fg⁶ 7d 7.3d 7.2d³ 7v* 7s*] stocky colt: useful handicapper: a really tough customer who won five of his fifteen races in 1976, at Haydock (two), Newcastle, York and Newmarket: successful in typical fashion on last-named course, making all and keeping on really well to beat Manilata ½ length in Haddenham Handicap in October: effective at 6f, and stays 9f: appears to act on any going but is particularly well suited by some give in the ground: suitable mount for an apprentice: suited by forcing tactics: tried in blinkers on twelfth start (had stiffish task): very game and genuine. *R. Hollinshead.*

JANES PAL 2 b.c. Pals Passage 115–Dellaree (Delirium 126) [1976 5d 6v] — first foal: sold twice as a yearling for 420 gns and 2,300 gns: dam never ran: unquoted when in mid-division in large fields of maidens at Newbury in the autumn. *D. Hanley.*

JANJAQ 3 gr.f. Polyfoto 124–Solviliana (Vilmorin) [1975 5d 5g 5f 1976 6d — 5.9g⁶ 5fg 5f 6f] compact filly: poor form in varied company. *G. Toft.*

JANTU 2 b.f. Deep Diver 134–Last Report 96 (Democratic 124) [1976 5fg 5s³ 81 5v⁴ 5v³] sixth foal: dam 6f to 1m handicapper: modest maiden: should stay 6f: acts on heavy ground. *G. Harwood.*

JAPORA 2 gr.f. Raffingora 130–Monogram 77 (Mon Fetiche 120) [1976 5fg* 100 5d 5f6 6fg⁶ 5fg³ 5fg 5g⁶] strong, good-quartered filly: second foal: 2,100 gns yearling: dam won at 1m: won maiden event at Nottingham in April by a length from Speed Trap: ran in some good-class races afterwards, putting up best efforts when 2 lengths sixth of 12 to Cramond in Queen Mary Stakes at Royal Ascot and 1½ lengths third of seven to Be Easy in Molecomb Stakes at Goodwood: finishes strongly over 5f but appeared not to stay when tried over 6f: acts on firm going and is probably unsuited by a soft surface. *N. Adam.*

358

Michael Sobell Handicap, York—Japsilk appears to win on merit from Minstrel Song but the placings are reversed in the stewards' room

JAPSILK 3 b.c. St Paddy 133–Geisha 88 (Shantung 132) [1975 5s 5f⁵ 6fg³ 7g⁶ 7fg² 9fg² 10g* 8d 1976 12f⁴ 10g* 12fg* 12fg* 16f* 14fg²] tall colt: quite a useful handicapper: in cracking form in first part of season and won at Salisbury, Brighton (twice), Chepstow and York: relegated to second place (appeared to us winner on merit) for hampering runner-up when beating Minstrel Song 1½ lengths on last-named course in June: effective from 1¼m to 2m: acts well on a firm surface: suitable mount for an apprentice: withdrawn lame, not under orders, at Goodwood in July and was not seen out again. *R. Hannon.* **92**

JARDINIER 2 b.c. Jefferson 129–Garden Green (Pinturischio 116) [1976 6fg 7fg⁵ 7f 8d] well-grown colt: quite modest form in maiden races: will be suited by 1m: swerved violently on leaving stalls on final outing and refused to race. *Doug Smith.* **80**

JARELLA 3 b.g. Another River 89–Judarona 78 (Swift Flight 101) [1975 6fg 5f⁵ 8g 1976 15.8f⁴ 12g] bad plater: wears bandages: blinkered final outing: sold 220 gns Doncaster November Sales. *K. Whitehead.* **—**

JARGAL 2 b.c. Amarko–Gale (Chamossaire) [1976 6g 7f 7v] attractive, well-made French-bred colt: fourth living foal: 50,000 francs yearling (approx. £5,300): dam, half-sister to high-class Hotfoot, won over 2m in Ireland: no worthwhile form in maiden races. *J. Dunlop.* **—**

JARULLAH 3 br.c. Sterling Bay–Jario (Pardal 130) [1975 5v 6g 1976 10g⁵ 16f⁶ 12f 12f⁶] poor maiden: blinkered last two outings. *G. Hunter.* **—**

JASMINE (FR) 2 ch.f. Jefferson 129–Valsania (Val de Loir 133) [1976 6f 9fg³] French-bred filly: first foal: dam ran only once: 4 lengths third to Identity in 20-runner maiden race at Wolverhampton in September: will stay 1½m. *Doug Smith.* **73**

JASON 2 b.c. Mummy's Pet 125–Manzanilla 88 (Major Portion 129) [1976 5g⁶ 5f² 5g 5fg* 5f 6fg 6f 8fg 6v⁵ 8v²] useful sort with a slightly dipped back: half-brother to smart Spanish Warrior (by Tamerlane), a winner at up to 1¼m: 3,400 gns yearling: dam won over 1m and 1¼m: won maiden race at Carlisle in May: ran moderately afterwards until final two outings, finishing fifth to Rush Bond in valuable seller at York and then putting up an excellent effort when 1½ lengths second to Catchword in nursery at Teesside, both in October: evidently **88**

359

suited by 1m: acts on any going but goes particularly well on heavy: blinkered fourth to seventh outings. *M. H. Easterby.*

JAVA RAJAH 3 ch.c. Jacinto–Sabana (Bryan G) [1975 8g⁶ 10f² 1976 10d⁶ 9d⁶ 10.5g² 12.5g* 12.5g² 12s*(dis) 12s 12v] good-looking American-bred French colt: half-brother to useful 1969 2-y-o Tom Gate (by Tom Fool), a winner at up to 1m at 3 yrs, and to several winners in U.S.A.: $40,000 yearling: dam, sister to champion racemare Cicada, won in U.S.A.: left his previous form way behind when eighth of 20 to Ivanjica in Prix de l'Arc de Triomphe at Longchamp in October: earlier successful in handicaps at Deauville and Longchamp: narrowly beat Kaole in very valuable Omnium on latter course in September but was later disqualified when traces of caffeine were found in his system: virtually pulled up in final 2f when last of 12 behind Mart Lane in very testing ground in St Simon Stakes at Newbury on final outing: suited by 1½m and will probably stay further: acts on any going but is evidently suited by soft. *A. Breasley, France.* **116**

JAY RIVER 2 br.c. Forlorn River 124–Jambo 82 (Babur 126) [1976 5f 5.1g 5d⁶ 7v] neat colt: plating-class maiden: should stay 7f but was tailed off on only attempt at trip: blinkered final outing. *J. Powney.* **67**

JAYSTAR 2 ch.f. Double-U-Jay 120–Crisp Star (Star Moss 122) [1976 5g 5f] only plating-class. *A. Dalton.* **—**

JAY TEE 2 br.f. Sit In The Corner–Forthcoming 69 (New Brig 120) [1976 5g 5f 7f⁶ 6fg³ 8.2h³ 5fg 7fg] lightly-built filly: poor plater: needs further than 5f and is suited by 1m: sold 280 gns Doncaster October Sales. *N. Angus.* **54**

JEAN D'ARGENT 2 gr.c. Birdbrook 110–Edict 51 (Privy Councillor 125) [1976 5g⁶ 6fg 7g⁴ 8s⁵ 10v³] workmanlike colt: first foal: 2,000 gns yearling: dam won two sellers at up to 1½m: in frame in maiden races at Kempton in August (6 lengths fourth to Gairloch) and Nottingham in October (1¾ lengths third to Pin Tuck): stays 1¼m: acts on heavy ground. *P. Cole.* **84**

JEBEL DRUSE 2 ch.c. Blue Streak 99–Strathtay 68 (Soueida 111) [1976 5fg⁵ 5f⁵ 6f³ 6f⁵] strong colt: first foal: 380 gns yearling: dam placed over 5f at 2 yrs: 4-length winner of 17-runner auction event at Wolverhampton in May: excellent third to Jump To It in £1,200 race at Leicester the following month: suited by 6f: acts on firm going: not seen out after June. *B. Hobbs.* **89**

JELLABY 3 ro.c. Pals Passage 115–Olanrose (Kythnos 126) [1975 5g² 6g* 6s* 6g* 1976 7f⁵ 7g² 7fg³ 8d* 7f* 7.2d² 8v* 8.2v⁴] big, strong, rangy, long-striding colt: ran well in all his races and developed into a smart performer: **117**

Askham Stakes, York—Jellaby gives Brian Taylor an armchair ride and runs out one of the easiest winners of the season

gained his victories in well-contested minor events at York in May and October and Goodwood in August: very impressive on both occasions at York, beating Ashbro Laddo by 3 lengths on first of them and Danestic by 7 lengths without coming off bridle on second: also in frame in James Lane 2,000 Guineas Trial at Kempton and Glenlivet Handicap at Newmarket in the spring and Sydney Sandon Handicap at Haydock and Prix Perth at Saint-Cloud in the autumn: raced on apparently slower ground in centre of course when fourth to Dominion in last-named event in November: stays 1m: acts on any going but clearly revels in the mud: genuine. *R. Price.*

JENE REPPIN 2 ch.f. Jimmy Reppin 131–Ranjitara (Right Boy 137) [1976 **79**
6g 6fg3 5.9f2 5.9fg 6g] useful-looking filly: second foal: 3,400 gns yearling: dam showed only poor form but is half-sister to two winners by Jimmy Reppin: 1½ lengths second of 16 to Red Seed in maiden event at Wolverhampton in August: stays 6f. *R. Jarvis.*

JENNY SPLENDID 2 br.f. John Splendid 116–Gay Maria (Tacitus 124) [1976 **101**
5f 6h 5f* 5.9f* 6g2 6g3 6s* 7d* 6s3] smallish filly: first foal: 520 gns yearling: dam unraced half-sister to very smart 1966 2-y-o Hambleden: proved a real bargain and won four races, maiden auction event at Doncaster and nurseries at Wolverhampton, Nottingham and Newmarket: scored most impressively by 8 lengths from Sequoia at Nottingham, and was clear from halfway when beating Movement by 1½ lengths in £2,000 event at Newmarket in October: stays 7f well: acts on any going but is extremely well suited by soft: genuine and most consistent. *J. Haine.*

JETADOR 4 b.f. Queen's Hussar 124–Swift Justice 98 (Court Martial) [1974 **59**
7d 6v 6s2 8s6 1975 7d 7d3 10f 12.2f 10f5 12g* 10fg* 13d 12g 12f* 1976 8fg 16f* 14f] light-framed filly: won handicap at Nottingham in June, beating Tight Rope ½ length: stays well: acts on firm going: not raced after early August. *W. Wightman.*

JET PATROL 3 ch.g. Jolly Jet 111–Stellario (Indian Hemp 124) [1975 5fg 6fg — §
8g 1976 10.8f 10.6d] seems of little account and temperamental into the bargain: sold 310 gns Ascot June Sales. *G. Hunter.*

JET PROPELLED 2 br.c. On Your Mark 125–Flat Impulse 75 (Meadow Court **62**
129) [1976 5s 5f4 5g4 5f 6fg 5h 7fg 5h] light-framed, unfurnished colt: plating-class maiden: should stay 7f: seemed totally unsuited by the hard ground on sixth outing (moved very badly to post): sold 210 gns Doncaster October Sales. *N. Robinson.*

JETWITCH 3 b.f. Lear Jet 123–Bestwitch 104 (Borealis) [1975 5h 8f 8f6 10g **56**
6g 6g 1976 8h6 8fg4 10.6d4] poor plater: stays at least 1m. *W. Haigh.*

JEUNE SOURIS 2 br.f. Chebs Lad 120–Souriciere 73 (Count Albany 99) [1976 —
5f] first foal: dam a sprinter: started slowly when tailed off in 25-runner maiden race won by Spring Dive at Thirsk in September. *J. Carr.*

JEWELLED TURBAN 2 ch.c. Mansingh 120–Chantry Pearl (Gulf Pearl 117) **95**
[1976 5s* 5h* 5d3 5d* 5s4 6fg3 5fg2 6fg2] useful-looking colt: first produce: 1,000 gns foal and resold twice as a yearling, for 1,300 gns and 2,900 gns: dam of little account: winner at Newcastle (beat Stephandre a length), Teesside and Catterick, on last-named course landing the odds a shade comfortably by ¾ length from Charley's Revenge: in frame on all his other starts, on seventh outing finishing length second to Beaumel Board in £2,000 race at Newcastle in July: stays 6f: acts on any going: badly behaved and got loose in paddock on last two outings and had to be taken long way round to post on final appearance. *R. D. Peacock.*

JIBE 3 ch.f. Double Jump 131–Riberta 89 (Ribot 142) [1975 N.R. 1976 —
7f 10f6 8f] first foal: 1,000 gns yearling: dam placed in 1970 Ribblesdale Stakes: well beaten in maiden company: sold, covered by Perdu, 920 gns Newmarket December Sales. *D. Hanley.*

JILL SOMERS 2 br.f. Will Somers 114 §–French Line 98 (Set Fair 129) [1976 **76**
6f 5f 5s 5s2 5s] sister to October Fair, a winner at up to 11f, and half-sister to three minor winners: 2,100 gns yearling: dam a sprinter: length second to Duke's Girl in 12-runner maiden race at Folkestone in October, easily best effort: acts on soft going. *R. Price.*

JIM COINER 4 b.g. Current Coin 118–Golden Windfall (High Treason 126) **67**
[1974 5fg 5g 6g 6g* 6g 7f 7.2g6 8s* 8s* 7v 1975 11.1v5 12v4 12.2g3 12g* 16f5 13f3 14g6 14fg5 1976 12f6 12.2g 10s3 11s5 13v3 12.5s*] quite a moderate handicapper: winner at Teesside in November: best form at up to 1½m: acts well on soft going: suitable mount for an apprentice. *R. Jarvis.*

361

Spillers Stewards' Cup, Goodwood—Jimmy The Singer is pursued by Delta Song (right), then come the blinkered grey Ribramble, Baildon (hoop on cap) and Broxted (light colours)

JIMMY THE SINGER 3 b.c. Jimmy Reppin 131–Solo Song 71 (Pinza 137) **104** [1975 7g 7g 6g 6s³ 6g² 1976 7fg 7g² 8d³ 6fg* 7g* 6fg³ 6g⁴ 6fg* 6fg 6f²] big, well-made colt: improved considerably on his early-season form which included victories in maiden race at Newmarket and handicap at Kempton, and on eighth outing won 17-runner Spillers Stewards' Cup at Goodwood in July decisively by a length from Delta Song: 1½ lengths runner-up to Honeyblest, the pair finishing clear of 12 others, in Great St Wilfrid Handicap at Ripon the following

Mrs Sidney Bates's "Jimmy The Singer"

month on final outing: best form at 6f although stays further: well suited by a sound surface: wears blinkers. *B. Lunness.*

JIMMY THE SPIV 2 b.c. Right Tack 131–Palgal (Le Prince 98) [1976 5f² 67 5g²] lengthy, unfurnished colt: first foal: dam won at up to 1½m in Ireland: second in sellers at Warwick in April and Goodwood in May, on latter course just failing to catch Laser Olivia: claimed for 2,100 gns after Goodwood race for export to Belgium and has won there. *G. Hunter.*

JIMS-DOUBLE 2 b.c. Double-U-Jay 120–Grandma 101 (Gilles de Retz 132) 71 p [1976 7f⁵ 8g] big, rangy colt: half-brother to smart middle-distance performer Jimsun (by Soleil II): dam won twice at 1½m: 25/1 and still not fully wound up when seventh of 13 to Royal Plume in £2,400 event at York in September: will do better in time. *Hbt Jones.*

JIN JANG 5 br.h. Val de Loir 133–Joy Land (Bold Ruler) [1974 6g* 8g⁶ 7s* 5v 86 5.5v⁴ 1975 6v⁶ 6.5v⁴ 7.8g⁵ 5s⁵ 1976 10fg² 6fg⁵ 6f⁶ 10f⁵ 10fg³ 10h* 9fg⁴ 10h* 10.1f* 10g* 10g 10.2g 12.2s] lightly-made ex-French horse: fair performer: winner at Pontefract, Folkestone, Windsor and Kempton within the space of a month in 1976: beat Modom in apprentice event on last-named course in August: best form in this country at around 1½m: acts on any going: sometimes dwells at start: sometimes sweats up: front runner: ran poorly last three starts, including in blinkers on final one. *R. Boss.*

JINKY JIM 2 b.c. Kibenka 119–Larcio (Lauso) [1976 5fg 5d² 5fg 5f³ 6f 8f 7fg 6v] 65 lengthy, lightly-made colt: placed in seller at Redcar in May and maiden race at Catterick in July, running creditably behind Hand Canter in latter event: should be suited by 6f+: blinkered penultimate outing. *S. Nesbitt.*

JINTY BELL 2 ch.f. Communication 119–Bright Bubble 62 (Star Moss 122) — [1976 5fg 5f] neat, light-framed filly: no worthwhile form, including in a seller. *T. Fairhurst.*

JOANNA SUPREME 2 br.f. John Splendid 116–Pictynna (Polic 126) [1976 — 5fg] fourth foal: dam ran only at 2 yrs: 12/1 when last of 15 in maiden race won by Brightelmstone at Salisbury in May. *T. Marshall.*

JOAN'S SONG 3 b.g. Crooner 119–Queen's Troop 88 (King's Troop 118) [1975 — 5v 5s 6fg 6g 1976 8fg 8fg 8fg 12fg 8s] plater: showed signs of a little ability at 2 yrs but was well beaten on all outings in 1976: should stay 1m: usually wears blinkers: sold out of J. Hill's stable 800 gns Ascot July Sales after second outing. *P. Ransom.*

JOAN'S WISH 2 b.c. Double Jump 131–Zoomie 78 (Pinza 137) [1976 5g 5d³ 5f 84 5f² 5fg³ 5f* 5h³ 5g 5.9fg² 5s⁵] second living foal: half-brother to 7f and 1m winner Sovereign Gold (by Grey Sovereign): 2,500 gns yearling: dam, winner at 1m and 9f, is half-sister to smart animals Blinis and Pithiviers: won £1,100 event at Bath in June by length from Brave Stroke: ran well when second of 23 to Princess Rose in nursery at Wolverhampton in September when blinkered first time but did not reproduce that form when again blinkered on final outing: will stay 7f: played up badly and was withdrawn under orders after rearing in stalls on third outing. *J. Hill.*

JOBINA 2 b.f. Town Crier 119–Swifter Justice 62 (King's Bench 132) [1976 78 5fg³ 5g 5d 5s⁵] useful-looking filly: second produce: 600 gns foal: dam selling handicapper: moderate maiden: favourite when 1¾ lengths fifth of 13 to No Tomorrow in maiden race at Nottingham in September: will be better suited by 6f+. *R. Vibert.*

JOB'S MILL 2 b.c. Blakeney 126–The Country Lane 90 (Red God 128 §) [1976 74 6fg 6g 6g⁶ 7fg] rangy, attractive colt: second foal: 8,600 gns yearling: dam won four times over 6f from six starts: quite a moderate maiden: should be suited by 7f+. *G. Balding.*

JOBURG SPECIAL 2 gr.f. Raffingora 130–Nautical Lady 69 (Star Moss 122) — [1976 5g 5s⁵ 5f⁴ 5f⁵] neat filly: beaten only about 5 lengths when last of four to Linguistic in maiden race at Edinburgh in July but was beaten a long way in seller at Hamilton later in week and is probably flattered by her Edinburgh run. *J. Berry.*

JOCKS BOND 2 br.c. Good Bond 122–Jocks Pearl 51 (Jock Scot 121) [1976 8d — 8s 6s 7s] lengthy, short legged colt: well behind in maiden and minor events in the autumn. *R. Armytage.*

JOCK'S NOVEL 6 b.h. Jock Scot 121–Bright Novel 79 (Borealis) [1974 N.R. — 1975 N.R. 1976 14fg] half-brother to some poor animals: dam showed quite

Ladbroke Chester Cup—John Cherry outclasses the opposition

moderate form at 2 yrs: well behind in amateur riders race at Salisbury in June, only outing. *S. Matthews.*

JOGGER 2 b.c. Sharpen Up 127–Shirini 74 (Tehran) [1976 5d 5d⁶ 5s² 5s⁴ 6s 8s] **79**
big, strong, workmanlike colt: half-brother to three winners, including useful French sprinter Fortinella (by Fortino II): 3,800 gns foal and resold 2,600 gns yearling: dam won over 1½m: in frame in end-of-season maiden races at Warwick (¾-length second of 18 to Military Queen) and Doncaster (3 lengths fourth to Jon George after dwelling): should be suited by 6f+. *C. Bewicke.*

JOHANNE 3 gr.f. Richboy 117–Miss Lauso 78 (Lauso) [1975 5d 5g 5g 5g 5f⁴ **—**
5h⁴ 6h³ 1976 8f 8g 10.6d⁴] strong filly: should stay 7f: acts on hard going. *J. Cousins.*

JOHN CHERRY 5 ch.g. Stage Door Johnny–Cerisette (My Babu 136) [1974 **125**
11g⁵ 16f* 14f² 14d⁴ 14g⁵ 16v* 16d* 1975 14d 18.4g⁶ 16fg* 16fg⁶ 14fg⁴ 16g* 18fg² 1976 15.5s⁵ 18.4s* 16g⁵ 16d* 18d*]
John Cherry proved unbeatable in long-distance handicaps in 1976 and his effortless victories under top weight in the Ladbroke Chester Cup in May and

SKF Cesarewitch Handicap, Newmarket—John Cherry cruises home under a record weight ahead of Belfalas (left) and Night In Town (noseband)

the SKF Cesarewitch at Newmarket in October were among the highlights of the season. At Chester the pace didn't warm up until it was far too late for the plodders in the field and John Cherry pulverised the opposition for finishing speed, winning without being off the bridle by three lengths, a margin that could have been much greater had his rider wished. Three of the fourteen who took on John Cherry at Chester also lined up against him in the SKF Cesarewitch more than five months later. John Cherry had a 6 lb penalty for a recent victory in the Joe Coral Newbury Autumn Cup which brought his weight in the Cesarewitch to 9-13, 7 lb more than the record weight carried to victory in the race by Grey of Falloden in 1964. Of those that had run in the Ladbroke Chester Cup, Night In Town, meeting John Cherry on terms two stone better, ran by far the best race against him at Newmarket to finish third. But nothing had the slightest chance with John Cherry. Few successes in the Cesarewitch can have been achieved more easily. It was positively impudent the way Piggott sat holding John Cherry tight by the head for much of the last half-mile while Carson on the leader Belfalas was kicking away two or three lengths in front of him. A furlong and a half out Piggott calmly eased John Cherry out and it was all over in no time. John Cherry was hardly doing more than cantering at the finish where he was five lengths ahead of Belfalas and eight ahead of Night In Town. John Cherry completed a double for his American owner last achieved in 1925; Mr Whitney's Intermission (like John Cherry, by the American stallion Stage Door Johnny) had won the Irish Sweeps Cambridgeshire a fortnight earlier.

		Prince John (ch 1953)	Princequillo
			Not Afraid
	Stage Door Johnny (ch 1965)	Peroxide Blonde (ch 1960)	Ballymoss
John Cherry			Folie Douce
(ch.g. 1971)		My Babu (b 1945)	Djebel
	Cerisette (ch 1967)		Perfume II
		Good News Cherry (ch 1963)	Intent
			Cherryville

John Cherry's performances against some of the best stayers were in sharp contrast to the way he performed in handicaps. The Gold Cup winner Sagaro gave him weight and a beating in the Prix de Barbeville at Longchamp in April as did Sea Anchor and Crash Course in the Henry II Stakes at Sandown in June.

Mr J. H. Whitney's "John Cherry"

In neither race could John Cherry finish in the frame. John Cherry's dam Cerisette was packed off to stud after failing to win in eight starts in the States as a two-year-old and produced John Cherry as her first foal. Two more of her offspring, the maiden three-year-old Please Turn Over (by Turn-to) and the promising staying two-year-old Cerua (by Nashua), were also raced in England in 1976. The third dam Cherryville is a half-sister to Secretariat and Sir Gaylord. John Cherry, who is best in blinkers, is said by Jeremy Tree to need an easy surface (he was off the course from June to September when firm-ground conditions prevailed). John Cherry changed hands in the autumn and was sent to H. T. Jones to be prepared for a hurdling campaign. *J. Tree.*

JOHNCIDIUM 2 b.c. John Splendid 116–Summer Sales 94 (Tropique 128) — [1976 5fg⁵] second foal: dam won over 6f as a 2-y-o: 5 lengths fifth of 10 to Aeras in minor event at Leicester in March: dead. *M. Salaman.*

JOHN GAY 3 ch.g. Jukebox 120–Ardria 76 (Major Portion 129) [1975 5s 5s* **80** 5g 5fg² 6fg² 6d⁴ 1976 7fg 7f 6d² 5s* 6v] leggy, light-framed gelding: quite a moderate handicapper: off course April to September but ran well on his return and won at Chepstow in October comfortably by a length from Cry No More: well beaten under a penalty on final outing: stays 6f: appears to act on any going but seems suited by some give in the ground. *J. Hill.*

JOHNGEE 2 br.g. John Splendid 116–La Fourragere 50 (Fortino II 120) [1976 — 5.9fg 8fg] leggy gelding: well behind in maiden race and a seller in midlands. *W. Wharton.*

JOHNJO 2 br.c. John Splendid 116–Ruddy Duck 84 (Dicta Drake 126) [1976 **74** 5fg² 5.3fg² 6g⁴ 5h³ 5fg⁴ 5g] tall, useful-looking colt: half-brother to four winners, including Ruddy Drake (by Goldhill), a moderate winner from 7f to 1½m: dam, sister to very useful stayer Chinatown, needed at least 1½m: placed in maiden races prior to running in valuable sellers on last two outings, putting up better effort when fourth of 17 to Quimay at York in August: best form at 5f but should stay further: blinkered last two outings. *J. Dunlop.*

JOHN JUNIOR 3 br.c. John Splendid 116–Junior Mistress 74 (Babur 126) — [1975 N.R. 1976 8fg 10.1fg 10.1fg 8fg] apparently of little account. *J. Holt.*

JOHN McNAB 4 ch.g. Whistling Wind 123–Efficiency (Pardao 120) [1974 — 5fg² 5g⁵ 7g² 7s* 8s 7g 1975 8d² 10s⁶ 11s⁴ 8.2g³ 13f² 16h 15f 12f⁵ 8.2h² 12f⁵ 12g 15s 12g⁴ 1976 10g⁴ 10s⁶ 13g 9f⁶ 10f⁴] strong gelding: stays 13f: acts on any going: has been tried in blinkers but has done better without them: inconsistent: winner in Jersey. *N. Angus.*

JOHNNIE BULL'S EYE 2 b.g. John Splendid 116–Sailing Dart 85 (Sailing — Light 119) [1976 7d 7fg 8s] well-grown gelding: poor plater: sold 250 gns Doncaster October Sales. *R. Bastiman.*

JOHNNIE GAMBLER 2 b.c. John Splendid 116–Susie Q (Ballyogan) [1976 — 5f 5g 5f 6h 5s 6s 7s] poor maiden: swerved and unseated rider on second outing: blinkered final appearance. *M. Bradley.*

JOHNNY TURNER 3 b.c. Realm 129–Wallflower 77 (Donore 119) [1975 5g* **83** 5fg* 6s⁶ 7fg⁶ 1976 8f 8fg 10g 10f⁶ 10f3] strong, compact, most attractive colt: not a good mover in his slower paces: good third to Fairman in handicap at Newmarket in August, final outing and easily best effort: stays 1½m: acts on firm going: blinkered last outing at 2 yrs and final start in 1976: ran badly fourth appearance: hurdling with D. Morley. *P. Walwyn.*

JOHNSHIELS 2 b.c. King's Troop 118–Sea-Hit 85 (Bleep-Bleep 134) [1976 — 5f 5g 5d] well-grown colt: in rear in small northern events: sold 280 gns Doncaster June Sales and exported to Sweden by B.B.A. *M. W. Easterby.*

JOHN WESLEY 4 ch.g. Hessonite 88–Villa Rosie 59 (Orbit 106) [1974 N.R. — 1975 N.R. 1976 12f 7f 8g 5s 5s] useless. *K. Stapleton.*

JOLLY GOOD 4 b.c. Jolly Jet 111–Rhodie (Rasper) [1974 7s⁶ 7fg⁴ 7g² 7s³ **122** 1975 10s* 10d* 12g³ 10.5d* 10.5fg⁴ 10g* 1976 10g* 9.7d 10fg 10g⁵ 12s* 10d 12v] Despite facing stiff tasks throughout 1976 Jolly Good never lost his zest for racing and managed to win two of his seven races, on both occasions prevailing where less stout-hearted individuals would have won lost.

Jolly Good was thrown in at the deep end, his first race of the season being the Westbury Stakes, a pattern race, at Sandown in April. Although he had shown good form in handicaps as a three-year-old, winning four races including

Westbury Stakes, Sandown—the indomitable Jolly Good regains the upper hand from Dominion (noseband)

the John Smith's Magnet Cup at York and the Peter Hastings Stakes at Newbury, Jolly Good looked to have too much on his plate, opposed by such as Anne's Pretender, Dominion, Record Run and Swell Fellow. He responded magnificently to the challenge. Setting a cracking pace from the start he had all the opposition except Dominion in trouble two furlongs from home. With the benefit of a previous outing and a pull of 8 lb, Dominion looked all set to smother his rival, but Jolly Good would have nothing of it. He battled on stoutly to beat Dominion by three quarters of a length and was almost six lengths clear of third-placed Record Run.

After Sandown Jolly Good proved difficult to place to advantage, and he was well beaten in his next three races which included the Prix Dollar at Longchamp, where he was eighth to Kasteel, and the P.T.S. Laurels Handicap at Goodwood. In the last-named it was hardly surprising that Jolly Good was beaten; he was conceding not less than 8 lb to any in a strong field, and among his opponents were good horses in Fool's Mate, Royal Match and Blaskette! Jolly Good's second win came in a strongly-contested minor race, the Hartfield Stakes, at Lingfield Park in September. On rain-soaked ground, which suits him ideally, he made all the running and showed far too much pluck in the finish for the Oaks runner-up Roses for the Star, who, getting 17 lb more than weight-for-age terms allow, was beaten two and a half lengths. On both his subsequent starts, the Champion Stakes at Newmarket and the St Simon Stakes at Newbury, Jolly Good was well down the field.

	⌠ Jolly Jet	⌠ Jet Action	⌠ Jet Pilot
		(ch 1963) { (ch 1951)	⌡ Busher
Jolly Good	⎨	⌡ La Joliette	⌠ Alycidon
(b.c. 1972)		(ch 1951)	⌡ Justina
		⌠ Rasper	⌠ Owen Tudor
	⌡ Rhodie	(br 1952) {	⌡ Red Sunset
	(br 1962)	⌡ Ria Mooney	⌠ Royal Charger
		(b 1952)	⌡ Conquest

Rhodie, Jolly Good's dam, is American bred. She raced only at two years, when she won four times at up to six furlongs from only five starts, and was rated 3 lb behind the leading filly of her year. Rhodie has also done extremely

367

well at stud. Jolly Good apart, she has had four foals to race, all of them winners, including the English winners Wilderness (by Herbager) and Rhodie Blake (by Blakeney).

Jolly Good is the best horse that Jolly Jet has sired. Jolly Jet was a good winner in America in 1966 when his six victories at distances up to nine furlongs were worth 122,000 dollars. The following season he raced in this country, picking up a minor race at Yarmouth and finishing a creditable fifth in both the Coronation Cup at Epsom and the Eclipse Stakes at Sandown Park. Before Jolly Good came along, Funny Man and Jolly Me were his most notable progeny.

Jolly Good has been sent to race in America, where there may well be better opportunities for him. A well-grown, good sort, he stays a mile and a half and is best suited by some give in the ground. *B. Hobbs.*

JOLLY JOE   2 ch.c. Jolly Jet 111–River Kwai (Sayajirao 132)   [1976 5g⁴ 5f² 5g³   **68** 6g³ 5g* 5.9f] workmanlike colt: half-brother to four minor winners: 1,800 gns yearling: dam ran only twice: came out best in close finish to maiden race at Hamilton in June: well beaten in nursery at Wolverhampton in August on only outing afterwards: will stay 1m. *K. Payne.*

JOLLY LUCKY   5 b.m. Jolly Jet 111–Lucky Pigeon (The Mongoose 108)   [1974 7g 8fg 9f³ 8.3fg³ 8.3s⁶ 8s 10.8v³ 10g 10v   1975 12fg⁴ 12.3g   1976 7fg 8fg⁵ 9fg⁵ 8s] strong, well-made mare: had stiffish tasks and showed no worthwhile form at 5 yrs: stayed 1½m: seemed to act on any going: had been tried in blinkers: dead. *P. Taylor.*

JOLLY SMOOTH   4 b.f. Jolly Jet 111–So Smooth (Pall Mall 132)   [1974 5g 5fg³   **67** 5g⁵ 6d⁴ 7g³ 7s⁴ 7.2s³ 8.2s*   1975 10fg 13h* 12f² 13f³ 11.7g   1976 10.6d 12f⁴ 12g³ 10f] leggy, light-framed filly: poor mover: stays 13f: acts on any going: blinkered last two starts. *M. H. Easterby.*

JOLLY TRIPPER   2 b.c. Tycoon II–Sunday Out 95 (Lord of Verona 120)   [1976   **71** 5d 5f 5d⁵ 6fg 6fg 8g] small colt: showed some ability, finishing seventh of 20 to Harriet Air in maiden race at Lanark in October: will probably stay middle distances. *W. Gray.*

JONA   2 br.c. Sweet Revenge 129–Glide 86 (Quorum 126)   [1976 6fg³ 6g* 7f² 8g   **111** 8g³ 7s] good sort: third foal: 5,000 gns yearling: dam a miler: finished clear of remainder when dead-heating with Bedlam Hill in eight-runner maiden race at Ayr in July: placed twice afterwards, putting up a much improved display when 1¾ lengths third of 13 to Bona-Mia in nursery at Newmarket in September: evidently better suited by 1m than shorter distances: acts on firm going and ran badly on soft on final outing. *J. Hindley.*

JON GEORGE   2 gr.c. Comedy Star 121–Romany Rose 93 (Grey Sovereign   **87** 128 §)   [1976 6fg 5v 5s* 7v⁴] strong colt: half-brother to three winners, including useful 5f to 7f winner Romany Music (by Tudor Melody): 4,400 gns yearling: dam, a sprinter, is sister to good sprinter Thyra Lee: put up a much improved performance when winning 13-runner maiden race at Doncaster in October by 1½ lengths from Seafields: should stay 7f: acts on soft going. *M. W. Easterby.*

JONLYN   3 br.g. Foggy Bell 108–Quite Enough (Quorum 126)   [1975 N.R.   1976   — 8h 10fg] first foal: dam of little account: in rear in maiden races at Beverley (burly) and Nottingham in July. *A. Bacon.*

JONSWALLOW   2 b.c. My Swallow 134–Pall Emma (Pall Mall 132)   [1976 6f   **73** 7d] half-brother to a winning plater: 3,000 gns yearling: dam ran only at 2 yrs: 33/1, never-dangerous eighth of 16 to The Czar in minor race at Yarmouth in September, second outing and better effort. *C. Brittain.*

JOSEPHINE EDWARDS   2 b.f. Saratoga Skiddy 113–Compression 74 (Como   — 120)   [1976 6s] fifth living foal: half-sister to 2¼m winner Aggression (by Fighting Charlie): dam won 5f seller at 2 yrs: unquoted, blinkered and apprentice ridden when well behind in 17-runner seller won by Stand On at Doncaster in October. *M. Naughton.*

JOSHLA'S LADY   2 ch.f. Joshua 129–Clifton Lady 90 (Arctic Prince 135)   **75** [1976 5g³ 5fg² 5fg³] rangy filly: half-sister to 1¾m winner David Fair (by Kalydon): dam won at 1m: placed in three early-season events, coming closest to success when failing by only a neck to beat Racing Fiend after dwelling at start at Warwick in April: will stay 1m. *W. Stephenson.*

JOSHUA'S DAUGHTER   3 b.f. Joshua 129–Legal Love 105 (King's Bench 132)   **61** [1975 N.R.   1976 8.2v 10v²] half-sister to The Happy Hooker (by Town

Crier), a useful winner at up to 1m: 880 gns yearling, resold 470 gns Ascot June Sales: dam, a sprinter, at her best as a 2-y-o: 33/1 when length second to Shepherd's Bar in claiming race at Leicester in November: stays 1¼m: acts on heavy ground: lost ground at start on both outings. *Mrs A. Finch.*

JOSS-STICK 2 b.c. Frankincense 120–Pearl Barley 79 (Pinza 137) [1976 7g **84** 7s⁵] lightly-made, quite attractive colt: fourth foal: half-brother to 3-y-o 1m winner Darley Dale (by Derring-Do): 2,400 gns yearling: dam second four times at up to 1¾m: prominent a long way when about 13 lengths fifth of 12 to Princess Tiara in Somerville Tattersall Stakes at Newmarket in October: will stay 1m: started slowly first outing. *B. Hills.*

J. O. TOBIN 2 br.c. Never Bend–Hill Shade 116 (Hillary) [1976 6fg* 6fg* **130** 7g* 8d³]
We freely admit that had J. O. Tobin's two-year-old career ended with his victory in the Laurent Perrier Champagne Stakes, we would have written him up with considerable confidence and no little enthusiasm for the 1977 classic races. Like everyone else, we were captivated by his display at Doncaster. It was breathtaking. Moving up on a tight rein below the distance, he mastered Durtal without Piggott's having to move a muscle and produced a tremendous burst of speed to go away and win in storming fashion by four lengths. And Durtal was no pushover. On her next appearance she was to defeat—in the absence of Cloonlara, Metair and Icena—the fastest fillies of her age that England and Ireland could muster against her, with a couple from France thrown in for good measure, in the William Hill Cheveley Park Stakes at Newmarket. No-one would deny her the right to be regarded as a smart filly. But Durtal did not look all that smart in the Champagne Stakes. In fact she was made to look pretty ordinary. It is this ability to make its opponents look much worse than they actually are which distinguishes the very good horse from the 'merely good' one. Tudor Minstrel had it, Sea-Bird II had it, and so, it appeared, had J. O. Tobin. That there could possibly be a better two-year-old seemed inconceivable.

After this brilliant performance the way seemed clear for J. O. Tobin to crown his two-year-old career, a career which had begun with a comfortable success in a maiden race at Newmarket in July and had been followed three weeks later by a very smooth and impressively-achieved win over Priors Walk and Tachypous in the Richmond Stakes at Goodwood, with a victory in the Grand Criterium. The French had a very good colt called Blushing Groom, who had won the Prix Robert Papin, the Prix Morny and the Prix de la Salamandre, but in the eyes of most English observers J. O. Tobin was invincible, 'the best two-year-old to have raced in this country for years', and Murless was even contemplating putting off his retirement so that he could bow out with a classic winner. But the French would have none of it. They might not have seen J. O. Tobin, or, to be precise, most of them might not have seen him, but what they had seen of their own champion had so impressed them that they made Blushing Groom an odds-on favourite. And they were right. Piggott, very wisely, tracked Blushing Groom in the early stages, and when that horse went into the lead on the turn, so J. O. Tobin attempted to go with him. At one point J. O. Tobin got to within a length and a half of the leader, but he couldn't hold on, and in the last furlong Blushing Groom went right away to beat him four lengths into third place. The bubble had burst.

What does one make of J. O. Tobin on this performance? Well those, of whom his trainer was one, who attributed his eclipse to failure to stay the mile were in a majority. Considering his breeding this is surprising, and had we

Fulbourn Maiden Stakes, Newmarket—J. O. Tobin beats the more experienced Chain of Reasoning

not seen the race such an explanation would be the last to occur to us. Other things being equal, one would expect a horse by Red God (Blushing Groom is a son of that stallion) to have more speed and less stamina in its make-up than one by Never Bend, and on top of that there is Hill Shade, J. O. Tobin's dam. Hill Shade won in good company at up to a mile and a quarter and to Crepello bred Mysterious, who won the Oaks at a mile and a half, as well, of course, as the One Thousand Guineas. If there were only breeding considerations to go upon, it would be reasonable to expect J. O. Tobin to get at least a mile and a quarter. But one can never be certain of these things. In reality J. O. Tobin is no more *certain* for instance to get a mile and a quarter than was Fairman, by Manacle out of a Floribunda mare, *certain* to be a sprinter; and when our expectation is not fulfilled, it does not show our thinking to be at fault, only that the less likely eventuality materialised. Our reading of the Grand Criterium is that J. O. Tobin, after showing the pace to get to a length and a half of Blushing Groom, *faltered* and allowed the other to go away again. He did not carry on right to the end as one who stayed the trip thoroughly would have done, and Amyntor, a horse with no pretension to the sort of speed J. O. Tobin showed against Durtal, made up a deal of ground on him in the closing stages to beat him by a head. We don't wish to imply that J. O. Tobin is a better horse than Blushing Groom or that he would have beaten him had he stayed the trip, but we are satisfied that there is nothing like the four lengths between them that the Grand Criterium suggests, and that Blushing Groom is therefore a little flattered by the result. One shouldn't leave the race without adding that J. O. Tobin looked a little light beforehand, and might perhaps have been not quite at his best.

J. O. Tobin (br.c. 1974)	Never Bend (b 1960)	Nasrullah (b 1940)	Nearco / Mumtaz Begum
		Lalun (b 1952)	Djeddah / Be Faithful
	Hill Shade (br 1965)	Hillary (br 1952)	Khaled / Snow Bunny
		Penumbra (b 1955)	Imperium / Moonrise

J. O. Tobin's connections could take some consolation in the knowledge that he had been beaten by a two-year-old of exceptional merit (we ignore Amyntor, who did not get into the Grand Criterium until J. O. Tobin had lost it) but inevitably his defeat served to knock some of the shine off him. Shortly after the William Hill Dewhurst Stakes Piggott was quoted in the *Daily Express* to the effect that The Minstrel would have 'murdered' J. O. Tobin. Quite possibly Piggott was merely indulging himself in a little exaggeration to empha- sise the fact that he believed The Minstrel to be the better colt; in which case, fair enough: if on the other hand it was a seriously considered remark meant to be taken seriously, it is, to us, so fantastic that we cannot possibly let it pass without comment. We have a very high opinion of The Minstrel, but so far as

Richmond Stakes, Goodwood—J. O. Tobin has no difficulty in beating Priors Walk and Tachypous (left)

Laurent Perrier Champagne Stakes, Doncaster—J. O. Tobin wins in tremendous style from Durtal

we are concerned the horse we saw ridden along to put four lengths between himself and an easing-down Saros in the Dewhurst Stakes would never in a million years have 'murdered' the one we saw winning the Champagne Stakes virtually on a tight rein. What the handicapper Mr Gibbs thinks may be judged from the fact that in the Two-Year-Old Free Handicap J. O. Tobin has to concede The Minstrel 8 lb.

A well-grown, impressive-looking individual with the stamp of quality, J. O. Tobin was sent back to the States on the retirement of Noel Murless. Murless, the most successful trainer in the history of British racing, sent out the winners of 1,430 races in a career dating back to 1935, was leading trainer nine times, and won a total of nineteen classics and £3,650,000 in win and place money. He did not believe in giving his classic hopes a hard time in their first season, and of the many champions to pass through his hands—Abernant, Petite Etoile, Crepello, Aunt Edith, St Paddy, Royal Palace for example—J. O. Tobin was only the second to top the Two-Year-Old Free Handicap. J. O. Tobin's breeding has already been mentioned, but we would like to add that his dam improved into one of the best of her sex after running unplaced in the Guineas and Oaks, and won three of her last four races; whilst Never Bend, who died early in 1977, was of course, the sire of Mill Reef. Several horses from J. O. Tobin's family have distinguished themselves in high-class company in America, and it will be surprising if J. O. Tobin does not do the same. The 1977 season in this country will be all the poorer without him. *N. Murless.*

JOYFUL GOD 3 ch.g. Green God 128–Sheer Joy (Major Portion 129) [1975 5s 5fg 6g 9fg⁵ 1976 10.8fg 8fg 7f 7g 6fg] lightly-made, quite attractive gelding: little worthwhile form in varied company, including selling, when trained by M. Jarvis and was sold 575 gns Ascot July Sales after fourth outing: said by former stable to be very wayward and ran out on first outing for new stable. *J. Murphy, Ireland.*   —

JOYFUL JET 3 b.f. Majetta 115–Joyful Queen (Sovereign Lord 120) [1975 6f 6f⁶ 6d 8v 1976 8h⁵] of no account. *C. Boothman.*   —

JOYFUL MAJOR 3 b.c. Major Portion 129–Lovely Alice (Galivanter 131) [1975 5s 5dg⁵ 5fg⁴ 7g 6g 6s 7g 1976 10.1fg 8.3f 8.3fg] useful sort in appearance but is only a plater: had some stiff tasks in 1976: ran very badly when tried in blinkers on last outing at 2 yrs. *A. Davison.*   —

JOYOUS IMP 2 ch.f. Green God 128–Carrick Castle 90 (Democratic 124) [1976 5f 5.3g 5f] no worthwhile form, including in sellers: sold 190 gns Ascot November Sales. *R. Akehurst.*   —

JOY'S MELODY 3 b.g. River Beauty 105–Vipinsor (Windsor Sun 116) [1975 N.R. 1976 6v 8v⁵] half-brother to two winners in Ireland and Italy: 500 gns foal, resold 190 gns yearling: dam ran only at 2 yrs: well beaten in plating company. *A. Smith.*   —

JUDY BURTON 2 b.f. Mummy's Pet 125–Judith 59 (Dumbarnie 125) [1976 5g] half-sister to three winners here and abroad, including useful 1m to 11f handicapper Coolmack (by Rise 'N Shine II): dam a sprinter: tenth of 12 to Sharpway in maiden race at Lanark in October. *J. Cousins.*

JUGE DE PAIX 2 br.c. Delta Judge–Egg Hunt (Blue Prince 123) [1976 5d* **116** 5.5g⁶ 8g* 8d² 8s⁵] American-bred French colt: brother to Eggy, rated equal second-best 2-y-o filly in U.S.A. in 1970 when winner at up to 8.5f, and half-brother to three minor winners: $75,000 yearling: dam won three times in U.S.A.: a smart colt who won two important races, finishing very strongly to win Prix du Bois at Longchamp in June by a head from Line Slippers, and getting the better of Shimnar in closing stages to win Prix des Foals at Deauville in August by ½ length: 2 lengths second to Command Freddy when giving 6 lb to most of 12-runner field in Group 3 Prix la Rochette at Longchamp in September, but ran nowhere near that form when remote fifth of six to Sporting Yankee in William Hill Futurity Stakes at Doncaster the following month: much better suited by 1m than sprint distances: possibly not at his best on very soft going. *A. Penna, France.*

JUKEBOX JURY 4 b.c. Jukebox 120–Cecilia Q.C. 89 (Counsel 118) [1974 **89** N.R. 1975 6s³ 5d* 5fg* 6g³ 5fg* 6g 5f² 5g⁶ 1976 5fg* 6fg 5.8f³ 5fg⁵ 6fg⁴ 6f* 6g] useful sort: quite a useful handicapper: successful at Kempton in April and Newmarket in August, on latter course beating Kiyoswanee 1½ lengths: effective at 5f and 6f, and promises to stay further: appears to act on any going: good mount for an apprentice: genuine and consistent but ran below his best on final outing: sold 4,100 gns Newmarket Autumn Sales. *Doug Smith.*

JUKE'S WALK 3 b.g. Jukebox 120–Camel Walk (Windsor Slipper) [1975 5s — 5s⁴ 5s⁶ 5s 5g⁵ 7f 6g⁵ 5f 1976 6f] leggy gelding: quite a moderate plater at 2 yrs: well beaten in better company on only outing in 1976 (April): should stay 7f: wore blinkers at 2 yrs. *S. Nesbitt.*

JULIETTE JONES 2 br.f. No Mercy 126–Bright Future 91 (Darius 129) **57** [1976 5fg 5g 6g 5g 5f⁴ 5f] workmanlike filly: plater: 4 lengths fourth of 11 to Gay Alice at Windsor in August: should stay 6f+: wears blinkers nowadays. *P. Cundell.*

JULI'S SON 2 ch.c. Joshua 129–Juli Girl 82 (Saint Crespin III 132) [1976 **74** 5f 5f² 5s 5f⁶ 5.9g² 7fg⁶ 5.9f⁵ 6f 8fg* 8s 7v] leggy colt: third foal: half-brother to fair 6f winner Gold Mark (by Jimmy Reppin): blinkered first time, won 23-runner race at Leicester in September comfortably by 1½ lengths from Velvet Circle: (bought in 950 gns) in rear in nurseries afterwards, once wearing blinkers: stays 1m well: acts on firm going and is probably unsuited by soft: sold 900 gns Ascot December Sales. *M. Tate.*

JUMPABOUT 6 ch.h. Double Jump 131–Sheer Joy (Major Portion 129) [1974 **105** d 10d² 10h² 10g* 8g 10fg² 10fg⁶ 9d⁶ 1975 10s 10fg* 10fg* 8f⁵ 10fg⁵ 10g³ 10d⁵ 1976 9g⁵ 10fg⁴ 10.5fg⁵ 10f³ 10g 10g 10.8s⁵] light-framed, lengthy horse: good mover: smart performer (rated 114) at 5 yrs: ran well on his first two starts in 1976, on second of them finishing 8 lengths fourth to Fool's Mate in P.T.S. Laurels Stakes at Goodwood in July: most disappointing afterwards: stays 1¼m: acts on easy going but is particularly well suited by top-of-the-ground conditions. *J. Sutcliffe.*

JUMP FOR JOY 3 ch.g. Double Jump 131–Jolly Jane (Jolly Jet 111) [1975 **46** 5f 5fg 5f 6d 6d 1976 5g 9fg³ 10f⁴ 8h⁵ 7f⁵ 6f²] dipped-backed gelding: plater: put up best effort when tried in blinkers final outing: best form at 6f: sold to M. Salaman 775 gns Ascot July Sales. *W. A. Stephenson.*

JUMPING HILL 4 gr.c. Hillary–Frequently (Decidedly) [1974 6g⁴ 1975 7v **119** 10.5d 8fg 9d* 8.2s² 1976 9fg⁴ 10g² 8s* 8f* 8fg² 9g] strong, well-made American-bred colt: very smart handicapper: did well at 4 yrs and put up a fine performance when winning sixteen-runner Royal Hunt Cup at Royal Ascot under 9-7, dominating race virtually throughout and going clear in final furlong to beat My Hussar 4 lengths: turned in another first-class effort when neck second to Silver Steel in Rose of York Handicap at York in August, battling on extremely gamely after coming under pressure 3f from home: successful earlier in season in well-contested event (also at York) and finished in frame in Earl of Sefton Stakes at Newmarket and Sandown Cup (both in April): stays 1¼m: acts on any going: well suited by forcing tactics: thoroughly genuine and consistent but ran moderately (sweated up) in Irish Sweeps Cambridgeshire at Newmarket in October (favourite under 9-11): sent to race in America. *N. Murless.*

JUMPS JUNIOR 2 b.c. Double Jump 131–Ellora 92 (Relic) [1976 5f 6f⁶ 8fg] — plain colt: behind in maiden races and a seller. *R. Hollinshead.*

JUMP TO IT 2 ch.c. Double Jump 131–Pie Eye 88 (Exbury 138) [1976 5f³ **92** 5s* 5d⁴ 6f* 6f⁴] strong, good sort: second foal: half-brother to fair 1975 2-y-o 1m winner Princess Pie Eye (by Prince de Galles): dam won over 9f: narrow

Royal Hunt Cup, Ascot—Jumping Hill provides Noel Murless with his last Royal Ascot winner. Chasing vainly are My Hussar and Yamadori

winner of maiden race at Chester in May and £1,200 event at Leicester the following month: creditable fourth in well-contested race at Pontefract later in June but was not seen out again: will stay 7f: acts on any going: blinkered final outing: genuine. *F. J. Houghton.*

JUNELLA 2 ch.f. Midsummer Night II 117–Potentilla 89 (Nearula 132) [1976 6fg⁶ 6fg² 6f³ 6g⁴ 8g] attractive filly: half-sister to several winners, including fairly useful stayer Potent Councillor (by Privy Councillor): 1,000 gns yearling: dam won over 13f: ran well in two maiden races at Newmarket, finishing 1½ lengths second to Etienne Gerard in July and 3 lengths third of 21 to Mecanopsis in August: will stay 1¼m. *T. Waugh.*   **81**

JUNIOR MISS 2 ch.f. Lorenzaccio 130–None-So-Pretty (Never Say Die 137) [1976 5f⁵ 5.9g⁶] first foal: 3,500 gns yearling: dam, who ran three times at 2 yrs, is daughter of half-sister to Display, Pourparler, Fleet and Democratie: showed only a little ability in maiden races at Windsor and Wolverhampton in August: may do better over middle distances. *P. Robinson.*   **—**

JUNKEY 2 ch.c. Swinging Junior 118–Tourney (Breakspear II) [1976 5fg⁶ 5s 5d³ 5f³ 5f³ 5.9f³ 5.9fg 5fg 6v] lengthy colt: in frame in maiden races and a nursery: stays 6f: blinkered last three outings: dwelt when well beaten in a seller on final outing: sold 1,200 gns Doncaster October Sales. *J. Edwards.*   **66**

JUSLUST 2 ch.c. Sky Gipsy 117–Darlinda 85 (Darius 129) [1976 8v] third produce: half-brother to useful 1974 2-y-o plater Smokey Clown (by Hill Clown), subsequently a winner in Belgium: 1,050 gns foal, resold 360 gns yearling: dam stayed 1¾m: dwelt and always behind in 13-runner maiden race won by Starlight Lad at Teesside in October. *R. Bastiman.*   **—**

JUSTAFANCY 3 ch.g. Royal Palace 131–Flights Fancy 95 (Worden II 129) [1975 N.R. 1976 16.1f⁶ 15.8g⁶] fourth foal: half-brother to two minor winners: 620 gns foal: dam a stayer: sixth in poor maiden races at Haydock (amateur riders event) in August and Catterick (looked rough in his coat) the following month. *G. Richards.*   **—**

JUST AMY 4 b.f. Song 132–Chinaberry (Shantung 132) [1974 5d³ 1975 5v 6v⁴ 5f 6g 8f 8.2d 9g⁶ 7g 8g² 8.2g⁵ 8d⁴ 1976 12fg 8f² 8g 10h⁴ 8f⁵ 7fg] unfurnished   **55**

filly: plater: won in Jersey in 1976: best at 1m: acts on firm going: ran well in blinkers ninth outing in 1975: in foal to Reliance II. *S. Norton.*

JUST FOR YOU 2 b.f. Decoy Boy 129–Wild Words 76 (Galivanter 131) [1976 **79**
5fg 5f* 6d] half-sister to two fairly useful winners, including 7f to 1¼m performer Debenture (by Tycoon II): 1,750 gns yearling: dam half-sister to very useful sprinter Sound Barrier: won quite well-contested minor event at Chepstow in May by ¾ length from Master Wrekin: not seen out again until September when behind in nursery at Windsor. *J. Hill.*

JUST FRED 3 br.c. Town Crier 119–Just Jenny 88 (Ennis 128) [1975 5d 5g⁵ **82**
5g⁴ 5fg⁴ 5f³ 5fg⁴ 5g⁶ 5f 5f⁶ 5g³ 5d² 6f⁴ 6g⁶ 1976 6fg 5.9fg⁴ 5f* 5fg² 5f² 5f³ 5d³ 5f⁶ 5h* 5fg⁶ 6g 5fg] strong, useful sort: moderate handicapper: game winner of maiden race at Beverley in April: ran well in many of his races afterwards and picked up a handicap at Carlisle in July: not certain to stay beyond 5f: appears to act on any going: best in blinkers: said by trainer to have dropped himself out after missing break on eighth outing. *R. Hollinshead.*

JUST JANIE 2 b.f. John Splendid 116–Crop (Acropolis 132) [1976 5g 5fg* 5f³ **84**
5g³] small, lengthy filly: first foal: 500 gns yearling: dam of little account: made all to win 28-runner maiden race at Windsor in June by 3 lengths from Johnjo: good third of 12 to Last Sale in nursery at Sandown in September: should stay 6f. *S. James.*

JUST JOLLY 5 b.m. Jolly Jet 111–Not for Portia 68 (King's Bench 132) **54**
[1974 10.1f 10.1fg 10g 14d 10.1g³ 10g² 12f* 11.7d² 14s 13s³ 12.2v² 16s²
12v² 1975 11.7g 17.7fg⁵ 1976 16f* 14fg³ 17.7f 16f⁶] big mare: won handicap at Nottingham in April by 3 lengths from Tantalos: stays very well: acts on any going: suitable mount for an apprentice. *P. Taylor.*

JUST REVENGE 4 ch.c. Compensation 127–Wise Counsel (Counsel 118) [1974 **86**
5g³ 5g* 6f³ 5fg⁴ 6fg 6g³ 6d⁶ 5s⁴ 1975 8fg* 8s⁴ 7.3s⁴ 7g 8fg² 8g 8.3fg³ 10f³ 9fg³ 8g
1976 10fg³ 8f² 9g 10fg* 11.7fg² 10g⁶ 10g⁴ 10s² 11s³ 10s³] robust colt: fair handicapper: won at Goodwood in May and ran creditably afterwards: stays 1½m: probably acts on any going: used to wear blinkers but didn't after third outing: sold to D. Barons 5,400 gns Newmarket Autumn Sales. *A. Corbett.*

JUST SHERWOOD 2 gr.f. Town Crier 119–Just Jenny 88 (Ennis 128) [1976 **85**
5v 5v 5s³] sister to winning 3-y-o sprinter Just Fred, and half-sister to two other winners: dam a sprinter: slow into stride but had every chance from distance when going down in a desperate finish to Miss Bagley and So Cutting in maiden race at Teesside in November: should win a race. *R. Hollinshead.*

JUST TEMPEST 3 ch.f. Caliban 123–February 84 (Will Somers 114 §) [1975 **50**
5g 6g 5g⁴ 5d⁶ 5f⁴ 5g² 5v 1976 6g⁴ 7g 5f 7fg 6f 6g 5s⁴ 7v² 8s⁴] plater: best form at up to 7f: changed hands 300 gns Doncaster October Sales. *L. Docker.*

K

KABAGOLD 2 br.c. Goldhill 125–Golden Palermo 70 (Dumbarnie 125) [1976 **82**
5fg³ 5f² 5fg³ 6s³ 5s* 5v*] neat colt: brother to a winning plater and half-brother to another: 680 gns yearling: dam won 5f seller at 3 yrs: won seller (no bid) at Haydock and claiming race at Leicester in space of four days at back-end of season: best form at 5f: seems to act on any going but is well suited by plenty of give in the ground. *W. A. Stephenson.*

KABRUF 3 b.f. Hopeful Venture 125–Consula 88 (Privy Councillor 125) [1975 **42**
7g 6f 7g⁶ 9fg⁴ 9g 1976 12fg 12.2d 8f³] tall, lengthy filly: quite a moderate plater: possibly does not stay 1½m. *N. Callaghan.*

KAFKA 6 b.h. Royal Palace 131–Bewilder 87 (Crepello 136) [1974 11g 12g 12.3g³ **87**
12d⁵ 10s 8g⁴ 11s² 10s* 1975 12d 10v⁵ 10s 10.4g² 10f³ 10f* 10h* 12.3g⁴ 10f 10.5fg⁶
1976 12g 10.6d 10fg 10d³ 10f⁵ 10f* 10f* 10g⁴ 10.5fg³ 10.2g⁴ 11g² 10.5v⁶ 12d⁵]
fair handicapper: successful at Lanark and Redcar in July, on latter course battling back gamely to head Affirmative close home: stays 1½m but best form at 1¼m: acts on any going: sometimes wears blinkers: sold 3,500 gns Newmarket Autumn Sales, reportedly for export to Sweden. *Denys Smith.*

KAFUE PARK 3 ch.c. Ragusa 137–Kew 110 (Princely Gift 137) [1975 6f* 7fg³ **110**
1976 8g* 12f* 10g⁴ 12fg² 12g 10fg² 11.7g³ 10g³] compact colt: overcame difficulties in running when winning £1,600 event at Liverpool in April and Hethersett Stakes at Brighton later in same month, on latter course leading close home to beat St Joles a head: runner-up in two good races at Goodwood afterwards, namely Predominate Stakes (beaten 4 lengths by General Ironside) and Extel Handicap

Arena Sports Advertising Stakes, Liverpool—Kafue Park finds the best turn of foot and beats Sweet Lad and Via Con Vente

(beaten a head by Il Padrone): out of his depth in Epsom Derby in between (nineteenth of 23): stays 1½m: goes well on fast ground: well suited by waiting tactics: sold to G. Peter-Hoblyn 23,000 gns Newmarket December Sales. *R. Price.*

KALA SHIKARI 3 br.c. Huntercombe 133–Vigour 72 (Vilmorin) [1975 5g 5fg³ **125** 6fg³ 5fg⁵ 5fg* 6s⁵ 6g* 6g* 1976 8s 5fg³ 6d³ 6g* 5d* 6fg 5fg⁶ 6g* 5s 5s²]

Ravi Tikkoo's decision to move some of his horses to France after the 1975 season met with mixed fortune. His horses amassed over £350,000 during the year, but his stable's activities will be centred on Belmont Park, New York, in 1977. Mr Tikkoo's main reason for leaving France after so short a stay was, we gathered, that he felt unwelcome in racing circles there, and he went so far as to say that he thought the French Jockey Club had victimized him by disqualifying his Haneena and Java Rajah after wins in valuable races. Consequently he decided to sell forty horses at the Deauville November Sales and send the rest of his horses in training to America. 'Top' price of 530,000 francs (approximately £63,850) at the sale was paid for the sprinter Kala Shikari. He was bought by a Mr Jones, apparently a close associate of Mr Tikkoo, and it is expected that Kala Shikari will be campaigning from Belmont Park in 1977.

The Tikkoo horses put life into the French sprint races. Of the seven major French sprints—the Prix de Saint-Georges, Gros-Chene, Maurice de Gheest, Meautry, Seine-et-Oise, l'Abbaye and Petit Couvert—only the Saint-Georges and the l'Abbaye went by without a Tikkoo horse finishing first or second. What's more, the only French-trained three-year-olds to finish in the first three in these seven major sprints were the Tikkoo-owned Kala Shikari and Arch Sculptor. Although Kala Shikari did not have much opposition from his own age group in France and was beaten on all his four visits to this country during 1976, he was probably as good as any English sprinter of his age. His best form in France, where he had three victories from five attempts at sprint distances, including in two pattern races, is much better than his thirds in the Palace House Stakes and the Duke of York Stakes and his seventh to Lochnager, after being baulked, in the July Cup.

Following a victory in a minor event, the Prix Cor du Chasse, at Maisons-Laffitte early in June, Kala Shikari contested the Prix du Gros-Chene at Chantilly eighteen days later. The Tikkoo stable fielded four of the nine runners —Kala Shikari, Arch Sculptor, Brave Panther and Harrapan Seal—but Polly Peachum started an odds-on favourite. For a time it looked as if the Tikkoo horses might fill the first four places and in the end Kala Shikari won by two lengths from Arch Sculptor, with Polly Peachum a head away third. In the Prix de Seine-et-Oise at Maisons-Laffitte three months later the stable again fielded four runners, Kala Shikari and Arch Sculptor being accompanied to post this time by Hittite Glory and Nagin. Unlike in the Gros-Chene, however, they filled three of the last four places, but Kala Shikari won the race, taking the lead from Vitiges at the distance and just holding off Raga Navarro by a short head with Mendip Man and Vitiges close up in third and fourth places.

The Prix du Petit Couvert at Longchamp in October was the final and decisive leg of the French sprint championship. Kala Shikari was opposed by Girl Friend, winner of the three good races that Kala Shikari did not contest (the

Saint-Georges, Maurice de Gheest and Meautry), and Mendip Man, who had dead-heated with Gentilhombre in the Prix de l'Abbaye when Kala Shikari had run unaccountably badly. Girl Friend started favourite to win her fourth pattern race of the season and did it in good style, depriving Kala Shikari of the lead inside the final furlong and beating him by two lengths.

Kala Shikari (br.c. 1973)	Huntercombe (b 1967)	Derring-Do (br 1961)	Darius
			Sipsey Bridge
		Ergina (br 1957)	Fair Trial
			Ballechin
	Vigour (gr 1961)	Vilmorin (gr 1943)	Gold Bridge
			Queen of the Meadows
		Pompienne (br 1953)	Éble
			Pomelane

Kala Shikari is the fourth and by far the best winning produce of Vigour, a winner of a six-furlong seller. Vigour's dam Pompienne who won at up to thirteen furlongs, is a sister to the Poule d'Essai des Pouliches winner Pomare. Kala Shikari, a 5,000 guinea yearling, is by Huntercombe, a better sprinter than Kala Shikari. Huntercombe has made a reasonably satisfactory start to his stud career, getting the very useful performers Hunting Prince and Sefton Court in his first crop, Kala Shikari, the Eclipse third and fourth, Radetzky and Arapaho, in his second, and the speedy two-year-olds Aspect, Ground Cover and Jameson in his third. However, the average price of his yearlings sold at public auction has halved in three years. Perhaps his change of location (he moved to the Greenmount Stud in the summer) will correspond with an upturn in his fortunes.

Kala Shikari made up into a powerful, strong, shapely colt. He acts on any going and is effective at five and six furlongs. He was well beaten when tried at a mile and is most unlikely to stay that distance. There should be plenty of opportunities for a good sprinter like him in America, provided he can adapt to the conditions. It will be interesting to see how he and his stablemates fare in their new surroundings. *A. Breasley, France.*

KALGOORLIE 3 ch.g. Goldhill 125–Copper Gold (Democratic 124) [1975 5f 5f⁶ 5f² 5f³ 6g² 6g 6g³ 7g² 7.2v⁶ 1976 8fg⁴ 8f 9fg 7.6fg*] strong, good-bodied gelding: made all when winning moderate 16-runner maiden race at Chester in September staying on by 3 lengths from Churchillian: stays 7f well: acts on any going: blinkered last two outings at 2 yrs and at Chester. *M. H. Easterby.* **85**

KALIPHA 2 ch.f. Lyphard 132–Kalise (Kashmir II 125) [1976 7.5s*] French filly: first foal: dam very useful at up to 9f in France: 7/1, put up an encouraging display in 14-runner newcomers event at Saint-Cloud in October, always holding a good place and coming through early in straight to win decisively by 2½ lengths: will probably stay 1¼m: likely to make a smart 3-y-o. *J. Cunnington, jnr, France.* **?**

KALLISSIMA 3 b.f. Tudor Melody 129–Matatina 132 (Grey Sovereign 128 §) [1975 4d² 4.5g 5s 6.5s³ 6.5s 1976 6fg² 7fg 8f* 7f 8.5g² 8fg³ 8fg 8f* 7fg⁶ 8.3d⁶ 7s] narrow ex-French filly: a twin: half-sister to Irish Sweeps Lincoln winner New Chapter (by Crepello) and useful 5f winner Miss Charisma (by Ragusa): dam top-class sprinter: won 17-runner maiden race at Thirsk in April and three-runner handicap at Brighton in August: stays 1m: acts on any going: has been tried in blinkers but does better without: sold 35,000 gns Newmarket December Sales, reportedly for export to Australia. *R. Boss.* **87**

KAMICIA 2 b.f. Kashmir II 125–Micia (Mincio 127) [1976 7d 9d* 8s*] **119**
The Criterium des Pouliches at Longchamp, France's only Group 1 race for two-year-old fillies, is as good a place as any to start looking for classic fillies. Of those to have run in it since its inception in 1969 Pampered Miss, Bold Fascinator and Allez France have gone on to win the Poule d'Essai des Pouliches; Prodice and Comtesse de Loir the Prix Saint-Alary; Rescousse and Allez France the Prix de Diane; Paysanne, Allez France and Paulista the Prix Vermeille; and Polygamy the Oaks. An interesting point here is that only Allez France was successful in the Criterium, so don't be surprised if the 1976 winner, Kamicia, good filly though she is, doesn't turn out to be the best in the field at three years.

Judging by her starting price of 32/1, it was a surprise that Kamicia proved the best of them at two years. She had beaten out only twice and, though she had won a minor race at Evry easily by four lengths on her second start, several of the others in the Criterium des Pouliches seemed to have much better form. Silk Slipper had won the Prix des Chenes by four lengths, up against colts;

Criterium des Pouliches, Longchamp—outsiders fill the first three places, victory going to Kamicia over Doha and Orchid Miss

Assez Cuite had been beaten only two lengths by Blushing Groom in the Prix de la Salamandre; Proud Event had run out an impressive winner of the hotly-contested Prix d'Aumale; and Anya Ylina, who started favourite, had created a most favourable impression when winning her only race. Kamicia quickly showed she had been grossly underrated by the punters. Her little-known jockey Flachi, riding a filly whose stamina was already well established, made the mile as severe a test as he could in the soft ground, dictating the pace. All the fancied fillies were in trouble early in the straight and Kamicia wasn't hard pressed from then on to hold off Doha, an even longer-priced outsider, by three lengths. To make all the running in such a race was a particularly fine effort by Kamicia, but we are doubtful whether the form of the race is as good as in previous years. Doha is without a win after eight races and the third horse, Orchid Miss, is still a maiden after five. Orchid Miss was beaten only three and three quarter lengths by Kamicia although the nearest she had come to winning previously was to finish a two-and-a-half-length second in a maiden race, and on her outing after the Pouliches she was beaten over seven lengths in the Prix des Reservoirs. The English filly Olwyn, also a maiden, was beaten less than six lengths into sixth place in the Pouliches.

Kamicia (b.f. 1974)	Kashmir II (br 1963)	Tudor Melody (br 1956)	Tudor Minstrel
			Matelda
		Queen of Speed (b 1950)	Blue Train
			Bishopscourt
	Micia (ch 1967)	Mincio (b 1957)	Relic
			Merise
		Furka (b 1954)	Tantieme
			Francia

Kamicia's pedigree suggests that she shouldn't be troubled by a mile and a quarter. Her dam, Micia, was placed over that distance but was a very disappointing filly, retiring without a win although she was beaten only about four lengths in the 1970 Poule d'Essai des Pouliches. Micia is making amends at stud; she has also produced the two-year-old winner Guest Artist (by Sword Dancer), who has since become one of the best young chasers in France. On the whole the family is a moderate one but another horse from it won a lot of money over jumps, Micia's half-brother Furlevant, who won the Grand Course de Haies des 4 Ans and was still winning good races as an eleven-year-old.

Kamicia has every right to be considered a live classic hope and could provide Kashmir II with his third French Guineas winner, following Moulines and Dumka. However, the results of some of the important fillies' races in France in the autumn were so difficult to make sense of that we wouldn't be at all surprised to see a little-known filly, a Flying Water or a Pawneese, come along and beat her. It's worth pointing out that very few of Daniel Wildenstein's string of over forty two-year-olds raced in 1976. Danseuse Etoile, one of his unraced fillies, was named as third favourite in the first ante-post list for the One Thousand Guineas and may well be a name to remember. *J. Laumain, France.*

KANDY BELLE 3 b.f. Hot Brandy 119–Sunny Belle (Windsor Sun 116) [1975   —
N.R. 1976 6g 8d] first foal: dam won selling hurdle: behind in seller at Leicester in June and amateur riders race at Yarmouth in September. *P. Allingham.*

K'ANG HSI 2 ch.c. Veiled Wonder–Nicona 89 (Nicolaus) [1976 5g6 5f3 5s* 5s5   84
7f4 7f5 6fg5 6f* 7f 6fg 6g5 8fg] useful-looking colt: half-brother to quite moderate 1m and 9f winner Tracona (by Track Spare): 550 gns foal, resold 920 gns

377

yearling: dam won four races at up to 1¼m: won maiden auction event at Doncaster in May and was always going well when winning eight-runner nursery at Redcar in August comfortably by 3 lengths from Sandbeck Song: has yet to show he stays 7f: acts on any going: none too consistent. *K. Payne.*

KARAFAIR 3 b.f. Karabas 132–Lynsted 79 (Big Game) [1975 N.R. 1976 — 8fg 8.2g 12.3fg 12.3f 8h 12v 8s⁵] of no account. *W. Murray.*

KARAKORUM 3 b.c. Realm 129–Focal 92 (Faubourg II 127) [1975 5f² 5fg³ 75 5fg⁴ 6g 5g⁵ 1976 7f* 7f⁴ 7g 8f] strong colt: good mover: won handicap at Warwick in April by 2 lengths from Baron Bunch: stays 7f: acts well on firm going: blinkered final outing at 2 yrs: sold 3,200 gns Ascot September Sales. *J. Nelson.*

KARANTINA 2 ch.f. Relko 136–Dorabella 88 (Rockefella) [1976 7s] sister — p to 1½m winner Relkotime, and half-sister to winners in France and Italy: dam, a winner over 9f and 1½m, is half-sister to Arietta and Anamnestes: 16/1, showed in front for over four furlongs when eighth of 19 to stable-companion Lady Oriana in maiden race at Newmarket in October: will do better over longer distances at 3 yrs. *B. Hills.*

KARELLA 2 b.f. Jukebox 120–Wise Counsel (Counsel 118) [1976 5fg* 5fg³ 5fg² 88 5.1fg³ 6fg⁴ 5g² 5g⁴ 5f⁴ 5fg 5s* 5d³] small, good-bodied filly: half-sister to three winners, including fairly useful 3-y-o Wickwell (by Wolver Hollow), successful at up to 1¼m: 3,300 gns yearling: dam plating-class half-sister to top 1963 2-y-o Talahasse: won maiden race at Leicester in March by 2 lengths from Brightelmstone and just got up to beat Fenny Boy when winning nursery at Warwick in October: probably stays 6f: acts on any going: blinkered twice, running creditably on first occasion but moderately on second: consistent. *A. Corbett.*

KARIS 2 ch.g. Keren 100–Madrina (Majority Blue 126) [1976 5d 5v] compact, — fair sort: second foal: dam ran only twice: in rear in October in minor event at Haydock (last of eight) and £1,800 maiden race at York. *T. Fairhurst.*

KASHIWA 4 ch.c. St Alphage 119–Trani (Nagami 124) [1974 5v³ 5d² 5s³ 115 5g* 5f² 6f² 7g⁶ 6s² 8s³ 6s⁵ 1975 5s⁴ 6d² 7v⁵ 7f³ 7g* 6fg² 7.9f* 9fg³ 10fg³ 8f² 9f*

Mr Phil Bull's "Karantina"

Baron T. de Zuylen de Nyevelt's "Kasteel"

7g² 7f² 9g² 6d² 8s 1976 9s⁴ 10g³ 8f* 6.3f³ 9f⁴ 8.6f² 9f* 6g* 7f* 8fg³ 8s⁵] ex-Irish colt: smart performer: enjoyed a fine season in 1976, winning four races, including two at Phoenix Park: put up a cracking performance when winning Herbertstown Stakes on that course in August, beating Grande Prairie and National Wish, the first three finishing 8 lengths clear of four others: favourite when gaining his final success, taking Turf Club Stakes at the Curragh in September by 2 lengths from Matagouri: very narrowly beaten when third of 25 to Floriferous in Irish Cambridgeshire on latter course later in month and when fifth to Serencia at Phoenix Park in October: effective at sprint distances and stays 1¼m: acts on any going: wears blinkers: suitable mount for an apprentice: consistent: to be trained by G. Pritchard-Gordon in 1977. *K. Prendergast, Ireland.*

KASHVILLE 4 bl.c. Kashmir II 125–Wold Lass 77 (Vilmorin) [1974 5g⁴ 5fg³ 5fg* 5s² 5d 5fg* 5s 1975 5d 6g² 5f 7f⁶ 8fg 6fg 5.8h² 6g⁵ 5f⁶ 5f* 5f⁵ 5fg² 1976 5.9g 5.9f 5f] attractive, well-made colt: lightly raced and no worthwhile form in 1976: acted on hard going and was not at his best on soft: at stud in Ireland. *M. Jarvis.* —

KASSANDROS 2 b.c. Shiny Tenth 120–Fruit and Nut 76 (Hard Sauce 131) 75
[1976 5f 5.9g 6f² 5h³ 5f³ 6d 7s] compact, deep-girthed colt: first foal: dam won over 6f at 2 yrs: quite a moderate maiden: suited by 6f but possibly does not stay 7f: blinkered last three outings, running respectably on first two. *J. Nelson.*

KASTEEL 4 b.c. King of the Castle–Esme (Le Haar 126) [1974 7d 8s* 10v⁵ 126
1975 8v⁶ 9.7v⁴ 10g² 9g³ 10g³ 10g* 10s* 12s 1976 10fg⁵ 10.5g² 9.7d* 10fg 10d²
11s* 12s] neat, attractive French colt: ran four excellent races in France at 4 yrs and is a considerably better horse than his only appearance in this country might suggest, when only eighth of nine to Trepan in Joe Coral Eclipse Stakes at Sandown in July (was almost certainly unsuited by firmish ground): had earlier won Prix Dollar at Longchamp by 2 lengths from El Rastro and finished short-head second of 11 to Infra Green in Prix Ganay on same course: subsequently ran second to Larkhill in Prix Gontaut-Biron at Deauville in August and won Prix Foy at Longchamp in September (made all and held off On My Way, rec

KAT

5 lb, by a short head): stays 11f (twice well beaten in Prix de l'Arc de Triomphe on only attempts at 1½m): acts on soft going. *J. de Choubersky, France.*

KATEBIRD 6 b.m. Birdbrook 110–Limena 67 (Pinza 137) [1974 9s 8f 7fg⁴ 6g² 7g 7d 6d 10fg 12.2s⁵ 12g 1975 8s 10g 1976 8g] poor performer: has poor forelegs: lightly raced since 1974: best form at sprint distances: acts on firm going: has worn blinkers. *P. Felgate.*

KATHALINKA 2 b.f. Galivanter 131–Tactless 91 (Romulus 129) [1976 5g⁵ 58 5f³ 5fg³ 6h⁵ 8s] plain, lengthy filly: poor mover: third in auction events at Beverley and Pontefract in the spring: only lightly raced subsequently: may stay beyond sprint distances. *J. Turner.*

KATIE GREY 3 gr.f. Pongee 106–Spotless 89 (Tehran) [1975 5d 5s⁵ 5g⁶ 6h³ 6fg 6g 8.2g 7f 1976 13.8g⁵ 12.2f⁵ 12g⁶ 13g⁶ 16fg⁵] small filly: plating-class maiden. *R. Titterington.*

KATIE LOUISE 4 ch.f. Florescence 120–Tilde §§ (Tropique 128) [1974 5g⁵ 5fg 5s⁶ 7s 1975 6s³ 6s 7s 8h 6g 7h 1976 12s] tall, leggy filly: poor plater: stays 6f: acts on soft going: well beaten when tried in blinkers: pulled up in amateur riders race at Doncaster in May on only outing at 4 yrs. *A. Smith.*

KATIE MAY 3 b.f. Busted 134–Cawston's Pride 131 (Con Brio 121) [1975 5s⁵ 98 5fg⁵ 5g 9g² 7g³ 7g* 1976 7fg³ 8fg 10g⁵ 8g* 8f⁶ 8g³ 8g] rangy filly: won minor event at Sandown in June comfortably by 2½ lengths from Caerinion: raced against good-class fillies in her other races, best efforts when third in Ladbroke Nell Gwyn Stakes and tenth in 1,000 Guineas, both to Flying Water at Newmarket and when fifth (had a poor run) to Sarania in Sandleford Priory Stakes at Newbury: stays 1¼m: acts on firm going: blinkered last four outings: sold 20,000 gns Newmarket December Sales. *F. Maxwell.*

KATMANDU 3 ch.g. Yellow God 129–Hunea (Hornbeam 130) [1975 5f 6f⁵ 6f 62 1976 8f 7f⁴ 10.4fg⁶ 11f² 8f³ 11g³ 8s³] handsome gelding: showed ability in varied company, including selling: needs at least 1m and stays 11f: has twice been tried in blinkers: sometimes wears bandages. *F. Carr.*

KATSINA 3 b.f. Jolly Jet 111–Holdfast 101 (Arco) [1975 N.R. 1976 8.2f 10.1f⁶ 54 8f⁴ 7g 7f³] half-sister to several winners at home and abroad, including very useful miler Motionless (by Midsummer Night II): dam a miler: ran best race when close-up third of nine to Abergwiffy in minor event at Lanark in September: should stay 1m: sometimes starts slowly. *W. Marshall.*

KAYMAY 4 b.f. Maystreak 118–Double K 72 (Goldhill 125) [1974 5s 5fg³ 5f⁴ 56 5f 1975 7d 6d² 5g⁶ 6fg⁴ 6h* 5f 5fg⁵ 8.2h* 6g* 8.2v 1976 7f 5f 6f 8f 7f⁶ 6f⁴ 6g⁵ 6f* 6h⁶ 8.2d] small filly: plater: showed only worthwhile form at 4 yrs when winning five-runner event at Newcastle in August by a short head from Peggy Jet: effective at 6f and stays 1m well: seems to act on any going: was tried in blinkers at 2 yrs: suitable mount for an apprentice: sometimes sweats up. *G. Wallace.*

KEELHAUL 3 b.f. Tyrant–On The Up (Graustark) [1975 6f⁵ 6d 1976 8f 76 12.2g³ 12f² 10.4fg* 11f³ 12s 12s² 12.2s³] strong filly: modest handicapper: won nine-runner maiden race at Chester in July by 2½ lengths from Chinar Tree despite edging left in final furlong: stays 1½m: seems to act on any going: blinkered third to fifth outings: sold 4,500 gns Newmarket December Sales. *B. Hills.*

KEEP PACE 4 ch.c. Tower Walk 130–Mossy 95 (Mossborough 126) [1974 5d⁶ — 6g⁶ 5s 1975 5.8g³ 6f⁴ 7fg 7f 8f² 8.3fg³ 8fg⁶ 8.3g 1976 10fg] neat, strong, good-bodied colt: quite a moderate performer (rated 72) at 3 yrs: has raced only once since: should stay further than 1m: acts on firm going: used to wear blinkers. *R. Armytage.*

KEIRA 2 ch.f. Keren 100–Cuddly Toy (Sovereign Lord 120) [1976 5fg 5fg³ 5d* 81 5g² 5f⁴ 7fg 6f 6h³ 5g² 5fg⁶ 5f³ 6v⁶ 8v] neat filly: third foal: dam of little account: won maiden event at Hamilton in the spring: ran best race afterwards when length second of nine to Whenby in apprentice nursery at Ayr in September: stays 6f: seems to need some give in the ground: blinkered seventh outing: occasionally sweats up. *T. Fairhurst.*

KEITH'S FRIDGE 4 b.c. Frigid Aire–Vernal Grass (Vilmoray 126) [1974 5f⁵ §§ 5f 6d 6d³ 7g⁴ 6s² 6s 1975 6s* 7v² 6s 7f* 7g⁴ 7g⁶ 7.2fg⁵ 7h 6g 8.2v 1976 7g² 7d⁶ 7f 7fg 8f 8g 9.4h⁵] compact, quite attractive colt: disappointing after first outing in 1976: stays 7f: acts on any going: sometimes wears blinkers: inconsistent, and definitely not one to trust: sweated up fifth start. *E. Collingwood.*

380

KELA HELENA 4 ch.f. probably Taken 64–Kela Halea (Little Buskins 119)   —
[1974 6d 1975 N.R. 1976 10f 5f 7g] of no account: sold 400 gns Ascot June
Sales. *J. Twibell.*

KELLYSTOWN 3 br.c. Sing Sing 134–Catch Fire 89 (Infatuation 129) [1975   **96**
5f⁶ 5g³ 5g² 5d² 5g* 1976 6fg 5s 5fg² 5fg⁵ 5d 6d] strong, good-looking colt:
creditable neck second to Self Satisfied at Brighton in May (blinkered first
time): ran well without them on next outing but was well beaten when tried
in them again on final outing (had stiff task): form only at 5f: acts on a firm and a
soft surface: sold to N. Callaghan 3,900 gns Newmarket Autumn Sales. *B.
Hobbs.*

KELSO BELLE 4 ro.f. Town Crier 119–Janabelle 101 (Gentle Art 121) [1974   **55**
5f 5d⁴ 5g 5s² 5s* 1975 7v 6s 5h⁴ 6g 5d* 5fg³ 5fg³ 6f² 6g³ 6g 6g⁴ 1976 6f⁵ 5f⁶]
strong, compact filly: best form at up to 6f: acts on any going: suitable mount for
an apprentice: exported to South Africa. *E. Weymes.*

KEMAL 5 b.h. Armistice 131–Ilrem (Prudent II 133) [1974 14g⁶ 12d⁵ 14g² **120**
12.5d³ 12.5d 12s³ 12s³ 15v⁴ 1975 15g* 12.5g³ 15.5g* 13g³ 20s² 24d⁴ 1976
15g* 20g² 15g² 20.9fg⁴ 20s⁵ 24s⁵] French horse: first foal: dam placed at 1m
at 2 yrs in France: good-class stayer at his best: ran a marvellous race on second
outing to finish 3 lengths second of 10 to Sagaro in Group 1 Prix du Cadran at
Longchamp in May: had previously won handicap at Maisons-Laffitte: odds on,
came home lame when fourth to Mr Bigmore in Goodwood Cup in July and ran
badly on his two subsequent starts, finishing last in Prix du Pont de Flandre
in September and Prix Gladiateur the following month, both won by Knight
Templar, at Longchamp: stays very well: acts on soft going. *M. Clement,
France.*

KENCO 7 ch.g. Espresso 122–Gedoparonija 88 (Right Boy 137) [1974 8.2fg⁵   **73**
8g⁴ 8s³ 9d⁴ 7fg* 8d 8.2d³ 8g³ 8s³ 1975 7v⁴ 8s² 8g³ 7g* 7.2fg* 7fg³ 8g* 7f³ 8f³ 8fg⁶
8s 7.2s⁶ 1976 7f 7fg 8g⁵ 7d³ 7f² 7f⁴ 8h² 8fg² 7f⁴ 7f] small gelding: quite a
moderate handicapper: ran creditably several times in 1976 and appeared to us to
be given great deal to do when second at Pontefract and Thirsk in July (seventh
and eighth outings): stays 1m well: has run respectably on soft ground but is
particularly well suited by a sound surface: has been tried in blinkers: evidently
needs to be held up. *W. Haigh.*

KENN TOWY 2 ch.f. Murrayfield 119–Telfi (Klondyke Bill 125) [1976 6fg]   —
half-sister to a winning 2-y-o plater: dam never ran: unquoted and apprentice
ridden when in rear in 12-runner maiden race won by Habeebti at Newmarket
in August. *A. Jarvis.*

KENNY'S PET 2 b.c. Knave to Play 79–Hyperina (Marine Corps) [1976 6h⁵]   —
small colt: first foal: 180 gns yearling: dam never ran: 33/1 when remote fifth of
seven to Grittle in maiden race at Pontefract in August. *E. Magner.*

KENTFORD 3 ch.c. Reform 132–Whitefoot 108 (Relko 136) [1975 N.R. 1976   —
8fg 9d 8fg 12f] strong, well-grown colt: second foal: half-brother to a minor
winner: dam won Musidora Stakes: well beaten in maiden company in the spring:
blinkered third outing: sold 660 gns Newmarket Autumn Sales. *H. Wragg.*

KENTISH PRIDE 8 b.g. Rosyth 94–Pride and Joy (Artist's Son) [1974 N.R.   **70**
1975 14g⁶ 12.5fg* 1976 10fg² 11.7f² 11.7fg⁵ 12d] big, rangy gelding: good
second in handicaps at Pontefract and Bath in April: would have stayed further
than 1½m: acted on firm going: dead. *B. Hanbury.*

KENTUCKY ROSE 3 ch.f. Tower Walk 130–Skyway 76 (Skymaster 126)   —
[1975 N.R. 1976 5f 9f] lengthy filly: last in maiden races at Beverley and
Wolverhampton in the spring: sold 220 gns Newmarket July Sales and resold 240
gns Doncaster October Sales. *D. Weeden.*

KENTUCKY WALTZ 2 b.c. Crepello 136–French Cream 110 (Faubourg II 127)   **66**
[1976 7g 7v 10v] neat colt: half-brother to four winners, including useful 1m
handicapper Loudoun Gale (by Klairon): 560 gns yearling: dam won Irish Oaks
and is half-sister to French Beige: seventh of 15 behind Chennel Lane in weakly-
contested maiden race at Leicester in October, second outing and best effort:
will stay 1½m. *H. Collingridge.*

KEREN PARK 2 b.g. Keren 100–Beautiful Sally (Sallymount 125) [1976 6g 7v]   —
strong, rangy gelding: behind in maiden race in August and minor event in
October, both at Newcastle: trained by W. A. Stephenson on first outing. *M.
Naughton.*

KERENSKI 3 gr.f. Keren 100–Lucy Jinks (Tudor Jinks 121) [1975 N.R. 1976   —
7g 12g] half-sister to Ezra (by Pongee), a winner at up to 13f, and quite useful

miler McIndoe (by Principal): dam never ran: in rear in minor event at Catterick and maiden race at Edinburgh in June. *T. Fairhurst.*

KERNEL ROSE 6 ch.h. Floribunda 136–Svenno 76 (Vilmorin) [1974 6g2 5fg* **69**
6g* 5g2 5fg6 6fg2 6s2 6f2 5f* 6d 6s2 6s 1975 6s 5d5 5fg4 6v5 5f2 5f* 6fg 6h* 6h2 6f*
5g* 6g5 7f 6fg4 6g3 5s 1976 5f3 5fg2] strong horse: ran well on both his starts at
6 yrs but wasn't raced after early May: stays 6f but possibly not 7f: acts on any
going, but goes particularly well on firm: good mount for an apprentice: has worn
blinkers but seems better without. *N. Angus.*

KEROUAILLE 2 br.f. Royalty 130–Morinda 87 (Matador 131) [1976 6fg3 7g 8s] **58**
half-sister to a minor 2-y-o winner by Sovereign Path: dam fair winner at 7f and
1m: never-dangerous 10 lengths third of six to Millionaire in minor event at
Windsor in September: will stay 1m: sold 310 gns Ascot November Sales. *B. Hobbs.*

KERRY BOLD 2 b.c. Derring-Do 131–Kerry Dancer 90 (Reliance II 137) [1976 **84**
5g 6g6 7fg6 8s3 8s] neat colt: first foal: dam won over 16.9f at 3 yrs: 8 lengths
third of eight to Night Before in minor event at Goodwood in September: will
stay 1¼m+: probably acts on any going. *D. Whelan.*

KERRY STREET 3 br.f. Dairialatan 111–Surrey Street (Whiteway 121) [1975 **—**
N.R. 1976 12g] leggy, light-framed filly: fourth foal: half-sister to smart
hunter chaser Stanhope Street (by Combat): dam won over hurdles: 33/1 when
seventh of 10 behind Turnpike in maiden race at Kempton in August. *V. Cross.*

KERTOSSEL 4 ch.g. Goldhill 125–Admiral's Quill 76 (Dicta Drake 126) [1974 **—**
5fg 6f 5fg 7g 7g 7.2d5 1975 7d 7s6 15.8fg2 12g3 11g5 12g6 10fg5 8h6 8f* 10f2 12g4
10h2 1976 8f] compact gelding: modest plater: ran only once at 4 yrs:
effective at 1m to 2m: acts on firm going: sometimes wears blinkers, and wore
them when successful: sold 575 gns Ascot November Sales. *G. Richards.*

KESAR QUEEN 3 b.f. Nashua–Meadow Saffron (High Perch 126) [1975 6g **117**
5f5 5g2 5g2 7f* 1976 8s* 8fg2 8fg3 10g5 8g2 8f* 8d4 8s 9.2s3 7s]
Kesar Queen provided her stable with its solitary success on English soil
in 1976 when she won the Coronation Stakes at Royal Ascot. In doing so she
underlined a fact that had become increasingly apparent—that the leading French
three-year-old fillies were superior to their counterparts on this side of the
Channel. Kesar Queen is a front runner who takes a great deal of pegging back.
Her characteristics were well exemplified by her performance at Royal Ascot
where she narrowly beat her compatriot Guichet, with the Irish One Thousand
Guineas runner-up Clover Princess two and a half lengths away in third place.
However in our opinion the result would almost certainly have been significantly
different had Guichet been ridden at all enterprisingly, for when Kesar Queen

*Coronation Stakes, Ascot—a French 1-2, with Kesar Queen (left)
pipping Guichet by a head*

was turning for home in front, travelling well within herself, Guichet had a lot to do. Guichet made splendid headway all the way up the straight, taking at least five lengths out of Kesar Queen in the last two furlongs, but had been asked just too much; she found an extra spurt close home beyond her and went down by a neck. Guichet's misfortune did not detract from a game and good performance by Kesar Queen, but it did underline a fine piece of jockeyship by Kesar Queen's rider Saint-Martin who has few equals.

Kesar Queen ran two other races in England. She was one of the five French challengers who dominated the One Thousand Guineas finish—the French fillies occupied five of the first seven places. After holding the lead until inside the last furlong Kesar Queen finished third, beaten a length and a neck by Flying Water and Konafa. In the Queen Elizabeth II Stakes at Ascot in September, Kesar Queen dropped away quickly in the straight and came home a well-beaten last of eight behind Rose Bowl. She didn't show her form, but she was slightly out of her depth.

Kesar Queen won only once in France; she won an early-season race at Evry, but although she wasn't up to beating the very best she usually acquitted herself with credit. In the Prix de la Grotte and the Prix Saint-Alary, both won by Riverqueen, Kesar Queen finished second and fifth respectively, beaten two and a half lengths each time. In the Prix de Sandringham, her last race before Royal Ascot, she was beaten a length by Guichet to whom she was conceding 2 lb. Whatever views are held on the result of the Coronation Stakes it must be admitted that there was not much between these two fillies at that stage of the season. But whereas Guichet trained off, Kesar Queen went on to finish in the frame in the Prix du Rond-Point won by Monsanto and the Prix de l'Opera won by Dona Barod.

Kesar Queen (b.f. 1973)	Nashua (b 1952)	Nasrullah (b 1940)	Nearco
			Mumtaz Begum
		Segula (b 1942)	Johnstown
			Sekhmet
	Meadow Saffron (b 1964)	High Perch (ch 1956)	Alycidon
			Phaetonia
		Meadow Music (b 1956)	Tom Fool
			Miss Grillo

Nashua was a top-class racehorse, winner of twenty-two races, including the Preakness Stakes and the Belmont Stakes, and he has sired the winners of well over fifty stakes races in America, including the champion handicap mare Shuvee, Diplomat Way, a good winner at up to nine furlongs and a successful stallion, and Bramalea and Nalee, good racemares both and dams of the classic winners Roberto and Meneval respectively. Kesar Queen's dam Meadow Saffron, a winner over a mile and a quarter as a three-year-old in Ireland, is a half-sister to the Irish Sweeps Derby and King George VI and Queen Elizabeth Stakes winner Meadow Court. Meadow Saffron's best runner prior to Kesar Queen was the stakes-placed winner Bold Saffron (by Bold Hour). The second dam Meadow Music, herself a winner in Ireland, is a daughter of Miss Grillo, a stakes winner in the United States after winning both the Argentine Derby and Oaks. Kesar Queen's style of racing almost inevitably imposes limitations on her stamina and a mile and a quarter is probably as far as she can be expected to stay. She acts on any going. Although she is inclined to sweat up before her races she looked in very good shape whenever we saw her, and certainly she runs her races out with great courage. She has been exported to the U.S.A. *A. Breasley, France.*

KEY OF THE KINGDOM   3 gr.f. Grey Sovereign 128 §–Lucky Key (Off Key 121)   —
[1975 5fg² 5fg* 5f² 6d   1976 7.3f 8d]   useful sort: showed very useful form as a 2-y-o: last in Fred Darling Stakes at Newbury (backward) and handicap at York in the spring: sold 20,000 gns Newmarket December Sales. *I. Balding.*

KEYPHONE   2 b.g. Siliconn 121–Keep At It (Larkspur 128)   [1976 6fg 6g 5g 8fg   **41**
7s³ 6s]   workmanlike gelding: poor plater. *P. Makin.*

KEZIA   2 b.f. Native Prince–Kessella (Le Levanstell 122)   [1976 6f 6fg⁶ 6d]   —
strong filly: fourth foal: half-sister to three winners, including 3-y-o Irish middle-distance winner Rathconrath (by Wolver Hollow): 1,800 gns yearling: no worthwhile form in maiden and minor events. *W. Elsey.*

KHARTOUM   4 b.g. Karabas 132–Freetown 96 (Crepello 136)   [1974 N.R.   —
1975 N.R.   1976 18s]   half-brother to two winners, including very useful stayer Tom Cribb (by Fighting Charlie): dam fairly useful miler: cost 2,000 gns at

Doncaster May (1975) Sales: 33/1 when well beaten in amateur riders maiden race at Doncaster in October, only outing. *I. Jordon.*

KIANDRA 2 gr.f. Baltus 98–Miss Monarch (Mr Potter 89) [1976 7s 6s 5v] — first foal: dam never ran: well beaten in end-of-season maiden races and a seller. *Dr A. Jones.*

KIDOLOGY 2 b.c. Tudor Music 131–Giftbearer (Princely Gift 137) [1976 5fg **79** 5s 5.1fg⁴ 5.1g 8g 7v²] half-brother to a minor winner: 2,100 gns foal, resold 1,550 gns yearling: dam won at 2 yrs in U.S.A.: no match for Hill's Double in minor event at Teesside in October but comfortably accounted for 11 others: will probably stay 1m: suited by heavy ground: blinkered third outing. *D. Weeden.*

KILAVEA 2 b.f. Hawaii–Special (Forli) [1976 5s*] American-bred filly: first **92 p** foal: $49,000 yearling: dam once-raced sister to outstanding 6f to 1m performer Thatch: odds on for six-runner newcomers race at Goodwood in September and made all to win unchallenged by 6 lengths from Salsa: a well-bred filly who looks sure to go on to better things over longer distances. *J. Dunlop.*

KILBAIGIE 4 b.c. Hill Clown–Dinah Moon (Hard Sauce 131) [1974 7s 6s 6v **57 d** 1975 6f 10fg 10.8f⁵ 10fg* 12f⁵ 12d 1976 12g³ 11.7fg 12f⁵ 17.1f 12f] leggy colt: good third to Comet Kohoutek in apprentice handicap at Ascot in May on reappearance but didn't reproduce that form: stays 1¼m well: tried in blinkers fourth start: sold 340 gns Ascot December Sales. *D. Dale.*

KILCARN LASS 3 b.f. Bold Lad (Ire) 133–Pride of Kilcarn 74 (Klairon 131) **74** [1975 6g⁶ 5.1g⁵ 6s 1976 8fg⁶ 8fg³ 6s* 6f² 6f³ 5f⁶] quite a modest performer: made all when winning minor event at Ayr in June by 3 lengths from Gold Topaz: best form at 6f: acts on any going. *G. Pritchard-Gordon.*

KILDOON 4 b.c. Kalydon 122–Lyndy Sue 70 (Major Portion 129) [1974 5g⁵ **77** 6s 7fg⁴ 7g³ 8d³ 7v 8s⁵ 1975 8.5d* 10d⁴ 10fg* 8f⁵ 11.7f 13g⁴ 12f 8.5fg* 1976 10fg⁶ 10fg⁶ 8.5g³ 8f⁴ 8g 10s] well-made colt: has a round action: quite a moderate handicapper: best form at up to 1¼m: seems to act on any going: has worn blinkers: sweated up on reappearance: sold 740 gns Newmarket Autumn Sales. *D. Whelan.*

KILGORIS 6 ch.g. Salvo 129–Mount Rosa 98 (Hill Gail) [1974 N.R. 1975 — N.R. 1976 15f] of no account. *L. Shedden.*

KILNAMEAL 3 br.c. Hard Man 102–Mexican Pink (El Gallo 122) [1975 7fg 8s — 8f⁵ 1976 9g 10g 8s] big colt: poor maiden. *L. Docker.*

KILROY VALUER 2 ch.c. Porto Bello 118–Drake's Image 66 (Dicta Drake 126) **84** [1976 6g 6d⁵] half-brother to Florica (by Floriana), a winner of sellers at up to 1¼m: dam stayed well: close-up fifth of 23 to Running Bull in maiden race at Newmarket in October: will stay 7f. *G. Hunter.*

KINBA 4 b.g. King's Troop 118–Funabashi (Venture VII 129) [1974 6s 1975 — 9v 8f 10.8f⁶ 1976 10fg] plating-class maiden: sold 1,000 gns Doncaster August Sales. *W. Stephenson.*

KING ALMARZAR 3 b.g. Czar Alexander 112–Great Aunt (Mourne 126) [1975 — 7fg 7g 6fg 1976 13fg⁶] neat, attractive American-bred gelding: no worthwhile form: needed race and tailed off on only outing in 1976 (April): sold 330 gns Ascot June Sales. *I. Walker.*

KING CHARLES 7 br.g. Le Levanstell 122–King's Victress (King's Bench 132) — [1974 15s 16v 10g⁵ 12s 1975 N.R. 1976 12g 14.7d 12f] of little account nowadays. *D. Plant.*

KING CONCORDE 7 gr.g. Sovereign Lord 120–French and English 67 (Djebe) — [1974 N.R. 1975 N.R. 1976 6d] formerly quite useful but none too genuine sprinter: has been tubed: in need of race when tailed off behind Breathing Exercise at Haydock in October, first outing on flat since 1973: acts on firm going: has sometimes worn blinkers and a tongue strap: has sometimes lost ground at the start. *P. Ransom.*

KING CROESUS 2 b.c. Green God 128–Scarcroft 66 (King's Bench 132) [1976 **108** 5f 5f* 5d⁵ 6g* 6s³] robust colt: half-brother to two winners, including useful sprinter Last Tango (by Be Friendly): 3,400 gns yearling: dam won at 7f: twice successful at Newmarket, picking up a maiden race in August (by short head from Stonewall Jack) and a £1,900 nursery in October (showed improved form to win going away by 3 lengths from Neil Diamond): finished well when close-up third to Casino Boy in nursery on same course later in month: probably better suited by 6f than 5f: acts on firm going but has shown better form with some give in the ground. *J. Hindley.*

KING CURRY 3 br.g. Space King 115–Aries Lady 71 (Damremont 120) [1975 —
N.R. 1976 12.5v⁵] first foal: 155 gns yearling: dam won four times at 7f and 1m:
50/1 when distant fifth of 15 to Chartered Course in maiden race at Teesside in
October. *M. Camacho.*

KING ELECT 2 ch.c. Frankincense 120–Short Sentence 114 (Court Martial) **106**
[1976 5.1fg* 6fg* 6fg³ 6f* 6fg³ 6fg* 6g] good-looking colt: half-brother to three
winners, including useful middle-distance winner Royal Display (by Right Royal
V): 5,600 gns yearling: dam very useful at 6f and 7f, and half-sister to Pardao:
odds-on winner at Yarmouth in May, June and July, and made all when beating
sole-opponent Champagne Willie cleverly by a neck in £1,900 event at Newmarket in August: also third in both Fenwolf Stakes at Ascot and July Stakes at
Newmarket but finished last of 11 in William Hill Middle Park Stakes at Newmarket in October when taking on best of his age: will stay 1m: acts on firm
going. *H. Cecil.*

KINGFISHER BLUE 12 b.g. French Beige 127–Windsor Charm 91 (Windsor **66**
Slipper) [1974 14g² 16fg² 16fg² 16f* 15g* 16g³ 20g 16.1fg* 15s* 16d³ 14.6g 17.4s
18d 1975 16d⁵ 15s 14.7f 17.7fg 18.4g⁶ 16.9f² 19f⁵ 16g³ 16f⁶ 16d² 16g⁵ 13g 1976
16.1d⁶ 16fg* 16f² 16fg⁶ 17f⁴ 16f³ 18f* 14.7f⁴ 20f⁴ 16.9f 18g⁵] quite a moderate
handicapper nowadays: kept on well when winning at Warwick in April and
Doncaster in July: needs a good test of stamina: acts on any going but is well
suited by firm: has worn blinkers: game and genuine: excellent mount for a boy.
D. Plant.

KING FLUSH 2 b.c. St Chad 120–Autumn Flush 57 (Rustam 127) [1976 6fg⁶ **79**
8g⁶ 8v] strong colt: second foal: 4,200 gns yearling: dam won over 1¼m: 50/1 for
£1,700 event at Doncaster in September on second outing but ran well, having a
lot to do turning into straight and then staying on (despite having none too clear
a run) to finish 9 lengths sixth of 10 to Royal Plume: unplaced in useful company
only subsequent outing: should be up to winning a small race in the north.
Hbt¹Jones.

KING GLAZEPTA 2 ch.c. Green God 128–Dark Melody (Tudor Melody 129) **72**
[1976 5h⁴ 5fg⁶ 5g 7g 5.9s 7s⁵ 8v] compact, useful-looking colt: good mover:
showed some ability in maiden race on first outing, but did not reproduce that
form and was well beaten in sellers on last two outings when blinkered: should
stay 7f: possibly unsuited by soft ground. *A. Jarvis.*

KING JAMIE 2 b.c. King Emperor–Effervescence II 103 (Charlottesville 135) —
[1976 5fg] half-brother to two winners, notably very smart French middle-
distance performer El Famoso (by Ragusa): dam won twice over 1¼m in France
and is half-sister to Zeddaan: 16/1 when behind in 20-runner maiden race won by
Ground Cover at Windsor in May. *J. Holt.*

KING JAY 3 b.c. King Emperor–Prima 75 (Alcide 136) [1975 5s 5f 6fg* 5g⁴ 6f⁵ ?
1976 7f⁶ 7fg³ 8g* 7.5g² 10s³ 7v² 6v²] neat, strong colt: won maiden race at
Newmarket in 1975: creditable sixth of ten to Relkino in Ascot 2,000 Guineas
Trial in April but folded up very quickly when favourite for eight-runner handicap at Epsom later in month: subsequently sent to race in Italy, where he won at
1m and ran very well in 6f pattern race: appears to act on any going: has worn
blinkers. *J. Winter.*

KING KAPPA 2 b.c. St Alphage 119–Dialora (Diatome 132) [1976 5g⁴] small, **70 p**
sturdy colt: second foal: closely related to very useful 3-y-o Heaven Knows (by
Yellow God), a winner at up to 1½m: 4,100 gns yearling: dam never ran: backed
from 25/1 to 8/1 when 11 lengths fourth of 25 to Song of Songs in maiden race at
Newbury in May, only outing: will probably stay further than sprint distances.
M. Smyly.

KINGLET 6 b.h. Pampered King 121–War Ribbon (Anwar 120) [1974 10d **92**
12f* 12fg² 14fg³ 12d² 1975 12d⁵ 12d⁶ 12fg 12f 14fg⁶ 14.6g⁶ 1976 12f* 12fg²
12fg² 12g²] neat horse: very good mover: fairly useful handicapper: ran on very
gamely when beating Paddy Jack a neck at Ascot in April: did well in his three
races afterwards including when second to Royal Match at York in August
on third start: stays 1¾m: probably acts on any going: genuine and consistent:
does best when ridden up with leaders. *R. Hern.*

KING MIDAS (USA) 6 br.h. Pieces of Eight 128–Rebecca M (King of the **69 d**
Tudors 129) [1974 10.2s 9f* 11d² 10fg⁶ 10g⁵ 10fg² 8g 10f⁶ 11g 10.2v* 12v⁴ 12d⁴
12v³ 1975 12d* 12s⁴ 11fg 1976 16s³ 15f 12g 13g⁶ 12.5v] poor handicapper: ran
his only worthwhile race in 1976 on reappearance: stays 2m: acts on any going:
sometimes wears blinkers and did so when successful at 5 yrs. *G. Richards.*

KING OAK 7 b.g. Royal Palm 131–Lily Oak 98 (Borealis) [1974 N.R. 1975 —
12s 12g 14f 8h 9h 1976 8g] of little account. *G. Wallace.*

KING OCAR 3 b.c. King's Troop 118–Ocarienne 105 (Ocarina 131) [1975 6g⁴ **78** 6f³ 7g 7f 1976 10f⁵ 10fg³ 10fg 6f³ 6f⁴ 6f³ 6f* 6f* 6f⁴ 7.6s² 6v] lightly-made colt: quite a moderate handicapper: comfortable winner of 17-runner maiden event at Nottingham in August: defied a 7-lb penalty when beating Tribal Festival a head at Yarmouth later in month: best form at 6f, although stays 1¼m: seems to act on any going: exported to Hong Kong. *M. Masson.*

KING OF MACEDON 2 br.c. Diatome 132–Regal Fountain 84 (Grey Sovereign **125** 128 §) [1976 5.5g* 5.5g* 5.5g⁵ 5g* 7s⁴ 5s⁵]
Foreign trainers may not have provided many winners in France in 1976 but the English and Irish breeding industries did very well over there. In addition to Gentilhombre and Dominion, other pattern race winners in France to have carried the GB or IRE suffix included Full of Hope, Sagaro, Red Lord, Infra Green and Mendip Man, who all won Group 1 races, Citoyen, Dona Barod and Knight Templar, who won Group 2 events; and El Rastro, Kala Shikari, Antrona, Son of Silver, Girl Friend, Larkhill, Command Freddy, Edinburgh and Silk Slipper, whose wins were in Group 3. Both Edinburgh and Silk Slipper belong to Sir Michael Sobell, as do two other leading two-year-olds, the French-bred pattern race winner Balteus and one of the fastest colts, King of Macedon.
Not many two-year-olds are put in against the top European sprinters in the Prix de l'Abbaye de Longchamp, and the last winner of that age was Farhana back in 1966, when, surprisingly, four of the five runners were two-year-olds. King of Macedon put up a very bold show in the race in 1976. After leaving the stalls behind most of the others, he came with a strong run from two furlongs out and kept on well to finish fifth behind Gentilhombre and Mendip Man, beaten only about a length. Just in front of King of Macedon was Girl Friend, winner of four top sprints during the year, and behind him he had Kronenkranich, who had won Baden-Baden's Goldene Peitsche, Faliraki, a close second in the William Hill Sprint Championship, and Kala Shikari, winner of both the Prix du Gros-Chene and the Prix de Seine-et-Oise.
Before the Prix de l'Abbaye King of Macedon had had five outings, winning three times and twice being soundly beaten by Blushing Groom. His first successes came in a race restricted to newcomers at Evry and the Prix Fast Fox at Maisons-Laffitte and it was his third race that provided his most important and impressive victory. As a 2/1-on favourite for the Prix de la Valle d'Auge at Deauville he was clearly expected to win well, and he drew clear from the distance to come home four lengths clear of Smoggy, with the rest well beaten off. Despite being allowed to ease up close home he returned the very fast time of 58 seconds, not much outside Nonoalco's course record.
King of Macedon's two defeats by Blushing Groom came in important races. In the Prix Robert Papin at Maisons-Laffitte in July he ran poorly, dropping out in the closing stages to finish fifth, over eleven lengths behind, but in the Prix de la Salamandre he ran creditably, making rapid headway to come within two furlongs to go, only to find his stamina giving out soon afterwards. At the line he was fourth, just over four lengths behind. It may be difficult to believe that a colt of King of Macedon's breeding doesn't truly stay seven furlongs, but that is how we saw it that day, and his cracking performances over five furlongs at Deauville and Longchamp suggest strongly that this is so.

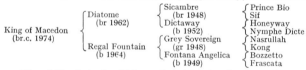

King of Macedon's sire, Diatome, showed top-class form over distances ranging from a mile and a quarter to nearly two miles, and his best sons, Margouillat and Steel Pulse, both stayed a mile and a half well. There is no shortage of stamina on this side of King of Macedon's pedigree and it seems that his dam has proved far more influential than his sire. Similar examples are not hard to find. That brilliant sprinter Abernant was by the Gold Cup winner Owen Tudor, the Cork and Orrery winner Welsh Saint was by St Paddy, the King George Stakes winner Laser Light was a son of Aureole and the top-class sprinter Deep Diver was by the Chester Vase winner Gulf Pearl. And there is Prince Tenderfoot, like King of Macedon bred by a stayer out of a Grey Sovereign mare; he showed form at five and six furlongs only.

King of Macedon's dam, Regal Fountain, won over a distance of around six furlongs as a three-year-old. Of her four previous foals three have won and two, Fount of Youth (by Sheshoon) and Creme Souffle (by Crepello), stayed middle distances. The grandam, Fontana Angelica, was a tough Italian filly who won sixteen times. There is certainly no reason on breeding why King of Macedon shouldn't stay at least a mile but he runs like a sprinter, and we expect six furlongs to be his best distance. King of Macedon has already shown he's a very good colt and it's possible he'll be even better as a three-year-old—he was a very late foal, so late that his first success was gained before he reached his second birthday. He acts on soft going. *J. Cunnington, jnr, France.*

KING OF SWING 5 gr.g. King's Leap 111–Primerva (Primera 131) [1974 12d **51** 8f 8g 6f* 8.3fg 1975 8fg 5.9f 10.1f 8h⁵ 6fg⁵ 6fg⁴ 6s 5g³ 6g² 6f 5g 1976 5.9g 5f⁵ 6f² 6s⁶ 6s] small gelding: fair plater on his day: ran well on third outing at 5 yrs: stays 1m: acts on firm going and is possibly unsuited by soft: used to wear bandages: wears blinkers: a difficult ride: inconsistent. *F. Yardley.*

KING REAY 3 ch.c. Straight King 98–Lady Reay (Queen's Hussar 124) [1975 — N.R. 1976 8h 11s 10.5fg 10g 7v] poor plater. *M. Naughton.*

KINGS BONUS 5 b.h. Kibenka 119–Hooked Heiress 74 (Hook Money 124) **103** [1974 8g 7f* 8fg³ 7g* 7g* 8.2f 8f 7.6g² 7g⁴ 8h* 8d⁵ 8g⁵ 8s⁵ 7s 7s² 1975 8fg* 8g² 7s 7.6g⁵ 7.2g⁴ 8f 7g⁵ 6g* 6f² 6g³ 6fg* 6d 6f² 7g³ 6g⁵ 1976 8g 6d* 6g³ 6g⁴ 6s* 6d² 6fg* 6f 6h⁴ 6fg⁵ 6s] tall horse: useful handicapper: successful at Haydock in April, Chester in May and York the following month: stays 1m but races mainly at 6f nowadays: acts on any going and on any track: excellent mount for an apprentice: tough, genuine and consistent: sold 4,600 gns Newmarket Autumn Sales. *R. Hollinshead.*

KING'S CAPER 3 ch.g. Saucy Kit 76–King's Caress 65 (King's Coup 108) **77** [1975 6f 6fg⁶ 8fg⁶ 6g⁵ 8f 1976 8s 8f⁶ 8f⁴ 8f* 7f² 9fg* 9f 8fg⁴] strong, rangy gelding: quite a moderate handicapper: winner at Ripon twice in the summer, on second occasion being kept going only with hands and heels to beat Trading a length: gave impression he was better suited by 1m and 9f than 7f: dead. *M. H. Easterby.*

KINGSCLIFFE 2 b.f. King's Troop 118–Palmyrrha 98 (Palestine 133) [1976 **66** 5.3g⁵ 5f³ 5s⁴ 5s⁵] half-brother to two winners, including fairly useful 1974 2-y-o 5f winner Pallbearer (by Weepers Boy): dam won over 5f at 2 yrs: quite moderate form: should stay 6f: sold 380 gns Ascot November Sales. *J. Dunlop.*

KING'S COMEDY 2 b.c. Comedy Star 121–Queen's Lane 107 (Tamerlane 128) **69** [1976 5d 6s 5h 5g 7.2f⁵ 7fg 8s 8v⁶] compact colt: plater: should stay 1m: best form on a firm surface: blinkered final outing. *W. A. Stephenson.*

KING'S CONFIDANT 2 ch.c. Most Secret 119–King's Caress 65 (King's Coup **71** 108) [1976 5d⁴ 5f⁶ 6g⁴ 7f³ 6f 6f] strong, muscular, good-bodied colt: second foal: half-brother to 3-y-o King's Caper (by Saucy Kit), a winner at up to 9f: dam, a plater, won over 6f and 1m at 3 yrs: quite a moderate maiden: stays 7f. *M. H. Easterby.*

KINGS DAY 2 b.f. Space King 115–Noonday Miss (Falls of Clyde 126) [1976 — 5.9f] fourth foal: dam of little account: last but one in nine-runner maiden race won by Ashen Light at Wolverhampton in August. *R. Whiston.*

KINGS DRUM 4 ch.c. Meldrum 112–My Request 72 (Sayajirao 132) [1974 5fg⁶ — 5h³ 7f⁶ 7fg³ 7d 8s⁴ 8.2d 8s² 7.2s³ 1975 9v 8.2s 10d³ 12g⁴ 12d 11fg* 12f² 12f² 11f* 16f³ 12h 1976 12s 12g] compact colt: lightly raced at 4 yrs: stays 1½m, but not 2m: acts on any going: does best in blinkers: good mount for an apprentice. *W. Wharton.*

KINGSFOLD TROOPER 2 b.c. King's Troop 118–Bella Lisa (River Chanter **92** 121) [1976 5fg 5f 5g³ 7s 5s*] small, sturdy, quite attractive colt: first foal: dam ran only three times: showed greatly improved form when finishing fast to win 11-runner nursery at Sandown in October by a neck from Abode: placed in seller on same course the previous month: best form at 5f but should stay further: acts on soft going. *A. Pitt.*

KING'S MESSENGER 5 br.h. King Log 115–Botany (Precipitation) [1974 — 11.7fg 10f 12g⁵ 12f² 12f³ 11g 14d² 16.9g⁵ 1975 12d 12f 1976 10f 9g 11.7fg 10.1fg⁴] compact horse: poor handicapper nowadays: needs at least 1½m: acts on firm going: sometimes wears blinkers and bandages. *M. Haynes.*

KING'S PALACE 3 gr.c. Sovereign Path 125–Crystal Palace 121 (Solar Slipper — 131) [1975 N.R. 1976 10.2s⁴] half-brother to numerous winners, including Royal Palace (by Ballymoss), Prince Consort (by Right Royal V) and Selhurst (by

Charlottesville): dam smart at 7f to 1¼m: very weak in market, stayed on in closing stages after a slow start when remote fourth of 17 to Flying Diplomat in maiden race at Doncaster in October, giving impression he would be suited by further: to be trained by H. Cecil. *N. Murless.*

KING'S RHAPSODY 5 br.g. Le Prince 98–Temptation (Milesian 125) [1974 10fg⁶ 10.8f³ 12f⁵ 14f² 14fg* 14g⁶ 8g⁵ 1975 N.R. 1976 12s] quite a moderate handicapper (rated 71) in 1974: having first outing since, finished well behind in apprentice event at Chepstow in October: suited by a test of stamina: acts on firm going: blinkered fifth start in 1974 and at Chepstow. *S. Mellor.* —

KINGS ROYALE 4 b.c. King's Troop 118–Fibula (King's Bench 132) [1974 6s⁶ 1975 7.6g² 6fg 6d² 5.8f* 6fg 7s 6g 1976 7g 8fg² 8s* 7g² 7fg* 8fg²] big, good sort of colt: fair handicapper: successful twice at Ayr, on second occasion beating Belle Vue ½ length in July: stays 1m: acts on any going: genuine and consistent: sold 1,100 gns Doncaster November Sales. *R. Price.* 89

KINGS SINGER 2 b.c. Taj Dewan 128–Singing Girl 96 (Sing Sing 134) [1976 6fg 8v 6s] workmanlike colt: half-brother to two winners by Petingo, very useful sprinter Tingo and smart French colt Tin Band, a winner at up to 1m: 260 gns yearling: dam a sprinter: eighth of 24 to The Czar in minor event at York in October, second outing and best effort: may stay further than 1m. *M. W. Easterby.* 75

KING ST CLARE 3 ch.c. Dike–Clariden 82 (Hook Money 124) [1975 6fg 8g 7g⁶ 6g³ 1976 6fg³ 7g 6d⁵ 8fg⁴] strong colt: quite a moderate maiden: should stay 1m: blinkered third outing: sold 1,700 gns Newmarket Autumn Sales. *W. Wharton.* 71

KING'S VERDICT 2 b.c. Lear Jet 123–Clean Verdict 109 (Whistler 129) [1976 5g 5f 5.8f³ 6fg*] third living foal: dam a sprinter, at her best as a 2-y-o: won 12-runner claiming race at Brighton in June: subsequently claimed for £1,000, reportedly for export to Belgium: stays 6f: blinkered third outing. *D. Keith.* 83

KING WILLI 3 b.c. Willipeg 112–Cressida Queen 84 (Troilus 101) [1975 5d³ 5s⁴ 5fg³ 5s⁵ 5f³ 6g 7g² 7g³ 1976 7f² 6g² 8s] strong colt and a good walker: not seen out until September when runner-up in minor event at Lanark and handicap at Ayr, putting up a good effort on latter course, but having no chance with runaway winner Sonnenblick: stays 7f and ran poorly when tried at 1m on final outing. *N. Angus.* 58

KING ZEUS 4 gr.g. Zeddaan 130–French Possession 107 (French Beige 127) [1974 N.R. 1975 8v² 10f* 8fg 8f⁴ 8g⁵ 8fg⁴ 1976 11g⁵ 10g 12g 8d] strong, good-bodied gelding: good mover: possibly best at distances short of 1½m: sometimes wore blinkers: dead. *J. Vickers.* —

KINSHASA 3 b.f. Swing Easy 126–Bisley (Polic 126 or Punchinello 97) [1975 5fg⁵ 5fg² 6g 5f* 5g 1976 7f 6f* 6fg² 5fg⁵ 6f⁴] lengthy filly: moderate handicapper: narrow winner at Windsor in May: stays 6f: acts on firm going: sweated up badly and ran moderately when tried in blinkers on fourth outing: bought by B.B.A. 4,800 gns Newmarket July Sales for export to New Zealand. *M. Stoute.* 82

KINTORE 4 b.g. Aberdeen 109–Dararole (Dara §§) [1974 N.R. 1975 8v⁵ 8s⁵ 8g 6h⁵ 6f⁵ 6fg⁴ 6f² 6f² 7g* 7f² 6g 1976 6g 7g* 7f* 8f⁴ 6f* 7fg⁴ 6g* 6f* 7g] quite a moderate handicapper: did really well at 4 yrs and won five times in the north: gained his last success when beating Gold Loom 1½ lengths at Ripon in August: stays 7f: acts on any track: has been tried in blinkers but does better without: acts on firm going: genuine and consistent. *J. W. Watts.* 82

KIREI 2 b.f. Will Hays (USA)–Farmers Daughter (Red Slipper 126 or Javelot 124) [1976 5f 5fg⁴ 5f] second produce: 480 gns foal: dam ran only three times: 6 lengths fourth of eight to Home Fire in minor event at Goodwood in September, best effort: will be suited by longer distances. *J. Dunlop.* 72

KIRK SELL 7 br.g. Goldhill 125–Wasdale 97 (Psidium 130) [1974 N.R. 1975 N.R. 1976 10g] of little account. *H. O'Neill.* —

KISSING AGAIN 2 ch.f. Maystreak 118–Kissing Grove (Midsummer Night II 117) [1976 5f 5f] strong filly: well behind in two races at Redcar in July and was sold 340 gns Doncaster September Sales. *P. Metcalfe.* —

KITHAIRON 5 br.h. Klairon 131–Gin-Ginger 72 (Happy Monarch 109) [1974 5s 7d 6fg⁴ 6fg² 7g⁴ 8f² 6f 11f³ 8fg⁶ 10g² 9fg² 8h⁶ 10g² 8fg³ 12g* 10s⁵ 8g⁵ 8s 1975 10.2g* 7v* 7s³ 11fg⁴ 9d 7f² 8f² 7f³ 10f⁶ 8.2f² 8d⁵ 7g² 7g² 8d² 8g² 8g⁶ 8f² 8g 8g 7fg 1976 7d* 8f³ 8f² 7fg 8f* 7.2d* 8f* 7g⁶ 8f⁶ 7fg⁵ 8fg⁵ 8.2g 7f⁶ 8f 7g 8.2s] workman-like horse: successful four times early in 1976, winning handicaps at Edinburgh 74

(two), Thirsk, and Haydock: most disappointing in second half of season and was
tailed off in a seller on final start: effective at 7f and stays 1½m: acts on any going:
sometimes wears blinkers: excellent mount for an apprentice. *K. Payne.*

KITTY FISHER 3 ch.f. Track Spare 125–Dictynna (Dickens 125) [1975 5s **41**
5d⁵ 5f³ 5h² 5fg³ 1976 8f⁴ 6g 7g⁶ 8g 7f 8f³ 7d 10d 8s⁵ 10v] neat, shapely filly:
poor plater: stays 1m: tried in blinkers seventh outing: usually starts slowly: sold
out of B. Hills's stable 340 gns Ascot July Sales after third start and was resold
for same sum at Newmarket Autumn Sales. *K. Ivory.*

KIYOSWANEE 5 gr.m. My Swanee 122–Anagram 76 (Vilmoray 126) [1974 **85**
5g 5fg 5fg 5f 6d* 6g³ 6fg* 6g* 6d⁴ 6v* 1975 6v³ 6g⁴ 6f² 6fg 6g 6g⁴ 6f 6d* 6d* 6s
1976 6g 6fg⁵ 6d 6g³ 5.1fg² 6f⁶ 6fg⁶ 6f² 6f² 5fg³ 6g 6g³ 6v] lengthy, attractive,
good-quartered mare: fair handicapper: placed several times at 5 yrs, final
occasion when 2 lengths third of 11 to Shuffling at Newmarket in September: best
form at 6f but runs as though she may well be suited by further: appears to
act on any going but is well suited by an easy surface: ran very badly final start.
J. Winter.

KLAIRE 2 ch.f. Klairon 131–Causerie 114 (Cagire II 122) [1976 7f* 7g⁶] half- **83**
sister to three winners, notably high-class stayer Proverb (by Reliance II): 2,400
gns yearling: dam stayed 1¼m: won nine-runner maiden race at Salisbury in July
by ½ length from Hora Royale: well-beaten sixth of seven to Leyburn Lady in
nursery at Wolverhampton the following month: will stay 1¼m. *R. Akehurst.*

KLAIREDE 4 b.f. Klairon 131–Welsh Bede 103 (Welsh Abbot 131) [1974 N.R. **42**
1975 6fg 8fg 5h 5.7f⁵ 5g 8f³ 8g 8g 8.2s⁶ 1976 6g³ 7fg 8fg⁴ 8g³] small filly:
selling handicapper: winner in Sweden in 1976: stays 1m. *D. Marks.*

KLAIRIO 4 br.c. Klairon 131–Fair Astrologer 81 (Relic) [1974 N.R. 1975 **86**
7s⁶ 7.6g² 1976 6fg⁵] strong colt: had stiff task and was not disgraced when
fifth of six to Boldboy in Ladbroke Abernant Stakes at Newmarket in April,
only outing since May 1975: will probably need 1m to be seen to best advantage:
sold 910 gns Newmarket July Sales. *M. Jarvis.*

KLAIRMAY 2 ch.f. Maystreak 118–Klaironga (Klairon 131) [1976 5g] first —
foal: dam never ran: 15/2 when last of 10 to Voleuse in seller at Nottingham in
July: sold 310 gns Doncaster September Sales. *M. H. Easterby.*

KLEPTES 3 b.g. Burglar 128–Dido's Grandaughter (By Thunder! 122) [1975 **75**
4g² 5.5g⁵ 9.5g⁵ 7v 1976 8f* 8g 10fg³ 8f 8f³ 10f⁶ 8s] tall gelding: brother to 6f
winner Heartbeat and half-brother to several other winners, including useful
middle-distance performer Barlasch (by Con Brio): dam never ran: made all
when beating Fly High a neck in maiden race at Brighton in May: in frame in
handicaps at Yarmouth afterwards: ran poorly last two outings: stays 1¼m:
usually wears blinkers but didn't when successful: sold 4,400 gns Newmarket
Autumn Sales. *J. Winter.*

KNARESBORO 4 b.c. Privy Seal 108–Princess Flora 64 (Floribunda 136) —
[1974 5g⁶ 6fg⁵ 8d² 6s 1975 8s⁵ 8fg⁵ 8f² 8g* 10f* 8.2d* 8fg⁵ 8.2v⁴ 1976 8f⁴ 8d]
strong colt: quite a moderate handicapper: ran better race at 4 yrs on reappearance: may stay further than 1¼m: appears to act on any going: sold 500 gns
Doncaster October Sales. *J. Hanson.*

KNIGHT MARSHALL 3 b.c. Paddy B 105–Miss Maxi (Martial 131) [1975 —
N.R. 1976 12g] plain colt: first foal: dam ran only twice: bit backward when
tailed off behind Island Mist in 14-runner maiden race at Lanark in May. *W.
Atkinson.*

KNIGHT TEMPLAR 6 br.g. King Log 115–Parthian Glance 120 (Parthia 132) **119**
[1974 10g² 11.7f* 12fg² 19fg⁵ 14s* 16d 18d 1975 10g² 12v* 16s* 12s² 12g³
16fg³ 12fg 14d⁵ 16g 16d* 18fg⁶ 1976 14s 15g⁵ 13g⁴ 17.5g* 15.5g² 15g³ 20s* 24s*]
strong gelding: useful handicapper when trained in England by R. Price: showed
improved form in France in 1976, winning three times at Longchamp, on third
occasion beating Forceful 5 lengths in Prix Gladiateur in October: had earlier won
handicap in May and Prix du Pont de Flandre in September, holding off Citoyen,
gave 7 lb, by 2 lengths in latter event: ran best other race when creditable third
to Hill Hawk in Grand Prix de Fontainbleau earlier in September: stays very
well: acts on any going: usually wears blinkers nowadays: possesses a useful
turn of foot for a stayer. *H. van de Poele, France.*

KNOCKMEALDOWN 2 b.c. Mountain Call 125–Mossy 95 (Mossborough 126) **70**
[1976 5fg 5f 5h² 6g 6g] useful-looking colt: hung badly right when 2 lengths
second of four to Geraghty Racing in maiden race at Pontefract in July: behind

in seller at Newmarket two months later: should stay 6f: wears blinkers: sold 880 gns Newmarket Autumn Sales. *A. Corbett.*

KNOCKROE 8 gr.g. Fortino II 120–Corbalton 103 (Milesian 125) [1974 N.R. **§§**
1975 N.R. 1976 12f 12fg 14.7f] very smart but temperamental performer (rated 122) in 1973: subsequently off course until May 1976 when finishing seventh of 15 to King Mousse in minor event at Limerick Junction in May: showed no interest in racing on his two outings in this country, on second occasion pulling himself up in early stages at Redcar in July (reportedly finished lame): effective from 1¼m to 1¾m: best suited by top-of-the-ground conditions: trained by A. Maxwell in Ireland until after second start. *J. Nelson.*

KOA RANGI 2 ch.c. Divine Gift 127–The Star of Sharon 73 (Midsummer Night **83**
II 117) [1976 5fg 5s 7s*] first foal: 1,400 gns yearling: dam won over 7f: 8-length winner of 17-runner seller at Chepstow in October (led all way): bought in for 625 gns afterwards: well suited by 7f and will stay 1m: acts on soft going. *D. Keith.*

KOBE 4 b.g. Relko 136–Geisha 88 (Shantung 132) [1974 5fg 6f 8s³ 7.2s 8v⁴ **—**
1975 11.1s⁶ 10.1f2 10g* 10fg 10f⁵ 10.2f⁴ 1976 8fg 10.8f⁶] small gelding: selling handicapper: should stay much further than 1¼m: acts on firm going: was tried in blinkers as a 2-y-o. *W. Charles.*

KOLYMA 2 b.f. Timmy My Boy 125–Kolamba (Klairon 131) [1976 5fg 6d 6fg⁵ **74**
7g⁴ 7fg² 7fg⁴ 7s] fair sort: French bred: half-sister to 1972 3-y-o 1¼m winner Platanus (by Pampered King): cost 6,000 francs as a yearling (approx. £640): dam won three times at up to 1¼m: showed ability in sellers at Goodwood and Deauville prior to finishing in frame in maiden races at Chester and Leicester in September: will stay 1¼m: acts on a firm surface and ran moderately on soft going on final outing. *G. Hunter.*

KONAFA 3 b.f. Damascus–Royal Statute (Northern Dancer) [1975 6g² 7g* **118**
8d⁵ 7fg⁴ 1976 7fg 8fg² 8g³ 10d]
Nothing Konafa did before or after the One Thousand Guineas bore the faintest resemblance to her performance in that race. She went to post for the One Thousand with credentials that suggested her starting price of 66/1 was far from generous: she had won a Yarmouth maiden race and finished a respectable fourth under top weight in a Newmarket nursery at two years but on the two occasions she had crossed swords with good fillies in the Argos Star Fillies Mile and the Nell Gwyn Stakes, she had been soundly beaten. In fact, in the Nell Gwyn she'd trailed in last of ten behind Flying Water, beaten the best part of twenty lengths. In the Guineas, however, Konafa raced close to Flying Water throughout. Three furlongs out Flying Water was last but one of the fourteen runners racing on the far side, with only Konafa behind her. Soon afterwards, as Flying Water moved through to deliver her challenge so too did Konafa. Konafa's storming run took her right through the field and she caught Kesar Queen close home and beat her a neck for second place, a length behind Flying Water. Whether Konafa would have troubled the winner with further to travel is debatable, but probably she would not: Saint-Martin on Flying Water was sitting as quiet as a mouse over the last furlong whereas Dettori on Konafa was riding most vigorously. Whatever one's views on that matter, there's no doubting that Konafa put up a tremendous performance.
The season went sour for Konafa after the Guineas. Apparently she went lame and lost condition. One by one the season's important races passed by without her, and she didn't race again until the autumn when she turned out twice at Newmarket, finishing third to Manilata and Early Dawn, both of whom were giving her weight, in the Severals Stakes and tailed-off last of nineteen behind Vitiges in the Champion Stakes.

	Damascus (b 1964)	Sword Dancer (ch 1956)	Sunglow Highland Fling
Konafa (b.f. 1973)		Kerala (b 1958)	My Babu Blade of Time
	Royal Statute (b 1969)	Northern Dancer (b 1961)	Nearctic Natalma
		Queen's Statute (b 1954)	Le Lavandou Statute

Konafa, an attractive, well-made filly, bred by Nijinsky's breeder E. P. Taylor, was bought for 57,000 dollars at the Saratoga Yearling Sales. She is a daughter of the top-class American horse Damascus who won twenty-one races, including the Preakness Stakes and the Belmont Stakes, and who was voted Horse of the Year in the United States in 1967. Damascus has made an extremely good start to his career as a stallion and in 1975 his runners earned a total of 1,328,554 dollars, an amount bettered only by the progeny of What A Pleasure. Konafa is the first foal of Royal Statute, a winner over five furlongs as a two-year-old. Royal Statute's dam Queen's Statute, an unraced sister to the smart miler Grand Statute, was imported to Canada in 1956 and has produced numerous good winners, including the leading Canadian middle-distance performer Dance Act and the Canadian Oaks winner Menedict. Konafa gives the impression that she should be well suited by distances longer than a mile. She has shown her best form on a firm surface. Clearly at her best she has the ability to win more races if connections stand by their intention of keeping her in training as a four-year-old, but it remains to be seen whether she will ever reproduce her One Thousand Guineas running, and in her end-of-season form she would be better employed at stud. *L. Cumani.*

KONRAD 3 br.c. Wolver Hollow 126–Tudor Lullaby (Tudor Melody 129) [1975 6fg⁴ 7g² 7g⁵ 7g² 7g 1976 8g 10g³ 10fg² 10f* 12h² 10h⁴ 10.5g⁶ 10g⁵ 10d] attractive colt: good mover: never in danger when winning maiden race at Pontefract in June by 5 lengths from Mister Rushton: good second to Double East in handicap at Lingfield later in month, going under by a head after a tremendous battle: stays 1½m: acts on hard ground (had plenty to do at weights when well beaten only outing on softish ground): sold 5,000 gns Newmarket Autumn Sales. *B. Hills.* **86**

KOST OF LIVING 2 br.c. Kibenka 119–Rising Prices (Royal Record II) [1976 5g⁵ 5v] first foal: dam of little account: behind in minor race at Leicester in May and all-aged event at Nottingham in October. *W. Stephenson.* **—**

KRASSATA 3 ch.f. Nijinsky 138–Bonnie Googie (Better Self) [1975 6fg* 6f 8g³ 1976 10f² 8g⁴ 11g³ 12g⁴ 12f³ 14fg⁶ 8g] well-grown American-bred Irish filly: sister to very useful Irish middle-distance winner Masqued Dancer, and half-sister to four winners in U.S.A.: $130,000 yearling: dam won at 2 yrs and 3 yrs in U.S.A.: fourth in both the Irish fillies classics at the Curragh, being beaten 4½ lengths by Sarah Siddons in 1,000 Guineas, looking sure to win when going clear well over 2f out but weakening in final furlong, and being beaten about 2½ lengths by Lagunette in Guinness Oaks after holding every chance in final 2f: also placed in well-contested Azalea Stakes at Phoenix Park, Group 3 race at Bremen and Brownstown Stakes at the Curragh: possibly finds 1m on sharp side and stays 1½m (sixth to Meneval in Irish St Leger when tried at 1¾m): acts on firm going: best form in blinkers. *D. Weld, Ireland.* **114**

KRIBIAN 3 ch.f. Kribi 110–Julie Anne (Tenterhooks 128) [1975 N.R. 1976 8fg] small filly: second foal: dam of little account: last of 17 in apprentice event won by Royal Major at Thirsk in July: sold 250 gns Doncaster October Sales. *K. Stapleton.* **—**

KRUGERRAND 3 b.f. Goldhill 125–Wether Fell (Klairon 131) [1975 5s 6f 6fg⁴ 5f⁴ 6d 1976 8f² 8f⁴ 9f* 11f⁶ 8.2g 7fg² 7f⁵ 8f⁶ 9fg⁵] strong filly: won minor event at Newcastle in April by a neck from Sousa, leading close home despite hanging quite badly: again wandered under pressure when 1¼ lengths second to Lorenzo Monaco in handicap at Wolverhampton in June: stays 9f but isn't certain to get 11f: acts on firm going: blinkered fourth and eighth outings: has given us impression that she isn't completely genuine. *R. D. Peacock.* **74**

KUANU 3 b.g. Kauai King–Tomboy 95 (Sica Boy 132) [1975 6fg 7g 8d 1976 12.2g³ 12f* 12g⁶ 13f 16f] big, powerful gelding: all out when winning at Beverley in April: stays 1½m: acts on firm going: ran well in blinkers on first outing but ran moderately in them on last two appearances: very one paced: sold 2,100 gns Newmarket September Sales, resold 720 gns Ascot December Sales. *Doug Smith.* **65**

KUNG FU 4 ch.c. Hul a Hul 124–Timeless (Only for Life 126) [1974 6d 7d 7.2g* 8s 8s³ 1975 12g² 11s² 11s² 12h* 14f* 14d³ 14f* 14fg* 15.5s 14g⁶ 1976 12fg²] big, strong colt: developed into a very useful animal at 3 yrs, winning four handicaps and finishing seventh of 16 to Henri le Balafre in French St Leger at Longchamp: ran well on only appearance at 4 yrs, finishing 1½ lengths second to Quite Candid in three-runner event at Lingfield in August: suited by 1½m and 1¾m, and will probably also be suited by longer distances: acts on any going but is reportedly considered best suited by top-of-the-ground conditions: genuine and consistent but has presumably had his training troubles and was sold only 1,900 gns Newmarket Autumn Sales. *M. Jarvis.* **106**

KUNPUU 5 b.h. French Beige 127–Green Velvet (Epaulette 125) [1974 8g 8g* **102**
10f 10g³ 8f³ 8.2d* 8s 8g³ 8.2s 1975 8d⁴ 10d* 10g² 10.5s⁵ 10fg 8f⁴ 10.5d 10f 9f² 8s³
9g 1976 10g³ 8g⁵ 10fg* 12d⁶ 12g³ 12fg⁴ 10fg 10.5fg⁶ 10g⁵ 11g³ 9g] well-made
horse: fairly useful handicapper: won Playboy Bookmakers Handicap at Newmarket in April by a length from Traquair: ran his best race afterwards when
2½ lengths third of 10 to Flame Tree in Ladbrokes Ayshire Handicap at Ayr in
September on tenth outing: stays 11f but has yet to prove he stays further: acts
on any going: best in blinkers: sold 7,400 gns Newmarket Autumn Sales. *F. J.
Houghton.*

KUSHBEHAR 3 br.f. Behistoun 131–Kushi 65 (Paridel 112) [1975 5g³ 5f³ —
6g* 6f 1976 6f 7g 7g 7.6fg 7.2g⁶ 6g⁶ 6v³] neat filly: rated 80 at 2 yrs but showed
little worthwhile form in 1976 and descended to selling company on last two
outings: sold to F. Wiles 660 gns Newmarket Autumn Sales. *F. Carr.*

KYLE KEEP 4 b.f. Ballymoss 136–Keep Going 113 (Hard Sauce 131) [1974 **73**
5f 6s⁶ 8s⁵ 6g² 8g⁶ 8s² 8g² 1975 10g⁶ 7v 10g³ 10f² 12f* 12f³ 12f⁶ 11g 1976 10g
13.3g⁵ 12f⁵ 10s] good sort: ex-Irish filly: won handicap at Limerick Junction in
1975: little worthwhile form in four outings in this country as a 4-y-o (including
in good-class company on first two): stays 1½m: probably acts on any going.
Dr A. Jones.

KYRIAKOS 3 b.c. Wolver Hollow 126–Crolly (Darling Boy 124) [1975 5fg 6f **65**
7d 8g² 7g 1976 8f 8.5fg⁴ 8fg 10.1f* 8.3fg⁵ 10fg] good sort: good mover: won
maiden race at Windsor in July by 1½ lengths from Snow Swan: stays 1¼m: acts
on firm going. *A. Pitt.*

L

LA BAMBOLA 3 ch.f. Be Friendly 130–Hatchettine 65 (High Hat 131) [1975 **95**
6g 6g² 7f³ 6s⁶ 6g² 7.2s³ 1976 7fg* 7fg⁴ 8fg⁵ 8f⁵ 8fg³ 10fg³ 10.6g 9g³ 10g 9g]
good-bodied filly: won maiden race at Newmarket in April by a short head from
Mistress Page: ran some good races afterwards, including when fifth of 16 to
Jumping Hill in Royal Hunt Cup at Royal Ascot in June: stays 1¼m: probably
acts on any going: blinkered eighth outing: often sweats up: genuine: sold
7,800 gns Newmarket December Sales. *R. Boss.*

LA BELLA 2 b.f. Northfields–La Dice 60 (Alcide 136) [1976 6fg 7d³ 8v] well- **85**
made, good sort: half-sister to a winner in Italy by Native Prince: 2,700 gns yearling: dam daughter of Italian 1,000 Guineas winner Ninabella: 2 lengths third
to Guama in 30-runner maiden race at Newbury in September: started favourite
for maiden race at Teesside the following month but finished well behind: should
stay 1¼m: possibly unsuited by heavy going. *P. Rohan.*

LA BONNE VIE 3 b.f. Galivanter 131–Time and Chance 96 (Supreme Court 135) —
[1975 5.3g 8g 1976 10fg 15.5h] small, fair sort: behind in maiden and minor
events. *S. Woodman.*

LA BRIGITTE 6 ch.m. Gulf Pearl 117–Hatton's Pearl (Pearl Orient) [1974 —
N.R. 1975 N.R. 1976 12.2s⁶ 12.5s] fair performer (rated 87) at 2 yrs: well
beaten in two races in late 1976, only outings since: has been to stud and produced a foal in 1975. *P. Felgate.*

LACE BASKET 3 ch.f. Silly Season 127–Miss Lollypop (St Paddy 133) [1975 **72**
5g 1976 8f² 10g 10f* 12fg 11.7f] lengthy filly: won maiden race at Folkestone
in May by 2½ lengths from Devil's Dike: stays 1¼m: acts on firm going. *G.
Harwood.*

LACEMAKER 3 b.f. Aztec 128–Seven Knots 95 (Blue Peter) [1975 N.R. 1976 —
12g⁶ 14d] half-sister to several winners, including good 1964 2-y-o Leonardo (by
Doutelle): 1,500 gns foal: dam a stayer: well beaten in maiden races at Salisbury
in May and Yarmouth in September: sold 400 gns Newmarket December Sales.
J. Bethell.

LACONIAN 4 b.g. Spartan General 109–Savilla (Le Sage 128) [1974 N.R. —
1975 N.R. 1976 12v] third foal: dam staying hurdler: last of 13 in minor
event won by Chance Belle at Lingfield in November, first outing on flat. *N.
Wakley.*

LA CONISTRANO 2 ch.f. Capistrano 120–Laconia 58 (Great Nephew 126) **86**
[1976 6fg 7f 6fg⁴ 6s] first foal: 3,000 gns yearling: dam half-sister to very useful
stayer Tudor Tale: put up easily best effort when about 5 lengths fourth to Metair
in well-contested minor event at Salisbury in September: should stay 7f. *B.
Swift.*

LA COURONNE 3 b.f. Blakeney 126–La Bastille (Nearco) [1975 6g 1976 **62**
10.8f⁵ 13.8d³ 12.2g³ 16.9f³ 16fg³ 14f⁵ 16f*] neat filly: possesses limited ability
but managed to win poor maiden race at Thirsk in September by 3 lengths from
Haunting Music: one paced and is suited by a test of stamina: ran poorly when
tried in blinkers on penultimate appearance: sold 7,000 gns Newmarket Autumn
Sales. *M. Stoute.*

LA CREOLE 2 ch.f. King's Company 124–Savannah (Ribot 142) [1976 6f 6fg —
5.1f 7g] half-sister to two minor winners: 1,300 gns yearling: dam never ran:
poor maiden: blinkered last two outings: sold 260 gns Ascot November Sales.
J. Winter.

LADY BAYFORD 2 ch.f. Calpurnius 122–Rain Bird (Klairon 131) [1976 5fg **63**
5fg⁶ 6fg] second foal: dam never ran: plating-class maiden: should be suited by
6f+. *J. Old.*

LADY BENTE 3 b.f. Realm 129–Maladie d'Amour 98 (Fidalgo 129) [1975 —
6fg⁴ 6g 5g* 6g⁴ 1976 7fg 7fg³ 8h] sparely-made filly: won maiden race at
Leicester in 1975: had stiff tasks at 3 yrs, best effort when 9 lengths third of eight
to Friendly Sound in handicap at Newmarket in June: should stay 1m+:
bought by B.B.A. 3,800 gns Newmarket July Sales for export to New Zealand.
J. Winter.

LADY CHANCELLOR 5 gr.m. Supreme Sovereign 119–Askadeelah (Petition —
130) [1974 8s 8f 10f 1975 9g 13.8f 9fg 1976 10f⁵] poor maiden: stays 1¼m:
sold 1,500 gns Doncaster October Sales. *R. Ward.*

LADY CONSTANCE 2 b.f. Connaught 130–Princely Maid 71 (King's Troop 118) **118**
[1976 5f⁵ 5f⁵ 5f 5f² 5fg² 6fg⁶ 5d* 7s* 7s]
  In a discussion on the leading two-year-old fillies, it is doubtful whether
many would give much thought to Lady Constance, a filly who began her career
running without distinction in moderate company at the minor meetings, and who
didn't get off the mark until her seventh racecourse appearance, when she encountered easy underfoot conditions for the first time and won a nineteen-runner
maiden event at Windsor in September by three lengths, after making all the
running. Even this performance didn't bespeak a great deal of merit in Lady
Constance, but there was plenty of merit attached to her win under a penalty in
the John Sutcliffe Trophy Nursery on soft going at Lingfield a week later, at least
there was the way she set about it. In front all the way from her draw one off the
rails, Lady Constance fought off a challenge from Fair Season in the last furlong
and stayed on strongly in the hands of her apprentice rider to win by a length
and a half. Fair Season went on to win the Horris Hill Stakes at Newbury,
whilst Casino Boy, who finished third, afterwards won a well-contested nursery
at Newmarket. Both were more than useful two-year-olds, but neither has much
chance at the weights with Lady Constance in the Free Handicap on the evidence
provided by this race at Lingfield, and nor has the Intercraft Solario Stakes
runner-up Mr Nice Guy, who was well back in fifth place. The fact that Lady
Constance was afterwards well beaten in the Somerville Tattersall Stakes might
have weighed with the official handicapper, but it doesn't weigh with us. Lady
Constance went off at a pace she hadn't a hope of maintaining for the full seven

*John Sutcliffe Trophy Nursery, Lingfield—the apprentice-ridden Lady Constance
wins from Fair Season*

furlongs, in addition to which she was ridden by an apprentice unable to claim his 7 lb. The logic in putting up claiming apprentices in races in which they are not entitled to draw their allowance escapes us. Whichever way you care to look at it, it doesn't make sense.

Lady Constance (b.f. 1974)	Connaught (b 1965)	St Paddy (b 1957)	Aureole
			Edie Kelly
		Nagaika (ch 1954)	Goyama
			Maim
	Princely Maid (b 1967)	King's Troop (b 1957)	Princely Gift
			Equiria
		Moss Maid (gr 1959)	Mossborough
			Jules Magic

The fourth foal of her dam and the second to race, Lady Constance, who cost 2,500 guineas as a yearling, is a half-sister to Pennina (by Great Nephew) a speedy two-year-old in this country in 1975 and a winner in France at up to seven and a half furlongs. Princely Maid raced only as a two-year-old, at which age she won in poor company over five furlongs at Thirsk. She is evidently much better as a broodmare than she showed herself to be on the racecourse. There is not much stamina in the family, and we don't expect Lady Constance, a free-running sort, to be effective beyond a mile. Her future is at the mercy of the elements, but judging from her Free Handicap mark she can hardly fail to win a race when she gets soft ground. *M. Salaman.*

LADY ESMERALDA 3 b.f. Karabas 132–Tiarella 84 (Democratic 124) [1975 5g⁵ 6g 6g⁵ 7v 6d 6g² 8g² 1976 11v* 10d³ 12d³ 10f 8h 10f⁵ 12f* 13g 12.2s] leggy, lightly-made filly: half-sister to Cesarewitch winner Shantallah: winner at Ayr in April (maiden race, easily) and Lanark in September (Ladbrokes Lanark Silver Bell Handicap, gamely by ¾ length from Heriot): should stay further than 1½m: acts on any going: ran poorly final outing. *J. Hanson.* — **78**

LADY ETON 2 b.f. Le Dieu d'Or 119–Toreadora 103 (Matador 131) [1976 5g 5fg* 5fg² 6fg* 6fg] tall, close-coupled filly: half-sister to three winners, including fair sprinter Pirator (by Pirate King): 1,600 gns yearling: dam stayed 1¼m: a useful filly who won at Newmarket in May (by a neck from newcomer Sunny Spring) and at Windsor the following month (three-runner £1,700 event by 2 lengths from Regency Bill): good second to Easy Landing in Kingsclere Stakes at Newbury in between but finished well behind that filly in Lowther Stakes won by Icena at York in August: will probably stay 7f. *R. Hannon.* — **106**

LADY FREEZE 2 b.f. Irish Ball 127–Deep Freeze 75 (Varano) [1976 7s⁶] French-foaled filly: first foal: dam, winner over 1¼m at 3 yrs, is half-sister to very useful miler Frigid Aire: unquoted, showed up for 4f when just under 9 lengths sixth of 20 to Brightly in maiden race at Newmarket in October: will do better over middle distances at 3 yrs. *B. Hills.* — **70 p**

LADY FURNISS 2 b.f. Crepello 136–Rely On Sue 75 (Reliance II 137) [1976 7g 7s] small filly: second foal: dam won over 1½m: tailed off in minor events at Lingfield and Sandown (slowly away) in the autumn. *D. Whelan.* — **—**

LADY GROSVENOR 3 b.f. Above Suspicion 127–Paloma Star 71 (Star Gazer 123) [1975 6f 7g 1976 8fg 15.8f] of no account. *K. Payne.* — **—**

LADY JADE 2 ch.f. Green God 128–Roll Out (Relko 136) [1976 5fg 5f 5s 5f 7g] useless. *P. Bevan.* — **—**

LADY JAY 3 ch.f. Double Jump 131–Straight Mistress (Straight Deal) [1975 5g⁶ 5fg 6g 7g 1976 7g⁴ 5fg 6fg⁵ 7fg 6fg³ 7d³ 10d 8s² 8s 8s²] light-framed filly: plater: runner-up at Wolverhampton and Teesside in the autumn: best at up to 1m: appears to act on any going: wears blinkers nowadays. *G. Smyth.* — **56**

LADY JIM 3 b.f. Jim J–Water Lady (Ambiorix 130) [1975 6.5g⁶ 7.5d 7g 1976 9f 8fg² 8f 8f⁵ 10f 9f⁴] American-bred filly: disappointing maiden: stays 1m: sweated up very badly when tried in blinkers. *R. Boss.* — **59**

LADY LAMBOURN 2 ch.f. Habitat 134–A Deux 80 (Crepello 136) [1976 6f 6fg³ 7fg*] strong filly: second foal: 9,600 gns yearling: dam placed from 6f to 1½m: won 12-runner maiden race at Ayr in July by ½ length from Mint: will probably stay further than 1m. *B. Hills.* — **82**

LADY-LE-GROS 2 gr.f. Seaepic 100–Sadie (Rise 'N Shine II) [1976 5d 5g 7f 5fg 9fg 8fg 6d 6v] plain filly: plating-class maiden: blinkered second and seventh outings. *S. Nesbitt.* — **56**

LADY MAE 3 ch.f. Behistoun 131–Miss Jeanette 91 (Sheshoon 132) [1975   **46**
N.R. 1976 14g 15.5s 18s³] third foal: dam game stayer: third of 13 to wide-
margin winner Quartic Melody in amateur riders maiden event at Doncaster in
October: evidently needs extreme distances. *D. Dale.*

LADY MASON 2 ch.f. Huntercombe 133–Russian Princess 99 (Henry the   **87**
Seventh 125) [1976 6d² 6d⁶] neat filly: half-sister to several winners, including
good French middle-distance stayer Paddy's Princess (by St Paddy) and useful
Tebaldi (by Astec): dam, half-sister to Connaught, won over 6f at 2 yrs: ran promisingly when 2 lengths second of 25 to Caerdeon Line in maiden race at Newmarket
in October: started favourite for similar event on same course later in month but
could finish only sixth of 22 to Rocket Symphony: will probably stay 1m. *P.
Walwyn.*

LADY MEDE 2 br.f. Runnymede 123–Dalton Lady (Sammy Davis 129) [1976   **74**
5g 5g⁶ 5g⁴ 5f 5s⁵ 6v 5v] leggy filly: first living foal: dam of little account: ran
best race when 4 lengths fifth of 13 to Selenis in maiden event at Nottingham in
September: not certain to stay beyond 5f: evidently suited by some give in the
ground. *V. Mitchell.*

LADY MERE 2 b.f. Decoy Boy 129–Wordrone (Worden II 129) [1976 5f 5fg*   **118**
6g* 5f² 6g* 8g⁴ 7s²]
This filly, who spent most of the season trained in the north of England
by Ernest Weymes, ran her best race when second at two lengths to the French
two-year-old Pharly in the Group 1 Prix de la Foret at Longchamp in October
on her final appearance: behind her at weight-for-age and sex were proven older
horses such as Manado, Monsanto, Full of Hope, Guichet and Kesar Queen,
the last-named of whom had been beaten about a length in the One Thousand
Guineas. But good as this performance by Lady Mere was, it did not earn her
many marks from Mr Gibbs, for in the Two-Year-Old Free Handicap Lady Mere is
to be found down among the 8-0 brigade, 21 lb below J. O. Tobin. Still 8-0 in
the Two-Year-Old Free Handicap represents a higher mark by far than does 8-0
in the Northern Free Handicap for two-year-olds, and only three have appearances
previously Lady Mere had been beaten by Trackally, a filly who has been given
8-0 in the Northern Free Handicap, in a four-horse minor event at Redcar!
The less said about that particular race, however, the better. Suffice to say
Lady Mere came out in the Tadcaster Stakes at York next time and beat fillies
much better than Trackally. And, what's more, beat them easily. Improving
smoothly below the distance, she quickly took up the running and forged clear to
beat Caelidh by three lengths, with Blackadder, Mielitta and Mummy's Darling
behind. This was good form, and Lady Mere bettered it in her last race for
Weymes, in the Argos Star Fillies' Mile at Ascot. Slowly out of the stalls in a race
run at a good strong gallop from the start, she was always having to work to keep
in touch, and in the circumstances did extremely well to get up into fourth place
at the post, only three lengths behind Miss Pinkie. Judging from her display in
the Prix de la Foret, she was unlucky not to have been more closely concerned in
the finish.

Lady Mere (b.f. 1974)	Decoy Boy (b 1967)	Tin Whistle (b 1957)	Whistler Sister Miles
		Scargill (ro 1955)	Vilmorin Foliage
	Wordrone (ch 1968)	Worden II (ch 1949)	Wild Risk Sans Tares
		Tyrone's Power (ch 1951)	Golden Cloud Sisterchase

Lady Mere is a useful-looking filly, and a good walker. Her dam, whose

Tadcaster Stakes, York—Lady Mere beats the favourite Caelidh

second foal she is, was no good on the racecourse and was sold, covered by High Table, for 600 guineas at the 1971 Newmarket December Sales. Tyrone's Power, the next dam, was no good on the racecourse or in the paddocks, and that Lady Mere should be a good racehorse is surprising, seeing that her sire Decoy Boy had little in two previous crops to recommend him as a stallion. On the question of stamina, it is difficult to come to any conclusions about Lady Mere. The dam's side of her pedigree suggests stamina, and in Snake Bite, from a Tehran mare, Decoy Boy has sired a winner at a mile and a half. But generally speaking most of Decoy Boy's stock seem to be sprinters like himself. Not that we need worry about Lady Mere's stamina so far as the One Thousand Guineas is concerned. She has already shown that she stays a mile well. *B. Hills.*

LADY MURRAY 2 br.f. Murrayfield 119–Impulsive Lady 83 (Quorum 126) — [1976 5fg 5fg 5fg] first foal: dam stayed 7f: no worthwhile form. *J. Holt.*

LADY OF DARIEN 4 b.f. Porto Bello 118–Pettifour 94 (Saint Crespin III 132) — [1974 6g⁵ 6d 6d 6s⁵ 1975 8g 10s 10f 8f 6f 8.2g 8.2d 12g 10s⁶ 1976 10v³] of little account: dead. *J. Pullen.*

LADY OF ELEGANCE 4 b.f. Blast 125–Vimarie 83 (Vimy 132) [1974 5f⁶ — 5f⁴ 5v³ 6d³ 8.2g² 6g² 7v 5s 1975 8g 8h⁶ 8f 1976 8.2d 15.8s] compact filly: of no account nowadays: sold 160 gns Doncaster October Sales. *F. Carr.*

LADY OF THE MOON 2 b.f. Crepello 136–Trip To The Moon 84 (Sicambre 135) **89** [1976 6d³ 7d] well-made, strong, deep-bodied filly: sister to two winners, including 1970 Derby fourth Great Wall, and half-sister to several other winners, including 1969 Derby fourth Moon Mountain (by Mourne): 16,000 gns yearling: dam ran only at 2 yrs: promising length third to Circlet in Blue Seal Stakes at Ascot in September (looked in need of race): 11/1 when seventh of 25 to Bessie Wallis in Houghton Stakes at Newmarket the following month: will stay 1½m. *P. Walwyn.*

LADY OF YORK 2 ch.f. Double-U-Jay 120–Sara's Star 70 (Sheshoon 132) **75** [1976 6fg 7fg⁴ 6g 7fg⁵ 7f 7g 8s] fourth foal: half-sister to three winners, including useful and very tough 3-y-o Venus of Stretham (by Tower Walk), a winner at up to 1m: showed a little ability in 7f events at Newmarket in July: should stay at least 1m. *G. Blum.*

LADY ORIANA 2 b.f. Tudor Melody 129–Merry Madcap 124 (Grey Sovereign **91 p** 128 §) [1976 7s*] half-sister to several winners here and in U.S.A., including useful 1m performer Dancing Cap (by Native Dancer) and stakes-placed 2-y-o 5f winner What a Sketch (by Gentle Art): 9,200 gns yearling: dam very smart sprinter: 8/1, led over 2f out and kept on well when winning 19-runner maiden race at Newmarket in October by a head from more-experienced Nicolene: may stay 1m: a good first effort, and sure to go on to better things. *B. Hills.*

LADY PEACEABLE 3 b.f. L'Homme Arme 111–Kali (Sayajirao 132) [1975 — 5v 5d⁴ 1976 8g] poor maiden. *G. Wallace.*

LADY RHAPSODY 2 b.f. Northern Dancer–Ankole 85 (Crepello 136) [1976 **101** 6g⁵ 6fg⁵ 7f² 8d³ 8s*] compact, good sort: sister to French 3-y-o middle-distance winner Lady Aires, and half-sister to several winners, including useful miler Horbury (by Sing Sing): dam won at up to 13f: put up good efforts when placed behind Triple First in valuable fillies races, finishing 4 lengths second in Waterford Candelabra Stakes at Goodwood in August and 3½ lengths third in May Hill Stakes at Doncaster the following month: short-priced favourite for 20-runner maiden race at Sandown in October and made much of running to win by 5 lengths from Bowshot with others well strung out: will stay middle distances: acts on any going. *F. J. Houghton.*

LADY SINGER 3 b.f. Lord Gayle 124–Ceol an Oir (Vimy 132) [1975 7g³ 7g* **116** 1976 7s² 7g² 8g³ 12g 10f* 12g 8f*(w.o.) 11.5g³ 10d⁵] Irish filly: sister to Yankee Gold, a smart winner in Ireland at up to 1½m, and half-sister to another winner: dam never ran: put up an excellent performance when about 5 lengths fifth of 19 behind Vitiges in Champion Stakes at Newmarket in October, finishing clear of those racing on disadvantageous stands side apart from fourth-placed Malacate: successful earlier in Pretty Polly Stakes at the Curragh in June by 2 lengths from Everything Nice and walked over for £2,300 event at Leopardstown in August: also placed four times, notably when 2 lengths third to Sarah Siddons in Irish 1,000 Guineas at the Curragh: stays 11f (unplaced in Epsom Oaks and Irish Guinness Oaks when tried at 1½m): acts on any going but is evidently well suited by a soft surface: blinkered last two outings: bandaged off-fore at Epsom: exported to U.S.A. *K. Prendergast, Ireland.*

LADY SPORT 2 br.f. Super Song 73–Angelorum (Mourne 126) [1976 5f 5f —
6fg] leggy, narrow filly: bad plater: swerved at halfway when apprentice ridden
and blinkered on final outing. *A. Jarvis.*

LADY VAL 2 b.f. Dike–Danabella (Dumbarnie 125) [1976 5v⁵ 5f] half- —
sister to four winners here and abroad, including fairly useful middle-distance
winner Rodney (by Saint Crespin III): 720 gns yearling: well behind in maiden
races at Ayr and Lanark in April. *M. Naughton.*

LAEN 3 ch.c. Yellow River 114–Gold Cypher 76 (Pardao 120) [1975 6s⁶ 8g **92** d
1976 8fg 12fg* 11.7fg* 16fg³ 16g 12s⁵ 13.3v⁴ 12v⁴] fair performer: won two-
horse maiden race at Lingfield and slowly-run three-runner handicap at Windsor
in July: stays 1½m and has yet to prove he stays further: probably acts on
any going with possible exception of heavy. *R. Price.*

LA FABOULEUSE 2 ch.f. Continuation 120–Gold Fable (Faberge II 121) **68**
[1976 5fg 5fg 5f 5d⁴ 5s] lightly-made filly: possesses a little ability: will stay
1m: trained by B. Hills on first three outings: sold 1,050 gns Newmarket Autumn
Sales. *C. Brittain.*

LA FURZE 2 b.f. Winden 109–Alladin Furze 54 (Dairialatan 111) [1976 5f —
5g 5f⁴ 6f] poor plater. *M. Stevens.*

LA GALLIA 4 b.f. Welsh Saint 126–Minouche (Faubourg II 127) [1974 7g 8s **65**
1975 8s 12.2f* 12f⁴ 14d 12g* 12f 1976 12f 12d 13.8g 12f* 12fg³ 12fg² 12f³
10g⁵ 12fg⁴ 13v] workmanlike filly: fairly useful plater: sweated up very badly
and was tailed off in early stages but finished very strongly when winning handicap (non-selling) at Pontefract in June from Clems Boy: has yet to show she
stays further than 1½m: acts on firm going. *P. Rohan.*

LA GARDE 2 ch.f. Alcide 136 or King's Troop 118–La Bastille (Nearco) [1976 **83**
7fg 7fg 7s⁴] strong, attractive filly: half-sister to several winners, mostly
stayers, including fairly useful 2m winner La Meme (by Pall Mall): 6,200 gns
yearling: dam never ran: made late progress when about 4 lengths fourth of
19 to Lady Oriana in maiden race at Newmarket in October: will probably stay
well. *B. Hobbs.*

LAGER BOY 3 ch.g. Whistling Wind 123–Priona (Primera 131) [1975 5f 7g —
1976 16f 17.7f 10f] no signs of ability, including in a seller. *Dr A. Jones.*

LAGUNETTE 3 b.f. Val de Loir 133-Landerinette (Sicambre 135) [1975 8g* **122**
10s 1976 10g⁴ 12g* 10.5d³ 12g* 12s* 12s]
     By the time that Lagunette had won the Irish Guinness Oaks French-
trained three-year-olds had made off with five of the seven classics French
stables had contested on this side of the Channel; only Wollow in the Two
Thousand Guineas and Northern Treasure in the Irish Two Thousand Guineas
had prevented their taking the other two. Crow, in the St Leger, improved
the account to six out of eight, and by the end of the season the overwhelmingly

*Irish Guinness Oaks, the Curragh—Lagunette is chased home by (left to right)
the blinkered Krassata (fourth), Acoma (fifth), Sarah Siddons (second)
and I've A Bee (third)*

superior strength of the French stables at the classic distances could not reasonably be disputed. The nature of their strength is amply illustrated by the fact
that they were able to win six out of eight classic races, against the very best
three-year-olds in training over here, without any assistance from Youth, Exceller
or Riverqueen. The French didn't always need their best; for example, they
were able to win the Irish Guinness Oaks with Lagunette, a better filly over
middle distances in all probability than any of her age trained in England or
Ireland, yet one, taken all round, behind Pawneese and Riverqueen.

The most surprising thing about the Irish Guinness Oaks was that Lagunette
did not start favourite to win it. The favourite, Acoma, had run only once
before, winning a race at Saint-Cloud restricted to newcomers by six lengths,
whereas Lagunette had won two of her four races, including a well-contested
race at Longchamp, the Prix des Tuileries, and had finished third to Pawneese
and Riverqueen in the Prix de Diane. The Prix de Diane looked easily the best
race for three-year-old fillies run in Europe up to that time; Lagunette had gone
down by only four and a half lengths to the winner, running on, and had beaten
such as Antrona, Sarah Siddons and Theia; what's more, she seemed certain to
be ideally suited by a return to a mile and a half from the ten and a half furlongs
of the Diane. On the book, Sarah Siddons, winner of the Irish One Thousand
Guineas and two lengths behind Lagunette in the Diane, seemed the only live
threat unless the form of the Italian Oaks winner Claire Valentine was better
than we appreciated. Lagunette won very well, by two lengths from Sarah
Siddons, after experiencing some difficulty in getting a run when switched off
the rails entering the second-last furlong, but she would have had a lot more to
do if Acoma could have found an opening on the rails in time. Claire Valentine,
never in serious contention, finished a creditable eighth.

Lagunette did not race again until taking part in the Prix Vermeille at
Longchamp in the autumn, by which time Sarah Siddons, Acoma, Pawneese
and Riverqueen had each won their only race since they last met Lagunette.
Sarah Siddons had won the Yorkshire Oaks by a head from African Dancer
(ninth in the Irish Guinness Oaks), Acoma had won the Prix de Minerve at
Evry by five lengths, Pawneese had beaten the colts in the King George VI and
Queen Elizabeth Diamond Stakes and Riverqueen, whose only defeat in six
races had been in the Diane, had won the Grand Prix de Saint-Cloud by half a
length from Ashmore. Acoma could not run in the Prix Vermeille because of
injury but Pawneese, Riverqueen and Sarah Siddons turned out against
Lagunette, starting at odds of 5/10, 2/1 and 24/1 respectively, while Lagunette
started at 14/1. Unfortunately, the race for the Prix Vermeille did not, as its
predecessors sometimes had done, give any indication as to which in its field
was the leading three-year-old filly over middle distances in Europe. Pawneese
and Riverqueen both ran so badly that the race lost much of its significance.
It did, though, show Lagunette the best in the field on the day, very narrowly
the best from Sarah Siddons, on whom Piggott replaced her regular jockey Roche.
Lagunette came with a strong challenge in the straight, and after a tremendous
battle with Sarah Siddons that looked as though it would first go one way and
then go the other, she held on by a margin officially given as a nose. Floressa,
well beaten by the first two in Ireland, finished a length behind in third place,
a length and a half ahead of Sweet Rhapsody. Neither Floressa nor Sweet
Rhapsody is consistent, but they ran well here, and their merit is sufficiently
well established to be used to measure the merit of the two in front of them.
By that measure, Lagunette and Sarah Siddons, good fillies though they are,
cannot seriously be regarded as in the same class as Pawneese and Riverqueen.
Lagunette had one more outing. Starting at 21/1, she never showed with a
chance in the Prix de l'Arc de Triomphe and trailed in a distant fourteenth,
well behind Pawneese and well ahead of Riverqueen, both of whom gave further
evidence that they had trained off completely.

Lagunette (b.f. 1973)	Val de Loir (b 1959)	Vieux Manoir (b 1947)	Brantome / Vieille Maison
		Vali (br 1954)	Sunny Boy III / Her Slipper
	Landerinette (ch 1953)	Sicambre (br 1948)	Prince Bio / Sif
		Lais (ch 1940)	Fantastic / Lady Chatterley

Lagunette, a sister to the 1968 Oaks winner La Lagune, was expected to
fetch the top price at the Polo Club sale on the eve of the Prix de
l'Arc de Triomphe, but she was led out 200,000 francs short of her reserve of

Prix Vermeille, Longchamp—Lagunette again beats Sarah Siddons, but this time only by a nose. Floressa is third, ahead of Sweet Rhapsody and Theia

three million francs (around £363,000). She has since been bought by Walter Haefner of the Moyglare Stud in Ireland and is to continue racing in France.

Both La Lagune and her dam, Landerinette, are now dead, the former after producing only two foals to race, the latter after producing four foals to race, of whom Lagunette is her last. There is probably little to choose between the best performances of La Lagune and Lagunette, although, remembering her tremendous five-length win in the Oaks we would incline to come down on the side of La Lagune, who was, incidentally, regarded as second- or third-best staying filly of her year in France after defeat behind Roseliere and Pola Bella in the Prix Vermeille. Landerinette, unraced, produced two other winners, a very useful jumper in France called Lord Risk (by Wild Risk) and the Prix Hocquart runner-up Exalte (by Exbury). The third dam Lady Chatterley bred the dual Grand Steeplechase de Paris winner Lindor. For readers interested in these things, we point out that the fourth dam of both Landerinette and her sire Sicambre is the French Guineas runner-up Saperlipopette.

Lagunette is a big, strong filly, in appearance similar to La Lagune. She is extremely well suited by a mile and a half, and will stay, and be suited by, longer distances. She acts well on soft going. She should win more races, but her future appears to be bound up with that of Pawneese; if Pawneese comes back to her best and Lagunette does not make more than the normal improvement, then Lagunette's opportunities in the best races could be limited. *F. Boutin, France.*

LAHAINA 3 ch.f. Hul a Hul 124–Crusheen (Typhoon 125) [1975 N.R. 1976 6g] strong filly: second foal: sister to Dancing Partner, a winner at up to 1m: 160 gns 2-y-o: dam ran twice at 2 yrs in Ireland: looked very backward indeed when behind in 17-runner seller won by Bendy Baby at Kempton in May: sold 380 gns Ascot September Sales. *W. Holden.* —

LAIS 2 b.f. Amber Rama 133–Folle Fete 73 (Vieux Manoir 132) [1976 5g 5fg 6fg2 7h4] neat, nippy sort: third reported foal: half-sister to 3-y-o Anemos (by Derring-Do), a very useful winner of five races at 2 yrs, and to a winner in Sweden: dam won over 1¼m in Ireland: 5 lengths second to odds-on Sailing Along in maiden race at Lingfield in July: should stay at least 7f: sold 4,500 gns Newmarket Autumn Sales. *P. Walwyn.* 68

LA JACA 2 br.f. Lauso–Corta Jaca (Tudor Jinks 121) [1976 5f6 5g6 6g] fourth foal: sister to 3-y-o Laujock: dam never ran: no worthwhile form, including in a Newmarket seller. *W. Stephenson.* 53

LA MAGNA 4 gr.f. Runnymede 123–La Garoupe 87 (Pirate King 129) [1974 5.1f2 5g* 6g2 5.1g* 5g6 5d3 5s4 1975 raced in Denmark 1976 5.8f6 7.6fg 8d 7g] useful performer (rated 104) as a 2-y-o: raced in Denmark in 1975 and showed little worthwhile form in this country at 4-y-o: should stay 1m+: probably acts on any going. *N. Guest.* —

LAMARA 2 b.f. Major Portion 129–Kutelamara 81 (Quorum 126) [1976 6g 7fg] half-sister to four winners, including fairly useful Montreal Boy (by Doon), a winner at up to 1½m: dam won over 1¼m: tailed off in maiden races at Windsor in August and Salisbury in September. *J. Holt.* —

LA MARSA 2 ch.f. Royalty 130–Laarne (Le Haar 126) [1976 5g 6fg 7fg 7s*] lengthy filly: first foal: dam ran only twice: favourite and dropped in class, had her field well strung out when winning 15-runner seller at Warwick in October by 6 lengths from Grey Blossom: sold to N. Callaghan 1,550 gns afterwards: will stay middle distances: acts on soft going. *I. Balding.* 82

LAM

LAMB 2 ch.f. Henry the Seventh 125–Heart of Gold 72 (Infatuation 129) [1976   —
7g 5s] well-made, good sort: good mover: half-sister to four winners, including
fair 1975 2-y-o 5f winner La Paz (by March Past): 800 gns yearling: dam stayed
2m: going on nicely at finish when seventh of 13 to Arctic Tribune in 5f maiden
race at Sandown in October: will stay 1¼m+. *M. Masson.*

LAMB'S TALE 3 b.f. March Past 124–Merry Yarn 64 (Aggressor 130) [1975 7d **102**
7g⁴ 1976 10g* 12g* 12g⁶ 12f³ 13.3g* 14.6g⁶] quite a useful filly: dam won over
2m: convincing winner of Morland Brewery Trophy (handicap) at Newbury in
July, beating Palmerston 2 lengths: successful earlier in maiden race at Sandown
and minor event at Salisbury, accounting for Primrose Bank on both occasions:
not disgraced when sixth of nine to African Dancer in Park Hill Stakes at Doncaster in September: stays well: acts on firm going: genuine and consistent.
M. Smyly.

LA MEME 4 b.f. Pall Mall 132–La Bastille (Nearco) [1974 N.R. 1975 8s 12f³ **78**
16fg2 13g2 16f* 12g5 16g* 16f³ 16g 16f* 1976 16fg³ 16fg5 16f⁴ 17.4g 16.1d]
rangy filly: needs a good test of stamina: acts on firm going: sold 5,000 gns
Ascot November Sales. *Denys Smith.*

LA MERLETTE 3 b.f. Balidar 133–La Chanteuse 81 (Hethersett 134) [1975   —
N.R. 1976 9f⁶ 7fg 8d 12fg 18s] seems to be of little account. *M. Tate.*

LAMINIA 2 ch.f. Midsummer Night II 117–Laroyso 87 (Lauso) [1976 6f⁶ **64**
5g³ 7g 7g 7s⁵ 6v] compact, good sort: plating-class maiden: will stay 1m: sold
1,050 gns Newmarket Autumn Sales. *M. Francis.*

LAMMERGEIER 3 ch.f. High Line 125–Dipper 108 (Donore 119) [1975 5s³   —
5d 7f³ 7fg5 7g 1976 11.1g 8fg 8s⁵ 8.2v⁵] leggy filly: half-sister to very smart
Chil the Kite (by Kalydon) but is of little account herself nowadays: ran poorly
when tried in blinkers at 2 yrs. *Mrs R. Lomax.*

LAMPSHADE 3 b.f. Hot Brandy 119–Lampo 91 (Infatuation 129) [1975 7g **63**
6d5 1976 10.1fg 10.1f³ 12g⁴] half-sister to smart 1m and 1¼m performer
Red Power (by Kibenka): dam a stayer: in frame in maiden races at Windsor
and Haydock in the summer: bred to stay 1½m but ran as though trip was
beyond her on final outing: sold 420 gns Ascot December Sales. *D. Morley.*

LANARK BIRK 3 ch.c. Cheval 117–Sealed Lips 65 (Privy Councillor 125) [1975 **70**
5fg 6g 5g5 5s6 5sg 5fg 5v5 1976 5v* 5fg4 6fg* 6g2 5g4 5h3 7f4 7f³ 8.2h6 5g 6v*]
quite a moderate handicapper: won at Ayr in April, Pontefract in May and
York (apprentice event) in October: had a very hard race when beating Lennoxlove gamely by 1½ lengths on last-named course: stays 7f (ran moderately
when tried at 1m): appears to act on any going but goes very well on heavy:
occasionally wears blinkers (did so at York) but does as well without: sweated
up when running below his best on sixth outing. *T. Craig.*

LANCASTERA 2 ch.f. Nodouble–Barite (Tom Fool) [1976 6.5g* 7s* 8s] **114**
American-bred French filly: third foal: 9,500 dollars yearling: dam unraced
daughter of stakes-winning half-sister to very smart Pattee Canyon: won a
maiden race at Deauville in August and looked a smart filly when beating
five useful winners decisively by 2 lengths in Prix de l'Obelisque at Longchamp
the following month: never-dangerous seventh behind Edinburgh in Prix des
Reservoirs at Longchamp in October but was giving weight away all round and
started none too well: will stay 1¼m. *C. Milbank, France.*

LANDED LADY 3 gr.f. Realm 129–Tiara III (Persian Gulf) [1975 5v* 5g4 5f   —
6fg5 6fg2 6g5 6s 1976 7fg 6fg] lightly-made filly: won maiden race at Newbury in 1975: had stiffish tasks on both outings at 3 yrs: should stay 7f: acts
on any going. *A. Corbett.*

LAND OF POINT 2 br.c. Pontifex (USA)–Asail (Atan) [1976 5d 5g5 5f **56**
5f³ 5fg 5d] leggy, quite useful sort: only poor form, including in a valuable
seller when blinkered. *D. Williams.*

LANDPOT 5 ro.h. Pinza 137 or Sayfar 116–Wizaller (King's Bench 132) [1974   —
10.1g 10.1g5 8.3fg4 8s³ 8s* 8d³ 10d2 10s* 12s 1975 8s 7s 8f 10.1g5 8.3s6 7g
7fg 8.3fg 8.3f 8g 10g5 10g 1976 12fg] small, compact horse: little worthwhile form since 1974: stays 1¼m: very well suited by soft going: sold 360 gns
Ascot November Sales. *J. Holt.*

LANDSCAPER 6 br.h. Linacre 133–Mary Monet (Monet 127) [1974 13g **56**
12fg 10.5f 7.6g³ 9g 8.2s4 7.6g6 10.4d6 6v³ 1975 13s 6v2 6g2 5h6 5.9fg6 7.6fg5
6g5 1976 6g5 6g2 6d³ 6f4 7.6fg³ 7f2 10.4fg] workmanlike horse: best at up
to 7f nowadays: acts on any going: suitable mount for an apprentice. *A. W.
Jones.*

400

LANDSLIDE 3 b.g. Birdbrook 110–Rock-On (Rockefella) [1975 5s 8g 1976 —
12d 12.3s] strong, compact gelding: seems not to possess much ability although
wasn't fully fit in two early-season outings in 1976: sold 1,000 gns Doncaster
May Sales. *G. Toft.*

LANE COURT 4 br.c. Tamerlane 128–Courtwell 110 (Court Harwell 130) **109**
[1974 6d3 6s6 7s4 8v2 7s6 1975 12f* 14f* 12f2 11f* 12fg* 14g 1976 15f3 12f
12g* 14fg 12f4 11.5g2 12s] strong, compact Irish colt: very useful performer: won
minor event under 10-5 at the Curragh in July, beating Brandon Hill a length:
also ran well when 1½ lengths second to Semenenko in Ulster Champion Stakes
at Down Royal in October: well beaten on both his outings in this country,
Bessborough Stakes at Royal Ascot and Tote-Ebor Handicap at York: stays
well: acts on any going, but seems particularly well suited by firm: suitable
mount for an apprentice. *D. Weld, Ireland.*

LANFINE 2 b.f. Hopeful Venture 125–Mitigation 91 (Milesian 125) [1976 **86**
7d 7g3 8s] neat, attractive filly: closely related to fairly useful 3-y-o Conciliation (by St Paddy), a winner over 6f and 7f as a 2-y-o, and half-sister to smart
middle-distance performer Colum (by Santa Claus): dam won at up to 1m:
4½ lengths third of 22 to Sin Timon in maiden race at Newmarket in October:
had every chance when remote seventh of 27 to Sporting Yankee in similar
event on same course later in month: should stay 1¼m. *B. Hobbs.*

LANGFORD BOY 3 ch.g. Decoy Boy 129–High Advice 86 (Counsel 118) [1975 **64**
N.R. 1976 8g 8f 10.1fg2 10s6 12v] well-grown gelding: quite a moderate
maiden: stays 1¼m. *S. Woodman.*

LANGTOFT PRINCE 3 ch.g. Pretendre 126–Toscanella (Tosco 126) [1975 —
N.R. 1976 10f5 12fg 16g] big gelding: slow maiden. *Hbt Jones.*

LANTAO LADY 2 ch.f. King's Troop 118–Singing Goddess 77 (Sing Sing 134) **63**
[1976 6g6 6f6] second foal: 1,400 gns yearling: dam stayed 1m at 2 yrs: sixth
in maiden races at Leicester in May and Brighton in August: will stay 7f. *N.
Adam.*

LANTERN BOY 3 ch.g. Double-U-Jay 120–Sudden Thought 98 (Pardal 130) **77**
[1975 7fg 1976 8g3 10f2 10f2 11d* 14fg5 12f3 14v5 13v] workmanlike gelding:
favourite, won moderate maiden contest at Hamilton in May: good third to
Plenty Spirit in handicap at Haydock in August, easily best effort afterwards
and was well beaten on last two outings: best form at up to 1½m: appears to
act on any going but gives impression that an easy surface suits him best. *F.
Carr.*

LANTERN LIGHT 2 ch.f. Le Levanstell 122–Crystal Light 114 (Never Say Die **86**
137) [1976 5.1f2 5f4 6d3 6d5] lengthy filly: half-sister to very smart sprinter
Street Light (by St Chad) and two very useful winners, including French 3-y-o
middle-distance performer Flash On (by Sea Hawk II): dam very useful over
1m at 2 yrs and is half-sister to Crocket: placed in maiden and minor events,
finishing 1½ lengths second to Colourful Connie at Yarmouth in August and
1¼ lengths third to Mrs McArdy at Redcar the following month: runs as if she
will be suited by 7f+. *J. Hindley.*

LANTONSIDE 4 ch.f. Royal Palace 131–Criffel 99 (Malhoa) [1974 N.R. 1975 —
11.1fg5 12d6 12f6 12g 12g 1976 7fg] neat filly: very disappointing since her
first outing at 3 yrs: blinkered final start in 1975. *P. Ashworth.*

LAOMEDONTE 4 ch.c. Raise A Native–Lost Message (Toulouse Lautrec) **116**
[1974 7s 7s* 8v3 1975 10g* 10g3 10v* 12v* 12g4 10v2 14g* 12g* 12fg 1976 10g4]
big, rangy ex-Italian colt: was rated 11 lb behind Bolkonski and Orange Bay
as a 2-y-o: improved a good deal in 1975, winning five races in Italy, notably
Gran Premio d'Italia, Italian St Leger and Gran Premio del Jockey Club:
ran promisingly (didn't particularly impress in paddock) when 5½ lengths
fourth of six to Anne's Pretender in Group 3 Brigadier Gerard Stakes at Sandown
in May, only outing at 4 yrs: stays 1¾m: acts on heavy going: suited by waiting
tactics: appeared unsuited by tight track when running moderately in Washington International at Laurel on final outing as a 3-y-o. *H. Cecil.*

LA RAINE 2 b.f. Majority Blue 126–Maritime 102 (Le Lavandou 111) [1976 **93**
5g* 5f2 6fg 6g 5g 6v] lengthy filly: half-sister to several winners, including
fairly useful 1974 2-y-o 5f winner Catch O'The Season (by Native Prince):
2,000 gns yearling: dam useful winner at 2 yrs: made all to win maiden race
at Lanark in May by 6 lengths and ran very well when 1½ lengths second to
Feudal Wytch in eight-runner Hilary Needler Trophy at Beverley the following
month: ran moderately afterwards, often in good company: should stay 6f:

probably unsuited by heavy ground: sweated up and ran badly on final outing. *M. Naughton.*

LARDANA 3 b.f. Burglar 128–Danabella (Dumbarnie 125) [1975 N.R. 1976 **65**
12.3s 12f⁵ 8fg 11d⁵ 11f 9g* 10g⁶ 10v] half-sister to three winners here and abroad, including quite useful middle-distance performer Rodney (by Saint Crespin III): 1,800 gns yearling: dam closely related to 1958 Cheveley Park winner Lindsay: put up easily best effort when 33/1 winner of 11-runner maiden race at Newcastle in August: evidently suited by 9f. *T. Craig.*

LARELLA 4 b.f. Linacre 133–Killala Bay (Larkspur 128) [1974 5h⁴ 5h* 1975 **51**
8s² 8g 8g⁶ 8.2g⁴ 8g⁵ 8g 6fg²(dis) 6f⁴ 7f⁵ 6fg 7g 7f 1976 5g⁴ 7g 7f* 8fg³ 8.3fg²
10.6g 8.2f³ 5f⁵ 8.2f⁶ 8.2d⁶ 5s² 7v 6d] compact filly: plater: bought in 460 gns after winning at Edinburgh in July by 1½ lengths from Tootal Boy: stays 1m: probably acts on any going: often wore blinkers at 3 yrs but does much better without them. *G. Wallace.*

LARGO BAY 3 b.f. Crozier 117–Bronze Seal 79 (Privy Councillor 125) [1975 **—**
N.R. 1976 13s⁵ 11f⁶ 8fg⁴] third produce: half-sister to a moderate animal: 740 gns foal: dam quite a moderate staying 2-y-o: plating-class maiden. *N. Angus.*

LARKHILL 4 ch.c. King's Troop 118–Everley 89 (Martial 131) [1974 5f² **118**
5g* 6fg* 5fg* 5s² 5d* 5v³ 1975 8.5s* 8v³ 9.5s⁴ 8d³ 10g* 8g⁶ 8g³ 8g⁴ 8.5g*
7s 1976 7.5g³ 7.5g⁴ 8g² 8g² 10d* 10g* 11s] ex-English colt: showed very useful form at 2 yrs when trained by N. Angus: raced in France subsequenty, winning minor events at Pau and Mont-de-Marsan and handicap at Maisons-Laffitte in 1975: showed improved form at 4 yrs and won handicap at Chantilly in June by 6 lengths and Group 3 Prix Gontaut-Biron at Deauville in August by 1½ lengths from Kasteel: only seventh to that horse in Prix Foy at Longchamp the following month: best form at 1¼m: seems to act on any going: exported to U.S.A. *M. Clement, France.*

LA ROCQUE 3 ch.f. Roan Rocket 128–Françoise 109 (French Beige 127) **62**
[1975 5fg 6g 6g 1976 6fg 8fg⁴ 10f⁴ 7.6fg 10.2s] rangy filly: best run at 1m but should stay further: sold 400 gns Newmarket December Sales. *G. Peter-Hoblyn.*

LASER LADY 2 b.f. Laser Light 118–Miss Nesta (Conspirator 114) [1976 5f* **96**
5g² 5d* 5fg² 5fg⁴ 5.9s 6s 5v³ 5v] small filly: half-sister to a minor 2-y-o winner by Will Somers and to a winner abroad: bought privately for 100 gns as a yearling: dam never ran: won minor event at Beverley in April and Wilkinson Memorial Stakes at York the following month, in latter race holding off Geopelia by ½ length: ran creditably on several of her other outings, wearing blinkers first time when 1¾ lengths third to Forlorn Scot in minor event at Teesside in October: again blinkered when running well below her best on final outing: should stay 6f: acts on any going: ridden by apprentice M. Wood when successful. *S. Norton.*

LASER OLIVIA 2 ch.f. Laser Light 118–Mary Theresa (Pall Mall 132) [1976 **77**
5g 5f³ 5g* 6f³ 5.1f⁶ 5f² 5fg* 5g⁴ 5g 5s] compact filly: second foal: half-sister to a winner in France: 400 gns yearling: dam Irish middle-distance maiden: made much of running when winning seller at Goodwood in May (no bid) and 13-runner nursery at Windsor in September: speedy and is unlikely to stay 6f: acts on firm going: goes well for apprentice S. Jarvis. *K. Ivory.*

LAST ATTEMPT 6 b.g. Pinicola 113–Spatterdash (Sunny Brae 121) [1974 **—**
N.R. 1975 N.R. 1976 7fg] probably of little account: dead. *B. Richmond.*

LAST DITCH 2 b.f. Ben Novus 109–Princess Fedora (Fedor II 107) [1976 8s] **—**
half-sister to a winner over jumps: dam ran only once on flat: tailed off in 19-runner maiden race won by Nordman at Sandown in October. *Mrs D. Oughton.*

Burmah-Castrol Ayr Gold Cup—Last Tango reverses Portland Handicap placings with Hei'land Jamie (right)

LAST SALE 2 ch.g. Royben 125–Tabarka (Dicta Drake 126) [1976 5f* 5f² 5f⁴ **96**
5h* 6f³ 6f⁵ 5g* 5g 5g³ 5v* 5d⁶] neat gelding: second foal: half-brother to winning
3-y-o sprinter Tabernacle (by Manacle): dam of little account: had a good season
and won at Bath (twice), Sandown and Newcastle: finished strongly when
beating Local Knowledge 1½ lengths in nursery at Sandown in September and
ran out a decisive 2-length winner from Star Attention in £1,600 event at Newcastle the following month: suited by a stiff 5f and will almost certainly stay 6f,
although his best form so far is at 5f: acts on any going. *G. Hunter.*

LAST TANGO 5 ch.h. Be Friendly 130–Scarcroft 66 (King's Bench 132) [1974 **103**
6g 5g⁴ 6g 5fg³ 5g* 5d² 5g² 5.8v⁴ 1975 5v⁵ 5g² 6fg² 5fg² 5d* 5f² 5g⁵ 5g³ 5d*
5g³ 5g⁵ 1976 5fg 5s² 5fg⁶ 5g³ 5g⁶ 5fg⁴ 5g 5.6g² 6g* 6s² 5s⁵] big, strong, good-
looking horse: useful handicapper: apprentice ridden and well backed, kept on
really well when winning Burmah-Castrol Ayr Gold Cup at Ayr in September
by 1½ lengths from Hei'land Jamie: had just failed to catch all-the-way winner
Hei'land Jamie in William Hill Portland Handicap at Doncaster the previous
week: stays 6f: acts on any going but is ideally suited by some give in the ground:
sometimes wears blinkers but does just as well without: sometimes loses ground
at start. *J. Sutcliffe.*

LAST TO LEAVE 3 gr.f. Captain's Gig–Mayo Blues 73 (Abernant 142) [1975 —
5f⁵ 6g⁴ 7.2s 1976 8f 7h] small filly: showed quite moderate form at 2 yrs but
ran poorly in 1976 and was sold 580 gns Newmarket Autumn Sales. *Doug
Smith.*

LAST WEEKEND 7 ch.g. Blast 125–Week End (Cash and Courage 116) [1974 —
8g⁶ 8.2fg² 11.2fg 10.2g⁶ 12g 8.2g⁴ 10s⁶ 8d* 13d² 11.2s* 9v³ 1975 8s 10.2g 10g⁴
9h 10f⁵ 10f 10.8g 1976 10f 10f 10f] poor plater: seemed to stay 13f: suited by a
soft surface: had been tried in blinkers: fell second outing: dead. *F. Wiles.*

LAST WINTER 6 b.g. Saint Crespin III 132–March Wonder 99 (March Past 124) —
[1974 8g 10g 10g 7g 8.3fg³ 7g 8d 8v 1975 10.1g* 8fg⁵ 10fg 1976 10.6d] selling
handicapper: bandaged and tailed off on only start in 1976: stays 1¼m: acts on
firm going: has run poorly in blinkers. *R. Akehurst.*

LAS VENTAS 3 b.f. Breton 130–Las Vegas (Hard Sauce 131) [1975 5s 7f 7.6g —
1976 7fg 10fg 12g] compact French-bred filly: poor mover: poor plater: covered
by Shiny Tenth. *D. Sasse.*

Mr R. B. Moller's "Laughing Girl"

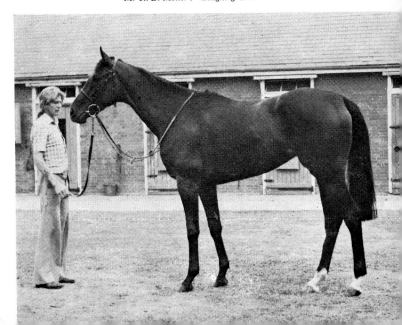

LAT

LATEST MODEL 2 b.c. Reform 132–Cover Girl (Edellic 124) [1976 6fg 6fg **115**
6g* 5g³ 6g] strong, well-made colt: brother to high-class sprinter New Model,
and half-brother to a winner: dam second in 1965 French 1,000 Guineas: had
his field well strung out when winning 15-runner maiden race at Newcastle in
August by 2½ lengths from Barny: put up a good effort when 1½ lengths third
of nine to He Loves Me in Harry Rosebery Challenge Trophy at Ayr the following
month but surpassed that run when finishing eighth of 11 to Tachypous in
William Hill Middle Park Stakes at Newmarket in October, weakening only
in last furlong after being up with leaders for much of way: stays 6f and will
get further. *R. D. Peacock.*

LAUGHING GIRL 3 b.f. Sassafras 135–Violetta III 110 (Pinza 137) [1975 **110**
N.R. 1976 7f⁵ 10g³ 10.5d⁶ 10g* 12g⁴ 12g 12fg² 14g⁴ 10g⁵ 12s] lengthy filly:
half-sister to numerous winners, notably Oaks runner-up Favoletta (by Baldric II)
and Irish 1,000 Guineas winner Favoletta (by Baldric II): dam dead-heated
in 1961 Cambridgeshire: won Lupe Stakes at Goodwood in May by ¾ length
from My Fair Niece: raced mainly in high-class fillies races afterwards, finishing
9¾ lengths fourth of 14 to Pawneese in Epsom Oaks (made up a lot of ground
in straight after being next to last at halfway), short-head second to Capricious
in Galtres Stakes at York (rallied gamely under pressure) and 5½ lengths fourth
to stable-companion African Dancer in Park Hill Stakes at Doncaster in September: probably finds 1¼m too short for her nowadays and stays 1¾m: possibly
not at her best on softish ground: blinkered last four appearances: got loose on
way to start on sixth outing. *H. Wragg.*

LAUGHING GODDESS 3 br.f. Green God 128–Gay Baby 101 (Galivanter 131) **92**
[1975 4g* 5g² 4.5g² 5g 5g² 5g³ 1976 8g 6f⁶ 8f⁴ 6d 6f* 5fg⁴ 5fg³ 6f* 5g] neat
ex-French filly: first foal: **3,000 gns** yearling: dam a speedy 2-y-o: showed quite
useful form and made all when winning handicaps at Yarmouth in July and
August under top weight: best form at 6f but probably stays 1m: acts on firm
going: trained until after first outing by P. Lallie: sometimes sweats up. *J.
Hindley.*

LAUJOCK 3 b.g. Lauso–Corta Jaca (Tudor Jinks 121) [1975 5.1f 7h* 7f 8fg **75**
1976 12f⁵ 12v* 12s] useful plater: well backed, won at York in October all out
by 2 lengths from Formland, the pair finishing clear of six others: bought in
2,300 gns afterwards: stays 1½m: acts on any going. *W. Stephenson.*

LAUMAL 2 ch.f. Lauso–Mallemoke 76 (Fairey Fulmar 124) [1976 5s] sister —
to moderate 1968 2-y-o Lucky Moke: dam ran only at 2 yrs: remote eleventh of
12 in maiden race won by Elton Abbess at Folkestone in October. *W. Stephenson.*

LAUREL LARK 3 ch.f. T.V. Lark–White Lie (Bald Eagle 119) [1975 7d 8g 8d⁴ **71**
1976 11.1g⁵ 10fg³ 12fg² 10g³ 12h³ 8f⁶ 9s² 10s³ 10.2s⁵] small American-bred
filly: quite a moderate maiden: should stay 1½m: best form on a sound surface:
trained most of season by C. Brittain: sold 22,000 gns Newmarket December
Sales. *D. Hanley.*

LA VALLIERE 3 b.f. Reform 132–La Mome 109 (Princely Gift 137) [1975 5fg —
5fg⁴ 5g² 5.9g 1976 10f 12g³ 12fg⁴ 11.5fg 13.9f⁴ 13g 16g⁴] poor maiden: best
form at 1½m: sold 2,500 gns Goffs September Sales. *R. Boss.*

LAVANTER 2 br.f. Galivanter 131–Flame Dancer 72 (Hop Bridge 87) [1976 **63**
5fg 6f 5fg⁵ 6v² 6s] lengthy filly: plater: ran best race when second of 19 to
wide-margin winner Rush Bond in valuable event at York in October: will stay
7f: suited by heavy ground. *J. W. Watts.*

LAVENDER LADY 2 ch.f. Porto Bello 118–Atlantica (Tulyar 134) [1976 5g —
7.2f 6g] leggy filly: behind in maiden and minor events. *A. Smith.*

LAVENGRO 3 gr.g. Crepello 136–Admonish 101 (Palestine 133) [1975 7fg **80**
1976 11f 11.7f* 12.2f² 14fg⁶] strong gelding: decisive winner of maiden race at
Bath in April: length second to Bagshot in minor event at Wolverhampton the
following month, easily better subsequent effort: should stay further than 1½m:
ran poorly in blinkers on final outing (July) and was sold 4,700 gns Newmarket
Autumn Sales. *R. Hern.*

LAVENTHYME 3 b.f. Royal Rhythm 78–Semicircle 89 (Your Fancy 106) —
[1975 N.R. 1976 8fg] half-sister to useful middle-distance winner Lavenette
(by No Worry) and useful hurdler Lavenanne (by Tacitus): dam moderate
2-y-o, but failed to train on: last of 15 behind Rout in maiden race at Salisbury
in June: sold 260 gns Ascot August Sales. *H. Collingridge.*

404

Doncaster Stakes—La Ville de Rire pulls out extra to hold off Mummy's Darling

LA VILLE DE RIRE 2 ch.c. Town Crier 119–French Laughter 96 (Gilles de **119**
Retz 132) [1976 5g² 6fg* 5.6f* 6g 6fg³ 5d² 6g⁶ 5s*]
    When trouncing modest opposition at Doncaster early in July La Ville de
Rire looked a good horse in the making, but it took him until his last three
outings to prove it. Encountering soft ground for the first time La Ville de
Rire showed substantial improvement in the Flying Childers Stakes at Doncaster.
In a field of good sprinters, he found no trouble in going the early pace and he
also kept on strongly in the last two furlongs, but he was unable to match the
finishing speed of Mandrake Major and was beaten a length. The William Hill
Middle Park Stakes run at Newmarket three weeks later confirmed La Ville
de Rire's improvement. With such as the Gimcrack winner Nebbiolo, Mandrake
Major and several other good two-year-olds in the field La Ville de Rire could
be given little chance of winning. However, he ran a most creditable race,
and after showing excellent pace throughout he was beaten only two and a half
lengths into sixth place behind Tachypous. On the evidence of these performances, and also of his last race, when he battled on tenaciously to beat the
much improved Mummy's Darling by a neck in the Doncaster Stakes over five
furlongs, La Ville de Rire is fully entitled to be regarded as one of the best
two-year-olds in the north, and in the Northern Free Handicap only Mandrake
Major and Haveroid were placed above him.

		Sovereign Path (gr 1956)	Grey Sovereign Mountain Path
	Town Crier (gr 1965)	Corsley Bell (b 1959)	Owen Tudor Dented Bell
La Ville de Rire (ch.c. 1974)		Gilles de Retz (b 1953)	Royal Charger Ma Soeur Anne
	French Laughter (b 1963)	Laughter (b 1959)	Pinza Gay's The Word

    La Ville de Rire cost only 2,300 guineas as a yearling. He is a brother to
the winning hurdler Happy Call, and a half-brother to another winning hurdler
and to a winner on the flat in Greece. His dam, French Laughter, quite a useful
winner at up to a mile, is a daughter of the lightly-raced Laughter, who comes
from a family which has produced many winners for Herbert Blagrave, including
Casque, Vitality Plus, Words and Music, Vital Match and Realist. La Ville
de Rire is effective at five and six furlongs and will probably stay further. A
game and consistent performer, he acts on firm going but seems better suited
by some give in the ground. *J. W. Watts.*

LAWRENCE JOHNSTON 3 ch.g. Lorenzaccio 130–Rose Arbour 106 (Pall **80**
Mall 132) [1975 6fg 7f* 7fg² 1976 7g 10fg 8f⁶ 8g⁴ 7.6g 8g 8s] rangy gelding:
had some stiff tasks in 1976 and showed worthwhile form only on third and
fourth outings: should stay further than 1m: sold to D. Barons 2,500 gns Newmarket Autumn Sales. *R. Jarvis.*

Mr P. W. Long's "Lazenby"

LAZENBY 4 b.g. Bleep-Bleep 134–Ardent Worker 88 (Buisson Ardent 129) **115**
[1974 5f 5f³ 5fg² 5g* 5s 5v² 5s⁶ 1975 5fg³ 7v² 5d* 6v² 5s 5f* 5f² 6f² 5fg* 6fg⁵
5g* 5g* 6g⁴ 5g* 1976 5s 6fg⁴ 5fg* 5fg 6f⁴ 5fg* 5g] strong gelding: smart
handicapper: put up a fine performance when winning Gosforth Park Cup at
Newcastle in June, recovering from a bad start (stumbled coming out of stalls)
to beat Gan On Geordie by a length: rather disappointing afterwards and
struggled to land the odds in minor event at Beverley in September (dwelt start):
has run creditably at 7f but is probably best at sprint distances: acts on any
going: blinkered last two outings: excellent mount for an apprentice. *M. W.
Easterby.*

LAZY BELLE 3 ch.f. Drone–Christmas Belle (Santa Claus 133) [1975 N.R. **73**
1976 7f 10fg⁶ 12f] attractive filly: good mover: first foal: dam Irish middle-
distance winner: ran well when just over 9 lengths sixth of 10 behind Spiranthes
in Pretty Polly Stakes at Newmarket in April but finished tailed-off last of
seven behind Catalpa in Ribblesdale Stakes at Royal Ascot in June on only
subsequent appearance: stud. *N. Murless.*

LEADING QUESTION 6 br.h. Klairon 131–Nice Dilemma 91 (Relic) [1974 **40**
8.2v⁴ 11.1s³ 8.2v* 1975 8.2s⁵ 8s³ 11s 8.2d 8f³ 8f 10fg 8g⁵ 11d⁴ 10.6fg 8f³ 1976
8fg³ 8fg] quite a modest plater: best form at up to 1m: acts on any going:
suitable mount for an apprentice: wears bandages. *S. Holland.*

LEADING ROSE 2 br.f. Scarlet Ruler 93–Anitra 104 (Borealis) [1976 6fg] —
June foal: half-sister to two winners, including fairly useful middle-distance
winner Trumpet Dance (by Klairon): dam won at 1½m: in rear in 15-runner
maiden race won by Etienne Gerard at Newmarket in July. *D. Ringer.*

LEATHER PANTS 2 ch.g. Jukebox 120–Nora's Sister (King's Leap 111) [1976 —
5fg 6d 8.2s 8s] tall gelding: poor plater: sold 310 gns Doncaster October Sales.
R. Bastiman.

LE CHAT 3 br.f. Burglar 128–Miss Mandy 92 (Mandamus 120) [1975 5v 5g* **92**
5fg² 6f* 6fg* 6fg⁶ 6g 1976 7fg 6fg 6g 6fg⁴] useful-looking filly: showed useful
form at 2 yrs: just over 4 lengths fourth to Net Call in handicap at Newmarket
in July, final outing and easily best effort in 1976: stays 6f well and may get
further: acts on firm going. *B. Hobbs.*

LE DAUPHIN 4 b.c. Sing Sing 134–Vauchellor 72 (Honeyway 125) [1974 5fg⁶ **57**
6g 6s 1975 8f² 8f² 8h² 10f⁴ 8.2s 9g 1976 8g 12fg³ 10.2g⁵ 8fg* 9g 7fg 8f⁵ 8f⁶
7.6fg 8g] poor handicapper: won apprentice event at Newmarket in April by
½ length from Brother Somers: stays 1¼m: acts on hard going: ran below his
best when tried in blinkers: sweated up eighth start. *P. Robinson.*

LE DEUX 3 b.c. Tudor Music 131–Pandora 75 (Crepello 136) [1975 6g 7d⁴ 7v⁶ **77**
1976 8.2f 7fg* 7fg 8f⁴ 8g⁶ 8f* 10fg 8.3g⁵] tall colt: quite a moderate handicapper:
dead-heated with Gimri at Epsom in April: gained an outright success when
beating Night Club 2 lengths at Brighton in August: stays 1m (ran moderately
when tried at 1¼m but had stiffish task): acts on firm going: best in blinkers.
J. Sutcliffe.

LEE ROSE 2 b.f. Shiny Tenth 120–Manor Born 71 (Canisbay 120) [1976 6fg] —
first produce: 280 gns foal: dam won 7f seller at 3 yrs: in rear in 12-runner
maiden race won by Sequoia at Nottingham in July. *H. Collingridge.*

LEGAL ADVICE 3 b.g. Lauso–Law Suit 85 (King's Bench 132) [1975 7g 8f⁶ 8fg **70**
1976 10fg 10.1fg 8fg² 11f⁶ 14fg*] rangy gelding: good walker: sold to D. Morley
4,200 gns after winning seller at York in July in good style by 4 lengths from
Terrine: suited by 1¾m: acts on a firm surface. *N. Callaghan.*

LEGAL EAGLE 4 b.c. Manacle 123–Judiciary 74 (Above Suspicion 127) [1974 **112**
5s* 5fg* 5g² 5g³ 6g² 6g* 6fg⁶ 6v 1975 8s⁴ 8g³ 8f² 7.3g⁴ 8fg² 7g* 8g* 1976
8.2g² 8d⁴ 8g³ 8d 10d 8.2v 8s 8s² 8v²] big, strong, deep-bodied ex-English colt:
very good performer (rated 126) at 3 yrs: raced in France in 1976 and ran well
against good-class opposition from time to time, although was not so good as in
1975: stayed 1m: acted on any going: sometimes wore blinkers: standing at Three
Gates Stud, Warwickshire, fee £300 n.f.n.f. *A. Paus, France.*

LEGAL LAIRD 2 ch.c. Murrayfield 119–Legal Mistress (Counsel 118) [1976 —
7s 7v⁶] first living foal: dam of no account: remote sixth to Forage in 15-
runner maiden race at Lingfield in November: started slowly first outing.
J. S. Evans.

LEGAL PLAY 4 ch.g. Weepers Boy 124–Foretell 63 (Fortino II 120) [1974 5s **54**
5fg 5.1g* 6s⁵ 6g 5.9s⁴ 1975 7s* 7s² 8s 7f* 7f³ 7.2fg 8f⁵ 1976 7f 8fg 8fg* 8.2fg
8f² 8g³ 7d 8s³] compact, workmanlike gelding: fair selling handicapper: easy
winner at Leicester in July (bought in 575 gns): stays 1m: acts on any going.
J. Hardy.

LEGATO 2 ch.f. Nice Music 115–Legal 72 (Petition 130) [1976 6f 7fg 8fg] —
leggy filly: half-sister to winners in Malaysia and Italy: dam placed over 1m:
gave indications of a little ability in maiden and minor events: should stay 1m.
S. Wainwright.

LE GURA 2 bl.f. Le Dieu d'Or 119–Parrullah (Valerullah 113) [1976 5g⁶ 5g³ **63**
5h³] compact, plating-class filly: third in maiden races at Lanark in May and
Pontefract in July: dead. *G. Richards.*

LEI 3 b.f. Hawaii–West Bramble (Krakatao 130) [1975 5f⁴ 5f* 5h³ 6fg* 6g* 6g⁶ **84**
1976 6g² 6g 6fg³] strong American-bred filly: won three races at 2 yrs but was
lightly raced in 1976 and showed only moderate form: stays 6f. *J. Dunlop.*

LE MAGICIEN 2 ch.c. Levanter 121–Midsummer Magic (Midsummer Night II **71**
117) [1976 5g 6fg⁴ 6h² 6g 6h⁶ 5f³] first foal: dam poor maiden: plater: in
frame at Lingfield (twice) and Folkestone: will stay 1¼m. *T. Gosling.*

LEMCO 2 b.c. Jefferson 129–Pomobar (Bobar II 127) [1976 7g] French-bred — p
colt: half-brother to two minor winners in France: dam won over 1¾m in France
and also over jumps: unquoted and extremely green when thirteenth of 23 to
Windy Sea in maiden race at Newmarket in October: will do better with more
experience. *Doug Smith.*

LE MELOS 3 ch.g. Levanter 121–Melos 88 (Hill Gail) [1975 N.R. 1976 12fg⁶ —
11f 14.7f⁶] big, workmanlike gelding: half-brother to three winners, including
fair 1973 2-y-o 5f performer Gail Performance (by Gala Performance): 2,700 gns
yearling, resold 4,100 gns Doncaster March (1976) Sales: dam ran only at 2 yrs:
only plating class. *D. Holmes.*

LEMON SORBET   2 br.f. Frigid Aire–Barrettstown Belle (Twilight Alley 133)   **68**
[1976 6fg 9fg 8fg⁶ 7g]   second foal: 980 gns foal: dam never ran: showed ability
in varied company, including selling: will stay 1¼m: blinkered last two outings:
sold 400 gns Newmarket Autumn Sales. *J. Hindley.*

LEND AN EAR   12 ch.g. Matador 131–Petronella 97 (Petition 130)   [1974 10g
10s⁶ 10.2g   1975 10fg 10.6fg 8f⁶ 10.8g 10g⁴ 12f³   1976 9g 10fg 10fg⁴]   poor
performer nowadays: stays 1½m: acts on any going: usually wears blinkers:
has sometimes lost ground at start. *I. Walker.*

LENNOXLOVE   3 b.f. Lear Jet 123–Green Edge 76 (Border Legend 119)   [1975   **70**
5g* 5fg³ 5f⁵ 7f⁶ 6g 8fg 5v   1976 7g⁶ 7d* 8fg⁴ 9fg⁶ 9f 8f⁵ 8fg 6v² 7v⁵ 6s⁶]   leggy
filly: 3 lengths runner-up to Oriental Star in handicap at Doncaster in May,
but was hampered in final furlong, and subsequently awarded race: carried 12 lb
overweight when very good second of 13 to Lanark Birk in apprentice handicap at
York in October: probably stays 1m: appears to act on any going but seems
particularly well suited by plenty of give in the ground: has worn blinkers but
does better without. *J. W. Watts.*

LEONI   3 b.f. King Log 115–Janie Mou 99 (Royal Charger)   [1975 N.R.   1976   **—**
8g 12fg⁶ 8fg 8s]   deep-girthed, good sort of filly: half-sister to three winners,
including useful stayer Anassa (by Pardal): dam useful 2-y-o, but deteriorated
temperamentally at 3 yrs: in rear in maiden races: sold 470 gns Ascot November
Sales. *R. Smyth.*

LEOPARD'S ROCK   2 b.c. Huntercombe 133–Reina Cristina 84 (Tamerlane 128)   **—**
[1976 5g 6f⁶]   small, robust colt: first foal: 3,100 gns yearling: dam won twice
over 11.7f at 3 yrs: little worthwhile form in maiden race at Sandown in July and
minor event at Salisbury in August. *J. Dunlop.*

LEPIDUS   6 b.g. Klairon 131–Timura 75 (Tamerlane 128)   [1974 8g 10g⁶ 10g*   **—**
9g³   1975 10v³ 12s 12s 11v   1976 12g]   strong, very attractive gelding: virtually
pulled up (heavily bandaged on both forelegs) on only outing in 1976: stays
1¼m: evidently acts on heavy going but best form on a sound surface. *P.
Rohan.*

LE PRETENDANT   2 b.c. Prince de Galles 125–Reine d'Etat 53 (High Hat 131)   **69**
[1976 7g⁶ 7v]   unfurnished colt: first foal: dam placed over 1½m: unquoted when
13 lengths sixth of 22 to Sin Timon in maiden race at Newmarket in October:
seemed unsuited by heavy going on next outing: will stay middle distances.
P. Robinson.

LERAZMA   3 b.g. Levanter 121–Razamataz (After Midnight 119)   [1975 N.R.   **—**
1976 12v² 10g 16d 17.7f]   plating-class maiden. *J. Hardy.*

LE RIFIFI   2 ch.c. Lorenzaccio 130–Bouboulina (Hornbeam 130)   [1976 6f   **—**
6g 7s 8s]   strong colt: no worthwhile form in maiden races: blinkered last
two outings. *D. Sasse.*

LE SOLEIL   2 ch.c. Roi Soleil 125–Mayo Blues 73 (Abernant 142)   [1976 6g   **73**
7s 7v]   third living produce: 4,100 gns yearling: dam best at sprint distances:
third favourite when seventh of 19 to Alltyre in minor event at Chepstow in
October, second and probably best effort. *R. Price.*

LET'EM HAVE IT   3 br.f. Le Levanstell 122–Tanndara (Venture VII 129)   **76**
[1975 8g 7g   1976 12.2fg 16g*]   robust filly: won maiden race at Thirsk in
May by 3 lengths from Please Turn Over: stays well: covered by Saritamer.
F. J. Houghton.

LETHINGTON   2 b.f. John Splendid 116–Divine Right 57 (King of the Tudors   **78**
129)   [1976 5f² 5f 5d² 6f² 6f³ 6g 6v]   leggy, light-framed filly: half-sister to
a winning plater: 400 gns yearling: dam needed at least 1½m: placed in varied
company, including selling, putting up best effort when 1½ lengths third of 15
to Mrs McArdy in nursery at Thirsk in September when apprentice ridden:
will stay beyond sprint distances: probably acts on any going. *J. W. Watts.*

LE TREIZE—See PEKINOIS

LET'S DANCE   2 b.f. Mansingh 120–Madame Birwood (Constable 129)   [1976   **76**
6d 6s² 7fg³ 6s⁵ 8v⁴ 6s]   third foal: half-sister to fairly useful 1975 2-y-o Cheeny
Boy (by Richboy): 860 gns foal and resold for 3,500 gns and 900 gns as a yearling:
quite a moderate maiden: stays 7f but seemed to find 1m on heavy ground too
far for her on penultimate outing: appears to act on any going. *Miss S. Hall.*

LETTERELLAN   2 ch.g. David Jack 125–Nicky's Vulgan (Vulgan 123)   [1976   **81**
6fg⁴ 6fg² 7f⁶]   second foal: dam won 2m bumpers race in Ireland: ran credit-

ably in maiden races at Newbury and Salisbury in June, going down by 2 lengths to Catiline in 16-runner event on latter course: ran poorly on final outing (July): will stay well. *G. Balding.*

LEVANSTRID 3 ch.f. Le Levanstell 122–Machastrid (Macherio) [1975 7g 6g 7g* 8s⁶ 1976 10g⁴ 10f⁵ 12f² 10g 16f 11f³ 16d 12s] lengthy filly: ran well when just over 4 lengths fifth of 12 to Gorse Bush in well-contested Azalea Stakes at Phoenix Park and when going under by a short head to Grey Tiger in handicap at Killarney in May: did not produce that form afterwards, and was tailed off behind General Ironside in Queen's Vase at Royal Ascot the following month: stays 1½m: acts on any going: sold 4,100 gns Newmarket December Sales. *P. Doyle, Ireland.* **108** d

LEVARAMOSS 3 b.c. Levmoss 133–Tandara (Tanerko 134) [1975 N.R. 1976 12fg 16g 15.5s²] big, rangy colt: half-brother to 1½m winner Crocodillo (by Crocket): 2,600 gns 2-y-o: dam poor maiden: put up easily best effort when neck second to Big Clive in maiden race at Folkestone in October: suited by a thorough test of stamina and plenty of give in the ground. *S. Ingham.* **63**

LEVEL PAR 3 b.c. Hallez 131–Aberdonia 71 (Alycidon 138) [1975 7g² 8s* 8g* 1976 10s 10.5s⁵ 12d⁵ 13s⁵ 10fg⁴ 8.2f* 13fg⁵ 10g² 8.2f* 8g] attractive colt: useful handicapper: winner at Hamilton in July and Haydock in August, on latter course beating Andy Rew in smooth fashion by 1½ lengths under 10-0: best form at up to 1¼m, although should stay further: appears to act on any going: sweated up fifth outing: lost his action completely and was pulled up lame behind on final outing. *N. Angus.* **108**

LEVENTIS 3 b.c. Le Levanstell 122–Ruta (Ratification 129) [1975 6g⁶ 8g⁵ 8g 1976 8f⁵ 10fg² 10f* 12fg⁵ 10.6d* 10fg 10f⁶] lightly-made, good sort of colt: won £1,100 event at Lingfield in May and valuable Bass Clubmen's Handicap at Haydock the following month, on latter course beating Seadiver 1½ lengths: very good fifth to General Ironside in Predominate Stakes at Goodwood in between: ran moderately on last two outings: not seen out after July: evidently stayed 1½m: acted on firm going but had a slightly round action and was probably better suited by some give in the ground: stud in Venezuela. *C. Brittain.* **98**

L'EVEQUE 5 ch.g. St Chad 120–Sans Sabots (Whistler 129) [1974 7.6g 8g 8fg* 8.2f⁵ 8g² 10s 8s 1975 10d 1976 9fg 7.6fg* 7fg 7f* 8.2fg* 8.2f* 7g] attractive gelding: returned to form in 1976 and won four handicaps, at Lingfield, Doncaster and Nottingham (two): stays 1m: acts on firm going. *J. Bethell.* **86**

LEVERANCIER 2 br.c. John Splendid 116–Levajok (Andrea Mantegna) [1976 5g 6fg⁴ 5.9g 7h 6f 6d 6g] useful-looking colt: little worthwhile form, including in sellers: blinkered fifth outing: sold 740 gns Newmarket Autumn Sales. *P. Makin.* **57**

LEVINDA 4 b.f. Le Levanstell 122–Palinda 117 (Palestine 133) [1974 N.R. 1975 10.1f⁵ 8g² 8fg⁶ 10s³ 10g* 10g² 12s⁴ 1976 11v 11g² 12.5v⁴ 12v* 12.2fg* 13f⁶ 12d⁴] neat, strong filly: successful at Cagnes-sur-Mer in March and Warwick the following month but not seen out after running below her best at Pontefract in late May: stays 1½m: probably acts on any going: suitable mount for an apprentice. *J. Dunlop.* **77**

LE VINGT-HUIT 4 b.c. Jukebox 120–Diamond Brooch 71 (Gilles de Retz 132) [1974 5g⁴ 5.1g* 5.3g² 1975 5s⁵ 5.9g⁴ 5f* 5fg⁴ 5fg² 5f⁴ 6f⁴ 5fg 1976 5fg³ 5d 5fg⁴ 5.3fg⁴ 5fg⁶ 5fg⁶] neat, quite attractive colt: fairly useful handicapper: mainly disappointing at 4 yrs although ran respectably on first and third outings: best at 5f, although has run respectably at 6f: acts well on firm going and is probably unsuited by soft: excellent mount for an apprentice: ran below his best when tried in blinkers on final outing at 3 yrs, although had a stiffish task at weights: sold 680 gns Ascot October Sales. *J. Sutcliffe.* **86**

LEWIS 3 b.g. Welsh Saint 126–Petal Princess 102 (Floribunda 136) [1975 N.R. 1976 12.2f 8.2g² 12fg⁵ 12f² 12.2fg] strong gelding: third foal: half-brother to two winners, including very useful 1974 2-y-o Hunting Prince (by Huntercombe): dam stayed 1m: runner-up in minor events at Haydock in May (beaten ¾ length by Lucastown) and Ripon in July (no chance with easy winner Du Maurier): ran poorly in his other races, once ruining his chance by swerving badly: stays 1½m. *F. Rimell.* **75**

LEYBURN LADY 2 ch.f. Ballyciptic 122–Recital (Botticelli 129) [1976 5f⁶ 5f³ 6g 5.9f² 5.9f⁵ 7g* 8f³ 8.2d 8s] leggy filly: half-sister to three winners, including Hollow Laughter (by Wolver Hollow), a fair performer at up to 1¾m: **73**

placed in sellers prior to showing much improved form to win seven-runner nursery at Wolverhampton in August by 2 lengths from Sylvia's Dream: much better suited by 7f and 1m than shorter distances: acts on firm going and is possibly unsuited by soft: claimed out of K. Payne's stable after fourth outing. *R. Ward.*

LEYLANDIA 3 b.f. Wolver Hollow 126–Potentilla 89 (Nearula 132) [1975 8g 1976 10.1fg 12f6 11.7fg4 13g3 16fg4 12.2s2 16.1v5 14d5] neat filly: in frame in maiden races and a handicap: best form at up to 13f. *J. Bethell.* **69**

LEZ 2 br.c. Keren 100–E.B.S. 100 (Infatuation 129) [1976 6fg 7fg6 8.2f 7v] well-grown colt: little worthwhile form in maiden and minor events. *W. A. Stephenson.* —

LIBERTY LASS 2 b.f. Caliban 123–Liberty Cry 98 (Democratic 124) [1976 6fg 6d 6s*] half-sister to two winners by Mandamus, including Liberty Lawyer, a fairly useful performer at up to 1m: dam a sprinter: attracted no bid after showing improved form to win nine-runner seller at Goodwood in September by a neck from Teeoff: will stay 1m: acts on soft going. *L. Hall.* **72**

LIBERTY LIGHT 3 ch.f. Henry the Seventh 125–Clouded Lamp 99 (Nimbus 130) [1975 5v* 5f3 5g4 5d4 5f 7.2v 1976 6f2 8f5 8g* 8.2d* 8g6 8f4 8fg] half-sister to very useful sprinter Irma Flintstone (by Compensation): won apprentice event at Ripon in May by 5 lengths from Startown and handicap at Hamilton later in month by ½ length from Fairman: didn't run up to her best afterwards but was only lightly raced: stays 1m well: acts on any going: ran badly when tried in blinkers at 2 yrs: ridden by claimer S. Eccles when successful. *T. Fairhurst.* **75**

LIBERTY QUEEN 3 gr.f. Runnymede 123-Queen Mab (Twilight Alley 133) [1975 N.R. 1976 12d] leggy filly: second foal: half-sister to fairly useful stayer Broughty Harbour (by Typhoon): dam ran only once: 20/1 when remote seventh of nine to Sanpello in maiden race at Ripon in June: sold 400 gns Doncaster October Sales. *R. D. Peacock.* —

LIBRA'S RIB 4 ch.c. Ribot 142–Libra 97 (Hyperion) [1974 6g5 6g* 7g4 1975 8s4 8g 10.5d4 12f2 15.5g 12g* 12f 12f2 12fg4 14.6g3 12s5 1976 12f3 12fg2 13.4s2 12g2 12f3 12.5g4 12s4 12fg3 13.3fg3] rather lightly-made, quite attractive American-bred colt: good mover: had some good efforts against top-class animals to his credit at 4 yrs, on fourth start finishing ½-length second to Quiet Fling in Coronation Cup at Epsom in June and being beaten about 4 lengths when third to Orange Bay in Hardwicke Stakes at Royal Ascot later in month: not disgraced in two valuable events abroad in July, finishing fourth to River-queen in Grand Prix de Saint-Cloud and to Windwurf in Grosser Preis von Nordrhein-Westfalen at Dusseldorf, but ran way below his best on last two appearances: should stay further than 1¾m: acts on any going but is well suited by top-of-the-ground conditions: wears blinkers nowadays. *F. J. Houghton.* **121**

LICHEN LADY 4 ch.f. Pardao 120–Moss Maiden 97 (Mossborough 126) [1974 N.R. 1975 10g* 12g 12g 1976 13fg 14g3 16d6] tall, rangy filly: probably stays 2m. *J. Bethell.* **59**

LIFE'S AMBITION 3 br.c. The Brianstan 128–Tickled Pink II (Arctic Star) [1975 6g5 6g 1976 8g5 8f 8f 8g2 8fg6 8g3 10g6 8s4 8s] small colt: stays 1m but probably not 1¼m: seems unsuited by very firm going: suitable mount for an apprentice. *W. Marshall.* **60**

LIESE 2 b.f. Umbrella Fella–Inja (Breakspear II) [1976 5g 5s 7v] well-made, attractive filly: first foal: dam ran only once: no worthwhile form in maiden races: very backward on first outing. *J. Bethell.* —

LIGHTER 3 b.c. Aureole 132–Raft 102 (Ragusa 137) [1975 6g2 1976 11f* 10.5s 12d2 13.3g4 12fg2 12fg2 12f*] big, tall, rangy colt: won maiden race at Newbury in April by a neck from Lost Chord and handicap at Goodwood in August by 3 lengths from Broken Record (made all): also first past post in handicap at Haydock in June but did not keep a straight course and was subsequently placed second for hampering runner-up Shangamuzo: well suited by 1½m and should stay further: acts on any going except perhaps really soft: sometimes wears blinkers but does as well without. *R. Hern.* **111**

LIGHT LAGER 4 ch.f. Crepello 136–St Pauli Girl 114 (St Paddy 133) [1974 6s2 7d3 1975 11.1g6 11.5f 11.1f2 12g2 12d* 12g4 16f2 1976 16fg6 14g3 16v3 **88**

Spring Maiden Stakes, Newbury—despite failing to keep a straight course Lighter resists the challenge of Lost Chord (left) by a neck. Macclesfield is third

14s² 14d²] rather lightly-built filly: ran creditably in most of her races at 4 yrs: stays 2m: best on an easy surface, but has run creditably on firm. *G. Pritchard-Gordon.*

LIGHT LAUGHTER 4 ch.f. Silly Season 127–Light Case 107 (Borealis) [1974 7g⁴ 6s⁶ 6s 1975 8s³ 10f* 10fg³ 10g* 10d* 1976 10fg³] strong, well-made filly: nice mover: fairly useful handicapper (rated 96) at 3 yrs: looked very much in need of the outing but nevertheless ran well when about 5 lengths third of eight to Bell-Tent at Sandown in June in only race in 1976: stays 1¼m: acts on any going: very genuine. *J. Nelson.* **85**

LIGHTNING 2 b.c. Kashmir II 125–Fidra (Sicambre 135) [1976 8.5g*] French colt: half-brother to three winners in France, including Skelda (by La Varende), a smart winner at up to 13f, and useful middle-distance filly Folle Enchere (by Exbury): dam won over 1¼m and is half-sister to top-class miler Soleil II: 2/1 on for nine-runner newcomers event at Longchamp in October and put up a highly promising display, taking lead easily 2f out and not being hard pressed to win by 1½ lengths from Conte Grande: will probably stay 1¼m: a very smart colt in the making. *F. Mathet, France.* **?**

LIGHT REIN 2 b.f. Sky Gipsy 117–Bridle 87 (Bivouac 114) [1976 6fg 5fg] smallish filly: first foal: dam, half-sister to Crooner, stayed 1m: behind in maiden races in July at Newmarket (£2,000 event) and Nottingham. *J. Bethell.* **—**

LIGHT THE FIRE 3 b.c. Frigid Aire–Cedar Valley (High Perch 126) [1975 7fg⁴ 7d 1976 11.1g⁶ 10fg] well-made colt: rated 95 at 2 yrs but seems only plating class nowadays. *J. Bethell.* **3**

LIKELY BOY 3 b.c. Jukebox 120–Epee (Cranach) [1975 5s⁶ 5g⁵ 5g 5f⁶ 5fg⁴ 6fg⁵ 6f* 7g³ 7g³ 6g⁶ 1976 7g 6f⁶ 6g 9g 10f 7g⁶ 8h³ 8fg⁴ 8f³ 8d] robust colt: quite a modest plater: seems to stay 1m: occasionally wears blinkers but does as well without: sold 600 gns Doncaster October Sales. *R. Bastiman.* **53**

LILAC WINE 6 ch.m. Will Somers 114 §–Extra Blue (The Cob) [1974 15s 16f³ 15g 12g⁴ 13f 12.3fg³ 12f⁴ 12g 12s 1975 N.R. 1976 10f⁵] poor staying handicapper (rated 51) in 1974: well beaten at Nottingham in June, only outing since: sold 450 gns Doncaster November Sales. *W. Haigh.* **—**

LILLIVANTER 2 ch.f. Levanter 121–Granite Lil 77 (Aberdeen 109) [1976 5f 5f 5s 5fg⁴ 5f² 6f² 6f⁶ 7f] quite a modest plater: stays 6f. *M. W. Easterby.* **55**

LILOY 5 b.h. Bold Bidder–Locust Time (Spy Song) [1974 7.5g³ 9g* 8g⁴(dis) 8s* 8g* 10v⁵ 1975 8g² 8d 10s* 1976 8g³ 8g⁴ 10fg*] American-bred French horse: showed much improved form when winning 11-runner Group 2 Prix d'Harcourt at Longchamp in April by 5 lengths from Ramirez and subsequent Prix Ganay winner Infra Green: not seen out afterwards: had earlier finished **124**

411

Chesham Stakes, Ascot—Limone takes over inside the last furlong from Brightelmstone and Regal Ray

in frame in Prix Edmond Blanc and Prix le Capucin at Saint-Cloud in March: stayed 1¼m: appeared to act on any going but was apparently well suited by a sound surface: blinkered second outing at 5 yrs: stud in Argentina. *A. Penna, France.*

LILY AUGUSTA 4 b.f. Typhoon 125–Ultra Violet 84 (Sunny Brae 121) [1974 **55** 7g* 7fg* 7f⁴ 8v 1975 8s⁶ 10fg⁵ 8f² 8.2f⁴ 10g² 1976 8f 8g 10fg⁵ 8f⁴ 8fg 9f⁵] poor performer: best form at up to 1m: acts on firm going and is possibly unsuited by soft: blinkered, bandaged and sweated up on first outing *Sir Mark Prescott.*

LILY LANGTRY 3 b.f. Prince de Galles 125–Intrusion 101 (Aggressor 130) **91** [1975 7fg 1976 7fg 10f* 10.8f² 12g² 12g* 14fg⁴ 14.7f² 14fg 11g 12g] smallish filly: half-sister to very smart stayer Mr Bigmore (by Mandamus): dam soft-ground stayer: won maiden race at Pontefract in April: showed much better form in handicaps afterwards, running Scallywag to 2½ lengths at Haydock and then scoring a most impressive 6-length win over Prince Pepe in Rosebery Memorial Stakes at Epsom in June: put up easily best subsequent effort when runner-up to Move Off in three-runner Redcar Gold Trophy Handicap the following month: will probably stay well: has won on firm going but has rather a round action and is probably much better suited by some give in the ground: unseated rider leaving stalls on penultimate outing. *P. Robinson.*

LILY TROTTER 2 b.f. Blakeney 126–Luscinia 73 (Sing Sing 134) [1976 6s⁴] **75 p** third foal: dam, half-sister to numerous winners, won over 1m: weak in market, ran well for a newcomer when 2½ lengths fourth of 20 to Nobodys Fool in minor race at Chepstow in October: will stay 1m+: should improve. *R. Hern.*

LIMONE 2 b.c. Relko 136–Palmavista 120 (Royal Palm 131) [1976 5g 5d³ **109 p** 6f*]
For Limone the season ended, as his trainer had prophesied that it would, with his success in the Chesham Stakes at Royal Ascot, which meant that he made only three appearances. However, he showed more than enough to suggest that he will make up into a pretty good horse over middle distances. Not much need be said about his first two appearances. He wasn't fancied on either occasion, but his third to Teddington Park and Showpiece in the Portsmouth Road Plate at Sandown in June represented a promising effort by a colt whose breeding and manner of racing suggested he needed further than five furlongs. He managed to keep these useful youngsters company until outpaced in the closing stages. In the Chesham Stakes Limone had six furlongs to travel, and it was the extra furlong that was his salvation. Brightelmstone, Regal Ray and Regency Bill all had the legs of him in the early stages, and it wasn't until approaching the final furlong that Limone got into top gear and began to make some impression. Finishing very strongly indeed, he swept into the lead well inside the last hundred yards to win by a length and a half. It would be foolish to pretend that Limone accomplished anything greatly out of the ordinary in this race, but Brightelmstone, Regal Ray and Regency Bill can all run, and it says a lot for a colt of Limone's breeding that he should be able to outpace them over six furlongs, even if it did take him practically the whole of the journey to do it.

It bears repeating that he promises to make up into a pretty good horse over middle distances.

		Tanerko	Tantieme
	Relko	(br 1953)	La Divine
	(br 1960)	Relance III	Relic
Limone		(ch 1952)	Folaire II
(b.c. 1974)		Royal Palm	Royal Charger
	Palmavista	(b 1952)	Pasquinade
	(ch 1961)	Galla Vista	Discovery
		(ch 1955)	Gallorette

A tall colt, who cost 14,500 guineas as a yearling, Limone is a son of the Derby winner Relko, most of whose stock require time and stay reasonably well, out of the Royal Palm mare Palmavista, a very useful miler who from three previous foals has bred Bigribo, a useful staying handicapper by Ribero. Gallorette, the third dam, won twenty-one races, including the Delaware Oaks, and is the grandam of the Jockey Club Cup winner Dancing Moss and the Irish St Leger winner White Gloves. Palmavista had pace, but the family, generally speaking, is a stout one, and distances of a mile and upwards will be required for Limone to be seen to best advantage as a three-year-old. He appears to act on any going. *G. Harwood.*

LIMPOPO 4 ch.g. Crepello 136–Zambesi 87 (Vimy 132) [1974 7d* 8s 1975 — 10d 8f² 10fg² 10g 10g* 10f³ 1976 10g 10.6d] tall, rangy gelding: well beaten both appearances at 4 yrs: suited by 1¼m and ran at 3 yrs as though longer distances would suit him extremely well: seems to act on any going: ran badly when tried in blinkers: sold out of E. Weymes' stable 820 gns Doncaster August Sales. *J. Berry.*

LINBALU 3 b.f. Linbuche 102–Babulass (Babu 117) [1975 5s 5fg⁵ 5fg 5f 7g 67 6f 6fg 9fg 10g 8g⁶ 10g³ 8v⁶ 1976 8f 12g⁶ 12.2d* 12f 12f⁶ 12fg] light-framed filly: plater: showed much improved form when winning easing up by 8 lengths at Catterick in May: sold out of P. Rohan's stable afterwards 1,650 gns and ran poorly in better company subsequently: stays 1½m: needs plenty of give in the ground: blinkered sixth outing at 2 yrs. *D. Holmes.*

LINCADE 3 b.c. Brocade Slipper 114–dam's name unregistered (Sir Mat) [1975 — N.R. 1976 7.6fg 12.2fg] small colt: well beaten in two maiden races: looks as though he has little future. *S. Brookshaw.*

LINCOLN FIELDS 3 ch.f. St Chad 120–Flaming Fields (Can) (New Providence) — [1975 N.R. 1976 8.2d 8s 10s] third foal: 260 gns yearling: dam won over 6f in North America: behind in maiden races in the autumn: covered by Shiny Tenth. *R. Boss.*

LINDEN DOLLY 3 ch.f. Gulf Pearl 117–Witty (Will Somers 114 §) [1975 6g 63 5.9g 1976 10.1fg 10.1f 8f⁵ 13fg⁶ 12f² 11.5d 10s² 12v⁵] first foal: 1,200 gns yearling: dam of little account: narrowly-beaten second in maiden races at Brighton in August (to General Augustus) and Folkestone in October (to River Mahwa): stays 1½m: acts on any going. *A. Pitt.*

LINDSELL 2 b.c. Charlottown 127–Mayfell 107 (Rockefella) [1976 5g 5f⁶ 82 5fg⁵ 7f² 6f* 6g⁴ 8s⁶] lightly-made colt: third foal: half-brother to a winner in Belgium: 500 gns yearling: dam won at up to 1½m: made all to win eight-runner nursery at Salisbury in August by a length from Red Ember: will stay 1¼m: acts on firm going: blinkered fourth and final outings, running creditably on former occasion. *R. Hannon.*

LINDWALL 2 br.c. Linacre 133–Dallowgill 77 (Darius 129) [1976 6d] fourth — foal: 2,000 gns yearling: dam won over 7f: unquoted when nineteenth of 22 to Rocket Symphony in maiden race at Newmarket in October. *R. Jarvis.*

LINGUISTIC 2 ch.f. Porto Bello 118–Linguist 90 (Mossborough 126) [1976 95 ? 5fg³ 6s 5h² 5f* 5fg* 5f⁴ 5fg] strong, quite attractive filly: first foal: dam, twice a winner over 1¼m, is half-sister to very smart miler Estaminet: easily landed the odds in four-runner maiden race at Edinburgh in July: improved greatly on that effort when winning nursery at Nottingham the following month by ¾ length from Rushley Bay but ran moderately on last two outings: should be suited by 6f +: possibly not at her best on soft going. *Sir Mark Prescott.*

LINKENHOLT 6 b.g. Reliance II 137–Tudor Gal 106 (Henry the Seventh 125) 76 [1974 12.2f⁵ 11.7fg 12h² 16f² 18.4fg* 19g 16s⁴ 16v⁶ 1975 18.4g 12f³ 16fg²

413

18.4g⁵ 12f² 16g⁶ 16d³ 1976 14fg³] big, rangy gelding: having his first outing since October 1975 when 6 lengths third of 17 to Buckie in handicap at Salisbury in September (apprentice ridden): lacks pace and stays very well: acts on any going. *P. Cole.*

LIN SLIPPER 3 b.g. Linacre 133–Tartan Slipper (Panaslipper 130) [1975 6fg 8s 7g 1976 10d 12.3fg⁶ 14.7d 15v 10.2s] compact gelding: no signs of ability. *P. Farrell.*

LINTHORPE 3 ch.g. Galivanter 131–Miss Ramuk 71 (Silver Kumar 112) [1975 5fg⁵ 5f 6fg 6f 7h 7f 8f 8g 8g 1976 12.3s 12f⁵ 8d⁶ 7d 9fg⁶ 10f⁵ 13.8f 13.8g] leggy gelding: poor plater: stays 7f, but is not certain to stay further (does not stay 1¾m): often wears blinkers: sold 380 gns Doncaster September Sales. *J. Calvert.*

LIONSMEAD 4 b.c. Levmoss 133–Hot Penny 105 (Red God 128 §) [1974 — N.R. 1975 9g 10.1s 12fg 1976 8fg] apparently of little account. *T. Craig.*

LIQUIDITY 3 ch.f. Richboy 117–Andromache 112 (Delirium 126) [1975 5fg⁶ 62 6g 5fg⁶ 6fg³ 5g 5g 8g 1976 8.5fg 7g 6g³ 6fg 5.3f⁴ 5h⁴ 5.8h⁵ 6f⁴ 7fg⁵] small, compact filly: modest plater nowadays: not certain to stay beyond 7f: sold 1,025 gns Ascot August Sales. *T. Gosling.*

LISA GREY 2 gr.f. Roan Rocket 128–Balisarda 82 (Ballymoss 136) [1976 5f] half-sister to two winners in France, including 1971 2-y-o 1m winner Balking (by Charlottown): 3,500 gns yearling: dam a staying half-sister to Derby runner-up Alcaeus: unquoted when ninth of 15 to Mandrake Major in maiden race at Newmarket in August: will be suited by much longer distances. *B. Lunness.*

LISBOA 2 b.f. Herero–Listigkeit (Alarich) [1976 5g 6f² 6g 7fg⁵] German-bred 78 filly: sire won 1962 German Derby: quite a moderate maiden: will stay middle distances. *C. Brittain.*

LISCANNOR LASS 2 br.f. Burglar 128–Ballyseedy 73 (Dicta Drake 126) 83 [1976 5fg⁶ 5f² 5fg² 5f⁶ 5fg 8v⁶ 6s³] neat filly: half-sister to two minor winners: dam won early-season 5f seller at 2 yrs: placed in maiden and minor events, finishing 1¾ lengths third of 24 to Tudor Jig at Teesside in November: not certain to stay 1m: acts on any going. *W. Gray.*

LITIGANT 4 ch.g. Aggressor 130–Barletta 106 (Tenerani 135) [1974 N.R. — 1975 10d⁵ 10.1s 10.1fg 12f⁶ 12s⁴ 12f² 10g⁶ 12f⁴ 1976 12.5v] small, sturdy gelding: seems to need at least 1½m: acts on any going: ran creditably when tried in blinkers. *Lady Herries.*

LITTLE BURGLAR 5 b.h. Burglar 128–Feather Ball 99 (Big Game) [1974 §§ N.R. 1975 6f 8h 8g² 6g 1976 5f 5h⁶ 5f 5f] plater: shows more temperament than ability nowadays and is best ignored. *F. Wiles.*

LITTLE CRACKER 2 b.f. Blast 125–Avonella 73 (Rockavon 120) [1976 5f 6h] light-framed filly: sister to useful sprinters Blastavon and Whoomph: 200 gns yearling: behind in maiden races at Edinburgh and Carlisle in the summer. *N. Robinson.*

LITTLE CYNTHIA 2 br.f. Wolver Hollow 126–Fazilka (Crepello 136) [1976 76 6f⁴ 6h²] neat, lightly-made filly: half-sister to two winners, including 9f to 1½m winner I'm Alright Jack (by Right Tack): 1,050 gns yearling: dam minor 11f winner in France: beaten 2 lengths when in frame in July in maiden race won by Pearl Haven at Yarmouth and in maiden auction event won by Movement at Redcar (odds on): will stay middle distances: gave impression at Redcar that easier ground would suit her better. *H. Cecil.*

LITTLE GADGE 2 b.g. Mandamus 120–Little Dora (Bounteous 125) [1976 65 5fg⁵ 5f² 6f 6h⁶ 7fg⁵ 8f⁴ 8.2h* 8fg⁶ 8s³ 8s] small gelding: attracted no bid after winning 10-runner seller at Hamilton in September by ¾ length from Grass Currency: will probably stay middle distances: seems to act on any going. *W. C. Watts.*

LITTLEGOOD LASS 5 b.m. Ron 103–High Fashion 74 (Distinctive 118) — [1974 N.R. 1975 N.R. 1976 10.1fg 10h⁶] probably of little account. *J. Webber.*

LITTLE GREY 2 gr.c. Kauai King–Kitty's Pet 59 (High Treason 126) [1976 — 5f] fourth foal: 240 gns foal and resold 180 gns yearling: dam won 6f seller at 3 yrs: tailed-off last of nine to Exposed in minor event at Lingfield in June. *J. Pullen.*

LITTLE MISCHIEF 3 b.c. probably Indigenous 121–Rockless 71 (Rockefella) — [1975 N.R. 1976 9g 8h 12g] evidently useless. *P. Buckley.*

LITTLE ROO 6 b.g. Rugantino 97–All Go 41 (Talgo 130) [1974 N.R. 1975 —
N.R. 1976 8fg] poor N.H. performer: well-beaten seventh of 10 to Chuconte
in amateur riders event at Salisbury in June, only outing on flat. *J. Cann.*

LITTLE RUN 6 ch.m. Silver Cloud 121–Roman Dawn 87 (Neron 121) [1974 **62**
7g⁴ 8f⁶ 5g⁶ 5s⁶ 6d² 5d³ 7g⁶ 1975 7s* 6g 7f* 6fg² 8g³ 6g⁴ 8fg 8.3g 1976 8f 7f*
7f⁵ 7 6fg² 5f⁶ 8g⁵ 7d² 6s⁴] compact mare: quite a moderate handicapper:
narrow winner at Chepstow in April: ran creditably afterwards, including in
sellers: stays 1m: acts on any going: usually wears blinkers: suitable mount
for an apprentice. *M. Tate.*

LITTLE TERN 3 gr.f. Sea Hawk II 131–Light Opera 101 (Vienna 127) [1975 **80**
5fg 5f² 5f* 6f³ 6g 7.6s 1976 7f 8f* 10fg² 10f³] small, sturdy filly: won handicap
at Goodwood in May by a head from Yunkel, having more in hand than winning
margin suggests: stays 1¼m: very well suited by firm ground: bought by B.B.A.
8,400 gns Newmarket July Sales for export to New Zealand. *J. Dunlop.*

LITTLE THRUSTER 2 ch.f. King's Company 124–Glimmer of Light (Only **89**
for Life 126) [1976 5fg 5g⁴ 5f6 6d² 6v] small, sturdy filly: second foal: dam
well beaten on only outing: 20/1 and apprentice ridden, put up easily best effort
when 1½ lengths second of 19 to Balante in nursery at Windsor in September:
will stay 1m: sold only 700 gns Newmarket Autumn Sales. *J. Tree.*

LITTLE TRADER 7 b.g. Constable 129–Kelso Girl (Royal Palm 131) [1974 —
N.R. 1975 N.R. 1976 12.5v] plating-class maiden: has run only once on
flat since 1972: form only at 5f: has been tried in blinkers. *W. C. Watts.*

LITTLE TRILBY 3 b.f. Tyrant–Petit Chapeau 84 (High Hat 131) [1975 5f⁵ **107**
5f⁴ 6f⁵ 5f² 5fg⁶ 6f³ 7fg* 1976 7f³ 8fg 7g 7f* 6.3f 8f³ 6.3g² 7f² 6f⁵ 6f⁵ 6f⁴ 8g]
third live foal: half-sister to 1½m winner Little Ditch (by Dike): 1,800 gns foal:
dam won twice over 1½m: won handicap at Phoenix Park in June by 2½ lengths
from Child of Grace: ran well on many of her other outings, including when
runner-up to Major Bee in handicap at the Curragh and to Wolverlife in £1,200
event also at Phoenix Park and when third to I've A Bee in Mulcahy Stakes
again at Phoenix Park: thirteenth of 25 behind Flying Water in 1,000 Guineas
at Newmarket: best form at 6f and 7f: acts on firm going. *J. M. Kennedy,
Ireland.*

LIVE SPARK 3 ch.g. Sky Gipsy 117–Gerda (Narrator 127) [1975 5g⁶ 5fg³ 5fg⁵ **56**
6f 7f 10g⁶ 1976 6f⁴ 10fg 10.1fg 8.3f 8fg 7g 6f 6f³ 10h² 10h² 10s⁶ 12s⁶ 10s] small
gelding: plater: bought in 420 gns after winning convincingly at Folkestone
in August: suited by 1¼m: best form on top-of-the-ground and acts on hard
going: has worn blinkers but does better without. *M. Goswell.*

LIVING FOR KICKS 2 br.f. Murrayfield 119–Enchanted Evening II (Sailor) —
[1976 5g 5fg 7f 8v 8g] fair sort: behind in maiden and minor events: trained
until after third outing by W. Wightman. *W. Haigh.*

LIVING LEGEND 3 b.f. Derring-Do 131–Leonora's Legend 83 (Rockefella) **86**
[1975 5d⁵ 5fg⁴ 6fg 6f² 6g 6f 6fg⁴ 6fg 7g³ 7g³ 7.6s 1976 8f* 8 5fg³ 10g 8.5g³ 8fg⁶
10f⁴ 8.3fg³ 7fg 8.3f* 8g 8s⁴ 7s] compact filly: fairly useful on her day and won
maiden race at Ascot in April and handicap at Windsor in August: made most
and rallied well when headed to beat Suited a short head on latter course: best
form at around 1m on a sound surface: ran moderately when tried in blinkers.
D. Whelan.

LIZANNA 2 b.f. The Brianstan 128–Barnie's Isle (Dumbarnie 125) [1976 5f **71**
7f⁴ 7.2f⁴ 9fg] strong, well-made filly: showed a little ability when fourth in
maiden race at Beverley in July and minor event at Haydock in August: not
certain to stay 9f. *J. Fitzgerald.*

LIZZIE EUSTACE 3 gr f. Firestreak 125–Bell Crofts 79 (Arctic Time 127) **53**
[1975 5f⁴ 5f 6h⁴ 7f 1976 6d 8g⁶ 9fg⁵ 10h² 7f⁶ 7fg⁵ 8.2h² 6g 8f² 13.8g⁴ 10d³ 10v]
small filly: plater: best form at up to 1¼m: occasionally wears blinkers. *I.
Jordon.*

LIZZYLYN 2 b.f. Tower Walk 130–True Dresden 58 (Vilmoray 126) [1976 **84**
5g⁶ 6fg 5.1f* 5g⁵ 6v] attractive, rangy filly: half-sister to two minor winners:
4,000 gns yearling: dam poor sprint maiden: got up close home to win seven-
runner maiden race at Yarmouth in August by a head from Fantasy Royale:
well beaten afterwards but had quite stiff tasks: should stay 6f: acts on firm
going. *C. Brittain.*

LLACCA 3 gr.f. Grey Love 103–Court Record (Court Feathers 120) [1975 N.R. —
1976 10.8f 5.9g 9f 8f 7g] first foal: dam poor novice hurdler: no sign of ability
in varied company: blinkered final outing. *J. Peacock.*

LLOYD ARDUA 3 b.g. Jimmy Reppin 131–Ardnahoe 67 (Big Game) [1975 5s² —
5v⁶ 5fg 5fg 5g⁶ 7g⁴ 8.2g⁶ 7g 5g⁴ 6f³ 5d³ 5v 1976 6fg⁴ 6g] leggy gelding: plater:
stays 7f and should get 1m: twice wore blinkers at 2 yrs: sold to R. Cambidge
920 gns Newmarket July Sales. *B. Lunness.*

LOBSTER POT 4 gr.f. Silver Shark 129–Bottalina (Botticelli 129) [1974 54
N.R. 1975 6s 8fg 8.2g³ 7fg 8.2f⁶ 8g⁵ 10s² 10.8g⁴ 12g³ 10f⁵ 1976 12f⁵ 12f³
16.1d 10.1fg⁴ 12fg] leggy, angular filly: poor handicapper: stays 1½m: probably
acts on any going: trained by H. Collingridge until after fourth outing. *N.
Adam.*

LOCAL 2 ch.g. Manacle 123–Princess Nefertiti (Tutankhamen) [1976 5v³ 5g* 86
5g⁵(dis) 5fg 5f* 5g⁴] compact, rather lightly-built gelding: third foal: half-
brother to a minor 2-y-o winner by Privy Seal: 900 gns foal, resold 1,650 gns
yearling: dam ran only twice: winner of maiden race at Catterick in June and
of minor event at Beverley in August, latter by ½ length from Ribbleston: will
stay 6f: wears blinkers nowadays. *J. Carr.*

LOCAL KNOWLEDGE 2 b.c. Sharpen Up 127–Indian Echo 106 (Kalydon 106
122) [1976 5g 5g* 5f⁴ 5fg² 5fg⁴ 6g³ 5g² 5d] small colt: half-brother to two
winners, including fair stayer Wovoka (by Appiani II): 3,200 gns yearling:
dam winner at 6f and 1m: made all when winning six-runner maiden race at
Epsom in June by 4 lengths from Midsummer: ran well afterwards, going down
by 1½ lengths to Last Sale under top weight in nursery at Sandown in September:
will probably stay 1m. *J. Sutcliffe.*

LOCHNAGER 4 br.c. Dumbarnie 125–Miss Barbara 87 (Le Dieu d'Or 119) 132
[1974 5g² 5g 5g* 5v⁴ 1975 6d 5fg* 5fg* 6fg* 6d³ 5g* 1976 5d⁵ 5f² 5g* 5f*
6fg* 5fg*]
     Is there such an animal as the ideal racehorse? In its report to the Jockey
Club on the pattern of racing the Norfolk Committee came up with the following
definition: 'The ideal racehorse has more speed than the best specialist sprinter
. . . . and is supreme over distances from one to one and three quarter miles
at three years old and upwards.' Alas, breeders did not get practical instruction
in the report on how to breed such a horse, but at least the definition squares
with our present racing programme which greatly favours a horse whose best
distance is a mile and a quarter to a mile and a half. In the minds of the vast
majority of racing people the ideal horse is the Derby winner or the winner of the
King George VI and Queen Elizabeth Stakes, the mile-and-a-half horse with pace.
It is this type of horse that earns most of the prestige and the prize money, and
almost every year one from among this specialist group is chosen as 'Horse of the
Year,' an award decided by a poll of forty leading racing writers.
     The Racecourse Association's presentation of an annual award for the
'Horse of the Year' was instituted in 1965, the year of Sea-Bird II. Since then
it has been won by Charlottown, Busted, Sir Ivor, Park Top, Nijinsky, Mill Reef,
Brigadier Gerard, Dahlia (two years in a row), Grundy and, in 1976, by Pawneese.
All those horses won either the Derby or the King George VI and Queen Elizabeth
Stakes, or both, in the years they were named 'Horse of the Year.' We can see
no harm in having a 'Horse of the Year' award; indeed anything that helps to
increase public interest in racing is to be commended. However, the award is
supposed to go each year to 'the best horse of any country to race in Britain',

*King's Stand Stakes, Ascot—Lochnager slams some of the best sprinters in Europe,
the blinkered Realty being his nearest rival*

not to the best mile-and-a-half horse. That Pawneese polled more than half the votes in 1976, a year when no horse dominated the middle-distance scene, is remarkable. In our opinion several horses that ran in Britain during the season showed form at a mile and a half at least the equal of that shown by Pawneese. And what of the sprinters, milers and stayers? Outstanding horses in these categories should merit serious consideration for the 'Horse of the Year' award too. In 1976, the sprinter Lochnager and the stayer Sagaro both stood out in their own sphere as a champion. Both came through the major racecourse tests for horses of their type undefeated, yet neither received more than a handful of votes from the racing writers.

The bias in European racing towards the middle-distance performers is wrong. There is no such animal as the ideal horse. There are simply horses; horses of different capabilities and different characters, horses with different requirements. All should have their opportunities; high-class races with substantial stakes should be provided for horses of all types. We have complained many times about the difference between the level of prize money offered for the top races for the various types of horses, and we warmly welcomed the sizeable increase in 1976 in the value of the races for the top sprinters. However, there is still no big stakes race for sprinters—no £40,000 'classic' event for five- or six-furlong horses. An offer by the William Hill Organization to sponsor a £30,000 sprint at York's August meeting was turned down by the Jockey Club on the recommendation of the Flat Race Planning Committee, although Hills were allowed to put up £20,000 for the Nunthorpe Stakes and to re-name it the William Hill Sprint Championship. The race carried a first prize of £18,660 making it the most valuable all-aged sprint run in Britain. England's two other major sprints also had their prize money jacked up, the first prize for the King's Stand Stakes going from £12,513 in 1975 to £16,424 and that for the July Cup from £9,474 to £12,258.

Lochnager swept the board in England's top races for sprinters, achieving a notable treble last achieved in 1949 by Abernant, the only other horse in the post-war era to have won the King's Stand Stakes, the July Cup and the Nunthorpe Stakes in the same season. Many's the year that the top sprint form fails to stand up from one race to the next. Top-class sprints can be something of a lottery, especially when a big field turns out: the heat is usually on from the break and a horse usually has little chance of overcoming a slow start; similarly, interference in running, however slight, can mean the difference between victory and defeat in a race over so short a distance. It may be that none of Lochnager's performances, taken singly, was exceptional, but his achievement in making a clean sweep of England's top weight-for-age sprints certainly was. And only tip-top performers run up a sequence of victories in the best races.

Lochnager was beaten only once in his last five starts as a three-year-old when he raced exclusively in handicaps. He made great strides in the summer and autumn to end the season on a handicap mark about 10 lb behind the best sprinters. Lochnager needed a couple of races before he was fully tuned up as a four-year-old. Outings in a handicap at York and a minor race at Thirsk helped to bring him to peak fitness for the Temple Stakes at Sandown at the end of May. It was here that Lochnager revealed the extent of the improvement he had made over the winter. He looked magnificent in the paddock and was impressive in the race, showing fine acceleration to go past the leaders Roman Warrior and Faliraki approaching the distance and then drawing clear to win by two lengths. On the strength of this performance Lochnager started short-priced favourite for the King's Stand Stakes at Royal Ascot. Once again he looked a picture beforehand and went out to give a sparkling display. He was with the leaders from the start and as soon as Hide moved on him at the distance he had his field settled in a matter of a few strides. Lochnager was challenged only by one of the twelve other runners, the French filly Realty, who got to within three quarters of a length of him in the closing stages. Lochnager held Realty comfortably in the last hundred yards and won most decisively.

By his victories at Sandown and Royal Ascot Lochnager proved his superiority over the best sprinters at five furlongs. The July Cup, his next race, showed him just as good at six. A persistent story went round Newmarket racecourse on July Cup day that all was not well with Lochnager, the ante-post favourite for the big race. He drifted in the market from 2/1, the best odds on offer on the morning of the race, to 3/1. Earlier in the week he had been the subject of one of the biggest ante-post gambles of the year. Any doubts about Lochnager's well-being were dispelled in the race; he ran on splendidly up the hill to hold on by three quarters of a length and a neck from the fast-finishing Three Legs and the Wokingham winner Import. Hide rode Lochnager

July Cup, Newmarket—harder this time, as Lochnager is strongly pressed by Three Legs (not on photograph) and Import

in the same way that he had at Sandown and Royal Ascot, setting him alight some way from home. After the July Cup Lochnager's trainer told us that this was not the correct way to ride the horse; in his opinion Lochnager would have been more impressive in his races had he been held up until the last furlong and then brought with a sharp run. However, we're sure Lochnager's trainer would agree that to keep a horse covered up until the last furlong is a policy liable to present difficulties in almost any sprint race. Perhaps the tactics adopted by Hide were not, in theory at any rate, ideal for a horse like Lochnager who, according to his trainer, tends to idle once he hits the front. However it is difficult to criticise riding that results in a horse's passing the post in front on every occasion that it really matters.

Lochnager's reputation was such that he was sent off with odds of 5/4 laid on him in the William Hill Sprint Championship at York in August. Of the ten that opposed Lochnager, eight had run in either the King's Stand Stakes or the July Cup and there seemed no sound reason why any of them should turn the tables on Lochnager, at any rate over five furlongs. Lochnager's stable-companion Polly Peachum and the 100/1-shot Clear Melody were the two other runners and, barring accidents, it was hard to envisage Lochnager's being beaten. But Lochnager did not have matters all his own way this time and, although

William Hill Sprint Championship, York—Lochnager puts the title 'Champion Sprinter' beyond all doubt, beating Faliraki (not on photograph), Polly Peachum and Three Legs (far side)

Mr C. F. Spence's "Lochnager"

victory decided the sprinters' championship conclusively in his favour, it was the least impressive of his four wins. Hide got down to work on Lochnager at the distance but he couldn't shake off Polly Peachum and the three-year-old Faliraki. Both made a great fight of it in the last furlong and Lochnager had to be driven right out to hold on. Faliraki, racing wide of Lochnager and Polly Peachum, was beaten only half a length; Polly Peachum was a neck behind Faliraki in third place with Three Legs, finishing almost as strongly as at Newmarket, breathing down the necks of the placed horses.

Lochnager (br.c. 1972)	Dumbarnie (br 1949)	Dante (br 1942)	Nearco
			Rosy Legend
		Lost Soul (b 1931)	Solario
			Orlass
	Miss Barbara (br 1961)	Le Dieu d'Or (br 1952)	Petition
			Gilded Bee
		Barbarona (br 1947)	Punt Gun
			Bessarona

It had been intended that Lochnager should run in the Prix de l'Abbaye de Longchamp in October before being retired, and the reasons for his absence from that race aren't clear. Perhaps he gave evidence at home of having lost his form or perhaps his connections thought the horse's reputation and value would be affected if he were to meet with defeat in France. Lochnager's best form is on a sound surface and there must have been a risk of his being beaten in the Prix de l'Abbaye for which the going was soft. Where does Lochnager stand when he is arrayed alongside the best sprinters of the post-war era? It may seem harsh to find fault with a horse with Lochnager's record but it is evident from a study of his performances that he was not a brilliant horse in the way that Abernant or Pappa Fourway were. Strictly on the book, he is not much in front of some of his contemporaries, and, truth to tell, his contemporaries were not a bright collection as top sprinters go. But if Lochnager did not win any of his races in

LOC

the devastating, runaway style of some earlier champion sprinters he did one thing that not many champion sprinters have done: he kept on winning. In this respect he *was* outstanding.

Lochnager, bought privately as a foal for a modest sum, proved a rare bargain. His value at the time of his syndication as a stallion was put at £260,000 (40 shares at £6,500 each). A salutary lesson for those who spend tens or even hundreds of thousands at the Yearling Sales in the hope of securing a high-class horse. Not that Lochnager would have fetched much at public auction as a foal or a yearling: he has an unfashionable pedigree. His sire Dumbarnie was a high-class sprinter but he had had limited success in a long period at stud before Lochnager arrived on the scene. Lochnager's dam Miss Barbara was a fair sprinter with whom Lochnager's trainer won six races. Miss Barbara has an undistinguished family background. Her dam Barbarona, who was too slow to get out of her own way, was by Punt Gun, an animal who gained his solitary success in three seasons' racing in a maiden race at Stockton, out of an unraced mare Bessarona. Lochnager's pedigree leaves something to be desired and his conformation too may not altogether satisfy the purist. He is a big, strong, good-bodied colt and a good walker but he lacks some of the quality one hopes to find in a horse of his sterling merit. Such things mattered not a jot so far as Lochnager's racing career was concerned but they assume importance when assessing his prospects as a stallion. He will stand his first season at the Easthorpe Hall Stud, Malton, Yorkshire in 1977. *M. W. Easterby.*

LOCHNESS LASS 2 br.f. Track Spare 125–Mascarade 58 (Pirate King 129) [1976 7fg 5s 6s] second foal: half-sister to 1975 2-y-o 5f winner Tribal Mask (by Tribal Chief): dam stayed 1¼m: well behind in maiden races at Salisbury, Bath and Chepstow in the autumn. *P. Cole.* —

LOCHRANZA 5 br.g. Highland Melody 112–Earall (Khalkis 127) [1974 8fg⁵ 8f² 8f⁶ 8g* 10g* 9fg⁵ 8fg* 12d* 12.3s 12.2s* 12s⁴ 1975 8s 11v⁵ 12f* 11g* 11g² 10g² 12.3f6 13d² 12s³ 12.2g³ 12.5fg6 1976 13v* 12.3d³ 12f6 12s³ 12f6 13.8g6 11fg⁵ 11fg² 10g³ 14fg⁵ 12g* 11g⁵ 12v² 12.2s² 12s⁵] fairly useful handicapper: winner at Ayr in April: ran creditably afterwards, and was awarded race after finishing 2½ lengths second to Empress Regent at York in September: stays 1¾m: acts on any going: has worn blinkers but does better without them: excellent mount for an apprentice: occasionally sweats up: tough, genuine and consistent: suited by forcing tactics. *J. Carr.* 89

LOCUS 3 ch.f. Dictus 126–Diello (Crepello 136) [1975 5s 6f⁴ 8g 8g³ 8d 7g 1976 10f² 8.5g⁵ 12f 11.7h⁴ 9.4h⁵] light-framed filly: ran well when second to Adorabella in handicap at Bath in May but is only plating class: stays 1¼m (ran moderately when tried at 1½m): blinkered final outing: sometimes bandaged on near-fore. *D. Hanley.* 68

LOGIC 2 gr.f. Lorenzaccio 130–Moonlight 101 (Djebe) [1976 5v 5v] half-sister to a minor winner and several poor animals: dam ran only at 2 yrs, when winner over 5f: ninth of 17 to Cedar Grange in all-aged event at Nottingham in October, first and better effort: should be suited by further: sold 320 gns Ascot December Sales. *G. Prichard-Gordon.* —

LOH 3 b.c. Realm 129–Sweet Mourne 85 (Mourne 126) [1975 6fg 7g² 7d* 7g³ 1976 7f² 8fg] compact colt: half-brother to fair 1974 2-y-o 6f winner Mountain of Mourne (by Mountain Call): dam sister to very useful stayer Suny-boy: showed very useful form in 1975, winning well-contested race at Ascot in the autumn and subsequently finishing good third in Somerville Tattersall Stakes at Newmarket: put up a good effort despite getting a little warm when running Relkino in to ¾ length in Ascot 2,000 Guineas Trial in April: ran well below his best in 2,000 Guineas at Newmarket later in month and was not seen out again (reportedly had a liver complaint): should stay 1m. *R. Akehurst.* 112 ?

LOINCLOTH 3 br.g. Native Prince–Cover Girl (Edellic 124) [1975 6fg 8.2g 1976 10fg 6g] lengthy gelding: half-brother to two good winners by Reform, namely New Model and 2-y-o Latest Model, but is only plating-class himself: taken down early to start when tried in blinkers on final outing (May). *M. Bradley.* —

LOIRE VALLEY 3 b.g. Donibristle 96–Pilicina (Milesian 125) [1975 7fg 8d 7.6g 1976 10.1g⁴ 10.1fg 10g 10s] plating-class maiden: sturdy, sturdy gelding: blinkered last two outings at 2 yrs. *R. Akehurst.* 54

LONDON GLORY 5 b.h. Pall Mall 132–Morgan le Fay 80 (Milesian 125) [1974 8g 7.6g6 8.2fg* 8g* 10g 8v* 1975 8fg 8s² 8g 8s* 8d⁴ 8g* 9g 8fg6 8v6 8g² 1976 92

420

10g 8g* 8g² 8g⁵ 8f 8.3f² 8g² 8.2f⁵ 9g*] rangy, attractive horse: useful handicapper: winner at Beverley in April and Wolverhampton in August, beating Calibration 1½ lengths on latter course: ran well in most of his other races, notably on seventh start when runner up to Strabo at Ascot in July: stays 1m: acts on any going. *V. Cross.*

LONDON GOD 3 ch.c. Pall Mall 132–Ambrosia 102 (Alcide 136) [1975 7g 8f² **106** 1976 10s* 12fg³ 11.7f* 10.6d6 10f* 12g² 12fg³ 10.5fg² 12.3g²] quite an attractive, lightly-made colt: developed into a useful handicapper and won at Newcastle (maiden event) in April, Windsor in May and Nottingham (slowly-run race) in June: creditable second to Blaskette in Falmouth Handicap at York in August on penultimate outing: stays 1½m: acts on any going: genuine and consistent. *M. Jarvis.*

LONDON ROSE 4 b.f. Pall Mall 132–Alamo Rose 71 (Crocket 130) [1974 5f **50** 7g 8s 1975 10f 10.1s 8f 8.3f6 8fg 12g 10.1fg⁴ 12s³ 12f6 17.1g⁴ 15.8g³ 11.1g 1976 12f⁴ 11.1f² 14fg² 15.5f* 15.5f³ 17.1h³ 14f⁵ 16g⁴ 18.1g] poor handicapper: beat Whistler's Lane a length at Folkestone in June: stays well: probably acts on any going: blinkered last two outings in 1975: suitable mount for an inexperienced rider. *D. Keith.*

LONDON SPIN 3 br.f. Derring-Do 131–Spin Out 97 (Pall Mall 132) [1975 **86** 5d6 5f6 7f² 8g 1976 8fg* 8f6 8fg 6d⁵ 7f* 8g⁴ 7.6g 8g6] ex-Irish filly: half-sister to quite useful 5f sprinter Troller (by Milesian): dam best at 5f: won maiden race at Leicester in March (made all) and handicap at Wolverhampton in August: good fourth to Welsh Flame in Devonshire Stakes at Doncaster the following month: stays 1m well: acts on firm going. *W. Marshall.*

LONDON SWEETHEART 2 b.f. Will Hays (U.S.A.)–St Pet (St Chad 120) — [1976 5fg] leggy, narrow filly: very bad mover: behind in 22-runner seller won by Ma Foi at Ripon in May: sold 290 gns Doncaster August Sales. *K. Payne.*

LONE GIRL 2 b.f. Pieces of Eight 128–Neamar (Nearula 132) [1976 5fg — 5f 5f] evidently of no account: sold 250 gns Doncaster October Sales. *J. Carr.*

LONG DROP 3 ch.f. Tower Walk 130–Lerdet 93 (Whistler 129) [1975 5d² **71** 5v* 5v³ 6fg² 7fg⁵ 5fg 6fg 7v 1976 5h6 5d6 7f6 8s² 7fg⁴ 7.6fg6 7g⁵ 7g³ 7g] quite a moderate handicapper: probably stays 1m: appears to act on any going: often wears blinkers. *T. Fairhurst.*

LONG LOVE 4 ch.g. Dike–Novitiate 97 (Fair Trial) [1974 8d 9s 8d 1975 **79** 10s 11.7s 10h² 12.2fg⁵ 12f6 12g³ 10f* 10f* 10fg⁴ 10.1fg 10f* 10g³ 11g² 10fg² 10s² 1976 10fg 10.6d³ 10h² 10f 10fg 10fg³ 10f 10f² 10fg² 10f* 10fg⁴ 10f* 10h² 10.1f⁴ 10g³ 10s 12.2s⁵] strong, well-made gelding: fair handicapper: winner at Yarmouth in July and Redcar in August, battling back gamely when beating Alison's My Girl ½ length on latter track: stays 1½m but best form at up to 1¼m: acts on any going: has worn blinkers but does better without: sold 6,000 gns Newmarket Autumn Sales: racing in U.S.A. *B. Hanbury.*

LOOK AT ME 3 ch.f. Runnymede 123–Miss Pink (Marshal Pil 108) [1975 — N.R. 1976 8g 6fg] half-sister to a winner in Belgium: dam never ran: seems only plating class. *W. Stephenson.*

LOOK NORTH 4 br.g. Le Dieu d'Or 119–Cecils 61 (Whistling Wind 123) [1974 — 5s* 5d² 5h² 6g6 5fg⁴ 5s 6v 1975 5g³ 7fg⁵ 6g 6g 1976 7g6 6fg6 8.3f] leggy gelding: plater: little worthwhile form since his 2-y-o days: best form at 5f: possibly best suited by a soft surface: sometimes wears blinkers but has run much better without them. *J. Harris.*

LOONG KOI 4 br.g. Negotiation–Young Mementa (Young Christopher 119) — [1974 6fg 6d⁴ 8d 7s 7d 1975 N.R. 1976 10.1g] of little account. *G. Balding.*

LOONSHIANG 3 ch.g. Be Friendly 130–Pochette (Worden II 129) [1975 6s **70** 1976 8fg⁵ 8g 8f 8d³ 8s⁵ 8s 10s³] compact, good sort of gelding: 3¾ lengths third of 12 to Estate Agent in maiden race at Teesside in November: stays 1¼m: blinkered fifth outing: sold to J. Haine 2,600 gns Doncaster November Sales. *R. Jarvis.*

LOOSE LADY 3 bl.f. Hard Man 102–Gloria Spy 57 (Epaulette 125) [1975 — N.R. 1976 8.2g 8f 6h] half-sister to quite moderate 1969 2-y-o I Spy (by Dunoon Star) and to two poor N.H. performers: dam of little account: in rear in varied company, including selling: dead. *L. Barratt.*

LOOSEN UP 3 b. or br.c. Never Bend–Dancing Hostess (Sword Dancer) [1975 **108** 8s⁴ 7.5s⁴ 7.5s³ 1976 8g⁵ 10s³ 11fg² 11.5g* 12g 12g 12g 11d⁵ 12s⁵ 12d⁵ 12s] tall American-bred French colt: half-brother to Palladium (by T.V. Lark), a sprinting stakes winner in U.S.A.: dam, who won over 6f in U.S.A., is half-sister to prolific stakes winners T.V. Commercial (by T.V. Lark) and Corraggioso (by Gallant Man): ran well in May when finishing 1½ lengths second to Malacate (gave 4 lb) in a handicap and then winning Prix de l'Avre by 2½ lengths from Saint Fort, both races at Longchamp: ran moderately afterwards but had some stiff tasks, including when seventeenth of 23 to Empery in Epsom Derby: probably stays 1¼m: usually wears blinkers. *A. Paus, France.*

LOPEZ 6 ch.g. Relko 136–Cuba 101 (Hyperion) [1974 16fg* 1975 16v⁴ 1976 14.7d⁴ 15.8g³ 15g² 15f* 18fg*] tall, lengthy gelding: improved steadily with his races in 1976 and won his last two races, at Edinburgh in July and Ripon the following month: won with more in hand than margin of ½ length suggests when beating Migelitto on last-named course (had difficulty getting a run but was always holding runner-up once in lead): needs a stiff test of stamina: acts on a firm and a soft surface: sweated up second outing. *W. A. Stephenson.* **77**

LORD CHAD 5 ch.g. St Chad 120–Molarina 100 (Denturius) [1974 5fg 7g 5s 5g⁶ 1975 6fg⁵ 5f 1976 5.9f 7d] well-made gelding: selling handicapper nowadays: stays 6f: acts on firm going: sometimes wears blinkers and wore a hood on final outing in 1975. *R. Supple.* —

LORD COMPOSER 3 br.c. Insubordination–In Harmony II (Brimstone 106) [1975 N.R. 1976 11s] American-bred colt: half-brother to four winners in Australia and to outstanding Norwegian 1974 2-y-o Royal Conductor (by Prince Royal II): dam winner three times in Australia: remote seventh of 12 behind Castle in Spain in maiden race at Ayr in May, only outing. *J. Mulhall.* —

LORD CON 4 ch.c. Connaught 130–Coriander 88 (Herbager 136) [1974 N.R. 1975 10fg 8g 8f 1976 8.3f 14fg⁵ 16d] big, strong colt: poor maiden. *J. Nelson.* —

LORD DAVID 8 br.h. Tesco Boy 121–The Veil 81 (Nimbus 130) [1974 8s⁴ 7.5g 9.8v 10.5g⁶ 10g³ 9g* 10g⁴ 9d⁶ 1975 10g* 1976 8f³ 10.4d³ 10g 10d² 9fg⁵ 8f³ 10f* 10h² 10g⁶] fairly useful performer: put up far and away his best effort of season on reappearance when close third to London Glory in handicap at Beverley in April: odds on, just failed to beat when trotting up in claiming race at Brighton in August: stays 1¼m: acts on any going: has been to stud and has sired a winner. *W. Marshall.* **95**

LORDEDAW 2 b.c. Lord Gayle 124–Umgeni Poort 109 (Botticelli 129) [1976 5s* 5g³ 5f* 6f² 7f² 6.3f⁴ 7f³ 8fg² 7g⁴ 6f*] useful-looking Irish colt: half-brother to several minor winners: 6,200 gns yearling: dam won at up to 1m at 2 yrs: won 17-runner maiden race at Naas in March easily by 4 lengths from Snap Happy, and put up an even better effort in £1,500 event at Leopardstown in June, scoring by a length from odds-on Rumson: placed afterwards in Coventry Stakes at Royal Ascot (short-headed by Cawston's Clown), Mullion Stakes at Leopardstown and National Stakes (5 lengths third of eight to Pampapaul) and Ashford Castle Stakes (2½ lengths second to Padroug) both at the Curragh, before carrying top weight to victory (apprentice ridden) in Birdcatcher Nursery at Naas in October: stays 1m: acts on any going. *K. Prendergast, Ireland.* **110**

LORD ELECT 3 ch.c. Lord Gayle 124–Polling Station 91 (Polly's Jet) [1975 6fg 6fg 5fg 7g 6g² 7g* 7.2v* 1976 8fg⁵ 9s² 8.2d 8f 8f² 8g² 8.2fg² 7.6g³ 8g⁶] strong, quite attractive colt: fair handicapper: usually finds one or two too good for him: stays 9f: acts on any going: sometimes wears blinkers: has given us impression that he is none too resolute. *J. Sutcliffe.* **87**

LORD HELPUS 3 ch.c. Green God 128–Velour (Golden Cloud) [1975 5g² 5s² 5fg* 6fg³ 5f³ 6h* 6f² 5d² 6g⁵ 1976 7fg⁴ 7.6s² 8.2d 8f2(dis) 8f* 8fg⁴ 8f³ 8fg⁶ 8g* 7d³ 7s³] tall, strong colt: ran very well in good-class handicaps in 1976, winning Welbred Stakes at Beverley in July by 1½ lengths from Gemina and Ripon Rowels the following month by ¾ length from Affirmative and finishing third in William Hill Gold Cup at Redcar (to Claudio Nicolai), Mark Lane Memorial Handicap at Doncaster (to Nearly New) and Cavendish Cup Stakes at Ascot (to Record Token): stays 1m: acts on any going: suitable mount for an apprentice: genuine and consistent: gives impression he is well suited by waiting tactics: sweated up and ran below his best on eighth outing. *B. Hills.* **111**

LORD JUSTICE 2 br.g. Lord Gayle 124–Divine Justice 79 (Sing Sing 134) [1976 5g 6fg 6fg⁴ 8s 8s 6s⁵ 6v⁶] sixth living produce: 440 gns foal: dam stayed 6f: 33/1 when about 2½ lengths fifth of 20 to Nobodys Fool in minor race at Chepstow in October, best effort: should stay further than 6f: seems to act on any going: wears blinkers. *M. McCourt.* **75**

LORD OF HOSTS 2 ch.c. Jimmy Reppin 131–Eureka 78 (Major Portion 129) [1976 5f 5fg 5fg 6d 5d 7s 7s 5v] poor plater. *C. James.* **60**

Ripon Rowels Handicap—Lord Helpus beats his seniors Affirmative and Court Lane

LORD OF LIGHT 3 ch.c. Aureole 132–Night Court 100 (Court Martial) [1975 —
N.R. 1976 12f] closely related to two winners, including very useful 1¼m to
2m performer St Ives (by St Paddy) and half-brother to two winners: 1,200 gns
yearling: dam, winner at 1m, is half-sister to Crepello, Honeylight and Twilight
Alley: unquoted and in need of race, went down to post very scratchily prior to
finishing tailed-off last behind Du Maurier in minor event at Ripon in July.
W. O'Gorman.

LORD OF MISRULE 2 gr.c. Supreme Sovereign 119–Mirth (Tamerlane 128) **79**
[1976 7s⁴ 7s 7v⁴] third foal: 1,600 gns yearling: dam never ran: apprentice
ridden when fourth in newcomers race and minor event at Lingfield at end of
season, being beaten 10 lengths by North Stoke in latter event: will stay 1m.
C. Dingwall.

LORD OF THE SILK 2 br.c. Lord Gayle 124–Taking Silk (Shantung 132) **101**
[1976 7g² 7d* 7.3v⁴] useful Irish colt: second foal: half-brother to winning
3-y-o plater North Two (by Stupendous): 7,400 gns yearling: dam, half-sister
to six winners, never ran: got up close home when winning 14-runner maiden
race at Fairyhouse in October by a neck from Aim: in frame on other outings,
going down by **3** lengths to odds-on Habitus in newcomers race at Phoenix
Park and finishing 6½ lengths fourth of nine to Fair Season in Horris Hill Stakes
at Newbury: will stay further than 1m: acts on heavy ground. *R. Annesley,
Ireland.*

LOR-E-ANA BIRD 3 gr.f. Birdbrook 110–Lady Magistrate 105 (Privy Coun- —
cillor 125) [1975 6g⁶ 1976 10g 10fg 7fg 7fg⁶ 7h⁵ 10.1d 8.2d] big, tall filly:
showed promise at 2 yrs but was well beaten on all outings in 1976: blinkered
second and third outings, swerving and unseating rider leaving stalls on latter
occasion: sold 310 gns Ascot December Sales. *M. Ryan.*

LORELENE 2 ro.f. Lorenzaccio 130–Cullen 80 (Quorum 126) [1976 7s³] **85 p**
sister to quite useful moderate Des and half-sister to two minor winners: 3,100 gns
yearling: dam a stayer: 25/1 and ridden by 7-lb claimer, made good headway
in final two furlongs when about 2¼ lengths third of 19 to Lady Oriana in maiden
race at Newmarket in October: will be suited by middle distances: should win
a race. *L. Cumani.*

LORENZO MONACO 3 br.c. Lorenzaccio 130–Moon Song 96 (Sing Sing 134) **86**
[1975 5fg⁵ 5f² 6fg⁶ 5.9g 5g⁶ 5.9g 1976 7g⁴ 6g⁶ 8fg³ 8d³ 7fg* 7.6fg* 7g* 8g 7.6fg
7g] smallish, lengthy colt: in excellent form in midsummer and won handicaps
at Wolverhampton, Chester (in good style by 6 lengths from Hayloft (Fr)) and
Ayr: defied a 10-lb penalty when beating Wigeon a head on last-named course
in July: stays 1m: best form on a sound surface: not disgraced when tried in
blinkers on final outing: sold 2,700 gns Doncaster October Sales and has been
exported to Hong Kong. *H. Williams.*

LORNY GIRL 2 b.f. Forlorn River 124–Achates 80 (Constable 129) [1976 5fg —
6f 7fg] lengthy filly: no worthwhile form in varied company, including selling.
K. Whitehead.

Lord Howard de Walden's "Lost Chord"

LOST BID 4 b.f. Fine Bid 106–Donova 92 (Devonian) [1974 N.R. 1975 8f — 10.6fg 9fg 1976 8fg] probably of no account. *S. Brookshaw.*

LOST CHORD 3 b.c. Busted 134–Magic Flute 124 (Tudor Melody 129) [1975 **116** 7g⁵ 1976 11f² 10f³ 11.1g* 12g² 12fg² 10fg² 12.3g* 14fg] powerful, well-made colt: wide-margin winner of 17-runner maiden race at Kempton in May and three-runner £3,000 event at Newcastle in August, on latter course coming home 10 lengths clear of London God (gave 10 lb): runner-up in three races in between, notably when running Meneval to 1½ lengths in Group 2 Gallinule Stakes at the Curragh: much better suited by 1½m than 1¼m (well beaten in Irish St Leger when tried at 1¾m): acts on firm going: sold privately for export to South Africa. *P. Walwyn.*

LOST SCENT 2 ch.c. Busted 134–Fragrant Morn 79 (Mourne 126) [1976 **85** 6fg⁶ 6g⁴ 7d⁵] lengthy, attractive colt: good mover: third foal: half-brother to smart 1973 2-y-o Alpine Nephew (by Great Nephew): 14,000 gns yearling: dam won over 5f at 2 yrs: 2 lengths fifth of 16 to The Czar in minor race at Yarmouth in September: raced in good-class races earlier and started favourite for Hyperion Stakes at Ascot on previous start (finished a moderate fourth): will stay 1m+. *R. Armstrong.*

LOT ONE 5 ch.m. Three Dons 91–Time Signal (Signal Act) [1974 11.7fg 16s⁶ — 12fg 8s* 8.3fg³ 8s 1975 N.R. 1976 12f⁶ 7f] selling handicapper (rated 72) in 1974: tailed off both outings since: apparently best at around 1m: acts on soft going: wears blinkers. *J. Long.*

LOTTO 3 br.f. Derring-Do 131–Lady Bingo (Match III 135) [1975 5g 6g 5.9f⁴ **83** 5g⁴ 6fg 1976 8fg³ 8g⁴ 7g* 7s³ 8s 8s³ 8.2s²] good-looking, well-made filly: won 14-runner maiden race at Kempton in August by 4 lengths from James Junior: ran well when placed in handicaps afterwards, going down by 2 lengths to Autumn Glow at Haydock in October: will stay further than 1m: seems to act on any going but is well suited by soft. *F. J. Houghton.*

Bunbury Cup, Newmarket—Lottogift wins going away from Berkeley Square and Stand to Reason

LOTTOGIFT 5 b.h. Charlottown 127–Charmaine's Gift 86 (Galivanter 131) **103**
[1974 9.2g⁶ 11s 10d 8.5f⁵ 8d⁵ 9g² 8.5f⁵ 7.3d⁶ 6fg⁶ 9d 8v⁶ 8s 1975 8v* 7s³ 8s⁵
7fg⁴ 8.5f² 8f² 8fg³ 10f⁵ 7g* 9g* 8.2s⁵ 10.6v 1976 8g 8s⁴ 10g³ 8.5g⁶ 8f 7fg* 7fg³
10fg 7fg 7d 7d 9g 10d] neat horse: useful handicapper: came from a long way
back when winning Bunbury Cup at Newmarket in July from Berkeley Square:
spoiled his chance by hanging left when close third to Fighting Lady at Newcastle later in month: stayed 1¼m: acted on any going: had been tried in blinkers
but seemed better without: suitable mount for an apprentice: genuine: stud in
Australia. *D. Hanley.*

LOUDLY 3 gr.c. Crooner 119–Quantity 77 (Quorum 126) [1975 5v² 5g³ 5f⁴ 5fg³ **78**
1976 7g 6f 8fg 8g⁴ 7g⁴ 8g* 8f* 7g⁶ 10s⁴ 8s⁶] strong, quite attractive colt: won
maiden race at Warwick (made most) and minor event at Thirsk in space of
five days, just holding on to beat Allan Water a head in latter event in September:
not certain to stay 1¼m: best form on a sound surface: sold to C. Davies 1,350 gns
Newmarket Autumn Sales. *B. Hills.*

LOUGHBORO' GEORGE 7 b.h. Kelly 122–Ogwen 117 (Abernant 142) [1974 —
8g⁵ 10f⁵ 7f* 7g³ 6g 1975 7s 7f 7f³ 7f 8f 7f 7f 8fg* 7g² 7.6g 1976 8fg 6f 5.9f⁵
8f 6h 5fg 7d 8g 6s 7v] big, strong horse: selling handicapper: stays 1m: acts on
firm going: best in blinkers: inconsistent: reportedly finished lame on second
outing. *Mrs L. Dingwall.*

LOUISE VALLIERE 3 b.f. St Paddy 133–Petit Trianon 93 (Princely Gift 137) **86**
[1975 6g* 6fg⁵ 8d 1976 9s 12d 12h⁴ 11.7f* 12fg⁶ 12fg⁶] quite attractive filly:
won handicap at Windsor in July by 2 lengths from Snow Swan: stays 1½m:
acts on firm going: sold 1,700 gns Newmarket December Sales. *M. Stoute.*

LOVEABLE ROGUE 2 b.c. Burglar 128–State Candy (Hardicanute 130) [1976 —
6f 5.1f 7f] useless. *R. Bastiman.*

LOVE ALWAYS 2 b.f. Be Friendly 130–Scattering 69 (Busted 134) [1976 5d —
5s 6d] first foal: 1,400 gns yearling: dam won over 1¼m and is half-sister to
Tribal Chief: behind in maiden races, finishing fifteenth of 22 to Rocket Symphony
at Newmarket in October on final outing. *P. Robinson.*

LOVE BEACH 2 ch.f. Lorenzaccio 130–Honeymoon House 89 (Honeyway 125) **75**
[1976 5fg 5.3f⁶ 9fg⁶ 8fg⁴ 7.2v] small, light-framed filly: half-sister to several
winners, including French 1,000 Guineas filly Fanghorn (by Crocket): quite a
moderate maiden: stays 1m: sold 280 gns Ascot December Sales. *B. Hills.*

LOVE FROM VERONA 2 b.c. Royal Palace 131–Julieta 108 (Ratification 129) **75 p**
[1976 7fg⁵] big, rangy colt: half-brother to several winners, including useful
middle-distance stayer Trustful (by Reliance II) and 3-y-o Insolvent (by Busted),
a winner over 1m at 2 yrs: 4,000 gns yearling: dam a sprinter: 12/1 and in need
of race when 6 lengths fifth of 20 to Main Event in maiden race at Leicester
in September: will probably stay middle distances: sure to improve and can win
a similar race. *B. Hills.*

LOVE ME TWO 2 b.f. Double Jump 131–Lilmi Love 82 (Miralgo 130) [1976 —
6d 5g 5g] second foal: dam won at 1¼m: no worthwhile form in maiden and
minor events. *M. Camacho.*

LOVE POTION 4 b.f. French Vine 111–Tiki (Technion 96) [1974 N.R. 1975 —
N.R. 1976 10.1f 12f⁴ 10.1fg 17.1s 15.5s] probably of no account. *D. Dale.*

LOVE ROCKET 4 gr.c. Roan Rocket 128–Maladie d'Amour 98 (Fidalgo 129) —
[1974 6fg 7g³ 7d 1975 10.1g 12f³ 10h² 10g* 10h* 10.1fg² 10fg³ 10g* 1976 10g]
strong, attractive colt: fair handicapper (rated 86) at 3 yrs: ran only once on
Flat in 1976: best form at 1¼m: acts on hard going: usually a front runner. *D. Nicholson.*

LOVESOME HILL 3 b.f. Murrayfield 119–Helen C (Counsel 118) [1975 8f 8g 46
6g 1976 8f 8g⁴ 10.6d⁵ 6h² 7f 6f³] lightly-made, narrow filly: plater: effective
at 6f and stays 1m (had stiff task when well beaten at 1¼m): sometimes wears
blinkers but does just as well without: sold 550 gns Doncaster September Sales.
Miss S. Hall.

LOVE STORY 3 b.f. Aureole 132–True Love 89 (Princely Gift 137) [1975 6d 79
1976 10s⁵ 10.5d³ 10.5fg⁵ 8fg² 8g* 8fg* 7h³ 10g⁶ 8s⁴ 8v⁵] neat filly: favourite,
won maiden race and minor event at Ayr in the space of five days in July,
holding on well to beat Mischief a head in latter race: also in frame in varied
company, including when 3 lengths third of eight to Everything Nice in Musidora
Stakes at York and when good fourth, apprentice ridden, to Yellow Boy in
handicap at Pontefract in October: probably needs further than 7f and stays
1¼m well: appears to act on any going: sweated up badly seventh outing: does
best when ridden up with pace: races with tongue tied down: sold 12,000 gns
Newmarket December Sales. *S. Hall.*

LOWANDER 2 ch.f. Counsel 118–No Profit (Epaulette 125) [1976 5f 5fg] —
eighth living produce: 150 gns yearling: dam of no account: last in May in
maiden auction events at Wolverhampton (hampered start) and Brighton.
R. Supple.

LOWLAND CAVALIER 3 ch.g. Bivouac 114–Honey Bun 109 (Honeyway 125) —
[1975 7g 8f 1976 12fg 12.2f⁵ 12.2fg 12v⁵ 10.2s⁶] plating-class maiden: seems
to stay middle distances. *R. Hollinshead.*

LOW LINDETH 2 br.g. Right Boy 137–Miss Scribbler 82 (Counsel 118) [1976 70
5f² 5f] lengthy, leggy gelding: quite a good walker: fourth foal: half-brother
to 1975 2-y-o 5f selling winner Durham Lad (by Tycoon II): 800 gns yearling:
4 lengths second to Slow Coach in maiden event at Warwick in April: behind
in similar event at Leicester two months later and was not seen out again.
D. Gandolfo.

LOWNDES SQUARE 3 ch.c. Pall Mall 132–Hyena (High Treason 126) [1975 65
6s⁴ 1976 8g⁵ 8g 10.1f³] attractive colt: reportedly hobdayed: showed a little
ability in maiden races: stays 1m (ran moderately when tried at 1¼m): started
very slowly second outing: sold 1,700 gns Ascot September Sales. *J. Tree.*

LOYAL DEED 2 b.g. Runnymede 123–Our Dark Lady 88 (Dumbarnie 125) 98
[1976 6fg 6f⁶ 7d 6fg³ 7s²] strong, good-bodied gelding: half-brother to several
winners, including fair miler Charlie's Pal (by Gratitude): dam a sprinter:
placed in 25-runner minor event at Redcar in September (1¼ lengths third to
Friendly Now) and nursery at Sandown the following month (beaten 5 lengths
by Frisco Bay but finished clear of seven others): stays 7f. *R. Jarvis.*

LUBA LOVE 3 ch.f. Midsummer Night II 117–Patient Sam 99 (Sammy Davis 42
129) [1975 5fg 5.1f 5fg 5.9f 5.1g 1976 6fg³ 7f³ 8.2f⁵ 6g 7fg 8f] poor plater:
has been tried in blinkers: sold 380 gns Ascot June Sales. *D. Weeden.*

LUCASTOWN 3 br.c. Charlottown 127–Lucasland 121 (Lucero 124) [1975 6fg⁴ 94
7fg² 7g² 1976 10s 9s⁴ 8.2g* 8f⁶ 8fg* 8g] medium-sized, strong-quartered colt:
showed useful form in varied company and scored comfortable wins in minor
events at Haydock in May and Doncaster in June: beat Gambling Gipsy 3
lengths on latter course: ran moderately in valuable ladies race at Ascot in July
and was not seen out again: promises to stay 1¼m: acts on any going. *M. Jarvis.*

LUCENT 2 b.f. Irish Ball 127–Lucasland 121 (Lucero 124) [1976 8fg* 8v² 8s*] 113
big, well-made filly: sixth foal: half-sister to 3-y-o 1m winner Lucastown (by
Charlottown): dam very smart sprinter and half-sister to So Blessed: won
seven-runner minor event at Goodwood in September by a short head from
Tanaka after a prolonged battle: went down by ¼ length to The Czar in 24-
runner minor event at York the following month but won 26-runner £2,200
event at Doncaster in November by 8 lengths from Never Say Guy: most
impressive at Doncaster, never looking in danger after taking lead three furlongs
out and staying on strongly to the post, and will stay further: seems to act on
any going. *R. Price.*

LUCKNOW 3 b.g. Taj Dewan 128–Jackyda 71 (Royal Palm 131) [1975 N.R. **53**
1976 10.1f 12g⁵ 10.1fg⁴ 10h⁴] big, workmanlike gelding: showed a modicum of
ability in maiden and minor events. *H. Smyth.*

LUCKY AMBITION 3 ch.g. Galivanter 131–Syringa 98 (Set Fair 129) [1975 —
5g 6f 1976 10f⁵ 8f 16f] neat gelding: plating-class maiden: not certain to
stay 2m. *J. W. Watts.*

LUCKY DATE 2 ch.c. Double Jump 131–Razia 97 (Martial 131) [1976 5f⁵ 5g **62**
5fg 6f 6g] lightly-made colt: plating-class maiden: sold out of J. Winter's
stable 820 gns Newmarket July Sales and was resold 1,150 gns Ascot October
Sales. *P. Mitchell.*

LUCKY DEVIL 3 b.c. Great Nephew 126–Good Fortune 65 (Native Prince) **65**
[1975 6fg 6fg 8.2g⁵ 8.2d 1976 12fg 12fg 12f³ 12fg⁴ 10.2fg⁵ 10f² 11.7h⁵ 11.7h*
12f⁴ 13s 12.2s 12s] lengthy colt: won maiden race at Bath in July by a length
from Mary Roan, making all: may well stay further than 1½m (never in race
when tried at 13f): best form on a sound surface: blinkered sixth and seventh
outings, running well on first occasion, but moderately on second: has given
impression he needs strong handling: trained until after ninth outing by R.
Price. *M. Salaman.*

LUCKY JOE 7 b.g. Shantung 132–Hormuz (Persian Gulf) [1974 N.R. 1975 —
12.5g 1976 12.2d 16f⁴] of little account nowadays: used to wear blinkers:
bandaged second start. *C. Boothman.*

LUCKY LARK 2 b.c. Birdbrook 110–Miss Gadabout 74 (Galivanter 131) [1976 **73**
5f 5f 5fg⁶ 5v⁴ 5s⁵] shapely colt: first foal: bought privately for 2,000 gns as
a yearling: dam stayed 1m: showed some promise in maiden races, finishing
fourth of 13 to Don in £1,800 event at York in October: will be suited by 6f+ :
the type to do better at 3 yrs. *M. W. Easterby.*

LUCKY MICKMOOCH 3 b.c. Blakeney 126–Lucky Janie 87 (Dual 117) [1975 **88**
7g⁶ 8g⁶ 7d 8f 1976 8f⁴ 10fg² 10fg³ 10g* 10.5fg⁴ 8.3f⁴ 8.3fg⁴ 12h* 12f² 12g²
14g⁶ 12s⁶] useful-looking colt: won maiden race at Epsom in June and handicap at Brighton in August: stays 1½m but has yet to show he stays 1¾m: acts
on hard ground and ran moderately on soft on final outing. *J. Winter.*

LUCKY OMEN 2 b.f. Queen's Hussar 124–Brass (Sovereign Path 125) [1976 **99**
5fg 5f* 6fg* 6g² 6v³] compact, well-made filly: half-sister to a winning plater
by Pinza: dam of no account: ran her best race when 1½ lengths second of
nine to Mofida in valuable Firth of Clyde Stakes at Ayr in September: successful
earlier in maiden race at Beverley and minor event at Chester: will stay 1m:
acts on any going. *C. Brittain.*

LUCKY PRIZE 2 b.c. Prevailing–Miss Christine 103 (Pall Mall 132) [1976 **80**
5f⁵ 5d* 5f³ 5g³ 5f⁴ 5s⁵ 6h⁴ 6f² 5f⁵ 5fg⁵] neat colt: first foal: dam at her best
at 2 yrs when winner over 5f: comfortable 3-length winner from Westgate
Sovereign in 10-runner maiden race at Edinburgh in April: in frame on several
of his other outings, going down by 1½ lengths to Christine Jane in £1,200 event
at Redcar in July: stays 6f: seems to act on any going: blinkered sixth outing:
sometimes sweats up. *F. Carr.*

LUCKY SEVENTEEN 4 b.c. So Blessed 130–Alcina (Alycidon 138) [1974 **68**
6g 6fg 7g 1975 7s⁶ 8.2g 11.5f 8g* 7g³ 8fg 9fg⁵ 8g³ 8.2s 1976 8g 8f* 10h³ 8fg³
10fg² 8g* 8f⁴ 10f² 10h⁶ 10g² 10.4fg⁶ 8d⁴] neat colt: quite a moderate handicapper: successful twice at Warwick, on second occasion beating Golden Gayle
4 lengths in amateur riders race in June: stays 1¼m: acts on firm going: ran
poorly when tried in blinkers. *D. Weeden.*

LUCKY SHOT 4 b.c. Reform 132–Photo Flash 119 (Match III 135) [1974 7g⁵ **95**
8d 8d⁴ 1975 11fg⁶ 10fg* 12f² 12g* 14fg³ 12s³ 1976 12g⁴ 16g 16fg⁴ 12g³ 14g*]
well-made colt: quite a useful handicapper: overcame difficulties in running
(hampered by a faller) to win at Sandown in July by 6 lengths from The Griggle:
looked most unlucky when about 2 lengths fourth of seven to Royal Orbit
on same course earlier, being badly checked when trying to challenge on inside,
but running on well in final furlong: stays 2m: acts on any going: genuine and
consistent. *S. Ingham.*

LUCKY SOVEREIGN (USA) 2 b.c. Nijinsky 138–Sovereign 129 (Pardao 120) **107**
[1976 5.6f 6g 5f² 6fg² 5g 7d⁴] strong, good-bodied colt: fifth foal: half brother
to very useful miler Flashy (by Sir Ivor): dam fastest 2-y-o filly of 1967 and
stayed 1m: still a maiden but took on smart animals on most of his outings
and has some useful efforts to his name: made Padroug pull out all the stops
when going down by a head to him in Acomb Stakes at York in August on

427

fourth outing, and ran well when about 10 lengths fourth of 11 to The Minstrel in William Hill Dewhurst Stakes at Newmarket in October: needs further than 5f and will stay 1m: acts on a firm and a soft surface: sure to win races at 3 yrs. *H. Wragg.*

LUCKY TOUCH 2 b.f. Tudor Music 131–Moonlight Story (Narrator 127) **74** [1976 5f2] second living foal: dam never ran: 25/1 and blinkered, failed by only a short head to catch Warrenward Park in seller at Folkestone in September: will be well suited by 6f+. *P. Haslam.*

LUCKY TRIX 2 b.c. Lauso–Hometrix 90 (Kalydon 122) [1976 5s 5fg5 **57** 5fg5 6f 7g] leggy, unfurnished colt: quite a moderate plater: best run at 5f but should be suited by further: blinkered first outing. *W. Stephenson.*

LUCKY WEDNESDAY 3 br.c. Roi Soleil 125–Pavlova (Fidalgo 129) [1975 **117** 5g4 5g* 6g* 8d5 1976 7s2 7s5 7f* 8d3 8g3] well-grown Irish colt: half-brother to four winners, including very useful middle-distance performer Kirov (by On Your Mark): 1,850 gns yearling: dam won over 1½m in Ireland: showed useful form in Ireland at 2 yrs: improved considerably in 1976 and after finishing 2½ lengths second to Wolverlife in Burmah-Castrol Trophy at Phoenix Park in March, won Group 3 Vauxhall Trial Stakes on same course the following month by a head from Sovereign Dice: put up an even better effort when length third to Northern Treasure and Comeram in Irish 2,000 Guineas at the Curragh in May but was then off course until October when going down to Serenica and Sandy Row in a desperate finish to Youghal Stakes at Phoenix Park: will stay 1¼m: acts on any going: to be trained in 1977 by H. Cecil. *C. Collins, Ireland.*

LUDOVIC 2 b.c. Prince Tenderfoot 126–Winter Rose (Santa Claus 133) [1976 **76** 5f3 5g3 5f5 5f6 5.9g3 6g3 5f6] small colt: fourth foal: 350 gns yearling: dam never ran: quite a moderate performer: stays 6f. *J. Haine.*

LUENGE 6 ch.g. Cavan–Li'l Filly (Li'l Fella) [1974 12v2 12s* 12g2 13g3 14g2 **113** 12.5g 12g 12v4 12.5s* 12v2 1975 12s 10.5g* 12s* 1976 15.5g2 13g2 11g6 12fg5] American-bred French gelding: very useful performer: ran best races in 1976 when runner-up behind Citoyen in Group 2 Prix Jean Prat at Longchamp in April, and Beau Buck in Group 3 La Coupe on same course the following month: reportedly completely unsuited by ground when well-beaten fifth to Smuggler in Princess of Wales's Stakes at Newmarket in July on final appearance: stays well: acts on heavy going: said to have been hampered on third outing. *A. Penna, France.*

LUKE SPLENDID 2 b.c. John Splendid 116–Fleur de Sol 64 (Vilmorin) [1976 **99** 5f 5f* 5f2 5d* 5f5 6h3 5f6 5.9fg3 5fg] useful-looking colt: half-brother to winning sprinter Fishy Tale (by Runnymede) and to a winner abroad: 520 gns yearling: dam placed over 7f at 2 yrs: won maiden auction race at Thirsk in April, and put up a very good display when making all to win minor event at Ripon in June by 1½ lengths from Maiden Grieve: excellent third of 23 to Princess Rose in nursery at Wolverhampton in September: stays 6f: possibly not at his best on very firm ground. *J. Etherington.*

LUKEWARM 3 b.g. Sahib 114–Coralanty (Star Signal 114) [1975 N.R. 1976 **66** 8.2f 10fg 16.1d6 16h5 16f* 14fg 12v] small gelding: third foal: dam winning hurdler: won weakly-contested maiden race at Warwick in July by a length from Wimberry: stays 2m: acts on firm going. *M. Smyly.*

LUNA REAL 3 gr.f. Roan Rocket 128–Soverena 98 (Sovereign Lord 120) **108** [1975 5s6 7.5g* 8s3 8d3 1976 8fg6 8fg6 9g5 10g 8g2 8v 9.2s6 9v4] French filly: half-sister to very useful middle-distance performer So Royal (by Tudor Melody): 8,200 gns yearling: dam, a sprinter, is half-sister to top-class sprinter Set Fair: showed very smart form at 2 yrs: placed only once in 1976 but ran well on occasions, notably when neck second to Anne Palatine in Prix de la Calonne at Deauville, when just over 8½ lengths sixth of 25 to Flying Water in 1,000 Guineas at Newmarket and when just over 7 lengths sixth of 12 to Dona Barod in Prix de l'Opera at Longchamp in October: stays 9f: appears to act on any going. *E. Bartholomew, France.*

LUNA'S DREAM 2 b.f. Breeders Dream 116–Lunawood 71 (Blast 125) [1976 **45** 5fg4 5f 8v] poor plater. *J. Hill.*

LUSH GOLD 4 br.f. Goldhill 125–Lush Pool 70 (Dumbarnie 125) [1974 5g6 **79** d 5d* 6d4 5d 1975 7d 6v 6d3 6f2 7f4 8f* 9g6 8g 8d* 8.2d5 8fg6 1976 8g2 7g4 8f6 8g 8d6 8f 8s3 8h5] compact, useful sort: ran respectably on her first three

428

starts at 4 yrs but was disappointing afterwards: stays 1m well: seems to act on
any going: usually wears blinkers. *M. H. Easterby.*

LUTEA 2 ch.c. Yellow God 129–Senthia (Parthia 132) [1976 5d 5g² 7f⁵ 5fg*   **72**
5g⁶ 5h⁶ 6h²] first foal: 1,450 gns yearling: dam won over 7f at 3 yrs in Ireland:
all out when winning seller at Newcastle in July in close finish with Baby Ben
and Kabagold: ran respectably in Scottish nurseries afterwards: should stay
1m: sold 500 gns Doncaster November Sales. *T. Craig.*

LUTOMER RIESLING 2 b.f. So Blessed 130–Bisley (Polic 126 or Punchinello   **91**
97) [1976 5g 5.1fg⁶ 5f* 5h* 5fg 6g⁴ 5d] lightly-built filly: third foal: half-
sister to winning 3-y-o sprinter Kinshasa (by Swing Easy): dam twice-raced
daughter of Park Hill winner Mitrailleuse: won maiden race at Warwick by
2 lengths from Home Fire and three-runner minor event at Redcar, both in July:
probably stays 6f: acts on hard ground. *M. Stoute.*

LYDIATE 2 gr.f. Tower Walk 130–Palotra 86 (Palestine 133) [1976 5f⁴ 5g   **77**
7.2fg⁶ 6f³ 5g⁴ 7g³ 6d 8g] leggy filly: first foal: dam won over 6f at 2 yrs: third
in maiden races at Redcar in August (to Firemaiden) and Ayr the following
month (to Nana's Queen): needs further than 5f and stays 7f. *R. D. Peacock.*

LYFORD CAY 12 ch.g. Alcide 136–Sonata 85 (Hyperion) [1974 16f³ 16fg   —
18.4g² 22.2fg 1975 16s² 1976 18.4s] quite a moderate out-and-out staying
handicapper: acts on firm going: has worn blinkers. *W. Swainson.*

LYNAUGHTER 2 br.c. Linacre 133–Harry's Daughter (Will Somers 114 §)   —
[1976 6g 7g 6d] robust colt: third foal: half-brother to useful 1974 2-y-o 6f winner
Alibita (by Above Suspicion): dam poor plater: behind in maiden races at
Goodwood and Newmarket (two) in the autumn. *R. Smyth.*

LYNCATHAL 3 br.f. Great Nephew 126–Alredo 61 (Whistler 129) [1975 5g⁴   **80**
5f 5f² 5fg² 6g³ 5s³ 1976 7g² 7g² 8h* 9fg 8f² 8g* 8h⁶] light-framed filly: won
maiden race at Beverley in July and then picked up a valuable prize when
winning six-runner Northern Goldsmiths' Handicap at Newcastle the following
month by a neck from Silver Steel: stays 1m: acts on hard ground: fell on
fourth outing: consistent. *W. Haigh.*

LYNWOOD SOVEREIGN 4 b.f. Connaught 130–Hypatia 84 (High Hat 131)   **86**
[1974 6g 6d 6fg* 7s⁶ 8g² 8s 1975 10g⁴ 10fg³ 8.5f 8fg⁶ 10f⁵ 10f* 14.6g³ 12g⁴
12g 1976 13.3g³ 12t² 12fg⁴ 12fg⁶ 12fg⁴] lightly-built filly: useful performer
on her day: often had stiff tasks but was very disappointing on final outing
(seemed to have a fair chance at weights): stays well: acts on firm going: blinkered
last four outings in 1975 and fourth start (tailed off). *C. Brittain.*

LYTHAM 4 b.g. Reliance II 137–Particule 117 (Vieux Manoir 132) [1974 7v 7s   **59**
7v 1975 10.1f 11.1fg⁴ 12f* 16f 1976 12.2f³ 12g³ 15.5f⁶] quite attractive,
strong, deep-girthed gelding: stays 1½m and should get further (had stiff task
on first attempt at 2m and broke down on third start): acts on firm going:
wears blinkers nowadays. *D. Kent.*

M

MA BELLE AMIE 3 b.f. Never Say Die 137–Twinkle (No Worry 105) [1975 6s   —
1976 12fg 12fg 12.2fg 16f] well beaten in minor event and maiden races:
blinkered final outing. *J. Powney.*

MACBAY 2 b.c. Diatome 132–Malva (Mourne 126) [1976 6f 7g 7fg 8g] second   **55**
foal: 3,800 gns yearling: dam second in French 1,000 Guineas: poor maiden. *D.
Sasse.*

MACCLESFIELD 3 ch.c. Shantung 132–Capital Charge 103 (High Treason 126)   **82**
[1975 N.R. 1976 11f³ 11g³] lengthy colt: half-brother to two winners,
including fairly useful 1m winner Cab (by Abernant): dam a sprinter: close-up
third to Lighter in maiden race at Newbury in April (finished strongly after being
slowly into stride and meeting with interference): odds on when 5 lengths third
of 13 to Rowe Residence in similar event on same course the following month:
will stay 1½m. *J. Tree.*

MACHINE 8 b.g. Tutankhamen–Princess Lee (Princely Gift 137) [1974 5.9g⁴   —
8f 12g⁴ 8g* 8.5d 8g 1975 8.2s 8s⁴ 5fg 8f⁵ 9f 10fg 1976 10.4fg] poor plater
nowadays: effective at sprint distances and stays well: best form on a sound
surface: ran poorly when tried in blinkers. *H. Morris.*

MACHRIHANISH 2 ch.f. King's Company 124–Celtic Sky 81 (Celtic Ash) **71**
[1976 5s 5g² 6g 5d 5.9s 6s] small filly: first produce: 220 gns foal, resold 420 gns
yearling: dam won over 7f at 2 yrs: length second of 10 to Taj Princess in maiden
auction event at Wolverhampton in June, best effort: had plenty on in nurseries
on last three outings, including when tried in blinkers on final start: should stay
7f. *E. Cousins.*

MACH TWO 3 ch.g. Henry the Seventh 125–Anglo Indian 86 (Alycidon 138) —
[1975 N.R. 1976 11g⁴ 10f⁶ 12g 15.8g 12g] plain gelding: brother to fairly
useful stayer Mark Henry and half-brother to another winning stayer: dam won
twice at 1½m: no worthwhile form in maiden races: blinkered last two outings.
W. Elsey.

MACKELLY 2 b.c. Irish Ball 127–Gala Honey 66 (Honeyway 125) [1976 7g **103 ?**
7v* 7d] half-brother to two minor winners: dam stayed 1½m: raced alone and
seemed to put up a very useful effort when winning 19-runner £1,300 event at
Newcastle in October, making all, being clear at halfway and drawing right away
to score by 10 lengths from Friendly Now, with the rest at least another 5 lengths
further back: 20/1 for William Hill Dewhurst Stakes at Newmarket later in month
and never got in a blow, finishing remote seventh of 11 to The Minstrel: will stay
at least 1¼m: goes very well on heavy ground. *C. Brittain.*

MACTAVISH 3 ch.f. St Alphage 119–Harmonet (Monet 127) [1975 5g 5fg 6f* —
6fg² 7f* 7s 8g 1976 8g 8f 10g] neat filly: won maiden race at Brighton and
nursery at Chester in 1975: ran moderately as a 3-y-o and was sold 480 gns
Newmarket Autumn Sales: not certain to stay 1m. *G. Hunter.*

MADAME CHOLET 2 br.f. Goldhill 125–March Moonlight 86 (March Past —
124) [1976 5fg] half-sister to four winners, including very useful sprinter
Blackbird (by Crooner): dam a miler: weak third favourite when ninth of 10 to
Mia Saint in minor event at Windsor in May, only outing. *P. Walwyn.*

MADAME STORACE 3 b.f. Illa Laudo 117–Foreverusa (Poona 116) [1975 —
N.R. 1976 10.2g] plain filly: fifth foal: half-sister to two winning hurdlers: dam
ran only three times: probably in need of race when tailed-off last of 12 to Amber
Valley in maiden race at Doncaster in September. *J. Turner.*

MADAM JANE 2 gr.f. No Mercy 126–Injaka 102 (Right Boy 137) [1976 5fg **55**
6fg³ 6fg 5d 7s 6s] lengthy filly: first foal: dam winner at up to 7f: 10 lengths
third of five to Sailing Along in maiden race at Lingfield in July: stays 6f. *R.
Hannon.*

MADAM VENTURE 2 b.f. Rajen 96–Lady Venture (Scottish Venture 106) —
[1976 5g] half-bred filly: swerved at start when tailed-off last of seven in seller
at Wolverhampton in May. *K. Bridgwater.*

MADANG 3 b.c. Habitat 134–Jellatina (Fortino II 120) [1975 N.R. 1976 6d* **116**
5v* 6d* 6g* 6g⁵ 5g* 5f⁶ 5fg⁵ 5fg 5g⁶] attractive ex-Italian colt: third foal: half-
brother to a poor animal by Hornbeam: 9,000 gns yearling: dam won over 9f in
Ireland: was one of the best sprinters in Italy and won four times at Rome and
once at Milan in first half of season: beat smart Giadolino (levels) by 5 lengths on
last-named course: started favourite for Group 3 Premio Melton at Rome but
could finish only fifth to Policrock (levels): looked really well in himself and
performed most creditably on first appearance in this country when about
5 lengths sixth of 13 to Lochnager in King's Stand Stakes at Royal Ascot in June:
failed to reproduce that form in King George Stakes at Goodwood, William Hill
Sprint Championship at York and Sir Gatric Stakes at Doncaster (never going
well): stays 6f: acts on any going: a taking individual. *L. Cumani.*

MAD BRAIN 3 br.c. The Brianstan 128–Mad Cap II 92 (Tyrone 130) [1975 5v⁴ **74**
5.9fg 5.9fg⁵ 5d 5g 1976 5.9fg² 6d* 7fg 6fg³ 6f 5s⁴ 6v] quite a moderate
handicapper: staying on when winning 10-runner maiden race at Newcastle in
April all out by a neck from Mr Metal: creditable fourth to Faridina in handicap
at Doncaster in October: should be suited by 7f: appears to act on any going:
blinkered last four outings. *J. Hardy.*

MAD CAREW 3 ch.c. Yellow God 129–Fair Darling 93 (Darling Boy 124) [1975 **73**
N.R. 1976 7fg⁵ 8.5fg* 8f⁶ 10fg⁵ 12f⁵] lengthy, useful sort of colt: fourth foal:
half-brother to Tudor Lord (by Tudor Music), winner at up to 1½m: dam best at
up to 1m: won nine-runner maiden race at Epsom in April by ¾ length from
De Milo: ran poorly afterwards in handicaps and a claiming race: stays 1m:
sold 1,150 gns Ascot August Sales. *S. Ingham.*

MA FOI 2 b.c. Most Secret 119–Rowin 71 (Sing Sing 134) [1976 5fg² 5fg* 6s⁴] **74**
leggy colt: fourth produce: half-brother to a minor winner: 100 gns foal: dam

stayed 1m: ran out a comfortable 4-length winner of 22-runner seller at Ripon in May and was sold out of M. H. Easterby's stable for 2,500 gns subsequently: not seen out again until October and was not disgraced in circumstances when fourth to wide-margin winner Burley in a Haydock nursery: may stay further than 6f: seems to act on any going. *H. Blackshaw.*

MAFTED 2 ch.c. Caruso 112–Virago Gray (Crown Again 96) [1976 5g 5f 7s] — lightly-built colt: first foal: dam never ran: no worthwhile form in varied company, including selling: started slowly second outing. *J. Hardy.*

MAGENTA 2 ch.f. Royal Gunner–None Sweeter 80 (Never Say Die 137) [1976 6g*] half-sister to two winners, including very useful stayer Close Combat (by Aggressor): 320 gns yearling: dam won at 1m: 25/1, showed up all way when winning 14-runner newcomers event at Goodwood in September by 1½ lengths from Celtic Goddess: a good first effort by a filly who should be well suited by longer distances. *N. Adam.*   **87 p**

MAGIC BLISS 2 ch.c. Sweet Revenge 129–Sultan's Slipper (Saint Crespin III 132) [1976 6d 6v 6v] third foal: half-brother to a minor 2-y-o winner by Runnymede: 3,100 gns yearling: dam ran only once: little worthwhile form in maiden races, finishing ninth of 16 to subsequently-disqualified Nampara Cove at Lingfield in November on final outing. *D. Keith.*   —

MAGIC LOVE 4 ch.f. Frankincense 120 or Elf-Arrow 117–Stormy Love 77 (Elopement 125) [1974 N.R. 1975 8s 11v 10.8s 10fg⁶ 10fg 10.1g⁴ 16s 12g³ 8g 1976 12.2fg] big, workmanlike filly: poor maiden: stays 1½m. *J. Holt.*   —

MAGIC NOTE 4 gr.c. Crooner 119–Magic Pin (Magic Red) [1974 5fg 5fg⁶ 5fg⁵ 7fg⁵ 5.3g⁴ 1975 6g⁶ 6f 5h⁶ 8.3fg² 8g⁵ 7.6g 1976 12.2fg 7fg] compact colt: plater: stays 1m: tried in blinkers on reappearance. *W. Williams.*   —

MAGIC RULER 3 b.c. Torullo 100–Kouli Khtar (Nordlys 94) [1975 6fg⁵ 7f 8g 8g⁵ 1976 10fg* 10fg 11.7fg] quite a modest performer: won maiden race at Salisbury in May by a neck from Ring Rose: stayed 1¼m: acted on a firm surface: ran well in blinkers last outing at 2 yrs: dead. *V. Cross.*   **76**

MAGIC SHOES 3 b.f. Henry the Seventh 125–Moira Shearer (Nearula 132) [1975 7fg⁶ 6g 1976 8fg 10.8f] leggy, sparely-made filly: plating class: sold 2,000 gns Newmarket July Sales: covered by Royal and Regal. *T. Waugh.*   —

MAGI-SU 2 b.f. Karabas 132–Winkie 112 (Bleep-Bleep 134) [1976 5g⁵ 5fg] tall, lengthy filly: half-sister to fairly useful sprinter Fulham Flirt (by Klairon): dam, at her best at 2 yrs, is half-sister to good sprinter Daylight Robbery: 3½ lengths fifth to Triple First in eight-runner maiden race at Sandown in May, first and better effort: should be suited by 6f+: not seen out after June. *T. Gosling.*   **74**

MAGNETIC 3 ch.f. Crewman–Romagna (Romulus 129) [1975 6g³ 5fg⁵ 7g² 7.2s⁴ 1976 7fg⁶ 10.1fg⁶ 10f² 8fg 8f² 8fg 8s 8s 8s] American-bred filly: disappointing maiden: 4 lengths second to Andy Rew in apprentice handicap at Bath in June, best effort: gives impression she needs further than 1m, and stays 1¼m: unsuited by soft ground: sold 5,000 gns Newmarket December Sales. *I. Balding.*   **62**

MAGNIFIQUE 3 b.g. Grand Roi 118–Port Margaret 91 (Gustator) [1975 N.R. 1976 12d] half-brother to several winners, including speedy 1959 2-y-o Sonomag (by Infatuation): 580 gns yearling: dam won over 5f: 20/1 when tailed off behind Sanpello in maiden race at Ripon in June: sold 350 gns at Doncaster Sales later in month. *M. H. Easterby.*   —

MAGNOLIA LAD 3 b.c. Mummy's Pet 125–Julita 87 (Rockavon 120) [1975 5f 5fg⁵ 6f* 6fg³ 7f² 6f² 7fg 5g* 5f⁵ 1976 5g⁶ 5g⁵ 6fg 6d 6f 5fg 6fg 8.2f⁴ 8fg] compact colt: creditable fifth to Bunny Boy in handicap at Doncaster in April but ran poorly afterwards: stays 7f but is probably better at shorter distances: wore blinkers at 2 yrs but ran best race at 3 yrs without. *W. Wharton.*   **90 d**

MAHADEO 3 b.c. Astec 128–More Mahal (Darbhanga) [1975 6g² 6g² 1976 7fg 10.1fg 10fg 12g⁴ 8f⁴ 10.1f* 8f 10g⁶ 10.8s⁴] useful-looking colt: first foal: dam won Danish 1,000 Guineas: won seven-runner maiden race at Windsor in August by 5 lengths from Claironcita: stays at least 1¼m (fourth in 1½m Danish Derby): probably acts on any going: sold 3,600 gns Newmarket Autumn Sales. *N. Guest.*   **75**

MAHAR 2 b.f. Highland Melody 112–Harmahal 79 (The Bug 135) [1976 5f 5fg 5d 6g² 8fg² 6s 6s] leggy filly: sister to 1975 2-y-o 5f winner Micjac: dam unreliable sprinter: runner-up in maiden races at Doncaster and Beverley in   **91**

September, putting up better effort on former course when beaten $\frac{3}{4}$ length by Sarasingh in 26-runner event: best form at 6f: looked and ran as if she was over the top on last two outings. *J. Calvert.*

MAHARANEE 2 ro.f. Sovereign Spitfire 81–Black Rage 91 (My Babu 136) **70** [1976 5fg 7h⁵ 7fg⁵ 8g 8.2s² 10v² 8.2v²] half-sister to three winners, including useful Handycuff (by Manacle), successful at up to 1m: dam moderate miler: runner-up in three sellers in the autumn, going down by $\frac{3}{4}$ length to Hard Luck at Nottingham in October on final outing: stays 1¼m: appears to act on any going: blinkered fourth appearance. *R. Akehurst.*

MAIDENFORM 3 b.f. King Emperor–Am Stretchin (Ambiorix 130) [1975 — 5v⁶ 5fg³ 5f³ 6g⁵ 6g² 6g* 6g³ 1976 7fg⁶ 8f⁵ 8.5g 7g 8g 10d] neat, strong, attractive filly: good mover: won nursery at Nottingham as a 2-y-o but was disappointing in 1976 (off course eleven weeks after third outing): possibly best at distances short of 1m: sold 3,100 gns Newmarket December Sales. *I. Balding.*

MAIDEN GRIEVE 2 ch.f. Miracle 116–Becalm 86 (Honeyway 125) [1976 5g⁴ **80** 5f* 5fg² 5d² 5g⁴ 5.6f³ 6fg² 6fg 6v 6v⁶] short-coupled filly: half-sister to 6f seller winner Peace and Quiet (by Meldrum): 450 gns yearling: dam stayed middle distances: won 15-runner maiden auction event at Pontefract in April by a length from Sovereign Brook: in frame five times afterwards and kept her form quite well, finishing excellent second to Star Attention in nursery at Ripon in August: will stay 1m: appears to act on any going: suitable mount for a boy. *S. Hall.*

MAIDEN'S PET 2 br.c. Mummy's Pet 125–Maiden's Prayer 71 (Petition 130) — [1976 5f 6fg 5g 8.2f 6v] workmanlike colt: in rear on all outings, including in a valuable seller: not certain to stay 1m: blinkered final outing. *M. W. Easterby.*

MAID FOR TWO 2 br.f. King's Troop 118–Tambresi 89 (Tamerlane 128) **67** [1976 5g⁴ 5fg³ 5fg⁵ 5f⁵ 5g] small, close-coupled filly: half-sister to 3-y-o middle-distance winner Tamingo (by Never Say Die): 920 gns yearling: dam won at 7f and 1m: showed form in varied company: behind in £1,900 seller at Sandown in September on final outing: should stay 1m. *S. Ingham.*

MAID OF WALES 4 b.f. Welsh Saint 126–Lady Captain (Never Say Die 137) **73** [1974 7s 7s 1975 6f³ 8f² 8f² 8f* 8f³ 12g³ 12g³ 1976 10.2g⁶ 12fg⁵ 8g³ 10.2fg² 10f⁴ 8h⁵] ex-Irish filly: useful performer at 3 yrs: didn't show the same form in this country in 1976: stays 1½m: acts on firm going: blinkered last two outings: sold 1,100 gns Newmarket September Sales. *W. Wharton.*

MAIN CHANCE 3 gr.f. Midsummer Night II 117–Grande Mere 87 (Grandmaster) **63** [1975 7.2s 5v 1976 6f 7.6s⁴ 9.4g 8f 9fg³ 10f 10.4fg⁶ 11.5d⁵ 11f* 10v 12v] shapely filly: led close home when winning 10-runner maiden race at Hamilton in September by a neck from Service Charge: stays 11f: acts on any going except heavy: wears blinkers: ran poorly last two outings. *W. Elsey.*

MAIN EVENT 2 gr.c. Birdbrook 110–Limena 67 (Pinza 137) [1976 5fg⁵ 5g⁵ **89** 6g 7g 7fg³ 7fg*] strong, good-topped colt: brother to 3-y-o Partridge Brook, a very tough and useful winner at up to 1¼m, and to a winning hurdler: 5,600 gns yearling: dam stayed 1½m: improved steadily and won 20-runner maiden race at Leicester in September all out by a head from Atwood: will stay 1¼m. *B. Swift.*

MAIN LINE 2 ch.c. High Line 125–Maizenrose 89 (Rustam 127) [1976 6fg 7fg] — second foal: half-brother to very useful 3-y-o sprinter Minstrel (by Crooner): dam stayed 1m: behind in maiden races at Newmarket in July. *J. Powney.*

MAI TAI 2 ch.f. Charlottown 127–Tulita 73 (Tudor Melody 129) [1976 7g 7s] — second foal: dam, half-sister to very speedy 1967 Irish 2-y-o Fatima's Gift, won over 6f: showed signs of a little ability in maiden races, finishing tenth of 20 to Brightly at Newmarket in October. *B. Hanbury.*

MAITLAND 4 br.c. Stupendous–Maintenon (Vandale) [1974 N.R. 1975 10g* **120** 12g* 12.5g* 12fg⁶ 12.5g⁵ 1976 12g* 12g* 12.5g] French colt: very smart performer: successful twice at Saint-Cloud at 4 yrs, beating Saquito 2½ lengths when winning Group 2 Prix Jean de Chaudenay in June on second occasion: not seen out after finishing seventh of eight to Riverqueen in Group 1 Grand Prix de Saint-Cloud the following month and has been sent to race in U.S.A.: stays 12.5f. *A. Penna, France.*

MAJESTIC BAY 2 b.c. Runnymede 123–Joie de Vie (Never Say Die 137) **83** [1976 5g² 6f 7fg² 6fg 7g⁵] big, strong colt: closely related to quite useful stayer Splice the Mainbrace (by Petition) and half-brother to several other winners: 4,100 gns yearling: dam unraced daughter of good stayer Sea Parrot: second in maiden races at Leicester and Ayr in the summer: came out best of stand-side group when about 10 lengths fifth of 23 to Windy Sea in maiden event at Newmarket in October: stays 7f. *V. Mitchell.*

MAJESTY 5 ch.h. Sir Ivor 135–Dolina (Saint Crespin III 132) [1974 8fg³ 10g² 12g³ 12f² 13.3g³ 12fg⁴ 12g* 12v³ 1975 12fg³ 13.3fg³ 12g⁵ 12fg² 12fg² 12s⁵ 12g* 1976 12fg² 14.7d³ 12f] rangy, good-looking horse, and a good mover: fair handicapper nowadays: not seen out after June in 1976: suited by 1½m or more: acts on any going: has worn blinkers. *M. Jarvis.* **88**

MAJOR BEE 6 ch.h. Majority Blue 126–Beelet (Royal Hamlet 115) [1974 5s 5h⁴ 5s⁴ 5fg⁴ 5fg³ 6.3fg 6.3g 5f 1975 6s 5d 5f 7.6f 5fg² 5f³ 5f 5g 5s 1976 5s⁶ 7f* 7g⁶ 7f³ 6.3f 7f* 9f 6.3g* 7f³ 5fg 5f² 6g⁵ 5s 8s⁶] lengthy, attractive horse: useful Irish handicapper: did well at 6 yrs, winning at Leopardstown, Phoenix Park and the Curragh, gaining his final success when beating Little Trilby 2 lengths on last-named course in July: narrowly beaten in Philips Electrical Rockingham Stakes at the Curragh the following month: made two appearances over here and ran creditably on second of them (lost all chance at start on first), finishing about 4 lengths fifth of 18 to Last Tango in Burmah-Castrol Ayr Gold Cup at Ayr in September: effective from 5f to 7f: acts on any going but is well suited by firm: has worn blinkers. *Sir Hugh Nugent, Ireland.* **104**

MAJOR FLORA 2 b.f. Major Portion 129–Peony (Psidium 130) [1976 7g 8v] small filly: behind in sellers at Newmarket and Leicester in the autumn. *R. Hannon.* **—**

MAJOR GREEN 5 b.h. Double-U-Jay 120–Breathalyser (Alcide 136) [1974 7fg³ 8g² 10f² 12fg⁴ 12g* 12s* 12s² 12s³ 1975 12v² 10s³ 12g 1976 12fg* 12f⁴ 16g² 13.3g* 12g³ 12fg² 12s 13.3fg⁵ 12g³ 16s⁵] rangy, good sort of horse: smart performer: turned in a fine effort when 3 lengths third of six to Quiet Fling in Group 1 Coronation Cup at Epsom in June: ran well on several of his other outings, winning minor event at Leicester in March and Aston Park Stakes at Newbury in May and finishing in frame in Paradise Stakes at Ascot, John Porter Stakes at Newbury, Princess of Wales's Stakes at Newmarket and Cumberland Lodge Stakes at Ascot (penultimate start, 6½ lengths behind Bruni, in Sep- **115**

Mr C. A. Blackwell's "Major Green"

tember): stays 2m: acts on any going: genuine, and consistent until running very badly on eighth and final appearance. *J. Winter.*

MAJOR ISLE 2 ch.f. Major Portion 129–Calleva (Worden II 129) [1976 5g 6g⁵ 7d 8s] big, strong filly: little worthwhile form in varied company. *W. Wightman.* —

MAJOR JOHN 3 b.c. Majority Blue 126–Amanda Jane 75 (Rustam 127) [1975 5g 6fg⁴ 5f* 5fg³ 5.3f⁴ 6s 6g 6d² 1976 5g 5f⁴ 6fg 6fg 6fg⁵ 6d 6f⁶ 6fg⁶ 6g⁵ 6f* 6fg² 6f³] small, sturdy colt: good walker: fairly useful handicapper: winner at Brighton in June: creditable second to Allez Britain at Windsor in August, better subsequent effort: stays 6f: probably acts on any going: wears blinkers nowadays. *W. Marshall.* **90**

MAJOR LANE 2 b.c. Capistrano 120–Tess 90 (Road House II) [1976 5g⁶] first living produce: 1,600 gns foal, resold 6,200 gns yearling: dam won over 5f and 6f at 2 yrs, and is half-sister to three very useful animals: 8/1, ran creditably when 10 lengths sixth of 18 to Tudor Lilt in maiden race at Leicester in June (flag start): refused to enter stalls at Salisbury the previous month: will stay 6f. *G. Hunter.* —

MAJOR PINTA 3 ch.g Major Portion 129–Drinka Pinta 101 (Court Feathers 120) [1975 6fg 1976 12fg 16.1v 10v⁴] fair sort: no worthwhile form, including in a seller. *P. Cundell.* —

MAJOR RAMA 3 b.c. Amber Rama 133–Shineberry 93 (St Paddy 133) [1975 6g 7g 7d 7g 1976 10g⁶ 10g 8g] well-made colt: plating-class maiden: tried in blinkers second outing. *G. Pritchard-Gordon.* —

MAJOR ROLE 6 ch.g. Major Portion 129–Ysolda 100 (Elopement 125) [1974 8d 10d⁶ 10fg 7.6g² 8fg⁶ 7s 14s⁶ 7.6v³ 1975 9g 8g² 8d* 10.6v* 1976 10g 10fg 7.6fg 7.3d 10s⁵ 10s² 8.2v* 12v] well-made, attractive gelding: moderate handicapper nowadays: narrow winner at Nottingham in October: put up his only other worthwhile display in 1976 (ran deplorably in three of his races) on sixth start when 4 lengths second to Gold Claim at Sandown earlier same month (had none too clear a run): stays 1½m well: suited by plenty of give in the ground: has worn blinkers but does better without: needs to be held up. *B. Swift.* **85**

MAJOR THOMPSON 2 ch.c. Brigadier Gerard 144–St Pauli Girl 114 (St Paddy 133) [1976 6fg] big, strong colt: half-brother to two winners, including fairly useful 1½m winner Light Lager (by Crepello): dam runner-up in 1,000 Guineas and Oaks: 14/1 and poorly drawn, started none too well and never got into race when in rear behind Pollerton in 20-runner Convivial Stakes at York in August: has plenty of scope and will do better at 3 yrs. *G. Pritchard-Gordon.* — p

MAKE A SIGNAL 3 ch.f. Royal Gunner–Look Out 84 (Vimy 132) [1975 7.2fg⁴ 7v³ 7g² 7.2v 1976 8d⁶ 11s⁴ 12.2f³ 10h² 11g* 9h⁶ 11h* 12v* 13v* 12v*] compact filly: won minor event at Ayr in August but really came into her own in the autumn when raced in blinkers, picking up handicaps at Hamilton, Nottingham and Leicester (two): made virtually all when beating Ben Donachan unchallenged by 4 lengths on last-named course in November: will stay further than 13f: acts on any going but is well suited by heavy. *S. Hall.* **76**

Irish Sweeps Derby, the Curragh—Malacate wins in clear-cut fashion from Empery and Northern Treasure

MALACATE 3 b.c. Lucky Debonair–Eyeshadow (My Babu 136) [1975 7.5g* **131**
8d⁶ 1976 11fg* 10.5g* 10g* 12g³ 12f* 12g⁵ 11d³ 10g* 10d⁴]
  The Irish Derby has grown in stature since the Irish Hospitals began their
sponsorship in 1962. Of the eight Epsom Derby winners and one Prix du
Jockey-Club winner to have contested the race in the past fourteen years all
except Santa Claus, Nijinsky and Grundy have gone away defeated; and in 1976
Empery, winner of the Epsom Derby and a better horse at the distance than any
three-year-old trained in England or Ireland, was beaten easily and entirely on
merit in the race by Malacate. Short of attracting Youth and possibly Twig Moss
from France, the Irish Sweeps Derby could not have had better colts in its field
at that stage of the season than Malacate and Empery.
  Malacate rose to the top in a very short space of time. Two months before
he ran third to Youth and Twig Moss in the Prix du Jockey-Club at Chantilly in
June he had begun the season in a handicap, the Prix des Epinettes at Longchamp, which he had won from Loosen Up and Rec The Toolhouse, giving 4 lb to
the runner-up and 5 lb to the third. Loosen Up, beaten a length and a half, and
Rec The Toolhouse were to be found towards the bottom of the previous season's
Handicap Optional, 22 lb and 24 lb respectively behind Manado. Malacate had
won one of his two races as a two-year-old, a maiden at Deauville; in the other he
had finished 20 lb behind French Swanee in sixth place in the Prix des Chenes,
four places in front of Rec The Toolhouse in the eleven-horse field. In the
period between his reappearance and his race in the Prix du Jockey-Club,
Malacate remained unbeaten. He won the Prix des Suresnes at Longchamp by
a length from Exceller and the Prix la Force, a pattern race over approximately
the same course, by a length and a half from the Poule d'Essai des Pouliches
fourth Start The Game with Happy New Year, Habitancum and Happy Tim, all
of whom had beaten Empery last time out, behind. On all three occasions
during the season Malacate was ridden for speed and he made a striking impression, closing fast very late-on after being held at the back. His third performance
was his best, for at the distance of around ten furlongs Start The Game and
company represented stronger opposition than Exceller, particularly as Exceller
was having his first outing of the year.
  Malacate again came from the back of the field in the Prix du Jockey-Club;
this time things didn't go so smoothly for him, though. He had the misfortune
to be carried very wide into the straight, and in a race run at a scorching pace he
then faced a tremendous task, especially as Youth was at least six lengths ahead
of him. He showed very fine acceleration, but so did Youth, and while Malacate
was passing opponent after opponent Youth sprinted into a clear lead halfway
up the straight, never to be challenged. Malacate, hard ridden, drew level with
Twig Moss and Ydja at the distance; then he could find no more, and he lost the
battle for second place by three parts of a length. Youth beat him by three and
three quarter lengths in the end. Malacate did not have the run of the race, but
there are no grounds for regarding him as an unlucky loser. Youth won by a
very decisive margin. Three months later Youth beat him on merit by just over
three lengths at level weights when the pair were first and third, separated by
Arctic Tern, in the Prix Niel, and Youth's overall record is better than Malacate's
too.
  Nevertheless, by the end of the July there existed some doubt as to whether
the result of the Prix du Jockey-Club gave a genuine indication of the relative
merit of the two horses. Malacate came out to account for Youth's stable-
companion Empery, without having to be shown the whip, in the Irish Sweeps
Derby and to finish in front of Youth in the King George VI and Queen Elizabeth
Diamond Stakes. Admittedly Youth could be excused his failure to secure a
better placing than ninth at Ascot after running very wide into the straight, yet it
had to be said that he never looked to be moving as easily as Malacate, who turned
for home ahead of him. Riding tactics on Malacate were changed after the Prix
du Jockey-Club, so presumably his connections took some of the blame upon
themselves for the manner of his defeat if not for the defeat itself. Malacate's
jockey gave no more start to good horses than he could reasonably avoid in the
Irish Sweeps Derby and in the King George, which is perhaps just as well seeing
that Oilfield in the first instance and Pawneese in the second ensured a strong
gallop. Malacate was never out of the first five for more than a few strides in a
seventeen-runner field at the Curragh, and (a far cry from Chantilly this!) he
raced in second place to Empery after Oilfield weakened early in the straight, with
only Hawkberry, Far North and Northern Treasure of the others threatening
danger. At Epsom Empery had managed to shake off such as Relkino, Oats and
Hawkberry in a similar position, although on much easier ground, but here he
hadn't the finishing speed to hold Malacate, who moved comfortably into the lead

Joe McGrath Memorial Stakes, Leopardstown—a smooth success for Malacate. Mart Lane (left) pips Niebo and Northern Treasure (obscured) for second place

a furlong and a half out and quickened to win by two and a half lengths. In the King George VI and Queen Elizabeth Diamond Stakes Malacate, starting fourth favourite behind Youth, Pawneese and Bruni at 13/2, kept up with the leaders all the way; he moved from third place to second as Ashmore began to tie up early in the straight and he held his place until a furlong from home. In the closing stages Bruni, Orange Bay and Dakota passed him, and he finished fifth, only two and a half lengths behind the winner.

Following his defeat by Youth in the Prix Niel at Longchamp in September Malacate missed the Prix de l'Arc de Triomphe in favour of the newly-instituted Joe McGrath Memorial Stakes run over a distance two furlongs shorter at Leopardstown. Considering the proximity of the new race to the Arc and to other big races that could foreseeably attract a similar type of entry, including such races as the Queen Elizabeth II Stakes and the Prix du Moulin de Longchamp run on the very same week-end as the Joe McGrath Memorial, the Irish authorities were perhaps lucky to get a foreign horse as good as Malacate in the line-up. However, he ruined the race as a contest, for there was nothing in Ireland to touch him. Malacate gave Piggott, deputising for the suspended Paquet, an armchair ride and won from Mart Lane, Niebo, Northern Treasure and Hawkberry after being handled with typical Piggott confidence. On this occasion Malacate began his run from about sixth position on the outside on the final turn and led, when his jockey allowed him, over a furlong out.

Malacate lost his only other race before being retired to stud, the Champion Stakes. Or did he? The way we look at the Champion Stakes and the way we would advise those thinking about using his services to look at the race, Malacate emerged as a winner as well as a loser. Certainly he finished only fourth behind Vitiges, Rose Bowl and Northern Treasure, but the first three all raced on faster ground on the other side of the track; conditions allowed him little chance against Vitiges, but in the well-contested race on the stand side he finished ahead after breaking last of all. To give some indication of the advantage the far-side runners enjoyed: the no-hoper Lottogift, slowly away on the far side and never at the races over there, managed to recover to a position almost level with the leaders of Malacate's group after going six furlongs. At this point Malacate was still in the rear, many lengths behind Vitiges and company. From then on he began to make progress; he led his group throughout the last two furlongs with only Lady Singer for company, and went down by around four lengths to Vitiges, a length and a half behind his old rival Northern Treasure. Malacate's merit was probably of much the same order as Vitiges'.

We can't suggest any measures to minimize the effect of the draw over the Rowley Mile that haven't been thought of before. Clearly some measure must be attempted when the fairness of a Grade One course is called into question and when huge sums of money—in stud fees, prize money and bets—are at stake on

Mme M-F. Berger's "Malacate" (P. Paquet)

the outcome of races like the Champion Stakes and the Guineas. Probably the only satisfactory solution will be to reduce the width of the course much more drastically than has already been done. If the course is to remain at its present width, then any improvement in the efficiency of the watering could prove beneficial; and if the difference in the nature of the ground between the two sides is always to be with us, to place the stalls as near to the far rail as possible would be a logical step. Even a field as large as the Champion field (nineteen runners) might not have divided if the stalls had been moved much further across than they actually were, especially when the advantage to be gained from racing on the far side had by then become fairly obvious to most people.

Malacate (b.c. 1973)	Lucky Debonair (b 1962)	Vertex (ch 1954)	The Rhymer
			Kanace
		Fresh as Fresh (b 1957)	Count Fleet
			Airy
	Eyeshadow (b 1959)	My Babu (b 1945)	Djebel
			Perfume II
		Pretty One (b 1947)	Bull Dog
			Irvana

Malacate has been retired to the Grangewilliam Stud, Maynooth, one of the Airlie Stud complex, after being syndicated with Captain Tim Rogers and Mme Felix Berger each taking a quarter of the shares. Shares were reportedly priced at £11,500, which is considerably below the reported price of a share in Empery. Malacate is American-bred, by the Kentucky Derby winner Lucky Debonair out of a mare by the imported Guineas winner My Babu, and was extremely well bought at 40,000 dollars as a yearling at the Keeneland Summer Sale. Mme Felix Berger paid almost twice as much two years earlier in the same sale-ring for her future Prix du Jockey-Club winner Caracolero, who was, incidentally, well beaten in the Irish Sweeps Derby. Lucky Debonair, not a fashionable stallion in the United States, was sold in 1975 for export to Venezuela. The dam, Eyeshadow, ran twice unplaced. She has produced seven winners in the States, none of them anywhere near so important as Malacate although Barbizon Jr. (by Barbizon) was placed in four stakes races; perhaps the most interesting of her winners are El Macho (by Forward Pass) who set a track record for a distance of three furlongs at Gulfstream Park, and One King (by the Wokingham winner Silver King) who set a track record for a mile at Tropical Park. Eyeshadow is a half-sister to a good winner called Cool Prince.

Malacate had a lot to like about him as a racehorse. He was one of the best of his age at a distance of a mile and a quarter as well as a mile and a half, he seemed to have the ability to act on any going and, to his credit, he could be relied on to give his running in France, Ireland or England, on any type of track. None could have been more dependable. In appearance he is a well-made, good sort of colt. *F. Boutin, France.*

MALAYSIAN RUBBER   2 ch.c. Saintly Song 128–Babuette 93 (Our Babu 131)   —
[1976 6g⁵]   half-brother to two winners, including fairly useful 1973 2-y-o 5f performer Burglar's Moll (by Burglar): 2,500 gns yearling: dam disappointing maiden at up to 1½m: beaten about 10 lengths when fifth of eight to dead-heaters Jona and Bedlam Hill in maiden race at Ayr in July: sold 800 gns Doncaster November Sales. *M. W. Easterby.*

MALIN COURT   3 br.f. Major Portion 129–Ritual 79 (Right Royal V 135)   **95**
[1975 7g* 7fg* 8g3   1976 8.2d² 9g* 10fg⁶ 8h* 8fg⁶ 12fg 10g⁴ 8g*]   leggy filly: clear-cut winner of £3,200 handicap at Ayr in September, beating Gemina 1½ lengths: had previously won weakly-contested minor events at Hamilton and Carlisle and taken on much stronger opposition on her other starts: probably stays 1¼m: appears to act on any going: sold 8,000 gns Newmarket Autumn Sales. *N. Angus.*

MALINOWSKI   3 b.c. Sir Ivor 135–Best in Show (Traffic Judge)   [1975 6f* 7fg² **123** 1976 8fg*]

We aren't a lot wiser about Malinowski's racing merit than we were at the end of 1975. His very easy win in maiden company and his second to Wollow in the William Hill Dewhurst Stakes on his only appearances as a two-year-old we took as revealing great potential rather than indicating outstanding ability. And his win by two and a half lengths from Oats in the Ladbroke Craven Stakes at Newmarket on his only appearance as a three-year-old came much too early in the year for one to be able to make other than a tentative appraisal of him on it. True enough he beat Whistlefield, Navigator, Seadiver, Over To You and Radetzky as well as Oats that day, but who can say for what their opposition counted at that stage of their careers and at that distance? Our feeling at the time was that Malinowski had not enhanced his classic prospects, winning in workman-like not spectacular style, and that he would be better suited by longer distances than a mile. He had to be ridden to master Oats, who did not get a clear run in the Dip.   A series of minor setbacks kept Malinowski off the course subsequently. His stable had 'the virus' and, most unusually, failed to supply a runner for any English classic.

One thing that did come to light about Malinowski during the season was that we did him an injustice in *Racehorses of 1975* by inferring that as the Irish handicapper allotted him a top weight in the Madrid Free Handicap lower than

Ladbroke Craven Stakes, Newmarket—Malinowski wins in workmanlike style from Oats, Whistlefield (far side), Navigator (No. 11) and Seadiver

any of the previous six O'Brien top weights the handicapper necessarily regarded him as a lesser horse. An upper limit of 9-7 to the handicap was fixed in 1975; there was no such restriction in the years when Apalachee, Thatch, Roberto, Minsky, Nijinsky and Sir Ivor were at the top.

Malinowski (b.c. 1973)	Sir Ivor (b 1965)	Sir Gaylord (b 1959)	Turn-to
			Somethingroyal
		Attica (ch 1953)	Mr Trouble
			Athenia
	Best in Show (ch 1965)	Traffic Judge (ch 1952)	Alibhai
			Traffic Court
		Stolen Hour (ch 1953)	Mr Busher
			Late Date

Malinowski's career as a four-year-old should be of great interest. His very return to the racecourse will be sufficient indication that his trainer expects him to win good races, and probably Malinowski will, over distances of a mile and a quarter or more. Malinowski's half-sister Star of Bagdad (by Bagdad) who raced in England gave the impression that she would have stayed a mile and a half. His dam, a stakes winner at up to seven furlongs, is a granddaughter of the champion handicap mare Late Date, whose victories included the Washington Park Championship over a mile and a quarter. Malinowski is a lengthy colt. He didn't impress in appearance—he still needed to furnish—when we last saw him but it was very early in the season then, and he did impress with the way he moved, both in the paddock and on the way to the start. He acts on firm going. *V. O'Brien, Ireland.*

MALLOW 3 ch.f. Le Dieu d'Or 119–Ruffino 99 (Como 120) [1975 5fg 5g 5f⁵ 5f³ **51** 5f 5f³ 5g 1976 5f⁵ 5h³ 6g⁶ 5f] compact filly: plating-class maiden: often wears blinkers. *E. Weymes.*

MAM'SELLE MARRON 2 ch.f. Quayside 124–Sultry One (Tropique 128) — **p** [1976 5g 7g] rangy, useful-looking filly: half-sister to three winners, notably very smart miler General Vole (by Songedor): 1,700 gns yearling: dam ran only twice: behind in maiden races at Sandown in May and Newmarket in October. *R. Jarvis.*

MANADO 3 b.c. Captain's Gig–Slipstream 85 (Sing Sing 134) [1975 5g* 6d **123** 7s* 8g* 1976 7g² 8fg 10.5g 6.5d⁴ 8d⁴ 8d³ 8s³ 7s³]
Manado, indisputably the best two-year-old in France and in all probability the best of his age in Europe in 1975, went through his second season without a win. He failed to live up to the high hopes we held for him yet, for all that, he wasn't a complete failure: he proved himself one of the best milers trained in France, with only Gravelines palpably his superior; moreover he ran only two moderate races from eight starts, in the Two Thousand Guineas and the Prix Lupin, and on both those occasions there were feasible explanations for his failure.
Manado went into winter quarters in 1975 defeated only once in four outings, in the Prix Morny in which he had ruined his chance by swerving badly racing into the last two furlongs. His victories that had earned him top weight in the Handicap Optional and had encouraged Captain Tim Rogers to purchase a half-share in him for a figure reputedly in excess of £250,000 had come in the Prix Yacowlef, the Prix de la Salamandre, in which he beat the Prix Morny winner Vitiges by a length, and the Grand Criterium, in which he had one and a half lengths to spare over Comeram. It's illuminating to have another look at the Criterium result in the light of what was achieved in 1976 by the horses who finished close up behind Manado. Comeram showed smart form but won only one race. He wasn't good enough to win the two classics he contested, the French and Irish Two Thousand Guineas. French Swanee, Pier and Kano, third, fourth and fifth past the post in the Grand Criterium, in which they all received a 6-lb beating from Manado, failed to muster a single victory between them as three-year-olds.
Manado started a well-supported second favourite at 4/1 for the Two Thousand Guineas at Newmarket in April. He had been beaten a length by Vitiges in the Prix Djebel at Maisons-Laffitte earlier in the month but by all accounts Manado had been far from fully tuned up on that occasion whereas Vitiges had had the benefit of a previous outing. It seemed reasonable to assume that wherever Vitiges finished in the Guineas, Manado would be at least upsides him. Vitiges ran a cracking race, accounting for all except Wollow, but Manado,

after appearing to be going well on the heels of the leader until after halfway, beat a hasty retreat in the closing stages and finished in ninth-of-seventeen position, some nine lengths behind Wollow and seven and a half lengths behind Vitiges. Evidently Manado was unsuited by the firmish ground. Manado's next run, in the Prix Lupin over an extended mile and a quarter at Longchamp in May, was no less disappointing but this time it was probably the trip that accounted for his failure to gain a place in the first six. According to his jockey, Manado was travelling easily entering the straight but gradually ran out of steam and, in his opinion, Manado was a miler. Manado was rested until August and was never again asked to tackle distances in excess of a mile.

Manado returned with the Prix Jacques le Marois at Deauville as his first major objective. In preparation he ran in the six-and-a-half furlong Prix Maurice de Gheest on the same course a week before the Marois, performed most creditably and finished close up behind Girl Friend, Arch Sculptor and Realty. However, Manado didn't manage to win the Jacques le Marois: equipped with blinkers for the first time he finished fourth to Gravelines and the dead-heaters Radetzky and Vitiges in that remarkable blanket finish. Manado's trainer considered that a later challenge might have brought success; nonetheless it was an excellent effort by Manado, arguably his best of the season. Manado ran his last three races at Longchamp and on each occasion finished third: to Monsanto and Nurabad in the Prix du Rond-Point in September, to Gravelines and Dona Barod in the Prix du Moulin later in the month and to the two-year-olds Pharly and Lady Mere in the Prix de la Foret in October. In the Rond-Point he ran without blinkers for the only time after Deauville and ran a little below his best; in the Foret he would probably have finished closer had he not been hampered by Lady Mere.

Manado (b.c. 1973)	Captain's Gig (br 1965)	Turn-to (b 1951)	Royal Charger
			Source Sucree
		Make Sail (br 1951)	Ambiorix
			Anchors Aweigh
	Slipstream (gr 1967)	Sing Sing (b 1957)	Tudor Minstrel
			Agin the Law
		Palestream (gr 1959)	Palestine
			Millstream

A good sort of colt, Manado replaces the now-deceased Petingo at the Simmonstown Stud, Co. Kildare at a fee of 1,750 guineas with the no foal concession. He is a half-brother to the modest sprinter Riverenegold (by Klondyke Bill). Manado's two-year-old half-brother by Habitat, Thaliard, finished a close-up second in Ireland on his only outing. The dam, Slipstream (by Sing Sing), won over a mile as a three-year-old and is a daughter of a winning half-sister to numerous winners, including the Goodwood Cup winner Medway and the good racemare Reel In. Although there is plenty of stamina on the dam's side of Manado's pedigree it wasn't entirely surprising to see Manado find a mile his limit. His sire Captain's Gig was essentially a speedy horse who won eight races from six furlongs to a mile. The fact that Manado stayed a mile so well as a two-year-old may be due to the fact that he matured early—we remember well how he overshadowed less precocious animals in the paddock before the Grand Criterium. That he reached the height of his powers earlier than most of his age goes some way to explaining his lack of success in 1976. Although we saw the best of Manado as a two-year-old, he was, as we said, a good three-year-old when racing at distances up to a mile on an easy surface. *F. Boutin, France.*

MANDALUS 2 br.c. Mandamus 120–Laminate 117 (Abernant 142) [1976 6g2 **106** 6f* 6f* 6g3 6g 7d2 7s*] strong colt: good mover: half-brother to a minor winner in Ireland and to a winner abroad: 4,800 gns yearling: dam smart 5f winner at 2 yrs: winner of maiden race at Nottingham in June (beat Sealed Brief very comfortably by 2 lengths) and minor events at Doncaster the following month (just got home from Weisshorn after seeming to be nearly brought down at halfway) and Catterick in October (trounced The Bowler by 6 lengths): suited by 7f, and may get further: acts on any going: slowly away on fifth outing: useful. *Sir Mark Prescott.*

MANDAMAY 2 ch.f. Royben 125–Miss Amanda (Never Say Die 137) [1976 5f — 5f 5f 5fg 5.9f] no worthwhile form, including in a seller: unseated rider and bolted prior to finishing last on final appearance (July). *J. Thorne.*

MANDATE 3 b.c. Manacle 123–Good Service 88 (Espresso 122) [1975 5s4 5g* **103** 5fg 6g 5g 5g 1976 8fg2 8fg* 8g2 8g* 7fg* 8g4 8f3 8f* 11f 8d] neat, strong, shapely colt: useful handicapper: won at Brighton and Leicester in May and Sandown in June: produced a good turn of speed and put up his best performance when beating Step Ahead by a length on last-named course: also successful at Ostend in August, picking up valuable Prix Chevalier de Stuers by ½ length from Andrang: stays 1m (had very stiff task when tried at 11f): acts on firm going: blinkered last outing at 2 yrs: genuine and consistent: out of his depth (Group 3 race at Cologne) on final appearance. *R. Hannon.*

MANDRAKE MAJOR 2 b.c. On Your Mark 125–Flattered 91 (Zarathustra 131) **122**
[1976 6g² 5f* 5d* 6g³]

One couldn't wish for a better indication of the quality of horse trained in the north than that provided by a direct comparison of the weights allotted in the Tote (The Two-Year-Old) and the Northern Free Handicaps. Year in and year out the mean of the Northern Free Handicap falls ten to fourteen pounds below that of the Tote Free Handicap, and the north's champion two-year-old is seldom recognised officially as being among the leading half-dozen two-year-olds of the season. 1976 was no exception. Mandrake Major, who topped the Northern Free Handicap, is to be found in tenth-equal place in the Tote Free Handicap, a stone behind J. O. Tobin.

Whether Mandrake Major was all of a stone behind J. O. Tobin or not (and we don't think he was) he showed himself to be a good two-year-old, and a speedy one. The Flying Childers Stakes, the season's only Group 1 race for two-year-olds run over five furlongs, fell to him at Doncaster in September on his third outing. And it wasn't handed to him on a plate. There were some fast youngsters in the field, and Mandrake Major, racing under the stand rails, had to work hard first to catch Song of Songs and then to fight off La Ville de Rire and Piney Ridge, before going on to win by a length.

On the evidence of his display in the Flying Childers Stakes one might have been tempted to say that Mandrake Major found five furlongs a shade on the sharp side, but only a speedy horse can win a well-contested and strongly-run Group 1 race over five furlongs, and it might perhaps give a better impression of Mandrake Major if we were to say that he is not a five-furlong sprinter pure and simple, and over six furlongs in the William Hill Middle Park Stakes at Newmarket on his next appearance he reproduced to the pound his form with La Ville de Rire when finishing a good third behind Tachypous and Nebbiolo. Coming from behind, he looked a threat in the Dip, only to find the first and second just too good in the last hundred yards. He was beaten a length and the same.

That Mandrake Major would train on into a two-year-old good enough to compete in top company was suggested by his performance on his first outing, when he finished second to Avgerinos in the Granville Stakes for newcomers at Ascot in July. Backed from 14/1 down to 7/1 in a field of seven, he led two furlongs out until collared near the finish. This proved to be useful form—Ad Lib Ra, Birkholm and Casino Boy were among those behind—and that Mandrake Major would improve was evident from his backward appearance in the paddock. Next time out saw him favourite at 11/8 on in the Isleham Maiden Stakes at Newmarket, and after getting behind in the early stages he stormed into the lead

Flying Childers Stakes, Doncaster—Mandrake Major keeps on strongly to hold off La Ville de Rire and Piney Ridge (No. 11)

inside the last furlong to win easily and impressively by three lengths.

Mandrake Major (b.c. 1974)	On Your Mark (ch 1964)	Restless Wind (ch 1956)	Windy City
			Lump Sugar
		Super Scope (ch 1958)	Swaps
			Weeber
	Flattered (br 1960)	Zarathustra (bl 1951)	Persian Gulf
			Salvia
		Flatter (ch 1947)	Rockefella
			Daring Miss

Thus Mandrake Major had four races as a two-year-old, and was never out of the first three. A well-grown, good sort of colt, who cost 16,500 guineas as a yearling, he is a half-brother to two winners, including the fairly useful middle-distance handicapper Huzzar (by Hardicanute). Flattered, a disappointing racemare placed at seven furlongs and a mile, is a half-sister to Flattering, the dam of the One Thousand Guineas winner Humble Duty. Mandrake Major's breeding (his sire, though essentially a speedy horse, won at up to eight and a half furlongs) gives him reasonable prospects of staying beyond six furlongs, but we fancy he'll turn out to be a sprinter. He appears to act on any going. *Denys Smith.*

MANHILL 3 br.c. Grisaille 115–Fiery Flo 78 (Firestreak 125) [1975 5f⁵ 5fg⁴ **64** 6f 1976 10.2fg 8g 8f⁶ 9.4h³ 7fg 6f²] plating-class maiden: ran best race over 6f. *R. Hollinshead.*

MANIFESTATION 4 b.f. Forli–Miss Midway (Reneged) [1974 N.R. 1975 **73** 10g² 8s 10.5d* 10.5s 1976 9fg 10.2g 8f⁶ 7.2d 7g 10f⁶ 11.7f*] big American-bred filly: useful performer when trained in France at 3 yrs by A. Penna: turned in by far her best effort in this country when winning seven-runner handicap at Windsor in August by ½ length from Persian King: stayed 1¼m: probably acted on any going: stud in South Africa. *P. Makin.*

MANILATA 3 b.f. Dancer's Image–Miss Sun Tan (Sunglow) [1975 5g* 5g* **115** 5.5g 1976 7.3f³ 8fg 6f⁵ 6fg² 6fg³ 6s⁶ 6g 8g* 7s²] well-made, good-quartered ex-German filly: sister to poor middle-distance performer Sleek and moderate French miler Unsolicited, and half-sister to a winner in U.S.A.: 5,000 gns yearling: dam a useful winner in U.S.A. and out of half-sister to Dan Cupid: successful at Dortmund and Cologne at 2 yrs: won Severals Stakes at Newmarket in October in good style by 1½ lengths from Early Dawn: had several other smart performances to her credit, including when close-up third under 9-7 to Sonnenblick in Wykeham Handicap at York in August and when ½-length second to Janes Joker in handicap at Newmarket in October: effective at 6f to 1m: acted on any going: sometimes gave trouble going into stalls: stud. *H. Wragg.*

MAN IN THE MOON 2 b.c. Buckpasser–Clear and Cold (Nearctic) [1976 6fg* **112** 6f* 7f² 6d⁴ 7s² 7d] strong, attractive, well-made American-bred colt: third foal: half-brother to a minor winner in U.S.A. by Olden Times: dam won seven times at up to 1m in U.S.A.: impressive winner of Fenwolf Stakes at Ascot in June and of three-runner Cock of the North Stakes at Haydock the following month, accounting for Great Oak on each occasion: second twice afterwards, going down by 2 lengths to Nice Balance when odds on for four-runner Seaton Delaval Stakes at Newcastle in August, but proving no match at weights for Saros (rec 14 lb) in £1,500 event at Goodwood the following month and being beaten 4 lengths: well-beaten eighth of 11 behind The Minstrel in William Hill Dewhurst Stakes at Newmarket in October: should stay 1¼m. *I. Balding.*

Tote Free Handicap, Newmarket—a well-timed challenge by Ron Hutchinson lands Man of Harlech (nearest camera) the winner by a neck from Pirate Dream

Mr Paul Mellon's "Man in the Moon"

MAN OF HARLECH 3 b.c. Welsh Pageant 132–Dauphine 102 (Pampered King **108**
121) [1975 6fg⁶ 6g* 6f* 7h* 7f³ 1976 7fg* 7.6fg⁴ 8fg 7.6g⁴ 10d⁶ 7s 7s⁶ 8s]
neat colt: good mover: dam genuine but rather one-paced stayer: put up a
smart performance when winning Tote Free Handicap at Newmarket in April by a
neck from Pirate Dream: reportedly coughing afterwards and didn't race again
until July but showed he had retained all his ability when very good fourth of
12 under top weight behind Yunkel in valuable Gatwick Handicap at Lingfield in
August on fourth outing: was below his best afterwards but was probably racing
on unsuitable ground: should stay middle distances (had stiffish task and was
never in race on only attempt at 1¼m): acts on hard going: should resume winning
ways as a 4-y-o. *J. Dunlop.*

MAN'S GLOW 4 b.g. Mandamus 120–Crimson Glow 89 (Firestreak 125) [1974 —
7d 6d 1975 8g 6f⁵ 6g⁴ 1976 10fg⁵] big, rangy gelding: plating class: tailed
off in handicap at Pontefract on only outing in 1976: best run at 6f, but should
stay 1m: sold 1,250 gns Ascot September Sales. *W. Stephenson.*

MANS-LIB 2 b.c. Caliban 123–Manerica (Mandamus 120) [1976 5fg 6fg 6fg —
6g 8fg 10v 8.2v] small colt: bad plater: wears blinkers nowadays. *A. Davison.*

MANTOP 4 b.c. Tamerlane 128–Final Bridge (Welsh Abbot 131) [1974 6g 6d **71**
8d 1975 8v⁴(dis) 10h³ 10.1fg⁴ 10.1f* 10.1fg 12g⁵ 12g⁴ 1976 12fg* 10fg⁴ 11.7fg³
12f² 12f* 10fg* 12fg⁴ 12fg 12g³ 14fg] small colt: did well at 4 yrs, winning at
Leicester (twice) and Ascot: may well stay further than 1½m: acts on firm going:
effective with or without blinkers: good mount for an apprentice. *C. Brittain.*

MANTRA 3 br.f. Tudor Melody 129–Zambesi 87 (Vimy 132) [1975 7g² 6f⁶ —
7fg⁴ 7g³ 7g⁶ 1976 9f³ 8d⁵ 9.4g 12.2g 8f 8.2v] useful sort: disappointing maiden:
often wears blinkers: left in stalls third outing: sold 1,100 gns Newmarket
December Sales. *E. Weymes.*

MANY COLOURS 10 b.g. Pinza 137–Colours 115 (Turbido) [1974 N.R. —
1975 N.R. 1976 8h⁶ 11g⁶] strong, dipped-backed gelding: has been fired:
quite a moderate handicapper in 1970: well beaten in two sellers since. *J. Cousins.*

443

MANZONI 4 bl.g. Murrayfield 119–Edwina Black 90 (High Treason 126) —
[1974 5fg 6s 6d⁴ 8s⁵ 6v⁴ 1975 10.8d⁴ 9fg 1976 13v] compact gelding: plating-
class on Flat but is a fair hurdler: stays at least 1m: blinkered only appearance in
1976. *D. Gandolfo.*

MAORI WARRIOR 2 b.c. Deep Diver 134–Maori Princess 91 (Linacre 133) 72 d
[1976 5g³ 5f² 5f³ 5f⁵ 5.3fg 5f] neat, sharp, early sort: placed in early-season
maiden races but did not progress and ran poorly in blinkers on penultimate
outing: possibly doesn't truly stay 5f: sold 825 gns Ascot July Sales. *G. Hunter.*

MAPLE SYRUP 3 ch.f. Charlottown 127–Sweet Solera 129 (Solonaway 128) 63
[1975 6g⁴ 6f² 7d 1976 10fg³ 12fg⁴ 10fg² 10.1fg² 10f³] rather lightly-built filly:
good mover: usually finds one or two too good for her: runs as though she will be
suited by 1½m+: possibly not at her best on an easy surface: ran respectably
when tried in blinkers on final outing. *J. Bethell.*

MAPLIN SANDS 3 br.f. Golden Dipper 119–Kermene 89 (Persian Gulf) [1975 —
N.R. 1976 8fg] second reported foal: half-sister to a minor winner: dam won at
1¼m and 11f: unquoted and ridden by 7-lb claimer when well-beaten eighth of 14
to Silver Yarrow in maiden race at Salisbury in June. *P. Cundell.*

MARCH 3 b.c. Highland Melody 112–Marking Ink 86 (Mark-Ye-Well) [1975 59
6f⁶ 6g⁴ 6g 8g 1976 5fg 5f⁴ 6fg⁵ 6g] big, strong colt: ran moderately behind
Walter in seller at Newcastle in August on final outing: gives impression that he
needs further than 5f but is not certain to stay 1m: blinkered first appearance:
bandaged off-hind third outing. *J. W. Watts.*

MARCHESANA 2 b.f. March Past 124–Tanisia 90 (Persian Gulf) [1976 6fg 6g⁶ 68
9fg 8g⁶] fifth produce: dam won twice at 1½m: showed a little ability in maiden
races. *R. Jarvis.*

MARCHING ON 2 b.c. Tudor Melody 129–Procession 118 (Sovereign Path 125) 90
[1976 5f⁴ 5g* 6d* 6d⁶] rangy, attractive colt: half-brother to moderate 1¼m
winner Captain's Escort (by Royal Palace): dam 5f sprinter: impressive winner
of two races in north, beating Silver Cygnet by 2 lengths despite being eased at
Carlisle in May, and running out a 5-length winner of 17-runner event at Ripon
the following month: not seen out again until September when 6 lengths sixth of
seven to Our Jimmy in £2,200 nursery at Ascot: will stay 7f: acts on a soft surface:
ridden by apprentice C. Nutter on last two outings. *Sir Mark Prescott.*

MARCH MEMORY 3 b.g. March Past 124–Memo (Faust 122) [1975 N.R. —
1976 7g 11s 13s⁴ 15f] probably of little account. *H. Bell.*

MARCH MORNING 3 b.g. Alcide 136–Grisella (Grey Sovereign 128 §) [1975 59
N.R. 1976 10g 16f³ 14fg² 13g⁴ 13fg⁴ 14f⁴ 16f² 14d 13.1f] second foal: 500 gns
yearling: dam won at 6f: showed a little ability in maiden races, on seventh
outing wandering about when coming off bridle (blinkered): ran moderately (not
blinkered) last two outings: stays 1¾m but possibly not 2m. *R. Supple.*

MARCHUNA 4 br.f. March Past 124–Sultry One (Tropique 128) [1974 6d 6fg 90
5.9fg⁵ 6s⁴ 8s² 8v 7s* 6d⁴ 1975 10g 8g 8g² 8g* 8.2d* 8d 8g 8.2v 1976 8.2f 8d⁶
8v* 8.2v 7.6v*] tall, leggy filly: fairly useful handicapper: winner at Leicester in
October and at Lingfield the following month: stays 1m: suited by a soft surface
and revels in the mud. *R. Jarvis.*

MARCO RICCI 4 b.c. Herbager 136–Double Drift (Double Jay) [1974 7d 112
1975 8s 10s 12g5 12g² 11fg* 12f² 12g6 14.7f* 14fg² 16g 1976 12f⁶ 16g* 16g³ 22.2f⁴
20.9fg⁶] tall, rangy American-bred colt: put up a very fine performance when
winning Paradise Stakes at Ascot in May by a neck from Major Green, making all
the running and keeping on exceptionally gamely under very strong driving: 4½
lengths third of six to Sea Anchor in Group 3 Henry II Stakes at Sandown the
following month: well beaten over extreme distances on last two appearances and
appears best at up to 2m: acts on firm going: has worn blinkers but does just as
well without: genuine and consistent: sent to race in America. *B. Hills.*

MARCUS GAME 6 br.g. Marcus Superbus 100–Miss Givens (Prince's Game 67) 67
[1974 8h⁵ 7g⁶ 7f⁴ 7fg⁴ 6f* 8g⁵ 6f* 7fg* 6h² 7d* 6d 8g 7fg² 6s 7s 1975 8g 7fg⁶ 6h
7.6g² 6f³ 7fg³ 7h² 7f² 7h² 8f 6g* 7f² 5f⁴ 6s² 6g⁴ 7fg² 7d 1976 6h³ 6h² 6f 6h 6h
7g 5fg⁴ 6s] strong gelding: quite a moderate handicapper nowadays: ran best
race at 6 yrs on seventh outing when fourth of 12 to Silver Camp at Beverley in
September: stays 1m but races mainly at shorter distances: acts on any going
but is ideally suited by top-of-the-ground conditions: excellent mount for a boy:
usually a very fast starter. *W. A. Stephenson.*

MARENNES BLUE 5 b.g. Majority Blue 126–Marennes 89 (Pearl Diver 130) —
[1974 7d² 7g⁶ 7g⁴ 6g* 6g⁶ 6g 6s² 6fg³ 1975 7f⁵ 7fg 7fg⁶ 7.6f⁵ 7g⁴ 7f² 7.2fg⁶ 7.2fg³

444

Mr Henry Keswick's "Mar Greig"

7g 6g 1976 8g] strong, compact gelding: fair handicapper: ran respectably in Irish Sweeps Lincoln on only start in 1976, having every chance until weakening inside final furlong: stays 7f well: acts on any going: sometimes wears blinkers. *G. Balding.*

MAR GREIG 2 ch.c. Habitat 134–Cananea (Majority Blue 126) [1976 5fg 5f **101** 5fg* 5g⁴ 6g⁴ 5g⁴ 6s] neat colt: first foal: 12,500 gns yearling: dam a useful winner at up to 9f in France: had field well strung out when winning maiden race at Leicester in July and beat odds-on Chain of Reasoning ¾ length in seven-runner minor event at Ayr later in month: respectable fourth in £2,600 nursery at Kempton and Harry Rosebery Challenge Trophy at Ayr afterwards: suited by 6f and should stay further. *P. Walwyn.*

MARHILL BELL 4 ch.g. Gala Performance–Caracasana **§§** (Whistler 129) — [1974 N.R. 1975 N.R. 1976 14f 14g] strong, compact gelding: probably of little account. *M. Goswell.*

MARIA ALEXANDRIA 4 b.f. Czar Alexander 112–Maria Helena 104 (Miralgo — 130) [1974 6fg 7g 8s³ 9g² 1975 8v² 10.8s* 10f 13f* 12.2fg⁴ 16h² 16.5fg* 16f² 1976 16f³ 18.4s 14fg³ 16fg⁵ 16g⁵ 16.9f⁵] well-made, useful-looking filly: quite a moderate handicapper: ran respectably on first and third outings at 4 yrs: stays very well: acts on any going. *J. Welch.*

MARIE LOUISE 3 b.f. King Emperor–Trinity Term 100 (Primera 131) [1975 **86** 6fg 7f⁶ 1976 8f⁶ 8f⁶ 7.6s* 7g* 7.6g 6fg² 7g] strong, robust, deep-bodied filly: good walker: made all when winning maiden race at Chester in May and minor event at Catterick (wandered badly in straight) the following month: good second to Power Girl in handicap on former course in September but ran moderately final outing: effective at 6f and may stay further than 1m: appears to act on any going: wears blinkers. *Doug Smith.*

MARIE'S BOY 2 b.g. Boreen (Fr) 123–Fiddle Dancer 72 (Fidalgo 129) [1976 **62** 5f⁵ 5g² 5.1fg* 5f⁶ 7f] fair sort: bought in 900 gns after narrowly winning seven-runner seller at Yarmouth in May: not seen out again until August and had very stiff tasks on his return: should stay middle distances. *K. Payne.*

MARIINSKY 2 b.f. Nijinsky 138–Iron Maiden 87 (Klairon 131) [1976 7d 7s] — p big, strong filly: third foal: dam, daughter of very useful half-sister to Royal Charger, ran only three times: ninth of 20 to Brightly in maiden race at Newmarket in October, second and better effort: will stay 1¼m: has the scope to do better in time. *H. Wragg.*

MARINERS GIRL 2 b.f. Communication 119–Grey Sport 71 (Court Feathers 79 120) [1976 5g 5g⁴ 5fg³ 5f⁶ 5s² 5f 5f² 5g* 5fg² 6s 5v²] light-framed filly: half-sister to a winning 2-y-o 5f plater by Bounteous: bought privately 975 gns yearling: dam a sprinter: won seller at Ayr in August easily by 6 lengths (afterwards changed hands for 800 gns): also runner-up four times in varied company, going down by a neck to Pandu in nursery at Edinburgh in September and by a short head to Kabagold in claiming event at Leicester in November: not certain to stay beyond 5f. *J. Berry.*

MARINSKY (USA) 2 b.c. Northern Dancer–Thong (Nantallah) [1976 7fg*] 99 p American-bred Irish colt: half-brother to outstanding miler Thatch (by Forli), very smart 7f and 1m winner Lisadell (also by Forli) and to King Pellinore (by Round Table), a high-class middle-distance performer both here and in U.S.A.: $225,000 yearling: dam stakes-placed sister to three high-class performers, including champion 2-y-o Moccasin: 7/2 on for 16-runner newcomers event at the Curragh in September and ran out an impressive 3-length winner from Milverton with four subsequent winners behind: will be suited by 1m+: comes from an outstandingly successful family and looks like enhancing its reputation even further. *V. O'Brien, Ireland.*

MARIO'S BOY 3 b.c. Song 132–Musical Game (Big Game) [1975 N.R. 1976 67 8fg⁵ 8.5fg⁶ 7fg² 6g⁵ 7g] tall colt: third foal: 500 gns yearling: dam ran only once: showed some ability, but was rather disappointing when co-favourite for seller at Kempton in May on final appearance: stayed 7f: dead. *P. Ashworth.*

MARIS PIPER 4 ch.c. Queen's Colour–Nuxia (Narrator 127) [1974 8.2d 8s⁵ — 8s 10s 1975 13d³ 12.2v* 16s² 12g² 16f* 12.2f² 16h* 16fg⁵ 14fg 16h* 15d² 1976 12s 12v] big, strong colt: fair handicapper (rated 86) at 3 yrs: no worthwhile form in two outings in 1976 (didn't reappear until October): stays very well: acts on any going: consistent: good mount for a lady rider: sometimes sweats up. *R. Hollinshead.*

MARITIME DIVER 2 b.f. Stephen George 102–Wild Duck 94 (Amour Drake 67 129) [1976 5fg⁵ 5f³ 5f⁵ 5g⁶ 5f³ 5s* 7f 5fg] compact filly: attracted no bid after winning nine-runner seller at Ayr in June: should stay 7f: acts on any going, but goes particularly well on soft: blinkered fourth outing: sold to T. Craig 460 gns Doncaster September Sales. *R. Supple.*

MARJANA 3 gr.f. Birdbrook 110–Nicoline 88 (Falls of Clyde 126) [1975 5s² 5f⁵ 70 5fg* 6f³ 5f 5d⁴ 5g⁶ 1976 5g 5f 8fg⁶ 6fg⁴] light-framed filly: didn't reproduce her 2-y-o form, although showed some ability on final outing: probably stays 6f: acts on any going. *M. Masson.*

MARJULSAR 2 gr.f. Mummy's Pet 125–Margo's Pal 91 § (Palestine 133) 63 [1976 5fg³ 5f⁴ 5g⁴ 5fg 5.8f⁶ 5s⁶] small, sturdy filly: in frame in maiden and minor events but showed only a little ability. *G. Beeson.*

MARKDAIL 2 b.c. On Your Mark 125–Dail Elith (Tamerlane 128) [1976 6f 76 6fg³ 6fg 6g⁴ 5.1g] well-made colt: good mover: half-brother to two winners, including useful 1975 2-y-o 5f performer Leinster House (by Manacle): 2,000 gns yearling: dam ran only twice: in frame in maiden races at Newmarket in July (4½ lengths third to Etienne Gerard) and Kempton in August: needs further than 5f and will stay 7f+. *J. Winter.*

MARKET FRESH 2 b.f. Tamerlane 128–Native Love 77 (Native Prince) 57 [1976 5f 5fg 5f³ 6f* 7h 7f 7h 6f 5g 5.9fg 5d] robust filly: sold out of M. H. Easterby's stable 900 gns after running out a very easy 4-length winner of seller at Nottingham in June: last on most of her subsequent outings: should stay further than 6f: wears blinkers nowadays. *S. Nesbitt.*

MARKET SAGE 3 ch.c. Porto Bello 118–Miss Pandit 85 (Panaslipper 130) 87 [1975 6fg² 6g* 7.2s² 7g⁶ 7f³ 1976 10fg 10h² 12fg³ 8g⁵ 10.8s 11v³ 12s] tall, good sort of colt: blinkered first time when good fifth of 12 (had little chance at weights)

MAR

to Manilata in Severals Stakes at Newmarket in October: again blinkered when
running moderately afterwards: stays 1¼m: acts on any going: rather inconsistent. *H. Collingridge.*

MARKET TOWN 3 ch.f. Roi Soleil 125–Sedelia (Saint Crespin III 132) [1975 —
5g 5f 6fg 5f 1976 12fg] of no account. *J. Hardy.*

MARK HENRY 5 ch.g. Henry the Seventh 125–Anglo Indian 86 (Alycidon 138) **76**
[1974 9d⁴ 10f⁴ 16f² 16f* 14f* 14g* 14fg 16s* 14d 1975 18.4g 14.7f 15g* 16fg 15g²
16fg³ 16f³ 14.6g⁵ 1976 16fg³ 16f² 16fg 15g 14.7f³ 16fg⁴ 16f³] lengthy gelding:
quite a moderate handicapper: ran respectably in some of his races at 5 yrs,
including on sixth start when 9½ lengths fourth to Coed Cochion at York in
August: one paced and is suited by long distances: acts on any going: probably
best when ridden up with leaders. *W. Elsey.*

MARK HUSH 3 b.g. Lauso–Spring Exploit (Exploitation 108) [1975 N.R. 1976 **101**
10s⁴ 16d* 16f 14fg* 16fg] leggy gelding: second foal: half-brother to fair 2m
winner The Froddler (by Philemon): dam unraced half-sister to top-class chaser
Domacorn: won maiden race at York in May by 5 lengths from Belfalas and
handicap on same course in July by 4 lengths from Dikusa: very well suited by
a test of stamina: acted on firm and a soft surface but was said to be unsuited
by very firm ground: ran moderately under a stiff weight on final outing: broke
a leg on the gallops in September: dead. *J. W. Watts.*

MARK'S BOY 6 b.g. Setay 105–Oh Boy (Pandemonium 118) [1974 13g 1975 —
16.1fg 1976 12h²] of little account on flat but is a fair hurdler. *Dr A. Jones.*

MARKS DAME 2 b.f. Continuation 120–Karo Dame (Tudor Melody 129) —
[1976 5g 5g 5fg] unfurnished filly: half-sister to some useful animals but showed
no worthwhile form in maiden and minor events. *S. Wainwright.*

MARK'S GEM 2 ch.f. On Your Mark 125–Susceptible 86 (Supreme Court 135) —
[1976 5v 8.2s] big filly: half-sister to minor winners here and in France:
cost 950 gns in March, 1976: dam needed 1¼m+: behind in end-of-season maiden
and minor events. *J. Mulhall.*

MARK'S LAD 2 ch.c. Chebs Lad 120–Bolton Girl 87 (Blue Lightning 114) —
[1976 5g 5d] plain, narrow, unfurnished, leggy colt: half-brother to very smart
sprinter Polly Peachum (by Singing Strand): 250 gns yearling: dam stayed
1½m: outpaced when in rear in maiden races at Catterick and Nottingham in
September. *V. Mitchell.*

MARKUS 14 br.g. Nimbus 130–Dolphinet 96 (Big Game) [1974 N.R. 1975 8g —
7g 1976 8v⁶] of no account. *B. Richmond.*

MARLBOROUGH LASS 2 ch.f. Quisling 117–Barby Road 62 (Tin Whistle 128) **47**
[1976 5f⁴ 5g³ 5fg 5g⁵] poor plater: sold 230 gns Doncaster June Sales. *K. Payne.*

MARMELO 2 b.f. Tudor Melody 129–Jaffa 103 (Right Royal V 135) [1976 6g] **71 p**
fourth foal: sister to French middle-distance winner Brave Tudor and half-
sister to high-class 2-y-o and miler Jacinth (by Red God): dam consistent stayer:
25/1, showed up 4f when twelfth of 30 in maiden race won by Rheola at Newmarket in September: should do better, probably over longer distances. *B. Hills.*

MARMORA BAY 3 br.f. Silly Season 127–Antigua Anthem 76 (Nashua) [1975 **73**
5f⁴ 5s² 6g² 6g⁵ 6fg³ 7f⁵ 1976 8f 10f⁴ 9f⁴ 8fg 8h³ 7h⁶ 7.6fg³ 7.6s 7s*] strong,
well-made, attractive filly: quite a useful 2-y-o: mainly disappointing in 1976
but won end-of-season maiden race at Wolverhampton by 5 lengths despite
wandering off a true line when clear: stays at least 9f: acts an any going: ran
badly in blinkers on fourth outing: finds little off bridle. *I. Balding.*

MAROCK MORLEY 2 b.f. Most Secret 119–Nasca 81 (King's Bench 132) **59**
[1976 5g 5g⁵ 5fg² 5fg³ 5d 5.1f⁴ 5g³ 5f⁴ 5f⁴ 5f] small filly: quite a modest plater:
will be suited by 6f: trained most of season by D. Yeoman. *W. Stephenson.*

MAROON 3 b.f. Roan Rocket 128–Mulberry Harbour 118 (Sicambre 135) **92**
[1975 N.R. 1976 7f⁴ 10g² 12f* 12fg 12g⁴ 16s*] compact filly: half-sister to
several winners, including useful 9f winner Crest of the Wave (by Crepello):
dam a stayer: odds on, made all when winning five-runner maiden race at Lingfield in June comfortably by 6 lengths from Omnia: continued to run creditably
and gained a further success when beating Cavalier's Blush 1½ lengths under
top weight in handicap at Warwick in October: stays 2m: acts on any going.
R. Hern.

447

MARQUIS DE SADE 3 br.c. Queen's Hussar 124–Sweet Charity 96 (Javelot **126** 124) [1975 6g* 6d² 8g   1976 10.5s⁶ 8g² 10fg* 12f* 14f* 14.6d]

A week before the St Leger Marquis de Sade appeared to have as a good a chance as any horse, and better than most, of winning the big race: he was ante-post favourite, at odds as short as 11/4 in one book.   He had improved enormously since running unplaced in the Observer Gold Cup on the same course as a two-year-old and, unlike many of his opponents, he appeared to have more improvement in him.   He had won his last three races, the Trafalgar House Handicap at Sandown, the King Edward VII Stakes at Royal Ascot and the March Stakes at Goodwood.   In the King Edward VII Stakes Marquis de Sade had beaten one of the best of the English-trained staying three-year-olds, Smuggler, by half a length at level weights; in the March Stakes, run over the Leger distance a fortnight before the Leger, he had won a five-horse contest pushed out from Roses for the Star, Scallywag and Tierra Fuego, with Spiranthes well behind.   Roses for the Star, receiving 11 lb, had been beaten one and a half lengths, Scallywag, receiving 8 lb, three lengths and Tierra Fuego, carrying the same as the winner, three and a half lengths.   The form of the March Stakes might not be as outstanding as it looks—Roses for the Star was becoming disappointing, Scallywag had been well beaten in his previous race, the Great Voltigeur, and Tierra Fuego hadn't raced since finishing a remote third in the King Edward VII Stakes—but the race was run at a true pace and we are satisfied to take the form at its face value, which makes Marquis de Sade's performance one of the best returned by an English-trained three-year-old over a distance of ground in a season when good staying performances by English-trained three-year-olds were scarce.

But Marquis de Sade did not win the St Leger; he didn't even get in the first six, and both Scallywag and Smuggler finished ahead of him.   He didn't run a race at all, and was unable to keep up when the pace increased after turning for home.   Why did he run so poorly?   In the form book, which is always the first and usually the best place to turn for an answer to such a problem, there is an obvious explanation to be found.   An investigation of Marquis de Sade's record shows straight away that his best form is on a firm surface.   His second to Night Vision in the Duke of Edinburgh Stakes in 1975, a race run on ground on the soft side of good, is nothing to write home about, and his sixth to Trasi's Son in the Mecca-Dante Stakes at York on the occasion of his only run on really soft is moderate form.

Another obvious explanation for his poor showing, one not to be found in the form book, is that he might not have been one hundred per cent fit.   At the start of the Leger week rumour was rife that Marquis de Sade had something wrong

King Edward VII Stakes, Ascot—Marquis de Sade (right) and Smuggler have the finish to themselves

March Stakes, Goodwood—Marquis de Sade has too much finishing speed for Roses for the Star and Scallywag

with him, and after his trainer had admitted that Marquis de Sade had coughed twice on the gallops on the Tuesday, the horse disappeared from some ante-post list and in others received a quote of 3/1 with a run. By Saturday confidence in him had so decreased that he started at 13/2, a price longer than that of Crow, General Ironside and Oats.

There you have the two most likely reasons for Marquis de Sade's poor showing. To that you could add a third—that he wasn't good enough to do much better. Which you favour depends to some extent on how well you know the horse. We would rule out number three without hesitation and, not being privy to every detail of Marquis de Sade's medical history, we would strongly suspect that the ground played the major part in his downfall. It is beyond reasonable doubt, we would think, that he is best on a sound surface.

Marquis de Sade (br.c. 1973)	Queen's Hussar (b 1960)	March Past (br 1950)		Petition	
				Marcelette	
		Jojo (gr 1950)		Vilmorin	
				Fairy Jane	
	Sweet Charity (b 1966)	Javelot (b 1956)		Fast Fox	
				Djaina	
		Phoenissa (b 1951)		The Phoenix	
				Erica Fragrans	

Marquis de Sade is the best horse to win at as long a distance as a mile and three quarters sired by Brigadier Gerard's sire Queen's Hussar. Queen's Hussar never raced beyond a mile. The dam, Sweet Charity, won four races, the longest of them a thirteen-furlong handicap at Alexandra Park. Her two previous foals, the winner Gymnast (by Red God) and the maiden Matia's (by Klairon or Runnymede) appeared to be sprinters, although Gymnast raced only as a two-year-old. The next dam was a sprinter, out of a mare who won at a mile and a quarter and ran as though longer distances would suit her. Phoenissa, a half-sister to the disqualified winner of the 1958 Washington International Tudor Era, bred several winners besides Sweet Charity, notably the Champion Stakes winner Lorenzaccio. Marquis de Sade's owner also owned Lorenzaccio, which may be one reason why he bought Marquis de Sade as a yearling (for 9,600 guineas). Marquis de Sade's prospects as a four-year-old are uncertain. If he comes back to his best he will be an interesting prospect. *R. Price.*

MARRAKESH 2 ch.g. Karabas 132–Telouet 90 (Sing Sing 134) [1976 6d⁴ 7d] — third living foal: half-brother to useful 3-y-o sprinter Derringo (by Derring-Do): dam ran only four times: showed promise when fourth of 15 to very easy winner Supernaculum in maiden race at Yarmouth in September: 11/1 when behind in 25-runner Houghton Stakes won by Bessie Wallis at Newmarket the following month. *B. Hobbs.*

MARSHALL 3 b.g. Town Crier 119–Changra 74 (Flush Royal 127) [1975 6f 1976 10s 12g⁵ 12g⁵ 12fg* 11s 10v⁵] strong gelding: good walker: favourite, won weakly-contested minor event at Edinburgh in September by ¾ length from Medodosusu: had stiff tasks in handicaps afterwards but was far from disgraced on final outing: stays 1½m: appears to act on any going. *M. W. Easterby.* **63**

MARTELLO PIRATE 6 ch.g. Barbary Pirate 91–Santa Marta 51 (Lavandin 128) [1974 8s² 8.2g* 10.1f³ 10g³ 10.1g⁵ 8.3fg 10d 10s⁴ 11.1s 1975 N.R. 1976 6g⁴ 13g⁴ 10f⁶ 7fg 10h² 7.6s] poor selling handicapper: needs further than 6f and probably stays 13f: acts on any going: usually wears blinkers. *R. Sturdy.* —

MARTIN STEPHEN 6 ch.g. Florescence 120–Tilde §§ (Tropique 128) [1974 **67**
5f 6f⁵ 6f⁴ 5g⁶ 6d⁵ 5fg 7fg⁴ 6g* 6s⁵ 7g 1975 N.R. 1976 5h* 5f² 5f 7f⁴ 6h⁴ 5s⁵]
quite a moderate handicapper: won six-runner apprentice handicap at Redcar in
July (made all) by 4 lengths from Peter Culter: stays 7f: seems to act on any
going: used to wear blinkers but didn't at 6 yrs: sold 500 gns Doncaster October
Sales. *G. Toft.*

MART LANE 3 b.c. Le Levanstell 122–Marians 95 (Macherio) [1975 7g* **125**
1976 10f³ 12g³ 12f 10g² 12v*]
     But for the presence of Malacate, Mart Lane would have been an appropriate
winner of the first running of the Group 1 Joe McGrath Memorial Stakes at
Leopardstown in September. The race commemorates the founder of the
Brownstown Stud which bred Mart Lane. Although Malacate beat Mart Lane
by one and a half lengths without being asked a serious question the race marked
the emergence of Mart Lane as a good-class racehorse; his determined last-furlong
challenge brought him second place from Niebo by a short head with Northern
Treasure half a length away in fourth place and Hawkberry a well-beaten fifth
of the eleven runners.
     We need not concern ourselves with Mart Lane's form before the
Joe McGrath Memorial. He'd run only four times, winning a newcomers event
at Phoenix Park on his solitary outing as a two-year-old and finishing third to
Meneval on his first two outings in 1976, in the Nijinsky Stakes at Leopardstown
in May and the Gallinule Stakes at the Curragh later in the month. Meneval
beat him very easily on both occasions, and in the Gallinule the English-trained
Lost Chord beat him by a length. On the one occasion Mart Lane had tackled
proven top-class opposition, in the Irish Sweeps Derby, he had toiled in the rear
all the way and had been beaten over twenty lengths by Malacate, with Northern
Treasure, Hawkberry and Niebo all a long way in front of him. It seems likely
that the firm ground caused Mart Lane's poor showing. Certainly when Mart
Lane won the St Simon Stakes at Newbury on his final outing of the season he
encountered ground that could hardly have been more dissimilar to that on the
Irish Sweeps Derby day, for to say that conditions at Newbury were desperate
is no exaggeration; the track was so wet it was barely raceable. The pace in
the St Simon, set by Jolly Good, Swell Fellow and Roses for the Star, was a
strong one, too strong in view of the conditions. Approaching the final turn
the field was well strung out and in normal circumstances Mart Lane, well back
in eighth place at that point, wouldn't have had a hope of catching the leaders,
but once in the straight he made relentless headway and took up the running
over two furlongs from home. From that point he had the race in his pocket
and crossed the line eight lengths ahead of an exhausted Roses for the Star,
with Illustrious Prince four lengths away in third. Most of the remaining
runners trailed in at walking pace, the finish bearing a close resemblance to
the end of some three-mile steeplechases.

Mart Lane (b.c. 1973)	Le Levanstell (b 1957)	Le Lavandou (b 1944)	Djebel
			Lavande
		Stella's Sister (ch 1950)	Ballyogan
			My Aid
	Marians (ch 1963)	Macherio (ch 1941)	Ortello
			Mannozza
		Damians (ch 1942)	Panorama
			Thirteen

     After the St Simon Stakes Mart Lane's trainer remarked that Mart Lane
would make up into a Cup horse in 1977. Should that prove so, we have a very
interesting prospect. After all, here is a horse who had the precocity to win
as a two-year-old, the speed to finish second to a horse of Malacate's ability
over a mile and a quarter and the stamina and determination to slog his way
through gruelling conditions over a mile and a half at Newbury. Mart Lane's
style of racing suggests he will be extremely well suited by distances in excess of
a mile and a half and that two miles or more will present no problems to him.
However, let's examine his pedigree. Le Levanstell who died in 1974 was a
sprint-bred miler who proved capable of getting animals who stay a great deal
better than himself. The best of Le Levanstell's stayers is Levmoss, winner of
the Prix de l'Arc de Triomphe, the Prix du Cadran and the Ascot Gold Cup as
a four-year-old. Levmoss, like Mart Lane, was Brownstown-bred and McGrath-
trained and, like Mart Lane, made rapid development in the latter stages of his
three-year-old career. However, by the end of his second season Levmoss had
already proved his ability to stay two miles and was more stoutly bred on his

St Simon Stakes, Newbury—Mart Lane revels in the heavy going and trounces Roses for the Star

dam's side. Mart Lane is the fifth living foal of his dam Marians, who won over five furlongs as a two-year-old and finished fourth in the Irish Guinness Oaks, but who appeared not to stay a mile and three quarters. Marians produced three other winners besides Mart Lane, the Irish Lincolnshire winner All in All (by Pall Mall) who seemed best at up to a mile and a quarter, the Irish Sweeps Derby winner Weavers' Hall (by Busted) who was well suited by a mile and a half and gave the impression he would have stayed further, and Never Merry (by Never Say Die) successful over a mile and a half in Ireland. The second dam Damians raced unsuccessfully over five furlongs at two years. In a long stud career she proved primarily an influence for speed, and produced many winners, including three smart performers by Ballyogan, namely the sprinters Ballydam and Sixpence and the Hunt Cup winner Continuation. On breeding there must be a shadow of doubt about Mart Lane's having the capacity to stay really long distances. Only time will tell. Whatever the limit of his stamina, this comparatively lightly-raced colt is almost certain to improve. Quite an attractive individual, he acts extremely well on heavy ground and is apparently unsuited by firm. *S. McGrath, Ireland.*

MARTYN ANDREW 4 b.g. Carlburg 78–Cacador's Darling (Cacador) [1974 N.R. 1975 N.R. 1976 10s 18s⁴] poor maiden: stays 2¼m. *J. Haine.* —

MARUSA 3 gr.f. Roan Rocket 128–Morinda 87 (Matador 131) [1975 6fg 1976 8fg 9.4g 8f³ 7f⁵] big filly: only poor form: sold to T. Marshall 840 gns Newmarket December Sales: blinkered first two outings. *Sir Mark Prescott.* 56

MARY CROONER 2 gr.f. Crooner 119–Mary Elaine 73 (Fastnet Rock 123) [1976 5fg 5fg⁴ 5f 6g 6fg 6d 6s] only poor form in varied company, including selling. *J. Holt.* 57

MARY ELIZABETH 3 b.f. Sahib 114–Tudor Request 87 (Tudor Minstrel 144) [1975 7.6g 1976 10.1f 8.3fg 10.1fg] seems of no account. *J. Hayward.* —

MARY GARDEN 3 b.f. Sahib 114–Bella Musica (Sing Sing 134) [1975 5fg³ 5h⁵ 5g 5s⁶ 6g² 6g⁵ 1976 6f 6f 6s⁵] useful sort: good walker and mover: will stay 1m: possibly best on a sound surface: sold 980 gns Doncaster August Sales. *H. Blackshaw.* —

MARY GREEN 2 b.f. Sahib 114–Codicil 95 (Prince Chevalier) [1976 5f 5g⁵ 7g² 7g 8s³ 10v³] shapely filly: half-sister to game and useful middle-distance handicapper Grandpa's Legacy (by Zeus Boy): dam won at up to 1¼m: fair maiden: stays 1¼m: acts on heavy ground. *P. Walwyn.* 81

MARY JUMP 6 b.m. Double Jump 131–Mary Murphy 85 (Aureole 132) [1974 10.4d 12g 10.2s 16.1v 1975 10f⁵ 13.4g⁵ 17.7f 1976 12f] poor maiden: not certain to stay beyond 1¼m. *W. Clay.* —

MARY MARINA 2 br.f. Captain's Gig–Casilda (Crepello 136) [1976 5d⁶ 5fg 7f⁵ 7.2f 8fg 8.2f⁵] shapely filly: only plating class: should stay 1m: tried in blinkers final outing. *M. W. Easterby.* 65

MARY McQUAKER 4 b.f. Acer 123–St Mary's Square 84 (Acropolis 132) [1974 7g⁵ 8s* 7s³ 1975 12h³ 12h⁶ 12f⁵ 13.8f⁵ 12h 16f⁶ 13.8g 1976 12g⁴ 13.8g⁵] fair sort: mainly disappointing since her first outing at 3 yrs: stays 1½m: acts on any going. *W. Gray.* 47

MARY ROAN 3 gr.f. Roan Rocket 128–Paul-Mary 107 (Pardao 120) [1975 **73**
5d⁶ 6d 1976 10f 11.7fg 10.1fg⁶ 11.7h² 10.2h³ 10fg² 10s⁵] quite a moderate
maiden: blinkered first time when 1½ lengths second of eight to Sunburst at
Salisbury in September, showing improved form: again blinkered when running
poorly only subsequent outing: stays 1½m: evidently unsuited by soft going:
sold 720 gns Newmarket Autumn Sales. *P. Walwyn.*

MA'S BABY 4 b.f. Ashford Lea 95–Babulass (Babu 117) [1974 5f 5fg² 5f 5f⁴
5g⁵ 5fg⁶ 5g* 5.9s² 5v² 1975 7v³ 6s⁶ 7s 6fg⁶ 6g 6fg 8g 6g 1976 7g 6g] leggy,
light-framed filly: one-time fair handicapper but has become disappointing: stays
7f: acts on any going: has run creditably for an apprentice but is probably better
suited by stronger handling nowadays. *S. Nesbitt.*

MASQUED DANCER 4 b.c. Nijinsky 138–Bonnie Google (Better Self) [1974 **99**
7g³ 6g² 8s³ 1975 10g³ 12fg 12g² 10f* 12g* 10d² 12g² 1976 12g² 12g⁶ 22.2f² 12f]
American-bred Irish colt: fairly useful performer: 2½ lengths second of 12 to
Coed Cochion in Queen Alexandra Stakes at Royal Ascot in June: had previously
finished second to Monksfield in apprentice race at Naas in April and sixth to
Yankee Gold in Royal Whip at the Curragh the following month: stays extremely
well: acts on any going: sold 16,500 gns Newmarket December Sales. *D. Weld,
Ireland.*

MASS 2 ch.f. Mansingh 120–Missa Luba (Silver Cloud 121) [1976 5fg⁵ 5f³ 5fg⁴ **61**
5fg⁵ 7fg] lengthy filly: in frame in maiden auction events: raced in sellers on
last two outings and gave impression that 6f is her trip: not seen out after July.
Miss S. Hall.

MASSMART 2 b.f. Decoy Boy 129–Cloudari (Pindari 124) [1976 5g 5fg 5f 5.3g —
5f 5g 5fg 10v] neat filly: bad plater: has worn blinkers: retained by stable
350 gns Ascot July Sales and resold 240 gns Ascot November Sales. *R. Supple.*

MASTER BILL 3 ch.g. Autre Prince 125–Fair Folly 93 (Fairford) [1975 7g —
1976 16.1f] half-brother to useful stayer Tumbled (by Pandofell): unseated
rider on only outing at 2 yrs: unseated rider on way to post when ninth of 11
behind Frisky Scot in maiden race (amateurs) at Haydock in August. *E.
Cousins.*

MASTER BUILDER 3 b.g. Song 132–Pamagilan 89 (Pall Mall 132) [1975 **60**
N.R. 1976 5.8h 5fg 5g 6fg 5.8f* 5s 6s 6v⁵] good sort: brother to a winning sprint
plater and half-brother to two minor winners: 820 gns foal and resold 130 gns
yearling and 420 gns 2-y-o: dam won over 5f at 2 yrs: blinkered first time and
dropped to selling company, made all when narrowly defeating stable-companion
The Headman at Bath in September: sold out of B. Swift's stable 900 gns afterwards: ran moderately on three outings for new stable, twice wearing blinkers:
should stay 6f: unsuited by soft ground. *A. W. Jones.*

MASTER CHAD 5 ch.g. St Chad 120–Good Spelling (Royal Hamlet 115) [1974 **65**
10.5f⁵ 9.4fg* 12fg³ 10d³ 10g 10s² 12.3s⁴ 12g 1975 13f³ 12g⁵ 11g² 11g* 12f² 10.6fg³
15g² 13g³ 11g⁶ 1976 12d³ 12.3f⁴ 12s⁴ 12g* 15.8g⁵ 15.8f* 12h³ 16fg⁴ 13g⁶ 12.2s⁴]
quite a moderate handicapper: successful at Carlisle in May and Catterick in
July: stays well: acts on any going: ran poorly when tried in blinkers: goes well
for apprentice S. Webster: sweated up eighth outing: sold 3,100 gns Newmarket
Autumn Sales. *R. D. Peacock.*

MASTER CUTTER 3 b.c. Hard Tack 111 §–Tailor Donore 83 (Donore 119) **94**
[1975 5g 5g³ 5f² 5g² 5f* 5f³ 5g* 5g² 1976 5s 5d² 5fg⁵ 5fg 5fg⁴ 5fg⁵ 5f] robust
colt: fairly useful sprint handicapper: good second of eight to Epsom Imp in
apprentice event at Haydock in June, best effort: will probably always be best at
5f: appears to act on any going: wears blinkers. *J. W. Watts.*

MASTER MARTON 3 b.c. Chebs Lad 120–Marton Lady 103 (March Past 124) **62**
[1975 5g 5d 5s⁵ 5g 5v 1976 5f³ 6d³ 5f² 6d⁵ 5fg⁵ 5g 5f³ 5fg³ 5f⁴ 5.9fg 5s⁴ 5v 6s]
small colt: poor mover: half-brother to very good 2-y-o Haveroid (by Tycoon II)
but is only a poor performer himself: best form at 5f: occasionally wears blinkers
but does better without. *F. Wiles.*

MASTER PETARD 4 b.c. Petingo 135–Miss Upward 77 (Alcide 136) [1974 **103** d
N.R. 1975 8s* 10s⁵ 10.5d 8g* 8f 10g² 9g 1976 8g⁴ 8g⁴ 10fg⁵ 12g⁵ 8g 12fg⁶ 7fg⁵]
strong, shapely colt: useful handicapper on his day: unreliable and seems none too
keen on racing nowadays: stays 1½m: acts on soft going and may be unsuited by
firm: sometimes wears blinkers: trained until after third outing by M. Jarvis:
not seen out after June. *R. Smyth.*

MASTER SKIPPER 4 b.c. Skymaster 126–Paris Princess 118 (Prince Chevalier) **82**
[1974 5g⁵ 5g² 5s* 7g³ 7g⁴ 6g² 6.3s⁶ 6g⁴ 5v³ 1975 8f² 8f⁵ 8f* 6f⁴ 8f³ 7f 1976 10f⁴

6f4] ex-Irish colt: had stiff tasks on both outings in this country at 4 yrs, finishing about 4½ lengths fourth of six to Raffindale in minor event at Lingfield in June on second of them: promises to stay 1¼m: probably acts on any going. *F. Muggeridge.*

MASTER'S SONG 2 ch.c. Huntercombe 133–Mezzo Soprano (Alcide 136) — [1976 5g 5g 5.1fg 5fg 5s 8v] evidently useless. *N. Adam.*

MASTER THIEF 5 ch.g. Pieces of Eight 128–Tudor Song (Tudor Minstrel 144) — [1974 10.5v 10.5g⁴ 10.5g 10.5g 1975 9g³ 10.5g 13s⁵ 12s* 12s⁴ 13g 12.5g 1976 14s⁶] ex-French gelding: cost 17,000 gns as a yearling: dam winner at 3 yrs in U.S.A. and half-sister to several good winners: won maiden race at Longchamp in 1975: having his first outing in this country when tailed off in strongly-contested minor event at Sandown in October (100/1): stays 1½m: acts on soft going: blinkered second and fourth outings at 3 yrs. *J. Welch.*

MASTER WREKIN 2 br.c. Sahib 114–Miss Wrekin 97 (Pardao 120) [1976 5g* 89 5f² 6f³ 6f* 6fg 6d⁵] strong, useful-looking colt: half-brother to useful stayer Peter Wrekin (by Lauso) and fairly useful winner Wrekinianne (by Reform): dam won over 5f at 2 yrs: winner of maiden race at Salisbury in May and minor event at Windsor two months later, on latter occasion scoring by 2½ lengths from Caroline's Melodie: excellent fifth of 19 to Balante in nursery at Windsor in September: will stay 7f: consistent. *F. Maxwell.*

MATERNAL 2 b.f. High Top 131–Mathilde 84 (Whistler 129) [1976 5f⁵ 6d* 93 5s* 6fg⁴ 6fg⁵ 6f] neat, well-made filly: half-sister to four winners, including speedy 1974 2-y-o Material (by Song) and useful sprinter Mink Mini (by Martial): dam at her best early on as a 2-y-o: won 17-runner minor event at Haydock in June and beat Bowsquare Lady comfortably by 2 lengths in four-runner race at Ayr later in month: not disgraced afterwards although was a bit below her best on final outing: will probably stay 7f. *E. Weymes.*

MATINALE 3 ch.f. Reliance II 137–At Dawn (Aggressor 130) [1975 7g 1976 72 11g⁵ 12g³ 16f³ 14fg⁶ 15.8g* 16v* 16v] fair sort: won poor maiden race at Catterick in September and handicap at Newcastle the following month, latter by 10 lengths from Pontresina: ran poorly final outing: stays very well. *B. Hills.*

MATNAT SABA 2 gr.c. Jukebox 120–Grandpa's Gift (Celtic Ash) [1976 6g 5g 63 5f² 6g⁵ 7s⁵ 7v] neat colt: showed ability in varied company, including selling, running best race when just over 4 lengths fifth of 10 to What-A-Secret in maiden race at Edinburgh in October: evidently suited by 7f: acts on any going: trained until after fourth outing by S. Ingham. *D. Weeden.*

MATSON GROUND 2 b.f. Galivanter 131–Silk Willoughby (Pirate King 129) — [1976 5fg 6d 6f] third foal: 360 gns yearling: dam unraced sister to very useful stayer Avast: no worthwhile form in maiden company in first half of season but still didn't look ready on final outing. *H. Blackshaw.*

MATSUI 3 b.f. Falcon 131–Minita (Guersant 129) [1975 5g 6g 6f 7g⁶ 8g⁶ 1976 46 8.2v⁴ 15.8f⁵ 12g 12g 11g³ 15f 13.8f² 14.7f⁴ 15.8f³ 15.8g 15.8s³] leggy filly: poor plater: stays well: blinkered eighth and last outings: bandaged ninth appearance. *T. Craig.*

MATSUSHIMA 3 ch.f. Yellow River 114–Muffet 75 (Matador 131) [1975 5f 53 5fg⁶ 6f² 6f⁵ 7s 1976 6f 6fg⁶ 6fg 7g⁶ 8g 7f⁶ 10.8g⁵ 10s⁵ 10s] small, sturdy filly: poor form, including in a seller: stays 11f: trained until after sixth start by Mrs F. Nagle. *H. Smyth.*

MAUREEN MHOR 2 br.f. Taj Dewan 128–Ritual 79 (Right Royal V 135) 70 [1976 7fg⁶ 7g⁴ 8g⁴] second foal: half-sister to useful 3-y-o Malin Court (by Major Portion), a winner at up to 9f: dam won over 7f at 2 yrs: fourth in maiden races at Ayr in August and September, starting second favourite on latter occasion and finishing 10 lengths behind Sultans Ruby: will stay 1¼m. *N. Angus.*

MAURITANIA 2 b.f. The Brianstan 128–Maurine 98 (Worden II 129) [1976 — 6d] strong filly: half-sister to several winners, including very useful middle-distance performer Belper (by Busted) and Musidora Stakes winner Lovers Lane (by Twilight Alley): dam useful at 1m and 1¼m: backward and weak in market, never showed behind Caerdeon Line in big field of maidens at Newmarket in October. *J. Dunlop.*

MAVERICK 8 b.g. Suki Desu 118–Lady Angus (Trouville 125) [1974 N.R. — 1975 N.R. 1976 8f⁶ 10h⁴] probably of little account. *H. Westbrook.*

MAXDEMCON 2 b.g. Le Dieu d'Or 119–Bella Juanita (Thirteen of Diamonds — 126) [1976 5fg 5g 5g 8fg] of no account: sold 320 gns Doncaster September Sales. *J. Turner.*

MAXIHOT 3 b.c. Hotfoot 126–Crash (Ballymoss 136) [1975 5s 5v⁵ 7g 7f⁴ 8f⁴ — 8f 10g 10g 1976 10.8fg6 10.8f⁶ 11.7f³ 10.1f] quite a moderate plater: probably stays 1¼m: blinkered final outing. *M. Bradley.*

MAXIMOVA 3 b.f. Sensitivo–Delray Dancer (Chateaugay) [1975 7f³ 1976 **80** 10g 11.1g³ 16fg⁵] big, rangy filly: seems desperately one-paced. *H. Cecil.*

MAXI'S TAXI 6 b.g. Klondyke Bill 125–Maggie's Pet 74 (Coronation Year 124) **97** [1974 5g* 6h 6g² 7g* 6g⁵ 6g 6fg² 6g* 5s² 6v* 6s 1975 5d⁴ 7f³ 6fg⁵ 1976 5g⁶ 7f⁵ 6fg* 7.6f⁶ 6f* 6fg 6fg⁴ 6f* 6g² 6v] lengthy gelding: quite a useful handicapper: successful three times at 6 yrs, including in Bretby Handicap at Newmarket in April and Home Ales Gold Tankard at Nottingham in June, in last-named event beating Ribramble a shade comfortably: gained his other win in apprentice race at Goodwood in August: stays 7f but possibly not much further: acts on any going: has been tried in blinkers: suitable mount for an apprentice: genuine and consistent. *M. Masson.*

MAYAB 3 b.f. Maystreak 118–Mablon 76 (Majority Blue 126) [1975 5fg³ 5g* **95** 5g² 5g* 5d 5d² 1976 5s 5d⁶ 6fg 5g* 5fg 5fg⁶ 6fg 5g] lightly-built filly: made virtually all when winning eight-runner handicap at Doncaster in June: ran moderately afterwards, twice wearing blinkers: probably better suited by 5f than 6f. *M. H. Easterby.*

MAY BECK 3 ch.f. Welsh Pageant 132–Gillamoor (Big Game) [1975 5fg³ 6d **109** 6g³ 5fg* 5g² 1976 6d⁴ 6fg² 6fg* 6fg² 6fg² 5.6g⁴ 6g⁶ 6d³] well-made, attractive filly: ran consistently well, showing useful form, and won handicap at Newmarket in July all out by a short head from Endless Echo: beaten less than 2 lengths when fourth of 11 to Hei'land Jamie in William Hill Portland Handicap at Doncaster in September: stayed 6f: acted on a firm and a soft surface: blinkered final outing: stud. *N. Murless.*

MAYBELLINE 3 ch.f. Weepers Boy 124–Edlin (Monet 127) [1975 5f 6fg* — 7f 1976 8g] plater: had stiff task only outing at 3 yrs: possibly does not stay 7f: sold 190 gns Ascot November Sales. *C. Dingwall.*

MAYBOY 2 b.g. Maystreak 118–Sicalaine 52 (Sica Boy 132) [1976 5g 6h 5f 5g] — useless: sold 230 gns Doncaster October Sales. *S. Nesbitt.*

MAY BRIDE 2 b.f. High Top 131–Madge (Tudor Melody 129) [1976 5g² 5g³ **80** 5fg² 5.8f² 5d³ 5s² 5v² 6g⁶ 5v] compact filly: second foal: half-sister to a winner in Italy by Tamerlane: 3,400 gns yearling: dam showed little worthwhile form in maiden races at 2 yrs: runner-up in five races, going down by 3 lengths to Scented Air in 20-runner maiden event at Leicester in October on final occasion: should stay 7f: acts on any going: blinkered second and third outings: sold 2,100 gns Newmarket December Sales. *J. Hill.*

MAYCROFT 3 b.g. Maystreak 118–Lingcroft 86 (Tutankhamen) [1975 N.R. — 1976 7g] neat gelding: first foal: dam showed fair form at 2 yrs: easy in market, dwelt when last of seven behind Black Jim in seller at Catterick in June. *E. Weymes.*

MAYFIELD MAGIC 2 b.f. Crooner 119–Zugela 90 (Zucchero 133 §) [1976 5d **53** 6g 6v 6s⁶] half-sister to three minor winners here and abroad: 600 gns foal and resold 700 gns yearling: dam a stayer: little worthwhile form, including in a valuable seller. *M. Camacho.*

MAY FOX 2 gr.f. Healaugh Fox–Aunt May 78 (Grey Sovereign 128 §) [1976 **67** 5g* 5f⁵ 5f⁶] half-sister to several winners, notably smart 6f to 1m winner Be Hopeful (by Roc du Diable) and Oaks runner-up Mabel (by French Beige), herself dam of May Hill: dam showed a little ability at 2 yrs: won 12-runner maiden race at Wolverhampton in May by ¾ length from Bayberry: beaten about 8 lengths by Billie's Pal on both outings afterwards, at Brighton and Chepstow: would have been suited by 6f+: retired to stud. *P. Walwyn.*

MAYHEM 3 b.g. Maystreak 118–Amaconda 83 (Dignitary 121) [1975 5fg⁴ 5g **58** 5d³ 5g⁴ 5f⁴ 9g 6d 7.2d 7fg 6v 1976 6d⁶ 6fg⁴ 10.6d² 8fg⁴ 7g 7.2fg⁴] lightly-made gelding: modest plater: stays 1¼m: often wears blinkers. *R. Ward.*

MAY HILL 4 b.f. Hill Clown–Mabel 113 (French Beige 127) [1974 6v* 1975 **106** 7.3v² 10.5s² 12f⁴ 12fg* 12fg* 14.6g* 12s³ 1976 16g³ 13.3g² 16.1d³ 12s⁴ 16s³] well-made, good-quartered filly: one of the best 3-y-o staying fillies in 1975, winning three races, including Yorkshire Oaks at York and Park Hill Stakes at Doncaster: ran creditably on first two outings at 4 yrs but finished lame when third to Mr Bigmore in Lymm Stakes at Haydock in May on third start, was off course until September and ran moderately in both her subsequent races: extremely well suited by a good test of stamina: seemed to act on any going except perhaps very firm: probably best on a galloping track: genuine: stud. *P. Walwyn.*

MAYMEDE 2 b.f. Runnymede 123–Eastwood Bounty 87 (Bounteous 125) **79** [1976 5d² 5d⁶ 5g³ 5f 7fg] third produce: sister to smart 1975 2-y-o Woodsome: 760 gns foal: dam, won five races, effective from 5f to 1¼m: placed in minor event at Newcastle in April (length second to Mofida) and maiden race at Haydock in May (kept on well to finish 3¾ lengths third to Faridetta): possibly does not stay 7f: acts on a soft surface: wears blinkers. *T. Fairhurst.*

MAYNOOTH 3 br.c. The Brianstan 128–Golden Storm 95 (Golden Cloud) **83** [1975 5f² 6g⁶ 5f* 5d* 6f³ 7v³ 5g 1976 5f 6fg⁴ 5f³] small, good-quartered colt: struggled to go early pace but stayed on well when 6 lengths third to Hot Bird in John Player Handicap at Redcar in July: will be suited by a return to 6f: acts on any going: trained until after first outing by I. Balding: exported to U.S.A. *W. Marshall.*

MAYO GIRL 3 b.f. Connaught 130–Montana Girl 110 (Ballymoss 136) [1975 6g **110** 1976 10.5d⁴ 12fg⁵ 14g⁵] big, rangy, rather round-actioned filly: half-sister to fair 1¼m winner Cholita (by St Paddy): dam, a miler, is daughter of sister to top-class sprinter Abelia: having first race since May when excellent fifth, beaten only just over 2 lengths, to Sarah Siddons in Yorkshire Oaks at York in August: occupied same position behind African Dancer in Park Hill Stakes at Doncaster the following month, but her run petered out in final 2f and was beaten about 10 lengths (possibly found trip too far): stays 1¾m: to be trained by H. Cecil. *N. Murless.*

MAY SONG 2 ch.g. Maystreak 118–Star Singer 94 (Umberto 118) [1976 5.9g **87** 7fg* 7fg 6f⁶ 8g] half-brother to several winners, including useful 1973 2-y-o 5f and 6f winner Brie (by Meldrum): dam a sprinter: had field well strung out when winning 13-runner maiden race at Chester in July by 2½ lengths from Haighall: suited by 7f but was well beaten when tried over 1m: sweated up and ran moderately on third outing. *A. Dickinson.*

MAYSWING 3 br.f. Maystreak 118–Khalswing (Khalkis 127) [1975 5d⁵ 5s³ **73** 6f³ 6h³ 6f⁵ 7f 6d⁵ 7.2s 8v³ 1976 8fg 10.6d* 12.2g⁶ 10.6d⁶ 8.2d² 8fg* 10f⁶ 9.4h⁴ 9h 8.2f⁵ 8s] leggy filly: won seller at Haydock in April (bought in 1,500 gns) and four-runner handicap at Leicester in June: stays 1½m well but possibly not 1½m: well suited by plenty of give in the ground, but acts on a firm surface: has won for an apprentice: none too consistent, and was running poorly in her later races. *R. Hollinshead.*

MAZURKA 2 br.f. Hotfoot 126–Somalia 96 (Alcide 136) [1976 5fg 5f⁵ 7fg⁶] **67** first foal: dam stayed well: 8 lengths sixth of 20 to Main Event in maiden race at Leicester in September: will be suited by middle distances. *P. Walwyn.*

McARTHUR PARK 2 br.f. Ben Novus 109–Souris 77 (Soueida 111) [1976 5g] **—** first foal: 200 gns yearling: dam won over 5f at 2 yrs: remote seventh of 10 to My Angel in minor event at Edinburgh in May, only outing. *T. Walker.*

MEADLANDS 3 br.f. Runnymede 123–Phyllida 89 (Pardal 130) [1975 5s* 5fg² **85** 5fg* 5f² 5h³ 5g³ 5fg 1976 5g 7d⁶ 6g⁶ 7f⁴ 8d 6f 7.6fg 7fg 6d 6v] sharp sort: creditable fourth to Solar Saint in handicap at Thirsk in May after having none too clear a run, but ran moderately afterwards: stays 7f: acts on any going: blinkered seventh, eighth and tenth (sweating and missed break) outings: suitable mount for an apprentice. *E. Collingwood.*

MEADOW BOND 2 b.f. Good Bond 122–Port Meadow 83 (Runnymede 123) **68** [1976 5.3g⁶ 6f⁴ 6f 5fg 5fg⁵ 5h 5.9g⁵ 6s] first foal: 420 gns yearling: dam probably stayed 1m: fair plater: stays 6f: changed hands 420 gns Doncaster September Sales. *W. Marshall.*

MEADOW BRIDGE 2 b.c. Busted 134–Arvonia (Charlottesville 135) [1976 **—** 7fg⁶] second foal: half-brother to useful 1974 2-y-o 5f winner Melody Hour (by Sing Sing): dam unraced daughter of Oaks runner-up West Side Story: 20/1 and backward when remote last of six to stable-companion Paddington in £1,600 event at Newmarket in July: to be trained by H. Cecil. *N. Murless.*

MEADOWCROFT 5 b.m. King Log 115–Chanette 89 (Epaulette 125) [1974 **59** 7d³ 8.5h⁴ 7g 7.2fg³ 7.2fg⁴ 10.6g 7fg⁵ 7fg 8.2g⁵ 1975 8.2d 12v 1976 8fg⁶ 6g³ 7g⁶ 7fg*] plater: favourite when winning at Yarmouth in June (no bid): stays 1m: acts on any going: has been tried in blinkers. *R. Hollinshead.*

MEADOW MONARCH 2 b.c. Meadow Mint 120–Souza Rose 80 (Songedor **87** 116) [1976 6fg* 7g⁴ 6s] second foal: dam a sprint plater: put up a really good effort for a newcomer when winning minor event at Thirsk in July by a head from Jewelled Turban: could finish only fourth of five, beaten 7½ lengths, to

Sealed Brief in £1,800 event at Newcastle the following month and had very stiff task in nursery on final outing: should stay 1m: acts on a firm surface. *E. Collingwood.*

MEADOW MOUSE 2 b.f. Calpurnius 122–Sleepy (Hereward the Wake 75) [1976 5f⁶ 5f 7g 6d] bad plater. *D. Hanley.* —

MEADOWS HOUSE 3 ro.g. Beau Garcon–Crossing (Le Haar 126) [1975 N.R. 1976 11s 12.2g 8f* 8fg⁶ 10fg⁶ 8g] workmanlike gelding: third foal: 200 gns yearing: dam won over 1¼m in France: plater: bought in 800 gns after winning at Edinburgh in June: ran badly afterwards: stays 1m: sold out of K. Payne's stable 1,150 gns Doncaster August Sales after fifth start and resold 650 gns same venue in November. *J. Berry.* **47**

MECANOPSIS 2 b.f. Major Portion 129–Opium 97 (Espresso 122) [1976 6fg³ 6f* 6g] smallish filly: first foal: dam won at up to 1½m: put up quite a useful effort when winning 21-runner maiden race at Newmarket in August, quickening well to draw away in final furlong and scoring by 3 lengths from St Petersburg: 10/1 for 15-runner Cheveley Park Stakes, again at Newmarket, the following month but finished only thirteenth to Durtal after showing up for long way: will be better suited by longer distances. *B. Hobbs.* **91**

MEDINA PRINCE 7 gr.g. Fortino II 120–Ad Adama (Palestine 133) [1974 N.R. 1975 N.R. 1976 12fg 8g] probably out little account. *J. Peacock.* —

MEDODOSUSU 3 b.f. The Brianston 128–Sage Warbler (Le Sage 128) [1975 5g 5fg 7v 8v 1976 7g 8f 8s 8f 6fg 6g 12g 16f 12fg² 12g²] useful-looking filly: plater: second in minor event and maiden race in Scotland: stays 1½m: trained most of season by R. Mason. *K. Oliver.* **59**

MEGALATOR 3 b.c. Blast 125–Groovy 86 (Sound Track 132) [1975 5g 5fg⁵ 6fg 6f⁶ 7fg⁴ 1976 5f 7g 8g 5f] smallish, sturdy colt: plating-class maiden: probably best at distances short of 7f (had very stiff tasks both outings over 5f in 1976). *N. Adam.* —

MEGAPHONE 3 b.g. Jukebox 120–Proud Meg (Proud Chieftain 122) [1975 N.R. 1976 7fg 6g 8s³ 10.2s6] strong gelding: third foal: 820 gns yearling: dam placed at 1¼m in Ireland: having first outing since May when 7½ lengths third of 19 to Pembi Chase in maiden race at Warwick in October, best effort: not certain to stay 1¼m: sold to J. Turner 2,300 gns Newmarket Autumn Sales. *F. J. Houghton.* —

MEG'S MANTLE 3 b.f. New Brig 120–Buzz About (Dara §§) [1975 N.R. 1976 15.8g³] half-sister to a winning hurdler: dam never ran: 33/1 and in need of outing, ran promisingly when 6½ lengths third of 14 to Matinale in maiden race at Catterick in September, coming from well behind and staying on without being able to quicken: may be up to winning a minor race over a distance of ground. *J. Fitzgerald.* **59**

MELADREAM 2 b.f. Breeders Dream 116–Damel 75 (Darius 129) [1976 5fg 7fg⁶ 6g 7s 6v³] neat filly: half-sister to quite useful staying handicapper Royal Fanfare (by March Past): dam needed at least 1½m: length third to subsequently-disqualified Nampara Cove in maiden race at Lingfield in November: should be suited by 7f: trained until after second outing by M. Jarvis. *N. Adam.* **81**

MELDORA 2 ch.f. Meldrum 112–Comdora 58 (Como 120) [1976 5fg 5f 6f⁴ 5f 5fg 7fg] strong filly: no worthwhile form, including sellers: gave trouble in stalls on first two appearances: blinkered final outing. *M. W. Easterby.* **58**

MELEX 2 b.f. Meldrum 112–Alexa (Runnymede 123) [1976 5f⁴ 6f⁴ 5.1f* 7h³ 6fg² 6h⁵ 5f⁴ 6f 5.9fg 6v 5d] compact filly: sold out of D. Williams' stable for 1,300 gns after showing improved form to win seller at Yarmouth in June: ran very well on next two outings, finishing second to In Haste in auction event at Newcastle in one of them: carried overweight in nurseries on last four outings: suited by 6f and 7f: blinkered penultimate appearance. *J. Powney.* **75**

MELGROVE WAY 2 ch.f. Miracle 116–Twice Shy (Lord of Verona 120) [1976 5d 6h⁴ 6f² 6v 6v 7g] modest plater: should be suited by 7f+: probably not at her best on heavy ground. *W. A. Stephenson.* **65**

MELODY PARADE 3 b.f. Tudor Melody 129–French Parade 113 (March Past 124) [1975 5.1f 5fg⁶ 6g⁶ 1976 8fg 6f 6g⁶ 8f⁵ 8d 9.2f³ 6v] well-bred but is only a plater: seems to stay 9f: possibly requires a sound surface: blinkered third and fourth outings: sold 420 gns Ascot November Sales. *M. W. Easterby.* **50**

MELODY RYDE 4 b.f. Shooting Chant–Persian Coach (Parthia 132) [1974 6fg² 6s² 6g⁵ 7s³ 7.2v* 1975 14fg⁴ 13.3g 12g⁶ 12v* 12g 13.3g² 16g⁵ 12g* 1976 **73**

12fg 12g⁵ 11.1g⁵ 12f⁴ 12fg³ 14f³ 12g² 14fg⁴ 12s² 12d² 12s² 12s²] compact filly: quite a moderate handicapper: ran well in the majority of her races at 4 yrs: needs at least 1½m: ideally suited by some give in the ground and goes very well on heavy going: consistent: sold 4,200 gns Newmarket Autumn Sales. *T. Gosling.*

MELPERION   2 ch.g. Meldrum 112–Fair Ellender (Sailing Light 119)   [1976   **65** 6h³ 8g 6fg 8.2f]   unfurnished gelding: only plating class.   *T. Fairhurst.*

MELROSE   3 b.g. Runnymede 123–Kildare Honey 79 (Khalkis 127)   [1975   **59** 5f⁵ 6d 5g⁵   1976 7g⁵ 9g⁴ 9g 10.2g 10g⁵ 8v³ 8s]   strong, good sort: good walker and mover: showed promise at 2 yrs and on first outing in 1976 but became very disappointing and ended season in plating company: probably stays 9f: sometimes bandaged off-fore: well beaten when tried in blinkers on final outing: changed hands 3,600 gns Doncaster November Sales. *S. Hall.*

MEMORY LANE   3 br.f. Never Bend–Milan Mill (Princequillo)   [1975 5fg*   **98** 6fg 6g³   1976 8.5fg* 12.3s⁵ 10fg 8g]   attractive, lengthy American-bred filly: very good mover: sister to Mill Reef: won six-runner Princess Elizabeth Stakes at Epsom in April decisively by 1½ lengths from Red Ruby: far from disgraced (having first outing since running very badly in Cheshire Oaks in May) when seventh of 10 to Roussalka in Nassau Stakes at Goodwood in July but ran moderately under a stiff weight on final appearance: should stay 1½m: possibly unsuited by soft ground: got worked up in stalls on second outing at 2 yrs. *I. Balding.*

MENDIP MAN   4 b.c. Manacle 123–Grandera 69 (Primera 131)   [1974 5h² 6f*   **123** 5g⁶   1975 8v² 8v⁵ 8v³ 6g* 7d² 7g 8g³ 6.5g 6g 5s³ 5d   1976 6s² 8d⁴ 5f⁴ 7d⁴ 5d⁴ 5g³ 5s* 5s]   ex-English colt: very smart sprinter: dead-heated for valuable Prix de l'Abbaye de Longchamp in October with English 3-y-o Gentilhombre, the pair coming out best in a driving finish with Raga Navarro and Girl Friend: in frame in most of his other races (put up his only moderate display on final start), notably when fourth in Prix de Ris-Orangis (behind El Rastro) at Evry in April and in Prix du Gros-Chene at Chantilly in June and when third in Prix de Seine-et-Oise at Maisons-Laffitte in September (both won by Kala Shikari): effective at 5f to 1m: acts on any going: game and genuine: exported to America. *A. Paus, France.*

Mr Paul Mellon's "Memory Lane"

MENEHAY 2 ch.f. Manacle 123–Anagola 64 (Queen's Hussar 124) [1976 **71**
5fg³ 5f⁵ 5g⁵ 5g⁵ 5f⁴ 5f⁴ 5s⁵ 5s 5s 5v⁵ 5v] small filly: first foal: dam of little
account: quite a moderate maiden: acts on any going. *R. Supple.*

MENEVAL 3 b.c. Le Fabuleux 133–Nalee (Nashua) [1975 8g² 1976 10g* **128**
10f* 12g* 14fg*]
No classic race in England, France or Ireland in 1976 was won with more
authority than that with which Meneval won the Irish St Leger. He hacked
up by eight lengths from General Ironside after the latter had led clear into the
straight. The Irish St Leger is usually one of the easiest of the classics open to
colts to win, and on this occasion Meneval, a 5/4-on shot, had considerably less to
do than did Crow at Doncaster (where General Ironside finished seventh) and
probably less to do than Exceller, who faced Sir Montagu in the Prix Royal-Oak.
Those that followed General Ironside home at the Curragh, Countess Eileen,
Red Invader, Midland Gayle, Krassata, Whistle for Gold, Finsbury, Navarre,
Lavache and the disappointing Lost Chord, in that order, represent nothing
out of the ordinary by classic standards, and it's possible that General Ironside,
running in blinkers for the first time, didn't show his very best form. But even
accepting in full the limitations of the opposition it is difficult to escape the
conclusion that Meneval is a top-class horse, or, at the very least, a top-class
horse in the making: he won so well.
Meneval has had very little racing, and he hasn't yet been seen outside
Ireland. The Irish St Leger was his first race for sixteen weeks and the last of
only four, all of them ending in a win for him, during the season. Winning the
Leger with Meneval after such a long spell off the course was another notable
training feat for Vincent O'Brien, who, incidentally, had considerably fewer
runners than usual in the season's big races mainly because of a virus infection
in the stable. Meneval's lengthy absence was said to be the result of his losing
his action after running in the Gallinule Stakes at the Curragh on May 29th;
he was then on the easy list until a late decision to go for the Irish St Leger
was taken. Meneval won the Gallinule Stakes, starting at 3/1 on, by a length
and a half from Lost Chord. The latter was probably the best horse Meneval
had met up to that time; earlier Meneval had won the Nijinsky Stakes at Leopardstown by a length from Whistling Deer, starting at 4/1 on, and the Ballysax
Stakes at the Curragh by four lengths from Emperor's Tailor, again at 4/1 on.
Piggott rode him in all his races; in every one he gave the impression that he
had a great deal in hand.

			Wild Risk	Rialto
	Le Fabuleux		(b 1940)	Wild Violet
	(ch 1961)		Anguar	Verso II
Meneval			(b 1950)	La Rochelle
(b.c. 1973)			Nashua	Nasrullah
	Nalee		(b 1952)	Segula
	(b 1960)		Levee	Hill Prince
			(ch 1953)	Bourtai

Meneval remains in training with the Prix de l'Arc de Triomphe as his
long-term objective. Although easily his best run is at a mile and three quarters,
he should experience little difficulty in coping with a return to the distance of
the Arc and other top middle-distance races; from what we have seen of him
he is not short of pace. His sire, Le Fabuleux, was well beaten in the Arc but
won the French Derby; his strong point was his ability to keep up a good gallop
for a long way. Le Fabuleux's list of European runners contains the French St
Leger winner Bourbon, the disqualified French St Leger winner Hallez, the Prix
Saint-Alary winner Lalika, the Oaks third La Manille and two horses, Bonami
and Dragoon, that might have won a classic had not their careers been ended by
injury. The Man o'War Stakes winner Effervescing is his best runner in the
U.S.A. On his dam's side Meneval could scarcely be better connected for a
middle-distance horse. His dam Nalee is a sister to the famous Shuvee, twice
champion handicap mare in the United States, winner of the then-record sum
for a mare of 890,445 dollars and winner of sixteen races including the Jockey
Club Gold Cup and the Coaching Club American Oaks. Nalee herself was a
high-class winner (she won three stakes) and is out of a top-class filly Levee,
the winner of the Monmouth Oaks, the C.C.A. Oaks and two other stakes races.
Levee is also the dam of the stallion Royal Gunner. Meneval is his dam's
seventh foal to reach the racecourse and, naturally enough in this family, her
seventh winner, the previous six all trained in the United States with at least
forty-one victories between them. Nalee's Folly (by Tom Fool) and Nalee's

Irish St Leger Stakes, the Curragh—Meneval hacks up from General Ironside

Man (by Gallant Man), stakes winners with nineteen victories and earnings of over 200,000 dollars between them, were probably her best before Meneval. When he came up as a yearling at the Keeneland Summer Sale Meneval made 170,000 dollars, a good figure even for Keeneland.

Meneval acts on firm going. He almost certainly has more than the normal amount of improvement in him, and he has more to recommend him than most of the leading three-year-olds of 1976 as a horse to follow in 1977. Let's hope that we see him in England. *V. O'Brien, Ireland.*

Mrs George F. Getty II's "Meneval"

459

MENIN 2 br.f. Silly Season 127–Verdun 82 (Relic) [1976 6g² 6fg⁴ 6f² 8fg³] **81** rather lightly-made filly: third living foal: 10,000 gns yearling: dam half-sister to good stayer Rally: moderate maiden: will stay 1¼m. *H. Cecil.*

MENSA 2 br.f. High Top 131–Intelligentsia 105 (Fortino II 120) [1976 5f 5fg⁴ **64** 5g⁶ 7fg 7fg³ 8v] first foal: dam won at up to 1m: 8 lengths third of 12 to Butterscotch in maiden race at Edinburgh in September: should stay 1m. *D. Weeden.*

MEPHISTO 2 bl.c. Blue Streak 99–Native Verse (Indigenous 121) [1976 6s] second foal: dam of little account: tailed-off last of 20 behind Nobodys Fool in minor race at Chepstow in October. *F. Freeman.*

MERCHANTMENS GIRL 2 br.f. Klairon 131–Polibede 98 (Polic 126) [1976 — 5v 6d] second foal: half-sister to useful 1975 2-y-o 5f and 6f winner Mabruk (by Manacle): 4,200 gns foal, a sprinter, is half-sister to very smart 5f sprinter Singing Bede: behind in large fields of maidens at Leicester and Newmarket in October. *K. Ivory.*

MERCHANT PRINCE 4 b.g. Hopeful Venture 125–Milonia (Tambourine II **46** 133) [1974 7g 8s 1975 10.8s 10g 7fg⁶ 8f 10f* 10fg⁵ 12f 1976 8g 10f⁴] neat gelding: stays 1¼m: acts on firm going: races with his tongue tied down: sold 210 gns Ascot June Sales. *M. Bolton.*

MERCHANT TUBBS 2 b.c. Great Nephew 126–Buff Beauty 92 (Mossborough **86** 126) [1976 7f 6d⁵ 6d 7v²] third foal: half-brother to winning 3-y-o stayer Cavalier's Blush (by King's Troop): dam well suited by a distance of ground: no match for runaway winner Forage in maiden race at Lingfield in November but finished 5 lengths clear of third horse: will probably stay well: evidently suited by some give in the ground. *H. Collingridge.*

MERCIFUL PROBLEM 3 b.c. No Mercy 126–Rose Blanche 89 (French Beige — 127) [1975 N.R. 1976 8.2d] third produce: half-brother to poor 1¼m winner Dandy Scot (by Behistoun): 960 gns foal, resold 210 gns yearling: dam won over 7f at 2 yrs: unquoted when behind in 17-runner maiden race won by Festival Hall at Haydock in October. *H. Wharton.*

MERCY'S GIRL 2 gr.f. No Mercy 126–Campagna (Romulus 129) [1976 5f 5fg⁵ **77** 6f⁴ 6f* 6fg 7.3d 8.2d] sturdy filly: second produce: half-sister to 1½m winner Camarina (by Aureole): 1,400 gns foal: dam won over 1¼m in France: got up close home to win eight-runner nursery at Windsor in August by a head from The Nadi Cat: should be suited by 7f+: acts on firm going. *M. McCourt.*

MERCY'S QUALITY 2 gr.c. No Mercy 126–Geology 74 (Rockavon 120) [1976 — 6fg 7g 7f 7.2f] big, strong, good-looking colt: fifth foal: dam stayed 1¼m: never-dangerous eighth of 13 to Fast Frigate in maiden race at Sandown in July, second outing and easily best effort. *G. Pritchard-Gordon.*

MERCY'S SCION 2 b.c. Queen's Hussar 124–Crowning Mercy (Supreme Court **66** 135) [1976 5s 5f 6g⁵ 6fg⁵ 8fg 8s] dipped-backed colt: half-brother to several winners, notably very smart 6f or 7f performer No Mercy (by Fortino II): showed a little ability in maiden and minor events: stays 1m: sold 1,200 gns Doncaster November Sales. *W. Wharton.*

MERGANSER 2 b.f. Most Secret 119–March Poulet (March Past 124) [1976 5f **71** 5g 8fg 6d 6v⁴ 6s⁵ 8v³ 7.2v] fourth reported produce: half-sister to three winners, including useful sprinter Golden Mallard (by Goldhill): quite a moderate maiden: stays 1m: acts on heavy ground: wears blinkers nowadays. *M. W. Easterby.*

MERITABLE 3 b.c. Round Table–Meritus (Bold Ruler) [1975 won twice at up **95** to a mile from eight starts in U.S.A. 1976 7f⁶ 8.5fg⁴ 10.4s 7g²] rather lightly-made colt: half-brother to champion 1976 American 2-y-o filly Sensational (by Hoist the Flag): dam, a stakes winner at 2 yrs in U.S.A., is sister to good American middle-distance horse Jungle Cove and half-sister to Oaks winner Long Look: won at Belmont and Aqueduct as a 2-y-o, including an allowance race: very creditable sixth to Wollow in Clerical, Medical Greenham Stakes at Newbury in April: ran best race afterwards when runner-up to Heracles in handicap at Epsom in June: should stay further than 1m. *I. Balding.*

MERITORIOUS 6 ch.g. Aureole 132–Parlez-vous 88 (Pardal 130) [1974 16f — 12.2g 17.7fg 1975 12h 1976 12g 14.7f⁵] of no account. *F. Dever.*

MERRY 3 ch.f. Jukebox 120–Gayness (Merry Boy) [1975 6g³ 5fg⁶ 6g³ 6g³ 6fg **52** 6s 7g⁴ 7.2s 1976 5v⁴ 6d 6fg 6s 6g⁵ 6f⁶ 5s⁶] quite a useful sort: only poor form: probably stays 7f: acts on any going: sold 600 gns Newmarket December Sales. *R. Mason.*

MERRY BRUMMEL 3 b.f. Beau Brummel–Merry Twirl (Turn-to) [1975 6g⁵ —
6g⁵ 5.1g² 5g 1976 6g 8fg 8g] well-grown filly: no worthwhile form at 3 yrs:
blinkered final outing: sold, covered by Dubassoff, 400 gns Newmarket December
Sales. *R. Jarvis.*

MERRY CRICKETER 6 ch.h. Double-U-Jay 120–Rose Bloom (Hook Money   **98**
124) [1974 6g⁶ 6g⁵ 6g⁴ 6g* 6f 7g 6s⁴ 6s* 6v³ 6s 1975 6s* 6g* 5.6g 6d 6d 7g
1976 6fg² 6fg 6fg 7.3d 6g 7s³ 7s⁶ 7s] leggy, strong-quartered horse: fairly useful
performer on his day: disappointing in 1976 apart from first and sixth outings:
stays 7f: seems to act on any going but is suited by some give in the ground:
retained by stable 420 gns Newmarket Autumn Sales. *A. Pitt.*

MERRY KERRY 7 ch.g. Quisling 117–Last Count (Final Score 113) [1974 11g   **97**
12f* 12g 12.3g* 13.3s 12g 12s 1975 10d 12fg 10f 1976 12fg⁴ 11.7fg 11g⁵ 12fg³
12f⁶ 12fg³ 12g² 12f* 14fg 12g* 12g* 16d³] big, handsome gelding: fairly useful
handicapper: winner three times in 1976, at Folkestone and Kempton in August
and at Doncaster the following month, on last-named course battling on well to
beat Palace Royal ¾ length: suited by 1½m and top-of-the-ground conditions
(didn't stay 2m on final start): sometimes wears bandages: sold 3,000 gns Newmarket Autumn Sales. *J. Sutcliffe.*

MERRY LEAP 3 b.f. Stephen George 102–French Court (Roi de Navarre II 123)   —
[1975 N.R. 1976 10.1f 10.1g 11.7fg⁶ 12s] second foal: 200 gns yearling: dam
never ran: well beaten in maiden and minor events at Windsor (apprentice ridden)
and ladies race at Chepstow. *M. McCourt.*

MERRY MEADOW 2 b.c. Meadow Mint 120–Glad Tidings 97 (Palestine 133)   **68**
[1976 6g⁶ 7s] quite attractive, tall, rangy colt: good walker: half-brother to a
winner in Denmark: 1,900 gns yearling: dam at her best at 2 yrs: 33/1, had a
stiff task for a newcomer in well-contested minor event at Kempton in August
but showed promise when sixth of nine to Adviser: third favourite for minor race
at Sandown in October but could finish only ninth of 12 to Sleeper: should stay
1m. *R. Price.*

MERRY MUSKATEER 2 ch.c. Jimmy Reppin 131–Ranjita 84 (Ballylinan 118)   **81**
[1976 5g⁵ 5s⁶ 6f 6h* 5fg³ 6fg⁶] big, strong colt: brother to consistent sprinter
Bien Etonne and half-brother to another winner: 5,600 gns yearling: dam a
sprinter: made all to win 10-runner maiden race at Carlisle in July by 2 lengths
from Eminence: put up a better effort in defeat at Newcastle later in month,
finishing 2 lengths third of six to Beaumel Board in £2,000 event after none too
good a run: ran moderately when favourite for a Ripon nursery in August and
was not seen out again: stays 6f well: acts on hard ground and is probably not
at his best on soft. *K. Payne.*

MERRY TUDOR 3 b.c. Tudor Music 131–Merry Mate 109 (Ballymoss 136)   **71**
[1975 7g 1976 11.1g 10fg 10.2fg 10g⁴ 10fg* 10h² 12f⁶ 10f²] big, rangy colt:
won five-runner maiden event at Ayr in July by 4 lengths from Jacyking: narrowly
beaten afterwards in handicap at Pontefract (by Acronym) and minor race at
Beverley (by sole opponent Bombe): best form at 1¼m: acts on hard ground:
wears blinkers: suited by forcing tactics: sold to I. Dudgeon 4,500 gns Newmarket
Autumn Sales. *M. Stoute.*

MESCALERO 4 ch.c. Tower Walk 130–Babucon 90 (My Babu 136) [1974   **57**
5fg⁴ 5g* 5f⁴ 5f⁵ 6fg³ 6fg 7.2g⁶ 6fg⁶ 1975 7d⁶ 7v⁶ 8d⁴ 8v³ 11f³ 11.7fg⁵ 10fg⁴ 12f³
9g⁵ 10fg⁵ 8.3fg⁴ 8d³ 1976 7fg⁴ 7g 8fg] useful sort: stays 11f, at least when
conditions aren't testing, but has yet to show he stays further: appears to act
on any going: suitable mount for an apprentice: trained by D. Marks until after
second outing. *G. Toft.*

MESOLONGI 2 b.c. Blakeney 126–River Run 111 (Chamossaire) [1976 7fg⁶   **86**
7fg⁴ 8fg² 8s⁶] neat colt: half-brother to several winners, including very useful
stayer Tiber (by Hugh Lupus): 6,000 gns yearling: dam a sprinter: 1½ lengths
second of 14 to Reppin Castle in maiden race at Beverley in September: had a
very stiff task when last in nursery on final outing: will stay middle distances.
C. Brittain.

MESSENGER BOY 5 b.g. Bleep-Bleep 134–Whistle Stop 114 (Whistler 129)   **90**
[1974 5g⁴ 8g⁴ 8fg* 1975 7f 6g* 8h⁵ 5.9fg² 7g² 7f 7g 7d³ 1976 5f³ 6v* 5f² 5g²
6g⁴ 6d* 7g³ 6s* 6g* 5g³ 6d] quite a useful handicapper: ran most consistently in
1976, winning four races, including three at Ayr: beat Indianira a short head
when gaining his last success at Ayr in July: effective at 5f to 1m: acts on any
going: excellent mount for an apprentice: genuine. *N. Angus.*

461

METAIR 2 ch.f. Laser Light 118–Treatisan 67 (Milesian 125) [1976 6f³ 5.3g* **118** 5f* 5fg³ 6fg* 5g*]

The 8-6 given to Metair in the Tote Free Handicap must have raised an eyebrow or two. She did not run in a pattern race nor in more than one race worth above £2,000 to the winner, but the handicapper has rated her second only to Durtal of the fillies, and a few pounds above the pattern race winners Ampulla, Cramond, Piney Ridge and Be Easy. The handicapper isn't far out with his rating in our opinion: there were few faster two-year-olds around.

Metair won four of her last five races, and only bad luck stopped her winning the other. She started favourite for the race she lost, a well-contested nursery at Goodwood in July, on the strength of comfortable wins in a maiden race at Brighton and in a minor event at Salisbury, but her chance went at the start when another horse swerved across her. By halfway she had recovered the lost ground but the effort of doing so proved too much in the final furlong and she finished third to Rahesh. Her two races afterwards showed how unlucky Metair had been. At Salisbury in September those useful fillies Silver Shoals, Great Memoirs, Stradey Park, Lady Constance and Great Flight proved no match for her and it was left to the newcomer Pas de Probleme, receiving a stone, to chase her home. A 7-lb penalty brought Metair's weight up to 9-0 in a nursery at Newmarket later in the month which made her top weight with Faridetta and Jameson. She started a bit tardily, but while several of the light weights had a barging match for the lead she made smooth progress along the rails, led halfway up the final hill and kept on strongly to win by half a length from First Swallow. This was a smart performance; the second was receiving over 20 lb and Faridetta, who had been beaten only narrowly by Be Easy when giving her weight in the Molecomb Stakes, was nearly four lengths behind in sixth place, apparently running up to her best.

Metair is a close-coupled filly and a good mover. She cost 1,600 guineas as a yearling, which might have seemed a high price if the only considerations to be made were that Laser Light's fee in 1973 was £148 and that Treatisan, her dam, cost only 380 guineas to buy in after winning a five-furlong seller at Redcar as a three-year-old. Treatisan had two living foals before Metair and both won; the first, a gelding by Cracksman, was a plater in this country who subsequently picked up several races in Belgium; the second, Eurocrat (by Gulf Pearl), showed quite useful form at two years before being sent to France where he won at up to a mile and a half. None of Treatisan's three winning half-brothers was anything out of the ordinary and her dam Treaty, a half-sister to the smart handicapper Tudor Treasure, was only a minor winner over six furlongs.

Metair has already shown she stays six furlongs well but there is no reason to anticipate her staying much further. Although we rate her highly among the fillies she still has some way to go before she can be considered up to winning a top sprint, and she will find races harder to come by at three years. She's genuine and consistent and acts on firm going. *W. Wightman.*

METEORITE 7 b.g. Star Moss 122–Rock Meal 85 (Rockefella) [1974 N.R. — 1975 N.R. 1976 13.4fg 12.2f] probably of no account. *S. Holland.*

MHAIRI DHU 2 b.f. Great Nephew 126–Control Tower 74 (Preciptic 122) **88** [1976 5f 7d 7s 6f²] strong filly: half-sister to four minor winners: dam a stayer: put up by far her best effort when length second of 12 to Unella in minor event at Pontefract in October: should stay 1¼m. *P. Walwyn.*

MIA BELLO 3 ch.f. Charlottown 127–Bianca Bellegra (Neebisch) [1975 8v³ — 1976 17.7f 16.1d 15f⁵ 10.4fg⁵ 14d⁴ 16.1d] plating-class maiden: should be suited by a test of stamina: sold to D. Williams 280 gns Doncaster November Sales. *R. Hollinshead.*

MIA CHILOE 3 b.f. Royal Palm 131–Polly Bellino 56 (Dadda Bert 95) [1975 — N.R. 1976 12d⁶ 16f] strong, robust filly: second living foal: half-sister to successful plater Archetto (by Arcticeelagh), a winner from 5f to 1¾m: dam won

Metair Freight Ltd's "Metair"

at 1¼m: well beaten in maiden race at Ripon and minor event at Nottingham in June but was still bit backward on latter course. *J. Hardy.*

MIA SAINT 2 ch.f. St Alphage 119–Acropolita Mia 75 (Acropolis 132) [1976 **87**
5g* 5fg* 5fg6 5fg* 5f* 5g3 5fg4] light-framed filly: first living foal: 900 gns yearling: dam won over 11.7f: proved well worth the 1,650 gns she cost to buy in after winning seller at Doncaster in March, adding further successes at Leicester and Windsor (two): good third of six to Brightelmstone in Acorn Stakes at Epsom in June, being beaten 3½ lengths: made much of running when gaining her wins: reportedly sold for export to U.S.A. *J. Hill.*

MICHAEL ARLEN 2 ch.c. Green God 128–Youee 66 (Buisson Ardent 129) **92**
[1976 5g2 5g* 5g3] lightly-made colt: fifth foal: half-brother to winning 3-y-o sprinter Power Girl (by Tyrant): 3,600 gns yearling: dam ran only at 2 yrs: won 10-runner event at Newbury in May very comfortably by 5 lengths from Colet Court: showed splendid initial speed on both other outings, eventually finishing 6 lengths second to Priors Walk at Kempton and 4½ lengths third to Royal Diver in Great Surrey Stakes at Epsom: sold 2,900 gns Newmarket September Sales. *J. Nelson.*

MICJAC 3 br.c. Highland Melody 112–Harmahal 79 (The Bug 135) [1975 5s **—**
5f 6h4 5fg* 6h2 5h2 5f 6d4 5d 6v 1976 8g 6f5 5f 7f 8d6 6f 10f6 8fg 10h4 11h5 12.2g 8s 7v] fair 2-y-o but showed little worthwhile form in 1976: not certain to stay 1m: possibly unsuited by very soft ground: has been tried in blinkers: retained by trainer 1,000 gns Doncaster November Sales. *J. Calvert.*

MICTED 5 ch.h. St Alphage 119–Dyne (Darius 129) [1974 N.R. 1975 6f5 6f4 **69**
5.8f6 6f2 7fg5 5.3g 5g5 5g* 6s6 1976 5.9f2 6f2 6f* 7fg4] lengthy horse: moderate handicapper: favourite when winning 11-runner handicap at Nottingham in June by a neck from White Emperor: stays 7f: acts on firm going: sold 200 gns Doncaster Autumn Sales. *R. Price.*

MID BEAT 3 b.c. Sir Ivor 135–Candida Gold 96 (Relic) [1975 6fg3 6fg* 6g **106**
1976 7fg3 7g 7.6g2 6fg 7f3 8d5 8g6 7s] strong, well-made, attractive American-bred colt: reportedly hobdayed: ran two cracking races, when close-up third to Man of Harlech in Tote Free Handicap at Newmarket in April and when 1¼ lengths second to Yunkel in valuable Gatwick Handicap at Lingfield in August:

463

was having first outing for four months on latter occasion: best form at 7f (not disgraced over 1m on sixth outing but appeared not to get trip next time out when wearing blinkers for first time): best form on a sound surface: far from consistent. *N. Vigors.*

MIDDLESTONE LADY 3 b.f. Falcon 131–Henco (High Hat 131) [1975 5f 8f³ 10g⁵ 8g 6g 1976 9fg 8h³ 10h³ 8h⁴ 10h² 15.8f⁶] small filly: plater: appeared to show improved form when runner-up to Moorman at Redcar in August: ran poorly only subsequent outing, when blinkered first time, and probably doesn't stay 2m. *W. A. Stephenson.*   **60**

MIDNIGHT CLEAR 2 ch.c. Mansingh 120–Christmas Fare 66 (Klondyke Bill 125) [1976 5f 5h* 5f 5g] compact, good-quartered colt: third foal: 1,500 gns yearling: dam of little account: all out when winning nine-runner maiden race at Folkestone in August by 1½ lengths from Communicate: had much stiffer tasks afterwards: acts on hard ground. *J. Winter.*   **81**

MIDNIGHT FLAME 4 br.g. Highland Melody 112–Flame Dancer 72 (Hop Bridge 87) [1974 5g 6fg 5fg 1975 7s 8g 6f 5.9fg* 5g⁶ 5g³ 1976 5f³ 5fg⁵ 5f⁶ 5f⁴ 5.9fg³ 5g 5g⁵ 5s] leggy gelding: poor handicapper: stays 6f: acts on firm going. *E. Weymes.*   **65**

MIDNIGHT MELODY 3 br.f. Linacre 133–Queen's Lane 107 (Tamerlane 128) [1975 7.2s 5v* 1976 10.6d 8f 8f 8.2v 8g 8.2s] neat, strongly-made filly: won maiden race at Haydock in November, 1975: well beaten at 3 yrs: should stay 1m+: acts well on heavy going. *J. Hanson.*   —

MIDSUMMER 2 br.f. My Swanee 122–Alison 73 (Abernant 142) [1976 5fg⁶ 5g² 5fg⁵ 5.3f⁴ 6fg² 6f² 6f 6s] half-sister to three minor winners: 2,100 gns yearling: dam, winner at up to 1¾m in Ireland, is sister to smart sprinter Ruthin: second in three maiden races, going down by 3 lengths to Cake Popper at Brighton in August on last occasion: will stay 1m: usually wears blinkers nowadays. *S. Ingham.*   **77**

MIDSUMMER MADNESS 3 ch.f. Silly Season 127–So Precious 100 (Tamerlane 128) [1975 6d 8v 1976 8f 7f² 7f² 8.2g³ 8f 10.2g⁵ 8.2f² 12g* 10v⁴] shapely filly: won 11-runner maiden race at Lanark in October by 4 lengths from Medodosusu: stays 1½m: best form on a sound surface, although wasn't entirely disgraced on heavy ground final outing: races with her tongue tied down. *S. Hall.*   **66**

MIDSUMMER STREAK 2 ch.c. Midsummer Night II 117–Flashlight 88 (Firestreak 125) [1976 5g 6fg 6fg 5d⁵ 7s] lengthy, workmanlike colt: fourth live foal: dam won over 6f at 2 yrs: ran easily best race when about 3½ lengths fifth of eight to Hedge School in minor event at Haydock in October: will stay 1m: evidently suited by some give in the ground. *H. Nicholson.*   **73**

MID-TERM 2 b.f. Quartette 106–Long Term 71 (Sing Sing 134) [1976 6f 6g] sister to moderate 1¼m winner Singlet: dam best at sprint distances: behind in maiden and minor events at Windsor in August, finishing last of 15 on second outing. *J. Holt.*   —

MIELLITA 2 b.f. King Emperor–Honey Match 98 (Match III 135) [1976 6fg* 6g⁴ 8g⁵] well-made, good-looking filly: third foal: half-sister to a winner in Germany by Sea Hawk II: 17,000 gns yearling: dam won over 1¼m and is half-sister to numerous good winners: gambled on, won 17-runner Selsey Stakes at Goodwood in July, not being unduly hard ridden to score by ½ length from Wedding Band: ran creditably in well-contested events at York (about 4 lengths fourth to Lady Mere) and Doncaster (2½ lengths fifth to Royal Plume) afterwards: will stay 1¼m. *B. Hills.*   **98**

MIGELITTO 4 ch.c. Lorenzaccio 130–Vivien 66 (Nearco) [1974 5s³ 6g 7.5f* 7v* 8s* 7.5s 1975 7v 12g* 12g³ 12g 12g⁵ 12g 12g² 1976 10.2g 16g 14d⁵ 13.8g³ 12fg⁶ 13s² 15g⁶ 12h² 13g⁴ 16fg 18fg² 18g⁴ 15g² 12s⁵ 12.2s³ 12s] strong colt: ex-Irish colt: quite a moderate performer: in frame in eight of his races at 4 yrs: stays well: acts on any going: sometimes wears blinkers: sold out of D. Weld's stable 900 gns Ascot January Sales. *M. Naughton.*   **76**

MIGHTY MAGGIE 2 b.f. Right Tack 131–Tesco Maid (Tesco Boy 121) [1976 7fg 8.2f²] second foal: dam won over 6f in Ireland: ¾-length second to Padovanna in 14-runner maiden race at Hamilton in September: stays 1m. *N. Angus.*   **77**

MIGHTY MOTH 2 b.c. Lear Jet 123–Treasure Flower 67 (Donore 119) [1976 5g 6fg] stocky colt: half-brother to four minor winners here and abroad: 540 gns yearling: dam stayed 1m: behind in minor event at Kempton in May (very backward) and maiden race at Newbury in June. *M. Haynes.*

MILBIL 4 br.g. Mandamus 120–Quolanta 81 (Quorum 126) [1974 5f 5fg 6s* — 7s² 8s 8v 1975 12g 6fg 7g 6g 1976 6v⁴ 10v] plater nowadays: should stay further than 7f: well suited by soft going: has run respectably in blinkers. *D. Chapman.*

MILD WIND 4 b.f. Porto Bello 118–Mile Cross 88 (Milesian 125) [1974 5g 6fg — 5d 6g 1975 6d 6f 1976 5h⁵ 6f⁴ 10d] of no account. *D. Chapman.*

MILE LANE 4 b.g. Tamerlane 128–Milesian Lady 85 (Milesian 125) [1974 N.R. — 1975 N.R. 1976 12f 8g 8fg 8f³ 8g] probably of little account. *W. Marshall.*

MILESIAN PRINCE 5 b.g. Milesian 125–Gentle Gael 97 (Celtic Ash) [1974 — 8.2fg 7f 7fg 7g 7g 8g⁵ 10g 10.8v 1975 10.2f 9fg⁵ 8f³ 8f² 5f⁶ 10d 8g 1976 10f⁶ 8.2s 12s 12s] lengthy gelding: poor performer: stays 1¼m: acts on firm going: has worn blinkers. *D. Hanley.*

MILESIAN STAR 7 ch.g. Star Moss 122–Milesian Lady 85 (Milesian 125) — [1974 N.R. 1975 N.R. 1976 12g³ 12.2g⁵ 14.7f³ 16.1fg³ 8g 8f] poor handicapper: stays well and probably finds 1m on short side: tried in blinkers at 2 yrs. *C. Tinkler.*

MILITARY MARCH 2 ch.f. Brigadier Gerard 144–Zither 72 (Vienna 127) — p [1976 6f⁵] half-sister to three winners, notably very smart middle-distance performer Zimbalon (by Ragusa): dam won at 1¼m: second favourite for 16-runner maiden race at Lingfield in June but finished only fifth, about 11 lengths behind Paddington: will be suited by middle distances. *R. Hern.*

MILITARY QUEEN 2 ch.f. Military 112–King's Desire (Souverain 135) [1976 **78** 6fg 6f 5fg 5s⁴ 5s*] leggy filly: second foal: dam won a point-to-point: won 18-runner maiden race at Warwick in October by ¾ length from Jogger, the pair finishing clear: should stay 6f+: unseated rider on third outing. *J. Spearing.*

MILK RIVER 2 br.f. Another River 89–Milk Hills (Arctic Time 127) [1976 8v] — sixth reported produce: dam never ran: 33/1 and backward, showed up until straight when behind in 12-runner minor event won by Applalto at Teesside in October. *W. A. Stephenson.*

MILLER'S LASS 2 b.f. Mill Reef 141–Prudent Girl 92 (Primera 131) [1976 6f **103** 7.5f* 7f²] Irish filly: second foal: 31,000 gns yearling: dam, a middle-distance winner, is half-sister to numerous winners, including St Leger winner Hethersett and very smart performers Proud Chieftain and Royal Prerogative: won 12-runner maiden plate at Gowran Park in August by 1½ lengths from Momentary Affair, the pair finishing clear: took on much better company in Park Stakes at Phoenix Park the following month and ran very well, being beaten only ½ length by All Serene after running wide into straight: will stay 1½m: a very useful filly in the making. *D. Weld, Ireland.*

MILLION 2 ch.c. Mill Reef 141–Lalibela 123 (Honeyway 125) [1976 7d] half- — p brother to three winners, including useful 1½m handicapper Mad Mahdi (by Hill Clown) and useful 11f and 13f winner Anadyomene (by Sea Hawk II): 202,000 gns yearling: dam won Cheveley Park Stakes and showed form only at sprint distances: weak 10/1 shot, pushed along most of way when thirteenth of 25 to Bessie Wallis in Houghton Stakes at Newmarket in October: did not impress us in paddock beforehand but should do better at 3 yrs. *R. Hern.*

MILLIONAIRE 2 br.c. Mill Reef 141–State Pension 112 (Only for Life 126) **108** [1976 6fg² 6fg² 6f* 6fg* 8d⁴] well-made, good-looking colt: second foal: half-brother to smart 1975 2-y-o 7f winner State Occasion (by Roan Rocket): dam second in Oaks: had his rivals well strung out when winning minor events at Haydock in August and Windsor the following month, on former course drawing right away to win by 12 lengths from Chichester Bird: got a bit stirred up in paddock and never looked dangerous when 8 lengths fourth of six to Gairloch in Royal Lodge Stakes at Ascot later in September: will stay middle distances: acts on firm going. *P. Walwyn.*

MILLIONDOLLARMAN 2 br.c. Connaught 130–Every Blessing 110 (Parthia **78** 132) [1976 5d⁶ 6f 8d⁶] compact, good sort: half-brother to fairly useful 1½m winner Pine Tree Hill (by Sir Ivor): 21,000 gns yearling: dam, winner at up to 8.5f, is half-sister to high-class stayer Die Hard: showed some promise on all his outings, and was having his first race for three months when never-dangerous 11 lengths sixth of 17 to Ad Lib Ra in maiden event at Newbury in September: will stay 1½m: may improve. *Mrs R. Lomax.*

MILLIPEDE 3 b.f. Military 112–Redouble 62 (Bounteous 125) [1975 7f 6g 6fg — 1976 10fg 7h⁴] of no account. *J. Leigh.*

Mrs D. McCalmont's "Millionaire"

MILL MISS 2 b.f. Typhoon 125–Lady Cortina 80 (Cortachy 107) [1976 5f³ — 5f⁶ 7s] beaten long way in poor races at Folkestone. *A. Neaves.*

MILLY MO 3 ch.f. Varano–Dundalk Rose (Sovereign Lord 120) [1975 N.R. — 1976 10.8f 10.1fg⁶] first foal: 210 gns yearling: dam Irish middle-distance handicapper: seems devoid of ability. *J. Spearing.*

MILVERTON 2 br.c. Royal Palace 131–Melodina 118 (Tudor Melody 129) **94** [1976 7fg² 8v²] Irish colt: second foal: 12,500 gns yearling: dam won over 5f at 2 yrs and stayed 1½m well: second favourite when 3 lengths second to odds-on Marinsky in 16-runner newcomers event at the Curragh in September: went down by a similar margin to Skelum in maiden race at Leopardstown the following month: will stay middle distances: sure to win races at 3 yrs. *C. Collins, Ireland.*

MIMIKA 3 ch.f. Lorenzaccio 130–Nytole 98 (Relko 136) [1975 5s⁴ 5g* 6fg³ 7g⁴ **73** 7fg⁵ 8.2g⁶ 7.2v 1976 12.2g 11.1f³ 12g⁵] light-framed, rather unfurnished filly: very good mover: quite a moderate handicapper: should stay 1½m: acts on firm going. *C. Brittain.*

MINED ILLUSION 2 ch.f. Pretense–Tanzanite (Mongo) [1976 5fg 6f 8g³ 8g* **91** 8s⁵ 8v 8s] first foal: dam stakes-placed winner at up to 1m in U.S.A.: won 12-runner maiden race at Leicester in September by 1½ lengths from Cape Race: beaten a long way on all outings afterwards and is probably unsuited by soft going: stays 1m. *B. Hanbury.*

MINERVINA 3 ch.f. King's Troop 118–Chopiniana 102 (Premonition 130) — [1975 5g 5f 1976 8fg 6f⁶ 6f 8fg] poor plater: sold 360 gns Ascot October Sales. *W. Wightman.*

MINEWA 4 gr.f. Phaeton 123–Shamirah (Charlottesville 135) [1974 7d 1975 — 11.1fg 14h⁵ 12g⁵ 16s⁵ 16.1d 1976 14fg] strong, workmanlike filly: only poor

466

form: tried in blinkers on only outing at 4 yrs: sold 1,500 gns Ascot June Sales: dead. *G. Balding.*

MINGALLES   2 b.f. Prince de Galles 125–Mingary 74 (Jock Scot 121)   [1976 5g   **65**
6h 7f 7h⁶ 7g³ 7g³]   fair sort: third in seller at Warwick in August and nursery at Lanark in October, putting up by far her best effort in latter race: will stay middle distances: started slowly on first outing, refused to enter stalls on next intended appearance and ran from flag starts afterwards: blinkered third outing. *D. Jermy.*

MINIBUS   3 b.f. John Splendid 116–Pleaseme 100 (Javelot 124)   [1975 5fg 5g⁴   **77**
5g 5.9g⁶   1976 6f² 6fg 6fg* 6f⁴ 7.2g 9fg 7s]   quite a moderate handicapper: winner at Windsor in June by 2 lengths from Shanghai Lady: suited by 6f: sold out of J. Dunlop's stable 2,000 gns Newmarket July Sales after fourth start and ran below her best afterwards. *R. Cambidge.*

MINIGIRL   2 b.f. Communication 119–Friendly Relations (Anwar 120)   [1976 5s   **68**
5fg 5f 6f⁴ 7fg 6v⁴ 6s 5s³]   light-framed filly: plater: ran best race when just over 2 lengths third to Kabagold at Haydock in October: stays 6f: probably acts on any going: wears blinkers nowadays: sold to D. Gandolfo 300 gns Doncaster November Sales. *J. Etherington.*

MINIGOLD   6 br.g. Goldhill 125–Minette 90 (Flush Royal 127)   [1974 6g² 10d⁴   **50**
7f 7g² 8.3fg* 6f³ 7g⁴ 7f⁶ 8.3fg⁴ 6d³ 6fg⁶ 8.2g* 10g* 8.3fg* 10g² 8g   1975 10g⁴ 12g 10fg 8g⁴ 9f 10.1fg⁵ 11.1g⁶ 8g   1976 10f² 8fg⁴ 8g 10s]   strong gelding: poor plater: well suited by 1¼m but appears not to stay further: acts on any going: sometimes wears bandages: blinkered final appearance. *A. Davison.*

MINO BOY   3 b.g. Decoy Boy 129–Pontesbury (Falls of Clyde 126)   [1975 5fg³   **78**
5g² 5fg² 5f³ 5g⁴ 5.9g*   1976 5.9g* 6d 6fg⁴ 7f 6f 6f]   strong, muscular gelding: won minor event at Wolverhampton in May by a length from Princess Silica: not disgraced when fourth of six to Gwent in handicap at Newbury the following month, best subsequent effort: stays 6f (ran moderately when tried at 7f but had stiffish task at weights): best form on a sound surface. *J. Etherington.*

MINSTER GIRL   2 b.f. First Phase 97–Bendy **§§** (Ben Hawke 94)   [1976 5f   **—**
10s]   probably useless. *T. Walker.*

MINSTER MELODY   2 br.f. Highland Melody 112–Denbigh Ward 81 (Blast 125)   **73**
[1976 5g³ 5d³ 5s⁶]   long-backed filly: second foal: dam won from 7f to 11f: quite a moderate maiden: will be suited by 6f+. *J. Cousins.*

MINSTREL   3 br.c. Crooner 119–Maizenrose 83 (Rustam 127)   [1975 5fg⁶   **110**
5.1g² 5.1g* 5s 5.3g*(dis) 5d⁴ 5g³ 5f*   1976 5g 5f* 5g⁴ 5fg 5g 5g² 5d*]   strong, well-made, good sort: dam stayed 1m: very useful handicapper: decisive winner at Newbury in April: had some stiff tasks afterwards until appearing to show much improved form (50/1) when 2½ lengths second to Athlete's Foot in strongly-contested Sir Gatric Stakes at Doncaster in September, finishing in front of such as Thrifty Trio, Polly Peacham and Music Boy: favourite, just got home in a close finish with Enchanted and Derringo in minor race at Newbury later in month: unsuited by really soft ground: sold 4,500 gns Newmarket Autumn Sales and was exported to Hong Kong. *J. Powney.*

MINSTREL SONG   3 b.c. Alcide 136–Helen Traubel 88 (Sing Sing 134)   [1975   **90**
6fg 7g 7.2fg⁴ 8.2g²   1976 12v* 12fg⁵ 12fg⁵ 14g³ 14fg* 14f² 16fg*]   good sort: half-brother to 4-y-o Noble Dancer (by Prince de Galles): fairly useful handicapper: winner at Hamilton (maiden race, by 15 lengths), York (on disqualification of Japsilk) and Thirsk: put up his best performance on last-named course in July when beating Two Swallows 2½ lengths despite hanging left on to rails: well suited by 2m: appears to act on any going. *W. Marshall.*

MINT   2 b.f. Meadow Mint 120–Painful Details (Shantung 132)   [1976 5f 5g⁴ 6d⁵   **91**
6fg⁵ 7fg² 7fg³ 8g³ 8g³]   well-grown, useful-looking filly: half-sister to two winners, including Beverley Boy (by Chebs Lad), quite a useful winner at up to 13f: 1,900 gns yearling: dam never ran: still a maiden but showed fairly useful form when tackling longer distances: stayed on well when creditable third in 1m nurseries won by Cosy Bar at York and by Revlow at Ayr, both in September: will stay middle distances. *W. Elsey.*

MINTAGE   2 b.c. Meadow Mint 120–Manera (Silly Season 127)   [1976 6fg*   **109**
6g* 6fg 7.3d*]   well-made colt: first produce: 1,000 gns foal, resold 1,050 gns yearling: dam never ran: won maiden race at Salisbury in June and ran out an impressive winner of 10-runner minor event at Kempton the following month: put up an excellent effort when gaining his third success, making all and holding

Marlborough Stakes, Newbury—Minstrel squeezes home from the blinkered Enchanted and Derringo

on really well to win 13-runner nursery at Newbury in September by a neck from Reclamation: will stay 1¼m: acts on a firm and a soft surface. *J. Dunlop.*

MINT CONDITION 2 b.g. Sovereign Gleam 117–Empress of Scotland (Ratifi-   **78** cation 129) [1976 6g 6d*] useful sort: half-brother to two winners, including quite useful 1m to 1¼m handicapper Empress of Britain (by Amber X): 440 gns yearling: dam a middle-distance performer: having first race for two months, looked very useful for a plater when winning 24-runner seller at Windsor in September by 1½ lengths from Double Light, the pair finishing clear: bought in 1,500 gns afterwards: will be suited by 1m+. *P. Cole.*

MINT IMPERIAL 3 b.f. Vaguely Noble 140–English Toffee (Sisters Prince)   **75** [1975 N.R. 1976 10g 12fg 12g 9v] big, good-looking American-bred filly: fourth foal: sister to Noblest Noble, placed in useful company at 1½m and 2m from three starts at 3 yrs: $35,000 yearling: dam won seven races at 2 yrs and 3 yrs, including stakes events: didn't fulfil the promise she showed in early-season maiden races and ran badly in maiden event at York in October on final outing: should stay well. *B. Hills.*

MINTON 4 ch.g. Crockett 130–Pretty Asset 100 (Galivanter 131) [1974 6fg 7v³   **49** 7v² 7g⁵ 1975 8f 11.7s 8fg⁵ 10h⁶ 10g 16f⁴ 12s⁶ 16s 1976 10f 8fg 10.1fg³ 10f* 10.6d 10f 10.1fg* 16.1h⁴] lengthy, attractive gelding: plater: bought in for 420 gns after winning at Folkestone in May and for 800 gns after beating Smart Shirley at Windsor in August: best at around 1¼m: acts on any going: sometimes wears blinkers but hasn't when successful. *P. Haslam.*

MIRACLES COTTAGE 3 b.f. Super Gay 101–Wendys Cottage (Cottage Son)   **—** [1975 N.R. 1976 12s 12v] sister to quite moderate novice hurdler/chaser Mr Darling: dam never ran: well beaten in end-of-season events at Chepstow and Lingfield. *D. Dale.*

MIREHOUSE 3 b.f. Huntercombe 133–Dundry Hill 95 (High Perch 126) [1975   **—** N.R. 1976 7f 6g 7g] big, rangy filly: second live foal: half-sister to 1m winner St Georges Hill (by Major Portion): dam won at up to 1¼m: unplaced in new-comers race at Newbury in April and maiden and minor races at Kempton in May: needs a lot more time. *W. Wightman.*

MISALLIANCE 2 b.f. Royal Palace 131–Costmary 108 (Grey Sovereign 128 §)   **86** [1976 6g⁴ 7d²] attractive filly: sister to fair 3-y-o 11f winner Castle in Spain, and half-sister to two 2-y-o winners, including useful 1971 5f to 7f winner Silly Billy (by Silly Season): dam won 14 races at up to 13.5f: put in best work in closing stages, after being under pressure 2f out, and ran on really well to finish

468

1¼ lengths second to Guama when favourite for 30-runner maiden race at Newbury in September: will be suited by middle distances. *J. Tree.*

MISCHIEF 3 gr.f. Sassafras 135–Princess Caroline 68 (Sovereign Path 125) **76** [1975 6g 7d 7.6g⁵ 1976 6s⁴ 6f³ 8fg² 12fg* 12f³ 11.7fg⁵] neat filly: got up close home when winning six-runner maiden race at Lingfield in August by a head from Ruscombe: suited by 1½m and may well stay further: ran moderately final start. *R. Price.*

MISCHIEFMAKER 2 ch.f. Calpurnius 122–Lucky Maid 85 (Acropolis 132) **73** [1976 5f⁶ 7.2f⁴ 8s* 7.2v] compact filly: half-sister to 1m and 1¼m winner Wheatclose (by Highland Melody): dam won over 1¼m: driven out when winning 18-runner seller at Redcar in October by a length from Velvet Circle: sold out of J. W. Watts's stable 820 gns afterwards: will stay further than 1m: acts on any going but is suited by soft. *D. McCain.*

MISCOU 3 b.f. Charlottown 127–Royal Justice 114 (Supreme Court 135) [1975 — 7f² 1976 8f⁴ 12fg 12d 10d 12g] neat filly: going on very well at finish when fourth to Living Legend in 1m maiden race at Ascot in April: subsequently disappointing over longer distances: probably unsuited by a soft surface: sold 10,000 gns Newmarket December Sales. *H. Wragg.*

MISFIELD 2 br.f. Sahib 114–Sauce Melba 90 (Hard Sauce 131) [1976 5fg⁴ **99** 5fg* 5d³ 5fg³ 5g* 5f³ 5fg 6g 6g⁴ 5fg³ 6v⁴ 5d] leggy filly: half-sister to two minor winners: 600 gns yearling: dam won over 5f at 2 yrs: winner of maiden race at Warwick in April and minor event at Leicester in May, on latter course beating Mummy's Darling by 1½ lengths: excellent fourth of 12 to Red Johnnie in £2,000 nursery at Leicester in September: best form at 6f: possibly not at her best on heavy ground. *R. Hollinshead.*

MISS BAGLEY 2 b.f. Laser Light 118–True Penny 67 (Relic) [1976 5.9g 5fg **85** 5f⁵ 5g⁵ 5d 5s 5s³ 5s 5v⁶ 5s*] fifth living foal: dam temperamental winner over 6f at 3 yrs: won 14-runner maiden race at Teesside in November, just coming out best in a desperate finish with So Cutting and Just Sherwood: should stay 6f: acts on soft going. *R. Hollinshead.*

MISS BELVEDERE 4 b.f. Remainder 106–Lilliberto (Umberto 118) [1974 5d² — 5fg³ 5g⁴ 5f⁶ 5s 5d 5g⁶ 1975 6v 5.9v⁵ 5v⁵ 5.9g 5f 5f³ 5h 5f 1976 5g 5h 5fg 7f 5fg⁶] bad plater: best form at 5f: acts on firm going: probably best in blinkers but didn't wear them at 4 yrs: sold 270 gns Doncaster October Sales. *S. Nesbitt.*

MISS CALETA 3 ch.f. Quayside 124–Blasllyn 88 (Blast 125) [1975 N.R. — 1976 16.1f] first foal: sold 1,100 gns at Doncaster January 1975 Sales: dam won over 5f at 2 yrs and stayed 1½m: seventh of 11 behind Frisky Scot in amateur riders maiden race at Haydock in August. *G. Richards.*

MISS CANDINE 2 ch.f. King Emperor–Picnic Party (Honeyway 125) [1976 **66** 5g 5fg 5d⁵ 6v 7s] well-made filly: half-sister to several winners, including speedy 1967 2-y-o Canteen (by King's Troop) and very useful sprinter Staincross (by Crocket): 2,300 gns yearling: dam a sprinter: showed only a little ability in maiden company. *B. Hills.*

MISS CARIBBEAN 2 gr.f. Sea Hawk II 131–Oserian 109 (Court Martial) **74** [1976 6fg⁶ 7.2f 7g⁵] strong, good-bodied filly: half-sister to several winners, notably very smart 1973 2-y-o Welsh Harmony (by Tudor Melody): dam stayed 1m: showed only a little ability: will probably stay 1¼m+. *Doug Smith.*

MISS CARVIN 2 b.f. Carvin 127–Lets Hope (One Count) [1976 7s] third — living produce: half-sister to two winners, notably very useful 3-y-o All Hope (by My Swallow): 2,900 gns yearling: dam won twice at around 1m at 3 yrs in Ireland: 20/1 when fifteenth of 20 to Brightly in maiden race at Newmarket in October. *M. Jarvis.*

MISS CHIRK 5 b.m. Hard Man 102–Ghost of the King 75 § (Fair Seller 126) — [1974 7.6d 5.9g 5.9s 1975 5h 5f 6f 7.6fg 5.9g 5g 1976 5g⁵ 6g] poor sprinter: sometimes sweats up: has worn blinkers. *M. James.*

MISS CONSTANCE 3 b.f. Calpurnius 122–Friendly Relations (Anwar 120) — [1975 6d 1976 5fg 7fg 8g³] compact filly: poor plater. *W. Wharton.*

MISS DALLAS 4 br.f. March Past 124–Blue Cheri 67 (Hook Money 124) [1974 **58** 6fg 1975 10fg 10.1fg 10.1g 10s 10.8g⁶ 1976 10f* 8.3d⁵ 8.2s 8s⁴] poor handi-capper: 25/1, showed vastly improved form when winning at Salisbury in August by a length from Track Hero: ran creditably afterwards: stays 1¼m: acts on any going. *G. Smyth.*

MISS DAMUS 3 br.f. Mandamus 120–Miracle Girl 75 (Sing Sing 134) [1975 6fg **65** 6f⁶ 8g 1976 12f 10.5s 8fg 9fg⁵ 8f³ 9g⁴ 7f⁴ 8s² 9s³ 8.2v*] strong filly: made all when winning maiden race at Nottingham in October by a length from Smithfield Lady: stays 9f: acts on heavy ground: form only in blinkers. *J. Etherington.*

MISS DEED 2 b.f. David Jack 125–Captive Flower 99 (Manacle 123) [1976 **83** 5g 5f⁶ 5.1f³ 5g⁵ 5fg 5s 5v⁵] first foal: 1,400 gns yearling: dam won twice over 5f at 2 yrs: ran well when fifth in apprentice nursery at Ayr in September to Whenby and minor event at Teesside the following month to Forlorn Scot: will be suited by 6f: best form with some give in the ground. *P. Robinson.*

MISS DIANE 2 b.f. Siliconn 121–Spaniard's Darling (Darling Boy 124) [1976 **70** 5f² 5f² 5f³ 6g³ 7f* 8f⁴ 8s] leggy filly: having first race for two months, won 10-runner seller at Wolverhampton in August (no bid): ran respectably in better company on next outing: stays 1m: appears to act on any going. *J. Hill.*

MISS DIKE 4 ch.f. Dike–Spoiled Wine (Pampered King 121) [1974 5g 5g 7.5f⁵ 7.5g⁵ 5s 1975 12f* 14f 12f⁶ 1976 12g 8g 12.2f] ex-Irish filly: no worthwhile form in three outings at 4 yrs in this country: stays 1½m: acts on firm going. *A. Jones.*

MISS DIVER 2 ch.f. Deep Diver 134–Modern Millie 95 (Milesian 125) [1976 **90** 5fg³ 5fg² 5s² 5fg³ 5fg³ 5f*5f² 5h² 5f² 5s⁵] neat, strong, attractive filly: third live foal: 6,200 gns yearling: dam won twice over 5f at 2 yrs: made all to win 12-runner maiden race at Lanark in July by 2½ lengths from Mariner's Girl: creditable second on next three outings, on last two being beaten only narrowly: only just stays 5f and is best suited by a firm surface: blinkered on fifth outing but is consistent: sold 7,000 gns Newmarket December Sales. *M. Jarvis.*

MISS DUBLIN 3 br.f. Tudor Melody 129–Miss Ireland 83 (Grey Sovereign 128 §) — [1975 6f³ 6fg³ 7g* 1976 7fg] sister to Irish Harmony, quite a useful winner at up to 11f: easy winner of 15-runner maiden event at Yarmouth in 1975: unimpressive in paddock and had stiff task when well beaten on only outing at 3 yrs: sold 6,600 gns Newmarket December Sales. *Doug Smith.*

MISS DUCAT 2 b.f. Pieces of Eight 128–Grass Skirt 77 (Native Prince) [1976 — 6g⁵ 6d] first foal: dam won over 5f at 3 yrs: remote fifth of 15 in seller won by Cedar Emerald at Lingfield in August, first outing. *J. Holt.*

MISS ELIZA 2 ch.f. Mountain Call 125–Merry Quip 73 (Petition 130) [1976 **101** 5d 6f² 6f*] leggy filly: half-sister to three winners, including very useful sprinter Sound Barrier (by Sound Track): 2,500 gns yearling: dam won at 7f and 1m: ran out a most convincing winner of 18-runner maiden race at Ripon in August, making all the running to beat Swift Sons by 7 lengths: will stay 7f: apprentice ridden last two starts. *S. Hall.*

MISS FANACKAPAN 4 b.f. Colonist II 126–Poosie Nansie (Combat 123) — [1974 N.R. 1975 N.R. 1976 14.7f⁶] fourth foal: dam, of little account, is half-sister to useful chaser Loyal Fort: backward, finished tailed off in maiden race at Redcar in August won by Pontresina, only outing on flat. *P. Buckley.*

MISS FILBERT 4 ch.f. Compensation 127–Money Matters 68 (Hook Money 124) **92** [1974 5fg⁴ 5f 7d² 6v³ 6s² 1975 7v⁵ 7v* 8s 7d* 7g² 7f⁶ 7fg² 7g* 6d 1976 8g⁵ 7.2d² 7fg 7fg² 7.6h⁵ 7g² 8g 8g 7.3d* 8g⁴ 7s] compact filly: quite a useful handi-capper: produced a fine turn of foot when winning at Newbury in September by 5 lengths from Star Walk: stays 1m but is possibly best at around 7f: acts on a firm surface but is particularly well suited by soft ground: genuine: ran disappointingly on final appearance. *D. Keith.*

MISS FRENCHY 3 ch.f. Exbury 138–Pytchley Princess 107 (Privy Councillor — 125) [1975 N.R. 1976 13.3fg 10fg] third living foal: half-sister to French minor 1¼m winner Hunting Man (by Mandamus): dam won at up to 1m: well beaten in maiden races at Newbury (tailed off) and Newmarket (last of 14) in June. *G. Smyth.*

MISS HARTNELL 2 ch.f. Ballymoss 136–Guernavaca 46 (Klairon 131) [1976 — 5fg 6v⁶] second foal: half-sister to a winner in Sweden by Mandamus: 1,500 gns yearling: dam appeared to stay 1¼m: beaten a long way in minor events at Goodwood and Newcastle in the autumn. *K. Payne.*

MISS HIGH PEAK 2 b.f. Decoy Boy 129–Lucky Slipper (Lucky Sovereign) — [1976 5g 5fg⁴] bad plater: sold 320 gns Doncaster May Sales. *K. Payne.*

MISS HILLSIDE 2 b.f. Frankincense 120–Shamrock's Beauty 79 (Primera **54** 131) [1976 5f 7s 8.2v] fourth foal: 1,050 gns yearling: dam stayed well: little worthwhile form in sellers: was gambled on second outing: should stay 1m. *J. Hill.*

MISS INIT 2 b.f. Balidar 133–Visitation 84 (Tarqogan 125) [1976 5fg 5fg³ **67**
5f 6g 5f² 6h²] workmanlike filly: first foal: 880 gns yearling: dam stayed 1¼m:
apprentice ridden when second in nurseries at Folkestone in August, going down
by only a neck to Bee Splendid on first occasion: stays 6f. *R. Smyth.*

MISSISSIPPI 2 br.c. Linacre 133–Missa 107 (Milesian 125) [1976 5s⁴ 5g⁶ 6g⁴ **102**
7f³ 7g² 6.3f³ 6f² 7g³ 6f* 8d⁵] small, quite well-made Irish colt: half-brother to
several winners, including very useful middle-distance performer Hymn (by
Aureole): dam won over 5f: won 23-runner minor event at Naas in October by a
length from Star of Erin: had some good efforts to his name in useful company
earlier, finishing third in both Mullion Stakes at Leopardstown and Anglesey
Stakes at the Curragh and finishing second in two other races: also ran well when
staying-on 1¼ lengths third of 17 to Royal Plume in £2,900 event at Ascot in
September: stays 1m: appears to act on any going. *Mrs D. Brewster, Ireland.*

MISS JIGGS 3 br.f. Blue Streak 99–Cushella (Dear Gazelle 113) [1975 5s 5.3g —
7s 1976 10fg 12f 8h⁴] of no account. *B. Wise.*

MISS KILO 4 b.f. King Log 115–Nearly Missed (Caudillo) [1974 5f 5.9fg 7v —
7g 7g 5v 1975 7v⁴ 9g 7.2g 10.4g 14fg 1976 16.1d⁵] poor plater *A. Jones.*

MISS KNIGHTSBRIDGE 2 gr.f. Sovereign Path 125–Miss London 95 (Pall **90**
Mall 132) [1976 5fg 5fg⁵ 5g⁶ 5d 5d* 6s⁴ 6v³ 5s⁴] rangy filly: second foal: half-
sister to fair 1975 2-y-o 5f winner Miss Chelsea (by Crocket): dam, who stayed 1m,
is half-sister to very useful miler Miss Paris (by Sovereign Path): won maiden
race at Haydock in October by 3 lengths from Friendly: creditable third to
Punto Banco in nursery at Nottingham later in month: should stay 1m: well
suited by some give in the ground: sometimes bandaged in front. *Doug Smith.*

MISS KUNG FU 3 b.f. Caliban 123–Kung Hei 94 (Road House II) [1975 5fg **70**
6fg 7g 7s⁵ 1976 8fg³ 7fg⁶ 8fg² 8g 6f² 6h² 5g⁴ 7g² 7s⁶ 6s⁵ 8v²] big, rangy
filly: placed in varied company: stays 1m: acts on any going: has run respectably in blinkers: sometimes sweats up. *R. Supple.*

MISS LA CREEVY 2 b.f. Hul a Hul 124–Hunter's Melody 70 (Off Key 121) **65**
[1976 5fg 6f 7g] half-sister to two winners in France: 2,000 gns yearling: dam a
staying half-sister to numerous winners: seventh of 16 in maiden race won by
stable-companion My Therape at Nottingham in July, first and best effort:
should be suited by 6f+. *M. Stoute.*

MISS MANDEVILLE 4 b.f. Runnymede 123–Royal Deb (Flush Royal 127) —
[1974 5f 5.8g 5s 1975 8g 1976 13.1s] seemingly of no account: sold 330 gns
Ascot November Sales. *D. Ancil.*

MISS MARS 2 b.f. Red God 128 §–Lavendula Rose 108 (Le Levanstell 122) **95**
[1976 5g⁵ 5g⁵ 5f 7s²] neat, strong filly: second foal: dam, third in Irish Guinness
Oaks, is half-sister to Wrekin Rambler: put up by far her best effort when 1½
lengths second of 19 to North Stoke in minor race at Chepstow in October: clearly
much better suited by 7f than 5f and will stay 1m: acts well on soft going. *R.
Price.*

MISS MELITA 5 b.m. Paveh 126–Look Out 84 (Vimy 132) [1974 12g 12g —
14fg 14fg⁵ 12s 1975 N.R. 1976 10d] of little account. *H. O'Neill.*

MISS MINNIE 2 ch.f. Majority Blue 126–Sumintra 82 (El Gallo 122) [1976 **57**
5g 5f⁴] neat filly: first foal: dam placed several times over 5f and 6f at 2 yrs:
5 lengths fourth of 12 to Geopelia in maiden race at Nottingham in April: sold
500 gns Newmarket Autumn Sales. *H. T. Jones.*

MISS MIRANDA 3 b.f. Caliban 123–Honey Palm 86 (Honeyway 125) [1975 —
6g 1976 7h⁴ 8h] poor maiden. *H. Smyth.*

MISS NICE 3 br.f. Le Levanstell 122–Light Grey 115 (Grey Sovereign 128 §) **66**
[1976 N.R. 1976 8fg 8g 8fg⁵ 6f 8h³ 8.2d³ 7s⁴ 7v] well-grown, attractive filly:
half-sister to very useful 6f and 7f winner Miss Scotland (by Henry the Seventh)
and to useful 1974 2-y-o Miss Monaco (by Crepello): ran probably best race when
3½ lengths third of 23 to Petrina in maiden race at Nottingham in September on
sixth outing: stays 1m: has sometimes dwelt at start: sold 3,600 gns Newmarket
December Sales. *Doug Smith.*

MISS PERT 2 b.f. Roan Rocket 128–Flirtigig 96 (Silly Season 127) [1976 5g* **93**
5fg⁴ 6fg* 6fg⁴] neat, lightly-built filly: first foal: dam won at 1m and 1½m: had
field well strung out when winning 15-runner maiden race at Salisbury in May
and made all to win minor event at Newmarket the following month by 1½ lengths
from Namara: favourite for both her other races but was well beaten each time:
suited by 6f, and will get further: blinkered last two outings: sold 8,600 gns
Newmarket Autumn Sales, reportedly for export to Australia. *P. Walwyn.*

MISS PINKIE   2 ch.f. Connaught 130–Picture Light 118 (Court Martial)   [1976 **121**
5g⁴ 7fg* 6fg* 7f³ 8g*]

Henry Cecil's disappointment at not being given J. O. Tobin to train in 1977 must have been offset to some extent by the knowledge that in Miss Pinkie, another horse originally trained by his father-in-law Noel Murless, he now has one of England's leading hopes of keeping the One Thousand Guineas at home.

Miss Pinkie was backward on her first appearance but her record afterwards of three wins, including in the Courage Stakes and the Argos Star Fillies' Mile, entitles her to be considered one of the best two-year-olds to have run over a trip in 1976. She was made an odds-on favourite for the Courage Stakes at York in July, having run out a most impressive all-the-way winner of one of the earliest seven-furlong races for two-year-olds, at Sandown eight days before. Although the distance at York was shorter Miss Pinkie quickly dispelled any doubts that she might find six furlongs on the sharp side, being bang up with the leaders under the stand rails until taking up the running two furlongs out. She looked beaten when headed a furlong later by Petinara but Petinara then went left, spoiling both her own chance and that of Swagger, the other main challenger, and Miss Pinkie rallied gamely under strong driving to get home by three quarters of a length. Many thought Swagger an unlucky loser but it was suggested strongly by events in a race later in the day that the ground she raced on in the centre of the course was quite a lot faster than that near the stands. In addition, Miss Pinkie carried 5 lb more than both the placed horses in the Courage Stakes, so the honours of the race were definitely hers.

Although Miss Pinkie had to give between 3 lb and 11 lb to five of the six other runners in the Waterford Candelabra Stakes at Goodwood in August, she again started favourite. For some reason the forcing tactics which had seemed to suit her so well at Sandown and York were dispensed with, and she was beaten. She came to have her chance approaching the final furlong but Triple First had her measure soon afterwards and Miss Pinkie was eased up close home, a man-oeuvre that cost her second place to Lady Rhapsody. Her jockey collected a £50 fine for easing her. Miss Pinkie was allowed to bowl along in front when she met Triple First again in the Argos Star Fillies' Mile at Ascot the following month, and only the maiden Dunfermline, in receipt of 8 lb, was able to get to her in the straight. Again Miss Pinkie showed commendable courage, battling on strongly after being headed for a stride or two about two furlongs out, and drawing half a length ahead by the line. Triple First, this time meeting her at level weights, was a length and a half further back in third place, a length ahead of the rather slow-starting Lady Mere who was possibly a little unlucky.

Miss Pinkie (ch.f. 1974)	Connaught (b 1965)	St Paddy (b 1957)	Aureole
			Edie Kelly
		Nagaika (ch 1954)	Goyama
			Naim
	Picture Light (b 1954)	Court Martial (ch 1942)	Fair Trial
			Instantaneous
		Queen of Light (b 1949)	Borealis
			Picture Play

Miss Pinkie, a tall, lengthy filly, is nothing special to look at but her breeding is impeccable. Her dam, Picture Light, was a granddaughter of the One Thousand Guineas winner Picture Play and a half-sister to Chandelier, the dam of Crockct, and to Crystal Palace, the dam of Royal Palace. Picture Light was no mean performer herself, numbering the Hungerford Stakes among her four wins at up to a mile, and did very well at stud; Miss Pinkie is her last foal and ninth winner. Six of the winners showed ability above average but none of the six stayed particularly well: Illuminous (by Rockefella) showed very useful

Courage Stakes, York—Miss Pinkie (left) regains the lead close home from Petinara and Swagger (right), whose placings are subsequently reversed

*Argos Star Fillies' Mile, Ascot—another sterling effort by Miss Pinkie,
who rallies to beat Dunfermline, with Triple First and Lady Mere
third and fourth*

form at up to a mile and a quarter; Photo Flash (by Match III) finished second
in the One Thousand Guineas but ran only once afterwards; Welsh Pageant (by
Tudor Melody) was a top-class horse at around a mile; Calshot Light (by Exbury)
put up some smart efforts at up to a mile and a quarter; and Father Christmas (by
Santa Claus) and Dazzling Light (by Silly Season) were both smart over seven
furlongs and a mile. Rockefella, Exbury and Santa Claus all stayed at least as
well as Miss Pinkie's sire, Connaught, so the chances are that she too will find a
mile and a quarter as far as she can manage, especially as the front-running tactics
which suited Connaught, Welsh Pageant and Father Christmas so well also seem
to bring out the best in Miss Pinkie. Her best chance of classic success would
seem to lie in the One Thousand Guineas. At this stage we regard Cloonlara as
the obvious choice for that race, but Miss Pinkie stands a good chance of running
into a place. She has yet to run on ground any softer than good. *N. Murless.*

MISS PLUMES 3 b.f. Prince de Galles 125–Money Matters 68 (Hook Money   **62**
124) [1975 5g 1976 10.1fg 12g 11.1g 8f⁵ 8h* 8.3fg⁶ 8g⁴ 10g³ 8.2d 8s] lightly-
made filly: bought in 900 gns after winning seller at Bath in July: improved a
good deal on that form when third to Wickwell in apprentice race at Leicester in
September but ran moderately in a seller next time out: evidently suited by
1¼m: acts on hard ground and is possibly unsuited by a soft surface: sold out of
D. Keith's stable 1,200 gns Ascot August Sales after seventh start. *J. Berry.*

MISS PRIDDY 2 br.f. Behistoun 131–Priddy Fair 108 (Precipitic 122) [1976 5g   —
5fg 5d] sister to a poor animal and half-sister to three winners, including very
useful 6f to 1¼m winner Priddy Maid (by Acropolis), the dam of Dibidale: 360 gns
yearling: in rear in minor events and a seller. *C. Boothman.*

MISS PRUDE 2 ch.f. Rum–Osse (Ossian II) [1976 5g 5f 5fg 5fg 6f² 6f⁴] small   **52**
filly: poor plater: stays 6f: sold to D. Williams 500 gns Ascot July Sales. *W.
Marshall.*

MISS QUAY 2 ch.f. Quayside 124–Halkissimo 61 (Khalkis 127) [1976 5fg 5f 5f]   —
second foal: sister to winning 3-y-o sprinter First Quay: dam won over 1m: in rear
in maiden and minor events in first part of season. *M. Tate.*

473

MISS QUILP 5 b.m. Canisbay 120–Estimator 89 (Dumbarnie 125) [1974 12g —
12fg^5 14fg 12fg 16v 11.1v^3 1975 13s 12s 13.4g 12.2fg^6 16d 18g 12v^5 1976 17.7f
17.1s 18s^2] very big, unfurnished mare: poor performer: seems to stay 2¼m:
sometimes wears blinkers. *A. Goodwill.*

MISS REASONING 2 b.f. Bold Reasoning–Pampered Miss 119 (Sadair) [1976 **108**
5d* 6g^5 7s^2] American-bred French filly: second foal: $93,000 yearling: dam
won French 1,000 Guineas and is half-sister to Empery: won five-runner newcomers event at Chantilly in June by a short neck from Line Slippers: showed she
is a very useful filly when about 5 lengths fifth of 11 to Blushing Groom in Prix
Morny at Deauville two months later but went down by 2 lengths to Lancastera
in minor event at Longchamp in September: will probably stay 1¼m. *F. Boutin,
France.*

MISS ROSETTA 4 b.f. Ballymoss 136–Russalka (Emerson) [1974 N.R. 1975 **59**
7s 10.1f 10g^6 14g^5 15fg^2 1976 17.7f 18.1g* 16.1d] lengthy, hollow-backed filly:
20/1, ran on well when winning 15-runner handicap at Yarmouth in September by
2½ lengths from Cumbernauld, only worthwhile form in 1976: suited by a really
stiff test of stamina: sold to M. Bradley 1,600 gns Newmarket Autumn Sales. *P.
Robinson.*

MISS SANDMAN 2 b.f. Manacle 123–Sandby 81 (Klairon 131) [1976 5f^4 5d^3 **86**
5f* 5f^6 6fg^3] useful-looking filly: half-sister to two 2-y-o winners, including fairly
useful 1975 5f and 6f winner Icica (by Frankincense) and to a winner in Norway:
2,700 gns yearling: dam won over 5f at 2 yrs: made all to land the odds in maiden
race at Pontefract in June: good third to Star Attention in nursery at Ripon in
August: suited by 6f: sold 2,600 gns Newmarket Autumn Sales. *M. Stoute.*

MISS SARA 3 b.f. Majetta 115–Sara Tal (Cagire II 122) [1975 7.2fg 1976 **63**
8fg^3 12fg 10.6g^6 15g^5 10.2s^4] strong filly: seems only plating class. *S. Hall.*

MISS SCANDALOUS 2 b.f. Firestreak 125–Scandal (Narrator 127) [1976 5g —
5fg 8d 10v 8v] leggy filly: poor plater. *D. Weeden.*

MISS SHANNON 2 ch.f Sassafras 135–Miss Ireland 83 (Grey Sovereign 128 §) **87**
[1976 5g* 6fg] half-sister to two winners by Tudor Melody, including quite
useful 6f to 11f winner Irish Harmony: dam won over 1m, and is half-sister to
very smart Welsh Harmony: put up a good first effort to win 24-runner maiden
race at Leicester in May by 2½ lengths from Risca: lost several lengths at start
and never recovered when last of seven to Ampulla in Cherry Hinton Stakes at
Newmarket in July, only subsequent outing: will stay 1m+. *Doug Smith.*

MISS VALENTINO 4 b.f. Rugantino 97–Lady Scandal (Tudor Bell) [1974 —
N.R. 1975 N.R. 1976 13.1s 12s 12s] probably of little account. *P. Makin.*

MISS VARIETY 2 br.f. Dike–Garzoni (Ribot 142) [1976 5fg 6fg 5f^2 5f 6f 7s 6v^6] **68**
neat filly: half-sister to a winner in France by Diatome: 3,500 gns yearling: quite
a moderate maiden: will be suited by middle distances: blinkered last two
outings: sold 1,900 gns Newmarket Autumn Sales. *N. Vigors.*

MISS WORDEN 6 ch.m. Worden II 129–Steal In (Phalorain 98) [1974 N.R. —
1975 10g^3 1976 15.5s] plater: stays 1¼m. *B. Wise.*

MISTER CHICKEN 4 b.g. probably Sermoney 91–Panyana 88 (Pandemonium **65**
118) [1974 5fg^4 6s 5d^4 6s^2 6d^3 6g 7fg 6v^6 1975 7s 8s 7.6g 7.2g 6f^4 7fg^5 7fg^3 7f
7g^2 6f* 7g^4 6g 6d^2 8g^6 1976 7f* 7fg^5 7.6fg^4 8f^4 7fg^3 8fg 10h^4 9fg^4 10fg^5 10.2s]
quite a moderate handicapper: successful at Thirsk in April, and ran well in most
of his races afterwards: stays 1¼m but best form at around 1m: acts on any going:
has been tried in blinkers but has done better without them: good mount for an
apprentice. *C. Crossley.*

MISTER GAYTIME 2 b.c. Galivanter 131–Up And At It 72 (Tamerlane 128) —
[1976 5fg 5.1fg^6 6fg 7f 5.9f] poor maiden. *G. Vergette.*

MISTER GEOFFREY 6 ch.h. Sheshoon 132–Eilan Aigas 93 (Counsel 118) **96**
[1974 12fg* 12f^2 14.7fg^6 15g^3 12fg^2 13s* 14.6g^5 1975 12v 13v* 14.7f^5 13.8f^3
12h* 13g* 16fg^3 14fg^4 12g 1976 12s 12f* 12f^5 12h* 14.7f^2 16g 14fg^2 12d*]
useful sort: very good mover: quite a useful handicapper: winner at Thirsk in
May: awarded race on disqualification of Halsall after finishing 3 lengths second
to that horse at Carlisle in July: ran creditably afterwards, and gained a further
success when beating Flame Tree and Warbeck in clear-cut fashion at Newmarket in October: effective at 1½m and stays 2m: acts on any going: has run
respectably in blinkers but didn't wear them in 1976: suitable mount for an
apprentice. *S. Hall.*

MISTER JOJO 3 gr.g. Joshua 129–Rosy Ribbon 83 (Donore 119) [1975 N.R. —
1976 6fg] half-brother to four winners, including quite useful sprinter De-

474

liverance (by Town Crier): dam won over 5f and is sister to very smart sprinter
Dondeen: needed run when behind in maiden race won by Bluehill at Leicester
in March. *J. Holt.*

MISTER QUILP 2 ch.c. Burglar 128–Palouci 59 (Palestine 133) [1976 5fg   **83**
5.1fg⁵ 5f⁴ 5f² 5fg 5.1g² 5v³ 5v⁴] useful-looking colt: good mover: half-brother
to fairly useful 1973 2-y-o Fair Wind (by Typhoon) and to French 3-y-o Aberdeen
Park (by Sheshoon), a good winner over 10.5f: 2,000 gns yearling: dam a plater:
good second to Self Portrait at Catterick in July and to Captain's Mate at
Yarmouth two months later: barely stays 5f and is consequently best served
by a sound surface: ran moderately when tried in blinkers on fifth outing. *T.
Molony.*

MISTER RUSHTON 4 b.c. Queen's Hussar 124–Gone Gay 86 (Crepello 136)   **74**
[1974 N.R. 1975 10f 11.5f 10.8g⁵ 12.5fg⁶ 1976 8fg⁴ 10fg² 10fg² 10f² 9f6 10fg*
10h² 10h* 10fg 8g⁴ 10d⁵ 10.2s⁵ 8v²] useful-looking colt: quite a moderate
performer: winner of handicap at Leicester in July and minor event at Pontefract
the following month: stays 1¼m: acts on any going: blinkered and coltish in
paddock on fourth and fifth starts. *P. Robinson.*

MISTER SCURRY 2 b.c. Be Friendly 130–My Paddy 83 (St Paddy 133)   —
[1976 6d 6fg] strong colt: fourth foal: 2,100 gns yearling: dam won over 7.5f
in Ireland and is daughter of Cheveley Park winner My Goodness Me: in rear in
maiden and minor events at Redcar in June (bit backward and finished last) and
September (dwelt). *L. Shedden.*

MISTER TACK 4 b.c. Right Tack 131–Tryphena (Sayajirao 132) [1974 6s   —
1975 12s² 12.2fg 16s⁶ 14f 12g 1976 12.2fg] lengthy colt: very disappointing
since first outing at 3 yrs: stays 1½m: seems to need some give in the ground:
sweated up when tried in blinkers third outing in 1975. *N. Wakley.*

MISTIGRI 5 b.h. Misti IV 132–Nyanga (Never Say Die 137) [1974 10.4g² 12f⁶   **121**
12fg 10g² 12s³ 14s* 12s⁴ 12f 1975 12s² 16s⁶ 20g⁴ 20f²(dis) 10fg* 12g 1976
15.5s² 15.5g 20g⁴ 20f⁴ 12g* 13.5d³ 12g⁴ 12.5v] strong, useful sort: smart performer: beat Good Point 1½ lengths in three-runner event at Saint-Cloud in July:
previously in frame in three top staying events won by Sagaro, finishing second
in Prix de Barbeville, fourth in Prix du Cadran (both at Longchamp) and fourth
in Gold Cup at Royal Ascot in June (on fourth start): 7 lengths third of six to
Ashmore in Prix de Reux at Deauville in August, best other effort: effective at
1¼m and stays extremely well: acts on any going: has worn blinkers (did so on
last five starts) but goes just as well without: a versatile individual. *C.
Bartholomew, France.*

MISTINA 2 ch.f. Grisaille 115–Alex M 69 (Kadir Cup 97 §) [1976 6d 6g 5fg 7s]   **52**
poor plater. *P. Rohan.*

MISTRAL ROSE 3 br.f. Typhoon 125–Rose of France 83 (Grand Roi 118)   —
[1975 5f⁶ 6f 6f 1976 6g] poor plater. *M. Bradley.*

MISTRESS CLARE 4 b.f. Prince de Galles 125–China Doll 92 (Guersant 129)   **88**
[1974 7g* 8s 1975 10.8d 11.1fg* 12f 12g⁶ 16h* 16g⁴ 16.5g³ 1976 14fg* 16g
16fg³ 14f³ 16g² 16h* 16v⁴ 14d] lengthy, well-made filly: good walker and good mover:
fairly useful handicapper: successful at Salisbury in May by 2½ lengths from
Realist: stays well: best form on a sound surface and acts on hard going: suitable
mount for an apprentice. *I. Balding.*

MISTRESS PAGE 3 ch.f. Welsh Pageant 132–Donna 118 (Donore 119) [1975   **77**
5fg³ 6g² 7g² 1976 7fg² 7.6s² 7g] big, rangy filly: found one too good for her in
four of her six races: very disappointing when tried in blinkers on final outing
(May): stays 7f: acts on a firm surface but gives impression that she is better
suited by an easy one. *H. Candy.*

MISTRESS SMITH 2 gr.f. Raffingora 130–Never in Tune 63 (Never Say Die   —
137) [1976 5g 5f] small filly: second foal: 800 gns foal: dam showed poor form
in varied company: in rear in Scottish maiden races in first half of season. *J.
Barclay.*

MISTY JOANNE 4 br.f. Foggy Bell 108–Tilly 64 (Le Levanstell 122) [1974   **52**
6g 6g 6fg 6s 1975 8v 10.8s 14f 10h 12f³ 13g³ 16fg⁶ 15.8f³ 13d³ 16g 15fg³ 10.6v³
1976 13.8g 12fg⁴ 13.8d⁴ 16f⁶ 13.8f² 14d² 12s⁶] poor maiden: ran best race at
4 yrs on sixth outing when 3 lengths second of 13 to Ventrex in handicap at
Yarmouth in September: stays well: acts on any going: sold to S. Underhill
1,500 gns Doncaster October Sales. *V. Mitchell.*

MISTY MISS 4 gr.f. Straight Lad 110–Heather Mist 73 (Airborne) [1974   —
N.R. 1975 N.R. 1976 14.7d⁶] strong filly: fourth foal: dam, quite moderate

at 2 yrs, won over fences: needed race when well-beaten sixth of 10 to Bustiffa in amateur riders event at Redcar in June, only outing. *N. Crump.*

MITEN DRINEN 2 ch.f. Divine Gift 127–Kindling (Psidium 130) [1976 5fg³ **63** 5g⁴ 5f²] small, lengthy filly: first foal: 560 gns yearling: dam ran only three times: in frame in auction events and a seller in first part of season: exported to Brazil by B.B.A. *B. Swift.*

MIXED MELODY 2 ch.f. Alcide 136–Harvest Melody 103 (Tudor Minstrel 144) **62** [1976 7g 7.2f⁶ 8g⁶] rangy filly: sister to smart stayer Flagon, and half-sister to another winner: 2,400 gns foal: dam won over 1½m: remote sixth in minor race at Haydock in August and maiden event at Ayr in September. *G. Richards.*

MIXED UP KID 2 b.f. Track Spare 125–Ward Mistress 58 (Worden II 129) [1976 6v 7s] unimpressive-looking filly: second foal: dam placed over 1¼m: in rear in maiden races at Newbury and Newmarket in October, finishing twelfth of 19 to Lady Oriana on latter course. *D. Marks.*

MOANING LOW 2 b.f. Burglar 128–Street Song 110 (Le Lavandou 111) [1976 **75** 5.1fg³ 5f³ 5f² 6g] half-sister to four winners, including smart sprinter Porto Bello (by Floribunda): dam very speedy at 2 yrs: quite a moderate maiden: should stay beyond 5f. *B. Hobbs.*

MODEL SOLDIER 2 ch.g. Military 112–Wood Anemone 83 (Tangle 121) [1976 **92** 5fg* 5f* 5fg 5fg⁵ 5.3f⁴ 5.3h³ 5f² 5fg³ 5g] useful-looking gelding: half-brother to 5f winners by Gang Warily and Ron: dam a sprinter: made all when winning seller at Warwick (bought in 550 gns) and minor event at Brighton (just held off The Dundass), both in April: also ran well in nurseries, being only narrowly beaten on sixth, seventh and eighth outings: will probably stay 6f: acts on hard ground: blinkered third outing (prominent when hampered at distance): genuine and consistent. *Miss N. Wilmot.*

MODERN TIMES 3 b.c. Royal Palace 131–Sans le Sou (Vimy 132) [1975 7fg **83** 1976 11f⁴ 14fg² 12fg* 12fg⁶ 12g] strong, well-grown colt: half-brother to Busted (by Crepello): won maiden race at York in July in impressive style, beating Rough River 4 lengths without coming off bridle: ran easily better subsequent race when creditable seventh of nine to Ivory Girl in Fitzwilliam Stakes at Doncaster in September: stays 1¾m: acts on a firm surface. *G. Pritchard-Gordon.*

MODIN 4 b.g. Appiani II 128–Epee (Cranach) [1974 6f 6f 1975 9s 12f 16h⁵ — 16fg 12f 14fg³ 16g⁵ 16f⁵ 15s 1976 12fg] compact gelding: plating-class staying maiden: has worn blinkers. *W. Atkinson.*

MODOM 5 b.m. Compensation 127–Dompas (Domaha) [1974 7.6g 6g 8g 6fg⁵ **62** 8g 8fg⁵ 8d³ 10v⁴ 10v² 10.6s⁴ 10.6v* 1975 8s⁴ 10.8d* 11.7g 10f 7g⁴ 10.2f³ 10.2f³ 12.2g² 12.2g² 10g* 12d*(dis) 1976 10fg 14fg 12g³ 12f⁴ 12f³ 10g⁴ 11.7fg⁴ 10fg³ 10g² 12g⁵ 12.2s 10s³] tall mare: moderate handicapper (rated 81) at 4 yrs: mainly disappointing in 1976: stays 1½m: acts on any going but is ideally suited by some give in the ground: has been tried in blinkers: needs to be held up and is a difficult ride. *W. Wightman.*

MOFIDA 2 ch.f. Right Tack 131–Wold Lass 77 (Vilmorin) [1976 5g 5fg² 5d* **111** 5d² 5d³ 6f² 7f³ 6fg* 6g⁵ 6f* 7g² 6g* 6d³ 6v* 6v³] attractive filly: half-sister to useful sprinter Kashville (by Kashmir II): 4,000 gns yearling: dam, a sprinter, is half-sister to Chebs Lad: a very tough filly who had a busy time after her first race, on the second day of the season, but steadily developed into a smart performer: won minor event at Newcastle in April and four of her last eight races, Black Duck Stakes at York (from Hot Heir), nursery at Newmarket (from Petinara), valuable Firth of Clyde Stakes at Ayr (from Lucky Omen) and £1,300 race at Newcastle (beat Caelidh a length, the pair finishing clear): best form at 6f: acts on any going: thoroughly genuine and consistent. *B. Hills.*

MOG 2 b.f. Mandamus 120–Nuit d'Or 87 (Doutelle 128) [1976 6f 7f⁶] second — foal: half-sister to a winning plater by Sky Gipsy: 1,400 gns yearling: dam stayed 1m: remote sixth of 13 to Bona-Mia in minor race at Salisbury in August: will stay 1m. *R. Smyth.*

MOGUL 2 b.c. Tamerlane 128–Queen's Secret 76 (Tutankhamen) [1976 5f⁶ **85** 5fg* 5fg⁵ 6g⁶ 6g 6g 7g 7s] shapely colt: good mover: first foal: 2,400 gns yearling: dam a sprinter: won four-runner minor event at Epsom in April by 1½ lengths from slow-starting Glensilver: well beaten in nurseries on last four outings: should be suited by 6f+: blinkered fourth outing (ran wide into straight). *B. Swift.*

MOHDANA 3 ch.f. Prince John–Mohmond (Jaipur) [1975 7f 1976 8.2f] — American-bred filly: half-sister to Deerslayer (by Tom Rolfe), a smart winner at

Mr Kalifa Sasi's "Mofida"

up to 1m, and to a winner in U.S.A. by Bagdad: dam unraced half-sister to four winners in U.S.A., including stakes-placed Narokan and Full of Fun: in rear in maiden races: needed race and did not impress in paddock only outing in 1976. *H. Cecil.*

MOLL FLANDERS 2 b.f. Frankincense 120–Calecho (Bleep-Bleep 134) [1976   **65**
5fg⁵ 5f⁴ 7h 6h 6g]   third foal: dam never ran: 3 lengths fourth of six to Wysboy in £1,000 event at Folkestone in May, best effort: possibly does not stay 7f: sold 480 gns Newmarket Autumn Sales. *G. Hunter.*

MOLLY'S BEAU 4 b.g. Sodium 128–Molly Belle (Molvedo 137) [1974 6f⁶ 6fg³   **57**
6g 8d⁵ 7g   1975 10.8d³ 14f 13f² 12f³   1976 10fg 12d⁴ 12fg² 12g⁴ 18.1g]   compact, well-made gelding: one paced and should stay long distances: seems to act on any going: sweated up on reappearance. *H. Collingridge.*

MOLLY'S LAD 2 ch.c. Chebs Lad 120–Lady Molly (King's Troop 118) [1976   **90**
5f 5fg⁶ 6f 6g³ 6fg² 6g⁵ 6s³ 6s]   strong colt: first foal: dam never ran: placed in minor events and ran well when 3 lengths fifth to Region in £1,600 race at Ayr in September: stays 6f, at least when conditions aren't testing: best form on a sound surface: will win a race in the north. *M. H. Easterby.*

MONARCH OILS 2 b.c. Hard Man 102–Gina Dene (Manicou) [1976 5f⁴ 5d⁴   **55**
5.9g 7f 5.9fg 6v 5v 5s]   poor plater: usually blinkered. *A. W. Jones.*

MONASTAR 3 gr.f. Sassafras 135–Petite Path 106 (Sovereign Path 125) [1975   **61**
6fg 7fg³ 7g   1976 8v⁴ 8fg⁴ 8fg 10.4fg⁵ 8fg³ 6g⁵ 8v⁴ 7s² 10s⁵ 8v³]   tall filly: needs further than 6f but has yet to show she stays 1¼m: acts on any going. *R. Mason.*

MON BEAUX 2 ch.c. Continuation 120–Affectionately 82 (Mark-Ye-Well)   —
[1976 6f 6d 6d]   half-brother to useful miler King Oedipus (by Gala Performance): 400 gns foal, resold 3,500 gns yearling: dam ran four times at 2 yrs: behind in large fields of maidens at Newmarket, finishing sixteenth of 22 to Rocket Symphony in October on final outing. *W. Marshall.*

MON CHAT 2 ch.c. Great Nephew 126–Kitten 102 (Pardal 130) [1976 5g 6g⁶   — §
7fg]   strong, good-looking colt: little worthwhile form: twice started slowly and

gave trouble at stalls on other appearance: blinkered final outing: one to be wary of. *R. Hern.*

MONEY BELT   3 ch.f. Richboy 117–Judolyn 82 (Canisbay 120)   [1975 5s 5fg 6g 5f 5g 6d 5g   1976 8f 8.2f⁴ 7fg 8.2d 10v]   poor maiden: best run at 1m: sold 460 gns Ascot November Sales. *C. Bewicke.*   —

MONEY BURNER   2 br.c. Crooner 119–Poinsettia 80 (Pinturischio 116)   [1976 5fg 6fg 5g³ 7.2f 8f]   small, chunky individual: quite a modest plater: should stay 1m: blinkered final outing. *G. Richards.*   57

MONEY IN   2 b.c. Jukebox 120–Lev Star (Le Levanstell 122)   [1976 6fg 7f⁶ 6g³ 7fg²]   tall, strong, close-coupled colt: brother to moderate 1974 2-y-o 6f winner Ray of Ollies: 3,600 gns yearling: dam never ran: 3 lengths third of 15 to Hyver Hill in maiden race at Kempton in August: favourite for 12-runner maiden event at Edinburgh the following month but lost ground by running wide into straight (was in lead at time) and was beaten 5 lengths into second place by Butterscotch: probably stays 7f. *W. Marshall.*   77

MONEY TO SPARE   2 b.c. Track Spare 125–Lucre 76 (Privy Councillor 125)   [1976 5g⁵ 6f 6g⁵ 7fg³ 8s* 7.2v²]   workmanlike colt: first foal: 950 gns yearling: dam stayed 1¼m: improved with distance and ran out a decisive 4-length winner from Erstung in 20-runner nursery at Pontefract in October: ran creditably under a penalty on final outing: will probably stay 1¼m: seems to act on any going, but goes particularly well on soft. *S. Hall.*   92

MON FLEUR   3 ch.f. Florescence 120–Turn Back (Match III 135)   [1975 5v⁴ 5fg 6f² 6g³ 5fg² 5g 6f 5g 5f⁶ 7f⁵ 5fg* 6g⁵ 7v⁵]   well-grown, leggy, unfurnished filly: plater: attracted no bid after winning all out at Beverley in September: evidently best at 5f: best form on a sound surface: ran well when tried in blinkers at 2 yrs: sold 400 gns Doncaster November Sales. *L. Shedden.*   50

MONHEGAN   8 b.g. Sea Hawk II 131–Rochetta 95 (Rockefella)   [1974 18g 17v⁶ 1975 N.R.   1976 16.1d 16fg⁴ 22.2f]   poor staying handicapper: acted on firm going: dead. *N. Crump.*   —

MONK'S CHANT   3 ch.c. Saintly Song 128–Princesse Moss (Mossborough 126)   [1975 6g 5.9f 6g² 8f* 8g⁶ 1976 7g 12g³ 10fg⁵ 8fg⁶ 12.2g⁵ 14f³ 14fg³ 12f⁴ 12f⁶]   small colt: poor mover: plater: best form at up to 1½m: acts on firm going: suitable mount for an apprentice: ran poorly final outing and was sold 1,800 gns Newmarket Autumn Sales. *P. Robinson.*   58

MONNIE BEE   3 ch.f. Pall Mall 132–Wild Bee (Hill Gail)   [1975 6f 5fg⁵ 5fg 1976 5.3f 8fg⁶ 7g]   sister to fair 1m to 1¼m handicapper Blitz: plating-class maiden: should stay at least 1m: blinkered final outing. *I. Walker.*   —

MONRUSHA   5 b.g. Ragusa 137–Montea (Seaulieu)   [1974 8g⁴ 8g⁵ 13.4g⁵ 10f⁶ 10.6g⁶ 10g* 10s⁴ 10.8v⁵ 10.6v 1975 13fg⁴ 14fg 14.6g 12d* 14g³ 12.2g 1976 12.3d* 12.3s³ 12f⁵ 12fg 12.2g 12d⁶ 12v⁴ 12s]   big, strong gelding: fair handicapper nowadays: beat Beverley Boy 2 lengths at Newcastle in April on reappearance: best form at up to 1½m and appears not to stay 1¾m: probably acts on any going: sometimes unreliable at start: most inconsistent. *F. Carr.*   83 d

MONSANTO   4 b.c. Breton 130–Moonmadness (Tom Fool)   [1974 7g³ 7.5v² 6.5v³ 7v⁴ 1975 7.5g² 8v* 8v* 8v³ 8v* 8g⁴ 8g² 1976 7d³ 8f⁴ 7g⁶ 8g² 8g² 10g* 8d* 8s⁵ 7s⁵]   strong, lengthy, good-bodied colt: smart performer: successful at Deauville in August (beat Twig a nose in Prix Ridgway) and at Longchamp the following month (held off stable-companion Nurabad by ½ length in Prix du Rond-Point): far from disgraced in his other races, running really well on fourth and fifth appearances when second in Prix Messidor at Maisons-Laffitte in July (1½ lengths behind Dona Barod) and in Prix Quincey, also at Deauville in August, (beaten 2½ lengths by Ellora): in frame earlier in Prix du Palais Royal at Longchamp in May (third to Gravelines) and Queen Anne Stakes at Royal Ascot (fourth to Ardoon): stays 1¼m: acts extremely well on heavy going and is probably unsuited by firm: genuine and consistent. *A. Penna, France.*   116

MONSEIGNEUR   2 ch.c. Graustark–Brown Berry (Mount Marcy)   [1976 8s² 9s⁴ 10s²]   American-bred French colt: brother to Avatar, a top-class winner at up to 1½m in U.S.A., and half-brother to several winners, including high-class middle-distance horse Unconscious (by Prince Royal II): dam a stakes winner: looked unlucky when short-head second to Amyntor in Prix de Fontenoy at Longchamp in September, seeming to have race won when taking lead but then hanging left and being caught on line: in frame in two pattern races afterwards, putting up better effort when ½-length second of seven to El Criollo in Prix de Conde at   122

Longchamp the following month: will be suited by 1½m: sure to win a good race. *F. Boutin, France.*

MONSIEUR MARRON 2 ch.c. Leander 119–Veronique 96 (Matador 131) **70** [1976 5g 6fg⁵ 6g⁵ 8g] strong, good-looking colt: half-brother to three winners, notably very smart 3-y-o sprinter Music Boy (by Jukebox): 7,400 gns yearling: dam a sprinter: showed a little ability: not certain to stay 1m. *G. Hunter.*

MONSIEUR SPOCK 6 ch.g. Tobrouk–Solar Song 98 (Solar Slipper 131) [1974 **66** 11.7g* 12g³ 11.7fg³ 14g³ 11.7g³ 11.7g³ 12g⁴ 1975 11.7f* 12fg⁵ 14fg² 11.7h⁴ 12g 12.2g⁴ 14g 1976 11.7fg⁶ 12g⁶ 12g⁵ 12fg³ 12f²] workmanlike gelding: ran best race at 6 yrs on final start when second of three to Perucio in handicap at Brighton in August: stays 1¾m: acts on firm going and is possibly not at his best on soft. *A. Pitt.*

MONTAGE 5 b.m. Polyfoto 124–Cream Jug 73 (King's Bench 132) [1974 N.R. — 1975 8f⁵ 8g⁵ 10f 12.2g 1976 12v] moderate plater (rated 64) in 1973: lightly raced and poor form on flat since. *S. Cole.*

MONTE ACUTO 2 ch.c. Mountain Call 125–Island Woman 76 (King's Troop **76** 118) [1976 5fg 5g 6fg 7g⁶ 5v⁶] strong, well-made, attractive colt: half-brother to 3-y-o 1¾m winner Iona and to 1m winner Burriana (both by Kalydon): 3,300 gns foal: dam, a sprinter, is half-sister to three very useful animals: showed a little ability in good-class maiden races: not certain to stay 7f: possibly unsuited by heavy ground: ran poorly in blinkers on final outing. *C. Brittain.*

MONTE BALDO 3 ch.g. Red God 128 §–Vilswitch 93 (Vilmorin) [1975 6g **66** 5fg 6fg⁵ 7d 1976 7fg 8fg⁴ 8fg 10f⁴ 8.5fg 8h² 8g⁴ 8fg] plater: stays 1m but possibly not 1¼m: blinkered fourth and fifth starts: ran moderately final outing: sold 4,000 gns Newmarket Autumn Sales. *G. Harwood.*

MONTE CECO 3 ch.g. Ragusa 137–Mountain Peak (Arctic Slave 116) [1975 7g **68** 8fg³ 8.2d 1976 10f⁴ 16f² 16f² 17.7f⁴ 15.5h⁵] attractive gelding: stays 2m (ran moderately when tried at 2¼m): possibly needs a sound surface: disappointing: sold 3,400 gns Ascot August Sales. *I. Balding.*

MONTESPAN 3 b.f. Roi Soleil 125–Stormy Venture (Arctic Storm 134) [1975 **83** 8d⁴ 8g 1976 9f⁶ 8fg³ 8g 8f* 8.2f⁶ 8s³ 8s⁴ 8s⁶] small, close-coupled filly: put up a good performance when winning handicap at Newcastle in August by 2½ lengths from Lyncathal: ran best race afterwards when third to Chum-Chum in similar event at Goodwood the following month: stays 1m: acts on any going. *R. Price.*

MONTREAL 6 br.h. Right Royal V 135–Montier (Crepello 136) [1974 N.R. — 1975 N.R. 1976 11g⁴] poor handicapper in 1973: well-beaten fourth of seven to Gold Claim at Edinburgh in May, only outing on flat since. *P. Farrell.*

MONTREAL BOY 5 gr.h. Doon 124–Kutelamara 81 (Quorum 126) [1974 8g³ **83** 8.5h² 7.6g* 10f³ 10g* 8g⁶ 10g² 13g² 12g² 14s⁵ 12g 1975 10v 10s⁴ 10f 12g⁴ 12g 10.5d 10.5fg 10.6fg 16g 12.2g⁶ 12g 12v 1976 14.6g⁴ 16s² 13g³ 13s⁴ 15.8g 15g³ 16.1d² 12.2v* 12s⁶] moderate handicapper: winner at Newcastle in October, leading 5f out and keeping on well to hold off Deep River by a neck: stays 2m: seems to act on any going: suitable mount for an apprentice: sometimes wears blinkers (did so at Newcastle). *J. Calvert.*

MONT ST MICHEL 5 b.h. Le Levanstell 122–Belille (Beau Prince 131) [1974 — 10f⁵ 11g 14s* 12s⁴ 1975 14.6fg² 16v³ 14f 16fg³ 16d⁴ 14g³ 16f 1976 16f⁵] lightly-made horse: made only one appearance at 5 yrs: suited by a good test of stamina: appears to act on any going. *A. Dalton.*

MONYMUSK 3 ch.f. Sky Gipsy 117–Sarum Lady 97 (Floribunda 136) [1975 **74** 5f 5f⁶ 5f 5f⁴ 5.3f 1976 6f* 6g² 6f* 5fg³ 6g* 6f⁴] quite a modest handicapper: showed improved form after winning seller at Brighton in April and won from small fields on same course in May and at Epsom in June: effective at 5f and 6f: acts on firm going: ran below her best final outing (June). *P. Calver.*

MOOMBA 2 ch.f. Song 132–French Twist 79 (Crocket 130) [1976 6fg 6g 5s²] **90** very attractive, full-quartered filly: third foal: half-sister to a winner in Norway: 4,000 gns yearling: dam placed over 5f at 2 yrs: kept on well when neck second to Waterbuck in maiden race at Haydock in October: should stay 6f. *G. Pritchard-Gordon.*

MOONBAY 3 b.f. Ovid 95–Evening Cruise 78 (Falls of Clyde 126) [1975 N.R. — 1976 9.4g⁴ 9fg 8h⁴ 13.8g⁶] lightly-made filly: poor plater. *W. Haigh.*

MOON BLINK 3 b.f. Breeders Dream 116–Strawberry Moon 97 (Midsummer **81**
Night II 117) [1975 5f 5f 5g² 5f³ 5g⁴ 5s² 6g* 6g⁵ 1976 7d 7s³ 7g⁴ 7f³] fair handicapper: stays 7f: probably acts on any going: consistent: withdrawn at start
(lame) on final appearance. *E. Weymes.*

MOON EXPRESS 2 b.f. Espresso 122–Mondsichel (Birkhahn) [1976 6fg² 7f* **93**
6h² 7f³ 7f² 8f* 8g⁴] compact fillv: half-sister to useful stayer Round the Moon
(by Henry the Seventh) and useful 1973 2-y-o Majordomo (by Major Portion):
dam won three times in Germany: easy 6-length winner of maiden race at Beverley
in July: ran creditably in nurseries afterwards and won one at Thirsk in September by 3 lengths from Revlow: will stay well: acts on firm going but seemed
unsuited by the hard ground on third outing. *J. Hindley.*

MOON GATE 2 b.c. Blue Streak 99–Kamitisi (Worden II 129) [1976 5fg 5d —
6f 7f] bad plater: has worn blinkers. *S. Nesbitt.*

MOON LAD 2 ch.c. Virginia Boy 106–Moon Lady 78 (Cash and Courage 116) **61**
[1976 5g³ 5d⁴ 5f 5f 6f⁶] first foal: dam won over 1m and 1¼m: in frame in maiden
races at Hamilton in May but descended to sellers on last two outings: stays 6f:
ran creditably in blinkers on final outing. *J. W. Watts.*

MOONLIGHT RAG 3 b.c. Ragusa 137–Strong Light 103 (Fortino II 120) **73**
[1975 8g 1976 12g⁵ 11g⁴] neat, quite attractive colt: showed ability in early-
season maiden races at Kempton and Newbury: will probably be suited by
further than 1½m. *H. Candy.*

MOON STEP 4 ch.c. Bribe 89–Moon Mist 91 (Golden Cloud) [1974 N.R. —
1975 16f 10f⁶ 12g 1976 12f 8f 9g] apparently of no account: sold 330 gns
Doncaster Autumn Sales. *K. Payne.*

MOONSTRIKE 4 b.g. Blast 125–Superior Complex 89 (Coronation Year 124) **62**
[1974 5g⁴ 1975 7.6g³ 8.5f² 10fg 10.4g³ 10fg 10.8f⁴ 10.1fg⁵ 8f 10.8g³ 9g² 1976
12fg⁵ 11.7fg 11.1g 12s³ 16.1s 11g* 10h³] lengthy, attractive gelding: won eight-
runner selling handicap at Ayr in July by 2½ lengths from Don Philipe (no bid):
stays 11f: has worn blinkers (didn't at Ayr). *P. Haslam.*

MOOR LANE 8 gr.g. Tin Whistle 128–Drip Dry 87 (Coronation Year 124) **59**
[1974 6h 6g 6f⁵ 6g⁶ 6f⁶ 6g 6g 6g 1975 6v 5.8g* 6f² 5g² 5.3f² 5f⁴ 5fg 5s 1976
6fg⁴ 6fg 6g 5g 5.8h⁵ 6d] one-time fair handicapper but showed little worthwhile
form in 1976 after his first outing: best at sprint distances: acts on hard going
and is not at his best on soft: sometimes wears blinkers: good mount for an
apprentice· very well suited by sharp track. *J. Nelson.*

MOORMAN 3 b.c. Chebs Lad 120–High Moor 104 (Sayajirao 132) [1975 5f 6f⁵ **64**
1976 9g 7.2g 8f⁶ 10h*] neat colt: plater: sold to H. Blackshaw 1,250 gns after
winning all out at Redcar in August: suited by 1¼m: acts on hard ground: has
been tried in blinkers but evidently does better without. *R. D. Peacock.*

MOQUERIE 3 b.f. Beaugency 126–Moqueuse (Saint Crespin III 132) [1975 **120**
8d² 8g 1976 10g² 12g* 10.5g⁵ 10.8g⁴ 10g⁵ 13.5g* 12s 12.5d² 10.5s] half-sister
to winning middle-distance stayer in France by Cadmus: dam won at up to 11f
in France: put up two very game performances in good-class fillies races, namely
when dead-heating with Sweet Rhapsody in Prix de Pomone at Deauville in
August and when neck second to Paint the Town in Prix de Royallieu at Longchamp in October: looked well beaten when headed turning into straight on
latter course but only just failed to pull race out of fire with determined last-
furlong rally: had earlier won maiden race at Saint-Cloud: stays 13f well: acts
on a soft surface: well suited by forcing tactics: ran below her best final appearance. *A. Head, France.*

MORAY 4 b.c. Prince Regent 129–Strike One (Match III 135) [1974 5fg 5f⁵ **75** d
7g⁵ 7d 8s 1975 12g⁴ 12g* 12.2f* 12f² 12f² 15.8fg* 13.8f³ 12f⁴ 1976 12f⁶ 12f⁵ 12h*
12f³ 13.8f⁵ 12fg⁶ 14.7f⁵ 16fg] neat colt: quite a moderate handicapper: made
all and stayed on strongly when winning four-runner event at Pontefract in July
unchallenged by 3 lengths from Don Fortune: ran moderately afterwards: stays
well: acts on hard going: sweated up second outing. *M. H. Easterby.*

MORE BUSINESS 6 ch.m. Money Business 84–Quintet (Tambourin) [1974 —
N.R. 1975 N.R. 1976 14fg 14f 16g] poor staying maiden. *J. Cann.*

MORE FRIENDLY 2 b.c. Be Friendly 130–Asturia 104 (The Phoenix) [1976
5f 5g] half-brother to several winners, notably Escorial (by Royal Palace),
a very useful performer at up to 1½m: sold twice as a yearling, for 1,000 gns and
250 gns: behind in maiden races at Windsor and Wolverhampton (auction event)
in first part of season. *J. Pullen.*

MORELIA 3 ch.f. Murrayfield 119–Sabot D'Or 112 (Princely Gift 137) [1975 **59**
5g 5f⁵ 7f* 7f⁵ 1976 8.2f 10.4s⁶ 11.1f⁶ 12.2g 12.2g⁶] small filly: poor handicapper:
seems to stay 11f. *P. Rohan.*

MORE MUSIC 5 b.h. Tudor Music 131–Morgaise 93 (Grey Sovereign 128 §) —
[1974 6g 5g 6g 8g³ 6g 8s 8s⁶ 1975 10.2d⁵ 9s⁵ 6f² 7f⁶ 7g 6f⁴ 8g 7f⁶ 7s⁵ 12s 1976
7f 6f] poor maiden: best form at up to 7f and is not bred to stay middle distances: retained 1,500 gns Newmarket April Sales. *J. Pullen.*

MORNING GREY 3 gr.c. Roan Rocket 128–Whispering II 111 (Whistler 129) **73**
[1975 5fg 6f⁶ 6fg 1976 5g 5fg* 6fg² 5g⁶ 6d] compact colt: quite a
moderate handicapper: winner at Salisbury in June: neck second to Pam's
Gleam at Nottingham the following month, best subsequent effort: stays 6f.
P. Cole.

MORNING LEE 2 br.g. Arctic Judge 94–Stacy Lee 95 (French Beige 127) **85**
[1976 5fg 5f⁴ 5f 6fg⁵ 7g⁵ 6fg 7g⁴ 8f⁶ 10v* 8.2v*] tall gelding: third foal: 350
gns yearling: dam, winner over 6f and 8.5f at 2 yrs, stayed 1¼m: showed much
improved form when winning two races in two days at Nottingham in October,
maiden event by a neck from Sovereign Fair starting at 25/1 and nursery (made
all) by 1½ lengths from Naughty Lass: will stay 1½m: evidently well suited by
heavy ground. *V. Cross.*

MORNING MISS 3 b.f. Golden Dipper 119–Madam Airlie 58 (Taboun 128) **59**
[1975 8g 7g 8v 1976 8g 10.8f 10f⁶ 16f 8.3fg³ 8f⁴ 7fg 8.3g* 9fg⁶] small, strong
filly: plater: apprentice ridden when winning by 5 lengths at Windsor in August:
attracted no bid afterwards: stays 1m. *D. Dartnall.*

MORNING MYSTERY 3 br.f. Right Boy 137–Nice Morning 77 (Tantieme 136) —
[1975 N.R. 1976 7.6fg 10s 8v] half-sister to a winner in Greece by Lucky
Brief: dam of little account: seems to possess little ability. *J. Bethell.*

MORNING PRINCESS 3 b.f. Prince Regent 129–Coming Morn (Ribot 142) **55**
[1975 N.R. 1976 10fg⁴ 12g⁵ 12f 10g 10fg 8fg⁴ 8.2f 8h 18s 10.6v] strong filly:
second foal: half-sister to fair Irish 1974 2-y-o Ardschull Boy (by Levmoss):
1,350 gns yearling: dam won over 1½m in Ireland: showed signs of some ability
on first and sixth starts but ran poorly on most of her other outings: should
stay 1½m: trained part of season by S. Ingham and N. Adam. *P. Bevan.*

MORTALLY OFFENDED 3 ch.f. Major Portion 129–Aggrieved (Aggressor 130) —
[1975 6f⁶ 1976 7h 9f 8h⁵ 11.5d] plating-class maiden. *K. Ivory.*

MORTCERF 2 b.c. Song 132–Cymbalita 79 (Tambourine II 133) [1976 6d —
6d] second living foal: dam won twice over 1m and stayed 1½m: in rear in
large fields of maidens at Newmarket in October, finishing fourteenth of 23 to
Running Bull on second occasion. *B. Hills.*

MOSSBERRY 3 ch.c. Welsh Pageant 132–Cranberry Sauce 119 (Crepello 136) **97**
[1975 N.R. 1976 8fg³ 7.6s⁴ 7f⁵ 10fg³ 8fg² 8g* 8g] well-grown, good sort of
colt: fourth foal: half-brother to two winners, including very smart Sauceboat
(by Connaught): dam best 1¼m filly of 1967: overcame difficulties in running
when winning handicap at Sandown in July under top weight by head from
Lord Elect, getting up close home under strong driving: had previously shown
useful form against strong opposition: stays 1¼m: best form on a sound surface:
brought wide when running below his best on final outing: sold 16,000 gns
Newmarket Autumn Sales and is to be trained by J. Etherington in 1977. *N.
Murless.*

MOSS RIVER 3 b.g. Forlorn River 124–Moss-Ralia 90 (Mossborough 126) —
[1975 5f 1976 8h] strong, workmanlike gelding: good walker: behind in minor
event at Ripon at 2 yrs and maiden race (needed run) at Beverley in July.
M. W. Easterby.

MOSSY PATH 3 ch.f. Ballymoss 136–Argentie (Sovereign Path 125) [1975 —
N.R. 1976 10h⁶ 12h⁵ 16f 11f⁵ 15v⁵] compact filly: poor mover: well beaten in
maiden races: blinkered last two outings. *J. Calvert.*

MOSSY STONE 3 b.c. Levmoss 133–Space Suit 100 (Roan Rocket 128) [1975 **85**
N.R. 1976 17.7f* 16g³ 17.1h²] good-looking, rangy colt: second produce:
half-brother to winning stayer Hill Station (by Sheshoon): 4,800 gns foal: dam won
over 1¼m: won maiden race at Wolverhampton in May, despite running green,
by 1¼ lengths from Blakewood: ran creditably both subsequent outings, on
final appearance being badly hampered and losing more ground than he was
beaten by when 3 lengths second to Homefield in handicap at Bath in August
(had stiffish task): stays very well: probably has further improvement in him
and should win more races as a 4-y-o, provided all goes well with him. *J. Nelson.*

MOST HIGH 3 b.c. Royal Orbit–High in the Sky (Above Suspicion 127) [1975 —
6fg 6g 8f 7g 1976 6fg 8v 6g 8h 12g 14fg 8g] poor maiden: blinkered final start.
B. Richmond.

MOTHER BROWN 4 b.f. Candy Cane 125–March Brown 90 (March Past 124) 95
[1974 7d 1975 8g* 8.5d³ 10g* 8.2f* 8d* 8fg⁴ 9g 8d⁵ 8.2v² 1976 8v 10g² 10g³
10g⁶ 8f² 10g⁵ 10h² 9g² 8fg* 8fg⁵ 8g⁴ 8g³ 8s*] neat filly: fairly useful handicapper:
successful at Goodwood in July and Brighton in October, on latter course leading
at halfway and running on well to beat Sunset Value 1½ lengths, the pair finishing
clear: stays 1¼m: acts on any going: sometimes sweats up profusely: badly
hampered on tenth outing (ran creditably): genuine and consistent. *J. Dunlop.*

MOTHER CAREY 3 b.f. Sea Hawk II 131–Catherine's Sister 96 (Petition 130) 72
[1975 6g 7g 7f 1976 12.2g⁴ 11.1f* 12.2g⁴ 12f* 12f*] small, compact filly: quite
a moderate handicapper: winner at Wolverhampton in May and Beverley and
Pontefract the following month: beat Snow Warning comfortably by 2 lengths
on last-named course after coming under whip some way out: stays 1½m: suited
by firm going: sold 6,200 gns Newmarket September Sales, reportedly for export
to Australia. *M. Stoute.*

MOUNTAIN CHILD 3 ch.f. Mountain Call 125–Mossgo 106 (Vigo 130) [1975 —
5g 5fg 5f⁵ 5fg⁴ 6g 6f⁵ 7v 1976 5d⁴ 5g] leggy filly: probably stays 6f: started
slowly first outing. *W. Marshall.*

MOUNTAIN CROSS 4 b.c. French Beige 127–Videmanette (High Perch 126) 73
[1974 N.R. 1975 10d² 10s 1976 16.1s* 14.7f² 13g⁵] 20/1 and sweating, won
17-runner maiden race at Haydock in June: close second to odds-on Sanpello in
minor event at Redcar later in month: stays well: acts on any going: off course
over two months before final appearance. *J. Fitzgerald.*

MOUNTAIN RESCUE 3 ch.f. Mountain Call 125–Succeed 85 (Parthia 132) 82
[1975 5s 6g³ 6fg² 6fg* 5g³ 1976 6g 8g⁵ 7.3g³ 7g³ 8fg⁴ 8g⁵ 8f²] neat filly: fair
handicapper: stays 1m: three times ran respectably in blinkers, including on
final appearance. *F. Walwyn.*

MOUNT IRVINE 4 b.g. Aureole 132–Picnic Party 85 (Honeyway 125) [1974 —
7.6v⁵ 1975 12g² 12f 12g* 15d² 13g* 15g* 14d⁴ 1976 16fg 16s] strong, good-
looking gelding: fairly useful performer at 3 yrs: had stiff tasks and pulled
extremely hard when well beaten on both outings in 1976: stays well: evidently
unsuited by firm going: reluctant to go into stalls on second and third outings
at 3 yrs: a very difficult ride. *C. Davies.*

MOUNT PELLE 2 ch.c. Crepello 136–Island Lore 100 (Court Martial) [1976 81
6fg⁵ 7f 8s⁵] half-brother to very smart 1½m horse Caliban (by Ragusa), useful
Alonso (by Ragusa) and 1967 2-y-o 5f winner Spanish Elm (by Matador): dam
won over 5f as a 2-y-o: having first race for three months, showed first worthwhile
form when 5 lengths fifth of 19 to Nordman in maiden event at Sandown in
October: better suited by 1m than shorter distances and will stay further:
acts on soft going. *G. Pritchard-Gordon.*

MOUNT SNOWDON 2 b.c. Polyfoto 124–Royal Solitude (Royal Challenger 64
129) [1976 5g 5g 7f⁵ 7h 7f⁵] big, rangy colt: good mover: only plating-class:
evidently stays 7f. *R. Hannon.*

MOUNT STREET 4 b.g. Connaught 130–Mecca II 90 (Exbury 138) [1974 —
6g* 7g* 7f* 8s 8g⁴ 6v² 1975 10d 8g⁶ 8f⁴ 8f* 10g⁴ 8f* 8.5fg⁶ 1976 10.2g 7fg
7fg 10fg 8f⁵ 8h⁴ 7fg] neat, quite attractive gelding: formerly quite a useful
handicapper: no worthwhile form on flat at 4 yrs (although won once over hurdles in
November): should stay 1¼m: acts on any going: blinkered three times in 1976:
probably best with strong handling. *S. Matthews.*

*Redcar Gold Trophy—Move Off has three lengths
to spare over Lily Langtry*

Zetland Gold Cup, Redcar—Move Off shows much improved form to beat Royal Match

MOVEMENT 2 b.f. Daring Display 129–Grindlewald 76 (Le Levanstell 122) **79**
[1976 5g² 5.1fg³ 6h* 6f 5.9fg 7d² 7v⁵] leggy filly: good mover: first foal: 920
gns yearling: dam won at up to 13f at 3 yrs: made most when winning seven-
runner maiden auction event at Redcar in July by 2 lengths from odds-on
Little Cynthia: kept on strongly when good 1½ lengths second to Jenny Splendid
in £2,000 nursery at Newmarket in October: will stay 1¼m: acts on any going.
L. Cumani.

MOVE OFF 3 ch.c. Farm Walk 111–Darling Do (Derring-Do 131) [1975 6fg **106**
8.2g* 8g⁶ 7g³ 7.2v³ 1976 12.2g² 10s³ 10f³ 12fg² 10d* 10.6d⁴ 10f² 10.5g⁶ 14.7f*
14fg⁴ 16g³ 17.4g³ 12.2s* 12s] light-framed colt: showed vast improvement on
his previous form when winning Zetland Gold Cup (handicap) at Redcar in May,
coming with a storming last-furlong rattle to beat Royal Match going away by
a length: afterwards ran most consistently in valuable handicaps in the north
and picked up three-runner Redcar Gold Trophy in July, coming home 3 lengths
clear of Lily Langtry: had 3 lengths to spare over Voucher Book when successful
in minor event at Catterick in October: effective at middle distances and stays
well: acts on any going: usually held up and has a fair turn of speed: suited by a
strong gallop. *J. Calvert.*

MOVIE IDOL 4 b.c. Silent Screen–Ambit (Ambiorix 130) [1974 N.R. 1975 **69**
8g 7.6g⁶ 8fg⁵ 6fg 6g³ 6fg 6d 1976 8fg 5.8h² 7f³ 6h* 5.9fg* 5.8f⁴ 6v⁵] quite
attractive American-bred colt: winner of handicaps at Carlisle in August and
at Wolverhampton the following month: best form at up to 7f: acts on any
going: blinkered fourth outing in 1975: sold 1,000 gns Ascot November Sales. *P.
Calver.*

MOVING ISLES 3 ch.f. Busted 134–Alaska Way 111 (Honeyway 125) [1975 **99**
N.R. 1976 7fg 10fg⁶ 10f² 10g* 12fg 10d⁴] lengthy filly: third living produce:
sister to a poor animal: dam won 1967 Acomb Stakes: battled on well when
winning maiden race at Ascot in July by 1½ lengths from Navigator: good fourth
to Renda in handicap at Newbury in September: should be well suited by 1½m+
(well beaten in Galtres Stakes on first attempt at trip): probably acts on any
going. *G. Pritchard-Gordon.*

MOVING PICTURE 2 b.f. Polyfoto 124–Frittenden (Sayajirao 132) [1976 **—**
5s⁵] fourth foal: sold twice as a yearling, for 1,250 gns and 1,400 gns: dam of
no account: drifted favourite for six-runner newcomers event at Goodwood in
September but dwelt and finished only remote fifth to Kilavea. *R. Price.*

MR BIGMORE 4 br.c. Mandamus 120–Intrusion 101 (Aggressor 130) [1974 **120**
6d 8s* 1975 8g⁴ 8s* 10g* 10f² 10.5d² 11v* 14g* 12g* 1976 12fg 14d² 16.1d*
20f⁵ 18.4fg* 20.9fg*].
The old saying that any lop-eared horse is an honest horse is inaccurate;
but anyone asserting its infallibility could be excused his error if the only lop-eared
horses of his acquaintance are of Mr Bigmore's kind. There are few gamer than
Mr Bigmore, who again returned a consistently high standard of performance
in 1976. The previous season he made great strides, winning five of his eight
races, rounding off his season with a fine win under a stiff weight in the Manchester
Handicap at Doncaster. Given the chance to tackle two miles plus at four years

483

of age he did even better, successfully competing against the best on weight-for-age terms.

Mr Bigmore's most important success in 1976 came in the Goodwood Cup. On form Kemal, runner-up to Sagaro in the Prix du Cadran, appeared to be Mr Bigmore's most dangerous opponent, the field being completed by Marco Ricci, Coed Cochion and the three-year-olds Ormeley and Belfalas, both tackling extreme distances for the first time. After Kemal had gone lame early in the straight, the finish developed into a duel between Mr Bigmore, who made most of the running, and Belfalas. Mr Bigmore was made to struggle by an opponent who found great improvement at the trip, but he had a length's advantage throughout the final furlong. Third-placed Coed Cochion finished twenty lengths behind Belfalas.

Mr Bigmore's other wins were not so hard-earned. In May he trotted up from Asama in a minor race at Haydock, and early in July he took the Chester Summer Handicap under 9-3, giving the Northumberland Plate winner Philominsky 19 lb and beating him gamely by one and a half lengths. In between these two victories he finished a creditable fifth, nine lengths behind Sagaro, in a very well-contested race for the Gold Cup. On his only other outing apart from his seasonal warm-up, Mr Bigmore, though no match for Bruni, kept on in typically dogged fashion to keep second place from Sea Anchor and Dakota in the Yorkshire Cup. After Goodwood a pulled muscle put out Mr Bigmore for the rest of the season.

Mr Bigmore (br.c. 1972)	Mandamus (br 1960)	Petition (br 1944)	Fair Trial / Art Paper
		Great Fun (br 1945)	Big Game / Merry Devon
	Intrusion (ch 1962)	Aggressor (b 1955)	Combat / Phaetonia
		Sun Lane (ch 1945)	Hyperion / Celestial Way

Intrusion, Mr Bigmore's dam, was an out-and-out stayer who revelled in the mud. She raced until she was five and won eight times. Lily Langtry, by Prince de Galles, was another of her offspring to do well on the racecourse in 1976, winning two races, including the Rosebery Memorial Handicap over

Chester Summer Handicap—top-weighted Mr Bigmore wins gamely from Philominsky

Goodwood Cup—Mr Bigmore keeps up the gallop in the face of a strong challenge from Belfalas

a mile and a half at Epsom. Mandamus, Mr Bigmore's sire, was a good-class handicapper at around a mile; he won the William Hill Gold Cup at Redcar as a five-year-old. The source for Mr Bigmore's name was, so his owner says, a local process-server, who a few years ago was a fairly frequent visitor to the Lambton establishment. So sympathetic and kind-hearted was the officer in the execution of his duties that he became not only a family friend but had a racehorse named after him. As a mandamus is a legal writ and Mr Bigmore is out of Intrusion, he is wittily named, is he not?

Mr Bigmore is a strong, attractive colt who is ideally suited by a thorough test of stamina. He acts on any going although his owner considers him best suited by an easy surface: he has run well for an apprentice. He remains in training and will, providing all goes well with him, be a force to be reckoned with in good long-distance races in 1977, although he is a few pounds behind the best stayers. *P. Robinson.*

MR BLUE 3 b.g. Bilsborrow 85–Crowned Beauty 83 (Coronation Year 124) [1975 6g 6g 1976 7g 8d] poor form, including in a seller: sold 410 gns Doncaster June Sales. *J. Vickers.* —

MR FORDETTE 4 ch.c. Gulf Pearl 117–Karen Chase 82 (Will Somers 114 §) [1974 N.R. 1975 7s 10f 8g 12fg* 11.7fg² 12g 14g⁵ 1976 12g³ 12fg* 13f³ 16g 11.1g⁴ 12fg 12fg⁴ 12fg⁴ 12g⁴ 12s* 12s³ 12s* 12s³ 12v³] well-made colt: quite a useful performer: winner three times at 4 yrs, at Newmarket in April, Lingfield in September and Folkestone in October, on last two courses beating Melody Ryde in close finishes: suited by 1½m but has yet to show he stays further (well beaten when tried over 2m): appears to act on any going: has twice worn blinkers, running badly on second occasion. *G. Harwood.* 86

MR GEMINI 2 b.c. Polyfoto 124–Golden Lass 62 (Golden Cloud) [1976 6g 5v 6v] half-brother to some poor animals: 1,500 gns yearling: dam of no account: behind in newcomers race and maiden races at the back-end. *C. Dingwall.* —

485

MR HIGGINS   3 ch.g. St Chad 120–French Line 98 (Set Fair 129)   [1975 5f 6g   **70**
1976 8f⁶ 7g³ 7fg* 8s⁵ 8.5fg² 7fg³ 8f] strong, sturdy gelding: won 19-runner
maiden race at Lingfield in May by 1½ lengths from Mario's Boy: probably stayed
1m: best form on a sound surface: broke a leg at Warwick in July and was
destroyed.   *N. Vigors.*

MR MANXMAN   3 b.c. Alcide 136–Not Suspect 76 (Above Suspicion 127)   **64**
[1975 N.R.   1976 11.7f⁴ 13.3fg 12f⁶ 13.1f⁴] half-brother to three winners,
including useful performer Go Grandly, a winner over 7f at 2 yrs, and fair stayer
Go Gracefully (both by Jolly Jet): dam appeared to stay 2m: about 5 lengths
fourth of 11 to Regalian in minor event at Bath in September, first outing for
almost three months and best effort: should be suited by a good test of stamina.
F. Maxwell.

MR MARLSBRIDGE   3 b.c. Prince de Galles 125–Nanaretta 116 (Narrator 127)   —
[1975 5s 6fg²(dis) 7g 6g³ 6f² 6fg 6g⁶ 8g 1976 12.2g⁶ 11d⁴ 8.2d 9fg 12f³ 14fg]
well-grown, leggy colt: ran well third outing but subsequently disappointed in
sellers: should stay 1¼m: sometimes wears blinkers nowadays.   *K. Payne.*

MR MEDE   2 b.c. Runnymede 123–Mrs Randy (Reneged)   [1976 5f 6fg 6f]   **62**
well-grown, rangy colt: good walker: showed signs of ability in maiden and
minor events.   *W. A. Stephenson.*

MR MELLORS   3 br.g. Precipice Wood 123–Lady C (Princely Gift 137)   [1975   **73**
6g 8.2d 1976 8fg³ 8s⁶ 10f⁵ 10g² 11.1f⁵ 10fg 10.6d 12s] lengthy gelding: has
ability, as he showed when runner-up to Chemin de Fer in handicap at Nottingham
in July, but was running badly in his later races and is not one to rely on: stays
1¼m.   *W. Wharton.*

MR METAL   3 b.c. Mummy's Pet 125–Lametta 94 (Alycidon 138)   [1975 5g 5g   **63**
5f³ 5g 1976 5f² 6d² 7g* 8s⁴ 8.5fg⁵ 7g⁵] good-looking, strong colt: won maiden
race at Edinburgh in May (well-backed favourite): descended to selling company
last two appearances: stays 1m: acts on any going: blinkered last two outings
at 2 yrs.   *K. Payne.*

MR MORRIS   2 b.c. Right Tack 131–Lady Sykes 76 (Sovereign Lord 120)   **81 §**
[1976 5g 5fg⁴ 5.3fg⁵ 6fg⁵ 7h³ 7f³ 6f³ 8g 8f² 8s⁶ 7.6v] compact colt: half-brother
to Guido Lord (by Linacre) and Giadolino (by Skymaster), both good winners in
Italy, and to a minor winner: 4,000 gns yearling: dam placed over 1m at 2 yrs:
ran well when fifth in July Stakes at Newmarket (to Sky Ship) and when head
second to Tudor Lilt in nursery at Bath but did not reproduce anything like
that form on his other starts: stays 1m: best form on top-of-the-ground conditions:
usually wears blinkers: inconsistent and unreliable.   *P. Haslam.*

MR MUSIC MAN   2 br.c. March Past 124–Merry Melody 68 (Counsel 118)   **98**
[1976 6fg 7fg⁴ 8g* 7fg 8s] small, useful-looking colt: second foal: 400 gns yearling: dam ran only at two years: kept on under hard driving to win 19-runner
maiden race at Goodwood in September by a neck from Elusive, the pair finishing
clear: respectable seventh of 17 to Royal Plume in well-contested race at Ascot
later in month, better subsequent effort: suited by 1m.   *E. Reavey.*

MR NICE GUY   2 gr.c. Murrayfield 119–Mead 93 (Honeyway 125)   [1976 5fg³ **107**
5f* 5fg⁴ 5fg* 5g* 6g* 5fg² 5f⁵ 6fg³ 6fg⁶ 7g² 7s⁵] leggy colt: half-brother to
three minor winners: 400 gns yearling: dam, 2-y-o 5f winner, is half-sister to
very smart sprinter Runnymede: proved a tremendous bargain, winning at
Newbury, Lingfield, Kempton and Epsom (Woodcote Stakes): brilliantly ridden
at Epsom, rallying very well under hard riding to catch newcomer Mandalus:
kept his form well afterwards, finishing good 3 lengths second of 10 to Avgerinos
in Intercraft Solario Stakes at Sandown in September on penultimate outing:
will stay 1m: consistent and exceptionally game.   *E. Reavey.*

MR PARK LANE   2 b.c. Continuation 120–Bella Fino (Major Portion 129)   **78**
[1976 6fg 6fg 7.2f⁶ 8fg⁴ 7d 7s⁴] strong, good-bodied, lengthy colt: fifth foal:
sold twice as a yearling, for 340 gns and 1,300 gns: dam won over 5f at 2 yrs in
Ireland: quite a moderate maiden: stays 1m.   *N. Callaghan.*

MR PLAYBIRDS   2 gr.c. Capistrano 120–Liesl (Pinza 137)   [1976 5fg 5s⁴ 6fg   **76**
7f 6f³ 7g⁴ 8fg³ 8s] workmanlike colt: fourth foal: sold twice as a yearling, for
500 gns and 3,100 gns: dam never ran: quite a moderate maiden: stays 1m.
N. Callaghan.

MR REPRESENTER   2 ch.c. Roan Rocket 128–Sweet Solera 129 (Solonaway   — p
128)   [1976 8.2s⁵] big, rangy colt: half-brother to three winners, including

Woodcote Stakes, Epsom—Mr Nice Guy gets up under extreme pressure to short-head Mandalus

useful French 6f and 9.5f winner Bon Appetit (by Major Portion) and fairly useful 1m and 1¼m winner Royal Shiraz (by Darius): 2,800 gns foal, resold 4,600 gns yearling: dam won six of her eight races, including 1,000 Guineas and Oaks: 12/1, got a bit above himself in paddock and then missed break when a remote staying-on fifth of 12 to Hot Grove in minor event at Haydock in October: will have learnt a good deal from this experience, has a lot of scope and should do much better at 3 yrs. *B. Hills.*

MR RESISTOR 3 br.g. Hotfoot 126–Welsh Coral 93 § (Welsh Abbot 131)   — §
[1975 5g⁴ 5f 6fg² 6fg 7g³ 7g³ 7f 7fg 8.2g   1976 10fg⁶ 10f 8fg 10.1f³ 10.1g³ 10.2f]
small, shapely gelding: has yet to show he stays 1¼m: twice ran badly in blinkers at 2 yrs, on one occasion losing a lot of ground at flag start: not one to trust: sold 680 gns Doncaster November Sales. *G. Peter-Hoblyn.*

MRS HIGGINS 2 b.f. Fine Blade 121–Change (Mourne 126)   [1976 5fg 5f 5fg   —
6f 6g⁶ 6d 7v 7s] unimpressive filly: poor mover: no worthwhile form in varied company. *P. Farrell.*

MRS MCARDY 2 b.f. Tribal Chief 125–Hanina 83 (Darling Boy 124)   [1976 **101**
5fg 5fg⁵ 5.6f⁵ 6f⁴ 5fg* 6f* 8g* 6d*] shapely, attractive filly: fourth reported
produce: dam stayed 1m: developed into a useful filly and won maiden race at Newcastle, nurseries at Thirsk and Doncaster (came from a long way back when winning £2,700 event comfortably by 1½ lengths from Fair Season) and minor event at Redcar: all out when beating Sarasingh by ¾ length in last-named event in September: effective at 5f to 1m: appears to act on any going: ridden by apprentice N. Crowther when successful. *M. W. Easterby.*

MRS TICKLE 3 b.r.f. Prince of Galles 125–Miss Twist 84 (Major Portion 129)   —
[1975 6fg 8.2d   1976 8f 7fg 5.8h] neat filly: apparently of no account. *I. Dudgeon.*

MRS WALMSLEY 2 b.f. Lorenzaccio 130–Riva 95 (Relic)   [1976 6fg 6h* 6s   **87**
8s 8s³] attractive, well-made filly: sister to 1974 2-y-o 5f winner Mary Mullen, and half-sister to smart 9f and 1½m winner Fisherman's Bridge (by Crepello): dam won over 6f and stayed 1m: won weakly-contested maiden race at Brighton in August by 3 lengths from Sally Lunn: fair third to Court House in nursery at Wolverhampton in October, best subsequent effort: probably stays 1m: slowly into stride first and third outings. *R. Price.*

MRS WIFE 2 ch.f. Royben 125–Palmaressa 80 (Royal Palm 131)   [1976 5fg   **80**
5fg⁶ 6fg³ 5fg 5g³ 7h* 6g⁵ 7g 6g⁵] small, strong filly: second foal: 1,950 gns yearling: dam won over 7f at 2 yrs: won seven-runner maiden race at Brighton in August by short head from Dastina: stays 7f: acts on hard ground. *R. Smyth.*

MR ZIMMERMAN   3 b.c. Mecode–mare's pedigree unknown   [1975 7g 6g   1976   —
10.8fg 8.2f 8g 12f]   useless.   *T. Healey.*

MUFF   3 b.f. Manacle 123–Queen's Fashion 78 (Queen's Hussar 124)   [1975 5fg⁶   §§
5s 5g 5fg 5.9f   1976 8d 6v]   light-framed filly: temperamental plater: wore
blinkers at 2 yrs.   *S. Nesbitt.*

MUJON   7 gr.h. Quorum 126–Persica 91 (Darius 129)   [1974 6g* 6g 6g³ 5.8f³   **81**
5.3f* 5.9g* 5.8g³ 6g 5g⁴ 5.8g 5g⁴ 6g 5.8v 5v⁶   1975 6s⁵ 5d⁵ 6g⁴ 6g⁶ 6g³ 6f³ 6h*
5f³ 6g* 5.8f³ 5.8f⁴ 5.9fg³ 6fg⁵ 5.8f   1976 7g² 7g 8fg² 6f* 5.9f* 7fg* 5.8h* 6f 6fg³
5v⁶]   deep-bodied horse: very good mover: moderate handicapper: successful
at Lingfield (twice), Wolverhampton and Bath within the space of three weeks
in midsummer, being ridden by claimer D. Moss on each occasion: best form
at up to 7f: acted on any going: had worn blinkers, but did at least as well without
them: standing at Chesterton Stud, Warwickshire, fee £98.   *P. Cundell.*

MULLION   4 b.g. Crocket 130–Tartar's Star 83 (Tamerlane 128)   [1974 N.R.   —
1975 9g 8f 10.1fg 10.8fg 8.2g 10f² 10g   1976 10g]   quite a modest plater: best
two runs at 1¼m: acts on firm going: sold 310 gns Ascot July Sales.   *M. Tate.*

MUMMY'S DARLING   2 b.f. Mummy's Pet 125–Wontell 80 (Buisson Ardent   **114**
129)   [1976 5fg 5g* 5g² 5fg* 5g² 6g⁵ 5s² 5v*]   small filly: seventh produce:
dam ran only at 2 yrs: won maiden race at Salisbury in May, Chesterfield Stakes
at Newmarket in July (produced a really good turn of foot to short-head Claddagh)
and minor event at Leicester in November: second in three other races, putting
up a really good effort on last occasion when failing by only a neck to catch
La Ville de Rire in Doncaster Stakes in October: best at 5f: has won on a firm
surface and goes very well on soft ground.   *R. Hannon.*

MUMMY'S PAL   2 b.f. Mummy's Pet 125–Palanna 87 (Pall Mall 132)   [1976   **78**
5fg³ 5f 5fg 5f⁵ 5g* 5d³ 6s⁴]   first foal: dam won over 6f at 2 yrs and stayed at
least 1m: led throughout when winning 14-runner maiden race at Catterick in
September by ¾ length from Signed On: fair third under a penalty in nursery
won by Star Attention at Redcar later in month: probably stays 6f: apprentice
ridden at Catterick.   *L. Shedden.*

MUMMY'S RASCAL   2 b.f. Mummy's Pet 125–Somalie II 76 (Silnet 131)   —
[1976 6s 5s 5s]   poor plater.   *Hbt Jones.*

MUMMY'S STAR   2 br.c. Mummy's Pet 125–Dycord 81 (Royal Record II)   **73**
[1976 6fg⁶ 7fg⁶ 7f⁶ 8s⁴]   strong, well-made, attractive colt: third produce:
780 gns foal, resold 3,000 gns yearling: dam won over 5f at 2 yrs: ran best race
when 13 lengths fourth of eight to Night Before in minor event at Goodwood
in September: stays 1m.   *G. Pritchard-Gordon.*

MUM'S ALIBI   2 b.c. Mummy's Pet 125–Caught-At-It 77 (Poaching 115)   —
[1976 5s 5fg 5f 5s]   strong, good-bodied colt: good walker: little worthwhile
form in maiden races: sold 820 gns Newmarket Autumn Sales.   *N. Adam.*

MUMS THE WORD   3 b.g. Mummy's Pet 125–Keruing (Quorum 126)   [1975   —
5f³ 5f² 5f³ 5f⁴ 5fg²   1976 5fg]   neat gelding: disappointing and is possibly none
too genuine: has worn blinkers: bought by B.B.A. 1,300 gns Ascot June Sales
for export to Belgium.   *J. Nelson.*

MURATA   2 ch.f. Be Friendly 130–Lady Anne Neville 97 (Right Boy 137)   [1976   **59**
5h⁵ 5g 6v 8g]   quite a modest plater: unlikely to stay 1m: sold 400 gns Newmarket December Sales.   *S. Hall.*

MURRAY AMOUR   2 b.f. Murrayfield 119–Amour-Propre (High Perch 126)   —
[1976 5d⁶ 5g 6f 5g⁶ 8f]   leggy, narrow filly: bad maiden.   *W. Murray*

MURRMATCH   4 br.c. Murrayfield 119–Lobinstown Pilgrim (Tyrone 130)   **93**
[1974 5g 5f* 5fg* 5g⁵ 6d* 7g⁴ 6g³ 6s³ 6d   1975 5s* 5d* 5s² 5fg³ 6g⁶ 5fg⁶ 5g* 5g³
5g³ 5g 5.6g 5d² 5g 5d³ 5g⁶   1976 6fg⁵ 6g⁴ 6g⁶ 6f² 5f 5g 5g 5g⁴ 5s³ 5v² 5s³]   sturdy
colt: very useful handicapper (rated 110) at 3 yrs: didn't show the same form
in 1976 although was well backed on three of his last four outings (ran respectably
on each of them): out of his depth on fifth start: best form at 5f but stays further:
acts on any going.   *R. Hannon.*

MUSCHIO   4 b.c. Tissot 131–Marinka (Alcide 136)   [1974 6s⁵ 5g⁴ 7.5s³ 8s⁵ 8g*   —
9.5s*   1975 10v* 10v* 10g⁵ 10s 10d   1976 10g 12fg⁶]   workmanlike ex-Italian
colt: showed quite useful form in Italy in 1974 and was rated 29 lb behind
Bolkonski in Italian Free Handicap: won two races in Italy as a 3-y-o but has

488

since been beaten in five races in this country, including on both starts in 1976: probably stays 1½m: acts on heavy going: wears blinkers. *L. Cumani.*

MUSH KABAD 2 b.g. Bold Lad (U.S.A.)–Persian Snow 68 (Tehran) [1976 **67** 6g 7g 6v⁶] big, strong, good sort: only plating class. *R. Jarvis.*

MUSICAL ECHO 3 ch.f. Double-U-Jay 120–Refrain (Crocket 130) [1975 **61** N.R. 1976 8fg 8f⁶ 8f 10.4fg⁴ 8f³ 10d 15v] big, lengthy filly: third foal: sister to Snake Dance, winner over 1¼m at 3 yrs and half-sister to fairly useful miler The Maltings (by Gala Performance): 1,400 gns yearling: dam won over 5f in Ireland: in frame in nine-runner maiden race at Chester in July (heavily-backed favourite) and apprentice maiden race at Yarmouth in August: probably stays 1¼m but not 15f: slipped up penultimate outing. *P. Robinson.*

MUSICAL LUCY 3 b.f. Jukebox 120–Drusilla 100 (Delirium 126) [1975 N.R. **58** 1976 8f 8f 8fg 7fg⁶ 8.2h³ 7f⁶ 11.5d 12g] well-grown filly: poor plater: not certain to stay 1½m. *W. Marshall.*

MUSICAL PIECE 4 b.f. Song 132–Piece or War (Martial 131) [1974 6fg 6fg³ **76** 5d² 6g 6g* 6d⁶ 1975 6g⁶ 6g² 6g⁴ 7f 6f³ 6f⁴ 5.3f⁶ 6fg⁴ 6g* 6d 5g 1976 6fg³ 6fg 6f 6s⁴ 5.1fg 5.9g* 6g⁵ 5h² 6fg² 5fg* 6f 5f 6h² 5.8f²] neat, good-bodied filly: quite a moderate handicapper: successful at Wolverhampton in June and Windsor the following month, on latter course beating Under Orders 2 lengths: best form at up to 6f: acts on any going: best in blinkers: pulled up twelfth outing (reportedly broke blood vessel) but ran creditably last two appearances. *B. Hanbury.*

MUSICAL PRINCE 3 br.c. Prince Consort 121–Toccata (Kythnos 126) [1975 **81** 7fg 1976 10.1f 10g 10.5fg 8fg² 8s*] strong, well-grown colt: ran well last two outings following a long absence and won 17-runner maiden race at Goodwood in September by 2 lengths from Guffaw: evidently suited by 1m but is bred to stay further: seems to act on any going: blinkered third appearance. *J. Bethell.*

MUSICAL PROGRESS 3 b.f. Paddy's Progress 113–Musical March 103 (March **—** Past 124) [1975 5g 1976 11.1g 16h 12f] fair sort: no signs of ability and was sold 300 gns Ascot September Sales. *D. Jermy.*

MUSIC BOY 3 ch.c. Jukebox 120–Veronique 96 (Matador 131) [1975 5s* 5fg* **118** 5d² 5fg* 5fg* 6fg* 5g² 1976 5d⁵ 5fg⁵ 5f 5fg⁵ 5fg* 5fg 5g] strong, muscular, sprint type: half-brother to fairly useful sprinter Princess of Verona (by King's Leap) and to another sprint winner by King's Leap: dam a sprinter: was one of fastest 2-y-o's of 1975 when he won five races, including Windsor Castle Stakes at Royal Ascot and C and G Gimcrack Stakes at York: nothing like so successful in his second season (said to have suffered from virus in first half of year), gaining his only success when making all and beating Polly Peachum by a neck in King George Stakes at Goodwood in July: put up easily best other efforts at 3 yrs when fifth of ten behind Polly Peachum in Palace House Stakes at Newmarket in April and about 5 lengths eighth of 13 behind Lochnager in King's Stand Stakes at Royal Ascot in June: stayed 6f although was a very speedy racehorse and ideally

King George Stakes, Goodwood—Music Boy resists the challenge of Polly Peachum

The Cheveley Park Stud's "Music Boy"

suited by 5f on top-of-the-ground: standing at Cheveley Park Stud, Newmarket, at £500 n.f.n.f. with 1st October concession. *B. Lunness.*

MUSIC LINE 3 b.c. Tudor Music 131–Next in Line (Our Babu 131) [1975 **69** 5fg 1976 7fg 8g 10h³ 10.1g⁵ 10s³ 10.2s] strong, well-made colt: showed ability, putting up a particularly good effort on fifth outing when 3 lengths third of nine to Blyth's Folly in minor event at Sandown in October: stays 1¼m: evidently suited by soft going. *F. Maxwell.*

MUSIQUE ROYALE 2 ch.f. Right Royal V 135–Musical (Prince Chevalier) **?** [1976 8.2s*] French filly: half-sister to Irish Sweeps Derby third Master Guy (by Relko): dam a useful winning daughter of 1,000 Guineas and Oaks winner Musidora: favourite for 17-runner newcomers race at Saint-Cloud in October and put up a highly promising display, disputing the lead all the way and drawing away to win by 4 lengths and 5 lengths: a very good middle-distance filly in the making. *F. Boutin, France.*

MUSTER LANE 2 gr.c. Sovereign Path 125–Welsh Mistress 113 (Abernant 142) **94** [1976 5fg 5g³ 6g² 7d] tall colt: half-brother to several winners, including smart 1975 French 2-y-o Charlie Man (by Habitat): 11,500 gns yearling: dam won four times over 5f: 1½ lengths third of nine to And Behold in maiden race at Kempton in May: not seen out again until September but ran very well on return, finishing 1½ lengths second of 14 to Region in £1,600 event: stays 6f well but had little chance when tried at 7f (William Hill Dewhurst Stakes). *H. T. Jones.*

MUSTON COPSE 2 ch.c. Track Spare 125–Goldella 60 (Golden Cloud) [1976 **86** 5g 6fg 7s 7v² 7s⁴] lengthy colt: half-brother to three minor winners: 2,300 gns yearling: dam of little account: 1½ lengths second of 15 to Chennel Lane in maiden race at Leicester in October: will probably stay 1m: acts on heavy going. *R. Akehurst.*

MY ANGEL 2 ro.f. St Alphage 119–Gay Charmaine 103 (Charlottesville 135) **81** [1976 5fg* 5fg² 5g* 5f 5g 5f⁵ 5.9fg 5d⁵] first foal: dam won over 6f at 3 yrs: won maiden race at Teesside in April and minor event at Edinburgh the following

490

month, on latter course holding off Laser Lady by a short head: off course two months afterwards and did not show her best form on her return but wasn't disgraced on last two outings: probably stays 6f: blinkered final appearance. *F. Carr.*

MY ANOUK 2 b.f. Comedy Star 121–Blue Ann 60 (Road House II) [1976 5fg **82** 5d³ 5f² 5g³ 5f 5v⁴ 5s⁶] short-coupled filly: half-sister to a winning plater by Weepers Boy: 500 gns yearling: dam a plater: off course over three months after fifth outing but ran well on her return, finishing 3 lengths fourth of eight to Forlorn Scot in minor race at Teesside in October: only just stays 5f: acts on any going but is evidently suited by heavy. *H. Blackshaw*

MY BOY TO 3 b.g. Runnymede 123–Grey Panther 91 (Right Boy 137) [1975 — 5s⁶ 5f 7f⁵ 8.2g 8g 6g 1976 8fg 11.7f⁵] plating-class maiden: not certain to stay beyond sprint distances and was beaten a long way on first attempt at 1½m. *P. Cole.*

MY CANDY 3 b.f. Lorenzaccio 130–Candy Gift 97 (Princely Gift 137) [1975 — 5fg 7h² 7f 1976 12fg 10.1f⁵ 10.1d 6v] small, narrow filly: plating-class maiden: should stay 1¼m. *P. Cole.*

MY CHARM 3 b.g. Welsh Abbot 131–Elsie's Choice (Stanmar 107) [1975 N.R. — 1976 10.1fg 6f 8f⁵ 7s] poor maiden *R. Supple.*

MY CHOPIN 5 ch.h. Manacle 123–Chopiniana 102 (Premonition 130) [1974 5g **83** 5g 5g* 5g* 5fg* 5g⁵ 1975 5d³ 5d³ 5f³ 5f² 6g⁵ 6fg⁶ 7.2g³ 1976 6g 6fg 6g⁴ 5fg 6fg⁵ 6d² 6f* 6fg⁴ 6fg⁵ 5f* 5f² 5fg⁴ 5f⁴ 5fg³ 6f² 5h*] strong, well-made, compact horse: moderate handicapper: successful at Ripon in June and at Hamilton in July and September: best at sprint distances: probably acts on any going: wears blinkers nowadays: genuine and consistent. *T. Fairhurst.*

MY COUSINS 2 br.f. My Swallow 134–Kawaakib (Crepello 136) [1976 8s] — half-sister to Beach Time (by Midsummer Night II), a winner over 1¼m in France at 3 yrs: 6,000 gns yearling: dam, who raced without success in France, is daughter of Irish Oaks winner Amante: unquoted and backward when behind in 28-runner maiden race won by Royal Boxer at Newmarket in October. *R. Jarvis.*

MY CRISSIE 2 b.f. Wolver Hollow 126–Vanilla (Vatellor) [1976 5.1f⁴ 7f 7g 7g] — of no account: sold 220 gns Newmarket Autumn Sales. *G. Blum.*

MY DARING BOY 2 b.c. Daring Display 129–Carcharus 80 (Silver Shark 129) **78** [1976 5fg⁶ 5f 5f 5fg⁵ 6f³ 7f 7s] neat colt: 1¾ lengths third of six to Pasaguarda in maiden race at Brighton in August, easily best effort: well beaten afterwards, including in a seller: best form at 6f: possibly unsuited by soft going: tried in blinkers on third outing: sold 210 gns Ascot December Sales. *J. Benstead.*

MY EAGLE 7 ch.h. Ballyciptic 122–Darrigle (Vilmoray 126) [1974 5.8fg 5.9f² **77** 6f 6h⁶ 5.8f* 5g² 5d² 8fg 5.8g* 5s 5g² 5.6d 6s 5.8v 1975 5.8g 5g* 5f 5f³ 5.8h⁴ 5.9f⁵ 5.8f 5g* 5g 5g* 5v⁶ 1976 7.2d³ 8g 5.8f 6g⁶ 5.8h 5fg³] strong, muscular horse: quite a moderate handicapper nowadays: best at 5f or 6f: acts well on firm going and is unsuited by very soft ground: usually wears blinkers: suitable mount for an apprentice: none too consistent: has won three times at Bath. *M. Stevens.*

MY FAIR NIECE 3 ch.f. Great Nephew 126–Oh So Fair (Graustark) [1975 6g* **97** 6f* 6d 1976 7fg 8fg 10g² 12g 12f³ 12fg⁴ 12fg³ 11g⁴ 10d*] lengthy, attractive filly: half-sister to 4-y-o Roussalka (by Habitat) and 2-y-o Etienne Gerard (by Brigadier Gerard): gained a well-deserved success when beating Dame Foolish by 7 lengths in minor event at Newmarket in October: had previously run well in good-class fillies races, gaining a place in Lupe Stakes at Goodwood in May (¾-length second to Laughing Girl), Ribblesdale Stakes at Royal Ascot in June (8 lengths third to Catalpa) and Galtres Stakes at York in August (5 lengths third to Capricious): also finished creditable fourth to Gunner B in Doonside Cup at Ayr the following month: stays 1½m: appears to act on any going. *B. Hobbs.*

MY FOLLY 2 b.f. Salvo 129–Brief Chorus 105 (Counsel 118) [1976 8fg] big — p filly: half-sister to three winners, including very useful stayer Brief Bay (by Canisbay) and useful 1975 2-y-o Donrae (by Don II): dam won at 1m and finished third in Yorkshire Oaks: unquoted, ridden by 7-lb claimer and looking burly, completely missed break and was tailed off until making some progress in straight when ninth of 12 to Vaguely in maiden race at Beverley in September: will stay well: will do much better in time. *W. Gray.*

MY HERO 7 b.h. Le Levanstell 122–Sistine (Botticelli 129) [1974 8d 8fg* 10h⁶ **83** 8f 8fg⁵ 8.5f* 8g 8g² 8fg⁶ 8g⁵ 8g⁴ 8.2d* 9d 8s⁶ 1975 8d 8g* 8g⁶ 8fg³ 8.5f⁶ 8f 10h⁴ 9g⁶ 9f⁶ 1976 9g⁶ 10g² 8.5g* 8f* 8h² 8fg⁴ 8g] fair handicapper: made a lot of running and battled on very gamely when winning at Epsom and Brighton in

June: stays 1¼m: acts on a soft surface but goes particularly well on a firm one: has been tried in blinkers: a splendid mount for a boy: very genuine and consistent but ran badly final outing. *R. Akehurst.*

MY HUSSAR 4 br.c. Queen's Hussar 124–Djenina 87 (Djebe) [1974 6d 6g⁵ **93** 5.8v* 6d³ 1975 7.3s⁵ 7f* 8fg² 8fg* 8f* 8g 9g 1976 8g 8f 8g 7fg 8g⁶ 8f² 7.6fg³ 8g⁶ 8f⁵ 8fg⁴ 9g] big, strong, well-made colt: fairly useful handicapper: had three creditable efforts to his name at 4 yrs, including when 4 lengths second of 16 to Jumping Hill in Royal Hunt Cup at Royal Ascot in June and when about 3 lengths fourth of 13 to Silver Steel in Rose of York Handicap at York in August: stays 9f: acts on any going: suitable mount for an apprentice: wears blinkers nowadays: virtually pulled up on eighth outing. *J. Sutcliffe.*

MY LADYBIRD 2 ch.f. My Swallow 134–Dame Judith 88 (Francis S) [1976 **—** 6fg 6f 5s 7s] neat filly: no worthwhile form in maiden and minor events. *D. Dale.*

MY LEVENT 2 b.c. Fighting Ship 121–Puffin 71 (Fastnet Rock 123) [1976 **66** 6fg 7fg 6f⁴ 7f] strong colt: showed a little ability when fourth of six to Freight Forwarder in minor event at Folkestone in July: will stay 1½m. *A. Dalton.*

MY MANDOLIN 3 gr.f. Mummy's Pet 125–Sheinter (Sheshoon 132) [1975 **48** 5s⁶ 6s⁴ 5f⁶ 5f³ 6d 7g 5d⁴ 5v² 1976 5f⁴ 5h 10fg 7fg 6d 5s 5s] lightly-made filly: ran poorly after first outing, including in sellers: evidently best at 5f: has worn blinkers. *O. O'Neill.*

MY MANON 3 b.f. Hard Tack 111 §–Chantarella (Typhoon 125) [1975 5g⁶ **47** 6fg⁵ 7g 1976 10.1fg 7.2g⁴ 7.2fg⁶ 8fg] tall, sparely-made filly: plater: promises to stay 7f: sometimes starts slowly: bolted before start on one occasion at 2 yrs. *G. Balding.*

MY MARK 4 b.f. On Your Mark 125–Q.E.D. (Montaval 129) [1974 5g 6s 1975 **—** 8g 10.6v 1976 9f 7fg 8.2f] probably of little account: sold 500 gns Doncaster November Sales. *J. Leigh.*

MY MERRY MAID 3 b.f. Will Somers 114 §–Tintale (Tin Whistle 128) [1975 **46** 6fg 7f 6g 6d 1976 8f* 8g⁴ 9fg] light-framed filly: easily won four-runner seller at Newcastle in April by a length from String-'em-along: bought in 680 gns afterwards: stays 1m: sold 420 gns Doncaster November Sales. *S. Hall.*

MY OLD MAN 2 ch.c. Most Secret 118–My Old Dutch 76 (Technion 96) [1976 **81** 5s 7fg 6f⁵ 6g³ 6fg 5v] strong colt: half-brother to three winners, including smart sprinter Dutch Gold (by Goldhill) and useful sprinter Dutch May (by Maystreak): dam won twice over 6f: blinkered, ran easily best race when 2½ lengths third of 15 to Latest Model in maiden race at Newcastle in August: again blinkered next start and was well beaten without them on final outing: stays 6f (missed break when tried over 7f). *M. W. Easterby.*

MY PATRIOT 3 b.c. Round Table–Spearfish (Fleet Nasrullah) [1975 7g 6g⁵ **76** 6fg² 1976 10f³ 10s] good-looking, well-made American-bred colt: didn't race as a 3-y-o until August and failed to fulfil the promise of his final outing in 1975: should stay at least 1m: possibly unsuited by soft going: ran badly when tried in blinkers on final outing. *N. Murless.*

MY PET INGO 2 ch.c. Petingo 135–Amassyna (Ragusa 137) [1976 8s 10d] **76** well-grown French-bred colt: second reported foal: dam unraced half-sister to good French stayer Misyaaf: showed signs of some ability in maiden races at Newmarket in October, finishing seventh of 12 to subsequently-disqualified Gunbad in second of these: apparently stays 1¼m. *B. Hills.*

MY POLYANNA 3 br.f. Polyfoto 124–Debnic 86 (Counsel 118) [1975 6fg **81** 1976 7fg 10fg² 10fg³ 10f³ 10.1f* 10f* 10f² 10.1fg² 10d* 12g² 10d² 12s³] neat filly: won maiden race at Windsor and two handicaps at Yarmouth, on latter course in September beating Nepotist ½ length: ran very well in her other races, particularly in Newmarket handicaps at the back-end, and was unplaced only once all season: stays 1½m: acts on any going: thoroughly genuine and consistent: has run well for an apprentice. *J. Hindley.*

MY RAFF 3 b.g. Raffingora 130–King's Fillet (King's Bench 132) [1975 5f 5fg³ **63** 5f⁴ 5d 5g 5s⁵ 1976 6fg 5fg* 5fg⁵ 5.8f* 5g⁵ 6f³ 5.7f⁵ 6fg 5.8h⁶ 5h² 5f³ 5g 5fg 8s] sprint handicapper: winner at Wolverhampton and Bath in the spring: stays 6f but is not certain to get 1m: suited by a sound surface: ran below his best under stiffish weights on last three outings. *M. Stevens.*

MYRRHMAID 3 b.f. Frankincense 120–Cute 75 (Hardicanute 130) [1975 N.R. **—** 1976 7fg 10fg] small filly: behind in maiden races at Wolverhampton (dwelt) in April and Yarmouth in May: sold 380 gns Newmarket Autumn Sales. *D. Thom.*

MY SAYANI 3 gr.f. Fleece 114–Sayarani 96 (Hard Tack 111 §) [1975 6g6 6h —
6d 1976 7g 7f 8.2d6 12g] no worthwhile form in Scottish maiden and minor
events. *N. Angus.*

MY SQUIRE 3 b.g. Cumshaw 111–Princess Diane III 84 (King's Coup 108) —
[1975 N.R. 1976 12v] big, strong gelding: second foal: half-brother to N.H.
performer Rudolpho's Verdict (by Perhapsburg): dam won at up to 1m: unquoted,
raced in touch until getting chopped off going into turn when distant seventh of
13 behind Touch of Class in maiden race at Newbury in October. *J. Benstead.*

MYSTERY VOICE 3 ch.c. Saintly Song 128–Spinneret (Persian Gulf) [1975 —
N.R. 1976 9fg 11f 12g] rangy colt: well behind in early-season maiden races:
sold 310 gns Doncaster October Sales. *H. Williams.*

MY SUNNY 4 ch.f. Grey Dawn II 132–Mabouba (Princely Gift 137) [1974 5fg —
5f4 5f5 5f 5f6 5g4 5f 5fg5 5s6 5s* 1975 6s 8.2fg3 8h3 9.4h2 9g6 8f3 13.8f* 10fg3 8g
1976 10g5] neat, compact American-bred filly: made only one appearance in
1976: well suited by a distance of ground nowadays but has run well over shorter
distances: acts on any going: best form in blinkers at 2 yrs, but has run well
without them since: good mount for a lady rider. *J. Calvert.*

MY THERAPE 2 b.f. Jimmy Reppin 131–Howrytuar 90 (Sound Track 132) **93**
[1976 5f4 5fg* 5f3 5g5] strong, shapely filly: not a good mover in her slower
paces: third living foal: 2,700 gns yearling: dam won at 5f to 7f: won maiden race
at Nottingham in July by 1½ lengths from Fragrant Coffee: ran creditably
afterwards, starting well-backed favourite when fifth to Noirima in nursery at
Goodwood in September: will be suited by 6f or more. *M. Stoute.*

MY WELLIE 3 b.c. Marcus Brutus 108–Snow Boots 62 (Marshal Pil 108) [1975 **75**
5v2 5v2 5s4 5g 5g 6f2 6f5 7f2 10g3 8g* 8fg6 1976 8fg5 12fg 10d4 10f4 10fg2 12h*
12f2 10f3 11h3 12fg5] neat colt: quite a moderate handicapper: won slowly-run
four-horse contest at Redcar in August all out by ½ length from Solatia, dis-
playing a good turn of foot: ran creditably next three outings but was disappointing when tried in blinkers final appearance: suited by 1½m and will stay further:
acts on any going: came from behind at Redcar and is considered by stable to be
best suited by such tactics. *W. C. Watts.*

N

NAGIN 4 ch.f. Pretense–Quilling (Princequillo) [1974 5s* 6g* 5f6 6s5 7s6 1975 **113**
8f 8h2 8f4 8d3 7f2 6f 6fg* 6d 6f* 6s2 5g 6g* 1976 6s3 5f5 6g* 7d 6f 5d3 6g3 6g3 6g 7g]
shapely, very attractive American-bred filly: smart performer: successful at
Evry in May: put up her best other performance at 4 yrs on seventh start, when
3 lengths third of 11 to Girl Friend in Prix de Meautry at Deauville in August:
ran moderately ninth appearance: best form at 6f but had run respectably at up
to 1m: acted on any going, but was particularly well suited by a sound surface:
visits Grundy. *A. Breasley, France.*

NAIVASHA 4 ch.g. Laser Light 118–Spirit (Conspirator 114) [1974 5s 5g 5fg2 —
5g* 6f* 6g4 6fg 7g3 6g5 7g 7v 1975 9g 7f 7g 10fg6 10h3 10f 10fg 12g6 1976 12fg6
10h] neat gelding: poor performer nowadays: evidently stays 1¼m but
apparently not 1½m: acts on any going: usually wears blinkers. *A. Potts.*

NAJD 2 ch.f. St Chad 120–Molarina 100 (Denturius) [1976 5.1f5 5d2 6d4 5s* **86**
6s3 5d] sister to a minor 2-y-o 5f winner, and half-sister to several winners,
including useful sprinter Queen of the Troops (by King's Troop): 1,700 gns
yearling: dam sister to Set Fair: odds on when winning 17-runner maiden race at
Bath in October by a neck from High Value: ran well on most of her other outings:
stays 6f: acts on soft going. *R. Boss.*

NAMARA 2 b.f. Pieces of Eight 128–Barlow Fold 99 (Monet 127) [1976 5fg **102**
6fg2 5g* 6fg* 5g3] half-sister to two minor winners here and to a winner in
Italy: 4,100 gns yearling: dam won over 5f at 2 yrs: odds-on winner of five-
runner maiden race at Ayr in July and had her six opponents well strung out when
winning £1,800 event at Windsor later in month by 5 lengths from Douvaine:
seemed to have good chance at weights in nursery at Lingfield in August but
ruined chance by starting slowly and was beaten 3 lengths into third place
behind Regal Flash: stays 6f well. *J. Hindley.*

NAMPARA COVE 2 ch.c. Fair Decision 93 §–Aspida (Honeyway 125) [1976 **88**
5fg 6v2] brother to winning sprinter Double Seven: 270 gns yearling: dam of
little account: 20/1, made all when first past post in 16-runner maiden race at
Lingfield in November, a short head in front of Songhurst: edged right in final

furlong and was subsequently placed second by stewards: will stay 1m. *B. Wise.*

NANAMO 2 ch.c. Sovereign Gleam 117 Caribe II (Tropique 128) [1976 5s 6f] — of no account: sold 550 gns Ascot August Sales. *Denys Smith.*

NANA'S QUEEN 2 b.f. Ridan–Nana's Girl 109 (Tin Whistle 128) [1976 6fg⁵ **84** 6g³ 6g² 6g 7g* 7v] leggy, sparely-made filly: third foal: half-sister to two winners, notably very smart 3-y-o Royal Boy (by Realm), a winner at up to 7f: dam, useful at up to 1m, is sister to very smart sprinter Tin King: forged clear from distance to win 21-runner maiden race at Ayr in September by 3 lengths from Helping Hand: well suited by 7f and will stay further: probably unsuited by heavy ground. *G. Pritchard-Gordon.*

NANTEQUOS 3 b.c. Tom Rolfe–Moccasin (Nantallah) [1975 7g³ 1976 9f* **108+** 9f*] American-bred Irish colt: half-brother to two winners by Round Table, namely top 1973 2-y-o Apalachee and very useful American colt Indian: dam, champion American 2-y-o filly of 1965, is sister to top-class performers Ridan and Lt Stevens, and Thatch's dam Thong: won minor event at Leopardstown in August (long odds on and made all) and Group 3 Whitehall Stakes at Phoenix Park the following month: comfortably accounted for Poacher's Moon (gave 6 lb) by 2½ lengths in latter event: will stay 1½m: a good-class colt in the making. *V. O'Brien, Ireland.*

NANTICIOUS 2 ch.f. Northfields–Nanette 100 (Worden II 129) [1976 6g 6g* **108** 8g*] Irish filly: half-sister to 3-y-o Tanella (by Habitat), a useful winner over 5f and 6f at 2 yrs: 11,000 gns yearling: dam won over 6f as a 2-y-o and stayed 1¼m: up with leaders all way when winning 16-runner maiden race at the Curragh in July by 4 lengths from Opening Flight: not seen out again until late-September when putting up a really good effort to win Silken Glider Stakes at Leopardstown by 2 lengths from Delicia: will stay 1½m: a very useful filly in the making. *D. Weld, Ireland.*

NANTUCKET 4 ch.c. Pall Mall 132–Argentessa 80 (Sing Sing 134) [1974 5g⁵ **85** 5g⁵ 5fg* 6d³ 6s⁴ 1975 6v 6f 7fg 7fg⁶ 7fg⁴ 6fg³ 6g⁴ 6f* 6d⁴ 5g² 6g* 1976 5g 6fg

Mr W. Haggin Perry's "Nantequos"

494

6g³ 7.6f* 7fg* 7fg 7.3d] smallish, lengthy colt: fair handicapper: successful at Lingfield in June and Sandown the following month, making all and holding on well on both occasions: stayed 1m: appeared to act on any going, except perhaps very soft: best in blinkers: sold 3,900 gns Ascot December Sales, and has been exported as a stallion to Australia. *Miss A. Sinclair.*

NAPOLEANA 2 br.f. King Emperor–Happy Music 84 (Hethersett 134) [1976 **85** p
6g⁵] quite attractive filly: second foal: half-sister to minor French 1¼m winner Nickelodeon (by Charlottesville): dam, suited by long distances, is daughter of Park Hill winner Cursorial: 20/1 for 30-runner maiden race at Newmarket in September but ran well, looking dangerous in the Dip and then weakening to finish 3 lengths fifth to Rheola: will stay at least 1m: sure to improve and will win races. *J. Winter.*

NARGIS 3 b.f. Busted 134–Swordblade 84 (Pall Mall 132) [1975 8f 1976 10g **79**
13.3fg² 12f³ 12f² 12fg 12.2s* 14d] lengthy filly: spreadeagled her field when winning moderate 10-runner maiden race at Wolverhampton in October: frequently ran as though she would be suited by a stiff test of stamina but was well beaten on her first attempt at 1¾m: acts on any going. *C. Brittain.*

NARLU MANI POUM 4 b.f. Sahib 114–Evening Flower (Crepello 136) [1974 —
5s 5f² 5fg⁴ 5f⁴ 5f⁶ 5.9fg⁵ 5g 5d 5fg 1975 6f 8f 7fg 8f⁶ 8fg 6g⁵ 5h 7f⁶ 5.9fg 5g 7fg 10d 1976 8fg 7g] light-framed filly: poor plater: best form at up to 7f: acts on firm going: ran badly when tried in blinkers. *B. Richmond.*

NARVIC WAY 4 br.g. Master Owen–Cottage Rule (Straight Rule 96) [1974 —
N.R. 1975 N.R. 1976 18s] second foal: dam point-to-pointer: 33/1 when well behind in amateur riders maiden race at Doncaster in October, only outing. *W. A. Stephenson.*

NASHITA 3 b.f. Nashua–Flor del Viento (Gulf Stream 120) [1975 6fg³ 7v³ —
1976 8d 8fg 8.2v 6s] American-bred filly: lightly raced and no worthwhile form at 3 yrs. *J. Mulhall.*

NASSA QUEEN 2 b.f. King Emperor–Palmetta (Pall Mall 132) [1976 6f] —
second foal: dam, half-sister to very useful Irish stayer Radiant Boy, won over 1½m in Ireland: unquoted when last of 17 finishers in minor event won by Swift Sons at Windsor in August. *B. Hanbury.*

NASSAU STREET 2 gr.c. Sea Hawk II 131–Drury Nell (Bold Lad (Ire) 133) —
[1976 6fg] small, strong colt: first foal: 11,000 gns yearling: dam, placed over 5f at 2 yrs in France, is half-sister to Typhoon: 16/1, not given an unduly hard race after being very slowly into stride when in rear in 14-runner maiden race won by Adviser at Goodwood in July, only outing. *H. Cecil.*

NATIONAL WISH 3 b.g. National–Somebody's Wish (Determine) [1975 5g **116** ?
5s³ 5g² 5g* 5f³ 6.3f* 6.3fg* 5fg* 1976 5f⁶ 6g⁶ 5f* 5f 5f 7.3fg 6f³ 5f⁴ 6f⁶ 5g] strong, deep-bodied, full-quartered American-bred Irish gelding: top weight, won handicap at Leopardstown in June by ¾ length from Paldamask: ran some

Mark Lane Memorial Handicap, Doncaster—Nearly New beats Scott Joplyn and then survives an objection

good races afterwards, notably when seventh of 13 (beaten less than 5 lengths) to Lochnager in King's Stand Stakes at Royal Ascot and when good fourth to Solo Venture in Philips Electrical Rockingham Stakes (handicap) at the Curragh in August: should stay further than 6f (ran below his best in Hungerford Stakes at Newbury when tried over 7.3f): probably acts on any going: best form in blinkers (ran moderately without them final appearance). *S. Murless, Ireland.*

NATION WIDE   3 b.c. Irish Ball 127–Misylda 100 (Faubourg II 127)   [1975 6fg   **75** 6g 6g   1976 8fg6 12.3s5 12.2g5 12fg4 16f2 16g* 12h4 16g6 14s3 16v2]   strong, attractive colt: quite a moderate handicapper: narrow winner from Piccadilly Etta at Newbury in July, but would undoubtedly have won by about a length had his jockey not dropped his hands close home: needs a really good test of stamina: acts on any going: ran creditably when blinkered last two outings: has run respectably for an apprentice. *H. Wragg.*

NATIVE SIOUX   3 b.f. Native Prince–Sweet Memory (Nashua)   [1975 5d 5g   — 1976 8f 6f6 8fg]   poor plater: blinkered last two outings: sold out of M. Masson's stable 320 gns Ascot July Sales after second appearance. *W. Williams.*

NAUGHTY B   2 b.c. Connaught 130–Busy Bee 95 (Appiani II 128)   [1976 6g   — 8d 8s]   powerful, rangy colt: first foal: 4,700 gns foal and resold for 9,600 gns as a yearling: dam, a winner over 1m at 2 yrs, is half-sister to several good winners: backward when behind in maiden races: blinkered final outing. *J. Sutcliffe.*

NAUGHTY LASS   2 ch.f. Run The Gantlet–Peaceful 92 (Crepello 136)   [1976   **82** 5fg5 5f5 5g4 5h4 7fg6 8g6 7d5 8fg2 7s2 8.2v2 7v]   light-framed filly: first foal: dam won over 9f and 1¼m: runner-up in nurseries at Redcar (beaten short head by Beau Brummie), Warwick and Nottingham: needs at least 7f and will stay 1¼m: acts on any going: sold 4,200 gns Newmarket December Sales. *H. Wragg.*

NAVIDAD   2 b.f. Porto Bello 118–Christmas Pageant (March Past 124)   [1976   — 5f 5g]   plain filly: pulled up after stumbling at start at Catterick in April: last of 17 in maiden race on same course in June. *M. Naughton.*

NAVIGATOR   3 ch.c. Exbury 138–Lovely Light 105 (Henry the Seventh 125)   **103** [1975 6fg 6fg3   1976 8fg4 8.5fg2 10.5s2 12f 10g2]   big, rangy colt: half-brother to smart middle-distance winner Moonlight Night (by Levmoss) and to useful 1973 2-y-o Plat du Jour (by Major Portion): showed useful form in good company, finishing 4½ lengths fourth of seven to Malinowski in Ladbroke Craven Stakes at Newmarket in April, 2 lengths second to Oats in Ladbroke Blue Riband Trial at Epsom later in month and 5 lengths second to Illustrious Prince in Glasgow Stakes at York in May: long odds on for maiden race at Ascot in July but was beaten 1½ lengths by Moving Isles: will probably stay 1½m (had stiff task only attempt at trip so far): goes well on a firm surface: had tongue tied down final outing at 2 yrs: sold only 2,300 gns Newmarket Autumn Sales. *N. Murless.*

NEARLY A HAND   2 ch.c. Busted 134–Petite Chou (Hook Money 124)   [1976   **85** 7g 10v2]   half-brother to fair 1975 2-y-o 5f winner Little Ditty (by Song): 5,600 gns yearling: dam won over 6f at 3 yrs in Ireland: finished strongly when length second of 17 to Pin Tuck in maiden race at Nottingham in October: will stay 1½m. *J. Hindley.*

NEARLY NEW   3 br.g. Derring-Do 131–Lydia II 79 (Neckar)   [1974 5g5 7g4   **102** 6g3 7g* 6f 7.6s3 8fg5 7fg5 7s 10d6 7d* 7s 7v3   1975 8d 8v2 7d2 7.6g6 8fg 7.6f3 7fg* 8f5 8g5 7g4 7s3 7g4 7.6s5   1976 7fg 7fg 7fg 7fg6 8g5 7.6h* 7.6fg* 7.2g4 7d* 7d6 8s 7v6]   quite attractive, well-made gelding: a good mover: useful handicapper on his day: won three good prizes worth over £19,000 in 1976, namely Queen Elizabeth Handicap in June and Watney Mann Stakes the following month, both at Lingfield, and Mark Lane Memorial Handicap at Doncaster in September: stays 1m: acts on any going: suitable mount for an apprentice. *B. Swift.*

NEASDEN BELLE   2 ch.f. Sovereign Path 125–Xanadu 86 (Zimone)   [1976   **66** 5g 7h 6g 7f 5d]   tall filly: seventh of 19 to Casino Boy in minor event at Lingfield in August, third outing and best effort: ran poorly in blinkers on final appearance. *D. Hanley.*

NEATLY ROYAL   3 ch.g. King's Troop 118–Compact (Counsel 118)   [1975 5.8f   **74** 1976 16h*]   half-brother to 2-y-o winners by Bleep-Bleep and Porto Bello: 300 gns yearling: dam unraced half-sister to Best Song: 50/1, won maiden race at Warwick in July by a neck from Impulsora: evidently suited by a test of stamina. *J. Nelson.*

496

NEBBIOLO 2 ch.c. Yellow God 129–Novara (Birkhahn) [1976 5f³ 5fg* 6f* **125** 5g* 7f* 6fg* 6g²]

In the ordinary way one would expect an Irish-trained two-year-old good enough to win five of his seven races, and to run second in the William Hill Middle Park Stakes at Newmarket, to be weighted within a pound or two of the top of the Irish Free Handicap. But 1976 was not, it seems, an ordinary year. At least it wasn't if we are to believe the Irish Free Handicap, for Nebbiolo, winner of the Eadestown Stakes at Naas, the Irish Chorus Stakes at Navan, the Curragh Stakes, the Arnott Stakes at Phoenix Park, the Gimcrack Stakes at York, and beaten only a length in the Middle Park Stakes, is to be found in the Irish Free Handicap no less than 13 lb behind the top horse, Cloonlara, 2 lb *more*, for instance, than the poundage he is set to receive from the top horse in the English Free Handicap, J. O. Tobin. Either the Irish handicapper has a very high opinion of the form shown by Cloonlara, or, as seems more likely, little was thought in official circles of the form represented by the Gimcrack Stakes and the Middle Park Stakes, two of the most famous events for two-year-olds in the Calendar. Even Padroug, whose activities were confined to relatively run-of-the-mill races such as the Acomb Stakes at York and the Ashford Castle Stakes at the Curragh, and who didn't exactly set the turf alight with his performance in either event, is deemed to have shown form in the order of 5 lb superior to that shown by Nebbiolo.

Is there any reason to believe that the fields for the Gimcrack Stakes and the Middle Park Stakes were below the standard one expects to see in these races? Well it must be admitted that Nebbiolo did not meet top-class opposition in the Gimcrack Stakes, for the very good reason that apart from J. O. Tobin and Cloonlara there was at the time precious little in the way of proven top-class opposition to be met. But Cawston's Clown, Royal Diver, Mr Nice Guy and And Behold were not bad horses by any means. Cawston's Clown had won the Coventry Stakes at Royal Ascot and two other races; Royal Diver, a speedy

Curragh Stakes—a win for Nebbiolo over the hard-ridden Captain James

colt, had won three races; Mr Nice Guy had been successful four times, and was to go on and finish a creditable second to Avgerinos in the Intercraft Solario Stakes; and And Behold, who had won at Kempton on his début, had run the July Stakes winner Sky Ship to a head at 6 lb in the Lanson Champagne Stakes at Goodwood. None of these four caused Nebbiolo the slightest bother. Cawston's Clown and Royal Diver disputed the lead in the early stages, at a pace which had Mr Nice Guy and And Behold in trouble after two furlongs and themselves in trouble two furlongs later. Nebbiolo then went on pursued by Forty Winks, and Curran on Nebbiolo had to get out his whip and ride his hardest before Nebbiolo raced away in the last hundred yards to win by two and a half lengths. The 100/1 outsider Whitby Jet stayed on through beaten horses to take third place, six lengths behind the runner-up. Any doubt about the value of Nebbiolo's performance was removed when Forty Winks ran an excellent second under 9-5 in the Harry Rosebery Challenge Trophy at Ayr. Not that there should have been any doubt. Cawston's Clown, Royal Diver, Mr Nice Guy and And Behold had been beaten much too far for the form reasonably to be anything but good and, thanks to the very strong pace set by Cawston's Clown and Royal Diver, Nebbiolo recorded a timefigure of 1.27 fast, which was to prove only three pounds slower than the season's best by a two-year-old— J. O. Tobin's 1.41 fast in the Laurent Perrier Champagne Stakes at Doncaster.

If Nebbiolo hadn't been faced with top-class opposition in the Gimcrack Stakes, he had a tough task awaiting him in the Middle Park Stakes. Of his ten opponents, Mandrake Major and La Ville de Rire had finished first and second respectively in the Group 1 Flying Childers Stakes at Doncaster, Anax and Adviser had occupied the first two places in the Group 2 Mill Reef Stakes at Newbury, Etienne Gerard, a highly-regarded Brigadier Gerard colt, had trounced some useful youngsters in the Clarence House Stakes at Ascot, Water Boy, from France, had run second to Blushing Groom in the Prix Morny, and Tachypous, who had run well in the Richmond Stakes at Goodwood, had a reputation which said he was overwhelmingly superior to Anax in home gallops. These were good horses by any standards, and as Nebbiolo began to inch ahead on the outside racing into the Dip he had them all beaten, or so it seemed, until one spotted Tachypous on the inside making up ground at a rate that was clearly going to get him to the post first. Nebbiolo struggled on bravely, but having already quickened into his top pace to take the lead, there was nothing he could do to prevent Tachypous from heading him just inside the last hundred yards.

By our reckoning Nebbiolo's performances in the Gimcrack Stakes and the Middle Park Stakes would entitle him to 8-13 in an average English Free Handicap. There is no question of his performances in Ireland coming up to this level. They don't. But then he usually had little to do. In the Irish Chorus Stakes, for instance, his principal rival Digitalis was set to concede him 8 lb. Nebbiolo won easily. Similarly in the Arnott Stakes Nebbiolo was opposed only by two moderate animals. Again he won easily. But over five furlongs Captain James, a very useful youngster in receipt of 4 lb, provided him with tough opposition in the Curragh Stakes, Nebbiolo having to put his best foot forward to hold on by a head as the other came at him strongly in the last furlong.

Nebbiolo (ch.c. 1974)	Yellow God (ch 1967)	Red God (ch 1954)	Nasrullah
			Spring Run
		Sally Deans (ch 1947)	Fun Fair
			Cora Deans
	Novara (b 1965)	Birkhahn (br 1945)	Alchimist
			Bramouse
		Norbelle (b 1957)	Norman
			Mirabelle

Nebbiolo's breeding—he is by the miler Yellow God out of a Birkhahn mare which won at a mile and a half—is not that of a colt likely to shine over five furlongs as a two-year-old, and he should have little difficulty in staying a mile. Novara has already bred a winner at up to that distance in Fair Cousin (by Great Nephew). Novara, who was the best two-year-old of her year in Germany, was sold at the end of her racing days by Mr Niels Schibbye supposedly for export to Canada, and she was carrying Nebbiolo when he purchased her back, for 16,000 guineas, at the 1973 December Sales. Mr Schibbye tried to sell Nebbiolo as a yearling, but the colt failed to reach his reserve (he was led out unsold at 1,900 guineas) so Mr Schibbye put him into training in Ireland with Kevin Prendergast. Until then he had never had a horse in training in the British Isles. A strong, good-bodied individual and a good mover, Nebbiolo has a little improvement to make before he can be regarded as in the top flight,

Gimcrack Stakes, York—Nebbiolo draws away from Forty Winks

and as he had a hard first season, and gave all that was in him to give in the Gimcrack Stakes and the Middle Park Stakes, it is not to be anticipated that he will make that improvement. But no two-year-old could give him points for toughness and consistency, and Nebbiolo can be expected to run well in the top races as a three-year-old even if he isn't good enough to win them. He acts on firm going. *K. Prendergast, Ireland.*

NEEDCOMBE 3 ch.f. Duneed 84–Heathcombe (Langton Heath 97) [1975 8g⁵ — 6g 7g⁶ 1976 12f⁴ 10fg] plating-class filly: should stay at least 1½m. *J. Thorne.*

NEEDLESS 2 b.f. Petingo 135–Never in Need (Never Say Die 137) [1976 6g⁵ **78** 6d⁵] attractive, lengthy filly: second foal: 3,800 gns yearling: dam twice-raced daughter of smart sprinter Patroness: fifth in September in newcomers race at Goodwood (3 lengths behind Magenta) and Blue Seal Stakes at Ascot (beaten 6½ lengths by Circlet): will be better suited by longer distances. *F. J. Houghton.*

NEIL DIAMOND 2 b.c. Mountain Call 125–Sweet Caroline 99 (Nimbus 130) **96** [1976 6d 6fg2 6f* 7fg 6f* 7g 6g² 6s⁶ 6v] useful-looking colt: half-brother to several winners, notably very smart French miler African Sky (by Sing Sing): 400 gns yearling: dam half-sister to Kalydon: proved a good buy, winning maiden auction event at Redcar in July and a £1,500 nursery at Haydock in August: showed improved form to win by 1½ lengths from Bobby Kempinski in latter race: creditable 3 lengths second to King Croesus in 10-runner nursery at Newmarket in October: evidently does not stay 7f: acts on any going but goes particularly well on firm: wears blinkers nowadays. *M. Jarvis.*

NEILIAN 2 b.c. Grisaille 115–Daughters Three 65 (Typhoon 125) [1976 5g⁴ **50** 5f⁵ 5d 5f 6f] light-framed colt: poor plater: should stay 6f: blinkered final outing. *A. Smith.*

NEKASIM 2 ch.c. El Cid 109–Bay Reel (Gratitude 130) [1976 7fg² 7fg 8s] **72** leggy colt: second foal: dam ran only twice, including in a seller: 6 lengths second of 12 to Calicourt in maiden race at Chester in September, best effort: should stay 1m. *E. Cousins.*

NELLIE CLARK 3 ch.f. Joshua 129–Jailbait 96 (Sing Sing 134) [1975 6d 6g⁵ **74** 1976 7fg⁶ 8fg⁵ 8g⁶ 8fg³ 8fg³ 8d* 8.2d*] fair sort: won weakly-contested amateur riders race at Yarmouth in September and 18-runner seller at Haydock the following month: bought in 1,900 gns on latter course: stays 1m well: acts on a firm and a soft surface: suitable mount for an inexperienced race rider. *G. Balding.*

NELLYKELLY 3 b.f. Polyfoto 124–Hunter's Melody 70 (Off Key 121) [1975 — 5g 5fg 1976 7.6s] poor mover: in rear in maiden races: sweated up and tailed off only outing at 3 yrs. *W. Wharton.*

NENITA 2 ch.f. Yellow God 129–Flatter Me (Palestine 133) [1976 5fg 6fg 6s³] **82** lengthy filly: half-sister to French middle-distance winner Fujikawa (by Pampered King) and to a winner in Venezuela by Will Somers: 1,500 gns yearling: dam ran only three times: showed first worthwhile form when 1¾ lengths third

499

of 11 to Port Ahoy in minor event at Pontefract in October: will be suited by 7f+: evidently needs some give in the ground. *P. Rohan.*

NEOSPRITE 2 b.f. Blue Streak 99–Nearust (Neron 121) [1976 6fg] half-sister —
to a winning hurdler: dam a selling hurdler: unquoted, showed up to past halfway
when in rear in 16-runner maiden race won by Sipit at Windsor in July. *D. Keith.*

NEPOTIST 3 b.c. Great Nephew 126–Dauntsey (Sea Hawk II 131) [1975 6fg **90**
6fg² 7g 7.3d 7g³ 1976 7f 9g³ 10g⁶ 10.1fg* 12fg* 10g* 12f⁵ 10d² 10g⁵] small,
quite attractive colt: good mover: won maiden race at Leicester and handicap at Sandown in the summer: just held on by ½ length
from Rout on last-named course: seemed to run out of stamina over 1½m on
seventh outing and is possibly better at 1¼m notwithstanding his victory on
fifth outing gained in a very slowly-run race: acts on a firm and a soft surface:
suited by forcing tactics: sold 6,200 gns Newmarket Autumn Sales for export
to South Africa. *P. Walwyn.*

NEPTUNIAN 2 ch.f. Royalty 130–Surfacing (Worden II 129) [1976 5d 5s 5s] —
lightly-made filly: first foal: dam never ran: in rear in end-of-season maiden
races: will be suited by middle distances: sold 800 gns Newmarket December
Sales. *W. Elsey.*

NESCIO 5 gr.g. Nelcius 133–Quality Girl (Quorum 126) [1974 10g 12fg 7fg⁵ —
7g³ 10.1fg³ 8g⁴ 10.1g* 10d⁴ 12s⁴ 10v³ 1975 N.R. 1976 10fg] moderate performer (rated 80) at 3 yrs: having first outing since when well behind at Leicester
in September: stays 1¼m: acts on any going: suitable mount for an apprentice.
D. Barons.

NESS POINT 3 b.c. Track Spare 125–Cheb's Image 100 (Anamnestes 118) **64**
[1975 5.1f 6f 1976 7g 6f⁴ 6g 8s 8v² 8d] poor maiden: ran easily best race when
4 lengths second to Prince Lambourn in claiming race at Leicester in October:
stays 1m: evidently suited by heavy ground. *D. Weeden.*

NET CALL 3 b.f. Song 132–Game All 109 (Alcide 136) [1975 6g* 6d² 1976 **108**
7fg⁵ 8g 6d 7.2d⁶ 7fg² 5g⁴ 6fg* 6fg 6f⁵] very attractive filly: apprentice ridden,
won handicap at Newmarket in July by ¾ length from May Beck: had performed
creditably against top-class opposition earlier in season when fifth to Flying
Water in Ladbroke Nell Gwyn Stakes also at Newmarket and when seventh of
10 to Riverqueen in Poule d'Essai des Pouliches at Longchamp on first two
starts: probably best at 6f, although stays further: best form on a sound surface:
blinkered fifth and sixth starts, running creditably on first occasion but losing her
chance at start on second: ran moderately last two outings. *R. Armstrong.*

NETHERLEIGH 2 b.f. Blast 125–Romero (Neron 121) [1976 5d⁶ 5f⁴ 5v 5s] —
sister to fairly useful 1972 2-y-o 5f winner Houston Control, and half-sister to
another winner: 1,000 gns yearling: poor form in maiden races but was off course
a long time after second outing. *E. Cousins.*

NETHERTON 3 b.c. Connaught 130–Tudor Romp 80 (Tudor Melody 129) **89**
[1975 6fg⁴ 6g³ 6fg⁵ 8s 10f⁵ 1976 12f* 12fg⁶ 12fg* 12g⁶ 16g⁶ 15g³] strong,
lengthy, useful sort: good walker: won maiden race at Thirsk and minor event
at Carlisle early in season: off course three months after fourth outing and ran
well following his return, notably when sixth of eight to Shangamuzo in Top
Rank Club Handicap at Newcastle in August (had very stiff task at weights):
evidently well suited by 2m: acts on firm going *R. D. Peacock.*

NETTLETON 2 b.f. Shiny Tenth 120–Flight Feathers (Ribocco 129) [1976 **64**
5g⁴ 5g 5f 5.3f 5s 7v] well-made French-foaled filly: beaten only a length by
May Fox at Wolverhampton on first outing but finished in rear on all outings
afterwards. *D. Marks.*

NEVER A LADY 2 ch.f. Pontifex (USA)–Camogie (Celtic Ash) [1976 5s 5f **112**
5f* 5g² 5f* 6.3f² 5g*] Irish filly: second foal: 560 gns yearling: dam unraced
daughter of leading 1963 2-y-o filly Mesopotamia and half-sister to Coin of Gold:
won £1,400 event at Phoenix Park in May and nurseries at the Curragh in August
and Leopardstown the following month, last-named by a length from First Up:
also runner-up in £1,200 event at Naas (to Athlete's Foot) and £1,700 event at
the Curragh (to Claire's Slipper): should stay 1m but showed best form at 2 yrs
at 5f: acts on firm going: sold 25,000 gns Newmarket December Sales. *C. Collins, Ireland.*

NEVER CARING 2 b.c. Silent Spring 102–Town Lass 73 (Weepers Boy 124) **66**
[1976 5f³ 5f 5g² 5g 5fg] quite a useful sort: started short-priced favourite for
seller at Wolverhampton in May but went down by a short head to Billie's Pal:
blinkered third and fourth outings: not seen out after June. *J. Nelson.*

NEVER DID 3 gr.c. John Splendid 116–Never Give Way (King's Bench 132) **63**
[1975 5g 5.9g⁵ 5g* 7g 1976 5fg² 7.6s 6g 5d 5fg⁵ 6h³ 6f 6g 8.2d 6v² 5s 6d⁶ 6s]
leggy colt: quite a modest handicapper: was racing mainly in selling company
at the back-end: should stay 7f: acts on any going: usually wears blinkers:
sweated up badly seventh outing: inconsistent. *R. Hollinshead.*

NEVER FLAP 2 ch.c. Never Say Die 137–Flipflap 87 (Fairey Fulmar 124) —
[1976 5s 5d] neat colt: in rear in sellers at Newcastle in April (backward) and
Hamilton in May: will need much further to show what little ability he may
possess. *V. Thompson.*

NEVERLAND 2 b.c. Caliban 123–Jolisu 110 (Welsh Abbot 131) [1976 6d 6g **51**
6d] poor plater: sold 280 gns Newmarket Autumn Sales. *G. Hunter.*

NEVER LIT UP 2 b.c. Never Say Die 137–Moonlit 93 (Mark-Ye-Well) [1976 — P
8s] half-brother to several minor winners: 650 gns foal, resold 2,000 gns yearling:
dam won at 7f: unquoted and in need of outing, put up a most promising performance when eighth of 26 to stable-companion Lucent in £2,200 event at
Doncaster in November, making significant headway in straight after being
behind early on: not knocked about unnecessarily here and has the makings of
a nice 3-y-o. *R. Price*

NEVER NEVER 3 b.g. King's Company 124–Hark Hark 75 (Sing Sing 134) —
[1975 5f 5fg³ 5fg⁴ 6f 1976 8fg 9.4g 8f] strong, compact, good-quartered
gelding: no worthwhile form as a 3-y-o and was sold 340 gns Doncaster October
Sales. *F. Carr.*

NEVER SAY BUST 2 ch.c. Busted 134–Nevetta 108 (Never Say Die 137) **73** p
[1976 6fg 8g⁴] rangy colt: poor mover: second foal: half-brother to 1973 2-y-o
7f winner Sandgrounder (by Reform): dam won four races from 6f to 9f: still
backward when 7½ lengths fourth of 12 to Jam in maiden race at Ayr in September: will be suited by 1¼m or more: will do better at 3 yrs. *R. D. Peacock.*

NEVER SAY GUY 2 ch.c. Never Say Die 137–Pasdeux 107 (Ballyogan) [1976 **92**
7d 7v⁵ 8s²] strong colt: half-brother to two 2-y-o winners, including fairly useful
1973 5f winner Sunblessed (by So Blessed): dam won twice over 5f at 2 yrs:
springer in market, kept on well in straight but had no chance with winner,
when 8 lengths second of 26 to Lucent in £2,200 event at Doncaster in November:
will probably stay middle distances. *S. Hall.*

NEVER SO LOVELY 2 ch.f. Realm 129–Lovely Lark (Larkspur 128) [1976 — p
5v] strong, quite attractive filly: closely related to Matsufuji Ehsu (by So
Blessed), a leading 2-y-o in Japan in 1974: 10,000 gns yearling: dam won over
7f in Ireland: started favourite for 17-runner maiden race at Leicester in
November but lost ground at start and never threatened to get into race thereafter, eventually finishing seventh to Be Royal: clearly quite well thought of
and should do better at 3 yrs. *M. Stoute.*

NEW CITY 3 b.c. Maystreak 118–Must Improve 47 (Lucky Brief 128) [1975 —
N.R. 1976 12.5g 16f⁵] unfurnished colt: first foal: dam, poor plater on flat,
was a fair hurdler: well beaten in maiden races at Teesside in April and Beverley
in May. *J. Berry.*

NEW DEAL 2 b.c. Reform 132–Darlene 117 (Dante) [1976 7fg³ 6fg⁶ 8g⁶] **91**
neat, shapely, attractive colt: brother to 3-y-o New Order, and half-brother to
several winners, including top-class middle-distance stayer Homeric (by Ragusa)
and very useful 1m to 1½m winner Dark Court (by Supreme Court): dam stayed
1½m: ran promisingly when 2¼ lengths third of 15 to Heronry in maiden race
at Newmarket in July: outpaced subsequently in quite valuable events at
Goodwood and York: will be suited by middle distances. *R. Hern.*

NEWGATE 3 b.c. Blakeney 126–Set Free 90 (Worden II 129) [1975 6fg 8d² **87**
7.3g⁵ 1976 10g⁵ 10.5s 12g 12fg⁶] neat, attractive colt: brother to Oaks and Irish
Guinness Oaks winner Juliette Marny: promising 4 lengths fifth of nine to Tierra
Fuego in White Rose Stakes at Ascot in May, leading until headed 1f out (would
have finished a couple of lengths closer had he not been eased when beaten): ran
moderately afterwards, on third outing being tried in blinkers: should stay 1½m:
sold 3,800 gns Newmarket Autumn Sales. *J. Tree.*

NEW HENRY 5 b.h. Henry the Seventh 125–Pampered Angel 97 (Pampered **80**
King 121) [1974 10f* 12fg³ 10.6g⁴ 10g⁶ 16fg³ 14fg 17.4s⁵ 16d 1975 13d* 15s²
13f⁴ 18g* 15g⁶ 18f⁴ 17.4d* 16s 1976 16.1d³ 16g⁵ 18d² 18.1g 16.1d 18d] lengthy
horse: moderate handicapper: good second of six to Tall Lad at Doncaster in May,
best effort: stays very well: acts on any going: blinkered final outing: genuine:
suited by forcing tactics: sold out of J. W. Watts's stable 500 gns Ascot July Sales
(after third outing). *P. Bevan.*

NEW MILLS 2 ch.c. Most Secret 119–Ruffino 99 (Como 120) [1976 6fg² 6g²   **79**
6f6 5f 5g⁵ 5d⁴ 6s] robust colt: half-brother to smart sprinter Bream (by Hornbeam) and to useful performers Meldrum, Saufina and Freeman (all by Hard
Sauce): dam a sprinter: did not fulfil the promise shown when 3 lengths second to
Northern Lady in maiden race at York on first outing, but ran creditably when
fourth in nursery won by Star Attention at Redcar in September on penultimate
start: better suited by 6f than 5f: blinkered final appearance. *E. Weymes.*

NEW ORDER 3 b.c. Reform 132–Darlene 117 (Dante) [1975 6fg⁴ 1976 8f² 10f⁴ **116**
10.4s⁴ 9g⁴ 11g] very attractive, well-made, deep-girthed colt: half-brother to
several winners, including top-class middle-distance stayer Homeric (by Ragusa)
and very useful 1m to 1½m winner Dark Court (by Supreme Court): dam stayed
1½m: showed himself a useful performer, running Umabatha to a short head in
maiden race at Newbury in April and finishing close-up fourth of nine to Tierra
Fuego in White Rose Stakes at Ascot the following month: creditable fourth to
Earth Spirit in Prix Jean Prat at Chantilly in June but broke a shoulder on final
appearance and was subsequently destroyed: would have stayed 1½m: was
possibly not at his best on soft going: trained until after third outing by R. Hern.
J. Cunnington, jnr, France.

NEW RIBBONS 3 b.f. Ribero 126–New Move 112 (Umberto 118) [1975 5d 6s   **79**
6g⁶ 1976 7g⁶ 10fg³ 10.1f 12d² 12fg⁴ 12f* 12h* 12f³ 12g 12s³ 12v] neat filly:
clear-cut winner of six-runner maiden race at Brighton in July, beating Golden
Lania 5 lengths: didn't have much in hand when landing the odds by 2 lengths
from Tilton Boy in small race at Carlisle later in month: seems to lack a turn of
foot and will be suited by further than 1½m: acts on any going: had stiff tasks
last three outings, running very well on second of them. *F. J. Houghton.*

NEW SEEKER 2 b.c. Busted 134–Sheet Music 91 (Monet 127) [1976 7g]   **— p**
useful-looking colt: fourth foal: dam won three 5f races at 2 yrs: unquoted and in
need of race when tenth of 22 to Sin Timon in maiden event at Newmarket in
October: will do better. *M. Stoute.*

NEW SUSPECT 4 ch.c. Above Suspicion 127–New Mover (Never Say Die 137)   **—**
[1974 N.R. 1975 N.R. 1976 18s] first foal: dam unraced daughter of very
useful 1960 2-y-o New Move: 25/1 when well beaten in amateur riders maiden
race at Doncaster in October, only outing. *J. Leigh.*

NEWTON'S FOLLY 2 b.c. Sky Gipsy 117–Salamanca (Honeyway 125) [1976   **—**
5g 5fg] plater: showed up 3f when eighth of 20 to Solchella at Thirsk in May,
second outing: retained by trainer 500 gns Doncaster June Sales: dead. *J.
Vickers.*

NICE AND FRIENDLY 2 b.g. Be Friendly 130–Sidam 79 (Psidium 130) [1976   **—**
6fg] half-brother to a minor winner by King's Leap: 1,000 gns yearling: dam
stayed well: in need of race when behind in 25-runner minor event won by
Friendly Now at Redcar in September: sold 440 gns Doncaster October Sales. *P.
Rohan.*

NICE BALANCE 2 b.c. High Echelon–Wiggle II (Rego 102) [1976 7fg³ 7f* 7s] **111**
strong, deep-bodied, good sort: American bred: half-brother to four winners,
including very smart 5f to 7.5f stakes winner Sir Wiggle (by Sadair) and useful 1m
and 13f winner Ambulation (by Vaguely Noble): $46,000 yearling: dam won 14
races in Australia and six races and $116,000 in U.S.A.: led at halfway and
battled on most courageously to win four-runner Seaton Delaval Stakes at Newcastle in August by 2 lengths from odds-on Man in the Moon (the second would
have been about a length closer had he not been eased close home): had earlier
put up another fine effort in Lanson Champagne Stakes at Goodwood, being

Seaton Delaval Stakes, Newcastle—Nice Balance upsets the odds-on Man in the Moon

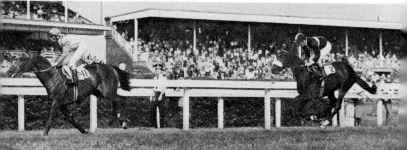

beaten only just over ½ length by Sky Ship: came under whip halfway up straight in Prix de la Salamandre at Longchamp in September and dropped out rapidly to finish last to Blushing Groom: will stay 1¼m: acts on firm going and is possibly unsuited by soft: very useful. *R. Price.*

NICE BREAK   2 br.c. Nice Music 115–Broken Half (Busted 134)   [1976 5s 7fg   **60**
6h² 7f⁴ 6f]   compact colt: plater: 4 lengths second to Grittle at Pontefract in August: should stay 1m: bandaged off-fore on last two outings.   *J. Etherington.*

NICE MATIN   2 ch.f. London Gazette 117–Fortuity (Fortino II 120)   [1976 7s]   **—**
quite attractive filly: first foal: dam lightly-raced maiden: unquoted, was bit slow to get going when tenth of 12 to Sleeper in minor event at Sandown in October, only outing.   *J. Nelson.*

NICE N'EASY   2 ch.c. Crooner 119–Young Mementa (Young Christopher 119)   **92**
[1976 8s* 8s]   fourth foal: half-brother to two winners abroad: dam never ran: put up a good first effort when winning 16-runner maiden race at Bath in October: never in race when well beaten in £2,200 event won by Lucent at Doncaster the following month: stays 1m well: acts on soft going.   *J. Nelson.*

NICE ROMANCE   4 ch.f. Varano–La Romantica III (Nagami 124)   [1974   **—**
N.R.   1975 8.5d⁵ 12f² 10g⁶ 12g* 14f²   1976 14.6g 12g 16f]   quite attractive filly: lightly raced and no worthwhile form at 4 yrs: very well suited by 1½m or more: acts on firm going: tried in blinkers on final appearance.   *S. Ingham.*

NICE VALUE   2 ch.c. Goldhill 125–Sinecure (Parthia 132)   [1976 5d 5.9g 6g 6fg⁵   **81**
5d³ 5v]   rangy colt: half-brother to 5f winner Super Track (by Track Spare): dam Irish maiden: took some time to come to hand, running best race when 3½ lengths third of 12 to Abode in maiden event at Nottingham in September: possibly better suited by 5f than 6f.   *E. Cousins.*

NICHOLA'S STAR   5 ch.m. Honour Bound 109–Stellelle (St Elmo 94)   [1974   **—**
N.R.   1975 N.R.   1976 16.1f]   first produce: dam never ran: tailed off throughout in bad maiden race at Haydock in August, only outing.   *M. Scudamore.*

Mrs W. Haefner's "Niebo"

NICOLENE 2 br.f. Nice Music 115–Rakene (Welsh Rake 118) [1976 5d 5.1fg **91**
7d⁵ 7g 7s³ 7s²]   robust filly: second produce: 740 gns foal, resold 820 gns yearling:
dam never ran: ran well in large fields of maidens in the autumn just failing by a
head to catch Lady Oriana in 19-runner event at Newmarket in October on final
outing: will stay 1m: acts on soft going. *I. Walker.*

NIEBO 3 ch.c. Arts and Letters–Firey Angel (Nashua) [1975 6f* 6.3fg* 6.3f* **125**
1976 7g⁴ 12f 11.5f² 8f* 8f6 10g³]   American-bred colt: closely related to two
minor winners in U.S.A. by Tom Rolfe and half-brother to several other winners:
very useful winner at 2 yrs: odds on, won Group 3 Desmond Stakes at the
Curragh in August in good style by 5 lengths from Raw Recruit: put up an even
better effort when just over 1½ lengths third of 11 to Malacate in Joe McGrath
Memorial Stakes at Leopardstown the following month: had earlier run respectably when tried at 1½m, finishing seventh of 17 to Malacate in Irish Sweeps Derby
at the Curragh and 2½ lengths third to Whistling Deer in Ulster Harp Derby at
Down Royal when tried in blinkers: hampered by winner in latter race and subsequently awarded second place on winner's disqualification: finished lame when
last of six behind Free State in Waterford Crystal Mile at Goodwood on only
appearance in this country: best form at up to 1¼m but stays 1½m: acts on firm
going: exported to California. *V. O'Brien, Ireland.*

NIGEL MARK 3 b.g. Yellow God 129–Baba Au Rhum (Big Game) [1975 6g **—**
1976 9v]   half-brother to two minor winners in France: 2,500 gns yearling: dam
very useful at around 1m in France: in need of race when well beaten in minor
events. *M. W. Easterby.*

NIGHT BEFORE 2 b.c. Vaguely Noble 140–Quick Flight (Herbager 136) **105 p**
[1976 6fg⁴ 8d² 8s*]
   Peter Walwyn said of Night Before after his win at Goodwood in September
'Pat Eddery tells me he's as good as Avgerinos. He's a lovely horse and did
it very easily, but he's very immature and will not race again this season'.
The handicapper also has a high opinion of the horse, giving him 8-5 in the Tote
Free Handicap, a pound more than his stable-companion Sporting Yankee
who won the £36,000 William Hill Futurity. We have rated him much less
highly, but think that Night Before has the makings of a very good three-year-
old.

   Night Before's win came in a minor event confined to horses that hadn't
won a race worth £1,500, or a race over a mile or more before September 5th.
Under the conditions he had to carry the same weight as Fast Frigate, the
winner of two races before finishing about nine lengths behind Avgerinos in the
Intercraft Solario Stakes. Once into the straight the pair had things to themselves, and Night Before went steadily clear to win easily by five lengths from
the hard-driven Fast Frigate. The soft ground suited him well.

   Night Before had raced twice earlier. In the Acomb Stakes at York
he seemed not to know what it was all about, but the experience wasn't wasted
on him; on his next outing he put up an excellent effort in a maiden race at
Newbury. In a seventeen-strong field it was 8/1 bar Ad Lib Ra and Night
Before, and the two of them dominated the finish, drawing right away from the
rest. It took Ad Lib Ra all his time to catch Night Before and at the line
there was a head between them.

Night Before (b.c. 1974)	Vaguely Noble (b 1965)	Vienna (ch 1957)	Aureole / Turkish Blood
		Noble Lassie (b 1956)	Nearco / Belle Sauvage
	Quick Flight (b 1966)	Herbager (b 1956)	Vandale / Flagette
		Grey Flight (gr 1945)	Mahmoud / Planetoid

   Night Before is a well-made, attractive colt who cost 70,000 dollars as
a yearling. He is the fourth foal of Quick Flight, who won a maiden race over
a mile at three years in the United States, and a half-brother to the moderate
Irish five-furlong to nine-furlong performer Never Linger (by Never Bend), a
three-year-old in 1976. Quick Flight was of no great stakes as a racehorse—her
total winnings came to a paltry 1,456 dollars and she was unplaced in thirteen of
her fourteen races—but she is exceptionally well bred. Herbager, her sire, won
the French Derby and sired numerous top-class winners, and Grey Flight must
rank as one of the most successful mares of all time. In the years from 1950
to 1969 Grey Flight produced fifteen foals, fourteen of which won. No less

than nine of her winners won stakes races, and her winners included Misty Morn, one of the best three-year-old fillies of 1955 and herself dam of the champion two-year-olds Successor and Bold Lad; What A Pleasure, a leading two-year-old of 1967 and champion sire in the States in 1975 and 1976; Misty Flight, one of the best two-year-olds in 1957 and sire of the winners of over 5,000,000 dollars; Misty Day whose offspring have won over 3,000,000 dollars; and the very smart Bold Queen, dam of one of the top 1976 American horses Intrepid Hero. Night Before has a lot to live up to, but we expect him to become a credit to his family, and he may well be a Derby horse. He is likely to need at least a mile and a quarter. *P. Walwyn.*

NIGHT CLUB 3 ch.g. Crooner 119–Promotion Year 81 (Damremont 121) **§§**
[1975 5f⁴ 5f² 6g² 6fg 6g* 7fg³ 7.3d⁶ 7g 1976 8.2f⁵ 7f³ 9g 10fg 8h 10fg⁴ 8f 8.2f⁴ 8f² 8h⁶ 18.1g] compact, strong-quartered gelding: possesses ability but is far from consistent: gives us impression that he needs further than 1m to be seen to advantage nowadays: wears blinkers: refused to race on fourth outing and virtually refused to race on last two appearances: pulled up seventh outing (badly hampered by faller). *C. Dingwall.*

NIGHT FLIER 2 ch.f. Midsummer Night II 117–Bluebottle 82 (Princely Gift 137) —
[1976 6g 7d] lengthy, lightly-made filly: half-sister to three winners, including fair handicapper Ephesian (by Runnymede), a winner at up to 7f: dam, half-sister to Hard Tack, won 5f seller at 2 yrs: unquoted when behind in minor event at Kempton in August (very green) and 30-runner maiden race at Newbury in September. *R. Hannon.*

NIGHT FRAME 3 ch.f. Midsummer Night II 117–Frame Up 66 (Alycidon 138) **54**
[1975 N.R. 1976 8f⁵ 10h² 10.1g⁶ 8.2d] half-sister to two minor winners here and to a winner in France: 2,700 gns foal, resold 400 gns yearling: dam ran only twice: only poor form: stays 1¼m: blinkered final outing: sold, covered by My Swallow, 2,200 gns Newmarket December Sales. *R. Jarvis.*

NIGHT GLOW 3 br.f. Firestreak 125–Enchanted Evening II (Sailor) [1975 5s **48**
5fg³ 5g⁴ 5f 5f* 6f³ 7f 6g 8g 7.2d 7g⁵ 8.2g⁴ 7d 1976 8fg⁵ 7f 8f 9fg 5f 5fg 6d 5s⁶ 6v] neat filly: plater: ran poorly most of her races in 1976: should stay 1¼m: tried in blinkers at 2 yrs: trained until after first outing by S. Nesbitt. *E. Collingwood.*

NIGHT IN TOWN 5 br.h. Ballyciptic 122–Dusky Evening (Chamier 128) [1974 **89**
13.3g* 12s² 12d³ 14fg⁵ 16d* 17.4s* 18d 1975 16s* 16f⁴ 22.2fg⁵ 14fg 16g 1976 16g 18.4s 18d⁶ 16g* 16fg³ 17.4g² 19s² 18d³ 14.6s²] lengthy horse: just a fair handicapper nowadays: won Brown Jack Stakes at Ascot in July, beating Asama a neck: finished strongly (may well have been closer had more use been made of his stamina) when 8 lengths third of 14 to John Cherry in SKF Cesarewitch at Newmarket in October on eighth outing: stays extremely well: seems to act on any going but is at his best with some give in the ground: tried in blinkers on third start. *I. Balding.*

NIGHT LINE 2 ch.c. Midsummer Night II 117–Quantas 91 (Roan Rocket 128) **74**
[1976 5fg 6fg⁵ 7fg 6fg 8d] leggy, narrow colt: first foal: 1,700 gns yearling: dam won over 6f at 2 yrs: quite a moderate maiden: should stay 1m. *S. Woodman.*

NIGHT MESSAGE 3 b.f. Midsummer Night II 117–Messenger Boat (Corres- —
pondent) [1975 N.R. 1976 8f 10f 12g] half-sister to three minor winners in U.S.A.: dam won one of her 22 starts in U.S.A.: apprentice ridden when behind in maiden races at Yarmouth (two) in the summer and Newmarket in September: sold, covered by My Swallow, 800 gns Newmarket December Sales. *P. Robinson.*

NIGHT MUSIC 2 b.f. Prince des Loges 73–Pirate's Mate 59 (Barbary Pirate 91) —
[1976 5f⁴ 5f] last in sellers and is evidently of no account: sold 165 gns Ascot December Sales. *K. Ivory.*

NIGHT NURSE 5 b.g. Falcon 131–Florence Nightingale 78 (Above Suspicion **82**
127) [1974 9f⁵ 8g 10s⁴ 9f* 8fg 9fg⁴ 1975 10h² 12g* 10 12fg²] well-grown gelding: Champion Hurdler and is no slouch on the Flat as he showed when ¾-length second of 14 to Dandy Scot in handicap at Beverley in September (looked in need of race), only appearance in 1976: will stay further than 1½m: acts on hard going: has worn blinkers, but does better without. *M. H. Easterby.*

NIGHT PORTER 2 b.c. Connaught 130–Bell Song 101 (Tudor Melody 129) **85 p**
[1976 7g 7s³] sturdy colt: third foal: half-brother to smart 1974 2-y-o filly Great Paul (by Great Nephew): dam stayed 1½m: still rather back backward, stayed on well when 2¾ lengths third of 12 to Sleeper in minor event at Sandown in October: will be suited by 1m+: probably has further improvement in him. *G. Pritchard-Gordon.*

NIGHT RETREAT 2 ch.c. Ridan–Not Forgotten 88 (Shantung 132) [1976 7f⁶ —
7.2f] first foal: 2,200 gns foal and resold for 1,150 gns as a yearling: tailed-off
last at Lanark in July (slowly away) and Haydock in August (jockey mistakenly
thought horse was lame): sold 460 gns Doncaster October Sales. *J. Edwards.*

NIGHT RUNNER 2 b.g. Midsummer Night II 117–Miss Damina 63 § (Psidium —
130) [1976 8s 5.9s] third living foal: dam poor plater at 2 yrs: behind in
maiden races at Bath and Wolverhampton in October. *H. Payne.*

NIGHT SKY 4 b.c. Star Moss 122–Pink Sky 86 (Midsummer Night II 117) [1974   **92**
5f9h 5h⁴ 5g* 6f* 6fg³ 6fg 7g* 7g² 8s³ 8s 8s 1975 10v⁴ 10d⁶ 10g² 11fg³ 12f⁶ 12g⁴
11.7f* 10f* 12fg³ 12f⁴ 11.7g² 12g⁶ 12g² 12s* 1976 12fg⁶ 12fg⁵ 12g⁴ 12f⁴] well-
made, short-legged colt: useful handicapper (rated 103) in 1975: didn't find his
best form (lightly raced) at 4 yrs: stays 1¼m: acts on any going and on any type
of track: suitable mount for an apprentice: ran slightly below his best when tried
in blinkers. *S. Ingham.*

NIGHT STORY 3 b.g. Roi Soleil 125–Bedside Story (Milesian 125) [1975 5d 5f —
6f 1976 8.2g⁴ 7fg 10.1f⁶ 10g] well-made, strong-quartered gelding: good
walker: only poor form in varied company, including a claiming race: blinkered
second outing: sold 400 gns Ascot December Sales. *S. Ingham.*

NIGHT VISION 3 ch.f. Yellow God 129–Nightingale II (Sicambre 135) [1975   **97**
6g⁴ 6d* 1976 7fg⁶ 8fg 8g⁵ 8.5g] strong, lengthy filly: half-sister to high-class
1¼m performer Take a Reef (by Right Tack): beat Marquis de Sade a short head
in 13-runner Duke of Edinburgh Stakes at Ascot in October, 1975, the pair
finishing clear: ran creditably in English and Irish 1,000 Guineas, finishing just
over 10 lengths eighth of 25 to Flying Water at Newmarket in April and 7 lengths
fifth to Sarah Siddons at the Curragh the following month: may well have stayed
further than 1m: struck into from behind in Ebbisham Handicap at Epsom in
June, suffered serious injuries to hind leg, including severed tendon, and was
retired to stud. *F. J. Houghton.*

NIKALI 3 ch.f. Siliconn 121–Lady Maggie (Distinctive 118) [1975 5g 5g 5g⁵ —
5.9g² 5s² 1976 6fg⁵ 5fg⁶ 5.8f⁶ 5fg 6h 6fg 5.9s⁵] tall, fair sort: ran poorly most
outings in 1976: best run at 6f (first outing). *R. Akehurst.*

NIKANCY 3 b.f. Castlenik 107–Ancypancy (Archive) [1975 8f 7.2s⁶ 8v 1976 —
10f 8.2g 8.2d 12g] unfurnished filly: should stay middle distances: ran
moderately when tried in blinkers on third start. *R. E. Peacock.*

NIKI NOVA 3 b.f. Ben Novus 109–Royal Heather (Indian Ruler 89) [1975   **35**
5g 5g³ 1976 8d 8f³ 8f 9fg 7f⁶ 7fg] small filly: poor plater: dead. *T. Craig.*

NIMBULLION 2 b.f. Gold Rod 129–Aquanimba (Acropolis 132) [1976 5g 5f 5f   **61**
5fg⁴ 5fg 5d² 5f⁴ 5f⁵ 6f⁶ 7f⁴ 6f 7fg² 7f² 7.2f 8f] small filly: modest plater: should
stay 1m: appears to act on any going: used to wear blinkers but does at least as
well without. *L. Shedden.*

NIPPY NORTH 2 ch.f. Northfields–Pretty Nippy (Delirium 126) [1976 5h⁵ —
5d⁶] small filly: in rear in early-season sellers. *K. Payne.*

NISBET-ANNE 3 ch.f. Alcide 136–Kilula 93 (Nearula 132) [1975 5fg² 7f² 7v   **64**
1976 8f 8g⁵ 8fg 8g⁵ 8fg⁴ 12g³ 10s⁴] small, unfurnished filly: ran best race in
apprentice event on fifth outing: should be well suited by middle distances but
has shown best form at up to 1m. *Denys Smith.*

NISWYTH 5 ch.g. Canisbay 120–Aberystwyth 92 (Abernant 142) [1974 7h⁶   **41**
7g 7g³ 7.6fg² 8f 10s 8h 7g⁵ 7g² 8s² 1975 9v⁴ 8s 7f² 7f 10g 1976 8g 8g⁵] quite
an attractive gelding: only poor form: acts on any going: sometimes wears
blinkers. *D. Hanley.*

NOAH'S ARK 3 ch.c. Busted 134–Rustling Waters 72 (Ballymoss 136) [1975 —
N.R. 1976 7fg 12fg 10g] strong, shapely colt: half-brother to very useful
middle-distance performer Shallow Stream (by Reliance II): dam disappointing
half-sister to St Leger winner Cantelo: weak in market all outings but showed
signs of ability: should stay 1½m: gives us impression he may need an easier
surface: rather coltish in paddock on final outing: sold 740 gns Newmarket
September Sales. *N. Murless.*

NOBLE BAY 4 b.c. Lord Gayle 124–Tackaway 77 (Hard Tack 111 §) [1974 —
5s⁵ 5fg 7v* 7g 7fg² 7g 8s⁴ 7.3d⁵ 8s* 8v⁶ 8s² 1975 12g³ 8v⁵ 10s² 10g* 10fg⁶ 12f
8g⁵ 10g³ 10g³ 10g 11d³ 10.6v 1976 12g 12fg⁵] rather a lightly-made colt:
useful handicapper (rated 103) at 3 yrs: made only two appearances in this
country in 1976: stays 11f: acts on a firm surface but has shown best form on an
easy one: exported to U.S.A. *G. Harwood.*

NOBLE DANCER   4 b.c. Prince de Galles 125–Helen Traubel 88 (Sing Sing 134) **125**
[1974 6d* 6s² 6g³, also won a race in Norway   1975 winner five times in Norway
including 12g* 9g* 14g*   1976 8f* 9f* 12g* 12s⁴ 12s 12s⁴]   ex-English colt: fairly
useful performer (rated 99) at 2 yrs in England when trained by G. Smyth: winner
five times (worth over £12,500) in Norway in 1975, including in Oslo Cup and
Norsk St Leger and was voted Horse of the Year: won his first three races at 4 yrs,
beating the best of the Norwegian 3-y-o's on third start when winning 1976 Oslo
Cup easily from Trainer's Seat: put up a wonderful effort on fourth appearance
when about 5 lengths fourth of 20 to Ivanjica in Prix de l'Arc de Triomphe at
Longchamp in October (would certainly have finished third had he not been
hampered): seventh to On My Way in Prix du Conseil de Paris over same course
later in month and well-beaten fourth to Youth in Washington D.C. International
at Laurel in November on only other outings: stays 1¾m: acts on any going but is
well suited by soft: racing in U.S.A.   *T. Dahl, Norway.*

NOBLE GAME   (U.S.A.)   4 br.c. Determine–Tit Willow (Fleet Nasrullah)   **75**
[1974 7s   1975 11.1g⁴ 12.2f² 12.2f* 15.5f* 16fg⁴ 18g 14g   1976 13v 12.3d 18.4s
14.7d 15g⁵ 15f² 12f² 15g³ 14.7f* 12g⁴ 13g⁴ 13f³]   well-made American-bred colt:
quite a moderate handicapper: heavily-backed second favourite, stayed on
well when winning at Redcar in August by ¾ length from Mister Geoffrey: stays
well: acts on firm going and is unsuited by heavy: sold to F. Winter 3,500 gns
Ascot October Sales.   *Denys Smith.*

NOBLE GUNNER   3 ch.c. Royal Gunner–Wontell 80 (Buisson Ardent 129)   **66**
[1975 5g⁵ 6fg 7d 6g 7g⁵   1976 10.1fg 10fg⁴ 8g 8f³ 7f⁵ 8g 9.5g⁵ 10.2v⁵ 11v⁴]   well-
made colt: good mover: inconsistent maiden: ran moderately in seller at Kempton
on sixth outing: subsequently raced in French provinces: apparently stays 11f:
often wears blinkers: trained in England by G. Peter-Hoblyn.   *P. Swann,
France.*

NOBLE PASSION   2 ch.f. Crooner 119–Moitie 80 (Vilmoray 126)   [1976 5s 5.3g   —
8g 7s]   half-sister to three winners, including fairly useful sprinter September (by
Blason): 1,000 gns yearling: in rear on all outings, including when tried in
blinkers in a seller on final outing: sold 250 gns Ascot November Sales.   *C.
Dingwall.*

NOBLE STAG   2 b.c. Native Prince–My Fawn 67 (Hugh Lupus 133)   [1976   **88**
6fg 6f⁶ 8g² 8v]   strong, attractive, lengthy colt: good mover: half-brother to
three winners, notably smart French stayer Chawn (by St Chad): 6,200 gns
yearling: dam once-raced half-sister to Knotty Pine: 3 lengths second to Sultans
Ruby in 12-runner maiden race at Ayr in September: suited by 1m.   *H. T.
Jones.*

NOBLE VENTURE   2 ch.c. Hopeful Venture 125–Grand Slam 65 (Fidalgo 129)   —
[1976 7g]   good-looking, rangy colt: half-brother to several winners here and in
France, including fairly useful sprinter Noble Native (by Indigenous): dam
disappointing: unquoted when in rear in 14-runner minor event won by Filipachi
at Kempton in August: looks the type to do better in time.   *C. Brittain.*

NOBODYS FOOL   2 b.c. Polyfoto 124–Nicaria 105 (Nearco)   [1976 5g 7g* 6s*   **100**
7s²]   neat colt: half-brother to several winners, including useful stayer Nicarion
(by Alcide): 8,000 gns yearling: dam stayed 1½m: won 21-runner maiden race at
Newmarket and 20-runner minor event at Chepstow, both in October, latter by
1½ lengths from Qui Va La: swerved badly in final furlong when 1½ lengths second
to Alltyre in minor event, also at Chepstow, later in month: will stay 1m: acts on
soft going.   *P. Walwyn.*

NO CAMPING   4 b.g. Bivouac 114–Sylvan Longville 72 (No Worry 105)   [1974   —
N.R.   1975 N.R.   1976 14fg]   first produce: dam showed quite moderate
form over middle distances at 4 yrs: well-beaten ninth of 19 to Eric Stuart in
amateur riders event at Salisbury in June, only outing on flat.   *F. Muggeridge.*

NO CARDS   2 gr.f. No Mercy 126–Queens to Open 75 (Darius 129)   [1976 5fg⁴   **94**
5.1fg* 5.1f⁴ 6f³ 5g⁴]   half-sister to two winners, including fairly useful miler Sea
Gem (by Gratitude): dam won at 1m: won maiden race at Yarmouth in June by
1½ lengths from Persistent Miss: put up her best effort though on final outing, running on to finish 2¾ lengths fourth to Metair in £1,800 nursery at Newmarket in
September: best form at 5f but should stay 7f: evidently well suited by some give
in the ground.   *G. Pritchard-Gordon.*

NO CONVENTIONS   2 ch.c. Balidar 133–Wet Powder (Above Suspicion 127)   **111**
[1976 5g³ 5f* 6f² 5fg* 5fg² 5fg⁶]   well-made, attractive colt: first foal: 5,000 gns
yearling: dam won at up to 13f in Ireland: winner of maiden race at Windsor in

May and minor event at Newmarket the following month, on latter course getting home by short head from Rocket Lancer: put up an excellent effort in £2,100 nursery at Goodwood in July, failing by only a short head to catch Rahesh, but was badly drawn when short-priced favourite for similar race at York the following month and could finish only sixth of 19 to Self Portrait: should stay 1m. *J Dunlop.*

NODDY OWEN 2 b.c. Shoolerville 121–Fearless Footsteps (Proud Chieftain 122) **61**
[1976 7s 7s 8v⁵] small colt: modest plater: probably stays 1m. *D. Marks.*

NOELETTA 3 ch.f. King's Leap 111–Benchers 109 (King's Bench 132) [1975 **61**
5s* 5h⁵ 6g² 6v   1976 6d 6g⁶ 9fg 8fg² 8.2f⁵ 10g*] lightly-built filly: plater: won claiming race at Kempton in August by a length from Great Things: stays 1¼m: appears to act on any going. *P. Rohan.*

NO FEAR 3 ch.f. Quayside 124–My Plucky Lady 64 (Cash and Courage 116) **91**
[1975 7fg⁵ 1976 8fg³ 12g² 12g² 10g 11f⁴ 10.2s*] small filly: tried in blinkers, won 10-runner maiden race at Doncaster by 7 lengths from Ferrybridge: stays 1¼m: acts on soft going. *E. Weymes.*

NOGLOW 4 ch.g. Busted 134–Vital Match 113 (Match III 135) [1974 N.R. **—**
1975 8g   1976 12fg² 12g 10fg⁴ 8g 12g⁵ 10g 8fg³] neat gelding: poor maiden: stays 1¼m: usually apprentice or lady ridden. *P. Cole.*

NO HAM 5 b.h. Wolver Hollow 126–Longford Abbess (Zarathustra 131) [1974 **—**
10d 1975 N.R. 1976 8fg 12.2g] of little account. *W. Haigh.*

NO HONESTLY 3 b.f. Hopeful Venture 125–Consequently 101 (Con Brio 121) **—**
[1975 6g 5.9g 1976 10.4fg 12fg 7s] well-grown filly: poor maiden. *S. Brookshaw.*

NO INTERFERENCE 3 b.c. Majetta 115–Delamere Princess 52 (King's Bench **—**
132) [1975 6h² 6h⁵ 8f⁵ 10g⁴ 8g⁵ 10g⁶ 1976 13.8f] quite a useful plater at 2 yrs: appears to stay 1¼m: sweating and in need of race on only outing in 1976. *A. Kemp.*

NOIRIMA 2 b.f. Right Tack 131–Noirmont Girl 95 (Skymaster 126) [1976 5fg⁴ **98**
5f* 6fg 5f⁶ 5g*] shapely filly: second foal: half-sister to winning hurdler Linsky (by Linacre): dam quite a useful sprinter: awarded minor race by stewards at Lingfield in June and put up easily best effort when leading close home to win 12-runner nursery at Goodwood in September by a head from Red Johnnie: should stay 6f: suited by some give in the ground. *B. Hobbs.*

NO JOKING 2 b.f. No Mercy 126–Free and Easy (Fr) 81 (Net 116) [1976 5fg⁴ **82**
5fg⁵ 6fg² 5.8h² 6g⁶ 5f* 6h⁵ 5.3h⁴] workmanlike filly: first foal: 780 gns yearling: dam stayed 1¼m: made all to win seven-runner maiden auction event at Folkestone in August by 1½ lengths from Colourful Connie: fair fourth to Sahib's Daughter in nursery at Brighton later in month: stays 6f, and should get further: not particularly consistent. *P. Cundell.*

NO MAN'S LAND 3 ch.f. Salvo 129–Land of Fire 99 (Buisson Ardent 129) **—**
[1975 N.R. 1976 12fg 14fg 16fg] rangy filly: second produce: dam stayed 1m: well beaten in maiden races: sold 780 gns Newmarket September Sales. *G. Pritchard-Gordon.*

NON DRINKER 3 br.c. Bold Reason–Reluctance (Rustam 127) [1975 5fg⁶ **63**
6fg 7f³ 1976 10fg 13fg³ 10fg⁶ 16.1d 8d2] rangy American-bred colt: effective at 1m and stays 13f: blinkered third appearance. *P. Cole.*

NONESUCH 2 ch.c. Royal Palace 131–Honeysuckle 96 (Darius 129) [1976 **68**
5fg 5d⁴ 6fg] half-brother to four winners, including smart sprinter The Bee (by Sammy Davis): 1,750 gns yearling: dam stayed 1¼m: 6½ lengths fourth of eight to Daring Dan in maiden race at Haydock in May: not seen out after June: should do better over longer distances. *M. W. Easterby.*

NO NO NANETTE 3 ro.f. Sovereign Path 125–Nuclea (Orsini 124) [1975 7g **118**
7s* 8s 8d   1976 8g* 9d* 8d 10g³ 10.5d³ 9.2s 10.5s*] half-sister to a winner in Germany: dam won at up to 9f in France: developed into a smart performer, winning handicap at Maisons-Laffitte, minor event at Evry and Group 3 Prix de Flore at Saint-Cloud: put up a particularly good effort in last-named event in October, scoring by 1½ lengths from Paint the Town: 2 lengths third to Theia in Prix de la Nonette at Longchamp the previous month, best other effort: stays 1¼m well: acts on soft going. *G. Bridgland, France.*

NON ROYAL 3 b.g. Fate 93–Star Princess 107 (Devon Prince 99) [1974 N.R. **—**
1975 N.R. 1976 8g] half-brother to novice hurdler Immortal King (by Never Say Die): dam useful sprinter: last of 20 behind Golden Gayle in amateur riders race at Newmarket in July, only outing: dead. *V. Lay.*

NONSENSE RHYME   3 b.f. Lear Jet 123–One Poem (La Varende 125)   [1975
5v 5d 8g   1976 10f⁶ 8g 12g 12f]   well beaten in varied company, including
plating.   *N. Angus.*

NOR BARS   4 b.c. Sing Sing 134–Mamzelle 85 (King's Troop 118)   [1974 5.8g*   **69**
5d 6d² 6g   1975 6s 6fg 5f³ 5.8h³ 6g⁴ 6fg⁴ 7f⁶ 5.8f 7g 5g⁶   1976 7fg 7f² 6fg* 7g⁶
6g 7f⁴ 6fg³ 6f⁵ 6f³ 5.8h³ 6fg² 5.9fg⁵ 5g 5s]   lengthy colt: won handicap at Windsor
in May and ran creditably in some of his races afterwards: stays 7f: seems to act
on any going: has worn blinkers but didn't at Windsor.   *S. James.*

NORDIC BEAUTY   2 b.f. Supreme Sovereign 119–Genoa (Milesian 125)   [1976   **66**
5f⁵ 5d⁵ 5h⁵ 7g 6s]   second foal: half-sister to a winner in Scandinavia by Runnymede: 7 lengths fifth of 11 to Stephandre in maiden race at Doncaster in May,
second outing and best effort: should stay 7f: blinkered third appearance.   *H.
Westbrook.*

NORDIC MAID   2 b f. Vent du Nord–Rama Lass (Jaipur)   [1976 6fg⁶ 7d⁴ 6d⁶   **84**
6s⁵]   neat American-bred filly: half-sister to a minor winner in U.S.A. by Noble
Commander: dam never ran: put up by far her best effort when staying-on 2
lengths fourth of 30 to Guama in maiden race at Newbury in September: needs
further than 6f and will be suited by 1m+.   *R. Armstrong*

NORDIC SALUTE   3 ch.f. Northern Dancer–Right of the Line 119 (King's   **96**
Troop 118)   [1975 6s⁵ 6d⁴   1976 10.1fg⁴ 8fg* 8h* 8h³ 8.3fg* 7fg³ 7g* 7g⁵]   very
attractive, strong, lengthy American-bred filly: had a good season and won
maiden race at Sandown and handicaps at Warwick, Windsor and Kempton:
very enterprisingly ridden when beating Jackoleon 1½ lengths on last-named
course in August: stays 1m: acts on hard ground: blinkered first outing:
genuine: lost chance when squeezed out turning into straight when well beaten on
last outing: reportedly exported to U.S.A.   *P. Walwyn.*

NORDMAN   2 b.c. Alcide 136–Nortia 123 (Narrator 127)   [1976 8g 7g⁵ 8s*]   **90**
half-brother to four winners, including quite useful middle-distance performers
Klemperer and Huzoor (both by Hethersett): 4,600 gns yearling: dam very smart
at around 1¼m: put up quite a useful effort when winning 19-runner maiden race
at Sandown in October by 2½ lengths from Bright Swan: will be suited by 1½m:
acts on soft going.   *R. Smyth.*

NORFOLK AIR   3 br.c. Blakeney 126–Melody Maid (Tudor Melody 129)   [1975   **122**
7g 8g*   1976 10g 12fg* 12g 12fg⁴ 12fg² 14.6d⁵ 10d]
　　　The build-up to the classics is often the most exciting feature of the first half
of the season and the results of the classic trials are still eagerly awaited and
analysed by pundits and punters alike in the search for pointers to the outcome
of the big races.   But some of the so-called classic trials are apt to be of doubtful
value.   Of the six Derby trials run over middle distances in England in 1976—
the Sandown Classic Trial, the Chester Vase, Dee Stakes, Lingfield Ladbroke
Derby Trial, Mecca-Dante Stakes and Predominate Stakes—only two fell! to
horses engaged in the Derby.   Three of the winners, Old Bill, Great Idea and
Trasi's Son, were never entered in the first place and one, General Ironside, had
already been withdrawn.   Only Riboboy and the Lingfield Derby Trial winner

*Ladbroke Derby Trial Stakes, Lingfield—an easy win for Norfolk Air
over Black Sabbath and Bluffer*

Norfolk Air were still engaged in the Derby when they won their respective races.

Norfolk Air's win in the Ladbroke Derby Trial at Lingfield was gained in very good style by four lengths, but two days after the race he was still on offer at 33/1 with one leading firm of bookmakers, the reason being that the second and third to him, Black Sabbath and Bluffer, were still maidens and the odds-on favourite Riboboy had put up a thoroughly mulish display. By Derby day, however, Norfolk Air's odds were down to 10/1, joint-second favourite, but he could not emulate his sire, and he finished twelfth behind Empery after being fifth into the straight. Norfolk Air was then aimed at the St Leger, taking in the Gordon Stakes at Goodwood and the Great Voltigeur Stakes at York on his way. At Goodwood he was held up a long way behind the front-running Smuggler, and in the circumstances did well to finish within a length of the winner albeit in fourth place. He also came from behind at York and he looked certain to score when producing a good turn of foot to go clear about a furlong out despite hanging to his left, but he was caught near the line by Hawkberry, the pair finishing four lengths clear of General Ironside. In contrast, Norfolk Air raced close to the leaders in the St Leger, never being much worse than sixth. He disputed the lead as the field entered the straight and had every chance, but in the last two furlongs he gradually weakened. In the end he was some ten lengths behind Crow in fifth place. On his only subsequent outing, in the Champion Stakes at Newmarket, Norfolk Air cut little ice and finished well behind.

Norfolk Air (br.c. 1973)	Blakeney (b 1966)	Hethersett (b 1959)	Hugh Lupus
			Bride Elect
		Windmill Girl (b 1961)	Hornbeam
			Chorus Beauty
	Melody Maid (b 1967)	Tudor Melody (br 1956)	Tudor Minstrel
			Matelda
		Moss Maiden (ch 1957)	Mossborough
			Swan Maiden

Norfolk Air is the second foal of the unraced Melody Maid. Her first foal Perfumed Lady (by Frankincense) showed only a little ability and was sold for 960 guineas at the 1975 Newmarket December Sales. Melody Maid's third foal Brave Ballard (by Derring-Do) did not run at two years but is in training with James Bethell. The second dam, Moss Maiden, won at up to two and a quarter miles. To a previous mating with Melody Maid's sire Tudor Melody she produced the Manchester Handicap winner Bugle Boy.

Norfolk Air has a good turn of foot and is ideally suited by waiting tactics. He should manage to win a race or two over middle distances in 1977 but we doubt if they will be top-class events. All his best form is on a sound surface, the only two races in which he encountered going softer than good being the St Leger and the Champion Stakes. Norfolk Air has given trouble at the start: he unseated his rider leaving the stalls on his first outing at two years and he lost an irretrievable amount of ground on his first appearance in 1976, but he seems reliable enough nowadays. *J. Dunlop.*

NORFOLK GIANT 2 b.c. Blakeney 126–Tinternell 96 (Tenerani 135) [1976 **86** 6fg² 6g 6d 8s⁴] neat, attractive colt: good mover: half-brother to three winners by Derring-Do, including fairly useful miler Gay Colour: dam a stayer: ran well for a newcomer when ½-length second to odds-on Hot Grove in four-runner minor event at Chester in July: put up easily best subsequent effort when fourth to Lucent in £2,200 event at Doncaster in November when tried in blinkers: will be suited by 1½m: probably acts on any going. *J. Bethell.*

NORFOLK ROYAL 4 br.f. Never Say Die 137–Zidda (Zarathustra 131) [1974 **69** N.R. 1975 N.R. 1976 12fg⁵ 12fg 12.5h² 14fg³ 10f⁴ 8f³ 10fg³ 13fg 17.7f³ 15.5h* 12g 12f* 14d] good sort: quite a moderate performer: won poor maiden race at Folkestone in August by 2 lengths from Collaborator: beat same horse into third place when winning handicap, also at Folkestone, the following month: effective at 1m and stays well: acts on hard going. *B. Hanbury.*

NORLYN ROSE 2 b.f. Sterling Bay–Bawnmore Rose (Hotspur 102) [1976 **52** 5h* 5d⁶ 5.6f⁶ 6f⁴ 7d] half-sister to a winning 2-y-o plater and to two winners abroad: 300 gns yearling: dam never ran: bought in for 820 gns after winning bad seller at Teesside in April: had very stiff tasks afterwards: should stay 6f+. *A. Bacon.*

NORTHERN BOY 2 gr.c. No Argument 107–Ladymarsh 71 (Vilmorin) [1976 **—** 5f 6fg 8.2f] strong, good-bodied colt: well beaten in maiden races: slowly away first outing: trained until after second start by S. Wainwright. *N. Adam.*

NORTHERN EAGLE 3 b.g. Northern Wizard 100–Delayed Cheers (Three —
Cheers 119) [1975 5f 5f 1976 12f] probably of no account. *J. Long.*

NORTHERN LADY 2 b.f. The Brianstan 128–Lady From Aske 82 (French **95**
Beige 127) [1976 5d 6fg* 6fg4 5f* 5fg5 5h* 6fg 5g6] quite attractive filly: first
foal: dam, second three times at 2 yrs, is sister to two useful stayers: won 18-
runner maiden race at York in June in grand style by 3 lengths from New Mills
and made all when gaining further successes at Redcar in July and August:
carried top weight in nursery on latter occasion and was all out to hold off
Sandbeck Song by ½ length after blinding her field for early pace: stays 6f.
J. W. Watts.

NORTHERN SHAMROCK 2 ch.c. Northfields–Orient Queen (King's Troop **95** p
118) [1976 7fg5 7g*] Irish colt: first living produce: 6,800 gns yearling:
dam won over 5f at 3 yrs in Ireland: looked a very useful colt in the making
when landing the odds in 13-runner maiden race at Fairyhouse in October,
drawing away from distance to win by 5 lengths from Lyleview King: will stay
1m: likely to go on to better things. *D. Weld, Ireland.*

NORTHERN SUN 3 b.f. Sunacelli 114–North Holme Queen (Phideas) [1975 —
N.R. 1976 8fg 10v] plain filly: seems of little account. *D. Williams.*

NORTHERN TREASURE 3 ch.c. Northfields–Place d'Etoile 93 (Kythnos 126) **126**
[1975 5v2 5g3 6f2 6f2 6.3fg2 6f* 7f* 5g2 6fg2 1976 5s3 7s3 7f4 6f2 8d* 12f3 12f*
10g4 10d3]
    Northern Treasure's victory in the Irish Two Thousand Guineas came as a
surprise, for nothing he had achieved in his thirteen previous races had suggested
he was within ten pounds of classic-winning standard, and he started at 33/1.
He had had a busy time of it as a two-year-old, being first seen out on April 5th
and not getting off the mark until five outings and three and a half months later.
He did not contest any of the top two-year-old races and there were a dozen
colts rated ahead of him in the Madrid Free Handicap in which he received 8-3.
Northern Treasure's four runs before the Guineas yielded four defeats. In the
race for the Madrid Free Handicap at the Curragh he was beaten over five lengths
by the top-weight Northern View and in the Vauxhall Trial Stakes at Phoenix
Park he finished fourth behind Lucky Wednesday, Sovereign Dice and Wolverlife,
the last-named pair giving him weight.
    The Irish Two Thousand Guineas had a 'for export' look about it, the first
five horses in the betting being trained outside Ireland. The favourite was
the French Two Thousand Guineas third Comeram; then came Northern Spring,
the top-rated Italian two-year-old of 1975, the Two Thousand Guineas fourth
Patris, Arapaho, who had made a favourable impression when winning two
maiden races in England, and The Chaplain, who had finished about two lengths
behind Comeram in the French Guineas. The most fancied of the Irish horses
were Northern View, Wolverlife, Lucky Wednesday and the Tetrarch Stakes
winner Poacher's Moon. The race provided the closest classic finish of the season.
After Arapaho, Poacher's Moon, Wolverlife, Northern Treasure and Comeram
had headed the closely-grouped seventeen-runner field for about six furlongs,
Comeram, Northern Treasure and Lucky Wednesday began to draw away with
the race between them. Lucky Wednesday cracked, and Northern Treasure
and Comeram fought out a stride-for-stride battle right up to the post, where
Northern Treasure had the better of it by a short head. A stewards inquiry
was announced but the placings remained unaltered. There were some hard-
luck stories, notably concerning Patris and Northern Spring who apparently
were badly hampered in the early stages, but nothing should detract from the
winner's game performance.
    Northern Treasure had a comparatively easy time of it afterwards, running
only four more races after having five in the space of two months at the beginning
of the season. He won only one of these four, but he ended the season with
his reputation enhanced. He put up a sterling performance to finish third to
Malacate and Empery in the Irish Sweeps Derby at the Curragh, only three
quarters of a length behind the Epsom Derby winner and a similar distance in
front of the Epsom Derby fourth, Hawkberry. In the light of this performance
the Blandford Stakes, run over the same course two months later, represented
a simple task for him and he had no difficulty in beating his four rivals, of whom
his stable-companion Whistling Deer followed him home.
    Northern Treasure's objectives in the autumn were the Joe McGrath
Memorial Stakes at Leopardstown and the Champion Stakes. At Leopardstown

Irish 2,000 Guineas Stakes, the Curragh—Northern Treasure (right), Comeram and Lucky Wednesday fight out an exciting finish

he was put firmly in his place once again by Malacate and didn't show his best form, being beaten also by Mart Lane and Niebo. In the Champion Stakes, ridden by Taylor instead of stable-jockey Curran who had the mount on Lady Singer, he ran his best race of the season. Never far behind the leaders on the far side, he was almost in line with Rose Bowl and Vitiges at the two-furlong pole, and he kept on well to finish third, less than three lengths behind the winner.

Northern Treasure (ch.c. 1973)	Northfields (ch 1968)	Northern Dancer (ch 1961)	Nearctic
			Natalma
		Little Hut (b 1952)	Occupy
			Savage Beauty
	Place d'Etoile (b 1967)	Kythnos (b 1957)	Nearula
			Capital Issue
		Etoile de France (b 1957)	Arctic Star
			Miss France

Northern Treasure is the second foal of Place d'Etoile who won the Pretty Polly Stakes at the Curragh and finished fifth in the Irish One Thousand Guineas. Her first produce, Etoile Grise (by Sea Hawk II) showed a little ability and was sold for 16,500 guineas at the December Sales. After Northern Treasure she produced Place Dauphine, a sister to Etoile Grise who was sold for 4,100 guineas as a yearling, and then a colt by Captain's Gig who was bought by Northern Treasure's trainer for 33,000 guineas at Goffs Premier Yearling Sales. Place d'Etoile's dam, Etoile de France, has produced five other winners, notably the stayers Irvine and Staralgo. The next dam Miss France was a very successful broodmare, numbering the Irish Derby winners Talgo and Fidalgo among her progeny.

Northern Treasure's sire Northfields has followed his half-brother Habitat by making a very successful start to his stud career. In his first crop he sired three horses who finished in the frame in a classic—Northern Treasure, Northern View and Oats; in his second he is represented by the Silken Glider Stakes winner Nanticious and the promising winners North Stoke and Northern Shamrock. In Northern Treasure he has sired a good and versatile colt, one able to run well at distances from five furlongs to a mile and a half, and able to act on any going. It said much for Northern Treasure's constitution and temperament that he was still improving at the end of his career. He is to be retired to the Newhaven Park Stud, New South Wales in 1977, having been purchased through the BBA (Ireland) in August for an undisclosed sum. *K. Prendergast, Ireland.*

NORTHERN VIEW 3 ch.c. Northfields–April Fancy (No Argument 107) **109**
[1975 6f 7g* 8g2 1976 7s3 7s* 7g3 8d4 9g 9g5 8v] first foal: 4,300 gns yearling: dam winner at up to 9f in Ireland: won Madrid Free Handicap at the Curragh in April in great style by 5 lengths from Extra La: good 4 lengths fourth to Northern

Treasure in Irish 2,000 Guineas on same course the following month: subsequently exported to Italy and was unplaced in three races: will stay 1¼m: acts on soft going: trained by S. Quirke in Ireland. *V. Bignami, Italy.*

NORTHGATE LASS 2 ch.f. Mansingh 120–Fiddlers Too 80 (Neron 121) **68** [1976 5g 5f⁴ 6h⁴ 5f 7fg 6v² 5v⁵ 5s] lightly-built, narrow filly: half-sister to three winners, including fairly useful 1975 2-y-o Carburton (by Runnymede): cost 1,250 gns Doncaster January 1976 Sales: dam won at 7f to 1½m: backed from 14/1 to 6/1, put up best effort when 2½ lengths second of 20 to Cathmaria in seller at Haydock in October: stays 6f: acts on any going. *S. Wainwright.*

NORTH STOKE 2 ch.c. Northfields–Mother 88 (Whistler 129) [1976 7g⁶ 7s* **105** 7v*] rangy colt: half-brother to two winners, including fairly useful middle-distance performer Balimar (by Ballymoss): 820 gns yearling: dam won over 5f at 2 yrs: won two races at end of season in the style of a useful performer, 19-runner minor event at Chepstow comfortably by 1½ lengths from Miss Mars and similar 15-runner race at Lingfield by 7 lengths from Peace Symbol: will stay at least 1m: acts on heavy going. *J. Dunlop.*

NORTH TWO 3 b.g. Stupendous–Taking Silk (Shantung 132) [1975 6fg **65** 1976 8.2d² 8.2g 12f⁴ 6g 9.2f*] first foal: 740 gns yearling: dam never ran: favourite, won five-runner seller at Hamilton in September by 3 lengths from Satasha (bought in 720 gns): should stay middle distances. *K. Payne.*

NORTON 4 gr.g. Prince Tenderfoot 126–Tiffany Case 72 (Never Say Die 137) **—** [1974 N.R. 1975 10f 1976 12.5v 10s] big, strong gelding: little worthwhile form in three races on flat. *M. W. Easterby.*

NORTON FALCON 3 gr.g. Birdbrook 110–Rogali 80 (Royal Avenue 123) **65** [1975 8fg⁵ 8s 1976 9f 9.4g⁶ 7f* 7g] lengthy gelding: good walker: won handicap at Doncaster in July by ¾ length from Pam's Gleam: well-backed favourite, finished lame on next outing two months later: suited by 7f: acts on firm going: sold 750 gns Doncaster October Sales. *M. H. Easterby.*

NOSTALGIA 3 b.f. Veiled Wonder–Claircelenda 68 (Robert Barker 125) **—** [1975 5g⁴ 5f² 7f⁴ 1976 7g 6f 7v 5s] no worthwhile form at 3 yrs, including in a Folkestone seller: sold out of R. Price's stable 500 gns Doncaster September Sales after second outing. *D. Plant.*

NO TOMORROW 2 ch.f. Will Somers 114 §–Spring Again (Primera 131) **80** [1976 5g 5fg 5fg 5d 5s* 6s⁶] neat filly: second foal: dam well behind in maiden races: 20/1, put up easily best effort when winning moderate maiden race at Nottingham in September going away by a length from Bitter Spare: should be well suited by 6f+: evidently needs soft going. *H. Williams.*

NO TURNING (USA) 3 b.c. Never Bend–Secret Story (Spy Song) [1975 6g* **112** 8g² 8s⁴ 1976 8s² 9.8fg² 9g³ 12g 12f] nice American-bred French colt: brother to a minor winner, and half-brother to three winners in U.S.A., notably smart 1962 2-y-o Catullus (by Roman): $48,000 yearling: dam, a winner at 2 yrs and 3 yrs, is half-sister to Royal Record II: placed in minor event at Saint-Cloud (beaten a short head by Wood Green), Prix de Guiche at Longchamp (beaten a length by Grandchant) and Prix Daphnis at Evry (close-up third to Happy New Year): fair seventh behind Empery in Epsom Derby but was well beaten in Irish Sweeps Derby (blinkered first time): appears to act on any going: exported to U.S.A. and has won an allowance race at Santa Anita. *F. Palmer, France.*

NOW HEAR THIS 2 br.c. Verbatim–Blackout 98 (Delirium 126) [1976 6fg³ **64** 7d 7fg 8s] half-brother to fair 1975 2-y-o Ebony Rock (by Rock Talk), and to two minor winners in U.S.A.; dam, winner twice over 6f at 2 yrs, is half-sister to smart miler Purple Haze: showed only a little ability in maiden and minor events: blinkered last two outings. *B. Hobbs.*

NUMA POMPILIUS 2 ch.c. Dr Fager–Nostrana (Botticelli 129) [1976 7d⁴ **116** 7g* 9s² 7.7s] American-bred French colt: half-brother to three winners in France, including very useful Ninfae (by St Paddy), a winner at up to 10.5f: dam won in Germany and is daughter of German 1,000 Guineas and Oaks winner Naxos, a half-sister to Neckar: won nine-runner maiden race at Deauville in August by a length from King Dash: put up better subsequent effort when failing by only a short head to catch all-the-way-winner Balteus in the Prix Saint-Roman at Longchamp in October: will stay at least 1¼m: acts on soft going. *G. Bridgland, France.*

NUNS FIFTEEN 3 ch.c. Roan Rocket 128–Zama Lake 68 (Mossborough 126) **60** [1975 8g 1976 8g⁶ 11f 8fg³ 8g³ 11.5fg⁶ 8f 9f* 8d 10.8s⁶ 12s] big colt: won seven-runner maiden race at Wolverhampton in August by 6 lengths from Quite Calm: stays 9f (has run poorly at longer distances): best form on a sound surface. *R. Hollinshead.*

NUNSTAR 3 b.g. Joshua 129–Mossy 95 (Mossborough 126) [1975 6g 6fg 1976 — 10.5s 16f6] strong, compact gelding: in rear in maiden races: should be suited by 1m+ but is not certain to stay 2m. *M. H. Easterby.*

NUROMA 3 b.f. Prince de Galles 125–Janabelle 101 (Gentle Art 121) [1975 5g5 — 5f2 5d3 5.8f2 6g 6g 6g3 1976 5fg4 6fg5 6fg6 5f 5f 5fg5 8.2d 8s 9s] rather unfurnished filly: little worthwhile form at 3 yrs and was tailed off when blinkered on final outing: evidently best at sprint distances. *M. Tate.*

NUTBROWN MAID 5 b.m. Sweet Story 122–Maid of Middleham 96 (Borealis) [1974 8h3 8f 9f 10g 9d 1975 12g 12v 1976 8.2v 13g 11g] of no account: sold 220 gns Doncaster October Sales. *G. Wallace.*

NUTHATCH 4 b.c. Levmoss 133–Meadow Pipit 103 (Worden II 129) [1974 **116** 7s4 8g* 1975 10v2 10s* 12fg 12f4 14g 1976 10g4 12g3 16g4 20f6 11.5g] good-looking Irish colt: smart performer: in frame against good-class opposition at 4 yrs, on third start finishing 6 lengths fourth of six to Sea Anchor in Group 3 Henry II Stakes at Sandown in June: well-beaten sixth to Sagaro in Gold Cup at Royal Ascot later in month: off course over three months before final appearance: should stay further than 2m: possibly needs some give in the ground, and acts on heavy going: sold 14,000 gns Newmarket December Sales. *J. Oxx, Ireland.*

O

OAKDENE 2 ro.g. My Swanee 122–Young Foolishness (Chantelsey 130) [1976 **65** 5f* 7h 6g] smallish, lengthy gelding: bought in for 1,000 gns after winning seller at Thirsk in April going away by 1½ lengths: not seen out again until August when in rear in nurseries at Redcar (probably needed race) and York (had little chance at weights): should be suited by 7f. *K. Payne.*

OAKLEY SUPREME 3 b.f. Gala Performance–Savannah (Ribot 142) [1975 — 5v6 5s 5g3 6g 6f4 5i* 1976 8fg 6g3 5f 6f] lightly-made filly: plater: little worthwhile form as a 3-y-o: missed break on last two outings. *D. Ringer.*

OATS 3 b.c. Northfields–Arctic Lace 106 (Arctic Chevalier) [1975 6s 7g* 1976 **126** 8fg2 8.5fg* 12g3 13.3fg2 14.6d4]

Oats showed admirable consistency during what was, for all that he raced only six times, a fairly demanding season for him, and although he only once managed to win he picked up prize money on all his starts, including third-place money in the Derby and fourth-place money in the St Leger, his two major objectives. He is a tough horse but lacks a turn of foot. This latter deficiency is always likely to prove a grave shortcoming, especially in any race less strenuously contested than the Derby and the Leger, and he may find difficulty in enhancing his reputation as a four-year-old.

Oats's best performances were probably his two in the classics: the strong pace at which the Derby and the St Leger were run favours a one-paced horse such as he. His form before the Derby did not measure up to that of Wollow, Vitiges and Empery, but his trainer made no secret of the fact that he considered him highly and he had obviously been trained for the Derby, missing the Guineas after winning the Ladbroke Blue Riband Trial at Epsom from Navigator, All Hope, Meritable and Radetzky. The distance of the Blue Riband, a mile, looked scarcely adequate for him—he had to work hard to get into the lead two furlongs from home—as it did also in the Ladbroke Craven Stakes at Newmarket two weeks earlier, where Eddery was already hard at work on him when they ran into trouble going into the Dip. Once clear of trouble, the horse ran on very strongly to take second place to Malinowski. In the Derby, Oats seemed to maintain his own strong gallop steadily right to the end. He was never far behind the leaders, he turned for home in sixth place and outstayed three of those horses in front of him without managing to look a serious threat to the other two, Relkino and Empery. Nevertheless Relkino held on to second place by only a head.

Oats had a very hard race in the Derby, coming under the whip two and a half furlongs out, and, if anything, he had a harder race on his next outing, in the Gordon Stakes at Goodwood in July. He is that sort of horse; he needs, and can stand, any amount of driving. Eddery was the only jockey that didn't allow

Smuggler too much rope in the Gordon Stakes, but even so, Oats had a lot of chasing to do in the straight and Eddery had to roust him along fully three furlongs out. For a long time the hard-pressed Oats made little impression on Smuggler (who is himself not the speediest of middle-distance performers) but once again he displayed his ability to maintain his gallop right through to the end; in the last furlong he gained ground with almost every stride and the finishing post came up just in time to save the flagging Smuggler from defeat.

In the paddock at Goodwood, Oats looked particularly well, almost too well after his eight-week absence from the course and he was given another race to tighten him up for the St Leger. His task in that warm-up race, the Geoffrey Freer Stakes at Newbury in August, seemed a difficult one even though he had only four opponents. He was meeting Dakota and Libra's Rib at weight-for-age, and Swell Fellow and Major Green on terms slightly worse than weight-for-age. The distance of around thirteen furlongs was in his favour but the small field and relatively slow pace were not. Oats had yet another hard chase, and Swell Fellow beat him by a head. The winner, who made all the running, quickened into a three-length advantage from Oats turning into the straight and although Oats drew almost level entering the final furlong after trying for at least three furlongs to catch up, Swell Fellow was able to hold on. Oats had every chance had he been good enough.

Oats started joint-favourite with General Ironside and Crow for the St Leger, which, on the face of it, doesn't say a great deal for the general opinion of the quality of the field, although it's true that he was widely expected to improve over the longer trip. However, it transpired that there was one horse in the field possessing top-class pace and that was Crow, who blinded the others, Oats included, for finishing speed. Oats, as always in defeat, went down fighting; he was beaten less than a length for third place by Scallywag, the best English-trained horse on the day.

The fact that Oats is short of pace doesn't necessarily mean that the further he goes the better he will get. He may not stay beyond a mile and three quarters; even if he does, he may not show to best advantage against top-class stayers in races as slowly run as some long-distance races are apt to be run nowadays.

Ladbroke Blue Riband Trial Stakes, Epsom—Oats has it sewn up from Navigator and All Hope

Mr A. D. G. Oldrey's "Oats"

Oats's pedigree doesn't give us all the help we need in assessing his stamina potential. His sire Northfields, a half-brother to Habitat, and a good winner at around nine furlongs, is a relatively unknown quantity as a stallion, his first crop being only three-year-olds in 1976. Among his winners in that first crop only the moderate Irish horse Le Grand Rouge has shown as much aptitude as Oats for staying. Oats's dam, whom one would have expected to have stayed middle distances, showed useful form at around a mile. Oats is her third foal; her only previous foal to have shown worthwhile form being Regent's Garden (by middle-distance horse Prince Regent) who stays at least fifteen furlongs. We estimate that Oats will stay further than a mile and three quarters, but are quite prepared to be proved wrong.

Oats (b.c. 1973)	Northfields (ch 1968)	Northern Dancer (ch 1961)	Nearctic
			Natalma
		Little Hut (b 1952)	Occupy
			Savage Beauty
	Arctic Lace (b 1966)	Arctic Chevalier (b 1957)	Arctic Star
			French Ballet
		Alace (b 1961)	Rapace
			Fair Alycia

Oats is a strong, attractive colt and a good mover; his fine looks and his appearance of tremendous physical well-being made a great impression on us throughout the season. Oats has run well on ground both on the firm side of good and the soft side of good but he has only once raced in public on very soft going (first time out as a two-year-old) and never on firm. His form on soft going was moderate, but this could well be the result of nothing more significant than his lack of experience, and one might well anticipate that the next time he runs on the soft he will show that he acts on it. In fact, one might expect, all else being equal, that soft going would suit him very well seeing that it would slow down the speedier types. Oats is a very genuine and most consistent racehorse.
P. Walwyn.

Valdoe Stakes, Goodwood—Obstacle beats the Derby runner-up Relkino and Red Regent (right)

OBEDE LIGHT   2 b.f. Fantastic Light 119–Obedience (Reliance II 137)   [1976   —
5fg 5d 6f]   small filly: well behind in sellers, ridden by girl apprentice each
time.   *D. Williams.*

OBSERVER ROYAL   2 b.f. King's Troop 118–High Spy 91 (High Treason 126)   —
[1976 6fg]   half-sister to a winning plater by Quorum: dam a sprinter: last of
15 in maiden race won by County Boy at Windsor in July, only outing.   *D. Underwood.*

OBSTACLE   3 ch.c. Dike–Miss Justice 87 (King's Bench 132)   [1975 5fg 6f³ 6g⁴   **110**
6fg⁵ 5.9f* 7d² 7g² 7fg*   1976 7fg 8g³ 8.2d⁴ 8g² 8fg³ 8fg⁵ 10g*]   compact, good
sort of colt: put up some good performances in 1976 and won Valdoe Stakes
at Goodwood in September by a length from Relkino (gave 9 lb): 1½ lengths
third to Trusted in Joe Coral Handicap at Ayr, best previous effort: suited by
1¼m: appears to act on any going: game and genuine, running his only poor race
on sixth outing.   *H. Candy.*

OCHIL HILLS STAR   3 b.c. Chebs Lad 120–Turkish Maid 58 (Menelek 114)   **72**
[1975 6f 7g⁵ 7g⁵ 6g⁴ 5fg⁵   1976 7g⁴(dis) 6g⁶ 8s⁵ 11f⁵ 8f* 8.2h² 10g² 8.2f]   quite a
moderate performer: dropped in class, won seller at Lanark in September with
a good deal in hand: bought in 720 gns afterwards: ran creditably in better
company on next two outings but was way below his best on final start: stays
1¼m: acts on hard ground.   *N. Angus.*

O'CONNA   3 b.c. I Say 125–Clip (Henry the Seventh 125)   [1975 5s⁶ 5v³ 5s⁶ 6h   —
1976 12.2fg 12fg 16.1v]   plain colt: plating-class maiden: possibly not at his
best on hard going.   *R. Cambidge.*

OCTOGENARIAN   3 b.c. Double-U-Jay 120–Red Ranger 102 (Red God 128 §)   **69**
[1975 5.3f³   1976 8g 8f⁴ 8h⁶ 7s]   neat colt: ran promisingly on first two outings
but was most disappointing when favourite for seller at Brighton in October on
final appearance, finishing well-beaten tenth of 12, and was sold 300 gns Ascot
November Sales.   *J. Dunlop.*

OCTOPUS   5 b.g. Major Portion 129–My Poppet 90 (My Babu 136)   [1974 8g²   —
10g² 8g 10s 10g² 11.7fg⁶ 12g⁵ 12d 12s³ 10.8v   1975 10.1f 10.1g 11fg 16f 12f³ 12f
12fg   1976 12fg⁶ 12f⁶ 10f⁶]   small, lengthy gelding: poor handicapper nowadays:
stays 1½m: acts on soft going, but is possibly best on a sound surface: sometimes
wears blinkers: wears bandages: twice slowly away when ridden by an amateur:
sold 320 gns Ascot December Sales.   *M. Haynes.*

OFFA'S DYKE   3 b.c. Adropejo 114–Nichucath (Nimbus 130)   [1975 N.R.   —
1976 7.6fg⁶ 12fg⁴ 16.1v]   first reported foal: dam ran only twice: distant fourth
of 15 to Ribo Pride in weakly-contested amateur riders event at Leicester in
September: tailed off in 18-runner maiden race won by Glenalema at Haydock
the following month.   *R. E. Peacock.*

OFFA'S MEAD   7 ch.g. Rathlin–Eridantini (Indigenous 121)   [1974 5g³ 5.8fg   **83**
5.9f 5.8f 5g 6fg 6d 6g* 5g³ 6g 5s⁴   1975 6v 5g² 6fg* 5h 5f⁶ 5h 5f 5f 6g 6s   1976
5.9fg² 5.8f* 5f 6fg 5g² 5.9g⁴ 5.8h² 5.8h* 5fg⁴ 5.9fg⁴ 5.8f³ 5s* 5s* 6s³]   neat
gelding: quite a moderate handicapper: had a fine season, winning at Bath
(twice), Warwick and Catterick: beat The Solostan 1½ lengths when winning on
last-named track in October: best at sprint distances: acts on any going: sometimes wears bandages: genuine and consistent.   *M. Bradley.*

OFFERING   4 b.f. Vaguely Noble 140–Trial Offer (Byland 119)   [1974 N.R.   —
1975 10.5d   1976 12fg 13.8d]   rangy ex-French filly: American-bred: well beaten

in minor event at Pontefract and maiden race at Catterick in 1976, but on both occasions gave us impression that she would be suited by a shorter trip: not raced after May. *M. Ryan.*

OFFLEY PRINCE 2 b.c. Prince Regent 129–Lifetime 89 (Darius 129) [1976 6d⁵ 6fg³ 8d 8v⁴ 8.2v] strong, robust colt: half-brother to fair 1975 2-y-o 5f winner Consistent (by Connaught): 825 gns yearling: dam won over 1¼m and is half-sister to Only for Life: in frame in minor events at Chester and York, putting up probably better effort when 2½ lengths third of 11 to Lucky Omen on former course in September: will stay further than 1¼m: seems to act on any going. *R. Hollinshead.* **86**

OH WELL 4 b.f. Sahib 114–Charline 93 (Charlottesville 135) [1974 5fg 5fg 6fg 5.8s⁶ 1975 6s⁶ 6f² 7fg 10h 8f⁴ 10.2f 6fg⁴ 8.2fg⁴ 8fg³ 8.2d³ 8g 1976 8fg² 8.3f⁴ 7f² 7fg 8fg⁵ 6h³ 6fg] small filly: plater: stays 1m, but apparently not 1¼m: seems to act on any going: suitable mount for an apprentice: blinkered last three outings. *P. Cundell.* **40**

OISIN 3 b.c. Bold Lad (U.S.A.)–Mudela (Sir Gaylord) [1975 N.R. 1976 10g* 10fg* 10g² 12g³ 14g⁴ 12fg² 12f* 12g³ 12s² 12v 12s] well-made colt: half-brother to two winners, including fair 1¼m and 1½m winner Tadorna (by Sea-Bird II): 3,200 gns yearling: dam useful winner in Italy and half-sister to Gyr: ran well in most of his races, winning maiden event at Folkestone in March and handicaps at Newmarket in April and Salisbury in July: beat Whistler's Lane by 7 lengths on last-named course: stays 1½m but apparently not 1¾m: acts on any going: excellent mount for an apprentice: well below his best on last two appearances but was probably feeling effects of his long season. *G. Harwood.* **86**

OISIN DUBH 4 b.c. Whistling Wind 123–Ebnal 79 (Umberto 118) [1974 6f 7.9g⁵ 7g 1975 8s* 9v* 8s* 10s* 9f 9g 8s⁶ 1976 9s* 12s* 10f⁴ 10v⁴ 8s⁴] Irish colt: useful performer: ran really well on first three outings at 4 yrs (all at Phoenix Park), winning well-contested Burmah Lincolnshire Trial Handicap (stormed home 6 lengths clear of Cnoch Bhui) and Rank Cup (by 4 lengths from Miralla), both in March, and finishing fourth under a stiff weight in handicap won by Spanish Doubloon in May: subsequently off course until October but wasn't disgraced in his last two races: effective at 1m and stays 1½m: acts on any going but is well suited by heavy ground. *C. Grassick, Ireland.* **105**

OKIE 3 b.f. Connaught 130–Fair Rosamond (Owen Tudor) [1975 5d 5g 7g⁶ 8d⁵ 1976 8fg 8fg⁴ 12g 10f⁵ 12f⁵] light-framed filly: plating-class maiden: best run at 1m. *R. Smyth.* **48**

OLD BILL 3 b.c. Busted 134–Country Path 101 (Mossborough 126) [1975 7fg 1976 11f 12.3d* 13.3g 14fg⁵ 14g⁴ 14v* 14.6s*] well-made, good-looking colt: **120**

Chester Vase—the outsider of the party Old Bill comes from behind to win from Ormeley, with Smuggler taking third place from Coin of Gold (left) and Broomley (rails)

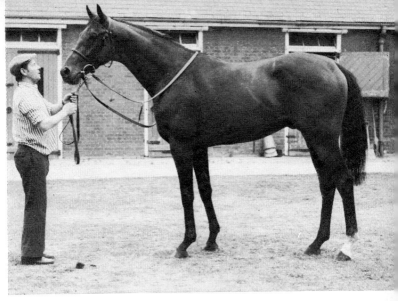

Mr R. B. Moller's "Old Bill"

second foal: closely related to disqualified 1m winner Garden Wall (by Crepello): dam, at her best on soft going, won at 1½m and 13f: 33/1, showed vastly improved form when winning Chester Vase in May by 2½ lengths from Ormeley, running a bit green but leading inside final furlong and running on strongly: lightly raced during the summer but came right back to his best when ground eased in the autumn and won handicaps at York and Doncaster in October: particularly impressive on latter course when making all and beating Night In Town easing up by 8 lengths: needs a good test of stamina and will be well suited by 2m+: said to require an easy surface, and revels in the mud: got a bit warm in paddock at Chester: should win good staying races as a 4-y-o when he has suitable ground conditions. *H. Wragg.*

OLD CARL 5 ch.g. Right Tack 131–Beuten (Sedan II) [1974 8s⁵ 8g 10f 10g 8s² —
8g² 8g 10s 10s 1975 9f⁵ 8g 7fg6 7h* 7f* 1976 8g 9fg 7v] big gelding: lightly
raced and no worthwhile form at 5 yrs: best at up to 1m: acts on any going.
W. Wharton.

OLD CHAD 5 b.g. St Chad 120–Graunuaile 116 (Proud Chieftain 122) [1974
10fg² 12fg* 12fg6 12f³ 11.2f* 12f² 12f6 12.2g⁵ 16d 1975 15.8d 1976 12s]
one-time moderate handicapper: has run only twice since 1974: suited by 11f
and 1½m but probably does not stay 2m: acts on firm going and seems unsuited
by soft. *K. Bridgwater.*

OLD COURT 2 b.c. Welsh Saint 126–Haughty 76 (Hugh Lupus 132) [1976 **98**
5d 6g² 7fg 7f* 7fg² 8g 8fg⁵ 8s* 8s⁵] rather leggy colt: poor mover: half-brother
to three winners, including French middle-distance winner Proud Heart (by
Astec): 2,900 gns yearling: dam placed over 9f in Ireland: carried right by
winner in final furlong when short-head second to Eminence in maiden race
at Lanark in July and was subsequently awarded race by stewards: made all
and showed much improved form when winning nursery at Edinburgh in October
unchallenged by 12 lengths from Catchword, but did not reproduce that form on
only subsequent outing. stays 1m: acts on any going but is very well suited by
soft. *W. Marshall.*

OLD CURRENCY 3 b.f. Lucky Brief 128–Vintage Coin (Old Wine 91) [1975 —
8g 8v 1976 10fg 14.7h⁴] plating-class maiden. *J. Leigh.*

OLDE YANK 3 b.c. Olden Times–Bold Flirt (Bold Ruler) [1975 5g 5g 1976 — 6fg 5g 6fg 5g] plating-class maiden. *N. Guest.*

OLD PARTNER 2 br.c. Roi Soleil 125–Musical Watch (Tudor Melody 129) — [1976 5g 6g⁵ 5fg⁶] compact colt: no worthwhile form, including in a seller, in this country: subsequently sent to race in Belgium and is a winner there. *J. Sutcliffe.*

OLD RARITY 3 b.c. Rarity 129–Papillio 78 (Pampered King 121) [1975 6f³ **75** 6g⁴ 5fg* 5f⁵ 5g⁶ 7f 1976 9fg⁶ 8.2d 8f 6fg] strong colt: needs further than 6f and will stay 1¼m+: ran best race on first outing: has raced with his tongue tied down: sold 500 gns Newmarket Autumn Sales. *Miss S. Hall.*

OLDTIMER 4 br.g. Sahib 114–Relic Star (Relic) [1974 5g 5fg 6f⁶ 1975 7.6g **57** 8g 7f 6f 6fg³ 8g⁴ 6g 6f⁶ 10g 1976 8fg 7f⁵ 7fg⁵ 6f* 8.3f* 7g] tall gelding: selling handicapper: successful at Brighton and Windsor at 4 yrs, being bought in for 920 gns on latter course: stays 1m: acts on firm going: wears blinkers nowadays. *L. Hall.*

OLIBANUM 3 ch.f. Frankincense 120–Makbuba 86 (Dumbarnie 125) [1975 5f — 5f 5fg 6f³ 7f⁵ 7f 1976 7g⁵ 7d] plater: suited by 7f: sometimes dwells at start. *Hbt Jones.*

OLIVARNIE'S DANDY 3 b.f. David Jack 125–Dick's Yarn 80 (Peter's Yarn — 106) [1975 5v 5s 5s 5s 5g 1976 8d] of no account: sold 250 gns Doncaster June Sales. *H. Wharton.*

OLWYN 2 b.f. Relko 136–Nantahala 84 (Nantallah) [1976 6fg⁵ 7f³ 7g⁴ 8s⁶] **106** strong, well-grown filly: second foal: 3,000 gns yearling: dam won over 1m at 3 yrs: 56/1 for valuable Criterium des Pouliches at Longchamp in October but ran remarkably well to finish sixth of 14, less than 6 lengths behind Kamicia: also ran very well earlier when 2 lengths third of eight to Card Player in £3,100 event at Newmarket in August: will probably stay 1½m: acts on any going. *R. Boss.*

OLYMPIAD 3 b.c. Charlottown 127–Amphora 110 (Ragusa 137) [1975 8g **72** 1976 11f 16g⁵ 14fg² 14fg⁴ 12fg] rangy colt: distinctly one paced and should be suited by 2m, although ran poorly only attempt at trip so far: ran best race when blinkered: pulled up (possibly lame) on final appearance: sold to M. Tate 600 gns Ascot October Sales. *J. Nelson.*

OLYMPIC VISUALISE 2 b.f. Northfields–Visualise 115 (Premonition 130) **84** [1976 6g 5v³ 6s² 7s² 6s⁵] strong filly: half-sister to fair sprinter Our Polly (by Henry the Seventh): dam smart winner over 5f and 6f at 2 yrs but disappointed afterwards: placed in end-of-season maiden races, on final occasion finishing 3 lengths second of 20 to Brightly at Newmarket in October: will stay 1m: acts on heavy going. *R. Jarvis.*

OMI 2 b.f. Hopeful Venture 125–Queens Port (Umberto 118) [1976 6d 7s] — sister to a poor animal and half-sister to two winners abroad: 600 gns yearling: dam never ran: in rear in end-of-season maiden races at Newmarket, finishing seventeenth of 19 to Lady Oriana on second occasion. *J. Powney.*

OMNIA 3 ch.f. Hill Clown–You All 99 (Alcide 136) [1976 10.5fg⁶ **80** 12f² 12.3f* 12fg 14g²] rangy filly: second foal: dam won at 1m and stayed at least 13f: won nine-runner maiden race at Newcastle in August gamely by a neck from Shuwaiman, the pair finishing clear of seven others: battled on most courageously when ¾-length second to Wounded Knee in minor race at York the following month: broke down on this occasion and was subsequently retired: stayed 1¾m: acted on firm going: sold 3,400 gns Newmarket December Sales. *N. Murless.*

ON COURSE 3 gr.g. Roan Rocket 128–Crescent Dart 103 (Sing Sing 134) **72** [1975 N.R. 1976 8fg⁵ 8f² 10fg² 10g⁵ 10g³] lengthy gelding: second foal: half-brother to Double Dart (by Songedor), a smart and consistent winner over 5f and 6f at 2 yrs: dam a very genuine sprinter: quite a moderate maiden: stays 1¼m well. *R. Hern.*

ONEDIN LINE 4 b.f. Cumshaw 111–Above the Line 86 (Above Suspicion 127) **43** [1974 5g 5fg⁴ 5f² 5s 6g 8s 8v 1975 8f 8.3s³ 7g⁴ 10fg² 10g 8g⁵ 10g⁴ 10d* 1976 10.1fg³ 10f 10g* 10.1fg⁴ 10h* 10v²] small filly: plater: winner at Leicester in May (bought in 675 gns) and Brighton in August (no bid): stays 1¼m: acts on any going: best in blinkers. *J. Benstead.*

ONE GLANCE 3 b.f. Sovereign Gleam 117–Sola (Golden Cloud) [1975 6fg 7f⁴ **69** 1976 8fg⁴ 7g 8fg* 7g³ 9g 8f² 8f 8.2s] quite an attractive filly: apprentice ridden, won eight-runner maiden race at Brighton in May comfortably by 4 lengths from Lady Jim: ran best subsequent race when runner-up to comfortable winner Kallissima in handicap on same course in August: stays 1m: wears blinkers: dwelt and had a poor run on final start. *R. Armstrong.*

ONES MINE 4 b.f. Compensation 127–La Music (Taboun 128 or Gilles de Retz 132) [1974 5h⁶ 6f⁴ 5.9fg 7g³ 7d 8v 1975 N.R. 1976 8g⁵ 10.1fg] moderate plater: stays 1m. *J. Thorne.* **40**

ONLY A MONKEY 6 b.g. Great Nephew 126–Belthorpe (Tanerko 134) [1974 11.7f 12g* 14.7f⁶ 13.1g* 14g⁶ 16.5g* 14s² 15.5s² 16.9s* 1975 16s 18f⁴ 15g³ 11.7f² 13g³ 1976 16.1d⁴] lengthy gelding: fair handicapper (rated 86) in 1975: made only one appearance at 6 yrs: stays well: acts on any going: suitable mount for an apprentice. *Lady Herries.* **—**

ONLY A PLUMBER 2 gr.c. Goldhill 125–Grey Parrot (Abernant 142) [1976 5fg 5g⁶ 5fg* 6fg 6fg⁶ 7s] lengthy colt: won three-runner seller at Nottingham in April all out by 1½ lengths from slow-starting Ma Foi: stays well: not certain to stay 7f: sold 575 gns Ascot December Sales. *P. Ashworth.* **69**

ONLY CHILD 4 br.f. Foggy Bell 108–Miss Adventure 79 (Tarqogan 125) [1974 5f⁵ 5f⁶ 5g⁴ 5f⁴ 1975 6f 8h⁶ 5fg 5d³ 6fg* 5f⁵ 5f⁴ 7f⁶ 7g³ 7fg⁶ 6g 1976 6g 7fg 5f 5f] compact, well-made filly: seems to act up to 7f: seems to act on any going: was tried in blinkers as a 2-y-o: suitable mount for an apprentice. *Denys Smith.*

ONLY FOR YOU 2 ch.f. Runnymede 123–Alice (Parthia 132) [1976 5g 5fg 5f 6d 6s² 5v] small, unfurnished filly: four lengths second of 17 to Stand On in seller at Doncaster in October: stays 6f: acts on soft going: blinkered last two outings: sold 250 gns Ascot November Sales. *I. Walker.* **66**

ON MY WAY 6 b.h. Laugh Aloud–Gracious Me (Tulyar 134) [1974 12v* 12.5g³ 12g³ 13g² 12.5g² 13.5g 10g* 12s 1975 10v² 12g³ 13v² 12.5g³ 12f⁴ 14.5g⁴ 12s² 12fg³ 1976 11s² 12s* 12s²] good sort of horse: didn't race until the autumn as a six-year-old but showed he had lost none of his dash, running excellent races when second in Prix Foy at Longchamp in September (beaten a head by Kasteel), winning Prix du Conseil de Paris on same course the following month (beat Beau Buck a length) and when 10 lengths second to Youth in Washington D.C. International at Laurel in November (hampered final bend but wouldn't have beaten winner): said by trainer to have been struck into when well beaten in Prix de l'Arc de Triomphe won by Ivanjica on only other start: best form at 1½m: acts on any going: very genuine and consistent. *N. Pelat, France.* **125**

ON SIGHT 3 ch.c. On Your Mark 125–Bon Mirage (Miralgo 130) [1975 5.9f 6g 7g 1976 8g³ 10f⁶ 10.8f³ 10fg⁶ 10.4s² 10g] rangy colt: stays 11f: evidently acts on any going: ran poorly when blinkered on final outing (June) and was sold 270 gns Doncaster October Sales. *H. Williams.* **68**

ON THE TURN 5 ch.m. Manacle 123–Walnut 81 (Rustam 127) [1974 5f* 5g⁴ 5g² 5fg⁵ 5d⁵ 5g 1975 5fg 5g⁴ 5g⁴ 5f 5f⁴ 5g 5f 5g 1976 5f⁶ 7g 5.9g 7f 5fg²] lightly-built mare: ran by far her best race at 5 yrs on final appearance: best at 5f: acts on firm going: has been tried in blinkers, including on penultimate outing in 1975. *B. Lunness.* **66**

ONWARD TAROO 6 b.h. Le Levanstell 122–Shushoe (Whitehall 116) [1974 10d* 14g* 12fg* 14fg⁵ 13s 13s³ 1975 12s⁴ 14.7f³ 14fg 12g² 14g* 1976 13s³ 18.4s³ 10f⁴ 10f⁴ 13g⁵ 12f] lengthy, rangy Irish horse: useful handicapper: made two appearances in this country in 1976, running well on first of them when 4½ lengths third of 15 to John Cherry in Ladbroke Chester Cup at Chester in May on second outing: last of five to Alverton in Bogside Cup at Ayr in September on penultimate start (had stiffish task at weights): stays well: acts on any going: sometimes wears blinkers. *P. Prendergast, Ireland.* **93**

ONWARD TSUBAME 5 b.h. Continuation 120–Darrigle (Vilmoray 126) [1974 8g 8g 6g³ 6g⁵ 7.2s 6s 8v 1975 13.8g*, 11fg⁵ 12.2f* 13f⁴ 12fg* 12g³ 13.8fg 12f³ 12g 1976 13g 12d⁴ 12.2f* 12.2d 12f⁵ 13.8f⁶ 12.2f 12g* 10g* 13f² 12s⁴] well-made individual: goes well at Catterick, and won on that course in April by a length from Halsall: ran moderately in his races in this country afterwards but won twice at Jersey (total value £1,600) in August: stays well: probably acts on any going: tried in blinkers at 2 yrs: front runner: not much of a battler: sold 1,000 gns Newmarket Autumn Sales. *F. Carr.* **60**

ON YOUR KNEES 2 b.c. On Your Mark 125–Orgy (Gilles de Retz 132) [1976 5fg 5gg³ 5fg² 5f* 5.9s³ 5s⁴ 5d²] compact colt: fourth foal: 480 gns yearling: dam won over 7f at 2 yrs in France: having first race for four months, showed improved form to win 13-runner maiden race at Bath in September by ¾ length **95**

521

from Sharpway: good second to Self Portrait in nursery at Newmarket the following month: will stay 7f: acts on any going. *D. Hanley.*

OPAL FANCY 2 b.f. Alcide 136 or Kibenka 119–Polinova 90 (Polic 126) [1976   **83** 6g 6d6] smallish, strong filly: putative sister to three winners, including fairly useful 1974 2-y-o 5f winner Opalenka: 920 gns yearling: dam 5f sprinter: unquoted, finished most creditable 4 lengths sixth of 25 to Caerdeon Line in maiden race at Newmarket in October: should win a race. *H. Collingridge.*

OPEN DOORS 4 ch.c. Quisling 117–Open Display (Pindari 124) [1974 5g 6g   — 1975 8s2 8g* 8.2g5 9fg4 11f2 11g6 12d 12g2 1976 12g6] tall colt: formerly quite a moderate handicapper: virtually pulled up only appearance at 4 yrs: stays 1½m: acts on any going. *F. Carr.*

OPEN SAFE 2 b.g. Burglar 128–Sweet Surprise 95 (Jolly Jet 111) [1976 5.3s5   **77** 5.9s4] first foal: dam won over 7f at 2 yrs: put up easily better effort when just over a length fourth of 18 to Fear Naught in maiden race at Wolverhampton in October: will probably stay 7f. *R. Price.*

OPIUM QUEEN 2 b.f. King's Troop 118–Poppy Time 77 (Hook Money 124)   **82** [1976 5f4 5f3 5g3 5d 5g3 5f 5g] compact filly: third produce: 2,500 gns yearling: dam stayed 1m: having first run for nearly three months, put up easily best effort when 3½ lengths third of 11 to Mrs McArdy in maiden race at Newcastle in August: will be better suited by 6f+. *J. Vickers.*

OPPRESSOR 2 gr.c. Tyrant–Shoofly 83 (Skymaster 126) [1976 5g 5f3 5g2   **80** 5fg 6h* 6f6 5fg 5f6 6f] tall, close-coupled colt: half-brother to 3-y-o middle-distance winner Saturnus (by Dike) and useful sprinter Shuffling (by St Chad) and to a winner in South Africa: 1,500 gns foal and resold 3,300 gns yearling: dam maiden sprinter: made all to win 15-runner maiden race at Chepstow in June by 3 lengths from East Plaistow: well suited by 6f: acts on hard going: lost chance by being bumped at start when blinkered seventh outing. *G. Hunter.*

OPTIMISTIC VIEW 5 b.g. Hopeful Venture 125–Cleobella (Panorama) [1974   — 10f3 1975 9s 1976 8fg 12.5v] of little account. *W. A. Stephenson.*

OPTIQUALITY 2 b.g. Decoy Boy 129–Lucky Pigeon (The Mongoose 108)   **72** [1976 5g 6f 8f5 8d6 7g 8d4] neat gelding: plater: blinkered first time, ran best race when 2½ lengths fourth of 14 to subsequently-disqualified East Plaistow in £1,400 event at Newmarket in October: stays 1m: acts on a soft surface. *P. Haslam.*

ORANGE BAY 4 b.c. Canisbay 120–Orange Triumph (Molvedo 137) [1974 7s*   **129** 7.5s* 7.5s2 1975 10g2 10g* 12s* 12v2 12g3 11.7fg* 1976 9fg3 12fg* 12f* 12g3 12v]

The Italian Derby winner Orange Bay, brought from Italy in the summer of 1975 to join Peter Walwyn's stable, earned a high reputation in this country as a four-year-old and showed himself to be a very good horse at a mile and a half. He won the Jockey Club Stakes at Newmarket and the Hardwicke Stakes at Royal Ascot and came a close third to Pawneese and Bruni in the King George VI and Queen Elizabeth Diamond Stakes, England's most important weight-for-age race for three-year-olds and upwards.

Orange Bay seemed to take some time to become acclimatised to English conditions and Walwyn gave him only one outing as a three-year-old, in a small race at Windsor in September, before putting him away for the winter. It was evident from Orange Bay's appearance in his early races as a four-year-old that he had done extremely well. The reader has only to compare the photograph of Orange Bay in *Racehorses of 1975* with the one reproduced with this commentary to see the tremendous physical development that Orange Bay made from three to four. He is now tall and handsome, every inch a high-class racehorse in appearance and one of the best-looking individuals in training; he was turned out in magnificent fettle each time we saw him.

Orange Bay was beaten by the smart four-year-olds Chil the Kite and Dominion in his first race as a four-year-old, the Earl of Sefton Stakes at Newmarket in April, giving weight away over a distance, odds short to show him to best advantage. Orange Bay won his next two races, both of them over a mile and a half, in courageous style. His narrow victory in the Jockey Club Stakes over Libra's Rib and Dakota, both of whom were in receipt of 7 lb, put Orange Bay on the map as one of the leading middle-distance performers in England. Orange Bay's trainer was reported to have said that the slow early pace at Newmarket did not suit his charge and with the heat on throughout he would probably have won more easily. We share the view that, at a mile and a half at

Jockey Club Stakes, Newmarket—Orange Bay holds off Libra's Rib, the blinkered Dakota and Fool's Mate

any rate, the stronger the gallop the better it suits Orange Bay. If Orange Bay has a chink in his armour it is that against good opposition he lacks finishing speed. He is by no means a one-pacer but he is not a horse that can be jumped from second gear to top in a matter of strides. The shorter the distance of the race and the better the class of horse opposing him the more important it is for Orange Bay that there should be a strong gallop from pillar to post.

In view of Walwyn's pronouncement after the Jockey Club Stakes it might have been expected that Orange Bay would be provided with a pacemaker in his next race, the Hardwicke Stakes, for which only five runners turned out. However, Orange Bay's trainer perhaps felt that a strong gallop would suit the odds-on favourite Bruni even better than Orange Bay. Bruni's best form before Royal Ascot had been at a mile and three quarters. In fact the fast pace set from the end of the first furlong to the half-mile marker by the Coronation Cup runner-up Libra's Rib and for the rest of the way by Orange Bay himself played a decisive part in Orange Bay's victory. Bruni, who gave away several lengths at the start, overhauled Orange Bay inside the final furlong but the effort of making up so much ground in a strongly-run race proved too much for him and he slowed near the line, enabling Orange Bay, who stuck to his guns admirably, to recover the lead in the shadow of the winning post. The pair were four lengths clear of Libra's Rib who brought home the rest of the field.

The King George VI and Queen Elizabeth Diamond Stakes is almost always run at a cracking pace and, with an established front runner like Pawneese in the field, there was no danger of a slow gallop in the race in 1976. It couldn't have been run better to suit Orange Bay and he ran superbly to finish third, beaten a length and a short head by Pawneese and Bruni, with the winners of the French Derby and the Irish Sweeps Derby among those behind. Only Bruni finished stronger than Orange Bay and both were making ground on Pawneese near the finish. Orange Bay's rider reported that his mount had been hampered by the French Derby winner Youth on the last bend. We must confess that this wasn't evident to our representatives on the course and, having run our copy of the film through several times, we can assure the reader that if Orange Bay met with interference it was only slight and was certainly not serious enough to have made the difference between Orange Bay's winning and losing. With this race the curtain effectively came down on Orange Bay's four-year-old career. After running deplorably in the Grosser Preis von Baden at Baden-Baden in September he wasn't seen out again. We were not at Baden-Baden so we don't know exactly what happened to Orange Bay; we understand, however, that his connections attribute Orange Bay's defeat to his failure to act on the very heavy ground. In this connection it is worth noting that Orange Bay was given a full preparation for the Prix de l'Arc de Triomphe but missed the race reportedly because the going was soft.

Looking back at Orange Bay's performances in Italy there is plenty of evidence that he can handle soft ground. As a two-year-old he ran on nothing else in public and ended the season rated close behind Start and Bolkonski in the Italian equivalent of the Free Handicap. Orange Bay was beaten only once in three starts at two and was widely considered an unlucky loser of the Gran Criterium in which he was beaten a head by Start after getting away tardily and being carried wide on the final turn. As a three-year-old Orange Bay's win on soft going in the Derby Italiano, for which he was odds on against home-trained opposition, was preceded by a two-length success over the English three-year-old Hobnob in the Premio Emanuele Filiberto, an important ten-furlong race. Hobnob won the Dante Stakes at York afterwards and showed other smart form during the season. After the Derby Italiano, in which only Pierre Curie finished within half a dozen lengths of Orange Bay, Orange Bay was placed in the Gran Premio d'Italia and the Gran Premio di Milano before being transferred from M. Benetti's stable. In the Gran Premio di Milano Orange Bay was about two lengths behind the German-trained Star Appeal who went on to take the Eclipse Stakes and the Prix de l'Arc de Triomphe.

Orange Bay is from the last crop sired in England by the Eclipse winner Canisbay before he was sent to stand in Italy. Orange Bay is the second foal of Orange Triumph who ran unplaced in a maiden race at Chester as a two-year-old on her only start. Her first and third foals are the fillies Tudor Trophy (by Henry the Seventh) and Tricy (by No Mercy), both winners in Italy. Orange Bay's grandam Orange won five races and bred four winners in Italy, including

Hardwicke Stakes, Ascot—touch and go between Orange Bay and Bruni. Libra's Rib is third

Dr Carlo Vittadini's "Orange Bay"

the smart stayer Ogaden and Oliveira, the dam of Orsa Maggiore, one of the best racemares bred in Italy in recent years. Orange was later brought to England where, after Orange Triumph, she bred the slow maiden Oratch who has since been successful at stud in Italy where she became the dam of Ovac, the winner of the Premio Parioli (Italian Two Thousand Guineas) in 1976. The third dam Fior d'Orchidea won the Oaks d'Italia and produced eight winners at stud including Oise, the winner of fifteen races including the Gran Premio di Milano, and Orvieto, the winner of the Gran Criterium.

Orange Bay (b.c. 1972)	Canisbay (ch 1961)	Doutelle (ch 1954)	Prince Chevalier
			Above Board
		Stroma (ch 1955)	Luminary
			Whoa Emma
	Orange Triumph (br 1965)	Molvedo (br 1958)	Ribot
			Maggi lina
		Orange (br 1954)	Dante
			Fior d'Orchidea

In view of Orange Bay's failure in Germany and his subsequent absence from the field for the Prix de l'Arc, any worthwhile assessment of his prospects as a five-year-old must wait until after his reappearance. However, if he can reproduce the form he showed in the King George VI and Queen Elizabeth Diamond Stakes there is no doubt he will again be a force to be reckoned with in the big races. It is even possible that he will turn out a better horse in 1977. His connections have been extremely patient with him and he has not had a lot of racing, which is all to the good so far as his future is concerned. It is on the cards that a mile and a half is not the limit of his stamina. However, if, as seems most probable, he is campaigned again at middle distances we should like to see him provided with a good pacemaker to ensure that his races are run at a strong enough gallop to suit him. *P. Walwyn.*

ORANGE GIN 3 ch.g. Virginia Boy 106–Bright Idea (Never Say Die 137) [1975 **66**
6fg⁴ 6fg 8.2g⁶ 8.2d 8g 8f 8v² 1976 10f 7fg 8g⁴ 11g² 9f* 10.1fg 10g 8s²] strong,
well-made gelding: narrow winner of maiden event at Wolverhampton in
August from Tzi-Tzi Girl: effective at 1m to 11f: acts on any going: wears
blinkers nowadays. *A. Corbett.*

ORBITMAN 3 ch.c. Skymaster 126–Gambola 105 (Exbury 138) [1975 5.1g⁶ **76**
8g 7fg* 1976 8fg 7d⁶ 7fg] robust colt: won maiden race at Teesside as a
2-y-o: well beaten at 3 yrs but had stiff tasks: would have stayed 1m: dead.
H. Cecil.

ORCHESTRA 2 ch.c. Tudor Music 131–Golden Moss 91 (Sheshoon 132) [1976 **114**
8g² 8d* 8s³] Irish colt: third live foal: dam middle-distance winner in Ireland:
14/1 when winning six-runner Beresford Stakes at the Curragh in October by
2 lengths from 4/1-on shot Artaius: put up another very useful effort when
6 lengths third of six to Sporting Yankee in William Hill Futurity Stakes at
Doncaster a week later: stays 1m well and will probably get further: acts on
soft going. *J. Oxx, Ireland.*

ORCHID MISS 2 b.f. Herbager 136–Stylish (Bold Ruler) [1976 6d⁴ 6.5g³ 7d² **113**
8s³ 8s] American-bred French filly: dam, who won three times at up to 6f at
3 yrs, is sister to two stakes winners and is daughter of half-sister to First Landing
and Hill Prince: still a maiden but finished third in two strongly-contested
fillies races, finishing 5 lengths behind Virgin in Prix du Calvados at Deauville
in August and 3¾ lengths behind Kamicia after starting none too well in Criterium
des Pouliches at Longchamp in October: favourite for 13-runner Prix des
Reservoirs at Longchamp later in October but could finish only eighth behind
Edinburgh: will stay at least 1¼m: acts on soft going. *F. Boutin, France.*

ORIENTAL ROCKET 2 ch.c. Roan Rocket 128–Zama Lake 68 (Mossborough **104**
126) [1976 7g⁵ 7fg* 7g³ 8g⁶ 7.3v] well-made colt: brother to 3-y-o 9f winner
Nuns Fifteen and fair middle-distance performer Matopo: dam placed over 13f:
won 18-runner maiden race at Newbury in August by ½ length: ran very well
when 4½ lengths third of 10 to Avgerinos in Intercraft Solario Stakes at Sandown
and when sixth to Bona-Mia in nursery at Newmarket, both in September,
but was well beaten in Horris Hill Stakes at Newbury the following month:
will stay middle distances: acts on a firm surface. *G. Smyth.*

ORIENTAL SLIPPER 5 b.m. Tycoon II–Panasolar (Solar Slipper 131) [1974 **59**
7f⁶ 8f⁴ 7f 10.1fg 11.7g 12.2fg⁶ 13g⁶ 1975 7s* 8f 8.3f⁴ 7f³ 8.2g* 8.3fg 8f³ 7g⁴
1976 7fg 7f⁵ 8fg² 7fg⁶ 8fg 7f³ 8.3fg* 8f²] smallish, strong mare: modest selling
handicapper: bought in 760 gns after winning at Windsor in July: best form
at up to 1m: acts on any going: sometimes wears blinkers and did so at Windsor:
suitable mount for an apprentice. *M. McCourt.*

ORIENTAL STAR 3 b.f. Falcon 131–Coming-of-Age 93 (Majority Blue 126) **94**
[1975 5d 5f* 1976 6fg² 6g 6fg² 7d² 7fg* 7fg⁴ 8g* 7fg* 9f 8g² 10g] big, lengthy
filly: quite a useful handicapper: in good form most of season and won at Doncaster (relegated to second for hampering runner-up, but was definitely winner
on merit), Leicester, Kempton and Goodwood: defied a 7-lb penalty on last-
named course in July, beating Star Walk gamely by a short head: stays 1m
(ran poorly over 1¼m): acts on a firm and a soft surface: very game and consistent:
twice slowly into stride. *M. Stoute.*

ORIENT BOY 2 br.c. Realm 129–Flapperette 92 (Hardicanute 130) [1976 **74**
5g 6fg⁶ 5f⁴ 5g⁴ 6f⁴ 6g³ 6fg 6d] strong colt: first foal: 6,000 gns yearling: dam,
half-sister to two very useful animals, won from 6f to 1m: quite a moderate colt:
will probably stay 7f. *M. Masson.*

ORMA 2 ch.f. Double Jump 131–Fran § (Acropolis 132) [1976 6g 6s⁶ 7v⁵] —
fair sort: half-sister to three winners, notably top-class sprinter Tudor Music
(by Tudor Melody): 11,500 gns foal: dam half-sister to High Top's dam Camanae
and Paulista's dam Petite Marmite: beaten some way in minor events at Pontefract and Teesside in October on last two outings. *M. Jarvis.*

ORMELEY 3 b.c. Crepello 136–Parmelia 118 (Ballymoss 136) [1975 6f 8fg* **102**
8s⁶ 7fg⁶ 10g³ 12.3d² 12fg⁴ 16f³ 15g 20.9fg⁵] very attractive, shapely colt:
good mover: in frame in Classic Trial at Sandown (third to Riboboy), Chester
Vase (second to Old Bill), Predominate Stakes at Goodwood and Queen's Vase at
Royal Ascot: 4 lengths third to General Ironside in last-named race: somewhat
disappointing last two outings, although had plenty on at weights: seemed to
find 2m his limit: appeared to act on any going: sometimes wore blinkers but
did as well without: sold 26,000 gns Newmarket December Sales for export to
Australia as a stallion. *P. Walwyn.*

ORMONDE PRINCESS 2 gr.f. Runnymede 123–Try Try Again 86 (King's —
Bench 132) [1976 5f 5f 7fg] small filly: poor plater. *W. Gray.*

ORNAMENTAL NIGHT 3 ch.c. Crocket 130–Queen of Twilight 107 (Off Key **75**
121 or Twilight Alley 133) [1975 N.R. 1976 7fg 10.1fg 8g 10s²] big boat of
a horse: first foal: 480 gns yearling: dam won at up to 1¾m, including Jockey
Club Stakes: showed first sign of ability when 3 lengths second of 12 to Estate
Agent in minor event at Teesside in November: will stay further than 1¼m.
W. Holden.

ORPHEAN 2 b.c. Double Jump 131–Skye Gem (Highland Melody 112) [1976 **89** d
5f* 5f* 5fg³ 5f³ 6v 6s⁶] lengthy, dipped-backed colt: first foal: dam ran only
once: well-backed favourite when winning maiden race at Nottingham and
minor event at Chepstow, both in April, on latter course beating Aeras by
¾ length: close-up third in minor events at Windsor the following month, finishing
behind Aeras each time: not seen out again until October and ran poorly in
sellers on his return: should stay 6f: possibly unsuited by soft going but seems
to have deteriorated: sold 700 gns Ascot December Sales. *R. Akehurst.*

OSCARS PRIDE 2 b.c. Paul Roy–Dee Time (Langton Heath 97) [1976 6g 9s] —
tailed-off last on both outings and is probably useless. *W. Charles.*

OSIRIS 2 b.c. Crepello 136–Magic Flute 124 (Tudor Melody 129) [1976 8g⁵ **85**
7g⁶] big, rangy colt: second foal: closely related to very useful middle-distance
3-y-o Lost Chord (by Busted): dam won Cheveley Park Stakes and was very
smart at up to 1m: showed ability in quite valuable events won by Royal Plume
at York and Ascot in September, being beaten about 8 lengths each time after
being prominent much of way: should win in the north. *E. Weymes.*

OSLO 3 b.c. Right Tack 131–Grischuna 103 (Ratification 129) [1975 6g 1976 **57**
6f 7g⁴ 13.1s³ 15.5s² 12v³ 16v⁶] leggy ex-Irish colt: half-brother to four winners,
including smart middle-distance stayer Chicago (by Fidalgo) and fairly useful
6f to 1½m winner Engadina (by Alcide): dam stayed 1m, and is half-sister to
Sovereign Path: showed ability, on fourth outing going down by a short head
to Past History in 12-runner maiden race at Folkestone in October: suited by
a good test of stamina: acts on soft going. *R. Hannon.*

OSSULTON 3 b.g. Tower Walk 130–Great Joy (Kythnos 126) [1975 7g 6fg **62**
8s 8.2g⁴ 1976 12.2g⁴ 10f 9g 12.2f³ 9g² 8.2d⁴ 11f³ 11g² 11f* 10f³] well-made
gelding: usually found one or two too good for him but managed to pick up a
moderate maiden race at Hamilton in July: has yet to show conclusively that
he stays 1½m: possibly unsuited by a soft surface: blinkered on fifth and sixth
outings, running creditably on first occasion but poorly on second. *K. Payne.*

OTTERDEN 2 br.f. Crooner 119–Orseniga 97 (Privy Councillor 125) [1976 —
5f⁶] second foal: 320 gns yearling: dam stayed at least 13f: remote last of six
to Wysboy in £1,000 event at Folkestone in May. *A. Neaves.*

OUDALIA 3 ch.f. Gala Performance–Ouda 111 (Traffic) [1975 5.9f* 6fg³ 6f³ **93**
6fg³ 6g* 1976 8fg 7g⁵ 6f⁵ 5.3f⁵ 6h² 6d* 6g⁴ 6d² 6v²] small filly: took some
time to find her form but was quite useful when she did, and spreadeagled her
field when winning 13-runner handicap at Yarmouth in September by 8 lengths
from Path of Gold: best at sprint distances: acted on any going but was well
suited by a soft surface: stud. *P. Walwyn.*

OUI MONSIEUR 2 b.g. Levanter 121–Melody Call 55 (Tudor Melody 129) **66**
[1976 7g⁵ 6g⁵ 8s⁶] quite attractive, lightly-made gelding: half-brother to four
minor winners: dam won 9f seller: ran promisingly in all races, finishing sixth
of 27 to Sporting Yankee in maiden event at Newmarket in October: will stay
further than 1m. *T. Gosling.*

OUR ANNIVERSARY 3 b.c. Irish Ball 127–Dorbe 80 (Tudor Melody 129) **88**
[1975 5g 8g 7g⁴ 7.6g⁴ 1976 8f⁶ 8.5fg³ 10fg* 12g 12fg³ 10.1fg 10d⁶] useful-
looking colt: won 11-runner maiden race at Salisbury in May by 1½ lengths
from Christchurch: had stiffish tasks in his subsequent races but ran creditably
when third of five to Sir Montagu in handicap at Salisbury in June: stays 1½m:
ran well in blinkers on final outing at 2 yrs. *R. Smyth.*

OUR BOOMERANG 2 ch.c. Lorenzaccio 130–Flash of Light 78 (Charlottesville —
135) [1976 8d] fair sort: third foal: 4,000 gns yearling: dam won over 1½m,
and is half-sister to Parthia: 20/1 when behind in 17-runner maiden race won by
Ad Lib Ra at Newbury in September. *J. Hill.*

OUR CHARLIE 4 br.c. Crossing The T–Tanglesum 81 (Entanglement 118) **99**
[1974 5f⁵ 5fg* 5.3g³ 1975 6d 6f* 6f³ 6d⁴ 5.6g⁶ 6d 5d 1976 6f⁶ 6fg⁵ 6f 7d⁵ 6g⁴]
big, useful sort: useful handicapper on his day: ran his best races at 4 yrs on

last two outings, on second of them finishing strongly when 3 lengths fourth of 11 to Shuffling at Newmarket in September: stays 7f: appears to act on any going: exported to America. *J. Dunlop.*

OUR EMILIE   3 b.f. The Brianstan 128–Stepney 83 (Lucky Brief 128)   [1975   — 5f 6g 6d⁶ 8v 5v   1976 8.3fg⁶]   poor plater: sold 420 gns Ascot August Sales. *J. Fitzgerald.*

OUR FRIEND   5 ch.g. Be Friendly 130–Vron 91 (Anwar 120)   [1974 7f⁵ 7.6g   — 10g⁵ 12g⁵ 16v*   1975 N.R.   1976 16f 14fg 17.7f]   tall, good-bodied gelding: tailed off both completed outings in 1976: refused to race and took no part on intended second appearance: stays well: acts on heavy going: tried in blinkers at 2 yrs: wears bandages. *P. Mitchell.*

OUR JADE   2 br.f. Forlorn River 124–Alice in Wonderland 78 (Worden II 129)   **56** [1976 5fg⁵ 5g 5fg 5fg]   lightly-built, unfurnished filly: struck us as lacking scope when fifth to Karella at Leicester in March and finished last on all subsequent appearances: started slowly when blinkered final outing: trained by P. Ashworth on first appearance. *A. Jarvis.*

OUR JANE   3 b. or br.f. Alloway Lad 103–Perelada 77 (Ben Hawke 94)   [1975   — N.R.   1976 11f 10g]   second foal: dam won over 5f: well beaten in maiden race and seller in Scotland in the autumn. *N. Angus.*

OUR JIMMY (U.S.A.)   2 br.c. Tom Rolfe–Flitter Flutter (Cohoes)   [1976 5g⁴   **116** 5g² 6fg* 6fg* 7g² 7fg⁵ 7f⁵ 7g⁴ 6d* 6d* 6v² 7v³]
    The self-evident fact about Our Jimmy is that as a two-year-old he was best at six furlongs on a yielding surface, and for his most noteworthy achievements in a busy season one has to look no further than his ninth, tenth and eleventh appearances, when he gained a splendid win under top weight of 9-0 in the Golden Gates Nursery at Ascot, gave Accelerate, from the powerful Walwyn stable, a stone and a half-length beating in the Marston Moor Stakes at York, and ran Hyver Hill, who was receiving 4 lb, to three quarters of a length in the Cottesmore Stakes at Leicester, in which race the speedy filly Mofida was ten lengths adrift in third place. This defeat by Hyver Hill marked the only occasion Our Jimmy was beaten at six furlongs in five races, as earlier in the season he had scored over the distance in maiden company at Newbury and in the Chesters Stakes at Newcastle, Crown Bowler running second to him in the latter event.
    But although Our Jimmy is well suited by a yielding surface, such conditions work against him when his stamina is stretched, and of his many unsuccessful attempts at seven furlongs, easily his least meritorious performance was his third on heavy going to Imperial Guard and the newcomer Atlantic Bridge in the Plaistow Stakes at Lingfield in November on his final appearance. Waited with, Our Jimmy looked to be going easily just in behind the leaders for most of the race, but there was no zip in his effort when he was asked to make his challenge, and no sooner had he got to grips with Imperial Guard, just inside the last furlong, than he dropped away again. He was beaten four lengths. This performance apart, Our Jimmy's form at seven furlongs was reasonable without being anything like as good as the best of his form at six

Chesters Stakes, Newcastle—Our Jimmy is pursued by Crown Bowler

furlongs. For instance, when fifth in the Fitzroy House Stakes at Newmarket in August on his sixth appearance, he was beaten only two and a half lengths by Card Player, to whom he was conceding 8 lb—by no means a bad effort, and at the weights he wasn't so far as all that off confirming his Chesters Stakes form with Crown Bowler, who finished second. It is not impossible that Our Jimmy will manage seven furlongs well enough to win over the distance as a three-year-old, but most unlikely that he will stay further.

Our Jimmy (U.S.A.) (br.c. 1974)	Tom Rolfe (b 1962)	Ribot (b 1952)	Tenerani
			Romanella
		Pocahontas II (br 1955)	Roman
			How
	Flitter Flutter (br 1966)	Cohoes (b 1954)	Mahmoud
			Belle of Troy
		Ellerslie (br 1954)	Nasrullah
			Effie B

An attractive colt, who cost 35,000 dollars as a yearling, Our Jimmy is a half-brother to three winners, of whom one, the Olden Times filly Chappelle Blanche, was successful in this country, winning a maiden event over six furlongs at Goodwood as a three-year-old. The dam Flitter Flutter stayed a mile, and as a son of the Preakness Stakes winner Tom Rolfe, Our Jimmy should, on the evidence of his breeding, do so too. But we are satisfied that Our Jimmy hasn't nearly so much stamina in him as his breeding suggests, and it is over six furlongs that we expect to see him run his best races. He is tough, genuine and consistent. *G. Harwood.*

OUR MANNY 7 b.g. Faberge II 121–Honeymoon (Honeyway 125) [1974 101 12g 12fg⁴ 12g³ 12g² 12g² 12g³ 1975 10s² 12g* 11fg³ 12fg 12f* 12g* 12f* 12fg* 14d² 12g⁶ 1976 12f 12f² 11.1g³ 12fg³] smart handicapper (rated 116) at 6 yrs: didn't run up to his best in 1976, although wasn't disgraced when second to Swell Fellow in minor event at Brighton in May and when third to Belper on same course the following month: stays 1¾m: acts on soft ground but is very well suited by firm: has worn blinkers: genuine and consistent: suited by waiting tactics. *G. Harwood.*

OUR PRIMROSE 2 b.f. Caliban 123–Kilula 93 (Nearula 132) [1976 5s 6fg 67 6f³ 8fg 6s 5s] shapely filly: only plating class: should stay 1m. *M. W. Easterby.*

OUR SHARON 2 br.f. Linacre 133–Queen Ursula 65 (Henry the Seventh 125) — [1976 7fg 7g] second reported foal: half-sister to a winner in Italy by Caspoggio: dam placed at up to 1¼m: in rear in September in maiden race at Salisbury (started slowly) and minor event at Lingfield (last of 19). *Mrs D. Oughton.*

OUR SONG 4 ch.f. Song 132–Hornton Grange 101 (Hornbeam 130) [1974 N.R. 70 1975 5v³ 5s⁵ 6f 5.8f⁴ 6fg² 5g⁶ 5.9g⁴ 5g 6g* 1976 6v* 6g³ 6g² 8f⁴ 6v⁶ 7v* 7v] lengthy filly: quite a moderate handicapper: successful at Hamilton in April and at Teesside in October: probably stays 1m: seems to act on any going but goes well in the mud: ran poorly when tried in blinkers: suitable mount for an apprentice. *Sir Mark Prescott.*

OUR SWALLOW 3 b.c. Le Levanstell 122–Our Girl 95 (Supreme Court 135) 104 [1975 7g 8d 8g⁶ 1976 9f* 10g⁵ 12fg* 16fg* 12fg³] good-looking colt: won maiden race at Teesside and handicaps at Thirsk and Lingfield (comfortably by ½ length from Assured, the pair finishing clear): creditable third to Bright Finish in well-contested minor event at Newmarket in July on final outing: suited by a test of stamina: acts well on a firm surface: was improving with racing but fetched only 1,700 gns when sold out of training at Newmarket Autumn Sales. *M. Jarvis.*

OUR SWANEE 5 gr.m. My Swanee 122–Safety Belt (Skymaster 126) [1974 — 6s 1975 5d 8f 1976 8g⁵ 8g 8f 5f 5f 8v] small mare: poor plater: best form at 5f: acts on firm going: has worn blinkers. *P. Poston.*

OUR TRAVELLING MAN 2 ch.c. Royben 125–Sombrilla (Big Game) [1976 81 5fg 5g 5g⁵ 6g* 6f⁴ 6fg³ 6d] lengthy, good-quartered colt: half-brother to three winners, including fair 1¼m winner Solar Flare (by Klairon): 650 gns yearling: showed improved form when winning 22-runner maiden auction event at Kempton in July by a neck from Telex Boy: ran creditably when in frame in nurseries at Salisbury afterwards: well suited by 6f. *J. Benstead.*

OUTBURST 4 br.f. Articulate 121–Delia's Tantrum (Rage Royal 78) [1974 57 N.R. 1975 9f⁵ 12.3f⁶ 12g 1976 12g⁴ 12d 15f⁴ 13.8f⁴ 13.8f³ 11h* 12fg⁴] poor staying handicapper: won eight-runner maiden race at Hamilton in August by 6 lengths from Service Charge: acts on hard ground. *T. Craig.*

OUTER CIRCLE 3 b.f. My Swallow 134–Saulisa 108 (Hard Sauce 131) [1975 — 5s² 5fg* 6f* 6fg* 6d⁴ 1976 7fg 8fg] lengthy, attractive filly: half-sister to very smart sprinter Saulingo (by Sing Sing): dam a very speedy 2-y-o winner: showed smart form in 1975, winning three races, including Princess Margaret Stakes at Ascot and Champion Trophy at Ripon, and finishing fourth to Pasty in William Hill Cheveley Park Stakes at Newmarket: pick of paddock when reappearing in Ladbroke Nell Gwyn Stakes at Newmarket in April but ran poorly (eighth of 10) behind Flying Water: nineteenth of 25 behind that filly in 1,000 Guineas on same course later in month: exported to U.S.A. *I. Balding.*

OUT OF DATE 2 b.f. David Jack 125–Breach of Promise 102 (Mandamus 120) **80 p** [1976 5f³] first living foal: dam a useful winner at up to 7f: unquoted, made a lot of late progress when 2 lengths third of 13 to King Croesus in maiden race at Newmarket in August: will stay at least 1m: should win a race. *P. Robinson.*

OUT OF DEPTH 2 ch.f. Deep Diver 134–Breide's Wood (Le Levanstell 122) — [1976 5g⁶ 5s] first foal: 3,800 gns yearling: dam won over 6f at 3 yrs in Ireland: well beaten in minor race at Haydock in August and maiden event at Doncaster in October. *E. Cousins.*

OUT OF SEASON 3 b.g. Frigid Aire–Game Coach (Big Game) [1975 5f 5f 5g **47** 5d 5g 1976 11.1g 8.2d 8g⁶ 7fg⁴ 8d⁵ 12fg³] close-coupled gelding: plating-class maiden: probably stays 1½m: wears blinkers nowadays: usually amateur ridden. *C. Bewicke.*

OUT OF THE BLUE 3 b.c. Sky Gipsy 117–Queen's Rhapsody 86 (Chanteur II **66** 135) [1975 5v⁴ 6g 1976 8fg 11g⁶ 7f³ 8h⁴ 8s 8s] strong French-foaled colt: third in seller at Newmarket in August: stays 1m: best form on a sound surface: trained until after fourth outing by J. Bethell. *B. Lunness.*

OUTPOINT 6 br.g. Fighting Charlie 127–Prim Dot (Primera 131) [1974 16g — 16.1fg 15s 13s⁵ 12v⁶ 1975 14.7s² 13v² 13g⁴ 12f⁴ 15g 1976 13v⁴] strong gelding: moderate handicapper (rated 81) at 5 yrs: well beaten only outing on flat in 1976, was sold to F. Winter 3,500 gns Ascot June Sales, and has subsequently done well over hurdles: stays 1¾m well: evidently acts on any going. *H. Collingridge.*

OUTRAGE 6 br.h. Crocket 130–Dynaminx 89 (Counsel 118) [1974 8s 8g **75** 7.6d⁵ 9g³ 10g 8.3fg⁶ 11g 1975 10g* 12g* 10f⁴ 10fg⁴ 10f* 10g* 12fg² 10f² 10.2g⁵ 10fg* 10.2g³ 1976 12g² 10f³ 11.7fg 12fg⁴ 12f² 10f² 10fg⁵] quite a moderate handicapper: ran his three best races in 1976 at Folkestone: stays 1½m: well suited by top-of-the-ground conditions although has run respectably on easy going: tried in blinkers at 3 yrs: excellent mount for an apprentice. *G. Harwood.*

OVERLOOK 2 b.c. Royal Palace 131–Whitefoot 108 (Relko 136) [1976 7g 7v⁴] **70 p** third foal: half-brother to 1¼m winner Whitey (by Sassafras): dam stayed at least 1½m: 12 lengths fourth of nine to Imperial Guard in minor event at Lingfield in November: will be suited by 1½m: the type to do better at 3 yrs. *H. Wragg.*

OVERSEAS 2 gr.f. Sea Hawk II 131–Fresh Start 103 (Busted 134) [1976 6v] — p first foal: dam won over 6f at 2 yrs: unquoted, showed early speed when thirteenth of 23 to Amity in maiden race at Newbury in October: likely to do better over longer distances. *F. Maxwell.*

OVERSEAS ADMIRER 2 b.c. High Top 131–Villa Marina 96 (Tudor Melody **86** 129) [1976 5fg³ 5.1fg² 5.3fg* 5fg⁴ 5f⁴ 5d⁴ 6g⁵ 5s] neat, compact colt: half-brother to four winners, including fairly useful 1970 2-y-o winner Mary Crocket (by Crocket): 5,000 gns yearling: dam a sprinter: odds on, made all to win maiden race at Brighton in June by 1½ lengths from Johnjo: good fourth of 13 to Song of Songs in Highclere Nursery at Newbury in September: stays 6f: well beaten when blinkered on final outing. *J. Winter.*

OVER THE MOON 4 ch.c. Double Jump 131–Sheer Joy (Major Portion 129) **53** [1974 6fg 7v 1975 8v⁵ 8g 10f 10f² 12g 10.1fg 10g 1976 10fg 10f 12f³ 17f³ 11d³ 10g² 12f³ 12f 15.5f⁵ 15f 13.4fg 10fg⁴ 7f⁶] neat colt: poor handicapper: stays 1½m but has yet to show conclusively that he stays further: probably acts on any going. *M. Stevens.*

OVERTOWN 4 gr.c. Raffingora 130–Tender Courtesan 90 (Primera 131) [1974 **111** 5fg* 5g* 5g² 5fg* 5g³ 5g² 6s⁵ 1975 5d⁵ 5fg 6g 5fg 6g 5f⁵ 5g² 5.6g⁴ 5d 1976 5.9fg⁴

5fg* 5d³ 5g⁶ 5fg* 6fg 6f² 5fg⁴ 6f⁵ 5.6g 6s] strong, really powerful colt: good mover: successful in Crocker Bulteel Handicap at Ascot in May and William Hill Sprint Handicap at Epsom the following month, finishing very strongly when beating Pennina a short head in latter event: also ran well in some of his other races, including on eighth start when 3 lengths fourth of 13 to High Award at York in August: stays 6f: possibly best suited by a sound surface but ran creditably on a soft one on third outing at 4 yrs: has been tried in blinkers: genuine and consistent. *R. Turnell.*

OVER TO YOU 3 ch.c. Buckpasser–Rose Bower (Princequillo) [1975 7g* 7fg* **102** 1976 8fg⁶ 10.5g 12g 12g⁵] attractive, well-made individual: good mover: won both his races in 1975, including Intercraft Solario Stakes at Sandown: well beaten in Craven Stakes at Newmarket, Prix Lupin at Longchamp and Prix Jean de Chaudenay at Saint-Cloud before finishing 5¼ lengths fifth of 10 to Crackao in Grand Prix de la Ville de Toulouse in June: stays 1½m: trained until after second outing by R. Hern. *J. Cunnington, jnr, France.*

OWEN GLYNDWR 3 br.c. Welsh Abbot 131–Arctic Crystal 82 (Arctic Star) **47** [1975 5g 6fg⁶ 8.2g⁶ 1976 10fg 12d 12f⁵ 16fg⁵ 16.1f² 12fg 18s⁵] neat colt: suited by 2m: acts on firm going (ran poorly on soft final outing). *P. Rohan.*

OWEN JONES 2 b.c. Tudor Melody 129–Crystal Palace 121 (Solar Slipper 131) **— p** [1976 7fg] handsome colt: half-brother to several winners, notably Royal Palace (by Ballymoss), Prince Consort (by Right Royal V) and Selhurst (by Charlottesville): dam smart at 7f to 1½m: looking very big and backward, very slowly into stride when last of nine to Prince Myshkin in maiden race at Sandown in July: not given at all a hard time once chance had gone and is sure to do a lot better in time: to be trained by H. Cecil. *N. Murless.*

P

PABABE 2 b.c. Busted 134–Glengarry 72 (High Hat 131) [1976 5fg 6g 7v] **—** small, strong colt: second foal: 4,400 gns yearling: dam half-sister to numerous winners, including Gwen: behind in maiden and minor events: should be suited by 1¼m+. *M. W. Easterby.*

PABLOND 5 b.h. Paveh 126–Blonde Bomb 72 (Worden II 129) [1974 7d 10f³ **—** 10g⁵ 10.6g⁵ 10g² 12g⁵ 12g⁴ 10s⁶ 1975 12d⁴ 10v² 12v³ 12s³ 14.7f* 13.8f* 1976 18d] stocky horse: quite a useful handicapper (rated 91) at 4 yrs: heavily bandaged when well beaten in SKF Cesarewitch at Newmarket on only start in 1976: stayed well: acted on any going: had worn blinkers: stud. *M. Francis.*

PACE ATTACK 2 ch.f. Barbary Pirate 91–Santa Marta 51 (Lavandin 128) **60** [1976 5g 6d 5.9f 6h⁴ 8fg 8s] fair sort: sister to a winning plater: dam won over 6f at 4 yrs: showed a little ability in maiden and minor events: should stay at least 1m: likely to do better in sellers. *R. Hollinshead.*

PADDINGTON 2 ch.f. Connaught 130–Key West 90 (Crepello 136) [1976 **107** 5fg 6f* 7fg* 6fg* 6fg⁴ 8d⁵] rangy filly: half-sister to three winners, including

Rous Memorial Stakes, Goodwood—Paddington wins comfortably from Stradey Park

very useful 6f and 7f winner Abbie West (by Abernant): dam stayed 1¼m: a useful filly who won at Lingfield, Newmarket and Goodwood, putting up an impressive display on last-named course when beating Stradey Park comfortably by a length in Rous Memorial Stakes: put up easily better subsequent effort when co-favourite for 13-runner Lowther Stakes at York in August, finishing 3 lengths fourth to Icena after being well behind at halfway: found 6f on sharp side at 2 yrs and should stay 1¼m+: acts on firm going and is possibly not at her best on soft: often sweats up profusely: to be trained by H. Cecil. *N. Murless.*

PADDY BE LUCKY   2 ch.c. Paddy B 105–Fiona F (Signal Point 104)   [1976 6f]   —
half-brother to a winning jumper: tenth of 19 to Fawn in maiden race at Ripon in August: fell and broke leg after passing post and was subsequently destroyed. *G. Richards.*

PADDY BOULER   3 br.g. Tiepolo II 121–Mistinguette 85 (My Babu 136)   [1975   **101**
7f⁶ 7f* 8g⁴ 7g³ 8d⁴   1976 10s² 12g* 12g⁵ 12g 16f 11.5f 12f² 12f⁶]   Irish gelding: won handicap at Naas in April under top weight: good fifth to Yankee Gold in Group 3 Royal Whip at the Curragh the following month but did not reproduce that form although had some stiff tasks: stays 1¼m (ninth of 14 to General Ironside in Queen's Vase at Royal Ascot only attempt at 2m): blinkered twice, virtually refusing to race on sixth outing but running respectably in them on next start: said to have cut his head in stalls and finished lame when well beaten on fourth appearance. *M. Kauntze, Ireland.*

PADDY JACK   5 ch.g. David Jack 125–Lucky Seven 79 (King's Bench 132)   **93**
[1974 8fg² 10g* 10f* 12f6 10g   1975 10g⁵ 11fg⁵ 12f³ 12d² 10g* 10fg² 12fg⁴ 10.5fg² 11v³ 12s* 12fg⁴ 11d⁴   1976 12g⁴ 12f² 14g⁵ 11g⁶ 12fg⁶ 11.7f³ 12h* 12h*(w.o.) 12fg* 12fg² 14g*]   tall gelding: fairly useful handicapper: winner at Redcar in July, Newmarket in August and Sandown the following month: held on very courageously when winning Sportsman Club Handicap on last-named course, beating Rowe Residence a neck despite going lame inside final furlong (broke sesamoid in near hind): stays 1¾m: acts on any going: genuine and consistent. *G. Smyth.*

PADDY'S DARLING   3 b.f. St Paddy 133–Hannah Darling 108 (Match III 135)   **73**
[1975 6fg   1976 16d⁶ 14fg⁴ 12g⁶ 12f* 10f³ 10.1fg³ 10fg]   leggy filly: showed first worthwhile form when winning maiden race at Folkestone in July by ½ length from General Augustus: twice ran respectably in handicaps afterwards: possibly finds 1¼m on sharp side and should stay further than 1¼m: acts on firm going. *C. Brittain.*

PADDY'S LASS   3 ch.f. St Paddy 133–Topolass 79 (Acropolis 132)   [1975 N.R.   —
1976 10fg 14f³]   second foal: dam won over 1¼m: remote last of three behind Glissando in maiden race at Salisbury in July: sold 500 gns Ascot August Sales. *P. Cundell.*

PADDY'S LUCK   4 gr.c. Cumshaw 111–Mary Paddy 100 (St Paddy 133)   [1974   **79**
5g⁴ 5f⁵ 5.3d⁵ 6fg 6g³ 7g⁵ 5s 6d 6s*   1975 7s² 6v* 7s² 6f⁵ 7fg³ 7g⁵ 8d 8.3fg⁴ 8fg⁵ 8g⁴ 8.3fg* 8g 8g³ 7.6s³   1976 7fg² 8f³ 7f⁶ 7fg⁶ 7f² 10h² 9g* 8g* 10fg 10h³ 8.3d³ 8g³ 10s⁴ 7.6v²]   small colt: quite a moderate handicapper: a grand mount for a boy and won apprentice handicaps at Kempton and Ascot at 4 yrs: stays 1¼m: acts on any going: does best in blinkers: genuine and consistent. *J. Benstead.*

PADDY'S TERN   2 b.f. St Paddy 133–Pardal Lassie (Pardal 130)   [1976 7fg 6f   —
8fg]   half-sister to several winners in U.S.A. and France: 2,700 gns yearling: dam a stakes-placed winner, is half-sister to high-class middle-distance filly La Bamba: in rear in maiden and minor events: sweated up first and third outings. *P. Wigham.*

PADDYSWITCH   2 ch.f. St Paddy 133–Vilswitch 93 (Vilmorin)   [1976 6g 5v]   —
half-sister to fairly useful sprinter Vilgora (by Raffingora): 1,000 gns yearling: dam a sprinter: well behind in minor event at Kempton in August and maiden race at Lingfield in November. *D. Whelan.*

PADOVANNA   2 gr.f. Allangrange 126–Pampatamy 75 (Immortality)   [1976   **79**
5f⁵ 5fg⁶ 6fg³ 8f 8.2f* 8s 8v]   well-grown filly: second foal: sold twice as a yearling, for 350 gns and 950 gns: dam placed at up to 1m: won 14-runner maiden race at Hamilton in September by ¾ length from Mighty Maggie: will probably stay 1½m: acts on firm going. *J. Calvert.*

PADROUG   2 b.c. Sir Ivor 135–Running Blue 115 (Blue Peter)   [1976 6.3g⁴ 6fg* **115**
8fg*]

Padroug made his first appearance on the racecourse in the Lagan Maiden
Stakes at the Curragh in July.   The market suggested there was no real confidence in his chance, and in finishing fourth, six lengths behind Pampapaul, he
doubtless acquitted himself as well as was expected.   Next, he was sent over to
this country for the Acomb Stakes, a maidens-at-closing event, at York in
August.   This time there was no question of his being unfancied.   Piggott was
aboard, and Padroug was a heavily-backed favourite.   As it happened it was
perhaps as well for Padroug that he was ridden by Piggott, for in a driving finish
over the last furlong he had to struggle hard to wear down Lucky Sovereign
close home and win by a head.   Lucky Sovereign went on to finish eighth of nine
in the Harry Rosebery Challenge Trophy at Ayr, and fourth of eleven, beaten ten
lengths by Padroug's stable-companion The Minstrel, in the William Hill
Dewhurst Stakes at Newmarket.   Lucky Sovereign did not get into the Free Handicap, the weights for which go down to 7-7.   Finally, Padroug was returned to
the Curragh in September for the recently-instituted Ashford Castle Stakes run
over a mile.   This distance suited Padroug much better than did the six furlongs
of the Acomb Stakes, and he came through strongly in the closing stages to win the
race readily by two and a half lengths from Lordedaw, with Slavonic, who was
receiving 7 lb from Padroug and 5 lb from Lordedaw, a length and a half away third.
For Lordedaw this was his fourth successive defeat since he had run Cawston's
Clown to a head in the Coventry Stakes at Royal Ascot, and for Slavonic his
first race since he had finished a poor eighth of ten in the Vernons Organisation
Plate at Doncaster: afterwards he was to finish seventh of nineteen, after losing
ground at the start, in a £690 nursery at Punchestown.

That in a nutshell was Padroug's record as a two-year-old.   Two points
emerge from it—(1) he ran in none of the races to which one is accustomed to look
for the best horses, and (2) his successes were gained from what by classic
standards must be regarded as modest opposition.   Admittedly Lordedaw's
second in the Coventry Stakes suggests he was a pretty good colt, but with such
as Majestic Bay, Gaelic God and Markdail close up, one didn't need the subsequent performances of Cawston's Clown, nor those of Lordedaw himself, to
indicate just how substandard a race that was.   Our rating for Padroug, based on
a strict interpretation of his form as we see it, suggests that 8-3 would be as
much as he would be entitled to in an average Free Handicap.   Astonishingly, he
has been given 9-1!   For the life of us we cannot understand how his form comes
to be assessed so highly.   Yaroslav's 9-5 in the 1971 Free Handicap was bad
enough, but he did at least win the Royal Lodge Stakes at Ascot.   Padroug's
mark seems ridiculous, to us at any rate.   We realise that these things are matters
of opinion, and that the official handicapper is just as likely to be right in his
assessment of Padroug's form as we are likely to be right in our assessment of
Padroug's form: that no one person has a monopoly on skill and good judgement
when it comes to the art of assessing the form of individual horses.   So it will be as
well if we put Padroug's 9-1 under the microscope, and examine its implication

Acomb Stakes, York—Padroug (far side) pokes his nose in front of Lucky Sovereign

relative to the marks received by the other two-year-olds in the Free Handicap. For the purposes of illustration, let us relate Padroug's Free Handicap mark to the marks received by The Minstrel (8-13), Avgerinos (8-8), Fair Season (8-5), Sporting Yankee (8-4) and Lady Mere (8-0).

At the risk of stating the obvious, the first thing Padroug's Free Handicap mark implies is that it is the opinion of the handicapper that Padroug's form was superior by 2 lb to that shown by The Minstrel in the Dewhurst Stakes, better by 7 lb than anything Avgerinos, winner of the Intercraft Solario Stakes, managed to accomplish, 10 lb better than Fair Season's form when winning the Horris Hill Stakes, 11 lb ahead of anything achieved by Sporting Yankee, who won the William Hill Futurity, and 15 lb in advance of Lady Mere's effort in running second in the Prix de la Foret. In other words it implies that it is the opinion of the handicapper that Padroug's form was good enough to suggest that he could have won the £37,000 William Hill Dewhurst Stakes (in the presumed absence of his stable-companion The Minstrel) by five lengths, the £5,000 Intercraft Solario Stakes by three to four lengths, the £11,000 Horris Hill Stakes by four lengths plus, and the £36,000 William Hill Futurity by five lengths. And what it implies he could have done to Manado, Kesar Queen and those other good French horses who contested the £27,000 Prix de la Foret, had he been able to run in that race, just doesn't bear thinking about

If we take the implication of Padroug's handicap mark a stage further, we deduce that it must be the handicapper's opinion that Padroug's form was good enough to suggest that of all the two-year-old colts who raced in England and Ireland during the course of the season, he is the one most likely to go on to success in a classic race, now that the Champagne Stakes winner J. O. Tobin has been sent to continue his career in the United States and with Godswalk almost certain to have stamina limitations. Well, all we can say is that Padroug most certainly did not perform at York in the Acomb Stakes in the manner of a horse who has the pace in him to win a classic race, whatever the heights to which he might rise eventually as a stayer, and from the points of view of possession of speed and of form at two years we must confess to a marked preference for his stable-companion The Minstrel. It is interesting to note that the majority of Vincent O'Brien's high-class two-year-olds and the best of his classic-winning colts were racing in events of greater importance than the Ashford Castle Stakes on their third appearance. It is true that Padroug might have contested the William Hill Futurity had he not fallen victim to the virus and we don't question that he is well thought of at home or that he might eventually show himself to be a really good colt—what we are objecting to is the horse's Free Handicap mark in relation to the form he showed on the racecourse. And we repeat, the form-book doesn't say he was the outstandingly good two-year-old his Free Handicap mark makes him out to be—the way we read it at any rate.

Another less obvious but more disturbing aspect of Padroug's unrealistic mark in the Free Handicap is that it implies a value on the horse out of all proportion to its achievements on the racecourse, in certain circumstances the consequences of which are only too apparent to need elaborating on here. We take no perverse pleasure in criticising what is, as we have said, just another person's opinion—we know only too well how wide of the mark we have been at times in our assessments of individual two-year-olds—but we would be failing in our duty as an unbiased observer not to speak our mind when we feel that the need arises.

Now that we have got that off our chest, it is time we returned to Padroug. No-one would deny that he is a very useful colt, and a promising one. A well-made individual, who cost 56,000 guineas as a yearling, he is a brother to the very smart middle-distance performer Sir Penfro, third in the 1974 Irish Sweeps Derby, and a half-brother to several other good winners, including Dominion Day (by Charlottesville) who won the 1967 Blandford Stakes at the Curragh. The dam Running Blue, a smart racemare, stayed a mile and a half, so with a Derby and Guineas winner as his sire, Padroug is bred to stay reasonably well. In all probability Padroug will need at least a mile and a quarter to be seen to best advantage as a three-year-old, and the chances of his emulating his dam, who won the Free Handicap in 1960, are about as bright as his chances of being allowed to run in the race. Which is to say he has no chance of emulating her at all. All the same, he is sure to win races. *V. O'Brien, Ireland.*

PADSKI 3 ch.g. St Paddy 133–No Relation 94 (Klairon 131) [1975 N.R. 1976 — 12f³ 12g 10.2s⁴] half-brother to fairly useful middle-distance handicappers Amicus (by Roan Rocket) and Warbeck (by Royal Palace): 460 gns yearling: dam stayed 1m: 8½ lengths fourth of 27 to Alvage in maiden race at Doncaster in November: should stay 1½m. *R. Hollinshead.*

PAGAN HOLE 2 b.c. Red God 128 §–Pin Hole 83 (Parthia 132) [1976 5f⁶ 5fg **62** 5s⁵] neat colt: first reported foal: dam won over 1¼m: little worthwhile form in maiden races but may do better over 1m. *B. Swift.*

PAGOS BOY 4 ch.c. Pago Pago–Nashville Cat (Fulcrum) [1974 6g⁵ 8s² 8d³ **97** 1975 8g⁵ 10.8s³ 10.1f² 10.1s* 10fg⁶ 10.1fg⁴ 8d* 8.3fg* 8f³ 8.3fg* 1976 8g 7fg 8.2g* 9fg* 8f 8fg² 8fg² 8fg⁴ 8fg³ 8.3d* 9g⁴ 8v* 8s] strong, good sort and a good walker: useful handicapper: successful at Haydock in May, Lingfield the following month and Newbury in October, on last-named course keeping on really well to beat The Happy Hooker: ran creditably most of his other outings, notably when short-head second to Bermondo at Windsor in September (awarded race after winner's disqualification), and when fourth, about 2½ lengths behind winner, to Intermission in Irish Sweeps Cambridgeshire at Newmarket in October: effective at 1m to 11f: acts on any going: game, genuine and consistent. *G. Harwood.*

PAHASKA 3 b.f. Wolver Hollow 126–Grace Note 104 (Parthia 132) [1975 7g **86** 6g* 1976 8fg³ 8fg 10.1fg³] quite attractive filly: moderate handicapper: not seen out after June: will probably stay 1½m: acts on a firm surface. *B. Hobbs.*

PAINT THE TOWN 3 b.f. Vaguely Noble 140–Belle de Nuit (Warfare) [1975 **121** 8s* 1976 8fg⁴ 8g⁵ 10.5g 12g³ 13d² 12g⁶ 12s* 12.5d* 10.5s² 12g*] American-bred French filly: half-sister to Tudor Gleeman (by Tudor Minstrel), a stakes-placed winner at up to 9f in U.S.A.: 350,000 francs yearling (approx. £32,000): dam, a smart winner at up to 7f, is half-sister to top 1953 American 2-y-o filly Evening Out: in good form in the autumn and won three of her last four races, a valuable handicap and Prix de Royallieu, latter by a neck from Moquerie, both at Longchamp, and Grand Prix de Nantes in November by 2 lengths from Condorcet: 1½ lengths runner-up to No No Nanette (rec 6 lb) in Prix de Flore at Saint-Cloud in between: ran well in fillies classics earlier in season, finishing fifth to Riverqueen in Poule d'Essai des Pouliches and sixth to Lagunette in Irish Guinness Oaks: stays 13f: appears to act on any going: a good filly. *J. Fellows, France.*

PAK LOK 2 b.c. Lord Gayle 124–Velour (Golden Cloud) [1976 6fg⁵ 5fg² 6fg⁵] **85** attractive, shapely colt: half-brother to four winners, including very useful 3-y-o miler Lord Helpus (by Green God): 3,700 gns yearling: dam half-sister to very useful Fleece: got outpaced at halfway but was going on very well in final furlong when 2½ lengths second of four to The Andrestan in Star Stakes at Sandown in July: finished only fifth to Sequoia when favourite for maiden race at Nottingham later in month and wasn't seen out again: should stay 1m *F. J. Houghton.*

PALACE PRINCE 5 b.g. Nantallah–Palace Dancer (Princequillo) [1974 **52** N.R. 1975 N.R. 1976 8fg⁴ 7fg² 6d 8v⁵ 8.2v 10s] American-bred gelding: showed ability in amateur riders races on first two outings (heavily backed on first of them) but was well beaten afterwards: stays 1m: possibly unsuited on a soft surface. *D. Chapman.*

PALACE ROYAL 3 b.g. Royal Palace 131–La Mirabelle 92 (Princely Gift 137) **89** [1975 6g⁶ 8.2g 1976 12d⁴ 12f* 12fg² 12g²] lengthy gelding: enterprisingly ridden when winning maiden race at Doncaster in July by 12 lengths from Nargis: runner-up on both his starts afterwards, going under by a neck to Bicoque in minor event at Newmarket later in month when blinkered first time, but not wearing blinkers when running Merry Kerry to ¾ length in handicap at Doncaster in September: will stay further than 1½m: acts on firm going. *R. Hern.*

PALAESTRINA 3 ch.g. Tudor Music 131–Plot (Never Say Die 137) [1975 5d **49** 5v⁵ 5s⁶ 5fg 6g 1976 7g³ 8h 8g³ 7fg⁵ 8fg⁶ 7d² 7g 8h] poor plater: stays 1m: ran moderately when tried in blinkers. *K. Payne.*

PALAMINE 2 b.c. Royal Palm 131–Stevie 79 (The Phoenix) [1976 5fg 5v* 5d⁶ **53**
5s 5h⁵ 5f] half-brother to three minor winners: had simple task when beating
slow-starting Harvest Boy in two-horse maiden race at Hamilton in April: behind
in nurseries on last two outings. *J. Hardy.*

PALASTAR 8 gr.h. Palestine 133–Star Dancer (Arctic Star) [1974 5.9f 10g⁴
8g* 8f⁶ 1975 N.R. 1976 8fg] poor handicapper (rated 65) in 1974: well beaten
in seller at Warwick in April, first outing since: stays at least 1m: acts on any
going: wears blinkers: suitable mount for an apprentice. *M. Stevens.*

PALATABLE 3 b.c. Tom Rolfe–Ameribelle (Amerigo 116 §) [1975 5g⁴ 6fg* 7g⁴ **102**
1976 7fg* 10s* 12fg³] good-looking colt: won two good early-season handicaps
in tremendous style, Crawfurd Handicap at Newmarket and X.Y.Z. Handicap
at Newcastle: completely outclassed his 14 rivals and defied a 6-lb penalty when
cruising home 5 lengths clear of Ginger Knit on latter course: odds on, appeared
not to stay trip in 1½m Predominate Stakes at Goodwood in May, finishing 5¾
lengths third to General Ironside: broke down badly soon afterwards: stays
1¼m: appears to act on any going. *J. Dunlop.*

PALAVER 2 ch.c. Crepello 136–Parlez-vous 88 (Pardal 130) [1976 5fg³ 6d³] **89**
closely related to useful 7f and 1¼m winner Gaelic (by Busted) and half-brother
to several winners, including very smart miler Estaminet (by Sovereign Path),
smart French middle-distance performer High Game (by High Hat) and very
useful 3-y-o middle-distance winner Amboise (by Royal Palace): dam won over
5f at 2 yrs: ran very well when 3 lengths third of nine to Swift Hussar in £1,200
event at Newmarket in May: favourite for 23-runner maiden race at Redcar the
following month but couldn't quicken in final furlong and finished 4 lengths
third to Whitby Jet: not seen out again: will probably stay 1½m. *H. Cecil.*

PAL DAN 6 b.g. Pall Mall 132–Faridane II (Dan Cupid 132) [1974 7s² 7g² **68**
7fg⁵ 7f⁶ 6f² 7f⁵ 6fg² 6f* 6g* 6g 6d³ 6g 6d 6s 6s 1975 6v⁶ 6fg² 6v⁶ 6fg* 7f² 6f⁶ 6fg*
6f³ 5h² 6g 1976 6g 7g 6f 6fg 7f 6f³ 7f² 8d 6s⁵ 8v] strong gelding: moderate
handicapper: ran best race in 1976 on eighth outing (backed at long odds):
effective from 5f to 1m: acts on any going but seems well suited by top-of-the-
ground conditions: ran poorly when tried in blinkers: suitable mount for an
apprentice: swerved badly at start tenth appearance: retained 1,350 gns
Doncaster March Sales. *H. Blackshaw.*

PALE SAINT 4 gr.g. St Paddy 133–Palestream 78 (Palestine 133) [1974 7s⁵ **70**
1975 8d 11.1fg 10f 10f² 10g² 12g⁴ 10.8g* 10s⁵ 1976 14g 10fg⁴ 10g³ 10h⁶ 10.1f²
9fg² 10fg⁴ 8s 10s] workmanlike gelding: quite a moderate handicapper: ran
best race at 4 yrs when 2 lengths second of nine to Solo Reign at Wolverhampton
in September on sixth outing: should stay further than 1¼m: acts on firm going.
A. Pitt.

PAL JOEY 2 b.c. Kauai King–Crag Bay 77 (Road House II) [1976 7g] lengthy **—**
colt: second foal: half-brother to St Severin (by Manacle), quite a useful
performer at up to 1¼m: dam, a plater, stayed 1¼m: unquoted and in need of race,
showed up 5f when seventeenth of 23 in maiden race won by Windy Sea at Newmarket in October. *H. Westbrook.*

PALL TAVI 3 b.c. Palmallet 95–Avreo (Aureole 132) [1975 5v 5s⁵ 5f⁵ 5g⁴ **44**
6g² 5g* 6f 1976 6v 6fg 6h⁵ 6f² 6fg⁶ 6f⁴ 8.2h⁴ 6g 8f⁵ 6v] poor plater: best form
at 6f: ran moderately on heavy ground on final outing: wears blinkers. *A.
Balding.*

PALM COURT JOE 3 b.g. Welsh Saint 126–Cis (Eudaemon 129) [1975 5f 5g⁶ **63**
6d⁶ 1976 5fg 5f⁴ 5f³ 6g⁴ 5f 6g² 5g⁶ 5s³ 5v 6s] stocky gelding: only a plater but
often ran creditably in better company, just failing to catch Cumnock Scouse in
maiden race at York in September: stays 6f: occasionally sweats up. *M.
Naughton.*

PALMERSTON 3 ch.c. Aureole 132–Hunting Bee (Honeyway 125) [1975 8g **101**
8.2d² 8g² 1976 12g³ 10fg³ 12.2g* 13.3g² 14fg³ 16f² 14s² 13.3v*] lengthy colt:
useful handicapper: placed on all his starts and won at Catterick in June:
subsequently showed better form and gained a further success when making all
to beat Snake Bite 7 lengths at Newbury in October: suited by a test of stamina:
acts on any going: consistent. *J. Dunlop.*

PALMVINNIA 3 b.f. Royal Palm 131–Whitestake 74 (Compensation 127) **97**
[1975 5s⁵ 5fg* 5v² 5fg* 5f³ 5h⁵ 5fg* 5g 1976 5s 5g⁴ 5fg² 5f* 5fg 5fg* 5g⁴
5fg²] quite a useful sort of filly: made all when winning at Wolverhampton in
August (handicap) and September (apprentice event): good ½-length second to
Lazenby in Raffingora Sprint Stakes at Beverley on final outing: not certain to

stay beyond 5f: acts well on a firm surface and is said to be unsuited by heavy going: blinkered fourth start: goes well for 7-lb claimer R. Barker. *J. Etherington.*

PALOMA NEGRO 2 br.c. Philip of Spain 126–Margaritina (Major Portion 129) —
[1976 5g 5f 5g 6h 6f⁶ 5f 5f] probably of little account. *J. Pullen.*

PAL'S BAMBINO 4 gr.c. Pals Passage 115–Shangara (Credo 123) [1974 5fg **106**
6g⁴ 8v 7s⁵ 6v³ 6d 1975 10.1g² 14f² 10f* 10.1fg³ 12f*(dis) 11.7fg* 12f* 12h*
11.7fg* 11.7fg⁴ 14.6g³ 16g² 14g² 18fg 1976 12fg³ 16g 12d 12f² 14fg* 13s⁴] big,
well-made colt: useful handicapper: made all when winning at Sandown in June
by 1½ lengths from Regal Step: stayed 2m: best form on a sound surface: wore
blinkers: genuine and consistent: sold 4,100 gns Newmarket December Sales:
stud in Ireland. *B. Hanbury.*

PALTARA 2 ch.f. Palmallet 95–Sarasail 58 (Hitting Away) [1976 5h 6f 5s 8.2v] —
bad plater: wears blinkers. *A. Balding.*

PALUSTRA 3 b.f. Irish Ball 127–Polly Moss 88 (Ballymoss 136) [1975 6f 6g² **104**
6f* 7fg⁶ 6fg⁵ 6d⁵ 1976 8f* 9g⁵ 8s³ 8f* 8f* 8f* 8g* 8g⁴ 8g² 8g⁴ 7s²] workmanlike
filly: useful handicapper: enterprisingly ridden when winning at Thirsk, Ripon,
Redcar (twice) and Pontefract: defied a 6-lb penalty when beating Andy Rew a
length in Websters Pennine Handicap on last-named course in August: creditable
second afterwards at Doncaster in September (to Silver Steel in Autumn Cup)
and Newmarket the following month (to Royfern in £2,200 race): best form at
up to 1m: acts on any going: genuine and consistent: sold 20,000 gns Newmarket
December Sales. *J. W. Watts.*

PAMPAPAUL 2 b.c. Yellow God 129–Pampalina 116 (Bairam II 101) [1976 **119**
5f² 6g² 6.3g* 6.3f² 7f* 8d²]

After Yellow God had had runners for two seasons it looked very much
as though their former owners had done the right thing when they sold him to
the Japanese in the summer of 1973. In 1974 seventeen two-year-olds by
Yellow God collected only £10,577 in win and place money, and in 1975 his
forty runners picked up only £13,519, a figure which left him way down the list
of leading sires. Nevertheless, at the time of the sale we thought the decision
to sell premature. Yellow God's first foals were keenly sought after; and
soon after his exportation his yearlings fetched a higher average price than nearly
all the other first-season sires. And now that his third crop has raced Yellow
God's departure is a matter for regret; he has got two of the best two-year-old
colts of 1976 in Nebbiolo and Pampapaul and ended the season the leading sire
of two-year-olds.

Pampapaul's contribution to his sire's total was £21,478, most of which
came from his success in the National Stakes at the Curragh on his fifth outing.
This race has long been established as one of Ireland's top two-year-old races—
Santa Claus, Sir Ivor and Roberto all won it—but its value has lagged behind
that of similar races in England and France. The 1975 running carried a first
prize of only £4,118 and the format of the race was changed in an attempt to
boost the prize money and, in so doing, to make the race of international appeal.
The 1976 race closed in March of that year but, to be eligible for entry to the
race, a horse had to have had a £20 subscription paid for it by its breeder before the
middle of December, 1975. In order to tempt the breeders to part with their
money, prizes of 5 per cent, 3 per cent and 2 per cent were introduced for the
breeders of the first three, and 698 subscriptions were received, supplementing
the entry fees by £13,960. The change of conditions may have worked from the
point of view of raising the prize money but the hoped-for foreign challengers
didn't materialise and even the powerful stables of O'Brien, Paddy Prendergast
and Weld had no runner. Yet with those very useful colts Captain James,
Roman Charger and Lordedaw among the eight runners the race still took
some winning, and Pampapaul put up a very smart, if erratic, performance.
Not for the first time, he showed that he's not the most tractable of characters,
being reluctant to enter the stalls, but once racing he was quickly up with the
leaders and took up the running two furlongs out. Hardly had Pampapaul gone
to the front than he veered sharply left, so sharply that he crossed the course and
hit the stand rails. Despite all this, he drew away to win by two and a half
lengths from the favourite Captain James, with Lordedaw the same margin
further away in third place.

Pampapaul's previous win had come in a maiden race on the same course
in July, when he proved troublesome at the start and also drifted left in the
closing stages. Blinkers were tried on him in his only race in between, again

Mr Hans Paul's "Pampapaul"

at the Curragh, in the Railway Stakes. This time he lost a few lengths at the start, and as he came through to challenge in the final furlong he was crossed by Roman Charger and lost any chance he might have had of winning. At the line Pampapaul was third, a short head and a length behind Brahms and Roman Charger; he was then moved up to second place by the stewards.

Pampapaul had been ridden in all five of his races in Ireland by John Corr but Tony Murray was given the mount when Pampapaul started favourite for the Royal Lodge Stakes at Ascot in September. Murray quickly got confirmation that his mount was no easy ride; Pampapaul pulled very hard in the early stages, when Card Player was upsides him in the lead, and it wasn't until Pampapaul was allowed to take a clear advantage that he started to race smoothly. The gallop was so strong that Sky Ship, Millionaire, Hot Grove and Card Player couldn't get to him in the straight. Only Gairloch, who had settled very well in the early stages, came through to challenge, and Pampapaul couldn't hold him in the final furlong. Gairloch beat him by three quarters of a length.

Pampapaul (b.c. 1974)			
	Yellow God (ch 1967)	Red God (ch 1954)	Nasrullah / Spring Run
		Sally Deans (ch 1947)	Fun Fair / Cora Deans
	Pampalina (br 1964)	Bairam II (b 1955)	Nearco / Bibi Toori
		Padus (br 1955)	Anwar / Cherry Way

Pampapaul is the fourth foal and second winner of Pampalina. The other winner, Pampapaul's three-year-old brother Pampagod, won a maiden race over a mile and a quarter at Navan and has also been placed over a couple of furlongs further. Provided he settles down, Pampapaul has a fair chance of staying one and a quarter miles. Pampalina's greatest asset was her stamina and she gained her most important success when running her field into the ground in the 1967 Irish Guinness Oaks. The grandam, Padus, needed at least a mile and a quarter and to the sprinter Hard Tack she produced the Free Handicap winner Short Commons, herself the dam of the one-time very smart miler Common Land and the promising 1976 two-year-old He Loves Me. Little else of note has come from this family in recent years. Pampapaul is a rangy, strong, good sort of colt, just the type to do well as a three-year-old. His probable early-season target is the Irish Two Thousand Guineas and he looks sure to figure prominently in that race. His prospects after that depend very much on how well he settles down. He seems to act on any going. *S. Murless, Ireland.*

PAMPERED SOVEREIGN 5 gr.g. Supreme Sovereign 119–Pampered Lil 70 — (Pampered King 121) [1974 6s 1975 8s⁴ 8g⁵ 9g* 8f 9fg⁶ 1976 14.7d⁵] leggy gelding: good walker: poor handicapper: stays 9f: possibly not at his best on firm going. *V. Thompson.*

PAMPHILOS 4 br.g. Khalkis 127–Pampered Anna (Pampered King 121) — [1974 N.R. 1975 N.R. 1976 10.2s 12s] second foal: dam an Irish N.H. mare: well behind in maiden races at Doncaster and Haydock in October. *J. Fitzgerald.*

PAMS GLEAM 3 ch.f. Sovereign Gleam 117–Itoldyouso (Trouville 125) [1975 **83** 5d⁴ 5s 5.9fg* 5h 6fg⁴ 6fg⁴ 5h 7.2fg 7f² 7f 7f⁶ 5.9g 6g 6g 5s 1976 8.2f 7f⁶ 8g⁵ 8g³ 8.2d 7fg³ 7fg³ 7f² 7fg² 6fg* 7.2g³ 6f* 5.9f² 7f⁴ 5.9fg² 7g³ 6d 7v⁵] leggy, good-bodied filly: a tough customer who stood up well to a busy season, running creditably in most of her races and winning handicaps at Nottingham in July and Catterick in August: good second to Song's First in amateur riders race at Wolverhampton two days after latter win when carrying 7-lb penalty: best form at 6f and 7f on a sound surface: genuine. *R. Hollinshead.*

PANALOGUE 3 b.f. King Log 115 or Grand Roi 118–Pandai 88 (Panorama) — [1975 7f 6g 6f 1976 8.2f 8h 8fg 8d] little worthwhile form in varied company, including selling, in first part of season: unseated rider leaving stalls on first outing. *A. Johnson.*

PANAMINT 2 b.c. Run The Gantlet–Panaview 103 (Panaslipper 130) [1976 8v **93** p 8s*] half-brother to several winners, notably Irish 1,000 Guineas winners Front Row (by Epaulette) and Black Satin (by Linacre) and Irish Sweeps Derby second Ragapan (by Ragusa): 47,000 gns yearling: dam won over 7f: short-priced favourite for 23-runner maiden race at the Curragh in November and put up a most impressive display, drawing away to win by 6 lengths and 5 lengths from Ragabash and Musical Sam: stumbled and unseated rider on previous outing: will stay 1½m: a very good colt in the making. *D. Weld, Ireland.*

PANARTIC 5 ch.m. Articulate 121–Panteleap (Tenterhooks 128) [1974 — N.R. 1975 N.R. 1976 12fg³ 14fg 13.4fg³ 17.7f] poor maiden: probably stays 1¾m. *F. Rimell.*

PANDA'S GAMBOL 3 ch.f. Richboy 117–Topless 67 (Epaulette 125) [1975 **60** 7g 7g 1976 8fg 8fg⁵ 8f² 8g 8fg⁶ 9f³ 10f⁴ 12fg²] good-looking filly: runner-up to Carn Grey Rock in claiming race at Leicester in September: probably stays 1½m. *G. Pritchard-Gordon.*

PANDU 2 b.c. Tribal Chief 125–Sparkling Pan (Panaslipper 130) [1976 5f* 5v* **104** 5f* 5d* 5g* 5f⁵ 5fg³ 5f² 5fg⁶ 5fg 5fg⁴ 5fg* 5v²] neat, strong, useful-looking colt: fifth foal: 1,050 gns yearling: dam won over 1m at 2 yrs in Ireland: a speedy colt who won at Teesside, Ayr, Catterick, Chester and Thirsk early in season: continued to show useful form on occasions afterwards and made all under top weight to win 13-runner nursery at Edinburgh in September by a neck from Mariners Girl: well suited by a sharp track and is not at his best over a stiff 5f: acts on any going: wears blinkers: sold 6,000 gns Newmarket Autumn Sales and exported to Hong Kong. *T. Fairhurst.*

PANEIPA 2 b.f. Green God 128–Pampered 109 (Abernant 142) [1976 5fg⁴ 5v] **57** half-sister to numerous winners in England and France, including smart French middle-distance winner Sybarite (by Royal Record II): 2,100 gns yearling: dam a sprinter: showed promise when fourth of 28 to Just Janie in maiden race at Windsor in June but wasn't seen out again until October and finished well beaten in a similar event at Leicester: sold 540 gns Newmarket Autumn Sales. *N. Adam.*

PANGLIMA 2 b.c. Tribal Chief 125–Caught-At-It 77 (Poaching 115) [1975 **93** 5g 5fg* 5g² 5f³ 5g* 5fg 5fg 5g 6v 1976 5g³ 5g³ 5d³ 5s³ 5fg 5d⁴ 5fg 5fg³ 5f⁵ 5f² 5g* 5g* 5v³] strong, workmanlike colt: fairly useful handicapper: made all when winning at Warwick (apprentice event) and Doncaster, on latter course apprentice ridden when beating Hot Bird by $\frac{3}{4}$ length in September (hung left final furlong): speedy and not certain to stay 6f: acts on firm going but has shown best form with some give in the ground: wears blinkers nowadays. *A. Goodwill.*

PANOMARK 4 ch.c. On Your Mark 125–Painter's Palate (Whistler 129)   [1974   **97** 5g* 5f* 6g3 5g3 6fg* 6fg3   1975 N.R.   1976 6g6 6f4 7.3fg 6f 5g] good-looking colt: showed smart form as a juvenile but was reported to have split a pastern in early 1975, and did not race at 3 yrs: having his first outing since August 1974 when 5$\frac{3}{4}$ lengths sixth of 12 to Solar in Hackwood Stakes at Newbury in July: had stiff tasks afterwards, and wasn't disgraced: best form at up to 6f: acted on any going: usually wore blinkers: dead. *J. Nelson.*

PANOREALM 3 ch.c. Realm 129–Suirelko (Relko 136)   [1975 5.1f* 5fg4 5s*   **96** 5d*   1976 6fg 6d 6d 5fg 7f4 7f4 7g* 7.6g* 7s6 7s] robust, good-quartered colt: quite a useful handicapper: won at Goodwood and Lingfield in September: made all and defied 5-lb penalty when comfortably accounting for Heracles on latter course: also ran several moderate races, including on last two outings: stays 7f well: acts on any going: suited by forcing tactics: a headstrong individual. *M. Stoute.*

PAPA NOEL 7 ch.g. Santa Claus 133–Ninabella (Buisson Ardent 129)   [1974   **—** N.R.   1975 N.R.   1976 16.1d5] looking very big and backward, wore bandages in front when tailed-off last in Lymm Stakes won by Mr. Bigmore at Haydock in May, only outing on flat since 1973. *F. Yardley.*

PAPERAID 2 b.f. March Past 124–Memo (Faust 122) [1976 5d6 5v] fourth   **—** foal: 170 gns yearling: dam never ran: little worthwhile form in maiden races in October at Haydock and Leicester (springer in market). *W. Wharton.*

PAPER CHASE 5 b.h. Current Coin 118–Following Breeze 119 (Umidwar)   **93** [1974 5s 6d4 7g5 7f5 8g4 10.6g2 10s* 10s 10g6 10s   1975 10g3 10.5s 10f2 10f* 12fg* 12f6 15g3 12f4 14fg 13g2   1976 8f 10fg4 10fg6 11g3 10g4 12fg* 12fg2 12.3fg6 12fg4 15g5 12f* 12fg5 12g*] lengthy, well-made horse: good mover: quite a useful handicapper: awarded race after finishing neck second to subsequently-disqualified Blagoslav (hampered third horse) in Durdans Handicap at Epsom in June: narrowly beaten when good second to Slim Jim in Newbury Summer Cup later in month: gained further successes in Operatic Society Challenge Cup at Brighton (by a head from Belper) and apprentice race at Kempton, both in August: stays 1$\frac{1}{2}$m and wasn't disgraced over 15f on tenth outing: acts on any going: twice sweated up. *G. Peter-Hoblyn.*

PAPER RICH 3 ch.c. Richboy 117–Paperback 94 (Hard Ridden 131)   [1975   **75** 5g 5.1f 5.1f4 6fg2 7g4 7g2 7g5 7f2 7f4 9fg6 7g2 7g6 7f*   1976 7g 7fg2 8.2f2 7fg 6f 8f4 8g 8d 8.2s5 8s2 7s] leggy colt: second in handicaps at Newmarket (to Palatable) and Nottingham (to Glorified) in April and Bath in October (to Calor): ran moderately in between: stays 1m well: acts on any going: often wears blinkers: suitable mount for an apprentice. *A. Goodwill.*

PAPER TIGER 3 br.c. Floriana 106–Speldhurst (Monet 127)   [1975 6s 7v 8g   **—** 1976 10.8fg5 12g 10g 10g] compact, good sort of colt: showed only sign of ability on final outing: not seen out after May. *P. Mitchell.*

PAPILLON 3 br.g. Maystreak 118–Gipsylass (Atlas 126) [1975 N.R.   1976   **—** 10f] lengthy, unfurnished gelding: poor mover: first foal: dam probably of little account: backward, tailed off all way behind Konrad in maiden race at Pontefract in June. *H. Wharton.*

PAQUITA 2 ch.f. St Paddy 133–Shaletta 89 (Shantung 132) [1976 6s] second   **—** foal: dam won over 6f at 2 yrs. slowly away and always behind in small race won by Nobodys Fool at Chepstow in October, only outing. *F. J. Wharton.*

PARALLEL 2 ch.c. High Line 125–Paripan (Pardao 120)   [1976 7g 7fg 8d4]   **79** p big, good-looking, rangy colt: good mover: third foal: dam, foaled in Denmark, never ran: ran easily best race when 5 lengths fourth of 16 to Tin Mine in maiden event at Newbury in September: will be suited by 1$\frac{1}{2}$m or more: the type to do better at 3 yrs. *F. J. Houghton.*

PARATUS 2 b.c. Firestreak 125–Condonna 92 (Constable 129) [1976 5g 5g   **59** 5fg2 5f 7f 6f3 7d 6s 6s 6s] compact colt: plater: claimed out of K. Whitehead's stable when $\frac{3}{4}$-length second of 20 to Solchella at Thirsk in May: has yet to show he stays 7f: trained by R. Hollinshead on fourth and fifth outings. *J. Powney.*

PARBLEU 7 br.g. Pardao 120–St Tropez 99 (Princely Gift 137) [1974 6g4 6f   **64** 6g 6g3 6g4 6fg3 6g6 6fg3 7.3d2 7g 6s2   1975 6s4 7d5 6g 6f2 6f5 6fg 6d 6f 6fg5   1976 6g5 6g6] well-built gelding: stayed 1m: acted on any going: sometimes wore blinkers: inconsistent and disappointing: dead. *M. Stevens.*

PARBOLD 3 b.f. Sassafras 135–Party Whip (Sica Boy 132) [1975 6g 6g 1976 **54**
5d³ 6f 5f⁶] narrow filly: plater: close-up third to Gershwin in maiden race at
Edinburgh in April, best effort: should be suited by a return to longer distances
than 5f: not seen out after May. *R. D. Peacock.*

PARENT 3 b.c. Great Nephew 126–Piragua 85 (Petition 130) [1975 6g⁶ 1976 **96**
8v* 9d* 10f* 10.6d] strong colt: good walker: dam won four times at 1¼m: won
maiden races at Ayr and Newcastle and handicap at Beverley, all in April, beating
What A Find impressively by a length on last-named course: took on much
stronger opposition when eighth of 11 to Leventis in Bass Clubmen's Handicap at
Haydock in June, only subsequent outing: will stay further than 1¼m: acts on
any going. *E. Weymes.*

PARKHOUSE LAD 3 b.g. John's Pride 56–mare's pedigree unknown [1975 **—**
N.R. 1976 8h 13.8g] half-bred gelding: useless. *D. Plant.*

PARK LASS 3 b.f. King Log 115–Sighted Unseen (Mincio 127) [1975 5.9fg **—**
5fg 5g 1976 8fg 10.6g] seemingly of no account. *R. Cambidge.*

PARK ROW 3 b.c. Sovereign Path 125–Front Row 111 (Epaulette 125) [1975 **80**
5.1f⁶ 7g⁴ 6g 8f⁶ 1976 8fg 10.1f³ 11.1g³ 12fg* 10.5fg³ 12fg² 12v] lengthy, attractive colt: half-brother to smart miler Long Row (by Linacre): won 18-runner maid-
en race at Lingfield in June by 6 lengths from Shuwaiman: ran creditably next
two outings, notably when third to Bright Finish in minor event at York after a
rough passage: off course three months afterwards and had stiff task and was well
beaten on final outing: stays 1½m. *R. Jarvis.*

PARKSIDE BOY 2 ch.c. Communication 119–Quisisana (Panaslipper 130) **69**
[1976 6f 5g 7fg² 8s⁵ 10s⁵ 6s⁴] compact colt: poor mover: fair plater: stays 1m
but probably not 1¼m: probably acts on any going. *G. Toft.*

PARK WALK 3 b.c. Derring-Do 131–Parradell 104 (Pandofell 132) [1975 5s **69**
5fg 6fg 7d 8g 7s³ 1976 7g 8fg⁴ 8f³ 7fg⁵ 8f] lengthy colt: quite a moderate
handicapper: had none too clear a run on last two outings: will probably stay
1¼m. *W. Wightman.*

PARLOR NOBLE 6 gr.h. Abernant 142–Pelisson (Zarathustra 131) [1974 **78**
6g² 7.5g* 6.5g⁵ 7.5g 1975 6v 12s 5f* 5h⁴ 6fg 1976 6v⁵ 7f² 8g⁵ 8f 8.2g 7v]
strong horse: moderate performer: disappointing after third outing in 1976:
effective at 5f and stays 1m: acts on hard going: sold 940 gns Newmarket Autumn
Sales. *S. Hall.*

PARNHAM PRINCE 2 b.c. Prince Regent 129–Zulu Lady (Proud Chieftain 122) **82**
[1976 7fg³ 7g] tall, lengthy colt: half-brother to useful Irish 5f and 7f winner
Zulu Queen (by Sovereign Path): 1,850 gns yearling: dam won from 5f to 7f in
Ireland: 3½ lengths last of three to Crucial Decision in £1,600 race at Lingfield in
July but ran well, chasing winner for 5f: last of eight to Catiline in Donnington
Castle Stakes at Newbury later in month and wasn't seen out again. *I. Balding.*

PARSIFAL b.c. Derring-Do 131–Sarsgrove 70 (Hornbeam 130) [1974 6d **86**
1975 11v* 12fg⁴ 12s⁶ 12g 10.6s² 1976 11.7fg⁶ 12g² 12fg⁶ 10g³ 10g* 10.5g*]
good-topped colt: fair handicapper: winner at Ayr in August and at York the
following month, on latter course making all and battling on resolutely to beat
Domitor ¾ length: stays 1½m: acts on heavy going: wears blinkers. *A. Corbett.*

PARTRIDGE BROOK 3 b.f. Birdbrook 110–Limena 67 (Pinza 137) [1975 5v² **109**
5s² 5g² 5f* 6d* 7f* 6fg* 7.2fg² 8g² 7f² 7g* 8g² 1976 10fg 8fg⁴ 10h⁶ 8h² 9f⁶ 8g⁵
10g* 9g⁶ 12s] well-made, good sort of filly: steadily came to hand and won
£2,400 handicap at Ascot in September by 1½ lengths from Primrose Bank: did best
of those racing on disadvantageous stand side when very good sixth of 29 to
Intermission in Irish Sweeps Cambridgeshire at Newmarket the following month:
stays 1¼m (well beaten when tried at 1½m): acts on any going: goes well for
apprentice N. Crowther. *M. W. Easterby.*

PASAGUARDA 2 gr.c. Runnymede 123–Irish Elegance 60 (French Beige 127) **91**
[1976 5f 6f* 6f⁵ 6fg⁴ 7.3d⁶ 7.2v³] neat colt: third foal: half-brother to two
winners, including French 1m and 1¼m winner Indian Head (by Derring-Do):
5,400 gns yearling: dam won at 1¼m: dwelt in six-runner maiden race at Brighton
in August but got up close home to win by a neck from Punto Banco: ran well
in nurseries subsequently: will stay 1m: acts on any going: sold 5,000 gns Doncaster November Sales and exported to Norway. *R. Price.*

PASCUALETE 3 br.c. Town Crier 119–False Evidence 53 (Counsel 118) [1975 **114**
6g⁶ 6g* 6g³ 1976 6fg* 6g² 5d² 5g* 6f³ 6g 5.6g] lengthy, attractive colt: good
mover: brother to top-class 1974 2-y-o Cry of Truth: dam placed over 1½m: won
handicap at Newmarket in April and minor event at Sandown in June, latter

by 2 lengths from Trigamy: good third to Gentilhombre in Cork and Orrery Stakes at Royal Ascot later in month: stays 6f: probably acts on any going: genuine and consistent but ran badly on sixth outing and had stiff task on final start. *P. Walwyn.*

PAS DE PROBLEME 2 b.f. Sir Gaylord–Queen's Parole (Worden II 129) **99** [1976 6fg² 6v⁵] fourth foal: dam, useful winner in France as a 2-y-o, is half-sister to Rock Roi: 6/1, took on several useful fillies in minor event at Salisbury in September and showed a deal of promise, having every chance at distance and being beaten only ¼ length by more-experienced Metair, the pair finishing 4 lengths clear: appeared to fly jump leaving stalls when favourite for £2,100 event at York the following month, but was soon racing up with leaders until finding little when let down 2f out: was not persevered with when beaten, and came home about 20 lengths behind subsequently-disqualified Picatina: will stay at least 1¼m: probably does not act on heavy ground: sure to win races when conditions are in her favour. *P. Walwyn.*

PASKO 5 b.g. Firestreak 125–New Moss (Mossborough 126) [1974 7fg 6.9f — 7.2fg⁵ 8f⁶ 10.4g 10fg 8fg 7fg⁶ 8.2g 10s³ 8s³ 10v⁴ 10v* 1975 8.2s 8s 7s 10d 8g 10g 1976 8f 8.2fg] of no account nowadays. *B. Richmond.*

PASQUABOND 3 ch.f. Good Bond 122–Chumba (Cambremer 132) [1975 5g 5f — 5fg 5f⁴ 7d 8f 6g 7g⁶ 1976 10.1fg 12g 8fg] poor maiden. *F. Muggeridge.*

PASSERINE 2 b.f. My Swallow 134–Marie Denise 68 (Dual 117) [1976 7fg 7.2f] tall, leggy filly: first foal: dam a stayer and quite a useful hurdler: in rear in minor events at Thirsk in July (missed break) and Haydock in August: looked to need more time at 2 yrs and may do better. *M. Camacho.*

PASSING GLORY 2 ch.f. Majority Blue 126–Apposite 83 (Relic) [1976 5fg 6g **68** 7g⁶ 7fg 7g 8d] lightly-made filly: half-sister to winners here and abroad: 500 gns yearling: dam won at 3 yrs in Italy: showed first sign of ability when sixth of 19 to Gairloch in maiden race at Kempton in August: showed nothing like that form in sellers on last two outings: not certain to stay 9f. *G. Pritchard-Gordon.*

PASS IT AROUND 2 b.c. Round Table–Dry Ice (Sir Gaylord) [1976 7fg⁶] — p American-bred colt: half-brother to three winners in U.S.A., including stakes-placed Cool Concept (by Swoon's Son): $80,000 yearling: dam unraced half-sister to two stakes winners: 7/1, showed up for over 4f when remote sixth of nine to Fair Season in minor event at Newmarket in July, only outing. *H. Cecil.*

PASS THE PORT 3 ch.c. My Swallow 134–Saint Shari 81 (Saint Crespin **98** III 132) [1975 5s 5g 6g 8.2g⁵ 7g⁶ 8.2d³ 8g* 7.6s² 1976 11.1fg² 12g* 12g⁴ 12.2g* 12fg* 12f² 13fg⁶ 11.7fg² 12f² 12g²] quite attractive colt: useful handicapper: a tough individual who kept his form and condition well and won at Doncaster, Wolverhampton and Ripon: also ran some good races in defeat, notably when short-head second to Ivory Girl in Fitzwilliam Stakes at Doncaster in September: stays 1⅝m well and has given impression he will stay further (ran below his best when tried at 13f but had stiffish task): probably acts on any going: blinkered fifth outing in 1975: genuine and consistent. *B. Hobbs.*

PAST HISTORY 3 br.g. March Past 124–Sanctuair (Sanctum 116) [1975 5d **57** 6f 7g 7d⁴ 7g 1976 10g 10fg 12fg³ 12fg³ 16h³ 15.5s*] compact gelding: having first outing since June, won maiden race at Folkestone in October by a short head from Oslo: stays 2m: acts on any going. *R. Smyth.*

PASTY 3 gr.f. Raffingora 130–Ma Marie 104 (My Babu 136) [1975 5f* 5fg* — 5f* 5fg* 6d* 1976 7.3f⁴ 8fg 8f 6fg⁶ 6fg] neat, well-made filly: sister to sprinter Raffmarie and half-sister to numerous winners, including useful stayer Q.C. (by Petition): dam stayed 1½m: was best of English 2-y-o fillies in 1975 and won all her five races, including Lowther Stakes at York and William Hill Cheveley Park Stakes at Newmarket: 3 lengths fourth to Rowantree in Fred Darling Stakes at Newbury in April: ran moderately afterwards in 1,000 Guineas (20th of 25 to Flying Water), Coronation Stakes (last of eight) and two handicaps (tried in blinkers on final outing) and seemed to have trained off: probably stayed 7f: probably acted on any going: stud. *P. Walwyn.*

PATCH 4 ch.c. St Paddy 133–Palatch 120 (Match III 135) [1974 5s⁴ 6g² **122** 8v* 7.5s⁵ 1975 8s⁵ 12g* 12g² 15.5g 12fg* 12g⁵ 1976 12f 10.5fg³ 11g⁵] big, strong, good-looking colt: one of best 3-y-o's of 1975, as he showed when finishing second to Val de l'Orne in French Derby at Chantilly: made only three appearances at

4 yrs, running his best race when 6 lengths third of seven to Wollow in Benson and Hedges Gold Cup at York in August: odds on, ran much below that form when well-beaten fifth of seven to Gunner B in Doonside Cup at Ayr the following month (subsequently found to have rapped a joint): extremely well suited by 1¼m and should have stayed further: acted on any going with the possible exception of very firm: suited by forcing tactics: genuine: standing at Raffin Stud Farm, Castletown, Meath. *P. Walwyn.*

PATER NOSTER 3 b.c. Green God 128–Meld's Relation (The Phoenix) [1975 **79** 7fg 1976 11f 16f* 16f2 16fg3] lengthy colt: won maiden race at Chepstow in April by 4 lengths from Monte Ceco: well suited by test of stamina: acts on firm going: apprentice ridden when successful: not seen out after June. *G. Harwood.*

PATH OF GOLD 3 b.g. Pall Mall 132–Gold Frame (Royal Serenade 132) [1975 **83** 5f 6fg 7g 6g2 6g3 6g4 6g2 1976 6g* 8g4 8g5 6f* 7g4 6d2 6g3 6v] workmanlike gelding: won maiden race at Nottingham in April and handicap at Salisbury in August: rallied to lead again close home when beating Allez Britain a short head on latter course: best form at 6f and has yet to show he stays 1m: acts on firm going. *M. Smyly.*

PATRIS 3 b.c. Petingo 135–Joyful 112 (Princely Gift 137) [1975 5g* 6f2 6fg **118** 7g4 6g3 1976 7f4 7g3 8fg4 8d 8.5g4 8f3 10fg 8fg 7g5 8d* 8s4]
The top two-year-olds of 1975 had a pretty lean time of it in 1976. Of the thirty two-year-olds rated at 8-8 and above in the Free Handicap, twenty-six ran in Europe in their second season and only nine of the twenty-six managed to win a race. This select group of nine was made up of five pattern race winners —Wollow, Music Boy, Gentilhombre, Smuggler and Relkino—plus Sarania, Royal Boy, Solar and Patris. It took Patris ten races to join the group, but he had been unlucky not to win much sooner. In the James Lane Two Thousand Guineas Trial at Kempton, Patris finished third, just over a length behind the winner Royal Boy, after being hampered when the winner veered across him in the final furlong. The subsequent stewards' inquiry left the placings unaltered, but after Patris had dead-heated with his stable-companion Radetzky for the St James's Palace Stakes at Royal Ascot another stewards' inquiry took a different course. After a stride-for-stride last-furlong battle, during which Patris had drifted a little to his left, the pair had finished a length in front of Earth Spirit, but Patris was subsequently relegated to third place for hampering Earth Spirit. In between these two races Patris put up an excellent performance in the Two Thousand Guineas, finishing fourth, only three and a half lengths behind Wollow.
If Patris had reproduced his Guineas running with any regularity he would surely have enjoyed a successful season, but in eight races after the Guineas he only twice finished in the first three and only once (at Royal Ascot) ran up to his best. When he did finally manage to get his head in front, in the Arlington Stakes at Newbury, he scrambled home from the disappointing All Hope after looking likely to win comfortably a quarter of a mile from home. Excuses may be made for one or two of his collection of miserable efforts during the year—he was reportedly badly hampered in the Irish Two Thousand Guineas and he did not stay the mile and a quarter of the Joe Coral Eclipse—but there are just too many poor races of his for all of them to be explained away. The fact of the matter is that Patris cannot be relied upon to reproduce his best form; he is inconsistent, and his inconsistency stands out all the more because he is such a very useful horse on his day.

		Petition	Fair Trial
	Petingo	(br 1944)	Art Paper
	(b 1965)	Alcazar	Alycidon
Patris		(ch 1957)	Quarterdeck
(b.c. 1973)		Princely Gift	Nasrullah
	Joyful	(b 1951)	Blue Gem
	(b 1962)	My Game	My Babu
		(br 1957)	Flirting

Petingo died early in the spring of 1976 after covering only a few mares. Patris is easily the best of his fourth crop although he does not measure up to the leading members of Petingo's previous crops—Satingo, English Prince and Three Legs. Patris is the second winner produced by Joyful who won the second of her only two starts as a two-year-old in the style of a very speedy filly, but who did not race again. Of her previous offspring, Grazia (by Aureole) also raced only at two years when she won over six furlongs, while the four-year-old Royal Heir (by Royal Palace) has raced only three times but has shown he possesses enough ability

*Arlington Stakes, Newbury—Patris is all out to beat All Hope,
Early Dawn and Danestic*

to win a race. Joyful is a half-sister to numerous winners, including Lady Seymour who won on both her starts at two years in Ireland in 1974, notably in the Phoenix Stakes, and who received 9-0 in the Madrid Free Handicap. Their dam My Game never ran, but is a half-sister to several good horses including the Eclipse winner Arctic Explorer. This is also the family of such horses as The Cobbler, Supreme Court, Cavo Doro, Saintly Song and Huntercombe.

A lengthy, good-quartered colt who cost 19,000 guineas as a yearling, Patris stays a mile and goes well on top-of-the-ground. It took him all his time to win a race as a three-year-old and, unless he turns over a new leaf, it is unlikely he will fare much better in 1977. *C. Brittain.*

PATRONELLIE 2 b.f. Veiled Wonder–Our Edith 86 (Will Somers 114 §) [1976 5s 5v] third foal: dam stayed really well: beaten long way in maiden races at Folkestone and Lingfield. *C. Benstead.* —

PAUL ALISON 4 ch.c. Whistling Wind 123–Jerusalem (Palestine 133) [1974 5f⁴ 5h² 5g* 5g² 5fg 5s⁶ 1975 5fg 6v² 7d⁴ 6d 7s 6d⁵ 6g 6fg 1976 5g⁴ 5.8f⁴ 6f⁴ 5.8h⁵ 6f 6h] compact colt: quite a moderate handicapper: stays 6f: seems to act on any going: sometimes wears blinkers but does just as well without them: fell final outing and was subsequently found to have broken a blood vessel. *A. Pitt.* **70**

PAULDENAM 5 ch.g. Henry the Seventh 125–Bright Future 91 (Darius 129) [1974 N.R. 1975 N.R. 1976 11.1g 7.6s 15.5s] of little account on flat nowadays. *R. Blakeney.* —

PAUL DIVER 2 ch.c. Deep Diver 134–Pink Foot 97 (Wilwyn 129) [1976 5s³] lengthy colt: half-brother to several winners, including fairly useful miler Cissbury Boy (by Galivanter): 10,500 gns yearling: dam stayed 1¼m: backward, made much of running when promising 3 lengths third of 13 to Arctic Tribune in maiden race at Sandown in October: sure to improve and win races at 3 yrs. *I. Balding.* **84 p**

PAUL GAUGUIN 3 br.c. Derring-Do 131–Ile de France 94 (French Beige 127) [1975 6g 5fg 7g 6g 1976 7fg 10g 8s 5s⁴ 5s] small, stocky colt: showed only semblance of ability when 4¾ lengths fourth of eight to John Gay in handicap at Chepstow in October: should stay 1m+: blinkered final outing. *W. Payne.* **56**

PAULOMAT 3 b.g. Welsh Saint 126–Rose Marullah 104 (Valerullah 113) [1975 N.R. 1976 8fg] well-grown gelding: unquoted, finished lame when seventh to Prince Murdoc in 14-runner minor event at Ripon in May: dead. *W. Haigh.* —

PAVE THE WAY 5 b.h. Paveh 126–Sailor Girl 100 (Hard Tack 111 §) [1974 8g⁶ 8g² 8.2f 10g⁵ 8.2g² 8d² 8.2g* 8d* 8g⁵ 10d⁴ 8v³ 8s³ 1975 8v⁴ 7f⁶ 8h³ 7fg⁴ 8.2g³ 8g³ 8fg* 7.3d 8g 1976 8fg 8g⁶ 8d 8fg 12.2s⁴ 8v] rangy horse and a good mover: disappointing since winning at Sandown in 1975: was tailed off on fourth outing: best form at 1m and has yet to show he stays further: acts on any going: suited by front-running tactics: blinkered final outing. *D. Weeden.* —

PAWNEESE 3 b.f. Carvin 127–Plencia (Le Haar 126) [1975 6.5fg² 7.5g⁴ **131** 1976 8g* 10.5g* 10.5g* 12g* 10.5d* 12g* 12s 12s]

The inability of the three-year-old fillies Pawneese and Riverqueen to show their form in the autumn was one of the biggest disappointments in a season that both had hitherto done much to vitalize. Pawneese's loss of form was the bigger disappointment, for she was the better filly; at her best she had the Prix Vermeille at her mercy and held as good a chance as any horse in the field of winning the Prix de l'Arc de Triomphe, but she ran poorly in both races. Two months earlier Pawneese had been regarded, with some justification, as the best middle-distance horse of either sex in Europe. At that time she had won six races in a row since the start of the season, and in an eight-week period she had performed prodigious feats. In the space of eight weeks she had won the Oaks, the Prix de Diane and the King George VI and Queen Elizabeth Diamond Stakes, trouncing the best fillies in England in the Oaks, inflicting on the Prix Saint-Alary winner Riverqueen in the Diane the first defeat of her career, and accounting for four classic winners, including the current French and Irish Sweeps Derby winners, in the King George, the last-named the most important race open to three-year-olds and upwards run in England.

The explanation for Pawneese's very disappointing showing in the autumn is probably to be found in either the nature of the programme she was asked to follow up to the end of July or the nature of the ground prevailing at Longchamp in the autumn. Despite her short rest after Ascot Pawneese might have been feeling the effects of her strenuous season when she returned to the racecourse, although her appearance as she walked round the paddock before the Prix Vermeille did not give the slightest hint that this might be so. She looked very well. The ground on which the Prix Vermeille and the Prix de l'Arc were decided was very soft—much softer than anything she had previously raced on, very different from the ground at Epsom and Ascot, and different even from that at Chantilly when she won the Diane, which was only just on the soft side of good. There must be, at the very least, a doubt about Pawneese's ability to handle the really soft going that seems to obtain at Longchamp nearly every autumn. Another season should resolve that doubt, for she will be in training in 1977 when, presumably, she will have the Arc as a greater priority than it was in 1976 and will be prepared accordingly. Her first objective is said to be the Coronation Cup; if she does manage to reproduce her best we can see nothing outside her own stable to stop her gaining it.

After Flying Water's easy win in the One Thousand Guineas her owner said he had another filly for the Oaks—Pawneese—and that Flying Water would go for the Prix de Diane, France's equivalent of the Oaks but run over a shorter distance. Pawneese already had the reputation of being the best filly in Penna's yard but she hadn't form anywhere near so good as Flying Water's. Her record as a two-year-old was nothing out of the ordinary and she had been beaten in

Oaks Stakes, Epsom—Pawneese wins in effortless fashion. Roses for the Star is a gallant second, followed by African Dancer, Laughing Girl (left) and Centrocon (partly obscured)

Prix de Diane, Chantilly—Pawneese wins from the hitherto-unbeaten Riverqueen. Lagunette finishes third

both her races. At three she had won the Prix la Camargo at Saint-Cloud as early as the second week in March and the Prix Penelope, a Group 3 race, on the same course later in the month. Her two performances at Saint-Cloud, while illustrating that she was progressing nicely, gave no indication that she was up to classic-winning standard, but two weeks after the Guineas she ran a first-rate trial for the Oaks in the Prix Cleopatre at Saint-Cloud, giving weight and a thorough beating to some useful fillies. She made all the running. Elise Ma Belle, a close second to the unbeaten Theia in the Prix Vanteaux and rated at 8-5 in the French Two-Year-Old Free Handicap, chased her home at a distance of two and a half lengths. Except for demonstrating that she stayed a mile and a half Pawneese couldn't have done much more to press her claim for the Oaks, and as her breeding shouted middle-distance stamina she looked a worthy favourite for Epsom. On the day she started the hottest favourite for the race since Valoris ten years earlier.

So superior was Pawneese to modest opposition at Epsom that she turned the Oaks into a procession. Her jockey Saint-Martin is not one to pay too much heed to convention when it comes to riding tactics, and finding himself at the head of affairs after only three furlongs without making any obvious effort to get there, he allowed Pawneese to make the best of her way home. The difference in ability between Pawneese and the rest had to be seen to be believed. There she strode at the top of the hill, lobbing along as if out for an exercise gallop, while the others laboured to keep up; she stretched out into a substantial lead in next to no time turning for home and did just enough to maintain her position. Without being asked seriously to race, she won by five lengths from the running-on Roses for the Star.

Easy race or not, to turn out Pawneese against Riverqueen and company over a shorter distance at Chantilly only nine days later seemed to be asking a great deal of her even in this age of high-speed travel. While Pawneese had been to Epsom and back Riverqueen had been rested, having had her last outing in the Prix Saint-Alary on May 23rd, in which she had beaten Theia, Flying Water and the third and fourth in the One Thousand Guineas too. Riverqueen had, in fact, done all that had been asked of her and had won the Poule d'Essai des Pouliches and two other races besides the Saint-Alary; she started favourite for the Prix de Diane at evens with Pawneese at only 18/10, so it looked very much a two-horse affair for all that eleven were taking part. Despite the shorter course of the Diane (about a furlong and a half under the Oaks's distance) Pawneese had no difficulty in leading all the way and she won just as impressively as at Epsom although by much less a margin. Again she quickened into a long lead early in the straight leaving Riverqueen, who is noted for her finishing speed, with an uphill task; and Riverqueen couldn't press home a challenge. Again Pawneese never had a serious question asked of her, but Riverqueen, swishing her tail under severe pressure, made a much better-looking second than Roses for the Star and closed to within a length and a half of Pawneese. The last Oaks winner to win the Prix de Diane was Fille de l'Air in 1864; the double is seldom attempted, and English fillies have had the chance to attempt it only in the last thirty years or so, since before then the Diane was closed to foreign competition.

Between the running of the Prix de Diane and the King George VI and Queen Elizabeth Diamond Stakes the results of two other races sent Pawneese's stock even higher. She already rated as one of the best Oaks winners for years. Riverqueen beat older colts in the Grand Prix de Saint-Cloud (among those behind her were Ashmore and the Coronation Cup winner Quiet Fling) and Lagunette, third in the Diane, beaten four and a half lengths, won the Irish Guinness Oaks from the Diane fifth Sarah Siddons. Not many fillies have won

546

the King George VI and Queen Elizabeth Stakes, nor have many front runners; and in addition the recent change in the weight-for-age allowance in the race gives an advantage of 3 lb to the older horses in our opinion, but there was no mistaking the confidence behind Pawneese. She started a strong second-favourite to Youth, who probably owed his market position to the fact that Malacate had gone on to beat the Derby winner Empery in Ireland after finishing third to Youth in the French Derby.

The only two winners of the King George VI and Queen Elizabeth Stakes before Pawneese to have led all the way were Nasram II, who needed to make the running and was a genuine racehorse only as long as he was in front, and Match III, who could run any sort of race asked of him. It will come as no great surprise to those who don't already know, to learn that Saint-Martin rode Match. Saint-Martin and his great contemporary Piggott are masters of the difficult art of waiting in front and have no equals in Europe today. The particular difficulty presented to a rider of a front runner in a middle-distance race of the highest class is that however strong the pace there is nearly always at least one horse in opposition able to stay in touch and produce a turn of speed towards the finish. Judging correctly what pace is best for one's own horse and worst for one's main rivals is the art. In Match's King George, Saint-Martin outwitted the opposition by dictating a slow gallop and then outsprinting Aurelius in the short straight; in Pawneese's King George, he set a fast gallop with her and judged her capabilities brilliantly, keeping just enough in reserve to see her home in comfort if not in ease. The difference in the quality of the opposition to Pawneese here to that in the Oaks was striking. Whereas at Epsom she had them all labouring with at least five furlongs to go, at Ascot she always had two or more horses moving well behind her and not so far behind at that, although it's true to say that she never looked in any danger of defeat. For a long way the main threat seemed likely to come from Malacate, who, unlike Riverqueen in the Diane and Orange Bay here, was able to quicken with Pawneese after a mile or so, and he stayed in contention until a furlong from home. Youth, who had never been moving particularly well, lost his chance by running very wide when in fourth place on the bend; Malacate finally weakened with a furlong to go, and the main challenges to Pawneese came very late in the day from three older horses, the slow-starting Bruni, Dakota, who was hanging badly left, and Orange Bay, who had begun to run on very strongly. All three were catching Pawneese at the finish but Saint-Martin, as we said, had judged the distance to a nicety and Pawneese got home by a length from Bruni. Afterwards the stewards took the unusual step of testing all ten runners; last-placed Duke of Marmalade's test proved positive.

Pawneese became only the fourth filly to win the King George VI and

King George VI and Queen Elizabeth Diamond Stakes, Ascot—Pawneese makes all the running and stays on strongly to beat the fast-finishing Bruni, with Orange Bay, Dakota (not on picture) and Malacate not far behind

M D. Wildenstein's "Pawneese"

Queen Elizabeth Stakes, following Aunt Edith, Park Top and Dahlia, the last-named of whom won the race twice and was the only one to equal Pawneese's feat of winning it as a three-year-old. Now is not the time to compare Pawneese with her three predecessors; there will be a more appropriate time when she has had the same chance to develop as they all had. It is appropriate, however, to give an appreciation of the value of her performance at Ascot. The King George VI and Queen Elizabeth Stakes is little behind the Prix de l'Arc de Triomphe as a test of a middle-distance horse, and it has the advantage of being run at a time of year when most of the contestants are at or near their best; and in most seasons it does not present the hazards of a very large field or very soft going that the Arc often presents. We would estimate that the merit of Pawneese's win in the King George is nearly as great as that of Ivanjica's in the Arc, in so doing accepting that Dakota, who was a better horse on his day than most allow, ran the race of his life to get within two lengths of Pawneese. On our estimate of Pawneese's merit, she emerges the best filly to have won the Oaks since Noblesse, and, apart from Petite Etoile, Noblesse and Bella Paola, as good an Oaks winner as there has been in the last thirty years. As a point of interest, she is regarded by her owner as behind Allez France, not surprisingly; amazingly, she is also regarded as behind the Irish Oaks favourite Acoma, who has now been retired through injury.

Pawneese (b.f. 1973)	Carvin (b 1962)	Marino (ch 1956)	Worden II / Buena Vista
		Coraline (b 1957)	Fine Top / Copelina
	Plencia (ch 1968)	Le Haar (ch 1954)	Vieux Manoir / Mince Pie
		Petite Saguenay (ch 1961)	Nordiste / Ballynash

Pawneese ran in only the Prix Vermeille and the Prix de l'Arc subsequently, finishing a well-beaten seventh of ten to Lagunette and a well-beaten eleventh of twenty to Ivanjica. In both races she was taken on for the lead—by River-queen's pacemaker Moquerie in the Vermeille and by Kasteel in the Arc—and

Vaux Gold Tankard, Redcar—Peaceful takes full advantage of the slow early pace and quickens away from Ribellaro

although she got to the front in both races by the time they reached the last turn, she went out like a light in the last two furlongs. Possibly the best way of beating Pawneese will be to put in a good pacemaker against her. And if a front-runner of the calibre of a High Hat or Vienna can be found (Kasteel can't be all that far behind them) then Pawneese could well be in as much trouble as Petite Etoile was in her day.

Pawneese's sire Carvin has sired little else of note; the Morny runner-up Rose de Saron is probably his second-best runner. He himself won very few races, but he was a rattling good horse and would have won more often had he not been foaled in the same year as Sea-Bird II, Reliance II and Diatome. He finished a short-head second to Diatome in the Washington International and a good third to Reliance and Diatome in the French Derby. Pawneese is her dam's first foal; the second, a filly by Don II called Patia, hasn't yet run. Plencia, the dam, won two races at around a mile and a half in France: she was a useful filly and is out of an unraced half-sister to four very well-known French horses in Montaval (the King George winner and Derby second), Paimpont (the Oaks second), Mourne and Moutiers. The third dam, Ballynash, won over sprint distances as a two-year-old.

We find ourselves at odds with the majority when expressing an opinion on Pawneese's conformation. Most people seem not to be taken with her appearance, but we think her very attractive. She has length, size, and a lovely head, and even though she has still room to fill out a little she has great quality. She will make up into a very beautiful broodmare. Let's hope we get another opportunity of seeing her before she goes to stud. *A. Penna, France.*

PAY ROLL 3 ch.f. Burglar 128–Sarsgrove 70 (Hornbeam 130) [1975 5g 5f 7h⁶ **74** 7.2fg⁵ 8f³ 1976 9f 10f⁶ 8fg² 8fg² 8fg⁵ 8f⁶ 8h² 7f* 7f* 7h² 8fg⁵ 7g⁶] strong filly: won handicaps at Lanark and Redcar in the summer, beating King's Caper a neck on latter course: stays 1m: acts on hard ground: wears blinkers: has a good turn of foot. *J.Etherington.*

P.C.'S RECORD 8 b.g. Royal Record II–Peaches and Cream (Pardal 130) — [1974 N.R. 1975 N.R. 1976 13f] plater (rated 63) in 1971: well-beaten last of seven behind Tilton Boy in handicap at Hamilton in September, only outing on flat since. *P. Arthur.*

PEACEFUL 5 ch.g. Crepello 136–Peace 113 (Klairon 132) [1974 8g⁴ 10fg⁴ **110** 14fg⁴ 12g² 13.3s 1975 12fg⁴ 12fg* 12fg* 12d² 12d² 1976 12fg* 12.3s⁴ 14.7d*

Old Newton Cup, Haydock—Peaceful (left) has the edge over Coin of Gold

12fg*] very useful performer: won three good handicaps before mid-season, Fraser Handicap at Kempton, Vaux Gold Tankard at Redcar and Old Newton Cup at Haydock: beat Coin of Gold a head when winning last-named event in July on final appearance: stays 1¾m: unsuited by very soft ground: ran poorly when tried in blinkers: good mount for an apprentice and goes well for S. Raymont: has a good turn of foot. *J. Tree.*

PEACEFUL VALLEY 2 ch.c. My Swanee 122–Mecara 90 (Gulf Pearl 117) **75** [1976 5g⁵ 5g 7f 7f⁴ 6f⁴] well-made colt: first foal: 4,600 gns yearling: dam, twice a winner over 5f at 2 yrs, is half-sister to smart Majetta: ran easily best race when 3 lengths fourth of 15 to His Master's Rocket in maiden event at Warwick in July, penultimate outing: will be suited by 1m. *J. Hill.*

PEACEFUL VENTURE 3 b.c. Irish Ball 127–Rue de la Paix (Abernant 142) **83** [1975 7g⁴ 6f 8g² 1976 8g⁴ 8g³ 10.4d⁴ 11.1g 10g³] strong colt: moderate maiden: put up best effort when fourth of 10 to Kafue Park in £1,600 event at Liverpool on first appearance: probably stays 1¼m: not seen out after July. *F. J. Houghton.*

PEACEFUL SYMBOL 2 ch.c. Sweet Revenge 129–Tortola § (Narrator 127) **99** [1976 5fg 7v* 7v²] half-brother to a winner in France: 5,800 gns yearling: dam lightly-raced half-sister to high-class stayer Almeira: won 16-runner maiden event at Leicester in October in good style, always going well and coming home 7 lengths clear of Hampshire despite being eased close home: proved no match for North Stoke in 15-runner minor race at Lingfield the following month and was beaten 2 lengths into second place: will stay at least 1m: acts well on heavy going: hampered at start first outing. *I. Balding.*

PEACH BLOSSOM 3 b.f. Blakeney 126–Picture Palace 83 (Princely Gift 137) — [1975 N.R. 1976 10g 10s⁶ 12v] neat filly: half-sister to several winners, including 1975 2,000 Guineas third Dominion (by Derring-Do), and good-class performers Prominent (by High Hat), Jeune Premier (by Primera) and Projector (by Hopeful Venture): dam won at 1¼m: showed up until turning for home when well beaten in maiden and minor events in the autumn. *J. Bethell.*

PEACHY 6 ch.m. Reliance II 137–Cheek to Cheek 99 (Alycidon 138 or Infatuation 129) [1974 10f 1975 N.R. 1976 12f⁵ 17.7f] of little account. *J. Welch.*

PEACOCK VAIN 2 ch.f. Shiny Tenth 120–Peacock Thread (Raeburn II) [1976 7s] fair sort: first foal: dam never ran: unquoted when remote eighth of 11 to Imperial Guard in minor event at Sandown in October, only outing. *R. Akehurst.*

PEAK PRINCESS 2 b.f. Charlottown 127–Jackies Joy (Skymaster 126) [1976 **62** 6f³ 5g³ 6fg* 8f⁶ 7g⁵] second foal: half-sister to fairly useful 3-y-o 9f and 1¼m winner Amber Valley (by Forlorn River): attracted no bid after winning seven-runner seller at Ayr in July by ¾ length from Bridgewater: stays 7f and shouldn't be troubled by 1m+: sold 240 gns Doncaster October Sales. *J. Hanson.*

PEARL CREEK 3 ch.f. Gulf Pearl 117–Molarina 100 (Denturius) [1975 N.R. 1976 6fg 5g] short-legged, compact filly: half-sister to six winners, including useful sprinter Queen of the Troops (by King's Troop): tailed off in early-season maiden races at Leicester and Sandown. *W. Wightman.*

PEARLDOR 2 b.c. Hotfoot 126–Pearlesque 88 (Gulf Pearl 117) [1976 5fg⁶ 6f⁶ **100 §** 6g⁴ 6g* 6fg 6g 7s* 6v] first foal: 2,800 gns yearling: dam won over 5f at 2 yrs from two starts and is sister to very useful animals Pearl Star and Seadiver: an inconsistent performer but is useful on his day and won a maiden race at Windsor and a nursery at Warwick, latter by 5 lengths from Naughty Lass: will stay at least 1m: suited by soft going: blinkered last two outings, running one very good race and one very bad: sold 6,200 gns Newmarket Autumn Sales and exported to Sweden. *P. Walwyn.*

PEARL HAVEN 2 gr.f. Raffingora 130–Pearl Harbour 83 (Martial 131) [1976 **93** 5f⁶ 5fg⁵ 6f* 6fg⁴ 5fg² 6g⁶] sturdy filly: third living foal: dam won over 6f at 3 yrs: won 12-runner maiden race at Yarmouth in July in close finish with Sound of the Horn: ran very well in nursery at Windsor in September, going down by only a head to Laser Olivia: stays 6f but put up her best effort over 5f: acts on firm going. *B. Hobbs.*

PEARL MINK (DEN) 5 ch.h. Prominer 125–Bouche Bee (Buisson Ardent 129) — [1976 6d 8g 8fg⁵ 7f 5.8h⁶ 6s] strong horse: placed in up to 7.5f in Denmark and Sweden in 1975: no form in varied company in this country, final race being a seller at Folkestone in October. *N. Guest.*

PEARL SHELL 3 gr.f. Gulf Pearl 117–Daystar 91 (Major Portion 129) [1975 **61** N.R. 1976 8fg 7fg² 6f³ 6fg] first foal: dam disappointing daughter of smart performer Alborada: placed in maiden races at Leicester and Brighton in the summer: was probably better suited by 7f than 6f: dead. *J. Dunlop.*

PEARLY 4 ch.f. Gulf Pearl 117–Jeannette (Whistler 129) [1974 5g 5f 7g⁶ 7g⁵ — 7g⁴ 8s* 8g 8s³ 1975 10v⁶ 12fg² 12d² 16f⁴ 16fg³ 13g* 13d 12d² 13.8g* 12g 1976 13f] compact filly: quite a moderate handicapper (rated 79) in 1975: made only one appearance at 4 yrs: stays well: appears to act on any going: suitable mount for an apprentice. *M. Tate.*

PEBBLE CROSSING 3 br.g. Falcon 131–Prelone 110 (Precipitation) [1975 — 5s 1976 11.7f⁶] lightly raced and no worthwhile form on flat: sold 750 gns Ascot June Sales: dead. *J. Hill.*

PEDLAR 2 br.c. Forlorn River 124–Street Hawker 74 (Ben Hawke 94) [1976 **90** 5fg⁵ 5g⁵ 5f⁶ 7fg² 7h² 7g 7g] leggy colt: brother to two winners in Norway and half-brother to three winners, including useful sprinter Kingshott (by Manacle): 5,000 gns yearling: dam of little account: second in maiden races, going down by a length to Qualuz in 10-runner event at Newmarket in July and by 4 lengths to Exploiteur at Brighton the following month: well beaten on last two outings: suited by 7f, and will probably stay 1m. *P. Ashworth.*

PEERLESS PRINCE 2 ch.c. Double Jump 131–Trenora 89 (Ballymoss 136) — [1976 5fg 7fg 5v³] neat, strong colt: first foal: dam won over 11f: 7½ lengths third of 17 to Cedar Grange in all-aged maiden race at Nottingham in October, best effort: should stay at least 1m: acts on heavy going. *G. Hunter.*

PEGGY JET 4 br.f. Willipeg 112–Barbary Falls 84 (Falls of Clyde 126) [1974 **67** 5f 5f⁴ 5fg 5f* 5fg 5fg 7fg 8s 6s 1975 6fg 7f² 7f* 7fg⁵ 8g³ 8f 8g 8f 8g 1976 8f² 8fg² 6fg* 6g* 6f² 8.2f⁶ 5fg² 6d²] neat, good-bodied filly: plater: successful at Ayr in July and August, attracting no bid on either occasion: stays 1m: seems to act on any going: suitable mount for an apprentice. *J. Carr.*

PEGGY WIG 2 gr.f. Counsel 118–Peg (Palestine 133) [1976 5g⁶] compact — filly: half-sister to fair 1968 2-y-o 5f winner Spinning Top (by Bleep-Bleep): dam never ran: never-dangerous 7 lengths sixth of nine to Great Flight in maiden race at Sandown in June, only outing. *J. Old.*

PEKINOIS (late LE TREIZE) 2 br.c. Virginia Boy 106–Magical Maid (Premoni- **77** tion 130) [1976 5fg 5f 6fg 6fg²] half-brother to three minor winners: 200 gns yearling: blinkered, ran best race when 2 lengths second to King's Verdict in claiming race at Brighton in June: claimed £1,100 afterwards and didn't race again. *J. Sutcliffe.*

PELLY RIVER 2 b.c. Yukon Eric–Placate 99 (Ratification 129) [1976 7fg 8s] — neat, attractive colt: seventh foal: dam a miler: unquoted when behind in large fields of maidens at Leicester and Sandown in the autumn. *A. Davison.*

PEMALA 3 b.f. Royal Palace 131–Colwyn Bay 81 (Klairon 131) [1975 N.R. — 1976 10.4fg 10.1d] plain filly: poor walker: second live foal: 540 gns yearling: dam won over 1¼m: tailed off in maiden races at Chester and Windsor in September. *M. Bradley.*

PEMBI CHASE 3 b.c. Welsh Saint 126–North Riding 74 (Big Game) [1975 **66** 7g 6fg 1976 10fg 10fg 8f³ 10s 8s* 10s] well-made colt: showed improved form when winning 19-runner maiden race at Warwick in October by 1½ lengths from Pippin Place: evidently suited by 1m but appears not to stay 1¼m: acts on soft going. *J. Powney.*

PENCHAND 3 ch.c. Hopeful Venture 125–The Country Lane 90 (Red God 128 §) **70** [1975 5g 6f 7fg⁵ 7g³ 9g⁵ 7fg⁵ 1976 10.4s 7f 8g⁵ 8.2f² 8g³ 14v⁴ 8s*] compact colt: ridden by 7-lb claimer when clear-cut winner of 18-runner maiden race at Warwick in October, beating Good Fellow 4 lengths: ran best previous race in a Haydock seller: stays 9f and is not certain to stay 1¾m: acts on any going: wears blinkers nowadays. *A. Goodwill.*

PENCRAIG 2 br.c. Klairon 131–Blind Date 91 (Twilight Alley 133) [1976 7d — 7v⁶] well-grown colt: half-brother to fair handicapper Glimmer of Hope (by Never Say Die), a winner at up to 1¾m: dam won over 7f from three starts: behind in autumn in Houghton Stakes at Newmarket and minor event at Ling-field (25/1, finished distant sixth to Imperial Guard). *J. Dunlop.*

PENCUICK JEWEL 2 b.f. Petingo 135–Fotheringay 101 (Right Royal V 135) — p [1976 7d] well-grown filly: half-sister to two winners, notably Ascot Gold Cup winner Ragstone (by Ragusa): dam won at 1m: unquoted and backward when eleventh of 25 to Bessie Wallis in Houghton Stakes at Newmarket in October: should stay 1¼m: likely to do better. *J. Dunlop.*

PENFORT 11 ch.g. Pendragon–Ring of Fortune 80 (River Prince) [1974 N.R. 1975 12g 12d 1976 14g] seems of no account nowadays. *H. O'Neill.* —

PENHALIGON 2 ch.c. Amber Rama 133–Ice Ballet 87 (Ballymoss 136) [1976 6fg] half-brother to fairly useful 1¼m winner Tanara (by Romulus) and to winning French stayer Spring Snow (by Reliance II): 1,950 gns yearling: dam a stayer: unquoted when last of 12 to Tudor Lilt in minor race at Lingfield in June, only outing. *S. Ingham.* —

PENHILL COTTAGE 3 ch.g. Goldhill 125–Dumana 96 (Dumbarnie 125) [1975 5f 7g 7g 1976 10.1fg⁵ 8f⁵] poor plater. *R. Keenor.* —

PENNINA 3 b.f. Great Nephew 126–Princely Maid 71 (King's Troop 118) [1975 5d* 5g* 5s* 5f² 6fg* 6g² 6f³ 5g* 6fg³ 1976 6f 8d 6s 5fg² 5fg² 11g² 7.5g* 8g 9.2g 6.5g* 7s*] sharp, good-quartered filly: runner-up in William Hill Sprint Handicap at Epsom (to Overtown) and Tote Sprint Trophy (to Rundontwalk) at Ascot in June when tried in blinkers: subsequently sent to race in France and won minor events at Biarritz-Bayonne, Toulouse and Bordeaux: best at 5f in England but has run respectably at up to 11f in France: acts on any going: genuine and consistent: trained by M. W. Easterby until after fifth outing. *M. Laborde, France.* **105**

PENNINE DEREK 2 ch.g. Fury Royal 108–Brandy Princess 66 (Salmon King 107) [1976 9s⁴] second foal: dam stayed 1m: 20/1 when close-up fourth of nine to Saratoga Kid in weakly-contested maiden race at Wolverhampton in October: will stay 1¼m+. *W. Wharton.* **72**

PENNY ARCADE 3 b.g. Polyfoto 124–Queen's Blossom 56 (King's Bench 132) [1975 5f 5d 5g⁶ 5.3f⁵ 5fg² 5fg* 1976 5fg 6f 5g⁶ 6g⁵ 5g² 5f] close-coupled gelding: 4 lengths second to Fragrant Cloud in handicap at Wolverhampton in August, first outing for three months and easily best effort: should stay 6f: sometimes sweats up: changed hands 550 gns Ascot July Sales and was sold 480 gns Doncaster September Sales. *W. Marshall.* **65**

PENNY CANDY 3 b.f. Tamerlane 128–La Viola (Guersant 129) [1975 N.R. 1976 9.4h⁶ 12f] neat, strong filly: half-sister to several winners, including Tivola (by Tiffauges), rated best 2-y-o filly in Italy in 1973: 2,000 gns yearling: dam won at up to 11.5f in France: tailed off in minor events at Carlisle and Ripon in the summer. *H. Bell.* —

PENNY GAMBLE 2 ch.f. Gambling Debt 98–Nickel Penny (Silver Cloud 121) [1976 5h 6f 9fg 8s 7s⁶ 7s] first foal: dam failed to complete course in five outings over hurdles: poor plater. *H. Nicholson.* —

PENNY GOD 3 b.f. Red God 128 §–Palestra 92 (Palestine 133) [1975 unbeaten in four races in Hungary, winning at up to 7f 1976 8d 6d 7f 7fg] attractive filly: half-sister to a winner in Brazil by Never Say Die: 6,200 gns foal, resold 4,300 gns as a yearling: dam stayed 7f: unbeaten in four starts as a 2-y-o and topped Hungarian Free Handicap: well beaten in varied company in this country: may stay 1m: blinkered third outing. *F. J. Houghton.* —

PENNY LEVY 2 ch.f. Levmoss 133–Bright Penny 73 (Skymaster 126) [1976 6d] second foal: 2,100 gns yearling: dam placed over 5f at 2 yrs: unquoted when last in 23-runner maiden race won by Rings at Newmarket in October. *R. Lunness.* —

PENNY POST 4 br.c. Balidar 133–The Game 80 (Petition 130) [1974 7g 6d* 1975 7g³ 6g* 7g* 6.5g 8g⁵ 1976 7fg 6d³ 7.2d⁵ 8f] strong, good-looking colt: very useful performer (rated 112) at 3 yrs: finished strongly when 3½ lengths third of nine to Sandford Lady in Spring Handicap at York in May, easily best effort in 1976 (ran moderately on final start): effective at 6f and 7f: acts on a soft surface: blinkered last three outings: dwelt at start on third appearance: not seen out after June. *J. W. Watts.* **100**

PENNY'S PET 2 b.f. Galivanter 131–Mamas Pet (Midlander 112) [1976 6f³ 7f⁴ 6g 5g⁵ 7g⁴ 8fg⁵ 6v⁴ 8v] rather plain filly: first foal: dam ran once on flat and finished tailed off in novice hurdles: in frame in varied company, including selling: stays 1m: sometimes sweats up. *Hbt Jones.* **75**

PEPONI 2 b.f. Petingo 135–Quondam (Relic) [1976 5f 6fg] first foal: sold twice as a yearling, for 620 gns and 1,600 gns: behind in minor events at Beverley in May and Ripon in August: broke leg on latter course and was destroyed. *L. Shedden.* —

PEPPERMINSKY 2 bl.g. Ben Novus 109–Czaremont 74 (Damremont 120) —
[1976 7s 10d] lightly-made gelding: half-brother to useful stayer Philominsky
(by Philemon): dam, winner of 1m seller, stayed well: in rear in autumn in minor
events at Sandown and Newmarket (last of 12). *W. Marshall.*

PERANKA 4 gr.c. Klairon 131 or Palestine 133–Garrucha 117 (Prince Taj 123) **99**
[1974 5f 5s 6g⁵ 5s* 1975 6v 5.9g* 5f* 5fg⁵ 5f³ 6g³ 5fg² 5.9fg² 1976 5g² 5fg 5d⁴
5s 5fg³ 5f² 6t 5fg⁵ 5fg² 5g⁴ 6fg⁶ 5.3f* 5fg⁶ 5g* 5g⁵] lightly-built colt: useful
handicapper: winner of minor event at Brighton (easily from Briar Patch) and
handicap at Kempton (beat Vilgora a shade cleverly), both in August): ran
creditably in most of his other races, notably on ninth and tenth outings, when in
frame at Newmarket (didn't get the best of runs on latter occasion): stays 6f:
acts on any going: ridden by L. Piggott on both occasions when successful at
4 yrs. *W. Marshall.*

PERBURY 3 gr.f. Grisaille 115–Peridot 95 (Faubourg II 127) [1975 6f 7g⁶ 7fg* **82**
7g 1976 8f⁵ 7g² 8.5g⁶ 7fg 8.3f⁴ 7g² 7g 7.6g] tall, lightly-made filly: runner-up
in handicaps at Kempton in May (to Jimmy The Singer) and August (to Star
Walk): ran moderately on most of her other starts: will stay further than 1m:
acts on firm going: unseated rider soon after start on seventh outing. *S.
Woodman.*

PERELLO 2 b.c. Crepello 136–Caballeria (Iron Liege) [1976 5.5d 7g⁴ 7d² 7g* **118**
10s⁶] French colt: half-brother to two winners, including 1974 French Oaks
fourth Capaddia (by St Paddy): dam, placed at 3 yrs, is daughter of Apollonia,
a top-class winner at 2 yrs and 3 yrs in France: won Group 3 Criterium de
Maisons-Laffitte in September by a head from Aigle Blanc after a hard struggle
from the distance: made running for a long way in Prix de Conde at Longchamp
the following month but lost chance when slipping on home turn, and finished
remote sixth behind odds-on El Criollo: should stay at least 1¼m. *G.
Bonaventure, France.*

PERFECT GENTLEMAN 3 gr.c. Breeders Dream 116–Pen Friend 90 (Vigo 130) **76 d**
[1975 N.R. 1976 8f 8g 10fg 6g* 6g 7fg⁶ 7h⁴ 6f 6h⁴] rangy colt: good walker:
half-brother to two winners, including fair sprinter Queen's Quill (by Sovereign
Lord): 3,200 gns yearling: dam best at 6f or 7f: won 18-runner maiden race at
Kempton in May by 3 lengths from River Belle: did not reproduce that form and
was tried in blinkers on penultimate appearance: best form at 6f. *P. Cole.*

PERFECT MARRIAGE 5 b.g. Falcon 131–Fei-Hoo 65 (Dionisio 126) [1974 **39**
6g* 8f⁴ 6fg² 6fg³ 6f⁴ 5s² 7fg² 6s 8d 1975 10f 8fg 8f 8f⁴ 7f 5.9fg 1976 6g² 8fg]
lengthy, plain gelding: plater nowadays: pulled up lame at Warwick in April on
second outing and wasn't seen out again: best form at up to 6f, but stays further:
seems to act on any going: has been tried in blinkers but has done better without
them. *R. Hannon.*

PERFECT MATCH 10 b.g. Poaching 115–Well Matched 79 (Niccolo Dell'Arca) —
[1974 10.8g 12.2d⁶ 12.3f⁶ 13g 12f² 12f⁶ 12fg³ 16g⁵ 12s⁴ 15s 12s⁴ 11s 12v⁴ 1975
N.R. 1976 12s] big gelding: poor stayer: acts on any going: has been tried
in blinkers. *J. Calvert.*

PERFECT PICTURE 2 b.f. Hopeful Venture 125–Photo Flash 119 (Match III **78**
135) [1976 6d 6v] big, strong French-foaled filly: half-sister to fairly useful
Lucky Shot (by Reform), a winner at up to 1¾m: dam, second in 1,000 Guineas,
is half-sister to Welsh Pageant: backward and rather nervous in paddock,
prominent for a long way in 25-runner maiden race won by Caerdeon Line
at Newmarket in October: very weak in market when behind in similar race
won by Amity at Newbury later in month: should do better over middle distances: to be trained by H. Cecil in 1977. *N. Murless.*

PERFECT SPARKLER 5 br.h. Above Suspicion 127–Sea of Gems (Princely **37**
Gift 137) [1974 6g 7f 10g 6d 10.1g⁶ 8d 6g 8s 9v⁴ 1975 8d 7f 8f 6f⁶ 7f⁴ 8fg 8g⁴
8g 1976 8f 8f 10h⁴ 12fg 10d 5s] poor plater: ran best race at 5 yrs on third
start: seems to stay 1¼m: probably acts on any going: best in blinkers. *Mrs
L. Dingwall.*

PERGAYLE 3 b.g. Lord Gayle 124–Mayhaw 98 (Parthia 132) [1975 N.R. —
1976 10h⁶] second foal: 500 gns yearling: dam stayed 7f: 50/1 and in need
of race, dwelt and finished well tailed off in six-runner minor event won by
Wickwell at Pontefract in July. *D. Holmes.*

PERICET 7 b.g. Atan–Pinochle 61 (Matador 131) [1974 6g 5fg 6fg* 5d³ 6g⁶ —
5fg² 6d² 5s* 5g 6s 5v 1975 6s³ 6g⁶ 6fg 5.1f⁵ 6fg 5g⁶ 6g⁴ 6f⁴ 5f² 5h⁴ 6f 6d³ 5g
6g 1976 7fg⁵ 6fg⁴ 6g 5fg 6fg 5g⁶ 6g⁵ 5.9f 8.3g⁴ 5fg³ 6s] neat gelding: has

been tubed: one-time useful handicapper but is a shadow of his former self nowadays and descended to sellers in 1976: probably stays 7f: acts on any going: sometimes wears blinkers but does just as well without: occasionally sweats up: needs firm handling: unreliable. *A. Corbett.*

PERIPLUS 4 br.f. Galivanter 131–Holiday Spirit 99 (Live Spirit 121) [1974 —
5g 5fg³ 5f³ 5f 6fg 5g 7g² 6s² 1975 7g 8h 8f⁴ 7f⁶ 7h 1976 12fg⁵ 10f] compact filly: poor performer: best form at up to 7f: acts on soft going and probably acts on firm: best form in blinkers. *W. Clay.*

PERIVAN GIRL 2 bl.f. Hotfoot 126–Saucy Jane 82 (Hard Sauce 131) [1976 —
5fg 5fg 6g6] quite attractive, good-bodied filly: good mover: half-sister to fair stayer C'est Afrique (by Behistoun): 1,550 gns yearling: dam a sprinter: showed a little ability in maiden races: will probably stay 1m. *S. Woodman.*

PERKASA 2 br.f. Huntercombe 133–Scots Twist (Tangle 121) [1976 5g   74
5f² 5d 5g 5f 5fg³ 5.9g 5f² 5.9fg 5g² 5s 5g 5s] strong filly: half-sister to three winners, including fairly useful sprinter Singing Scot (by Songedor): 2,300 gns yearling: dam never ran: an inconsistent filly but occasionally showed ability, and in September finished second in maiden races at Thirsk (to Spring Dive) and Catterick (to Simple Gifts): form only at 5f: acts on firm going and is probably unsuited by soft: well beaten in blinkers on last two outings, one of them in a seller. *T. Fairhurst.*

PERMALITE 2 ch.c. Laser Light 118–Stickpin 74 (Gulf Pearl 117) [1976   64
5fg 5g⁵ 6fg⁴ 6g 7.3d] lengthy colt: June foal: first produce: 600 gns yearling: dam placed over 5f and 7f at 2 yrs: showed a little ability, finishing 7 lengths fourth of 15 to Haighall in maiden race at Windsor in July: had very stiff tasks in nurseries on next two outings: stays 6f and may get further: sold 160 gns Ascot November Sales. *R. Akehurst.*

PERQUAY LADY 2 br.f. Quayside 124–Perfect Lady 85 (Sovereign Lord 120) —
[1976 5fg 5d 7s 10v 8.2v] bad plater: wears blinkers: sold 300 gns Doncaster November Sales. *S. Norton.*

PERSEVERING 3 b.f. Blakeney 126–Pertinacity 106 (Aggressor 130) [1975   95
7d² 1976 10fg 13.4fg* 12fg 12fg 15.8fg* 15g* 16g* 14s⁴] neat filly: improved throughout season and won twice at Chester (maiden race and handicap) and once at Ayr and Newmarket: put up particularly good efforts on last two courses, beating Rowe Residence 1½ lengths in minor event on former and getting home all out by a length from Ventrex in a handicap on latter: needs further than 1½m and stays 2m: acts on a firm and a soft surface. *J. Bethell.*

PERSIAN BREEZE 4 b.c. Whistling Wind 123–Persian Pie (Tamerlane 128) —
[1974 5fg* 5f* 5g⁴ 5fg² 5fg³ 5v* 5s* 5g* 1975 5d³ 5g 5f⁴ 6fg 8g³ 6d* 5fg* 5.6g 6v 6s³ 5g³ 1976 7h⁵ 6f⁶ 6g] useful sort: smart performer (rated 115) in 1975: had stiff tasks in his three races at 4 yrs and was well beaten: did all his winning at up to 6f but ran creditably on only attempt at 1m: acted on any going: showed a tendency to hang left: blinkered penultimate start at 3 yrs: genuine: to stand at Eaton House Stud, Lincolnshire at a fee of £350. *N. Angus.*

PERSIAN KING 6 b.g. Tamerlane 128–Gilboa 113 (Palestine 133) [1974 10d⁵   69
8d* 10d⁵ 8.2s⁵ 8.2v⁴ 1975 8f* 7.6g 8g³ 1976 10g² 10.2g⁶ 12d* 10fg² 11.7f²
10.4fg⁵ 12s⁴] strong, compact gelding: quite a moderate handicapper: 3-length winner at Doncaster in May and ran creditably afterwards: stays 1½m: acts on any going: has worn bandages: trained by W. Wharton until after third outing: suitable mount for apprentice or lady rider. *N. Guest.*

PERSIAN PRAYER 2 b.f. So Blessed 130–Bibi Mah 108 (Tehran) [1976   — p
5g] lightly-made filly: half-sister to several winners, including very smart sprinter Jukebox (by Sing Sing) and Abassi (by Abernant), useful winner over 5f at 2 yrs: dam, middle-distance performer, is half-sister to Lord of Verona: not knocked about unnecessarily when seventh of 14 to Mummy's Pal in maiden race at Catterick in September: looked to be in need of outing that day, and should do better, probably at around 1m. *R. D. Peacock.*

PERSIAN REAPER 2 ch.c. Weepers Boy 124–Narsia (Narrator 127) [1976   55
5fg 5g⁶ 5g 5.9f 8fg 7s 10s⁶ 8.2v] plater: sweated up when 11 lengths sixth of 13 to Sleigh Bells at Pontefract in October: probably stays 1¼m. *A. Jarvis.*

PERSIAN SWALLOW 2 b.f. My Swallow 134–Persian Music (Hugh Lupus 132   77
or Tamerlane 128) [1976 7d 6g] lengthy filly: second produce: 4,900 gns foal, 5,400 gns yearling: dam never ran: unquoted when about 6 lengths eighth of

30 to Rheola in maiden race at Newmarket in September, second outing: will stay 1m. *P. Haslam.*

PERSISTENT MISS 2 b.f. Continuation 120–Milveagh 92 (Milesian 125) **77**
[1976 5.1fg² 5s 5v] unfurnished filly: third foal: half-sister to two 2-y-o winners, including fair 1975 6f winner Eagle Hill (by Tudor Music): 2,000 gns yearling: dam won at up to 1m: 20/1, put up a good first effort when 1½ lengths second to No Cards in 13-runner maiden race at Yarmouth in June: not seen out again until end of season and was well beaten on both outings: should be suited by 1m. *G. Pritchard-Gordon.*

PERUCIO 5 b.g. Super Sam 124–Insouciante 71 (No Worry 105) [1974 N.R. **96**
1975 10.8s² 12g 10g* 12s⁵ 1976 10f* 10f* 10fg* 10g* 10fg* 12f*] rangy gelding: improved tremendously in 1976 and was unbeaten in six handicaps, including five at Brighton: gained his final success when beating Monsieur Spock 1½ lengths on that course in August: stays 1½m: acts on any going: genuine and consistent: front runner. *R. Akehurst.*

PETALCA 3 b.f. Dewan–Alcazar 94 (Alycidon 138) [1975 6s* 1976 8fg **78**
10g⁶ 10fg⁵ 12f² 10g⁴ 10g 10.6d* 12v] attractive American-bred filly: half-sister to top-class miler Petingo (by Petition): won minor event at Haydock in October by 8 lengths from Upavon: best form at 1¼m: acts on soft going and is possibly unsuited by firm. *C. Brittain.*

PETALINA 2 b.f. Mummy's Pet 125–Florintina 104 (Floribunda 136) [1976 **93**
5fg 5fg⁶ 5h* 5fg⁶ 6fg⁵ 6f 5f⁵ 5s³] useful-looking, well-made filly: first foal: dam won at 7f and 1m: got up close home to beat Diorina in eight-runner £1,400 maiden race at Warwick in July: creditable sixth to Be Easy in Molecomb Stakes at Goodwood later in month and was not disgraced when 2½ lengths third to Karella in nursery at Warwick in October on final outing: appears not to stay 6f: seems to act on any going. *P. Cole.*

PETALLOT 2 b.c. Mummy's Pet 125–Shallot (Sheshoon 132) [1976 6d 7v] **—**
well-grown colt: half-brother to three winners here and abroad, including 7f to 1½m winner Grey Diamond (by Aberdeen): behind in maiden races at Yarouth and Leicester, latter a weakly-contested event. *J. Harris.*

PETARD 2 b.f. Mummy's Pet 125–Tackard 87 (Hard Tack 111 §) [1976 112
5fg* 5f* 5f³ 5fg*] lightly-built filly: third foal: half-sister to winning sprint plater Tack Rule (by Counsel): dam won over 6f at 2 yrs: improved with racing and won minor events at Newcastle and Ripon (hung right) in August and nursery at Beverley the following month: put up a splendid effort under top weight in last-named event, winning by 1½ lengths from Whenby despite having again hung right (would have won by considerably further had she kept a straight course): 1½ lengths third of six to Imperial Jade in quite well-contested event at Thirsk in between: may well stay 6f: apprentice ridden at Ripon and Beverley. *W. C. Watts.*

PETA'S ECHO 2 b.f. Mountain Call 125–Peta's Bay 67 (I Say 125) [1976 **—**
6fg 5s] second foal: 520 gns yearling: dam, winner over 7f, is half-sister to high-class 1m to 1¼m horse Gold Rod: behind in minor event at Salisbury in September (last of 11) and maiden race at Warwick the following month: sold 250 gns Ascot December Sales. *R. Akehurst.*

PETE MURRAY 2 ch.c. Murrayfield 119–Petemoss (Bounteous 125) [1976 **—**
5fg 5f⁴ 5.1fg⁴] half-brother to useful 3-y-o stayer Black Sabbath but is only a plater himself: not seen out after May. *D. Ringer.*

PETER CRAIG 2 b.c. Siliconn 121–Stafford's Gold (March Past 124) [1976 **—**
6fg 8.2h] first foal: 200 gns yearling: long way behind on both outings, including in a seller at Hamilton. *P. Metcalfe.*

PETER CULTER 4 br.c. Sky Gipsy 117–Gloaming 94 (High Treason 126) **70**
[1974 5fg⁵ 5f³ 5g² 5g⁴ 5fg* 5.9g⁴ 5s³ 6v* 6d 7g⁶ 7.2v 1975 7d 6s³ 7v 6d 6s 7f 5f⁴ 5g⁴ 7g 6g² 6f* 6g* 7h³ 6d⁴ 1976 7g 6fg² 6h² 6h² 6h* 6f⁶ 5h² 6h* 6f⁶ 7f 6g⁶ 5fg⁵ 6v] strong colt: not a good mover: quite a moderate handicapper: winner at Carlisle in July and at Pontefract in August: stays 7f: acts on any going: sometimes wears blinkers: sometimes has his tongue tied down: trained by J. Mulhall until after twelfth outing. *S. Norton.*

PETER GRIMES 3 b.c. Tudor Melody 129–Martinetta 77 (Ballymoss 136) **71**
[1975 6g⁵ 1976 7fg³ 7g³ 10f* 12d 10fg⁴ 10.8g] strong, good-bodied, shapely colt: odds on, ridden out to win maiden race at Ayr in May by ¾ length from Irish Prince: had stiff tasks in handicaps afterwards: stays 1¼m. *G. Pritchard-Gordon.*

PETERHOF 4 ch.g. Royal Palace 131–Raymonda 106 (Primera 131) [1974 —
6fg 6g⁵ 8d⁴ 1975 12g 10.1fg⁵ 10f² 14d³ 8fg*(dis) 10f² 12g* 10.2g 12.5g⁴ 12v⁵
1976 10g] lengthy gelding: fairly useful handicapper at his best: had only one
outing on flat in 1976 and is better known as a hurdler nowadays: seems to stay
1¾m: best form on a sound surface: ideally suited by strong handling. *M. W.
Easterby.*

PETER THE GREAT 4 ch.c. Great Nephew 126–Ship Yard 107 (Doutelle 128) **44**
[1974 7g⁶ 7g 7.3s 1975 12s 10s 10f 12g 1976 12fg² 13.8g⁴ 15.5f³ 15.5f⁴] strong
colt: poor handicapper: probably stays 2m: sold to C. Dingwall 1,150 gns Ascot
October Sales. *J. Dunlop.*

PETER WREKIN 4 b.c. Lauso–Miss Wrekin 97 (Pardao 120) [1974 7s 8d²
1975 11s³ 12f* 12.2fg* 12fg* 14.7f* 12g* 1976 16d] strong, sturdy colt: was
said to be regarded as a good-class animal, and won last five of his six races as a
3-y-o, but never took on good-class opposition: did take on good-class opposition
on only outing in 1976, finishing eighth of nine to Marco Ricci in Paradise Stakes
at Ascot in May (bandaged): subsequently reported to have broken down:
should stay 2m: acts on any going. *F. Maxwell.*

PETILIA 3 ch.f. Petingo 135–Lioba 80 (Alcide 136) [1975 7g 1976 8f 10fg 10f* **83**
12v] quite a modest performer: got up close home when winning five-runner
maiden race at Yarmouth in August by ½ length from Doubly Hopeful: should
stay 1½m+ (had stiff task when tried at trip): sold to J. Hardy 2,600 gns
Newmarket December Sales. *C. Brittain.*

PETINARA 2 ch.f. Hul a Hul 124–Shadow Queen (Darius 129) [1976 5fg⁶ 5d² **106**
5fg² 5g* 6fg³ 6fg³ 6f² 6f²] shapely filly: good walker: fourth living foal: half-
sister to a winner in Italy by Prince Tenderfoot: dam of little account: odds on,
scraped home by a head from Gradiva in 13-runner maiden race at Doncaster
in June: also placed behind useful fillies in several other races, on final outing
finishing neck second to Bodensee in 13-runner nursery at Goodwood in August:
will stay 1m: consistent: used to be a difficult ride but did nothing wrong when
blinkered on last two outings. *B. Hanbury.*

PETIPA 3 b.f. Habitat 134–Twaddle II (Tim Tam) [1975 6fg³ 5fg* 6f* 6d **113**
1976 7fg⁶ 6.3d* 6f 6fg 6f²] well-made, most attractive filly: won Greenlands
Stakes at the Curragh in May by ¾ length from Willy Willy: ran below her best
in Cork and Orrery Stakes at Royal Ascot (tailed off) and July Cup at Newmarket
(blinkered first time) but ran respectably when 1½ lengths second (odds on and
again blinkered) to Child of Grace in minor event at Naas in July: stays 7f
(creditable sixth to Man of Harlech in Tote Free Handicap at Newmarket only
attempt at trip) and should stay further: appears to act on any going. *P.
Prendergast, Ireland.*

PETITE CASE 2 gr.f. Upper Case–Petite Path 106 (Sovereign Path 125) [1976 **76**
5g 5g⁴ 5fg⁴ 6g 5s³ 5v] fourth foal: half-sister to two winners by Track Spare:
dam won Queen Mary Stakes and Ayr Gold Cup: quite a modest filly: should be
well suited by 6f or more: whipped round at start on first outing. *R. Mason.*

PETIT ECLAIR 3 ch.f. Major Portion 129–Cafe au Lait 97 (Espresso 122) **94**
[1975 5fg⁶ 7f³ 7g* 8f³ 1976 8.2g³ 12h² 12fg⁵ 10.8g 10.8s* 10v²] lightly-made
filly: won minor event at Warwick in October by a neck from Bright Fire, the
pair finishing clear: ridden by 7-lb claimer when creditable second to easy
winner Amber Valley in handicap at Teesside later in month: stays 11f: acts on
any going but seems best with plenty of give in the ground. *Doug Smith.*

PETITE DOUTELLE 5 ch.m. Percy Dear–Notafella (Willowdale 112) [1974 **46**
5fg 1975 N.R. 1976 12f 8g 8fg³ 7fg 12g³ 10.4fg 14d⁴ 13v 12s⁶] poor staying
maiden: has worn blinkers. *M. Ryan.*

PETITE SOURIS 4 b.f. Chebs Lad 120–Langton Girl 90 (Langton Abbot) **66**
[1974 5f⁶ 5f* 5f⁵ 6g² 7s⁵ 6fg⁴ 6fg² 7d² 6d² 6g² 7g 1975 8s 7g* 7f³ 6h³ 8f 8d⁴ 8f³
7f³ 8.2fg⁴ 8g⁶ 8g 1976 8f 7fg 8f 7f 7f³ 8f² 7f⁵ 7f³ 8f² 7g² 8g⁴ 8v³] lightly-made
filly: poor handicapper nowadays: stays 1m: seems to act on any going: usually
wears blinkers. *J. Carr.*

PETITIONER 3 b.c. Petingo 135–French Cream 110 (Faubourg II 127) [1975 —
6g⁵ 1976 8g] narrow, leggy colt: remote seventh of 15 to Arapaho in maiden
race at Sandown in April (appeared to finish lame): will stay 1¼m: sold 340 gns
Newmarket July Sales and has since won in Denmark. *C. Brittain.*

PETIT PRETENDRE 5 ch.h. Pretendre 126–Little Rapide 90 (Rapace 130) **88**
[1974 12g 12g 16f* 14g⁴ 14fg 16s² 16d 14d⁵ 1975 16d² 16d* 18f² 16g 18fg 14g⁵
1976 14fg* 16g⁶ 16fg² 16fg² 18.1g] strong, rangy horse: fairly useful handi-

capper: made all when winning four-runner event at Newmarket in May: also ran creditably on third and fourth outings (didn't get best of runs on second occasion when 1½ lengths second to Royal Orbit at Sandown in July): suited by a good test of stamina: acts on any going: pulled up lame final outing: sold 1,150 gns Doncaster November Sales. *R. Jarvis.*

PETLADY 2 ch.f. Petingo 135–Lovely Lady 81 (Never Say Die 137) [1976 6g² **81** 6g* 8g] lightly-made filly: third foal: half-sister to fairly useful 3-y-o stayer Sanpello (by Crepello) and to Great Lad (by Great Nephew), a winner at up to 1¼m: 6,600 gns yearling: dam stayed 1½m and is half-sister to St Pauli Girl: disputed lead all way and stayed on really well when winning 15-runner maiden race at Kempton in August by a length from Alltyre: out of her depth when seventh of eight to Miss Pinkie in Argos Star Fillies' Mile at Ascot the following month: should stay 1¼m+. *C. Brittain.*

PETRA GIRL 2 b.f. Mummy's Pet 125–Fast Pleasure 90 (Sound Track 132) — [1976 5fg⁵ 5g⁶] leggy, unfurnished filly: third foal: half-sister to two winners, including Smart Sheila (by King's Leap), a very useful winner at 2 yrs: 800 gns yearling: dam a sprinter: little worthwhile form in early-season maiden races. *W. C. Watts.*

PETRINA 3 b.f. Petingo 135–Shandon Belle 114 (Hook Money 124) [1975 6g⁶ **87** 1976 8h⁵ 8.2d* 8v* 8s] rangy, rather leggy filly: dam won Irish 1,000 Guineas: never in much danger when winning 23-runner maiden race at Nottingham in September and five-runner minor event at Newcastle the following month, latter by 6 lengths from Flying Diplomat: ran no sort of a race under a penalty on final outing: stays 1m: acts on heavy ground. *H. Cecil.*

PETRINA'S VISION 2 br.f. Breeders Dream 116–Metaphor 79 (Nimbus 130) — [1976 6fg 5f] half-sister to several minor winners: well behind in seller at Nottingham in July and maiden race at Bath in September: sold 250 gns Ascot October Sales. *J. Hill.*

PETROGRAD 2 br.c. Manacle 123–Clear Whistle 80 (Tin Whistle 128) [1976 **59** 5g 5f⁵ 5g* 5f⁴ 6f 7f 6g⁶ 5.9fg] tall, leggy colt: made all to win three-runner seller at Leicester in April (bought in 870 gns): well behind in nurseries on last four outings: not certain to stay 7f: blinkered third to seventh outings. *N. Callaghan.*

PETRONISI 2 ch.c. Petingo 135–White Bunnie (Exbury 138) [1976 6g⁴ 7g² **95** 7d⁵] rangy colt: second foal: 9,400 gns yearling: dam won over 1¼m in France: second favourite, ran on well when length second of 23 to Windy Sea in maiden race at Newmarket in October: 33/1, never looked dangerous when remote fifth to The Minstrel in 11-runner William Hill Dewhurst Stakes on same course later in month: will stay 1¼m. *C. Brittain.*

PETS FIRST 3 b.g. Mummy's Pet 125–Cawkwell Lady 72 (Premonition 130) **72** [1975 5d 5d 5g* 5h⁵ 5f⁶ 6fg 1976 5fg* 5fg⁴ 5h* 6f³ 5g 6fg* 5fg 5f² 5g³] work-manlike gelding: quite a moderate handicapper: successful at Warwick and Teesside in April and Leicester in July: all out to beat Fleur d'Amour a head on last-named course: stays 6f: acts on hard going: often wears blinkers but usually does as well without. *J. Hardy.*

PETTITS LANE 3 br.c. Gala Performance–Pure Fantasy (Above Suspicion — 127) [1975 N.R. 1976 12f⁵ 12.2f⁶ 11h⁴ 8.2h 10g 8.2f] third living foal: half-sister to a winning Irish stayer by Hul a Hul: 220 gns yearling: dam maiden Irish stayer: only plating class. *P. Poston.*

PETULIA 3 br.f. Petingo 135–Peta's Bay 67 (I Say 125) [1975 5fg 7g² 6f⁴ 6g — 1976 7g 8fg 10.2g 8.2d⁴ 7s] lengthy filly: should stay 1m: sold 1,500 gns Newmarket December Sales. *J. Bethell.*

PEWTER SPEAR 3 ch.c. Gyr 131–Klairette (Klairon 131) [1975 5d⁴ 5v⁴ 5f 5f **63** 5fg⁴ 7fg⁴ 7fg⁶ 5.1g³ 6g⁵ 6d* 5g³ 5d⁵ 6v 1976 6f 8f³ 7g³ 7g⁴ 7fg 7g 7fg 6g⁶] leggy colt: only a modest plater nowadays and did not run up to his best after fourth outing: probably stays 1m but seems better at shorter distances: has twice worn blinkers: pulled up seventh outing (thought to have gone lame but was in fact all right): sold 1,500 gns Doncaster August Sales. *K. Payne.*

PHAEDRA'S TALE 2 ch.f. Richboy 117–Fergus Lily 73 (Ennis 128) [1976 5fg — 5f 8fg 7s] bad plater: blinkered fourth outing. *C. Dingwall.*

PHANTOM BIRD 2 br.c. Falcon 131–Gardinela (Tanavar 118) [1976 6v 5.9s] — second foal: 160 gns yearling: dam never ran: behind in the autumn in £2,000 event at Leicester and maiden race at Wolverhampton. *W. Marshall.*

557

*Prix de la Foret, Longchamp—Pharly takes this important event from
English challenger Lady Mere; then come Manado, Kronenkranich
and Monsanto*

PHANTOM LAD 4 b.g. probably Ledsam Lad 79–Olives Girl (St Xavier 77) —
[1974 N.R. 1975 7f 8f 12f 10d⁵ 12.2g 12s 1976 12s 8g 16.1fg] probably of
no account. *B. McMahon.*

PHARLY 2 ch.c. Lyphard 132–Comely (Boran) [1976 7.5g⁴ 7g² 7.5g² 7g* 7s*] **126**
    Pharly failed to reveal any evidence of outstanding merit when he tackled
two-year-old opposition, but his performance in the Prix de la Foret, a £27,000
Group 1 race run over seven furlongs at Longchamp in October, put him in the
top flight of French juveniles, and only Blushing Groom was placed above him
in the French Two-Year-Old Free Handicap.   Open to all ages, the Prix de la
Foret attracted Manado, the best French two-year-old of 1975 but a disappointment at three, although he had run well in top company from time to time;
Monsanto, whose two successes included one over Manado in the Prix du Rond-
Point; Full of Hope, who had defeated Ivanjica when winning the Prix d'Ispahan
and Gravelines when winning the Prix du Chemin de Fer du Nord; Kesar Queen,
winner of the Coronation Stakes at Royal Ascot and third in the One Thousand
Guineas; Guichet, a head behind Kesar Queen at Ascot but a winner of three
races, including the Prix de Sandringham, in which she had beaten Kesar Queen
by a length; Kronenkranich, a pretty good German four-year-old who had
finished close-up sixth in the Prix de l'Abbaye de Longchamp; and the English
two-year-old filly Lady Mere.   Monsanto was accorded the position of favourite,
and Pharly started at just under 4/1, hardly a generous price for a horse whose
best form was a two-and-a-half-length win, when receiving weight from the
runner-up, in an event of no particular importance on the course less than two
weeks previously, and who before that had been beaten in ordinary maiden
company at Deauville (twice) and Maisons-Laffitte.   Kesar Queen made the
running, but was done with soon after halfway.   Shortly afterwards Pharly
established a definite advantage, and although Lady Mere came with a good run
from the distance, Pharly stretched out well to hold her off by two lengths,
Manado finishing well into third place, a length and a half behind Lady Mere.
An emphatic triumph for first-season horses!

Pharly (ch.c. 1974)	Lyphard (b 1969)	Northern Dancer (b 1961)	Nearctic / Natalma
		Gooted (ch 1960)	Court Martial / Barra II
	Comely (ch 1966)	Boran (ch 1960)	Mourne / Bethora
		Princesse Comnene (ch 1961)	Beau Prince II / Commemoration

    Pharly, who cost 140,000 francs (approximately £15,000) as a yearling, is
bred to be a good horse.   A son of Lyphard, a top-class performer in France
at up to a mile and a quarter and sire of Durtal, he is a half-brother to Comeram
(by Amber Rama), one of the leading French two-year-olds of 1975 and beaten
a short head in the Irish Two Thousand Guineas.   Pharly is as good a horse as
Comeram, and should he meet his engagement here in the Two Thousand
Guineas, The Minstrel and Tachypous will find it no easy job to beat him.
Pharly's dam, Comely, a very useful middle-distance performer, is out of a
half-sister to the Grand Prix de Paris winner Armistice, and Pharly will probably
stay at least a mile and a quarter.   He acts well on soft going.   *J. Cunnington,
jnr, France.*

PHILADELPHIA STORY 2 b.c. Decoy Boy 129–Nelson Touch 94 (Prince **67**
Chevalier) [1976 5.1fg⁶ 5f 6g 5g 7g 6v³] fair sort: half-brother to three winners,
including very useful middle-distance performer Trafalgar (by Pardal): 1,500
gns yearling: dam middle-distance performer: about 4 lengths third of 20 to
newcomer Cathmaria in seller at Haydock in October: should stay 7f: sold
2,100 gns Newmarket Autumn Sales. *Doug Smith.*

PHILHOPE 5 b.g. Fleece 114–Molvitesse 75 (Molvedo 137) [1974 8g⁴ 8g⁶ 8s **—**
11g⁴ 10g⁴ 10g 12s 1975 N.R. 1976 8g] plater: well beaten at Edinburgh in
May, only outing on flat since his 3-y-o days. *H. Bell.*

PHILIP GREEN 4 b.g. Space King 115–This and That (Fedor II 107) [1974 **—**
5fg⁵ 5f 7f⁵ 8s 8s² 8s² 7s⁴ 10s 1975 12.2d³ 12s³ 16s⁴ 14g³ 12.3fg² 12d 12h* 12g³
10f⁵ 1976 12.2d 12f] compact gelding: stays 1¾m: seems to act on any going:
suitable mount for an apprentice. *W. Gray.*

PHILMARNIE 4 ch.f. Klondyke Bill 125–Relax 73 (Seminole II) [1974 7g 6d **51**
8s 7s 1975 9.4g 10h 10f³ 7g³ 8f* 9fg⁵ 8fg* 8g⁶ 8f⁵ 8g 7g 7fg 8g 1976 10fg⁶ 8d*
10.6d³ 10f³ 7f⁴ 8f³ 7f² 10.6g⁵ 8f* 7g 8.2d] plater: successful at Pontefract in
May and Beverley in August, on latter course beating Gay Pat 2½ lengths (no
bid): stays 1¼m but is best at around 1m: appears to act on any going: ran
below form when tried in blinkers: suitable mount for an apprentice: missed
break on tenth outing. *A. Smith.*

PHILMONT 4 gr.f. Philemon 119–Czaremont 74 (Damremont 120) [1974 7d **—**
6f⁵ 7g⁵ 7s 7v³ 7s⁶ 1975 11.1s² 8g² 10.1g⁴(dis) 10f 13.3fg 14d³ 16f 16.1fg 10g⁵
1976 16fg 13v] small filly: plating class: best form at up to 11f, but should
stay long distances: acts on soft going: trained by S. Norton until after first
outing. *J. Leigh.*

PHILOMINSKY 5 b.h. Philemon 119–Czaremont 74 (Damremont 120) [1974 **97**
10.2s⁶ 12g* 12g 11.7fg* 11g⁴ 11f⁵ 14.8fg⁶ 13.3g³ 12v 16s 1975 18.4g⁴ 16.1g*
13.3fg 16fg 16fg³ 19f⁶ 16g⁵ 18fg 1976 18.4s⁵ 20f 16fg* 18.4fg²] robust
horse: fairly useful handicapper on his day: stayed on dourly when winning
11-runner Joe Coral Northumberland Plate at Newcastle in June by 1½ lengths
from Crash Course: creditable second to Mr Bigmore under a penalty at Chester
the following month: suited by a stiff test of stamina: probably acted on any
going: dead. *W. Marshall.*

PHILOTIMO 2 br.f. Prevailing–Lake Shore Drive (Master Owen) [1976 6fg] **—**
workmanlike filly: second foal: dam a prolific winner on flat at up to 2m, and
over hurdles in Ireland: unquoted, showed up well in group on far side when
eleventh of 27 to Home Fire in maiden race at Newbury in August, only outing.
P. Cundell.

PHLEEZ 3 gr.c. Above Suspicion 127–Following Breeze 119 (Umidwar) [1975 **89**
6s 7s 1976 11f 11.1g 12g* 12g] strong, well-made colt: won 19-runner maiden

*Joe Coral Northumberland Plate, Newcastle—Philomsky makes the most of the weight
concession from Crash Course. The blinkered Grinling Gibbons is third*

race at Salisbury in May all out by a head from Rickadoo: out of his depth only
outing afterwards (Epsom Derby): stays 1½m. *R. Smyth.*

PHLOX 4 b.f. Floriana 106–Mainstream (River Chanter 121) [1974 5fg 5h* 5.3f² **74**
6fg⁶ 6fg² 5g* 5fg* 5s 5s 1975 5fg⁵ 5f⁴ 5fg³ 5fg 6g 5fg 5g 5fg⁶ 7g⁵ 1976 5.9fg
5.8f³ 6fg 5.9f 5g* 5.3fg³ 5g 5fg] neat filly: quite a moderate handicapper:
made virtually all when winning at Kempton in May by ½ length from Sicasanta:
well beaten afterwards: best form at 5f: acts on hard going and is probably not
at her best on soft: blinkered final start. *R. Akehurst.*

PHOENIX ROSE 2 b.f. Frankincense 120–Rose de Mai 63 (Romulus 129) **85**
[1976 5g⁵ 6h³ 6g⁵ 8fg 8s⁶ 6s² 7v³ 6s²] half-sister to quite moderate 1974 2-y-o
7f winner Phoenix House (by Jolly Jet): 420 gns yearling: dam ran only at 2
yrs: placed in varied company, on last outing going down by a short head to
Song Book in seller at Newmarket in October: has yet to show she stays 1m:
acts on any going. *M. Naughton.*

PHOTO BELLE 2 b.f. Polyfoto 124–Belvedere 71 (Royal Hamlet 115) [1976 **111**
5g⁵ 5f* 5f* 5s² 5f³ 5f⁴ 5g⁶ 5g 5g⁴ 5v* 5s³] useful Irish filly: half-sister to two
minor winners: 320 gns yearling: dam sister to useful 7f and 1m handicapper
Royal Unity: made all when clear-cut winner in May of 23-runner auction event
at Phoenix Park and of £1,400 race at Leopardstown: ran well on most of her
other outings and gained another success at Leopardstown in October, giving
weight to 19 others and scoring by 2½ lengths from Back Bailey: will stay 6f:
acts on any going. *S. Quirke, Ireland.*

PHRED 3 ch.c. Continuation 120–Phrygia (Mossborough 126) [1975 5v 5d 5f³ **59**
5g⁵ 6fg 7d 6g 1976 12f 10f⁵ 11.7fg³ 10.8g 10.4fg⁶ 12g⁶ 17.1s 16s 8s⁴] lengthy
colt: best form at up to 1¼m: often wears blinkers but does as well without.
Dr A. Jones.

PHYLICA 2 ch.f. Pieces of Eight 128–Waltzing Matilda (Sound Track 132) **70**
[1976 5f⁴ 5f² 5.1f⁶ 9fg] French-foaled filly: half-sister to two winners in France
and closely related to useful middle-distance performer Mobola (by Mincio):
1,900 gns yearling: dam, half-sister to Roan Rocket, placed over 1m at 3 yrs
in Ireland: stayed on, after being hopelessly outpaced in early stages, to finish
4 lengths second of 13 to Hutton Barns in maiden race at Catterick in August:
needs further than 5f but seemed not to stay when tried over 9f. *R. Boss.*

PHYL'S BOY 4 b.g. Dutch Rider 77–Pride of Clyde 64 (Falls of Clyde 126) —
[1974 N.R. 1975 N.R. 1976 10s] big gelding: eighth produce: dam moderate
plater at 2 yrs: 33/1 when well beaten in minor event at Nottingham in September
(needed race), only outing. *J. Peacock.*

PIBER 2 ch.f. Saintly Song 128–Lipizza (Acropolis 132) [1976 5fg 7fg 7g] **53**
first foal: dam lightly-raced daughter of very smart 1952 2-y-o Pirouette: behind
on all outings, including in a Newmarket seller: sold 840 gns Newmarket Autumn
Sales. *J. Dunlop.*

PICATINA 2 b.f. Welsh Pageant 132–Miss Charisma 104 (Ragusa 137) [1976 **94**
6fg 6v*(dis) 6v⁵] good sort: second produce: half-sister to a winning hurdler by
Sing Sing: 22,000 gns foal: dam, daughter of top-class sprinter Matatina, won
over 5f at 2 yrs: won £2,100 event at York in October by ½ length from Silver
Shoals, going clear over 1f out, only to tire in final furlong and come off a true
line near finish, interfering with third horse: subsequently disqualified and
placed last: short priced favourite for 23-runner maiden race at Newbury later
in month but was at a big disadvantage in racing alone on far side, and weakened
to finish 7 lengths fifth to Amity after leading for 5f: should stay 1m. *C. Brittain.*

PICCADILLY ETTA 5 ch.m. Floribunda 136–Carteretta 100 (Chanteur II **66**
135) [1974 7fg 10g 10g³ 10g⁶ 12s² 12s 12.2s* 13.8s* 14.7s* 12.3v² 14.6s⁶ 1975
13g⁵ 16d 14f⁶ 15.8f* 14.6fg³ 18g³ 16g* 16d⁶ 14g 16f⁴ 1976 16fg 16fg* 17.7f
14fg⁴ 16f² 16f³ 16fg* 16g² 14f² 16fg⁴] strong mare: quite a moderate handicapper: goes well at Lingfield and won twice there in 1976, on second occasion
beating sole opponent Tamashoon by 4 lengths in July: stays very well: acts
on any going: suitable mount for an amateur. *B. Lunness.*

PICCADILLY LINE 3 b.g. Northfields–Little Miss Muffet 102 (Tourment 132) **76**
[1975 7.2fg 7d⁶ 7.6g 1976 10.1fg 10f³ 11.1g 12fg⁶ 10.2fg³ 11g² 10fg² 10fg²
12v] compact gelding: quite a modest maiden: usually finds one or two too
good for him: ran poorly final outing and either doesn't stay 1½m or is unsuited
by heavy ground. *G. Peter-Hoblyn.*

PICCINA 2 ch.f. Grisaille 115–Abask (Henry the Seventh 125 or Abernant 142) —
[1976 6fg 5f] small filly: first foal: dam of little account: in rear in sellers at

Goodwood in July and Wolverhampton in August: will be hard pressed to win a race judging by her size: sold to H. Bell 280 gns Doncaster September Sales. *W. Marshall.*

PICCOLO MARAT 2 b.c. Be Friendly 130–Path Dancer 94 (Sovereign Path 125) [1976 6f⁵ 8s² 10v⁴] well-made colt: half-brother to two minor winners: 4,200 gns foal: dam winning half-sister to Roan Rocket: having first outing since June, failed by a short head to catch Billion (U.S.A.) in maiden race at Bath in October: favourite when moderate fourth to Morning Lee in similar race at Nottingham later in month: suited by 1m but seemed not to stay 1¼m at 2 yrs. *L. Cumani.* **88**

PICKPOCKET 3 ch.g. Golden Dipper 119–Light Spark 73 (Twilight Alley 133) [1975 8g 7s 1976 7f g 8.5fg⁴ 7fg] well-made gelding: poor plater. *B. Swift.* **—**

PICKWOOD SUE 3 gr.f. Right Boy 137–Lucky Deal 93 (Floribunda 136) [1975 5s 5g 5f 5f² 5h² 5g⁵ 5fg⁵ 5h 8f 6g⁵ 6d⁵ 1976 8fg 8g 7g 5f² 5f* 5h⁴ 5f 5g 5fg 5s 5s⁵] small filly: quite a modest handicapper: ridden by 7-lb claimer when winning at Beverley in July by a neck from Hot Bird and when excellent fourth to Jamar on same course later in month: showed form only once afterwards: stays 6f but is unlikely to stay 1m: appears to act on any going: best in blinkers. *J. Leigh.* **66**

PICK YOUR OWN 2 b.g. No Mercy 126–Karen Scott (Our Babu 131) [1976 5g 5v³ 5d⁶] big, rangy, lengthy gelding: second foal: half-brother to quite moderate 1975 2-y-o Virginia Girl (by Virginia Boy): dam, placed over 5f at 2 yrs, is half-sister to high-class sprinters Silver Tor and Prince Tor: showed ability in early-season events even though he looked short of peak fitness. *E. Cousins.* **64**

PICTURE 3 ch.f. Lorenzaccio 130–Jojo 103 (Vilmorin) [1975 6d² 6g² 6fg* 1976 6g 8f⁴ 5.6g] leggy, narrow filly: half-sister to very smart miler Queen's Hussar (by March Past): won maiden race at Windsor in 1975: creditable seventh of 12 to Solar in Hackwood Stakes at Newbury in July but ran moderately when odds on for minor event at Brighton the following month and had stiff task when tried in blinkers on final outing: best form at sprint distances but is bred to stay further: wore a bandage behind on last appearance. *R. Hern.* **84**

PICTURE POST 2 b.c. Polyfoto 124–Dance Mistress (Javelot 124) [1976 5f 5f 5h] first foal: 800 gns yearling: dam moderate Irish middle-distance maiden: looked a short-runner in three early-season outings, including in a seller. *M. W. Easterby.* **39**

PIETY 2 ch.f. Gulf Pearl 117–Piragua 85 (Petition 130) [1976 5g 5d² 6fg 8s] rangy filly: half-sister to 3-y-o Parent (by Great Nephew), a useful winner at up to 1¼m, and to a minor 2-y-o winner: dam won four times at 1¼m: 2 lengths second of eight to Daring Dan in maiden race at Haydock in May: well beaten afterwards but was off course four months after third outing: should stay 1m: blinkered final outing: sold 3,700 gns Newmarket Autumn Sales. *H. Candy.* **80**

PIKELLA 4 ch.f. Sica Dan 116–Never Ella (Never Dwell 89) [1974 5f 5fg 5g 5s 1975 5.9v 6f 5h³ 5f³ 5g⁶ 6g 5g⁵ 1976 6g 5h 5g⁴ 5fg 5s 5s 5v] poor plater: best at 5f: acts on hard going. *V. Mitchell.* **—**

PIKEY 5 b.g. Polyfoto 124–Dixie Rose (Le Dieu d'Or 119) [1974 8f⁴ 8d³ 8fg* 10s² 8.5g³ 10g² 10s⁴ 10d³ 10v⁴ 1975 10g² 10f³ 12f³ 1976 8g³ 10fg⁵ 8g] workmanlike gelding: probably stays 1¼m: acts on any going: genuine: good mount for an apprentice. *W. Stephenson.* **52**

PILLAR-BOX 3 b.c. So Blessed 130–Pilamenon 90 (Parthia 132) [1975 6g⁶ 7f² 1976 10f² 12fg 9fg⁴ 10g³ 10.1fg⁶ 8f* 8h* 8d 8d⁴ 7s⁵] quite a useful performer: won maiden race at Yarmouth in July and handicap at Pontefract in September: had to battle hard to beat The Truant a neck on latter track: best form at 1m but stays 1½m: acts on hard going and was not entirely disgraced on soft on last two appearances: ran moderately when tried in blinkers on fifth outing: sold 5,800 gns Newmarket Autumn Sales. *H. Cecil.* **92**

PINACLE 3 b.g. Manacle 123–Miss Pippin (Damremont 120) [1975 5s³ 5g* 8f 8fg 1976 8f⁵ 6g 6h⁴ 6f⁶] plater: not certain to stay 1m: often wears blinkers. *J. Vickers.* **51**

PINARS BOY 2 b.c. St Chad 120–Royal Escape 94 (King's Bench 132) [1976 6f⁵ 5f³ 7fg⁴ 8s 8v] lengthy, angular colt: half-brother to three winners, including very useful miler Mendi (by Gratitude): 500 gns yearling: dam won over 7f at 2 yrs: quite a moderate maiden: should stay 1m: acts on firm going. *A. Smith.* **72**

PINCHOW   5 br.h. Shantung 132–Spare Filly 95 (Beau Sabreur 125)   [1974 11fg* —
13.4g² 12f³ 15s² 12g* 12d⁴ 12.3s³   1975 10d² 12s³ 10.5s* 9g⁶ 10.2fg³ 10.2g* 10g⁴
10g 10.5fg⁵ 10.2g   1976 12v³]   tall horse: quite a useful handicapper (rated 94)
in 1975: remote third of four to Galahad II at Lingfield in November on only
start at 5 yrs: effective at 1¼m and stays well: seems to act on any going: wears
blinkers: possibly requires front-running tactics to be seen to advantage.   *D.
Kent.*

PINEWOOD GRANGE   3 b.g. Sing Sing 134 or Caliban 123–Charlotte Stuart 87   66
(Doutelle 128)   [1975 7g 10g   1976 10.8f 12.2f 10fg⁶ 12f⁶ 14f² 14f² 12f 13s⁵ 16v⁴]
useful-looking gelding: stays well: wears blinkers nowadays: trained until after
seventh outing by C. Brittain.   *T. Kersey.*

PINEY RIDGE   2 ch.f. Native Prince–Makeacurtsey (Herbager 136)   [1976 **116**
5f⁵ 5f* 5d³ 5f² 5g* 5d³ 6g⁵]

It looks as though Piney Ridge's trainer is using to full advantage the
wealth of experience he must have gained as assistant to Vincent O'Brien, Toby
Balding and the late Bill O'Gorman.   He sent over only two two-year-olds from
Ireland in 1976; the first, Tyranny, had been unplaced three times in useful
company but, in blinkers for the first time, he ran out a five-length winner of a
maiden auction race at the Epsom Derby meeting, landing a nice touch in the
process; the second, Piney Ridge, won a pattern race, was placed in two others
and established herself among the best fillies.

Piney Ridge made her first appearance here in the Queen Mary Stakes at
Royal Ascot.   Her starting price of 14/1 seemed about right: she had run three
times, winning only a maiden race at Navan and being beaten over five lengths
by Godswalk when 25/1 for the Marble Hill Stakes at the Curragh.   She came
very close to winning the Queen Mary though, leading at halfway and proving
very difficult to peg back when strongly challenged in the last furlong.   Cramond
caught her close home to win by a head but Piney Ridge held on to second place
by a neck from Easy Landing.

Piney Ridge raced exclusively in this country afterwards, her next race
being the National Stakes at Sandown in July.   This was also the next race for
Easy Landing and what a battle they had!   Easy Landing looked the likely
winner when heading Piney Ridge going into the final furlong but in the closing
stages Piggott really got to work on Piney Ridge.   She received twelve mighty
cracks of the whip and, showing wonderful courage, got up in the very last stride
to get the verdict by a head.   The Andrestan, giving the pair of them 7 lb, was
four lengths behind in third place.   There can be little doubt that Piggott's
riding turned defeat into victory, and an important victory at that; Piney

*National Stakes, Sandown—a desperate struggle between Piney Ridge (right)
and Easy Landing*

Mr M. C. Throsby's "Piney Ridge"

Ridge is worth a good bit more as the winner of the National Stakes than if she had finished an honourable second.

Our immediate reaction was that it would take Piney Ridge a long time to recover from her race in the National Stakes. We were wrong; she was back again seven weeks later for the Flying Childers Stakes at Doncaster and showed that her enthusiasm hadn't been dampened in the slightest. Co-favourite with her in the nine-strong field was Mandrake Major who had been gambled on from 6/1 to 7/2. Mandrake Major took up the running a furlong and a half out and, hard as she tried, Piney Ridge was unable to peg him back after being held up, and she went down by a length. La Ville de Rire also beat her, but by only a short head; Easy Landing was among the backmarkers. Piney Ridge's last outing of the season came in the William Hill Cheveley Park Stakes at Newmarket. This was her first attempt at six furlongs and she seemed to find the extra distance against her, fading in the final furlong to finish fifth of fifteen to Durtal, beaten about six lengths.

Piney Ridge (ch.f. 1974)	Native Prince (b 1964)	Native Dancer (gr 1950)	Polynesian
			Geisha
		Sungari (br 1948)	Eight Thirty
			Swabia
	Makeacurtsey (b 1967)	Herbager (b 1956)	Vandale
			Flagette
		Courtesy (b 1952)	Nasrullah
			Highway Code

Piney Ridge cost 7,000 guineas as a yearling and her strenuous first season brought in nearly twice that amount. Her connections have probably been shrewd to have exploited her to the full, for it seems she won't stay the One Thousand Guineas distance; and her appearance—she's a lightly-made, rather hollow-backed filly—suggests that she may not improve as much as some of her contemporaries. She'll be a very valuable broodmare though, coming as she does from a highly successful American family.

Piney Ridge is the first living foal of Makeacurtsey who was placed three times from fifteen starts in the United States. Several of Makeacurtsey's half-brothers and half-sisters did much better than she; Knightly Manner was a high-class grass horse from a mile to thirteen furlongs, Respected was a very useful three-year-old filly and Dignitas, a smart stakes winner, has done well at stud in Australia. Two of Makeacurtsey's half-sisters have produced very smart animals when mated to Herbager, Makeacurtsey's sire. Respected is the dam of Forage, a very good stakes winner at up to nine furlongs, and Continue is the dam of a similar animal called List. Another of Continue's foals by Herbager is a filly called Chain who briefly held the British record for a broodmare sold at auction when she fetched 84,000 guineas at the 1976 Newmarket December Sales. Piney Ridge's sire is a strong influence for speed; his five wins as a two-year-old in the States were all at distances shorter than six furlongs. A lot was expected of Native Prince at stud—a colt from his second crop sold for 117,000 guineas, a price which remained a record for four years—but he never sired a top-class horse and was exported to Australia in 1975. Piney Ridge, one of the best and gamest two-year-old fillies of 1976, is probably his best offspring. She seems to act on any going. *M. Kauntze, Ireland.*

PINK TANK 3 b.c. Wolver Hollow 126–Pinks (Pink Flower) [1975 7g 7.2fg⁶ **74** 9fg 6g 8v⁵ 1976 7s 8.2d⁵ 8fg² 7g* 7g⁶] quite a moderate handicapper: blinkered first time when scoring by ½ length from Belle Vue at Warwick in June (made all): ran moderately when again blinkered on only subsequent start: should stay 1¼m: sold 5,800 gns Newmarket Autumn Sales. *E. Cousins.*

PINTARY 3 b.f. Military 112–Pin Perle (Round Up) [1975 N.R. 1976 12f⁵ — 12g] fourth foal: dam poor novice hurdler: tailed-off last in minor event at Salisbury and amateur riders race at Kempton in August. *J. Cann.*

PIN TUCK 2 b.c. High Top 131–Somersweet 70 (Celtic Ash) [1976 5f 6g⁶ 6fg⁴ **87** 6fg 8g 7fg⁴ 8s 8g⁵ 10v*] small colt: first foal: 980 gns yearling: dam won over 13f: eased close home when winning 17-runner maiden race at Nottingham in October by a length from Nearly A Hand: very well suited by a test of stamina at 2 yrs and will stay 1½m: goes well on heavy ground and has run respectably on firmish. *W. Marshall.*

PIP-A-LONG 2 gr.c. Long Till 112–Orange Town (Metropolis 96) [1976 5f 6g **69** 8g 8s] third foal: dam a plater, stayed 1¼m: ran on when seventh of 19 to Mr Music Man in maiden race at Goodwood in September, third outing and best effort: will stay at least 1¼m. *R. Smyth.*

PIPPA'S PRIDE 2 ch.c. Red God 128 §–Time and Again 81 (Silly Season 127) **76** [1976 5g 5fg 6g⁵ 6fg⁴ 5fg] lightly-built colt: second foal: 1,100 gns foal and resold 1,300 gns yearling: dam stayed 1¼m: ran well in two 6f races, including when 2 lengths fourth of 13 to Virginia Lad in valuable seller at Goodwood in July when sweating: evidently better suited by 6f than 5f, and will probably stay further. *G. Harwood.*

PIPPIN PLACE 3 ch.g. Darling Boy 124–Jefferson Court (King's Bench 132) **60** [1975 N.R. 1976 10d 8s² 10.2s] first reported foal: dam ran only twice: 33/1 when 1½ lengths second of 19 to Pembi Chase in maiden race at Warwick in October, the pair finishing clear, only worthwhile form: should stay middle distances. *H. Collingridge.*

PIRATE BELL 7 b.h. Barbary Pirate 91–Crimson Belle 80 (Red God 128 §) [1974 14fg⁵ 12.3g³ 14.7fg 12f 12h* 12fg* 11.2f² 12g³ 11.7fg⁴ 1975 11.7g 11.7f 12f² 12fg⁶ 12g* 12f⁴ 12h² 12h³ 12fg 1976 13g⁵ 12s⁶] quite a useful handicapper (rated 90) in 1975: raced mainly in Jersey in 1976, winning three times: fifth in amateur riders race at Craon in September: 25/1 when well-beaten sixth of 11 to Raratonga in handicap at Folkestone in October on only appearance in this country at 7 yrs: stays well: acts on any going but seems best suited by top-of-the-ground conditions: suitable mount for an apprentice: sometimes wears blinkers. *S. Arthur, Jersey.*

PIRATE DREAM 3 b.c. Breeders Dream 116–Pampered Angel 97 (Pampered **117** King 121) [1975 5f 5fg⁵ 6fg² 7fg* 7g² 7f³ 7g⁵ 6s 1976 8g* 7fg² 7g⁶ 7fg 7f 8g* 10fg] well-made, good-looking colt: won minor race at Doncaster in March by 3 lengths from Silver Steel: put up a splendid effort when neck second to Man of Harlech in Tote Free Handicap at Newmarket the following month, but disappointed somewhat subsequently until winning Brighton Mile Handicap in June by ½ length from Obstacle: stays 1m (well beaten when tried at 1¼m): acts on firm going: blinkered fourth and last two outings: exported to U.S.A. *D. Keith.*

PITBOY 3 br.c. Will Somers 114 §–Golden Darling 86 (Darling Boy 124) **91** d
[1975 5g 5v⁵ 5d* 6d³ 7g² 6fg* 6fg 6g⁴ 6s 1976 7g* 7d 6fg 6d² 7f⁵ 6d 5f⁵ 6f 6fg
6g 7v 6s] strong colt: quite a useful handicapper at his best: successful at
Doncaster in March all out by a neck from Glorified: creditable second to
Dolphin Safari at York in May but ran well below his best afterwards and seems
to have deteriorated: finds 5f on sharp side nowadays and stays 7f well: suited
by an easy surface. *F. Carr.*

PIT HILL PETE 3 ch.g. Whistlewood 109–High Spirits (Live Spirit 121) [1975 —
N.R. 1976 8f⁴ 7f⁵ 10v] useless. *D. Chapman.*

PLACID PET 2 b.f. Mummy's Pet 125–Rennett 109 (King's Bench 132) [1976 —
5fg⁵ 5g] half-sister to useful sprinter Tribal Feast and 3-y-o 6f winner Tribal
Festival (both by Tribal Chief): 5,000 gns yearling: dam stayed 1¼m: never
dangerous in maiden races at Epsom in April and Wolverhampton in May. *N.
Callaghan.*

PLASTIC CUP 2 b.g. Jukebox 120–Miss Melanie (Hard Ridden 131) [1976 5fg⁶ **86**
5g⁵ 5g⁴ 6g⁴ 5f⁶ 6s 8s] tall, useful-looking gelding: first produce: 2,000 gns foal:
dam won 2m bumpers race in Ireland: creditable fourth to Mr Nice Guy in eight-
runner Woodcote Stakes at Epsom in June: off course over four months subsequently: better suited by 6f than 5f, and will probably stay further (had stiff
task over 1m). *D. Hanley.*

PLATTE PRINCESS 2 ch.f. King's Company 124–Naranja 81 (Roan Rocket **85**
128) [1976 5fg 5g* 5f⁴ 5f³ 6d 7s] well-made filly: second foal: 3,400 gns
yearling: dam won over 1m: quickened nicely when winning 14-runner maiden
race at Kempton in May by 3 lengths from Colombe: fair third to Exposed in
minor event at Lingfield the following month and was not seen out again until
September: should be suited by 6f or more: sold 2,900 gns Ascot December
Sales and exported to Trinidad. *Miss A. Sinclair.*

PLATTY 3 b.g. Goldhill 125–Maltam 64 (Royal Record II) [1975 5g 5g 5f —
6fg 1976 11.1fg] bad plater. *R. Clay.*

PLAY FOR GOLD 2 ch.f. Gold Rod 129–Replay (Double-U-Jay 120) [1976 —
5f] second foal: dam lightly-raced half-sister to very useful Penny Post: eighth
of nine in seller at Bath in May: sold 150 gns Newmarket Autumn Sales. *Miss N.
Wilmot.*

PLEASE TURN OVER 3 b.c. Turn-to–Cerisette (My Babu 136) [1975 N.R. **74**
1976 8fg 12g 11.7f⁶ 16g² 16.1d 16fg² 16f 16.1v] tall, leggy American-bred
colt: half-brother to high-class stayer John Cherry (by Stage Door Johnny):
second in maiden races at Thirsk in May and York in June: suited by a test
of stamina: probably requires a sound surface: ran deplorably seventh outing
and was subsequently off course well over three months, but performed little
better on his return: sold 3,300 gns Newmarket Autumn Sales. *B. Hills.*

PLEASURE GARDEN 4 b.g. Jolly Jet 111–Pleasaunce 84 (Petition 130) **74**
[1974 6fg 6fg 7d⁶ 8d 1975 8g 6fg⁶ 6f⁵ 5g³ 5f² 5g³ 5g³ 5f* 5fg⁴ 5g²
6d 1976 5f 5g⁴ 5f 5fg⁵ 7f² 7g 6f* 7f 7f 8d³] strong, lengthy gelding: fair
handicapper: successful at Newmarket in August by 1½ lengths from Kiyoswanee: stays 7f: best form on a sound surface and acts on firm going: best in
blinkers: hampered eighth outing: sold 1,900 gns Newmarket Autumn Sales.
H. Collingridge.

PLEDGE 3 br.c. Rarity 129–Boucle 86 (Princely Gift 137) [1975 6fg³ 7g 8d⁵ **95**
7g³ 1976 7fg 7.6s* 8fg³ 8g 8g⁵ 7.6g⁶] strong, good-looking colt: good walker:
well backed, showed much improved form when winning well-contested minor
event at Chester in May going away by 4 lengths from Lord Helpus: did not
reproduce that form, but was off course three months after next outing: should
stay further than 1m: evidently requires plenty of give in the ground to be
seen to best advantage. *H. Candy.*

PLENTY SPIRIT 3 ch.c. Jimmy Reppin 131–Holiday Spirit 99 (Live Spirit **99**
121) [1975 6f 6g 7g² 7d* 6fg 1976 7d 11f* 10d⁶ 10f⁶ 14fg³ 13fg* 12fg⁶ 12f*
12g⁶ 13g² 12g⁵ 12s] big, rangy colt: won handicaps at Ayr in May and July,
latter by 4 lengths from Tutu, and at Haydock in August: finished clear of
remainder when length second of five to Alverton in Bogside Cup, also at
Ayr, in September: probably stays 1¾m: appears to act on any going except,
perhaps, soft: said to be best on a galloping course: none too consistent. *W.
Gray.*

POACHER'S MOON 3 b.c. Roi Soleil 125–Messene 109 (Ballyogan) [1975 **124**
6f³ 6f² 7f* 6.3f² 8g³ 1976 7f⁶ 7g* 8d 9f 8fg³ 8f⁴ 9f² 8s⁶] lengthy, good sort

of colt: half-brother to three winners, including very useful stayer Pardner (by Pardao): dam very useful at up to 1¼m: ran race of his life (66/1) when third, beaten a length and a head, to Wollow and Free State in Sussex Stakes at Goodwood in July, coming from a long way back on home turn and finishing very strongly (had very little room in last 100 yards): had put up best previous performance when winning Group 3 Tetrarch Stakes at the Curragh in April by a neck from Wolverlife: did not reproduce the Goodwood form, finishing fourth to Free State in Waterford Crystal Mile, also at Goodwood, 2½ lengths second to Nantequos in Whitehall Stakes at Phoenix Park and sixth to Rose Bowl in Queen Elizabeth II Stakes at Ascot in September: stays 9f: acts on firm going and is probably unsuited by soft. *S. McGrath, Ireland.*

POCKET HERCULES 3 b.c. Baldric II 131–Altesse Royale 126 (Saint Crespin III 132) [1975 6f* 6g⁶ 1976 7g³] neat colt: first foal: dam won 1,000 Guineas, Oaks and Irish Guinness Oaks: won 15-runner maiden race at Brighton in September, 1975: 2½ lengths third to Asa Yolson in £1,200 event at Folkestone in March, only outing: exported to Australia. *P. Walwyn.*   **76**

POINT ONE 2 b.c. Shiny Tenth 120–Sheinter (Sheshoon 132) [1976 5f 6h⁶ 6h⁴ 6d⁵ 7fg] workmanlike colt: quite a moderate plater: should stay 1m. *R. Bastiman.*   **56**

POLICROCK 3 ch.c. Crocket 130–Acropolitan (Acropolis 132) [1975 5g² 5v* 6g* 6g* 5.5g³ 6d 7g* 8v 8g⁵ 1976 7v* 8g² 6g* 6f 6g 8v 6v³] Italian colt: first reported produce: 900 gns foal and resold 800 gns yearling: dam twice-raced half-sister to very useful stayer Crystal Clear: showed very useful form as a 2-y-o, winning four races, including Criterium di Roma, and finishing good third to Vitiges in Prix Robert Papin at Maisons-Laffitte: was officially rated 11 lb behind top-rated 2-y-o Northern Spring: winner at Rome in March and May, on second occasion beating fast filly Lipsia by 2 lengths with Madang fifth in Group 3 Premio Melton: third, beaten 2 lengths and ½ length, to 2-y-o My Royal Prima and ex-English King Jay in Premio Umbria on same course in November: eighth in Cork and Orrery Stakes at Royal Ascot (to Gentilhombre) and Prix de Meautry at Deauville (to Girl Friend) in between: probably stays 1m: acts on heavy going but is said to be well suited by a sound surface: wears blinkers: sweating at Royal Ascot. *A. Perrone, Italy.*   **?**

POLICY LAD 4 b.g. Polyfoto 124–Life Insurance 87 (Prudent II 133) [1974 6g 5g⁵ 5.1g⁴ 6s⁴ 5.9v* 1975 7d⁵ 10fg⁶ 7fg 7f² 7g⁵ 7f² 7g 7d 1976 7f⁴ 8fg 7fg 7f] poor handicapper: has yet to show he stays further than 7f: acts on any going: blinkered final outing. *H. Collingridge.*   **50**

POLIFOX 3 b.f. Healaugh Fox–Poliwog (Polic 126) [1975 5g⁴ 5fg 5s 5g 6g⁶ 5v 1976 6fg 5f⁶ 6g 8fg 8fg 5h⁶] neat filly: poor plater. *J. Spearing.*   **—**

Convivial Stakes, York—Pollerton wins very impressively from Viscount

POLLENKA 3 br.f. Reliance II 137–Polana (Botticelli 129) [1975 N.R. **122**
1976 10g* 10.8g³ 10g² 10.5d* 9.2s² 10.5s⁵ 8.2v*] French filly: first foal: dam
won at up to 1m in France: won newcomers event at Saint-Cloud in May and
minor event at Chantilly in September: supplemented these gains when accounting for useful opposition at Saint-Cloud in November: also placed in two pattern
races, Prix Fille de l'Air (length third to Gramy) also at Saint-Cloud and Prix
de l'Opéra at Longchamp: put up a good effort in latter event, running Dona
Barod to ¾ length, the pair finishing 4 lengths clear: will probably stay 1½m:
acts on heavy ground: a good filly. *A. Klimscha, France.*

POLLERTON 2 b.c. Rarity 129–Nilie (Relko 136) [1976 6f 6f³ 6fg*] Irish **101**
colt: second foal: dam won over 7f at 3 yrs in Ireland and is daughter of Musidora winner Arctic Melody: improved greatly on his Irish form when running
out a very impressive winner of 20-runner Convivial Stakes at York in August,
soon bowling along some way clear of his rivals and keeping on to score by
2 lengths from Viscount: not seen out again: will stay 1¼m: a smart colt in
the making. *P. Prendergast, Ireland.*

POLLY PEACHUM 5 b.m. Singing Strand–Bolton Girl 87 (Blue Lightning 114) **121**
[1974 5fg² 5g² 6f³ 5g* 5g² 5s² 5.6d 5s⁴ 1975 6s⁴ 5f* 5fg³ 6f² 6g³ 5fg³ 5g* 5f*
1976 6g⁵ 6f³ 5fg* 5f² 5f* 5d³ 5fg² 5fg³ 5g⁴]
    Interviewed at Goodwood during the season Mick Easterby, never the most
reticent of trainers, confirmed his apparent readiness to take a chance at the
bottom end of the market. 'Aye, I like cheap 'osses', he said. No wonder! Of
the five sprinters that contributed handsomely towards his becoming leading
trainer in the north, Lochnager, Indianira, Sweet Nightingale, Lazenby and
Polly Peachum, none reportedly cost their trainer more than 2,000 guineas. Of
the five Polly Peachum, who has now been retired to stud, was one of the cheapest
and best, in merit second only to Lochnager. In four seasons Polly Peachum,
bought for just 440 guineas as a yearling, ran twenty-nine times, winning on eight
occasions and finishing in the first four on another eighteen, for prize money in
excess of £35,000.
    Polly Peachum was kept very busy in the first half of the season. Before the
end of June she ran six times, including twice in France. Following a couple of
runs which brought her to peak fitness she was sent to Newmarket to contest the
Palace House Stakes, run over five furlongs on Two Thousand Guineas day. Polly
Peachum was all the rage in the market, being backed down to 11/10 in a field
that included Kala Shikari, Three Legs and Music Boy. Despite giving her
supporters a few anxious moments by dwelling, she came through strongly in the
closing stages and won going away by three quarters of a length from Faliraki,
who in turn was followed home by Kala Shikari and Three Legs. After Newmarket, apart from taking in a minor event at Beverley which she won as she
pleased from Peranka, Polly Peachum engaged top-class opposition for the
remainder of her season. Although she failed to win again she was far from
disgraced, gaining places in the Prix de Saint-Georges at Longchamp, the Prix du
Gros-Chene at Chantilly, the King George Stakes at Goodwood and the William
Hill Sprint Championship at York. In the last-named race, Polly Peachum ran
as well as she had done all season, finishing third, beaten less than a length by
Lochnager. Those behind her included Three Legs, Gentilhombre, Roman
Warrior and Music Boy.

		⎰ Sing Sing	⎰ Tudor Minstrel
	⎰ Singing Strand	⎱ (b 1957)	⎱ Agin the Law
	⎱ (br 1963)	⎰ Blue Palm	⎰ Royal Palm
Polly Peachum		⎱ (b 1958)	⎱ Bluefin
(b.m. 1971)		⎰ Blue Lightning	⎰ Blue Peter
	⎰ Bolton Girl	⎱ (b 1952)	⎱ Sun Petal
	⎱ (ch 1964)	⎰ Heckley Gem	⎰ Dara
		⎱ (ch 1956)	⎱ Casserole

    By Singing Strand out of a mare by Blue Lightning, Polly Peachum is
hardly bred in the purple, and in purchasing her at all her trainer showed both
judgement and nerve. Because of a back injury Singing Strand never raced.
He died in 1975 having covered only a handful of mares in several years at stud
and has never sired anything else remotely as good as Polly Peachum. Bolton
Girl, the dam, raced until she was five, winning six races at up to a mile and a half
in the north. Heckley Gem, Bolton Girl's dam, managed to win a seller over
a mile and a half on what proved to be her last outing on the flat. Before
retirement she had an unsuccessful spell over hurdles. Both of Bolton Girl's

Palace House Stakes, Newmarket—Polly Peachum storms past Faliraki

foals to race since Polly Peachum, Lady Chairman (by Tycoon II) and Mark's Lad (by Chebs Lad), have so far failed to distinguish themselves on the racecourse.
  Although Polly Peachum didn't quite run up to her best in her two races over six furlongs as a five-year-old she stayed that trip really well, as she proved when second to Import in the highly competitive Spillers' Stewards Cup at Goodwood in 1975. A well-made mare, Polly Peachum acted on any going and was very genuine and consistent. She has been tested in foal to Workboy. *M. W. Easterby.*

POLYEYE 2 ch.f. Polyfoto 124–Goldeneye 91 (Aureole 132) [1976 5fg 5f — 5f] neat, strong filly: second foal: dam won at up to 1½m: looked in need of race when behind in minor events at Ripon in May and August (went down

Mrs A. Mears's "Polly Peachum"

to start poorly): swerved badly at start and unseated rider on third outing. *G. Toft.*

POLYPONDER 2 ch.f. Barbizon–Second Thought (Sailor) [1976 4g* 5g³ **124** 6g⁶ 5s 5s³] American-bred French filly: sister to two successful animals in U.S.A., including Second Bar, a very smart stakes winner at up to 1m: dam unplaced in five outings: won five-runner newcomers event at Saint-Cloud in May by 2 lengths: off course four months after second outing and took on top-class older sprinters on return, finishing 4½ lengths sixth to Kala Shikari in Prix de Seine-et-Oise, 4 lengths seventh to dead-heaters Mendip Man and Gentilhombre in Prix de l'Abbaye de Longchamp and 2¼ lengths third to Girl Friend in Prix du Petit Couvert: should stay 1m: acts on soft going: smart. *J. Cunnington, France.*

PONMAYSOUL 4 b.g. Pongee 106–Daisy May (Dara **§§**) [1974 6f 6g 8g — 1975 8g 8.2g 5h 7g 12g 7g 7fg* 8g⁵ 1976 5f 8g 8g⁵] leggy gelding: selling handicapper: stays 7f: started slowly three times in 1975. *N. Robinson.*

PONTRESINA 3 ch.f. Ballymoss 136–Privas (Preciptic 122) [1975 6fg 7.2s **68** 1976 12fg 12fg 11.5fg³ 12.2g² 12f² 12.2f* 12h³ 14.7f* 16fg² 16v² 16v⁶] strong, very attractive filly: won maiden race at Catterick in July and minor event at Redcar the following month, latter decisively by 4 lengths from Emperor of Ghana: lacks pace and needs a test of stamina to be seen to advantage: evidently acts on any going: not disgraced when tried in blinkers on seventh outing. *M. Stoute.*

PONTYLAY 2 b.c. Pontifex (U.S.A.)–Lay Lady Lay (Celtic Ash) [1976 6v] — second foal: half-brother to winning 1975 2-y-o plater Welsh Villain (by Welsh Saint): 2,600 gns yearling: dam well beaten in three Irish maiden races: tailed-off last of 22 in maiden race won by Good Company at Newbury in October. *D. Keith.*

POOL MONEY 3 b.c. Caliban 123–Rosecon 66 (Typhoon 125) [1975 5f 5g⁴ **69** 6fg² 6g 6g³ 5f⁶ 1976 6fg 6v* 6fg⁶ 6d 7fg⁶] robust colt: showed improved form to win maiden race at Hamilton in April by 10 lengths from Copper: should stay further than sprint distances: well suited by testing conditions but seems to act on any going. *J. Hardy.*

POOP 3 ch.f. Jim J–Line of Battle (Quadrangle) [1975 N.R. 1976 9g⁵] — first foal: 2,100 gns yearling: dam, from a good American family, won over 6f at 3 yrs: weak in market when just over 12 lengths fifth of six to Bartolozzi in newcomers race at Wolverhampton in May, only outing. *J. Hindley.*

POP A LONG 2 b.c. Baldric II 131–Popkins 120 (Romulus 129) [1976 5fg⁴ **84** 5fg⁴] small, strong, compact American-foaled colt: third foal: half-brother to a minor winner by Crepello and to 3-y-o middle-distance winner Bobbins (by Bold Lad, Ire): dam very smart winner at up to 10.5f: promising fourth in maiden races at Newmarket in April (7 lengths behind Card Player) and May (beaten 4 lengths by Lady Eton in 23-runner event), on each occasion showing plenty of speed: looked a useful colt in the making but didn't race again: should stay 1¼m. *H. Wragg.*

POPOV 2 ch.c. Hill Clown–Moss Call 70 (Mossborough 126) [1976 5fg⁵ 6f⁴ — 5f] small colt: first foal: dam placed over 1m: well beaten on all outings. *D. Whelan.*

POPSI'S POPPET 3 ch.f. Hill Clown–Popsie's Pride (Border Legend 119) **89** [1975 6g 8g 1976 12.2fg² 12g 10fg 16.7f³ 16fg* 16.9f² 13.3g 16fg* 16fg 16g⁵ 14s] strong filly: showed vastly improved form and ran out one of easiest winners we saw all season when beating Please Turn Over by 10 lengths in maiden race at York in June: gained another wide-margin success when beating Sea Kestrel in handicap at Lingfield in August: needs long distances: acts on firm going: got above herself in paddock at York and gave trouble before going into stalls on seventh appearance. *M. Haynes.*

POPPY LANSDOWNE 2 b.f. Levmoss 133–Petal Princess 102 (Floribunda 136) — p [1976 7v⁵] half-sister to two winners, including very useful 1974 2-y-o Hunting Prince (by Huntercombe): dam stayed 1m: 50/1 when remote fifth of nine to Imperial Guard in minor event at Lingfield in November, only outing. *B. Hills.*

PORCUPINE PIE 3 b.c. Illa Laudo 117–Smoke Tree (Tit for Tat II) [1975 **76** 5d⁴ 5v* 5s 5g⁵ 6fg 5g 5g⁵ 7.2fg⁶ 5d 6g 6d 6g 1976 8 2g* 7f* 7f* 8fg⁴ 7d⁴ 8fg³ 8f³ 7.6g⁵ 10g] workmanlike colt: in good form early in season and won handicaps at Nottingham, Warwick and Wolverhampton: ran easily best race afterwards when close third to Thieving Demon in Charlton Stakes (handicap) at Goodwood in July: suited by 7f and 1m (had stiff task when well beaten at 1¼m): acts on any going. *H. Westbrook.*

PORT AHOY 2 ch.f. Petingo 135–Guiding Light 78 (Crepello 136) [1976 6f⁵ 7g* 6s*] third foal: half-sister to 1974 2-y-o 7f winner Strovili (by Reform): 15,500 gns yearling: dam middle-distance maiden: made virtually all when winning 16-runner maiden race at Yarmouth in September by 1½ lengths from Princesse du Rhone: all out to win 11-runner minor event at Pontefract in October by ¾ length from Phoenix Rose: will stay 1¼m+: acts on soft going. *M. Stoute.*   **93**

PORTALLA 2 b.f. Porto Bello 118–Artalla 79 (Nantallah) [1976 5.3g 5f³ 5f⁶ 6g 6d³ 7s 10v] second foal: dam moderate at 2 yrs: plater: best run at 5f (on third outing): ran poorly in blinkers on sixth outing and dwelt on next. *W. Marshall.*   **72**

PORTAL LAD 2 b.c. Native Prince–Golden Darling 86 (Darling Boy 124) [1976 6fg 5fg² 6f³ 6fg 5fg* 5g³ 5g³ 6s 5d] lengthy colt: half-brother to fair 3-y-o Pitboy (by Will Somers), a winner at up to 7f: 1,200 gns yearling: dam won over 5f at 2 yrs: showed much improved form when winning 12-runner nursery at Chester in September by 3 lengths from Westgate Sovereign: third in nurseries at Ayr and Newmarket afterwards, being beaten 2 lengths by Metair in £1,800 event on latter course after swerving very badly right in final furlong: best at 5f: acts on a firm surface. *F. Carr*   **94**

PORTAL PRINCE 2 b.c. Crowned Prince 128–Torrefranca (Sicambre 135) [1976 6fg 7fg 8v] big colt: half-brother to two winners, including useful 1973 2-y-o 6f winner Sabrewing (by Petingo): 5,600 gns yearling: dam, twice a winner over 1¼m, is half-sister to Carlemont: little worthwhile form in maiden and minor events but looked unsuited by Chester course on second outing: should stay 1¼m. *F. Carr.*   **—**

PORTELLA 3 b.f. Porto Bello 118–Lords Lady (Lord of Verona 120) [1975 5.8f⁵ 5fg⁵ 5g² 6fg⁶ 5f 6f⁴ 5.9g 5g⁵ 5.9g 6g⁴ 1976 6g⁴ 6f2(dis) 6d³ 5.7f⁶ 7fg 6fg³ 5.8h⁴ 6f⁵ 6fg 6f 5.8f 6d 5s] strong filly: may stay 1m: acts on firm going: wears blinkers nowadays: became very bad at the start, twice refusing to race and twice starting very slowly and is one to leave alone. *F. Freeman.*   **§§**

PORTE MONNAIE 2 b.f. Ribero 126–Madame Recamier 92 (Relic) [1976 6fg 7fg 7fg 8s] neat, strong, attractive filly: first foal: dam won twice over 1¼m at 3 yrs: poor maiden: blinkered final outing: sold 380 gns Ascot December Sales. *P. Walwyn.*   **62**

PORT-LE-BOY 3 b.g. Richboy 117–Port-le-Dor (Le Dieu d'Or 119) [1975 6fg⁵ 6d 6d⁶ 6g 1976 8fg³ 7d 7g² 7g²] neat gelding: modest plater: creditable second of 16 to Go About at Doncaster in June on final outing: stays 1m: ran badly in blinkers on second start: sold 300 gns Doncaster October Sales. *A. Bacon.*   **61**

PORTMAN SQUARE 4 b.g. Charlottown 127–Tinted (Kythnos 126) [1974 6d 8s⁴ 1975 12g 11.5g 12.2g⁵ 16.1d 1976 12f⁵ 16g 18s⁵] lengthy gelding: poor staying maiden. *W. Wharton.*   **48**

PORT-OF-VERONA 2 ch.f. Porto Bello 118–Lords Lady (Lord of Verona 120) [1976 5fg 5f 6f 7.2f⁴ 5g 7fg 6v] plater: ran best race when fourth of 14 to Gala Lad after making running for long way at Haydock in August: probably needs further than 5f. *D. Williams.*   **61**

PORTOMORE 2 ch.c. Porto Bello 118–Tomore 77 (Chanteur II 135) [1976 6d] half-brother to a winning plater and two winners abroad: 1,400 gns yearling: dam won over 1½m: in need of run when behind in 23-runner maiden race won by Whitby Jet at Redcar in June, only outing. *J. Carr.*   **—**

PORTO RICO 4 ch.g. Appiani II 128–Vron 91 (Anwar 120) [1974 7g 8s 1975 12s 16f 12.2f⁶ 9.4h³ 12f⁵ 9f³ 12.3g² 12h² 12.2d* 12h 12f 1976 11.7f] strong, sturdy gelding: quite a moderate performer (rated 74) at 3 yrs: always behind on only outing in 1976: stays 1½m: acts on hard going: usually wears blinkers: sometimes sweats up badly. *J. Gibson.*   **—**

PORTOS 2 b.c. Balidar 133–Tea Cosy (Astec 128) [1976 6d] first foal: 7,800 gns yearling: dam poor Irish maiden: 20/1 when in rear in 23-runner maiden race won by Running Bull at Newmarket in October, only outing. *J. Winter.*   **—**

PORTRAYAL 3 ch.g. Porto Bello 118–Zimbie 97 (Zimone) [1975 5v⁶ 5s⁵ 5g² 5f³ 5f³ 6f 1976 6d 5f³ 5f³ 7f 6f* 6f 6f 5f⁵ 5g 6v] compact gelding: plater: won   **55**

at Catterick in July (no bid): stays 6f and ran moderately when tried at 7f: acts on firm going and is possibly unsuited by heavy: has been tried in blinkers but does at least as well without: sold out of K. Payne's stable 370 gns Doncaster May Sales after second outing. *D. Chapman.*

PORT ROYAL 3 gr.c. King's Troop 118–Porto Novo (Sovereign Lord 120) **85**
[1975 5s 6f* 1976 7f 6fg5 6fg 6v 6s] lengthy colt: rated 99 at 2 yrs: creditable fifth of 16 behind Broxted in handicap at Newmarket in April: off course a long time after next outing and was well beaten on both his subsequent races although had very stiff task in first of them: stays 6f: acts on firm going. *S. Ingham.*

PORT SIDE 4 ch.g. Porto Bello 118–Lady Anita 72 (Como 120) [1974 5f 5g **49**
1975 8s6 7s 9fg5 10f 11.7f 1976 8fg2 8g 10.1fg 8s] plater: second to Fast Mover at Leicester in March, best effort at 4 yrs: best form at up to 9f. *H. Nicholson.*

POSITIVE DREAM 3 ch.f. Jimmy Reppin 131–Marialaina 79 (No Worry 105) **80**
[1975 5v 5d* 5fg2 5f 6f6 6g3 6g 1976 7g 8.5fg4 7f2 8d5] big, strong filly: good walker: 2½ lengths runner-up to Porcupine Pie in handicap at Warwick in April: not seen out after early June: evidently stays 1m: appears to act on any going. *W. Marshall.*

POT HUNTER 3 ch.g. Mountain Call 125–Raglin (Ragusa 137) [1975 5s5 5g **56**
7f 6f* 7f6 1976 7g 7f4 7f5 8d4 10g5 10.8f3 10h4 10g6] workmanlike gelding: plater: evidently stays 1¼m: appears to act on any going: wears blinkers. *J Hardy.*

POT LUCK 5 ch.h. Hopeful Venture 125–Flibbertigibbet 97 (Klairon 131) **95**
[1974 8.2fg4 10fg2 12fg* 12fg* 10d2 14fg* 12s4 12g 1975 N.R. 1976 14.6g 12f3 13f* 12fg3 12f2 12d 14f3 13.3fg4 16fg6 14.6fg3 16fg 12fg5] useful handicapper: had a busy time in 1976 and ran twelve times before the end of July: won at Nottingham under 10-0 in April on third appearance: stays well: acts on a soft surface but is well suited by top-of-the-ground conditions: game and genuine. *T. Marshall.*

POTTERON 7 b.g. probably Mr Potter 89–Honorine (Rigolo 126) [1974 N.R. **—**
1975 N.R. 1976 9g5 13.4fg 11g5 8fg] probably of no account. *R. Cambidge.*

POUGATCHOF 2 br.c. Impressive–Igraine (Round Table) [1976 5f* 6fg2 8g4 **106**
8d4 8s] strong, medium-sized, deep-bodied French colt: American bred: particularly good mover: first foal: $11,000 yearling: dam unraced half-sister to high-class French sprinter Realty: put up a good first effort when winning maiden race at Maisons-Laffitte in June by 3 lengths from Bartan: in frame afterwards in three important events, finishing 4 lengths second to Sky Ship when favourite for July Stakes at Newmarket and fourth in Prix des Foals at Deauville and Prix la Rochette at Longchamp: stays 1m: exported to U.S.A. *R. de Tarragon, France.*

POUND NOTE 3 b.g. Pals Passage 115–Gainsvale (Valerullah 113) [1975 **—**
N.R. 1976 10v] workmanlike gelding: fourth produce: 980 gns foal, resold 1,000 gns yearling and 160 gns Doncaster October (75) Sales: dam never ran: dwelt and in need of run when remote seventh of 14 to Shepherd's Bar in claiming race at Leicester in November, only outing. *J. Hardy.*

POWDERHALL 4 ch.f. Murrayfield 119–Broken Doll 91 (Relic) [1974 5fg4 5f5 **74**
6fg5 6g 6v4 1975 6s5 6f 7fg3 8g2 8f2 8fg4 10g2 10.8g2 8g* 10g* 12s2 1976 10f 10h5 10.8h* 10g4 9f2 10f3 10.4fg2 10fg6 10.6d* 10d] neat filly: winner of handicap at Warwick in July: held her form pretty well subsequently, gaining another success when winning amateur riders event at Haydock in October by 5 lengths from Sixfiveseven: effective at 7f and stays 1¼m really well: acts on any going: ran badly when tried in blinkers at 2 yrs: slowly into stride fourth outing: didn't enjoy the best of runs on eighth start. *H. Williams.*

POWER AND GLORY 5 ch.h. Sky Gipsy 117–Fridoline 99 (Sing Sing 134) **80**
[1974 6.5g6 6.5v* 6.5g2 5f* 6d* 6fg 6f5 6fg3 6f 6d5 6s6 6d2 6v6 6v3 1975 6s 6g 6f 6fg4 5.9f* 6d* 5h 1976 5g 5fg 6g 5s6 6v2 5v3 6v 6v*] lengthy horse: fair handicapper on his day: held off The Solostan in game fashion when winning at Lingfield in November: needs 6f nowadays: acts on any going. *D. Marks.*

POWER CASEMAKER 2 b.c. Meadow Mint 120–Nippy (Road House II) **59**
[1976 5fg6 6fg6 5f 6g] lightly-made colt: blinkered when eighth of 22 to Our Travelling Man in maiden auction event at Kempton in July, fourth outing and best effort: sold 850 gns Ascot August Sales. *D. Jermy.*

POWER GIRL 3 ch.f. Tyrant–Youee 66 (Buisson Ardent 129) [1975 5f⁴ 6g 6d 77 1976 6f⁶ 6g 6fg 5g* 6fg* 6d 6v⁴ 6v] small, rather lightly-built filly: well backed when winning maiden race at Kempton in August and handicap at Chester the following month: defied 7-lb penalty when beating Marie Louise ½ length on latter course: stays 6f: appears to act on any going. *N. Callaghan.*

PRE CATALAN 2 ch.c. My Swallow 134–Meadow Princess 85 (Meadow Court 62 129) [1976 6fg 6g 7s 7g] second living foal: half-brother to 11f winner Royal Russet (by Roan Rocket): 3,000 gns yearling: dam stayed 1½m: plating-class maiden: sold 380 gns Ascot November Sales. *B. Hobbs.*

PRECENTOR 3 b.g. Ragusa 137–Chanter 112 (Chanteur II 135) [1975 N.R. 77 1976 12g 14v² 15v*] tall gelding: shows a lot of knee action: half-brother to several winners here and abroad, including smart German middle-distance performer Irish Star (by Relko) and good Spanish horse My Mourne (by Mourne): dam, very useful winner over 1m as a 2-y-o, needed at least 1½m as 3 yrs: fulfilled promise shown against stronger opposition when winning weakly-contested maiden race at Teesside in October by 7 lengths from Formland with the rest well strung out: stays well: acts on heavy going. *W. Elsey.*

PRECIOUS IMAGE 2 ch.f. Double Jump 131–Golden Shot 73 (Miralgo 130) 68 [1976 5f⁵ 5f² 5s² 5f²] small filly: second foal: half-sister to 1975 2-y-o Naughty Pigeon (by Willipeg), a winner twice over 5f: dam seemed to stay 2m: runner-up in sellers at Beverley, Newcastle and Thirsk in April but wasn't seen out afterwards: best run on soft ground. *M. W. Easterby.*

PRECIOUS PAL 8 b.g. Precipitant 113–Odearest (Le Lavandou 111) [1974 — N.R. 1975 N.R. 1976 12f 10f] tailed off in poor company on both outings on flat and is probably of no account: sold 680 gns Doncaster Autumn Sales. *R. Page.*

PRECIPITOUS 4 b.c. Precipice Wood 123–Debra C 72 (Combat 123) [1974 7d — 8d 1975 N.R. 1976 18s] probably of no account. *A. Davison.*

PREEMA 2 b.f. Gala Performance–Primeapple (Primera 131) [1976 5d] — third foal: half-sister to a winning sprint plater by Runnymede: dam of little account: behind in 19-runner maiden race won by Lady Constance at Windsor in September, only outing. *P. Makin.*

PREFERENCE 3 ch.f. Sky Gipsy 117–Fearless Lady 92 (Privy Councillor 125) — [1975 5g³ 5fg 6g 5g 5g 1976 7g 6f 11.5fg] no worthwhile form in maiden and minor events in first part of season: blinkered second outing. *J. Harris.*

PRELATE 3 b.g. Prince de Galles 125–Leila (Grey Sovereign 128 §) [1975 — N.R. 1976 10f⁵ 10.2g] very tall, leggy gelding: half-brother to two winners, including moderate stayer and useful hurdler Tussaud (by Tyrone): dam of little account: showed a little ability on first outing but was then off course a long time and was well beaten on only subsequent outing (dwelt). *Miss S. Hall.*

PREMIER BOND 3 ch.f. Good Bond 122–Sailing 109 (Douttelle 128) [1975 90 6g 6d 6s 1976 7g⁴ 8f⁵ 8g² 8g* 10g 8s³ 8s² 8fg 8g² 8f² 6g 8fg⁴] rangy filly: much improved in 1976 and won minor event at Ayr in May by 2 lengths from Sienna: good second to Indianira in handicap on same course in July: stays 1m well (well beaten in Lupe Stakes on only attempt at 1¼m) and probably finds 6f too sharp: much better suited by an easy surface than a firm one: sometimes wears blinkers but seems better without. *R. Supple.*

PRETSEL 2 ch.c. Sky Gipsy 117–Sound Honour 94 (Sound Track 132) [1976 64 5f 5fg 5d] useful-looking colt: half-brother to useful 1973 2-y-o Streak of Honour (by Firestreak): 1,900 gns foal, resold 2,600 gns yearling: dam a sprinter: seventh of 19 to Right of Light in maiden race at Salisbury in September, second outing and best effort. *A. Pitt.*

PRETTY GIRL 2 ch.f. Double-U-Jay 120–Gold Standard 98 (Quorum 126) 78 [1976 6d 5.9s³] half-sister to a winner in Belgium by Entanglement: 200 gns yearling: dam, winner over 5f at 2 yrs, is half-sister to very smart sprinter Monet: 33/1 when length third of 18 to Fear Naught in maiden race at Wolverhampton in October: will probably stay 1m. *H. Westbrook.*

PRETTY USEFUL 2 ch.f. Firestreak 125–Idyll-Liquor (Narrator 127) [1976 78 5g 5g 6g 5fg⁵ 6h³ 6fg⁴] light-framed filly: fourth foal: dam ran over hurdles: quite a moderate maiden: should be suited by middle distances. *G. Vergette.*

PREVAILING LOVE 3 b.f. Prevailing–Nadia (Democratic 124) [1975 5g 5s 5f⁴ 78 5f² 5f⁴ 6fg 5h³ 6g 5f² 1976 5fg 5f 5g 5f* 5f⁴ 5fg² 6f 5f² 5f 5fg 5g⁵ 5s] robust filly: clear-cut winner of 19-runner maiden race at Beverley in June, beating

Pickwood Sue 3 lengths: creditable second to Shackle in handicap at Redcar in August, best subsequent effort: form only at 5f: acts on firm going: blinkered eighth outing at 2 yrs: suitable mount for an apprentice: not particularly consistent. *A. Bacon.*

PRIAM PRINCE 3 b.g. Grisaille 115–Linton Spring 84 (Khalkis 127) [1975 5f 5s⁶ 7g 1976 8fg] of no account. *T. Gosling.* —

PRICE REVIEW 2 b.g. Frigid Aire–Delfgirl (Immortality) [1976 5g 8d] strong gelding: half-brother to Irish 1½m winner Decoy (by Florescence): 800 gns yearling: dam won over 8.5f in Ireland: tailed off in maiden auction event at Kempton in April: not seen out again until October when in rear in £1,400 seller at Newmarket. *G. Peter-Hoblyn.* —

PRIDE OF HATTON 2 b.f. Gulf Pearl 117–Hattons Pearl (Pearl Orient) [1976 5f 5f 5f] a very small filly who was well beaten on all outings and has little future as a racehorse. *P. Wigham.* —

PRIDE OF PENROSE 3 br.f. Good Bond 122–Mona's Own (Entanglement 118) [1975 7f 6f 7f 8g 8d² 1976 8f 8h³ 10.8f⁴ 8f* 10g] plater: bought in 675 gns after winning three-runner event at Bath in September (made all): best form at 1m: probably acts on any going. *J. Hill.* **54**

PRIESTCROFT BOY 3 b.g. Chebs Lad 120–Alfreda 78 (Fidalgo 129) [1975 5f 6f² 7g 6g² 1976 7f 7.2g² 8f³ 8f² 8f⁴ 8fg³ 7f⁶ 8f⁵ 8fg⁶ 8d³] fair sort: dropped in class and well-backed favourite when third of 14 to Fairy Caravan in seller at Redcar in September on final outing: stays 1m: appears to act on any going: blinkered last three outings: has worn a bandage on near-fore. *M. H. Easterby.* **69**

PRIESTLAW 4 ch.c. Busted 134–Castle Mona 78 (Sound Track 132) [1974 6fg⁶ 7fg* 7fg⁶ 1975 7f 7.6g⁴ 7g 10.2g³ 8g 7g 7f 1976 10.2g² 10f⁶] lengthy, useful sort: good walker: fair performer: second to Gunner B in minor race at Doncaster in March, better effort at 4 yrs: stays 1¼m: acts on firm going: not raced after April and was sold 3,200 gns Newmarket Autumn Sales. *R. Armstrong.* **85**

PRIMA SLIP 3 b.g. Saratoga Skiddy 113–Primasilia 76 (Romulus 129) [1975 N.R. 1976 12.2f] big gelding: first foal: dam stayed 1m at 2 yrs but showed little form afterwards: tailed off in maiden race won by Fontresina at Catterick in July. *J. Fitzgerald.* —

PRIMA TEMPO 2 b.f. Capistrano 120–Javelot's Dancer (Javelot 124) [1976 5fg⁴ 5.1f² 5g² 6g⁴ 5fg²] lightly-made filly: second foal: 400 gns yearling: dam never ran: second in sellers at Yarmouth, Sandown and Edinburgh: claimed for £900 after finishing 2 lengths runner-up to Elaine Mary on last-named course in September (blinkered): stays 6f. *P. Haslam.* **72**

PRIME MISTRESS 3 b.f. Skymaster 126–Primed (Primera 131) [1975 5fg⁵ 6g 7v⁵ 1976 6g 6g 7g] lengthy, useful sort: showed a little ability at 2 yrs but was well beaten on all outings in 1976, including in a seller: should stay 1m: has been tried in blinkers, including on second outing: sold 400 gns Ascot June Sales. *D. Keith.* —

PRIMER 4 ch.g. Prominer 125–Bellaria (Djebe) [1974 N.R. 1975 9g 9fg³ 8f² 8f³ 7f* 6f 7f³ 7fg⁶ 7.6g⁵ 8g 8.2d⁶ 1976 7f* 7f⁵ 8f⁵] strong gelding: quite a moderate handicapper: won 17-runner seller at Kempton in May by 3 lengths from Jack Jiggs: suited by 7f or more: acts on firm going: sold 1,250 gns Doncaster August Sales and resold for 520 gns Ascot September Sales. *D. Morley.* **70**

PRIMONATO 3 ch.c. Native Prince–Vaguely Related (Pall Mall 132) [1975 5v⁶ 5f² 5fg* 6fg² 5.9f² 6d 1976 8.2f 8.2g 9g 7d⁵ 7fg 7g 7s* 7s* 7s⁴ 7s 8s] compact colt: 25/1, put up easily best effort when winning handicap at Goodwood in September in clear-cut fashion by 4 lengths from Fleur d'Amour: should stay 1m: acts on any going: trained until after fourth outing by J. Hardy. *R. Akehurst.* **90**

PRIMROSE BANK 3 b.f. Charlottown 127–Neptune's Daughter 76 (Neptunus 132) [1975 7d⁵ 1976 10g² 12g² 12g* 12fg⁵ 12g⁵ 10g² 11v 12v⁶] lengthy, attractive filly: hacked up by 5 lengths from Hardirondo in maiden race at Brighton in June and turned in an excellent effort when 1½ lengths second of seven to Partridge Brook in £2,400 handicap at Ascot in September: stays 1½m: best form on a sound surface: bandaged in front at Ascot. *F. Maxwell.* **91**

PRIMROSE DAY 2 b.f. The Brianstan 128–J'Accuse (I Say 125) [1976 5fg⁴ 5f²] light-framed, unfurnished filly: second foal: 780 gns yearling: dam twice-raced half-sister to top-class miler The Creditor: in frame in small, early-season events at Newmarket and Folkestone. *J. Winter.*

PRINCE ARDENT 4 br.g. Prince Regent 129–Kazannka (Wild Risk) [1974 N.R. 1975 12v⁶ 16s 14f 12f 13g² 1976 12.2f] poor handicapper: stays 13f. *W. Clay.*

PRINCE BLAKEANA 2 b.c. Prince Regent 129–Blakeana (Only for Life 126) [1976 6fg 7fg 6v] second foal: dam well behind in all races: behind in maiden races but had every chance 2f out on last two outings, on final one finishing ninth of 22 behind Good Company at Newbury: should stay well. *J. Winter.*

PRINCE CARL 2 b.c. Connaught 130–Maladie d'Amour 98 (Fidalgo 129) **99** [1976 6fg⁵ 7fg* 7fg³ 7fg² 8g² 8g³ 8fg⁴] well-made, good-bodied colt: half-brother to two winners, including fair middle-distance performer Love Rocket (by Roan Rocket): dam a stayer: made most of running when winning nine-runner maiden race at Ayr in July by a length from Majestic Bay: creditable second in two nurseries afterwards, but has been only narrowly by Downholme at Newcastle in August and going down by 1½ lengths to Cosy Bar at York the following month after getting behind in early stages: will be suited by 1½m+: consistent but is not the easiest of rides. *J. Hindley.*

PRINCE CARLOS 3 br.g. Don Carlos–Princess Penella (Prince Chevalier) — [1975 N.R. 1976 9fg 11g 12d 12.3fg⁵ 15f⁴] poor maiden. *W. Marshall.*

PRINCE DOWA 2 b.c. Prince Regent 129–Redowa 60 (Red God 128 §) [1976 — p 8d] big, well-made colt: brother to very smart middle-distance performer Red Regent, and half-brother to two winners, including fairly useful sprinter Ballydowa (by Ballymoss): dam sister to St Alphage and Yellow God: unquoted and very much in need of race, showed excellent speed to race up with leaders for 6f when remote seventh of 16 to Tin Mine at Newbury in September: likely to make a good middle-distance 3-y-o. *J. Nelson.*

PRINCE GABRIEL 2 b.c. Graustark–Francine M (Sir Gaylord) [1976 7d] — p lengthy, well-made, very attractive American-bred colt: half-brother to a minor winner in U.S.A. by Prince John: $55,000 yearling: dam a stakes winner of 10 sprint races: unquoted when fifteenth of 25 in Houghton Stakes won by Bessie Wallis at Newmarket in October: a very likeable individual who will do better at 3 yrs. *J. Tree.*

PRINCE GLEN 3 ch.g. Henry the Seventh 125–Latter Head (Saint Crespin III **43** 132) [1975 5v 5fg⁵ 5.9f 10g 8g 1976 11.1fg² 13g 15.8f² 12.2d⁶] workmanlike gelding: poor plater: stays well: often wears blinkers: bought by B.B.A. 260 gns Doncaster June Sales for export to Sweden. *J. Hardy.*

PRINCE HENHAM 3 b.g. Prince Tenderfoot 126–Pagan Chorus 68 (Polic 126) **76** [1975 6fg 6g 5.3g 6g 5v 1976 6fg* 6f⁵ 7f 6fg⁶ 5d 7f⁵ 6fg* 8fg* 10f⁵ 10fg* 8s⁴ 10d⁴] useful plater: successful three times at Newmarket, on third occasion beating Noeletta 2 lengths (bought in 2,100 gns), and once at Beverley (non-selling handicap): stays 1¼m well: suited by a firm surface but has run respectably on a soft one: sometimes wears blinkers but does as well without. *N. Callaghan.*

PRINCE LAMBOURN 3 br.g. Prince de Galles 125–Red Favourite 101 (Flori- **68** bunda 136) [1975 6f² 6f² 6g⁴ 8f² 7d 7g 7g⁴ 7f³ 1976 7g 8g 10g⁴ 8f⁴ 8.3f⁴ 6f⁶ 8v*] narrow, light-framed gelding: plater: made all when winning seven-runner claiming race at Leicester in October: stays 1m but possibly not 1¼m: acts on any going: tried in blinkers on fourth and sixth outings: sold 2,900 gns Newmarket Autumn Sales. *P. Cole.*

PRINCE LANCING 2 b.c. Prince Regent 129–Semblance (Aureole 132) [1976 **88** 8s⁴ 7s⁵] third foal: dam never ran: unquoted when just over 5 lengths fourth of 27 to stable-companion Sporting Yankee at Newmarket in October, leading far-side group 2f out and not being given a hard race when held: looked very promising on this effort but could finish only 8½ lengths fifth of 19 to North Stoke when odds on for minor event at Chepstow later in month: will be suited by middle distances. *P. Walwyn.*

PRINCE LAUSO 4 b.g. Lauso–Who-Done-It 98 (Lucero 124) [1974 6f⁴ 6d² 6s **61** 1975 10f 8fg⁶ 8f* 8f² 7f⁴ 8f⁶ 8fg* 8g 8f 8g⁴ 1976 8fg 8f 8d⁵ 8s⁵ 8h 8f⁶ 8fg* 8.2f 8g 8v⁶] strong gelding: won handicap at Edinburgh at 4 yrs (backed at long odds): seems to need at least 1m to be seen to best advantage: best form on a firm surface: suitable mount for an apprentice: sweated up fifth outing: blinkered sixth, seventh, eighth and tenth starts. *W. A. Stephenson.*

PRINCE LOG 2 b.c. King Log 115–Fairy First 54 § (Fairey Fulmar 124) —
[1976 5fg] brother to very useful 7f to 1½m winner King Frog: tailed off in
maiden race won by Lady Eton at Newmarket in May: dead. *W. Marshall.*

PRINCE LUTHER 2 b.c. Reform 132–Princess Jasmine 84 (King of the Tudors —
129) [1976 5g 5fg] compact, fair sort: half-brother to French Vine (by French
Beige), a very useful winner at up to 1½m: 300 gns yearling: behind in big
fields for maiden auction events at Kempton in April and Salisbury
in May: sold 210 gns Ascot August Sales. *C. Dingwall.*

PRINCELY 3 b.g. St Paddy 133–Noctiluca (Cernobbio 123 or Dark Tiger) 87
[1975 6fg 6fg⁴ 8.2d 8.2g 1976 8.2f 10.8f⁴ 12fg² 12fg² 12d⁴ 11.7fg* 11s² 11.7fg*
12.3fg* 13fg⁴ 12.3fg³ 12g] fairly useful handicapper: won at Windsor (twice) in
June and Chester the following month, putting up best effort when beating
Carnlea House a short head on latter course: stays 1½m well (did not run up to
his best when tried at 13f): seems to act on any going: blinkered on fourth and
fifth starts, running creditably on former occasion but poorly on latter. *M.
Stoute.*

PRINCELY BEAU 2 ch.c. Sassafras 135–Top Park (Gulf Pearl 117) [1976 5g 84
7g 7s⁶] small colt: first foal: 3,000 gns yearling: dam, sister to very useful
Seadiver, won over 7f at 2 yrs in France: showed some promise in all his races,
racing up with leaders for a long way when about 13 lengths sixth of 12 to Princess
Tiara in Somerville Tattersall Stakes at Newmarket in October: will stay 1¼m.
R. Akehurst.

PRINCELY CALL 2 ch.c. Dike–Hunea (Hornbeam 130) [1976 7fg 7f⁵ 8s 8s] 62
fourth foal: 1,400 gns yearling: dam lightly-raced daughter of half-sister to
high-class stayer Exar: plating-class maiden: should be suited by a test of
stamina. *G. Smyth.*

PRINCELY CHIEF 4 br.c. Chieftain–Corner Garth 102 (Solonaway 128) [1974 78
5.8v 6v 1975 8v 8.2g 8fg² 1976 12f² 12.5h* 12d³ 11s³ 9.4h* 9f* 9h³ 10.6f*]
strong, well-made American-bred colt: did well after landing the odds in poor
maiden race at Teesside in April, winning handicaps at Carlisle and at Wolverhampton and minor race at Haydock: effective at 9f and stays 1½m: acts on
soft going but is particularly well suited by top-of-the-ground conditions: game,
genuine and consistent. *J. Etherington.*

PRINCE MANDARIN 6 ch.h. Le Dieu d'Or 119–Ballerine 99 (Borealis) [1974 61
6d² 7h⁴ 6f³ 6g² 5v 1975 5.8g 6f 6g⁵ 6fg⁶ 6fg³ 6d³ 5f⁴ 6g³ 6d 6s 6g 7d 8g 1976 6g³]
big, shapely horse: ran respectably on only outing in 1976: possibly needs further
than 5f and stays 7f: acts on any going except perhaps very soft: sold 320 gns
Doncaster August Sales. *Miss S. Hall.*

PRINCE MELODY 3 br.g. Prince de Galles 125–Tula Melody 71 (Tudor Melody 64
129) [1975 6g 5v 1976 11f 12g 9.4h³ 12fg 12f² 9g] tall gelding: has given
impression he will stay much further than 9f but ran moderately when tried
at 1½m: ran badly in blinkers on final outing. *W. A. Stephenson.*

PRINCE MILO 3 b.g. Native Prince–Milosun 79 (Milesian 125) [1975 N.R. —
1976 15v] strong gelding: third foal: half-brother to very useful 1973 Irish
2-y-o winner Milly Whiteway (by Great White Way): dam ran only at 2 yrs:
backward when last of 10 in maiden race won by Precentor at Teesside in
October. *H. Blackshaw.*

PRINCE MURDOC 3 br.c. Tudor Melody 129–My Advantage 89 (Princely Gift 81
137) [1975 6g 6f 8g³ 1976 8f 8fg* 8g* 9f³ 8.3f⁵ 8f 8d] small, useful-looking
colt: won minor events at Ripon in May and Leicester in June, on latter course
showing improved form when blinkered first time, beating Life's Ambition
4 lengths: blinkered on all outings afterwards, running creditably on first but
moderately on others: stays 9f: acts on a firm surface: sold 2,100 gns Newmarket
Autumn Sales. *M. Stoute.*

PRINCE MYSHKIN 2 br.c. Levmoss 133–Harissa (Tudor Melody 129) [1976 93
6fg 7fg* 7g 8g] lengthy colt: fourth foal: 6,000 gns yearling: dam placed from
5f to 1m in Ireland: made all and kept on extremely well under pressure when
winning nine-runner maiden race at Sandown in July by neck from newcomer
Sea Boat: had quite a stiff task at weights in nursery on final outing: should
stay 1½m. *N. Callaghan.*

PRINCE OASIS 6 ch.g. Mossborough 126–Miss Loveridge 88 (Alcide 136) —
[1974 14.7g⁵ 12g 1975 N.R. 1976 12fg⁵] workmanlike gelding: poor staying
maiden. *J. Hanson.*

PRINCE OF DUNOON 10 b.g. Dunoon Star 110–False Impression (Turkhan) —
[1974 N.R. 1975 7f⁶ 5f⁵ 1976 6h⁵ 5.9f] probably of little account nowadays.
L. Barratt.

PRINCE OF JARVA 2 b.c. Native Prince–Javatina 87 (Javelot 124) [1976 **90**
5s³ 5f³ 5fg⁴ 6g² 6s⁶] rather leggy colt: third living foal: half-brother to a winner
in France and to a winner over hurdles: 2,700 gns yearling: dam, winner at
up to 1½m, is sister to smart miler Presto: having first race for four months, put
up easily best effort when length second of 10 to Broon's Secret in £3,400 nursery
at Ayr in September: will stay 1m: possibly needs a sound surface. *Denys Smith.*

PRINCE OF LIGHT 4 b.g. Laser Light 118–Royal Escape 94 (King's Bench **83**
132) [1974 5f 6d 7g⁶ 1975 6s⁵ 8s* 8.2g⁶ 7g² 7fg³ 8h* 9.4g³ 7g⁵ 9h* 10fg⁴ 8h*
8g² 8g³ 8g⁵ 10f* 1976 10fg³ 8fg 8fg² 8fg* 12f⁴ 9fg³ 8h* 9fg² 8fg 8v⁶ 10d⁶ 8.2v⁴
7s 8s⁵] fair handicapper: successful at Pontefract in May and Carlisle the
following month: best form at up to 1¼m: acts on any going with the exception
of heavy: suitable mount for an apprentice: genuine and consistent: runs well
on tracks with an uphill finish. *Denys Smith.*

PRINCE OF PLEASURE 3 b.g. Saintly Song 128–Counsel's Opinion 83 **78**
(Counsel 118) [1975 5g 6fg 6fg 6f⁶ 8v⁴ 1976 12f⁴ 16d³ 14fg⁶ 16fg 14f³ 15.8fg³
14d* 13s⁴] leggy, light-framed gelding: won 13-runner maiden race at Yarmouth
in September by 2½ lengths from Rare One with rest of field well strung out:
evidently stays well: acts on any going: blinkered fourth outing: none too
consistent. *N. Callaghan.*

PRINCE PEPE 3 b.c. Prince Regent 129–Peperonia (Prince Taj 123) [1975 **100**
6fg³ 7v³ 8g* 1976 10s⁵ 10fg² 12g² 12f⁵ 10f* 12fg* 12fg⁴] well-made, good-
bodied, attractive colt: useful handicapper: a genuine animal who is well suited
by forcing tactics, as he showed when winning Watney Special Stakes at Lingfield
in July, pulling out extra in closing stages to beat sole opponent Park Row by a
length: ran well earlier and won two-horse event at Brighton by a wide margin:
stays 1½m: acts on any going: hurdling with K. Oliver. *P. Walwyn.*

PRINCE QUAY 2 ch.c. Quayside 124–Princess Lorna 63 (Royal Palm 131) **75**
[1976 7fg 8s 8s] half-brother to four winners, notably very smart Irish sprinter
Sandy Row (by Blast) and useful sprinter Ginnies Pet (by Compensation):
4,100 gns yearling: dam won at 1m: 13 lengths seventh of 28 to Royal Boxer in
maiden race at Newmarket in October, second outing and best effort. *H.
Collingridge.*

PRINCE'S MATE 3 b.f. Prince Regent 129–King's Mate 91 (King's Bench 132) —
[1975 8g 1976 12d 14d] tall, lengthy filly: no worthwhile form in maiden
races. *J. Nelson.*

PRINCESS ARIBA 2 ch.f. King Emperor–Palariba 88 (Ribot 142) [1976 —
7.2fg] lengthy filly: half-sister to two minor winners: 1,700 gns yearling: dam
won at 1m: backward when pulled up lame at Haydock in July on only appearance. *M. James.*

PRINCESS BLANCO 2 b.f. Prince Regent 129–Whitewood 74 (Worden II **76**
129) [1976 6fg 6g 7fg 7g⁵ 7s⁵] big filly: half-sister to two winners, including
quite useful out-and-out stayer Amberwood (by Amber Light): dam ran only
at 2 yrs: quite moderate: should stay well. *J. Benstead.*

PRINCESSE DU RHONE 2 ch.f. Lorenzaccio 130–Princess Bonita 113 (Native **82**
Prince) [1976 7g² 8fg* 7d⁵] strong, lengthy, quite attractive French-foaled
filly: first produce: 10,000 gns 2-y-o: dam, very useful at 2 yrs and 3 yrs, stayed
1m: fulfilled promise shown when runner-up to Port Ahoy in maiden race at
Yarmouth in September when winning similar event at Beverley later in month
by a short head from Catchword: creditable fifth of 13 to Jenny Splendid in
£2,000 nursery at Newmarket in October: stays 1m. *R. Boss.*

PRINCESS GERRARD 2 b.f. Brigadier Gerard 144–Vital Error 105 (Javelot **66**
124) [1976 5g 5g 5fg⁴ 7g 5h³] small, lightly-built, quite attractive filly:
half-sister to fairly useful 1972 2-y-o 7f winner Miss Carefree (by Hill Clown)
and to several winners in France: dam useful at up to 7f: possesses only a little
ability: should stay at least 1m: blinkered fifth outing. *F. J. Houghton.*

PRINCESS GREEN 2 ch.f. Green God 128–Frontier Princess 66 (Crocket 130) **56**
[1976 5g 5fg⁵ 5f³ 7f⁴ 6f 7fg 6v] poor plater: suited by 7f. *F. Carr.*

PRINCESS JACQUELINE 4 gr.f. Whistling Wind 123–Palouranna (Palestine **115**
133) [1974 5g⁴ 5v* 6v* 6v* 5v* 6s 1975 5g² 7v³ 6s² 5g² 5g* 5s* 5v* 6g³ 5g³
5g* 6v³ 7.5g* 1976 5v* 5g* 5g* 5f 6.5d] very attractive Italian filly: third

foal: dam never ran: a very tough and consistent performer who won five of her
12 races at 3 yrs, racing against the best sprinters in Italy: clearly retained
all her ability and won her first three races in 1976, on third start beating Lord
Mark (gave 3 lb) in Premio Bersaglio at Milan: well beaten in King's Stand
Stakes at Royal Ascot in June (showed speed 3f) and in Prix Maurice de Gheest
at Deauville in August subsequently: effective at sprint distances and stays
7.5f: acts on heavy going: moved short to post at Ascot. *A. Perrone, Italy.*

PRINCESS MODESTY 3 gr.f. Lord Gayle 124–Palouranna (Palestine 133) **66**
[1975 5.1f 6g   1976 8fg 9.4g³ 8.2g² 8s³ 8f⁴ 8g⁴ 7g* 8fg]   strong, compact filly:
won apprentice handicap at Ayr in August by ½ length from Tiruler: effective
at 7f and should stay 1¼m: acts on any going: trained until after second appearance by R. Jarvis. *N. Angus.*

PRINCESS OF VERONA 4 b.f. King's Leap 111–Veronique 96 (Matador 131) **82**
[1974 5g* 5d⁶ 5s² 5s⁶   1975 6f 7.3s⁶ 7g 6fg 5f* 5g 5g⁵ 5d 5g⁶ 5s² 5g³   1976 5fg²
5g² 5fg* 5g⁴ 5g⁵ 5s⁶ 5v 5s⁶ 5s]   rangy, useful-looking filly: fair handicapper:
ran on strongly when winning at Newbury in August by ¾ length from September
Sky: very good fifth of nine to Athlete's Foot in Sir Gatric Stakes at Doncaster
the following month, best subsequent effort: best at 5f: acts on any going:
sometimes starts very slowly. *V. Cross.*

PRINCESS PIXIE 2 b.f. Royal Captive 116–Dane Girl 78 (Hornbeam 130) **106**
[1976 5f 6f² 5f* 5f* 5g 5g]   strong Irish filly: third foal: dam middle-distance
maiden: won maiden plate at Down Royal in July by a neck and put up a useful
performance in £1,300 event at Phoenix Park the following month, running on
well to score by 2 lengths from odds-on Fairhaven Lady: last of nine to He Loves
Me in Harry Rosebery Challenge Trophy at Ayr in September on next outing:
should stay 1m: ridden by apprentice J. Coogan when successful. *P. Woods,
Ireland.*

PRINCESS ROSE 2 br.f. Manacle 123–Rose Castle 65 (Acropolis 132)   [1976 **74**
5g 5fg⁴ 5f 6g 5f² 6h² 5.9fg* 6s⁵]   neat filly: second foal: 1,450 gns yearling:
dam stayed 1¼m: second in sellers prior to winning 23-runner nursery at Wolverhampton in September by a length from Joan's Wish: will stay 1m: acts on
hard going. *G. Smyth.*

PRINCESS SILICA 3 ch.f. Siliconn 121–Princess Lorna 63 (Royal Palm 131) **61**
[1975 5s 5d 5f 6g 5.9f⁵ 5fg⁶ 5f²   1976 5fg⁵ 5fg 5.9g² 5f⁵ 5fg⁶ 5.8f⁶]   robust filly:
length second to Mino Boy in minor event at Wolverhampton in May, best
effort: off course long time after fourth outing and was well beaten on her return,
including in a seller: stays 6f: blinkered last four outings: sold 580 gns Doncaster
October Sales. *H. Williams.*

PRINCESS TAVI 2 gr.f. Sea Hawk II 131–Tikki Tavi 92 (Honeyway 125)   —
[1976 8s]   half-sister to three winners, including useful 1m to 1¼m performer
Duration (by Only for Life): dam a sprinter: unquoted when last of 19 to
Nordman in maiden race at Sandown in October, only outing   *N. Adam.*

PRINCESS TIARA 2 b.f. Crowned Prince 128–Paris Label (One Count) [1976 **111 p**
7s*]
    We said in *Racehorses of 1972* that Crowned Prince looked a very fine
prospect indeed as a stallion. The appearance of his first few runners in 1976
has done nothing to show otherwise, for among his runners were the Cherry
Hinton Stakes winner Ampulla, the Anglesey Stakes runner-up Irony, the very
promising Tamanaco, the French winners Montaperti and Vivaraes, and, perhaps
the most promising of all, Princess Tiara.
    Princess Tiara had only one outing as a two-year-old and she seemed to
have been pitched in at the deep end in the Somerville Tattersall Stakes at
Newmarket in October. Preferred to her in the betting were Elland Road, who
had gone down only narrowly to Royal Plume at Ascot the previous month, and
the Gimcrack Stakes second Forty Winks. At 10/1 Princess Tiara started at the
same price as Teddington Park and Lady Constance, the latter the winner of the
most valuable nursery of the season on her previous outing. In the early stages
it looked 100/1 against Princess Tiara's winning; she ran green, getting a long way
behind as Lady Constance made the running, but she really found her stride in
the last quarter mile and came through in impressive fashion to hit the front well
inside the final furlong. So fast was she travelling that at the line she was a
length clear of the runner-up Baudelaire and six lengths clear of Forty Winks in
third place. The rest were well strung out. A length's beating of Baudelaire,
when in receipt of 8 lb, is form some way behind the best but she is certain to

improve; she looked distinctly backward before the race and showed in it how inexperienced she was.

Princess Tiara (b.f. 1974)	Crowned Prince (ch 1969)	Raise A Native (ch 1961)	Native Dancer
			Raise You
		Gay Hostess (ch 1957)	Royal Charger
			Your Hostess
	Paris Label (b 1958)	One Count (br 1949)	Count Fleet
			Ace Card
		Thorn Wood (b 1942)	Bois Roussel
			Point Duty

Princess Tiara's dam, Paris Label, spent her first fourteen years in the United States, winning nine of her thirty-eight starts and producing six winners from six runners. This isn't as impressive a record as it sounds, for though her foals were by such good stallions as Nashua and Herbager none of them was placed in a stakes race and four were successful in claiming races. That a mile was the longest distance any of them won over is due probably more to the shortage of longer races in America than to any lack of stamina; Paris Label's sire, One Count, won the Jockey Club Gold Cup over two miles and her half-sister, Thicket, was the dam of that top-class long-distance horse Hornbeam. Thorn Wood, Princess Tiara's grandam, was a half-sister to the Park Hill Stakes winner Traffic Light. This is the family of those very good stayers Ambiguity, Sodium and Craighouse. The distance of the One Thousand Guineas should suit Princess Tiara well, and we wouldn't like to say at this stage that the Oaks distance will be beyond her. Whether she's good enough to stand a chance in either race it is impossible to tell on the evidence of her one run but she certainly looks a good filly in the making. *J. Hindley.*

PRINDOWA 3 b.g. Prince Regent 129–Redowa 60 (Red God 128 §) [1975 6s 1976 10f⁶ 10.1f 10g] brother to very smart middle-distance winner Red Regent but seems of no account himself and was tried in blinkers on final outing: sold 720 gns Ballsbridge November Sales. *R. Supple.*

PRINENA 2 b.f. Prince Tenderfoot 126–Serena Rose 76 (Hethersett 134) [1976 5f 7f 6g 6fg⁴ 6g 6f] quite a moderate plater: ran best race when blinkered final outing. *J. Etherington.* 58

PRINIA 3 b.f. On Your Mark 125–I Will (I Say 125) [1975 5g⁴ 6g⁶ 6g 6g⁶ 6g⁴ 6s 1976 7fg² 7fg³ 8f⁵ 10fg* 10fg⁵ 10.1fg⁶ 10fg] neat filly: won 15-runner maiden race at Nottingham in July by a length from Piccadilly Line: stays 1¼m and has given impression she will be suited by 1½m. *B. Hobbs.* 77

PRIORS WALK 2 ch.c. Pals Passage 115–Sister Paddy (Miralgo 130) [1976 5g* 5fg* 6fg² 5fg⁵] tall, narrow colt: first live foal: bought privately for 1,500 gns as a yearling: dam never ran: won maiden race at Kempton in April and £1,800 Garter Stakes at Ascot in May in style of a very useful 2-y-o, on both occasions breaking quickly and keeping up a very strong gallop throughout: put up by far his better subsequent effort when 1½ lengths second of five to very comfortable winner J. O. Tobin in Richmond Stakes at Goodwood in July, leading until distance and keeping on well: probably found 5f too sharp for him by end of season and will stay 1m: taken down early to start on last two outings, having taken charge of rider when withdrawn at Royal Ascot. *R. Hannon.* 111

PRIORY GIRL 3 b.f. Rugantino 97–Colonia (Colonist II 126) [1975 N.R. 1976 11.1g 11.1g 12fg 12g 10d 7.6s] compact filly: first foal: dam poor N.H. mare: poor maiden. *J. O'Donoghue.* —

PRIORY LAD 4 gr.c. Hopeful Venture 125–Green Valley 92 (Abernant 142) [1974 N.R. 1975 8d 10d 11s 14g 12fg 12g 1976 12s] big colt: poor maiden. *J. O'Donoghue.* —

PRIVATEER 10 br.g. Pirate King 129–Pretty Cage 110 (Cagire II 122) [1974 6g 5.9g⁶ 5.3g 1975 6f 5h 5f² 5.3f⁴ 5.8f² 5fg² 5.8f⁵ 1976 6g⁴ 6fg] formerly a useful, genuine and consistent sprint handicapper: not the force he was but still retains some of his ability and ran respectably on first appearance in 1976: acts on any going. *W. Wightman.* 54

PRIVATE LINE 3 ch.c. Queen's Hussar 124–Zingaline 112 (Abernant 142) [1975 6fg 7g² 7g³ 7d* 7g⁶ 1976 6g* 7fg⁵ 6fg 6d³ 6f 6f⁶ 6g⁵ 7.2d⁵ 8v³ 6s] tall colt: not a good mover: useful sprinter: won handicap at Kempton in April by a neck from Pascuale: good third to Ubedizzy in William Hill North-Western Stakes at Haydock the following month: had some stiffish tasks afterwards, on 101 penultimate outing finishing well-beaten third to Jellaby in minor event at York in October: effective at 6f and 7f and should stay 1m: well suited by an easy surface and ran moderately on firm ground fifth and sixth starts. *C. Brittain.*

PRIVATE WELL 5 ch.m. Privy Seal 108–Rydewell (Blast 125) [1974 10f 11.7g 10f3 10g2 12g* 12g* 12fg3 11.7s3 1975 12f3 12f 10f4 11.7f 12fg 11.7h3 11.7fg4 1976 10.1fg4 12.2f3 12g 17.1f*] small mare: poor walker: poor handicapper: apprentice ridden when winning at Bath in May by 3 lengths from London Rose: stays well: acts on any going: sometimes wears blinkers. *P. Cole.*   **59**

PRIVY CONSORT 2 b.c. Prince Consort 121–Sweet Councillor (Privy Councillor 125) [1976 8g] big, strong colt: second foal: half-brother to very smart 3-y-o Gunner B (by Royal Gunner), a winner from 6f to 1½m: dam never ran: 14/1 and backward, dwelt when well behind in 12-runner maiden race won by Jam at Ayr in September. *G. Toft.*   **—**

PRIZE BINGO 5 b.g. Gustav 121–Quits 71 (Tit for Tat II) [1974 9.4fg 16g 12f6 8s 1975 12s 10f 13.8fg 1976 16f5 16h] of little account. *D. Holmes.*   **—**

PROFIT LINE 2 gr.c. St Paddy 133–Zingaline 112 (Abernant 142) [1976 5.9g 7h 7s5 5v4] half-brother to three winners, including useful 3-y-o Private Line (by Queen's Hussar) and smart middle-distance performer Recalled (by Crepello): bought privately 200 gns as a yearling: showed ability in plating company, finishing 4½ lengths fourth to Kabagold in claiming race at Leicester in November: best form at 5f but should stay further. *H. Westbrook.*   **69**

PROGRESSIONAL 3 br.g. Paddy's Progress 113–Supernal 50 (Supreme Court 135) [1975 N.R. 1976 10.6g] first reported foal: dam stayed 2m: unquoted and ridden by 7-lb claimer, started slowly and was always tailed off when last of nine behind Schloss in maiden race at Haydock in August. *D. Nicholson.*   **—**

PROMINENT 9 b.g. High Hat 131–Picture Palace 83 (Princely Gift 137) [1974 11g2 10g5 10.5fg 12g* 10d 11s* 10.6v6 1975 10d6 10fg4 12f5 10.5d3 10f4 12g2 12d5 1976 10.2g4 11.7f6 10f* 10f2 10fg2 10.8h4 10fg4 10.4fg3 10fg 10.5v5 10.2s] just a fair handicapper nowadays: successful at Goodwood in May by 1½ lengths from Burleigh and ran creditably in most of his races afterwards: stays 1½m: acts on any going: genuine and consistent: good mount for an apprentice: sometimes sweats up: unseated rider and bolted before start on second outing. *J. Bethell.*   **87**

Garter Stakes, Ascot—Priors Walk beats the newcomer Teddington Park

PROPOSE 2 b.f. Tamerlane 128–Miss Twomey (Will Somers 114 §) [1976 5d 6s 6f] of no account. *J. Barclay.*

PROSECUTE 5 bl.g. Prove It–Double Face (Double Jay) [1974 8g⁴ 10g⁵ 12s   **58** 10.2fg 7fg 1975 12s 12f⁶ 8g⁶ 1976 12h* 10.2f⁴ 12fg] leggy American-bred gelding: won handicap at Chepstow in June: well beaten afterwards: stays 1½m: acts on hard going: has twice run moderately in blinkers: sold out of C. Hassell's stable 850 gns Doncaster January Sales. *Dr A. Jones.*

PROSEN 7 b.g. Welsh Rake 118–Princess Palm (King of the Jungle) [1974 N.R. 1975 11fg 10fg 10fg 10f 12f 10g 12g 1976 12g⁵ 14g 15.5s 10s] of no account nowadays. *J. O'Donoghue.*

PROSPECT RAINBOW 4 ch.c. Tudor Music 131–King's Victress (King's   **78** Bench 132) [1974 6fg 6fg⁶ 5g* 6g² 7.3d* 7d⁵ 1975 7v⁶ 7s³ 8g 8.2g 8fg⁴ 12f 10g⁵ 8g³ 8g 1976 8g⁵ 9g⁵ 8fg* 7fg] smallish, workmanlike colt: lightly raced at 4 yrs but managed to win 16-runner handicap at Salisbury in June: stays 1m: best on an easy surface: ran poorly when tried in blinkers on last outing at 3 yrs: broke down final start. *J. Winter.*

PROSPERITY 2 ch.f. Sovereign Path 125–So Precious 100 (Tamerlane 128)   **72 p** [1976 5s] second foal: half-sister to 3-y-o 1½m winner Midsummer Madness (by Silly Season): dam won at up to 1¼m and stayed 1½m: 25/1, ran respectably when seventh of 13 to Jon George in maiden race at Doncaster in October, making late progress: will be suited by 1m or more: likely to improve and win a race. *S. Hall.*

PROUD EVENT 2 br.f. Proud Clarion–Sports Event (T.V. Lark) [1976 7d*   **109+** 8s* 8s] American-bred French filly: fourth foal: half-sister to fairly useful 7f or 1m performer Sportsky (by Nijinsky) and to two stakes winners by Noholme II, namely Anono, a very useful winner at up to 1½m, and Vagabonda, a very useful winner at up to 9f in France and U.S.A.: dam, a stakes winner at up to 1m, is half-sister to Empery and French 1,000 Guineas winner Pampered Miss: successful twice at Chantilly, winning newcomers event in July by 2½ lengths and hotly-contested Prix d'Aumale in September: beat nine other previous winners in impressive style in latter race, leading 2f out and not being at all hard pressed to beat Powderhound a length: third favourite for Criterium des Pouliches at Longchamp in October but ran disappointingly and finished in rear behind Kamicia: will stay 1¼m: better than her Pouliches run suggests. *M. Clement, France.*

PROUD FELIX 3 b.c. St Alphage 119–Carlingford (Sayajirao 132) [1975 5v*   **84** 5d² 5g⁵ 5f³ 7f³ 7g⁶ 5g* 5g⁶ 5g² 6v 1976 5g⁴ 5f⁶ 6fg 5fg⁶ 5d 5g 8s⁵] neat colt: good mover: fair handicapper nowadays: stays 1m: has been tried in blinkers but seems better without: sold 2,100 gns Newmarket Autumn Sales. *N. Vigors.*

PROUD PATHAN 4 b.c. Tribal Chief 125–Athanatos (Never Say Die 137)   — [1974 6d⁶ 6g³ 7d* 7f² 7.2g 7v* 7v³ 1975 7v³ 8s 7s⁴ 7.3s 8f⁵ 7.6f* 10f⁴ 8f* 7.6g³ 8h* 8h² 8fg² 8s² 8d 1976 7.2g 8fg] well-made colt: fairly useful and consistent handicapper (rated 94) in 1975: no worthwhile form in two outings at 4 yrs (not raced after August) and was sold 1,100 gns Newmarket Autumn Sales. *D. Sasse.*

PROVERBIAL 3 ch.f. Mountain Call 125–Causerie 114 (Cagire II 122) [1975   **58** 6f⁶ 7f 7g⁴ 1976 7g⁴ 8fg 10f 10.1fg⁶ 9g³ 10.1fg6 8.3d 8g⁶] sparely-made filly: half-sister to high-class stayer Proverb (by Reliance II) but is only a poor performer herself: probably stays 9f: trained until after fourth outing by C. Brittain: sold 3,100 gns Newmarket December Sales. *D. Hanley.*

PROVING FLIGHT 2 b.f. Sky Gipsy 117–Versification 91 (Dante) [1976 6f 6s] half-sister to several winners, including fairly useful stayer Foretelling (by Premonition): dam middle-distance handicapper: in need of outing when in rear in maiden race at Catterick in August (missed break) and minor event at Pontefract in October (hampered start). *R. D. Peacock.*

PSALVE 4 br.g. Salvo 129–Meadow's Alley (St Paddy 133) [1974 N.R. 1975   **68** 11v⁵ 8g⁶ 10s² 8f⁴ 8fg 8f 8fg² 8fg⁴ 9fg* 8.2fg 10g² 10g 12g 1976 8g 9fg 8d⁶ 12fg³ 12.2d² 12d* 12f* 12.3fg 16g 10.4fg* 12.2g⁶] big, deep-girthed gelding: quite a moderate handicapper: successful at Pontefract in May, Edinburgh the following month and Chester in September, on last course staying on well to win valuable ladies race by a head from Powderhall: has yet to show he stays further than 1½m: seems to act on any going: wears blinkers. *D. Sasse.*

PSIDERIC 5 ch.m. Psidium 130–Glamorous 71 (King of the Tudors 129) [1974   — 11.2f 12f 12f 1975 10s 8f 1976 14fg] of no account: sold 330 gns Doncaster March Sales. *J. Old.*

PSOMMA 7 b.m. Psidium 130–White Flame (Venture VII 129) [1974 N.R. —
1975 N.R. 1976 6g 8fg 12.2f 10.6g 15.5h⁴ 10h 10d] of little account. *K. Sturdy.*

PTERIDIUM 2 ch.f. Royal Palm 131–Paphinia (Hook Money 124) [1976 5f —
5fg 5f⁵ 6g] robust filly: first foal: dam never ran: unquoted when behind in
maiden races: not raced after July. *W. Wharton.*

PUB CRAWL 7 br.g. Road House II–Oloviedis (Maravedis) [1974 N.R. 1975 **39**
8v⁶ 6fg 8h⁴ 8g⁶ 8f 1976 11d⁴ 8g⁴] poor performer nowadays: evidently stays
1m: acts on hard going: has worn blinkers and sometimes wears bandages.
J. Vickers.

PUBLICANS FOLLY 3 br.g. Cheveley Lad 105–Viola 97 (Tudor Minstrel 144) —
[1975 5fg⁴ 5f 5fg⁵ 5g 5g 6v 1976 8f 7h⁶] poor maiden: should stay 6f+:
blinkered final outing in 1975. *M. Goswell.*

PUB SPY 2 ch.c. On Your Mark 125–Chanfrin 86 (Chamossaire) [1976 6s⁵ 7f* **104**
6f* 6h* 7g² 7d⁴] strong, attractive colt: half-brother to three minor winners
and some winning jumpers: 1,500 gns foal, 2,900 gns yearling: dam stayed 1½m:
caused an upset in nine-runner minor race at Newcastle in August on third
outing, making all and staying on stoutly to win by 1½ lengths from 11/2-on shot
Avgerinos: also successful in small races at Lanark and Hamilton: 9/4-on for
£1,800 event at Newcastle, again in August, but looked a bit lean in paddock
and went down by a length to clever winner Sealed Brief after seeming to be
going the better at halfway: stays 7f but gives impression 6f suits him better:
acts well on firm ground and is possibly not at his best on soft. *N. Angus.*

PUEBLO 4 br.g. Astec 128–Pertinacity 100 (Aggressor 130) [1974 N.R. 1975 **68**
11v⁶ 13.3fg² 12fg² 13g⁴ 12g³ 12g² 12g³ 1976 14g 14f⁵ 16.1d² 12g* 14g³ 12.2s]
useful-looking gelding: won maiden race at Haydock in August by a head from
Ice King: stays well: has worn blinkers and did so at Haydock: sold to F. Winter
7,200 gns Newmarket Autumn Sales. *J. Bethell.*

PULCINELLA 2 b.f. Shantung 132–Romella (Romulus 129) [1976 5s³ 7v⁵] **72**
third foal: half-brother to Firemiss (by Firestreak), a winner of a 5f seller at
2 yrs: 5,200 gns yearling: dam never ran: ran respectably when 6 lengths third
of six to Kilavea in newcomers event at Goodwood in September, making steady
progress after a slow start: co-favourite for minor race at Lingfield in November
but was never dangerous and finished fifth of 15 to wide-margin winner Forage:
should stay middle distances. *R. Price.*

PUNTABELLA 3 gr.f. Town Crier 119–Fiddle Dancer 72 (Fidalgo 129) [1975 —
5d 5d⁶ 1976 7f⁶ 8.2d 12f³ 11h] neat filly: poor maiden: sold 430 gns Doncaster
September Sales. *H. Bell.*

PUNTA BRAVA 2 br.c. Mummy's Pet 125–Old Scandal 72 (Elopement 125) —
[1976 5f 6f⁵ 7d 6d] evidently not of much account. *N. Adam.*

PUNTO BANCO 2 br.c. Sweet Revenge 129–Ol Arabel (Relic) [1976 6g⁶ 6g³ **97**
5g⁶ 6f² 6g 7fg⁶ 6g⁴ 7s 6v*] strong, short-legged colt: half-brother to three
winners, including very useful 1967 sprint 2-y-o The Rift (by Major Portion):
dam showed moderate form at sprint distances: 20/1 when winning 19-runner
nursery at Nottingham in October by 2 lengths from Sky Jump: stays 6f well

*Wansbeck Stakes, Newcastle—a surprise result, as Pub Spy floors the odds
on Avgerinos*

but possibly not 7f: acts on any going but goes particularly well on heavy: blinkered seventh outing and when successful: none too consistent. *C. Brittain.*

PURPLE HAZE 2 br.g. Meadow Mint 120–Sageway 82 (Le Sage 128) [1976 **52** 7fg⁵ 7f 7f⁵ 7fg⁶ 6h⁶] neat gelding: only poor form in sellers: sold 350 gns Doncaster November Sales. *K. Payne.*

PUTTY MEDAL 2 b.c. Galivanter 131–Decoration (Petition 130) [1976 5d **53** 7.2f 7fg 6g 8s] big colt: little worthwhile form, including in a seller. *D. McCain.*

PUT UP 3 ch.f. Communication 119–Bella Piccolina (Neckar) [1975 5v 5s 5s 5.9fg 1976 6fg] of no account: sold 300 gns Doncaster November Sales. *L. Barratt.*

PUZZI 3 gr.f. Dancer's Image–Sally's Market (To Market) [1975 5f⁵ 6g⁶ 6g⁴ 1976 7g⁶ 6d] American-bred filly: should be suited by 1m+: ran poorly final outing (May): exported by B.B.A. to New Zealand. *J. Dunlop.*

PYEGORA 3 gr.f. Raffingora 130–Pisces 115 (Polic 126) [1975 N.R. 1976 5fg] first foal: dam a smart sprinter: 20/1 when behind in maiden race won by Walter at York in June, only outing. *M. Stevens.*

PYTCHLEY GIRL 2 b.f. Prince de Galles 125–Intrusion 101 (Aggressor 130) [1976 5g 5.9g] sister to fairly useful 3-y-o middle-distance winner Lily Langtry and half-sister to very smart stayer Mr Bigmore (by Mandamus): 300 gns foal: dam soft-ground stayer: unquoted when behind in large fields of maidens at Leicester in May and Wolverhampton in June. *J. Hardy.*

Q

QUALITY BLAKE 2 br.f. Blakeney 126–Quoff 98 (Quorum 126) [1976 5g⁵ 6f³ **85** 6g⁴] attractive, well-made filly: half-sister to three winners, including useful 1974 2-y-o Cresset (by Henry the Seventh): 7,800 gns yearling: dam a miler: unquoted and having first race for three months, put up best effort when 3 lengths fourth of 30 to Rheola in maiden event at Newmarket in September: will be well suited by 1¼m+. *B. Hobbs.*

QUALUZ (FR) 2 br.c. Royal Palace 131–Fardo 86 (Tudor Melody 129) [1976 **93** 5fg⁶ 7fg³ 7fg* 7f 8g] big, rather hollow-backed, unattractive colt: first foal: dam won over 7f at 3 yrs: won 20-runner maiden race at Newmarket in July by a length from Pedlar: last in strongly-contested event on same course the following month and had a very stiff task with top weight in nursery at Doncaster in September: should stay 1¼m. *H. Wragg.*

QUARTIC MELODY 4 b.c. Quartette 106–Melody Call 55 (Tudor Melody 129) **57** [1974 7g⁵ 6g 6d 8s² 8.2s² 8v⁵ 10s³ 1975 12v⁶ 12v³ 12s³ 12g 10g² 10.1fg² 10.1fg² 12f³ 13f² 12g² 12g 12s³ 1976 12fg⁶ 12g² 16f⁴ 17.1f³ 16h² 15.5f 15.5h⁴ 15.5h³ 16g⁵ 15.5s³ 18s*] strong, sturdy colt: trotted up in weakly-contested amateur riders maiden race at Doncaster in October: lacks pace and stays well: acts on any going: ran badly in blinkers on sixth start: sold to R. Hannon 1,000 gns Ascot November Sales. *T. Gosling.*

QUEEN ADELAIDE 3 ch.f. Alcide 136–Success 107 (Arctic Prince 135) [1975 **75** 7g 1976 12.2fg⁵ 10f³ 12f⁴] unfurnished filly: sister to Observer Gold Cup and Dante Stakes winner Approval: in frame in maiden races in first part of season: will be suited by a really good test of stamina. *J. Winter.*

QUEEN ALEXANDRIA 4 ch.f. Czar Alexander 112–Ya (Selim Hassan) [1974 **—** 5f 1975 N.R. 1976 11.7h] probably of little account. *G. Francis.*

QUEEN ANNE 3 br.f. Faraway Son 130–Napolitana (Kaiseradler) [1975 6f² **77** 6g* 8d⁶ 1976 8g³ 10fg⁶] good-bodied French-bred filly: creditable third of eight to Katie May in minor event at Sandown in June, better effort: should be suited by further than 1m. *J. Nelson.*

QUEEN LUCILLE 3 br.f. King of the Castle (U.S.A.)–Lucy 83 (Sheshoon 132) **46** [1975 N.R. 1976 6d³ 7g⁶ 9.2f⁴] poor plater: best run at 6f. *J. Cousins.*

QUEEN OF NAVARRE 3 ch.f. Double-U-Jay 120–La Reine Margot 76 (Pam- **—** pered King 121) [1975 N.R. 1976 12g] first foal: dam, quite moderate at 2 yrs, is half-sister to high-class French filly Paulista: unquoted when in rear in 19-runner maiden race won by Phleez at Salisbury in May, only outing: exported by B.B.A. to New Zealand. *J. Dunlop.*

QUEEN OF THE SUN 3 ch.f. Roi Soleil 125–Winbeam (Hornbeam 130) **58**
[1975 6fg 5g 5d⁶ 1976 8fg 5.8h 6fg⁵ 6fg³ 7f 6fg⁵ 5.8f³ 6s] moderate plater:
best form at 6f: seemingly not at her best on soft ground: blinkered last three
outings: sold to A. Davison 1,000 gns Newmarket Autumn Sales. *P. Makin.*

QUEEN'S CAPE 3 ch.c. Queen's Hussar 124–Roquelaure 98 (Abernant 142) —
[1975 N.R. 1976 9fg⁵ 10g] well-grown colt: first foal: dam won at 1m: co-
favourite when remote fifth of 10 to Tamingo in newcomers race at Wolverhampton in April (bit backward): unquoted, finished last of 15 to Sousa in
better race at Nottingham later in month: dead. *B. Hobbs.*

QUEEN'S HARMONY 4 b.f. Tudor Music 131–Blood Royal (Princely Gift 137) **47**
[1974 5v 5v² 1975 5g 6g⁵ 6g 8g 1976 8fg⁶ 8f] light-framed filly: best form at
up to 6f: acted on heavy going and was possibly unsuited by firm: dead. *P. Robinson.*

QUEEN'S JESTER 4 ch.g. Hill Clown–Queens to Open 75 (Darius 129) [1974 —
5f⁶ 6s 1975 N.R. 1976 8g⁵ 5.1fg 8g 8fg] seemingly of little account. *G. Pritchard-Gordon.*

QUEEN'S MELODY 6 br.m. Highland Melody 112–Society Queen (King of —
the Jungle) [1974 8f⁶ 8fg⁴ 1975 N.R. 1976 12.5g⁶ 8g] poor maiden: wears
blinkers. *Miss S. Hall.*

QUEEN SONIA 2 b.f. King's Company 124–Milonia (Tambourine II 133) **76**
[1976 5f 5fg² 5d⁶ 7h 7f³ 8fg²(dis) 8s⁴ 8s⁴] small filly: third foal: half-sister to
two winners, including very useful 1975 5f to 1m winner Allez Allostock (by
Welsh Saint): 1,000 gns yearling: dam ran only once: in frame in a maiden
auction event and nurseries, finishing creditable fourth of 20 to Money To Spare
at Pontefract in October on final outing: will probably stay 1½m: acts on any
going: has shown a tendency to hang right. *J. W. Watts.*

QUEEN'S TREASURE 6 b.m. Queen's Hussar 124–Catchy Lyric (Eastern —
Lyric 114) [1974 16g 17.1g⁴ 16f⁴ 13.1g³ 17.1g³ 16g 16d⁴ 19s 18.1g² 16.9s 1975
17.1h² 12f³ 16f² 17.1f 1976 16f] workmanlike mare: very one paced and is
suited by long distances: acts on any going: bandaged and always behind in
only race in 1976. *V. Cross.*

QUEEN SWALLOW 3 br.f. Le Levanstell 122–Sovereign Help 98 (Sovereign —
Lord 120) [1975 6f 6fg⁴ 5g 5g 5g 5s 1976 8f⁵ 8f 6fg 5.9f⁶ 5.8h 16f⁶] compact
filly: probably stays 1m (ran abysmally over 2m on final outing): sometimes
wears blinkers. *F. Rimell.*

QUEENS WORD 2 ch.f. Lexicon 104–Queen's Blossom 56 (King's Bench 132) —
[1976 5fg 5g] of no account: sold 290 gns Ascot July Sales. *W. Marshall.*

QUEEZY 4 b.f. Lear Jet 123–Qualm 91 (Royal Palm 131) [1974 5f³ 5g² 5g* —
5f² 6g⁵ 1975 6g 5f² 6fg² 6fg⁶ 5fg 6g 1976 8.3d 8.2s 6s⁶] big, lengthy filly:
one-time fair handicapper: well beaten at 4 yrs, including in a seller: stays 6f
well: acts on firm going: ran poorly when tried in blinkers on last outing at 2 yrs.
O. O'Neill.

QUELUZ 3 ch.g. Royal Palace 131–Pampas Flower 80 (Pampered King 121) **77**
[1975 7g 7g* 8f* 8v 8g 1976 12g 11f⁴ 8.2g⁴] quite an attractive gelding:
should stay 1½m: acts on firm going and appears unsuited by heavy ground.
E. Weymes.

QUENELLE 3 gr.f. Roan Rocket 128–Queen of Arisai 73 (Persian Gulf) [1975 **62**
5.9f 7d³ 7f³ 7s 6g² 6g 1976 8.2f 10.1fg⁴ 9f³ 8f⁶ 10.1fg⁴ 8.2fg] smallish, robust
filly: sister to smart filly Catherine Wheel but is only plating class; probably
stays 1¼m: ran moderately when blinkered on final outing. *H. Candy.*

QUESTA NOTTE 5 b.m. Midsummer Night II 117–Quentilla 90 (Star Moss 122) **93**
[1974 6fg* 6g² 6fg* 6g 6fg* 6s⁴ 1975 7s³ 6s³ 6fg* 6fg 6f 1976 6f⁴ 6g 6s] neat
mare and a very good mover: fairly useful handicapper: having first outing for
over a year when about 2 lengths fourth of five to Jukebox Jury at Newmarket
in August: creditable seventh of 18 to Last Tango in Burmah-Castrol Ayr Gold
Cup at Ayr the following month, better subsequent effort: stays 7f: acts on any
going: goes very well for apprentice C. Rodrigues: genuine and consistent.
B. Hobbs.

QUEUEING 4 b.c. Prince des Loges 73–Pink Inn (Lavandin 128) [1974 6f⁴ 5.3g —
6fg 7v 1975 8.3fg 6f⁶ 6g 7fg 1976 7f 8g] of no account. *N. Wakley.*

QUIBALA 2 b.f. Crepello 136–Quita II 105 (Lavandin 128) [1976 7s⁵] half-sister to three winners, including top-class sprinter Realm (by Princely Gift): dam won Lingfield Oaks Trial and is half-sister to Prix de l'Arc de Triomphe winner Oroso: 14/1, ran promisingly when 7 lengths fifth of 20 to Brightly in maiden race at Newmarket in October, having every chance 2f out: a useful staying filly in the making: to be trained by H. Cecil. *N. Murless.*   **74 p**

QUICK HALF 4 b f. Quorum 126 or Caliban 123–Railway Hill (Guersant 129) [1974 N.R. 1975 10s 8.2g 8h⁵ 8h³ 10.4g⁶ 10fg⁴ 12f⁵ 10.6s⁶ 16.1d⁴ 12s⁶ 10.6v⁵ 1976 12s⁵] leggy filly: slow maiden. *D. McCain.*   **—**

QUICK NOTE 2 ch.f. On Your Mark 125–Pure Fiction 68 (Narrator 127) [1976 5g³ 6g 6f² 8g] sister to 7f and 1m winner Story Teller: 800 gns yearling: dam of little account: placed in auction events at Ripon in April and Redcar in July: tailed-off last in nursery at York in September but had a lot to do at weights: should stay 1m: sold 1,600 gns Newmarket Autumn Sales. *J. W. Watts.*   **66**

QUICK RESULT 5 br.g. Moyrath Jet–Tudor Trial (Falls of Clyde 126) [1974 12g⁶ 6f³ 6f⁵ 7s* 1975 10f⁴ 9f 14.7f⁶ 10fg 10fg 8g 1976 12fg⁴ 12g 8fg⁶] ex-Irish gelding: poor performer: evidently stays 1¾m: acts on any going: suitable mount for an apprentice: sold 900 gns Ascot July Sales. *Mrs J. Pitman.*   **46**

QUICK RETORT 2 gr.c. Swing Easy 126–Rebuke (Princely Gift 137) [1976 5f 5fg⁵ 5f³ 6fg² 5f² 5d² 6d⁴] tall, close-coupled colt: third foal: 8,000 gns yearling: dam once-raced half-sister to Remand: second in maiden races, on last occasion starting favourite for 25-runner event at Newbury in September but being caught in final furlong and beaten a length by Union Card: again favourite when fourth of 25 to Caerdeon Line in similar contest at Newmarket in October: suited by 6f and may get further. *W. Wightman.*   **90**

QUICKS-THE-WORD 2 br.c. Sharpen Up 127–Rose Garden (Sovereign Path 125) [1976 5s 5fg⁶ 6fg⁵ 7f* 7f⁶ 6f³ 7fg] half-brother to fairly useful 1973 2-y-o Kuroshio (by Firestreak), a winner at up to 7.2f: 2,300 gns foal: dam ran only once: made all and showed improved form to win six-runner minor event at Beverley in July by a head from Briareus: not seen out after August: well suited by 7f: best in blinkers. *M. W. Easterby.*   **77**

QUICK THINKING 5 br.m. Will Somers 114 §–Fast Act (Rullahgeelah 112) [1974 7d* 8f 8.2fg³ 9fg* 8g 8.2s⁶ 9g³ 8.2g* 8s⁶ 1975 8.2s³ 8s² 8g 8.2fg⁵ 10fg⁵ 1976 10.2s 10v] strong mare: poor mover: well beaten in two apprentice handicaps at 5 yrs: stays 9f: seems to act on any going: sold 700 gns Doncaster November Sales. *W. Haigh.*   **—**

QUIET 5 ch.g. Salvo 129–Night Appeal 99 (Petition 130) [1974 10fg 14fg 16s³ 16s² 13v* 16d³ 14d* 1975 14.6fg⁴ 16v* 14d* 16g⁶ 16f 16.1g² 14fg⁴ 16fg 16g² 17.1g³ 18fg 1976 14.6g³ 16g⁶ 16fg⁵ 14fg⁶ 16g⁴ 14g⁵ 16g 18.1g⁴ 16d⁶ 17.1s* 13v⁴] small gelding: quite a moderate handicapper nowadays: heavily-backed favourite, beat Rushmere by ¾ length at Bath in October: also ran well on first and final starts: stays very well: needs plenty of give in the ground to be seen to best advantage: blinkered last two outings. *G. Smyth.*   **62**

QUIET AFFAIR 3 br.f. Prince Regent 129–Cease Fire 112 (Martial 131) [1975 7fg⁵ 6g 6d² 1976 8v 8s⁴ 8g 6.5g³ 7.5s⁵ 8.2f³ 7g⁴ 8g 6g⁶ 8.2fg 8f⁴] strong, compact filly: quite a modest performer: may stay further than 1m. *J. Dunlop.*   **73**

QUIET FLING 4 b.c. Nijinsky 138–Peace 113 (Klairon 131) [1974 7d² 1975 9d⁶ 13.3fg* 12f 14d* 14fg 12g* 14g² 1976 12f* 12g* 12.5g⁶ 10.5fg⁶]   **122**
This big, tall, rangy American-bred colt was successful in the first two of his four races as a four-year-old; victories in the John Porter Stakes at Newbury in April and the Coronation Cup at Epsom in June established him among the best middle-distance performers trained in England in 1976. When we saw Quiet Fling in the paddock at Newbury it was evident that he had been given plenty of work; he looked in peak condition and moved extremely well on the way to post. Piggott had him close up all the way in the race and he showed a useful turn of speed to take the lead with about two furlongs to go. The French-trained Rouge Sang and Libra's Rib chased him home. Libra's Rib proved Quiet Fling's most formidable opponent in the Coronation Cup, in which one of the French challengers Val du Fier broke down and the other Infra Green was struck into. Quiet Fling, who was made favourite, lay last until approaching the straight and then produced a good finishing run which carried him past Libra's Rib and into the lead a furlong out. Piggott kept Quiet Fling going

Coronation Cup, Epsom—Quiet Fling (left) gains his most notable win at the expense of Libra's Rib, Major Green and Zimbalon

with hands and heels to win by half a length, with the John Porter Stakes fourth Major Green two and a half lengths away third. The form shown by Quiet Fling in these two races is some way below top classic form as we know it and he ran without distinction against Riverqueen, Ashmore and company in the Grand

Mr J. H. Whitney's "Quiet Fling"

Prix de Saint-Cloud in July. Libra's Rib also ran in this event and came in fourth, about half a length and two places ahead of Quiet Fling.

Quiet Fling (b.c. 1972)	Nijinsky (b 1967)	Northern Dancer (b 1961)	Nearctic
			Natalma
		Flaming Page (b 1959)	Bull Page
			Flaring Top
	Peace (ch 1966)	Klairon (b 1952)	Clarion III
			Kalmia
		Sun Rose (ch 1960)	Mossborough
			Suntime

Quiet Fling had only one more outing, finishing sixth of seven in the Benson and Hedges Gold Cup over ten and a half furlongs at York in August. His trainer informed us that the horse jarred himself in the race but, even if Quiet Fling had been at his absolute best, it must be doubted whether he would have given the three-year-olds Wollow and Crow, who finished first and second, much trouble. It came as something of a surprise to us to find Quiet Fling running over ten and a half furlongs at this stage of his career. Judged on his running we should have expected Quiet Fling to have been suited ideally by further than a mile and a half as a four-year-old. Among his performances at a mile and three quarters in the previous season was a very good second to Caucasus in the Irish St Leger on his final outing. However, it is evident that Quiet Fling's connections do not regard him as a stayer and we are told that a similar programme to that which he had as a four-year-old has been mapped out for Quiet Fling in 1977. The magnificent stud record of Quiet Fling's dam Peace, who is also the dam of Peaceful and Intermission, is described in the commentary on the latter. Quiet Fling, who is an impressive mover, acts on any going. *J. Tree.*

QUILLET 5 br.g. Quorum 126–Lobster Quadrille 79 (Neptunus 132) [1974 10fg³ 11.7fg 10s⁶ 10g⁶ 10s 10.8v 1975 12s 1976 12.2fg] big, lengthy gelding: poor maiden. *T Healey.*

QUIMAY 2 b.f. Maystreak 118–Querl 66 (Quorum 126) [1976 5f⁴ 5h² 6f² 5fg*] 77
well-made filly: first foal: dam stayed 1m: won 17-runner £2,000 seller at York in August going away by 2 lengths from Imari: bought for 2,450 gns afterwards, reportedly for export to Sweden: will stay 1m: sometimes sweats up. *M. H. Easterby.*

QUINTON 3 br.f. Ribocarre 118–Quickshot 91 (Abernant 142) [1975 N.R. —
1976 8fg 10.1f⁶ 10f] French-bred filly: half-sister to five winners here and abroad, including smart French 6f to 1m winner Quebracho (by Shantung): 40,000 francs (approx £3,600) yearling: dam won over 5f at 2 yrs: little worthwhile form in maiden company: sold 660 gns Newmarket Autumn Sales. *J. Dunlop.*

QUITE A LAD 3 gr.g. Precipice Wood 123–Alan's Pet 79 (Grey Sovereign 128 §) —
[1975 N.R. 1976 10.1fg 10g] fourth foal: half-brother to a winning hurdler: dam a miler: well beaten in maiden race at Windsor (started slowly) and minor event at Lingfield in September. *P. Taylor.*

QUITE CALM 3 b.f. Blast 125–Ocean Song (Fortino II 120) [1975 N.R. —
1976 9f² 10g⁶ 9fg] lightly-made filly: fourth foal: half-sister to 1972 2-y-o plater Expressity (by Espresso): dam of little account: 6 lengths second to Nuns Fifteen in seven-runner maiden race at Wolverhampton in August: well beaten afterwards, including when tried in blinkers in a seller (favourite) on final outing: probably stays 9f. *N. Vigors.*

QUITE CANDID 3 b.c. Candy Cane 125–Suspense 83 (Anwar 120) [1975 6g² 116
7g⁴ 7d* 7d² 1976 12fg² 12fg⁴ 10fg* 12fg* 12g 12g⁵ 12v⁶] well-made, good-looking colt: good walker and particularly good mover: showed smart form and won five-runner Surplice Stakes at Goodwood in July by 2½ lengths from Lost Chord and three-runner £2,500 event at Lingfield in August by 1½ lengths from Kung Fu: in frame in Warren Stakes at Epsom (runner-up to Smuggler) and Ladbroke Derby Trial at Lingfield (fourth to Norfolk Air) earlier but was well beaten in high-class company (Cumberland Lodge Stakes and St Simon Stakes) afterwards: stays 1½m: appears to act on any going. *R. Price.*

QUITO 3 b.c. So Blessed 130–Quita II 105 (Lavandin 128) [1975 6g 6f* 5g² 6f⁵ 82
1976 6fg⁴ 6g 6f² 6fg⁶] lengthy colt: closely related to top-class sprinter Realm (by Princely Gift): 1½ lengths second to Monymusk in four-runner handicap

at Brighton in May, best effort: should stay 7f: dwelt and ran moderately final
outing (May). *J. Winter.*

QUI VA LA 2 b.c. Klairon 131–Quenilda 101 (Fair Copy) [1976 6fg² 7h³ 6fg **89**
7fg* 7s* 6s²] half-brother to numerous winners, including smart 5f to 7f performer Quy (by Midsummer Night II): dam a sprinter: apprentice ridden, beaten
on merit by 1¼ lengths by Nobodys Fool in small race at Chepstow in October:
had earlier won maiden race at Edinburgh and all-aged event at Folkestone:
will stay 1m: acts on any going: genuine and consistent. *Sir Mark Prescott.*

QUIZAIR 7 ch.h. Quisling 117–Amber Breeze (Arctic Storm 134) [1974 8d* 8g⁵ **93**
8g⁴ 8g⁶ 8g² 8d* 8h* 8g* 8g³ 8fg⁶ 8s 8v 1975 8d 8g 8f* 8f⁴ 8f³ 8fg⁴ 8fg* 8v 8g
1976 8g² 8f² 8g 8f 8fg² 8.2g² 8s⁶ 8s] small, attractive horse: good mover: fairly
useful handicapper: didn't manage to win in 1976 but had three good efforts to his
credit, finishing second at Doncaster in March (length behind The Hertford in
Irish Sweeps Lincoln), Beverley the following month (didn't get best of runs) and
Newmarket in July (4 lengths behind Tiger Trail): stays 1m: acts on any going
except very soft: suitable mount for an apprentice. *R. Jarvis.*

QUORTIS 3 b.c. Ortis 127–Queen of the Winds (Borealis) [1975 6f⁵ 7g 8g⁵ **72**
8g³ 10g⁴ 1976 12.5g³ 12fg 12g 16f* 16f⁵ 16f⁶] strong colt: won six-runner
maiden race at Beverley in May by 8 lengths from Haunting Music: suited by
long distances: acts on firm going: ran badly final outing (June). *W. Marshall.*

R

RACHMANINOFF 2 b.c. Northern Dancer–True Blue (Jester) [1976 6f² 6d²] **106**
rather leggy American-bred Irish colt: fourth foal: half-brother to winners by
Imbros and Dancer's Image in U.S.A.: $45,000 yearling: dam stakes-placed
winner at up to 1m: beaten favourite on both outings, going down by 2½ lengths
to Laughing River in 18-runner maiden race at the Curragh in August and failing
by a neck, despite very strong driving, to catch Carriage Way in £2,500 event
at Doncaster the following month: exported to U.S.A. *V. O'Brien, Ireland.*

RACING FIEND 2 ch.g. Sky Gipsy 117–Royal Rosette 66 (Pardao 120) [1976 **73**
5fg* 5f⁶ 6f⁴ 6fg 6fg] well-grown gelding: second foal: 360 gns yearling: dam
stayed 1¼m: finished strongly to beat Joshla's Lady a neck in 15-runner maiden
race at Warwick in April: will stay 1m: slowly away on fourth outing and wore
blinkers on fifth: sold 1,200 gns Ascot September Sales. *T. M. Jones.*

RACQUEL BOLTON 2 b.f. Burglar 128–Mrs Flurry 97 (Fairey Fulmar 124) **64**
[1976 5d 5f 7f⁵ 6f] small, unfurnished filly: half-sister to successful out-and-out
stayer Cathy Jane (by Lauso): sold twice with dam as a foal for 1,000 gns: dam
won at 1¼m and 1½m: only plating class: unimpressive in paddock at Redcar in
August and did not race again. *J. W. Watts.*

RADETZKY 3 br.c. Huntercombe 133–Selina Fair 94 (Hugh Lupus 132) [1975 **123**
5fg² 5f⁵ 5fg⁴ 6fg* 6fg⁴ 7fg⁴ 1976 8fg 8.5fg⁵ 10.4s² 12g 8f* 10fg² 8d² 8f³ 10d]
Dead-heats and disqualifications were a recurring feature of Radetzky's
season. On no less than three occasions the camera showed that Radetzky
had dead-heated, for second place in the Dee Stakes at Chester and the Prix
Jacques le Marois at Deauville and for first place in the St James's Palace Stakes
at Royal Ascot. Twice he benefited from a disqualification: in the St James's
Palace he became outright winner when Patris, the horse with whom he shared
the photo, was relegated to third place for hampering Earth Spirit, and in the
Joe Coral Eclipse Stakes at Sandown Radetzky was promoted from third place
to second place when Trepan lost the race on technical grounds.
When Radetzky was at the top of his form he was a very difficult opponent
to beat, a match for all but the best, yet on the evidence of his first two runs,
when he trailed in last of seven behind Malinowski in the Ladbroke Craven Stakes
at Newmarket and last of five, beaten over thirty lengths, behind Oats in the
Ladbroke Blue Riband Trial Stakes at Epsom, he could hardly have been fancied
to cut much ice in any company. By the time of the St James's Palace Stakes,
however, Radetzky had gone a long way towards redeeming his reputation.
After a thrilling duel with Gunner B in the Dee Stakes, both were touched off
on the post by Great Idea and in the Derby Radetzky kept close company with
Vitiges until dropping away in the straight to finish a fair tenth of twenty-three
behind Empery. We're not for a moment suggesting that either run was anything like Radetzky's best form but both were a vast improvement on his first two
performances.
At 16/1 Radetzky was nonetheless one of the outsiders in the eight-runner

St James's Palace Stakes, Ascot—Radetzky (left) dead-heats with his stable-companion Patris but becomes outright winner on the latter's disqualification. The favourite Earth Spirit (extreme right) finishes third

field for the St James's Palace Stakes a fortnight after Epsom. On settling down Radetzky was leading from Take Your Place and Trust A Native, with the first and second favourites Earth Spirit and Red Lord held up at the back of the field. He continued to hold the advantage until he was joined a furlong from home by his stable-companion Patris; from there it was a ding-dong battle all the way to the line.

Although Radetzky didn't win again he continued to run extremely well, and on his next three appearances he gained a place in the Eclipse Stakes, the Prix Jacques le Marois and the Waterford Crystal Mile. In the Eclipse he showed himself a good horse at a mile and a quarter; it took Trepan and Wollow to beat him. Radetzky was beaten two lengths and four lengths by the first two, but finished six lengths clear of the next horse, Anne's Pretender. In the Marois he shared second place with Vitiges, inches behind the top-class horse Gravelines. And in the Waterford Crystal Mile at Goodwood three weeks after Deauville, Radetzky was beaten only a short head and three lengths by the Sussex Stakes runner-up Free State, to whom he was conceding 9 lb, and the revitalized Boldboy. Unfortunately, Radetzky could not reproduce this form in the Champion Stakes; he ran poorly, and after showing up for some way dropped out to finish tailed off behind Vitiges.

Radetzky (br.c. 1973)	Huntercombe (b 1967)	Derring-Do (br 1961)	Darius / Sipsey Bridge	
		Ergina (br 1957)	Fair Trial / Ballechin	
	Selina Fair (b 1964)	Hugh Lupus (b 1952)	Djebel / Sakountala	
		Raggoty Ann (br 1954)	Bright News / Costume	

By the sprinter Huntercombe Radetzky is the fifth reported foal of Selina Fair, a winner over six furlongs as a two-year-old and over a mile and a quarter at three. She produced three winners before Radetzky, the useful stayer Party Time (by Parthia) and the moderate performers Bladon (by High Hat), who needed at least a mile and a half, and Fnopp (by Crocket), who seemed to stay a mile and a quarter. The second dam Raggoty Ann, a half-sister to the Cesarewitch winner French Design, was a fairly useful performer at up to two miles. Radetzky appeared to find a mile and a half too far for him in the Derby and was never again asked to race over the distance. He seems equally effective at a mile and a mile and a quarter though, and he appears to act on any going. A leggy colt, he is rather highly strung and on his first outing in 1976 he became very upset in the stalls, but he ran his races out genuinely—at least he did when he was on top form. Radetzky does not possess a really sharp turn of finishing speed, and for that reason he does best when allowed to race up near the front. *C. Brittain.*

RADIANT MORN 3 b.c. Be Friendly 130–El Galgo 64 (Miralgo 130) [1975 **84** d 6f⁴ 5f* 5g   1976 6g 9g⁶ 10fg³ 10f³ 12f⁴ 12f³ 8h⁴] rangy colt: best run at 1¼m: acts on firm going: ran poorly in blinkers on last two outings *J. Nelson.*

RADIO BRACELET   2 b.f. Manacle 123–Lady Spy 80 (Spy Well 126)   [1976 5s⁵]   —
first foal: dam second twice over 7f at 2 yrs: last of five in seller at Ayr in May,
only outing. *N. Angus.*

RADIO OXFORD   2 b.f. Blakeney 126–Radio Caroline 109 (Sing Sing 134)   **66 p**
[1976 6fg⁵ 6g]   leggy filly: half-sister to four winners, including French 3-y-o
Caroline's Tern (by Sea Hawk II) and useful miler Bustello (by Busted): dam a
miler and sister to very smart French miler African Sky: showed speed to halfway
when remote fifth of eight to Padroug in Acomb Stakes at York in August: 10/1
for 30-runner maiden race won by Rheola at Newmarket the following month
but finished behind: should do better over longer distances. *J. W. Watts.*

RADIO SPORT   3 ch.f. Town Crier 119–Devon Night 100 (Midsummer Night II   —
117)   [1975 N.R.   1976 8fg 8g 6f⁵ 8fg⁵ 8g]   sturdy filly: little worthwhile form
in varied company, including selling: wears bandages. *R. Hannon.*

RADSTONE   4 b.g. Raffingora 130–Kateld (Supreme Court 135)   [1974 5d⁴ 6fg⁴   **43**
5d⁴ 5g³ 5.3g 5d⁶ 6s 8v   1975 6s 6f⁵ 6f³ 5f 5.3f 5h⁴ 8g⁶ 5g² 5f³ 6fg 5f 8.2g⁴ 5.9fg²
5g⁶ 8g   1976 7fg 5f⁶ 6g² 6f³ 5f 6f³ 6fg 8fg⁶ 8f⁶]   compact gelding: plater: good
third of 11 to Red Lever in non-seller at Folkestone in June on fourth outing,
easily best run at 4 yrs: best form at up to 6f and probably doesn't stay further:
acts on firm going: well beaten when tried in blinkers, including on final start:
inconsistent: missed break on reappearance and started slowly fifth outing: sold
480 gns Ascot December Sales. *M. Stevens.*

RAFFERION   2 b.f. Raffingora 130–Auxiliary (Aureole 132)   [1976 5f 5fg 6fg   **68**
7fg 7g 7g 8d]   half-sister to Mannix (by Carnoustie), a winner on flat and over
jumps in France: possesses some ability but was well beaten in sellers at Newmarket on last two outings: stays 7f: often wears bandages and wore blinkers on
final appearance. *B. Lunness.*

RAFFIA SET   3 b.c. Raffingora 130–Sue Set 99 (Set Fair 129)   [1975 5g 5fg⁴ 5f   **99**
6f⁶ 5g 5fg² 5f* 5.3g*   1976 5f⁶ 5fg² 5s⁶ 5g³ 5fg⁶ 5fg⁴ 6f³ 6h³ 5g⁴ 5g 5d⁴ 5g² 5v³]
strong, well-made, full-quartered colt: put up some useful performances in good
handicaps, notably when second at Ascot in May (to Overtown) and September
(to Derringo) but also ran some moderate races and is inconsistent: stays 6f:
best form on a sound surface, and acts well on firm going: has been tried in
blinkers. *W. Wightman.*

RAFFINDALE   4 gr.c. Raffingora 130–Wharfedale 88 (Wilwyn 129)   [1974 5g²   **111**
5f* 5g* 6fg⁴   1975 5h⁵ 5d²   1976 5g³ 5fg⁶ 6d⁵ 6fg* 6f*]   fine, big colt: useful performer: presumably had training troubles in 1975 and ran only twice: returned
to form at 4 yrs and won minor events at Brighton in May and Lingfield the
following month, starting odds-on when beating Walk By comfortably by 3
lengths at Lingfield: stays 6f: acts on any going: exported to Australia. *R. Price.*

RAFFIN FAIR   2 gr.f. Raffingora 130–Fairabunda 59 (Floribunda 136)   [1976   —
5fg]   second foal: half-sister to 3-y-o Fairman (by Manacle), a winner at up to
1½m: last of nine in seller at Warwick in April, only outing. *J. Holt.*

RAFFINGO   2 b.c. Raffingora 130–Evening Shoe 111 (Panaslipper 130)   [1976   **86**
5g² 5f* 5f⁴ 5g]   useful-looking colt: brother to 1974 2-y-o 5f winner Vibration
and closely related to useful sprinter Grey Shoes (by Grey Sovereign): 2,800 gns
foal, resold 1,000 gns as a yearling: dam third in Irish 1,000 Guineas: having
first race for four months, won 11-runner maiden event at Windsor in August
by 2½ lengths from odds-on Wild Diver: ran creditably afterwards: will probably
stay 6f: trained by F. J. Houghton on first appearance. *V. Cross.*

RAFFINITE   3 b.c. Raffingora 130–Queen's Rock 85 (Souverain 135)   [1975 5g   —
5d   1976 6fg 5f 6f⁴ 5f 5g 5h]   small, compact colt: little worthwhile form in
varied company, including selling: blinkered final outing: sold 240 gns Ascot
July Sales. *M. Stevens.*

RAFFINROSE   2 br.c. Raffingora 130–Acre Light (Linacre 133)   [1976 5fg³   **76**
6fg 5h]   useful-looking colt: first foal: dam poor plater: ran easily best race
when 5 lengths third of eight to Claddagh in minor race at Sandown in June:
not seen out after August: appeared not to stay when tried over 6f. *P. Ashworth.*

RAFFIN'S BOY   2 b.c Raffingora 130–Midnight Hour 91 (Hyperion)   [1976 5g⁶   **53**
5f³ 5g⁵ 7h⁶]   quite a moderate plater: had little chance when tried over 7f but is
not certain to stay that far: sold 650 gns Ascot August Sales. *R. Hannon.*

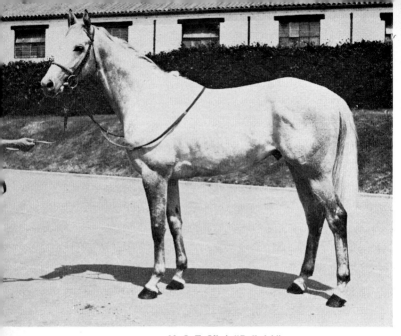

Mr C. T. Olley's "Raffindale"

RAFFONDO 2 gr.f. Raffingora 130–Rotondo (Royal Buck) [1976 5g 5g 5fg³ **68**
5fg³ 6fg 7f⁶ 7.2f⁶ 5fg² 5g] small filly: fair plater: length second to Another
Warrior in 17-runner seller at Ripon in August: appears to stay 7f but ran best
race at 5f. *M. H. Easterby.*

RAFKA 2 b.f. Raoul 87–Lucy Wood (Manuchehr 97 §) [1976 6fg] tailed off —
in seller and is probably of no account. *J. O'Donoghue.*

RAGATINA 3 b.f. Ragusa 137–First Round 97 (Primera 131) [1975 N.R. 1976 —
10g 9d⁶ 8g² 8s 10s] ex-French filly: second foal: half-sister to Tuparamaro (by
Astec), a useful winner at up to 1¼m in England and France: dam won at up to
1½m: odds on when ¾-length second to Touch of Spring in three-runner maiden
race at Warwick in August: will stay 1½m. *B. Hills.*

RAGERAY 4 b.c. King Emperor–Mona Louise 109 (Chamier 128) [1974 N.R. **51**
1975 10g 10g 12g 12g⁶ 9s⁶ 1976 12fg⁴ 12fg⁵ 12g⁴ 12.2d⁶ 10fg⁵] ex-Irish colt:
ran creditably on three of his five outings at 4 yrs, on final outing finishing about
5 lengths fifth of seven to Charlie M at Yarmouth in June: stays 1½m: usually
wears blinkers: sold 640 gns Newmarket September Sales. *M. Ryan.*

RAGGEN 3 ch.g. Firestreak 125–Saucy Moll 94 (Hard Sauce 131) [1975 5v⁵ —
5s 6fg⁶ 6f² 6f* 6fg⁵ 7f 6g 1976 12fg 10d 8f 8f 11fg² 12v⁶] strong sort: fair performer at 2 yrs but has deteriorated and showed little worthwhile form in 1976,
including in a seller on final outing: should stay 1½m: sometimes wears blinkers:
seemed best on a galloping track at 2 yrs: sold to C. Dingwall 1,100 gns Ascot
October Sales. *Hbt Jones.*

RAGING CALM 4 b.f. Salvo 129–Heavenly Gift (Sanctum 116) [1974 N.R. —
1975 12.3g 10fg 10fg⁵ 1976 12f 10g 16.1d 16.1fg 20f] of little account. *J.
Etherington.*

RAGOTINA 3 ch.c. Ragusa 137–Meld 128 (Alycidon 138) [1975 N.R. 1976 **89**
10g² 10fg⁵ 12fg⁴ 10.1f* 11.7fg² 10g³ 14s*] compact, good sort of colt: half-
brother to four winners, including Derby winner Charlottown (by Charlottesville):

dam won 1,000 Guineas, Oaks and St Leger: said to have split a pastern as a 2-y-o: put up a very promising display when head second to Tierra Fuego in White Rose Stakes at Ascot in May but subsequently proved very disappointing (only scrambled home in maiden event at Windsor in August) until winning 10-runner handicap at Newmarket in October by ¾ length from Palmerston: suited by 1¾m and should stay 2m: best form on an easy surface: appeared to shirk the issue on second outing. *Doug Smith.*

RAGUSA BAY 3 b.c. Ragusa 137–Ash 102 (Hornbeam 130) [1975 N.R. **69** 1976 12g 12fg 16f⁵ 13g 12g 15.8g⁵ 13.1s³ 16.1v² 16v*] quite a moderate handicapper: showed improved form when racing in testing conditions and won handicap at Nottingham in October by ½ length from Cavalier's Blush: stays well: wears blinkers: sold 4,800 gns Newmarket Autumn Sales. *F. J. Houghton.*

RAHAT 2 b.g. Pieces of Eight 128–Netherside 73 (Alcide 136) [1976 7.2f **76** 8d⁵] attractive gelding: third foal: dam, sister to very useful middle-distance stayer Nearside, lacked pace: nearest at finish when 6 lengths fifth of 16 to Tin Mine in maiden race at Newbury in September: will stay 1½m: sold 2,800 gns Newmarket Autumn Sales. *R. Hern.*

RAHESH 2 b.f. Raffingora 130–Destiny Day 109 (Tim Tam) [1976 5g² 6d³ **111** 5fg² 5fg* 6g⁴ 5fg* 5f* 5d² 6g] neat, strong, good-looking filly: half-sister to 6f seller winner United (by Merger) and to a winner in North America: dam a useful winner over 5f at 2 yrs: had a fine season, winning a maiden race at Chester and nurseries at Goodwood (£2,100 event) and Nottingham: very good second to Song of Songs in valuable Highclere Nursery at Newbury in September but did not show her best form when eleventh of 15 to Durtal in William Hill Cheveley Park Stakes at Newmarket later in month: best form at 5f: appears to act on any going. *P. Cundell.*

RAIL TICKET 2 gr.c. Shoolerville 121–Royal Command 84 (Arctic Prince 135) **65** [1976 5f 5fg⁶ 5fg 5g⁴ 5fg 6fg 6f⁶ 6f] small, compact colt: showed some ability when 2 lengths fourth to Swaynes Lady in auction event at Wolverhampton in June but was twice well beaten in sellers afterwards: form only at 5f: sometimes wears blinkers. *M. McCourt.*

RAINBEAU FELLA 2 b.c. Umbrella Fella–Belle (Continuation 120) [1976 — 5fg 6fg] first foal: 700 gns yearling: dam apparently of little account: behind in maiden races at Windsor and Salisbury in June. *J. Pullen.*

RAINDIKE 3 ch.f. Dike–Alizarina (Ragusa 137) [1975 7g 6f⁶ 9fg 1976 — 8fg⁶ 8.2d⁵ 12s⁶ 12g³ 12f⁴] poor maiden: heavily-backed favourite (blinkered first time) for selling handicap at Haydock in July on final outing but ran badly: should stay 1½m. *J. Berry.*

RAISE YOU 2 ch.g. Saintly Song 128–Queen Flush (Twilight Alley 133) [1976 — 9s 7s⁵ 10v] rangy gelding: third foal: dam showed only poor form: no worthwhile form in maiden and minor events. *L. Shedden.*

RAJAHMELA 3 br.g. Sahib 114–Henrietta (Henry the Seventh 125) [1975 — 5g 6g 8.2d 1976 10.8fg 12.2f⁴ 12fg⁶ 16f] big, strong gelding: about 7 lengths fourth of 13 to Bagshot in minor event at Wolverhampton in May, only sign of ability: pulled up lame final outing (June). *R. Hollinshead.*

RAJAL 3 ch.g. Calpurnius 122–Gay Life 72 (Zeus Boy 121) [1975 5v* 5v⁵ 5f **72** 7.2d 1976 8f⁵ 8.2g² 9fg 8.2d² 8d⁶] neat gelding: runner-up in handicap at Hamilton in June (to Gold Flight) and 18-runner seller at Haydock in October (beaten ½ length by Nellie Clark): will stay 1½m: acts on any going: sold 1,950 gns Doncaster November Sales. *S. Hall.*

RAJMATAJ 5 br.g. Taj Dewan 128–Radio Caroline 109 (Sing Sing 134) [1974 — 7d 10f 8.5g 10g* 12g 10.1d 10v⁴ 9d 10s⁶ 1975 11.7g³ 8f⁵ 12g² 12fg² 1976 16g 16d] big, workmanlike gelding: poor handicapper: needs further than 1m and stays 1½m: acts on a firm surface: has been tried in blinkers. *M. Haynes.*

RAMADAN 3 ch.c. Amber Rama 133–Gift Token 107 (Firestreak 125) [1975 **97** 5s³ 5f* 5fg² 7f² 7g⁴ 7fg* 8s² 1976 7fg 10fg 8g 10g⁶ 8g 6d⁴] rated 109 at 2 yrs: put up easily best effort in 1976 when fourth of nine to Bowling Alley in handicap at Newmarket in October: probably stays 1m (well beaten but had stiff tasks when tried at 1¼m): seems to act on any going: sold out of J. Nelson's stable 4,000 gns Newmarket September Sales after third outing. *T. Marshall.*

RAMAVIS 3 b.f. Raffingora 130–Corrida 96 (Matador 131) [1975 5.9f 5g — 1976 6fg 5fg] behind in maiden races in the Midlands. *W. Stephenson.*

RAMPHIS 3 b.g. Welsh Saint 126–Another Daughter 106 (Crepello 136) [1975 — 6fg 1976 10.1fg 8g⁵ 8.2d] strong, lengthy gelding: seems only plating class: sold 500 gns Ascot December Sales. *M. Ryan.*

RAMPION 3 b.c. Pall Mall 132–Wild Thyme 63 (Galivanter 131) [1975 5g⁴ **105** 5g⁶ 5fg* 6g² 6g* 1976 6g⁴ 7fg 6fg⁴ 6fg 5g⁵ 5g] strong, well-made colt: useful handicapper: good 2 lengths fifth of nine behind Peranka at Kempton in August: ran moderately on only subsequent outing: best form at sprint distances although should stay 1m: sometimes wears blinkers: trained until after fourth start by J. Tree. *N. Adam.*

RAMPSBECK 3 b.f. Marcus Superbus 100–Signet 76 (Cagire II 122) [1975 — N.R. 1976 12g 9.4h⁵] lengthy filly: second foal: dam, quite moderate at 2 yrs, won over hurdles: plating-class maiden. *W. Atkinson.*

RAMUK'S QUEEN 5 ch.m. Queen's Hussar 124–Miss Ramuk 71 (Silver Kumar — 112) [1974 8.2f⁴ 8f 8d 7g⁴ 8.3fg* 1975 8g 10.6fg⁴ 12f³ 1976 10v⁶] leggy mare: poor handicapper: made only one appearance in 1976: suited by 1¼m and 1½m: acts on firm going: has been tried in blinkers but does better without: suitable mount for an apprentice. *W. Marshall.*

RAMZANI 4 ch.c. Levmoss 133–Crystal Drop (Saint Crespin III 132) [1974 — 7s 1975 12.3f³ 10f 1976 12s 12s] long-backed colt: poor maiden: will be suited by a good test of stamina. *D. Jermy.*

RANAWAY 2 ch.f. St Paddy 133–Giveaway (Princely Gift 137) [1976 7s — 8s] second produce: 600 gns foal: dam, well beaten in four races, is half-sister to very smart Darling Boy: long way behind in end-of-season events at New-market and Doncaster. *C. Brittain.*

RANDA 2 b.f. Welsh Saint 126–Petite Amourette (Hautain 128) [1976 7v] — fourth produce: half-sister to a winner in Italy and to 1975 2-y-o seller winner Tender Prince (by Prince Tenderfoot): 2,600 gns yearling: dam never ran: 50/1 when distant seventh of nine to Imperial Guard in minor event at Ling-field in November. *B. Hills.*

RANDOM LIGHT 4 bl.g. Bluerullah 115–Persian Highlight 93 (Tehran) [1974 — 5g 5f 5.9g6 7g⁵ 8d⁶ 1975 N.R. 1976 8v⁴ 11d⁶ 14fg 10.2h⁵] poor plater: sold out of K. Payne's stable 700 gns Doncaster May Sales. *W. Williams.*

RANDY SCOTT 3 b.c. Hard Man 102–Celtic Star 78 (Star Gazer 123) [1975 **43** 5f 7g 5d 1976 6fg² 10.6d 8f⁴ 6h 10h⁴ 8h⁴] poor plater: probably needs a sound surface: ran poorly last two outings, being tried in blinkers on second occasion. *K. Payne.*

Sun Chariot Stakes, Newmarket—Ranimer is too good for Duboff

RANIMER 3 br.f. Relko 136–Anahita 80 (Persian Gulf) [1975 6.5g2 7.5d2 **118**
6.5s* 1976 9g2 8g3 10g2 8s2 10g* 8.2v6]
    The Sun Chariot Stakes at Newmarket in September joined the imposing
list of English races won by a French challenger in 1976. It was won not as was
widely anticipated by Antrona, but by a less well-known filly, Ranimer, who was
allowed to take her chance in the race because the French fillies throughout
the year had proved so overwhelmingly superior to their English counterparts.
Half the Sun Chariot runners carried penalties for winning a pattern race, but
Ranimer was not one of them. Her only success had been in a Saint-Cloud
maiden race as a two-year-old. She had been placed in all her other races and
shown herself a very useful filly, but Guichet and Kesar Queen had both given
her weight and a beating in the Prix de Sandringham at Longchamp and Antrona
had beaten her comfortably by two lengths at levels in the Prix de Malleret on the
same course. From the way she came home at Newmarket, it is highly likely
that Ranimer would still have won the Sun Chariot even with a penalty: she ran
rings round her field, producing a great run from two furlongs out and drawing
away on the hill to beat Duboff by two and a half lengths, with Sauceboat four
lengths further away in third place. Ranimer ran once after Newmarket, in the
Prix Perth at Saint-Cloud in November. She wasn't disgraced, taking into account that she had been returned to a shorter trip, and she finished sixth of
fifteen, just under eight lengths behind Dominion.

		Relko	Tanerko	Tantieme
Ranimer (br.f. 1973)		Relko (b 1960)	Tanerko (br 1953)	Tantieme La Divine
			Relance III (ch 1952)	Relic Polaire
		Anahita (b 1959)	Persian Gulf (b 1940)	Bahram Double Life
			Nadika (b 1948)	Nosca Adoli

    If Ranimer remains in training, and we understand that to be the plan, let's
hope she is given the opportunity of racing over a mile and a half or more. In
our opinion she is certain to be ideally suited by distances longer than she has so
far tackled. At Newmarket she finished with great zest; nothing in the race
was moving better over the last furlong, and her form at a mile and a quarter
is markedly superior to her form at a mile. Ranimer's pedigree is that of a filly
whom one could confidently anticipate staying long distances. Her sire won the
Prix Royal-Oak over fifteen furlongs as a three-year-old and is primarily an
influence for stamina. Her dam Anahita is a half-sister to the Ascot Gold Cup
winner Pandofell and to Red Marine who needed long distances. Anahita, a
daughter of a mare who stayed at least fifteen furlongs, was woefully slow and
needed at least a mile and three quarters as a four-year-old at which age she did
the bulk of her racing. At stud she has produced three winners apart from
Ranimer. Two of them, Soothing and Gay Anita, who both won over a mile
and a quarter, were by the fast racehorses Gentle Art and Galivanter respectively.
We await Ranimer's first attempt at a mile and a half or more with great interest.
P. Head, France.

RANKSBOROUGH 4 br.c. Relko 136–Heath Rose 124 (Hugh Lupus 132)   —
[1974 7g 7s* 8g6 1975 10f* 14d3 10s2 12d4 1976 12fg 16.1d4] very big,
long-striding colt: smart performer (rated 117) at 3 yrs: well beaten in Jockey
Club Stakes at Newmarket and Lymm Stakes at Haydock in 1976: should
stay 2m: acts on any going: not seen out after May and was sold only 900 gns
Newmarket December Sales. *H. Candy.*

RANTZESTHER 2 ch.f. Bally Russe 113–Guardian Oak 34 (The Eunuch 103)   **66**
[1976 6f4 7g 8.2s] big filly: second reported live foal: dam won 1m seller: showed
signs of ability on first outing but was well beaten subsequently. *D. McCain.*

RAPIDE 2 ch.c. Gulf Pearl 117–Donine (Soleil II 133) [1976 6g 7g 7fg3 7fg3   **84**
6s] robust colt: half-brother to French 1m winner Kashmine (by Kashmir II):
1,150 gns yearling: dam never ran: third in maiden races in September at Chester
and Leicester (2 lengths behind Main Event in 20-runner event): will stay 1¼m.
I. Walker.

RAPPORT 3 ch.c. Porto Bello 118–Radiant Princess 81 (Primera 131) [1975   **56**
6fg 6fg4 5g 6s 1976 6g 6g 7g 7g3 7fg 7f] tall, useful-looking colt: ran best race
when third to Sierra Verde in seller at Brighton in June: will stay 1m: tried in
blinkers second outing. *W. Wightman.*

RAR

RARATONGA 3 b.g. Ribero 126–Wake Island 101 (Relic) [1975 7fg 8d 8g* 7g⁵ **86**
1976 12g* 12g 12g 12f⁵ 12g⁵ 12s³ 12s* 14s⁵] neat gelding: won Yellow Pages
Spring Handicap at Leicester in April all out by 3 lengths from Stilton after leading
all way: ridden with a good deal more restraint when successful in similar race
at Folkestone in October, beating Keelhaul 2 lengths: ran poorly four of his five
outings in between, once wearing blinkers: stays 1½m (ran below his best when
tried over 1¾m): suited by some give in the ground: sold out of H. Candy's stable
1,900 gns Ascot July Sales after fourth start. *M. Goswell.*

RARE AWARD 3 ch.f. Reliance II 137–High Order 102 (Hugh Lupus 132) **64**
[1975 N.R. 1976 10s 14fg⁴ 10d³ 10s² 10.2s] tall filly: fourth foal: half-sister
to a minor winner in France: dam, sister to Hethersett, won over 9f in France:
showed some ability in varied company, finishing 4 lengths second to Wolver
Valley in maiden race at Newmarket in October: will stay well. *J. Hindley.*

RARE BEAUTY 2 b.f. Rarity 129–Pretty Patch 81 (Golden Cloud) [1976 5f 6fg⁵ **90**
6fg⁶ 7g² 8.2v] half-sister to five winners, including good Italian miler Pripjat (by
Faberge II): 2,500 gns yearling: dam moderate over 5f at 2 yrs: ran easily best
race when 2½ lengths second of 19 to Best Offer in minor event at Lingfield in
September: better suited by 7f than shorter distances, and should stay 1m. *T.
Waugh.*

RARE ONE 3 b.c. Rarity 129–Glad News (Ballymoss 136) [1975 7g 1976 10g **74**
12.2f³ 14fg⁴ 12g⁴ 14d²] quite a moderate performer: placed in minor event at
Wolverhampton in May (close-up third to Bagshot) and maiden event at Yarmouth in September (2½ lengths second to Prince of Pleasure with rest of field
well strung out behind): stays 1¾m: appears to act on any going. *M. Stoute.*

RARE TRIAL 3 b.c. Rarity 129–Trial By Fire 91 (Court Martial) [1975 7g² **99**
1976 7s 9f* 10.4s⁶ 8f⁶ 9f³ 10g] well-made colt: half-brother to very useful stayer
Deep Run (by Pampered King), and to fair 1m winner Fils du Feu (by Levmoss):
20,000 gns yearling: dam won at 1m: won maiden race at Mallow in April: second
favourite, one of first beaten when remote sixth of nine to Great Idea in Dee
Stakes at Chester in May: off course three months subsequently and ran well on
his return, finishing 2½ lengths third to Nantequos in Whitehall Stakes at Phoenix
Park and eighth of 11 to Malacate in Joe McGrath Memorial Stakes at Leopardstown after making a lot of the running, both in September: should stay 1¼m:
acts on firm going and is possibly unsuited by soft. *P. Prendergast, Ireland.*

RASHID 2 ch.c. Gulf Pearl 117–Conspiring 73 (Conspirator 114) [1976 5fg⁶ 7g **71**
8s] brother to fairly useful 6f winner Mon Parnes and half-brother to Prince
Chad (by St Chad), a very useful performer at up to 1m: 2,800 gns yearling:
dam won 6f seller at 2 yrs: showed signs of ability in maiden races at Newmarket,
on third outing showing up well for over 6f when eighth of 28 to Royal Boxer in
October. *B. Hobbs.*

RASTI 5 b.h. Ray–Stillula (Cranach) [1974 8g 8fg 10g⁵ 10fg⁵ 12f⁶ 10g² 14d* 14g **—**
12s* 12g⁵ 14s* 16d² 1975 15.5v 16s² 21f⁵ 14d 16d⁴ 1976 13.3g⁶ 16g] strong,
good-looking horse: smart handicapper at his best but has been lightly raced and
rather disappointing since his 3-y-o days: stays very well: needs an easy surface
and goes extremely well on soft ground: has been tried in blinkers but is better
without them: suitable mount for an apprentice: front runner: bandaged both
outings at 5 yrs. *P. Mitchell.*

RATAMATAZ 2 b.c. Shiny Tenth 120–Water Rat 83 (Hard Tack 111 §) **88**
[1976 5g² 5fg³ 5g³] lightly-made colt: second foal: half-brother to winning 3-y-o
stayer Baby Rat (by Reliance II): dam won at up to 9f: placed in early-season
maiden and minor events, finishing 8 lengths third of 25 to Song of Songs at
Newbury on last outing: should stay at least 7f. *D. Marks.*

RATES A NAP 3 b.f. Galivanter 131–Golden Mall (Pall Mall 132) [1975 8f **—**
1976 7fg 8fg] strong filly: plating-class maiden: sold 500 gns Newmarket Autumn
Sales. *J. Hardy.*

RAVEL 4 b.c. Levmoss 133–Ravie (Relko 136) [1974 7d 1975 8v 10.2g³ 10.4d* **95**
10fg* 12f⁵ 11v 1976 8f 8g⁵ 10.4d⁵ 10.5v 10.2s] strong, attractive colt: showed
very useful form as a 3-y-o: most disappointing in 1976 and was tailed off on last
three outings (off course over four months before fourth appearance): should
stay 1½m+: appears to act on any going: trained by B. Hills until after third
start. *M. W. Easterby.*

RAVELSTON 2 b.c. Northfields–Rubella (Buisson Ardent 129) [1976 5fg⁵ **88**
5g⁴ 6g² 5fg⁴ 5d²] small, useful-looking colt: half-brother to three winners, in-

594

cluding speedy 1975 2-y-o Alacriter (by Mountain Call): 7,000 gns yearling: dam ran only once: ran well in maiden races and failed by only a head to catch Jacado at Nottingham in September on final outing: should stay 1m. *I. Balding.*

RAVENSBOURNE 3 br.c. Siliconn 121–Suzy Wong II 71 (Mincio 127) [1975 **61** 5fg 1976 9f 8s 8s 8s³ 10v⁴] poor handicapper: gambled on, showed only worthwhile form when 4 lengths third to Fairy Caravan at Chepstow in October: stays 1m: acts on soft going. *R. Akehurst.*

RAVER 3 ch.f. Runnymede 123–Tropical Fruit (Tropique 128) [1975 5d 6h³ **57** 5.1f2 6fg⁵ 5f³ 5fg² 5g⁶ 5f2 6g 5g⁶ 1976 6v³ 5f⁵ 5f2 6g 5f 6g 5g 5fg⁵] plain, workmanlike filly: plater: stays 6f: acts on any going: ran poorly last three outings, twice wearing blinkers. *A. Balding.*

RAW DEAL 2 ch.c. Don II 123–Mrs Binks (Whistling Wind 123) [1976 6g 6d] — third foal: half-brother to smart sprinter Divine King (by Divine Gift): 15,000 gns yearling: dam never ran: in middle division in newcomers event at Lingfield in September and 22-runner maiden race at Newmarket in October. *A. Corbett.*

RAY OF OLLIES 4 ch.g. Jukebox 120–Lev Star (Le Levanstell 122) [1974 5g **41** 6f2 6g* 7g⁵ 8s⁶ 7.2s 7g 1975 7s⁵ 7g 8g⁶ 10fg⁵ 10fg 9g² 7fg 10d⁶ 1976 8fg⁵] strong gelding: stays 9f: has been tried in blinkers: disappointing: sold 550 gns Ascot June Sales for export to Sweden. *F. Carr.*

READJUST 2 ch.c. Arts and Letters–Allies Serenade (Royal Serenade 132) **108** [1976 5f* 5f2 7f³ 6.3f* 6f2 5g⁵] American-bred Irish colt: half-brother to a minor winner by Dr Fager in U.S.A.: $20,000 yearling: dam very useful stakes winner at up to 1m: won maiden race at Leopardstown and Anglesey Stakes at the Curragh: beat Irony by a length in latter event: short-head second to Star of Erin in nursery at Navan in September and ran creditably under 9-7 when about 2½ lengths fifth of seven to First Up in similar company at Phoenix Park the following month: bred to stay 1¼m+: acts on firm going: very useful. *P. Prendergast, jnr, Ireland.*

READ'S BOY 3 br.g. Richboy 117–Al Be Lucky 87 (March Past 124) [1975 — 6g⁵ 6fg 1976 10.4fg] of no account. *P. Milner.*

REALIST 8 br.g. Reliance II 137–Words and Music 112 (Worden II 129) [1974 **80** 13.3g⁵ 16fg 14s⁶ 14s* 14.6s⁵ 1975 14f2 16fg⁶ 20f 16g 14g* 14fg³ 16g⁵ 14g 1976 14fg²] big gelding: fair handicapper: creditable second at Salisbury in May on only outing in 1976: stays very well: acts on any going: has often worn bandages. *H. Blagrave.*

REALLY AGLOW 3 br.f. Reliance II 137–Moon Glow (Right Royal V 135) — [1975 5s⁶ 5f 8g 10g 1976 12.2fg 14fg 15.8g 12.2s] poor maiden: tailed off when tried in blinkers on final outing. *R. Vibert.*

REALMS OF GOLD 2 br.f. Realm 129–Scollop 70 (Grey Sovereign 128 §) **64** [1976 5g⁵ 5.9f³ 5g] unfurnished filly: half-sister to winners here and abroad: 4,000 gns yearling: dam won over 1m: well-backed favourite when 3¾ lengths third of nine to Ashen Light at Wolverhampton in August: last of 11 in similar company at Newcastle later in month and didn't race again. *M. Jarvis.*

REALM TREE 2 b.f. Realm 129–Bay Tree (Fr) (Relko 136) [1976 5g³ 5fg² 5g³ **81** 5g⁴ 7fg⁴ 6f* 6fg³] compact filly: first foal: bought privately for 2,000 gns as a yearling: dam won over 1½m in Ireland at 3 yrs: won eight-runner maiden race at Hamilton in July by a head from Why Bird: blinkered first time when close-up third to Virginia Lad in valuable seller at Goodwood later in month: should stay beyond 6f. *B. Hills.*

REALTY 4 ch.f. Sir Ivor 135–Reveille II (Star Kingdom 131) [1974 6s⁵ 4.5s* **124** 5g* 1975 5g* 6g* 5s* 6g³ 6d* 5s 5d* 1976 5f³ 7d 5f2 6.5d³ 6g⁵] big, strong, very attractive American-bred French filly: top-class sprinter: didn't manage to win at 4 yrs (made only five appearances) but nevertheless turned in a cracking effort when strong-finishing ¾ length second to Lochnager in King's Stand Stakes at Royal Ascot in June: also placed in two important events won by Girl Friend, finishing third in Prix de Saint-Georges at Longchamp in May and Prix Maurice de Gheest at Deauville in August: not raced after finishing about 4 lengths fifth to that filly in Prix de Meautry on last-named course later in August: best at sprint distances: acts on any going: wears blinkers. *C. Datessen, France.*

REAPER'S GOLD 2 b.c. Yukon Eric–Rich Harvest (Bounteous 125) [1976   —
7fg] fourth living foal: dam never ran: well behind in nine-runner minor
event won by Fair Season at Newmarket in July, only outing. *B. Lunness.*

REASBY 2 gr.f. Aglojo 119–Try Hard (Quorum 126) [1976 5g⁴ 5f 5f 6f] **41**
lengthy filly: poor plater: sold 480 gns Newmarket Autumn Sales. *W. Wharton.*

REBEC 4 b.c. Tudor Melody 129–Parmelia 118 (Ballymoss 136) [1974 6fg⁴ 8d² **96**
1975 8v* 10s 8.2g* 1976 7fg 8s² 8g⁶ 8f] lengthy, quite attractive colt: fairly
useful performer: ran well when ¾-length second to Jumping Hill in strongly-
contested handicap at York in May, staying on well in final ¼m after being
behind in early stages: disappointed on both subsequent outings and wasn't
seen out after finishing well behind in Royal Hunt Cup at Royal Ascot in June
(tried in blinkers): runs as though he will stay further than 1m: acts on heavy
going: coltish in paddock on reappearance: sold 3,400 gns Newmarket Autumn
Sales. *H. Cecil.*

REBEL PATRON 4 ch.f. Aberdeen 109–I Wonder Why 95 (Pearl Diver 130)   —
[1974 5g 6fg 6g 7.2d 8s* 7s 8s 7v 1975 N.R. 1976 10v] quite a moderate
performer (rated 71) at 2 yrs: has run only once since (well behind in seller
at Nottingham in October): stays 1m: evidently suited by soft going. *B.
Richmond.*

RECAPTURE 2 ch.f. Sassafras 135–Fusil 105 (Fidalgo 129) [1976 8s] half-   **— p**
sister to 1,000 Guineas winner Full Dress II (by Shantung) and smart staying
fillies Reload (by Relko), Boulette (by Nasram II) and Grenadiere (by Right
Royal V): dam stayed 1½m: 16/1 when behind in 27-runner maiden race won
by Sporting Yankee at Newmarket in October: should do better over long
distances at 3 yrs. *H. Wragg.*

RECKLESS LAD 3 b.c. Sky Gipsy 117–Lady in Trouble 112 (High Treason 126) **43**
[1975 5fg 6g 6fg 5f 5.1g⁶ 5v 1976 6fg 6fg⁵ 8.2f⁴ 10.1fg 10g] bad plater: wears
blinkers. *G. Vergette.*

RECLAMATION 2 ch.c. Roan Rocket 128–Nerissa 117 (Court Martial) [1976 **111**
6g* 6f⁴ 7.3d²] tall, rather lightly-built colt: half-brother to three winners,
including very speedy 1968 2-y-o Red Rose Prince (by Henry the Seventh)
and 1975 2-y-o Venetian Palace (by Royal Palace): dam smart 5f sprinter:
put up a good first effort when leading well inside final furlong to beat Golden
Vow a short head in maiden race at Newmarket in July: ran very well in nurseries afterwards, putting up a particularly fine effort when neck second of 13
to Mintage at Newbury in September: will stay 1m: sure to win more races.
P. Walwyn.

RECORD RUN 5 b.h. Track Spare 125–Bench Game (King's Bench 132) **119**
[1974 9d* 8fg* 10g* 9fg* 10fg³ 10f² 10.6g* 10g* 10fg 10d* 1975 10v 10.4g*
10f* 10f* 10g* 10g2* 10fg 1976 10g³ 10g² 11f* 12g] well-made horse:
one of the top middle-distance performers in 1975, winning six of his eigh
races, including Prince of Wales Stakes at Royal Ascot: lightly raced at 5 yrs,
and gained his only success when winning Grosser Hansa-Preis at Hamburg
in July by 2½ lengths from Kandia: third in Westbury Stakes at Sandown,
second in Premio Presidente della Repubblica at Rome and seventh in King
George VI and Queen Elizabeth Diamond Stakes at Ascot on only other outings:
probably stayed 1½m: did win on softish ground but was extremely well suited
by firm: acted on any track: thoroughly game, genuine and consistent:
pulled up lame after a gallop in August and was retired to Waterloo House
Stud, Mallow, County Cork at a fee of 500 gns. *G. Pritchard-Gordon.*

RECORD TOKEN 4 ch.c. Jukebox 120–Bare Costs (Petition 130) [1974 6v³ **128**
6s* 6v* 6v* 1975 6v* 8g⁶ 8fg* 8f⁵ 7.3g 1976 8f⁴ 7fg* 7.2d* 8f² 7g 7.3fg² 7d⁴
7d* 6v*]
   In mid-October it was announced that Record Token would stand at the
Limestone Stud, Lincolnshire, in 1977; shares in him were advertised at £1,750.
At the time £1,750 a share seemed a fair price. Record Token had shown good
form and was thoroughly dependable, he was physically a most attractive individual, and he had a decent pedigree. All that he really needed to ensure a
healthy interest in his services, so far as one could judge, was a big-race win to his
name. Less than two weeks later Record Token put the matter straight, beating
some of the season's leading sprinters in the Vernons Sprint Cup at Haydock.
   Although Record Token had shown his ability to act on any going he had
always given us the impression that he was ideally suited by some give in the

Cavendish Cape Handicap, Ascot—Pat Eddery drives Record Token home ahead of Scott Joplyn

ground.   In the Vernons, where he had the opportunity of racing over six furlongs on really soft ground for the first time since his early three-year-old days, Record Token put up a high-class performance.   Taking up the running on the stand side nearly three furlongs from home he ran on strongly to defeat Hillandale by a length.   Behind Hillandale came Be Tuneful, Royal Boy, Girl Friend and Gentilhombre.   Although Record Token's win at Haydock was, in point of merit, the best of his career, he was no less effective over seven furlongs or a mile, at which distances he had few superiors in the country.

Two of Record Token's three other wins in 1976 came in good seven-furlong handicaps at Ascot.   In May he took the Top Rank Club Victoria Cup by a length and a half from Rhodomantade and in September, in the Cavendish Cape Handicap, he produced a tremendous turn of finishing speed to beat Scott Joplyn by three quarters of a length.   Scott Joplyn, receiving 18 lb more than weight-for-age from Record Token, was well clear of the rest of a strong field headed by Lord Helpus.

The highlight of the first part of Record Token's season was his clashes with Ardoon.   Three times the pair of them fought stirring finishes to good races, and although Ardoon twice came out the better—he beat Record Token by a neck in both the Queen Anne Stakes at Royal Ascot and the Hungerford Stakes at Newbury—Record Token came out on top by a much more decisive margin in their other meeting.   With the ground in his favour in the John of Gaunt Stakes

Vernons Sprint Cup, Haydock—Record Token concludes a successful year, beating Hillandale (noseband) and Be Tuneful

Sir Herbert Ingram's "Record Token"

at Haydock, Record Token readily took Ardoon's measure at the distance and drew away to win by two and a half lengths.

Record Token (ch.c. 1972)	Jukebox (b 1966)	Sing Sing (b 1957)	Tudor Minstrel
			Agin the Law
		Bibi Mah (b 1955)	Tehran
			Mulier Magnifica
	Bare Costs (b 1965)	Petition (br 1944)	Fair Trial
			Art Paper
		Bootless (b 1951)	The Cobbler
			Careless Nora

Record Token is the third foal of the unraced Bare Costs. Her other representatives on the racecourse Costerini, by Soderini, and Gallico, by El Gallo, have both been successful, Gallico having won four times over sprint distances, including twice in 1976. Bare Costs is out of Bootless, a fairly useful sprinting daughter of the brilliantly speedy Careless Nora, winner of the Nunthorpe in 1948. Record Token also comes from a speedy family on his sire's side, being a son of the Sing Sing horse Jukebox. Jukebox was a good sprinter on his day, his victories including one in the Spillers' Stewards Cup. Music Boy and Reelin Jig are his best other winners, from three crops. Record Token was a better racehorse than was his sire, and a more versatile one, too. His departure to stud leaves a gap in the ranks of the older horses that won't easily be filled. *P. Walwyn.*

RED AMBION 4 ch.g. Hotfoot 126–Cherry Traces (Escart III) [1974 5f3 — 6g*(dis) 7g4 7g 6v6 6v3 6v3 1975 10.1g2 11.7fg 1976 12fg3 10.1fg 15.5f 15.5f5] lengthy gelding: poor handicapper: stays 1½m: probably acts on any going: blinkered third start: pulled up final outing. *A. Davison.*

598

REDANCER   3 br.g. Rubor 88–Last of Fluff (Lord of Verona 120)   [1975 N.R.   —
1976 10f]   second foal: dam never ran: broke a leg and was destroyed in minor
event at Ripon in August.   *G. Richards.*

RED BEAM   4 ch.g. Laser Light 118–Chamazette (Entanglement 118)   [1974   **77**
6fg 6fg* 6d2 5s* 5v* 5g2 5v4   1975 6v5 6g3 6f3 8f 8f5 6d 6fg6 6g   1976 6f3 6fg4
6s5 6f4]   lengthy, rangy gelding: quite a useful handicapper (rated 94) at 3 yrs:
didn't show the same form in 1976: stays 6f: acts on a firm surface but has shown
best form on soft ground.   *W. Wharton.*

RED BENDEL   3 ch.f. Yellow God 129–Whistling Star 81 (Whistler 129)   [1975   —
5g 5d5 5g 5g   1976 5.9s 5s 5v5]   quite moderate at 2 yrs: well beaten in all-
aged maiden races at end of season: should stay 6f.   *R. Akehurst.*

RED BOW   2 ro.c. Red God 128 §–Miss Vicki 94 (Roan Rocket 128)   [1976   —
5fg5]   strong colt: second foal: 7,200 gns yearling: dam won twice over 5f
at 2 yrs: distinctly in need of race, was bit slowly into stride when 9 lengths
fifth of six to The Andrestan in minor event at Lingfield in May: looked sure
to do better but wasn't seen out again.   *Miss A. Sinclair.*

RED BRIGAND   7 b.g. Red God 128 §–La Brigantine (Astrophel)   [1974   **89**
10d* 10fg 10g2 10g 10d* 10.2g 10s2   1975 8v4 10fg6 10f3 10g3 11d   1976 10g
10g6 10fg 10fg4 10g* 10g2 10s 10.6v5]   strong gelding: fair handicapper: successful at Kempton in July, beating Track Hero 5 lengths: odds on, went down by
3 lengths to Gold Claim at Sandown later in month (subsequently off course
until October): best form at 1¼m: acts on any going: suited by front-running
tactics: good mount for an apprentice.   *H. Blagrave.*

RED CHRIS   2 b.c. Red God 128 §–Christingle (Santa Claus 133)   [1976 6d   **69** p
6d 6d]   June foal: first produce: 3,500 gns yearling: dam ran only once: 33/1
and apprentice ridden, ran best race on final outing when about 8 lengths eighth
of 23 to Running Bull in maiden race at Newmarket in October: should be
suited by 1m.   *M. Jarvis.*

RED COUNSEL   3 ch.f. Counsel 118–Desert Inn (Martial 131)   [1975 5g 5fg*   **61**
5fg6 5f5 6f3 7f   1976 6g 6g 7g 6f3 6f* 6h5 6f2 6v5 7v]   leggy filly: plater: changed
hands 800 gns after winning all out at Folkestone in August: good second to
Dame Clara in handicap on same course the following month: should stay
1m: best form on a sound surface.   *R. Supple.*

RED CRYSTAL   2 b.f. Realm 129–How Much (Palestine 133)   [1976 6f*   **87**
6g 6g]   closely related to fairly useful Flower Man (by Floribunda), a winner
at up to 7f, and half-sister to three minor winners: 4,300 gns yearling: dam of
little account: made all to win eight-runner maiden race at Yarmouth in June
comfortably by 2½ lengths from Lisboa: last in a much better race at Ayr in
September and had quite a stiff task when tailed off in nursery at Newmarket
the following month.   *M. Jarvis.*

RED DAWN   6 ch.h. Red God 128 §–African Dawn 72 (Chanteur II 135)   [1974   **56**
5.8fg 6f 6g 6fg* 6f2 7.2g3 6s5 6d4 6g2 7d5 7.2g4 7.6d3 7fg6 6g   1975 7g5 8.2g5
6g5 7g 6h2 7f3 7.6g 5f5 6g2 7f 5.9fg 6f3 7f 6d   1976 6g 6h 6f* 7fg3 7g3 7h5]
neat horse: won four-runner apprentice handicap at Hamilton in July by 3
lengths from Dutch Martyr: stays 7f well: acts on hard going: wears blinkers
nowadays.   *C. Crossley.*

RED DOG   3 b.g. The Brianstan 128–White Net   §   (Monet 127)   [1975 5.8h   **76**
6fg6 5f6 5.9f3 6g* 6g   1976 8f 7s 7.3g6 7fg5 7fg 8f4 6h* 6fg3 6f6 6h3 6d6]   small,
sturdy gelding: quite a moderate handicapper: winner at Carlisle in July:
promises to stay 1m: acts on hard ground: wears blinkers nowadays.   *D.
Hanley.*

RED EMBER   2 b.f. Richboy 117–My Pal (Welsh Abbot 131)   [1976 5fg 5f5   **62**
6fg3 6h* 6fg5 5.3f4 6f2 6f5 6fg 8f 7s]   lengthy filly: attracted no bid after making
all to win four-runner seller at Lingfield in June by 1½ lengths: creditable second
to Lindsell in nursery at Salisbury in August: suited by 6f but is not certain
to stay further.   *M. Haynes.*

RED FOX   4 ch.g. Red God 128 §–China Maid 79 § (Tehran)   [1974 6g 5s 5.8v   **76**
1975 6f6 8f 8h* 7f 10.8f2 10fg 7s5 8g4   1976 7fg4 10fg4 7g4 7g 7fg2 8h* 7fg*
8f2 7f6 8.3d]   small, useful-looking gelding: quite a moderate handicapper:
successful at Pontefract (made all) and Thirsk (beat Tiruler a length in apprentice
race) in July: stays 1¼m: well suited by a sound surface and acts on
hard going: wears blinkers: sold 1,350 gns Ascot December Sales.   *P. Makin.*

RED FRAME 3 ch.c. Red God 128 §–Silver Frame (Niccolo Dell'Arca) [1975   **64**
7f⁵ 7fg 8.2d 8g   1976 9f⁶ 8f⁶ 10fg 16g]   small, strong colt: plating-class maiden:
best run at 1m: sometimes has tongue tied down: not seen out after May. *J.
Leigh.*

REDHEAD 3 ch.f. Hotfoot 126–Alyba 87 (Alycidon 138) [1975 5f 5f 6g 1976   **66**
10g 11.1f 14fg⁵ 11.5fg⁵ 10g⁵ 12fg² 9fg* 12v]   small, sturdy filly: plater: sold
out of H. Wragg's stable 2,000 gns after winning all out at Newcastle in August:
effective at 9f and stays 1½m: acts on a firm surface and ran poorly on heavy
ground on final outing: tried in blinkers on fifth appearance. *M. W. Easterby.*

REDHILL LADS 3 ch.g. Lolly Tree 97–Pauline 89 (Denturius) [1975 6f 6g   **—**
5f   1976 6f 6d 7d⁴ 9fg]   leggy gelding: bad plater: blinkered last two outings.
S. Nesbitt.

RED INVADER 3 b.c. Brave Invader–Wavy Navy (Hardicanute 130) [1975   **110**
6f 7.5f* 6f² 8g 8g⁴   1976 10s⁴ 12f⁵ 12g⁶ 13.5g* 12f* 12g³ 13.5g⁴ 14f* 12f* 12.8f*
14fg⁴]   Irish colt: first foal: dam won three races in Ireland at up to 1m: had a
very successful season, winning handicaps at Dundalk, Phoenix Park (two), Gowran Park and Wexford: ridden by 5-lb claimer at 10·1 when comfortably landing
odds laid on him on last-named track in August: started fourth favourite
for Irish St Leger and was not disgraced in finishing 13½ lengths fourth of 11
to runaway winner Meneval: stays 1¾m: acts on firm going: wears blinkers nowadays. *K. Prendergast, Ireland.*

RED JESTER 5 b.g. Silly Season 127–Red Goddess 84 (Red God 128 §) [1974   **—**
10.5f⁴ 10d   1975 N.R.   1976 11.1g 12s 14fg]   poor maiden nowadays: bandaged
all outings. *G. Balding.*

RED JOHNNIE 2 ch.c. Red God 128 §–Corbara II (Marino) [1976 5g* 5fg³   **100**
5g⁴ 5d 5f³ 5fg⁵ 5fg⁶ 5g² 6g* 6g⁴]   small, stocky colt: good mover: brother to two
winners, notably very useful 5f to 9f winner Tickled Pink, and half-brother to a
winner: 3,200 gns yearling: dam won over 9f in France: won 18-runner Brocklesby
Stakes at Doncaster in March by short head from Flaming Temper and stayed
on to win £2,000 nursery at Leicester in September by a neck from Breast Stroke:
stays 6f well and may get further: did not seem suited by blinkers on fourth
outing. *C. Brittain.*

RED LETTER DAY 2 b.f. Crepello 136–Red Velvet 114 (Red God 128 §)   **97**
[1976 6g* 6fg 8g⁵]   neat, attractive filly: good walker and mover: second foal:
sister to very useful 1974 2-y-o Red Cross: dam, half-sister to Lord David, showed
very useful form at 2 yrs: put up an impressive performance when winning nine-
runner Virginia Water Stakes at Ascot in July, quickening in really good style
in final furlong and soon going clear to beat Petlady by 2½ lengths: beaten after
in pattern races, on final outing finishing 9 lengths fifth of eight to Miss Pinkie
in Argos Star Fillies' Mile at Ascot in September: stays 1m. *P. Walwyn.*

RED LEVER 4 ch.g. Le Levanstell 122–Ruby Laser 122 (Red God 128 §) [1974   **75**
6s³ 6v² 1975 7g³ 7g 8fg³ 8d 1976 7fg 6fg⁴ 5.3fg⁵ 6f* 6f⁵ 8g² 7.6v]   powerful,
good-looking gelding: favourite when winning 11-runner minor race at Folkestone
in June all out from Vrondi: effective at 6f and stays 1m: seems to act on any
going: has shown a marked tendency to hang and is not one to rely on. *J.
Dunlop.*

RED LIGHT DISTRICT 2 ch.c. Red God 128 §–Censorship (Prince John)   **92**
[1976 6fg⁵ 6f² 5.1g 6s* 7v² 6s]   compact sort: first foal: 5,600 gns yearling: dam
won over 1m at 2 yrs and 3 yrs in U.S.A. and is daughter of best 1953 2-y-o filly
Sixpence: won 13-runner minor event at Redcar in October going away by 4
lengths from Forlorn Scot: had rest of field well strung out when 5 lengths runner-
up to Tudor Jig in similar race at Teesside later in month: better at 6f than 5f,
and probably stays 7f: acts on any going. *L. Cumani.*

RED LORD 3 b.c. Red God 128 §–Dame de Grace (Armistice 131) [1975 5g³   **124**
6.5g* 8g³ 7s³ 1976 8s 8fg* 8g* 9g⁶ 8f⁶]
The Poule d'Essai des Poulains, the French equivalent of the Two Thousand
Guineas, was won for the third time in five years by Alec Head's stable. The
latest winner, Red Lord, followed in the footsteps of Riverman (1972) and Green
Dancer (1975); he won with greater ease than either of his predecessors, yet when
it comes to an overall assessment of the respective merits of the three Red Lord
must be considered some way inferior to the others. Riverman and Green Dancer
were right at the top of the tree as two-year-olds and both went on to register
further high-class performances after their victories in the Poulains. Not so

Poule d'Essai des Poulains, Longchamp—Red Lord wins from Roan Star, Comeram (far side), Empery (obscured) and Arctic Tern

Red Lord. Smart though his two-year-old form was, including a victory in the Prix des Planches at Deauville and a third to Earth Spirit in the Criterium de Maisons-Laffitte, it qualified him only for a weight of 8-6 in the 1975 French Two-Year-Old Free Handicap, a stone behind the top-rated Manado, on the same mark incidentally as another subsequent classic winner, Youth. Red Lord raced only twice after the Poulains, and on both occasions ran way below his best.

Red Lord reached the zenith of his racecourse achievement within the space of a week in April. Following a dismal showing behind Arctic Tern in the Prix de Fontainebleau on his seasonal début he scored an easy win from second-class opposition in the Prix de la Butte Mortemart at Longchamp; six days later he took the Poulains on the same course in even more convincing style. Although Manado and Vitiges, the two top-rated French two-year-olds of 1975, missed the race in favour of the English Two Thousand Guineas, the field for the Poule d'Essai des Poulains was a representative one. Arctic Tern and Roan Star, both high-class colts at two years and first and second respectively in the Prix de Fontainebleau, were first and second favourites. The Parrish-owned pair Comeram and French Swanee, neither of whom had turned in very inspiring first runs of the season but both of whom had shown very good form in 1975, were coupled together as third choice in the betting. Empery, having his first run of the season, the ex-English Hittite Glory, The Chaplain, smart winner of the Prix Montenica, and three others comprised the remainder of the opposition to Red Lord who started at odds of approximately 11/2. The race was pretty straightforward. Comeram made the running from Empery with Red Lord well in touch in fifth place. Turning for home the field was still well grouped, with Red Lord and Arctic Tern beginning their challenges simultaneously and Roan Star also making headway. Shortly afterwards it became merely a battle for the minor placings as Red Lord found a turn of speed that took him clear from below the distance. Roan Star finished second, two and a half lengths behind Red Lord, with Comeram a short head away third. Empery battled on to be fourth, half a length further back, a short neck in front of Arctic Tern. It isn't easy to evaluate the result. On the credit side Comeram subsequently ran consistently well in seven-furlong and one-mile races, losing the Irish Two Thousand Guineas by a whisker. Arctic Tern proved most inconsistent through the season but he did show high-class form from time to time. Empery, of course, went on to greater things at Epsom—clearly on French Two Thousand Guineas day, having his first run of the season over an inadequate trip, he can hardly be considered the horse he was later in the year. On the debit side, runner-up Roan Star went from bad to worse, as did Tystan who finished a creditable eighth. However, taking everything into account, we are convinced that Red Lord's performance was that of a high-class colt.

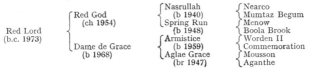

			⎧ Nearco
	⎧ Red God	⎧ Nasrullah	⎨ Mumtaz Begum
	(ch 1954)	(b 1940)	⎧ Menow
Red Lord	⎨	⎩ Spring Run	⎨ Boola Brook
(b.c. 1973)		(b 1948)	
		⎧ Armistice	⎧ Worden II
	⎩ Dame de Grace	(b 1959)	⎨ Commemoration
	(b 1968)	⎨ Aglae Grace	⎧ Mousson
		(br 1947)	⎩ Aganthe

The same cannot be said of Red Lord's two subsequent efforts. He started at 5/2 on for the Prix Jean Prat at Chantilly in June, but never looked like winning at any stage and came home sixth of nine, over five lengths behind all-the-way winner Earth Spirit. It was a similar story in the St James's Palace

Stakes at Royal Ascot nine days later. Last of eight on the turn for home with a great deal to do, Red Lord made little headway and could finish only sixth behind the dead-heaters Radetzky and Patris. Again Red Lord finished about five lengths behind Earth Spirit who was third past the post. Red Lord wasn't seen out again. He has been retired to the Haras du Petit Tellier, Argentan.

Red Lord was bred by William Hill Studs and was sold for 18,000 guineas as a yearling. By the outstanding stallion Red God, he is the first foal of Dame de Grace who won a mile-and-a-half maiden race at Saint-Cloud on the second of her only two starts. The dam comes from a high-class family, being a sister to the French Oaks fourth Aglae (the dam of the French Derby winner Val de l'Orne) and a half-sister to the Prix de l'Arc de Triomphe winner Soltikoff. The grandam Aglae Grace was also a high-class racemare, winner of the French Oaks. Red Lord has the conformation and the pedigree one likes to see in a prospective stallion. A well-made colt, he stayed a mile and appeared to act on any going, except going as firm as that at Ascot. He may have stumped himself up in the St James's Palace Stakes, and there may be some significance in the fact that this was his last race. *A. Head, France.*

RED LUPUS   2 b.f. Red God 128 §–Santa Lucia (Hugh Lupus 132)   [1976 5f 6g 6d]   neat filly: poor maiden: sold 620 gns Doncaster October Sales. *A. Balding.*   —

REDOUBLED   2 b.c. Swing Easy 126–Pallah (Palestine 133)   [1976 5f 6fg⁵]   brother to 3-y-o Corderay, and half-brother to four winners, including useful 1969 2-y-o Tefcros (by Crocket): 11,000 gns yearling: dam of little account: 4½ lengths fifth of nine to Cosy Bar in maiden race at Newmarket in June: not seen out again. *J. Dunlop.*   **79**

RED QUIVER   2 ch.c. Red God 128 §–Wedding Cake 81 (Amour Drake 129)   [1976 6fg⁵ 5fg 6h² 8fg³ 8s⁶]   good sort: half-brother to four winners, including smart 1965 2-y-o Procession (by Sovereign Path): 3,800 gns foal, resold 4,300 gns yearling: dam, half-sister to Constable, won 5f seller at 2 yrs: quite a moderate maiden: stays 1m: probably acts on any going: sold 4,300 gns Newmarket Autumn Sales. *M. Jarvis.*   **80**

RED REEF   8 ro.g. Goose Creek 116–Red Sea 94 (Fairway)   [1974 16f² 18h⁴ 16fg⁴ 18fg² 16f 16g* 19g 16g³ 17v⁴ 16.2v* 18d 16.1v*   1975 16s 16v 16g⁴ 16.1g⁶ 14fg² 16fg 16.1g³ 15s* 15.8fg* 16f   1976 14v⁴ 14s 14d]   strong gelding: poor staying handicapper nowadays: acts on any going: ideal mount for an apprentice: suited by front-running tactics: bandaged first outing. *I. Balding.*   —

RED REGENT   4 b.c. Prince Regent 129–Redowa 60 (Red God 128 §)   [1974 6g³ 7g* 7v³   1975 8g³ 10.4g* 10g* 12fg 10f⁵ 10f⁵ 11.7fg* 10g⁵   1976 10fg* 13.4s³ 10f² 10g* 12s² 12g* 10g* 10g³ 10d⁶]   **123**

Over the last two years several good European horses have continued their racing careers in America with notable success. Snow Knight, the 1974 Derby winner, ended the 1975 season the leading grass horse in the U.S.A., and in 1976 two colts formerly trained by Vincent O'Brien, the Irish St Leger winner Caucasus and King Pellinore, second in both the Irish Sweeps Derby and Doncaster St Leger, made a big impact on the American racing scene. In view of their achievements it was only to be expected that other good horses would follow, especially after the sharp fall in the value of sterling, and among those that have been sent to continue their racing career in the United States are Bruni, Anne's Pretender, Jolly Good, Chil the Kite and Red Regent, the last-named just about the best middle-distance handicapper in England. By the time he came to leave for America, Red Regent wasn't far behind the very best horses running outside handicaps either: on his final outing he finished a most creditable sixth to his new stable-companion Vitiges in the Champion Stakes at Newmarket.

Red Regent's two appearances in handicaps in 1976 resulted in highly impressive victories for him. In April he turned the Ladbroke City and Suburban Handicap at Epsom into a procession, having the race in his pocket a long way from home and eventually beating Blaskette by four lengths. He was giving Blaskette 16 lb. At Sandown in September, in the Don Zoilo Handicap, Red Regent handed out the same treatment to a strong field, racing clear entering the final furlong, and beating a decent three-year-old, The Tista, who was receiving 25 lb more than weight-for-age, by four lengths.

The tasks that Red Regent faced in the remainder of his races at four years were varied. In July he was sent over to Germany for the Concentra-Pokal des Deutschen Investment-Trust, a pattern race in Frankfurt worth over £11,000,

Ladbroke City and Suburban Handicap, Epsom—top weight Red Regent wins handsomely from Blaskette

and won comfortably. The following month saw him running in the Copa de Oro de San Sebastian in Spain, a race one might have expected him to have won, but he was beaten a length on soft going. Later in August he won the Moet and Chandon Silver Magnum at Kempton.

The Moet and Chandon Silver Magnum, usually run over the Derby course and distance, is the most prestigious race for amateur riders in this country, and is usually a competitive affair. In 1975, for example, the finish was fought out by decent horses in Lane Court, Fool's Mate, Night Sky and Laurentian Hills. However in 1976, when hard ground at Epsom caused the meeting to be transferred to Kempton Park, the race was no contest. Red Regent was opposed by four horses little better than platers. He started at 11/2 on and cantered in by twenty lengths. It's not altogether surprising that the race was so poorly contested; it was worth only £2,400 to the winner in 1976. Nowadays races of twice that value are weekly occurrences. The Moet and Chandon can only be restored to its former position as one of the leading international events for amateur riders by trebling the prize money and possibly altering some of the conditions; steps have already been taken in this direction.

Red Regent (b.c. 1972)	Prince Regent (br 1966)	Right Royal V (br 1958)	Owen Tudor
			Bastia
		Noduleuse (b 1954)	Nosca
			Quemandeuse
	Redowa (ch 1964)	Red God (ch 1954)	Nasrullah
			Spring Run
		Sally Deans (ch 1947)	Fun Fair
			Cora Deans

Red Regent also ran well in defeat in both his other races in which the ground was in his favour, when chasing home Rose Bowl in the Clive Graham

Stakes at Goodwood and when finishing a close third to Obstacle and the Derby runner-up Relkino in the Valdoe Stakes over the same course and distance.

Red Regent is from the first crop of the 1969 Irish Sweeps Derby winner Prince Regent. With three generations representing him on the racecourse Prince Regent, who stands at the Collinstown Stud in Ireland, can be seen to have made an excellent start to his stud career, his progeny having won races over all sorts of distances and in at least six countries. Easy Regent and Count in France, Regal Ray in Ireland, and Brightelmstone in England are other notable winners that he has sired. Redowa, Red Regent's dam, is by Red God. Although a full sister to Yellow God and St Alphage, Redowa only once gave any indication of merit on the racecourse, when winning a selling handicap over five furlongs as a three-year-old. Her two other winners are Rigadoon (by Aberdeen) and Ballydowa (by Ballymoss) the last-named a fairly useful sprinter on her day.

Although Red Regent has twice won over a mile and a half, he has put up his very best performances over a mile and a quarter. He is a good-actioned individual, who is ideally suited by top-of-the-ground conditions, and he is unsuited by really soft ground. A strong colt and a thoroughly genuine performer who was still improving at the end of his four-year-old campaign, Red Regent should do well in America. *P. Walwyn.*

RED ROGUE 3 ch.c. Firestreak 125–Brogue 81 (Panaslipper 130) [1975 5s 5f 6g 6f² 6g² 5f² 6g* 8f³ 7g* 7g⁴ 7.6s 1976 8f⁵ 11.7f⁶ 10g 11.7f 10fg 8.3g² 9fg³ 10s³ 8s] light-framed colt: poor mover: plater: probably stays 1¼m: seems to act on any going: blinkered third and fifth outings: sold to Denys Smith 1,500 gns Newmarket Autumn Sales. *M Haynes.* **60**

RED RUBY 3 b.f. Tudor Melody 129–Ruby Laser 122 (Red God 128 §) [1975 6g³ 7f* 7d⁴ 6g² 1976 8.5fg² 8.5g* 8fg² 8fg² 8h²] tall, rangy, useful-looking filly: good mover: half-sister to smart sprinter Laser Light (by Aureole): game winner of Ebbisham Handicap at Epsom in June, beating Kallissima ½ length: runner-up on all her other outings, going down by 1½ lengths to Memory Lane in Princess Elizabeth Stakes at Epsom in April and being beaten only narrowly on her last three appearances, by Duboff in Child Stakes at Newmarket, Thieving Demon in Charlton Stakes Handicap at Goodwood and Stirling Castle in £2,200 handicap at Brighton: stays 1m well: appears to act on any going: suited by forcing tactics: most consistent. *J. Dunlop.* **113**

RED SAINT 6 b.g. St Alphage 119–Red Sails 87 (Vilmorin) [1974 N.R. 1975 N.R. 1976 10s 9g 14.7f⁶ 7v] of no account. *M. Naughton.* **—**

RED SEED 2 ch.c. Red God 128 §–Alcina (Alycidon 138) [1976 7fg⁴ 7f³ 5.9f* 6g² 6g] strong colt: half-brother to several winners, including useful stayer Pride of Alcide (by Worden II): 3,700 gns yearling: dam unraced sister to Alcide: put up a smooth display when making all to win 16-runner maiden event at Wolverhampton in August by 1½ lengths from Jene Reppin: looked to be going the best for much of way when 4 lengths second to Disc Jockey in minor race at Newcastle later in month: stays 7f, and should get further: reportedly exported to Norway. *M. Jarvis.* **88**

RED SHIELD 2 b.c. So Blessed 130–Sing a Song 115 (Sing Sing 134) [1976 5fg* 5.1fg* 5f² 5.1f³] neat, early sort: second foal: dam very speedy: kept on well to win 19-runner maiden race at Thirsk in May and held off Hot Heir by ¾ length in minor race at Yarmouth later in month: ran creditably on both subsequent outings but wasn't seen out after July: will stay 6f. *T. Waugh.* **99**

RED SHIRT 3 ch.g. Murrayfield 119–Phydorine (Vilmorin) [1975 5s⁶ 1976 8f 6fg 6fg] leggy, light-framed gelding: well beaten in varied company, including in a claiming race. *B. Wise.* **—**

RED SUN 4 b.c. Aureole 132–Ribina II 85 (Ribot 142) [1974 7s 7d³ 8s³ 1975 10v* 12g³ 12fg* 13.3g² 14f⁴ 14fg⁵ 12s² 12g 11d⁵ 1976 11s² 12g⁵ 12g* 12g⁴ 12v³ 10g 11.7fg⁵] big, strong, attractive colt: fairly useful handicapper: successful at Cagnes-sur-Mer in February: ran respectably when fifth of 10 to Busted Fiddle at Windsor in May on second of only two appearances in this country in 1976: stays well: seems to act on any going. *J. Dunlop.* **95**

RED TUNE 2 ch.f. Red God 128 §–Born Friendly (Takawalk II 125) [1976 5fg 5fg6 5fg² 5f² 5g 5f 5s] plater: well-beaten second in two poor races: of no account. *A. Pitt.* **34**

REELIN JIG 3 b.f. Jukebox 120–Reelin Bridge (New Day) [1975 5s⁴ 5s² 5g 5f⁶ 5f² 5f* 5fg⁴ 5f⁵ 5f³ 5g⁵ 5f⁴ 5s 1976 5s⁴ 5s² 5f* 5g* 5f* 5f⁴ 5f² 5f⁴ 5f* 5f] third produce: 400 gns foal: dam won over 1½m in Ireland at 5 yrs: completed **114**

her hat-trick when winning Group 3 Ballyogan Stakes at Leopardstown in June
by 2 lengths and a neck from Willy Willy and Rev Counter: had earlier been
successful in minor events at Navan and the Curragh and subsequently made all
when winning handicap at Mallow in August under top weight: 2 lengths second
to Thrifty Trio in Stackallen Stakes at Phoenix Park in July: has raced exclusively at 5f, although should stay further: acts on any going: occasionally
wore blinkers at 2 yrs: genuine and consistent: goes well for apprentice M. J.
Kinane: one of the best Irish sprinters. *L. Browne, Ireland.*

REFERENDUM 3 b.c. Reform 132–Hitesca 110 (Tesco Boy 121) [1975 6fg 6g³ **85**
6g⁴ 1976 8g² 10s 8s² 8fg* 8fg² 9f] strong, compact colt: made all when winning
Harp Lager Handicap at York in July by 5 lengths from Fir's Hill, changing his
legs in last 2f as though none too happy on the firmish ground: runner-up in minor
events on three of his other outings, going down by a length to Roman Fantasy
later in month on last of them: should stay 1¼m. *S. Hall.*

REFORMATORY 2 b.c. Crepello 136–Parolee 88 (Sing Sing 134) [1976 6v⁵] **— p**
brother to very useful 3-y-o miler Trusted, and half-brother to two minor winners:
dam a sprinter: 14/1, showed promise when about 10 lengths fifth of 22 behind
Good Company in maiden race at Newbury in October, being well placed for most
of way: should be suited by 1m+: sure to do better and will win races. *J.
Dunlop.*

REFORMIST 2 ch.c. Reform 132–Lagoa (Mossborough 126) [1976 5fg 5f] **—**
third foal: 640 gns yearling: dam never ran: behind in sellers at Wolverhampton
(very much on toes) and Nottingham (blinkered and dwelt at start), both in
April. *N. Vigors.*

REGAL BINGO 10 gr.g. Proud Chieftain 122–Miss Wong 102 (Democratic 124) **—**
[1974 5.9f³ 6f² 5.8f 5g 5fg 5fg³ 7fg² 5fg 7fg 6g 1975 7g⁶ 5f 6fg 5.9g⁶ 6h 5f 5.9fg
5f⁴ 1976 5h 5fg 5.9f 8.3g⁶] poor sprint handicapper: acts on any going:
has worn blinkers but does better without: frequently sweats up: inconsistent.
F. Freeman.

REGAL FLASH 2 ch.c. King's Company 124–Fiery Riband (Firestreak 125) **97**
[1976 5g² 5g³ 5fg² 5.8h* 6fg² 5g* 5fg 5g* 6g⁶ 5g 5g⁴] small, quite lengthy colt:
fourth living foal: half-brother to a winner in Greece: 360 gns yearling: dam
never ran: proved a very shrewd buy and won at Bath, Kempton and Lingfield:
made all when winning £1,600 nursery on last-named course in August by a
short head from Mummy's Darling: well beaten in nurseries afterwards: should
stay 7f: genuine *E. Reavey.*

REGAL GUARD 2 b.f. Realm 129–Inner Guard (King's Bench 132) [1976 **60**
5g⁵ 5f⁴] lightly-made filly: half-sister to several winners, including useful
sprinter Tin Guard (by Tin Whistle): dam of little account: only plating class
on two early-season runs. *B. Hills.*

REGALIAN 3 b.g. Prince Regent 129–Wishful Thinking 104 (Petition 130) **79**
[1975 8d³ 7g 1976 12g² 10.2g³ 12g⁴ 13.1f* 13.1s*] rangy gelding: favourite
when winning minor events at Bath in September and October, gaining second
victory by 5 lengths from Charlotte's Den: stays 13f: acts on any going: wears
blinkers nowadays. *R. Hern.*

REGAL JESTER 3 ch.g. Hopeful Venture 125–Arnisdale (Aggressor 130) **—**
[1975 N.R. 1976 12fg] second live foal: 500 gns yearling, resold 800 gns
2-y-o: dam, unplaced in five starts in France at 3 yrs, is daughter of 1,000 Guineas
winner Happy Laughter: 12/1 and in need of race when in rear in weakly-
contested 15-runner amateur riders event at Leicester in September. *S. Mellor.*

REGAL RAY 2 b.f. Prince Regent 129–Red Laser 95 (Red God 128 §) [1976 **107**
5s⁵ 6g* 6f³ 6f* 6g⁶] leggy Irish filly: first foal: dam 5f sprinter and closely
related to very speedy Ruby Laser: a very useful filly who won at the Curragh
in April, May and August, gaining most important success on last occasion
when scoring by a length from All Serene in eight-runner Moyglare Stud Stakes:
met her two defeats in this country but ran creditably both times, finishing
1½ lengths third to Limone in Chesham Stakes at Royal Ascot in June and
6½ lengths sixth of 15 to Durtal in William Hill Cheveley Park Stakes at Newmarket in September: suited by 6f and may get further. *R. Annesley, Ireland.*

REGAL ROCKET 4 b.c. Roan Rocket 128–Omentello 91 (Elopement 125) **76**
[1974 7d 1975 9fg 14g⁴ 14f 16f 14fg² 16g* 16f* 16fg* 18g⁶ 1976 14fg⁴ 16s⁵
16fg⁴ 14fg² 22.2f 16.1f⁴] strong colt: possibly didn't stay extreme distances:
probably acted on any going: sold 1,900 gns Newmarket Autumn Sales: at stud
in Ireland. *G. Pritchard-Gordon.*

REGAL ROMANCE 3 b.f. Prince Tenderfoot 126–Bright Match 72 (Match III 135) [1975 5g⁴ 5d⁴ 1976 7.6s⁶ 7g² 8f³ 8fg² 8f* 7f⁵] well-made filly: won 12-runner maiden race at Salisbury in August gamely by a short head from True Prince: should stay 1¼m: acts on firm going. *R. Hern.* **82**

REGAL STEP 4 b.f. Ribero 126–Right Royal Time (Right Royal V 135) [1974 6fg 1975 10d⁶ 10d 13.4g² 17.7f* 14.7f* 12g* 14fg6 16f* 14g* 14g³ 1976 16g⁵ 18.4s 16g² 16fg² 16fg 18.4fg⁶ 16fg⁶ 16g 17.4g* 19s⁴ 18d] lengthy filly: fairly useful handicapper: beat Night In Town in great style when winning Eglinton and Winton Memorial Handicap at Ayr in September by 7 lengths: looked a little unlucky (swerved quite badly at distance) when good second to Rising Falcon in H. S. Persse Memorial Handicap at Kempton in May on third start: mainly disappointing on her other appearances: well suited by a good test of stamina: acted on firm going: blinkered fifth outing: sold to Irish National Stud 10,500 gns Newmarket December Sales. *F. J. Houghton.* **96**

REGAL TUDOR 3 b.g. Darling Boy 124–Tudor Style 98 (Owen Tudor) [1975 5g 5g⁶ 6fg³ 6fg 7g³ 7f³ 7fg⁶ 8v 8g⁵ 7fg⁵ 7.2v 1976 8d² 12.3s³ 12.2f² 10.5s⁶ 11d² 12s³ 10fg² 12f² 9fg⁴ 10fg⁶ 9g² 11s⁶ 12g⁶] good-topped, round-barrelled gelding: usually finds one or two too good for him: stays 1½m: acts on any going: has been tried in blinkers but does better without. *N. Robinson.* **67**

REGAL VIEW 2 ch.f. Royal Palace 131–Outlook 110 (Ballymoss 136) [1976 6d 8s 7s] well bred but is only a bad plater. *V. Cross.* **—**

REGENCY BILL 2 br.c. Royalty 130–Gold Bloom 72 (Klondyke Bill 125) [1976 5fg* 5d³ 5f* 5fg* 5g³ 6g* 6f⁶ 5fg² 6fg* 5.1f* 5fg³ 6fg²] leggy colt: half-brother to three winners, including useful 1975 2-y-o River Bloom (by Forlorn River): 1,500 gns yearling: dam a sprinter: an admirably tough individual who was well rewarded for his consistency, winning at Leicester, Pontefract, Newmarket, Epsom, Chester and Yarmouth: picked up quite a valuable prize at Epsom, beating Heronry ½ length in Carew Stakes, and got home by a neck from Beaumel Board in well-contested event at Yarmouth in July: again ran well when length second to Fife and Drum in Washington Singer Stakes at Newbury in August: effective at 5f and 6f, and may stay further: probably not at his best on a soft surface: thoroughly genuine and consistent: exported to Trinidad. *G. Hunter.* **108**

Carew Stakes, Epsom—Regency Bill beats Heronry and Town and Country

REGENCY GENERAL 2 b.g. Royal Palace 131–Heath Rose 124 (Hugh Lupus **81**
132) [1976 6fg² 7g 6d] big gelding: half-brother to three winners, including
1972 Middle Park Stakes winner Tudenham (by Tudor Melody) and Ranksborough (by Relko), a smart winner at up to 1¼m: 520 gns yearling: dam very
smart at up to 1½m: ran creditably for a newcomer in six-runner minor event
at Windsor in September, proving no match for long odds-on winner Millionaire
but finishing well clear of remainder: behind in Newmarket maiden races afterwards: will stay 1½m: acts on a firm surface. *H. Collingridge.*

REGENCY PRINCESS 3 br.f. Prince Regent 129–Romany Girl 103 (Worden —
II 129) [1975 8f 8g 1976 12.2fg 10f 12.2fg] first foal: dam won at up to
13f in Ireland: behind in maiden races: will need long distances to show to
advantage: sold 1,300 gns Newmarket July Sales. *W. Wharton.*

REGENT DANCER 3 b.g. Prince Regent 129–Balsania (Baldric II 131) [1975 **49**
6g³ 6fg⁶ 7fg 8f 1976 7.6fg⁶ 10g 8g 12.2fg³ 12.2f⁵ 12.2f⁴ 12g⁶ 10g⁵] unfurnished
gelding: poor maiden: stays 1½m: sometimes wears blinkers: sold to D. Barons
1,650 gns Newmarket Autumn Sales. *D. Hanley.*

REGENT PRINCESS 2 br.f. Prince Regent 129–Boxing Miss (Gallant Man) —
[1976 5f⁴ 7f 9fg] lengthy filly: first foal: dam a stakes-placed winner at up to
1m in U.S.A.: no worthwhile form in maiden races: sold to R. Hollinshead for
340 gns Doncaster October Sales. *F. Carr.*

REGENT'S GARDEN 4 b.g. Prince Regent 129–Arctic Lace 106 (Arctic **101**
Chevalier) [1974 5f⁶ 5fg 6fg³ 6g³ 7d³ 8g 1975 12s* 12f³ 12.3g* 16g 12d³ 13.3g*
14g⁴ 1976 12.3d⁶ 12d⁵ 14.7d⁵ 15g 13g 15g* 12s] big, lengthy gelding:
useful handicapper on his day: odds on, won hands down from weak opposition
in amateur riders race at Ayr in September: mainly disappointing on his other
outings: stays well: acts on soft going and seems unsuited by firm. *S. Hall.*

REGINA WILHELMINA 4 ch.f. Privy Seal 108–Princess Nefertiti (Tutan- **44**
khamen) [1974 5g 5f* 5f 6fg 6d⁵ 5d³ 7v⁶ 6g 1975 6fg 7fg 5f 6f⁵ 6fg 6g² 6fg
6fg 6d 1976 7f 6f³ 7f 6f 5h³ 6s⁵] selling handicapper: stays 6f: acts on firm
going: inconsistent: lost all chance by rearing up at start on fourth appearance
(blinkered). *A. Dalton.*

REGION 2 br.c. Realm 129–Lullaby 109 (Relko 136) [1976 6fg 7g² 6g*] **97**
well-made colt: third foal: dam stayed 1½m: put in a strong late run to
win £1,600 event at Ayr in September going away by 1½ lengths from Muster
Lane: will stay 1m: should make a useful 3-y-o. *P. Walwyn.*

REHEARSAL 3 b.c. Reform 132–Harlequinade 80 (Klairon 131) [1975 5g² 5g* **99**
6f⁴ 5d⁴ 1976 7fg 7.6s³ 10d² 8f] attractive, lengthy sort: good mover: ruined
his chance by hanging when going under by a head to Amboise in minor event
at Redcar in May: tried in blinkers on only subsequent outing (June) and
gave impression he needs further than 1m nowadays: stays 1¼m: probably
acts on any going. *R. Hern.*

REIGATE 2 ch.f. Salvo 129–Azalea (Abernant 142) [1976 7v] half-sister —
to a winner in Germany: 200 gns yearling: dam of no account: 33/1, had every
chance 2f out when distant seventh of 15 to Forage in minor event at Lingfield
in November. *A. Neaves.*

REINE BEAU 6 b.g. Queen's Hussar 124–Beauatire 86 (Beau Sabreur 125) **73**
[1974 12g⁴ 12fg³ 14g² 16d* 16s* 15.5s* 19g* 19fg* 18d² 1975 18.4g 16f⁶ 20f
19f 14d⁴ 18fg 1976 12g 16fg 16g 16g 19fg⁶ 16g⁵ 19s 17.1s³] well-made
gelding: not the force he was and ran his only worthwhile race in 1976 on final
outing when 3¾ lengths third of 14 to Quiet in handicap at Bath in October:
now needs further than 1½m and stays extremely well: acts on any going:
has worn blinkers: good mount for an apprentice. *G. Beeson.*

RELATIVE EASE 5 ch.h. Great Nephew 126–Glider 82 (Buisson Ardent 129) **93**
[1974 8g 7fg 6s² 6g 5fg³ 6g² 6g³ 5s⁵ 5s⁵ 5g 6d⁶ 1975 6v⁴ 5d* 6fg⁴ 5fg⁵ 5g⁴ 5f⁶
5g 6f 5g⁴ 5h⁶ 6g³ 5f² 5f 6h⁵ 5f⁶ 5f³ 5f 5f 1976 5f* 5f* 5g* 5f* 5f* 5f⁵ 6f⁵ 5fg⁵
5g² 5g] leggy horse: fairly useful handicapper: did well at 5 yrs and reeled
off five wins before mid-season (three of them at Edinburgh), including four
apprentice events, gaining last win when getting better of Song's First in a
tight finish at Edinburgh early in July: best form at 5f: acts on any going:
has worn blinkers but does better without: usually ridden by claimer J. Ward: ran
badly final start. *T. Fairhurst.*

RELIANT WONDER 2 br.f. Aureole 132 or Reliance II 137–Fifehead Wonder —
76 (Vilmorin) [1976 5v⁴ 5f] half-sister to three minor winners: 400 gns foal:
dam a plater: well beaten in minor events at Ayr and Brighton in April. *G.
Wallace.*

Ascot 2,000 Guineas Trial Stakes—Relkino is in command from Loh

RELKINO 3 b.c. Relko 136–Pugnacity 117 (Pampered King 121) [1975 6g* **123**
6g⁵ 1976 7f* 8fg⁶ 12g² 10fg 12fg⁵ 10g² 10d]

Relkino's season divides into two strikingly contrasting parts. In the first
part, which ends with his fine second to Empery in the Derby, everything
progressed smoothly—a win from Loh in the Ascot Two Thousand Guineas Trial,
a fair sixth to Wollow in the Guineas and then a display in the Derby that
augured well for the rest of the season. He was at least as promising a three-
year-old as his former stable-companion Bustino was at the same stage; which
is to say that he was highly promising. But thereafter nothing went right.
He was thoroughly outpaced in the Joe Coral Eclipse Stakes, so much so that he
failed to overhaul his pacemaker Arapaho; he finished only fifth, beaten by three
of the horses he had beaten at Epsom, when returned to a mile and a half in the
Great Voltigeur Stakes; he ran respectably, though not with the distinction one
would expect of a Derby second, in the Valdoe Stakes at Goodwood, and ended
the year by finishing only eleventh of twenty in the Champion Stakes.

What is to be made of him? Well, at the risk of stating the obvious, the
first thing to be said is that Relkino is moderate as Derby seconds go. And he
finished second in a weakly-contested Derby. Having said that, we still have to
try to explain why he failed to gain even a place in three of the four races he
contested after the Derby. There is no entirely convincing explanation to be
found, but the probability is that he finds a mile and a quarter, the distance of
three of his four races after the Derby, on the sharp side for him, especially
against horses as good as he met in the Eclipse and the Champion Stakes. There
is also a possibility that he didn't progress at the same rate as some of his
opponents, if he progressed at all, in the second half of the season; and there is
also a possibility that he is no longer as keen on racing as he was when he resolutely
held Empery to three lengths in the Derby after a hard struggle all the way home
from Tattenham Corner. Relkino appeared to buckle down to his task in the
Valdoe Stakes, in which he went down by a length to the useful three-year-old
Obstacle, giving him 9 lb, yet he still might be a horse that does his best only
when he has a mind to. However, regular readers should know by now that
we are reluctant to suggest a horse is lacking in enthusiam when another
explanation for his actions is feasible. The only race in which Relkino gave the
prime impression of being half-hearted about his work was the Voltigeur, in which
he dropped out after Norfolk Air deprived him of the lead a furlong and a half
out. He could, perhaps, be excused his failure to achieve a higher placing than
eleventh in the Champion Stakes on the grounds that, in being drawn number-one,
he had the worst possible draw. In that race he was beaten two furlongs out
after showing up well from the start.

Relkino (b.c. 1973)	Relko (b 1960)	Tanerko (br 1953)	Tantieme La Divine
		Relance III (ch 1952)	Relic Polaire
	Pugnacity (b 1962)	Pampered King (b 1954)	Prince Chevalier Netherton Maid
		Ballynulta (b 1953)	Djebel Ballisland

Relkino's dam, Pugnacity, was a grand racemare although she deteriorated
as a four-year-old; she gave her running under all sorts of conditions and showed

Lady Beaverbrook's "Relkino"

the speed to win in good company at five furlongs and the stamina to get a mile
and a quarter. She never tackled a distance beyond a mile and a quarter.
Her best wins were in the Lowther Stakes at York, the Falmouth Stakes at
Newmarket and the King George Stakes at Goodwood. She has proved a grand
broodmare too. All her five foals of racing age have won; they are, in order of
seniority, Souvran (by Sovereign Path), Sky Messenger (by Saint Crespin III),
Hard Fighter (by Habitat), Relkino and the two-year-old Royal Boxer (by
Royal Palace), and are all winners of note, although none of the older horses was
as good, or stayed as well, as Relkino. Pugnacity's dam was a sprinter and a
daughter of the very speedy Ballisland. Pugnacity produces good-looking
animals, and Relkino, who cost 58,000 guineas as a yearling, is very attractive
and moves very well. The dam's next foal, now named Hills Treble (by
Blakeney), fetched 50,000 guineas as a yearling. Relkino stays a mile and a
half, and he acts on firm going. *R. Hern.*

RELTHORNE 6 b.g. Relic–Hawthorn III (Prince Bio) [1974 8s⁶ 8fg 8f 7fg² **41**
7g² 8g⁴ 7g² 8g* 1975 N.R. 1976 8f⁶ 7f³ 8h³ 9h⁵] poor performer nowadays:
stays 1m: used to wear blinkers. *N. Robinson.*

REMENHAM 3 b.g. Henry the Seventh 125–Livonia 74 (Linacre 133) [1975 —
5s 7f 8s 7.6g 10g 1976 12g 16f] seems of no account. *D. Jermy.*

REMEZZO 2 ch.c. Ribero 126–Camina Bay 109 (Whistling Wind 123) [1976 — p
6fg] rangy, useful sort: good walker: second foal: dam, a winner over 5f and 6f
at 2 yrs, is half-sister to very smart Folle Rousse: 33/1, missed break completely
when seventh of eight to Padroug in Acomb Stakes at York in August, only
outing: should do better. *C. Brittain.*

RENDA 3 ch.f. Gulf Pearl 117–Highland Reel (Sword Dancer) [1975 5g 6f³ **103**
6f² 7f² 8fg* 8.2d³ 7fg² 1976 10fg⁴ 10g⁵ 10fg⁵ 10fg² 11.1f* 10d* 10d] well-
made, useful sort: useful handicapper: steadily came to hand and won at Wolverhampton in August and Newbury the following month: made all and held on
very well when beating Home Waters by ¾ length on latter course: will be suited
by 1½m: appears to act on any going. *B. Hobbs.*

REPIQUE 2 b.c. Jimmy Reppin 131–Winning Bid 93 (Great Captain) [1976 6g³ **113**
6fg⁴ 8v³] strong, attractive colt: half-brother to several winners, notably St
Leger winner Peleid (by Derring-Do) and Eclipse winner Coup de Feu (by White
Fire III): dam a stayer: in frame on all outings, battling on extremely well under
pressure when just over ⅓-length third of 24 to The Czar in minor event at York
in October, first outing for 10 weeks: will stay at least 1¼m: well suited by heavy
going: sure to win races if not tried too highly   *W. Elsey.*

REPPIN CASTLE 2 ch.c. Jimmy Reppin 131–Castle Rough 96 (Counsel 118)   **90**
[1976 6f⁴ 6fg 8g⁵ 8fg* 8v⁶] lengthy colt: half-brother to three winners, including
Cwm Castell (by Celtic Ash), a fair winner over 5f and 7f at 2 yrs: 480 gns yearling:
dam won at 5f and 6f: driven out when winning 14-runner maiden race at
Beverley in September by 1½ lengths from Mesolongi: suited by 1m: probably
acts on any going.   *A. Smith.*

RERICO 3 b.g. Rarity 129–Tudor Heather 87 (Tudor Melody 129) [1975 5f   **87** d
5.9fg² 5h* 6g³ 5fg² 6fg³ 5f 6d³ 1976 6d⁶ 7fg² 8f 7f⁶ 7.2f 8fg] sturdy, robust
gelding: good walker: appeared to show improved form when neck second to
Oriental Star in handicap at Leicester in June but ran poorly afterwards: should
stay 1m: probably acts on any going: sold to S. Cole 700 gns Doncaster November
Sales.   *W. Wharton.*

RESIN 3 b.g. Frankincense 120–Love Seat (King's Bench 132) [1975 5s 5s*   **81**
5g⁶ 6fg* 6f⁶ 6f² 8v⁴ 1976 8fg³ 6f⁴ 7g 6d* 6f 5f⁴ 6g* 6f² 6f⁴ 6g⁶ 6g⁵ 6v⁵ 6s³]
lengthy gelding: moderate handicapper: won at Redcar (Norseman Lager Handicap) in May and Ayr in July: creditable second to Crusty Shah at Redcar later
in month and was not disgraced afterwards: stays 1m but seems better at shorter
distances: acts on any going: suitable mount for an apprentice.   *M. W. Easterby.*

RETHINK 4 br.c. Hauban 132–White Flame (Venture VII 129) [1974 5s 5g*   **63**
7g 7g 7v 1975 10v³ 10s² 9g⁴ 10fg³ 11.7fg 14g⁴ 13d⁶ 13g* 12f⁵ 12.5g 1976 13f²
12.2f* 12s 12f³ 14f³ 12g³] poor handicapper: 5-length winner from Greek
Monarch at Warwick in April: stays 1¾m: acts on any going but seems well
suited by top-of-the-ground conditions: has twice worn blinkers but not when
successful.   *A. Dalton.*

REVE 3 b.g. Forlorn River 124–Evergreen (Buisson Ardent 129) [1975 5d 6fg   **43**
7s 1976 8.2f 8fg³ 8f 8s 8s] leggy, light-framed gelding: bad plater: blinkered
final outing: sold 450 gns Doncaster November Sales.   *W. Wharton.*

REVEL PRINCE 3 br.g. Richboy 117–Atalanta Queen 79 (Premonition 130)   —
[1975 N.R. 1976 8.2f 10.8f 16f 16f⁶ 17.7f] seemingly of no account on form
shown in maiden races in first part of season but may do better on easier ground.
M. Stevens.

REVENGE IS SWEET 2 ch.c. Sweet Revenge 129–Lindylee 99 (Grey Sovereign   **74**
128 §) [1976 5f 5f 5h⁶ 5.9f⁴ 6f 5fg⁴ 7.2v 7g] strong colt: half-brother to several
winners, notably very useful miler Dalry (by Hethersett): cost 2,100 gns Doncaster January 1976 Sales: dam useful at 2 yrs: quite a moderate maiden: well
beaten over 7f and evidently doesn't stay that far: possibly unsuited by heavy
ground.   *N. Adam.*

REVERTIS 5 ch.g. Milesian 125–Persiana (Persian Gulf) [1974 7f² 11g 12g⁴   **76**
12s* 1975 14.6fg 12.3v⁴ 13f⁵ 12.5fg 12.5g 1976 12.3d 12.3f² 12d³ 12g⁵ 12f⁵
16.1d 12v² 12.5v 12.5s³] well-made, good-looking gelding and a good walker:
quite a moderate handicapper: ran best race in 1976 on final appearance: stays
1½m: acts on any going: usually wears bandages in front nowadays: blinkered
fourth start and last two outings: sold 400 gns Ascot December Sales.   *T. Craig.*

REVLOW 2 br.c. Wolver Hollow 126–Velvet Sheen 92 (Linacre 133) [1976 6d   **103**
6fg 7f² 7g* 8f² 8g* 8g⁵ 8s² 7.2v*] second foal: 480 gns yearling: dam won at up
to 1m: did very well in nurseries after winning a maiden race at Ayr in August,
making all to win Jack Jarvis Memorial Nursery on same course and a £1,400 event
at Haydock: came home 4 lengths clear of Money to Spare in last-named race:
stays 1m very well and is likely to stay 1¼m: acts on any going but has shown best
form with some give in the ground: genuine and consistent.   *M. H. Easterby.*

RHEIDOL VALLEY 3 b.f. Siliconn 121–March Rose 87 (March Past 124)   —
[1975 N.R. 1976 8.2d 10.6v] half-sister to three winners, including fairly useful
stayer Soldier Rose (by Galivanter): 200 gns 2-y-o: dam fair 1¼m to 1½m handicapper: last in maiden races at Haydock in October.   *D. McCain.*

RHEOLA 2 b.f. Welsh Pageant 132–Native Treasure 94 (Native Prince) [1976   **93**
5fg 6fg² 5g³ 6fg³ 6fg² 6g*] well-grown, rangy filly: first foal: 2,600 gns yearling:
dam won over 5f at 2 yrs: placed several times in good-class maiden company

Yellow Pages Whitsun Cup, Sandown—Rhodomantade (centre) inches out Marquis de Sade and the blinkered Yamadori

prior to making all to win 30-runner maiden event at Newmarket in September by 1½ lengths from Chartered Lady: will probably stay 7f. *W. Wightman.*

RHODIE BLAKE 3 b.f. Blakeney 126–Rhodie (Rasper) [1975 7g* 1976 10g⁴] **101** good-bodied, attractive filly: half-sister to very smart middle-distance performer Jolly Good (by Jolly Jet): dam, a leading American 2-y-o filly in 1964, won four of her only five starts: not extended when winning at Newmarket at 2 yrs: ran a fine race (possibly in need of run) when 2¾ lengths fourth of nine to Sarania in Sandleford Priory Stakes at Newbury in May: would have stayed further than 1¼m: said to have split a sesamoid bone and has been retired to stud. *B. Hobbs.*

RHODOMANTADE 5 b.h. Blast 125–Rhodia (Parthia 132) [1974 12g⁶ 10f⁴ **110** 8g² 8f³ 8d⁴ 8d* 8s⁶ 8g* 8v⁴ 8s² 1975 7s* 8g⁵ 8f 7.6g⁴ 7fg* 7.2fg⁵ 8fg⁴ 7d* 9g 7g² 8d⁴ 1976 8g 7fg² 8g⁴ 8g* 8f 8fg⁵ 7fg² 8f 8g⁴ 7g³ 7.2d* 7v² 8v] very useful handicapper: ran on very gamely under strong pressure when beating Marquis de Sade and Yamadori in a tight finish for Yellow Pages Whitsun Cup at Sandown in May: picked up another good prize when winning Sydney Sandon Handicap at Haydock in October, beating Jellaby 4 lengths: finished excellent second under a penalty to Jane's Joker at York later in month: best at 7f or 1m: acts on any going: genuine: tried in blinkers on reappearance. *P. Makin.*

RHODRES 2 b.c. Welsh Pageant 132–Chemise 75 (Shantung 132) [1976 6g 7s⁴] **81 P** good-bodied, short-legged colt: first foal: dam won over 1¼m at 3 yrs: weak in market and having first race for over two months, really caught our eye when about 5 lengths fourth of 12 to Sleeper in minor event at Sandown in October, running on in very good style in straight without being given an unnecessarily hard time: will be suited by 1m+: the type to do very well at 3 yrs. *J. Dunlop.*

RHODYMENIA 2 b.f. Siliconn 121–Rhodia (Parthia 132) [1976 6g 5f³] **58** tall, useful-looking filly: third foal: half-sister to two winners by Blast, notably very useful 7f and 1m performer Rhodomantade: dam once-raced half-sister to Champion Hurdle winner Saucy Kit: moderate third to No Joking in maiden auction event at Folkestone in August: sold 1,000 gns Newmarket Autumn Sales. *P. Makin.*

RHONDDA PRINCE 4 b.c. Native Prince–Monet Royal 79 (Monet 127) [1974 **57** 6s 5s² 6d⁵ 7g² 7s⁴ 8d 8d⁶ 1975 8g 8d 5s² 12.2fg 6v⁵ 6f² 5g⁴ 5fg² 6fg² 6f⁶ 6fg* 7g 6g 1976 5f⁵ 6fg³ 7f⁵ 6f² 6g 6d 6h⁴ 5f⁵ 6fg⁵ 5h* 5.9f] big colt: bought in 970 gns after winning seller at Pontefract in August by 2 lengths from Cortown Lady: best at 5f to 7f: acts on any going: successful with and without blinkers *K. Payne.*

RIAL 2 b.g. Goldhill 125–Persian Empress (Palestine 133) [1976 5fg⁵ 6fg 6d⁶] **67** useful sort: half-brother to two minor winners: 8,000 gns yearling: dam lightly-raced half-sister to Tamerlane: showed signs of ability in minor races. *M. Stoute.*

RIBAC 2 b.c. Ribero 126–Bacchanalia 94 (Nearco) [1976 7s⁶ 7g 10d³] closely **89** related to useful 1970 2-y-o Revellarie (by Romulus), and half-brother to several other winners, notably very smart middle-distance filly Shebeen (by Saint Crespin III): 11,000 gns yearling: dam a stayer: blinkered when 2½ lengths third of 12 to subsequently-disqualified Gunbad in minor event at Newmarket in October: will need a stiff test of stamina. *P. Walwyn.*

RIBARBARO 3 b.c. Charlottown 127–Ribasha (Ribot 142) [1975 7fg⁶ 6g³ 8g **97** 1976 12.3s* 12g* 10fg⁴ 13.4s³ 14g² 13f* 12.3fg³ 15.8f³ 16fg* 16f* 16g⁴] useful-looking French-foaled colt: had a successful season, winning apprentice maiden race at Newcastle and handicaps at Ripon (easing up by 6 lengths), Nottingham, Newcastle and Thirsk: beat Palmerston 2 lengths in £2,000 event on last-named course in September: needs further than 1¼m to be seen to advantage and stays 2m well: has won on soft going but is much better suited by a sound surface: sometimes sweats up: suited by forcing tactics. *M. Stoute.*

RIBARIA 2 ch.f. Ribero 126–Relcia 92 (Relko 136) [1976 7s] third foal: half- **—** sister to 3-y-o middle-distance winner Welsh Relic (by Welsh Pageant): dam stayed well: 16/1 when eleventh of 19 to Lady Oriana in maiden race at Newmarket in October: should stay well. *Doug Smith.*

RIBBLE ROUSER 3 ch.c. Marcus Brutus 108–Ribble Reed 75 (Bullrush 106) **73** [1975 5d⁴ 5s⁶ 5v³ 5g⁴ 6f⁶ 6f⁴ 7f* 7f² 7f* 8f* 8v² 8g³ 1976 8.2d⁵ 8f 9g 12fg⁵ 13.8f² 12f⁶ 13h* 12.2g] light-framed, unfurnished colt: blinkered first time, made all when winning three-runner minor event at Hamilton in September by a neck from Willie Ormond: ran badly when again blinkered on final start: stays 1¾m: acts on any going. *W. C. Watts.*

RIBBLESTON 2 b.f. The Brianstan 128–Ribble Reed 75 (Bullrush 106) [1976 **75** 5g 5h² 5g⁴ 5d⁴ 6g 5f² 6fg 7g 7s⁶ 5v⁴] neat filly: second foal: half-sister to 3-y-o Ribble Rouser (by Marcus Brutus), a winner at up to 13f: dam a sprint plater: in frame in early-season minor events and ran well when apprentice ridden in minor race at Beverley in August, finishing ½-length second to Local: appears not to stay beyond 5f: acts on hard going and ran moderately in a seller on heavy. *W. C. Watts.*

RIBELLARO 4 b.c. Riboccare 118–Dianella (Aureole 132) [1974 6fg⁵ 7d² 7s⁴ **111** 8g* 8s 7s⁶ 1975 12s³ 10.4g² 10g² 10g⁴ 12f² 12f² 14fg 12f² 12g⁴ 14g² 12g³ 14g⁶ 10.6v² 1976 12fg⁵ 12d* 14.7d² 12f⁵ 16fg⁶ 15g² 14.7f³] neat, attractive colt: won David Dixon Gold Cup at York in May by 3 lengths from Ahdeek: did well in some of his other races, including when fifth of eight, beaten less than 2 lengths, to Orange Bay in Jockey Club Stakes at Newmarket in April on reappearance and when neck second to Grey Baron in Tennent Trophy at Ayr in July: well suited by 1½m or more: acts on any going and on any track: has run well both in blinkers and without them: genuine and consistent but ran moderately final outing (last of three). *C. Brittain.*

David Dixon Gold Cup, York—Ribellaro masters Ahdeek inside the last furlong

RIBERRY 2 b.c. Ribero 126–Blaeberry 100 (Hook Money 124) [1976 7fg 6v²] **88**
half-brother to useful middle-distance performer Great Ball (by Major Portion):
2,100 gns yearling: dam won at up to 1m: ran well when 2 lengths second of 22 to
Good Company in maiden race at Newbury in October, running on in good style in
closing stages: should stay at least 1¼m: acts on heavy going. *R. Smyth.*

RIB LAW 2 b.c. Ribero 126–Turkhan Law (Turkhan) [1976 5g⁶ 6d 6fg³ 6fg⁵ **74**
7f⁴ 7g⁵ 7f⁴ 8f*] strong, useful sort: good walker and mover: half-brother to
several winners, notably very smart 1m to 1¼m handicapper Hardy Scot (by
Hard Sauce): 660 gns yearling: dam half-sister to Ebor winner Hyperion Kid:
won eight-runner nursery at Lanark in September, being hard driven to lead last
strides and beating Darwen Lad by ½ length: will stay well: acts on firm going:
wears blinkers. *T. Fairhurst.*

RIBOBOY 3 b.c. Ribot 142–Slapton Sands (First Landing) [1975 7g* 7f* 7g **112**
1976 10g* 12fg 12g 10g 13.5g] good-looking, rangy colt: very good mover: ran
out a decisive 2 lengths winner of Classic Trial at Sandown in April from Take
Your Place: sweated up in Ladbroke Derby Trial at Lingfield (odds on) and
Epsom Derby (tried in blinkers) and ran a thoroughly sour race on each occasion,
finishing last at Epsom: subsequently transferred from R. Hern's stable and ran
creditably for new trainer, finishing seventh in Prix Eugene Adam at Saint-Cloud
in July (to Crow) and in Grand Prix de Deauville the following month (to
Ashmore): will stay 1¾m: acts on firm going. *A. Paus, France.*

RIBOFLEUR 3 b.f. Ribero 126–Harbour Flower 105 (Hethersett 134) [1975 **74**
6fg 1976 10fg⁴ 12.2fg³ 14g² 12fg³] lengthy filly: ran best race when length
second to Hardirondo in 12-runner maiden race at Sandown in July: evidently
suited by a test of stamina. *G. Pritchard-Gordon.*

RIBOMINE 4 br.g. Riboccare 118–Firenza Mia (Vigo 130) [1974 N.R. 1975 **—**
16f 12.2g 12g 1976 10f] poor handicapper: should stay long distances. *A.
Neaves.*

RIBO PRIDE 3 b.f. Ribero 126–Pride of India 73 (Orsini 124) [1975 7f 1976 **77**
10.8f³ 12g³ 12f⁵ 16.1d² 13.4fg² 14g⁶ 14f⁵ 15.8fg 12fg* 13s⁶ 12s⁶] fair sort: 10-
length winner of weakly-contested 15-runner amateur riders event at Leicester
in September: stays 2m: sometimes wears blinkers (did so at Leicester): sold
2,500 gns Newmarket December Sales. *F. J. Houghton.*

RIBOSA 2 b.c. Ribero 126–Rosaura 105 (Court Martial) [1976 5g 6fg 6fg³ 6fg* **96**
8s⁶] half-brother to three winners, including quite useful middle-distance handicapper De Musset (by Alcide): 2,300 gns yearling: dam, a sprinter, is daughter of
1,000 Guineas winner Belle of All: having first race for over two months, showed
improved form when leading well inside final furlong to win 15-runner nursery at
Salisbury in September by 1½ lengths from Teddington Park: stays 1m, and
should get further: seems to act on any going. *R. Smyth.*

RIBRAMBLE 4 gr.g. Ribero 126–Bramble 85 (Sound Track 132) [1974 5g 5g³ **90**
6g⁴ 7g² 7d² 6fg² 8s⁶ 1975 8v 8v 6fg² 5.3f⁶ 5.8f* 6f² 5.3f⁵ 5f² 5g⁴ 5g* 6d² 6fg*
1976 6fg 5fg⁴ 6f³ 6f² 6fg³ 6f⁶] strong, robust gelding: good walker: fair handi-
capper: ran creditably in three good handicaps at 4 yrs, gaining places in
Wokingham Stakes at Royal Ascot (behind Import), Home Ales Tankard at
Nottingham (1½ lengths second to Maxi's Taxi), both in June and Spillers
Stewards' Cup at Goodwood the following month (beaten 2 lengths by Jimmy
The Singer): best at up to 7f: seems to act on any going: effective with and
without blinkers: suitable mount for an apprentice: genuine and consistent. *L.
Cumani.*

RICCIOLA 3 ch.f. Stage Door Johnny–Gay West (Chateaugay) [1975 N.R. **66**
1976 8g 8.5g³ 8g 8g⁵ 12g³ 12v² 12s⁴ 10.2s³] American-bred filly: first foal: 2,500
gns foal, resold 5,400 gns yearling: dam won over 6f at 3 yrs: raced in Italy first
four outings, finishing third at Milan in April: in frame in maiden races on all four
outings in this country, coming closest to success when neck second to Chance
Belle at Leicester in October: stays 1½m: acts on heavy ground: sold 1,300 gns
Newmarket December Sales. *L. Cumani.*

RICCO BOY 3 b.c. Falcon 131–Reel of Silk 86 (Shantung 132) [1975 7.5s⁶ **121**
8g⁴ 9d* 1976 10.5g² 10.5fg⁶ 8g² 9g² 9.2g³ 8d 8s* 8s² 10d] French colt: half-
brother to winning stayer Tvashtri (by Native Prince): 6,200 gns yearling: dam
won at 1¼m and 15f: gained a well-deserved success when making all to win
£5,500 Prix d'Automne at Longchamp in September by 5 lengths from Ranimer:
has some fine efforts to his name in pattern races, finishing runner-up in Prix de
la Jonchere at Longchamp (beaten a neck by Avaray), Prix Jean Prat at

Chantilly (failed by a nose to catch Earth Spirit) and Queen Elizabeth II Stakes (went down by 4 lengths to impressive winner Rose Bowl), third in Prix d'Ispahan at Longchamp (to Full of Hope) and seventh of 19 to Vitiges in Champion Stakes at Newmarket in October: stays 1¼m well: appears to act on any going but is suited by an easy surface: had plenty to do when tried in blinkers on sixth outing. *A. Paus, France.*

RICH BLACK 2 br.f. David Jack 125–Full Sutton 73 (Hardicanute 130) [1976 —
5h⁶ 5d 6g] small filly: bad plater. *F. Wiles.*

RICHELLO 3 b.c. Ribocco 129–Hiello II (Vertex) [1975 6fg⁵ 5d⁴ 1976 10s 10.4d —
6g 8g⁶ 8fg 12s⁵] workmanlike colt: showed a little ability on fourth outing: off course a long time afterwards and was well beaten on his return, including when tried in blinkers on final start, and seems to be of little account nowadays: should stay 1¼m: sold 625 gns Ascot December Sales. *K. Payne.*

RICHEST 3 ch.f. Richboy 117–Lovable 84 (Miralgo 130) [1975 6g 1976 8fg **72**
8g 8fg⁵ 8s] good sort: just over 3 lengths fifth of 14 to Cockade in maiden race at Salisbury in September, only worthwhile form: should stay further than 1m (dam stayed 2m): possibly unsuited by soft going: trained until after third outing by I. Balding: sold 720 gns Newmarket December Sales. *M. Jarvis.*

RICH GOLD 3 ch.c. Richboy 117–Flying Spear 94 (Breakspear II) [1975 N.R. —
1976 8d 5v 10s] strong colt: little worthwhile form in varied company, including selling. *F. Wiles.*

RICHMEDE 3 gr.c. Runnymede 123–Scilly Isles 54 (Silly Season 127) [1975 —
8.2d 8g 7g 1976 5f 7f 7h 10v] small, light-framed colt: no worthwhile form, including in a claiming event. *M. Bradley.*

RICHMOND HILL 2 gr.f. Highland Melody 112–Cathays Park (Reliance II 137) **86**
[1976 5d 6f 7fg⁵ 6f* 6g 7g] small filly: first foal: dam, of little account, comes from same family as Manado: made all when winning 16-runner maiden race at Catterick in August by 3 lengths from Quimay: in rear in nurseries afterwards: comes from a stamina-packed female line and should stay at least 1m: blinkered final outing. *J. W. Watts.*

RICHO'S FANCY 2 b.c. Track Spare 125–Pat's Fancy 82 (Falcon 131) [1976 —
5g 5g 5g] first foal: dam stayed 7f: very backward when behind in maiden races at Salisbury (last of 13) and Newbury in May: fell on third outing. *P. Taylor.*

RICKY'S DREAM 2 br.c. Breeders Dream 116–Enough (Rustam 127) [1976 **67**
5fg 6d 6g 6d⁴ 7v] fair sort: springer in market, ran easily best race when about 10 lengths fourth of 11 to Friendly Now in maiden race at Yarmouth in September: should stay 1m: will probably win a seller. *J. Hardy.*

RICKADOO 3 b.f. Round Table–War Khal (Khaled) [1975 7f⁴ 8f² 1976 10.1fg **85**
12g² 16.1d⁵ 13.1h* 11f* 13.1h* 12fg⁵ 13.1f² 12fg* 12g] well-made, good sort: fair handicapper: winner at Bath (twice) and Hamilton (minor event) in July and Salisbury (apprentice race) in September: stayed 13f but probably not 2m: acted on hard ground: stud. *P. Walwyn.*

RIDING LEA 3 b.f. Healaugh Fox–Grey Sport 71 (Court Feathers 120) [1975 **56**
8g 7fg 7fg 1976 10fg⁵ 12.2f³ 9g⁵] workmanlike filly: stayed 1½m: retained by trainer 820 gns Doncaster May Sales: dead. *Denys Smith.*

RIESLING 4 b.c. Ragusa 137–Glass House 88 (Court Martial) [1974 7fg 7d **56**
7g³ 8.2s⁵ 1975 12s 11.7s 12g 10f³ 11.5g⁴ 12g 12.2g* 1976 8g⁴ 12g 10g 12.2d⁴ 13.8g² 13.8fg³ 14d³ 12fg 16.1d⁴] small colt: poor mover: stays 1¾m: possibly unsuited by very firm ground: sometimes wears blinkers: sold 2,400 gns Newmarket Autumn Sales. *R. Armstrong.*

RIEVAULX ABBEY 2 ch.f. Double Jump 131–Gold Pin 96 (Pinza 137) [1976 **61**
5d⁵ 6fg 5fg 7fg 7g 8v⁶] rangy filly: half-sister to seven minor winners: 4,100 gns yearling: dam won at 6f and stayed 1m: plating-class maiden: should stay 1m. *M. W. Easterby.*

RIGGED AND READY 2 b.c. Right Tack 131–Sea Mew (Sammy Davis 129) **80**
[1976 5d⁵ 5d 5.9s⁵ 7v] strong, good-looking colt: first produce: 500 gns foal, resold 560 gns yearling: dam unraced daughter of Yorkshire Oaks winner Sea Parrot: moderate maiden: stays 6f and should get further: blinkered last two outings. *H. Collingridge.*

RIGHT BEAUTY 3 b.f. Right Boy 137–Miss Barbara 87 (Le Dieu d'Or 119) —
[1975 5v 5fg⁶ 5g⁵ 5fg² 5f⁶ 5f⁵ 1976 6g 5fg] lengthy filly: half-sister to top-class sprinter Lochnager (by Dumbarnie) but is only a plater herself: ran respectably in blinkers on final outing (June). *M. W. Easterby.*

RIGHT OF LIGHT 2 ch.c. Tyrant–Daisy June (Epaulette 125) [1976 5g³ 6f **96**
5f³ 5fg* 6v⁴ 5s⁶] lightly-built colt: half-brother to Carlos of Kilnaboy (by
Appiani II), a winner over 2¼m in Ireland: 2,900 gns yearling: dam won at 1m
in Ireland: showed a good turn of foot to draw clear when winning 19-runner
maiden race at Salisbury in September by 4 lengths from Friendly Goddess: ran
as though 6f was too far when remote fourth of six to Our Jimmy in £2,600 event
at York the following month but is bred to stay 1m. *P. Makin.*

RIGHT SHARP 2 gr.c. Right Boy 137–Kailblades 107 (Anwar 120) [1976 6f **—**
5d 6v 5v] useless. *J. Mulhall.*

RIGHT SO 3 ch.g. Falcon 131–Nectis (Honeyway 125) [1975 5g³ 6f* 7f³ 7f⁴ **92**
6.3g³ 7.5g⁴ 8d 1976 12g⁴ 10g 8g* 8f 8f³ 10fg⁵] useful sort: ex-Irish gelding:
half-brother to three winners, including useful 1972 Irish 2-y-o Mellifont (by
Hook Money): 600 gns yearling: dam placed over 1m at 3 yrs in Ireland: showed
useful form at 2 yrs: won handicap at the Curragh in May by a short head from
Frankly Yours: subsequently transferred from R. Annesley's stable, putting up
best effort when 4½ lengths third of nine to Huntsman's Leap in minor event at
Windsor in July: had stiff tasks on other two outings in this country: promises
to stay 1½m: acts on firm going. *I. Walker.*

RIGHT TACTICS 5 b.g. Right Tack 131–King's Victress (King's Bench 132) **—**
[1974 8.2fg 10f 10f 12d 16g 1975 8fg 10.2g⁴ 17.7f 1976 8fg 12g] of little
account. *C. V. Miller.*

RIGHT VALE 2 b.f. Right Tack 131–Ebvale (Relic) [1976 5g⁶ 5g⁶ 5f 5g 5d⁵ **47**
5f⁴ 5f] sharp sort: no worthwhile form, including in sellers: blinkered final
start. *W. Marshall.*

RIGHT VIEW 3 b.f. Right Tack 131–Sky Valley 101 (Skymaster 126) [1975 **—**
5fg³ 5d* 5s³ 5g 6h⁴(dis) 1976 6g 5f 5f 5g⁵ 8.2s 8s] compact, quite well-made
filly: won maiden race at Liverpool in 1975: not seen out until the summer and
showed little worthwhile form. *W. Wharton.*

RIGTON EMPRESS 3 b.f. Tycoon II–Rigton Caprice 69 (Straight Deal) [1975 **58**
8fg⁶ 1976 9g 8h 12g⁶ 14.7f⁶ 16f 15.8f* 11h⁵] plater: bought in 1,100 gns after
winning all out at Catterick in August: suited by long distances: hampered and
brought down on first outing. *J. Turner.*

RINGED AUREOLE 3 ch.f. Aureole 132–Ring Time II 100 (Pardal 130) [1975 **77**
7.2fg 1976 12.2fg³ 12f* 12.2f* 12fg⁴ 12g⁴ 12f* 16f* 14g*] leggy, sparely-made
filly: only a modest performer but had a very successful season and won five times,
maiden race at Lanark, minor events at Catterick and Ostend and slowly-run
amateur riders events at Beverley and Goodwood: beat Cartwright 2 lengths on
last-named course in September: stays well: acts on firm going. *Sir Mark
Prescott.*

RING LEADER 2 br.c. Bold Lad (Ire) 133–Circus 89 (Vilmorin) [1976 5d **104**
5g² 5fg* 5f* 5g⁴ 5f³] strong, quality-looking, good sort: half-brother to
three winners, including Ringmistress (by Nantallah), a very useful stakes
winner in U.S.A.: 18,000 gns yearling: dam, half-sister to top-class 1m to 1½m
horse Pipe of Peace, was best at 5f: favourite when winning 18-runner maiden
race at Leopardstown and four-runner minor event at Phoenix Park, both in
June, on latter course landing the odds by 10 lengths from Violet Shadow: not
seen out again after finishing 10 lengths third to Cloonlara in Phoenix Stakes in
August: should stay 6f: useful. *L. Browne, Ireland.*

RING OF FIRE 4 b.g. St Chad 120–Gay Wren (Arctic Star) [1974 5fg 1975 **55**
10.8s* 10s* 10f4 1976 12fg⁵ 12f] quite a moderate handicapper (rated 75) at
3 yrs: ran poorly on second of only two outings in 1976: probably stays 1½m:
best form on soft going. *C. Dingwall.*

RING ROSE 3 br.f. Relko 136–Heath Rose 124 (Hugh Lupus 132) [1975 6g **86**
6fg⁵ 7f 1976 10.8f⁵ 10fg² 10.1f* 10g² 10f 11.7f³ 12.2f* 12g* 12.3fg² 12s⁴ 14s⁵]
quite attractive filly: ran creditably in most of her races, picking up maiden event
at Windsor in May and handicaps at Wolverhampton and Kempton in August,
quickening well when beating Darcy 8 lengths on last-named course: suited by
1½m and may well stay further: ran below her best on last two outings and
evidently needs a sound surface. *H. Candy.*

RINGS 2 b.f. Realm 129–Wild Wings 89 (Skymaster 126) [1976 5fg³ 6g⁴ 6g³ **104**
6d*] quite an attractive filly: second foal: half-sister to 1974 2-y-o 6f winner
Swiss Roll (by Burglar): 15,000 gns yearling: dam a sprinter: a useful filly, as
she showed when strong-finishing 5 lengths third of 15 to Durtal in William Hill

Cheveley Park Stakes at Newmarket in September: short-priced favourite for 23-runner maiden race on same course the following month and came through approaching final furlong to win by ¾ length from newcomer Call of the Deep: stays 6f well. *J. Hindley.*

RINGS AND THINGS 2 b.f. Upper Case–Sum Toy (Chieftain) [1976 5f 5g 5f3 72 5.3g3 5fg4 5.3f3 5s] sturdy filly: second foal: 2,400 gns yearling: dam won at around 1m in Ireland and France: quite a moderate filly: in frame in maiden races and a nursery: not bred to be a 5f specialist and should stay at least 1m. *R. Smyth.*

RIP KIRBY 2 br.c. Sweet Revenge 129–Kathie 87 (Zucchero 133 §) [1976 5g 57 6f 5fg 5v 5s] quite a moderate plater: should stay 6f: seems to act on any going: ran creditably in blinkers on final outing. *D. Williams.*

RIPPLING 3 br.f. Derring-Do 131–Running River 77 (Crocket 130) [1975 5h* — 5g2 5g* 6d* 6g2 1976 7fg] dipped-backed filly: showed useful form in 1975 and won maiden race at Pontefract and nurseries at Newmarket and York: broke a leg at Newmarket in April and was subsequently destroyed: stayed 6f well: acted on any going: had a good turn of foot. *M. Stoute.*

RISCA 2 b.f. Right Tack 131–Tarara 117 (Tamerlane 128) [1976 5g2 5s6 6s 5v] 78 closely related to useful 1967 2-y-o Miss Tarara (by Hard Tack) and half-sister to three other 2-y-o winners: dam, very useful sprinter, won at 5f and 6f: 2½ lengths second to Miss Shannon in 24-runner maiden race at Leicester in May: not seen out again until end of season and ran poorly last two outings: will be suited by 6f: possibly needs a sound surface. *R. Viberi.*

RISING FALCON 4 ch.c. Gyr 131–Alpine Bloom 123 (Chamossaire) [1974 8d 98 7v6 1975 11v 11fg2 10h* 12g2 12f* 12f2 12fg4 16g 13.3g6 1976 14fg* 16fg2 16g* 15g4 14fg 16g* 18d] tall, well-made colt: quite a useful handicapper: winner three times in 1976, at Newmarket in April, Kempton the following month (put up a good performance to win valuable H. S. Persse Memorial Handicap from Regal Step) and Sandown in September (quickened impressively to beat Sea Kestrel 6 lengths): favourite and looking exceptionally well, beaten a long way from home when thirteenth of 14 to John Cherry in SKF Cesarewitch at Newmarket the following month (reportedly unsettled at start): stays 2m: best form on a sound surface: suitable mount for an apprentice. *J. Dunlop.*

RISING RHYTHM 2 b.c. Jukebox 120–Hill Time (Hill Gail) [1976 5g 6d 7f 73 8fg] well-grown, workmanlike colt: half-brother to 1½m winner The Suestan (by Ballyciptic), and to a fairly useful winner in Italy: 200 gns foal, and resold 1,500 gns yearling: dam won over 6f in Ireland at 2 yrs: showed a little ability in maiden and minor events: stays 7f: blinkered fourth outing. *S. Norton.*

RISING STAR 2 b.f. St Paddy 133–Rave Notice (Princequillo) [1976 7g 7g] — half-sister to several winners here and in the U.S.A., including smart middle-distance stayer Laurentian Hills (by Hill Rise) and 1966 Irish Sweeps Lincoln winner Riot Act (by Ribot): dam ran three times at 2 yrs in U.S.A.: behind in maiden races at Yarmouth in September (dwelt) and Newmarket in October (tailed-off last of 23). *R. Armstrong.*

RITZY DREAMER 2 ch.f. High Line 125–Golden Thoughts 86 (Golden Cloud) — [1976 5f 5f 7fg 7f 7fg] poor filly: blinkered fourth outing. *R. Murphy.*

RIVALYNN 3 b.g. Forlorn River 124–Glasllyn 60 (Linklater) [1975 5fg 6h — 5fg 5f 1976 8f 8f6 6g] tall gelding: no worthwhile form, including when blinkered in a seller on final outing: sold 1,025 gns Ascot December Sales. *W. A. Stephenson.*

RIVER ALN 3 b.g. Swing Easy 126–Princess Dido 63 (Sayajirao 132) [1975 — N.R. 1976 9v 10s] half-brother to two minor winners: 4,500 gns foal, resold 1,500 gns yearling: dam won over 1m at 3 yrs: well beaten in maiden and minor events at end of season. *H. Blackshaw.*

RIVER BELLE 3 ch.f. Divine Gift 127–Sham Alarm (Chamier 128) [1975 5d 5f 72 5s4 5s6 1976 6g2 7g4 7g* 8s 7v3] good sort: ex-Irish: half-sister to 1972 2-y-o 5f winner Evie (by Takawalk II): won minor race at Ayr in September by ¾ length from Miss King Fu: creditable third (spoilt chance by hanging) to Our Song in apprentice handicap at Teesside the following month: has given impression she will be suited by further than 7f but was well beaten on only attempt at 1m: trained by I. Walker until after second outing. *T. Craig.*

RIVER BLOOM 3 br.c. Forlorn River 124–Gold Bloom 72 (Klondyke Bill 125) 94 [1975 5s* 5f3 6d2 5f3 6fg3 6g3 6d 1976 7g 7d3 7s4 6fg3 6d2] useful-looking colt:

ran well when placed at Newcastle in April (third to Dunmurry Boy in Northern Free Handicap) and Newmarket (third to Gwent in Great Eastern Handicap) and Redcar (beaten ½ length by Resin in Norseman Lager Handicap) in May: stayed 7f: acted on any going: genuine and consistent: dead. *J. Etherington.*

RIVER BLUE 4 br.c. Forlorn River 124–Assignation (Twilight Alley 133) [1974 6s* 1975 7v² 8g 8.5fg 1976 10d⁴] tall, rather narrow colt: showed useful form in good company in 1975: having first outing for 11 months when 8 lengths fourth of six to Great Ball in six-runner minor event at Pontefract in May: probably stayed 1¼m: acted on heavy going: dead. *W. Stephenson.* —

RIVER DANE 2 ch.f. Tyrant–Audrey Joan 118 (Doutelle 128) [1976 4.5g* 5.5g* 5.5g² 6g⁴] smart French filly: fourth living foal: dam, half-sister to Irish 1,000 Guineas winner Cloonagh, was a smart winner of both her starts at 2 yrs and won Portland Handicap at 3 yrs: winner of newcomers event at Saint-Cloud in June and minor race at Maisons-Laffitte the following month, in latter race putting up an excellent effort to win by 2 lengths from Guile Princess: subsequently took part in two highly competitive events, proving that she is a very fast filly when ¾-length second to Blushing Groom in Prix Robert Papin at Maisons-Laffitte, finishing at least 8 lengths clear of nine other previous winners: did not run up to that form in Prix Morny at Deauville in August, being beaten 4¾ lengths into fourth place behind Blushing Groom, and wasn't seen out again: should be suited by 6f but isn't certain to stay 1m. *A. Paus, France.* 118

RIVER EAMONT 2 b.f. Another River 89–Hyper Rose 62 (Pinza 137) [1976 5f] third foal: sister to fairly useful 3-y-o sprinter River Petterill: dam, a plater, best at 1m: in need of race when always behind in 13-runner maiden event won by Hutton Barns at Catterick in August. *G. Richards.* —

RIVER HENHAM 3 br.g. Forlorn River 124–Aleta 71 (Montaval 129) [1975 5g 5g 6g 6fg 8v⁴ 1976 8fg 8f 8.5fg⁶ 10fg 6f⁶ 6f 10.4fg] well-made, useful-looking gelding: plater: rated 77 at 2 yrs but showed no worthwhile form in 1976: sometimes wears blinkers: trained until after sixth outing by N. Callaghan. *S. Cole.* —

RIVERLITE 3 br.g. Another River 89–Hyperlite 72 (Bleep-Bleep 134) [1975 N.R. 1976 11f⁵] half-brother to two winners, including useful miler Drakensberg (by Fury Royal): dam ran only at 2 yrs: just under 8 lengths fifth of 10 to —

Mr Robert Sangster's "River Dane" (L. Piggott)

Hydrographic in maiden race at Edinburgh in June: broke a leg near finish and was subsequently destroyed. *W. A. Stephenson.*

RIVER MAHWA 3 b.f. Yellow River 114–Mahwa 82 (Match III 135) [1975 **64** 5g 7f 8d 8g 1976 8fg 8fg 10.1d⁶ 10s* 8v⁴] small filly: showed much improved form when winning maiden race at Folkestone in October by a neck from Linden Dolly: fourth in claiming race at Leicester later in month, running as though she needs further than 1m: will stay well: evidently suited by soft going: trained until after second outing by Mrs F. Nagle. *M. Haynes.*

RIVER MIST 4 br.g. Foggy Bell 108–River Moy (Niagara Falls 104) [1974 7g — 6g⁴ 8d⁵ 1975 9.4g⁶ 9.4g² 10d³ 12f⁴ 12.5fg² 12v 1976 12f⁶ 12s 16.1d] big gelding: poor maiden: stayed 1½m: seemed to act on any going: dead. *R. Cambidge.*

RIVER PETTERILL 3 b.f. Another River 89–Hyper Rose 62 (Pinza 137) **89 d** [1975 5v⁶ 5d⁴ 5fg 5f* 5g 6f² 5g² 1976 6f* 8g⁴ 6d² 5g 6h 6f 6g 6f 6s] fair sort: won handicap at Catterick in April by ½ length from Rhondda Prince: runner-up in similar event on same course the following month: showed no worthwhile form afterwards and has deteriorated: stays 6f: appears to act on any going: blinkered final start. *G. Richards.*

RIVERQUEEN 3 b.f. Luthier 126–Riverside (Sheshoon 132) [1975 8.2d* **128** 1976 8fg* 8g* 10g* 10.5d² 12.5g* 12s 12s]

It took Pawneese to end this outstanding filly's run of victories that began in a race restricted to newcomers at Saint-Cloud in the autumn of 1975. Pawneese beat her on merit by a length and a half in the Prix de Diane at Chantilly in June, nine days after the Oaks. Before taking part in the Prix de Diane Riverqueen had won the Prix Saint-Alary from the unbeaten Theia and the One Thousand Guineas fourth Antrona, the Poule d'Essai des Pouliches (the equivalent of the One Thousand Guineas) from Suvannee, who had received a rating of 8-11 in the French Two-Year-Old Free Handicap, and the Prix de la Grotte from Kesar Queen, subsequently third in the Guineas, and Antrona. Riverqueen was so highly regarded in France that she started favourite at even money to beat Pawneese and nine others in the Prix de Diane.

Little need be detailed of Riverqueen's races before the Diane: the fact that she was widely expected to account for Pawneese, who had won by five lengths and four at Epsom, speaks volumes for her. The Prix Saint-Alary was the most important race she had won, for although the Pouliches is the equivalent of the One Thousand Guineas in France, the Saint-Alary is always held in higher regard; and she was harder pressed in that race than in either of the previous two. She won both the Grotte and the Pouliches with ease after being waited with, by two and a half lengths from Kesar Queen and by three lengths from Suvannee respectively, whereas in the Saint-Alary, facing the best field of three-year-old fillies assembled in Europe up to that stage of the season, she had to fight hard to get the better of Theia by three quarters of a length. Theia, 9-0 in the Two-Year-Old Free Handicap and winner as a three-year-old of the Prix Vanteaux, pressed Riverqueen strongly after the latter had gone ahead from Kesar Queen a furlong and a half from home in a fast-run race; and so did Antrona and Suvannee, who also finished very close up. Flying Water, said to have been in season, finished only seventh and never looked dangerous.

Riverqueen couldn't get to grips with Pawneese in the Prix de Diane. Some blamed her jockey Head for setting her too much to do, but the fact of the matter is that Pawneese, not Head, set Riverqueen too much to do. When front-running Pawneese quickened turning for home, as she had done at Epsom, Riverqueen was left stranded, and although Riverqueen made good ground under severe pressure, swishing her tail, Pawneese had so much in hand that her jockey was able to ease up in the last half-furlong. There isn't much doubt that Riverqueen ran right up to her form: behind her again were Theia and Antrona, and third-placed Lagunette went on to win the Irish Guinness Oaks from fifth-placed Sarah Siddons showing just how good was the form of the French middle-distance fillies.

Riverqueen and Pawneese did even more than Lagunette and Sarah Siddons to illustrate how competitive a race the Prix de Diane had been. Before the Irish Guinness Oaks was run, Riverqueen had won the Grand Prix de Saint-Cloud from a field of older colts, and a week after the Irish Guinness Oaks Pawneese won the King George VI and Queen Elizabeth Diamond Stakes. The field that faced Riverqueen at Saint-Cloud was not so strong as that which

Poule d'Essai des Pouliches, Longchamp—an impressive triumph by Riverqueen

faced Pawneese at Ascot, but it was a strong one nevertheless; all the colts had good form, although one of them, Ashmore, the co-favourite with his stable-companion Maitland, hadn't been out since finishing sixth to Grundy in the previous year's King George, and another, Citoyen, is best served by a longer distance when conditions are as fast as they were that day at Saint-Cloud. No three-year-old filly had won the Grand Prix de Saint-Cloud and only three fillies, Corrida, Banassa and Dahlia, had ever won it since its institution in 1904 as the Prix du President de la Republique. There were no three-year-old colts in the field. Youth and Malacate were in reserve for Ascot and Grand-chant, an unlucky fifth to Youth in the French Derby, had to be pulled out with a sprained fetlock a few days before the event.

Riverqueen won by half a length from the previous year's runner-up Ashmore, who went on to finish eighth behind Pawneese at Ascot three weeks later. Citoyen, coming back to a mile and a half after his third to Sagaro in the French Gold Cup, had to make the running to stand any chance in this company, and he led at a fast gallop, with Riverqueen eventually settling down in fifth place behind Maitland, Libra's Rib and Ashmore after racing second early on. Turning for home Maitland, winner of the Prix Jean de Chaudenay over approximately the same course the previous month, surprisingly began to find Citoyen's pace too hot for him, and with Libra's Rib showing his customary lack of acceleration in this type of company, Riverqueen and Ashmore on her inside gradually began to get on top. Citoyen was left behind when the pace quickened in the last two furlongs, and in the end Riverqueen was not hard pressed to win the race, having more in hand of Ashmore than the official margin might suggest. Tip Moss, third to Kasteel and El Rastro in the Prix Dollar and fifth to Infra Green in the Ganay, finished strongly to take third here without ever being the slightest threat. Quiet Fling, the Coronation Cup winner, never got in the hunt; he beat only Maitland and a disappointing Beau Buck.

Neither Riverqueen nor Pawneese did herself justice in the autumn. They ran in the same two races, the Prix Vermeille and the Prix de l'Arc de Triomphe, and were unrecognisable as the same fillies who had played such a major part in the European season up to the end of July. Riverqueen was said to have beaten Ivanjica at level weights on the gallops before the Prix Vermeille but no-one who saw the Prix Vermeille would have given credence to the story even if he had done so earlier. Riverqueen finished last but one

Prix Saint-Alary, Longchamp—Riverqueen wins from Theia, Antrona and Suvannee

*Grand Prix de Saint-Cloud—Riverqueen accounts for the older horses Ashmore,
Tip Moss, Libra's Rib, Citoyen and Quiet Fling*

behind Lagunette, beating only her pacemaker Moquerie and finishing eight
lengths behind Pawneese, who was herself at least eleven lengths adrift of the
winner. In the Arc she trailed in seventeenth of twenty, virtually in another
parish to Ivanjica. It's possible that both Riverqueen and Pawneese were over
the top in the autumn after their hard season, it's also possible that neither is
suited by the really soft going they encountered for the only times in their
careers in the Vermeille and the Arc. On their form of the summer Pawneese
and Riverqueen had the Vermeille sewn up between them, and both would
have gone close in the Arc.

Riverqueen
(b.f. 1973)
{
  Luthier
  (br 1965)
  {
    Klairon
    (b 1952)
    {
      Clarion III
      Kalmia
    }
    Flute Enchantee
    (b 1950)
    {
      Cranach
      Montagnana
    }
  }
  Riverside
  (b 1966)
  {
    Sheshoon
    (ch 1956)
    {
      Precipitation
      Noorani
    }
    Renounce
    (b 1957)
    {
      Big Game
      Refreshed
    }
  }
}

Each of the first three in the Grand Prix de Saint-Cloud was by Luthier,

Mme A. Head's "Riverqueen"

the most successful French-bred stallion standing in France at present. Unlike his three runners in the Grand Prix, Luthier did not get a mile and a half; he showed as much when beaten favourite for the 1968 French Derby. He stayed almost that distance though. Among the races he won were the semi-classic Prix Lupin and the Prix Jacques le Marois; in the latter he trounced some of the best milers in France. Riverqueen's dam, Riverside, did stay a mile and a half; in fact she won a good race over thirteen furlongs, the Prix de Royallieu. She also won a lesser race at a mile and a half and two at ten furlongs, and in addition she ran third to Saraca in the Prix Vermeille and fourth to Karabas in the Prix du Conseil Municipal. Although by the French horse Sheshoon, Riverside was bred in England and comes from a family well-known over here; she was purchased as a yearling at Newmarket for 8,400 guineas. Her half-brother is Double-U-Jay, a good horse at a mile and a mile and a quarter, and her grandam is Refreshed, third in the One Thousand Guineas and a half-sister to the Guineas winner Festoon. Riverside had two foals before Riverqueen, the very useful middle-distance colt Riverking (by Le Fabuleux) and a minor winner, a filly by Sir Ivor called Riverstar.

Riverqueen, a good-looking filly, stays in training. There are worthwhile middle-distance races to be won with her, especially in France, if she comes back to her best, but she looks like having to take on Pawneese again so she won't have things all her own way. *C. Datessen, France.*

RIVERSIDE INN 2 b.c. Mandamus 120–Bernie's Auction (Rockavon 120) [1976 5.9f] half-brother to a winning plater: 120 gns foal, resold 260 gns yearling: tailed-off last of seven in maiden race won by Honey Bowl at Wolverhampton in August: sold 500 gns Ascot August Sales. *Denys Smith.* —

RIVER SIRENE 3 b.f. Another River 89–La Sirene (Pinturischio 116) [1975 6g 8v 1976 12.5v] unfurnished filly: no worthwhile form in maiden and minor events: was not seen out until October in 1976. *J. W. Watts.* —

RIVOCK 2 ch.c. Most Secret 119–Uncharted 77 (Rock Star 129) [1976 5f 5f 6g² 7fg³ 8fg⁵] short-coupled colt: showed first worthwhile form when ½-length second of 12 to Gold Bar in £1,500 seller at Haydock in August: had stiff task when remote third to Bedford Lodge in nursery at Chester the following month: should stay 1m: bandaged near-fore final start. *M. H. Easterby.* **71**

RIVOLI 7 b.g. Ragusa 137–Gift Token 107 (Firestreak 125) [1974 14.6s 16g* 1975 16g 1976 13.3fg] fairly useful handicapper on his day: pulled up lame at Newbury in June on only outing in 1976: stays 2m: best form on a sound surface: presumably difficult to train. *G. Peter-Hoblyn.* —

RIYALIM 2 br.f. Pieces of Eight 128–Bualim (Khalkis 127) [1976 6f⁶ 7fg 7g] half-sister to two winners in France, namely middle-distance performer Taking Off (by Snob II) and very useful 3-y-o sprinter Baradaan (by Habitat): 3,400 gns yearling: dam placed at up to 10.5f in France: little worthwhile form in maiden races: sold 750 gns Ascot November Sales. *G. Pritchard-Gordon.* —

ROADHEAD 3 br.g. Doon 124–Chantabelle 81 (Chantelsey 130) [1975 8g⁶ 10g 1976 11.5fg 12g³ 12.2fg* 12fg 16v⁵] rangy gelding: well-backed favourite, won 17-runner maiden race at Wolverhampton in September by ¾ length from Glenalema: ran moderately under stiffish weights in handicaps afterwards: suited by 1½m. *R. Jarvis.* **68**

ROAMING CLOUD 2 b.c. Galivanter 131–Nephopolis (Acropolis 132) [1976 5d 6fg 7f⁵ 7v] well-made colt: second living foal: cost 30,000 francs as a yearling (approx £3,200): dam poor French maiden: quite a moderate maiden: stays 7f: ran poorly on heavy ground on fourth outing. *G. Hunter.* **77**

ROAMING MINSTREL 3 br.g. Bing II–Gipsy Legend 87 (Border Legend 119) [1975 N.R. 1976 8s 10.2s 10s³] fourth foal: cost 1,700 gns Doncaster May Sales: dam needed at least 1½m: made some late progress when 11 lengths third of 14 to Chartered Course in minor event at Teesside in November: will be suited by 1½m+. *R. Hollinshead.* —

ROAN STAR (USA) 3 ro.c. Al Hattab–Hail a Star (Hail to Reason) [1975 5g² 5.5g* 5.5g⁴ 6d 6d⁵ 6.5g* 7d* 1976 8s² 8g² 10.5g⁴ 12g 10g] American-bred French colt: second foal: dam won over 7f in U.S.A.: showed high-class form as a 2-y-o and won Prix de la Foret at Longchamp: ¾-length second to Arctic Tern in Prix de Fontainebleau at Longchamp in April and 2½ lengths second to Red Lord in Poule d'Essai des Poulains (French 2,000 Guineas) on same course later in month: never better than final position when 6 lengths fourth of 12 to Youth in Prix Lupin, also at Longchamp, in May: subsequently well beaten in Prix du **118**

Jockey-Club and Prix Eugene Adam: best form at up to 1m: acts on soft going: has been tried in blinkers but does better without: trained until after fourth outing by R. Poincelet. *M. Zilber, France.*

ROANTOP 2 ch.f. Roan Rocket 128–Topolass 79 (Acropolis 132) [1976 5fg⁶ **71** 8s 7s] tall, lengthy filly: third foal: 3,100 gns yearling: dam won over 1¼m: finished well when 2½ lengths sixth of 12 to Elm in minor event at Lingfield in May: not seen out again until October when behind in large fields at Sandown and Newmarket (last of 20). *S. Ingham.*

ROAN VALLEY 3 ro.f. Carrara–Right of Alys 77 (Right Boy 137) [1975 N.R. — 1976 12f⁵ 15.5s] second foal: dam won over 5f at 2 yrs: well beaten in maiden races at Brighton in August and Folkestone in October. *B. Wise.*

ROAST CHESTNUT 6 ch.g. Red God 128 §–Armande 92 (High Treason 126) — [1974 7s³ 7f⁴ 8f⁴ 7fg⁶ 7f 7d³ 8g 8d⁶ 7s 1975 6g 1976 6g 7fg 10s 7g 9g 7f⁶] poor handicapper: best at 7f: acts on any going but is well suited by soft: has worn blinkers: slipped up in only race in 1975: none too genuine and probably not a suitable mount for a lady. *D. Williams.*

ROBB RIAN 4 gr.g. Right Boy 137–Superiority 88 (Djebe) [1974 5fg 5g⁶ 6d — 7g 8s⁴ 1975 10f⁵ 10f* 10.1fg* 10fg² 10.1fg* 12f 12.2g 1976 10.6d⁴] tall gelding: won three maiden races in 1975: ran very promisingly when finishing 4½ lengths fourth of 11 to Tiger Trail in handicap at Haydock in April but not seen out again: stays 1¼m but not 1½m: acts on firm going: was tried in blinkers as a 2-y-o. *J. Hardy.*

ROBETTE 3 ch.f. King Bob–Merok (Eastern Venture 107) [1975 N.R. 1976 **52** 9g² 9f 7g⁶ 8.5fg] neat filly: third foal: half-sister to useful 9f and 1¼m winner Blaskette (by Blast): plater: probably stays 9f. *N. Vigors.*

ROBIN BROOK 2 b.c. Birdbrook 110–Charity Parade 67 (March Past 124) **83** [1976 5f 5f 5d² 7f³ 6f 6g⁴] compact colt: first foal: 1,050 gns yearling: dam sister to useful miler Smartie and very useful sprinter French Parade: placed in maiden auction events at Redcar in May and Doncaster in July: put up moderate displays on last two outings, hanging badly on first and wearing blinkers on next: will stay 1m: appears to act on any going: possibly needs strong handling. *M. W. Easterby.*

ROBIN JOHN 4 gr.g. Pongee 106–Little Wren (Doudance 99) [1974 5f⁴ 5f 5f² **60** 5f* 6fg 6fg 5d⁴ 8g 7.2s 7g 5d 6g* 1975 8fg 5g 6fg 6g³ 6f 7fg² 6fg 6d 1976 8.2v⁵ 11d² 8g 8fg 10fg² 15g 8h* 9.4h³ 8f* 8fg⁴ 10f³ 8h³ 9h⁴ 8h²] smallish, lengthy gelding: plater: winner at Carlisle (apprentice event) and Edinburgh, both in July, being bought in for 480 gns on latter course: stays 11f: probably acts on any going with exception of very soft: used to wear blinkers. *T. Craig.*

ROBINSCOURT 2 ch.c. Red God 128 §–Right Royal Time (Right Royal V — 135) [1976 5f] half-brother to useful stayer Regal Step (by Ribero): 2,000 gns yearling: dam, a winner in Italy, is half-sister to very useful 1m to 1¼m filly Haymaking: 20/1 when behind in 25-runner maiden race won by Spring Dive at Thirsk in September, only outing. *Denys Smith.*

ROBIN'S SONG 2 b.c. Saintly Song 128–Casual (Solar Slipper 131) [1976 **87** 6f 7.2f² 8v²] useful-looking colt: half-brother to useful 1m winner Daisy Chain (by Darius): 500 gns yearling: dam twice-raced half-sister to top-class sprinter Abadan: second in minor events at Haydock in August and Teesside (length behind Applalto) in October: will probably stay 1¼m. *J. W. Watts.*

ROCK BRANDY 5 ch.m. Alba Rock 107–dam's name unregistered [1974 N.R. — 1975 N.R. 1976 6d 12.2s] of no account. *M. Bradley.*

ROCKEATER 2 ch.f. Roan Rocket 128–Sea Lichen 106 (Ballymoss 136) [1976 **84** 6fg 6g 6g⁶ 6d] useful-looking filly: half-sister to two winners, including fair miler Patula (by Petingo): dam fourth in 1,000 Guineas: ran easily best race when about 3 lengths sixth of 30 to Rheola in maiden race at Newmarket in September: will be suited by 1m: got stuck in stalls and took no part on second outing. *H. Wragg.*

ROCKERY 2 b.f. Track Spare 125–Rose Rock 95 (Court Harwell 130) [1976 7fg **86** 7d 8s² 8s³] compact filly: half-sister to useful stayer Sisodan (by Never Say Die): dam stayed at least 1¼m: placed in maiden events at Bath and Newmarket in October, on latter course putting up a good effort when 4¾ lengths third of 27 to Sporting Yankee: will stay 1¼m: acts on soft going. *R. Smyth.*

ROCKERY (FR) 2 gr.f. Roan Rocket 128–Header 78 (High Hat 131) [1976 5fg³ **101** 6g* 6g] lengthy filly: second foal: dam moderate half-sister to good stayer Charlton: put up a smooth performance when winning nine-runner minor event at

Kempton in August, leading about 1f out and coming home 2 lengths clear of Great Memoirs: ran very well in better company on other outings, finishing 3½ lengths third to Haraka in St Hugh's Stakes at Newbury and 7 lengths seventh of 15 to Durtal in William Hill Cheveley Park Stakes at Newmarket: will be suited by 1m+. *I. Balding.*

ROCKETANIA 3 ro.f. Roan Rocket 128–Ruritania (Pampered King 121)   **69**
[1975 5v⁵ 5s³ 5fg⁵ 5f⁵ 6g 6f 6f 6g 5g³ 5d³   1976 6fg³ 6fg² 6fg² 6g 6fg 6g⁴ 6fg 6f⁴ 7.6fg⁴ 10.1d 8.2d 8.2d⁶] useful-looking filly: placed at Leicester (maiden race), Warwick (minor event) and Windsor (handicap) in the spring: best form at 6f and does not stay 1¼m: ran moderately when tried in blinkers: sold 800 gns Ascot November Sales. *C. V. Miller.*

ROCKET FIRE 2 ro.c. Roan Rocket 128–Tudor Story 96 (Henry the Seventh   —
125) [1976 6fg] first foal: dam, half-sister to very smart Sweet Story, stayed well: tailed off in maiden race won by Truce of Oman at Salisbury in June: sold 260 gns Newmarket September Sales. *J. Nelson.*

ROCKETINA 2 gr.f. Roan Rocket 128–Victorina 121 (The Phoenix) [1976 6v]   —
sister to useful 1973 French 2-y-o Roanina, and half-sister to five winners: dam won 1962 Stewards' Cup: 8/1 when last of 16 in minor event won by Songhurst at Lingfield in November. *I. Balding.*

ROCKET LANCER 2 ch.c. Roan Rocket 128–Colony 93 (Constable 129) [1976   **75**
5g 5fg² 5g⁶ 5fg 5fg⁵ 5d] rangy colt: half-brother to two winners, including fairly useful 1969 2-y-o Louisiana (by Royal Record II): 820 gns foal, resold 1,600 gns yearling: dam won over 5f at 2 yrs: moderate maiden: ran best race when short-head second to No Conventions in minor event at Newmarket in June: put up a poor effort on final outing: should stay beyond 5f: acts on a firm surface. *A. Corbett.*

ROCKET'S PAL 2 ch.c. Vilmoray 126–Equine (Eudaemon 129) [1976 5g 5f   —
5.9g] strong, workmanlike colt: unquoted when behind in maiden races. *M. Bradley.*

ROCKET SYMPHONY 2 gr.c. Roan Rocket 128–Climbing Rose 81 (Pirate   **99 p**
King 129) [1976 6d 6d*] useful sort of colt: third foal: half-brother to two winners in Scandinavia: 5,600 gns yearling: dam won over 5f at 2 yrs: put up a splendid performance in 22-runner maiden race at Newmarket in October, making all and drawing away in impressive fashion to win by 4 lengths from Fairly Hot: should stay at least 1m: a smart colt in the making. *R. Price.*

ROCK FOLLY 2 b.f. Siliconn 121–Conita 94 (Constable 129) [1976 5f 5fg 5s 5s   —
5s] neat filly: no worthwhile form, including in a seller: blinkered final outing: sold 350 gns Ascot November Sales. *P. Makin.*

ROCKORAMA 3 gr.c. Double-U-Jay 120–Quarry (Quorum 126) [1975 6g 6g*   **88**
6f⁴ 7fg² 6v   1976 7fg 7fg⁵ 7g 10f³ 10f* 11g* 10f³ 10f⁵ 10g⁴ 11.7d⁵] lengthy colt: made all when winning handicaps at Folkestone and Ayr in the summer: stays 11f: acts on firm going: ran poorly when tried in blinkers. *M. Stoute.*

ROCK SIGNAL 10 b.g. Rockavon 120–Heliographic 100 (Coup de Lyon) [1974   **65**
7f⁶ 6g⁴ 7f* 7f² 7.2g 7fg³ 7.2s² 7g⁵ 7s 6s   1975 7f⁵ 7.2fg² 7fg 7g⁴ 7fg³ 7g⁶ 7f⁴ 7.2fg⁴ 7f* 8g³ 7fg³   1976 7fg 7f³ 7g⁵ 7f 7fg 7f 7f] poor handicapper nowadays: stays 1m but is better at shorter distances: seems to act on any going except heavy: has worn blinkers: moved short to post on sixth start. *R. D. Peacock.*

ROCKY FOX 2 ch.c. Healaugh Fox–Rocky Dart (Master Rocky 106) [1976   —
5fg 6fg] small colt: well behind in July in maiden race at Leicester and seller at Nottingham. *J. Spearing.*

RODADO 4 ch.g. Crepello 136–Rosario 80 (Nearco) [1974 8s⁴   1975 11d² 12g³   —
16s* 14d² 13.3g* 14fg 17.4d³ 16g   1976 13g⁶] strong, good sort of gelding: quite a useful handicapper in 1975: ran only once at 4 yrs: needed a good test of stamina: had a round action and probably needed some give in the ground to be seen to best advantage: very game: dead. *E. Weymes.*

RODA HAXAN 2 ch.f. Huntercombe 133–Kamiyaana (Charlottesville 135)   **67**
[1976 5f 5.1fg⁴ 5g⁶ 6g⁶ 5fg 6d 5d 5s] light-framed filly: first living produce: 1,500 gns yearling: dam unraced half-sister to Habat: only plating class: will stay 1m: started slowly on first outing and reared up and fell in stalls before third appearance. *N. Guest.*

RODERICK DHU 3 b.g. Mountain Call 125–Vhairi 115 (Narrator 127) [1975   —
6fg 6fg⁵   1976 8f⁴ 10g 9v 8s] well-made gelding: no worthwhile form: blinkered final outing: sold 1,200 gns Doncaster November Sales. *W. Elsey.*

RODMAN 2 b.c. Relko 136–Neptune's Daughter 76 (Neptunus 132) [1976 8s⁴]   **75** p
big, workmanlike colt: third foal: half-brother to fairly useful 3-y-o 1¼m winner
Primrose Bank (by Charlottown) and fair 1974 2-y-o 5f winner Madrisa (by
Bold Lad, Ire): dam won over 9f and is half-sister to very smart 1966 French
2-y-o Tiepolo II: 16/1, finished well after being very slowly into stride when 11
lengths fourth of 20 to Lady Rhapsody in maiden race at Sandown in October:
should develop into a useful stayer. *F. Maxwell.*

ROD OF GOLD 2 b.f. Gold Rod 129–Canwell 75 (Canisbay 120) [1976 5f 6f]   —
neat filly: having first race for four months when in rear in seller at Nottingham in
August. *J. Hardy.*

ROI-DES-TOITS 2 b.c. Roi Soleil 125–Raise the Roof (Raise You Ten 125)   **88** ?
[1976 5f⁵ 5f⁴ 5s⁴ 5fg⁵ 6g* 5f 6f] robust, useful-looking colt: first living foal: 2,200
gns yearling: dam won at up to 17f in Ireland: made all to win 17-runner maiden
race at Haydock in August by a neck from Nana's Queen, the pair finishing well
clear: showed nothing like that form in any of his other races and finished last of
15 in nursery at Thirsk on final appearance: bred to stay 1¼m. *E. Collingwood.*

ROI RIG 3 ch.g. Roi Soleil 125–Sovereign Comment (Sovereign Path 125) [1975   —
5d 5s⁶ 7g 10f 1976 13s] big, tall gelding: had stiff task and was well tailed off
on only outing (September): stays 1¼m. *W. Stephenson.*

ROLFE 3 b.c. Tom Rolfe–Lighted Lamp (Sir Gaylord) [1975 6s 7d 8g⁴ 1976   **77**
8f 8.2f 8h⁵ 8f⁴ 10f* 10fg³ 11.1f³ 10.1fg* 11v²] small American-bred colt: won
maiden race at Brighton in July and handicap at Windsor in September, latter by
a length from My Polyanna: went under by a head to Bright Fire in handicap at
Newbury the following month, the pair finishing clear of five others: would have
stayed 1½m: acted on any going: tried in blinkers third outing: standing at
Herridge Stud Farm, Wiltshire. *F. J. Houghton.*

ROLLESTON 2 ch.c. Communication 119–Chamolive 56 (Poaching 115) [1976   **92**
5fg⁴ 5fg⁴ 5fg 6f⁵ 7f⁴ 7f 8.2d 7s² 8s*] leggy colt: first foal: dam won over hurdles
and fences: improved steadily and won 20-runner maiden race at Warwick in
October by 2 lengths from Sovereign Ford, after making most of the running:
stays 1m well: acts on any going. *W. Marshall.*

ROLLICKING ROSIE 2 b.f. Roll of Honour 130–Colour Bar (Majority Blue 126)   —
[1976 5g⁴ 5g⁶ 7fg 5g] small filly: second foal: dam won over 5f at 2 yrs in Ireland:
no worthwhile form in Scottish maiden races: sold 600 gns Newmarket Autumn
Sales. *N. Angus.*

ROLL ME OVER 2 br.g. Hopeful Venture 125–Elaine 90 (Mossborough 126)   **73** p
[1976 7s³] good walker: half-brother to several winners, notably very useful
stayer Hornet (by Hornbeam): dam middle-distance performer: showed promise
when 7½ lengths third of five to Mandalus in minor event at Catterick in October,
soon recovering after dwelling at start and racing in touch against more
experienced animals for some way: will be suited by middle distances: should do
better. *S. Hall.*

ROLUS 7 gr.g. Romulus 129–Flag Ship 93 (Grey Sovereign 128 §) [1974 10fg   —
8g 8fg* 10fg 7fg 8g 11s 8fg 8d³ 8g⁵ 10.6v 1975 11s 8fg⁴ 8.2d⁴ 1976 10.6g]
strong gelding: inconsistent selling handicapper: stays 1¼m: unsuited by very soft
ground: has worn blinkers and bandages: slowly away and tailed off only start
in 1976. *D. Chapman.*

ROMANCE AT SEA 3 ch.f. Tobin Bronze–Live It Up II (Never Say Die 137)   **77**
[1975 N.R. 1976 8fg³ 11g⁵ 7g³ 8fg⁴ 8fg 8fg² 8fg* 8s 8g²] rangy, deep-girthed
American-bred filly: half-sister to a minor winner: cost $11,500 at Florida 2-y-o's
in Training Sales: dam never ran: won eight-runner minor event at Leicester in
August, beating Blyth's Folly a head: creditable second to Abercata in 19-runner
handicap at Lanark in October: best form at up to 1m but should stay further: ran
below her best when tried in blinkers on fifth outing and when racing on soft
ground on eighth appearance: sold 5,200 gns Newmarket Autumn Sales. *R.
Armstrong.*

ROMAN CHARGER 2 ch.c. Sallust 134–Robusta (Saint Crespin III 132) [1976   **116**
5d 6g³ 6f* 6.3f³ 7f⁴] Irish colt: half-brother to four winners, including fairly
useful sprinter Air Power (by Skymaster): 3,500 gns yearling: dam never ran:
put up a very good effort when winning 20-runner Tyros Stakes at the Curragh
in June, coming home 3 lengths clear of Laughing River with the rest at least 5
lengths further back: in frame in two good races afterwards, putting up better
effort when short-head second to Brahms in Railway Stakes at the Curragh
(veered left in final furlong and was moved down to third place by stewards):
will stay 1m+. *J. Oxx, Ireland.*

ROMAN FANTASY 3 b.g. Calpurnius 122–Manilla II 74 (Mourne 126) [1975 **87**
5g⁵ 6g 1976 6fg⁶ 8.2f² 8g* 8fg* 10.6g⁵ 9f⁴ 8f²] strong gelding: won maiden
race at Kempton and minor event at Ayr in July, on latter course beating
Referendum most decisively by a length: best form at 1m: acts on a firm surface:
gives impression he needs a man on his back. *G. Pritchard-Gordon.*

ROMAN GOD 4 ch.c. Appiani II 128–Rose of Tralee 114 (Buisson Ardent 129) —
[1974 5g⁶ 7fg⁶ 6fg 7d 6d⁴ 6g³ 7s 7v³ 7s 1975 6f 7fg 10f⁶ 10f* 12f⁴ 12.2f⁴ 13d
1976 12f⁵ 12g 14fg⁶] well-made colt: poor handicapper: stays 1½m well: acts on
firm going: has been tried in blinkers but seems better without them nowadays:
sold 680 gns Newmarket Autumn Sales. *J. Benstead.*

ROMAN WARRIOR 5 ch.h. Porto Bello 118–Colliers 85 (Skymaster 126) **126**
[1974 7d 6f² 6f* 7g 6g* 6s³ 5v⁴ 6v⁵ 1975 5f² 5fg* 6g⁴ 6g* 7.3g⁶ 5fg⁴ 6d* 6g* 6fg²
6v² 1976 6f* 6d⁴ 5g² 6fg⁴ 6fg* 5fg 6g]
Following his splendid 1975 campaign, highlighted by memorable wins in the
Canada Dry Shield, the Burmah Castrol Ayr Gold Cup, both at Ayr, and the
Diadem Stakes at Ascot (where he dead-heated with Swingtime), many tipped
Roman Warrior to be leading sprinter in 1976. And, after Roman Warrior had
beaten Honeyblest, giving him 7 lb, in the Thirsk Hall Stakes at Thirsk in April
on his seasonal reappearance, who would have said they were wrong? Less than
three weeks earlier Honeyblest had nearly won the Ladbroke Abernant Stakes at
Newmarket. However, after Thirsk Roman Warrior won only one of his six
races. Roman Warrior's second win of the season was gained in the Canada Dry
Shield at Ayr in July. Set, as usual in handicaps, to concede lumps of weight
all round, he ran on really well to defeat Gershwin and Rundontwalk by three
quarters of a length, in the process registering his third victory in the race.
Three times Roman Warrior took on Lochnager and three times he proved
unable to beat him, putting up his best effort against that horse when a close
fourth in a competitive race for the July Cup at Newmarket. Apart from his
second outing, when he ran disappointingly behind the ex-Italian colt Three Legs
in the Duke of York Stakes at York, Roman Warrior's only other race of the
season was in the Ayr Gold Cup. At Ayr, on his final appearance on a racecourse,
he started at the ridiculously short odds of 3/1. His bold backers knew their fate
two furlongs out as Roman Warrior, conceding upwards of 15 lb, began to weaken.
He finished eighth, about six lengths behind the winner Last Tango.

Roman Warrior (ch.h. 1971)	Porto Bello (ch 1965)	Floribunda (b 1958)	Princely Gift
			Astrentia
		Street Song (b 1956)	Le Lavandou
			Theme Song
	Colliers (ch 1963)	Skymaster (ch 1958)	Golden Cloud
			Discipliner
		Turkish Blend (br 1945)	Sir Walter Raleigh
			Lady Turk

Roman Warrior is the best of three winners that his dam, Colliers, has

Thirsk Hall Stakes—Roman Warrior shows his fighting qualities and beats Honeyblest

produced. Colliers, a fair performer at up to a mile and a quarter on the flat, was also successful over hurdles. Her two-year-old Warrior's Sister (by Hunter-combe) showed promise in 1976. Roman Warrior, although capable of running well at five furlongs as he showed when second to Lochnager in the Temple Stakes at Sandown on his third outing of the season, was unquestionably best at six furlongs. He was game, genuine and consistent and acted on any going. He was syndicated at £2,000 per share and is to stand at the Sturt Farm Stud, Burford, Oxfordshire at a fee of £500 or £750 with the October 1st concession. Roman Warrior, an enormous, strong, lengthy horse, was, as we said in *Race-horses of 1975*, a colossus of a horse with a heart to match. *N. Angus.*

ROMAN WAY 6 b.h. In Reality–Latin Walk (Roman Tread) [1974 6fg* 6f³ 7g² 6f² 5fg 6f⁴ 6s² 6d² 6g⁴ 6g* 6s 1975 6g 6f 6g² 6fg⁵ 6f⁵ 6f⁶ 6f 6fg 5f⁵ 8g 6g 5g 6g 6s 1976 8f⁶ 7f⁴ 7g³ 8g² 8f² 7fg⁴ 8g⁵ 8f 6f³ 6fg* 6v⁶] sturdy, short-legged American-bred horse: fair handicapper nowadays: won apprentice event at Windsor in September: stays 1m: acts on any going: sometimes wears blinkers. *R. Hannon.* **85**

ROMANY CHARTER 3 ch.c. Runnymede 123–My Gipsy Moth 81 (Aggressor 130) [1975 5g³ 5g² 6fg² 7g 7g⁵ 6fg² 5fg⁶ 8.2g² 8g³ 7.2v 1976 9.4g² 8.2g⁴ 9.4h⁴ 8h⁵ 9fg⁶] moderate performer (rated 81) at 2 yrs: runner-up in maiden race on first outing but became disappointing and ran poorly in a seller on last outing in this country: has reportedly been placed since in Belgium: stays 9f: wears blinkers: puts little heart into racing. *R. D. Peacock.* **62**

ROMANY LIGHT 2 b.g. Sky Gipsy 117–Clouded Lamp 99 (Nimbus 130) [1976 6d 7s] strong, lengthy gelding: half-brother to several winners, including very useful sprinters Irma Flintstone (by Compensation) and Canton Silk (by Runnymede): 1,100 gns foal and resold 1,400 gns yearling: dam a miler: behind in large fields at Newmarket and Chepstow in October. *Sir Mark Prescott.* **—**

ROMARGLEN 2 b.f. Varano–Forest Love (Super Sam 124) [1976 5.9f] first foal: 400 gns yearling: dam never ran: tailed-off last of 16 to Red Seed in maiden race at Wolverhampton in August, only outing. *G. Vergette.* **—**

ROMNEY CHASE 3 b.g. Breeders Dream 116–Marcida 85 (Alcide 136) [1975 7g 8fg 8f 8g 1976 12.3s 13.8d 14.7f⁴ 15f* 16fg³ 14.7f⁴] dipped-backed gelding: won maiden race at Edinburgh in July by ½ length from Tinkletoes: slow and is suited by long distances and strong handling: wears blinkers nowadays: sold to R. Lamb 2,200 gns Doncaster September Sales. *J. Etherington.* **59**

RONDA BOY 3 ch.g. Green God 128–Vron 91 (Anwar 120) [1975 5f³ 6g 5f⁵ 5g 5f 8fg 8f² 1976 8fg 10.8f⁵ 10fg 7g⁵ 7f 8g 8f³ 10fg⁵ 8fg⁵ 8.2d⁵] strong gelding: quite a moderate maiden: stays 1m: acts on firm going: has been tried in blinkers: occasionally sweats up: often wears a bandage on off-hind. *B. Lunness.* **69**

RONDO CAPRICCIOSO 2 b.c. Set to Music 106–Killybegf 49 (Falls of Clyde 126) [1976 6f 6h⁶] workmanlike colt: fourth reported foal: dam of little account: always well behind in maiden races at Catterick and Carlisle in August. *S. Norton.* **—**

RONDO'S BOY 8 ch.g. Continuation 120–Rondone (Fighting Don) [1974 7s 8g 8g* 8fg 8g 8g* 7f³ 8fg* 8d² 8s 8g⁵ 7fg 10.2g 1975 6s⁶ 7v⁶ 8.2d 7f 10h² 8h⁴ 8h³ 8g² 11d⁶ 12.2f 12h⁵ 8g 10.2g² 1976 12g 10f 10f 8f⁴ 8fg⁵ 8fg 10.6g³ 10f] selling handicapper: poor mover: probably doesn't stay further than 1¼m: acts on any going except really soft: has worn blinkers: suitable mount for an apprentice: dwelt start sixth outing. *W. Murray.* **45**

RONKSLEY 2 ch.c. Daring Display 129–Running Cedar (Bryan G) [1976 5fg 6fg 6fg 6f⁴ 7f⁴ 6f 8f 7fg³ 8s] plater: just over 7 lengths third to runaway winner Supreme Penny in 26-runner event at Redcar in September, best effort: stays 7f: sometimes wears blinkers but does just as well without: sold to S. Holland for 700 gns Doncaster October Sales. *R. D. Peacock.* **62**

RON'S LASS 5 ch.m. Ron 103–Cheering Crowds 75 (Entente Cordiale 119) [1974 8g 6g⁴ 7h 7g⁶ 8fg 8d⁵ 8v⁵ 1975 6fg 7f² 9f³ 8.3fg 12.2fg 1976 8.2fg] tall mare: poor plater: probably stays 9f but is not certain to stay 1½m: acts on any going but goes particularly well on firm: has worn bandages. *M. Bradley.* **—**

RONSON AVENUE 7 ch.g. Ron 103–Rosemary Road (The Dane or Fair Map) [1974 12.2fg³ 18fg³ 16d⁴ 16s 18d 1975 16d* 17.7fg 17.1f 16.9f⁴ 16fg⁴ 1976 16fg⁵ 16f⁶] poor handicapper: needs further than 1½m and stays very well: seems to act on any going. *M. Tate.* **51**

ROOM SERVICE 2 b.c. Silly Season 127–Tabulator (Never Say Die 137) [1976 6g 6f] brother to High Season, a useful winner at up to 1½m, and half-brother to another winner: 1,750 gns yearling: dam won over 1m and 1¼m in France: behind in maiden races at Newmarket in July and August: should be suited by 1¼m+. *G. Harwood.*

RORY'S ROCKET 3 gr.f. Roan Rocket 128–Cantadora 107 (Matador 131) **110** [1975 5v³ 5d 5f* 6fg³ 5f* 6g² 5f⁴ 5fg⁶ 1976 8fg 6fg* 5fg 5fg]   fair sort: sister to 1¼m winner Apologetic: dam a sprinter: won Queen Mary Stakes at Royal Ascot in 1975 in impressive fashion by 4 lengths from Enchanted when trained by P. Ashworth: ran best subsequent race when winning handicap at York in July under top weight by a length from Gold Cheb: had stiff tasks afterwards: unlikely to stay beyond 6f: well suited by a sound surface. *J. Dunlop.*

ROSALINA 4 b.f. Porto Bello 118–Saucy Talina (Hard Sauce 131) [1974 5v **64** 1975 9s 8.2g 8f⁵ 8h 8f 7fg⁵ 8g* 7f* 8f⁴ 8f 7g 1976 7fg 8f 7fg³ 7f 8h² 8g 8g⁵ 8.2s] big filly: placed in apprentice handicaps at Yarmouth in June and Redcar in August: stays 1m well: acts on hard going. *V. Mitchell.*

ROSCOMMON 3 ch.g. Connaught 130–Photo Flash 119 (Match III 135) [1975 — 7g³ 1976 8g⁵]   big, rangy gelding: 5 lengths third of four to Rhodie Blake in £1,000 event at Newmarket in July, 1975, only outing at 2 yrs: second favourite, outpaced in first half of race but was running on well in closing stages, giving impression he would be suited by middle distances, when 12 lengths fifth of 15 to Arapaho in maiden race at Sandown in April: not seen out again and was sold to H. T. Jones 3,100 gns Newmarket September Sales. *N. Murless.*

ROSEANNE 3 b.f. St. Paddy 133–Rosie Wings 102 (Telegram II 120) [1975 **68** 8v 1976 10f³ 12g⁴ 12d² 13s² 13fg³ 12f* 12fg³ 16v]   half-sister to several winners, including Derby third Mount Athos (by Sunny Way) and smart sprinter John Splendid (by Sing Sing): dam a stayer: landed odds by 7 lengths in bad maiden contest at Lanark in July: stays 13f (tailed off over 2m): acts on any going except perhaps heavy: one paced. *S. Hall.*

ROSE BOWL 4 b.f. Habitat 134–Roseliere 127 (Misti IV 132) [1974 6s² 5d* **131** 6s³ 5v⁵ 1975 7v* 8g⁴ 8f² 8d² 8s* 10fg* 1976 10.5g⁴ 10f* 10f³ 8d* 10d² 12s⁵] Rose Bowl's record is a very fine one, especially for a filly. As a three-year-old her record at a mile all but measured up to that of Europe's leading specialist miler, the Two Thousand Guineas winner Bolkonski, and in 1976 only Wollow had better form at a mile than Rose Bowl. And in both seasons Rose Bowl demonstrated that she had few superiors at a mile and a quarter. Rose Bowl is that rare bird, a filly capable of beating the best of the opposite sex at the regulation 3 lb allowance. There have been a larger number than usual of such fillies in Europe in recent seasons, but history shows clearly that very few top fillies are good enough to hold their own against the best colts. And for a filly to do well in the top races as a four- or five-year-old is even more rare; of the high-class fillies that stay in training after the age of three not many match or better their earlier achievements. Probably the most famous examples of those that have done so in the past decade are Park Top, Allez France, Dahlia, Lianga, Comtesse de Loir and, in the most recent season, Ivanjica and Rose Bowl.

Rose Bowl came back to the course almost as good as ever she left it at three. She ended a magnificent season as a three-year-old on a very high note, winning the Queen Elizabeth II Stakes over a mile and the Champion Stakes over a mile and a quarter. These victories made up for her most unfortunate defeat in the One Thousand Guineas and her narrow failure against Bolkonski in the Sussex Stakes. With Bolkonski and most of the other top milers retired to stud, Rose Bowl had only the new generation of three-year-olds to worry about in the best all-aged mile races in 1976. Unfortunately, it was late-September before Rose Bowl ran in a race over a mile. She was off the course throughout the summer, a casualty of the firm ground at Royal Ascot where she jarred herself when running way below her best in the Prince of Wales Stakes over a mile and a quarter. Rose Bowl's earlier races, the Prix Ganay at Longchamp and the newly-instituted Clive Graham Stakes for four-year-olds at Goodwood, had also been over a similar distance. We did not see the Prix Ganay in which Rose Bowl was a close fourth, beaten less than a length by the winner Infra Green. At Goodwood a fortnight later Rose Bowl won most impressively. She disposed of Red Regent and Anne's Pretender by four lengths and five with three lesser lights in their parish. The Clive Graham Stakes may build into a useful pattern race in years to come as it provides a much-needed opportunity for the high-class mile-and-a-quarter horse in May.

After an absence of more than three months Rose Bowl reappeared in the Queen Elizabeth II Stakes at Ascot, where she was due to clash with the three-

Queen Elizabeth II Stakes, Ascot—Rose Bowl wins the race even more impressively than in 1975. Ricco Boy and Dominion fill the places

year-old Wollow. Wollow had established himself as England's best miler during the summer, adding the Sussex Stakes to his triumph in the Two Thousand Guineas. When Wollow was withdrawn from the Queen Elizabeth II Stakes after overnight rain had softened the going, the race seemed at the mercy of Rose Bowl—always provided she was at her best after her lengthy lay-off. She returned to the track in a blaze of glory, running right away from a good-class field which included the three-year-olds Thieving Demon and Patris, third and fourth in the Two Thousand Guineas, and Poacher's Moon, third in the Sussex Stakes. Rose Bowl shot to the front two furlongs out after turning for home on the outside of the two leaders, the four-year-old Dominion and Patris. The French three-year-old Ricco Boy fought his way past Dominion and Patris in the straight but was never a threat to Rose Bowl who went by the post with Carson patting her neck and easing her to a canter. The winning distance was four lengths; there was another three lengths to Dominion and a further five to the fourth-placed dead-heaters Patris and Thieving Demon. On her only sub-sequent outing in England Rose Bowl made a valiant attempt to win the Champion Stakes at Newmarket for the second year in succession. She looked all over a winner after going ahead on the favoured far side in the last quarter of a mile but the outsider Vitiges came along to catch her well inside the last furlong and beat her by a neck.

Rose Bowl (b.f. 1972)	Habitat (b 1966)	Sir Gaylord (b 1959)	Turn-to / Somethingroyal
		Little Hut (b 1952)	Occupy / Savage Beauty
	Roseliere (br 1965)	Misti IV (br 1958)	Medium / Mist
		Peace Rose (gr 1959)	Fastnet Rock / La Paix

On her way to visit the top stallion Vaguely Noble in Kentucky, Rose Bowl stopped off at Laurel to run in the Washington International. It was the only race she ran at a mile and a half and she failed to reproduce her best form; Carson reported that she didn't stay. Rose Bowl should be a goldmine at stud. Her racing record is outstanding and her pedigree is first-class—she is by the champion miler and top sire Habitat out of Roseliere who was the best middle-distance filly of her generation in France. Roseliere, who won the Prix de Diane and the Prix Vermeille, comes from a very stout family. Roseliere's brother Pamir was an out-and-out stayer and another brother Les Roseaux won the French Champion Hurdle in 1976. Peace Rose, their dam, is also responsible for another long-distance performer, the Queen Alexandra Stakes winner Peacock.

628

Rose Bowl, a strong, robust, attractive filly, had a good turn of foot and acted on any going. She was a genuine and consistent filly and one of the best of her sex at a mile and a mile and a quarter seen in Europe in the post-war years. *F. J. Houghton.*

ROSEHETTA 2 b.f. Hul a Hul 124–Merry Coin (Current Coin 118) [1976 — 5fg 7g 5g] plain filly: first foal: 220 gns yearling: dam won over 6f in Ireland at 3 yrs: well behind in maiden races: slowly away third outing. *P. Bevan.*

ROSE LEE 2 b.f. Sky Gipsy 117–Freda Rose 103 (Sheshoon 132) [1976 7f] sister to a moderate animal, and half-sister to two winners, including fair middle-distance filly Great Freda (by Great Nephew): cost 800 gns Ascot January 1976 Sales: dam won over 7f and 1m at 2 yrs: eleventh of 13 to Bona-Mia in minor event at Salisbury in August, only outing. *P. Mitchell.*

ROSELLIO 2 gr.c. Roan Rocket 128–Maruka 70 (Abernant 142) [1976 5.9g³ 78 5s⁵] first foal: dam won over 5f at 2 yrs: ran better race on first outing when 3 lengths third to Gusty's Gift in maiden race at Wolverhampton in August: suited by 6f and may stay further. *Sir Mark Prescott.*

ROSE MELODY 2 b.f. Tudor Melody 129 Rambling Rose 118 (Silly Season 94 127) [1976 5.1fg⁶ 7fg² 7h* 7f* 7f 8g] quite attractive filly: first foal: dam smart sprinter and half-sister to good-class French performer Rose Laurel: odds-on winner of minor event at Beverley in July, beating Christine Jane 1½ lengths, and improved on that effort when winning five-runner £1,700 event at Redcar later in month by ¾ length from odds-on Big Treat: in rear in nurseries on last two outings: suited by 7f but is not certain to stay 1m: sold 15,000 gns Newmarket December Sales. *H. T. Jones.*

ROSE OF BAYDON 2 gr.f. Lord David 121–Paulownia (Palestine 133) [1976 62 5g² 5fg⁵ 5f* 5fg⁵ 6d 8f] small, light-framed filly: half-sister to fairly useful 1975 2-y-o Steel King (by King's Company): won seller at Chepstow in April by a neck from Miss Diane (no bid): well behind in better company the following month and was not seen out again until September when in rear in nurseries. *Mrs R. Lomax.*

ROSE OF FRANCE 8 b.m. Grand Roi 118–Treasure Flower 67 (Donore 119) 35 [1974 N.R. 1975 N.R. 1976 13g 12g 10f⁴ 8fg⁶ 8g 10f 12h⁴] of little account nowadays. *D. Jermy.*

ROSE PETITE 4 br.f. Negotiation–Tiny Rose 73 (Palestine 133) [1974 7g 37 6fg 8.2g* 8s 8g 1975 8v⁶ 10d³ 8g 10s 10fg³ 10h 12g⁶ 8f* 8.2h² 8h³ 8f³ 8g⁵ 9g⁴ 1976 8g 10fg 10f 8.2fg⁴ 8f³ 10h* 10d 10v] neat filly: poor mover: plater: bought in 600 gns after winning at Pontefract in September by 2 lengths from Tidal Dance: stays 1½m: acts on firm going: ran below form when tried in blinkers: trained by K. Whitehead until after seventh outing. *J. Mulhall.*

ROSES FOR THE STAR 3 ch.f. Stage Door Johnny–Libra 97 (Hyperion) 114 [1975 7fg* 1976 7fg 10g³ 12g² 12f² 12fg³ 12fg³ 14f² 14.6g² 12s² 14s* 12v²] It's not difficult to imagine the feeling of relief that prompted Roses for the Star's trainer to remark 'Thank God for that!' after his filly had gained her solitary success as a three-year-old when she beat Grey Baron, who was giving her lumps of weight, by three lengths in a minor race at Sandown in October. It had, after all, looked as though Roses for the Star, winner of the Houghton Stakes on her only outing as a two-year-old, might well go through her entire second season without a win. She had been placed in eight of her nine previous races, including the Oaks, the Ribblesdale Stakes, the Yorkshire Oaks and the Park Hill Stakes, but in her last race before Sandown she had been tried in blinkers and had looked to have had enough for the season when beaten two and a half lengths by Jolly Good, from whom she was receiving a stone more than weight-for-age-and-sex. Roses for the Star's victory at Sandown, where she again wore blinkers, didn't please everyone—she had to struggle—but three days later in the St Simon Stakes at Newbury she put up a performance in very trying conditions which gave her detractors little to crab. Once more wearing blinkers, she took up the running fully seven furlongs from home and held the advantage until headed by Mart Lane halfway up the straight. Mart Lane drew clear and beat her eight lengths but she accounted for her other ten rivals easily, having four lengths to spare over third-placed Illustrious Prince. The remainder included Jolly Good.

Roses for the Star's main problem was her lack of finishing speed. The first opportunity she had of racing over a suitable distance was in the Oaks, in which she started a 33/1-shot. Benefiting greatly from the strong pace, she chased Pawneese hard from a long way out and although she never threatened the winner she was a clear second-best at the line, four lengths ahead of African Dancer with Laughing Girl and Centrocon a little further back in fourth and fifth places. The first four home after Pawneese at Epsom joined battle again in the Park Hill Stakes at Doncaster in the autumn. This time Roses for the Star was no rank outsider—she started 9/4 favourite in spite of the fact that African Dancer had beaten her in the Yorkshire Oaks the previous month. On that occasion they had filled the places behind Sarah Siddons but Roses for the Star had had a bad run and in most people's opinion, including our own, was an unlucky loser. In the Park Hill though, African Dancer and Roses for the Star reproduced their Yorkshire Oaks running almost to the pound and Roses for the Star, who this time had every chance, finished second, two lengths ahead of third-placed Centrocon who reversed the Oaks form with Laughing Girl. In between Epsom and Doncaster Roses for the Star put up one other particularly good performance, when runner-up to Marquis de Sade in a St Leger trial, the March Stakes at Goodwood in August, but was well below her best when soundly beaten by Catalpa in the Ribblesdale Stakes at Royal Ascot and by Smuggler and Major Green in the Princess of Wales's Stakes at the Newmarket July meeting.

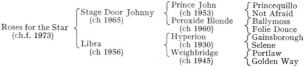

	Stage Door Johnny (ch 1965)	Prince John (ch 1953)	Princequillo Not Afraid
Roses for the Star (ch.f. 1973)		Peroxide Blonde (ch 1960)	Ballymoss Folie Douce
	Libra (ch 1956)	Hyperion (ch 1930)	Gainsborough Selene
		Weighbridge (ch 1945)	Portlaw Golden Way

Roses for the Star is by Stage Door Johnny, sire of the autumn-double winners Intermission and John Cherry, out of the Hyperion mare Libra. Libra is a winning half-sister to the high-class two-year-olds of the 'fifties Gloria Nicky (by Alycidon) and Edmundo (by Owen Tudor). As a broodmare Libra has a magnificent record. To Ribot she has produced Ribocco and Ribero, both of them Irish Sweeps Derby and St Leger winners, and Libra's Rib, and in 1976 she had a promising two-year-old by Droll Role called Ad Lib Ra representing her. Ad Lib Ra won a good-class maiden race over a mile and doubtless in 1977 he will improve a good deal when given the opportunity of racing over a mile and a half or more. Roses for the Star has been retired. A rangy filly, she was well suited by a thorough test of stamina and acted on any going. She must be worth a fortune as a broodmare. *F. J. Houghton.*

ROSE TRACK 4 b.c. Track Spare 125–Camp Follower 90 (Darius 129) [1974 **69** 5g 5f 1975 5d2 7.6g 6f4 6f5 5.8f6 6f6 6f3 6fg 6g* 6f* 7g2 5g 6d3 1976 7fg4 7f6 8f* 8fg5 7.6s3] modest handicapper: successful at Pontefract in June by ½ length from Hard Held: stays 1m: seems to act on any going: wore blinkers at 2 yrs. *L. Cumani.*

ROSETTE BLEU 3 b.c. Roll of Honour 130–Colour Bar (Majority Blue 126) **57** [1975 8g 8v 1976 12d2 16d 12d] poor maiden: stays 1½m but possibly not 2m: sold 280 gns Ascot September Sales. *W. Wharton.*

ROSEY'S RAGUSA 2 b.f. Ragusa 137–January 68 (Aggressor 130) [1976 — 5d 7.2f 6fg] half-sister to 1975 2-y-o 5f winner Gala Season (by Gala Performance): bought privately 2,500 gns yearling: dam, a plater, won at up to 1m: well behind in maiden and minor events. *R. Ward.*

ROSSELLA BELLA 3 br.f. Balidar 133–Sunbreak (Golden Cloud) [1975 5fg **60** 5g 5d 1976 6g 6f 8g 8.3f6 6f3 6fg2 7fg2 7f2 6fg2 7d4 6v2 6s4 6d] plater: has been fired: runner-up at Newmarket (twice), Leicester, Windsor and Haydock: seems to stay 1m: acts on any going: blinkered eleventh and twelfth outings, running well on first occasion but moderately on second: has raced with her tongue tied down. *G. Hunter.*

ROSSIAN 2 br.f. Silent Spring 102–Sherbet (Zarathustra 131) [1976 6f 7g] — fourth produce: half-sister to Talk of the Town (by Town Crier), a useful performer at up to 1m: dam won over 1m in Ireland: behind in large fields of maidens at Newmarket in August and Yarmouth in September. *N. Guest.*

ROSTOV 2 b.c. Charlottown 127–Plotina 114 (Hugh Lupus 132) [1976 7f² **95**
7g² 8g² 8g²] well-grown, rather leggy colt: half-brother to quite useful stayer
Rapid Pass (by Ribero) and to useful 7f and 1m handicapper Panama Canal
(by Crocket): 900 gns yearling: dam won at up to 1½m: second on all four
outings: went down by a length to Royal Plume in Sancton Stakes at York
in September on third appearance and by 2½ lengths to Jam in maiden race
at Ayr later in month (would have been a fair bit closer to Jam had his rider
kicked on when leading on bridle 3f out): will stay at least 1½m. *J. W. Watts.*

ROSY HAZE 3 b.f. Laser Light 118–Autumn Flush 57 (Rustam 127) [1975 **56**
N.R. 1976 8fg 8g² 10g⁵] light-framed filly: first foal: bought privately as
a yearling for 600 gns: dam won over 1½m: 5 lengths second to Galadriel in
four-runner seller at Wolverhampton in August: seems better suited by 1m
than 1¼m. *P. Robinson.*

ROSY JINKS 5 b.m. Rosyth 94–Sally Jinks (Tudor Jinks 121) [1974 N.R. —
1975 N.R. 1976 12g] probably of no account. *D. Plant.*

ROTA 2 ch.f. Reliance II 137–Lucy Jane (Palestine 133) [1976 6v] lightly- —
built filly: half-sister to useful jumper Vaguely Attractive (by Attractive): dam
ran only once: missed break when always behind in 23-runner maiden race
won by Amity at Newbury in October. *W. Wightman.*

ROUGE ETOILE 3 b.f. Star Moss 122–Vigia 100 (Tornado) [1975 6f 5g 7s⁴ **66**
1976 8g 9f⁵ 8fg³ 8g⁶] useful-looking filly: will be suited by a test of stamina:
acts on any going. *V. Cross.*

ROUGE SANG 4 b.c. Bold Bidder–Red Damask (Jet Action) [1974 N.R. **116**
1975 10g* 12g* 1976 12g* 12g⁶ 12f² 12g³ 12g* 12s 12g³ 12s⁶] well-made,
attractive American-bred colt: half-brother to a smart stakes winner: dam
winning half-sister to good stallion Speak John: beat Art Style ½ length when
winning Gran Premio di Milano at San Siro in June: had previously been successful at Maisons-Laffitte and also finished second to Quiet Fling in John Porter
Stakes and third to Tip Moss in Grand Prix d'Evry: never in race when well
beaten in valuable Grosser Preis von Nordrhein-Westfalen at Dusseldorf won by
Windwurf on sixth outing (reportedly completely unsuited by the ground):
subsequently sold out of A. Penna's stable, raced in America and dead-heated for
fourth place behind Effervescing in Group 1 Man o' War Stakes at Belmont Park
in October on first outing for new stable (subsequently moved up to third):
stays 1½m: acts on firm going. *M. Zilber, France.*

ROUGH RIVER 3 b.c. Forlorn River 124–Stormy Love 77 (Elopement 125) **78**
[1975 5s 7f³ 8fg 8g 1976 12g 10.5fg 12fg² 14.7f² 12h* 14fg⁴ 14g⁶ 12fg²] leggy
colt: wide-margin winner of five-runner maiden race at Pontefract in August:
probably stays 1¾m: acts on hard ground: wears blinkers: seems best when
allowed to make running. *Hbt Jones.*

ROUGH SHOOT 2 b.f. King's Troop 118–Daydreamer 78 (Star Gazer 123) **72**
[1976 5.1f 5f 5s 5s⁵] third foal: sister to moderate 3-y-o Fire Plan and half-
sister to a winner in Belgium: dam won 1m seller: showed first worthwhile
form when just over 3½ lengths fifth of 18 to Brave Prince in maiden race at
Warwick in October: will stay 1m: sold 440 gns Newmarket Autumn Sales.
J. Winter.

ROUNCEVAL 2 ch.f. Ridan–Poplin 122 (Vilmorin) [1976 7s] half-sister —
to two winners here and abroad, including Fleece (by Palestine), a very useful
performer at up to 7f: 3,000 gns yearling: dam one of fastest 2-y-o's of her year:
7/1 when seventh of 10 to What-A-Secret in maiden race at Edinburgh in
October, only outing. *J. Fitzgerald.*

ROUND SIXTY THREE 3 ro.g. Fleece 114–Cloudari (Pindari 124) [1975 5d —
5s 5f 7g 5g⁶ 6g 7g 7fg⁶ 8v² 1976 8h 9g 11s 12.2g 10s⁵] workmanlike gelding:
rated 87 at 2 yrs but showed no worthwhile form in 1976: was off course a long
time after penultimate outing: suited by heavy ground at 2 yrs: has worn blinkers.
H. Blackshaw.

ROUNDTOWN 3 gr.g. Connaught 130–Fairy Ring 91 (Quorum 126) [1975 **73**
7fg⁶ 7d 1976 11f 13.4s⁶ 16fg⁶ 12.3f³] strong, lengthy gelding: half-brother to
very smart 2-y-o Fair Season (by Silly Season) but is only quite moderate
himself: should stay 1½m+ but appeared to find 2m beyond him on third outing.
I. Balding.

*Nassau Stakes, Goodwood—Lester Piggott is at his most brilliant on Roussalka who hits the front near the post. Sauceboat (**dark sleeves**) is again second, followed by Silken Way and Spiranthes (right)*

ROUSSALKA 4 b.f. Habitat 134–Oh So Fair (Graustark) [1974 5.1f* 5f² **123** 6fg* 6fg* 6g* 6s⁴ 1975 7v 10.5s 8f* 8g² 10f* 8d³ 10.2g² 10g 1976 8.5g⁵ 8fg⁴ 10fg*]

Ground conditions were ideal for Roussalka for the greater part of the season but we saw very little of her; she ran only three times. Nevertheless, we saw enough of her to be able to say that she was just about as good as ever, which is to say she was for the third year running one of the leading fillies in the country. On her final outing she won the Nassau Stakes at Goodwood from Sauceboat for the second time. Roussalka needed two races to put her right; in the second of those races, the Child Stakes at Newmarket, she finished a promising fourth to Duboff. Although Roussalka as a four-year-old was just about as good as ever, she found Sauceboat much harder to beat in the 1976 Nassau Stakes than she did in the race the previous season. In 1975 Piggott on Roussalka had been able to indulge in a cat and mouse game in the straight, and after he had pounced well inside the last furlong Roussalka had gone on to win hard-held by a length. In 1976 it took Piggott at his brilliant best to get Roussalka home by half a length. After losing a good place coming down the hill into the straight Roussalka came to the three-furlong pole looking beaten, with at least six horses in front of her, and two furlongs later her chance of success looked far from bright although she had managed to move closer to the leaders. By this time Sauceboat had hit the front with the race apparently at her mercy. But Piggott had other ideas. Switching his whip to his left hand he gave Roussalka several hefty cracks, rode her right out for the line and the filly very gamely found just enough to take her into the lead near the finish. Sauceboat was receiving 3 lb.

Roussalka (b.f. 1972)	Habitat (b 1966)	Sir Gaylord (b 1959)	Turn-to
			Somethingroyal
		Little Hut (b 1952)	Occupy
			Savage Beauty
	Oh So Fair (b 1967)	Graustark (ch 1963)	Ribot
			Flower Bowl
		Chandelle (b 1959)	Swaps
			Malindi

A strong, robust filly by Habitat, Roussalka has such a high stud value that it was a surprise to find her in training as a four-year-old. However, the Nassau Stakes was worth over £13,000 to the winner, more than double its worth two years earlier, so to argue that her owner did the wrong thing with her would be very difficult. She has now been retired. Roussalka's dam is a granddaughter of a sister to a famous stallion and a daughter of a half-sister to another, for Malindi is a full sister to Nasrullah and Chandelle is a half-sister to Prince Taj. The dam, Oh So Fair, was prominently represented by two other foals during 1976, Roussalka's half-sister My Fair Niece (by Great Nephew) and her half-brother Etienne Gerard (by Brigadier Gerard). Roussalka was equally effective at a mile and a mile and a quarter. She was extremely well suited by top-of-the-ground conditions. *H. Cecil.*

ROUSSILLON 4 br.c. Porto Bello 118–Baltic Exchange 97 (Vilmorin) [1974 — 5g⁶ 6fg 6g 8d 1975 8.2g 7.6g 1976 12f⁶ 12f⁶] poor maiden: has run respectably over 1m: finished lame on second outing at 4 yrs. *M. Bradley.*

ROUT 3 b.f. Irish Ball 127–Fair Nicolle 106 (Niccolo Dell'Arca) [1975 N.R. **86** 1976 8fg* 10g²] light-framed filly: half-sister to several winners here and abroad, including high-class French 1m to 1½m performer Montevideo II (by Honeyway): dam useful miler: 8/1, put up an excellent first effort when winning 15-runner maiden race at Salisbury in June, finishing very strongly to lead close home and beat Regal Romance by a head: ran a similar sort of race when failing by ½ length to catch Nepotist in handicap at Sandown the following month (possibly unlucky and would have won in a few more strides): will stay 1½m. *B. Hills.*

ROWANA FAIR 2 b.f. Jukebox 120–Carnmore (Breakspear II) [1976 5f 5fg⁴ **57** 5fg⁵ 5fg 5f*] short-backed filly: won bad seller at Folkestone in June and was bought in for 420 gns. *R. Hannon.*

ROWANTREE 3 b.f. Silly Season 127–Calvine 94 (Prince Chevalier) [1975 6g **103** 6fg* 6d³ 1976 7.3f* 8fg 8f 10fg 10f* 8g⁴] lengthy, deep-bodied filly: sister to high-class 7f and 1m performer Martinmas: dam stayed 1½m: 20/1, won Fred Darling Stakes at Newbury in April by ½ length from Solar, leading well inside final furlong: far from impressive when winning five-runner minor event at Salisbury in August from vastly inferior animals: well beaten in high-class fillies races on other starts, including 1,000 Guineas (finished last): stays 1¼m: appears to act on any going. *I. Balding.*

ROWE RESIDENCE 3 b.c. Royal Palace 131–Lucyrowe 125 (Crepello 136) **99** [1975 7g 10f⁴ 1976 11g* 11fg³ 13.3g³ 14fg² 14g² 15g²] strong, really good sort of colt: good mover: made virtually all when winning maiden race at Newbury in May by 2½ lengths from Du Maurier: ran creditably in handicaps on next four outings, including when finishing third to Lamb's Tale in Morland Brewery Handicap at Newbury and when second to Iona in Melrose Handicap at York, but was a most disappointing favourite when beaten 1½ lengths by Persevering in minor race at Ayr in September on final outing: lacks pace and will be well suited by 2m+: shows a good deal of knee action and may do better with more give in the ground: sold to I. Wardle 4,600 gns Newmarket December Sales. *P. Walwyn.*

ROXBURGH BELLE 2 gr.f. Meldrum 112–Nottingham Belle 78 (Chanteur II **79** 135) [1976 7f*] half-sister to four winners here and abroad, including useful 6f or 7f handicapper Janabelle (by Gentle Art): dam a miler: put up a good effort for a newcomer when winning nine-runner minor event at Edinburgh in July, running on to beat Star Role ½ length with rest well strung out behind: not seen out again: will stay 1m. *E. Weymes.*

Fred Darling Stakes, Newbury—a hard-fought contest ends with Rowantree the winner from Solar, Manilata (left) and the grey Pasty

Col J. Berry's "Rowantree"

ROXMEAD 2 gr.c. Runnymede 123–Roxanne (Sheshoon 132) [1976 5fg 5.3fg] —
first foal: dam well behind in maiden races: behind in maiden races at Windsor and
Brighton in June. *D. Kent.*

ROXWELL 2 gr.c. Roan Rocket 128–Thereby 99 (Star Moss 122) [1976 7fg **90**
7.2f2 7d6] big, rangy colt: half-brother to two winners, including very useful
sprinter Captive Dream (by Sing Sing): 5,000 gns yearling: dam won at up to 1m:
neck second to Bowerbird in 13-runner minor event at Haydock in August: 6
lengths sixth of 16 to The Czar in similar race at Yarmouth in September: will
stay 1m: can win a maiden race. *N. Callaghan.*

ROYAL ANDRIAN 2 br.g. Mummy's Pet 125–Vacation 102 (Remainder 106) —
[1976 5g 5.9g 5g] light-framed gelding: first foal: dam won twice over 5f at 2
yrs: in rear in small races. *E. Cousins.*

ROYAL ARTIST 2 b.f. Manacle 123–Royal Academy 99 (Golden Cloud) [1976 **55**
5f 6fg 6g 5fg 7fg] half-sister to four winners, including 3-y-o Jackoleon (by
Major Portion): 1,500 gns yearling: dam a sprinter: little worthwhile form in varied
company, including selling. *M. W. Easterby.*

ROYAL AUDITION 2 b.c. Comedy Star 121–Consideration (Primera 131) **79**
[1976 5f 6fg 6f 5g 8fg3 7g3 8.2v 7v*] compact colt: improved in autumn and,
after being placed in sellers, won an 18-runner nursery at Leicester in November
under a light weight: stays 1m, and may get further: seems to act on any going:
blinkered sixth and seventh outings: suitable mount for a boy. *C. Dingwall.*

ROYAL BALLY 4 b.f. Bally Russe 113–Little But Royal 76 (King's Troop 118) **61**
[1974 5f 6f 7g6 7f2 7g4 8d4 8s6 8s5 7.2v 8g5   1975 7v6 10.4g6 10.6g* 12fg5   1976
13g 10.6d5 12.2f3 12.3s 10g6 8d3 10f 12.5v 12.5s] poor handicapper nowadays:
tailed off when pulled up at Chester on fourth outing: stays 1½m: acts on firm
going: blinkered sixth and seventh outings. *D. Plant.*

ROYAL BANNER 3 ch.g. Royal Gunner–Pronuba (Sica Boy 132) [1975 6g 6g **64**
1976 12.3s 12f6 8g3 12g* 13f6 12f5 12f4 13.8g2] plater: attracted no bid after
winning 16-runner event at Thirsk in May all out by 3 lengths from Bariole:
probably stays 1¾m: wears blinkers. *Hbt Jones.*

634

ROYAL BLAST 3 b.f. Royal Palm 131–Balandra Star 92 (Blast 125) [1975   —
N.R.   1976 7f 7fg 6g 10.1fg 10f⁴ 10.1d 10s]   small, fair sort of filly: poor maiden.
H. O'Neill.

ROYAL BLUE 3 b.c. Straight King 98–Blue Parrot 71 (Pando 118) [1975 8g   —
8v 1976 6v⁴ 6g 7d⁵ 5f 6h 8f⁴] of no account. *T. Walker.*

ROYAL BOFF 3 gr.f. King's Company 124–Tiffany Case 72 (Never Say Die 137)   **62**
[1975 6fg 6g 5g³ 6g* 1976 7f⁵ 8fg⁵ 7g 10fg⁴ 6g⁵ 6d] slightly hollow-backed
filly: very good mover: not disgraced in early-season handicaps: off course four
months afterwards, putting up better effort on her return when fifth of 17 to
Touch of Silver in well-contested seller at Ayr in September: best form at up to
1m: had stiff task when tried in blinkers on final outing. *P. Cole.*

ROYAL BOXER 2 b.c. Royal Palace 131–Pugnacity 117 (Pampered King 121) **101 p**
[1976 8s* 7.3v⁶] very good-looking colt: fifth foal: half-brother to four winners,
including Derby runner-up Relkino (by Relko) and useful 7f and 1m performer
Hard Fighter (by Habitat): 26,000 gns yearling: dam smart from 5f to 1¼m: 20/1,
made most of running on stands side, and was clear coming to final furlong, when
winning 28-runner maiden race at Newmarket in October by 3 lengths from
Honegger without apparently being asked for any effort by his jockey: favourite
for nine-runner Horris Hill Stakes at Newbury a week later but was hard ridden
early in straight and could finish only sixth to Fair Season, beaten about 20
lengths: will stay at least 1¼m: certainly much better than his Newbury running
would suggest and may be unsuited by really soft ground. *P. Walwyn.*

ROYAL BOY 3 ch.c. Realm 129–Nana's Girl 109 (Tin Whistle 128) [1975 **123**
5g* 5d* 5f² 6g² 5g* 6g* 6g⁵ 1976 7f⁵ 7g* 8fg 5f 6fg⁵ 6f³ 6g³ 6g³ 7v³ 6v⁴]
As we anticipated he might, Royal Boy made up into a better three-year-
old than he was a two-year-old, even though he added only one race to the
four he collected in his first season. And as far as most people were concerned,
he was more than a shade fortunate to keep the one race he did win, for no
sooner had he taken the lead on the outside in the James Lane Two Thousand
Guineas Trial Stakes at Kempton in April, than he went sharply over towards
the far rails, severely hampering Patris, who had to be snatched up. Thomas
changed his whip hand, straightened Royal Boy up, and the colt ran on strongly
to pass the post a length ahead of Jellaby, with the unfortunate Patris a head
away in third place. Still, who would begrudge Royal Boy the one piece of
good fortune to come his way. There is little doubt that he performed with
a good deal more consistency afterwards than did Patris, even if he did fail
to make much of a show over a mile (too far) and over five furlongs (not far
enough) on his next two appearances.
Thereafter Royal Boy was raced exclusively over six furlongs except for
one more attempt at seven furlongs, and he always acquitted himself with
credit. When third in the Ayr Gold Cup, he finished in front on the stand
side of the course; when fourth in the Vernons Sprint Cup he was beaten only
two lengths by Record Token, and was staying on really well. Royal Boy's
failing, apart from the obvious one that he is not up to beating high-class performers on level terms, is that he finds six furlongs a shade on the sharp side,
gets behind, and invariably finds himself with a lot to do. Unfortunately,
ground conditions were very testing when he ran over seven furlongs, in the
Brown's Diamond Handicap at York in October, and lack of the necessary
stamina prevented him from getting to grips with the all-the-way winner Janes
Joker and Rhodomantade in the last furlong. Not that it was a bad effort
on his part to finish in front of horses like Frankie, Shuffling and Berkeley
Square on handicap terms.

		Princely Gift	Nasrullah
	Realm	(b 1951)	Blue Gem
	(b 1967)	Quita II	Lavandin
Royal Boy		(b 1962)	Eos
(ch.c. 1973)		Tin Whistle	Whistler
	Nana's Girl	(b 1957)	Sister Miles
	(b 1967)	Shandrim Queen	Dilawarji
		(br 1948)	Shandrim Lass

In 1977 we would like to see Royal Boy embarked on a programme similar
to that which Creetown pursued so successfully in 1976. In handicap company
over seven furlongs on courses like Brighton and Epsom he will always be
difficult to beat. A neat, strong and attractive colt, Royal Boy is a half-
brother to the useful miler Velvella (by Right Tack). He acts on any going.

James Lane 2,000 Guineas Trial Stakes, Kempton—Royal Boy wins from Jellaby (left), the unlucky Patris, and Asa Yolson (right)

Blinkers were tried on him in his last four races, and judging by the way he performed he will be wearing them again as a four-year-old. *M. Jarvis.*

ROYAL BRANCH   2 br.c. King Log 115–Mim-Joa 56 (Welsh Abbot 131)   [1976   —
5f 5f 5.3f 6h 5f]   of no account.   *R. Wilson.*

ROYAL BUDGET   2 b.c. Pall Mall 132–Our Girl 95 (Supreme Court 135)   [1976   66
5fg 6d 6h⁶ 7v]   quite good-looking colt: brother to very useful miler Lucky Shoes
and half-brother to several winners, including smart stayer Knotty Pine (by
Tambourine II): dam, middle-distance performer, is half-sister to smart American
horse Sir Ribot: ran poorly after showing signs of ability on first outing: moved
down very poorly indeed on hard ground on third outing.   *M. Jarvis.*

ROYAL CHASE   3 ch.f. Royal Palace 131–Indian Game 104 (Big Game)   [1975   —
7g   1976 10.1fg]   half-sister to Oaks second Maina (by St Paddy): lightly raced
and no worthwhile form.   *T. Waugh.*

ROYAL COMMUNIQUE   2 gr.c. Communication 119–By Appointment 82   61
(Henry the Seventh 125)   [1976 5fg⁵ 5fg⁴ 5g³ 6fg² 6fg 6g 5v⁶]   early sort:
moderate plater: stays 6f: seems to act on any going: inconsistent and wore
blinkers on sixth start.   *R. Hannon.*

ROYAL DARWIN   4 b.f. Royal Palm 131–Darwin Tulip (Campaign 106 or   —
Pirate King 129)   [1974 5fg* 7f 5fg⁵ 6g 5s   1975 7s 5v⁴ 6g⁶ 6fg² 5f⁴ 6h⁴ 6f* 6g⁵
1976 6v⁵ 8g]   sprint plater: appears to act on any going: does best in blinkers:
sold 400 gns Newmarket July Sales.   *B. Richmond.*

ROYAL DECLARATION   2 b.f. Breeders Dream 116–Vital Word 82 (Worden   78
II 129)   [1976 7g 6g 8s 8g²]   leggy filly: second foal: 500 guineas yearling: dam won
over 1m at 3 yrs: ran best race when ¾-length second of 20 to Harriet Air in minor
event at Lanark in October: will stay 1½m.   *D. Thom.*

ROYAL DIVER   2 gr.c. Deep Diver 134–Hakoah (Palestine 133)   [1976 5f² 5fg*   108
5g* 5g* 5f⁴ 5fg² 6fg⁴ 5f⁴]   sharp, active sort: half-brother to several winners,
including useful 5f to 7f winner Spanish Prince (by Don II): 2,700 gns yearling, resold
8,400 gns yearling: dam won over 9f in France: odds-on winner of three races,
gaining most valuable success on fourth outing when beating Song of Songs by 2½
lengths in Great Surrey Stakes at Epsom in June: again odds on for £1,800 event
at Windsor in July but failed by ½ length to catch The Andrestan: had to be
snatched up in final furlong when about 2 lengths fourth of six to Imperial Jade

636

Great Surrey Stakes, Epsom—Royal Diver beats Song of Songs and Michael Arlen (right)

in quite well-contested minor event at Thirsk in September: best form at 5f: bandaged off-hind at Thirsk. *R. Hannon.*

ROYAL DOON 4 ch.g. Doon 124–City Carriage 88 (Counsel 118) [1974 5fg 5g — 6d3 6fg 6d6 7g5 7d 7s6 1975 7f* 10fg3 10g4 8g* 1976 8g 7fg 7fg 7f 7f 8.2fg4 7f] big, tall gelding: no worthwhile form at 4 yrs: best form at up to 1m: acts on firm going: blinkered fifth and final starts. *T. Waugh.*

ROYAL FANFARE 4 br.c. March Past 124–Damel 74 (Darius 129) [1974 6s **90** 7v 1975 10f4 10f2 14d* 15fg2 14g* 13.3g 12s3 1976 13g* 14g* 16fg2 14f* 11g2] strong, useful-looking colt: showed improved form at 4 yrs and won minor event at Liverpool in April and handicaps at Sandown (also in April) and Goodwood (the following month): battled on very gamely when beating True Song ½ length on last-named course: subsequently sent from R. Price's stable to France: stays well: acts on any going: game, genuine and consistent. *P. de Watrigant, France.*

ROYAL FLARE 3 b.f. Welsh Pageant 132–Catherine Wheel 116 (Roan Rocket — 128) [1975 6f6 7d 1976 10g] lengthy filly: showed a lot of promise on first outing at 2 yrs but finished last on her only two appearances afterwards. *B. Hobbs.*

ROYAL FLIP 2 b.f. Double Jump 131–Regal Trial 93 (High Treason 126) **79** [1976 5fg 5f5 7g 8v2] third living foal: 1,000 gns yearling: dam best at 6f or 7f: improved in the autumn and went down by only a neck to Starlight Lad in minor event at Teesside in October: evidently suited by 1m, and may stay further: suited by some give in the ground. *R. Price.*

ROYAL HAND 2 b.c. Realm 129–Buffy (French Beige 127) [1976 5fg2 5d* 6f6 **96** 6g 5fg 5d] attractive, well-made colt: second foal: half-brother to a winner at up to 11f in France by Native Prince: 8,400 gns yearling: dam won over 6f at 2 yrs in Ireland: favourite for well-contested event at Haydock in May and made all to win by ½ length from Jameson: mainly disappointing afterwards: stays 6f: acts on a firm and a soft surface: blinkered fifth outing. *M. Jarvis.*

ROYAL HIT 3 b.g. King's Troop 118–Well Scored 104 (Final Score 113) [1975 — 5s 5d 8d 1976 12.5s] neat gelding: no worthwhile form in varied company but had very stiff task on only outing in 1976 (November): blinkered second outing at 2 yrs. *A. W. Jones.*

ROYAL HIVE 2 b.f. Royal Palace 131–Come on Honey 94 (Never Say Die 137) **77** [1976 7s3 7s5] attractive, well-made, good-bodied filly: half-sister to high-class middle-distance stayer Attica Meli (by Primera): dam daughter of 1,000 Guineas winner Honeylight: ran promisingly when 7 lengths third of 11 to Imperial Guard in minor event at Sandown in October: favourite for 19-runner maiden race at Newmarket later in month but weakened in closing stages and finished only fifth, about 7 lengths behind Lady Oriana: will be suited by 1¼m or more: to be trained by H. Cecil in 1977. *N. Murless.*

637

ROYAL IDOL 2 b.c. Royal Captive 116–Lesanne (Faberge II 121) [1976 5fg — 6fg 7fg] strong colt: fourth foal: half-brother to a winner abroad: 1,500 gns yearling: behind in maiden races but still looked short of peak fitness on final outing, in July: sold 300 gns Doncaster November Sales. *B. Lunness.*

ROYAL JOHN 2 br.c. John Splendid 116–Royal Bit (King's Troop 118) [1976   **82** 6fg⁴ 6fg⁵] strong, well-made, good-looking colt: good mover: third foal: brother to a plating-class animal: 1,600 gns foal: dam unraced half-sister to smart French animals Some Crack and La Troublerie: showed promise on both outings: took some time to get going in £2,000 maiden race at Goodwood in July but stayed on really strongly, finishing 7 lengths fifth of 14 to Adviser: will stay 1m: sure to win a race. *J. Dunlop.*

ROYAL KASHMIR 2 b.c. Kashmir II 125–Romardia 75 (Romulus 129) [1976 — 5f⁶ 5f 7h] bad maiden. *J. Edmunds.*

ROYAL LEGACY 4 b.c. Prince de Galles 125–Inheritance 81 (Compensation 127) — [1974 N.R. 1975 8g 8f* 1976 10fg 10fg 12f⁶ 8d] poor handicapper nowadays: best form at 1m: acts on firm going: sold to G. Blum 2,200 gns Newmarket Autumn Sales. *P. Robinson.*

ROYAL LEGEND 2 b.c. Le Levanstell 122–Eminence Grise 85 (Grey Sovereign 128 §) [1976 8s] half-brother to three winners here and abroad, including smart French middle-distance stayer El Mina (by Reliance II): dam, half-sister to Bounteous, won over 6f at 3 yrs on only outing: unquoted when behind in £2,200 event won by Lucent at Doncaster in November. *W. Elsey.*

ROYAL LILT 2 b.c. Dadda Bert 95–Irish Lilt (Highland Melody 112) [1976   **46** 5fg⁵ 5f⁶ 5h³ 5d 5f⁶] small colt: bad plater. *J. Hardy.*

ROYAL LINE 2 ch.f. Henry the Seventh 125–Blue Line 98 (Blue Peter) [1976   **51** 5d 6f 7f⁵ 8f] leggy filly: half-sister to some good winners but possesses very little ability herself: wears blinkers. *M. H. Easterby.*

ROYAL MAJOR 3 ch.g. Majority Blue 126–Majestic 86 (Buisson Ardent 129)   **73** [1975 5g⁵ 6f⁶ 5g⁴ 5.9g 1976 8fg⁶ 8s⁴ 8fg⁴ 8f³ 8fg* 10fg³ 8s 8.2s] strong, well-grown gelding: heavily-backed favourite when winning 17-runner apprentice race at Thirsk in July by ¾ length from Emperor of Ghana: stays 1m (seemed not to stay 1¼m on sixth outing): acts on a firm surface. *W. A. Stephenson.*

ROYAL MATCH 5 ch.h. Sovereign Path 125–Shortwood 90 (Skymaster 126) **117** [1974 8.2fg³ 8g² 8g⁶ 7g² 8g* 8f² 7d⁶ 8fg⁶ 8fg³ 8.3fg² 8.2s* 8fg* 8s² 8s³ 10s 1975 10fg⁵ 9f⁵ 10fg² 10.2g* 9g 10g* 11g* 11d⁶ 10.6v⁴ 1976 10g* 10g² 10g* 11g* 10g* 10d² 12f* 12fg⁴ 10fg² 12fg* 11.7g* 12g⁴]
   One would have to go a long way to find a tougher or more genuine racehorse than Royal Match. He developed into a smart performer as a five-year-old and his seven victories, all of them in handicap company, were handsome reward for a season's honest endeavour. He won his first race, the valuable Littlewoods Spring Cup at Liverpool, when the season was barely a week old and continued to run regularly until the end of September by which time he had earned for his owner £31,259 in first-prize money alone. The handicappers never managed to

Littlewoods Spring Cup, Liverpool—Royal Match pulls away from Immortal Knight

Ultramar Jubilee Stakes, Kempton—a 10-lb penalty fails to halt Royal Match's winning run. This time the runner-up is Wephen

get a full hold on Royal Match and after Liverpool he kept himself in the limelight with victories in the Sandown Cup in April; the London Gold Cup at Newbury and the Ultramar Jubilee Stakes at Kempton in May; the Bessborough Stakes at Royal Ascot; and the Great Yorkshire Handicap at York and the Quortina Challenge Cup at Windsor in August. Royal Match tasted defeat only three times in handicap company in 1976, each time finishing second and on at least two occasions looking an unlucky loser.

Royal Match was, needless to say, well handled by his trainer who kept the horse bright and fresh throughout the season and had him cleverly ridden; Thomas, who was on Royal Match in all his races, usually managed to save him for a well-timed late run which resulted in the horse's winning races narrowly when he could probably have won by much further. Horses who can produce winning form ridden in this manner may defeat the handicapper several times before their full merit is discovered. Royal Match's good turn of finishing speed made him a formidable opponent in handicap company, but on the two occasions that he ran against high-class horses in weight-for-age races he was beaten. He could manage only a fairly distant fourth place in the Princess of Wales's Stakes at Newmarket in July and the Cumberland Lodge Stakes at Ascot in September.

		Grey Sovereign (gr 1948)	Nasrullah / Kong
	Sovereign Path (gr 1956)	Mountain Path (b 1948)	Bobsleigh / Path of Peace
Royal Match (ch.h. 1971)		Skymaster (ch 1958)	Golden Cloud / Discipliner
	Shortwood (b 1966)	Go Honey (b 1955)	Mustang / Honeysuckle

Royal Match is a strong, well-made horse who did extremely well physically as a five-year-old. He is the first foal of the sprinter Shortwood who subsequently bred the smart Tranos (by Caliban), runner-up in the 1974 Horris Hill Stakes. Royal Match's grandam Go Honey won over a mile in Ireland. She is the dam of a number of fairly useful performers including the sprinters Sweet Frenzy and Goabundle and the out-and-out stayer Cossall. Royal Match stayed a mile and a half and acted on any going. He has now been retired to the Irish National Stud, Tully, County Kildare, at a fee of £500 with the live-foal concession. *R. Jarvis.*

ROYAL MESSAGE   2 ch.f. Town Crier 119–Blue Queen 54 (Majority Blue 126)   **56**
[1976 5fg⁶ 5f² 5fg 5fg⁶ 5g 7g 8fg 8s]   leggy filly: sister to speedy 1974 2-y-o Queens
Message and half-sister to 3-y-o Semper Nova and useful 1m to 1¼m winner
Findon Lad (both by Right Boy): 1,750 gns yearling: dam, a poor plater, is half-
sister to top-class sprinter Sandford Lad: 2 lengths second to easy winner Linguistic in four-runner maiden race at Edinburgh in July, easily best effort:
not certain to stay beyond sprint distances: blinkered final outing.   *W. A.*
Stephenson.

ROYAL ORBIT   4 b.g. Taj Dewan 128–Fleeting Morn (Ribot 142)   [1974 6g⁵   **69**
8d 8d⁶   1975 10s² 12g² 12.2f3 12fg* 12f* 12f² 13g²   1976 12s 14f⁴ 13.3fg 16fg*]
useful sort: quite a moderate handicapper on his day: not seen out after winning
seven-runner event at Sandown in July by 1½ lengths from Petit Pretendre: stays
well: appears to act on any going: has been tried in blinkers.   *S. Ingham.*

ROYAL PENGUIN   2 ch.c. Tyrant–Painter's Palate (Whistler 129)   [1976   **78** p
5.1fg³ 6d]   strong, attractive colt: half-brother to two speedy 2-y-o winners,
including very useful 1974 performer Panomark (by On Your Mark): 12,000 gns
yearling: dam ran only twice: with leaders to distance when 7½ lengths third of six
to Abs in maiden race at Yarmouth in June: not seen out again until October
when seventh in 23-runner maiden race won by Rings at Newmarket: likely to do
better at 3 yrs.   *B. Hanbury.*

ROYAL PLUME   2 b.c. Welsh Pageant 132–Whipped Cream 77 (Alycidon 138)   **111**
[1976 7fg 7f³ 8g* 8g* 7g*]
   On his first outing Royal Plume, ridden by the apprentice M. Bohannon,
started at 33/1, dwelt leaving the stalls, and finished seventeenth of twenty
behind Qualuz in a maiden event at Newmarket in July.   Which says all that
needs to be said about that race.   Not much need be said about his next race
either.   Again apparently little fancied, Royal Plume was unable to go with
Welsh Dancer and Jona over the last furlong of the Dickens Stakes at Yarmouth
a fortnight later, and had to be content with third place, only three lengths
behind the winner but not all that far in front of some decidedly modest animals—
Roaming Cloud, Money In and Avec Amour, for example.
   Just over three weeks later Royal Plume gave his first real show, in the
Sancton Stakes over a mile at York, where he was ridden by Piggott.   For a

SGB Stakes, Ascot—Royal Plume (near side) runs on stoutly to hold off Elland Road

first prize of £2,400 the field was a poor one, so poor in fact that Royal Plume, despite having little worthwhile form to his credit, was favourite at 9/2, with Rostov second favourite at 5/1 and Cupid's Dew at 11/2. They finished in their market order, Royal Plume going to the front at the distance and staying on strongly under hard driving to hold off Rostov by a length, with Cupid's Dew, who had made much of the running, two lengths behind Rostov.

For his fourth outing Royal Plume was sent to Doncaster nine days afterwards for the Vernons Organisation Plate, run over a mile on the round course. Slavonic, Town and Country, Spartiatis, Mielitta and Whitby Jet, to name the best of his opponents, were better horses than Rostov and Cupid's Dew, but again Royal Plume started favourite. And he proved himself a worthy one, though only after a struggle. Racing into the last furlong Royal Plume had to battle hard to wrest the lead from Spartiatis, and with Spartiatis fighting back bravely and Whitby Jet putting in a good run on the outside, there was no respite right up to the line. The verdict was half a length and the same.

Which brings us finally to the seven-furlong SGB Stakes at Ascot in September. Conceding weight to all but one of his sixteen opponents and racing over a distance one could be excused for thinking would prove a shade sharp for him, Royal Plume was always well placed in a race run at a good strong gallop, took it up from Elland Road entering the last furlong and battled on gamely to retain a narrow advantage to the post. Mississippi, Imperial Guard, Caporello and Chain of Reasoning were among those behind. This is very useful form. Rostov and Cupid's Dew wouldn't have got anywhere near Royal Plume in this race.

Thus Royal Plume closed his two-year-old career with three hard races in a little over three weeks, and it says a lot for his courage and constitution that he should come back a better horse each time. If he continues as a three-year-old the progress he was showing in the September of his first season there is no telling where he'll end up! But it is not seriously to be expected that Royal Plume will make it right to the top at three years, for although he stays pretty well and is obviously a good fighter, his lack of top-class pace is evident: all the courage in the world won't get him out of the trouble his deficiency in speed is likely to get him into if he tries to match strides with classic colts. All the same, he looks certain to win races as a three-year-old.

Royal Plume (b.c. 1974)	Welsh Pageant (b 1966)	Tudor Melody (br 1956)	Tudor Minstrel
			Matelda
		Picture Light (b 1954)	Court Martial
			Queen of Light
	Whipped Cream (ch 1962)	Alycidon (ch 1945)	Donatello II
			Aurora
		Nagaika (ch 1954)	Goyama
			Naim

A big, strong colt, Royal Plume is a son of the top-class miler Welsh Pageant out of a disappointing Alycidon half-sister to that good horse Connaught and the promising 1976 two-year-old The Czar. Stamina is the family's long suit, and Royal Plume, a half-brother to the lightly-raced stayer Thomas Jefferson (by Charlottesville), will stay at least a mile and a quarter. He will be trained in 1977 by Henry Cecil. *N. Murless.*

ROYAL PRINCESS 2 br.f. Meadow Mint 120–Gold Court 79 (Gentle Art 121) **81**
[1976 5fg 5f⁶ 5d 5f⁵ 5f* 5fg² 5fg] compact filly: fourth foal: dam, who won over 5f at 2 yrs, is closely related to good sprinter Monet: showed much improved form when making all to win nine-runner maiden race at Catterick in July by 5 lengths from Templa: confirmed this performance when 5 lengths second to Hand Canter in 20-runner event at Ripon the following month but finished last of 19 in nursery on final outing: should stay 6f. *H. Wharton.*

ROYAL PURSUIT 3 br.g. King's Leap 111–Hunting Moon 85 (Tudor Minstrel **—**
144) [1975 5f 5f⁶ 5f⁴ 5fg* 5h 5f³ 5.9g 5d⁵ 1976 8.2f 8f 7f 6fg⁶ 6d⁵ 5s] strong, compact gelding: won maiden race at Liverpool in 1975 and was rated 82 but showed no worthwhile form at 3 yrs. *H. Wharton.*

ROYAL REVENGE 2 ch.c. Sweet Revenge 129–Oversight (Tudor Melody 129) **68**
[1976 5d⁴ 5g⁶ 7fg⁶ 5fg] strong, lengthy colt: didn't fulfil the promise he showed on first outing: started slowly when last of 17 in valuable seller at York on final appearance: not certain to stay 7f. *K. Payne.*

ROYAL ROMEO 2 br.c. Royal Captive 116–Denromo 85 (Denturius) [1976 **76**
5f 5fg 5d⁴ 6f² 7f* 6f³ 8f 7.2d³] useful-looking colt: half-brother to two 2-y-o

winners: sold twice as a yearling, for 500 gns and 950 gns: dam won over 6f at 2 yrs: all out when winning 13-runner maiden auction event at Doncaster in July by ¾ length from Revlow: well suited by 7f but disappointed when heavily backed in 1m nursery: probably acts on any going. *J. Carr.*

ROYAL RUSSE 3 br.f. Bally Russe 113–Little But Royal 76 (King's Troop 118) —
[1975 7.2fg 8f 9g 1976 16g] big, lengthy filly: poor maiden. *D. Plant.*

ROYAL SET 5 br.h. Sovereign Path 125–Nisette (Black Tarquin 136) [1974 —
12d⁴ 12g 11.7fg⁵ 12g² 10fg³ 10d⁵ 12d 11.7d⁴ 13v 10.8v⁶ 14.6s 1975 10s⁵ 10g⁶
10fg⁴ 10f* 12d⁴ 11.7fg 1976 11g] strong horse: quite a moderate handicapper
(rated 70) at 4 yrs: made only one appearance in 1976 (had stiffish task): stays
1½m: acts on firm going and seems unsuited by heavy: sometimes wears blinkers.
H. Bell.

ROYAL SOUND 2 br.f. Royalty 130–Sing High 85 (Sound Track 132) [1976 —
7g] tall filly: half-sister to two winners, including quite useful 1970 2-y-o 6f
and 7f winner Thief Lane (by Mandamus): 720 gns yearling: dam stayed 1m:
looked nowhere near ready when behind in 21-runner maiden race won by Nana's
Queen at Ayr in September, only outing. *F. Carr.*

ROYAL TACTIC 3 ch.f. Right Tack 131–Pardal Lassie (Pardal 130) [1975   **62**
N.R. 1976 8f 10d⁶ 8.2d³ 8v⁵ 10.6v⁴] half-sister to several winners in France
and U.S.A.: 2,800 gns yearling: dam a stakes-placed winner in U.S.A.: in frame
in maiden races at Haydock in October but was beaten some way on both
occasions. *G. Pritchard-Gordon.*

ROYAL TANNER 3 ch.g. Royal Palm 131–Elsie Tanner (Buckhound 117) —
[1975 5g 5f 6g 6fg⁴ 5f³ 5g 7g 1976 7g 8.2f 6d] sturdy gelding: bad plater:
has been tried in blinkers: sold 440 gns Ascot July Sales. *T. Kersey.*

ROYALTINA 4 b.f. Nos Royalistes 119–Chiltern Miss 85 (Hook Money 124) —
[1974 N.R. 1975 N.R. 1976 10.1fg] second foal: dam won at up to 1m: well
behind in 14-runner maiden race at Windsor in June won by Veracious, only
outing. *D. Barons.*

ROYFERN 4 br.c. Sing Sing 134–Follow Elizabeth 101 (Cagire II 122) [1974   **99**
5g* 6g² 7fg²(dis) 5d 1975 5d² 6d³ 5fg* 6fg² 5fg 6g 6d* 6d 6fg⁵ 8d 1976 6fg⁴
6fg⁴ 6g* 6g⁴ 6f 7fg⁴ 7g 7fg* 6f² 7d⁴ 7s*] attractive colt: quite a useful handicapper: successful at Newbury in May, Goodwood in July and Newmarket in
October, on last-named course finishing strongly to beat Palustra a length: stays
7f: acts on any going: suitable mount for an apprentice nowadays. *J. Benstead.*

ROY ROSE 2 b.f. Royben 125–Whistling Rose (Tin Whistle 128) [1976 6h] —
second foal: dam never ran: in rear in 15-runner maiden race won by Oppressor
at Chepstow in June, only outing. *M. Killoran.*

ROY'S REP 2 gr.f. Cumshaw 111–Composure 87 (Alycidon 138) [1976 5.9f⁶   **53**
6fg³ 8v] leggy filly: well-backed favourite for sellers at Wolverhampton and
Nottingham in July, on latter course finishing 4½ lengths third of 10 to The
Nadi Cat: not seen out again until November: should stay 1m. *J. Hill.*

ROZEL BUOY 4 ch.c. Laser Light 118–Pretest 87 (Premonition 130) [1974 — §
5f 5f² 5fg³ 6fg* 6g² 6g* 6d² 6d* 6v⁴ 1975 7s⁵ 7g 7fg² 7f⁴ 7.6f² 7g⁴ 7g* 8s² 8fg
1976 7fg 7fg³ 8s 7g⁴ 7fg 8g³ 7fg⁶ 7g 8g⁵] strong colt: very good mover: one-time
very smart handicapper: ran respectably when third at Ascot on second and
sixth outings in 1976 but showed little enthusiasm for racing on most of his other
starts at 4 yrs: best at distances short of 1m: acted on any going: sweated up
and unseated rider leaving paddock before fourth outing: trained by S. Ingham
until seventh start: wore a muzzle on eighth outing: sold 3,600 gns Newmarket
December Sales: stud in Ireland. *S. Hall.*

RUBYDAR 4 br.c. Balidar 133–Margaret's Ruby (Tesco Boy 121) [1974 5s⁴   **80**
5fg³ 5fg 5g⁶ 5fg⁵ 5d² 5s 1975 5v² 6s² 6v² 5g* 5g² 6fg* 6fg³ 5g² 5g² 5g² 5v⁴
1976 6g 6fg 5d³ 6g² 7f 6f⁴ 5fg⁶] useful sort: fair handicapper: effective at 5f
and 6f but appears not to stay further: seems to act on any going: usually wears
blinkers: sometimes sweats up: genuine. *M. H. Easterby.*

RUDDING RUMOUR 3 b.g. Mummy's Pet 125–Aequanimitas (Infatuation 129) —
[1975 N.R. 1976 8s 8.2f 9f 9g 7.6fg] stocky gelding: no worthwhile form in
maiden and minor events: blinkered final outing: sold 420 gns Doncaster September Sales. *R. Mason.*

RUDDY DRAKE 5 b.g. Goldhill 125–Ruddy Duck 84 (Dicta Drake 126) [1974 —
7s 12fg³ 10f 10.6f* 14d⁵ 11.7fg* 14fg 12d³ 1975 10d⁴ 11s⁴ 1976 12g⁶] compact
gelding: stays 1½m well: appears to act on any going: good mount for a boy.
W. Marshall.

Mr D. D. Prenn's "Rudella"

RUDDY SAM 3 br.g. Goldhill 125–Ruddy Duck 84 (Dicta Drake 126) [1975 **79**
N.R. 1976 10.6g⁵ 10f 14.7d*] useful sort: brother to two winners, including
Ruddy Drake, a moderate winner from 7f to 1½m, and half-brother to another
winner: 2,800 gns yearling: dam needed at least 1½m: 33/1, showed first worthwhile form when upsetting long odds-on shot Wounded Knee by ½ length in
minor event at Redcar in September: suited by a test of stamina. *M. H.
Easterby.*

RUDELLA 2 b.f. Raffingora 130–Goldarella (Goldhill 125) [1976 5g⁵ 5g* 6g³ **95**
6g] strong filly: first foal: dam never ran: made all and won 10–runner maiden
race at Lingfield in August by 3 lengths from Careless Princess: creditable
third of nine to Rockery (Fr) in minor event at Kempton later in month, being
beaten 2½ lengths: stays 6f. *J. Winter.*

RUE D'OR 5 b.g. Rugantino 97–Dierama (Schapiro 99) [1974 N.R. 1975 **—**
N.R. 1976 12s] second foal: dam of no account: 33/1 when well beaten in
apprentice event at Chepstow in October, only outing. *O. O'Neill.*

RUMSON 2 br.c. Amazing–Erin Blu (Noor 123) [1976 5s⁶ 5f³ 5d* 5f² 6g] **104**
well-grown American-sired Irish colt: brother to two winners in U.S.A., including
Amazing Man, a very smart stakes winner at up to 7f at 2 yrs, and half-brother
to Irish 3-y-o 1½m winner Vaguely Blue (by Vaguely Noble): dam a minor winner
in U.S.A.: made all when comfortably winning 12-runner maiden race at the
Curragh in May by 1½ lengths from Glenturret: went down by a length to Lordedaw when odds on for five-runner event at Leopardstown in June and was
not seen out again until October when 50/1 for William Hill Middle Park Stakes
at Newmarket (finished ninth of 11 to Tachypous): should stay 1m. *M. Fogarty,
Ireland.*

RUMSTAR 2 ch.f. Rum–Madam Nick 92 (Espresso 122) [1976 5f⁵ 5f⁶ 6h⁵ 5f⁶ **59**
6f⁴ 5fg 8fg] fair sort: plater: ran best race when 3 lengths fourth of 18 to Swing
Right at Ripon in August: probably needs further than 5f and should stay 1m:
blinkered sixth outing. *M. W. Easterby.*

*Tote Sprint Trophy, Ascot—northern-trained horses finish first and second.   Rundontwalk
beats Pennina, with Codebreaker (left) and Bill's Song close up*

RUNDONTWALK 3 ch.c. Takawalk II 125–Trinacria (Relic) [1975 5g² 5s* **111**
5f* 6fg² 5g⁴ 5v⁵ 1976 5d² 6g* 5s⁴ 6d⁴ 5fg* 5fg⁵ 5fg 6g] small, strong, robust
colt: picked up a valuable prize when beating Pennina by a length in 14-runner
Tote Sprint Trophy at Ascot in June: had earlier dead-heated with Gold Loom
in William Hill Handicap at Ripon: equally effective at 5f and 6f: acts on any
going, with possible exception of heavy: ran below his best last three outings,
sweating up on second of them. *G. Richards.*

RUN FOR THE ROSES 2 br.c. Captain's Gig–Bonnie Blue (Majority Blue 126) **—**
[1976 5f 6d] second foal: 2,000 gns yearling: dam never ran: unquoted when
behind in maiden races at Bath and Newmarket in the autumn. *G. Hunter.*

RUNNING ACCOUNT 2 b.f. Double Jump 131–Dandy's Cash 81 (Fastnet **76**
Rock 123) [1976 5fg⁴ 5fg² 6fg] half-sister to fair 1969 2-y-o 5f winner Loot
of India (by Pindari): 740 gns yearling: dam moderate over 5f at 2 yrs: ran
best race when length second to Foden's Eve in 23-runner maiden auction event
at Salisbury in May: exported to Belgium by B.B.A. and is a winner there.
P. Ashworth.

RUNNING BULL 2 br.c. Prince Tenderfoot 126–Windfield Lily (Hard Tack **91 p**
111 §) [1976 6d*] half-brother to Irish St Leger winner Conor Pass (by
Tiepolo II) and useful 1975 Irish 2-y-o 5f winner Lace Curtain Lil (by Whistling Wind):
16,000 gns yearling: dam prolific winning Irish sprinter: appeared with a big
reputation and started short-priced favourite when winning 23-runner maiden
race at Newmarket in October: led over 2f out but ran a bit green and got home
by only a short head and a head from Haco and Gerard: may stay 1m: sure
to do much better. *H. Cecil.*

RUNNING JUMP 4 ch.c. Runnymede 123–High Acres (High Perch 126) [1974 **88**
5f* 5f⁴ 5g³ 6g³ 5d* 5s 1975 6v⁶ 5s⁴ 6g⁵ 6d* 5fg³ 6d⁴ 7g⁶ 6g⁴ 1976 6v³ 7fg 8s⁵
8.2g⁴ 7d² 8fg² 7f³ 7fg² 8fg 7d] well-made colt: fair handicapper nowadays:
didn't win a race in 1976 but ran well from time to time, on sixth outing finishing
second to Janes Joker in Dobson Peacock Handicap at Newcastle in June and
going down narrowly to Fighting Lady on same course the following month: stays
1m: acts on any going: suitable mount for a boy: ran below his best last two
outings: sweated up sixth start. *J. W. Watts.*

RUNNING SCARED 4 gr.c. Supreme Sovereign 119–Balfeighan (Arctic Time **54**
127) [1974 7.6v⁴ 1975 8v³ 10g³ 9g⁴ 10g⁴ 8g 1976 12fg³ 12fg³ 17.7f² 16.1d³
15f³ 14fg] strong colt: stays well: acts on any going: blinkered last two outings
in 1975: very useful hurdler. *A. Pitt.*

RUNNYBELLE 2 ch.f. Runnymede 123–Persian Belle 77 (Darius 129) [1976 **76**
5g 5tg⁴ 5fg³ 6fg⁵ 6f 6g 5v⁶] fourth foal: 2,300 gns yearling: dam, half-sister
to Welsh Rake, won over 5f at 2 yrs: in frame in maiden races at Salisbury
in June and Lingfield (1½ lengths third to Trumpet Call) in July: possibly does
not stay 6f: blinkered fifth outing: sold 1,400 gns Doncaster November Sales
and exported to Norway. *R. Price.*

RUSCOMBE 3 b.f. Blakeney 126–Templecombe 74 (Derring-Do 131) [1975 **76**
N.R. 1976 10fg 10fg⁴ 10.4fg 12fg² 10.1f² 10.1d² 10.2s] attractive filly: first
foal: dam disappointing sister to top-class sprinter Huntercombe: runner-up
in maiden races at Lingfield and Windsor (two): stays 1½m: ran poorly when
tried in blinkers on third outing: sold 4,000 gns Newmarket December Sales.
J. Bethell.

RUSH BOND 2 b.c. Good Bond 122–Rushkey (Bullrush 106) [1976 5f 5f* **94**
6f* 5h² 6f 6h² 6h⁴ 6g⁴ 5.9fg 6v*] lightly-made, fair sort: third foal: half-
brother to a winner in Hungary: dam never ran: won maiden and minor events
at Warwick and Nottingham in first half of season: co-favourite for valuable
seller at York in October and showed he is much better than the usual plater,
coming home a long-looking 8 lengths clear of Lavanter in a 19-strong field:
sold to H. Blackshaw for 2,800 gns afterwards: well suited by 6f and will stay
further: acts on any going. *B. Hills.*

RUSHLEY BAY 2 b.f. Crooner 119–Vicki Ann (Floribunda 136) [1976 6fg⁴ **87**
5f* 5fg² 5f* 5d⁶ 5g²] tall filly: first foal: dam of little account: easy winner
of maiden race at Folkestone in July and beat Model Soldier a head in nursery
at Goodwood the following month: outclassed by winner when runner-up to
Brave Lass in nursery at Ascot in September: should stay 6f. *H. Westbrook.*

RUSHMERE 3 br.c. Blakeney 126–Omentello 91 (Elopement 125) [1975 7d **92**
8g 10g* 1976 12g⁵ 12fg⁴ 14g⁵ 14f* 14fg² 16g* 19s³ 17.1s²] strong, compact,
deep-girthed colt: quite a useful handicapper: won at Salisbury in August
and Lingfield in September, making all to beat Hardirondo 3 lengths on latter
course: stays well: acts on any going: blinkered last three outings: game: sold
to J. Gifford 6,400 gns Ascot October Sales. *P. Walwyn.*

RUST BOROUGH 4 b.g. Star Moss 122–Abernisia (Abernant 142) [1974 6d **—**
7g 6v 7s* 1975 7v 8s 8h 8g⁵ 12d 7fg³ 8g 1976 12.5s] leggy gelding: plater:
best form at up to 7f: appears to act on any going. *A. Doyle.*

RUSTHALL 3 ch.g. Midsummer Night II 117–French Seam 80 (French Beige **74**
127) [1975 6fg 6f 5.1f³ 7g* 7f² 7fg⁵ 7s² 1976 8fg³ 8f⁵ 12g³ 11fg⁵ 7.6fg³ 8g
7f³] well-made gelding: good mover: quite a moderate handicapper: effective
at 7f and promises to stay 1½m: acts on any going: trained until after second
outing by P. Haslam. *G. Hunter.*

RUTLOW 2 ch.c. Yellow God 129–Turnbeam (Hornbeam 130) [1976 5fg **101**
5g 6fg³ 7g⁶ 7g³ 7f 7g 8s*] sturdy colt: second foal: half-brother to a winner
in Sweden: 1,700 gns yearling: dam won at 2 yrs in Sweden: 25/1 for £1,800
nursery at Bath in October and showed greatly improved form, getting up close
home by short head from Atwood: clearly very well suited by 1m and
soft going: trained by M. Francis on first seven outings: exported to Singapore.
P. Haslam.

RUY LOPEZ 4 br.c. Timmy Lad 130–Lisabella (Right Royal V 135) [1974 5g **—**
6f⁵ 8.2d 9g 8d⁶ 8s² 10s³ 1975 9v 12s⁶ 12g⁴ 16f³ 16.1fg² 1976 12fg 22.2f]
well-made colt: poor handicapper: stays well: acts on any going: probably
best in blinkers: tailed off when pulled up on final start. *P. Buckley.*

RYAN'S PROPHET 2 b.c. Firestreak 125–Tajlette (Prince Taj 123) [1976 **54**
6fg 6fg 7f 8s 7v] third reported foal: cost 360 gns Ascot January 1976 Sales:
dam ran only twice: in rear in maiden and minor events. *J. Pullen.*

RYE GRASS 2 b.f. Ribero 126–Grasper 105 (Galivanter 131) [1976 5d⁴ 6d] **71**
half-sister to French 7f and 1m winner My Sniff (by Royal Palm): 3,900 gns
yearling: dam a speedy 2-y-o: second favourite and pick of paddock, did not
move well on way to post prior to finishing about 5 lengths fourth of 14 to
Miss Knightsbridge in maiden race at Haydock in October: well placed for a
long way in 23-runner maiden race won by Rings at Newmarket later in month:
may do better at around 1m. *F. J. Houghton.*

RYHALL GRANGE 4 ch.f. Grand Roi 118–Recce (Donore 119) [1974 6g⁵ 7d **47**
8d³ 1975 12v³ 12g⁴ 16s⁵ 14f⁴ 14f⁵ 13g 15.5f² 16h⁶ 1976 12g 12g 12h³ 10.2s]
rangy filly: poor staying maiden: acts on firm going: blinkered three times at
3 yrs. *C. Brittain.*

RYMER 5 b.h. Reliance II 137–Piave (Alcide 136) [1974 10g² 12g 8f² 8g* 10fg³ **105**
8d² 9d⁴ 1975 10d² 10fg* 10f⁴ 10fg 8f 10d² 1976 10g⁶ 10f⁴ 11g² 12g⁶] well-
made, robust, good-looking horse: good mover: very smart performer (rated
121) at 4 yrs: made only four appearances in 1976 and didn't show the same
form, putting up his best effort when ½-length second of seven to Gunner B
in Doonside Cup at Ayr in September, closing fast on winner in final furlong:
stays 11f well: seems to act on any going. *H. Blagrave.*

S

SABALA 3 b.f. Tribal Chief 125–Svenno 76 (Vilmorin) [1975 5s⁶ 5s 6f³ 7g²   **83** 7h* 6fg⁵ 8f² 8g⁵ 8g² 1976 6g³ 6f* 6f⁴ 7fg⁴ 7f 7g³ 7g] rangy filly: won handicap at Chepstow in June, beating Bluehill by ¾ length: stays 1m well: evidently needs a sound surface. *H. Candy.*

SABANTE 3 b.g. Varano–Sans Sabots (Whistler 129) [1975 5g 7f 1976   — 12.3s 12f] of no account. *P. Metcalfe.*

SABARAK 3 ch.g. Karabas 132 Town House 91 (Pall Mall 132) [1975 5g   **77** 6f 6g 7g 7f⁵ 8.2g 6g 1976 10fg⁵ 12.2f⁵ 13f³ 12fg⁴ 12f* 16f* 14g] big, rangy gelding: won maiden race at Redcar (made all to beat solitary opponent) and handicap at Nottingham in August (well-backed favourite when beating Blake-wood 1¼ lengths): stays 2m: acts on firm going: ran moderately when blinkered last two outings at 2 yrs. *P. Rohan.*

SABI 2 b.c. Crooner 119–Quits 71 (Tit for Tat II) [1976 6v] third produce: — half-brother to Irish 1m winner Torrent (by Galivanter): 960 gns foal, resold 1,500 gns yearling: dam won over 6f at 2 yrs: easy in market when tenth of 16 to subsequently-disqualified Nampara Cove in maiden race at Lingfield in November. *R. Price.*

SACCHARUM 3 ch.c. Shantung 132–Waltzing Matilda (Sound Track 132)   — [1975 7g 1976 12d 10.1fg 13s] big, strong colt: slow maiden: sold 350 gns Ascot December Sales. *W. Holden.*

SACKBUT 3 b.c. Relko 136–Harpsichord 96 (Ocarina 131) [1975 6f 7.2g 7g⁵ 7g 8fg 1976 12fg⁶ 12f 16f 10.2s] strong colt: should stay middle distances (heavily-backed favourite but well beaten when tried at 2m): blinkered last outing at 2 yrs. *M. W. Easterby.*

SADDLERS QUEEN 3 ch.f. Silver Cloud 121–Zan Cloud (Golden Cloud) [1975   **58** 5g 5.9fg 6fg⁴ 7f⁶ 1976 8h²] quite a moderate plater at 2 yrs: good second of eight to Bird Cherry in maiden race at Chepstow in June (flag start): suited by 1m: was bad at the start in 1975 (withdrawn not under orders, when blinkered on last appearance at 2 yrs). *V. Cross.*

SADEDAB 3 br.c. Badedas 81–June Clare (Fairwell) [1975 5.9f 6f 6f 7f 7g   **47** 6g 1976 7f 10fg⁵ 15.8s⁶ 11.1s³ 10v⁵] poor plater: best run at 11f. *J. Edmunds.*

SAD ERIC 2 b.c. Yukon Eric–La Tristesse 88 (Exploitation 108) [1976 8s   — 8s 7v] half-brother to a winning hurdler: dam a stayer: no signs of ability in varied company in the autumn. *A. Davison.*

SAFE ANCHORAGE 3 ch.f. Quayside 124–Tomore 77 (Chanteur II 135)   **53** [1975 5g 6f 7g⁵ 7g³ 8g 1976 8f 8fg 8fg 11f 8fg³ 12f³ 13.8g] workmanlike filly: plater: stays 1½m: sometimes sweats up: wears bandages: moved very badly to post and ran poorly on final outing. *K. Whitehead.*

SAFETY CATCH 7 br.h. King's Troop 118–Natural Caution 71 (Big Game)   — [1974 7f⁶ 7fg³ 8f³ 7f⁵ 7g* 7fg 7s 7v⁵ 1975 7fg 8.3fg 5.8f⁶ 7f 7f³ 8g 1976 7fg] neat horse: poor handicapper: stays 1m: acts on any going. *V. Cross.*

SAGARO 5 ch.h. Espresso 122–Zambara 82 (Mossborough 126) [1974 12g*   **129** 10.5g⁴ 12.5g* 15d* 15.5s* 11s³ 12s 1975 15.5v² 20g³ 20f* 12.5 15g⁴ 13.5g 1976 15.5s* 15.5g⁴ 20g* 20f*]

How good a Gold Cup winner is Sagaro? The probability is that he's the best since Levmoss and, as the state of the going is immaterial to Sagaro, it is certain to take an exceptional horse to beat him at Royal Ascot in 1977 when, all being well, he will attempt to make racing history by winning the Gold Cup for a third time. Sagaro was emphatically the best of a vintage collection of out-and-out stayers in 1976. The form of the Gold Cup looks very good: the winner Sagaro, who didn't race after the Gold Cup, had previously won the Prix du Cadran easily by three lengths; the Gold Cup runner-up Crash Course franked the form when narrowly beaten with 10-0 on his back in the Joe Coral Northumberland Plate on his only subsequent outing; the third Sea Anchor went through the remainder of the season undefeated, winning the Goodwood Stakes under the record weight of 10-0, and the Doncaster Cup; and the fifth home Mr Bigmore also won his two later races, a valuable handicap at Chester (carrying 9-13) and the Goodwood Cup. The gelding John Cherry, debarred from running in the Gold Cup, but defeated convincingly by Sagaro, Sea Anchor and Crash Course in races before Royal Ascot, paid some handsome

tributes to the best stayers during the season, notably when cantering away with the Ladbroke Chester Cup and the SKF Cesarewitch under big weights.

With the benefit of hindsight, there's no doubt that the Gold Cup took more winning than it did in 1975 when Sagaro trotted up from the subsequently-disqualified Mistigri and the Prix du Cadran winner Le Bavard. But such was Sagaro's reputation by the time the Gold Cup came round again that he started at 15/8 on, the seventh horse to start at odds on in the Gold Cup in the post-war era. Of these seven only Caracalla in 1946, Arbar in 1948 and Sagaro have been successful. Sagaro came to Royal Ascot on the crest of a wave, having swept aside all the best French stayers in the Prix du Cadran (the French Gold Cup) at Longchamp in May. He had also won the Prix de Barbeville in the first week in April, before suffering a surprising defeat in the Prix Jean Prat later in the same month. Paquet rode Sagaro in these three events but Piggott, who had partnered the horse in the Gold Cup a year earlier, took the mount at Royal Ascot. The Irish St Leger winner Mistigri, runner-up in the Prix de Barbeville and fourth in the Cadran, was the only French-trained runner to take on Sagaro in the Gold Cup. The home challenge would have been greatly strengthened had Bruni been allowed to take his chance but, with him out of the way, Sagaro looked unbeatable. Sagaro has an excellent turn of finishing speed for a horse that stays so well and the connections of the home-trained contingent rightly realised that a slow early pace in the Gold Cup would play right into his hands. The nine-year-old Barton Mills was put in the race as pacemaker for Crash Course and took the field along at a good pace for two miles. Mistigri was then sent on and was still at the head of affairs on the final turn where the confidently-ridden Sagaro was four lengths behind the leader with only Barton Mills behind him. First Sea Anchor and then Crash Course battled his way to the front but it was obvious early in the straight that Piggott was having an armchair ride, and as soon as Sagaro was given his head he showed easily the best acceleration, drawing up to the leaders on the outside at the distance and going ahead inside the final furlong to win in very smooth style by a length. Crash Course was second, two lengths in front of Sea Anchor with Mistigri three lengths away fourth and Mr Bigmore a further three lengths back in fifth place. Sagaro thus became only the second dual Gold Cup winner since the war, emulating Fighting Charlie who won in 1965 and 1966. Sagaro is also only the fourth horse in the post-war era to win the Gold Cup and the Prix du Cadran in the same season. Arbar in 1948, Levmoss in 1969 and Lassalle in 1973 are the others.

It is sad that Sagaro was not seen out again after Royal Ascot: for the top-class out-and-out stayer the season effectively ends with the Gold Cup. The Goodwood Cup, the Doncaster Cup and the Jockey Club Cup are the only pattern races in England at two miles or more after June and none is worth more than half the value of the Gold Cup. The French, who are popularly supposed to cater for their stayers much more adequately than we do, are as guilty as we are in not giving stayers a square deal. They have only two pattern races all season over a distance of two miles or more, the Prix du Cadran and the Prix Gladiateur, run over three miles in October.

Twenty years ago the owner of the Gold Cup winner collected £11,555; Sagaro's owner picked up £19,179 in 1976. In 1956 the first prize for the Prix du Cadran was approximately £7,150; Sagaro's win was worth £34,965. The prize money for the Cadran has kept pace with inflation much better than that offered for the Gold Cup but the standing of both races has fallen as the pattern of racing has been contracted around the mile and a quarter to mile and a half centre. The big middle-distance events have increased in value much more

*Gold Cup, Ascot—Sagaro has no difficulty winning for the second year running.
Crash Course and Sea Anchor (left) come out best of his rivals*

sharply than any other group of races in the past twenty years. Then, the
Derby had a first prize of £17,282; in 1976 it was £111,825. The first prize
for the French Derby has grown from approximately £17,000 to £110,835 in
the same period. In 1956 the Grand Prix de Paris, run over one mile seven
furlongs, was the most valuable race for three-year-olds in France with a first
prize of around £25,000 but it has now been overtaken in value by the French
Derby; in 1976 the winner of the Grand Prix earned £98,522. The Coronation
Cup, well behind the Gold Cup in importance in 1956 when it was worth £2,691,
carried a £21,420 first prize in 1976. Similarly the prize money for the Prix
Ganay, the French equivalent of the Coronation Cup, has overtaken that
offered for the Prix du Cadran, climbing from about £4,000 in 1956 to £46,620
twenty years later. Europe's two major all-aged weight-for-age races, the
Prix de l'Arc de Triomphe and the King George VI and Queen Elizabeth Stakes,
have also fared well, the former jumping from around £29,500 to £144,928 and
the latter from £23,727 to £81,508 in the period under review.

And it isn't just a question of the top-class races: there is an imbalance
about the pattern of racing as a whole. Two-year-old racing in England is
heavily weighted in favour of the sprint-bred horse (almost 80 per cent of races
are at five furlongs or six) and racing for three-year-olds and older horses is
weighted in favour of the miler and the middle-distance performer (almost 60 per
cent of all races are at a mile to a mile and a half). The William Hill Futurity
(founded as the Timeform Gold Cup) and one or two other races now provide
good opportunities for staying two-year-olds, but the provision of these races,
small number though they are, has not been matched by a corresponding
widening of the spread of distances over which the races for older horses are
run. Only 6 per cent of races are at two miles or over; only one in eight at
distances beyond a mile and a half. All the really big stakes for older horses
are at a mile, a mile and a quarter or a mile and a half, with the single exception
of the St Leger, a race which is open only to three-year-olds. In 1976 the first prizes
for England's three most important all-aged weight-for-age races for out-and-out
stayers, the Gold Cup, the Goodwood Cup and the Doncaster Cup did not, together, amount to the prize money won by Wollow in either the Eclipse Stakes
or the Benson and Hedges Gold Cup, or by Vitiges in the Champion Stakes.

English racing enjoys at least three important advantages over its French
and American cousins. One is the charm and variety of its racecourses;
another is the presence of a live betting market provided by the bookmakers;
and a third is the wider range of distances over which racing takes place.
American racing favours the sprinter-miler to excess and in France the opportunities for top-class sprinters and stayers are more restricted than they are
in England. To our mind variety is the spice of racing-life and, if variety in
the range of distances over which we race in Britain is to be maintained, the
drift towards breeding for speed at the expense of stamina must be halted.
And there is only one effective way to encourage the breeding of staying horses
and the *racing* of them at the distances over which they are most effective:
and that is to promote a sufficient number of races over distances long enough

to reward stamina. With this must come much increased Levy Board support not only for the Cup races but also for the important sprint races for older horses. Merit of any kind deserves its reward, and it is up to the turf authorities to see it gets it.

Some increase in the number of good long-distance races open to horses above the age of three is also desirable. York's important August meeting should stage a big all-aged weight-for-age race over two miles; more importantly, the St Leger should be opened up to older horses. The St Leger would be a magnificent race then, bringing top-class stayers of all ages into battle. And it would provide the best older stayers with a really worthwhile opportunity in the second half of the season. Sagaro's win in the Gold Cup, Sea Anchor's superb weight-carrying performance in the Goodwood Stakes and John Cherry's breathtaking victories in the Chester Cup and the Cesarewitch were among the highlights of the season and provided fitting reminders of the marvellous entertainment that can be provided by good stayers.

		Acropolis (ch 1952)	Donatello II / Aurora
Sagaro (ch.h. 1971)	Espresso (ch 1958)	Babylon (b 1940)	Bahram / Clairvoyante III
	Zambara (b 1966)	Mossborough (ch 1947)	Nearco / All Moonshine
		Grischuna (b 1959)	Ratification / Mountain Path

Commercial breeders apparently aren't interested in the shapely, good-looking Sagaro, hence the reason for his being in training again in 1977. Breeding's loss is racing's gain. It is rare to see a stayer of Sagaro's quality in these times of so-called progress. Most top-class horses are denied the opportunity to show their worth over long distances; nowadays even potentially brilliant out-and-out stayers, such as Bruni and Bustino, are campaigned at middle-distances at which all the big money, not to mention the prestige, is to be won. *F. Boutin, France.*

SAGE 3 b.c. Sheshoon 132–White Flame (Venture VII 129) [1975 6g 8g 7g 8v³ 1976 12g³ 16d⁵ 14fg⁵ 13fg² 12fg³ 12v⁴ 12s⁵] compact colt: best form at up to 13f: probably acts on any going. *C. Bewicke.* **68**

SAHIB'S DAUGHTER 2 b.f. Sahib 114–Roman Nose 95 (Nosca) [1976 5fg⁴ 5fg* 5f* 5g⁶ 5fg³ 5.3h* 5g³ 5d] smallish, compact filly: half-sister to several minor winners: 1,050 gns yearling: dam won over 6f at 2 yrs: had a good season and won at Epsom, Goodwood and Brighton, on last-named course doing very well to win a nursery in August after losing ground at start: beaten only narrowly when third of 12 to Noirima in nursery at Goodwood the following month: will stay 6f: acts on hard ground: very much at home on sharp tracks: trained by P. Ashworth in first part of season. *P. Cole.* **88**

SAILCLOTH 2 b.c. Shantung 132–Pertinacity 106 (Aggressor 130) [1976 7g] compact, robust colt: half-brother to two winners, including useful 3-y-o stayer Persevering (by Blakeney): dam, middle-distance performer, is half-sister to very smart Petty Officer: unquoted, showed promise when tenth of 21 to Nobodys Fool in maiden race at Newmarket in October: will do better with time and longer distances: sold to W. Hastings-Bass 5,200 gns Newmarket December Sales. *J. Bethell.* **79 p**

SAILING ALONG 2 ch.f. Crooner 119–First Sail 74 (Vilmorin) [1976 5f 5fg² 5g⁴ 6f² 6fg* 6g 7f* 7.3d] attractive, well-made filly: half-sister to three winners, including smart 1967 Irish 2-y-o The Viscount (by Whistling Wind): 2,100 gns yearling: dam a sprinter: easy winner of maiden race at Lingfield in July and showed improved form in 12-runner nursery at Newmarket the following month, just holding off Bow-Wow to win by a short head: suited by 7f: acts well on firm going and is possibly unsuited by an easy surface. *H. Candy.* **104**

SAILLE DECEIT 2 gr.f. Grisaille 115–Lutescens (Skymaster 126) [1976 5g 5fg 5f⁶ 6f⁴ 6h 7f 5fg] very small, light-framed filly: worthless plater. *E. Magner.* **43**

SAILOR'S FROLIC 5 b.m. Deck Hand–Tumble and Toss (Rough 'n Tumble) [1974 6fg* 6fg 7h 6g⁵ 6g³ 6g* 6f* 6f 6fg⁶ 5f⁴ 5g⁴ 6g 6d 1975 6f 6f² 5.8h⁵ 6fg² 6d⁵ 7f⁶ 6d 6fg³ 5g 6g* 1976 6f⁶ 6h* 5.9fg] light-framed filly: made only three appearances in 1976, winning handicap at Pontefract in September on second of **67**

them: stays 6f but possibly not 7f: best form on a sound surface: sold 3,300 gns Newmarket December Sales. *W. Marshall.*

SAINT BRELADES 2 b.c. St Chad 120–Boucle 86 (Princely Gift 137) [1976 —
6fg 7s] half-brother to useful 3-y-o 7.6f winner Pledge (by Rarity) and two minor winners: 1,550 gns yearling: dam a sprinter: last in maiden race at Newbury in June (started slowly) and minor event at Lingfield in September: sold 300 gns Ascot November Sales. *G. Balding.*

SAINTHILL 3 ch.f. St Alphage 119–Hill Queen 75 (Djebe) [1975 N.R. 1976 —
7s] sister to top-class sprinter Sandford Lad, and half-sister to three other winners: dam stayed 1¼m: 16/1 when well-beaten ninth of 16 behind Marmora Bay in maiden race at Wolverhampton in October. *R. Price.*

SAINT JUST 2 b.c. St Paddy 133–High Fidelyty (Hautain 128) [1976 7fg 8d] **74**
attractive, deep-girthed colt: second foal: half-brother to a middle-distance winner in France by Ribero: 3,000 gns yearling: dam won in Italy: ran better race on first outing when seventh of 17 to Gairloch in minor event at Goodwood in September: should be suited by middle distances. *B. Hobbs.*

SAINTLY GESTURE 2 ch.f. Saintly Song 128–Gedoparonija 88 (Right Boy **73 d**
137) [1976 5d² 5d 6g 6f 7g] lengthy filly: half-sister to three winners, including fair miler Kenco (by Espresso): 1,700 gns yearling: ¾-length second to Sandicroft in maiden event at Haydock in April: well beaten in varied company afterwards (off course a long time after second outing), including in a valuable seller, and no longer seems to be of any account: sold 800 gns Doncaster October Sales. *R. Bastiman.*

SAINTLY SINNER 2 ch.f. St Alphage 119–Miss Rousse (Blue Chariot) [1976 **64**
5fg⁵ 5fg⁶ 5f³ 5g] strong, shapely filly: held up for first time, ran best race when length third of 12 to May Fox in maiden event at Wolverhampton in May: sold 550 gns Ascot July Sales. *B. Hobbs.*

SAINTLY SPIRE 4 ch.c. St Chad 120–The Tower (High Treason 126) [1974 —
5fg⁵ 6fg 1975 8fg 5.9v 6s 1976 10h 8fg] of little account: dead. *J. Berry.*

SAINT MICHELLE 2 b.f. Saintly Song 128–Lochville 83 (Charlottesville 135) —
[1976 5.1fg 5.9g 5g 5g 5fg] bad plater: blinkered final outing: sold 420 gns Newmarket Autumn Sales. *D. Thom.*

SAINT MOTUNDE 3 ch.f. Tyrant–Saint Veronica (Saint Crespin III 132) **62**
[1975 5g 6g³ 6f 6d² 7f³ 7s 7g³ 8d 1976 8f⁴ 10fg⁵ 6f 8fg⁶ 8.3fg 6f³] fair sort: rated 84 at 2 yrs but became disappointing and raced in sellers on last three outings: should stay 1m: appears to act on any going: often wears blinkers: sold 520 gns Newmarket September Sales. *S. Woodman.*

SALAD DAYS 4 b.g. Pardao 120 or Salvo 129–Leila (Grey Sovereign 128 §) —
[1974 N.R. 1975 14.7f⁴ 12.3f² 1976 16.1d] strong gelding: lightly raced and only poor form: should be suited by long distances. *Miss S. Hall.*

SALIAN 2 ch.c. Salvo 129–Sooner or Later (Sheshoon 132) [1976 8g 8d⁵ 8s] **79**
good-looking colt: second foal: half-brother to 3-y-o 1½m winner Solatia (by Kalydon): dam lightly raced: showed up quite well all way when 10 lengths fifth of 17 to Ad Lib Ra in maiden race at Newbury in September and when eighth of 27 to Sporting Yankee in similar company at Newmarket the following month: will be suited by 1½m or more. *J. Hindley.*

SALINJA 2 gr.f. No Mercy 126–Cansanta 96 (Canisbay 120) [1976 5h 5.1f] first —
foal: dam won twice over 5f at 2 yrs: last in August in maiden races at Folkestone (slowly away) and Yarmouth: sold 320 gns Newmarket Autumn Sales. *B. Hanbury.*

SALLOW 2 ch.c. Sallust 134–Mega Fawn 87 (Sound Track 132) [1976 5f 6d 5d²] **82**
second foal: 2,100 gns yearling: dam won twice over 5f at 2 yrs: 3 lengths second of 12 to Abode in maiden race at Nottingham in September: should stay 6f. *G. Pritchard-Gordon.*

SALLY BOWLES 2 br.f. Blakeney 126–Raven's Wing 75 (Nearula 132) [1976 **87**
6d⁴ 7d⁶] neat filly: half-sister to several winners, including smart sprinter Nevermore (by Sing Sing): 7,400 gns yearling: dam lightly-raced sister to very useful miler Lindrick: showed up well all way and kept on, without being knocked about unnecessarily, when 1½ lengths fourth of seven to Circlet in Blue Seal Stakes at Ascot in September: 12/1, ran well on stand side when 10 lengths sixth of 25 to Bessie Wallis in Houghton Stakes at Newmarket the following month: will be suited by 1m+: will win a race. *B. Hills.*

SALLY BREEN 2 ch.f. Sallust 134–Aubreen (Crepello 136) [1976 6s 6s] half- —
sister to two winners, including quite useful 7f winner Esau (by Major Portion):
dam ran only twice: 20/1, showed speed for 4f when ninth of 13 to High Value in
maiden race at Chepstow in October, second outing. *E. Cousins.*

SALLY JANE 7 b.m. Royal Palm 131–Susan 88 (Hard Tack 111 §) [1974 6fg —
5g 6d² 6s³ 5fg⁵ 6s 8v 6s³ 1975 5f⁴ 5f 5f⁵ 5g 1976 5f 6g 7g 7f⁵ 5fg 7f 5fg 7v]
small, strong mare: poor handicapper: best at up to 6f: acts on any going: has
worn blinkers: suitable mount for an apprentice: has raced with her tongue tied
down. *J. Mulhall.*

SALLY LUNN 2 ch.f. Frankincense 120–Bread and Butter (Gratitude 130) **78**
[1976 5fg 5g 6fg⁶ 6h² 8fg⁶] leggy, lightly-made filly: third foal: half-sister to two
winners, including useful sprinter Hovis (by Blast): dam of little account:
moderate filly: 3 lengths second to Mrs Walmsley in five-runner maiden race at
Brighton in August: suited by 6f but is not certain to stay 1m. *R. Smyth.*

SALO 2 ch.c. St Chad 120–Seul 69 (Faberge II 121) [1976 5s 5fg 7.2f²] first **78**
foal: 3,800 gns yearling: dam won over 7f at 2 yrs: well backed when 3 lengths
second of 14 to Gala Lad in seller at Haydock in August: will be suited by 1m.
J. W. Watts.

SALOPIA 2 b.g. Decoy Boy 129–Pinochle 61 (Matador 131) [1976 5fg 6g 5g] —
strong gelding: backward when well beaten in varied company, including a
valuable seller: sold 350 gns Ascot December Sales. *P. Ashworth.*

SALOTE 2 b.f. Forli–Queen of Orient (Round Table) [1976 5fg⁶ 6fg³ 6fg⁵] **79**
lightly-built American-bred filly: second foal: dam, half-sister to smart middle-
distance performer Shady Character, is daughter of sister to Bold Ruler: favourite
for £2,000 maiden race at Newmarket in July but was beaten 2 lengths into third
place by Icena: moderate fifth to Miellita in similar race at Goodwood later in
month: will stay 1¼m. *R. Hern.*

SALSA 2 b.f. Funny Fellow (USA)–Restless Haste (Restless Native) [1976 **72 p**
5s²] first foal: 2,700 gns yearling: dam won five races, including a claiming
event, at up to 1m in U.S.A.: chased Kilavea all way when 6 lengths second to
that filly in six-runner newcomers race at Goodwood in September: will be
better suited by longer distances. *F. J. Houghton.*

SALTIRE 2 b.f. Royal Palm 131–Berryfield Beauty 62 (Gratitude 130) [1976 —
5g 5g⁴ 5s⁴ 5h³ 5f⁴] neat filly: seems devoid of ability. *N. Angus.*

SALTY MISS 3 bl.f. Typhoon 125–Sally Scott 95 (Quorum 126) [1975 N.R. —
1976 8fg 11d] of little account: sold 370 gns Ascot June Sales. *J. Berry.*

SALUTE THE LAW 5 b.g. Counsel 118–Parade 97 (March Past 124) [1974 8d⁶ —
8.2fg⁵ 8g* 8fg 10.4g* 10.6g 12.2fg⁵ 12f⁵ 1975 N.R. 1976 10fg 12g 12g 12fg⁶ *
10.8h 10.4fg⁴ 10fg] poor handicapper: best form at up to 1¼m: probably
acts on any going. *C. V. Miller.*

SAMABELLE 2 br.f. Salmon King 107–Belle of Acrum 56 (Faubourg II 127) —
[1976 5g 6f 5f] neat filly: no sign of ability in maiden and minor events. *L.
Shedden.*

SAMATAJ 3 br.f. Taj Dewan 128–Belisama 71 (High Treason 126) [1975 N.R. —
1976 10.1d] third foal: 420 gns yearling: dam stayed 1m: started slowly when
tailed off in maiden race won by Blyth's Folly at Windsor in September: sold
400 gns Ascot October Sales. *H. Payne.*

SAMBROOK 3 ch.g. Amber Light 114–Mainstream (River Chanter 121) [1975 **60**
6fg 7d 7g 1976 8g 9f⁶ 10fg⁵ 10.1f⁵ 10g⁴ 9s⁵ 10v² 10v⁵] modest plater: suited
by 1¼m: acts on any going. *R. Akehurst.*

SAM BROWNE 4 b.c. Double Jump 131–Sam's Song 99 (Narrator 127) [1974 —
5g 6d* 7.2g 1975 7s 7f 8fg⁵ 10fg 1976 15f⁶] big, tall, lengthy colt: not
certain to stay 15f: seems to act on any going. *J. Hardy.*

SAMBURU 3 b.c. Attractive 72–Inyanga 90 (Lord of Verona 120) [1975 N.R. —
1976 12v⁵ 10s 12fg] of little account. *N. Robinson.*

SAM CADE 5 br.g. Faberge II 121–Wanderly Wagon (Road House II) [1974 —
8g 8g⁶ 5.3fg⁴ 5g 6g 1975 8f³ 7f³ 7fg² 7f 8.2g² 8.3f* 8.2fg* 8fg⁵ 8g 1976 7fg
8fg] small, compact gelding: plater: stays 1m: acts on any going: sold 480
gns Ascot June Sales for export to Sweden. *M. Smyly.*

SAME AS TOM 3 b.c. Candy Cane 125–Delfgirl (Immortality) [1975 N.R. —
1976 9f⁴ 8fg 7g⁵ 10d⁶ 6f 8g 8d 10.5v] plating-class maiden: should stay 1¼m. *P.
Farrell.*

SAMMY SOUZA 2 b.g. Double-U-Jay 120–Robert's Carol 69 (Sing Sing 134) —
[1976 6g 5fg 5s⁵] second foal: 500 gns yearling: dam won over hurdles: showed
first sign of ability when about 8 lengths fifth of 18 to Military Queen in maiden
race at Warwick in October: should stay 6f+. *W. Payne.*

SAMOA TAN 5 b.m. Pago Pago–Tan Jane (Summer Tan) [1974 7fg 10s 10g⁶
7fg 10f² 11.5g 10.6s 1975 10.1fg* 10g⁴ 12h 12g 1976 12g] well-made
American-bred mare: ran only once at 5 yrs: best at 1¼m and evidently doesn't
stay 1½m: acts on any going, except perhaps hard: has twice worn blinkers:
has run respectably for a lady rider. *D. Dale.*

SANAARA'S PEARL 2 ch.c. Gulf Pearl 117–Sanaara (Mourne 127) [1976   75
5fg⁶ 6s³ 7fg⁶ 7fg 8v] strong, compact colt: second reported foal: half-brother
to useful plater Beechwood Lad (by Skymaster), successful at up to 15f: 400
gns foal and resold 450 gns yearling: dam never ran: 3 lengths third of 14 to
Sir Lord in maiden race at Ayr in June: off course subsequently until September
and did not reproduce that form: should stay middle distances: tried in blinkers
final outing. *W. Haigh.*

SAN BERNADINO 2 b.c. Kaiseradler–Sporada (Masetto) [1976 6fg⁴ 6fg²   85
6d⁵] American-foaled German-bred colt: first foal: dam won four races in
Germany: showed promise in two maiden races at Newmarket, chasing home
5-length winner Habeebti in second of them: odds on for maiden event at
Yarmouth in September but ran disappointingly behind very easy winner Supernaculum: will stay 1½m. *R. Armstrong.*

SAN CELSO 4 ch.g. Appiani II 128–St Cecilia 113 (Milesian 125) [1974 N.R.
1975 12f⁶ 12f³ 12f³ 12g 12g² 14g³ 1976 13g] ex-Irish gelding: appeared to
stay 1¾m: had been tried in blinkers: dead. *D. McCain.*

SANDBECK LADY 2 ch.f. Pentland Firth 125–Miss Camie 65 (Flyover 109)   52
[1976 5d 6v⁵ 6s 5s] compact filly: poor plater: will be suited by 7f+: ran
respectably in blinkers on final outing. *A. Doyle.*

SANDBECK SONG 2 ch.f. Song 132–Fair Martyr 88 (Saint Crespin III 132)   70
[1976 5fg⁵ 5s 5f³ 5h* 6fg³ 5h² 6f² 6f 6f⁴ 5fg] robust filly: first live foal: 300
gns yearling: dam stayed 7f: won maiden auction event at Carlisle in June
all out by ⅜ length from Ben Hall: ran several good races afterwards, finishing
second in two nurseries at Redcar in August: stays 6f well: possibly needs a
sound surface, and acts on hard going: blinkered eighth outing: suitable mount
for an apprentice. *A. Doyle.*

SANDEWAN 3 b.f. Taj Dewan 128–Stockingful (Santa Claus 133) [1975 N.R.
1976 8h 12fg] first foal: dam once-raced half-sister to smart miler Richboy:
backward and ridden by 7-lb claimer when behind in maiden race at Teesside
in April: pulled up only subsequent outing (September). *N. Adam.*

SANDFORD LADY 4 b.f. Will Somers 114 §–Hill Queen 75 (Djebe) [1974   116
N.R. 1975 5d 6fg* 7fg³ 5.8f* 6g² 1976 5f² 6g* 6d* 6f⁵ 7.6h⁵ 6f 6g* 6d*]
good-bodied, strong-quartered filly: half-sister to Sandford Lad: smart handi-
capper: successful at Nottingham, York (twice, on second occasion winning
Playboy Bookmakers Trophy in September impressively from stable-mate Delta
Song) and Haydock (final outing, beat 2-y-o Gradiva rather cleverly by ¾ length in
Vernons Sprint Trial): best form at sprint distances: appears to act on any going:
bought by Ashleigh Stud. *R. Price.*

SANDFORTH LYNNE 3 b.f. Healaugh Fox–Eagle Dora 96 (Star Gazer 123) —
[1975 N.R. 1976 7g 8f² 8f] poor plater: unseated rider first outing. *M.
Naughton.*

SANDICROFT 2 b.c. Mountain Call 125–Ember Grill 84 § (Indigenous 121)   78
[1976 5f⁴ 5d* 5d³ 5f* 5g² 5f 6d 5g⁵ 5s³ 5f 6fg 5f] big, strong colt: third foal:
1,700 gns yearling: dam won over 5f at 2 yrs but then disappointed badly:

Spring Handicap, York—Sandford Lady beats Kings Bonus

all out when winning maiden race at Haydock and minor event at Newcastle in April: pulled up on sixth and final outings: dead. *K. Payne.*

SANDMAN 3 b.g. So Blessed 130–Golden Dusk (Aureole 132) [1975 N.R. 1976 8s] fourth foal: 700 gns 2-y-o, resold 3,000 gns Doncaster May Sales: dam unraced half-sister to Crepello, Twilight Alley and Honeylight: unquoted when in rear in maiden race won by Pembi Chase at Warwick in October. *A. Johnson.* —

SANDRAY'S PALACE 2 ch.f. Royal Palace 131–Sandray 99 (Sheshoon 132) [1976 10v 10d] half-sister to a winner over jumps: 2,100 gns foal: dam a stayer: led 7f when eighth of 12 to subsequently-disqualified Gunbad in £2,100 event at Newmarket in October, second outing. *C. Brittain.* — p

SANDWICH BAY 3 br.g. Sterling Bay–Tivoli (Faubourg II 127) [1975 6g 1976 6g 6f 6f] leggy, light-framed gelding: seems devoid of ability. *A. Neaves.* —

SANDY SEA 2 b.f. Be Friendly 130–Vivid Blue 74 (Aegean Blue 110) [1976 5g 5d⁵ 5f 5g] plain filly: little worthwhile form: blinkered final outing. *E. Collingwood.* —

SANEDTKI 2 b.f. Sallust 134–Fortlin 95 (Fortino II 120) [1976 5d³ 8g 8.5s* 8s²] half-sister to a winner in Belgium: 1,150 gns yearling: dam, winner of four races at 2 yrs, stayed 7f: won eight-runner maiden race at Longchamp in September by ½ length from Lestelie: went down by a length to Edinburgh in Group 3 Prix des Reservoirs on same course the following month: stays 1m well: blinkered first outing. *O. Douieb, France.* **115**

SANGRAIL 3 b.f. Porto Bello 118–Saucy Queen 110 (Hard Sauce 131) [1975 5fg 5fg⁴ 5g* 5f³ 5d² 1976 5fg⁵ 5fg⁴ 5fg⁴ 6f* 5h* 5.3f³] small filly: quite a useful handicapper: apprentice ridden when winning at Brighton and Bath in the summer, latter by 4 lengths from My Raff: stays 6f: acts on any going: blinkered last three outings: exported to Hong Kong. *R. Turnell.* **92**

SANGUINE 3 ch.c. Sanctus II–Vanga (Rockavon 120) [1975 6g 6g 8.2d⁵ 1976 12g 10f⁴ 10fg³ 10f* 10f* 10g⁴ 12g² 12.2g* 12s⁵] neat colt: won two three-runner contests at Yarmouth in August (maiden event and handicap) and handicap at Catterick the following month: led a long way out but kept on well when beating Gone On by 4 lengths with rest of field well strung out on latter course: ran well in between especially when fourth of eight (beaten just over 3 lengths) to Arapaho (gave 3 lb) in £1,700 minor event at Sandown: stays 1½m well: acts on firm going and ran very badly on soft on final outing. *B. Hanbury.* **94**

SANPAUL 3 br.c. Galivanter 131–Ivy B 72 (Denturius) [1975 5d⁶ 5g 6f 6f⁴ 6fg⁶ 7g 10g² 8g⁴ 1976 10.8f 8f³ 8g⁶ 10.1fg⁶ 8.3f⁶ 10f⁴ 10.1fg³] lengthy colt: plater: stays 1¼m: has run respectably when tried in blinkers: lacks pace: trained until after sixth outing by R. Hannon. *P. Haslam.* **61**

SANPELLO 3 ch.c. Crepello 136–Lovely Lady 81 (Never Say Die 137) [1975 7.2fg⁵ 8s² 1976 12d* 14.7f* 16fg²] good-bodied colt: won nine-runner maiden race at Ripon in June in devastating style, cruising home 15 lengths clear of Slap Happy: ran better subsequent race in defeat, when 1½ lengths second to Shanga-muzo in minor event at Newcastle later in month: landed odds in small race at Redcar in between but was not particularly impressive and is possibly not at his best on very firm going: stays well. *Miss S. Hall.* **87**

SANS FAIRE RIEN 2 b.f. Tycoon II–Late Pension 58 (Compensation 127) [1976 7f 6h 6f⁵ 6d⁴ 5fg⁵ 5g⁶] sturdy filly with bad fore-legs: modest plater: stays 6f: blinkered fourth and fifth outings. *D. Williams.* **59**

SANS ROYALE 2 ch.f. Royalty 130–Sans Peur (Nimbus 130) [1976 6fg 6h⁴ 8fg] plain, unfurnished filly: well behind in maiden and minor events. *L. Shedden.* —

SANTANA 2 b.g. Pall Mall 132–Alamo Rose 71 (Crocket 130) [1976 5.1g⁵ 6g² 6v 7s] neat gelding: third foal: brother to a staying plater: 600 gns yearling: dead-heated for second place, 2 lengths behind Burley, in 21-runner seller at Newmarket in September: should be suited by 7f: probably unsuited by heavy ground. *R. Boss.* **79**

SARAGUSA 4 ch.g. Aggressor 130–Sugar Sugar (Midsummer Night II 117) [1974 7fg 8v 1975 8s⁴ 7s⁶ 7.6g 8.2g 8g 10fg² 1976 12fg* 14fg⁷ 14fg³ 12f³ 10.6f² 12t⁵] quite a moderate performer: 5-length winner of maiden event at Kempton in April on reappearance: ran creditably in handicaps in some of his races after-wards but performed very poorly on final outing: stays 1¾m: probably acts on any going: slowly away when tried in blinkers. *H. Westbrook.* **65**

SARAH DOON 3 ch.f. Doon 124–Autumn Princess (Sica Boy 132) [1975 —
N.R. 1976 9fg 10g 9f 8g⁶ 8fg 8.2v 8v⁶] neat filly: fifth foal: dam of little
account: little worthwhile form in maiden and minor events. *A. Jarvis.*

SARAH LOUISE 5 b.m. Double-U-Jay 120–Jane Shaw (Galivanter 131) [1974 **43**
N.R. 1975 N.R. 1976 8fg 12fg 8.2fg⁶] of little account nowadays. *S.
Holland.*

SARAH SIDDONS (FR) 3 b.f. Le Levanstell 122–Mariel 122 (Relko 136) [1975 **122**
7g* 1976 7g² 8g* 10.5d⁵ 12g² 12fg* 12s²]
    The Irish-trained challengers at the three-day York August meeting ex-
celled themselves, reaping a harvest of six of the important races; Padroug won
the Acomb Stakes, Nebbiolo the Gimcrack Stakes, Sarah Siddons the Yorkshire
Oaks, Hawkberry the Great Voltigeur Stakes, Pollerton the Convivial Stakes
and Capricious the Galtres Stakes. The last four in this list were trained by
Paddy Prendergast who has had a remarkable record of success at the fixture
over the years. Prendergast's tally was his best at the meeting since 1954 when
he celebrated the lifting of a ban on the running of his horses in this country by
winning the Prince of Wales's Stakes with Panalley, the Nunthorpe Stakes with
My Beau, the Great Voltigeur Stakes with Blue Sail (whose running in the
previous year's Cornwallis Stakes had provoked the ban) and the Rous seller with
Gipsy Rover. Let's recall a few of the many first-class racehorses that have represented Prendergast's stable at York since the early 'fifties: the Gimcrack winners
Windy City, The Pie King, Paddy's Sister and Young Emperor; the Lowther
winners Royal Duchy, Kathy Too, La Tendresse and Pourparler; the Nunthorpe
winner Floribunda; the Voltigeur winner Ragusa; the Galtres winner Patti.
Sarah Siddons isn't so good as some of her predecessors but she's every bit as
genuine as any of them and was extremely impressive in appearance as are most
of the runners from her stable. Anyone wanting to know what a well-turned-
out horse looks like, should make the effort to see a few of Prendergast's runners
as soon as the opportunity arises.
    Sarah Siddons was undoubtedly the best three-year-old filly trained in
either England or Ireland. After a pipe-opener in the Athasi Stakes at the
Curragh Sarah Siddons ran five times. In the races where she encountered no
French challenge—the Irish One Thousand Guineas and the Yorkshire Oaks—
she was successful; in the races where she was opposed by one or other of the
best of the French fillies, Pawneese, Riverqueen and Lagunette, she ran with
great credit but she wasn't up to winning. Had Lagunette not been in the
field for the Irish Guinness Oaks and the Prix Vermeille, Sarah Siddons would
have added both those very important races to her laurels. In what terms
would we have been talking about her then?
    Sarah Siddons had to work hard for her victory in the Irish One Thousand
Guineas at the Curragh in May. Two furlongs from home, when she came under
pressure, we wouldn't have given a great deal for her chance, but by the furlong-
pole she was still in the race, and as Krassata began to fade out Lady Singer, Clover
Princess and Sarah Siddons raced for the post in line abreast. In the last fifty
yards it was Sarah Siddons who found the vital final spurt, and she crossed the
line a length in front of Clover Princess who beat Lady Singer by the same margin
for second place. It was a third win in the race for a stable previously successful
with Gazpacho in 1963 and Wenduyne in 1969. Sarah Siddons was returned to
the Curragh nine weeks later for the Irish Guinness Oaks. In the interim she
had been sent over to Chantilly for the Prix de Diane in which she had finished

*Irish 1,000 Guineas Stakes, the Curragh—Sarah Siddons is pursued by Clover Princess,
Lady Singer and Krassata (left)*

strongly to take fifth place behind Pawneese, Riverqueen, Lagunette and Antrona. Lagunette had finished two lengths and a short head in front of Sarah Siddons in the Diane and it was difficult to envisage a reversal of that form in the Irish Oaks. After all, Lagunette was improving every bit as fast as Sarah Siddons and was just as likely to be suited by the extra furlong and a half. Sarah Siddons beat all except Lagunette, but the latter was a decisive winner by two lengths with the fast-finishing I've A Bee taking third place, half a length behind Sarah Siddons.

Well deserved compensation awaited Sarah Siddons in the Yorkshire Oaks, although when the thirteen-runner field turned for home she had only three behind her and compensation looked a long way distant. Switched to the outside, she began an inexorable challenge which a furlong out had taken her into fifth place, with African Dancer, Centrocon, Roses for the Star and Mayo Girl still to be overhauled. Staying on, Sarah Siddons struck the front on the line and beat African Dancer by a head, with Roses for the Star a length away third. I've A Bee, a heavily-backed favourite to reverse Irish form with Sarah Siddons, trailed in last of all. In spite of his filly's splendid win on fast ground Sarah Siddons' trainer steadfastly maintained, as he had done all season, that she would do even better on soft ground. Sarah Siddons' final run of the season, in the Prix Vermeille at Longchamp just over a month after York, showed that his observations had foundation. Sarah Siddons took the field in the Vermeille with her connections hopeful rather than confident about her managing even a place; not surprisingly, since Pawneese, Riverqueen and Lagunette were again in opposition. Sarah Siddons however, ridden by Piggott for the first time, ran the race of her life; she looked to have the race won when coming through under pressure to head Lagunette inside the last furlong but the stout-hearted French filly rallied to regain the lead on the line and beat her by a whisker. Floressa, who had been trounced in the Irish Oaks, showed her running there to be all wrong and took third place, a length behind Sarah Siddons. Pawneese and Riverqueen performed so poorly that their performances in the Vermeille in relation to Sarah Siddons are meaningless, but the fact remains that Sarah Siddons finished a good deal closer to Lagunette than she had done in their two previous encounters. One obvious explanation for the improvement in Sarah Siddons is the soft ground, another the presence of Piggott on Sarah Siddons' back for the first time. We mean no disrespect to the filly's regular partner, Roche, who is one of the best riders in Ireland and whose handling of Sarah Siddons in her previous races had been exemplary, but Piggott at his best is, in our opinion, worth several pounds more to a horse than any jockey riding in Europe with the exception of Saint-Martin and the ride he gave Sarah Siddons in the Vermeille was one of the first water.

Sarah Siddons (b.f. 1973)	Le Levanstell (b 1957)	Le Lavandou (b 1944)	Djebel
			Lavande
		Stella's Sister (ch 1950)	Ballyogan
			My Aid
	Mariel (b 1968)	Relko (b 1960)	Tanerko
			Relance III
		Ela Marita (ch 1961)	Red God
			Fantan II

Sarah Siddons did extremely well physically during the season and developed

Yorkshire Oaks, York—Sarah Siddons leads close home to beat African Dancer (noseband)

into a strong, lengthy, attractive filly. She's a very well-bred one too, being by Le Levanstell out of Mariel, a very smart, genuine and consistent racemare who won three races, including Ireland's Pretty Polly Stakes and who finished in the frame in three classics, the Irish One Thousand Guineas, which she lost by a neck to Favoletta, the Epsom Oaks and the Irish Oaks. Mariel's dam, Ela Marita, was no slouch either on the racecourse; she won the Fred Darling Stakes and the Musidora Stakes. Furthermore Ela Marita is a half-sister to Ragusa; as she cost only 500 guineas as a yearling, she must rank as one of the bargains of all time! Unfortunately Mariel is now dead; she produced only two more foals after Sarah Siddons, fillies by Exbury and Mill Reef, the former named Never Forget. Sarah Siddons should make an excellent replacement for Mariel when she is eventually retired to the paddocks, but that won't be for a while yet. She remains in training in 1977. Four-year-old fillies, even good ones, are more often than not difficult to place, particularly on this side of the Channel, but it is in Sarah Siddons' favour that she hasn't been overraced and that she was getting better throughout her second season. She is better suited by a mile and a half than shorter distances and there's every likelihood she will stay further if called upon to do so. She acts on a firm surface, but seems particularly well suited by an easy one. Like her dam Sarah Siddons is a thoroughly game and consistent animal. *P. Prendergast, Ireland.*

SARANIA 3 b.f. Sassafras 135–Persian Apple (No Robbery) [1975 6s* 6d* 1976 10g* 12g⁶ 8f⁵ 10g 8g⁶] attractive filly: sister to a winner in Spain: dam won over sprint distances in U.S.A.: won both her races at 2 yrs, Blue Seal Stakes at Ascot and Malton Stakes at York: quickened well in closing stages to beat Centrocon 1½ lengths when winning Sandleford Priory Stakes at Newbury in May: failed to reach the frame afterwards in Epsom Oaks (second favourite, never near leaders and possibly unsuited by course when sixth of 14 to Pawneese), Coronation Stakes at Royal Ascot (tried in blinkers when 5½ lengths fifth of eight to Kesar Queen), Joe McGrath Memorial Stakes at Leopardstown (seventh of 11 to Malacate) and Youghal Stakes at Phoenix Park (never nearer than sixth to Serencia): needs further than 1m and should stay 1½m: acts on soft going: a smart filly at her best: trained until after Royal Ascot by J. Tree. *S. Murless, Ireland.* **112**

SARASINGH 2 ch.f. Mansingh 120–Gold Ribbon 106 (Blast 125) [1976 6g* 6d² 6v] rangy, attractive filly: first foal: 3,100 gns yearling: dam won over 7f and 1m at 2 yrs: 33/1, won 26-runner maiden race at Doncaster in September going away by ¾ length from Mahar: ¾-length second to Mrs McArdy in minor event at Redcar later in month, better subsequent effort: will probably stay 7f. *B. Hanbury.* **93**

SARATOGA KID 2 b.g. Saratoga Skiddy 113–Tsing Ling (Eastern Lyric 114) [1976 8fg⁴ 9s*] half-brother to a winner in Germany: dam never ran: favourite, won nine-runner maiden race at Wolverhampton in October by 1½ lengths from Cavewoman despite slipping and losing ground on final turn: stayed well at 2 yrs and is likely to get middle distances as a 3-y-o. *J. W. Watts.* **75**

SARATOGA MAID 3 ch.f. Saratoga Skiddy 113–Bridle Track (Sound Track 132) [1975 N.R. 1976 7f 10f 10f³] small filly: of no account. *B. Wise.* —

SARCEN 5 ch.g. Gustav 121–Littlestone 59 (Tamerlane 128) [1974 9g* 9f⁵ 9fg³ 8f² 8g⁴ 8d 9g 8.2g 8s 1975 9f⁶ 8h² 8h⁴ 9.4h* 8g* 7h⁵ 9fg 12.2f⁴ 1976 8f 8h 10h⁵ 8f³ 8f 7g 8fg] workmanlike gelding: poor performer nowadays: best form at up to 9f and seems not to stay further: seems to need a sound surface and acts on hard going: has been tried in blinkers but does better without. *Hbt Jones.* **54**

SAREALM 3 b.f. Realm 129–Caftan 88 (Kashmir II 125) [1975 N.R. 1976 6fg 6g] small, light-framed filly: first foal: dam stayed 1½m: behind in maiden race and seller at Leicester: sold 260 gns Goffs September Sales. *B. Hills.* —

SARNI PASS 2 b.c. Bold Bidder–Mountain Drive (Buckpasser) [1976 5f] American-bred colt: first foal: dam, half-sister to top-class but inconsistent Ribofilio, never ran: started slowly when last of 11 in minor event won by Top Soprano at Goodwood in August: dead. *G. Hunter.* —

SARONG 4 b.f. Taj Dewan 128–Sharondor 84 (Matador 131) [1974 6s 6d⁵ 1975 8g 10f 8g* 10s² 1976 8fg⁵ 8g 8.2v] strong, deep-bodied filly: little worthwhile form in three races in 1976: stays 1¼m: best form on an easy surface: saddle slipped (unseated rider) on second outing. *I. Walker.* —

SAROS 2 b.c. Sassafras 135–Rose Copse (Floribunda 136) [1976 7s* 7d²]   **120 p**
  Saros appeared in public for the first time, at Goodwood in September, with a reputation which said he was the best of his age in a stable which had sent out such good two-year-old winners as Avgerinos and Adviser, and in a field of twelve he was made a hot favourite for the Limekiln Stakes over seven furlongs, only the very useful Buckpasser colt Man in the Moon, from whom Saros was receiving a stone, being seriously backed to beat him. Saros proved much too good at the weights for Man in the Moon, mastered him without a struggle, and raced away to win easily by four lengths and seven. After this most promising display Saros came in for a deal of support to upset the Irish 'hot-pot' The Minstrel in the William Hill Dewhurst Stakes at Newmarket. They went 12/1 bar the pair in a field of eleven. The race went according to expectation, The Minstrel and Saros drawing out with the issue between them entering the last two furlongs, and The Minstrel showing the better pace from the foot of the hill to win ridden out but not touched with the whip by four lengths; Saros, who had had to be pushed along at halfway, was given an easy time of it in the last half-furlong. Without raising classic hopes, this was a good performance by Saros. The Minstrel is a top-class colt of considerable pace, and Saros clung on well and made a fight of it until The Minstrel's superior speed took him away in the closing stages. Saros is no slouch himself, and granted normal improvement, which he is practically certain to make, he is bound to win good races as a three-year-old.

		Sheshoon	Precipitation
	Sassafras	(ch 1956)	Noorani
Saros	(b 1967)	Ruta	Ratification
(b.c. 1974)		(b 1960)	Dame d'Atour
		Floribunda	Princely Gift
	Rose Copse	(b 1958)	Astrentia
	(b 1969)	Maryland Wood	Honeyway
		(ch 1962)	Margaret Ann

  Let's take a look now at Saros' pedigree. We think it is an interesting one, interesting because it features on the one side a French Derby and St Leger winner who had the pace to beat Nijinsky in the Prix de l'Arc de Triomphe, and on the other side a well-related mare by the top-class sprinter Floribunda. Sassafras, who retired to stud in 1971, has made a successful start to his career as a stallion. He has already given us a French St Leger winner in Henri le Balafre, and those of his stock to have done well in England and Ireland include the smart 1975 two-year-old winners Galway Bay and Sarania, and the useful three-year-old fillies Sassalya and Laughing Girl. Though most of his produce stay, Sassafras is by no means a sire of 'sluggards'. Floribunda, Saros' maternal grandsire, is not noted as a broodmare sire, but then we don't suppose he has produced many fillies from families as famous as that to which Maryland Wood belongs. Maryland Wood is a direct descendant of the 'flying' Mumtaz Mahal, ancestress among others of Nasrullah and Royal Charger, two of the most influential stallions in North America. Saros had only to show himself to be some sort of racehorse—and he has already done more than that—to be virtually assured of patronage somewhere as a stallion. One would have thought that a filly by Floribunda would have had marked stamina limitations, but on the second of two appearances at three years (she won over four and a half furlongs as a two-year-old) Rose Copse was beaten only a head over an extended mile, and we'll be surprised if Saros, Rose Copse's first foal and a strong, good-looking colt who cost 11,000 guineas as a yearling, fails to stay at least a mile and a quarter. He acts well on soft going. *P. Walwyn.*

SARPEDON 4 b.c. My Swanee 122–Pampered Belle (Pampered King 121)   —
  [1974 7s⁶ 7s 10s² 1975 8v 10f 12f 11fg 11g³ 12g⁶ 8fg* 10g² 1976 10s⁶] useful sort: ran only once on flat in 1976: possibly best at around 1m, although has run respectably over longer distances: appears to act on any going: usually wears blinkers (didn't at 4 yrs): suitable mount for an apprentice. *R. Smyth.*

SARSA 2 gr.f. Sassafras 135–Grisella 89 (Grey Sovereign 128 §)   [1976 6g 5s 6v]   —
  leggy filly: third foal: dam won over 6f at 2 yrs: behind in large fields of maidens in the autumn: slowly away second outing. *J. Sutcliffe.*

SASSHAI 2 b.f. Sassafras 135–Ashaireez (Abernant 142)   [1976 7d 6v] tall,   —
  useful-looking filly: third foal: half-sister to fair 1975 2-y-o 6f winner Taiseera (by Northfields): dam twice-raced daughter of Irish Oaks winner Amante: behind

657

in large fields of maidens at Newbury in September (fifteenth of 30 to Guama) and October (tailed off). *B. Hills.*

SATASHA   3 br.f. Sahib 114–Tartown 89 (Gratitude 130)   [1975 5fg 7fg 6d⁴   **53** 1976 6d 7g 8f 6f⁵ 7g 8.2h⁶ 9.2f² 9v⁴ 10g⁴ 8s³]   poor plater: probably stays 1¼m: seems to act on any going: often wears blinkers: sold 260 gns Doncaster November Sales.   *T. Craig.*

SATIATE   2 br.c. Mansingh 120–Feasting (Sayajirao 132)   [1976 5d 5f]   strong-   **—** quartered, useful-looking colt: well beaten in maiden race at Sandown and minor event at Lingfield, both in June: sold 270 gns Ascot August Sales.   *J. Sutcliffe.*

SATIN DOLL   3 ch.f. St Alphage 119–Piccola Luce (Soderini 123)   [1975 N.R.   **§§** 1976 8f 8f³ 10f]   possesses little ability and is temperamental into the bargain.   *F. Carr.*

SATIRICAL   2 ch.f. Sheshoon 132–Whirlbird 78 (The Pelican)   [1976 6g 7g]   **—** half-sister to five winners, including Gyropolis (by Acropolis), a useful winner at up to 1½m: 1,700 gns yearling: dam stayed 1¼m: behind in maiden races at Windsor in August and Newmarket in October.   *S. Woodman.*

SATURDAY   3 b.f. St Paddy 133–Satu (Primera 131)   [1975 N.R.   1976 10s]   **—** third living foal: dam smart performer at up to 10¾f in France: third favourite, never showed when eighth of 12 to Wolver Valley in maiden race at Newmarket in October: sold 1,500 gns Newmarket December Sales.   *N. Murless.*

SATURN SUN   3 ch.g. Skymaster 126–Red Madonna 84 (Red God 128 §)   [1975   **—** 5.1f 6g 5d³ 6g 7fg³ 6g   1976 6g 6g]   strong gelding: plater: stays 7f: has been tried in blinkers.   *D. Keith.*

SATURNUS   3 ch.c. Dike–Shoofly 83 (Skymaster 126)   [1975 5.9fg 5fg² 6fg²   **93** 7fg² 7.3d² 7d   1976 10.1fg 10.1fg* 10g² 10.1fg² 10f* 12g⁶ 10fg* 10g 10g]   rangy colt: good mover: put up easily his best performance when winning £2,500 handicap at Lingfield in August by a length from subsequently-disqualified Air Trooper: ran well on most of his previous outings, winning at Windsor (maiden event) and Lingfield (handicap): gives impression he will stay further than 1½m (hampered when tried at 1½m): appears to act on any going: ran below his best last two outings.   *R. Akehurst.*

SAUCEBOAT   4 b.f. Connaught 130–Cranberry Sauce 119 (Crepello 136)   [1974   **119** 6fg 6fg*   1975 8g* 10f² 12fg⁵ 8d 8d*   1976 8g*(dis) 8.5g² 8f 8fg⁵ 10fg² 8g* 10g³] Sauceboat's initial outing as a four-year-old came at Newbury in May in the Lockinge Stakes, a Group 2 pattern race with a first prize of £12,244. Starting at 16/1 and ridden by the good 3-lb claimer R. Fox, who was unable to draw his allowance because of the value of the race, Sauceboat came from behind to beat the French challenger El Rastro by a length and a half with Dominion a short head away third and Ardoon a further length and a half behind in fourth place.   To most observers on the stands Sauceboat appeared an impressive and most convincing winner and the objection by El Rastro's rider for 'crossing about two furlongs out' was greeted with general amazement.   The film taken with the patrol camera confirmed that Sauceboat veered to the left when making her

Lockinge Stakes, Newbury—Sauceboat finishes ahead of El Rastro (right) and Dominion but is disqualified for causing interference

Strensall Stakes, York—no problems this time as Sauceboat draws away from Island Degree and Katie May

challenge and interfered with El Rastro; after a lengthy deliberation, the stewards found that Sauceboat's rider had ridden carelessly and, in accordance with rule 153 of the Rules of Racing, Sauceboat was disqualified and placed last.

The first part of rule 153 states that a horse must be disqualified (placed last) 'if his rider causes interference in any part of a race by dangerous, reckless, careless or improper riding.' Few who had the opportunity to view the patrol film took issue with the stewards for disqualifying Sauceboat under rule 153 as it stands. Equally, however, it seemed the opinion of the majority that Sauceboat was probably the best horse in the Lockinge Stakes field on the day. That she was deprived of the race highlighted once again the unfairness of rule 153. To use disqualification as an instrument of discipline is bad policy. If jockeys transgress the rules they should be fined or suspended and the size of the fine or the duration of the suspension should match the seriousness of the offence. The rider of Sauceboat received no fine, no period of suspension, only a caution. Any suggestion that he received lenient treatment because he was an apprentice is surely invalid. Fox was an experienced rider and in fact needed only one more winner to lose his right to claim. You see similar cases every season in which salutary disciplinary action against the jockey does not accompany disqualification. It is quite improper and highly undesirable for horses or their owners to be deprived of races won on merit as a means of disciplining jockeys. Alterations to placings should never be made unless the interference, in the opinion of the stewards, affects the result. To argue against this because it would impose an embarrassing responsibility upon the stewards is illogical: stewards already have embarrassing responsibilities on their shoulders, they can't escape them. Such a consideration should not be allowed to cloud the issue which is simply this, that depriving the owner of a race won on merit is no way to discipline a jockey.

Sauceboat's connections had to wait until September before a bona-fide victory came the way of their filly. The Strensall Stakes at York presented Sauceboat with her easiest opportunity of the season and she took it without turning a hair, cantering in front of her three rivals most of the way and having to be only hand ridden in the closing stages to win by four lengths from Island Degree. An extremely hard race in the Diomed Stakes at Epsom in June on her second outing seemed to knock some of the stuffing out of Sauceboat and she never reproduced that form we the form she showed in the Lockinge Stakes. At Epsom Piggott gave her a severe ride to get her to within a short head of the winner All Friends. Two months later it was Piggott, riding Roussalka, who denied Sauceboat victory in the Nassau Stakes at Goodwood. Sauceboat, with Fox in the saddle, looked sure to win when going ahead a furlong out but Piggott rode a magnificent finish on Roussalka to catch Sauceboat near the line. Sauceboat gained her only other placing in the Sun Chariot Stakes at Newmarket on her final outing.

Sauceboat (b.f. 1972)	Connaught (b 1965)	St Paddy (b 1957)	Aureole / Edie Kelly
		Nagaika (ch 1954)	Goyama / Naim
	Cranberry Sauce (gr 1964)	Crepello (ch 1954)	Donatello II / Crepuscule
		Queensberry (gr 1957)	Grey Sovereign / Blackberry

Sauceboat, a rangy, lengthy filly and a very good mover, has a fine future as a broodmare. She has an excellent pedigree—her sire Connaught won the Eclipse and was second in Sir Ivor's Derby and her dam Cranberry Sauce was the best filly in England at a mile and a quarter in 1967. Sauceboat too showed her best form at up to a mile and a quarter, and she acted on any going. *N. Murless.*

SAUVE QUI PEUT 2 b.c. The Brianston 128–Save Us 70 (Darius 129) [1976 **94** 5f 5fg³ 5f* 6g 6f² 6f² 7.2g³ 8g] compact, useful-looking colt: half-brother to two minor winners: 380 gns foal, resold 2,800 gns yearling: dam of little account: odds on, won four-runner maiden race at Folkestone in May by ¾ length from Tudor Lilt: creditable third to Eminence in £2,200 nursery at Haydock in August: stays 7f well but is not certain to stay 1m: ran poorly at Epsom on fourth outing. *G. Hunter.*

SAW DOCTOR 3 b.g. Brave Invader–Beaushu (Beau Sabreur 125) [1975 **110** N.R. 1976 10g 10f* 12.8f* 10f* 16f*] half-brother to a winner in Italy by Ballyciptic: 1,000 gns foal, resold 1,100 gns yearling: dam won over 9f in Ireland: an improving performer who won his last four races, apprentice maiden event at Navan and handicaps at Wexford and the Curragh (two, one an apprentice event): beat Borallez a head, the pair finishing 6 lengths clear, on last-named track in September: stays well: acts on firm going: probably has further improvement in him and could develop into a smart staying 4-y-o. *K. Prendergast, Ireland.*

SAYCHETTE 4 br.f. I Say 125–Cuccetta 78 (Punchinello 97) [1974 5f⁴ 6fg **46** 5.9fg 6g 7g* 7.2g³ 8s 7.2v⁵ 1975 8g 7f³ 7fg 8g 8f⁴ 9fg⁴ 10g⁶ 9g³ 8g* 1976 12.2d⁵ 10f* 16f⁶] leggy filly: well backed, won 11-runner seller at Beverley in June by ¾ length from Africa Star (no bid): stays 1¼m: acts on firm going: suitable mount for an apprentice. *P. Wigham.*

SAYF 2 ch.c. Sir Ivor 135–Treacle 86 (Hornbeam 130) [1976 7d] American- **—** bred colt: brother to 3-y-o Ivory Girl, a useful winner at up to 1½m, and half-brother to three winners: 29,000 gns yearling: dam, half-sister to Darling Boy won twice at 1¼m: unquoted when twenty-second of 25 in Houghton Stakes won by Bessie Wallis at Newmarket in October. *M. Masson.*

SAYGRACE 3 br.f. So Blessed 130–Mange Tout 125 (Galivanter 131) [1975 **—** 5fg⁵ 7d 1976 8.2g 8.2v] tall, close-coupled filly: no worthwhile form in maiden and minor events: tried in blinkers on first outing when trained by P. Cundell: sold 4,000 gns Newmarket December Sales. *G. Pritchard-Gordon.*

SAYIDA 5 br.m. Kalydon 122–Princess Saj (Sayajirao 132) [1974 10f 12d 10fg⁴ **§§** 12d 12.2s 1975 N.R. 1976 12f⁶] plater (rated 65) in 1974: has twice refused to race, including on reappearance in 1976, and is definitely not to be trusted. *S. Matthews.*

SAZERAC 2 ch.c. Tarbes 125–Kirmidian (Bold Bidder) [1976 5.9f⁵ 7fg⁴ 8d³] **82** attractive, well-made colt: first foal: dam won over 4.5f at 2 yrs in France and is half-sister to smart Bold Pirate and French Derby third Gunter: ran best race

when 4 lengths third of 16 to Tin Mine in maiden race at Newbury in September:
suited by 1m and will stay further: acts well on a soft surface. *A. Johnson.*

SCABBARD 2 b.c. Cornish Prince–Cross Quill (Princequillo) [1976 6f³ 6g] **90**
American-bred Irish colt: half-brother to two winners in U.S.A. and to Irish 7f
and 1½m winner Bend a Bow (by Never Bend): $40,000 yearling: dam won at
4 yrs and is sister to Cheveley Park winner Crimea II: ran well in 18-runner
maiden race at the Curragh in August, finishing 2¾ lengths third to Laughing
River: second favourite for £1,600 event at Ayr the following month but was
under whip and beaten soon after halfway, eventually finishing moderate
seventh of 14 to Region: a likeable individual who is better than his Ayr run
would indicate. *P. Prendergast, jnr, Ireland.*

SCALDED CAT 5 ch.g. probably Negotiation–Winged Rebel (High Treason 126) —
[1974 N.R. 1975 N.R. 1976 8fg 10f³ 10h] light-framed gelding: poor maiden:
stays 1¼m. *B. Wise.*

SCALLYWAG 3 gr.c. Sea Hawk II 131–Scammell § (Dante) [1975 10f* 1976 **127**
12g* 12fg⁶ 14f³ 14.6d³]
This very big, long-striding, immature stayer whose size prevents his being
satisfactorily accommodated in an ordinary starting stall, whose length of stride
makes a galloping track highly desirable for him and whose lack of maturity and
abundance of stamina would, in normal circumstances, lead one to believe that
his best performances were still in front of him, ran the race of his life in the
St Leger on his final outing. Finding conditions more suitable than at any time
since he had won a race Across the Flat at Newmarket on his only outing as a
two-year-old, Scallywag came out best of the English-trained runners at Doncaster and finished third to Crow and Secret Man. He seemed at full stretch
from a long way out, showing none of the winner's ability to find another gear,
but he plugged on very gamely, beat Oats by three quarters of a length and was
little more than two lengths behind Crow.

This was a much better performance than his third to Marquis de Sade in
the March Stakes at Goodwood (where probably neither the small field nor the
track suited him) and his sixth to Hawkberry in the Great Voltigeur Stakes at
York (where he probably needed the outing as well as finding the trip, against
such opposition, on the sharp side for him). It was his best performance since
giving lumps of weight and a beating to second-class opposition in the John Davies
Handicap at Haydock in May. Scallywag had only the four races during the
season, so he is still relatively inexperienced. He would have run in the King
Edward VII Stakes at Royal Ascot, where he would, no doubt, have found
Marquis de Sade much too quick for him over a mile and a half on firm going; but
he couldn't be persuaded to enter his stall. His trainer subsequently had a strap

*John Davies Handicap, Haydock—Scallywag creates a favourable impression,
giving weight and a beating to Lily Langtry*

made that would replace the rear doors of the stall and allow Scallywag more room, and so far the device has done the trick.

Scallywag's future is none too secure, however. He isn't an easy horse to get fit and he has had trouble with his wind. He was tubed after Goodwood and there was also a plan, since shelved, to have him hobdayed during the winter; with a tubed horse it's usually a question of seeing how he goes from one race to the next. Scallywag is the first tubed horse we can recall doing well in the top company. If he keeps his form he should be a good prospect over two miles or more.

Scallywag (gr.c. 1973)	Sea Hawk II (gr 1963)	Herbager (b 1956)	Vandale
			Flagette
		Sea Nymph (gr 1957)	Free Man
			Sea Spray
	Scammell (b 1956)	Dante (br 1942)	Nearco
			Rosy Legend
		Always (b 1943)	Solario
			Court of Appeal

Sea Hawk, Scallywag's sire, gets hardly anything that doesn't stay well or promise to stay well. Scammell, Scallywag's dam, was apparently no good on the racecourse and was sold for 160 guineas after three outings as a two-year-old, on one of which she refused to start. She was a well-bred filly, by Dante out of a Solario mare who won races at eleven furlongs, a mile and a half and two miles, and she has been a great success at stud. She has produced six winners besides Scallywag, the stayer Scapegrace (by Vandale), the middle-distance winners Scamp (by Pan II), Silk II (by Counsel) and Vernier (by High Hat) and the milers Downy Bird (by Mourne) and Scabbard (by King's Bench). The last-named remained in training over a very long period; at his best he was useful, and as a three-year-old finished close third in the Cork and Orrery Stakes.

Scallywag has won on firm going, but he ran his best race on softish ground in the Leger and he is the type of horse that one would expect to be ideally suited by some give in the ground. There is temperament in Scallywag's family but he is a genuine racehorse, and his starting-stall troubles seem to be due entirely to the fact that he is too big to be fitted comfortably into a stall. *B. Hobbs.*

SCANDALOUS (FR) 2 b.f. Fireside Chat 122–Spylia (Spy Well 126) [1976 **66** 5g 5g 7d 8s 6d] lengthy filly: half-sister to a middle-distance winner in France by Riboccare: dam a plater at 2 yrs in France: beaten only just over 9 lengths when eleventh of 23 to Running Bull in maiden race at Newmarket in October, last outing and best effort. *D. Marks.*

SCARCELY BLESSED 2 b.f. So Blessed 130–Parsimony 121 (Parthia 132) **100** [1976 5fg* 5s³] very good-looking, well-made filly: good mover: first foal: dam, best at 6f, won July Cup and is half-sister to Mummy's Pet: had quite a barging match with Home Fire when beaten ½ length by that filly in £2,000 maiden race at Goodwood in July, and was subsequently awarded race by stewards: not seen out again until late–October when running well to finish 4 lengths third of nine to La Ville de Rire in Doncaster Stakes: will stay 6f: appears to act on any going: could make a very useful sprinter at 3 yrs. *F. J. Houghton.*

SCARLET MONARCH 2 b.c. Communication 119–Flowering Trees (Ennis 128) **75** [1976 5g 5.9g 7f⁴ 8g 7g 8.2d 7v⁴] tall, good sort: third foal: dam of little account: fourth in minor event at Salisbury in August and maiden race at Leicester in October, putting up easily better effort when beaten 4 lengths by Fast Frigate on former course: evidently suited by 7f but is not certain to stay 1m: blinkered final outing. *D. Dale.*

SCARLET SISTER 2 b.f. Hallez 131–Storm Widow 84 (Technion 96) [1976 **73** 5fg³ 5d 5g³ 6g] half-sister to three winners here and abroad, including very useful 1975 2-y-o Scattered Scarlet (by Hotfoot): 720 gns yearling: dam won at 5f and 1m when racing as Simba: third in maiden race at Windsor and auction event at Wolverhampton (2¼ lengths behind Taj Princess) in first part of season: should be suited by 1m+. *W. Stephenson.*

SCARLET THREAD 3 b.f. Joshua 129–Roedean 56 (Big Game) [1975 6g 7f **75** 6fg³ 1976 8d 8.2d² 9v* 10s⁴ 10v*] tall filly: wide-margin winner of maiden events at York and Lingfield in the autumn: stays 1¼m: ran respectably on a firm surface at 2 yrs but has shown her best form in the mud. *M. Francis.*

SCATTERED SCARLET 3 b.c. Hotfoot 126–Storm Widow 84 (Technion 96)   **90**
[1975 5s⁶ 5d⁴ 5f* 6fg* 6fg* 6d* 6h* 7g⁵   1976 10.5s 5fg 6fg⁵ 6fg² 6f⁵ 5f² 5g³ 6g
6v 6v]   shapely, attractive colt: showed very useful form as a 2-y-o when trained
by M. W. Easterby, winning five races, including Fenwolf Stakes at Ascot
(dead-heated) but is only quite a useful handicapper nowadays: should stay
further than 6f (dam won at 1m): appears to act on any going except perhaps
heavy: ran below his best last three outings, being tried in blinkers on final
appearance. *W. Stephenson.*

SCATTER GUN 2 b.c. Run The Gantlet–Covey 114 (Rustam 127) [1976   —
6fg⁶]   half-brother to 1975 2-y-o 6f winner Still Flying (by Klairon): dam ran
only at 2 yrs when very useful over 5f: unquoted when never-dangerous sixth
of seven to Hot Grove in Champagne Stakes at Salisbury in June, only outing:
sold 500 gns Newmarket September Sales. *J. Tree.*

SCENTED AIR 2 b.f. Derring-Do 131–Rose Dubarry 127 (Klairon 131) [1976   **92 p**
5v*]   first foal: dam fastest 2-y-o filly of 1971: 16/1, put up a promising display
when winning 20-runner maiden race at Leicester in October, quickening well
1f out to draw 3 lengths clear of May Bride: should stay 1m: acts on heavy
going: a useful filly in the making. *T. Waugh.*

SCHLOSS 3 b.f. Busted 134–Schonbrunn 100 (Blue Peter) [1975 6fg⁶ 7g 1976   **87**
10g⁶ 12d⁶ 10.2fg⁴ 10.6g* 10g² 10fg² 10.5v* 10d³]   well-made, attractive filly:
showed much improved form in second part of season and won maiden race
at Haydock in August (by 6 lengths) and £4,000 apprentice handicap at York
in October by 5 lengths from Croisette: should stay 1½m: acts well on heavy
going but is not inconvenienced by a firm surface: sold 10,500 gns Newmarket
December Sales. *J. W. Watts.*

SCHOLEAAGIAL 2 b.f. Shoolerville 121–Corokea (Roc du Diable 125) [1976   **78**
5f 5g 7h⁴ 6g² 6f⁵ 6d 7s*]   half-sister to a minor winner: 640 gns yearling: dam
never ran: blinkered first time when winning 16-runner seller at Warwick in
October by a short head from Dalal (no bid): stays 7f: ran moderately when
apprentice ridden on fifth outing. *R. Hannon.*

SCHOOL FOR LOVERS 2 b.c. Alcide 136–Peribo 71 (Con Brio 121) [1976   —
7s 6v]   second foal: 800 gns yearling: dam won over 5f at 2 yrs: unquoted
when behind in minor event at Lingfield in September and 22-runner maiden
race at Newbury in October. *M. Masson.*

SCHOOLHOUSE DALE 3 b.f. Reform 132–Croomedale (Alcide 136) [1975   **72**
7.5s³ 7g⁶ 8.5s   1976 8fg⁵ 10s² 10.4d⁵ 12g² 12f³ 10f⁴ 12.2f² 12fg* 12.3g³ 10g]
ex-French filly: favourite and blinkered first time when trotting up from Wall
Hill in moderate maiden contest at Thirsk in July (value of win 10 lengths):
blinkered both outings afterwards (had stiff tasks): will stay further than 1½m:
acts on any going. *W. Elsey.*

SCIMONE 3 ch.c. Amber Rama 133–Swingtime 108 (High Treason 126) [1975   **59**
5g 7d* 8.2g   1976 10f⁵ 10s 10f⁴ 11f 10fg 12f⁵ 14fg]   compact colt: bought
out of H. Cecil's stable 2,800 gns after winning seller at Newmarket in 1975:
did not show anything like that form at 3 yrs in varied company but is not
certain to stay middle distances: possibly needs some give in the ground: not
seen out after July. *F. Carr.*

*Crown Plus Two Apprentice Championship Final, York—Walter Wharton brings home
Schloss clear of Croisette (noseband) and Fir's Hill*

SCOPS OWL 2 b.f. Amber Rama 133–Padante 101 (St Paddy 133) [1976 **108**
5f* 5fg³ 6f] neat, rather lightly-built Irish filly: half-sister to three winners
at up to 1m, including useful Irish sprinter Stunning and useful middle-distance
performer Decimo (both by Stupendous): dam best at up to 1m: won six-
runner maiden race at Leopardstown in July by a neck from Swatchel: ran
well against stronger opposition at York the following month, finishing 1¼
lengths third of seven to Haveroid in Prince of Wales's Stakes, but finished
only seventh of eight behind Regal Ray in Moyglare Stud Stakes at the Curragh
later in month: should stay 6f. *P. Prendergast, Ireland.*

SCORE 3 b.g. Dike–Opening Chorus (Tudor Minstrel 144) [1975 7g 8g 10f **74**
1976 12fg⁴ 12.3s⁴ 10.1f⁵ 12g³ 16f* 12fg 14fg⁴] strong gelding: made most
when winning maiden race at Nottingham in June when blinkered first time:
had stiffer tasks afterwards when again blinkered but nonetheless ran poorly:
stays 2m: acts on any going: sold to G. Blum 2,600 gns Newmarket July Sales.
J. Hindley.

SCORPIO MAID 2 ch.f. Crooner 119–Esquire Maid 86 (Aureole 132) [1976 **59**
5fg 5fg 5fg⁶ 5.1fg 7fg³ 7f 8g 7fg 7g] strong filly: 3¼ lengths third of six to
Witton Wonder in seller at Newmarket in July, best effort: suited by 7f:
blinkered at Newmarket and on last two outings: lost ground at start on first
two outings: sold 320 gns Newmarket Autumn Sales. *D. Thom.*

SCORTON GIRL 3 ch.f. Frankincense 120–Scorton Green 84 (Above Suspicion **71**
127) [1975 5v³ 5g² 6fg³ 6g⁴ 5g 1976 8d 6f³ 6g² 5g³ 5f 5f⁶ 5fg⁶ 6f 6f* 7g⁵ 6d]
lightly-made filly: came from some way back when winning maiden race at
Haydock in August by ¾ length from Fragrant Cloud (Fr.): bred to stay at least
1m but best form at 6f: probably acts on any going: sold 820 gns Newmarket
Autumn Sales. *Denys Smith.*

SCOTCH BONNET 3 b.f. Supreme Sovereign 119–Glengarry 72 (High Hat —
131) [1975 N.R. 1976 8fg⁶ 8.2f⁶] good sort: first foal: dam, half-sister to
1,000 Guineas runner-up Gwen, ran only at 2 yrs: well-beaten sixth in maiden
races at Sandown and Haydock in the summer. *F. Maxwell.*

SCOTLAND THE BRAVE 6 ch.g. Bold Lad (Ire) 133–Scotch Corner II (Cohoes) —
[1974 16fg 16fg 1975 N.R. 1976 14g] evidently of no account nowadays.
M. Goswell.

SCOT NAT. 3 b.g. Song 132–Uranda 93 (King's Troop 118) [1975 5g 5g 5fg⁴ —
5v³ 1976 6g] small gelding: fairly useful plater at 2 yrs: tailed off on only
outing in 1976 (June): should stay 6f: probably acts on any going. *D. Kent.*

SCOTS LAIRD 2 br.c. Sit In The Corner–Kling Kling 68 (Hook Money 124) —
[1976 6g 5.9g 8s 7s] second foal: dam won over 7f: well behind in maiden
and minor events: blinkered final outing. *C. Dingwall.*

SCOTTISH DEVICE 3 b.c. Highland Melody 112–Gorgeous Device 88 (Falls —
of Clyde 126) [1975 5fg⁵ 1976 6d 5.9s 5s 8.2s] well-built colt: no worthwhile
form: sold 380 gns Doncaster November Sales. *E. Cousins.*

SCOTTISH MANDATE 3 bl.g. Mandamus 120–Anner Loch 73 (Flamenco) **78**
[1975 N.R. 1976 12g³ 16fg* 14g⁴ 16.1d* 16s] good sort: quite a good mover
and a good walker: brother to 1971 Irish 2-y-o 5f winner Mandaloch and to a
winner over hurdles: 1,800 gns yearling, resold 2,800 gns 3-y-o: dam, useful N.H.
performer, is half-sister to top-class chaser Lochroe: won maiden race at Nottingham in August and apprentice handicap at Haydock in October, latter by 2
lengths from Montreal Boy: stays well: acts on a firm and a soft surface but ran
moderately on really soft going on final outing. *G. Harwood.*

SCOTT JOPLYN 3 b.c. Tower Walk 130–Lady's Walk (Pall Mall 132) [1975 **108**
6g 6f⁵ 6f* 1976 7.6s⁵ 7.3g* 7g³ 7f³ 7.6h³ 8fg 7.6g⁶ 7.3fg⁴ 7f² 7d² 7s²] lengthy,
good-looking colt: won handicap at Newbury in May by ½ length from Gimri:
put up some very good performances afterwards, including when in frame in
Jersey Stakes at Royal Ascot (third of 12 to Gwent), Hungerford Stakes at
Newbury (fourth of 15 to Ardoon), Mark Lane Memorial Handicap at Doncaster
(1½ lengths second to Nearly New after being chopped off and having to be
switched in final furlong) and Cavendish Cape Handicap at Ascot (runner-up
to Record Token): should stay 1m: acts on any going: consistent, running
only moderate race when tried in blinkers on sixth outing, but raced much too
freely on way to post and run is best ignored. *C. Brittain.*

SCRAPALOT 2 b.c. Welsh Pageant 132–Ramatuelle (King's Bench 132) [1976 **73** p
6g⁶] half-brother to four winners by Abernant at up to 1¼m: cost 1,500 gns
at Newmarket April (76) Sales: dam half-sister to top-class 1½m horse Wilwyn:

unquoted when 8 lengths sixth of 18 to Greenjacket in newcomers event at Lingfield in September: will be suited by longer distances: likely to do better. *J. Benstead.*

SCUTARI   4 b.c. St Paddy 133–Tirana 101 (Ragusa 137)   [1974 N.R.   1975   **74** 9g 8.2g 12.2f² 12g* 12h² 12.2fg² 12f² 12fg⁴ 16f³   1976 15.8g 16f³ 16s 16fg* 12.3fg 16f² 16h* 14.7f³ 20f³ 16.9f⁶]   strong colt: quite a moderate handicapper: successful at Nottingham in April and Beverley in July, on latter course beating Dandy Scott a neck: stays well: acts on hard going and is probably unsuited by soft.   *F. Carr.*

SEA ANCHOR   4 ch.c. Alcide 136–Anchor 106 (Major Portion 129)   [1974 8d   **128** 8d²   1975 11s² 10f* 12f* 12fg⁴ 12fg² 14.6g   1976 14d³ 16g* 20f³ 19fg* 18g*] Had not the 1976 flat-racing season boasted a thorough stayer of Sagaro's exceptional quality, Sea Anchor would have had good claims to be regarded as the best horse to race over extreme distances in Britain.   He was one of the best of as fine a collection of out-and-out stayers as seen in a single season for a long time.   In an excellent campaign Sea Anchor won the Henry II Stakes at Sandown in June, the Goodwood Stakes under a record weight in July and the Doncaster Cup in September.   His only genuine defeat (he was backward on his first outing) came in the Gold Cup in which he was a very good third to the five-year-olds Sagaro and Crash Course at level weights.   Under an international agreement the weight-for-age allowance between four-year-olds and older horses was abolished before the start of the 1976 flat season.   Using Timeform's scale of weight-for-age, which gives a four-year-old 4 lb less to carry against an older horse over two and a half miles in June, Sea Anchor comes out of the Gold Cup with even greater credit.

Sea Anchor's two-length victory in the Henry II Stakes over a three-parts fit Crash Course left Sea Anchor's connections undecided for a time about whether to run the horse next in the Hardwicke Stakes or the Gold Cup.   At the start of the season a middle-distance programme was contemplated for Sea Anchor who had shown good form at a mile and a half as a three-year-old, winning the King Edward VII Stakes and then finishing fourth in the Irish Sweeps Derby and second in the Great Voltigeur Stakes.   However, despite Sea Anchor's poor show when tried in blinkers in the St Leger on his final outing, his stable had always firmly believed he would be best served by long distances.   It was decided that Sea Anchor should take his chance in the Gold Cup; he ran exceptionally well to go down by only a length and two lengths to Sagaro and Crash Course after holding the lead briefly early in the straight. Sea Anchor had not been entered for the Goodwood Cup, the entries for which close in April, and his next outing came in the Goodwood Stakes, a handicap

Goodwood Stakes—Sea Anchor (left) wins under 10-0 and sets a weight-carrying record for the race.   Albrighton is second, followed by Asama

Doncaster Cup—Sea Anchor wins from Coed Cochion

in which he had top weight of 10-0. Sea Anchor wiped the floor with his seven rivals; only the second top-weight Albrighton, in receipt of 17 lb, was anywhere near him at the finish. No horse had won the Goodwood Stakes with more than 9-7 on his back since Glaucus, who was successful under 9-8 in 1835. Sea Anchor's memorable victory overshadowed that of the Gold Cup fifth Mr Bigmore in the Goodwood Cup the next day. By the time the Doncaster Cup came along most of the best out-and-out stayers either had been retired or were on the easy list. Sea Anchor started long odds on but the Queen Alexandra Stakes winner Coed Cochion gave him a run for his money, sticking gamely to him in the straight; at the line Sea Anchor had only three quarters of a length to spare over Coed Cochion.

Sea Anchor (ch.c. 1972)	Alcide (b 1955)	Alycidon (ch 1945)	Donatello II
			Aurora
		Chenille (br 1940)	King Salmon
			Sweet Aloe
	Anchor (ch 1966)	Major Portion (ch 1955)	Court Martial
			Better Half
		Ripeck (br 1959)	Ribot
			Kyak

Sea Anchor's excellent record in the long-distance races could hardly be expected to commend him highly as a stallion to today's fashion-conscious commercial breeders in Europe, and in November came the news that Sea Anchor had been exported to stand at stud in New Zealand. A big, good-looking, rangy colt, and a good mover, Sea Anchor acted on any going and was a game, genuine and consistent racehorse. His dam Anchor, a useful seven-furlong winner, comes from a good family and is a half-sister to the smart sprinter Fluke and the high-class stayer Buoy. *R. Hern.*

SEA BOAT 2 b.c. Royal Palace 131–Anchor 106 (Major Portion 129) [1976 **92** 7fg² 7fg³ 8g³] good-looking colt: half-brother to two winners, notably high-class 1¼m to 19f winner Sea Anchor (by Alcide): dam useful half-sister to high-class stayer Buoy: placed in maiden races at Sandown, Newbury and Ayr (odds on), on last named course finishing 4½ lengths third of 12 to Sultans Ruby in September: will stay 1½m+. *R. Hern.*

SEADIVER 3 ch.c. Gulf Pearl 117–Whispering Star 78 (Sound Track 132) **112** [1975 7g³ 7g* 7.3g² 1976 8fg⁵ 7g 8fg 10.6d² 10f³ 10fg⁵ 10g⁴ 12s⁶] shapely colt: good mover: ran well in first part of season, finishing eighth to Wollow in 2,000 Guineas at Newmarket and placed in two valuable handicaps, Bass-Clubmen's Handicap at Haydock (1½ lengths runner-up to Leventis) and Andy Capp Handicap at Redcar (1¾ lengths third to Gunner B): ran moderately on next outing and was off course some time afterwards: did not run up to his best on his return, but was not disgraced when fourth to Obstacle in Valdoe Stakes at Goodwood in September: stays 1¼m well (ran badly over 1½m but isn't certain to stay trip): appears to act on any going. *M. Ryan.*

SEADORA 5 b.m. Sea Hawk II 131–Abadora (Abernant 142) [1974 10fg 10f³ **47** 10fg 12fg³ 12f² 1975 9g 12f 10h 1976 10.1fg 12.2f⁴ 10.6d 8fg³ 10f³ 12f⁶ 8.2fg* 9f³ 10h³ 8g] small mare: plater: narrow winner at Nottingham in July (no bid): effective at 1m and stays 1½m: acts on firm going: suitable mount for an apprentice. *M. Bradley.*

SEA FABLE 3 b.f. Typhoon 125–Sea Baby (Babur 126) [1975 5f 5fg 5fg **51** 5g 5.3g 6g 1976 7fg 7f 6g 8g 6f⁴ 7f 6fg⁴ 7f⁴ 6s⁶ 6d⁵] poor plater: should stay further than 6f. *J. Benstead.*

SEAFIELDS 2 ch.c. Northfields–Rose of Tralee 114 (Buisson Ardent 129) [1976 **83** 6f 5f 6g⁵ 8g 6fg⁵ 5v⁴ 7d 5s² 6s 8s] workmanlike colt: half-brother to three minor winners: 840 gns yearling: dam very speedy at 2 yrs: ran well when blinkered first time, failing by 1½ lengths to hold off Jon George in 13-runner maiden race at Doncaster in October: far from disgraced in nursery when again blinkered on next outing: best at sprint distances: seems to act on any going except perhaps very firm. *P. Farrell.*

SEA FREIGHT 2 b.c. Sea Hawk II 131–Burning Love 78 (Buisson Ardent 129) — [1976 8s] half-brother to several winners, including fairly useful 1968 2-y-o 5f winner Oristano (by Proud Chieftain): 3,100 gns yearling: dam half-sister to very smart Le Cordonnier: 12/1, always well behind when seventh of eight to Night Before in minor event at Goodwood in September. *R. Price.*

SEAGO 2 b.c. Blakeney 126–Royal Case 89 (King's Bench 132) [1976 5fg 5g 8s **69** 8s 8.2s⁴ 8s] stocky colt: half-brother to quite useful miler Royal Ziska (by Aggressor): 1,700 gns yearling: dam a sprinter: showed some ability, finishing remote fourth of 12 to Hot Grove in minor event at Haydock in October: suited by 1m and will probably stay further: acts on soft going: had stiff task when tried in blinkers on final outing. *D. Ancil.*

SEA HEADRIG 3 b.c. Double-U-Jay 120–King's Victress (King's Bench 132) **65** [1975 6h⁵ 6f² 7d³ 6g 8v 1976 8v 8d³ 10s 8fg⁵ 13fg⁵ 10fg⁴ 8.2h* 12fg³] leggy colt: won five-runner seller at Hamilton in August: sold for 900 gns subsequently and was not disgraced in non-seller on first outing for new stable: probably stays 1½m: probably acts on any going. *T. Craig.*

SEA KESTREL 5 gr.m. Sea Hawk II 131–Rising Wings (The Phoenix) [1974 **68** 10f⁵ 14fg 12d 12d⁵ 16g⁴ 16s⁴ 16g⁴ 13v 1975 10.8s 12f² 14fg³ 12f³ 16g* 16fg* 16fg⁴ 16g⁵ 16g² 14g² 1976 16fg³ 16fg³ 16f* 22.2f³ 16f⁴ 16f² 16g² 18g³ 14s] robust, well-made mare: quite a moderate handicapper: apprentice ridden when winning at Lingfield in June: turned in fine efforts when 6½ lengths third of 12 to Coed Cochion in Queen Alexandra Stakes at Royal Ascot and when 8¾ lengths third of four to Sea Anchor in Doncaster Cup in September: stays extremely well: acts on any going: sometimes wears blinkers, but does just as well without. *Mrs R. Lomax.*

SEALED BRIEF 2 ch.c. Most Secret 119–Well Matched 79 (Niccolo Dell'Arca) **98** [1976 5f 5g³ 6f² 7fg 7g* 7g⁴] rangy colt: half-brother to several winners, including fair miler Branded (by Meldrum): 3,300 gns yearling: dam won at 1m: put up a good effort when winning £1,800 event at Newcastle in August by a length from odds-on Pub Spy, and would have won by about 3 lengths but for being eased close home: creditable fourth under a penalty in nursery won by Cake Popper at Goodwood the following month: will stay 1m: acts on firm going: retained by trainer 9,400 gns Newmarket Autumn Sales. *N. Adam.*

SEALEGATION 2 b.f. Seaepic 100–Dear Madam (Darling Boy 124) [1976 7f⁶ **56** 7g⁶ 9fg 8.2s⁵ 10v 8.2v⁵] first foal: dam won a selling hurdle: fifth in two sizeable fields of platers at Nottingham in the autumn: should stay further than 1m: acts on soft going. *J. Spearing.*

SEA LEGS 3 b.c. Sea Hawk II 131–Anchor 106 (Major Portion 129) [1975 6f 7g 1976 12g 12.3fg⁴ 11.7h³ 16fg² 16g⁴] good-looking colt: half-brother to high-class 1¼m to 19f winner Sea Anchor (by Alcide) but is only quite a moderate maiden himself: needs a test of stamina: wears blinkers: has given us impression he is none too genuine. *R. Hern.* **70**

SEALETTE 3 ch.f. Huntercombe 133–Sealing-Wax (Crepello 136) [1975 5g 5g³ 5g³ 6g² 1976 7fg⁵ 7.6s 8fg⁴ 7g 6s³ 5fg 6f 6g³ 6fg³ 8.2d⁶ 7s 8s³ 10s⁴] light-framed filly: good walker: disappointing maiden: probably stays 1¼m: sold 2,900 gns Newmarket December Sales. *J. Winter.* **60**

SEALOVE 2 b.f. Seaepic 100–Miss Tamworth (Remainder 106) [1976 5g 5f 5fg³ 5.1fg] bad plater. *B. Richmond.* **—**

SEAMARK 2 ch.c. On Your Mark 125–Nicest (Sheshoon 132) [1976 5g 5fg² 5f* 5d 5fg⁵ 5g³ 6fg³ 6fg 6f 7g³ 8v³ 8s⁶] workmanlike colt: good mover: half-brother to N.H. performer Nice Palm (by Royal Palm) and to a winner in Brazil: 2,000 gns yearling: dam won over 2m in Ireland: won three-runner maiden race at Nottingham in April by 3 lengths from Felice: good third to Charley's Revenge in £2,200 nursery at Newmarket in July: best form at up to 6f (beaten quite a long way when third in nurseries over further): acts on firm going: wears blinkers. *A. Goodwill.* **95**

SEA MINOR 2 b.f. Nice Music 115–Sea Magic (Hardicanute 130) [1976 5.1fg 5f 5.9f⁵ 7g⁵ 8fg 7s 10s 8v] bad plater: blinkered third and fifth outings. *H. Westbrook.* **48**

SEA MINSTREL 2 b.c. Seaepic 100–Lunar Hornpipe 75 (Mossborough 126) [1976 6f³ 6f 8d 8s] first foal: dam a stayer: 50/1 when third of nine to wide-margin winner Adviser in minor event at Salisbury in August: seventh of 18 to Swift Sons in similar race at Windsor on next outing: should stay middle distances: possibly unsuited by a soft surface. *R. Armytage.* **67**

SEA NATIVE 2 b.f. Faristan 123–Noble Native 98 (Indigenous 121) [1976 5.1fg² 5v³] leggy, quite attractive filly: second foal: dam stayed 1m: in frame in maiden races, finishing ¾-length second to Beriosova at Yarmouth in May and 6 lengths third of 17 to Be Royal at Leicester in November: will stay 6f+: seems to act on any going. *C. Brittain.* **82**

SEA PUSSY 2 b.f. Proud Clarion–Knightside (Graustark) [1976 7g] first foal: dam won over 6f at 3 yrs in U.S.A., and is half-sister to very smart stakes winner Garwol: 16/1 when behind in 19-runner minor event won by Best Offer at Lingfield in September: should do better. *B. Hills.* **— p**

SEA QUEEN 2 b.f. Ribomar 108–Oulton Princess 61 (Sing Sing 134) [1976 7fg] fourth live foal: dam showed poor form over 5f at 2 yrs: tailed off in 15-runner maiden race won by Eulalie at Salisbury in September: sold 340 gns Ascot October Sales. *Mrs A. Finch.* **—**

SEA RAIDER 2 gr.c. Sea Hawk II 131–Betula 89 (Hornbeam 130) [1976 7s 7d⁴] good-looking colt: half-brother to two minor winners, including 3-y-o Bird Cherry (by Falcon): 1,100 gns foal, resold 5,200 gns yearling: dam won at up to 1¼m: ran with promise when 7 lengths fourth of 25 to Bessie Wallis in Houghton Stakes at Newmarket in October, holding every chance 2f out but then weakening: will stay 1½m+: slowly away first outing: will win races. *R. Price.* **91**

SEA ROSE 4 b.f. Hardicanute 130–Santa Rosa 80 (Persian Gulf) [1974 N.R. 1975 7v 10d² 10f² 10f 11.1f* 12g⁴ 1976 9g 10f⁵ 10.8h⁶] attractive, close-coupled filly: little worthwhile form in 1976: suited by a longer distance than 1¼m: seems to act on any going. *H. Candy.* **63**

SEA SWIFT 2 b.c. Seaepic 100–Dantette (Dumbarnie 125) [1976 6f] fourth living produce: dam apparently of little account: unquoted when last of 11 to Brown Mint in minor event at Windsor in July. *T. Marshall.* **—**

SEATON SANDS 5 ch.g. El Ruedo 91–Darting Light (Sailing Light 119) [1974 7g 8d 1975 7d⁶ 8s* 11s² 10h 13fg⁶ 12g⁵ 1976 10g] poor selling handicapper: stays 11f: acts on soft going and possibly not at his best on hard. *J. Turner.* **—**

SEA VENTURE (FR) 3 br.f. Diatome 132–Knighton House 113 (Pall Mall 132) [1975 6g* 7d 8g⁴ 1976 7f⁴ 10fg 10.5g 10.8g⁵ 12g] strong, lengthy, very attractive French-foaled filly: raced only in good-class fillies races, putting up easily best efforts when fourth to Gilding in Ascot 1,000 Guineas Trial in April and when about 2 lengths fifth to Gramy in Prix Fille de l'Air at Saint-Cloud in June: stays 1¼m: trained until after second outing by R. Hern. *J. Cunnington, jnr, France.* **96**

SECRET MAN   3 b.c. Breton 130–Secret Harbour 83 (Ribot 142)   [1975 8.2v³ **128**
1976 12s* 12g* 15d* 15.5g² 13.5d* 14.6d²]

Secret Man was beaten only twice as a three-year-old, on both occasions
by a top-class colt in a Group 1 race: Exceller beat him four lengths in the

Grand Prix de Paris and Crow beat
him by half that margin in the St
Leger. Secret Man was brought
along steadily. As a two-year-old
he ran only once, finishing third in a
newcomers race at Saint-Cloud late
in the season. His victories as a
three-year-old came in minor races
over a mile and a half at Evry and
Saint-Cloud in the spring and, later
in the season, in much more important contests, the Prix de l'Esperance at Longchamp and the Prix
de Menneval at Deauville. At both
Longchamp and Deauville he was
marginally superior to Campero,
with second-rate opposition well
beaten off.

At 15/2 Secret Man was fifth
choice behind Crow, General Ironside, Oats and Marquis de Sade in
the wide-open St Leger betting.
After racing in the rear of the 15-
runner field for over a mile Secret
Man began a forward move. He
came wide off the home turn and
was soon delivering his challenge in
the centre of the track. Two furlongs out he came through to tackle

M J. Lagardere's "Secret Man"
(P. Paquet)

Crow who had still not been asked
a serious question, but as Secret
Man began to tire he hung sharply
to his left and came very close
indeed to giving Crow a hefty bump.
Soon afterwards Saint-Martin let out a reef on Crow who quickly put paid to
Secret Man, but the latter was strong enough to hold on to second place by a
neck from Scallywag. This was Secret Man's best performance in what turned
out to be his last race. He was sent over to Newmarket during December
Sales week and in a deal negotiated by Susan Piggott he was sold to a syndicate
to replace the ex-Henry Cecil horse Element at stud in Jamaica.

		Relko (b 1960)	Tanerko / Relance III
Secret Man (b.c. 1973)	Breton (br 1967)	La Melba (b 1957)	Chanteur II / Mary Tavy
	Secret Harbour (b 1968)	Ribot (b 1952)	Tenerani / Romanella
		Patrina (b 1960)	Olympia / Bonnet Ann

Secret Man is by Breton who died in 1973. Breton was the best two-year-
old in France in 1969 but ran only three times in his second season before being
retired to stud. His best representative apart from Secret Man has been
Monsanto. Secret Man is the first foal of Secret Harbour who stayed a mile and
a half and won twice in this country as a three-year-old before being bought
out of Denys Smith's stable for 8,000 guineas at the December Sales in 1971.
Secret Harbour is a half-sister to a winning sprinter in the United States called
Comfrey. The second dam, Patrina, who ran only twice, is a half-sister to
two smart winners in United States, Picador and Capeador. Secret Man was
well suited by a strong test of stamina and acted well on soft going. He must
be one of the best horses ever to have been exported to the Caribbean from
Europe. *F. Boutin, France.*

SECRET MISSION   2 ch.f. Most Secret 119–Mahyre 88 (Relic)   [1976 5f 5fg⁶ **62**
6v 6s 5s]   well-grown, lengthy filly: first foal: dam won twice over 5f at 2 yrs:

seventh of 14 to Miss Bagley in minor event at Teesside in November, final outing and best effort: unseated rider at start on fourth appearance: changed hands 450 gns Doncaster September Sales. *M. H. Easterby.*

SECRET ROSE 2 br.f. Most Secret 119–Rosemarkie 75 (Goldhill 125) [1976 5fg 5s⁴] fair sort: little worthwhile form in sellers at Thirsk (favourite for 20-runner event) and Ayr, both in May: wears blinkers: sold 310 gns Doncaster August Sales. *M. H. Easterby.* **47**

SECRET STAKE 2 ch.f. Most Secret 119–Whitestake 74 (Compensation 127) [1976 5d 5fg⁶ 5fg⁵ 5f 5g 5s⁶] strong, compact filly: second foal: half sister to quite useful 3-y-o sprinter Palmvinnia (by Royal Palm): 2,400 gns yearling: dam won 5f seller at 2 yrs: only plating-class on form so far. *J. Etherington.* **56**

SECURITY COUNCIL 3 b.g. Realm 129–Miss Maverick 76 (Vilmorin) [1975 5f⁵ 7d⁶ 5f 5f³ 7f 1976 6f⁶ 6f] plating-class maiden: not certain to stay 7f. *W. Payne.* **59**

SEDITION 4 b.c. Tower Walk 130–All England 93 (St Paddy 133) [1974 5g 6s⁵ 6fg 1975 N.R. 1976 10.1f 8f⁵ 10.1fg⁵] of little account. *Mrs D. Oughton.* —

SEED CORN 2 ch.f. Charlottown 127–Rosambre 107 (Sicambre 135) [1976 6s] half-sister to a moderate mile winner: 760 gns foal: dam, who showed form only at 6f, is daughter of 1,000 Guineas runner-up Rosalba: unquoted when behind in 24-runner minor event won by Tudor Jig at Teesside in November: should do better over longer distances at 3 yrs. *W. Elsey.* — p

SEGURO 2 b.c. Tombeur–L'Espionne (Moutiers 127) [1976 7d⁶ 9d* 10v²] French colt: dam won three times over hurdles and races at 3 yrs in France: won 17-runner maiden race at Evry in October by 1½ lengths from Funny Hobby: stayed on to finish 6 lengths second of nine in Group 2 Criterium de Saint-Cloud the following month but had no chance with very easy all-the-way winner Conglomerat: will stay at least 1½m: acts on heavy going. *G. de Mola, France.* **117**

SELBORNE 2 br.c. Royal Captive 116–Miss Jones 61 (March Past 124) [1976 5d 5h⁶ 5g 6f⁶ 7f⁴ 7f²] sturdy, deep-bodied colt: claimed after finishing 3 lengths second of 12 to Darwen Lad in seller at Redcar in July: stays 7f: blinkered third outing. *J. Etherington.* **63**

SELENIS 2 ch.f. Huntercombe 133–Living Free 81 (Never Say Die 137) [1976 5fg 5d³ 5s* 5v²] compact filly: first foal: dam stayed 1½m and is half-sister to Free State: sweated up before winning 9-runner maiden race at Nottingham in September by 1½ lengths from May Bride: no match for Mummy's Darling in minor event at Leicester in November: will be suited by 6f+: acts on heavy ground. *F. J. Houghton.* **95**

SELF PORTRAIT 2 ch.c. Jukebox 120–Cress (Crepello 136) [1976 5d 5s 5f* 5fg* 5f* 5g⁵ 5d*] useful-looking colt: first living produce: 1,300 gns yearling: dam ran only three times: enjoyed an excellent season and won four of his last five races, maiden event at Catterick in July, £2,000 nurseries at York and Beverley in August (scored impressively both times) and nursery at Newmarket in October: favourite and put up a useful performance to beat On Your Knees 1½ lengths in last-named event: twice hampered by swerving horses and in circumstances ran well when fifth to Metair in another nursery at Newmarket in between: will stay 6f: appears to act on any going. *Denys Smith.* **106**

SELF SATISFIED 3 br.f. Great Nephew 126–Solo Performance 109 (Sing Sing 134) [1975 5fg⁴ 5fg² 5fg² 5h² 5.1g⁴ 5f* 1976 5g 5fg* 5f⁶ 5fg⁴ 5g⁴ 5g² 5fg² 5s² 5s⁵] lightly-made filly: quite a useful handicapper: made all when beating Kellystown a neck at Brighton in June: runner-up at Catterick, Redcar and Wolverhampton in the autumn: should stay 6f: acts on any going: suited by a sharp track. *Doug Smith.* **91**

SELHAM 3 b.f. Derring-Do 131–Lavington 64 (Ratification 129) [1975 N.R. 1976 9g² 8fg* 8fg⁵ 11s³ 11g⁴] shapely filly: won maiden race at Carlisle in May by 2 lengths from Miss Kung Fu: found little off bridle when third of five to Alhib in handicap at Ayr the following month and possibly finds 11f in testing conditions too far for her. *Sir Mark Prescott.* **71**

SELICA 3 ch.f. Salvo 129–Azalea (Abernant 142) [1975 7g 7.6g 1976 11.1g 12fg 7f] probably of no account. *A. Neaves.* —

SELINAS GOLD 2 ch.f. Goldhill 125–Selenas Girl (Forlorn River 124) [1976 5s⁴ 5h² 5fg 6f⁶] neat filly: bad plater: sold out of M. H. Easterby's stable 440 gns Doncaster May Sales after third outing. *W. Clay.* **47**

SELLBOB 2 b.g. Red God 128 §–Roman Twilight (Romulus 129) [1976 **83**
5g 5g 5fg 5d⁴] well-made gelding: second living produce: half-brother to a
winner in Italy by Welsh Saint: 3,000 gns yearling: dam placed at 2 yrs in
Ireland: having first race for over two months, put up best effort when 3½
lengths fourth of 25 to Union Card in maiden event at Newbury in September:
will stay 6f+: evidently suited by a soft surface. *P. Rohan.*

SELOCHROME 2 ch.f. Blast 125–Resurgence (Runnymede 123) [1976 6g —
7s 8v] bad plater. *F. Wiles.*

SELSDON 2 b.c. The Brianstan 128–Anjonic 56 (Le Levanstell 122) [1976 **54**
5fg³ 5f³ 5f⁵ 6fg⁶] quite a moderate plater: should stay 6f. *P. Ashworth.*

SEMENENKO 3 b.c. Vaguely Noble 140–Carrozza 120 (Dante) [1975 7g² 8g* **111**
1976 7f 11.5g* 12v⁴] well-made American-bred colt: half-brother to Matahawk's
dam Carromata and to four winners, including moderate 1½m winner Battle
Wagon (by Never Say Die), a leading sire in New Zealand, and Irish 1¼m winner
Camilla Edge (by Alcide), dam herself of Bonne Noel and Tender Camilla:
102,000 dollars yearling: dam won 1957 Oaks: showed useful form as a 2-y-o:
having first outing since finishing seventh of 13 behind Lucky Wednesday
in Vauxhall Trial Stakes at Phoenix Park in April, won £2,800 Ulster Champion
Stakes at Down Royal in October by 1½ lengths from Lane Court with Lady
Singer (gave 7 lb) a length away third: had difficulty going early pace and got
well behind but was staying on well in closing stages when remote fourth of
12 behind Mart Lane in St Simon Stakes at Newbury later in month: will be
suited by further than 1½m: a very smart performer in the making. *V. O'Brien,
Ireland.*

SEMPER NOVA 3 gr.c. Right Boy 137–Blue Queen 54 (Majority Blue 126) **104**
[1975 5fg 1976 8f3 8fg* 8f 7.6g 10g⁵ 8fg⁴] lengthy, useful-looking colt: good
mover: won 21-runner maiden race at Newbury in April on bridle by 5 lengths
from Welsh Flame: not disgraced on last two outings, finishing just over 6
lengths fourth of five to Dominion in strongly-contested minor event at Goodwood in September on second of them: probably stays 1¼m but seems better at
1m: acts on a firm surface. *R. Price.*

SENATOR SAM 3 gr.c. Meldrum 112–Pinnacle 70 (High Perch 126) [1975 **89**
5s 5s⁶ 5g⁵ 5f³ 6fg* 7f* 6g* 7.2fg* 7g* 7fg⁴ 8v* 1976 7fg 10s 9s 8.2f⁴ 8fg⁵]
stocky, attractive colt: dam best at up to 1½m: won six of his last seven races
as a 2-y-o, sometimes carrying big weights in nurseries: did not reproduce that
form in 1976 but didn't look fully wound up on first three outings and had a
stiff task on final appearance (July): should stay 1¼m: acts on any going. *J. W.
Watts.*

SENORA 3 b.f. Formentor 102–Santarima 74 (Romney II) [1975 5.9f 5g —
6fg 1976 12.2f] useless. *F. Dever.*

SEPTEMBER SKY 5 ch.m. Sky Gipsy 117–September 91 (Blason 109) [1974 **88**
5fg 5g³ 5g* 5fg⁴ 5fg* 5.3g⁴ 5d² 5v² 5s³ 5s* 1975 5g⁴ 5d 6fg⁴ 6d 5g* 5f 5g 5fg
5g² 5g 5d 5g 5v* 1976 5g 5fg⁶ 5d 5s³ 5fg 5g* 5g⁴ 5fg² 5g] rangy mare: fair
handicapper: apprentice ridden, made all and held on very gamely when
winning at Sandown in July: good third to Future Forest in Amoco Handicap at
Doncaster in May and good second to Princess of Verona at Newbury in August:
speedy and is best at 5f: probably acts on any going but has shown best form on
soft: not particularly consistent. *G. Balding.*

SEQUOIA 2 ch.f. Sassafras 135–La Lidia 78 (Matador 131) [1976 5.1fg⁴ **87**
6fg* 7g³ 6s²] half-sister to three winners, including fairly useful 7f and 1¼m
winner Sinzinbra (by Royal Palace) and 3-y-o 1½m and 1¾m winner Wounded
Knee (by Busted): dam, who won at up to 13f, is half-sister to Irish Derby
winner Your Highness: put up a good display when winning 12-runner maiden
race at Nottingham in July by 1½ lengths from Daring **March**: ran creditably
in nurseries afterwards: will stay 1¼m: seems to act on any going. *H. Cecil.*

SEREENA 4 gr.f. Continuation 120–Glen Wood 54 (King's Bench 132) [1974 —
5f 5g 5g 1975 8fg 1976 8g] of no account. *W. Clay.*

SERENCIA 3 b.f. Great Heron 127–Serendip (Sing Sing 134) [1975 7g⁶ 6g² **114**
7.5d² 1976 7s* 7g* 8g 8f3 8g* 6d] Irish filly: first foal: dam never ran: won
maiden race at Naas and Group 3 Athasi Stakes at the Curragh, holding on
well under pressure to beat Sarah Siddons by ¾ length on latter course in April:
well beaten when second favourite for Irish 1,000 Guineas, also at the Curragh,
the following month but came back to form with a splendid performance in
Youghal Stakes at Phoenix Park in October, coming out best in a desperate

finish with Sandy Row and Lucky Wednesday: always behind when last but one to Star Bird in eight-runner Challenge Stakes at Newmarket later in month and probably finds 6f too sharp for her: stays 1m well: seems to act on any going: sold 18,000 gns Newmarket December Sales. *S. Quirke, Ireland.*

SERGEANT BIBOT 4 br.c. Blakeney 126–Banning (Crafty Admiral) [1974 — 7s² 7d 8s* 1975 8s 10.2g* 10.4d 12g⁴ 16f 1976 12fg] neat, attractive colt: fairly useful performer (rated 94) at 3 yrs: has made only one appearance since June 1975 (ran as if something was wrong with him when tailed off at Kempton in April) and is evidently difficult to train: should stay well: acts on soft going: ran very freely when tried in blinkers: probably unsuited by track when disappointing at Chester on third outing at 3 yrs: sold 1,400 gns Newmarket July Sales. *P. Walwyn.*

SERGEANT JIM 2 b.g. Major Portion 129–Military Miss 72 (Martial 131) — [1976 8g] second foal: dam winning 6f plater: unquoted when behind in 19-runner maiden race won by Mr Music Man at Goodwood in September. *J. Holt.*

SERNOK 2 b.g. My Swallow 134–Collateral 100 (Compensation 127) [1976 67 5s⁵ 6f⁴] first foal: 3,000 gns yearling: dam effective at 6f to 1m: about 5 lengths fourth of eight to Realm Tree in maiden race at Hamilton in July: will stay 7f. *E. Cousins.*

SEROGAN 7 br.g. Blueroy 93–Silvia Aurora (Preciptic 122) [1974 11.7s⁶ 14s³ — 1975 10s⁴ 12.2f⁵ 1976 12fg 17.1h] strong, good sort: poor handicapper: stays well: seems to act on any going. *D. Gandolfo.*

SERPENTINE 2 b.f. Charlottown 127–Strip The Willow 79 (Native Dancer) 75 [1976 6g⁴ 6g 7d] small, strong, attractive filly: third foal: half-sister to two winners, notably very smart 7f and 1m filly Joking Apart (by Jimmy Reppin): dam unplaced in five outings: 5½ lengths fourth of nine to Red Letter Day in Virginia Water Stakes at Ascot in July, best effort: will stay 1m: not disgraced when tried in blinkers on final outing. *I. Balding.*

SERVICE CHARGE 3 b.f. Quayside 124–Lady Harnham 88 (Sovereign Lord 67 120) [1975 5g 1976 6s 11f⁴ 12.2f² 11h² 10h³ 11f² 10v³] quite a moderate performer: placed in varied company, including selling: suited by 1½m: acts on hard ground: not much of a battler. *Denys Smith.*

SETALITE 3 ch.f. Red God 128 §–Feeval 96 (Alcide 136) [1975 5fg 5g 8g² 60 1976 11g⁴ 10.1fg³ 10f⁵ 10.2s⁶] lengthy, rather lightly-made filly: stays 11f. *P. Walwyn.*

SETARBAR 5 br.m. French Beige 127–Queen of the Moss (Mossy Face 98) — [1974 N.R. 1975 N.R. 1976 9f 9g 12f⁴] evidently of little account. *E. Magner.*

SET SQUARE 2 b.g. Lorenzaccio 130–Russian Dancer 98 (Red God 128 §) 65 [1976 6fg 6g⁴ 6g⁶] second foal: brother to 3-y-o Via Con Vente, a useful winner at up to 1¼m: 1,250 gns yearling: dam stayed 1¼m: showed a little ability in a maiden race and a seller: will stay 1¼m. *Mrs R. Lomax.*

SEVEN THE QUADRANT 6 b.h. Javelot 124–Farandole II (Deux pour Cent) 83 [1974 14fg 16.1f⁴ 20g 16fg⁵ 15s⁶ 22.2fg 19fg⁶ 19s² 16s² 18d⁴ 16v³ 1975 16v³ 12g⁴ 16fg² 14fg³ 16fg² 14fg² 15g⁵ 19f⁴ 16f* 16g³ 19s³ 18fg 1976 14fg⁶ 18.4s² 20f 16f⁶] small horse: moderate handicapper: ran well when 3 lengths second of 15 to John Cherry in Ladbroke Chester Cup at Chester in May: lacks pace and needs a really good test of stamina to be seen to best advantage: acts on any going: suitable mount for an apprentice: has been tried in blinkers: not the stoutest of battlers: sold to S. Nesbitt 800 gns Doncaster November Sales. *R. Price.*

SEVENTH MOON 2 ch.c. Henry the Seventh 125–Pamoon 79 (Sheshoon 132) — [1976 8fg 8v] well-grown, lengthy colt: fourth foal: brother to fair miler Hepash, and half-brother to two winners: dam won at 1½m: in rear in maiden race at Beverley (dwelt) and 24-runner minor event at York in the autumn: retained by trainer 620 gns Doncaster November Sales. *W. Gray.*

SEVEN WINDS 2 ch.c. Whistling Wind 123–Sunday's Child (Nice Guy 123) 67 [1976 5fg³ 5f⁴ 6d 6f⁴ 6fg 7f⁵ 6d 8s 8g] strong, lengthy colt: third produce: half-brother to a prolific winner in Italy by Current Coin: 1,000 gns foal, resold 4,800 gns yearling: dam won over 6f at 3 yrs in Ireland: showed a little ability in varied company: seems to stay 1m: blinkered seventh and final outings. *B. Lunness.*

SHABA 4 br.c. Shantung 132–Miba 109 (Ballymoss 136) [1974 6fg 8s 7d 7v* — 1975 12s² 13.4g⁵ 12fg⁴ 14g* 1976 14fg 12g 16f⁶] quite a moderate handicapper: stays very well: acts on heavy going: has run well both with and without blinkers:

apparently suited by forcing tactics: finished lame final outing: sold 2,000 gns Newmarket Autumn Sales. *P. Haslam.*

SHACKLE 4 ch.c. Manacle 123–Aberystwyth 92 (Abernant 142) [1974 5f2 5f4 **98** 5g* 5fg4 6d 6d4 5d* 5s 1975 5s 5fg* 5f3 5fg5 5g* 5f 5fg2 5fg3 5g 5g 1976 5f6 5fg5 5d 5fg2 5.1fg3 5fg3 5fg3 5g* 5f* 5fg 5g 5g* 5v 5s] well-made, useful sort: useful handicapper: winner at Newmarket, Redcar and Ayr in 1976, putting up a fine effort on last-named course when making all to beat Clintwood 3 lengths: best at 5f: has won on a soft surface but seems best on a sound one: has won with and without blinkers: sometimes sweats up: well beaten last two outings. *M. Jarvis.*

SHADY DESIRE 3 ch.f. Meldrum 112–Red Doon 61 (Blason 109) [1975 5g **81** 5g3 5f4 5f 5g3 5h* 5g* 5g3 6fg6 5fg5 7f2 7.2s2 7f* 7.2d3 8fg2 7d 1976 6f 9g4 7g 9g 8d6 8.2g3 8f3 7f3 10f2 8f 9fg4 8f6 10v2 8s2 10.2s 8v*] small filly: quite a moderate handicapper: won at Teesside in October, coming with a strong run to beat Mister Rushton: best at up to 9f: acts on any going: sometimes has tongue tied down: often wears blinkers: said by trainer to require waiting tactics. *T. Fairhurst.*

SHADY GREY 3 gr.f. Frigid Aire–Gamerullah 85 (Grey Sovereign 128 §) [1975 **—** 5s 5f6 6f 1976 6fg] leggy, light-framed filly: poor maiden: dwelt only outing (April): sold 400 gns Ascot December Sales. *D. Keith.*

SHADY HILL 3 b.f. Hillary–Penumbra (Imperium) [1975 N.R. 1976 8g 10f3] **82** lightly-made, rather small American-bred filly: sister to high-class 1m and 1¼m filly Hill Shade and half-sister to two winners, including very smart Shady Fellow (by Sir Gaylord): dam useful winner in U.S.A.: beaten just over ½ length when third of five to Petilia in maiden race at Yarmouth in August: will probably stay 1½m: exported to U.S.A. *N. Murless.*

SHAKA 2 ch.c. Bold Lad (U.S.A.)–Mobola (Mincio 127) [1976 5f] first foal: **—** 2,200 gns yearling: dam useful French sprinter: unquoted, showed up for 3f when behind in 15-runner maiden race won by Mandrake Major at Newmarket in August. *R. Boss.*

SHAKE THE HAND 2 b.c. Klairon 131–Ragirl (Ragusa 137) [1976 6g 7g] **—** good-bodied colt: third foal: half-brother to very useful 3-y-o middle-distance winner Il Padrone (by St Paddy) and to useful sprinter Fats Waller (by Sing Sing): 3,400 gns yearling: dam unraced half-sister to high-class miler Lucyrowe: behind in maiden race at Kempton in August (backward) and £2,900 event at Ascot the following month. *J. Sutcliffe.*

SHANDREDHAN 2 br.c. St Paddy 133–Scammel § (Dante) [1976 10d] half- **—** brother to numerous winners, including high-class 3-y-o Scallywag (by Sea Hawk II) and useful miler Scabbard (by King's Bench): dam ran only three times: 6/1 when last but one in £2,100 event won by subsequently-disqualified Gunbad at Newmarket in October. *B. Hobbs.*

SHANGAMUZO 3 ch.c. Klairon 131–French Fern 118 (Mossborough 126) **108** [1975 7d 7g 8g5 1976 11.1g* 12d* 12f* 16fg* 13.3g5 14fg3 16g* 18g4 16s2] big, well-made colt: enjoyed a fine season and won five times, maiden race at Kempton, handicap at Haydock (on disqualification of Lighter), King George V Stakes (handicap) at Royal Ascot (by a neck from Tutu) and minor event and Top Rank Club Handicap at Newcastle: stayed on well to lead in final furlong when beating Alverton 1½ lengths in last-named event in August: also ran well when placed in Tote-Ebor Handicap at York (third to wide-margin winner Sir Montagu) and Jockey Club Cup at Newmarket (8 lengths second to Bright Finish): stays very well: acts on any going: very genuine and consistent. *G. Hunter.*

SHANGHAI LADY 3 ch.f. Crocket 130–China Maid 79 § (Tehran) [1975 5f5 **82** 6f6 7fg3 6g 5g* 6g6 1976 6fg* 6fg 6fg2 6f* 6g2 6fg* 5f3 5.9fg] strong, lengthy filly: good mover: won handicaps at Windsor in May and July and Ripon in August: made all and held well to beat Skiddy River all out in a tight finish on latter course: better suited by 6f than 5f: acts on firm going. *P. Cole.*

SHANTALLAH 4 b.c. Levmoss 133–Tiarella 94 (Democratic 124) [1974 7g 6d **108** 1975 8g4 12v* 12.3g* 15d5 14.6g2 14g3 18fg* 1976 12fg6 20g 16s4 14.6s3] lengthy colt: good-class stayer (rated 121) at 3 yrs, winning three races, notably Chester Vase and SKF Cesarewitch at Newmarket: didn't show the same form at 4 yrs and ran by far his best race in 1976 on reappearance, when sixth of eight to Orange Bay in Jockey Club Stakes at Newmarket in April, never troubling leaders but being beaten less than 6 lengths by the winner: pulled up in Prix du

King George V Stakes Ascot—Shangamuzo (right) comes with a strong run to beat Tutu. Lamb's Tale finishes third ahead of Beau Dutch

Cadran at Longchamp the following month and was subsequently off course until October when finishing tailed off behind Bright Finish in Jockey Club Cup at Newmarket (refused to race until other runners had gone nearly a furlong) and remote third to Old Bill in White Rose Handicap at Doncaster: very well suited by a stiff test of stamina: probably acts on any going: blinkered at Doncaster. *R. Jarvis.*

SHANTOGAN 3 b.g. Tarqogan 125–Shangara (Credo 123) [1975 5s 5s 6h6 7g 1976 11.7fg 16h 10.2h3] neat gelding: poor plater: occasionally wears blinkers. *D. Underwood.*   —

SHAPIRO VERDE 2 br.f. Frankincense 120–Double Handful 96 (Major Portion 129) [1976 5fg] half-sister to three minor winners: dam a sprinter: weak 12/1-shot when seventh of 10 to Mia Saint in minor event at Windsor in May. *W. Stephenson.*   —

SHARDIA 2 ch.f. Shantung 132–Zardia 96 (Zarathustra 131) [1976 7.2f*] leggy filly: half-sister to Irish 1½m and 1¾m winner Miss Freckles (by Roan Rocket): 2,500 gns foal: dam middle-distance stayer: impressed us when winning 11-runner minor event at Haydock in August, making a steady recovery from a slowish start and leading inside final furlong to win going away by 3 lengths from Robin's Song: bound to improve with this race behind her and is a very useful staying filly in the making. *B. Hobbs.*   **91 p**

SHARI SWALLOW 2 b.c. My Swallow 134–Saint Shari 81 (Saint Crespin III 132) [1976 7g 8g 5.9s] rangy colt: brother to useful 3-y-o Pass the Port but showed no ability in varied company himself. *G. Blum.*   —

SHARON'S BOY 3 b.c. Crozier 117–Della's World 68 (Atlas 126) [1975 7g 1976 13.1f] lightly raced and no worthwhile form: sold 350 gns Ascot November Sales. *V. Cross.*   —

SHARP 2 ch.c. Sharpen Up 127–Swift Harmony 107 (Elopement 125) [1976 5g6 5f3 5fg 5h4] half-brother to two winners, including Harmonise (by Reliance   **80**

674

II), a very useful performer at up to 1¼m: dam middle-distance handicapper: quite a moderate maiden: probably needs further than 5f and will stay 7f: ran poorly in blinkers on third outing: not seen out after July. *R. Hern.*

SHARPWAY 2 ch.f. Good Bond 122–Sharp Work 110 (Beau Sabreur 125) **79** [1976 5s 5fg 5fg³ 5f² 5g* 6v] June foal: half-sister to three winners in Italy: 600 gns yearling: dam very useful from 5f to 7f at 2 yrs in England, and also won five times in Italy: made all to win 12-runner maiden race at Lanark in October by a short head from Heavenly Choir: had very stiff task on only subsequent outing: should stay at least 7f: wears blinkers. *D. Sasse.*

SHARRAD'S WAY 2 gr.c. Lear Jet 123–Lady Patient (Dumbarnie 125) [1976 **68** 5g⁶ 5fg⁵ 6f⁵ 7f³ 7g⁴ 8g⁶ 7g] strong, robust colt: showed ability in varied company, including selling: stays 7f but possibly not 1m: sold 1,800 gns Newmarket Autumn Sales. *Sir Mark Prescott.*

SHATIN 2 b.f. Dike–Kung Hei 86 (Road House II) [1976 6g 5s] third foal: — 400 gns yearling: dam a sprinter: behind in maiden auction event at Kempton in July (very backward) and maiden race at Lingfield in September (last of 12). *R. Supple.*

SHEILA'S BOY 2 b.c. Master Spiritus–Poladell (The Dell 94) [1976 6fg] first — foal: dam unraced granddaughter of Grand National winner Sheila's Cottage: tailed-off last in maiden race won by Cosy Bar at Newmarket in June. *A. Dalton.*

SHELAHNU 3 ch.c. Dike–Petronella 97 (Petition 130) [1975 5fg⁴ 6fg⁶ 7g **110** 7g² 7.6s* 7.2v⁵ 1976 10fg² 10fg³ 10g² 10f² 10f² 10fg⁶ 12fg³ 10g² 12g* 12s²] attractive, shapely colt: very useful handicapper: enterprisingly ridden when winning at Goodwood in September by 5 lengths from Lucky Mickmooch: placed on all but one of his other starts, finishing runner-up six times, putting up best effort when beaten 3 lengths by stable-companion Gale Bridge, the pair finishing 7 lengths clear, in William Hill November Handicap at Doncaster: stays 1½m: acts on any going but is well suited by soft: usually wears blinkers nowadays: often pulls hard for his head. *R. Price.*

SHELTON SONG 3 ch.f. Song 132–La Speranza (Princely Gift 137) [1975 **59** N.R. 1976 5g⁶ 6fg⁵ 5s] neat filly: half-sister to two winners here and abroad, including fair 1974 2-y-o Raccoon (by Right Tack): dam once-raced half-sister to very smart milers The Creditor and Pinched: showed a little ability on first two outings: stays 6f: possibly not at her best on soft going. *J. Holt.*

SHEPHERD'S BAR 3 ch.g. Double Jump 131–Barlow Fold 99 (Monet 127) **59** [1975 6g 6g 1976 8s 10v*] plating-class gelding: well-backed second favourite, showed first signs of ability when winning claiming race at Leicester in November by a length from Joshua's Daughter, staying on well after being off bridle a long way out: will stay 1½m: suited by heavy ground. *P. Rohan.*

SHEREEN 2 ch.c. Boreen (Fr) 123–Shevara 64 (Sheshoon 132) [1976 6f⁵ 6g **70** 8.2f⁴ 7s² 5s⁶] fourth foal: half-brother to three winners, including fairly useful sprinter Russian Dandy (by Right Boy): 1,000 gns yearling: dam lightly raced: quite a moderate maiden: needs much further than 5f and should stay 1¼m+: acts on any going. *W. Gray.*

SHERIC BOY 3 b.g. Decoy Boy 129–La Caline 57 (Soderini 123) [1975 5s⁶ 5f* **68** 5.3f² 5h⁴ 6fg⁴ 5.9f⁴ 6fg² 6g⁶ 7s 6g³ 6g 7g 1976 5fg⁴ 5f 6f² 6g 6fg* 5.9f 6g 5.8h 6fg 8.3f⁵ 8.2d 7s 8s] workmanlike gelding: fair plater: won claiming race at Brighton in May: ran very well against stiff opposition on seventh outing but was well beaten afterwards: best form at up to 6f: sometimes wears blinkers. *R. Hannon.*

SHERIDAN'S DAUGHTER 4 ch.f. Majority Blue 126–Dandy Brush 82 (Will — Somers 114 §) [1974 5v⁴ 6v⁵ 1975 9v 12.2f 12f² 12f⁴ 10f* 12g² 10g³ 1976 10.2s⁶] compact, strong, good-bodied filly: tailed off only outing in 1976: stays 1½m well: probably acts on any going. *G. Cottrell.*

SHERNDEN 3 ch.c. Runnymede 123–Belinda Pocket 84 (Pampered King 121) — [1975 5g² 5f* 5fg³ 5fg⁴ 5.1g³ 5fg⁴ 5.3f⁶ 5g⁶ 6g 1976 6f⁵ 6fg] well-made colt: very good mover: showed fair form at 2 yrs: well beaten in a seller and claiming race in first part of season: should stay 6f: acts well on firm going: blinkered second outing and was sold 1,900 gns afterwards for export to Belgium. *G. Balding.*

SHESHEEN 4 gr.f. Lauso–Golden Lima 67 (Kalydon 122) [1974 7fg 7g 8v 10s — 1975 11.1v⁴ 16.9f² 14g³ 16h² 16g 1976 16f⁵ 17.7f⁵] narrow, leggy filly: good walker: poor handicapper: stays well: acts on hard going: suitable mount for an apprentice: changed hands 1,600 gns Doncaster October Sales. *W. Stephenson.*

SHIMMY DANCER 3 b.f. Hul a Hul 124–Gay Biddy 48 (Khalkis 127) [1975 — N.R. 1976 7g 8.2f] first foal: dam, poor plater, ran only at 2 yrs: seemed only plating class: dead. *W. Wharton.*

SHIMNAR 2 b.c. Baldric II 131–Shiraza (Twilight Alley 133) [1976 5.5d* **115** 5g* 8g²] smart French colt: half-brother to two winners in France, including very useful 3-y-o Sharazar (by Silver Shark), a winner at up to 6f at 2 yrs: dam a very useful performer at up to 13f: won newcomers race at Evry in June and well-contested event at Vichy the following month but got home only by a head from Garofalo in a very close finish to latter race: ran very well when tried over 1m in Prix des Foals at Deauville in August, being up with leaders all way and going down by only ½ length to Juge de Paix: not seen out afterwards: will stay at least 1¼m. *F. Mathet, France.*

SHINE ON 4 ch.f. Silver Cloud 121–Gunnhildr 65 (Hill Gail) [1974 5s³ 5s² 5g² **80** 6fg* 7g² 8g 1975 9g⁵ 9s⁵ 8f² 10f⁶ 8d 8d⁵ 8g 1976 10.2g 7g* 7d² 8f⁶ 8d 8f³ 8.2g³ 7g³ 7g² 8fg² 10.4fg² 8fg* 10.5v 8.2v⁶ 8v] strong filly: quite a moderate handicapper: won at Teesside in the spring and ran creditably in several of her races afterwards, gaining a further success at Beverley in September when holding off Sir Pelleas by 1½ lengths: should stay 1¼m: acts on any going, except perhaps heavy: suitable mount for an apprentice: genuine and consistent. *Denys Smith.*

SHINING LOVE 3 br.f. John Splendid 116–Never Rust (Rustam 127) [1975 5f — 6fg 1976 6g] evidently of no account: sold 160 gns Ascot November Sales. *R. Supple.*

SHINTIN 3 br.f. Le Dieu d'Or 119–Moreland Brandy 74 (Cash and Courage 116) — [1975 8.2g 1976 7g⁶ 7g 7fg 7d] bad plater: sold 525 gns Ascot November Sales. *W. Wharton.*

SHINY'S FIRST 2 b.f. Shiny Tenth 120–Eirlys 90 (Elopement 125) [1976 5f] — half-brother to a winning plater and to a winner abroad: dam ran only twice: unquoted, dwelt when behind in 15-runner maiden race won by Mandrake Major at Newmarket in August. *N. Callaghan.*

SHIRLEYS GIRL 2 gr.f. Veiled Wonder–Princess Flora 64 (Floribunda 136) **78** [1976 5g³ 5f⁵ 6g 5fg⁶ 5h⁵ 5fg³] neat filly: half-sister to two winners, including fair 1m to 1¼m handicapper Knaresboro (by Privy Seal): dam of little account: quite moderate: has had tongue tied down: will be suited by 6f. *B. Hanbury.*

SHIRTY BOY 3 b.c. King's Leap 111–Aspidistra 86 (Royal Palm 131) [1975 **65** 5s 5s* 6f 7g 5f* 5h⁴ 5g⁵ 1976 7d 10f 8g 6g 7g⁴ 5f⁶ 8h³ 7f³ 8h* 6g 10.4fg] strong, compact colt: sold out of K. Payne's stable 580 gns after winning seller at Carlisle in July: stays 1m: acts on any going: sometimes wears blinkers but has done better without: suitable mount for an apprentice. *T. Fairhurst.*

SHOOTING SEASON 2 b.f. Silly Season 127–Tumbledown 75 (Relic) [1976 **80** 7g³ 7g³ 8g⁶] attractive, rangy filly: good mover: half-sister to two winners, including useful middle-distance performer Young Arthur (by Darling Boy): 4,100 gns yearling: dam daughter of useful stayer Tamper: favourite on first two outings but could finish only third each time, being beaten 3½ lengths by Taffytina in £2,100 event at Newmarket in July and 2½ lengths by Port Ahoy in maiden race at Yarmouth two months later: out of her depth when tried over 1m but should stay that distance. *H. Cecil.*

SHOP STEWARD 2 b.c. Fleece 114–Heron's Strike (Combat 123) [1976 7f — 7g 8.2s] useless. *J. H. Peacock.*

SHORE CAPTAIN 4 b.g. Skymaster 126–West Virginia (Charlottesville 135) **74** [1974 6g 6fg⁵ 6s³ 6d 1975 8g⁴ 9f* 8g⁴ 10fg³ 10.1fg* 10f* 12g² 10g³ 1976 11.7f 10fg³ 9g⁵ 10f⁴ 10.8h³ 10g* 10h³ 10f⁴] strong gelding: quite a moderate handicapper: successful at Newbury in July by ½ length from Bright Fire: stays 1½m really well: acts on hard going: sold to M. Scudamore 4,800 gns Ascot October Sales. *J. Dunlop.*

SHORTBREAD 3 b.f. Crisp and Even 116–Astoria 92 (Derring-Do 131) [1975 **104** 6g 7fg* 7g² 1976 7f⁵ 8fg 10g⁵ 10fg³ 10f² 12f* 12g² 11g⁴ 11g³ 10.5s⁶] neat filly: placed at Newbury (third to Silken Way in Twyford Stakes) and Brighton (runner-up to Honey Blossom in handicap) when trained by J. Bethell: subsequently sent to race in Scandinavia, and narrowly won a sponsored conditions event at Oslo in August: runner-up in Norsk Oaks on same course and finished 6 lengths fourth to Swell Fellow in Goteborgs Stora Pris at Aby in September prior to finishing very good sixth (beaten just under 5 lengths) to No No Nanette in Prix de Flore at Saint-Cloud in October: stays 1½m: seems to act on any going: wears blinkers nowadays. *B. Olsson, Norway.*

SHORT SEA 2 ch.c. Shiny Tenth 120–Lease Lend 96 (Cash and Courage 116) **86** [1976 5g⁶ 5f² 5f⁴ 5s 6d⁴] half-brother to a winning 2-y-o plater by Soueida: 1,050 gns foal, resold 3,000 gns as a yearling: dam a sprinter: in frame in maiden races, finishing just over ½-length fourth of 23 to Running Bull at Newmarket in October: stays 6f. *A. Pitt.*

SHORT TERM 3 b.g. Hardicanute 130–Red Rag (Ragusa 137) [1975 6fg³ **76 d** 5f 6fg* 6f⁶ 8f⁵ 8f* 8.2d 1976 12.2g* 11.1fg* 12g⁵ 12fg³ 12.2g 10.8f⁶] smallish gelding: won early-season handicaps at Catterick and Wolverhampton: stays 1½m well: acts on firm going: has won with and without blinkers: ran poorly final outing (July). *J. Hardy.*

SHOWBOARD 2 b.c. One For All–Atwitter (Battlefield) [1976 7fg] neat, **— p** attractive American-bred colt: half-brother to several winners in U.S.A., notably smart stakes winner Aglimmer (by Grey Dawn II): $40,000 yearling: dam ran only three times: 25/1 showed up for over 4f when behind in 18-runner maiden race won by Oriental Rocket at Newbury in August: will do better at 3 yrs. *J. Tree.*

SHOWMAN'S FAIR 13 b.g. Fidalgo 129–Reef Knot (Blue Peter) [1974 12.2f² **—** 12g⁵ 12.2fg² 12f⁴ 12g* 12fg⁶ 12g* 13.8f 12g⁶ 12s 12.2g 13d⁶ 1975 12.2fg 12fg 12g⁴ 12f⁶ 12fg 10g⁵ 12f 1976 12d 12fg⁶] poor selling handicapper nowadays: stays 1¾m: well suited by a sound surface: good mount for a boy: tailed off both outings in 1976. *D. Williams.*

SHOWPIECE 2 b.c. Daring Display 129–Magic Thrust 102 (Zarathustra 131) **100** [1976 5d² 6fg⁴ 6fg⁶ 6g* 6g⁵ 8g] dipped-backed colt: good mover: half-brother to two winners, including high-class German 3-y-o middle-distance performer Sharper (by Sea Hawk II): dam showed best form at up to 1m: ran very well to win £2,600 nursery at Kempton in August by ½ length from The Sign Centre after looking to have a fair bit to do at halfway: fair fifth to Broon's Secret in similar event at Ayr the following month: should be suited by 1m: badly hampered third outing. *R. Hern.*

SHOW STEALER 2 b.c. Quayside 124–Chequered Flag 70 (King's Troop 118) **82** [1976 5g⁵ 7f⁶ 5g* 6v] second foal: half-brother to Vital Statistics (by Keren), winner over 5f at 2 yrs in 1975: dam won over 5f as a 2-y-o: made all and held off Green Turtle Diver by a short head, despite flashing tail under pressure, when winning 21-runner seller at Ayr in September (no bid): form only at 5f but should stay further. *Denys Smith.*

SHOW STOPPER 2 b.f. Habitat 134–Careysville 79 (Supreme Court 135) **70 p** [1976 5fg 5g³] big, well-made filly: half-sister to Irish 3-y-o 9f winner Brazos (by Bold Lad, Ire) and to a winner abroad by Sovereign Path: 12,500 gns yearling: dam lightly-raced half-sister to 1961 Coronation Stakes winner Aiming High: ran promisingly when 5¾ lengths third of nine to Be Easy in maiden race at Kempton in July, having every chance 1f out but then finding lack of peak fitness telling against her: will stay 1m: probably has further improvement in her. *G. Harwood.*

SHRIKE 2 b.c. Whistling Wind 123–Nonstopnell 92 (Arctic Time 127) [1976 5fg **63** 5fg] brother to very useful 1970 2-y-o Windstorm, and half-brother to two other winners: 620 gns yearling: dam won twice over 1m in Ireland: behind in maiden races at Salisbury in May (auction event) and June: sold 440 gns Ascot September Sales. *G. Harwood.*

SHUFFLING 5 ch.g. St Chad 120–Shoofly 83 (Skymaster 126) [1974 8.2fg **93** 6fg* 7g⁵ 7f⁴ 7g⁵ 6d³ 6d* 6g² 6d* 6s* 6g* 6s* 6v* 1975 7v 7s 6g⁶ 6fg 6g 6g 6f 6d 6g 6g* 6g³ 7f 6s* 1976 6d 6fg⁶ 6fg³ 6fg⁶ 6g³ 6g 6g* 7v 6s⁴ 7s³ 5s] compact gelding: fairly useful handicapper: generally at his best in the autumn, and came with a great rattle to peg back Maxi's Taxi and Kiyoswanee when winning at Newmarket in September: creditable fourth to Hillandale at Doncaster the following month, best subsequent effort: stays 7f but best form at 6f: has won on a firm surface but is particularly well suited by soft ground: has been tried in blinkers: sometimes wears bandages: excellent mount for an apprentice. *W. Wharton.*

SHUKRAN 3 b.f. Illa Laudo 117–Contourno (Continuation 120) [1975 5fg* **66** 5g⁴ 5f* 6f⁴ 7fg⁴ 8fg² 8f⁴ 8g² 8.2g* 7.2v] 1976 9g 8f 8f 9fg 7f³ 8f⁵ 6g⁴ 12fg] well-made filly: quite a useful performer at 2 yrs but is only quite moderate nowadays and ran in a seller on penultimate outing: stays 1m: possibly unsuited by heavy ground: best form at 3 yrs in blinkers. *M. W. Easterby.*

SHUSH 2 b.c. Diplomat Way–Yell Aloud (Laugh Aloud) [1976 5f⁴ 4s² 5s* 6f² **100** 6fg³ 6fg⁴] lengthy, good sort: American-bred: first foal: dam won at up to 6f in U.S.A., including a claiming event: ran on gamely to win 15-runner maiden race at Doncaster in May by neck from Viva Zapote: ran well afterwards, going down by only a short head to Brown Mint in minor event at Windsor in July and finishing 2¾ lengths third to Abs in seven-runner New Ham Stakes at Goodwood later in month, but was not seen out after early August: will stay 7f: acts on any going. *H. Candy.*

SHUWAIMAN 3 b.c. Alcide 136–Kentucky Blues 83 (Royal Record II) [1975 **82** N.R. 1976 11.1g 12fg² 12.3f² 10g* 10f² 12v⁵ 11v⁵] strong, attractive colt: second produce: 2,600 gns foal, resold 4,000 gns yearling: dam showed ability over sprint distances at 2 yrs: won maiden race at Sandown in September by 1½ lengths from Candid Queen: stays 1½m: acts on firm going and is unsuited on heavy ground. *R. Price.*

SHY MELD 3 ch.f. Meldrum 112–Twice Shy (Lord of Verona 120) [1975 5fg **62** 5f* 6g³ 5.9f⁶ 5g 1976 6v² 7d 6fg* 10.6d³ 9g 9.4h² 6h²] smallish, strong filly: plater: attracted no bid after winning all out at Carlisle in May: apprentice ridden when good second in non-selling handicaps at Catterick in July: stays 9f: acts on any going: takes a strong hold. *G. Richards.*

SIBARD 3 b.g. Quayside 124–Gold Empress 76 (Coronation Year 124) [1975 — N.R. 1976 10.1f] half-brother to very useful 1m to 1¼m handicapper Owen- boliska (by Compensation): 420 gns yearling: dam a stayer: last of 11 in maiden race at Windsor in July: sold 360 gns Ascot December Sales. *D. Gandolfo.*

SIBERIAN TIGER 2 b. or br.c. Sir Ivor 135–Tiger Lily II (Endeavour II) ? [1976 8v*] American-bred French colt: half-brother to fairly useful 1973 2-y-o 5f winner Belle Tigresse (by Jaipur), smart 1974 French 2-y-o 7f winner Win Tiger (by Restless Wind) and to a winner in U.S.A.: 36,000-dollar yearling: dam very useful winner of three races from 5f to 1m in France: favourite for 19-runner newcomers event at Maisons-Laffitte in November and put up a very promising effort, always being well placed and coming home 6 lengths clear: will stay 1¼m: bound to go on to better things. *F. Boutin, France.*

SICA LIGHT 2 b.g. Fantastic Light 119–Madame Roland (Sica Boy 132) **72** [1976 5f 6d 6d³ 6fg 6s 10s 8v⁵ 8v] strong gelding: ran best race when 4 lengths third of 12 to Gala Lad in claiming race at Haydock in June: disappointing afterwards, including in sellers, running easily best subsequent race in minor event on penultimate outing: seems to stay 1m but probably not 1¼m: sweated up when tried in blinkers on sixth outing: sold 600 gns Ascot December Sales. *Miss S. Hall.*

SICASANTA 4 ch.g. Sica Dan 116–Christmas Rush (Klondyke Bill 125) [1974 **70** 5.8g 5v³ 6s⁶ 6v 1975 5.9v* 6f 5fg 5f⁵ 5g* 5f⁵ 5f² 5g* 5g* 5g 1976 5g 6g 5g² 5.3fg² 5g³ 5f 5fg⁵ 5.9fg 5s² 5s² 5s 5s⁶] quite a moderate handicapper: placed several times at 4 yrs, final occasion when ¾-length second of 14 to Offa's Mead at Warwick in October: stays 6f: acts on any going: effective with or without blinkers: suitable mount for an apprentice: consistent. *P. Cundell.*

SIDIANA 2 b.f. Porto Bello 118–Petticoat (Primera 131) [1976 5g 5d 5f] — § well-grown, leggy filly: behind throughout in maiden races at Carlisle in May (hampered at start) and Redcar in June (started slowly): refused to race in seller at Ripon in August and is evidently not one to trust. *M. W. Easterby.*

SIENNA 3 b.f. Richboy 117–Saufina 106 (Hard Sauce 131) [1975 5f⁵ 6g² 6g* **94** 6f² 6f* 6fg³ 6d³ 1976 6f 8g² 6fg 6f⁶ 8f⁴ 6fg 6fg⁴] strong, shapely filly: good mover: tried in blinkers, came off fourth best in very close finish to handicap won by Shanghai Lady at Ripon in August on final outing: stays 1m: acts on firm go- ing. *E. Weymes.*

SIERRA VERDE 3 gr.g. Runnymede 123–Eastern Miss (Eastern Lyric 114) **64** [1975 5s² 5f² 5f³ 7g⁵ 7f⁵ 6g⁵ 6g 5f³ 1976 10.1fg 10g⁶ 7g* 6f² 7h] plater: bought in 850 gns after winning at Brighton in June: creditable second to Briarvanter in better company at Salisbury the following month: best form at up to 7f: ran poorly when blinkered on seventh start in 1975. *Mrs R. Lomax.*

SIGNARY 2 ch.f. Behistoun 131–Syringa 98 (Set Fair 129) [1976 5g⁶ 6s⁵] — half-sister to two winners, including quite useful 1968 2-y-o 5f winner Galtonia (by Galivanter): dam stayed 1½m: showed a little ability in maiden company in Scotland: slowly into stride first outing: will stay 1½m. *J. W. Watts.*

SIGNED ON 2 b.c. Saintly Song 128–Sealed Contract 76 (Runnymede 123) **84** [1976 5f 5g² 5s³] strong, compact colt: first foal: 720 gns yearling: dam won over 5f at 2 yrs: placed in the autumn in maiden races at Catterick (¾-length second to Mummy's Pal) and Doncaster (beaten 1½ lengths by Jon George): will stay 6f: acts on soft going. *W. Haigh.*

SILENT WALK 3 b.g. Tower Walk 130–Jais 94 (Grey Sovereign 128 §) [1975   **50** 5g 5f³ 5g⁵ 7f 7.2fg 1976 6v⁶ 8.2f³ 10f³ 8.2g⁶] strong sort: plater: evidently stays 1m but possibly not 1¼m: sold 720 gns Doncaster May Sales. *K. Payne.*

SILETTE 2 ch.f. Siliconn 121–Merok (Eastern Venture 107) [1976 6v] leggy   — filly: fourth foal: half-sister to useful middle-distance performer Blaskette (by Blast): 1,700 gns yearling: dam poor N.H. performer: unquoted when eleventh of 23 to Amity in maiden race at Newbury in October: withdrawn after refusing to enter stalls at Newmarket earlier in month. *N. Vigors.*

SILICONN STAR 2 ch.c. Siliconn 121–Brush Off 72 (Arctic Star) [1976 5g]   — half-brother to quite useful hurdler Southern Darling (by Darling Boy): bought privately for 450 gns as a yearling: dam a plater: 14/1 when in rear in 14-runner minor event won by Birkholm at Haydock in August. *W. A. Stephenson.*

SILIKAR 2 ch.f. Burglar 128–Queen Plum (Pampered King 121) [1976 5f 5h   — 6f 6f] bad plater: blinkered final outing. *P. Buckley.*

SILKEN JANE 2 ch.f. Continuation 120–Laos Silk (Lauso) [1976 5g 6g 7f⁴ 9fg   **62** 8f] big, lengthy filly: second foal: half-sister to Irish 3-y-o 1½m winner Muslin Rags (by Santamoss): 700 gns yearling: dam won over 5f in Ireland at 2 yrs: only plating class: should stay 1m. *A. Pitt.*

SILKEN WAY 3 ch.f. Shantung 132–Boulevard 114 (Pall Mall 132) [1975 N.R. **103** 1976 10fg* 10fg³ 12fg] lengthy, deep-girthed filly, with a nice, long stride: first foal: dam, half-sister to Sun Prince, won Princess Margaret Stakes at 2 yrs and showed useful form at up to 1m in France at 3 yrs: put up an excellent performance on her début, coming from a long way back to win well-contested Twyford Stakes at Newbury in June by ¾ length from better-fancied stable-companion Crofting: confirmed that she is a useful filly when excellent 2 lengths third of 10 to Roussalka in Nassau Stakes at Goodwood the following month but ran moderately behind Sarah Siddons (Fr) in Yorkshire Oaks at York in August on only subsequent outing: stays 1¼m well: acts on a firm surface. *R. Hern.*

SILKETT 3 ch.g. Crocket 130–Shot Silk 110 (High Treason 126) [1975 N.R.   — 1976 7.6fg] half-brother to five winners, notably very speedy 1966 2-y-o Rose of Tralee (by Buisson Ardent): 300 gns yearling: dam very speedy 1962 2-y-o: 25/1 and very backward when tailed-off last of 16 in maiden race at Chester in September. *L. Barratt.*

SILK SEEKER 3 b.c. Shantung 132–Time of Hope 98 (Matador 131) [1975   — N.R. 1976 11f 12g 10fg³ 8fg] compact, short-legged colt: showed only sign of ability when 6½ lengths third of 11 to Our Anniversary in maiden race at Salisbury in May: will probably stay further than 1¼m: wears blinkers. *S. Ingham.*

SILK SLIPPER 2 b.f. Prince Tenderfoot 126–Fine Soie (Le Fabuleux 133) **116** [1976 5d⁶ 7g* 8s* 8s⁴] leggy, rather light-framed French filly: half-sister to 3-y-o 1m winner Eastern Silk (by Zeddaan): dam lightly-raced daughter of sister to Ascot Gold Cup winner Wallaby II: won a maiden race at Clairefontaine in August by 2½ lengths and improved greatly on that form in Group 3 Prix des Chenes at Longchamp the following month, coming through in straight to win unchallenged by 4 lengths from Water Boy: second favourite for 14-runner Criterium des Pouliches at Longchamp in October but finished only fourth, beaten 4½ lengths by Kamicia: will probably stay at least 1¼m: suited by soft going. *J. Cunnington, jnr, France.*

SILS MARIA 3 ch.f. Midsummer Night II 117–Tanara 93 (Romulus 129) [1975   — 5s 5g⁶ 6fg⁶ 6f² 7g 7fg 7g⁴ 9g 1976 10.8f 8fg 8f 8g⁴ 10s] neat, useful sort: poor plater: occasionally wears blinkers. *A. W. Jones.*

SILVERA 2 b.f. Ribero 126–Silver Bede 79 (Silver Cloud 121) [1976 6fg 7f⁶ 8fg³ **73** 5s 5s] third foal: dam, who stayed 1m, is half-sister to very smart sprinter Singing Bede: quite a moderate maiden: 8 lengths third to Lucent in minor event at Goodwood in September, best effort: suited by 1m and probably finds 5f too sharp for her. *C. Brittain.*

SILVER CAMP 4 b.f. Silver Shark 129–Royal Camp 91 (Sovereign Path 125) **73** [1974 5fg² 5fg⁴ 5g 6s 5.9v⁶ 1975 7.6g 5fg² 5fg² 5g 5fg² 5d⁴ 5g 5f² 5g* 5fg* 5g 5g* 5g 5g⁴ 1976 5f 5g 5g⁵ 5fg* 5g⁶ 5g⁴ 5h³ 5f⁶ 5fg⁶ 5f³ 5f³ 5fg⁵ 5fg 6g⁵ 5fg* 5s⁵ 5s² 6s] light-framed filly: quite a moderate handicapper: winner at Newmarket in May and Beverley in September, on latter course beating Two Ronnies 4 lengths: best

679

at 5f: acts on any going: suitable mount for an apprentice: slowly away on fifth start: inconsistent. *R. Mason.*

SILVER CHIEF   2 ro.c. Tribal Chief 125–Wroth Silver 79 (Tenterhooks 128)   **80**
[1976 5g 5f³ 6g 6d 6g] sturdy colt: good walker: half-brother to useful 1971 2-y-o 7f and 1m winner Gold Ribbon (by Blast): 420 gns foal, resold 2,000 gns yearling: dam best at 1¼m: 5½ lengths third of 15 to odds-on Mandrake Major in maiden race at Newmarket in August: stays 6f. *W. Marshall.*

SILVER CYGNET   2 gr.f. My Swanee 122–Moral (Aureole 132)   [1976 5fg 5f²   **71**
5g² 6g² 6g⁴ 6f⁵ 6g 7g] small, compact filly: half-sister to a minor 2-y-o winner by Red God: 900 gns foal: dam of little account: runner-up in maiden and minor events, going down by 2½ lengths to Lady Mere at Catterick in June on third occasion: off course two months subsequently and did not reproduce her best form: should stay 1m. *T. Fairhurst.*

SILVER GLEAM   3 gr.f. Silver Shark 129–Nishat (Sayajirao 132)   [1975 N.R. 1976 8.2d 8s⁴ 10s] rangy filly: half-brother to three winners, including useful French 1m winner Spanish Fort and useful 1971 2-y-o Jakim (both by Fortino II): dam stayed at least 1¼m: well beaten in back-end maiden races. *G. Pritchard-Gordon.*

SILVER RING   2 gr.f. Royal Captive 116–La Garoupe 87 (Pirate King 129)   **59**
[1976 5g 6h⁴ 7h 8s 7v] poor maiden: form only at 6f but should stay further (dam won over 16.9f): blinkered last two outings: trained by J. Hill on first three appearances. *G. Balding.*

SILVER SEAL   2 bl.c. Privy Seal 108–Silver Yarn (Peter's Yarn 106)   [1976   **84**
5g² 5f⁵ 5f⁵ 6g* 6f⁴ 6f⁶ 7g6] big, rangy colt: third foal: dam a point-to-pointer: having first race for two months, showed much improved form to win 11-runner maiden race at Doncaster in June by 2 lengths from New Mills: excellent fourth to Catiline in £2,100 event at Newbury the following month but was well beaten on both outings afterwards: will stay at least 1m: seems to need a straight course and strong handling to show to best advantage. *N. Adam.*

SILVER SHOALS   2 b.f. Mill Reef 141–Double Treasure (Rough 'n Tumble)   **98**
[1976 5g² 6fg³ 5s* 6v*] lengthy, light-framed American-bred filly: half-sister to fair performer King's Honour (by Majestic Prince), a winner at up to 1¼m, and to a winner in U.S.A.: dam, placed once from eight starts, is sister to a stakes-placed winner: won 12-runner maiden race at Lingfield in September by 4 lengths from Careless Princess: ½-length second to Picatina in £2,100 event at York the following month, but was subsequently awarded race on winner's disqualification for hampering another horse: will stay 1¼m: probably acts on any going but is well suited by some give in the ground. *I. Balding.*

SILVERSMITH   3 gr.c. Silver Shark 129–La Connaisseuse 78 (King's Bench 132)   **78**
[1975 5d⁴ 4.5g⁵ 6g⁴ 7g   1976 7fg² 8fg⁵ 10.1f² 10g* 14.8fg³ 13.3g⁶ 10.5g⁴ 10d⁴ 14s³] compact ex-French colt: won very slowly-run minor race at Leicester in May by a short head from Tolmiros: subsequently in frame in varied company in England and France: seems to stay 1¾m. *Doug Smith.*

SILVER STEEL   3 gr.c. Double-U-Jay 120–Holme Lacy 88 (March Past 124)   **114**
[1975 6g⁵ 6g³ 7v² 6g³ 7.3g   1976 8g² 9d² 9s* 10d³ 8f 9fg² 8fg* 8g² 8g* 8s 9g 8s⁴] deep-bodied colt: very useful handicapper: had a fine season and won three times, Sledmere Handicap at York in May by 2 lengths from Lord Elect, Rose of York Handicap in August by a neck from Jumping Hill and Autumn Cup at Doncaster in September by 1½ lengths from Palustra: very creditable seventh of 29 under 9-0 to Intermission in Irish Sweeps Cambridgeshire at Newmarket but was well beaten when taking on some of the best milers in Prix du Moulin de Longchamp in October: effective at 1m to 1¼m: acts on any going with possible exception of very firm: genuine and consistent. *C. Brittain.*

SILVER STRAND   5 gr.g. Silver Shark 129–Right Boy (Right Boy 137)   —
[1974 10.2s⁵ 10fg⁴ 8fg 10fg* 10g⁶ 8.2fg⁴ 12fg* 14v⁴ 14d⁶ 12g² 12s⁵   1975 12d² 12s 12s⁶ 12f⁴(dis) 12fg³ 16f³ 10g⁵   1976 13g 12s 14fg⁵ 12g⁴] strong, rangy gelding: little worthwhile form on flat in 1976: stays 2m: seems to act on any going: has worn blinkers: inconsistent and not much of a battler, and probably needs to be held up until last possible moment: sold 2,300 gns Ascot August Sales. *R. Hollinshead.*

SILVER SWALLOW   3 gr.f. My Swallow 134–Fingerofortune 100 (Fortino II   —
120) [1975 N.R.   1976 8g] fourth living foal: 5,000 gns yearling: dam won at up to 7f: 50/1 and in need of race when well-beaten eighth of 12 behind Pirate Dream in minor race at Doncaster in March, only outing. *M. W. Easterby.*

Rose of York Handicap—Silver Steel (left) catches Jumping Hill (rails) and Court Lane near the post

SILVER TEMPEST 2 gr.g. Impecunious–Chinchilla Cat (Silver Kumar 112) — [1976 7g 8d 8s] big, lengthy gelding: good mover: well behind in maiden and minor events. *P. Mitchell.*

SILVER TINKLE 4 ch.c. Jukebox 120–Silver Phantom 82 (Right Boy 137) 79 [1974 5d 5f⁶ 5fg² 5f⁴ 6s² 5g² 5g 5d³ 6d 5v⁴ 1975 6g 6f⁶ 5f 5h* 5h* 6fg* 6f⁶ 7f⁵ 6h² 6g⁴ 6g² 6g* 5g 1976 5f² 6g³ 5s³ 6f³ 6f⁴ 7f] strong, useful sort: good walker: quite a moderate handicapper: ran creditably most outings at 4 yrs although didn't manage to win: best at up to 6f: acts on any going: wears blinkers: tough and consistent: sold 1,350 gns Newmarket Autumn Sales. *M. H. Easterby.*

SILVER YARROW 3 gr.f. Birdbrook 110–Silvery Arches 82 (Petition 130) 77 [1975 6g 5.1fg⁴ 5g⁶ 7g⁵ 1976 8fg* 8f⁵ 10fg⁶ 8f*] shapely filly: won 14-runner maiden race at Salisbury in June and handicap at Yarmouth in August, on latter course showing improved form when hacking up by 7 lengths from Ebb and Flo: best form at 1m. *G. Pritchard-Gordon.*

SIMMERING 3 b.c. Ribero 126–Spring Fever 110 (Botticelli 129) [1975 7g 8.2d* 1976 12fg⁵ 9f] half-brother to tip-top middle-distance handicapper Fool's Mate (by Busted): won maiden race at Nottingham in 1975 by 2 lengths from Palmerston: when beaten under stiff weights in handicaps at Newmarket in April and Ripon (looked burly and was tailed off) in August: should stay 1½m+: trained until after first outing by H. Cecil. *E. Weymes.*

SIMM'S PIMMS 3 b.f. David Jack 125–Campari 103 (Bleep-Bleep 134) [1975 — 8g 1976 8fg 10fg 12.2g 14d] seems to be of little account. *P. Robinson.*

SIMON GEE 5 ch.g. Ballyciptic 122–Fishfinger (Golden Cloud) [1974 8g⁶ — 7f⁶ 10g³ 10g* 9g⁶ 9f⁶ 10g 1975 9g 10g 1976 10g] ex-Irish gelding: won maiden race in 1974: 33/1 when well behind in apprentice race at Leicester in September, first outing in this country: stays 1¼m. *S. Norton.*

SIMON SLINGSBY 3 b.c. Ballymoss 136–Star Trophy 63 (Umberto 118) 77 [1975 7g* 8v³ 8.2d* 8g³ 1976 10s 12h³ 12g⁶] big, strong, lengthy colt: won small race at Lingfield and nursery at Nottingham in 1975: only lightly raced at 3 yrs, putting up best effort when third of four, beaten just over 3 lengths, to shorter-priced stable-companion Double East in handicap at Lingfield in June: should stay 1½m: probably not at his best on heavy ground: not an ideal mount for a boy. *R. Price.*

SIMPLE GIFTS 2 ch.c. Miracle 116–Tammy's Princess 78 (Tamerlane 128) 82 [1976 5g 5f⁶ 6f³ 5g* 7.2v] workmanlike colt: second reported foal: half-brother

681

to 3-y-o 1m winner The Truant (by The Brianstan): dam stayed 1¼m: won 14-runner maiden race at Catterick in September ridden out by 1½ lengths from Perkasa: should stay 1m. *Denys Smith.*

SIMPSON JERSEY 2 br.c. Highland Melody 112–Leisure Hour (Persian Gulf) **79** [1976 5f³ 7g⁵ 7v] useful-looking colt: fourth foal: dam never ran: finished well when 2½ lengths third of eight to Self Portrait in maiden race at Catterick in July: well beaten in Laurent Perrier Champagne Stakes at Doncaster and maiden race at Leicester afterwards: probably unsuited by heavy ground. *N. Adam.*

SINARTRA 3 b.f. Connaught 130–Silkwood 95 (Shantung 132) [1975 5f⁵ — 1976 8fg 11.5fg] poor maiden. *H. Westbrook.*

SINDAB 5 b.h. Gallup Poll or Aberdeen 109–Sind 108 (Darius 129) [1974 **82** 8f² 8f* 7f* 8.2f 7.2fg³ 7g³ 7g³ 7g² 8.2g³ 7fg³ 6s³ 1975 7v* 7.6g³ 7g⁶ 7f⁶ 8g² 7fg⁴ 7g⁶ 8h³ 7f³ 7h* 8f³ 7f³ 8f³ 7.2s 1976 7g⁵ 6fg 6s⁵ 8f* 7fg³ 8g 8f* 8f⁴ 10h* 8h⁴ 10g⁵ 10f⁴ 8fg⁵ 8.2f³] strong, compact horse: fair handicapper: ran well at Beverley in 1976 and won three of his five races there: stays 1¼m and probably finds 6f on short side nowadays: acts on any going: sometimes wears blinkers but does just as well without. *J. W. Watts.*

SINGAPORE FLING 3 ch.g. Caruso 112–Triarder 43 (Hard Ridden 131) [1975 — 5s² 5s 5f² 5g 5fg⁶ 6fg 7g⁶ 5g⁶ 5g⁵ 5g 6d² 5v 1976 8h 8fg⁶ 7.2g 5g 10v] lengthy, plain gelding: plater: stays 6f: acts on any going: blinkered eighth and eleventh outings at 2 yrs: inconsistent: sold out of K. Payne's stable 620 gns Doncaster June Sales after fourth outing. *F. Wiles.*

SINGING PRINCE 3 br.g. Prince Regent 129–Singapation (Sing Sing 134) — [1975 N.R. 1976 6g] heavily-built gelding: third foal: half-brother to a minor winner in Ireland by Hard Tack: dam won twice over 5f at 2 yrs in Ireland: 25/1 when last of 18 in maiden race at Kempton in May: sold 310 gns Ascot October Sales. *J. Benstead.*

SINGING SAINT 4 b.g. Welsh Saint 126–Singapation (Sing Sing 134) [1974 — 5g 7g 1975 10.8d² 10fg 10.2f⁵ 1976 16.1d] neat gelding: plater: stays 1¼m: probably needs some give in the ground: ran poorly when tried in blinkers. *Mrs A. Finch.*

SINGING SPAN 2 b.f. Crooner 119–Long Bridges 93 (Court Martial) [1976 — 5g⁵ 5g 7f] leggy, unfurnished, narrow filly: well beaten in Scottish maiden races. *N. Robinson.*

SINGLET 4 b.c. Quartette 106–Long Term 76 (Sing Sing 134) [1974 5g³ 5f² — 5g 6fg⁶ 6g³ 7fg 7g 1975 8g⁵ 10.1fg⁵ 10f* 10f⁶ 10h² 10g 10d 8g 1976 10fg 9fg⁶ 12.2f⁵ 11.7f⁵ 10d 8g⁶] strong, useful sort of colt: disappointing at 4 yrs: well suited by 1¼m and evidently stays 1½m: acts well on firm going: trained by N. Vigors until after fourth outing. *J. Holt.*

SIN TIMON 2 br.c. Captain's Gig–Ilsebill (Birkhahn) [1976 7g⁴ 7g*] lightly- **102 p** built colt: half-brother to 1m winner Treasury Bill (by Red God): 4,400 gns yearling: dam won in Germany and is half-sister to two German classic winners: favourite for 22-runner maiden race at Newmarket in October and won in the style of a very useful colt, always going well, taking lead at halfway and coming home with his jockey looking round 3 lengths clear of Sporting Yankee who raced on opposite (stands) side of course: will stay 1m: won with something in hand at Newmarket and will go on to better things. *J. Hindley.*

SIPIT 2 ch.f. Sharpen Up 127–Chacachacare (Gulf Pearl 117) [1976 5fg 5f² 5g² **86** 6g⁴ 6fg* 6f² 6g⁵ 5.9s] first foal: 860 gns yearling: dam well beaten in four races: won 16-runner maiden race at Windsor in July by ½ length from Eulalie: caught on line when short-head second of 18 to Swift Sons on same course the following month: will stay 7f: acts on firm going and may be unsuited by soft. *W. Payne.*

SIR ABU 2 b.c. Sahib 114–Ceol Abu (Vimy 132) [1976 5fg 6d⁴ 7h 6g⁶ 7.2f* **82** 7.3d 8s³] narrow colt: half-brother to two winning hurdlers: dam of little account: attracted no bid after gamely winning 12-runner seller at Haydock in August: creditable third of 20 to Money to Spare in nursery at Pontefract in October: will stay middle distances: acts on any going: very slowly into stride on penultimate outing. *P. Rohan.*

SIR DESTRIER 3 br.g. Sir Gaylord–Ruby of Iran (Cosmic Bomb) [1975 6fg — 1976 8s 8s⁴ 10.2s 10.2s] strong, rangy, attractive gelding: showed some ability in early-season maiden races in Ireland: off course long time afterwards, finishing tailed off in similar company at Doncaster at end of season, once wearing blinkers: sold out of M. Vance's stable 3,300 gns Goffs September Sales. *R. E. Peacock.*

SIRETTE   3 b.f. Great Nephew 126–Sea Swift 89 (Sea-Bird II 145)   [1975 N.R.   —
1976 10fg⁶ 10f 8f³ 8.2d 7s]   lightly-made filly: first foal: dam won over 1¼m:
9½ lengths third of seven to runaway winner Eastern Silk in maiden race at
Goodwood in August, best effort: should stay 1¼m: tried in blinkers final outing:
sold 1,300 gns Newmarket Autumn Sales. *M. Stoute.*

SIR GALIVA   2 b.c. Galivanter 131–Seaside (Mossborough 126)   [1976 5s 5g⁴   **77**
5.1fg⁵ 5f² 7fg⁴ 5.1g 5d³ 6d 6s]   big colt: first foal: dam won over 1½m
placed over 1¾m: had anything but a clear run when 2 lengths second of 11 to
Tin Miner in maiden race at Ripon in June: not seen out again until September
and did not reproduce his best form: should stay 1m.   *R. Hollinshead.*

SIR JASPER   3 ch.c. Lord Gayle 124–Rosy Gleam 74 (Golden Cloud)   [1975   —
N.R.   1976 13.3fg⁶ 12fg⁶]   half-brother to four winners, including useful 1½m
winner Red Canute (by Hardicanute) and leading Venezuelan horse Senador
(by Sound Track): 680 gns yearling: dam won over 7f at 3 yrs: put up a creditable
first effort when 9 lengths sixth of 13 to Sunbelt in maiden race at Newbury in
June: well beaten in weakly-contested amateur riders event at Leicester three
months later and was sold to M. Tate only 200 gns Ascot December Sales.   *F.
Maxwell.*

SIR LORD   2 gr.g. Lord Gayle 124–Miss Pimm 88 (Gentle Art 121)   [1976 5s²   **83**
5d² 6s* 7f³ 8fg]   lightly-built gelding: half-brother to 2-y-o winners in Ireland
and Italy: 800 gns yearling: dam won over 5f at 2 yrs: won maiden race at Ayr
in June by 2½ lengths from Let's Dance: should stay 7f: acts well on soft ground
and is probably not at his best on a firm surface: reportedly exported to Singapore.
P. Rohan.

SIR MONTAGU   3 ch.c. Connaught 130–Coy Lady (Damremont 120)   [1975   **122**
6fg 7g⁴   1976 11f⁶ 10fg² 10g* 11fg² 12fg* 12g* 12fg* 14fg* 15.5s²]
    Sir Montagu's rapid improvement in midsummer resulted in that normally
most competitive of handicaps, the Ebor, being turned into a procession.   When
the weights for the Tote-Ebor were published Sir Montagu had won two of his
previous three races, a maiden event at Sandown by six lengths and a three-year-
old handicap at Salisbury under 8-4 but had been beaten when odds on for a five-
runner handicap at Newbury in between.   His weight of 7-4 did not appear harsh
but there was then nothing in his record to suggest he would start the shortest-
priced favourite for the Ebor since Arctic Vale thirteen years earlier.   Within
a week of the publication of the weights Sir Montagu had scored two decisive
victories, netted his connections more than £6,000 and made the 7-lb penalty he
had incurred for the Tote-Ebor look a mere trifle.   In the Sandringham Handicap at Ascot he won virtually unchallenged from the older horses Warbeck

Tote-Ebor Handicap, York—Sir Montagu turns the race into a procession

and So They Say and six days later, in the William Hill Southern Handicap at Goodwood, he carried a 4-lb penalty and came home five lengths clear of the useful Lighter. A rise in the weights left Sir Montagu with 8-0 to carry in the Tote-Ebor, the weight a good-class three-year-old would have to carry in a normal year. From the moment he took the lead just over three furlongs from home the race was as good as over. Nothing even looked remotely like getting anywhere near him and he sauntered past the post eight lengths clear of Alverton whose first defeat in six outings this was.

Only a horse on the fringe of classic standard could have won the Tote-Ebor in such devastating style and Sir Montagu was given his chance to take on the best in the Prix Royal-Oak (French St Leger) at Longchamp in September. Here he carried the colours of Paul de Moussac who had bought Sir Montagu for a sum reported to be in excess of £80,000 after York. He made a handsome and speedy contribution towards his purchase price, even though his winning run was brought to an end. Sir Montagu led briefly turning into the straight at Longchamp and although he could not hold the Grand Prix de Paris winner Exceller he kept second place by half a length from Adam van Vianen and survived a subsequent objection from the latter's jockey. Sir Montagu lost no caste in defeat—Exceller is a top-class staying colt—and he received only a beating similar to that Exceller had handed out to the subsequent Doncaster St Leger runner-up Secret Man in the Grand Prix de Paris. Incidentally, the Prix Royal-Oak is going to be run in late-October in 1977 to avoid a clash with the St Leger which has been thought to be detrimental to both races.

Sir Montagu (ch.c. 1973)	Connaught (b 1965)	St Paddy (b 1957)	Aureole / Edie Kelly
		Nagaika (ch 1954)	Goyama / Naim
	Coy Lady (gr 1963)	Damremont (ch 1947)	Dogat / Wild Violet
		Village Maid (gr 1954)	Vilmorin / Elephant Bird

Sir Montagu is the first winner on the flat produced by Coy Lady. Of her previous four foals, Potter's Lad (by Sailing Light) won over hurdles and Pinnacle (by High Perch) showed a little ability on the flat and is the dam of the useful 1975 Northern two-year-old Senator Sam (by Meldrum). Since visiting Connaught, Coy Lady has been to Meldrum, Foggy Bell and Calpurnius and had foals by the last two. Coy Lady ran only as a two-year-old when down the back in all her three races, but she is a sister to the useful seven-furlong to ten-furlong handicapper Le Garcon.

A strong, compact colt and a good mover, Sir Montagu was bought for 4,500 guineas as a yearling. He stays very well and he will probably get further than two miles as a four-year-old. He seems to be able to act on any going. *R. Price.*

SIR NIGEL 5 b.g. Sir Gaylord–Arta (Mr Trouble) [1974 12g 16f 1975 N.R. — 1976 10.1f 18.1g] seemingly of no account. *J. Powney.*

SIROCCO SIREN 7 b.m. Barbary Pirate 91–Dedicated (Merry Boy) [1974 — 11.7g 12fg⁵ 10.6g 1975 10g⁵ 10f 12f 12fg⁶ 10.2g⁴ 1976 12s] bad plater. *R. Sturdy.*

SIR PELLEAS 4 b.c. Sahib 114–Bella Musica (Sing Sing 134) [1974 6s 6v 66 1975 7.6g 8.2g 8f⁶ 8.2g⁵ 6g 1976 10f⁴ 8.2g² 8g 8f* 11.7f⁶ 8g* 8fg² 8.2s³ 10s²] sturdy colt: winner twice at Yarmouth in 1976, on second occasion beating Blues Again 3 lengths in apprentice handicap in September: best form at 1m but stays 1¼m: acts on any going. *M. Stoute.*

SIR PERCIVAL 3 b.c. Blakeney 126–Kerkithalis 98 (Acropolis 132) [1975 7g 62 7fg 8g 1976 12fg 16.1d 12.2g* 12fg 12f⁵ 12g] small colt: put up easily best effort when winning handicap at Warwick in July by 3 lengths from Pontresina: stays 1½m: sold 2,000 gns Newmarket Autumn Sales. *C. Brittain.*

SISTER MOON 4 b.f. Great Nephew 126–Vestal Fire 87 (Match III 135) — [1974 N.R. 1975 12g 10.6v 1976 12g 12.3fg] evidently of little account. *G. Peter-Hoblyn.*

SISTER SAINT 3 b.f. Welsh Saint 126–Jackie's Sister (Hard Tack 111 §) [1975 84 5d 5fg² 5fg 1976 5fg² 5fg 5.9s 5v] plain filly: ran well when 1½ lengths second to Pets First in handicap at Warwick in April: not seen out again until September and ran poorly on her return: should stay 6f. *N. Adam.*

SISTER TO BEN 4 ch.f. Stephen George 102–Alex M 69 (Kadir Cup 97 §)   **35**
[1974 5g³ 5f* 7d⁴ 5fg   1975 7g⁵ 7fg 6g⁵ 7h   1976 5g 6g⁶ 5g 6g]   plain filly: plater:
stays 7f: seems to act on any going: frequently starts slowly: blinkered third
start: sold 500 gns Doncaster August Sales. *K. Payne.*

SIXFIVESEVEN 9 ch.g. Henry the Seventh 125–Word Perfect (Worden II 129)   **64**
[1974 7f* 7f* 8h² 7fg⁵ 7d 7g 7.2s 7s   1975 7v 7s 7g⁵ 7f³ 7f   1976 8f⁴ 15g⁴ 10.6d²
8g 10v 7v]   poor handicapper nowadays: creditable second to Powderhall in
amateur riders race at Haydock in October: appears to stay 15f: acts on firm
going and a soft surface: usually wears blinkers: sometimes loses ground at start.
D. Thom.

SIZZLER 2 b.f. Blakeney 126–Death Ray 100 (Tamerlane 128) [1976 6fg 7g 8s   **62**
8s]   small filly: half-sister to three winners, including useful middle-distance
handicappers Hired Assassin (by Hook Money) and Open Fire (by Aggressor):
dam a miler: showed a little ability on first two outings: should stay 1m. *J.
Bethell.*

SKATER'S WALTZ 2 bl.f. Nice Music 115–Progress (March Past 124) [1976   **64**
5g³ 5h⁵ 6v]   small filly: first foal: 920 gns yearling: dam showed only poor form
on flat but won a point-to-point: narrowly-beaten third of seven to Jolly Joe in
maiden race at Hamilton in June: off course a long time after next start and was
well beaten in a seller on her return: should stay 6f. *E. Collingwood.*

SKELUM 2 b.c. Ragusa 137–Wise Countess (Count Amber) [1976 7fg⁴ 8v*] **101 p**
fourth foal: half-brother to 7.6f winner Penny Halfpenny (by Sir Ivor): dam won
at up to 1¼m in France: put up a good performance when winning 10-runner
maiden race at Leopardstown in October by 3 lengths from Milverton: will stay
1½m: started slowly first outing: a very useful colt in the making. *M. Kauntze,
Ireland.*

SKERRY WOOD 3 b.f. Timber King 95–Enniskerry 85 (Royal Hamlet 115)   **—**
[1975 N.R.   1976 12.5v 10s]   neat filly: second reported produce: brother to a
winning plater: dam stayed 1m: well behind in end-of-season maiden events at
Teesside. *J. Calvert.*

SKIDDY RIVER 3 ch.f. Saratoga Skiddy 113–Lady River § (Clear River 114)   **83**
[1975 5f 5h⁶ 5fg⁴ 5h⁴ 5fg³ 5f² 7f⁴ 6g 5g* 5g⁴   1976 8f 8f⁵ 8fg³ 10g⁵ 6fg² 6f⁵ 8h⁵
7g 6s* 6s⁴]   small, light-framed filly: apprentice ridden, won handicap at Redcar
in October by 1½ lengths from Gold Loom: best form at 6f: acts on any going:
changed hands 1,200 gns Doncaster August Sales. *J. Calvert.*

SKIDLID 2 br.f. Daring Display 129–Mon Chapeau (High Hat 131) [1976 5g⁶   **48**
5h⁴]   poor maiden: sold 260 gns Ascot November Sales. *R. Vibert.*

SKIN DEEP 3 b.f. Prevailing–Vanity Case 77 (Counsel 118) [1975 6fg 5f 6f 5f⁴ **106**
6f* 5f* 5f³ 6f*   1976 7s 5f* 5d* 6f* 6g 5f 5s³]   well-made, attractive, good sort
of filly: third foal: half-sister to two winners, including fairly useful 1973 2-y-o
Frigid Case (by Frigid Aire): 1,500 gns foal: dam middle-distance stayer: developed into a useful sprinter, winning handicaps at Leopardstown and the
Curragh in May and at Phoenix Park the following month: ran below her best
on next two outings, including when tenth of 12 to Solar in Hackwood Stakes
at Newbury in July, but returned to her best when creditable third to Wolverlife
in handicap at the Curragh in November: stays 6f: probably acts on any going:
suitable mount for an apprentice: sold 12,500 gns Newmarket December Sales.
M. Connolly, Ireland.

SKINNY DIP 2 br.f. Deep Diver 134–Dusky Evening (Chamier 128) [1976   **—**
6v 6s]   half-sister to numerous winners, including useful stayer Night In Town
(by Ballyciptic) and useful middle-distance performer Spur On (by Larkspur):
9,500 gns yearling: dam never ran: showed a little ability in end-of-season maiden
races: sold 4,900 gns Newmarket Autumn Sales. *I. Balding.*

SKI SHOP 3 b.c. Crocket 130–Oh So Sweet 90 (Ballymoss 136) [1975 6fg 7fg⁶   **78**
1976 10.8fg 10.8f* 10f* 10g³ 12g⁴ 10g⁴ 10.1fg*]   tall, lengthy colt: in good form
in first part of season, trotting up in maiden race at Warwick and apprentice
event at Chepstow, both in April, and making all and just holding off Saturnus
in handicap at Windsor in June: stays 11f: acts on firm going: suitable mount
for an apprentice. *P. Cole.*

SKY JUMP 2 ch.c. Double Jump 131–Damascus Sky (Skymaster 126) [1976   **93 ?**
5g 5fg 5g⁴ 5s² 6v²]   strong colt: second foal: dam ran four times unplaced:
runner-up in nurseries at Folkestone and Nottingham in October, racing on
apparently faster ground and appearing to show improved form when beaten
2 lengths by Punto Banco in nursery on latter course: had earlier finished fourth
to Imari in £1,900 seller at Sandown: stays 6f: acts on heavy ground. *B. Swift.*

July Stakes, Newmarket—Sky Ship draws away from Pougatchof

SKY SHIP 2 ro.c. Roan Rocket 128–Bedeni 100 (Parthia 132) [1976 5g* 6fg* **114** 7fg* 8d⁵]

Few people have been more successful in the breeding of high-class stayers over the last twenty or so years than Mr Dick Hollingsworth. His Ark Royal, Cutter, Kyak, Hermes, Mariner, Torpid, Buoy and Sea Anchor, all descendants of that exceptional broodmare Felucca, won numerous top races between them but it wasn't until 1976, when Sky Ship won the July Stakes at Newmarket, that Mr Hollingsworth won a really important race for two-year-olds.

Although Sky Ship had won a maiden race at Salisbury on his only outing, four of the five other runners were preferred to him in the betting at Newmarket. Favourite was the French colt Pougatchof, the winner of his only start. Perhaps some backers were put off Sky Ship by the way he moved on the way to the start; he hardly strode out at all and seemed completely unsuited by the firmish going.

Lanson Champagne Stakes, Goodwood—Sky Ship is driven out to beat And Behold (right), with Nice Balance (left), Cosy Bar, Our Jimmy (centre) and the grey The Don in close attendance

He also looked ill-at-ease on the ground in the first half of the race, but the picture changed soon afterwards; Sky Ship came through to join Pougatchof in the lead about a furlong out and then drew away in good style on meeting the rising ground to win by four lengths.

It seemed clear from the way that Sky Ship finished at Newmarket that he would be well suited by longer distances than six furlongs and three weeks later he started odds on for the seven-furlong Lanson Champagne Stakes at Goodwood. Again, he didn't stride out at all well on the way to the start although this time he had no difficulty holding a good place. He looked to have taken a decisive advantage when he headed the pace-setting And Behold about two furlongs out but that colt rallied so well that Sky Ship's jockey had to ride his hardest to get home by a head. This was a very game display by Sky Ship and a smart one too, for he was giving between 6 lb and 14 lb to all but one of the seven other runners.

Sky Ship's owner immediately said that his horse would need a long rest. It was the end of September, two months later, before Sky Ship had his next race in the Royal Lodge Stakes at Ascot, where he started second favourite to the Irish colt Pampapaul. Things were different this time; he faded soon after the turn into the straight and trailed home fifth of six behind Gairloch. The distance of the race, a mile, can't be blamed for his failure—he wouldn't have won at six furlongs or seven furlongs either—and the likely cause of his poor showing, could be, ironically, that he wasn't at his best on the softish ground, the very ground that his action had suggested would suit him.

Sky Ship (ro.c. 1974)	Roan Rocket (ro 1961)	Buisson Ardent (b 1953)	Relic
			Rose o'Lynn
		Farandole II (gr 1947)	Deux pour Cent
			Faramoude
	Bedeni (ch 1969)	Parthia (b 1956)	Persian Gulf
			Lightning
		Cutter (b 1955)	Donatello II
			Felucca

Sky Ship is the first foal of Bedeni who has therefore made speedy amends for a disappointing racing career. Her performance first time out as a three-year-old was sufficiently promising for her to start a short-priced favourite for the

Mr R. D. Hollingsworth's "Sky Ship"

Lingfield Oaks Trial but she ended her racing days still a maiden and she wore both a hood and blinkers on her final appearance. She was bred well enough for anything; her sire was the Derby winner Parthia and her dam, Cutter, won the Park Hill Stakes and the Yorkshire Cup. Several of Cutter's foals showed very good form: Torpid finished second in the French St Leger and the Ascot Gold Cup, Tepukei won the White Rose Stakes, and Sloop, a brother to Bedeni, won the Craven Stakes and finished second to Hopeful Venture in the Princess of Wales's Stakes. Another of Cutter's winners, a moderate filly called Cutle, is the dam of the Irish Two Thousand Guineas winner Sharp Edge.

Stamina is certainly the strong suit of the family and Sky Ship should stay a mile and a half. Good though his form was at two years, it does not entitle him to be considered a live classic candidate and his appearance–he's a neat and not very imposing individual—doesn't suggest he will improve abnormally. *R. Hern.*

SKY'S SUNNY 3 ch.f. Dewan–Naphalia (Swaps) [1975 6.5g* 8s⁶ 1976 8s* 8s⁴ 8g³ 6g³ 8g⁶ 8d] American-bred French filly: second foal: half-sister to a minor winner in U.S.A. by Graustark: $50,000 yearling: dam unraced half-sister to very smart Hail The Pirates and very smart 1964 American 2-y-o Candalita: showed smart form at 2 yrs: 3-length winner of minor event at Cagnes-sur-Mer in February: put up a much better effort in 11-runner Poule d'Essai des Pouliches at Longchamp in April, finishing third, beaten 3 lengths and a neck, to Riverqueen and Suvannee: creditable third to Nagin in well-contested Prix de Bonneval at Evry the following month, best subsequent effort: will stay at least 1¼m: acts on soft going: ran freely when tried in blinkers on final outing. *C. Milbank, France.* **114**

SKYS THE LIMIT 4 ro.c. Galivanter 131–Apex 72 (Donore 119) [1974 5s 7g 1975 9g⁵ 7d⁴ 10.1s 10.1f³ 1976 10s⁶] compact colt: plating-class maiden: apparently suited by longer distances than 7f: not seen out until October at 4 yrs when well beaten in amateur riders event (had very stiff task). *Mrs D. Oughton.* **—**

SLAP HAPPY 3 b.g. Chebs Lad 120–Keep Happy 62 (Skymaster 126) [1975 6f 6g 1976 12d² 13g 13fg⁵ 14.7h* 16f⁶ 14d] neat gelding: scraped home in poor race at Redcar in August: stays well: acts on hard ground. *J. Hardy.* **52**

SLASHER 2 gr.g. Ballymoss 136–Princess Caroline 68 (Sovereign Path 125) [1976 7v] second foal: half-brother to 3-y-o 1½m winner Mischief (by Sassafras): dam, only plating class, comes from same family as Faberge II and Turbo Jet: 20/1, showed speed for 4f when ninth of 15 to easy winner North Stoke in minor event at Lingfield in November. *M. Smyly.* **—**

SLAVONIC 2 b.c. Derring-Do 131–Hornton Grange 101 (Hornbeam 130) [1976 6g 7.5f² 8.6f* 8g 8fg³ 7.5g] neat Irish colt: second foal: half-brother to quite moderate Our Song (by Song), a winner at up to 7f: 13,000 gns yearling: dam won at up to 1m: led from halfway when winning 17-runner minor event at Galway in July by 1½ lengths from Dike Wine: in rear behind Royal Plume at Doncaster in September but ran well in blinkers when 4 lengths third of eight to Padroug in Ashford Castle Stakes at the Curragh later in month: will stay 1¼m: again blinkered when slowly away on final outing. *D. Weld, Ireland.* **99**

SLEEPER 2 br.c. Track Spare 125–Railway Hill (Guersant 129) [1976 5g 5fg⁶ 6fg⁴ 6g 5d 7s*] strong, good sort: half-brother to three minor winners: dam won over 5f in Ireland: put up easily best effort when winning 12-runner minor event at Sandown in October by ¾ length from Vaguely, making most of running and rallying in very game style under hard riding: clearly better suited by 7f than shorter distances, and will stay 1m: acts well on soft going. *R. Smyth.* **92**

SLEEPER KING 7 ch.h. King's Leap 111–Astrimache (Macherio) [1974 8s⁵ 10d 8d 7g 5s⁶ 9v 1975 8g 1976 13g⁶ 10f 12.2f] of no account. *F. Dever.* **—**

SLEIGH BELLS 2 b.g. Saintly Song 128–Snow Goose (Santa Claus 133) [1976 6fg 8s 10s*] well-made gelding: good walker: first foal: dam unraced half-sister to very useful middle-distance horse Dieu Soleil: all out when winning 13-runner seller at Pontefract in October by 1½ lengths from Son Tom: sold 1,800 gns afterwards, reportedly for export to Scandinavia. *S. Hall.* **73**

SLICK CHICK 2 b.f. Shiny Tenth 120–Ibis 96 (Tamerlane 128) [1976 5fg 5f⁵ 5.1fg 7f⁵ 7h³ 7f² 8f 8s⁴ 8v* 7.6v⁶] first foal: dam won over 6f at 2 yrs: made virtually all and had seven-strong field strung out a long way behind her when winning nursery at Newbury in October by 8 lengths from Billion (U.S.A.): stays 1m well: has run respectably on hard going but is clearly very much a mudlark: suitable mount for an apprentice. *R. Hannon.* **89**

SLIDE OVER BABY 4 b.f. Super Game–Gold Caress (Solidarity) [1974 5v⁶ — 1975 N.R. 1976 10f 12f 11d 13.8g 16f 16fg⁶ 10v⁶] of no account: trained by F. Wiles until after sixth outing. *M. Camacho.*

SLIM JIM 4 ch.c. Silly Season 127–Gay Life 72 (Zeus Boy 121) [1974 5g³ 6g² **102** 6s³ 7g* 7s⁴ 8s* 8g 1975 8v 10fg⁴ 8fg 10fg* 10g* 9fg⁴ 10g⁶ 9g 1976 10g 10g³ 11.7fg³ 12fg* 12fg⁶ 11.7f⁴ 12f³ 12g⁴ 13g³ 12d⁴] useful sort: fairly useful handicapper: narrow winner of Newbury Summer Cup in June, beating Paper Chase a neck: didn't show the same form afterwards and ran poorly last two outings: stays 1½m: seems to act on any going: blinkered ninth outing. *I. Balding.*

SLOANE RANGER 2 ch.f. Sharpen Up 127–Andun Lassy 79 (Khalkis 127) **84** [1976 5fg⁴ 5f⁵ 6s⁵ 6g² 5.9f⁶ 7f⁴ 7g* 8.2d* 7.2v* 8s⁴ 7.2v⁶] lengthy filly: third foal: half-sister to World's Worse (by Frankincense), a winner over 1¼m in Ireland: 840 gns yearling: dam stayed 1½m: bought in 900 gns after trouncing her field in 17-runner seller at Warwick in August and proved herself well worth the money, winning nurseries at Nottingham and Haydock: accounted for Glazepta Rework in both races, being more impressive when making all to beat him by a long-looking six lengths on latter course in October: stays 1m well: acts on firm going but is evidently very well suited by some give in the ground: blinkered fourth and fifth outings, running creditably on first occasion. *D. Hanley.*

SLOW COACH 2 ch.c. Shiny Tenth 120–Shano 58 (Shantung 132) [1976 5f 5f* **88** 5fg⁴ 5fg² 5g⁶ 6fg⁵ 7s 6s 6s⁵] first foal: dam showed best form at sprint distances: won maiden race at Warwick in April by 4 lengths from Low Lindeth: put up several good efforts afterwards, including in nurseries on last two outings: stays 6f: acts on any going. *D. Marks.*

SMAILHOLM LAD 3 gr.g. Alloway Lad 103–Dotty Belle (Coronation Year 124) — [1975 6g 1976 10f] lightly raced and no sign of ability: sold 900 gns Doncaster November Sales. *H. Bell.*

SMART KID 3 b.c. Duneed 84–Penstemon (Pendragon) [1975 N.R. 1976 — 10h⁵ 11.7h⁶] second foal: dam never ran: never near to challenge when 7½ lengths fifth of nine to Gloom in apprentice event at Chepstow in June, first outing and easily better effort. *J. Thorne.*

SMART SHIRLEY 4 b.f. Assembly Man–Discretion (Buisson Ardent 129) **42** [1974 5fg 6fg³ 7g* 1975 7s² 8.5s⁴ 8g² 8f 7f 7.6f⁴ 6fg 11.7g³ 10.2f 1976 16f 11.7fg 12.2f 10.1fg²] lengthy filly: plater nowadays: stays 1½m: suited by some give in the ground: seems to act on any track: suitable mount for an apprentice. *G. Balding.*

SMIDDLY HILL 6 b.h. Crepello 136–Bracey Bridge 115 (Chanteur II 135) **51** [1974 10h 17.1f 13.1g 12d⁶ 16g⁴ 14s 1975 N.R. 1976 12fg⁴ 12h⁶ 16.1fg² 15.8f³] burly horse: poor handicapper nowadays: stays well: probably acts on any going: disappointing. *M. Scudamore.*

SMILE OF FORTUNE 4 b.g. Graustark–Prides Profile (Free America) [1974 — N.R. 1975 8fg 13f* 13g³ 1976 10d] quite a moderate performer (rated 75) at 3 yrs: better known nowadays as a hurdler: will probably stay 2m. *J. Gifford.*

SMILING 4 b.f. Silly Season 127–Costmary 108 (Grey Sovereign 128 §) [1974 **53** N.R. 1975 7v⁵ 10d⁵ 12f⁵ 12d⁴ 12g² 12v³ 1976 13.8g³] rangy filly: stays well: probably acts on heavy going: bandaged only outing at 4 yrs. *W. Wharton.*

SMITH 4 gr.g. Raffingora 130–Charybdis (Chanteur II 135) [1974 5g⁶ 5fg **85** 1975 6fg* 7f 6fg² 7g⁴ 6g⁶ 8g⁵ 7g 1976 6f 5.9f⁴ 6h* 6h⁵ 6d⁵ 8s³ 7s⁴ 8v⁴] strong gelding: fair handicapper: won minor event at Brighton in August by ¾ length from Oudalia: stays 1m: acts on any going: suitable mount for an amateur: sweated up fifth start: had a poor run on fourth outing: sold 4,100 gns Newmarket Autumn Sales. *R. Jarvis.*

SMITHFIELD LADY 3 b.f. Balidar 133–Sky Green (Skymaster 126) [1975 5s **63** 7d 7g 7.6g⁵ 7f⁵ 1976 8fg 11.1g 8fg 8.2f³ 8f 8s³ 9v³ 8v² 8.2v² 8v⁴] big, rangy filly: best form at 1m: seems to act on any going: ran moderately in blinkers on final outing. *R. Akehurst.*

SMOGGY 2 b.c. Run The Gantlet–Loose Cover 106 (Venture VII 129) [1976 **115** 5d⁵ 5g² 7d* 7g⁵ 7g²] smart French colt: half-brother to several winners, including useful miler Silk and Satin (by Charlottown) and American stakes winner Canterbury Tale (by Exbury): 15,500 gns foal: dam a miler: fulfilled promise shown in two good-class races when winning maiden race at Chantilly in September by a head from Perello: not disgraced afterwards, finishing close-up fifth to that horse in Criterium de Maisons-Laffitte later in month and then going down by 2½ lengths to Pharly in minor event at Longchamp in October: will stay 1¼m. *A. Head, France.*

SMOKEY ANGEL 2 gr.f. Swing Easy 126–Abaddon 109 (Abernant 142) [1976 **74** 5fg³ 5g³ 5fg 5f⁵ 6fg⁶ 6fg 6g³ 5g⁶ 5g⁵ 5s] small filly: half-sister to three useful winners, including 1m and 1½m winner St Angelina (by St Paddy): dam won over 6f as a 2-y-o: quite modest form in varied company, including selling: stays 6f: acts on firm going: wears blinkers nowadays: sold 410 gns Ascot November Sales. *G. Balding.*

SMOOTH DISPLAY 2 ch.c. Daring Display 129–Idylle (Dan Cupid 132) **91** [1976 6f⁵ 6d² 8s] stocky colt: third foal: half-brother to fairly useful 1½m winner Bellium (by Bon Mot III): 1,200 gns yearling: dam won small race over 9f in France: ran promisingly on first two outings, on second finishing neck second of 11 to Friendly Now in maiden event at Yarmouth in September, pair coming home well clear: well beaten in similar company at Newmarket the following month: should be suited by 1m+. *W. Marshall.*

SMUGGLER 3 ch.c. Exbury 138–Hiding Place 109 (Doutelle 128) [1975 **123** 6f* 7g* 7s 1976 12fg* 12.3d³ 12g 12f² 12fg* 12fg* 14.6d⁶]
'Smuggler was stopped twice. He is certain to beat all those in front of him when he meets them in the St Leger.' So said his jockey Frankie Durr after the Derby, yet Smuggler had gone to post the longest priced of trainer Hern's three runners and had come home in eighth place, some thirteen lengths behind Empery. Unfortunately for Durr as well as for Smuggler's connections, when the St Leger came around the drought had ended and the ground was riding on the soft side. Soft conditions are no good for Smuggler—he had been well beaten in similar conditions in the Prix de la Salamandre and the Chester Vase—and he dropped away in the Leger after holding a prominent position to the two-furlong marker, eventually finishing sixth, nearly a dozen lengths behind Crow. Oats, the only horse that ran in the St Leger to have finished in front of Smuggler at Epsom, finished a close-up fourth.

Smuggler's four other runs in his second season were on a firm surface; he won three of them and went down only narrowly in the other. A well-backed odds-on shot in the Warren Stakes at Epsom in April on his reappearance, Smuggler had to be ridden to get the better of Quite Candid but in the end won going away by five lengths. Two months later in the King Edward VII Stakes at Royal Ascot he just came off the worse after a long-drawn-out struggle with Marquis de Sade. Incidentally, the third horse Tierra Fuego finished five lengths further behind him here than at Epsom. At about this time attempts were made to obtain a pacemaker for Smuggler, but when these came to nothing front-running tactics were adopted with him in the Princess of Wales's Stakes at Newmarket and the Gordon Stakes at Goodwood. At Newmarket he was soon bowling along ahead of the French horse Luenge, and when challenged by the Coronation Cup third Major Green and the Oaks runner-up Roses for

Princess of Wales's Stakes, Newmarket—Smuggler is never headed. Major Green finishes second

Lord Porchester's "Smuggler"

the Star he had enough in reserve to draw away again and win by five lengths. At Goodwood it was a much closer call. With half a mile to run, the very enterprisingly ridden Smuggler had a five-length advantage over Oats, with General Ironside and Norfolk Air languishing well back. Although his lead was gradually reduced by Oats from then on, he had been allowed to set up just too commanding an advantage to be caught, and battling on courageously he held off Oats by a short head, with General Ironside and Norfolk Air breathing down their necks. It hardly ever makes sense to give a horse as good as Smuggler so much start.

Smuggler (ch.c. 1973)	Exbury (ch 1959)	Le Haar (ch 1954)	Vieux Manoir
			Mince Pie
		Greensward (b 1953)	Mossborough
			Stargrass
	Hiding Place (ch 1963)	Doutelle (ch 1954)	Prince Chevalier
			Above Board
		Jojo (gr 1950)	Vilmorin
			Fairy Jane

A rangy colt, Smuggler is the fifth foal and winner of his dam Hiding Place, the best of whose previous offspring were the smart Disguise (by Klairon), winner of the Horris Hill Stakes, and the Royal Hunt Cup winner Camouflage (by March Past). Hiding Place was a useful performer at around a mile and numbered the Nell Gwyn Stakes among her successes. She is a half-sister to numerous winners produced by Jojo, most notably the brothers Queen's Hussar and Scots Fusilier and the Cheveley Park Stakes third Grey Goose. Jojo's final foal, Picture, became her twelfth to win on the flat when successful at Windsor in 1975.

A very genuine and consistent battler who is well suited by front running tactics, Smuggler will take some pegging back on fast going in all but the highest class as a four-year-old. He almost certainly needs at least a mile and a half—he was not asked to race at a shorter distance in 1976—and is worth another chance over a longer trip. *R. Hern.*

691

SNACK TIME 2 ch.c. Dike–Petite Marmite 110 (Babur 130) [1976 7g 8s]   **69** p
rangy colt: half-brother to top-class French middle-distance filly Paulista (by Sea
Hawk II) and smart French stayer Caribo (by Sassafras): 1,500 gns yearling:
dam very useful miler: showed promise in large fields of maidens at Newmarket
in October, running on to finish eighth of 23 to Windy Sea and being prominent for
5f when fifteenth of 27 to Sporting Yankee: sure to do better. *B. Hills.*

SNAKE BITE 3 b.c. Decoy Boy 129–Bavizud (Tehran) [1975 6g 6fg 6g⁶ 5v⁶   **85**
1976 10fg⁴ 12g* 12g⁵ 13.1f² 12.2s* 13.3v² 12v] strong colt: won maiden race at
Ripon in August: improved a good deal on that form when winning 12-runner
handicap at Warwick in October by 3 lengths from Ebb and Flo: stays 13f: acts
on any going but is evidently well suited by soft: ran poorly final outing. *G.
Harwood.*

SNAKE DANCE 4 ch.f. Double-U-Jay 120–Refrain (Crocket 130) [1974 6fg   **—**
6g⁴ 7g 8.2d⁴ 7g² 7.2v 1975 10.4g 10.6g⁵ 8.2fg⁴ 8g³ 10.4g⁴ 10fg* 8f² 10f 10g⁴ 8f⁶
1976 10v 8fg 8g 8f 12.2g4] strong, useful sort: no worthwhile form at 4 yrs: best
form at 1¼m: acts on firm going, and may not be at her best on heavy: good
mount for an apprentice or lady rider: sold out of E. Cousins' stable 1,200 gns
Newmarket July Sales. *I. Wardle.*

SNAPPER 3 b.c. Forlorn River 124–Davina (Darius 129) [1975 6fg 6f⁴ 6fg⁶   **—**
8g² 7fg 8.2g 1976 10g⁶ 12fg⁵ 12g 16fg⁴ 16.9f⁵ 10.1fg³] well-made colt: good
walker: plater: probably stays 1¼m (had stiff task when tried at 1½m and ran
moderately over 2m, including when tried in blinkers): sold 1,100 gns Ascot
August Sales. *S. Ingham.*

SNOW BARON 2 ch.c. Midsummer Night II 117–Lenton Rose 66 (Aggressor 130)   **—** p
[1976 8s] big, well-made colt: first foal: 6,400 gns yearling: dam, winner of 2m
amateur riders event, is half-sister to Derby winner Snow Knight: unquoted, gave
trouble going into stalls and was slowly into stride, but made steady progress up
the straight when tenth of 20 to Lady Rhapsody in maiden race at Sandown in
October: sure to come on a lot as a result of this experience and will do much
better at 3 yrs. *J. Nelson.*

SNOW DANCER 3 ch.f. Huntercombe 133–Ice Ballet 87 (Ballymoss 136)   **—**
[1975 N.R. 1976 7f 8f 14fg⁶] good-looking filly: half-sister to fairly useful 1¼m
winner Tanara (by Romulus) and to winning French stayer Spring Snow (by
Reliance II): 12,500 gns yearling: dam a stayer: no worthwhile form in maiden
races in first part of season: sold 1,100 gns Newmarket December Sales. *M. Jarvis.*

SNOW HOPE 3 b.g. Coliseum 116–Snow Dell (Constable 129) [1975 N.R.   **—**
1976 8s 10s] fifth foal: half-brother to sprint plater Now Lad (by Blandford
Lad): dam probably of little account: slowly into stride and always behind when
ninth of 12 to Churchillian in maiden race at Edinburgh in October: pulled up on
next outing. *N. Robinson.*

SNOW JUMP 2 ch.f. King's Leap 111–No Scent 63 (Narrator 127) [1976 5f 5fg   **—**
5f 5d 5fg] of no account. *L. Shedden.*

SNOW MOUNTAIN 4 ch.f. Mountain Call 125–Vital Word 82 (Worden II 129)   **—**
[1974 6fg 1975 7.6g 7fg⁵ 7fg⁶ 8f⁴ 10.1fg 10f⁴ 10.1fg 10fg³ 10f³ 10s 10.6v⁴ 1976
16fg 16.1d] big, rangy filly: has ability but is inconsistent and disappointing:
evidently stays 1¼m, but is not certain to get 2m: possibly unsuited by soft going.
M. Stevens.

SNOW STAR 3 b.c. Crisp and Even 116–L'Etoile 73 (Faubourg II 127) [1975   **66**
8.2d 1976 12f⁴ 16fg* 16f 16s⁴ 16v⁴] half-brother to two winners, including fair
1968 2-y-o 5f winner Star-Call (by Bleep-Bleep): won weakly-contested maiden
race at Thirsk in July by ½ length from La Couronne: stays well: appears to act
on any going: sometimes wears bandages. *J. Bethell.*

SNOW SWAN 3 b.g. Charlottown 127–Raven's Wing 75 (Nearula 132) [1975   **59**
5f 6g 8.2d 8g 10g 1976 12g 17.7f 12g⁴ 12fg 10.1fg 10.1f² 11.7f² 10.1fg* 11.1f⁶]
lightly-built gelding: won maiden race at Windsor in July by ½ length from
Claironcita despite hanging badly left in final furlong: should stay further than
1½m: blinkered last appearance at 2 yrs: sold 1,250 gns Newmarket Autumn Sales.
P. Cole.

SNOW VENTURE 3 ch.g. Hopeful Venture 125–Snowfall II (Migoli 132) [1975   **62**
6g 7g 1976 16g 12d 12f 12f² 10.6g³ 12g 15.8g 13s] tall gelding: plating-class
maiden: best run at 1¼m: sometimes sweats up: sold 940 gns Doncaster October
Sales. *R. Hollinshead.*

SNOW WARNING 3 ch.c. Sky Gipsy 117–Cold Storage 110 (Never Say Die 137)   **64**
[1975 6g 7f 1976 9g⁵ 10.5s 12fg⁶ 12.2g³ 12g⁴ 12f² 13.8i*] big, strong colt: made

SOL

all when winning two-horse handicap at Catterick in July by a length from Stilton: will probably stay further than 1¾m: acts on firm going: usually wears blinkers but did not at Catterick: sold 1,300 gns Newmarket Autumn Sales. *W. Elsey.*

SNOWY M 3 gr.g. Supreme Sovereign 119–Royal Alba 69 (Royal Record II) [1975 5s 1976 7f‡ 10s] well-grown gelding: lightly raced and no worthwhile form. *W. Stephenson.* —

SNUG 3 ch.f. Midsummer Night II 117–Monamolin 109 (Golestan 127 §) [1975 5s 5g 5g 1976 5.8f³ 8f⁴ 5.8h² 5.8h 5.8f] lightly-made filly: stays 6f (had stiff task when well beaten at 1m). *F. Walwyn.* 64

SOBHIA 2 ch.f. Silly Season 127–La Colline 97 (Acropolis 132) [1976 6fg³ 7f⁵] neat filly: half-sister to several minor winners: 3,100 gns yearling: dam won over 7f and 1m at 2 yrs: second favourite for 20-runner Convivial Stakes at York in August and ran well for a newcomer, soon showing up and keeping on under pressure from halfway to finish 5 lengths third to Pollerton: again well backed in Waterford Candelabra Stakes at Goodwood later in month but finished only 10 lengths fifth of seven to Triple First after leading for over 4f: will stay 1m. *B. Hills.* 85

SO BRIGHT 3 ch.f. King's Company 124–Red Skies 84 (Skymaster 126) [1975 5fg³ 6d³ 5g* 6g 7.2s 1976 6g⁶ 6f⁶ 5fg 6g] rangy, rather sparely-made filly: won maiden race at Lanark in 1975: had stiff tasks prior to finishing seventh of 17 behind Touch of Silver in well-contested seller at Ayr in September on final outing: stays 6f: sold 500 gns Newmarket December Sales. *J. W. Watts.* —

SOCIAL CONTRACT 3 b.c. Hopeful Venture 125–Dilly 89 (Princely Gift 137) [1975 N.R. 1976 10g⁴ 10s³] lengthy colt: second foal: dam placed at 5f: in frame on both his outings in September, finishing 3¾ lengths third of 20 to Claironcita in minor event at Nottingham: may stay further than 1¼m. *H. Cecil.* 82

SOCIAL DRINKER 2 ch.c. Diplomat Way–Fighting Colleen (Irish Ruler) [1976 5f 5f⁵ 5g] quite a useful sort: good mover: showed ability in maiden race at Ayr in May, but ran poorly when favourite for a seller two months later and was not seen out again: blinkered last two outings. *F. Carr.* 63

SOCIETY REEF 3 br.f. Easter Island 101–Donasville (Don Carlos) [1975 N.R. 1976 11.7f 11g 12g 10.1d⁵ 8.2d 12v] big, tall filly: first foal: dam never ran: should stay 1½m: pulled up lame final outing. *E. Fisher.* —

SOCKBURN 2 b.c. My Swallow 134–Blue Bird 84 (Majority Blue 126) [1976 6g 6f 7.2f 8v 8v⁶] big, strong colt: first foal: dam stayed 1¼m: little worthwhile form but was springer in the market on final outing: has twice been slow into stride and swerved badly at start on another. *M. Camacho.* 69

SO CUTTING 2 b.f. So Blessed 130–Swordblade 84 (Pall Mall 132) [1976 5.3s³ 5s² 6s² 5s²] half-sister to several winners, including useful 5f to 7f winner Don Quixote (by Galivanter): 3,400 gns yearling: dam won over 5f at 2 yrs and is half-sister to very smart 1¼m horse Tacitus: runner-up in end-of-season maiden and minor events, going down by a short head to Miss Bagley at Teesside in November: stays 6f: acts on soft going. *R. Price.* 85

SOETNOS 2 ch.f. St Paddy 133–Miss Rocket 88 (Roan Rocket 128) [1976 6g 6d 8v³] well-grown filly: first foal: 720 gns yearling: dam won over 1m from only three starts: creditable 3 lengths third of 12 to Applalto in minor event at Teesside in October: will stay 1¼m: acts on heavy ground. *W. Elsey.* 79

SOFI 2 br.f. Adropejo 114–Bahia Castle (Turenne) [1976 5.1fg 6f 5f] of no account. *A. Dalton.* —

SOLAIRE 3 b.f. Roi Soleil 125–Crimson Velvet 89 (Above Suspicion 127) [1975 5s 5g 6f 6g 8v⁴ 1976 10f³ 13.4s 10fg⁵ 11g⁵ 12.3f 9g⁶ 10.6v⁶ 10.2s] small, neat filly: stays 11f: acts on any going: blinkered sixth outing: sold 350 gns Ascot December Sales. *W. Elsey.* 61

SOLAMBA 4 b.c. Aggressor 130–Dear Sol (Dear Gazelle 113) [1974 6s 1975 10.8s 11.5f 10.8fg 10f³ 1976 15.5h] of little account. *D. Dale.* —

SOLAR 3 ch.f. Hotfoot 126–L'Anguissola 102 (Soderini 123) [1975 5s 5fg* 6f² 6g² 7d³ 6fg* 6d³ 1976 7d 7.3f² 8fg 10g³ 12g 8fg² 7fg³ 6g* 7.3fg⁶ 8g² 8g⁵] well-made filly: half-sister to smart sprinter Walk By (by Tower Walk): dam stayed at least 1¼m: one of the leading 2-y-o fillies in 1975: gained her only success in 1976 in well-contested Hackwood Stakes at Newbury in July, coming with a well-timed late run to beat Wolverlife by ¾ length: ran well in many of her 108

693

other races, including when placed in Fred Darling Stakes (½-length second to Rowantree) and Sandleford Priory Stakes (2¼ lengths third to Sarania) on same course and when ninth of 25 to Flying Water in 1,000 Guineas at Newmarket: effective at 6f to 1¼m (well-beaten eleventh of 14 in Epsom Oaks, only attempt at 1½m): acts on any going: genuine: often wears blinkers, but does just as well without. *W. Wightman.*

SOLAR BRIGHT 2 gr.f. Right Boy 137–Solebar (Star Combine 109) [1976 **82**
5g* 5f3 5g2 5fg4] light-framed filly: first foal: dam poor hurdler: bought in 720 gns after making all to win seller at Teesside in April: in frame in better company subsequently, going down by ¾ length to Beaumel Board in minor event at Ripon in May: looked a bit light at Pontefract later in month and was not seen out again: will probably stay 6f. *G. Toft.*

SOLAR CRESCENT 4 br.f. Stupendous–Star of Gold 102 (Nimbus 130) [1974 **37**
5f 6f 5g 6g 6g4 7.2g 7v2 5s 6s 6v 1975 7d* 8v4 7g 6g 8g 7g 1976 7g5 8f6 10fg3 8d5 10.6d5 11g4 10h6 12fg5 10d 15.8s4 12.5v] leggy filly: plater: stays 1¼m but appeared not to stay 2m on tenth outing: acts on heavy going: has been tried in blinkers but seems to do just as well without: inconsistent. *A. Doyle.*

SOLAR ROSE 3 ch.f. Solar Topic 97–Wild Tudor (Tudor Treasure 119) [1975 **—**
5fg 5f 1976 6g 5f5 5f] small, lengthy filly: no worthwhile form in varied company, including selling. *T. Molony.*

SOLAR SAINT 3 ch.g. St Alphage 119–Luna (Milesian 125) [1975 5g 5f 5g5 **70**
5f3 5f6 5g6 6g 8g3 8g4 1976 7f* 7f2 8g2 7f* 8f 6fg6 8f 7f 6g2 6g 8d2 6v4 7v3] fairly useful selling handicapper: blind in near eye: successful in early-season contests at Beverley (no bid) and Thirsk (non-seller): stays 1m: acts well on firm going and is possibly not at his best on heavy. *W. Gray.*

SOLATIA 3 ch.f. Kalydon 122–Sooner or Later (Sheshoon 132) [1975 6g 7fg **75**
1976 12fg4 12f* 12fg3 12h2 12f5 12g] smallish, rather lightly-built filly: none too impressive when landing odds in slowly-run poor maiden race at Beverley in July: showed better form when second to My Wellie in handicap at Redcar but ran poorly under stiff weights on last two starts: will stay further than 1½m. *M. Jarvis.*

SOLCHELLA 2 b.c. Welham 94–Dear Sol (Dear Gazelle 113) [1976 5g 5g2 **77**
5f 5fg* 6g 5v3] leggy, unfurnished colt: third foal: 400 gns yearling: won 20-runner seller at Thirsk in May (bought in 1,300 gns) by ¾ length from Paratus:

Mrs F. C. B. Fleetwood-Hesketh's "Solar"

off course five months after next outing but showed much improved form on his return when 1½ lengths third to Kabagold in claiming event at Leicester in November: will stay 1m: acts on a firm surface but is clearly well suited by heavy ground: blinkered last three outings. *R. Stubbs.*

SOLDIER QUEEN 2 b.f. Queen's Hussar 124–French Frolic 78 (Prince **67** Chevalier) [1976 5g 5fg⁵ 5f 5f 5d] fair sort: half-sister to three minor winners: dam lightly raced: about 8 lengths fifth of 14 to Blackadder in maiden race at Salisbury in June, only worthwhile form: will stay 1m: tried in blinkers fourth outing: sold 1,000 gns Newmarket December Sales. *D. Whelan.*

SOLDIER ROSE 4 br.c. Galivanter 131–March Rose 87 (March Past 124) **83** [1974 7g² 7g⁴ 1975 11.1fg² 10fg⁵ 11.7f* 12fg⁴ 12s* 12g* 14g* 1976 16g⁴ 14s] strong, useful-looking colt: useful handicapper (rated 101) at 3 yrs: made only two appearances in 1976 and still looked in need of race on second of them: stays very well: acts on any going: very genuine. *R. Price.*

SOLDIERS FIELD 4 br.g. Queen's Hussar 124–Mow Meadow (Acropolis 132) **—** [1974 5fg 5fg² 5fg 6g³ 7g 6g 1975 8g 7.2g⁶ 10h 10h² 8fg⁴ 12v 1976 12f 12.5h⁵] tall gelding: bad maiden nowadays: stays 1¼m: acts on hard going: used to wear blinkers (didn't at 4 yrs). *F. Wiles.*

SOLE AGENT 2 b.f. King's Company 124–Two Fast 78 (Dual 117) [1976 **73** 5g 5fg² 5fg² 5f³] strong filly: first foal: 1,300 gns yearling: dam won over 1m at 2 yrs: in frame in early-season maiden and minor events: will be suited by 6f: exported by B.B.A. to South Africa. *B. Swift.*

SOLECISM 3 b.g. Roi Soleil 125–Gipsy Twist (Babur 126) [1975 6g 6g⁵ 6g **65** 6f* 1976 6fg 7f 6d⁵ 6d⁵ 6v 6v⁶ 8d⁴] fair plater: probably stays 1m. *R. Jarvis.*

SOLEFFIC 2 br.g. Rheffic 129–Solitude 129 (Nosca) [1976 5g 6fg] very **—** well bred but cost only 1,600 gns as a yearling and showed very little ability. *A. Jarvis.*

SOLENTOWN 4 br.f. Town Crier 119–Solensister 100 (Ennis 128) [1974 5s **49** 5fg 6d⁶ 6fg 6g⁶ 7d 1975 6s⁶ 8.2g⁴ 8f⁶ 8.2g 1976 10s 18s²] tall, leggy filly: only poor form: evidently stays 2¼m. *J. Spearing.*

SOLO DIVER 2 br.c. Deep Diver 134–Solo Girl (Como 120) [1976 5fg 5g **53** 5f 6g 6f] only poor form, including in a seller: blinkered third outing: sold 380 gns Doncaster September Sales. *M. H. Easterby.*

SOLO REIGN 3 b.f. Space King 115–Honerone 85 (Sammy Davis 129) [1975 **82** 6f 6fg² 7g² 8fg³ 7d² 7.2v 1976 8fg³ 8f⁵ 7.2fg* 8.2fg³ 8.2g⁵ 8.2h* 8f⁶ 8h⁴ 9fg* 10fg 10.2s 12s*] light-framed filly: retained 1,100 gns after winning seller at Haydock in July: proved well worth it, winning handicaps at Hamilton, Wolverhampton and Newmarket afterwards, last-named in October by 1½ lengths from Big Clive: stays 1¼m: acts on any going: swerved at start at Haydock: trained first two outings by J. W. Watts: sold 2,300 gns Doncaster November Sales. *R. Hollinshead.*

SOLO SPY 4 b.g. Allangrange 126–Inki Dinki (Rustam 127) [1974 5s* 5fg² **—** 5fg⁶ 6f 1975 6v³ 7s 6s⁶ 8v 9fg 6f 7f 6fg 7fg 6g 6g⁶ 1976 7g⁴ 8g 7g 6f] worthless plater nowadays. *F. Wiles.*

SOME FELLA 4 br.g. Will Somers 114 §–Jasperella (Sayajirao 132) [1974 **35** 5s⁵ 5g⁴ 5g⁵ 6f⁴ 5g² 5f² 7g⁵ 1975 5v 5s6 6f⁴ 5f 5g 7fg⁶ 1976 8f³] well-made gelding: plater: stays 1m: acts on firm going: has worn blinkers. *D. Chapman.*

SOME NIGHT 4 b.c. Galivanter 131–Penitent 85 (Sing Sing 134) [1974 5g **—** 5s⁵ 5v 1975 5.9g6 6s* 5f* 5g⁴ 5s 6g 1976 5.9g] big, attractive colt: moderate handicapper (rated 84) at 3 yrs: made only one appearance in 1976: stays 6f: acts on any going. *R. Akehurst.*

SOMERSEL 5 ch.g. Will Somers 114 §–Chamousel (Chamossaire) [1974 11g **61** 10fg⁵ 10v 12g² 10v³ 1975 12v⁶ 10s 12f 14fg 12.2fg² 12g⁵ 12.2g² 10g² 10.2g* 1976 10f⁵ 12f 10h⁴ 10fg² 10f⁶] fair sort in appearance but is only a poor handicapper: stays 1½m: best form on a sound surface. *G. Balding.*

SOMERVILLE QUEEN 5 ch.m. Clear Run 109–Royal Queen (Manicou) [1974 **62** N.R. 1975 N.R. 1976 9g 10.1fg 10fg* 8.2f² 9fg⁶] quite a moderate handicapper: 33/1 when winning at Nottingham in July by 2½ lengths from Persian King: creditable second to L'Eveque on same course the following month, better subsequent effort: stays 1¼m: acts on firm going. *J. Spearing.*

SON EMINENCE 2 br.c. Sovereign Path 125–Frauenzimmer (Masetto) — [1976 5fg 6f⁶ 7f⁴ 8g] rangy, useful sort: French bred: first foal: 75,000 francs yearling (approx. £8,000): dam a very useful middle-distance winner in France, and sister to smart out-and-out stayer Faux Monnayeur: little worthwhile form in varied company. *Denys Smith.*

SONETTA 2 br.f. Captain's Gig–Londonderry Air 84 (Ballymoss 136) [1976 **70** 5f⁴ 6g] half-sister to two winners, including useful 1m winner Persian Market (by Taj Dewan): 24,000 gns yearling: dam won over 5f from three starts at 2 yrs: well-backed favourite, stayed on well when 5½ lengths fourth of 13 to King Croesus in maiden race at Newmarket in August: second favourite for 30-runner maiden event the following month, again at Newmarket, but could finish only thirteenth behind Rheola: should stay 1m. *M. Jarvis.*

SONG BOOK 2 b.f. Saintly Song 128–Warrior Queen 95 (King's Bench 132) **85** [1976 7s 7s⁵ 6v 6s*] half-sister to two winners, including middle-distance per- former French Warrior (by French Beige): 2,600 gns yearling, resold 350 gns at 2 yrs: dam middle-distance performer: bought in 950 gns after winning seller at Newmarket in October by a short head from Phoenix Rose: will be suited by 1m: acts on soft going. *L. Hall.*

SONGFUL 3 b.f. Song 132–Baroda Glory (Palestine 133) [1975 5g² 5f⁶ 7d **55** 1976 5.8f² 5d⁶ 5fg 6fg⁶ 5.8f 5s 8s] useful-looking filly but is only a poor per- former: stays 6f. *W. Wightman.*

SONG GOD 3 b.f. Red God 128 §–Carol Song (Sing Sing 134) [1975 5d 5f² **83** 5g* 5g⁵ 5h⁴ 6fg⁵ 5d* 5g⁶ 1976 5g 6fg⁴ 6d 6fg 6fg³ 5fg 6fg 6fg⁵ 6d 6d 6d⁵ 6v] strong, compact filly: moderate handicapper: ran well when fourth of 16 to Broxted at Newmarket in April and when third of 13 to Ubedizzy in William Hill Trophy at York in June: had some stiff tasks afterwards: stays 6f: probably acts on any going: suitable mount for an apprentice: sold out of D. Holmes's stable 8,400 gns Doncaster March Sales: occasionally misses break. *R. Hollinshead.*

SONGHURST 2 b.c. Jimmy Reppin 131–Ardnahoe 67 (Big Game) [1976 **88** 5fg 5s⁶ 6v*] brother to modest 1975 2-y-o Lloyd Ardua: dam sister to useful stayer Whisky Poker: short-head second to Nampara Cove in maiden race at Lingfield in November, but was subsequently awarded race after a stewards' inquiry: will stay 1m: acts on heavy going. *D. Whelan.*

SONG OF DIXIE 2 ch.c. My Swanee 122–Welsh Lullaby 80 (Henry the — Seventh 125) [1976 7d] strong colt: second foal: 3,000 gns yearling: dam won at 11f and 1¼m: unquoted and very backward when behind in 25-runner Houghton Stakes won by Bessie Wallis at Newmarket in October. *B. Lunness.*

Highclere Nursery Handicap, Newbury—Joe Mercer keeps Song of Songs (left)
up to the mark to beat Rahesh

SONG OF SONGS 2 b.c. Song 132–Soltera 100 (Matador 131) [1976 5f³ **116**
5g* 5g² 5d⁴ 5d*]
  Few English-trained two-year-olds had as much early pace as Song of
Songs, and his trouncing of a large field of maidens from an unfavourable draw
at Newbury in May was a joy to watch. He showed so much speed from the
stalls that he was able to cross in front of the field from one side of the course
to the other, and he had the race sewn up before halfway even though the
experienced Our Jimmy and Ratamataz were among the opposition. He won
by four lengths from Our Jimmy. Song of Songs improved afterwards, and
on his final outing he put up one of the best performances of the season in a
nursery when he won the Highclere Nursery over the same course and distance
in September by a head from Rahesh. Giving weight all round, he disputed
the lead throughout and held on most gamely in the face of Rahesh's strong
finish. Song of Songs lost both his races in between, having reasonable excuse
for doing so on each occasion. He was kicked badly at the start of the Great
Surrey Stakes at Epsom, and he was having his first outing for three months
when contesting the Flying Childers Stakes at Doncaster. His speed was
missing at Epsom, but at Doncaster he led a good field for three and a half
furlongs before finishing fourth to Mandrake Major, beaten about four lengths.

			(Tudor Minstrel
		(Sing Sing	(Agin the Law
	(Song	((b 1957)	
	((b 1966)	(Intent	(Vilmorin
Song of Songs	(	((gr 1952)	(Under Canvas
(b.c. 1974)	(	(Matador	(Golden Cloud
	(Soltera	((ch 1953)	(Spanish Galantry
	((ch 1962)	(No Appeal	(Court Martial
		((ch 1948)	(Orasolfa

  Song of Songs is a half-brother to the one-mile winner Reform Bill (by Reform)
and even more closely related to Sing a Song (by Sing Sing), a very speedy
two-year-old winner in 1970. His sire, dam and maternal grandam were all
sprinters, his dam Soltera a useful one and his grandam No Appeal a very
useful one. Song stayed six furlongs but Soltera and No Appeal were five-
furlong specialists, and there is very little doubt that Song of Songs will always
be best at five furlongs. He is a neat, attractive colt, and a genuine one. *S.
Ingham.*

SONG OF THE TOWER 2 b.c. Tower Walk 130–Medium Rare (Larkspur 128) —
[1976 6fg 6f⁴ 7v 7v] workmanlike colt: poor maiden. *D. Williams.*

SONG'S FIRST 4 b.f. Song 132–Uranda 93 (King's Troop 118) [1974 5g 5fg⁶ **82**
5g 5v 6g³ 1976 6s 6g 5f 5h* 8f 5fg⁵ 1976 5f² 5f³ 5f 5fg* 5fg⁴ 5f³ 5s² 5f³ 5f³
5.9g 5f² 5f² 5f⁴ 5fg* 5d⁵ 5f⁵ 5.9f* 5f* 5fg*] neat filly: fair handicapper: a
grand little performer who kept her form really well and won five times, last three
in space of seventeen days: stays 6f (had a lot to do when well beaten over 1m):
acts on hard going: suitable mount for an apprentice or amateur rider: effective
with or without blinkers: game, genuine and consistent. *S. Nesbitt.*

SONIC SOUND 2 b.c. Galivanter 131–Grey Gal (Grey Sovereign 128 §) [1976 —
5.6f 6fg 5f] attractive colt: brother to two winners, including useful sprinter
Grey Autumn, and half-brother to three winners here and abroad: 7,200 gns
yearling: dam won over 5f in France at 2 yrs: showed a little ability on second
outing, finishing seventh of 15 to Etienne Gerard in maiden race at Newmarket
in August. *R. Armstrong.*

SONNENBLICK 3 b.c. Song 132–Cutlass Bay 68 (King's Bench 132) [1975 **110**
6f* 6f* 7fg 1976 7fg 7d⁴ 8d 6fg² 6fg² 6fg* 7d 6g* 6d²] big, strong, rangy,
useful sort: ran well when put back to racing at 6f and won handicaps at York
in August (Wykeham Handicap by ½ length from May Beck) and Ayr in September (trounced his opposition, winning without being extended by 7 lengths):
also runner-up in three good handicaps, Canada Dry Shield at Ayr, Northumberland Sprint Trophy at Newcastle and Top Deck Handicap at Redcar: narrowly
failed to defy a 7-lb penalty when beaten by Briarvanter in last-named event:
best form at 6f but stays 7f: appears to act on any going. *G. Richards.*

SON OF RAGUSA 4 ch.c. Ragusa 137–Lovely Virginia (Aggressor 130) [1974 —
5f* 6fg⁵ 7d⁵ 5g* 6v² 1975 7v⁴ 9s³ 12g 10h² 12h³ 8h² 9g 12f 1976 10.5g]
robust colt: has been fired: fair handicapper in 1975: tailed off in only race at
4 yrs: best at up to 1¼m: acts on any going. *J. Calvert.*

Wykeham Handicap, York—Sonnenblick wins all out from May Beck. The horse on the far side is Hayloft who finishes fourth

SON OF SILVER 5 ch.h. Silver Cloud 121–Now What 109 (Premonition 130) **118**
[1974 8fg³ 8g 10.5f⁵ 1975 8.2s² 10v* 9s* 9.2v⁵ 9.8d² 8g* 9.2g 8g* 8g 8s² 10fg⁵ 8s 1976 10fg⁴ 8g⁶ 8d³ 7g* 8s] very tall ex-English horse: good mover: half-brother to 2,000 Guineas winner Mon Fils (by Sheshoon): showed himself a very smart performer in 1975, winning four races, including Prix Messidor, and turning in an excellent effort to finish about 3 lengths fifth to Rose Bowl in Champion Stakes at Newmarket: lightly raced at 5 yrs but ran well on three occasions, on fourth outing coming out best in a blanket finish to Prix de la Porte Maillot at Longchamp in June, beating Comeram a nose: stayed 1¼m: probably acted on any going: game front runner: standing at King Edward's Place Stud, Wiltshire, at a fee of £750 no foal, no fee. *A. Paus, France.*

SON'S DREAM 2 br.c. Bill Hickock–Petranelly (Brocade Slipper 116) [1976 — 6g 6f] first foal: dam never ran: behind in minor events at Lingfield and Windsor in August. *J. Dunlop.*

SONSIE 2 b.f. Tudor Melody 129–Sonia 86 (Worden II 129) [1976 5fg 6f — 6fg] quite attractive, close-coupled filly: half-sister to French 3-y-o middle-distance winner Hadley Wood (by Pretendre): 5,000 gns yearling: dam won over 1½m: behind in maiden races: blinkered final outing (July). *G. Harwood.*

SON TOM 2 b.c. Welsh Saint 126–Armeria 111 (Persian Gulf) [1976 5s⁵ 5f **70** 6fg 6f⁴ 7.2f 8f 8fg 8.2s 8s⁶ 10s²] well-grown colt: plater: stayed on when 1½ lengths second of 13 to Sleigh Bells at Pontefract in October: will stay 1½m: acts on any going. *K. Payne.*

SORBONNE 4 b.g. Alcide 136–Lyoness (Milesian 125) [1974 5g³ 5f² 5g⁴ 6fg² — 6f² 6f⁴ 7g² 7g 1975 11s 10.8d 8s 7fg 6f³ 5.9f 6f³ 6f 7f 1976 8fg 5f²] poor plater: second to Craigellachie in 10-runner handicap at Ostend in July: best form at up to 7f: acts on firm going: sometimes wears blinkers and did so on reappearance: trained by F. Rimell until after first outing. *J. Tierney.*

SOSANNAH 2 b.f. So Blessed 130–Hannah Darling 108 (Match III 135) [1976 **75** 5s³ 6s⁵] third foal: half-sister to 3-y-o middle-distance winner Paddy's Darling (by St Paddy): 3,800 gns yearling: dam second in Irish 1,000 Guineas and stayed 1½m: 5½ lengths third of 12 to Silver Shoals in maiden race at Lingfield in September, better effort: will stay 1m. *J. Dunlop.*

SO SHARP 3 b.c. So Blessed 130–Cutle 86 (Saint Crespin III 132) [1975 6g² **106** 1976 10.4d* 10.6d 10fg* 10.6fg³ 12f⁴] attractive colt: half-brother to Irish 2,000 Guineas winner Sharp Edge (by Silver Shark): dam winner at up to 13f: won minor event at Chester in May and handicap at Newmarket in July: creditable third to Chemin de Fer in £4,000 handicap at Haydock the following month, losing a tremendous amount of ground on turn but staying on well in straight: may stay further than 1½m: probably acts on any going. *R. Hern.*

698

Mrs A. Wettermark's "So Sharp"

SOSPECHA 3 b.f. So Blessed 130–Karenina 95 (Silver Shark 129) [1975 **77**
5d⁴ 6f³ 6f³ 1976 8fg* 8f² 8fg³ 8fg 8s³ 8.2s⁴] neat filly: half-sister to 2-y-o
Sultans Ruby (by Royal Palace): won 16-runner maiden race at Thirsk in May
by a length from Canicule: off course over three months after third outing but
ran well when third to Grey Sail in handicap at Redcar in October: will probably
stay further than 1m: acts on any going. *P. Rohan.*

SOSUE ME 2 br.f. Judgable–Place to Place (No Robbery) [1976 5g 5f 7f³ 7h³ **76**
7g* 8.2v⁴] compact, strong American-sired filly: first foal: dam, a winner at
up to 6f in U.S.A., ran until she was a 5-y-o: favourite when winning 21-runner
seller at Newmarket in September by 1½ lengths from It's Bubbles (bought in
2,600 gns): should stay 1m: best form on top-of-the-ground. *P. Cole.*

SO THEY SAY 4 b.c. So Blessed 130–Amorella 106 (Crepello 136) [1974 6g 7g² **76**
8d⁶ 7v³ 1975 8v⁵ 7v⁵ 10.1f 10fg⁵ 12g² 11.7fg⁴ 12g* 11.7fg³ 10d⁶ 12v⁴ 12g⁵ 16s⁶
1976 14g 11.7fg² 12g* 11.1g² 12g⁴ 12g³] strong colt: quite a moderate handicapper: successful at Kempton in May by 2½ lengths from Chasseur: very well
suited by 1¼m and 1½m, and may well stay further, although he has yet to show
he stays 2m: appears to act on any going: suited by front-running tactics: sold
400 gns Newmarket Autumn Sales. *J. Benstead.*

SOTTO IL VULCANO 2 b.c. Right Tack 131–Splendidly (Luminary 132) **97**
[1976 6d⁵ 7g 7.3v³] strong colt: closely related to three winners by Hard Tack,
notably very useful miler Tack On: 6,000 gns foal: dam half-sister to very useful
middle-distance stayer Shackleton: put up by far his best effort when 6 lengths
third of nine to Fair Season in Horris Hill Stakes at Newbury in October: will
be suited by 1m: evidently well suited by heavy going. *L. Cumani.*

SOTUTA 2 ch.f. Sovereign Bill 105–Mayella 100 (Aggressor 130) [1976 5f 5f 6fg **58**
5f 5f 5s 6s] third foal: dam best at up to 1¼m: poor maiden. *F. Freeman.*

SOUDNO 3 ch.c. Ribero 126–Sucu Sucu 73 (Tudor Jinks 121) [1975 7g⁵ **84**
1976 6s⁶ 8f² 10f² 10f³ 7g* 10f* 8.2h³] half-brother to three winners, including
smart miler Redundant (by Busted): 8,600 gns foal: resold 8,800 gns yearling:

dam a sprinter: odds on when winning maiden race at Limerick in July and minor event at Lanark in September: comfortably accounted for weak opposition on latter course: ran moderately in minor event at Hamilton four days later (again odds on): stays 1¼m: acts on firm going but is possibly unsuited by hard ground. *M. Vance, Ireland.*

SOULOU 3 b.c. Barbary Pirate 91–Shizuka 83 (Tacitus 124) [1975 6f 1976 — 12f⁵ 8f⁵ 12v] poor maiden. *R. Sturdy.*

SOUNDING ARCH 3 ch.c. Whistling Wind 123–Florence Nightingale 78 — (Above Suspicion 127) [1975 5fg⁵ 7fg² 7g* 1976 7g 10.4s 10fg] lengthy colt: good mover: won £1,800 maiden race at Doncaster in 1975 staying on from Loh: only lightly raced and had stiff tasks at 3 yrs: should stay 1¼m+: sold 6,200 gns Ascot October Sales. *P. Walwyn.*

SOUND JIFF 5 ch.h. Never Say Die 137–Sound Number 103 (Sound Track 132) 77 [1974 8.5g⁵ 7f³ 7g⁶ 8fg² 8fg² 7.3g⁶ 6g³ 8d 8g⁶ 6d⁵ 11.7s⁴ 10.1d 10d 10.8v 12s⁴ 10g⁶ 1975 8g* 7s* 7f² 7g³ 8fg* 8f 8f⁶ 7fg⁶ 8fg 1976 7fg⁶ 7f 7fg³ 7fg³ 7.2d⁶ 8fg* 8fg³ 7f* 7g⁴ 7f* 7f² 7fg³ 8.3d] strong, compact horse: quite a moderate handicapper: had another successful season and won at Newbury and Yarmouth in June and at Salisbury in August, on last course beating Chukaroo ¾ length: best form at up to 1m: acts on any going: genuine: ran below his best when tried in blinkers: good mount for an apprentice: sometimes wears bandages. *R. Hannon.*

SOUND OF THE HORN 2 ch.f. Mountain Call 125–Aldona 96 (Mossborough 81 126) [1976 5.1fg⁵ 6f² 6fg⁵ 6g⁶ 5g⁶ 8s⁵] third foal: 5,200 gns yearling: dam, winner over 7f at 3 yrs, is half-sister to top-class 1960 2-y-o Kathy Too: neck second to Pearl Haven in maiden race at Windsor in August: effective at 5f and stays 1m. *Doug Smith.*

SOUNDS GOOD 4 b.c. Laser Light 118–Eden (Gulf Pearl 117) [1974 5fg* 5f² 65 5v 5g 6d 1975 6s⁵ 7v 6fg 6g³ 6f⁵ 8.2f² 8fg 8.2f⁴ 7g⁴ 8f³ 12h⁵ 12g⁴ 13.8g² 10fg 1976 15.8g 10v* 10g³ 10s³ 12.5s] strong colt: 10-length winner of apprentice handicap at Ayr in April: stays 1¾m: acts on any going: wears blinkers nowadays: off course over five months before final appearance. *Denys Smith.*

SOUSA 3 br.c. March Past 124–Sandarey 94 (Darius 129) [1975 6g 8g 1976 97 10g* 9f² 10g 10s⁴ 7fg² 7f⁴ 8f* 7.2g* 8g* 8g⁶ 7s] tall, fine-looking, rangy colt: good mover and good walker: enjoyed an excellent season, winning maiden race at Nottingham and handicaps at Yarmouth, Haydock and Kempton: put up an excellent performance on last-named course in August, finding a really good turn of speed to beat Chop-Chop 2 lengths: effective at 7f to 1¼m: possibly unsuited by soft going. *M. Stoute.*

SOUTH OF ALASKA 2 b.c. Yukon Eric–Lisnabrin (Straight Lad 110) [1976 — 6fg 8s] fourth foal: 115 gns yearling: dam never ran: in rear in maiden races at Salisbury in June (tailed off) and Bath in October. *J. Cann.*

SOUTH TODAY 2 ch.c. Sky Gipsy 117–Night Lark (Larkspur 128) [1976 — 7v 7s] small, strong colt: half-brother to winning 1973 2-y-o Next Step (by March Past): 800 gns foal: dam ran only twice: behind in maiden company at Leicester and Chepstow in October: wears blinkers. *D. Sasse.*

SOVEREIGN BROOK 2 gr.c. Sovereign Path 125–Charletta 67 (Charlottesville 64 135) [1976 5g⁵ 5fg² 5f² 5f⁶ 5s 5d⁴ 6fg] lightly-built colt: plater: second in seller at Wolverhampton and maiden auction event at Pontefract (beaten a length by Maiden Grieve), both in April: ran badly final outing (July): should be suited by 6f: possibly needs a sound surface. *K. Payne.*

SOVEREIGN CHIEF 2 gr.c. Tribal Chief 125–Sovereign Star 101 (Joan's Star 75 112) [1976 5fg 6f³ 6fg⁴ 5d⁴ 6s⁴] useful-looking colt: good walker: half-brother to a minor winner by Lucky Brief: dam won seven races from 5f to 1m: in frame in maiden and minor events, finishing 5 lengths fourth of 13 to Red Light District at Redcar in October: runs as though he will stay 7f+: acts on any going. *M. W. Easterby.*

SOVEREIGN CLOUD 2 b.c. Lucky Sovereign–Malarise 60 (Pall Mall 132) — [1976 5g 6fg 7g] attractive, well-made colt: second reported living foal: brother to moderate 1975 2-y-o 5f winner Tengarlos: 1,550 gns yearling: dam, poor handicapper, stayed 1¼m: made no show in sizeable fields of maidens but was only seen out from time to time. *G. Hunter.*

SOVEREIGN DICE 3 gr.c. Supreme Sovereign 119–Knocknagrena (Worden II 117 129) [1975 N.R. 1976 6s* 7s* 7f²] half-brother to several winners here and abroad, including quite moderate 1970 2-y-o Neat Trick (by Takawalk II): 2,500 gns foal: dam placed at up to 1¼m in Ireland: showed himself to be one of the best performers in Ireland in his early-season races, winning maiden event at Naas by 8 lengths and Group 3 Gladness Stakes at the Curragh by 5 lengths, and going down by only a head to subsequent Irish 2,000 Guineas third Lucky Wednesday (rec 7 lb), with Wolverlife (rec 3 lb) and Northern Treasure (rec 7 lb) third and fourth, in Group 3 Vauxhall Trial Stakes at Phoenix Park in April: not seen out again: will probably stay 1¼m: acts on any going: sold 15,500 gns Newmarket December Sales. *S. Quirke, Ireland.*

SOVEREIGN FAIR 2 ch.c. Sovereign Gleam 117–Kals Angel 68 (Kalydon 122) **65** [1976 7d 8fg 8s] half-brother to two winners, including Irish 3-y-o Engage (by Whistling Wind) a useful winner at up to 1m at 2 yrs: 500 gns yearling: dam won 7f seller: seventh of 14 to Reppin Castle in maiden race at Beverley in September, second outing and only sign of ability: sold 1,500 gns Newmarket Autumn Sales. *B. Hanbury.*

SOVEREIGN FORD 2 b.c. Sovereign Path 125–Florrie Ford 79 (Kelly 122) **87** [1976 5fg⁵ 5fg 7h⁴ 7g² 7f⁴ 8g 8g 8.2d 8s² 10v² 7.6v³] useful-looking colt: first living foal: 4,100 gns yearling: dam won over 6f at 2 yrs: runner-up in minor event at Sandown in July (blinkered, beaten 4 lengths by Fast Frigate) and maiden races in October at Warwick and Nottingham: well beaten in between, three times wearing blinkers: stays 1¼m: suited by heavy ground: inconsistent. *C. Brittain.*

SOVEREIGN LANE 2 b.c. Wolver Hollow 126–Wonder Star (Royal Palm 131) **79** [1976 5fg 6fg 6g³ 8f² 8g 8s] workmanlike colt: half-brother to useful 1968 2-y-o 6f winner Chellice (by Proud Chieftain): 5,400 gns yearling: dam won over 5f at 2 yrs: ran best race when getting up close home to win eight-runner maiden race at Bath in August by a neck from Cabin Boy, but was moved down to second by stewards: ran poorly afterwards: stays 1m: acts on firm going. *G. Hunter.*

SOVEREIGN'S ESCORT 2 gr.c. Supreme Sovereign 119–Jean Amour 88 **80** (Delirium 126) [1976 5d⁶ 7fg 7g] neat colt: third foal: half-brother to a winner in Malaya: dam middle-distance winner: showed promise when sixth of 12 to Rumson in maiden race at the Curragh in May when trained by R. Annesley: did not reproduce that form in sizeable fields of maidens at Newbury and Kempton in August. *S. Ingham.*

SOVEREIGN SILVER 2 gr.c. Sovereign Path 125–Silver Talisman (Silver **106** Shark 129) [1976 5s⁵ 5s 5f 7.9f² 8fg³ 8g* 8d⁴ 7s⁶] Irish colt: first foal: dam a useful winner over 5f and 6f at 2 yrs in Ireland from only three starts: off course most of summer but put up several useful efforts in nurseries on return, winning one at Thurles in October by 2½ lengths under 9-7: ridden by girl apprentice unable to claim 5-lb allowance when 6¼ lengths fourth to Orchestra in Beresford Stakes at the Curragh on penultimate outing: stays 1m: probably acts on any going. *S. McGrath, Ireland.*

SOYEZ FERME 4 ch.g. Majestic Prince–Charvak (Alcibiades 95) [1974 6g 7g — 7d 1975 9v 12.2g⁵ 14f³ 16f³ 1976 12g] attractive, well-made American-bred gelding: poor maiden: needs a good test of stamina: acts on firm going: heavily bandaged on fore-legs on only outing in 1976 (August). *G. Smyth.*

SPACER 4 b.g. Space King 115–Aldon 75 (Donore 119) [1974 N.R. 1975 — 12.2g 1976 12fg⁵] probably of little account. *D. McCain.*

SPACE SHIP 2 b.c. Captain's Gig–Alta-Vista (Skymaster 126) [1976 5s⁴ 6f* **105** 6.3f³ 7.5g³ 6.3s] Irish colt: half-brother to two winners, notably very useful 7f and 1m performer Fabvista (by Faberge II): 5,400 gns yearling: dam never ran: won 17-runner maiden race at Navan in June by a head from Uncle Pokey, the pair finishing clear: third subsequently in Goff's Stakes at the Curragh and £2,400 nursery at Gowran Park, running well under top weight in latter race when beaten 2¾ lengths by Snap Happy: will be suited by 1m: acts on firm going. *D. Weld, Ireland.*

SPADE GUINEA 3 ch.c. Golden Dipper 119–Chilcombe Belle 75 (Robert **104** Barker 125) [1975 6fg³ 6fg* 8s³ 1976 7f 7g 8g² 10fg 8g 10fg³ 8fg⁴ 10fg 8g⁴ 9g] strong, lengthy colt: put up a smart performance when winning 19-runner Convivial Stakes at York as a 2-y-o: ran well in many of his races in 1976, including when placed in good handicaps at Sandown, running Free State to 4 lengths in Esher Cup in April and finishing third to Marquis de Sade in Trafalgar House Handicap in June, and when seventh of 13 to Il Padrone in Extel Handicap at Goodwood in July: stays 1¼m: appears to act on any going. *W. Marshall.*

SPANISH AIR 3 b.c. Tudor Melody 129–Lerida 119 (Matador 131) [1975 5f⁶ **115**
5d³ 6f² 5fg* 5v⁴ 5g² 1976 6d² 6fg 6g⁵ 5fg³ 5g 5g³] strong, shapely colt: brother
to high-class 1971 2-y-o Philip of Spain: smart handicapper: placed at Haydock
in May (second to Ubedizzy in William Hill North-Western Stakes), York in
August (third to High Award) and Ascot in September (third to Derringo):
stays 6f, but is a speedy animal and is probably best at 5f: acts on a firm and a
soft surface: best in blinkers (ran moderately without them on fifth start): sold
to B.B.A. N. Murless.

SPANISH BARON 2 ch.g. Song 132–La Speranza (Princely Gift 137) [1976 **77** p
5g*] June foal: half-brother to two minor winners: 4,100 gns yearling: dam
once-raced half-sister to high-class miler The Creditor: favourite for 10-runner
maiden race at Edinburgh in June and justified the confidence, winning by
½ length from Humbie: will stay 6f. S. Hall.

SPANISH DOUBLOON 6 b.h. Supreme Sovereign 119–Big Bertha 75 (Herbager **110**
136) [1974 10g 10g⁵ 10g* 8f⁶ 9s² 10.7s 10s 1975 10f 8f⁵ 9f 1976 10f* 10f*
9fg⁴ 10f³ 9f³ 12f² 10f²] Irish horse: smart performer: winner twice at Phoenix
Park in 1976, beating Grey Tiger a length when winning well-contested Double
Diamond Handicap in May on second outing: did well afterwards, on final start
finishing good second to Hawkberry in Mulhuddart Stakes (also at Phoenix Park)
in August: stays 1½m: acts on any going: genuine and consistent. S. Murless,
Ireland.

SPANISH LAMP 2 br.f. Don Carlos–Lantern (Relic) [1976 6d 6v⁶ 5s] light- —
framed filly: sister to two winners, including fairly useful middle-distance winner
Spanish Lantern: cost 520 gns at Ascot January 1976 Sales: dam, a twin, never
ran: well behind in maiden and minor events: needs further than sprint distances
to show any ability she may possess. P. Farrell.

SPANISH LANTERN 5 b.m. Don Carlos–Lantern (Relic) [1974 7.6g³ 8g³ —
10d* 12fg⁶ 12g* 10s⁶ 10d 12s 1975 14s 12d 10g 10g 10fg³ 10fg³ 14fg² 14fg⁶
12g 14g⁵ 1976 14s 12f⁴ 12f⁴ 12f] light-framed mare: quite a moderate handicapper (rated 75) in 1975: didn't run up to her best at 5 yrs: stays 1¾m: appears
to act on any going: has been tried in blinkers. M. Goswell.

SPANISH NUN 5 ch.m. El Ruedo 91–Zabbotina (Welsh Abbot 131) [1974 **58**
5f⁶ 5g⁴ 5fg 5f 5.9fg⁶ 5g³ 5g⁴ 5.8g² 5g 6g⁴ 5g² 5.8v² 5.9s 5v⁴ 5s⁴ 1975 6v 5.8g 6f
6f³ 5h⁵ 5.8f 5.8f 5f⁴ 6fg* 6g⁴ 6g³ 6f 1976 6g³ 5f⁶ 6g⁶ 8h² 10f* 9h 13f⁶ 8g] strong
mare: plater: narrow winner from Story Teller at Lanark in July (bought in
640 gns): stays 1¼m: acts on any going: suitable mount for an apprentice:
slowly into stride on second outing. G. Wallace.

SPANISH PARADE 12 b.g. Vigo 130–Ceremonial 89 (March Past 124) [1974 —
8fg 7fg³ 8f* 7fg* 8g* 8fg 8s³ 1975 7s 1976 8f⁴ 8f] poor plater nowadays:
having only his third outing since 1974 when pulled up lame behind Eve at
Yarmouth in August: stays 1m: acts on any going: usually wears blinkers: has
won eight times at Yarmouth. R. Akehurst.

SPANISH SINGER 3 b.f. Crooner 119–Majorca II (Caldarium) [1975 5f 5fg —
1976 10fg⁶ 9f 8f 10.1d] poor maiden. W. Payne.

SPANISH TRICK 3 b.g. Ballyciptic 122–Pinochle 61 (Matador 131) [1975 —
N.R. 1976 8s 12s] half-brother to useful sprint handicapper Pericet (by Atan):
dam ran only at 2 yrs: 20/1, made late headway when remote seventh of 19 to
Tudor Wynk in maiden race at Chepstow in October: started slowly first outing.
R. Turnell.

SPARKATION 2 ch.f. Communication 119–Light Spark 73 (Twilight Alley 133) **59**
[1976 6g 5f 5f 6d 7v 6s⁵] strong filly: well-beaten fifth of 17 in seller won by
Stand On at Doncaster in October. L. Shedden.

SPARKENBROKE 3 b.g. Busted 134–Piccadilly Lil 92 (Pall Mall 132) [1975 —
N.R. 1976 8f 8g 11g] rangy gelding: first foal: 2,900 gns yearling: dam won
over 6f as a 2-y-o: behind in maiden races at Newbury (two) and Sandown in
first part of season: sold 460 gns Ascot December Sales. W. Wightman.

SPARKLING SPREE 3 ch.f. Roan Rocket 128–Shopping Spree 88 (Takawalk —
II 125) [1976 8f] first living foal: dam won over 5f as a 2-y-o: first foal:
tailed-off last of 11 behind Bright Decision in maiden race at Yarmouth in June:
sold 480 gns Newmarket September Sales and resold 400 gns Doncaster November
Sales. G. Pritchard-Gordon.

SPARTIATI   2 b c. Le Levanstell 122–Narcotic (Narrator 127)   [1976 5fg   **98**
6fg⁴ 8g² 8s]   well-grown, good sort: half-brother to two winners here and abroad,
including useful sprinter Fine Silver (by Silver Shark): 16,000 gns yearling:
dam, middle-distance winner in Ireland, is daughter of 1,000 Guineas winner
Hypericum: put up a useful effort when going down by only ½ length to Royal
Plume in £1,700 event at Doncaster in September: co-favourite for 28-runner
maiden race at Newmarket the following month but ran poorly, finishing only
fifteenth behind Royal Boxer: will stay 1¼m: possibly not suited by soft ground.
C. Brittain.

SPEED TRAP   2 br.f. Pontifex–Traffic Offence 61 (Traffic Judge)   [1976 5g³   **76**
5f² 5f² 5s* 5d³ 6h⁵ 5h⁶ 5fg]   leggy filly: half-sister to four winners, including
useful 1971 2-y-o 5f winner Light Jumper (by Red God): dam half-sister to smart
Stoned: made all and just held on when winning £1,500 seller at York in May
by a head from newcomer Sir Lord: respectable third of nine to Luke Splendid
in minor event at Ripon the following month, best subsequent effort: should
stay 6f: acts on any going.   *M. H. Easterby.*

SPEY   3 b.f. Jimmy Reppin 131–Marsajac 74 § (Zucchero 133 §)   [1975 N.R.   **88**
1976 10.4fg² 12g*]   rangy filly: half-sister to two winners, including useful
middle-distance handicapper Silver Doctor (by Salvo): bought privately for
700 gns as a yearling: dam, temperamental middle-distance winner, is daughter
of Oaks third Reel In: put up an impressive performance when winning 13-runner
maiden race at Newmarket in September, going well clear from over 2f out and
scoring unchallenged by 8 lengths from Dancing Hill: well suited by 1¼m and
may well stay further.   *F. J. Houghton.*

SPINNINGDALE   2 gr.f. Good Bond 122–Sapphire Melody 89 (Tudor Melody   **54**
129)   [1976 5fg 6g 5.3f⁵]   fourth produce: 220 gns foal: dam won over 5f at
2 yrs: blinkered when 7 lengths fifth of seven to The Triplets in claiming race
at Brighton in August.   *D. Morley.*

SPIRANTHES   3 b.f. Vaguely Noble 140–Shenow (Eternal Bim)   [1975 6g 8d* **101**
8g   1976 10g* 12fg² 12g 10fg⁴ 12fg 14f⁵]   lengthy American-bred filly: dam, a
leading 2-y-o in U.S.A. in 1967, won at up to 7f: won Pretty Polly Stakes at
Newmarket in April going away by ¾ length from Everything Nice after getting
behind early on (value of win 2 lengths): subsequently finished in frame in
Oaks Trial at Lingfield (appeared not to handle track too well and was beaten
1½ lengths by Heaven Knows) and Nassau Stakes at Goodwood (3 lengths fourth
to Roussalka, staying on in grand style in straight after being well behind on
home turn): stays 1½m: acts on a firm and a soft surface.   *J. Dunlop.*

SPIRIT OF ECSTASY   5 ch.m. Pardao 120–Susiana (Darius 129)   [1974 10f   **—**
9.4fg⁴ 10g 12h⁴ 8.2g²   1975 13s 12s 8f 10.2f 8f³ 7f 8.2g⁴ 8h² 8f 10g³ 7g* 10g 10g
1976 8g 10g 10f 13g]   neat mare: modest plater: best form at up to 1¼m, but
seems to stay 1½m: acts on hard going: sometimes wears blinkers: not raced
after April.   *B. Richmond.*

SPLENDECHO   3 br.c. John Splendid 116–Calecho (Bleep-Bleep 134)   [1975   **—**
5d⁵ 5s² 5s⁴   1976 6f 10h]   leggy colt: quite a moderate maiden at 2 yrs but
finished tailed off on both outings in 1976: sold 250 gns Ascot July Sales.   *G.
Hunter.*

SPLENDID   2 b.f. John Splendid 116–Hunting Bee (Honeyway 125)   [1976 6g]   **—**
half-sister to 3-y-o Palmerston (by Aureole), a winner at up to 13f, and to a
winner abroad: 420 gns yearling: apprentice ridden when tailed-off last of 21 to
Burley in seller at Newmarket in September: sold 380 gns Newmarket Autumn
Sales.   *Sir Mark Prescott.*

SPLENDID SUMMER   2 gr.c. John Splendid 116–Rue Talma § (Vigo 130)   **71**
[1976 5g 5fg 6g⁵ 8g⁵ 7s 7s⁶ 7v]   strong colt: half-brother to a winner in Austria:
660 gns yearling: dam left at start on three of her four outings: showed some
ability in maiden and minor events: evidently stays 1m.   *P. Ashworth.*

SPOOFER   3 b.g. Pretendre 126–Pussy Pelmet 93 (Right Boy 137)   [1975 7f   **61**
6fg 7f 6g⁶ 8f* 8.2g   1976 8fg⁴ 12g 12.2d 10fg³ 10f² 10h* 7f⁴ 10h 10g*]   plater:
winner at Pontefract in July (sold out of G Blum's stable 920 gns) and Leicester
in September (sold 875 gns): stays 1¼m but possibly not 1½m: possibly needs a
sound surface, and acts on firm going: has won with and without blinkers.   *A.
Bacon.*

SPORTING YANKEE   2 b.c. Vaguely Noble 140–Sale Day (To Market)   [1976 **123** 7g² 8s* 8s*]

Had Dick Francis written a novel about an owner who bought his first horse, took over the sponsorship of one of Europe's most valuable races for two-year-olds and then won his own race, critics would have said the scenario was too far fetched. Admittedly such a plot does stretch the bounds of probability but this is just about what happened in 1976 when the William Hill Futurity Stakes was won by Sporting Yankee, one of the three yearlings bought by William Hill Racing Limited in 1975 after the Jockey Club began to allow horses to run under company names.

The William Hill Futurity, run first as the Timeform Gold Cup and then as the Observer Gold Cup, is usually one of the most strongly contested two-year-old races of the season. However, the field in 1976 was the smallest in the race's history—and the six runners very nearly became five when the plane carrying Valinsky from Ireland burst three tyres on landing. Perhaps it's because there were only six runners, more than any other reason, that some people have taken the view that Sporting Yankee is below the standard usually required to win this race. Whatever the reason, we think that his mark of 8-4 in the Free Handicap, 17 lb less than J. O. Tobin, is unjustifiably low.

There may have been only six runners for the Futurity but they included Valinsky and another Irish colt Orchestra, as well as the French challenger Juge de Paix. All three had smart form to their credit. Valinsky, an exceptionally well-bred colt, had run out a most impressive five-length winner on his only outing; Orchestra had won the Beresford Stakes, one of Ireland's most important races for two-year-olds; and Juge de Paix had also shown he was well suited by a mile by winning the Prix des Foals at Deauville and then finishing a highly creditable second in the Prix la Rochette. Valinsky started favourite at odds on and Sporting Yankee was much preferred in the betting to the other two English runners, the Ayr winner Sultans Ruby and the useful maiden Atwood, both of whom started at 66/1. Sporting Yankee led early on but then allowed Sultans Ruby to set the pace until just after halfway when he moved back into the lead. Valinsky and Juge de Paix were already struggling and

William Hill Racing Ltd's "Sporting Yankee"

only Orchestra, out in the centre of the course, ever looked likely to trouble the two leaders. He was unable to get to them though and Sporting Yankee kept on gamely under pressure to win by two lengths from Sultans Ruby, with Orchestra four lengths further away. Valinsky and Juge de Paix were so well beaten that it seemed probable that they were unsuited by the very soft going. This doesn't necessarily mean that Sporting Yankee's performance was not up to scratch though, and before the form is condemned out of hand it is worth comparing the time of the Futurity with that of a nursery run over the same course and distance an hour later. Most of the runners in the nursery had shown decent form, were of proven stamina and four of them had shown they were at home on soft ground. With three front runners in the field, the nursery was run at a fast pace but the winner's time was a good bit slower than that put up by Sporting Yankee who carried 6 lb more.

Sporting Yankee
(b.c. 1974)
- Vaguely Noble (b 1965)
  - Vienna (ch 1957)
    - Aureole
    - Turkish Blood
  - Noble Lassie (b 1956)
    - Nearco
    - Belle Sauvage
- Sale Day (b 1965)
  - To Market (ch 1948)
    - Market Wise
    - Pretty Does
  - Hasty Girl (b 1951)
    - Princequillo
    - In Love

Sporting Yankee had raced only twice before the Futurity. Evidently he wasn't exactly a picture of good health after his journey over from the U.S.A. as a yearling and, as he was very tall, he was given plenty of time. It wasn't until early in October that he had his first race, against a large field of maidens at Newmarket, and he ran most encouragingly; the favourite Sin Timon beat him three lengths, but Sporting Yankee drew a long way clear of the group on the disadvantageous stand side. He soon went one better, running out an impressive winner of a twenty-seven-runner maiden race at the next Newmarket meeting. Again he raced on the stand side and after going well all the way he drew clear in the final two furlongs, with his jockey simply pushing him with

Chesterton Maiden Stakes, Newmarket—Sporting Yankee is clear of the leaders on the far side who are (left to right) Eastern Spring, Rockery and Prince Lancing

*William Hill Futurity Stakes, Doncaster—Sporting Yankee stays on well to beat
Sultans Ruby and Orchestra*

hands and heels, to win by four lengths from Eastern Spring. The next horse
to finish on the winner's side was a very long way behind.

Whatever opinion is held of Sporting Yankee's form as a two-year-old, there
are two good reasons to expect him to improve on it at three years. First, his
immaturity and his physical scope for development; even when he won the
Futurity he still looked rather weak and gangling, but he gives the impression
that with time he could be an imposing individual. Second, his pedigree; this
is more the pedigree of a top-class middle-distance horse than anything else.
It's true that his sire, Vaguely Noble, won the 1967 Observer Gold Cup and has
already sired Noble Decree, winner of the 1972 race, and Mississipian, second
in 1973, but both he and the majority of his best runners improved after their
two-year-old days. Of those that spring to mind, Dahlia was rated 10 lb below
the top in the French Free Handicap, Nobiliary 14 lb, Empery 10 lb and Exceller
13 lb; Royal and Regal, winner of the Florida Derby in 1973, was rated 21 lb
below the top in the Experimental Handicap of the previous year; Ace of Aces
didn't run as a two-year-old and Duke of Marmalade had only one outing.

Sporting Yankee is the second foal of Sale Day and a half-brother to Malan-
drino (by Drone) who won three small races as a three-year-old. Sale Day was
seen out only twice at two years but more than made up for lost time the following season, when she won nine of her twenty-five starts. Among the races she
won were the Falls City Handicap over a mile and the Spinster Stakes over a
furlong further and she was rated among the best fillies of her year. Sale Day didn't
do so well at four years, winning only three of her twenty-three starts, but she was
still very useful. Although her career of fifty races seems extremely arduous by
our standards, it pales in comparison with the record of her dam, Hasty Girl,
whose one hundred and twelve outings resulted in eleven wins and forty places
over a period of six seasons. Hasty Girl's strenuous efforts on the racecourse
didn't adversely affect her stud career; she produced ten foals in twelve years
and all eight of those to race were winners. They weren't all ordinary either,
for she was the dam of Hurry To Market, a brother to Sale Day, who was named
the champion two-year-old of 1963 in two of the three year-end polls in the
States.

Sporting Yankee is a colt whose main asset is stamina. He will probably

706

need at least a mile and a quarter and will do better at even longer distances. His trainer made it clear very early in the day that he doesn't regard him as a Guineas horse, and at the same time expressed doubts as to whether the Epsom course will suit Sporting Yankee's long-striding action. The Irish Sweeps Derby, therefore, looks a likely target and Sporting Yankee will probably be brought along in a manner similar to the stable's English Prince who won that race in 1974. If he improves, as he is virtually certain to, Sporting Yankee looks sure to do well as a three-year-old, and William Hill Racing Ltd isn't likely to regret turning down a six-figure offer made for him in November. There is little to lose —he has already repaid much of the 90,000 dollars he cost as a yearling—and everything to gain. *P. Walwyn*

SPORTSKY 4 b.c. Nijinsky 138–Sports Event (T.V. Lark) [1974 6g 7d² 1975 **93**
10s 10fg⁶ 8g³ 10fg³ 8fg 7g* 1976 8d 7.6d² 7fg* 7fg³ 7f* 7fg² 7g² 8fg⁶ 7.6fg* 7g*]
tall, quite attractive American-bred colt: dam half-sister to Empery: had a good season and won at Goodwood, Newcastle, Chester and Ayr: beat Fearless Boy in a blanket finish on last-named course on final outing in September: best form at 7f or 1m: seemed to act on any going: usually came with a late run and had a fine turn of foot: sold to South Australia as a stallion. *C. Brittain.*

SPRINGBOARD 3 b.f. Silly Season 127–Header 78 (High Hat 131) [1975 **56**
5fg 5.8f⁴ 1976 10.1fg 12f⁴ 10fg³ 10.2h² 10.1g² 10.1d] first foal: dam half-sister to good stayer Charlton: runner-up in maiden races at Bath and Windsor in August: probably stays 1½m: acts on hard ground and ran moderately on dead on final outing: sold 4,000 gns Newmarket December Sales. *I. Balding.*

SPRING CRUISE 7 b.g. Silly Season 127–Snowdrop 83 (Falls of Clyde 126) —
[1974 N.R. 1975 10g³ 1976 8h⁵ 11g] selling handicapper nowadays: should stay further than 1¼m. *J. Barclay.*

SPRING DIVE 2 ch.c. Deep Diver 134–Fortunes Lady 93 (Fortino II 120) **94**
[1976 5fg⁴ 5f⁵ 5f* 5d² 5s³ 5v⁶] big, strong colt: first foal: 11,500 gns yearling: dam won twice at around 1m: won 25-runner maiden race at Thirsk in September by 2 lengths from Perkasa: placed subsequently in nurseries at Redcar (creditable second to Star Attention) and Sandown: acts on any going. *M. Jarvis.*

SPRING FLING 4 b.g. Crooner 119–Gay Frolic 83 (Coalition 110) [1974 7d —
6g⁵ 5g⁵ 7s 6s 6v 1975 9.4g 8fg 8h 10.6fg 8g 10f⁴ 9.4g* 10d* 10d 1976 10g]
strong well-made gelding: ran only once at 4 yrs: stays 1¼m. *W. A. Stephenson.*

SPRING FROLIC 3 ch.c. Silly Season 127–Gigi 85 (Acropolis 132) [1975 6fg **93**
6fg 8s 1976 12fg⁶ 12g* 12fg* 12g⁵ 12g⁶ 14fg² 12fg*] powerful colt: quite a useful handicapper: winner at Kempton (maiden race), Newmarket and Newbury: picked up a valuable prize on last-named course in August when beating Lighter decisively by a length: seems to stay 1¾m: acts well on a firm surface. *J. Sutcliffe.*

SPRINGHILL 2 b.c. Sallust 134–Marsville (Trouville 125) [1976 5f 6g*] Irish **121 ?**
colt: second live foal: dam won over 7f and 1m in Ireland: disputed lead all way when winning £1,400 event at the Curragh in June by 1½ lengths from Pampapaul, with the other 12 runners, headed by Roman Charger, at least 6 lengths further away: looked likely to take some beating in the top races on this performance but wasn't seen out again: will stay 1m. *C. Collins, Ireland.*

SPRING LANE 4 b.f. Acer 123–Saucy Councillor 64 (Privy Councillor 125) —
[1974 5d 5fg 5f 7g⁴ 7f³ 7f³ 8s⁴ 1975 13.8d² 12s 12.2f 12fg 1976 12.5g 10f]
narrow filly: of no account nowadays. *G. Toft.*

SPRING SEASON 2 b.c. Silly Season 127–Gay Life 72 (Zeus Boy 121) [1976 **62**
5g 7fg 8s] brother to very useful Slim Jim, a winner at up to 1½m, and half-brother to 1975 2-y-o 5f winner Rajal (by Calpurnius): dam won at up to 1m: little worthwhile form in maiden races but was seen out only infrequently. *I. Balding.*

SPRING STORM 3 br.f. March Past 124–Sultry One (Tropique 128) [1975 **74**
N.R. 1976 7g⁵ 8f³ 8f³ 8fg² 9f⁴ 10.4fg* 10g⁵ 8.2s* 10.2s⁵ 10d] tall, lightly-built filly: sister to Marchuna, a winner at up to 1m, and half-sister to very smart miler General Vole (by Songedor): dam ran only twice: won maiden race at Chester and apprentice handicap at Nottingham in September: blinkered first time, beat Westward Leading going away by 6 lengths in latter event: stays 1½m: acts on any going but seems well suited by soft: ran poorly last two outings when again blinkered. *R. Jarvis.*

SPRING WILLOW 3 br.f. Willowick–March Round 65 (March Past 124) [1975 —
5s 5fg⁵ 5f 5f 1976 6h 8f] leggy filly: poor plater: should stay 1m: sold 240 gns Doncaster August Sales. *K. Payne.*

SQUASH (FR) 3 b.c. Tarbes 125–Sentimental (Cavan) [1975 7.8v* 1976 9g³ **119** 10fg⁶ 9.2g⁶ 10.5g⁵ 12g⁴ 13g* 12d* 13d* 12s 12.5v³] French colt: dam unraced half-sister to smart middle-distance performer Wittgenstein: improved a good deal in the autumn and won handicap at Evry (by 10 lengths) plus quite valuable conditions events at Chantilly and Longchamp, latter in October in good style by 4 lengths: took on better company afterwards, finishing only eighth to On My Way in Prix du Conseil de Paris at Longchamp but putting up a much better effort when narrowly beaten by Carvalin and Beau Buck in valuable Grand Prix de Marseille: stays 13f well: acts on heavy ground: smart. *A. Penna, France.*

SQUIRES VINE 4 b.g. Hard Man 102–Armagnac 72 (Golestan 127 §) [1974 **61** d 5g 5fg 5fg 6fg* 6f³ 7s 5g 5.9s⁵ 1975 8s 7v² 7s⁶ 8g* 8.2g* 7fg* 7f⁴ 8f 7g 8.2g⁵ 7g⁴ 10f 8f 1976 8g 8.2v³ 12g² 12g 16f⁴ 13fg⁵ 17.1h 14d⁵ 12.2s⁶ 12s⁴ 13v] compact gelding: poor handicapper nowadays: best at up to 1¼m: appears to act on any going: has been tried in blinkers but has done better without them: suitable mount for an apprentice. *A. Jarvis.*

STAB 2 ch.c. Habitat 134–Star Story 117 (Red God 128 §) [1976 5g 5f* 6fg² **95** 6g⁴ 6fg³ 6d⁴ 7s] strong, robust colt: brother to Habitation, a useful performer at up to 7f, and half-brother to fairly useful 7f winner Genesis (by Ribero): 13,000 gns yearling: dam prolific winner at 5f and 6f: won 18-runner maiden race at Leicester in June by neck from Heath Wood: in frame on most of his other outings, best effort when short-head second to La Ville de Rire in minor event at Newcastle later in June: suited by 6f, and should stay 7f: acts on firm going: wears blinkers nowadays: pulled up on début. *P. Walwyn.*

ST ALBANS 2 b.c. Sovereign Path 125–The Maid (Milesian 125) [1976 7g 7s³ **90** 7s⁴] good-looking, well-made colt: third foal: half-brother to a winner in Norway: 6,200 gns yearling: dam won over 6f at 2 yrs in Ireland: in frame in minor events at Lingfield (6 lengths third to close finishers Crown Bowler and Swagger) and Chepstow (5½ lengths fourth to Alltyre) in October: will stay 1m. *B. Hanbury.*

STALBEC 3 b.f. Forlorn River 124–Genetic Art (Bleep-Bleep 134) [1975 N.R. — 1976 8s 8.2v⁴] half-sister to fairly useful plater Mary Louise (by Tiger), a winner at up to 9f: 260 gns yearling: dam never ran: remote fourth of 13 to Miss Damus in maiden race at Nottingham in October. *Mrs J. Pitman.*

STALEY HAL 2 ch.c. My Swanee 122–Golden Number (Goldhill 125) [1976 **70** 5g 5d 6g 7f 6h⁵ 7fg⁴ 8f³(dis) 7fg⁶ 8s] neat colt: plater: ran well when narrowly-beaten third to dead-heaters Boom Quay and Eightsome in 22-runner event at Thirsk in September but hung left and was disqualified: suited by 7f and 1m: best form on top-of-the-ground conditions. *Hbt Jones.*

STALYBRIDGE 3 b.f. The Brianstan 128–Shirley Bridge 83 (Vilmoray 126) **74** [1975 5f 6fg⁵ 7g* 7g* 7fg³ 7g⁴ 7f⁵ 1976 10f³ 8f⁴ 9fg 10f] useful sort: quite a moderate handicapper: stays 1¼m: acts on firm going but gives impression that some give in the ground may suit her better: ran moderately in blinkers on last two outings. *Hbt Jones.*

STANAURE 3 b.c. Aureole 132–Castania (Orsini 124) [1975 7g 8g 1976 11g **81** 12fg⁵ 10.5g⁵ 12.5g³ 12g⁴ 11g⁴ 18d 12v⁶] big, tall French-bred colt: about 2 lengths fifth of six to Bicoque in minor race at Newmarket in July: in frame subsequently in France, including in the provinces: will probably stay further than 1½m (had no chance at weights when well beaten in SKF Cesarewitch). *C. Brittain.*

STAND ASIDE 3 b.c. probably Dory 66–Iona Star (Glen of Stars) [1975 N.R. — 1976 12fg 9.2f] useless. *G. Wallace.*

STAND ON 2 ro.c. Cumshaw 111–Benign 67 (King's Bench 132) [1976 5g⁵ 6d **83** 7fg 6g⁶ 6f 5f 8g⁶ 6s* 6s] half-brother to two winners, including Jaffa Speed (by Pall Mall), a useful performer at around 7f in France: 420 gns foal: dam won 8.5f seller: dropped in class, made all and showed much improved form when winning 17-runner seller at Doncaster in October by 4 lengths from Only for You (no bid): had stiff task final outing: best form: clearly well suited by soft ground: usually blinkered nowadays: sold 1,200 gns Doncaster November Sales. *J. Carr.*

STAND TO REASON 3 br.c. The Brianstan 128–The Advocator 80 (Counsel **113** d 118) [1975 5g³ 5fg* 5fg² 6f* 6f² 6f* 6fg² 7s 1976 7f⁴ 8fg 8f 7fg³ 6fg 7.6g] smallish, lengthy colt: dam won over 1½m: was a smart 2-y-o when he won three races, notably Richmond Stakes at Goodwood: put up creditable efforts when in frame in Clerical, Medical Greenham Stakes at Newbury in April (fourth to Wollow) and Bunbury Cup Handicap at Newmarket in July (just over 2 lengths third to Lottogift): out of his depth in 2,000 Guineas at Newmarket (eleventh to Wollow) and St James's Palace Stakes at Royal Ascot in between but ran poorly in Stewards' Cup at Goodwood (tried in blinkers and well-backed second favourite) and valuable handicap at Lingfield afterwards and is not the force he was: stays 7f: acts well on firm going and is possibly not at his best on soft. *B. Hills.*

ST ANTHONY 2 b.c. Upper Case–Greek Gift (Acropolis 132) [1976 5fg 6fg 6d⁶] second foal: dam twice-raced half-sister to very smart Rocky Royale: well beaten in maiden races: sold to I. Dudgeon 1,050 gns Newmarket Autumn Sales. *D. Whelan.* —

STANWICK MAID 2 b.f. Siliconn 121–Llynian 81 (Ballylinan 118) [1976 5d 5g* 5f³ 5g 5g² 5d⁶] second living foal: 850 gns yearling: dam won six races in Belgium and one over 5.5f in France: won 17-runner maiden race at Catterick in June in close finish with Fibeel: excellent second to Hand Canter in nursery at Ripon in August: will stay 6f: acts on firm going and ran moderately on dead on final outing (heavily-backed favourite). *M. W. Easterby.* 82

STAR ATTENTION 2 b.f. Northfields–Star Relation (Star Gazer 123) [1976 5d 5g³ 5g³ 5d 6fg 6fg⁵ 6fg* 6f⁵ 6g⁶ 7g 5d* 6g⁶ 5v² 6d⁵ 5s] unfurnished filly: second foal: 940 gns yearling: dam Irish maiden: twice successful in nurseries, winning at Ripon in August and making all to score by 2½ lengths from Spring Dive at Redcar the following month: had some other good efforts to her name and put up a really fine display when taking on very smart horses in Challenge Stakes at Newmarket in October, finishing about 7 lengths fifth of eight behind Star Bird although carrying 5 lb overweight: speedy and is unlikely to stay beyond 6f: acts on any going but goes very well on softish ground: did not impress in appearance towards end of season but kept her form well. *P. Farrell.* 91

STAR BIRD 3 gr.f. Birdbrook 110–Wagon Star 90 (Three Star II 101) [1975 5.5g³ 7fg² 8d⁶ 8s 8.2v 1976 7.5g³ 8g 7g 6.5d* 7g* 7g⁵ 6g² 7g 6d*] French filly: half-sister to several winners, including useful 1964 2-y-o Welsh Star (by Welsh Abbot): dam ran only at 2 yrs, when smart plater: 20/1, showed vastly improved form when winning eight-runner Challenge Stakes at Newmarket in October from some very smart sprinters, probably benefiting from racing alone in centre of course on seemingly faster ground, and making most of running to beat Be Tuneful and Boldboy by ½ length and the same: had done most of her racing previously in handicaps, picking up one at Evry in July and running the useful Dacani to 1½ lengths in another at Deauville the following month: also successful in a minor event at Clairefontaine earlier in August, beating Blue Spark a short head: best at up to 7f: acted on a firm and a soft surface: stud. *P. Lallie, France.* 121

STARLIGHT LAD 2 br.g. Willipeg 112–Star of Light 85 (Counsel 118) [1976 6f 8g 8fg⁵ 8v 8v* 8s] well-grown gelding: first foal: dam won over 9f and also over hurdles: 20/1, showed improved form when winning 13-runner minor event at Teesside in October all out by a neck from Royal Flip: had stiff task only subsequent outing: stays 1m well: suited by heavy ground. *W. Gray.* 80

STAR MAGIC 2 b.c. Comedy Star 121–Typhelia 79 (Typhoon 125) [1976 5f 5fg 6fg] well-grown colt: first foal: 650 gns yearling: dam won from 5f to 1m: behind in maiden races in the midlands. *J. Hardy.* —

STAR MUSIC 2 ch.c. Nice Music 115–Nelstar (Nelcius 133) [1976 5fg 5f⁴ 5.8f 5f 7fg 6d 8.2s 7s 7s⁴] plater: suited by 1m: evidently acts on soft going. *M. Bradley.* 63

STAR OF AUREOLE 2 ch.c. Aureole 132–Rigoletta (Ragusa 137) [1976 6d 9s⁵ 10v 7v] second foal: half-brother to 3-y-o Gilda (by Connaught), a winner of a 1m seller: bought privately as a yearling for 200 gns: dam lightly-raced half-sister to several good winners: led briefly in final furlong when close-up fifth of nine to Saratoga Kid in maiden race at Wolverhampton in October, easily best effort: will stay 1½m: blinkered first three outings. *H. Westbrook.* 75

STAR OF ISRAEL 4 br.g. So Blessed 130–Silkwood 95 (Shantung 132) [1974 N.R. 1975 9g 8s 7f³ 8.3fg⁴ 8f⁵ 8fg* 8g⁶ 1976 9fg 8s] compact gelding: plater: runs as though he needs at least 7f and will stay further than 1m: probably acts on any going. *S. Brookshaw.* —

STAR OF WONDER 2 br.c. Typhoon 125–Star of Bethlehem 77 (Arctic Star) [1976 6d⁴ 6h³ 8fg] neat colt: half-brother to a winning stayer by Reliance II: 1,800 gns yearling: dam a staying half-sister to Eclipse winner Khalkis: in frame in maiden races at Redcar and Chepstow (4½ lengths third of 15 to Oppressor), both in June: off course three months afterwards and ran moderately on his return: should be suited by 1m. *Sir Mark Prescott.* 64

STAR PENNY   4 b.f. Current Coin 118–Sirrenetta (Star Gazer 123)   [1974 5fg   **64**
6g* 7d² 7g³ 8s³   1975 12g⁵ 10g⁴ 9fg 8f⁶ 8fg⁶ 8g 8g³   1976 8g 10g³ 10v⁴ 12h⁵]
well-made filly: mainly disappointing at 4 yrs: best form at up to 1m but stays
1¼m: possibly needs an easy surface and is suited by soft going.   *T. Fairhurst.*

STAR PRINCE   2 ch.c. Realm 129–Welsh Star 102 (Welsh Abbot 131)   [1976   **78 p**
6d⁶ 5v⁶]   strong, lengthy, good-bodied colt: half-brother to four winners,
including useful miler Welsh Pearl (by Gulf Pearl) and quite useful 3-y-o 7f
winner Star Walk (by Tower Walk): 17,500 gns yearling: dam won three times
over 6f at 2 yrs: in need of race, had every chance If out in eight-runner Ribero
Stakes at Doncaster in September but sprawled after jumping shadow and was
then allowed to come home in his own time, eventually finishing sixth to Carriage
Way: raced on unfavourable stand side when remote sixth of 13 to Don in
£1,800 maiden race at York the following month (eased right up once chance
had clearly gone): an attractive individual who is almost certainly better than
he has had chance to show so far.   *M. Jarvis.*

STAR QUERY   3 br.f. Willywonty 100–Star Truce 90 (Conspirator 114)   [1975   **50**
6g 5g⁶   1976 6g 5f 6fg 5g 6d⁴ 5s⁶]   neat filly: showed a little ability in minor
and maiden events in the autumn: gives impression she may stay further than
6f: suited by a soft surface: sold 410 gns Ascot November Sales.   *D. Weeden.*

STAR ROLE   2 gr.c. Town Crier 119–Rosa Lewis 65 (Relic)   [1976 5f 7f² 6f³]   **80**
well-grown, lengthy colt: half-brother to three winners, including sprinter
Gullible Joe (by Tycoon II): 600 gns foal, resold 1,500 gns yearling: dam maiden
miler: had rest of field well strung out when ½-length second of nine to Roxburgh
Belle in minor event at Edinburgh in July: moderate third to Realm Tree at
Hamilton later in month and was not seen out again: will stay 1m.   *G. Toft.*

STAR'S SALUTE   2 b.c. Sallust 134–Sterna (Neckar)   [1976 7.5g*]   half-   **?**
brother to several winners, notably top-class middle-distance horse Star Appeal
(by Appiani II): dam placed six times at 3 yrs in Germany: put up a pleasing
first effort when winning 18-runner maiden race at Punchestown in October,
leading in final furlong and holding off Dr T.J. by ¾ length: will stay 1¼m:
likely to go on to better things.   *K. Prendergast, Ireland.*

STAR TACK   4 b.f. Right Tack 131–Vanilla (Vatellor)   [1974 6fg 5s   1975 8g   **—**
1976 5.8h 5.3f 5.3h⁵ 5g 10s 10s]   seems of little account.   *M. Tate.*

STARTINGO   2 ch.c. Petingo 135–Pearl Star 110 (Gulf Pearl 117)   [1976 6g³   **86**
7g]   first foal: 1,400 gns yearling: dam game performer at up to 7f and is sister
to very useful Seadiver: 20/1, ran on when 1½ lengths third of 14 to Magenta
in newcomers event at Goodwood in September: third favourite when eleventh
of 21 behind Nobodys Fool in maiden race at Newmarket the following month:
will stay 1m.   *I. Walker.*

STARTOWN   4 gr.c. Town Crier 119–Artemesia 56 § (Martial 131)   [1974 6g   **75**
6g⁶ 5.9v⁵   1975 8g 9v⁴ 8v* 10.4g⁴ 10f⁴ 8fg 8g⁵ 8f   1976 8g 8g² 9g⁴ 7g⁴ 10h⁶
8fg* 8f⁶ 8f* 8.2s⁴ 10d⁶]   big colt: quite a moderate performer: won seller at Ayr
in July by 1½ lengths from Peggy Jet: also a winner at Ostend in August: seems
to stay 1¼m: acts on any going: suitable mount for an inexperienced race-rider:
sold out of R. Hollinshead's stable 1,300 gns Doncaster January Sales and was
trained by S. Wainwright until after seventh outing.   *P. Rohan.*

STAR WALK   3 br.f. Tower Walk 130–Welsh Star 102 (Welsh Abbot 131)   **96**
[1975 5d⁶ 5fg² 6g⁵ 6f²   1976 7fg⁴ 7g² 7g² 7fg² 7fg* 7fg² 7fg* 7g* 7.3d² 7s⁵]
neat filly: won maiden race at Leicester in July and showed a good turn of
speed when winning handicaps very comfortably at Newbury and Kempton in
August, scoring by 3 lengths both times: stays 7f: consistent but ran below her
best on soft going on final outing: sold 22,000 gns Newmarket December Sales,
presumably for export to U.S.A.   *H. Candy.*

STARYLLIS GIRL   3 ch.f. Star Moss 122–Double Handful 96 (Major Portion   **67**
129)   [1975 5g 5fg   1976 8f 8.5fg⁵ 8f³ 8fg 8fg⁵ 5h* 7fg³ 6f² 6fg⁵ 7g⁴ 7f]   big
filly: good mover: ¾-length winner of apprentice maiden race at Bath in July:
effective at 5f to 1m: acts on hard ground: had stiff task when tried in blinkers
on final outing: sold 1,650 gns Newmarket Autumn Sales.   *R. Smyth.*

STATE OCCASION   3 gr.c. Roan Rocket 128–State Pension 112 (Only for Life   **—**
126)   [1975 6g³ 7.6g* 7.3g*   1976 10.6d 10fg⁶ 10fg]   strong, well-made colt:
improved rapidly at 2 yrs and won Horris Hill Stakes at Newbury on final
outing: lightly raced and had stiff tasks in 1976 but did not run up to his best:
sold 13,000 gns Newmarket December Sales and is to stand at stud in Australia.
P. Walwyn.

STATEROOM 3 ch.g. Habitat 134–Ship's Biscuit 96 (Doutelle 128) [1975 **74** N.R. 1976 5fg³ 8fg³ 8g 5g⁵] strong, shapely gelding: brother to unreliable 1m winner Captain's Table: dam a middle-distance performer: has a good deal of ability, as he showed when third in maiden races at York in June (2¾ lengths behind Walter) and Newcastle later in month (3½ lengths behind Ground Work) but ran poorly on last two outings, once wearing blinkers, and is not one we would care to trust: has given impression he will stay further than 1m: sold to H. T. Jones 3,500 gns Newmarket September Sales. *J. Tree.*

STATFOLD PRIDE 3 br.f. Precipice Wood 123–Pride of Statfold (Compensa- — tion 127) [1975 8v 1976 8fg 10.8f 12.2f⁶ 10f 10fg] strong filly: plating-class maiden. *W. Wharton.*

STAY HAPPY 3 br.g. Hapanui 67–Doma Lass (Domaha) [1975 5g 5fg 5f 7f 7f — 8f 5.9g 8g 1976 8s] useless. *B. McMahon.*

STAY WITH ME 2 b.c. Royal Captive 116–Alea-Yacta (Javelot 124) [1976 **77** 5fg⁶ 6fg⁶ 5f 5g⁶ 5s²] neat, sturdy, robust colt: half-brother to useful Rio Alta (by My Swanee), a winner at up to 1½m: 1,500 gns yearling: dam ran four times unplaced in Ireland: showed ability in varied company, including selling, finishing 2 lengths second to Brave Prince in 18-runner maiden race at Warwick in October: will stay 7f. *W. Marshall.*

ST BARNABAS 6 b.h. Silver Shark 129–Nutting Grove 95 (Crepello 136) — [1974 8d 10g* 11g⁵ 10f4 9f⁵ 10g² 11g⁵ 10.6g² 9fg⁵ 10.4d 10s⁵ 1975 10f 1976 8.2v 12v] strong horse: lightly raced and no worthwhile form since 1974: stays 1¼m: appears to act on any going: has been tried in blinkers: sometimes wears a tongue strap: needs to be held up and doesn't find much off bridle. *Mrs A. Finch.*

ST BEES 3 ch.f. Calpurnius 122–Marisa 78 (Matador 131) [1975 7f 7g 6d 6g — 1976 5fg 7h⁵ 6f 6f 10f 15.8g] of no account. *M. Naughton.*

ST BRIAVELS 2 ch.c. Sovereign Path 125–Ambrosia 102 (Alcide 136) [1976 **74** 6fg 7fg 7s⁵] good-looking, well-made colt: half-brother to useful 3-y-o middle-distance winner London God (by Pall Mall) and fairly useful stayer Lotus Eater (by Le Levanstell): 15,000 gns yearling: dam, winner at 1m, is half-sister to Hethersett, Proud Chieftain and Royal Prerogative: showed ability in maiden and minor races, finishing 11½ lengths fifth of 12 to Saros in £1,500 event at Goodwood in September: will stay 1¼m. *G. Pritchard-Gordon.*

ST CHARLES 2 b.c. Tower Walk 130–Tricia (St Paddy 133) [1976 5s 5h⁵ — 5g 5g⁶ 6v] compact colt: poor maiden: well beaten in valuable seller at York on final outing. *K. Payne.*

STEEL AURA 2 b.c. Pontifex (U.S.A.)–Auster 80 (Aureole 132) [1976 7h 7g — 8g] last in maiden races on first two outings, unseated rider leaving stalls when blinkered on third and is seemingly of little account. *Dr A. Jones.*

STEEL BAND 2 br.c. Riverman 131–Sainte Colline (Sanctus II 132) [1976 **115** 6s* 7d³ 7g* 7g⁶ 7g⁵] French colt: first foal: 120,000 francs yearling (approx. £12,900): dam a smart performer from 1½m to 13f: won maiden race at Chantilly in July and Prix des Ventes at Deauville the following month, putting up an excellent effort in latter race when beating Pharly by 3 lengths: also ran well in two good-class races, finishing close-up third to Darkeino in Criterium de Bernay at Deauville and being beaten only 3 lengths by Perello in Group 2 Criterium de Maisons-Laffitte when giving weight to all the first five: will stay middle distances. *F. Boutin, France.*

STEEL BLUE 3 b.g. Majority Blue 126–Unharmed (Breakspear II) [1975 — N.R. 1976 11f] fair sort: second foal: dam never ran: unquoted when last of 19 in maiden race won by Lighter at Newbury in April. *H. Williams.*

STEEL CITY 2 ch.c. Sharpen Up 127–Tantau's Delight 77 (Tantieme 136) **73** [1976 6fg 7.2f⁴ 7v³] half-brother to three minor winners: 2,000 gns yearling: dam won over 7f at 2 yrs: in frame in minor events at Haydock in August and Lingfield in November (remote third to Forage): will be suited by 1m: acts on any going. *C. Dingwall.*

STELLA SOLARIS 2 ch.f. Fine Blade 121–Newsy Nook (Bright News) [1976 **55** 5s 5s³ 6g⁶ 7g] half-sister to several winners, including very useful sprinter Close Call (by Whistler): 720 gns yearling: dam won in Ircland at 2 yrs: only plating class: should stay 7f: sold 900 gns Ascot October Sales. *Denys Smith.*

STELLENBOSCH 3 b.c. Mountain Call 125–Peach Stone (Mourne 126) [1975 **84** 6g 1976 9g³ 8g* 8f 8g² 8g³ 8g⁵ 8g 10.6d⁵] rangy colt: won apprentice event

STE

at Kempton in May in runaway style by 7 lengths from Roman Way: placed in handicaps afterwards, on fifth outing going under in desperate finish in race won by Mossberry at Sandown in July: stays 9f (didn't run up to his best on only attempt at 1¼m but gave impression trip will not be beyond him): ran poorly when tried in blinkers on penultimate outing. *R. Armstrong.*

STEP AHEAD 5 b.h. Continuation 120–Schull (Yorick II 127) [1974 7g⁵ 103
8g 7f* 7g 6f⁶ 8g⁴ 7g³ 7s* 7.6v* 1975 7s 7fg* 7fg⁵ 6fg 7.6g² 7g⁶ 8g³ 8fg² 7g 8g
8g³ 7f³ 1976 8f 7fg 7fg* 7.6d⁵ 7g* 7fg² 7.6h² 7g³ 7fg⁴ 7.2g³ 7h* 7d] tall
horse: useful handicapper: an admirably consistent front-runner who races with tremendous gusto and won at Epsom, Kempton (Saxon House Handicap) and Brighton in 1976: stays 1m: acts on any going: does best in blinkers: game and genuine: good mount for an apprentice. *P. Cole.*

STEPHANDRE 2 b.f. Derring-Do 131–Brushover 88 (Molvedo 137) [1976 94
5s² 5d² 5d* 5f] second living foal: half-sister to fairly useful middle-distance stayer Mischievous (by Le Mesnil): 4,100 gns yearling: dam fair winner at 11f: odds on, made all to win 11-runner maiden race at Doncaster in May by ½ length from Petinara: also ran very well in defeat going down by a neck to As Blessed in £1,700 event at York and finishing eighth of 12 to Cramond in Queen Mary Stakes at Royal Ascot (eased right up when badly hampered in final furlong): will stay 1m: acts on any going. *T. Fairhurst.*

STEPHEN FRANCIS 2 ch.c. Stephen George 102–Sweet Silhouette 79 (Setay 79
105) [1976 5fg 6fg 5.1f*] fourth foal: sold privately for 500 gns as a yearling and resold same sales for 380 gns: dam won over hurdles: showed first worthwhile form when winning five-runner maiden auction event at Yarmouth in July by 1½ lengths from Hey Willie: should be suited by 6f+. *R. Supple.*

STEPPING STONES 3 b.f. Stephen George 102–Road Star 52 (Road House –
II) [1975 5f 6fg 6g 1976 11.1g 10.8f 7f 8fg 10h] useless. *W. Charles.*

STEP YOU GAILY 3 b.f. King's Company 124–Schull (Yorick II 127) [1975 –
7g 8.2g³ 1976 8f 11.1f 10s⁴ 7s 10s⁶] quite moderate at 2 yrs but showed no worthwhile form in 1976. *Sir Mark Prescott.*

STERLING CLOUD 2 b.c. Sterling Bay–Fiery Cloud (Golden Cloud) [1976 –
5f 7fg] neat colt: half-brother to several winners, including fairly useful sprinter Villa Marina (by Tudor Melody): sold for 400 gns both as a foal and a yearling: well behind in maiden races at Wolverhampton in May and Chester in September. *P. Bevan.*

STERLING GOLD 3 b.g. Sterling Bay–Denver Song (Chanteur II 135) [1975 60
N.R. 1976 7fg⁵ 8f³] neat, strong gelding: half-brother to a winner in Peru: 2,400 gns foal, resold 1,800 gns yearling: dam of little account: showed ability on both his outings in May, being a fast-finishing fifth of 19 to Mr Higgins in maiden event at Lingfield and 5½ lengths third of five to Gold Flight in minor race at Chepstow: subsequently exported to Belgium and is a winner there. *J. Dunlop.*

STETCHWORTH LAD 4 ch.c. Allangrange 126–Queen of Connemara (Prince –
Chevalier) [1974 7fg⁴ 6fg 8s³ 1975 8v* 10d² 10g³ 12f* 1976 16.1f⁵] rangy, slightly dipped-backed colt: showed himself a useful handicapper and won at Newmarket and Epsom at 3 yrs: finished lame at Newmarket in August (first race for 14 months), only appearance since: should stay well: acts on any going: suitable mount for an apprentice. *P. Robinson.*

STEVE WONDER 4 b.g. Stephen George 102–Traquita (Mosquito II 110) –
[1974 7d 7g 7d 1975 N.R. 1976 17.1f] probably of no account. *Dr A. Jones.*

STEWART LINDSAY 3 b.f. Chebs Lad 120–Little Singer (Sing Sing 134) –
[1975 5v 5v 5s 5fg 5h 5f 1976 6g 5f] probably useless. *S. Nesbitt.*

STIFF SENTENCE 2 bl.f. Sweet Revenge 129–Soft Collar 99 (Quorum 126) 79
[1976 6f 6fg 7d 6d⁵] compact, good-quartered filly: half-sister to four winners, including fairly useful 7f winner Trotty (by King's Troop): 3,000 gns yearling: dam a sprinter: 5½ lengths fifth of 22 to Rocket Symphony in maiden race at Newmarket in October: stays 6f. *B. Swift.*

STILL WINDY 3 gr.c. Whistling Wind 123–Apoplexy (Quorum 126) [1975 69
5d 5v 5fg⁶ 5fg⁵ 5fg³ 6fg⁴ 5h² 5f⁵ 6g³ 6d⁴ 7g³ 7g² 7f* 7.2v 1976 8.2d⁴ 8.2f⁴ 12g⁴
10.4s⁴ 12fg³ 10s² 10f⁴ 8f⁴ 8h³ 10fg³ 10.8f⁵ 9f³ 8.2fg⁴ 11.1f² 10.8g⁴ 12.3fg⁴ 12g⁵
12fg] useful sort: quite a modest handicapper: only twice out of frame in a very busy season: stays 1½m: acts on any going except very soft: tough and consistent. *R. Hollinshead.*

STILTON 3 b.g. Blue Streak 99–Brocette 60 (Brocade Slipper 116) [1975 **86**
5.1f 7f⁶ 7g² 8f* 8.2g* 8f⁶ 8d⁴ 8g⁴ 1976 8fg² 10fg⁵ 12g² 13.4s 12.3fg² 12f² 13.8f²]
fair handicapper: second at Newmarket, Leicester, Newcastle, Brighton and
Catterick (two-horse race) in first half of season: evidently stays 1½m: appears
to act on any going. *N. Callaghan.*

STINGO 3 ch.c. Petingo 135–Dryad (Panorama) [1975 N.R. 1976 8fg **—**
10.2fg 11.5d] well-grown colt: half-brother to numerous winners, notably
1,000 Guineas winner Glad Rags (by High Hat) and very smart sprinter Victorina
(by The Phoenix): 10,500 gns yearling: dam a sprinter: well beaten in newcomers and maiden races: sold 860 gns Newmarket Autumn Sales. *M. Jarvis.*

STIRLING CASTLE 4 gr.c. Royal Palace 131–Betty Burke 95 (Prince **94**
Chevalier) [1974 7fg 7g* 6g⁵ 8g⁴ 6d 1975 8fg 8fg³ 7g* 8g⁴ 8fg* 8s⁴ 7g⁶ 1976
8f 7fg 10fg⁵ 8fg² 8h* 7h² 8g⁵ 8g³ 8g³ 9g] strong, powerful colt: fairly useful
performer: short-headed sole-opponent Red Ruby in handicap at Brighton in
August: stays 1m: acts on a firm surface and ran respectably on only outing on
soft: used to wear blinkers but didn't after fourth appearance at 4 yrs. *G.
Harwood.*

ST JOLES 3 b.c. Welsh Saint 126–Gleniffer Braes (Hard Tack 111 §)] [1975 **106**
7f⁴ 7fg* 7fg* 8s³ 8g³ 1976 8g² 12f² 12.2d⁶ 10fg* 10h³ 12fg⁵ 11g² 11g³] leggy
colt: showed improved form when winning strongly-contested Durham Stakes at
Newcastle in June, never looking in much danger of defeat in straight and beating
Crofting by ¾ length: also ran well when runner-up in Roseberry Stakes at
Teesside (beaten ½ length by Claudio Nicolai), Hethersett Stakes at Brighton
(beaten a head by Kafue Park in slowly-run race) and Furstenberg-Rennen at
Baden-Baden (beaten 1¾ lengths by German Derby fourth Tuttlinger): 6 lengths
third to Swell Fellow in Goteborgs Stora Pris at Aby in September (reportedly
hampered on final turn): stays 1½m: extremely well suited by a sound surface:
genuine, but ran below his best fifth and sixth starts. *B. Hills.*

STOLEN-SECRET 2 b.f. Burglar 128–B and D 99 (Princely Gift 137) [1976 **—**
6g] leggy, unfurnished, sparely-made filly: closely related to very smart
sprinter Singing Bede (by Sing Sing) and half-sister to four winners: 4,400 gns
yearling: dam, a sprinter, is half-sister to Miss Stephens, dam of top-class sprinter

Mrs F. N. Phillips Browne's "St Joles"

Deep Diver: 33/1 and dwelt when behind in 26-runner maiden race won by Sarasingh at Doncaster in September. *W. Gray.*

STONEWALL JACK 2 b.c. Illustrious–Surfboard Betty (Bold Commander) **90**
[1976 6h3 5fg6 5f2 5g5 5v5 5d] strong, well-made, grand-looking American-bred colt: brother to a minor winner in U.S.A. and half-brother to another: dam never ran: went down by only a short head to King Croesus in 13-runner maiden race at Newmarket in August and ran well when fifth to He Loves Me in Harry Rosebery Stakes at Ayr the following month: had very stiff task on final outing: acts on firm going and is probably unsuited by heavy. *H. T. Jones.*

STOP THE MUSIC 3 b.f. Welsh Saint 126–Musical Chairs 65 (Pinza 137) **75**
[1975 6g4 6f4 1976 10f3 10g 12g4 16.1v3 16v] very attractive filly: good third to Il Padrone in maiden race at Nottingham in April: off course a long time after next outing and did not reproduce her best form, starting a heavily-backed favourite on her return: best run at 1¼m: sold 1,350 gns Ascot November Sales. *B. Hobbs.*

STORMALONG 2 br.c. Swing Easy 126–Golden Storm 95 (Golden Cloud) **80 p**
[1976 6g5] half-brother to four winners, including useful 7f and 1m performer Apple King (by Birdbrook): 2,100 gns foal and resold 6,300 gns as a yearling: dam a sprinter: weak 9/1 shot, showed up quite well when 6 lengths fifth of 18 to Greenjacket in newcomers event at Lingfield in September: will do better. *B. Hills.*

STORMER 8 b.h. Arctic Storm 134–Final Bloom 104 (Final Score 113) [1974 **55**
7h5 8g* 7g 8g6 6s6 1975 8.2s4 8g 7fg 8g* 8fg 7f* 8g 10g* 10g 8.2g* 8d6 8g 1976
8.2v 8fg6 8.2g 10g4 10f4 8f4] strong, short-backed horse: quite a moderate performer (rated 78) at 7 yrs: didn't show the same form in 1976: stayed 1¼m: best form on a sound surface and acted on firm going: occasionally wore blinkers: inconsistent: stud. *W. Marshall.*

STORMY AFFAIR 3 br.g. Prevailing–Romancing 82 (Romulus 129) [1975 **76**
5g 6g5 6fg4 7fg 7.3d* 7.2s5 7d 8d3 1976 8f5 9fg 10d 10h5 8f6 8f4 8s5 8s6 8.2s3] smallish, lengthy gelding: showed quite useful form as a 2-y-o but is only quite moderate nowadays: probably stays 1¼m: best form with some give in the ground: blinkered sixth outing. *M. H. Easterby.*

STORMY PRINCESS 4 ch.f. Ballymoss 136–Urugano 101 (Buisson Ardent 129) **68**
[1974 8d 7s3 1975 8g 10fg6 10f5 10fg4 10g2 12v4 1976 10g3 12fg5 10d2 13.1s* 12s2 12.5v4 12v3] quite a moderate performer: won poor maiden race at Bath in October by 7 lengths from Striker: length second of five to Bugle Boy in apprentice event at Pontefract later in month: stays 13f: acts on heavy going. *N. Callaghan.*

STORMY SUMMER 2 ch.c. Lord Gayle 124–Rose Allana (Final Score 113) **92**
[1976 5g2 5s* 6f6 7f3 6fg5 8f4 8g2 8v2] good mover: fourth foal: 1,000 gns yearling: dam sister to six winners: sold out of K. Payne's stable for 1,700 gns after winning eight-runner seller at Newcastle in April by 2 lengths from Precious Image: ran creditably afterwards, on penultimate start putting up a fine effort under 7 lb overweight when 3 lengths second to Revlow in valuable nursery at Ayr in September: suited by 1m: probably acts on any going. *Denys Smith.*

STORY TELLER 5 ch.h. On Your Mark 125–Pure Fiction 68 (Narrator 127) **51**
[1974 7d4* 5f5 8f* 5.8g 7fg4 7f2 8.2g6 7g 1975 8f 7f 1976 8g2 8g 7g 10f2 12h2 11h6] strong, compact, good-bodied horse: plater: ran best race in 1976 on fourth outing: stays 1¼m but has yet to show conclusively that he stays further: appears to act on any going: has been tried in blinkers: bandaged last two outings. *M. Stevens.*

STORY WRITER 5 b.m. Sweet Story 122–Bonny May (Neron 121) [1974 **49**
10d5 8s 8v 1975 11h* 12g3 1976 12d 13g5 15f] poor handicapper nowadays: stays 1½m: acts on hard going. *W. Atkinson.*

ST PETERSBURG 2 b.c. Royal Palace 131–La Paiva 92 (Prince Chevalier) **85 p**
[1976 5g2 6f2] big, rangy colt: half-brother to several winners, notably Brigadier Gerard (by Queen's Hussar): dam effective at 1m to 1¼m: second in maiden races, going down by a head to unlucky-in-running Anax at Sandown in July and having every chance when beaten 3 lengths by Mecanopsis in 21-runner event at Newmarket the following month: will be well suited by middle distances: looked the type to need a lot more time but will make a very useful performer eventually. *H. Candy.*

STRABO 3 b.c. Tudor Melody 129–Bandarilla 116 (Matador 131) [1975 6fg2 **116**
6fg 6g* 1976 7fg 8g4 9s6 8.5g 8f* 8g* 8g5] very good-looking colt: half-brother to top-class miler Sallust (by Pall Mall): improved considerably in

Britannia Stakes, Ascot—waiting tactics pay off with Strabo (left) who wins in a close finish with the subsequently-disqualified Lord Helpus (right), Free State and the blinkered Game Lord

the summer and is a smart handicapper: won two valuable handicaps at Ascot, Britannia Stakes at the Royal meeting by a head from subsequently-disqualified Lord Helpus and Blacknest Stakes in July by 1½ lengths from London Glory: fifth of seven to Ellora in Prix Quincey at Deauville only subsequent outing: stays 1m well: acts on firm going: wears blinkers: suited by waiting tactics. *R. Hern.*

STRADEY PARK 2 br.f. Murrayfield 119–Flying Spear 94 (Breakspear II) **103**
[1976 6fg⁵ 5g* 6fg² 5fg 6g⁵ 6fg 5g] big, useful-looking filly: second foal: dam won over 5f at 2 yrs: won 10-runner maiden race at Newbury in July by a length from Aunt Betty: afterwards ran well in two quite valuable events, finishing length second to Paddington in Rous Memorial Stakes at Goodwood and about 3 lengths fifth to Anax in Champion 2-y-o Trophy at Ripon: will stay 7f. *R. Hannon.*

STRAE BRIDGE 2 b.c. Reform 132–Nasira 94 (Persian Gulf) [1976 5d 5s 6v⁵] **72**
neat, attractive colt: brother to very smart 5f to 7f performer Glen Strae and half-brother to three other winners: dam won at up to 1m: showed promise in maiden races in the autumn, finishing 5 lengths fifth of 16 to subsequently-disqualified Nampara Cove at Lingfield in November: will stay 7f. *R. Price.*

STRAFFORD GYPSY 2 ch.f. Sky Gipsy 117–Euclea 81 (Epaulette 125) [1976 —
5h 5fg 5fg 8f 6v 6s 8v] poor plater. *L. Shedden.*

STRAIGHT ARROW 5 ch.g. On Your Mark 125–Sylvan Wood (Red God 128 §) **95**
[1974 6f 6g 7g⁴ 7.9g 6g* 7f⁶ 7f⁶ 6s⁵ 7.5s⁴ 1975 8d 7g 10f² 8f* 6f⁴ 7f⁵ 8f³ 8.7f³ 9f 7g* 8g 9g 10g³ 8s 1976 7g⁶] fairly useful ex-Irish handicapper: successful at Naas and the Curragh in 1975: had stiff task in only race at 5 yrs when running respectably in Sanyo Stakes won by Boldboy at Doncaster in September: effective at 6f and stays 1¼m: acts on any going: bolted on way to start and was withdrawn, not under orders, on intended reappearance (April): sold out of W. Robinson's stable 4,300 gns Goffs February Sales. *B. Swift.*

STRAIGHT COURSE 2 br.f. My Swallow 134–True Course II (Sea Charger 129) — p
[1976 6f 6fg] big, rangy filly: sister to a winner in South Africa and half-sister to several winners, including fairly useful miler Southwark Star (by Midsummer Night II): 6,200 gns yearling: dam placed in U.S.A.: unquoted when behind in maiden races at Lingfield in June and Goodwood in July. *W. Wightman.*

STRAIGHT CUE 5 b.h. Never Bend–Greencloth (Court Martial) [1974 7d 8g **53**
5g⁶ 8s³ 7.6v 8s 1975 7f³ 7g³ 8fg⁵ 7f⁴ 7f⁶ 8fg 1976 7f* 8fg] quite attractive, though lightly-made horse: apprentice ridden when winning selling handicap at Brighton in May (no bid): best form at up to 7f: acts on firm going: wears blinkers nowadays: inconsistent: sold 2,400 gns Ascot June Sales. *G. Balding.*

STRAIGHT PALM 2 b.g. Straight King 98–Rose Palm 73 (Bleep-Bleep 134) —
[1976 6d 6s 7v 6s] compact gelding: no worthwhile form in varied company, including selling. *D. Chapman.*

STRAIGHT PHASE 3 br.f. probably First Phase 97–Straight Forward (Ortho- —
dox) [1975 N.R. 1976 12g 12.5v] half-sister to several winners, including useful miler Straight King (by King's Coup): dam of little account: behind in maiden races at Lanark and Teesside (still burly) in October. *M. Naughton.*

STRANGE LOVE 2 b.c. Sir Gaylord–Servilia (Aureole 132) [1976 7g⁶ 8v⁵ 8s] **82**
compact, good sort: French-bred: good mover: half-brother to a minor 2-y-o

winner in France by Kashmir II: dam twice-raced half-sister to top-class French horses Snob and Sigebert: showed a little ability on all three outings, taking some time to get going each time and then running on without ever reaching a challenging position: will be suited by 1¼m+. *P. Walwyn.*

STRATHCLYDE 2 b.c. March Past 124–Grecian Bridge 90 (Acropolis 132) [1976 6d] leggy, lengthy colt: brother to good-class 1m to 1¼m performer Roy Bridge, and half-brother to moderate 1¼m winner Monemvasia (by Sovereign Path): 6,200 gns yearling: dam comes from same family as Edmundo and Ribocco: unquoted when last but one in 23-runner maiden race won by Rings at Newmarket in October. *J. Dunlop.* —

STRATHOYKEL 5 b.m. Aberdeen 109–Gold Bloom 72 (Klondyke Bill 125) [1974 5f2 5.8g* 5fg2 5fg 5g* 5g4 5.8v 1975 5.8g5 6g4 6f6 5.8h2 5.9f3 6h 5.8f4 5.8f* 7.6fg2 7fg3 6g* 5.8f3 8f6 1976 6g2 7fg2 7f3 7f3 8f2 8h3 10h3 7f2 8fg5] lightly-made mare: quite a moderate handicapper: placed in most of her races at 5 yrs but weakened very quickly when tried over 1¼m and is best at up to 1m: acts on hard going, and is probably unsuited by soft. *Sir Mark Prescott.* **76**

STRAWBERRY LADY 2 ro.f. Capistrano 120–Fairmile 65 (Milesian 125) [1976 5g 6f 6g 7g 7fg] rangy filly: good mover: second foal: 1,000 gns yearling: dam stayed 1½m: seventh of 26 to Supreme Penny in seller at Redcar in September, final outing and best effort: will stay 1m. *K. Payne.* —

STREAK 4 b.c. Runnymede 123–Baby Tracey 71 (Pinza 137) [1974 5d 5h* 5fg2 5fg* 5f* 5g* 5s3 1975 5g 5fg3 5f6 5fg 5g3 6f4 5fg4 5.6g5 5d2 1976 5.9fg3 5fg4 5fg4 6fg2 6f 6f5] strong, lengthy, attractive colt: very smart performer at 2 yrs (rated 119), winning four races including National Stakes at Sandown and Windsor Castle Stakes at Royal Ascot: didn't manage to win in two subsequent seasons (although ran several good races in 1975) and seemed to us to have lost some of his enthusiasm for racing as a 4-y-o: stayed 6f: acted well on firm going and was probably not at his best on soft: well beaten when tried in blinkers: not raced after June: standing at Benham Stud, Newbury at a fee of £300. *J. Sutcliffe.* **97**

STREAKER KING 3 b.c. King's Troop 118–Grey Streak 85 (Palestine 133) [1975 5fg 5g 6g5 1976 8fg3 8d2 10fg4 8s* 8f* 8f5 9f 8fg4] attractive, well-made colt: won maiden race at Ayr in June and minor event at Redcar the following month: blinkered first time on latter course and made all to beat Bright Decision 1½ lengths: blinkered next two outings but ran best subsequent race without them on final start: suited by 1m and possibly does not stay 1¼m: appears to act on any going. *R. Price.* **86**

STREAKY RITA 3 b.f. Blue Streak 99–Native Senorita (Indigenous 121) [1975 N.R. 1976 8s] first foal: dam well beaten in novice hurdles: started slowly when tailed off in maiden race won by Penchand at Warwick in October. *G. Gadd.* —

STREET CHOIR 3 ch.g. Jolly Jet 111–Miss Monet 80 (Monet 127) [1975 6f6 5fg 5g2 5d* 5s2 6g3 1976 6g5 6f 6fg5 6h6 6g] narrow gelding: poor mover: won seller at Ayr in 1975 and ran creditably in better company: not so good at 3 yrs, running best races on first and third outings: very well suited by soft going at 2 yrs and is probably unsuited by very firm. *Denys Smith.* **68**

STRIKER 4 b.g. Taj Dewan 128–Miss Match (Match III 135) [1974 6v 7.3s 1975 10.2g2 12f2 10fg3 10fg5 1976 12fg 7f 8fg5 7f 8fg* 13.1s2] rangy gelding: quite a moderate performer: favourite, won 12-runner seller at Salisbury in September by 10 lengths from Bali Breeze and was subsequently sold out of H. Blagrave's stable 1,500 gns: stays 13f: probably acts on any going: ran below his best when tried in blinkers final outing at 2 yrs. *J. Thorne.* **66**

STRING-'EM-ALONG 3 br.c. Hotfoot 126–Captious 97 (Sunny Brae 121) [1975 8fg 1976 9f5 8f 12f4 15.8f3 8f2 12g5 12.2f6] poor plater: apparently effective from 1m to 2m: not seen out after May. *K. Payne.* **54**

ST RIOCH'S BOY 3 ch.g. Richboy 117–Irish Halo (Macherio) [1975 N.R. 1976 7fg 9f 8g 8g3 10f* 7h*] compact gelding: fifth foal: half-brother to Green Ice (by Frigid Aire), winner of a bumpers race in Ireland: 340 gns yearling: dam won at 1½m in Ireland: winner of maiden race and minor event at Folkestone in the summer: beat Bridstow 1½ lengths in latter race in August, giving impression that 7f is an absolute minimum for him: will probably stay further than 1¼m: acts on hard ground. *M. Masson.* **76**

ST SEVERIN 4 b.c. Manacle 123–Crag Bay 77 (Road House II) [1974 5fg4 5fg4 6g2 6g3 5v* 5s4 1975 6f3 6g 6h3 6fg5 6g3 7.6s 1976 5f 7fg2 6fg 7fg 8d* **71**

716

8g³ 10f⁴ 7h³ 8f³ 10 4fg* 7g⁵ 10.6d 10d 8 2v] quite a moderate handicapper: successful at Redcar in June and Chester in September, beating Shine On a length in apprentice event on latter course: effective at 7f and stays 1¼m: acts on any going: ran well below his best when tried in blinkers: sweated up seventh outing. *D. Weeden.*

ST TEILO 2 b.c. Welsh Saint 126–Igea (Asterios) [1976 6fg 6g] lengthy colt: — half-brother to two middle-distance winners in Ireland and France: sold twice as a yearling, for 200 gns and 3,800 gns: dam won three races in Germany at 3 yrs: remote eighth in maiden races at Windsor in July and Kempton in August: will be suited by longer distances. *N. Vigors.*

ST TORBAY 3 b.c. St Paddy 133–Torbay (Hill Prince) [1975 5d⁶ 9fg⁶ 10f **46** 1976 14fg 14fg² 12.2f⁵ 16f⁶ 15.5s] poor maiden on form but changed hands 2,200 gns Doncaster November Sales. *W. Stephenson.*

ST TRYST 4 ch.g. St Chad 120–Risky Tryst (Court Harwell 130) [1974 6fg — 6fg 7fg 7g⁶ 8d² 8s² 1975 10s³ 10s⁵ 10.6g² 12.2f² 10.8fg 12f* 12fg² 12f³ 11.7g 12s 1976 15.8g 12.2f⁶ 12fg] strong, compact gelding: has run poorly since winning maiden race at Beverley in 1975: stays 1½m: acts on any going: has been tried in blinkers: off course over 4 months before final start (looked distinctly burly). *N. Crump.*

STUCK UP 2 ch.f. Upper Case–Sealing-Wax (Crepello 136) [1976 6s⁵] half- **71** p sister to two winners, including useful sprinter Latin Melody (by Tudor Melody): dam unraced daughter of Yorkshire Oaks winner Sea Parrot: 9/2 when just over 6 lengths fifth of 12 to Chartered Lady in maiden race at Chepstow in October: will stay 1m. *Sir Mark Prescott.*

STUFF AND NONSENSE 2 b.f. Crooner 119–Silk II 102 (Counsel 118) [1976 — p 7s] lengthy filly: half-sister to three minor winners: dam middle-distance performer: unquoted, showed some promise when eighth of 12 to Sleeper in minor event at Sandown in October. *J. Tree*

STUPENDOUS BOY 6 br.g. Stupendous–Rock Snake 76 (Rockefella) [1974 — N.R. 1975 N.R. 1976 12g 12s] poor maiden: stays 1½m: extremely well suited by some give in the ground: wears bandages. *J. Powney.*

SUBALTERN 4 gr.g. Right Boy 137–Jaunty (Le Haar 126) [1974 8s 7v* 7v⁶ **74** 1975 7v⁵ 8f² 8.3s 10g 10g* 10d² 1976 10d 10.2s² 10v² 12s*] big gelding: quite a moderate performer: successful at Leicester in November: stays 1½m well: acts on any going but goes well in the mud: suitable mount for a boy: wears blinkers. *C. Dingwall.*

SUBALTERN (N.Z.) 6 br.g. Bellborough 122–Jaycee (Super) [1976 12s] New — Zealand-bred gelding: winner over 7f and 1¼m in his native country: 12/1 when well behind in ladies race at Chepstow in October, first appearance on flat in this country. *S. Mellor*

SUBMARINA 2 ch.c. Deep Diver 134–Aswellas 93 (Le Levanstell 122) [1976 — 6v 6d] first foal: dam won three times over 7f at 2 yrs and is half-sister to very useful animals Burlington Boy and Dunmurry Boy: behind in 22-runner maiden races at Newbury (tailed off) and Newmarket (blinkered) in October. *B. Hills.*

SUBTLE QUEEN 3 ch.f. Stephen George 102–Endless Questions (Never Say — Die 137) [1975 N.R. 1976 6g 10.1f 10.1fg⁶ 7g⁶ 8.2d 8.2d 8v] strong, short-legged filly: fifth reported foal: half-sister to two winners in Belgium: dam apparently of little account and her daughter appears to be no better. *C. Bewicke.*

SUCCESSOR 7 ch.g. Great Nephew 126–Loidien 95 (Ribot 142) [1974 10d* **63** 12f* 10g* 10h* 8fg² 10fg² 7.6v² 10v 8s 1975 10d³ 10f² 10f² 10fg⁵ 10.6s⁶ 1976 10d 12s³] quite a moderate handicapper on his day: ran only twice on Flat in 1976: stays 13f and finds 1m on sharp side: acts on any going: has worn blinkers: good mount for a lady rider. *R. Turnell.*

SUCKI BABY 2 b.f. Grisaille 115–Tin Foil 74 (Tin Whistle 128) [1976 5f 5d] — bad plater: sold 200 gns Doncaster August Sales. *A. Balding.*

SUDDEN SURRENDER 2 br.f. The Brianstan 128–Grange Park 73 (Derring- — Do 131) [1976 6f 5fg⁶ 5s 5v 5v] first foal: cost 310 gns Doncaster January 1976 Sales: dam poor maiden: no worthwhile form, including in a seller: unseated rider and bolted before first outing: trained by M. Tate on first two appearances. *J. Hardy.*

SUFFICIENCY 5 b.g. Quorum 126–Persian Lamb 108 (Rustam 128) [1974 9s⁶ — 12fg 8fg 8g 10v 10g⁶ 1975 N.R. 1976 12f⁶ 12.2g] useless. *J. Turner.*

SUFFRAGETTE 3 b.f. Reform 132–Triumphantly (Bold Ruler) [1975 N.R. **107**
1976 7f*] well-made, attractive filly: first foal: dam won four races at up to
1m in U.S.A.: 20/1, moved poorly to post for 20-runner newcomers race at
Newbury in April but came back much better, running on steadily under strong
driving to lead inside final furlong and beat Intermission and apparently better-
fancied stable-companion Honeypot Lane by 2 lengths and 5 lengths: not seen
out again but was allotted 8-7 in 3-y-o Free Handicap and is probably a very
useful performer: will stay 1¼m. *R. Hern.*

SUGAR BOY 4 ch.g. Darling Boy 124–Rising Gold (Rise 'N Shine II) [1974 —
5g 5.8g 1975 8.3tg 1976 7fg] of no account. *D. Hanley.*

SUGAR COOKIE 2 ch.f. Crepello 136–Ship's Biscuit 96 (Doutelle 128) [1976 **71**
6g 6f³ 6fg 7g] neat filly: good mover: half-sister to three quite useful winners,
including miler Captain's Table (by Habitat): dam middle-distance performer:
apprentice ridden when 4½ lengths third of eight to Cake Popper in maiden race
at Brighton in August, best effort: will stay 1½m: reared as stalls opened on
first outing. *J. Tree.*

SUGAR LAD 4 ch.g. St Alphage 119–Demerara 83 (Democratic 124) [1974 N.R. —
1975 N.R. 1976 11.1g] second foal: half-brother to a moderate performer
in France by Breakspear II: 8,000 gns yearling: dam stayed 1m: bandaged,
pulled up 5f out in amateur riders race won by Irish Harmony at Kempton
in May, only outing. *A. Davison.*

SUGAR MOSS 7 b.g. Star Moss 122–Sugar Sauce 94 (Hard Sauce 131) [1974 —
7h 7fg 7g 8f 7fg⁴ 7f 7s⁵ 8g⁴ 8s² 10g* 8s³ 10v⁵ 1975 7.6g 7s 8f⁴ 8f⁵ 8.3g 10g²
7.6s 1976 7f 8f⁶] poor handicapper nowadays: stays 1¼m: acts on any going:
inconsistent. *J. Edmunds.*

SUITED 3 b.c. Right Tack 131–Amara (Sanctus II 132) [1975 5d 5g⁶ 7.2g* **70**
7.2fg 7g⁴ 8.2d 1976 8.2d² 8.2g⁵ 9g³ 10g³ 10g⁵ 10f⁴ 10g 8f* 8.2fg² 8.3f² 8g²
8.8g²] unfurnished colt: quite a modest handicapper: blinkered first time
when winning at Warwick in July, overcoming difficulties in running and getting
up close home to beat Yellow Boy ½ length: again blinkered when runner-up
at Nottingham and Windsor the following month: subsequently transferred
from F. J. Houghton's stable to French provinces and was runner-up in minor
events at Lyon in October (not blinkered): stays 1¼m: appears to act on any
going. *P. Swann, France.*

SULTANS RUBY 2 ch.c. Royal Palace 131–Karenina 95 (Silver Shark 129) **118**
[1976 6d³ 6f⁵ 8g* 8s²]
It would seem fair to assume that owner-trainer Jack Hanson has a habit
of thinking his geese are swans if one judged him solely by the starting prices of
most of his runners in pattern races in 1976. His Frankie started at 200/1 for
the Two Thousand Guineas and 75/1 for the Derby, Desert Warrior was the 33/1
outsider in the Flying Childers Stakes and Sultans Ruby went off at 66/1 in the
six-runner William Hill Futurity Stakes. In two of these races though, his
horses fully justified his decision to run; Frankie missed third place in the
Guineas by less than a length, and Sultans Ruby, in finishing second in the
Futurity, collected the very worthwhile sum of £10,774.
A look at Sultans Ruby's form soon reveals why he was a rank outsider
at Doncaster. He had raced three times, finishing a five-length third to Card
Player at Haydock and a well-beaten fifth to Limone at Royal Ascot before
winning a maiden race at Ayr in convincing fashion. As his race at Ayr was his
first for three months it was reasonable to expect improvement but even so his
opponents Valinsky, Orchestra and Juge de Paix all seemed to have much better
form. Sultans Ruby beat them well though, and in game fashion too. As
nobody else was keen to go on in the testing conditions, Sultans Ruby's jockey
sent him to the front. By halfway Sporting Yankee had drawn alongside and
soon took a decisive lead but Sultans Ruby rallied well to fend off Orchestra and
kept on so strongly that he was going up on the winner in the closing stages.
Sporting Yankee beat him by two lengths. The others were well strung out
behind.
Sultans Ruby is a rangy, good sort of colt. He cost 8,400 guineas as a
yearling which seems a reasonable price for a colt by a Derby winner, albeit an
unfashionable one, out of a mare from a high-class staying family. He is the
second foal of Karenina, who ran only at two years when successful in two of her
four races, and a half-brother to the winning miler Sospecha (by So Blessed).
The grandam, Varinia, was a good filly who won the Oaks Trial at Lingfield, but
she was short of acceleration and usually found one or two too good for her.

She has proved a strong influence for stamina at stud and in addition to Karenina she has produced Tudormead, a winner at up to seventeen furlongs, to Tudor Melody; Amber Sun, who stays a mile and a half, to that fast horse Amber Rama; and Pigsticker, who stays at least eleven furlongs, to the miler Derring-Do. Varinia is a half-sister to the Park Hill Stakes winner Collyria and to Visor, the dam of the good long-distance horse Raise You Ten.

Sultans Ruby (ch.c. 1974)	Royal Palace (b 1964)	Ballymoss (ch 1954)	Mossborough / Indian Call
		Crystal Palace (b 1956)	Solar Slipper / Queen of Light
	Karenina (b 1968)	Silver Shark (gr 1963)	Buisson Ardent / Palsaka
		Varinia (b 1963)	Charlottesville / Eyewash

Both Sultans Ruby's breeding and style of running suggest that he will need at least a mile and a quarter at three years. His dam went particularly well in the mud and, although it's far too soon to be dogmatic about Sultans Ruby's capabilities, it is worth remembering that he put up easily his best effort on very soft ground and was well beaten on his only outing on firm. If his trainer adopts a fighting policy with him, as seems likely, Sultans Ruby will find races hard to come by at three years but don't dismiss him out of hand—he's a smart colt. *J. Hanson.*

SUMMER BLOOM 2 b.f. Silly Season 127–Rosalie II 66 (Molvedo 137) [1976 6fg] lightly-made, leggy filly: half-sister to French 1½m winner Rosala (by Diatome), subsequently a good winner in Scandinavia: dam won at 1¼m: 16/1 when behind in 27-runner maiden race won by Home Fire at Newbury in August. *R. Hern.* —

SUMMER MOSS 2 ch.f. Ballymoss 136–Summer Love 60 (Silver Cloud 121) [1976 5f⁶ 5g 7g] plain filly: half-sister to fairly useful 1973 2-y-o winner Hayloft (by Bold Lad Ire) and to a winner abroad: dam won over 1¼m: no worthwhile form in maiden races: off course May to September. *G. Richards.* —

SUMMER OAK 3 b.f. Willipeg 112–Green Oak (Rustam 127) [1975 5g 5v 1976 6f 7g 7.2g⁶ 6d⁶ 5f⁵ 6h³ 5f 6f⁴ 8fg] bad plater: stays 6f. *J. Cousins.* 42

SUMMER SAINT 2 b.c. Welsh Saint 126–Summer's Lease (Soderini 123) [1976 7fg 7.2f 6g 8g 8.2f⁶] useful-looking colt: second foal: 2,100 gns yearling: dam won over 1½m in Ireland: showed a little ability in maiden races: will probably stay middle distances. *N. Angus.* 67

SUMMER SERENADE 5 br.m. Midsummer Night II 117–Solensister 100 (Ennis 128) [1974 8.2fg 10g 7g⁶ 7d 8fg⁵ 7g 8d² 9s⁴ 8.2s⁶ 10.8v⁴ 11.1v* 1975 8f 10fg 10.2g 8g⁶ 10d 10g² 10g² 1976 14d 10s⁵ 10v⁵] plater at 4 yrs: not seen out until September in 1976 and was well beaten in better company: stays 11f: acts well on heavy going and is possibly unsuited by firm: sometimes wears blinkers but didn't when successful. *J. Powney.* —

SUMMER WONDER 4 b.f. Crozier 117–Gretna Wonder 46 (Elopement 125) [1974 N.R. 1975 10.1g 8fg 8h 8g 10.1g 1976 8.3f* 8fg 12f 10.1fg*] strong, compact filly: plater: successful twice at Windsor at 4 yrs, on second occasion (June) being sold for 1,900 gns after beating Goldania a length: stays 1¼m: acts on firm going. *V. Cross.* 63

SUNBELT 3 b.c. Baldric II 131–Costa Sola 87 (Worden II 129) [1975 6g 1976 10fg⁵ 12f² 13.3fg* 12fg⁵ 12s* 13.3v⁵] most attractive looking colt: half-brother to top-class miler Sun Prince (by Princely Gift): decisive winner of 13-runner maiden race at Newbury in June, beating Nargis by 1½ lengths: wore blinkers on all outings afterwards, putting up a good effort when winning handicap at Goodwood in September by 2 lengths from Oisin: ran badly final outing: suited by a test of stamina: appears to act on any going except perhaps heavy: somewhat lacking in pace and is suited by being sent on some way from home in his races: sold 15,000 gns Newmarket December Sales. *R. Hern.* 83

SUNBIRD 3 br.f. Tudor Melody 129–Seaswan 104 (Sea-Bird II 145) [1975 6g* 1976 8g 8f⁴ 8fg] very attractive filly: very good mover: won 29-runner maiden race at Newbury as a 2-y-o in good style from Picture: pick of paddock, started favourite for Irish 1,000 Guineas at the Curragh in May but ran badly, finishing well tailed off behind Sarah Siddons: put up a much better effort when 5½ lengths fourth of eight to Kesar Queen in Coronation Stakes at Royal Ascot 103

Ecchinswell Maiden Stakes, Newbury—Sunfish wins cleverly from Gerard

in June but confirmed that she has more than her share of temperament when trailing in last of nine behind Duboff in Child Stakes at Newmarket the following month (raced alone and caved in without a struggle) and was not seen out again: evidently stays 1m. *R. Hern.*

SUNBURST 3 ch.f. Porto Bello 118–Silk Tabard (Court Harwell 130) [1975   **76**
6s 6s⁴ 1976 10fg⁴ 10.1fg⁵ 8fg² 7fg³ 8g 10f² 8f² 10fg* 10d 8s* 10v⁴] compact filly: won maiden race at Salisbury in September by 1½ lengths from Mary Roan and handicap at Chepstow the following month by ¾ length from Winged Typhoon: placed in varied company earlier, putting up a good effort on sixth outing when making Rowantree pull out all the stops in minor event on former course in August: stays 1¼m: acts on any going. *G. Balding.*

SUNDAY MARKET 3 ch.f. Double Jump 131–La Maffia (Mourne 126) [1975   **—**
6g 7g⁶ 1976 7fg 8f 11.5fg] rangy filly: stays 7f: sold 900 gns Newmarket July Sales. *J. Winter.*

SUN DEVIL 2 ch.c. Galivanter 131–Tyrona 76 (Tyrone 130) [1976 5fg 6g   **66**
7f 7f 6f 8fg] workmanlike colt: fourth foal: 780 gns yearling: dam placed at up to 1m at 2 yrs: plating-class maiden: best run at 6f. *M. Jarvis.*

SUNFISH 2 b.c. Mill Reef 141–Costa Sola 87 (Worden II 129) [1976 6fg 6g*] **93 p**
attractive, shapely colt: half-brother to 3-y-o 1½m and 13f winner Sunbelt (by Baldric II) and three other winners, notably top-class miler Sun Prince (by Princely Gift) and smart filly Boulevard (by Pall Mall): dam, winner over 1½m, is daughter of Park Hill winner Sunny Cove: won 10-runner maiden race at Newbury in July by ¾ length from Gerard, taking that colt's measure 1f out and from then on being made to do just enough to win: will stay 1½m: looked sure to hold his own in better class races (seemed to have quite a lot of improvement still in him) but was not seen out again. *R. Hern.*

720

SUNFLIGHT 3 ro.f. Precipice Wood 123–Redinza (Red God 128 §) [1975 **62**
5f 1976 8.2f⁵ 8g 12g⁴ 11.1g⁴ 10d* 10s⁵ 12v⁴] quite a modest performer:
showed considerably improved form when winning selling handicap at Nottingham in September by 6 lengths from Grey Presto: sold out of B. McMahon's
stable 1,300 gns afterwards and was not disgraced on both her runs in better
company for her new stable: stays 1½m: evidently suited by some give in the
ground. *G. Smyth.*

SUNHAT 2 br.c. Roi Soleil 125–Lucem 96 (Guersant 129) [1976 7g 7g⁵ 8s³] **84**
good-bodied, useful-looking colt: half-brother to four winners, including fairly
useful 1967 2-y-o 5f and 1m winner Coonbeam (by Crocket): 4,000 gns yearling:
dam won at up to 1¼m: favourite when 3½ lengths third of 19 to Nordman in
maiden race at Sandown in October: stays 1m: acts on soft going. *P. Walwyn.*

SUNNY SPRING 2 ch.c. Realm 129–Lady Gaston 76 (Pall Mall 132) [1976 **97**
5fg² 5f* 5.5g³ 5d] second living foal: 10,000 gns yearling: dam, winner over
5f at 2 yrs, is half-sister to smart animals Cyrus and Right of the Line: odds
on, won six-runner Windsor Castle Stakes at Royal Ascot in June without any
difficulty, making all to beat Desert Warrior by 3 lengths: not disgraced when
taking on leading French 2-y-o's in Prix Robert Papin at Maisons-Laffitte
the following month, finishing 8½ lengths third to Blushing Groom, but ran
poorly in Flying Childers Stakes at Doncaster in September (looked a bit lean,
was reluctant to go down to start and was tailed off most of way): will stay
6f. *L. Cumani.*

SUNNY WONDER 5 ch.h. Floribunda 136–Sunshine Wonder 107 (Lord Mayor **–**
111) [1974 5.8g 5fg 1975 6fg⁶ 6g 6f 1976 5.8h⁶] neat, strong, muscular
horse: bad sprint plater nowadays: tailed off when tried in blinkers on final
outing at 4 yrs: acts on firm going: sold 460 gns Ascot August Sales. *V. Cross.*

SUNSET SONG 3 b.f. Song 132–Crimson Glow 89 (Firestreak 125) [1975 **82**
5fg 5g² 5fg* 5d² 5h³ 5fg 6fg⁶ 6s 1976 5s 7f 6fg 7f 6g⁴ 8f 6g² 6g³ 6v⁶] useful
sort: ran easily best race when neck second to Gresham Girl in handicap at
Ripon in August: subsequently failed to run up to that form in well-contested
sellers at Ayr and Newcastle: stays 6f but probably not 7f: acts on any going
with the possible exception of very soft: wears blinkers nowdays. *J. Carr.*

SUNSET VALUE 4 br.g. Current Coin 118–Elected 74 (Red God 128 §) [1974 **80**
5d 5h⁶ 5f² 5.9fg⁶ 5.8g 5d 1975 7d³ 8g* 7fg² 7fg⁶ 8d 7s⁵ 7g² 8g³ 8g⁴ 1976
7fg* 7f² 7f⁵ 7fg² 9g⁶ 7fg³ 7f² 7h* 7f* 8s²] strong, well-grown gelding: moderate
handicapper: successful at Warwick, Brighton (amateur riders event) and
Folkestone: best form at up to 1m but wasn't disgraced over 9f on fifth start:
appears to act on any going: good mount for an inexperienced race-rider.
A. Pitt.

SUNSHINE LIE 2 b.c. Shiny Tenth 120–Liebeslust (Mangon) [1976 5g **71**
5f⁵ 6f⁵ 7.2f⁵ 7fg⁵] well-made colt: half-brother to several winners here and in
Germany, including useful stayer Vishvamitra (by Mossborough): 1,450 gns
yearling: dam won twice at 2 yrs in Germany: quite a moderate maiden: should
stay 1m. *M. Camacho.*

SUNSHUN 2 br.c. Manacle 123–Gay Soleil 75 (Soleil II 133) [1976 5f 5fg **71**
5fg⁴ 5d³ 5f⁵ 5f*] neat colt: bought in 675 gns after winning eight-runner

*Windsor Castle Stakes, Ascot—Sunny Spring has no difficulty putting paid
to Desert Warrior and Captain's Mate*

seller at Beverley in July by 2½ lengths from Habbershaw: appears to act on any going. *M. W. Easterby.*

SUPER CAVALIER 3 ch.c. Tower Walk 130–Ennel (Seminole II) [1975 5g⁵ 5fg* 6f² 6g* 5fg* 6fg 6g⁶ 1976 7f² 8fg 7.3fg⁵ 8f⁵ 7fg³ 7s 6d⁴] strong, shapely colt: won two important races for 2-y-o's in 1975, July Stakes at Newmarket and National Stakes at Sandown but was a stone behind best of his age: failed to win a race in 1976 but had three good efforts to his name, finishing 1½ lengths second to Wollow in Clerical, Medical Greenham Stakes at Newbury in April, fifth of 15 to Ardoon in Hungerford Stakes on same course in August and 4½ lengths third to Boldboy in Sanyo Stakes at Doncaster the following month: off course over three months after first outing: best form at up to 7f on a sound surface: sold 25,000 gns Newmarket December Sales and is to stand at stud in Argentina. *G. Hunter.* **111**

SUPER DANCER 2 b.f. Taj Dewan 128–Derry Lass (Derring-Do 131) [1976 7d] strong filly: second foal: dam unraced half-sister to Derby winners Blakeney and Morston: unquoted, showed promise in 25-runner Houghton Stakes at Newmarket in October, finishing eighth to Bessie Wallis: will stay 1½m: likely to do better. *J. Bethell.* **72 p**

SUPER DART 2 ch.c. Straight King 98–Pallian (Anton 106) [1976 7f⁶ 7f 6h⁵ 6fg 7s] useless. *T. Walker.* **—**

SUPER JENNIE 3 ch.f. Stephen George 102–Kasada-Da (Tacitus 124) [1975 5f³ 5.9f⁶ 7f 7fg⁶ 7d 7g² 1976 8f 12.2fg⁴ 13.4fg⁵ 13fg* 12f* 16g² 14fg 12d 14s] fair performer: clear-cut winner of maiden race at Nottingham in July and minor event at Salisbury in August: stays well: form only on top-of-the-ground conditions: trained when successful by D. H. Jones. *M. Salaman.* **80**

SUPER KELLY 4 gr.c. Supreme Sovereign 119–Kelly Green (Kelly 122) [1974 5fg 5d⁵ 5fg² 5g* 5.3f³ 6s* 6g* 6g 7v² 1975 7d² 7s³ 7g² 6f² 7fg² 8f² 8d* 6.5g 8g⁶ 7.3d 7g 1976 8f 6fg⁶ 7fg² 7g³ 7g⁵ 7.2g⁶ 7f 7.3d 6g 8v³] good-topped colt: formerly a useful handicapper but was most disappointing after finishing ½-length second of 11 to Sportsky at Goodwood in May on third outing: stays 1m: acts on any going: blinkered sixth and ninth starts. *A. Corbett.* **81**

SUPER LOVE 3 br.g. Stupendous–Lilmi Love 82 (Miralgo 130) [1975 6f 8g 1976 12.2s 10.2s] robust, quite useful sort but seems not to possess much ability. *N. Adam.* **—**

SUPERMOLL 4 b.f. Super Slip 86–Mollie's First 59 (Songedor 116) [1974 5f 5g⁶ 5fg⁴ 6fg 6fg² 7s* 7s⁴ 7.2g 8s⁴ 8s² 1975 8g 8v 12s 11.1fg 10fg 10g⁴ 10.6fg² 10.4f⁶ 12g* 13d 14g 12g 10.6s⁴ 12g⁵ 1976 12g 15f⁶ 11fg 12fg 16d 12v] poor handicapper nowadays: no worthwhile form in 1976: stays 1½m: appears to act on any going: good mount for an apprentice: inconsistent: sometimes sweats up. *R. Mason.* **—**

SUPERNACULUM 2 gr.g. Supreme Sovereign 119–Perpelia (Red God 128 §) [1976 7fg 6g⁴ 6d* 6fg²] unfurnished gelding: half-brother to middle-distance winner Grindelwald (by Le Levanstell): 7,600 gns yearling: dam of little account: put up a very good performance in 15-runner maiden event at Yarmouth in September, winning by 10 lengths from Fleur de Flandre: finished strongly when ½-length second to Friendly Now in 25-runner minor event at Redcar later in month: will stay 1m: acts on a firm and a soft surface: wears blinkers. *H. Cecil.* **106**

SUPER PLUIT 2 b.c. Pluit 102–Tell-A-Lady (Supertello 128) [1976 7v] fifth reported produce: dam novice hurdler: very slowly away and was always tailed off when last of 12 behind Tudor Jig in minor event at Teesside in October. *W. Haigh.* **—**

SUPER PRINCESS 3 br.f. Falcon 131–Aficionada 87 (Infatuation 129) [1975 5f⁴ 6fg⁴ 7f* 7.2fg³ 8g 1976 7.3g 10.6d 10f⁵ 8f⁴ 8g 7fg⁶ 10.8g] useful-looking filly: showed fair form at 2 years: had some stiff tasks in 1976 but is only quite a moderate performer nowadays: may stay middle distances: acts on firm going: blinkered last two outings: has occasionally started slowly. *G. Hunter.* **73**

SUPER SIX 3 b.g. Henry the Seventh 125–Pleasantry (Right Royal V 135) [1975 8.2d 8g 1976 12d 12v] lengthy gelding: poor maiden. *J. Bethell.* **—**

SUPER SPLASH 5 b.h. Impressive–Grey Flood (Intentionally) [1974 8g 7g 5g* 5g⁵ 5g* 5.8g⁶ 5f* 1975 6.5v* 6s* 7s 6fg 7g⁵ 6g⁶ 6d 5d 5g⁵ 5g⁴ 6s 1976 7fg] big American-bred horse: one-time useful handicapper: made only one appearance in 1976 and was well beaten: probably needs further than 5f nowadays and stays 7f: acts on any going but best form with some give in the ground: has been tried in blinkers: suitable mount for an apprentice: sold 760 gns Newmarket Autumn Sales. *Mrs N. Whitfield.*

SUPER SYMPHONY 2 b.c. Dike–Pascha 82 (Saint Crespin III 132) [1976 **87** 5g⁵ 5d 7fg⁴ 8s⁵] tall, useful-looking colt: third produce: 1,500 gns foal, resold twice as a yearling for 3,000 gns and 4,000 gns: dam stayed well: having first race for three months, put up best effort when 6 lengths fourth of 17 to Gairloch in minor event at Goodwood in September: will stay middle distances: acts on a firm surface. *G. Hunter.*

SUPER TROJAN 6 b.g. Super Sam 124–Phrygia (Mossborough 126) [1974 **69** 10d 11.7fg 10g 14g* 12g 16g 14g² 11.7g⁶ 16v⁵ 14s* 16v⁵ 1975 16s* 16v 14d³ 14fg⁴ 16fg⁵ 16g 16d⁶ 14g⁴ 12v² 1976 14g⁶ 14fg³ 14g³ 16g⁴ 16.1d³ 12v³] rather lightly-made gelding: quite a moderate handicapper: ran best race in 1976 on fifth outing: stays 2m: revels in the mud: suitable mount for an apprentice: sometimes wears blinkers. *J. Cann.*

SUPREME HALO 6 ch.g. Starry Halo 122–Pyrola 87 (Psidium 130) [1974 **79** 12g 12d⁴ 16v⁵ 16v* 14.6s³ 1975 16s² 12d² 12g⁴ 18fg⁵ 1976 12g* 18fg² 12s⁵] strong gelding: quite a moderate handicapper nowadays: narrow winner at Folkestone in March: creditable second of four to True Lad in Great Metropolitan Handicap at Epsom the following month: subsequently off course until October: ideally suited by a good test of stamina: acts on any going: has been tried in blinkers but does as well without: suitable mount for an apprentice: genuine and consistent: good N.H. performer. *R. Smyth.*

SUPREME PENNY 2 b.f. Good Bond 122–Princess Pin 69 (Pindari 124) **78** [1976 5f⁵ 5f³ 5f⁵ 5f⁶ 5g³ 7fg* 7v⁴] half-sister to a winning sprinter in Ireland by Highland Melody: 500 gns yearling: dam half-sister to good stayer Lomond: well-backed favourite, won 26-runner seller at Redcar in September in good style by 7 lengths from Parkside Boy (bought in 950 gns): not disgraced in better company on final outing: will stay at least 1m: acts on any going. *S. Wainwright.*

SUPREME VISTA 3 b.g. Supreme Sovereign 119–Alta-Vista (Skymaster 126) **61** [1975 7f 6fg 1976 7fg 8fg 7f² 7fg 7fg⁵ 8f⁴ 8fg⁵ 8f 8f* 8fg 12.5s²] very big gelding: won six-runner maiden race at Yarmouth in August by a neck from For Keeps: creditable ¾-length second to Jim Coiner in handicap at Teesside in November: evidently stays 1½m: acts on any going: ran moderately when tried in blinkers on ninth outing. *B. Lunness.*

SURPRISE EVENT 4 br.g. Galivanter 131–Reaward 78 (Ratification 129) **57** [1974 6s 6d 6s 1975 8fg⁶ 7f 9fg³ 10g* 10fg⁵ 12g² 1976 12fg 10f 11.7fg 10g³] rangy gelding: plater: stays 1½m: best form on a sound surface: sold to D. Jermy 550 gns Ascot October Sales. *W. Holden.*

SUVANNEE 3 b.f. Versailles–Synaldo (Tantieme 136) [1975 8g* 8s² 8d* **115** 1976 8g² 10g⁴] French filly: closely related to Irish Guinness Oaks runner-up Lastarria (by Right Royal V): high class 2-y-o, winning two of her three races and being awarded second place in Criterium des Pouliches: came up against Riverqueen on both her outings in 1976, finishing 3 lengths runner-up to her in Poule d'Essai des Pouliches and just over a length fourth to her in Prix Saint-Alary, with Theia and Antrona between them, both at Longchamp in May: sustained an injury soon afterwards and was taken out of training: suited by 1¼m: acted on soft going: was one of the best fillies in France in 1976. *F. Boutin, France.*

SUVIEL 4 b.g. Arctic Judge 94–Farani 69 (Tenerani 135) [1974 N.R. 1975 — N.R. 1976 8f²(dis) 10.1fg] poor maiden: disqualified and placed last after finishing 2½ lengths second of seven to Sir Pelleas in poor maiden race at Yarmouth in August (jockey failed to draw correct weight), first outing and better effort. *J. Powney.*

SWAGGER 2 b.f. Prominer 125–Twaddle II (Tim Tam) [1976 5g⁶ 5fg* 6fg² **107** 6g² 6fg 7s²] lightly-made filly: half-sister to three winners, notably smart Irish 3-y-o sprinter Petipa (by Habitat): dam placed at 1½m in France: kept on strongly when winning 15-runner maiden race at Salisbury in June by 2½ lengths from Rahesh: beaten ¾ length in two good-class fillies events the following month, looking bit unlucky when third to Miss Pinkie in Courage Stakes at York (moved up a place by stewards afterwards) and keeping on well when runner-up to Al Stanza in Princess Margaret Stakes at Ascot: went down by a short head

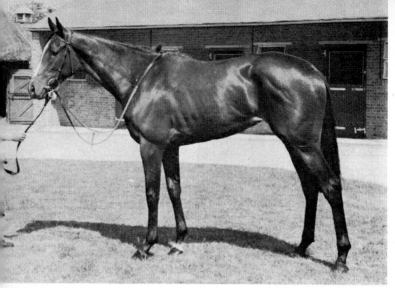

Mrs J. R. Mullion's "Swagger"

SWAGMAN 9 b.g. Cracksman 111–Mistrust (Rustam 127) [1974 5g 7h 7g   **64**
8g² 7s³ 8g² 8g⁴ 8s³ 8fg⁵ 7g   1975 7f⁶ 7s 8f 7f⁶ 7f⁵ 7f⁴ 8g* 8d 7f² 8f 7g³   1976 7f
7g⁴ 7fg 7f* 9g³ 7g⁴ 8f⁴] strong, workmanlike gelding: 2½-length winner of nine-
runner seller at Brighton in July (no bid): stays 1m: best form on a sound
surface: ideal mount for a boy. *H. Smyth.*

SWAKARA 3 b.f. Porto Bello 118–Persian Lamb 108 (Rustam 127) [1975 5d⁶   **83**
5f⁴ 5s⁴ 5g* 6g 5g²   1976 8f⁶ 7s⁵ 8d³ 8fg⁴ 8.2d 7fg⁵ 8f⁶ 8f³ 7f² 8f 7f 8fg⁴ 6d* 6v*
5s* 6v² 6v*] well-made filly: in fine form in the autumn and won minor event at
Nottingham and handicaps at Wolverhampton and Leicester (two, one an
apprentice event): comfortably defied a 7-lb penalty when beating Fleur d'Amour
3 lengths on last-named course on final outing in November: had looked an
unlucky loser on her previous appearance: stays 1m but has done all her winning
at sprint distances: acts on any going but is very well suited by some give in
the ground: genuine. *R. Hollinshead.*

SWALLOW GIRL 3 b.f. My Swallow 134–Jeunesse (Prince Bio) [1975 5g 5d⁵   **76**
1976 8fg 8fg 9f⁵ 10.5fg 12.2g* 11.7fg⁵] quite a useful sort: beat sole opponent
Bally Tudor by 5 lengths in minor event at Warwick in June: stays 1½m. *P.
Robinson.*

SWALLOW HILL 2 b.c. My Swallow 134–Hillowton (Mister Gus) [1976 6f⁴ 7g⁵   **80**
7g] lightly-made, good sort: half-brother to two winners, including quite
useful 1969 2-y-o 5f winner Harrow on the Hill (by Thinking Cap): dam, half-
sister to three stakes winners, won twice at 4 yrs in U.S.A.: shaped well in useful
maiden company, finishing ninth of 21 to Nobodys Fool at Newmarket in
October: will be suited by 1m. *P. Robinson.*

SWALLOW PRINCE 2 b.c. My Swallow 134–Princess Gretel 97 (The Phoenix)   **67 p**
[1976 6d] half-brother to three winners, including quite useful middle-distance
performer Hansel's Nephew (by Fidalgo): dam a miler: 14/1 when eighth of 22
to Rocket Symphony in maiden race at Newmarket in October: will stay 1m.
N. Guest.

SWALLOWSON 3 ch.c. My Swallow 134–Dame Judith 88 (Francis S) [1975   **—**
N.R. 1976 10fg 8g 8g 8fg] big, well-made colt: fourth foal: half-brother to

a winner in Ireland: dam won over 5f at 2 yrs: no worthwhile form in maiden company. *D. Dale.*

SWANEE BELLE 3 gr.f. My Swanee 122–Pampatamy 75 (Immortality) [1975 — N.R. 1976 9fg⁶ 10.8f 12.2s] plain, long-backed filly: first foal: 1,000 gns yearling: dam placed at up to 1m: no worthwhile form in maiden company: sold 1,200 gns Newmarket Autumn Sales. *J. Hardy.*

SWANEE MUSIC 3 gr.f. My Swanee 122–Showboat 80 (Sing Sing 134) [1975 — 5.1f³ 5f³ 6g 6fg 5.8f 1976 7fg 6g] poor plater: blinkered fourth outing in 1975: sold 350 gns Ascot June Sales. *P. Robinson.*

SWAN MAID 2 ch.f. My Swanee 122–Mile Cross 88 (Milesian 125) [1976 5f⁵] — lengthy filly: second live foal: 1,200 gns yearling: dam best at up to 1m: distant last of five to Sahib's Daughter in auction event at Goodwood in May. *S. Ingham.*

SWAN VALLEY 2 gr.g. My Swanee 122–Christmas Eve 86 (Rockefella) [1976 — 8d 6s 7s] strong, close-coupled gelding: half-brother to useful stayer Christmas Joy (by Darling Boy) and useful 1971 2-y-o Cansanta (by Canisbay): 2,500 gns yearling: dam middle-distance performer: no worthwhile form in maiden and minor events. *J. Hill.*

SWATCHEL 2 b.c. Virginia Boy 106–Hill Dancer (Hill Gail) [1976 5s³ 5f⁵ **107** 5f² 5f² 5f² 5f* 5f*] Irish colt: third foal: half-brother to a winning hurdler: dam unraced half-sister to Irish 1,000 Guineas winner Royal Danseuse: made all when winning at Limerick Junction in August (maiden plate by 5 lengths) and September (nursery under top weight by 4 lengths): second three times previously, on last occasion going down by a neck to Scops Owl in maiden race at Leopardstown: speedy but should stay at least 6f. *S. McGrath, Ireland.*

SWAYNES LADY 2 b.f. St Alphage 119–Gun Running (Derring-Do 131) [1976 **76** 5f⁶ 5f⁴ 5f⁴ 5fg⁴ 5g* 5g³ 5fg 5f* 5.3h 5fg] very small filly: first foal: 400 gns yearling: dam second five times from 6f to 1m in Ireland at 3 yrs: twice a winner at Wolverhampton, picking up a maiden auction event in June and putting up an excellent effort to score by a length from Laser Olivia in nursery in August: ran poorly final outing: will stay 6f. *T. Marshall.*

SWEET AFTON 4 b.f. Above Suspicion 127–Spending Spree (Delirium 126) — [1974 5f⁵ 5h 8d 7s 8.2d 1975 10d⁶ 12d 12.2f 12f 15g 1976 12f 15g] of no account. *T. Craig.*

SWEET AND SHINY 3 ch.f. Siliconn 121–Sharp and Sweet (Javelot 124) — [1975 5g 5fg 1976 7.6s] neat filly: lightly raced and no worthwhile form in maiden races. *M. Tate.*

SWEET AND UGLY 2 b.f. High Table 105–Guid Tassie 66 (French Beige 127) — [1976 5f 6h 7f 7f 6h⁵] small, unimpressive filly: of no account. *W. Murray.*

SWEET ANICE 7 ch.m. Goldhill 125–Menith Wood (Lancewood) [1974 N.R. — 1975 N.R. 1976 8fg] of little account: dead. *J. Leigh.*

SWEET BELLA 2 ch.f. Sweet Revenge 129–Belle Royale 89 (Right Royal V 135) — [1976 5.1fg] first foal: dam, a winner at up to 1½m, is daughter of 1962 Irish 1,000 Guineas winner Shandon Belle: 33/1 when in rear in 13-runner maiden race won by No Cards at Yarmouth in June. *H. Cecil.*

SWEET CHAMPAGNE 4 b.f. Sweet Story 122–Shamiana (Fortina) [1974 — N.R. 1975 N.R. 1976 12s 18s] evidently useless. *D. Williams.*

SWEET DOUGH 4 gr.f. Reindeer 124–Pastina 92 (March Past 124) [1974 5f — 5f⁵ 5g³ 7g³ 7g⁶ 7d 8s 5g⁴ 6g 1975 12g 16f⁴ 9g² 12f⁶ 15.8g⁴ 12g⁶ 10g⁴ 1976 12fg⁵] neat, light-framed filly: plater: best form at up to 1¼m, although ran respectably over 2m on fifth outing in 1975: apparently best in blinkers (didn't wear them on only start at 4 yrs). *P. Buckley.*

SWEET HORTENSE 3 b.f. King's Troop 118–Innovation 80 (Immortality) **58** [1975 5f 7g³ 6f 7fg 8d 1976 8fg 8g 8fg⁶ 11.7f 14f 10s] strong, attractive filly: quite a moderate plater: best run at 1m and is not certain to stay much further: blinkered final outing at 2 yrs. *L. Hall.*

SWEET LAD 3 b.c. Don II 123–Lovesick (Sicambre 135) [1975 6d⁵ 6fg 6s² **100** 1976 8g² 8.5fg* 10f 9f* 9.4h* 8f* 10f³ 9fg³] rangy colt: developed into a useful animal and gained comfortable wins in minor events at Epsom, Ripon, Carlisle and Beverley in the summer, on each occasion making all: ran well in handicaps afterwards, finishing good third to Game Lord in £4,000 event at Newcastle in July on final outing: stays 1¼m: probably acts on any going: retained by trainer 6,600 gns Newmarket April Sales: exported to U.S.A. *B. Hills.*

Singleton Handicap, Goodwood—Sweet Nightingale regains her form and beats Amun' Ra a neck

SWEET NICOLE 4 b.f. Sweet Story 122–Gay Nicole (Harbour Pilot 83) [1974 — N.R. 1975 N.R. 1976 16.1d 16f 12f] of little account. *R. Hollinshead.*

SWEET NIGHTINGALE 3 br.f. Swing Easy 126–Cabaret 74 (Sammy Davis 129) [1975 5v³ 5s 5s* 5h* 5d² 5fg* 5f* 5fg² 6d² 1976 5d 5f⁶ 6fg 5fg⁶ 5fg* 6g] strong filly: very useful and consistent at 2 yrs: put up easily her best effort and showed she retained all her ability when winning Singleton Handicap at Goodwood in July by a neck from Amun' Ra: best form at 5f but should stay further: acts on any going but is particularly well suited by a firm surface. *M. W. Easterby.* **109**

SWEET NO 2 br.f. No Mercy 126–Sweet Flight 81 (Falcon 131) [1976 5g 5f 6f 7g] small, lightly-made filly: no worthwhile form in maiden and minor events: sold 420 gns Ascot August Sales. *M. Masson.* —

SWEET PORT 2 b.f. Quayside 124–Sweet Sweet 71 (Bleep-Bleep 134) [1976 6fg 6fg⁵] third foal: half-sister to fair 1973 2-y-o Deidi (by French Beige), a winner at up to 6f: dam a sprinter: well behind in maiden races in the summer: sold 380 gns Ascot September Sales. *J. Sutcliffe.* —

SWEET RECLAIM 4 ch.c. Compensation 127–Sharp and Sweet (Javelot 124) [1974 5f⁵ 5fg³ 6g* 6fg³ 6g* 6g⁵ 6s² 6v* 1975 8d 7fg³ 7f 8fg⁵ 10g³ 9fg⁵ 10fg⁴ 10.2g 10d 8g* 10s 1976 7fg⁵ 10fg 9g³ 10fg² 8fg³ 8fg³ 8.3g* 8g² 8g* 9g 8s⁴] fairly useful handicapper: in good form in second half of season and won at Windsor in August and at Ascot the following month, on latter course keeping on well to beat Chop-Chop ½ length: good second to The Goldstone at Sandown in between: effective at 7f and stays 1¼m: acts on a firm surface but best form on soft ground (moved very feelingly to post on second start): started very slowly when tried in blinkers: genuine and consistent. *T. Waugh.* **97**

SWEET SPOT 2 ch.c. St Chad 120–Sweet Perfume (Parthia 132) [1976 5d³ 6s 6f³ 5g 5g⁶ 7g⁵ 6h⁴] modest plater: should stay 1m: ran poorly when blinkered on fifth outing. *N. Angus.* **60**

SWEET SWALLOW 3 ch.c. My Swallow 134–Senna (Sica Boy 132) [1975 7fg 1976 8f 11g⁶ 10fg 10fg* 12fg⁴ 12.2f⁴ 10.8g³] tall, rather lightly-built colt: 20/1, made all when winning six-runner maiden race at Newmarket in July by 1½ lengths from Welsh Relic: good third to Buck's Club in handicap at Warwick the following month: stays 11f (ran respectably on first attempt at 1½m but **96**

moderately on second): acts on a firm surface: trained until after second outing
by I. Balding. *P. Robinson.*

SWEET VENEER 2 ch.c. Siliconn 121–Sharp and Sweet (Javelot 124) [1976 **67**
5f 5f 5f6 5.1g 7s 7v] strong, compact colt: 8 lengths sixth of 13 to King Croesus
in maiden race at Newmarket in August, only sign of ability: should stay 7f:
ran poorly in blinkers on final outing. *T. Waugh.*

SWEET VIOTA 2 ch.f. Sweet Revenge 129–Viota 86 (Klairon 131) [1976 5s —
10v] seemingly of little account. *W. Charles.*

SWEET VIXEN 3 ch.f. Derek H 97–Renardeau 80 (Reynard Volant 125) [1975 —
N.R. 1976 12.2g 8fg] sister to fair hurdler Aldaniti: dam a stayer: well beaten in
maiden races at Catterick and Thirsk in the summer. *J. Carr.*

SWEET WALK 2 ch.f. Balidar 133–Lucky Janie 87 (Dual 117) [1976 5f2 5f3 5g5 **83**
6g4 5h3 6fg 5g4 6v3 6s*] neat, strong filly: half-sister to 3-y-o middle-distance
winner Lucky Mickmooch (by Blakeney) and moderate 1¼m winner Lucky-So-So
(by Lauso): 1,450 gns foal: dam won from 5f to 1m: won 17-runner seller at Doncaster in October (no bid) by 4 lengths from Heavenly Song: stays 6f well: acts
on any going: wore a hood on last two outings: sold 2,400 gns Newmarket Autumn
Sales. *T. Fairhurst.*

SWELL FELLOW 5 b.g. Giolla Mear 113–Nonnie (Dumbarnie 125) [1974 12g2 **118**
12d2 11g* 10d* 11s* 1975 10s* 12d2 10f2 10.5d 1976 10g5 12f* 10g6 10fg2
13.3f* 11g3 11g* 12v]
    Swell Fellow had almost as many races in his fourth season as in his two
previous seasons put together, and to the four races he had already won he added
three more, the £2,000 Brighton Festival Stakes, in which he was apprentice
ridden to a length and a half victory over Our Manny, the Group 2 Geoffrey
Freer Stakes at Newbury, where after making all the running he held on to win
by a head from Oats for a prize of almost £12,500, and the £4,400 Goteborgs
Stora Pris at Aby in Sweden, which race he picked up by two lengths from the
German six-year-old Honduras, with St Joles five lengths away third.
    The Geoffrey Freer Stakes represents Swell Fellow's most notable triumph,
and in addition to the Derby third Oats he had behind him Libra's Rib, brother
to Ribocco and Ribero and third in the 1975 St Leger, Dakota, beaten less than
two lengths into fourth place in the King George VI and Queen Elizabeth

*Geoffrey Freer Stakes, Newbury—the enterprisingly-ridden Swell Fellow
holds the challenge of Oats*

Diamond Stakes, and Major Green, a good third in the Coronation Cup. Not bad for a 3,800-guinea yearling by the Irish St Leger winner Giolla Mear out of an unraced Dumbarnie half-sister to the hurdler Rosyth!

Swell Fellow (b.g. 1971)	Giolla Mear (b 1965)	Hard Ridden (b 1955)	Hard Sauce
			Toute Belle II
		Iacobella (b 1955)	Relic
			Jacopa Bellini
	Nonnie (br 1962)	Dumbarnie (br 1949)	Dante
			Lost Soul
		Rossenhall (b 1949)	Chamossaire
			Grace Abounding

And although he will be six in 1977, Swell Fellow, a light-bodied gelding, almost certainly has plenty of winning left in him yet. He has had comparatively little racing for one of his years, he has a useful turn of finishing speed, he is not beholden to the ground, he can adapt himself to the demands of any racecourse, he can give his running for an apprentice, and he is as game and as honest as they come. What more could one want from any racehorse? *J. Hindley.*

SWIFT FALCON 5 b.g. Falcon 131–Musical Watch (Tudor Melody 129) [1974 **75** 5f³ 6g 6d⁴ 5.8g 7.6g 7fg² 8.5d² 8s³ 1975 7s 7f³ 7s* 8fg³ 1976 10v² 8f⁴] sturdy, well-made gelding: quite a moderate handicapper: ran well in two apprentice events at 5 yrs: probably stays 1¼m: acts on any going: sometimes wears blinkers: sold to J. Berry 3,600 gns Ascot June Sales. *W. A. Stephenson.*

SWIFT HUSSAR 2 b.c. Queen's Hussar 124–Berga (Baldric II 131) [1976 **104** 5fg³ 5d⁴ 5fg* 5d⁵ 6fg² 6g⁴ 6g³ 6s 6s⁶] close-coupled, useful-looking colt: second foal: 3,100 gns yearling: dam won 5f seller at 2 yrs in France: started well for first time when winning £1,200 event at Newmarket in May by 1½ lengths from newcomer Royal Hand: ran very well when in frame subsequently in two nurseries at Newmarket and in well-contested minor event won by Adviser at Kempton: suited by 6f, and will get further: best form on a sound surface: ran well below his best in blinkers on final outing. *C. Brittain.*

SWIFTLY 4 ch.c. Sailing Light 119–Brocatelle 71 (Brocade Slipper 116) [1974 **—** 5g 5fg 6f 5s⁵ 1975 7f⁴ 6f³ 5f 6h² 7.2fg³ 6f⁴ 8f² 8f* 8g 1976 8.2f 8g] compact colt: plater: effective at 6f to 1m, and may stay further: acts on hard going: ran well both in blinkers and without them in 1975 (didn't wear them at 4 yrs). *R. Stubbs.*

SWIFT MARINA 3 b.f. Birdbrook 110–Fair Marina 93 (Hethersett 134) [1975 **64** N.R. 1976 7fg 7g 8f 8f⁵ 7fg 6f 7f 7fg 7f* 8s] rangy filly: showed much improved form when making all to win seller at Newmarket in August by 4 lengths from Rosella Bella (no bid): well beaten in much better company on only subsequent outing: stays 7f: acts on firm going: blinkered sixth outing: has occasionally made a slowish start: suitable mount for an apprentice: sold 1,100 gns Newmarket Autumn Sales. *W. Holden.*

SWIFT SENSATION 2 b.c. My Swallow 134–Orange Sensation 69 (Floribunda **106** 136) [1976 5g 6f 6g⁶ 7.5f* 7g*] Irish colt: second living foal: half-brother to moderate 6f winner Astronomical (by Highland Melody): 5,000 gns yearling: dam placed at up to 7f at 2 yrs: improved steadily and won a maiden race at Gowran Park in July and a nursery at Leopardstown the following month: finished well to catch lightly-weighted Ball Night when winning by ¾ length in latter race: will stay 1m: acts on firm going. *L. Browne, Ireland.*

SWIFT SONS 2 br.c. Polyfoto 124–La Roquette (Sammy Davis 129) [1976 **83** 5fg⁶ 5g⁶ 5f 5f⁴ 6f² 6f* 6g⁶ 5fg] strong colt: first foal: 1,600 gns yearling: dam never ran: showed improved form when winning 18-runner minor event at Windsor in August by short head from Sipit: had stiffish tasks in nurseries afterwards: will stay 7f: acts on firm going. *W. Marshall.*

SWINGING GIRL 2 ch.f. Swing Easy 126–Mansi (Pardao 120) [1976 5f² 5fg³ **80** 5g³ 6f] strong, shapely filly: first foal: 3,000 gns yearling: dam won over 7f at 2 yrs in France: ran well when second to Heckle in maiden race at Newbury in April: did not reproduce that form and was not seen out after June: should stay 6f. *A. Corbett.*

SWINGING TRIBE 3 b.c. Swing Easy 126–Tribal Chant (Native Dancer) **91** [1975 5g* 5f² 7f² 7g² 6g 1976 7s 7s 7.2d⁴ 8fg³ 10fg 8g⁵ 7f⁶ 8h* 7f³ 8g³ 7.3d 8s 7s] useful-looking ex-Irish colt: half-brother to French middle-distance winner Gone Native (by Graustark): dam won over 6f as a 2-y-o: won minor event at Brighton in August in runaway fashion by 6 lengths from Balidon: ran respectably, often faced with stiff tasks, in many of his other races in this country: stays 1m: possibly unsuited by very soft ground: blinkered second start: trained first two outings by D. Weld: sold 5,000 gns Newmarket Autumn Sales. *C. Brittain.*

SWING RIGHT 2 br.f. Swing Easy 126–Ever Joyful (Aureole 132) [1976 **69**
5f⁶ 5.1fg³ 5fg³ 6g 6fg² 6f* 7d⁶ 6s⁵ 5v⁴] lightly-made filly: bought in 1,250 gns after winning seller at Ripon in August by a length from Melgrove Way: better suited by 6f than 5f, and should stay 7f: acts on any going. *R. Supple.*

SWING THROUGH 3 br.c. Swing Easy 126–Senta 103 (Chanteur II 135) **89**
[1975 7fg⁴ 7fg⁵ 7g² 7fg 1976 10.5s³ 10fg* 10.5fg² 12f⁵ 10.5fg 10fg² 14fg 12f³ 14.6d² 10.5v⁴ 12s⁴] tall, narrow colt: fair performer: won 15-runner maiden race at Yarmouth in May: ran well when runner-up in strongly-contested minor event at York (to Bright Finish) and handicap at Newmarket (to Tiger Trail) afterwards but became none too consistent: probably stays 1¾m: appears to act on any going: tried in blinkers on fifth and tenth outings but has done better without. *C. Brittain.*

SWITCHBACK 2 b.g. Red God 128 §–Romanova (Queen's Hussar 124) [1976 **76**
5fg⁶ 5fg³ 5f³ 5g⁴ 5g⁴ 6fg 5fg⁴ 6fg 6g³ 7f 6g³ 6g⁴ 7.6v] dipped-backed gelding: plater: narrowly-beaten third of 14 to Eastern Romance at Goodwood in September: should stay 7f: not particularly consistent. *R. Smyth.*

SWOONER 2 b.c. Crooner 119–Suju 73 (Hard Tack 111 §) [1976 5f 6f] plain —
colt: apprentice ridden when behind in sellers at Ripon in August: sold 200 gns Doncaster September Sales. *W. Haigh.*

SWOPPIE 2 b.f. Bivouac 114–Indaca (Pinza 137) [1976 6d] neat filly: half- —
sister to winners in Italy and Scandinavia: 420 gns yearling: dam won twice in Italy: unquoted when behind in 17-runner minor event won by Mrs McArdy at Redcar in September: lacks scope. *J. W. Watts.*

SWORD RULER 4 br.c. Damascus–Firm Defense (Bold Ruler) [1974 8d³ 7.5v **?**
8v 1975 8s 8g* 8fg 9g³ 8g² 9g⁵ 1976 8g 7.5g 10.5fg⁴ 10.5g⁵ 11.7f⁴] American-bred ex-French colt: first foal: dam never ran: won handicap at Evry at 3 yrs and ran creditably on third and fourth outings in France in 1976: 40/1, finished 4½ lengths behind Amboise when last of four in slowly-run minor event at Windsor in August on first appearance in this country: last trained in France by A. Bates. *D. Gandolfo.*

SYCAMORE GRANGE 3 ch.c. High Line 125–Recce (Donore 119) [1975 —
N.R. 1976 10s⁵ 10v 10.2s] fair sort: fifth foal: dam never ran: about 9 lengths fifth of nine to Blyth's Folly in minor event at Sandown in October: pulled up on next outing (bit slipped through mouth) and dwelt on final start. *C. Brittain.*

SYGNOME 3 b.f. Precipice Wood 123–P's and Q's (Pinza 137) [1975 6f⁵ 1976 **53**
12.2fg 13g 16f³ 16.1v 10.2s] poor staying maiden. *C. Brittain.*

SYLVAN D'OR 3 ch.f. Songedor 116–Sylvanite 86 § (Rockefella) [1975 —
5s 5s 5s² 5f 5h³ 5f⁴ 5f⁶ 5g³ 5g* 6g 6v⁴ 1976 5fg⁵ 6f⁴] neat filly: won nursery at Edinburgh in 1975: didn't run up to her best in two early-season outings: stays 6f: acts on any going. *V. Mitchell.*

SYLVAN GLADE 4 gr.g. Shooting Chant–Sidalgo (Fidalgo 129) [1974 N.R. —
1975 7f⁵ 7f⁴ 7f⁶ 7f² 7f* 7f 6v 5s 1976 8fg 10.4fg] moderate ex-Irish handicapper: well beaten in amateur riders race at Salisbury in June and ladies race at Chester in September (tailed off): stays 7f: acts on firm going. *D. Dartnall.*

SYLVIA'S DREAM 2 b.f. Sahib 114–Point of View (Vilmorin) [1976 5f⁵ 6fg* **83**
7g² 7f 6d 5.9s* 6v² 6v⁵] half-sister to a minor winner by Taste of Honey: 380 gns foal, resold 420 gns yearling: dam placed over 10.8f: bought in 680 gns after landing a gamble in 10-runner seller at Windsor in June: ran well in nurseries afterwards and won one at Wolverhampton in October by 2½ lengths from Victa: stays 7f: acts on a firm surface but goes particularly well on very soft going. *J. Hill.*

SYLVIA'S GIFT 3 ch.g. Charltown 127–Sea Treasure 93 (Princely Gift 137) —
[1975 6g 1976 8s] no worthwhile form in maiden company: tailed off only outing at 3 yrs. *J. Hill.*

729

SYLVIAS STAR 2 br.f. Forlorn River 124–Aleta 71 (Montaval 129) [1976 **64**
5g² 5f 5s⁴] light-framed filly: 2 lengths second of nine behind Cambridge Star
in maiden race at Folkestone in March: did not reproduce that form, including in
a seller: trained by P. Ashworth on first two outings: exported to Norway. *J.
Berry.*

SYNDICATE QUEEN 2 b.f. Galivanter 131–Grasp 117 (Torbido) [1976 5f 6g —
5g 5g] small, sharp sort: behind on all outings, including in sellers: blinkered final
start: sold 225 gns Doncaster October Sales. *P. Cole.*

T

TABERNACLE 3 b.g. Manacle 123–Tabarka (Dicta Drake 126) [1975 5fg 5f³ **61**
5g* 5fg 6g⁴ 6d³ 7g 6g⁶ 6v⁵ 1976 5fg 6d³ 5f 6fg 7fg⁵ 6fg³ 8d 5f⁵ 8d⁶ 6d* 6v 6v 6s²]
leggy, lightly-made gelding: all out when winning 14-runner minor event at
Nottingham by a length from Tribal Festival: also placed in varied races,
including a Newmarket seller: best form at 6f, although stays 7f: seems to act on
any going: suitable mount for an apprentice. *K. Bridgwater.*

TACHYPOUS 2 b.c. Hotfoot 126–Stilvi 126 (Derring-Do 131) [1976 5fg **128**
5fg* 6f 6fg³ 6g*]
    Through no fault of his own Tachypous lacked the consistency of per-
formance one likes to see in a horse of the highest class, but his victory in the
William Hill Middle Park Stakes at Newmarket in October on his final appearance
established him beyond doubt as a very good colt, and he was retired for the
season in our eyes England's main hope of winning the Two Thousand Guineas,
and no forlorn hope at that either. Tachypous' troubles stemmed from the fact
that he went down with the virus in mid-season: he ran no sort of race at all
when favourite for the Coventry Stakes at Royal Ascot on his third appearance,
and was still below his best when J. O. Tobin and Priors Walk beat him on his
return to the course in the Richmond Stakes at Goodwood. Apart from these
two races, Tachypous did nothing wrong, if one is prepared to overlook his failure
to make much of a show when eighth, upsides Royal Budget, in the Ashley
Maiden Stakes at Newmarket in May on his début.
    A 15/2 chance from 3/1 on the Ashley Maiden Stakes, Tachypous was
supported at 2/1 to beat previous winners Mr Nice Guy, Tribal King and Model
Soldier in a field of five for the Berkshire Stakes at Newbury under three weeks
later, and whatever it was he didn't know at Newmarket he showed in this race
he had since learned thoroughly by having his opponents stone cold as he moved
up on the bridle to dispute the lead two furlongs from home. The moment he was
given his head—racing into the last furlong—Tachypous strode clear to win most
impressively by five lengths. Few who saw his victory doubted that he was
potentially a very good two-year-old, and with his virus troubles behind him and
with reports circulating to the effect that he had proved overwhelmingly superior
to the Mill Reef Stakes winner Anax in home gallops, Tachypous was backed
down to co-favouritism with Etienne Gerard in the Middle Park Stakes. In a
race which included the Gimcrack Stakes winner Nebbiolo, the first and second
in the Flying Childers Stakes, Mandrake Major and La Ville de Rire, the first
and second in the Mill Reef Stakes, Anax and Adviser, and the second in the

*William Hill Middle Park Stakes, Newmarket—Tachypous comes storming up the hill to beat
Nebbiolo (No. 8), Mandrake Major, Adviser (far side) and Anax*

Mr G. L. Cambanis' "Tachypous"

Prix Morny, Water Boy, in addition to Etienne Gerard, who had slammed some pretty useful youngsters in the Clarence House Stakes, Tachypous looked to be in serious trouble in the early stages. Try as he might, he couldn't produce in this company the pace necessary to hold his place, and it wasn't until they were fairly well into the last two furlongs that he began to get into the fight. But from the moment he started to improve there was hardly a doubt that he was going to get up and win, and he came through very strongly in the last one hundred yards to beat Nebbiolo by a length, with Mandrake Major the same distance away third.

			Firestreak		Pardal
		Hotfoot	(br 1956)		Hot Spell
		(br 1966)	Pitter Patter		Kingstone
Tachypous			(br 1953)		Rain
(b.c. 1974)			Derring-Do		Darius
		Stilvi	(br 1961)		Sipsey Bridge
		(b 1969)	Djerella		Guersant
			(ch 1960)		Djeretta

A rangy, extremely attractive colt, who looks every inch a high-class performer, Tachypous is the first foal of that fine mare Stilvi, a very fast sprinter who beat Deep Diver in the 1972 King George Stakes at Goodwood. In terms of merit Tachypous is every bit as good as Stilvi was, but he lacks her brilliant speed, as may be judged from the fact that he needed practically the whole of six furlongs to assert himself in the Middle Park Stakes. So far as his future is concerned, this is a good sign, for the indications are that Tachypous has inherited a measure of stamina through his sire Hotfoot, a very good middle-distance performer. We expect Tachypous to stay a mile at least, and over that distance to be a greater force than he showed himself to be over six furlongs in the Middle Park Stakes. As we intimated earlier, he has a good chance of winning the Two Thousand Guineas; The Minstrel and Pharly are two he has to beat. *B. Hobbs.*

TACKLING 4 b.c. Hard Tack 111 §–Sweet Rose Nose (Infatuation 129) [1974 **70**
5d 5fg 6v 1975 7s 6s³ 6f⁶ 8f³ 6d 10g⁵ 1976 10.1fg³ 10.1fg²] workmanlike colt:

731

quite a moderate maiden: placed twice at Windsor at 4 yrs: stays 1¼m: seems to act on any going: suitable mount for an apprentice. *R. Akehurst.*

TACK RULE 4 b.f. Counsel 118–Tackard 87 (Hard Tack 111 §) [1974 5s⁴ 5s* 5g 1975 6s 6g³ 6fg⁶ 6f⁵ 7f² 7h⁴ 8f⁶ 8g⁶ 6g* 1976 7f 6fg] small, very light-framed filly: plater: best at up to 7f: acts on any going: suitable mount for an apprentice: hampered at halfway on second outing. *W. C. Watts.* —

TACORINDA 3 br.f. Takawalk II 125–High Corinda 85 (High Treason 126) [1975 5.9g 1976 6f 5g⁶] no worthwhile form in maiden races. *E. Cousins.* —

TAFFINA 2 ch.f. Rangitikei–Startup 65 (Stardust) [1976 5h] third reported foal by a thoroughbred sire: dam moderate plater: last of 11 in maiden race at Bath in July, only outing. *M. Bradley.* —

TAFFYTINA 2 b.f. Caerdeon 98–Tina II (Tulyar 134) [1976 5g* 5fg³ 6fg⁴ 7g* 7g² 7f⁴] good-looking, strong filly: good mover: half-sister to smart performers Ovaltine (by Match III) and Guillotina (by Busted), and to outstanding brood-mare Pristina (by Petition): dam never ran: won 21-runner maiden race at Newbury in May and put up a good effort to win £2,100 event at Newmarket two months later, beating Crucial Decision 1½ lengths despite swerving right at start: in frame in good-class races on other outings, notably when 2 lengths fourth to Ampulla in Cherry Hinton Stakes at Newmarket and excellent length second to In Haste in Heronslea Stakes at Ayr: will probably stay 1¼m: genuine and consistent. *P. Walwyn.* **106**

TAIKUN'S MELODY 5 gr.h. Tycoon II–Melody Call 55 (Tudor Melody 129) [1974 10g² 11g² 10f² 12g* 12fg² 1975 10g⁶ 12g 14g⁶ 11d 12s⁴ 1976 14fg 12s 15.5s³] compact horse: poor handicapper nowadays: best form on an easy surface: usually wears bandages in front. *T. Gosling.* —

TAJ GIRL 3 br.f. Taj Dewan 128–Palestream 78 (Palestine 133) [1975 5s⁴ 5s² 6fg 8g⁶ 1976 7f 12fg⁴ 12f* 12g³ 12s⁵ 12v] fair plater: winner at Newmarket in August, beating Grey Mountain 3 lengths (bought in 2,300 gns): not disgraced in better company afterwards: stays 1½m: acts on any going. *W. Stephenson.* **68**

Mr Louis Freedman's "Taffytina"

TAJ PRINCESS   2 b.f. Taj Dewan 128–Pink Velvet (Petingo 135)   [1976 5f 5g² **78** 5fg 5g* 6fg⁵ 7s⁶ 7.6v⁵]   small, sturdy filly: first produce: 740 gns foal, resold 540 gns yearling: dam never ran: made all to win 10-runner maiden auction event at Wolverhampton in June by a length from Machrihanish: weakened after 6f on last two outings and has yet to prove she stays 7f.   *P. Taylor.*

TAKE AIM   3 ch.g. Firestreak 125–Take a Chance 107 (Rockefella)   [1975 N.R. **80** 1976 9g* 9g² 12g 10.2f⁵ 13fg⁶ 12h³ 12f⁶ 13s]   compact gelding: brother to fairly useful 1½m winner Seaport: 400 gns yearling: dam won from 5f to 1½m: said to have been hobdayed: won maiden race at Ripon in April by 1½ lengths from Selham: effective from 9f to 13f: acts on firm going: inconsistent.   *J. W. Watts.*

TAKE A LAKER   2 gr.c. Grand Roi 118–Meadow Grass 86 (Pampas Grass)   **56** [1976 5f 5f⁴ 6fg 6fg 5g]   light-framed colt: brother to very useful 1½m to 1¾m winner Royal Park but showed only poor form himself: may do better over distances more in keeping with his breeding.   *R. Smyth.*

TAKEARISK   3 br.c. Baldric II 131–Fall in Love 126 (Swaps)   [1975 N.R. **88** 1976 8g⁶ 8fg*]   good-looking, strong, short-legged French-bred colt: fifth foal: brother to two minor winners in France: 105,000 francs foal (approx £9,000): dam, from a good family, was a high-class 2-y-o in 1964: won 21-runner maiden race at Goodwood in May by a length from The Sentry despite running green: will probably stay further than 1m: exported by B.B.A. to New Zealand.   *R. Price.*

TAKE IT EASY   5 ch.g. Great Nephew 126–Red Sea 70 (Zimone)   [1974 6s 6fg   **63** 6f⁵ 6g 7g 6g 5h² 8s² 8v* 10v* 10s* 10v⁴   1975 8s 12f³ 9.5g³   1976 10g 12s⁴ 10s⁶ 11.1s*]   plater: sold to M. Tate 775 gns after winning at Wolverhampton in October by 5 lengths (apprentice ridden): stays 11f: acts well on heavy going: has worn a hood and blinkers, but does better without them.   *Miss N. Wilmot.*

TAKE YOUR PLACE   3 b.c. Round Table–Zonah (Nasrullah)   [1975 7g* 7g* **112** 8g*   1976 10g² 10.5s⁴ 8f⁵]   tall, rather lightly-made colt: good mover: brother to top-class middle-distance American mare Drumtop: 125,000 dollars yearling: dam a winner in U.S.A.: won all three races as a 2-y-o, notably Observer Gold Cup at Doncaster (by a head from Earth Spirit): somewhat disappointing in 1976: odds on for first two outings but went under by 2 lengths to Riboboy in Classic Trial at Sandown and ran well below his best when fourth of 11 to Trasi's Son in Mecca-Dante Stakes at York: about 2½ lengths fifth of eight to Radetzky in St James's Palace Stakes at Royal Ascot in June, final outing and probably best effort: stays 1¼m: possibly unsuited by soft ground: exported to U.S.A. and is in training with R. Laurin.   *H. Cecil.*

TAL   2 b.c. Appiani II 128–Matubelle (Jolly Jet 111)   [1976 5fg 5g⁵ 6g 7f 8g⁶ 8s²]   **83** well-made colt: first foal: dam won over 1½m in France and is half-sister to very smart Soderini: moderate maiden: ran best race when ¾-length second of 16 to Wester Win in maiden event at Bath in October: will stay at least 1½m: evidently best suited by soft going.   *S. Ingham.*

TALAREA   4 b.f. Takawalk II 125–Nemea 98 (Ommeyad 120)   [1974 N.R.   **74** 1975 6f⁶ 8g 6d 5g² 5d⁵ 5g 5g   1976 7fg⁴ 6f² 6g⁵ 5fg* 5.9fg 5s]   lengthy, useful-looking filly: quite a moderate handicapper: winner at Salisbury in September: stays 7f: appears to act on any going.   *M. Masson.*

TALL LAD   7 b.g. Twilight Alley 133–Diamond Rock 81 (Chamossaire)   [1974   **81** 16s³ 16g²   1975 N.R.   1976 14.6g 15f³ 16s* 16fg³ 16g² 18d*]   tall, strong gelding: fair handicapper: successful at Newcastle in April and Doncaster the following month: not seen out after winning by ¾ length from New Henry on last-named course: needs long distances: acts on any going: has worn bandages: suitable mount for a boy.   *Denys Smith.*

TALLULAH   3 ch.f. Richboy 117–Zulaika 75 (Worden II 129)   [1975 7g 6g   **59** 1976 12f 8f 8f⁴ 11f 7fg⁴ 8fg⁶ 8f* 10g 8.2s]   big, lengthy filly: only a poor per-former but won five-runner apprentice maiden event at Yarmouth in August by ¾ length from Fintalex: best form at 7f or 1m but runs as though she should be suited by further: acts on firm going.   *R. Bastiman.*

TAMALAN   3 b.f. John Splendid 116–Sylvan Rose (Quorum 126)   [1975 5s⁴ 5s³   — 5fg² 5g² 5f⁵ 5fg⁵ 5f 5fg   1976 7f⁵ 6d]   light-framed filly: has been tubed: showed some ability at 2 yrs but was well beaten in 1976: has plenty of early pace and may be best at 5f.   *T. Fairhurst.*

TAMALINDEN TILLIA   2 b.f. Linden Tree 127–Carina 98 (Tamerlane 128)   — [1976 5d 6s]   lengthy filly: half-sister to a winning plater in France by Le

Fabuleux: dam won over 5f at 2 yrs: unquoted when in rear in autumn in small races at Haydock (dwelt) and Chepstow. *H. Nicholson.*

TAMANACO 2 ch.c. Crowned Prince 128–Vela 123 (Sheshoon 132)   [1976 7s²]   **91** P
well-made colt: second foal: 15,000 gns yearling: dam high-class 2-y-o in France in 1969: 14/1, ran very promisingly when 3 lengths second to more-experienced Imperial Guard in 11-runner minor event at Sandown in October, being made to do only enough to hold second place once winner clearly had his measure: will stay 1½m: a very well-bred colt who looks sure to do a lot better. *R. Price*

TAMARISCIFOLIA 2 b.c. Ridan–War Lass 100 (Whistler 129)   [1976 5d⁵ **104**
5f* 5g³ 5f* 5f⁴]   Irish colt: half-brother to minor winners by Palestine and Charlottesville: 2,800 gns foal: dam won twice over 5f at 2 yrs: won 18-runner maiden plate at Mallow in June and landed the odds by ½ length from Fairhaven Lady in minor event at Phoenix Park in July: also in frame in two good races, finishing 2½ lengths third to Nebbiolo (gave 7 lb) in Curragh Stakes and 10 lengths fourth to Cloonlara in Phoenix Stakes: not seen out after August: should stay beyond 5f: blinkered final outing. *J. Murphy, Ireland.*

TAMASHOON 4 b.g. Sheshoon 132–Tamanoir (Vieux Manoir 132)   [1974 **69** §
N.R. 1975 17.7fg² 16s⁴ 13g⁴ 18g* 16s 12g³ 1976 15.8g² 15f* 13f 13g⁴ 14g⁴
17f² 17.7f⁶ 16fg² 15.5g⁴ 20g 16g 16.1d]   poor handicapper: successful at Teesside in April: ran creditably in some of his races afterwards, but refused to race on last two starts (blinkered final appearance) and clearly has a mind of his own nowadays: needs a test of stamina: best form on a sound surface, and may be unsuited by soft going. *P. Mitchell.*

TAMINGO 3 b.c. Never Say Die 137–Tambresi 89 (Tamerlane 128)   [1975 **67**
N.R. 1976 9fg* 10.2f² 12f³ 8fg⁶ 9g 8.2d 10f⁶ 9g³ 10f⁴ 11f* 12f³ 12f³ 10f⁵ 12fg⁴
10.8g 10f⁴]   workmanlike colt: second foal: 700 gns yearling: dam won at 7f and 1m: won newcomers race at Wolverhampton in April and three-runner handicap at Edinburgh in July: performed moderately on most of his other outings, including when tried in blinkers on one occasion: stays 1½m: acts on firm going: has worn a tongue strap. *M. Stevens.*

TAMMY'S GIRL 2 br.f. Tamerlane 128–Shimmering C 60 (Privy Councillor 125)   **60**
[1976 5fg⁶ 5f³ 5f 6fg² 6g⁶ 7f³ 5fg 6d⁶ 6v]   neat filly: placed in sellers at Warwick, Windsor and Wolverhampton: should stay 1¼m: blinkered eighth outing. *M. McCourt.*

TAMPA 3 b.c. Amber Rama 133–Caliante (Hugh Lupus 132)   [1975 5s* 6f³ **93**
7fg² 7.3g 1976 7g 8d 8g* 8fg⁴ 12fg 8s⁶ 7s³]   lengthy, light-framed colt, and a good mover: showed smart form at 2 yrs: put up easily best effort in 1976 when winning Excelsior Diamond Stakes (ladies race) at Ascot in July, making virtually all and holding off Welsh Flame by ¾ length: stays 1m well (ran badly under a very stiff weight over 1½m): best form on a sound surface: sold 7,000 gns Newmarket December Sales: exported to U.S.A. *P. Cole.*

TAMSIN 2 br.f. Tamerlane 128–Beach Belle (Raise You Ten 125)   [1976 5g 5g² **60**
5f 7h⁶ 7f 7.2f 8fg 7s]   sharp sort: showed a little ability on two of her early-season runs but was well beaten in sellers on last few outings: blinkered sixth outing: sold 330 gns Doncaster October Sales. *J. Edwards.*

TANAKA 2 b.f. Tapalque 126–Nyanga (Never Say Die 137)   [1976 6f³ 8fg²]   **99**+
half-sister to high-class 1¼m to 2½m performer Mistigri (by Misti IV): dam won twice at 1¼m in France: odds on for seven-runner minor event at Goodwood in September but went down by a short head to Lucent after a really good last-furlong battle: will need at least 1¼m and should stay well. *P. Walwyn.*

TANARO 2 b.c. High Top 131–Nellie (Sing Sing 134)   [1976 7s]   big, strong   **– p**
colt: half-brother to two 2-y-o winners, including 1975 6f winner Peta (by Petingo), and to two winners abroad: 18,000 gns yearling: dam, placed at 2 yrs, is half-sister to numerous winners: unquoted and very much in need of race, faded in straight when remote seventh of 11 to Imperial Guard in minor event at Sandown in October: likely to do much better at 3 yrs. *B. Swift.*

TANDLE HILL 2 b.c. Blast 125–Patel 101 (Constable 129)   [1976 5g]   half-   **–**
brother to a winning plater: dam a sprinter: backward when in rear in 14-runner maiden event at Ripon in April, only outing. *Hbt Jones.*

TANELLA 3 b.f. Habitat 134–Nanette 100 (Worden II 129)   [1975 5g* 5h² **100**
5.6g³ 6fg* 6fg² 7g 1976 6f⁵ 7s 6fg 7fg⁶ 6f⁵ 6f³ 6f³]   shapely, attractive, good-

bodied filly: useful handicapper: will stay 1m: acts on firm going and did not move particularly well to post on soft ground on second outing: tried in blinkers on fifth appearance. *M. Jarvis.*

TANTALOS 4 ch.g. Sayfar 116–Tantalizing (Polly's Jet) [1974 7v 7fg 7g 7s 8d 1975 10.5g⁶ 10.4g⁵ 9fg³ 10.4f² 12g 12f* 12d 12d⁴ 12g⁶ 1976 12fg³ 16f² 14g⁴ 12g 17.7f 12fg³ 14.5f] compact gelding: poor handicapper: stays 2m: acts on firm going: suitable mount for an apprentice. *R. Mason.*   **52**

TANWEN 2 gr.f. Firestreak 125–Riccardi 68 (Roan Rocket 128) [1976 5g 6h⁶ 5h⁵ 8s 7s 7v⁶] first produce: 420 gns foal: dam ran only at 2 yrs: showed a little ability in maiden and minor events: stays 7f and should get 1m. *D. Dartnall.*   **72**

TAPSALTERRIE 2 br.c. On Your Mark 125–Circumstance 72 (Bleep-Bleep 134) [1976 5fg 5f 5f⁴] of no account: sold 240 gns Ascot June Sales. *M. Smyly.*   **—**

TARACROSS 4 b.c. Tamerlane 128–Harolds Cross 111 (Tudor Jinks 121) [1974 5g³ 7s 7g 5s² 1975 7d⁵ 6s² 5d² 6s* 5.8f³ 6g³ 6g 6d 5g 1976 8s 6s⁴] rangy colt: ran only twice at 4 yrs: best form at sprint distances: acts on any going: excellent mount for an apprentice. *M. Stevens.*   **64**

TARRADEEN 5 ch.g. Aberdeen 109–Tarragon (Javelot 124) [1974 10g 8f⁴ 8fg 1975 N.R. 1976 7f] of little account. *M. Killoran.*   **—**

TARROPEKE 2 gr.c. Good Bond 122–Pen Friend 90 (Vigo 130) [1976 8g 8.2f 8s] strong, deep-bodied, robust colt: good walker: half-brother to three winners, including 3-y-o 6f winner Perfect Gentleman (by Breeders Dream): 1,600 gns yearling: dam best at 6f or 7f: well beaten in maiden races at Ayr (very backward), Hamilton and Newmarket (14/1): a taking individual who looks capable of a good deal better. *Denys Smith.*   **— p**

TARTAN RIVER 2 br.c. Another River 89–Tarsets (Firestreak 125) [1976 5g 8g] neat colt: second live foal: dam ran only once: never troubled leaders in maiden race at Catterick in September (burly) and minor event at Lanark in October. *W. A. Stephenson.*   **—**

TARTAR PRINCE 9 ch.g. Fury Royal 108–Royal Cham (Chamossaire) [1974 15.5f³ 16.1fg² 22.2fg 1975 N.R. 1976 16d⁵ 13v⁶ 14d³] fair handicapper (rated 89) in 1974: not raced again until September 1976 but showed he still retains some of his ability when third to Unsuspected at Newmarket in October: stays very well: appears to act on any going: has twice worn blinkers. *T. Waugh.*   **77**

TARTE NORMANDE 2 br.f. Continuation 120–Apple Brandy 100 (Arctic Prince 135) [1976 5g] half-sister to several winners, including useful middle-distance performers Honfleur and Black Velvet (both by Hethersett): 1,000 gns yearling: dam won over 5f at 2 yrs: behind in 24-runner maiden race at Leicester in May, only outing: sold 700 gns Newmarket Autumn Sales. *J. Powney.*   **—**

TAW VALLEY 3 b.g. Siliconn 121–Senecio 76 (Sammy Davis 129) [1975 5s 5v⁵ 5s 6g 1976 8.3f 5g 5h] sprint plater: no worthwhile form in 1976, including when tried in blinkers: refused to race on final outing. *J. Hill.*   **—**

TAX DONATION 2 br.f. Don II 123–Surtax (Helioscope) [1976 5.1fg 7fg 5.3f² 6h⁴ 5.1f⁴] lightly-made filly: plater: 3 lengths second of seven to The Triplets in claiming race at Brighton in August, best effort: should stay 1m: sold 350 gns Ascot October Sales. *J. Winter.*   **63**

TEABAG 6 b.g. Ragusa 137–Singapura 103 (Grey Sovereign 128 §) [1974 N.R. 1975 N.R. 1976 18.1g] useless. *P. Arthur.*   **—**

TEARS OF JOY 2 ch.g. Doon 124–Royal Tears 55 (Weepers Boy 124) [1976 5g 5g 6fg 6fg 7fg 7s] second foal: dam won 7f seller at 3 yrs: plating-class maiden: will stay 1m. *R. Smyth.*   **68**

TEASE 2 b.g. Maystreak 118–Playful 56 (Right Boy 137) [1976 6s] first foal: dam of little account: 25/1 when behind in 24-runner minor event won by Tudor Jig at Teesside in November. *W. Elsey.*   **—**

TEASIE FORMULA TOO 2 br.f. Comedy Star 121–First Gain (Psidium 130) [1976 6fg² 6h⁴] plater: 1½ lengths second of four to odds-on Huleh Valley at Yarmouth in June: ran badly at Lingfield later in month: sold 400 gns Ascot July Sales. *A. Pitt.*   **50**

TEASING WIND 5 ch h. Whistling Wind 123–Agla (Preciptic 122) [1974 7fg 8fg 9fg⁴ 9.4fg² 10g⁴ 8f² 9g⁶ 10.2v³ 8s⁵ 10g⁴ 12s⁶ 1975 10f 12fg⁴ 12h⁵ 12d 17.1f 1976 8.2fg⁶] lengthy, well-grown horse: poor handicapper nowadays: seems to stay 1½m: acts on any going: suitable mount for an apprentice: has been tried in blinkers. *D. H. Jones.*   **—**

TEDDINGTON PARK 2 b.c. Mill Reef 141–Hecla 117 (Henry the Seventh 125) **107 §**
[1976 5fg² 5d* 6f⁵ 6fg⁶ 6fg² 6g⁶ 7s] very attractive colt: good mover: second
foal: half-brother to 1975 2-y-o 6f winner Handa (by Roan Rocket): 75,000 gns
yearling: dam, a smart performer over 6f at 2 yrs, is half-sister to very speedy
fillies Mange Tout and Rose Dubarry: odds on, made all and put up a very
smooth performance indeed when beating Showpiece by 2½ lengths in 10-runner
maiden event at Sandown in June: subsequently didn't fulfil the high hopes held
of him but is a useful colt, as he showed when second of 15 under top weight in
nursery won by Ribosa at Salisbury in September: should stay 1m: gave the
impression on occasions of being none too genuine and wore blinkers on fifth
and sixth outings: exported to U.S.A. *I. Balding.*

TEEOFF 2 b.f. Forlorn River 124–Golf Ball (Persian Gulf) [1976 5f 6f 6g² **74**
6s² 8s 8s 8v²] small filly: half-sister to very useful Irish performer Bunkered
(by Entanglement), winner from 6f to 1¼m: dam won over 10.5f in France:
close-up second in sellers at Goodwood (two) and Leicester: stays 1m and may
get further: suited by some give in the ground and acts on heavy going. *R.
Jarvis.*

TELAKA 3 b.f. Fair Decision 93 §–Cuckmere Queen 60 (Perfect Sovereign) —
[1975 N.R. 1976 8.2f 13fg] plain filly: fourth foal: dam won poor 5f seller
at 2 yrs: well beaten in maiden races at Nottingham in the summer. *W. Clay.*

TELESTAR 2 b.c. Irish Ball 127–Fair Rosamond (Owen Tudor) [1976 5g **71**
6fg 6fg 7f⁴ 8f 8s 10v⁵] half-brother to three winners, including very useful
miler Ros Rock (by Rockefella): 2,100 gns yearling: dam unraced half-sister
to Best Song: only plating class: should stay 1¼m. *W. Wightman.*

TELEX BOY 2 b.c. Communication 119–Samia 73 (Galivanter 131) [1976 **76**
5f⁵ 5fg 5f⁴ 5.3fg³ 6g² 6fg 6g] compact colt: third foal: 700 gns yearling: dam
poor maiden: quite moderate: neck second of 22 to Our Travelling Man in maiden
auction event at Kempton in July: last in nursery at Windsor on next outing:
stays 6f well: sold 420 gns Ascot November Sales. *W. Wightman.*

TELL MICHELLE 2 b.f. Tell–Madam Michelle (Francis S) [1976 7g⁶ 7s⁶] **79**
attractive American-bred filly: half-sister to stakes-placed Alota Calories (by
Candy Spots), successful at up to 1m: dam, unplaced in five starts, is half-sister

Mrs Eric Phillips' "Teddington Park"

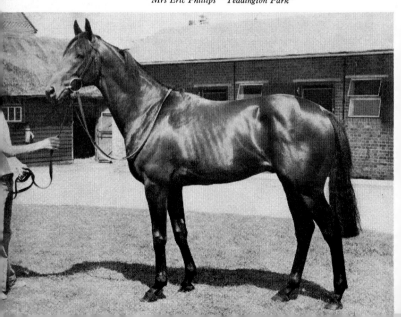

to several good winners, including Paris Review: showed promise when sixth in large fields of maidens at Newmarket in October, being beaten 7 lengths by Nobodys Fool and 8 lengths by Lady Oriana: will stay middle distances: likely to improve and win races. *B. Hanbury.*

TEMPEST 2 ch.f. Caliban 123–Pinwave 82 (Pinza 137) [1976 5f 5f 8f 8.2h4] **57** neat, short-coupled filly: half-sister to useful 3-y-o 1¼m winner Wire Up (by Firestreak): quite a moderate plater: will stay 1½m+: sold 420 gns Ascot November Sales. *Denys Smith.*

TEMPEST GIRL 3 b.f. Caliban 123–Scorton Court 65 (Le Levanstell 122) **68** [1975 6g 6g 1976 10.8fg 10.4d6 10fg 13.4fg4 10.4fg3 10fg4] strong filly: in frame in maiden races: best form at 1¼m: acts on a firm and an easy surface. *H. Nicholson.*

TEMPLA 2 b.f. Green God 128–Tin Saint 99 (Tin Whistle 128) [1976 5d 5fg5 **74** 5f2 5f2 5h3 5g3 5.9fg 5s4] neat filly: in frame in maiden races, running well when 3¾ lengths fourth of 13 to Selenis at Nottingham in September: stays 6f: acts on any going. *W. Wharton.*

TEMPTING PRINCE 2 b.g. Le Prince 98–Temptation (Milesian 125) [1976 **64** 7f 7h 8v4] brother to a moderate winning stayer: favourite and sweating when 1½ lengths fourth of 14 to Grey Blossom in seller at Leicester in November. *B. Swift.*

TENNIS BALL 2 gr.f. Charlottown 127–Some Tune 96 (Tin Whistle 128) [1976 **61** 5g 5f 5.8f2 5fg 5s] third live produce: 2,700 gns yearling: dam won over 5f at 2 yrs and is sister to very speedy Decoy Boy: ran best race when 2 lengths second to Jackie's Promise in seller at Bath in June: off course three months afterwards and was then well beaten in non-sellers: should stay 1m. *J. Hill.*

TERRAN ROYAL 3 br.f. Right Royal V 135–Pen-Emma 112 (Pindari 124) — [1975 N.R. 1976 9f 12d6 10f] half-sister to quite useful sprinter Pol Na Chree (by Princely Gift) and to a winner in France by Stupendous: 520 gns yearling: dam at her best at 2 yrs, when winner at 6f: well beaten in early-season maiden races. *L. Shedden.*

TERREGLES 6 br.g. Bargello–Punchestown Lass (King Hal) [1974 12f 16g2 — 16g* 16f3 14g 16g2 17v3 1975 16f4 1976 14.7f 12f3 12.2f4] ex-Irish gelding: poor staying handicapper: slipped and unseated rider on reappearance (amateur riders event): acts on firm going: has been tried in blinkers. *J. Cousins.*

TERRINE 3 br.c. Klairon 131–Elaine 90 (Mossborough 126) [1975 6f 8fg 7g **63** 7g3 8g4 8v5 1976 11v3 12f4 16g 14fg2 15.8f5 15.8f4 12f6] compact colt: modest plater: ran poorly last two outings: stays 1¾m: best form on a sound surface: occasionally wears blinkers: sold 3,100 gns Newmarket Autumn Sales. *S. Hall.*

TERVEY BOY 2 b.c. Major Portion 129–Beryl's Song 86 (Sing Sing 134) [1976 — 6fg 6v 6d] first foal: dam showed fair form as a 2-y-o: behind in large fields of maidens. *W. Wightman.*

THATCHED HOUSE LAD 3 b.g. Frigid Aire–Final Slipper (His Slipper) — [1975 5s 5g 6h3 5g 7h 1976 13.8g 11v4 10f5 15.8f6] light-framed gelding: poor plater: often wears blinkers: sold 320 gns Doncaster May Sales. *M. Naughton.*

THATS CHAR-LOTTE 2 ch.f. Virginia Boy 106–Straw Lady (Set Fair 129) **51** [1976 6f 7g 7s6] lightly-made, useful-looking filly: fifth foal: 140 gns yearling: dam never ran: little worthwhile form. *R. Hannon.*

THE ANDRESTAN 2 br.c. The Brianstan 128–Nimble Gate 64 (Nimbus 130) **112** [1976 5fg 5fg* 5d4 5f3 5fg* 5g3 5fg* 5fg2 5d5] strong, well-made, very taking individual: half-brother to a winning plater by Remainder: 600 gns foal, resold 2,300 gns yearling: dam won 5f seller at 2 yrs: a very useful and speedy 2-y-o who won at Lingfield, Sandown (Star Stakes) and Windsor: put up a fine effort on last-named course in £1,800 event in July, leading 2f out and holding off odds-on Royal Diver by ½ length: also placed in three good races, finishing 6½ lengths third to Godswalk in Norfolk Stakes at Royal Ascot, 4 lengths third to Piney Ridge (rec 7 lb) in National Stakes at Sandown, and length second to Haveroid in Prince of Wales's Stakes at York: will stay 6f: probably not at his best on an easy surface: thoroughly genuine. *J. Sutcliffe.*

THE ASSASSINATOR 4 gr.g. Runnymede 123–Consuelo 81 (Donatello II) **51** [1974 6fg 6fg 7g 7s 7s3 8v5 1975 7v3 8g5 7d2 7fg6 8f 8g5 10d5 1976 8fg3] light-framed gelding: plater: ran well on only outing at 4 yrs: probably stays 1m but not 1¼m: seems to act on any going: sold 310 gns Ascot April Sales. *R. Akehurst.*

THE AUCTIONEER 2 br.c. Mansingh 120–Rose's Leader (Damremont 120) **70**
[1976 5fg 6fg 5f5 6g6] rangy colt: ran best race when about 3 lengths fifth to
Trossachs in maiden race at Folkestone in July: ran poorly in seller on next
appearance and wasn't seen out again: possibly does not stay 6f: blinkered last
two outings. *J. Sutcliffe.*

THE BAKER 6 ch.g. Super Sam 124–Azizah (Zarathustra 131) [1974 13g5 16g **82**
12g4 10f2 10d* 10g 10g* 10.2g4 10d2 1975 11.7f 10f 10h* 10fg2 10fg4 10f 1976
10h3 10f6 10h5] well-made gelding: quite a moderate handicapper nowadays:
ran creditably on reappearance: best form at 1¼m, although stays much further:
probably acts on any going: has been tried in blinkers: unseated rider and
galloped riderless before start on final outing. *D. Gandolfo.*

THE BLEEZAR 2 br.g. So Blessed 130–Sky Hostess 72 (Skymaster 126) [1976 —
6f5 6h3 6s 6s] first foal: dam tough performer at around 1m: no worthwhile form
in maiden and minor events. *J. Turner.*

THE BOWLER 2 b.c. Bold Lad (Ire) 133–Jabula 99 (Sheshoon 132) [1976 **96**
5fg3 5fg2 5f* 5d6 5g4 7f* 7f* 8g5 8fg3 7s2] strong, useful sort: half-brother to
quite useful 1971 2-y-o 5f winner Tudabula (by Tudor Melody): 5,400 gns yearling: dam winner at up to 1½m: won maiden event at Bath in April and showed a
return to form when beating Rostov a neck in minor race at Redcar in July:
gained another win at Catterick later in July, scoring by 1½ lengths from Wayland
Prince: ran respectably afterwards: will probably stay 1¼m: seems to act on any
going: blinkered fourth outing (ran moderately). *B. Hills.*

THE BROTHERS 3 b.g. Forlorn River 124–Sombrilla (Big Game) [1975 5g5 **75**
5g6 5g2 5f 5d 1976 8.2g 9f 7f* 6f* 6h2 6g4 6d] useful plater: winner twice at
Redcar in July (bought in 700 gns on second occasion): creditable second to
Movie Idol in non-selling handicap at Carlisle the following month: effective at
6f and 7f: acts on hard ground: blinkered final outing in 1975: has worn a muzzle.
W. Haigh.

THE CORAL HORSE 2 ch.c. Lorenzaccio 130–Willowtale 103 (Olein's Grace **73**
127) [1976 5fg 7fg 7g] well-grown, lengthy colt: good mover: half-brother
to three winners, including useful stayer Sea Tale (by Sea Hawk II): bought
privately for 5,000 gns as a yearling: dam won at up to 1¼m in Ireland: showed
ability on first outing but was then well beaten in maiden races: should be suited
by middle distances. *H. T. Jones.*

THE CULSTAN 2 b.c. The Brianstan 128–Gimima 54 (Narrator 127) [1976 5g —
5.8f5] poor plater. *J. Sutcliffe.*

THE CZAR 2 ch.c. Royal Palace 131–Nagaika 117 (Goyama 127) [1976 7f 7f4 **117**
7d* 8v*]
A top-notch racehorse who has been given every chance at stud, Royal Palace
has been most disappointing as a sire. With the exception of the very smart filly

Leyburn Stakes, York—The Czar wins from Lucent (far side) and Repique

Antrona and to a lesser degree of Sultans Ruby, runner-up to Sporting Yankee in the William Hill Futurity, none of his stock has revealed outstanding merit on the racecourse. But in Royal Boxer and The Czar Royal Palace has two nice colts from good racemares who could do well in 1977, The Czar having the better form at two years. And even The Czar, a half-brother to that good horse Connaught, suffers, it seems, from a touch of the 'slows', for it wasn't until he was provided with a test of stamina on soft ground on his last two outings that he really showed what he could do. Making his third appearance on the racecourse, The Czar won the Monument Stakes, a £1,500 race, at Yarmouth in September by half a length and the same from Elland Road and Great Oak, the latter of whom was conceding him 10 lb. This was useful form, and better was to follow. In the Leyburn Stakes, run over a mile under extremely testing conditions at York the following month, The Czar battled on gamely over the last two furlongs to hold off Lucent and Repique in a driving finish during the course of which the three horses came right away from the rest of the field. The merit of The Czar's performance here was underlined a month later when Lucent hacked up under similar conditions from a field which included Bow-Wow, Whitby Jet, Forage and Welsh Dancer in the Guys and Dolls Stakes at Doncaster.

		Royal Palace (b 1964)	Ballymoss (ch 1954)	Mossborough
The Czar (ch.c. 1974)				Indian Call
			Crystal Palace (b 1956)	Solar Slipper
				Queen of Light
		Nagaika (ch 1954)	Goyama (ch 1943)	Goya
				Devineress
			Naim (ch 1946)	Amfortas
				Nacelle

The Czar's dam, Nagaika, who wasn't far short of classic standard, stayed well: she won the Solario Stakes over seven furlongs as a two-year-old, and the Princess Royal Stakes at a mile and a half as a three-year-old. In addition to Connaught, Nagaika has bred Court Sentence (by Court Martial) who won the St James's Palace Stakes over a mile at Ascot on his only appearance at three years, and several other winners, including The Czar's full sister Empress of Russia, who won at a mile and a half. The Czar is a much better racehorse than was Empress of Russia, but he is not in Connaught's class nor likely to be. A mile will be too short for him as a three-year-old, but in handicap or second-class company over distances or under conditions which call for stamina and a stout, fighting heart he should never be left out. It will be as well to remember that he has yet to show his form on firm ground. *T. Waugh.*

THE DANSTAN 3 br.f. The Brianstan 128–Flame Dancer 72 (Hop Bridge 87) **63** [1975 5fg⁶ 5g⁶ 6g 5fg* 5g⁶ 6fg 6f 1976 6fg³ 5fg³ 6h⁵ 6f³ 6fg⁵ 6f³ 6h⁴ 7g 6v] small, sturdy filly: good third to Pams Gleam in handicap at Catterick in August: stays 6f: acts on firm going: ran moderately in blinkers on second and third outings. *J. W. Watts.*

THE DON 2 gr.c. Busted 134–Donna 118 (Donore 119) [1976 7fg⁶ 7g 7s⁵] **95** well-made, attractive colt: brother to useful 1972 2-y-o Busted Flush, and half-brother to numerous winners, notably 1,000 Guineas runner-up Gwen (by Aber-nant): 21,000 gns yearling: dam smart at up to 7f: 20/1, took some time to get going but then ran on well to finish 3½ lengths sixth of eight to Sky Ship in Lanson Champagne Stakes at Goodwood in July: didn't fulfil the promise of that run and again took some time to find his stride when 9 lengths fifth behind Imperial Guard in minor event at Sandown in October: will be suited by 1¼m+. *J. Dunlop.*

THE DUNDASS 2 b.c. Amber Rama 133–Khazaeen (Charlottesville 135) [1976 **89** 5fg 5fg* 5f² 5fg² 5fg* 5f⁵ 7f²] sharp sort: first foal: 700 gns yearling: dam unraced half-sister to very smart French colt Afayoon: winner of seller at Wolver-hampton in April (bought in 900 gns) and minor event at Brighton the following month: close-up second in three other races, going down by ½ length to Danish King in minor race at Brighton in July on final outing: will stay at least 1m: consistent *R. Hannon.*

THE DURCOTT 2 br.c. Irish Ball 127–Miss Jeanette 91 (Sheshoon 132) [1976 **67** 6h⁵ 7f⁵ 6g 8s 10v⁶] lengthy colt: third foal: dam game stayer: only plating class: should stay well: trained by G. Hunter first three outings. *D. Dale.*

THE FIXING 2 br.c. Pieces of Eight 128–Bright Spark 65 (White Fire III) **80** [1976 5.1g⁴ 6fg⁴ 6fg⁶ 8.2d 7d⁶] light-framed filly: first foal: dam, poor maiden, is half-sister to smart animals Ovaltine and Guillotina: moderate maiden:

blinkered first time, ran creditably when sixth of 13 to Jenny Splendid in £2,000 nursery at Newmarket in October on last outing: suited by 7f and should stay at least 1m: probably acts on a firm and a soft surface: sold 2,200 gns Newmarket Autumn Sales. *B. Hobbs.*

THE FLYING FILLY 3 b.f. My Swallow 134–Nettling 85 (Vimy 132) [1975 7g 1976 10f 12fg 16d 12g⁵ 16f³] plating-class maiden: ran easily best race on final outing and is evidently suited by a test of stamina: blinkered last two appearances: sold 1,000 gns Newmarket September Sales. *T. Molony.* **56**

THE FOUR HUNDRED 3 gr.g. Pall Mall 132–Dark Dolores 83 (I Say 125) [1975 5f 6fg³ 6fg 6g 1976 6fg 8fg³ 10fg³ 8f* 10.2h² 12h³ 11.7d⁴ 8d*] lengthy gelding: won maiden race at Bath in June and claiming event at Newmarket in October, latter by 4 lengths from Friendly Builder: best form at up to 1¼m: appears to act on any going: blinkered penultimate appearance. *H. Williams.* **81**

THE FRUMMER 3 b.g. Prince Tenderfoot 126–Blue Saree (Sayajirao 132) [1975 5d 5fg 5g 1976 8fg 6fg² 8fg*] strong gelding: dead-heated with Fly High in maiden race at Brighton in June: stays 1m: acts on a firm surface. *R. Smyth.* **70**

THE FUZZ 2 ch.c. Frankincense 120–Clytemnestra 81 (Bullrush 106) [1976 5fg 5fg 5f⁵ 6fg³ 6g 6v] good-looking colt: good mover: third foal: half-brother to 3-y-o 1¼m winner Grecian Bond (by Good Bond) and very useful sprinter King of Troy (by King's Troop): 3,100 gns yearling: dam a sprinter: length third of 15 to Pearldor in maiden race at Windsor in August: last in nurseries at Leicester on both outings afterwards: stays 6f well. *B. Swift.* **81**

THE GARDEN 2 ch.f. Gulf Pearl 117–Miss Holborn (Pall Mall 132) [1976 7g 7s³] sister to two winners, including useful 1m and 1¼m winner Saffron Hill: 4,200 gns yearling: dam sister to very smart sprinter Holborn: about 3 lengths third of 20 to Brightly in maiden race at Newmarket in October: will probably stay 1¼m. *Doug Smith.* **83**

THE GOD DAUGHTER 2 b.f. Balidar 133–Squirrel 91 (White Fire III) [1976 5g⁶ 5f 7fg² 7g³ 7g⁵ 8.2f 8v⁵ 8g⁴ 8v⁴] compact filly: first reported foal: dam won twice over 6f at 2 yrs: in frame in a Newmarket seller and northern maiden races: beaten just over 3 lengths when fourth of 20 to Harriet Air at Lanark in October: stays 1m: wears blinkers: trained by K. Payne on first three outings. *T. Craig.* **73**

THE GOLDSTONE 4 ch.g. Murrayfield 119–Delph 89 (Final Score 113) [1974 5g 5g⁵ 6g⁵ 5s⁵ 6fg⁴ 5.8s 7s⁴ 7s* 6d⁴ 7.3s 1975 7d⁴ 7s⁵ 8s⁴ 6s 5f⁵ 6f³ 7f 6fg⁵ 6g⁶ 8g² 8g* 8g⁵ 7d* 1976 8g 7g 7f⁵ 7.6f⁵ 7fg⁵ 7g⁴ 8f 7f 8f* 8g* 7fg⁵ 8g 8.2v² 8s 8s³] strong, compact gelding: fair handicapper on his day: won ladies race at Goodwood in August (valuable Waterford Rosebowl Handicap) by 2 lengths from Esprit d'Or, hanging badly left inside final furlong: ran on well when beating Sweet Reclaim ¾ length at Sandown the following month: stays 1m well: acts on any going: ran respectably when tried in blinkers: suitable mount for an inexperienced race-rider. *W. Wightman.* **86**

THE GRANDSON 5 br.g. Prince Hansel 118–Raggoty Ann 93 (Bright News) [1974 10.8g⁵ 10.8fg² 10fg³ 10g⁵ 1975 8v³ 10f 10g² 12f³ 8fg⁵ 1976 7f 12fg] compact gelding: poor handicapper: possibly finds 1m on fast ground on sharp side for him but has yet to prove he stays 1½m: appears to act on any going: best in blinkers (didn't wear them in 1976). *J. Gibson.* **—**

THE GRIGGLE 5 b.g. Crocket 130–Tamatha (Ridan) [1974 10d⁶ 12fg 12fg² 14s³ 14g* 12g* 1975 16d 1976 12f³ 14g² 16.9f*] lengthy gelding: very good mover: quite a moderate handicapper: well-backed second favourite, made all when winning at Wolverhampton in August by 2½ lengths from Hill Station: stays well: acts on firm going: good mount for an amateur. *G. Harwood.* **69**

THE GUVNOR 4 gr.c. Sahib 114–Right Beam 62 (Right Boy 137) [1974 5g³ 5g* 6g 6g² 7.3d 5s⁶ 1975 6v⁴ 6g 5.8f* 6g 6fg⁶ 6v⁵ 7d 7g 1976 7d⁴ 7.6fg⁴ 7fg 8g⁴ 6s* 7fg 7f³ 8f* 7fg³ 8fg 8.2f 8f 8fg] tall, strong colt: moderate handicapper: successful at Doncaster in May and Edinburgh in July: stays 1m: acts on any going: no worthwhile form last four outings (blinkered final appearance). *W. Marshall.* **81**

THE HAND 3 ch.c. Song 132–La Foire II 90 (Arabian) [1975 6fg 5g⁶ 6fg² 1976 7fg 7fg² 7s² 8f* 8f* 12g³ 12fg²] strong, muscular colt: good mover: won maiden race at Doncaster in July (unimpressively landed the odds) and amateur riders race at Newmarket the following month (unchallenged by 10 lengths): **103**

placed on all but one of his other starts, including when very good short-head second to Fighting Lady in Glenlivet Handicap at Newmarket and when respectable third to Ivory Girl in Fitzwilliam Stakes at Doncaster in September: effective at 7f to 1½m: possibly best suited by a sound surface (didn't go down particularly well on soft ground on third outing and ran slightly below his best after a slowish start). *J. Hindley.*

THE HAPPY HOOKER 5 gr.m. Town Crier 119–Legal Love 105 (King's Bench 132) [1974 7f 6g 7fg 6g² 8s⁴ 7fg³ 7s² 8s 7s* 8.2v* 1975 8s* 7v* 8s³ 7g* 8fg⁵ 8f 8f 7.2fg³ 7.2fg* 7.3d* 7.2s* 8.2d³ 8.2s 1976 8f⁵ 7fg⁴ 8g* 8.2g⁵ 8.5g² 8.2f² 8fg⁶ 7fg* 7.3d⁵ 9g 8.2v 8v²] big mare: useful handicapper: winner twice at 5 yrs, beating London Glory a short head in Ayr 400th Anniversary Handicap in May and Chukaroo the same margin when successful at Salisbury in September: had some other good efforts to her credit, including when dead-heating for eighth place behind Intermission in Irish Sweeps Cambridgeshire at Newmarket in October on tenth outing: stays 9f: acts on any going but goes particularly well in the mud: ran poorly when tried in blinkers: very game, genuine and consistent. *P. Cundell.* **94**

THE HEADMAN 3 br.g. Tribal Chief 125–July Mist 79 (High Treason 126) [1975 5d² 5s* 5s² 5fg² 5g⁶ 6d⁶ 6fg 6g⁵ 6d 5g⁵ 1976 6g³ 6fg 6fg 7fg 7h 6fg 6h⁵ 5.9fg 5.8f² 7s* 8v 6.5g] compact gelding: plater nowadays: attracted no bid after winning narrowly at Brighton in October when trained by B. Swift: subsequently ran unplaced in non-selling company at Lyon: stays 7f: acts on any going: wears blinkers. *P. Swann, France.* **71**

THE HERTFORD 5 b.g. Supreme Sovereign 119–Emerald Velvet 76 (Sheshoon 132) [1974 7s* 8.5g⁴ 8fg 7g 8g 8.3fg⁵ 7.6g 1975 8.3fg 8d⁴ 8g* 8v* 7f⁶ 1976 8g* 8g* 8f 7fg⁶ 8g⁵ 8fg⁵ 8g⁶ 9g²] strong, attractive gelding: useful handicapper: produced a good turn of foot when winning Irish Sweeps Lincoln at Doncaster in March (by a length from Quizair) and William Hill Easter Handicap on same course the following month (beat Ardoon ¾ length): ran by far his best subsequent race and put up a cracking effort into the bargain, when going down by the narrowest of margins to Intermission in Irish Sweeps Cambridgeshire at Newmarket in October, just failing to catch winner: stays 9f: evidently acts on any going: sometimes loses ground at the start. *B. Swift.* **107**

THEIA 3 b.f. Caro 133–Cavadonga (Dan Cupid 132) [1975 6g* 6.5d* 8s* 1976 9.5fg* 10g² 10.5d⁶ 10g³ 10.5d* 12s⁵ 9s⁴ 10d] French filly: fourth foal: half-sister to three winners, including useful stayers Pallante (by Taj Dewan) and Astreus (by Sheshoon): dam ran only at 2 yrs when successful over 6f: best 2-y-o filly in France in 1975 and was unbeaten in three races, including Criterium des Pouliches at Longchamp: picked up two Group 3 events at Longchamp in 1976, Prix Vanteaux in April by a head from Elise Ma Belle and Prix de la Nonette in September by ⅓ length from Antrona: put in her place however by the best French fillies, finishing ¾-length second to Riverqueen in Prix Saint-Alary, just over 2½ lengths fifth to Lagunette in Prix Vermeille and 5 lengths fourth to Dona Barod in Prix de l'Opera, all also at Longchamp and **117**

Irish Sweeps Lincoln Handicap, Doncaster—The Hertford produces a good turn of foot to beat Quizair and Galiano (No. 5)

Mr B. Shine's "The Hertford" (G. Lewis)

when about 7 lengths sixth to Pawneese in Prix Diane at Chantilly: never seen with chance when ninth of 19 behind Vitiges in Champion Stakes at Newmarket in October on only appearance in this country: evidently stays 1½m: appears to act on any going. *R. Touflan, France.*

THE LAIBON 2 b.g. Lorenzaccio 130–Isadora Duncan (Primera 131) [1976   —
7g 8s] compact gelding: first foal: 6,000 gns yearling: dam placed at 3 yrs in France: beaten some way in minor event at Kempton in August and Sandown in October. *M. Jarvis.*

THE MAGI 3 b.g. Frankincense 120–Borage 77 (Cagire II 122) [1975 7fg 7d 7g   —
1976 14fg 8s] compact gelding: no worthwhile form in varied company but had stiff tasks in 1976. *H. Payne.*

THE MALTINGS 5 ch.g. Gala Performance–Refrain (Crocket 130) [1974 6g²   —
8f* 8g* 8g² 8f² 8f³ 8g* 9d 10.2g³ 7v   1975 8fg² 10d⁶ 12s 8g⁶ 7f⁵ 8fg* 8fg⁵ 8g⁶
9f⁴ 12h² 10fg⁵ 8g 8g   1976 7f] formerly quite a useful handicapper: well beaten since eleventh outing in 1975: evidently stays 1¼m: acts on hard going and has run creditably once on softish ground: sometimes dwells at start: carries his head rather high. *C. Davies.*

THE MINSTREL 2 ch.c. Northern Dancer–Fleur (Victoria Park) [1976 6f* **130**
7g* 7d*]
This is where we say that it is our opinion that the leading two-year-olds of 1976 were a better collection than their 1975 counterparts, and that The Minstrel, the unbeaten winner of the William Hill Dewhurst Stakes, was the equal of any two-year-old in England and Ireland, with Blushing Groom his only superior in France. By our reckoning, The Minstrel gave a first-class display when winning the Dewhurst Stakes, and in the likely absence of Blushing Groom and with J. O. Tobin in the States, he is the one they all have to beat in the

William Hill Dewhurst Stakes, Newmarket—The Minstrel, neck outstretched, wins in good style from Saros

Two Thousand Guineas. How he comes to receive only 8-13 in the Two-Year-Old Free Handicap we cannot imagine.

The Minstrel, a flashy chesnut with four white feet, came to this country in October for the Dewhurst Stakes the winner in the previous month of two races in Ireland, the Moy Stakes for maidens over six furlongs at the Curragh and the Group 3 Larkspur Stakes over seven furlongs at Leopardstown. Such was his reputation that he was made a 9/4 on favourite for the Moy Stakes, despite the presence in a field of twelve of Mississippi, beaten only a length in the Group 3 Anglesey Stakes on his previous appearance. Mississippi was good enough to win most maiden races and he was good enough here to beat the rest of the Moy Stakes field by twelve lengths, but he was no match at all for The Minstrel, who raced right away from him inside the last two furlongs to win in two-year-old course record time by five lengths. The Minstrel ran to a rating of 116, which is a very high figure indeed for a two-year-old racing for the first time. He did not run to 116 in the Larkspur Stakes, but then he didn't have to. Captain James, the best of his seven opponents in a field which included the Coventry Stakes runner-up Lordedaw, was conceding him 5 lb, and Piggott, who was riding The Minstrel for the first time, was quite content to let the colt come through smoothly in the last furlong to win by a length.

On the strength of these performances The Minstrel was all the rage for the Dewhurst Stakes, at £37,195.70 the country's most valuable race for first-season horses. Of his ten opponents, only Saros, who had created a favourable impression when spreadeagling a fair-sized field at Goodwood on his only previous appearance, was seriously backed to beat him. Like Wollow in 1975, The Minstrel was in last place as they settled down, but he made up ground smoothly and quickly approaching the last two furlongs, drew out with Saros soon afterwards, and raced clear up the hill to win ridden along but not touched with the whip by four lengths, Crown Bowler being the same distance behind Saros in third place.

It is worth noting that the Dewhurst Stakes has recently become an excellent guide for the following year's classics. Since 1969 it has been won by Nijinsky (Two Thousand Guineas, Derby and St Leger), Mill Reef (Derby), Grundy (Irish Two Thousand Guineas and Epsom Derby) and Wollow (Two Thousand Guineas), whereas in the eight preceding years not one Dewhurst Stakes winner went on to success in a classic race. The Minstrel's prospects of continuing the Dewhurst's fine run would seem to be distinctly bright. Saros might fairly be regarded as an unknown quantity, but we have a sufficiently high opinion of Crown Bowler to be satisfied that the administration of an eight-length beating to that colt at seven furlongs represents an achievement of the first magnitude. And whereas Wollow's time in 1975 compared unfavourably with that of the winner of the Tattersall Nursery, The Minstrel's was very good indeed—equivalent to a timefigure value of 1.27 fast, a figure well up to classic-winning standard.

The Minstrel is a full brother to the French three-year-old Far North, a temperamental colt who became very strung up before the start of the Irish Sweeps Derby, in which he finished a fair fifth behind Malacate. Judging from his exemplary behaviour before the Dewhurst Stakes, The Minstrel has none of the temperamental flaws in his make-up which afflict his brother, and as the latter stays a mile and a half, The Minstrel, therefore, must have good prospects of doing so too. Against that, it should be borne in mind that whereas Far

743

North needed nine furlongs on testing ground to be seen to best advantage as a two-year-old, The Minstrel was able to put up a smart performance over six furlongs on firm going on his first racecourse appearance: unquestionably he is much the speedier animal of the two. So, as usual, we must turn to the pedigree to see what indication of stamina is to be found there.

The Minstrel (ch.c. 1974)	Northern Dancer (b 1961)	Nearctic (br 1954)	Nearco
			Lady Angela
		Natalma (b 1957)	Native Dancer
			Almahmoud
	Fleur (b 1964)	Victoria Park (b 1957)	Chop Chop
			Victoriana
		Flaming Page (b 1959)	Bull Page
			Flaring Top

The Minstrel's sire Northern Dancer, sire of Nijinsky, failed to stay a mile and a half in the Belmont Stakes, and apart from Nijinsky most of his best offspring to race in Europe—Lyphard, Northern Taste, Northern Gem and Broadway Dancer, for example—have shown their best form at up to a mile and a quarter. Fleur, The Minstrel's dam, is a half-sister to Nijinsky: she won at only up to a mile, but her breeding suggests that she should have stayed at least a couple of furlongs further: both her sire, the 1960 Canadian Horse of the Year Victoria Park, and her dam, Flaming Page, were successful in the mile-and-a-quarter Queen's Plate. Judging from his pedigree, we should say that there is no room for doubt that The Minstrel will stay a mile and a quarter, but that it is by no means so certain that he will stay a mile and a half. In which case the Two Thousand Guineas would seem to be the race most likely to provide him with success in a classic. Granted normal luck in running, The Minstrel will be hard to beat at Newmarket. *V. O'Brien, Ireland.*

THE MUSTARD CLUB 2 ch.f. Gold Rod 129–Emma Lass 78 (Sky Gipsy 117) **72**
[1976 5g 5g 5fg6 5d 5f2 5f4] small filly: first foal: 720 gns yearling: dam won over 5f at 2 yrs: held up first time, ran easily best race when 1½ lengths second of nine to Trossachs in maiden race at Folkestone in July: sold 960 gns Newmarket Autumn Sales. *G. Blum.*

THE NADI CAT 2 gr.c. My Swanee 122–Tabatha (Soderini 123) [1976 5f **77**
5.3fg 6g 6fg* 6f2 7g6] neat colt: first foal: 580 gns yearling: dam won over 7f at 2 yrs in Ireland: showed much improved form when winning 10-runner seller (no bid) at Nottingham in July by 2 lengths from Swing Right: narrowly beaten by Mercy's Girl in nursery at Windsor the following month: should stay at least 1m: acts on firm going. *J. Sutcliffe.*

THE NADI ROYALE 5 gr.h. My Swanee 122–Bamford Queen (Rise 'N Shine II) **92**
[1974 6d 7h5 7g 6g 7g3 7.2fg3 7g* 7.6g3 8fg* 8g3 7g 7s 1975 8v5 8s 8g3 8fg 9fg4 8g* 8fg3 9fg5 8v5 1976 9fg 8g3 8g6 8.5g4 8fg* 8h* 8fg3] light-framed horse: good mover: fairly useful handicapper: successful at Sandown and Bath, both in July: had earlier run very well when 1¾ lengths third of 12 to The Hertford in William Hill Easter Handicap at Doncaster in April: stays 1m but possibly not 9f: needs a sound surface: has worn blinkers but is better without: game. *J. Sutcliffe.*

THE OLD PRETENDER 5 ch.h. King's Leap 111–Angelique (Hill Gail) **89**
[1974 7g3 6s* 7d2 7g6 6s3 6s 6d 1975 7fg3 6g 7.3d6 6d6 7g 6s 1976 5g3 6g* 6fg2 6g* 6fg* 7g* 7fg* 6g* 7f2 8g3 6f3 6f6 7s6 7s 8s] good-quartered horse: has been tubed: fairly useful handicapper: had a tremendous run in first half of season, winning at Ripon (twice), Thirsk, Leicester, Yarmouth and Doncaster, being apprentice ridden on each occasion: effective at 5f and stays 1m: appears to act on any going: acts on any track: ran below his best when tried in blinkers: genuine and consistent: excellent mount for a boy. *R. Armstrong.*

THE OLD RECTORY 2 br.g. Supreme Sovereign 119–Jungle Drum 107 —
(Delirium 126) [1976 5fg 6d 5d] fair sort: half-brother to quite moderate sprinter Bushed (by Entanglement): 760 gns yearling: dam a sprinter: blinkered, led 4f when behind in 24-runner seller won by Mint Condition at Windsor in September, second outing: had stiffer task on next outing (not blinkered). *M. Salaman.*

THE PUKAAR BELL 2 gr.g. Town Crier 119–Hethabella 62 (Hethersett 134) —
[1976 5s 5s 6v] compact gelding: third foal: 2,700 gns yearling: dam won over 1½m: made no show in maiden and minor events. *J. Sutcliffe.*

THERAPEON 2 b.c. One For All–Burlington (Tim Tam) [1976 7s⁴ 8s 10d⁵]   **82**
strong, lengthy American-bred colt: third foal: 15,500 gns yearling: dam half-
sister to top-class miler Faraway Son and very smart Liloy: showed moderate
form in good-class company, finishing 7 lengths fifth to subsequently-disqualified
Gunbad in £2,100 event at Newmarket on final outing: will stay 1½m. *P.
Walwyn.*

THE REAL ME 2 b.f. Realm 129–Kiss Me 82 (Tamerlane 128) [1976 5fg 6g⁵   **50**
5.9f] small, light-framed filly: poor plater: blinkered third outing. *B. Hills.*

THE RYLES 3 ch.c. Jukebox 120–Second Bloom 64 (Double Jump 131) [1975   **88**
5f⁶ 5f* 5f² 6fg³ 6f 8fg 8v⁵ 8g* 8g⁴ 7d⁵ 1976 8fg⁴ 8f² 9g* 8d* 8d* 8s⁴ 10h⁴ 9f
8g⁶ 8v³ 8s] strong, robust colt: fair handicapper: winner at Pontefract and
Ripon (twice), beating Igloo Fire in good style by 4 lengths on latter course in
June: ran best race afterwards when highly respectable third to Handycuff
at Newcastle in October: stays 9f well: acts on any going: wears blinkers: sold
8,600 gns Newmarket Autumn Sales and has been exported to U.S.A. *Miss
S. Hall.*

THE SCHEMER 3 ch.g. Divine Gift 127–Idle Chatter (Romulus 129) [1975   **45**
5f 6f² 6g⁵ 6f⁶ 6g⁴ 7f 6d 1976 6d⁶ 9fg 6h⁵ 7f 8d 6v] sturdy gelding: bad plater:
evidently a sprinter: blinkered fourth outing. *H. Blackshaw.*

THE SENTRY 3 br.c. So Blessed 130–Wide Awake 95 (Major Portion 129)   **79**
[1975 6g 1976 8fg⁶ 8fg² 10g³ 10fg³ 12fg⁵ 12g³] lightly-built, useful-looking
colt: quite a moderate maiden: stays 1¼m but evidently not 1½m. *H. Candy.*

THE SERGEANT 4 br.c. King's Troop 118–Sincerity 91 (Soderini 123) [1974   **—**
5f³ 7g⁴ 6d* 8s⁴ 8.2s⁴ 1975 7v* 9s² 10g 10.6s 1976 8d] rangy colt:
quite a useful handicapper (rated 96) at 3 yrs: pulled up lame at Newcastle in
April on only outing in 1976: stays 1¼m: acts on a firm surface but is particularly
well suited by a soft one: bandaged at Newcastle. *J. Carr.*

THE SIGN CENTRE 2 ch.c. St Alphage 119–Silver Bullion (Silver Shark 129)   **96**
[1976 5g 5g⁶ 5f* 6fg³ 6g² 6fg³ 6g² 6g] compact, quite attractive colt: second
foal: 2,000 gns yearling: dam unraced half-sister to very useful sprinter Smooth:
all out to win 13-runner maiden race at Nottingham in June by a head from
Callimoor: subsequently ran well on most of his outings, including when ½-length
second to Showpiece in £2,600 nursery at Kempton in August, but was very
disappointing when favourite for similar event on same course later in month:
stays 6f. *J. Sutcliffe.*

THE SOLOSTAN 6 b.g. El Gallo 122–Polling Station 91 (Polly's Jet) [1974   **80**
6s 7g 5.3fg⁶ 6f⁶ 5g 5v⁶ 6s* 6v* 1975 5v* 6s* 6g³ 5g⁴ 6fg 5f⁵ 5g⁵ 5f 1976 5g
5f⁴ 5s* 6v³ 5s² 6v³ 6v²] compact gelding: quite a moderate handicapper: well-
backed second favourite when winning at Goodwood in September: ran creditably
afterwards: stays 6f: acts on any going: often wears bandages but has not worn
them when successful. *J. Sutcliffe.*

THE STREAKER 5 br.g. Kabale 103–Daily Help (Vic Day 126) [1974 N.R.   **—**
1975 N.R. 1976 12g] half-brother to winning Irish middle-distance stayer
Dailyaide (by Shackleton): dam, sister to champion hurdle winner Anzio, of
little account: tailed off in amateur riders race at Leicester in April, only outing.
D. Williams.

THE TANK 2 b.c. Mansingh 120–Machella 93 (Crepello 136) [1976 5g 5f³   **68**
5g⁵ 6fg 6f³] strong, compact colt: quite a moderate maiden: form only at 5f:
blinkered fifth outing. *P. Haslam.*

THETIS 3 b.f. King Emperor–Etoile de France (Arctic Star) [1975 6d 1976   **—**
11g 12g] big, strong filly: half-sister to several winners, including the stayers
Irvine (by Sea Hawk II) and Staralgo (by Miralgo) and quite useful Place
d'Etoile (by Kythnos), the dam of Northern Treasure: no worthwhile form in
maiden races: sold 5,800 gns Newmarket Autumn Sales. *M. Smyly.*

THE TISTA 3 b.g. Sahib 114–Winding River 101 (Entanglement 118) [1975   **100**
5f* 6f² 7g 6f⁴ 6fg⁶ 8f* 7g³ 1976 8f² 8fg² 8f 10fg* 10fg⁵ 10g² 10d² 9g⁵] lightly-
made gelding: useful handicapper: successful at Lingfield in July: runner-up
in strongly-contested handicaps at Sandown and Newbury afterwards, putting
up a particularly good effort when 2 lengths second to Chil the Kite in Peter
Hastings Stakes at Newbury in September: good fifth of 29 to Intermission
in Irish Sweeps Cambridgeshire at Newmarket the following month: stays
1¼m well: appears to act on any going: blinkered fifth outing at 2 yrs: consistent.
H. Candy.

THE

THE TRIPLETS 2 gr.f. Roan Rocket 128–Achnanellan 85 (Abernant 142) **85**
[1976 5fg 5g⁶ 5f⁵ 5fg 5.3f* 5s³ 6s⁶] good sort: sister to a minor sprint winner,
and half-sister to two other minor winners: 2,500 gns yearling: dam stayed
1¼m: made all, and showed much improved form, when winning seven-runner
claiming race at Brighton in August by 3 lengths from Tax Donation: should
stay beyond sprint distances: acts on any going: blinkered fourth and fifth
outings: sold 2,200 gns Ascot December Sales and exported to Barbados. *R.
Hannon.*

THE TRUANT 3 b.c. The Brianstan 128–Tammy's Princess 78 (Tamerlane **78**
128) [1975 5fg⁷ 6f⁴ 6f⁴ 5g⁵ 5g 1976 6v³ 5d² 6d⁴ 6d⁴ 7f⁶ 8f* 7f² 8f* 7f⁵ 8h²
8d 8s] strong colt: quite a moderate handicapper: won maiden race at Lanark
in July: carried left by Denaneer when second to that horse at Ripon the following month and was subsequently awarded race: suited by 7f and 1m: best form
on a sound surface. *Denys Smith.*

THE VERGER 3 b.c. The Parson 119–Miss Moneypenny (High Treason 126) **60**
[1975 8f 1976 8fg⁵ 16d 6d 8.2d 5s³ 5s³ 5s⁵] plating-class maiden: easily best
form at 5f and does not stay long distances. *R. Supple.*

THE VIRGINIAN 3 b.g. Virginia Boy 106–Florist (Floribunda 136) [1975 **—**
N.R. 1976 6fg 5.9fg⁵ 5g 6fg⁴ 6g⁵ 6fg 6fg 6d] well-made gelding: first foal:
dam tailed off in a 2-y-o seller on only outing: modest plater: stays 6f: sometimes
wears bandages. *J. Sutcliffe.*

THE WHEEL 2 ch.c. Green God 128–Rosameen 51 (Breakspear II) [1976 **—**
5s⁴ 6d 7v] first produce: 1,000 gns foal, resold 4,000 gns yearling: gave little
indication of ability: dead. *A. Pitt.*

THE WHITE TOWER 3 ch.g. Tower Walk 130–Caroline of York 55 (Saint **—**
Crespin III 132) [1975 N.R. 1976 6g 10g³ 8s 8s] second foal: 500 gns yearling,
resold 300 gns 2-y-o: dam a stayer: 25/1 when remote last of three to Turnpike
in minor event at Goodwood in September. *J. Haine.*

THE YELLOW GIRL 2 ch.f. Yellow God 129–Faa Paa (Skymaster 126) [1976 **—**
6d 6d] strong, robust filly: sister to 3-y-o Yellow Boy, a fairly useful winner
at 1m, and half-sister to a winner in Greece: sold twice as a yearling, for 1,050
gns and 2,200 gns, and resold as a 2-y-o for 2,800 gns: dam won over 7f at 2
yrs: in middle division in maiden races won by Rings and Running Bull at
Newmarket in October. *G. Pritchard-Gordon.*

THIEF 2 ch.c. Burglar 128–Lovely One 65 (Ballymoss 136) [1976 5g⁵] first **—**
foal: bought privately 200 gns as a yearling: dam stayed 1¼m: 11 lengths fifth
of 16 to Fenny Boy in maiden race at Salisbury in May: sold 200 gns Ascot
December Sales. *F. Maxwell.*

THIEVING DEMON 3 b.c. Burglar 128–Hell's Angels 109 (Hook Money 124) **118**
[1975 5d⁶ 5f³ 5f² 6f* 6f* 6f⁵ 6fg 1976 7f 8fg³ 7d⁶ 7f 7g* 8fg* 7.3fg³ 8s⁴]
Thieving Demon, whose two-year-old form earned him a weight of 8-3 in
the Free Handicap, with sixty horses rated his superior and who had been
trounced by Wollow in the Clerical, Medical Greenham Stakes, not surprisingly
started one of the outsiders for the Two Thousand Guineas at 66/1, at longer
odds than Mon Fils from the same stable had started when successful in the
race in 1973. Thieving Demon was unable to emulate Mon Fils and was beaten
fair and square by Wollow and Vitiges, but he ran a very fine race, coming late
on the scene to deprive Patris of third place by a short head. After the Guineas
we thought that the proximity of Thieving Demon didn't say a great deal for
the form of the race, but he did enough later in the season to prove that he is
indeed a smart miler. In the space of ten days in July he netted £5,645 for
victories in the Fen Ditton Stakes at Newmarket and the Charlton Handicap
at Goodwood. In the former race, a newly-established seven-furlong contest,
Thieving Demon looked in trouble at halfway but came through under pressure
to beat that good sprinter Honeyblest going away by two lengths; at Goodwood
under top weight of 9-5 he struck the front a furlong out and just managed to
hold the determined last-furlong challenge of the Child Stakes runner-up Red
Ruby, to whom he was conceding 5 lb; in another few strides he would have been
beaten. Thieving Demon was now again in the form he had shown in the
Guineas and on his next appearance he ran with credit in the strongly-contested
Hungerford Stakes at Newbury. Turning into the straight he had only two of
his fourteen rivals behind him, when he started to make up ground he found
himself badly boxed in, and not until inside the last furlong could he get clear.
Then he really began to motor, but it was too late—Ardoon had gone beyond
recall and won by a neck from Record Token, and Thieving Demon was two

746

Mrs D. Goldstein's "Thieving Demon" (F. Durr)

lengths away in third place. In two of his other races, the Prix du Palais Royal at Longchamp and the Queen Elizabeth II Stakes at Ascot, Thieving Demon encountered soft going, and although in neither race was he disgraced he ran sufficiently below his best form to suggest he was not at his best on the ground. His only bad run was in the Jersey Stakes at Royal Ascot for which he started favourite and toiled in the rear all the race. Probably a bad knock at the start had a lot to do with the way he ran that day.

Thieving Demon (b.c. 1973)	Burglar (b 1966)	Crocket (ch 1960)	King of the Tudors / Chandelier
		Agin the Law (b 1946)	Portlaw / Revolte
	Hell's Angels (b 1962)	Hook Money (ch 1951)	Bernborough / Besieged
		Luminant (b 1951)	Nimbus / Bardia

Burglar, one of the best sprinters around in 1969, has proved a disappointment as a stallion and in 1976 he was exported to Tasmania. Thieving Demon is one of the few good horses he has sired. Hell's Angels was a very useful sprinter who won five races, including the Blue Seal Stakes at Ascot as a two-year-old, in three seasons on the racecourse. However, before Thieving Demon none of her three foals to race possessed any great measure of ability. The second dam Luminant, a one-paced individual, managed to win over a mile. She has produced several winners, easily the best of them being Hell's Angels' brother, the good sprinter Daylight Robbery. Thieving Demon is a rangy colt and a good walker. He stays a mile and is well suited by a sound surface. *R. Hannon.*

THIRTY DAYS 2 ch.c. Sky Gipsy 117–September 91 (Blason 109) [1976 — 5f⁶] brother to fairly useful 5f sprinter September Sky: dam a sprinter: started slowly when remote sixth of nine to Exposed in minor event at Lingfield in June, only outing. *G. Balding.*

THOMAS BLOOD 2 ch.c. Burglar 128–Proxy 104 (Quorum 126) [1976 5fg — 5fg 6s] of no account. *M. Ryan.*

THOMSON 2 gr.c. Roan Rocket 128–Third Slip 87 (Delirium 126) [1976 **90** 5fg⁴ 5s 6fg⁶ 7f 7f* 7g² 8g] fair sort: brother to a disappointing animal, and half-brother to useful middle-distance performer Hully Gully (by Emerson): dam 5f sprinter: showed much improved form in five-runner maiden race at Brighton in August, winning by 2½ lengths from Tinder Box despite swerving left in final furlong: creditable second to Gleaming Wave in nursery at Warwick later in month: better suited by 7f than shorter distances and should get 1m: ran moderately in blinkers on fourth outing. *G. Pritchard-Gordon.*

THOMSON'S POLICY 2 b.c. Jukebox 120–Reelin Bridge (New Day) [1976 **65** 7g 8s⁶] small, sturdy colt: brother to very useful Irish 3-y-o sprinter Reelin Jig: dam won over 1½m: never nearer when remote sixth of 20 to Lady Rhapsody in maiden race at Sandown in October: wears blinkers. *P. Haslam.*

THORGANBY BELLA 2 b.f. Porto Bello 118–Miracle Girl 75 (Sing Sing 134) — [1976 5fg 5fg⁴] strong filly: half-sister to two winners, including quite useful 1973 2-y-o Patrizio (by St Paddy): dam ran only at 2 yrs: 7 lengths fourth of eight to Petard in minor event at Newcastle in August. *M. W. Easterby.*

THORGANBY LAD 2 ch.c. Frankincense 120–Red Robe 97 (Supreme Court **61** 135) [1976 5fg 6f 6v 6s] compact colt: quite a moderate plater: blinkered fourth outing. *M. W. Easterby.*

THORNHILL FANCIFUL 2 gr.f. Jimmy Reppin 131–Suzygail (Amber X 133) **70** [1976 6v⁵ 5g⁴ 5v*] first foal: 190 gns yearling: sold to H. Blackshaw for 730 gns after winning 15-runner seller at Teesside in October by ½ length from Yarlsba: bred to be suited by 1m+: acts on heavy going. *T. Craig.*

THORNTON BAY 3 br.f. Major Portion 129–True Pardal (Pardal 130) [1975 **59** 5d 5s 6h⁵ 5fg 7f 8.2f* 8g 1976 9g 12f⁵ 12f⁴ 10.6g⁶ 8f³ 10d 10v*] leggy filly: plater: easy 7-length winner at Leicester in November (no bid): seems to stay 1½m: acts on any going. *J. Cousins.*

THREE LEGS 4 br.c. Petingo 135–Teodora (Hard Sauce 131) [1974 5g² 5g* **128** 5g* 6g 8g³ 7.5g 1975 5g* 6g* 8g² 8g² 8g⁵ 6v* 6g² 5g* 6g³ 1976 5fg⁴ 6d* 6f 6fg² 6.5d⁵ 5fg⁴ 6g⁶]
Although Three Legs won only one race, his cracking efforts in three of the top sprint races entitle this ex-Italian colt to be rated one of the leading sprinters of 1976, in point of merit probably second only to Lochnager.

We were most impressed with Three Legs when we saw him for the first time, at Newmarket in April. A big, lengthy colt, he looked on the backward side in the paddock and in the circumstances put up a highly pleasing display to finish a close fourth to Polly Peachum in the Palace House Stakes. A couple of weeks later Three Legs fulfilled that promise with a fine win in the Duke of York Stakes at York, where he came through strongly in the final furlong to win by two and a half lengths from Broxted.

In three of his five races after York Three Legs turned in first-class efforts, particularly when he finished second to Lochnager in the July Cup at Newmarket. Outpaced early on in the July Cup and still last at halfway, Three Legs made up a tremendous amount of ground in the closing stages to get within three quarters of a length of Lochnager; we estimated that in the final two furlongs

Duke of York Stakes, York—Three Legs is followed home by Broxted and Kala Shikari

he made up at least four lengths on the winner. No mean achievement this, especially when one considers the quality of sprinter that he passed in the latter part of the race: Import, Roman Warrior, Be Tuneful and Gentilhombre were four of the eight that Three Legs had behind him at the finish.

Three Legs next ran in the Prix Maurice de Gheest over six and a half furlongs at Deauville in August. Following a good fifth to Girl Friend there he lined up for the William Hill Sprint Championship over the minimum trip at York later in August. At York Three Legs performed in an almost identical manner to the way he had done at Newmarket. After being thoroughly outpaced early on, he was flying at the finish and was beaten only just over a length by Lochnager into fourth place. In his only other races of the season, the Cork and Orrery Stakes and the Diadem Stakes, both run over six furlongs at Ascot, Three Legs performed inexplicably badly and he wasn't seen out again after trailing in last of those to finish behind Honeyblest in the Diadem Stakes in September.

Three Legs (br.c. 1972)	Petingo (b 1965)	Petition (br 1944)	Fair Trial
			Art Paper
		Alcazar (ch 1957)	Alycidon
			Quarterdeck
	Teodora (br 1963)	Hard Sauce (br 1948)	Ardan
			Saucy Bella
		Tellastory (gr 1957)	Tulyar
			King's Story

Three Legs's dam Teodora is out of the Tulyar mare Tellastory. Raced in Italy Teodora won once and finished third in the Italian Oaks. Of her three foals to race Three Legs is her best, although Tell Me Why (by Molvedo) has done well in Italy. Three Legs has never won over a distance longer than six furlongs but he has good form in Italy over a mile; he ran one of his best races over there when second to Baly Rockette in the 1975 Premio Resegone over that distance. We are sure that Three Legs needs further than five furlongs and might well be suited by a return to longer distances than six furlongs. Three Legs appears to act on any going except, perhaps, very firm, although at one time he gave the impression that an easy surface suited him ideally. He stays in training. *L. Cumani.*

THREE MUSKETEERS 3 br.g. Sovereign Gleam 117–Kalympia (Kalydon 122)   — [1975 5s 5s⁶ 5g 5v 8g 1976 10s⁴ 7.5g⁵ 8f⁴ 8fg 10.2s] ex-Irish gelding: first foal: 1,700 gns yearling: dam ran only twice: fourth in handicap at Navan in March and maiden race at Yarmouth in July: stays 1½m: often wore blinkers in Ireland but hasn't in this country: trained until after second outing by T. Costello. *W. Wharton.*

THREE-ONE-THREE 5 br.g. Native Prince–French Line 98 (Set Fair 129)   **41** [1974 12g 10f⁶ 11.2f 8g 5fg³ 5.8g 6g 1975 8s⁴ 5d 6g 6f⁴ 7f⁵ 5.9f 8g 7h 5f⁴ 5.3g 1976 5f 5f⁵ 5g⁴ 6d⁶ 5f⁵ 6g⁵ 10f 8h² 9h] lengthy gelding: poor handicapper: stays 1m and has run respectably over 5f: evidently acts on any going. *P. Poston.*

THRIFTY TRIO 4 b.f. Groton–Good Landing (First Landing)   [1974 5s 6f* **116** 7g⁵ 6fg⁴ 5g⁴ 1975 5s 5g* 6f² 6.3f* 5f* 5f* 6f* 6fg* 5f 1976 5f² 5fg⁴ 5f⁴ 5f* 5fg 5f* 5fg⁵ 5g³ 5.6g] most attractive American-bred Irish filly: smart sprinter: successful twice at Phoenix Park at 4 yrs, on second occasion beating Arun River (rec 24 lb more than w.f.a.) a length in August: also ran creditably in her two races against Lochnager, finishing about 4 lengths behind him when fourth in King's Stand Stakes at Royal Ascot on third outing and less than 3 lengths when fifth in William Hill Sprint Championship at York in August: also ran twice at Doncaster in September in space of three days putting up by far better effort on first occasion (ran very badly on second) when 4 lengths third to Athlete's Foot in Sir Gatric Stakes (had rather a poor run): stays 6f: acts on firm going: wears blinkers: suitable mount for an apprentice: genuine and consistent but ran very poorly (dropped out as if something had gone wrong with her) on fifth outing: racing in U.S.A. *D. Weld, Ireland.*

TIA POLLY 2 ch.f. King's Leap 111–Blue Polly (Blue Water)   [1976 5fg 5f   — 5g 5fg] tall, close-coupled filly: half-sister to several winners over sprint distances, notably very smart Great Bear (by Star Gazer): dam never ran: no worthwhile form in maiden races. *W. Wightman.*

TIBS EVE 3 b.c. Ribero 126–Venette (Epaulette 125)   [1975 5f⁴ 6fg³ 7f³ 8g²   **96** 1976 8s⁴ 10s³ 12f³ 12.2f* 12f* 14.6d 14g³] rangy, useful sort of colt: half-brother to useful Irish middle-distance winner Valleymount (by Ballyciptic): dam won over 5f at 2 yrs in Ireland: won maiden race at Wexford (odds on) and apprentice handicap at the Curragh in August: close-up third to Midland Gayle in handicap at Leopardstown the following month: 66/1, showed up until straight when remote twelfth to Crow in 15-runner St Leger at Doncaster in between: stays 1¾m: acts on any going. *S. McGrath, Ireland.*

TID 5 b.g. Raeburn II–Irish Rising 71 (St Paddy 133) [1974 11.2d 12fg 9f⁴ 8f* 7fg² 7.2d⁵ 7g⁵ 8g⁴ 8g* 9g³ 10g⁴ 7g 8d 1975 7d³ 7fg³ 8f² 8h² 8g² 7f² 8.2g⁵ 8h⁵ 6g 1976 8g² 8g*] neat gelding: selling handicapper: sold for 1,500 gns after winning at Edinburgh in May: finds 6f too sharp for him and is best at around 1m: probably acts on any going: suitable mount for an apprentice: usually wears blinkers. *Hbt. Jones* **50**

TIDAL DANCE 3 br.f. Hardicanute 130–Dance Away (Red God 128 §) [1975 5f 6g⁵ 6f 7f⁶ 8.2g³ 9fg 8.2d 8g 8fg 1976 9f 8f⁴ 8f⁶ 8f⁴ 10.1f⁴ 10.8f* 10.2h² 8fg 10.8g 10h² 10s 8d 10v⁴] neat filly: plater: bought in 1,500 gns after winning at Warwick in July: probably needs further than 1m and stays 11f: best form on top-of-the-ground conditions: ran poorly when tried in blinkers on eleventh start. *E. Reavey.* **65**

TIERRA FUEGO 3 b.c. Shantung 132–Argentina 115 (Nearco) [1975 6fg⁵ 8fg² 1976 8f⁴ 10f* 12g 12f³ 14f⁴ 14.6d 12g] well-made, useful-looking colt: half-brother to very smart Averof (by Sing Sing), a winner at up to 1¼m, and good stayer Falkland (by Right Royal V): dam stayed 1½m: stayed on really well under strong driving when winning nine-runner White Rose Stakes at Ascot in May by a head and the same from Ragotina and Lost Chord: beaten some way on next two outings, Epsom Derby (eleventh of 22 to Empery) and King Edward VII Stakes at Royal Ascot (10½ lengths third to Marquis de Sade): got much nearer to Marquis de Sade and put up an excellent performance in March Stakes at Goodwood in August, giving weight to all but winner but being beaten only 3½ lengths into fourth-of-five placing: reportedly cut his near-hind leg when tailed-off last in Doncaster St. Leger the following month: will stay 2m: acts on firm going. *C. Brittain.* **113**

TIGER TRAIL 4 b.c. Great Nephew 126–Indian Game 104 (Big Game) [1974 6fg 8d² 1975 11.1g* 10.5g⁴ 10fg* 10f⁴ 12d³ 10g⁴ 10d⁴ 10g⁵ 1976 10.6d* 10g 10.5d⁴ 9g* 8fg* 10fg* 10g* 7.3d⁴ 10v⁴] attractive, well-made colt: good mover: fairly useful handicapper: did really well at 4 yrs, winning at Haydock, Newmarket (twice) and Kempton (twice): gained his final win in Playboy Stakes on last-named course in August, beating Balidon by 1½ lengths (eased considerably in final furlong): stays 11f and possibly finds 7f a little on short side: appears to act on any going with possible exception of heavy: does best when ridden up with leaders: hurdling with R. Turnell. *N. Murless.* **98**

TIGHT ROPE 4 b.f. Tower Walk 130–Alcohol (Alcide 136) [1974 5d 6s 1975 10d 10d⁶ 10fg⁴ 10fg⁴ 10s³ 10g⁴ 10f⁴ 12v 1976 16f⁵ 16f* 16f2²] quite well-made filly: stayed on well when winning poor maiden race at Beverley in June by 7 lengths from Dandy Scot: creditable second to Jetador in handicap at Nottingham later in month: stays well: seems to act on any going: blinkered last three **64**

White Rose Stakes, Ascot—barely a length covers the first four who are (right to left) Tierra Fuego, Ragotina, Lost Chord and New Order

outings in 1975: sweating on reappearance: sold 2,500 gns Newmarket July Sales. *R. Boss.*

TILTIL 2 ch.c. Tiepolo II 121–Late Appeal (Palestine 133) [1976 7f] first — foal: dam poor maiden in Ireland: apprentice ridden when in rear in 15-runner minor event won by Welsh Dancer at Yarmouth in August, only outing. *C. Brittain.*

TILTON BOY 3 br.g. Meldrum 112–Portavia (Darling Boy 124) [1975 7fg⁵ **78** 8.2g⁶ 1976 9f⁶ 10f⁵ 8.2d⁴ 11f² 12g* 11f³ 12h² 12f* 13fg 13f* 12.3v⁴] strong gelding: won maiden race at Edinburgh in June and handicaps at Hamilton in July and September: will probably stay further than 13f: acts on hard ground (well beaten only outing on heavy): swerved and unseated rider on ninth start. *T. Craig.*

TIMALEX 2 ch.c. Goldhill 125–Cuccetta 78 (Punchinello 97) [1976 5f 5d⁵ **65** 5g² 5f⁵ 5s 5f² 5fg 5f⁶ 5fg] strong colt: second in maiden race at Catterick in June (length behind Local) and seller at Hamilton the following month (beaten 4 lengths by Ceppo when odds on): blinkered first and eighth outings: broke blood vessel on seventh appearance: inconsistent. *K. Payne.*

TIMANDAMUS 9 br.g. Mandamus 120–Petite Rita 76 (Lighthouse II) [1974 — N.R. 1975 8g 8h 1976 10fg⁶ 8f] of no account. *T. Kersey.*

TIMBO 9 gr.g. Quorum 126–Gamble In Gold 125 (Big Game) [1974 N.R. **45** 1975 N.R. 1976 11d³ 15g³ 15f³ 15fg⁴] poor handicapper: stays well: best form on firm going. *F. Carr.*

TIM DING 7 b.g. Celtic Ash–Marvedo 76 (Molvedo 137) [1974 16fg* 18h* — 13.3g⁶ 20g³ 16fg⁴ 22.2fg 19g 1975 18d 18.4g 20f³ 12.2g 16d⁵ 16f⁵ 1976 12f 17.1f 16f⁴ 12f⁶] neat, smallish, deep-bodied gelding: ran poorly in 1976 and appears a light of former days: lacks a turn of foot and needs a really thorough test of stamina: has run respectably on softish ground but is ideally suited by top-of-the-ground conditions: usually wears blinkers. *Mrs L. Dingwall.*

TIME AND LIFE 3 ch.f. Arts and Letters–Colonia (Cockrullah 115) [1975 **?** N.R. 1976 10g⁴ 12f⁵ 9v* 11.5g 10g*] good-looking filly: American-bred: half-sister to very useful Sun Colony (by Sunrise Flight), a stakes winner in U.S.A.: $55,000 yearling: dam a prolific winner in the Americas: showed some ability on first two outings in this country when trained by L. Cumani, being beaten about 14 lengths into fifth place behind Catalpa in Ribblesdale Stakes at Royal Ascot: subsequently sent to race in Italy and won there twice, putting up an excellent performance when winning Group 2 Premio Lydia Tesio at Rome in October by a short head from Italian Oaks runner-up Sierra Morena, the pair finishing 7 lengths clear: best form at up to 1¼m: acts on heavy ground. *S. Cumani, Italy.*

TIMELY GIFT 2 b.f. Frankincense 120–Free Time 89 (Sayajirao 132) [1976 **78** 5g 5g 6d 7g 6g 6d 6s⁴] tall, light-framed filly: half-sister to three winners, including fairly useful 7f to 1¼m winner Impromptu (by My Swanee): dam won over 5f at 2 yrs and is half-sister to High Line: ran easily best race on final outing, finishing 2½ lengths fourth to High Value in a Chepstow maiden event: should stay at least 1m: evidently well suited by soft going. *D. Thom.*

TIMERAH 4 b.c. Olden Times–Rahmana (Tamerlane 128) [1974 7d 7g 1975 **53** N.R. 1976 8g* 8fg⁶ 10fg] American-bred colt: won 11-runner amateur riders maiden race at Ripon in May by 2½ lengths from Highview Lord: well beaten both outings afterwards: stays 1m. *F. J. Houghton.*

TIMJON RIXIM 4 ch.g. Beau Chapeau–Roll By (Rabirio) [1974 N.R. 1975 — N.R. 1976 18s³] half-brother to winning chaser Beau By (by Beau Tudor): dam never ran: 33/1, showed a glimmer of ability when 10¾ lengths third of 13 to Brother George in amateur riders maiden race at Doncaster in October, first outing on flat: promising hurdler. *A. Wates.*

TIM LECHEREO 2 b.c. Derring-Do 131–Pilamenon 90 (Parthia 132) [1976 **78 p** 6f³] second foal: half-brother to 3-y-o 1m winner Pillar-Box (by So Blessed): 5,400 gns yearling: dam won over 1m and 1¼m from three starts: ran promisingly when 5 lengths third behind previous winners Brown Mint and Shush in 11-runner minor event at Windsor in July but wasn't seen out again: will be suited by 1m+. *J. Hindley.*

TIMOTHY JON 6 b.g. Tacitus 124–Court Circles (Flush Royal 127) [1974 **44** N.R. 1975 10.1f 1976 10f⁵ 8g⁴] poor maiden: showed a little ability when about 4½ lengths fourth of six to Flying Bridge in seller at Warwick in August: sold 1,000 gns Doncaster October Sales. *O. O'Neill.*

TINACEDE 2 b.f. Nicky's Double 90–Intercede 67 (Woodcut 114) [1976 7f 7f] —
half-sister to two minor winners: dam, a plater, won at 11f: behind in maiden
race at Beverley and minor event at Redcar, both in July: sold 240 gns Doncaster
October Sales. *T. Walker.*

TINDER BOX 2 b.c. Silly Season 127–Quickmatch 89 (Match III 135) [1976 **84**
5g 5f³ 7h² 7h² 7f²] attractive colt: second foal: dam best at 1m: runner-up to
Big Treat at Warwick and Bath in July: odds on for five-runner maiden race
at Brighton the following month but again finished second, beaten 2½ lengths
by Thomson: will stay middle distances: blinkered last two outings. *I. Balding.*

TINGANGA 5 ch.g. Be Friendly 130–Hatrique 66 (High Hat 131) [1974 8g⁴ —
7f* 6f   1975 7s 6fg⁵ 7f⁵ 7.6g 7fg* 7g³ 7f 7f 8.2g   1976 8.2v⁴] leggy gelding:
made only one appearance at 5 yrs: stays 1m: acts on firm going: inconsistent.
E. Cousins.

TINGRITH 2 b.c. Mandamus 120–Mary Stuart 92 (High Treason 126) [1976 —
5d 6v] neat colt: half-brother to three winners, including fair 1974 2-y-o 7f
winner Sandy's Girl (by Grand Roi): 300 gns yearling: dam fairly useful 2-y-o:
unquoted when behind in large fields of maidens at Newbury in the autumn.
W. Payne.

TINKLETOES 3 gr.f. Falcon 131–Twinkletoes 86 (Royal Challenger 129) **63**
[1975 6f 6fg⁶ 6fg   1976 8f 12f 12d 16f³ 15f² 15.8f* 16fg⁴] strong filly: sister
to fairly useful stayer Man Alive: won handicap at Catterick in July by 2 lengths
from Wings of Spring: ran badly under a penalty later in month and was not
seen out again: suited by firm ground and a test of stamina: wears blinkers
nowadays. *M. Camacho.*

TIN MINE 2 b.c. Blakeney 126–Guessing Game 87 (Doutelle 128) [1976 7g 8d*] **90 p**
quite attractive, sturdy, short-legged colt: half-brother to three winners here
and abroad, including 1973 2-y-o 5f winner Shirwani (by Major Portion): 13,000
gns yearling: dam won over 1m from only three starts: quickened well at
distance when winning 16-runner maiden race at Newbury in September by a
length from Billion (U.S.A.): will be suited by 1½m or more: likely to go on to
better things. *M. Stoute.*

TIN MINER 2 br.c. Prince de Galles 125–Myna Tyna 85 (Blast 125) [1976 5g³ **82**
5g⁴ 5f* 6fg 5fg 6s] neat colt: third foal: dam, winner over 5f at 2 yrs, is half-
sister to good stayer Lomond: made all to win 11-runner maiden race at Ripon
in June by 2 lengths from Sir Galiva: should stay at least 6f: acts well on firm
going. *M. W. Easterby.*

TINSLEY GREEN 2 b.f. So Blessed 130–Gossops Green (Crepello 136) [1976 **85**
5g⁶ 5s² 5v*] big, attractive filly: half-sister to very useful 6f to 1¼m winner
Golden Thorn (by Floribunda): dam never ran: short-priced favourite, led
close home to win maiden race at Lingfield in November by a neck from Careless
Princess, and thereby provided a fitting ending to Noel Murless' magnificent
career as a trainer: will stay 1m: acts on heavy going: to be trained by H. Cecil
in 1977. *N. Murless.*

TINTORETTO 5 b.h. Ribot 142–White Paper (Honeyway 125) [1974 8g³ **90**
12fg² 10f³ 11.1g² 12g* 10s* 12s²   1975 13g² 12s⁵ 10g² 12.3f⁵ 10fg* 10g² 9d³
1976 10g⁵ 8f 9g* 10f⁶ 8g⁶ 8fg⁴ 10f² 9f⁵ 10g³ 8f⁴ 11f 10.2s* 10s³ 10s⁴] attractive
American-bred horse: fairly useful handicapper: winner at Wolverhampton
in May and Bath in October (apprentice race): mainly disappointing on his
other starts: almost certainly finds 1m too short for him nowadays and stays
1½m: probably acts on any going: has been tried in blinkers but does better
without: well suited by front-running tactics: sold 7,000 gns Newmarket Autumn
Sales. *G. Harwood.*

TIRULER 5 b.g. Fair Ruler–Tituba (Prophets Thumb) [1974 5f⁵ 7g 7g 8fg 6g* **64**
6f² 6g 6g⁴ 6v   1975 7f³ 7f 8.2g⁴ 11v 10.8g   1976 10fg⁵ 10fg⁶ 10f 6h³ 7fg² 7g²
7f 6h⁶ 6g] well-made American-bred gelding: poor handicapper nowadays:
effective at 7f and stays 1¼m: acts on firm going: sweated up when tried in
blinkers on third start: sold 1,000 gns Newmarket Autumn Sales. *I. Walker.*

TITLE TRAIL 3 br.c. Tribal Chief 125–Rubbish (Major Portion 129) [1975 **55**
N.R.   1976 5.9fg⁶ 6fg 5.9g³ 6f⁵ 6f⁶ 7f⁶ 7f⁴ 8f⁵] compact colt: second produce:
1,900 gns foal, resold 1,500 gns yearling: dam ran only twice: poor maiden:
stays 7f (ran poorly over 1m): sold 360 gns Newmarket Autumn Sales. *A.
Johnson.*

TITUS 2 gr.g. Boreen (Fr) 123–Regency Girl 89 (Right Boy 137) [1976 6f⁶ **43**
5f 5g⁵ 7.2f 6s] small, strong gelding: poor plater: sold 450 gns Ascot December
Sales. *T. Craig.*

TOBIQUE 2 ch.c. Connaught 130–Ship Yard 107 (Doutelle 128) [1976 7g³ 7g³] **91** big, rangy, long-striding colt: half-brother to three winners, notably outstanding middle-distance stayer Bustino (by Busted) and high-class stayer Oarsman (by Aureole): 25,000 gns yearling: dam won over 7f and 1m at 2 yrs: showed promise on both outings, finishing 1½ lengths third to Filipachi in minor race at Kempton in August and 4½ lengths third of 14 to Caporello in £1,900 event at Sandown the following month: will need at least 1¼m: to be trained by R. Hern at 3 yrs: sure to win races. *I. Balding.*

TOGETHERNESS 2 ch.c. Shiny Tenth 120–Bernina (Prudent II 133) [1976 — 5.9g 5f 6g 7fg 5s] no worthwhile form in maiden and minor events: sold 480 gns Ascot November Sales. *D. Marks.*

TOLLESBURY 3 b.f. St Chad 120–Shushan 77 (Darius 129) [1975 6f 1976 **57** 16f 12g 11h 11f³ 10v³ 10s⁶] poor maiden: stays 11f: acts on firm going. *P. Poston.*

TOLMIROS 4 gr.c. Lorenzaccio 130–Chysanthia (Ballymoss 136) [1974 N.R. **99** 1975 8g 10g* 10s* 1976 10g⁶ 10.5d² 10g² 9fg³] lengthy colt: didn't fulfil promise shown on first two starts at 4 yrs: stays 1¼m: appears to act on any going: sold 3,700 gns Newmarket Autumn Sales. *B. Hobbs.*

TOMAROSA 2 ch.f. Mountain Call 125–Fair Songstress 100 (Compensation 127) **75** [1976 5f 5g⁵ 5g³ 5g 6d⁴ 6g⁶ 7s⁴] well-made filly: first produce: 1,050 gns foal, resold 1,100 gns yearling: dam stayed 1m well: ran best race when 4 lengths fourth of 19 to Balante in nursery at Windsor in September on fifth outing: well suited by 6f: sold 2,000 gns Newmarket Autumn Sales. *R. Smyth.*

TOMBOLA 2 b.c. Bold Lad (Ire) 133–Abanilla 115 (Abernant 142) [1976 5f — 5.9g 5f] a very well-bred colt but showed no worthwhile form, including when blinkered, and was sold for 460 gns Ascot July Sales. *J. Dunlop.*

TOMMY LAD 3 b.g. Sahib 114–Honey Wax 105 (Ennis 128) [1975 N.R. — 1976 10fg 15.8g] tailed off in maiden races at Ripon in August and Haydock the following month: sold 660 gns Ascot November Sales. *G. Richards.*

TOMMYS HOPE 3 b.c. Military 112–Shropshire Lyric (Eastern Lyric 114) **90 d** [1975 5f 5fg⁵ 7f⁴ 7.2fg* 8f² 7f⁵ 1976 8s* 8.2d⁶ 8s* 8fg 7.2g 8.2v] robust colt: won handicaps at Ayr in May and June: ran badly afterwards: stays 1m: best form on soft going. *S. Hall.*

TOMMY'S OWN 3 ch.c. Richboy 117–Hay-Hay 62 (Hook Money 124) [1975 — 5g 5f 5f 6f⁴ 7f 7f 8f 1976 6g] small colt: no worthwhile form: has worn blinkers. *B. Richmond.*

TOM TALLIS 4 b.g. Tudor Music 131–Skyline 78 (Major Portion 129) [1974 **44** 5d 5fg⁶ 7d 7g 8s 9g⁶ 9s⁵ 8s⁵ 1975 12.2v 10g 16f⁴ 12s² 12f⁵ 13g⁵ 12d 1976 12fg² 13g⁵ 14g] leggy, short-backed gelding: plater: stays 1½m: acts on any going: sold 270 gns Ascot May Sales. *R. Akehurst.*

TONY 4 br.g. Pongee 106–Lilt 52 (Drumbeg 94) [1974 5f⁵ 5f² 6fg⁴ 7g³ 7g⁵ 7d³ **89** 8g³ 7fg⁵ 1975 8g* 8.2g³ 10g⁶ 10fg 8g* 12.2f² 13d* 12.2g* 1976 12s⁶ 12f³ 14.7d⁶ 12fg⁴ 12f⁴ 12.2g³ 12d⁴ 14v² 12 2s* 12v²] compact gelding: good walker: fairly useful handicapper: ran consistently in second half of season and gained a well-deserved success when beating Lochranza 7 lengths at Catterick in October: stays well: acts on firm going but is particularly well suited by an easy surface: good mount for an apprentice: genuine: sweated up third and sixth outings. *E. Weymes.*

TONY STEPHEN 4 gr.g. Supreme Sovereign 119–Narita 86 (Narrator 127) — [1974 N.R. 1975 10f 1976 12v⁶] probably of little account. *J. Mulhall.*

TOOTAL BOY 4 ch.c. Seafront–Pleshy Mount (Sallymount 125) [1974 7g⁶ 5f **49** 8d 7s 7s 1975 8h⁴ 8f⁴ 8f 8h 7f 8g 1976 8f 8g 7g⁴ 6g⁵ 5g⁵ 6g 7g⁴ 7f² 7f 6f⁶ 8f 6d 8.2d 8s*] plater: 33/1-winner at Warwick in October: stays 1m: acts on any going: has been tried in blinkers. *F. Wiles.*

TOP FORM 3 gr.g. Reform 132–Grisetta 103 (Grey Sovereign 128 §) [1975 — 6g 8.2d 1976 12d⁵ 12g] tall, leggy gelding: poor maiden: refused to race on second outing (April): sold to A. Smith 680 gns Newmarket Autumn Sales. *C. Brittain.*

TOPI 3 ch.g. Hotfoot 126–Cap Estel 104 (Fortino II 120) [1975 5g 6fg 5f⁴ 6fg⁵ **51** 6fg⁴ 6d 5s⁵ 1976 7g 8f⁵ 6g 6fg⁵ 6fg⁴ 5h⁶ 6f³] big, good-looking gelding: stays 6f: acts on firm going: usually wears blinkers nowadays. *H. Smyth.*

TOP LEVEL 4 b.c. Tower Walk 130–Feyre Eleyne (King's Troop 118) [1974 **75** 6g⁵ 7s² 7s⁴ 1975 7v² 7s* 8g² 10g 8f* 7fg 10fg⁵ 8g⁴ 1976 8g 8g⁴ 8fg 7.6fg³ 7fg⁵ 7fg] big, rangy colt: mainly disappointing at 4 yrs: stays 1m: acts on any going: blinkered third and final starts: sold 720 gns Doncaster August Sales. *N. Callaghan.*

TOPLING 2 b.f. High Top 131–Heather Grove (Hethersett 134) [1976 6fg⁶ **81** 6f³ 7fg* 7g⁶ 7d 8v] strong, good-bodied filly: good mover: half-sister to very useful sprinter Meiwa King (by Sing Sing): 8,400 gns yearling: dam French middle-distance maiden: won 15-runner maiden race at Salisbury in September by 1½ lengths from Wedding Band: had stiff tasks in nurseries on last two outings: suited by 7f and should stay at least 1m. *R. Jarvis.*

TOP OF THE TREE 3 ch.f. Lorenzaccio 130–Top of the Milk 115 (King of the **66** Tudors 129) [1975 N.R. 1976 8f 7g⁴ 8.2d 9v⁶ 10.2s 10s⁶ 10.2s] unfurnished filly: half-sister to two winners here and abroad, including useful miler Double Cream (by Klairon): dam won at up to 1m: seems only plating class: blinkered last two outings: sold 1,200 gns Ascot November Sales. *W. Elsey.*

TOPPING 5 b.g. Alcide 136–Tudor Top 104 (Tudor Minstrel 144) [1974 11g — 11g⁶ 12d 13g⁶ 14s² 14s 12s² 1975 12s 14g 1976 12.2fg⁶] lengthy gelding: quite moderate at 3 yrs: lightly raced and no form since: acts on soft going: wears blinkers. *K. Ivory.*

TOPS LOVE 2 b.f. Dike–Golden Hind 90 (Aureole 132) [1976 7g] half-sister — to two winners, including useful miler Mahler (by Great Nephew): 4,200 gns yearling: dam, half-sister to several good winners, needed at least 7f at 2 yrs: 14/1 when behind in 18-runner maiden race won by Unella at Yarmouth in September. *B. Hanbury.*

TOP SOPRANO 2 b.f. High Top 131–Land of Song 82 (Sing Sing 134) [1976 **89** 5f* 5fg⁶] second foal: 7,000 gns yearling: dam, half-sister to out-and-out stayer Celtic Cone, won over 5f at 2 yrs: made very good progress in final ¼m when winning 11-runner minor event at Goodwood in August by 2 lengths from Lady Constance: odds on for similar event on same course the following month but again got outpaced in early stages and could finish only 9 lengths sixth of eight to Home Fire: will be suited by 7f and 1m. *P. Walwyn.*

TOP STRAIGHT 4 b.c. Acer 123–Long Range 82 (March Past 124) [1974 6d⁶ **87** 7fg⁶ 7d² 8.2d⁴ 7g² 8d 1975 10f³ 11.5f³ 14f² 16fg² 14g³ 14.7g² 16s 1976 18fg² 16fg³ 12fg* 14fg* 14.6fg² 14f* 14f* 14fg 14g] rangy colt: fair performer: successful in minor event at Pontefract and three handicaps at Yarmouth in 1976, gaining his last win when beating odds-on-opponent Piccadilly Etta 7 lengths on last-named course in July: stays well: appears to act on any going: wears blinkers. *T. Waugh.*

TORLONIA 4 ch.f. Royal Palace 131–Relcia 92 (Relko 136) [1974 N.R. **§§** 1975 7v³ 8g 14f 16fg 16.9f³ 16f³ 11.1fg 16f 1976 8fg 16g] fair sort in appearance but is a thorough jade, and is best left alone. *J. Edmunds.*

TORNADO PRINCE 4 br.g. Typhoon 125–Dail Elith (Tamerlane 128) [1974 **80** 7d 7d 7g 10s⁵ 10s 1975 10.1f 8s⁶ 7.2g* 9f* 8g⁶ 9g² 11.7fg⁵ 10g² 10g² 10fg* 10f 10fg³ 1976 12g² 10g* 10fg* 12f 10fg⁵ 10fg⁴ 10.4fg⁴ 10d²] lengthy gelding: quite a moderate handicapper: easy winner at Teesside (apprentice handicap) and Pontefract, both in April: stays 1½m: seems to act on any going: good mount for an apprentice or amateur rider: suited by front-running tactics. *N. Callaghan.*

TOTOWAH 2 b.c. Biskrah 121–Scotts (Orthodox) [1976 7g 8s] strong, — robust colt: half-brother to several minor winners, including fairly useful 1967 2-y-o 5f and 6f winner Row Barge (by Zeus Boy): dam showed no worthwhile form: in middle division in maiden races won by Sin Timon and Sporting Yankee at Newmarket in October: sweated up and was very green in paddock on first outing. *M. Jarvis.*

TOUCH OF CLASS 3 br.c. Tudor Melody 129–Parida 90 (Pardao 120) [1975 **81** 7g 7fg 6f⁴ 1976 7f 7g 8.2f⁶ 7f⁶ 8g⁵ 12fg⁴ 12g⁶ 10.2g⁴ 13s 12v* 12s*] small, strong colt: good walker: made all when winning two races in the space of three days in October, maiden event at Newbury (by 8 lengths) and ladies race at Chepstow (by 2 lengths from Hipparion): stays 1½m well: acts on heavy ground: best form in blinkers: sometimes gets hot in paddock: sold to J. Gifford 7,200 gns Newmarket Autumn Sales. *H. Wragg.*

TOUCH OF GOLD 4 ch.c. Golden Dipper 119–Keep in Touch (Rockavon 120) — [1974 5g* 5h* 5fg² 5fg⁶ 6fg² 1975 7v⁵ 8.5d⁴ 8g 6g 6g⁶ 6f⁶ 7g 7g³ 8f⁵ 8f* 8fg² 8fg⁵

8fg⁴ 10d⁴ 9g 9d⁵ 1976 10.2g³ 10fg³] robust, good-quartered colt: good walker and mover: very useful handicapper at 3 yrs (rated 112): ran respectably on second of two outings in this country in 1976, finishing 9 lengths third of eight to Red Regent in Ladbroke City and Suburban Handicap at Epsom in April: best form at up to 1m although has run respectably at 1¼m: best form on a sound surface and acts on hard going: exported to U.S.A. where he was subsequently successful. *W. Marshall.*

TOUCH OF SILVER 3 ch.c. Siliconn 121–Keep in Touch (Rockavon 120) **78**
[1975 6fg⁶ 6g² 6g³ 7g³ 7.6g 1976 7g 7fg 8s⁴ 8.2d 7g 6f* 6f⁶ 6g* 6s 8g 6s] well-made, good sort: won maiden race at Brighton in August and well-contested seller at Ayr the following month (sold out of G. Balding's stable 2,500 gns): stays 7f, but is not certain to stay further: apparently does not act on soft going: usually wears blinkers nowadays. *T. Craig.*

TOUCH OF SPRING 3 ch.f. King's Troop 118–Lady Carina 92 (Ocarina 131) **65**
[1975 7d 6g⁵ 1976 7fg 12g 8g 8g*] lengthy, fair sort: won three-runner maiden race at Warwick in August by ¾ length from Ragatina: stays 1m: sold to P. Kelleway 760 gns Newmarket Autumn Sales. *P. Makin.*

TOUGHIE 9 b.g. Hard Ridden 131–Jini 110 (Nosca) [1974 N.R. 1975 13s —
12s 12g 12h 20g 16h 1976 16f⁶] of no account nowadays. *M. Naughton.*

TOUR DE FORCE 4 b.g. Cornish Prince–Doubledoor (Sir Gaylord) [1974 7s³ **76**
7d⁵ 8s⁴ 1975 8g 11g 8g* 10.1fg* 10f² 12g* 12f² 1976 10f⁴ 12fg³ 12s 12fg² 12d 12g² 16g⁶ 12fg³ 12s 12v* 12s⁵ 12v] big, strong, rangy American-bred gelding: made all when beating Revertis 2½ lengths in handicap at Haydock in October: had run creditably in some of his earlier races, including on sixth outing (second in Prix Xandover at Ostend in August) and eighth start (third in apprentice race at Salisbury the following month): suited by 1½m nowadays and should stay further: acts on any going: ran creditably when tried in blinkers at 2 yrs. *I. Balding.*

TOWER-BIRD 4 b.c. Tower Walk 130–Misquote (Quorum 126) [1974 7g³ —
6g² 7.5s² 6s⁴ 1975 10s* 8s³ 12s² 10f³ 10f² 12fg⁵ 13.4f² 11f* 12f* 12g* 14g 12fg³ 1976 10g⁶ 12g 8v⁶] strong colt: very useful handicapper as a 3-y-o when trained in Ireland by D. Weld: well beaten all outings (had very stiff tasks against good horses on first two starts) in England in 1976: stays 13f: acts on any going. *J. Webber.*

TOWER KING 3 b.g. So Blessed 130–Follow Elizabeth 101 (Cagire II 122) —
[1975 6h³ 5f 1976 8h] leggy gelding: showed a little ability at 2 yrs but was well beaten on only outing in 1976: dead. *S. Nesbitt.*

TOWER MOSS 3 gr.g. Tower Walk 130–Katie Moss (Fortino II 120) [1975 —
5f 6g 5g 1976 6f 10f] of no account. *A. Neaves.*

TOWN AND COUNTRY 2 b.c. Town Crier 119–First Huntress 64 (Primera 131) **105**
[1976 5fg* 6g³ 6g* 8g⁴ 7.3v] tall colt: second foal: half-brother to 1m winner Chasseur (by Queen's Hussar): dam of little account: a useful colt who won a newcomers event at Goodwood in May and five-runner Hyperion Stakes at Ascot two months later, on latter course finding extra in final furlong to go clear and beat Champagne Willie 1½ lengths: creditable fourth of 10, beaten only a length, behind Royal Plume in £1,700 event at Doncaster in September, but ran badly in Horris Hill Stakes at Newbury the following month: stays 1m well: acts on a firm surface and is possibly unsuited by heavy going. *R. Hern.*

TOWN FARM 4 b.c. Tycoon II–Brush's Choice (Robson's Choice 105) [1974 **78**
6g 7d² 7s² 7s² 7d⁴ 8s² 1975 8v² 7v 7g 7.3s³ 8g² 8fg* 7s³ 8d² 7g² 10s⁴ 8.2v 1976 8g 7fg 8f 7g* 8g 7g 7g⁵ 8fg⁶ 7.6s⁴ 8.2d⁴ 7.6v³] compact colt: quite a moderate performer: led last stride when winning 17-runner apprentice handicap at Newbury in May from Mujon: stays 1¼m: appears to act on any going: wears blinkers nowadays: sold to M. Tate 1,000 gns Ascot November Sales. *P. Taylor.*

TOWN GIRL 5 br.m. Town Crier 119–Jane Somers 64 (Will Somers 114 §) **59**
[1974 6g 6g* 6d* 8fg² 7.6v⁴ 1975 8f⁴ 7.6f 8g 1976 7g³ 5.9g 8g 7g 8v⁵ 8.2v] leggy mare: stays 7f: probably requires an easy surface to be seen to best advantage: blinkered fourth and fifth outings: disappointing. *W. Wharton.*

TOWN ROSE 2 b.f. David Jack 125–Brush's Choice (Robson's Choice 105) **61**
[1976 5fg⁶ 8s 7s] leggy, light-framed filly: half-sister to fairly useful miler Town Farm (by Tycoon II): dam apparently of little account: showed only a little ability in maiden and minor events. *R. Akehurst.*

TOWNSONG 2 b.c. Town Crier 119–Toccatina 79 (Bleep-Bleep 134) [1976 6fg 6g 8g 7s 7g 6d] third foal: 2,500 gns yearling: dam a sprinter: plating-class maiden: stays 7f. *D. Weeden.*   —

TOWY MELODY 2 b.f. Stephen George 102–Sweet Minuet (Setay 105) [1976 5f 5s] second living foal: sister to 3-y-o Hargrave Rogue, a winner at up to 1m: dam ran once on flat and over hurdles: in rear in maiden races at Bath in September and October. *R. Wilson.*   —

TRACKALLY 2 ch.f. Track Spare 125–Casually 78 (Cash and Courage 116) [1976 5fg5 5d2 5f2 5f* 5f4 5g* 5g3] strong, compact filly: third reported live foal: half-sister to fairly useful 1m to 1½m winner Privy Case (by Privy Councillor): dam 1¼m performer: made much of running to win minor event at Ripon in June and £1,700 nursery at Ayr in August, on latter course rallying gamely to beat Double Secret a head: bred to stay at least 1m: appears to act on any going. *E. Collingwood.*   **95**

TRACK ANNA 3 ch.f. Track Spare 125–Pixie Jet 105 (Polly's Jet) [1975 5d 5f 6f6 5fg4 5g2 5g* 5f* 5f4 6g4 5d 6g 10fg 5f5 5f* 6d4 6g3 6fg4 5fg4 6f2 6g 5h4 5fg4 6d 5s4 6v6 6s] compact filly: won seller at Ayr in May by 1½ lengths from Raver (no bid): ran creditably in better company afterwards, including when neck second to Pams Gleam in handicap at Catterick in August: stays 6f: evidently acts on any going: ran respectably when tried in blinkers. *L. Shedden.*   **67**

TRACK BELLE 2 b.f. Track Spare 125–Ring True 80 (Gulf Pearl 117) [1976 5f 5g 5d 5f 5fg4 5g3 5fg3 5f4 5fg4 5d 6g 5v 7s4] well-made filly: first foal: dam won over 7f at 3 yrs: put up easily her best effort when 4 lengths seventh of 12 to Cramond in Queen Mary Stakes at Royal Ascot in June on fourth start and is only moderate on the balance of her form: stays 7f: acts on any going. *R. Mason.*   **78**

TRACK BLUES 2 b.f. Track Spare 125–Gypsy Blues 70 (Bing II) [1976 7f6 7.2f 8g 8.2s] first foal: dam won at up to 1½m: well behind in sellers and a maiden race. *R. Mason.*   —

TRACKERS HIGHWAY 5 b.h. Track Spare 125–Panderwick 69 (Pandemonium 118) [1974 7g3 7fg6 10fg 7g5 7.3g5 7h4 7g5 8fg* 8fg2 8s 1975 8v5 8fg 8fg6 8fg 7g 8s 8g6 8g 8g6 1976 8g 7fg6 8g 8g 7d] strong, well-grown horse: just a moderate handicapper nowadays: beaten about 4 lengths when creditable sixth of 14 to Record Token in Top Rank Club Victoria Cup at Ascot in May (lady ridden), best effort at 5 yrs: stays 1m but apparently not 1¼m: acts well on hard ground and is unsuited by soft going: used to wear blinkers, but didn't in 1976: off course nearly four months before fourth outing: sold 720 gns Newmarket December Sales. *R. Mason.*   **81**

TRACK EVENT 3 b.g. Track Spare 125–Smoking Room (Pall Mall 132) [1975 5s 5g 5v 5f 6f 7f5 6g 6g 1976 8d6 10f4 8.2g 12.2d 9g 10f* 10.8f2 11.1f4] lengthy, workmanlike gelding: poor mover: plater: won at Beverley in July (made all) by 1½ lengths from Spoofer: sold out of K. Payne's stable 950 gns afterwards and ran respectably for new stable in better company: best form at around 1¼m: has worn blinkers but does better without: suitable mount for a boy: retained by trainer 900 gns Ascot October Sales. *G. Blum.*   **62**

TRACK HERO 5 b.h. Track Spare 125–Brave Heart 90 (Never Give In) [1974 7fg 8g 10.1g6 8d 8g3 8fg* 7fg3 8.3s4 8.3g4 8v 8g 1975 8s 9v3 8s* 7.6g4 8fg* 10f2 10g 1976 9fg 7fg* 7fg4 10g3 7fg 8fg 10g2 10f2 10g5 8fg2 10fg 8v] big, rangy horse: quite a moderate handicapper: successful at Salisbury in May and ran creditably in most of his races afterwards: stays 1¼m: acts on any going: suitable mount for an apprentice: sometimes sweats up: tailed off final appearance. *J. Benstead.*   **69**

TRACK MINSTREL 7 br.g. Track Spare 125–Diddled (Tudor Minstrel 144) [1974 9f* 8f3 8g5 8h* 8g 8g3 8s* 8fg6 7.2s 8fg2 9d3 8s5 1975 8d 8g6 8s 9g 10fg2 9f2 8f5 10g 10fg* 9fg* 10g5 9d* 7g 10.2g4 1976 7.6d 9fg6 10.2fg5 8fg4 8fg 8.2f4 8fg6 9fg 8fg] strong, compact gelding: most disappointing in 1976: probably needs further than 7f and stays 1¼m: acts on any going: good mount for a lady: far from consistent: sold 800 gns Doncaster Autumn Sales. *R. Mason.*   **61**

TRACK STAR 2 ch.c. Track Spare 125–Fiery Comet 82 (Star Moss 122) [1976 5f4 5f 5.3fg3 5fg 5.3f6] fair sort: good walker: first foal: 1,550 gns yearling: dam, half-sister to brilliantly speedy Sica Dan, placed at up to 7f: in frame twice at Brighton, being beaten only 3½ lengths when third to Overseas Admirer in June after starting slowly and being badly hampered 1f out: ruined chance by veering very sharply left on penultimate outing and dwelt on last: not one to trust. *G. Balding.*   **68 §**

TRADING 3 b.f. Forlorn River 124–Part Exchange 78 (Faubourg II 127) **74**
[1975 5f 6fg 1976 7.2g³ 7g³ 8h⁴ 8f² 8.2fg* 9fg² 8f² 8h³] light-framed filly:
improved after being placed in sellers on first two outings and won handicap at
Nottingham in July by ¾ length from Lord Elect: suited by 1m and 9f and may
well stay further: has worn bandages: suitable mount for an apprentice: consistent: trained until after second outing by N. Guest. *W. Holden.*

TRAFFIC LEADER 15 b.g. Traffic Judge–Party Leader (Eternal Bull) [1974 **61**
11g⁴ 8g² 8.2fg* 7fg* 7g* 5g⁴ 6f 8g² 8fg⁶ 1975 7s⁵ 7g 7f 1976 7f⁴ 8f⁵] plater:
a grand veteran who still had a little ability as he showed when fourth of eight to
Larella at Edinburgh in July: effective at 5f to 1½m: acted on any going: wore
blinkers: has been retired. *H. Bell.*

TRAITORS GAIT 2 ch.f. Tower Walk 130–Miss McWorden 75 (Worden II 129) —
[1976 6g] half-sister to three winners, including fairly useful out-and-out
stayer Mr McMandy (by Mandamus): dam a stayer: unquoted, started slowly
when last of 30 in maiden race won by Rheola at Newmarket in September: sold
to T. Craig 340 gns Doncaster November Sales. *R. Jarvis.*

TRANBY 5 b.g. Wynkell 88–Sheelagh's Babu 59 (Babu 117) [1974 9f 9f 5g⁴ **55**
5.8g 1975 N.R. 1976 12f² 10.1fg 12h⁶ 13.1s⁴] leggy, unfurnished gelding:
slow maiden: stays 13f: probably acts on any going. *H. Payne.*

TRANSFORM 6 br.g. Reform 132–Empetrum 98 (Premonition 130) [1974 —
13f² 12g 16g 12g 1975 N.R. 1976 14fg⁴] fair handicapper (rated 88) in 1974:
blinkered when creditable fourth of 14 at Salisbury in May, first outing since:
stays 1¾m: acts on firm going. *D. Gandolfo.*

TRAPANI 2 ch.f. Ragusa 137–Epona 98 (Le Levanstell 122) [1976 6fg 7d] —
quite attractive, small, lengthy filly: first foal: dam won over 5f at 2 yrs in
Ireland: unquoted when behind in large fields of maidens at Newbury in August
and September (led on stand side for over 4f). *I. Balding.*

TRAQUAIR 7 b.g. Klairon 131–Brandina (Never Say Die 137) [1974 11g* **92**
10g 11g⁶ 12f 12g⁴ 12g* 10g³ 10fg⁵ 10fg⁴ 8s* 9d³ 9v* 1975 8d 10g² 10d⁶ 8fg
10g⁶ 8g 10g 10f 1976 10g⁴ 10fg² 10f³ 9g* 9fg² 10g²] strong, well-developed
gelding: fairly useful handicapper: quickened in good style when winning seven-
runner event at Kempton in May by ½ length from Fighting Brave: ran creditably
afterwards, but wasn't raced after June: stays 1¼m: acts on any going but is
particularly well suited by some give in the ground. *J. Dunlop.*

TRASI'S SON 3 ch.c. Pretendre 126–Trasi Girl 115 (Le Levanstell 122) [1975 **108**
5.9f 7f⁴ 9fg³ 8.2d² 8g* 1976 10fg* 10.5s* 10.6d³ 12f⁶ 10d] well-grown colt:
50/1, put up a much improved performance in Mecca-Dante Stakes at York in
May, making all and holding on gamely to win by ¾ length from Gunner B: had

*Mecca-Dante Stakes, York—rank outsider Trasi's Son makes every yard of the running,
with Gunner B the only opponent to throw down a serious challenge. Behind come
Dutch Treat, Take Your Place and Level Par (noseband)*

made all and won unchallenged in handicap at Epsom the previous month: fair third of 11 to Leventis in Bass Clubmen's Handicap at Haydock in June: well beaten under stiff weights in valuable handicaps at Royal Ascot (King George V Stakes) and Newbury (Peter Hastings Stakes, virtually tailed off): reportedly found to be lame after Newbury: should stay further than 1¼m: appears to act on any going: extremely well suited by enterprising riding tactics: genuine. *M. Tate.*

TRAVELLING SECRET   2 b.f. Mummy's Pet 125–Copper Gold (Democratic   **77** 124)   [1976 5d³ 5g⁴ 5g³ 5h* 5f³ 6fg 6f]   neat filly: half-sister to 3-y-o 7.5f winner Kalgoorlie (by Goldhill) and to two other minor winners: 2,500 gns yearling: dam won over 6f in Ireland as a 2-y-o: stayed on well to win 10-runner maiden race at Pontefract in July by a length from Linguistic: remote third of 10 to Northern Lady in minor event at Redcar later in month, and finished in rear in two nurseries in August: possibly doesn't stay 6f: appears to act on any going. *M. H. Easterby.*

TREAD SOFTLY   2 br.f. High Flown 117–Two Slippers (Solstice 118)   [1976 6f⁶   **65** 6f 6d³ 7d⁵ 7s]   Swedish-bred filly: fair sort: hard-ridden third of 15 behind very easy winner Supernaculum in maiden race at Yarmouth in September: will stay middle distances. *N. Guest.*

TREAMOON   2 br.f. Sahib 114–Hunter's Treasure 69 (Tudor Treasure 119)   **69** [1976 5fg 5.9s]   second foal: dam, winner over 1m on flat, was a very useful hurdler: 16/1 when seventh of 18 to Fear Naught in maiden race at Wolverhampton in October: will be suited by 1m. *E. Cousins.*

TREBLE EVENT   2 ch.f. Decoy Boy 129–Search 79 (High Perch 126)   [1976 5g   **73** 7f 5f 5f 5g⁵ 6d 5v 5s⁶]   half-sister to two winners, including very useful Irish 3-y-o sprinter Grande Prairie (by No Mercy): bought privately 475 gns foal: dam won at 1½m: quite moderate: ran best race on final outing, on soft going: blinkered penultimate appearance. *J. Calvert.*

TREBLE JUMP   2 ch.c. Double Jump 131–Homecomings (Primera 131)   [1976   **80** 5g 5f² 5f² 6d 5h 6g² 7g 6v]   workmanlike colt: first produce: 500 gns foal: dam poor maiden: apprentice ridden, showed first form for some time and put up easily best effort when ¾-length second to Cedar Emerald in nursery at Warwick in August: had stiff task when tried at 7f but should stay that far: acts on firm going: sold 4,000 gns Newmarket Autumn Sales. *W. Wharton.*

TREE BREEZE   5 ch.m. Farm Walk 111–Gay Breeze (Con Brio 121)   [1974   **71** 10f 12h² 8s 9v²   1975 10.5s 10f 8g 10f⁴ 10g 9g 10f³ 10g⁵ 12h³ 12.2f⁶ 10f⁶ 11g⁴ 8g   1976 15.8g* 13v³ 16s⁴ 12.2f⁴ 15f² 14fg² 15.8g² 15g* 16f* 15.8f² 14.7f⁴ 15.8fg⁴ 16fg⁴]   smallish, light-framed mare: ran creditably in 1976 and won at Catterick in March, Edinburgh in June and Beverley in July: stays 2m: acts on any going: has been tried in blinkers: bandaged on reappearance. *Miss S. Hall.*

TREIGN   2 b.c. Track Spare 125–Smart Sovereign 72 (Smartie 102)   [1976 5g   **61** 7g 10v⁴]   neat colt: 7 lengths fourth of 16 to Habbersupreme in seller at Leicester in October: evidently stays 1¼m: sold to M. Bradley 1,500 gns Newmarket Autumn Sales. *P. Haslam.*

TREKKELO   4 br.f. Pals Passage 115–Vipinsor (Windsor Sun 116)   [1974 5g⁶   — 5d   1975 10.2h 5f 10.8g   1976 12.2f 10d 8s 10.2s]   of no account. *F. Yardley.*

TRENCHERMAN   2 ch.c. Ballymoss 136–L'Anguissola 102 (Soderini 123)   — [1976 10v 8s]   third foal: half-brother to smart 3-y-o Solar (by Hotfoot) and very useful sprinter Walk By (by Tower Walk): 3,400 gns yearling: dam won three 6f races at 2 yrs, but disappointed at 3 yrs: behind in end-of-season events at Nottingham (started slowly) and Doncaster (33/1). *W. Wightman.*

TREPAN   4 br.c. Breakspear II–Quiriquina (Molvedo 137)   [1974 7.5d* 9s² 9s⁶   **133 ?** 9v²   1975 9v* 8v* 10.5s⁵ 8g 8d² 8g* 10d* 8s⁶   1976 8g² 8s³ 8s⁴ 9.2g* 10f*(dis) 10fg*(dis) 10.5fg 10s⁴ 12s]

A nine-days' wonder has been memorably analysed as being made up of three days' amazement, three days' discussion of details and three days' subsidence. Surprisingly, the Trepan dope cases managed far to exceed the statutory nine days' hold on the attention of the racing public. The disqualification, after positive dope tests, of the French-trained Trepan from two important English victories set in train a series of sensational stories in the Press. The top French trainer Francois Mathet was reported to have told a leading British journalist: 'Horses are being "doped" throughout Chantilly. I know what is used and how it is being done.' Although Mathet claimed that his words had been distorted, the statement was followed up by other reporters. Several

*Prince of Wales Stakes, Ascot—the first of Trepan's controversial victories,
as he slams Anne's Pretender*

stories, all of them seemingly based on hearsay and rumour, appeared in the ensuing weeks alleging that some French trainers were giving drugs to healthy racehorses to promote better performance. It was also alleged that some French horses were being given transfusions of their own blood before races, an act which, it was claimed, temporarily improved their performance. The epidemic of stories about 'treatment,' as it came to be known, seemed to have been pretty well exhausted by the end of the season. Racing has been left largely unchanged by them which is perhaps the most illuminating comment on the nature of the publicity that surrounded the Trepan episode.

Trepan was disqualified by the Stewards of the Jockey Club from the Prince of Wales Stakes at Royal Ascot and the Joe Coral Eclipse Stakes at Sandown, and his trainer fined a total of £1,250, after traces of a stimulant were found in his system after each event. Both cases were dealt with at a Jockey Club inquiry in London on August 12th. The traces of caffeine and theobromine in the urine sample taken from Trepan at Royal Ascot were attributed by the horse's trainer, Francois Boutin, to a dose of the diuretic (urinary) drug Hepatorenal, which was given to Trepan mistakenly by a stable employee only twenty-four hours before the race. Boutin said that he gave some of his runners a diuretic before they raced but he emphasised that this was normally given at least three days beforehand. Boutin was fined £1,000 in connection with the positive test on Trepan at Royal Ascot; the Stewards accepted Boutin's explanation of the source of the illegal substances but found him in breach of rules 53 and 200 of the Rules of Racing, both of which deal with the administration of illegal substances to racehorses. The Stewards imposed the maximum fine of £500 on Boutin for each breach of the rules; the stable employee concerned was also fined £100. The sample taken from Trepan after his victory in the Joe Coral Eclipse Stakes, a Group 1 pattern race, contained traces of theobromine. The source of the theobromine in the Sandown sample was not established at the inquiry. Boutin claimed that Trepan received no medication whatever during the two and a half weeks between the Prince of Wales Stakes and the Eclipse. In fining Boutin only £250 in connection with the Sandown case, the Stewards seem to have been influenced by the possibility that traces of theobromine could have remained in Trepan's system during the period between the two races.

Although the Stewards of the Jockey Club announced that they took a serious view of the Trepan cases, it is clear from the punishment imposed that they regarded the offences as technical. Boutin, a trainer of the highest international repute, was no more branded a cheat than was Peter Walwyn when the 1971 Gold Cup winner Rock Roi was disqualified after traces of oxyphenbutazone, a metabolite of phenylbutazone, were found in a routine urine sample taken

759

Joe Coral Eclipse Stakes, Sandown—Trepan puts up another performance worthy of a champion to beat Wollow. Radetzky finishes third

after the race. The Stewards had it within their power to declare Boutin a disqualified person in Britain; they could also have asked the French authorities to withdraw his licence to train.

The Jockey Club rule on doping is unequivocal and there was never any doubt, once the results of the dope tests were announced, that Trepan would be disqualified from both races at the subsequent Jockey Club inquiry. Rule 180(ii) of the Rules of Racing states that a horse *shall* be disqualified if *any* amount is found of any substance which is not a normal nutrient and which by its nature could affect a horse's racing performance. It is irrelevant that the amount may have been so small that it could not have had any effect on a horse's performance. Trainers must, therefore, ensure that no residue of any drug is left in a horse's system at the time of racing. The rate at which drugs are excreted from the system varies from horse to horse. After the Rock Roi case, and several others like it, the Royal College of Veterinary Surgeons advised veterinarians that if they discontinued the administration of anti-inflammatory drugs such as phenyl-butazone not less than eight days before racing they should cater for 'all but the most exceptional case.' With certain other types of drugs the elimination time can run into weeks. The use of diuretics may help to clear the system but some of these drugs too contain substances which are regarded as illegal.

In France and Ireland the relevant rules are very similar to those in Britain, while in certain parts of North America horses may run when under treatment with certain pain-killing drugs, such as phenylbutazone. It has been suggested that the rules in Europe are out of date and that lists of permissible and prohibited drugs should be drawn up. The Turf Authorities in Europe are adamant that, for the good of the integrity of racing and breeding, the present strict rules must stay. Most racing people wholeheartedly agree. We have seen it suggested that the French interpret the relevant rule more leniently than the British. It may well be that the use of drugs which help horses to be brought to, and maintained at, peak fitness is much more widespread in France than anywhere else in Europe. But, of course, the use of such drugs is not in itself illegal; the rules are only transgressed if traces of drugs are found at the time of racing. And there is no evidence that the French are turning a blind eye to the illegal use of drugs. In 1976 a leading trainer in France was fined 20,000 francs (about £2,400), just short of the maximum permissible fine, when a dope test proved positive on one of his important winners.

No-one can afford to be complacent about so serious a matter as doping but we can't help feeling that the burst of outrage in the British Press about the so-

760

called 'treatment' of French horses was just sour grapes. Trepan was the only one, out of a fairly large number of French-trained runners in Britain or Ireland in 1976, that was disqualified under the anti-doping rules; Trepan's trainer himself won tip-top races with Sagaro, Malacate and Lagunette, all of whom were dope-tested as a matter of routine after their victories.

Trepan won both the Prince of Wales Stakes and the Eclipse Stakes in storming fashion, on each occasion his time being a record for the course. There is no doubt that on these performances, particularly the one in the Eclipse Stakes, in which Trepan beat Wollow by two lengths, Trepan can be regarded as a top-class racehorse, worthy of a rating of 133. But his performances at Royal Ascot and Sandown were a sharp advance on the others in his career, none of which would entitle him to a position in the first rank of Europe's middle-distance performers, and on his only other outing in England he finished last in the Benson and Hedges Gold Cup at York in August over a similar distance and on similar going to that he encountered in the Eclipse. Trepan's only victory in six races in France in 1976 came in a handicap at Longchamp in May, less than three weeks before Royal Ascot, when he carried 9-8 and won by four lengths. After York he finished only fourth of seven to Ivanjica in the Prix du Prince d'Orange and only thirteenth behind the same filly in the Prix de l'Arc de Triomphe, both races being run on soft ground. He was placed on a mark 10 lb behind Ivanjica in the Handicap Libre, the French Free Handicap, but was not included in the British official handicap for four-year-olds and upwards published at the end of the season.

	Breakspear II	Bold Ruler	Nasrullah
	(br 1961)	(b 1954)	Miss Disco
Trepan		Pocket Edition	Roman
(br.c. 1972)		(br 1944)	Never Again
	Quiriquina	Molvedo	Ribot
	(b 1966)	(br 1958)	Maggiolina
		La Chaussee	Tyrone
		(ch 1961)	Flying Colours

Trepan is a big, good-looking colt. His sire Breakspear II, who was a miler, raced for three seasons in the U.S.A. and won eight of his thirty-seven starts;

Mr R. Schafer's "Trepan" (P. Paquet)

the most successful horse sired by Breakspear is the very good French miler El Rastro. Trepan's dam Quiriquina failed to gain a place in five starts; her only other foal to race is Oncle Tom (by Blue Tom), a winner at up to eleven furlongs in France. Trepan's grandam La Chaussee was a half-sister to many good winners in France including Le Mesnil, the best two-year-old colt of 1962 and runner-up to Exbury in the Prix de l'Arc de Triomphe the following year, and Fontenay, a rattling good two-year-old, who subsequently won the Prix Ganay. Trepan stays a mile and a quarter and acts on any going, although he is, apparently, particularly well suited by top-of-the-ground conditions. He is usually held up. *F. Boutin, France.*

TREVOR BOYO 2 b.c. Malvasia 108–Copious (River Chanter 121) [1976 5fg 5g] first foal: dam ran only once: well behind in maiden races at Windsor in May and Leicester (last of 17) in June: wears blinkers. *K. Bridgwater.*

TREWENOL 2 ch.f. Goldhill 125–Flash of Dawn 89 (Pendragon) [1976 5f 5f6 6h 6fg 5f] of no account: sold 320 gns Ascot July Sales. *R. Wilson.* —

TRIBAL DUEL 3 b.c. Tribal Chief 125–Button Boots 78 (Panaslipper 130) **66** [1975 5g4 5h4 6f* 5g4 5g6 6v 1976 6d 5f4 6s5 6f6 5f4 6f4 6f 6s 7v6] small colt: rated 82 at 2 yrs: not so good but had some stiffish tasks in 1976, including in a seller: should stay 7f: acts on any going. *E. Collingwood.*

TRIBAL FESTIVAL 3 b.f. Tribal Chief 125–Rennet 109 (King's Bench 132) **65** [1975 6fg 6f5 5g 1976 5fg 5.3f6 5.8h6 5fg4 6f3 6f2 6fg* 6d2 5s] light-framed filly: favourite, when winning 16-runner maiden event at Goodwood in September by 1½ lengths from Broken Date: stays 6f: appears to act on any going with possible exception of really soft. *N. Callaghan.*

TRIBAL KING 2 b.c. Tribal Chief 125–Harmony Thyme 73 (Sing Sing 134) **90** [1976 5g5 5fg* 5fg4 5fg3 5fg3 5fg] leggy colt: first foal: 4,000 gns yearling: dam won over 5f at 2 yrs: clear throughout when 4-length winner from Cambridge Star in minor race at Newmarket in April: third afterwards in Berkshire Stakes at Newbury (5½ lengths behind Tachypous) and minor event at Newmarket: coltish in paddock when blinkered on sixth outing, in July, and wasn't seen out again. *R. Hannon.*

TRIBAL SONG 3 b.f. Tribal Chief 125–Burytown (Sammy Davis 129) [1975 **51** 6fg 6s 7g* 7g6 1976 7g 5.9f 6f3 5g6 9fg5 5.8f5] well-made filly: good mover: poor plater: well suited by 7f but is not certain to stay further: ran moderately in blinkers on final outing: sold 725 gns Ascot October Sales. *J. Hill.*

TRIBULATION 4 br.f. Highland Melody 112–Qadar (Sir d'Orient 90) [1974 — 6g* 6g4 5g4 5d6 5s 7v* 1975 7f3 6f3 7f* 7fg6 7.6g5 8g 1976 7g] leggy, rather unfurnished filly: ran only once at 4 yrs: best form at up to 7f: acts on any going: suitable mount for an apprentice. *Sir Mark Prescott.*

TRICIA'S TREASURE 4 gr.f. My Swanee 122–Suku 80 (Light Thrust 114) **73** [1974 5g 5fg* 5g6 5g 1975 6f 5g 5g 1976 5.9f 8f 7fg 6d 6s* 6s3] lengthy filly: made all when winning 11-runner selling handicap at Folkestone in October by a length from Youngest Child (bought in 500 gns): stays 6f and should get further: appears to act on any going: trained by A. Pitt until after second outing: sold 250 gns Ascot November Sales. *R. Hannon.*

TRIESTE 2 ch.f. Porto Bello 118–Mynah Mo (Darius 129) [1976 6g 6v] strong — filly: second foal: dam ran only twice: behind in large fields of maidens at Newmarket in September and Newbury in October. *Doug Smith.*

TRIGAMY 3 br.f. Tribal Chief 125–Polyandrist 92 (Polic 126) [1975 5d3 5g* **110** 5g* 1976 7f 5fg 5f* 5g2 5fg 5fg3 5g 5v*] neat filly: good mover: useful sprinter: won minor event at Thirsk in May by 2½ lengths from Lochnager (gave a stone more than w.f.a.), having only to be kept up to her work with hands and heels: 2 lengths second to Pascualete in minor event at Sandown the following month: ran moderately afterwards until running out a most impressive 7-length winner from Enchanted in similar event at Haydock in October: speedy and may always be best at 5f: acts on any going. *R. Price.*

TRIGGER 2 ch.g. Military 112–Ambition 61 (Petition 130) [1976 6f 8g 5g 6g **52** 8d] bad plater. *D. Thom.*

TRILLIUM 10 ch.g. Psidium 130–Grecian Palm 78 (Royal Palm 131) [1974 — 5g* 5h 5f2 5fg 5fg5 5fg3 5fg6 5g 5d6 1975 5g 5g6 5.1f 6fg5 6g4 5f5 5.9fg 5g 1976 5g 5.9f 6v 6v] poor handicapper nowadays: best at 5f: acts on any going but is very well suited by a soft surface: has been tried in blinkers. *G. Pritchard-Gordon.*

TRINGA 5 b.m. Reform 132–Royal Tucson 87 (Henry the Seventh 125) [1974 **81**
8g³ 10.1d² 8.3g 8s* 8v⁴ 1975 8s³ 8f² 8f² 8h³ 8h⁶ 10f* 10.2g 10f⁶ 8f⁵ 8g³ 10f⁴
1976 10fg 8f⁴ 8f* 8f⁴ 10f² 10h³ 8.2f³ 8f* 9fg² 8fg] neat mare: quite a moderate
handicapper: successful at Warwick in April and Lanark in July: stayed 1¼m:
acted on any going: had run well in blinkers but didn't wear them when successful: sold privately out of J. Hardy's stable Ascot June Sales (after fourth start):
dead. *S. Nesbitt.*

TRIOLE 2 ch.f. Charlottown 127–Wind Break 81 (Borealis) [1976 6g 8s⁴ 7s] **64**
sister to winning stayer Charente and to a winner in Italy, and half-sister to
three other winners: 500 gns yearling: dam won over 7f at 2 yrs: showed a little
ability: will be suited by a test of stamina. *D. Kent.*

TRIPLE FIRST 2 b.f. High Top 131–Field Mouse 108 (Grey Sovereign 128 §) **117**
[1976 5g* 5f⁵ 6fg⁵ 7fg* 7f* 8d* 8g³]
We complained in our commentary on Polygamy in *Racehorses of* 1973 that
the British racing programme lacked one important test—a valuable mile race
for two-year-old fillies. Thankfully, the Argos Star Fillies' Mile at Ascot seems
now to be providing that test although its value to the winner in 1976 was less than
a quarter of the prize carried by the French equivalent, the Criterium des Pouliches, and there are now also quite valuable races for staying fillies at Goodwood
and Doncaster.
The need for these races could hardly have been better illustrated than by
Triple First's career. Her form in her first three races was no more than useful;
after putting in a spectacular late run to win a maiden race at Sandown in May
she finished only fifth in the Queen Mary Stakes at Royal Ascot, beaten two
lengths by Cramond, and in the Cherry Hinton Stakes at Newmarket, where
Ampulla beat her four lengths. Clearly she wasn't up to beating the best of her
sex over five and six furlongs but up to 1974 her trainer would probably have
had to continue running a filly of her type in similar races, as the only alternatives
for her over long distances were nurseries and races for which colts were also
eligible.
Now that he had three worthwhile prizes to aim at, her trainer wasted no
time in trying Triple First over longer trips. After a none too impressive win in
a minor race at Thirsk she ran in the Waterford Candelabra Stakes at Goodwood
and showed much improved form, coming through to hit the front approaching
the final furlong and then striding out in fine style to win by four lengths. The
fast-finishing Lady Rhapsody snatched second place from the favourite Miss
Pinkie who would have beaten her but for being eased close home. A fortnight
later Triple First started second favourite to Paddington in the May Hill Stakes at
Doncaster. This time she made the running at a steady pace, quickened well
coming to the final two furlongs and then battled on in splendid style to get home
by half a length from Dunfermline who had looked to be going the better for much
of the way up the straight. Lady Rhapsody, reproducing her Goodwood form,
was third.
Triple First was made favourite for the Argos Star Fillies' Mile although
giving Dunfermline 8 lb, a pound more than at Doncaster, and although she was
meeting Miss Pinkie on terms 7 lb worse than at Goodwood. She was unable to

May Hill Stakes, Doncaster—Triple First keeps Dunfermline at bay

beat them at these weights and it was all she could do to get into a challenging position a furlong out. At the line she was two lengths behind the all-the-way winner Miss Pinkie.

Triple First (b.f. 1974)	High Top (br 1969)	Derring-Do (b 1961)	Darius
			Sipsey Bridge
		Camanae (b 1961)	Vimy
			Madrilene
	Field Mouse (gr 1964)	Grey Sovereign (gr 1948)	Nasrullah
			Kong
		Meadow Song (b 1953)	Nitgal
			Singing Grass

Triple First is a well-made, quite attractive filly who cost 7,800 guineas as a foal and 11,000 guineas when resold the following year. She is from the first crop of the Two Thousand Guineas winner High Top who has made a very encouraging start to his stud career, siring seven other winners including Blackadder. High Top never raced beyond a mile, and since Triple First's dam, Field Mouse, gained all her six wins over five furlongs it's a little surprising that Triple First needed at least seven furlongs to show her best at two years. However there is stamina further back in Field Mouse's pedigree—her dam, Meadow Song, won twice over a mile and a quarter and is a half-sister to Never Say Die—and the best of her three previous winners is the useful Asama (by Ribero) who stays long distances. Although Triple First stayed a mile so well at two years that's no reason to expect her to stay much further at three. There are more races for fillies of her type than there are for sprinting fillies of similar ability and she should continue to do well. She is thoroughly genuine and consistent, seems to act on any going, has an excellent turn of foot but can make her own running if need be, and has won on all types of track. In all, an admirable filly. *M. Stoute.*

TRIPOLI 3 ch.f. Great Heron 127–Mega Fawn 87 (Sound Track 132) [1975 — 6g 6d 1976 8f] attractive filly: lightly raced but has shown definite signs of ability. *B. Hills.*

TROLLER 6 ch.g. Milesian 125–Spin Out 97 (Pall Mall 132) [1974 7h 5.8fg 38 5.9f 5g3 5fg5 5g 5fg5 8s2 1975 6g 7f4 8f 12f6 1976 7f2 8fg4 7fg 5g 7f6 7f6] lengthy, short-legged gelding: plater nowadays: stays 1m: probably acts on any going: suitable mount for an apprentice. *J. Hayward.*

TROOPERS TREASURE 2 b.f. King's Troop 118–Balfour Lass 81 (My — Smokey 125) [1976 5g] half-sister to winning 3-y-o sprinter Cry No More (by Weepers Boy) and to a winning plater: 1,000 guineas yearling: dam stayed 1¾m: seventh of 15 to Miss Pert in maiden race at Salisbury in May, only outing: dead. *A. Johnson.*

TROOPETTE 4 b.f. King's Troop 118–Crepinette 64 (Saint Crespin III 132) — [1974 5f* 5g5 5d* 5d5 6v 1975 7g 7f6 6f5 10f3 10f 9f2 8f3 8fg2 8f5 8g 8f 1976 8g 8fg 8f4 7fg] smallish, strong, lengthy, good-quartered filly: quite a moderate performer at 3 yrs but didn't find her form in 1976: stays 1¼m: seems to act on any going except perhaps very heavy ground: wears blinkers. *W. O'Gorman.*

TROSSACHS 2 ch.c. Tower Walk 130–Special Branch 83 (Acer 123) [1976 5g4 101 5g 5h5 5f* 6h* 5.9fg 6s 6v4 7.6v*] neat colt: second foal: half-brother to a winner in Belgium by Balidar: dam won twice over 5f at 2 yrs: won at Folkestone in July and August and put up a game display to hold off Gleaming Wave by a neck in nursery at Lingfield in November: will stay 1m: acts on any going: not disgraced when blinkered on third outing. *J. Dunlop.*

TROTALONG THOMAS 2 b.c. Tompion–Fleeting Lady (Fleet Nasrullah) 64 [1976 5fg 6fg5] first foal: 480 gns yearling: dam, second three times in France from 6f to 1m, is daughter of $145,000 earner Lady Larue: 3 lengths fifth of 11 to Frisco Bay in seller at Leicester in July: not seen out again: should be suited by 1¼m+. *T. Marshall.*

TROTTY 5 b.g. King's Troop 118–Soft Collar 99 (Quorum 126) [1974 8.2fg4 — 7g* 7f3 7f* 7g5 7.6s2 7g3 7g 7.6v* 7d6 1975 7v 7f 7g3 7fg6 7g* 7g 7f 1976 10f 7fg 7f 6f5 7d] well-grown gelding: seems of little account nowadays. *A. Dalton.*

TRUCE OF OMAN 2 ch.c. Gulf Pearl 117–Cease Fire 112 (Martial 131) [1976 108 5g 6fg2 6fg* 6fg3 6fg* 7g4 6fg6 6g*] neat, attractive colt: half-brother to a winner in Italy by Silly Season and to 7f and 1¼m winner Verity's Request (by Prince Regent): 8,600 gns yearling: dam 6f sprinter: made all to land the odds in 16-runner maiden race at Salisbury in June and two-runner £1,600 event at

Leicester the following month: gained another success when top weight in eight-runner nursery at Lingfield in September and put up a very useful performance, coming home a length clear of Bodensee: best form at 6f: possibly needs some give in the ground to show to best advantage: sold privately for export to North America. *P. Walwyn.*

TRUE DIVER 2 b.c. Deep Diver 134–Elsa 103 (Migoli 132) [1976 6f 7v] useful-looking colt: half-brother to two minor winners: 6,200 gns foal and resold for 4,700 gns as a yearling: dam a miler: well behind in minor event at Newmarket in August and maiden race at Leicester in October (eased when beaten). *M. Stoute.* —

TRUE LAD 6 b.g. Straight Lad 110–Telado (Telegram II 120) [1974 N.R. 1975 16s 16.1fg² 22.2fg⁴ 16d 1976 18fg* 16fg] big gelding: beat Supreme Halo 5 lengths when winning four-runner Great Metropolitan Handicap at Epsom in April on reappearance: tailed off on second start (had stiffish task): stays extremely well: acts on a firm surface: refused to start (flag) until field had gone a furlong when tailed off on first outing in 1975, and is apparently something of a funny customer. *W. Swainson.* 76

TRUE PRINCE 3 b.c. Prince Tenderfoot 126–Twilight Tear (Ragusa 137) [1975 6g⁴ 6g 7.6g² 1976 8.2f² 8f⁴ 8.2f³ 8g³ 8f² 8h* 10f* 8d 8.2s⁶] lightly-made colt: won maiden race at Brighton in August (made short work of three vastly inferior animals) and three-runner minor event at Folkestone the following month (enterprisingly ridden when beating Shuwaiman 1½ lengths): stays 1¼m: best form on a sound surface: wears blinkers nowadays. *P. Walwyn.* 85

TRUE SHOT 3 ch.c. On Your Mark 125–Rain Water 83 (Nimbus 130) [1975 6s⁴ 6g⁴ 7s³ 1976 8f* 9s³ 10g* 10.5fg³ 10fg⁴ 10fg² 12f⁴ 10g⁴] well-made, good-looking colt: winner of maiden race at Ascot and handicap at Sandown: put up two good efforts in July, when just over 1½ lengths third of nine to Bold Pirate in John Smith's Magnet Cup (handicap) at York and 5 lengths fourth to Chil the Kite in Land of Burns Stakes at Ayr, but ran below his best last two starts: stays 1¼m: acts on any going: sold privately after final outing to D. Underwood. *R. Price.* 105

TRUE SONG 7 ch.h. Relko 136–Soldier's Song 104 (Court Martial) [1974 12v² 16v⁴ 12g³ 1975 12s⁵ 1976 14f² 20f²] rangy horse: fair handicapper: had only two outings on flat in 1976 but ran well on both of them, on second finishing 1½ lengths second of 10 to Tudor Crown in Ascot Stakes at Royal Ascot in June: stays well: acts on any going: has been tried in blinkers: game. *D. Underwood.* 84

TRUE WORD 4 b.g. Blakeney 126–Gospel Truth 95 (Above Suspicion 127) [1974 N.R. 1975 10g² 9.4g* 11.7f* 14d* 16h³ 15.8fg² 1976 12d² 15.8g* 18.4fg³] quite a useful handicapper: decisive winner of 10-runner apprentice handicap (heavily-backed favourite) at Catterick in June, being ridden with only hands and heels to beat Tree Breeze 2½ lengths: well-beaten third to stable-companion Mr Bigmore at Chester the following month: stays well: appears to act on any going: suitable mount for an apprentice: consistent. *F. Robinson.* 88

TRULY YOURS 3 br.f. So Blessed 130–Yours Sincerely 94 (Above Suspicion 127) [1975 5g⁵ 5s* 5g* 1976 7g 6fg 7fg⁵ 6fg 6fg⁶ 10g³ 10.6d⁴] strong, good-looking filly: fairly useful handicapper: evidently stays 1¼m: appears to act on any going: blinkered fifth outing: has had tongue tied down. *S. Hall.* 91

TRUMANIA 2 b.f. Silly Season 127–True Delirium 87 (Delirium 126) [1976 5fg⁵ 5d⁵ 7f⁵ 9fg⁴ 8fg³] leggy, narrow filly: half-sister to three winners, including useful 5f to 1m winner Mons Madness (by Hill Clown): 3,000 gns yearling: dam fair at 2 yrs: quite a modest performer: looked lean but ran creditably when third to runaway winner Vaguely in 12-runner maiden race at Beverley in September: stays 9f: sold 1,800 gns Newmarket December Sales. *H. Cecil.* 71

TRUMPET BLOWER 2 b.c. Joshua 129–Finlandian 63 (Acropolis 132) [1976 6g 8s 7v] big, strong colt: half-brother to several winners, including fairly useful middle-distance performer Finmoss (by Mossborough): 1,300 gns foal, resold 1,550 gns yearling: dam temperamental sister to smart stayer Acrophel: beaten some way in maiden and minor events. *M. Francis.* —

TRUMPET CALL 2 ch.f Joshua 129–Long Days 92 (Bleep-Bleep 134) [1976 5.3g² 5fg* 6f⁵] third living foal: dam won over 5f at 2 yrs, only season to race: kept on gamely when winning five-runner maiden race at Lingfield in July by short head from Cake Popper: not raced after August: should stay 6f. *H. Candy.* 81

TRUST A NATIVE 3 b.c. Raise A Native–Primary 112 (Petition 130) [1975 5.5d* 1976 7g⁶ 7.5g³ 8f 6.5d⁵ 6.5g³ 8g⁵ 8g 7s 8s⁵ 6.5d] American-bred French 108 colt: in frame only twice in ten starts, being beaten just over a length into third place by The Chaplain in Prix Montenica at Maisons-Laffitte in April and occupying same place in Prix Hampton at Evry in July, 5 lengths behind Arch Sculptor: has also several respectable efforts in handicaps to his name but was out of his depth in St James's Palace Stakes at Royal Ascot when last of eight to Radetzky on only outing in this country: stays 1m: acts on heavy ground: often wears blinkers. *J. Fellows, France.*

TRUSTED 3 ch.c. Crepello 136–Parolee 88 (Sing Sing 134) [1975 6s⁵ 8.2d* **109** 8d⁵ 1976 10fg² 10fg² 8fg* 8fg* 10fg⁴ 8f⁴] big, rangy colt: picked up two valuable races in July, namely William Hill Silver Vase at Newmarket by ½ length from Free State and Joe Coral Handicap at Ayr by ½ length from Pagos Boy (made most): fair fourth in Extel Handicap at Goodwood and William Hill Gold Cup at Redcar subsequently: best form at 1m: acts on a firm and a soft surface: sweated up final outing (August). *J. Dunlop.*

TRUSTFUL 5 b.g. Reliance II 137–Julieta 108 (Ratification 129) [1974 12g **80** 12g² 12f* 12g⁵ 12g 12s 1975 12s⁴ 12g* 8g³(dis) 8f² 12g⁶ 14fg* 1976 14g³ 16g⁵] strong, rangy gelding: ran promisingly on reappearance when about 3½ lengths behind Paddy Jack in three-runner Sportsman Club Handicap at Sandown in September: didn't reproduce that form when last of five behind Tug of War at Ascot later in month on only subsequent start: stays 1¾m: possibly requires a sound surface and acts on firm going: ran very freely and was well beaten when tried in blinkers. *S. Mellor.*

TRUST VIEW 2 b.f. Sahib 114–Mollie (I Say 125) [1976 5g* 7h 8fg] leggy **62** filly: first produce: 520 gns foal, resold 740 gns yearling: dam poor maiden: attracted no bid after winning eight-runner seller at Carlisle in May: well beaten afterwards in nurseries at Redcar in August and September but had stiff tasks: should be suited by 7f. *K. Payne.*

TRY ROCKING 4 b.f. Tycoon II–Rock-On (Rockefela) [1974 N.R. 1975 8v⁴ **—** 10s⁵ 12f 8g 12f⁴ 1976 8g 8f] strong filly: of little account. *A. Bacon.*

TRYSULL 2 b.f. Swinging Junior 118–Tinker Lass (Tin Whistle 128) [1976 5s **—** 5f 5f⁵] bad plater. *R. Ward.*

TSAREVICH 3 gr.c. Iron Ruler–Hibernate 87 (Arctic Prince 135) [1975 5.1f* **79** 6f² 6fg 1976 10g⁴ 10.4s⁵ 8f⁶ 10f³] leggy, lightly-made colt: American-bred: quite a moderate handicapper: co-favourite and top weight when fifth of 12 to Grecian Bond at Chester in May, best effort: probably stays 1¼m: sold 580 gns Goffs September Sales. *M. Vance, Ireland.*

TSTNAN 3 ch.g. Yellow River 114–Miss Rosa 102 (Rustam 127) [1975 6s 7g **—** 1976 10g 11.7f 18s] bad maiden: sold out of Mrs F. Nagle's stable 560 gns Ascot June Sales. *J. Twibell.*

TUDOR BANQUET 2 ch.c. Grisaille 115–Cantelle 66 (Canisbay 120) [1976 5f **—** 7fg 6f] neat colt: blinkered first and third outings and started slowly on second: trained by K. Whitehead on first two appearances: sold 210 gns Doncaster October Sales. *S. Nesbitt.*

TUDOR CHEAT 5 br.g. Tudor Music 131–Royal Escape 94 (King's Bench 132) **46** [1974 7d⁵ 7d³ 5fg³ 8h* 9fg⁶ 8.2g² 8fg⁶ 14g⁶ 10g³ 11.2s³ 11.1s² 10v² 1975 N.R. 1976 8v* 11d* 13g³ 10f 8g 8fg 10f 8.2fg] lengthy, light-framed gelding: selling handicapper: successful at Ayr in April and Edinburgh later the same month (co-favourite, awarded race after stewards inquiry), being bought in for 480 gns on latter course: stayed 11f: acted on any going: used to wear blinkers: dead. *B. Richmond.*

TUDOR CROWN 5 b.h. Tudor Music 131–Crownless (Royal Challenger 129) **85** [1974 8.5fg² 8g* 8g² 8g² 10g* 10.5s³ 12d⁴ 12v⁵ 12v* 1975 12s* 12g* 12fg³ 12f 12f² 14g² 12g² 12f 14g⁴ 12s⁵ 12d⁴ 12fg² 12g³ 12s² 12v 1976 12.3d⁵ 12f 20g 20f*] strong, good sort of horse: fair handicapper: 66/1, stunned Royal Ascot racegoers when winning Ascot Stakes in June, setting up a clear lead from start and battling on most courageously to beat True Song and stable-companion Coed Cochion: not seen out subsequently: stays extremely well: acts on any going: sometimes wears blinkers and did so at Ascot: well suited by front-running tactics: genuine and consistent. *J. Hindley.*

TUDOR DAWN 3 ch.f. Tudor Treasure 119–Montash (Doubtless II 111) [1975 **—** N.R. 1976 12.2s] first foal: dam poor N.H. performer: tailed off in maiden race won by Nargis at Wolverhampton in October. *R. Edwards.*

Ascot Stakes—66/1-shot Tudor Crown is never headed. True Song is a good second followed by the favourite (and stable-companion of the winner) Coed Cochion, and Grinling Gibbons (striped cap)

TUDOR DEB   2 br.f. Tudor Music 131–Gay Baby 101 (Galivanter 131)   [1976   **68**
5fg³ 5fg⁴ 5f* 6d]   small filly: won nine-runner seller at Bath in May by 2 lengths
from Miten Drinen: bought in 750 gns subsequently: not certain to stay 6f. *G. Hunter.*

TUDOR FLAME   4 b.c. Sing Sing 134–Slag 92 (Mossborough 126)   [1974 7d⁶   **—**
6g⁴ 7d* 6d   1975 8.2s² 12v⁵ 8d 6f 7g 7f⁶ 8g⁵ 8.2g⁴ 7.2fg   1976 10s 10s]   very
tall colt: poor handicapper nowadays: evidently stays 1m: acts on soft going:
has been tried in blinkers: dwelt start reappearance. *M. Stevens.*

TUDOR JEWEL   8 ch.g. Henry the Seventh 125–Diamond Wedding (Never   **68**
Say Die 137)   [1974 8g⁵ 9f⁴ 10g⁴ 10g³ 6f* 8g 6g⁵ 10f⁵ 8g   1975 7s⁶ 6g*   1976 6f³
7fg 6f 6f⁵ 10f 10f⁴ 7.6v⁵]   light-framed gelding: ran his best race of 1976 on
reappearance: stays 1¼m but is effective at much shorter distances: best form on a
sound surface: has worn blinkers but does at least as well without. *B. Wise.*

TUDOR JIG   2 b.c. Tudor Melody 129–Conflagration 86 (Privy Councillor 125)   **99**
[1976 5d 6d 5fg 5f⁵ 8v 7v* 6s*]   rangy colt: third foal: half-brother to a minor
2-y-o winner by Birdbrook: dam won at up to 1m: in good form at end of season
and won two minor events at Teesside, beating Red Light District by 5 lengths in
October and Alexanda the Great by a length in 24-runner race in November:
stays 7f well, and should get 1m: acts on any going but goes particularly well on
heavy. *M. W. Easterby.*

TUDOR KING   2 b.c. Henry the Seventh 125–Schonbrunn 100 (Blue Peter)   **—**
[1976 7fg]   brother to fairly useful 1m and 1¼m winner Austria, and half-brother
to several other winners: dam won at 1m: remote seventh of 11 in maiden race
won by Qui Va La at Edinburgh in September. *J. W. Watts.*

TUDOR LILT   2 ch.c. Tudor Music 131–Eriskay 78 (Romulus 129)   [1976 5g⁶   **102**
5f² 5g* 6fg* 6fg⁴ 7fg² 7g⁴ 7f⁶ 8f*]   well-made colt: third foal: brother to Caltra,
a useful winner over 7f at 2 yrs in Ireland in 1975: 3,100 gns yearling: dam stayed
1¼m: won at Leicester and Lingfield in June and put up an excellent effort under
top weight to win 17-runner nursery at Bath in September by a head from Mr
Morris: suited by 1m: acts on firm going: genuine: to U.S.A. *J. Hindley.*

TUDOR LINK   2 b.f. Manacle 123–Royal Tucson 87 (Henry the Seventh 125)   **77**
[1976 5d⁴ 5f³ 6fg 6fg⁴ 5.1f³ 6fg 6g 7.2v⁵]   leggy filly: half-sister to three winners,
including quite useful 1975 2-y-o Tucsedo (by Northfields), a winner in Italy
subsequently: 4,100 gns yearling: dam placed at up to 9f: in frame in maiden
races, finishing 2½ lengths third of nine to Colourful Connie at Yarmouth in
August on fifth outing: probably stays 7f: seems to act on any going: sold 2,000
gns Newmarket December Sales.   *R. Armstrong.*

TUDOR LORD   5 b.h. Tudor Music 131–Fair Darling 93 (Darling Boy 124)   **62**
[1974 8f³ 10f 8f⁵   1975 10v 10s* 9d⁴ 9.4h² 8g³ 10.1fg³ 8.3fg² 9f⁶ 8.2g² 8g   1976
10f³ 12.2f 10.2s 12.5s]   strong, lengthy horse: didn't run up to his best after
first outing at 5 yrs (off course over five months before third start): stays 1¼m:
evidently acts on any going, but is probably best served by a sound surface:
blinkered first two outings: sold out of D. Morley's stable 2,500 gns Doncaster
May Sales.   *T. Craig.*

TUDOR MAESTRO   4 ch.g. Tudor Music 131–Blonde Bomb 72 (Worden II 129)   **—**
[1974 5g 5g 5g 6s 8d* 6s³ 7.2v   1975 7v 11s 10g 8f⁶ 8fg⁵ 8g⁵ 8f² 8g⁶   1976 8.2v²]
moderate handicapper (rated 80) at 3 yrs: 12 lengths second to Croisette at
Hamilton in April on only outing in 1976: stays 1m: acts on any going: has run
creditably both with and without blinkers (wore them on reappearance):
inconsistent: sold 920 gns Newmarket July Sales.   *Denys Smith.*

TUDOR MANSION   2 b.c. Tudor Melody 129–Private View 74 (Derring-Do 131)   **77**
[1976 8d 7v]   lengthy, lightly-made colt: second foal: half-brother to a winner
in Spain: 1,650 gns yearling: dam stayed 1m: never-dangerous seventh of 17 to
Ad Lib Ra in maiden race at Newbury in September: never showed in weakly-
contested maiden race won by Chennel Lane at Leicester in October.   *I. Walker.*

TUDORRIO   2 b.c. Shoolerville 121–Demi Nuage 83 (Silver Cloud 121)   [1976   **62**
5g 6f 7.2f 6s 5v⁶ 5s⁵]   neat colt: moderate plater: stays 6f, and should get
further: acts on any going: ran creditably in blinkers on final outing.   *J.
Etherington.*

TUDOR SET   2 b.c. Tudor Melody 129–My Game (My Babu 136)   [1976 5g 6g   **82**
5s 6s³]   brother to very useful 1974 Irish 2-y-o Lady Seymour, and half-brother
to numerous winners: 2,400 gns yearling: dam unraced half-sister to Eclipse
winner Arctic Explorer: ran best race when 2½ lengths third to Song Book in
seller at Newmarket in October: should stay 1m: blinkered last two outings.
W. Holden.

TUDOR SLIPPER   4 ch.c. Henry the Seventh 125–Snow Slipper (Panaslipper   **74**
130)   [1974 5fg 6fg 7g 7d² 7.3d²   1975 8v⁴ 11.7g² 10fg 12fg 12d 16g 10g 10s* 10g*
10fg⁴ 10s³   1976 10fg 12fg* 13fg 12f* 14f⁴ 14fg⁶ 12fg³ 12.2s]   lengthy colt: quite
a moderate handicapper: successful at Newmarket in June (apprentice event)
and Ripon in August, on latter course beating My Wellie ½ length: best form at
up to 1½m: acts on any going: sold out of R. Price's stable 3,400 gns Doncaster
March Sales.   *W. O'Gorman.*

TUDORS RUNABOUT   3 gr.f. Galivanter 131–Tudor Wench 72 (Tudor Jinks   **—**
121)   [1975 5s 5f 5f 5.8h 7fg 6g⁶ 8f⁴ 7g 8d   1976 8fg 10g⁵ 12fg]   bad plater: has
worn blinkers.   *R. Wilson.*

TUDOR VELVET   4 b.f. Tudor Music 131–Shot Silk 110 (High Treason 126)   **—**
[1974 N.R.   1975 7s 7fg 8fg   1976 8fg⁶ 8fg 10f 12f6]   lengthy filly: plater: has
shown little sign of ability: sold 700 gns Newmarket Autumn Sales.   *P.
Robinson.*

TUDOR WAKE   2 ch.c. Tudor Music 131–Wake 85 (Never Say Die 137)   [1976   **52**
5f 5fg⁵ 5fg]   showed only poor form in sellers and didn't race after August.
M. W. Easterby.

TUDOR WYNK   3 br.g. Wynkell 88–Wandering Rose (Tudor Minstrel 144)   **76**
[1975 6fg 6g 6g⁵ 6fg 6g⁵ 8f² 8d   1976 8g 7.6fg⁵ 8fg 10.2s³ 12s*]   workmanlike
gelding: won 19-runner maiden race at Chepstow in October by 10 lengths from
Brave Elbow: suited by middle distances: acts on any going: blinkered last
outing in 1975.   *H. Nicholson.*

TUG OF WAR   3 ch.c. Reliance II 137–Pirate Queen 77 (Pirate King 129)   **98**
[1975 7f 7g 7fg² 8d 8g 8g⁴   1976 12fg⁶ 12f⁴ 12fg* 16f 12f* 15.5f² 14fg* 12g⁴ 16g*
18d⁴ 16v⁵].   quite a useful handicapper: winner at Brighton (twice), Goodwood
and Ascot: put up easily his best performance on last-named course in September
when scoring unchallenged by 4 lengths (eased right up inside final furlong) from
Mistress Clare: far from disgraced when fourth of 14 to most impressive winner
John Cherry in SKF Cesarewitch at Newmarket the following month: suited

by long distances: appears to act on any going, except perhaps heavy. *D. Whelan.*

TULLY 2 b.c. Tudor Melody 129–La Milo 87 (Hornbeam 130) [1976 7g⁴ 7g²] **96**
well-made, good-bodied colt: sixth foal: half-brother to five winners, notably top-class middle-distance performer Admetus (by Reform) and smart 1970 2-y-o Laristan (by Tamerlane): dam won at around 1½m: disputed lead most of way when 2½ lengths second of 14 to Caporello in £1,900 event at Sandown in September: will stay at least 1¼m: certain to win races. *R. Hern.*

TUMBAH 3 gr.g. Shantung 132–Some Tune 96 (Tin Whistle 128) [1975 N.R. 1976 11g⁶ 10g 9v 12g] big, strong gelding: second live produce: 1,100 gns foal: dam, fairly useful winner over 5f at 2 yrs, is sister to very speedy Decoy Boy: no worthwhile form in maiden and minor events but has been backward. *G. Richards.*

TUMBLING DICE 3 br.g. Gay Don 111–Sodeska (Fric 128) [1975 5s⁵ 5g 5f 6g 7d 10g⁴ 1976 9fg 14g 12fg 12g 15.5s] big, fair sort: plater: stays 1¼m. *A. Davison.*

TUNIS 3 ro.c. Henry the Seventh 125–Lebanon 87 (Palestine 133) [1975 5s³ **62** 6f 5fg 6f 6g 1976 8fg 8f 10f⁶ 11.7fg 10.1g 8fg 6s 6s*] plater: 33/1 and apprentice ridden, showed vastly improved form when winning at Folkestone in October (no bid): should stay 1m but isn't certain to stay 1½m: acts on soft going: has sometimes worn blinkers but is evidently better without. *T. Gates.*

TURK 4 ch.g. Native Prince–Devon Chimes (Devonian) [1974 5d⁵ 5fg⁵ 5s 7s **65** 1975 6f 5.3g 6d 5g 5g² 1976 12f⁴ 10fg 16f⁴ 6f²] compact gelding: plater: 1½ lengths second to Yellow Watch in seller at Yarmouth in July: form only at up to 6f: blinkered second and third starts: sold 700 gns Doncaster November Sales. *R. Carter.*

TURKEY TROT 4 b.g. Great Heron 127–Solar Song 98 (Solar Slipper 131) **58** [1974 6g*(dis) 6g² 7g³ 7g⁴ 7s² 7s⁶ 6v* 1975 7v 10s 7g 5h 7fg⁴ 6fg* 6g² 6f 8g 1976 8g⁴ 8g²] tall gelding: selling handicapper: ran creditably on his two outings in this country in 1976: best form at up to 1m, but should stay further: seems to act on any going: sometimes wears blinkers but does just as well without them: exported to Sweden where he was subsequently successful. *P. Buckley.*

TURMOIL 6 b.g. Primera 131–Kilula 93 (Nearula 132) [1974 8g 10f⁶ 8.3fg 1975 10s⁵ 1976 12g⁴ 10f³ 15g] of no account. *A. Pitt.*

TURNKEY 5 gr.h. Tudor Melody 129–Bolting 108 (King's Bench 132) [1974 — 6g* 5fg⁶ 6fg⁵ 6fg³ 6g 5fg⁵ 5.6d² 5d* 1975 5fg 5fg 5f 6f³ 5g 1976 5.9fg 5fg⁶] strong horse: very useful sprinter in 1974, but was mainly disappointing after: effective at 5f and 6f: probably acted on any going: tried in blinkers on final start: at stud in South Africa. *R. Price.*

TURNPIKE 3 ch.c. Sheshoon 132–Following 91 (Royal Palm 131) [1975 7g⁶ **92** 7g⁶ 1976 11f 12fg² 16f 14g³ 12g* 10g* 10.6d⁵] attractive, good-looking, rangy colt: good mover: enterprisingly ridden when winning maiden race at Kempton in August and three-runner minor event at Goodwood the following month: best form at up to 1½m but has given impression he will be suited by a good test of stamina (out of his depth on only attempt at 2m): bandaged in front on fourth outing. *I. Balding.*

TURN THE CORNER 2 b.f. Sit In The Corner–Buckskin Annie (Maharaj **57** Kumar 124) [1976 5g 6f* 6f] neat, light-framed filly: half-sister to useful 1969 2-y-o Ickford (by Counsel): dam won over 6f in Ireland on her only start: bought in 1,750 gns after staying on to win nine-runner seller at Ripon in July by neck from stable-companion Firby: had quite a lot to do at weights when last in nursery on next outing: should stay 1m. *M. W. Easterby.*

TURO 2 b.c. Captain's Gig–Sams Daisy 91 (Super Sam 124) [1976 7g 7d⁵] big, **83 p** strong colt: second foal: half-brother to quite useful 3-y-o Autoway (by Astec), a winner over 7f at 2 yrs: 3,000 gns yearling: dam won over 6f from three starts: unquoted and still backward, caught our eye when 10 lengths fifth of 25 to Bessie Wallis in Houghton Stakes at Newmarket in October, making good late progress to come out best of group on stands side: will stay 1¼m: a tailing individual who looks sure to do much better. *B. Hanbury.*

TUSCANY 3 br.f. Sterling Bay–Tuolpukka 75 (High Hat 131) [1975 6g⁴ — 6g 1976 8g] tall, leggy Swedish-bred filly: fourth foal: half-sister to two winners in Sweden, including Tuola (by High Flown), placed in Swedish 1,000 Guineas and Oaks and Danish Oaks: dam, stoutly bred, showed quite modest form at 2 yrs: won maiden race in Sweden as a 2-y-o: 33/1 when last of eight to Katie May in minor race at Sandown in June, only outing in this country: sold 840 gns Newmarket Autumn Sales. *N. Guest.*

TUTORIAL 3 b.c. Tudor Melody 129–Yelda 109 (Crepello 136) [1975 6g³ 1976 8fg² 8g⁴ 10.1fg² 9f* 10f² 10fg* 10g⁴ 10fg² 12g* 12v²] fair performer: won maiden race at Lingfield and two handicaps at Leicester: apprentice ridden when gaining second success on latter course in September by a length from Ebb and Flo: stays 1½m: acts on any going: consistent: sold 6,400 gns Newmarket Autumn Sales, reportedly to race in Norway. *R. Armstrong.* **88**

TUTU 3 ch.f. Ballymoss 136–Final Orders (Prince John) [1975 8g⁴ 1976 8g⁴ 12.2fg* 12g* 12f* 12f² 14.8fg² 13fg² 12fg* 12g*] tall, well-grown, unfurnished filly: improved greatly during the year and ended it a very useful performer: won maiden race at Wolverhampton and handicaps at Kempton and Lingfield in first half of season: put up a most impressive performance on last-named course in June, defying a 4-lb penalty with ridiculous ease (beat Breeze Wagon by a good deal further than official margin of 12 lengths) and breaking course record in process: kept her form and condition extremely well afterwards and gained further good-style successes in minor event at Beverley (by 5 lengths from The Hand) and handicap at Newmarket (beat My Polyanna by 2 lengths, defying a 4-lb penalty), both in September: stays 1¾m: acts well on firm going: a thoroughly game, genuine and consistent individual: exported to U.S.A. *B. Hobbs.* **110**

T.V. SUNDAY 4 br.c. T.V. Lark–Rope Yarn Sunday (Royal Charger) [1974 7g 7d 1975 12v³ 12s⁵ 16.1fg* 16f² 14fg* 21f³ 13f* 16fg* 15.5s 1976 12f 16g⁵ 18.4s 16g 12g⁶ 18g⁶] close-coupled, good sort of colt: American-bred: showed useful form in 1975, winning four races and finishing third in Goodwood Cup: little worthwhile form at 4 yrs and ran very poorly in his last few races: needs long distances: acts on firm going and is probably unsuited by soft: trained by B. Hills until after fourth start (blinkered): off course over three months between fifth and sixth outings. *N. Vigors.* **—**

TWENTY-TWO CARAT 4 b.c. Grey Sovereign 128 §–Bean Feast (Hornbeam 130) [1974 7g 1975 10s 10g⁵ 10fg⁶ 10f 12f² 16s 1976 16f] attractive, shapely colt: disappointing maiden: stays 1½m: has been tried in blinkers: sold 1,200 gns Doncaster August Sales. *R. Price.* **—**

TWIDALE 3 ch.g. Twilight Alley 133–Leadendale Lady 90 (Damremont 120) [1975 N.R. 1976 12.2f⁶ 16g⁶ 16fg] neat gelding: half-brother to two winners, including quite useful stayer Sufficient (by Quorum): 700 gns yearling: dam game and genuine 1m to 1½m handicapper: showed a little ability in maiden events in first part of season: sold 550 gns Doncaster November Sales. *J. W. Watts.* **65**

TWIG MOSS 3 b.c. Luthier 126–Top Twig (High Perch 126) [1975 8s 8v³ 1976 8.5s* 8.5g² 10v* 10fg² 11g* 12f³ 12g² 10.5fg⁵ 12s] lengthy, attractive French colt: third foal: brother to good-class French middle-distance 4-y-o Tip Moss and half-brother to very smart 1m to 1½m performer Twig (by Hul a Hul): 100,000 francs (approx £9,000) yearling: dam last in both her races: developed into a high-class performer, on seventh start going down by 3 lengths to Youth in Prix du Jockey-Club at Chantilly in June with subsequent Irish Sweeps Derby winner Malacate ¾ length away third: successful earlier in two minor events at Cagnes-sur-Mer (both in good style) and Group 2 Prix Noailles at Longchamp (beat Caron by ¾ length): also placed in Prix de Courcelles (½-length second to Avaray) and Prix Hocquart (1¼ lengths third to Grandchant), both at Longchamp: ran below his best on last two outings, finishing about 10 lengths fifth to Wollow in Benson and Hedges Gold Cup at York and beating only two home in Prix de l'Arc de Triomphe: stays 1½m: acts on any going: sure to win more races if returning to his best as a 4-y-o. *C. Milbank, France.* **124**

TWINKLING BOOTS 2 b.c. Military 112–Road Star 52 (Road House II) [1976 5fg 5f 6fg 8fg 8s 10v] useless. *W. Charles.* **—**

TWIST OF LEMON 3 b.f. Northfields–Zest (Crepello 136) [1975 6d 7f 1976 10g 12g 11g³ 11.7h⁶ 10f² 11.1g*] lightly-made filly: half-sister to three winners, including Oaks winner Ginevra (by Shantung): odds on, made all when 5-length winner of weakly-contested maiden race at Wolverhampton in August: stays 11f: acts on firm going: sold, covered by Silly Season, 17,500 gns Goffs November Sales. *I. Balding.* **64**

TWO BELLS 4 b.f. Foggy Bell 108–Belle of Acrum 56 (Faubourg II 127) [1974 5f⁴ 5f⁵ 5d 5d³ 5s 5s⁴ 6d 1975 8.2f⁴ 8g* 8fg 8f³ 9f* 10fg 9f* 8.2g³ 8f⁵ 1976 12f³ 11g⁶ 9g⁴ 12.2d 8f⁵ 9.4h² 9fg* 8h⁵ 8h³ 10g² 8f³ 8fg 10.6d] compact filly: **63**

won apprentice handicap at Newcastle in July by ¾ length from Tringa and kept her form well afterwards: effective at 1m and stays 1½m: acts on firm going: consistent: suitable mount for a lady rider. *Denys Smith.*

TWO FOR JOY 6 b.m. Double-U-Jay 120–Minouche (Faubourg II 127) [1974 **46** 12.2d⁴ 12.2f³ 15g⁴ 13.8f² 13.8s⁴ 1975 12.2fg² 10fg³ 1976 15.8g⁴] unfurnished mare: probably needs further than 1¼m and stays well: probably acts on any going: suitable mount for an apprentice. *P. Rohan.*

TWO GOOD 4 ch.f. Double Jump 131–Righteous Girl 93 (Right Boy 137) **64** [1974 5f 5g² 5g² 5g² 6fg² 6g³ 6s⁴ 1975 6s² 6f 7fg 6fg 7d³ 7f 8.2d 8g³ 8.2g³ 8d* 1976 7f 8fg 8g³ 10g⁶ 8g 8fg 10.8h 9g² 11.7fg³ 8f* 10g⁶ 10.4fg⁵ 10d⁵ 8g² 8.2s 10d] strong-quartered filly: won nine-runner apprentice handicap at Salisbury in August by 2 lengths from Red Fox: stays 1½m but is probably best at around 1m: appears to act on any going: sometimes wears blinkers (didn't at Salisbury): sold 500 gns Newmarket Autumn Sales. *F. J. Houghton.*

TWO RONNIES 4 b.g. Carnival Dancer 113–Little Singer (Sing Sing 134) **64** [1974 5s* 5g⁶ 5f 6h 5fg 5fg⁵ 5g² 5fg⁴ 5fg³ 5g 5.9g* 5d 5v⁵ 1975 5g⁵ 5s* 5v² 5d 6v³ 5fg 6f* 5f⁵ 6g³ 5f² 6f³ 6f* 6h 6fg⁶ 6g 6fg 5f⁶ 5fg 5d⁴ 5g 5g 1976 5f⁶ 6d⁵ 6s⁴ 6g 6g 5.9f 6d 6f³ 5f⁶ 5fg² 5s* 6d] neat, compact gelding: favourite, sold out of M. H. Easterby's stable 680 gns after winning seller at Edinburgh in October by 1½ lengths from Larella: mainly disappointing beforehand: stays 6f: acts on any going: suitable mount for an apprentice: sometimes awkward at start and sometimes sweats up: trained by S. Nesbitt until after eighth start. *J. Etherington.*

TWO SWALLOWS 3 gr.c. My Swallow 134–Two Blues 95 (Kingsway) [1975 **84** 6d⁴ 7g⁵ 6g 6fg³ 7g 1976 7g 8f³ 9d³ 10.5s⁴ 12d* 12f³ 13fg³ 16fg² 14f² 16f⁵ 16fg 18d] big, strong colt: won maiden race at Doncaster in May by 5 lengths from New Ribbons: subsequently placed in handicaps: stays well: acts on firm going but is well suited by some give in the ground. *G. Toft.*

TWO TOGETHER 3 b.g. Great Nephew 126–Gertie Millar 104 (Larkspur 128) — [1975 7.2fg* 7fg⁶ 7.2s 1976 10g 8g 8d] useful-looking gelding: won maiden

Mr R. Brooke's "Twig Moss"

race at Haydock in 1975: not seen out until September and wore bandages when tailed off on all outings, including when tried in blinkers in a claiming event: is probably no longer of any account. *I. Walker.*

TWYNLYNE LASS 3 b.f. Stupendous–Pretty Cage 110 (Cagire II 122) [1975 — 5v⁶ 5f 5g⁶ 5.9f 7g 9fg 1976 8f 10.1fg] of little account. *M. Bradley.*

TYNWALD MILLS 2 ch.c. Henry the Seventh 125–Not Suspect 76 (Above 57 Suspicion 127) [1976 6fg 8g 7s 8v⁵] stocky colt: little worthwhile form, including in a seller: will probably need a test of stamina. *R. Hollinshead.*

TYRANNOS 3 ch.c. Tyrant–Orange Sash (Sica Boy 132) [1975 N.R. 1976 — 8fg⁶ 10s 10.2g⁶] big, strong, good-topped colt: third reported foal: dam never ran: gave signs of possessing a little ability but was off course a long time after second outing. *G. Pritchard-Gordon.*

TYRANNY 2 ch.c. Tyrant–Persian Gal 68 (Persian Gulf) [1976 5f 5f 5g 6fg* 6f] 88 Irish colt: half-brother to three winners, including useful 1m to 1¾m winner Levantine (by Le Levanstell): 820 gns yearling: dam half-sister to very speedy 1968 2-y-o Flying Legs: blinkered, showed improved form and had field well strung out when winning 11-runner maiden auction event at Epsom in June by 5 lengths from No Joking: ran without blinkers when last of eight to Nebbiolo in Irish Chorus Stakes at Navan later in month: not seen out again: should stay 1¼m. *M. Kauntze, Ireland.*

TYRO DON 5 ch.g. Weepers Boy 124–Tailor Don 103 (Fighting Don) [1974 8g — 1975 7g 1976 12h⁶ 12fg⁶ 8v⁴ 18s 12s] stocky gelding: probably of little account. *J. Calvert.*

TYRUS 3 b.g. Tyrant–Zaraway 102 (Honeyway 125) [1975 5v 6f 6f 7g 6g 5fg 66 5fg 1976 12f² 8h 10f³ 13.8f⁶ 8h* 8fg* 10h 8h 8d] plater: winner at Redcar in July and Ripon in August: bought in 1,100 gns on latter course: best form at up to 1¼m and evidently doesn't stay 1¾m: acts on hard ground: wears blinkers: ran poorly last three outings: trained until final outing by P. Buckley. *E. Collingwood.*

TZI-TZI GIRL 4 b.f. Sovereign Path 125–Toots 66 (Will Somers 114 §) [1974 75 7d 1975 7g³ 1976 8f³ 7f 7fg² 7f⁵ 8f³ 9f² 8f 8g⁵ 6v⁴] big, rangy filly: odds on, headed close home when runner-up to Orange Gin in maiden race at Wolver- hampton in August on sixth outing: stays 1m: acts on firm going: trained by M. Ryan until after fourth outing: ran poorly seventh start: performed respectably in blinkers on final appearance: sold 1,250 gns Newmarket December Sales. *N. Adam.*

U

UBEDIZZY 3 b.c. Carnival Dancer 113–Ermyn Lass 64 (Ennis 128) [1975 5v 119 5fg 5f 5f⁴ 6f* 5g² 6g³ 6v² 1976 6f* 6f* 5f* 6g⁵ 6d³ 6fg² 6d* 6fg* 6f 6s 6v 5s*]

Ubedizzy's improvement during the course of his second season was phe- nomenal; by the end of 1976 he had improved on his two-year-old form by going on for 35 lb and it was Ubedizzy's exploits which were largely responsible for his trainer's enjoying his best flat season. Nesbitt believes firmly that the horse was created to run, and that it is better employed keeping fit on the racecourse than on the home gallops. Nesbitt's methods have not always met with universal approval but the simple fact is that racehorses can earn their keep only on the racecourse. Of course some horses are tougher and more durable than others, and in this respect, Nesbitt has been fortunate to be in charge of as hardy a pair of customers as Ubedizzy and Clear Melody, the latter of whom retains his enthusiasm despite having raced seventy times in four seasons. Ubedizzy's very strenuous campaign would have finished some horses but not he. Ubedizzy kept going and right at the back-end, in a handicap at Doncaster, he put up his best performance. His top weight of 10-0 was reduced by 7 lb, the allowance claimed by his apprentice rider Andrew Crook, but even so his chances of beating in-form sprinters Faridina, Alanrod, Walter and the Ayr Gold Cup winner Last Tango seemed none too bright, and he started at 25/1. However, after racing prominently all the way he ran on with great courage to take the lead near the finish and beat Walter by a neck, with Alanrod two lengths away in third place. A magnificent performance!

All five of Ubedizzy's other victories came in the first half of the season. By the end of April he had completed a hat-trick in handicaps at Pontefract, Thirsk and Beverley, twice being ridden by the apprentice Crook, and then, after a brief

William Hill North-Western Stakes, Haydock—Ubedizzy shows much improved form to beat Spanish Air

spell when it seemed as though the handicapper might be catching up with him, he improved further to pick up two valuable prizes, the William Hill North-Western Stakes at Haydock and the William Hill Gold Trophy at York. At Haydock Ubedizzy won all out by a neck from Spanish Air, a leading two-year-old of the previous season, who was having his first outing of 1976 and from whom Ubedizzy was receiving 4 lb. The pair met again in the William Hill Trophy, the highlight of the Timeform Charity Day meeting and a race which in previous years has been won by the good sprinters Some Hand, Alphadamus, Roman Warrior and Be Tuneful. Spanish Air started a short-priced favourite to reverse Haydock form with Ubedizzy despite the fact that Ubedizzy was meeting him on terms 5 lb better. From his number-one draw Ubedizzy was soon up with the leaders and after taking up the running two furlongs from home he drew clear of his twelve rivals and at the post had one and a half lengths to spare over Gold Cheb; Spanish Air was over three lengths further back in seventh place. Timeform Charity Day in aid of Cancer Relief has been held every year since 1971 and has proved an unqualified success, not only as a fund-raiser for a most worthwhile cause but also simply as a day's racing, despite its proximity to Royal Ascot. Over the six years, the Charity Day meetings have made £216,918, the bulk of which has gone to Cancer Relief, and 161,632 race-goers have passed through the turnstiles. 1976 was a particularly good year in every respect: a record £46,442 was raised and the crowd witnessed three of the

William Hill Trophy Handicap, York—the most valuable event on Timeform Charity Day which raised a record £46,442 for Cancer Relief. Ubedizzy accounts for Gold Cheb

Mr J. Finlayson's "Ubedizzy"

races falling to really good horses, Intermission (Vernons Plate), Bright Finish (Daniel Prenn Plate) and Ubedizzy.

Misfortune overtook Ubedizzy after York. Firstly he went down with the cough and then he was found to have heat in a leg, and he didn't race again until late-August. In none of his first three races after his return, the Great St Wilfrid Handicap at Ripon, a handicap at Doncaster and the Vernons Sprint Cup at Haydock, did Ubedizzy have much chance, apparently, at the weights, but more important he hadn't recovered peak fitness. Had he been in the same form he was in for his final outing there's no doubt he would have made much more of a show.

Ubedizzy (b.c. 1973)	Carnival Dancer (b 1957)	Native Dancer (gr 1950)	Polynesian / Geisha
		Confetti (ch 1942)	War Admiral / Galady II
	Ermyn Lass (ch 1963)	Ennis (b 1954)	Golden Cloud / First House
		Rye Girl (ch 1949)	Blue Water / Brosna

Ubedizzy, who joined Nesbitt early in 1976 after spending his two-year-old days in the care of Harry Blackshaw, did extremely well physically from two years to three years, developing into a strong, compact colt. He is the fifth foal of the undistinguished five-furlong winner Ermyn Lass who before Ubedizzy had produced three modest platers and the fairly useful sprinter Dizy Dave, all of them by Carnival Dancer. Ermyn Lass is closely related to Red Alert's dam Ashton Jane, a winner over five furlongs, and is a half-sister to Red Idol who won over five furlongs in this country and was subsequently a prolific winner at up to a mile in the United States. The second dam, Rye Girl, won a five-furlong seller and is a half-sister to several sprint winners, including the brilliantly fast filly Crimson who won the Lowther Stakes in 1953. Ubedizzy stays six furlongs well, acts on any going and is a suitable mount for an apprentice. He ended his second season about as good as were those other northern stalwarts Lochnager and Roman Warrior at the same stage of their careers, although it remains to be seen whether he will make the same progress that they made as four-year-olds. Whether Ubedizzy makes it to the top or not, we are sure that this tough, game and genuine colt will acquit himself with credit in 1977. *S. Nesbitt.*

UGO 4 ch.c. Mountain Call 125–Bicolor 72 (French Beige 127) [1974 6g 6fg 7s⁶ **62** 1975 8d 9g 8g⁶ 8f⁴ 10fg⁵ 8g 10.1fg⁴ 10fg⁵ 1976 9fg* 11.7fg 10.6d 8fg³] big, strong colt: plater: made all when winning at Kempton in April (blinkered): seems to stay 1¼m: has run respectably both with and without blinkers. *R. Hannon.*

ULSTER 2 b.c. Connaught 130–Camisole 94 (Psidium 130) [1976 7fg 7h 8g] — tall colt: half-brother to two minor winners here and abroad: 6,400 gns yearling: dam won over 6f as a 2-y-o: in rear in maiden races, finishing tailed off on third outing. *P. Haslam.*

UMABATHA 3 b.c. Nijinsky 138–Hardiesse 117 (Hornbeam 130) [1975 7fg⁴ **100** 1976 8f*] strong, good-bodied colt: good mover: half-brother to two winners, including useful stayer Dubrovnik (by Ragusa): dam smart at up to 1½m: looked to have done well since his 2-y-o days (when he finished very promising fourth in Houghton Stakes) and showed a good deal of courage when winning maiden race at Newbury in April by a short head from New Order: not seen out again: will stay 1½m+. *H. Candy.*

UNBIASED 11 bl.g. Klairon 131–Impartial 91 (Big Game) [1974 7f 8g² 7g³ **56** 8f² 7g⁴ 8.2s² 7g⁴ 8g³ 10d 1975 8g 7s 8d 10fg⁶ 10f⁶ 1976 7f 9g 8f⁶ 8g 10v] one-time quite moderate handicapper: little worthwhile form in 1976: seems to stay 1¼m: acts on any going: wears blinkers: excellent mount for a boy. *Doug Smith.*

UNCLE CYRIL 5 ch.g. I Say 125–Aunt Jane (Le Levanstell 122) [1974 12h⁵ — 12g⁴ 11g⁶ 16g⁵ 14d⁵ 13.3g 12d⁵ 1975 16s 1976 14.6g⁵ 16fg] strong gelding: no worthwhile form since his three-year-old days: stays well: has run poorly in blinkers. *S. Matthews.*

UNCLE JACK 3 ch.g. Midsummer Night II 117–Cowlam 81 (Alcide 136) [1975 — 6f 7g 8g 1976 10.2g 15.8f 8fg 10g 15f 13.8f] strong, compact gelding: poor plater: sometimes wears blinkers. *R. Bastiman.*

UNCLE JOE 3 b.c. Burd Alane–Gay Niece (Sir Gaylord) [1975 7fg 6f 7g⁵ 8f² 8g **62** 1976 10s 10.4s 8f³ 8f⁴ 8h⁵ 8f² 7fg* 7f 8fg] strong American-bred colt: favourite, ran out a decisive winner of 22-runner amateur riders maiden race at Leicester in July: best form at up to 1m: acts on firm going: sold to F. Walwyn 5,600 gns Ascot December Sales. *A. Johnson.*

UNCLE JOHN 4 b.g. Falcon 131–Papillio 78 (Pampered King 121) [1974 6fg⁵ — 5fg* 7d* 8g 8s⁵ 1975 8g 8g* 9.4h* 9h² 10g⁵ 8g⁴ 11s⁵ 12.2g⁵ 1976 10h 8fg 8g 10f 9.4h⁴ 12.2f⁶ 13g] neat gelding: poor handicapper nowadays: best form at up to 9f: appears to act on any going. *W. Atkinson.*

UNCOMMITTED 2 b.f. Buckpasser–Lady Be Good (Better Self) [1976 6d⁵ **101** 7g* 6g] tall, lengthy American-bred French filly: half-sister to numerous winners in U.S.A., including smart animals Disciplinarian, Full of Hope, In Hot Pursuit (all by Bold Ruler) and Discipline (by Princequillo): dam a very useful stakes winner at 2 yrs: looked a good filly in the making when winning eight-runner maiden race at Deauville in August by 4 lengths from Troja: 12/1 3-runner William Hill Cheveley Park Stakes at Newmarket the following month but could never get to leaders and was beaten 7 lengths into equal-seventh place behind Durtal: should stay middle distances. *F. Boutin, France.*

UNDER ORDERS 4 b.g. On Your Mark 125–Fadmoor (Primera 131) [1974 **75** 6g 7.5s 8v 1975 10g 6s⁴ 8g² 8g⁶ 10g 8g* 1976 8v4 6.5s⁶ 6.5g⁵ 6.5g² 5g* 6d² 6fg⁶ 6g 5f⁴ 5fg² 5fg⁶ 6g* 6v³ 6v* 6s³] lengthy gelding: quite a moderate handicapper: successful at Folkestone in March, Leicester in September and at Nottingham the following month: effective at 5f to 1m: appears to act on any going: wears blinkers. *C. Bewicke.*

UNDER PRESSURE 2 ch.g. Red God 128 §–Glamouna (Spy Well 126) [1976 — 6fg 6g 7s 6s] first foal: 2,600 gns yearling: well beaten in varied company, including selling: sold 280 gns Ascot November Sales. *I. Walker.*

UNELLA 2 gr.f. Hallez 131–Aunt Fannie (Fortino II 120) [1976 5.1fg 6f⁵ 6g⁵ **98** 7g* 6v² 6s* 6s⁴] fair sort: half-sister to moderate 1975 2-y-o 1m winner Fantail (by St Chad): dam unraced half-sister to top French hurdler Hardatit: successful in 18-runner maiden race at Yarmouth in September and 12-runner minor event at Pontefract the following month, on latter course being kept up to her work to score by a length from Mhairi Dhu: also ran very well when ½-length third to Picatina in £2,100 event at York in between and would have gone close to winning but for being hampered (was moved up a place on winner's disqualification): will stay middle distances: acts on heavy ground. *W. O'Gorman.*

UNION CARD 2 ch.c. Good Bond 122–Season Ticket (Silly Season 127) [1976 5f⁶ 5d* 6v⁵] tall colt: first foal: dam never ran: won 25-runner maiden race at Newbury in September by a length from Quick Retort: never quite got going pace when remote fifth of six to Our Jimmy in £2,600 event at York the following month: should stay 1m. *G. Hunter.* **93**

UNITED 3 b.g. Merger–Destiny Day 109 (Tim Tam) [1975 5g 6fg 6h² 6fg⁶ 6fg⁵ 6g* 6g5 6g 1976 6g³ 7g³ 8.3fg 8g 7f⁵] fair sort: plater: best form at up to 7f: blinkered fifth outing in 1975. *Miss N. Wilmot.* **62**

UNSUSPECTED 4 b.f. Above Suspicion 127–Chevanstell (Le Levanstell 122) [1974 5.1s⁴ 6g² 8d* 8.5s⁴ 7s 1975 8s* 10g⁶ 10g 10fg* 10f² 10g* 10fg5 11.7g⁶ 1976 10fg 10.5d³ 12g² 12fg* 12fg5 12h⁴ 12f³ 12fg² 12fg4 14f* 14d 14g* 14d*] neat filly: fairly useful handicapper: had a good season, winning at Leicester, Yarmouth and Newmarket (twice): stays 1¾m well: acts on any going: has a good turn of foot: genuine. *R. Jarvis.* **91**

UPANISHAD 3 b.f. Amber Rama 133–Blue Shadow 97 (Crepello 136) [1975 5g 6fg4 1976 7fg 10g 9f 10g 10fg² 11.7fg5 12f³ 10fg³ 12.3f⁶ 10f* 10.1fg 12g] tall, attractive filly: quite a moderate handicapper: showed improved form when winning at Beverley in August by ½ length from Bustello: probably stays 1½m: acts on firm going: wears blinkers nowadays: inconsistent: sold 10,500 gns Newmarket December Sales. *H. Wragg.* **75**

UPAVON 3 b.f. Goldhill 125–Everley 89 (Martial 131) [1975 5v⁶ 5h⁶ 5fg²(dis) 5g* 5h* 6fg4 5d 5g 1976 7d 5fg 6s 5fg³ 5h 5h³ 10g4 10.6d² 8g³] leggy filly: moderate handicapper: stays 1¼m: apparently needs a sound surface: sometimes sweats up: sold 3,000 gns Newmarket Autumn Sales. *N. Angus.* **81**

UPPER ECHELON 4 b.c. On Your Mark 125–Nagakanya 76 (Dionisio 128) [1974 6s 1975 7s⁵ 10f 8f 8g² 9g⁵ 1976 13.8g⁶ 8g³] plating-class maiden: stays 1m: best form in blinkers. *M. Camacho.* **40**

UPSTAIRS 2 gr.f. Raffingora 130–Brief Note 92 (Counsel 118) [1976 5g4 5g⁶ 5g⁶ 5.3g 5f³ 5f³ 5.3f⁶ 5h 6g³ 6fg 7s⁶] strong, sturdy filly: third foal: half-sister to Piercing Note (by Bleep-Bleep), a winner over 6f: dam needed at least 1¼m: quite a moderate filly: probably stays 7f: suited by some give in the ground: wears blinkers. *B. Swift.* **70**

URRAY HARRY 3 b.c. Decoy Boy 129–Star-Call 90 (Bleep-Bleep 134) [1975 5g 5s³ 5s* 5g² 5g² 5g³ 5h² 6d² 6g⁵ 5fg 5g4 5g³ 5s⁶ 1976 5g² 5f* 5f⁵ 5d4 5s* 5g⁵] strong, compact colt: developed into a useful handicapper and won at Ascot in April, a shade comfortably by 1½ lengths from Codebreaker, and York in May: put up his best performance when beating Future Forest by 4 lengths on latter course: speedy and is better suited for 5f than 6f: acts on any going but revels in the mud: ran moderately when tried in blinkers at 2 yrs: genuine and consistent: raced only once after York, and was sold 3,000 gns Newmarket Autumn Sales. *R. Hollinshead.* **105**

V

VAGUELY 2 ch.f. Bold Lad (Ire) 133–Vaguely Mine 90 (Silly Season 127) [1976 5fg5 6g² 6fg4 8g4 8fg* 7s²] lengthy, attractive filly: first foal: dam, half-sister to St Leger winner Provoke, won at up to 1½m: decisive winner of 13-runner maiden race at Beverley in September, being kept up to her work to beat Mahar by 7 lengths: battled on gamely when ¾-length second to Sleeper in 12-runner minor event at Sandown the following month: may well stay 1¼m: probably acts on any going. *R. Hern.* **92**

VAGUELY JAMES 2 ch.c. Jimmy Reppin 131–Vaguely Hopeful 65 (Fortino II 120) [1976 6f³ 7f² 7f² 8f³ 8g² 8s³] second foal: half-brother to 3-y-o 1m and 1¼m winner Doubly Hopeful (by Double Jump): 3,900 gns yearling: dam ran only three times: placed in all his races, running really well in nurseries at Yarmouth in September and Brighton in October on last two outings: beaten only ½ length by Rutlow in £1,800 event on latter course: suited by 1m: acts on any going but is particularly well suited by some give in the ground: blinkered last two outings. *M. Stoute.* **93**

VAIN PURSUIT 2 ch.f. Run The Gantlet–Inkless (Epaulette 125) [1976 5g4 5f4 6fg 7fg5] useful-looking filly: half-sister to two winners, including smart **75**

1972 2-y-o Kwang Su (by Astec), subsequently a winner at 1¼m: sold twice as a yearling, for 5,000 gns and 8,200 gns: dam won over 9f in Ireland: fourth in maiden races, being beaten 2 lengths by Great Flight at Sandown in June and 4 lengths by Lutomer Riesling at Windsor in July: ran badly on next outing and had little chance at weights on final: form only at 5f but is bred to stay middle distances. *Doug Smith.*

VALACE 2 br.g. Linacre 133–Almondvale (Valerullah 113) [1976 10v] third — living foal: dam of little account: dwelt when ninth of 16 to Habbersupreme in seller at Leicester in October. *D. Hanley.*

VALBAR 2 ch.f. Meldrum 112–Aquagold (Goldhill 125) [1976 6f 7f 6f] bad — plater: sold 350 gns Ascot August Sales. *W. A. Stephenson.*

VAL D'ISERE 3 ch.f. Mountain Call 125–Dilettante 108 (Dante) [1975 6fg⁴ **63** 6g 6g 1976 9f² 10g 12g⁵] deep-girthed, strong-quartered filly: well-backed co-favourite when ½-length second of 23 to Blue Rag in maiden race at Wolverhampton in May, first and easily best effort: stays 9f: sometimes wears blinkers. *J. Winter.*

VAL DU FIER 4 b.c. Bon Mot III 132–Vali (Sunny Boy III) [1974 8g² S.5d³ **?** 8v 1975 10f 10v⁵ 12.2g* 10.5g* 10.5s⁶ 12g⁴ 15.5g 10g⁴ 1976 12g* 12g⁶ 10g 12g] big, very attractive ex-French colt: very good mover: half-brother to French Derby winner Val de Loir: won twice at 3 yrs and ran two good races in top-class company, finishing fourth in French Derby and Prix Eugene Adam: easy winner of Prix Sea-Bird at Saint-Cloud in May on reappearance at 4 yrs, beating Hunza Dancer 2½ lengths: virtually pulled up when last of six to Quiet Fling in Coronation Cup at Epsom the following month (finished lame): subsequently last in Valdoe Stakes at Goodwood and Cumberland Lodge Stakes at Ascot, when serving quarantine over here: stayed 1½m: acted on heavy going: trained by A. Penna until after Epsom: exported to New Zealand as a stallion by B.B.A. *J. Dunlop.*

VALIANT MAID 3 ch.f. Dieu Soleil 111–Maid Valiant (No Comment 117) [1975 — N.R. 1976 8fg 9.4g] small filly: first foal: dam winning hurdler: behind in maiden races at Carlisle in May. *B. Wilkinson.*

VALINSKY 2 b.c. Nijinsky 138–Valoris 120 (Tiziano) [1976 8g* 8s⁴] half- **117** brother to three winners, notably Irish Guinness Oaks second Vincennes (by Vieux Manoir) and Epsom Oaks runner-up Val's Girl (by Sir Ivor): dam won Irish 1,000 Guineas and Epsom Oaks, and is half-sister to French Derby winner Val de Loir: odds on for 14-runner maiden race at Leopardstown in September and spread-eagled his field, coming home 5 lengths clear of subsequent Beresford Stakes winner Orchestra, with others at least 10 lengths further behind: again odds on in six-runner William Hill Futurity Stakes at Doncaster the following month but was beaten early in straight and finished only 14 lengths fourth to Sporting Yankee, some way behind third-placed Orchestra: will stay at least 1½m: clearly not at his best on very soft ground. *V. O'Brien, Ireland.*

VALISE D'OR 2 b.f. Blakeney 126–Musical Gift 99 (Princely Gift 137) [1976 — 8v 7s] first foal: 600 gns yearling: dam stayed 6f: in rear in large fields at York and Newmarket in October. *J. Fitzgerald.*

VALLEY OF DIAMONDS 2 ch.f. Florescence 120–Sacred Honey (Honeyway **74** 125) [1976 5g 5fg⁵ 5f 5fg 6d*] tall, lengthy filly: showed improved form when winning 13-runner seller at Yarmouth in September by ¾ length from Dulcidene and was bought in for 975 gns: suited by 6f: evidently acts well on a soft surface. *W. Wharton.*

VALRAIN 3 b.g Cheval 117–Quite a Storm 87 (Quorum 126) [1975 5s 5g 5s — 6f² 6h 7g⁵ 6g 7f 7.2fg 8.2f⁴ 10g 8g 1976 12g] neat, compact gelding: plater: tailed off only outing in 1976: should stay 1¼m: has worn blinkers: sold 320 gns Doncaster May Sales. *M. Naughton.*

VALUATION 3 ch.g. Gulf Pearl 117–Arbitrate 107 (Arbar 135) [1975 6fg⁴ **105** 1976 12fg* 12fg⁵ 12g⁴ 16f² 15.5g 16fg* 12s²] smallish, compact gelding: won maiden race at Newmarket in April by 4 lengths from Bagshot but was far from impressive when accounting for two moderate rivals in minor event at Beverley in September: ran two excellent races in between, finishing fourth under a very stiff weight to Beau Dutch in handicap at Newmarket in May and 2 lengths second to General Ironside in Queen's Vase at Royal Ascot in June: out of his depth in Grand Prix de Paris at Longchamp and was no match for Dutch Treat in minor event at Redcar in October on final appearance: probably needs further than 1½m nowadays and is very well suited by a good test of stamina: acts on firm going: usually wears blinkers nowadays. *R. Hern.*

VALUE ADDED 3 b.f. Abermist 85–Value 95 (Grandmaster) [1975 N.R. —
1976 8fg 10.1fg 12s] last in maiden races on all outings, including when tried in
blinkers, and is of little account. *S. James.*

VANISH 4 b.f. Decoy Boy 129–Valentina Rose 85 (Red God 128 §) [1974 5s —
5v⁵ 5s 6d² 1975 N.R. 1976 7fg 7g 8fg] of little account nowadays. *D.
Gandolfo.*

VANISHING ACT 3 ch.f. Stage Door Johnny–Eastern Princess (Nasrullah) **101**
[1975 N.R. 1976 10f6 9.5g* 10g² 10f⁶ 12f* 12f* 12g 12fg⁵ 12f*] shapely,
American-bred Irish filly: half-sister to several winners in U.S.A., including
smart stakes winner Shady Character (by Graustark): $67,000 yearling: dam
stakes-placed sister to outstanding American racehorse and sire Bold Ruler:
won maiden race at Dundalk and handicaps at Mallow (by 8 lengths), the
Curragh (beat strong field) and Galway: beat Cill Dara 2 lengths on last-named
course in September: not disgraced when taking on stronger company in Irish
Guinness Oaks (well there to 2f out) and Galtres Stakes at York (fifth of 17 to
Capricious): much better suited by 1½m than shorter distances and will stay
further: acts on firm going. *D. Weld, Ireland.*

VANITY GAY 2 b.f. Sahib 114–Sevantha 80 (Henry the Seventh 125) [1976 5f **73**
5f 5.3f³ 5f⁵ 5.9g] neat filly: first foal: dam ran only twice: showed a little
ability in maiden races and a nursery: ran moderately in blinkers on final outing:
sold 440 gns Newmarket Autumn Sales. *H. Candy.*

VANZETTA 3 b.c. Welsh Saint 126–Prefer (Preciptic 122) [1975 5g 6g 9g 8f **46**
8f⁴ 1976 8v 8d 10f⁴ 7g 7g 8f² 8g 8fg⁵ 7fg] bad plater: best run at 1m: has
twice worn blinkers but seems to do better without. *T. Craig.*

VARDES 2 b.g. Sahib 114–Prima Santa 86 (Guersant 129) [1976 10v] half- —
brother to useful hurdler/chaser Tabasco Time (by Tacitus): dam won over 5f at
2 yrs: 14/1 when behind in 17-runner maiden race won by Pin Tuck at Nottingham in October. *P. Cole.*

VARMETER 2 b.g. Varano–Sweet Success 81 (Privy Councillor 125) [1976 8v —
8v] leggy gelding: first foal: dam won 6f seller at 2 yrs: behind in minor events
at York and Teesside in October. *M. Camacho.*

VARSITY MATCH 7 ch.g. Double Jump 131–Bluecourt 103 (Court Martial) **51**
[1974 10.2g 8g 6v² 1975 6f³ 5.9fg 6s⁵ 10g⁵ 1976 8fg 5.9f 7fg³ 8f 6h⁵] narrow,
lightly-made gelding: poor selling handicapper: stays 7f: acts on any going:
suitable mount for an apprentice: has twice worn blinkers (ran poorly in them
on first occasion). *M. Ryan.*

VEILADY 2 gr.f. Veiled Wonder–Jacobean Lady (Tudor Jinks 121) [1976 5fg —
5.9g] narrow filly: half-sister to fair miler All Love (by No Argument): dam
never ran: well behind in maiden races in Midlands: started slowly on first outing.
W. Clay.

VEILISA 2 b.f. Veiled Wonder–Mielisa 66 (Tehran) [1976 5fg³ 5h⁵ 5.9f 5g 5s³ **77**
5s³ 5g³] light-framed filly: half-sister to a minor 2-y-o winner: 280 gns foal: dam
won at 1m: quite moderate: third in four maiden races, last two in Scotland:
appears to act on any going. *N. Adam.*

VELOUTINE 2 gr.f. No Mercy 126–Tassel (Ragusa 137) [1976 5g 5f⁶ 6f 7.2f **62**
7fg⁴ 8v⁴] robust, quite useful-looking filly: has a round action: moderate plater:
stays 1m: seems to act on any going. *Denys Smith.*

VELVELLA 4 br.c. Right Tack 131–Nana's Girl 109 (Tin Whistle 128) [1974 **84**
6g 6d² 6g² 6fg* 6d⁵ 8g 1975 8s⁶ 7d² 6d⁴ 7f³ 6f⁶ 7fg⁶ 8f* 8g* 9g 1976 8v 10g³
9fg⁵ 10f⁴] strong, well-made, attractive colt with a good, easy action: useful
handicapper (rated 102) at 3 yrs: lightly raced (not seen out after April) and
didn't recapture his best form in 1976: best form at 1m although has run
respectably over 1¼m: seems to act on any going: has been tried in blinkers. *J.
Nelson.*

VELVET BOY 2 b.g. Shantung 132–Amara (Sanctus II 132) [1976 5fg⁵ 8g⁵ **79**
8fg² 10v 6s] lengthy gelding: third foal: half-brother to 3-y-o Suited (by Right
Tack), a winner at up to 1m: 400 gns yearling: dam minor winner at 9f and 1¼m
from four starts in France: 1½ lengths second to Acquittal in 14-runner maiden
race at Beverley in September, best effort: stays 1m, and should stay middle
distances at 3 yrs: possibly not at his best on soft going. *A. Smith.*

VELVET CIRCLE 2 b.f. Majority Blue 126–Damaring (Saidam) [1976 5s 5fg **70**
6f 7fg 7.2f 8f³ 8fg² 8s² 10v] leggy, unfurnished filly: plater: showed improved
form at 1m and stayed on well when length second of 18 to Mischiefmaker at

Redcar in October on eighth outing: seemed not to stay when tried over 1¼m (favourite): acts on any going. *M. Camacho.*

VENETIA 3 b.f. Song 132–Americana II (Hill Prince) [1975 5s 5d⁴ 5g³ 6g **6s** 63 1976 6fg⁴ 8f 5fg 7fg 6f⁶ 10s 7s] big, rangy filly: 8½ lengths fourth to Jimmy The Singer in maiden race at Newmarket in May, first and easily best effort: should stay further than 6f. *J. Powney.*

VENETIAN PALACE 3 b.f. Royal Palace 131–Nerissa 117 (Court Martial) — [1975 7f⁴ 8d⁶ 7.2s* 1976 8f 12f³] half-sister to very speedy 1968 2-y-o Red Rose Prince (by Henry the Seventh): won maiden race at Haydock at 2 yrs: last on both outings in 1976 and probably needed some give in the ground to show her form: stayed 7f and would probably have got 1m: bought by B.B.A. 2,100 gns Newmarket July Sales for export to New Zealand. *P. Walwyn.*

VENETICO 3 ch.c. Great Nephew 126–Fair Charlotte 87 (Charlottesville 135) 77 [1975 7d 7g 1976 11f⁵ 10.4d 10.2fg²] well-made colt: good fifth to Lighter in maiden race at Newbury in April: hung away from rails under pressure when beaten 4 lengths by Bobbins in similar event at Doncaster in June, easily better subsequent effort: will probably stay 1½m: seems to need a sound surface. *C. Brittain.*

VENEZ-VITE 3 b.f. Vitriolic–Paris or Bust (Francis S) [1975 N.R. 1976 56 10.1fg 108f*. 10g³ 11.7d 10.8s] American-bred filly: second foal: half-sister to a winner in U.S.A. by Chieftain: $20,000 yearling: dam winner over 5f at 3 yrs in U.S.A.: beat sole opponent Fire Plan ¾ length in maiden race at Warwick in August: stays 11f: acts on firm going: sold 4,600 gns Newmarket December Sales. *F. J. Houghton.*

VENO STAR 3 b.f. Varano–Veno (Macherio) [1975 N.R. 1976 8fg⁵ 9.4h 10s] — probably of little account. *M. Naughton.*

VENSAYO 3 ch.g. I Say 125–Venazia 72 (Vienna 127) [1975 N.R. 1976 8f — 12.2fg 13.1s 6s 6v] third foal: half-brother to a winner in Jersey: dam stayed 1¼m: little worthwhile form in varied company. *D. H. Jones.*

VENTREX 3 b.f. Henry the Seventh 125–Terex (Khalkis 127) [1975 8f 1976 95 14fg² 12fg 14g⁵ 16g* 14d* 16g² 14s⁶] lengthy, fair sort of filly: improved considerably in the autumn and won maiden race at York and handicap at Yarmouth, latter by 3 lengths from Misty Joanne: well-backed favourite when creditable second to Persevering in handicap at Newmarket in October: suited by long distances: acts on a firm and a soft surface but ran moderately when soft going on final outing. *C. Brittain.*

VENTURA BOY 2 br.c. Jukebox 120–Vanity Case 77 (Counsel 118) [1976 5f⁶ 73 5s⁴ 6g 5fg 5s 5s] half-brother to three winners, including 3-y-o Irish sprinter Skin Deep (by Prevailing): 4,600 gns yearling: dam middle-distance stayer: showed ability on second outing, in May, but was well beaten afterwards. *V. Mitchell.*

VENTURION 2 b.c. Hopeful Venture 125–Snow Rum (Quorum 126) [1976 5g — 5f 5fg 7f 8s] sturdy, short-legged colt: behind in maiden and minor events. *V. Cross.*

VENTURUS 2 b.c. Hill Clown–Malvina 82 (Fidalgo 129) [1976 7fg 5d 5.9s²] 84 workmanlike colt: half-brother to a minor winner by Charlottown: dam placed over 5f at 2 yrs: neck second of 18 to Fear Naught in maiden race at Wolverhampton in October: will stay 1½m: acts on soft going: withdrawn under orders on second outing after going down in stalls. *E. Cousins.*

VENUS OF STRETHAM 3 b.f. Tower Walk 130–Sara's Star 70 (Sheshoon 132) 93 [1975 5v 5fg* 5f* 5f⁴ 6f* 5fg⁶ 6g² 6d⁴ 6fg* 6h² 6fg* 6g* 7g* 6f³ 1976 8g* 8g⁴ 7g⁶ 8f* 7f⁴ 8fg⁵ 7fg 8f⁵ 7s] lightly-made filly: quite a useful performer: won seven races at 2 yrs, five of them at Catterick: won two more races in 1976, well-contested minor events at Doncaster in March and Beverley in June: creditable fourth of 12 to Gwent in Jersey Stakes at Royal Ascot but ran well below her best afterwards: stays 1m well: acts well on firm going and is not at her best on soft: wears blinkers: occasionally sweats up. *G. Blum.*

VERACIOUS 3 ch.f. Astec 128–Gospel Truth 95 (Above Suspicion 127) [1975 86 N.R. 1976 10.1fg⁴ 10.1fg* 11.7f⁵ 12fg 16f³ 11.7d* 13s² 12s² 16v⁵] quite an attractive filly: second foal: half-sister to quite useful staying handicapper True Word (by Blakeney): dam stayed well: narrow winner of maiden event and handicap at Windsor: also first past post (probably winner on merit) in handicap at Nottingham in September, 1½ lengths ahead of Winslow Boy, but hung badly left in final furlong, hampering runner-up and was subsequently placed second: effective at 1¼m and stays 2m: acts on any going. *J. Dunlop.*

VERBOSITY 2 b.g. Communication 119–Diamond Talk (Counsel 118) [1976 **81** 5f⁴ 8s³] second foal: brother to Communicant, fairly useful 5f 2-y-o winner in 1975: dam never ran: in frame in maiden races at Windsor in August and Bath in October (4½ lengths third of 16 to Nice N'Easy): stays 1m. *F. Maxwell.*

VERONICA HERON 2 br.f. Crooner 119–Vahine 72 (Umberto 118) [1976 6d² **73** 6fg 7f² 6fg⁶ 7h⁴ 8.2d⁶ 8s] tall, leggy filly: half-sister to several winners abroad and to Irish 3-y-o middle-distance stayer Mr Kildare (by Hill Clown): 1,950 gns yearling: dam won at 1m and 1¼m: quite a modest maiden: well suited by 1m, and will probably stay further: appears to act on any going. *W. Elsey.*

VERONICA TELLI 4 b.f. Charlottown 127–Primed (Primera 131) [1974 8.2s 8v 1975 N.R. 1976 12.2g 12fg 13.4fg 10s 10.8s] probably of no account. *P. Felgate.*

VIA CON VENTE 3 ch.c. Lorenzaccio 130–Russian Dancer 98 (Red God 128 §) **89** [1975 6fg⁴ 6g 6g* 7g² 1976 8g³ 10s 12f³ 10fg* 8g 10fg 10.1fg 8fg] lightly-made colt: enterprisingly ridden when winning handicap at Brighton in May gamely by ¾ length from Bines Bridge: ran moderately afterwards: probably stays 1½m: possibly unsuited by soft going. *Mrs R. Lomax.*

VIBRATE 3 b.f. Charlottown 127–Easy to Love 90 (Infatuation 129) [1975 — 7fg⁶ 7.2s 1976 8fg 8fg⁶ 11.7fg⁶ 10fg 10g⁵ 10.1d 10.2f] light-framed filly: good sixth of 21 to Roses for the Star in Houghton Stakes at Newmarket in October, 1975, but did not fulfil that promise: blinkered final outing: trained until after fourth appearance by C. Brittain: disappointing. *D. Hanley.*

VICLA 4 b.f. Vijay 109–Clara Bow 90 (Solar Slipper 131) [1974 5f 1975 10d — 8.3fg 10fg 12s 1976 14g] of no account: sold 220 gns Ascot August Sales. *R. Akehurst.*

VICTA 2 ch.f. Northfields–Mithril (Princely Gift 137) [1976 5g 5f² 5g⁵ 5.9g⁴ **79** 5fg⁵ 6d⁶ 5.9s² 6v³ 7v] third reported foal: 1,600 gns yearling: dam won over 9f in Ireland: quite a moderate filly: placed in the midlands, on last occasion finishing creditable third to Cestrefeld in nursery at Leicester in October: should stay at least 1m: acts on any going. *R. Hollinshead.*

VICTORIA BLUE BOY 2 gr.c. Blue Streak 99–Tamblast (Tamerlane 128) **67** [1976 5fg 5d 5s 5f² 5fg 5f⁵ 6f³ 5fg] neat, strong, stocky colt: plater: ran well when third to stable-companion Brave Hunter at Nottingham in August: probably better suited by 6f than 5f and should stay further: acts on firm going: none too consistent. *W. Marshall.*

VICTORIA LUDORUM 2 ch.f. Sassafras 135–All Souls 96 (Saint Crespin III — 132) [1976 5.3f] first foal: dam won over 9f and 1¼m in Ireland: last of seven to Angelos in maiden race at Brighton in July, only outing. *J. Nelson.*

VICTORIAN HABIT 3 ch.f. Habitat 134–Victorian Era (High Hat 131) [1975 — 5s⁶ 5s* 5s⁴ 6g³ 6f⁴ 8g 1976 10s 10fg] well-grown, rather leggy filly: won maiden race at Ascot in 1975: behind in valuable early-season handicaps at Newcastle and Lingfield (tried in blinkers): should stay 1¼m. *B. Hobbs.*

VICTORY HILL 2 b.f. Goldhill 125–Valiant Victress (Nulli Secundus 89) [1976 — 5g] fourth foal: dam never ran: started slowly when last of 10 to Rudella in maiden race at Lingfield in August. *D. Kent.*

VIDKUN 4 ch.g. Quisling 117–Angelique (Hill Gail) [1974 5fg⁶ 5g² 5s³ 5s⁵ — 1975 8.2g² 8g* 8g³ 7.2fg* 6f 6v² 8.2d 1976 8f⁶ 8d 7fg 8d⁴ 8s] big gelding: poor handicapper: stays 1m: appears to act on any going: ran creditably when tried in blinkers: suitable mount for an apprentice: brought down final start. *Denys Smith.*

VIDO 5 br.m. Vimadee 120–Waveney May 67 (High Perch 126) [1974 N.R. — 1975 N.R. 1976 14s] first reported produce: dam won over 1¼m: 100/1 when well tailed-off in strongly-contested minor event won by Roses for the Star at Sandown in October. *J. Webber.*

VIGREY 3 gr.f. Supreme Sovereign 119–Vi 90 (Vilmorin) [1975 6g 5h 6g² 7v² **73** 7.2s² 1976 8f 10s⁵ 12.2fg⁶ 12.2f* 10fg 9f 10.6d 12v⁵] big, rangy filly: blinkered first time, won maiden race at Catterick in July by a neck from Schoolhouse Dale: ran poorly afterwards, twice wearing blinkers, including in a York seller: stays 1½m: acts on any going: sold 2,400 gns Newmarket Autumn Sales. *J. Etherington.*

VIKING LADY 3 br.f. John Splendid 116–Brush's Choice (Robson's Choice 105) —
[1975 6f² 5.8f⁵ 5g⁵ 6g 6g 1976 6fg⁵ 7fg 6g 7g 7s 8d] poor form in varied company, including a claiming event: sold 250 gns Ascot December Sales: dead.
R. Akehurst.

VIKING SPIRIT 6 b.g. Faberge II 121–Glancie (Krakatao 130) [1974 12f* —
14d* 11.7fg³ 15.8g⁴ 12d³ 10d 1976 12g⁶ 12fg⁵ 14.7d] workmanlike
gelding: stays well: probably acts on any going: has been tried in blinkers:
suitable mount for a lady rider. *S. Mellor.*

VILA REAL 5 gr.m. Town Crier 119–Goldelope (Elopement 125) [1974 8f 8fg —
5.9fg 5g 5.8g 7f 7d⁴ 8.2g³ 7g 8s 8v³ 7s⁶ 7g* 6v⁴ 10d⁴ 1975 7d⁴ 8s 10fg³ 8h⁴ 8h⁶
8g³ 7fg 7h³ 8fg³ 8f² 7.6fg 8f* 8fg⁶ 8g² 7g* 8.2s* 7d 1976 8f 8f 7fg] compact mare:
quite a useful selling handicapper at 4 yrs: no worthwhile form in 1976: stays
1¼m: acts on any going: suitable mount for an apprentice: unseated rider leaving
stalls on second outing. *R. Hollinshead.*

VILGORA 4 b.c. Raffingora 130–Vilswitch 93 (Vilmorin) [1974 5f³ 5fg⁶ 5g   92
5s³ 5d 5s² 5s² 5s 1975 5d 5fg 5g⁶ 7f² 5fg³ 5h⁵ 7d² 8f⁴ 5f² 6d⁴ 5.8f 5.9g³ 5g*
5g 5g⁶ 1976 5g² 5f* 5f* 5f 5g* 5g⁴ 5f² 5g* 5h* 5fg* 6fg* 5f² 5f² 5fg 5fg 5g² 5g⁵ 5f³
5g* 5g⁵ 5v 5v⁴ 5s] really strong colt: a remarkably tough individual who
won eight races at 4 yrs, including five in the north: ran on well when gaining his
final success, beating Gallico 1½ lengths at Goodwood in September: best form at
up to 6f: acts on any going: has run well both with and without blinkers: suitable
mount for a lady rider: most genuine and consistent: missed break on fourteenth
start. *M. Stevens.*

VILLAGE GREEN 4 b.c. Taj Dewan 128–Gossops Green (Crepello 136) [1974 —
N.R. 1975 12.3g 16fg 12f⁵ 1976 12.5g 8g⁴ 12s⁶ 13.4fg] well-grown colt: poor
maiden: tried in blinkers on third start: sold 2,300 gns Ascot September Sales.
F. Carr.

VILLAGE IDOL 2 br.f. Blakeney 126–Ile de France 94 (French Beige 127)   72 p
[1976 6g⁵ 6fg⁴] neat filly: third foal: dam, half-sister to good 1964 2-y-o
Leonardo, won at up to 7f: showed signs of ability in maiden races at Newbury in
July and Nottingham (fourth of 13 to Dumbunny) in August: may do better
over 1¼m+. *G. Harwood.*

VILLAGE SWAN 2 gr.c. My Swanee 122–Loweswater 74 (Saint Crespin III 132)   87
[1976 5g⁶ 6fg 6fg⁴ 6g³ 6fg⁴ 7g 7.3d³] compact, good sort: first produce: sold
privately for 500 gns as a foal, resold 1,500 gns yearling: dam won over 1½m:
moderate colt: ran on when good third to Mintage in nursery at Newbury in
September, final outing: should stay 1¼m. *R. Hannon.*

VINEPARK PARADE 2 b.f. Impecunious–Fernhill Melody 88 (Golden Cloud) —
[1976 6d 5s 6s] quite a useful-looking filly: half-sister to a winning hurdler:
dam 5f sprinter: behind in maiden and minor events but needed race on first two
outings. *G. Vergette.*

VIOLENCELLO 2 b.c. Philip of Spain 126–Tatty Head 76 (Queen's Hussar 124)   45
[1976 5g⁵ 5d 5h 5h⁵] small colt: bad plater: wears blinkers: sold 170 gns
Doncaster August Sales. *A. Balding.*

VIOLET HONEY 2 b.f. St Paddy 133–Oh So Sweet 90 (Ballymoss 136) [1976   81
6g⁶ 6g³ 8fg⁴] lengthy, attractive American-foaled filly: half-sister to fair 3-y-o
middle-distance winner Ski Shop (by Crocket): dam, placed from 1m to 1½m, is
sister to smart 1m to 1½m horse Sweet Moss: moderate filly: should stay at least
1½m. *B. Hills.*

VIRGIN 2 gr.f. Zeddaan 130–Vahinee (Mourne 126) [1976 5g* 6.5g* 7s⁶] 114
French filly: half-sister to four winners in France, notably very smart but
short-lived Dragoon (by Le Fabuleux): dam won at 2 yrs: won a minor race at
Clairefontaine and strongly-contested Prix du Calvados at Deauville in August:
drew clear from distance in latter race to win by 2½ lengths and the same from
Doha and Orchid Miss, who went on to finish second and third in Criterium des
Pouliches: co-second favourite for Prix de la Salamandre at Longchamp in
September but was always behind and finished only sixth of eight, nearly 9
lengths behind Blushing Groom: will stay at least 1m. *J. Cunnington, France.*

VIRGINIA COURT 2 ch.f. Lord David 121 or Virginia Boy 106–Hiatus 87 —
(High Treason 126) [1976 5d 6g 5v] well-made filly: third foal: 2,500 gns
yearling: dam best at 5f: behind in large fields of maidens: backward first two
outings. *Doug Smith.*

VIRGINIA GIRL 3 ch.f. Virginia Boy 106–Karen Scott (Our Babu 131) [1975 — 5h 6fg 5d 6g 5g⁵ 5fg² 5v 1976 8fg] strong filly: plater: well beaten in better company (needed race) on only outing at 3 yrs: probably stays 6f: acts on firm going: wore blinkers at 2 yrs: sold 270 gns Doncaster June Sales. *M. H. Easterby.*

VIRGINIA LAD 2 b.c. Virginia Boy 106–Florist (Floribunda 136) [1976 5fg **81** 5fg² 6fg*] strong colt: second foal: dam ran only once at 2 yrs: won valuable 13-runner seller at Goodwood in July by ½ length from Comtec, coming with a great run in final furlong: sold 3,500 gns afterwards and subsequently won in Belgium. *J. Sutcliffe.*

VIRGINIA SLIM 2 b.c. Virginia Boy 106–Firenza Mia 65 (Vigo 130) [1976 5fg] brother to very useful 3-y-o 5f performer Virginia Wade: in rear in 15-runner maiden race at Warwick in April: dead. *B. Swift.*

VIRGINIA WADE 3 gr.f. Virginia Boy 106–Firenza Mia 65 (Vigo 130) [1975 **112** 5.1f² 5fg⁴ 5h* 5f² 5h* 5fg* 5fg² 5fg* 5g⁵ 1976 5d³ 5fg* 5fg⁶ 5fg⁶] compact filly: half-sister to Just Because (by Midsummer Night II), winner of a 2¼m amateur riders event: dam ran only at 2 yrs: put up a splendid performance when winning six-runner Ladbroke Club Handicap at Epsom in April under 9-4, soon having opposition off bit and beating Gallico by a length: seen out only twice subsequently and ran poorly, being tried in blinkers on final outing: has blistering early pace, and is ideally suited by 5f, top-of-the-ground and a sharp track. *Doug Smith.*

VIRGINIA WOLF 2 br.c. Virginia Boy 106–Eyerini (Soderini 123) [1976 5fg 5g **80** 5fg 6fg⁴ 6g 6g 8.2s*] quite a good sort: showed greatly improved form when winning 22-runner seller at Nottingham in September by 6 lengths from Maharanee, and was bought in for 1,000 gns: clearly much better suited by 1m than sprint distances and goes very well on soft going. *G. Smyth.*

VISCOUNT 2 b.c. Realm 129–Sunflower 96 (Paveh 126) [1976 5g² 6fg² 6g³] **95** impressive-looking colt: first foal: dam won three times over 1m at 3 yrs: ran well on all outings, including when 2 lengths second of 20 to Pollerton in Convivial Stakes at York in August and when 1½ lengths third in £1,600 event won by Region at Ayr the following month: runs as though 7f will suit him: sure to win races. *S. Hall.*

VISHVAMITRA 4 b.c. Mossborough 126–Liebeslust (Mangon) [1974 7d 7v 8d **95** 1975 14fg⁶ 14.7f⁴ 16.1d* 14.7g* 14f⁴ 1976 16s 12.3f³ 15f* 13s² 14.7f* 16.1fg* 12v⁵] neat colt: fairly useful handicapper: well-backed favourite when winning at Ayr in May and when trotting up in amateur riders event at Redcar the following month: awarded race on disqualification of Wee Robin after finishing ½-length second to that horse at Haydock in July: well suited by long distances: acts on any going: ran badly final appearance. *S. Hall.*

VITAL HUNTER 3 b.c. Huntercombe 133–Vital Error 105 (Javelot 124) **107** [1975 5.5g* 7g⁵ 6d⁶ 1976 8g³ 9.8fg⁵ 9g⁶ 8d⁴ 6.5d 8d* 7.5g² 10g² 14.6d 12g³ 11.5v] strong, robust French colt: half-brother to four winners here and in France, including useful middle-distance performer Major Busted (by Busted): dam useful at up to 7f: won ladies race and finished runner-up in handicaps at Deauville in August: performed with credit earlier against much stronger opposition, including when close-up sixth to Happy New Year in Prix Daphnis at Evry: 200/1, made running until past halfway when thirteenth to Crow in 15-runner Doncaster St Leger in September: best form at around 1m to 1¼m: acts on a firm and a soft surface: trained for St Leger by H. Cecil. *E. Bartholomew, France.*

VITIGES 3 ch.c. Phaeton 123–Vale (Verrieres 131) [1975 5.5g² 5.5g* 6d* **132** 5.5g* 6d* 7s² 8g⁵ 1976 10.5s 7g* 8fg² 12g⁶ 10g⁶ 8d² 6g⁴ 10d*]
Vitiges' win by a neck from Rose Bowl in the Champion Stakes maintained the race's reputation for producing the unexpected. Vitiges started at 22/1. He could be given little more than an outside chance of winning, good horse that he was and for all that he seemed likely to benefit from the opportunity of racing on the softish ground that his high action suggests will always suit him best. The opposition appeared too strong for him, especially over the distance of ten furlongs. Of his eighteen opponents in what was the hottest field to turn out for any race over the distance in England in 1976, the three-year-olds Crow, Malacate, Northern Treasure and Wollow had won a classic, and the four-year-old Rose Bowl, winner of the Champion Stakes the previous year, had given every indication that she was fast approaching her best.
On the other hand Vitiges, since beating Manado in the seven-furlong Prix

Mme M. Laloum's "Vitiges" (G. Rivases)

Djebel 'classic trial' at Maisons-Laffitte in the spring, had gone five races without a win, which is a long losing sequence for a horse with pretensions to winning the Champion Stakes. In two of those races, the Guineas and the Derby, he had finished a place and a length and a half behind Wollow; and in another, the Prix Eugene Adam, he had finished five places and over five lengths behind Crow who subsequently left that form behind. Of course, there was some doubt whether Crow was fully effective any longer at a mile and a quarter but there was more doubt whether Vitiges was capable of showing his best form at the trip. Although Vitiges is by the thorough stayer Phaeton his record suggested strongly that he was best at a distance up to a mile, a free-running type most at ease when allowed to bowl along in front. As a two-year-old he showed far more speed than stamina; he showed top-class speed, winning the best two sprints in France for horses of his age, the Prix Robert Papin and the Prix Morny. Tackling longer distances he was beaten by Manado in the seven-furlong Prix de la Salamandre and the one-mile Grand Criterium, running creditably in the former but disappointing, apparently outstayed after being ridden with restraint, in the latter. As a three-year-old Vitiges had three outings over distances greater than a mile before running in the Champion Stakes, and he didn't earn a penny by his efforts. A very disappointing last of nine to Youth in the Prix Greffulhe, a moderate sixth to Crow in the Eugene Adam and a creditable sixth of twenty-three to Empery in the Derby was his record. Each time the tactics were the same, blazing away at the head of the field; there was no compromise at Epsom where he lasted in front for a mile and a quarter. In testing conditions in the Greffulhe, on his first appearance of the season, he blew up soon after halfway; in the Eugene Adam he disputed the lead to the distance.

In the shorter races during the season Vitiges' front-running tactics had always paid a dividend: second place in the Two Thousand Guineas, second place in the one-mile Prix Jacques le Marois and fourth place in the six-furlong Prix de Seine-et-Oise, besides his win in the Djebel. One of the most memorable aspects of a pretty straightforward running of the Two Thousand Guineas was the sight of Vitiges striding out with wonderful freedom at the head of the seventeen-strong field, setting a very lively gallop. He came under hard driving

Champion Stakes, Newmarket—Vitiges catches Rose Bowl near the finish. Northern Treasure is a good third

about two furlongs from home and remained hard driven to the post, but only Wollow, who went on below the distance and won comfortably in the end, ever looked likely to get to him. In the Marois Vitiges led everywhere except where it counted most: in an astonishingly tight finish Gravelines scraped home by a head and Radetzky got up to share second-place spoils, just in front of a line of high-class horses stretched across the course. In the Seine-et-Oise, his last race before the Champion Stakes, Vitiges made a return to sprinting encouraging enough to foster the idea that he had been racing out of his distance at a mile and a quarter or more: he led some of France's speediest horses for almost five furlongs before giving way to Kala Shikari, Raga Navarro and Mendip Man. The winner, Kala Shikari, beat him by less than a length.

And so to the Champion Stakes, in which we saw a different and better Vitiges than the one we had expected. Surprisingly, it was Vitiges' new stable-companion Red Regent, not Vitiges himself, who set about forcing the pace on the far side of the course. Vitiges, it transpired, had been fitted with a softer bit and taught to settle down in the short time he had been with Peter Walwyn since being transferred from the French stable of his long-time trainer Philippeau; far from pulling for his head, he proved perfectly willing to be dropped in behind, and he did not begin to make his challenge until passing the Bushes, around two furlongs out, at which point Rose Bowl was about to deprive Red Regent of the lead, and it was obvious from the stands that the best of the far-side group had easily the advantage over the stand-side group led by Malacate. Producing a strong run under pressure, Vitiges gradually wore down Rose Bowl and went ahead near the finish, with the far-side runner, Northern Treasure, two and a half lengths further back in third place and four of the other five horses who raced on that side of the track among the first ten home.

The race for the Champion Stakes called further into question the fairness of the Rowley Mile course as a test when a big field splits into two groups: the television camera showed the larger division on the stand side—and it included Wollow and Crow besides Malacate—soon at a clear disadvantage and remaining so, although Malacate and fifth-placed Lady Singer did make good ground over the last two furlongs. Throughout the season, but particularly at the Houghton meeting, there had been more than a suspicion that conditions were slower on the stand side, and the position is clearly unsatisfactory as long as there exists the shadow of a doubt about the soundness of the result of a race as important as the Champion Stakes. Nevertheless even if the most pessimistic view of the result is taken and all the stand-side runners are discounted, Vitiges' performance is still clearly an outstanding one, easily the best of his career and one that places him firmly in the top half-dozen horses in Europe. He beat a tip-top filly in Rose Bowl fair and square.

With such an improved and outstanding performance to his credit Vitiges, who remains in training with Walwyn, is a tremendous prospect, perhaps the most interesting horse in the country. If he should improve further, as well he might in present hands, he could probably have any race over his distance at his mercy; if he should do no more than reproduce his Champion form he would be extremely difficult to beat. And now that he has shown that he is not the hard-pulling miler almost everyone thought him to be, but is instead a horse amenable to restraint who gets a mile and a quarter with ease, more options are open to his trainer with him. There is the real possibility that Vitiges, ridden as he was in the Champion Stakes, will get a mile and a half, the distance of the King George VI and Queen Elizabeth Stakes and Prix de l'Arc de Triomphe, in which he could renew rivalry with Crow. He is an interesting horse is he not?

Just one cautionary note here though. Another dry summer may limit Vitiges' opportunities of reproducing his very best form. Vitiges' high knee action was very marked on both occasions he went to post at Newmarket, and most horses that display such a round, pounding gallop prove best suited by a soft surface; usually the softer the ground the better they perform. Now Vitiges is not a horse for whom cut in the ground is essential—on his only outing on ground any firmer than good he showed excellent form in the Guineas and stretched out really well, as we said—but it is almost certainly no coincidence that he gave his best running when conditions were on the soft side. A cautionary note that others have raised, that Vitiges is allegedly unable to act well round a turn, we view with scepticism. True, most of his best results have come on a straight track—the Rowley Mile, the straight mile at Deauville, the straight seven at Maisons-Laffitte—but he rounded the turn at Longchamp smoothly enough in the Prix de la Salamandre and he simply flew round Tattenham Corner in the Derby.

Vitiges (ch.c. 1973)	Phaeton (gr 1964)	Sicambre (br 1948)	Prince Bio
			Sif
		Pasquinade (gr 1957)	Vandale
			Mademoiselle Paganini
	Vale (ch 1959)	Verrieres (b 1953)	Palestine
			Serre Chaude
		Calliopsis (ch 1954)	Prince Chevalier
			Calluna

Vitiges looks the part: he is a grand stamp of animal, as was his sire and also his half-sister Virunga (by Sodium), the latter seen over here at York, where she finished second to Mysterious in the Yorkshire Oaks, and Newmarket, where she set the pace for Allez France in the Champion Stakes. Virunga, by a stayer as is Vitiges, gained all her four wins over a distance of a mile and a quarter; she gave the impression she was best at that trip although she did stay a mile and a half. The two other winners by stayers out of the dam are Vallarta (by Sheshoon) who won over a mile and a half and Varig (by Pan II) who won twice at a mile and a quarter. The dam, Vale, a useful winner at six furlongs and nine furlongs, was the daughter of a miler.

With a losing sequence as long as his during the season, Vitiges was in some danger of having his generosity questioned by that regrettably large section of the racing fraternity which doesn't seem capable of recognising merit in anything less than a winner, but fortunately he seemed to escape criticism. Had Vitiges been so criticised, we would have been delighted to have refuted such a libel. He is a really genuine battler, and the riding tactics employed in most of his races before he came to England gave him ample opportunity to show as much. He will do well as a four-year-old. In the autumn the information was disclosed that Vitiges had been syndicated at 187,000 francs (approximately £23,000) a share, and would stand at the Someries Stud, Newmarket, in 1978. *P. Walwyn.*

VITORIA 3 ch.f. Salvo 129–Valentina Rose 85 (Red God 128 §) [1975 6h 7d 1976 10h] seems devoid of ability: sold 360 gns Ascot August Sales. *D. Gandolfo.* —

VIVACISSIMO 3 b.g. Fortissimo 111–Kith-n-Kin 90 (Kythnos 126) [1975 10g 1976 12g4 16d 11.1g 11.7fg4 8fg 15.5h6] light-framed, lengthy gelding: poor maiden: stays 1½m but possibly not 2m: had stiff task when tried in blinkers on fifth outing. *M. Francis.* 64

VIVA ZAPOTE 2 ch.c. Sweet Revenge 129–Persona Grata 88 (Petition 130) [1976 5fg4 5s2] half-brother to several winners, notably very useful 1969 2-y-o Long Till (by Fidalgo): 740 gns foal, resold 3,200 gns yearling: dam won over 6f at 2 yrs: ran well on both outings, finishing 3 lengths fourth to Swift Hussar in £1,200 event at Newmarket and neck second to Shush when favourite for 15-runner maiden race at Doncaster: not seen out after May: will stay 6f. *B. Hanbury.* 89

VOLEUSE 2 b.f. Burglar 128–Prime Beauty (Primera 131) [1976 5g 5s⁶ 5g⁴ 5h⁴ **65** 5g* 5.9s] small filly: half-sister to two minor winners: 200 gns yearling: dam disappointing middle-distance maiden: attracted no bid after making all to win 10-runner seller at Nottingham in July by 2 lengths from Dashing David: not seen out again until October when last of 12 in nursery at Wolverhampton: should stay 6f: sold to T. Marshall 540 gns Newmarket December Sales. *F. Maxwell.*

VOUCHER BOOK 3 ch.f. Good Bond 122–Concession Day 79 (Will Somers **96** 114 §) [1975 5f 6g 6f⁶ 8.2d³ 8fg* 1976 9g⁶ 12f* 13.8f* 12f* 12fg* 12s² 12.2s² 12.5v²] robust filly: developed into quite a useful handicapper, winning at Catterick in July (minor event) and August and Thirsk (apprentice event) and Redcar (slammed Rough River by 7 lengths) in September: runner-up in all her three subsequent races, going down in a driving finish with Grey Aglow at Teesside in October: stays 1¾m: acts on any going: good mount for an apprentice: genuine and consistent. *S. Hall.*

VRONDI 4 ch.c. Welsh Rake 118–Jevington 102 (Fairey Fulmar 124) [1974 **78** 5g⁵ 6g 8s 5s 1975 5d² 7.6g⁶ 5f⁶ 5.3f⁴ 5s 1976 6fg⁶ 6fg³ 6f⁵ 7fg² 6f² 5f³ 6f² 7g³ 5.3f⁴ 7h² 5.3h* 8d 6d 6v⁴] tall colt: thereabouts in most of his races at 4 yrs and gained a well-deserved success when trotting up in maiden race at Brighton in August: best form at up to 7f: seems to act on any going: genuine and consistent: suitable mount for an apprentice: blinkered sixth outing. *B. Wise.*

VULRORY'S STAR 4 ch.f. Negotiation–Vulrory (Vulgan 123) [1974 N.R. — 1975 N.R. 1976 10.1fg 14fg 13.1s 18s] slow maiden. *M. McCourt.*

W

WAGON LADY 2 br.f. Double Jump 131–Sonella 81 (High Treason 126) [1976 **58** 5g⁶ 5s³ 5fg⁶ 5f³ 5g²] plater: 1¾ lengths second to Trust View at Carlisle in May: should stay 6f: probably acts on any going: blinkered last two outings: sold 230 gns Doncaster June Sales. *M. W. Easterby.*

WAGON MASTER 3 ch.g. Birdbrook 110–Covered Wagon 74 (Klondyke Bill — 125) [1975 7g 8f 1976 10.4d 8s 5fg 8f⁶ 5f 5fg 6f 8s] strong gelding: poor

Mrs F. C. B. Fleetwood-Hesketh's "Walk By"

maiden: blinkered penultimate appearance: sold out of R. Mason's stable 1,000 gns Ascot September Sales after seventh outing. *D. H. Jones.*

WALK AROUND 4 ch.g. Farm Walk 111–Leger Bar 63 (French Beige 127) **78**
[1974 5f 6f 7g⁴ 7s⁶ 7.2s² 7s⁵ 1975 8s³ 8g² 10f* 10fg* 9.4h*(dis) 12fg³ 10f² 10.6s⁴ 1976 12.3f⁵ 10g³ 10f* 10f² 10f* 12f² 12fg⁵ 12.3f*] quite a moderate handicapper: successful at Beverley (twice) and Newcastle, on latter course short-heading Court Circus: extremely well suited by 1¼m and 1½m, and will stay further: acts on any going: ran well in blinkers at 2 yrs, but has done best without them since: races with his head held very high and is a difficult ride. *W. Haigh.*

WALK BY 4 b.f. Tower Walk 130–L'Anguissola 102 (Soderini 123) [1974 5g⁴ 5g* **108**
6g⁴ 6s* 6s 1975 7s⁶ 8g 6d 6fg 5fg² 7g⁶ 5f⁴ 6d² 5.6g* 5d³ 1976 5fg 6f² 6f 5fg³ 6f]
lengthy, good-topped filly: useful sprinter: ran well when about 3½ lengths third to Music Boy in Group 3 King George Stakes at Goodwood in July, running on strongly after losing a prominent position in early stages: heavily-backed favourite and apparently well in at weights, never going well when well beaten in Great St Wilfrid Handicap at Ripon in August won by Honeyblest, only subsequent start: best at sprint distances: acts on any going. *W. Wightman.*

WALL HILL 3 br.c. Goldhill 125–Tarramee 66 (Tarqogan 125) [1975 5fg 5f 7f **57**
8d⁵ 1976 9.4g 12g⁶ 12fg² 16f² 12f⁴ 12fg³] poor form in varied races, including a claiming event: stays 1½m and seemed not to get 2m on fourth outing. *P. Rohan.*

WALNUT TREE 2 b.f. Run The Gantlet–Lavender Girl 92 (Petition 130) —
[1976 6d 6v] strong filly: half-sister to several useful winners, notably smart stayer Realistic (by Reliance II): dam a sprinter: unquoted when ninth of 23 to Amity in maiden race at Newbury in October, second outing: should be suited by 1m+. *H. Blagrave.*

WALTER 3 ch.g. Chebs Lad 120–Goldwis 94 (Golden Cloud) [1975 N.R. **89**
1976 6d² 7f³ 6g² 5fg* 5h² 6fg³ 6f⁵ 6g* 6g⁶ 6v* 6s³ 5s²] strong, compact gelding: won 18-runner maiden race at York in June by 2 lengths from Aboma and sellers at Newcastle in August and October (bought in 1,200 gns after winning by 7 lengths from New Did): is a cut above plating class and has several creditable efforts to his name in handicap company, just failing to hold off Ubedizzy at Doncaster in November: best form at 5f and 6f: acts on any going. *M. H. Easterby.*

WALTHAM LAD 3 br.g. Grisaille 115–Spatula (Epaulette 125) [1975 5f 6fg 7g —
1976 8g] of no account. *W. Wharton.*

WANDERING WAYS 2 ch.f. Will Somers 114 §–Jungle Jewel (Kingstone) **53**
[1976 6g 6s 7s 7s] bad plater: blinkered fourth outing: sold 500 gns Newmarket Autumn Sales. *D. Sasse.*

WAN LI 2 b.c. Great Heron 127–Kokuwa (Klairon 131) [1976 5f 5s³ 5s* 6d⁵ **73**
8.2d 8v⁵] neat, useful-looking colt: second living foal: half-brother to a winning plater by Florescence: 500 gns yearling: dam never ran: won five-runner seller at Ayr in May by 4 lengths and was bought in for 2,200 gns: ran creditably in nursery on penultimate outing and stays 1m: possibly unsuited by heavy going: trained by K. Payne on first four outings. *T. Molony.*

WANLOCKHEAD 5 b.h. Wolver Hollow 126–Exultation (Chamier 128) [1974 **95**
8d⁵ 8.5g* 8fg* 8g⁶ 8g⁵ 8fg³ 8s 1975 10d³ 8v² 9g 7.6f⁶ 10fg 9d⁵ 8f 8d 8fg 1976
10g³ 10fg 8f 9g⁶ 10fg] lengthy horse: good walker: ran very promisingly on reappearance, when 1¼ lengths third of seven to Blaskette in Daily Mirror

Hue-Williams Plate, York—Walter has more finishing speed
than Aboma and Stateroom (right)

Handicap at Epsom in June: most disappointing in his later races, finishing last on three of his subsequent starts: stays 1¼m: acts on any going: blinkered last outing: sold 1,300 gns Newmarket Autumn Sales. *D. Sasse.*

WANWETH GIRL 2 b.f. Crooner 119–Odessa 80 (Umberto 118) [1976 5g³ **58**
5f* 5f 5d 7h⁶ 7f 8f 8fg 8s 8v] leggy filly: 360 gns foal, resold 300 gns yearling: dam won over 1¼m: won seller at Beverley (no bid) in April by 2 lengths: in rear on all outings afterwards: missed break when tried in blinkers on penultimate start: should be suited by 7f+. *L. Shedden.*

WARBECK 4 b.c. Royal Palace 131–No Relation 94 (Klairon 131) [1974 5f **93**
5fg⁵ 7fg 1975 8v³ 10s* 8g³ 8f* 10fg² 10.5fg* 10d³ 12g 1976 12g⁶ 12fg 12d⁴ 10d⁶ 12.3fg* 12h³ 8g² 11g⁴ 12d* 12v* 12d³] small colt: quite a useful handicapper: winner three times at 4 yrs, at Newcastle in June, Ascot in September and York the following month: found a good turn of foot to beat Lochranza a neck on last-named course: stays 1½m and should get further: acts on any going: wears blinkers: ran below his best when lady ridden: sold to R. Armstrong 7,400 gns Newmarket Autumn Sales. *H. Wragg.*

WARM SLIPPER 3 ch.f. King's Company 124–Margaret's Slipper 70 (Pana- —
slipper 130) [1975 N.R. 1976 8fg] second produce: 3,200 gns foal, resold 3,300 gns yearling: dam won over 1¼m: tailed-off last in seven-runner minor event won by Colombade at Newmarket in July. *M. Stoute.*

WARMSPUNS JOY 2 br.f. Tycoon II–Warmspun 86 (Specific 103) [1976 **69**
5g⁶ 5fg⁴ 5fg 5f 5g 5g 7f² 7g 8fg⁶ 5.9s] second foal: half-sister to fair 1975 2-y-o 6f winner Miss Warmspun (by Saratoga Skiddy): dam won over 5f and 6f at 2 yrs: fair plater at her best: going well when hampered by slipping saddle on penultimate appearance: suited by 7f+: acts on firm going: blinkered fifth and sixth outings. *J. Hardy.*

WARREN ROSE 3 ch.f. Amber Light 114–Rock Dandy (Master Rocky 106) —
[1975 5f 6g* 1976 8g 7fg 5.3f⁴] lightly-built, narrow filly: won 12-runner minor event at Chepstow in November, 1975: no worthwhile form at 3 yrs and was sold 300 gns Ascot August Sales. *B. Swift.*

WARRENWOOD PARK 2 br.c. Comedy Star 121–Nearly Safe 76 (Neron 121) **77**
[1976 5f 6fg 6fg 6f⁴ 6f 5f* 6g³ 6s] half-brother to Caerlaverock (by Weepers Boy), a minor winner at up to 7f: dam won over 1m: well-backed favourite and dropped in class, showed first worthwhile form when winning 13-runner seller at Folkestone in September by short head from Lucky Touch (bought in 980 gns): respectable third in nursery at Lingfield later in month: should stay 1m: acts on firm going. *B. Lunness.*

WARRIOR'S SISTER 2 b.f. Huntercombe 133–Colliers 85 (Skymaster 126) **92**
[1976 5g² 6g³ 5s²] half-sister to three winners, notably top-class sprinter Roman Warrior (by Porto Bello): dam stayed 1¼m: seemed to have every chance when third of nine to Mofida and Lucky Omen, beaten 1½ lengths and ¾ length, in valuable Firth of Clyde Stakes at Ayr in September: seemed to have an outstanding chance in minor event at Edinburgh the following month, but went down by 1½ lengths to Docket: suited by 6f and runs as though she will stay further: possibly not at her best on soft ground. *N. Angus.*

WASHINGTON GREY 3 gr.c. Siliconn 121–Helgonet (Soueida 111) [1975 —
6fg 5f 1976 5.3h⁴ 6v] strong colt: particularly good mover: no worthwhile form in varied company: slowly away on first outing and was bandaged near-fore on second: sold to P. Mitchell 500 gns Doncaster November Sales. *R. Price.*

WASSENAAR ROSE 2 b.f. Sky Gipsy 117–Molly Polly (Molvedo 137) [1976 —
5.9f] half-sister to fairly useful 1974 2-y-o 5f winner Fair Parrot (by Sahib) and to a winner in Italy: dam won five races in Italy: last of nine after starting slowly in maiden race at Wolverhampton in August. *J. Gibson.*

WATCH-BEAR 4 b.c. Sassafras 135–Agar's Plough 122 (Combat 123) [1974 —
7fg² 7g 7d³ 1975 12v 12v 9s 8fg 10.1f⁶ 8.3fg 10.8f* 10.1fg³ 10fg* 10.1fg² 10g 1976 12fg 12f² 10f⁴ 10fg] strong, lengthy colt: quite a moderate handicapper: sometimes starts slowly, and did so when second to easy winner Charles Martel in four-runner event at Pontefract in April: probably stays 1½m: acts on firm going: best in blinkers: none too consistent: bought by B.B.A. for export to New Zealand. *Doug Smith.*

WATERBECK MAID 3 ch.f. Ra (U.S.A.) 92–Mobberley Maid (Phebus 99) —
[1975 N.R. 1976 8s 12.2f⁶ 10f 14.7f] plain filly: well beaten in maiden races, finishing last in three of them, and is of little account. *M. Naughton.*

WATER BOY 2 ch.c. Timmy My Boy 125–Dame des Ondes (Neptunus 132) **116**
[1976 5g* 6d* 6.5d* 6g² 8s² 6g] smart French colt: first foal: 150,000 francs
yearling (approx. £16,000): dam a smart performer at 2 yrs and 3 yrs in France,
winning from 6f to 9.5f, and comes from a highly successful family: won at
Chantilly, Evry and Deauville on first three outings, picking up his most valuable
prize on last-named course in August when winning seven-runner Prix des
Yearlings by 2 lengths from Doha (rec 6 lb): also ran well when 3 lengths second
of 11 to Blushing Groom in Prix Morny at Deauville later same month but
proved no match for Silk Slipper, to whom he was giving 7 lb, in Prix des Chenes
at Longchamp in September and went down by 4 lengths: did not take the eye
in paddock prior to finishing seventh of 11 to Tachypous in William Hill Middle
Park Stakes at Newmarket in October: should stay 1¼m: suited by a soft surface.
F. Boutin, France.

WATERBUCK 2 ro.f. The Axe II 115–Abyssinia 84 (Abernant 142) [1976 6g² **91**
6d⁵ 5s*] useful-looking filly: American bred: sister to three winners, including
very smart American performer Al Hattab, and half-sister to several other
winners: $50,000 yearling: dam won over 5f at 3 yrs: had more in hand than
short-head margin would suggest when winning 12-runner maiden race at
Haydock in October from Moomba: should stay at least 1m. *J. Dunlop.*

WATERGATE 3 ch.g. Hopeful Venture 125–Freetown 96 (Crepello 136) [1975 **73**
6g 7d⁶ 7g 8g 8f 1976 12fg⁵] big, strong gelding: quite a moderate maiden:
sweated up a bit on only outing (April): will stay beyond 1½m. *B. Hobbs.*

WAVELAND 2 ch.c. Song 132–Fair Winter 111 (Set Fair 129) [1976 5g] fair —
sort: closely related to a winning plater by Sing Sing, and half-brother to two
other winners: 240 gns foal, 950 gns yearling: dam very useful at up to 1¼m:
eighth of 15 to Local in maiden even at Catterick in June, only outing. *K.
Whitehead.*

WAX FRUIT 3 b.f. John Splendid 116–Pyracantha 68 (Firestreak 125) [1975 **79**
5f⁶ 6g* 6f* 7d² 5.9g² 1976 7g⁵ 6f 6f] attractive, well-made filly: quite a
moderate handicapper nowadays: acts on firm going and is possibly not at her
best on a soft surface: sold 1,000 gns Newmarket July Sales. *J. Dunlop.*

WAYLAND PRINCE 2 b.g. Autre Prince 125–What A Carry On (Mr Cavendish) **87**
[1976 5f³ 5f³ 6d 7.2fg² 6h* 7f² 7fg 6f⁵] useful-looking gelding: second foal
by a thoroughbred sire: dam never ran: won four-runner minor event at Carlisle
in July by 4 lengths from odds-on Moon Express: did not get best of runs when
1½ lengths second to The Bowler in similar race at Catterick later in month:
stays 7f well, and will get at least 1m: best form on a sound surface: started
slowly when blinkered on final outing. *M. H. Easterby.*

WAYWARD MAN 3 b.c. Manacle 123–Wayward Damsel (Pay Up) [1975 **62**
N.R. 1976 8fg⁶ 6f 6fg⁴ 7s 9s⁶] half-brother to several winners, including
very useful stayer Cornuto (by Firestreak) and some very useful jumpers:
dam a chaser: about 2 lengths fourth of 16 to Tribal Festival in maiden race at
Goodwood in September, easily best effort: should stay 1m: sold 5,100 gns
Doncaster November Sales. *R. Price.*

WEALTH TAX 2 b.c. New Policy–Rand (Bryan G) [1976 6g 7g] lightly-made **71 p**
American-sired colt: fourth produce: 2,500 gns foal: dam half-sister to very
smart French filly Gazala II: showed a little ability in September in newcomers
event at Goodwood and £2,900 race at Ascot (did not stride out at all well on
way to start). *B. Hills.*

WEARWELL 2 b.c. Frigid Aire–Put Right 61 (Mandamus 120) [1976 7fg —
7f 6f 6d] bad plater: blinkered third outing: sold 200 gns Ascot December
Sales. *A. Dalton.*

WEDDING BAND 2 b.f. Sir Gaylord–Babble On 79 (Acropolis 132) [1976 **77 ?**
5fg³ 6fg⁴ 6fg² 7fg² 8g] strong, attractive filly: half-sister to several minor
winners: 17,000 gns yearling: dam, sister to Espresso, won at up to 11f: in
frame in £2,000 maiden races in July on second and third outings, finishing
2¾ lengths fourth to Icena at Newmarket and going down by ½ length to Miellita
at Goodwood: did not run anywhere near her best form when favourite for
maiden event at Salisbury in September, finishing 1½ lengths second to Topling:
by far her best efforts at 6f but is bred to stay at least 1m. *I. Balding.*

WEE ANNA 3 ch.f. Weepers Boy 124–Khairaana (Sheshoon 132) [1975 **56**
5g 5g³ 5.9g⁴ 1976 6f⁵ 5g⁵ 5fg 5s⁵ 6v³] poor maiden: best run at 6f: sold to
W. R. Williams 700 gns Ascot November Sales. *Doug Smith.*

WEEPER'S STAR 4 b.f. Weepers Boy 124–Etoile Royale 93 (Sovereign Lord — 120) [1974 6s 5v⁶ 5v 1975 6s 6s 6fg⁶ 6fg 8.3f 7f 1976 12fg] of no account. *Miss N. Wilmot.*

WEE ROBIN 4 b.g. Le Levanstell 122–Boundary 90 (Ballymoss 136) [1974 **65** N.R. 1975 12f⁶ 14f* 13f² 12f³ 12f* 12f* 16g⁵ 15d⁴ 1976 12fg 9g 16.1fg⁴ 16h³ 12f³ 15.8f⁵ 15.8fg⁶ 12fg] poor handicapper: disqualified and placed fourth (wandered about very badly in straight) after winning nine-runner amateur riders race at Haydock in July by ½ length from Vishvamitra: also performed creditably on fifth appearance but ran badly on four of his outings, including on last three: stays well: acts on firm going: good mount for an apprentice: blinkered fifth and sixth starts: most inconsistent. *Denys Smith.*

WEIGH-IN FIRST 3 b.f. Bally Russe 113–Way Up (Three Wishes 114) [1975 **47** 5d⁵ 5v⁴ 5s 6fg 7.2g 7f 6fg 6g 6f 5f 1976 13.8g 12d⁴ 15.8f*] plater: bought in 600 gns after winning comfortably at Catterick in April: suited by 2m: acts on firm going: tried in blinkers at 2 yrs. *D. Plant.*

WEISSHORN 2 b.f. Maystreak 118–Asicion 89 (Above Suspicion 127) [1976 **79** 6f² 5g 6g] unfurnished filly: second foal: dam won three times over 5f and 6f at 2 yrs: ran easily best race when neck second of 11 to odds-on Mandalus in minor event at Doncaster in July, keeping on really strongly under pressure: probably needs further than 5f and should stay 1m. *M. H. Easterby.*

WELBECK LADY 3 b.f. Sweet Story 122–Thoughtful Light 85 (Borealis) — [1975 5.1f 7g 6g 6g 1976 7g 8.2d 8s] compact filly: bad plater: bandaged last two outings: sold 400 gns Newmarket December Sales. *V. Mitchell.*

WELCH SOLDIER 2 b.c. Easter Island 101–Flying Nun 66 (Welsh Abbot 131) **77** [1976 5fg 5f 7f³ 7f³ 6h² 6f³] second foal: dam won over 5f at 2 yrs: placed in maiden and minor events, on last occasion finishing 4 lengths third of 16 to Richmond Hill at Catterick in August: was badly drawn here and missed the break, but for which he would have gone close: will stay 1m. *J. Etherington.*

WELCOME GUEST 3 b.c. Sir Ivor 135–Miss Flirt (My Babu 136) [1975 **81** 8g⁴ 1976 11g⁴ 12d 13.3fg] attractive, well-made American-bred colt: half-brother to two minor winners in U.S.A.: 7,000 gns yearling: dam won at 2 yrs: just under 6 lengths fourth of 13 to Rowe Residence in maiden event at Newbury in May: ran poorly afterwards: stays 11f: not seen out after June: sold to M. Francis 2,000 gns Newmarket Autumn Sales. *H. Cecil.*

WELCOME HONEY 4 b.f. Be Friendly 130–Crystal Stream (Pardal 130) [1974 **49** 6g 5.1g⁴ 5.1g 1975 8d 10.1fg 8f 5g 6g 8g* 8f³ 1976 9fg 7f 7f 8.3f⁵ 8fg] compact filly: poor handicapper: stays 1m: has been tried in blinkers: suitable mount for an apprentice: sold 360 gns Ascot October Sales. *W. Wightman.*

WELLINGTON GIRL 2 br.f. Tribal Chief 125–Cloudy (Nyrcos 130) [1976 **62** 5g 5d 5f³ 5h 6fg] neat, light-framed filly: second foal: sister to a poor plater and is only plating class herself. *W. Gray.*

WELL OFF 2 gr.f. Welsh Pageant 132–Rockney 84 (Roan Rocket 128) [1976 — 6fg 6g 7g] small filly: second foal: dam, winner over 5f at 2 yrs, is half-sister to very useful miler Aberdeen: behind in maiden and minor events: sold 1,500 gns Newmarket Autumn Sales. *H. Candy.*

WELL SET UP 3 b.g. On Your Mark 125–Nell Gwyn 102 (Whistler 129) [1975 — 5f 1976 6g] no worthwhile form in maiden company: dead. *H. Candy.*

WELLS FARGO 6 b.g. Cracksman 111–Pretty Show (Ossian II) [1974 12g² — 10.2s* 1975 8g⁵ 1976 12.2s] neat gelding: has been hobdayed: quite a moderate handicapper in 1974: lightly raced since and was well beaten on only start in 1976: stays 1½m: acts on soft going. *C. Bewicke.*

WELLSPRINGS LASS 3 ch.f. Ben Novus 109–Alex M 69 (Kadir Cup 97 §) **59** [1975 5d⁶ 5v² 5g 6f³ 5f 5f⁴(dis) 5fg 1976 6f²] short-coupled filly: good second (had a far from clear run) to Ubedizzy in nine-runner handicap at Thirsk in April but was not seen out again: suited by 6f and should stay further: acts on any going. *H. Blackshaw.*

WELLSWOOD 3 b.g. Frigid Aire–Send 110 (Infatuation 129) [1975 N.R. — 1976 8f] half-brother to two winners, including smart sprinter Communication (by Bleep-Bleep): 1,700 gns yearling: dam a sprinter: unquoted when in rear in 21-runner maiden race won by Allan Water at Ripon in August. *G. Toft.*

WELSH ARBOUR 2 b.f. Welsh Pageant 132–Rose Arbour 106 (Pall Mall **63**
132) [1976 5g 7d 6g 6s] lightly-made, fair sort: third foal: half-sister to two
2-y-o winners, including useful 1974 6f winner Ramadour (by Amber Rama):
dam useful at up to 1m: little worthwhile form in maiden races: blinkered
fourth outing. *P. Walwyn.*

WELSH DANCER 2 br.c. Welsh Pageant 132–Come Dancing (Can) 91 (Northern **96**
Dancer) [1976 7fg 7f* 8s] third foal: half-brother to very smart 3-y-o stayer
General Ironside (by Sea Hawk II): 18,000 gns yearling: dam stayed 1m: odds
on, made all and held off Jona by a neck in 15-runner minor event at Yarmouth
in August: not seen out again until final day of season when well beaten in £2,200
event won by Lucent at Doncaster: should stay 1m: acts on firm going. *H.
Cecil.*

WELSH DRAGON 8 b.h. Welsh Abbot 131–Suzy Wong II 71 (Mincio 127) **70**
[1974 11d 10g 8f* 7f* 10fg 8g3 10.1g4 8.3g 7g 1975 7s5 8g2 7.6g 8f6 7fg6 7f*
7f2 7f2 7f5 7.6g 1976 7f3 8fg3 7fg 7f2 7f* 7g 10h] quite a useful selling handicapper on his day: successful at Folkestone in July (no bid): effective at 7f
and stays 1¼m: acts well on firm going: suitable mount for an apprentice:
has been tried in blinkers: pulled up lame final outing. *T. Gates.*

WELSH DRESSER 5 br.m. Welsh Rake 118–Dollar Princess II (America) —
[1974 11.1g 10.1fg 8d 7g 6g 5g 10v 1975 N.R. 1976 15.5s] of no account.
H. O'Neill.

WELSH FLAME 3 br.f. Welsh Pageant 132–Electric Flash 85 (Crepello 136) **106**
[1975 6d6 1976 7fg3 8fg2 10fg5 8f* 8g2 8.2fg* 8f* 8g* 9g] shapely filly: won
maiden race at Pontefract in June, handicaps at Nottingham and Newmarket
in August and Devonshire Stakes at Doncaster the following month: made her
field look very ordinary in last-named race, quickening clear in final furlong
with her jockey looking round to win as she pleased by 2½ lengths from Island
Degree: appeared to have excellent chance at weights in Irish Sweeps Cambridgeshire at Newmarket in October but ran poorly from an unfavourable
draw: best form at 1m, although has given impression she would stay further:
acts on firm going: has run well for a lady rider. *B. Hobbs.*

*Devonshire Stakes, Doncaster—Welsh Flame wins as she pleases from Island Degree
and Gale Bridge*

WELSH FRIEND 2 gr.c. Grisaille 115–Radio City (Bleep-Bleep 134) [1976   **94**
5g⁴ 5fg* 5f⁵ 5fg] half-brother to very useful 6f and 7f winner Welsh City (by
Maestoso): dam poor plater: made all, and had his four opponents well strung
out, when winning minor event at Brighton in May by 6 lengths from Slow
Coach: showed nothing like that form on either subsequent outing. *J. Nelson.*

WELSH HERO 2 br.c. Welsh Advocate 86–Tibbee (Nulli Secundus 89) [1976   **47**
5.9f 5g⁴ 5f 8.2s 7s] bad plater: blinkered fifth outing. *J. H. Peacock.*

WELSH JEWEL 2 br.f. Welsh Pageant 132–King's Gem 88 (King's Troop 118)   **72**
[1976 6fg 5f³ 5f⁴ 6g 5v] useful-looking filly: good mover: half-sister to fairly
useful 1972 2-y-o African God (by Runnymede) and to French 3-y-o 1m winner
Legemme (by Le Levanstell): dam a sprinter: in frame in maiden races at
Warwick and Catterick in August: should stay at least 6f. *J. Winter.*

WELSH PRINCESS 3 b.f. Welsh Saint 126–Procina 69 (Prince Bio) [1975   —
6d 1976 8f] narrow filly: lightly raced and no sign of ability: sold 1,300 gns
Newmarket September Sales. *W. Wharton.*

WELSH REASON 3 b.c. Welsh Saint 126–Sweet Reason (Elopement 125)   **75**
[1975 5g 8g⁵ 7s² 1976 8g⁶ 7.3g 7.2g* 8s⁶] attractive, sturdy colt: bandaged in
front and moved very poorly to post when winning seller at Haydock in May,
showing great courage to score all out by ¾ length from Priestcroft Boy: sold out of
P. Walwyn's stable 2,400 gns afterwards: badly hampered on only outing for new
stable (June): should stay 1m+: well suited by soft going. *K. Payne.*

WELSH RELIC 3 br.c. Welsh Pageant 132–Relcia 92 (Relko 136) [1975 6fg 6g   **84**
7g 1976 8f 10fg² 10f* 10.6g⁴ 12f* 12f 12g⁶ 13.3v³] useful-looking colt: won
maiden race at Yarmouth in July and minor event at Ripon the following month,
latter by a head from Bombardier: had stiff tasks afterwards but ran creditably on
final outing: stays 13f: evidently acts on any going. *Doug Smith.*

WELSH STREAK 2 b.c. Welsh Saint 126–Fire Bell (Firestreak 125) [1976   **80**
6fg 6g⁵ 6g⁴ 6g³ 7.3d 7g 8s] workmanlike colt: half-brother to 1975 2-y-o 5f
winner Kings Fire (by King's Leap): dam, who raced without success in France,
is half-sister to very useful stayers Aegean Blue and Khalekan: quite a modest
maiden: should stay 1m: sold 1,600 gns Newmarket Autumn Sales. *J. Benstead.*

WELSH TREATY 4 b.g. Welsh Saint 126–Treaty 86 (Ratification 129) [1974   —
5g 6g⁴ 6d⁴ 6g 6d³ 1975 7fg 10g² 10g³ 10.8f² 10fg* 12.3g³ 1976 12fg 10.6f⁴]
rangy gelding: good mover: poor handicapper nowadays: appears not to stay a
stiff 1½m: seems to act on any going: has been tried in blinkers. *G. Pritchard-
Gordon.*

WELTHI 3 b.g. probably Welsh Abbot 131–Thisbe (Midsummer Night II 117)   **57**
[1975 6s 7v⁵ 7.6g³ 8g 1976 10g⁴ 10fg 12fg 10.1fg⁴ 12g² 14g⁴ 12fg²] big gelding:
stays 1¾m: usually wears blinkers but has shown form without: suitable mount
for an amateur rider: seems desperately one paced. *M. Francis.*

WENALLT RED KNIGHT 3 b.c. Furzebreck 62–Mays Request (Compensation   —
127) [1975 N.R. 1976 10fg 10.1f 12.2fg] half-bred colt: apparently of little
account: blinkered last two outings, running out on first of them. *D. H. Jones.*

WENDOVER LAD 3 b.g. Bluerullah 115–Bright Talk (Bright News) [1975   **46**
5d 5g⁵ 6f⁶ 5f* 1976 6fg⁴ 6f 6g 7f⁵ 6f⁶ 6f⁴ 6h2] small, compact gelding: plater:
ran best race on final outing (August): will stay 1m: acts on hard ground. *A. Pitt.*

WENLOCK EDGE 5 b.m. King Log 115–Porringer (Vigo 130) [1974 N.R.   —
1975 12.2fg 1976 11.1g 8g 8g] of little account: sold 360 gns Ascot July Sales.
M. James.

WENNING 2 b.f. Nice Music 115–La Cage Doree 92 (Le Dieu d'Or 119) [1976   —
6fg 6g 7v 8.2s] neat filly: fourth foal: dam ran only at 2 yrs, when winner at 5f
and 6f: in rear in varied company. *J. Calvert.*

WEPHEN 4 br.c. Great Nephew 126–Courgette 73 (Gilles de Retz 132) [1974   **97**
5g 5g 5f² 5s 8g 7v⁴ 7g³ 7.2v* 1975 8s⁶ 10.2g 10.4g⁵ 8g* 8f³ 8fg 8f⁴ 10g* 10fg²
10f² 12g⁵ 12f³ 10g 1976 10g 11.7fg 10g² 10d⁴ 10d* 10fg* 10h*] compact colt:
fairly useful handicapper: successful at Ripon (beat Lord David very easily in
Joe Coral Handicap), Salisbury (Gwen Blagrave Memorial Stakes) and Chepstow,
all in June: had earlier finished very good second to Royal Match in Ultramar
Jubilee Handicap at Kempton in May: has run respectably over an easy 1½m but
is possibly better at shorter distances: acts on any going: genuine and consistent: suitable mount for an apprentice: front runner. *P. Cole.*

ESLEYAN 3 b.f. Great Nephew 126–Never Angel 78 (Never Say Die 137)   —
[1975 5g 6g 7g⁴ 8g 8.2g 1976 12g 11f 12v] poor maiden: should stay middle

distances: blinkered last two outings: sold 420 gns Doncaster November Sales.
M. Camacho.

WESLEY BOAT 2 b.f. Forlorn River 124–Ever Grateful 95 (King's Bench 132) **77**
[1976 6g 5s⁶ 5v⁴] sister to winning 3-y-o sprinter Four Lawns and half-sister to
some moderate animals: 700 gns foal, resold 940 gns yearling: dam fairly useful
at 6f and 7f: ran best race when 7 lengths fourth of 17 to Be Royal at Leicester in
November. *D. Marks.*

WESTACRE FOLLY 2 ch.f. Privy Seal 108–Why Dorrit (Question) [1976 7g] —
smallish, lengthy filly: second foal: dam well beaten on both outings: in need
of race when last of 22 to Sin Timon in maiden race at Newmarket in October.
N. Callaghan.

WEST BEAUTY 2 b.f. Willipeg 112–Film Fan (Fast Fox 123) [1976 5fg] —
light-framed filly: half-sister to a minor winner: 170 gns yearling: moved badly
to post when behind in 22-runner seller at Ripon in May. *T. Molony.*

WESTBROOK 2 b.g. Sweet Revenge 129–Marcia (Mark-Ye-Well) [1976 5g 5f² **89**
5f* 5fg* 5f 5g 5fg] strong gelding: half-brother to a winner in France and to a
winner in Belgium: 2,400 gns yearling: dam rated leading filly of her generation at
2 yrs in Norway: won maiden race at Ayr and minor event at Pontefract in May:
ran badly on next outing, was subsequently off course for three months and was
then well beaten in nurseries: will stay 6f: lost chance at start on fifth outing.
L. Shedden.

WESTERLANDS PRIVET 2 ch.f. Yellow River 114–Westerlands Priestess 103 —
(Acropolis 132) [1976 7s] second foal: dam won over 6f at 2 yrs: 20/1 when in
rear in 19-runner maiden race won by Lady Oriana at Newmarket in October.
B. Hills.

WESTERN TYRANNY 2 ch.f. Tyrant–West Iran (Zarathustra 131) [1976 5s⁴ **108**
5s² 5g² 6f* 5f* 5f*] Irish filly: half-sister to two winners, including fairly useful
1974 2-y-o 6f winner Persilla (by Silver Shark): 2,500 gns yearling: dam won over
1¼m and 2m in Ireland: won 12-runner maiden event at Navan in June by short
head from newcomer Sallail, the pair finishing 10 lengths clear: subsequently beat
Swatchel when winning minor events at Leopardstown, beating him far more
easily on first occasion: not raced after July: will stay 1m: acts on any going:
wears blinkers. *K. Prendergast, Ireland.*

WESTERN WHORLS 4 gr.g. Fleece 114–Crystal Clear 113 (Chamossaire) **66**
[1974 N.R. 1975 12v 1976 12s² 12s] half-brother to very useful stayer
Chiseldon (by Worden II): dam won at up to 2m: backed at long odds when
length second of 14 to Burleigh at Chepstow in apprentice race in October, better
effort at 4 yrs. *R. Hannon.*

WESTER WIN 2 gr.f. Ragusa 137–St Cecilia 113 (Milesian 125) [1976 5f 5f 7f⁴ **82**
7fg 7d 8fg 8s* 7s 8s] leggy filly: half-sister to two winners, including Irish 9f and
1¼m winner All Souls (by Saint Crespin III): 540 gns yearling: dam very useful
sprinting 2-y-o: only moderate: won 16-runner maiden race at Bath in October
by ¾ length from Tal: ran creditably in nursery on final outing: should stay 1¼m:
acts on any going: blinkered on second outing. *R. Boss.*

WESTGATE GIRL 2 ch.f. Huntercombe 133–Bowling Green (Ballymoss 136) **85**
[1976 6g* 7.2f³ 7.2v⁶] lengthy filly: sister to useful sprint winner Vanda Diana,
and half-sister to two winners, including Wotdyknow (by Reliance II), a winner
over 1⅛m: sold twice as a yearling, for 960 gns and 1,900 gns respectively: dam
placed at up to 13f in Ireland: won nine-runner maiden race at Ayr in August
by a length from Avitus: 3¼ lengths third of 13 to Bowerbird in minor event at
Haydock later in month, better subsequent effort: will stay 1m: acts on firm
going. *E. Collingwood.*

WESTGATE SOVEREIGN 2 br.f. Sovereign Path 125–Lerdet 93 (Whistler **89**
129) [1976 5f⁶ 5d² 5g* 5d⁴ 5d⁵ 5fg⁴ 5fg² 5s] third foal: half-sister to two 2-y-o
winners, including fairly useful 1974 6f winner Port Tack (by Right Tack): sold
twice as a yearling, for 1,400 gns and 3,000 gns: dam a sprinter: made all to win
14-runner maiden race at Ripon in April by ½ length from La Ville de Rire: off
course three months after fifth outing and ran well in two nurseries afterwards:
will be suited by 6f. *E. Collingwood.*

WESTWARD LEADING 5 b.g. Frankincense 120–Teflon 80 (Pan II 130) [1974 **61**
12fg 8.2g 10g 7g 8d* 7s* 8v⁴ 6v³ 8.2v³ 1975 8s 7s 7fg 8.3f 6fg 8f⁵ 8fg 10d* 10g*
1976 8g⁵ 10f⁵ 7fg² 7f 8f⁵ 8f² 8.2fg³ 7d* 8.2s²] light-framed gelding: selling handicapper: bought in 675 gns after winning at Yarmouth in September by 1½ lengths

from Little Run: stays 1¼m: probably acts on any going: blinkered second outing and fifth start (dwelt). *A. Bacon.*

WESTWOOD BOY 2 br.c. Saintly Song 128–Sunshine Holyday 96 (Three Wishes 114) [1976 5g³ 5f⁶ 6f³ 6g⁴ 7fg⁴ 7h² 8f 8fg² 8v*] robust colt: first foal: 600 gns yearling: dam stayed very well: in frame on most of his outings prior to winning eight-runner nursery at Newcastle in October by 7 lengths from Stormy Summer: will stay at least 1½m: acts on hard going and goes very well indeed on heavy. *W. Gray.* **93**

WHAT A FIND 3 ch.c. Hul a Hul 124–Brig O'Doon 57 (Shantung 132) [1975 5v⁶ 5v 5g 6fg 7g² 7g* 8fg³ 1976 8g 10f* 10f² 10g³] workmanlike colt: fair handicapper: ran two good races at Beverley in April, beating Hopeful Bloom by ½ length and then finishing creditable second to easy winner Parent: will probably stay 1½m: acts on firm going: seems best in blinkers nowadays: not seen out after early June. *J. Hardy.* **86**

WHAT A PICTURE 4 br.f. My Swanee 122–Lady Matador 108 (Matador 131) [1974 5g 5d 5g⁵ 5d² 5g 5d⁴ 5s² 5fg* 1975 5fg 5f³ 5f⁶ 5fg 5.3f 5f* 5f³ 5g² 5f⁵ 5g 5g⁴ 5g⁶ 1976 5fg² 5.1g 5g³ 5f² 5fg⁵ 5f² 5g*] stocky filly: had some good efforts to her credit at 4 yrs and gained a well-deserved success when winning at Catterick in September by ¾ length from Self Satisfied: well suited by a sharp 5f: acts on any going: wears blinkers: bolted before start when apprentice ridden on third outing in 1975, but subsequently ran well: sold 3,500 gns Newmarket December Sales. *P. Makin.* **68**

WHAT-A-SECRET 2 ch.c. Most Secret 119–Diddy Duck 53 (Dicta Drake 126) [1976 5f 7s* 8g] half-brother to a winning hurdler: dam best at 1m: ran on strongly when winning 10-runner maiden race at Edinburgh in October by 1½ lengths from Shereen: 12/1 when behind in 20-runner minor event at Lanark later in month: suited by 7f and should stay 1m. *W. A. Stephenson.* **73**

WHEATCLOSE 5 b.g. Highland Melody 112–Lucky Maid 85 (Acropolis 132) [1974 8g⁶ 12s² 10d* 1975 10.2g* 10v* 10d* 8.2s* 8g³ 1976 8g] strong, lengthy gelding: much improved at 4 yrs, winning four early-season apprentice handicaps: beaten favourite for first race of season, only outing in 1976: best form at up to 1¼m although stays further: goes well in the mud. *M. W. Easterby.* **—**

WHENBY 2 br.g. Prevailing–Sea Music 108 (Atan) [1976 5g⁴ 5s 5d* 5f 5fg 5g⁵ 5g* 5fg² 5f* 6v] robust, good-quartered gelding: first foal: 300 gns yearling: dam won eight races over 5f and 6f at 2 yrs: showed improved form after winning a seller at Redcar in May (bought in 1,900 gns) and won nurseries at Ayr (apprentice event, gambled on) and Hamilton in September: should stay 6f: seems to act on any going except perhaps heavy: missed break and never going well final outing. *M. W. Easterby.* **81**

WHEN'S KID 2 b.c. Saratoga Skiddy 113–When 76 (Our Babu 131) [1976 8.2h] first foal: dam best at sprint distances: started slowly when tailed-off last of 10 in seller at Hamilton in September. *D. Williams.* **—**

WHICKER'S WORLD 8 b.g. Bivouac 114–Helen C (Counsel 118) [1974 8fg⁴ 8f 8fg³ 1975 N.R. 1976 8.3g⁵] poor handicapper: stays 1m but not 1¼m: acts on firm going and a soft surface: suitable mount for an apprentice. *D. Jermy.* **—**

WHIFFERING 3 ch.g. Whiffenpoof 97 §–Havering (Gilles de Retz 132) [1975 7d 5.9g 1976 8.2f 9f⁶ 8.3d] of little account. *R. Vibert.* **—**

WHINNEY BRAE 2 b.g. Major Portion 129–Prim Dot (Primera 131) [1976 6g 8v 7v³] half-brother to two winners, including useful stayer Outpoint (by Fighting Charlie): dam unraced daughter of useful stayer Dotterel: showed ability in maiden and minor events won by useful animals: should stay middle distances: may do better at 3 yrs. *J. W. Watts.* **77**

WHIPALASH 2 b.f. Stephen George 102–Whipand 83 (Supreme Court 135) [1976 5fg 5g 5d 5s⁴ 5v⁶ 6s] sister to two minor 2-y-o winners, and half-sister to three others: dam disappointing half-sister to Connaught: quite a moderate maiden: should stay at least 7f. *C. Bewicke.* **73**

WHIP FINISH 2 b.f. Be Friendly 130–Party Whip (Sica Boy 132) [1976 5g* 5g⁶ 5g* 5f⁶ 6g] tall filly: good walker and mover: half-sister to a 2-y-o winner over 1m in France by Kashmir II: 500 gns yearling: dam twice-raced half-sister to Liberal Lady and Be Careful: won 16-runner auction event at Ripon in April and 18-runner minor race at Catterick the following month, on latter course making all to beat Bee Bumble by 2½ lengths: had stiff tasks on last two outings: should stay at least 6f: acts well on a soft surface. *R. D. Peacock.* **77**

WHIRLITZER 4 ch.c. Jukebox 120–Gentle Katie 84 (Anwar 120), [1974 5d 7s **62** 6s 1975 5d 6f* 6s 6f⁴ 7f 7f⁴ 8.3fg⁵ 8.3fg⁴ 6fg 8g² 8fg⁵ 8g² 8g 8d 8g* 8g³ 7d 1976 7f 8g⁶ 7.6fg² 8fg² 7fg 7f⁴ 8.2f³ 8f³ 8fg⁴ 8.3d 8v 10s] well-grown, strong colt: good mover: inconsistent but capable of showing form on his day: stays 1m: well suited by a sound surface and acts very well on firm going: suitable mount for an apprentice or lady rider: occasionally wears blinkers. *A. Pitt.*

WHIRLOW GREEN 5 b.g. Crocket 130–Word from Lundy 93 (Worden II 129) **89** [1974 7.2f³ 7fg 8f 10fg⁶ 12fg 8fg² 9g* 8g³ 10g 10s 1975 10v 7f* 8.2f² 7f⁵ 7g* 7f⁶ 7f 7f² 7f 7g 1976 7fg³ 6fg⁵ 7fg⁴ 10fg* 9fg⁴ 10.2fg* 10f* 10.2f* 10f⁶ 9f⁶ 10.2g⁵ 10f³ 10.2s²] fairly useful handicapper: a game front runner who did well in 1976, winning twice at Yarmouth and Doncaster: kept his form well and turned in another good effort on final outing when ½-length second of 16 to Firesilk at Doncaster in October: stays 1¼m well: acts on any going: wears blinkers. *J. Winter.*

WHISKEY MOUNTAIN 3 b.f. Bold Hour–Touch the Clouds (My Babu 136) **89** [1975 5g³ 1976 7g* 7g] lengthy American-bred filly: impressive winner of nine-runner maiden race at Goodwood in May, beating Regal Romance by 3 lengths: ran poorly in minor event at Kempton later in month and was not seen out again: will stay at least 1m: sold 4,800 gns Goffs November Sales. *I. Balding.*

WHISPERING GRACE 13 br.g. Articulate 121–The Duchess of Berwick (Berwick) **71** [1974 14g* 12g³ 14.7f⁴ 15g⁵ 14.7g* 14.6fg² 18g⁶ 14.6s* 1975 14.6fg³ 14s 12s⁴ 14.7f 14.7f³ 14.6fg² 13g* 13d⁴ 14g⁴ 13g⁶ 14g 1976 15f⁵ 15f⁶ 12g³] a grand old-timer who still possesses a fair amount of ability as he showed when 5 lengths third of eight to subsequently-disqualified Empress Regent at York in September (looked in need of outing, his first for nearly four months): best form at around 1¾m, although stays further: acts on any going: front runner: genuine. *N. Crump.*

WHISTLANGO 4 ch.f. Whistling Wind 123–Joan's Gallery (Sunny Way 120) — [1974 6fg 6d 1975 N.R. 1976 9fg] of no account. *M. Bradley.*

WHISTLEFIELD 3 ch.c. Roan Rocket 128–Nettlebed 84 (Hethersett 134) **116** [1975 7fg³ 8d* 8s* 1976 8fg³] strong, well-made colt: good walker and mover: brother to 2-y-o Gairloch: dam won at 7f and was placed at up to 1½m: wide-margin winner of last two of his three races as a 2-y-o, maiden event at Newbury and Kinrara Stakes at Goodwood: outstanding in paddock for Ladbroke Craven Stakes at Newmarket in April and ran very well to finish third to Malinowski and Oats, beaten 2½ lengths and ½ length: looked set for a good season but was not seen out again: will stay at least 1¼m: appears to act on any going. *R. Price.*

WHISTLER'S LANE 6 b.h. Whistling Wind 123–Scarlet Sash 75 (Umidwar) **54** [1974 12g 1975 N.R. 1976 15.5f² 12f²] poor handicapper: backed at long odds, finished length second of eight to London Rose at Folkestone in June: stays well: acts on firm going: ran below his best when tried in blinkers. *I. Wardle.*

WHISTLER'S PRINCESS 2 b.f. King Emperor–Fille Sifflante §§ (Whistler — 129) [1976 6g] half-sister to two winners by Gulf Pearl, including French 3-y-o Gulf Ring, a winner at up to 1½m: 920 gns yearling: dam temperamental half-sister to Queen Mary Stakes winner Grizel: tailed-off last of 18 to Reclamation in maiden race at Newmarket in July. *I. Walker.*

WHISTLING BERNIE 3 ch.g. Whistling Wind 123–Bernie 94 (Beau Sabreur **57** 125) [1975 5h⁶ 5h⁶ 6g 6d 1976 8fg 12g 10g² 9v⁶ 10v³] robust gelding: plater: stays 1¼m. *H. Wharton.*

WHISTLING DEER 3 ch.c. Whistling Wind 123–Lindear 80 (Vigo 130) [1975 **117 ?** 5s* 5g⁴ 5fg 6.3fg² 6.3f³ 7g³ 8g* 8d³ 1976 7s⁶ 7s⁶ 7g⁵ 10f² 12g 8f⁴ 9f⁵ 11.5f³ 12f⁴ 8f⁴ 12f² 13f] Irish colt: showed very useful form as a 2-y-o, winning two races, including Beresford Stakes at the Curragh: failed to win a race in 1976 but was first past post in Ulster Harp Derby at Down Royal in July, 1½ lengths and a length in front of Captain Memory and Niebo only to be placed third for hampering Niebo, after a stewards inquiry: runner-up in Nijinsky Stakes at Leopardstown (beaten a length by Meneval) in May and Blandford Stakes at the Curragh (went down by 3 lengths to stable-companion Northern Treasure) in August: fifteenth of 23 to Empery in Epsom Derby: slipped and lost a lot of ground when odds on for final outing: stays 1½m: acts on any going. *K. Prendergast, Ireland.*

WHISTLING HARD 2 b.f. Whistling Wind 123–Hardihood (Hard Ridden 131) **70** [1976 5fg⁶ 6fg 7g⁵ 7g⁶] half-sister to a 2-y-o winner in Italy: 420 gns foal, resold

3,000 gns yearling: 6 lengths fifth of 18 to Unella in maiden race at Yarmouth in September: blinkered when sixth of 21 in £1,600 seller won by Sosue Me at Newmarket later in month: stays 7f. *B. Hanbury.*

WHISTLING SCOT 2 ch.c. Whistling Wind 123–Princess Esra 70 (Pampered **67** King 121) [1976 5g³ 6fg] tall, leggy colt: third foal: 1,000 gns yearling: dam won 5f seller at 2 yrs: 4½ lengths third of four behind Charley's Revenge in minor event at Doncaster in April: not seen out again until late-September when in mid-division in 25-runner minor event won by Friendly Now at Redcar. *A. Balding.*

WHISTLING SWAN 6 b.g. Whistling Wind 123–Pavlova (Fidalgo 129) [1974 — 7.6g² 8g⁵ 8.2fg* 8g 8fg 7g² 1975 8g⁵ 11.7g 10g 8fg 1976 10g⁵] strong, shapely gelding: one-time fair handicapper but has shown little worthwhile form since his 4-y-o days: best form at up to 1m: acts on firm going: has run well in blinkers. *K. Ivory.*

WHITBY JET 2 ch.c. Be Friendly 130–That's Better (Mourne 126) [1976 **102** 5f 6d* 5fg⁴ 6fg³ 6fg³ 8g³ 7d* 8s⁵] strong colt: second foal: sold twice as a yearling, for 1,750 gns and 2,300 gns: dam won over 5f at 2 yrs: successful at Redcar in June and September, winning £1,600 event by ½ length from Mandalus on latter occasion despite hanging right in last 2f: also had some other good efforts to his name, finishing highly creditable 8½ lengths third to Nebbiolo in Gimcrack Stakes at York on fifth outing and staying on well when beaten a length by Royal Plume in £1,700 event at Doncaster on next: stays 1m well: perhaps not at his best on very soft going: tends to get behind in early stages. *J. Calvert.*

WHITE EMPEROR 4 ch.c. Great White Way–La Romana (Pardao 120) [1974 **71** 5f⁵ 5f³ 5f⁴ 5fg² 5fg² 6g 5f⁴ 5d 5d⁵ 5s⁶ 5v 1975 6s 5v⁵ 6g² 6fg⁴ 6f² 7.2fg⁵ 6g* 6f³ 7g 5f* 5g² 5g 6g 6f⁴ 1976 5f⁴ 5f* 5f² 5f⁵ 5fg³ 5g² 6f² 5g⁶ 6h* 5.8h⁴ 5f 5.8h³ 5f³ 5.9f³ 5f* 5f² 5f* 6h³ 5fg³ 5s] small, strong colt: quite a moderate handicapper: enjoyed a successful season, winning four races in the north, beating Fragrant Cloud a length at Lanark in September when gaining his last win: particularly well suited by a stiff track but acts on any: best form at up to 6f: acts on firm going: has been tried in blinkers: suitable mount for an apprentice: genuine and consistent. *R. Hollinshead.*

WHITE LANCER 2 b.c. Brigadier Gerard 144–Couloir 114 (Court Martial) — p [1976 5d] half-brother to four winners, including useful milers Coulomb (by Crepello) and Miss Glen (by Abernant): dam at her best at 2 yrs when very useful over 5f: 10/1, backward and green when never-dangerous eighth of 25 to Union Card in maiden race at Newbury in September: should do better at around 1m. *H. Candy.*

WHITE MINK 4 br.g. Barbary Pirate 91–Princess Zarina (Prince Chevalier) — [1974 6fg 7v 8v 8s 1975 10.8s 8g 8f 14g 10g 8g 1976 8fg] of little account. *R. Sturdy.*

WHITE WONDER 4 wh.c. Mont Blanc II 99–Checkendon 109 (Relic) [1974 **9** 7g⁵ 1975 11v⁵ 11.7g 7fg² 8h 6f² 6fg² 6f 6f 6d 6g⁴ 6d* 1976 6fg* 6g² 6g⁴ 6g² 6s³ 6f* 5.8f* 6f³ 6fg³ 6f⁴ 7.6fg⁴ 7fg⁶] fair handicapper: ran most consistently in 1976, gaining wins at Pontefract, Chepstow and Bath: stays 7.6f but is possibly best at up to 6f: acts on any going: suitable mount for an apprentice. *P. Cole.*

WHITSUNCELLI 6 ch.g. Sunacelli 114–dam's name unregistered [1974 N.R . — 1975 13s⁵ 12d 12s 1976 12.5v⁴ 12s] poor maiden. *M. Naughton.*

WHO CARES 2 ch.c. Pall Mall 132–Florinda 91 (Maharaj Kumar 124) [1976 8g⁴ **88** 5fg³ 6d⁵ 6g⁴ 7g² 8.2d 8s 7.2v⁴] lengthy colt: brother to Pallinda, fairly useful 2-y-o 6f winner in 1970, and half-brother to several other winners, notably very useful sprinter Smokey Haze (by Majority Blue): 2,000 gns yearling: dam won over 6f as a 2-y-o: moderate maiden: ran best race when length second of 13 to Cake Popper in nursery at Goodwood in September: suited by 7f but is not certain to be as effective at 1m: acts on heavy ground: sold 4,600 gns Newmarket Autumn Sales. *G. Harwood.*

WHY BIRD 2 gr.f. Birdbrook 110–Freddie Why (Primera 131) [1976 6h⁵ 6h⁴ 6f² **78 §** 6g 8g 7s] lightly-built filly: first foal: dam of little account: ran easily best effort when head second to Realm Tree in maiden race at Hamilton in July: should stay 1m (had stiffish task when tried at distance): apprentice ridden on first two outings, missing break once and swerving badly left on other occasion, and clearly needs strong handling: ran moderately in blinkers on final outing: unreliable. *N. Angus.*

WICKWELL 3 b.c. Wolver Hollow 126–Wise Counsel (Counsel 118) [1975   **89**
6fg 6f⁴ 7d* 7fg³ 7g²(dis) 7f* 8g 8d   1976 10f⁵ 10h* 8g⁶ 8h³ 10f⁴ 10g* 10.2s] strong,
compact colt: decisive winner of minor race at Pontefract in July and apprentice
event at Leicester in September, on latter course beating Burleigh by 3 lengths:
stays 1¼m well: appears to act on any going. *F. Maxwell.*

WIDNEY WONDER 3 b.c. Jimmy Reppin 131–Avonella 73 (Rockavon 120)   **65**
[1975 5fg 5.8f⁴ 8.2g   1976 6d⁴ 7f 8fg 7g 8h² 8fg² 8f³ 8.3fg⁵ 9fg²] rangy colt:
plater: runner-up three times in the summer: stays 9f: acts on hard ground:
blinkered final outing: not a particularly genuine individual. *G. Hunter.*

WIGEON 3 ch.f. Divine Gift 127–Wanda Drake (Canisbay 120) [1975 5f   1976   **80**
8f² 8fg* 8.2g³ 8f* 8g* 7g² 8f⁵ 8f³ 8.2v 7v⁴] neat filly: won maiden race at Thirsk
in May and minor events at Leicester and Edinburgh the following month:
narrowly beaten by Lorenzo Monaco in handicap at Ayr in July but did not run up
to her best afterwards: may stay further than 1m: acts on firm going. *W.
Elsey.*

WIGGED 6 b.g. Delta Judge–Bantu (Double Jay)   [1974 10g 8h⁵ 7fg 7fg⁶ 7g⁵   **50**
8d⁶   1975 10s 10g⁴ 10g⁶ 6f 7fg⁵ 8f² 8.3fg 10fg 7g 8fg² 8g⁶ 8g   1976 8g⁴ 8fg⁴ 8fg⁵
8fg 7f³ 7f⁶ 7h⁴ 8fg] poor handicapper: stays 1m: acts on hard going and is
possibly unsuited by soft: wears blinkers. *J. Old.*

WILD DIVER 2 ch.c. Deep Diver 134–Wild Honey 89 (Gentle Art 121) [1976   **82**
5fg² 5g⁵ 5f²] medium-sized, lengthy colt: half-brother to a winning plater:
6,000 gns yearling: dam won over 5f and is half-sister to two very speedy fillies:
odds on when second in newcomers event at Goodwood in May (beaten 2 lengths
by Town and Country) and maiden race at Windsor in August (went down by
2⅓ lengths to Raffingo): almost certainly a short runner: sold to H. Bell for 3,500
gns Newmarket Autumn Sales. *J. Tree.*

WILD EASTER 4 br.f. Punchinello 97–Spotless 89 (Tehran) [1974 5h 5fg   **46**
5f⁴ 5f⁵ 6fg 7d⁵ 7g   1975 12s⁴ 8g³ 9g² 9.4g 10f⁶ 8h³ 8g⁶ 8.2h⁵ 8g 8f   1976 8d 9g⁶
9g⁴ 6h⁴ 6h 7f 8h] lightly-made filly: poor mover: poor handicapper: stays 9f:
acts on hard going: moved badly to post on final outing. *R. Titterington.*

WILD IMAGINATION 2 b.f. Decoy Boy 129–My Pink Parrot (Pirate King 129)   **67**
[1976 5s 5fg⁴ 5d 6f⁴ 5fg* 6fg 5f 5.9fg] neat filly: first foal: 1,000 gns yearling:
dam never ran: bought in 3,400 gns after justifying favouritism in seller at Newcastle in June, getting up to beat Baby Ben a neck: twice finished last subsequently: stays 6f. *K. Payne.*

WILD ROCKET 2 gr.c. Cratloe Rocket 95–Wildacre 69 (Will Somers 114 §)   **54**
[1976 5f 5g 5f 5f³ 5.8f 6g 6f⁵ 7s 7s] poor plater: refused to race on first outing:
blinkered sixth and seventh appearances. *M. Bradley.*

WILD SPRING 2 b.c. Ribero 126–Nelion 102 (Grey Sovereign 128 §) [1976   **79** p
10d⁶] half-brother to three winners here and abroad, including high-class stayer
Recupere (by Reliance II): 21,000 gns yearling: dam ran only at 2 yrs, when
winner at 6f and 1m: showed promise when about 9 lengths sixth of 12 to
subsequently-disqualified Gunbad in £2,100 event at Newmarket in October,
holding every chance 2f out: will probably stay well: likely to improve. *L.
Cumani.*

WILD TIME 2 br.c. Breeders Dream 116–Midsummertime (Midsummer Night II   **72**
117) [1976 5fg 5f³ 5f⁶ 6h⁶ 5s 7v⁴] compact, well-made colt: first foal: dam
never ran: creditable 2 lengths third of five behind previous winners Beaumel
Board and Last Sale in small race at Folkestone in May: didn't reproduce that
form until blinkered in a nursery at Leicester in November: probably needs at
least 7f: acts on any going. *H. Smyth.*

WILLIAM PITT 6 b.g. Reform 132–Seascape 118 (Naucide) [1974 12g 12g   **—**
10v⁴ 12g   1975 10v* 10s 10g   1976 12f⁴] light-framed gelding: quite a useful
performer (rated 99) in 1975: remote fourth of six to Kinglet in handicap at
Ascot in April on only start on flat at 6 yrs: stays 1½m, but best form at 1¼m: acts
well on heavy going: best in blinkers nowadays. *S. Ingham.*

WILLIE DOBSON 2 b.c. Hul a Hul 124–Country Music (Red God 128 §)   **85**
[1976 5fg² 5f* 5f* 5fg 5g⁴] rather leggy colt: first foal: 160 gns yearling: dam
won over 6f at 2 yrs in Ireland: bought in 820 gns after outclassing his field in
seller at Nottingham in April: took on much stronger opposition in minor
event at Beverley the following month and again won well, coming home 3
lengths clear of Liscannor Lass: not seen out after May: will stay 6f. *G.
Peter-Hoblyn.*

WILLIE MAY 3 b.g. Extra–Bens Lucy (Gang Warily 109) [1975 5g 6f 7d 6f — 6g 7g 10g 8g 8d 1976 14g⁶ 12.2f⁵ 11.1s⁶ 10v] poor plater: has worn blinkers. *R. Wilson.*

WILLIE ORMOND 4 br.c. Blakeney 126–Kerkithalis 98 (Acropolis 132) [1974 **70** 6f⁶ 6s* 8.2s³ 7.2v³ 1975 7v⁵ 10s² 11s³ 9d⁵ 7f⁵ 8g⁴ 10f* 10g² 8f² 10g* 10f² 12g* 15g 13d³ 13g 12.2g⁴ 1976 10v⁵ 12d⁶ 13g⁵ 12f³ 11s 12.3fg³ 12g³ 20f² 13g³ 16fg² 13h² 12.2g 13f⁴] small colt: fair handicapper at his best but is disappointing, and is possibly none too keen: probably stays 2m, but best form at up to 13f: acts on any going: possibly unsuited by a sharp track: sold 925 gns Ascot December Sales. *N. Angus.*

WILLIE OWEN 4 b.g. Bright Year 67–Chandelle 54 (Rising Light) [1974 N.R. — 1975 N.R. 1976 15.5s⁴ 18s⁶] probably of little account. *G. Harwood.*

WILLINGS HOPE 4 br.f. Chestergate 111–Millards (Pollards 104) [1974 8d **65** 1975 10.1f 10.1s* 10g⁴ 10fg 10f⁴ 8.3fg⁴ 8fg 1976 11.7fg 9g 8g* 7fg⁶ 10g³ 10g³ 7f 8.3g⁴] small, sturdy filly: heavily backed, made all when winning apprentice handicap at Sandown in June by a short head from Brother Somers: stays 1¼m: seems to act on any going: suitable mount for an apprentice. *P. Mitchell.*

WILLOW BECK 4 b.g. Farm Walk 111–Swale 85 (Dionisio 126) [1974 N.R. — 1975 N.R. 1976 12.5h⁶] of no account. *P. Buckley.*

WILL'S STAR 8 ch.g. Dunoon Star 110–Will's Girl 76 (Will Somers 114 §) **72** [1974 6g 6fg 6f⁵ 6g* 5fg 6g² 6s³ 6f⁴ 6g 5v 1975 6v 6g⁵ 6s³ 5fg* 5g* 5fg* 5.9g* 5f² 5h⁵ 5.9fg* 6fg² 5g³ 5g² 6g 5s 1976 6fg⁴ 6s³ 5.9g 5f³ 5fg 5.9fg] quite a moderate sprint handicapper: stays 6f: probably acts on any going: good mount for an apprentice: genuine. *L. Barratt.*

WILLYBOY 4 b.g. Willipeg 112–Northern Democracy 56 (Democratic 124) **53** [1974 5fg⁵ 5f 5g⁵ 5g⁶ 5g* 5g⁵ 6s³ 1975 6h⁶ 6h³ 7f 7g* 8f⁵ 8fg³ 10f² 10g³ 8g³ 1976 8f⁵ 8g³ 8g⁴ 7f³ 8fg² 8h² 8h* 7f⁴] neat, strong gelding: plater: successful at Carlisle in July by 2½ lengths from Spanish Nun (bought in 680 gns): stays 1¼m: probably acts on any going: suitable mount for an apprentice. *J. Etherington.*

WILLY WILLY 5 b.m. Whistling Wind 123–Milly (Milesian 125) [1974 6s* 8g **108** 6f³ 8s² 5g² 6f* 6.3g² 5g* 5f 5g³ 6s 5g² 6g* 5v⁴ 1975 5s 6g³ 5g* 5g² 6fg* 5fg⁴ 5fg³ 5fg² 5f⁵ 6d 5s 1976 6g* 6.3d² 5fg² 6f⁴ 5f³ 5f⁵ 6f⁶ 5g⁵ 6d⁴] neat mare: very smart sprinter (rated 124) at 4 yrs: didn't show the same form in 1976, although won in good company at Phoenix Park in May and finished fair fourth to Gentil-hombre in Cork and Orrery Stakes at Royal Ascot: best at sprint distances: acts on any going: genuine: sold for export to America 17,500 gns Goffs November Sales. *R. McCormick, Ireland.*

WILMORE 5 b.g. Super Sam 124–Torrish 79 (Jock Scot 121) [1974 7d 8h⁴ 8g⁴ — 9s* 8d* 10g 10.2g* 1975 8s⁶ 8s 10fg 12fg 12fg 10.6fg 10.2g* 10fg 12.5fg* 12d* 1976 12fg⁶ 16.1d 13v 12v] workmanlike gelding: little worthwhile form in 1976: stays 1½m: appears to act on any going: wears blinkers: good mount for an apprentice. *W. Wharton.*

WILSPOON HOLLOW 3 gr.f. Wolver Hollow 126–Chinchilla II (Sicambre 135) **64** [1975 5f⁶ 5g 7g 6g 1976 8fg 10f 12f 9v⁴ 12v⁶ 10.6v² 10s⁴] leggy filly: runner-up to wide-margin winner Ferrybridge at Haydock in October: should stay 1½m: sometimes wears blinkers but does at least as well without. *M. Camacho.*

WILY KIM 3 br.f. Healaugh Fox–Kimolina (Ki Myth 96) [1975 5v 5s⁶ 6fg — 7.2fg 8f 7g⁵ 5v 1976 8fg 7f⁴ 8f 10.1fg 16f] small filly: not seen out after June. *W. Marshall.*

WIMBERRY 3 ch.f. Hotfoot 126–Blaeberry 100 (Hook Money 124) [1975 5fg **64** 5f⁴ 6g⁴ 6f 6fg⁵ 6fg⁴ 8g⁴ 1976 8.2g 8f⁶ 12f³ 13.1h² 11.7h² 16f² 15.5h 13.1f⁴ 13.1f³ 16s⁵] staying maiden: runner-up in two maiden events and a handicap in July: usually wears blinkers (ran creditably without them on sixth outing but badly without them on next). *P. Cundell.*

WIND 2 ch.f. Tom Rolfe–Whirled 116 (Globemaster) [1976 6g 6d⁶ 7s] lengthy, **80** very attractive American-bred filly: half-sister to French 3-y-o Power Drive (by Iron Ruler), a winner at around 1m, and to a winner in Ireland: dam a smart miler: showed ability in large fields of maidens at Newmarket in the autumn, on second outing finishing 9 lengths sixth of 23 to Rings: will stay 1¼m: the type to do better at 3 yrs. *P. Walwyn.*

WINDING TRACK 2 b.c. Track Spare 125–Winding River 101 (Entanglement **66**
118) [1976 6g 7f 8d 8s⁶] tall, close-coupled colt: second foal: half-brother to
fairly useful 3-y-o The Tista (by Sahib), a winner at up to 1¼m: dam won from
5.8f to 1¼m: showed first sign of ability when 7 lengths sixth of 16 to Wester Win
in maiden race at Bath in October: will stay 1½m: sold 1,600 gns Newmarket
Autumn Sales. *H. Candy.*

WINDMILL BOY 4 b.g. Typhoon 125–Milltown Lass (Panaslipper 130) [1974 —
7v 6s 1975 8v 10d 7f 6g³ 6f 7fg 12f 10g 8g² 10d* 1976 8g 9fg] close-coupled
gelding: plater: not raced after April: stays 1¼m: best form on an easy surface:
suitable mount for an apprentice. *H. Nicholson.*

WINDRUSH 8 b.g. Acropolis 132–Ogygia 69 (Pinza 137) [1974 N.R. 1975 —
N.R. 1976 16g 14fg 16g⁶] useful stayer (rated 106) in 1971: no form in three
races in 1976: acts on any going: has worn blinkers. *J. Gifford.*

WIND SWALLOW 2 ch.f. My Swallow 134–Windstorm 110 (Whistling Wind123) —
[1976 5g 5f] small filly: first foal: dam best at 5f and 6f: in rear in maiden races at
Teesside and Newcastle in April. *M. W. Easterby.*

WINDY SEA 2 br.f. Sea Hawk II 131–Wind Goddess (Whistling Wind 123) **105**
[1976 7g* 7d³] big filly: half-sister to two winners, including smart 1974 2-y-o
Windy Glen (by Wolver Hollow): dam won over 5f in Ireland as a 2-y-o: 20/1 and
burly, led 2f out when winning 23-runner maiden event at Newmarket in
October decisively by a length from Petronisi: ran well when giving weight away
all round in 25-runner Houghton Stakes on same course later in month, finishing
4 lengths third to Bessie Wallis: will probably stay 1¼m. *B. Hanbury.*

WINDY SPOT 2 br.c. Silly Season 127–Lonely Leopardess 80 (Pardal 130) **73**
[1976 6f 7h³ 7fg] half-brother to three winners here and abroad: 5,000 gns foal,
resold 2,100 gns yearling: dam won at 1¾m: 7 lengths third to Exploiteur in nine-
runner maiden race at Brighton in August, best effort: should stay 1½m. *D.
Morley.*

WINGED DAGGER 7 b.g. Falcon 130–Gay Natasha 105 (Prince Chevalier) **68**
[1974 N.R. 1975 11.7g³ 10f 12f⁴ 10g 7f* 7f 6g 10g⁶ 1976 12.2fg³ 11.7f* 11.7fg²
10g 11.7f³ 13.1f* 10f] quite a moderate handicapper: successful at Bath in
April and September, on latter occasion holding off Rickadoo in last 100 yds
despite going lame near finish: stays 13f: seems to act on any going: used to
wear blinkers but didn't in 1976: game and genuine. *J. Old.*

WINGED TYPHOON 4 b.f. Typhoon 125–Winged Rebel (High Treason 126) **62**
[1974 5f⁴ 5fg² 6g 5d⁶ 1975 7g⁴ 6g* 6f 6f 7.6f² 6g² 7fg 7.6g 7.6s² 1976 10f⁵ 6fg⁵
6f⁶ 7f⁵ 8fg⁶ 8s² 8.2v² 7v³] lightly-made, attractive filly: ran well most outings
at 4 yrs: stays 1m: acts on any going, but is particularly well suited by some
give in the ground: suitable mount for an apprentice: trained by B. Wise until
after fourth outing. *V. Cross.*

WINGS OF SPRING 3 b.c. Silent Spring 102–Longwings 75 (Vimy 132) [1975 **66**
6s 8g 1976 10fg⁶ 12g 16f³ 16h³ 15.8f² 16fg³ 13.1f⁵ 17.1s⁵ 15.5s⁵] light-framed
colt: evidently suited by a test of stamina: possibly needs a sound surface: often
sweats up: well beaten in blinkers last two outings but carried 10 lb overweight
on first of them. *P. Cole.*

WIN-LASS 2 br.f. Whistling Wind 123–Blue Lagoon 60 (Forlorn River 124) **74**
[1976 5d⁵ 5d⁵ 7fg 6h⁴ 6f³ 6f³ 6g⁶ 7s⁴] leggy filly: first foal: sold twice as a
yearling for 550 gns and 1,100 gns: dam placed twice over 1m: put up best
efforts on fifth and sixth outings, finishing third in minor event at Newcastle in
August and in 15-runner nursery at Haydock later same month: stays 6f but is
not certain to stay further: blinkered final outing. *G. Toft.*

WINNICENSE 2 br.f. Frankincense 120–Corral 73 (Big Game) [1976 5f 5g 5d **72**
6g⁵ 7g 8.2f³ 7s 7v 6s] useful-looking filly: good walker: half-sister to 1m winner
Eleanor Rigby (by Sound Track): 260 gns foal: dam plating-class miler: just under
3 lengths third of 14 to Padovanna in maiden race at Hamilton in September,
easily best effort: best form at 1m: unseated rider on leaving stalls on second
outing: ran moderately in blinkers on seventh appearance. *J. Etherington.*

WINNING DREAM 2 gr.c. Breeders Dream 116–My Diana 94 (Sovereign Path **85**
125) [1976 5g 5f⁵ 5fg* 6f 6f] compact, strong-quartered colt: half-brother to
1m seller winner Guilsborough Grey (by Court Fool): 620 gns yearling: dam a
sprinter: made all to win maiden auction event at Brighton in May by 4 lengths
from On Your Knees: showed nothing like that form on any of his other outings,
including when blinkered on final appearance: should stay 6f. *P. Haslam.*

WINSAN   3 b.f. Maystreak 118–Sapphire Signal (Bleep-Bleep 134)   [1975 5g 6g   —
7fg   1976 5f 5f 5.9s 5s]   poor maiden: blinkered first three outings.   *A. Doyle.*

WINSCOMBE   4 b.c. Blakeney 126–Ergina 101 (Fair Trial)   [1974 N.R.   1975   **55 §**
8s 9fg 10g² 10g³   1976 12s 8g³ 8g 8fg²]   neat colt: poor maiden: blinkered,
appeared to us to shirk issue when well-beaten second to Esprit D'or in amateur
riders maiden race at Thirsk in July: stays 1¼m: not one to trust.   *S. Mellor.*

WINSLOW BOY   3 ch.g. Salvo 129–Open Court (Court Martial)   [1975 8d 7s   **74**
1976 11f 10fg 16g2 14d³ 13s* 16v]   tall, lengthy gelding: 1½ lengths second to
Veracious in handicap at Nottingham in September, but was hampered inside
final furlong and subsequently awarded again: suited by a test of stamina and will
stay really long distances: acts on soft going.   *G. Smyth.*

WINTERTOUR   3 ch.f. Barron's Court–Autumn Fire (Silly Season 127)   [1975   **58**
N.R.   1976 6fg 7g⁶ 5f⁵ 8f⁶ 10.8f⁴ 12h⁴ 10h* 12f 10s]   well-made filly: third foal:
half-sister to Takamaka (by El Gallo), a winner at up to 1¼m in France: dam never
ran: won weakly-contested maiden race at Folkestone in August by 2 lengths
from Night Frame: stays 1¼m (ran moderately when tried at 1½m): possibly
unsuited by soft going: sold 1,000 gns Newmarket Autumn Sales.   *H. T. Jones.*

WIRE UP   3 b.f. Firestreak 125–Pinwave 82 (Pinza 137)   [1975 7g⁵ 7.2s⁵ 8v   **98**
1976 10.8f² 10f* 12g]   sturdy filly: favourite, won minor event at Folkestone in
May by 2 lengths from Ginger Ken: ran a remarkable race to finish eighth of 14
to Pawneese in Epsom Oaks the following month and is evidently useful: suited by
middle distances: acts on firm going: exported by B.B.A. to Brazil.   *H.
Westbrook.*

WISPY VISION   3 ch.f. Gulf Pearl 117–Dandy Brush 82 (Will Somers 114 §)   **66**
[1975 6f⁵ 6g 7v 6g⁶ 7.2s   1976 8v⁵ 8f* 10f⁵ 10.4s 7g³ 7d³ 8.2d⁴ 9f⁴ 7.2g]   quite a
moderate handicapper: won at Lanark in April: ran creditably when in the frame
afterwards, including in amateur riders race: stays 1¼m: appears to act on any
going with the exception of very soft.   *E. Cousins.*

WISTANWICK   3 b.g. Salvo 129–Miss Peseta 95 (Sovereign Path 125)   [1975   **45**
5g⁶ 6fg⁵ 7.2g 6h⁴ 9g 6v   1976 12f² 12f⁵ 16f 12.2g⁵ 10.4fg 13.8f⁵ 10f]   tall gelding:
bad plater: probably stays 1¾m.   *A. W. Jones.*

WISTFUL LADY   2 ch.f. Dike–Wish 106 (Whistler 129)   [1976 8fg 8v⁵]   half-
sister to three winners by Ballymoss, including useful miler Wishing Stone:
4,200 gns yearling: dam a sprinter: remote fifth to Starlight Lad in minor event at
Teesside in October.   *J. Etherington.*

WITCHES BROOM   4 b.c. Divine Gift 127–Lupreno 69 (Hugh Lupus 132)   **69**
[1974 5f 5.6g³ 5g* 7d 7s⁵ 5.9g³ 6s   1975 7d 5v² 6s* 6fg* 6fg⁴ 6f² 6fg⁵ 6f 6f⁵ 5g
1976 5f² 6v² 6f⁵ 5.9g³ 5f 6g² 5s³ 6v]   small colt: quite a moderate handicapper:
best at up to 6f: acts on any going: best in blinkers.   *J. Hardy.*

WITHIN THE LAW   2 b.c. Sharpen Up 127–Escape 93 (Gilles de Retz 132)   —
[1976 5f 5d 5f⁶]   plain, lengthy colt: half-brother to smart performer Escapologist
(by Derring-Do), a winner at up to 1¼m: dam won over 6f at 2 yrs: little
worthwhile form: not seen out after June: blinkered third outing.   *L. Shedden.*

WITH RESPECT   3 ch.g. Song 132–Dominica 71 (Tyrone 130)   [1975 N.R.   —
1976 10f 12f 8h³]   ex-Irish gelding: third produce: 6,000 gns foal, resold 4,700 gns
yearling and 400 gns 2-y-o: dam, winner at 1¼m, is half-sister to good 1m to 1¼m
handicapper Executor: short-priced favourite for three-runner seller at Redcar in
July on only appearance in this country but finished tailed off after making
running to halfway.   *K. Payne.*

WITTON WONDER   2 b.c. Lear Jet 123–Paddygrino (St Paddy 133)   [1976   **70**
5s 5f⁵ 6fg 5.1f³ 7fg*]   plater: sold for 2,600 gns after winning seller at Newmarket
in July by 2½ lengths: subsequently won in Belgium: stays 7f well.   *C. Brittain.*

WOBURN   2 b.c. Crepello 136–Plunder 77 (Tamerlane 128)   [1976 5g 6g 6g 5s⁶]   —
fair sort: third foal: dam twice-raced sister to useful middle-distance filly So
Precious: showed only a little ability in maiden and minor events: not bred to be
a sprinter and will need at least 1m at 3 yrs: blinkered third outing.   *C. Bewicke.*

WOGAN'S WAGER   5 ch.h. Behistoun 131–Storm Widow 82 (Technion 96)   —
[1974 10fg 10.4g 14fg 16g 13g 10g 12s⁶   1975 13g⁴ 12v³   1976 12.5v 12.5s]   poor
maiden.   *J. Leigh.*

WOLLOW 3 b.c. Wolver Hollow 126–Wichuraiana (Worden II 129) [1975 6g* **132**
7g* 7g* 7fg* 1976 7f* 8fg* 12g⁵ 10fg* 8fg* 10.5fg* 10d]
Now that Wollow has been retired with as full a season behind him as is
necessary to be able to assess him with confidence, it is evident that he was
neither as outstanding nor as ordinary a top-class horse as most people seemed
to believe at one time or other during the year. Wollow was, unfortunately, a
martyr to the need facing most commentators to exaggerate merit on the
principle that the bigger the celebrity the bigger the news value, as well as to the
perfectly understandable longing among racing men for a great horse to appear
on the racecourse. First the subject of wildly exaggerated plaudits after an
unbeaten run of six races, one of those races the Guineas, he fell victim to downright disparagement when, in the Derby and the Eclipse, he didn't live up to his
reputation. Fortunately his trainer persevered with him, and although Wollow
was well beaten late in the season in the Champion Stakes he had done enough
by then, in winning the Sussex Stakes and the Benson and Hedges Gold Cup, to
show his worth.
We cannot regard Wollow as his trainer is said to regard him, the equal of
Bolkonski; to do so would be to regard him an exceptionally good miler. He
never accounted for opposition quite as good as that which Bolkonski beat when
winning the Guineas from Grundy and the Sussex Stakes from Rose Bowl and
Lianga, nor did he ever beat slightly lesser opposition in such a manner as to
suggest that he might be Bolkonski's equal. Nevertheless Wollow, on the
evidence of his performance in the Sussex Stakes and the Benson and Hedges
Gold Cup, particularly the latter, is, in all fairness, deserving of a higher mark
in the Three-Year-Old Handicap than the one he got which put him 9 lb behind
the best in a normal year, 10 lb behind Grundy and 5 lb behind Bolkonski.
Readers of *Racehorses of 1975* will require little reminding (neither do we!)
that Wollow received no exaggerated plaudits from us as a two-year-old. If
anything, his merit was underestimated and Manado's overestimated, but we still
refuse to allow that Wollow's defeats of Solitary Hail in the Laurent Perrier
Champagne Stakes and of Malinowski in the William Hill Dewhurst Stakes, his
best performances at two, deserved all the superlatives heaped on them. There
was sufficient evidence to show that Wollow was the best two-year-old to have
raced in England, but none, at that time, to show that he was a champion.
One couldn't take exception to anything about Wollow's performance in the
Clerical, Medical Greenham Stakes at Newbury in April on his reappearance. It
was a thoroughly convincing trial for the Guineas, of especial significance
coming the day after Vitiges had turned the tables on Manado in the Prix Djebel
and four days after Malinowski had won the Ladbroke Craven Stakes by two and
a half lengths from the highly-regarded Oats. Wollow made decent three-year-
olds look small in the paddock. Exceptionally well in himself in the paddock,
he came from behind and had the race at his mercy from the moment his jockey
let him down on the outside of the field about two furlongs from home. He soon
took the lead and nothing could trouble him, not even the hard-ridden Super
Cavalier or Gentilhombre, both of whom were receiving 5 lb. Super Cavalier had
received a weight of 8-7 in the Two-Year-Old Free Handicap, Gentilhombre 8-12,

*Clerical, Medical Greenham Stakes, Newbury—Wollow enhances his classic prospects by
outclassing the opposition, the best of which are Super Cavalier, Gentilhombre
(striped sleeves) and Stand to Reason (right)*

2,000 Guineas Stakes, Newmarket—Wollow is too good for the French challenger Vitiges. Fighting out third place are (right to left) Thieving Demon, Patris and Frankie

and the next two home, Stand to Reason and Duke Ellington, weights of 8-13 and 8-11 respectively. It was not to be expected at this stage of the season that all or any of the runners in the Greenham would be near their best, but it was difficult to look beyond Wollow as the best hope the home side had against Vitiges and Manado (who was widely expected to improve more than Vitiges) in the Two Thousand Guineas. The main threat to the big three, if there was to be one, seemed on looks and form to be posed by Relkino, a 58,000-guinea yearling who had won the Ascot Two Thousand Guineas Trial from another Guineas runner, Loh; and paddock inspection revealed no other likely source of danger. There were several nice horses in a Guineas parade unimpressive by classic standards, but none that hadn't already been considered.

Wollow did all that was necessary to win; no more, no less. He kept in touch from the start in the seventeen-runner field, took the lead below the distance after Vitiges had made the running and quickened clear up the hill to win by a length and a half, his jockey content to leave him alone in the last furlong although a furlong earlier he had cracked him hard with the whip. Once racing began in earnest, only Wollow seemed likely to beat Vitiges, and once Wollow struck the front only Vitiges seemed likely to get back at him. Manado, second favourite at 4/1 to Wollow's even money, found nothing in the last three furlongs and finished only ninth, apparently unsuited by the firmish going.

With horses like Thieving Demon in third place and Frankie in fifth, both of them quite close up, the form of the Guineas, then as now, did not look all that hot, but even if one still had reservations about Wollow's invincibility there seemed no particular reason why one's worst fears should be confirmed in his next race, the Derby. After all, he was still meeting horses only of his own age and none of his opponents at Epsom had, on the face of it, a better record than Vitiges, although many of the runners, as in every Epsom Derby field, seemed to be improving rapidly. Empery, an improving horse if ever there was one, had been beaten three times in as many starts during the season and seemed not to be as good as his stable-companion Youth. Could not Wollow also be expected to improve, especially at this distance? Of course he could; his pedigree and style of racing said as much! And was not the fast ground, almost as fast as that for the Guineas, in his favour? Probably the main concern about him was the inexperience of his jockey, Dettori, round Epsom. Dettori had ridden his first race over the course only an hour earlier, on Fool's Mate in the Daily Mirror Handicap, and had encountered the most common of the Epsom bogeys, running out of room on the inside around the furlong pole.

Well, Wollow did meet with his first defeat, but let's say straight away that he didn't show his form, for all that he ran the same race with Vitiges as he had done at Newmarket, in fifth place finishing a length and a half up on the French horse. All kinds of reasons have been advanced for Wollow's performance, including a very belated one that he twisted a hind shoe, but the most likely reason is the one right under the nose of anyone who saw the Derby. Wollow did not get the run of the race. He was chopped off then bustled along, chopped off then bustled along, then bustled along again. Stop; start; stop; start—he never had chance to settle, and must have used up precious reserves before he even reached the bottom of Tattenham Hill in an unpromising ninth place. By the time he had succeeded in moving up to fifth on the outside approaching the distance, he had run out of steam, and although he kept on well enough thereafter to keep within five lengths of Empery it was noticeable that he was making no ground on fourth-placed Hawkberry. His finishing burst of the previous two races had vanished. Wollow's unsettled and unsettling passage through the first mile or so of the Derby makes it unsafe to draw any firm conclusion on whether he stayed the distance; it's a pity, academically speaking, that he never had another chance to show his capabilities at a mile and a half. He was, as we said, expected to be well suited by the trip. However, his connections must have anticipated at the very least that shorter distances would suit him best, for they next ran him in the Joe Coral Eclipse Stakes at Sandown in July, and by the end of the season it could not be argued with any justification that they had done wrong by Wollow in taking the course they did.

Wollow failed to cope with Trepan in the Eclipse but he ran creditably after making things difficult for himself by giving away ground at the start of a race run in course-record time and after having things made more difficult for him by his jockey's tactics of switching wide into the straight while the winner stuck to the inside rail. Wollow recovered most of the ground lost at the start (about four or five lengths) rather quickly, possibly too quickly for his own good, and he turned into the straight in front of Trepan. Once Trepan had struck the front a furlong and a half out it was clear that he was too good for Wollow; and Wollow,

Sussex Stakes, Goodwood—Wollow beats Free State (left) and Poacher's Moon. The other horse in the picture is Dominion

Benson and Hedges Gold Cup, York—a splendid effort by Wollow, who convincingly beats the subsequent St Leger winner Crow. Patch heads the chasing group

two lengths behind at the finish but four lengths ahead of the next horse, Radetzky, was not subjected to unnecessarily hard punishment. Despite Wollow's not having the run of the race, we would have no hesitation in regarding Trepan as the better horse if it were not for the fact that Trepan subsequently failed his test for dope. The Stewards of the Jockey Club disqualified Trepan and awarded first prize to Wollow, which made a difference of nearly £27,000 to the latter's impressive final earnings total of £200,790.

There was no Trepan in the Sussex Stakes at Goodwood later in July. The opposition was nowhere near so strong as that which Bolkonski faced in the race twelve months earlier but it was strong enough, with Dominion and tip-top handicappers like Free State and Ardoon in the field, to measure Wollow by on his return to racing at a mile. Wollow had plenty in hand at the finish, which he reached a length ahead of Free State, a little more ahead of the improved Poacher's Moon, around four lengths ahead of Ardoon and around six ahead of Dominion. Particularly impressive was the manner in which he swept to the front two furlongs out with Dettori sitting comfortably, and thereafter he never seemed likely to be caught, although Poacher's Moon came with a rattle up a narrow gap on the inside towards the end. What was not impressive about Wollow was his appearance: he now looked light about the body and very much on the leg.

Later in the season Wollow's connections were accused of pursuing a less than fighting policy when they withdrew him from the Queen Elizabeth II Stakes at Ascot on the morning of the race after rain turned the ground softer than the trainer considered suitable for him. Such an accusation was grossly unfair. After winning the Sussex Stakes with Wollow his shareholders, who had paid £31,000 a share after the Guineas, could have been forgiven if they had retired the horse there and then; he had re-established himself yet he looked as though he needed a rest. Instead, they boldly sought out the first available opportunity of another meeting with Trepan and risked defeat by other top horses, among them Empery, in the Benson and Hedges Gold Cup at York in August. As things turned out Wollow did not have to face Empery—the Derby winner was withdrawn only hours before the race—and he faced a Trepan well below his best; but Wollow still put up a very fine performance in winning the race by a length. Looking slightly more himself in the paddock than at Goodwood, he jumped out of the stalls as keenly as he had ever done, settled down in third place to Patch and kept his place in the seven-horse field until quickening impressively once again into a clear lead soon after passing the two-furlong marker. Crow was the only one to give Wollow a race over the last furlong, and judging by Dettori's air of confidence he didn't give him any more trouble than Free State had at Goodwood, but Crow was probably not quite the horse here that he was in the autumn. The pair finished a long way clear of the others.

Some of those who criticised Wollow's trainer for withdrawing him at Ascot might have had second thoughts when they saw Wollow's performance in his first and only race on ground any softer than good, in the Champion Stakes. He started a heavily-backed favourite, was never in the hunt, finished fifteenth of nineteen behind his old rival Vitiges, and in company with Crow was well beaten by the leader on his own side of the course, Malacate. He might not have been good enough to win the Champion Stakes at his best, but this was not Wollow at his best. Probably he was over the top; possibly the ground was against him, certainly the draw was, although an unfavourable draw does not excuse such a poor showing.

Wollow (b.c. 1973)	Wolver Hollow (b 1964)	Sovereign Path (gr 1956)	Grey Sovereign
			Mountain Path
		Cygnet (b 1950)	Caracalla II
			Mrs Swan Song
	Wichuraiana (ch 1963)	Worden II (ch 1949)	Wild Risk
			Sans Tares
		Excelsa (ch 1949)	Owen Tudor
			Infra Red

Wollow has been retired to the Banstead Manor Stud, Newmarket. He will probably be a magnificent animal to look at out of training. Early on in his three-year-old days he seemed all set to develop into a fine-looking racehorse: he always had a noble head on him and carried it, and himself, with the air of a champion, but he never quite managed to fill out to his tall frame for all that he was beginning to put on weight again in the autumn. He was a very fine mover, though.

To the breeder Wollow has a lot to recommend him, not least his pedigree, which traces on the tail-female side to the famous Black Ray, his fourth dam, who had no less than nineteen consecutive foals and a well-nigh immeasurable influence, mainly for good, on the Stud Book. One of Black Ray's many winners was Infra Red, third dam of Wollow, fourth dam of Mill Reef and a sister to the dam of Khaled. Infra Red, who ran fourth in the One Thousand Guineas, produced four winners including Wollow's grandam Excelsa, the winner of six races in Ireland and runner-up in the Irish Champion Stakes as a three-year-old. One of Excelsa's foals was the top-class stayer Exar (by Arctic Prince); another, Wollow's dam Wichuraiana who did not maintain the family tradition, failing to win and showing only modest form. Wichuraiana, by Worden II, the

Mr C. d'Alessio's "Wollow"

maternal grandsire of other recent classic winners Grundy and Juliette Marny, produced two winners before Wollow, the French filly Dyna Mia who managed to win at a mile and a quarter though by the sprinter High Treason, and the staying hurdler Birdcage Walk, by the Guineas winner Pall Mall. At stud since 1970, Wollow's sire, the Eclipse winner Wolver Hollow (trained by Henry Cecil, incidentally), has produced the Irish Two Thousand Guineas winner Furry Glen, Charlie Bubbles, successful over a mile and a half in the Hardwicke Stakes; and Windy Glen, Wolverlife and Wanlockhead, all placed in pattern races.

Although Wollow showed his best form at up to a mile and a quarter, had the speed to win top-class mile races on fast ground and acted extremely well on firm going, it would be as well to bear in mind when his runners start to appear and have to be assessed, that he never gave incontrovertible evidence that he did not stay a distance of a mile and a half or that he was unsuited by softish going. Wollow's record leaves no doubt that he was easily the best horse of his age trained in England (leaving aside the latecomer Vitiges) during 1976, a period when admittedly there was a dearth of good three-year-olds in the country. Thanks mainly to Wollow, Henry Cecil became leading trainer for the first time, narrowly turning the tables on Peter Walwyn after finishing runner-up to him in 1975. Cecil, who has handled such good horses as Falkland, Parthenon, Relay Race and Roussalka besides Wollow, Bolkonski and Wolver Hollow in a space of only eight years, succeeds Noel Murless at Warren Place in 1977. *H. Cecil.*

WOLVERLIFE 3 b.c. Wolver Hollow 126–Miralife 103 (Miralgo 130) [1975 7g⁴ **115** 6g² 1976 7s* 7f³ 8g² 8d 12g⁴ 7f² 8f² 6g² 7f* 7.3fg 6d* 5s*] tall colt: second foal: half-brother to Irish 1,000 Guineas winner Miralla (by Allangrange): dam, third in Irish 1,000 Guineas, stayed at least 9f: won Burmah-Castrol Trophy at Phoenix Park in March by 2½ lengths from Lucky Wednesday: runner-up in four races afterwards, narrowly going down in Tetrarch Stakes (to Poacher's Moon) and French Furze Stakes (to Gododin) both at the Curragh and acquitting himself well in Jersey Stakes at Royal Ascot (beaten a length by Gwent) and Hackwood Stakes at Newbury (went under by ¾ length to Solar): easily landed odds in minor event at Phoenix Park in August from Little Trilby prior to showing improved form when winning last two races, Kildare Sprint Stakes by 2½ lengths from Sandy Row in October and handicap under top weight of 9-12 in November, both at the Curragh: effective from 5f to 1m and was not disgraced when fourth to Meneval in Gallinule Stakes when tried at 1½m: acts on any going: suitable mount for an apprentice: genuine and consistent. *Sir Hugh Nugent, Ireland.*

WOLVER VALLEY 3 b.f. Wolver Hollow 126–Our Dark Lady 88 (Dumbarnie **72** 125) [1975 5g 6fg 7g² 7.2d⁵ 8v² 1976 8f³ 10fg⁶ 10g⁶ 8v³ 10s* 10s²] tall filly: won 12-runner maiden race at Newmarket in October by 4 lengths from Rare Award: stays 1¼m: acts on any going: blinkered third outing. *R. Jarvis.*

WONG WAY GIRL 4 br.f. Kibenka 119–Suzy Wong II 71 (Mincio 127) [1974 **85** 5f 5fg 5g* 6s² 6d* 1975 7f² 7g⁵ 7fg³ 7f 7s* 7s 7g 7.6s 1976 7fg 7.2d⁴ 8fg⁴ 7g* 7f 7.3d³ 8v 7.6v⁴] lengthy, light-framed filly: fair handicapper: made all when winning at Sandown in July, keeping on gamely to beat Miss Filbert 2½ lengths: should stay at least 1m but seems best at around 7f: acts on any going: suitable mount for an apprentice. *R. Akehurst.*

WOODDITTON 9 b.g. Molvedo 137–Title Deed 118 (Supreme Court 135) — [1974 10s⁵ 9f⁵ 10fg⁴ 14.6g³ 12g² 12fg⁵ 1975 10fg⁶ 12f⁵ 16h 16g 1976 12fg⁴ 16.1d 10d 12v] poor handicapper: seems to stay 1¾m: acts on a firm and a soft surface: excellent mount for a boy. *H. Wragg.*

WOOD GROVE 2 gr.c. Sovereign Path 125–Boscage 104 (Queen's Hussar 124) — [1976 7g 7fg] sturdy colt: first foal: 17,500 gns yearling: dam won three races at 2 yrs, and stayed 1m: last in September in £1,900 event at Sandown (backward) and minor race at Goodwood: stumbled on first outing. *B. Swift.*

WOODSOME 3 br.f. Runnymede 123–Eastwood Bounty 87 (Bounteous 125) — [1975 5g* 5s* 5s* 5h⁴ 6d* 6fg⁵ 6d* 5g³ 1976 7fg⁴ 6d 6d⁵ 7f] smart filly at 2 yrs, winner of five of her eight races: fourth of 10 to Flying Water in Ladbroke Nell Gwyn Stakes at Newmarket in April: did not reproduce that form in England but subsequently won a stakes race in U.S.A.: stays 7f: well suited by some give in the ground at 2 yrs. *T. Fairhurst.*

WOODY WOODPECKER 2 b.c. Reliance II 137–Tangleberry (Entanglement — 118) [1976 10v] second living produce: dam won over 13f in Ireland: un-quoted when behind in 17-runner maiden race won by Pin Tuck at Nottingham in October. *C. Dingwall.*

WOOLBAGS 2 ch.f. Fleece 114–Bintags (Bindy 86) [1976 5f 6fg⁶ 6g] bad — plater. *N. Vigors.*

WOOL BRIDGE 2 b.f. Fleece 114–Shirley Bridge 83 (Vilmoray 126) [1976 7f 6f — 8fg 6s] workmanlike filly: good walker: poor maiden. *Hbt Jones.*

WOOLLEY 2 b.f. Wolver Hollow 126–Authenticated (Above Suspicion 127) — p [1976 6g] half-sister to several winners here and abroad, including winning French middle-distance stayer Be Truthful (by Behistoun): 4,600 gns yearling: dam won over 9f in Ireland: unquoted when in rear in 30-runner maiden race won by Rheola at Newmarket in September: should stay 1¼m. *P. Robinson.*

WORD OF HONOUR 4 b.g. Reliance II 137–Parolee 88 (Sing Sing 134) [1974 73 N.R. 1975 10.1fg⁴ 10f* 10f² 1976 10g 8g 10f* 10fg 8g⁶ 10d 10s* 10s*] quite a moderate performer: winner at Folkestone in July and on same course and Chepstow in October: stays 1¼m: acts on any going: suitable mount for an apprentice or lady rider: sweated up and ran wide fourth outing. *J. Dunlop.*

WORTH A CHANCE 2 b.f. Hopeful Venture 125–Tevere 104 (Romulus 129) — [1976 7v] second foal: half-sister to Irish 3-y-o 9f winner Richard G (by Double Jump): dam won from 5f to 1m: unquoted and apprentice ridden when last to finish in minor event won by Forage at Lingfield in November. *B. Swift.*

WORTHY STAR 3 gr.g. Grisaille 115–Saucy Tyrol 81 (Hard Sauce 131) [1975 61 5v 5s 5s⁶ 5fg 5fg⁶ 5g 5g³ 7h⁴ 5f⁵ 6g² 5f⁵ 6g² 5f⁵ 6fg 1976 5f 6d⁵ 6fg 6d 6d² 5g 5f² 6h* 5f³ 6f* 6fg² 6f 6f⁵] small gelding: modest plater: won at Carlisle in June (bought in 660 gns) and Hamilton in July (no bid): effective at 5f to 7f: appears to act on any going: used to wear blinkers: ran badly final outing (August). *S. Nesbitt.*

WOTTON LASS 2 b.f. Space King 115–Tilstina (Dionisio 126 or Autumn Gold 70 101) [1976 5fg 6f² 6g 6g 7fg 5s] fourth foal: bought privately for 450 gns as a yearling: dam placed over hurdles: showed a little ability in maiden and minor events: should stay 1½m: blinkered last two outings. *D. Barons.*

WOUNDED KNEE 3 ch.f. Busted 134–La Lidia 78 (Matador 131) [1975 7f 78 1976 12f* 14g* 14.7d² 16v⁶ 16v³] rather leggy filly: won minor events at Newmarket in August and York in September, on latter course beating Omnia by ½ length, the pair finishing clear: long odds on, seemed beaten on merit when ½-length second to Ruddy Sam in similar company at Redcar later in September: creditable third to Cavalier's Blush in handicap at Lingfield in November, easily better subsequent effort: stays 2m: acts on any going: sold 9,000 gns Newmarket December Sales. *H. Cecil.*

WRAPPITS 2 b.c. King's Company 124–Sunningdale Sandy 53 (Sea Hawk II — 131) [1976 5fg 5d] strong colt: second foal: half-brother to 1975 2-y-o 5f winner Balidale (by Balidar): 740 gns foal and resold 1,700 gns yearling: dam daughter of very speedy Rose of Tralee: behind in maiden race at Thirsk and auction event at Redcar, both in May. *K. Payne.*

WRAYS MEADOW 2 b.f. Runnymede 123–Red Meadow (Tyrone 130) [1976 54 5fg⁵ 5f⁴ 6f 6f 6h 6g 6d 6g] compact filly: only poor form, including in sellers: stays 6f: blinkered fifth and seventh outings: sold 350 gns Ascot October Sales. *G. Blum.*

WREKIN RHYTHM 3 b.g. Song 132–Miss Wrekin 97 (Pardao 120) [1975 — 5f⁶ 5fg² 5.9f⁵ 6d 7.2d 1976 7.6fg 10.2g] strong gelding: showed quite moderate form at 2 yrs but was well beaten in maiden races in September, 1976: should stay beyond sprint distances: blinkered final outing at 2 yrs: sold to S. Holland 500 gns Doncaster November Sales. *R. Murphy.*

WRENS HILL 6 ch.h. Double Jump 131–Trotification 73 § (Ratification 126) 93 [1974 5g 5f 6f 5d² 5fg⁶ 5g* 6d⁵ 5g* 5.6d 5v³ 5s* 1975 5v³ 5v⁶ 5f 5f⁴ 5d 5g 1976 5.9fg* 5g⁶ 6g 5s 5fg⁴ 5g* 5fg³ 5f 5g] lengthy, lightly-made horse: fairly useful performer: favourite, finished in tremendous style when beating Derringo a neck at Ascot in July: had previously won minor event at Wolverhampton in April and also ran creditably on fifth and seventh outings: ran his best races at 5f but stayed further: acted on any going, but was at his best with some give in the ground: needed a lot of driving: stud in Ireland. *J. Winter.*

WRIBBEN HALL 3 b.g. Forlorn River 124–Swifter Justice 62 (King's Bench 41 132) [1975 5fg⁶ 7fg 6g 7g 1976 8f 7f 7g³ 8fg⁶ 7.2fg 7.6fg 8f⁵ 7.6fg] bad plater: stays at least 7f. *A. W. Jones.*

807

WRIGGLING 4 ch.f. Weepers Boy 124–Balfour Lass 81 (My Smokey 125) —
[1974 6g⁴ 7d³ 7fg⁵ 6fg³ 6s 8g 6s⁶ 1975 7fg 8h 11.1fg⁶ 10.8f 9fg 1976 12.2f 13.8d
8fg 10.8f] compact filly: poor plater nowadays. *R. Cambidge.*

WYCHWOOD 2 br.f. Brigadier Gerard 144–Eastwood 81 (Shantung 132) [1976 — p
6v] tall, lengthy filly: half-sister to two winners, namely Milon (by Milesian),
winner of 1m seller, and Maplewood (by Major Portion), a winner over 7f at
2 yrs: dam, a stayer, is half-sister to Hornbeam: unquoted, missed break and
never got into race when behind in 23-runner maiden event won by stable-
companion Amity at Newbury in October: immature at 2 yrs and should do
better, probably over 1¼m+. *R. Hern.*

WYSBOY 2 br.c. Tudor Melody 129–Shapely 84 (Parthia 132) [1976 5g 5g²   84
5f* 5fg⁵ 6fg] workmanlike colt: second foal: 12,000 gns yearling: dam stayed
1¾m: won £1,000 event at Folkestone in May by 2 lengths from newcomer Happy
Combination: ran moderately afterwards and wore blinkers when last of 11 in
nursery at Newmarket in July: should stay at least 1m. *G. Harwood.*

Y

YAGODA 3 gr.f. Saratoga Skiddy 113–Baronova (Impeccable 130) [1975 6g   60
7f² 6f² 6g 6g 1976 7g 8d⁵ 12f 12f² 13.8f⁴ 8h² 8h* 13.8g 10g⁴ 10g⁶ 10v] modest
plater: sold out of J. W. Watts's stable 820 gns after scoring with something in
hand at Carlisle in August: stays 1½m and has twice run below her best when
tried over 1¾m: acts on hard ground and ran poorly on heavy on final outing:
has worn blinkers but does better without. *J. Berry.*

YAHABIBI 2 br.g. Sahib 114–Sister Deb 78 (Welsh Abbot 131) [1976 5.9s 6d]   63
second reported live foal: dam, quite a moderate 2-y-o in this country, subsequently won in Scandinavia: showed ability when ninth of 22 to Rocket Symphony
in maiden race at Newmarket in October, second outing. *M. Smyly.*

YAMADORI 4 ch.c. Mountain Call 125–Village 91 (Charlottesville 135) [1974   97
6fg 6fg⁵ 5.3g⁵ 6d⁴ 1975 6s 7s* 8d³ 7.6g* 8g* 8fg* 7g² 8fg 8f³ 8g* 10f 8g³ 8h²
9g 9.2d 8g* 1976 8g 8f² 7fg 8g² 10g⁴ 8g³ 8f³ 8fg³ 9fg* 8fg⁵ 8.2g² 8fg 8.3g² 8g⁵
9fg³ 8g* 9g 8s²] strong, muscular colt: good walker: made all when winning
three-runner handicap at York in July: managed to find one or two too good
for him in most of his other races but finished in good style when winning
amateur riders race at Ascot in September by 4 lengths from Red Lever: best at
around 1m: acts on any going: usually wears blinkers (didn't at York): a funny
customer who often takes some time to warm up in his races but has a good
turn of finishing speed: wears a tongue strap. *F. J. Houghton.*

YANDINA 2 b.g. Sit In The Corner–November (Firestreak 125) [1976 5f 5f 5d   36
5f³ 6f 5.9f 5h 5fg 5fg 5s] short-backed gelding: bad plater: sometimes wears
blinkers: sold 200 gns Doncaster October Sales. *R. Ward.*

YANKEE GOLD 4 gr.c. Lord Gayle 124–Ceol an Oir (Vimy 132) [1974 7s 6g* 113
1975 8g* 14g⁵ 10g* 10d* 1976 7s² 10g* 12g* 12f⁴] Irish colt: brother to Lady
Singer: very useful performer: won two important events at the Curragh in 1976,
namely Group 2 Ballymoss Stakes in April and Group 3 Royal Whip the following
month (beat Radiant Boy on each occasion): remote fourth of five to Orange Bay
in Hardwicke Stakes at Royal Ascot in June on final appearance: stays 1½m (well
beaten in Irish St Leger on only attempt at 1¾m): acts on soft going: blinkered
third and fourth starts. *J. Oxx, Ireland.*

YARLSBA 2 br.c. Mummy's Pet 125–Mahtessa 79 (Gentle Art 121) [1976 5g 7v   71
5v² 6s] neat colt: second foal: dam won over 5f at 2 yrs: ½-length second to
Thornhill Fanciful in seller at Teesside in October, best effort and only outing in
plating company. *E. Collingwood.*

YDJA 3 br.c. Djakao 124–Yverdon (Sicambre 135) [1975 7v 9s³ 10s⁵ 10v 120
1973 10.5g 12g⁵ 12g⁴ 15.5g⁴] French colt: half-brother to several minor winners
in France: 17,000 francs (approx £1,560) yearling: dam lightly-raced half-sister
to 1,000 Guineas runner-up Yami: still a maiden but put up two splendid performances in June, finishing 5¼ lengths fourth of 18 to Youth (started at 90/1) in
Prix du Jockey-Club at Chantilly and 9½ lengths fourth of nine to Exceller in Grand
Prix de Paris at Longchamp: reportedly injured in running at Longchamp and
was not seen out again: stays 2m: trained first outing by A. Badel. *G. Delloye,
France.*

YEA VERILY 4 b.f. Mountain Call 125–Veritas (Rockefella) [1974 5g⁴ 6g 5v²   —
1975 6s 5.8f 1976 7g] of little account nowadays. *P. Calver.*

YELLOW BOY 3 ch.c. Yellow God 129–Faa Paa (Skymaster 126) [1975 7g   **87**
7g³ 8v* 1976 8.2s* 8f² 7.6fg⁴ 8f² 8.2h² 8fg³ 8v² 8s*] useful sort: good walker:
fair handicapper: won at Haydock in April from Suited with a good deal more in
hand than 1½-length margin indicates: ran creditably afterwards and gained a
further success when beating Indian Warrior 2 lengths at Pontefract in October:
stays 1m well: acts on any going but has done all his winning in the soft: genuine
and consistent: sold to D. Nicholson 9,600 gns Newmarket Autumn Sales. *M.
Jarvis.*

YELLOW BRICK ROAD 4 b.g. Great White Way–Mam'zelle Dolly (Saint   —
Crespin III 132) [1974 5g 5f⁶ 1975 10.8s 10.1g 8g 10f⁵ 1976 10f 10f⁵ 10g]
plater: stays 1¼m: acts on firm going. *A. Pitt.*

YELLOW COLL 3 ch.g. Yellow River 114–Collina 88 (Matador 131) [1975 5d   —
7d 5.3g 1976 6g 5g 9g] rangy gelding: no worthwhile form in varied company,
including selling. *Mrs F. Nagle.*

YELLOW FIRE 3 ch.g. Yellow God 129–Glorious Light 53 (Alcide 136) [1975   **50**
5f 7f 8d⁶ 1976 8f 12f 12g³ 15v³] strong gelding: third in seller at Thirsk in May
(well-backed favourite) and maiden event at Teesside in October (in need of race
and beaten a long way by Precentor): stays at least 1½m. *P. Rohan.*

YELLOW GLEN 2 ch.c. Yellow God 129–Glencarrig (Skymaster 126) [1976   **67**
5d 5s² 5f 5g⁴ 5d 6s] big, strong colt: third foal: brother to a moderate animal:
680 gns yearling: dam won over 5f at 3 yrs in Ireland: in the frame in maiden
races at Doncaster in May (favourite for auction event) and Catterick in
September: should stay 6f. *M. H. Easterby.*

YELLOW PRINCE 4 b.c. Yellow God 129–Persian Lamb 108 (Rustam 127)   —
[1974 5f³ 5h³ 5f* 5fg 6g 6g⁴ 5g⁴ 5g² 5d⁴ 5d⁵ 5s* 1975 5fg² 5g* 5s² 6g 5fg 5f
6fg⁶ 5fg⁴ 5g⁶ 5f³ 6f³ 5d 5g 5g² 5s 1976 5.9f] lengthy, quite attractive colt:
quite a useful handicapper (rated 93) in 1975: had only one outing at 4 yrs:
best at 5f: acts on any going: suitable mount for an apprentice: sometimes sweats
up: none too consistent. *M. Stevens.*

YELLOW SPOTS 2 ch.c. Yellow God 129–Pot de Creme 68 (Candy Spots)   —
[1976 6fg 5d 7s] workmanlike colt: first reported foal: dam stayed well: in rear
in maiden and minor events. *L. Barratt.*

YELLOW STAR 3 ch.g. Yellow God 129–Blond Star (Tin Whistle 128) [1975   —
N.R. 1976 7f 6g 10g] no worthwhile form, including in sellers. *G. Wallace.*

YELLOW VINE 4 b.f. Behistoun 131–Princess Jasmine 84 (King of the Tudors   —
129) [1974 N.R. 1975 8fg 13g 14.7f⁴ 12f⁴ 12g 15.8f⁵ 12v 1976 12fg 10s 10v
10s] poor maiden: stays 1¾m: acts on firm going. *W. Elsey.*

YELLOW WATCH 3 ch.c. Yellow God 129–Stop Watch (Big Game) [1975   **70**
6fg 6fg⁴ 6f² 1976 5.9fg³ 7g 6fg⁴ 5d³ 5fg 6f*] well-made, good sort of colt:
dropped in class, won seller at Yarmouth in July by 1½ lengths from Turk,
making all: sold 925 gns afterwards: should stay 1m: appears to act on any going:
wears blinkers nowadays. *H. Collingridge.*

YENTALA 2 b.f. Upper Case–Charity Concert 80 (Vimy 132) [1976 6fg 7f⁴ 6h²   **75 ?**
7g⁶ 7s] strong, attractive filly: half-sister to several useful winners, including
Kensington High (by Be Friendly) and miler Wild Root (by Tudor Melody):
4,000 gns yearling: dam won over 1¼m, and is half-sister to fastest 1956 2-y-o
Skindles Hotel: stayed on to get within ¼ length of hard-held Aspect in six-runner
minor event at Pontefract in September: remote sixth of 16 to Port Ahoy in
maiden race at Yarmouth later in month: should stay 1¼m. *B. Hanbury.*

YEOMAN 7 b.g. Queen's Hussar 124–Freeholder 95 (Pinza 137) [1974 7fg 7g⁶   **83**
7f⁴ 8g* 10s⁶ 8s² 8v* 1975 7s³ 8f* 8f* 8fg⁴ 8g 8g³ 8d 1976 8fg³ 8g⁵ 8fg⁴ 9g⁴ 8g²]
fair handicapper: didn't manage to win in 1976 but ran well in most of his
races, notably when second to Paddy's Luck in apprentice handicap at Ascot
in July (had great difficulty in getting a run and looked an unlucky loser): best
at 1m: acts on any going: sometimes wears blinkers: excellent mount for a boy
and has won four times for S. Raymont: hung badly right fourth start. *J. Tree.*

YEOVIL 2 b.f. Sir Gaylord–Sunda II (Tropique 128) [1976 8v*] French filly: **?**
half-sister to several winners, including Solitude II (by Gratitude), a smart winner
at around 1¼m in France, and Calypso Boy (by Tudor Melody), a fairly useful
performer from 1¼m to 1¾m: 310,000 francs yearling (approx £33,000): dam won
twice over 13f in France: odds on for eight-runner newcomers event at Maisons-
Laffitte in November and completely dominated her field, going clear from the
distance to win by 4 lengths and 6 lengths: wore blinkers here: will stay 1½m:
certain to go on to much better things. *A. Head, France.*

YES LOVE 2 ch.f. On Your Mark 125–Margaret's Ruby (Tesco Boy 121) [1976 **94** 5fg⁴ 5g² 5f* 5fg² 5f³ 5g] strong, good-quartered, useful-looking filly: second foal: half-sister to fairly useful sprinter Rubydar (by Balidar): 4,800 gns yearling: dam won over 5f in Ireland at 2 yrs: made all and was always toying with opposition when winning maiden race at Redcar in July very easily by ½ length from Avitus: dead. *B. Hanbury.*

YINKA 2 ch.f. Rarity 129–My Idea (Floribunda 136) [1976 7fg³ 7g⁴ 8s] half- **80** sister to two winners, including very smart out-and-out stayer King Levanstell (by Le Levanstell): 2,400 gns yearling: dam maiden Irish sprinter: in frame in September in maiden and minor events, finishing well when 2 lengths third to Eulalie at Salisbury and being beaten over 6 lengths when fourth of 19 to Best Offer at Lingfield: in rear in 27-runner maiden race won by Sporting Yankee at Newmarket the following month: should be suited by 1m. *S. Woodman.*

YMIRKHAN 2 ch.f. Kashmir II 125–Yverda (Dan Cupid 132) [1976 5.5d² 6s² **115** 7g* 8s 8s³] French filly: second foal: half-sister to French 1975 2-y-o 7f winner Yeoman du Roi (by King's Troop): dam, a minor winner over 1¼m, is daughter of 1,000 Guineas runner-up Yami: close-up second on first two outings and won a minor event at Evry in September by 2 lengths: ran well in Criterium des Pouliches and Group 3 Prix des Reservoirs, both at Longchamp in October, in latter race finishing just over a length third to Edinburgh: will stay 1¼m: acts on soft going. *C. Bartholomew, France.*

YOM KIPPUR 4 b.c. Frankincense 120–Snowdrop 82 (Falls of Clyde 126) **54** [1974 6g⁶ 6s 8s 1975 8.2g 8g 7f 10fg 10g 1976 8fg 10.1fg² 10.1fg* 10f³ 12f³ 10f³ 10.8h⁵] plater: successful at Windsor in May by a length from Galadriel and ran creditably in non-sellers afterwards: stays 1½m: acts on a firm surface: has been tried in blinkers. *J. Spearing.*

YOOHOO 2 ch.g. Mountain Call 125–Dreamy Idea 68 (Double Jump 131) **82** [1976 5f 5f* 6f⁶ 6h* 7g 8fg⁴ 7g⁴] light-framed gelding: first foal: 1,000 gns yearling: dam ran only twice at 2 yrs: sold out of R. Jarvis's stable 2,000 gns after winning 20-runner seller at Ripon in August: had other four runners well strung out when successful in nursery at Hamilton the following month: stays 1m: acts on hard going. *D. Williams.*

YORKER 3 b.c. Twilight Alley 133–Java Rose 85 (Javelot 124) [1975 N.R. **—** 1976 11g⁶ 12g] neat colt: third foal: half-brother to a winner in Italy and to a winning plater (both by Starry Halo): 1,700 gns foal, resold 1,800 gns as a yearling: dam best at up to 7f: about 14 lengths sixth of 13 behind Rowe Residence in maiden race at Newbury in May, first and better effort: wears bandages. *I. Balding.*

YOUNG BLADE 2 b.c. Sharpen Up 127–Reita 87 (Gilles de Retz 132) [1976 **—** 5g 5g 6g 5fg 5f 5s] small, close-coupled colt: half-brother to two winners, including 3-y-o Homeboy (by King's Troop): dam a miler: behind in maiden and minor events, twice finishing last. *F. Walwyn.*

YOUNG BOB 3 ch.c. Amber Rama 133–Habbari 104 (St Paddy 133) [1975 **84** 5f 5g⁵ 8s 1976 8h² 8fg* 7d² 6f* 6g 7g⁶ 6d⁶] first foal: dam useful at up to 1m: won maiden race at Carlisle in May and handicap at Redcar the following month: put up a good performance on latter course when beating Clintwood by a length: off course three months afterwards but ran respectably on his return: stays 1m but gives impression that he is better at sprint distances: appears to act on any going. *J. Hanson.*

YOUNG DESIGNER 2 br.c. Philip of Spain 126–Tantilly 66 (Tanavar 118) **61** [1976 5f⁶ 5f* 5d] leggy colt: first foal: dam needed a test of stamina: bought in 1,250 gns after winning seller at Wolverhampton in May by a length: in rear in better company later in month. *K. Payne.*

YOUNGEST CHILD 4 ch.f. Compensation 127–Tetroana 85 (Palestine 133) **68** [1974 N.R. 1975 8f 5g 5g 1976 7fg 8g 6g 6s² 6d* 7v] poor handicapper: bought in 850 gns after winning seller at Newmarket in October (apprentice ridden): evidently best at 6f on soft ground. *W. Holden.*

YOUNG JANE 2 b.f. Frankincense 120–Saint-Cyr 73 (Set Fair 129) [1976 **74** 5d 7fg⁴ 6f⁴ 8f 7g⁵ 6g 8v³] leggy filly: second foal: half-sister to 1974 2-y-o 5f winner Fair Saint (by Bleep-Bleep): dam, a plater, stayed 9f: quite modest form in varied company: stays 1m: acts on any going: ran creditably when apprentice ridden on final outing but gave impression she'd have done even better with stronger handling. *Miss S. Hall.*

YOUNG PIP 3 ch.c. Huntercombe 133–Meadow Pipit 103 (Worden II 129) **90**
[1975 7g 7s⁶ 1976 7fg 10.1fg⁵ 11.1g⁴ 9f⁴ 10fg* 10g* 10.1fg⁴ 10g*] quite attractive colt: won maiden race at Newmarket and minor event at Ripon in August and
handicap, also at Newmarket, in September: had a length to spare over fast-
finishing Chemin de Fer in last-named event: may well stay 1½m: blinkered
third and fourth outings. *M. Jarvis.*

YOUNG ROMANCE 3 br.f. King's Troop 118–Spring Romance 83 (Silly —
Season 127) [1975 N.R. 1976 8fg] first foal: dam a sprinter: in need of race,
pulled up after a furlong in maiden race won by Sospecha at Thirsk in May, only
outing. *S. Nesbitt.*

YOUNG SOVEREIGN 3 b.f. Baldric II 131–Sovereign 129 (Pardao 120) **69**
[1975 5s 5g 5s⁶ 1976 8fg⁵ 6d⁶ 6fg³ 8f² 8d 8.2d] neat, well-made filly: half-sister
to very useful miler Flashy (by Sir Ivor) but is only quite moderate herself: probably stays 1m: sometimes bandaged on off-hind: sold 5,400 gns Newmarket
December Sales. *H. Wragg.*

YOUNG THOMAS 6 ch.g. Celtic Ash–Cobette 75 (The Cobbler 130) [1974 —
N.R. 1975 N.R. 1976 12f 14.7d⁶] workmanlike gelding: poor handicapper:
stays at least 2m. *J. Hanson.*

YOUR LOVE 2 b.f. Blakeney 126–Nylon Pirate 80 (Derring-Do 131) [1976 6f] —
first foal: 740 gns yearling: dam won over 1m: 20/1 when never-dangerous
seventh of 13 to Habeebti in minor event at Newmarket in August, only outing.
B. Hanbury.

YOUTH 3 b.c. Ack Ack–Gazala 124 (Dark Star) [1975 8s* 9s² 1976 10.5s* **135**
10.5fg* 10.5g* 12g* 12g 11d* 12s³ 13s* 12s*]
The joint syndication of the French Derby winner Youth and the Epsom
Derby winner Empery for six million dollars each before the month of June was
out, understandably provoked adverse comment. The syndication seemed premature and the price paid ridiculously high, especially when both horses were
beaten in their next race, Youth only ninth of ten to Pawneese in the King George
VI and Queen Elizabeth Diamond Stakes and Empery only second to Malacate
in the Irish Sweeps Derby. And their proposed retirement to stud at the end of
the season threatened to rob racing of two of its most interesting prospects before
either had had the opportunity to prove himself fully. But still, what people do
with their money is their affair, within the law of the land and the rules of racing,
and if they choose to gamble (and a gamble the syndication certainly was) that is
their business. In the end things turned out much more favourably for the bold
investors than seemed possible at the end of July. While Empery never raced
again after the Irish Sweeps Derby, never got the chance to show his powers
over the longer distances that would have suited him ideally and never looked
remotely worth six million dollars of anyone's money as a racehorse, Youth won
three of his four races after Ascot, including the Canadian International Championship by four lengths and the Washington International by ten; he also
finished a creditable third behind Ivanjica and Crow in the Prix de l'Arc de
Triomphe, and if his presence on the racecourse as a four-year-old will be sorely
missed, he at least retired with few fields still left to conquer and retired with a
record for the season better than any other colt trained in Europe in 1976. His
earnings as a three-year-old amounted to £361,035.
There was seldom a time during the season when Youth didn't seem superior
to his stable-companion Empery; perhaps the only period in which he didn't
appear to have the edge was in the few days between the Epsom Derby and the
French equivalent, the Prix du Jockey-Club run at Chantilly. As two-year-olds,
there was little to choose between them; both were lightly raced, and at the end
of their first season Empery received a rating of 8-10 in the French Free Handicap,
10 lb less than top-weighted Manado, and Youth, who won a race restricted to
newcomers and finished second to Far North in the Prix Saint-Roman at Longchamp, received 8-6.
Youth did everything asked of him at three in his preparation for the Prix
du Jockey-Club. Whereas Empery lost all his three races before Epsom,
Youth won all his before Chantilly, the Prix Greffulhe, the Prix Daru and the
Prix Lupin, in the last-named having the improving Empery two lengths behind
in third place. The three races that Youth won in the spring, all of them at
Longchamp incidentally, are recognised as classic trials in France; they are
important, the Lupin, carrying a first prize of almost £60,000, especially so,
although the turnout for the Lupin would probably be even more important if the
Prix Hocquart, another trial, were run two or three weeks earlier than it is now.

Prix Lupin, Longchamp—Youth is the master of Arctic Tern and Empery

Among those taking part in the Hocquart, run only a week before the Lupin, had been Grandchant and Twig Moss, who were to show prominently in the Prix du Jockey-Club. Youth started at 5/2 on, along with Empery and the pacemaker Oilfield, for the Prix Lupin, opposed principally by the French Two Thousand Guineas runner-up Roan Star, Manado, the Guineas fifth Arctic Tern and the English trained Danestic, who had finished second to Youth in the Prix Daru. Youth had been very impressive in the Daru and had won by four lengths; he had had more trouble with Velino and Yule Log in the Prix Greffulhe on his first outing of the season, in which he had finished strongly to win by a length and a half. Youth won the Lupin by three parts of a length from Arctic Tern and won well enough, despite a rumour that Arctic Tern was some way behind Far North at home, to convince us that he would be good value against Wollow should it be decided to send him and not Empery to Epsom. Arctic Tern had been a top-class two-year-old, and so had Roan Star, who finished fourth in the Lupin.

Following Empery's win at Epsom—he was chosen ahead of Youth for Epsom primarily because he was expected to be able to handle the track the better—Youth's prospects in the Prix du Jockey-Club were brighter than ever, although he started at longer odds (19/10 coupled with Oilfield) than did Wollow at Epsom. The three-year-old colts in France, as in England, at this stage of the season were generally considered a motley collection and many regarded the fillies Pawneese and Riverqueen in front of the best of them; but, as we said, Youth had done all that was asked of him, which was something that could be said of few of his seventeen opponents at Chantilly. Admittedly Youth's stamina had to be taken on trust, and although the balance of probabilities in his pedigree and his style of running came down in his favour there was still a doubt whether he would get a mile and a half. His half-brother Mississipian, a close fourth in the race two years earlier, stayed the trip, but Mississipian was by Vaguely Noble, a much less speedy type than Youth's sire Ack Ack and one more likely, so far as could be foretold (Ack Ack's first runners were only three-year-olds) to sire staying horses. The dam Gazala, the French Oaks winner, was well beaten in the Prix Vermeille on her only attempt at a mile and a half but was found to be coughing afterwards. Ack Ack stayed at least a mile and a quarter, although he did all his winning at shorter distances until he reached his last season, at five years.

Youth proved ideally suited by a mile and a half. He ran out one of the most impressive recent winners of the Prix du Jockey-Club despite the fact that, as is only to be expected in a classic with as many as eighteen runners taking part, some of the opposing jockeys returned with hard-luck stories to tell. Youth won an extremely fast-run race virtually unchallenged by three lengths from Twig Moss, a horse that had begun the season with a victory in the south at Cagnes-sur-Mer in February and had improved tremendously to take the Prix Noailles and to finish third to Grandchant in the Hocquart. Grandchant was the unluckiest horse at Chantilly; he finished fifth after having a very poor run; ninth-placed Arctic Tern and Twig Moss were slightly hampered in the straight and third-placed Malacate was left with a great deal to do from the home turn, but all this takes little of the shine off Youth's performance. He thoroughly trounced the opposition such as it was (fourth-placed Ydja had been unplaced, receiving weight, in a handicap for three-year-olds at Longchamp on his previous outing). Kept in the first five from the start, pulling over all those who ever got in front of him (only Oilfield, Arctic Tern, Ydja and the strongly-fancied Wildenstein runner Cheraw), Youth swept into the lead around two furlongs out and ran on very powerfully at full throttle to the finish.

Malacate's subsequent win in the Irish Sweeps Derby and Ydja's running behind Youth's stable-companion Exceller in the Grand Prix de Paris, on top of Youth's unblemished record for the season, did enough, apparently, to persuade the majority that he had a better chance than any of his distinguished opponents in the King George VI and Queen Elizabeth Diamond Stakes at Ascot the following month. Youth started a 15/8 favourite and ran poorly. He was never moving with the ease and freedom of the front-running Pawneese, and coming into the home turn he appeared to be experiencing a little difficulty in holding fourth place behind Pawneese, Ashmore and Malacate. Rounding the turn he came so wide that he forfeited whatever chance he held; he finished up in last-but-one position, more than ten lengths behind the winner, failing to reach the frame for the only time in his career. Head, who rode Youth, has a record from relatively few rides in England that contrasts sharply with his brilliant record in France, and it's extraordinary how often he has made elementary errors on admittedly difficult courses such as Epsom and Ascot.

That Youth did not get a fair chance to show his worth was one of two very unsatisfactory aspects of the King George (Bruni's slow start was the other), and what the form amounted to, with Dakota fourth and Coin of Gold a relatively close-up sixth, was anyone's guess. Whether, in more favourable circumstances, Youth would have been able to quicken in the straight as he had done at Chantilly, will always be a matter for conjecture, but it scarcely seems conceivable that at anywhere near his best he would have failed to get in the shake-up.

Head, who had ridden Youth in all his races in 1976, did not ride him again. He was out of action when Youth next ran, ridden by Piggott, in the Prix Niel at Longchamp in September and was claimed for Ivanjica when Youth ran, ridden by Pyers, in the Arc; the Canadian Sandy Hawley, who had the remarkable total of 515 winners in 1973, rode Youth on his two starts in North America, on the second of which, in the Washington International, Head was again aboard Ivanjica. The importance of jockeyship to top-class horses has sometimes been questioned, for such horses have a habit of winning so well that it often seems that any competent rider would suffice for them, but even with horses as good as Youth the rider can be faced with one or more difficult problems in the course of a race. At Ascot, Head suddenly and apparently unexpectedly found himself landed with the major problem of getting Youth round a turn not very much different from the last turn at Longchamp and Chantilly, and before he had solved it the race had slipped out of his grasp.

Piggott had a different problem in the Prix Niel: that of deciding the best way of coping with a fast finisher like Malacate in a small field short of a recognised pacemaker in a race run over a distance of eleven furlongs. Besides the King George fifth Malacate, Youth's opponents were the inconsistent Arctic Tern, receiving 4 lb from Youth and Malacate, the Prix de la Cote Normande winner Iron Duke, who was receiving 4 lb and was well suited by this sort of distance, and the rank outsider Loosen Up. Piggott solved his problem in the way that might have been expected of the great jockey. He made sure that each of his three main rivals would have to come from behind him if they were going to win, and had Youth in front for all the journey except for the time when Loosen Up quickened the pace and led on sufferance coming down the hill. After regaining the lead Youth had to fight off Arctic Tern and Malacate in the straight, Arctic

Prix du Jockey-Club, Chantilly—Youth wins impressively from Twig Moss and Malacate

Canadian International Championship Stakes, Woodbine—Youth is in no danger

Tern being the more persistent, but when rousted along in the last furlong Youth lengthened his stride and won going away by three parts of a length.

Pyers had been in the unenviable position of both preceding and following Piggott on some of Mr Bunker Hunt's good horses in the past, and he found himself in the hot seat again when Piggott chose to ride Bruni in the Prix de l'Arc de Triomphe. No-one could have given Youth, co-favourite with Exceller, a better ride than Pyers did in the Arc: he rode the text-book race, keeping him in third place to Pawneese and Kasteel until taking the lead and sprinting for home soon after the turn. That Youth was caught, as he was first by Crow and then by Ivanjica, was no fault of jockey or horse but only that on the day the horse wasn't good enough. Youth, challenged by several other opponents in the straight, ran on very gamely to the finishing line, which he reached five lengths behind Ivanjica, who had had a much less strenuous season than he, and three lengths behind Crow, who was the only three-year-old colt to have any reasonable claim to being Youth's equal at a mile and a half, and that only on the strength of this performance. Youth's running in the Arc we regard as being a shade below his best; he did better in North America we are sure. It is no use looking for excuses for him in the Arc—there aren't any—and had he not run afterwards he would have been rated inferior to Crow. To excuse his defeat on account of the soft going seemed mistaken at the time and a downright nonsense at the end of the year.

Tackling American horses on their own ground always used to appear a hazardous enterprise with horses straight over from Europe, especially so late in the season. There are obvious difficulties to be overcome, not least the effects of travelling and the change of environment. But recently there have been enough instances of European horses doing well over there to make the enterprise seem straightforward, if not child's play. On his way to join Empery at stud, at Gainesway Farm in Kentucky, Youth ran in the Canadian International Championship over thirteen furlongs on turf at Woodbine (Toronto) on October 23rd, a weight-for-age race won two years earlier by his stable's Dahlia, and then, on November 6th, in the Washington International at Laurel in Maryland, a race won by Dahlia in 1973 and by the stable's Nobiliary in 1975.

Youth lost potentially dangerous opponents in Toronto when the Irish St Leger winner of 1975 Caucasus, a big winner in the States as a four-year-old, was scratched after being cast in his box, and when the French horse Maitland was scratched after a disappointing gallop; but despite starting at odds on he still faced strong opposition, the pick on his record the recent Man o' War Stakes winner Effervescing, an American-trained three-year-old. Among the nine other runners was the ex-French horse Kamaraan, who had been brought back to racing from stud duties and who was retired again after bowing a tendon in running. Youth won very impressively, making ground through the race to go third approaching the last turn, taking over from Effervescing and Kamaraan into the straight and dominating the field thereafter. The American outsider Improviser, a four-year-old and the winner of two handicaps at Gulfstream in the spring, came out second best, seven lengths in front of third-placed Effervescing. An interesting feature of Youth's race was that he had been up to overtaking good horses on the fairly sharp last bend (a left-handed bend, unlike those at Ascot, Longchamp, and Chantilly) and although his momentum threatened to take him wide, he was in command in a few strides.

The first three in the Canadian International Championship were invited to run at Laurel but only Youth accepted. Effervescing, the last remaining representative of the United States was due to run but did not, ostensibly because he re-injured a hip during a preparatory gallop but more likely because the trainer thought the ground too soft to risk him on. Youth himself was pronounced fit to run only at around eleven o'clock on the morning of the race, having cut his off-hind heel early in the week. Except for the presence of the Japanese-trained Fujino Pahshia (by Parthia out of a Die Hard mare) who had been at Laurel for two months preparing for the race, and the Brazilian-trained Janus (by Pardallo) the International might well have been taking place in Europe. Besides Youth the only other runners were Ivanjica, co-favourite with Youth, Rose Bowl, Noble Dancer, On My Way and the German horse Windwurf, winner of the Preis von Europa.

We thought that Rose Bowl would be well suited by a mile and a half but not so—not in this, her last race, at any rate. In the very testing conditions she dropped behind from the last turn, at which point Youth was brought to make his challenge on the outside. Hawley at this stage and thereafter looked to be sat on easily the best horse in the race, but he took an unnecessary risk. Upon passing Ivanjica and On My Way to go into the lead, Hawley brought Youth sharply across to the running rail, much sooner than safety allowed, and caused On My Way to check in his stride; then he ran right away from the field, and at the finish he had ten lengths to spare over On My Way, third to Nobiliary in 1975, and slightly more to spare over third-placed Ivanjica, who obviously did not give her Arc running. After long deliberation the stewards, in their charity, allowed the result to stand, possibly because the race was an international event, more likely because the foul did not affect the outcome of the race. 'French' runners, all of whom had been bred in the United States, the winner in Maryland, the second in Virginia and the third in Kentucky, filled the first three places—a notable achievement despite the absence of North American-trained runners. Probably the best of the home-trained grass horses, incidentally, was none other than the former inmate of Vincent O'Brien's stable King Pellinore, who instead of tackling Youth stayed in California for the Champions Invitational Handicap at Santa Anita and picked up a winner's purse of 240,000 dollars, almost two and a half times Youth's winnings at Laurel. No European-trained horse put up a better performance in 1976 than did Youth at Laurel, although the conditions the race was run under (very soft going, late in the season on an American track) make one stop short of giving him anything like full value for the winning distance.

Youth (b.c. 1973)	Ack Ack (b 1966)	Battle Joined (b 1959)	Armageddon
			Ethel Walker
		Fast Turn (b 1959)	Turn-to
			Cherokee Rose
	Gazala (br 1964)	Dark Star (br 1950)	Royal Gem
			Isolde
		Belle Angevine (br 1957)	L'Amiral
			Bella II

Youth's owner has said that he used the stallion Ack Ack, American Horse of the Year as a five-year-old, primarily because the horse showed speed through-

Washington D.C. International, Laurel—a scintillating performance by Youth, who finishes well clear of On My Way and Ivanjica (rails)

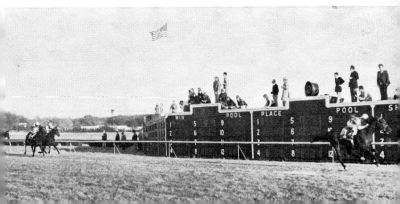

out a long career, although Mr Hunt admitted to being not 'all that crazy about him' at the time he used him. Both before visiting Ack Ack and since, Gazala has been covered by Vaguely Noble and by him produced, in Mississipian, a horse very similar to Youth, although not quite so good. Mississipian, now also at stud in the United States, stayed so well that as a two-year-old he won the Grand Criterium in the mud from Nonoalco and finished second to Apalachee in the Observer Gold Cup, and at three he won the Prix Niel from Mount Hagen and Sagaro, and finished in the frame in the Irish Sweeps Derby as well as the French Derby. He also finished ninth of twenty behind Allez France in the Prix de l'Arc de Triomphe, and a close second in the French Guineas and the Lupin. A full brother to Mississipian fetched 550,000 dollars at the Keeneland Yearling Sales and is in training in Ireland with O'Brien. An earlier full sister, the unraced Double Classic, was sold out of training for 30,000 guineas at the December Sales in 1973.

Youth's dam won the Poule d'Essai des Pouliches (the French One Thousand Guineas) and three other races, including the Criterium de Maisons-Laffitte at two and the Prix de la Grotte at three, as well as the Prix de Diane, the French Oaks. She had an outstanding turn of finishing speed. Gazala's sire, Dark Star, won at up to a mile and a quarter, the distance over which he gained his most important victory in the Kentucky Derby. Her dam was a winner in France, and so was her grandam; Belle Angevine at thirteen furlongs, Bella II at around a mile. Bella II, her grandam, produced ten foals to race from twelve in all, among them the Grand Prix de Saint-Cloud and Grand Prix de Marseille winner Burgos (he dead-heated with Oroso at Saint-Cloud) and the stakes winner Bell Hop, the latter of whom became a stallion in Argentina.

In appearance Youth is a strong, very lengthy colt, too long in the back and too rawboned to be described as attractive. In action, though, he was impressive, and had fine powers of acceleration that might not have been suspected in one with as raking a stride as his. He acted on a surface as firm as that which prevailed on the day the Prix Daru was run (his only appearance on ground any firmer than good) but obviously soft going suited him exceptionally well. To his credit he had all the consistency and enthusiasm for racing that top-class horses ideally should possess; his unfortunate defeat at Ascot, the low point of his career, now looks very insignificant indeed in comparison with the sum of his achievements. One of his first duties in his new career will be to cover Dahlia.
M. Zilber, France.

Mr N. B. Hunt's "Youth"

YOU WOULD 2 b.f. Athens Wood 126–Fearless 77 (Derring-Do 131) [1976 5s **64**
7v⁴] first foal: dam won over 7f at 3 yrs: distant fourth of 14 finishers in minor
event won by Forage at Lingfield in November. *J. Bethell.*

YUKON FLASH 2 b.c. Yukon Eric–Headliner (Pampered King 121) [1976 —
5fg⁵] neat, good-quartered colt: second foal: dam ran only once: always toiling
when remote fifth of six in maiden race won by Fulbeck at Newmarket in April.
A. Davison.

YUKON TRAIL 3 br.g. Yukon Eric–Ranjitara (Right Boy 137) [1975 5v⁵ —
6g 1976 8s 9f 12f⁶] well-grown gelding: little sign of ability in maiden
company: bandaged near-fore final outing: sold 370 gns Ascot August Sales and
resold 500 gns Doncaster November Sales. *W. Elsey.*

YULE LOG 4 b.g. Firestreak 125–Christmas 86 (Santa Claus 133) [1974 5g⁵ **63**
5g 6fg⁵ 7g⁵ 7d³ 8s² 8v 8.5s² 8v³ 7v⁴ 7v⁵ 1975 8g 10fg 7f³ 6fg 1976 16f* 17.7f*]
poor handicapper: successful at Warwick in April and Wolverhampton the
following month: stays well: acts on any going: used to wear blinkers, but
didn't in 1976: suitable mount for an apprentice. *O. O'Neill.*

YUNG CHENG 2 ch.g. Politico 124–Contourno (Continuation 120) [1976 —
5g 5f] small gelding: in rear in auction event at Ripon in April and seller at
Wolverhampton in May: sold 200 gns Doncaster September Sales. *K. Payne.*

YUNKEL 3 b.c. Amber Rama 133–March Wonder 99 (March Past 124) [1975 **105**
5g² 5f 5fg³ 5fg* 7g⁶ 6f⁵ 6d* 7fg⁴ 7.3d 6g⁴ 1976 7fg 6fg³ 8f² 7g² 7.6f² 7.6fg⁵ 7.6g*
8g 7.6g⁴ 9g 7s] strong, useful sort: good mover: ran well in handicaps and
picked up a valuable prize at Lingfield in August when beating Mid Beat 1½
lengths in Gatwick Handicap: not disgraced under 8-9 behind Intermission in
Irish Sweeps Cambridgeshire at Newmarket in October when tried in blinkers:
promises to stay further than 1m: seems to act on any going with possible
exception of really soft: suitable mount for an apprentice. *R. Smyth.*

Z

ZAB 6 b.h. Baldric II 131–Zelfana (Philius II 132) [1974 14fg⁶ 14g 14.6g* —
1975 13.4d2 16f* 20f 13.3g⁴ 1976 16g⁴ 13.3g⁴] attractive French-bred horse:
smart performer: won Henry II Stakes at Sandown in 1975: well-beaten fourth at
Ascot and Newbury at 6 yrs, on last-named course finishing 13½ lengths behind
Major Green in six-runner Aston Park Stakes in May: stays 2m (ran moderately
at 2¼m in Gold Cup at Royal Ascot): acts on any going. *M. Jarvis.*

ZABRISKIE POINT 2 b.f. Irish Ball 127–Wonder Belle 118 (Faubourg II 127) **68**
[1976 5f 6g⁵ 6f 7fg⁶ 9fg⁵ 7fg 10v⁵] neat filly: half-sister to two winners here and
abroad: 620 gns yearling: dam smart performer at 1m and 1¼m: only plating
class: will stay 1½m. *R. Hollinshead.*

ZALITZING 2 b.c. Fleet Nasrullah–Native Love (Raise A Native) [1976 **110**
5g* 7g* 7g 6.5s³] American-bred French colt: second foal: $21,000 yearling:
dam won at up to 6f at 3 yrs in U.S.A., and is half-sister to three smart winners:
twice a winner at Clairefontaine, winning a maiden race in July by 4 lengths and
Prix Georges de Kerhallet the following month by 2 lengths from River Sleep: put
up better subsequent effort when dead-heating with Lone Escape for third place,
about 1¾ lengths behind Aerosol, in Prix Eclipse at Saint-Cloud in October: will
stay 1m. *R. de Tarragon, France.*

ZARAJEFF 3 gr.g. Jefferson 129–Asha Vahista (Zarathustra 131) [1975 7.5f² —
8g* 1976 10.2f³ 8fg⁶ 8f 12fg⁵] tall, short-backed French-foaled gelding: half-
brother to a winner in France: dam won twice in Ireland at 2 yrs: won at Sterre-
beek in Belgium at 2 yrs: had stiff tasks in 1976, but led for nearly 1¼m when
remote fifth of 11 to Rickadoo in apprentice handicap at Salisbury in September:
should stay middle distances. *B. Swift.*

ZARZAITINE 3 br.g. Murrayfield 119–Finesse 87 (Miralgo 130) [1975 5f 5f 6g **88**
6s⁶ 6g* 1976 10g⁴ 12fg⁴ 12.3fg* 10fg² 13fg² 12fg⁴ 14fg⁵ 12g³] robust gelding:
fair handicapper: comfortable winner at Newcastle in June: also first past post
at Nottingham the following month, 1½ lengths ahead of Ardent Portion, but was
subsequently placed second because his rider hit the other horse: stays 13f: acts
on a firm surface. *G. Peter-Hoblyn.*

ZEBAK 3 gr.c. Zeddaan 130–Babble On 79 (Acropolis 132) [1975 6fg 5g 6g **74**
1976 7fg⁶ 8d² 8fg 7g 8h* 10s⁵] strong French-foaled colt: far from consistent,
but won moderate 10-runner maiden event at Pontefract in September by a

length from Alvage despite hanging left under pressure: should stay 1¼m:
ran freely when tried in blinkers on third outing. *H. Wragg.*

ZELENKO 2 b.c. Welsh Pageant 132–Another Daughter 106 (Crepello 136)   **93**
[1976 6d⁴ 7g²]   attractive, well-made, good sort: half-brother to two winners,
including 1973 2-y-o 6f winner Stogumber (by Habitat): 36,000 gns yearling:
dam, half-sister to Great Nephew, won over 1m at 2 yrs: favourite for 21-runner
maiden race at Newmarket in October and ran well, going down by 2½ lengths to
Nobodys Fool: will be suited by 1m+. *R. Hern.*

ZELOSO 2 b.c. Henry the Seventh 125–Grenfilt 83 (Sheshoon 132) [1976 8v]   **—**
third foal: half-brother to two poor animals: dam won over 7f at 2 yrs: distinctly
burly, missed break when last of 13 to Starlight Lad in minor event at Teesside
in October. *R. D. Peacock.*

ZIMBALON 4 b.c. Ragusa 137–Zither 72 (Vienna 127) [1974 N.R. 1975 8s⁵   **118**
10.4g* 12g* 10.6fg* 12f* 10.5d⁶ 10g 10fg 1976 10g* 13.4s* 12g⁴] strong, attractive colt: good mover: won four races as a 3-y-o, including King George V Stakes
at Royal Ascot: did well physically from 3 to 4 yrs and showed even better form,
winning Rosebery Handicap at Kempton in April and four-runner Ormonde
Stakes (Group 3) at Chester the following month: trounced three good-class
opponents on last-named occasion, storming into the lead turning for home and
beating Libra's Rib (gave 8 lb) 7 lengths: somewhat disappointing when 4½
lengths fourth of six to Quiet Fling in Group 1 Coronation Cup at Epsom in June,
finding no extra pace 2f from home after having every chance: stays 13f: acts on
any going: disappointed on final outing at 3 yrs when tried in blinkers: has a fine
turn of foot: sold to race in U.S.A. *R. Hern.*

ZINOV 2 gr.c. Drone–Crafty Jo (Crafty Admiral) [1976 8d* 7.7s⁴] American-   **113**
bred French colt: half-brother to several winners in U.S.A., including Decimator
(by What A Pleasure), a very useful stakes winner at up to 1m at 2 yrs: 21,000
dollars yearling: dam won a 6f claiming race at 3 yrs: won six-runner newcomers
race at Longchamp in September by 1½ lengths from He's a Gent: 17/1 for Prix
Thomas Bryon at Saint-Cloud the following month but ran well, always holding

Mr R. D. Hollingsworth's "Zimbalon"

a good place, leading halfway up straight and being beaten 4 lengths into fourth place behind General: stays 1m and may get further: trained by R. de Tarragon on first appearance: to be trained by D. Weld. *J. Audon, France.*

ZIOBIA 3 br.f. Tribal Chief 125–Ibozia 73 (Mossborough 126) [1975 5g⁶ 5g³ **63** 5s 5g 1976 7fg⁵ 7f³ 6g 8g 7f 5.3h³ 6f] lightly-built filly: poor form in varied company: stays 7f. *C. Bewicke.*

ZIP FASTENER 5 gr.g. Silver Shark 129–Safety Fast 76 (Abernant 142) — [1974 8g³ 10f 10.4g³ 12f⁴ 12.3g 12s² 12.3d* 12g³ 12.3s² 1975 N.R. 1976 13g⁵] lengthy gelding: fairly useful handicapper in 1974: having first outing since when fifth to Royal Fanfare in minor event at Liverpool in April: stays 1½m: acts on any going *F. Rimell.*

ZIPPERDI-DOO-DAH 4 b.c. Shooting Chant–Spring Bonnet (Cash and Courage **61** 116) [1974 5d 6fg 6d 7s 5s* 5s 5v 1975 6s⁴ 6s 7g 6fg² 7g 6f 6fg² 6fg⁴ 6fg 6fg 10g 6f 1976 6g* 6g³ 6fg 5.9f³ 6g² 5.9g⁵ 7f 6fg⁴ 6s³ 6s² 6d⁴] strong, workmanlike colt: fairly useful plater: narrow winner at Folkestone in March (no bid): ran creditably most outings afterwards: stays 6f well: appears to act on any going: wears blinkers: suitable mount for an apprentice. *J. Benstead.*

ZOMAAR 3 b.f. Silly Season 127–Arkadia 74 (Larkspur 128) [1975 N.R. **58** 1976 9fg⁴ 10s 11g 16.1d 13s⁶ 10fg 11f³ 13fg 16fg 10f⁵] poor maiden: ran easily best race over 11f. *D. Thom.*

ZOROASTER 3 gr.c. Zeddaan 130–Persina (Tamerlane 128) [1975 6g⁴ 6f* — 1976 7f 9s 5d⁶ 5v⁵] strong colt: particularly good walker: won New Ham Stakes at Goodwood on second of only two outings as a 2-y-o, beating Spanish Air in style of a very useful animal: did not reproduce that form in 1976 but had very stiff tasks in first two races, Clerical, Medical Greenham Stakes at Newbury and handicap at York (got unsettled in the stalls) and was subsequently off course four months: should stay further than sprint distances. *B. Hills.*

ZOUAVE 2 br.c. Zeddaan 130–Menai 100 (Abernant 142) [1976 5h] half- — brother to two winners: dam, half-sister to Canisbay, appeared not to stay 6f: tenth of 11 to Aberoan in maiden race at Bath in July: sold 480 gns Ascot August Sales. *I. Balding.*

Mr Phil Bull's "Zoroaster"

TIMEFORM
HORSE OF THE YEAR
1976

YOUTH

TIMEFORM CHAMPIONS OF 1976

Horse of the Year
YOUTH
Rated at 135

3 b.c. Ack Ack–Gazala (Dark Star)
Owner Mr N. B. Hunt   *Trainer* M. Zilber

Best Two–year–old colt
BLUSHING GROOM
Rated at 131

2 ch.c. Red God–Runaway Bride (Wild Risk)
Owner H. H. Aga Khan   *Trainer* F. Mathet

Best Two–year–old filly
CLOONLARA
Rated at 130

2 b.f. Sir Ivor–Fish-Bar (Baldric II)
Owner Mr J. A. Mulcahy   *Trainer* V. O'Brien

Best Sprinter
LOCHNAGER
Rated at 132

4 b.c. Dumbarnie–Miss Barbara (Le Dieu d'Or)
Owner Mr C. F. Spence   *Trainer* M. W. Easterby

Best Miler
WOLLOW
Rated at 132

3 b.c. Wolver Hollow–Wichuraiana (Worden II)
Owner Mr C. d'Alessio   *Trainer* H. Cecil

Best Middle–distance horse
YOUTH
Rated at 135

3 b.c. Ack Ack–Gazala (Dark Star)
Owner Mr N. B. Hunt   *Trainer* M. Zilber

Best Stayer
SAGARO
Rated at 129

5 ch.h. Espresso–Zambara (Mossborough)
Owner Mr G. A. Oldham   *Trainer* F. Boutin

1976 STATISTICS

The following tables show the leading owners, trainers, breeders, jockeys, horses and the sires of winners during the 1976 season. Except for the list of sires, which relates to racing in both England and Ireland, these statistics refer only to racing under Jockey Club Rules. The tables are reproduced by permission of *The Sporting Life*.

OWNERS

		Horses	Races Won	Stakes £
1.	Mr D. Wildenstein	5	10	244,500
2.	Mr C. d'Alessio	3	9	169,819
3.	Mr N. B. Hunt	5	6	123,384
4.	Mr J. H. Whitney	7	20	107,398
5.	Mr R. Sangster	8	11	84,109
6.	Mr C. F. Spence	1	4	53,342
7.	Mr G. L. Cambanis	2	5	52,437
8.	Mr C. A. B. St George	9	13	49,977
9.	Mr H. J. Joel	15	29	45,789
10.	Mr R. D. Hollingsworth	5	11	45,463
11.	Mr G. A. Pope, jnr	3	8	43,889
12.	William Hill Racing Ltd	2	4	39,145

TRAINERS

		Horses	Races Won	Stakes £
1.	H. Cecil	24	52	261,301
2.	P. Walwyn	61	110	260,112
3.	A. Penna	4	6	240,819
4.	R. Price	47	83	198,749
5.	R. Hern	46	69	153,298
6.	B. Hobbs	30	55	144,080
7.	B. Hills	35	60	113,180
8.	M. Zilber	1	1	111,825
9.	M. W. Easterby	29	53	111,711
10.	C. Brittain	37	53	102,617
11.	M. Stoute	29	62	91,499
12.	J. Dunlop	29	48	88,012

BREEDERS

		Horses	Races Won	Stakes £
1.	Dayton Ltd	5	10	232,599
2.	Mr N. B. Hunt	6	8	166,775
3.	Tally Ho Stud	1	5	166,389
4.	Mr J. H. Whitney	7	18	84,115
5.	Mr E. A. Dandy	1	4	53,342
6.	Mr R. D. Hollingsworth	5	11	45,463
7.	Mr H. J. Joel	14	29	45,111
8.	Mr G. A. Pope, jnr	3	8	43,889
9.	Cragwood Estates Inc	3	7	40,791
10.	Societe Aland	1	3	40,318
11.	Herve de la Heronniere	1	1	38,609
12.	Mr E. P. Taylor	1	1	37,195

JOCKEYS

			1st	2nd	3rd	Unpl	Total Mts	Per Cent
1.	P. Eddery	..	162	139	102	400	803	20·17
2.	W. Carson	..	138	142	106	479	865	15·95
3.	B. Taylor ..		108	76	69	306	559	19·32
4.	E. Hide ..	..	103	93	101	378	675	15·26
5.	J. Mercer ..		98	87	85	304	574	17·07
6.	M. L. Thomas		90	73	75	423	661	13·62
7.	L. Piggott	..	87	68	51	196	402	21·64
8.	G. Starkey	..	73	49	58	282	462	15·86
9.	P. Cook ..	..	66	75	66	376	583	11·32
10.	G. Lewis ..		65	64	53	285	467	13·92
10.	E. Johnson	..	65	63	53	311	492	13·21
12.	B. Raymond		58	61	56	307	482	12·03

HORSES

		Races Won	Stakes £
1.	Wollow (3 yrs), b.c. by Wolver Hollow—Wichuraiana ..	5	166,389
2.	Pawneese (3 yrs), b.f. by Carvin—Plencia ..	2	131,625
3.	Empery (3 yrs), b.c. by Vaguely Noble—Pamplona II ..	1	111,825
4.	Crow (3 yrs), ch.c. by Exbury—Carmosina ..	1	53,638
5.	Lochnager (4 yrs), b.c. by Dumbarnie—Miss Barbara	4	53,342
6.	Flying Water (3 yrs), ch.f. by Habitat—Formentera ..	2	43,310
7.	Durtal (2 yrs), b.f. by Lyphard—Derna II ..	3	40,318
8.	Vitiges (3 yrs), ch.c. by Phaeton—Vale ..	1	38,609
9.	Sporting Yankee (2 yrs), b.c. by Vaguely Noble—Sale Day ..	2	38,019
10.	The Minstrel (2 yrs), ch.c. by Northern Dancer—Fleur ..	1	37,195

SIRES OF WINNERS

		Horses	Races Won	Stakes £
1.	Wolver Hollow (1964), by Sovereign Path ..	18	34	192,362
2.	Vaguely Noble (1965), by Vienna ..	7	9	166,323
3.	Carvin (1962), by Marino ..	1	2	131,625
4.	Habitat (1966), by Sir Gaylord ..	15	20	87,513
5.	Lucky Debonair (1962), by Vertex..	1	2	86,746
6.	Le Levanstell (1957), by Le Lavandou	15	23	77,703
7.	Exbury (1959), by Le Haar ..	4	7	75,612
8.	Yellow God (1967), by Red God ..	20	29	72,961

THE FREE HANDICAPS

TWO-YEAR-OLDS OF 1976

The following are the weights allotted in the Tote Free Handicap published on 25th November. The race is to be run over seven furlongs at Newmarket on 13th April, 1977.

J. O. Tobin	9	7	Easy Landing	8	0
Godswalk	9	2	Sultans Ruby	8	0
Padroug	9	1	Mummy's Darling	8	0
Gairloch	8	13	Al Stanza	8	0
The Minstrel	8	13	Paddington	8	0
Tachypous	8	12	Card Player	8	0
Nebbiolo	8	10	No Conventions	7	13
Durtal	8	8	Be Easy	7	13
Avgerinos	8	8	Town and Country	7	13
Saros	8	7	Baudelaire	7	13
Hot Grove	8	7	Mr Nice Guy	7	13
Mandrake Major	8	7	Crown Bowler	7	13
Haveroid	8	6	In Haste	7	12
Icena	8	6	Imperial Guard	7	12
Metair	8	6	Claddagh	7	12
Fair Season	8	5	The Andrestan	7	12
Night Before	8	5	And Behold	7	12
Ad Lib Ra	8	5	Great Oak	7	12
Sky Ship	8	5	Nice Balance	7	12
Anax	8	5	Man in the Moon	7	12
Adviser	8	5	Haraka	7	12
Etienne Gerard	8	4	As Blessed	7	12
Miss Pinkie	8	4	Song of Songs	7	12
Sporting Yankee	8	4	Royal Diver	7	12
La Ville de Rire	8	4	Princess Tiara	7	12
Royal Plume	8	3	Faridetta	7	11
Forty Winks	8	3	Latest Model	7	11
Cawston's Clown	8	3	Blackadder	7	11
Priors Walk	8	3	King Elect	7	11
Our Jimmy	8	3	Petard	7	11
Ampulla	8	3	Habeebti	7	11
Brave Lass	8	2	Lady Constance	7	11
Limone	8	1	Casino Boy	7	11
Cramond	8	1	Bessie Wallis	7	10
Millionaire	8	1	Swagger	7	10
Birkholm	8	1	Catiline	7	10
Piney Ridge	8	1	Oriental Rocket	7	10
Sunny Spring	8	1	Whitby Jet	7	10
Athlete's Foot	8	0	Champagne Willie	7	10
Hyver Hill	8	0	Fife and Drum	7	10
Lady Mere	8	0	Scarcely Blessed	7	9
Triple First	8	0	Rocket Symphony	7	9

Cosy Bar	7	9	Great Flight		7	8
Brightelmstone	7	9	Pollerton		7	8
Lucent	7	9	Teddington Park		7	8
The Czar	7	9	Mrs McArdy		7	7
Great Memoirs	7	9	Pub Spy		7	7
Rings	7	9	Taffytina		7	7
Rockery (Fr)	7	9	Fast Frigate		7	7
Local Knowledge	7	9	Aspect		7	7
Mofida	7	8	Mandalus		7	7
Rudella	7	8	Home Fire		7	7
Lady Eton	7	8	Rahesh		7	7
Jameson	7	8	Region		7	7

THREE-YEAR-OLDS OF 1976

The following handicap, published on 25th November, is for information only. The figure shown after the name of the highest weighted horse represents the official assessment of its merit against a norm of 100.

Vitiges, 96	10	0	Gwent		8	12
Pawneese	9	11	Pascualete		8	12
Wollow	9	9	Relkino		8	12
Crow	9	8	Tierra Fuego		8	12
Empery	9	8	Caljobo		8	11
Mart Lane	9	7	Catalpa		8	11
Free State	9	6	Lost Chord		8	11
Malinowski	9	6	Patris		8	11
Radetzky	9	5	Sarah Siddons		8	11
Sir Montagu	9	5	Thieving Demon		8	11
Bright Finish	9	4	Virginia Wade		8	11
Gentilhombre	9	4	African Dancer		8	10
Marquis de Sade	9	4	Pirate Dream		8	10
Scallywag	9	4	Quite Candid		8	10
Flying Water	9	3	Ranimer		8	10
Oats	9	3	Ubedizzy		8	10
Old Bill	9	3	Jellaby		8	9
Smuggler	9	3	Roses for the Star		8	9
Broxted	9	2	Sarania		8	9
Hawkberry	9	2	Strabo		8	9
Music Boy	9	2	Coin of Gold		8	8
Riboboy	9	2	Amboise		8	7
Gunner B	9	1	Centrocon		8	7
Kesar Queen	9	1	Danestic		8	7
Norfolk Air	9	1	Fluellen		8	7
Royal Boy	9	1	Intermission		8	7
Delta Song	9	0	Suffragette		8	7
Grey Baron	9	0	Dutch Treat		8	6
Star Bird	9	0	Illustrious Prince		8	6
General Ironside	8	12	Minstrel		8	6

Red Ruby	..	..	8	6	Lamb's Tale	..	..	7	13
Claudio Nicolai		..	8	5	Partridge Brook		..	7	13
Heaven Knows		..	8	5	So Sharp	..	..	7	13
Laughing Girl		..	8	5	Umabatha	..	..	7	13
Manilata	..	..	8	5	Beau Dutch	..	..	7	12
Rory's Rocket	..	..	8	5	Du Maurier	..	..	7	12
Rundontwalk	..	..	8	5	Man of Harlech		..	7	12
Shangamuzo	..	..	8	5	Pass the Port		..	7	12
Trigamy	..	..	8	5	Rowe Residence		..	7	12
Arapaho	..	..	8	4	Sweet Lad	..	..	7	12
Capricious	..	..	8	4	Bluffer	..	..	7	11
Everything Nice		..	8	4	Glorified	..	..	7	11
Ivory Girl	..	..	8	4	Great Idea	..	..	7	11
Kafue Park	..	..	8	4	Lucastown	..	..	7	11
Net Call	..	..	8	4	Private Line	..	..	7	11
Obstacle	..	..	8	4	The Hand	..	..	7	11
Palatable	..	..	8	4	True Shot	..	..	7	11
Sweet Nightingale		..	8	4	Welsh Flame	..	..	7	11
Tutu	..	..	8	4	Brands Hatch	..	..	7	10
Valuation	..	..	8	4	Double East	..	..	7	10
May Beck	..	..	8	3	Fall to Pieces	..	..	7	10
Silken Way	..	..	8	3	Frankie	..	..	7	10
Trasi's Son	..	..	8	3	Leventis	..	..	7	10
Gale Bridge	..	..	8	2	Palustra	..	..	7	10
Gilding	..	..	8	2	Rowantree	..	..	7	10
Ippolyti	..	..	8	2	Semper Nova	..	..	7	10
Lighter	..	..	8	2	Amun' Ra	..	..	7	9
London God	..	..	8	2	Fighting Lady		..	7	9
Lord Helpus	..	..	8	2	Lily Langtry	..	..	7	9
Mark Hush	..	..	8	2	Scott Joplyn	..	..	7	9
Memory Lane		..	8	2	Spring Frolic	..	..	7	9
Move Off	..	..	8	2	Aliante	..	..	7	8
Our Swallow	..	..	8	2	Ashabit	..	..	7	8
Sonnenblick	..	..	8	2	Bagshot	..	..	7	8
Spiranthes	..	..	8	2	Black Sabbath		..	7	8
St Joles	..	..	8	2	Broken Record		..	7	8
Urray Harry	..	..	8	2	Dikusa	..	..	7	8
Ashbro Laddo		..	8	1	Honey Blossom		..	7	8
Belfalas	..	..	8	1	My Fair Niece	..	..	7	8
Future Forest		..	8	1	Parent	..	..	7	8
Level Par	..	..	8	1	Renda	..	..	7	8
Prince Pepe	..	..	8	1	Caribbean	..	..	7	7
Shelahnu	..	..	8	1	Delayed Action		..	7	7
Silver Steel	..	..	8	1	Guido Fawkes		..	7	7
Solar	..	..	8	1	Honeypot Lane		..	7	7
Il Padrone	..	..	8	0	Mandate	..	..	7	7
Jimmy The Singer		..	8	0	Palmvinnia	..	..	7	7
Katie May	..	..	8	0	Ribarbaro	..	..	7	7
Plenty Spirit	..	..	8	0	Tug of War	..	..	7	7
Trusted	..	..	8	0	Yunkel	..	..	7	7

FOUR-YEAR-OLDS AND UPWARDS OF 1976

The following handicap, published on 25th November, is for information only. The figure shown after the name of the highest weighted horse represents the official assessment of its merit against a norm of 100.

Sagaro, 96	10	0	Overtown	8	9
Bruni	9	12	Peaceful	8	9
Lochnager	9	12	Roussalka	8	9
Orange Bay	9	12	Creetown	8	8
Rose Bowl	9	10	Battlecry	8	7
John Cherry	9	7	Harem	8	7
Sea Anchor	9	6	Sauceboat	8	5
Three Legs	9	6	Flame Tree	8	4
Honeyblest	9	5	Pal's Bambino	8	4
Polly Peachum	9	5	Hei'land Jamie	8	3
Red Regent	9	5	Ahdeek	8	2
Anne's Pretender	9	4	Berkeley Square	8	2
Jolly Good	9	4	Ribellaro	8	2
Roman Warrior	9	3	Albrighton	8	0
El Rastro	9	2	Alverton	7	13
Mr Bigmore	9	2	Echo Summit	7	12
Quiet Fling	9	2	The Hertford	7	12
Ardoon	9	1	Belper	7	11
Boldboy	9	1	Blaskette	7	11
Chil the Kite	9	1	Hard Attack	7	11
Fool's Mate	9	1	Don Fortune	7	10
Record Token	9	1	King's Bonus	7	10
Zimbalon	9	1	Rhodomantade	7	10
Raffindale	9	0	Grinling Gibbons	7	9
Coed Cochion	8	12	Janes Joker	7	9
Dominion	8	12	Last Tango	7	9
Duboff	8	12	Merry Kerry	7	9
Hillandale	8	12	Peranka	7	9
Import	8	12	Philominsky	7	9
Jumping Hill	8	12	Slim Jim	7	9
Swell Fellow	8	12	Horseguards	7	8
Bold Pirate	8	11	Lottogift	7	8
Major Green	8	11	Tiger Trail	7	8
Royal Match	8	11	Mister Geoffrey	7	7
All Friends	8	10	Nearly New	7	7
High Award	8	10	Regal Step	7	7
Lazenby	8	10	Rising Falcon	7	7
Marco Ricci	8	10	Shackle	7	7
Sandford Lady	8	10			

THE IRISH FREE HANDICAP

TWO-YEAR-OLDS OF 1976

The following are the weights allotted in the Madrid Free Handicap published on 25th November. The race is to be run over seven furlongs at the Curragh on 2nd April, 1977.

Cloonlara	9	7	Scops Owl	7	4
Godswalk	9	0	Success At Last	7	4
Padroug	8	13	Magyar Melody	7	4
The Minstrel	8	11	Star Of Erin	7	4
Pampapaul	8	10	Delicia	7	4
Nebbiolo	8	8	Autocratic	7	3
Orchestra	8	5	Ball Night	7	3
Captain James	8	5	Snap Happy	7	2
Lordedaw	8	2	Fairhaven Lady	7	2
Roman Charger	8	2	Mr Philosopher	7	2
Annacloy	8	0	Zelos	7	2
Rumson	7	13	Height Of Season	7	2
Piney Ridge	7	13	In The Clover	7	1
First Up	7	13	Uncle Pokey	7	1
Athlete's Foot	7	12	Yemshik	7	1
Readjust	7	12	Pat's Swallow	7	1
Regal Ray	7	11	Impious	7	1
Photo Belle	7	11	Gilwanigan	7	1
Sovereign Silver	7	11	Abbot's Walk	7	1
Ring Leader	7	11	Lady La Mancha	7	1
Digitalis	7	11	Sal	7	0
Glenturret	7	10	Evergreen Cedar	7	0
Irony	7	10	Commi Bug	7	0
Never A Lady	7	10	Phoenisian Pride	6	13
Claire's Slipper	7	9	Oakland	6	13
All Serene	7	8	Aristocracy	6	13
Nanticious	7	8	Sweet Mint	6	13
Western Tyranny	7	8	Great Sound	6	13
Slavonic	7	8	Moment To Remember	6	12
Princess Pixie	7	7	Opening Flight	6	12
Tamariscifolia	7	7	Lady Margaret	6	12
Swatchel	7	7	Mussorgsky	6	12
Laughing River	7	7	Hint-Hint	6	12
Run For Cover	7	6	Dike Wine	6	12
Haraka	7	6	Sallail	6	12
Swift Sensation	7	6	Welsh Steel	6	12
Space Ship	7	5	Lady Laura	6	12
Miller's Lass	7	5	Taj	6	12
Gallant Welsh	7	5	Rue Balzac	6	12
Mississippi	7	5	Fetching	6	11
Jeremy Fisher	7	5	Flower Grange	6	11
Quick J	7	5	Contalanco	6	11

Twilight God	..	6	11	Momentary Affair	..	6	8
Ida	..	6	11	Clodin Na Maun	..	6	8
Spaghetti Sauce	..	6	10	Gala Display ..	..	6	8
Musco	..	6	10	Dream World	..	6	8
Jean Fabre ..	..	6	10	Classic Line ..	..	6	8
House Bug ..	..	6	10	High Hollow ..	..	6	7
Borsalino ..	..	6	10	Lost Cove	..	6	7
Garonne ..	..	6	10	Kingly Sway ..	..	6	7
Reindeer Moss	..	6	10	Monaco Prince	..	6	7
Granny's Whistle	..	6	10	Independent Miss	..	6	7
Kenhora	..	6	10	Northern Wind	..	6	7
Soon Enough ..	..	6	10	Molto Vivace ..	..	6	7
Palm Bay ..	..	6	10	Bit Of The Holly	..	6	7
Asante Sana ..	..	6	10	Katayeff ..	..	6	7
Grateful King ..	..	6	10	Reign Supreme	..	6	7
Captain Gores	..	6	10	South Wind ..	..	6	7
Road Runner ..	..	6	9	Captain's Beauty	..	6	7
Sweet Rosaleen	..	6	9	Playfields ..	..	6	7
Rue Del Peru	..	6	9	Leapallez ..	..	6	7
Eiger Sanctions	..	6	9	Fir Sprig ..	..	6	7
Back Bailey ..	..	6	9	Schotia ..	..	6	7

THE FRENCH FREE HANDICAPS
TWO-YEAR-OLDS OF 1976

The following are the weights allotted in the Handicap Optional, published on 10th December. The race was run over a mile at Saint-Cloud on 26th February, 1977.

Blushing Groom	9	13	Guile Princess	8	7
Pharly	9	6	Proud Event	8	7
Amyntor	9	5	Rip Off	8	7
J. O. Tobin	9	5	Champ Libre	8	7
General	9	4	Virgin	8	7
Conglomerat	9	4	Lillan	8	7
King of Macedon	9	2	Le Despote	8	7
El Criollo	9	1	Miss Reasoning	8	7
Alpherat	9	1	Concerto Barocco	8	7
Water Boy	9	1	Bold Lady	8	7
Kamicia	9	0	Steel Band	8	7
Monseigneur	9	0	Lone Escape	8	6
Hermodore	9	0	Watership Down	8	6
Haneena	9	0	Rhino	8	6
Lady Mere	8	13	Oestrine	8	6
Assez Cuite	8	13	Alcaban	8	6
Edinburgh	8	13	Double Lane	8	5
Polyponder	8	13	Powderhound	8	5
Doctor's Choice	8	11	Rexana	8	5
Juge de Paix	8	11	Gamble On Gold	8	5
Blanc Rivage	8	11	Casaque	8	5
Seguro	8	10	Obolensky	8	5
Perello	8	10	Angarius	8	5
Balteus	8	10	Borodine	8	5
Numa Pompilius	8	10	Duchino	8	5
Lancastera	8	10	Istre	8	5
Silk Slipper	8	10	Bold Glow	8	5
French Venture	8	10	Damire	8	5
Zalitzing	8	10	Jaborandi	8	4
Manicero	8	9	Garofalo	8	4
Corviglia Boy	8	9	Countom	8	4
Doha	8	9	Bien Elevee	8	4
Command Freddy	8	9	Line Slippers	8	3
Zinov	8	9	Mefio	8	3
Shimnar	8	9	Mirkash	8	3
Aigle Blanc	8	9	Quiet Zone	8	3
Aerosol	8	9	Hatha	8	3
Sanedtki	8	9	Captain's Queen	8	3
Ymirkhan	8	9	Sunny Spring	8	3
River Dane	8	8	Adorant	8	3
Orchid Miss	8	8	Un Soleil	8	3
Darkeino	8	8	Silgar	8	3
Black Sulphur	8	8	Shanizadeh	8	3
Smoggy	8	8	Blondinette	8	3
Beaune	8	8	Armor	8	3

Champagne Girl	..	8 2	Guichardiere ..	..	7 12
Ogabi	..	8 2	Dungaree Doll..	..	7 12
Egmont.. ..	..	8 2	Blanat	..	7 11
Deep Deep ..	..	8 2	Franpote ..	..	7 11
Diligo ..	..	8 2	Joyeux Noel ..	..	7 11
Frosty Eskimo	..	8 2	Toubib ..	..	7 10
Pougatchof ..	..	8 2	Comtesse d'Ouilly	..	7 10
Irodos	..	8 0	Fabuleux Jane	..	7 10
River Sleep ..	..	8 0	Holiway ..	..	7 10
Man Alive ..	..	8 0	Catus	..	7 10
San Trop ..	..	8 0	Maximan ..	..	7 10
Abala	..	8 0	Jaldic	..	7 10
Silken Image	..	8 0	Fred the Ferryman	..	7 10
Tigre Cupide ..	..	8 0	Loco Mio ..	..	7 10
Jour Jack ..	..	8 0	Mandrake ..	..	7 9
Kapicua ..	..	7 13	Miramas ..	..	7 8
Gracious Djakao	..	7 13	Rasalhague ..	..	7 8
Calculus ..	..	7 13	Anida	..	7 8
Sharp Rocket ..	..	7 12	Itza	..	7 8
Nanterre ..	..	7 12	Bet On Belle ..	..	7 3
Solicitor ..	..	7 12	Calling	..	7 3
Le Royal Tor	..	7 12	Dey	..	7 1
Picketer ..	..	7 12	Scorched Earth	..	7 1
Bold Burglar ..	..	7 12	Fagness ..	..	6 13
Pockley ..	..	7 12	Beautiful Model	..	6 13
Kom Ombo ..	..	7 12			

THREE-YEAR-OLDS AND UPWARDS OF 1976

The following are the weights allotted in the Handicap Libre, published on 14th October. The race was run over 1½m at Longchamp on 24th October, 1976. The age of the horse appears in brackets, and the weight-for-age (between three-year-olds, and four-year-olds and upwards) is 4 lb.

Ivanjica (4) F ..	..	10 10	Full of Hope (6)	..	9 13
Ashmore (5) ..	..	10 4	Maitland (4) ..	..	9 13
Gravelines (4) ..	..	10 3	Trepan (4) ..	..	9 13
Youth (3) ..	..	10 3	Twig Moss (3)..	..	9 13
Noble Dancer (4)	..	10 2	Beau Buck (5) ..	..	9 12
Sagaro (5) ..	..	10 2	Olmeto (4) ..	..	9 12
Crow (3) ..	..	10 2	Rose Bowl (4) F	..	9 12
Citoyen (4) ..	..	10 1	Riverqueen (3) F	..	9 12
Liloy (5) ..	..	10 1	Admetus (6) ..	..	9 11
Kasteel (4) ..	..	10 0	Campo Moro (8)	..	9 11
Empery (3) ..	..	10 0	Dona Barod (4) F	..	9 11
Exceller (3) ..	..	10 0	Duke of Marmalade (5)		9 11
Malacate (3) ..	..	10 0	Ellora (4) ..	..	9 11
Pawneese (3) F	..	10 0	On My Way (6)	..	9 11
El Rastro (6) ..	..	9 13	Ramirez (5) ..	..	9 11

Name			Name		
Tip Moss (4)	9	11	Beau Dad (4)	9	4
Val du Fier (4)	9	11	Franconian (5)	9	4
Zein (4)	9	11	Such (5)	9	4
Condorcet (4)	9	10	Acoma (3) F	9	4
Infra Green (4) F	9	10	Campero (3)	9	4
Kemal (5)	9	10	Earth Spirit (3)	9	4
Knight Templar (6)	9	10	Lodovico (3)	9	4
Larkhill (4)	9	10	Moquerie (3) F	9	4
Libra's Rib (4)	9	10	Pollenka (3) F	9	4
Mistigri (5)	9	10	Sweet Rhapsody (3) F	9	4
Son of Silver (5)	9	10	Biloxi (4)	9	3
Twig (5)	9	10	Cavalcadour (4)	9	3
Lagunette (3) F	9	10	Gentil Dauphin (5)	9	3
French Hollow (4)	9	8	My Last Sovereign (4)	9	3
Hunza Dancer (4)	9	8	Shamsan (7)	9	3
Mittainvilliers (4)	9	8	Caron (3)	9	3
Tajeslie (5)	9	8	Happy Tim (3)	9	3
Arctic Tern (3)	9	8	Squash (3)	9	3
Grandchant (3)	9	8	Alluvium (4)	9	2
Radetzky (3)	9	8	Blue Vermillion (4)	9	2
Sarah Siddons (3) F	9	8	Gun Captain (4)	9	2
Secret Man (3)	9	8	Oreste (4)	9	2
Vitiges (3)	9	8	Prince Balthazar (5)	9	2
Ydja (3)	9	8	Comeram (3)	9	2
Luenge (6)	9	7	Elise Ma Belle (3) F	9	2
Mendip Man (4)	9	7	Guichet (3) F	9	2
Monsanto (4)	9	7	Indus Warrior (3)	9	2
Rouge Sang (4)	9	7	Kesar Queen (3) F	9	2
Saquito (4)	9	7	Nuclear Pulse (3)	9	2
Sea Sands (4) F	9	7	Ranimer (3) F	9	2
Iron Duke (3)	9	7	Tyrant's Vale (3) F	9	2
Manado (3)	9	7	Velino (3)	9	2
Brinkmanship (5)	9	6	Count Down (4)	9	1
Carolina Moon (4) F	9	6	Grand Trianon (4)	9	1
Djarvis (5)	9	6	Ile Flottante (4)	9	1
Gramy (5) F	9	6	Lanargo (4)	9	1
Kervic (5)	9	6	Sissoo (4)	9	1
Nurabad (4)	9	6	Uppercut (4)	9	1
Antrona (3) F	9	6	Far North (3)	9	1
Avaray (3)	9	6	Gold Nugget (3)	9	1
Diagramatic (3)	9	6	Nillaos (3)	9	1
Floressa (3) F	9	6	Roan Star (3)	9	1
Red Lord (3)	9	6	Fabliau (5)	9	0
Sir Montagu (3)	9	6	Royal Family (4) F	9	0
Suvannee (3) F	9	6	Valpolar (5)	9	0
Theia (3) F	9	6	Cheraw (3)	9	0
Fee du Lac (7) F	9	5	French Friend (3)	9	0
Inis Gloire (4)	9	5	Java Rajah (3)	9	0
Adam Van Vianen (3)	9	5	No No Nanette (3) F	9	0
Paint the Town (3) F	9	5	Pandour (3)	9	0
Ricco Boy (3)	9	5	Sharper (3)	9	0

Name			Name		
Sky's Sunny (3) F	9	0	Cap Martin (4)	8	7
Rise and Flight (4)	8	13	Show Boy (4) ..	8	7
Danestic (3)	8	13	Avril Cinq (3) ..	8	7
Empty Jest (3)	8	13	Beau Charles (3)	8	7
From Exile (3)..	8	13	Brouhaha (3) ..	8	7
Happy New Year (3) ..	8	13	Fashion Lad (3)	8	7
Wood Green (3)	8	13	Mescalero (3) ..	8	7
Zamp (3)	8	13	Raj Mahal (3)	8	7
Carvalin (4)	8	11	Sharazar (3)	8	7
Mendham (4) ..	8	11	Ohrid (6)	8	6
Mon Tapis (6)	8	11	Rebel God (5)	8	6
Satsuki (6)	8	11	Blue Mambo (3)	8	6
Surf (4)..	8	11	Echo (3) F	8	6
Anne Palatine (3) F	8	11	Hollygood (4)	8	5
Doll Dreams (3) F	8	11	Crackle (3)	8	5
Flash On (3) F	8	11	La Marelle (3) F	8	5
Fresnay (3)	8	11	Lady And Co (3) F	8	5
Kano (3)	8	11	Prosperantes (3)	8	5
No Turning (3)	8	11	Santalino (3)	8	5
Right Minx (3) F	8	11	Glorieuse (3) ..	8	4
Noces de Saphir (4)	8	10	Le Grand Monarque (3)	8	4
Quart de Vin (4)	8	10	Low Castle (3) F	8	4
Red Sun (4)	8	10	Saint Fort (3)	8	4
Rue de la Paix (4)	8	10	Sigune (3) F	8	4
Sebastiano (6) ..	8	10	Stella Reale (3) F	8	4
Fulgus (3)	8	10	Titra (6) F	8	3
Khalida (3) F ..	8	10	Caldrague (3) ..	8	3
Loveliest (3) F..	8	10	Come Up Smiling (3) F	8	3
Pamlico Gal (3) F	8	10	Djazir (3) F	8	3
Rose of Stanbul (3) F..	8	10	Spring Pear (3) F	8	3
Start The Game (3) F	8	10	Potiche (3) F	8	2
Tar Sienpre (3)	8	10	Spim (3)	8	2
Last Refrain (4)	8	9	In The Balance (4) F ..	8	0
Nord (4)	8	9	Caminel (3)	8	0
French Scandal (3)	8	9	Kaole (3)	8	0
Habitancum (3)	8	9	Dernier Tango (3)	7	13
Loosen Up (3)	8	9	Chere Madame (3) F ..	7	12
New Order (3)..	8	9	Pigsticker (3)	7	12
Versailles Prince (3) ..	8	9	Levy (4)	7	11
Via Venise (3) F	8	9	Fair Shake (3) F	7	10
Yule Log (3) ..	8	9	Montesquieu (3)	7	10
Extramidable (4)	8	8	Balakhirev (4)	7	7
Tourron (4)	8	8	Princess Mistletoe (4) F	7	6
Aberdeen Park (3)	8	8	Edictus (3)	7	3
Air du Nord (3)	8	8	Fine Danse (3) F	7	1
Crackao (3)	8	8	Musquaro (3) ..	7	1
Crispette (3) F..	8	8	Kamandah (3) F	7	0
Dacani (3) F ..	8	8	Hasty Whirl (3)	6	13
Imogene (3) F	8	8	Rimac (3)	6	13
Starina (3) F ..	8	8			

RACING ABROAD

1   PRIX PENELOPE   (3y)
1m 2½f

£11,655   Saint-Cloud 27 March

Pawneese 8-11
  YSaint-Martin 1
Loveliest 8-11 AGibert....2.2
Khalida 8-11 HSamani..1½.3
Lady and Co 8-11
  GRivases 1½.4
Ancholia 8-11 PPaquet....2½.5
Edition Nouvelle 8-11
  ELellouche..........s.hd.6
Princesse Flor 8-11
  APerrotta nk.7
Low Castle 8-11
  J-CDesaint ½.8
Ricabie 8-11 WPyers 8.9
Kashmirosa 8-11
  MPhilipperon 6.10
Janylou 8-11 JTaillard 0
Frenetique 8-11 FHead......0

24/10 PAWNEESE, 4/1 Khalida, Ricabie, 21/4 Ancholia, 17/2 Lady and Co, 9/1 Edition Nouvelle, 16/1 Frenetique, 22/1 Low Castle, 23/1 Princesse Flor, 26/1 Kashmirosa, 29/1 Loveliest, 39/1 Janylou.

D. Wildenstein (A. Penna) 12rn 2m 19.4 (Good).

2   PRIX GREFFULHE   (3y)
1m 2½f

£23,310   Longchamp 4 April

Youth 9-2 FHead..........1
Velino 9-2 YSaint-Martin.1½.2
Yule Log 9-2 LPiggott...1½.3
Versailles Prince 9-2
  PPaquet 1½.4
Comeram 9-2 WPyers.....5.5
Adam van Vianen 9-2
  JMercer 4.6
Iron Duke 9-2 J-CDesaint..8.7
Pier 9-2 ALequeux.......2½.8
Vitiges 9-2 GRivases......¾.9

2/1 Comeram, 4/1 Velino, Vitiges, 42/10 YOUTH, 33/4 Versailles Prince, 12/1 Iron Duke, 19/1 Pier, 22/1 Yule Log, 30/1 Adam van Vianen.

N. B. Hunt (M. Zilber) 9rn 2m 20.7 (Soft).

3   PRIX DE
FONTAINEBLEAU (3y) 1m

£11,655   Longchamp 4 April

Arctic Tern 9-2
  MPhilipperon 1
Roan Star 9-2 WCarson...¾.2

Wood Green 9-2
  WPyers 1½.3
Raj Mahal 9-2 GRivases...2.4
Sardo 9-2 PPaquet........4.5
Monsieur Dian 9-2
  SLeonardos 6.6
Red Lord 9-2 FHead.....1½.7
Kala Shikari 9-2
  YSaint-Martin 2½.8

5/4 Roan Star, 26/10 ARCTIC TERN, 25/4 Kala Shikari, 29/4 Sardo, 33/4 Red Lord, 19/2 Wood Green, 17/1 Raj Mahal, Monsieur Dian.

Mrs J. S. Knight (J. Fellows) 8rn 1m 45 (Soft).

4   PRIX DE BARBEVILLE
1m 7½f

£11,655   Longchamp 4 April

Sagaro 5-9-4 PPaquet......1
Mistigri 5-9-4 LPiggott..2½.2
Campo Moro 8-9-2
  RJallu ¾.3
Citoyen 9-9-0 GRivases....2.4
John Cherry 5-8-12
  GLewis 2.5
Beau Geste 4-8-12
  YJosse 2.6
Carvalin 4-8-12
  J-CDesaint 2.7
Prince Balthazar 5-8-12
  APerrotta..............4.8
Alluvium 4-8-12
  ELellouche..........s.nk.9
Good Point 4-8-12
  AGibert s.hd.10
Fair World 8-9-0
  MPhilipperon 0
Thoreau 5-8-12 FHead......0

6/4 Citoyen, 51/10 SAGARO, 15/2 Campo Moro, 9/1 Mistigri, 10/1 Good Point, 11/1 Thoreau, 15/1 Alluvium, 17/1 Carvalin, Fair World, 18/1 John Cherry, 37/1 Prince Balthazar, 40/1 Beau Geste.

G. A. Oldham (F. Boutin) 12rn 3m 33.1 (Soft).

5   PRIX DE RIS-ORANGIS 1m

£11,655   Evry 8 April

El Rastro 6-9-2
  GDubroeucq 1
Full of Hope 6-9-2
  WPyers 1.2
Trepan 4-9-2 PPaquet....¾.3
Mendip Man 4-9-2
  AGibert 1.4

839

Mark Anthony 4-9-2
  ALequeux ½.5
Dona Barod 4-8-13
  MPhilipperon ½.6
Brinkmanship 5-9-2
  FHead ¾.7
Ellora 4-9-2 JTaillard......2.8
Girandole 4-8-13 PAlafi....3.9
Girl Friend 4-8-13
  J-PLefevre 2.10

5/4 Full of Hope, 4/1 Trepan, 17/4 Brinkmanship, 53/10 EL RASTRO, 13/1 Dona Barod, 21/1 Mendip Man, Mark Anthony, 30/1 Girl Friend, 36/1 Girandole, 57/1 Ellora.

D. Wildenstein (A. Penna) 10rn 1m 39.6 (Dead).

6   PRIX IMPRUDENCE (3y) 7f

£4,662   Maisons-Laffitte 9 April

Guichet 9-2 PPaquet 1
Come Up Smiling 9-2
  GRivases ½.2
Twelve O'Clock 9-2
  J-CDesaint 3.3
Pretty Gift 9-2 JTaillard ..nk.4
Imogene 9-2 WPyers 6.5
Mardi Gras Rose 9-2
  J-PLefevre ¾.6
La Moisson 9-2
  YSaint-Martin 10.7

19/10 GUICHET, 2/1 Imogene, 15/4 La Moisson, 4/1 Come Up Smiling, 10/1 Twelve O'Clock, 21/1 Mardi Gras Rose, 22/1 Pretty Gift.

Mrs M. Miller (F. Boutin) 7rn 1m 27 (Good).

7   PRIX DJEBEL (3y)   7f

£4,662   Maisons-Laffitte 9 April

2 **Vitiges** 9-2 GRivases.......1
  Manado 9-2 PPaquet 1.2
  Sharazar 9-2 HSamani...5.3
  Tystan 9-2 MPhilipperon.hd.4
  Trois Quarts 9-2 FHead....2.5
  Trust a Native 9-2 WPyers.1.6
  Big Bazar 9-2 ALequeux...6.7
  Troms 9-2 AGibert......½.8

5/10 Manado, 52/10 VITIGES, 23/4 Sharazar, 9/1 Trust a Native, 14/1 Trois Quarts, 16/1 Troms, 22/1 Tystan, 27/1 Big Bazar.

Mme M. Laloum (G. Philippeau) 8rn 1m 25.8 (Good).

8   PRIX D'HARCOURT 1m 2f

£23,310   Longchamp 11 April

Liloy 5-9-0 YSaint-Martin..1
Ramirez 5-9-4 PPaquet...5.2
Infra Green 4-8-10
  JTaillard............s.hd.3
Son of Silver 5-9-0
  LPiggott hd.4
Kasteel 4-9-0 GRivases...1½.5
Ivanjica 4-9-1 FHead......2.6

Tajeslie 5-8-11 AGibert...2½.7
My Brief 7-9-2 AMurray...1.8
Henri le Balafre 4-9-4
  HSamani ¾.9
Sea Sands 4-8-13
  MPhilipperon 4.10
Condorcet 4-8-11
  J-CDesaint 0

5/4 Ivanjica, 15/4 Ramirez, 51/10 LILOY, 27/4 Kasteel, 13/1 Henri le Balafre, 19/1 Condorcet, 24/1 Infra Green, 25/1 Tajeslie, 26/1 Son of Silver, 27/1 Sea Sands, 49/1 My Brief.

D. Wildenstein (A. Penna) 11rn 2m 2.8 (Good to Firm).

9   PRIX DE LA GROTTE (3y) 1m

£11,655   Longchamp 11 April

Riverqueen 9-2 FHead.....1
KesarQueen 9-2
  YSaint-Martin 2½.2
Antrona 9-2 PPaquet.....2.3
Paint the Town 9-2
  MPhilipperon 1.4
Rose of Stanbul 9-2
  LPiggott s.hd.5
Luna Real 9-2 JTaillard...1½.6
Anne Palatine 9-2
  HSamani ¾.7
Dacani 9-2 J-CDesaint ..s.hd.8
Hopeful Bindy 9-2
  AMurray 2.9
Ricarelle 9-2 AGibert....2½.10
Poundcake 9-2 WPyers......0

7/4 Antrona, 4/1 Paint the Town, 54/10 RIVERQUEEN, 13/2 Anne Palatine, 15/2 Kesar Queen, 17/2 Poundcake, 16/1 Rose of Stanbul, 18/1 Luna Real, 33/1 Dacani, 41/1 Ricarelle, 57/1 Hopeful Bindy.

Mme A. Head (C. Datessen) 11rn 1m 39.6 (Good to Firm).

10 PRIX DARU (3y) 1m 2½f

£23,310   Longchamp 19 April

2* **Youth** 9-2 FHead........1
  Danestic 9-2 PEddery....4.2
  French Scandal 9-2
  YJosse 1½.3
  Aberdeen Park 9-2
  WPyers ½.4
2 Pier 9-2 HSamani........hd.5
  Ricco Boy 9-2
  LPiggott 2.6
  Artonius 9-2 GRivases....4.7
  Far North 9-2
  MPhilipperon ½.8
  Mouron Rouge 9-2
  ALequeux 1½.9
  All Majesty 9-2
  PChelef 15.10

17/10 YOUTH, 5/2 Far North and All Majesty, 17/4 French Scandal,

Aberdeen Park, 21/4 MouronRouge, 11/1 Ricco Boy, 18/1 Artonius, 19/1 Pier, 22/1 Danestic.

N. B. Hunt (M. Zilber) 10rn 2m 9.8 (Good to Firm).

11 PRIX VANTEAUX (3y)
1m 1½f

£11,655 Longchamp 19 April

Theia 9-2 FHead...........**1**
Elise Ma Belle 9-2
  AGibert hd.**2**
Sweet Rhapsody 9-2
  PPaquet............1½.**3**
Pamlico Gal 9-2
  GDubroeucq ½.4
1² Loveliest 9-2 LPiggott ..s.hd.5
La Jolie Femme 9-2
  MPhilipperon 1½.6
Spring Pear 9-2
  J-CDesaint 2½.7

Evens THEIA, 5/2 Pamlico Gal, 15/4 Sweet Rhapsody, 11/1 Loveliest, 15/1 Elisa Ma Belle, 16/1 La Jolie Femme, 27/1 Spring Pear.

Baroness de Lopez-Tarragoya (R. Touflan) 7rn 2m 4.6 (Good to Firm).

12 PRIX DE GUICHE (3y)
1m 1¾f

£11,655 Longchamp 19 April

Grandchant 9-2
  MPhilipperon **1**
No Turning 9-2
  J-CDesaint 1.**2**
7³ **Kano** 9-2 GRivases.......2.**3**
Sharazar 9-2 HSamani....nk.4
Vital Hunter 9-2
  JTaillard hd.5
French Swanee 9-2
  YJosse ns.6
Habitancum 9-2
  AMurray 1½.7
3 Sardo 9-2 PPaquet........½.8
Happy New Year 9-2
  GDubroeucq hd.9
3³ Wood Green 9-2 WPyers..3.10
Laelius 9-2 MDelmas.......0
Westos 9-2 J-PLefevre......0
Apres Demain 9-2
  PEddery 0
3 Monsieur Dian 9-2
  SLeonardos 0

2/1 Kano and Laelius, 5/2 No Turning, 17/4 French Swanee and Wood Green, 15/2 Sharazar, 19/2 Apres Demain, 13/1 GRAND-CHANT, 19/1 Sardo, 33/1 Habitancum, 35/1 Monsieur Dian, 36/1 Vital Hunter, 58/1 Happy New Year, 70/1 Westos.

Mme P. Ribes (J. Cunnington, jnr) 14rn 2m 1.3 (Good to Firm).

13 GRAND PRIX D'EVRY
1½m

£17,482 Evry 24 April

Tip Moss 4-9-2 JDupin.....**1**
Saquito 4-9-0 FHead.....½.**2**
Rouge Sang 4-9-0
  GDubroeucq s.nk.**3**
Franconian 5-9-0
  MPhilipperon s.nk.4
Dhaubasix 5-9-2 AGibert.1½.5
Nord 4-9-2 MDepalmas...½.6
Sissoo 4-9-0 ELellouche..1½.7
Shamaraan 4-9-0 HSamani 2½.8
Beau Buck 5-9-2 J-CDesaint 2.9
Greycliff 4-9-0 PPaquet..10.10

2/1 Beau Buck, 13/4 Shamaraan, 9/2 Rouge Sang, 13/2 Saquito, 29/4 Dhaubasix, 13/1 Sissoo, 15/1 Franconian, 18/1 Greycliff, 26/1 TIP MOSS, Nord.

P. Guichou (N. Pelat) 10rn 2m 38.2 (Good to Firm).

14 POULE D'ESSAI DES
POULAINS (3y) 1m

£34,965 Longchamp 25 April

3 **Red Lord** 9-2 FHead.......**1**
3² **Roan Star** 9-2 WCarson.2½.**2**
2 **Comeram** 9-2 WPyers.s.hd.**3**
  Empery 9-2 LPiggott......½.4
3* Arctic Tern 9-2
  MPhilipperon s.nk.5
Marbret 9-2 RJallu......1½.6
The Chaplain 9-2
  J-CDesaint s.hd.7
7 Tystan 9-2 HSamani.....hd.8
Tepozteco 9-2 PPaquet.....2.9
12 French Swanee 9-2 YJosse.2.10
Hittite Glory 9-2 PDurr....11

9/4 Arctic Tern, 15/4 Roan Star, 9/2 Comeram and French Swanee, 54/10 RED LORD, 13/2 Empery, 10/1 Tepozteco, 15/1 The Chaplain, 24/1 Hittite Glory, 31/1 Tystan, 41/1 Marbret.

J. Wertheimer (A. Head) 11rn 1m 42.3 (Good).

15 PRIX NOAILLES (3y) 1m 3f

£23,310 Longchamp 25 April

Twig Moss 9-2 AMurray....**1**
Caron 9-2 MPhilipperon..½.**2**
Pandour 9-2 AGibert.....¾.**3**
Avaray 9-2 FHead........¾.4
2³ Yule Log 9-2 LPiggott.....½.5
Tom Fine 9-2 ALequeux..½.6
10 Pier 9-2 APerrotta........½.7
Pappagallo 9-2 WPyers..s.hd.8
Robertissimo 9-2
  PPaquet...........s.hd.9
Roselier 9-2 YJosse.......2.10
Lancret 9-2 ABadel.........0
Be There 9-2 GDubroeucq...0

Evens Avaray, 11/2 Yule Log, 6/1
Pandour, 11/1 Caron, Roselier, 12/1
TWIG MOSS, Pier, Robertissimo,
18/1 Tom Fine, 26/1 Pappagallo,
51/1 Lancret, 72/1 Be There.

R. Brooke (C. Milbank) 12rn
2m 20.5 (Good).

16 PRIX JEAN PRAT 1m 7½f

£17,482   Longchamp   25 April

4	**Citoyen** 4-9-0 GRivases	1
	Luenge 6-8-12	
	GDubroeucq	.........2½.2
4³	**Campo Moro** 8-9-2	
	RJallu	...............2.3
4★	Sagaro 5-9-4 PPaquet	.....2½.4
	Monde Soyeux 4-8-12	
	ABadel	..............3.5
	Lysimaque 4-8-12 HSamani	2.6
4²	Mistigri 5-9-4 LPiggott	....10.7
	Aldebaran 5-8-12 AGibert.1½.8	
4	Fair World 8-9-0	
	MPhilipperon	.........4.9
	Etincelbury 4-8-12	
	JTaillard	.............8.10

Evens Sagaro, 11/2 Campo Moro,
Mistigri, 64/10 CITOYEN, 15/2
Luenge, 15/1 Aldebaran, 16/1
Fair World, 20/1 Lysimaque, 41/1
Monde Soyeux, 58/1 Etincelbury.

Baron de Rede (J. de Choubersky)
10rn 3m 23.2 (Good).

17 PREMIO PARIOLI (3y) 1m

£23,570   Rome   11 April

	Ovac 9-2 SFancera	1
	Kruger 9-2 VPanici	.......¾.2
	Roberto Guiscardo 9-2	
	LBietolini	.............2.3
	Norberto 9-2 MAndreucci..1.4	
	Filomaco 9-2 GDoleuze	....2.5
	Jinnetti 9-2 CDeMonte	....2.6
	Rocambole 9-2 EMazzoni..2.7	
	Gim Toro 9-2 DCampeis..1½.8	
	Casteggio 9-2 GGuignard..½.9	
	Deimos 9-2 GDettori	.....1.10
	Scellino 9-2 GFois	11
	Fiumicino 9-2 MMassimi...12	

6/4 Deimos, 7/2 Casteggio, 4/1
Filomaco, 5/1 Roberto Guiscardo,
11/2 Kruger, 6/1 OVAC, 10/1
Scellino, 18/1 Norberto, 30/1 Fiumicino, 33/1 Jinnetti, 40/1 Gim Toro,
100/1 Rocambole.

Scuderia Metauro (U. Pandolfi)
12rn 1m 42 (Good).

18 PREMIO EMANUELE
FILIBERTO (3y) 1¼m

£18,070   Milan   18 April

	Duchamp 9-2 GDettori	1
	Le Michel 9-2 LBietolini..¾.2	
	Sir Bull 9-2 RFestinesi	....1.3
	Mahr 9-2 VPanici	........1½.4

	Crespin Gunner 9-2	
	PAgus	.................1.5
	Wolfermann 9-2 ADiNardo.8.6	
	Chirone 9-2 CWigham	.....3.7
	Shiseido 9-2 JMassard	.....2.8
	Sciro 9-2 GVerricelli	......3.9
	Amber Return 9-2	
	AVincis	.............10.10

6/4 DUCHAMP, 7/2 Mahr, 5/1 Sir
Bull and Amber Return, 8/1 Le
Michel and Chirone, 9/1 Sciro, 10/1
Wolfermann, 12/1 Shiseido, 15/1
Crespin Gunner.

Scuderia Cieffedi (S. Cumani)
10rn 2m 4.2 (Firm).

19 PREMIO REGINA ELENA
(3y) 1m

£23,570   Rome   25 April

	Dir El Gobi 8-11	
	GDoleuze	1
	Giannina 8-11 BTaylor...5.2	
	Miss Benedicta 8-11	
	SAtzori	...............½.3
	Rosina Schindler 8-11	
	MAndreucci	.........1½.4
	Amerusa 8-11 RSannino...½.5	
	Sagan 8-11 GDettori	......6.6
	Lipsia 8-11 SFancera	.....1½.7
	Native Fleet 8-11	
	LBietolini	.............12.8
	Leda Sterling 8-11	
	RFestinesi	.........left.9

2/1 DIR EL GOBI, 9/4 Amerusa,
5/2 Sagan, 11/4 Rosina Schindler,
3/1 Leda Sterling, 10/1 Giannina,
12/1 Miss Benedicta, 14/1 Lipsia,
100/1 Native Fleet.

Razza di Vedano (F. Regoli) 9rn
1m 44.4 (Heavy).

20 POULE D'ESSAI DES
POULICHES (3y) 1m

£34,965   Longchamp   2 May

9★	**Riverqueen** 9-2 FHead	1
	Suvannee 9-2 PPaquet	....3.2
	Sky's Sunny 9-2	
	GDubroeucq	.....nk.3
	Start the Game 9-2	
	AMurray	.........hd.4
9	Paint the Town 9-2	
	MPhilipperon	.......¾.5
6★	Guichet 9-2 LPiggott	....ns.6
	Net Call 9-2 WCarson	....3.7
11	Pamlico Gal 9-2	
	YSaint-Martin	.........8.8
6³	Twelve O'Clock 9-2	
	J-CDesaint	.............5.9
	Sweet Habitat 9-2	
	GRivases	.............ns.10
	Jurassic 9-2 WPyers	......p.u.

8/10 RIVERQUEEN, 19/4 Pamlico
Gal, 29/4 Suvannee, 10/1 Paint the
Town, 12/1 Jurassic, 13/1 Guichet,
14/1 Start the Game, 25/1 Twelve

842

O'Clock, 33/1 Sweet Habitat, 46/1 Net Call, 49/1 Sky's Sunny.

Mme A. Head (C. Datessen) 11rn 1m 38.6 (Good).

21 PRIX GANAY 1m 2½f
£46,620   Longchamp   2 May

8³	**Infra Green** 4-8-13	
	JTaillard	1
8	**Kasteel** 4-9-2 GRivases. s.hd.	2
8	**Ivanjica** 4-8-13 FHead...nk.	3
	Rose Bowl 4-8-13	
	WCarson	½.4
13*	Tip Moss 4-9-2 JDupin.s.hd.	5
8²	Ramirez 5-9-2 PPaquet....	3.6
	Free Round 4-9-2 WPyers..	1.7
8	Henri le Balafre 4-9-2	
	HSamani	s.hd.8
	Hunza Dancer 4-9-2	
	AGibert	nk.9
	Irish Star 4-9-2	
	GStarkey	2.10
	Easy Regent 4-9-2	
	GDubroeucq	11

5/2 Ramirez, 13/4 Rose Bowl, 4/1 Ivanjica, 10/1 Henri le Balafre, Easy Regent, 11/1 Free Round, 12/1 INFRA GREEN, Kasteel, 15/1 Tip Moss, 52/1 Hunza Dancer, 58/1 Irish Star.

Mme J. Pochna (E. Bartholomew) 11rn 2m 14.8 (Good).

22 PRIX DU MUGUET 1m
£11,655   Saint-Cloud   6 May

5	**Ellora** 4-9-0 FHead	1
5*	**El Rastro** 6-9-2	
	YSaint-Martin	ns.2
5²	**Full of Hope** 6-9-0	
	WPyers	1½.3
5³	Trepan 4-9-0 PPaquet..s.nk.4	
5	Dona Barod 4-8-9	
	MPhilipperon	½.5
8	Son of Silver 5-9-2	
	LPiggott	hd.6
5	Mark Anthony 4-9-2	
	AMurray	hd.7
	Blacksmith 4-8-10	
	GDubroeucq	½.8
	Lanargo 4-8-10 ALequeux.½.9	
5	Brinkmanship 5-9-2	
	GDoleuze	3.10
	Kronenkranich 4-9-2	
	DRichardson	0
	Irena 4-8-11 AGibert	0
	Impulsivo 4-8-8 JPall	0
	Royal Family 4-8-5	
	GRivases	0

3/1 El Rastro, Son of Silver, 11/2 Full of Hope, 7/1 Trepan, 37/4 Blacksmith, 12/1 Lanargo, 13/1 Brinksmanship, 20/1 Mark Anthony, 22/1 Dona Barod, 23/1 Royal Family, 25/1 Impulsivo, 30/1

Irena, 35/1 Kronenkranich, 37/1 ELLORA.

R. N. Tikkoo (A. Breasley) 14rn 1m 37.8 (Good).

23 PRIX DAPHNIS (3y) 1m 1f
£9,324   Evry   8 May

12	**Happy New Year** 9-2	
	J-CDesaint	1
12	**Habitancum** 9-2	
	ALequeux	½.2
12²	**No Turning** 9-2 AMurray nk.3	
	Happy Tim 9-2 PAuge....½.4	
14	Empery 9-2 FHead	½.5
12	Vital Hunter 9-2	
	JTaillard	hd.6
	Rec the Toolhouse 9-2	
	AGibert	hd.7
12	Sharazar 9-2 HSamani....¾.8	
12	Monsieur Dian 9-2	
	SLeonardos	3.9
	Indus Warrior 9-2	
	YSaint-Martin	½.10
	Power Drive 9-2 PPaquet....0	
14	French Swanee 9-2 WPyers..0	
14	Tystan 9-2 MPhilipperon....0	

6/4 Empery, 6/1 No Turning, 29/4 French Swanee, 31/4 Sharazar, 9/1 Vital Hunter, 19/2 Rec the Toolhouse, 12/1 Indus Warrior, 13/1 Power Drive 21/1 Tystan, 30/1 Happy Tim, Monsieur Dian, 33/1 HAPPY NEW YEAR, 53/1 Habitancum.

W. R. Hawn (J. Cunnington) 13rn 1m 52.2 (Good).

24 PRIX HOCQUART (3y) 1½m
£23,310   Longchamp   9 May

12*	**Grandchant** 9-2	
	MPhilipperon	1
	Lodovico 9-2 ELellouche.¾.2	
15*	**Twig Moss** 9-2 AMurray.½.3	
	From Exile 9-2	
	J-CDesaint	2.4
	Almo 9-2 GRivases....½.5	
	Levantome 9-2 FHead....½.6	
	Val du Diable 9-2	
	APerrotta	3.7
15	Lancret 9-2 ABadel......1½.8	
	Loredo 9-2 PPaquet....10.9	

6/4 GRANDCHANT, 11/4 Twig Moss, 7/1 From Exile, 8/1 Lodovico, Levantome, 11/1 Almo, 13/1 Loredo, 25/1 Val du Diable, 33/1 Lancret.

Mme P. Ribes (J. Cunnington, jnr) 9m 2m 35.3 (Firm).

25 PRIX DE SAINT-GEORGES 5f
£10,489   Longchamp   9 May

5	**Girl Friend** 4-8-13	
	J-PLefevre	1

Polly Peachum 5-9-5
EHide ns.2
Realty 4-9-8 RJallu.......1.3
5 Mendip Man 4-9-2
LPiggott 1½.4
Nagin 4-9-5
YSaint-Martin hd.5
Baradaan 3-8-8 HSamani.1½.6
Widerhall 4-9-2 AGibert..¾.7
9 Dacani 3-8-8 J-CDesaint.d.h.7
Diffusion 3-8-11 FHead...½.9
Harem 4-9-5 AMurray...¾.10
Gold Nugget 3-8-8 WPyers.11

9/4 Nagin, 5/2 Realty and Diffusion, 17/4 Mendip Man, 25/4 Polly Peachum, 7/1 Gold Nugget, 12/1 Baradaan, 13/1 Dacani, 15/1 GIRL FRIEND, Widerhall, 35/1 Harem.

D. W. Molins (P. Lallie) 11rn 56.6 sec. (Firm).

26 IRISH 1,000 GUINEAS (3y)
1m

£22,596.50 The Curragh 14 May
Sarah Siddons 9-0
CRoche 1
Clover Princess 9-0
TCarmody 1.2
Lady Singer 9-0 GCurran.1.3
Krassata 9-0 WSwinburn..2½.4
Night Vision 9-0
FMorby 2½.5
Bellavanta 9-0 RCarroll...nk.6
Glanoe 9-0 GDettori.....2½.7
Galana 9-0 LPiggott....3.8
Capricious 9-0
MKennedy 1.9
Flower Petals 9-0
GMcGrath ½.10
Serencia 9-0 DHogan...1½.11
I've A Bee 9-0 TMurphy ...12
Sassalya 9-0 RFParnell......13
Sunbird 9-0 JMercer.......14

11/4 Sunbird, 4/1 Serencia, 9/2 SARAH SIDDONS, 5/1 Galana, 10/1 I've A Bee, Krassata, 14/1 Night Vision, 25/1 Glanoe, Lady Singer, 33/1 Flower Petals, 66/1 Clover Princess, 100/1 others.

Mrs J. R. Mullion (P. J. Prendergast) 14rn 1m 43.2 (Good).

27 IRISH 2,000 GUINEAS (3y)
1m

£30,444.50 The Curragh 15 May
Northern Treasure 9-0
GCurran 1
14³ **Comeram** 9-0 LPiggott s.hd.2
Lucky Wednesday 9-0
CRoche 1.3
Northern View 9-0 JRoe...3.4
14 The Chaplain 9-0
AMurray ¾.5
Dunmurry Boy 9-0
JSeagrave 6.6

Rhenus 9-0 JCorr.........6.7
Festive Morn 9-0 TMurphy ¼.8
Poacher's Moon 9-0
GMcGrath 1½.9
Wolverlife 9-0 RFParnell.½.10
Brandon Hill 9-0
RCarroll 1¼.11
Arapaho 9-0 JMercer....2½.12
Patris 9-0 WCarson......4.13
Gododin 9-0 MKennedy.1½.14
Captain Memory 9-0
WSwinburn..........10.15
Tampa 9-0 BRaymond 16
Northern Spring 9-0
GDettori...............17

2/1 Comeram, 5/1 Northern Spring, 7/1 Patris, 15/2 Arapaho, 10/1 The Chaplain, 14/1 Northern View, 18/1 Wolverlife, 20/1 Lucky Wednesday, Poacher's Moon, 22/1 Festive Morn, 25/1 Dunmurry Boy, 33/1 NORTHERN TREASURE, 40/1 Tampa, 66/1 Rhenus, 100/1 others.

A. D. Brennan (K. Prendergast) 17rn 1m 42.8 (Dead).

28 PRIX CLEOPATRE (3y)
1m 2½f

£11,655 Saint-Cloud 15 May
1★ **Pawneese** 8-13
YSaint-Martin 1
11² **Elise Ma Belle** 8-7
AGibert 2½.2
Flash On 8-7 RJallu......2.3
1 Low Castle 8-7
GDubroeucq ns.4
Moquerie 8-7 FHead....¾.5
1³ Khalida 8-7 HSamani...nk.6
20 Paint the Town 8-11
JTaillard 5.7
Daisy Mae 8-7 J-CDesaint 1½.8
11³ Sweet Rhapsody 8-7
PPaquet 1½.9
Cavalerie Legere 8-7
GRivases 3.10
9 Rose of Stanbul 8-13
ALequeux 0
Fiquefleur 8-7 J-PLefevre...0
Sea Venture 8-7
MPhilipperon 0

9/10 PAWNEESE, 17/4 Elise Ma Belle, 29/4 Sweet Rhapsody, 9/1 Khalida, Paint the Town, 12/1 Moquerie, 21/1 Daisy Mae, 28/1 Low Castle, Rose of Stanbul, 35/1 Sea Venture, 36/1 Cavalerie Legere, 61/1 Fiquefleur, 62/1 Flash On.

D. Wildenstein (A. Penna) 13rn 2m 16 (Good).

29 PRIX LUPIN (3y) 1m 2½f
£58,275 Longchamp 16 May
10★ **Youth** 9-2 FHead 1
14 **Arctic Tern** 9-2
MPhilipperon ¾.2

23 **Empery** 9-2 WPyers......1.3
14² Roan Star 9-2
    YSaint-Martin 4.4
15³ Pandour 9-2 AGibert....½.5
10² Danestic 9-2 PEddery....½.6
7² Manado 9-2 PPaquet.....2.7
15 Yule Log 9-2 LPiggott....1½.8
15 Pier 9-2 APerrotta........2.9
    Over to You 9-2 JMercer.½.10
    Oilfield 9-2 ALequeux.......0
    Val de Soie 9-2
    GDubroeucq 0

4/10 YOUTH, Empery and Oilfield, 4/1 Roan Star, 31/4 Manado, 16/1 Arctic Tern, 17/1 Danestic, 18/1 Pandour, 22/1 Yule Log, 37/1 Val de Soie, 45/1 Pier, 53/1 Over to You.

N. B. Hunt (M. Zilber) 12rn 2m 13.6 (Good).

30 PRIX DE LA JONCHERE
    (3y) 1m
£13,986 Longchamp 16 May
15 **Avaray** 9-1 FHead.........1
10 Ricco Boy 8-7 LPiggott..nk.2
    Fulgus 8-7
    YSaint-Martin s.nk.3
    Blue Mambo 8-7
    J-CDesaint ½.4
12 Sardo 8-7 PPaquet......1½.5
    Yeoman du Roi 8-7
    ALequeux......s.nk.6
23 Monsieur Dian 8-11
    SLeonardos ¾.7
    Bert the Sea Wave 8-7
    WPyers 4.8
    Pahlot 8-7 GDubroeucq..¾.9
23 Tystan 8-7 MPhilipperon.½.10

6/4 AVARAY, 13/4 Fulgus, 11/2 Pahlot, 13/2 Ricco Boy, 11/1 Bert the Sea Wave, 15/1 Sardo, 16/1 Yeoman du Roi, 17/1 Monsieur Dian, 21/1 Tystan, 22/1 Blue Mambo.

J. Wertheimer (A. Head) 10rn 1m 40.7 (Good).

31 PRIX SAINT-ALARY (3y)
    1¼m
£40,792 Longchamp 23 May
20★ **Riverqueen** 8-11 FHead....1
11★ **Theia** 8-11 HSamani......¾.2
9³ **Antrona** 8-11 LPiggott.s.nk.3
20² Suvannee 8-11 PPaquet..nk.4
9² Kesar Queen 8-11
    AMurray 1½.5
    Bienvenida 8-11
    MPhilipperon ½.6
    Flying Water 8-11
    YSaint-Martin 2.7
    Prix 8-11 WPyers........2.8
28 Rose of Stanbul 8-11
    ALequeux 5.9

9 Poundcake 8-11
    SLeonardos 10.10

Evens RIVERQUEEN, 2/1 Flying Water, 11/2 Theia, 10/1 Suvannee, 13/1 Prix and Poundcake, 24/1 Antrona, 25/1 Kesar Queen, 32/1 Bienvenida, 51/1 Rose of Stanbul.

Mme A. Head (C. Datessen) 10rn 2m 7.1 (Good).

32 PRIX DU CADRAN 2¼m
£34,965 Longchamp 23 May
16 **Sagaro** 5-9-2 PPaquet......1
    Kemal 5-9-2
    YSaint-Martin 3.2
16★ **Citoyen** 4-9-2 GRivases..¾.3
16 Mistigri 5-9-2 LPiggott...¾.4
21 Henri le Balafre 4-9-2
    HSamani.........s.nk.5
    Coed Cochion 4-9-2 PCook.2.6
16 Monde Soyeux 4-9-2
    ABadel 10.7
    Tudor Crown 5-9-2
    AKimberley dist.8
    Le Bavard 5-9-2 AGibert.p.u.0
    Shantallah 4-9-2 BTaylor.p.u.0

21/10 SAGARO, 9/4 Citoyen, 11/2 Le Bavard, 6/1 Kemal, 13/2 Henri le Balafre, 12/1 Mistigri, 19/1 Monde Soyeux, 22/1 Shantallah, 49/1 Coed Cochion, 98/1 Tudor Crown.

G. A. Oldham (F. Boutin) 10rn 4m 20.3 (Good).

33 PRIX LA FORCE (3y) 1¼m
£11,655 Longchamp 23 May
    Malacate 8-11 PPaquet.....1
20 **Start the Game** 8-6
    AMurray 1½.2
23 **Happy Tim** 8-9 BTaylor.1½.3
23² Habitancum 8-9
    ALequeux ns.4
3 Raj Mahal 8-9 GRivases.nk.5
23★ Happy New Year 8-13
    J-CDesaint s.hd.6
    Tonofras 8-9
    YSaint-Martin 1½.7
29 Oilfield 8-9 WPyers.......½.8

8/10 MALACATE, 7/2 Tonofras, 21/4 Start the Game, 9/1 Habitancum, 12/1 Happy New Year, 13/1 Happy Tim, 17/1 Oilfield, 22/1 Raj Mahal.

Mme M-F. Berger (F. Boutin) 8rn 2m 11.9 (Good).

34 PRIX DE L'ESPERANCE
    (3y) 1m 7f
£11,655 Longchamp 30 May
    Secret Man 8-11 PPaquet...1
    Campero 8-11 FHead...hd.2
    Fresnay 8-11 J-CDesaint..4.3

Beau Charles 8-11
GChirurgien ½.4
Selante Stanelta 8-11
WPyers ½.5
Avril Cinq 8-11
J-PLefevre s.nk.6
Tar Sienpre 8-11
YSaint-Martin 1½.7
Carvello 8-11 GLewis ns.8
Dom Bethune 8-11
GDubroeucq...........4.9
Sure Death 8-11 AGibert.6.10
Aubrac 8-11 JTaillard.......0
Bops 8-11 MPhilipperon.....0

13/10 SECRET MAN, 11/2 Beau Charles, 13/2 Dom Bethune, 15/2 Campero, 17/2 Tar Sienpre, 12/1 Fresnay, 14/1 Selante Stanelta, 17/1 Carvello, 19/1 Sure Death, 30/1 Aubrac, 37/1 Avril Cinq, 38/1 Bops.

J.-L. Lagardere (F. Boutin) 12rn 3m 21 (Dead).

---

35   PRIX DOLLAR   1m 1¾f

£29,137   Longchamp   30 May
21²   **Kasteel** 4-9-0 AMurray.....1
22²   **El Rastro** 6-9-3
       YSaint-Martin 2.2
21   **Tip Moss** 9-3
       J-CDesaint ½.3
22³   Full of Hope 6-9-0
       WPyers ½.4
22   Dona Barod 4-8-9
       MPhilipperon s.hd.5
21   Ramirez 5-9-6 PPaquet..hd.6
21³   Ivanjica 4-9-3 FHead......2.7
       Jolly Good 4-9-0 GLewis.1½.8
22*   Ellora 4-9-0 GRivases...s.nk.9
21   Free Round 4-9-3
       GDubroeucq..........2.10
       Wronsky 4-9-0 HSamani....0
22   Irena 4-8-11 AGibert.......0

27/10 KASTEEL, 3/1 Ivanjica, 6/1 Ramirez, 13/2 El Rastro, 15/2 Tip Moss, 19/2 Full of Hope and Free Round, 11/1 Jolly Good, 20/1 Dona Barod, 25/1 Wronsky, 26/1 Ellora, 39/1 Irena.

Baron T. de Zuylen (J. de Choubersky) 12rn 2m 5.9 (Dead).

---

36   PRIX DU PALAIS ROYAL
       7f

£11,655   Longchamp   30 May
       Gravelines 4-9-4
       YSaint-Martin 1
25*   **Girl Friend** 4-9-4
       J-PLefevre 2.2
       Monsanto 4-9-7 WPyers..1½.3
25   Mendip Man 4-9-4
       AGibert 1½.4
       Baly Rockette 4-9-10
       AMurray ½.5

Thieving Demon 3-8-8
       FDurr s.nk.6
14   Marbret 3-8-8 RJallu 1½.7
       Blue Spark 3-8-8
       ESauvaget ½.8
25³   Realty 4-9-7 FHead hd.9
25   Nagin 4-9-1 PPaquet nk.10
       Ouialco 3-8-5
       MPhilipperon 11

2/1 Realty, 5/2 GRAVELINES and Monsanto, 23/4 Blue Spark and Nagin, 6/1 Girl Friend, 27/4 Thieving Demon, 31/4 Marbret, 12/1 Mendip Man, 27/1 Ouialco, 34/1 Baly Rockette.

D. Wildenstein (A. Penna) 11rn 1m 25.7 (Dead).

---

37   PRIX DE SANDRINGHAM
       (3y) 1m

£12,315   Longchamp   3 June
20   **Guichet** 9-0 PPaquet.......1
31   **Kesar Queen** 9-2 FHead..1.2
       Ranimer 8-10 AGibert....2.3
25   Dacani 8-12 APerrotta.....2.4
       J'Habite en France 8-8
       J-CDesaint 1½.5
20³   Sky's Sunny 9-2 AMurray.1½.6
1   Edition Nouvelle 8-12
       ELellouche 3.7
       Babylone Lady 8-8
       VPanici 3.8

5/4 Kesar Queen, 19/10 GUICHET, 9/2 Ranimer, 35/4 Sky's Sunny, 15/1 J'Habite en France, 26/1 Babylone Lady, 32/1 Edition Nouvelle, 34/1 Dacani.

Mrs M. Miller (F. Boutin) 8rn 1m 40.5 (Good).

---

38   PRIX JEAN PRAT   (3y)
       1m 1f

£24,630   Chantilly   6 June
       Earth Spirit 9-2
       YSaint-Martin 1
30²   **Ricco Boy** 9-2 LPiggott..ns.2
30³   **Fulgus** 9-2 PPaquet......1½.3
       New Order 9-2
       MPhilipperon 1.4
33   Happy New Year 9-2
       J-CDesaint 2.5
14*   Red Lord 9-2 FHead ½.6
24   From Exile 9-2 HSamani.s.hd.7
33²   Start the Game 8-13
       AMurray ns.8
       Sol Dewan 9-2 AGibert...hd.9

4/10 Red Lord, 33/10 EARTH SPIRIT, 11/1 Ricco Boy, 12/1 Fulgus, 15/1 From Exile, 16/1 Start the Game, 23/1 Happy New Year, 25/1 Sol Dewan, 42/1 New Order.

D. Wildenstein (A. Penna) 9rn 1m 51.5 (Good).

39 PRIX DU JOCKEY-CLUB
(3y) 1½m

£110,835   Chantilly   6 June

29★ **Youth** 9-2 FHead **1**
24³ **Twig Moss** 9-2 AMurray..3.**2**
33★ Malacate 9-2 PPaquet ¾.3
Ydja 9-2 DEstienne......1¼.4
24★ Grandchant 9-2
MPhilpperon.........hd.5
33³ Happy Tim 9-2 BTaylor..2½.6
24 Loredo 9-2 MDepalmas....2.7
33 Oilfield 9-2 ALequeux ¾.8
29² Arctic Tern 9-2 GRivases.2½.9
29 Pandour 9-2 AGibert ½.10
29 Pier 9-2 APerrotta 0
2² Velino 9-2 WPyers..........0
29 Yule Log 9-2 GDubroeucq...0
29 Roan Star 9-2 WCarson.....0
10 Aberdeen Park 9-2
LPiggott 0
10³ French Scandal 9-2
HSamani 0
24² Lodovico 9-2 J-CDesaint 0
Cheraw 9-2 YSaint-Martin...0

19/10 YOUTH and Oilfield, 5/1
Cheraw, 23/4 Grandchant, 15/2
Arctic Tern, 8/1 Malacate, 13/1
Aberdeen Park and French Scandal,
14/1 Lodovico, 19/1 Velino, 36/1
Twig Moss, Pandour, 38/1 Roan
Star, 58/1 Yule Log, 65/1 Happy
Tim, 67/1 Pier, 90/1 Ydja, Loredo.

N. B. Hunt (M. Zilber) 18rn
2m 27.4 (Good).

40 PRIX DU LYS   (3y) 1½m

£12,315   Chantilly   6 June

Exceller 9-2 GDubroeucq...**1**
Brouhaha 9-2 PPaquet....6.**2**
15² Caron 9-2 MPhilpperon.nk.3
Saint Fort 9-2 J-CDesaint.1½.4
10 Mouron Rouge 9-2
ALequeux ½.5
Four Spades 9-2 AMurray..6.6
12³ Kano 9-2 GRivases......1½.7
Count 9-2 LPiggott 6.8

19/10 EXCELLER, 11/4 Caron,
Kano, 29/4 Mouron Rouge, 8/1
Saint Fort, 12/1 Count, 29/1
Brouhaha, 30/1 Four Spades.

N. B. Hunt (F. Mathet) 8rn
2m 28.8 (Good).

41 PRIX JEAN DE
CHAUDENAY   1½m

£30,517   Saint-Cloud   7 June

Maitland 4-9-2
YSaint-Martin **1**
13² Saquito 4-9-2 FHead.....2.**2**
8 **Condorcet** 4-9-2
AGibert 1½.3
34² Campero 3-8-1
GDubroeucq s.nk.4

16³ Campo Moro 8-9-4
RJallu hd.5
Diagnostic 3-8-4
PPaquet 3.6
Battle Song 5-9-4 WPyers..8.7
29 Over to You 3-8-3
MPhilpperon 6.8

9/10 MAITLAND, 4/1 Saquito,
6/1 Battle Song, 7/1 Diagnostic, 9/1
Campo Moro, 13/1 Campero, Over
to You, 18/1 Condorcet.

D. Wildenstein (A. Penna) 8rn
2m 28.1 (Good).

42 DERBY ITALIANO (3y) 1½m

£55,625   Rome   16 May

Red Arrow 9-2 WCarson...**1**
Jerez 9-2 GDettori.....3½.**2**
Gallio 9-2 MCipolloni..3½.3
17² Kruger 9-2 VPanici......2.4
Malherbe 9-2 MAndreucci.½.5
17³ Roberto Guiscardo 9-2
LBietolini ½.6
19★ Dir El Gobi 8-11
GDoleuze 1½.7
18 Wolfermann 9-2 SAtzori ..2.8
17 Norberto 9-2 GPisa......1½.9
19 Leda Sterling 8-11
RFestinesi............1.10
Linceo 9-2 ATortorella......0
Dioscuro 9-2 CWigham......0
17 Fiumicino 9-2 CMarinelli....0
Rheometer 9-2 GPucciatti...0
Nanteuil 9-2 OPessi.........0
Tricesimo 9-2 APattera......0
17 Filomaco 9-2 GGuignard....0
18 Sciro 9-2 GVerricelli........0
17 Deimos 9-2 RAntonuzzi.....0
17★ Ovac 9-2 SFancera........0
17 Casteggio 9-2 MMassimi...21

6/4 Malherbe and Nanteuil, 2/1
Dir El Gobi and Casteggio, 5/1
Gallio, 10/1 Ovac, 14/1 Jerez,
15/1 RED ARROW, 18/1 Leda
Sterling, 33/1 Rheometer, 40/1
Roberto Guiscardo, 50/1 Sciro,
100/1 Dioscuro, Norberto, Filomaco, Deimos, Tricesimo, Wolfermann, Fiumicino.

Scuderia Diamante (A. Pandolfi)
21rn 2m 29.4 (Good).

43 OAKS D'ITALIA (3y) 1m 3f

£34,765   Milan   23 May

Claire Valentine 8-11
GFois **1**
Sierra Morena 8-11
CForte ¾.**2**
42 **Dir El Gobi** 8-11
GDoleuze 5.3
19 Sagan 8-11 GDettori....hd.4
Simpaty 8-11 MMattei...2½.5
Lady Beck 8-11
GGuignard s.hd.6
Giaguara 8-11 VDiMaggio.2.7

847

Gabella 8-11 LBietolini...1½.8
19 Rosina Schindler 8-11
MAndreucci 1.9
Love You 8-11 VPanici..1½.10
Marmellata 8-11
ADiNardo 3.11
Gaiana 8-11 MCipolloni..3.12
2/1 CLAIRE VALENTINE, 3/1
Sierra Morena and Gaiana, 7/2
Lady Beck, 4/1 Dir El Gobi, 6/1
Sagan, 7/1 Rosina Schindler, 10/1
Marmellata, 20/1 Love You, 25/1
Gabella, 30/1 Simpaty, 33/1 Gia-
guara.

Razza Ascagnano (G. Miliani)
12rn 2m 18.2 (Good).

44 PREMIO PRESIDENTE
DELLA REPUBLICA 1½m

£31,605 Rome 27 May

Shamsan 7-9-6 LBietolini..1
Record Run 5-9-6 EEldin.1.2
Duke of Marmalade 5-9-6
SFancera..............2.3
15 Robertissimo 3-8-4
GDoleuze 7.4
Gino Trojan 4-9-4 BJovine.2.5
Bahadir 6-9-6 APuca....1½.6
Oltre il Fiume 3-8-4
GDettori 2½.7
Paulus Potter 4-9-4 GPisa..3.8
Magibrook 4-9-4 OPessi...3.9
Marcus 4-9-4 RAntonuzzi.3.10

4/5 Record Run, 6/4 Duke of
Marmalade and Marcus, 7/1
Bahadir, 8/1 Robertissimo, 9/1
SHAMSAN, 10/1 Magibrook, 12/1
Oltre il Fiume, 20/1 Paulus Potter,
33/1 Gino Trojan.

Scuderia Bierregi (V. Bignami)
10rn 2m 4 (Good).

45 GRAN PREMIO
D'ITALIA (3y) 1½m

£38,245 Milan 2 June

42* Red Arrow 9-2 VPanici...1
Art Style 9-2 ADiNardo.d.h.1
42³ Gallio 9-2 MCipolloni...1½.3
2 Versailles Prince 9-2
PPaquet 5.4
18² Le Michel 9-2 LBietolini..1½.5
18 Mahr 9-2 SAtzori........2.6
42² Jerez 9-2 SFancera.......2.7
Coltinger 9-2 GFois......2½.8
42 Casteggio 9-2 GDoleuze...3.9
Diogene 9-2CWigham 4.10

5/4 Coltinger, 11/5 ART STYLE,
9/4 RED ARROW, 4/1 Versailles
Prince, 9/2 Jerez, 11/2 Gallio, 6/1
Le Michel and Diogene, 10/1
Mahr, 12/1 Casteggio.

Red Arrow—Scuderia Diamante
(A. Pandolfi). Art Style—Scuderia
La Cascina (G. Benetti) 10rn
2m 29.4 (Firm).

46 PRIX DU CHEMIN DE
FER DU NORD 1m

£12,315 Chantilly 10 June

35 Full of Hope 6-9-4 WPyers..1
36* Gravelines 4-9-4
YSaint-Martin nk.2
22 Son of Silver 5-9-4
LPiggott ¾.3
22 Lanargo 4-9-2 ALequeux..1½.4
Mister Dip 5-8-12
RJallu s.hd.5
35 Ellora 4-9-4 FHead.......½.6
8/10 Gravelines, 37/10 FULL OF
HOPE, 5/1 Son of Silver, 10/1
Ellora, 15/1 Mister Dip, 22/1
Lanargo.

C. F. Delecroix (G. Delloye) 6rn
1m 38.4 (Dead).

47 PRIX DE DIANE (3y) 1m 2½f

£86,205 Chantilly 13 June

28* Pawneese 9-2
YSaint-Martin 1
31* Riverqueen 9-2 FHead..1½.2
Lagunette 9-2 PPaquet...3.3
31³ Antrona 9-2 LPiggott.....2.4
26* Sarah Siddons 9-2
CRoche s.hd.5
31² Theia 9-2 GDubroeucq...½.6
28² Elise Ma Belle 9-2
AGibert ¾.7
28³ Flash On 9-2 RJallu...s.hd.8
31 Prix 9-2 WPyers..........1.9
Denia 9-2 GRivases......½.10
31 Bienvenida 9-2
MPhilipperon 11
Evens Riverqueen, 18/10 PAWN-
EESE, 19/4 Theia, 15/1 Antrona,
22/1 Denia, 23/1 Prix, 28/1 Lagunette, 30/1 Elise Ma Belle, 50/1
Sarah Siddons, 54/1 Flash On,
71/1 Bienvenida.

D. Wildenstein (A. Penna) 11rn
2m 9 (Dead).

47A GRAN PREMIO DI
MILANO 1½m

£54,230 Milan 20 June

13³ Rouge Sang 4-9-6
YSaint-Martin 1
45* Art Style 3-8-6
ADiNardo 1½.2
44³ Duke of Marmalade
5-9-8 SFancera ¾.3
21 Irish Star 4-9-6 GStarkey.2½.4
45 Le Michel 3-8-6 GDettori.2.5
Rue de la Paix 4-9-6
JMassard 2.6
45³ Gallio 3-8-6 MCipolloni...4.7
Aubry 3-8-6 TizianaSozzi..4.8
Firehorn 5-9-8 FDessi.....4.9

6/4 Art Style, 7/4 ROUGE SANG,

4/1 Duke of Marmalade, 6/1 Gallio, 8/1 Irish Star, 10/1 Le Michel, 15/1 Rue de la Paix, 66/1 Firehorn, 100/1 Aubry.

D. Wildenstein (A. Penna) 9rn 2m 29.4 (Good).

48 PRIX DU GROS-CHENE 5f

£11,083   Chantilly   22 June

3 **Kala Shikari** 3-9-0
   YSaint-Martin **1**
   Arch Sculptor 3-8-10
   AMurray 2.2
25² **Polly Peachum** 5-9-5
   EHide hd.3
36 Mendip Man 4-9-2
   LPiggott ¾.4
   Brave Panther 3-8-10
   PSimonin 1.5
   Harrapan Seal 3-8-7
   AGibert 1.6
9 Anne Palatine 3-8-7
   GDubroeucq s.nk.7
25 Diffusion 3-8-13 FHead....¾.8
   Gyrmiss 3-8-9 ABadel.....5.9
9/10 Polly Peachum, 2/1 KALA SHIKARI, Arch Sculptor, Brave Panther, Harrapan Seal (all grouped), 17/4 Mendip Man, 35/4 Anne Palatine, 9/1 Diffusion, 32/1 Gyrmiss.

R. N. Tikkoo (A. Breasley) 9rn 1m 2.2 (Dead).

49 IRISH SWEEPS DERBY
(3y) 1½m

£66,016   The Curragh   26 June

39³ **Malacate** 9-0 PPaquet......**1**
29³ **Empery** 9-0 LPiggott....2½.2
27* **Northern Treasure** 9-0
   GCurran ¾.3
   Hawkberry 9-0 CRoche....¾.4
10 Far North 9-0 WPyers...2½.5
27 Brandon Hill 9-0
   RFParnell nk.6
   Niebo 9-0 TMurphy......5.7
   Navarre 9-0 TCarberry...2½.8
   Finsbury 9-0 RCarroll.....2.9
39 Oilfield 9-0 ALequeux....4.10
23³ No Turning 9-0
   AMurray hd.11
   Decent Fellow 9-0
   WSwinburn 1½.12
   Mart Lane 9-0
   GMcGrath 2.13
   Riot Helmet 9-0
   MissJMorgan 4.14
   Talarias 9-0 DHogan.....4.15
   King Mousse 9-0
   MKennedy 6.16
   Imperial Fleet 9-0 JRoe..12.17
4/5 Empery, 5/1 MALACATE, 9/1 Far North, 10/1 Northern Treasure, Hawkberry, Niebo, 20/1 Mart Lane, 33/1 No Turning, 40/1 Decent

Fellow, 100/1 Brandon Hill, Oilfield, 200/1 others.

Mme M-F. Berger (F. Boutin) 17rn 2m 31.2 (Firm).

50 PRIX DE MALLERET (3y)
1½m

£14,778   Longchamp   27 June

47 **Antrona** 8-11 PPaquet......**1**
37³ **Ranimer** 8-11 AGibert....2.2
   Floressa 8-11 J-PLefevre..¾.3
   Doll Dreams 8-11
   YSaint-Martin ½.4
6 Imogene 8-11 WPyers.....3.5
47 Denia 8-11 GRivases.....2½.6
9 Luna Real 8-11
   AMurray 6.7
28 Low Castle 8-11
   J-CDesaint 6.8
1 Lady and Co 8-11 FHead...¾.9
31 Rose of Stanbul 8-11
   ALequeux 2.10
   Noah's Acky Astra 8-11
   LPiggott 11
9/10 ANTRONA, 21/4 Ranimer, 6/1 Doll Dreams, 15/2 Imogene, 12/1 Denia, 13/1 Low Castle, 14/1 Floressa, 22/1 Luna Real, 29/1 Lady and Co, 31/1 Rose of Stanbul, 38/1 Noah's Acky Astra.

G. A. Oldham (F. Boutin) 11rn 2m 7 (Good).

51 GRAND PRIX DE PARIS
(3y) 1m 7½f

£98,522   Longchamp   27 June

40* **Exceller** 8-11
   YSaint-Martin **1**
34* **Secret Man** 8-11
   PPaquet 4.2
40³ **Caron** 8-11
   MPhilipperon 1½.3
39 Ydia 8-11 DEstienne......4.4
24 Levantome 8-11 FHead....4.5
   Blue Marlin 8-11 GRivases.1.6
34³ Fresnay 8-11 J-CDesaint...½.7
   Valuation 8-11 JMercer...10.8
39 Yule Log 8-11 LPiggott....nk.9
4/10 EXCELLER, 15/4 Secret Man, 12/1 Ydia, Valuation, 13/1 Fresnay, 17/1 Caron, 22/1 Levantome, 24/1 Blue Marlin, 34/1 Yule Log.

N. B. Hunt (F. Mathet) 9rn 3m 20.5 (Good).

52 PRIX D'ISPAHAN 1m 1½f

£36,946   Longchamp   27 June

46* **Full of Hope** 6-9-6 WPyers..**1**
35 **Ivanjica** 4-9-5 FHead....2½.2
38² **Ricco Boy** 3-8-9LPiggott..½.3
35² El Rastro 6-9-6
   YSaint-Martin 1.4
35 Ramirez 5-9-6 PPaquet..s.nk.5
38³ Fulgus 3-8-9 MPhilipperon.¾.6

849

Evens El Rastro, 7/2 Ivanjica, 4/1 Ramirez, 13/2 Ricco Boy, 71/10 FULL OF HOPE, 11/1 Fulgus.

C. F. Delecroix (G. Delloye) 6rn 1m 54.4 (Good).

53 PRIX DE LA PORTE MAILLOT 7f

£14,778   Longchamp   27 June

46³	**Son of Silver** 5-9-4 AGibert	1
27²	**Comeram** 3-8-8 LPiggott	ns.2
	My Last Sovereign 4-9-2 ALequeux	s.nk.3
	Boldboy 6-9-2 JMercer	nk.4
36²	Girl Friend 4-9-1 J-PLefevre	s.nk.5
36³	Monsanto 4-9-2 YSaint-Martin	½.6
	Karanas 3-8-8 J-LKessas	s.nk.7
	Record Token 4-9-2 PEddery	s.nk.8
	Folie de Grandeur 5-9-2 YJosse	s.nk.9
	Raga Navarro 4-9-7 PPaquet	½.10

9/4 Comeram, 15/4 Record Token, 9/2 Monsanto, 11/2 Girl Friend, 13/2 SON OF SILVER, 37/4 Folie de Grandeur, 12/1 Raga Navarro, 15/1 Boldboy, 25/1 My Last Sovereign, 30/1 Karanas.

Mrs J. Davis (A. Paus) 10rn 1m 21.6 (Good).

54 GRAND PRIX DE SAINT-CLOUD 1m 4½f

£70,922   Saint-Cloud   4 July

47²	**Riverqueen** 3-8-6 FHead	1
	Ashmore 5-9-8 WPyers	½.2
35³	**Tip Moss** 4-9-8 PPaquet	2.3
	Libra's Rib 4-9-8 WCarson	¾.4
32³	Citoyen 4-9-8 GRivases	½.5
	Quiet Fling 4-9-8 LPiggott	nk.6
41*	Maitland 4-9-8 YSaint-Martin	3.7
13	Beau Buck 5-9-8 J-CDesaint	5.8

Evens Ashmore and Maitland, 19/10 RIVERQUEEN, 31/4 Quiet Fling, 8/1 Tip Moss, 33/4 Citoyen, 15/1 Beau Buck, 30/1 Libra's Rib.

Mme A. Head (C. Datessen) 8rn 2m 34.9 (Good).

55 PRIX MAURICE DE NIEUIL 1m 4½f

£17,731   Saint-Cloud   14 July

41³	**Condorcet** 4-9-0 PPaquet	1
41²	**Saquito** 4-9-2 FHead	2.2
	Gramy 5-9-3 J-CDesaint	½.3
	Admetus 6-9-0 MPhilipperon	½.4
39	Cheraw 3-8-3 GDubroeucq	s.nk.5
41	Battle Song 5-9-6 AMurray	2.6
54³	Saint Fort 3-8-0 AGibert	2½.7
	Tip Moss 4-9-6 YSaint-Martin	4.8
34	Tar Sienpre 3-8-3 ALequeux	1½.9
34	Carvello 3-8-0 J-PLefevre	4.10
	Loosen Up 3-8-5 LPiggott	11

5/4 Tip Moss, 13/4 Saquito, 19/4 Admetus, 8/1 Cheraw, 39/10 CONDORCET, 19/1 Gramy, Saint Fort, 20/1 Battle Song, 23/1 Loosen Up, 35/1 Tar Sienpre, 61/1 Carvello.

P. Le Blan (J. Laumain) 11rn 2m 39.2 (Good).

56 IRISH GUINNESS OAKS (3y) 1½m

£31,559   The Curragh   17 July

47³	**Lagunette** 9-0 PPaquet	1
47	**Sarah Siddons** 9-0 9-0 CRoche	2.2
26	**I've A Bee** 9-0 LPiggott	½.3
26	Krassata 9-0 JRoe	s.hd.4
	Acoma 9-0 YSaint-Martin	hd.5
28	Paint the Town 9-0 MPhilipperon	2½.6
	Countess Eileen 9-0 TCarmody	s.hd.7
43*	Claire Valentine 9-0 GFois	¾.8
	African Dancer 9-0 RFParnell	hd.9
26	Sassalya 9-0 TMurphy	½.10
26³	Lady Singer 9-0 GCurran	hd.11
	Laughing Girl 9-0 AMurray	1.12
50³	Floressa 9-0 J-PLefevre	2.13
	Vanishing Act 9-0 WSwinburn	1½.14
	Ceili Mor 9-0 RCarroll	¾.15
26	Flower Petals 9-0 GMcGrath	8.16
	Karabice 9-0 PBoothman	3.17
	Mingoon Bell 9-0 ASofley	8.18

9/4 Acoma, 3/1 LAGUNETTE, 4/1 Sarah Siddons, 12/1 I've A Bee, 16/1 Laughing Girl, 20/1 Paint the Town, 25/1 African Dancer 33/1 Claire Valentine, Floressa, Krassata, Lady Singer, 50/1 Ceili Mor, Countess Eileen, Vanishing Act, 250/1 others.

M. Berghgracht (F. Boutin) 18rn 2m 33.1 (Good).

57 PRIX EUGENE ADAM
(3y) 1¼m

£23,640   Saint-Cloud   18 July

	Crow 8-9 YSaint-Martin....	**1**
30*	**Avaray** 8-13 FHead ...s.hd.	**2**
	French Friend 8-9	
	WCarson	.2.3
39	Happy Tim 8-11 YJosse...¼.4	
39	Arctic Tern 8-13	
	MPhilipperon ½.5	
7*	Vitiges 8-11 GRivases 2½.6	
	Riboboy 8-13 LPiggott ...nk.7	
	Zamp 8-13 PSimonin......2.8	
39	Pandour 8-9 AGibert.....nk.9	
	Dom Sully 8-11	
	GDubroeucq 2½.10	
	Quest 8-11 PPaquet........0	
33	Habitancum 8-11	
	AMurray 0	
51	Yule Log 8-9 J-CDesaint....0	
39	Roan Star 8-9 WPyers......0	

13/4 Arctic Tern, 39/10 CROW, 21/4 Vitiges, 13/2 Roan Star, 15/2 Avaray, 12/1 French Friend, Happy Tim, Pandour, Dom Sully, 19/1 Habitancum, 23/1 Quest, 25/1 Zamp, 36/1 Riboboy, 39/1 Yule Log.

D. Wildenstein (A. Penna) 14rn 2m 8.5 (Good).

58 PRIX MESSIDOR   1m

£14,184   Maisons-Laffitte   22 July

35	**Dona Barod** 4-8-6	
	MPhilipperon...........	**1**
53	**Monsanto** 4-9-0	
	YSaint-Martin 1½.2	
46²	**Gravelines** 4-9-0	
	WPyers ¾.3	
53²	Comeram 3-8-2	
	AMurray 3.4	
	Duboff 4-9-1 EHide......nk.5	
22	Royal Family 4-8-6	
	GRivases 1½.6	
53	Raga Navarro 4-9-4	
	PPaquet s.nk.7	
53³	My Last Sovereign 4-8-9	
	AGibert hd.8	
46	Lanargo 4-8-9	
	JTaillard ½.9	
	Falusi 4-8-9 J-CDesaint...2.10	
	Dealer's Ace 4-9-0	
	GDubroeucq 0	
53	Folie de Grandeur 5-8-9	
	YJosse 0	
	Uppercut 4-8-9 J-LKessas...0	

6/4 Monsanto and Gravelines, 7/2 DONA BAROD, 4/1 Comeram, 12/1 Dealer's Ace, 16/1 Folie de Grandeur, 19/1 Lanargo, 21/1 Duboff, My Last Sovereign, 24/1 Falusi, 25/1 Raga Navarro, 35/1 Royal Family, 37/1 Uppercut.

A. Blasco (J. Cunnington, jnr) 13rn 1m 40.6 (Good).

59 PRIX ROBERT PAPIN (2y)
5½f

£23,640   Maisons-Laffitte   25 July

	Blushing Groom 8-11	
	HSamani...............	**1**
	River Dane 8-9	
	GWMoore ¾.2	
	Sunny Spring 8-11	
	GDettori 8.3	
	Egmont 8-11 GDoleuze....¾.4	
	King of Macedon 8-11	
	MPhilipperon 2.5	
	Juge de Paix 8-11	
	YSaint-Martin 1½.6	
	Philipotte 8-9 ABadel......2.7	
	Super Bowl 8-11	
	MDepalmas 4.8	
	Man Alive 8-11	
	J-CDesaint 1½.9	
	Boldtrapsky 8-11	
	LPiggott ¾.10	
	Tanairdo 8-11 BRipert 0	
	Lady Kinz 8-9 APerrotta....0	

5/2 Juge de Paix,32/10BLUSHING GROOM, 21/4 Boldtrapsky, 11/2 King of Macedon, 17/2 Super Bowl, 15/1 River Dane, 16/1Sunny Spring, 18/1 Lady Kinz, 19/1 Man Alive, 21/1 Egmont, 37/1 Tanairdo, 60/1 Philipotte.

H. H. Aga Khan (F. Mathet) 12rn 1m 4.8 (Good).

60 PRIX DE MINERVE (3y)
1½m

£9,112   Evry   29 July

56	**Acoma** 8-7 YSaint-Martin..	**1**
50	**Lady and Co** 8-7	
	WPyers 5.2	
	Naughty Marcia 8-7	
	GDubroeucq 1½.3	
1	Princesse Flor 8-7 ABadel...4	
	Sigune 8-7 FHead..........5	
28	Khalida 9-0 HSamani...s.hd.6	
	Sifana 8-7 APerrotta.....2.7	
28	Sea Venture 8-7	
	MPhilipperon 10.8	

7/10 ACOMA, 17/4 Sigune, Khalida, 17/2 Naughty Marcia, 13/1 Sifana, 14/1 Lady and Co, 20/1 Sea Venture, 22/1 Princesse Flor.

Sigune finished fourth, a short head behind Naughty Marcia, and a neck in front of Princesse Flor, but was put down a place after a stewards' inquiry.

D. Wildenstein (A. Penna) 8rn 2m 34.3 (Good).

61 PRIX D'ASTARTE   1m

£11,390   Deauville   31 July

	Carolina Moon 4-9-2	
	YSaint-Martin 1	

58* **Dona Barod** 4-9-8
    MPhilipperon 2.2
58 **Royal Family** 4-9-2
    GRivases ....$\frac{3}{4}$.3
    Tyrant's Vale 3-8-13
    FHead ....2$\frac{1}{2}$.4
1   Frenetique 3-8-8
    GDoleuze ....$\frac{1}{2}$.5
37* Guichet 3-9-1 PPaquet...2$\frac{1}{2}$.6
    No No Nanette 3-8-10
    HSamani 3.7
37 Sky's Sunny 3-8-8
    AMurray 5.8
50 Imogene 3-8-8 WPyers....4.9

2/1 Guichet, 4/1 Dona Barod, 46/10
CAROLINA MOON, 5/1 Tyrant's
Vale, 7/1 Imogene, 12/1 No No
Nanette, 16/1 Sky's Sunny, 17/1
Royal Family, 19/1 Frenetique.

Mme A. Speelman (M. Clement)
9rn 1m 42 (Dead).

62 PRIX MAURICE DE
    GHEEST   6$\frac{1}{2}$f
£10,250   Deauville   1 August
53 **Girl Friend** 4-9-3
    GDubroeucq 1
48² **Arch Sculptor** 3-8-8
    YSaint-Martin 1.2
36 **Realty** 4-8-8 FHead hd.3
29 Manado 3-8-7 PPaquet ...hd.4
    Three Legs 4-9-6
    LPiggott hd.5
    Be Tuneful 4-8-8
    AKimberley ....$\frac{3}{4}$.6
25 Gold Nugget 3-8-7
    MPhilipperon ....$\frac{3}{4}$.7
    Princess Jacqueline 4-9-1
    GDoleuze 2.8
    Tarik 6-8-11 AGibert....hd.9

9/4 Manado, 3/1 Realty, 4/1 Arch
Sculptor, 56/10 GIRL FRIEND,
19/2 Three Legs, 10/1 Tarik, 13/1
Gold Nugget, 16/1 Be Tuneful,
21/1 Princess Jacqueline.

D. W. Molins (P. Lallie) 9rn
1m 23.2 (Dead).

63 PRIX KERGORLAY 1m 7f
£17,084   Deauville   1 August
54 **Citoyen** 4-9-8 GRivases....1
    Olmeto 4-9-6 PPaquet....3.2
57³ **French Friend** 3-8-7
    LPiggott 2.3
4   Prince Balthazar 5-9-4
    ABadel 4.4
    Stand Hill 3-8-9 AMurray.10.5

13/10 CITOYEN, 2/1 Olmeto,
French Friend, 12/1 Prince Balthazar, Stand Hill.

Baron de Rede (J. de Choubersky) 5rn 3m 9.40 (Dead).

64 PRIX DE MENNEVAL (3y)
             1m 5$\frac{1}{2}$f
£9,112   Deauville   7 August
51² **Secret Man** 9-4 PPaquet....1
41 **Campero** 9-4 WPyers..s.nk.2
    Air du Nord 9-1
    LPiggott 6.3
34 Beau Charles 9-1
    GChirurgien nk.4
55 Carvello 8-12 GDubroeucq.4.5
    Fils Royal 8-12
    MPhilipperon 8.6

6/10 SECRET MAN, 2/1 Campero,
9/1 Air du Nord, Fils Royal, 11/1
Beau Charles, 15/1 Carvello.

J-L. Lagardere (F. Boutin) 6rn
3m 4.2 (Dead).

65 PRIX JACQUES LE
    MAROIS   1m
£28,474   Deauville   8 August
58³ **Gravelines** 4-9-2
    GWMoore 1
    Radetzky 3-8-8 WCarson.hd.2
57 **Vitiges** 3-8-8 GRivases..d.h.2
62 Manado 3-8-8 PPaquet...hd.4
46 Ellora 4-9-2 AMurray....hd.5
57² Avaray 3-8-8 FHead....s.hd.6
52 El Rastro 6-9-2
    YSaint-Martin nk.7
62* Girl Friend 4-8-13
    GDubroeucq 1.8
61* Carolina Moon 4-8-13
    ALequeux 3.9
52* Full of Hope 6-9-2
    WPyers ....$\frac{1}{2}$.10
58 My Last Sovereign 4-9-2
    AGibert 0
61² Dona Barod 4-8-13
    MPhilipperon 0
52³ Ricco Boy 3-8-8 LPiggott....0

2/1 GRAVELINES and El Rastro,
5/1 Full of Hope, 21/4 Vitiges, 6/1
Avaray, 13/2 Manado, 9/1 Dona
Barod, 12/1 Girl Friend, 22/1 Ricco
Boy, 24/1 Radetzky, 41/1 Carolina
Moon, 46/1 Ellora, 66/1 My Last
Sovereign.

D. Wildenstein (A. Penna) 13rn
1m 35.1 (Dead).

66 PRIX DE LA COTE
    NORMANDE   (3y)   1$\frac{1}{4}$m
£13,667   Deauville   12 August
2   **Iron Duke** 8-9 HSamani....1
55 **Cheraw** 8-9
    YSaint-Martin ....1$\frac{1}{2}$.2
47 **Theia** 8-10 GDubroeucq..$\frac{3}{4}$.3
57 Zamp 8-9 AMurray......1$\frac{3}{4}$.4
    Great Idea 8-13
    GWMoore s.hd.5
38 Happy New Year 8-13
    J-CDesaint ....$\frac{1}{2}$.6

Emeric 8-9 GRivases......2.7
49 Far North 8-9MPhilipperon¾.8
44 Robertissimo 8-13
GDoleuze 6.9
Lac Ontario 8-9
ALequeux 1½.10
30 Monsieur Dian 8-9
SLeonardos 11
5/4 Theia, 4/1 Cheraw, Far North,
11/1 Great Idea, 13/1 Lac Ontario,
15/1 Emeric, 17/1 IRON DUKE,
19/1 Zamp, 21/1 Robertissimo,
24/1 Happy New Year, 35/1
Monsieur Dian.

G. Tournier (F. Palmer) 11rn
2m 4 (Good).

67 PRIX DE MEAUTRY   6f
£10,250   Deauville   12 August
65 **Girl Friend** 4-9-3
GDubroeucq **1**
62² **Arch Sculptor** 3-8-9
YSaint-Martin ½.2
36 Nagin 4-8-13 AMurray...2½.3
Cetosca 5-9-2 J-CDesaint.ns.4
62³ Realty 4-9-3 FHead.......½.5
Hillandale 4-9-0 GLewis..1½.6
37 Dacani 3-8-8 APerrotta......7
Policrock 3-9-0 GDoleuze...8
Lord Bend 3-8-9
GWMoore 9
65 My Last Sovereign 4-9-2
AGibert 10
50 Rose of Stanbul 3-8-10
ALequeux 11
19/10 GIRL FRIEND, 2/1 Arch
Sculptor, Nagin, Lord Bend
(grouped), 3/1 Realty, 10/1 My
Last Sovereign and Rose of Stanbul,
13/1 Cetosca, 21/1 Dacani, 25/1
Policrock, 27/1 Hillandale.

D. W. Molins (P. Lallie) 11rn
1m 11.8 (Good).

68 PRIX GONTAUT-BIRON
1¼m
£13,667   Deauville   14 August
Larkhill 4-8-11
YSaint-Martin **1**
35★ Kasteel 4-9-4 AMurray..1½.2
Blue Vermillion 4-8-11
GWMoore s.nk.3
52 Ramirez 5-9-6 PPaquet....3.4
Ile Flottante 4-9-2
GDoleuze ½.5
58 Duboff 4-9-1 EHide.......½.6
9/10 Kasteel, 29/10 LARKHILL,
7/2 Ramirez, 9/1 Ile Flottante,
Duboff, 11/1 Blue Vermillion.

Mse L. Moratalla (M. Clement)
6rn 2m 4.8 (Good).

69 PRIX MORNY   (2y)   6f
£28,474   Deauville   15 August
59★ **Blushing Groom** 8-11
HSamani **1**
Water Boy 8-11 PPaquet..3.2
Alpherat 8-11
GDoleuze nk.3
59² River Dane 8-8 LPiggott..1½.4
Miss Reasoning 8-8
GWMoore hd.5
Obolensky 8-11
ALequeux s.hd.6
Rhino 8-11 FHead 2½.7
Adorant 8-11 WPyers ¾.8
Haneena 8-8
YSaint-Martin ½.9
59 Man Alive 8-11
GRivases 1½.10
Top Streak 8-11
GDubroeucq 11
Evens BLUSHING GROOM, 5/1
Water Boy, 7/1 Obolensky, Haneena
10/1 River Dane, 12/1 Rhino, 18/1
Miss Reasoning, 19/1 Adorant, 44/1
Alpherat, 45/1 Man Alive, 73/1
Top Streak.

H. H. Aga Khan (F. Mathet) 11rn
1m 12.4 (Good).

70 PRIX QUINCEY   1m
£11,390   Deauville   22 August
65 **Ellora** 4-9-4 AMurray......**1**
58² **Monsanto** 4-9-4
YSaint-Martin 2½.2
66 **Happy New Year** 3-8-12
J-CDesaint ½.3
68 Ile Flottante 4-9-6
GDoleuze 1½.4
Strabo 3-8-12 JMercer....2½.5
22 Brinkmanship 5-9-6
ALequeux s.nk.6
Melion 3-8-10 GWMoore.hd.7
5/4 Monsanto, 28/10 ELLORA, 5/1
Brinkmanship, 6/1 Happy New
Year, 8/1 Strabo, 18/1 Ile Flottante,
29/1 Melion.

R. N. Tikkoo (A. Breasley) 7rn
1m 38.6 (Good).

71 GRAND PRIX DE
DEAUVILLE   1m 5½f
£28,474   Deauville   29 August
54² **Ashmore** 5-9-8
YSaint-Martin **1**
Diagramatic 3-8-6
GDubroeucq 4.2
47A³ **Duke of Marmalade** 5-9-8
SFancera s.nk.3
Beau Dad 4-9-0
GWMoore............¾.4
21 Hunza Dancer 4-9-0
AMurray 1½.5
2 Adam van Vianen 3-8-4
AGibert 1.6

853

57 Riboboy 3-8-6 LPiggott....¾.7
55 Tip Moss 4-9-5 FHead....5.8
    Avance 4-9-0 WPyers.....2.9
63² Olmeto 4-9-2 PPaquet....8.10
    American Patrol 3-8-6
    J-CDesaint.............11

5/4 Diagramatic, 22/10 ASHMORE, 8/1 Tip Moss, Avance, 12/1 Duke of Marmalade, 13/1 Olmeto, 18/1 Hunza Dancer, 19/1 Beau Dad, 26/1 American Patrol, 33/1 Riboboy, 59/1 Adam van Vianen.

D. Wildenstein (A. Penna) 11rn 2m 59 (Good).

72 PRIX RIDGWAY   1¼m
£9,112   Deauville   29 August
70² Monsanto 4-9-0
    YSaint-Martin 1
    Twig 5-9-4 GDoleuze....nk.2
55 Admetus 6-9-0
    MPhilipperon.........ns.3
8 Tajeslie 5-9-4 AGibert.....½.4
57 Happy Tim 3-8-10
    BTaylor nk.5
70³ Happy New Year 3-9-0
    J-CDesaint 2½.6
57 Dom Sully 3-8-8
    GDubroeucq 5.7
68 Ramirez 5-9-0 PPaquet.....8
    Chavin 5-9-0 GWMoore......9

17/10 MONSANTO, 4/1 Happy Tim, 5/1 Admetus, Ramirez, 7/1 Twig, 11/1 Dom Sully, 14/1 Happy New Year, Chavin, 18/1 Tajeslie.

D. Wildenstein (A. Penna) 9rn 2m 12.3 (Good).

73 PRIX NIEL   (3y)   1m 3f
£13,699   Longchamp   5 September
39* Youth 9-4 LPiggott........1
57 Arctic Tern 9-0
    MPhilipperon ¾.2
49* Malacate 9-4 PPaquet..2½.3
66* Iron Duke 9-0
    HSamani 4.4
55 Loosen Up 8-12 AGibert.10.5

8/10 YOUTH, 7/4 Malacate, 13/2 Arctic Tern, 31/4 Iron Duke, 32/1 Loosen Up.

N. B. Hunt (M. Zilber) 5rn 2m 22 (Dead).

74 PRIX DE LA NONETTE
          (3y) 1m 2½f
£13,699   Longchamp   5 September
66* Theia 8-11 GDubroeucq...1
50* Antrona 8-11 PPaquet...½.2
61 No No Nanette 8-9
    YSaint-Martin 1½.3
47 Elise Ma Belle 8-9
    AGibert nk.4
60 Sifana 8-9 J-CDesaint....4.5

8/10 Antrona, 23/10 THEIA, 9/2 No No Nanette, 7/1 Elise Ma Belle, 11/1 Sifana.

Baroness de Lopez-Tarragoya (R. Touflan) 5rn 2m 17.4 (Dead).

75 PRIX DU ROND-POINT   1m
£11,415   Longchamp   5 September
72* Monsanto 4-9-0
    YSaint-Martin 1
    Nurabad 4-9-0 WPyers...½.2
65 Manado 3-8-9 PPaquet.s.hd.3
37² Kesar Queen 3-8-10
    GWMoore ¾.4
65 Carolina Moon 4-8-13
    MPhilipperon ¾.5
62 Gold Nugget 3-8-9
    LPiggott 5.6
    Mittainvilliers 4-9-0
    ALequeux ½.7
67 My Last Sovereign 4-9-0
    AGibert ½.8

Evens Manado. 16/10 MONSANTO and Nurabad, 7/2 Kesar Queen, 14/1 Carolina Moon, 18/1 Mittainvilliers, 24/1 Gold Nugget, 41/1 My Last Sovereign.

D. Wildenstein (A. Penna) 8rn 1m 39.4 (Dead).

76 PRIX FOY   1m 3f
£13,698   Longchamp   12 September
68² Kasteel 4-9-2 GRivases.....1
    On My Way 6-8-12
    AGibert s.hd.2
71 Tip Moss 4-9-2 JDupin..2½.3
54 Beau Buck 5-9-0
    J-CDesaint 2.4
72 Tajeslie 5-8-12
    MLecaplain 2.5
55* Condorcet 4-9-2 PPaquet..1½.6
68* Larkhill 4-9-0
    YSaint-Martin 6.7
13 Nord 4-8-12 GDubroeucq.10.8
    D'Aniane 5-8-9
    SLeonardos dist.9

18/10 KASTEEL, 13/4 Larkhill, 7/2 Condorcet, 19/4 On My Way, 33/4 Tip Moss, 13/1 Beau Buck, 19/1 Tajeslie, 43/1 Nord, 95/1 D'Aniane.

Baron T. de Zuylen (J. de Choubersky) 9rn 2m 22.5 (Soft).

77 PRIX ROYAL-OAK   (3y)
          1m 7½f
£51,370   Longchamp   12 September
51* Exceller 9-2 GDubroeucq ..1
    Sir Montagu 9-2 BTaylor.4.2
71 Adam van Vianen 9-2
    LPiggott ½.3
64 Beau Charles 9-2
    ALequeux 5.4

66　Zamp 9-2 YSaint-Martin . . 3.5
　　Bold Bird 9-2 PPaquet 8.6
　　Nuclear Pulse 9-2
　　　　AMurray b.d.0
2/10 EXCELLER, 9/2 Zamp and
Nuclear Pulse, 13/2 Sir Montagu,
15/1 Bold Bird, 19/1 Adam van
Vianen, 34/1 Beau Charles.

N. B. Hunt (F. Mathet) 7rn
3m 33.8 (Soft).

78　PRIX DE LA
　　SALAMANDRE　(2y)　7f
£28,539 Longchamp 12 September
69*　Blushing Groom 8-11
　　　HSamani 1
　　Assez Cuite 8-8 GRivases . 2.2
69³　Alpherat 8-11
　　　YSaint-Martin ¾.3
59　King of Macedon 8-11
　　　MPhilipperon 1¼.4
　　Sunday Guest 8-11
　　　PPaquet 1½.5
　　Virgin 8-8 J-CDesaint 3.6
　　Doha 8-8 GDubroeucq 5.7
　　Nice Balance 8-11 BTaylor . 1.8
3/10 BLUSHING GROOM, 9/1
King of Macedon, Virgin, 11/1
Alpherat, 12/1 Sunday Guest, 18/1
Nice Balance, 23/1 Doha, 30/1
Assez Cuite.

H. H. Aga Khan (F. Mathet) 8rn
1m 24.8 (Soft).

79　IRISH ST LEGER (3y) 1¾m
£15,842　The Curragh　18 Sept.
　　Meneval 9-0 LPiggott 1
　　General Ironside 9-0
　　　FDurr 8.2
56　Countess Eileen 8-11
　　　TCarmody 3.3
　　Red Invader 9-0 GCurran . 2¼.4
　　Midland Gayle 9-0
　　　PBoothman ¾.5
56　Krassata 8-11
　　　WSwinburn s.hd.6
　　Whistle For Gold 9-0
　　　RCarroll ¾.7
49　Finsbury 9-0 CRoche 4.8
49　Navarre 9-0
　　　TMurphy 1½.9
　　Lavache 9-0 JRoe 4½.10
　　Lost Chord 9-0 FMorby . nk.11
4/5 MENEVAL, 9/2 Lost Chord,
5/1 General Ironside, 12/1 Red
Invader, 20/1 Krassata, 33/1 Coun-
tess Eileen, 40/1 Finsbury, Navarre,
50/1 Whistle For Gold, 100/1
Lavache, Midland Gayle.

Mrs George F. Getty II (V.
O'Brien) 11rn 3m 2.1 (Good to
Firm).

80　PRIX ALY KHAN　　6f
　　　　(Amateur riders)
£2,854　Evry　18 September
67　Hillandale 4-10-12
　　　NHenderson 1
67　Lord Bend 3-9-13
　　　Ray Hutchinson 2.2
　　Reine de Chypre 3-9-10
　　　TClout 1½.3
　　Allez Paris 4-10-1 PAdda . hd.4
　　Lt Hobson 6-10-1
　　　FTurner ½.5
36　Ouialco 3-9-12 DBoutier . . ½.6
50　Noah's Acky Astra 3-10-7
　　　GSauque 1½.7
　　Amadou 4-9-13
　　　GdeChevigny 1½.8
　　Blackbird 4-10-2 LSward . . ½.9
48　Brave Panther 3-10-10
　　　CdeAsis Trem hd.10
　　Baldock 3-10-7 GForien 11
9/4 Amadou, 29/10 HILLAN-
DALE, 11/4 Lord Bend and
Brave Panther, 33/4 Blackbird,
13/1 Allez Paris, Ouialco, 14/1
Reine de Chypre, Baldock, 18/1
Lt Hobson, 22/1 Noah's Acky
Astra.

E. Widner (D. Keith) 11rn
1m 16.4 (Dead).

81　PRIX VERMEILLE (3y) 1½m
£68,490 Longchamp 19 September
56*　Lagunette 9-2 PPaquet 1
56²　Sarah Siddons 9-2
　　　LPiggott ns.2
56　Floressa 9-2 J-PLefevre . . 1.3
28　Sweet Rhapsody 9-2
　　　PEddery 1¼.4
74*　Theia 9-2 GDubroeucq . . . nk.5
　　Empty Jest 9-2
　　　MPhilipperon ¾.6
47*　Pawneese 9-2
　　　YSaint-Martin 8.7
50　Denia 9-2 GRivases 5.8
54*　Riverqueen 9-2 FHead 3.9
28　Moquerie 9-2 RJallu 6.10
5/10 Pawneese, 2/1 Riverqueen and
Moquerie, 14/1 LAGUNETTE,
16/1 Theia, 24/1 Sarah Siddons,
36/1 Denia, 44/1 Empty Jest,
56/1 Floressa, 58/1 Sweet Rhapsody.

M. Berghgracht (F. Boutin) 10rn
2m 40.2 (Soft).

82　PRIX DES CHENES (2y) 1m
£11,415 Longchamp 19 September
　　Silk Slipper 8-6
　　　MPhilipperon 1
69²　Water Boy 9-1 PPaquet . . . 4.2
　　Borodine 8-9 FHead 2.3
　　Duchino 8-9 ALequeux . . . hd.4
　　Manicero 8-12
　　　GDubroeucq hd.5

Black Sulphur 9-1 WPyers.2.6
69 Man Alive 8-9 GRivases.s.nk.7
Concerto Barocco 9-1
J-PRoman ¾.8
Pougatchof 8-9 LPiggott..10.9

7/4 Water Boy, 3/1 Borodine, 6/1 Duchino, 13/2 Pougatchof, 82/10 SILK SLIPPER, 12/1 Black Sulphur, 13/1 Manicero, 15/1 Concerto Barocco, 36/1 Man Alive.

Sir M. Sobell (J. Cunnington, jnr) 9rn 1m 45.8 (Soft).

---

83 PRIX DU PRINCE
   D'ORANGE   1¼m

£11,415 Longchamp 19 September

52² Ivanjica 4-8-10 FHead.....1
8   Sea Sands 4-8-10
    ALequeux 4.2
72² Twig 5-8-13 GDubroeucq.¾.3
22 Trepan 5-8-13 PPaquet...nk.4
21* Infra Green 4-9-2
    MDepalmas 1.5
23 Indus Warrior 3-8-7
    YSaint-Martin 2.6
    Kervic 5-8-13
    MPhilipperon 1½.7

14/10 IVANJICA, 11/4 Trepan, 13/2 Twig, 27/4 Indus Warrior, 15/2 Infra Green, 22/1 Sea Sands, 40/1 Kervic.

J. Wertheimer (A. Head) 7rn 2m 16.3 (Soft).

---

84 PRIX DE SEINE-ET-OISE
   6f

£9,132 Maisons-Laffitte 20 Sept.

48* Kala Shikari 3-9-6 FHead..1
58 Raga Navarro 4-9-8
    PPaquet s.hd.2
48 Mendip Man 4-9-8
    AGibert ¾.3
65³ Vitiges 3-9-6 GRivases..hd.4
67* Girl Friend 4-9-5
    J-PLefevre 2.5
    Polyponder 2-7-13
    GDubroeucq 1½.6
67² Arch Sculptor 3-9-6
    YSaint-Martin hd.7
    Casaque 2-8-0 JDupin   6.8
14 Hittite Glory 3-9-6
    AMurray 1.9
67³ Nagin 4-9-5 PSimonin....½.10

Evens Vitiges, 22/10 KALA SHIKARI, Arch Sculptor, Hittite Glory, Nagin (all grouped), 3/1 Girl Friend, 16/1 Polyponder, Casaque, 17/1 Mendip Man, 19/1 Raga Navarro.

R. N. Tikkoo (A. Breasley) 10rn 1m 13.5 (Good).

---

85 CRITERIUM DE
   MAISONS-LAFFITTE
   (2y)   7f

£11,415 Maisons-Laffitte 23 Sept.

    Perello 8-7 GRivases......1
    Aigle Blanc 8-7 ABadel..hd.2
78 Doha 8-4 AGibert........¾.3
    Bold Glow 8-7 WPyers....¾.4
    Smoggy 8-7 FHead.....s.hd.5
    Steel Band 8-11 AMurray.1½.6
    Darkeino 8-11
    MPhilipperon 2.7
    Zalitzing 8-11 HSamani....1.8

9/4 Bold Glow, 7/2 Steel Band, 4/1 Darkeino, 9/2 Smoggy, 8/1 Zalitzing, 82/10 PERELLO, 11/1 Doha, 30/1 Aigle Blanc.

M. Boussac (G. Bonnaventure) 8rn 1m 27.5 (Good).

---

86 JOE McGRATH
   MEMORIAL STAKES   1¼m

£20,730 Leopardstown 25 Sept.

73³ Malacate 3-8-9 LPiggott....1
49 Mart Lane 3-8-9
    GMcGrath 1½.2
49 Niebo 3-8-9 TMurphy..s.hd.3
49³ Northern Treasure 3-8-9
    GCurran ¾.4
49 Hawkberry 3-8-9 CRoche..5.5
49 Decent Fellow 3-8-9
    WSwinburn 2½.6
    Sarania 3-8-6 JCorr.....2½.7
    Rare Trial 3-8-9
    KFCoogan 3.8
49 Imperial Fleet 3-8-9
    DHogan...........5.9
    Ballyglass 3-8-9 JRoe...2.10
    Charles Stewart 4-9-3
    MKennedy 8.11

4/5 MALACATE, 100/30 Northern Treasure, 6/1 Hawkberry, 12/1 Niebo, 25/1 Decent Fellow, Mart Lane, 33/1 Sarania 100/1 others.

Mme M-F. Berger (F. Boutin) 11rn 2m 7.6 (Good).

---

87 PRIX DU PONT
   DE FLANDRE   2½m

£6,849 Longchamp 26 September

    Knight Templar 6-9-0
    WPyers 1
63* Citoyen 4-9-6 GRivases...2.2
    Biloxi 4-9-0 RJallu.......8.3
    Quart du Vin 4-9-2
    ALequeux 6.4
32² Kemal 5-8-12
    YSaint-Martin 20.5
    Forceful 9-8-12
    J-CDesaint 20.6

6/4 Kemal, 2/1 Citoyen, 4/1 Quart

du Vin, 99/10 KNIGHT TEMP-
LAR, 11/1 Biloxi, Forceful.

P. G. Richards (H. Van de Poele)
6rn 4m 27.7 (Soft).

88 PRIX DU MOULIN
    DE LONGCHAMP   1m
£28,539 Longchamp 26 September

65*	**Gravelines** 4-9-2	
	YSaint-Martin	1
65	**Dona Barod** 4-8-13	
	MPhilipperon	2½.2
75³	**Manado** 3-8-12 LPiggott.1½.3	
65	Avaray 3-8-12 FHead	1½.4
75*	Monsanto 4-9-2 WPyers	¾.5
70*	Ellora 4-9-2 AMurray	2½.6
38*	Earth Spirit 3-8-12	
	GDubroeucq	10.7
	Silver Steel 3-8-12	
	WCarson	½.8
53	Son of Silver 5-9-2	
	AGibert	5.9

7/10 GRAVELINES, Monsanto,
Earth Spirit (grouped), 3/1 Avaray,
6/1 Manado, 10/1 Ellora, 16/1 Son
of Silver, 18/1 Dona Barod, 23/1
Silver Steel.

D. Wildenstein (A. Penna) 9rn
1m 42 (Soft).

89 LA COUPE DE
    MAISONS-LAFFITTE 1¼m
£13,698 Maisons-Laffitte 30 Sept.

73	**Iron Duke** 3-8-11	
	HSamani	1
83³	**Twig** 5-9-1 GDubroeucq..1.2	
76	**Condorcet** 4-9-5 FHead...2.3	
	Inis Gloire 4-8-11	
	ALequeux	1½.4
75	Mittainvilliers 4-9-1	
	WPyers	1½.5
72³	Admetus 6-8-11	
	MPhilipperon	1½.6
40	Kano 3-8-5 GRivases	½.7
72	Happy Tim 3-8-5	
	J-PLefevre	8.8
63³	French Friend 3-8-5	
	AMurray	1½.9
83	Indus Warrior 3-8-11	
	PSimonin	1.10
	Popayan 6-9-5 APerrotta....0	
	Top Gear 4-8-11	
	YSaint-Martin	0
29	Danestic 3-8-5 RJallu	0
	Antietam 3-8-5 J-CDesaint..0	

4/1 Mittainvilliers, 9/2 Twig, 6/1
Kano, 15/2 Top Gear, 9/1 IRON
DUKE, Admetus, 10/1 Antietam,
13/1 Happy Tim, 14/1 Inis Gloire,
15/1 Condorcet, 16/1 French Friend,
22/1 Danestic 38/1 Popayan, 50/1
Indus Warrior.

G. Tournier (F. Palmer) 14rn
m 8.7 (Heavy).

90 PRIX DE L'ABBAYE DE
    LONGCHAMP   5f
£18,116 Longchamp 3 October

	Gentilhombre 3-9-10	
	TMcKeown	1
84³	**Mendip Man** 4-9-10	
	AGibert	d.h.1
84²	**Raga Navarro** 4-9-10	
	FHead	hd.3
84	Girl Friend 4-9-7	
	J-PLefevre	nk.4
78	King of Macedon 2-8-8	
	MPhilipperon	¾.5
22	Kronenkranich 4-9-10	
	JJednaszewski	2½.6
84	Polyponder 2-8-6	
	J-CDesaint	½.7
	Faliraki 3-9-10 PEddery...1.8	
84*	Kala Shikari 3-9-10	
	YSaint-Martin	nk.9
	Nassy 2-8-5 RJallu	5.10

2/1 Faliraki, 4/1 Kala Shikari, 9/2
King of Macedon, 11/2 Raga
Navarro, 6/1 Girl Friend, 31/4
MENDIP MAN, 12/1 Kronen-
kranich, 30/1 Nassy, 38/1 GENTIL-
HOMBRE, 44/1 Polyponder.

Gentilhombre—T. Robson (N.
Adam). Mendip Man—Mrs J. Davis
(A. Paus) 10rn 1m 0.3 (Soft).

91 CRITERIUM DES
    POULICHES   (2y)   1m
£24,155 Longchamp 3 October

	Kamicia 8-9 FFlachi	1
85³	**Doha** 8-9 AGibert	3.2
	Orchid Miss 8-9 FHead...¾.3	
82*	Silk Slipper 8-9	
	MPhilipperon	¾.4
	Guile Princess 8-9	
	JTaillard	1.5
	Olwyn 8-9 JMercer	nk.6
78²	Assez Cuite 8-9	
	GRivases	s.hd.7
	Countom 8-9 AMurray...hd.8	
	Powderhound 8-9	
	HSamani	hd.9
	Ymirkhan 8-9 ALequeux..1.10	
	Anya Ylina 8-9 LPiggott.....0	
	Anida 8-9 GDubroeucq.....0	
	Proud Event 8-9	
	YSaint-Martin	0
	Al Stanza 8-9 WCarson	0

3/1 Anya Ylina, 13/4 Silk Slipper,
7/2 Proud Event, 21/4 Assez Cuite,
13/1 Guile Princess, 20/1 Powderhound, 26/1 Ymirkhan, 31/1
KAMICIA, 33/1 Orchid Miss,
47/1 Al Stanza, 52/1 Doha, 55/1
Anida, 56/1 Olwyn, 95/1 Countom.

Mme H. Rabatel (J. Laumain)
14rn 1m 49.7 (Soft).

92 PRIX DE L'ARC
DE TRIOMPHE 1½m
£144,928 Longchamp 3 October

83★ **Ivanjica** 4-9-1 FHead......**1**
57★ **Crow** 3-8-11
    YSaint-Martin **2.2**
73★ **Youth** 3-8-11 WPyers.....**3.3**
    Noble Dancer 4-9-4
    GLewis s.nk.**4**
    Bruni 4-9-4 LPiggott.....1½.**5**
76 Beau Buck 5-9-4
    J-CDesaint ½.**6**
83 Infra Green 4-9-1
    MDepalmas ¾.**7**
    Java Rajah 3-8-11 FDurr...**5.8**
76² On My Way 6-9-4 AGibert..¾.**9**
76★ Kasteel 4-9-4 GRivases..hd.**10**
81 Pawneese 3-8-8 PEddery..5.**11**
73² Arctic Tern 3-8-11
    MPhilipperon ½.**12**
83 Trepan 4-9-4 JMercer...10.**13**
81★ Lagunette 3-8-8
    ALequeux 6.**14**
81³ Floressa 3-8-8
    J-PLefevre s.hd.**15**
71³ Duke of Marmalade 5-9-4
    GDoleuze 5.**16**
81 Riverqueen 3-8-8 RJallu..5.**17**
39² Twig Moss 3-8-11
    AMurray 10.**18**
77★ Exceller 3-8-11
    GDubroeucq t.o.**19**
    Dakota 5-9-4 ABarclay..t.o.**20**

2/1 Youth and Exceller, 5/2 Bruni,
21/4 Crow and Pawneese, 71/10
IVANJICA and Riverqueen, 14/1
On My Way, 19/1 Trepan, 21/1
Lagunette, 23/1 Noble Dancer,
Arctic Tern, 54/1 Twig Moss, 56/1
Beau Buck, 64/1 Kasteel, 66/1
Duke of Marmalade, 75/1 Java
Rajah, 99/1 Infra Green, Dakota,
Floressa.

J. Wertheimer (A. Head) 20rn
2m 39.4 (Soft).

93 PRIX DE L'OPERA 1m 1¼f
£18,116 Longchamp 3 October

88² **Dona Barod** 4-8-13
    MPhilipperon **1**
    Pollenka 3-8-9 AGibert...¾.**2**
75 **Kesar Queen** 3-8-12
    AMurray **4.3**
81 Theia 3-8-12
    GDubroeucq s.nk.**4**
    Victory Tune 3-8-9
    YSaint-Martin 1½.**5**
50 Luna Real 3-8-9
    MDepalmas 2.**6**
43 Lady Beck 3-8-9 LPiggott.ns.**7**
61 Guichet 3-8-9 FHead......½.**8**
74³ No No Nanette 3-8-9
    HSamani 1½.**9**
83² Sea Sands 4-8-13
    ALequeux 2.**10**

61³ Royal Family 4-8-13
    GRivases **0**
    Torisca 4-8-13 APerrotta....**0**
5/2 Sea Sands, 36/10 DONA
BAROD, 4/1 Theia, 19/4 Victory
Tune, 14/1 Pollenka, Guichet, 17/1
No No Nanette, 20/1 Royal Family,
21/1 Kesar Queen, 23/1 Lady Beck,
50/1 Torisca, 55/1 Luna Real.

A. Blasco (J. Cunnington, jnr)
12rn 2m 2.2 (Soft).

94 GRAND CRITERIUM (2y)
1m
£60,386 Longchamp 10 October

78★ **Blushing Groom** 8-11
    HSamani **1**
    Amyntor 8-11
    GRivases **4.2**
    J. O. Tobin 8-11
    LPiggott hd.**3**
78³ Alpherat 8-11
    GDubroeucq **3.4**
    He's A Gent 8-11
    J-CDesaint **2.5**
85 Darkeino 8-11
    MPhilipperon **4.6**
    Command Freddy 8-11
    YSaint-Martin ¾.**7**
    Ziethen 8-11 JMercer....6.**8**
78 Sunday Guest 8-11 FHead.**3.9**
    Azimut 8-11 ALequeux...½.**10**

8/10 BLUSHING GROOM, 5/4
J. O. Tobin, 5/1 Command Freddy
and Azimut, 27/1 He's A Gent, 28/1
Amyntor, 31/1 Sunday Guest, 35/1
Alpherat, Darkeino, 85/1 Ziethen.

H. H. Aga Khan (F. Mathet) 10rn
1m 44.7 (Dead).

95 PRIX DE ROYALLIEU
1m 4½f
£14,493 Longchamp 10 October

56 **Paint the Town** 8-7
    MPhilipperon **1**
81 **Moquerie** 8-10 FHead ..nk.**2**
74 **Elise Ma Belle** 8-7
    AGibert 1½.**3**
81 Empty Jest 8-7
    GDubroeucq **2.4**
55³ Gramy 9-3 J-CDesaint...nk.**5**
60 Khalida 8-7 HSamani....1½.**6**
    Mohawk Princess 8-8
    YSaint-Martin s.hd.**7**
56 African Dancer 9-0
    AMurray s.nk.**8**
81 Sweet Rhapsody 8-10
    LPiggott 6.**9**

11/4 Gramy, 7/2 PAINT THE
TOWN, African Dancer, 6/1 Elise
Ma Belle, 29/4 Sweet Rhapsody,
12/1 Khalida, 16/1 Moquerie,
Empty Jest, Mohawk Princess.

Mrs P. Augustus (J. Fellows) 9rn
2m 52.6 (Dead).

96 PRIX DU CONSEIL DE PARIS 1½m

£36,231 Longchamp 17 October

92	**On My Way** 6-9-4 AGibert	1
92	**Beau Buck** 5-9-4 J-CDesaint	1½.2
55²	**Saquito** 4-9-0 FHead	½.3
92	Arctic Tern 3-9-1 MPhilipperon	s.nk.4
89³	Condorcet 4-9-6 FFlachi	2½.5
95	Gramy 5-9-3 HSamani	1.6
92	Noble Dancer 4-9-11 LPiggott	1.7
	Squash 3-8-8 YSaint-Martin	¾.8
32	Monde Soyeux 4-9-2 ABadel	2.9
89	Kano 3-9-1 GRivases	½.10
87²	Citoyen 4-9-11 YJosse	0
71²	Diagramatic 3-8-13 GDubroeucq	0
64²	Campero 3-8-13 WPyers	0
73	Loosen Up 3-8-10 AMurray	0

33/10 ON MY WAY, 9/2 Noble Dancer, 5/1 Saquito, 21/4 Squash, 7/1 Beau Buck, 15/2 Diagramatic, 11/1 Arctic Tern, 24/1 Monde Soyeux, 28/1 Condorcet, 32/1 Citoyen, 37/1 Kano, 38/1 Campero, 40/1 Gramy, 98/1 Loosen Up.

X. Beau (N. Pelat) 14rn 2m 36.6 (Soft).

97 PRIX DE CONDE (2y) 1¼m

£12,077 Longchamp 17 October

	El Criollo 8-11 WPyers	1
	Monseigneur 8-11 FHead	½.2
	Rip Off 8-11 J-CDesaint	4.3
	Le Despote 8-11 ABadel	3.4
91	Powderhound 8-8 MPhilipperon	5.5
85*	Perello 8-11 GRivases	3.6
	Niroun 8-11 HSamani	fell

8/10 EL CRIOLLO, 15/4 Perello, 21/4 Monseigneur, 7/1 Niroun, 11/1 Le Despote, 13/1 Rip Off, 14/1 Powderhound.

S. Sokolow (R. Carver) 7rn 2m 16.7 (Soft).

98 PRIX DE FLORE (3y) 1m 2½f

£12,077 Saint-Cloud 18 October

93	**No No Nanette** 8-9 YSaint-Martin	1
95*	**Paint the Town** 9-1 MPhilipperon	1½.2
	La Marelle 8-12 J-CDesaint	1½.3
81	Denia 8-9 GRivases	s.nk.4
93²	Pollenka 8-9 AGibert	1.5
	Shortbread 9-1 AMurray	¾.6

95² Moquerie 9-1 FHead ... ¾.7
Stella Reale 8-9 ABadel ... s.nk.8

95	Sweet Rhapsody 9-1 ALequeux	4.9
92	Floressa 9-1 J-PLefevre	6.10
74	Sifana 8-9 GDubroeucq	11

7/4 Pollenka, 4/1 Floressa, 21/4 Paint the Town, 6/1 Moquerie, 76/10 NO NO NANETTE, 14/1 Denia, 16/1 La Marelle, 17/1 Sweet Rhapsody, Sifana, 36/1 Stella Reale, 42/1 Shortbread.

Comtesse M. Batthyany (G. Bridgland) 11rn 2m 16.3 (Soft).

99 PREMIO FREDERICO TESIO 1m 3f

£18,076 Milan 19 September

47A	**Gallio** 3-8-9 MCipolloni	1
	Eran 3-8-9 CForte	1.2
	Aliante 3-8-9 GDettori	½.3
	Veio 6-9-2 SFancera	1½.4
	Strasburgo 4-9-2 ADiNardo	hd.5
42	Kruger 3-8-9 VPanici	½.6
70	Ile Flottante 4-9-2 GDoleuze	½.7
44*	Shamsan 6-9-2 GFois	1.8
39	French Scandal 3-8-9 WCarson	½.9
	Saint Paul 6-9-2 RSannino	1.10
77	Zamp 3-8-9 AMurray	1.11

4/1 Veio, 5/1 Eran, 11/2 Aliante, 6/1 Zamp, 13/2 Shamsan, 7/1 Strasburgo, 8/1 French Scandal, 12/1 GALLIO, 14/1 Ile Flottante, 20/1 Kruger, 25/1 Saint Paul.

Razza Ticino (I. Gabbrielli) 11rn 2m 18.4 (Soft).

100 ST LEGER ITALIANO (3y) 1¾m

£14,316 Milan 3 October

99*	**Gallio** 9-3 MCipolloni	1
	Black Marlin 9-3 PPerlanti	1.2
	Nagala 9-3 MMattei	5.3
99²	Eran 9-3 CForte	¾.4
56	Claire Valentine 8-13 GFois	2.5
47A	Aubry 9-3 Tiziana Sozzi	2.6
	Blu Veronese 9-3 PAgus	4.7
	Gay Petrol 9-3 ADiNardo	6.8

3/5 GALLIO, 9/2 Claire Valentine and Blu Veronese, 5/1 Eran, 10/1 Gay Petrol, 14/1 Black Marlin, 15/1 Nagala, 33/1 Aubry.

Razza Ticino (I. Gabbrielli) 8rn 3m 15 (Very Heavy).

101 PREMIO LYDIA TESIO
1¼m

£25,307   Rome   9 October

Time and Life 3-8-7
  GDettori 1
43² **Sierra Morena** 3-8-7
  CForte s.hd.2
  Osipowics 3-8-7
  ADiNardo 7.3
42 Leda Sterling 3-8-7
  RFestinesi 3½.4
  Cupina 3-8-7 CWigham...1½.5
  Alchiara 3-8-7 AParravani..½.6
  Diala 4-9-0 GPucciatti.....2.7
43³ Dir El Gobi 3-8-7
  GDoleuze 3.8
43 Simpaty 3-8-7 SFancera...2.9
  Vouille 3-8-7 OPessi......6.10

2/1 Dir El Gobi and Vouille, 5/2 Sierra Morena, 4/1 Osipowics, 5/1 Leda Sterling, 6/1 Cupina, 10/1 Simpaty, 12/1 TIME AND LIFE, 14/1 Diala, 33/1 Alchiara.

Scuderia Cieffedi (S. Cumani) 10rn 2m 7.6 (Good).

102 GRAN CRITERIUM (2y)
1m

£31,815   Milan   10 October

Sirlad 8-11 ADiNardo......1
Tommy Barban 8-11
  VPanici 2½.2
Capo Bon 8-11
  GDoleuze ½.3
Stateff 8-11 SAtzori.....1½.4
Charleroi 8-11 CForte.....2.5
Oltre il Colle 8-11
  NMulas 2.6
Corot 8-11 MCipolloni....1½.7
Truewer 8-11 GDettori....2.8
Quadrano 8-11 SFancera...2.9
Reason to Love 8-11
  MMattei 4.10

2/1 SIRLAD, 3/1 Capo Bon, 7/2 Stateff, 6/1 Truewer, 7/1 Reason to Love, 8/1 Charleroi, 9/1 Oltre il Colle, 12/1 Quadrano, 14/1 Tommy Barban, 18/1 Corot.

Razza La Tesa (G. Benetti) 10rn 1m 44.8 (Soft).

103 GRAN PREMIO DEL
JOCKEY CLUB 1½m

£50,615   Milan   17 October

92 **Infra Green** 4-9-2
  GDoleuze 1
101² **Sierra Morena** 3-8-8
  VPanici 1½.2
92 **Duke of Marmalade**
  5-9-5 RSannino.......hd.3
100³ Nagala 3-8-11 MMattei...1½.4
47A Rue de la Paix 4-9-5
  ADiNardo ½.5
100★Gallio 3-8-11 MCipolloni.1½.6

99 Veio 6-9-5 SFancera......½.7
100² Black Marlin 3-8-11
  PPeranti 2.8
100 Eran 3-8-11 CForte......3.9
  Mousquetaire 4-9-5
  FBarrix 4.10

7/10 INFRA GREEN, 5/2 Gallio, 7/1 Duke of Marmalade, 10/1 Sierra Morena, 12/1 Mousquetaire, 14/1 Veio, 15/1 Rue de la Paix and Nagala, 20/1 Eran, 25/1 Black Marlin.

Mme J. Pochna (E.Bartholomew) 10rn 2m 35.6 (Heavy).

104 CANADIAN
INTERNATIONAL
CHAMPIONSHIP 1m 5f

£69,878 Woodbine 23 October

92³ **Youth** 3-8-5 SHawley.......1
  Improviser 4-9-0
  JCruguet 4.2
  Effervescing 3-8-5
  ACordero, jnr 7.3
Tiny Tinker 3-8-5 JFell...1½.4
Kamaraan 5-9-0 EMaple...½.5
Chintain 7-9-0 LDuffy...3½.6
Erwin Boy 5-9-0
  RTurcotte ns.7
Pampas Host 4-9-0
  GPeichoto 1.8
Good Port 6-9-0 RGrubb..1.9
Detrimental 5-9-0
  CLoseth 4½.10
Crackle 3-8-5 AGomez....p.u.

20/21 YOUTH, 4/1 Effervescing, 5/1 Erwin Boy, 17/2 Kamaraan, 19/2 Tiny Tinker, 23/1 Crackle, 24/1 Good Port, 25/1 Improviser, 77/1 Chintain, Pampas Host, Detrimental.

N. B. Hunt (M. Zilber) 11rn 2m 48 (Soft).

105 PRIX DU PETIT
COUVERT 5f

£10,869 Longchamp 24 October

90 **Girl Friend** 4-9-7
  J-PLefevre 1
90 **Kala Shikari** 3-9-10
  YSaint-Martin 2.2
90 **Polyponder** 2-8-6
  J-CDesaint nk.3
48 Diffusion 3-9-7 FHead.....1.4
  Haveroid 2-8-8
  TMcKeown nk.5
90³ Raga Navarro 4-10-0
  PPaquet ¾.6
90★ Mendip Man 4-10-0
  AGibert ½.7
67 Dacani 3-9-7 ALequeux....4.8

22/10 GIRL FRIEND, 13/4 Kala Shikari, Raga Navarro, 11/2 Mendip Man, 17/2 Haveroid, 12/1

Diffusion, 14/1 Polyponder, 27/1 Dacani.

D. W. Molins (P. Lallie) 8rn 59.1 sec (Soft).

106 PRIX DE LA FORET   7f

£30,192   Longchamp   24 October

	Pharly 2-8-5 MPhilipperon	..**1**
	Lady Mere 2-8-2	
	WCarson	..2.2
88³	**Manado** 3-9-11 LPiggott	.1½.3
90	Kronenkranich 4-9-12	
	JJednaszewski	........1.4
88	Monsanto 4-9-12	
	YSaint-Martin	........½.5
65	Full of Hope 6-9-12	
	WPyers	..............2.6
93	Guichet 3-9-7 PPaquet	.....3.7
93³	Kesar Queen 3-9-7	
	AMurray	..............3.8

9/4 Monsanto, 3/1 Manado, Full of Hope, 39/10 PHARLY, 12/1 Kesar Queen, 14/1 Guichet, 15/1 Kronenkranich, 26/1 Lady Mere.

A. Blasco (J. Cunnington, jnr) 8rn 1m 26 (Soft).

107 PRIX GLADIATEUR   3m

£14,493   Longchamp   24 October

87*	**Knight Templar** 6-9-2	
	WPyers	................**1**
87	**Forceful** 9-9-2 YJosse	.....5.2
13	**Shamaraan** 4-9-2	
	HSamani	..............1.3
	Aracena 5-9-2 ABadel	...s.hd.4
87	Kemal 5-9-2	
	YSaint-Martin	.........8.5

8/10 KNIGHT TEMPLAR, 5/2 Shamaraan, 3/1 Kemal, 10/1 Aracena, 14/1 Forceful.

P. G. Richards (H. Van de Poele) 5rn 5m 49.4 (Soft).

108 PRIX THOMAS BRYON (2y)   7¾f

£9,662   Saint-Cloud   30 October

	General 8-7 GDubroeucq	...**1**
	Doctor's Choice 8-4	
	ALequeux	...........1½.2
	Hermodore 8-7	
	J–CDesaint	.........s.hd.3
	Zinov 8-7 HSamani	.....2½.4
84	Casaque 8-7 JDupin	5
	Granlieu 8-7	
	MPhilipperon	6
	Numa Pompilius 8-7	
	FHead	................½.7
82	Concerto Barocco 8-11	
	J–PRoman	...........½.8
	Silgar 8-7 GRivases	.......½.9
85²	Aigle Blanc 8-7 ABadel	...5.10
82	Black Sulphur 8-13	
	YSaint-Martin	0

Balsamo 8-7 PPaquet........0
Saint Irial 8-7 AGibert......0

5/10 GENERAL, 33/4 Numa Pompilius, 10/1 Aigle Blanc, 12/1 Granlieu, 23/1 Black Sulphur, 17/1 Zinov, 20/1 Hermodore, 22/1 Silgar, 23/1 Casaque, 27/1 Concerto Barocco, 38/1 Doctor's Choice, 52/1 Balsamo, 76/1 Saint Irial.

Granlieu finished fifth, a short head behind Zinov, and 1½ lengths ahead of Casaque, but was put down a place after a stewards' inquiry.

Baron G. de Rothschild (F Mathet) 13rn 1m 41.6 (Soft).

109 PREMIO TEVERE   (2y)   1m

£23,860   Rome   4 November

	Baudelaire 8-11 PEddery	...**1**
	Hasty Reply 8-11	
	PPaquet	.............2½.2
	My Royal Prima 8-11	
	GFois	.................5.3
94	Alpherat 8-11 GDoleuze	...½.4
	Sangineto 8-11 GDettori	.1½.5
	Friendly Now 8-11	
	GPucciatti	............2.6
	Heristal 8-11 CWigham	....2.7
	Cutino 8-11 GPLigas	....1½.8
102	Quadrano 8-11 RSannino	..3.9
	Water Front 8-11	
	SFancera	............3.10
	Castelsilano 8-11 MGallo	..4.11

6/4 Alpherat and Friendly Now, 3/1 BAUDELAIRE, 5/1 Hasty Reply, 6/1 My Royal Prima, 8/1 Sangineto, 10/1 Heristal, 12/1 Quadrano, 14/1 Water Front, 16/1 Cutino, 25/1 Castelsilano.

F. Sasse (D. Sasse) 11rn 1m 47.6 (Very Heavy).

110 CRITERIUM DE SAINT CLOUD   (2y)   1¼m

£12,077   Saint-Cloud   6 November

	Conglomerat 8-11	
	PPaquet	................**1**
	Seguro 8-10	
	YSaint-Martin	.........6.2
	Istre 8-9 RJallu	..........2.3
	Jour Jack 8-9	
	APerrotta	.............3.4
97*	El Criollo 8-13 WPyers	...1½.5
	Hartebeest 8-6	
	MPlanard	...............6.6
	Pockley 8-9 AMurray	......3.7
97	Le Despote 8-9 ABadel	...10.8
	Dom Alaric 8-9	
	GDubroeucq	.........20.9

Evens El Criollo, 9/2 Dom Alaric, 57/10 CONGLOMERAT, 7/1

Seguro, 10/1 Istre, 12/1 Hartebeest, 14/1 Le Despote, 18/1 Pockley, 24/1 Jour Jack.

J. Ternynck (F. Boutin) 9rn 2m 17.5 (Heavy).

111 WASHINGTON D.C. INTERNATIONAL   1½m

£61,728   Laurel   6 November

104*	**Youth** 3-8-8 SHawley	...... **1**
96*	**On My Way** 6-9-1 AGibert	 2
92*	**Ivanjica** 4-8-12 FHead	..ns.3
96	Noble Dancer 4-9-1 LPiggott	...6.4
21	Rose Bowl 4-8-12 WCarson	...3.5
	Fujino Pahshia 5-9-1 SOhsaki	...4.6
	Windwurf 4-9-1 JJednaszewski	...24.7
	Janus 4-9-1 GAlmeida	...p.u.

9/5 YOUTH, Ivanjica, 15/2 Noble Dancer, 17/2 On My Way, 10/1 Janus, 13/1 Rose Bowl, Fujino Pahshia, 37/1 Windwurf.

N. B. Hunt (M. Zilber) 8rn 2m 46.2 (Soft).

112 PRIX PERTH   1m ¼f

£12,077 Saint-Cloud 13 November

	Dominion 4-8-11 GStarkey	...... **1**
89	**Mittainvilliers** 4-8-13 ALequeux	...2½.2
61	**Tyrant's Vale** 3-8-8 FHead	...¾.3
	Jellaby 3-8-9 BTaylor	...1½.4
96	Arctic Tern 3-8-13 MPhilipperon	...3.5
50²	Ranimer 3-9-0 GDubroeucq	...hd.6
	Dauphin du Roi 3-8-9 J-CDesaint	...3.7
98	Denia 3-8-6 GRivases	...2.8
106	Full of Hope 6-9-6 WPyers	...8.9
	North Cumberland 3-8-9 HSamani	...4.10
88	Earth Spirit 3-9-3 YSaint-Martin	...0
	Honduras 6-9-1 RSuerland	...0
105	Raga Navarro 4-8-11 PPaquet	...0
	Legal Eagle 4-8-11 ABadel	...0
84	Arch Sculptor 3-8-9 AMurray	...0

9/4 Arctic Tern, 19/4 Full of Hope, 31/4 Earth Spirit, 17/2 Raga Navarro, 11/1 Jellaby, Ranimer, Seguro, 12/1 Dauphin du Roi, 13/1 Tyrant's Vale, 14/1 Mittainvilliers, 16/1 Honduras, 18/1 DOMINION, 21/1 Denia, 31/1 Arch Sculptor, 62/1 Legal Eagle, 99/1 North Cumberland.

Mrs P. Wright (I. Balding) 15rn 1m 49.5 (Heavy).

113 PREMIO CHIUSURA   7f

£14,460   Milan   14 November

42	**Ovac** 3-9-5 SFancera	...... **1**
102²	**Tommy Barban** 2-7-13 VPanici	...1½.2
	West 3-9-5 ADiNardo	...½.3
	Alceo 3-9-5 GVerricelli	...1.4
	Ingegner Preside 3-9-5 Tiziana Sozzi	...½.5
102	Oltre il Colle 2-7-13 NMulas	...½.6
	Start 4-9-8 PPerlanti	...hd.7
42	Deimos 3-9-5 AVincis	...½.8
	Old Soldier 3-9-5 PAgus	..hd.9
19²	Giannina 3-9-2 MDepalmas	...1.10
	Twinkling Star 4-9-8 SAtzori	...½.11
	Paddy's 4-9-8 GFois	...½.12
	El Birillo 3-9-5 CPanici	..2½.13
	Ship Reason 3-9-5 GDettori	...1½.14

2/1 OVAC, 3/1 Start, 4/1 Tommy Barban, 7/1 Paddy's, 8/1 West, 12/1 Oltre il Colle, 16/1 Twinkling Star, 20/1 Deimos, 25/1 Ship Reason, 33/1 Giannina, El Birillo, Ingegner Preside, Alceo, 66/1 Old Soldier.

Scuderia Metauro (U. Pandolfi) 14rn 1m 31.2 (Very Heavy).

114 PREMIO ROMA   1¾m

£36,155   Rome   21 November

103³	**Duke of Marmalade** 5-9-0 RSannino	...... **1**
103	**Gallio** 3-8-7 MCipolloni	..1½.2
47A	**Le Michel** 3-8-7 CWigham	...s.hd.3
103	Rue de la Paix 4-9-0 CForte	...s.hd.4
71	Hunza Dancer 4-9-0 YSaint-Martin	...3.5
103	Nagala 3-8-7 GPucciatti	...8.6

Evens Hunza Dancer, 2/1 DUKE OF MARMALADE, 4/1 Gallio, 5/1 Le Michel, 11/2 Rue de la Paix and Nagala.

Scuderia Eleonora (M. Bertini) 6rn 3m 12.8 (Very Heavy).

INDEX TO RACING ABROAD

864

867

TRAINERS

The following is a list of trainers who held a flat licence in 1976. Quarters and telephone numbers are given beneath the trainer's name. The racecourse nearest to their quarters is shown in italics.

Adam, N. M. *Leicester*
Melton Mowbray
    (Waltham-on-the-Wolds 878)
Akehurst, R. P. J. *Newbury*
Lambourn   (Lambourn 71850)
Allingham, P. B. *Windsor*
Luton   (Offley 337)
Ancil, D. I. *Warwick*
Banbury   (Sulgrave 316)
Angus, N. J. *Ayr*
Ayr   (Ayr 66232)
Armstrong, R. W. *Newmarket*
Newmarket (Newmarket 3333/4)
Armytage, R. C. *Newbury*
East Ilsley   (East Ilsley 203)
Arthur, P. J. *Windsor*
Singleborough   (Winslow 2085)
Ashworth, P. H. *Epsom*
Epsom   (Epsom 20336)
    (Home—Burgh Heath 5450)
Atkinson, W. *Carlisle*
Carlisle   (Carlisle 25649)
Bacon, A. W. *Doncaster*
Retford   (Retford 2638)
Bailey, P. G. *Newbury*
Wantage   (Childrey 288)
Balding, A. *Doncaster*
Doncaster (Doncaster 710221)
Balding, G. B. *Salisbury*
Weyhill   (Weyhill 2278)
Balding, I. A. *Newbury*
Kingsclere (Kingsclere 298210)
Barclay, A. T. *Carlisle*
Annan   (Annan 2815)
Barclay, James *Ayr*
Ayr   (Joppa 226)
Barons, D. H. *Salisbury*
Kingsbridge   (Loddiswell 326)
Barratt, L. J. *Chester*
Oswestry (Queen's Head 209)
Bastiman, R. *York*
Wetherby   (Wetherby 2901)
Beeson, E. E. G. *Brighton*
Newhaven (Peacehaven 3304)
Bell, C. H. *Carlisle*
Hawick   (Denholm 278)
Benstead, C. J. *Epsom*
Epsom   (Ashtead 73152)
Berry, J. *Carlisle*
Lancaster   (Forton 791179)
Bethell, J. D. W. *Newbury*
Whatcombe (Chaddleworth 372)
Bevan, P. J. *Wolverhampton*
Kingstone
    (Dapple Heath 647 or 670)
Bewicke, C. *Newbury*
Didcot (Rowstock 333 and 355)
Blackshaw, H. F. *Catterick*
Middleham (Middleham 3295)
Blagrave, H. H. G. *Bath*
Beckhampton   (Avebury 345)
    (Home—Avebury 218)

Blakeney, R. E. *Folkestone*
Ashford   (Charing 2667)
Blum, G. *Newmarket*
Newmarket (Newmarket 2734)
Bolton, M. J. *Brighton*
Felcourt (Dormans Park 403)
Boothman, C. *Pontefract*
South Milford
    (South Milford 682481)
Boss, R. *Newmarket*
Newmarket (Newmarket 3286)
Bradley, J. M. *Chepstow*
Chepstow (Chepstow 2486)
Bridgwater, K. S. *Warwick*
Solihull (Knowle 77026)
Brittain, C. E. *Newmarket*
Newmarket (Newmarket 3739
    and 4347)
Brookshaw, S. J. *Wolverhampton*
Ternhill   (Ternhill 272)
Callaghan, N. A. *Newmarket*
Newmarket (Newmarket 4040)
Calver, P. *Goodwood*
Cherlton (Bramdean 527)
Calvert, J. B. *Thirsk*
Hambleton   (Sutton 373)
Camacho, M. J. C. *York*
Towton (Tadcaster 3294)
Cambidge, B. R. *Wolverhampton*
Shifnal
    (Weston-under-Lizard 249)
Candy, H. D. N. B. *Newbury*
Wantage   (Uffington 276)
Cann, J. F. *Bath*
Cullompton (Cullompton 2284)
Carr, E. J. *Thirsk*
Hambleton   (Sutton 288)
Carr, F. *York*
Malton   (Malton 2695)
Carter, R. *Newmarket*
Swaffham (Gooderstone 226)
Cecil, H. R. A. *Newmarket*
Newmarket (Newmarket 2192)
    (Home—Cheveley 730300)
Chapman, D. W. *Thirsk*
Stillington (Easingwold 21683)
Charles, W. *Warwick*
Warwick (Warwick 43878)
Chesmore, Mrs S. M. P. *Hamilton*
Glasgow   (Drymen 596)
Clarkson, H. *Ripon*
Harrogate   (Sawley 229)
Clay, R. H. *Wolverhampton*
Market Drayton
    (Market Drayton 4736)
Clay, W. *Nottingham*
Uttoxeter (Uttoxeter 2068)
Cole, P. F. I. *Newbury*
Lambourn (Lambourn 71632)
Cole, S. N. *Leicester*
Newport Pagnell (Newport Pagnell
    611149)

Collingridge, H. J. *Newmarket*
Newmarket (Newmarket 5454)
Collingwood, E. E. *Catterick*
Middleham (Coverdale 653)
Cottrell, L. G. *Bath*
Cullompton (Kentisbeare 320)
Cousins, E. *Chester*
Tarporley (Little Budworth 316)
Cousins, J. H. E. *Haydock*
Carnforth (Carnforth 3058)
Craig, T. *Edinburgh*
Dunbar (Dunbar 2583)
Cross, R. F. *Newcastle*
Alnwick (Chatton 2471)
Cross, V. B. *Salisbury*
Stockbridge (Stockbridge 515)
Crossley, C. C. *Chester*
Wirral (Neston 2382)
Crump, N. F. *Catterick*
Middleham (Leyburn 3269)
Cumani, L. M. *Newmarket*
Newmarket (Newmarket 61569
and 5432)
Cundell, P. D. *Newbury*
Compton (Compton 267/8)
Dale, D. *Epsom*
Farnham (Headley Down 3464)
Dalton, A. *Newmarket*
Newmarket (Newmarket 3741)
Dartnall, D. J. A. *Chepstow*
Chepstow (Tinterne 415)
Davies, C. H. *Chepstow*
Chepstow (Chepstow 2876)
Davison, A. R. *Lingfield*
Caterham (Caterham 43857)
Dent, A. *Doncaster*
Market Rasen (Market Rasen 3689)
Dever, F. *Nottingham*
Newark (Mansfield 870276)
Dickinson, A. E. *Haydock*
Gisburn (Gisburn 227)
Dingwall, C. B. J. *Newbury*
East Ilsley (East Ilsley 253)
Dingwall, Mrs L. E. *Salisbury*
Poole (Canford Cliffs 708165)
Docker, L. O. J. *Lanark*
Cleghorn (Carstairs 277)
Doyle, D. A. *York*
Wetherby (Wetherby 2420)
Dudgeon, I. M. *Salisbury*
Warminster
(Codford St Mary 477)
Dunlop, J. L. *Goodwood*
Arundel (Arundel 882194)
(Home—Arundel 882106)
Easterby, M. H. *York*
Malton (Kirby Misperton 600)
Easterby, M. W. *York*
Sheriff Hutton (Sheriff Hutton 368)
Edmunds, J. *Wolverhampton*
Wythall (Wythall 822334)
Edwards, D. R. *Wolverhampton*
Shrewsbury (Hodnet 374)
Edwards, J. A. C. *Wolverhampton*
Leominster (Kingsland 533)
Elsey, C. W. C. *York*
Malton (Malton 3149)

Etherington, J. *York*
Malton (Malton 2842)
Evans, J. S. *Salisbury*
Liss (Blackmoor 253)
Fairhurst, T. *Catterick*
Middleham (Middleham 3362)
Farrell, P. J. *Newcastle*
Belmont (Durham 67428)
Felgate, P. S. *Nottingham*
Aslockton (Whatton 50335)
Finch, Mrs A. *Salisbury*
Shaftesbury (East Knoyle 305)
Fisher, W. E. *Bath*
Chewton Mendip
(Chewton Mendip 283)
Fitzgerald, J. G. *York*
Malton (Malton 2718)
Forster, T. A. *Newbury*
Letcombe Bassett (Wantage 3092)
Francis, M. E. D. *Epsom*
Coldharbour (Dorking 6223)
Francis, W. D. *Chester*
Malpas (Tilston 208)
Freeman, F. G. *Bath*
Bath (Box 2456)
Gadd, G. J. *Bath*
Calne (Calne 814723)
Gandolfo, D. R. *Newbury*
Wantage (Wantage 3242)
Gates, T. l'A. *Brighton*
Lewes (Lewes 4250)
Gibson, J. H. *Chepstow*
Cheltenham (Cheltenham 30302)
Gifford, J. T. *Brighton*
Findon (Findon 2226)
Gilbert, J. C. *Warwick*
Winchcombe
(Winchcombe 602194)
Gillam, T. A. *Ripon*
Boroughbridge
(Boroughbridge 2592)
Goodwill, A. W. *Newmarket*
Newmarket (Newmarket 3218)
Gosling, T. *Epsom*
Epsom (Epsom 22080)
Goswell, M. O. *Goodwood*
Horsham (Slinfold 728)
Gray, W. H. *Beverley*
Beverley (Beverley 882490)
Guest, W. N. *Newmarket*
Newmarket (Culford 852 or 333)
Haigh, W. W. *York*
Malton (Malton 4428)
Haine, J. *Chepstow*
Haresfield (Hardwicke (Glos.) 256)
Hall, L. A. *Salisbury*
Winchester (Winchester 880341)
Hall, N. *Wolverhampton*
Burton-on-Trent
(Barton-under-Needwood 2279)
Hall, S. *Catterick*
Middleham (Leyburn 3350)
Hall, Miss S. E. *Catterick*
Middleham (Coverdale 223)
Hanbury, B. *Newmarket*
Newmarket (Newmarket 3193)
(Home—Wickhambrook 396)

Hanley, D. L. *Newbury*
Lambourn (Lambourn 71700)
Hannon, R. M. *Newbury*
East Everleigh
(Collingbourne Ducis 254)
Hanson, J. *York*
Wetherby (Wetherby 2841)
Hardy, J. *Nottingham*
Staunton (Long Bennington 212)
Harris, J. L. *Leicester*
Melton Mowbray (Harby 60671)
Harwood, G. *Goodwood*
Pulborough (Pulborough 2335)
Haslam, P. C. *Newbury*
Lambourn (Lambourn 71696)
Hassell, C. M. *Newmarket*
Newmarket (Exning 321)
Haynes, M. J. *Epsom*
Epsom (Burgh Heath 51140)
Hayward, J. E. *Epsom*
Ewhurst (Ewhurst 507)
Head, R. A. *Newbury*
Lambourn (Lambourn 71411)
Hern, W. R. *Newbury*
West Ilsley
(East Ilsley 219 and 251)
Herries, Lady *York*
York
(Holme-on-Spalding Moor 203)
Hill, C. J. *Bath*
Barnstaple (Barnstaple 2048)
Hills, B. W. *Newbury*
Lambourn (Lambourn 71548)
Hindley, J. J. *Newmarket*
Newmarket (Newmarket 4141)
Hobbs, B. R. *Newmarket*
Newmarket (Newmarket 2129)
Holden, W. *Newmarket*
Newmarket (Exning 384)
Holland, S. F. *Wolverhampton*
Shrewsbury (Cressage 392)
Hollinshead, R. *Wolverhampton*
Upper Longdon (Armitage 490298)
Holmes, D. H. *York*
Malton (Malton 2140 and 2740)
Holt, L. J. *Newbury*
Tunworth (Long Sutton 376)
Houghton, R. F. J. *Newbury*
Blewbury (Blewbury 850480)
Hunter, G. H. *Newbury*
East Ilsley (East Ilsley 250)
Ingham, S. W. H. *Epsom*
Headley (Ashtead 72859)
Ivory, K. T. *Windsor*
Radlett (Radlett 6081)
James, C. J. *Newbury*
Newbury (Great Shefford 280)
James, M. B. C. *Chester*
Whitchurch (Whitchurch 3155)
James, S. S. *Newbury*
East Ilsley (East Ilsley 248)
Jarvis, A. P. *Warwick*
Withybrook (Wolvey 566)
Jarvis, M. A. *Newmarket*
Newmarket (Newmarket 2915)
Jarvis, W. J. R. *Newmarket*
Newmarket (Newmarket 2677)

Jermy, D. C. *Epsom*
Carshalton (01-668 3765)
Johnson, J. A. T. *Newbury*
Lambourn (Lambourn 71368)
Jones, A. W. *Chester*
Oswestry (Oswestry 59720)
Jones, Dr A. *Chester*
Swansea (Clydach 3504)
Jones, D. H. *Chepstow*
Pontypridd
(Newton-Llantwit 2515)
Jones, E. *Wolverhampton*
Hednesford (Hednesford 2721)
Jones, Hbt *York*
Malton (Malton 2630)
Jones, H. T. *Newmarket*
Newmarket (Newmarket 4884)
(Home—Exning 260)
Jordon, I. D. *Newcastle*
Newcastle-on-Tyne
(Newcastle-on-Tyne 869143)
Keenor, R. F. *Bath*
Chulmleigh (Chulmleigh 432)
Keith, D. *Salisbury*
Winchester (Winchester 880808)
Kemp, A. R. *Catterick*
Richmond (East Layton 397)
Kennard, L. G. *Bath*
Bishops Lydeard
(Bishops Lydeard 432550)
Kent, D. W. J. *Goodwood*
Chichester (West Ashling 231)
Kersey, T. *Doncaster*
West Melton (Rotherham 873166)
Killoran, M. *Chepstow*
Cheltenham (Coberley 344)
Kindersley, G. *Newbury*
Newbury (Great Shefford 301)
Lamb, C. R. *Newcastle*
Seahouses (Seahouses 260)
Lay, V. M. *Warwick*
Broughton (Banbury 3209)
Leigh, J. P. *Doncaster*
Willoughton (Hemswell 210)
Lomax, Mrs R. A. *Newbury*
Baydon (Aldbourne 288)
Long, J. E. *Folkestone*
Elham (Elham 229)
Lunness, B. W. *Newmarket*
Newmarket (Newmarket 3926)
Magner, E. *Doncaster*
Doncaster (Doncaster 49787)
Makin, P. J. *Newbury*
Ogbourne Maisey
(Marlborough 2973)
Marks, D. *Newbury*
Lambourn (Lambourn 71767)
Marshall, T. C. *Newbury*
Lambourn (Lambourn 71025)
Marshall, W. C. *Newmarket*
Newmarket (Newmarket 61574)
Mason, R. E. G. *Leicester*
Guilsborough (Guilsborough 381)
Masson, M. J. *Brighton*
Lewes (Lewes 4984)
Matthews, S. G. *Salisbury*
Romsey (West Wellow 22254)

Maxwell, W. F. *Newbury*
Lambourn (Lambourn 71653)
McCain, D. *Liverpool*
Birkdale (Southport 66007
or 69677)
McCourt, M. *Newbury*
Letcombe Regis (Wantage 4456)
McMahon, B. A. *Wolverhampton*
Tamworth (Tamworth 62901)
Mellor, S. T. E. *Newbury*
Lambourn (Lambourn 71485)
Metcalfe, P. E. A. *Thirsk*
Oldstead (Coxwold 278)
Miller, C. J. V. *Warwick*
Stratford-on-Avon
(Alderminster 296 or 232)
Milner, G. P. *Chester*
Cuddington (Whitchurch 3527)
Mitchell, P. *Epsom*
Epsom (Ashtead 73729)
Mitchell, V. J. *Doncaster*
Worksop (Worksop 85163)
Molony, T. *Leicester*
Melton Mowbray
(Wymondham 273)
Morley, M. F. D. *Newmarket*
Bury St Edmunds (Culford 278)
Morris, H. *Chester*
Bangor-on-Dee
(Overton-on-Dee 349)
Morris, Miss S. O. *Salisbury*
Chard (Chard 3187 and 3379)
Muggeridge, F. M. *Salisbury*
Romsey (West Wellow 22430)
Mulhall, J. *York*
York (York 66321)
Murless, C. F. N. *Newmarket*
Newmarket (Newmarket 2024)
(Home—Newmarket 2387)
Murphy, R. G. R. *Wolverhampton*
Wellington (Telford 42209)
Murray, W. F. *Catterick*
Middleham (Leyburn 2220)
Naughton, M. P. *Catterick*
Richmond (Richmond 2803)
Neaves, A. S. *Folkestone*
Eastling (Eastling 274)
Nelson, J. P. *Newbury*
Lambourn (Lambourn 71391)
Nesbitt, S. *Ripon*
Ripon (Boroughbridge 2037)
Nicholson, D. *Warwick*
Stow-on-the-Wold
(Stow-on-the-Wold 30417)
Nicholson, H. C. D. *Warwick*
Prestbury (Cheltenham 28763)
Norton, S. G. *Doncaster*
Barnsley (Silkstone 8497)
O'Donoghue, J. *Lingfield*
Reigate (Reigate 45241)
O'Gorman, W. A. *Newmarket*
Newmarket (Newmarket 3330)
Old, J. A. B. *Salisbury*
Salisbury (Fontmell Magna 648)
Oliver, J. K. M. *Edinburgh*
Hawick (Denholm 216)
O'Neill, H. *Warwick*
Rugby (Rugby 3205)

O'Neill, O. *Warwick*
Cheltenham (Bishops Cleeve 3275)
Oughton, Mrs D. R. *Brighton*
Findon (Findon 2113)
Palmer, S. T. *Nottingham*
Bottesford (Bottesford 42767)
Payne, H. W. *Bath*
Wells (Wells 72419)
Payne, W. J. *Newbury*
Eastbury (Lambourn 71722)
Peacock, J. H. *Wolverhampton*
Lawton
Peacock, R. D. *Catterick*
Middleham (Leyburn 3291)
Peacock, R. E. *Chester*
Tarporley (Tarporley 2716)
Peter-Hoblyn, G. H. *Newbury*
Marlborough (Marlborough 2417)
Pitman, Mrs J. S. *Newbury*
Lambourn (Lambourn 71714)
Pitt, A. J. *Epsom*
Epsom (Epsom 25034)
Plant, D. G. *Chester*
Wirral (051-327 6469)
Poston, P. J. *Newmarket*
Newmarket (Newmarket 2319)
Potts, A. W. *Beverley*
Barton-on-Humber
(Saxby All Saints 750)
Powney, J. *Newmarket*
Newmarket (Newmarket 3343)
Prescott, Sir Mark *Newmarket*
Newmarket (Newmarket 2117)
Price, H. R. *Brighton*
Findon (Findon 2388)
Pritchard-Gordon, G. A.
Newmarket
Newmarket (Newmarket 2824)
(Home—Newmarket 4685)
Pullen, J. R. F. *Ascot*
Church Crookham
(Aldershot 850567)
Ransom, P. B. *Wolverhampton*
Wigmore (Wigmore 253)
Reavey, E. J. B. *Newbury*
East Hendred (East Hendred 297)
Richards, G. W. *Carlisle*
Penrith (Greystoke 392)
Richmond, B. A. *Doncaster*
Wellingore (Lincoln 810578)
Rimell, T. F. *Warwick*
Kinnersley (Severn Stoke 233)
Ringer, D. S. *Newmarket*
Newmarket (Newmarket 2653)
Robinson, G. N. *Newcastle*
Beal (Beal 237)
Robinson, P. J. *Newmarket*
Newmarket (Newmarket 2090)
(Home—Stetchworth 414)
Rohan, H. P. *York*
Malton (Malton 2337/8)
Ryan, M. J. *Newmarket*
Newmarket (Newmarket 4172)
Salaman, M. *Chepstow*
Crickhowell (Crickhowell 810362)
Sasse, D. J. G. *Newbury*
Lambourn (Lambourn 71902)

871

Scudamore, M. J.   *Wolverhampton*
Hoarwithy   (Carey 253)
Shedden, L. H.   *York*
Wetherby   (Wetherby 2122)
Simpson, Mrs J. B.   *Catterick*
Heighington   (Aycliffe 2263)
Sinclair, Miss A. V.   *Brighton*
Lewes   (Lewes 6619)
   (Home—Lewes 3851)
Smith, A.   *Beverley*
Beverley   (Beverley 882520)
Smith, Denys   *Newcastle*
Bishop Auckland
   (Bishop Auckland 3317)
Smith, Douglas   *Newmarket*
Newmarket
   (Newmarket 2036 and 2841)
Smyly, R. M.   *Newbury*
Lambourn   (Lambourn 71408)
Smyth, G. R.   *Brighton*
Lewes   (Lewes 4581)
Smyth, H. E.   *Epsom*
Epsom   (Epsom 23664)
   (Home—Epsom 21446)
Smyth, R. V.   *Epsom*
Epsom   (Epsom 20053)
Spearing, J. L.   *Warwick*
Alcester   (Bideford-on-Avon 2639)
Stapleton, K. G.   *Ripon*
Skipton   (Skipton 2703)
Stephenson, W.   *Newmarket*
Royston   (Royston 43386)
Stephenson, W. A.   *Newcastle*
Bishop Auckland   (Rushyford 213)
Stevens, A. G. M.   *Bath*
Chippenham   (Box 2777)
Stoute, M. R.   *Newmarket*
Newmarket   (Newmarket 3801)
Stubbs, R. W.   *Teesside*
Darlington   (Darlington 56877)
Sturdy, R. C.   *Salisbury*
Shrewton   (Shrewton 222)
Supple, R. H.   *Lingfield*
Dartford   (Longfield 3915)
Sutcliffe, J. R. E.   *Epsom*
Epsom   (Ashtead 72825)
Swainson, W. J. H.   *Warwick*
Bredon   (Bredon 332)
Swift, B. C.   *Epsom*
Headley
   (Leatherhead 77209 and 77308)
Tate, F. M.   *Warwick*
Kidderminster
   (Chaddes ey Corbett 243)
Taylor, P. M.   *Newbury*
Upper Lambourn
   (Lambourn 71667)
Thom, D. T.   *Newmarket*
Newmarket   (Exning 288)
Thompson, V.   *Newcastle*
Alnwick   (Embleton 272)
Thorne, J.   *Bath*
Bridgwater   (Holford 216)
Tinkler, C. H.   *Thirsk*
Thirsk   (Upsall 336)
Titterington, R.   *Carlisle*
Penrith   (Skelton 363)

Toft, G.   *Beverley*
Beverley   (Beverley 885105)
Tree, A. J.   *Newbury*
Beckhampton   (Avebury 204)
   (Home—Avebury 244)
Turnell, A. R.   *Newbury*
Ogbourne Maisey
   (Marlborough 2542)
Turner, J. A. M.   *York*
Boston Spa   (Boston Spa 843324)
Underhill, S.   *Warwick*
Alcester   (Bideford-on-Avon 3714)
Underwood, D. B.   *Sandown*
Bramley   (Bramley (Surrey) 3147)
Vallance, G. R. A.   *Bath*
Bishops Cannings   (Cannings 285)
Vergette, G. M.   *Leicester*
Market Deeping
   (Market Deeping 342226)
Vibert, R. J.   *Newbury*
East Hendred   (East Hendred 247)
Vickers, J. R. P.   *Catterick*
Darlington
   (Dinsdale 2450 and 2438)
Vigors, N. A. C.   *Newbury*
Lambourn   (Lambourn 71657)
Wainwright, S.   *York*
Malton   (Malton 4334)
Wakley, N. J. W.   *Bath*
Taunton   (Churchstanton 253)
Walker, I. S.   *Newmarket*
Newmarket
   (Exning 219 and Newmarket 2457)
Walker, T. F.   *York*
Flaxton   (Flaxton Moor 314)
Wallace, G.   *Leicester*
Grantham   (Knipton 312)
Walwyn, F. T. T.   *Newbury*
Lambourn   (Lambourn 71555)
Walwyn, P. T.   *Newbury*
Lambourn   (Lambourn 71347)
Ward, R. C.   *Doncaster*
Doncaster   (Doncaster 700574)
Wardle, I. P.   *Bath*
East Harrington   (Wells 73167)
Watts, J. W.   *Catterick*
Richmond   (Richmond 2081)
   (Home—Richmond 2287)
Watts, W. C.   *Beverley*
Bridlington   (Bridlington 3719)
Waugh, T. A.   *Newmarket*
Newmarket   (Newmarket 2233)
Webber, J. H.   *Warwick*
Mollington   (Cropredy 226)
Weeden, D. E.   *Newmarket*
Newmarket   (Newmarket 5050)
Welch, J. T.   *Ascot*
Ascot   (Ascot 22395)
Westbrook, H. C.   *Newmarket*
Newmarket   (Newmarket 3657)
Weymes, E.   *Catterick*
Leyburn   (Coverdale 229)
Wharton, H.   *Doncaster*
Doncaster   (Doncaster 54126)
Wharton, W.   *Leicester*
Melton Mowbray
   (Waltham-on-the-Wolds 258)
   (Home—Melton Mowbray 5225)

Whelan, D.   *Epsom*
 Epsom   (Epsom 22763)
   (Home—Epsom 21482)
Whiston, W. R.   *Wolverhampton*
 Market Drayton   (Hodnet 203)
Whitfield, Mrs N.   *Goodwood*
 Petworth   (Graffham 258)
Wigham, P.   *York*
 Malton   (Rillington 332)
Wightman, W. G. R.   *Goodwood*
 Upham (Bishop's Waltham 2565)
Wiles, F. J.   *Pontefract*
 Wakefield   (Flockton 468)
Wilkinson, B. E.   *Catterick*
 Middleham   (Middleham 3385)
Williams, D. H.   *York*
 Bishopthorpe   (York 28693)
Williams, H. F.   *Newbury*
 Lambourn   (Lambourn 71423)
Williams, W. R.   *Bath*
 Buckfastleigh (Buckfastleigh 3590)
Wilmot, Miss N. E.   *Ascot*
 Binfield   (Bracknell 3326)
Wilson, R.   *Newbury*
 Lambourn   (Lambourn 71636)
Winter, F. T.   *Newbury*
 Lambourn   (Lambourn 71438)

Winter, J. R.   *Newmarket*
 Newmarket   (Newmarket 3898)
Wise, B. J.   *Brighton*
 Polegate   (Polegate 3331)
Woodman, S.   *Goodwood*
 Chichester (Chichester 527136)
Wragg, H.   *Newmarket*
 Newmarket   (Newmarket 2328)
Yardley, F.   *Wolverhampton*
 Kidderminster
   (Chaddesley Corbett 273)
Yeoman, D.   *Newmarket*
 Comberton

The following also held a licence for
part of the year:
Blackwell, G.
Buckley, P. J. C.
Corbett, T. A., The Late
Cundell, F. L.
Francis, G. T.
Healey, T. W.
Nagle, Mrs F.
Payne, K.
Simpson, R.
Whitehead, K. C.

JOCKEYS

The following is a list of jockeys who held a flat licence in 1976. The figures
in brackets show the number of winners each jockey has ridden in this country
during the past three seasons, 1974, 1975 and 1976, in that order. The
telephone numbers and riding weights are added, where known.

Appleton, D. N. (—:—:0).... 8 2
Apter, E. R. (20:25:19)....... 7 10
 c/o Beverley 885041
Askew, H. C. (—:0:0)........ 8 0
 c/o Rushyford 213
Atkinson, D. J. (2:1:0)....... 7 13
 Great Shefford 288
Bailey, R. C. (—:—:1)....... 8 9
 c/o Weyhill 2278
Balding, J. (1:2:0).......... 8 4
 Doncaster 710096
Baldock, Mrs C. E. (—:—:0) 7 10
Barclay, A. M. (18:40:21).... 8 2
 Thirsk 23209
Baxter, G. E. (34:65:44)...... 7 12
 Lambourn 71320
Bentley, W. (6:2:5).......... 7 9
 Leyburn 2289
Birch, M. (13:33:48)......... 7 12
 Malton 3885
Bodman, G. A. (0:0:0)....... 7 12
 Rockbourne 388
Bond, A. M. (36:69:46)....... 7 12
 c/o Newmarket 2192
Bray, M. J. (2:3:1).......... 7 10
 c/o Wetherby 2122
Bridge, T. G. M. (1:0:1)...... 8 0
 c/o Longfield 3915
Brown, L. G. (14:10:6)....... 7 13
 Malton 2631
Butler, K. R. (1:0:0)......... 7 7
 Winchester 880310

Cain, T. (21:16:7)........... 7 10
 01-640 9061
Carson, W. F. H.
 (129:131:138) 7 10
 Newmarket 3623
Chan, C. C. (Patrick)
 (—:0:0) 7 7
Cook, P. A. (34:56:66)....... 7 11
 Newbury 200893
Cousins, A. M. (3:17:5)...... 8 1
 Leyburn 3417
Cullen, D. (29:18:10)........ 7 7
 Goring-on-Thames 2440
Curant, J. A. (22:7:3)........ 7 12
 c/o Weyhill 2278
Curant, R. D. (1:0:10)....... 7 12
 Lambourn 71937
Davies, R. F. (—:—:0)....... 9 0
 Hodnet 368
Douglass, G. W. (—:—:0).... 8 0
Dudley, J. (—:—:0).......... 8 2
Duffield, G. P. (49:26:50).... 7 10
 Stetchworth 544
Durr, F. (39:79:44).......... 8 0
 Newmarket 730363
Dwyer, C. A. (4:5:17)........ 8 1
 Malton 3471
Eagleton, Mrs M. R. (0:0:0). 8 5
Eccleston, C. H. (29:15:29)... 7 7
 York 21374
Eddery, P. J. J. (148:164:162). 8 2
 Cheltenham 28763

Egan, J. R. (4:3:0).......... 8 0
Exning 547
Eldin, E. (45:34:49)......... 8 2
Newmarket 3217
Elliott, R. P. (6:—:9)....... 8 0
Newbury 43472
Elliott, R. S. (3:1:1)........ 8 0
c/o Avebury 204
Ellis, J. (0:—:0)............. 7 2
Ellison, G. E. (—:—:0)...... 8 0
Ferguson, R. J. (3:0:3)...... 7 1
Newmarket 2004
Flint, A. (—:0:—)........... 8 7
c/o Coverdale 653
Fox, Robert (—:0:0)........ 8 0
c/o Weyhill 2278
Francois, C. G. A. (0:0:0).... 8 0
c/o Bishop's Waltham 2565
Germon, M. (1:2:3)......... 8 0
Worthing 207920
Giles, M. S. (0:0:0).......... 8 0
c/o Newmarket 2196
Glover, K. F. (—:—:0)....... 7 10
Goodwill, Miss L. M. (1:0:0). 8 0
c/o Newmarket 3218
Gray, D. J. (23:28:13)........ 8 0
Leyburn 2148
Guest, D. E. (0:0:1)......... 7 12
Newmarket 5453
Hall, A. G. (—:—:0).......... 8 2
Hancock, M. J. (0:—:0)...... 8 4
Hawkins, J. K. M. (—:—:0)... 8 0
c/o Hednesford 2721
Haynes, P. D. (—:—:0)...... 8 13
West Ashling 429
Hayward, J. E. (1:—:0)...... 8 4
Ewhurst 507
Hedley, B. F. (—:—:1)....... 8 0
Malton 3749 or 2511
Henry, B. (—:2:4)........... 8 0
Beverley 882520
Hide, E. W. G. (137:78:103)... 8 1
Malton 2132
Higgins, J. J. (7:6:2)......... 7 12
North Grimston 272
Hinds, H. W. (—:—:0)....... 8 2
Holmes, K. M. (—:—:0)..... 8 7
Hornsby, H. M. (—:—:0).... 8 0
Hutchison, B. A. (—:—:0)... 9 0
Hutchinson, Richard (7:10:1) 7 10
c/o Ayr 66232
Hutchinson, Ron. R.
(62:59:56) 7 12
Reigate 42132 and 48817
Ives, T. A. (26:24:48)........ 8 4
Malton 3994
Jago, B. (11:2:10)............ 7 10
Epsom 21025
Jenkinson, I. P. (8:7:7)...... 7 4
c/o Epsom 20053
Jesse, W. A. (5:0:1).......... 7 0
Lambourn 71767
Johnson, E. (55:57:65)....... 7 8
Buckland 603
Kelsey, T. (2:0:0)........... 8 5
c/o Bishop Auckland 3317
Kettle, M. (14:9:10)......... 7 11
Fordham 696

Kimberley, A. A. (38:37:35).. 8 1
Newmarket 3267
Knowles, E. E. (0:0:0)....... 7 13
Lappin, T. W. (20:17:13)..... 7 12
c/o Leyburn 2477
Leason, K. M. (12:9:18)...... 7 7
c/o Dunbar 2583
Lee, B. (0:0:0).............. 7 5
c/o Malton 2842
Leonard, C. S. (3:0:1).. ..... 7 0
c/o Dorking 6223
Lewis, G. (84:89:65)......... 8 1
Burgh Heath 51225
Lewis, K. (16:25:19)......... 7 2
c/o Armitage 490298
Logie, J. (0:0:0)............. 8 0
Lowe, J. J. (13:31:47)........ 7 4
Old Catterick 8340
Lynch, J. (19:24:46).......... 7 12
Wantage 3682
Maclean, T. J. (—:—:0)...... 8 5
Madden, P. J. (8:7:9)........ 8 3
Newmarket 750603
Maitland, D. (17:7:7)........ 7 5
Newmarket 61615
Marshall, R. C. (19:27:22)... 8 2
c/o Newmarket 61574
Matthias, J. J. (24:18:21)..... 8 2
c/o Kingsclere 298210
McEntee, P. M. (—:—:0).... 8 9
c/o Lambourn 71850
McIntosh, N. (0:1:0)........ 7 0
c/o Dunbar 2583
McKay, D. J. (19:9:18)....... 7 5
Great Shefford 237
McKeown, T. P. (19:25:22)... 7 8
Newmarket 61589
McNamee, C. J. (—:—:0).... 8 0
Mercer, J. (70:93:98)........ 8 4
Hermitage 200306
Millman, B. R. (3:2:0)....... 8 7
c/o Box 2777
Moore, G. M. (—:0:1)....... 8 4
c/o Boroughbridge 2037
Morby, F. (34:43:30)........ 8 0
Newbury 42610
Moriarty, J. (—:2:0)......... 8 0
c/o Winchester 880808
Morris, D. W. (0:0:0)........ 8 9
Stetchworth 493
Moss, C. J. T. (15:26:18)..... 7 13
Long Buckby 842489
Murray, A. P. (84:88:4)...... 7 12
Chantilly 457 1298
Naughton, Mrs A. M. (0:0:0) 7 12
Richmond 2803
Noble, D. (1:1:3)............ 7 5
c/o Findon 2388
O'Gorman, W. A. (—:4:2)... 8 12
Newmarket 3330
Oldroyd, G. R. (2:16:9)...... 8 3
Bridlington 79712
O'Leary, P. (0:0:0).......... 7 9
01-979 6046
O'Neill, J. J. (1:2:0)......... 9 0
c/o Greystoke 392
Owen, R. J. (—:0:0)......... 8 1
East Knoyle 305

Parkes, L. C. (12:5:6) 7 3
Malton 2845
Perkins, P. (8:3:1) 7 13
Romsey 512670
Perks, S. J. (27:6:16) 7 11
Hednesford 4836
Piggott, L. K. (143: 113: 87) . . 8 5
Newmarket 2584
Procter, B. T. (4:1:1) 8 2
East Ilsley 369
Ramshaw, G. (10:16:14) 8 1
Burgh Heath 53611
Raymond, B. H. (46:73:58) . . . 8 2
Newmarket 730387
Reader, R. W. D. (3:0:0) 7 7
Norwood Hill 246
Rogers, T. (6:3:4) 7 12
Thatcham 63047
Rouse, B. A. (22:20:34) 7 11
Epsom 22140
Ryan, D. (8:5:5) 8 2
Crishall 466
Salmon, S. E. W. (37:35:22) . . 7 4
Malton 4285
Seagrave, J. (53:45:50) 8 3
Malton 2692
Senior, A. (0:0:0) 8 0
c/o Harby 60671
Sexton, G. C. (10:14:12) 7 12
Newmarket 4367
Stainsby, R. I. (0:0:0) 7 10
c/o Cressage 392
Starkey, G. M. W. (42:42:73) 8 5
Mildenhall 714672
Stead, D. (0:0:0) 8 4
Steel, P. J. B. (0:0:0) 8 11
c/o Clydach 3504
Still, R. W. (4:4:7) 7 4
Newmarket 750755
Storey, F. (1:0:0) 8 2
c/o Newmarket 730300
Street, R. (2:9:10) 7 5
c/o Lambourn 71548
Taylor, B. (64:49:108) 8 4
Stetchworth 515 or 530

Thomas, M. L. (62:58:90) 7 8
Mildenhall 713916
Thornley, A. W. (0:0:0) 7 0
c/o Baschurch 374
Tinkler, C. H. (0:3:0) 8 11
Upsall 336
Tinkler, N. D. (1:0:0) 9 4
Upsall 336
Tippling, A. A. (1:0:0) 7 12
c/o Leyburn 3254
Tulk, P. F. (8:0:24) 8 0
Aycliffe 5769
Waldron, P. (43:36:33) 7 12
Newbury 43620
Wargen, L. S. (2:1:0) 8 4
Newmarket 3707
Weaver, R. I. (—:—:0) 7 12
Hungerford 2190
Welsh, G. (0:0:0) 7 10
c/o Rushyford 213
Wilkins, L. F. (0:0:0) 8 0
c/o Long Sutton 376
Williams, C. N. (6:5:3) 8 0
Lambourn 71454
Williams, J. A. N. (0:—:0) 9 0
Clydach 3407
Williams, M. (3:0:0) 8 10
c/o Chepstow 2846
Wilson, E. (0:0:0) 8 5
c/o Little Budworth 316 . . . . .
Wilson, J. M. (14:1:1) 8 0
Mogador 2010
Yeoman, Mrs M. M. (—:0:0) 8 7

The following relinquished their
licences during the season:

Alexander, S. R.   James, P. A.
Ball, C. A.   Keane, A. F.
Becker, R.   Marshall, E. T.
Cadwaladr, G. E.   Nicholson, W. J. C.
Carson, T. W.   Skilling, J. F.
Foster, R. D.   Tate, J. W.
Gauntlett, C.   Willey, D. M.
Gilbert, Miss A.   Wilson, P.
Guest, R.   Yates, D. I.

APPRENTICES

The following list shows the employer and riding weight of every apprentice who held a licence at the end of the 1976 season, and the number of winners he or she had ridden in this country up to the end of the 1976 season, wins in apprentice races being recorded separately.

Apprentices under 24 years of age may claim 7 lb until they have won 10 races, 5 lb until they have won 50 races and 3 lb until they have won 75 races. Apprentice races are excepted in all these cases. The claim may be exercised in all handicaps and selling races, and in all other races with guaranteed prize money of not more than £2,500.

The allowance each apprentice is entitled to claim is shown in brackets.

Addie, L. W. (7) 1 ap......... 8 0
(N. Angus)
Allsopp, R. M. (7).......... 7 10
(W. Wharton)
Anderson, W. J. (7).......... 7 12
(J. Nelson)
Armstrong, I. S. (7) 1 ap..... 7 2
(B. Hills)
Atkinson, P. (7)............. 6 11
(P. Walwyn)
Auld, A. (7)................. 7 4
(M. Jarvis)
Baker, R. W. (5) 25+6 ap.... 7 10
(W. Wightman)
Ballantine, H. (5) 36+6 ap... 7 3
(H. Smyth)
Balmer, A. McC. (7)........ 7 0
(Denys Smith)
Banner, M. A. (7) 7 6
(B. Lunness)
Barker, R. S. (7) 3+2 ap..... 7 4
(J. Etherington)
Barrett, W. (7) 2............. 7 9
(S. Matthews)
Beecroft, M. C. (7).......... 7 0
(W. Murray)
Belton, G. (7)............... 7 5
(I. Balding)
Bennett, B. (7).............. 9 0
(J. W. Watts)
Bennett, J. (7).............. 7 0
(K. Payne)
Black, J. (7)................. 7 7
(R. Armstrong)
Blake, A. M. (7)............. 8 0
(I. Balding)
Blanks, J. M. (7)............ 7 7
(A. Pitt)
Bleasdale, J. (5) 13+6 ap..... 7 8
(S. Hall)
Bodley, K. M. (7)............ 7 6
(H. Candy)
Bohannan, M. J. (7)......... 8 4
(N. Murless)
Booth, K. J. (7)............. 5 10
(D. Holmes)
Boud, W. M. (7)............. 7 7
(J. O'Donoghue)
Boughton, J. H. (7).......... 7 7
(T. Marshall)
Bowker, R. A. (7) 1 ap....... 7 9
(N. Callaghan)
Bowley, R. G. (7)............ 7 7
(B. Hobbs)
Bowness, C. J. (7)........... 7 0
(P. Taylor)

Boyfield, A. R. (7)........... 7 7
(Miss N. Wilmot)
Bradbury, E. (7)............. 7 8
(C. Brittain)
Brannick, N. (7)............. 7 2
(R. Mason)
Breeze, N. B. (7)............ 7 4
(J. Peacock)
Brown, J. M. (7)............. 7 5
(P. Rohan)
Bruce, E. A. (7)............. 7 0
(E. Magner)
Brydon, G. (7).............. 7 5
(G. Harwood)
Cade, R. M. (7)............. 8 0
(I. Walker)
Cain, P. (7) 1+2 ap.......... 8 7
(S. Hall)
Callaghan, R. J. (7).......... 7 7
(G. Smyth)
Cameron, T. (7)............. 7 0
(R. Jarvis)
Carter, P. D. (7)............ 7 0
(S. Ingham)
Cartmill, R. A. (7).......... 7 2
(M. Jarvis)
Chadderton, P. T. (7)....... 6 9
(C. Bewicke)
Chaddock, N. A. (7)......... 8 3
(G. Pritchard-Gordon)
Charlton, S. F. (7) 9+5 ap... 8 7
(D. Williams)
Charnock, L. (5) 35+4 ap.... 7 0
(Denys Smith)
Cheshire, M. T. (7).......... 6 0
(I. Balding)
Christie, C. M. (7) 3+1 ap... 7 9
(N. Angus)
Clark, J. R. (7).............. 7 3
(W. A. Stephenson)
Clarke, P. (7) 1 ap........... 6 7
(J. W. Watts)
Clayton, D. R. (7)........... 8 7
(W. Wightman)
Clotworthy, B. J. (7) 2+2 ap. 7 12
(N. Adam)
Cochrane, R. (5) 11+4 ap.... 8 2
(B. Hills)
Codgell, P. (7).............. 7 10
(P. Haslam)
Cole, C. R. G. (7)........... 7 7
(R. Hannon)
Collins, J. F. (7)............. 8 7
(R. Hollinshead)
Colquhoun, P. R. (7) 2 ap.... 7 9
(I. Walker)

876

Cooney, D. E. (7) 4 ap....... 7 8
(F. Carr)
Corney, G. A. (7) 1.......... 7 11
(R. Armstrong)
Corrigan, R. (7)............ 7 10
(K. Payne)
Court, P. J. (7).............. 7 6
(D. Keith)
Cox, I. G. (7)................ 9 1
(H. T. Jones)
Crawford, I. R. (7).......... 7 7
(S. Ingham)
Cressy, A. P. (5) 16+8 ap.... 7 10
(G. Harwood)
Crick, Miss S. E. (7)......... 7 7
(J. Benstead)
Crook, A. (7) 5+2 ap........ 7 12
(S. Nesbitt)
Crossley, B. G. (7).......... 6 7
(R. Armstrong)
Crowther, N. (5) 39+7 ap.... 7 11
(J. Hindley)
Curley, F. J. (7) 4+3 ap...... 6 12
(P. Poston)
Dale, G. (7)................. 8 0
(H. Nicholson)
Dalton, P. T. (7)............ 8 7
(J. Etherington)
d'Arcy, L. M. (7)............ 6 7
(F. Carr)
d'Arcy, P. W. (7) 1+3 ap..... 7 8
(G. Toft)
Darley, K. P. (7)............ 6 4
(R. Hollinshead)
Davies, N. (7)............... 7 10
(P. Robinson)
Davies, T. G. (7) 6+4 ap..... 8 0
(W. A. Stephenson)
Dewar, M. D. (7)............ 8 2
(S. Ingham)
Dineley, D. B. (3) 51+13 ap.. 7 8
(P. Cole)
Dinwoodie, R. J. (7)......... 7 9
(R. Smyth)
Dixey, V. (7)................ 7 2
(P. Haslam)
Dixon, A. (7)................ 7 7
(M. Naughton)
Dodds, S. W. (7)............ 7 0
(Sir Mark Prescott)
Douthwaite, G. (7) 1+1 ap... 7 0
(S. Nesbitt)
Duffy, G. J. (7).............. 6 0
(H. Wragg)
Dunlop, V. A. (7) 1+3 ap..... 7 10
(N. Angus)
Eccles, S. (5) 18+7 ap........ 7 5
(K. Payne)
Eden, G. H. (7).............. 7 7
(Miss N. Wilmot)
Edmondson, R. J. 127+4 ap.. 8 6
(P. Cole)
Elderfield, W. G. (7)......... 7 0
(R. Jarvis)
Emes, I. M. (5) 12+3 ap...... 7 12
(C. Dingwall)
Emmerson, P. (7)............ 7 2
(K. Payne)

Fairhurst, A. (7)............ 7 0
(T. Fairhurst)
Fenwick, J. A. (7)............ 6 7
(W. A. Stephenson)
Fisher, Miss J. (7).......... 6 11
(F. Dever)
Fitzgerald, E. F. (7) 3 ap..... 7 5
(R. Smyth)
Fitzgerald, S. S. P. (7)....... 7 4
(B. Swift)
Ford, D. P. A. (7)........... 6 7
(M. Jarvis)
Ford, D. R. J. (7) 1 ap........ 6 7
(M. Jarvis)
Fox, R. D. S. 96+8 ap....... 7 4
(H. Nicholson)
Franks, A. (7)............... 6 13
(R. Price)
Freeman, S. (5) 11+2 ap..... 7 10
(J. Calvert)
Gardiner, D. J. (7).......... 7 0
(M. Bradley)
Gengan, T. (7).............. 6 13
(M. Haynes)
Gibson, S. G. (7)............ 8 7
(D. Sasse)
Giles, M. J. (7)............. 8 7
(R. Hollinshead)
Gillespie, D. F. (5) 21........ 7 6
(J. Dunlop)
Gleaves, P. A. (7) 1.......... 8 0
(K. Whitehead)
Gosney, G. (7) 6+2 ap....... 7 9
(H. Wragg)
Gould, M. R. (7)............ 7 0
(J. Dunlop)
Grant, D. (7)............... 7 10
(M. McCourt)
Gray, E. J. (7) 1+1 ap........ 7 1
(B. Swift)
Greaves, D. W. (7).......... 7 0
(D. Marks)
Greensmith, J. J. (7)......... 6 12
(R. Hollinshead)
Griffiths, A. (7)............. 8 3
(C. V. Miller)
Guest, G. A. (7)............. 7 12
(N. Guest)
Gunn, G. P. (7) 8+1 ap...... 7 12
(W. Holden)
Hall, S. A. (7)............... 6 9
(K. Stapleton)
Hamblett, P. A. (7).......... 7 5
(E. Collingwood)
Hamblett, S. (7)............. 6 13
(E. Collingwood)
Hamill, T. (7)............... 7 7
(J. Dunlop)
Hamilton, J. F. (7).......... 6 11
(R. Hern)
Hannigan, L. (7)............ 7 5
(J. Hill)
Harraway, M. E. (7)......... 7 9
(M. Stevens)
Hawes, K. (7) 1 ap........... 7 9
(R. Hern)
Hawkes, C. A. (7)........... 8 7
(B. Swift)

877

Haynes, J. C. (7) 1 ap........ 6 12
(R. Hollinshead)
Higgins, E. M. (7)........... 7 12
(P. Buckley)
Hill, S. C. (7) 2 ap........... 7 4
(W. Stephenson)
Hirst, Miss K. L. (7)......... 7 13
(Miss S. Hall)
Hives, S. K. (7) 8+8 ap....... 8 3
(W. Stephenson)
Holland, A. (7) 3 ap.......... 7 10
(P. Haslam)
Hood, B. (7) 8+1 ap......... 7 11
(J. Etherington)
Hood, S. J. (7)............... 7 8
(H. Candy)
Hopkins, A. C. (7) 1 ap....... 7 8
(R. Armstrong)
Hopley, D. J. (7).............. 7 2
(R. Hollinshead)
Horton, S. P. (7) 1 ap 8 0
(P. Rohan)
Houlker, S. (7).............. 7 7
(J. Berry)
Houston, H. McG. T. (7)
1+2 ap................... 6 6
(C. Brittain)
Howard, P. T. (7) 1 ap....... 6 7
(R. Hern)
Howes, C. R. (7) 7 0
(J. Sutcliffe)
Howie, D. D. (7) 8 0
(P. Cundell)
Hyslop, S. (7)............... 7 7
(A. Jarvis)

Innes, S. (7)................ 7 13
(P. Cole)

Jacques, B. T. (7)............ 6 6
(R. Smyth)
Jarvis, S. J. (7) 3+1 ap 6 0
(A. Jarvis)
Johnson, Ian (7)............. 7 10
(Hbt Jones)
Johnson, Ian E. (3) 72+7 ap.. 7 13
(H. Nicholson)
Johnson, M. (7).............. 7 10
(Doug Smith)

Kalis, S. A. (7).............. 7 10
(M. Stevens)
Kear, J. L. (7)............... 8 0
(M. Bradley)
Keenan, W. D. (7)............ 8 0
(W. A. Stephenson)
Keightley, S. L. (7)........... 7 4
(W. Stephenson)
Keltie, W. (7) 1+1 ap........ 7 7
(T. Craig)
Kitaszewski, S. (7)........... 6 4
(E. Reavey)

Lake, P. M. (7) 8 0
(S. James)
Langfrey, P. (7).............. 7 0
(S. Ingham)
Laws, S. D. (7) 6 7
(G. Toft)
Laybourn, P. (7) 1 ap 7 7
(Denys Smith)

Lingham, J. J. (7)............ 6 5
(B. Hobbs)
Lintott, D. J. (7)............. 8 0
(M. Smyly)
Little, D. (7)................ 7 9
(N. Angus)
Little, R. (7)................ 7 10
(T. Craig)
London, R. (7).............. 7 7
(P. Ashworth)
Lundie, I. S. (7)............. 7 12
(W. Wightman)
Lynch, J. D. (7).............. 7 0
(R. Smyth)
Lynch, P. B. (7).............. 7 7
(B. Swift)
MacInnes, Miss M. (7)....... 7 7
(G. Wallace)
Madden, J. (7) 1............. 7 8
(H. Candy)
Major, C. T. (7).............. 7 3
(W. Marshall)
Malham, M. S. T. (7)........ 6 7
(D. Marks)
Malone, T. A. (7)............ 7 8
(J. Hindley)
Marsh, G. J. (7).............. 7 7
(G. Harwood)
McBride, G. (7) 1+1 ap...... 7 0
(N. Angus)
McCubbin, F. A. (7)......... 7 10
(A. Pitt)
McCutcheon, P. (7)......... 7 3
(S. Woodman)
McDermott, P. M. (7)....... 7 1
(D. Peacock)
McGee, P. J. (7)............. 7 12
(W. O'Gorman)
McGlynn, J. (7)............. 6 11
(C. Boothman)
McGregor, J. P. (7).......... 7 12
(P. Ashworth)
McIlfatrick, C. (7).......... 7 7
(J. Bethell)
McKay, A. (7) 1 ap........... 7 7
(T. Craig)
McKay, R. D. (7) 2.......... 7 5
(E. Reavey)
McKechnie, M. (7) 2 ap...... 7 7
(I. Balding)
McKeown, W. A. P. (7) 1 ap.. 7 2
(D. Ringer)
McKevitt, V. (7)............. 7 2
(A. Johnson)
McLaughlin, J. F. S. (7) 1 ap. 7 5
(B. Lunness)
McLean, G. J. (7) 1 ap........ 8 2
(P. Cundell)
Menzies, N. (7).............. 7 7
(R. Bastiman)
Miller, M. M. (5) 12+9 ap.... 7 9
(R. Armstrong)
Montgomery, S. J. (7)....... 7 0
(J. Benstead)
Moore, J. B. (7).............. 7 10
(W. Haigh)
Moore, P. D. (7) 1 ap........ 8 7
(R. Hollinshead)

Morgan, K. E. (7) 7 10
(I. Walker)
Morris, P. P. (7) 1 ap 6 12
(F. J. Houghton)
Moss, D. E. (7) 3 + 6 ap 7 9
(P. Cundell)
Muddle, R. J. (5) 18 + 1 ap 7 10
(S. Ingham)
Murphy, P. M. (7) 7 4
(K. Ivory)
Nalepa, J. E. (7) 7 9
(C. Bewicke)
Nesbitt, H. A. (7) 5 12
(S. Nesbitt)
Newton, H. (7) 1 + 1 ap 7 4
(A. Balding)
Nicholls, D. (5) 19 + 8 ap 7 9
(R. Bastiman)
Nickson, K. (7) 1 ap 8 0
(P. Walwyn)
North, R. K. G. (7) 7 5
(M. Ryan)
Nuttall, M. J. (7) 5 + 3 ap 7 12
(Doug Smith)
Nutter, A. (7) 2 ap 7 7
(J. Bethell)
Nutter, C. (7) 5 + 4 ap 7 7
(Sir Mark Prescott)
O'Connell, A. V. F. (7) 6 7
(D. Marks)
O'Connor, M. G. (7) 8 3
(J. Berry)
O'Donoghue, T. A. (7) 7 10
(R. Hollinshead)
Ollivier, C. G. (7) 1 . . . . 6 5
(R. Vibert)
O'Ryan, T. (5) 42 + 10 ap 7 10
(M. H. Easterby)
Oxland, R. (7) 2 . . . . 7 13
(R. Boss)
Paisley, P. (7) 1 ap 7 7
(Dr A. Jones)
Parkin, S. J. (7) 1 . . . . 8 2
(L. Shedden)
Parr, S. (7) 6 0
(H. Wragg)
Patterson, P. J. A. (7) 7 9
(H. Wragg)
Payne, S. M. (7) 5 0
(I. Balding)
Pearson, S. C. (7) 7 0
(W. Elsey)
Peirson, S. (7) 7 10
(D. Nicholson)
Phillips, J. (7) 7 7
(Mrs L. Dingwall)
Pinnington, K. (7) 2 ap 7 3
(H. Smyth)
Plant, R. S. T. (7) 7 7
(D. Plant)
Powell, A. (7) 8 0
(H. Wharton)
Price, N. (7) 7 7
(J. Bethell)
Proud, A. (7) 1 . . . . 7 0
(M. W. Easterby)
Quinn, D. O. (7) 8 2
(G. W. Richards)

Radford, A. J. (7) 6 0
(E. Collingwood)
Raymont, S. J. (5) 10 + 4 ap . . . 7 5
(J. Tree)
Reid, J. A. (3) 66 + 3 ap 7 10
(C. Bewicke)
Reilly, B. A. (7) 2 + 2 ap 8 2
(I. Balding)
Richardson, B. (7) 7 0
(D. Sasse)
Richardson, S. R. (7) 8 0
(J. Gifford)
Richardson, T. C. (7) 7 10
(J. Nelson)
Riley, M. J. (7) 1 ap 7 5
(N. Robinson)
Roberts, B. (7) 7 7
(S. Nesbitt)
Robertson, Peter (7) 7 0
(R. Akehurst)
Robinson, A. N. (7) 7 4
(N. Robinson)
Robinson, P. A. (7) 1 . . . . 8 4
(W. Gray)
Rodrigues, C. (5) 22 + 2 ap 6 8
(B. Hobbs)
Ross, K. R. (7) 1 + 2 ap 6 12
(J. Dunlop)
Round, K. (7) 7 0
(Hbt Jones)
Rowe, J. (7) 2 + 4 ap 7 5
(H. Nicholson)
Roxburgh, D. (7) 7 0
(W. Wightman)
Ruddick, M. (7) 7 0
(R. Mason)
Rutledge, J. (7) 7 10
(I. Balding)
Rutter, P. J. (7) 7 5
(G. Blum)
Sanders, T. F. (7) 7 8
(W. Stephenson)
Sands, W. A. (7) 6 7
(C. Brittain)
Sapcote, P. (7) 7 3
(R. Bastiman)
Savigar, A. V. (7) 7 7
(R. Murphy)
Scaysbrook, S. P. (7) 8 0
(A. Jarvis)
Scott, D. C. (7) 7 9
(M. Smyly)
Shalloe, M. W. (7) 6 12
(Sir Mark Prescott)
Sharpe, B. (7) 7 7
(I. Balding)
Shaw, H. (7) 7 7
(J. Spearing)
Shearer, B. (7) 1 . . . . 6 11
(H. T. Jones)
Sheppard, C. (7) 4 ap 7 11
(R. Hannon)
Shrimpton, P. R. E. (7) 7 3
(R. Hollinshead)
Simmonite, C. A. R. (7) 2 . . . . 7 5
(M. Masson)
Simpson, Paul (7) 7 2
(R. Simpson)

Simpson, Philip (7)........ 6 11
(T. Walker)
Simpson, R. (7)............. 7 8
(L. Cumani)
Sims, D. J. (7).............. 6 7
(P. Cundell)
Skeats, G. H. (7)............ 7 10
(J. Cousins)
Skingle, A. T. (7)............ 7 4
(A. Jarvis)
Smith, A. J. (7)............. 6 7
(J. W. Watts)
Smith, K. (7)................ 7 12
(Doug Smith)
Snaith, W. J. (7) 2 + 1 ap...... 9 0
(B. Swift)
Sorby, K. (7)................ 7 12
(R. Hern)
Southern, R. (7)............. 7 7
(H. Westbrook)
Spendlove, S. (7) 1 ap........ 7 7
(H. Nicholson)
Spiller, G. V. (7) 1 ap........ 6 10
(P. Walwyn)
Stanford, Mrs J. (7)......... 7 0
(D. Williams)
Steed, P. C. (7) 3 + 1 ap...... 7 4
(R. Hollinshead)
Stiff, M. (7) 2 ap............. 7 4
(G. Harwood)
Stockton, J. (7)............. 7 10
(J. Turner)
Storey, C. V. (7) 1........... 7 4
(L. Shedden)
Stroud, C. P. (7)............ 7 12
(D. Dale)
Styring, S. E. (7)............ 7 10
(S. Hall)
Supple, K. R. (7)............ 7 10
(R. Supple)
Sutton, S. A. (7)............ 8 3
(J. Benstead)
Swales, J. A. (7)............ 6 7
(J. W. Watts)
Sykes, D. (7)................ 6 10
(G. Pritchard-Gordon)
Tasker, P. W. (7)............ 6 4
(P. Robinson)
Taylor, G. (7)............... 7 0
(J. Bethell)
Taylor, M. (7)............... 7 0
(R. Price)
Thomas, R. (7).............. 7 7
(Dr A. Jones)
Thompson, J. M. (7) 1....... 8 0
(M. Jarvis)
Tindle, A. J. (7)............. 7 7
(J. Hanson)
Tompkins, J. J. (7) 1 ap....... 7 7
(A. Johnson)
Troop, N. (7) 3 ap........... 8 0
(P. Rohan)
Tudway, S. R. (7)............ 7 0
(G. Hunter)
Tyas, M. E. (7).............. 8 0
(R. Bastiman)
Tyldsley, J. S. (7)............ 7 3
(M. Smyly)

Wainwright, J. S. (7) 1....... 7 4
(S. Wainwright)
Wall, T. R. (7) 1 ap.......... 8 7
(F. Maxwell)
Walsh, T. (7) 5 + 7 ap........ 7 9
(M. W. Easterby)
Walton, T. P. (7)............ 6 7
(D. Plant)
Ward, J. (7) 1 + 5 ap......... 7 10
(T. Fairhurst)
Ward, P. (7)................. 7 2
(G. Blum)
Watt, J. (7)................. 7 3
(J. Hindley)
Webb, A. (7)................ 8 10
(D. Nicholson)
Webster, S. (3) 55 + 3 ap...... 7 0
(T. Fairhurst)
Wernham, R. A. (3) 63 + 3 ap. 7 11
(H. Nicholson)
Westhead, T. (7) 2 ap........ 7 5
(B. Hobbs)
Westhead, W. (7)............ 7 0
(E. Weymes)
Wharton, W. J. (7) 7 + 7 ap... 6 8
(H. Nicholson)
Whelan, T. M. (7) 3 + 6 ap.... 8 0
(P. Robinson)
Whitehouse, P. A............ 7 7
(D. Nicholson)
Whitworth, A. P. (7)........ 7 10
(D. Holmes)
Wigham, M. (7) 7 + 4 ap...... 7 0
(R. Hollinshead)
Wigham, R. (7).............. 8 0
(N. Adam)
Willard, D. (7).............. 8 4
(P. Cundell)
Williams, K. (7) 6........... 8 0
(K. Payne)
Wilson, B. J. (7) 1 + 2 ap...... 7 12
(H. Wragg)
Wilson, M. (7).............. 6 0
(I. Balding)
Winter, P. D. (7) 1 + 2 ap..... 7 9
(G. Balding)
Wood, M. (7) 3.............. 7 4
(S. Norton)
Woods, V. V. (7) 2.......... 6 4
(R. Hannon)
Woodward, J. M. (7) 2 + 1 ap. 7 12
(V. Mitchell)
Woollard, R. G. (7) 1 ap..... 7 0
(P. Taylor)
Wooley, S. J. (7)............. 7 0
(E. Collingwood)
Wragg, G. E. (7)............ 8 0
(H. Wragg)
Wright, G. W. (7)........... 6 5
(F. J. Houghton)
Wright, K. (7)............... 9 7
(H. T. Jones)
Yates, C. A. (7)............. 8 3
(Doug Smith)
Young, P. J. (5) 24 + 14 ap.... 7 8
(P. Robinson)
Young, S. (7) 1 ap........... 7 0
(P. Robinson)

P. T. FAWCETT

(Caterers) Ltd.,
The Racecourse, York.

YORK 24225

Sole CATERERS at the following racecourses:—

> Beverley
> Catterick
> Pontefract
> Ripon
> Thirsk
> Wetherby
> York (County Stand &
>   Tattersalls Enclosure)

> Also: Gimcrack Banqueting Suite,
>   York Racecourse.
>   Dinner Dances, Weddings,
>   Conferences.

Quotations given for Outside Catering.

AYR

Scotland's Premier Racecourse

FLAT MEETINGS 1977

Monday and Tuesday	April 4 and 5
Saturday and Monday (Silver Jubilee Day)	May 7 and 9

The William Hill Scottish Handicap, 6f (£6,000)
The Balmoral Castle Stakes, 3-y-o, 1m (£5,000)

Saturday	May 28
Friday and Saturday	June 17 and 18

The Belleisle Stakes, 2-y-o only, 5f (£4,000)

Saturday, Monday and Tuesday	July 16, 18 and 19

The Joe Coral Handicap, 1m (£6,000)
The Tennent Trophy (Handicap), 1m 7f (£10,300)
The Strathclyde Stakes, 2-y-o only, 6f (£5,000)

Friday and Saturday	July 22 and 23

The Canada Dry Shield (Handicap), 6f (£6,000)
The Roman Warrior Shield, 2-y-o maidens, 5f (£2,000)
The Land of Burns Stakes, 1m 2f (£5,000)

Tuesday and Wednesday	August 2 and 3

The Heronslea Stakes, 2-y-o 7f (£4,000)

THE WESTERN MEETING

Wednesday, Thursday, Friday and Saturday	September 21, 22, 23, 24

The Doonside Cup, 1m 3f (£10,000)
The Ladbroke Leisure Nursery Handicap, 6f (£5,000)
The Ladbroke Ayrshire Handicap, 1m 3f (£10,000)
The Harry Rosebery Challenge Trophy, 2-y-o, 5f (£7,000)
The Burmah-Castrol Ayr Gold Cup, 6f (£15,000)
The Ladbroke Stratchclyde Handicap, 1m (£5,000)
The Eglinton and Winton Memorial Handicap, 2m 1f (£5,000)
The Bogside Cup, 1m 5f (£5,000)
The Firth of Clyde Stakes, 2-y-o fillies, 6f (£5,000)

Total Amount of Added Prize Money
for 1977 Flat £258,000

Ayr is one of Britain's best equipped and leading racecourses.
Free Stabling and Accommodation for Lads and Girls.
Landing facilities for Helicopters in Centre of Course.
A Watering System ensures reasonable Going at all times.

Further Particulars from

W. W. McHarg	Racecourse Office,
General Manager and Secretary	2 Whitletts Road,
and Joint Clerk of the Course.	Ayr.

Telephone: Ayr 64179

CHARACTERISTICS OF RACECOURSES

ASCOT.—The Ascot round course is a right-handed, triangular circuit of 1m 6f 34yds, with a run-in of 3f. There is a straight mile course, over which the Royal Hunt Cup is run, and the Old mile course which joins the round course in Swinley Bottom. All races shorter than a mile are decided on the straight course. From the 1½-mile starting gate the round course runs downhill to the bend in Swinley Bottom, where it is level, then rises steadily into the turn into the straight, from where it is uphill until less than a furlong from the winning post, the last hundred yards being more or less level. The straight mile is slightly downhill from the start and then rises to the 5f gate, after which there is a slight fall before the junction with the round course. Despite the downhill run into Swinley Bottom and the relatively short run-in from the final turn, the Ascot course is galloping in character; the turns are easy, there are no minor surface undulations to throw a long-striding horse off balance, and all races are very much against the collar over the last half-mile. The course is, in fact, quite a testing one, and very much so in soft going, when there is a heavy premium on stamina. In such circumstances races over 2 miles to 2¾ miles are very severe tests. Group 1.
DRAW: On occasions it has seemed that high numbers have had a considerable advantage on the straight course and on other occasions it has seemed that low numbers have had a considerable advantage. An analysis of results since the course was reconstructed in 1954 disclosed that slightly more than half the winners have come from the high numbers.

AYR.—The Ayr round course is a left-handed, oval track, about twelve furlongs in extent, with a run-in of half a mile. Eleven-furlong races start on a chute which joins the round course after about a furlong. There is a straight six-furlong course of considerable width. The course is relatively flat, but there are gentle undulations throughout, perhaps more marked in the straight. It has a good surface and well-graded turns, and is a fine and very fair track, on the whole galloping in character. Group 1.
DRAW: In races over seven furlongs and a mile a low number is desirable. On the straight course the draw is ordinarily of little consequence.

BATH.—The Bath round course is a left-handed, oval track, just over a mile and a half in extent, with a run-in of nearly half a mile. There is an extension for races over five furlongs and five furlongs and 167 yards. The run-in bends to the left, and is on the rise all the way. The mile and the mile and a quarter courses have been designed to give over a quarter of a mile straight at the start, and the track generally is galloping rather than sharp. The course consists of old downland turf. Group 3.
DRAW: Low numbers have an advantage over the sprint course and in races at up to a mile on the round course.

BEVERLEY.—The Beverley round course is a right-handed, oval track, just over a mile and three furlongs in extent, with a run-in of two and a half furlongs. The five-furlong track bends right at halfway. The general galloping nature of the track is modified by the downhill turn into the straight and the relatively short run-in. The five-furlong course is on the rise throughout, and so is rather testing even in normal conditions; in soft going it takes some getting, particularly for two-year-olds early in the season. Group 3.
DRAW: High numbers have an advantage over the five-furlong course.

BRIGHTON.—The Brighton course takes the shape of an extended 'U' and is 1½ miles in length. The first three furlongs are uphill, after which there is a slight descent followed by a slight rise to about four furlongs from home; the track then runs more sharply downhill until a quarter of a mile out, from where it rises to the last hundred yards, the finish being level. The run-in is about 3½ furlongs, and there is no straight course. This is essentially a sharp track. While the turns are easy enough, the pronounced gradients make Brighton an unsuitable course for big, long-striding horses, resolute gallopers or round-actioned horses. Handy, medium-sized, fluent movers, and quick-actioned horses are much more at home on the

CHESTER RACES
1977

MAY MEETING
Tuesday, May 3rd   CHESTER VASE
Wednesday, May 4th   CHESTER CUP
Thursday, May 5th   164th DEE STAKES

SUMMER MEETING
Friday (Evening), July 8th
(probable time of first race 6.30 p.m.)
Saturday, July 9th

SEPTEMBER MEETING
Friday, September 2nd
Saturday, September 3rd

**For further particulars please apply to
Secretaries, Chester Race Company Ltd.,
29 Eastgate Row North, Chester (Tel. 28301).**

course. There are no opportunities for long-distance plodders at Brighton. Group 2.

DRAW: In sprint races a low number is advantageous, and speed out of the gate even more so.

CARLISLE.—Carlisle is a right-handed, pear-shaped course, just over a mile and a half in extent, with a run-in of a little more than three furlongs. The six-furlong course, of which the five-furlong course is a part, the mile course, and the mile and a half course start on three separate off-shoot extensions. For the first three furlongs or so the course runs downhill, then rises for a short distance, levelling out just beyond the mile post. From there until the turn into the straight the course is flat, apart from minor undulations. The six-furlong course, which bears right soon after the start, and again at the turn into the straight, is level for two furlongs, then rises fairly steeply until the distance, from which point it is practically level. The track is galloping in character, and the six-furlong course is a stiff test of stamina for a two-year-old. Group 4.

DRAW: High numbers have an advantage which is more marked in the shorter races.

CATTERICK.—The Catterick round course is a left-handed, oval track, measuring one mile and 180 yards, with a run-in of three furlongs. The five-furlong course bears left before and at the junction with the round course. From the seven-furlong starting gate the round course is downhill almost all the way, and there is a sharp turn on the falling gradient into the straight. The five-furlong course is downhill throughout, quite steeply to start with, and less so thereafter. Catterick is an exceedingly sharp track with pronounced undulations of surface, and it is therefore an impossible course for a big, long-striding animal. Experience of the track counts for a great deal, and jockeyship is of the utmost importance. Group 4.

DRAW: A low number gives a slight advantage over five furlongs, and a much more definite one on the six and seven-furlong course but a quick start is essential whatever the draw. A slow beginner on the inside is almost certain to be cut off.

CHEPSTOW.—The Chepstow round course is a left-handed, oval track, about two miles in extent, with a run-in of five furlongs. There is a straight mile course, over which all races up to a mile are run. The round course has well-marked undulations, and the straight course is generally downhill and level alternatively as far as the run-in, thereafter rising sharply for over two furlongs, and then gradually levelling out to the winning post. Notwithstanding the long run-in and general rise over the last five furlongs, this is not an ideal galloping track because of the changing gradients. Group 3.

DRAW: High numbers have a slight advantage on the straight course.

CHESTER.—Chester is a left-handed, circular course, only a few yards over a mile round, the smallest circuit of any flat-race course in Great Britain. It is quite flat and on the turn almost throughout, and although the run-in is nearly straight, it is less than two furlongs in length. The Chester Cup which is invariably run at a very strong gallop all the way, is a testing race demanding exceptional stamina and is always won by an out-and-out stayer. Apart from extreme distance events, such as the Cup and other 2¼m races, the course is against the long-striding, resolute galloper and greatly favours the handy, medium-sized, sharp-actioned horse. Group 2.

DRAW: A low number is of great importance in races at up to seven and a half furlongs and a quick beginning is essential. It is virtually impossible to overcome a slow start over sprint distances.

DONCASTER.—Doncaster is a left-handed, pear-shaped course, over 15 furlongs round and quite flat, except for a slight hill about 1½ miles from the finish. There is a perfectly straight mile, and a round mile starting on an off-shoot of the round course. The run-in from the turn is about 4½ furlongs. This is one of the fairest courses in the country, but its flat surface and great width, its sweeping turn into the straight, and long run-in, make it galloping in character, and ideal for the big, long-striding stayer. Group 1.

DRAW: The draw is of no importance on the round course, but on the straight course horses drawn in the high numbers have an advantage.

EDINBURGH.—The Edinburgh round course is a right-handed, oval track, nearly a mile and a quarter in extent, with a run-in of half a mile. There is a straight five-furlong course. The track is flat, with slight undulations and a gentle rise from the distance to the winning post. The turns at the top end of the course and into the straight are very sharp, and handiness and adaptability to negotiate the bends is of the utmost importance. The big, long-striding, cumbersome horse is at a distinct disadvantage on the round track, especially in races at up to a mile and three furlongs, but to a lesser extent in races over longer distances. Group 4.

DRAW: High numbers have an advantage in seven-furlong and mile races.

EPSOM.—Epsom is a left-handed, U-shaped course, $1\frac{1}{2}$ miles in extent, with an interior unfenced track, known as the Metropolitan course, used only in $2\frac{1}{4}$-mile races. In these races the horses start at the winning post and proceed the reverse way of the course, branching off to the right just before reaching Tattenham Corner and rejoining the course proper just over $8\frac{1}{2}$ furlongs from the winning post. The Derby course is decidedly uphill for the first half-mile, level for nearly two furlongs and then quite sharply downhill round the bend to Tattenham Corner and all the way up the straight until approaching the final furlong, from where there is a fairish rise to the winning post. The run-in is less than four furlongs. The 7f and 6f courses start on tangential extensions. The 5f course is quite straight and sharply downhill to the junction with the round course. Races over $2\frac{1}{4}$ miles are, of course, true tests of stamina, and races over $1\frac{1}{2}$ miles can also be testing if the pace over the first uphill four furlongs is strong, as it frequently is in the Derby. Otherwise the track is not really testing in itself, and races up to $8\frac{1}{2}$ furlongs are very sharp indeed, the sprint courses being the fastest in the world. Owing to its bends and pronounced downhill gradients, Epsom favours the handy, fluent-actioned, medium-sized horse: big horses sometimes handle the course well enough, but cumbersome horses, long-striding gallopers, or those with pronounced 'knee-action' are not suited to it and are frequently quite unable to act upon it, especially when the going is firm or hard. Any hesitation at the start or slowness into stride results in considerable loss of ground over the first furlong in sprint races. For this reason Epsom is no course for a green and inexperienced two-year-old, slow to realise what is required. Group 1.

DRAW: In races up to eight and a half furlongs a low number is advantageous, but quickness out of the gate is of far greater importance, particularly in five-furlong, six-furlong and seven-furlong races.

FOLKESTONE.—The Folkestone round course is a right-handed, pear-shaped track, about ten and a half furlongs in extent, with a run-in of two and a half furlongs. There is a straight six-furlong course. The course is undulating, with the last part slightly on the rise, but notwithstanding its width, the easy turns and the uphill finish, it is by no means a galloping track. Group 4.

DRAW: Low numbers have a slight advantage on the straight course.

GOODWOOD.—The Goodwood track consists of a nearly straight 6f course, with a triangular right-handed loop circuit. The Goodwood Cup, about 2m 5f, is started by flag in front of the stands: the horses run the reverse way of the straight, branch left at the first or lower bend, go right-handed round the loop and return to the straight course via the top bend. Races over 2m 3f, $1\frac{3}{4}$m and $1\frac{1}{2}$m are also run on this course, but 1m races rejoin the straight course via the lower bend. Although there is a 5f run-in for races of $1\frac{1}{4}$ miles and upwards, the turns and, more specially, the pronounced downhill gradients from the turn make Goodwood essentially a sharp track, favouring the active, handy, fluent mover rather than the big, long-striding horse. This is of lesser importance in 2m 3f and 2m 5f races, where the emphasis is on sound stamina, and of greater importance in the shorter distance races, particularly in sprints and especially when the going is on top. The 5f course is one of the fastest in the country. Group 1.

DRAW: A high number is regarded as advantageous in sprint races, but the advantage is not great. Alacrity out of the gate is certainly of importance in five-furlong races.

HAMILTON.—The Hamilton track is a perfectly straight six-furlong course, with a pear-shaped, right-handed loop, the whole being a mile and five furlongs in extent from a start in front of the stands, round the loop and back to the winning post. The run-in is five furlongs. The turns are very easy, and the course is undulating for the most part, but just over three furlongs from the winning post there are steep gradients into and out of a pronounced hollow, followed by a severe hill to the finish. Group 3.

DRAW: Middle to high numbers are thought to have a slight advantage in races over the straight course.

HAYDOCK.—Haydock is a left-handed, oval-shaped course, about 13 furlongs round, with a run-in of 4½ furlongs, and a straight 5-furlong course. Races of 6 furlongs and 1½ miles start on tangential extensions to the round course. This course is rather galloping in character, with a rise of twenty-one feet throughout the straight. Group 1.

DRAW: Horses drawn in the low numbers are regarded as having an advantage in races of six, seven and eight furlongs. On the straight course the draw is of no consequence when the going is sound, but when it is soft, horses racing under the stands rails (high numbers) seem to be favoured.

KEMPTON.—Kempton is a right-handed, triangular course, just over 13 furlongs round. The nine-furlong Jubilee course starts on an extension to the round course. Sprint races are run over a separate diagonal course. The Kempton track is perfectly flat with normal characteristics, being neither a sharp track nor a galloping one. Group 1.

DRAW: The draw is of no particular consequence.

LANARK.—The Lanark round course is a right-handed, oval track, a mile and a quarter in extent, with a run-in of three and a half furlongs. There is a straight five-furlong course. The course is perfectly flat, and the turns are very easy, but being only a mile and a quarter round, it is hardly ideal for a big, long-striding horse. Group 4.

DRAW: The draw is of no great consequence.

LEICESTER.—The Leicester round course is a right-handed, oval track, nearly two miles in extent, with a run-in of five furlongs. The straight mile course, on which all races of up to a mile are run, is mainly downhill to halfway, then rises gradually for over two furlongs, finishing on the level. The course is well-drained, the bends into the straight and beyond the winning post have been eased and cambered, and the track is galloping. For two-year-olds early in the season it poses quite a test of stamina. Group 3.

DRAW: High numbers have an advantage in races at up to a mile and the advantage seems to be more marked when the going is on the soft side.

LINGFIELD.—The Lingfield round course is a left-handed loop, which intersects the straight course of seven furlongs and 140 yards nearly half a mile out and again less than two furlongs from the winning post. The run-in is not much more than three furlongs. For nearly half its length the round course is quite flat, then rises with easy gradients to the summit of a slight hill, after which there is a downhill turn to the straight. The straight course has a considerable downhill gradient to halfway, and is slightly downhill for the rest of the way. The straight course is very easy, and the track as a whole is sharp, putting a premium on speed and adaptability, and making relatively small demands upon stamina, though this does not, of course, apply to races over two miles. The mile and a half course, over which the Derby Trial is run, bears quite close resemblance to the Epsom Derby course. Group 2.

DRAW: On the straight course high numbers have a slight advantage in normal conditions but when the going is heavy low numbers are favoured.

LIVERPOOL.—The flat-race course at Liverpool is a left-handed, oval-shaped circuit of 11 furlongs, with a straight run-in of 4f. There is a separate straight course which runs diagonally across the main circuit over which all 5f races are decided. The course is perfectly flat throughout and is somewhat galloping in character, but owing to the short circuit it is not ideal for horses lacking a turn of speed. Group 3.

DRAW: In large fields horses drawn in the low numbers in six-furlong and mile races are regarded as having an advantage.

RACING FIXTURES 1977
HAYDOCK PARK

JANUARY
7th & 8th Fri & Sat.*
Gamekeepers' Chase (Friday). Tote Northern Chase; Philip Cornes Hurdle; Merseyside Hurdle (Saturday).

22nd Sat.*
Embassy Premier Chase Final; Embassy Hurdle.

FEBRUARY
9th & 10th Wed. & Thurs.*
Malcolm Fudge National Trial Chase (Wednesday). The Premier Long Distance Hurdle (Thursday).

MARCH
4th & 5th Fri. & Sat.*
White Rabbit Handicap Chase (Friday). Greenall Whitley Breweries Chase; Victor Ludorum Hurdle (Saturday).

APRIL
6th & 7th Wed. & Thurs.
Field Marshal Stakes; Steve Donoghue Stakes (Wednesday). Fred Archer Handicap; Herbert Jones Handicap (Thursday).

MAY
27th & 28th Fri. & Sat.
John Davies Handicap; Cambrian Soft Drinks Point-to-Point Final (Friday). Gus Demmy Stakes; Cecil Frail Handicap (Saturday).

JUNE
3rd & 4th Fri (Evening) & Sat.
Manchester Handicap; Red Rose Amateur/Lady Riders Handicap (Friday). Bass Clubmen's Handicap; John of Gaunt Stakes; Be Friendly Handicap (Saturday).

JULY
1st & 2nd Fri. & Sat.
Cock of the North Stakes; Gt. Central Handicap (Friday). Lancashire Oaks; Old Newton Cup; Rose of Lancaster Stakes; Sporting Chronicle Handicap (Saturday).

AUGUST
5th & 6th Fri. & Sat.
Matthew Peacock Handicap; Lilburne Nursery (Friday). Joe Coral Handicap; Harvey Jones Handicap (Saturday).

24th & 25th Wed. & Thurs.
Buggins Farm Nursery; Cavalier Handicap (Wednesday). Colonel Ashton Handicap; Restoration Stakes (Thursday).

OCTOBER
Sept. 30th & 1st Fri. & Sat.
Preston Handicap; Outland Handicap (Friday). Brooke-Bond-Oxo Handicap; Crown Plus Two Apprentice Handicap; Sydney Sandon Handicap (Saturday).

12th & 13th Wed. & Thurs.
Walnut Stakes; Maple Nursery (Wednesday). Rowan Nursery; Silver Birch Stakes (Thursday).

28th & 29th Fri. & Sat.
Claude Harrison Trophy; Southport Nursery (Friday). Vernons Sprint Cup Morecambe Handicap (Saturday).

DECEMBER
Nov. 30th & 1st Wed. & Thurs.*
Sundew Pattern Chase; Northern Pattern Hurdle (Wednesday). Garswood Pattern Hurdle (Thursday).

PARTY BOOKINGS
Special discounts for advance-booked parties of 25 plus. Catering in private dining-room.

Full particulars from:

THE SECRETARY
HAYDOCK PARK RACECOURSE
NEWTON-LE-WILLOWS WA12 0HQ
MERSEYSIDE

Phone: Ashton-in-Makerfield 77345

ADMISSION
County Stand	..	..	..	£4·00
Juniors (16-21)	..	..	..	£2·00
Tattersalls..	..	..	..	£2·50
Pensioners and Juniors (16-21)				£1·25
Newton Stand	..	..	..	£1·00
Pensioners and Juniors (16-21)				50p
Children free			Car Parks	FREE

***National Hunt Racing**

All information is published in good faith at the start of the season, and Haydock Park Racecourse reserve the right without notice to make any alteration to the programme, prices or other details.

RIPON RACES

1977 FIXTURES

WEDNESDAY 13th APRIL

SATURDAY 7th MAY
R. W. Armstrong Memorial Cup £2,500

WEDNESDAY 18th MAY

WEDNESDAY 1st JUNE
(*Derby Day*) *Joe Coral Stakes* £2,000

WEDNESDAY 22nd JUNE
(Evening meeting)

SATURDAY 16th JULY
Hornblower Stakes £2,500

MONDAY 1st AUGUST

SATURDAY 13th AUGUST
Charity Day

SATURDAY 20th AUGUST
Great St Wilfrid Handicap £10,000

BANK HOLIDAY MONDAY
Ripon Rowels Stakes £3,000
Champion Two Year Old Stakes £2,500

TUESDAY 30th AUGUST

**Bring the whole family for a
day out in the country**

NEWBURY.—The Newbury round course is a left-handed, oval track, eighty feet wide and about a mile and seven furlongs in extent, with a run-in of nearly five furlongs. There is a straight mile course, which is slightly undulating throughout. Races on the round mile and over the extended seven furlongs start on an extension from the round course. Notwithstanding the undulations this is a good galloping track, and excellent arrangements have been made for watering the course. Group 1.
DRAW: A high number is a fairly considerable advantage over the straight course.

NEWCASTLE.—Newcastle is a left-handed, oval-shaped course of 1m 6f in circumference. There is also a straight course, over which all races of seven furlongs or less are run. The course is decidedly galloping in character, and a steady climb from the turn into the straight makes Newcastle a testing track, particularly for two-year-olds early in the season. Ability to see the journey out thoroughly is most important. Group 1.
DRAW: The draw is of no particular consequence.

NEWMARKET ROWLEY MILE COURSE.—The Cesarewitch course is two and a quarter miles in extent, with a right-handed bend after a mile, the last mile and a quarter being the straight Across the Flat. From the Cesarewitch start the course runs generally downhill to a sharp rise just before the turn. There are undulations throughout the first mile of the straight, then the course runs downhill for a furlong to the Dip, and uphill for the last furlong to the winning post. This is an exceedingly wide, galloping track, without minor irregularities of surface, so it is ideal for the big, long-striding horse, except for the descent into the Dip, which is more than counterbalanced by the final hill. Ability to see the trip out thoroughly is absolutely essential. Group 1.
DRAW: There is no material advantage.

NEWMARKET SUMMER COURSE.—The Newmarket Summer course is two miles and twenty-four yards in extent, with a right-handed bend at halfway, the first mile being part of the Cesarewitch course, and the last the straight Bunbury Mile. The course runs generally downhill to a sharp rise just before the turn. There are undulations for the first threequarters of a mile of the straight, then the course runs downhill for a furlong to a dip, and uphill for the last furlong to the winning post. This is an exceedingly wide, galloping track, ideal for the big, long-striding horse, except for the descent into the dip which is more than counterbalanced by the final hill. Ability to see the trip out thoroughly is essential. Group 1.
DRAW: The draw confers little advantage.

NOTTINGHAM.—The Nottingham round course is a left-handed, oval track, about a mile and a half in extent, with a run-in of four and a half furlongs. The course is flat and the turns are easy. Group 3.
DRAW: High numbers are slightly preferred over the straight course.

PONTEFRACT.—Pontefract is a left-handed track, a mile and a half in extent occupying three-parts of an oval. There is no straight course, and the run-in is only just over two furlongs. There are considerable gradients and a testing hill over the last three furlongs. The undulations, the sharp bend into the straight, and the short run-in disqualify it from being described as a galloping track, but there is a premium on stamina. Group 3.
DRAW: A low number is advantageous particularly over five furlongs but it becomes a decided disadvantage if a horse fails to jump off well.

REDCAR.—Redcar is a narrow, left-handed, oval track, about a mile and threequarters in extent, with a run-in of five furlongs, which is part of the straight mile course. The course is perfectly flat with normal characteristics, and provides an excellent gallop. Group 2.
DRAW: The draw confers no advantage.

RIPON.—The Ripon course is a right-handed, oval circuit of 13 furlongs, with a run-in of 5f, and a straight 6f course. Owing to the rather cramped bends and the surface undulations in the straight, the Ripon track is rather sharp in character. Group 2.
DRAW: On the straight course the draw is of no importance but in races on the mile course, horses drawn in the high numbers seem to have an advantage.

SALISBURY.—The Salisbury track is a right-handed loop course, with a run-in of seven furlongs, which, however, is not straight, for the mile course, of which it is a part, has a right-handed elbow after three furlongs. For races over a mile and threequarters horses start opposite the Club Enclosure, and running away from the stands, diverge to the left, and go round the loop. The course, which is uphill throughout the last half-mile is galloping and rather testing. Group 2.
DRAW: High numbers have a slight advantage in five- and six-furlong races.

SANDOWN.—Sandown is a right-handed, oval-shaped course of 13 furlongs, with a straight run-in of 4f. There is a separate straight course which runs across the main circuit and over which all 5f races are decided. From the 1½m starting gate, the Eclipse Stakes course, the track is level to the turn into the straight, from where it is uphill until less than a furlong from the winning post, the last hundred yards being more or less level. The 5f track is perfectly straight and rises steadily throughout. Apart from the minor gradients between the main winning post and the 1½m starting gate, there are no undulations to throw a long-striding horse off balance, and all races over the round course are very much against the collar from the turn into the straight. The course is, in fact, a testing one, and over all distances the ability to see the trip out well is of the utmost importance. Group 1.
DRAW: The draw is of no particular consequence, but on the five-furlong course high numbers have a considerable advantage in big fields when the ground is soft.

TEESSIDE.—The Teesside track, known until 1967 as Stockton, is a left-handed course, nearly a mile and threequarters in extent, with a run-in of half a mile. The five- and six-furlong courses start on separate tangential extensions, the five-furlong track joining the round course on a left incline after a furlong, and the six-furlong track being so laid out as to give a straight start of two furlongs before the bend to the run-in. The turns are sweeping and easy, and the course is perfectly flat, but it is rather a sharp track, and for a flat course it is very fast indeed when the going is firm. The premium is always upon speed. Group 4.
DRAW: A low number is a fairly considerable advantage in five- and six-furlong races, and is also advantageous in seven-furlong and mile races.

THIRSK.—The Thirsk round course is a left-handed, oval track, just over a mile and a quarter in extent, with a run-in of half a mile. There is a straight six-furlong course, which is slightly undulating throughout. The round course itself is almost perfectly flat, but though the turns are relatively easy and the ground well levelled all round, the track is on the sharp side, and by no means ideal for a horse that requires time to settle down, and time and space to get down to work in the straight. Group 2.
DRAW: High numbers have an advantage on the straight course.

WARWICK.—Warwick is a broad, left-handed, oval track, just over a mile and threequarters in extent, with a run-in of about three and a half furlongs. There is no straight course, the five-furlong course having a left-hand elbow at the junction with the round course. Mile races start on an extension from the round course, the first four and a half furlongs being perfectly straight. This is a sharp track, with the emphasis on speed and adaptability rather than stamina. The laboured galloper is at a disadvantage, especially in races at up to a mile. Group 4.
DRAW: A low number is advantageous in races up to mile, but a quick beginning is even more important.

WINDSOR.—Windsor racecourse, laid out in the form of a figure eight, is 12½ furlongs in extent. In races of around 1½ miles both left-handed and right-handed turns are encountered, but in races over 1m 70 yds only right-handed turns are met. The last five furlongs of the course are straight, except for a slight bend to the right three furlongs from the finish. The six-furlong start is now on an extension of this straight. Although perfectly flat throughout, the bends make this track rather sharp in character. However, as there is a nearly straight 5f run-in the relative sharpness of the track is of no consequence in the longer races. Big, long-striding horses which normally require a more galloping course are at little or no disadvantage over these trips.

The course gives spectators a very good view of the racing, since the runners are broadsides on to the stands for all but about 20 yards of the circuit, and all starts are in sight of the stands. Group 3.

DRAW: In five- and six-furlong races horses drawn in the high numbers have an advantage provided they start well enough to be able to avoid being squeezed out or impeded at the slight right-hand elbow in the straight.

WOLVERHAMPTON.—The Wolverhampton round course is a left-handed, pear-shaped or triangular track, just over a mile and a half in extent, with a run-in of five furlongs. There is a straight course of five furlongs and 190 yards. The course is level throughout, with normal characteristics. Group 4.

DRAW: The draw confers no advantage.

YARMOUTH.—The Yarmouth round course is a narrow, left-handed, oval track, about thirteen furlongs in extent, with a run-in of five furlongs. There is a straight mile course. Apart from a slight fall just before the run-in, the track is perfectly flat, with normal characteristics. Group 3.

DRAW: High numbers have a slight advantage on the straight course.

YORK.—York is a left-handed, U-shaped course, 2 miles in extent, and quite flat throughout. There is also a perfectly flat straight course, over which all 5f and 6f races are run. The run-in from the turn is nearly 5 furlongs. This is one of the best courses in the country, of great width throughout and with a sweeping turn into the long straight. The entire absence of surface undulations makes it ideal for a long-striding, resolute galloper, but it is really a splendid track, bestowing no great favours on any type of horse. Group 1.

DRAW: The draw is of no consequence.

THE HOLLINS STUD

Mr. Phil Bull welcomes enquiries regarding the purchase of any of the following bloodstock.

Further details can be obtained from Phil Bull, The Hollins, Warley, Halifax, West Yorkshire. Telephone: Calder Valley (0422 83) 2387.

HORSES IN TRAINING

Zoroaster 4 gr.c. Zeddaan–Persina
Karantina 3 ch.f. Relko–Dorabella
Philodantes 2 b.c. Connaught–Sweet Sauce
Fiordiligi 2 ch.f. Tudor Melody–Dorabella
Rietta 2 b.f. Amber Rama–Relza

YEARLINGS OF 1977

b.c. Blakeney–Alcarelle (Alcide)
Foaled March 15
b.c. Relko–Sweet Sauce (Hard Sauce)
Foaled April 22

FOALS DUE 1977

Connaught–Relza (Relko)
Due April 4
Brigadier Gerard–Dorabella (Rockefella)
Due May 1

MATINGS FOR 1977

Berganza visits Relko
Dorabella visits Silly Season
Sweet Sauce visits Connaught
Relza visits Welsh Pageant
Connarca visits Amber Rama

BROODMARES

BERGANZA b. (1961) Grey Sovereign–Lady Electra (Fairway)
DORABELLA ch. (1961) Rockefella–Anne of Essex (Panorama)
SWEET SAUCE b. (1963) Hard Sauce–Dictavelle (Vatellor)
RELZA b. (1967) Relko–Berganza (Grey Sovereign)
CONNARCA ch. (1972) Connaught–Orarca (Arctic Prince)

Stallion Section

Timeform Ratings quoted in the Stallion Section are those which appeared in the 'Racehorses' annuals except where otherwise stated.

INDEX

Balliol

Bay, 1969, by WILL SOMERS—VIOLET BANK by THE PHOENIX

Top Sprinter Own-Brother to Balidar

Winner of 6 races, £16,947 (3-4 years: 6-8f), including Cork and Orrery Stakes, Royal Ascot (by 5 lengths), Abernant Stakes, Newmarket, and Yellow Pages Autumn Cup, Doncaster; placed 6 times, including 2nd Nunthorpe Stakes (length to SANDFORD LAD), Palace House Stakes (head to BRAVE LAD beating HOME GUARD, WORKBOY and BOLD AND FREE), etc.; 3rd July Cup, Newmarket (to THATCH and PITSKELLY).

He is own-brother to BALIDAR (leading European sprinter and sire of BOLKONSKI, 2,000 Guineas, Sussex Stakes etc. in 1975). WILL SOMERS has sired the winners of over £200,000. His dam, VIOLET BANK, has already bred 2 outstanding sprinters.

Good Fertility. First runners 1977.

Enquiries to BBA (Ireland) Ltd.
51 Lansdowne Road, Dublin 4.   Tel: 686222
**Standing at Hollywood Rath Stud,
Mulhuddart, Co. Dublin, Ireland**
Enquiries at the stud to **C. Grassick.**
Tel: Dublin 383746/383890

TOP-CLASS RACEHORSE & PATTERN RACE SIRE

BALLYCIPTIC

Chesnut, 1962 Preciptic—Ballytickle

Won 3 races, £1,589, at 3 years, including Whitehall Stakes and
Nobber Stakes; 2nd (sh hd) in Champion Stakes, Newmarket,
(sh hd) in Peter Hastings Stakes, Eclipse Stakes, Queen Elizabeth
II Stakes, etc., also won Queen Anne Stakes but was disqualified.

Half-brother to 6 winners including **SOLARTICKLE** (3 races, also
sire of winners), **BALLYMARTIAL** (Madrid Free Handicap),
SHOOTING CHANT (6 races, $55,126; now at stud in Japan),
etc. His dam was three-parts sister to **MAFOSTA** (4 races in
Ireland; 14 races in U.S.A.; sire).
Sire of the winners of more than 140 races and over £170,000 including
BALLYHOT (Royal Palace Stakes, Prix de la Ville de Trouville,
St Simon Stakes etc.), **ASSERTIVE** (Ballymoss Stakes, Curragh
and Irish Cambridgeshire), **CIDER WITH ROSIE** (SKF Cesare-
witch), **NIGHT IN TOWN** (Paradise Stakes 1975), **MY EAGLE**
(8 races) and good winners over the jumps including **CALL THE
TUNE** (four wins in 1975/6).   FULL 1967—76

Enquiries to: **Joseph McGrath, Brownstown Stud,
Curragh, Co. Kildare.**   (Tel: Curragh 41303)

Standing at Old Fairyhouse Stud, Ratoath, Co. Meath.
The property of a partnership

BE FRIENDLY

Ch. 1964 **SKYMASTER—LADY SLIPTIC (PRECIPTIC)**

Champion sprinter and European record holder when retired to stud in 1970. Winner of 12 races and placed 9 times. Stakes won £43,880.

AVERAGE FERTILITY OVER 85%

Sire to date of the winners of 106 races, Value over £160,000, including 24 individual winners in 1976. His winners include **AS FRIENDLY** (6 races), now sire in Australia, and **BE TUNEFUL** (5 races, £15,000, including Challenge Stakes, Newmarket), **LADY ICE** (4 races), **LAST TANGO** (3 races including 1976 Ayr Gold Cup), and **BE EASY** (Molecomb Stakes 1976), etc. His yearlings have averaged 5,220 guineas for 58 of his first three crops sold at auction.

Enquiries to: **F. E. HILLMAN**
as above. **DUBLIN (01) 256152**

903

Bluerullah beats Bold Lad (rec 8 lb) in the Lockinge Stakes, Newbury

At Brownstown Stud, Curragh, Co. Kildare

BLUERULLAH

Brown 1963 *Valerullah-Windsor Blue* (*Windsor Slipper*)

Winner of eight races from two to five years, including the Lockinge Stakes (1m.), Newbury, beating **Bold Lad** (see above), the Hennessy Handicap, the Whitehall Handicap, Phoenix Park (with **Busted** third, beaten 4 lengths), etc. He was placed 10 times including second to **Tesco Boy** in Variety Club Stakes, Sandown, third to **Busted** in the Coronation Stakes, Sandown, third to **Reform** in the Sussex Stakes, Goodwood, and third to **Emerilo** and **Wolver Hollow** (btn. nk., sh. hd.) in the Cambridgeshire carrying 9 st. 1 lb., Newmarket. Total stakes earned £12,400.

His winning dam has bred winners including **Blue Chevalier** and **Vale Blue** (£6,318). The next dam, **Arctic Blue,** is half-sister to **Arctic Prince** (winner of the Derby, successful sire and maternal grandsire of **Park Top, Santa Claus, Approval,** etc.).

Bluerullah is sire of **Blue Barrier**, **Hippie Blues, San Rullagh, Bluehel, Blue Town Thanks**, **Wendover Lad, Blue Bangle, Chinrullah, Our Ollie, Ingegner Preside** (4 races in Italy), **Adrianos** (£5,736 in Greece) and **Amvresens** (£5,250 in Greece) with few runners.

Enquiries to: **Joseph McGrath,**
Brownstown Stud, Curragh, Co. Kildare.
(Tel: Curragh 41303)

BRIGADIER GERARD

Sire in his first season of General, unbeaten winner of Prix Thomas Bryon (Gp. III), and Prix Louvre (in almost a second faster time than Blushing Groom in the Grand Criterium the same day); Etienne Gerard, won Clarence House Stks, Pegasus Stks; Imperial Guard, won Granby Stks, Plaistow Stks; Gerard, 2nd, 3rd and twice 4th; Brig of Ayr, beaten $\frac{1}{2}$ length in her only race; Actal, beaten a head and a short neck in France, her only race; Princess Gerrard, placed 3rd and 4th.

Standing at the Egerton Stud, Newmarket.

From the painting by Madeline Selfe.

BUSTED

Bay, 1963, by CREPELLO out of SANS LE SOU, by VIMY

European Champion of 1967
Unbeaten 'Horse of the Year'

LEADING SIRE (Races Won) in **1974**
2nd LEADING SIRE (Races Won) in **1975**
LEADING SIRE (58 Races Won) in **1976**
LEADING SIRE (35 Individual Winners) in **1976**

With six crops of runners, Busted has sired the winners of 224 races value £682,582 including **BUSTINO** (St Leger, Coronation Cup, Great Voltigeur, 2nd King George and Queen Elizabeth Stakes), **WEAVERS' HALL** (Irish Sweeps Derby and £67,757), **VALUTA** (Prix Kergorlay, Prix Maurice de Nieuil and over £30,000), **GUILLOTINA** (Prix de Royallieu), **BOG ROAD** (Gallinule Stakes, Ballymoss Stakes, 2nd Prix Ganay, total £37,419), **CHEVELEY PRINCESS** (Ascot 1,000 Guineas Trial, Nassau Stakes, Sun Chariot Stakes), **CRASH COURSE** (Doncaster Cup 1975, March Stakes, Goodwood, Ascot Stakes, Top Rank Club Stakes), **FOOL'S MATE** (PTS Laurels Stakes, Bessborough Stakes, Old Newton Cup), **OLD BILL** (Chester Vase) £3,500, **BUSS, L' EAULNE, SILK BUDS, BELPER, CURTAINS, GAELIC, BROXTED, KATIE MAY, LOST CHORD, DU MAURIER, ALIANTE,** etc.

Full at £3,500 for 1977

His fertility was 90.38% for 1974 coverings and 89.65% for 1975 coverings
Yearlings averaged 12,600 gns in 1976

At SNAILWELL STUD, NEWMARKET
The property of Snailwell Stud Co. Ltd.

Apply: **ANTHONY W. EARL, The Manager, Moulton Paddocks**
Newmarket. Telephone: (0638) 2867

THE CLASSIC WINNING SON OF WOLVER HOLLOW

Furry Glen

The Property of Senator P. McGrath

Furry Glen wins the Irish 2,000 Guineas from Pitcairn. Cellini is third, then comes Red Alert.

Furry Glen won five races £31,757, from 5 to 9 furlongs, at 2 and 3 years, including Gr I Irish Two Thousand Guineas, beating PITCAIRN, CELLINI, RED ALERT, etc. Gr III Whitehall Stakes, Marble Hill Stakes, Mullion Stakes; also placed 2nd in Gr II Gallinule Stakes (btn sh hd), and Gr III Vauxhall Trial Stakes (btn hd), and 3rd in Gr II Coventry Stakes, Royal Ascot, and Gr III Larkspur Stakes.
By the Champion Sire of 1976; also sire of **WOLLOW,** etc. **FURRY GLEN** is half-brother to 3 winners; his dam is own-sister to CARTIER (16 races). Grandam won 4 races, and comes from the family of DELIRIUM (leading sprinter and successful sire).

Wolver Hollow (b. 1964)	Sovereign Path	Grey Sovereign
		Mountain Path
FURRY GLEN (b. 1971)	Cygnet	Caracalla II
		Mrs Swan Song
Cleftess (br. 1956)	Hill Gail	Bull Lea
		Jane Gail
	Cleft	Lighthouse II
		Rift

Full 1975 and 1976
First Crop are Yearlings in 1977
His foals averaged 2,000 gns at Goff's November Sales 1976
Enquiries to: Joseph McGrath (as above). Tel.: Curragh 41303

AT THE NATIONAL STUD, NEWMARKET

GRUNDY

Chesnut, 1972, by GREAT NEPHEW out of WORD FROM LUNDY by WORDEN II

GRUNDY was head of the Two- and Three-Year-Old Handicaps. Unbeaten winner of 4 races at two years, including William Hill Dewhurst Stakes, Newmarket (Group I), by six lengths and the Champagne Stakes, Doncaster (Group II). Champion of Europe at three years, winning the Derby (Group I) by three lengths, the Irish Derby (Group I) by two lengths, the Irish 2,000 Guineas (Group I), by one-and-a-half lengths and the King George VI and Queen Elizabeth Diamond Stakes, Ascot (Group I), by half-a-length, in 2.36 seconds better time than the previous record for the race.

GRUNDY, in his first season at stud, had thirty-two of his thirty-three mares tested in foal.

GRUNDY earned a new European record of £326,421 for an English-trained horse.

Apply: The Director, The National Stud, Newmarket, Suffolk CB8 0XE
(telephone: Newmarket 3464)

KEITH FREEMAN (BLOODSTOCK) LTD.,
Pettus House, Elm Hill, Norwich, Norfolk NR3 1HS
(telephone: Norwich 27773 or 21307)

HABAT

Grey, 1971

by HABITAT out of ATREVIDA by SUNNY BOY III

HABAT was the leading English Two-Year-Old of 1973 when winning the Berkshire Stakes, Newbury by five lengths, the Norfolk Stakes, Royal Ascot (Group III), by six lengths, the Mill Reef Stakes, Newbury (Group II) by five lengths and the Middle Park Stakes, Newmarket (Group I), by two-and-a-half lengths. As a three-year-old he won the 2,000 Guineas Trial Stakes, Ascot (Group III) by one-and-a-half lengths and second in the Sussex Stakes, Goodwood (Group I). Total earnings, £49,636.

The leading son of Habitat, HABAT traces through Kalamoun's grandam Palariva, and Nasrullah's sister, Rivaz, to Mumtaz Mahal. HABAT in his second season at stud, had 42 mares tested in foal by the end of the season.

Full 1975, 1976 and 1977 at £1,500

Apply: The Director, The National Stud, Newmarket, Suffolk CB8 OXE
(Telephone: Newmarket 3464)
or: Keith Freeman (Bloodstock) Ltd., Pettus House, Elm Hill, Norwich, Norfolk NR3 1HS
(Telephone: Norwich 27773 or 21307)

Standing at

COTSWOLD STUD

MANOR FARM, LOWER SLAUGHTER, CHELTENHAM, GLOUCESTERSHIRE, GL54 2HP

The property of Mr JOHN A. McDOUGALD

IDIOT'S DELIGHT

Bay 1970   Silly Season—Dolphinet (Big Game)

A spreadeagling seven lengths win for Idiot's Delight under top-weight in the Follifoot Handicap at York.

IDIOT'S DELIGHT won 5 races, value £9,905, from 6f to 1¼m, including the Fenwolf Stakes, Ascot (on his first outing as a 2-y-o), the Brighton Mile Challenge Trophy, the Falmouth Handicap at York and the Follifoot Handicap at York. He was also 3rd of 36 in the Irish Sweeps Cambridgeshire carrying 9-2, beaten only two necks and 'making up an enormous amount of ground in closing stages after being virtually last of those racing on far side 2f out, and did not have a particularly clear run when challenging' (*Timeform*, Nov 1975).

IDIOT'S DELIGHT is the best son of SILLY SEASON, the leading 7-10f horse of 1965 who has sired the winners of over £300,000.

IDIOT'S DELIGHT's dam, Dolphinet, has bred several other winners including the Queen Anne Stakes winner Good Match.

Fee £175 (special concessions to winners and dams of winners)

Full 1976

Enquiries to: FRANK HAYDON, as above
Telephone: Bourton-on-the-Water 20973 and 20288

913

Jukebox

Bay 1966, by SING SING—BIBI MAH by TEHRAN

Record Token crowns a fine season with a win in the Vernons Sprint Cup.

A top sire in 1976

Sire in 1976 of 27 winners of 46 races, £90,576 at home and abroad including the leading 3-y-o's **Record Token** (Vernons Sprint Cup, Group 2, Victoria Cup, John of Gaunt Stakes, etc.), **Music Boy** (King George Stakes, Group 3) and **Reelin Jig** (Ballyogan Stakes, Group 3).

Winner of 6 races and £9,495 from 2-4 years including the Stewards' Cup, Sceptre Stakes (beating Decoy Boy and Raffingora). He was placed 11 times and rated by Timeform as 'A very smart sprinter . . . very genuine and consistent.'

He is by the deceased **SING SING** whose sons at stud also include **SONG, MANACLE, MUMMYS PET**, etc. and he is the only son at stud in Ireland by this fine sprint sire.

FULL FOR 1977

Standing in 1977 at Haras du Manoir Saint-Georges, Coudray-Rabut, 14130
Pont L'Eveque, France.

TIMEFORM HORSE OF THE YEAR 1969

LEVMOSS

Bay 1965, LE LEVANSTELL – FEEMOSS (BALLYMOSS)

The only horse ever to win
THE PRIX DE L'ARC DE TRIOMPHE
THE ASCOT GOLD CUP AND
THE PRIX DU CADRAN

Own brother to SWEET MIMOSA winner of French Oaks, 1970

With 4 crops Levmoss has sired the winners of more than **80** races
and almost **£200,000**. In 1975 he was **second leading pattern
race sire.** Sire of five pattern race winners in 1975; MOON-
LIGHT NIGHT (Musidora Stakes), NUTHATCH (Nijinsky Stakes),
SHANTALLAH (Chester Vase), MOSS TROOPER (Prix Kergorlay),
RAVEL (Dee Stakes) and sire in 1976 of the top Italian 2-y-o
DUCHAMP (Premio Emanuele Filiberto, Group 2)

Enquiries: **Joseph McGrath, Brownstown Stud, Curragh,
Co. Kildare. (Tel: Curragh 41303)
or Dr. Urban at the stud.**

915

916

AT UPEND STUD, NEWMARKET

NO MERCY

Grey, 1968, by
FORTINO II out of CROWNING MERCY by SUPREME COURT

NO MERCY, as a two-year-old won 4 races, at 5 and 6 furlongs, leading throughout on every occasion and as a three-year-old won Prix de Meautry, Deauville (Group III), 6 furlongs, in record time, again leading throughout and Totalisator Free Handicap, Newmarket, 7 furlongs.

NO MERCY, sire of winners with his first crop, including GENTILHOMBRE, 5½ races, including Prix de l'Abbaye de Longchamp (Group I) and Cork and Orrery Stakes, Royal Ascot (Group III), earnings, £23,489. Also sire of 7 individual winners, including CROWNING ISSUE, winner in Ireland of Hennessy Handicap, value £4,748.

NO MERCY was full 1972 to 1976 with 39 mares tested in foal this year.

The property of a syndicate

Apply: Keith Freeman (Bloodstock) Ltd., Pettus House, Elm Hill, Norwich, Norfolk NR3 1HS
(Telephone: Norwich 27773 or 21307)

918

Northfields (U.S.A.)

Chesnut, 1968, by NORTHERN DANCER—LITTLE HUT by OCCUPY

An excellent season with his first crop of 3-y-o's
NORTHFIELDS is sire from his first two crops of **NORTHERN TREASURE** (Irish 2,000 Guineas Group 1, Blandford Stakes Group 2, 3rd Irish Derby Group 1, 3rd Champion Stakes Group 1 and £48,613), **OATS** (Blue Riband Stakes Group 3, 2nd Geoffrey Freer Stakes Group 2, 3rd Epsom Derby Group 1 and £30,975), **NORTHERN VIEW** (Madrid Free Handicap, 4th Irish 2,000 Guineas Group 1), **NANTICIOUS** (Silken Glider Stakes Group 3), **TUCSEDO, MISS KISSFIELD** and the winners of over £120,000. A stakes-winner of 7 races from 5½ to 9 furlongs at 2 and 3 years including the LOUISIANA DERBY and HAWTHORNE DERBY. He was placed second 4 times and was third in the American Derby etc.
Total stakes earned $195,035.
He is by NORTHERN DANCER, sire in Europe of NIJINSKY and LYPHARD, and is half-brother to HABITAT.

FULL FOR 1977

On Your Mark

Chesnut, 1964, by RESTLESS WIND—SUPERSCOPE by SWAPS

1976 - best season ever

Winner at 2 years of the Windsor Castle Stakes, Great Surrey Stakes, etc., and winner in the U.S.A. of $22,440.

His sire RESTLESS WIND, has sired winners in the U.S.A. of nearly $3 million including Champion 2-y-o filly PROCESS SHOT.

He is out of the Queen Mary Stakes winner WEEBER. This is the family of PRINCE REGENT, WHISTLER, NEVER SAY DIE and EXAMPLE and is entirely free from any strain of PHALARIS.

Sire in 1976 of the winners of 37 races and £78,934; his best winners included MANDRAKE MAJOR (Flying Childers Stakes Group 1 and £22,514), LORD MARK (15 wins, £33,921 in Italy), NOBLE MARK (Duke of York Stakes Group 3, Curragh Stakes Group 3, Phoenix Stakes Group 2 and £14,567), FIDDLERS DREAM (Prix la Fleche, and £11,187), GAN ON GEORDIE (£10,674), CHUM CHUM and PANOMARK.

PIECES OF EIGHT

Brown, 1963 by RELIC out of BABY DOLL by DANTE

From Fairway winning the Eclipse Stakes and Champion Stakes in 1928 and 1929 to BRIGADIER GERARD winning in 1971 and 1972, only four horses had won both races, including PIECES OF EIGHT. He was allotted 9 st. 10 lbs. in the Three Year Old Free Handicap, above the winners of the 2,000 Guineas, 1,000 Guineas, Derby and Oaks.

PIECES OF EIGHT returned to England in 1973 and his first crop include Namara (2 races and £3,075) and two other winners, to August 1st. His yearlings in 1976 averaged £8,725.

PIECES OF EIGHT has averaged over 40 mares in his 4 seasons at stud in England.

The property of a syndicate

Apply: KEITH FREEMAN (BLOODSTOCK) LTD., PETTUS HOUSE, ELM HILL, NORWICH, NORFOLK NR3 1HS
(Telephone: Norwich 27773 or 21307)

Pitskelly

Brown, 1970, PETINGO—FRENCH BIRD by GUERSANT

Top stakes-winner
—excellent first crop of foals

PITSKELLY won 4 races over 7 furlongs at 2, 3 and 4 years including the Totalisator Free Handicap, Newmarket, Jersey Stakes, Ascot and Bunbury Cup, Newmarket. He was second to **THATCH** in the July Cup and third to **TARGOWICE** and **KALAMOUN** in the Prix Thomas Bryon.

A tough consistent stakes-winning son of top miler and Champion Sire PETINGO from the same family as RIGHT STRATH, PRINCELY STRATH.

Excellent first crop of foals 1976. Excellent fertility.

Enquiries to BBA (Ireland) Ltd., 51 Lansdowne Road, Dublin 4.
Tel: Dublin 686222
Standing at Dowdstown House Stud,
Maynooth, Co. Kildare.

Enquiries at the stud to
Sean Collins, M.R.C.V.S.,
Tel: Dublin 288081 or 286004

Standing at SANDLEY STUD, Gillingham, Dorset
(Gillingham 2696)

PORTO BELLO

Ch 1965 by FLORIBUNDA - STREET SONG (LE LAVANDOU)

A Leading Sire in 1975 & 1976
1975 21 winners of 45 races, £83,259
1976 24 winners of 42 races, £81,263

PORTO BELLO's principal winners include **ROMAN WARRIOR** (Gr 3 Diadem Stakes 1975 and £43,830), **IMPORT** (Stewards' Cup, Wokingham Stakes 1976 and £29,463), **CRAMOND** (Gr 2 Queen Mary Stakes 1976) and **GIANNINA** (in Italy 1976)

PORTO BELLO won 9 races, £15,717, including Gr 3 New (Norfolk) Stakes, Royal Ascot, Lonsdale Stakes, Hyde Park Stakes, Epsom, and Summer Solstice Purse, Hialeah Park in new record time for 5½f of 62.8 secs.

Enquiries to Secretaries to the Syndicate:
British Bloodstock Agency,
ALTON HOUSE,
NEWMARKET, SUFFOLK.
TEL: 0638 5021   TELEX 817157

923

PRINCE DE GALLES 16h

(brown 1966 by Welsh Abbot—Vauchellor by Honey-way)

PRODUCTION

HIS 41 WINNERS INCLUDE THE NOTABLE PERFORMERS

NOBLE DANCER (Best horse ever in Scandinavia, Fourth Prix de l'Arc de Triomphe and Washington D.C. International), **BESSIE WALLIS** (Houghton Stakes) and **LILY LANGTRY**

PERFORMANCE

WON FIVE RACES—only three times out of the frame in 18 starts.

DUAL CAMBRIDGESHIRE WINNER—with record top weight on second occasion.

HOLDER 9f RECORD AT NEWMARKET.

DEFEATED SONG, BURGLAR, BE FRIENDLY over 6 furlongs.

SECOND VERNONS SPRINT CUP (Gr. II) to Tudor Music.

SECOND WILLS MILE (Gr. II) to Humble Duty.

SECOND PRIX DU PALAIS ROYAL (Gr. III) to Yellow God.

SECOND PETER HASTINGS STAKES, 10f, to Hotfoot.

THIRD QUEEN ELIZABETH II STAKES (Gr. II) to Welsh Pageant and Gold Rod.

PRINCE DE GALLES STANDS AT KING EDWARD'S PLACE STUD, WANBOROUGH, SWINDON, WILTS.
Tel: Wanborough 230/347

Enquiries to:
Raymond Barnes (Bloodstock) Ltd.
57 High Street, Newmarket
Tel: (0638) 2855

or **Rustons & Lloyd, 136 High Street Newmarket. Tel: (0638) 3044**

Standing at Ashleigh Stud, Clonee, Co. Dublin

Prince Tenderfoot

Bay 1967 Blue Prince — La Tendresse (Grey Sovereign)

Principal Winners:

LORD HENHAM	Hialeah Turf Cup, Group 2.
FALIRAKI	Norfolk Stakes, Group 2, 2nd Wm Hill Sprint Championship.
TENDER CAMILLA	Railway Stakes, Group 3, Moyglare Stud Stakes, Group 3.
ICING	Argos Star Fillies Mile, Group 3.
DUKE ELLINGTON	Harry Rosebery Trophy, also 2nd Middle Park Stakes, Group 1.
SILK SLIPPER	Prix des Chenes, Group 3.
ATHLETE'S FOOT	Sir Gatric Stakes, Doncaster.

Prince Tenderfoot was one of the leading two-year-olds of 1969 when he was rated only 3 lb below Nijinsky in the Irish Free Handicap. He won Coventry Stakes, Royal Ascot, Leopardstown Stakes, Curragh, etc.

His sire **Blue Prince** is a leading sire in the USA, sire of KLING KLING (Champion Grass Horse 1970) and FOUR-AND-TWENTY (Santa Anita Derby, Hollywood Derby).

His dam **La Tendresse** was the fastest 2-y-o of 1961 and is a half-sister to seven winners.

Syndicate secretaries:

THE ANGLO-IRISH AGENCY LTD., 16 OLD BOND STREET, LONDON W.1. 01-493 2613 or 1197. Cables: Anglirish, London. **ISIS**

Red God

Chesnut 1954   **NASRULLAH-SPRING RUN (MENOW)**

Blushing Groom confirms his position as Champion 2-y-o of Europe by thrashing English Champion J. O. Tobin in the Grand Criterium.

Red God has been one of the outstanding sires of the past decade, siring the winners of over £1,000,000 throughout the world.   Hardly a season goes by without Red God figuring high in the stallion lists:

1968   2nd Leading Sire of two-year-olds in Europe, including **FOLLE ROUSSE** (9-3 Free H'cap)

1969   The Leading Sire of two-year-olds in Great Britain and Ireland including **YELLOW GOD** (9-1 Free H'cap)

1970   Sire of the top three-year-old miler **YELLOW GOD** (2nd 2,000 Guineas) and the top two-year-old **SUPERNATURAL** (9-7 Irish Free H'cap)

1971   Sire of the Champion Sprinter **GREEN GOD**

1972   Sire of the Champion two-year-old **JACINTH** (top Free H'cap)

1973   Sire of 21 individual winners in England and Ireland including **JACINTH** and **SILVER GOD**

1974   Sire of 18 individual winners in England and Ireland including **RED ALERT** (Spillers' Stewards' Cup, Jersey Stakes)

1975   His son **GREEN GOD** was 2nd leading first-season sire

1976   Sire of the Champion European 2-y-o **BLUSHING GROOM** and the French 2,000 Guineas winner **RED LORD** with over £200,000 in stakes.   **YELLOW GOD** leading sire of 2-y-o's (money won).

FULL FOR 1977

Enquiries to: **BBA (Ireland) Ltd.,**
51 Lansdowne Road,
Dublin 4.   Tel: 686222.

ISIS

Standing at Loughtown Stud, Donadea,
Co. Kildare, Ireland.   Tel: Naas 69115.

AT BEECH HOUSE STUD, NEWMARKET

RIBERO

Bay, 1965 (16.1½ h.h.) by RIBOT out of LIBRA by HYPERION

RIBERO, winner of Irish Sweeps Derby (Group 1), beating Sir Ivor by two lengths and St. Leger (Group 1), also a winner at two years. Own-brother to RIBOCCO.

RIBERO is sire of the winners of over £185,000 from 1973 to August, 1976.

RIBERO's first four crops of yearlings averaged over £10,000.

The property of a syndicate.

FULL 1970 to 1976.

Apply: Keith Freeman (Bloodstock) Ltd., Pettus House, Elm Hill, Norwich, Norfolk NR3 1HS

(Telephone: Norwich 27773 or 21307)

927

ROAN ROCKET

(Grey 1961 by Buisson Ardent out of Farandole II
by Deux Pour Cent)

WINNER OF 5 RACES AND £34,258 UP TO A MILE AT TWO, THREE AND FOUR YEARS

RATED ONLY 3lb BEHIND SANTA CLAUS ON THE 1964 THREE-YEAR-OLD FREE HANDICAP

CONSISTENTLY SUCCESSFUL

Sire of the winners of at least 270 races and £334,854 including in 1976 more top Two-Year-Olds SKY SHIP and GAIRLOCH

Roan Rocket stands at the Dunchurch Lodge
Stud, Newmarket, at a fee of £1,050, mare
in foal 1st October.

Apply Raymond Barnes (Bloodstock) Ltd.,
57 High Street, Newmarket. Tel.: 2855
or The Secretary, Dunchurch Lodge Stud,
Newmarket. Tel.: 2115.

ROYAL AND REGAL

Bay or Brown 1970 Vaguely Noble-Native Street (Native Dancer)

Champion Florida-bred horse 1973. Won six races at 2 and 3 years including Florida Derby (beating Forego, U.S. Champion 1975 and 1976 and 3rd leading money winner of all time to Kelso and Round Table), Bahamas Stakes, etc. His dam won 10 races, $236,808 including Kentucky Oaks, Sorority Stakes, Astoria Stakes, Jasmine Stakes. He is by the sensational **VAGUELY NOBLE**, Leading Sire in the British Isles in 1973 and 1974, sire of **DAHLIA** (King George VI and Queen Elizabeth Stakes, twice, Irish Oaks, Washington International, Benson & Hedges Gold Cup, twice, Grand Prix de Saint-Cloud, the leading European stakes-earner), **NOBILIARY** (Washington International), **EMPERY** (Epsom Derby), **EXCELLER** (Grand Prix de Paris, Prix Royal-Oak), **ACE OF ACES** (Sussex Stakes), **MISSISSIPIAN, NOBLE DECREE** etc.

FULL each season since going to stud
Fertility estimate (Stallion Review 1976) 79.5% live foals

Standing at Ballygoran Stud
Maynooth, Co. Kildare, Ireland
Enquiries to Dr. J. O'Driscoll
Tel. Dublin 286264
or Kildare 21220

Standing at Wyld Court Stud, Hampstead Norreys,
NEWBURY, Berkshire

SARITAMER

gr 1971 by DANCER'S IMAGE—IRISH CHORUS

SARITAMER— **TIMEFORM'S CHAMPION
SPRINTER of 1974**

SARITAMER— **won 8 races, £27,054 (5 Pattern
Races)**

SARITAMER— **by a Classic winner out of a
brilliantly fast filly, who is closely
related to Pistol Packer, Noblesse,
Attivo and Where You Lead.**

Fee: £1,500 or £2,000 no foal no fee

FULL 1975-77

FERTILITY (foals of 1976) 87·09%

Enquiries to
D. V. Dick, Wyld Court Stud (Hermitage 201487)

Telex 849425

Standing at **BALLYLINCH STUD**, Thomastown,
Co. Kilkenny

SASSAFRAS

bay, 1967, by SHESHOON - RUTA, by RATIFICATION

Henri le Balafre, by SASSAFRAS, winning the Prix Royal-Oak

THE OUTSTANDING YOUNG CLASSIC SIRE

With just 3 crops Sassafras is sire of the winners of over £250,000,
including FLORESSA (Gr. 3 Prix Royaumont; 3rd Prix Vermeille,
1976), HENRI LE BALAFRE (Gr. 1 Prix Royal-Oak, Gr. 1 Premio
Roma), FOUR SPADES (Prix des Yearlings, Deauville, and
£9,149), SARANIA (Sandleford Priory Stakes, 1976), GALWAY BAY
(Gr. 2 Coventry Stakes, Royal Ascot, Hyperion Stakes, etc.),
HOKUEI ONE (3 races, £19,547 in Japan), LAUGHING
GIRL, COUNTESS EILEEN, SAROS, etc.

SASSAFRAS who was rated **135** by Timeform, won **6 races**,
£249,540 at **2** and **3** years, from **7** to **15½** furlongs. He beat Nijinsky
in the Prix de l'Arc de Triomphe, and also won the Prix du Jockey
Club and the Prix Royal-Oak.

Full 1971-1977 Fertility: 78.12% (foals of 1976)

Enquiries:
British Bloodstock Agency
Alton House, Newmarket, Suffolk
Tel: 0638 5021   Telex 817157
or The Manager Ballylinch Stud, Thomastown, Co. Kilkenny.
Tel: Kilkenny (056) 24217

933

SONG

Bay 1966 by SING SING – INTENT

Champion Sprinter 1969

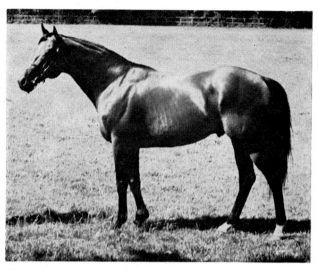

From his first three crops, **SIRE of 32 INDIVIDUAL WINNERS of 73 RACES,** and total stakes over £110,000 at home and abroad.

1974—**SIX two-year-old winners.**

1975—**Joint leading sire of two-year-olds** standing in England with **ELEVEN individual winners.**

1976—**SIX two-year-old winners** of 13 races from 11 runners, ★ and **thirteen 3 & 4 y.o. winners of 26** races, total stakes over £70,000.

★(Due to limited covering season in 1973 after leg fracture).

SONG'S notable winners with total earnings include: SONNENBLICK, £8,059; ENCHANTED, £8,105; SONG'S FIRST, £5,474; BILL'S SONG, £4,103; NET CALL, £3,324; and MUSICAL PIECE, £4,413 at home; also, BRER RABBIT, £21,860; SATIN SONG, £3,185 in South Africa; PIPER, course record holder in Oslo; and GREEK SONG, £9,504, incl. Norsk Kriterium.

Fee for 1977 is £800 or £1,000 NFNF (1st October terms)

Fully booked every season 1970-1976

Consistently high fertility

Enquiries to: **Miss Audrey Westerdick, Littleton Stud, Winchester, Hants.** Winchester (0962) 880210.

Sovereign Path

Grey, 1956, by GREY SOVEREIGN—MOUNTAIN PATH by BOBSLEIGH

Establishing himself as a sire of sires

Sire of the winners of more than 600 races and over £1,000,000 including **Humble Duty** (8 races £63,696, including 1,000 Guineas, Coronation Stakes, Sussex Stakes and Cheveley Park Stakes), **Wolver Hollow** (Eclipse Stakes), **Town Crier** (Victoria Cup, Queen Anne Stakes), **Estaminet** (Northern Goldsmiths Handicap under 10.0), **Spanish Express** (Middle Park Stakes), **Petite Path** (Queen Mary Stakes, Ayr Gold Cup), **Supreme Sovereign** (Lockinge Stakes), **Hunters Path** (National Stakes), **Warpath** (Extel Centenary Handicap) and **Royal Match** (7 races, £44,899).

His sons are also becoming prolific sires—
Wolver Hollow (sire of **Wollow**, 2,000 Guineas, Benson & Hedges Gold Cup, Sussex Stakes etc. in 1976, **Furry Glen**, Irish 2,000 Guineas winner), **Town Crier** (sire of **Cry of Truth**, best 2-y-o filly 1974), **Supreme Sovereign** (sire of **Nocturnal Spree**, 1,000 Guineas and **Mark Anthony** a leading Irish 2-y-o in 1974 and conqueror of Grundy in 1975), **Sovereign Edition** (a leading sire in Australia in 1976).

FULL 1977

**Enquiries to BBA (Ireland) Ltd.,
51 Lansdowne Road, Dublin 4.
Tel: Dublin 686222**
Standing at Burgage Stud, Leighlinbridge,
Co. Carlow, Ireland.

Steel Heart

Bay, 1972, by **HABITAT-A.1.** by **ABERNANT**

Winner of 5 races £66,661 including William Hill Middle Park Stakes Group 1, C & G Gimcrack Stakes Group 2, Duke of York Stakes Group 3, Goldene Peitsche, Baden Baden Group 3; 2nd William Hill Dewhurst Stakes Group 1 (to GRUNDY) and **July Cup Group 2** (to LIANGA).

By European Sire of the decade HABITAT, whose offspring include FLYING WATER (1,000 Guineas), ROUSSALKA (Coronation Stakes, Nassau Stakes twice), HITTITE GLORY (Middle Park and Flying Childers Stakes), ROSE BOWL (Champion Stakes, Queen Elizabeth Stakes twice), HABAT (Middle Park, Mill Reef and Norfolk Stakes).

Out of A.1. by ABERNANT dam of 6 winners including CHILI GIRL (Star Stakes Group 3), AMPULLA (Cherry Hinton Stakes, Group 3 at 2, 1976). She herself is half-sister to 9 winners including TAITTINGER (Princess Margaret Stakes) and to the dam of Top Miler and Sire SUPREME SOVEREIGN (Sire of NOCTURNAL SPREE, MARK ANTHONY, etc.).

TARQOGAN

Brown, 1960, Black Tarquin-Rosyogan

TARQOGAN won the Cambridgeshire, the Chesterfield Cup and four other races. Placed 14 times, including second Lincolnshire, third King George VI and Queen Elizabeth Stakes, Cambridgeshire, Eclipse Stakes, also fourth, including Derby Stakes, Irish Sweeps Derby, Prix Ganay, etc.

HIGHLY SUCCESSFUL SIRE UNDER BOTH RULES

Sire of the winners of more than 130 races, and over £100,000 including 13 2-y-o winners and a Royal Ascot winner on the Flat.

A LEADING SIRE OF JUMPERS IN 1976

Sire of the winners of 70 races and £50,000 including BLACK ANDREW (Stone's Ginger Wine Chase, Sandown, Geoffrey Gilbey Memorial Chase, Newbury and 3 other races), ROMANOGAN, CONTRAPTION and many other winners and runners of high promise.

FULL 1967-76

Tower Walk

Bay, 1966, by HIGH TREASON—LORRIKEET by PEARL DIVER

The leading sire of 1975

With just 3 crops to race, sire of the winners of 84 races and over £130,000, and a leading sire of 2-y-o's in 1975. His best winners include **SUPER CAVALIER** (National Stakes, July Stakes), **WALK BY** (Portland Handicap), **NAGWA** (13 races at 2 years), **TOWER BIRD** (4 races), **CREETOWN, WESTERN JEWEL** (5 races in England including Cornwallis Stakes, 2nd Prix Robert Papin), **VENUS OF STRETHAM** (7 races at 2 years) and in Italy **RED GIFT** (6 races, £16,554).

Winner of 7 races from 2-4 years, £40,480, including National Stakes, Nunthorpe Stakes and the Prix de l'Abbaye de Long-champ. At 4 years won the Palace House Stakes. Also placed second in 2,000 Guineas.

He is from a family noted for producing tough, sound and consistent horses which includes Horse of the Year for 1975, **GRUNDY.**

Enquiries to **BBA (Ireland) Ltd.**
51 Lansdowne Road, Dublin 4.
Tel: Dublin 686222
Standing at Woodpark Stud, Dunboyne,
Co. Meath, Ireland.
Tel: Dublin 255225

940

Winner of the Italian Derby by the sire of **DERRING-DO**

VARANO

Bay, 1962
Darius–
Varna II

Winner of **7** races, value **£15,974,** including Italian Derby (equalling the record time, beating Ben Marshall and Marco Visconti).

His dam, **VARNA II** (the top-priced broodmare at 1966 December Sales), won 5 races at 2 and 3 years, and comes from a great Italian Classic family.

Sire of the winners of more than 85 races and over £65,000 including Count Varano, Princess Varano, Celtic Twilight, Pink Posy, Arctic Vagabond, Kilboy, Came True, Crafty Codger and Varano Gem. Also sire of the winners of 40 races over the sticks including Classic Gem, Renvyle, Slievereagh etc.

FULL 1968-1976
(Property of Mr. Joseph McGrath)

All enquiries to:
Joseph McGrath, Brownstown Stud,
Curragh, Co. Kildare.
(Tel: Curragh 41303)

Standing at Nidd Hall Stud, Ripley, Harrogate, Yorkshire

WARPATH

by SOVEREIGN PATH, from a dam line that produces leading sires

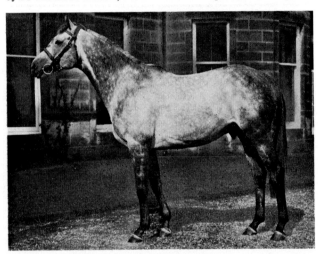

WARPATH won 4 races, £18,217 (9-10f) including Scottish and Newcastle Breweries H. Stakes in record time (beating Ginevra, won Oaks), Extel Centenary Stakes, Goodwood and Doonside Cup (beating Klairvimy and Star Ship, both Royal Ascot winners); 3rd (beaten neck and ¾ length to Gift Card and Scottish Rifle, levels) in Prince of Wales Stakes, Royal Ascot and Cumberland Lodge Stakes, Ascot; 5th (beaten about 2 lengths, by Our Mirage) in Great Voltigeur Stakes, York.

Rated 125 (Timeform 1st October 1973)
"good sort of colt; very good walker; genuine and consistent"
37 mares tested in foal in 1974.   40 mares tested in foal in 1975.
39 mares tested in foal in 1976.

Dam: ARDNEASKEN WON at 3 yrs; WARPATH is her first foal.   Dam of DAKOTA (7 races and over £41,848; won as a two-year-old and three successive races in 1974 including King George V Stakes, Royal Ascot in record time; in 1975 won St. Simon Stakes, Newbury, Tennent Trophy, Ayr and Ebor Handicap, York, 4th King George VI and Queen Elizabeth Stakes, 1976), SHOSHONI (Royal Caledonian Hunt Cup), CHEYENNE (Jorrocks Stakes, Redcar), her first four foals.   Grandam: ALICE DELYSIA WON at 3 yrs; dam of winners including MY HEART, leading sire of Two-Year-Olds in Australia; half-sister to GAY TIME, ELOPEMENT and CASH AND COURAGE, all successful sires, and to MISTRESS GWYNNE (3 wins, grandam of JACINTH), also to FLATTER (grandam of HUMBLE DUTY, 1,000 Guineas and £67,171).

Applications to:

The Secretary, Nidd Hall Stud, Ripley, Harrogate.
Tel: Harrogate 770065 or 770159

Windjammer (USA)

Bay, 1969, by RESTLESS WIND—CROWDING IN by MISTER GUS

Outstanding 2-y-o in U.S.A.
First Crop of yearlings in great demand

Won 6 races and $102,783 including Breeders Futurity, Group 3 (by 5l) and Kentucky Jockey Club Stakes (by 7l). In the Experimental Handicap of 1971 (American Free Handicap for two-year-olds) he was allotted only 7 lb less than RIVA RIDGE (winner of Kentucky Derby and Belmont Stakes).

A good-looking quality horse by Restless Wind (sire of On Your Mark, and a leading sire in the U.S.A.), he is a full-brother to RACING ROOM (won 9 races and $159,800), half-brother to JOE NAMATH (won 7 races and $58,000).

First Crop of yearlings were in great demand in 1976 and made up to 12,000 gns. FULL 1977

At *WOODDITTON STUD*
Newmarket
CONNAUGHT

Bay 1965
by ST PADDY out of NAGAIKA by GOYAMA

Sire of the winners of £93,372 to date including SAUCE-BOAT (Child Stakes Gr. III), ASTERINA (Seaton Delaval Stakes, Gr. III), SIR MONTAGU (Ebor Handicap, 2nd French St Leger 1976), CONNAUGHT SQUARE, MISS PINKIE (3 races, £9,894 including Argos Star Fillies Mile, Group 3), PADDINGTON (3 races, £5,848, at 2 years 1976 including Rous Memorial Stakes), MOUNT STREET, LADY CONSTANCE, etc.

Syndicated

WELSH PAGEANT

Bay 1966
by TUDOR MELODY out of PICTURE LIGHT by COURT MARTIAL

Sire from his first 2 crops of the winners of £68,662 to date, including GWENT (Jersey Stakes, Royal Ascot, Gr. III), AVGERINOS (Granville Stakes, Ascot), MAN OF HAR-LECH (Tote Free Handicap), COIN OF GOLD, MOSS-BERRY, HUNTSMAN'S LEAP, MAY BECK, ROYAL PLUME, etc.

Syndicated

Applications for Nominations should be made to:
C. F. N. MURLESS
Woodditton Stud, Newmarket, Suffolk CB8 9SR
Tel. Stetchworth 271 or 441

AIRLIE STALLIONS 1977

In the past two seasons **297** Airlie-sired horses have won **757** races and over **£2,100,000**. This includes **23** winners of **37** pattern races.

For the stallions listed in the following pages apply to:

Captain A. D. D. Rogers,
Airlie Stud,
Lucan,
County Dublin,
Irish Republic.
Tel: Dublin 280267.

CROWNED PRINCE

Champion 2-y-o of 1971 above HIGH TOP, DEEP DIVER, SUN PRINCE, SHARPEN UP, SALLUST, etc.   Winner of Dewhurst S, Gr I by 5 lengths, and Champagne S, Gr II beating European Champion RHEINGOLD on both occasions.

Stud Record.   **First Runners 1976.**   Sire of 7 winners of 8 races, £32,163. From his first crop sire of AMPULLA (Cherry Hinton S, Gr III, third Champagne S, Gr II, £12,687), PRINCESS TIARA (Somerville Tattersall S, her only start, beating Baudelaire, Premio Tevere, Gr II), IRONY (winner, placed Beresford S, Gr II, Larkspur S, Gr II, Anglesey S, Gr III), VIVARES (Prix Bratome), DUCHESSE DE LOIR, MONTAPERTI, GIUSTINA AVIANA, etc.   Fertility 94·44% (Foals of 1976).

CROWNED PRINCE	Raise A Native (ch 1961)	Native Dancer	Polynesian
			Geisha
		Raise You	Case Ace
			Lady Glory
	Gay Hostess (ch 1957)	Royal Charger	Nearco
			Sun Princess
		Your Hostess	Alibhai
			Boudoir

His sire RAISE A NATIVE has already produced the winners of over $4,700,000 including EXCLUSIVE NATIVE (currently second on leading sires and leading sires of 2-y-o's lists in America) and SON ANGE (a leading first crop sire in 1976).
CROWNED PRINCE is full-brother to MAJESTIC PRINCE, winner of Kentucky Derby, Preakness S, Santa Anita Derby, $414,200 and half-brother to stakes-placed BETTY LORRAINE dam of CARACOLERO (French Derby and over £350,000).

Stands at Airlie Stud, Lucan, Co. Dublin.
Enquiries to Capt. A. D. D. Rogers, at the stud (tel. Dublin 280267).

DANCER'S IMAGE

Champion Canadian 2-y-o (winner and placed in 12 of 15 starts). At 3 years won Kentucky Derby (disq), Wood Memorial S, Governor's Gold Cup, etc. Total stakes $359,236.
Stud Record   **First Runners 1972.**   Sire of the winners of 235 races, £894,438.
His best winners include SARITAMER (July Cup, Gr II, Cork and Orrery S, Gr III, Diadem S, Gr III), LIANGA (Prix Jacques le Marois, Gr I, July Cup, Gr II, Prix de l'Abbaye, Gr I, Vernons Sprint Cup, Gr II, Prix Robert-Papin, Gr I, Prix Maurice de Gheest, Gr III), GODSWALK (Norfolk S, Gr III) and the American Stakes winners SMOOTH DANCER, FLEET IMAGE, SHERBY, GALA IMAGE, VICTORIAN IMAGE, etc.

	Native Dancer (gr 1950)	Polynesian	Unbreakable
			Black Polly
		Geisha	Dixcovery
DANCER'S			Miyako
IMAGE			
	Noor's Image (b 1953)	Noor	Nasrullah
			Queen of Baghdad
		Little Sphinx	Challenger II
			Khara

His sire is NATIVE DANCER winner of 21 of 22 races including Belmont and Preakness S. Sire of KAUAI KING (Kentucky Derby, Preakness S), RAISE A NATIVE (Champion and sire of Champions), DAN CUPID (sire of SEA BIRD), NATIVE CHARGER (Florida Derby, a leading sire), and Champion fillies HULA DANCER, NATIVE STREET and SECRET STEP.
His dam NOOR'S IMAGE is out of a sister to grandam of HABITAT and NORTHFIELDS.

Standing at Haras du Quesnay, Vauville, 14800 Deauville, France.

Apply: M. Alec Head, tel: Paris 457 0101, or Capt. A. D. D. Rogers, Airlie Stud, Lucan, Co. Dublin (tel. Dublin 280267).

Airlie
Grangewilliam
Simmonstown
Williamstown
Ballyowen
Baroda
STUDS

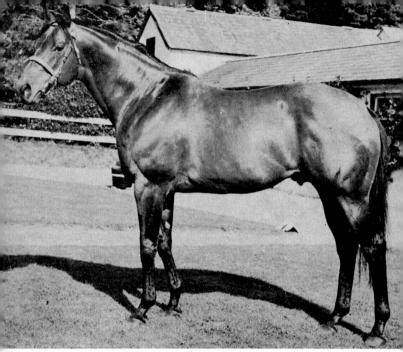

HABITAT

CHAMPION EUROPEAN MILER OF 1969 when winner of Prix du Moulin de Long-champ, Gr I, Lockinge S, Gr II, Prix Quincey, Gr III and Wills Mile, Gr III.

Stud Record   First Runners 1973.   Sire of 115 winners of 177 races, £733,170.
Sire in 1976 of HABITONY (a leading 2-y-o in U.S.A. winning Norfolk S, Gr I), Sunny Slope S, Gr III and £66,596), ROSE BOWL (Queen Elizabeth II S, Gr II, twice, Champion S, Gr I), FLYING WATER (1,000 Guineas, Nell Gwyn S, Gr III), ROUSSALKA (Nassau S, Gr II, twice, Coronation S, Gr I, etc.), MADANG (a leading Italian sprinter), etc. Previous winners include HITTITE GLORY, HABAT and STEEL HEART, all winners of Gr I, Middle Park S, BITTY GIRL (Queen Mary S, Gr II, Lowther S, Gr III), HOT SPARK (Flying Childers S, Gr I), HAMADA (Prix de la Porte Maillot, Gr III), etc. Fertility 90% (foals of 1976).

		Turn-to	Royal Charger
	Sir Gaylord		Source Sucree
	(b 1959)	Somethingroyal	Princequillo
HABITAT			Imperatrice
		Occupy	Bull Dog
	Little Hut		Miss Bunting
	(b 1952)	Savage Beauty	Challenger II
			Khara

By SIR GAYLORD winner of 10 races, Sire of SIR IVOR (Champion at 2 and 3 years, winning Epsom Derby, Washington International, etc., a leading sire). Out of LITTLE HUT also dam of NORTHFIELDS (Louisiana Derby, classic sire with his first crop) and GUEST ROOM (SW of $172,954).

Stands at Grangewilliam Stud, Maynooth, Co. Kildare.

Apply: Capt. A. D. D. Rogers, Airlie Stud, Lucan, Co. Dublin. (tel. Dublin 280267).

Airlie
Grangewilliam
Simmonstown
Williamstown
Ballyowen
Baroda

STUDS

MALACATE

Winner of 6 races, £141,051 including Irish Sweeps Derby, Gr 1 (see above beating Empery, Epsom Derby), Joe McGrath Memorial, Gr I (beating Northern Treasure, Irish 2,000 Guineas), Prix la Force, Gr III and Prix de Suresnes (beating dual classic winner Exceller). Third French Derby, Gr I, Prix Niel, Gr 3 and fourth Champion S, Gr 1.

Stud Record

Malacate retires to stud in 1977.

MALACATE	Lucky Debonair (b 1962)	Vertex	The Rhymer / Kanace
		Fresh as Fresh	Court Fleet / Airy
	Eye Shadow (b 1959)	My Babu	Djebel / Perfume II
		Pretty One	Bull Dog / Irvana

By LUCKY DEBONAIR winner of Kentucky Derby, Santa Anita Derby, Blue Grass S, Santa Anita H, etc. and $370,960. Sire of the winners of over $1,500,000 including MALACATE, PEPENDOR (Prix Maurice de Gheest, Gr III), DRESDEN DOLL (Demoiselle S, Gr II), CITY GIRL (Alcibiades S, Gr II), etc.

Out of EYE SHADOW dam of 7 other winners including BARBIZON JR ($79,860) and half-sister to COOL PRINCE (Sussex Turf H, sire). Her dam is half-sister to NO STRINGS (Modesty S, dam of the successful sires GLOBEMASTER, $355,423 including Wood Memorial, Gr 1, NAIL, Champion 2-y-o and MITO sire of the winners of over $3,000,000). Immediate family of PROUD DELTA (leading 4-y-o filly in U.S.A., 1976) and GREEK ANSWER ($274,700 including Arlington-Washington Futurity, Gr I). His pedigree is free of Hyperion and Phalaris for five generations.

Stands at: Grangewilliam Stud, Maynooth, Co. Kildare

Apply: Capt. A. D. D. Rogers, Airlie Stud, Lucan, Co. Dublin (tel. Dublin 280267).

MANADO

CHAMPION FRENCH 2-y-o OF 1975, rated above YOUTH (French Derby, Washington International, Canadian International, etc.), EMPERY (Epsom Derby), VITIGES (Champion S, Prix Robert-Papin), EXCELLER (Grand Prix de Paris, Prix Royal-Oak), etc. Winner of Grand Criterium, Gr I, Prix de la Salamandre, Gr I, Prix Yacowlef (by 8 lengths), third Prix du Moulin, Gr I, Prix de la Foret, Gr I, Prix de Rond-Point, Gr III and fourth Prix Jacques le Marois, Gr I (beaten two heads). Total earnings £100,545. Timeform considered his form to be 'the best of any 2-y-o colt who raced in England, France or Ireland in 1975' and he was their HIGHEST RATED 2-y-o OF 1975.
Stud Record
Manado retires to stud in 1977.

MANADO	Captain's Gig (b/br 1965)	Turn-to	Royal Charger
			Source Sucree
		Make Sail	Ambiorix II
			Anchors Aweigh
	Slipstream (ITY) (gr 1967)	Sing Sing	Tudor Minstrel
			Agin the Law
		Palestream	Palestine
			Millstream

By CAPTAIN'S GIG winner of 8 races, $205,312 including Jim Dandy S, Gr III, second rated 2-y-o of his year. Sire of the winners of over 50 races, £160,000 from only two European crops.
Out of SLIPSTREAM a winner who is out of a winning half-sister to MEDWAY (Goodwood Cup, Gr III), REEL IN (Nassau S, Gr II, third Oaks), MILADY (Ribblesdale S, Gr II), etc. Third dam MILLSTREAM an own-sister to LIVE LETTERS (Yorkshire Oaks, Gr I) is ancestress of DR KNIGHTON (Will Rogers S, Gr II, sire), PRINCELY SON (Vernons Sprint Cup, Gr II), RICCO BOY (a leading French miler, 1976), etc.

Stands at: Simmonstown Stud, Celbridge, Co. Kildare.
Apply: Capt. A. D. D. Rogers, Airlie Stud, Lucan, Co. Dublin (tel. Dublin 280267).

Airlie
Grangewilliam
Simmonstown
Williamstown
Ballyowen
Baroda
STUDS

NONOALCO

Winner of 7 races from 10 starts including Prix Morny, Gr I (in record time from LIANGA)
Prix de la Salamandre, Gr I, Prix Yacowlef (by 8 lengths in record time) at 2 years and
2,000 Guineas, Gr I (beating GIACOMETTI, Champion S., etc.), Prix Jacques le Marois,
Gr I and Prix du Rond-Point, Gr III (beating LIANGA) at 3 years.   Total earnings
£148,255.   Timeform said of him 'an exceptionally brilliant 2-y-o' and 'a top class miler.
He lacks none of the qualities to be found in the better class North American bred colts,
which breeders are rightly attracted to in increasing numbers nowadays.'
Stud Record
First runners 1978
Fertility 100% (foals of 1976).

		Nearco	Pharos
	Nearctic		Nogara
	(br 1954)	Lady Angela	Hyperion
NONOALCO			Sister Sarah
		Hasty Road	Roman
	Seximee		Traffic Court
	(ch 1966)	Jambo	Crafty Admiral
			Bank Account

Sire, NEARCTIC winner of 21 races, $152,384 and Canadian Horse of the Year.   Sire
of the winners of over $7,000,000 including NORTHERN DANCER (Kentucky Derby,
Champion at 2 and 3 years and sire of NIJINSKY), Champion 2-y-o COOL RECEPTION,
ICECAPADE (Saranac S, Gr II, $256,400), etc.
Dam, SEXIMEE a winner out of a winning half-sister to NANCY JR (Kentucky Oaks).
Family of SECRETARIAT, SIR GAYLORD, EMPERY, etc.

Stands at: Airlie Stud, Lucan, Co. Dublin
Apply: Capt. A. D. D. Rogers, Airlie Stud, Lucan,
Co. Dublin (tel. Dublin 280267).

Airlie
Grangewilliam
Simmonstown
W Hamstown
Ballyowen
Barada
STUDS

SANDFORD LAD

CHAMPION EUROPEAN SPRINTER OF 1973 when unbeaten winner of Nunthorpe S, Gr II, King George S, Gr III and Prix de l'Abbaye de Longchamp, Gr I, beating ABERGWAUN (leading sprint filly), MOUBARIZ (Champion sprinter, 1974), MARBLE ARCH (Champion Irish 2-y-o filly), SAULINGO, etc. Also winner of 3 races and including Prince of Wales's S, and placed second beaten ⅛ length at 2 years, all his starts. Rated 133 by Timeform (1973 annual) and was their HIGHEST RATED SPRINTER OF 1973. ONLY TOP SPRINTER TO REMAIN UNBEATEN AT 3 YEARS IN THE LAST TWENTY YEARS.

Stud Record: First Runners 1977. Full since retiring to stud in 1974. His first crop yearlings sold for up to **12,500 gns** in 1976. Fertility 91·66% (Foals of 1976).

SANDFORD LAD	St Alphage (ch 1963)	Red God	Nasrullah
			Spring Run
		Sally Deans	Fun Fair
			Cora Deans
	Hill Queen (b 1958)	Djebe	Djebel
			Catherine
		Home Rule	Norseman
			Motherland

ST ALPHAGE his sire is own-brother to YELLOW GOD, Champion Sire of 2-y-o's in 1976. His grandsire RED GOD is sire in 1976 of European Champion BLUSHING GROOM and GREEN GOD (leading sire of 2-y-o's—number of winners—1976).

His dam HILL QUEEN has also bred the good sprint filly SANDFORD LADY winner of the Vernons Sprint Trial and £12,518. Her third dam is FAIR ISLE winner of 1,000 Guineas and own-sister to FAIRWAY and PHAROS.

Stands at Airlie Stud, Lucan, Co. Dublin.
Apply: Capt. A. D. D. Rogers, Airlie Stud, Lucan,
Co. Dublin (tel. Dublin 280267).

SIMBIR

Unbeaten at 2 years after winning his only 2 starts including the Gr II Grand Criterium de Saint-Cloud. Joint-Second rated on the French 2-y-o Handicap above ALLEZ FRANCE, ROSE LAUREL, KALAMOUN, EL RASTRO, DAHLIA, THATCH, AFRICAN SKY, CAVO DORO, etc. On his only start at 3 years he was beaten a neck by Rose Laurel in the Gr II Prix Daru. Unfortunately he split a pastern in his final preparation for the French Derby. Timeform said of him 'of all the 2-y-o colts raced in 1972 none appeals more as a prospective classic winner than SIMBIR.'

Stud Record   **First Runners 1977.**   Full since retiring to stud in 1974. Yearlings from his first crop averaged **5,020** gns and fetched up to **20,000** gns. Fertility 86·84% (Foals of 1976).

		Prince Bio
Shantung	Sicambre	Sif
(b 1956)		Hyperion
	Barley Corn	Schiaparelli
SIMBIR		Vandale II
	Herbager	Flagette
Hevea		Prince Chevalier
(b 1961)	Princess Reine	Kingscavil

Own-brother to SARACA, leading 3-y-o filly of her year in France winner of Prix Vermeille, Prix Saint-Alary and £102,000. He is by SHANTUNG twice Europe's leading sire with such offspring as FELICIO, CANADEL II, GINEVRA, FULL DRESS, LACQUER, etc. Out of HEVEA, who in addition to SIMBIR and SARACA has produced stakes-placed LYCEE. This is the family of leading sires and stakes winners DERRING-DO, HETHERSETT, PROUD CHIEFTAIN, PIRATE KING, PAMPERED KING, DROLL ROLE, etc.

(ISIS)   **Stands at Baroda Stud, Newbridge, Co. Kildare.**
Apply: Capt. A. D. D. Rogers, Airlie Stud, Lucan, Co. Dublin (tel. Dublin 280267).

Airlie
Grangewilliam
Simmonstown
Williamstown
Ballyowen
Baroda
STUDS

TARGOWICE

Highest-weighted 2-y-o in France 1972 when unbeaten winner of Prix Fontenoy, Prix Eclipse, Gr III and Prix Thomas Bryon, Gr III. He twice met KALAMOUN (French 2,000 Guineas, Prix Lupin, Jacques le Marois) and twice beat him, giving him 7 lb in the Thomas Bryon. Winner in 1973 of Prix Djebel and Prix Pontarme. Total stakes earned £26,262.

Stud Record
First runners 1977.
Full since retiring to stud in 1974.
Yearlings from his first crop have made up to **11,500 gns** in 1976.
Fertility 88·57% (Foals of 1976)

TARGOWICE	Round Table (b 1954)	Princequillo	Prince Rose
			Cosquilla
		Knights Daughter	Sir Cosmo
			Feola
	Matriarch (b/br 1964)	Bold Ruler	Nasrullah
			Miss Disco
		Lyceum	Bull Lea
			Colosseum

By ROUND TABLE multiple Champion and Horse of the Year in USA and leading sire there in 1972. His best offspring include Champions DRUMTOP, HE'S A SMOOTHIE, APALACHEE, BALDRIC, FLIRTING AROUND, etc.
Out of MATRIARCH winner and dam of 4 winners including TARGOWICE'S own-sister RONDEAU (National Stallion S, Colleen S and over $100,000) from her first 4 runners. She is out of an own-sister to LEA LARK dam of Champion 2-y-o filly LEALLAH.

Stands at: Simmonstown Stud, Celbridge, Co. Kildare.
Apply: Capt. A. D. D. Rogers, Airlie Stud, Lucan, Co. Dublin (tel. Dublin 280267).

TUMBLE WIND

Winner of 9 races (5½f-12f), $249,175 including Haggin and Westchester S Gr II (at 2 years), Hollywood Derby, Gr 1, Argonaut S. Gr II, San Vincente S, Gr III, etc. Second Hollywood Juvenile Championship, Gr II and Santa Anita Derby, Gr I.   Course record breaker for 1½m at Santa Anita.

Stud Record (U.S.A. foals)
First runners 1972.   Sire of the winners of 63 races, $315,010.
His best winners include WINDY CHEYENNE (Hollywood Nursery S, $20,000 added, 1976), DRIFTIN ALONG (La Habras S) and stakes placed SANDS AFFAIR.
Stud Record (European foals)
Yearlings from his first European crop sold for up to **16,000 gns** and averaged over 5½ times his fee.
Fertility 80·55 % (Foals of 1976)

		Windy City II	Wyndham
	Restless Wind		Staunton
	(ch 1956)	Lump Sugar	Bull Lea
TUMBLE WIND			Sugar Run
		Endeavour II	British Empire
	Easy Stages		Himalaya
	(b 1953)		Kiev
		Saturday Off	Mexican Tea

His sire RESTLESS WIND has sired the winners of over $3,000,000 including PROCESS SHOT (Champion 2-y-o filly, $463,200), WINDJAMMER (Keeneland Breeders Futurity, Kentucky Jockey Club S) and ON YOUR MARK (a noted sire of fast 2-y-o's).   This is a male line renowned for speed and precocity.

His dam EASY STAGES is own-sister to the dam of HUL A HUL, sire of record breaking 2-y-o Chamozzle.   Third dam Mexican Tea is also third dam of classic fillies FLYING RYTHM (Hollywood Oaks) and FLYING LILL (Kentucky Oaks).

Stands at: Baroda Stud, Newbridge, Co. Kildare
Apply: Capt. A. D. D. Rogers, Airlie Stud, Lucan,
Co. Dublin (tel. Dublin 280267).

Airlie
Grangewilliam
Simmonstown
Williamstown
Ballyowen
Baroda

STUDS

TYRANT

Stakes winner 13 races, $197,706 including Salvator Mile, Gr III, Carter H, Gr II, Delaware Valley H, Second Withers S, Gr II, to Horse of the Year ACK ACK.

Stud Record

First runners 1975

Sire of the winners of 60 races and £110,982.

His leading winners include the high-class French fillies TYRANT'S VALE (£25,750) and FRENETIQUE (£17,766), RIVER DANE (£19,358, second Prix Robert-Papin, Gr I to Blushing Groom), AMERUSA (6 races, £11,532), FLAMING TEMPER (£6,490, third Grand Criterium International d'Ostend) and LITTLE TRILBY (won, third Mulcahy Fillies S, Gr III). Sire in 1976 of 14 2-y-o winners more than any other stallion standing in England or Ireland.

Fertility 92·10% (Foals of 1976).

		Nasrullah	Nearco
	Bold Ruler		Mumtaz Begum
	(b 1954)	Miss Disco	Discovery
TYRANT			Outdone
		My Babu	Djebel
	Anadem		Perfume II
	(b 1954)		Panorama
		Anne of Essex	Queen of Essex

He is by BOLD RULER who has been Champion sire 8 times and who maintains his dominance in 1976 as virtually every American Champion of 1976 is a son or grandson or by a son or grandson of this great patriarch. His dam ANADEM won Great Surrey Foal S and is dam of 6 other winners including stakes winners L'AIGLON and CROWNED KING. She is half-sister to Champion European miler ROMULUS.

Stands at: Haras d'Etreham, Tour-en-Bessin, 14400 Bayeux, France
Apply: Comte R. de Chambure tel: Paris 722 6516 or 770 8929 or Capt. A. D. D. Rogers, Airlie Stud, Lucan, Co. Dublin (tel. Dublin 280267).

COOLMORE CASTLE HYDE

AND ASSOCIATED STUD FARMS

COOLMORE—
JOHN MAGNIER (CLONMEL 31298; TELEX 8695)
BOB LANIGAN

CASTLE HYDE—
GAY O'CALLAGHAN (FERMOY (025) 31689;
TELEX 8470)

STALLIONS:

ARCH SCULPTOR	PRINCE HANSEL
DEEP DIVER	RAGAPAN
DEEP RUN	RED ALERT
GAY FANDANGO	RHEINGOLD
HOME GUARD	SAULINGO
LAURENCE O	SUN PRINCE
MOUNT HAGEN	THATCH
	VARANO

ARCH SCULPTOR

**Bay 1973, by Habitat ex Money for Nothing
by Grey Sovereign**

Won 2 races and £17,802 at two
and three years.   Second in Prix
du Gros-Chene (Gr3), Prix Maurice
de Gheest (Gr3) and Prix de
Meautry (Gr3) and fourth in Wm
Hill Middle Park Stakes (Gr1).

He is half-brother to **Mummy's Pet**
(*a leading sire of 2-y-o's in 1975 & 1976*)
and **Parsimony** (*July Cup*).

Arch Sculptor is by the brilliant
stallion Habitat.

Habitat	Sir Gaylord	Turn-to
		Somethingroyal
	Little Hut	Occupy
ARCH		Savage Beauty
SCULPTOR		
	Grey	Nasrullah
Money for	Sovereign	Kong
Nothing		Honeyway
	Sweet	Farthing
	Nothings	Damages

COOLMORE
CASTLE HYDE
AND ASSOCIATED STUD FARMS

Will stand his first season at GRANGE STUD in 1977
Gay O'Callaghan
Tel: Fermoy (025) 31689.   Telex: 8470

GAY FANDANGO

Ch. 1972, by Forli ex Gay Violin by Sir Gaylord

Won 2 races and £15,443 at three years, his only season to race. **Won Waterford Crystal Mile (GR3)** (*beating Rose Bowl, Roussalka, Mark Anthony etc.*), **and Jersey Stakes (GR3), Royal Ascot.** **Also second in Queen Elizabeth II Stakes (GR2), Royal Ascot** (*to Rose Bowl and beating Anne's Pretender, Bolkonski, etc.*). **Also placed fourth in his first start, Irish 2,000 Guineas (GR1)** (*beaten 3½ lengths by Grundy*) **and in Prix du Rond-Point (GR3),** Longchamp. **ALL HIS STARTS.** **Timeform 132.**

		Aristophanes	Hyperion
	Forli		Commotion
		Trevisa	Advocate
GAY FANDANGO			Veneta
		Sir Gaylord	Turn-To
	Gay Violin		Somethingroyal
		Blue Violin	First Fiddle
			Blue Lu

COOLMORE
CASTLE HYDE
AND ASSOCIATED STUD FARMS

Stands at COOLMORE
—John Magnier or Bob Lanigan
Tel: Clonmel 31298.   Telex: 8695

MOUNT HAGEN

Ch. 1971 by Bold Bidder ex Moonmadness by Tom Fool

Won 4 races and £64,870, at two
and three years.
His wins included **Prix du Moulin
de Longchamp** (*beating Lianga,
Nonoalco, Ace of Aces, etc.*), **Prix de
Fontenoy by 8 lengths** (*from
Caracolero*), **and Prix de Fontaine-
bleau.**
Also placed four times including
**Eclipse Stakes, Sussex Stakes
and Grand Criterium.**
**Third rated two year old in the
Handicap Optional.**
Timeform 127.
Half-brother to MONSANTO.
His first crop are yearlings in
1977.

	Bold Ruler	Nasrullah
Bold Bidder		Miss Disco
	High Bid	To Market
MOUNT HAGEN		Stepping Stone
	Tom Fool	Menow
Moonmadness		Gaga
	Sunset	Hyperion
		Fair Ranger

COOLMORE
CASTLE HYDE
AND ASSOCIATED STUD FARMS

**Stands at COOLMORE - John Magnier or Bob Lanigan
Tel: Clonmel 31298.   Telex: 8695**

RED ALERT

Ch. 1971 by Red God ex Ashton Jane by Gratitude

Won 5 races and £19,413 at two
and three years.
His wins included Jersey Stakes,
Royal Ascot, Spillers Stewards
Cup and Enniskillen Stakes.
Also placed four times including
Norfolk Stakes (*to Habat*),
Anglesey Stakes (*to Saritamer*) **and
Tetrarch Stakes** (*to Cellini*).
Timeform 127.
His first crop will be yearlings
in 1977.

		Nasrullah	Nearco
	Red God		Mumtaz Begum
		Spring Run	Menow
RED ALERT			Boola Brook
		Gratitude	Golden Cloud
	Ashton Jane		Verdura
		Rye Girl	Blue Water
			Brosna

COOLMORE
CASTLE HYDE
AND ASSOCIATED STUD FARMS

**Stands at CASTLE HYDE STUD - Gay O'Callaghan
Tel: Fermoy (025) 31689. Telex: 8470**

SAULINGO

Bay 1970 by Sing Sing ex Saulisa by Hard Sauce

Won 6 races and £17,387 at two
and three years.
His wins included Prix du Gros-
Chene, Chantilly (5 *furlongs in* 58.4*s*)
Temple Stakes, Sandown and
Tattersalls Yorkshire Stakes.
Also placed three times including
New Stakes, Royal Ascot and
Norfolk Stakes, Doncaster.
Rated 8 st 13 lb, on Free Handi-
cap—equal rating to SANDFORD
LAD.   Timeform 122.
His first crop of yearlings made
up to 15,500 gns.

		Tudor	Owen Tudor
	Sing Sing	Minstrel	Sansonnet
			Portlaw
		Agin the Law	Revolte
SAULINGO			
		Hard Sauce	Ardan
	Saulisa		Saucy Belle
		L.S.D.	Lighthouse
			Styrian Dye

COOLMORE
CASTLE HYDE
AND ASSOCIATED STUD FARMS

**Stands at CASTLE HYDE STUD - Gay O'Callaghan
Tel: Fermoy (025) 31689. Telex: 8470**

RHEINGOLD

Bay 1969 by Faberge ex Athene by Supreme Court

Won 9 races and £357,033 at two,
three and four years.
His wins included **Prix de L'Arc
de Triomphe, Grand Prix de
Saint-Cloud** *(twice)*, **Prix Ganay**
and **Dante Stakes.**
Also placed 5 times including
Epsom Derby *(to Roberto by a short
head)*, **Dewhurst Stakes** *(to
Crowned Prince)*, **and King George
VI and Queen Elizabeth Stakes**
(to Dahlia).   **Timeform 137.**
His first crop of yearlings ave-
raged £17,746
His only yearling sold in the
U.S.A. made £36,500

	Princely Gift	Nasrullah
Faberge II		Blue Gem
	Spring	Legend of France
	Offensive	Batika
RHEINGOLD		
	Supreme	Persian Gulf or
	Court	Precipitation
Athene		Forecourt
	Necilia	Nearco
		Cecily

COOLMORE
CASTLE HYDE
AND ASSOCIATED STUD FARMS

**Standing at COOLMORE - John Magnier or Bob Lanigan
Tel: Clonmel 31298.   Telex: 8695**

SUN PRINCE

Ch. 1969 by Princely Gift ex Costa Sola by Worden II

Won 4 races and £47,644 at two, three and four years.
His wins included three wins at Royal Ascot in successive years, Coventry Stakes, St. James' Palace Stakes and Queen Anne Stakes. In France he won the Prix Robert Papin.
Also placed in 6 races including 2,000 Guineas, Eclipse Stakes and Sussex Stakes.
Timeform 128.
His first crop of yearlings fetched up to 32,000 gns.

	Nasrullah	Nearco
Princely Gift		Mumtaz Begum
	Blue Gem	Blue Peter
SUN PRINCE		Sparkle
	Worden II	Wild Risk
Costa Sola		Sans Tares
	Sunny Cove	Nearco
		Sunny Gulf

COOLMORE
CASTLE HYDE
AND ASSOCIATED STUD FARMS

Stands at CASTLE HYDE STUD - Gay O'Callaghan
Tel: Fermoy (025) 31689. Telex: 8470

THATCH

Bay 1970 by Forli ex Thong by Nantallah

Won 7 races and £40,277 at two and three years. His wins included Probationers Stakes, St. James' Palace Stakes (*by 15 lengths from Owen Dudley*), **July Cup and Sussex Stakes** (*by 3 lengths from Jacinth*). **Also placed fourth in Prix Morny and 2,000 Guineas. Timeform 136. His dam, THONG, is own sister to Ridan** (*13 races $635,074*), **Lt. Stevens** (*9 races $240,949*) **and Moccasin** (*Champion filly and dam of Apalachee*).

	Aristophanes	Hyperion
Forli		Commotion
	Trevisa	Advocate
THATCH		Veneta
	Nantallah	Nasrullah
Thong		Shimmer
	Rough Shod	Gold Bridge
		Dalmary

COOLMORE CASTLE HYDE
AND ASSOCIATED STUD FARMS

Leading first season sire 1976 & 4th highest in the yearling averages. His first crop of yearlings averaged £24,971.

Stands at COOLMORE-John Magnier or Bob Lanigan Tel: Clonmel 31298.   Telex: 8695

DERISLEY WOOD STUD LTD.
Newmarket

EUROPEAN CHAMPION TWO-YEAR-OLD IN 1970
MY SWALLOW
(Le Levanstell-Darrigle-Vilmoray)
SIRE OF 22 WINNERS OF 32 RACES 1976

AMERICAN DERBY WINNER
DUBASSOFF
(Sea Bird-Love Lyric-Prince Chevalier)
FIRST RUNNERS 1977

MIDSUMMER NIGHT II
(Djeddah-Night Sound-Mahmoud)

**Enquiries to: A. W. JOHNSON, ESQ.,
Derisley Wood Stud Ltd.,
Tel: NEWMARKET 730055**

iRish NATiONAL STUD

FOR 1977 SEASON

ROYAL MATCH (Ch. 1971)
Sovereign Path Grey Sovereign
Mountain Path
Shortwood Skymaster
Go Honey
Winner of thirteen races
including Littlewoods Spring
Cup, Sandown Cup, Bessborough
Stakes, Great Yorkshire
Handicap.
Fee: £500 – Special Live Foal.

CRASH COURSE (B. 1971)
Busted Crepello
Sans Le Sou
Lucky Stream Persian Gulf
Kypris
Winner of Doncaster Cup,
Top Rank Club Handicap, Ascot
Stakes.
Fee: £250 – Special Live Foal.

SALLUST (Ch. 1969)
Pall Mall Palestine
Malapert
Bandarilla Matador
Interval
Winner of Richmond Stakes,
Diomed Stakes, Prix de la Porte
Maillot, Goodwood Mile,
Sussex Stakes, Prix du Moulin
de Longchamps. Track record
holder for 1 mile – Goodwood
and Longchamp.
Fee: £2,200 – Special Live Foal.

LINACRE (Bl. 1960)
Rockefella Hyperion
Rockfel
True Picture Panorama
Verity
Winner of Irish 2,000 Gns.,
Queen Elizabeth II Stakes,
Whitehall Stakes, Prix de la
Porte Maillot, Scarborough
Stakes and two other races.
Fee: £100 – Special Live Foal.

LORD GAYLE (B. 1965)
Sir Gaylord Turn To
Somethingroyal
(dam of Secretariat)
Sticky Case Court Martial
Run Honey
Winner of eight races, once
unplaced, including William
Hill Gold Cup, Mitre Stakes,
Ripon Rowels, Prix Perth.
Fee: £1,250 – Special Live Foal.

TUDOR MUSIC (Br. 1966)
Tudor Melody Tudor Minstrel
Matelda
Fran Acropolis
Madrilene
Winner of International
Richmond Stakes, Gimcrack
Stakes, July Cup, Cork and
Orrery Stakes, Vernon Sprint Cup
Fee: £600 – Special Live Foal.

Terms and Conditions.

The terms for all stallions include a special live foal concession.
All stallions are included in the Irish Stallion Incentive Scheme and will be limited to 45 mares per season.
The service fee becomes payable on 15th October, 1977 unless a veterinary certificate of barrenness is produced on or before that date.

TEPUKEI (B. 1970)
Major Portion   Court Martial
Better Half
Cutter   Donatello II
Felucca
Winner of three races including White Rose Stakes, 1¼ miles; Placed second twice from seven starts. Total stakes £6,286.
Fee: £200 – (live foal).
Breeding on free range 1977.

GIOLLA MEAR (B. 1965)
Hard Ridden   Hard Sauce
Toute Bell II
Jacobella   Relic
Jacopa Bellini
Winner of Players Navy Cut Stakes, Desmond and Gallinule Stakes, Irish St. Leger.
Fee: £200 – Special Live Foal.

AFRICAN SKY (B. 1970)
Sing Song   Tudor Minstrel
Agin The Law
Sweet Caroline   Nimbus
Lackaday
Winner of his only two starts at 2 years. Winner at three years of Prix Fontainbleau. (1600m Longchamp) beating KALAMOUN; Prix Palais Royal (1400m Longchamp), Prix Quincey (1600m) Deauville beating SPARKLER; Prix de la Foret (1400m Longchamp). Total stakes £63,300.
Fee: £2,000 – Special Live Foal.

For further information and application forms:– APPLY The Manager,
Irish National Stud Co. Ltd.,
Tully, Kildare.
Telephone: 21251/21301/21377.
Telex: 31770.

Stallions?
Agencies?
Bookmakers?
Racecourses?
Stud Farms?
Transport?
Sporting Publications?
Veterinary Products?
etc.

why not advertise in

RACEHORSES OF 1977

Published early next March

THE STALLION REVIEW

Europe's principal breeding guide

**FULL DETAILS, PEDIGREES
and PHOTOGRAPHS of over 250 of
the best stallions in Europe**

The fourteenth edition of
the Stallion Review (1977)
is available from:

**Stallion Review, 26 Charing Cross Road,
London, W.C.2. Tel. 01-836 0461 ext. 36**

THE
EQUINE RESEARCH STATION
OF THE
ANIMAL HEALTH TRUST

Depends on voluntary contribution to maintain and, if possible, extend its investigations of problems of health and disease in horses and ponies of all types.

Donations will be gratefully acknowledged by:—

The Secretary,

EQUINE RESEARCH STATION
BALATON LODGE
NEWMARKET

Telephone: Newmarket 2241

2,000 GUINEAS 1916–1976

Year	Winner and S.P.	Second	Third	Rns
1916	Clarissimus (100/7)	Kwang-Su	Nassovian	17
1917	Gay Crusader (9/4)	Magpie	Athdara	14
1918	Gainsborough (4/1)	Somme Kiss	Blink	13
1919	The Panther (10/1)	Buchan	Dominion	12
1920	Tetratema (2/1)	Allenby	Paragon	17
1921	Craig an Eran (100/6)	Lemonora	Humorist	26
1922	St Louis (6/1)	Pondoland	Captain Cuttle	22
1923	Ellangowan (7/1)	Knockando	D'Orsay	18
1924	Diophon (11/2)	Bright Knight	Green Fire	20
1925	Manna (100/8)	St Becan	Oojah	13
1926	Colorado (100/8)	Coronach	Apple Sammy	19
1927	Adam's Apple (20/1)	Call Boy	Sickle	23
1928	Flamingo (5/1)	Royal Minstrel	O'Curry	17
1929	Mr Jinks (5/2)	Cragadour	Gay Day	22
1930	Diolite (10/1)	Paradine	Silver Flare	28
1931	Cameronian (100/8)	Goyescas	Orpen	24
1932	Orwell (evens)	Dastur	Hesperus	11
1933	Rodosto (9/1)	King Salmon	Gino	27
1934	Colombo (2/7)	Easton	Badruddin	12
1935	Bahram (7/2)	Theft	Sea Bequest	16
1936	Pay Up (11/2)	Mahmoud	Thankerton	19
1937	Le Ksar (20/1)	Goya II	Mid-day Sun	18
1938	Pasch (5/2)	Scottish Union	Mirza II	18
1939	Blue Peter (5/1)	Admiral's Walk	Fairstone	25
1940	Djebel (9/4)	Stardust	Tant Mieux	21
1941	Lambert Simnel (10/1)	Morogoro	Sun Castle	19
1942	Big Game (8/11)	Watling Street	Gold Nib	14
1943	Kingsway (18/1)	Pink Flower	Way In	19
1944	Garden Path (5/1)	Growing Confidence	Tehran	26
1945	Court Martial (13/2)	Dante	Royal Charger	20
1946	Happy Knight (28/1)	Khaled	Radiotherapy	13
1947	Tudor Minstrel (11/8)	Saravan	Sayajirao	15
1948	My Babu (2/1)	The Cobbler	Pride of India	18
1949	Nimbus (10/1)	Abernant	Barnes Park	13
1950	Palestine (4/1)	Prince Simon	Masked Light	19
1951	Ki Ming (100/8)	Stokes	Malka's Boy	27
1952	Thunderhead II (100/7)	King's Bench	Argur	26
1953	Nearula (2/1)	Bebe Grande	Oleandrin	16
1954	Darius (8/1)	Ferriol	Poona	19
1955	Our Babu (13/2)	Tamerlane	Klairon	23
1956	Gilles de Retz (50/1)	Chantelsey	Buisson Ardent	19
1957	Crepello (7/2)	Quorum	Pipe of Peace	15
1958	Pall Mall (20/1)	Major Portion	Nagami	14
1959	Taboun (5/2)	Masham	Carnoustie	13
1960	Martial (18/1)	Venture VII	Auroy	17
1961	Rockavon (66/1)	Prince Tudor	Time Greine	22
1962	Privy Councillor (100/6)	Romulus	Prince Poppa	19
1963	Only for Life (33/1)	Ionian	Corpora	21
1964	Baldric II (20/1)	Faberge II	Balustrade	27
1965	Niksar (100/8)	Silly Season	Present II	22
1966	Kashmir II (7/1)	Great Nephew	Celtic Song	25
1967	Royal Palace (100/30)	Taj Dewan	Missile	18
1968	Sir Ivor (11/8)	Petingo	Jimmy Reppin	10
1969	Right Tack (15/2)	Tower Walk	Welsh Pageant	13
1970	Nijinsky (4/7)	Yellow God	Roi Soleil	14
1971	Brigadier Gerard (11/2)	Mill Reef	My Swallow	6
1972	High Top (85/40)	Roberto	Sun Prince	12
1973	Mon Fils (50/1)	Noble Decree	Sharp Edge	18
1974	Nonoalco (19/2)	Giacometti	Apalachee	12
1975	Bolkonski (33/1)	Grundy	Dominion	24
1976	Wollow (evens)	Vitiges	Thieving Demon	17

1,000 GUINEAS 1916–1976

Year	Winner and S.P.	Second	Third	Rns
1916	Canyon (9/2)	Fifinella	Salamandra	10
1917	Diadem (6/4)	Sunny Jane	Nonpareil	14
1918	Ferry (50/1)	My Dear	Herself	8
1919	Roseway (2/1)	Britannia	Glaciale	15
1920	Cinna (4/1)	Cicerole	Valescure	21
1921	Bettina (33/1)	Petrea	Pompadour	24
1922	Silver Urn (10/1	Soubriquet	Golden Corn	20
1923	Tranquil (5/2)	Cos	Shrove	16
1924	Plack (8/1)	Mumtaz Mahal	Straitlace	16
1925	Saucy Sue (1/4)	Miss Gadabout	Firouze Mahal	11
1926	Pillion (25/1)	Trilogy	Short Story	29
1927	Cresta Run (10/1)	Book Law and Endowment dead-heated		28
1928	Scuttle (15/8)	Jurisdiction	Toboggan	14
1929	Taj Mah (33/1)	Sister Anne	Ellanvale	19
1930	Fair Isle (7/4)	Torchere	Sister Clover	19
1931	Four Course (100/9)	Lady Marjorie	Lindos Ojos	20
1932	Kandy (33/1)	Thorndean	Safe Return	19
1933	Brown Betty (8/1)	Fur Tor	Myrobella	22
1934	Campanula (2/5)	Light Brocade	Spend a Penny	10
1935	Mesa (8/1)	Hyndford Bridge	Caretta	22
1936	Tide-way (100/30)	Feola	Ferrybridge	22
1937	Exhibitionnist (10/1)	Spray	Gainsborough Lass	20
1938	Rockfel (8/1)	Laughing Water	Solar Flower	20
1939	Galatea II (6/1)	Aurora	Olein	16
1940	Godiva (10/1)	Golden Penny	Allure	11
1941	Dancing Time (100/8)	Beausite	Keystone	13
1942	Sun Chariot (evens)	Perfect Peace	Light of Day	18
1943	Herringbone (15/2)	Ribbon	Cincture	12
1944	Picture Play (15/2)	Grande Corniche	Superior	11
1945	Sun Stream (5/2)	Blue Smoke	Mrs Feather	14
1946	Hypericum (100/6)	Neolight	Iona	13
1947	Imprudence (4/1)	Rose O'Lynn	Wild Child	20
1948	Queenpot (6/1)	Ariostar	Duplicity	22
1949	Musidora (100/8)	Unknown Quantity	Solar Myth	18
1950	Camaree (10/1)	Catchit and Tambara dead-heated		17
1951	Belle of All (4/1)	Subtle Difference	Bob Run	18
1952	Zabara (7/1)	La Mirambule	Refreshed	20
1953	Happy Laughter (10/1)	Tessa Gillian	Bebe Grande	14
1954	Festoon (9/2)	Big Berry	Welsh Fairy	12
1955	Meld (11/4)	Aberlady	Feria	12
1956	Honeylight (100/6)	Midget II	Arietta	19
1957	Rose Royale II (6/1)	Sensualita	Angelet	20
1958	Bella Paola (8/11)	Amante	Alpine Bloom	11
1959	Petite Etoile (8/1)	Rosalba	Paraguana	14
1960	Never Too Late II (8/11)	Lady in Trouble	Running Blue	14
1961	Sweet Solera (4/1)	Ambergris	Indian Melody	14
1962	Abermaid (100/6)	Display	West Side Story	14
1963	Hula Dancer (1/2)	Spree	Royal Cypher	12
1964	Pourparler (11/2)	Gwen	Petite Gina / Royal Danseuse	18
1965	Night Off (9/2)	Yami	Mabel	16
1966	Glad Rags (100/6)	Berkeley Springs	Miliza II	21
1967	Fleet (11/2)	St Pauli Girl	Lacquer	16
1968	Caergwrle (4/1)	Photo Flash	Sovereign	14
1969	Full Dress II (7/1)	Hecuba	Motionless	13
1970	Humble Duty (3/1)	Gleam	Black Satin	12
1971	Altesse Royale (25/1)	Super Honey	Catherine Wheel	10
1972	Waterloo (8/1)	Marisela	Rose Dubarry	18
1973	Mysterious (11/1)	Jacinth	Shellshock	14
1974	Highclere (12/1)	Polygamy	Mrs Tiggywinkle	15
1975	Nocturnal Spree (14/1)	Girl Friend	Joking Apart	16
1976	Flying Water (2/1)	Konafa	Kesar Queen	25

THE DERBY 1916–1976

Year	Winner and S.P.	Second	Third	Rns
1916	Fifinella (11/2)	Kwang-Su	Nassovian	10
1917	Gay Crusader (7/4)	Dansellon	Dark Legend	12
1918	Gainsborough (8/13)	Blink	Treclare	13
1919	Grand Parade (33/1)	Buchan	Paper Money	13
1920	Spion Kop (100/6)	Archaic	Orpheus	19
1921	Humorist (6/1)	Craig an Eran	Lemonora	23
1922	Captain Cuttle (10/1)	Tamar	Craigangower	30
1923	Papyrus (100/15)	Pharos	Parth	19
1924	Sansovino (9/2)	St Germans	Hurstwood	27
1925	Manna (9/1)	Zionist	The Sirdar	27
1926	Coronach (11/2)	Lancegaye	Colorado	19
1927	Call Boy (4/1)	Hot Night	Shian Mor	23
1928	Felstead (33/1)	Flamingo	Black Watch	19
1929	Trigo (33/1)	Walter Gay	Brienz	26
1930	Blenheim (18/1)	Iliad	Diolite	17
1931	Cameronian (7/2)	Orpen	Sandwich	25
1932	April the Fifth (100/6)	Dastur	Miracle	21
1933	Hyperion (6/1)	King Salmon	Statesman	24
1934	Windsor Lad (15/2)	Easton	Colombo	19
1935	Bahram (5/4)	Robin Goodfellow	Field Trial	16
1936	Mahmoud (100/8)	Taj Akbar	Thankerton	22
1937	Mid-day Sun (100/7)	Sandsprite	Le Grand Duc	21
1938	Bois Roussel (20/1)	Scottish Union	Pasch	22
1939	Blue Peter (7/2)	Fox Cub	Heliopolis	27
1940	Pont l'Eveque (10/1)	Turkhan	Lighthouse II	16
1941	Owen Tudor (25/1)	Morogoro	Firoze Din	20
1942	Watling Street (6/1)	Hyperides	Ujiji	13
1943	Straight Deal (100/6)	Umiddad	Nasrullah	23
1944	Ocean Swell (28/1)	Tehran	Happy Landing	20
1945	Dante (100/30)	Midas	Court Martial	27
1946	Airborne (50/1)	Gulf Stream	Radiotherapy	17
1947	Pearl Diver (40/1)	Migoli	Sayajirao	15
1948	My Love (100/9)	Royal Drake	Noor	32
1949	Nimbus (7/1)	Amour Drake	Swallow Tail	32
1950	Galcador (100/9)	Prince Simon	Double Eclipse	25
1951	Arctic Prince (28/1)	Sybil's Nephew	Signal Box	33
1952	Tulyar (11/2)	Gay Time	Faubourg II	33
1953	Pinza (5/1)	Aureole	Pink Horse	27
1954	Never Say Die (33/1)	Arabian Night	Darius	22
1955	Phil Drake (100/8)	Panaslipper	Acropolis	23
1956	Lavandin (7/1)	Montaval	Roistar	27
1957	Crepello (6/4)	Ballymoss	Pipe of Peace	22
1958	Hard Ridden (18/1)	Paddy's Point	Nagami	20
1959	Parthia (10/1)	Fidalgo	Shantung	20
1960	St Paddy (7/1)	Alcaeus	Kythnos	17
1961	Psidium (66/1)	Dicta Drake	Pardao	28
1962	Larkspur (22/1)	Arcor	Le Cantilien	26
1963	Relko (5/1)	Merchant Venturer	Ragusa	26
1964	Santa Claus (15/8)	Indiana	Dilettante II	17
1965	Sea-Bird II (7/4)	Meadow Court	I Say	22
1966	Charlottown (5/1)	Pretendre	Black Prince II	25
1967	Royal Palace (7/4)	Ribocco	Dart Board	22
1968	Sir Ivor (4/5)	Connaught	Mount Athos	13
1969	Blakeney (15/2)	Shoemaker	Prince Regent	26
1970	Nijinsky (11/8)	Gyr	Stintino	11
1971	Mill Reef (100/30)	Linden Tree	Irish Ball	21
1972	Roberto (3/1)	Rheingold	Pentland Firth	22
1973	Morston (25/1)	Cavo Doro	Freefoot	25
1974	Snow Knight (50/1)	Imperial Prince	Giacometti	18
1975	Grundy (5/1)	Nobiliary	Hunza Dancer	18
1976	Empery (10/1)	Relkino	Oats	23

THE OAKS 1916–1976

Year	Winner and S.P.	Second	Third	Rns
1916	Fifinella (8/13)	Salamandra	Market Girl	7
1917	Sunny Jane (4/1)	Diadem	Moravia	11
1918	My Dear (3/1)	Ferry and Silver Bullet	dead-heated	15
1919	Bayuda (100/7)	Roseway	Mapledurham	10
1920	Charlebelle (7/2)	Cinna	Roselet	17
1921	Love in Idleness (5/1)	Lady Sleipner	Long Suit	22
1922	Pogrom (5/4)	Soubriquet	Mysia	11
1923	Brownhylda (10/1)	Shrove	Teresina	12
1924	Straitlace (100/30)	Plack	Mink	12
1925	Saucy Sue (30/100)	Miss Gadabout	Riding Light	12
1926	Short Story (5/1)	Resplendent	Gay Bird	16
1927	Beam (4/1)	Book Law	Grande Vitesse	16
1928	Toboggan (100/15)	Scuttle	Flegere	13
1929	Pennycomequick (11/10)	Golden Silence	Sister Anne	13
1930	Rose of England (7/1)	Wedding Favour	Micmac	15
1931	Brulette (7/2)	Four Course	Links Tor	15
1932	Udaipur (10/1)	Will o' the Wisp	Guidecca	12
1933	Chatelaine (25/1)	Solfatara	Fur Tor	14
1934	Light Brocade (7/4)	Zelina	Instantaneous	8
1935	Quashed (33/1)	Ankaret	Mesa	17
1936	Lovely Rosa (33/1)	Barrowby Gem	Feola	17
1937	Exhibitionnist (3/1)	Sweet Content	Sculpture	13
1938	Rockfel (3/1)	Radiant	Solar Flower	14
1939	Galatea II (10/11)	White Fox	Superbe	21
1940	Godiva (7/4)	Silverlace II	Valeraine	14
1941	Commotion (8/1)	Turkana	Dancing Time	12
1942	Sun Chariot (1/4)	Afterthought	Feberion	12
1943	Why Hurry (7/1)	Ribbon	Tropical Sun	13
1944	Hycilla (8/1)	Monsoon	Kannabis	16
1945	Sun Stream (6/4)	Naishapur	Solar Princess	16
1946	Steady Aim (7/1)	Iona	Nelia	10
1947	Imprudence (7/4)	Netherton Maid	Mermaid	11
1948	Masaka (7/1)	Angelola	Folie II	25
1949	Musidora (4/1)	Coronation V	Vice Versa II	17
1950	Asmena (5/1)	Plume II	Stella Polaris	19
1951	Neasham Belle (33/1)	Chinese Cracker	Belle of All	16
1952	Frieze (100/7)	Zabara	Moon Star	19
1953	Ambiguity (18/1)	Kerkeb	Noemi	21
1954	Sun Cap (100/8)	Altana	Philante	21
1955	Meld (7/4)	Ark Royal	Reel In	13
1956	Sicarelle (3/1)	Janiari	Yasmin	14
1957	Carrozza (100/8)	Silken Glider	Rose Royale II	11
1958	Bella Paola (6/4)	Mother Goose	Cutter	17
1959	Petite Etoile (11/2)	Cantelo	Rose of Medina	11
1960	Never Too Late II (6/5)	Paimpont	Imberline	10
1961	Sweet Solera (11/4)	Ambergris	Anne la Douce	12
1962	Monade (7/1)	West Side Story	Tender Annie	18
1963	Noblesse (4/11)	Spree	Pouponne	9
1964	Homeward Bound (100/7)	Windmill Girl	La Bamba	18
1965	Long Look (100/7)	Mabel	Ruby's Princess	18
1966	Valoris (11/10)	Berkeley Springs	Varinia	13
1967	Pia (100/7)	St Pauli Girl	Ludham	12
1968	La Lagune (11/8)	Glad One	Pandora Bay	14
1969	Sleeping Partner (100/6)	Frontier Goddess	Myastrid	15
1970	Lupe (100/30)	State Pension	Arctic Wave	16
1971	Altesse Royale (6/4)	Maina	La Manille	11
1972	Ginevra (8/1)	Regal Exception	Arkadina	17
1973	Mysterious (13/8)	Where You Lead	Aureoletta	10
1974	Polygamy (3/1)	Furioso	Matuta	15
1975	Juliette Marny (12/1)	Val's Girl	Moonlight Night	12
1976	Pawneese (6/5)	Roses for the Star	African Dancer	14

ST LEGER 1916–1976

Year	Winner and S.P.	Second	Third	Rns
1916	Hurry On (11/10)	Clarissimus	Atheling	5
1917	Gay Crusader (2/11)	Kingston Black	Dansellon	3
1918	Gainsborough (4/11)	My Dear	Prince Chimay	5
1919	Keysoe (100/8)	Dominion	Buchan	10
1920	Caligula (100/6)	Silvern	Manton	14
1921	Polemarch (50/1)	Franklin	Westward Ho	9
1922	Royal Lancer (33/1)	Silurian	Ceylonese	24
1923	Tranquil (100/9)	Papyrus	Teresina	13
1924	Salmon-Trout (6/1)	Santorb	Polyphontes	17
1925	Solario (7/2)	Zambo	Warden of the Marches	15
1926	Coronach (8/15)	Caissot	Foliation	12
1927	Book Law (7/4)	Hot Night	Son and Heir	16
1928	Fairway (7/4)	Palais Royal II	Cyclonic	13
1929	Trigo (5/1)	Bosworth	Horus	14
1930	Singapore (4/1)	Parenthesis	Rustom Pasha	13
1931	Sandwich (9/1)	Orpen	Sir Andrew	10
1932	Firdaussi (20/1)	Dastur	Silvermere	19
1933	Hyperion (6/4)	Felicitation	Scarlet Tiger	14
1934	Windsor Lad (4/9)	Tiberius	Lo Zingaro	10
1935	Bahram (4/11)	Solar Ray	Buckleigh	8
1936	Boswell (20/1)	Fearless Fox	Mahmoud	13
1937	Chulmleigh (18/1)	Fair Copy	Mid-day Sun	15
1938	Scottish Union (7/1)	Challenge	Pasch	9
1939	No race			
1940	Turkhan (4/1)	Stardust	Hippius	6
1941	Sun Castle (10/1)	Chateau Larose	Dancing Time	16
1942	Sun Chariot (9/4)	Watling Street	Hyperides	8
1943	Herringbone (100/6)	Ribbon	Straight Deal	12
1944	Tehran (9/2)	Borealis	Ocean Swell	17
1945	Chamossaire (11/2)	Rising Light	Stirling Castle	10
1946	Airborne (3/1)	Murren	Fast and Fair	11
1947	Sayajirao (9/2)	Arbar	Migoli	11
1948	Black Tarquin (15/2)	Alycidon	Solar Slipper	14
1949	Ridge Wood (100/7)	Dust Devil	Lone Eagle	16
1950	Scratch II (9/2)	Vieux Manoir	Sanlinea	15
1951	Talma II (7/1)	Fraise du Bois II	Medway	18
1952	Tulyar (10/11)	Kingsfold	Alcinus	12
1953	Premonition (10/1)	Northern Light II	Aureole	11
1954	Never Say Die (100/30)	Elopement	Estremadur	16
1955	Meld (10/11)	Nucleus	Beau Prince	8
1956	Cambremer (8/1)	Hornbeam	French Beige	13
1957	Ballymoss (8/1)	Court Harwell	Brioche	16
1958	Alcide (4/9)	None Nicer	Nagami	8
1959	Cantelo (100/7)	Fidalgo	Pindari	11
1960	St Paddy (4/6)	Die Hard	Vienna	9
1961	Aurelius (9/2)	Bounteous	Dicta Drake	13
1962	Hethersett (100/8)	Monterrico	Miralgo	15
1963	Ragusa (2/5)	Star Moss	Fighting Ship	7
1964	Indiana (100/7)	Patti	Soderini	15
1965	Provoke (28/1)	Meadow Court	Solstice	11
1966	Sodium (7/1)	Charlottown	David Jack	9
1967	Ribocco (7/2)	Hopeful Venture	Ruysdael II	9
1968	Ribero (100/30)	Canterbury	Cold Storage	8
1969	Intermezzo (7/1)	Ribofilio	Prince Consort	11
1970	Nijinsky (2/7)	Meadowville	Politico	9
1971	Athens Wood (5/2)	Homeric	Falkland	8
1972	Boucher (3/1)	Our Mirage	Ginevra	7
1973	Peleid (28/1)	Buoy	Duke of Ragusa	13
1974	Bustino (11/10)	Giacometti	Riboson	10
1975	Bruni (9/1)	King Pellinore	Libra's Rib	12
1976	Crow (6/1)	Secret Man	Scallywag	15

1977 FLAT RACING FIXTURES

† Denotes evening meeting

March

24 Thur. Doncaster
25 Fri. Doncaster
26 Sat. Doncaster
28 Mon. Leicester
29 Tues. Leicester
30 Wed. Catterick, Folkestone
31 Thur. Teesside

April

1 Fri. Warwick, Teesside
2 Sat. Ascot
4 Mon. Ayr, Wolverhampton
5 Tues. Ayr, Wolverhampton
6 Wed. Haydock, Hamilton
7 Thur. Haydock
9 Sat. Kempton, Doncaster, Newcastle
11 Mon. Kempton, Newcastle, Nottingham, Warwick
12 Tues. Newmarket, Warwick
13 Wed. Newmarket, Ripon
14 Thur. Newmarket, Lanark
15 Fri. Newbury, Beverley
16 Sat. Newbury, Beverley
18 Mon. Brighton, Nottingham, Edinburgh
19 Tues. Epsom, Nottingham
20 Wed. Epsom, Pontefract
21 Thur. Epsom, Pontefract
22 Fri. Sandown, Thirsk, Leicester
23 Sat. Sandown, Thirsk
25 Mon. Bath, Warwick
26 Tues. Newmarket, Nottingham, Chepstow
27 Wed. Newmarket, Catterick
28 Thur. Newmarket, Teesside
29 Fri. Newcastle, Beverley
30 Sat. Ascot, Beverley

May

2 Mon. Wolverhampton, Edinburgh
3 Tues. Chester, Windsor†
4 Wed. Chester, Salisbury
5 Thur. Chester, Salisbury
6 Fri. Lingfield, Carlisle
7 Sat. Lingfield, Ayr, Ripon, Bath
9 Mon. Ayr, Windsor†
10 Tues. York, Brighton
11 Wed. York, Brighton
12 Thur. York, Folkestone
13 Fri. Newbury, Thirsk
14 Sat. Newbury, Thirsk, Hamilton†
16 Mon. Windsor†, Pontefract, Wolverhampton
17 Tues. Goodwood, Wolverhampton, Hamilton
18 Wed. Goodwood, Ripon
19 Thur. Goodwood

20 Fri. Newmarket, Kempton†
21 Sat. Newmarket, Kempton†, Thirsk
23 Mon. Hamilton, Folkestone
24 Tues. Salisbury, Lanark
25 Wed. Brighton, Catterick
26 Thur. Brighton, Carlisle
27 Fri. Sandown, Haydock, Pontefract†
28 Sat. Sandown, Haydock, Ayr
30 Mon. Lingfield, Leicester, Edinburgh†
31 Tues. Lingfield, Hamilton†

June

1 Wed. Epsom, Ripon
2 Thur. Epsom
3 Fri. Epsom, Haydock†, Catterick
4 Sat. Epsom, Haydock, Doncaster, Catterick
6 Mon. Sandown, Redcar, Doncaster, Leicester, Chepstow
7 Tues. Sandown, Redcar, Leicester, Chepstow
8 Wed. Newbury, Beverley†, Yarmouth
9 Thur. Newbury, Beverley, Yarmouth
10 Fri. York, Kempton
11 Sat. York, Kempton, Leicester†, Bath
13 Mon. Windsor†, Nottingham, Edinburgh†
14 Tues. Royal Ascot, Hamilton
15 Wed. Royal Ascot, Lanark
16 Thur. Royal Ascot, Beverley
17 Fri. Royal Ascot, Ayr
18 Sat. Ascot, Redcar, Ayr, Warwick†
20 Mon. Brighton, Pontefract, Wolverhampton†
21 Tues. Brighton, Pontefract
22 Wed. Salisbury, Ripon†, Yarmouth
23 Thur. Salisbury, Newcastle, Yarmouth
24 Fri. Lingfield, Newcastle†, Doncaster
25 Sat. Newmarket, Lingfield, Newcastle, Doncaster†, Chepstow
27 Mon. Windsor†, Thirsk, Nottingham
28 Tues. Nottingham, Folkestone
29 Wed. Brighton, Yarmouth, Carlisle
30 Thur. Brighton, Yarmouth, Carlisle

July

1 Fri.   Sandown, Haydock, Beverley†
2 Sat.   Sandown, Haydock, Beverley, Bath, Nottingham†
4 Mon. Windsor†, Pontefract, Edinburgh, Wolverhampton†
5 Tues. Newmarket, Warwick, Lanark
6 Wed. Newmarket, Doncaster†, Catterick
7 Thur. Newmarket, Doncaster†, Brighton
8 Fri.   York, Lingfield, Chester†
9 Sat.   York, Lingfield, Chester, Salisbury, Carlisle†
11 Mon. Leicester†, Edinburgh, Folkestone
12 Tues. Kempton, Beverley, Leicester†
13 Wed. Kempton, Redcar
14 Thur. Redcar, Bath, Nottingham†, Hamilton†
15 Fri.   Newbury, Hamilton†
16 Sat.   Newbury, Newmarket, Ayr, Ripon
18 Mon. Ayr, Pontefract, Windsor†
19 Tues. Ayr, Folkestone
20 Wed. Sandown†, Yarmouth, Catterick, Lanark
21 Thur. Sandown, Yarmouth, Catterick, Lanark
22 Fri.   Ascot, Ayr
23 Sat.   Ascot, Ayr, Newcastle, Warwick†
25 Mon. Newcastle, Bath, Windsor†, Nottingham†
26 Tues. Goodwood, Redcar
27 Wed. Goodwood, Redcar
28 Thur. Goodwood, Redcar, Carlisle
29 Fri.   Goodwood, Newmarket†, Thirsk
30 Sat.   Goodwood, Newmarket, Thirsk, Windsor†

August

1 Mon. Ripon, Bath, Wolverhampton†, Folkestone, Wolverhampton
2 Tues. Ayr, Redcar, Brighton, Wolverhampton
3 Wed. Ayr, Brighton, Pontefract
4 Thur. Brighton, Pontefract, Warwick
5 Fri.   Newmarket, Haydock, Lingfield, Redcar
6 Sat.   Newmarket, Haydock, Lingfield, Redcar
8 Mon. Newcastle, Windsor†, Nottingham
9 Tues. Newcastle, Folkestone
10 Wed. Salisbury, Yarmouth, Catterick
11 Thur. Salisbury, Yarmouth, Catterick

12 Fri.   Newbury
13 Sat.   Newbury, Ripon Wolverhampton
15 Mon. Windsor, Leicester
16 Tues. York, Folkestone
17 Wed. York, Brighton
18 Thur. York
19 Fri.   Kempton, Hamilton†
20 Sat.   Kempton, Ripon, Nottingham
22 Mon. Windsor
23 Tues. Brighton
24 Wed. Haydock, Beverley, Yarmouth
25 Thur. Haydock, Beverley, Yarmouth
26 Fri.   Goodwood, Newmarket
27 Sat.   Goodwood, Newmarket, Newcastle, Windsor†
29 Mon. Epsom, Newcastle, Ripon, Wolverhampton, Warwick, Chepstow
30 Tues. Epsom, Ripon, Warwick, Chepstow
31 Wed. York, Bath

September

1 Thur. York, Carlisle
2 Fri.   Sandown, Chester, Thirsk
3 Sat.   Sandown, Chester, Thirsk, Lanark
5 Mon. Windsor, Nottingham
6 Tues. Pontefract, Folkestone
7 Wed. Doncaster, Salisbury, Hamilton
8 Thur. Doncaster, Salisbury
9 Fri.   Doncaster, Goodwood
10 Sat. Doncaster, Goodwood
12 Mon. Goodwood, Wolverhampton
13 Tues. Yarmouth
14 Wed. Windsor, Beverley, Yarmouth
15 Thur. Beverley, Yarmouth
16 Fri.   Newbury, Catterick
17 Sat.   Newbury, Catterick
19 Mon. Leicester, Bath, Edinburgh
20 Tues. Lingfield, Leicester
21 Wed. Ayr, Lingfield
22 Thur. Ascot, Ayr
23 Fri.   Ascot, Ayr
24 Sat.   Ascot, Ayr, Redcar
26 Mon. Goodwood, Nottingham, Hamilton
27 Tues. Goodwood, Nottingham
28 Wed. Newmarket, Brighton
29 Thur. Newmarket
30 Fri.   Haydock

October

1 Sat.   Newmarket, Haydock
3 Mon. Wolverhampton, Bath, Edinburgh, Folkestone
4 Tues. Newcastle, Brighton
5 Wed. Lingfield
6 Thur. York, Lingfield

7 Fri.	Ascot, York		22 Sat.	Doncaster, Newbury
8 Sat.	Ascot, York		24 Mon.	Nottingham, Chepstow,
10 Mon.	Pontefract, Warwick			Teesside
11 Tues.	Redcar, Warwick		25 Tues.	Nottingham, Teesside
12 Wed.	Haydock, Folkestone		28 Fri.	Haydock, Newmarket
13 Thur.	Newmarket, Haydock		29 Sat.	Haydock, Newmarket
14 Fri.	Newmarket, Catterick		31 Mon.	Leicester
15 Sat.	Newmarket, Catterick			
17 Mon.	Leicester, Edinburgh			
18 Tues.	Sandown, Leicester,			**November**
	Chepstow, Lanark		1 Tues.	Lingfield, Leicester
19 Wed.	Sandown, Redcar		3 Thur.	Teesside
20 Thur.	Newbury, Wolverhampton		5 Sat.	Doncaster
21 Fri.	Doncaster, Newbury			

ERRATA & ADDENDA
"RACEHORSES OF 1975"

Auction Ring	first form figure 6g<u>*</u>
August	third form figure 8.2g²
Charities	Chari<u>te</u>s
Crash Course	P 181—Sultry <u>Da</u>y
Doonside	dam is Easter<u>b</u>ury
Minstrel	disqualified at <u>Brighton</u>
Mount Carmel	additional form figure 16g <u>three</u> races
Palatable	sire of dam is Ameri<u>go</u>
Psalve	second form figure 8<u>g</u>⁶
Saturnus	half-<u>brother</u>
Sempa Nova	Semp<u>er</u> Nova
Shesheen	is a grey
Snow Venture	maiden race at <u>Newmarket</u>
Vitoria	sire is Salvo

INDEX TO ADVERTISEMENTS

A race can just as easily be lost up in the air as down on the ground

You know and we know that a horse can have an unhappy ride on its way from one course to another. The most hair raising moment for a horse is on take off and landing. That's when they're likely to panic unless you know what you're doing.

A good travelling groom judges his horse before he gets it on the aircraft.
A bad travelling horse taken good care of can become a good travelling horse.

Horses are like some high flying humans, they like reassuring!

Lep grooms know exactly what to do very often before they have to do it, and that's good especially for your mares travelling abroad from their home stud.

We know more about horses in transit than anyone else because we've been transporting horses for a lot longer and a lot farther than anyone else.

We arrange the insurance, customs documentation, transport to and from airports, where there's always plenty of supervision. We also have our own grooms on every flight and they know about it every time your horse blinks *and* why.

At Lep we take care to get your horses there.

For moves to Europe by air, talk to Bill Palmer or Tom Toller on extension 44/45.

Long distance hauls talk to John Bidwell or Christopher Mahoney on extension 41.

Sea and road to Europe please talk to Gina Garner or Jane Savill on extension 42/43.

Lep Bloodstock Ltd,
Caroline House,
55-57 High Holborn,
London WC1V 6DX.
Tel: 01-236 5050

Telex:
Lep Bld
LDN 23459